2019

THE AWARD WINNING GOLDEN BEER

TOP PERFORMING GOLDEN ALE ON THE MARKET*

SILVER WINNER OF THE DBS DESIGN EFFECTIVENESS AWARDS 2018

WINNER OF BEST INTEGRATED CAMPAIGN IN THE 2017 BEER AND CIDER MARKETING AWARDS

WINNER OF THE GROCER CAMPAIGN OF THE YEAR 2016

*CGA OPMS 30/12/2017 drinkaware.co.uk for the facts

#FINDYOURMOUNTAIN

SEARCH 'WAINWRIGHTGOLDENBEER'

WWW.WAINWRIGHTGOLDENBEER.CO.UK

Wainwright
THE GOLDEN BEER

The Good Pub Guide 2019

Edited by Fiona Stapley

Associate Editor: Patrick Stapley
Managing Editor: Fiona Wright
Editorial Assistants: Annabel Lees,
Kyle Farrell
Founded by Alisdair Aird in 1982

EBURY PRESS
LONDON

Please send reports on pubs to:

The Good Pub Guide
FREEPOST RTXY–ZCBC–BBAZ, Stream Lane, Sedlescombe, Battle TN33 0PB

or **feedback@goodguides.com**

or visit our website: **www.thegoodpubguide.co.uk**

If you would like to advertise in the next edition of *The Good Pub Guide*, please email **goodpubguide@tbs-ltd.co.uk**

10 9 8 7 6 5 4 3 2 1

Published in 2018 by Ebury Press, an imprint of Ebury Publishing

Ebury Press, an imprint of Ebury Publishing
20 Vauxhall Bridge Road,
London, SW1V 2SA

Text © Ebury Publishing 2018
Maps © PerroGraphics 2018
Fiona Stapley has asserted her right to be identified as the author of this Work in accordance with the Copyright, Designs and Patents Act 1988

All rights reserved. No part of this publication may be reproduced, stored in a retrieval system, or transmitted in any form or by any means, electronic, mechanical, photocopying, recording or otherwise, without the prior permission of the copyright owner.

www.eburypublishing.co.uk

Penguin Random House is committed to a sustainable future for our business, our readers and our planet. This book is made from Forest Stewardship Council® certified paper.

To buy books by your favourite authors and register for offers, visit www.penguin.co.uk

Typesetter: Integra
Designer: Jerry Goldie Graphic Design
Project manager and copy editor: Cath Phillips
Proofreader: Tamsin Shelton
Good Pub Guide icons: William Collins

Printed and bound in Great Britain by Clays Ltd, Elcograf S.p.A.

ISBN 9781785038686

Contents

DISCOVER
INDIVIDUAL INNS

EAT,
DRINK
AND
SLEEP

Our eclectic traditional inns in stunning settings, all offer excellent food and service, a fine range of hand pulled beers and a great cellar of wine. Each Individual Inn offers a welcoming environment, with delightful settings, cosy bars and eating areas with real Inn charm. All the Inns have the advantage of lovely accommodation, or try our luxury bunkhouse!

MASONS ARMS
THE WHEATSHEAF INN
LUMLEY FEE BUNKHOUSE

The Fountaine Inn
THE WHEATLEY ARMS

Visit... individualinns.co.uk

INDIVIDUAL INNS

Wherever you want your visit to the pub to take you, we've got the venue to fit your bill and make the most of your experience.

From rural landscapes with top quality dining, to live music venues with good old fashioned boozers in between, our eclectic mix of pubs are just the ticket to your perfect outing.

Each pub has its own individuality, fuelled by character and charm, to ensure you have the best experience no matter who you're with.

With pubs across Somerset, Bristol, Bath, Gloucester and Wiltshire, there's something for everyone. So, why not pop in and say hello, we'd love to see you!

Join the Butcombe Loyalty Club and get £5 to spend in any of our managed pubs* today! Head to ButcombeLoyaltyClub.com to register.

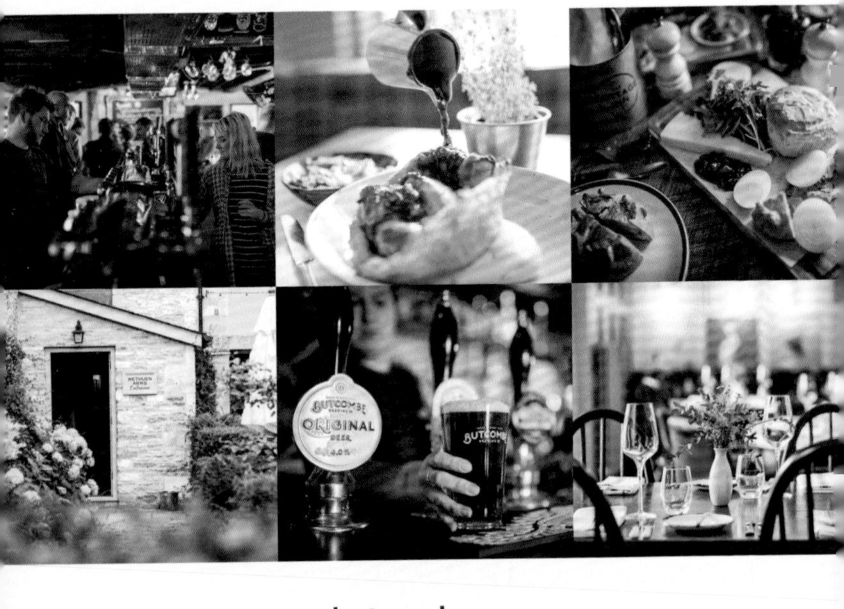

butcombe.com

butcombe  @butcombebrewery  butcombe

*For a list of our managed pubs, head to butcombe.com/managed.

Introduction & The Good Pub Guide Awards 2019

Pass the food dictionary

Pubs and food now go hand in hand – and for many people, eating out means heading for an inn where they know they'll get a good meal in a cheerful, relaxed atmosphere. And this can be anything from breakfast and brunch to morning coffee and full afternoon tea to interesting tapas-style nibbles and cuisines that range from pub classics through popular Mediterranean-style dishes to unusual and sometimes unknown Korean dishes. But have some pub chefs gone too far with their adventurous ideas by using ingredients that many of us have never heard of?

Here at *The Good Pub Guide* we spend a lot of time looking at menus and, while this enterprising food can be exciting and delicious, we can be baffled by the descriptions and products used. If you're eating out, do you really want to have to keep asking the waiter to explain a dish or search on your mobile phone before you can order something? How many of us have heard of crosnes, fattoush, fregola, ful, kabsa, katsuobushi, keta, kirmizi biber, matbucha, nduja, persillade, shimeji, succotash, tataki and verjus? And what are choucroute, monk's beard, pangritata and pastille? Do you want your dish adorned with carrot fluff, edible sand, seaweed dust, fish foam – or even a 'soil' made of black pudding? The best-known chefs in the *Guide* are not fans of overly complicated dishes that contain fancy ideas for the sake of it, but prefer to let the first class quality of their cooking speak for itself. In the 37 years of *The Good Pub Guide's* existence, many food fads have come and gone but what stands fast is honest cooking using first rate, local, seasonal ingredients (but maybe ones that we can recognise!).

Use them or lose them

It seems only a short time ago that we were surprised when the price of a pint of beer reached, and then tipped over, £3. This year has been the first time that we've regularly come across real ales that cost £4 and above, and this, together with the certainty of forthcoming price rises for meals, means pub customers are going to have to dig deeper into their pockets.

But before we complain too strongly, spare a thought for the poor publicans who are trying their best to absorb price increases before passing them on to customers. Margins are being continually squeezed and profits eroded.

Business rates are the killer. One top landlord tells us that the rates for one of his pubs have recently risen from £36,000 per year to £63,000 and for another from £36,000 to £78,000. Another publican says one of his pubs experienced a whopping 425% hike. The situation can also be challenging for leaseholders. A London pub we've known and loved for many years had to shut its doors when the rent went from £90,000 to £250,000.

Other factors include the increase in the national minimum and living wages, the 3% addition to the government pension, rising food prices, and the actual day-to-day costs of running a pub (apart from the wages bill): builders, cleaners, gardeners, electricians, costly new kitchen equipment, refurbishments – the list is endless.

Pubs have been part of the British way of life for hundreds of years and our landlords and landladies need our support more than ever. If paying a bit extra for our drinks and meals makes the difference between hostelries surviving or closing, then it will be money well spent, even though we may huff and puff a bit.

Drinks: the search for fair prices and top quality

Our national survey of beer prices shows a huge £1.07-a-pint difference in the cost of a pint of ale between Shropshire and Herefordshire, the cheapest areas, and London, the most expensive. The average price for a pint of beer in Britain is now £3.69. How does your area rank? Here are the details, in average price order from cheapest upwards:

Bargain beer
Shropshire, Herefordshire, Staffordshire, Yorkshire, Northamptonshire

Fair-priced beer
Wales, Northumbria, Worcestershire, Derbyshire, Dorset,

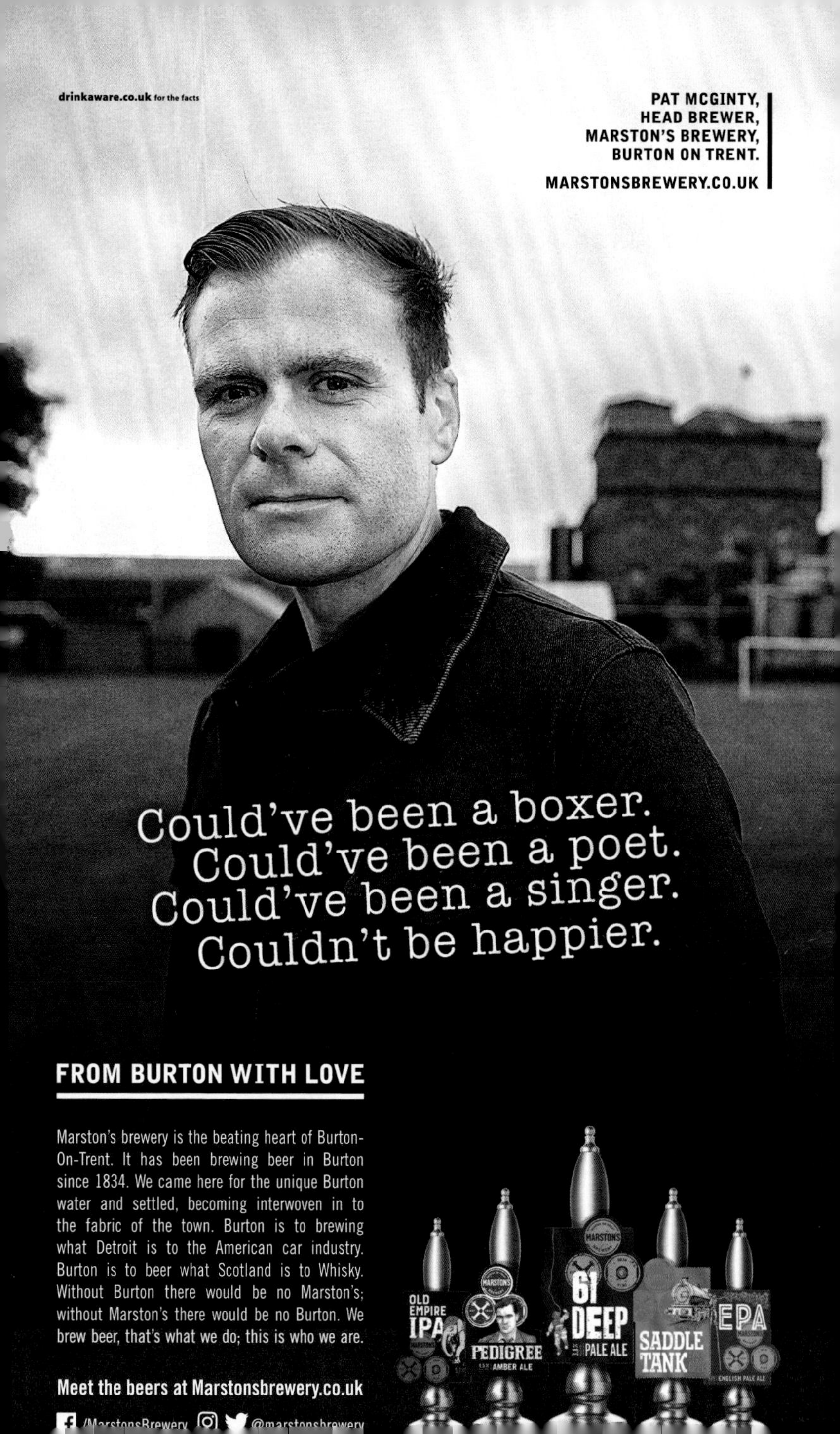

PAT MCGINTY,
HEAD BREWER,
MARSTON'S BREWERY,
BURTON ON TRENT.

MARSTONSBREWERY.CO.UK

Could've been a boxer.
Could've been a poet.
Could've been a singer.
Couldn't be happier.

FROM BURTON WITH LOVE

Marston's brewery is the beating heart of Burton-On-Trent. It has been brewing beer in Burton since 1834. We came here for the unique Burton water and settled, becoming interwoven in to the fabric of the town. Burton is to brewing what Detroit is to the American car industry. Burton is to beer what Scotland is to Whisky. Without Burton there would be no Marston's; without Marston's there would be no Burton. We brew beer, that's what we do; this is who we are.

Meet the beers at Marstonsbrewery.co.uk

Cheshire

Average-priced beer
Cumbria, Leicestershire, Lancashire, Suffolk, Bedfordshire, West Midlands, Somerset, Lincolnshire, Devon, Warwickshire, Cornwall, Nottinghamshire, Norfolk, Cambridgeshire, Essex, Isle of Wight, Wiltshire, Gloucestershire, Hampshire

Expensive beer
Scotland, Scottish Islands, Buckinghamshire, Oxfordshire, Kent, Sussex, Berkshire

Top-whack beer
Hertfordshire, Surrey, London

Tring Brewery was founded in 1992 by Richard Shardlow (an experienced brewer whose background included working for Greene King, Ruddles and Devenish), who was then joined in 2000 by Andrew Jackson from Whitbread. Most of the staff working at the brewery live in Tring itself, so there's a real sense of camaraderie, and as a company they're proud of their location and surrounding countryside. The public, unsurprisingly, enjoyed their ales and as demand grew they moved to bigger premises in 2010. They supply around 200 outlets and have a delivery radius of 60 miles.

The brewing process uses water filtered through the chalk of the surrounding Chiltern Hills, the best British barley and hops carefully sourced from across the world, each one selected for the unique character it brings to a beer. And, of course, yeast. They offer ten core beers, a monthly special and five seasonal choices.

But apart from the quality of Tring's beers, it's the unusual names that people recognise. And with every name there's a connection to local wildlife, folklore or literature. Names include Brock, Colley's Dog, Fanny Ebbs Summer Ale, Moongazing, Santa's Little Helper, Tea Kettle Stout and, perhaps their most famous, Side Pocket for a Toad (a Hertfordshire saying for something that is useless).

They hold bargain-priced brewery tours twice a month on Saturday mornings (01442 890721 – pre-booking essential), which includes tasting samples or a bottle to take home.

For their hard work and commitment – and excellent beers, of course – **Tring** is our **Brewery of the Year 2019**.

You'll find this year's Top Ten Beer Pubs are spread across

THE ORANGE TREE

THORNHAM

Norfolk's best just
keeps getting better

01485 512213

www.theorangetreethornham.co.uk

TRADITIONAL VILLAGE INN
with RESTAURANT & ROOMS
Ideally situated to explore Dartmoor
National Park & the South Hams
www.ANCHORINNUGBOROUGH.co.uk

theSHIP AT DUNWICH
A traditional coastal inn

Home-cooked food | well-kept ales | cosy bedrooms, some with views across the sea or marshes | beer garden | coastal walks | dogs are very welcome

www.shipatdunwich.co.uk
info@shipatdunwich.co.uk

St James Street, Dunwich,
Nr Southwold, Suffolk, IP17 3DT
01728 648219

the country: the **Bhurtpore** in Aston and **Mill** in Chester (both in Cheshire), **Beer Hall at Hawkshead Brewery** in Staveley (Cumbria), **Tom Cobley** in Spreyton (Devon), **Fat Cat** in Norwich (Norfolk), **Malt Shovel** in Northampton (Northamptonshire), **Halfway House** at Pitney (Somerset), **Fat Cat** in Ipswich (Suffolk), **Nags Head** in Malvern (Worcestershire) and **Harp** in central London. All these pubs keep an exceptional number of real ales in tip top condition, but it's Colin Keatley's collection of 32 beers at the **Fat Cat** in Norwich that makes it our **Beer Pub of the Year 2019**.

You will typically save yourself 43p a pint if you drink at one of the own-brew pubs in this edition of *The Good Pub Guide*. Our Top Ten Own-Brew Pubs are the **Brewery Tap** in Peterborough (Cambridgeshire), **Drunken Duck** near Hawkshead, **Watermill** at Ings and **Brown Horse** in Winster (all Cumbria), **Church Inn** at Uppermill (Lancashire), **Grainstore** in Oakham (Leicestershire), **Dipton Mill Inn** at Diptonmill and **Ship** at Newton-by-the-Sea (both Northumbria), **Gribble Inn** at Oving (Sussex) and **Weighbridge Brewhouse** in Swindon (Wiltshire). Our **Own-Brew Pub of the Year 2019** is the **Grainstore** in Oakham.

A total of 384 of the Main Entry pubs in this edition hold one of our Wine Awards, meaning that they keep a very special and carefully chosen selection of wines. This year's Top Ten are the **Old Bridge Hotel** in Huntingdon (Cambridgeshire), **Acorn** in Evershot (Dorset), **Inn at Whitewell** at Whitewell (Lancashire), **Olive Branch** in Clipsham (Leicestershire), **Woods** in Dulverton (Somerset), **Duncombe Arms** at Ellastone (Staffordshire), **Unruly Pig** in Bromeswell and **Crown** in Stoke-by-Nayland (both Suffolk), **The Inn West End** in West End (Surrey) and **Griffin** in Felinfach (Wales). The charming and exceptionally knowledgeable Paddy Groves reckons he could put 1,000 wines up on the bar and will open any of them (with a value of up to £100) for just a glass – **Woods** in Dulverton is our **Wine Pub of the Year 2019**.

You'll be sure to find an extraordinarily wide choice of malt whiskies in our Top Ten Whisky list: the **Bhurtpore** in Aston (Cheshire), **Acorn** in Evershot (Dorset), **Red Fox** at Thornton Hough and **Worsley Old Hall** in Worsley (both Lancashire), **Black Jug** in Horsham (Sussex), **Pack Horse** at Widdop (Yorkshire), **Old Orchard** on the outskirts of west London, and **Bow Bar** in Edinburgh, **Bon Accord** in Glasgow and **Sligachan Hotel** on the Isle of Skye (Scotland). Now with over 400 malts to choose from, the **Bon Accord** in Glasgow is our **Whisky Pub of the Year 2019**.

So many pubs now stock an incredible number of gins that we thought the time had come to mention them too. Our inaugural Top

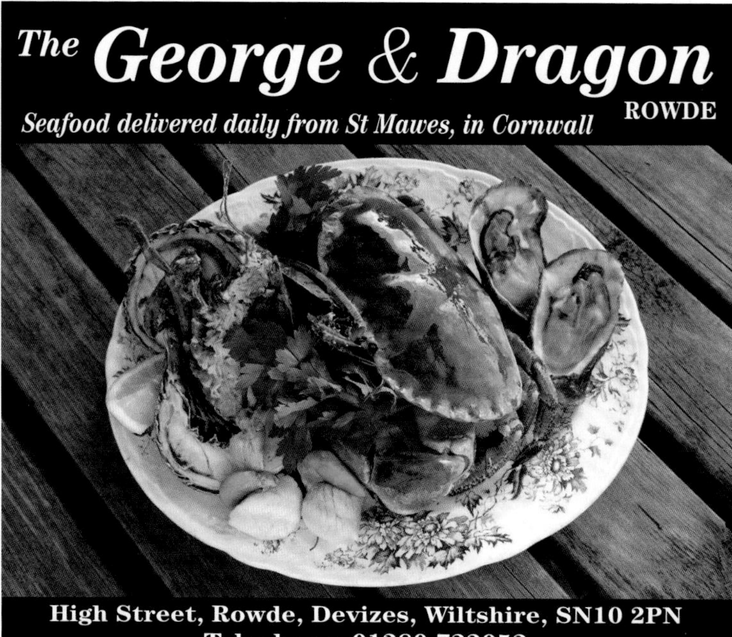

Ten Gin Pubs are the **Bhurtpore** in Aston, **Architect** in Chester and **Cholmondeley Arms** in Cholmondeley (Cheshire), **Brown Horse** in Winster (Cumbria), **Mill House** at North Warnborough (Hampshire), **Red Fox** in Thornton Hough (Lancashire), **Maytime** in Asthall (Oxfordshire), **Fox** at Chetwynd Aston (Shropshire), **Oakley** at Brewood (Staffordshire) and **Falcon** at Warmington (Warwickshire). For offering a mind-boggling collection of 400-plus gins, the **Cholmondeley Arms** in Cholmondeley is our **Gin Pub of the Year 2019**.

The best pubs in town and country

We're so lucky to still be able to find pubs in this modern world that don't change to suit fashions in décor or food and that remain quite unpretentious and honest. This year's Top Ten Unspoilt Pubs are the **White Lion** in Barthomley (Cheshire), **Barley Mow** in Kirk Ireton and **Flying Childers** in Stanton in Peak (Derbyshire), **Fountain Head** in Branscombe (Devon), **Square & Compass** at Worth Matravers (Dorset), **Harrow** in Steep (Hampshire), **Black Horse** at Caythorpe (Nottinghamshire), **Crown** in Churchill (Somerset), **Birch Hall** at Beck Hole (Yorkshire) and **Olde Mitre** in central London. The cottagey **Flying Childers** in Stanton in Peak is our **Unspoilt Pub of the Year 2019**.

A country pub conjures up roaring fires, honest food and a genuine welcome for both you and your dog after a walk. Our Top Ten Country Pubs are the **White Horse** in Hedgerley and **Crown** in Little Missenden (Buckinghamshire), **Brace of Pheasants** at Plush (Dorset), **Royal Oak** at Fritham (Hampshire), **Althorp Coaching Inn** at Great Brington (Northamptonshire), **Royal Oak** in Cardington (Shropshire), **Black Horse** in Clapton-in-Gordano (Somerset), **Hatchet** in Lower Chute (Wiltshire), **Fleece** in Bretforton (Worcestershire) and **Harp** in Old Radnor (Wales). For over 90 years the same friendly family have been running the charming **Crown** in Little Missenden, and it is our **Country Pub of the Year 2019**.

Town pubs are often just as popular for morning coffee or afternoon tea as they are for a pint – but they must offer a genuine welcome to strangers. Our Top Ten Town Pubs are the **Punter** in Cambridge (Cambridgeshire), **Old Courthouse** in Cheltenham (Gloucestershire), **Wykeham Arms** in Winchester (Hampshire), **Bank House** in King's Lynn (Norfolk), **Victoria** in Durham

(Northumbria), **Woodstock Arms** in Woodstock (Oxfordshire), **Lion & Pheasant** in Shrewsbury (Shropshire), **Old Green Tree** in Bath (Somerset), **Old Joint Stock** in Birmingham (Warwickshire) and **Babbity Bowster** in Glasgow (Scotland). With its lively atmosphere, flamboyant interior, all-day popular food and even its own theatre, the **Old Joint Stock** in Birmingham is our **Town Pub of the Year 2019**.

To stay overnight in a lovely bedroom at a pub or inn means you just have to totter down to the bar if you want a drink or a meal: perfect. Almost 300 – 292, in fact – of our pubs hold one of our Stay Awards and many are in stunning locations or in historic buildings. Our Top Ten Inns are the **Drunken Duck** near Hawkshead (Cumbria), **Rock** at Haytor Vale (Devon), **Kings Head** in Bledington (Gloucestershire), **Wellington Arms** in Baughurst (Hampshire), **Inn at Whitewell** near Whitewell (Lancashire), **Lord Crewe Arms** at Blanchland (Northumbria), **Luttrell Arms** in Dunster (Somerset), **Cat** in West Hoathly (Sussex), **Blue Lion** in East Witton (Yorkshire) and **Bear** in Crickhowell (Wales). Surrounded by glorious countryside and with an excellent restaurant and own-brewed beer, the **Drunken Duck** near Hawkshead is our **Inn of the Year 2019**.

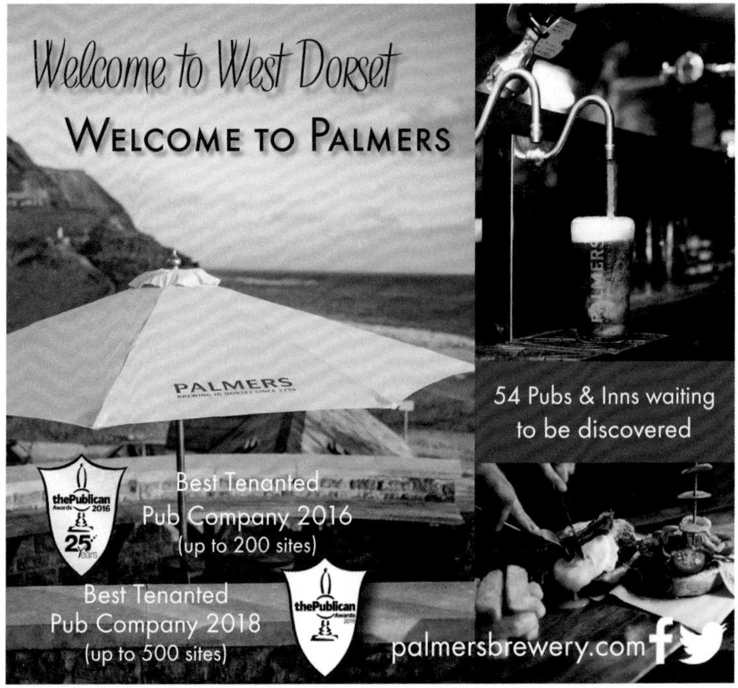

Looking for value and taste

It's quite a feat managing to keep main course dishes at £11 or under, but 64 pubs among our Main Entries have done that. Our Top Ten Value pubs are the **Drake Manor** in Buckland Monachorum (Devon), **Digby Tap** in Sherborne (Dorset), **Yew Tree** at Lower Wield (Hampshire), **Church Inn** at Uppermill (Lancashire), **Dipton Mill Inn** at Diptonmill (Northumbria), **Old Castle** in Bridgnorth (Shropshire), **Black Horse** at Clapton-in-Gordano (Somerset), **Blue Boar** in Aldbourne (Wiltshire), **Crown & Trumpet** in Broadway (Worcestershire) and **Maltings** in York (Yorkshire). For its wide choice of very fair value food, the **Old Castle** in Bridgnorth is our **Value Pub of the Year 2019**.

We are incredibly lucky to have such gifted chefs providing wonderful food in so many of our pubs – which makes the task of whittling them down to just ten a difficult task. But this year's Top Ten Dining Pubs are the **Pheasant** in Keyston (Cambridgeshire), **Wellington Arms** in Baughurst (Hampshire), **Stagg** in Titley (Herefordshire), **Assheton Arms** at Downham (Lancashire), **Olive Branch** in Clipsham (Leicestershire), **Martins Arms** at Colston Bassett (Nottinghamshire), **Plough** at Kingham (Oxfordshire), **White Horse** in Sibton (Suffolk), **Red Lion** in East Chisenbury (Wiltshire) and **Griffin** in Felinfach (Wales). Chef proprietor Emily Watkins cooks inspirational food from an exceptional menu – the **Plough** at Kingham is **Dining Pub of the Year 2019**.

The best of the very best

Our new entries come from right across the country and range from little country taverns to smart dining pubs and even to character bars in civilised hotels. Our Top Ten New Pubs are the **Pint Shop** in Cambridge (Cambridgeshire), **Millbrook** at South Pool (Devon), **Masons Arms** in Meysey Hampton (Gloucestershire), **Dog** in Wingham (Kent), **Greyhound** in Letcombe Regis (Oxfordshire), **George** in Norton St Philip (Somerset), **Weeping Willow** in Barrow (Suffolk), **George** in Shipston-on-Stour (Warwickshire), **Wheatsheaf** at Chilton Foliat (Wiltshire) and **Wild Swan** in Minskip (Yorkshire). In a bustling Cotswold village, the **Masons Arms** in Meysey Hampton is our **New Pub of the Year 2019**.

To be among the elite of publicans running some of the best pubs in the country, you have to be a pretty special person. Our Top Ten Licensees are **Philip and Lauren Davison** of the Fox in Peasemore (Berkshire), **Mary Short** of the Barley Mow in Kirk

Ireton (Derbyshire), **John Vereker** of the Bell at Horndon-on-the-Hill (Essex), **Kathryn Horton** of the Ostrich in Newland (Gloucestershire), **Tim Gray** of the Yew Tree in Lower Wield (Hampshire), **Norman and Janet Whittall** of the Three Horseshoes at Little Cowarne (Herefordshire), **Paddy Groves** of Woods in Dulverton (Somerset), **Colin and Teresa Ombler** of the Bell in Welford-on-Avon (Warwickshire), **Rob and Liz Allcock** of the Long Arms in South Wraxall (Wiltshire) and the **Key family** of the Nags Head in Usk (Wales). Their dedication and care for both their pub and their customers make **Colin and Teresa Ombler** of the **Bell** in Welford-on-Avon our **Licensees of the Year 2019**.

A prestigious award indeed, the Pub of the Year pulls together the best pubs in the country. This year they are the **Cock** at Hemingford Grey (Cambridgeshire), **Bell** at Horndon-on-the-Hill (Essex), **Kings Head** in Bledington (Gloucestershire), **Wykeham Arms** in Winchester (Hampshire), **Olive Branch** at Clipsham (Leicestershire), **Rose & Crown** in Snettisham (Norfolk), **Lord Crewe Arms** in Blanchland (Northumbria), **Swan** in Swinbrook (Oxfordshire), **Woods** in Dulverton (Somerset) and **Bell** in Welford-on-Avon (Warwickshire). A first class, pretty pub in a delightful village, the **Cock** at Hemingford Grey is our **Pub of**

TOP TEN PUBS 2019

(in county order)

Cock in Hemingford Grey (Cambridgeshire)

Bell at Horndon-on-the-Hill (Essex)

Kings Head in Bledington (Gloucestershire)

Wykeham Arms in Winchester (Hampshire)

Olive Branch at Clipsham (Leicestershire)

Rose & Crown in Snettisham (Norfolk)

Lord Crewe Arms in Blanchland (Northumbria)

Swan in Swinbrook (Oxfordshire)

Woods in Dulverton (Somerset)

Bell in Welford-on-Avon (Warwickshire)

Ridley Inns

Characterful, family-run pubs with great food

The Cock

Old Uckfield Road (A26), Near Ringmer, BN8 5RX

Food served 7 days a week lunchtime and evening and all day Sunday until 8.30pm

Large Garden and Sun Terrace
Log Fire in Winter
Roasts served all day Sunday
Open all day on Bank Holidays
Vegetarian Menu always available (5 choices)
Real Ales incl. Harveys and other locally sourced micro breweries
Home Cooked Food - something for every taste, diet and budget!

tel: 01273 812040

www.cockpub.co.uk

The Highlands Inn

Eastbourne Road, Ridgewood, Uckfield, TN22 5SP

Food served 7 days a week lunchtime and evening and all day Sunday until 7.30pm

Sports Bar showing all BT and Sky Sports fixtures with special Sports Bar menu
Formal Restaurant area with seating for 120 covers and separate Restaurant Bar Area
Real Ales incl. Harveys and other locally sourced micro breweries
Extensive selection of wines by the glass
Large Sun Trap Garden with al fresco Dining
Live music on Bank Holiday Sundays

tel: 01825 762989

www.highlandsinn.co.uk

www.ridleyinns.co.uk

VIEW FROM THE FRONT

'Make Beer not War'

By **Jaega Wise**

Cask or keg? Keg or cask? With CAMRA voting to be the voice of cask beer rather than all beer, the divide between the two has never seemed greater than at any time during my career. There are some who will drink only cask, and who defend it with an almost religious fervour. Others will touch only keg, and are baffled by the interest in the warm, flat pint held dear by so many. Then there are those who sit on the fence. A little of this and a bit of that. I love both.

Cask beer is a British institution. It's as British as stilton cheese and Melton Mowbray pork pies. Nowhere else in the world is cask beer found in every village, every town, every city across a country. Live beer – brewed, packaged, stillaged and served using methods that are hundreds of years old.

Some beer styles work incredibly well on cask. It's cool in temperature and naturally carbonated for a gentle fizz. The complexity and depth of flavour from live beer is hard to beat. I would challenge anyone to find a better format for 'best bitter', or 'midlands pale ale', than in cask. It just works.

But there is a battle going on in craft breweries all across the country. To cask or not to cask? One of the main arguments is price. Publicans want to pay a low price for cask beer, just as drinkers expect a low price for their cask pint. For many brewers, profit margins for keg, bottle or can beers are higher because these demand a higher price. For many craft breweries, cask is a low-margin product.

The dispensing of cask beer requires space, expertise, time and care. For some, keg is simply a better option. A keg is a pressurised container, where gas goes in and beer comes out. The beer is as the brewer intended, and the quality is generally less variable than with cask beer. Any venue can serve good keg beer. As long as you're cleaning your lines regularly, have the temperature under control and have a technician to call when equipment inevitably breaks down, you'll be fine. Cask, on the other hand, requires careful planning and loving care. As drinkers we all know the bliss of a well-kept pint of cask beer, and the horrors when it goes wrong. As a brewer, I dread a cask of my lovingly brewed beer ending up as vinegar in someone's glass.

But keg beer has its downsides too. It's expensive for the drinker. There is a tolerance towards higher prices in the keg world that doesn't exist in cask beer. This leads to experimental (and expensive) styles. All those hops in that NEIPA (New

England India Pale Ale) don't come cheap! And high prices can make beer quite inaccessible. Beer for the few, not beer for the many. Here, there is a very real risk of class division. One of the things that I love most about beer is its accessibility. You can drink the best beer in the world: the best rated beers on the planet are often only a little more expensive than those from your local brewery, unlike wine or whisky where most people (myself included) will never be able to afford even a sip of the world's best. I hate to think of a day when the best beers in the world are the preserve of the privileged few.

A balance is clearly needed. If you want to sell a heavily hopped DIPA (Double IPA), then selling it in thirds-of-a-pint is advisable. If you're going to brew it, then have something else in your core range that is affordable. And I mean really affordable, not 'affordable housing' level affordable. Something an ordinary person on an ordinary wage could buy.

With so many pros and cons to both cask and keg beer, the superiority of either is frankly nonsense. Why does one have to triumph over the other or be locked in a perpetual battle, like something out of a Marvel movie? Beer is the ultimate social drink, it has the power to build bridges between us. I, for one, am going to continue loving both.

Jaega Wise is head brewer of east London-based microbrewery **Wild Card Brewery**. Combining expertise in engineering, mathematics, logistics and a love of all things beer, she has been leading the brewing team at Wild Card since 2012. Hailing from Nottingham, Jaega holds a chemical engineering degree and has worked in water treatment and international chemical trading. She is a member of the Institute of Chemical Engineers and regularly brews with the ladies of Project Venus, which aims to promote women in brewing through education and collaborative brewing. Jaega is also a television presenter, appearing most recently on Channel 5's *The Wine Show* and Channel 4's *The Ultimate Shopping List*.

Favourite pub Chequers, High Street, London E17.
This is one of the most relaxing pubs I've been to. It's the kind of place where you sit at the bar and make conversation with a stranger. Enjoying a pint of excellent beer, normally from breweries in east London, is a key part of its appeal.

Foraging: The new food trend

By **Mark Price**

It takes a lot to change people's eating habits. When I was in charge of Waitrose I commissioned research that concluded that the average number of products eaten by customers was 250, in spite of the fact that we sold around 20,000 food lines, and launched thousands of new ones each year.

One of our most primal instincts is to eat food that we know to be safe. It's why we tend to put the same items in our shopping basket at the supermarket, use the same pubs and restaurants and pick the same things on the menu. It's also why recommendations, like those given here in *The Good Pub Guide*, are so important to us. I therefore suspect you either have to be naturally courageous or need a good shove to try the new trend to eat foraged food. Globally, the year 2000 marked the point when more people lived in cities than in the countryside. Of course, it happened much sooner than that in the UK. With that move comes a disconnection for many people with where their food comes from and how it is produced.

I remember as a child in the 1960s foraging on family picnics for berries, fruits, flowers, nettles and mushrooms to take home to brew or cook with. I remember from back then, and I still believe it now, that things seem to taste better if you pick them yourself, or consume them locally.

When I moved to Dorset a number of years ago, I decided to reawaken my inner forager. I went on a seashore forage in Studland Bay run by Fore Adventure, and another with the River Cottage cookery school hunting for mushrooms. You can find details of both online, and many more similar courses are

Mark Price's wild mushrooms on toast

1. Grill the wild mushrooms you've collected along with several rashers of streaky bacon.
2. Once the bacon is crispy, remove from the grill and cut into small pieces.
3. Place the mushrooms and bacon on a freshly toasted and buttered slice of granary bread.
4. Crumble cheshire cheese on top.
5. Heat under the grill for a minute.

shooting up across the country. For me, one of the greatest dishes is wild mushrooms on toast – especially if you've picked the mushrooms yourself.

If you'd like to save the time and money involved in taking a course, foraging and then cooking for yourself, there are many talented chefs who are working to give you a taste of your local forest, countryside and seashore. There are also a few pubs that encourage you to explore something new, which is, of course, actually very old.

The **Verulam Arms** in St Albans, Herts, has an excellent reputation. The team based there organise foraging walks where you learn about what to pick, and afterwards they cook what you've gathered. Alternatively, you can opt for the à la carte menu, which changes constantly with the seasons depending on what can be foraged. I'd recommend the local hunted game and also do try the beers brewed on-site. Near the pub is the fine Norman cathedral, and before that was built the town was an important Roman centre – called Verulamium. The food eaten back then would probably have been remarkably similar to the 'fayre' served in the pub today, although I suspect not as well or as lovingly prepared and presented.

If you want to try a taste of what's been naturally harvested from the seashore, there's the **Anchor Inn** in Chideock, near Seatown in Dorset. The head chef is a foraging and wild food fan and it shows, with both land and sea covered on the menu. Nestling by the sea, it's the nicest place to enjoy local cask beers and food on a lovely sunny day. I'm lucky it's close enough to home that I can pop there for lunch. Bliss.

Mark Price grew up with a father who was a grocer turned confectionery wholesaler and a mother who was a frenetic baker. It's therefore no surprise that he spent 17 happy years working at Waitrose; for the last nine years he was managing director of the company. He prided himself on trying every new line that Waitrose sold – over the course of nearly two decades, this considerably expanded both his knowledge of food and his waistline!

Favourite pub Peat Spade, Longstock, Hampshire.
This has been one of my favourite pubs for nearly three decades. It's had a number of reincarnations, from selling fish and chips in the early 1980s that was so large it was referred to as 'whale and chips' to more refined dining these days. Delicious it is too. There's also a lovely secluded garden for a sunny day.

Sherry: A long-awaited comeback?

By **Beanie Geraedts-Espey**

The UK's love affair with sherry is long-standing and deep-rooted – Shakespeare is just one of countless British luminaries who refer to it in their writing with great affection – so why has it fallen from favour in recent years and is it true that a comeback is finally just around the corner?

Beginning at the beginning, there are records dating as far back as the 12th century of shipments of wine to the British Isles from 'Sherish', the Moorish name for the town of Jerez de la Frontera, in the heart of the 'Sherry Triangle'. However, it took almost 100 years before trade began in earnest, when the Spanish king, Alfonso X – having reclaimed the city from the Moors – entered into a bartering agreement with the English king, Henry I, to promote their respective national products: English wool for Spanish sherry wine. Business boomed and the Jerez vineyards became such an important source of wealth for the Spanish kingdom that a royal decree in 1402 prohibited the uprooting of even a single vine.

The export of sherry gave rise to some of the leading characteristics of this style of wine, notably fortification with grape spirit to prevent spoiling during lengthy sea voyages and, later, the unique ageing method known as the Solera system, which ensured a product that was consistent in quality and flavour year after year. Before long, sherry had become so popular in the UK that, as with port, British companies were setting up home in the region to oversee production. In 1796 an importer by the name of Harveys was established, before going on to blend and launch one of the enduring sherry brands in the UK market: Harveys Bristol Cream.

To this day, sweeter styles of sherry, such as the chestnut-hued Harveys Bristol Cream or the pale cream Croft Original, account for 85% of sherry consumption in the UK, though tastes are changing as younger consumers turn away from sweeter drinks in favour of crisper, fresher alternatives – nowhere seen more clearly than in the stratospheric rebirth of gin. Spain is, in fact, Europe's leading market for gin – their elaborate 'gintonic' culture is an inspiration – but Spain has also now succeeded the UK as the largest single market for sherry, and it's on the rise. The reason? Some 85% of sherry consumed in Spain is dry: bone-dry finos and manzanillas.

Fino sherry, like its cousin manzanilla, has all the hallmarks of a contemporary classic here in the UK too. A food-loving, appetite-whetting wine, it pairs brilliantly with traditional bar snacks such as nuts, olives and charcuterie, as well as heartier staples, such as fish and chips and risotto. Naturally low in residual sugars (comparable to champagne), which appeals to the growing body of health-conscious consumers, it is also far lower in alcohol than most consumers think, at 15% ABV.

The UK's changing relationship with alcohol is demonstrated by the increasing number of drinkers looking for low- or no-alcohol options. As a fortified wine that is more robust than most white table wines, sherry, in general, and fino, in particular, can offer up their services to a large number of fun and more elaborate low-alcohol spritz options. Soda, tonic, lemonade and ginger ale all work brilliantly with fino, and look delicious when properly garnished.

XECO Ginger

75ml XECO Fino
75ml Schweppes Ginger Ale
2 dashes of peach bitters

Combine together in a rocks glass, over ice, and garnish with a lemon twist.

XECO Cobbler

50ml XECO Amontillado
25ml lime juice
15ml sugar syrup
Summer fruits and herbs

Muddle fruits and herbs together in the bottom of a highball glass, add the other ingredients and churn with ice. Garnish with lots of fruit and an optional dash of soda.

It's still early days, but the tide is definitely turning as more and more younger consumers wise up to the richness of sherry, its history and its pedigree, but most of all its versatility.

Beanie Geraedts-Espey began her career – and her love affair with sherry – at González Byass in Jerez, Andalucía. After pursuing a career in marketing at L'Oréal and later Chanel, Beanie returned to the wine and spirits industry, taking over from her father as managing director of family business The Last Drop Distillers in 2014. Following the sale of the company, Beanie co-founded **XECO Wines** with two fellow 'fino-fiends'; they sold their first bottle in September 2017.

Favourite pub close to home Fox & Grapes, Wimbledon Common, London SW19.
Favourite pub further afield Bull on Bell Street, Henley-on-Thames, Oxfordshire.

10 Ingredients of a Good Pub

By **Guy** and **Sal Martin**

Here are the 10 things we think make a really decent pub:

1. Kerb appeal… our hanging baskets are to die for!
2. Friendly, welcoming staff.
3. Good food.
4. Good beer.
5. Fab atmosphere and good regulars, including plenty of characters.
6. Free house, so a good choice of beer.
7. Cleanliness… especially the toilets.
8. Village community spirit.
9. Characterful – 'quirky' definitely sums up mine!
10. Plenty of history. We have 166 Squadron memorabilia in ours, the RAF bomber squadron that was based in the village during the war.

Sal Martin is the licensee of the **Marrowbone & Cleaver**, Kirmington, Lincolnshire – so named because half of it was used as a butcher's shop back in the old days. The latest volume of memoirs from her brother, motorcyle racer and TV presenter **Guy Martin**, is published in autumn 2018.

Favourite pub The Marrowbone & Cleaver, of course. It's been our local since we've been old enough to drink, so it's how a pub should be in our eyes: full of good memories with plenty more to come in the future!

What is a Good Pub?

We hear about possible new entries in this *Guide* from our many thousands of correspondents who keep us in touch with pubs they visit – by post, by email at feedback@goodguides.com or via our website, www.thegoodpubguide.co.uk. These might be places they visit regularly (and it's their continued approval that reassures us about keeping a pub as a full entry for another year) or pubs they have discovered on their travels and that perhaps we know nothing about. And it's from these new discoveries that we make up a shortlist, to be considered for possible inclusion as new Main Entries.

What marks a pub out for special attention could be an out of the ordinary choice of drinks – a wide range of real ales (perhaps even brewed by the pub), several hundred whiskies, a remarkable wine list, interesting spirits from small distillers or proper farm ciders and perries. It could be delicious food (often outclassing many restaurants in the area) or even remarkable value meals. Maybe as a place to stay it's pretty special, with lovely bedrooms and obliging service. Or the building itself might be stunning (from golden-stone Georgian houses to part of centuries-old monasteries or extravagant Victorian gin-palaces) or in a stunning setting, amid beautiful countryside or situated by water.

Above all, what makes a good pub is its atmosphere. You should feel at home and genuinely welcomed by the landlord or landlady – it's their influence that can make or break a pub. It follows from this that a lot of ordinary local pubs, perfectly good in their own right, don't earn a place in the *Guide*. What makes them attractive to their regulars could make strangers feel a bit left out.

Another point is that there's not necessarily any link between charm and luxury. A basic unspoilt tavern may be worth travelling miles for, while a too smartly refurbished dining pub may not be worth crossing the street for.

The pubs featured as Main Entries do pay a fee, which helps to cover the *Guide*'s production costs. But no pub can gain an entry simply by paying this fee. Only pubs that have been inspected anonymously, and approved by us, are invited to join.

Using the *Guide*

The Counties

England has been split alphabetically into counties. Each chapter starts by picking out the pubs that are currently doing best in the area, or are specially attractive for one reason or another.

The county boundaries we use are those for the administrative counties (not the old traditional counties, which were changed back in 1976). We have left the new unitary authorities within the counties that they formed part of until their creation in the most recent local government reorganisation. Metropolitan areas have been included in the counties around them – for example, Merseyside in Lancashire. And occasionally we have grouped counties together – for example, Rutland with Leicestershire, and Durham with Northumberland to make Northumbria. If in doubt, check the Contents pages.

Scotland, Wales and London have each been covered in single chapters. Pubs are listed alphabetically (except in London, which is split into Central, East, North, South and West), under the name of the town or village where they are. If the village is so small that you might not find it on a road map, we've listed it under the name of the nearest sizeable village or town. The maps use the same town and village names, and additionally include a few big cities that don't have any listed pubs – for orientation.

We list pubs in their true county, not their postal county. Just once or twice, when the village itself is in one county but the pub is just over the border in the next-door county, we have used the village county, not the pub one.

Star ★

Really outstanding pubs are awarded a star, and in one case two: these are the aristocrats among pubs. The stars do NOT signify extra luxury or specially good food – in fact, some of the pubs that appeal most distinctively and strongly are decidedly basic in terms of food and surroundings. The detailed description of each pub shows what its particular appeal is, and this is what the stars refer to.

Food Award

Pubs where food is really outstanding.

Stay Award

Pubs that are good as places to stay at (obviously, you can't expect the same level of luxury at £60 a head as you'd get for £100 a head). Pubs with bedrooms are marked on the maps as a square.

Wine Award 🍷
Pubs with particularly enjoyable wines by the glass – often a good range.

Beer Award
Pubs where the quality of the beer is quite exceptional, or pubs that keep a particularly interesting range of beers in good condition.

Value Award £
This distinguishes pubs that offer really good value food. In all the award-winning pubs, you will find an interesting choice at around £11.

Recommenders
At the end of each Main Entry we include the names of readers who have recently recommended that pub (unless they've asked us not to use their names).

Important note: the description of the pub and the comments on it are our own and not the recommenders'.

Also Worth a Visit
The Also Worth a Visit section at the end of each county chapter includes brief descriptions of pubs that have been recommended by readers in the year before the *Guide* goes to print and that we feel are worthy of inclusion – many of them, indeed, as good in their way as the featured pubs (these are picked out by a star). We have inspected and approved nearly half of these ourselves. All the others are recommended by our reader-reporters. The descriptions of these other pubs, written by us, usually reflect the experience of several different people.

The pubs in Also Worth a Visit may become featured entries in future editions. So do please help us know which are hot prospects for our inspection programme (and which are not!), by reporting on them. There are report forms at the back of the *Guide*, or you can email us at feedback@goodguides.com, or write to us at

The Good Pub Guide, RTXY–ZCBC–BBAZ, Stream Lane,
Sedlescombe, Battle TN33 0PB.

Locating Pubs
To help readers who use digital mapping systems we include a postcode for every pub. Pubs outside London are given a British Grid four-figure map reference. Where a pub is exceptionally difficult to find, we include a six-figure reference in the directions. The Map number (Main Entries only) refers to the maps at the back of the *Guide*.

Motorway Pubs

If a pub is within four or five miles of a motorway junction we give special directions for finding it from the motorway. The Special Interest Lists at the end of the book include a list of these pubs, motorway by motorway.

Prices and Other Factual Details

The *Guide* went to press during the summer of 2018, after each pub was sent a checking sheet to get up-to-date food, drink and bedroom prices and other factual information. By the summer of 2019 prices are bound to have increased, but if you find a significantly different price please let us know.

Breweries or independent chains to which pubs are 'tied' are named at the beginning of the italic-print rubric after each Main Entry. That generally means the pub has to get most if not all its drinks from that brewery or chain. If the brewery is not an independent one but just part of a combine, we name the combine in brackets. When the pub is tied, we have spelled out whether the landlord is a tenant, has the pub on a lease, or is a manager. Tenants and leaseholders of breweries generally have considerably greater freedom to do things their own way, and in particular are allowed to buy drinks including a beer from sources other than their tied brewery.

Free houses are pubs not tied to a brewery. In theory they can shop around, but in practice many free houses have loans from the big brewers, on terms that bind them to sell those breweries' beers. So don't be too surprised to find that so-called free houses may be stocking a range of beers restricted to those from a single brewery.

Real ale is used by us to mean beer that has been maturing naturally in its cask. We do not count as real ale beer that has been pasteurised or filtered to remove its natural yeasts.

Other drinks. We've also looked out particularly for pubs doing enterprising non-alcoholic drinks (including good tea or coffee), interesting spirits (especially malt whiskies), country wines, freshly squeezed juices and good farm ciders.

Bar food usually refers to what is sold in the bar; we do not describe menus that are restricted to a separate restaurant. If we know that a pub serves sandwiches, we say so – if you don't see them mentioned, assume you can't get them. Food listed is an example of the sort of thing you'd find served in the bar on a normal day.

Children. If we don't mention children at all, assume that they are not welcome. All but one or two pubs allow children in their garden if they have one. 'Children welcome' means the pub has told us that it lets them in with no special restrictions. In other cases, we report exactly what arrangements pubs say they make for children. However, we have to note that in readers' experience some pubs make restrictions that they haven't told us about (children allowed only if eating, for example). If you find this, please let us know, so that we can clarify with the pub concerned for the next edition.

The absence of any reference to children in an Also Worth a Visit entry means we don't know either way. Children's Certificates exist, but in practice children are allowed into some part of most pubs in this *Guide* (there is no legal restriction on the movement of children over 14 in any pub). Children under 16 cannot have alcoholic drinks. Children aged 16 and 17 can drink beer, wine or cider with a meal if it is bought by an adult and they are accompanied by an adult.

Dogs. If Main Entry licensees have told us they allow dogs in their pub or bedrooms, we say so; absence of reference to dogs means dogs are not welcome. If you take a dog into a pub you should have it on a lead. We also mention in the text any pub dogs or cats (or indeed other animals) that we've come across ourselves, or heard about from readers.

Parking. If we know there is a problem with parking, we say so; otherwise assume there is a car park.

Credit cards. We say if a pub does not accept them. We also say if we know that a pub tries to retain customers' credit cards while they are eating. This is a reprehensible practice, and if a pub tries it on you, please tell them that all banks and card companies frown on it – and please let us know the pub's name, so that we can warn readers in future editions.

Telephone numbers are given for all pubs if possible.

Opening hours are for summer; we say if we know of differences in winter, or on particular days of the week. In rural areas, many pubs may open rather later and close earlier than their details show (if you come across this, please let us know – with details). Pubs are allowed to stay open all day if licensed to do so. However, outside cities many pubs in England and Wales close during the afternoon. We'd be grateful to hear of any differences from the hours we quote.

Bedroom prices normally include a full english breakfast (if available), VAT and any automatic service charge. If we give just one price, it is the total price for two people sharing a double or twin-bedded room for one night. Prices before the '/' are for single occupancy, prices after it for double.

Meal times. Bar food is commonly served between the hours of 12-2 and 7-9, at least from Monday to Saturday. We spell out the times if they are significantly different. To be sure of a table it's best to book before you go. Sunday hours vary considerably from pub to pub, so it's advisable to check before you leave.

Disabled access. Deliberately, we do not ask pubs about this, as their answers would not give a reliable picture of how easy access is. Instead, we depend on readers' direct experience. If you are able to give us help about this, we would be particularly grateful for your reports.

Website, iPhone and iPad

You can read and search *The Good Pub Guide* via our website (www.thegoodpubguide.co.uk), which includes every pub in this *Guide*. You can also write reviews and let us know about undiscovered gems. The *Guide* is also available as an app for your iPhone or iPad and as an eBook for your Kindle.

Changes during the year – please tell us

Changes are inevitable during the course of the year. Landlords change, and so do their policies. We hope that you will find everything just as we say, but if not please let us know. You can email us at feedback@goodguides.com or use the Report Forms section at the end of the *Guide*.

Editors' acknowledgements

We could not produce the Guide without the huge help we have from the many thousands of readers who report to us on the pubs they visit, often in great detail. Particular thanks to these greatly valued correspondents: Richard Tilbrook, Chris and Angela Buckell, Tony and Wendy Hobden, R K Phillips, Brian and Anna Marsden, Edward Mirzoeff, Neil and Angela Huxter, Steve Whalley, Ian Herdman, Ann and Colin Hunt, Roger and Donna Huggins, Gerry and Rosemary Dobson, Clive and Fran Dutson, Peter Meister, Simon Collett-Jones, Susan and John Douglas, Michael Butler, Michael and Jenny Back, Tony and Jill Radnor, Tracey and Stephen Groves, Paul Humphreys, Sara Fulton and Roger Baker, John and Sylvia Harrop, Ian Phillips, David Hunt, Mrs Margo Finlay and Jörg Kasprowski, Dr J Barrie Jones, Michael Doswell, David Jackman, John Wooll, Guy Vowles, Theocsbrian, Pete and Sarah, David Lamb, Roy Hoing, Dave Braisted, Giles and Annie Francis, Mike and Mary Carter, John Saville, Christian Mole, Mr and Mrs P R Thomas, John Evans, Katharine Cowherd, B and M Kendall, John Beeken, Revd R P Tickle, GSB, Tina and David Woods-Taylor, M G Hart, Mike and Eleanor Anderson, S G N Bennett, R L Borthwick, Gene and Kitty Rankin, Hugh Roberts, Phil and Jane Hodson, Nigel and Jean Eames, Les and Sandra Brown, Stephen Funnell, Simon King, Dr and Mrs A K Clarke, Richard Kennell, Nick and Meriel Cox, Hunter and Christine Wright, Celia Caulkin, Roy and Gill Payne, John and Eleanor Holdsworth, Janet and Peter Race, Andrew Low, Dr D J & Mrs S C Walker, David and Doreen Beattie, Mike Kavaney, Sheila Topham, Graham and Elizabeth Hargreaves, Simon, Darren and Jane Staniforth, Chris Taylor, Martin Day, Dr Matt Burleigh, Pat and Tony Martin, W K Wood, Jason Caulkin, Brian Glozier, Keith Smith, Margaret and Peter Staples, Michael Sargent, Mrs J Ekins-Daukes, Stuart Doughty, Peter and Anne Hollindale, Dr K Nesbitt, Helene Grygar, Philip J Alderton, Jamie and Sue May, Sue Parry-Davies, Richard Cole, Dr Martin Owton, Ian and Rose Lock, M J Winterton, Derek Stafford, Sally Anne and Peter Goodale, Dave Snowden, Miss B D Picton, S Holder, Kevin Chesson, Graham and Carol Parker, Minda and Stanley Alexander, Denis and Margaret Kilner, Penny and Peter Keevil, John Pritchard, S F Parrinder, Colin and Pat Honey, Lewis Canning, Lesley Broadbent, M and GR, Mrs Edna Jones, Peter Harrison, David and Sally Frost, Adrian Johnson, Mrs Zara Elliott, Dr and Mrs J D Abell, Derek and Sylvia Stephenson, Gail Plews, Mike and Margaret Banks, Nigel and Sue Foster, John and Sheila Lister, David and Judy Robison, Michael and Sheila Hawkins, Ian Tanner, Stephen Funnell, Bob and Margaret Holder, David and Sally Cullen, D W Stokes, Malcolm and Sue Scott, Peter Smith and Judith Brown, David Fowler, DHV, Martinthehills, Alistair Forsyth, Eddie Edwards, Mark Kerrigan, Dr A J and Mrs B A Tompsett, Mrs P Sumner, Robert Lester, Dr Malcolm McDonald, Phillip Rosendale, Rob Nash, Alan Johnson, David and Stella Martin, Richard Tingle, Michael Dudding, Michael Massey, Patric Curwen, Ian Malone, Peter Johnson, Callum Whaley, Colin McLachlan, Christopher and Elise Way, Tony and Caroline Elwood, Franklyn Roberts, Barry Collett, Alan Cowell, Barbara and Phil Bowie, Mr and Mrs D J Nash, Michael Heuck, Jane Durrant, I D Barnett, Judith Ambrose, Tim and Ann Hunt, Nigel Cowdery, David Nash, Revd Michael Vockins, Dr Peter Crawshaw, Helen and Brian Edgeley, Liz Bell, Carol Borthwick, Colin Bateman, Mike and Marion Higgins, Pete Newton, Eric Joseph, John Hunter Wright, Peter L Harrison, D and NF, Martin Hartog, John Walker, David Bird, Colin and Angela Boocock, Phil and Helen Holt, D J and P M Taylor, B and F A Hannam, Mike Buckingham, Tom and Ruth Rees, Frank and Joan Carruthers, Philip Saunders, David Eberlin, Paul and Helen Busby, J A Snell, Richard and Penny Gibbs, Peter Kirkman, Chris Elford, Robert Coleshill, Dr Stuart Jenkins, John and Sharon Hancock, Patricia and Gordon Tucker, M A Borthwick, Marianne and Peter Stevens, V Brogden, Mrs P R Sykes, Nick Borst-Smith, Malcolm and Pauline Pellatt, Christopher Acomb, L and A Haywood, Gerald and Brenda Culliford, Mr and Mrs Ted Hollingworth, Gordon and Margaret Ormondroyd, Malcolm Phillips, Gerry and Pam Pollard, Barrie and Mary Crees, Graham Orpwood, Alun and Jennifer Evans, Professor James Burke, Angela and Steve Heard, David Twitchett, R and M Thomas, Baz Manning, Paul Faraday, Jill Webster.

Many thanks, too, to Fiona Gorringe at The Book Service for her cheerful dedication. And particularly to John Holliday of Trade Wind Technology, who built and looks after our all-important database.

Fiona Stapley

ENGLAND

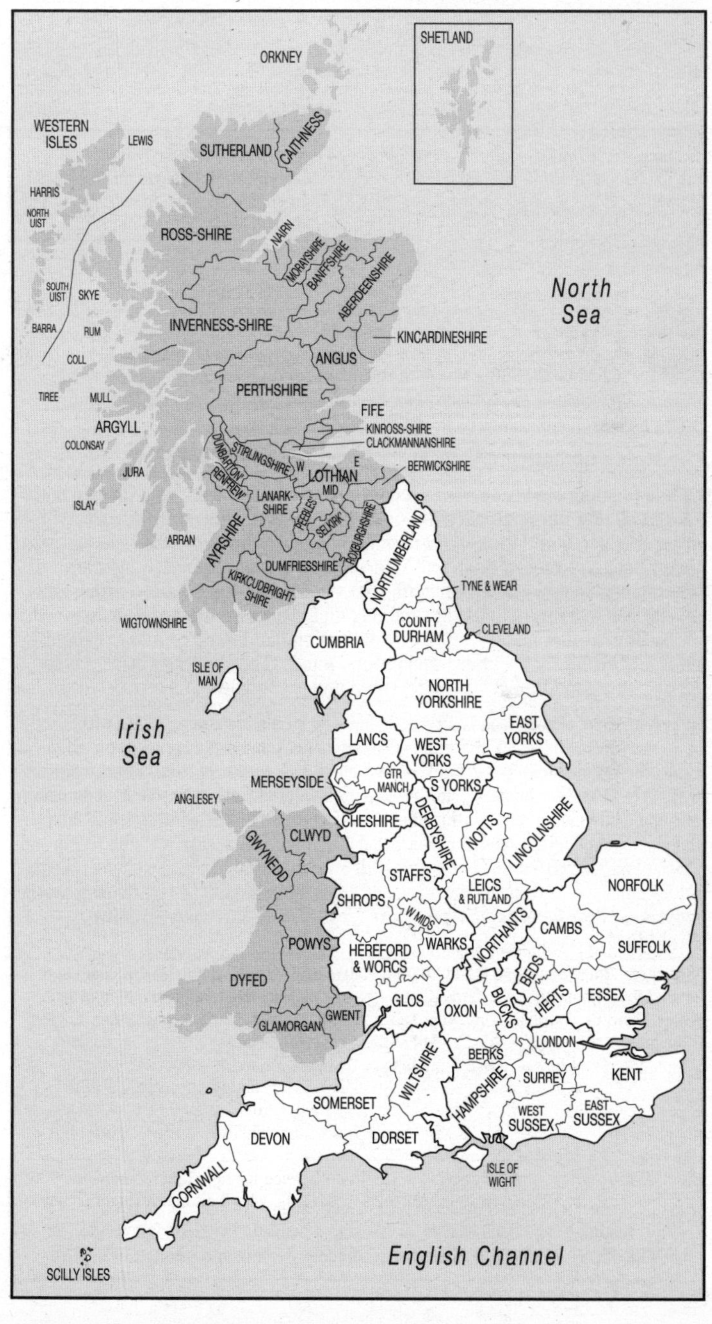
SHETLAND
ORKNEY
WESTERN ISLES
LEWIS
SUTHERLAND
CAITHNESS
HARRIS
NORTH UIST
ROSS-SHIRE
NAIRN
MORAYSHIRE
BANFFSHIRE
ABERDEENSHIRE
North Sea
SOUTH UIST
SKYE
BARRA
RUM
INVERNESS-SHIRE
KINCARDINESHIRE
COLL
ANGUS
TIREE
MULL
PERTHSHIRE
FIFE
KINROSS-SHIRE
CLACKMANNANSHIRE
ARGYLL
COLONSAY
STIRLINGSHIRE
DUNBARTON
W
E
LOTHIAN
MID
BERWICKSHIRE
JURA
RENFREW
LANARK-SHIRE
ISLAY
PEEBLES
SELKIRK
ROXBURGHSHIRE
ARRAN
AYRSHIRE
NORTHUMBERLAND
DUMFRIESSHIRE
KIRKCUDBRIGHT-SHIRE
TYNE & WEAR
WIGTOWNSHIRE
COUNTY DURHAM
CLEVELAND
CUMBRIA
ISLE OF MAN
NORTH YORKSHIRE
EAST YORKS
Irish Sea
LANCS
WEST YORKS
GTR MANCH
MERSEYSIDE
S YORKS
ANGLESEY
DERBYSHIRE
NOTTS
LINCOLNSHIRE
CHESHIRE
CLWYD
GWYNEDD
STAFFS
NORFOLK
LEICS & RUTLAND
SHROPS
W MIDS
CAMBS
POWYS
HEREFORD & WORCS
WARKS
NORTHANTS
SUFFOLK
BEDS
DYFED
BUCKS
HERTS
ESSEX
GLOS
OXON
GWENT
GLAMORGAN
LONDON
BERKS
WILTSHIRE
KENT
SURREY
HAMPSHIRE
SOMERSET
WEST SUSSEX
EAST SUSSEX
DEVON
DORSET
ISLE OF WIGHT
CORNWALL
English Channel
SCILLY ISLES

Bedfordshire

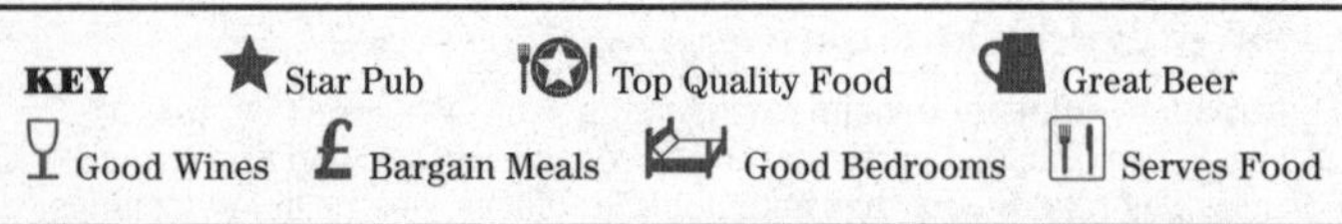

BEDFORD TL0550 Map 5

Park

(01234) 273929 – www.theparkbedford.co.uk

Corner of Kimbolton Road (B660) and Park Avenue, out past Bedford Hospital; MK40 2PA

Civilised and individual oasis – a great asset for the town

This bustling place appeals to a wide group of customers who drop in and out all day. There are all sorts of seating areas to choose from, each with appealing décor and thoughtful touches: a more or less conventional bar with heavy beams, panelled dado and leaded lights in big windows, a light and airy conservatory sitting room with easy chairs well spread on a carpet, and an extensive series of softly lit rambling dining areas, carpeted or flagstoned. Wells Bombardier and a guest from Maldon on handpump and an excellent choice of wines by the glass; background music. The sheltered brick-paved terrace has good timber furniture, some under canopies, and attractive shrubs.

Some sort of good food is served all day: sharing boards; crab cocktail with bloody mary jelly, cucumber and whipped avocado, duck and pistachio terrine with rhubarb chutney, sweet potato and coconut curry with coriander raita, steak in ale pie, corn-fed chicken caesar salad, slow-cooked pork belly with sticky cheek, fondant potato and apple and cider gravy, whiting fillet with king prawn broth, leeks, samphire and linguine, and puddings such as rhubarb and ginger nut cheesecake with lime syrup and sherbert and double chocolate brownie with chocolate sauce; they also offer a two- and three-course weekday lunchtime menu and weekend breakfasts (9-11am). *Benchmark main dish: steak burger with toppings and frites £13.50. Two-course evening meal £21.00.*

Little Gems Country Dining Pubs ~ Manager Matt Jackson ~ Real ale ~ Open 11.30am-11.30pm (midnight Thurs, Fri); 9am-midnight Sat; 9am-10.30pm Sun ~ Bar food 12-3, 6-9.30; 12-10 Fri; 9am-10pm Sat; 9am-8pm Sun ~ Restaurant ~ Children in one bar and restaurant ~ Dogs allowed in bar ~ Wi-fi *Recommended by Belinda Stamp, Adam and Natalie Davis, Sandra and Neil White, Edward Edmonton*

Please tell us if the décor, atmosphere, food or drink at a pub is different from our description. We rely on readers' reports to keep us up to date: feedback@goodguides.com, or (no stamp needed) The Good Pub Guide, FREEPOST RTXY–ZCBC–BBAZ, Stream Lane, Sedlescombe, Battle TN33 0PB.

IRELAND TL1341 Map 5

Black Horse

(01462) 811398 – www.blackhorseireland.com

Off A600 Shefford–Bedford; SG17 5QL

Bedfordshire Dining Pub of the Year

Contemporary décor in old building, first class food, good wine list and lovely garden with attractive terraces; bedrooms

Our readers enjoy their visits to this family-run 17th-c inn very much, with warm praise in particular for the excellent food and fine choice of drinks. The relaxing bar has inglenook fireplaces, beams in low ceilings and timbering, with Adnams Bitter, Fullers London Pride and Sharps Doom Bar on handpump, 28 wines by the glass from a well described list, a dozen malt whiskies, Weston's cider and good coffee from the long green-slate bar counter; staff are courteous and helpful. There are leather armchairs and comfortable wall seats, a mix of elegant wooden and high-backed leather dining chairs around attractive tables on polished oak boards or sandstone flooring, original artwork and fresh flowers; background music. French windows open from the restaurant on to various terraces with individual furnishings and pretty flowering pots and beds. The chalet-style bedrooms (just across a courtyard in a separate building) are comfortable and well equipped; continental breakfasts are included and taken in your room. The Birch at Woburn is under the same ownership.

Imaginative food from seasonal menus includes lunchtime ciabattas and pub classics plus southern-fried pork cheeks with carrot jam and red cabbage slaw, salmon terrine wrapped in smoked salmon with pickled cucumber, bacon and black pudding salad with mozzarella and mustard vinaigrette, tofu and mediterranean vegetable filo parcel with shallot and baby spinach salad, tuna steak with mango salsa, pork tenderloin glazed with honey and chilli with a beetroot and potato rösti and pickled fennel and burnt apple jus, cod loin on sweetcorn and pea risotto with lemon oil, and puddings such as a crème brûlée and a soufflé of the day; they also offer a two- and three-course set menu (not Friday evenings or weekends). *Benchmark main dish: lager-battered fish and triple-cooked chips £13.95. Two-course evening meal £23.00.*

Free house ~ Licensee Darren Campbell ~ Real ale ~ Open 12-3, 6-11; 12-11 Sat; 12-6 Sun ~ Bar food 12-2.30, 6.15-9.45; 12-5 Sun ~ Restaurant ~ Children welcome ~ Wi-fi ~ Bedrooms: /£89.95 *Recommended by Alison and Tony Livesley, Alison and Dan Richardson, M G Hart, Graham and Carol Parker, Beverley and Andy Butcher*

WOBURN SP9433 Map 4

Birch

(01525) 290295 – www.birchwoburn.com

3.5 miles from M1 junction 13; follow Woburn signs via A507 and A4012, right in village then A5130 (Newport Road); MK17 9HX

Well run dining establishment with focus on imaginative food and drinks, plus attentive service

You'll find a good mix of both regulars and visitors in this edge-of-town pub, all keen to enjoy the thoughtful choice of food and drinks. The several individually and elegantly furnished linked rooms have contemporary décor and furnishings. The upper dining area has high-backed leather or wooden dining chairs around tables on stripped and polished floorboards. The lower part occupies a light and airy conservatory with a pitched glazed roof, ceramic floor tiles, light coloured furnishings, original artwork and fresh flowers; background music. The bustling bar is similarly furnished and has a few high bar stools against the sleek, smart counter where they serve Adnams Bitter and Sharps Doom Bar on handpump, 15 good wines by the glass, a dozen malt whiskies and quite a few teas and coffees; background music. There are tables out on a sheltered deck, and in summer the front of the pub has masses of flowering hanging baskets and tubs. This is sister pub to the Black Horse at Ireland.

Interesting food using seasonal, local ingredients includes lunchtime ciabattas, fishcake of the day with crispy onion stack and lemon butter sauce, chicken and thyme croquettes with crispy leeks and lemon hollandaise, spiced chickpea and sweet potato strudel with fennel and chicory salad and pomegranate dressing, duo of lamb (roasted cannon and slow-braised shoulder) with chorizo croquettes, shallot purée, roast cherry tomatoes and red wine jus, hake fillet with pea purée, smoked salmon velouté and saffron creamed potatoes, duck breast with parisienne potatoes and fennel and orange reduction, and puddings such as chocolate and caramel tart with Guinness ice-cream and a soufflé of the day; they also offer a two- and three-course set menu (weekday lunchtimes). *Benchmark main dish: griddled sea bass fillet with mango salsa £15.95. Two-course evening meal £25.00.*

Free house ~ Licensee Mark Campbell ~ Real ale ~ Open 12-3, 6-11; 12-6 Sun ~ Bar food 12-2.30, 6.15-9.45; 12-5 Sun ~ Restaurant ~ Children welcome ~ Wi-fi *Recommended by Lindy Andrews, Daniel King, Jeff Davies, Michael Sargent, Graham and Carol Parker, Sandra and Neil White*

WOOTTON TL0046 Map 4

Legstraps

(01234) 854112 – www.thelegstraps.co.uk

Keeley Lane; MK43 9HR

Bustling village pub with a nice range of food from open kitchen, local ales and wines by the glass

Just a few minutes' drive from Bedford, this is popular for its top quality food, though there are plenty of drinkers too, and you'll get a genuine welcome from the efficient staff. The low-ceilinged bar has an elegant feel with contemporary and comfortable upholstered chairs around all sizes of table, big flagstones, a woodburning stove in a brick fireplace with a leather sofa and box wall seats to either side, and leather-topped stools against the pale planked counter. They keep Sharps Doom Bar and Wychwood Hobgoblin on handpump, good wines by the glass and quite a few gins; background music, TV and board games. The dining rooms have bold paintwork, similar furnishings to the bar, polished bare boards and flower prints on one end wall with butterflies wallpaper on another.

Up-to-date food from a thoughtful menu using daily-fresh fish and local produce includes lunchtime sandwiches, mussels with shallots, tarragon and cider, ham hock terrine with chutney, mushroom and root vegetable bourguignon, thai chicken, quinoa and pinto bean and aberdeen angus burgers, spiced duck breast with dauphinoise potatoes and port sauce, beef casserole with herb dumplings, chicken breast stuffed with pistachio and sage with white wine and pancetta sauce, and puddings such as a cheesecake of the week and caramelised lemon tart; they also offer a weekend brunch (11-4). *Benchmark main dish: catalan fish stew £18.00. Two-course evening meal £21.00.*

Free house ~ Licensee Ian Craig ~ Real ale ~ Open 12-11; 12-8 Sun; closed one week Jan ~ Bar food 12-9; 12-5 Sun ~ Restaurant ~ Children welcome ~ Dogs allowed in bar ~ Wi-fi *Recommended by Chantelle and Tony Redman, Alice Wright, Belinda Stamp*

Also Worth a Visit in Bedfordshire

Besides the fully inspected pubs, you might like to try these pubs that have been recommended to us and described by readers. Do tell us what you think of them: feedback@goodguides.com

AMPTHILL TL0337

Albion (01525) 634857

Dunstable Street; MK45 2JT Drinkers' pub with up to 12 well kept ales including local B&T and Everards, real ciders and a perry, friendly knowledgeable staff, no food apart from lunchtime rolls; monthly folk night and other live music; dogs welcome, paved beer garden, open all day. *(Daniel King)*

AMPTHILL TL0338

Prince of Wales (01525) 840504

Bedford Street (B540 N from central crossroads); MK45 2NB Attractive red-brick town house (perhaps more bar-brasserie than traditional pub); comfortable stylish furnishings and modern prints on mainly cream walls, slightly sunken flagstoned area with log fire leading to part-panelled dining room with dark leather chairs around mix of sturdy tables, also plenty of church candles and big burgundy leather armchairs and sofas at low tables on bare boards, quite a choice of well liked food from lunchtime sandwiches and snacks up, Wells Bombardier and Eagle, several wines by the glass, efficient friendly service; background music; children and dogs (in bar) welcome, picnic-sets on two-level lawn, more on terrace by car park, five bedrooms, open all day (till 5pm Sun). *(Maggie and Matthew Lyons, Susan and Tim Boyle)*

BEDFORD TL0549

Castle (01234) 353295

Newnham Street; MK40 3JR Modernised 19th-c two-bar pub; Courage, Wells, Youngs and guests, generous helpings of enjoyable good value pubby food from baguettes up, some themed evenings, friendly helpful service; Mon open mike night; children welcome, no dogs inside at meal times, courtyard garden, five bedrooms, open all day, no evening food weekends. *(Jane Rigby)*

BEDFORD TL0450

Wellington Arms (01234) 308033

Wellington Street; MK40 2JX Friendly no-frills backstreet corner local, a dozen well kept ales including Adnams and B&T, real cider/perry and good range of continental beers, wooden tables and chairs on bare boards, lots of breweriania; no food or mobile phones, some live music; seats in backyard, open all day from midday and perhaps at its best in the evening. *(S Holder)*

BIDDENHAM TL0249

Three Tuns (01234) 354847

Off A428; MK40 4BD Refurbished part-thatched village dining pub with bar, lounge and restaurant extension, good varied choice of food from traditional favourites up, well kept Greene King ales and plenty of wines by the glass, efficient friendly service; children welcome, spacious garden with picnic-sets, more contemporary furniture on terrace and decked area, open all day. *(Sandra and Neil White)*

BLETSOE TL0157

Falcon (01234) 781222

Rushden Road (A6 N of Bedford); MK44 1QN 17th-c building with comfortable opened-up bar, low beams and joists, seating from cushioned wall/window seats to high-backed settles, woodburner in double-aspect fireplace, snug with sofas and old pews, panelled dining room, popular food from pub standards and burgers up (plenty of gluten-free choices), Charles Wells ales and decent choice of wines by the glass, friendly service; background music, daily papers; children welcome, decked and paved terrace in lovely big garden down to the Great Ouse, open (and food) all day. *(Adam Jones)*

BOLNHURST TL0858

★**Plough** (01234) 376274

Kimbolton Road; MK44 2EX Stylishly converted Tudor building with thriving atmosphere, charming professional staff and top notch cooking from chef-landlord (must book Sat night), Adnams and a couple of interesting guests, over a dozen wines by the glass from good carefully annotated wine list (including organic vintages and plenty of pudding wines), maybe home-made summer lemonade and tomato juice, airy dining extension, log fires; children welcome, dogs in bar, attractive tree-shaded garden with decking overlooking pond, remains of old moat, closed Sun evening, Mon and for two weeks after Christmas. *(Michael Sargent, Peter Andrews, Mike Buckingham)*

BROOM TL1743

Cock (01767) 314411

High Street; from A1 opposite Biggleswade turn-off, follow 'Old Warden 3, Aerodrome 2' signpost, first left signed Broom; SG18 9NA Friendly and unspoilt 19th-c village-green pub; four changing ales tapped from casks by cellar steps off central corridor (no counter), proper cider and enjoyable traditional home-made food such as steak and kidney pudding, also themed nights and meal deals, original latch doors linking one quietly cosy little room to the next (four in all), low ceilings, stripped panelling, farmhouse tables and chairs on old tiles, open fires, games room with bar skittles and darts; children and dogs welcome, picnic-sets on terrace by back lawn, camping field, open all day, no food Sun evening. *(Rosie and John Moore)*

CARDINGTON TL0847

Kings Arms (01234) 838533
The Green; off A603 E of Bedford; MK44 3SP Spacious Mitchells & Butlers village dining pub with refurbished linked areas; extensive choice of enjoyable food from light lunches up including a vegan menu, meal deal Tues and Weds evenings, Sharps Doom Bar and a couple of guests from well stocked bar, helpful friendly service; background music; children and dogs (in bar) welcome, disabled facilities, modern tables and chairs on front terrace, picnic-sets under willows to the side, open (and food) all day. *(Revd R P Tickle)*

CLOPHILL TL0838

Stone Jug (01525) 860526
N on A6 from A507 roundabout, after 200 metres, second turn on right into backstreet; MK45 4BY Secluded old stone-built local (originally three cottages), cosy and welcoming with traditional old-fashioned atmosphere, well kept B&T, Otter, St Austell and a couple of guests, popular good value pubby lunchtime food (not Sun, Mon), various rooms around L-shaped bar, darts in small games extension; background music; children and dogs welcome, roadside picnic-sets and pretty little back terrace, open all day Fri-Sun, closed Mon lunchtime. *(Adam Jones)*

FLITTON TL0535

White Hart (01525) 862022
Village signed off A507; MK45 5EJ Village dining pub under new family management; front bar with dark leather tub chairs around low tables, contemporary leather and chrome seats at pedestal tables, steps down to good-sized, simply furnished back dining area with dark wooden floorboards, a real ale or two such as local B&T, good popular food (booking advised); children and dogs (in bar) welcome, neatly kept garden with teak furniture on tree-shaded terrace, 13th-c church next door, open all weekends (Sun till 8pm), closed Mon. *(John Gibbon, Andrea and Philip Crispin, Mark Morgan, Charles Todd)*

GREAT BARFORD TL1351

Anchor (01234) 870364
High Street; off A421; MK44 3LF Open-plan pub by medieval arched bridge and church; good sensibly priced food from snacks up, Charles Wells ales and guests kept well, friendly staff, river views from main bar, back restaurant where children allowed; background music; picnic-sets in front looking across to Great Ouse, three bedrooms, open (and food) all day weekends. *(Steve Todd)*

HAYNES TL1041

Greyhound (01234) 381239
Northwood End Road; MK45 3QD Refurbished and extended 17th-c country pub, good food including sharing plates, pub favourites and grills (lunchtime carvery only Sun till 4pm), four changing ales and a couple of ciders, friendly staff; quiz every other Thurs; children welcome, garden with play area and boules, open all day, food all day Sat. *(S Holder)*

HENLOW TL1738

Crown (01462) 812433
High Street; SG16 6BS Modernised beamed dining pub with good choice of popular food including children's menu, well kept Caledonian Deuchars IPA, Courage Directors and a guest, lots of wines by the glass, friendly helpful staff, woodburners (one in inglenook); quiet background music, free wi-fi, daily newspapers; terrace and small garden, five well appointed bedrooms in converted stables, open (and food) all day, breakfasts and Sat brunch for non-residents. *(Jane Rigby)*

HENLOW TL1738

★**Engineers Arms** (01462) 812284
A6001 S of Biggleswade; High Street; SG16 6AA Traditional 19th-c village pub with ten well kept changing ales and half a dozen proper ciders/perries, also bottled belgian beers and good choice of wines/gins, helpful knowledgeable staff, snacky food such as rolls; comfortable carpeted front room with old local photographs, bric-a-brac collections and nice open fire, smaller tiled inner area and another carpeted one; beer/cider/country wine festivals, music nights, sports TVs; dogs allowed in bar, plenty of outside seating, open all day (till 1am Fri, Sat). *(Stuart Burns)*

HOUGHTON CONQUEST TL0342

Chequers (01525) 404853
B530 towards Ampthill; MK45 3JP Refurbished roadside country dining pub (Little Gems); enjoyable fairly pubby food from pizzas and burgers up, three real ales and plenty of wines by the glass, friendly helpful service; children welcome, garden with play area, open (and food) all day, weekend brunch from 9am. *(Steve Todd)*

HOUGHTON CONQUEST TL0441

Knife & Cleaver (01234) 930789
Between B530 (old A418) and A6, S of Bedford; MK45 3LA Updated and extended 17th-c village dining pub opposite church; good variety of well liked food from separate bar and restaurant menus, extensive choice

of wines by the glass including champagne, Charles Wells ales and a guest, friendly staff; free wi-fi; children welcome, no dogs inside, nine chalet bedrooms arranged around courtyard and garden, good breakfast, free charging of electric cars for guests, open all day from 7.30am for breakfast. *(Sandra and Neil White)*

HUSBORNE CRAWLEY SP9635

White Horse (01525) 280565
Mill Road, just off A507; MK43 0XE Open-plan village pub arranged around central servery, three real ales and good reasonably priced home-made food (vegetarians and special diets well catered for), friendly attentive staff, beams, wood and quarry-tiled floors, some stripped brickwork and woodburner; live jazz every other Mon, free wi-fi; children and dogs (in bar) welcome, tables outside, lovely hanging baskets, open (and food) all day, till 8pm (6pm) Sun. *(Mike Hickling)*

LITTLE GRANSDEN TL2755

Chequers (01767) 677348
Main Road; SG19 3DW Welcoming village local in same family for over 60 years and keeping its 1950s feel; simple bar with coal fire, darts and framed historical information about the pub, interesting range of own-brewed Son of Sid ales, step down to cosy snug with another fire and bench seats, comfortable back lounge with fish tank, no food apart from excellent fish and chips Fri evening (must book); open all day Fri, Sat. *(Adam and Natalie Davis)*

MAULDEN TL0538

Dog & Badger (01525) 860237
Clophill Road E of village, towards A6/A507 junction; MK45 2AD Attractive neatly kept bow-windowed cottage; enjoyable food (booking advised weekends) including gluten-free choices, sharing boards, pizzas and grills, set lunch Mon-Sat and other deals, friendly service, beams and exposed brickwork, high stools on bare boards by carved wooden counter serving Charles Wells and guests, mix of dining chairs around wooden tables, double-sided fireplace, steps down to two carpeted areas and restaurant; background music, maybe Sun quiz, sports TV; children welcome, no dogs inside, tables and smokers' shelter in front, garden behind with sturdy play area, open all day Fri-Sun. *(Grant Simons)*

MILTON BRYAN SP9730

Red Lion (01525) 210044
Toddington Road, off B528 S of Woburn; MK17 9HS Refurbished red-brick village dining pub; Greene King ales and a guest, several wines by the glass, cocktails and good range of gins, well liked nicely presented food from bar snacks and sharing boards up, Weds steak night, Thurs burgers, good friendly service, central bar with dining areas either side, beams and open fire; children and dogs welcome, pretty views from big garden, open all day Sat, till 7pm Sun. *(Daniel King)*

NORTHILL TL1446

★**Crown** (01767) 627337
Ickwell Road; off B658 W of Biggleswade; SG18 9AA Prettily situated village pub dating from the 17th c; cosy flagstoned bar with copper-topped counter, heavy low beams and bay window seats, woodburner here and in restaurant with modern furniture on light wood floor, steps up to another dining area with exposed brick and high ceiling, good brasserie-style food (not Sun evening) including lunchtime baguettes/panini, Greene King and guests, plenty of wines by the glass, prompt friendly service; soft background music; children welcome, no dogs inside, tables out at front and on sheltered side terrace, more in big back garden with play area, open all day Fri and Sat, till 7pm Sun. *(Steve Todd)*

OAKLEY TL0053

★**Bedford Arms** (01234) 822280
High Street; MK43 7RH Updated 16th-c village inn (sister to the Hare & Hounds in Old Warden); interesting contemporary décor in several interconnected rooms, pubbiest part with wooden furniture on bare boards, flower prints and a woodburner, four cosy, individually decorated rooms lead off, one has farmhouse chairs and a cushioned pew beside a small fireplace, another very much Victorian in style, Wells Eagle and a couple of guests, up to 40 wines by the glass and well regarded food (not Sun evening, Mon), stone-floored dining rooms with tartan-covered seating or wicker chairs, airy conservatory; daily papers, TV, darts and board game; children welcome till 7pm, dogs in bar, pretty garden, open all day (till 8pm Sun). *(Holly and Tim Waite, Elise and Charles Mackinlay, Lucy and Giles Gibbon, Peter Andrews)*

ODELL SP9657

Bell (01234) 910850
Off A6 S of Rushden, via Sharnbrook; High Street; MK43 7AS Popular and welcoming thatched village pub; several comfortable low-beamed rooms around central servery, log fire and inglenook woodburner, good reasonably priced home-made food (not Sun evening, booking

Post Office address codings confusingly give the impression that some pubs are in Bedfordshire, when they're really in Buckinghamshire or Cambridgeshire (which is where we list them).

advised) including Mon steak, Tues pie and Thurs curry nights, well kept Greene King, guest ales and good selection of wines/gins, friendly helpful young staff; children and dogs welcome, big garden backing on to river, handy for Harrold-Odell Country Park, open all day. *(Revd R P Tickle)*

OLD WARDEN TL1343

Hare & Hounds (01767) 627225
Village signposted off A600 S of Bedford and B658 W of Biggleswade; SG18 9HQ Sister dining pub to the Bedford Arms at Oakley; four cosy rooms, log fire in one, inglenook woodburner in another, tweed upholstered chairs at light wood tables on stripped wood, tiled or carpeted floors, prints and old photographs including aircraft in the Shuttleworth Collection (just up the road), popular food using local ingredients from sharing boards up, two Charles Wells ales, a guest beer and several wines by the glass, cocktails, friendly attentive service; background music; children welcome, garden stretching up to pine woods behind, nice thatched village and good local walks, open all day, no food Sun evening. *(Grant Stevens)*

RAVENSDEN TL0754

★**Horse & Jockey** (01234) 772319
Village signed off B660 N of Bedford; pub at Church End, off village road; MK44 2RR Pleasantly modern pub decorated in olive greys and deep reds; leather easy chairs in bar with wall of old local photographs, Adnams Southwold, a couple of guests and over 20 wines by the glass, bright dining room with chunky tables and high-backed seats, good food from shortish but varied menu including weekday set lunch, friendly service; background music, board games, free wi-fi; children welcome, dogs in bar (limited dining space), modern tables and chairs under parasols on sheltered deck, a few picnic-sets on grass, handsome medieval church nearby, open till 6pm Sun, closed Mon. *(Adam Jones)*

RISELEY TL0462

Fox & Hounds (01234) 709714
Off A6 from Sharnbrook/Bletsoe roundabout; High Street, just E of Gold Street; MK44 1DT Modernised village pub dating from the 16th c; low beams, stripped boards and imposing stone fireplace, Wells Bombardier and Eagle, steaks cut to weight and other food including daily specials and takeaway fish and chips, separate dining room; children and dogs (in bar) welcome, seats out in front and in back garden with terrace, open (and food) all day weekends. *(Michael Sargent)*

SALFORD SP9339

Swan (01908) 281008
Not far from M1 junction 13 – left off A5140; MK17 8BD Popular Edwardian country dining pub (Peach group), well liked food from sandwiches and deli boards to dry-aged steaks, also fixed-price lunchtime menu Mon-Sat, ales such as Greene King and Hook Norton, good range of wines, gins and cocktails, friendly accommodating staff, updated interior with drinking area to right of central servery, sofas and leather chairs on wood floor, restaurant to left with modern country cottage feel and window view into kitchen; background music; children welcome, dogs in bar, seats out on decking, open (and food) all day. *(S Holder)*

SHEFFORD TL1439

Brewery Tap (01462) 628448
North Bridge Street; SG17 5DH No-nonsense L-shaped bar notable for its well kept/priced B&T ales brewed nearby and guest beers; bare boards and low ceiling, beer bottle collection and other brewerania, simple lunchtime food, friendly helpful staff; darts and dominoes; children (in family area) and dogs welcome, picnic-sets out behind, open all day. *(Daniel King)*

SHILLINGTON TL1234

Crown (01462) 711667
High Road, S end; SG5 3LP Recently revamped by same owners as the Chequers at Westoning; emphasis on good food in smart comfortable surroundings from sandwiches, sharing plates and well priced weekday set lunch up, also a cosy bar area serving ales such as Otter and Purity along with excellent range of wines, whiskies and gins, large restaurant/conservatory, cheerful enthusiastic staff; children and dogs welcome, garden tables, open all day, food all day weekends. *(Dr Matt Burleigh)*

SHILLINGTON TL1232

Musgrave Arms (01462) 711286
Apsley End Road, towards Pegsdon and Hexton; SG5 3LX Friendly 16th-c low-beamed village local; well kept Greene King ales and enjoyable home-made food (not Sun evening, Mon), log fire; quiz first Weds of month; children and dogs welcome, big back garden with play area, camping, open all day. *(Sophie Ellison)*

SOULDROP SP9861

Bedford Arms (01234) 781384
Village signposted off A6 Rushden–Bedford; High Street; MK44 1EY Village pub dating from the 17th c; cosy low-beamed bar with snug and alcove, Black Sheep, Greene King IPA and three guests, several wines by the glass, tasty well priced pubby food, cottagey dining area has more low beams, broad floorboards and woodburner in central fireplace, also roomy mansard-ceilinged part with big inglenook; table skittles, shove-ha'penny and darts; children and dogs (in bar) welcome, garden tables, open all day Fri-Sun, closed Mon. *(Steve Todd)*

STEPPINGLEY TL0135

French Horn (01525) 720122
Off A507 just N of Flitwick; Church End; MK45 5AU Comfortable dining pub next to church; linked rooms with stippled beams, standing posts and wall timbers, two inglenooks (one with woodburner), eclectic mix of chesterfields, leather armchairs, cushioned antique dining chairs and other new and old furniture on flagstones or bare boards, Greene King IPA and a changing guest, good range of wines by the glass and malt whiskies, well liked freshly made food (all day weekends) served by friendly staff, elegant dining room; background music, TV, free wi-fi; children and dogs (in bar) welcome, seats outside overlooking small green, open all day (till 1am Sat). *(Rosie and John Moore)*

STOTFOLD TL2136

Fox & Duck (01462) 732434
Arlesey Road; SG5 4HE Welcoming roadside pub-restaurant with light modern interior; good variety of enjoyable generously served food from lunchtime ciabattas and bar snacks up, Greene King IPA, a guest ale and over a dozen wines by the glass, friendly accommodating staff, separate coffee lounge; Mon poker night, free wi-fi; children welcome, big enclosed garden with play area, open all day, no evening food Sun, Mon. *(Jane Rigby)*

STUDHAM TL0215

Red Lion (01582) 872530
Church Road; LU6 2QA Character community pub with hands-on landlord and friendly staff; public bar and eating areas filled with pictures and bits and pieces collected over many years, house plants, wood flooring, carpeting and old red and black tiles, open fire, ales such as Adnams, Fullers, Greene King and Timothy Taylors, enjoyable pubby food (not Sun, Mon or Tues evenings); background music, quiz/curry night first Tues of month; children and dogs welcome, green picnic-sets in front under pretty window boxes, more on side grass, play house, open all day. *(Jim Studd)*

SUTTON TL2247

★**John O'Gaunt** (01767) 260377
Off B1040 Biggleswade–Potton; SG19 2NE Friendly bustling village pub just up from 14th-c packhorse bridge and ford: beams and timbering, red-painted or pretty papered walls, local artwork for sale, flagstoned bar with leather seats and sofas around ships' tables, open fire and hood skittles, Adnams and Woodfordes ales, local cider and 12 wines by the glass, good food cooked by landlord-chef (Thurs fish and chips), dining rooms with mix of furniture on bare boards, woodburner; background music, free wi-fi; children and dogs (in bar) welcome, seats in sheltered garden, pétanque, closed Sun evening, Mon (open lunchtime bank holiday Mon, then closed Tues). *(Peter Pilbeam)*

TILSWORTH SP9824

Anchor (01525) 211404
Just off A5 NW of Dunstable; LU7 9PU Comfortably modernised 19th-c red-brick village pub; good food (not Sun evening) from *MasterChef* finalist including tasting menus, Greene King ales, friendly attentive service, dining conservatory; children welcome, picnic-sets in large garden, open all day weekends, closed Mon and Weds lunchtimes and all day Tues. *(Jane Rigby)*

TOTTERNHOE SP9721

Cross Keys (01525) 220434
Off A505 W of A5; Castle Hill Road; LU6 2DA Restored thatched and timbered two-bar pub below remains of a motte and bailey fort; low beams and cosy furnishings, good reasonably priced food (all day Sat, not Sun, Mon evenings) from sandwiches/baguettes up, well kept ales such as Adnams Broadside, Greene King IPA and Sharps Doom Bar, dining room; quiz first Weds of month, TV; children and dogs (in bar) welcome, good views from attractive big garden, plenty of walks nearby, open all day Fri-Sun. *(Ross Balaam)*

TURVEY SP9452

Three Cranes (01234) 881365
Off A428 W of Bedford; MK43 8EP Renovated stone-built village pub on two levels, good food (not Sun evening) from sandwiches and sharing boards to daily specials, up to five well kept ales, friendly staff; children and dogs welcome, secluded tree-shaded garden, five bedrooms, open all day. *(Mrs Margo Finlay, Jörg Kasprowski)*

TURVEY SP9352

★**Three Fyshes** (01234) 881463
A428 NW of Bedford; Bridge Street, W end of village; MK43 8ER Well maintained early 17th-c beamed village pub; big inglenook with woodburner, mix of easy and upright chairs around tables on tiles

'Children welcome' means the pub says it lets children inside without any special restriction. If it allows them in, but to restricted areas such as an eating area or family room, we specify this. Places with separate restaurants often let children use them, and hotels usually let children into public areas such as lounges. Some pubs impose an evening time limit – let us know if you find one earlier than 9pm.

or ancient flagstones, Marstons Pedigree, Sharps Doom Bar and a couple of guests, decent choice of wines, good italian food including selection of small plates, friendly attentive staff, carpeted side restaurant; background music; children and dogs (in bar) welcome, charming garden with decking overlooking bridge and mill on the Great Ouse (note the flood marks), car park further along the street, open all day, no food Sun evening, Mon. *(Adam and Natalie Davis)*

WESTONING SP0332

Chequers (01525) 712967
Park Road (A5120 N of M1 junction 12); MK45 5LA Updated 17th-c thatched village pub under same owners as the Crown at Shillington; enjoyable food including good value set lunch, steak night Weds, seafood evening Thurs, beers such as Adnams, Otter and Purity, good choice of wines by the glass and of other drinks, various teas/coffees, helpful friendly service, low-beamed front bar and good-sized stables restaurant; free wi-fi; children and dogs welcome, courtyard tables, open all day from 9am (10am weekends) for breakfast. *(Daniel King)*

WOBURN SP9433

Bell (01525) 290280
Bedford Street; MK17 9QJ Traditional and comfortable with small beamed bar and longer bare-boards dining lounge up steps, enjoyable good value food, Greene King, guest beers and several gins, friendly helpful service; background music; children and dogs welcome, back terrace, hotel part across busy road, handy for Woburn Abbey/Safari Park, open (and food) all day. *(Jim Studd)*

Berkshire

BRAY SU9079 Map 2

Crown

(01628) 621936 – www.thecrownatbray.co.uk

1.75 miles from M4 junction 9; A308 towards Windsor, then left at Bray signpost on to B3028; High Street; SL6 2AH

Ancient low-beamed pub with 16th-c features in open-plan rooms, highly regarded food, real ales and seats in the large garden

Of course, the main emphasis here is on dining (not surprising given that the owner is Heston Blumenthal) but there's a friendly, welcoming little bar area with high stools around an equally high table, simple tables and chairs beside an open fire and regulars who drop in for a chat and a drink. They keep Courage Best and Directors, a beer named for the pub and a quickly changing guest on handpump and around 18 wines by the glass. The snug rooms have panelling, heavy old beams – some so low you may have to mind your head – plenty of timbers at elbow height where walls have been knocked through, a second log fire and neatly upholstered dining chairs and cushioned settles; board games. The newly designed garden, complete with an outdoor kitchen and bar, is open from May to September.

Rewarding food includes a lunchtime sandwich of the day and ploughman's, king prawn cocktail with rye bread, a trug of seasonal vegetables with bagna càuda, burger with pastrami, smoked cheese, mustard, pickles and fries, roast salmon fillet with crushed potatoes and bois boudran sauce, braised ox cheek with champ mash, turnip tops, mushrooms and caramelised onions, chargrilled hereford sirloin steak with marrowbone sauce, chocolate ganache with Grand Marnier, cocoa nib and blood orange sorbet and sticky toffee pudding with vanilla ice-cream; they also offer a Sunday supper club between September and April. *Benchmark main dish: confit duck leg with braised red cabbage and blackberry sauce £20.90. Two-course evening meal £28.00.*

Star Pubs & Bars ~ Tenant Matt Larcombe ~ Real ale ~ Open 11.30-11; 12-10 Sun ~ Bar food 12-2.15 (2.45 Sat), 6-9.15 (9.45 Fri, Sat); 12-5.45 Sun ~ Children welcome ~ Dogs allowed in bar ~ Wi-fi *Recommended by Dr and Mrs A K Clarke, Barry and Daphne Gregson, Susan Eccleston, John and Claire Masters, Simon Collett-Jones, Audrey and Andrew Nichols*

Please keep sending us reports. We rely on readers for news of new discoveries, and particularly for news of changes – however slight – at the fully described pubs: feedback@goodguides.com, or (no stamp needed) The Good Pub Guide, FREEPOST RTXY–ZCBC–BBAZ, Stream Lane, Sedlescombe, Battle TN33 0PB.

CHIEVELEY SU4574 Map 2

Crab & Boar

(01635) 247550 – www.crabandboar.com

North Heath, W of village; RG20 8UE

Stylish inn with a welcoming atmosphere, good drinks choice, imaginative food and charming staff; seats outside; well equipped bedrooms

This is a nice place to stay in comfortable, well equipped bedrooms which have fine country views and private courtyards; five even have their own hot tub. The civilised interconnecting bars and dining rooms are smartly furnished and one end of the L-shaped bar is light and airy with tall green leather chairs lining a high shelf, a couple of unusual, equally high tables with garden planter bases, a contemporary chandelier and stools lining the shabby-chic counter. Here they keep West Berkshire Good Old Boy and Mr Chubbs and Wells Bombardier on handpump, 12 good wines by the glass and a dozen gins and a dozen malt whiskies. The other end of this bar is cosier, with leather armchairs and sofas facing one another across a low table in front of a woodburning stove in a large fireplace; background music and TV. The first room leading off has beams and timbering, tartan-upholstered stall seating and leather banquettes, and framed race tickets on the walls. Dining rooms, linked by timbering and steps, are decorated with old fishing reels, a large boar's head, photos and prints, with an eclectic mix of attractive chairs and tables on bare floorboards or carpet; an end room is just right for a private party. In the garden are elegant metal or teak tables and chairs on gravel and grass; there's also a fountain and an outside bar.

As well as breakfasts (7.30-9.30am; 8-10am weekends), the impressive modern food includes sandwiches and pub favourites plus citrus-cured trout with pickled fennel, caviar and yoghurt, duck terrine with foie gras and pear and red onion chutney, spinach lasagne, salt-aged pork cutlet with red sauerkraut, smoked apple purée and wholegrain mustard, sole meunière with brown shrimps, roasted brussels sprouts and brown butter foam, beer brine roasted chicken with creamy barley, nduja sausage and curly kale, and puddings such as chocolate brownie with caramelised banana and a choice of ice-cream and warm honey cake with lemon cream, baked apple and camomile ice-cream; they also offer a two- and three-course set weekday lunch. *Benchmark main dish: burger in a potato and onion bun with toppings and fries £16.00. Two-course evening meal £34.00.*

Free house ~ Licensee Roger Swain ~ Real ale ~ Open 7.30am-11pm; 8am-11pm (10.30pm Sun) Sat ~ Bar food 12-2, 6.30-9.30; 12-3, 6.30-8.30 Sun ~ Restaurant ~ Children welcome ~ Dogs allowed in bar and bedrooms ~ Wi-fi ~ Bedrooms: /£110 *Recommended by R K Phillips, Brian and Susan Wylie, Alison and Dan Richardson, Mr and Mrs D J Nash, Cecily and Steven Evans, Belinda and Neil Garth*

CURRIDGE SU4871 Map 2

Bunk

(01635) 200400 – www.thebunkinn.co.uk

Handy for M4 junction 13, off A34 S; RG18 9DS

Bustling pub with attractive bar and dining rooms, good modern food and seats outside; bedrooms

An extended pub on the edge of a village and a well thought-of all-rounder. The atmosphere is bustling and friendly and there's a good mix of customers. The bar has chunky wooden armchairs and a sofa facing one another before an open fire, leather-seated wall banquettes, and farmhouse chairs and stools around pine tables on wide boards. More stools line the counter where they keep Upham Punter and Tipster and a couple of guest ales and good wines by the glass; background music and board games. The candlelit dining room has painted, wooden and high-backed leather chairs around a mix of tables, rustic stable door partitioning, a pale green dado with mirrors and artwork on brick walls above, fresh flowers and little plants in pots; there's also a spacious dining conservatory. Outside, terraces (heated in chilly weather) have tables and chairs and picnic-sets under parasols. Bedrooms are well equipped and comfortable. The pub is well placed for Newbury Racecourse.

Food using local, seasonal produce is interesting and includes lunchtime sandwiches and pub classics plus sharing boards, crispy duck pancakes with sticky rhubarb and chilli, cucumber and spring onion, king prawns in garlic butter with toasted sourdough, stir-fried vegetables with mushroom broth and noodles (you can add trout, chicken or beef), maple syrup baby back rib chops with coleslaw, smoked haddock rarebit with basil mash and tomato salad, soft herb-coated lamb rump with wholegrain mustard crushed potatoes and rosemary sauce and puddings. *Benchmark main dish: beer-battered fish and chips £13.95. Two-course evening meal £26.00.*

Upham ~ Manager Sophie Lee ~ Real ale ~ Open 7am-midnight; 7.30am-midnight Sat; 8am-11pm Sun; may open at 9am if not busy in winter ~ Bar food 12-2.30 (3 Sat), 6-9.30; 12-8 ~ Restaurant ~ Well behaved children welcome ~ Dogs allowed in bar and bedrooms ~ Wi-fi ~ Occasional live music; quiz monthly Sun evening ~ Bedrooms: £109/£119 *Recommended by William Pace, Caroline and Oliver Sterling, James and Becky Plath, Cliff and Monica Swan, Anna and Mark Evans*

HARE HATCH SU8077 Map 2

Horse & Groom

(0118) 940 3136 – www.brunningandprice.co.uk/horseandgroom

A4 Bath Road W of Maidenhead; RG10 9SB

Spreading pub with attractively furnished, timbered rooms, enjoyable food and seats outside

A former coaching inn on what was the main road to Bath, this place has been offering sustenance to customers for 300 years. There are plenty of signs of great age in the interconnected rooms and much of interest too: beams and timbering, a pleasing variety of well spread individual tables and chairs on mahogany-stained boards, oriental rugs and some carpet to soften the acoustics, and open fires in attractive tiled fireplaces. Also, a profusion of mainly old or antique prints and mirrors, book-lined shelves, house plants and daily papers. Well trained, courteous staff serve a splendid range of drinks including a good changing range of 15 wines by the glass, Brakspears Bitter and Oxford Gold, Jennings Cumberland and Wychwood Dirty Tackle and Hobgoblin on handpump, two farm ciders, 75 gins and 60 malt whiskies; background music and board games. A sheltered back garden has picnic-sets while the front terrace has teak tables and chairs under parasols.

An interesting choice of food includes sandwiches, red pepper and goats cheese pannacotta with pickled vegetables, moroccan-style briouats (pastry parcels) filled with chicken, manchego cheese and chorizo with an orange salad, broccoli, leek and blue cheese quiche with crème fraîche potato salad, crispy beef in sweet chilli dressing on oriental salad leaves with shredded mouli radish and cashew nuts, chicken, ham and leek pie, king prawn, sea bass and monkfish laksa with rice noodles, peanuts and pak choi, and puddings such as apple and mixed berry crumble with vanilla custard and triple chocolate brownie with chocolate sauce. *Benchmark main dish: braised lamb shoulder with dauphinoise potatoes and rosemary gravy £18.95. Two-course evening meal £21.00.*

Brunning & Price ~ Manager John Nicholson ~ Real ale ~ Open 11.30-11 ~ Bar food 12-9.30 (10 Fri, Sat) ~ Children welcome ~ Dogs allowed in bar ~ Wi-fi *Recommended by DHV, George Sanderson, Max Simons, Sally and David Champion, John and Mary Warner*

HURLEY SU8382 Map 2

Hurley House

(01628) 568500 – www.hurleyhouse.co.uk

A4130 SE, just off A404; SL6 5LH

Elegant, up-to-date hotel with friendly bar, smart dining rooms, local ales and fine wines, excellent food and seats in pretty gardens; bedrooms

A rather smart boutique hotel has risen from what was once the Red Lion pub. It's been done with great style, and while, of course, the main emphasis is on the ten very comfortable, well equipped bedrooms and highly regarded restaurant, at its heart is a proper bar that our readers enjoy. Here, you're genuinely welcomed for just a drink and a chat and the atmosphere is gently upmarket but informal. It's a big open-plan room with different seating areas: chairs against the counter where friendly staff serve Rebellion IPA and West Berkshire Good Old Boy on handpump and good wines by the glass, green leather chesterfields grouped in the centre, armchairs (leather or wooden) in front of a woodburning stove, and cushioned wall seats and dining chairs around wooden tables down one wall. There are slate and granite floor tiles, large chrome storm lanterns with lit church candles, grey paintwork and contemporary lighting and touches of oak; background music and board games. Dining rooms have a clubby feel with green button-back leather banquettes and mustard-yellow dining chairs, candles on tables and in more lanterns and occasional paintings of vegetables. In the carefully landscaped gardens you'll find plenty of seats and tables set out on gravel underneath huge parasols.

Creative food uses premium local produce and includes bar snacks and a two- and three-course set lunch plus scorched mackerel with pink fir potato and cucumber, duck liver parfait with red onion chutney, porcini mushroom tortellini with butter roasted crosnes (also known as chinese or japanese artichokes), butternut squash, turnip leaves and cheese, lamb rump with japanese turnip, shepherd's pie and mint, stone bass with cockles, sea lettuce and celeriac, and puddings such as milk chocolate and banana double-decker with banana ice-cream and jamaican ginger sponge with caramel mousse and marmalade ice-cream; they also offer breakfasts (7-11.30am; from 8am weekends) and afternoon tea. *Benchmark main dish: tapas dishes £13.50. Two-course evening meal £30.00.*

Free house ~ Licensee Nathan Unwin ~ Real ale ~ Open 12-11; 12-6 Sun; closed Sun evening ~ Bar food 12-2.30, 6.30-9.30; 12.30-4 ~ Restaurant ~ Children welcome ~ Dogs allowed in bar ~ Wi-fi ~ Live music Fri evening from 7.30pm ~ Bedrooms: /£180 *Recommended by Susan and John Douglas, Daphne and Robert Staples, Geoff and Ann Marston, Brian and Sally Wakeham*

INKPEN SU3764 Map 2

Crown & Garter

(01488) 668325 – www.crownandgarter.co.uk

Inkpen Common: Inkpen signposted with Kintbury off A4; in Kintbury turn left into Inkpen Road, then keep on into Inkpen Common; RG17 9QR

Carefully run country pub with modern touches blending with original features, enjoyable food and seats outside; bedrooms

Dating from the 17th c and surprisingly substantial for somewhere so remote-feeling, this was once used by James II on his way to visit his nearby mistress. You'll find a friendly welcome from the hands-on landlady and the spreading bar area has wooden stools against the counter where they serve Ramsbury Gold, West Berkshire Good Old Boy and a guest on handpump, ten wines by the glass and a dozen malt whiskies; leading off here is a snug area with leather armchairs by an open fire in a raised brick fireplace. Throughout there's an assortment of upholstered dining chairs grouped around simple tables on pale floorboards, cushioned wall seating and armchairs, old suitcases, mirrors and modern artwork on contemporary paintwork and wallpaper that depicts bookcases (in the smart restaurant); background music. The front terrace has seats and tables under parasols. The comfortable bedrooms are in a separate single-storey L-shaped building around an attractive garden. There's also a separate coffee shop (which becomes a private dining space in the evening). Disabled access.

Highly regarded food includes lunchtime ciabattas and pub staples plus duck and game terrine with orange purée and carrot chutney, fresh tuna tartare, vegetable curry with home-made chutney, sea bass with cavolo nero and lemon and caper sauce, venison pave with baby turnips, cauliflower purée and wild mushroom sauce, slow-cooked pork belly with fennel potato rösti, savoy cabbage, apple purée and red wine jus, and puddings such as chocolate fondant with walnut ice-cream and banana parfait with crumble, toffee sauce and lime cream chantilly. *Benchmark main dish: beer-battered fish and chips £14.50. Two-course evening meal £25.00.*

Honesty Group ~ Licensee Romilla Arber ~ Real ale ~ Open 11-11 ~ Bar food 12-3, 6.30-9 ~ Restaurant ~ Children welcome ~ Dogs allowed in bar ~ Wi-fi ~ Bedrooms: £105/£130
Recommended by Angela and Steve Heard, Joe and Belinda Smart, David and Judy Robison, Jim King

INKPEN SU3564 Map 2

Swan

(01488) 668326 – www.theswaninn-organics.co.uk
Lower Inkpen; coming from A338 in Hungerford, take Park Street (first left after railway bridge); RG17 9DX

Country pub with rambling rooms, traditional décor, real ales and plenty of seats outside; comfortable bedrooms

This much extended pub is owned by local, organic beef farmers, so not only is the meat used in their cooking top quality, but you can buy their produce and ready-made meals and groceries in the interesting farm shop next door. The rambling beamed rooms have homely corners, traditional pubby furniture, eclectic bric-a-brac and two log fires, and there's a flagstoned games area plus a cosy restaurant. Butts Jester and Traditional and a local guest ale on handpump, several wines by the glass and home-made sloe gin; cribbage, shut the box and board games. The bedrooms are quiet and comfortable. There are picnic-sets arranged on tiered front terraces overlooking a footpath.

Using their own produce, the popular food includes sandwiches, a trio of smoked fish with horseradish cream, chicken liver pâté, aubergine, tomato and mozzarella layers with parmesan, home-made sausages with mash and gravy, thai green chicken curry, beef stroganoff, organic steaks, and puddings such as mixed fruit crumble and chocolate fudge cake. *Benchmark main dish: organic burgers with toppings and chips £10.95. Two-course evening meal £20.00.*

Free house ~ Licensees Mary and Bernard Harris ~ Real ale ~ Open 12-2.30, 7-11; 12-11 Sat; 12-4 Sun; closed Mon, Tues, evening Sun; all January ~ Bar food 12-2 (3 weekends), 7-9 ~

Restaurant ~ Children welcome ~ Wi-fi ~ Bedrooms: £80/£85 *Recommended by D J and P M Taylor, Jamie Green, Amy Ledbetter, Mike Swan, Charles Todd, Jim and Sue James*

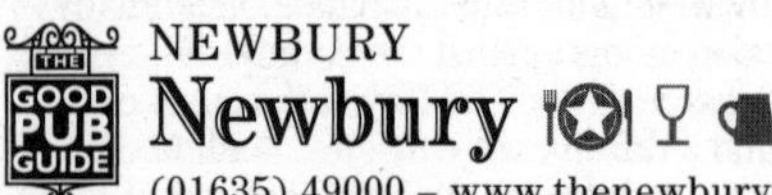

NEWBURY SU4767 Map 2

Newbury

(01635) 49000 – www.thenewburypub.co.uk

Bartholomew Street; RG14 5HB

Lively pub with a thoughtful choice of drinks, good food and plenty of bar and dining space

There are lots of different seating areas here to suit whichever mood you're in, from a rooftop terrace with a cocktail bar, a pizza oven and an electric folding canopy roof to a downstairs courtyard with seats and tables. The bar (renovated in 2018 to make it lighter and more inviting) has an assortment of wooden dining chairs around sturdy farmhouse and other solid tables on bare boards, comfortable leather sofas, big paintings, church candles and an open fire. They keep a fantastic choice of drinks: a beer named for them (from Greene King), Timothy Taylors Landlord and Upham Punter, Silver Blaze and Tipster on handpump, 20 malt whiskies, 28 wines (including champagne and sparkling) by the glass, an extensive cocktail list (using their own-made gin) and a fine range of coffees and teas (including tea grown in Cornwall). The light and airy dining rooms have wall benches and church chairs around more rustic tables on more bare boards, local artwork and an open kitchen; background music and board games.

From a diverse menu and sourcing their produce with great care, the pleasing food includes sandwiches and pub classics plus duck parcel with chilli, apple glaze and crispy capers, corn-fed chicken terrine with shiitake mushrooms, truffle, spring onions and chutney, ricotta gnocchi with courgette carpaccio, toasted pine nuts, lemon and rocket pesto, venison loin with rösti potato, confit swede and chocolate and blackberry jus, cod with shaved fennel, pickled beets, radish, satsuma, dill and lemon gel, and puddings such as chocolate nemesis with lime ice-cream and gin and tonic trifle; they also offer an express two- and three-course set lunch and a Saturday brunch (10am-12). *Benchmark main dish: pork belly with spring onion mash, chorizo quail egg, bacon and black pudding £16.50. Two-course evening meal £22.50.*

Greene King ~ Lease Peter Lumber ~ Real ale ~ Open 12-11.30; 10am-2am Sat; 12-10.30 Sun ~ Bar food 12-3, 5-9; 10-9 weekends ~ Restaurant ~ Children welcome ~ Dogs allowed in bar ~ Wi-fi ~ Open mike Thurs evening, plus Fri, Sat in summer *Recommended by Charles Welch, Diane Abbott, Geoff and Ann Marston, Katherine Matthews, Millie and Peter Downing*

PEASEMORE SU4577 Map 2

Fox

(01635) 248480 – www.foxatpeasemore.co.uk

4 miles from M4 junction 13, via Chieveley: keep on through Chieveley to Peasemore, turning left into Hillgreen Lane at small sign to Fox Inn; village also signposted from B4494 Newbury–Wantage; RG20 7JN

Friendly downland pub on top form under its expert licensees

For regular customers this is a favourite but we get plenty of enthusiastic reports from first-timers too. What will strike you immediately is the genuinely warm and personal welcome you'll get from the first-class, professional licensees; they know their pub and they care about their customers. The long bare-boards bar has strategically placed high-backed settles (comfort guaranteed by plenty of colourful cushions), a warm woodburning stove in a stripped-brick chimney breast and, for real sybarites, two luxuriously carpeted end areas, one with velour tub armchairs. Friendly, efficient, black-clad staff serve West Berkshire Good Old Boy and a couple of changing guests on handpump, 16 wines by the glass and summer farm cider; background music. This is downland horse-training country, and picnic-table sets at the front look out to the rolling fields beyond the quiet country lane – on a clear day you can see as far as the Hampshire border hills some 20 miles south. There are more picnic-sets on a smallish sheltered back terrace. There are good surrounding walks.

Reliably good food includes open sandwiches, crispy fried brie with mixed berry compote, ham hock and caper terrine with piccalilli, a choice of omelettes, mixed bean and vegetable suet pudding with roast tomato sauce, local sausages with onion gravy and mash, rack of barbecue ribs with coleslaw, chicken breast with wild mushroom and tarragon risotto and truffle oil, skate wing with samphire and caper brown butter, and puddings such as lemon and raspberry cheesecake and caramelised apple tarte tatin. *Benchmark main dish: steak and kidney pie £12.95. Two-course evening meal £18.95.*

Free house ~ Licensees Philip and Lauren Davison ~ Real ale ~ Open 12-2.30, 6-11; 12-11 Sat; 12-6 Sun; closed Mon, Tues ~ Bar food 12-2, 6-9; 12-3, 5.30-9 Sat; 12-4 Sun ~ Children welcome ~ Dogs allowed in bar ~ Wi-fi *Recommended by David and Judy Robison, Nigel and Sue Foster, Sally and David Champion, Maggie and Matthew Lyons, Tracey and Stephen Groves, Ian Herdman*

RUSCOMBE SU7976 Map 2

Royal Oak

(0118) 934 5190 – www.burattas.co.uk

Ruscombe Lane (B3024 just E of Twyford); RG10 9JN

Wide choice of food at welcoming pub (known locally as Buratta's) with interesting furnishings and paintings and local beer and wine

Although the carpeted bars here are open-plan, they're carefully laid out so each area is fairly snug but still feels part of the action. A good variety of furniture runs from dark oak tables to big chunky pine ones with mixed seating to match; the two sofas facing each other are popular. Contrasting with the old exposed ceiling joists, mostly unframed modern paintings and prints decorate the walls, which are painted in grey and white. Binghams (the brewery is just across the road) Twyford Tipple, Fullers Front Row and London Pride and Woodfordes Nice Try on handpump, 14 wines by the glass (they stock wines from the village's Stanlake Park vineyard), 14 malt whiskies, six gins and attentive service. Picnic-sets are ranged around a venerable central hawthorn in the garden behind (where there are ducks and chickens); summer barbecues. The pub is on the Henley Arts Trail. Do visit the friendly landlady's antiques and collectables shop, which is open during pub hours.

A changing choice of food includes sandwiches and pub staples, sharing platters, tempura prawns with sweet chilli dip, gin-infused chicken liver parfait with orange and cranberry dressing, thai vegetables with noodles, lamb kidneys with bacon, mushroom and red wine sauce, sea bass with chive cream sauce and basil and balsamic tomatoes, venison steak with redcurrant and rosemary sauce and puddings. *Benchmark main dish: black pudding tower with bacon and peppercorn sauce £14.00. Two-course evening meal £22.00.*

Enterprise ~ Lease Jenny and Stefano Buratta ~ Real ale ~ Open 12-3, 6-11; 12-4 Sun; closed Sun and Mon evenings ~ Bar food 12-2.30, 7-9.30; 12-3.30 Sun ~ Restaurant ~ Children welcome ~ Dogs welcome ~ Wi-fi *Recommended by Paul Humphreys, Barry and Daphne Gregson, Andrew and Michele Revell, Stuart and Natalie Granville, Mandy and Gary Redstone*

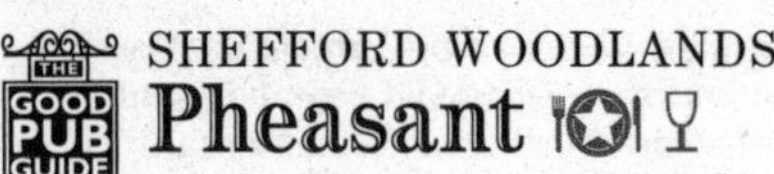

SHEFFORD WOODLANDS SU3673 Map 2

Pheasant

(01488) 648284 – www.thepheasant-inn.co.uk

Under 0.5 miles from M4 junction 14 – A338 towards Wantage, first left on B4000; RG17 7AA

Bustling bars, a separate dining room, highly thought-of food and beer and seats outside; bedrooms

A perfect escape from the nearby M4, this is just right for a drink or a meal. The various interconnecting bar rooms have been carefully refurbished with contemporary paintwork, lots of antiques and plenty of horse-related prints, photographs and paintings; there are elegant wooden dining chairs and settles around all sorts of tables, big mirrors here and there, leather banquettes and stools, and a warm fire in a little brick fireplace. One snug little room has attractively upholstered armchairs and sofas. A smashing range of drinks includes 36 gins, 15 vodkas, ten rums, 26 malt whiskies, cocktails and interesting liqueurs – plus a beer named for the pub (from Banks's), Marstons Pedigree, Ramsbury Gold and Ringwood Best on handpump and quite a few good wines by the glass from a decent list. There's also a separate dining room; background music. Seats in the garden have attractive views. The 11 individually decorated and well equipped modern bedrooms are in a separate extension, and breakfasts are tasty.

Popular food from a thoughtful menu includes sandwiches, confit duck rillettes with caper and gherkin salad, beetroot-cured salmon with horseradish crème fraîche and bloody mary sorbet, spiced roast cauliflower with red lentils, pickled carrot and coconut sauce, beer-battered fish and chips, pork belly with bubble and squeak, black pudding and apple syrup and red wine sauce, three-bone rack of lamb with turnip and potato dauphinoise and rosemary jus, and puddings such as iced banana parfait with toffee sauce, honey-roast granola, caramelised bananas and a white chocolate crisp and chocolate and hazelnut torte with chocolate crumble, raspberry coulis and hazelnut ice-cream. ***Benchmark main dish: roast cod with bacon and mussel broth, charred leeks and kale £18.00. Two-course evening meal £21.00.***

Free house ~ Licensee Jack Greenall ~ Real ale ~ Open 11-11 (10.30 Sun) ~ Bar food 12-3, 6-9.30; 12-5, 6-9 Sun ~ Children welcome ~ Dogs allowed in bar and bedrooms ~ Wi-fi ~ Bedrooms: /£110 *Recommended by Nick Higgins, Patti and James Davidson, William and Sophia Renton, Peter L Harrison, Mr and Mrs P R Thomas, Dr and Mrs A K Clarke*

SONNING SU7575 Map 2

Bull

(0118) 969 3901 – www.bullinnsonning.co.uk

Off B478, by church; village signed off A4 E of Reading; RG4 6UP

Pretty timbered inn in attractive spot, plenty of character in old-fashioned bars, friendly staff and good food; bedrooms

As ever, reports from our readers are very positive. A lovely old black and white timbered inn, it looks its finest in early summer when the wisteria is flowering and the hanging baskets are at their best. Inside, there's plenty of character: two old-fashioned bar rooms have low ceilings and heavy beams, cosy alcoves, leather armchairs and sofas, cushioned antique settles and low wooden chairs on bare boards, and open fireplaces. Fullers HSB and London Pride and several guest ales on handpump served by helpful staff, 16 good wines by the glass, cocktails and a farm cider. The dining room has a mix of wooden chairs and tables, rugs on parquet flooring and shelves of books; TV. The refurbished bedrooms are lovely but they do get booked up well in advance. If you bear left through the ivy-clad churchyard opposite, then turn left along the bank of the river, you come to a very pretty lock. The Thames Valley Park is close by.

From seasonal menus the fine food includes smoked salmon with horseradish cream, buffalo mozzarella with heritage beetroot, orange and pumpkin seed salad, beer-battered haddock and chips (they also offer takeaways), duck with braised baby gem, bacon, peas, pressed potato and jus, roast hake with brown crab cannelloni with sweet potatoes and avocado salsa, and puddings such as balsamic roast plums with vanilla and coconut yoghurt and passion-fruit brûlée; they also offer themed food evenings. *Benchmark main dish: steak in ale pie £15.00. Two-course evening meal £22.00.*

Fullers ~ Managers Sian and Jason Smith ~ Real ale ~ Open 10am-11pm; 12-10.30 Sun ~ Bar food 12-9.30 (8.30 Sun); 12-3, 6-9 in winter ~ Restaurant ~ Children welcome ~ Dogs allowed in bar ~ Wi-fi ~ Live local artist and tribute evenings ~ Bedrooms: /£119
Recommended by Frank and Marcia Pelling, Penny and David Shepherd, Susan and John Douglas, Gordon and Patricia Gorringe, Barbara and Phil Bowie

SWALLOWFIELD SU7364 Map 2

George & Dragon

(0118) 988 4432 – www.georgeanddragonswallowfield.co.uk
Church Road, towards Farley Hill; RG7 1TJ

Busy country pub with enjoyable bar food, real ales, friendly service and seats outside

Head here for lunch before or after an enjoyable four-mile walk that starts and ends at this pub (see the pub website for details). You'll need to book a table in advance as it's extremely popular. The long-serving licensees are attentive and friendly and the various comfortable and easy-going interconnected rooms have plenty of character: beams (some quite low) and standing timbers, a happy mix of nice old dining chairs and settles around individual wooden tables, rugs on flagstones, lit candles, a big log fire and country prints on red or bare brick walls; background music. Ringwood Razorback, Sharps Doom Bar and Youngs Bitter on handpump, quite a few wines by the glass and several gins and whiskies. There are picnic-sets on gravel or paving in the garden.

A wide choice of good quality food includes lunchtime ciabattas, whole baked camembert with chilli and apricot glaze, grilled prawns with garlic mayonnaise, wild mushroom, tarragon and stilton filo parcels on creamy garlic spinach, smoked haddock with sage rarebit, bacon crust, roast sweet potato and parsley sauce, calves liver with bubble and squeak, pancetta and red wine sauce, herb-marinated butterflied chicken breast with sautéed potatoes, grilled chorizo and goats cheese salad with a mustard and tarragon dressing, and puddings such as triple chocolate brownie with dark chocolate sauce and seasonal fruit crumble with vanilla ice-cream. *Benchmark main dish: half shoulder of lamb £15.50. Two-course evening meal £24.00.*

Free house ~ Licensee Paul Dailey ~ Real ale ~ Open 12-11 (midnight Sat) ~ Bar food 12-2.30, 7-9.30 ~ Restaurant ~ Children welcome ~ Dogs allowed in bar ~ Wi-fi
Recommended by Rosie and John Moore, Colin and Daniel Gibbs, Susie and Spencer Gray, Catherine and Daniel King

Bedroom prices are for high summer. Even then you may get reductions for more than one night, or (outside tourist areas) weekends. Winter special rates are common, and many inns reduce bedroom prices if you have a full evening meal.

WHITE WALTHAM SU8477 Map 2

Beehive

(01628) 822877 – www.thebeehivewhitewaltham.co.uk

Waltham Road (B3024 W of Maidenhead); SL6 3SH

Berkshire Dining Pub of the Year

Attractive village pub with welcoming staff and excellent food and drinks choice; seats in garden with table service

Exceptionally good food cooked by the landlord is the main draw here, though the atmosphere is bustling and friendly and there's a thoughtful choice of drinks too. To the right of the entrance are several comfortably spacious areas with leather chairs around sturdy tables, while to the left is a neat bar brightened up by cheerful scatter cushions on built-in wall seats and captain's chairs. Impeccable, friendly staff serve Rebellion IPA, Sharps Doom Bar and Timothy Taylors Landlord on handpump, 20 wines by the glass from a good list and farm cider; background music. An airy dining room has glass doors opening on to the front terrace where teak seats and picnic-sets take in the rather fine view. The bigger back garden has plenty of seats and tables and the village cricket field is opposite. Disabled access and facilities.

Impressive food includes local snails with garlic butter and gorgonzola, grilled octopus with capers, paprika and lemon vinaigrette, tagliatelle with wild mushrooms, artichokes, cherry tomatoes, parmesan cream and garlic crumbs, chicken, ham and leek pie, lemon sole with cucumber, mussels, dill and lemon butter sauce, rib of beef with persillade tomatoes, braised shallots, chips and béarnaise sauce (for two to share), slow-cooked duck with creamed potatoes and roasting juices, and puddings such as banana and toffee millefeuille and chocolate fondant with toffee sauce and coffee ice-cream; they also offer a two- and three-course set lunch. *Benchmark main dish: peppered haunch of wild venison with creamed spinach, celeriac purée and sauce poivrade £26.00. Two-course evening meal £25.00.*

Enterprise ~ Lease Dominic Chapman ~ Real ale ~ Open 11-2.30, 5-11; 12-11 Sat; 12-6 Sun ~ Bar food 12-2.30, 6-9.30 (10 Fri, Sat); 12-4 Sun ~ Restaurant ~ Children welcome ~ Dogs allowed in bar ~ Wi-fi *Recommended by Dr and Mrs A K Clarke, Gerald and Brenda Culliford, Alison and Tony Livesley, Mary and Douglas McDowell, DHV, Louise and Simon Peters, Cecily and Steven Evans*

WOOLHAMPTON SU5766 Map 2

Rowbarge

(0118) 971 2213 – www.brunningandprice.co.uk/rowbarge

Station Road; RG7 5SH

Canalside pub with plenty of interest in rambling rooms, six real ales, good quality food and lots of outside seating

This pub's fine position by a swing bridge on the Kennet & Avon Canal guarantees plenty of customers in warm weather, but this is helped along by a fantastic drinks choice and brasserie-style food. Six rambling rooms with beams and timbering are connected by open doorways and knocked-through walls. The décor is gently themed to represent the nearby canal with hundreds of prints and photographs (some of rowing and boats) and oars on the walls, as well as old glass and stone bottles in nooks and crannies, big house plants and fresh flowers, plenty of candles and several open fires; the many large mirrors create an impression of even more space. Throughout there are antique dining chairs around various nice old tables, settles, built-in cushioned wall seating, armchairs, a group of high stools around a huge wooden barrel table, and rugs on polished boards, stone tiles or carpeting. Friendly, helpful staff serve Phoenix Brunning & Price Original plus Red Cat Prowler Pale, Stonehenge Spire Ale, Tring Side Pocket for a Toad and West Berkshire Maharaja IPA on handpump, 20 wines by the glass, 90 gins and 65 malt whiskies; background music and board games. A decked terrace has wooden chairs and tables and you'll find picnic-sets among trees by the water.

From an appetising menu the modern food includes sandwiches, teriyaki salmon with wasabi crème fraîche and chilli salad, smoked duck and beetroot salad with raspberry vinegar, aubergine, pea and lemon risotto, pork tenderloin with braised pig cheek, sweet potato purée, fondant potato and red wine jus, guinea fowl ballotine with sage stuffing, cauliflower purée and black pudding fritter, sea trout fillet in sage and bacon butter with roasted squash and celeriac, braised lamb shoulder with dauphinoise potatoes and rosemary gravy, and puddings such as dark and white chocolate brownie with vanilla ice-cream and crème brûlée. *Benchmark main dish: beer-battered cod and chips £13.45. Two-course evening meal £20.00.*

Brunning & Price ~ Manager Stuart Groves ~ Real ale ~ Open 12-11; 12-10.30 Sun ~ Bar food 12-9.30 (10pm Fri, Sat) ~ Restaurant ~ Children welcome ~ Dogs allowed in bar ~ Wi-fi *Recommended by Ian Herdman, Andrew and Michele Revell, Brian and Susan Wylie, Louise and Simon Peters*

YATTENDON SU5574 Map 2

Royal Oak

(01635) 201325 – www.royaloakyattendon.co.uk

The Square; B4009 NE from Newbury; right at Hampstead Norreys, village signed on left; RG18 0UG

Civilised old inn with beamed and panelled rooms, imaginative food and seats in pretty garden; bedrooms

Many customers are here for the pleasing food, though you're more than welcome to drop in for just a drink. The charming bar rooms have beams and panelling, an appealing mix of wooden dining chairs around interesting tables, some half-panelled wall seating, rugs on quarry tiles or wooden floorboards, plenty of prints on brick, cream or red walls, lovely flower arrangements and four log fires; background music and TV. As the West Berkshire brewery is actually in the village, the Good Old Boy, Maggs Mild and Mr Chubbs on handpump are on tip top form; the 12 wines by the glass are well chosen. Under the trellising in the walled back garden are wicker armchairs and tables and they have picnic-sets under parasols at the front; boules. This is a comfortable place to stay and the light, attractive bedrooms overlook the garden or village square; breakfasts are good. The pub is only ten minutes from Newbury Racecourse and so it can get pretty busy on race days.

First class seasonal dishes includes sandwiches, beetroot and orange-cured salmon gravadlax with wasabi crème fraîche, sweet and sticky char siu pork spare ribs with spring onion and chilli, butternut squash, coconut and chilli laksa with coriander and lime, pork and herb schnitzel with cider apple sauce, 12-hour slow-roasted lamb shoulder with garlic roast potatoes and lamb jus, rib on the bone with béarnaise sauce, and puddings such as fig, rhubarb and kirsch crumble with vanilla ice-cream and chocolate fondant with salted caramel ice-cream; they also offer a two- and three-course set weekday lunch and afternoon tea. *Benchmark main dish: roasted red duck laksa with lime and coriander, toasted peanuts and rice noodles £20.00. Two-course evening meal £27.00.*

Free house ~ Licensee Rob McGill ~ Real ale ~ Open 11-11 (midnight Sat); 12-10.30 Sun ~ Bar food 12-2.30, 6.30-9.30; 12-3, 6-9.30 Sat; 12-3.30, 6-9 Sun ~ Children welcome ~ Dogs welcome ~ Wi-fi ~ Bedrooms: /£99 *Recommended by Nick Sharpe, Andrew Lawson, Brian and Sally Wakeham, Mary Joyce, John Ledbury*

Also Worth a Visit in Berkshire

Besides the fully inspected pubs, you might like to try these pubs that have been recommended to us and described by readers. Do tell us what you think of them: feedback@goodguides.com

ALDWORTH SU5579

★**Bell** (01635) 578272

A329 Reading–Wallingford; left on to B4009 at Streatley; RG8 9SE Unspoilt and unchanging village pub in same family for over 250 years; simply furnished panelled rooms, beams in ochre ceiling, old photographs and ancient one-handed clock, woodburner, glass-panelled hatch serving well kept Arkells, West Berkshire and a monthly guest, Upton cider and nice house wines, good value rolls, ploughman's and winter soup, traditional pub games; no mobile phones or credit cards; well behaved children and dogs welcome, seats in quiet cottagey garden by cricket ground, animals in paddock behind pub, maybe Christmas mummers and summer morris, closed Mon (open lunchtime bank holidays), can get busy weekends. *(Maggie and Matthew Lyons)*

ALDWORTH SU5579

Four Points (01635) 578367

B4009 towards Hampstead Norreys; RG8 9RL Attractive 17th-c thatched roadside pub with low beams, standing timbers and panelling, nice fire in bar with more formal seating area to the left and restaurant at back, popular good value home-cooked food (all day weekends) from baguettes up, bargain lighter lunch deal Mon-Fri, local Two Cocks and Wadworths 6X, friendly helpful young staff; children and dogs (in bar) welcome, garden over road with play area, open (and food) all day weekends. *(William Pace)*

ASHMORE GREEN SU4969

Sun in the Wood (01635) 42377

B4009 (Shaw Road) off A339, right to Kiln Road, left to Stoney Lane; RG18 9HF Updated and extended 19th-c dining pub; enjoyable food from stone-baked pizzas and pub favourites up, Thurs grill night, Wadworths ales and several wines by the glass, friendly helpful staff, spacious interior with light open feel, small side conservatory; background music, quiz nights; children and dogs (in bar) welcome, decked terrace and woodside garden, open all day Sat, till 4pm Sun. *(Cliff and Monica Swan)*

ASTON SU7884

★**Flower Pot** (01491) 574721

Off A4130 Henley–Maidenhead at top of Remenham Hill; RG9 3DG Roomy red-brick country pub with nice local feel, snug traditional bar and airy back dining area, lots of stuffed fish and other taxidermy, milk churn stools and roaring log fire, four well kept ales such as Brakspears and Ringwood, enjoyable reasonably priced food (not Sun evening) from baguettes to fish and game, friendly service; vocal parrot called Paddy; very busy with walkers and families at weekends, dogs allowed in some parts, picnic-sets in big orchard garden with country views, Thames nearby, three bedrooms, open all day weekends. *(Susan and John Douglas)*

BARKHAM SU7866

Bull (0118) 976 2816

Barkham Road; RG41 4TL Traditional pub run by friendly thai family; opened-up carpeted interior with dining area to one end, half a dozen ales such as Gales, Rebellion, Sharps and Timothy Taylors, popular food including good south-east asian choices; Mon quiz; children welcome, open all day (till 7pm Sun). *(Darren and Jane Staniforth)*

BEECH HILL SU6964

Elm Tree (0118) 988 3505

3.3 miles from M4 junction 11: A33 towards Basingstoke, turning off into Beech Hill Road after about 2 miles; RG7 2AZ Five rooms, one with blazing fire, and nice rural views especially from more modern barn-style restaurant and conservatory, much enjoyed food (not Sun evening) from varied menu, prompt friendly service, well kept ales such as Ringwood and Timothy Taylors, good choice of wines by the glass and decent coffee; children and dogs welcome, disabled access/loo, tables on heated front deck with palms, open all day. *(Louise and Simon Peters)*

BEENHAM SU5868

Six Bells (0118) 971 3368

The Green; RG7 5NX Extended red-brick Victorian village pub with good food from landlord-chef including imaginative additions to standard pub menu, well kept West

Berkshire Good Old Boy, Sharps Doom Bar and a guest, friendly staff, two bar areas with armchairs and winter fires, dining conservatory; board games; children welcome at lunchtime, four bedrooms, closed Sun evening, Mon lunchtime. *(John Pritchard)*

CHAPEL ROW SU5769

Bladebone (0118) 971 4000

Centre of village; RG7 6PD Renovated red-brick village pub with very good well presented food cooked by landlord-chef, ales from Sharps and West Berkshire, good range of wines and gins, friendly helpful young staff, small conservatory overlooking terrace and garden; children and dogs welcome, open all day, no food Sun evening, Mon. *(Jeff Davies)*

CHARVIL SU7776

Lands End (0118) 934 0700

Lands End Lane/Whistley Mill Lane near Old River ford; RG10 0UE Welcoming 1930s Tudor-style pub; generous helpings of enjoyable reasonably priced food from baguettes to popular Sun roasts (best to book), well kept Brakspears Bitter, a guest beer and a dozen wines by the glass, helpful accommodating staff, open-plan bar with log fire, separate restaurant; children welcome, no dogs inside, sizeable garden with terrace picnic-sets, open all day Sun till 9pm. *(Charlie Stevens)*

CHEAPSIDE SU9469

Thatched Tavern (01344) 620874

Off A332/A329, then off B383 at Village Hall sign; SL5 7QG Civilised dining pub with a good deal of character and plenty of room for just a drink; well liked up-to-date food (can be pricey) along with more traditional choices and weekday set lunch, lots of wines by the glass including champagne from extensive list, Fullers London Pride, a beer named for the pub and a guest ale, big inglenook log fire, low beams and polished flagstones in cottagey core, three smart dining rooms off; children welcome, dogs in bar, tables on terrace and attractive sheltered back lawn, handy for Virginia Water, open (and food) all day, busy on Ascot race days. *(Stuart and Natalie Granville)*

CHIEVELEY SU4773

★**Olde Red Lion** (01635) 248379

Handy for M4 junction 13 via A34 N-bound; Green Lane; RG20 8XB Welcoming village pub with three well kept Arkells beers and good varied choice of generously served food at reasonable prices, friendly attentive service, low-beamed carpeted bar with log fire, extended back restaurant; background music, TV; children and dogs welcome, wheelchair accessible throughout, small garden, five bedrooms in separate building, open all day weekends. *(John and Enid Morris)*

COOKHAM SU8985

★**Bel & the Dragon** (01628) 521263

High Street (B4447); SL6 9SQ Smartly updated 15th-c inn; heavy beams, log fires and simple country furnishings in two-room front bar and dining area, hand-painted cartoons on pastel walls, more modern bistro-style back restaurant, emphasis on good food (separate bar and restaurant menus) including weekend brunch, Rebellion IPA and a local guest, plenty of wines by the glass from extensive list, cocktails; children welcome, dogs in bar, well tended garden with tables on paved terrace, play area, five bedrooms, Stanley Spencer Gallery almost opposite, open all day, food all day Sun. *(Theocsbrian)*

COOKHAM SU8885

★**White Oak** (01628) 523043

The Pound (B4447); SL6 9QE Modernised red-brick restauranty pub with highly regarded interesting food including good value set menus, large back area and several other parts set for eating, front bar serving ales such as Greene King and good choice of wines by the glass, friendly efficient service; free wi-fi; children welcome, sheltered back terrace with steps up to white wirework tables on grass, closed Sun evening, otherwise open all day. *(Mike Swan)*

COOKHAM DEAN SU8785

★**Jolly Farmer** (01628) 482905

Church Road, off Hills Lane; SL6 9PD Refurbished 18th-c pub owned by village consortium; linked beamed rooms with open fires, five well kept ales such as Rebellion and Timothy Taylors, Weston's cider and good choice of wines by the glass, popular fairly pubby food including wood-fired pizzas, pleasant attentive service; occasional live music; well behaved children and dogs welcome, tables out in front and on side terrace, garden with big play area, open all day. *(Belinda and Neil Garth)*

COOKHAM DEAN SU8785

Uncle Toms Cabin (01628) 483339

Off A308 Maidenhead–Marlow; Hills Lane, towards Cookham Rise and Cookham; SL6 9NT Welcoming small-roomed local with simple sensitively modernised interior, four well kept mainstream ales and plenty of wines by the

We mention bottled beers and spirits only if there is something unusual about them – imported belgian real ales, say, or dozens of malt whiskies; so do please let us know about them in your reports.

glass, good reasonably priced food cooked by owner-chef, low beams (and doorways), wood floors and grey-green panelling, gleaming horsebrasses, open fire; children in eating areas, dogs in bar, seats out at front and in sheltered sloping back garden, peaceful country setting, open all day Sat, closes 9pm Sun and Mon. *(Mandy and Gary Redstone)*

CRAZIES HILL SU7980

Horns (0118) 940 6041
Warren Row Road, off A4 towards Cockpole Green, then follow Crazies Hill signs; RG10 8LY Welcoming 16th-c beamed village pub with landlord-chef's good food from lunchtime baguettes and traditional favourites up, Brakspears ales kept well and nice choice of wines by the glass, friendly helpful service, four rooms including raftered barn restaurant; children welcome, dogs in bar, big garden with play area and summer barbecues, open all day Fri and Sat, till 7pm Sun, closed Mon (Tues after bank holiday). *(Paul Humphreys)*

DATCHET SU9877

Royal Stag (01753) 584231
Not far from M4 junction 5; The Green; SL3 9JH Ancient beamed pub next to church overlooking green; well kept Fullers London Pride and three Windsor & Eton ales, enjoyable food including good Sun roasts, friendly staff; Tues quiz; children and dogs welcome, seats outside, open (and food) all day. *(Charlie Stevens)*

EAST GARSTON SU3676

★**Queens Arms** (01488) 648757
3.5 miles from M4 junction 14; A338 and village signposted Great Shefford; RG17 7ET Friendly slate-roofed inn at the heart of racehorse-training country; opened-up bar with antique prints (many jockeys), wheelbacks around well spaced tables on bare boards, well kept Ramsbury, Sharps and a beer badged for them, plenty of wines by the glass, lighter dining area with more prints, good food from sandwiches and traditional choices up (not Sun evening), friendly obliging staff; background music, TV for racing, newspapers including *Racing Post*, free wi-fi; children and dogs (in bar) welcome, seats on sheltered terrace, 12 attractively decorated bedrooms, good surrounding downland walks, fly fishing and shooting can be arranged, open all day. *(Mr and Mrs P R Thomas, Michael Sargent)*

EAST ILSLEY SU4981

Crown & Horns (01635) 281545
Just off A34, about 5 miles N of M4 junction 13; Compton Road; RG20 7LH Welcoming brick and tile pub in horse-training country; rambling beamed rooms with log fires, enjoyable home-made food from sandwiches, pizzas and pub favourites up, Thurs steak night, five real ales and over a dozen wines by the glass, friendly staff; background music; children, dogs and muddy boots welcome, tables in pretty courtyard, modern bedroom extension, open all day and busy on Newbury race days. *(Susie and Spencer Gray)*

EASTBURY SU3477

Plough (01488) 71312
Centre of village by stream; RG17 7JN Popular old whitewashed village dining pub with very good food from chef-proprietor, a couple of changing ales and over 20 gins, friendly efficient staff, open-plan interior with some modern touches including large back restaurant, two-way log fire; children welcome, dogs in bar, tables out on front deck, open all day Sun, closed Mon. *(Michael Doswell)*

ETON SU9677

George (01753) 861797
High Street; SL4 6AF Welcoming 18th-c corner pub just back from Thames bridge; traditional beamed interior with settles, pews and other wooden furniture on bare boards, open fire, half a dozen Windsor & Eton beers (tasting trays) from ornately carved oak counter, ample helpings of enjoyable pubby food, friendly helpful service; quiz every other Tues; children and dogs welcome, decked back terrace with seating booths, eight bedrooms, open (and food) all day, kitchen shuts 7pm Sun. *(Kiara Maher)*

FINCHAMPSTEAD SU7963

Queens Oak (0118) 996 8567
Church Lane, off B3016; RG40 4LS Welcoming country pub named for an oak planted by Queen Victoria on green opposite; largely open-plan interior refurbished by present licensees, well kept Brakspears and other Marstons-related beers, enjoyable food (all day weekends) from pub favourites up; Sun quiz, some live music; children, walkers and dogs welcome, good-sized garden with play area, open all day. *(Cliff and Monica Swan)*

FRILSHAM SU5573

Pot Kiln (01635) 201366
From Yattendon take turning S, opposite church, follow first Frilsham signpost, but just after crossing motorway go straight on towards Bucklebury ignoring Frilsham signposted right; pub on right after about 0.5 miles; RG18 0XX Tucked-away red-brick country dining pub with good food including signature local game; various eating areas and small bare-boards bar with woodburner, West Berkshire ales, several wines by the glass and maybe a couple of real ciders; free wi-fi; children and dogs welcome, unobstructed views from seats in big suntrap garden, outside pizza oven, nice walks in nearby woods, open all day Sat, till 5pm Sun, closed Tues; plans for expansion including bedrooms. *(Jeff Davies)*

HENLEY SU7682

★**Little Angel** (01491) 411008
Remenham Lane (A4130, just over bridge E of Henley); RG9 2LS Civilised dining pub, more or less open-plan but with distinct modernised seating areas, bare boards throughout, little bar with leather cube stools, tub and farmhouse chairs, other parts with mix of dining tables and chairs, artwork on Farrow & Ball paintwork, popular modern food (all day weekends) from sharing plates up, Brakspears ales and several wines by the glass including champagne, pleasant attentive service, airy conservatory; background music; well behaved children allowed, dogs in bar, tables on sheltered floodlit back terrace overlooking cricket pitch, open all day. *(Tom and Ruth Rees, Gus Swan)*

HOLYPORT SU8977

George (01628) 628317
1.5 miles from M4 junction 8/9, via A308(M)/A330; The Green; SL6 2JL Attractive 16th-c pub on picturesque village green with duck pond, colourful history and plenty of old-world charm; open-plan low-beamed interior, cosy and dimly lit, with nice fireplace, good food from lunchtime baguettes and pub favourites up, well kept Fullers London Pride and a couple of Rebellion ales, nice wines from sound list, friendly helpful service; background music, quiz first Mon of month; children and dogs (in bar) welcome, picnic-sets on pretty terrace, closed Sun evening, Mon. *(William Pace)*

HUNGERFORD SU3368

Hungerford Arms (01488) 682154
High Street; street parking opposite; RG17 0NB Horseracing-themed pub with open-plan interior stretching back from the smallish bow-windowed façade; bare boards and some low beams, open fire at the back, Greene King Old Speckled Hen, Timothy Taylors Landlord and a beer badged for the pub from island servery, decent choice of wines and enjoyable food from sandwiches, wraps and pizzas up, friendly staff; background music, TVs for racing; children welcome, small sheltered back courtyard, open all day. *(Mike and Mary Carter)*

HUNGERFORD SU3368

John O'Gaunt (01488) 683535
Bridge Street (A338); RG17 0EG Welcoming 16th-c town pub with modernised beamed interior; enjoyable generously served food from lunchtime sandwiches/wraps up, six well kept mainly local ales including own microbrews (tasting trays available), good bottled range too and local cider, efficient cheerful service; children and dogs welcome, small sheltered garden, open all day, food all day Sun. *(David Shaw)*

HUNGERFORD SU3368

Three Swans (01488) 682721
High Street; RG17 0LZ Refurbished former coaching inn, bright and welcoming, with panelled bar serving three well kept ales such as Black Sheep and Ramsbury, Somersby's cider, plenty of wines by the glass and cocktails, good food from snacks and pizzas up, helpful friendly service, large split-level restaurant and coffee shop; children and dogs (in bar) welcome, some tables out at front, more in part-covered courtyard behind, 25 bedrooms, open all day from 7am (8am weekends) for breakfast. *(Kristin Warry, Tony and Wendy Hobden)*

HUNGERFORD NEWTOWN SU3571

Tally Ho (01488) 682312
A338 just S of M4 junction 14; RG17 0PP Traditional red-brick beamed pub owned by the local community, friendly and welcoming, with good food (not Sun evening) from baguettes to specials and popular Sun lunch (rare roast beef), four well kept local ales such as Ramsbury and West Berkshire, log fire; occasional music and quiz nights, free wi-fi; children and dogs welcome, a couple of picnic-sets out in front, more tables on side terrace, three bedrooms, open all day. *(Cecily and Steven Evans)*

HURLEY SU8281

Dew Drop (01628) 315662
Small yellow sign to pub off A4130 just W; SL6 6RB Old flint and brick pub tucked away in nice woodland setting, shortish choice of food including good lunchtime sandwiches, Brakspears and a guest ale, two adjoining rooms (one with piano), log fire; free wi-fi; children and dogs welcome, pleasant views from back garden, good local walks, open all day Sat, till 6pm Sun, closed Mon. *(Paul Humphreys, Simon Collett-Jones)*

HURST SU7973

★**Castle** (0118) 934 0034
Church Hill; RG10 0SJ Popular old dining pub next to bowling green and owned by church opposite; very good well presented food (not Sun evening, Mon) from fairly priced varied menu including daily specials (Fri fish night), three well kept changing ales and plenty of wines by the glass, friendly staff, beams, wood floors and old brick nogging, some visible wattle and daub, woodburners; children and dogs (in bar) welcome, garden picnic-sets, open all day weekends, closed Mon lunchtime. *(DHV, Paul Humphreys)*

HURST SU8074

Green Man (0118) 934 2599
Off A321 just outside village; RG10 0BP Partly 17th-c pub with enjoyable food from sandwiches, sharing plates and pub favourites up, a couple of well kept Brakspears ales and a guest, several wines

by the glass, friendly service, bar with dark beams and standing timbers, cosy alcoves, wall seats and built-in settles, hot little fire in one fireplace, old iron stove in another, dining area with modern sturdy wooden tables and high-backed chairs on solid oak floor; children and dogs welcome, sheltered terrace, picnic-sets under spreading oak trees in large garden with play area, open all day, food all day weekends. *(Paul Humphreys)*

KINTBURY SU3866

★**Dundas Arms** (01488) 658263
Village signposted off A4 Newbury–Hungerford about a mile W of Halfway; Station Road – pub just over hump-back canal bridge, at start of village itself; RG17 9UT Handsome early 19th-c inn (being fully refurbished as we went to press) on pretty canal islet next to River Kennet; Ramsbury Gold, local cider and 14 wines by the glass from bar counter decorated in old pennies, imaginative menu using seasonal local produce, various dining areas including cosy snug, Potting Shed with floor-to-ceiling glass overlooking the garden and main restaurant in classic country style, there's also a private dining room at the back; children welcome, riverside terrace and mature garden with outside bar, eight well appointed country house-style bedrooms. *(Ian Herdman, Jack Trussler, Daniel King, Maggie and Matthew Lyons, Tracey and Stephen Groves)*

KNOWL HILL SU8178

Bird in Hand (01628) 826622
A4, handy for M4 junction 8/9; RG10 9UP Now owned by Wadworths and refurbished; roomy interior with beams, panelling, parquet floor and log fire in main area, four real ales and enjoyable reasonably priced food including some specials, restaurant; background music; children welcome, tables on front terrace and garden, bedrooms (some in separate block), open (and food) all day. *(John Pritchard)*

LAMBOURN SU3175

Hare (01488) 71386
aka Hare & Hounds; Lambourn Woodlands, well S of Lambourn itself (B4000/Hilldrop Lane); RG17 7SD Rambling 17th-c beamed restaurant-pub with well liked fairly priced food from lunchtime sandwiches/baguettes to good Sun roasts, several small linked rooms including a proper bar with ales such as Ramsbury and Sharps, friendly efficient service; background music, TV; children and dogs (in one part) welcome, garden behind, open all day (till 8pm Sun). *(Michael Sargent)*

LITTLEWICK GREEN SU8379

Cricketers (01628) 822888
Not far from M4 junction 9; A404(M) then left on to A4 – village signed on left; Coronation Road; SL6 3RA Welcoming old-fashioned village pub in charming spot opposite cricket green (can get crowded); three well kept Badger ales and good choice of wines by the glass, enjoyable pub food (not Sun evening) from lunchtime sandwiches to specials, traditional interior with three linked rooms, wood and quarry-tiled floors, huge clock above woodburner in brick fireplace; background music, TV; children and dogs welcome, pretty hanging baskets and a few tables out in front behind picket fence, open all day. *(D J and P M Taylor)*

MAIDENHEAD SU8582

Pinkneys Arms (01628) 630268
Lee Lane, just off A308 N; SL6 6NU Refurbished dining pub with good food from weekly changing menu (can be pricey), pizzas only Mon and Tues, well kept ales (mainly Rebellion) and decent wines, friendly efficient service; outside gents', barn function room; children and dogs welcome, big garden, closed Mon lunchtime, otherwise open all day from midday. *(Susie and Spencer Gray)*

MAIDENS GREEN SU9072

★**Winning Post** (01344) 882242
Follow signs to Winkfield Plain W of Winkfield off A330, then first right; SL4 4SW Gently civilised 18th-c inn with open-plan beamed rooms (some leather crash pads); main flagstoned bar area has tub chairs, a long cushioned settle and stools by counter serving two Upham ales and good wines by the glass, bare boards dining rooms to the left, some huge wall photos of horses, tartan banquettes, bowler-hat lights and woodburner, good well presented interesting food, friendly service, also back room 'Winning Enclosure' with more horse-racing pictures and large raised fireplace; TV, free wi-fi; children and dogs (in bar) welcome, part-covered terrace and rather smart conical smokers' hut, quiet bedrooms facing garden, handy for Ascot and Henley, open (and food) all day, kitchen shuts 7.30pm Sun. *(Angela and Steve Heard, Sylvia and Phillip Spencer, Monty Green, Mike Kavaney)*

MARSH BENHAM SU4267

Red House (01635) 582017
Off A4 W of Newbury; RG20 8LY Attractive thatched dining pub with good imaginative food from french chef-owner, also lunchtime sandwiches and pub favourites, steak nights Tues and Fri, fish and chips Thurs, friendly efficient service, well kept West Berkshire ales and a guest, lots of wines by the glass, afternoon teas, roomy bar with wood or flagstone floors, logburner, separate restaurant, good cheerful service; background music; children and dogs welcome, terrace and long lawns sloping to River Kennet water meadows, open (and food) all day. *(Ian Herdman, David and Judy Robison)*

MIDGHAM SU5566

Coach & Horses (0118) 971 3384
Bath Road (N side); RG7 5UX
Comfortable main-road pub with good choice of enjoyable food from baguettes up including lunchtime offers, cheerful efficient service, Fullers London Pride and West Berkshire Good Old Boy, flagstoned bar with sofa by brick fireplace, steps up to small half-panelled carpeted dining area with country-style furniture, second dining room; children welcome, garden behind, closed Sun evening and Mon (including bank holidays). *(Charlie Stevens)*

NEWBURY SU4767

Lock Stock & Barrel
(01635) 580550 *Northbrook Street; RG14 1AA* Modern pub approached down small alleyway and popular for its canalside (River Kennet) setting; low ceiling, light wood or slate flooring and painted panelling, lots of windows overlooking canal, varied choice of enjoyable sensibly priced food all day from sandwiches up, well kept Fullers/Gales beers, efficient friendly staff; occasional live music, free wi-fi; children welcome, outside seating including suntrap roof terrace looking over a series of locks towards handsome church, moorings, open all day (till midnight Fri, Sat). *(Louise and Simon Peters)*

OLD WINDSOR SU9874

Oxford Blue (01753) 861954
Crimp Hill Road, off B3021 – itself off A308/A328; SL4 2QY Fully refurbished 19th-c restaurant-pub; highly regarded upscale food (not cheap) from proprietor-chef, well kept local ales and good wines from extensive list, friendly professional service; well placed with open country views, terrace tables, open till 6pm Sun, closed Mon, Tues. *(Jackie Bird)*

PALEY STREET SU8676

★**Royal Oak** (01628) 620541
B3024 W; SL6 3JN Attractively modernised and extended 17th-c restauranty pub owned by Sir Michael Parkinson and son Nick; highly regarded british cooking (not cheap) and most here to eat, good service, dining room split by brick pillars and timbering with mix of well spaced wooden tables and leather chairs on bare boards or flagstones, smallish informal beamed bar with woodburner, leather sofas and cricketing prints, Fullers London Pride and wide choice of wines by the glass including champagne; background jazz; children welcome (no pushchairs in restaurant), seats outside among troughs of herbs, closed Sun evening. *(Mandy and Gary Redstone)*

PANGBOURNE SU6376

Elephant (0118) 984 2244
Church Road; RG8 7AR Handsome inn with decorative elephants of all sizes in bars, dining room and seating areas; main bar has flagstone floor, log fire and antler chandeliers, leather-backed stools around counter serving West Berkshire, Sharps, a couple of real ciders and 16 wines by the glass, good choice of enjoyable food from lunchtime sandwiches to steaks cooked on an open fire, afternoon teas, friendly service; background music; children and dogs (in bar) welcome, big back garden with giant chess set and rattan-style sofas on raised terrace, individually styled bedrooms, open all day. *(Michael Napier, Monty Green, David and Leone Lawson)*

READING SU7173

Alehouse (0118) 950 8119
Broad Street; RG1 2BH No-frills drinkers' pub with nine well kept quickly changing ales, craft kegs, lots of different bottled beers and real ciders/perries; small bare-boards bar with raised seating area, hundreds of pump clips on walls and ceiling, corridor to several appealing panelled rooms, some little more than alcoves, no food; open all day. *(William Pace)*

READING SU7273

Fishermans Cottage
(0118) 956 0432 *Kennet Side – easiest to walk from Orts Road, off Kings Road; RG1 3HJ* White-painted pub tucked away in housing estate by canalised River Kennet; good food including tapas and paella, four interesting changing ales along with various craft beers, friendly service, modern interior with airy conservatory; children and dogs welcome, picnic-sets out by towpath, beach hut-style booths on back decking, open all day, kitchen closes 7pm Sun and all Mon. *(Tony Hobden)*

READING SU7073

Nags Head 07765 880137
Russell Street; RG1 7XD Fairly basic mock-Tudor drinkers' pub just outside town centre attracting good mix of customers; a dozen well kept changing beers and 14 ciders, baguettes and pies (roasts on Sun), open fire, darts and cribbage; background and occasional live music, TV for major sporting events (busy on Reading FC match days); suntrap beer garden, open all day. *(William Pace)*

READING SU7173

★**Sweeney & Todd** (0118) 958 6466
Castle Street; RG1 7RD Pie shop with popular bar-restaurant behind (little

We say if we know a pub allows dogs.

changed in over 30 years); warren of private period-feel alcoves and other areas on various levels, enjoyable home-made food including their range of good value pies, cheery service, small bar with four well kept ales such as Adnams and Hook Norton, Weston's cider and decent wines; children welcome in restaurant area, closed Sun evening and bank holidays, otherwise open (and food) all day. *(Robin James, John Pritchard)*

SHINFIELD SU7368

Black Boy (0118) 988 3116

Shinfield Road (A327); RG2 9BP Refurbished Barons group pub; contemporary beamed interior with bow-windowed front bar and spreading back restaurant, painted half-panelling, some high tables and lots of booth seating, modern artwork and a couple of gas woodburners, three real ales including Greene King and good range of wines/gins, popular food from baguettes and sharing plates through burgers and pub favourites up, efficient helpful staff; background music; children welcome, back terrace with own bar and various covered seating areas, open all day. *(Darren and Jane Staniforth)*

SHINFIELD SU7367

★Magpie & Parrot (0118) 988 4130

2.6 miles from M4 junction 11, via B3270; A327 just SE of Shinfield on Arborfield Road; RG2 9EA Unusual homely little roadside cottage with two cosy spic and span bars, warm fire and lots of bric-a-brac (miniature and historic bottles, stuffed birds, dozens of model cars, veteran AA badges and automotive instruments), Fullers London Pride and a local guest from small corner counter, weekday lunchtime snacks and evening fish and chips (Thurs, Fri), hospitable landlady; no credit cards or mobile phones; pub dogs (others welcome), seats on back terrace and marquee on immaculate lawn, open 12-7.30 (later some Thurs nights when live jazz), closed Sun evening. *(Jackie Bird)*

SHURLOCK ROW SU8374

★Shurlock Inn (0118) 934 9094

Just off B3018 SE of Twyford; The Street; RG10 0PS Recently refurbished and extended 17th-c village dining pub (part of the tiny Rarebreed group – see Plough at Cobham, Surrey); popular food from bar snacks and sharing plates up including signature steaks, well kept ales such as Sharps, Rebellion and local Stardust, nice wines from shortish list and interesting gin range, friendly knowledgeable staff, log fire in double-sided fireplace, restaurant with open-view kitchen; background music; children and dogs (in bar) welcome, black metal furniture on terrace, lawned garden with picnic-sets and fenced play area, open (and food) all day, kitchen closes 6.30pm Sun. *(Tony and Jill Radnor, Simon Collett-Jones)*

SULHAMSTEAD SU6269

Spring (0118) 930 3440

Bath Road (A4); RG7 5HP Old barn conversion with spacious bar and balustraded upstairs dining area under rafters, good variety of popular food from interesting sandwiches up, three real ales including Fullers and West Berkshire, nice range of wines by the glass, friendly efficient staff; children welcome, plenty of seats outside, open all day. *(Daphne Veale)*

SUNNINGHILL SU9568

Belvedere Arms (01344) 870931

London Road; SL5 7SB Refurbished dining pub on edge of Virginia Water and Windsor Great Park, wide choice of good interesting food including Weds evening set menu, ales such as Fullers, Hogs Back and Sharps, friendly helpful service; children and dogs welcome, nice outside seating area with stream, open (and food) all day. *(Ian Phillips)*

SUNNINGHILL SU9367

Carpenters Arms (01344) 622763

Upper Village Road; SL5 7AQ Restauranty village pub run by french team, good authentic french country cooking, not cheap but they do offer a reasonably priced set lunch (Mon-Sat), nice wines including house pichets, Sharps Doom Bar; no children in the evening, terrace tables, open all day, food all day Sun, booking advised. *(John Hunter Wright)*

SUNNINGHILL SU9367

Dog & Partridge (01344) 623204

Upper Village Road; SL5 7AQ Bright contemporary décor and emphasis on good freshly made food from lunchtime sandwiches up including some vegan choices, friendly helpful staff, Fullers, Sharps and a guest, good range of wines; background music; children and dogs welcome, disabled facilities, part-covered courtyard garden with central fountain, closed Mon, otherwise open all day, food till 6pm Sun. *(Mike Swan)*

THEALE SU6471

Bull (0118) 930 3478

High Street; RG7 5AH Modernised and extended old red-brick inn; large bar with tiled floor and dark half-panelling, carpeted dining area behind with banquettes, generous helpings of enjoyable food including specials delivered by dumb-waiter from upstairs kitchen, three or four well kept

All *Guide* inspections are anonymous. Anyone claiming to be a *Good Pub Guide* inspector is a fraud. Please let us know.

Wadworths ales, friendly efficient staff; background and some live music, quiz nights; children and dogs welcome, seats outside, open (and food) all day. *(John Pritchard)*

THEALE SU6471

Fox & Hounds (0118) 930 2295
2 miles from M4 junction 12; follow A4 W, then first left signed for station, over two roundabouts, then over narrow canal bridge to Sheffield Bottom; RG7 4BE Large Wadworths pub with enjoyable reasonably priced pubby food (not Sun evening) from baguettes to specials, five well kept ales, Weston's cider, decent wines and coffee, friendly efficient service, L-shaped bar with dividers, traditional mix of furniture on carpet or bare boards including area with modern sofas and low tables, two open fires; pool and darts, Sun quiz; children and dogs welcome, outside seating at front and sides, lakeside bird reserve opposite, open all day Fri-Sun. *(John Pritchard)*

THREE MILE CROSS SU7167

Swan (0118) 988 3674
A33 just S of M4 junction 11; Basingstoke Road; RG7 1AT Smallish traditional pub built in the 17th c and later a posting house; four well kept ales including Loddon and Timothy Taylors, enjoyable fairly standard home-made food at reasonable prices, friendly efficient staff, two beamed and panelled bars, inglenook with hanging black pots, old prints and some impressive stuffed fish; large well arranged outside seating area behind, near Madejski Stadium and very busy on match days, closed Sun evening, otherwise open all day. *(John Pritchard)*

WALTHAM ST LAWRENCE SU8376

★**Bell** (0118) 934 1788
B3024 E of Twyford; The Street; RG10 0JJ Welcoming 14th-c village local with well preserved timbered interior, good home-made food marked on blackboard from bar snacks up, cheerful attentive service, five well kept mainly local beers including Loddon, up to eight real ciders and plenty of wines by the glass, also good choice of whiskies, two compact connecting rooms, another larger one off entrance hall, warming log fires, daily newspapers; children and dogs welcome, pretty back garden with terrace and shady trees, open all day weekends, no evening food Sun-Tues. *(Simon Collett-Jones)*

WARGRAVE SU7878

Bull (0843) 289 1773
Off A321 Henley–Twyford; High Street; RG10 8DE Low-beamed 15th-c brick coaching inn run well by hospitable landlady; five smallish interconnected rooms, main bar with inglenook log fire, two dining areas (one up steps for families), good traditional home-made food from baguettes up, three well kept ales including Brakspears Bitter, friendly attentive staff; background music, free wi-fi; well behaved dogs welcome, walled garden behind, four bedrooms, open all day weekends, no evening food Sun, Mon. *(DHV, Simon Collett-Jones)*

WEST ILSLEY SU4782

Harrow (01635) 281260
Signed off A34 at E Ilsley slip road; RG20 7AR Appealing and welcoming family-run country pub in peaceful spot overlooking cricket pitch and pond; Victorian prints in deep-coloured knocked-through bar, some antique furnishings, log fire, good choice of enjoyable sensibly priced home-made food (not Sun or Mon evenings), well kept Greene King ales and nice selection of wines by the glass, afternoon teas; children in eating areas, dogs allowed in bar, big garden with picnic-sets, more seats on pleasant terrace, handy for Ridgeway walkers, may close early Sun evening if quiet. *(M and GR)*

WINDSOR SU9676

Carpenters Arms (01753) 863739
Market Street; SL4 1PB Popular Nicholsons pub rambling around central servery; good choice of well kept ales and several wines by the glass, reasonably priced pubby food from sandwiches up including range of pies, friendly helpful service, sturdy pub furnishings and Victorian-style décor with two pretty fireplaces, family areas up a few steps, also downstairs beside former tunnel entrance with suits of armour; background music, sports TV; no dogs, tables out on cobbled pedestrian alley opposite castle, no nearby parking, handy for Legoland bus stop, open (and food) all day. *(Jackie Bird)*

WINDSOR SU9676

Two Brewers (01753) 855426
Park Street; SL4 1LB In shadow of Windsor Castle with three cosy unchanging rooms around central servery, well kept ales such as Fullers London Pride, St Austell Tribute and Sharps Doom Bar, good choice of wines by the glass and enjoyable freshly made food (not Fri-Sun evenings) from shortish mid-priced menu, friendly efficient service, thriving old-fashioned pub atmosphere, beams, bare boards and open fire, enamel signs, posters and old photographs; background music, daily papers; no children inside, dogs welcome, tables and attractive hanging baskets out by pretty Georgian street next to Windsor Great Park's Long Walk, open all day. *(William Pace)*

WINDSOR SU9576

Vansittart Arms (01753) 865988
Vansittart Road; SL4 5DD Friendly three-room Victorian local with cosy corners and open fires, well kept Fullers/Gales beers, big helpings of enjoyable good value home-made food (all day weekends); background music,

sports TV, pool, free wi-fi; children and dogs welcome, part-covered beer garden, open all day. *(Jackie Bird)*

WOODSIDE SU9270

Rose & Crown (01344) 882051
Woodside Road, Winkfield, off A332 Ascot–Windsor; SL4 2DP Recently refurbished dining pub, beamed bar with wood flooring and logburner, other areas set for their enjoyable food from sandwiches and pub favourites up including deals and good Sun roasts, attentive friendly service, well kept Timothy Taylors Landlord and a guest; background music; children and dogs (in bar) welcome, tables out at front and in side garden, smallish car park (parking in lane can be tricky), open all day, food all day weekends. *(Simon Collett-Jones)*

WRAYSBURY TQ0174

George (01784) 482000
Windsor Road (B376); TW19 5DE Revamped beamed dining pub with good fairly priced food from lunchtime sandwiches up (special diets catered for), three real ales and plenty of wines by the glass, friendly helpful service, mix of wooden farmhouse-style furniture on bare boards, wall lanterns and painted half-panelling, armchairs by open fire; background music; children and dogs welcome, decked terrace with modern rattan tables and chairs, open all day, food all day Sun. *(Maggie Lay)*

WRAYSBURY TQ0074

Perseverance (01784) 482375
High Street; TW19 5DB Welcoming old community village pub ('the Percy'); enjoyable good value home-made food from sandwiches up including weekday set lunch and Weds steak night, well kept Otter Ale and three guests, real cider, decent choice of wines by the glass and interesting selection of gins, friendly helpful staff, beams and log fires (one in inglenook); Thurs quiz, live music Sun afternoon, darts; children (till 9pm) and dogs welcome, nice back garden with pizza oven, open all day (till 8pm Sun), food all day Sat. *(Jeff Davies)*

Post Office address codings confusingly give the impression that some pubs are in Berkshire, when they're really in Buckinghamshire, Oxfordshire or Hampshire (which is where we list them).

Buckinghamshire

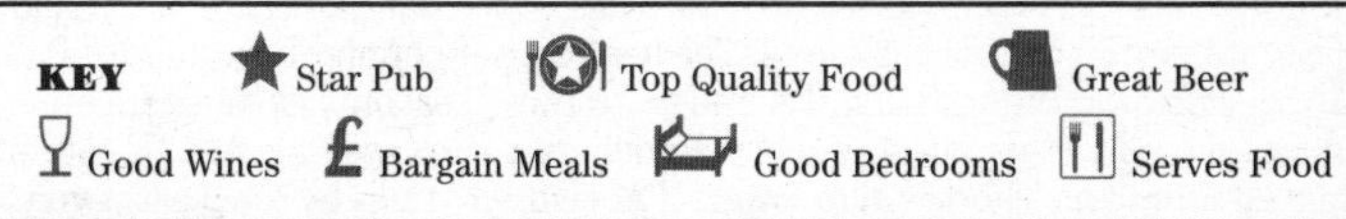

ADSTOCK SP7330 Map 4

Old Thatched Inn

(01296) 712584 – www.theoldthatchedinn.co.uk

Main Street, off A413; MK18 2JN

Thatched dining pub with keen landlord, friendly staff, five real ales and good food

This well run and pretty thatched dining pub is in an attractive village surrounded by rolling farmland. The small front bar area has low beams, sofas on flagstones, high bar chairs and an open fire. A dining area leads off with more beams and a mix of pale wooden dining chairs around miscellaneous tables on a stripped wooden floor; background music. The enthusiastic landlord keeps Black Sheep, Fullers London Pride, Gun Dog Jack's Spaniels, Hook Norton Hooky and Sharps Doom Bar on handpump, 18 wines by the glass, a dozen malt whiskies and 15 gins. A modern conservatory restaurant at the back has well spaced tables on bare boards. The sheltered terrace has plenty of tables and chairs under a gazebo.

Contemporary and attractively presented, the interesting food includes sandwiches, baked camembert studded with rosemary and garlic, prawn cocktail, daily fresh fish specials, calves liver with bacon and red wine gravy, chicken with potato gnocchi, chorizo and tomatoes, ginger ale braised pork belly with potato purée and pickled apples, braised lamb shoulder with smoked tomato and pepper ragoût, lemon and thyme potatoes and salsa verde, and puddings such as white chocolate pannacotta with poached rhubarb and sticky toffee pudding with crystallised ginger and cinnamon ice-cream and caramel sauce. *Benchmark main dish: roasted duck with celeriac and potato rösti, anise carrot purée and duck sauce £15.50. Two-course evening meal £20.00.*

Free house ~ Licensee Andrew Judge ~ Real ale ~ Open 12-11; 12-9 Sun ~ Bar food 12-2.30, 5-9; 12-8 Sun ~ Restaurant ~ Well behaved children welcome ~ Dogs allowed in bar ~ Wi-fi

Recommended by Graham and Carol Parker, Dave Braisted, Richard Kennell, Jess and George Cowley, Sophie Ellison, Paul Faraday

AYLESBURY SP8113 Map 4

Kings Head

(01296) 718812 – www.kingsheadaylesbury.co.uk

Kings Head Passage (off Bourbon Street), also entrance off Temple Street; no nearby parking except for disabled; HP20 2RW

Fine old town centre pub with civilised atmosphere, good local ales (used in the food too) and friendly service

It's quite a surprise to come across this little gem, tucked away as it is in a modern town centre. The handsome 15th-c building (owned by the National Trust) is only partly a pub, the rest being the tourist information office, an oak-panelled dining room and conference rooms. The Farmers Bar is three timeless rooms that have been restored with careful and unpretentious simplicity: stripped boards, cream walls with minimal decoration, gentle lighting and a variety of seating which includes upholstered sofas and armchairs, cushioned high-backed settles and some simple modern pale dining tables and chairs dotted around. Most of the bar tables are of circular glass, supported on low cask tops. The neat corner counter has Chiltern Pale Ale, Beechwood Bitter, Black IPA and up to three seasonal guest beers on handpump plus other guests such as Redchurch Paradise Pale Ale, Roosters Ragged Point and Thornbridge Jaipur IPA; also, 11 wines by the glass, two farm ciders and some interesting bottled beers. Service is friendly and there's no background music or machines. The atmospheric medieval cobbled courtyard (said to be the oldest in England) has teak seats and tables, some beneath a pillared roof; summer barbecues and live events. Disabled access and facilities.

Tasty, pubby food includes lunchtime sandwiches, sharing platters, burgers with toppings, coleslaw and sauce, cumberland sausage with chips, chicken caesar salad, beef in ale pie, and puddings such as apple crumble and bakewell slice. *Benchmark main dish: beer-battered haddock and chips £10.50. Two-course evening meal £15.00.*

Chiltern ~ Manager George Jenkinson ~ Real ale ~ Open 11-11; 12-10.30 Sun ~ Bar food 11.30-3, 5-9 (not Mon or Tues evenings); 11.30-9 Fri, Sat; 12-6 Sun ~ Restaurant ~ Children welcome away from bar ~ Wi-fi *Recommended by Graham and Carol Parker, David and Charlotte Green, Robin and Anne Triggs, Dr J Barrie Jones*

BOVINGDON GREEN SU8386 Map 2

Royal Oak

(01628) 488611 – www.royaloakmarlow.co.uk

0.75 miles N of Marlow, on back road to Frieth signposted off West Street (A4155) in centre; SL7 2JF

Buckinghamshire Dining Pub of the Year

Civilised dining pub with nice little bar, a fine choice of wines by the glass, real ales and imaginative food

Most customers are here to enjoy the enticing, seasonal food but they do keep Rebellion IPA on handpump alongside a guest such as Rebellion Roasted Nuts, 33 wines by the glass (including sparkling wine, champagne and pudding wines), 41 gins and 15 malt whiskies. Staff are helpful and impressively efficient even when really pushed. The low-beamed, cosy snug, closest to the car park, has three small tables and a woodburning stove in an exposed brick fireplace (with a big pile of logs beside it). Several other attractively decorated areas open off the central bar with half-panelled walls variously painted in pale blue, green or cream (the dining room ones are red). Throughout there's a mix of church chairs, stripped wooden tables and chunky wall seats, with rugs on the partly wooden, partly flagstoned floors, co-ordinated cushions and curtains, and a bright, airy feel. Thoughtful extra touches enhance the tone: a bowl of olives on the bar, carefully laid-out newspapers and fresh flowers or candles on the tables. Background music. A sunny terrace with good solid tables leads to an appealing garden with pétanque, ping pong, badminton and swing ball; there's also a smaller side garden and a kitchen herb garden. They have a tipi for private events.

First class modern food includes crayfish cocktail sliders with fennel and kohlrabi slaw, wild mushroom pannacotta with candied walnuts, tarragon oil and celeriac purée, chickpea and sweetcorn bhajis with roast romanesco, pickled cauliflower and curried popcorn, sea bass with basil gnocchi, caramelised fennel, black olives and charred tomato oil, chargrilled 28-day dry-aged rib-eye steak with skinny fries and roast garlic and béarnaise butter, guinea fowl with creamed celeriac, fondant potato, greens and truffle jus, and puddings such as baked chocolate and tonka bean soup with honeycomb ice-cream and warm carrot and walnut cake with toffee sauce and cream cheese sorbet. *Benchmark main dish: bubble and squeak with oak-smoked bacon, a free-range poached egg and hollandaise £13.25. Two-course evening meal £23.00.*

Salisbury Pubs ~ Manager James Molier ~ Real ale ~ Open 11am-midnight; 12-11 Sun ~ Bar food 12-2.30, 6.30-9.30; 12-3, 6.30-10 Fri, Sat; 12-9 Sun ~ Restaurant ~ Children welcome ~ Dogs allowed in bar ~ Wi-fi *Recommended by Guy Henderson, Mary and Douglas McDowell, Sally Anne and Peter Goodale*

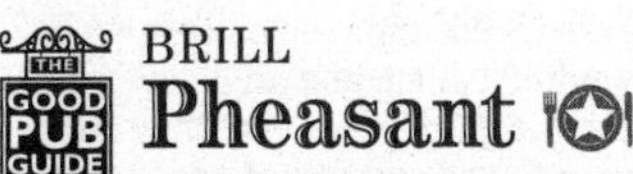

BRILL SP6514 Map 4

Pheasant

(01844) 239370 – www.thepheasant.co.uk

Windmill Street; off B4011 Bicester–Long Crendon; HP18 9TG

Long-reaching views, a bustling bar with local ales, attentive staff and tasty food; bedrooms

Our readers love their visits here and their reports are full of enthusiastic praise for all aspects of this well run inn. The interior is more or less open-plan, with a raftered bar area, leather tub seats in front of a woodburner, and a good mix of customers – including chatty, friendly regulars. Brains Rev James, Vale Brill Gold and a beer named for the pub on handpump and a dozen wines by the glass are served by charming, attentive staff. Dining areas have high-backed leather or dark wooden chairs, attractively framed prints and books on shelves; background music. There are plenty of seats and tables on the decked area and in the garden with marvellous views over the windmill opposite (one of the oldest post windmills still in working order) and into the distance across five counties. Bedrooms are comfortable and two are in the former bakehouse; good views and nearby walks too. Roald Dahl used to drink here, and some of the tales the locals told him were worked into his short stories.

Particularly good food includes smoked salmon and cream cheese roulade with fennel and dill, an antipasti sharing plate, chicken caesar salad, honey-roasted ham and free-range 'the works', local sausages with confit onions and gravy, curried tiger prawns and indian bread, venison loin with creamy truffle mash, black pudding and gravy, scallops with thermidor sauce and fries, sirloin steak with a choice of sauce, and puddings such as stem ginger sticky toffee pudding with toffee sauce and vanilla ice-cream and warm bakewell tart; they also offer a weekday takeaway menu. *Benchmark main dish: steak in ale pie £14.00. Two-course evening meal £20.50.*

Free house ~ Licensee Marilyn Glover ~ Real ale ~ Open 12-11 (midnight Fri, Sat); 12-10 Sun ~ Bar food 12-2.30, 6-9; 12-5 Sun ~ Children welcome ~ Dogs allowed in bar ~ Wi-fi ~ Bedrooms: £85/£110 *Recommended by John Evans, Alison and Graeme Spicer, Canon Michael Bourdeaux, Neil and Angela Huxter, Gerry and Rosemary Dobson, Graham and Carol Parker*

A star symbol after the name of a pub shows exceptional character and appeal. It doesn't mean extra comfort. And it's nothing to do with exceptional food quality, for which there's a separate star-on-a-plate symbol. Even quite a basic pub can win a star, if it's individual enough.

BRILL SP6513 Map 4

Pointer

(01844) 238339 – www.thepointerbrill.co.uk

Church Street; HP18 9RT

Carefully restored pub in a pretty village with rewarding food, local ales and interesting furnishings; bedrooms

Four new restful, pretty bedrooms have been opened up in a red-brick cottage opposite this handsome village inn. The stylish bar has low beams, windsor chairs, elegant armchairs and sofas with brocaded cushions, open fires or woodburners in brick fireplaces and animal-hide stools by the counter. A beer named for the pub (from the XT Brewing Company), Vale Gravitas and a guest from Rebellion on handpump, 11 wines by the glass, a dozen gins, 28 malt whiskies, and friendly, attentive staff. The airy and attractive restaurant has antique Ercol chairs around pale oak tables, cushioned window seats, rafters in a high vaulted ceiling and an open kitchen. French windows open on to the sizeable garden. Do visit their own butchers next door where they sell home-reared beef and free-range pork, free-range eggs, home-baked bread and home-made pies, sausage rolls and so on (open 2.30-6.30pm Wednesday-Friday, 9am-2.30pm Saturday). Tolkien is said to have based the village of Bree in *The Lord of the Rings* on this pretty village.

Impressive food using meat from their own farm and other seasonal, local produce includes pub classics, as well as crab on toast with avocado, fennel and orange, beetroot and pear salad with goats curd, wild mushroom risotto with aged parmesan, Torbay sole with roasted salsify, spinach and beurre noisette, venison haunch with butternut squash, red onion and pear, ox tongue with carrot and swede and red wine sauce, and puddings such as caramel and hazelnut parfait with chocolate nougat and treacle tart with poached rhubarb and vanilla ice-cream; they also offer a two- and three-course set lunch (Tuesday-Friday). *Benchmark main dish: rare-breed slow-roasted suckling pig with apple and scrumpy sauce £22.00. Two-course evening meal £35.00.*

Free house ~ Licensees David and Fiona Howden ~ Real ale ~ Open 12-11.30 (midnight Sat); 12-9 Sun; closed Mon and first week Jan ~ Bar food 12-2.30, 6.30-9.30; 12.30-4.30 Sun ~ Restaurant ~ Children welcome ~ Dogs allowed in bar and bedrooms ~ Wi-fi ~ Bedrooms: /£180 *Recommended by Brian Glozier, John Harris, Jim King, Camilla and Jose Ferrera, Peter and Alison Steadman*

BUTLERS CROSS SP8407 Map 4

Russell Arms

(01296) 624411 – www.therussellarms.co.uk

Off A4010 S of Aylesbury, at Nash Lee roundabout; or off A413 in Wendover, passing station; Chalkshire Road; HP17 0TS

Attractive old pub in quiet village with access to Chiltern hills; good food, local ales, friendly landlord and seats on sunny terrace

After a walk in the nearby Chilterns come to this brick and flint former coaching inn for lunch. The simply furnished bar has stools and chairs around polished tables on new pale floorboards, tartan curtains, fresh flowers, an open fire with logs piled high to both sides and a woodburning stove in an inglenook fireplace; there's also a contemporary restaurant area. Well kept Brakspears Bitter, Chiltern Beechwood Bitter and Rebellion Zebedee on handpump, 17 wines by the glass and artisan gins, all served by welcoming staff; background music and board games. French windows lead to a suntrap terrace with teak furniture and there are steps up to the garden with picnic-sets. This was the servants' quarters for nearby Chequers, the prime minister's country retreat.

Interesting, seasonal food includes goats cheese mousse with golden beetroot, pomegranate and a yoghurt crisp, grilled mackerel with apple, kohlrabi, squid ink and dill oil, potato and truffle gnocchi with wild mushrooms and a parmesan crisp, a pie of the day, braised lamb shoulder with shepherd's pie, mousseline potatoes and lamb sauce, sea trout with crab-crushed potatoes and salsa verde, chicken suprême with king oyster mushroom, bacon, leeks and thyme jus, and puddings such as mixed berry and caramelised white chocolate pavlova. *Benchmark main dish: braised pork belly with black haggis croquette, cauliflower and jus £17.95. Two-course evening meal £24.00.*

Free house ~ Licensee James Penlington ~ Real ale ~ Open 11-11 (midnight Sat); 12-9 Sun; 12-6 Sun in winter; closed Mon ~ Bar food 12-2.30, 6.30-9; 12-4 Sun ~ Children welcome ~ Dogs allowed in bar ~ Wi-fi *Recommended by Lorna and Jack Mulgrave, Holly and Tim Waite, Simon and Sue Lamb, Sally and Brian Turner*

FORTY GREEN SU9291 Map 2

Royal Standard of England

(01494) 673382 – www.rsoe.co.uk

3.5 miles from M40 junction 2, via A40 to Beaconsfield, then follow sign to Forty Green, off B474 0.75 miles N of New Beaconsfield; keep going through village; HP9 1XT

Full of history and character, with fascinating antiques in rambling rooms, and good choice of drinks and food

This ancient pub has enormous appeal, both in the layout of the building itself and in the fascinating collection of antiques which fills it. It's been trading for nearly 900 years and there's a leaflet documenting its long history which is really worth a read. The rambling rooms have some fine old features to look out for: huge black ship's timbers, lovely worn floors, carved oak panelling, roaring winter fires with handsomely decorated iron firebacks and cluttered mantelpieces; there's also a massive settle apparently built to fit the curved transom of an Elizabethan ship. Nooks and crannies are filled with a collection of antiques, including rifles, powder-flasks and bugles, ancient pewter and pottery tankards, lots of tarnished brass and copper, needlework samplers and richly coloured stained glass. Belhaven 80/- Ale, Chiltern Pale Ale, Rebellion IPA and Windsor & Eton Conqueror and Guardsman on handpump, a carefully annotated list of bottled beers, 11 malt whiskies, seven gins, farm ciders, perry, somerset brandy and 19 wines by the glass. You can sit outside in a neatly hedged front rose garden or under the shade of a tree; look out for the red gargoyle on the wall facing the car park. The inn is used regularly for filming television programmes such as *Midsomer Murders*.

A wide choice of food includes lunchtime baguettes and toasties, whitebait, devilled kidneys on fried bread, chicken caesar salad, home-made sausages with mash and onion gravy, chicken, leek and mushroom or fish pie, butternut squash and bean burger with pickles and chips, steak and kidney pudding, pork belly with red cabbage, bubble and squeak and apple sauce, rib-eye steak with pepper or blue cheese sauce, and puddings such as hot chocolate pudding with ice-cream and crème brûlée. *Benchmark main dish: beer-battered fish and chips £14.75. Two-course evening meal £20.00.*

Free house ~ Licensee Matthew O'Keeffe ~ Real ale ~ Open 11-11 ~ Bar food 12-9.30 ~ Children welcome ~ Dogs welcome ~ Wi-fi *Recommended by Martin and Sue Neville, Charlie May, Selwyn Jones, Mrs Edna Jones*

FULMER SU9985 Map 2

Black Horse

(01753) 663183 – www.theblackhorsefulmer.co.uk

Village signposted off A40 in Gerrards Cross, W of junction with A413; Windmill Road; SL3 6HD

Appealingly reworked dining pub, friendly and relaxed, with up-to-date food, exemplary service and pleasant garden; bedrooms

Once found, this is a place that customers tend to return to on a regular basis. Usefully open all day, it's an extended 17th-c pub with a proper bar in the middle and two cosy areas to the left: low black beams, rugs on bare boards, settles and other solid pub furniture and several open log fires. Greene King IPA, Timothy Taylors Landlord and a guest such as Sharps Sea Fury on handpump, 21 wines by the glass and 22 malt whiskies; staff are friendly and efficient even when pushed. Background music, TV. The main area on the right is set for dining and leads to the good-sized suntrap back terrace where there's a summer barbecue bar. The two bedrooms are stylish and well equipped. The church is next door and this is a charming conservation village.

All-day country cooking (with just an hour's break in the morning) includes sandwiches, sharing boards, crab cakes with roasted corn, chilli and coriander dressing and popcorn, baked camembert to share with pineapple chutney, wild mushroom risotto with truffle oil, smoky barbecue ribs with coleslaw and skinny fries, halibut and haricot bean cassoulet, confit duck leg with balsamic and bacon lentils and orange jus, and puddings such as passion-fruit brûlée and steamed date pudding with banana caramel sauce and vanilla ice-cream. *Benchmark main dish: beer-battered haddock and chips £14.75. Two-course evening meal £20.00.*

Greene King ~ Lease Jane Gaunt ~ Real ale ~ Open 8am-11pm; 12-10.30 Sun ~ Bar food 8am-11am, 12-9.30; 12-7 Sun) ~ Restaurant ~ Children welcome ~ Dogs allowed in bar ~ Wi-fi ~ Bedrooms: /£120 *Recommended by R K Phillips, Ian Phillips, Anne and Ben Smith, Andrew and Michele Revell*

GRANBOROUGH SP7625 Map 4

Crown

(01296) 670216 – www.thecrowngranborough.co.uk

Winslow Road; MK18 3NJ

Extended coaching inn that's perfect in good weather with several seating areas and an outside bar, and cosy in winter with open fires

In warm weather you can sit on cushioned rattan-style sofas on the terrace, at wooden tables and chairs under parasols on gravel or at picnic-sets on grass (where there's also a climbing frame); summer barbecues. Inside, the main bar is a long room with painted beams, high chairs at the counter and at elbow tables and a fire at one end; a second bar has leather tub chairs, more painted beams and a comfortable feel. Fullers London Pride, Gun Dog Scrum Dog, Sharps Doom Bar and Vale Brill Gold on handpump, 12 wines by the glass and 30 gins, served by friendly staff. The restaurant is a lovely room with high ceilings and oak beams, farmhouse and other chairs around solid tables on wooden boards and a woodburning stove in a sizeable fireplace; a smaller room is more intimate and similarly furnished.

Interesting food includes sandwiches, ham hock terrine with mustard piccalilli, prawn and crayfish cocktail, daily fresh fish specials, duck leg hash with parsnip purée and an egg, burger with toppings and triple-cooked chips, smoked haddock mac and cheese with parmesan crumble, chicken breast with mushroom gnocchi and artichoke purée, 10oz rib-eye steak with pepper sauce and puddings. *Benchmark main dish: local sausages with bubble and squeak and braised red cabbage £13.50. Two-course evening meal £20.00.*

Free house ~ Licensee Andy Judge ~ Real ale ~ Open 12-11 (5-9 Mon); 12-8 Sun; closed Mon lunchtime ~ Bar food 12-2, 5-9; 12-6 Sun; not Mon ~ Restaurant ~ Children welcome ~ Dogs allowed in bar ~ Wi-fi *Recommended by John and Abigail Prescott, Nicola and Nigel Matthews, Peter Pilbeam, Mandy and Gary Redstone, Mick Allen, Graham and Carol Parker*

GREAT MISSENDEN SP9000 Map 4

Nags Head

(01494) 862200 – www.nagsheadbucks.com

Old London Road, E – beyond Abbey; HP16 0DG

Well run and pretty inn with beamed bars, an open fire, a good range of drinks and modern cooking; bedrooms

It's the tempting food that draws most customers in to this pub, formerly three 15th-c cottages. There's a low-beamed area on the left, a loftier part on the right, a mix of small pews, dining chairs and tables on carpet, Quentin Blake prints on cream walls and a log fire in a handsome fireplace. Rebellion IPA and a couple of guests such as Chiltern Beechwood Bitter and Malt Missenden Pale Ale on handpump from the unusual bar counter (the windows behind face the road), 25 wines by the glass from an extensive list, 15 malt whiskies, 20 gins and half a dozen vintage Armagnacs. As well as an outside dining area beneath a pergola, there are seats on the extensive back lawn. Beamed bedrooms are well equipped and comfortable, and the breakfasts are very good. Roald Dahl used this as his local and the Roald Dahl Museum & Story Centre is just a stroll away.

Creative food includes pub classics as well as ham hock, wrapped in seaweed leaf with a fried quail egg, piccalilli cream and toast, white crab and home-smoked salmon with chive cream and blinis, a risotto of the day, cod fillet with a herb crust and tomato broth with beluga lentils and yellow split peas, lamb steak with wholegrain mustard jus and wilted wild rocket, duck breast and confit leg with black fig jus, and puddings such as white chocolate and raspberry jelly cheesecake with mixed berry and Chambord compote and bourbon vanilla crème brûlée. *Benchmark main dish: veal kidneys in creamy brandy sauce £16.95. Two-course evening meal £20.00.*

Free house ~ Licensee Adam Michaels ~ Real ale ~ Open 12-11 ~ Bar food 12-2.30, 6.30-9.30; 12-7 Sun ~ Restaurant ~ Children welcome ~ Dogs allowed in bar ~ Wi-fi ~ Bedrooms: £90/£95 *Recommended by Gerry and Rosemary Dobson, Dan and Nicki Barton, Amanda Shipley*

HEDGERLEY SU9687 Map 2

White Horse ★ £

(01753) 643225 – www.thewhitehorsehedgerley.co.uk

2.4 miles from M40 junction 2; at exit roundabout take Slough turn-off following alongside M40; after 1.5 miles turn right at T junction into Village Lane; SL2 3UY

Convivial old place with lots of beers, home-made lunchtime food and a cheery mix of customers

Everybody loves the fact that as an old-fashioned and charming country gem, this place does not change at all. Most are here to enjoy the fine range of real ales, which might include Rebellion IPA and up to seven daily changing guests, sourced from all over the country and tapped straight from casks kept in a room behind the tiny hatch counter. Their Easter, May, Spring and August bank holiday beer festivals (they can get through about 130 beers during the May event) are highlights of the local calendar. This marvellous range of drinks extends to craft ales in cans or bottles, three farm ciders, 12 wines by the glass, a dozen malt whiskies and winter mulled wine. The cottagey main bar has plenty of unspoilt character with beams, brasses and exposed brickwork, low wooden tables, standing timbers, jugs, ballcocks and other bric-a-brac, a log fire and a good few leaflets and notices about village events. A little flagstoned public bar on the left has darts, shove-ha'penny and board games. A canopied extension leads out to the garden where there are tables, lots of hanging baskets and occasional barbecues; a few tables in front of the building overlook the quiet road. Good walks nearby and the pub is handy for the Church Wood RSPB reserve.

Lunchtime-only bar food includes good sandwiches, a salad bar with home-cooked quiches and cold meats, changing hot dishes such as soup, sausage or lamb casserole, and proper puddings such as plum sponge and bread and butter pudding. *Benchmark main dish: pie of the day £7.50.*

Free house ~ Licensees Doris Hobbs and Kevin Brooker ~ Real ale ~ Open 11-2.30, 5-11; 11-11 Sat; 12-10.30 Sun ~ Bar food 12-2 (2.30 weekends) ~ Children allowed in canopied extension area ~ Dogs allowed in bar ~ Wi-fi *Recommended by Len and Lilly Dowson, Val and Malcolm Travers, Tom and Lorna Harding, Susan and John Douglas, Rod Wilson, V Brogden*

LITTLE MARLOW SU8787 Map 2

Queens Head

(01628) 482927 – www.marlowslittlesecret.co.uk

Village signposted off A4155 E of Marlow near Kings Head; bear right into Pound Lane cul-de-sac; SL7 3SR

Pretty tiled cottage with good food and ales, friendly staff and appealing garden

Head for the church if you want to find this charmingly tucked-away country pub. The friendly, unpretentious main bar has simple but comfortable furniture on polished boards and leads back to a sizeable squarish carpeted dining extension with good solid tables. Throughout are old local photographs on cream or maroon walls, panelled dados painted brown or sage, and lighted candles. On the right is a small, quite separate, low-ceilinged public bar with Rebellion IPA and Sharps Doom Bar on handpump, several wines by the glass, quite a range of whiskies and good coffee; neatly dressed efficient staff and unobtrusive background music. On summer days, the front garden is a decided plus, though not large: sheltered and neatly planted, it has teak tables and quite closely arranged picnic-sets, and white-painted metal furniture in a little wickerwork bower.

Tempting food includes lunchtime sandwiches, ham hock and baby vegetable terrine with home-made piccalilli, scallops on sweetcorn pancakes with red pepper coulis, spicy bean burger with a rich virgin mary sauce, crispy pork and tiger prawn thai broth with chili bread, crispy cabbage and sesame dipping sauce, corn-fed chicken with sweet potato hash, black pudding purée, glazed shallots and jus, braised shin of beef with oxtail ravioli with potato purée, baby carrots and sun-dried tomatoes, and puddings such as earl grey tea crème brûlée and fruit trifle. *Benchmark main dish: beer-battered fish and chips £12.50. Two-course evening meal £15.00.*

Punch ~ Lease Daniel O'Sullivan ~ Real ale ~ Open 11-11; 11-10 Sun ~ Bar food 12-2.30, 6.30-9.30; 12-4, 6.30-9.30 weekends ~ Restaurant ~ Children welcome ~ Wi-fi *Recommended by Bernard Stradling, Anne Taylor, Alexandra and Richard Clay, Simon Collett-Jones, Alexander and Trish Cutter*

LITTLE MISSENDEN SU9298 Map 4

Crown £

(01494) 862571 – www.thecrownlittlemissenden.co.uk

Crown Lane, SE end of village, which is signposted off A413 W of Amersham; HP7 0RD

Long-serving licensees and pubby feel in little country cottage, with several real ales and straightforward food; attractive garden

Of course, the regulars love it here but there's a proper welcome for visitors too from the friendly family who've run this place for more than 90 years. It's a traditional brick cottage with bustling bars that are more spacious than they might first appear – and immaculately kept. There are old red floor tiles on the left, oak parquet on the right, built-in wall seats, studded red leatherette chairs and a few small tables and a winter fire. Otter Bitter and St Austell Tribute with a couple of quickly changing guests on handpump or tapped from the cask, farm cider, summer Pimms and several malt whiskies; darts and board games. A large attractive sheltered garden behind has picnic-sets and other tables, and there are also seats out in front. Bedrooms are in a converted barn (continental breakfasts in your room only). Dogs may be allowed inside if well behaved. No children. The interesting church in the pretty village is well worth a visit.

Honest lunchtime-only food (not Sunday) includes their famous bucks bite, a big choice of sandwiches with home-made chutney, cornish pasty with baked beans, generous salads and smoked haddock and spring onion or cod and bacon fishcakes with a sweet chilli dip. *Benchmark main dish: pie of the day £8.75.*

Free house ~ Licensees Trevor and Carolyn How ~ Real ale ~ Open 11-2.30, 6-11; 12-3, 7-10.30 Sun ~ Bar food 12-2; not Sun ~ Wi-fi ~ Bedrooms: /£85 *Recommended by David Lamb, Edward May, Peter and Emma Kelly, Caroline and Oliver Sterling, William and Sophia Renton*

LONG CRENDON SP6908 Map 4

Eight Bells

(01844) 208244 – www.8bellspub.com

High Street, off B4011 N of Thame; car park entrance off Chearsley Road, not 'Village roads only'; HP18 9AL

Good beers and sensibly priced seasonal food in nicely traditional village pub with charming garden

This old place became a licensed pub in 1607 when it was called the Five Bells. Once the church had three more bells installed in 1771, the inn changed its name. The little bare-boards bar on the left has Marstons Pedigree, Rebellion Smuggler, XT Four and a guest beer on handpump, 16 wines by the glass, 14 gins and summer cider; service is cheerful. A bigger low-ceilinged room on the right has a log fire, daily papers and a pleasantly haphazard mix of tables and simple seats on ancient red and black tiles; one snug little hidey-hole is devoted to the local morris men who are frequent visitors. Board games, TV and background music. The small back garden is a joy in summer when there are well spaced picnic-sets among a colourful variety of shrubs and flowers; aunt sally. The interesting old village is known to many from TV's *Midsomer Murders*. Sister pub is the Black Boy in Oving.

Traditional food includes generous sandwiches, crispy baby squid with chorizo jam, goats cheese and red pepper bonbons, pizzas with lots of toppings, steak and mushroom in ale pie, oriental noodles with stir-fry vegetables, ham and free-range eggs, cod loin with garlic pesto spaghetti, mixed grill, and puddings such as chocolate brownie with chocolate sauce and mango possett with meringue; Tuesday is pie night and Thursday is burger specials. *Benchmark main dish: burger with toppings and skinny fries £13.25. Two-course evening meal £20.00.*

Free house ~ Licensee Paul Mitchell ~ Real ale ~ Open 12-11; 12-10 Sun ~ Bar food 12-9; 12-4 (pizzas till 8) Sun ~ Restaurant ~ Children welcome ~ Dogs welcome ~ Wi-fi ~ Regular events; see website *Recommended by Peter Brix, Martin Jones, Elizabeth and Bill Humphries, Jill and Dick Archer, Gerry and Rosemary Dobson*

OVING SP7821 Map 4

Black Boy

(01296) 641258 – www.theblackboyoving.co.uk

Off A413 N of Aylesbury; HP22 4HN

Partly 16th-c pub with friendly owners, popular food, local ales and lovely views from spacious garden

A popular, friendly pub, this has dining rooms and a bar that are linked by brick arches with beams, log fires (one in a huge inglenook), wooden chairs around tables of all sizes on bare boards or original black and red tiles, sofas and settles with scatter cushions, books on shelves and various prints and photos on pale walls. Friendly staff serve Chiltern Beechwood Bitter, Ringwood Boondoggle and XT Four on handpump, 16 wines by the glass, farm cider and a specialist gin menu with lots of mixers. Seats and tables on spacious sloping lawns and a raised terrace behind this 16th-c brick and timbered pub have expansive views of the Vale of Aylesbury; not surprisingly, it's best to arrive early on a sunny day. Sister pub is the Eight Bells in Long Crendon.

Good food includes generous sandwiches and sharing boards, crispy duck salad with hoisin sauce, pork bonbons with apple sauce, pizzas, burgers with toppings, vegetable enchilada, steak and kidney pie, butterflied sea bass with stir-fried vegetables, mixed grill, and puddings such as vanilla pannacotta with red wine poached fig and black forest tiramisu; all main courses are available as takeaway options. *Benchmark main dish: chicken with pepperonata sauce and parmentier potatoes £13.95. Two-course evening meal £21.00.*

Free house ~ Licensee Paul Mitchell ~ Real ale ~ Open 12-11; 12-6 Sun; closed Sun evening ~ Bar food 12-9; 12-4 Sun ~ Restaurant ~ Children welcome ~ Dogs welcome ~ Wi-fi *Recommended by Chloe and Tim Hodge, Martine and Fabio Lockley, Miles Green*

Also Worth a Visit in Buckinghamshire

Besides the fully inspected pubs, you might like to try these pubs that have been recommended to us and described by readers. Do tell us what you think of them: feedback@goodguides.com

AMERSHAM SU9597

Elephant & Castle (01494) 721049
High Street; HP7 0DT Twin-gabled local with good value tasty food including sharing plates, stone-baked pizzas and burgers, quick friendly service, three well kept ales such as St Austell from U-shaped counter, low-beams, woodburner in large brick fireplace, conservatory; garden behind, children and dogs welcome, open (and food) all day. *(Mick Allen)*

AMERSHAM SU9597

Kings Arms (01494) 725722
High Street; HP7 0DJ Picture-postcard timbered inn (dates from the 1400s) in charming street, lots of heavy beams and snug alcoves, big inglenook, Brakspears, Rebellion and a guest, over a dozen wines by the glass and good range of enjoyable food from sandwiches up, afternoon teas, friendly helpful service, restaurant; children and dogs (in bar) welcome, 34 bedrooms,

garden behind, open all day, food all day weekends. *(Simon Collett-Jones)*

AMERSHAM SU9597

Swan (01494) 727079

High Street; HP7 0ED Mitchells & Butlers pub-restaurant on two floors; contemporary bar with comfortable chairs and low tables, decent choice of enjoyable food from sharing plates up including children's menu, well kept beers such as Fullers and Rebellion, several wines by the glass; tables out on front cobbles and in nice garden behind, open (and food) all day. *(Rob Harrison)*

ASHERIDGE SP9404

Blue Ball (01494) 758305

Braziers End; HP5 2UX Small open-plan country pub with light airy décor, generous helpings of enjoyable good value food cooked to order including daily specials, well kept Courage Directors, Fullers London Pride and Youngs Bitter, real cider, friendly landlady and staff; children (till 6pm) and dogs welcome, large well maintained back garden, good Chilterns walking country, open all day, no food Sun or Mon evenings. *(Mrs P Sumner, Brian Smith, Roy Hoing)*

ASTON ABBOTTS SP8519

Royal Oak (01296) 681262

Off A418 NE of Aylesbury; Wingrave Road; HP22 4LT Welcoming part-thatched beamed pub, up to four real ales and generous helpings of enjoyable reasonably priced food; children welcome, sunny back garden, bedrooms, quite handy for Ascott House (NT). *(David Lamb)*

ASTON CLINTON SP8811

Bell (01296) 632777

London Road; HP22 5HP Comfortably refurbished old Mitchells & Butlers village inn-restaurant; good choice of enjoyable food from sandwiches and sharing boards up, vegan choices, Adnams Southwold, Fullers London Pride, and a couple of guests, plenty of wines by the glass including champagne, friendly efficient service; children welcome, tables out under trees, 11 bedrooms, car park across road, open (and food) all day from 8am. *(David Lamb)*

ASTWOOD SP9547

Old Swan (01234) 391351

Main Road; MK16 9JS Part thatched 17th-c village pub with warm cosy atmosphere, good food cooked by chef-landlord, well kept Fullers London Pride and a guest such as Sharps, nice selection of wines, friendly helpful service, beams and gleaming flagstones, inglenook woodburner, china collection, two attractive dining areas; children welcome, large garden, closed Sun evening, Mon and Tues. *(Nigel Cowdery, S Holder)*

AYLESBURY SP8114

Hop Pole (01296) 482129

Bicester Road; HP19 9AZ Friendly well looked after end of terrace pub brewing its own Aylesbury Brewhouse beers, also guests such as Vale and traditional cider, enjoyable fairly priced food including sharing platters and grills, back restaurant; seats out at front behind metal fence, open all day Fri-Sun, closed Mon lunchtime. *(Pesto)*

BEACHAMPTON SP7736

Bell (01908) 418373

Main Street; MK19 6DX Big low-beamed pub with pleasant view down attractive streamside village street, updated bar and dining area divided by woodburner, popular food including weekday offers, up to four changing ales, good friendly service; children welcome, large garden with paved terrace, open all day (till 8pm Sun), closed Mon. *(Graham and Carol Parker, Jess and George Cowley)*

BEACONSFIELD SU9588

Hope & Champion (01494) 685530

M40, Beaconsfield Services; HP9 2SE UK's first pub (Wetherspoons) in a motorway service area; spacious spotlessly clean modern interior on two floors, five real ales including Sharps Doom Bar and enjoyable food from breakfast on, good fast service; TVs, free wi-fi; children welcome, no dogs inside, disabled access to ground floor only, seats out overlooking lake with fountain, open (and food) all day from 6am. *(Ross Balaam)*

BEACONSFIELD SU9490

Royal Saracens (01494) 674119

1 mile from M40 junction 2; London End (A40); HP9 2JH Former coaching inn with striking timbered façade and well updated open-plan interior; bar area with comfortable seating on wood or tiled floors, massive beams and timbers in one corner, log fires, wide choice of enjoyable food from sandwiches and sharing plates up, evening fixed-price menu (Mon, Tues) for two including bottle of wine, well kept ales such as Fullers London Pride and Sharps Doom Bar, craft kegs and plenty of wines by the glass, friendly young staff, large back restaurant; children welcome, modern furniture and seating booths in sheltered courtyard, open (and food) all day, busy at weekends when best to book. *(Tim and Mary Thomson)*

Real ale may be served from handpumps, electric pumps (not just the on-off switches used for keg beer) or – common in Scotland – tall taps called founts (pronounced 'fonts') where a separate pump pushes the beer up under air pressure.

BLEDLOW RIDGE SU7997

Boot (01494) 481499

Chinnor Road; HP14 4AW Welcoming village pub with fresh modern décor; good food from sandwiches, sharing plates and pub favourites up, well kept Rebellion ales and Sharps Doom Bar, several wines by the glass from extensive list, dining room with exposed rafters and large brick fireplace; background music; children and dogs welcome, terrace and sizeable lawned garden, closed Mon, otherwise open all day (till 8pm Sun). *(David Lamb)*

BOURNE END SU8987

Bounty (01628) 520056

Cock Marsh, actually across the river along the Cookham towpath, but shortest walk – still over 0.25 miles – is from Bourne End, over the railway bridge; SL8 5RG Welcoming take-us-as-you-find-us pub tucked away in outstanding setting on bank of the Thames and accessible only by foot or boat; collection of flags on ceiling and jumble of other bits and pieces, well kept Rebellion ales from boat counter, basic standard food including children's meals, back dining area, darts and bar billiards; background music inside and out; dirty dogs and muddy walkers welcome, picnic-sets with parasols on front terrace, play area to right, open all day in summer (may be boat trips), just weekends in winter and closes early if quiet. *(Tony and Wendy Hobden)*

BUCKINGHAM SP6933

Villiers (01280) 822444

Castle Street; MK18 1BS Pub part of this large comfortable hotel with own courtyard entrance; big inglenook log fire, panelling and stripped masonry in flagstoned bar, beers from Hook Norton and Black Sheep, reliably good food from shortish menu, afternoon tea, competent friendly staff, sofas and armchairs in more formal front lounges, restaurant with two large tropical fish tanks; children welcome till 9pm, no dogs, terrace tables, open all day. *(Caroline and Oliver Sterling)*

CHALFONT ST GILES SU9895

Ivy House (01494) 872184

A413 S; HP8 4RS Old brick and flint coaching inn with U-shaped bar, wood or tiled floors, log fire, Fullers ales and a guest back beamed and flagstoned restaurant serving tasty home-made food, friendly staff; background and some live music, quiz Thurs, free wi-fi; children welcome, some seats out under covered front part by road, pleasant terrace and sloping garden, five comfortable bedrooms, good hearty breakfast, open all day (till 8pm Sun). *(Tracey and Stephen Groves)*

CHEARSLEY SP7110

Bell (01844) 208077

The Green; HP18 0DJ Cosy traditional thatched and beamed pub on attractive village green; Fullers beers and good wines by the glass, enjoyable sensibly priced home-made food (not Sun or Mon evenings), efficient friendly service, inglenook with big woodburner; quiz (first Sun of month), bingo (first Tues); children in eating area, dogs welcome, plenty of tables in spacious back garden with heated terrace and play area. *(David Lamb)*

CHENIES TQ0198

Bedford Arms (01923) 283301

2 miles from M25 junction 18; A404 towards Amersham, then village signposted on right; Chesham Road; WD3 6EQ Country-house hotel with bright modernised front bar, good food here or in more formal oak-panelled restaurant (all day Sun), efficient staff, Fullers London Pride, Tring Side Pocket for a Toad and a guest, decent choice of wines by the glass; tables on attractive front terrace and in lovely garden behind with mature oaks, 18 bedrooms, enjoyable walks, open all day. *(Graham and Pam Winton, Richard Kennell)*

CHESHAM SP9604

Black Horse (01494) 784656

Vale Road, N off A416 in Chesham; HP5 3NS Extended and recently refurbished black-beamed country pub; well liked pubby food (all day Sat, till 8pm Sun) from sandwiches up, Charles Wells ales and guests, good friendly service, inglenook log fire; Tues quiz; children and dogs welcome, picnic-sets out in front and on back lawn, closed Mon, otherwise open all day. *(Monty Green)*

CHESHAM SP9501

Queens Head (01494) 778690

Church Street; HP5 1JD Popular corner pub with two traditional beamed bars, scrubbed tables and log fires, Fullers ales and a guest kept well, good thai food along with modest range of pub staples, restaurant, friendly staff and chatty locals; sports TV, quiz Thurs, free wi-fi; children and dogs welcome, tables in small courtyard used by smokers, next to little River Chess, open all day. *(Graham Smart)*

CLIFTON REYNES SP9051

Robin Hood (01234) 711574

Off back road Emberton–Newton Blossomville; no-through road; MK46 5DR Stone-built 16th-c village pub with welcoming licensees and good friendly service, nice range of well liked food including wood-fired pizzas, three real ales such as St Austell and decent wines, dark beams, woodburner in small lounge's inglenook, dining conservatory; bar billiards and darts; children and dogs (in bar) welcome, back garden with terrace and summer barbecues, riverside walks to Olney, closed Mon. *(Nigel Cowdery, Philip Randell)*

COLESHILL SU9594

★Harte & Magpies (01494) 726754
E of village on A355 Amersham–Beaconsfield, by junction with Magpie Lane; HP7 0LU Busy roadside pub with open-plan interior; collection of pews, high-backed booths and distinctive tables and chairs making for plenty of snug corners, candles in bottles and lots of old patriotic prints, ales such as Chiltern and Rebellion, several wines by the glass and popular food from baguettes and pizzas up; children (except on live music evenings) and dogs welcome, picnic-sets on terrace by wisteria-draped tree, more tables in big sloping garden with sturdy wooden play area, classic car meeting (second Tues of month Apr-Sept), good surrounding walks, open (and food) all day, Sun till 9.30pm (8pm). *(David Lamb, Edward Edmonton, Brian and Susan Wylie)*

COLNBROOK TQ0277

Ostrich (01753) 682628
1.25 miles from M4 junction 5 via A4/B3378, then 'village only' road; High Street; SL3 0JZ Historic timbered inn (12th-c origins) with gruesome history – tales of over 60 murders; recently refurbished interior blending modern furnishings with oak beams and open fireplaces, three Shepherd Neame ales and good choice of wines, enjoyable sensibly priced food from sandwiches and pub favourites up, friendly service, restaurant; quiz first Sun of month; children welcome, 11 bedrooms, teak furniture in courtyard, open (and food) all day including breakfast/brunch for non-residents. *(Sophie Ellison)*

CUDDINGTON SP7311

★Crown (01844) 292222
Spurt Street; off A418 Thame–Aylesbury; HP18 0BB Recently refurbished thatched cottage with two low-beamed linked rooms and big inglenook log fire, well kept Fullers and guests and enjoyable fairly priced food (not Sun evening) from burgers up (special diets catered for), friendly service, two-room back dining area with country kitchen chairs around mix of tables; children and dogs (in bar) welcome; neat side terrace with modern furniture and planters, picnic-sets in front, open all day weekends. *(Graham and Carol Parker, David Lamb)*

DENHAM TQ0487

Green Man (01895) 832760
Village Road; next to the Swan; UB9 5BH Welcoming 18th-c red-brick pub in centre of this lovely village; modernised beamed bar with flagstones and log fire, five well kept ales including Rebellion and Sharps, good choice of popular food from baguettes up, cheerful efficient service, conservatory dining extension; free wi-fi; children and dogs welcome, pretty hanging baskets out at front, sunny back terrace and garden, open all day. *(David Lamb)*

DENHAM TQ0487

★Swan (01895) 832085
Village signed from M25 junction 16; UB9 5BH Wisteria-clad Georgian dining pub (Little Gems group); stylishly furnished bars with nice mix of antique and old-fashioned chairs at solid tables, heavily draped curtains, log fires, Rebellion IPA and a guest, good sensibly priced wine list and decent range of spirits, well liked food (all day Fri-Sun) including blackboard specials and Sat brunch from 9.30am, friendly efficient staff; background music, daily papers, free wi-fi; children and dogs (in bar) welcome, extensive floodlit back garden with sheltered terrace, open all day. *(Edward Mirzoeff)*

DINTON SP7610

Seven Stars (01296) 749000
Signed off A418 Aylesbury–Thame, near Gibraltar turn-off; Stars Lane; HP17 8UL Pretty 16th-c community-owned pub run by french landlady and popular locally; inglenook bar, beamed lounge and dining room, well kept Fullers, Rebellion and Vale, extensive wine list on two blackboards, good fairly priced food cooked to order from pub staples up including some french influences, friendly service; children welcome, no dogs inside, tables in sheltered garden with terrace, pleasant village, closed Sun evening. *(Graham and Carol Parker, David Lamb)*

DORNEY SU9279

Palmer Arms (01628) 666612
2.7 miles from M4 junction 7, via B3026; Village Road; SL4 6QW Modernised and extended dining pub in attractive conservation village, good popular food (best to book) from snacks and pub favourites to more restauranty dishes, friendly efficient service, Greene King ales kept well, lots of wines by the glass (interesting list) and good coffee, open fires in civilised front bar and back dining room; background music, daily newspapers; children and dogs (in certain areas) welcome, disabled facilities, terrace overlooking mediterranean-feel garden, enclosed play area, nice riverside walks nearby, open (and food) all day. *(Minda and Stanley Alexander, I D Barnett)*

A star symbol before the name of a pub shows exceptional character and appeal. It doesn't mean extra comfort. Even quite a basic pub can win a star, if it's individual enough.

DORNEY SU9279

Pineapple (01628) 662353
Lake End Road: 2.4 miles from M4 junction 7; left on A4 then left on B3026; SL4 6QS Nicely old-fashioned pub handy for Dorney Court (where the first english pineapple was grown in 1661); shiny low Anaglypta ceilings, black-panelled dados, leather chairs around sturdy country tables (one very long, another in big bow window), woodburner and pretty little fireplace, china pineapples and other decorations on shelves in one of three cottagey carpeted linked rooms on left, Fullers London Pride, Sharps Atlantic and a guest, huge variety of signature sandwiches, roasts on Sun; background music, open mike night last Weds of month, games machine; children and dogs welcome, rustic seats on roadside verandah, round picnic-sets in garden, fairy-lit decking under oak tree, open (and food) all day; some refurbishment planned. *(Mick Allen)*

EASINGTON SP6810

★**Mole & Chicken** (01844) 208387
From B4011 in Long Crendon follow Chearsley, Waddesdon signpost into Carters Lane opposite indian restaurant, then turn left into Chilton Road; HP18 9EY Creeper-clad dining pub with opened-up beamed interior; cream-cushioned farmhouse chairs around oak and pine tables on flagstones or tiles, a couple of dark leather sofas, church candles and good winter log fires, Chiltern ales, several wines by the glass and quite a few malt whiskies from slabby-topped counter; interesting modern food along with more affordable pubby dishes and set menu, good service; background music, free wi-fi; children welcome, no dogs inside, seats on raised terrace and decked area with fine views, simply but elegantly furnished bedrooms, open all day from 7.30am (8am weekends). *(Richard Kennell, Beth Aldridge, Patricia and Anton Larkham, Alison Nicholls, Graham and Carol Parker)*

EMBERTON SP8849

Bell & Bear (01234) 711565
Off A509 Olney–Newport Pagnell; High Street; MK46 5DH Old stone-built village pub with good interesting food cooked by landlord-chef including set lunch and tapas-style bar menu (Weds-Sat), four well kept changing ales, craft beers, real cider and good selection of other drinks, friendly efficient staff, bar with log fire and hood skittles, restaurant; well behaved children welcome, muddy boots and dogs in bar, garden tables, open all day Fri-Sun, closed Mon lunchtime, no food Sun evening to Tues lunchtime. *(Jim Studd)*

FINGEST SU7791

★**Chequers** (01491) 638335
Off B482 Marlow–Stokenchurch; RG9 6QD Ancient white-shuttered brick and flint pub with unspoilt public bar plus other neatly kept old-fashioned rooms with large open fires, horsebrasses, pewter tankards and pub team photographs, beers from Brakspears and Jennings, traditional cider, decent wines by the glass and several malt whiskies, enjoyable country cooking, smart back dining extension; board games, free wi-fi; children and dogs welcome, tables on terrace and in big beautifully tended garden with fine views over the Hambleden Valley, good walking country and opposite interesting church with unique twin-roofed Norman tower, open all day weekends, closed Mon. *(Isobel Mackinlay, Donald Allsopp, Lenny and Ruth Walters)*

FLACKWELL HEATH SU8889

Crooked Billet (01628) 521216
Off A404; Sheepridge Lane; SL7 3SG Steps up to cosily old-fashioned 16th-c pub; Brakspears and Youngs ales, reasonably priced traditional lunchtime food including sandwiches, charming landlord and friendly staff, eating area spread pleasantly through alcoves, low black beams and good open fire; lovely cottagey garden with nice views (beyond road), walks nearby. *(Mick Allen)*

FRIETH SU7990

Prince Albert (01494) 881683
Off B482 SW of High Wycombe; RG9 6PY Cottagey Chilterns local with low black beams and joists, high-backed settles, big black stove in inglenook and log fire in larger area on right, decent lunchtime food from sandwiches up (also Fri and Sat evenings – they ask you to book on Sat), well kept Brakspears ales, friendly service; quiz every other Tues, folk night last Weds of month; children and dogs welcome, nicely planted informal side garden with views of woods and fields, good walks, open all day. *(Peter and Emma Kelly)*

GAWCOTT SP6831

Crown (01280) 822322
Hillesden Road; MK18 4JF Welcoming 16th-c black-beamed village pub, popular good value food including notable fish pie, carvery Weds and Sun, three well kept ales such as Sharps Doom Bar from herringbone brick counter, restaurant area; background and some live music, Sky TV, pool; children welcome, long back garden with swings, open all day (till 9pm Mon, 10pm Tues), no food Sun evening, Mon. *(Philip Kingsbury)*

GERRARDS CROSS TQ0089

★**Three Oaks** (01753) 899016
Austenwood Lane, just NW of junction with Kingsway (B416); SL9 8NL Civilised dining pub facing Austenwood Common; two-room front bar with fireside bookshelves, tartan wing armchairs, sturdy wall settles and comfortable banquettes, well kept Fullers, Rebellion and several

wines by the glass, dining part with three linked rooms, popular highly regarded food including short set menu, attentive friendly young staff; soft background music, free wi-fi; children welcome, sturdy wooden tables on flagstoned side terrace, open all day. *(Simon Collett-Jones, David Lamb, John Evans)*

GREAT BRICKHILL SP9029

Red Lion (01525) 261715

Ivy Lane; MK17 9AH Recently refurbished roadside village pub; enjoyable fairly traditional food including lunchtime sandwiches, real ales from Caledonian and Tring and maybe a local guest, good friendly service, log fire in small bar, restaurant with woodburner; background music, quiz Sun evening; children and dogs welcome, lovely views over Buckinghamshire and beyond from enclosed back lawn, closed Mon, otherwise open all day, no food Sun evening. *(William and Sophie Renton)*

GREAT HAMPDEN SP8401

★**Hampden Arms** (01494) 488255

W of Great Missenden, off A4128; HP16 9RQ Friendly village pub opposite cricket pitch; comfortably furnished rooms (back one more rustic with big woodburner), well kept Rebellion IPA and a couple of guests, local cider and several wines by the glass from small corner bar, enjoyable reasonably priced pubby food including one or two greek dishes, cheerful efficient service; quiz third Weds of month; children and dogs welcome, seats in tree-sheltered garden, good Hampden Common walks, open all day Sun. *(David Lamb)*

GREAT KINGSHILL SU8798

★**Red Lion** (01494) 711262

A4128 N of High Wycombe; HP15 6EB Welcoming village pub across from cricket green; contemporary décor and relaxed informal atmosphere, well cooked locally sourced brasserie-style food including fixed-price menu (Tues-Fri lunchtime, Tues-Thurs early evening), local beers such as Rebellion and good value wine list, 'lobby' and cosy little flagstoned bar with leather tub chairs by log fire, spacious candlelit dining room; well behaved children welcome, a few seats out at front and behind, closed Sun evening, Mon. *(David Lamb)*

GREAT MISSENDEN SP8901

★**Cross Keys** (01494) 865373

High Street; HP16 0AU Friendly and relaxed village pub dating from the 16th c; unspoilt beamed bar divided by standing timbers, traditional furnishings including high-backed settle, log-effect gas fire in huge fireplace, well kept Fullers ales and often an unusual guest, enjoyable fairly priced food (not Sun evening) from burgers up (special diets catered for), cheerful helpful staff, spacious beamed restaurant; free wi-fi; children and dogs welcome, picnic-sets on back terrace, open all day. *(Monty Green)*

GROVE SP9122

★**Grove Lock** (01525) 380940

Pub signed off B488, on left just S of A505 roundabout (S of Leighton Buzzard); LU7 0QU Overlooking Grand Union Canal and usefully open all day; open-plan with lofty high-raftered pitched roof in bar, squashy brown leather sofas on oak boards, eclectic mix of tables and chairs including butcher's block tables by bar, big open-standing log fire, steps down to original lock-keeper's cottage (now three-room restaurant area), enjoyable food from sandwiches to daily specials, Fullers ales and lots of wines by the glass; background music, Tues quiz, free wi-fi; children and dogs welcome, seats on canopied deck and waterside lawn by Lock 28. *(David Lamb)*

HAMBLEDEN SU7886

★**Stag & Huntsman** (01491) 571227

Off A4155 Henley–Marlow; RG9 6RP Friendly brick and flint pub in pretty Chilterns village; chatty locals in busy little bar, built-in cushioned wall seats and simple furniture on bare boards, Rebellion IPA, Sharps Doom Bar and a couple of guests, several wines by the glass, sizeable open-plan room with armchairs by woodburner, dining room with good mix of wooden tables and chairs, hunting prints and other pictures on floral wallpaper, popular food from breakfast on, good service; background music, free wi-fi, darts; children and dogs (in bar) welcome, country garden and nice walks nearby, comfortable bedrooms, open all day. *(Susan and John Douglas, DHV, Paul Humphreys)*

HUGHENDEN VALLEY SU8697

★**Harrow** (01494) 564105

Warrendene Road, off A4128 N of High Wycombe; HP14 4LX Small cheerful brick and flint roadside cottage surrounded by Chilterns walks (leave muddy boots in porch); traditionally furnished with tiled-floor bar on left, black beams and joists, woodburner in big fireplace, pewter mugs, country pictures and wall seats, similar but bigger right-hand bar with sizeable dining tables on brick floor, carpeted back dining room, tasty good value pub food (all day Sat, till 6pm Sun) from sandwiches and baked potatoes up, Courage Best, Fullers London Pride and a guest, quick friendly service; Tues quiz; children and dogs welcome, disabled access, picnic-sets out in front, play area, open all day. *(David Lamb)*

If you know a pub is ever open all day, please tell us.

HYDE HEATH SU9300

Plough (01494) 774408
Off B485 Great Missenden–Chesham; HP6 5RW Small prettily placed pub with freshened-up bare-boards bar and carpeted dining extension, popular good value food (more emphasis on fish since recent change of management), Fullers London Pride and a couple of guests, efficient service, real fires and cosy friendly atmosphere; picnic-sets on green opposite, open all day Fri-Sun, closed Mon lunchtime, no food Sun evening-Tues. *(David Lamb)*

ICKFORD SP6407

Rising Sun (01844) 339238
E of Thame; Worminghall Road; HP18 9JD Pretty thatched local under new management; cosy low-beamed bar, friendly staff and regulars, Adnams, Black Sheep, Marstons and a weekly guest, enjoyable reasonably priced home-made food (just sandwiches and baked potatoes at lunchtime apart from Sun roasts), log fire; Tues quiz; children, walkers and dogs welcome, pleasant garden with picnic-sets and play area, handy for Waterperry Gardens, open all day Fri-Sun, no food Sun evening, Mon, Tues. *(David Lamb)*

IVINGHOE SP9416

Rose & Crown (01296) 668472
Vicarage Lane, off B489 opposite church; LU7 9EQ Cosy 17th-c red-brick pub doing well under newish management; good food at sensible prices from sandwiches up, well kept Sharps, Tring and three local guests, friendly efficient service; children and dogs welcome, a couple of tables out at front, sunny beer garden behind, pleasant village, open all day, no food Sun evening, Mon. *(Andrew Hetherington)*

IVINGHOE ASTON SP9518

Village Swan (01525) 220544
Aston; signed from B489 NE of Ivinghoe; LU7 9DP Village-owned pub run by bulgarian couple; traditional beamed interior with open fire, enjoyable home-made food (not Sun evening) from varied menu including some bulgarian dishes, three real ales and nice wines by the glass; quiz first Mon of month, sports TV, free wi-fi; children, walkers and dogs welcome, covered outside area and garden, handy for Ivinghoe Beacon and Icknield Way, open all day weekends, closed Mon and weekday lunchtimes. *(Graham Smart)*

LACEY GREEN SP8200

Black Horse (01844) 345195
Main Road; HP27 0QU Friendly mix of customers at this two-bar beamed country local; popular good value home-made food (not Sun evening, Mon) from baguettes up, breakfast from 9am Tues-Sat, four real ales including Brakspears and nice choice of wines by the glass, quotations written on walls, inglenook woodburner; darts, sports TV, free wi-fi; children and dogs welcome, picnic-sets in garden with play area and aunt sally, open all day Thurs-Sun, closed Mon lunchtime. *(Roy Hoing)*

LACEY GREEN SP8201

Pink & Lily (01494) 489857
A4010 High Wycombe–Princes Risborough, follow Loosley sign, then Great Hampden, Great Missenden sign; HP27 0RJ Friendly updated 18th-c pub in pretty setting; enjoyable food from sandwiches and traditional choices up, four changing mainly local ales and several wines by the glass, pubby furniture and open fire in airy main bar, cosier side areas and conservatory-style extension with big arches, small tap room with built-in wall benches on red tiles, framed Rupert Brooke poem about the pub (he used to drink here) and broad inglenook, games room; occasional background music, free wi-fi; children, dogs and muddy walkers welcome, big garden with heated deck, futuristic glass pods, play area and barbecue, open all day. *(Roy Hoing)*

LACEY GREEN SP8100

Whip (01844) 344060
Pink Road; HP27 0PG Hilltop local with mix of simple traditional furnishings in smallish front bar and larger downstairs dining area, popular generously served pubby food including range of home-made pies, six interesting well kept ales (May beer festival with live music), traditional ciders, friendly helpful staff; background music, sports TV, free wi-fi; children and dogs welcome, tables in charming sheltered garden looking up to windmill, open all day, no food Sun evening. *(Robert Watt, Tracey and Stephen Groves)*

LEY HILL SP9901

★**Swan** (01494) 783075
Village signposted off A416 in Chesham; HP5 1UT Friendly well looked-after pub – once three 16th-c cottages; character main bar (some steps) with original features including low beams, standing timbers, antique range and inglenook log fire, nice mix of furniture and collection of old local photographs, St Austell Tribute, Timothy Taylors Landlord and Tring Side Pocket for a Toad, several wines by the glass and tasty reasonably priced food, raftered dining section with french windows to terrace and lawn; children welcome till 9pm, pretty summer hanging baskets and tubs, common opposite with cricket pitch and a nine-hole golf course, closed Sun evening, Mon; for sale so may be changes. *(Tim and Marty Thomson)*

LITTLE KINGSHILL SU8999

Full Moon (01494) 862397
Hare Lane; HP16 0EE Picturesque brick and flint village pub with popular food from sandwiches up including Tues steak night

and Weds burger night, well kept Adnams, Fullers London Pride, Youngs and a guest, nice wines, friendly helpful service from busy staff, traditional beamed and quarry-tiled bar with open fire, bigger dining room; Thurs quiz, TV; children and dogs welcome, circular picnic-sets out at front, lawned garden with swings, good walks. *(David Lamb)*

LITTLE MISSENDEN SU9298

Red Lion (01494) 862876

Off A413 Amersham–Great Missenden; HP7 0QZ Unchanging pretty 17th-c cottage with long-serving landlord; small black-beamed bar, plain seats around elm pub tables, piano squashed into big inglenook beside black kitchen range packed with copper pots, kettles and rack of old guns, little country dining room with pheasant décor, well kept Greene King IPA, Skinners Betty Stogs and Tring Side Pocket for a Toad, fair-priced wines, pubby food; live music Sat; children welcome, dogs in bar, picnic-sets out in front and on grass behind wall, back garden with little bridge over River Misbourne, two bedrooms, open all day Fri-Sun. *(Roy Hoing)*

LITTLEWORTH COMMON SP9386

Blackwood Arms (01753) 645672

3 miles S of M40 junction 2; Common Lane; SL1 8PP Traditional little 19th-c brick pub tucked away in lovely spot on edge of beechwoods (features in the film *My Week with Marilyn*); sturdy mix of furniture on bare boards, roaring log fire, enjoyable home-made food (not Sun evening) from open sandwiches up, well kept Brakspears and guests (regular beer festivals), interesting selection of wines, friendly accommodating staff; free wi-fi; children and dogs welcome, hitching rail for horses, nice garden and good local walks, closed Mon, otherwise open all day (till 8pm Sun). *(Ross Balaam, Mark Wilson)*

LITTLEWORTH COMMON SU9386

Jolly Woodman (01753) 644350

2 miles from M40 junction 2; off A355; SL1 8PF Lived-in red-brick country pub with three well kept changing ales and generous helpings of reasonably priced home-made food from blackboard menu, rambling multi-level beamed and timbered areas including snug, collection of old tools and other bric-a-brac, central woodburner; children and dogs welcome, small front terrace and nice garden, good site by Burnham Beeches, closed Sun evening, Mon (except for monthly jazz nights – see website), otherwise open all day. *(David Lamb)*

LUDGERSHALL SP6617

Bull & Butcher (01844) 238094

Off A41 Aylesbury–Bicester; bear left to The Green; HP18 9NZ Nicely old-fashioned country pub continuing well under present friendly management; bar with low beams in ochre ceiling, pews and wheelback chairs on dark tiles or flagstones, inglenook woodburner, Greene King IPA and Old Speckled Hen plus a guest, enjoyable fairly priced pubby food including themed nights and popular Sun lunch (booking advised), back dining room; children and dogs welcome, picnic-sets on pleasant front terrace, play area on green opposite, circular walks from the door, open (and food) all day Fri and Sat, till 8pm Sun, closed Mon and lunchtime Tues. *(David Lamb)*

MAIDS MORETON SP7035

Wheatsheaf (01280) 822903

Main Street, just off A413 Towcester–Buckingham; MK18 1QR Attractive 17th-c thatched local with spotless low-beamed bar, bare boards and tiled floors, two inglenooks, four well kept ales including Tring Side Pocket for a Toad, good fairly pubby food, friendly service, conservatory restaurant; dogs allowed in bar, seats on front terrace, hatch service for pleasant enclosed back garden, closed Mon, otherwise open all day. *(Jess and George Cowley)*

MARLOW SU8586

Coach No phone

West Street; SL7 2LS Sister dining pub to Tom Kerridge's Hand & Flowers; very well liked food (tapas-style helpings, no bookings) from open kitchen with rotisserie, good helpful service, compact interior with modern décor, bar area serving up to four changing ales and nice wines by the glass (maybe local fizz) from pewter-topped counter; silent TVs; open all day from 8am for breakfast. *(Tracey and Stephen Groves)*

MARLOW SU8486

★**Hand & Flowers** (01628) 482277

West Street (A4155); SL7 2BP Restaurant-pub owned by celebrity chef Tom Kerridge; nice informal atmosphere in three linked beamed rooms all set for dining, high-backed leather-seated chairs and wall seats around chunky tables, bare boards or flagstones, fresh flowers and candles, first class food (not cheap and must book long in advance), professional service, conservatory bar with four real ales including one named for them, lots of wines by the glass from good list and specialist gins; children welcome, comfortable character bedrooms, Thames walks nearby, closed Sun evening. *(Richard Tilbrook, Simon Collett-Jones)*

MARLOW SU8586

Two Brewers (01628) 484140

St Peter Street, first right off Station Road from double roundabout; SL7 1NQ 18th-c red-brick beamed pub set just back from the river; enjoyable fairly pubby food from snacks up, good value lunchtime set menu, friendly helpful service, three well kept Rebellion ales, Fullers London Pride and a dozen wines by the glass, various dining areas including upstairs room and cellar restaurant; free wi-fi; children and dogs welcome, seats outside, open (and food) all day, kitchen closes 5pm Sun. *(Simon Collett-Jones)*

MARLOW BOTTOM SU8588

Three Horseshoes (01628) 483109
Signed from Handy Cross roundabout, off M40 junction 4; SL7 3RA Much extended former coaching inn under friendly management; well kept Rebellion ales and enjoyable reasonably priced food including pizzas, beams and log fires, comfortable traditional furnishings on different levels; background music; children and dogs (in bar) welcome, big back garden, good walks nearby, open all day, till 6pm Sun. *(Tracey and Stephen Groves, Roy Hoing)*

MEDMENHAM SU8084

Dog & Badger (01491) 579944
A4155, opposite the church; SL7 2HE Renovated low-beamed roadside bar-restaurant with contemporary décor; good if not cheap food from open kitchen, local ales such as Rebellion, plenty of wines by the glass and good selection of other drinks including cocktails, friendly helpful staff; children and dogs (in bar) welcome, terrace tables, herb garden, six stylish bedrooms in separate building, open all day from 7am for breakfast (8am weekends). *(Peter and Emma Kelly)*

MILTON KEYNES SP8737

Swan (01908) 679489
Newport Road, Woughton on the Green; MK6 3BS Spacious and picturesque timber-framed Chef & Brewer overlooking village green; beamed interior with good log fires and nice nooks and corners, enjoyable food from their usual extensive menu, Greene King ales and good wine choice; children welcome, plenty of seating in large garden, footpaths to nearby lakes, open (and food) all day. *(Graham and Carol Parker)*

NEWPORT PAGNELL SP8743

Cannon (01908) 211495
High Street; MK16 8AQ Friendly little bay-windowed drinkers' pub serving four well kept reasonably priced ales, carpeted half-panelled interior with interesting military theme, gas woodburner in central fireplace, room behind for live music and comedy nights; Tues quiz, TV, juke box; seats in small backyard, open all day. *(William and Sophie Renton)*

NEWTON LONGVILLE SP8431

Crooked Billet (01908) 373936
Off A421 S of Milton Keynes; Westbrook End; MK17 0DF Revamped brick and thatch pub under new management; comfortably updated beamed interior with inglenook log fires, good range of enjoyable food (they add a service charge) including daily specials, a beer badged for the pub along with Greene King Abbot and two guests, decent choice of other drinks; quiz first Mon of month; children and dogs (in bar) welcome, nice garden with plenty of seating, open all day, food all day Fri, Sat, till 5pm Sun. *(Mike Hickling)*

OLNEY SP8851

Bull (01234) 711470
Market Place/High Street; MK46 4EA Former 17th-c coaching inn recently reopened by Apostrophe group after devastating 2016 fire; spacious well renovated interior, Wells, Youngs and guests from generously stocked bar, decent choice of enjoyable food from sandwiches and deli boards up, sky-lit dining room with open kitchen, friendly young staff; children and dogs welcome, disabled loo (others upstairs), 12 bedrooms, tables in courtyard and big back garden, open (and food) all day from 7am (8am weekends) for breakfast. *(Dr J Barrie Jones)*

OLNEY SP8851

★**Swan** (01234) 711111
High Street S; MK46 4AA Cosy little pub with beamed and timbered linked rooms; popular good value food from british tapas through pub favourites and burgers to blackboard specials, up to six well kept/priced ales and plenty of wines by the glass from good list, friendly attentive service, cheery log fires, small back bistro dining room (booking advised); courtyard tables, open all day (till 9pm Sun). *(Gerry and Rosemary Dobson, Michael Sargent)*

PENN SU9093

★**Old Queens Head** (01494) 813371
Hammersley Lane/Church Road, off B474 between Penn and Tylers Green; HP10 8EY Stylish old pub with open-plan rooms; well spaced tables, a modicum of old prints and comfortably varied seating on flagstones or broad dark boards, stairs up to attractive two-level raftered dining room, well liked food (special diets catered for) including Sat brunch from 9.30am, Greene King ales, lots of wines by the glass and good choice of other drinks including 18 gins, friendly efficient service, log fire in big fireplace; background music, daily papers, free wi-fi; children and dogs (in bar) welcome, sunny terrace overlooking church, picnic-sets on sheltered L-shaped lawn; beechwoods of Common or Penn Woods close by, open all day. *(Tracey and Stephen Groves)*

PENN SU9093

★**Red Lion** (01494) 813107
Elm Road, B474; HP10 8LF Bustling 16th-c pub opposite the village duck pond (sister to the Royal Standard of England at Forty Green – see Main Entries); various bar rooms and mix of furniture including cushioned mate's chairs, settles and rustic

tables with candlesticks, homely sofas and armchairs, rugs on ancient parquet or old quarry tiles, fantastic collection of british empire prints and paintings, windowsills and mantelpieces crammed with staffordshire dogs, plates and old bottles, hop-strung beams, woodburner in big fireplace, Chiltern, Rebellion and a guest, real cider, good choice of wines by the glass and well liked home-made pubby food; TV for major sports, shove-ha'penny, board games; children and dogs welcome, seats on front terrace and small side garden, open all day; still for sale last we heard. *(John Pritchard, Tracey and Stephen Groves)*

PENN STREET SU9295

★**Hit or Miss** (01494) 713109

Off A404 SW of Amersham, keep on towards Winchmore Hill; HP7 0PX Welcoming traditional village pub; heavily beamed main bar with leather sofas and armchairs on parquet flooring, horsebrasses and open fire, two carpeted rooms with interesting cricketing and chair-making memorabilia, more sofas, wheelback and other dining chairs around pine tables, good interesting food (highish prices) including daily specials, Badger ales; background music, free wi-fi; children and dogs (in certain areas) welcome, picnic-sets on terrace overlooking own cricket pitch, parking over the road, open all day. *(Roy Hoing)*

PENN STREET SU9295

Squirrel (01494) 711291

Off A404 SW of Amersham, opposite the Common; HP7 0PX Friendly sister pub to nearby Hit or Miss; open-plan bar with flagstones, log fire and mix of furniture including comfortable sofas, reasonably priced home-made pubby food from baguettes up (not Sun evening, Mon), good children's meals too, up to five well kept ales such as Rebellion, Tring, Vale and XT, various craft beers and a proper cider, bric-a-brac and cricketing memorabilia (village cricket pitch is opposite), sweets in traditional glass jars; live acoustic music Fri, monthly quiz; dogs welcome, covered outside deck with sofas, logburner and own servery, play area in big back garden, lovely walks nearby, closed Mon lunchtime, otherwise open all day. *(David Lamb, Roy Hoing)*

PRESTWOOD SP8799

★**Polecat** (01494) 862253

170 Wycombe Road (A4128 N of High Wycombe); HP16 0HJ Smallish civilised rooms opening off low-ceilinged bar, rugs and assorted tables and chairs on bare boards or red tiles, various stuffed animals (white polecats in one cabinet), good open fire, five real ales including Malt and Rebellion, 30 wines by the glass and quite a few gins, large helpings of good tasty food; free wi-fi; children and dogs (in bar) welcome, attractive big garden with colourful hanging baskets and tubs, large play area, picnic-sets under parasols on neat front grass beneath fairy-lit pear tree, open all day in summer, till 6pm Sun; major refurbishment planned. *(Tracey and Stephen Groves, Roy Hoing)*

PRINCES RISBOROUGH SP8104

Red Lion (01844) 344476

Whiteleaf, off A4010; OS Sheet 165 map reference 817043; HP27 0LL Comfortably worn-in 17th-c family-owned pub in charming village; Sharps Doom Bar and a couple of guests, reasonably priced pubby food including popular steaks, flowers on tables, log fire, friendly service; traditional games; children, walkers and dogs welcome, seats in garden behind, extensive views over to Oxfordshire, four bedrooms, open all day weekends, closed Mon. *(Jim Studd)*

QUAINTON SP7420

George & Dragon (01296) 655436

The Green; HP22 4AR Traditional flower-decked brick pub by village green; five well kept mainly local ales, Weston's cider and good choice of reasonably priced food including blackboard specials and bargain OAP lunch Tues, friendly efficient staff, split-level bar, coffee shop, post office facility Weds; quiz nights and darts; children welcome, tables outside with good view of windmill, handy for Buckinghamshire Railway Centre, open all day Sat, closed Mon. *(David Lamb, Graham and Carol Parker)*

SEER GREEN SU9691

★**Jolly Cricketers** (01494) 676308

Chalfont Road, opposite the church; HP9 2YG Bustling red-brick Victorian pub with two parquet-floored bar rooms, woodburner in each, cushioned window seats, farmhouse and antique-style dining chairs around bare wood or painted tables, old cricketing photos, prints and bats, Rebellion, Vale and three guests, 16 good wines by the glass and 20 malt whiskies, well liked interesting food served by pleasant helpful young staff, separate restaurant; background and some live music, quiz last Sun of month, TV, free wi-fi, board games; dogs and muddy boots in main bar, picnic-sets on back terrace, handsome wisteria at front (also note the ironic pub sign), open all day (till midnight Fri, Sat), food all day Sun till 6pm. *(Tracey and Stephen Groves, David Lamb)*

SKIRMETT SU7790

★**Frog** (01491) 638996

From A4155 NE of Henley take Hambleden turn and keep on; or from B482 Stokenchurch–Marlow take Turville turn and keep on; RG9 6TG Pretty pub in Chilterns countryside; public bar with log fire, prints on walls, cushioned sofa and leather-seated stools on wood floor, high chairs by counter, Rebellion IPA and guests, 18 wines by the glass including champagne, 24 malt whiskies, two dining rooms in different styles – one light and airy with country kitchen furniture, the other more formal with dark red walls, smarter furniture and candlelight, good interesting food cooked by chef-landlord from baguettes and deli boards up, attentive prompt service; background music; children and dogs (in bar) welcome, side gate to lovely garden with unusual five-sided tables, attractive valley views and farmland walks, Chiltern Valley Winery & Brewery nearby, three bedrooms, closed Sun evening mid Sept to mid May. *(Graham Smart)*

STOKE GOLDINGTON SP8348

★**Lamb** (01908) 551233

High Street (B526 Newport Pagnell–Northampton); MK16 8NR Chatty village pub with friendly helpful licensees, up to five ales including Tring, real ciders and good range of wines, generous helpings of enjoyable home-made food (all day Sat, not Sun evening) from baguettes to good value Sun roasts, lounge with log fire and sheep decorations, two small pleasant dining rooms, darts and table skittles in public bar; may be soft background music, TV; children and dogs welcome, terrace and sheltered garden behind with play equipment, bedrooms in adjacent cottage, closed Mon lunchtime, otherwise open all day (till 7pm Sun). *(Mick Allen)*

STOKE MANDEVILLE SP8310

★**Bell** (01296) 612434

Lower Road; HP22 5XA Relaxed red-brick pub with airy open-plan interior; wood and slate floors, painted beams, mix of chairs, wall settles and rustic benches around medley of tables, drawings, maps and hunting prints above dark blue dado, woodburner, good freshly made food (all day Fri-Sun) from varied daily-changing menu, Wells Bombardier and Youngs Bitter, plenty of wines by the glass, friendly service; background music, board games; free wi-fi; children and dogs (in bar) welcome, picnic-sets on side terrace and in garden with weeping silver birch, open all day. *(David Lamb, Nicola and Stuart Parsons, Kerry and Guy Trooper, Tracey and Stephen Groves)*

STONY STRATFORD SP7840

Crown (01908) 262888

Market Square; MK11 1BE Former coaching inn refurbished under newish owner-chef; various areas arranged around central servery, bare boards, some stripped stonework and interesting modern artwork, back dining room, good food including tapas and range of burgers, special diets catered for, ales such as Adnams and Sharps Doom Bar, friendly staff; background and some live music; picnic-sets on brick terrace, open all day Sat, till 7pm Sun, closed Mon. *(Caroline and Oliver Sterling)*

THE LEE SP8904

★**Cock & Rabbit** (01494) 837540

Back roads 2.5 miles N of Great Missenden, E of A413; HP16 9LZ Overlooking village green and run by same friendly italian family for over 25 years; much emphasis on their good italian cooking including popular Weds evening pasta deal, Greene King, Sharps and a beer named for the pub, plush-seated lounge, cosy dining room and larger restaurant; children welcome, dogs in bar, seats on verandah, terraces and lawn, good walks, open all day weekends. *(John Evans, Roy Hoing)*

THE LEE SP8904

★**Old Swan** (01494) 837239

Swan Bottom, back road 0.75 miles N of The Lee; HP16 9NU Friendly tucked-away country pub, mainly 16th-c with attractively furnished linked rooms; heavy beams, flagstones and old quarry tiles, high-backed antique settles and window seats, log fire in inglenook cooking range, good food (not Sun evening, Mon) from sensibly short menu, Chiltern, Sharps and a guest such as Rebellion, several wines by the glass; free wi-fi; children and dogs (in bar) welcome, big, spreading back garden with picnic-sets and contemporary seating around rustic tables, play area, surrounding walks and cycling routes, open all day Fri and Sat, till 7pm Sun, closed Mon lunchtime; extension/building works still planned. *(Peter Pilbeam, Emma Scofield, Richard Kennell)*

TINGEWICK SP6532

Royal Oak (01280) 848373

Main Street; MK18 4NN Modernised village pub with good fairly priced food including Sun carvery, a couple of Sharps ales, welcoming helpful staff; children and dogs allowed, seats out at front and in garden behind, open all day, no food Sun evening. *(Adam Catlin)*

TURVILLE SU7691

★**Bull & Butcher** (01491) 638283

Valley road off A4155 Henley–Marlow at Mill End, past Hambleden and Skirmett; RG9 6QU Popular 16th-c black and white pub in pretty village (famous as film and TV location); two traditional low-beamed rooms with inglenooks, wall settles in tiled-floor bar, deep well incorporated into glass-topped table, Brakspears ales kept well and decent wines by the glass, enjoyable good value locally sourced food cooked by chef-landlord, friendly staff; background music; children

Pubs close to motorway junctions are listed at the back of the book.

and dogs welcome, seats by fruit trees in attractive garden, good walks (Chiltern Way runs through village), open all day weekends and can get very busy. *(Peter Pilbeam)*

WADDESDON SP7316

Long Dog (01296) 651320
High Street; HP18 0JF Renovated village pub with good food from open-view kitchen including lunchtime baps, friendly accommodating service, well kept ales and nice choice of wines by the glass, bar area with open fire; background music, live jazz every other Tues; children and dogs welcome, tables out front and back, very handy for Waddesdon Manor (NT), open all day, food all day weekends. *(Graham Smart)*

WEEDON SP8118

★**Five Elms** (01296) 641439
Stockaway; HP22 4NL Cottagey thatched pub with two welcoming little bars; low beams and log fires, ample helpings of good fairly priced food cooked by landlord (best to book), nice wines, interesting range of gins and a well kept ale such as XT Four, cheerful helpful service, old photographs and prints, separate compact dining room; games such as shove-ha'penny; children welcome (no under-9s in restaurant), dogs in bar, pretty hanging baskets and a few picnic-sets out in front, attractive village, closed Sun evening and lunchtimes Mon, Tues. *(Emma Scofield)*

WENDOVER SP8609

Village Gate (01296) 623884
Aylesbury Road (B4009); HP22 6BA Modernised country pub with interconnecting rooms; tartan-carpeted bar has woodburner in brick fireplace, red leather tub seats around log tables and high leather chairs against unusually decorated counter, St Austell Tribute, Sharps Doom Bar and a guest, several wines by the glass, other rooms laid for eating, one down steps with high raftered ceiling, good interesting food from lunchtime sandwiches up, efficient service; live music Fri evening; children and dogs (in bar) welcome, outside seating including raised deck, long-reaching country views, open all day; for sale as we went to press, so may be changes. *(David Lamb)*

WEST WYCOMBE SU8394

George & Dragon (01494) 535340
High Street; A40 W of High Wycombe; HP14 3AB Rambling hotel bar in preserved NT Tudor village; massive beams and sloping walls, big log fire, three well kept Rebellion ales along with St Austell Tribute, good range of wines and enjoyable food from shortish menu, prompt friendly service; children and dogs (in bar) welcome, tables in nice garden, ten bedrooms (magnificent oak staircase), handy for West Wycombe Park (NT) and the Hell-Fire Caves, open all day, meals 12-6 Sun. *(Jim Studd)*

WESTON TURVILLE SP8510

Chequers (01296) 613298
Church Lane; HP22 5SJ Comfortably updated dining pub with low 16th-c beams, flagstones and large log fire, very good up-to-date food from chef-owner in bar or restaurant including set lunch, friendly helpful staff, well kept ales such as Rebellion and Sharps, wide choice of wines by the glass; children (no under-6s after 4pm) and dogs (away from dining areas) welcome, tucked away in attractive part of village, tables on large front terrace, closed Sun evening to Tues lunchtime, otherwise open all day. *(Roger and Penny Gudge, Penny Dathan, Jayne Muir, David Alexander, Michael Cookson, Ian Usher)*

WESTON UNDERWOOD SP8650

Cowpers Oak (01234) 711382
Signed off A509 in Olney; High Street; MK46 5JS Wisteria-clad village pub with enjoyable home-cooked food (special diets catered for) from bar snacks up, Mon burger and Tues pie nights, well kept real ales including Woodfordes Wherry, several wines by the glass, friendly helpful staff, beams, painted panelling and some stripped stone, nice mix of old-fashioned furnishings, two open fires, restaurant behind; background music, Mon quiz; children and dogs welcome, small suntrap front terrace, more tables on back decking and in big orchard garden, fenced play area, open all day weekends (till 9pm Sun). *(William and Sophie Renton)*

WHELPLEY HILL SP9501

White Hart (01442) 833367
Off B4505 Bovington–Chesham; HP5 3RL Cosy tile-hung village pub with enjoyable home-made food (till 5pm Sun), well kept interesting beers and good selection of other drinks, friendly accommodating service, log fires; background music; children and dogs welcome, seats out at front and in big back garden, nice local walks, open all day, can get crowded at weekends. *(Mick Allen)*

WINCHMORE HILL SU9394

Plough (01494) 259757
The Hill; HP7 0PA Village pub-restaurant with good italian food from wood-fired pizzas up (landlord is from Campania); flagstones, low beams and open fires, linked dining area with polished wood floor, real ales and imported lagers, nice coffee, little shop selling italian wines and other produce; children welcome, tables on terrace and lawn, pleasant walks nearby, open all day. *(John Evans)*

WINCHMORE HILL SU9394

Potters Arms (01494) 726222
Fagnall Lane; HP7 0PH Welcoming 17th-c pub close to village green; ales such as Brakspears and Ringwood, enjoyable pubby

food (not Sun evening) from sandwiches and panini up, good helpful service, some black beams, leather sofa and armchairs by inglenook log fire; popular comedy night last Thurs of month; children welcome, tables in fenced front garden, four bedrooms, open all day Sat, till 7pm Sun. *(Monty Green)*

WINSLOW SP7627

Bell (01296) 714091

Market Square; MK18 3AB Fine old coaching inn, comfortable and atmospheric, with reasonably priced food including range of pies in beamed bar and popular carvery restaurant, Greene King ales, friendly welcoming staff, snug with historical photos and log fire; courtyard tables, 39 bedrooms (some with four-posters), open all day. *(Sophie Ellison)*

WOOBURN COMMON SU9187

★Chequers (01628) 529575

From A4094 at Bourne End roundabout, follow for Wooburn, then straight over next roundabout into Kiln Lane; OS Sheet 175 map reference 910870; HP10 0JQ Bustling hotel with friendly low-beamed main bar, second bar to the left and light and airy restaurant; good range of well liked food from sandwiches, wraps and some pubby choices up, three Rebellion ales, Wells Bombardier and a dozen wines by the glass from good list, fair range of whiskies and brandies too; background music, TV, free wi-fi; children and dogs (in bar) welcome, spacious garden set away from the road, comfortable bedrooms, open (and food) all day. *(David Lamb, R K Phillips)*

Post Office address codings confusingly give the impression that some pubs are in Buckinghamshire, when they're really in Bedfordshire or Berkshire (which is where we list them).

Cambridgeshire

BALSHAM TL5850 Map 5

Black Bull

(01223) 893844 – www.blackbull-balsham.co.uk

Village signposted off A11 SW of Newmarket, and off A1307 in Linton; High Street; CB21 4DJ

Pretty thatched pub with bedroom extension – a good all-rounder – and with well regarded food, too

A good mix of both locals and visitors are welcomed into this 17th-c inn by the friendly landlord. The beamed bar spreads around a central servery where they keep Adnams Ghost Ship, Crafty Beers Carpenters Cask, Greene King IPA and Woodfordes Wherry on handpump, 22 wines by the glass from a good list, 15 malt whiskies, draught lager and interesting juices. Dividers and standing timbers break up the space, which has an open fire (with leather sofas in front of it), floorboards and low black beams in the front part; furniture includes small leatherette-seated dining chairs. A restaurant extension (in a listed barn) has a high-raftered oak-panelled roof and a network of standing posts and steel ties. The front terrace has teak tables and chairs by a long, pleasantly old-fashioned verandah and there are more seats in a small sheltered back garden. Smart, comfortable bedrooms are in a neat single-storey extension. This pub has the same good owners as the Red Lion at Hinxton.

Interesting food includes sandwiches and baguettes, pub classics including a pie board plus smoked haddock fishcake with chilli and lime mayonnaise, goats cheese cheesecake with tomato jam and rosemary vinaigrette, aubergine and chickpea tagine with honey-roasted sweet potato and cucumber dressing, corn-fed chicken breast with asian vegetables and noodle broth, venison haunch with slow-braised venison profiterole, carrot purée, roast celeriac and a reduction, and puddings such as chocolate fondant with salted caramel and white chocolate sorbet and orange jelly, saffron and cardamom pannacotta with lemon curd. *Benchmark main dish: steak in ale pie £14.00. Two-course evening meal £22.00.*

Free house ~ Licensee Alex Clarke ~ Real ale ~ Open 7.30am (8.30am Sat)-11pm; 8.30am-10.30pm Sun ~ Bar food 12-2, 6.30-9; 12-2.30, 6.30-9.30 Fri, Sat; 12-3, 6-8 Sun ~ Restaurant ~ Children welcome ~ Dogs allowed in bar and bedrooms ~ Wi-fi ~ Bedrooms: £99/£129

Recommended by Carol and Barry Craddock, Caroline Prescott, Guy Henderson, Gerry and Pam Pollard, Lee and Jill Stafford, Mrs Margo Finlay, Jörg Kasprowski, M and GR

If we know a featured-entry pub does sandwiches, we always say so – if they're not mentioned, you'll have to assume you can't get one.

CAMBRIDGE TL4458 Map 5

Pint Shop

(01223) 352293 – www.pintshop.co.uk

Peas Hill; CB2 3PN

Busy, lively, chatty place with fine drinks and food – great fun

This was a house in the mid 19th c and E M Forster once lived here. It later became university offices and in 2013 was revamped and opened up as a pub on two floors. A fantastic range of drinks and up-to-date tasty food ensure the place is always packed with customers of all ages. The bar and dining rooms are simply furnished with wooden tables and chairs and cushioned wall seating on parquet floors, industrial-style lamps hanging from the ceiling and bird prints lining the walls; background music. Efficient, friendly staff keep Adnams Ghost Ship and Southwold, Marble Pint, Oakham JHB and a guest on handpump, up to 17 craft ales, a good choice of wines and around 60 gins. There are a couple of upstairs dining rooms, similarly furnished, and a split-level, canopy-covered courtyard with chunky picnic-sets and fairy lights. The pub is handy for the Cambridge Arts Theatre and the Corn Exchange. Wheelchair access and loos.

Extremely popular food includes scotch eggs, british cured meats and cheeses, gin-cured sea trout with buttermilk pancakes, lancashire cheese, parsnip and hazelnut croquettes with stout mayonnaise, coal-baked flatbread kebabs (north african-style squash and leek with crispy chickpeas or charred mackerel with confit lemon), charcoal spit-roast chicken and pork belly, charcoal-grilled curries, stone bass and lamb chops, good dry-aged steaks, and puddings such as butterscotch chocolate pot with sesame brittle and gin and gooseberry sorbet. *Benchmark main dish: devilled lamb shoulder kebab £12.00. Two-course evening meal £18.00.*

Free house ~ Licensee Jack Etherington ~ Real ale ~ Open 12-11 (midnight Thurs, Fri); 11am-midnight Sat; 11-11 Sun ~ Bar food 12-10 (10.30 Thurs, Fri); 11-10.30 Sat (10 Sun) ~ Restaurant ~ Children welcome ~ Dogs welcome *Recommended by Gary and Marie Miller, Margo and Derek Peters, Graeme and Sally Mendham*

CAMBRIDGE TL4459 Map 5

Punter

(01223) 363322 – www.thepuntercambridge.com

Pound Hill, on corner of A1303 ring road; CB3 0AE

Good enterprising food in relaxed and interestingly furnished surroundings

You'll find a cheerful and chatty mix of customers here and plenty of nice nooks and crannies in which to sit. The rambling and informal linked rooms have quite a bit of character, with paintings, antique prints, old dark floorboards and a pleasing choice of seating such as pews, elderly dining chairs and Lloyd Loom easy chairs. One prized corner is down a few steps, behind a wooden railing. The scrubbed tables feature candles in bottles or assorted candlesticks, and staff are quick and friendly. There's also a raftered dining barn, similar in style, with more pictures on papered walls and a large rug on dark flagstones. Oakham Citra, Sharps Doom Bar, Turpins Meditation and a guest beer on handpump and eight wines by the glass; board games and background jazz music. The flagstoned and mainly covered former coachyard has tables and picnic-table sets. This is sister pub to the Punter in Oxford.

Enjoyable seasonal food includes tiger prawns in passata with garlic and parmesan croutons, oregano and mozzarella pizzadilla, portobello mushrooms with goats cheese, pesto and grilled polenta, crab and chilli tart with sweet potato fries, lamb steak with couscous and herb butter, duck breast with herb tabbouleh and orange dressing, beef bourguignon, and puddings such as pear and blackberry crumble with vanilla ice-cream and white chocolate mousse. *Benchmark main dish: beer-battered fish and chips £12.50. Two-course evening meal £18.00.*

Star Pubs & Bars ~ Lease Sarah Lee ~ Real ale ~ Open 12-11; 12-11.45 Sat ~ Bar food 12-3, 5.30-9 (10 Fri); 12-10 Sat; 12-9 Sun ~ Children welcome ~ Dogs welcome ~ Wi-fi
Recommended by Richard Tilbrook, Lyn and Freddie Roberts, Christopher Mannings, Donald Allsopp, Martin and Sue Neville, Edward Edmonton

DUXFORD TL4746 Map 5

John Barleycorn

(01223) 832699 – www.johnbarleycorn.co.uk
Handy for M11 junction 10; right at first roundabout, then left at main village junction into Moorfield Road; CB22 4PP

Traditional, pretty pub with friendly staff, an enjoyable atmosphere, good, interesting food and seats outside; bedrooms

A charming former coaching inn, this has the appearance of the perfect English country pub. It's thatched and shuttered and, as it dates from the 17th c, has a lot of character where the standing timbers and brick pillars create alcoves and different drinking and dining areas. There are heavy beams and nice old floor tiles, a log fire, all manner of seating from rustic cushioned settles and plain wooden dining chairs to some rather fine antique farmhouse chairs and quite a mix of wooden tables. Plenty to look at too – pub and air force memorabilia, china plates and old clocks, copper pans and plenty of pictures and paintings on blue or pale yellow walls. Greene King Abbot and IPA and guests such as Sadlers Peaky Blinder and Wadworths Bishops Tipple on handpump and ten wines by the glass; background music. The front terrace has picnic-sets beside pretty hanging baskets while the back garden has more picnic-sets among flowering tubs and shrubs. This is a comfortable place to stay; the bedrooms are in a converted barn. The pub was used by the brave young airmen of Douglas Bader's Duxford Wing during World War II and the Imperial War Museum Duxford is close by. Easy wheelchair access from the back car park.

Reliably good food includes lunchtime sandwiches and ploughman's, grazing boards, baked camembert infused with garlic and rosemary with red onion marmalade, moules marinière, mushroom risotto, steak burger with toppings and coleslaw, peppered fillet steak strip salad with honey and mustard dressing, local venison haunch with horseradish mash and redcurrant jus, lamb rump with crushed rosemary potatoes and raspberry jus, and puddings such as cheesecake of the week and a changing crème brûlée. *Benchmark main dish: pie of the day £11.95. Two-course evening meal £19.50.*

Greene King ~ Tenant Nicholas Kersey ~ Real ale ~ Open 11-11; 11-10.30 Sun ~ Bar food 12-3, 5-9; 12-3, 5.30-8.30 Sun ~ Restaurant ~ Children welcome ~ Dogs allowed in bar ~ Wi-fi ~ Bedrooms: /£99.50 *Recommended by Simon King, Minda and Stanley Alexander, Nicola and Holly Lyons, Monica and Steph Evans, David Fowler, Catherine and Daniel King*

Please let us know what you think of a pub's bedrooms: feedback@goodguides.com or (no stamp needed) The Good Pub Guide, FREEPOST RTXY–ZCBC–BBAZ, Stream Lane, Sedlescombe, Battle TN33 0PB.

ELTON TL0894 Map 5

Crown

(01832) 280232 – www.crowninnelton.co.uk

Off B671 S of Wansford (A1/A47), and village signposted off A605 Peterborough–Oundle; Duck Street; PE8 6RQ

Pretty pub with interesting food, several real ales, well chosen wines and a friendly atmosphere; stylish bedrooms

A chef-patron and his friendly staff run this lovely golden-stone thatched pub. The softly lit, beamed bar has leather and antique dining chairs around a nice mix of chunky tables on bare boards, an open fire in a stone fireplace and good pictures and pubby ornaments on pastel walls. The beamed main dining area has fresh flowers and candles, and similar tables and chairs on stripped wooden flooring; there's a modern circular dining extension too. High bar chairs against the counter are popular with locals, and they keep a house beer (from Kings Cliffe Brewery), Greene King IPA, Oakham JHB and two quickly changing guests on handpump, well chosen wines by the glass and farm cider; background music and TV. There are tables outside on the front terrace, and Elton Mill and Lock are nearby. Bedrooms are smart, comfortable and well equipped and the breakfasts are especially good. To find the pub (it's on the edge of this charming village), follow the brown sign towards Nassington.

Appealing food cooked by the landlord includes sandwiches, crab and smoked salmon cocktail, ham hock croquettes with apple and chilli jam, a choice of omelettes, spinach and ricotta ravioli with tomato sauce and parmesan, stone-baked pizzas, free-range belly pork with crispy bacon hash brown, apple purée and cider sauce, fish pie topped with cheddar and herb mash, chicken breast wrapped in pancetta with sautéed potatoes, wild mushrooms and tarragon sauce, and puddings such as Baileys crème brûlée and chocolate bread and butter pudding with chocolate sauce and pistachio ice-cream. *Benchmark main dish: burger with toppings and french fries £12.95. Two-course evening meal £20.00.*

Free house ~ Licensee Marcus Lamb ~ Real ale ~ Open 12-10.30 (11 Sat); 12-9 Sun; closed one week Jan ~ Bar food 12-2 (3 Sun), 6.30-9; not Sun evening, not Mon except for residents ~ Restaurant ~ Children welcome ~ Dogs allowed in bar ~ Wi-fi ~ Bedrooms: £80/£140

Recommended by Caroline and Steve Archer, Charlie Stevens, Elise and Charles Mackinlay, John Harris, Ian Herdman, Chris and Sophie Baxter, W K Wood

GREAT WILBRAHAM TL5558 Map 5

Carpenters Arms

(01223) 882093 – www.carpentersarmsgastropub.co.uk

Off A14 or A11 SW of Newmarket, following The Wilbrahams signposts; High Street; CB21 5JD

Inviting village pub with traditional bar, own-brew beers, highly regarded food in both the bar and the back restaurant; nice garden

Their own ales, brewed at a local farm unit by the enthusiastic Mr Hurley, are Crafty Beers Carpenters Cask, Sauvignon Blonde and Sixteen Strides on handpump and they keep a carefully chosen wine list (strong on the Roussillon region). The low-ceilinged village bar on the right is properly pubby with bar billiards, a woodburning stove in a big inglenook, copper pots and iron tools, and cushioned pews and simple seats around solid pub tables on floor tiles. Service is spot-on: thoughtful, helpful and cheerful. Background music, darts and board games. On the left, a small cosy carpeted dining area has another big stone fireplace and overflowing bookshelves;

this leads through to a sitting area with comfortable sofas and plenty of magazines. The light and airy extended main dining room has country kitchen chairs around chunky tables. A huge honeysuckle swathes the tree in the pretty back courtyard and, further on, an attractive homely garden, with fruit and vegetables, has circular picnic-sets shaded by tall trees.

The landlady makes everything in-house and it's extremely good: orange, fennel pollen and dill-cured salmon with fennel and orange salad, pear and stilton bake, slow-roast pork belly with creamy mash, braised red cabbage and apple cider sauce, burger with triple-cooked chips and beer-battered onion rings, tartiflette (potatoes, onion and bacon baked with reblochon cheese), sea trout suprême with spinach and hollandaise sauce, and puddings such as a crumble of the day and lemon tart; their cheeses come from East Anglia and they now offer a two- and three-course set lunch. *Benchmark main dish: chicken breast stuffed with mushrooms, bacon and onion in a creamy brandy and mushroom sauce £14.50. Two-course evening meal £20.00.*

Free house ~ Licensees Rick and Heather Hurley ~ Real ale ~ Open 11.30-3, 6.30-11; 11.30-4 Sun; closed Sun evening, Mon, Tues ~ Bar food 12-2, 7-9; 12-3 Sun ~ Restaurant ~ Children welcome ~ Wi-fi *Recommended by Chris Bell, Sally and Lance Oldham, Julie and Andrew Blanchett, Cecily and Steven Evans, Robert and Diana Ringstone*

THE GOOD PUB GUIDE

HEMINGFORD GREY TL2970 Map 5

Cock

(01480) 463609 – www.cambscuisine.com/the-cock-hemingford

Village signposted off A14 eastbound, and (via A1096 St Ives road) westbound; High Street; PE28 9BJ

Imaginative food in pretty pub with extensive wine list, four interesting beers, a bustling atmosphere and a smart restaurant

'A first class pub with wonderful food and drink,' says one of our readers with enthusiasm; we agree, as do so many other customers. They've sensibly kept the public bar on the left for drinking only: an open woodburning stove on a raised hearth, bar stools, wall seats and a carver, and steps leading down to more seating. Adnams Southwold, Brewsters Hophead and Oldershaw Grantham Stout on handpump, 20 wines by the glass mainly from the Languedoc-Roussillon region and Cromwell cider (made in the village). Other bar rooms have white-painted or dark beams and lots of contemporary pale yellow and cream paintwork, church candles, artworks here and there, and a really attractive mix of old wooden dining chairs, settles and tables. In marked contrast, the stylishly rustic restaurant on the right (you must book to be sure of a table) is set for dining, with pale wooden floorboards and another woodburning stove. There are seats and tables among stone troughs and flowers on the terrace and in the neat garden, and pretty hanging baskets. This is a delightful village on the River Ouse. Sister pubs are the Crown & Punchbowl at Horningsea, Three Horseshoes in Madingley and Tickell Arms in Whittlesford (all in Cambridgeshire).

Excellent, imaginative food includes lunchtime sandwiches (not Sunday), grilled mackerel with blood orange, chicory and toasted almonds, pigeon breast with gingerbread leg, smoked bacon and popcorn, home-made sausages with mash and a choice of sauce, shallot and blue cheese polenta tart with salsify and balsamic dressing, clam tagliatelle with saffron, chilli, garlic and lemon, lamb rump with lamb shoulder sausage roll, braised gem and lamb sauce and puddings such as pistachio-crusted apple tart with malt ice-cream and chocolate and passion-fruit bavarois with yoghurt sorbet; Tuesday is steak night and they also offer a two- and three-course weekday set lunch. *Benchmark main dish: duck breast with rhubarb, sloe gin gel, butternut squash croquette, duck and orange sauce £17.50. Two-course evening meal £25.00.*

Free house ~ Licensees Oliver Thain and Richard Bradley ~ Real ale ~ Open 12-3, 6-11; 12-11 Sat; 12-10.30 Sun ~ Bar food 12-2.30, 6.30-9; 12-2.30, 6-9.30 Fri, Sat; 12-8 Sun ~ Restaurant ~ No children after 6pm ~ Dogs allowed in bar ~ Wi-fi *Recommended by Paul Farraday, Monty Green, Rosie and John Moore, Mrs Margo Finlay, Jörg Kasprowski, Barbara and Phil Bowie, Sarah and David Gibbs*

HINXTON TL4945 Map 5

Red Lion

(01799) 530601 – www.redlionhinxton.co.uk

2 miles off M11 junction 9 northbound; take first exit off A11, A1301 N, then left turn into village – High Street; a little further from junction 10, via A505 E and A1301 S; CB10 1QY

16th-c pub with friendly staff, interesting bar food, real ales and a big landscaped garden; comfortable bedrooms

This is a nice place to stay in well equipped, pretty bedrooms in a separate flint and brick building; breakfasts are good. The low-beamed bar has a relaxed, friendly atmosphere, oak chairs and tables on bare boards, two leather chesterfield sofas, an open fire and an old wall clock. You'll find their own-label Red & Black Ale (from the local Nethergate Brewery) plus Adnams Ghost Ship, Woodfordes Wherry and a guest such as Crafty Beers Sauvignon Blonde on handpump, 22 wines by the glass, 15 malt whiskies and first class service. An informal dining area has high-backed settles, and the smart restaurant (with oak rafters and traditional dry peg construction) is decorated with various pictures and assorted clocks. In warm weather, there's plenty of seating outside with teak tables and chairs on one terrace, huge parasols on a second terrace by the porch and picnic-sets on grass. There's also a dovecote and nice views of the village church. The Imperial War Museum at Duxford is close by. They also own the Black Bull in Balsham just up the road.

Creative food includes lunchtime sandwiches and hot baguettes and pub classics plus duck livers with confit rhubarb and celeriac purée, cod cheeks with fermented cabbage and peanuts, cauliflower medley with compressed apple and gruyère rarebit, guinea fowl breast with smoked potatoes and pomegranate, soused mackerel with black quinoa and turnip tartare, venison loin with snails and boulangère potatoes, and puddings such as sticky toffee pudding with butterscotch sauce and vanilla ice-cream and banana parfait with tonka bean and whisky. *Benchmark main dish: game pie with garlic mash £14.00. Two-course evening meal £23.00.*

Free house ~ Licensee Alex Clarke ~ Real ale ~ Open 7.30am-11pm; 8.30am-10.30pm (11pm Sat) Sun ~ Bar food 12-2, 6.30-9; 12-2.30, 6.30-9.30 Fri, Sat; 12-3, 6-8 Sun ~ Restaurant ~ Children welcome ~ Dogs allowed in bar ~ Wi-fi ~ Bedrooms: £109/£139 *Recommended by Alison and Dan Richardson, Patti and James Davidson, Peter L Harrison, Charlotte and William Mason, Mrs J Ekins-Daukes*

HORNINGSEA TL4962 Map 5

Crown & Punchbowl

(01223) 860643 – www.cambscuisine.com/the-crown-and-punchbowl

Just NE of Cambridge; CB25 9JG

Impressive food and thoughtful drinks choice in carefully refurbished old inn with seats outside; bedrooms

Reliably well run and with consistent praise from our readers, this is a carefully refurbished and extended 17th-c inn. Original features and character have been maintained and the beamed bar has a woodburning stove in a brick fireplace, leather banquettes and rustic old chairs, stripped boards, terracotta walls and an attractively carved counter where they serve freshly carved ham and home-made pickles. Behind the bar they keep Brewsters Hophead, Milton Pegasus and maybe a changing guest tapped from the cask and 20 wines by the glass (with a focus on the Languedoc-Roussillon region), home-made punches (alcoholic and non-alcoholic), lavender lemonade and local cider. The timbered dining room has leather cushioned chairs around wooden tables on pale boards, wall panelling and candlelight. Another conservatory-style room has large windows and ceramic light fittings (a nod to the village's history as a centre for Roman pottery). There are country seats out in front of the pub, while the five guest bedrooms upstairs are well equipped, light and comfortable. Sister pubs are the Cock at Hemingford Grey, Three Horseshoes in Madingley and Tickell Arms in Whittlesford (all in Cambridgeshire).

Food is first class and includes cod cheeks with spicy sausage, pease pudding, lemon thyme crumb and garlic chives, wild boar ragôut with pappardelle and cheese, shallot, celeriac and red kidney bean roast with leek and turnip purée, home-made sausages with mash and a choice of sauce, skate wing with pineapple, shiitake mushrooms, leek, cabbage and tomato broth, duck leg wellington wrapped in mash with wild mushroom velouté, and puddings such as coconut and lime posset with passion-fruit and kiwi compote and peanut butter parfait with apricot purée and milk chocolate peanut cluster; they also offer a two- and three-course set menu (not Friday evening, all day Saturday, lunchtime Sunday); Tuesday is steak night. *Benchmark main dish: steaks with chips and a choice of sauce £22.00. Two-course evening meal £24.00.*

Free house ~ Licensees Oliver Thain and Richard Bradley ~ Real ale ~ Open 12-3, 6-11.20; 12-11.20 Sat; 12-10.30 Sun ~ Bar food 12-2.30, 6.30-9; 12-2.30, 6-9.30 Fri, Sat; 12-3, 6.30-8.30 Sun ~ Restaurant ~ Children welcome ~ Dogs allowed in bar ~ Wi-fi ~ Bedrooms: /£120

Recommended by Scott and Charlotte Havers, Penny and David Shepherd, Mrs Margo Finlay, Jörg Kasprowski, M and GR, Mike Benton

HUNTINGDON TL2471 Map 5

Old Bridge Hotel

(01480) 424300 – www.huntsbridge.com

1 High Street; ring road just off B1044 entering from easternmost A14 slip road; PE29 3TQ

Proper bar in Georgian hotel with a splendid range of drinks, first class service and excellent food; individually styled bedrooms

On the edge of town and beside the river sits this lovely, civilised hotel. It's run with thought and great care, and our readers love it. At the heart of the place is a proper pubby little bar with a wide mix of customers, a log fire, comfortable sofas and low wooden tables on polished floorboards, and Adnams Southwold, Nene Valley Blond Session Ale and a guest on handpump. They also have an exceptional wine list (up to 30 by the glass in the bar) and a wine shop where you can taste a selection of wines before you buy. Food is available in the big airy restaurant with floor-to-ceiling windows overlooking the garden, or in the bar/lounge. There are seats and tables on the terrace by the Great Ouse, and they have their own landing stage. Bedrooms are luxurious (some overlook the water) and breakfasts excellent.

Imaginative food includes sandwiches, king prawns with samphire and garlic butter, venison terrine with spiced apple chutney, butternut squash tart with sage oil, goats cheese and crispy baby carrot salad, confit duck pudding with king oyster mushrooms and foie gras sauce, sea trout fillet with lobster butter, monks beard and griddled new potatoes, guinea fowl with confit chips and wild mushroom fricassée, chargrilled aberdeenshire steak with triple-cooked chips, caesar salad and peppercorn sauce (carved in the kitchen unless requested otherwise), and puddings such as lemon tart with blackberry sorbet and chocolate fondant with prune ripple ice-cream; they also offer morning coffee, afternoon teas and all-day snacks. *Benchmark main dish: steak sandwich with caramelised onions, grain mustard and fries £12.95. Two-course evening meal £26.00.*

Huntsbridge ~ Licensee John Hoskins ~ Real ale ~ Open 11am-11.30pm ~ Bar food 12.15-2.15, 6.15-9.15 (10 Fri, Sat) ~ Restaurant ~ Children welcome ~ Dogs allowed in bar and bedrooms ~ Wi-fi ~ Bedrooms: £99/£168 *Recommended by Roy Shutz, Jennifer and Nicholas Thompson, Peter and Caroline Waites, Liz and Mike Newton, Michael Sargent, Christopher Mannings*

KEYSTON TL0475 Map 5

Pheasant

(01832) 710241 – www.thepheasant-keyston.co.uk

Just off A14 SE of Thrapston; brown sign to pub down village loop road, off B663; PE28 0RE

Cambridgeshire Dining Pub of the Year

Smart but friendly country dining pub with appealing décor and attractive garden

Once found, customers tend to return here frequently. Since it's a charming thatched building serving exceptional food in civilised surroundings, that's not surprising. The main bar has pitched rafters high above, with lower dark beams in side areas. The central serving area has padded stools beside the leather-quilted counter and dark flagstones, with hop bines above the handpumps for Adnams Southwold, Digfield Fools Nook and a guest beer, and a tempting array of 14 wines (including champagne and prosecco) by the glass; service by neat staff is attentive and courteous. Nearby are armchairs, a chesterfield, quite a throne of a seat carved in 17th-c style, other comfortable seats around low tables, and a log fire in a lofty fireplace. The rest of the pub is mostly red-carpeted with dining chairs around a variety of polished tables, large sporting prints, some hunting-scene wallpaper and lighted candles and tea-lights. The attractively planted and well kept garden behind has tables on the lawn and terrace, and there are picnic-sets in front. This is a quiet farming hamlet.

The landlord cooks the appealing food: sandwiches and pub classics plus red mullet with puy lentils, celeriac purée, pickled apple and dill, corn-fed coronation chicken terrine with apricot chutney, curried chickpeas with coconut basmati, carrot and lime pickle, red onion relish and onion bhaji, chargrilled pork fillet with potato rösti, confit swede, smoked bacon, tarragon and grain mustard, wild black bream with gnocchi, jerusalem artichokes, beetroot and cockles, and puddings such as spiced tea pannacotta with marinated pineapple and coconut biscuit and arabian orange cake with chocolate ice-cream and cinnamon raisins; they also offer a two- and three-course set menu (not Saturday evening or Sunday). *Benchmark main dish: twice-cooked blade of scotch beef with fondant potatoes and bourguignon sauce £19.00. Two-course evening meal £22.00.*

Free house ~ Licensee Simon Cadge ~ Real ale ~ Open 12-3, 6-11; 12-11 Sat; 12-5 Sun; closed Sun evening, Mon; first two weeks Jan ~ Bar food 12-2 (2.30 Fri, Sat), 6.30-9.30; 12-3.30 Sun ~ Restaurant ~ Children welcome ~ Dogs allowed in bar ~ Wi-fi *Recommended by Rupert and Sandy Newton, Max Simons, Michael Sargent, Peter Andrews, Rona Mackinlay, Douglas Power, Dave Braisted*

MADINGLEY TL3960 Map 5

Three Horseshoes

(01954) 210221 – www.cambscuisine.com/three-horseshoes

High Street; off A1303 W of Cambridge; CB23 8AB

Pretty thatched pub with excellent food and wines, charming staff and seats in the garden

There's a gently civilised but informally friendly atmosphere in this pleasing thatched pub, where both drinkers and diners feel welcome, and the décor throughout is light and attractive. The bare-boards bar has high-backed cushioned settles and a mix of nice old dining chairs around wooden tables, prints on pale paintwork and a woodburning stove. From the bar counter, friendly, courteous staff serve Adnams Southwold and a changing ale from Nene Valley on handpump and several good wines by the glass. The airy conservatory restaurant, overlooking the garden, has rattan-style and pale wooden chairs around plain tables on quarry tiles and parquet flooring, a long, brown button-back wall banquette and another woodburning stove. At the front of the building are solid benches and tables, and the sunny back terrace and lawn have picnic-sets and teak tables and chairs. Sister pubs are the Cock in Hemingford Grey, Crown & Punchbowl in Horningsea and Tickell Arms in Whittlesford (all in Cambridgeshire).

Appealing food includes sandwiches, crayfish cocktail, game terrine with pear chutney, jerusalem artichoke and sage risotto with ricotta, sausages and mash with onion gravy, steak and wild mushroom pudding with red wine sauce, duck breast with pearl barley and port reduction, gilt-head bream with white bean stew, spinach and salsa verde, manhattan steak (for two to share) with peppercorn sauce and chips, and puddings such as rice pudding croquettes with apple and star anise compote and dark chocolate and peanut fondant with banana ice-cream and salted caramel. *Benchmark main dish: guinea fowl breast with thyme potato cake and creamed baby chard £16.50. Two-course evening meal £25.00.*

Free house ~ Licensee Oliver Thain ~ Real ale ~ Open 12-3, 6-11; 12-10.30 Sun ~ Bar food 12-2.30, 6.30-9; 12-2.30, 6-9.30 Fri, Sat; 12-3, 6-8 Sun ~ Restaurant ~ Children welcome ~ Dogs allowed in bar ~ Wi-fi *Recommended by Muriel and Spencer Harrop, Alexandra and Richard Clay, Patricia and Anton Larkham, Mark and Mary Setting, George Sanderson, Melanie and David Lawson*

PETERBOROUGH TL1899 Map 5

Brewery Tap £

(01733) 358500 – www.thebrewery-tap.com

Opposite Queensgate car park; PE1 2AA

Fantastic range of real ales including their own brews, popular thai food and a lively, friendly atmosphere

It may be an unusual combination, but the popular thai food and the particularly good own-brewed real ales consistently draw in many happy customers. The building itself is interesting too – a striking modern conversion of an old labour exchange. Open-plan and contemporary, it has an expanse of light wood and stone floors and blue-painted iron pillars holding up a steel-corded mezzanine level. Stylish lighting includes steel-meshed wall lights and a giant suspended steel ring with bulbs running around the rim. A band of chequered floor tiles traces the path of the long sculpted pale wood bar counter, which is boldly backed by an impressive display of bottles in a ceiling-high wall of wooden cubes. There's also a comfortable downstairs area, a big-screen TV for sporting events, background music and regular live bands and comedy nights. A two-storey glass wall divides the bar from the brewery, giving fascinating views of the two-barrel brew plan from which they produce their own Oakham Bishops Farewell, Citra, Inferno, JHB and seasonal ales; also, guest ales, quite a few whiskies and several wines by the glass. It gets very busy in the evening.

The incredibly popular thai food includes set menus and specials, as well as tom yum soup, chicken, beef, pork, prawn, duck and vegetable curries, stir-fried crispy chilli beef, talay pad cha (prawns, squid and mussels with crushed garlic, chilli and ginger), various noodle dishes, all sorts of salads and stir-fries and five kinds of rice. *Benchmark main dish: pad thai noodles £8.90. Two-course evening meal £17.00.*

Own brew ~ Licensee Jessica Loock ~ Real ale ~ Open 12-11 (1am Fri, 2am Sat); 12-10.30 Sun ~ Bar food 12-2.30, 5.30-10.30; 12-10.30 Fri, Sat; 12-3.30, 5.30-9.30 Sun ~ Restaurant ~ Children welcome during food service times only ~ Dogs allowed in bar ~ Wi-fi ~ Live band last Fri of month; DJs Sat evening *Recommended by Lorna and Jack Mulgrave, Paddy and Sian O'Leary, Peter and Emma Kelly*

STILTON TL1689 Map 5

Bell

(01733) 241066 – www.thebellstilton.co.uk

High Street; village signposted from A1 S of Peterborough; PE7 3RA

Fine coaching inn with character bars, popular food, thoughtful drinks choice and seats in a pretty courtyard; bedrooms

A lovely example of a 17th-c coaching inn, this is on the old Great North Road between London and York. Our favourite spot remains the neatly kept right-hand bar which has a great deal of character: bow windows, sturdy upright wooden seats on flagstone floors, a big log fire in a handsome stone fireplace, partly stripped walls with large prints of sailing and winter coaching scenes, and a giant pair of blacksmith's bellows. This room has been opened up with the bistro to create a bar-cum-dining area with a bustling, chatty atmosphere. Grainstore Red Kite, Greene King IPA and Old Speckled Hen, Oakham Bishops Farewell and a guest from Digfield on handpump, several malt whiskies, 14 wines by the glass, 11 gins and farm cider; service is helpful and welcoming. Other rooms include a residents' bar and a restaurant; background music, board games and TV. Through the fine coach arch is a very pretty sheltered courtyard with tables, and a well that dates from Roman times. The bedrooms mix old-world charm with modern facilities and three are on the ground floor.

Enjoyable food includes sandwiches, chicken liver parfait with date and apple chutney, smoked haddock bake, mushroom and stilton quiche with apples, kohlrabi, stilton beignets and mushroom ketchup, beer-battered haddock and chips, pork, leek and stilton sausages with gravy and mash, venison loin with butternut squash, juniper berries and truffle, slow-cooked beef with goose fat roast potatoes and cranberry and red wine jus, and puddings such as clementine, polenta and almond cake with fennel, yoghurt and honey and lemon posset with ginger, rhubarb and meringue. *Benchmark main dish: lamb stew with stilton cheese dumplings £16.60. Two-course evening meal £25.00.*

Free house ~ Licensee Liam McGivern ~ Real ale ~ Open 12-2.30, 6-11 (5-11 Fri); 12-midnight Sat; 12-10.30 Sun ~ Bar food 12-2.15 (2.30 Sat), 6-9; 12-3, 6-8.30 Sun ~ Restaurant ~ Children welcome ~ Wi-fi ~ Bedrooms: £89.50/£115 *Recommended by Andrew Lawson, John and Delia Franks, Jeff Davies, Lance and Sarah Milligan*

There are report forms at the back of the book.

SUTTON GAULT TL4279 Map 5

Anchor

(01353) 778537 – www.anchor-inn-restaurant.co.uk

Bury Lane off High Street (B1381); CB6 2BD

Charming candlelit inn with beamed rooms, excellent food, real ales and a thoughtful wine list; bedrooms

Although space for drinks here may be limited at weekends, you can drop in at other times for a chat and a pint from the quickly changing choice of ales from Milton, Nethergate, Oldershaw and Three Blind Mice on handpump or one of the dozen or so wines by the glass. The four heavily timbered rooms are stylishly simple and civilised, with two log fires, and antique settles and wooden dining chairs around scrubbed pine tables set with candles and nicely spaced on gently undulating floors. Service is helpful and friendly. There are seats outside and you can walk along the high embankment where the bird-watching is good. This is an enjoyable place to stay in comfortable, well equipped bedrooms that overlook the river, and the breakfasts are very good.

First class modern food includes pigeon breast with honey-roasted apricot, kale and bacon, smoked salmon and mackerel roulade with orange semi-gel, cucumber and poached rhubarb, rare-breed beef in ale pie with horseradish mash, roasted butternut squash stuffed with peanuts, sunblush tomatoes, red onion and spinach, topped with goats cheese, chicken suprême with saffron risotto balls, pak choi, carrot purée and spicy coconut cream sauce, cod suprême with pea and leek risotto, pickled courgette and shrimp and caper butter, and puddings such as dark chocolate brownie with lemon curd and fig sorbet and elderflower pannacotta with biscuit crumbs and pink champagne and raspberry sorbet; they also offer a two- and three-course set lunch. *Benchmark main dish: local lamb rump with dauphinoise potatoes, kalettes and mint jus £19.00. Two-course evening meal £26.00.*

Free house ~ Licensee Kasia Marciniak ~ Real ale ~ Open 12-11 ~ Bar food 12-2, 7-9; 12-2.30, 6-9.30 Sat; 12-3.30, 6.30-8.30 Sun ~ Restaurant ~ Children welcome ~ Wi-fi ~ Bedrooms: £59.50/£79.50 *Recommended by Martin and Clare Warne, Brian Glozier, Sabina and Gerald Grimshaw, Phil and Jane Villiers, Andy and Rosemary Taylor*

THORNEY TL2799 Map 5

Dog in a Doublet

(01733) 202256 – www.doginad.co.uk

B1040 towards Thorney; PE6 0RW

Country inn with produce from own farm, tasty food and local ales, friendly service and seats outside; bedrooms

Head here after enjoying one of the many nearby walks. Much emphasis is placed, of course, on the enjoyable food but the bar has sofas, comfortable seats and an open fire and Angles Ales Feral Nun, Kings Cliffe No.10 and Tom Woods Bomber County on handpump, 15 wines by the glass and three farm ciders. The restaurant leads off and has an open kitchen, solid wooden dining chairs around farmhouse tables, prints on red-painted walls and a monthly live pianist; background music and bar games. A deli counter offers their own produce and treats from further afield too. Outside, there are brightly painted picnic-sets under a gazebo. The eight bedrooms have vaulted ceilings and their own balconies, and they also have a campsite. The River Nene and one of the biggest lock gates in Europe are just across the road.

Free-range eggs, home-grown vegetables and home-reared pigs are provided from their small farm for the well regarded food: king prawns with chilli and black garlic butter, devilled lamb kidneys with cream and parsley, sticky black bean udon noodles with chunky vegetables and herbs (also with chicken or beef), maple and thyme gammon with a duck egg, sesame lamb with thai salad (papaya, watercress, lemongrass, mint, coriander and roasted peanuts), aged steak with oxtail and peppercorn ragoût, confit egg yolk, field mushrooms and roast tomato, and puddings such as sticky toffee pudding with brandy butterscotch sauce, vanilla bean ice-cream and salted caramel popcorn and eton mess (raspberry, strawberry and tonka bean-infused chantilly cream with meringue). *Benchmark main dish: trio of home-made sausages with onion marmalade £14.00. Two-course evening meal £20.00.*

Free house ~ Licensees John McGinn and Della Mills ~ Real ale ~ Open 12-11; 12-10 Sun; closed Mon and Tues lunchtimes ~ Bar food breakfast 8-10am (9-10am weekends); 12-9 ~ Children welcome ~ Dogs allowed in bar and bedrooms ~ Wi-fi ~ Bedrooms: £60/£70
Recommended by Peter Brix, Edward Nile, Donald Allsopp, Charlie Stevens, Lenny and Ruth Walters

UFFORD TF0904 Map 5

White Hart

(01780) 740250 – www.whitehartufford.co.uk
Main Street; S on to Ufford Road off B1443 at Bainton, then right; PE9 3BH

Lots of interest in bustling pub, bar and dining rooms, good food and extensive garden; bedrooms

This is a nice place to stay, with four of the comfortable bedrooms in the pub, two in a converted cart shed and four more in the Old Brewery. What was a former farm is now a relaxing, welcoming inn with plenty of drinking and dining space. The bar has an easy-going atmosphere, farm tools and chamber-pots, scatter cushions on leather benches, some nice old chairs and tables, a woodburning stove, exposed stone walls and stools against the counter where they serve Grainstore Red Kite, Oakham JHB and a guest ale on handpump, 22 wines by the glass and 21 gins. There's also an elegant beamed restaurant and an airy Orangery; background music, board games and TV. In warm weather, the three acres of gardens at the back are a huge bonus – they include a sunken dining area with plenty of chairs and tables, picnic-sets on grass, steps to various peaceful corners and lovely flowers and shrubs.

Quite a choice of pleasing food includes sandwiches, chicken liver parfait with red onion marmalade, beetroot-cured salmon with dill dressing, goats cheese and butternut squash wellington with walnut salad and red pimento dressing, local pork sausages with bacon and onion gravy, peppered chicken suprême in a white wine sauce with sautéed potatoes, local pheasant casserole with creamy mash, chargrilled steaks with chips and a choice of sauce, and puddings such as chocolate brownie with chocolate sauce and cinammon and calvados pannacotta. *Benchmark main dish: salmon en croûte with spinach and salsa verde filling and dill and lime sauce £14.95. Two-course evening meal £19.00.*

Free house ~ Licensee Sue Olver ~ Real ale ~ Open 10am-10.30pm; 10am-midnight Sat; 10am-9pm Sun ~ Bar food 12-2.30, 6-9; 12-9.30 Sat; 12-8 Sun ~ Restaurant ~ Children welcome ~ Dogs allowed in bar and bedrooms ~ Wi-fi ~ Bedrooms: /£80 *Recommended by David and Leone Lawson, Matt and Hayley Jacob, Caroline Sullivan, Dr Simon Innes*

THE GOOD PUB GUIDE

WHITTLESFORD TL4648 Map 5

Tickell Arms

(01223) 833025 – www.cambscuisine.com/the-tickell-whittlesford
2.4 miles from M11 junction 10: A505 towards Newmarket, then second turn left signposted Whittlesford; keep on into North Road; CB22 4NZ

Light and refreshing dining pub with good enterprising food and pretty garden

With creative modern food and a fine choice of drinks served by neatly dressed, friendly staff, this pub is a winner. And there are some fine architectural features that are really worth looking at in the bars and dining rooms. The L-shaped bar has bentwood stools on floor tiles, ornate cast-iron pillars, a woodburning stove and (under bowler-hatted lampshades over the counter) Bishop Nick 1555, Brewsters Hophead, Nene Valley Release the Chimps and Milton Pegasus on handpump, 20 fairly priced wines by the glass including champagne, and farm cider. There are also three porcelain handpumps from the era of the legendarily autocratic regime of the Wagner-loving former owner Kim Tickell. Tables in the dining room vary from sturdy to massive, with leather-cushioned bentwood and other dining chairs and one dark pew, and fresh minimalist décor in palest buff. This opens into an even lighter limestone-floored conservatory area, partly divided by a very high-backed ribbed-leather banquette. A side terrace has comfortable tables, and the secluded garden beyond has pergolas and a pond. Sister pubs are the Cock in Hemingford Grey, Crown & Punchbowl at Horningsea and Three Horseshoes in Madingley (all in Cambridgeshire).

Assured cooking from a seasonal menu includes sandwiches, duck parcel with sweet and sour cucumber and sweet soy and ginger dressing, cod cheeks with roast squash, artichoke purée, artichoke crisps and beetroot fondant, roast cauliflower risotto, sausages and mash with caramelised onions and red wine sauce, whole lemon sole with crushed potatoes and caper and lemon butter, slow-cooked pork belly with mac and cheese and red wine sauce, and puddings such as cambridge burnt cream and chocolate fondant with chocolate crumb and raspberry ice-cream; steak night is Tuesday, and they also offer a two- and three-course set menu (not Friday evening, not Saturday, not Sunday lunchtime). *Benchmark main dish: sea bream with vegetable lasagne and truffle potato £17.50. Two-course evening meal £25.00.*

Free house ~ Licensees Oliver Thain and Max Freeman ~ Real ale ~ Open 12-3, 6-11; 12-11 Sat; 12-10 Sun ~ Bar food 12-2.30, 6.30-9; 12-2.30, 6-9.30 Fri, Sat; 12-3, 6-8 Sun ~ Restaurant ~ Children welcome ~ Dogs allowed in bar ~ Wi-fi *Recommended by Sally Harrison, Gail and Frank Hackett, Katherine and Hugh Markham, Louise and Oliver Redman, Jill and Hugh Bennett*

Also Worth a Visit in Cambridgeshire

Besides the fully inspected pubs, you might like to try these pubs that have been recommended to us and described by readers. Do tell us what you think of them: feedback@goodguides.com

ABBOTS RIPTON TL2377

Abbots Elm (01487) 773773
B1090; PE28 2PA Open-plan thatched dining pub reconstructed after major fire; highly rated food from snacks and bar meals to interesting restaurant dishes using locally sourced and home-grown produce, extensive choice of wines by the glass including champagne, three well kept ales, good friendly service; children and dogs welcome, four bedrooms, open all day Sat, till 4pm Sun, closed Mon. *(Colin James)*

BARRINGTON TL3849

Royal Oak (01223) 870791
Turn off A10 about 3.7 miles SW of M11 junction 11, in Foxton; West Green; CB22 7RZ Rambling thatched Tudor pub with tables out overlooking classic village green; heavy low beams and timbers, mixed furnishings, Greene King IPA and guests, Aspall's and Thatcher's ciders, enjoyable food from pub favourites up, good wine list, friendly helpful service, airy dining conservatory; background music, free wi-fi; children and dogs welcome, classic car club meeting first Fri of month. *(Lenny and Ruth Walters)*

BARTLOW TL5845

Three Hills (01223) 890500
Off Camps Road, signed Ashdon, S Walden; CB21 4PW Attractively refurbished 17th-c inn; very good well presented food including cheaper bar

menu and two-course lunch, friendly accommodating service, several real ales such as Crafty Beers and Woodfordes, cosy beamed bar, restaurant and snug with log fire; children and dogs welcome, terrace and garden running down to little River Granta, six well appointed bedrooms (four in separate building), picturesque village with interesting hill forts nearby, closed Sun evening and Mon lunchtime, bar food only Mon. *(Ted Hawkes)*

BOURN TL3256

★Willow Tree (01954) 719775

High Street, just off B1046 W of Cambridge; CB23 2SQ Light and airy dining pub with relaxed informal atmosphere despite the cut-glass chandeliers, sprinkling of Louis XVI furniture and profusion of silver-plated candlesticks; accomplished restaurant-style cooking (all day Sun till 8pm), Woodfordes and a local guest, well chosen wines and inventive cocktails, friendly staff; live jazz Sun evening; children welcome, smart tables and chairs on back deck, grassed area beyond car park with fruit trees, huge weeping willow and tipi, open all day. *(John Saville)*

BOXWORTH TL3464

Golden Ball (01954) 267397

High Street; CB23 4LY Attractive partly thatched 16th-c village pub with pitched-roof bar, restaurant and small conservatory, emphasis on good fairly priced food from baguettes through pubby choices and grills to blackboard specials, friendly attentive service, well kept Charles Wells ales, good wine and whisky choice; free wi-fi; children welcome, nice garden and heated terrace, pastures behind, 11 quiet bedrooms in adjacent block, open all day, food till 7pm Sun. *(Andy and Rosemary Taylor)*

BRAMPTON TL2170

Black Bull (01480) 457201

Church Road; PE28 4PF 16th-c and later with updated low-ceilinged interior, stripped-wood floor and inglenook woodburner in split-level main bar, restaurant with light wood furniture on tiles, popular well priced pubby food including range of pies, four real ales, friendly efficient staff; free wi-fi; children and dogs (in bar) welcome, garden with play area, open (and food) all day, till 9pm (4pm) Sun. *(Jill and Hugh Bennett)*

BRANDON CREEK TL6091

★Ship (01353) 676228

A10 Ely–Downham Market; PE38 0PP Lovely spot for this 17th-c pub at confluence of the Great and Little Ouse rivers; carefully modernised central bar with substantial stonework in sunken former forge area, big log fire one end, woodburner the other, interesting old fenland photographs/prints along with local artwork for sale. Adnams Southwold and a couple of guests, proper cider and good choice of wines, enjoyable food (all day weekends) including range of home-made pies, cosy snug, restaurant overlooking the rivers; live music or quiz first Fri of month, board games, free wi-fi; children and dogs (in bar) welcome, outside seating making most of the waterside position, moorings, closed Mon, otherwise open all day; for sale as we went to press. *(Nick Higgins, Susan and Callum Slade)*

BRINKLEY TL6254

Red Lion (01638) 508707

High Street; CB8 0RA Old country pub set back from the road; painted beams, bare boards and inglenook log fire, Woodfordes Wherry and a couple of guests (plans for on-site microbrewery), good sensibly priced food from sandwiches up including some themed nights and Sun brunch, friendly service, restaurant; free wi-fi; children and dogs (in bar) welcome, picnic-sets on lawn, closed Sun evening, Mon lunchtime, Tues and Weds. *(Casey Duncan)*

BROUGHTON TL2877

★Crown (01487) 824428

Off A141 opposite RAF Wyton; Bridge Road; PE28 3AY Attractively tucked-away mansard-roofed dining pub opposite church; fresh airy décor with country pine tables and chairs on stone floors, some leather bucket seats and sofa, good well presented food (special diets catered for) from lunchtime sandwiches and pub favourites up, friendly service, real ales such as Mauldons, restaurant; background music; children and dogs welcome, disabled access and facilities, tables out on big stretch of grass behind, open all day Sun till 6pm, closed Mon. *(Gary and Marie Miller)*

BUCKDEN TL1967

★George (01480) 812300

High Street; PE19 5XA Handsome and stylish Georgian-faced hotel with bustling informal bar, fine fan beamwork, leather and chrome chairs, log fire, Adnams Southwold and a changing guest from chrome-topped counter, lots of wines including champagne by the glass, teas and coffees, popular brasserie with good modern food served by helpful enthusiastic young staff, also bar meals; background music; children and dogs welcome, tables under large parasols on pretty sheltered terrace with box hedging, 12 charming bedrooms named after famous Georges, smallish car park (free street parking), open all day. *(Michael Sargent)*

BURWELL TL5867

Anchor (01638) 743970

North Street; CB25 0BA Recently revamped 18th-c dining pub with good imaginative food cooked by chef-owner, a couple of Greene King ales, a guest beer and plenty of wines by the glass from interesting list, helpful friendly service, restaurant, snug with books and board games; background music; children welcome till 9pm, dogs in bar, sunny garden backing on to small river, closed Mon and Tues, no food Sun evening. *(Ted Hawkes)*

CAMBRIDGE TL4458

Anchor (01223) 353554
Silver Street; CB3 9EL Pub-restaurant in beautiful riverside position by punting station, popular with tourists and can get very busy; fine river views from upper dining room and suntrap terrace, five well kept beers and plenty of wines by the glass, good variety of food from open sandwiches up, friendly service; background music and some Pink Floyd memorabilia (the band had early associations with the pub); children and dogs welcome, open (and food) all day. *(Tony Scott)*

CAMBRIDGE TL4658

★**Cambridge Blue** (01223) 471680
85 Gwydir Street; CB1 2LG Friendly little backstreet local with a dozen or more interesting ales (some tapped from the cask – regular festivals), also six craft kegs, 200 bottled beers, up to seven ciders and over 70 whiskies, enjoyable well priced home-made food including seasonal specials, extended bar area with lots of breweriana and old advertising signs, attractive conservatory; free wi-fi; children and dogs welcome, seats in back garden bordering cemetery, open (and food) all day and can get very busy weekends. *(Casey Duncan)*

CAMBRIDGE TL4459

Castle (01223) 353194
Castle Street; CB3 0AJ Adnams range and interesting guest beers in bare-boards bar and other pleasantly simple rooms including snug and quieter upstairs area, good choice of pub food from sandwiches and snacks to blackboard specials, efficient friendly staff; background music, free wi-fi; children and dogs welcome, part-covered walled back courtyard, open all day and very busy Fri, Sat evenings. *(Casey Duncan)*

CAMBRIDGE TL4658

Clarendon Arms (01223) 778272
Clarendon Street; CB1 1JX Welcoming backstreet corner local; pubby furniture on flagstones or bare boards, lots of pictures including local scenes, step down to back bar, Greene King ales and enjoyable home-made food from snacks to Sun roasts, friendly helpful service; free wi-fi; children and dogs welcome, wheelchair access with help, seats in sunny back courtyard, open all day, no food Sun evening. *(Ted Hawkes)*

CAMBRIDGE TL4657

Devonshire Arms (01223) 316610
Devonshire Road; CB1 2BH Welcoming Milton-tied pub with two busy linked bars, their well kept ales and guests, real cider, also great choice of bottled beers, decent wines and a dozen malts, enjoyable good value food (not Sun evening) from sandwiches and pizzas to grills, creaky wood floors, mix of furniture including long narrow refectory tables, architectural prints and steam engine pictures, woodburner in back bar; wheelchair access, handy for the station, open all day. *(Casey Duncan)*

CAMBRIDGE TL4458

★**Eagle** (01223) 505020
Benet Street; CB2 3QN Once the city's most important coaching inn; rambling rooms with two ancient mullioned windows and the remains of possibly medieval wall paintings, two fireplaces dating from around 1600, lovely worn wooden floors and plenty of pine panelling, dark red ceiling left unpainted since World War II to preserve the signatures of british and american airmen made with Zippo lighters, candle smoke and lipstick, well kept Greene King ales including Eagle DNA (Crick and Watson announced the discovery of DNA's structure here in 1953) and two guests, decent choice of enjoyable food served efficiently considering the crowds; children welcome, disabled facilities, heavy wooden seats in attractive cobbled and galleried courtyard, open all day. *(Tony Scott)*

CAMBRIDGE TL4558

Elm Tree (01223) 502632
Orchard Street; CB1 1JT Traditional one-bar backstreet drinkers' pub with welcoming atmosphere, ten well kept ales including B&T and Charles Wells, good range of continental bottled beers plus local cider/perry, friendly knowledgeable staff, no food, nice unspoilt interior with breweriana and other memorabilia; some live music; wheelchair access, a few tables out at the side, open all day. *(Jim Studd)*

CAMBRIDGE TL4559

Fort St George (01223) 354327
Midsummer Common; CB4 1HA Picturesque old pub (reached by foot only) in charming waterside position overlooking ducks, punts and boathouses; good value pubby food including traditional Sun lunch, well kept Greene King ales and decent wines by the glass, cheerful service, interior extended around old-fashioned Tudor core with oars on beams, historic boating photographs and open fire; free wi-fi; children and dogs welcome, wheelchair access via side door, lots of tables outside, open (and food) all day. *(Ted Hawkes)*

CAMBRIDGE TL4558

Free Press (01223) 368337
Prospect Row; CB1 1DU Unspoilt little backstreet pub with interesting décor including old newspaper pages and printing memorabilia (was printshop for a local paper); Greene King IPA, Abbot and Mild plus regularly changing guests, good range of

wines by the glass, 25 malt whiskies and lots of gins and rums, tasty good value food, log fire, friendly atmosphere; TV for major sports, board games; children and dogs (in bar) welcome, wheelchair access, small sheltered paved garden behind, open all day.
(John Wooll)

CAMBRIDGE TL4557

Live & Let Live (01223) 460261

Mawson Road; CB1 2EA Popular backstreet corner pub with friendly relaxed atmosphere; five well kept ales including Nethergate and Oakham, proper cider and over 120 rums, snacky food, panelled interior with sturdy varnished tables on bare boards, some steam railway and brewery memorabilia, old gas light fittings, cribbage and dominoes; dogs welcome, disabled access awkward but possible, closed Wed and Thurs lunchtimes. *(Casey Duncan)*

CAMBRIDGE TL4458

Mill (01223) 311829

Mill Lane; CB2 1RX Fairly compact old pub in picturesque spot overlooking mill pond (punt hire); seven mainly local ales and proper cider from plank-topped servery, reasonably priced food such as burgers, opened-up bar with bare boards, quarry tiles and some exposed brickwork, mix of old and new furniture including pews and banquettes, snug panelled back room; radiogram playing vinyl, Mon quiz, sports TV, free wi-fi; children welcome, open (and food) all day. *(John Wooll)*

CAMBRIDGE TL4458

Mitre (01223) 358403

Bridge Street, opposite St Johns College; CB2 1UF Popular Nicholsons pub close to the river and well placed for visiting the colleges; spacious rambling bar on several levels, good selection of well kept ales and reasonably priced wines by the glass, their usual food including range of pies, efficient friendly service; background music, free wi-fi; children welcome, disabled access, open (and food) all day. *(John Saville)*

CAMBRIDGE TL4559

Old Spring (01223) 357228

Ferry Path; car park on Chesterton Road; CB4 1HB Extended Victorian pub, roomy and airy, with enjoyable home-made food from traditional choices up, friendly efficient service, well kept Greene King IPA, Abbot and four guests, plenty of wines by the glass and good coffee, mix of seating including sofas on bare boards, log fires, conservatory; background music; well behaved children welcome, no dogs inside, disabled facilities, seats out at front and on large heated back terrace, open all day, food all day Sun.
(Jim Studd)

CASTOR TL1298

Prince of Wales Feathers

(01733) 380222 *Peterborough Road, off A47; PE5 7AL* Friendly stone-built local with half a dozen well kept ales including Castor, craft beers and proper cider/perry, good value food cooked by landlady (not Sun evening), Thurs steak night, open-plan interior with dining area to the left; Sat live music, Sun quiz, pool, TV; children and dogs welcome, disabled facilities, attractive front terrace, another at the back with large smokers' shelter, open all day, till late weekends. *(Sarah and David Gibbs)*

CATWORTH TL0873

Racehorse (01832) 710123

B660, S of A14; PE28 0PF Welcoming 19th-c village pub with enjoyable food from sandwiches/panini and sharing boards up, three well kept changing ales and good choice of wines, whiskies and gins, cheerful helpful service, smallish bar connecting to more spacious dining areas, log fire, deli/coffee shop; some live music, pool, TV; children and dogs welcome, café-style tables outside, five bedrooms in converted stables, closed Sun evening, otherwise open all day (till 10pm Mon-Thurs); may be for sale.
(Guy and Caroline Howard)

CONINGTON TL3266

White Swan (01954) 267251

Signed off A14 (was A604) Cambridge–Huntingdon; Elsworth Road; CB23 4LN Quietly placed 18th-c red-brick country pub; well kept Adnams and guests tapped from the cask, nine wines by the glass and good freshly made food (not Mon, Tues or evening Sun), friendly attentive service, traditional bar with tiled floor and log fire, restaurant extension, some old photographs and local artwork; children and dogs welcome, big front garden with play area, open all day. *(Jill and Hugh Bennett)*

DUXFORD TL4745

Plough (01223) 833170

St Peters Street; CB22 4RP Popular early 18th-c thatched pub, clean bright and friendly, with enjoyable home-made food from shortish reasonably priced menu, Adnams, Everards and guests kept well, also a craft keg and four ciders/perries, friendly helpful service, woodburner in brick fireplace; children and dogs welcome, handy for IWM Duxford, open all day, no food Sun evening. *(Casey Duncan)*

ELLINGTON TL1671

Mermaid (01480) 891106

High Street; PE28 0AB Popular village dining pub dating in part from the 14th c; highly praised imaginative food (not Sun

We say if we know a pub has background music.

evening) from owner-chef including interesting tapas menu and plenty for vegetarians/vegans, a couple of Greene King ales and a guest from brick counter, several wines by the glass (good list), friendly obliging young staff, beams (some hiding coins left by US airmen), country furniture, woodburner, smallish dining rooms; background music (turned off on request); garden overlooking church, no proper car park, open all day weekends (till 8pm Sun), closed Mon. *(Roy Shutz, Mike and Mary Carter)*

ELSWORTH TL3163

George & Dragon (01954) 267236

Off A14 NW of Cambridge, via Boxworth, or off A428; CB23 8JQ Neatly kept dining pub in same group as the Eaton Oak at St Neots and Rose at Stapleford; panelled and carpeted main bar opening on left to slightly elevated dining area with woodburner, garden room overlooking attractive terraces, more formal restaurant on right, wide choice of popular food including speciality fish/seafood, set menus and other deals, Greene King ales, a guest beer and decent range of wines, friendly service; steps down to loos, free wi-fi; children welcome, dogs in bar, open (and food) all day Sun. *(Michael and Jenny Back)*

ELSWORTH TL3163

Poacher (01954) 267722

Brockley Road; CB23 4JS Welcoming 17th-c thatched and beamed corner local; well kept Woodfordes Wherry, St Austell Tribute and a couple of guests from tiny servery, good reasonably priced traditional food (not Sun evening), friendly service, painted pine furniture on bare boards or tiles, open fire; background and some live music, monthly quiz, TV; children and dogs welcome (they have two huskies), a few picnic-sets out in front, more in back garden, good walks, open all day weekends. *(Jim O'Leary)*

ELTON TL0893

Black Horse (01832) 280591

Overend; B671 off A605 W of Peterborough and A1(M); PE8 6RU Honey-stone beamed dining pub with nicely updated and opened-up interior; popular generously served food cooked by owner-chef, friendly accommodating service, four real ales including Digfield, Greene King and a beer badged for them, decent wines; children welcome, dogs in bar, terrace and garden with views across to Elton Hall park and village church, open (and food) all day. *(Christopher Mobbs)*

ELY TL5479

Cutter (01353) 662713

Annesdale, off Station Road (or walk S along Riverside Walk from Maltings); CB7 4BN Beautifully placed riverside pub with bar, dining lounge and restaurant, enjoyable food from sandwiches and wraps up, friendly helpful service, well kept Adnams, Sharps, Woodfordes and a guest from boat-shaped counter, nice wines by the glass and decent coffee, good views from window seats and terrace; children welcome, no dogs inside, moorings, open all day from 9am (food from midday). *(John Saville)*

ELY TL5480

Lamb (01353) 663574

Brook Street (Lynn Road); CB7 4EJ Good choice of food in popular hotel's panelled lounge bar or restaurant, friendly welcoming staff, Greene King ales and plenty of wines by the glass; children and dogs welcome, close to cathedral, 31 clean comfortable bedrooms, good breakfast (for non-residents too), open (and food) all day. *(Andy and Rosemary Taylor)*

ETTON TF1406

Golden Pheasant (01733) 252387

Just off B1443 N of Peterborough, signed from near N end of A15 bypass; PE6 7DA Former Georgian farmhouse (a pub since 1964) refurbished under welcoming new owners; spacious bar with open fire, good choice of real ales and other drinks, well liked food served by friendly staff, back restaurant; TV; children welcome, no dogs inside, big tree-sheltered garden with play area, on Green Wheel cycle route, closed Sun evening, Mon, otherwise open all day. *(Ted Hawkes)*

FEN DRAYTON TL3468

Three Tuns (01954) 230242

Eastbound on A14, take first exit after Fenstanton, signed Fen Drayton and follow to pub; westbound on A14 exit at junction 27 and follow signs to village on Cambridge Road; High Street; CB24 4SJ Well preserved thatched pub under new management; three more-or-less open-plan rooms with heavy moulded Tudor beams and timbers, log fires, mix of burgundy cushioned stools, nice old dining chairs and settles in bar, red-patterned carpet in dining room, Greene King IPA, Old Speckled Hen and a couple of guests, 14 wines by the glass, enjoyable pubby food including blackboard specials, friendly service; some quiz and live music nights; children and dogs (in bar) welcome, back garden with covered dining area and play equipment, open all day Sat, till 4pm Sun, closed Mon lunchtime. *(Gordon and Margaret Ormondroyd, Stephen Funnell)*

FOWLMERE TL4245

★**Chequers** (01763) 208558

High Street (B1368); SG8 7SR Popular 16th-c coaching inn with split-level rooms, long cushioned wall seats, dining chairs around dark tables, inglenook woodburner, good food from traditional choices up served by friendly staff, Greene King, two guests and plenty of wines by the glass, attractive upstairs beamed and timbered dining room with interesting moulded plasterwork above one fireplace, spacious conservatory; monthly quiz Sun; children welcome, dogs in bar, picnic-sets on paved terrace and lawn, four bedrooms, open all day Sat, till 9pm Sun. *(Tim Price)*

GRANTCHESTER TL4355

★Blue Ball (01223) 846004

Broadway; CB3 9NQ Traditional bare-boards free house rebuilt in 1900 on site of much older pub (cellars remain); welcoming licensees (there's a list of publicans back to 1767), a couple of real ales such as Adnams and Woodfordes, Aspall's ciders and decent choice of wines by the glass, affordably priced wholesome food, good log fire; some live music, traditional games including shut the box and ring the bull, newspapers and lots of books; children and dogs welcome, tables on small terrace with lovely views to Grantchester Meadows, two comfortable bedrooms, nice village, open all day (till 8pm Sun). *(Andy and Rosemary Taylor)*

GRANTCHESTER TL4355

Red Lion (01223) 840121

High Street; CB3 9NF Comfortable and spacious thatched pub with attractively modernised open areas including pitched-roof dining room, beams, timbers and panelling, popular food from shortish varied menu, well kept ales such as Nene Valley, Greene King, Oakham and Woodfordes, lots of wines by the glass and some interesting gins including Cambridge distilled nearby, friendly service (can slow at busy times); background music; children, dogs and muddy boots welcome, sheltered terrace and good-sized lawn with play area, easy walk to river, open (and food) all day. *(Clive and Fran Dutson)*

GRANTCHESTER TL4455

Rupert Brooke (01223) 841875

Broadway; junction Coton Road with Cambridge–Trumpington Road; CB3 9NQ Smartly presented restauranty pub; contemporary wood-clad extension at front with big windows, elegant dining chairs around polished tables on bare boards, back bar area and two-level restaurant, brasserie-style food from open kitchen including set lunch, over 20 wines by the glass and a couple of real ales such as Milton and Woodfordes, afternoon tea (not Sun), good friendly service, upstairs club room and roof terrace; free wi-fi; children and dogs (in bar) welcome, open all day (till 7pm Sun), breakfast from 9am Mon-Sat. *(Mrs Margo Finlay, Jörg Kasprowski)*

GREAT ABINGTON TL5348

Three Tuns (01223) 891467

Off A1307 Cambridge–Haverhill, and A11; CB21 6AB Peacefully set 16th-c beamed village pub; low-backed settles on stripped-wood floors, open fires, good authentic thai food (traditional roast on Sun), three well kept changing ales, welcoming landlord and friendly efficient staff; garden picnic-sets, nine well appointed bedrooms in modern block, open all day weekends. *(Mrs Margo Finlay, Jörg Kasprowski)*

GREAT CHISHILL TL4239

Pheasant (01763) 838535

Follow Heydon signpost from B1039 in village; SG8 8SR Old split-level pub under newish management; beams, timbers, flagstones and open fires, welcoming friendly staff, a house beer from Nethergate and a couple of other beers from herringbone brick counter, enjoyable food including some blackboard specials, small dining room; children and dogs welcome, nice secluded back garden with small play area and pétanque, open all day weekends. *(Jill and Hugh Bennett)*

HADDENHAM TL4675

Three Kings (01353) 749080

Station Road; CB6 3XD Popular 17th-c village pub; enjoyable home-made food from sandwiches and pub favourites up including good Sun roasts and Thurs curry night, well kept Greene King IPA and guests, friendly welcoming staff, log fire; children and dogs allowed, back courtyard, open all day, food all day weekends. *(Tim Price)*

HAIL WESTON TL1662

Royal Oak (01480) 716712

High Street; just off A45, handy for A1 St Neots bypass; PE19 5JW Picturesque thatched pub (recently reopened by local consortium after long closure) in pretty village near Grafham Water; cosy interior with beams, flagstones and inglenook log fire, four real ales and good reasonably priced home-made food from sandwiches and sharing boards up, restaurant; background music (live every other Weds), Sun quiz; children and dogs (in bar) welcome, picnic-sets in garden with sandpit, good circular walks (ask for details), closed Mon and Tues, otherwise open all day, no food Sun evening. *(Michael Sargent)*

HARDWICK TL3758

Blue Lion (01954) 210328

Signed off A428 (was A45) W of Cambridge; Main Street; CB23 7QU Attractive 18th-c split-level dining pub; good generously served food from landlord-chef using local ingredients, can eat in bar or extended dining area with conservatory, Greene King IPA and guests, friendly efficient young staff, beams and timbers, leather armchairs by copper-canopied inglenook; children welcome, pretty little front garden, more seats on decking and lawn with play area, handy for Wimpole Way walks, open all day (food all day weekends). *(Casey Duncan)*

HELPSTON TF1205

Blue Bell (01733) 252394
Woodgate; off B1443; PE6 7ED Extended and refurbished 17th-c stone pub, enjoyable food from sharing plates and pub favourites up, four well kept ales including a house brew from local Star, good range of wines and gins, friendly staff; children and dogs welcome, four bedrooms, open all day weekends, no food Sun evening, John Clare's cottage next door (open Fri, Sat and Mon). *(Anna Morrish)*

HEMINGFORD ABBOTS TL2870

Axe & Compass (01480) 463605
High Street; village signposted off A14 W of Cambridge; PE28 9AH Spacious old thatched pub in nice village; simple beamed public bar with mate's chairs and stools around wooden tables on ancient floor tiles, woodburner in snug, main room has more beams and standing timbers, tweed tartan-patterned chairs and armchairs and cushioned wall seating around nice old tables on wood floors, local photographs and another woodburner in small brick fireplace, Adnams, Sharps and Timothy Taylors Landlord, local cider and 12 wines by the glass, well liked seasonal food (all day Sat, not Sun evening), long dining extension; background music (live first Fri of month), quiz Tues, board games, free wi-fi; well behaved children and dogs (in bar) welcome, disabled facilities, garden with fenced play area, river walks, open all day. *(Mrs Margo Finlay, Jörg Kasprowski, Ted and Mary Bates, Miranda and Jeff Davidson)*

HEYDON TL4339

★**King William IV** (01763) 838773
Off A505 W of M11 junction 10; SG8 8PW Rambling dimly lit rooms with fascinating rustic jumble (ploughshares, yokes, iron tools, cowbells and so forth) along with copperware and china in nooks and crannies, some tables suspended by chains from beams, central log fire, Fullers, Greene King and Timothy Taylors, good choice of highly rated food including several vegetarian options, helpful staff; background music; children and dogs (in bar) welcome, teak furniture on heated terrace and in pretty garden, four bedrooms in separate building, open (and food) all day weekends. *(Colin James)*

HISTON TL4363

★**Red Lion** (01223) 564437
High Street, off Station Road; 3.7 miles from M11 junction 1; CB24 9JD Impressive choice of draught and bottled beers along with traditional cider/perry (festivals Easter/early Sept); ceiling joists in L-shaped main bar packed with beer mats, pump clips and whisky-water jugs, also fine collection of old brewery advertisements and enamel signs, enjoyable traditional food (not Fri, Sun evenings) including a gluten-free menu, cheerful efficient service, log fires, comfortable brocaded wall seats, matching mate's chairs and pubby tables, extended bar on left (well behaved children allowed here) with darts, TV and huge collection of beer bottles; mobile phones discouraged, no dogs inside; disabled access/facilities, picnic-sets in neat garden, limited parking, four bedrooms, open all day. *(Lenny and Ruth Walters)*

HOUGHTON TL2772

Three Jolly Butchers
(01480) 463228 *A1123, Wyton; PE28 2AD* Popular 17th-c beamed pub with wide choice of enjoyable home-made food from bar and restaurant menus, friendly accommodating service, well kept ales including Greene King, inglenook woodburner; background and live music, quiz nights, sports TV; well behaved children and dogs (in bar) welcome, covered back terrace with pool table, picnic-sets in large garden down to River Ouse (own moorings), pretty village and handy for Houghton Mill (NT), open (and food) all day, kitchen closes 4pm Sun. *(Mike Kavaney)*

KIMBOLTON TL0967

New Sun (01480) 860052
High Street; PE28 0HA Pink-painted village pub with cosy low-beamed front lounge, standing timbers, exposed brickwork, comfortable seats by log fire, narrower locals' bar serving Charles Wells ales, several wines by the glass and decent range of gins, ample helpings of enjoyable food including tapas, friendly service, traditionally furnished dining room and airy conservatory leading to terrace with smart furniture under giant umbrellas; background music, piano; well behaved children welcome away from bar, dogs allowed in bar, open all day, no food Sun or Mon evenings. *(Peter Andrews, Richard Kennell)*

LEIGHTON BROMSWOLD TL1175

Green Man (01480) 890238
Signed off A14 Huntingdon–Kettering; PE28 5AW Cosy traditional village pub with origins from the 13th c; four well kept changing ales and enjoyable good value food, friendly long-serving landlady, heavy low beams, inglenook log fire; northants skittles; children welcome, picnic-sets outside, closed Sun evening, Mon. *(Guy and Caroline Howard)*

LITTLE SHELFORD TL4551

Navigator (01223) 843901
2.5 miles from M11 junction 11: A10 towards Royston, then left at Hauxton, The Shelfords signpost; CB2 5ES

You can send reports directly to us at feedback@goodguides.com

Attractive little 16th-c village pub with bar and small restaurant, beams, painted panelling and some exposed brickwork, open fire, good authentic thai food (not Sun), mainstream ales and decent wines, friendly prompt service; children welcome, some picnic-sets outside, closed Sat lunchtime and Sun evening. *(Esther and John Sprinkle)*

NEWTON TL4349

★**Queens Head** (01223) 870436
2.5 miles from M11 junction 11; A10 towards Royston, then left on to B1368; CB22 7PG Lovely traditional unchanging pub run by same welcoming family for many years – lots of loyal customers; peaceful bow-windowed main bar with crooked beams in low ceiling, bare wooden benches and seats built into cream walls, curved high-backed settle, paintings and big log fire, well kept Adnams ales tapped from the cask, farm cider and simple food such as soup and sandwiches, small carpeted saloon, traditional games including table skittles, shove-ha'penny and nine men's morris; children on best behaviour allowed in games room only, dogs welcome, seats out in front by vine trellis. *(Casey Duncan)*

OFFORD D'ARCY TL2166

Horseshoe (01480) 810293
High Street; PE19 5RH Extended former 17th-c coaching house with two bars and restaurant; emphasis on their good food including popular Sun carvery, Sharps Doom Bar, a couple of guests and well chosen wines, friendly helpful service, beams and inglenooks; children welcome, dogs in snug (not Sun), lawned garden with play area, open all day Sat, till 9.30pm Sun. *(Tim Studd)*

ORWELL TL3650

Chequers (01223) 207840
Town Green Road; SG8 5QL Village dining pub with good food (not Tues or Sun evenings) from pub favourites up including popular themed nights, well kept ales and decent choice of wines by the glass, friendly helpful staff; children and dogs (in bar) welcome, disabled facilities, handy for Wimpole Hall (NT), open all day Fri and Sat, till 8pm Sun, closed Mon. *(Jim O'Leary)*

PAMPISFORD TL4948

★**Chequers** (01223) 833220
2.6 miles from M11 junction 10: A505 E, then village and pub signed off; Town Lane; CB22 4ER Traditional neatly kept old pub with low beams and comfortable old-fashioned furnishings, booth seating on pale ceramic tiles in main area, low step down to bare-boards part, four real ales such as Greene King IPA and Woodfordes Wherry, well liked fairly priced pubby food including Sun carvery, good friendly service; TV, free wi-fi; children and dogs welcome, picnic-sets in small garden lit by black streetlamps, parking can be tricky, open all day (till 4pm Sun). *(Sarah and David Gibbs)*

PETERBOROUGH TL1998

★**Charters** (01733) 315700
Town Bridge, S side; PE1 1FP Interesting conversion of dutch grain barge moored on River Nene; sizeable timbered bar on lower deck with up to a dozen real ales including Oakham (regular beer festivals), restaurant above serving good value south-east asian food, lots of wooden tables and pews; background music, live bands (Fri and Sat after 10.30pm, Sun from 3.30pm); children welcome till 9pm, dogs in bar, huge riverside garden (gets packed in fine weather), open all day (till 1am Fri, Sat). *(Lenny and Ruth Walters)*

PETERBOROUGH TL1897

Coalheavers Arms (01733) 565664
Park Street, Woodston; PE2 9BH Friendly old-fashioned little flagstoned local near football ground and busy on match days; half a dozen well kept ales and good range of bottled beers, traditional cider and several malt whiskies, basic snacks; Sun quiz, free wi-fi; dogs welcome, pleasant garden behind, open all day Fri-Sun, closed lunchtime Mon-Weds. *(Ted Hawkes)*

PETERBOROUGH TL1898

Drapers Arms (01733) 847570
Cowgate; PE1 1LZ Roomy open-plan Wetherspoons in converted 19th-c draper's; ten well kept ales and their usual good value food served all day, prompt friendly service; TV, free wi-fi; children welcome, open from 8am and can get very busy Fri, Sat evenings. *(Ted Hawkes)*

REACH TL5666

Dykes End (01638) 743816
From B1102 follow signpost to Swaffham Prior and Upware; village signposted; CB25 0JD New owners for this 17th-c pub in attractive spot next to church and village green; traditional bar simply furnished with kitchen chairs and heavy pine tables on dark boards, smarter furniture in panelled section to the left, step down to carpeted part with small servery, ales such as Adnams, Crafty Beers and Timothy Taylors, several wines by the glass, decent pubby food (not Sun evening, Mon), more dining space in refurbished upstairs room; well behaved children and dogs welcome, picnic-sets on front grass, good walks at nearby Devil's Dyke, open all day weekends, closed Mon lunchtime. *(Peter Brix, Toby Jones, Mark Morgan, Mike Swan)*

ST IVES TL3171

Oliver Cromwell (01480) 465601
Wellington Street; PE27 5AZ Homely two-bar pub in little street just back from the river; enjoyable good value lunchtime

food such as steak and kidney pudding, half a dozen well kept changing ales, proper ciders and good choice of wines, friendly staff; background music (live Thurs), quiz first Tues of the month (not summer); small back terrace, open all day. *(Dave and Jan Pilgrim)*

ST NEOTS TL1761

Eaton Oak (01480) 219555
Just off A1, Great North Road/Crosshall Road; PE19 7DB In same group as the George & Dragon at Elsworth and Rose at Stapleford; wide choice of popular food including grills, fresh fish and good value weekday set menu, Wells and Youngs ales plus a guest, friendly helpful service, plenty of nooks and crannies in older part, two front snugs, light airy dining area and conservatory; free wi-fi; children and dogs (in bar) welcome, disabled access and loo, tables out under parasols, flowering tubs and hanging baskets, smokers' shelter, nine bedrooms, open all day (breakfast for non-residents); up for sale so may be changes. *(Michael and Jenny Back)*

STAPLEFORD TL4651

Rose (01223) 843349
London Road; M11 junction 11; CB22 5DG Comfortable sister dining pub to the Eaton Oak at St Neots and George & Dragon at Elsworth, good choice of popular fairly pubby food including set menus and Mon/Tues early-bird deal, friendly uniformed staff, Courage Directors, Youngs Best and Wells Bombardier, small low-ceilinged lounge with inglenook woodburner, roomy split-level dining area; steps up to lavatories; picnic-sets on back grass, open (and food) all day weekends. *(Ted Hawkes)*

SWAFFHAM PRIOR TL5663

Red Lion (01638) 745483
B1102 NE of Cambridge; High Street; CB5 0LD Comfortable and welcoming 17th-c pub with well kept Batemans and guests, a dozen wines by the glass and enjoyable reasonably priced home-made food, helpful friendly staff, beams, old quarry tiles and brick fireplace, historic local photographs; quiz third Sun of month, darts, TV; children welcome, picnic-sets in back garden, interesting church and priory, open all day Sat, till 8pm Sun (later on quiz nights), closed lunchtimes Mon and Tues (no food those days). *(David Bird)*

THRIPLOW TL4346

Green Man (01763) 208855
3 miles from M11 junction 10; A505 towards Royston, then first right; Lower Street; SG8 7RJ Welcoming little roadside pub owned by the village; good food from shortish daily changing menu along with blackboard tapas, four well kept ales and decent wines by the glass, efficient friendly service; free lift home for local evening diners (must book); children and dogs welcome, picnic-sets on small grassy triangle in front, two circular walks from the pub, closed Mon, otherwise open (and food) all day, till 7pm (6pm) Sun. *(Colin James)*

WHITTLESFORD TL4648

Bees in the Wall (01223) 834289
North Road; handy for M11 junction 10 and IWM Duxford; CB22 4NZ Village-edge local with comfortably worn-in split-level timbered lounge, polished tables and country prints, small tiled public bar with old wall settles, darts, decent good value food from shortish menu, well kept Adnams Lighthouse and one or two guests, open fires; background and live music including folk club second Tues of month, small TV for major sports; children welcome, no dogs, picnic-sets in big paddock-style garden with terrace, bees still in the wall (here since the 1950s), closed all day Mon, lunchtimes Tues-Thurs (and Sat in winter), no food Sun evening or Tues. *(Casey Duncan)*

Post Office address codings confusingly give the impression that some pubs are in Cambridgeshire, when they're really in Bedfordshire, Lincolnshire, Norfolk or Northamptonshire (which is where we list them).

Cheshire

ALDFORD SJ4259 Map 7

Grosvenor Arms ★

(01244) 620228 – www.brunningandprice.co.uk/grosvenorarms

B5130 Chester–Wrexham; CH3 6HJ

Spacious place with impressive range of drinks, wide-ranging imaginative menu, good service, suntrap terrace and garden

For a sizeable pub, the various chatty bars here have plenty of interest and individuality. Spacious cream-painted areas are sectioned by big knocked-through arches with a variety of floor finishes (wood, quarry tiles, flagstones, black and white tiles), and the richly coloured turkish rugs look well against these natural materials. Good solid pieces of traditional furniture, plenty of pictures and attractive lighting keep it all cosy. A handsome room has tall bookshelves lining one wall and they keep a good selection of board games. Well trained, attentive staff serve Phoenix Brunning & Price Original, Weetwood Eastgate and Timothy Taylors Landlord with guests such as Salopian Lemon Dream and Titanic Mild from a fine-looking bar counter, and they offer 20 wines by the glass, more than 80 whiskies, 30 gins and farm cider. The airy, terracotta-floored conservatory – lovely on summer evenings – has lots of gigantic low-hanging flowering baskets and chunky pale wood garden furniture. It opens out to a large elegant suntrap terrace and a neat lawn with picnic-sets; the village green is opposite.

Rewarding food includes sandwiches and pub classics, baked camembert with plum and ginger chutney, dried fruits and smoked almonds, pumpkin tortellini with spaghetti vegetables and lemon and herb butter sauce, chicken caesar salad, steak in ale pudding, cheese, potato and onion pie with paprika-spiced baked beans, chicken with lemon thyme risotto, roasted cherry tomatoes and herb pesto, moroccan-spiced lamb with chilli baked plums, raisin dressing and mint yoghurt, sea bass with caper and dill potato cake and salsa verde, and puddings such as triple chocolate brownie with chocolate sauce and crème brûlée. *Benchmark main dish: smoked haddock kedgeree with poached egg £9.50. Two-course evening meal £21.00.*

Brunning & Price ~ Manager Justin Realff ~ Real ale ~ Open 11-11; 12-10.30 Sun ~ Bar food 12-9.30; 12-9 Sun ~ Children welcome ~ Dogs allowed in bar ~ Wi-fi ~ Acoustic night monthly *Recommended by Mike and Wena Stevenson, Michael and Sarah Lockley, John and Mary Warner, Peter and Emma Kelly, Nik and Gloria Clarke*

Anyone claiming to arrange, or prevent, inclusion of a pub in the *Guide* is a fraud. Pubs are included only if recommended by readers and if our own anonymous inspection confirms that they are suitable.

ALLOSTOCK SJ7271 Map 7

Three Greyhounds Inn

(01565) 723455 – www.thethreegreyhoundsinn.co.uk

4.7 miles from M6 junction 18: A54 E then fork left on to B5803 into Holmes Chapel, left at roundabout on to A50 for 2 miles, then left on to B5082 towards Northwich; Holmes Chapel Road; WA16 9JY

Relaxing, civilised and welcoming, with enjoyable food and drink all day

Drop in here after visiting Shakerley Mere nature reserve which is just across the road. The rooms are linked by open doorways and décor throughout is restful: candles and soft lighting, thick rugs on quarry tiles or bare boards, and dark grey walls (or interesting woven wooden ones made from old brandy barrels) hung with modern black-on-white prints. There's an appealing variety of wooden dining chairs, cushioned wall seats, little stools and plenty of plump purple scatter cushions around all sorts of tables; do note the one made from giant bellows. A smashing choice of drinks includes 15 interesting wines by the glass, over 50 brandies and six local cider brandies, a farm cider and Three Greyhounds Bitter (named for the pub from Weetwood) plus quickly changing guests such as Byley Bomber, Caledonian Deuchars IPA, Storm Bosley Cloud and Tatton Blonde on handpump; unobtrusive background music and board games. Above the old farm barns is a restored private dining and party room called the Old Dog House. The big side lawn has picnic-table sets under parasols, with more tables on a decked side verandah with a Perspex roof. The pub is owned by Tim Bird and Mary McLaughlin of Cheshire Cat Pubs & Bars.

Enterprising food includes sandwiches, tandoori-spiced scallops with mint yoghurt, mango jam and crispy onion rösti, field mushrooms with shallots, cognac and cream on toasted seed bread, smoked haddock, salmon and spinach fish pie, puy lentil, wild mushroom, carrot and shallot in ale pie, chicken, coconut and lemongrass curry with pineapple salsa, calves liver with bacon, onions and mustard mash, venison loin with celeriac fondant and tangy cumberland sauce, and puddings such as sticky toffee pudding with rum and raisin ice-cream and milk chocolate and peanut butter brownie with vanilla ice-cream. *Benchmark main dish: chicken, ham and leek pie £13.95. Two-course evening meal £19.00.*

Free house ~ Licensee Dominic Gottelier ~ Real ale ~ Open 12-11; 12-10.30 Sun ~ Bar food 12-9 (9.30 Fri, Sat) ~ Children welcome until 7pm ~ Dogs allowed in bar ~ Wi-fi ~ Live music every second Fri *Recommended by John and Mary Warner, Caroline Prescott, Barry and Daphne Gregson, Jim King, Dr and Mrs A K Clarke*

ASTON SJ6146 Map 7

Bhurtpore ★ £

(01270) 780917 – www.bhurtpore.co.uk

Off A530 SW of Nantwich; in village follow Wrenbury signpost; CW5 8DQ

Warm-hearted pub with some unusual artefacts and an excellent range of drinks, especially real ales; big garden

Not surprisingly, it gets pretty busy here (especially at weekends) with customers keen to try the fantastic choice of drinks. They keep around 11 constantly changing real ales from all over the country that might include Abbeydale Coffee & Hazelnut Baby Stout, Acorn Barbe Rouge IPA, Coastal Triton, Mobberley Maori, Moorhouses Pendle Witches Brew, Ringwood Fortyniner, Roosters By 'Eck, Salopian Avarice, Stonehouse Futility, Turning Point Rising Tide and Wye Valley Goddess. You'll also find dozens of unusual bottled beers and fruit beers, a great many bottled ciders and perries and farm cider, over 100 different whiskies, 100 gins, 20 vodkas, 22 rums, carefully selected soft drinks and a dozen wines by the glass from a good list. The pub name commemorates the 1826 siege of Bhurtpore (a town in India) during which local landowner Sir Stapleton Cotton (later Viscount Combermere) was commander-in-chief. The connection with India also explains some of the quirky artefacts in the carpeted lounge bar – look out for the sunglasses-wearing turbanned figure behind the counter. There are also good local period photographs and some attractive furniture in the comfortable public bar; board games, pool, TV and games machine.

As well as their popular half a dozen curries (including a vegetarian one), the tasty food includes sandwiches and baguettes, smoked haddock in a cheese and leek sauce wrapped in a herb pancake, spicy lamb samosas with yoghurt and mint dip, steak and kidney in ale pie, beer-battered haddock and chips, lasagne, specials such as chicken in a creamy stilton and bacon sauce, breaded cheese and leek cakes on dijon mustard sauce, quarter lamb shoulder in mint and sherry, and puddings such as sticky toffee pudding with vanilla ice-cream and warm chocolate fudge cake. *Benchmark main dish: beef, stilton and red wine pie £12.50. Two-course evening meal £16.50.*

Free house ~ Licensee Simon George ~ Real ale ~ Open 12-11.30 (midnight Fri, Sat); 12-11 Sun ~ Bar food 12-2, 7-9; 12-9.30 Fri, Sat; 12-9 Sun ~ Restaurant ~ Children welcome ~ Dogs allowed in bar ~ Wi-fi ~ Folk third Tues of the month *Recommended by Nick Sharpe, Jo Garnett, Donald Allsopp, Buster and Helena Hastings, Charles Fraser, Christopher Mannings*

BARTHOMLEY SJ7752 Map 7

White Lion £

(01270) 882242 – www.whitelion-barthomley.co.uk

M6 junction 16, B5078 N towards Alsager, then Barthomley signed on left; CW2 5PG

Timeless 17th-c thatched village tavern with classic period interior, up to half a dozen real ales and good value lunchtime food

Charming, unchanging and very much part of the local community, you'll feel quite at home here very quickly. The bar has a blazing open fire, heavy oak beams dating from Stuart times, attractively moulded black panelling, prints of Cheshire on the walls, latticed windows and uneven wobbly old tables. Up some steps, a second room has another welcoming open fire, more oak panelling, a high-backed winged settle and a paraffin lamp hinged to the wall; shove-ha'penny. Local societies make good use of a third room. Banks's Sunbeam, Jennings Cocker Hoop and Sneck Lifter, Marstons Saddle Tank and Wainwright and a guest beer on handpump and eight wines by the glass served by genuinely friendly staff. The gents' are across an open courtyard. In summer, seats on cobbles outside offer nice views over the pretty village. The early 15th-c red sandstone church of St Bertoline (where you can learn about the Barthomley massacre) is worth a visit.

Traditional lunchtime-only food is good value: sandwiches and baguettes, various hotpots, sausage and mash with onion gravy, and puddings such as bread and butter pudding. *Benchmark main dish: steak in Guinness pie £8.95.*

Marstons ~ Tenant Katy Hollins ~ Real ale ~ Open 12-11 (10.30 Sun) ~ Bar food 12-2 Mon, Tues; 12-3 Weds-Sun ~ Children welcome away from bar counter ~ Dogs welcome ~ Wi-fi ~ Quiz first Tues of the month *Recommended by Mike and Wena Stevenson, Heather and Richard Jones, John Harris, John Saville, Dr and Mrs A K Clarke, Andrew Wall, Buster May*

The symbol shows pubs that keep their beer unusually well, have a particularly good range or brew their own.

BOSTOCK GREEN SJ6769 Map 7

Hayhurst Arms

(01606) 541810 – www.brunningandprice.co.uk/hayhurstarms

London Road, Bostock Green; CW10 9JP

Interesting pub with a marvellous choice of drinks, a wide choice of rewarding food, friendly staff and seats outside

This handsome place was built in 1845 as Reading Rooms for the locality. It's been cleverly converted and extended, incorporating the former stables and coach house, to create a large and interesting pub. The long main bar is divided into different dining areas by elegant supporting pillars, and it's light and airy throughout: big windows, house plants, bookshelves, standard lamps, metal chandeliers and prints, old photographs and paintings arranged frame-to-frame above wooden dados. The varied dark wooden dining chairs are grouped around tables of all sizes on rugs, quarry tiles, wide floorboards and carpet, and three open fireplaces have big mirrors above them, with hefty leather armchairs to each side. A couple of cosier rooms lead off; background music and board games. Phoenix Brunning & Price Original and Weetwood Eastgate Ale with guests such as Merlin Gold, Spitting Feathers Empire IPA, Stockton New World Order and Wolf Straw Dog on handpump, 25 wines by the glass, 70 malt whiskies and 25 gins; staff are efficient and courteous. The outside terrace has good quality tables and chairs under parasols, and the village green opposite has swings and a play tractor.

Good, up-to-date food includes sandwiches and pub favourites plus seared scallops with crispy ham fritters and pea purée, cider-braised pig cheek with colcannon cake, crispy bacon and scrumpy sauce, cheese, potato and onion pie with wholegrain mustard sauce, warm crispy beef salad with sweet chilli dressing and chilli roasted cashew nuts, chicken breast with mushroom, spinach and tarragon pasta topped with parmesan, malaysian fish curry with cardamom and lime rice, and puddings such as triple chocolate brownie with chocolate sauce and honeycomb ice-cream and crème brûlée. *Benchmark main dish: steak in ale pie £13.95. Two-course evening meal £21.50.*

Brunning & Price ~ Manager Christopher Beswick ~ Real ale ~ Open 11-11 (10.30 Sun); 11-10.30 Sun ~ Bar food 12-9 (9.30 Fri, Sat) ~ Children welcome ~ Dogs allowed in bar ~ Wi-fi *Recommended by Dr Peter Crawshaw, Sabina and Gerald Grimshaw, Nik and Gloria Clarke, Sally and Brian Turner, John and Lorna Chew, Tim and Mary Thomson*

BUNBURY SJ5658 Map 7

Dysart Arms

(01829) 260183 – www.brunningandprice.co.uk/dysart

Bowes Gate Road; village signposted off A51 NW of Nantwich; and from A49 S of Tarporley – coming in this way on northernmost village access road, bear left in village centre; CW6 9PH

Civilised chatty dining pub with thoughtfully laid-out rooms, enjoyable food and a lovely garden with pretty views

A splendid choice of drinks and interesting food continue to draw in praise for this well run country pub and a meandering series of knocked-through rooms manage to keep a cosy but still very sociable atmosphere. Each room (some with open fires) is nicely furnished with an appealing variety of well spaced sturdy wooden tables and chairs, a couple of tall filled bookcases and just the right amount of carefully chosen bric-a-brac, properly lit pictures and plants. Flooring ranges from red and black tiles to stripped boards and some carpet. Phoenix Brunning & Price Original and Weetwood Best Bitter with guests such as Hawkshead Iti, Salopian Oracle and Timothy Taylors Landlord and Ram Tam are served on handpump alongside a good selection of 20 wines by the glass, 60 gins and around 30 malt whiskies; background music and board games. There are sturdy wooden tables on the terrace and picnic-sets on the lawn in the neatly kept and slightly elevated garden, and the views of the splendid church at the end of this pretty village and the distant Peckforton Hills beyond are lovely.

Brasserie-style food includes sandwiches and pub classics plus wild mushrooms on toasted sourdough with a poached egg and tarragon hollandaise, crispy five-spice pork belly on oriental puy lentils with pickled ginger and hoisin, venison and pear pie with piccalilli, chicken curry with bombay potatoes and sweet potato pakora, braised lamb shoulder with dauphinoise potatoes and sticky red cabbage, sea bass with braised fennel, sunblush potato cake and black olive salsa, and puddings such as apple and blackberry pie with custard and salted caramel cheesecake. *Benchmark main dish: local sausages and mash with onion gravy £11.45. Two-course evening meal £18.95.*

Brunning & Price ~ Manager Daniel Rose ~ Real ale ~ Open 11-11 (10.30 Sun) ~ Bar food 12-9 (9.30 Fri, Sat) ~ Children welcome ~ Dogs allowed in bar ~ Wi-fi *Recommended by Mike and Wena Stevenson, Scott and Charlotte Havers, Sophia and Hamish Greenfield, Mark Morgan*

BURLEYDAM SJ6042 Map 7

Combermere Arms

(01948) 871223 – www.brunningandprice.co.uk/combermere

A525 Whitchurch–Audlem; SY13 4AT

Roomy and attractive beamed pub successfully mixing a good drinking side with imaginative all-day food

Consistently well run and highly enjoyable, this is a good all-rounder where you'll get an equally nice welcome whether you want a drink and a chat or a full meal. The place has been cleverly extended without losing too much character and there are plenty of nooks and crannies in the rambling yet intimate-feeling rooms. Attractive and understated, they're filled with all sorts of antique cushioned dining chairs around dark wood tables, rugs on wood (some old, some new oak) and stone floors, prints hung frame-to-frame on cream walls, bookshelves and open fires. Friendly, efficient staff serve Phoenix Brunning & Price Original and Weetwood Cheshire Cat Blonde Ale and guests such as Salopian Shropshire Gold, Sharps Doom Bar and Timothy Taylors Boltmaker on handpump, 60 gins, 40 malt whiskies, 15 wines by the glass from an extensive list and two farm ciders; board games and background music. Outside there are good solid wood tables and picnic-sets in a pretty, well tended garden.

Rewarding food includes sandwiches and pub classics plus deep-fried cornish brie with sweet red pepper marmalade, scallops with cauliflower purée, black pudding fritters and apple dressing, crispy beef salad with sweet chilli and cashew nuts, cheese, potato and onion pie with carrot purée and red wine jus, malaysian chicken curry with sticky coconut rice, sea bass with tomato, chorizo and butterbeans and watercress sauce, and puddings such as sticky toffee pudding with toffee sauce and raspberry bakewell tart with raspberry compote. *Benchmark main dish: braised lamb shoulder with dauphinoise potatoes and rosemary gravy £17.25. Two-course evening meal £21.00.*

Brunning & Price ~ Manager Lisa Hares ~ Real ale ~ Open 11-11; 11-10.30 Sun ~ Bar food 12-9 (9.30 Fri, Sat) ~ Restaurant ~ Children welcome ~ Dogs allowed in bar ~ Wi-fi *Recommended by Michael Butler, Dr Simon Innes, Jack Trussler, Chris Stevenson, Sally and David Champion, Dan and Belinda Smallbone, Gail and Arthur Roberts*

BURWARDSLEY SJ5256 Map 7

Pheasant ★

(01829) 770434 – www.thepheasantinn.co.uk

Higher Burwardsley; signposted from Tattenhall (which itself is signposted off A41 S of Chester) and from Harthill (reached by turning off A534 Nantwich–Holt at the Copper Mine); follow pub's signpost up hill from Post Office; OS Sheet 117 map reference 523566; CH3 9PF

Cheshire Dining Pub of the Year

Fantastic views and enjoyable food at this clever conversion of an old heavily beamed inn; good bedrooms

The excellent food is one of the mainstays here, but the friendly, helpful staff also offer Weetwood Best, Cheshire Cat Blonde Ale and Eastgate and a guest such as Pheasant Gold (named for the pub, also from Weetwood) on handpump, 13 wines by the glass, ten malt whiskies and local farm cider. The attractive low-beamed interior is airy and modern-feeling in parts, and the various separate areas have nice old chairs spread spaciously on wooden floors and a log fire in a huge see-through fireplace; quiet background music and daily newspapers. From picnic-sets on the terrace, you can enjoy one of the county's most magnificent views right across the Cheshire plains; on a clear day with the telescope you can see as far as the pier head and cathedrals in Liverpool. Comfortable, character bedrooms are in the main building or an ivy-clad stable wing and make a great base for exploring the area. There are plenty of surrounding walks and the scenic Sandstone Trail along the Peckforton Hills is nearby. Sister pubs are the Fishpool in Delamere and Bears Paw in Warmingham.

Imaginative food includes sandwiches and sharing boards (until 6pm), seared scallops with roasted cauliflower purée, spiced black pudding, golden raisins, apple and air-dried ham, breaded camembert with fig jam, candied walnuts, nasturtium pesto and brioche croutons, moroccan-spiced pearl couscous with spinach, charred peppers and mint yoghurt and goats cheese wrapped in crispy filo pastry, roasted corn-fed chicken breast with potato galette, green kale, chestnuts and wild mushroom and thyme boudin, sea bass fillet with cauliflower and chilli couscous, sautéed king prawns and salted fennel and parsley purée, venison haunch with bubble and squeak, game faggot, blackberries, chocolate and red wine sauce, and puddings such as white chocolate and passion-fruit cheesecake, Baileys caramel sauce and clotted cream ice-cream and warm cherry and almond tart with kirsch jelly and toasted almond and cherry crumble ice-cream; they also offer brunch (9-12.30, not Sunday). *Benchmark main dish: steak in ale pie £14.95. Two-course evening meal £23.00.*

Free house ~ Licensee Andrew Nelson ~ Real ale ~ Open 11-11 (10.30 Sun) ~ Bar food 12-9.30 (10 Fri, Sat; 9 Sun) ~ Restaurant ~ Children welcome ~ Dogs welcome ~ Wi-fi ~ Bedrooms: £115/£125 *Recommended by Sylvia and Phillip Spencer, Matt and Hayley Jacob, Rosie and John Moore, Guy Henderson, Lesley and Brian Lynn, Gwendoline and Ralph Mason*

CHESTER SJ4066 Map 7

Albion ★ £

(01244) 340345 – www.albioninnchester.co.uk

Albion Street; CH1 1RQ

Strongly traditional pub with comfortable Edwardian décor and captivating World War I memorabilia; pubby food and good drinks

Sadly, the charming Mr and Mrs Mercer have decided to retire after running this special pub for over 40 years; they hope that as many of their loyal customers as possible will be able to visit them before they leave in mid 2019. An absorbing collection of World War I memorabilia has been collected throughout the time they've been here and this is an officially listed site of four war memorials to soldiers from the Cheshire Regiment. The peaceful rooms have large engravings of men leaving for war and similarly moving prints of wounded veterans, as well as flags, advertisements and so on. Also, leatherette and hoop-backed chairs around cast-iron-framed tables, lamps, an open fire in the Edwardian fireplace and dark floral William Morris wallpaper (designed on the first day of World War I). You might even be lucky enough to hear the vintage 1928 Steck pianola being played; there's an attractive side dining room too. The cats Charlie and Rosie appear after food service has finished. There's Sharps Sea Fury and Youngs London Gold on handpump, new world wines, fresh orange juice, organic bottled cider and fruit juice, over 25 malt whiskies and a good selection of rums and gins. Bedrooms are small but comfortable and furnished in keeping with the pub's style (free parking for residents and a bottle of house wine if dining). An attractive way to reach the place is along the city wall, coming down at Newgate/Wolfsgate and walking along Park Street. No children. Please note: if the pub is quiet they may close early, so it's best to ring ahead and check.

The generously served 'trench rations' include club and doorstep sandwiches, corned beef hash with pickled red cabbage, fish pie with cheese topping, boiled gammon and pease pudding with parsley sauce, haggis and tatties, and lambs liver, bacon and onions with cider gravy. *Benchmark main dish: curry of the day £10.00. Two-course evening meal £15.00.*

Punch ~ Lease Mike and Christina Mercer ~ Real ale ~ Open 11-2.30 (3 Sat), 5-11; best to phone for Sun ~ Bar food 12-2.30, 5-8 (8.30 Sat) ~ Dogs allowed in bar ~ 1920s swing monthly ~ Bedrooms: £85/£95 *Recommended by David and Leone Lawson, John and Delia Franks, David H Bennett, Steve Whalley, Richard Tilbrook*

CHESTER SJ4066 Map 7

Architect

(01244) 353070 – www.brunningandprice.co.uk/architect
Nicholas Street (A5268); CH1 2NX

Lively pub by the racecourse with interesting furnishings and décor, attentive staff, a good choice of drinks and super food

You'd better arrive early on race days (there are views over Roodee Racecourse) to be sure of a table. It's almost a place of two halves connected by a glass passage. The pubbiest part, with a more bustling feel, is the garden room where they serve Phoenix Brunning & Price Original and Weetwood Eastgate alongside guests such as Big Hand Seren, Conwy Spring Chicken, Tatton Blonde and Titanic Lifeboat and Plum Porter on handpump, 18 wines by the glass, 74 whiskies, 170 gins and farm cider. Throughout there are elegant antique dining chairs around a mix of nice old tables on rugs or bare floorboards, hundreds of interesting paintings and prints on green, cream or yellow walls, house plants and flowers on windowsills and mantelpieces, and lots of bookcases. As well as a friendly, easy-going atmosphere, you'll also find open fires, armchairs in front of a woodburning stove or tucked into cosy nooks, candelabra and big mirrors; background music and board games. Big windows and french doors look over a terrace, where there are plenty of good quality wooden seats and tables under parasols.

Enterprising food includes sandwiches, king prawns with chorizo, rocket and chipotle sauce, garlic and rosemary baked camembert with fruit chutney, chicken caesar salad, sweet potato, aubergine and spinach malaysian curry with coconut rice, steak in ale pudding with mustard mash, sea bass with crab croquette, pea purée and oven-dried cherry tomatoes, warm crispy beef salad with sweet chilli dressing and cashew nuts, venison haunch with fondant potato, beetroot purée, bacon, savoy cabbage and blackberry sauce, and puddings such as crème brûlée and hot waffle with caramelised banana, toffee sauce and honeycomb ice-cream. *Benchmark main dish: beer-battered fish and chips £13.45. Two-course evening meal £19.75.*

Brunning & Price ~ Manager Alan Porlock ~ Real ale ~ Open 10.30am-11pm (11.30pm Sat); 10.30-10.30 Sun ~ Bar food 12-9.30 (10 Fri, Sat); 12-9 Sun ~ Children welcome ~ Dogs allowed in bar ~ Wi-fi *Recommended by Michael Butler, Peter Pilbeam, Isobel Mackinlay, Alfie Bayliss, Mungo Shipley, David Phillips, Richard Tilbrook*

CHESTER SJ4166 Map 7

Mill £

(01244) 350035 – www.millhotel.com

Milton Street; CH1 3NF

Big hotel with huge range of real ales, good value food and cheery service in sizeable bar; bedrooms

Converted from an old mill, the large, modern hotel here straddles either side of the Shropshire Union Canal, with a glassed-in bridge connecting the two sections. A big surprise is that they stock up to a dozen real ales on handpump (in fact, they get through more than 2,000 guest beers a year). Weetwood Best and Mill Premium (brewed for them by Coach House) are available all the time, with guests such as Castle Rock Harvest Pale and Oakham JHB; also, a dozen wines by the glass, two farm ciders and 20 malt whiskies. You'll find a real mix of customers in the neatly kept bar which has some exposed brickwork and supporting pillars, slate-effect wallpaper, contemporary purple/grey upholstered seats around marble-topped tables on light wooden flooring, and helpful, friendly staff; a glass-walled dining extension has been added. One comfortable area is reminiscent of a bar on a cruise liner; quiet background music and unobtrusively placed big-screen sports TV. Bedrooms are comfortable and rather smart.

There are several different menus, but the bar food includes sandwiches, whitebait, warm camembert cheese with sticky onion topping, spinach and ricotta tortellini in tomato sauce, rack of ribs with coleslaw, a stir-fry of the day, breadcrumbed chicken breast filled with brie, leek and pine nut stuffing and tarragon sauce, king prawns and fillet steak with a choice of sauce and parmesan fries, and puddings such as banoffi cheesecake and eton mess. *Benchmark main dish: beer-battered fish and chips £11.95. Two-course evening meal £16.00.*

Free house ~ Licensee Chris Gould ~ Real ale ~ Open 10am-midnight; 11am-midnight Sun ~ Bar food 12-10 ~ Restaurant ~ Children welcome ~ Wi-fi ~ Live jazz Mon ~ Bedrooms: £74/£98 *Recommended by Peter Brix, John and Delia Franks, Lee and Jill Stafford, Mark and Sian Edwards, Darrell Barton, Alister and Margery Bacon*

CHESTER SJ4166 Map 7

Old Harkers Arms

(01244) 344525 – www.brunningandprice.co.uk/harkers

Russell Street, down steps off City Road where it crosses canal; CH3 5AL

Well run canalside building with a lively atmosphere, fantastic range of drinks and extremely good food

The splendid position here means you can still watch boats on the Shropshire Union Canal from the tall windows that run the length of the main bar. The striking industrial interior with its high ceilings is divided into user-friendly spaces by brick pillars. Walls are covered with old prints hung frame-to-frame, mixed dark wood furniture is set out in intimate groups on stripped-wood floors, there's a wall of bookshelves above a leather banquette at one end, and the attractive lamps lend some cosiness; board games. Cheerful staff serve Phoenix Brunning & Price Original and Weetwood Cheshire Cat Blonde Ale with guests such as Castle Rock Harvest Pale, Hawkshead Windermere Pale and Titanic Plum Porter on handpump, 150 malt whiskies, 24 wines from a well described list, 30 gins and nine farm ciders. There was indeed a Mr Harker who once ran a canal-boat chandler's next door to this building.

High standards of cooking include sandwiches and pub classics, plus prawn and chorizo salad with courgette spaghetti and lime and coriander crème fraîche, chicken liver pâté with red onion marmalade, honey-glazed bacon chop with fried egg, smoked haddock and salmon fishcakes with tomato and spring onion salad, aubergine, potato and okra curry with lime rice, chicken schnitzel with wild mushroom spinach and marjoram tagliatelle, beef fillet with slow-cooked ox cheek, horseradish mash and pedro ximénez sherry jus, and puddings such as rhubarb and ginger trifle with pistachio granola and triple chocolate brownie with chocolate sauce. *Benchmark main dish: braised lamb shoulder with dauphinoise potatoes and rosemary gravy £17.25. Two-course evening meal £20.00.*

Brunning & Price ~ Manager Paul Jeffery ~ Real ale ~ Open 10.30am-11pm; 10am-10.30pm Sun ~ Bar food 12-9.30; 10-9.30 Sat; 10-9 Sun ~ Dogs allowed in bar ~ Wi-fi *Recommended by Simon Collett-Jones, David H Bennett, Andy and Louise Ramwell, Daniel King, William Pace, Amy Ledbetter*

CHOLMONDELEY SJ5550 Map 7

Cholmondeley Arms

(01829) 720300 – www.cholmondeleyarms.co.uk

Bickley Moss; A49 5.5 miles N of Whitchurch; SY14 8HN

Former schoolhouse with a decent range of real ales and wines, well presented food and sizeable garden; bedrooms

Interesting food, a fine range of drinks and a genuine welcome continues to keep customers more than happy here. There's a lot to look at too – the bar rooms have lofty ceilings and tall Victorian windows plus huge old radiators and school paraphernalia (hockey sticks, tennis rackets, trunks and so forth), armchairs by a fire with a massive stag's head above, big mirrors and all sorts of dining chairs and tables on warmly coloured rugs over bare boards; fresh flowers, church candles and background music. As well as an extraordinary number of gins (400 and counting), you'll find Cholmondeley Best (from Weetwood) and three guests such as Coach House Gunpowder Strong Mild, Merlin Avalon and Woods Shropshire Born N Bred on handpump and 15 wines by the glass. A sizeable lawn (which drifts off into open countryside) has plenty of seating and there's more in front overlooking the quiet road. The bedrooms are in the old headmaster's house opposite and named after real and fictional teachers; the pictures dotted about actually did belong to former headmasters. Cholmondeley Castle Gardens are nearby. The pub is owned by Tim Bird and Mary McLaughlin of Cheshire Cat Pubs & Bars.

Highly enjoyable food includes sandwiches, king prawn, scallop and crab cocktail with cucumber, gin and tonic jelly, crispy lamb salad with red pepper and feta couscous and rosemary yoghurt dressing, celeriac, parsnip and beetroot crumble with a creamy wholegrain sauce, wild boar and pheasant faggots with roasted squash, chorizo and lentil cassoulet, chicken breast stuffed with apricot and red pepper with roast tomato and tarragon sauce, cod loin with chive mash and warm tartare cream sauce, and puddings such as orange and passion-fruit cheesecake and coconut ice-cream and salted caramel brownie with vanilla ice-cream. *Benchmark main dish: steak and kidney pie £14.50. Two-course evening meal £22.50.*

Free house ~ Licensee Timothy Moody ~ Real ale ~ Open 11-11; 12-11 Sat; 12-10.30 Sun ~ Bar food 12-9.15 (9.45 Fri, Sat); 12-8.45 Sun ~ No under-10s after 7pm ~ Dogs welcome ~ Wi-fi ~ Live music every fortnight ~ Bedrooms: £85/£100 *Recommended by R T and J C Moggridge, Audrey and Paul Summers, Margo and Derek Peters*

COTEBROOK SJ5765 Map 7

Fox & Barrel

(01829) 760529 – www.foxandbarrel.co.uk

A49 NE of Tarporley; CW6 9DZ

Attractive building with stylishly airy décor, an enterprising menu and good wines

You'll get a warm welcome from the friendly staff here and although there is, of course, much emphasis on the excellent food, drinkers feel quite at home on the high chairs against the bar counter or on the cushioned benches and settles. A beer named for the pub plus guests such as Black Sheep Golden Sheep, Bollington Oat Mill Stout and Weetwood Mad Hatter are served on handpump, alongside 16 wines by the glass from a good list. A big log fire dominates the bar while a larger uncluttered beamed dining area has attractive rugs and an eclectic mix of period tables on polished floorboards, with extensive wall panelling hung with framed old prints. The front terrace has plenty of smart tables and chairs under parasols; at the back, there are picnic-sets on grass and some nice old fruit trees. There's a large car park at the front.

Carefully crafted food includes sandwiches (until 6pm), local gin and beetroot-cured salmon with whipped avocado and sweet mustard, hand-rolled lobster ravioli with pickled fennel, samphire and lobster sauce, bubble and squeak with mushroom duxelles, a poached egg and red pepper cream, omelette arnold bennett, ox cheek suet pudding with red wine sauce, chicken breast with creamed cabbage, confit potatoes and crispy home-made black pudding, roasted halibut with curried mussel and vegetable cream and sticky rice, and puddings such as steamed damson sponge with almond ice-cream and raspberry millefeuille. *Benchmark main dish: beer-battered haddock and chips £13.95. Two-course evening meal £18.90.*

Free house ~ Licensee Gary Kidd ~ Real ale ~ Open 12-11 ~ Bar food 12-9 ~ Children welcome ~ Dogs allowed in bar ~ Wi-fi *Recommended by Colin and Daniel Gibbs, Robin and Anne Triggs, Mike Swan, Selwyn Jones, Amanda Shipley*

DELAMERE SJ5667 Map 7

Fishpool

(01606) 883277 – www.thefishpoolinn.co.uk

Junction A54/B5152 Chester Road/Fishpool Road, a mile W of A49; CW8 2HP

Something for everyone in extensive, interestingly laid-out pub, with a good range of food and drinks served all day

Great style and wit have been used in the clever layout here, which combines a big, cheerful open main section plus plenty of other snug and intimate smaller areas, and the décor and furnishings are unusual and varied. A lofty central area, partly skylit and full of contented diners, has a row of booths facing the long bar counter, and numerous other tables with banquettes or overstuffed small armchairs on pale floorboards laid with rugs; then comes a conservatory overlooking picnic-sets on a flagstone terrace, and a lawn beyond. Off on two sides are many rooms with much lower ceilings, some with heavy dark beams, some with bright polychrome tile or intricate parquet flooring: William Morris wallpaper here, dusky paintwork or neat bookshelves there, sofas, armchairs, a fire in an old-fashioned open range, lots of old prints and some intriguing objects including carved or painted animal skulls; background music. Weetwood Best, Cheshire Cat Blonde Ale and Eastgate plus a guest named for the pub (from Beartown) on handpump, 13 wines by the glass, ten malt whiskies and farm cider; unobtrusive background music and upstairs lavatories. Sister pubs are the Pheasant in Burwardsley and the Bears Paw in Warmingham.

Food is good and includes sandwiches (until 6pm), poached and smoked chicken rillettes with red onion chilli and mango salsa, salted cod brandade with crispy pea and mint cake, a soft poached egg and chive butter sauce, grilled salmon caesar salad, roasted vegetable and pine nut strudel with pepper and oregano sauce and tapenade, wood-fired pizzas, 12-hour braised sticky beef short ribs with onion and thyme purée and thyme jus, king prawn thai green curry, and puddings such as orange-scented crème caramel with caramel oranges, candied zest and Cointreau sorbet and apple tart with calvados custard; they also offer afternoon tea (weekdays 2.30-5pm; you must pre-book). *Benchmark main dish: lamb tagine £15.50. Two-course evening meal £20.00.*

Free house ~ Licensee Andrew Nelson ~ Real ale ~ Open 11-11 ~ Bar food 12-9.30; 12-10 Fri, Sat; 12-9 Sun ~ Restaurant ~ Children welcome ~ Dogs allowed in bar ~ Wi-fi *Recommended by Lindy Andrews, Patrick and Emma Stephenson, John Harris, Colin and Daniel Gibbs, Jim King*

KETTLESHULME

SJ9879 Map 7

Swan

(01663) 732943

B5470 Macclesfield–Chapel-en-le-Frith, a mile W of Whaley Bridge; SK23 7QU

Charming 16th-c pub with enjoyable food, good beer and an attractive garden

A lovely place, this is a pretty white cottage clad in wisteria. The interior is snug and cosy, with latticed windows, very low dark beams hung with big copper jugs and kettles, timbered walls, antique coaching and other prints and maps, ancient oak settles on a turkish carpet and log fires; the dining room has an open kitchen. Marstons Bitter on handpump with a couple of guest beers such as Hawkshead Windermere Pale and Wincle Waller, ten wines by the glass, 30 gins and a dozen malt whiskies served by courteous, friendly staff. The front terrace has teak tables, while another two-level terrace has further tables and steamer benches under parasols. The pub is handy for walks in the relatively unfrequented north-west part of the Peak District National Park.

Lots of fresh fish on the menu includes bouillabaisse, smoked haddock kedgeree, dover sole with brown shrimp and caper butter and gurnard with mussels, wild mushrooms, smoky bacon and tarragon fricassée; they also offer sandwiches, camembert fondue, potted beef with balsamic onions, wild mushroom and truffle oil risotto, moroccan-style lamb and apricot tagine, beef bourguignon, free-range duck breast with sweet and sour morello cherry sauce, steaks cooked in their new Josper oven, and puddings such as chocolate torte with salted caramel ice-cream and orange and treacle sponge pudding. *Benchmark main dish: beer-battered fish and chips £13.95. Two-course evening meal £26.00.*

Free house ~ Licensee Robert Cloughley ~ Real ale ~ Open 12-11 (midnight Sat); 4-8 Mon; 12-8 Sun; closed Mon lunchtime ~ Bar food 12-8.30; 12-4 Sun; no food Mon ~ Restaurant ~ Children welcome ~ Dogs allowed in bar ~ Wi-fi *Recommended by Celia and Geoff Clay, Kerry and Guy Trooper, Thomas Green, Stuart and Natalie Granville, Chloe and Michael Swettenham*

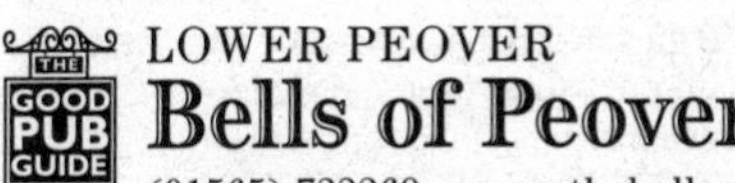

LOWER PEOVER SJ7474 Map 7

Bells of Peover

(01565) 722269 – www.thebellsofpeover.com

Just off B5081; The Cobbles; handy for M6 junction 17; WA16 9PZ

Wisteria-covered pub in pretty setting with real ales and interesting food; lots of seating areas in the garden

In warm weather there's plenty of space outside this lovely old pub: there are seats on a front terrace overlooking the black and white 14th-c church, rattan-style furniture under a pergola on a side decked area and a spacious lawn with picnic-sets spreading down through trees all the way to a little stream. Inside, the various rooms have beams, panelling and open fires that contrast cleverly with contemporary seating ranging from brown leather wall banquettes with scatter cushions to high-backed upholstered or leather dining chairs around an assortment of tables on bare boards; plenty of prints, paintings and mirrors on the walls. Robinsons Cumbria Way, Dizzy Blonde and Unicorn on handpump and several wines by the glass served by helpful, friendly staff; background music.

Well presented food includes lunchtime sandwiches, chicken liver pâté with apple, blackberry, spiced pear and shallot chutney, spicy king prawns with coriander and garlic butter, smoked haddock kedgeree with a poached egg, chilli and black pepper crème fraîche, stuffed aubergine with couscous, baba ganoush, sweet potato rösti, baby vegetables and crispy egg, prawn linguine with chilli and garlic, thai green curry with a choice of chicken, halloumi, prawn and tofu, a pie of the day, duck breast with sesame and chilli pak choi, saffron and coriander cocotte potatoes, berry purée and hot and sour jus, and puddings such as vanilla crème brûlée and dark chocolate and Cointreau marquis with orange sorbet and italian meringue. *Benchmark main dish: sea bass fillets with rosemary gnocchi, french-style peas, pea purée and pancetta £16.95. Two-course evening meal £22.00.*

Robinsons ~ Real ale ~ Open 12-11 ~ Bar food 12-9 (9.30 Fri, Sat; 8 Sun) ~ Restaurant ~ Children welcome ~ Wi-fi *Recommended by Hilary Forrest, Martin and Sue Neville, Nicola and Nigel Matthews, Rosie and Marcus Heatherley, Steve Whalley, Helene Grygar*

MACCLESFIELD SJ9271 Map 7

Sutton Hall

(01260) 253211 – www.brunningandprice.co.uk/suttonhall

Leaving Macclesfield southwards on A523, turn left into Byrons Lane signposted Langley, Wincle, then just before canal viaduct fork right into Bullocks Lane; OS Sheet 118 map reference 925715; SK11 0HE

Historic building set in attractive grounds, with a fine range of drinks and well trained, courteous staff

Considering this former convent is nearly 500 years old, it's highly impressive that some fine original features have been carefully restored and incorporated into the fabric of an up-to-date pub. The hall at the heart of the building is especially noteworthy, in particular the entrance space. There's a charming series of rooms (a bar, a library with books on shelves and a raised open fire and dining areas) divided by tall oak timbers: antique oak panelling, warmly coloured rugs on broad flagstones, bare boards and tiles, lots of pictures placed frame-to-frame and two more fires. Background music and board games. The atmosphere is nicely relaxed and a good range of drinks includes Phoenix Brunning & Price Original and Wincle Lord Lucan and guests such as Bass, Brightside Manchester Skyline and Timothy Taylors Boltmaker and Landlord on handpump, 18 wines by the glass from an extensive list, 65 malt whiskies and 50 gins; service is attentive and friendly. The pretty gardens have spaciously laid-out tables (some on their own little terraces), sloping lawns and fine mature trees.

Modern bistro-style food includes sandwiches, coconut crumbed king prawns with papaya and chilli dipping sauce, chicken liver pâté with plum and ginger chutney, salmon, smoked haddock and prawn pie, warm, crispy beef salad with cashew nuts and sweet chilli dressing, superfood salad with quinoa, roast sweet potato, charred tenderstem broccoli and toasted almonds, game suet pudding, lemon and thyme chicken breast with chorizo croquette and tomato jus, and puddings such as passion-fruit and vanilla pannacotta and sticky toffee pudding with toffee sauce. *Benchmark main dish: braised lamb shoulder with dauphinoise potatoes and gravy £16.95. Two-course evening meal £21.00.*

Brunning & Price ~ Manager Syd Foster ~ Real ale ~ Open 11-11 (10.30 Sun) ~ Bar food 12-9.30 (9 Sun) ~ Restaurant ~ Children welcome ~ Dogs allowed in bar ~ Wi-fi
Recommended by Mike and Wena Stevenson, John Wooll, Dan and Nicki Barton, Katherine and Hugh Markham, Gus Swan, Ian Duncan, Brian and Anna Marsden

MOBBERLEY SJ7879 Map 7

Bulls Head

(01565) 873395 – www.thebullsheadpub.co.uk
Mill Lane; WA16 7HX

Terrific all-rounder with interesting food and drink and plenty of pubby character

Once customers find this particularly well run, cheerful pub they tend to return on a regular basis. Several rooms are furnished quite traditionally but with just a touch of modernity, and there's an unpretentious mix of wooden tables, cushioned wall seats and chairs on fine old quarry tiles, black and pale grey walls contrasting well with warming red lampshades, and pink bare-brick walls and pale stripped-timber detailing; also, lots of mirrors, hops, candles and open fires. A fine range of drinks includes a beer or two named for the pub (from Weetwood), Weetwood 1812 Overture and guests from breweries such as Front Row, Merlin, Storm and Wincle on handpump (useful tasting notes too), 15 wines by the glass, around 100 whiskies and local gins. Background music and board games, and their website lists regular themed food evenings, quizzes, live music and so forth. Dogs get a warm welcome (they're allowed in the snug) with friendly staff dispensing doggie biscuits from a huge jar; a circular walk to and from the pub is mentioned on the website. There are seats outside in the big garden. The pub is owned by Tim Bird and Mary McLaughlin of Cheshire Cat Pubs & Bars.

Pleasing food includes sandwiches, seafood crockpot in creamy dill and white wine sauce, sharing boards, sausages of the day with shallot gravy, mixed bean and red pepper burger with tomato and caramelised onion chutney, bacon chop with thyme and mustard and black pudding croquette, hake fillet with roast sweet potatoes, courgettes and spinach and mango and coriander sauce, lamb stew with scallion mash, 10oz 28-day-aged rib-eye steak with a choice of sauces, and puddings such as irish whiskey sticky toffee pudding with honeycomb ice-cream and dark chocolate brownie with chocolate sauce and mint choc chip ice-cream. *Benchmark main dish: steak in ale pie £13.95. Two-course evening meal £19.00.*

Free house ~ Licensee Barry Lawlor ~ Real ale ~ Open 12-11; 12-10.30 Sun ~ Bar food 12-9.30 (9 Sun) ~ Children welcome but no under-10s after 7pm ~ Dogs allowed in bar ~ Wi-fi ~ Live duo Fri monthly; jazz first Sun of month *Recommended by Mike and Wena Stevenson, David and Charlotte Green, Martine and Lawrence Sanders, Dr and Mrs A K Clarke*

MOBBERLEY SJ7980 Map 7

Church Inn ★

(01565) 873178 – www.churchinnmobberley.co.uk

Brown sign to pub off B5085 on Wilmslow side of village; Church Lane; WA16 7RD

Nicely traditional, friendly country pub with bags of character; good food and drink

Good, enjoyable food and a thoughtful range of drinks draw plenty of chatty customers to this stylish and pretty brick pub. The small, snug interconnected rooms have all manner of nice old tables and chairs on wide floorboards, low ceilings and plenty of candlelight. The décor in soothing greys and dark green, with some oak-leaf wallpaper, is perked up by a collection of stuffed grouse and their relatives, and a huge variety of pictures; background music. Friendly, efficient young staff serve Battlefield Saxon Gold, Mallorys Mobberley Best (George Mallory, lost near Everest's summit in 1924, is remembered in the church with a stained-glass window), Pennine Amber Necker and Tatton Church Ale-Alujah on handpump, and unusual and rewarding wines, with 12 by the glass; wine tastings can be booked in the upstairs private dining room. The sunny garden snakes down to an old bowling green with lovely pastoral views and a side courtyard has sturdy tables and benches. They give out a detailed leaflet describing a good four-mile circular walk from the pub, passing sister pub the Bulls Head en route. Dogs are welcomed in the bar with not just a tub of snacks on the counter, but maybe even the offer of a meaty 'beer'. The mainly medieval and Tudor St Wilfrid's Church is opposite. The pub is owned by Tim Bird and Mary McLaughlin of Cheshire Cat Pubs & Bars.

Imaginative food includes sandwiches, chicken terrine with morel mushroom truffle, lime-cured stone bass with fennel and grapefruit salad, miso caramel and crispy noodles, venison burger with braised red cabbage and chips, monkfish with crab tortellini, coconut crab bisque and saffron mash, pork belly with fennel-crusted cheek, glazed salsify and dauphinoise potatoes, duck breast and confit leg with orange gel and Cointreau jus, and puddings such as treacle tart with brown bread ice-cream and dark chocolate, marshmallow and white chocolate ganache with marshmallow ice-cream. *Benchmark main dish: whole roasted flat fish of the day with caper butter sauce £15.95. Two-course evening meal £20.00.*

Free house ~ Licensee Simon Umpleby ~ Real ale ~ Open 12-11 (10.30 Sun) ~ Bar food 12-9.15 (9.45 Fri, Sat); 12-8.30 Sun ~ Children welcome but no under-10s after 7pm ~ Dogs allowed in bar ~ Wi-fi *Recommended by John Watson, Dr and Mrs A K Clarke, Jacqui and Alan Swan, Martine and Fabio Lockley*

MOBBERLEY SJ7879 Map 7

Roebuck

(01565) 873939 – www.roebuckinnmobberley.co.uk

Mill Lane; down hill from sharp bend on B5085 at E edge of 30mph limit; WA16 7HX

Refurbished inn with a lot of individuality in bar and bistro, good range of drinks, enjoyable food and pretty multi-level garden; boutique-style rustic bedrooms

This place is very 'auberge' in style with plenty of quirky touches – you'll find old shutters, reclaimed radiators, wood panelling and stripped brickwork, big gilt-edged mirrors, copper cooking pots and red and brick floor tiles. There's an open fire in the bar, chunky leather armchairs, lots of scatter cushions, an old trunk as a table, a two-way woodburner and an eclectic collection of art and photographs. Friendly staff serve Buck

Bitter (named for the pub from Weetwood) and Deer Beer (from Dunham Massey) on handpump, a dozen wines and champagne by the glass, and a fine collection of liqueurs and aperitifs. The authentic-looking bistro has pots of herbs and candles in bottles on simple tables, café-style chairs and long leather wall banquettes; background music. To get to the garden you walk through the 'potting shed': upper and lower terraces, gazebos, herb beds and seats that range from rattan or elegant metal chairs to wooden benches and straightforward tables under parasols on decking or flagstones. The front of the building has a mediterranean feel with gnarly olive and standard box trees, flowering window boxes and a couple of benches. The shabby-chic bedrooms have much character and colour and some have log burners; good breakfasts. A walking route is suggested on the website. The pub is owned by Tim Bird and Mary McLaughlin of Cheshire Cat Pubs & Bars.

Highly rewarding food includes sandwiches, crispy confit duck rolls with hoisin sauce, french onion soup with gruyère croûte, sharing boards, wild mushroom and spinach crêpe, stone-baked pizzas, thyme-roasted baby chicken with madeira sauce, beef bourguignon, lamb burger with grilled halloumi and onion chutney, sweet and sour spiced tempura monkfish, lamb chops in a mint marinade with hasselback potatoes, charred onions and sour cream, and puddings such as crème caramel and crêpes suzette with Grand Marnier syrup; they also offer a weekend brunch (10am-noon). *Benchmark main dish: 35-day-aged steak with café de paris butter £16.00. Two-course evening meal £22.00.*

Free house ~ Licensee Dana Randall ~ Real ale ~ Open 12-11; 12-10.30 Sun; closed Mon lunchtime ~ Bar food 12-3, 5.30-9.15 (9.45 Fri); 12-9.45 Sat; 12-9 Sun ~ Children welcome but no under-10s after 7.30pm; not in bedrooms ~ Dogs allowed in bar ~ Wi-fi ~ Bedrooms: £115/£130 *Recommended by Adam Bellinger, Sarah Roberts, Alice Wright, Frank and Marcia Pelling, Malcolm and Pauline Pellatt, Dr and Mrs A K Clarke, Martin Cawley*

MOTTRAM ST ANDREW SJ8878 Map 7

Bulls Head

(01625) 828111 – www.brunningandprice.co.uk/bullshead

A538 Prestbury–Wilmslow; Wilmslow Road/Priest Lane; E side of village; SK10 4QH

Smashing country dining pub with a thoughtful range of drinks and interesting food, plenty of character and well trained staff

At the heart of this sizeable dining pub is a bustling bar offering a large and thoughtful choice of drinks served by cheerful, efficient staff. But perhaps the star feature is the dining zone at the far end. Four levels stack up alongside or above one another, each with a distinctive décor and style, from the informality of a sunken area with rugs on a tiled floor, through a comfortable library/dining room to another with an upstairs conservatory feel and the last, with higher windows and more of a special-occasion atmosphere. The rest of the pub has an appealing and abundant mix of old prints and pictures, comfortable seating in great variety, a coal fire in one room, a blazing woodburning stove in a two-way fireplace dividing two other rooms and an antique black kitchen range in yet another. Phoenix Brunning & Price Original and guests such as Lancaster Amber, Shiny 4 Wood, Wincle Sir Philip and Wold Top Ursa Minor on handpump, around 20 wines by the glass, 50 malt whiskies, 50 gins and several ciders, and an attractive separate tea-and-coffee station with pretty blue and white china cups, teapots and jugs. Also, background music, daily papers and board games. The lawn has plenty of picnic-sets beneath cocktail parasols.

High quality food includes sandwiches and pub classics plus goats cheese filo parcel with cumberland sauce, confit duck leg and spring onion croquette with plum sauce, venison and juniper meatballs with pasta and red wine sauce, sweet potato, cauliflower and chickpea tagine with lemon and coriander couscous, pork trio (pulled pork suet pudding, confit belly and braised cheek) with black pudding boulangère, sea bass with crayfish and chive risotto and pea and ham velouté, and puddings such as bread and butter pudding with apricot sauce and lemon meringue roulade with raspberry sorbet; they also offer weekend brunch (9.30-11.30am). *Benchmark main dish: sea bass with crayfish risotto £17.25. Two-course evening meal £20.00.*

Brunning & Price ~ Manager Andrew Coverley ~ Real ale ~ Open 11-11; 11-10.30 Sun ~ Bar food 12-9.30 (9 Sun) ~ Children welcome ~ Dogs allowed in bar ~ Wi-fi *Recommended by Mike and Wena Stevenson, Jacqui and Alan Swan, Chloe and Tim Hodge, James and Sylvia Hewitt, Lyn and Freddie Roberts, W K Wood*

NETHER ALDERLEY SJ8576 Map 7

Wizard

(01625) 584000 – www.thewizardofedge.co.uk

B5087 Macclesfield Road, opposite Artists Lane; SK10 4UB

Bustling pub with interesting food, real ales, a friendly welcome and relaxed atmosphere

Just a few minutes from lovely walks along Alderley Edge (a dramatic red sandstone escarpment with fine views), this is a popular pub with seats and tables in the sizeable back garden that are just right for a relaxing lunch after a hike. The various rooms, connected by open doorways, are cleverly done up in a mix of modern rustic and traditional styles. There are beams and open fires, antique dining chairs (some prettily cushioned) and settles around all sorts of tables, rugs on pale floorboards, prints and paintings on contemporary paintwork and decorative items ranging from a grandfather clock to staffordshire dogs and modern lampshades. A beer named for the pub (from Beartown), Jennings Bitter and Storm Beauforts Ale on handpump, 11 wines by the glass and farm cider; background music and board games. The pub is part of the Ainscoughs group.

Good food includes lunchtime sandwiches, whitebait with lime mayonnaise, ham hock, grain mustard and caper terrine with pickled red onion salad, borlotti bean and quinoa burger with their own sauce and onion rings, cumberland sausage and mash with red onion gravy, beer-battered fish and chips, a pie of the day, sea bass with crushed potatoes and fresh tomato dressing, and puddings such as steamed lemon sponge with lemon curd mascarpone and vanilla crème brûlée; they also offer a two- and three-course set menu. *Benchmark main dish: rare-breed beef burger with toppings, onion rings and chips £13.50. Two-course evening meal £20.00.*

Free house ~ Licensee Jamie Hurst ~ Real ale ~ Open 12-11; 12-8 Sun ~ Bar food 12-2.30, 6-9; 12-9 Sat; 12-7 Sun ~ Children welcome ~ Dogs welcome ~ Wi-fi *Recommended by Susan Eccleston, Andrew Vincent, Charles and Maddie Bishop, Graham Smart*

SANDBACH SJ7560 Map 7

Old Hall

(01270) 758170 – www.brunningandprice.co.uk/oldhall

1.2 miles from M6 junction 17: A534 – ignore first turn into town and take the second – if you reach the roundabout double back; CW11 1AL

Lovely hall-house with impressive original features, plenty of drinking and dining space, six real ales and imaginative food

This is a glorious 17th-c manor house with many fine original architectural features, particularly in the room to the left of the entrance hall. This is much as it's been for centuries, with a Jacobean fireplace, oak panelling and priest's hole, and it leads into the Oak Room, divided by standing timbers into two dining areas with heavy beams, oak flooring and reclaimed panelling. Other rooms in the original building have hefty beams and oak boards, three open fires and a woodburning stove; the cosy snugs are carpeted. The Garden Room is big and bright, with reclaimed quarry tiling and exposed A-frame oak timbering, and opens on to a suntrap back terrace with teak tables and chairs among flowering tubs. Throughout, the walls are covered with countless interesting prints, there's an appealing collection of antique dining chairs and tables of all sizes, and plenty of rugs, bookcases and plants. From the handsome bar counter, efficient and friendly staff serve Phoenix Brunning & Price Original and March Hare, Timothy Taylors Boltmaker and Three Tuns XXX with guests such as Abbeydale Moonshine, Beartown Full Bodied Ruby Bear and Salopian Half Life on handpump, 16 good wines by the glass, 50 malt whiskies, 20 gins and farm cider; board games. There are picnic-sets provided in front of the building beside rose bushes and clipped box hedging.

Enterprising food includes sandwiches, moroccan-spiced chicken thighs with lemon couscous, apricot, date and pomegranate salad, a charcuterie board, smoked haddock fishcake with a poached egg and chive and caper sauce, cauliflower, red pepper and chickpea curry with red onion and sweet potato bhaji, chicken breast stuffed with buffalo mozzeralla, sunblush tomatoes and garlic sauce, slow-cooked warm crispy beef salad with satay sauce, pickled ginger and lotus root crisps, and puddings such as sticky toffee pudding with toffee sauce and cherry and almond tart with boozy cherries and clotted cream ice-cream; they also offer a weekend brunch menu (9-11.30am). *Benchmark main dish: slow-cooked ox cheek bourguignon with roast garlic and parsley mash and roasted carrots £16.75. Two-course evening meal £20.00.*

Brunning & Price ~ Manager Chris Button ~ Real ale ~ Open 11-11; 12-10.30pm Sun ~ Bar food 12-9.30; 9am-10pm Sat; 9am-9pm Sun ~ Restaurant ~ Children welcome ~ Dogs allowed in bar ~ Wi-fi *Recommended by Mike and Wena Stevenson, Hugh Roberts, Paul Scofield, Dr and Mrs A K Clarke, John Harris, Emily and Toby Archer*

SWETTENHAM SJ7967 Map 7

Swettenham Arms 

(01477) 571284 – www.swettenhamarms.co.uk

Off A54 Congleton–Holmes Chapel or A535 Chelford–Holmes Chapel; CW12 2LF

16th-c country pub in a fine setting with shining brasses, five real ales and tempting food

For over 25 years, the same welcoming licensees have been running this lovely country pub. It's a former nunnery and the three interlinked dark beamed areas are nicely traditional with individual furnishings on bare floorboards or a sweep of fitted turkey carpet. There's also a polished copper bar, three woodburning stoves, plenty of shiny brasses and a variety of old prints including military, hunting, old ships, reproduction Old Masters and so forth. Friendly efficient staff serve Black Sheep Best, Hydes Original Bitter, Tatton Best, Marstons Wainwright and Timothy Taylors Landlord on handpump, 14 wines by the glass, 15 malt whiskies and Addlestones cider; background music. Outside at the back there are tables on a lawn that merges into a lavender meadow; croquet and children's games in good weather. They hold classic car and vintage motorbike events in the summer,

'Children welcome' means the pub says it lets children inside without any special restriction. If it allows them in, but to restricted areas such as an eating area or family room, we specify this. Some pubs may impose an evening time limit. We do not mention limits after 9pm as we assume children are home by then.

and can also host civil ceremonies in the grounds or the newly refurbished suite. Do visit the interesting village church which dates in part from the 13th c. You can walk in the pretty surrounding countryside or in the nearby Quinta Arboretum.

Food is very good and uses the best quality local produce: sandwiches (until 5.30pm), duck confit and chicken terrine with golden raisin and cognac purée, prawn cocktail, spinach, ricotta and caramelised red onion cannelloni, beef stroganoff, gammon and duck egg with creamy cheese sauce, thai green chicken curry with king prawns and scallops, pheasant breast and braised leg and thigh with a red wine and rosemary sauce, salmon with a herb crust, spring onion mash and white wine and pancetta sauce, and puddings such as chocolate and walnut brownie with vanilla ice-cream and vanilla cheesecake with blackcurrant compote. *Benchmark main dish: steak and mushroom in ale pie £14.00. Two-course evening meal £20.00.*

Free house ~ Licensees Jim and Frances Cunningham ~ Real ale ~ Open 11.30am-11pm ~ Bar food 12-9 (8 Sun) ~ Restaurant ~ Children welcome ~ Dogs allowed in bar ~ Wi-fi
Recommended by Mike and Wena Stevenson, Margaret McDonald, Tom and Lorna Harding, Mark and Sian Edwards

THELWALL SJ6587 Map 7

Little Manor

(01925) 212070 – www.brunningandprice.co.uk/littlemanor
Bell Lane; WA4 2SX

Restored manor house with plenty of room, lots of interest, well kept ales and tasty bistro-style food; seats outside

With well kept ales served by consistently helpful young staff and highly regarded food, you can't fail to enjoy your visits to this big, handsome 17th-c house. The six beamed rooms are linked by open doorways and standing timbers to create plenty of nooks and crannies, and there's so much to look at. Flooring ranges from rugs on bare boards through carpeting to some fine old black and white tiles, and an appealing variety of seats includes antique dining chairs around small or large, circular or square tables plus leather armchairs by open fires (note the lovely carved wooden one); background music. Lighting is from metal chandeliers, wall lights and standard lamps, and the décor includes hundreds of intriguing prints and photos, books on shelves and old glass and stone bottles on windowsills and mantelpieces; fresh flowers and house plants too. Phoenix Brunning & Price Original, Hawkshead Windermere Pale, Merlin Excalibur, Mobberley Boom Juice and HedgeHopper and Tatton Blonde on handpump, around 15 wines by the glass, 60 gins and 60 whiskies. In fine weather you can sit at the chunky teak chairs and tables on the terrace; some of them are under a heated shelter.

Up-to-date food choices include sandwiches, pulled pork terrine with apple purée and crackling, prawn cocktail, crispy duck salad with hoisin, watermelon and cashews, puy lentil, aubergine and sweet potato moussaka with black olive dressing, steak and kidney suet pudding, fish pie with french-style peas, steak burger with toppings, coleslaw and chips, braised lamb shoulder with rosemary gravy, and puddings such as dark chocolate pannacotta and wild cherry sorbet and sticky toffee pudding with toffee sauce and vanilla ice-cream. *Benchmark main dish: beer-battered cod and chips £13.75. Two-course evening meal £21.00.*

Brunning & Price ~ Manager Jill Dowling ~ Real ale ~ Open 10.30am-11pm; 10.30-10.30 Sun ~ Bar food 12-9.30 ~ Children welcome ~ Dogs allowed in bar ~ Wi-fi *Recommended by Mike and Wena Stevenson, Hilary Forrest, Michael Butler, Alison and Michael Harper, Steve Whalley, Mandy and Gary Redstone*

WARMINGHAM SJ7161 Map 7

Bears Paw

(01270) 526317 – www.thebearspaw.co.uk

School Lane; CW11 3QN

Nicely maintained and extensive Victorian inn with enjoyable food, half a dozen real ales and seats outside; bedrooms

Our readers enjoy staying in the well equipped bedrooms here and breakfasts are very good indeed. Downstairs, each of the spreading, interlinked bar rooms have plenty of individual character but we particularly like the two little sitting rooms with panelling, fashionable wallpaper, bookshelves and slouchy leather furniture comfortably arranged beside woodburning stoves in magnificent fireplaces; stripped wood flooring and a dado keep it all informal. An eclectic mix of old wooden tables and some nice old carved chairs are well spaced throughout the dining areas, with lofty windows providing a light and airy feel and lots of big pot plants dotted about. There are stools at the long bar counter where cheerful, efficient staff serve Beartown Bears Paw (named for the pub), Bear Ass and Bluebeary and Weetwood Best and Eastgate on handpump, 13 wines by the glass, 17 malt whiskies and local cider; background music. A small front garden by the car park has seats and tables. This is sister pub to the Pheasant in Burwardsley and the Fishpool at Delamere.

Food is reliably good and includes sandwiches, baps and wraps (until 6pm; not Sunday), sharing boards, salmon and smoked haddock fishcake with a soft poached egg and hollandaise, confit duck leg and prosciutto with damson jelly, ginger nut crumb, pickled radish and fine herb salad, smoked wild mushroom, thyme and parmesan tagliatelle, garam masala-spiced monkfish tail with braised baby gem, turmeric potatoes, pak choi, coriander shoots and a chorizo and lentil dressing, pork belly with sticky pig cheek, white and black pudding fritter, caramelised apple, roasted celeriac, confit cabbage and cider jus, venison haunch and confit shin cannelloni with smoked white onion purée, crispy shallots and port jus, and puddings such as rhubarb and ginger cheesecake with strawberry compote and rhubarb sorbet and double chocolate brownie with dark chocolate sauce and pistachio ice-cream. *Benchmark main dish: steak in ale pie £14.50. Two-course evening meal £25.00.*

Free house ~ Licensee Andrew Nelson ~ Real ale ~ Open 12-11 (midnight); 12-8 Sun ~ Bar food 12-9.30; 12-10 Fri, Sat; 12-9 Sun ~ Restaurant ~ Children welcome ~ Dogs welcome ~ Wi-fi ~ Bedrooms: £95/£105 *Recommended by Katherine Matthews, Ivy and George Goodwill, Karl and Frieda Bujeya, Bob and Melissa Wyatt*

WHITELEY GREEN SJ9278 Map 7

Windmill

(01625) 574222 – www.thewindmill.info

Brown sign to pub off A523 Macclesfield–Poynton, just N of Prestbury; Hole House Lane; SK10 5SJ

Extensive relaxed country dining bar with big sheltered garden and enjoyable food

After a nearby walk, many customers come here for lunch. Most of the place is given over to dining tables, mainly in a pleasantly informal, painted base/stripped top style, on bare boards. The interior spreads around a big bar counter, its handpumps serving Storm Bosley Cloud and guests from breweries such as Adnams, Mobberley, Roosters and Weetwood; also, eight wines by the glass served by friendly and helpful staff. One area has several leather sofas and fabric-upholstered easy chairs; another by a log fire in a huge brick fireplace has more easy chairs and a suede sofa; background music. The spreading lawns, surrounded by a belt of young trees, provide plenty of room for well spaced tables and picnic sets, and even a maze to baffle children. Middlewood Way (a sort of linear country park) and Macclesfield Canal (Bridge 25) are just a stroll away.

A thoughtful choice of good food includes sandwiches and sharing boards, crisp corned beef hash cake with a poached egg and home-made brown sauce, smoked haddock, ricotta and spinach fishcakes, cheese, potato and spring onion pie with chive cream sauce, lamb and mint burger with tzatziki and onion rings, garlic chicken with fondant potato and bacon jus, pork belly with black pudding, honey apples and cider and golden raisin jus, and puddings such as caramelised plum and anise crumble with anglaise sauce and chocolate and raspberry tart with salted caramel ice-cream. *Benchmark main dish: beer-battered fresh haddock £11.00. Two-course evening meal £21.50.*

Mitchells & Butlers ~ Lease Peter and Jane Nixon ~ Real ale ~ Open 12-11 (10 Sun) ~ Bar food 12-2.30, 5-9.30; 12-9.30 Sat; 12-8 Sun ~ Restaurant ~ Children welcome ~ Dogs allowed in bar ~ Wi-fi *Recommended by Buster May, Barbara Brown, Daniel King, Sandra and Miles Spencer, Belinda and Neil Garth*

Also Worth a Visit in Cheshire

Besides the fully inspected pubs, you might like to try these pubs that have been recommended to us and described by readers. Do tell us what you think of them: feedback@goodguides.com

ALLGREAVE SU9767

Rose & Crown (01260) 227232
A54 Congleton–Buxton; SK11 0BJ
Welcoming 18th-c roadside pub in remote upland spot with good Dane Valley views and walks; renovated beamed rooms, wood floors and log fires, good local food from bar and restaurant menus including daily specials, half a dozen well kept ales such as Jennings, RedWillow and Wincle from wood-clad servery; children and dogs welcome, lawned garden taking in the views, three bedrooms. *(Michael Butler)*

ALPRAHAM SJ5759

Travellers Rest (01829) 260523
A51 Nantwich–Chester; CW6 9JA
Timeless four-room country local in same family for three generations; friendly chatty atmosphere, well kept Tetleys and Weetwood, no food, leatherette, wicker and Formica, some flock wallpaper, fine old brewery mirrors, darts and dominoes; may be nesting swallows in outside gents'; dogs welcome, back bowling green, 'Hat Day' last Sun before Christmas when locals don unusual headgear, closed weekday lunchtimes (opens 6.30pm). *(Gail and Arthur Roberts)*

ASHLEY SJ7784

Greyhound (0161) 871 7765
3 miles S of Altrincham; Cow Lane; WA15 0QR Extended red-brick Lees pub, their well kept ales, decent wines and good choice of tasty reasonably priced food, friendly service, greyhound-theme décor and some old photos of nearby Tatton Hall (NT), wood floors, central woodburner; fortnightly quiz Tues, darts; children and dogs (in bar) welcome, seats out on lawn and terrace, handy for the station, open (and food) all day. *(Hilary Forrest)*

ASTBURY SJ8461

Egerton Arms (01260) 273946
Village signposted off A34 S of Congleton; CW12 4RQ New licensees for this 16th-c village pub; Robinsons ales, decent range of wines and enjoyable fairly pubby food in beamed bar or restaurant with central fireplace, friendly helpful service; children welcome, no dogs inside, seats on terrace and grass, play area, pretty spot with church opposite and Little Moreton Hall (NT) nearby, bedrooms, open all day. *(Mike and Wena Stevenson)*

BARBRIDGE SJ6156

Barbridge Inn (01270) 528327
Just off A51 N of Nantwich; CW5 6AY
Spacious open-plan family dining pub by lively marina at junction of Shropshire Union and Middlewich canals, enjoyable food from snacks and sharing boards to steaks served by friendly staff, three Weetwood ales including one rebadged for the pub and one or two guests, conservatory; background music; dogs allowed in a couple of areas, waterside garden with enclosed play area, moorings, open (and food) all day. *(Dave Braisted)*

BARTON SJ4454

★**Cock o' Barton** (01829) 782277
Barton Road (A534 E of Farndon); SY14 7HU Stylish contemporary décor in bright open skylit bar, cocktails, plenty of wines by the glass and up to four real ales including Stonehouse, Fri happy hour till 7pm, good choice of well liked up-to-date food served by neat courteous staff, beamed restaurant areas; background music; children welcome (free main course for them on Sun), tables in sunken heated inner courtyard with canopies and modern water feature, picnic-sets on back lawn, 14 bedrooms, open (and food) all day from 8am for breakfast. *(Andrew Wall)*

BIRKENHEAD SJ3386

Refreshment Rooms
(0151) 644 5893 *Bedford Road E; CH42 1LS* Bow-fronted former 19th-c refreshment rooms for the Mersey ferry; three rooms with interesting collection of old photographs and other memorabilia, good selection of mainly local ales such as Liverpool Organic, Peerless and a house beer from Lees (HMS Conway), Rosie's welsh cider and a couple of interesting lagers, good competitively priced home-made food including set deals, friendly prompt service; children and dogs welcome, beer garden at back with play area, open (and food) all day. *(Sandra and Miles Spencer)*

BOLLINGTON SJ9377

Church House (01625) 574014
Church Street; SK10 5PY Friendly traditional village pub on edge of the Peak District – a good place to start or end a walk; well liked home-made food including good value set lunch, efficient friendly service, three well kept ales such as Adnams, nice open fire, separate dining room; children and clean dogs welcome, small beer garden, five comfortable competitively priced bedrooms, good breakfast, open all day weekends (food all day Sun). *(John and Lorna Chew)*

BOLLINGTON SJ9477

Poachers (01625) 572086
Mill Lane; SK10 5BU Stone-built village local prettily set in good walking area, comfortable and welcoming, with tasty pub food (all day Sun, not Mon) including bargain lunches, well kept Storm, Weetwood and three guests such as local Happy Valley, efficient friendly service, log fire and woodburner; charity quiz last Sun of month; children and dogs (towels and treats) welcome, sunny back garden, open all day weekends, closed Mon lunchtime. *(Christopher Mannings)*

BOLLINGTON SJ9377

Vale (01625) 575147
Adlington Road; SK10 5JT Friendly tap for Bollington brewery in three converted 19th-c cottages; their full range and a couple of guests (tasters offered), real ciders, enjoyable food (all day weekends) including range of locally made pies and daily specials, helpful efficient service, interesting photos, newspapers and books, roaring fire; dogs welcome, picnic-sets out behind overlooking cricket pitch, near Middlewood Way and Macclesfield Canal, open all day Fri-Sun. *(Mike and Wena Stevenson)*

BOLLINGTON CROSS SJ9177

Cock & Pheasant (01625) 573289
Bollington Road; SK10 5EJ Refurbished 18th-c red-brick Vintage Inn at edge of village; their usual good value food including weekday set menus and other deals, real ales such as Sharps Doom Bar, craft beers and plenty of wines by the glass, pleasant helpful young staff, beams and open fire; children welcome, plenty of outside seating (some under cover), play area, good local walks, open all day. *(John Wooll)*

BROOMEDGE SJ7086

Jolly Thresher (01925) 752265
Higher Lane; WA13 0RN Spacious well appointed dining pub with enjoyable food including daily specials and good value set lunch (not Dec), well kept Hydes, lots of wines by the glass and good choice of other drinks, restaurant and dining conservatory; background music, Tues quiz, free wi-fi; children and dogs (in bar) welcome, disabled access, tables on front terrace and in garden behind, open (and food) all day. *(Ian Duncan)*

BROXTON SJ4858

Egerton Arms (01829) 782241
A41/A534 S of Chester; CH3 9JW Large neatly kept mock-Tudor dining pub; old polished furniture on wood or carpeted floors, lots of prints and books, log fires, wide choice of popular food from sandwiches and pub favourites up, four well kept changing beers and plenty of wines by the glass, efficient friendly staff; children and dogs welcome, wheelchair access, big garden with decking and play area, open all day. *(Amy Ledbetter)*

BURTONWOOD SJ5692

Fiddle i'th' Bag (01925) 225442
3 miles from M62 junction 9, signposted from A49 towards Newton-le-Willows; WA5 4BT Eccentric 19th-c country pub (not to everyone's taste) crammed with bric-a-brac and memorabilia, three well kept changing ales and enjoyable uncomplicated home-made food (cash only), friendly staff and pub cat; may be nostalgic background music; children welcome, open all day weekends. *(Jim and Mary Thomson)*

CHELFORD SJ8175

★**Egerton Arms** (01625) 861366
A537 Macclesfield–Knutsford; SK11 9BB Cheerful rambling old village pub; beams and

nice mix of furniture including carved settles and a couple of wooden porter's chairs, grandfather clock, Copper Dragon and up to six guests, several wines by the glass, popular food including range of burgers, stone-baked pizzas and signature steaks, restaurant, steps down to little raftered games area with pool, darts and sports TV; background music (live last Fri of month including traditional jazz), quiz last Thurs; children and dogs welcome, picnic-sets on canopied deck and slate terrace, toddlers' play area, adjoining deli/ coffee shop, open (and food) all day. *(John Watson)*

CHESTER SJ4065

★**Bear & Billet** (01244) 311886
Lower Bridge Street; CH1 1RU Handsome 17th-c timber and lattice-windowed Market Town Tavern (an inn since the 18th c); Okells beers and three changing guests, belgian/american imports plus good selection of wines and gins, reasonably priced pubby food including range of burgers, efficient service, beamed bar with wood floor and panelling, open fire, scenes of old Chester in back dining part, further rooms above; quiz night and upstairs folk club (both Sun), sports TVs; children and dogs welcome, courtyard seating, open (and food) all day), kitchen closes 7pm Sun. *(David H Bennett, Dave Braisted, Michael Butler)*

CHESTER SJ4066

Boathouse (01244) 328709
The Groves, off Grosvenor Park Road; on River Dee five-minute walk from centre; CH1 1SD Modernised pub on site of 17th-c boathouse with great River Dee views; well priced pubby food from sandwiches and sharing plates up, Lees ales and decent choice of wines by the glass; Weds quiz, free wi-fi; children welcome, dogs outside only, disabled access/facilities, tables and painted beach huts on paved terrace overlooking the water, little bridge to floating seating area, bedrooms, open (and food) all day. *(Richard Tilbrook)*

CHESTER SJ4065

★**Brewery Tap** (01244) 340999
Lower Bridge Street; CH1 1RU Tap for Spitting Feathers brewery in interesting Jacobean building with 18th-c brick façade, steps up to lofty barrel-vaulted bar (former great hall) serving a couple of their well kept ales, five guest beers, a local cider and good choice of wines, hearty home-made food using local suppliers including produce from Spitting Feathers farm (rare-breed pork), pews and other rustic furniture on flagstones, tapestries on walls, large carved red-sandstone fireplace, also smaller plainer room; children and dogs welcome, no wheelchair access, open (and food) all day. *(Charles Fraser)*

CHESTER SJ4166

Cellar (01244) 318950
City Road; CH1 3AE Laid-back Canal Quarter bar with six well kept ales, craft beers and interesting selection of imports, decent wines and cocktails too, happy hour till 9pm weekdays, limited snacky food, basement bar for private functions; sports TVs; closed Mon-Thurs till 3pm, otherwise open noon till late. *(David H Bennett)*

CHESTER SJ4066

Coach House (01244) 351900
Northgate Street; CH1 2HQ Modernised 19th-c coaching inn by town hall and cathedral; comfortable lounge with central bar, well kept Thwaites and a couple of guests, decent choice of wines and other drinks, enjoyable fairly priced home-made food including daily specials from semi-open kitchen, afternoon teas, prompt friendly service; children and dogs welcome, tables out in front, eight bedrooms, good breakfast, open (and food) all day, kitchen closes 7pm Sun. *(Michael Butler, David H Bennett)*

CHESTER SJ4065

Cross Keys (01244) 344460
Duke Street/Lower Bridge Street; CH1 1RU Small Victorian corner pub with ornate interior, dark panelling, etched mirrors and stained-glass windows, button-back leather wall benches and cast-iron tables on bare boards, open fire, well kept Joules ales and a guest, sensibly priced pubby food, friendly service, upstairs function room; free wi-fi; no dogs inside, seats out in front, closed Mon and Tues, otherwise open all day. *(William Pace)*

CHESTER SJ4066

Olde Boot (01244) 314540
Eastgate Row N; CH1 1LQ Lovely 17th-c Rows building; long narrow bar with heavy beams, dark woodwork, oak flooring and flagstones, old kitchen range in lounge beyond, settles and oak panelling in upper area, well kept/priced Sam Smiths beers, cheerful service and bustling atmosphere; no children. *(Michael Butler)*

CHESTER SJ4066

Pied Bull (01244) 325829
Upper Northgate Street; CH1 2HQ Old beamed and panelled coaching inn with roomy open-plan carpeted bar, good own-brewed ales (brewery tours) along with guests and nice wines, enjoyable fairly priced traditional food from sandwiches and baked potatoes up, friendly staff and locals, imposing stone fireplace with tapestry above, divided inner dining area; background music, TV, machines; children welcome, tables under parasols on enclosed terrace, handsome Jacobean stairs to 13 bedrooms, open (and food) all day. *(David H Bennett, William Pace)*

CHESTER SJ4066

Telfords Warehouse (01244) 390090

Tower Wharf, behind Northgate Street near railway; CH1 4EZ Large converted canal building with half a dozen well kept interesting ales and good variety of fairly priced food from sandwiches and snacks up, friendly efficient young staff, bare boards, exposed brickwork and high ceiling, big wall of windows overlooking the water, some old enamel signs and massive iron winding gear in bar, steps up to heavily beamed area with sofas, artwork and restaurant; late-night live music, bouncers on the door; tables out by canal, open all day (till late Weds-Sun). *(David H Bennett)*

CHURCH MINSHULL SJ6660

Badger (01270) 522348

B5074 Winsford–Nantwich; handy for Shropshire Union Canal, Middlewich branch; CW5 6DY Modernised 18th-c coaching inn in pretty village next to church; good food from sharing boards and pub favourites up, well kept ales such as Tatton, Titanic and Weetwood, Thatcher's cider, interesting range of wines and spirits, friendly helpful staff, bar with old quarry tiles, opened-up lounge/dining area leading to conservatory, woodburners; background music, free wi-fi; children and dogs (in bar) welcome, paved terrace with rattan-style furniture, five bedrooms, good breakfast, open (and food) all day. *(Sandra and Miles Spencer, Tony Hobden)*

COMBERBACH SJ6477

Spinner & Bergamot

(01606) 891307 *Warrington Road; CW9 6AY* Comfortable 18th-c beamed village pub named after two racehorses; good home-made food (smaller helpings available for some main courses), well kept Robinsons ales and nice choice of wines, friendly service, pitched-ceiling timber dining extension, two-room carpeted lounge and tiled-floor public bar where dogs allowed, log fires, some Manchester United memorabilia; unobtrusive background music, Mon quiz, sports TV; children welcome, small verandah, picnic-sets on sloping lawn, bowling green, open all day (food all day Sun). *(Mike and Wena Stevenson)*

CONGLETON SJ8659

Horseshoe (01260) 272205

Fence Lane, Newbold Astbury, between A34 and A527 S; CW12 3NL Former 18th-c coaching inn set in peaceful countryside; three small carpeted rooms with decorative plates, copper and brass and other knick-knacks (some on delft shelves), mix of seating including plush banquettes and iron-base tables, log fire, well kept predominantly Robinsons ales, popular hearty home-made food at reasonable prices, good daily specials, friendly staff and locals; children welcome, no dogs, rustic garden furniture, adventure play area with tractor, good walks. *(Nik and Gloria Clarke)*

CONGLETON SJ8662

Young Pretender (01260) 273277

Lawton Street; CW12 1RS Same ownership as the Treacle Tap in Macclesfield; one room (former shop) divided into smaller areas with local artwork on display, half a dozen well kept interesting ales and good selection of international draught/bottled beers, enjoyable food from snacks up including range of locally made pies; various events such as Sun quiz, live music and film nights; children (till 8pm) and dogs welcome, open (and food) all day. *(Karl and Frieda Bujeya)*

COTEBROOK SJ5765

Alvanley Arms (01829) 760200

A49/B5152 N of Tarporley; CW6 9DS Welcoming roadside coaching inn, 17th-c behind its flower-decked Georgian façade, with updated beamed rooms, Robinsons ales, several wines by the glass and good choice of other drinks, well liked fairly priced food from pubby menu, friendly helpful service; background music, free wi-fi; children welcome, disabled access, garden with deck and large pond, pleasant walks, seven comfortable bedrooms, good breakfast, open (and food) all day. *(Malcolm and Pauline Pellatt)*

CREWE SJ7055

Borough Arms (01270) 748189

Earle Street; CW1 2BG Drinkers' pub with up to ten well kept changing ales (maybe own microbrews), also good choice of continental beers and a couple of real ciders, friendly staff and regulars, two small rooms off central bar and downstairs lounge; occasional sports TV; picnic-sets on back terrace and lawn, open all day Fri-Sun, closed lunchtime other days. *(Emily and Toby Archer)*

CREWE SJ7055

Hops (01270) 211100

Prince Albert Street; CW1 2DF Friendly and relaxed belgian café-bar on two floors; huge range of continental bottled beers (some also on draught), eight interesting ales and good range of ciders, snacky lunchtime food (Weds-Sat), proper coffee; children and dogs welcome, disabled access/facilities, seats out at front, closed Mon lunchtime, otherwise open all day. *(William Pace)*

DISLEY SJ9784

White Horse (01663) 762397

Buxton Old Road, car park down Ring O'Bells Lane by pub; SK12 2BB Proper straightforward pub popular with locals and well looked after by friendly hard-working licensees, four Robinsons ales and good value tasty food (all day weekends); free wi-fi;

children welcome, no dogs inside, handy for Lyme Park (NT), open all day. *(Steve Whalley)*

DISLEY SJ9784

White Lion (01663) 762800
Buxton Road (A6); SK12 2HA Welcoming pub at east end of village; up to nine well kept changing ales and enjoyable food (not Mon) including good home-made pies, friendly efficient staff; quiz nights; dogs welcome in one part (food for them too), closed Mon lunchtime, otherwise open (and food) all day. *(Christopher Mannings)*

EATON SJ8765

★**Plough** (01260) 280207
A536 Congleton–Macclesfield; CW12 2NH Cosy and welcoming village pub with beams, leaded windows and exposed brickwork, cushioned wooden wall seats and comfortable armchairs on red-patterned carpet, a couple of snug alcoves, woodburner in big stone fireplace, Storm, Charles Wells and a couple of guests, ten wines by the glass from decent list and 20 malt whiskies, well liked food including sandwiches and good value set lunch (Mon-Thurs), friendly efficient staff, heavily raftered barn function room (moved here from Wales); background music (live Thurs), board games and occasional TV, free wi-fi; children and dogs (in bar) welcome, disabled access, big tree-filled garden with tables set for dining on covered deck, fine views of Peak District fringes, appealingly designed bedrooms in converted stable block, open (and food) all day. *(William and Ann Reid, Steve Whalley)*

FADDILEY SJ5852

Thatch (01270) 524223
A534 Wrexham–Nantwich; CW5 8JE Attractive thatched and timbered dining pub under welcoming new management; low beams and open fires, raised room to right of bar, back barn-style dining room, Salopian Shropshire Gold, Timothy Taylors Landlord and a guest, popular traditional food from lunchtime sandwiches up, friendly helpful service; background music, free wi-fi; children and dogs (in bar and snug) welcome, nice country garden with play area, open all day. *(Gail and Arthur Roberts)*

GAWSWORTH SJ8869

★**Harrington Arms** (01260) 223325
Off A536; Congleton Road/Church Lane; SK11 9RJ This unspoilt three-storey building is still part of a working farm; low 17th-c beams, tiled and flagstoned floors, snug corners and open fires, counter in narrow space on right serving Robinsons ales, a guest beer and good selection of wines and whiskies, several unpretentious rooms off with old settles and eclectic mix of tables and chairs, lots of pictures on red or pale painted walls, well liked hearty food from hot and cold sandwiches to daily specials, friendly relaxed atmosphere; background music (live folk Fri), free wi-fi; children and dogs (in bar) welcome, benches out on small front cobbled area, more seats in garden overlooking fields, lane leads to one of Cheshire's prettiest villages, open all day weekends. *(Mike and Wena Stevenson, Michael Butler)*

GOOSTREY SJ7770

Crown (01477) 532128
Off A50 and A535; CW4 8PE Extended and opened-up 18th-c red-brick village pub refurbished under new management; beams and open fires, small conservatory, good choice of enjoyable fairly pubby food including bargain lunch menu, up to five well kept Marstons-related ales, lots of wines by the glass, cocktails, friendly efficient service from young aproned staff; children and dogs welcome, picnic-sets outside, close to Jodrell Bank, open (and food) all day. *(Ian Duncan)*

GRAPPENHALL SJ6386

Parr Arms (01925) 212120
Near M6 junction 20 – A50 towards Warrington, left after 1.5 miles; Church Lane; WA4 3EP Renovated black-beamed pub in picture-postcard setting with picnic-sets out on cobbles by church, more tables on small canopied back terrace, good reasonably priced food from ciabattas and sharing plates to blackboard specials, well kept Robinsons from central bar, log fires; children and dogs (in one area) welcome, open (and food) all day. *(Alister and Margery Bacon)*

GREAT BUDWORTH SJ6677

★**George & Dragon** (01606) 892650
Signed off A559 NE of Northwich; High Street opposite church; CW9 6HF Characterful building dating from 1722 (front part is 19th-c) in delightful village; Lees ales kept well and plenty of wines by the glass, good choice of enjoyable home-made food from sandwiches and pub favourites to specials, dark panelled bar with log fire, grandfather clock and leather button-back banquettes, back area more restauranty with wood floors and exposed brickwork, tables around central woodburner, some stuffed animals and hunting memorabilia; children and dogs (in bar) welcome, picnic-sets outside, open (and food) all day. *(Mike and Wena Stevenson)*

KNUTSFORD SJ7776

Dun Cow (01565) 633093
Chelford Road; outskirts of Knutsford towards Macclesfield; WA16 8RH Comfortably opened-up country dining pub arranged around central servery; modern décor with cosy alcoves and log fires, popular food (smaller appetites catered for) from sandwiches to daily specials, well kept Robinsons ales, friendly caring service; children and dogs welcome, good disabled access, tables on paved front and back terraces, open (and food) all day. *(Tom Cosgrove)*

KNUTSFORD SJ7578

Lord Eldon (01565) 652261

Tatton Street, off A50 at White Bear roundabout; WA16 6AD Traditional red-brick former coaching inn with four comfortable rooms (much bigger inside than it looks), friendly staff and locals, beams, brasses, old pictures and large open fire, well kept Tetleys and a couple of guests, no food; music and quiz nights, darts; dogs welcome, back garden but no car park, handy for Tatton Park (NT), open all day. *(Charles Fraser)*

KNUTSFORD SJ7578

Rose & Crown (01565) 652366

King Street; WA16 6DT Beamed and panelled 17th-c inn with bar and Chophouse restaurant, well liked food from sandwiches (till 6pm), snacks and sharing plates up, a couple of changing ales, plenty of wines by the glass and some interesting gins, good friendly service; children and dogs (in bar) welcome, terrace tables, nine bedrooms, open (and food) all day. *(Martin Cawley)*

LANGLEY SJ9471

★ Leather's Smithy (01260) 252313

Off A523 S of Macclesfield; OS Sheet 118 map reference 952715; SK11 0NE Isolated stone-built pub in fine walking country next to reservoir; well kept Theakstons and two or three guests, lots of whiskies, good food from sandwiches to blackboard specials, efficient friendly service, flagstoned bar and carpeted dining areas, beams, log fire and interesting local prints/photographs; unobtrusive background music; children welcome, no dogs inside but muddy boots allowed in bar, picnic-sets in garden behind and on grass opposite, lovely views, open all day weekends (till 8pm Sun). *(Mike and Wena Stevenson)*

LITTLE BOLLINGTON SJ7387

Swan with Two Nicks

(0161) 928 2914 *2 miles from M56 junction 7 – A56 towards Lymm, then first right at Stamford Arms into Park Lane; use A556 to get back on to M56 westbound; WA14 4TJ* Extended red-brick village pub with good choice of enjoyable generously served food from sandwiches and baked potatoes up, well kept ales including Dunham Massey and a house beer from Coach House, decent wines and coffee, efficient service, beams, knick-knacks and log fire, back restaurant; children and (particularly) dogs welcome, tables outside, attractive hamlet by Dunham Massey (NT) deer park, walks by Bridgewater Canal, open (and food) all day. *(Mike and Wena Stevenson)*

LITTLE BUDWORTH SJ5867

Cabbage Hall (01829) 760292

Forest Road (A49); CW6 9ES Restauranty pub (part of the Pesto chain) specialising in good tapas-style italian food (piattini), drinkers catered for in comfortable bar with real ales and decent wines by the glass, also italian-style afternoon teas, efficient friendly staff; children welcome, garden tables, open (and food) all day. *(Andrew Wall)*

LITTLE BUDWORTH SJ5965

Egerton Arms (01829) 760424

Pinfold Lane; CW6 9BS Welcoming 18th-c family-run country free house, enjoyable home-made food including wood-fired pizzas and range of burgers, six well kept local ales including Thwaites Original, good selection of bottled beers and interesting cocktails; weekend live music; children and dogs welcome, seats out in front and in garden behind overlooking cricket pitch, walks from the door, handy for Oulton Park racetrack, closed Mon (except bank holidays), otherwise open all day (from 3pm Tues, Weds, Thurs in winter). *(Ian Duncan)*

LITTLE LEIGH SJ6076

Holly Bush (01606) 853196

A49 just S of A533; CW8 4QY Brick and timbered 17th-c thatched pub; good choice of enjoyable well priced food including several vegetarian options, very friendly helpful staff, Tetleys and a couple of mainstream guests, bar with open fire, restaurant extension; Sun quiz; children welcome, no dogs inside, wheelchair access, courtyard tables and garden with play area, 14 bedrooms in converted back barn, open all day weekends (food all day Sun). *(Mike and Wena Stevenson, Dr A McCormick)*

LOWER WHITLEY SJ6178

Chetwode Arms (01925) 640044

Just off A49, handy for M56 junction 10; Street Lane; WA4 4EN Rambling low-beamed dining pub dating from the 17th c; good food including range of exotic meats cooked on a hot stone, early-bird deal till 7pm (6pm Fri, Sat), welcoming efficient service, solid furnishings all clean and polished, small front bar with warm open fire, four real ales and good wines by the glass; well behaved children allowed but best to ask first, limited wheelchair access, tables outside along with tipi and own bowling green, open from 5.30pm (1-9pm Sun), closed Mon in winter. *(John and Lorna Chew)*

LYMM SJ7087

Barn Owl (01925) 752020

Agden Wharf, Warrington Lane (just off B5159 E); WA13 0SW Popular comfortably extended pub in nice setting

It's very helpful if you let us know up-to-date food prices when you report on pubs.

by Bridgewater Canal; Marstons Lancaster Bomber and Wainwright, Thwaites Original plus three guests, decent wines by the glass, good choice of affordably priced traditional food including weekday OAP menu and Sun carvery, efficient service even when busy, friendly atmosphere; children and dogs (in one part) welcome, disabled facilities, moorings (space for one narrowboat), open all day. *(Mike and Wena Stevenson)*

LYMM SJ6886

Church Green (01925) 752068

Higher Lane; WA13 0AP Popular dining pub owned by celebrity chef Aiden Byrne; food can be very good from restauranty dishes to more affordable pubby choices, also children's menu, Caledonian and a guest beer, carefully chosen wines and interesting gins, various dining areas including conservatory; background music; disabled access/facilities, pretty garden with heated side deck, open (and food) all day, breakfast from 9am at weekends, kitchen shuts 7pm Sun. *(Emily and Toby Archer)*

MACCLESFIELD SJ9173

Snow Goose (01625) 619299

Sunderland Street; SK11 6HN Quirky laid-back bar with feel of an alpine ski lodge; well kept ales such as Storm, several craft beers and good range of wines, unusual food including meze, bare-boards interior on three levels, woodburners, local artwork for sale, piano; background and live music, board games; children and dogs welcome, balcony overlooking back garden, open all day and can get very busy. *(Amy Ledbetter)*

MACCLESFIELD SJ9173

Treacle Tap (01625) 615938

Sunderland Street; SK11 6JL Simply furnished little bare-boards bar in former shop (same owners as the Young Pretender in Congleton); three interesting mainly local ales and good selection of bottled beers (particularly belgian and german), other drinks too, short menu including meat/cheese platters and tasty local pies; regular events such as Sun quiz, foreign language evenings, photography club and a stitch'n'bitch night; children welcome till 8pm, open (and food) all day Fri-Sun, from 4pm other days. *(Emily and Toby Archer)*

MOBBERLEY SJ8179

Plough & Flail (01565) 873537

Off B5085 Knutsford–Alderley Edge; at E end of village turn into Moss Lane, then left into Paddock Hill Lane (look out for small green signs to pub); WA16 7DB Extensive family dining pub tucked down narrow lanes; low-beamed bar with chunky cushioned chairs and stripped tables, flagstones and panelled dado, sofas in wood-floored side area, Lees ales, good choice of wines by the glass and popular food including daily specials, comfortable airy dining room and conservatory; background music, free wi-fi; heated terraces with teak tables, picnic-sets on neat lawns, play area, open (and food) all day. *(W K Wood)*

NANTWICH SJ6452

★Black Lion (01270) 628711

Welsh Row; CW5 5ED Cosy old black and white pub with plenty of character, beams, timbered brickwork, bare boards and stone floors, open fire, good food (not Sun evening, Mon) from short but varied menu, four well kept Weetwood ales and a couple of guests, good friendly service, upstairs rooms with old wooden tables and leather sofas on undulating floors; children and dogs welcome (courtyard Hop Room only in the evening), open all day weekends (when it can get very busy), closed Mon lunchtime. *(Brian and Anna Marsden, Tony Hobden)*

NANTWICH SJ6552

Vine (01270) 619055

Hospital Street; CW5 5RP Black and white fronted pub dating from the 17th c, modernised interior stretching far back with steps and quiet corners, woodburner, four well kept ales including Hydes, popular good value food from fairly pubby menu (till 6pm Sun), friendly staff and locals, raised seating areas; background music, sports TVs, darts; children and dogs welcome, small sunny outside seating area behind, open all day. *(William Pace)*

NESTON SJ2976

Harp (0151) 336 6980

Quayside, SW of Little Neston; keep on along track at end of Marshlands Road; CH64 0TB Tucked-away little two-room country local; five well kept ales such as Holts and Timothy Taylors, decent choice of bottled beers, wines by the glass and some good malt whiskies, enjoyable simple pub food (not Sun evening) including Tues curry night, log fire, pale quarry tiles and simple furnishings, interesting old photographs, hatch servery to lounge; children and dogs allowed, garden behind and picnic-sets up on front grassy bank facing Dee Marshes and Wales, glorious sunsets with wild calls of wading birds, good walks, open all day. *(John and Lorna Chew)*

NORLEY SJ5772

Tigers Head (01928) 788309

Pytchleys Hollow; WA6 8NT Friendly little village local near Delamere Forest; enjoyable good value home-made food, five well kept Marstons-related ales and over 30 gins including their own Second Son, tap room and lounge, upstairs skittle alley/function room; pool, darts, sports TV; children and dogs welcome, some seating out in front, more on paved terrace behind, bowling green, open all day Fri and Sat, till 9.30pm Sun, 8.30pm Mon, closed lunchtimes Mon-Thurs. *(Tim and Mary Thomson)*

PARKGATE SJ2778

Boathouse (0151) 336 4187
Village signed off A540; CH64 6RN Popular 1920s black and white timbered pub with attractive linked rooms, good choice of enjoyable food from sandwiches and snacks up, cheerful attentive staff, well kept Hydes and guests (cheaper on Mon), several wines by the glass, big conservatory with great views to Wales over silted Dee estuary (RSPB reserve), may be egrets and kestrels; children and dogs (in bar) welcome, seats out on decking, open (and food) all day. *(Mike and Wena Stevenson)*

PARKGATE SJ2778

Ship (0151) 336 3931
The Parade; CH64 6SA Far-reaching estuary views from hotel's bow-windowed bar; well kept Brimstage Trappers Hat, Marstons Pedigree and guests, several wines by the glass, over 50 whiskies and interesting range of gins, good reasonably priced home-cooked food including sandwiches (until 5pm), daily specials and popular Sun roasts, friendly service, log fire; children welcome, no dogs inside, a few tables out at front and to the side, 25 bedrooms, open (and food) all day. *(Emily and Toby Archer)*

PEOVER HEATH SJ7973

★**Dog** (01625) 861421
Wellbank Lane; the pub is often listed under Over Peover instead; WA16 8UP Well renovated traditional country pub with intimate rooms (sister to the Ship at Styal); good variety of popular generously served food (all day weekends), five ales including Weetwood, decent choice of wines by the glass and malt whiskies, friendly efficient staff; children welcome, dogs in tap room, picnic-sets out at front and in pretty back garden, can walk from here to the Jodrell Bank Discovery Centre and Arboretum, six bedrooms, open (and food) all day. *(Mike and Wena Stevenson)*

PLUMLEY SJ7275

Golden Pheasant (01565) 722125
Plumley Moor Road (off A556 by the Smoker Inn); WA16 9RX Refurbished country pub with roomy interior; enjoyable food from sandwiches up including good value weekday set lunch, well kept Lees ales and plenty of wines by the glass, friendly helpful staff; background music, Tues quiz, free wi-fi; children and dogs (in bar area) welcome, spacious garden with play area, nine bedrooms (two with four-posters), open (and food) all day. *(Mike and Wena Stevenson)*

POYNTON SJ9483

Boars Head (01625) 876676
Shrigley Road N, Higher Poynton, off A523; SK12 1TE Welcoming red-brick Victorian country pub with enjoyable good value home-made food including speciality pies, four well kept ales such as Black Sheep and Theakstons, warm woodburner; quiz last Thurs of month; children, walkers and dogs welcome, next to Middlewood Way and close to Macclesfield Canal moorings, also handy for Lyme Park (NT), open all day weekends. *(David Walker)*

POYNTON SJ9283

Cask Tavern (01625) 875157
Park Lane; SK12 1RE Busy recently refurbished Bollington pub with five of their well kept ales and a guest, craft beers, real ciders and several wines by the glass including draught prosecco, friendly staff, some snacky food; fortnightly quiz Mon; dogs allowed, open all day Fri-Sun, from 4pm other days. *(William Pace)*

PRESTBURY SJ8976

Legh Arms (01625) 829130
A538, village centre; SK10 4DG Beamed inn with divided-up bar and lounge areas; enjoyable food from sandwiches and traditional choices to daily specials, weekend set lunch, Robinsons ales and decent wines by the glass, soft furnishings, ladder-back chairs around solid dark tables, brocaded bucket seats, stylish french prints and italian engravings, two-way log fire and woodburner, cosy panelled back part with narrow offshoot; background music in one area, daily papers; children and dogs welcome, seats on heated terrace, eight bedrooms, good breakfast, open (and food) all day. *(Nik and Gloria Clarke)*

STYAL SJ8383

Ship (01625) 444888
B5166 near Ringway Airport; SK9 4JE Popular 17th-c beamed pub under same ownership as the Dog at Peover Heath; good variety of well liked food, ales such as Dunham Massey, Timothy Taylors and Weetwood, plenty of wines by the glass, friendly helpful service, lots of alcoves and snugs, some stripped brickwork and painted panelling, open fire; children welcome, seats out at front and on back terrace, attractive NT village with good walks on the doorstep, open (and food) all day. *(Jeremy King, Mike and Wena Stevenson, John Watson)*

SUTTON SJ9469

★**Ryles Arms** (01260) 252244
Hollin Lane, Higher Sutton; SK11 0NN Popular dining pub in fine countryside; very good food from extensive menu including signature grills, ales such as Black Sheep and Wincle, decent wines and several whiskies, pleasant décor, hill-view dining room with french windows to terrace; children welcome, good bedrooms in converted barn, open all day. *(Malcolm and Pauline Pellatt)*

SUTTON SJ9273

Sutton Gamekeeper (01260) 252000
Hollin Lane; SK11 0HL Updated beamed

village pub with good freshly made food from interestingly varied menu, Dunham Massey, Wincle and a guest, good friendly service, warm open fire; children welcome, well behaved dogs in bar, metal furniture in fenced garden behind, closed Mon (except bank holidays), otherwise open all day till 10pm, food all day weekends (till 7pm Sun). *(Ian Duncan)*

TARPORLEY SJ5562

Swan (01829) 733838

High Street, off A49; CW6 0AG Elegant Georgian fronted inn (building actually dates from the 16th c) with rambling linked areas, beams and open fires, good food from sandwiches and snacks through pub favourites up, some main dishes available in smaller helpings, Weetwood ales and a couple of guests, lots of wines by the glass, efficient friendly staff; children and dogs (in bar) welcome, tables outside, 16 charming bedrooms, open (and food) all day. *(Amy Ledbetter)*

WESTON SJ7352

White Lion (01270) 587011

Not far from M6 junction 16, via A500; CW2 5NA Renovated 17th-c black and white inn; low-beamed lounge bar with slate floor, standing timbers and inglenook woodburner, popular food here or in restaurant, three well kept ales including Salopian, cocktail bar; background music; children allowed in eating areas, dogs in bar, lovely garden with bowling green (not owned by the pub), 17 comfortable bedrooms, open all day. *(Andrew Wall)*

WHITEGATE SJ6268

Plough (01606) 889455

Beauty Bank, Foxwist Green; OS Sheet 118 map reference 624684; off A556 just W of Northwich, or A54 W of Winsford; CW8 2BP Comfortable country pub with bar and extended dining area; good home-made food (best to book) from panini and baked potatoes up, cheerful efficient service, four well kept Robinsons ales and plenty of wines by the glass; background music, free wi-fi; no under-14s inside, well behaved dogs allowed in tap room, disabled access, picnic-sets out at front and in back garden, colourful window boxes and hanging baskets, popular walks nearby, open (and food) all day. *(John and Lorna Chew)*

WILDBOARCLOUGH SJ9868

Crag (01260) 227239

Village signed from A54; bear left at fork, then left at T junction; SK11 0BD Old stone-built pub in charming little sheltered valley below moors (good walk up Shutlingsloe for great views); enjoyable generously served home-made food including weekday OAP deal and Sun carvery, three well kept local beers, genuinely friendly staff, old-fashioned feel with plates on delft shelving, various stuffed animals, open fires; children, walkers and dogs (food for them) welcome, terrace with covered smokers' shelter, may open all day in summer, just weekends till 5pm out of season, but best to check; some refurbishment planned as we went to press. *(Charles Fraser)*

WILMSLOW SJ8481

Old Dancer (01625) 530775

Grove Street; SK9 1DR Mock Tudor-fronted pub on pedestrianised street; bare-boards interior with simple wooden furniture and padded wall benches, some striking murals, five well kept changing local ales, craft beers and a proper cider, decent coffee and good value food such as sandwiches, sharing platters and pies, friendly staff, second bar/function room upstairs (not always open); regular events including film night (Weds), traditional games, free wi-fi; children and dogs welcome, seats out in front, open all day (till 1am Fri, Sat). *(M Hamilton)*

WINCLE SJ9665

★**Ship** (01260) 227217

Village signposted off A54 Congleton–Buxton; SK11 0QE Friendly 16th-c stone-built country pub; bare-boards bar leading to carpeted dining room, old stables area with flagstones, beams, woodburner and open fire, good generously served food (not Sun evening) from varied well priced menu, three Lees ales and several wines by the glass, quick attentive service; children and dogs welcome, tables in small side garden, good Dane Valley walks, open all day. *(Guy Vowles, Malcolm and Pauline Pellatt, Roger and Donna Huggins)*

WRENBURY SJ5947

Dusty Miller (01270) 780537

Cholmondeley Road; village signed from A530 Nantwich–Whitchurch; CW5 8HG Converted 19th-c corn mill with fine canal views from terrace and series of tall glazed arches in bar; spacious feel with banquettes, oak settles and wheelback chairs around mix of tables, old lift hoist up under the rafters, Robinsons beers, proper cider and good food (all day weekends), friendly staff; background music, free wi-fi; children and dogs welcome, disabled access/loos, farm shop, closed Mon, otherwise open all day. *(Gail and Arthur Roberts)*

Post Office address codings give the impression that some pubs are in Cheshire, when they're really in Derbyshire (and therefore included in that chapter) or in Greater Manchester (see the Lancashire chapter).

Cornwall

ANTONY SX4054 Map 1

Carew Arms

(01752) 814440 – www.carewarms.com

Off A374; PL11 3AB

Renovated village pub with linked bar and dining rooms, imaginative food, well kept ales, good wines by the glass and downstairs farm shop

There's certainly a buzzing atmosphere here now that the old downstairs skittle alley has been transformed into a store-cum-farm-shop with a small café at one end (and a woodburning stove). The pub itself has interconnected dining rooms with wide floorboards, painted farmhouse and other sturdy chairs around rustic wooden tables, wide stripped floorboards and immaculate pale paintwork; décor is minimal and includes a few pieces of artwork dotted about. There's also an open fire. High chairs line the bar counter (and the tables here are reserved for those wanting just a drink and a chat) where they keep St Austell Tribute and a guest from Keltek or Phoenix on handpump and ten wines by the glass served by courteous staff. There's also an upstairs loft room for private hire.

Local, seasonal produce is at the heart of the first class food: local mussels with shallots, garlic, sea beet and white wine, smoked duck breast with pickled rhubarb and watercress salad, fishcake with warm tartare sauce, seasonal root vegetable crumble with citrus greens, corn-fed chicken with caesar croquette and anchovies, lemon sole with pickled cockles and sea greens, aged rib-eye steak with garden herb salsa and crunchy chips, and puddings such as salted caramel and rum chocolate pot with honeycomb and tonka bean crème brûlée with granola and orange and cranberry sorbet. *Benchmark main dish: local pork belly with seasonal slaw and apple £15.50. Two-course evening meal £21.00.*

Free house ~ Licensee Tremayne Carew Pole ~ Real ale ~ Open 12-11; 12-10 Sun; closed Mon and Tues except for bank holidays ~ Bar food 12-2.30 (3 Sun), 6-9 ~ Restaurant ~ Children welcome ~ Dogs allowed in bar ~ Wi-fi ~ Quiz monthly Sun *Recommended by Jane Rigby, Frances Parsons, Matt and Hayley Jacob, Peter L Harrison, Catherine and Daniel King, George and Alison Bishop*

BOSCASTLE SX0991 Map 1

Cobweb

(01840) 250278 – www.cobwebinn.com

B3263, just E of harbour; PL35 0HE

Plenty of interest in cheerful pub, several real ales and friendly staff

This popular pub is close to the tiny steeply cut harbour and the pretty village. The two interesting bars have quite a mix of seats (from settles and carved chairs to more pubby furniture), heavy beams hung with hundreds of bottles and jugs, lots of pictures of bygone years, and cosy log fires; the atmosphere is lively, especially at peak times. They keep four real ales such as St Austell Tribute, Tintagel Cornwalls Pride and Harbour Special and a guest beer on handpump, decent wines by the glass, a local cider and a dozen malt whiskies; games machine, darts and pool. The restaurant is upstairs. There are picnic-sets and benches outside, some under cover; dogs must be kept on a lead. A self-catering apartment is for rent.

Quite a choice of tasty food includes sandwiches and baguettes, whitebait with a citrus dip, creamy garlic and chive mushrooms, chicken caesar salad, mexican beef chilli with tortilla chips and sour cream, a choice of pizzas (available to take away too), vegetarian pasty with chips, home-cooked ham and egg, sausages with mustard mash and caramelised onion gravy, a curry of the day, mixed grill, and puddings. *Benchmark main dish: steak in ale pie £11.95. Two-course evening meal £18.00.*

Free house ~ Licensee Adrian Bright ~ Real ale ~ Open 10.30am-11.30pm (midnight Sat); 11-11 Sun ~ Bar food 11.30-2.30, 5.15 (6 in winter)-9.30 ~ Restaurant ~ Children welcome ~ Dogs allowed in bar ~ Wi-fi *Recommended by David Appleyard, Alan and Alice Morgan, Andrew Vincent*

CONSTANTINE SW7328 Map 1

Trengilly Wartha

(01326) 340332 – www.trengilly.co.uk

Nancenoy; A3083 S of Helston, signposted Gweek near RNAS Culdrose, then fork right after Gweek; OS Sheet 204 map reference 731282; TR11 5RP

Well run inn surrounded by big gardens with a friendly welcome for all, and popular food and drink; bedrooms

The long-serving owners run this bustling country place with great care and thought and our readers enjoy their visits very much. The long, low-beamed main bar has a sociable feel (especially in the evening when locals drop in), all sorts of tables, chairs and settles, a woodburning stove, lots of pump clips, and cricket team photos and bats on the walls. Penzance Potion No 9, Sharps Doom Bar and a changing guest beer on handpump, lots of wines by the glass, 80 malt whiskies and 11 gins. Leading off the bar is the conservatory family room and there's also a cosy bistro. The six acres of gardens are well worth a wander and offer plenty of seats and picnic-sets under large parasols. The cottagey bedrooms are comfortable and breakfasts highly regarded, and as the inn is not far from the Helford River and tucked away on a peaceful hillside, you'll find good nearby walks.

As well as lunchtime sandwiches (their seasonal crab is good), the well regarded food includes chicken liver pâté with home-made chutney, beetroot and walnut salad topped with goats cheese, chickpea and vegetable curry, cajun-marinated pork with spicy mayonnaise, hungarian goulash, steak and mushroom in ale pie, whole plaice with lemon butter, local steaks with trimmings and chips, and puddings that include local ice-cream. *Benchmark main dish: fish medley (three different fish fillets) with dauphinoise potatoes and pesto sauce £16.50. Two-course evening meal £21.00.*

Free house ~ Licensees Will and Lisa Lea ~ Real ale ~ Open 11-3.15, 6-11; 11-11 Sat; 12-11 Sun ~ Bar food 12-2.15, 6.30-9.30 ~ Restaurant ~ Children welcome away from bar area ~ Dogs allowed in bar and bedrooms ~ Wi-fi ~ Live music Weds and Sun evenings ~ Bedrooms: £77/£84 *Recommended by Colin Humphreys, Mike and Sarah Abbot, Andrew and Ruth Simmonds, Victoria and James Sargeant, Dr Geoff Butts, Sophie and James Collier, Sandra and Miles Spencer*

DEVORAN SW7938 Map 1

Old Quay

(01872) 863142 – www.theoldquayinn.co.uk

Devoran from new Carnon Cross roundabout A39 Truro–Falmouth, left on old road, right at mini roundabout; TR3 6NE

Light and airy bar rooms in friendly pub with four real ales, good wine, imaginative food and seats on pretty back terraces; bedrooms

Walkers, cyclists and even horse riders enjoy this convivial place as it's just 50 metres from the coast-to-coast Portreath to Devoran Mineral Tramways cycle path. The easy-going, roomy bar has an interesting 'woodburner' set halfway up one wall, a cushioned window seat, wall settles and a few bar stools around just three tables on stripped boards, and bar chairs by the counter. Black Sheep, Sharps Atlantic and Doom Bar and Skinners Betty Stogs on handpump and good wines by the glass (including prosecco). Off to the left is an airy room with pictures by local artists (for sale), built-in cushioned wall seating, plush stools and a couple of big tables on the dark slate floor. To the other side of the bar is another light room with more settles and farmhouse chairs, attractive blue and white striped cushions and more sailing photographs; darts and board games. As well as benches outside at the front looking down through the trees to the water, there's a series of snug little back terraces with picnic-sets and chairs and tables. The two bedrooms (one faces the quay, the other overlooks the garden) have shared facilities. Nearby parking is limited unless you arrive early. There is wheelchair access through a side door.

They use carefully sourced, very local produce for the pleasing food that includes lunchtime sandwiches and pub classics plus moules marinière, oxtail and wild mushroom risotto, mackerel fillets on seafood linguine, southern-fried marinated tofu with slaw and fries, lamb stroganoff, fish pie topped with cheesy mash, and puddings such as peanut cheesecake with chocolate ice-cream and peanut brittle and red and white wine-poached pear with elderflower sorbet and praline. *Benchmark main dish: peppered rib-eye steak with black pudding hash and a poached egg £21.00. Two-course evening meal £20.00.*

Punch ~ Tenants John and Hannah Calland ~ Real ale ~ Open 11-11 ~ Bar food 12-3, 6-9 ~ Restaurant ~ Children welcome ~ Dogs allowed in bar ~ Wi-fi ~ Bedrooms: £65/£85

Recommended by Jean P & Myriam Alderson, Peter and Emma Kelly, Lee and Jill Stafford, Sally Harrison, Liz and Mike Newton

GURNARDS HEAD SW4337 Map 1

Gurnards Head Hotel

(01736) 796928 – www.gurnardshead.co.uk

B3306 Zennor–St Just; TR26 3DE

Interesting inn with lots of wines by the glass, good inventive food and fine surrounding walks; comfortable bedrooms

Impressive food and drink plus comfortable bedrooms keep our readers coming back here on a regular basis. It's a civilised but informal place with open fires, work by local artists on bold, strong paintwork, books on shelves, fresh flowers, and all manner of wooden dining chairs and tables and sofas on stripped boards or rugs. St Austell Tribute, a beer named for the pub (from Cornish Chough) and a local guest on handpump, 14 wines by the glass or carafe and a couple of ciders; background music, darts and board games. The large back garden has plenty of seats. Well appointed bedrooms have views of the rugged moors or the Atlantic which is just 500 metres away. This is under the same ownership as the Old Coastguard in Mousehole (also in Cornwall) and the Griffin at Felinfach (Wales).

Enticing modern food includes mussels with lemongrass, coconut and lime leaf broth, pork rillettes with marmite butter and chutney, duck leg with spiced lentils and stir-fried broccoli, lamb breast with merguez sausage, cucumber, yoghurt and chickpeas, rump of beef with red onion, tomatoes and hash brown, ray wing with tomato, olive, caper and samphire, and puddings such as treacle tart with raspberry compote and cappuccino mousse with amaretto sabayon; they also offer a two- and three-course set lunch. *Benchmark main dish: cod with taramasalata, almonds and za'atar £18.00. Two-course evening meal £22.00.*

Free house ~ Licensees Charles and Edmund Inkin ~ Real ale ~ Open 10am-11pm; closed first week Dec ~ Bar food 12-2.30, 6 (6.30 Sun)-9 ~ Restaurant ~ Children welcome ~ Dogs allowed in bar and bedrooms ~ Wi-fi ~ Bedrooms: £105/£125 *Recommended by Andrew and Michele Revell, Patricia and Gordon Thompson, Angela and Steve Heard*

HALSETOWN TL5038 Map 1

Halsetown Inn

(01736) 795583 – www.halsetowninn.co.uk

B3311 SW of St Ives; TR26 3NA

Quite a mix of customers in bustling pub with local ales and wine suppliers, bold, often elaborate food and easy-going atmosphere

It's important to the licensees of this quirky little stone pub that they run the place with environmental awareness (they use green energy and recycle as much as possible) and offer a strong commitment to local producers, which range from farmers and fishermen to the local tea plantation. As well as the snug bar (liked by locals for a pint and a chat), there are simply furnished dining areas with an old range and a woodburning stove, an eclectic collection of wooden dining chairs and mismatched tables on quarry tiles, cushioned settles, candles and fresh flowers. Artwork and murals are bold and contemporary, with many of the pieces created by local artists. Skinners Betty Stogs on handpump, 12 wines by the glass, a dozen malt whiskies, 35 gins and cider; background jazz. The front terrace has a few picnic-sets.

Robust cooking using seasonal ingredients includes sandwiches, mussel, haddock, smoked bacon and sweetcorn chowder, lamb keema flatbread with mango and red chilli salsa and tomato and cucumber raita, mushroom ragoût with crispy parmesan polenta balls and cavolo nero, slow-roasted pork belly with a stew of fennel, potato, cannellini beans, harissa, preserved lemon, black olive and tomatoes, confit duck leg with squash, parsnip and caramelised onion mash and orange and star anise sauce, and puddings such as apple and berry crumble with coconut sorbet and sticky toffee pudding with toffee pecan sauce and banana ice-cream; they also offer a two- and three-course set lunch (not Sunday). *Benchmark main dish: hake with laksa butter and an asian crab salad £15.50. Two-course evening meal £22.00.*

Free house ~ Licensee Julia Knight ~ Real ale ~ Open 12-2, 5-11; 12-9 Sun ~ Bar food 12-2, 6-9; 12-3 Sun ~ Restaurant ~ Children welcome ~ Dogs welcome ~ Wi-fi *Recommended by Matt and Hayley Jacob, Donald Allsopp, David Appleyard, Greta and Gavin Craddock, Sabina and Gerald Grimshaw*

Please tell us if the décor, atmosphere, food or drink at a pub is different from our description. We rely on readers' reports to keep us up to date: feedback@goodguides.com, or (no stamp needed) The Good Pub Guide, FREEPOST RTXY–ZCBC–BBAZ, Stream Lane, Sedlescombe, Battle TN33 0PB.

HELFORD SW7526 Map 1

Shipwrights Arms

(01326) 231235 – www.shipwrightshelford.co.uk

Off B3293 SE of Helston, via Mawgan; TR12 6JX

17th-c waterside inn with seats on terraces, attractively decorated bars, friendly service and tasty food

In warm weather try to arrive early to bag one of the seats on the various terraces that drop down from this thatched pub to the water's edge; the lovely view of the beautiful wooded creek is at its best at high tide. There's pontoon mooring and a foot-ferry from Helford Passage. The bars have quite a nautical theme, with old navigation lamps, ship models, boat wallpaper, appropriate artworks and even the odd figurehead; antique pine and oak furniture sits on slate or bare-boarded floors and cushioned window seats have pretty cushions. Stools line the counter where they keep St Austell Tribute and a guest such as Skinners Porthleven on handpump, 14 wines by the glass, 14 gins and 26 rums; there's an open fire in winter. There are good surrounding walks, including a long-distance coast path that goes right past the door of the pub.

Cooked by the landlord using very local produce, the good food includes sandwiches (until 4pm), smoked mackerel pâté, goan seafood curry, spinach, mushroom and blue cheese lasagne, steak burger with toppings, coleslaw and chips, hake fillet with pistachio and parmesan crumb, celeriac mash and lemon cream sauce, steak tagliata (sirloin steak on griddled aubergine, courgettes and sunblush tomatoes topped with basil and pine nuts), and puddings such as dark chocolate and caramel crème brûlée and strawberry eton mess; their outside pizza oven is much used in good weather. *Benchmark main dish: local fish and chips £12.95. Two-course evening meal £19.00.*

Free house ~ Licensee Lindsey Evans ~ Real ale ~ Open 11-11; 12-11 in winter ~ Bar food 12-3, 6-9; 12-9 in summer ~ Restaurant ~ Children welcome ~ Dogs welcome ~ Wi-fi ~ Live music most Sun afternoons *Recommended by Mrs L Gustine, Robert and Diana Ringstone, Greta and Gavin Craddock, Usha and Terri Patel*

HELSTON SW6522 Map 1

Halzephron

(01326) 240406 – www.halzephron-inn.co.uk

Gunwalloe, village about 4 miles S but not marked on many road maps; look for brown sign on A3083 alongside perimeter fence of RNAS Culdrose; TR12 7QB

Bustling pub in lovely spot with tasty bar food, local beers and good nearby walks; bedrooms

Many of our readers have been coming here for years, it's that kind of reliable place. But maybe not so reliable 500 years ago, when it was well known as a smugglers' haunt. The bar and dining areas are neatly kept and have an informal, friendly atmosphere, some fishing memorabilia, comfortable seating, a warm winter fire in a woodburning stove and a good range of drinks: Rebel Penryn Pale Ale, Sharps Doom Bar and Skinners Porthleven on handpump, nine wines by the glass, 41 malt whiskies and summer farm cider. The dining gallery seats up to 30 people; board games. Picnic-sets outside look across National Trust fields and countryside. The pretty bedrooms have country views. Church Cove with its sandy beach is nearby, Gunwalloe fishing cove is just 300 metres from the pub and there are lovely coastal walks in both directions.

Fresh, seasonal food includes lunchtime sandwiches and ploughman's, seafood chowder, garlic-baked camembert with redcurrant jelly, butternut squash and leek crumble, ham and free-range eggs, white crabmeat in thermidor sauce topped with melted cheese, free-range chicken breast strips in wild mushroom and crème fraîche sauce with basmati rice, duck breast with cherry brandy sauce and anna potatoes, surf and turf (steak topped with king prawns), and puddings. *Benchmark main dish: daily fresh fish dish £14.95. Two-course evening meal £21.00.*

Free house ~ Licensee Claire Murray ~ Real ale ~ Open 11-11; 12-10.30 Sun ~ Bar food 12-2.30 (3 Sun), 6-9 ~ Restaurant ~ Children welcome ~ Dogs allowed in bar and bedrooms ~ Wi-fi ~ Bedrooms: £55/£95 *Recommended by Sophia and Hamish Greenfield, Frank and Marcia Pelling, Guy Henderson, Andrew and Michele Revell*

LANLIVERY SX0759 Map 1

Crown

(01208) 872707 – www.thecrowninncornwall.co.uk

Signposted off A390 Lostwithiel–St Austell (tricky to find from other directions); PL30 5BT

Chatty atmosphere in nice old pub, with traditional rooms and well liked food and drink; bedrooms

This place has been catering for travellers since it was built in the 12th c, and customers today are made just as welcome as they were all those hundreds of years ago. It's a pretty white-painted long house with a great deal of character. The main bar has a good mix of both locals and visitors, a woodburning stove in a huge fireplace, traditional settles on big flagstones, church and other wooden chairs around all sorts of tables, old Cornwall photographs and boarded ceilings with beams. Sharps Doom Bar and Skinners Porthleven on handpump, several wines by the glass and local cider. A couple of other rooms have high-backed black leather dining chairs and built-in cushioned pews, there's another (smaller) woodburning stove and a simply furnished conservatory; darts. The porch has a huge well with a glass top and the quiet, pretty garden has picnic-sets. The bedrooms (in separate buildings) are clean and comfortable and overlook the rustic garden; breakfasts are good. The Eden Project is a ten-minute drive away.

Reasonably priced tasty food includes lunchtime sandwiches and pub classics, baked brie topped with red onion chutney, lamb koftas with mint yoghurt, spicy mixed bean hotpot, ham and eggs, lamb with garlic and thyme sautéed potatoes and red wine and mint jus, guinea fowl breast with mushroom and onion sauce and crushed herb potatoes, red mullet fillets on pea and basil risotto with a lemon and dill dressing, and puddings. *Benchmark main dish: chicken breast on chorizo risotto with chilli, lime and coriander dressing £11.75. Two-course evening meal £22.00.*

Free house ~ Licensee Nigel Wakeham ~ Real ale ~ Open 11.30-11; 12-10.30 Sun ~ Bar food 12-2.30, 6-9 ~ Restaurant ~ Children welcome away from bar ~ Dogs allowed in bar and bedrooms ~ Wi-fi ~ Bedrooms: /£95 *Recommended by Bob and Margaret Holder, Tracey and Stephen Groves, Ian Herdman, Dr and Mrs F McGinn, Adam and Natalie Davis, Belinda and Neil Garth*

LONGROCK SW5031 Map 1

Mexico Inn

(01736) 710625 – www.themexicoinn.co.uk

Riverside; old coast road Penzance–Marazion; TR20 8JB

Granite-stone pub with rustic charm, seasonal food cooked by both licensees and a merry atmosphere

This cheerful pub is the sort of place where everyone chats to everyone else, and customers include walkers with their dogs, windsurfers, locals in for a pint and a natter, and families meeting up for the popular Sunday lunches. The open-plan rooms include one with leather tub chairs and a chesterfield sofa around a woodburning stove, as well as dining rooms with wheelback and wooden chairs around nice antique tables on bare boards, bold aqua-green and orange paintwork, bookshelves, and stools against the counter where they serve St Austell Tribute, Skinners Betty Stogs and Lushingtons and maybe a guest from Phoenix on handpump, several wines by the glass, local gin, farm cider and home-made pink lemonade and ginger beer; background music, darts and board games. At the front are a few picnic-sets and they've extended the back garden to include the terrace and a large area growing herbs; there are more seats here too.

The licensees, enthusiastic chefs, cook the good, seasonal food from a sensibly short menu: ham hock and celeriac fritters with a soft boiled egg and piccalilli, salt and pepper crispy squid with asian-style salad, spiced chickpea burger with swiss cheese, relish and pickles, bratwurst sausage with pancetta and pork belly with braised sauerkraut, hake fillet with jerusalem artichokes and celeriac, hazelnuts and a red wine and shallot dressing with parsley oil, and puddings such as vanilla crème brûlée with pink rhubarb and steamed chocolate pudding with espresso custard. *Benchmark main dish: beer-battered fish and chips £12.50. Two-course evening meal £19.00.*

Free house ~ Licensee Tom Symons ~ Real ale ~ No credit cards ~ Open 11.30-11.30 (midnight Sat); 12-11 Sun ~ Bar food 12.30-2.30, 6.30-9; 12.30-2.30, 5.30-8 Sun ~ Restaurant ~ Children welcome ~ Dogs allowed in bar ~ Wi-fi ~ Regular live bands *Recommended by Nicola and Stuart Parsons, Robin and Anne Triggs, Serena and Adam Furber, Heather and Richard Jones, David Appleyard, Millie and Peter Downing*

LOSTWITHIEL SX1059 Map 1

Globe

(01208) 872501 – www.globeinn.com

North Street (close to medieval bridge); PL22 0EG

Traditional local with interesting food and drink, friendly staff and suntrap back courtyard

---

You'll get a genuinely warm welcome here as well as a thoughtful choice of good food and drink. The unassuming and friendly bar, which is long and narrow, has a mix of pubby tables and seats, local photographs on pale blue plank panelling at one end and nice, mainly local prints (for sale) on walls above a coal-effect stove at the snug inner end; there's also a small front alcove. The ornately carved bar counter, with comfortable leatherette stools, dispenses Sharps Own, Skinners Betty Stogs and a local guest on handpump, ten reasonably priced wines by the glass, 20 malt whiskies and two local ciders; background music, darts, board games and TV. The sheltered back courtyard is not large but has some attractive and unusual plants, and is a real suntrap (with an extendable awning and outside heaters). You can park in several of the nearby streets or the (free) town car park. The 13th-c church is worth a look and the ancient river bridge, a few metres away, is lovely.

Pleasing food includes moules marinière, prawn cocktail, vegetarian roast with red onion, mushroom and port sauce, gammon with pineapple and a free-range egg, chilli con carne, sausages with mash and onion gravy, a pie of the week, slow-roasted lamb with mash and gravy, and puddings such as ginger and black treacle sponge and caramel apple pie with local clotted cream. *Benchmark main dish: fresh fish dish of the day £12.95. Two-course evening meal £20.00.*

Free house ~ Licensee William Erwin ~ Real ale ~ Open 12-11 (midnight Fri, Sat) ~ Bar food 12-9 ~ Restaurant ~ Children welcome ~ Dogs allowed in bar ~ Wi-fi ~ Live music alternate Fri evenings ~ Bedrooms: /£70 *Recommended by Gavin and Helle May, Buster May, Sheila Topham, R K Phillips, Vibekke Böhl, Len and Lilly Dowson, Peter Brix*

THE GOOD PUB GUIDE

MOUSEHOLE SW4726 Map 1

Old Coastguard

(01736) 731222 – www.oldcoastguardhotel.co.uk

The Parade (edge of village, Newlyn coast road); TR19 6PR

Lovely position for civilised inn with an easy-going atmosphere, good choice of wines and first rate food; bedrooms

On a warm day the rather special garden here is hard to beat. There are tropical palms and dracaena, a path leading down to rock pools and seats on the terrace looking over to St Michael's Mount and the Lizard. Inside, the bar rooms have boldly coloured walls hung with paintings of sailing boats and local scenes, stripped floorboards and an atmosphere of informal but civilised comfort. The Upper Deck houses the bar and the restaurant, with a nice mix of antique dining chairs around oak and distressed pine tables, lamps on big barrel tables and chairs to either side of the log fire, topped by a vast bressumer beam. St Austell Tribute and a guest from Cornish Crown on handpump, 14 wines by the glass or carafe, a big choice of gins, vodkas and whiskies, a farm cider and a good choice of soft drinks. The Lower Deck has glass windows running the length of the building, several deep sofas and armchairs, and shelves of books and games; background music. The comfortable bedrooms look over the sea. This is sister pub to the Gurnards Head (also Cornwall) and the Griffin at Felinfach (Wales).

Up-to-date brasserie-style food includes grilled mackerel with horseradish and beetroot relish, roasted quail with carrots, maple syrup and hazelnuts, gurnard with jerusalem artichokes and café de paris butter, crisp red wine salsify with a duck egg, turnips and lentil dressing, guinea fowl with boulangère potatoes, black pudding, apple and parsley sauce beef cheek with mash, roasted celeriac and red wine jus, and puddings such as vanilla crème brûlée and rhubarb and lemon verbena trifle; they also offer a two- and three-course set menu. *Benchmark main dish: fish stew £14.00. Two-course evening meal £19.50.*

Free house ~ Licensees Charles and Edmund Inkin ~ Real ale ~ Open 8am-11pm ~ Bar food 12.30-2.30, 6.30-9 (9.30 Fri, Sat) ~ Restaurant ~ Children welcome ~ Dogs allowed in bar and bedrooms ~ Wi-fi ~ Live jazz Sun ~ Bedrooms: £105/£140 *Recommended by Rosie and Marcus Heatherley, Louise and Anton Parsons, Mark and Sian Edwards, Miranda and Jeff Davidson*

MYLOR BRIDGE SW8137 Map 1

Pandora

(01326) 372678 – www.pandorainn.com

Restronguet Passage: from A39 in Penryn, take turning signposted Mylor Church, Mylor Bridge, Flushing and go straight through Mylor Bridge following Restronguet Passage signs; or from A39 further N, at or near Perranarworthal, take turning signposted Mylor, Restronguet, then follow Restronguet Weir signs, but turn left down hill at Restronguet Passage sign; TR11 5ST

Idyllically placed waterside inn with lots of atmosphere in beamed and flagstoned rooms, and all-day food

On a quiet day at high tide, it would be hard to beat this medieval thatched pub's sheltered waterfront position, best enjoyed from picnic-table sets in front or on the long floating jetty – you'll need to arrive early to bag a seat. Rambling, interconnected rooms have low beams, beautifully polished big flagstones, cosy alcoves, cushioned built-in wall seats and pubby tables and chairs, three large log fires in high hearths (to protect them against tidal floods) and maps, yacht pictures, oars and ships' wheels; church candles help with the lighting. There's also a back cabin bar with pale farmhouse chairs, high-backed settles and a model galleon in a big glass cabinet. St Austell HSD, Proper Job, Trelawny and Tribute on handpump, 17 wines by the glass and 18 malt whiskies. Upstairs, the attractive dining room has exposed oak vaulting, dark tables and chairs on pale oak flooring and large brass bells and lanterns. Because of the pub's popularity, parking is extremely difficult at peak times; wheelchair access.

Some sort of good food is offered all day: sandwiches (until 5pm), a seafood sharing board, tempura king prawns with saffron aioli, roasted portobello mushroom with an olive caponata stuffing and carrot rösti, beer-battered fish and chips, halloumi burger with toppings and chips, lambs liver and bacon with blue cheese bubble and squeak and red wine jus, local mussels with cream, ginger, honey and spring onions, stuffed saddle of lamb with bacon boulangère potatoes and mint purée, and puddings such as tiramisu and dark chocolate and coconut soufflé. *Benchmark main dish: fish pie £13.50. Two-course evening meal £20.00.*

St Austell ~ Tenant John Milan ~ Real ale ~ Open 10.30am-11pm ~ Bar food 10.30am-9.30pm ~ Restaurant ~ Children welcome away from bar area ~ Dogs allowed in bar ~ Wi-fi
Recommended by IAA, HMW, Maria Sansoni, Graeme and Sally Mendham, Amanda Shipley, Franklyn Roberts, Martine and Lawrence Sanders, Justine and Neil Bonnett

PENZANCE — SW4730 Map 1

Turks Head

(01736) 363093 – www.turksheadpenzance.co.uk

At top of main street, by big domed building turn left down Chapel Street; TR18 4AF

Bustling atmosphere in well run pub with popular food and beer

We always get enthusiastic reports from our readers about this lively town pub. The bar has old flat irons, jugs and so forth hanging from the beams, pottery above the wood-effect panelling, wall seats and tables and a couple of elbow-rests around central pillars; background music and board games. Sharps Doom Bar, Skinners Betty Stogs and Sennen and a guest such as Bath Gem on handpump, ten wines by the glass, a dozen gins and 12 malt whiskies. The suntrap back garden has big urns of flowers, seats under a giant parasol and a barbecue. There's been a Turks Head here for over 700 years – though most of the original building was destroyed by a Spanish raiding party in the 16th c.

Well liked food includes sandwiches, barbecue-glazed chicken wings, seafood tapas sharing plate, butternut squash, spinach and five-bean lasagne, burgers with toppings and skin-on fries, lasagne, beer-battered fresh fish of the day and chips, lambs liver and bacon with mustard mash and red wine and onion jus, local steaks with a choice of four sauces, and puddings. *Benchmark main dish: seafood pie £14.95 Two-course evening meal £20.00.*

Punch ~ Lease Jonathan and Helen Gibbard ~ Real ale ~ Open 11.30-11.30 (midnight Sat); 12-11 Sun ~ Bar food 12-2.30, 6-10 ~ Restaurant ~ Children welcome ~ Dogs welcome ~ Wi-fi *Recommended by Chris Stevenson, John and Mary Warner, Andrew Stone, Alan Johnson, Paul Faraday, Ivy and George Goodwill*

We accept no free drinks or meals and inspections are anonymous.

PERRANUTHNOE SW5329 Map 1

Victoria

(01736) 710309 – www.victoriainn-penzance.co.uk

Signed off A394 Penzance–Helston; TR20 9NP

Cornwall Dining Pub of the Year

Carefully furnished inn with interesting food, a friendly welcome, local beers and seats in pretty garden; bedrooms

The imaginative food cooked by the chef-landlord is obviously a big draw here, but plenty of customers drop in for a drink and a chat after a walk. The L-shaped bar has various cosy corners, exposed joists, a woodburning stove and an attractive array of dining chairs around wooden tables on oak flooring; the restaurant is separate. Sharps Doom Bar and guests such as Cornish Crown Helter Skelter and Shiver Me Timbers on handpump and over ten wines by the glass; background music and board games, and the pub spaniel is called Monty. The pretty tiered garden has seats and tables. Bedrooms are cosy and breakfasts tasty. The South West Coast Path and the beaches of Mount's Bay are close by.

Enticing food cooked by the landlord includes lobster bisque with scallops, mussels, parmesan and aioli, truffle whipped goats cheese with beetroot and 14-year-old balsamic, lentil and chickpea dhal with cauliflower steak, toasted coconut, lime pickle and yoghurt, beef, mushroom and Guinness suet pudding, confit duck leg with root vegetable mash, braised red cabbage, croquette, parsnip purée and rosemary jus, plaice with capers, asparagus, leeks and tomato butter sauce, and puddings such as sticky ginger pudding with toffee sauce and ginger ice-cream and chocolate délice with passion-fruit and yoghurt sorbet; they also offer a three-course set lunch. *Benchmark main dish: confit pork belly with crispy ham croquette, apple and thyme purée and crackling £17.00. Two-course evening meal £22.00.*

Free house ~ Licensee Nik Boyle ~ Real ale ~ Open 12-11; 12-4.30 Sun; 12-3, 5.30-11 Tues-Sat in winter; closed Sun evening, winter Mon ~ Bar food 12-2, 6.15-9; 12-3 Sun ~ Restaurant ~ Children welcome but not in bedrooms ~ Dogs allowed in bar ~ Wi-fi ~ Bedrooms: /£95 *Recommended by Sally Melling, Martine and Lawrence Sanders, Millie and Peter Downing, Sophie and James Collier, Sally and Brian Turner*

POLGOOTH SW9950 Map 1

Polgooth Inn

(01726) 74089 – www.polgoothinn.co.uk

Well signed off A390 W of St Austell; Ricketts Lane; PL26 7DA

Welcoming pub in small village, plenty of space for eating and drinking, cornish ales, well liked food and seats on big front terrace

The spreading, linked rooms in this spacious old pub have dark beams and timbering, open fires and woodburning stoves. Seating ranges from high-backed settles to tartan upholstered dining chairs, banquettes to nice farmhouse seats (all around wooden tables on carpet), and there are old agricultural tools and photos on painted or exposed-stone walls. St Austell Cornish Best, HSD, Proper Job, Tribute and a seasonal guest on handpump, good wines by the glass and a gin menu. A dining extension with country kitchen furniture has a modern woodburner against a black brick wall, contemporary lighting and french doors to the terrace. They have picnic-sets on grass (some under an awning), separate dining booths and a kitchen garden where they grow herbs and salads and keep chickens. The Lost Gardens of Heligan are nearby.

High quality food includes sandwiches, scallops with cauliflower purée, hog's pudding and red wine glaze, slow-roasted pig cheeks with beetroot and sage mash and a treacle glaze, thick-cut ham and eggs, timbale of local white crab with chive mayonnaise, rack of ribs with pickled slaw and rustic chips, thai fish curry, superfood salad with either chicken, chilli salmon or courgette fritters, and puddings such as tiramisu and sticky toffee pudding with toffee sauce; they also offer breakfasts (7.30-10am Friday and Saturday). *Benchmark main dish: fish pie £14.50. Two-course evening meal £22.00.*

St Austell ~ Tenants Alex and Tanya Williams ~ Real ale ~ Open 11-11; 11am-midnight Fri, Sat ~ Bar food 12-9.30 ~ Restaurant ~ Children welcome ~ Dogs allowed in bar ~ Wi-fi ~ Live music summer Sun afternoons *Recommended by Peter Pilbeam, Colin and Daniel Gibbs, David and Charlotte Green, Isobel Mackinlay*

POLKERRIS SX0952 Map 1

Rashleigh

(01726) 813991 – www.therashleighinnpolkerris.co.uk

Signposted off A3082 Fowey–St Austell; PL24 2TL

Lovely beachside spot with sizeable sun terrace, five real ales and quite a choice of food

Once you've discovered this pub, you're sure to come back. In winter, it's cosy and warm, while in summer the seats on the front terrace have a wonderful view towards the far side of St Austell and Mevagissey bays. The bar has comfortably cushioned chairs around dark wooden tables at the front, and similar furnishings, local photographs and a winter log fire at the back. Dartmoor Legend, Padstow Windjammer, Sharps Sea Fury, Skinners Betty Stogs, Timothy Taylors Landlord and Tintagel Arthur's Ale on handpump, nine wines by the glass, two farm ciders and organic soft drinks; background music. All the tables in the restaurant have a sea view. There's plenty of parking in either the pub's own car park or the large village one. A fine beach with a restored jetty is a few steps away, as is the local section of the South West Coast Path (renowned for its striking scenery).

Decent food includes sandwiches, sticky cajun chicken, baked camembert with cranberry sauce, a trio of local sausages with mash and red onion gravy, steak in ale pie, hake in spicy tomato and spinach sauce with sautéed potatoes, slow-roast pork belly with wholegrain mustard and cider gravy, specials such as local mussels, wild mushroom risotto and barbecue pulled beef, and puddings. *Benchmark main dish: beer-battered cod and chips £9.95. Two-course evening meal £16.00.*

Free house ~ Licensees Jon and Samantha Spode ~ Real ale ~ Open 11-11 (10 winter) ~ Bar food 12-3, 6-9; snacks 3-5 ~ Restaurant ~ Children welcome ~ Dogs allowed in bar *Recommended by Geoff and Ann Marston, Patti and James Davidson, Ian Herdman, Serena and Adam Furber*

POLPERRO SX2050 Map 1

Blue Peter

(01503) 272743 – www.thebluepeterinn.com

Quay Road; PL13 2QZ

Friendly pub overlooking harbour with fishing paraphernalia, real ales and carefully prepared food

There's a good mix of customers of all ages in this bustling little harbourside pub, though families must use the upstairs room. The atmosphere is easy-going and friendly and traditional furnishings include a small winged settle and a polished pew, wooden flooring, fishing regalia, photographs and pictures by local artists, lots of candles and a solid wood bar counter. St Austell Tribute and Sharps Own plus guests such as Cornish Crown SPA, Fish Key Hip Hop and Hanlons Yellowhammer on handpump and a growing choice of gins and rums served by the helpful, long-serving licensees. One window seat looks down on the harbour, while another looks out past rocks to the sea. Background music and board games. There are seats on the terrace outside and more in an amphitheatre-style area upstairs. The pub gets crowded at peak times.

Fair priced food includes lunchtime sandwiches (the crab is popular) and wraps plus daily fresh fish specials, chicken liver pâté with red onion chutney, crispy salt and pepper squid with sweet chilli dipping sauce, honey and cider roasted ham with a poached egg and pineapple chutney, chicken tikka masala, a pie of the day, chickpea and vegetable burger with chips, and puddings. *Benchmark main dish: beer-battered fish and chips £11.50. Two-course evening meal £18.00.*

Free house ~ Licensees Steve and Caroline Steadman/Rob and Rebecca Hawkes ~ Real ale ~ Open 11-11; 12-10.30 Sun ~ Bar food 12-2.30, 6-8.30; 12-9 in high season ~ Children in upstairs family room only ~ Dogs welcome ~ Wi-fi ~ Live music Fri, Sat 9pm *Recommended by Tracey and Stephen Groves, Max Simons, Sally and David Champion, Colin Gooch, Anne Roots, Ian Herdman, Vibekke Böhl*

PORT ISAAC SX0080 Map 1

Port Gaverne Inn

(01208) 880244 – www.portgavernehotel.co.uk

Port Gaverne signposted from Port Isaac and from B3314 E of Pendoggett; PL29 3SQ

Bustling small hotel with a proper bar and real ales, well liked food in several dining areas and seats in the garden; bedrooms

The individually furnished and comfortable bedrooms here have plenty of character, though the stairs up to most of them are fairly steep (staff will carry your luggage). The chatty bar has low beams, flagstones and carpeting, some exposed stone, a big log fire and Bath Gem, St Austell Proper Job and Tribute, Skinners Betty Stogs and Timothy Taylors Landlord on handpump, 20 wines by the glass, 40 gins, 30 malt whiskies and farm cider. The lounge has some interesting old local photographs. You can eat in the bar or in the 'Captain's Cabin' which is a little room where everything is shrunk to scale (old oak chest, model sailing ship, even the prints on the white stone walls). There are seats and tables under parasols at the front, with more in the terraced garden. This is a lovely spot just back from the sea and the inn is surrounded by splendid clifftop walks.

Popular food includes lunchtime sandwiches, local mussels in creamy cider, sage and onion sauce, smoked ham hock and black pudding terrine with apple and vanilla chutney, roast pumpkin salad with whipped ricotta, chicory marmalade and toasted seeds and grains, faggots with bubble and squeak mash, balsamic shallots and mint gravy, roast chicken, stuffed leg, pancetta, chestnuts, parsnips and fresh truffle, turbot fillet with grilled leeks, mussels and seaweed and dill butter, and puddings such as sticky ginger cake with butterscotch sauce and rum and raisin ice-cream and earl grey set cream with poached pears and chocolate sorbet; they also offer a two- and three-course set lunch. *Benchmark main dish: beer-battered haddock and chips £14.00. Two-course evening meal £21.00.*

Free house ~ Licensee Jackie Barnard ~ Real ale ~ Open 11-11 ~ Bar food 12-2.30, 5-9.30 ~ Restaurant ~ Children welcome ~ Dogs welcome ~ Wi-fi ~ Bedrooms: /£170 *Recommended by Charlie May, Celia and Rupert Lemming, Freddie and Sarah Banks, Selwyn Jones, Abigail Slater*

PORTHLEVEN SW6225 Map 1

Ship

(01326) 564204 – www.theshipinnporthleven.co.uk

Mount Pleasant Road (harbour) off B3304; TR13 9JS

Welcoming harbourside pub with fantastic views, pubby furnishings, real ales and tasty food and seats on terrace

In clement weather, the seats and tables in the terraced garden here make the most of the sea view, and at night the harbour is interestingly floodlit. Both the bustling bar and dining room share these views. There are open fires in stone fireplaces, quite a mix of chairs and tables on flagstones or bare boards, beer mats and brasses on the ceiling and walls, and various lamps and pennants. Sharps Cornish Coaster and Doom Bar, Skinners Porthleven and changing guests such as Penzance Brisons Bitter and Tintagel Harbour Special on handpump, farm cider and eight wines by the glass; background music. They also have a cosy, traditionally furnished and separate function room.

Tasty food includes lunchtime sandwiches, crispy salt and pepper squid with sweet chilli sauce, ham hock with pickled vegetables and mustard mayonnaise, spicy cajun chicken burger with avocado salsa, mussels in creamy cider sauce with fries, chestnut mushroom, new potato, halloumi and feta bake, salmon with crushed herby potatoes and fennel cream, steak in ale stew, good local steaks, and puddings. *Benchmark main dish: fish pie £11.95. Two-course evening meal £18.00.*

Free house ~ Licensee Christian Waite ~ Real ale ~ Open 11am-midnight ~ Bar food 12-2.30, 6-9; no food Sun evening Jan-Mar ~ Well behaved children welcome away from bar ~ Dogs welcome ~ Wi-fi ~ Occasional live music *Recommended by Clifford Blakemore, Francis and Mandy Robertson, Melanie and David Lawson, Alan Johnson, Guy Henderson*

ST IVES SW5441 Map 1

Queens

(01736) 796468 – www.queenshotelstives.com

High Street; TR26 1RR

Bustling inn just back from the harbour with a spacious bar, open fire, real ales and tasty food; bedrooms

When in this busy seaside town, our readers make their way here for a drink or a meal – and it's handy for the harbour. The open-plan, spreading bar has a relaxed atmosphere, all sorts of wooden chairs around scrubbed tables on bare floorboards, tartan banquettes on either side of the Victorian fireplace, a wall of barometers above a leather chesterfield sofa and some brown leather armchairs; also, fresh flowers and candles on tables and on the mantelpiece above the open fire. Red-painted bar chairs line the white marble-topped counter where they serve St Austell Proper Job and Tribute on handpump, eight wines by the glass (including a local one), a good choice of gins and rums and farm cider; background music, board games and TV for sports events. Bedrooms are attractive, airy and simply furnished, with cornish artwork on the walls and some period furniture. The window boxes and hanging baskets are quite a sight in summer.

Bedroom prices are for high summer. Even then you may get reductions for more than one night, or (outside tourist areas) weekends. Winter special rates are common, and many inns reduce bedroom prices if you have a full evening meal.

Championing local produce, the food includes sandwiches (until 3pm), tiger prawn, saffron, parsley and parmesan risotto, chicken liver pâté with chutney, vegetable lasagne, pulled pork burger with smoked cheddar and relish, sausages and mash with onion gravy, moules frites, beef stew with dumplings, rib-eye steak with trimmings and onion rings, and puddings such as chocolate brownie with rum and raisin ice-cream and apple, raisin and cinnamon crumble with vanilla ice-cream. *Benchmark main dish: beer-battered fish and chips £11.00. Two-course evening meal £18.00.*

St Austell ~ Tenant Neythan Hayes ~ Real ale ~ Open 10.30am-11pm ~ Bar food 12-2.30, 6-9.30 (12-3, 6-10 high season); 12-9 (6 in winter) Sun ~ Children welcome ~ Dogs allowed in bar ~ Wi-fi ~ Open mike Wednesday evening, live bands Sat evening ~ Bedrooms: £139/£179 *Recommended by Hilary and Neil Christopher, Pauline and Mark Evans, Rosie and John Moore, Alan Johnson, Julian Richardson*

ST MAWGAN SW8765 Map 1

Falcon

(01637) 860225 – www.thefalconinnstmawgan.co.uk

NE of Newquay, off B3276 or A3059; TR8 4EP

Friendly, creeper-covered stone inn with a cosy, simply furnished bar and dining room, real ales, good food and seats in spacious garden; bedrooms

Dating in part from the 16th c, this handsome place has been a village inn since 1758. The bar has a log fire in the big fireplace, farmhouse chairs and cushioned wheelbacks around an assortment of tables on patterned carpet, antique coaching prints and falcon pictures, and stools against the counter where friendly staff serve Dartmoor Jail Ale and Legend and a guest such as Pennine Natural Gold on handpump, several wines by the glass and 30 gins and 30 malt whiskies; background music and darts. A compact stone-floored dining room is similarly furnished. The pretty garden has a wishing well, a cobbled front courtyard and a lawn with picnic-sets. Bedrooms are comfortable.

Well liked food includes sandwiches, scallops and pork belly with tomato salsa, baked goats cheese with beetroot and watercress salad, falafel and halloumi burger with toppings, sausage and mash with onion gravy, baked hake with thai mango salad, barbecue pulled pork sliders with coleslaw and chips, steaks with trimmings and a choice of sauce, and puddings such as chocolate and hazelnut torte and toffee apple mini tarts with toffee sauce and vanilla ice-cream. *Benchmark main dish: steak in ale pie £11.50. Two-course evening meal £19.00.*

Free house ~ Licensees Steph and Jaimey Lomax ~ Real ale ~ Open 11-3, 5.30-11; 11am-midnight Fri, Sat; 12-11 Sun ~ Bar food 12-2.30, 6-9 ~ Restaurant ~ Children welcome away from the bar ~ Dogs allowed in bar ~ Wi-fi ~ Bedrooms: £65/£95 *Recommended by Anne Taylor, Philip J Alderton, Edward Nile, Peter Brix, Toby Jones*

ST MERRYN SW8874 Map 1

Cornish Arms

(01841) 532700 – www.rickstein.com/eat-with-us/the-cornish-arms

Churchtown (B3276 towards Padstow); PL28 8ND

Bustling pub with lots of cheerful customers, bar and dining rooms, real ales, good pubby food, friendly service and seats outside

If you wish to eat here during peak times, you must book a table in advance as it's extremely popular with holidaymakers. The main door leads into a sizeable informal area with a pool table and plenty of cushioned wall seating; to the left, a light, airy dining room overlooks the terrace. There's an upright modern woodburner, photographs of the sea and former games teams, and pale wooden dining chairs around tables on quarry tiles. This leads to two more linked rooms with ceiling joists; the first has pubby furniture on huge flagstones while the end room has more cushioned wall seating, contemporary seats and tables and parquet flooring. There's also a dining room to the back. St Austell Proper Job, Trelawny and Tribute on handpump, 12 wines by the glass, a local gin and a farm cider, friendly service, background music, board games and TV; they hold a beer and mussel festival every March. The window boxes are pretty and there are picnic-sets on a side terrace and on grass.

Reliably good food includes lightly curried crab mayonnaise, devilled kidneys on toast, burger with toppings and chips, tomato and blue cheese tart, sea bass with fennel mayonnaise, wild mushroom risotto, moules frites, local rump steak with tomato, thyme and shallot salad, and puddings such as a cheesecake and a crumble of the day. *Benchmark main dish: beer-battered cod and chips £13.95. Two-course evening meal £21.50.*

St Austell ~ Tenant Siebe Richards ~ Real ale ~ Open 11.30-11 ~ Bar food 12-3, 5-9; 12-8 Sun ~ Children welcome ~ Dogs welcome ~ Wi-fi *Recommended by Peter and Emma Kelly, Alfie Bayliss, Adam Jones, Colin and Daniel Gibbs*

ST TUDY SX0676 Map 1

St Tudy Inn

(01208) 850656 – www.sttudyinn.com

Off A391 near Wadebridge; PL30 3NN

Well run pub with several bars and dining rooms, good wines by the glass, first class food and seats outside

The excellent modern food cooked by the landlady is, of course, what most customers are here for. But this is no straightforward dining pub: they keep a good choice of drinks such as Sharps Doom Bar and a beer named for the pub on handpump, 25 wines by the glass and a couple of ciders. It's a welcoming and attractive place, and the main bar has a leather armchair beside a log fire in a raised fireplace (fairy lights on the bressumer beam), beer-cask seats, chairs and cushioned window seats by a mix of tables on floor slates, and stools against the wooden counter. The dining rooms are relaxed and informal with dark farmhouse, wheelback and elegant wooden chairs and tables on bare boards or rugs, a second fireplace, fresh flowers and candlelight; background music. There are picnic-sets under parasols at the front and more seats in the garden.

Cooked by the landlady, the imaginative food includes figs with honey, ticklemore cheese, honey and almonds, mussels with shallots, white wine, cream and parsley, shoulder of lamb with couscous, spinach and aubergine, a vegetable risotto of the day with courgette flowers and parmesan, line-caught mackerel with honey, spinach and horseradish cream, pork belly with mash and red wine sauce, monkfish with saffron, cream and rocket, sirloin steak with garlic, tarragon butter and rustic chips, and puddings such as chocolate mousse with vanilla seeded ice-cream and treacle tart with clotted cream. *Benchmark main dish: fish stew £16.00. Two-course evening meal £23.00.*

Free house ~ Licensee Emily Scott ~ Real ale ~ Open 11am-midnight; 11-10 Sun ~ Bar food 12-2.30, 6.30-9; not Sun evening ~ Restaurant ~ Children welcome ~ Dogs allowed in bar ~ Wi-fi *Recommended by Caroline Prescott, Lindy Andrews, Guy Henderson, Gordon and Patricia Gorringe, Simon and Sue Lamb*

TREBURLEY SX3477 Map 1

Springer Spaniel

(01579) 370424 – www.thespringerspaniel.co.uk

A388 Callington–Launceston; PL15 9NS

Cosy pub with highly popular food, friendly staff and a genuine welcome for all

An easy-going little bar in a friendly 18th-c pub, this has beams, antlers and a few copper pans on an exposed stone wall above a woodburning stove, books on shelves, pictures of springer spaniels, a rather fine high-backed settle and other country kitchen chairs and tables and old parquet flooring. Dartmoor Jail Ale and St Austells Tribute on handpump, ten good wines by the glass (including sparkling), home-made cocktails and a growing collection of gins; background music. A dining room has more bookcases, candles and similar tables and chairs, and stairs lead up to the main restaurant; a second woodburner is set into a slate wall with a stag's head above it. Outside in the small enclosed, paved garden are picnic-sets.

Good, interesting food includes sandwiches, torched mackerel with rhubarb, radish and dill, ham hock terrine with leeks, pineapple and piccalilli, deconstructed cheese and onion pasty, sausages and mash, burger with toppings and skinny fries, lamb shoulder with pea, celeriac and garlic, bream with crab bisque, apple and fennel, sirloin steak with garlic purée, and puddings such as chocolate délice with coffee, yoghurt and honeycomb and coconut rice pudding with raspberry jam. *Benchmark main dish: beer-battered fish and chips £14.00. Two-course evening meal £20.00.*

Free house ~ Licensee Victoria Martin ~ Real ale ~ Open 12-3, 5-11.30; 12-11.30 Sat, Sun ~ Bar food 12-3, 6-9; 12-9 Sun ~ Restaurant ~ Children welcome ~ Dogs allowed in bar ~ Wi-fi

Recommended by Isobel Mackinlay, Edward May, Hazel Hyde

TREVAUNANCE COVE SW7251 Map 1

Driftwood Spars

(01872) 552428 – www.driftwoodspars.co.uk

Off B3285 in St Agnes; Quay Road; TR5 0RT

Friendly inn with plenty of history, own microbrewery, a wide range of other drinks and popular food; nearby beach; bedrooms

Being close to a dramatic cove and beach, it can get busy here at peak times. Three small bars are timbered with massive ships' spars (the masts of great sailing ships, many of which were wrecked along this coast over the years), and furnishings include dark wooden farmhouse and tub chairs and settles around tables of different sizes, padded stools by the counter, old ship prints, lots of nautical and wreck memorabilia and woodburning stoves; table football. It's said that an old smugglers' tunnel leads from behind the bar up through the cliff. The modern dining room overlooks the cove. On handpump, they have their own Driftwood Alfies Revenge, Blackheads Mild, Lou's Brew and Spars with a guest such as Tintagel Merlins Muddle (they also hold three beer festivals a year), plus 25 malt whiskies, ten rums, seven gins and several wines by the glass. Staff are knowledgeable and friendly. The summer hanging baskets are pretty

The star-on-a-plate award, distinguishes pubs where the food is of exceptional quality. The knife-and-fork symbol just means the pub serves food.

and there are seats in the garden. Bedrooms are attractive and comfortable and have views of the coast.

Quite a choice of well regarded food includes lunchtime sandwiches and platters, local brie studded with garlic and rosemary and ale and red onion jam, crispy fried whitebait with lemon mayonnaise, spiced sweet potato and black bean burger with toppings and smoked tomato relish, chicken with pea and pancetta risotto, fish and coconut curry, slow-roast pork belly with parsnip purée, baby apples and potato fondant, and puddings such as lemon tart with gin and tonic sorbet and pistachio and yoghurt pannacotta with blackberries and granola. *Benchmark main dish: mussels cooked in ale and fennel £13.95. Two-course evening meal £19.00.*

Own brew ~ Licensee Louise Treseder ~ Real ale ~ Open 11-11; 11am-midnight Sat; 11-10.30 Sun ~ Bar food 12-2.30, 6 (5 in summer holidays)-9; 12-8 Sun ~ Restaurant ~ Well behaved children welcome away from main bar ~ Dogs welcome ~ Wi-fi ~ Live music some weekends (phone to check) ~ Bedrooms: £55/£95 *Recommended by David Thorpe, Nicola and Holly Lyons, Daniel King, Dr A McCormick*

WADEBRIDGE SW9972 Map 1

Ship

(01208) 813845 – www.shipinnwadebridge.co.uk

Gonvena Hill, towards Polzeath; PL27 6DF

One of the oldest pubs in town, with beams and open fires, carefully refurbished bars, real ales and good, seasonally changing food

As this was once owned by a shipbuilding family, there is plenty of nautical memorabilia on the rough whitewashed walls in the bar. Seating ranges from leather button-back wall banquettes to a collection of wooden dining chairs, stools and window seats topped with scatter cushions; also, flagstone or bare-boarded floors, books on shelves, church candles and open fires. High chairs line the counter where attentive staff serve Coastal Poseidon Extra, Otter Bitter and Sharps Doom Bar on handpump and 12 wines by the glass (they hold a wine club on the first Tuesday of the month); background music. There are two dining areas, one with high rafters and brass ship lights. The small, sunny decked terrace outside has seats and tables.

Well executed food includes sandwiches of the week, local crab with curried mayonnaise, pickled carrot and coriander, smoked ham hock terrine with pineapple pickle, shrimp caesar salad with bacon and brioche croutons, basil gnocchi with pesto, spinach, broad beans and parmesan, moules frites, chicken ballotine with sautéed potatoes, asparagus purée, spinach, mushrooms and madeira, herb-crusted cod loin with courgettes, tomatoes, orange and pine nuts, rib-eye steak with fat chips, shallots and a choice of three sauces, and puddings such as lemon posset with gooseberry compote and a flapjack and eton mess. *Benchmark main dish: 12-hour slow-cooked pork £15.75. Two-course evening meal £21.00.*

Punch ~ Tenants Rupert and Sarah Wilson ~ Real ale ~ Open 12-2.30, 5-11; 12-10 Sun ~ Bar food 12-2 (3 Sun), 5-9 (9.30 Fri, Sat); no food Sun evening except high season ~ Children welcome ~ Dogs allowed in bar ~ Wi-fi ~ Wine club first Tues of month, folk club last Tues of month *Recommended by Lindy Andrews, Jamie Green, Buster May, James and Sylvia Hewitt, Trish and Karl Soloman, Lorna Eaketts-Rogers, Nicola and Stuart Parsons*

Please keep sending us reports. We rely on readers for news of new discoveries, and particularly for news of changes – however slight – at the fully described pubs: feedback@goodguides.com, or (no stamp needed) The Good Pub Guide, FREEPOST RTXY–ZCBC–BBAZ, Stream Lane, Sedlescombe, Battle TN33 0PB.

Also Worth a Visit in Cornwall

Besides the fully inspected pubs, you might like to try these pubs that have been recommended to us and described by readers. Do tell us what you think of them: feedback@goodguides.com

ALTARNUN SX2280

Kings Head (01566) 86241
Five Lanes; PL15 7RX Old mansard-roofed beamed village pub; two or three west country ales and generous helpings of reasonably priced pubby food from sandwiches up including popular Sun carvery, carpeted lounge set for dining with big log fire, slate floor restaurant and public bar with another fire, friendly staff and ghost of former landlady Peggy Bray; background music; children and dogs welcome, picnic-sets on front terrace and in small raised garden, comfortable bedrooms, big breakfast, open (and food) all day, handy for A30.
(Dr D J and Mrs S C Walker)

ALTARNUN SX2083

★**Rising Sun** (01566) 86636
NW; village signed off A39 just W of A395 junction; PL15 7SN Tucked-away 16th-c pub with traditionally furnished L-shaped main bar, low beams, slate flagstones and coal fires, well kept Penpont St Nonnas, Skinners Lushingtons and guests, real cider and nice wines by the glass, highly rated food including local seafood and daily specials, good crab sandwiches too, efficient friendly service, restaurant; background music, pool, free wi-fi; well behaved children and dogs (in bar) welcome, seats on suntrap terrace and in garden, pétanque, camping field, nice village with beautiful church, open all day weekends. *(Sandra and Miles Spencer)*

BLISLAND SX1073

★**Blisland Inn** (01208) 850739
Village signposted off A30 and B3266 NE of Bodmin; PL30 4JF Traditional old-fashioned local with convivial landlord (usually in shorts) and friendly staff; six well kept west country ales (some tapped from the cask) including two badged for the pub from Sharps, also proper cider and fruit wines, generous helpings of tasty food cooked by landlady, beams and ceiling covered in pump clips and collection of mugs, beer-related posters and other memorabilia, carpeted lounge with several barometers, toby jugs on beams, also a family room with pool and table skittles; background and regular live music; dogs welcome, picnic-sets out on front grass overlooking village green, close to Camel Trail cycle path, open all day (till midnight Sat), no food Sun evening. *(Julian Richardson, Peter Brix, Ian Herdman, Malcolm and Madeline Ashton)*

BODINNICK SX1352

Old Ferry (01726) 870237
Across the water from Fowey; coming by road, to avoid the ferry queue, turn left as you go downhill – car park on left before pub; PL23 1LX 17th-c inn just up from the river with lovely views from terrace, dining room and some of its 12 comfortable bedrooms; traditional bar with nautical memorabilia, old photographs and woodburner, back room hewn into the rock, well kept Sharps ales and at least one guest, nice wines, good food from lunchtime sandwiches up including daily specials and children's menu, friendly french landlord and helpful staff; free wi-fi; good circular walks, lane by pub in front of ferry slipway is extremely steep and parking limited, open (and food) all day. *(Sabine and Gerald Grimshaw)*

BOSCASTLE SX0990

★**Napoleon** (01840) 250204
High Street, top of village; PL35 0BD Welcoming 16th-c thick-walled cottage at the top of this steep quaint village (fine views halfway up); cosy rooms on different levels, slate floors, oak beams and log fires, interesting Napoleon prints and lots of knick-knacks, good food from daily changing menu in bar areas or small evening restaurant, well kept St Austell ales tapped from the cask, decent wines and coffee, traditional games; background music (live Fri, sing-along Tues), sports TV, free wi-fi; children and dogs welcome, small covered terrace and large sheltered garden, open all day. *(Peter Brix)*

BOSCASTLE SX0991

Wellington (01840) 250202
Harbour; PL35 0AQ Old hotel's long beamed and carpeted bar, good varied choice of fairly priced food including vegan menu (other special diets catered for), cornish ales kept well, nice coffee and cream teas, roaring log fire, upstairs gallery area and separate evening restaurant with more upmarket menu; Weds folk night, quiz first Mon of month; children and dogs (in bar) welcome, big secluded garden, bedrooms and apartments in adjacent mill, Museum of Witchcraft and Magic nearby, open all day, food all day weekends. *(Andrew and Michelle Revell)*

BOTALLACK SW3632

Queens Arms (01736) 788318
B3306; TR19 7QG Honest welcoming old pub with good home-made food including local fish/seafood and meat sourced within

3 miles, well kept Sharps, Skinners and guests, friendly service, log fires (one in unusual granite inglenook), dark wood furniture, tin mining and other old local photographs on stripped-stone walls, family extension; dogs welcome, tables out in front and pleasant back garden, wonderful clifftop walks nearby, lodge accommodation, open all day. *(Dr D J and Mrs S C Walker)*

BREAGE SW6128

Queens Arms (01326) 564229
3 miles W of Helston just off A394; TR13 9PD Welcoming corner pub with long part-carpeted bar, plush banquettes and woodburner at each end, up to eight well kept ales and good home-made pubby food (all day Sun) including daily specials, small restaurant with another woodburner, pool and darts in games part; background music (live first Sun of month), quiz nights, sports TV, free wi-fi; children and dogs welcome, seats outside under cover, barbecue and play areas, two bedrooms (also caravan pitches), farmer's market last Sat of month, interesting medieval wall paintings in church opposite, open all day. *(Mr and Mrs John Clifford)*

CADGWITH SW7214

★**Cadgwith Cove Inn** (01326) 290513
Down very narrow lane off A3083 S of Helston; no nearby parking; TR12 7JX Friendly little pub in fishing cove with lovely walks in either direction; simply furnished front rooms with bench seating on parquet, log fire, local photos and nautical memorabilia, big back bar with huge fish mural, well kept Otter, Sharps, Skinners and a guest from Atlantic, popular food including local fish/seafood (can be pricey) and good Sun lunch; background music, folk night Tues, local singers (sea shanties) Fri, TV, darts and board games; children and dogs welcome, front terrace overlooking old fishermen's sheds, comfortable bedrooms with sea views, coastal walks, open all day. *(Griffiths family, David Eberlin, Canon Michael Bourdeaux)*

CALSTOCK SX4368

Tamar (01822) 832487
The Quay; PL18 9QA Cheerful and relaxed 17th-c local opposite the Tamar with its imposing viaduct; dark stripped stone, flagstones, tiles and bare boards, pool room with woodburner, more modern back dining room, good generous straightforward food and summer cream teas, well kept Sharps Doom Bar and other west country ales such as Exeter Avocet, reasonable prices and friendly service; some live music; children (away from bar) and well behaved dogs welcome, nicely furnished terrace, heated smokers' shelter, hilly walk or ferry to Cotehele (NT). *(Tracey and Stephen Groves, Dave Braisted)*

CHAPEL AMBLE SW9975

Maltsters Arms (01208) 812473
Off A39 NE of Wadebridge; PL27 6EU Country pub-restaurant with good food including Sun lunchtime carvery, friendly accommodating staff, Sharps ales and Weston's cider, log fire, beams, stripped stone and painted half-panelling, modern back extension; music and quiz nights; children and dogs (on slate-floored area) welcome, seats outside. *(Serena and Adam Furber)*

CHARLESTOWN SX0351

Harbourside (01726) 67955
Part of Pier House Hotel; PL25 3NJ Glass-fronted split-level warehouse conversion alongside the recently refurbished Pier House Hotel (also worth a visit), great spot looking over classic little harbour and its historic sailing ships; St Austell ales and guests, popular reasonably priced food including sandwiches and pizzas, friendly efficient service; live music every other Sat, sports TVs, pool; children and dogs welcome, interesting film-set conservation village with shipwreck museum, good walks, parking away from pub, open (and food) all day. *(Dr A McCormick)*

CHARLESTOWN SX0351

Rashleigh Arms (01726) 438024
Charlestown Road; PL25 3NJ Modernised early 19th-c inn with public bar, lounge and dining area; five well kept St Austell ales, three guests and good wine choice, popular fairly priced food including burger menu and Sun carvery, quick friendly service; background music, fortnightly live bands Fri, trad jazz second Sun of month, free wi-fi; children welcome, dogs in bar, disabled facilities, front terrace and garden with picnic-sets, eight bedrooms (some with sea views), ten more in nearby Georgian house, Grade II listed car park (site of old coal storage yards), short walk to attractive harbour with tall ships, open (and food) all day. *(Toby Jones)*

COMFORD SW7339

Fox & Hounds (01209) 820251
Comford; A393/B3298; TR16 6AX Rambling low-beamed roadside pub; stripped stone and painted panelling, mix of old and new furniture including some comfortable leather seating, rugs on flagstones, woodburners, good range of well liked freshly made food from pub favourites up, daily specials and Sun carvery, well kept St Austell ales, good friendly service; background music, pool and darts; children and dogs (in bar) welcome, disabled facilities, nice floral displays at front, picnic-sets in back garden, open all day weekends. *(Trevor Burgess)*

COVERACK SW7818

Paris (01326) 280258
The Cove; TR12 6SX Comfortable Edwardian seaside inn above harbour in beautiful fishing village; carpeted L-shaped bar serving well kept St Austell ales and Healey's cider, large relaxed dining room with white tablecloths and spectacular bay views, wide choice of enjoyable food from sandwiches to good fresh fish, Sun lunchtime carvery, helpful cheery staff, model of namesake ship (wrecked nearby in 1899); popular Weds quiz, pool, free wi-fi; children and dogs welcome, more sea views from garden and six bedrooms, limited parking. *(Sally Harrison)*

CRACKINGTON HAVEN SX1496

Coombe Barton (01840) 230345
Off A39 Bude–Camelford; EX23 0JG Extended old inn in beautiful setting overlooking splendid sandy bay (fine sunsets); much enjoyed food from shortish fairly priced menu (booking advised), three rotating cornish ales and good choice of other drinks, efficient friendly service; background and some live music, quiz nights, sports TV, pool and darts; children welcome, dogs in bar, picnic-sets on side terrace, lovely cliff walks, roomy bedrooms, open all day. *(Jim Slattery, Andrew Low)*

CRAFTHOLE SX3654

★**Finnygook** (01503) 230338
B3247, off A374 Torpoint road; PL11 3BQ This popular 15th-c coaching inn suffered a bad fire in Dec 2017 and was closed for renovations as we went to press – news please. *(David and Sally Cullen)*

CROWS NEST SX2669

Crows Nest (01579) 345930
Signed off B3264 N of Liskeard; OS Sheet 201 map reference 263692; PL14 5JQ Characterful and welcoming little 17th-c pub; well kept St Austell ales, decent wines and good home-made food including daily specials, bowed beams hung with hops, stirrups, brasses and so forth, exposed stonework and big log fire, chatty locals; outside loos; children and dogs welcome (pub dog is Sully), picnic-sets on terrace by quiet lane, handy for Bodmin Moor walks, open all day weekends. *(David and Charlotte Green)*

CUBERT SW7857

★**Smugglers Den** (01637) 830209
Off A3075 S of Newquay; TR8 5PY Big open-plan 16th-c thatched pub tucked away in small hamlet; good locally sourced food and up to four beers (May pie and ale festival), several wines by the glass, friendly staff, neat ranks of tables, dim lighting, stripped stone and heavy beam and plank ceilings, west country pictures and seafaring memorabilia, steps down to part with huge inglenook, another step to big side dining room, also a little snug area with woodburner and leather armchairs; background and occasional live music; children and dogs welcome, small front courtyard and terrace (both decked) with nice country views, sloping lawn and play area, camping opposite, open all day. *(P and J Shapley, R K Phillips)*

DULOE SX2358

Plough (01503) 262556
B3254 N of Looe; PL14 4PN Popular restauranty pub with three country-chic linked dining rooms all with woodburners, dark polished slate floors, a mix of pews and other seats, good fairly priced food using locally sourced produce (must book weekends), reasonably priced wines, well kept St Austell, Sharps and summer guests, Cornish Orchards' cider, friendly helpful service; unobtrusive background music; children and dogs welcome, picnic-sets out by road, closed Tues lunchtime. *(Tracey and Stephen Groves, Anne Roots)*

EDMONTON SW9672

★**Quarryman** (01208) 816444
Off A39 just W of Wadebridge bypass; PL27 7JA Welcoming busy family-run pub adjoining small separately owned holiday courtyard complex; three-room beamed bar with interesting decorations including old sporting memorabilia, fairly pubby food from shortish menu with good individual dishes such as sizzling steaks and portuguese fish stew, quick friendly service, well kept Exeter Avocet, Padstow May Day and Skinners Lushingtons, seven wines by the glass; sports TV; well behaved children and dogs (on slate-floored area) allowed, disabled access (but upstairs lavatories), picnic-sets in front and courtyard behind, self-catering apartment, open all day. *(Isobel Mackinlay)*

EGLOSHAYLE SX0071

Earl of St Vincent (01208) 814807
Off A389, just outside Wadebridge; PL27 6HT Pretty flower-decked beamed dining pub with over 200 working antique clocks (many chiming), also golfing memorabilia, art deco ornaments, old pictures and rich furnishings, enjoyable home-made food from sandwiches to steaks, St Austell ales and Healey's cider; background music, outside loos; well behaved children allowed, no dogs inside, lovely garden. *(Paul Faraday)*

FALMOUTH SW8132

5 Degrees West (01326) 311288
Grove Place; TR1 4AU Modern split-level open-plan bar with mixed furnishings including squashy sofas and low tables on stripped wood floors, log fire in driftwood-effect fireplace, local artwork, enjoyable food from snacks to grills, five real ales, three ciders and good choice of other drinks including cocktails, back dining area; background and live music, free wi-fi; children

and dogs welcome, disabled facilities, seats out at front and on sheltered back terrace, open (and food) all day. *(Peter Brix)*

FALMOUTH SW8032

Beerwolf (01326) 618474
Bells Court (opposite Marks & Spencer); TR11 3AZ Stairs up to intriguing old pub-cum-bookshop hidden down little alley in centre of town; a former working men's club with raftered ceilings and eclectic mix of furniture on bare boards, good range of well kept changing beers and ciders, decent coffee, no food but can bring your own, friendly laid-back atmosphere; games including table tennis and pinball, free wi-fi; children and dogs welcome, a few picnic-sets outside, open all day. *(Peter Brix)*

FALMOUTH SW8033

Boathouse (01326) 315425
Trevethan Hill/Webber Hill; TR11 2AG Two-level pub with buoyant local atmosphere, four well kept beers featuring some smaller cornish brewers such as Black Rock, Dynamite Valley and Padstow, good range of other drinks, enjoyable home-made food including fresh fish/seafood, friendly service; background and live music; children and dogs (in bar) welcome, tables outside, upper deck with awning and fantastic harbour views, closed weekday lunchtimes in winter, otherwise open all day. *(Sally Harrison)*

FALMOUTH SW8132

★**Chain Locker** (01326) 311085
Custom House Quay; TR11 3HH Busy recently refurbished 16th-c pub in fine spot by inner harbour; St Austell ales, guest beers and nice wines by the glass, good food from sandwiches and sharing plates to local fish/seafood, friendly service, bare-boards and flagstone bar keeping its nautical theme with plenty to look at, woodburners, upstairs restaurant (they have a lift) with two new balconies taking in the views; background music, Tues quiz; well behaved children and dogs (in bar) welcome, quayside tables under parasols, six well appointed boutique bedrooms, open all day from 8am. *(Peter Brix)*

FALMOUTH SW8033

★**Chintz Symposium** (01326) 617550
High Street/Brewery Yard; TR11 2BY Upstairs bar with Alice in Wonderland-inspired décor, welcoming and relaxed and run by two brothers; wood floors, rafters, comfortable plain furniture and hot little stove, plenty of quirky features including pitched ceiling decorated with patchwork of wallpaper and prints, a gold room hidden behind a bookcase and loos with dinosaur and circus-tent themes; a couple of changing local ales, plenty of bottled beers, Healey's cider and 15 wines by the glass from carefully chosen list, also good range of spirits (some cornish ones), cheese and charcuterie boards, friendly service; live music and other events, board games; children and dogs (theirs is Pig) welcome, roof terrace, open all day weekends, from 5pm Mon, 2pm Tues-Fri; the Hand craft beer bar is below. *(IAA, HMW, Maria Sansoni)*

FALMOUTH SW8132

Front (01326) 212168
Custom House Quay; TR11 3JT Welcoming bare-boards quayside drinkers' pub; great changing selection of well kept ales, some tapped from the cask from hop-strewn barrel-fronted counter, also foreign beers and ciders/perries, friendly knowledgeable staff, no food but can bring your own (fish and chip shop above), good mix of customers; seats outside, open all day. *(Sally Harrisom, Toby Jones)*

FALMOUTH SW8032

Seven Stars (01326) 312111
The Moor (centre); TR11 3QA Quirky 17th-c local, unchanging, unsmart and not for everybody; friendly atmosphere with chatty regulars, up to six well kept ales tapped from the cask including Bass, Sharps and Skinners, quiet back snug; no food or mobile phones; dogs welcome, corridor hatch serving roadside courtyard, open all day. *(Toby Jones)*

FALMOUTH SW8032

Working Boat (01326) 314283
Greenbank Quay, off Stratton Place; TR11 2SP Part of the Greenbank Hotel set down by one of the up-river piers (town centre is a brisk ten minutes' walk); interior on varying levels with big windows overlooking the water, dark green walls and stripped plank wainscoting, some nautical touches and many interesting Falmouth pictures, black-tile or board floors, tables with candles in bottles, Skinners, St Austell and a couple of other real ales, decent wines by the glass and good fairly priced food, friendly efficient service; background music, quiz nights; tables out overlooking the natural harbour, another good bar and restaurant in the hotel, open all day. *(Peter Brix)*

FLUSHING SW8033

Royal Standard (01326) 374250
Off A393 at Penryn (or foot-ferry from Falmouth); St Peters Hill; TR11 5TP Compact pub just back from the waterfront with bistro-bar feel, enjoyable fairly priced blackboard food, local ales and decent wines by the glass, friendly helpful staff; background and live music; children and dogs welcome, picnic-sets on small front terrace, garden behind with harbour views, open all day. *(Geoff and Anne Marston)*

FLUSHING SW8033

Seven Stars (01326) 374373
Trefusis Road; TR11 5TY Old-style waterside pub with welcoming local atmosphere; good selection of well kept

ales (third-pint tasters available), pubby food including Mon evening fish and chips, coal fire, separate dining room; darts and pool; children and dogs welcome, pavement picnic-sets, great views of Falmouth (foot-ferry across), open all day. *(Geoff and Anne Marston)*

FOWEY SX1251

Galleon (01726) 833014

Fore Street; from centre follow car-ferry signs; PL23 1AQ Superb spot by harbour and estuary, good beer range (local/national) and decent choice of wines, popular food from extensive reasonably priced menu, friendly staff, slate-floor bar with modern décor, lots of solid pine and exposed stone, lofty river view dining area; live bands Fri night, projector TV, pool, free wi-fi; children welcome, disabled facilities, attractive waterside terrace and sheltered courtyard, seven bedrooms (two with estuary view), open all day. *(David Appleyard)*

FOWEY SX1251

★**King of Prussia** (01726) 833694

Town Quay; PL23 1AT Handsome quayside building with roomy upstairs bar, bay windows looking over harbour to Polruan, enjoyable food from ciabattas and deli boards up, St Austell ales and sensibly priced wines, friendly helpful staff, side restaurant; background music, free wi-fi; children and dogs welcome, partly enclosed outside seating area, six pleasant bedrooms (all with views), open all day. *(David and Charlotte Green)*

FOWEY SX1251

Lugger (01726) 833435

Fore Street; PL23 1AH Centrally placed St Austell pub with good mix of locals and visitors (can get very busy); up to three of their well kept ales in spotless front bar with nautical memorabilia, small back dining area, generous helpings of enjoyable good value food including local fish, friendly helpful staff, children welcome, pavement tables, open all day. *(Caroline Prescott)*

FOWEY SX1251

★**Ship** (01726) 832230

Trafalgar Square; PL23 1AZ Bustling 16th-c beamed pub with open fire in bare-boards bar, maritime prints, nauticalia and other bits and pieces, St Austell ales and good wines by the glass, steps up to dining room with big stained-glass window, well liked interesting food along with pub favourites and sandwiches; background and live music; children and dogs welcome, bedrooms (some oak-panelled), open all day. *(Edward Nile)*

GERRANS SW8735

Royal Standard (01872) 580271

The Square; TR2 5EB Friendly little local (less touristy than nearby Plume of Feathers in Portscatho), narrow doorways linking plainly furnished carpeted rooms, a couple of well kept cornish ales, Sharps cider and Skinners lager, short choice of well chosen wines, enjoyable pub food from sandwiches to local fish, old photographs on white plaster or black boarded walls, brass shell cases and kitchen utensils, woodburner; children welcome away from bar, disabled access, sunny beer garden, opposite interesting 15th-c church (rebuilt in 19th c after fire), self-catering apartment. *(Theocsbrian)*

GOLANT SX1254

Fishermans Arms (01726) 832453

Fore Street (B3269); PL23 1LN Partly flagstoned small waterside local with lovely views across River Fowey from front bar and terrace, good value generous pubby food and up to four well kept west country ales, friendly service, log fire, interesting old photographs; fortnightly quiz Tues; children and dogs welcome, pleasant garden, open all day in summer (all day Fri-Sun, closed Mon in winter). *(Ian Herdman)*

GRAMPOUND SW9348

Dolphin (01726) 882435

A390 St Austell–Truro; TR2 4RR Friendly St Austell pub with their well kept ales and decent choice of wines, good generous pub food (not Mon), two-level bar with black beams and some panelling, polished wood or carpeted floors, pubby furniture with a few high-backed settles, pictures of old Grampound, woodburner; Tues quiz, darts, pool, TV; children welcome, dogs in bar, wheelchair access from car park, beer garden, good smokery opposite, handy for Trewithen Gardens, open all day weekends, closed Mon lunchtime. *(Julian Richardson)*

GWEEK SW7026

Black Swan (01326) 221502

Village signed from A394 at Edgcumbe; TR12 6TU Welcoming village pub with large open-plan beamed bar, woodburner in big stone fireplace, well kept ales such as St Austell and Skinners, enjoyable reasonably priced food from sandwiches and light meals up, good friendly service, roomy back restaurant; pool, TV; children and dogs welcome, picnic-sets out at the side, short walk from seal sanctuary, four bedrooms, open all day. *(David Appleyard)*

GWITHIAN SW5840

Red River (01736) 753223

Prosper Hill; TR27 5BW Stone-built one-room village pub with several well kept ales and eclectic range of popular generously served food, welcoming friendly staff; background and acoustic live music, quiz nights, free wi-fi; children and dogs welcome, picnic-sets in small garden across road, near dunes, beach and coastal path, open all day summer, closed Mon in winter. *(Craig Burkinshaw)*

HELFORD PASSAGE SW7626

★**Ferryboat** (01326) 250625
Signed from B3291; TR11 5LB Busy old pub in lovely position by sandy beach (can book seats on terrace in advance); bar with farmhouse and blue-painted kitchen chairs, built-in cushioned wall seats and stripped tables on grey slates, woodburner, St Austell Proper Job, Tribute and a guest, real cider and a dozen wines by the glass, good food including local fish/seafood, friendly service, arched doorway to games room with pool and darts; some live music, free wi-fi; children and dogs (in bar) welcome, summer ferry from Helford village across the water, can also hire small boats and arrange fishing trips, walk down from car park is quite steep, open (and food) all day. *(Julian Richardson)*

HELSTON SW6527

★**Blue Anchor** (01326) 562821
Coinagehall Street; TR13 8EL Many love this no-nonsense, highly individual, 15th-c thatched pub; quaint rooms off corridor, flagstones, stripped stone, low beams and well worn furniture, ancient back brewhouse still producing distinctive Spingo ales including Middle, a very strong Special and Bragget made with honey and herbs, no food but can bring your own (good pasty shop nearby), family room, traditional games and skittle alley, friendly local atmosphere; regular live music, Mon quiz; back garden with own bar, four bedrooms in house next door, generous breakfast, open all day. *(Peter Johnson)*

HESSENFORD SX3057

Copley Arms (01503) 240209
A387 Looe–Torpoint; PL11 3HJ Friendly 17th-c village pub popular with passing tourists; focus on enjoyable reasonably priced food from bar snacks to grills in linked carpeted areas, well kept St Austell ales and nice choice of wines, variety of teas and coffee, log fires, tables in cosy booths in one part, sofas and easy chairs in another; background and some live music, Thurs quiz; children and dogs (in bar) welcome, a few roadside picnic-sets by small River Seaton, fenced play area, five bedrooms, open all day. *(Sabine and Gerald Grimshaw)*

HOLYWELL SW7658

St Pirans (01637) 830205
Holywell Road; TR8 5PP Great location backing on to dunes and very popular with holidaymakers; well kept ales such as St Austell and Sharps, decent wines and enjoyable food from sandwiches and pub favourites up, cream teas, friendly helpful staff; children and dogs welcome, tables on large back terrace, open all day, but closed out of season and Mon in Apr. *(Edward Nile)*

HOLYWELL SW7658

Treguth (01637) 830248
Signed from Cubert, SW of Newquay; TR8 5PP Ancient whitewashed stone and thatch pub near large beach; cosy low-beamed carpeted bar with big stone fireplace, bigger dining room at back, three real ales and popular food cooked by landlord-chef, friendly service; regular live music, Weds quiz, pool; children and dogs welcome, handy for campsites and popular with holidaymakers, open all day weekends. *(Toby Jones)*

KINGSAND SX4350

Devonport (01752) 822869
The Cleave; PL10 1NF Lovely bay views from front bar of this popular pub, well kept changing local ales and good food including local fish/seafood, nice sandwiches and afternoon teas too, friendly efficient service even at busy times, light airy modern décor, warming log fire; occasional live music, free wi-fi; children and dogs welcome, tables out by sea wall, closed Tues during term time. *(David and Charlotte Green)*

LANIVET SX0364

Lanivet Inn (01208) 831212
Truro Road; PL30 5ET Welcoming old stone pub with long L-shaped bar, dining end with woodburner and generous helpings of popular good value food (best to book) from sandwiches/wraps to daily specials, St Austell ales and a guest, friendly efficient service; background and live music, fortnightly quiz Tues, pool, darts and TV; children and dogs (in bar) welcome, seats out at front and in fenced garden, handy for Saints Way trail, unusual pub sign recalling days when village supplied bamboo to London Zoo's pandas, open all day weekends. *(Andrew and Michelle Revell)*

LELANT SW5436

Watermill (01736) 757912
Lelant Downs; A3074 S; TR27 6LQ Mill-conversion family dining pub; working waterwheel behind with gearing in dark-beamed central bar opening into brighter airy front extension, upstairs evening (and Sun lunchtime) restaurant, Sharps Doom Bar, Skinners Betty Stogs and a guest, enjoyable food served by friendly staff; live music Fri, quiz night Weds, free wi-fi; dogs welcome, good-sized pretty streamside garden, open all day. *(Alan Johnson)*

LIZARD SW7012

Top House (01326) 290974
A3083; TR12 7NQ Neat clean pub with friendly staff and regulars; tasty food from sandwiches and snacks up including fresh fish, children's meals and cream teas, well

If we know a pub has an outdoor play area for children, we mention it.

kept St Austell ales and guests, lots of good local sea pictures, fine shipwreck relics and serpentine craftwork (note the handpumps), warm log fire; folk music Mon; dogs welcome in bar, disabled access, sheltered terrace, eight bedrooms in adjoining building (three with sea views), good coastal walks, open all day in summer, all day weekends winter. *(Toby Jones)*

LIZARD SW7012

Witchball (01326) 290662

Lighthouse Road; TR12 7NJ Small friendly beamed pub popular with locals and visitors (booking recommended in season), good food from sandwiches and pizzas to fresh fish/seafood, well kept ales such as Cornish Chough, St Austell and Skinners, cornish cider, cheerful helpful staff; Sat quiz; children and dogs welcome, front terrace, open all day summer, closed winter lunchtimes Mon-Wed. *(Clifford Blakemore)*

LOSTWITHIEL SX1059

Earl of Chatham (01208) 872269

Grenville Road; PL22 0EP Traditional 16th-c split-level pub with beams, bare stone walls and open woodburner, generous helpings of enjoyable home-made food including popular Sun lunch, St Austell ales and nice choice of wines, friendly staff; children and dogs welcome, terrace picnic-sets, bedrooms, open all day. *(Sally Harrison)*

LOSTWITHIEL SX1059

Royal Oak (01208) 872552

Duke Street; PL22 0AG Welcoming old pub continuing well under present licensees; St Austell Tribute, Sharps Doom Bar and guests, traditional cider, several wines by the glass and a gin menu, good generously served pub food including Sun carvery, amiable helpful staff, bar, lounge and evening dining area, open fires; background and live music (Fri), free wi-fi; children welcome, dogs in bar (theirs is Radar), terrace picnic-sets under large willow, six comfortable clean bedrooms, open all day. *(Sandra and Miles Spencer)*

LUDGVAN SW5033

White Hart (01736) 740175

Off A30 Penzance–Hayle at Crowlas; TR20 8EY Ancient stone-built village pub, friendly and welcoming, with three west country beers tapped from the cask and good home-made food including blackboard specials, small unspoilt beamed rooms with wood and stone floors, nooks and crannies, woodburners; background music, quiz first Weds of month; children and dogs welcome, back garden with decked area, interesting church next door, open all day, no food Sun evening in winter. *(Toby Jones)*

MANACCAN SW7624

New Inn (01326) 231301

Down hill signed to Gillan and St Keverne; TR12 6HA Refurbished part-thatched community-owned pub in attractive village setting; opened-up bar area with painted beam-and-plank ceiling, exposed stonework and blue/grey half-panelling, cushioned wall benches and other fairly traditional furniture on flagstones, log fire, garden room opening on to small terrace, up to three well kept changing ales (often Dartmoor Legend), good home-cooked food served by friendly staff; children and dogs welcome, open all day Fri-Sun, evening meals only Fri and Sat out of season. *(Christopher Mobbs)*

MARAZION SW5130

Godolphin Arms (01736) 888510

West End; TR17 0EN Revamped and extended former coaching inn with wonderful views across to St Michael's Mount; light contemporary décor and modern furnishings, well liked food from sandwiches and sharing plates up, St Austell and Skinners ales, lots of wines by the glass and good coffee, friendly staff; children welcome, beachside terrace and upper deck, ten stylish bedrooms (most with sea view, some with balconies), good breakfast, open all day from 8am. *(Edward Nile)*

MARAZION SW5130

Kings Arms (01736) 710291

The Square; TR17 0AP Old one-bar pub in small square, comfortable, cosy and welcoming with warm woodburner, good well presented food (best to book) including local fish from regularly changing menu, well kept St Austell ales, friendly helpful staff; children and dogs welcome, sunny picnic-sets out in front, open all day. *(Alan Johnson)*

MAWGAN SW7025

Ship (01326) 221240

Churchfield, signed off Higher Lane; TR12 6AD Former 18th-c courthouse in nice setting near Helford River on the Lizard peninsula; high-ceiling bare-boards bar with woodburner in stone fireplace, end snug and raised eating area, emphasis on landlord's good food including local fish/seafood and seasonal game (best to book), takeaway fish and chips Tues, well kept ales and decent wine list, cheerful helpful young staff; well behaved children and dogs welcome, garden picnic-sets, closed lunchtimes and all day Sun, Mon. *(Roger Burton)*

MAWNAN SMITH SW7728

Red Lion (01326) 250026

W of Falmouth, off former B3291 Penryn–Gweek; The Square; TR11 5EP Old thatched and beamed pub with cosy series of dimly lit rooms including raftered bar; enjoyable food from light lunches to daily specials, friendly helpful service, well kept ales such as Bath Gem, St Austell Tribute and Skinners Betty Stogs, plenty of wines by the glass and good selection of rums, woodburner in huge stone fireplace, country and marine pictures, stoneware bottles/flagons and some other bric-a-brac; children (away from bar) and dogs welcome, disabled access, picnic-sets outside, handy for Glendurgan (NT) and Trebah gardens, open all day. *(David and Charlotte Green)*

MENHERION SX2862
Golden Lion (01209) 860332
Top of village by reservoir; TR16 6NW Newish management for this tucked-away little stone dining pub in nice spot by Stithians Reservoir; beamed bar and snug, woodburner, well kept St Austell ales, decent wines by the glass and local gin, good choice of tasty well presented food, friendly welcoming staff, restaurant with lake view; children and dogs welcome, wheelchair access using ramps, disabled loo, attractive garden with play area, good walks, camping, open (and food) all day. *(Trevor Burgess, Peter Johnson)*

METHERELL SX4069
Carpenters Arms (01579) 351148
Follow Honicombe sign from St Anns Chapel just W of Gunnislake A390; Lower Metherell; PL17 8BJ Steps up to heavily black-beamed village local; huge polished flagstones and massive stone walls in cosy bar, carpeted lounge/dining area, three well kept ales such as St Austell, Sharps and Timothy Taylors Landlord, good reasonably priced food (not lunchtimes Mon-Thurs) cooked by landlord including stone-baked pizzas Mon and Fri evenings, friendly staff and regulars; live music, free wi-fi; children and dogs welcome, front terrace, farmers' market and brunch first Sat of month, handy for Cotehele (NT), open all day Fri-Sun, from 2pm other days. *(Peter Brix)*

MEVAGISSEY SX0144
★**Fountain** (01726) 842320
Cliff Street, down alley by Post Office; PL26 6QH Popular low-beamed fishermen's pub; slate floor, some stripped stone and a welcoming coal fire, old local pictures, well kept St Austell ales and good reasonably priced food including local fish/seafood, friendly staff, back bar with glass-topped pit (the remains of an old fish-oil press), small upstairs evening restaurant; children and dogs welcome, pretty frontage with picnic-sets, three bedrooms, open all day in summer. *(Paul Faraday)*

MEVAGISSEY SX0144
Kings Arms (01726) 843904
Fore Street; PL26 6UQ Small welcoming local tucked away behind the harbour; good varied choice of ales and other drinks from slabby-topped wooden counter, landlord's well liked interesting food including home-smoked fish and own-baked bread; background and maybe some acoustic live music, board games; children and dogs welcome, opening times can vary. *(Paul Faraday)*

MEVAGISSEY SX0144
Ship (01726) 843324
Fore Street, near harbour; PL26 6UQ 16th-c pub with interesting alcove areas in big open-plan bar, low beams and flagstones, nautical décor, woodburner, fairly priced pubby food (small helpings available) from sandwiches to good fresh fish, well kept St Austell ales, cheery uniformed staff; background and some live music, Tues quiz, games machines, pool; children and dogs (in the bar) welcome, five bedrooms, open all day (food all day in summer). *(R K Phillips)*

MITCHELL SW8554
★**Plume of Feathers** (01872) 510387
Off A30 Bodmin–Redruth, by A3076 junction; take southwards road then first right; TR8 5AX Popular 16th-c coaching inn with appealing contemporary décor (same management as the Lewinnick Lodge in Newquay); several linked bar and dining rooms, stripped beams and standing timbers, local artwork on pastel walls, painted dados and two open fires, good food from sandwiches up with some emphasis on fish, Weds steak night, Sharps, Skinners and St Austell ales, several wines by the glass, impressive dining conservatory with central olive tree; background music; children (away from bar) and dogs welcome, picnic-sets under parasols in well planted garden areas, comfortable stable-conversion bedrooms, open all day from 8am. *(R J Herd, GSB, R K Phillips)*

MITHIAN SW7450
★**Miners Arms** (01872) 552375
Off B3285 E of St Agnes; TR5 0QF Cosy old stone-built pub with traditional small rooms and passages, pubby furnishings and open fires, fine old wall painting of Elizabeth I in back bar, good choice of popular reasonably priced food from sandwiches/baked potatoes up, St Austell, Sharps and Skinners kept well, friendly helpful staff; background music, board games; children and dogs (in bar areas) welcome, seating in sheltered front cobbled forecourt, back terrace and garden, open (and food) all day. *(Serena and Adam Furber)*

MORWENSTOW SS2015
Bush (01288) 331242
Signed off A39 N of Kilkhampton; Crosstown; EX23 9SR Newish licensees for this 13th-c beamed pub in fine spot near coastal walks and surfing beaches; character bar with traditional pubby furniture on flagstones, horse tack and copper knick-knacks, woodburner in stone fireplace, two St Austell ales and a guest, real cider and several wines by the glass, reasonably priced pubby food from sandwiches up, friendly

staff, various dining rooms, one with second woodburner, another overlooking garden and its heated dining huts; background and some live music, fortnightly quiz Weds; children and dogs (in bar) welcome, bedrooms with sea views and a self-catering cottage, open (and food) all day. *(Sophie Ellison, Charles Todd, Julian Thorpe, Malcolm and Madeline Ashton)*

MOUSEHOLE SW4626

★**Ship** (01736) 731234

Harbourside; TR19 6QX Busy harbourside pub with opened-up main bar; black beams and panelling, built-in wooden wall benches and stools around low tables on granite flagstones, sailors' fancy ropework, cosy open fire. St Austell ales and several wines by the glass, straightforward pubby food; maybe background music, free wi-fi; children and dogs (in bar) welcome, bedrooms above or in next-door cottage (some overlooking the sea), best to park at top of this pretty village and walk down (traffic in summer can be a nightmare), Christmas harbour lights also worth seeing, open all day. *(Julie Swift, Peter and Emma Kelly, Simon and Alex Knight, Alan Johnson, Harriet Mitchell)*

NEWLYN SW4629

★**Tolcarne** (01736) 363074

Tolcarne Place; TR18 5PR Refurbished 17th-c quayside pub with highly rated food from chef-landlord, much emphasis on local fish/seafood (menu changes daily) and must book, friendly efficient service, St Austell Tribute, Skinners Betty Stogs and maybe a local microbrew; live jazz Sun lunchtime; children and dogs welcome, terrace (harbour wall cuts off view), good parking. *(Jan)*

NEWQUAY SW8061

Fort (01637) 875700

Fore Street; TR7 1HA Massive pub in magnificent setting high above surfing beach and small harbour; full St Austell range and decent food from sandwiches and baked potatoes up, friendly staff coping well at busy times, open-plan areas divided by balustrades and surviving fragments of former harbourmaster's house, good solid furnishings from country kitchen to button-back settees, soft lighting, games part with two pool tables, excellent indoor children's play area; great views from long glass-walled side section and sizeable garden with multi-level terrace and further play areas, open (and food) all day. *(Alan Johnson)*

NEWQUAY SW8061

Lewinnick Lodge (01637) 878117

Pentire headland, off Pentire Road; TR7 1QD Modern flint-walled bar-restaurant built into bluff above the sea – big picture windows for the terrific views; light airy bar with wicker seating, three or four well kept ales and plenty of wines by the glass, spreading dining areas with contemporary furnishings on light oak flooring, popular bistro-style food from shortish menu, good service and pleasant relaxed atmosphere; children and dogs (in bar) welcome, modern seats and tables on terraces making most of the stunning Atlantic views, ten bedrooms, open all day; same management as the Plume of Feathers in Mitchell. *(Isobel Mackinlay)*

PADSTOW SW9175

★**Golden Lion** (01841) 532797

Lanadwell Street; PL28 8AN Old inn dating from the 14th c; cheerful black-beamed locals' bar and high-raftered back lounge with plush banquettes, well kept Sharps Doom Bar, Skinners Betty Stogs and a guest, simple reasonably priced bar lunches including good crab sandwiches, evening steaks and fresh fish, friendly staff, coal fire and woodburner; pool in family area, background music, sports TV; dogs welcome, colourful floral displays at front, terrace tables, three good bedrooms, open all day (no food Sun evening). *(GSB)*

PADSTOW SW9175

Harbour Inn (01841) 533148

Strand Street; PL28 8BU Attractive old-school pub just back from the harbour and a quieter alternative; long room with nautical bric-a-brac, pubby furnishings including some high-backed settles, comfy sofas in front area, piano and woodburner, well kept St Austell ales and enjoyable generously served traditional food, friendly helpful staff; children and dogs welcome, open all day. *(Edward Nile)*

PADSTOW SW9175

London (01841) 532554

Lanadwell Street; PL28 8AN Intimate proper fishermen's local with lots of pictures and nautical memorabilia, mix of tables, chairs and built-in benches, friendly ex-merchant navy landlord, half a dozen well kept St Austell ales and decent choice of malt whiskies, good value bar food including fresh local fish, back dining area (arrive early for a table), two log fires; background and some live music; children and dogs welcome, four comfortable reasonably priced bedrooms named after boats, open all day. *(Sally Harrison)*

PAUL SW4627

Kings Arms (01736) 7311224

Mousehole Lane, opposite church; TR19 6TZ Beamed local with cosy bustling atmosphere, enjoyable sensibly priced pub food from baked potatoes and basket

If you report on a pub that's not a featured entry, please tell us any lunchtimes or evenings when it doesn't serve bar food.

meals up, well kept St Austell ales, Healey's cider and good selection of gins; live music including bluegrass on Tues; children welcome, dogs in one bar, a few picnic-sets out in front, five bedrooms, open all day in summer. *(Toby Jones)*

PELYNT SX2054

Jubilee (01503) 220312

B3359 NW of Looe; PL13 2JZ Beamed village inn dating from the 16th c; enjoyable locally sourced food from sandwiches and sharing boards up, well kept St Austell ales, Healey's cider and decent range of other drinks including cornish rum and gin, friendly helpful staff, spotless interior with interesting Queen Victoria mementoes (pub renamed in 1897 to celebrate her diamond jubilee), some handsome antique furnishings, log fires under copper canopies, separate bar with winter pool table and darts; children and dogs welcome, disabled facilities, large terrace, 11 comfortable bedrooms, open all day (food all day in summer, all day weekends winter). *(Paul Faraday)*

PENDEEN SW3834

North (01736) 788417

B3306, opposite the school; TR19 7DN Friendly little creeper-clad village pub set back from the road; well kept St Austell ales and popular food including range of curries and good Sun roasts, single bar with interesting tin-mining memorabilia, upstairs restaurant looking over fields to the sea; children and dogs welcome, boules in big back garden, bedrooms and camping, good walks nearby, open all day. *(Dr D J and Mrs S C Walker)*

PENDOGGETT SX0279

Cornish Arms (01208) 880335

B3314; PL30 3HH Old beamed coaching inn under newish ownership; traditional oak settles on front bar's polished slate floor, well kept Sharps ales, a guest beer and several wines by the glass from good list, around 30 gins, enjoyable food (all day weekends, not Mon lunchtime) including sandwiches and interesting burgers, friendly efficient service, comfortably spaced tables in dining room with wooden floor, proper back locals' bar with woodburner; children and dogs (in bars) welcome, disabled access, distant sea view from terrace, seven bedrooms, open all day. *(Andrew Low)*

PENELEWEY SW8140

★Punch Bowl & Ladle

(01872) 862237 *B3289; TR3 6QY* Thatched dining pub dating from the 15th c; very enjoyable freshly made food from sandwiches to daily specials, four St Austell ales, Healey's cider and good wine and whisky selection, helpful friendly service, dark beams, some white-painted stone walls and oak panelling, rustic bric-a-brac and big sofas, steps down to lounge/dining area, restaurant; soft background music, quiz second and fourth Sun of month, free wi-fi; children (away from bar) and dogs welcome, wheelchair access (not from small side terrace), handy for Trelissick Garden (NT), open all day. *(Jean P & Myriam Alderson)*

PENZANCE SW4730

Admiral Benbow (01736) 363448

Chapel Street; TR18 4AF New owner for this wonderfully quirky two-floor pub, still packed with interesting nautical paraphernalia and full of atmosphere; St Austell Proper Job, Sharps Doom Bar and a west country guest, friendly staff, cosy corners and log fire, downstairs restaurant in captain's cabin style (new chef being recruited as we went to press), second bar upstairs and nice view from back room; children and dogs (in some areas) welcome, open all day. *(Julian Richardson)*

PENZANCE SW4730

Crown (01736) 351070

Victoria Square, Bread Street; TR18 2EP Friendly little backstreet corner local with neat bar and back snug, own Cornish Crown beers and several wines by the glass, no food but can bring your own; live acoustic music Mon, quiz Tues, board games; children and dogs welcome, a few seats out in front, open all day. *(Julian Richardson)*

PENZANCE SW4729

Dolphin (01736) 364106

Quay Street, opposite harbour after swing-bridge; TR18 4BD Old stone-built pub with enjoyable good value food including fresh fish, up to four well kept St Austell ales and good wines by the glass, roomy bar on different levels, nautical memorabilia and three resident ghosts; pool and darts; children and dogs welcome, pavement picnic-sets, three comfortable bedrooms with sea/harbour views, no car park (public one not far away), handy for Scillies ferry, open (and food) all day. *(Edward Nile)*

PERRANARWORTHAL SW7738

Norway (01872) 864241

A39 Truro–Penryn; TR3 7NU Large beamed pub with half a dozen linked areas, good choice of food including daily specials and Sun carvery, Tues burger night and other themed evenings, St Austell ales and several wines by the glass, cream teas, good friendly service, open fires, panelling and mix of furniture on slate flagstones, restaurant; background music, free wi-fi; children and dogs welcome, tables outside, four bedrooms, open (and food) all day. *(Usha and Terri Patel)*

PERRANWELL STATION SW7739

Royal Oak (01872) 863175

Village signposted off A393 Redruth–Falmouth and A39 Falmouth–Truro; TR3 7PX Traditional chatty village pub, carpeted black-beamed bar with paintings by local artists, candlelit tables in snug room behind, big fireplace, St Austell Proper Job, Sharps Doom Bar, Skinners Lushingtons and a guest, proper cider and several wines by the glass, hearty helpings of enjoyable home-cooked food including specials, good friendly service; free wi-fi; children and dogs (in bar) welcome, picnic-sets out at front, more seats in back garden, good surrounding walks, open all day weekends. *(Sandra and Miles Spencer)*

PHILLEIGH SW8739

★**Roseland** (01872) 580254

Between A3078 and B3289, NE of St Mawes just E of King Harry Ferry; TR2 5NB In small hamlet handy for the King Harry Ferry and Trelissick Garden (NT); two cosy black-beamed bar rooms, one with flagstones, the other carpeted, wheelbacks and built-in red cushioned seats, horsebrasses, interesting old photographs and some framed giant beetles, woodburner, tiny lower area liked by locals, side restaurant too, well kept Skinners Betty Stogs, Sharps Doom Bar and a guest, nice wines by the glass and enjoyable home-made food, friendly helpful service; folk night first Weds of month (not summer), free wi-fi; children and dogs (in bar) welcome, seats on pretty paved front terrace, may open all day weekends in high season. *(Mr and Mrs Richard Osborne, R and S Bentley, Phil and Jane Villiers)*

POLPERRO SX2051

Crumplehorn Mill (01503) 272348

Top of village near main car park; PL13 2RJ Converted mill and farmhouse keeping beams, flagstones and some stripped stone, snug lower bar leading to long main room with cosy end eating area, well kept cornish ales, wide choice of popular food from snacks to blackboard specials (booking advised), friendly efficient service, log fire; children and dogs welcome, outside seating and working mill wheel, bedrooms and self-catering apartments, open all day. *(Serena and Adam Furber)*

POLPERRO SX2050

Three Pilchards (01503) 272233

Quay Road; PL13 2QZ Small low-beamed local behind fish quay; generous helpings of reasonably priced food from baguettes to good fresh fish, well kept St Austell Tribute, up to four guest beers and decent wines by the glass, efficient obliging service even when busy, lots of black woodwork, dim lighting, simple furnishings, open fire in big stone fireplace; weekend live music; children and dogs welcome, picnic-sets on terrace up steep steps (lovely views), open all day. *(Sally Harrison)*

POLRUAN SX1250

★**Lugger** (01726) 870007

The Quay; back roads off A390 in Lostwithiel, or foot-ferry from Fowey; PL23 1PA Popular and friendly waterside pub; steps up to cosy beamed bar with open fire and woodburner, well kept St Austell ales, good freshly cooked food (they'll cater for special diets) from bar snacks to daily specials including local fish/seafood, Sun carvery, restaurant on upper level; quiz and live music nights; children, dogs and boots welcome, not suitable for wheelchairs, good local walks, limited nearby parking (steep hill to main car park), open all day. *(Caroline Prescott)*

PORT ISAAC SW9980

★**Golden Lion** (01208) 880336

Fore Street; PL29 3RB Popular well positioned 18th-c pub keeping friendly local atmosphere in simply furnished old rooms; bar and snug with open fire, window seats and balcony tables looking down on rocky harbour and lifeboat slip far below, upstairs restaurant, enjoyable food including good local fish, well kept St Austell ales from well stocked bar, amiable helpful staff; background music, pool, darts; children and dogs welcome, dramatic cliff walks, open all day. *(Julian Richardson)*

PORTHALLOW SW7923

Five Pilchards (01326) 280256

SE of Helston; B3293 to St Keverne, then village signed; TR12 6PP Sturdy old-fashioned stone-built local in secluded cove right by shingle beach; lots of salvaged nautical gear, interesting shipwreck memorabilia and model boats, woodburner, four real ales such as St Austell, Bays, Dartmoor and Exeter, a nearby cider and enjoyable reasonably priced food including local fish, friendly chatty staff, conservatory; children and dogs welcome, seats out in sheltered yard, sea-view bedrooms, open all day Sun, closed in winter Mon lunchtime and Tues. *(Geoff and Anne Marston)*

PORTHLEVEN SW6325

Atlantic (01326) 562439

Peverell Terrace; TR13 9DZ Friendly buzzy pub in great setting above the harbour; good value tasty food including bargain OAP lunch (Mon, Weds, Fri) and other deals, ales such as St Austell and Skinners from boat-shaped counter, Weston's cider, big open-plan lounge with well spaced seating and cosier alcoves, good log fire in granite fireplace, carpeted dining room with trompe l'oeil murals; live music/entertainment Sat evening, Mon quiz, TV for major sports, darts, free wi-fi; children and dogs welcome, lovely bay views from raised front terrace, open all day. *(David Appleyard)*

PORTHLEVEN SW6225

Harbour Inn (01326) 573876

Commercial Road; TR13 9JB Large neatly kept pub-hotel in outstanding harbourside setting; expansive lounge and bar with dining area off, big public bar, well kept St Austell ales and good range of pubby food, carvery Wed lunchtime and Sun, well organised friendly service; unobtrusive background music (live Sat), Thurs quiz, free wi-fi; children and dogs (in bar) welcome, picnic-sets on spacious quayside terrace, 15 well equipped bedrooms (some with harbour view), good breakfast, open all day. *(Paul Faraday)*

PORTHTOWAN SW6948

★**Blue** (01209) 890329
Beach Road, East Cliff; car park (fee in season) advised; TR4 8AW Popular easy-going bar (not a traditional pub) by stunning beach attracting customers of all ages; big picture windows looking across terrace to huge expanse of sand and sea, wicker and white chairs around pale tables on grey-painted floorboards, cream or orange walls, ceiling fans and some large ferns, ales from St Austell, Sharps and Skinners, several wines by the glass, cocktails and shots, various coffees, hot chocolates and teas, all-day food from 10am brunch on including nachos with toppings, burgers, superfood salads and stone-baked pizzas; background music (live Sat evening), free wi-fi; children and dogs welcome, open all day (till midnight Fri, Sat), closed Mon-Thurs evenings in winter. *(Edward May, Karl and Frieda Bujeya, Martine and Fabio Lockley)*

PORTLOE SW9339

Ship (01872) 501356
At top of village; TR2 5RA Cheerful traditional local in charming fishing village; L-shaped bar with tankards hanging from beams, nautical bric-a-brac, local memorabilia and an amazing beer bottle collection, straightforward pubby tables and chairs on red carpet, open fire, St Austell ales, cider/perry and six wines by the glass, generously served food from shortish menu; background music, sports TV, darts, free wi-fi; children and dogs (in bar) welcome, sloping streamside garden across road, comfortable bedrooms, beach close by. *(Paul Faraday)*

PORTSCATHO SW8735

Plume of Feathers (01872) 580321
The Square; TR2 5HW Largely stripped-stone coastal village pub with some sea-related bric-a-brac and pictures in two comfortable linked areas, also small side bar and separate restaurant, St Austell ales and enjoyable reasonably priced pubby food, friendly staff; background music, free wi-fi; children, dogs and boots welcome, disabled access (steps to restaurant and gents'), picnic-sets out under awning, lovely coast walks, open all day in summer (and other times if busy). *(Edward Nile)*

ROCK SW9375

★**Mariners** (01208) 863679
Rock Road; PL27 6LD Modern dining pub with huge windows taking in the lovely estuary views; light spacious bar with slate flooring and bare stone or painted walls, contemporary metal chairs and wall seats around pale wood-topped tables, old black and white photos and modern prints, highly regarded food from open kitchen, well kept Sharps ales and good wines by the glass, similarly furnished upstairs restaurant with balcony; background music (live every second Sun in summer), TV; children and dogs welcome, seats on front terrace (or can sit on sea wall), open all day. *(Jill and Dick Archer, Alan and Linda Blackmore)*

ROSUDGEON SW5529

Falmouth Packet (01736) 762240
A394; TR20 9QE Comfortably modernised old pub with bare-stone walls, slate/carpeted floors and open fire, good food using local produce (booking advised), own pickles, relishes etc for sale, well kept Penzance ales and guests, family run with good friendly service, conservatory; children and dogs welcome, wheelchair access, picnic-sets out at front and on paved back terrace, self-catering cottage, open all day (till 6.30pm Sun), closed Mon in winter. *(Nick and Sylvia Pascoe)*

RUAN LANIHORNE SW8942

★**Kings Head** (01872) 501263
Village signed off A3078 St Mawes Road; TR2 5NX Country pub in quiet hamlet with interesting church nearby; relaxed small bar with log fire, Skinners and a guest, maybe farm cider, very well liked food especially local fish/seafood, dining area to the right divided in two, lots of china cups hanging from ceiling joists, cabinet filled with old bottles, hunting prints and cartoons, separate restaurant to the left; background music; well behaved children allowed in dining areas, dogs in bar only, terrace across road and nice lower beer garden, walks along Fal estuary, closed winter Sun evening and Mon; for sale, so may be changes. *(Julian Richardson)*

SENNEN COVE SW3526

Old Success (01736) 871232
Cove Hill; Cove Road off A30; TR19 7DG Glorious Whitesand Bay view from the terraced garden or inside this seaside hotel; beamed bar with lifeboat and other nautical memorabilia, log fire, St Austell ales from plank-fronted servery, enjoyable food including fresh local fish, friendly helpful staff; background and some live music; children and dogs welcome, 14 comfortable bedrooms (good breakfast), four self-catering apartments, popular with surfers, open all day. *(Roger and Donna Huggins)*

ST BREWARD SX0977

Old Inn (01208) 850711
Off B3266 S of Camelford; Churchtown; PL30 4PP Broad slate flagstones, low oak beams, stripped stonework and two massive granite fireplaces dating from the 11th c, ales such as Sharps Doom Bar, proper ciders

and several wines by the glass, enjoyable good value food including popular Sun carvery, roomy extended restaurant with tables out on deck; background music, darts, pool, free wi-fi; children and dogs welcome, moorland behind (cattle and sheep wander into the village), open all day in summer. *(Alan McQuilan)*

ST DOMINICK SX4067

Who'd Have Thought It

(01579) 350214 *Off A388 S of Callington; PL12 6TG* Large comfortable country pub with popular reasonably priced home-made food (booking advised) including gluten-free and vegan choices, well kept St Austell ales, a guest beer and good value wine list, friendly competent service, superb Tamar views especially from conservatory, beams and open fire; live music and quiz nights; children and dogs (in bar) welcome, garden tables, handy for Cotehele (NT), open all day. *(John Evans)*

ST EWE SW9746

Crown (01726) 843322

Pub signed from Kestle and Polmassick; PL26 6EY Tucked-away 16th-c village pub with thoroughly traditional décor; low black-painted beams, big slate flagstones and carpet, two fireplaces decorated with shiny horsebrasses, china in glazed corner cupboards, wheelback chairs, pews and a splendid high-backed settle, four St Austell ales kept well and good value food from light lunchtime dishes up, also bargain OAP lunch Fri, back overflow dining room up steps; children and dogs welcome, disabled access/facilities, very handy for Lost Gardens of Heligan. *(IAA, HMW, Maria Sansoni)*

ST ISSEY SW9271

Ring o' Bells (01841) 540251

A389 Wadebridge–Padstow; Churchtown; PL27 7QA Traditional slate-clad 18th-c village pub with open fire at one end of beamed bar, pool table the other, well kept Courage Best, St Austell Tribute, Sharps Doom Bar and Skinners Betty Stogs, good choice of wines and whiskies, friendly service, enjoyable sensibly priced food (own vegetables and pork) in long narrow side dining room; live music; children and dogs welcome, decked courtyard with pretty hanging baskets and tubs, three bedrooms, car park across road, open all day weekends and can get packed in summer. *(Sally Harrison)*

ST IVES SW5140

Golden Lion (01736) 797935

Market Place, next to church; TR26 1RZ Refurbished 19th-c two-room pub with friendly relaxed atmosphere, Skinners Betty Stogs and guests, proper ciders, enjoyable good value pubby food from sandwiches and baked potatoes up; live music and quiz nights, sports TV; children and dogs welcome, beer garden behind, open all day. *(Alan Johnson)*

ST IVES SW5140

Lifeboat (01736) 794123

Wharf Road; TR26 1LF Thriving family-friendly quayside pub with decent choice of generously served food including fresh fish/seafood, well kept St Austell ales, spacious interior with harbour-view tables and cosier corners, nautical theme including lifeboat pictures, friendly helpful staff; background music, sports TV, darts; no dogs inside, disabled access/facilities, open (and food) all day. *(Peter Brix)*

ST IVES SW5441

Pedn Olva (01736) 796222

The Warren; TR26 2EA Hotel rather than pub, but has well kept reasonably priced St Austell ales in roomy bar, fine views of sea and Porthminster beach (especially from tables on roof terrace), all-day bar food and separate restaurant, good service; comfortable bedrooms. *(Alan Johnson)*

ST IVES SW5140

★Sloop (01736) 796584

The Wharf; TR26 1LP Popular low-beamed, panelled and flagstoned harbourside inn, bright St Ives School pictures and attractive portrait drawings in front bar, booth seating in back bar, good choice of food from sandwiches and baguettes to lots of fresh local fish, quick friendly service even though busy, well kept ales such as Greene King Old Speckled Hen and Sharps Doom Bar, good coffee, upstairs evening restaurant; background and live music, TV; children in eating area, beach view from roof terrace and seats out on cobbles, bedrooms, open all day (breakfast from 9am), handy for Tate gallery. *(P and J Shapley, Alan Johnson)*

ST IVES SW5140

Union (01736) 796486

Fore Street; TR26 1AB Popular and friendly low-beamed local, roomy but cosy, with good value food from sandwiches to local fish, well kept Sharps Doom Bar and Weston's Old Rosie cider, decent wines and coffee, small hot fire, leather sofas on carpet, dark woodwork and masses of ship photographs; background music; dogs welcome. *(Alan Johnson)*

ST JUST IN PENWITH SW3731

Kings Arms (01736) 788545

Market Square; TR19 7HF Friendly pub with three separate carpeted areas, granite walls, beamed and boarded ceilings, open fire, shortish menu of good home-made food (not Sun evening in winter), well kept ales and

We say if we know a pub has background music.

decent coffee; background music, Weds quiz, free wi-fi; children and dogs welcome, tables out in front, open all day. *(Alan Johnson)*

ST JUST IN PENWITH SW3731

★**Star** (01736) 788767
Fore Street; TR19 7LL Low-beamed two-room local with friendly landlord and relaxed informal atmosphere; five well kept St Austell ales, no food (can bring your own lunchtime sandwiches or pasties), dimly lit main bar with old mining photographs on dark walls, ceiling covered in flags, coal fire; nostalgic juke box, live celtic music Mon, open mike Thurs, darts and euchre; tables in attractive backyard with smokers' shelter, open all day. *(Paul Faraday)*

ST KEW SX0276

★**St Kew Inn** (01208) 841259
Village signposted from A39 NE of Wadebridge; PL30 3HB Popular 15th-c beamed pub next to village church; unchanging slate-floored bar with fire in old black range, two dining areas including neat restaurant with stone walls, winged high-backed settles and other traditional furniture on tartan carpet, log fire in stone fireplace, St Austell ales from cask and handpump, gin menu, well liked food (not Sun evening in winter) from lunchtime baguettes to good Sun lunch, friendly attentive service; live music every other Fri; children away from bar and dogs welcome, pretty flowering tubs and baskets outside, picnic-sets in garden over road, open all day in summer. *(David and Charlotte Green)*

ST MAWES SW8433

Idle Rocks (01326) 270771
Tredenham Road; TR2 5AN Civilised waterfront hotel by edge of harbour; pleasant small bar area and separate lounge, two-tier restaurant looking on to terrace and sea, Sharps Doom Bar (bottled beers only in winter) and decent wines by the glass, good food from bar snacks up, friendly helpful staff; well behaved dogs (but no small children) allowed on sun terrace, smallish bedrooms overlooking the water are the best bet, open all day. *(R K Phillips)*

ST MAWES SW8433

★**Rising Sun** (01326) 270233
The Square; TR2 5DJ Light and airy pub across road from harbour wall; bar on right with end woodburner and sea-view bow window, rugs on stripped wood and a few dining tables, sizeable carpeted left-hand bar and conservatory, well prepared tasty food from local fish to good steaks, cream teas, well kept St Austell ales and nice wines by the glass, friendly young staff, buzzy atmosphere; background music, free wi-fi; children and dogs welcome, awkward wheelchair access, picnic-sets on sunny front terrace, comfortable bedrooms, open (and food) all day. *(Phil and Jane Villiers)*

ST MAWES SW8533

St Mawes Hotel (01326) 270170
Marine Parade; TR2 5DN Harbourside hotel's relaxed bar-restaurant; bare boards and simple furnishings, woodburner, enjoyable food from small plates and pizzas up, St Austell Tribute and a summer guest, nice wines and good italian coffee, more room upstairs with sofas, scatter-cushion wall seats and second woodburner, small balcony overlooking the sea, friendly helpful young staff; children welcome, a few tables out in front, good if not cheap bedrooms (lovely views), open all day. *(Phil and Jane Villiers)*

TINTAGEL SX0588

Olde Malthouse (01840) 770461
Fore Street; PL34 0DA Restored 14th-c beamed pub with inglenook bar and restaurant, good generously served food (booking advised) from ciabattas up, well kept local ales including Tintagel, friendly helpful service; some live music, free wi-fi; children and dogs welcome, tables on roadside terrace, bedrooms, good walks, closed Sun, otherwise open all day, may shut Nov-Mar. *(Usha and Terri Patel)*

TOWAN CROSS SW4078

Victory (01209) 890359
Off B3277; TR4 8BN Comfortable and welcoming roadside local with four real ales including Skinners and enjoyable well priced food, good helpful service, nice unfussy country décor and warm relaxed atmosphere; pool and euchre; children and dogs welcome, beer garden, camping, handy for good uncrowded beaches, open all day. *(Caroline West)*

TREBARWITH SX0585

Port William (01840) 770230
Trebarwith Strand; PL34 0HB Lovely seaside setting with glorious views and sunsets, waterside picnic-sets across road and on covered terrace, maritime memorabilia and log fires inside, enjoyable food from sandwiches and baked potatoes to daily specials (they may ask to swipe a card before you eat), St Austell ales; background music; children and dogs welcome, eight well equipped comfortable bedrooms, open all day. *(John Ledbury)*

TREEN SW3923

★**Logan Rock** (01736) 810495
Just off B3315 Penzance–Land's End; TR19 6LG Cosy traditional low-beamed bar with good log fire, well kept St Austell ales and tasty pub food from sandwiches and pasties to nice steaks, small back snug with collection of cricketing memorabilia (welcoming landlady eminent in county's cricket association), family room (no under-14s in bar); dogs welcome on leads, pretty split-level garden behind with covered area, good coast walks including to Logan Rock

itself, handy for Minack Theatre, open all day in season and can get very busy. *(David Appleyard)*

TREGADILLETT SX2983

★ **Eliot Arms** (01566) 772051
Village signposted off A30 at junction with A395, W end of Launceston bypass; PL15 7EU Creeper-covered pub with series of small rooms, interesting collections including 72 antique clocks, 700 snuffs and hundreds of horsebrasses, also barometers, old prints and shelves of books/china, fine mix of furniture on Delabole slate from high-backed settles and chaises longues to more modern seats, open fires, well kept St Austell Tribute, Wadworths 6X and a scottish house beer, big helpings of enjoyable pubby food, friendly staff and chatty locals; background music, darts, games machine; children and dogs welcome, outside seating front and back, lovely hanging baskets and tubs, two bedrooms, open all day. *(Alan McQuilan)*

TREGONY SW9244

Kings Arms (01872) 530202
Fore Street (B3287); TR2 5RW Light and airy 16th-c village coaching inn; long traditional main bar and two beamed and panelled front dining areas, St Austell ales, Healey's cider/perry and nice wines, enjoyable sensibly priced pub food using local produce, tea and coffee, prompt service and friendly chatty atmosphere, two fireplaces, one with huge cornish range, pubby furniture on carpet or flagstones, old team photographs, back games room; children and dogs welcome, disabled access, tables in pleasant suntrap garden. *(A E Forbes)*

TREMATON SX3960

Crooked Inn (01752) 848177
Off A38 just W of Saltash; PL12 4RZ Friendly family-run inn down long drive; open-plan bar with lower lounge leading to conservatory (lovely views), beams, straightforward furnishings and log fire, cornish ales and decent wines by the glass, good choice of popular freshly made food from doorstep sandwiches to daily specials, helpful service; children and dogs welcome, terrace overlooking garden and valley, play area, roaming ducks and other animals, 15 bedrooms, open all day. *(John Evans)*

TRURO SW8244

★ **Old Ale House** (01872) 271122
Quay Street; TR1 2HD City-centre tap for Skinners brewery, five of their ales plus guests (some from casks behind bar), west country ciders and several wines by the glass including country ones, tasty food from snacks and sharing plates up, good cheerful service, dimly lit beamed bar with engaging mix of furnishings, sawdust on the floor, beer mats on walls and ceiling, some interesting 1920s bric-a-brac, life-size cutout of Betty Stogs, daily newspapers and free monkey nuts, upstairs room with table football; juke box, live music Mon and Sat evenings; children (away from bar) and dogs welcome, open all day. *(Alan Johnson)*

TRURO SW8244

White Hart (01872) 277294
New Bridge Street; TR1 2AA Compact old city-centre pub with nautical theme (aka Crab & Ale House); friendly staff and locals, up to five well kept ales including Fullers London Pride, St Austell Tribute and Sharps Doom Bar, good reasonably priced traditional lunchtime food; background music, weekend live music/discos, quiz Thurs; children and dogs welcome, open all day (till 2am Fri, Sat). *(Alan Johnson)*

TYWARDREATH SX0854

New Inn (01726) 813901
Off A3082; Fore Street; PL24 2QP Welcoming 18th-c local in nice village setting, St Austell ales and guests including Bass tapped from the cask, good food (not Sun evening, Mon or Tues) in back restaurant and conservatory, friendly relaxed atmosphere; some live music; children and dogs welcome, large secluded garden behind with play area, open all day. *(Sandra and Miles Spencer)*

WAINHOUSE CORNER SX1895

Old Wainhouse (01840) 230711
A39; EX23 0BA New licensees as we went to press for this popular roadside pub – reports please; main flagstoned bar with attractive built-in settle and stripped rustic farmhouse chairs around mix of tables, beams hung with old tools, horse tack, copper pans and so forth, large woodburner, simpler room off and dining room with high-backed chairs around pale wooden tables and another woodburner, Sharps beers, food has been good; children and dogs (in bar) welcome, picnic-sets on side grass, bedrooms looking towards the sea, South West Coast Path close by, open all day. *(Jim King, Justine and Neil Bonnett, R K Phillips, Andrew Low)*

WATERGATE BAY SW8464

Beach Hut (01637) 860543
B3276 coast road N of Newquay; TR8 4AA Great views from bustling modern beach bar appealing to customers of all ages; planked walls, cushioned wicker and cane armchairs around scrubbed wooden tables, corner snugs with banquettes and tile-topped tables, weathered stripped-wood floor and unusual sloping bleached-board ceiling, big windows and doors opening to glass-fronted deck with retractable roof, three real ales including Skinners, decent wines by the glass and lots of coffees and teas, enjoyable modern food served by friendly young staff; background music; dogs welcome in bar, easy wheelchair access, open all day from 9am (10.30am-5pm in winter). *(Caroline Prescott)*

ZELAH SW8151

Hawkins Arms (01872) 540339
A30; TR4 9HU Homely 18th-c beamed local; up to four well kept ales such as Bays, St Austell and Skinners, tasty generously served food from sandwiches to blackboard specials, friendly staff, woodburner in stone fireplace, restaurant; occasional live music and quiz nights; children and dogs welcome, back and side terraces, three bedrooms. *(Peter Brix, Sally Harrison)*

ZENNOR SW4538

★**Tinners Arms** (01736) 796927
B3306 W of St Ives; TR26 3BY Friendly welcome and good food from sandwiches to fresh local fish; long unspoilt bar with flagstones, granite, stripped pine and real fires each end, back dining room, well kept St Austell, Skinners and a house beer (Zennor Mermaid) from Sharps, farm cider, sensibly priced wines and decent coffee, helpful staff coping well at busy times, nice mix of locals and visitors; Thurs folk night; children, muddy boots and dogs welcome, tables in small suntrap courtyard, lovely windswept setting near coast path and church with 15th-c carved mermaid bench, bedrooms in building next door, open all day. *(Phil and Jane Villiers)*

ISLES OF SCILLY

ST AGNES SV8808

★**Turks Head** (01720) 422434
The Quay; TR22 0PL One of the UK's most beautifully placed pubs with idyllic sea and island views from garden terrace, can get packed on fine days; good food from pasties to popular fresh seafood (best to get there early), well kept ales such as Skinners Betty Stogs, proper cider, friendly licensees and good cheerful service; children and dogs welcome, closed in winter, otherwise open all day. *(Nigel Morton)*

ST MARTIN'S SV9116

Seven Stones (01720) 423777
Lower Town above Lawrence's Flats; TR25 0QW Stunning location and sea and islands views from this long single-storey stone building (the island's only pub); welcoming atmosphere and enjoyable food from sandwiches to local fish, well kept St Austell, Sharps and Skinners, five wines by the glass; some film and live music nights; children and dogs allowed, lots of terrace tables, wonderful walks, open all day in summer (Weds, Fri and Sat evenings, all day Sun till early evening in winter). *(Miranda and Jeff Davidson)*

ST MARY'S SV9010

Atlantic Inn (01720) 422323
The Strand; next to but independent from Atlantic Hotel; TR21 0HY Spreading and hospitable dark bar with well kept St Austell ales and popular pubby food including children's menu, sea-view restaurant, low beams, hanging boat and other nauticalia, mix of locals and tourists – busy evenings, quieter on sunny lunchtimes; background and live music, pool, darts, games machines, free wi-fi; dogs welcome in bar, nice raised verandah with wide views over harbour, bedrooms in adjacent hotel. *(Millie and Peter Downing)*

ST MARY'S SV9010

Mermaid (01720) 422701
The Bank; TR21 0HY Splendid picture-window views across town beach and harbour from back restaurant extension, dimly lit bar with lots of seafaring relics and ceiling flags, woodburner, steps down to second bar with stone floor and boat counter, enjoyable sensibly priced food including children's choices, Sun carvery, Ales of Scilly, Sharps and Skinners; background and some live music, pool, fruit machine; dogs welcome in bars, open all day and packed Weds and Fri when the gigs race. *(Millie and Peter Downing)*

ST MARY'S SV9110

Old Town Inn (01720) 422301
Old Town; TR21 0NN Nice local feel in welcoming light bar and big back dining area, wood floors and panelling, good freshly made food (not Mon-Weds in winter) from daily changing menu, up to four well kept ales including Ales of Scilly and Sharps Doom Bar, great range of ciders; live music including monthly folk club, cinema in back function room, pool and darts; children and dogs welcome, wheelchair access, tables in garden behind, three courtyard bedrooms, handy for airport, open all day in season (from 5pm weekdays, all day weekends in winter). *(Millie and Peter Downing)*

TRESCO SV8815

★**New Inn** (01720) 423006
New Grimsby; TR24 0QG Handy for ferries and close to the famous gardens; redecorated main bar with comfortable sofas, banquettes, planked partition seating and farmhouse tables and chairs, a few standing timbers, boat pictures, collection of old telescopes and model yacht, pavilion extension with wicker seats on blue-painted floors, Ales of Scilly and Skinners, a dozen good wines by the glass, quite a choice of spirits and several coffees, enjoyable not especially cheap food including daily specials; background music, board games, darts and pool; children and dogs (in bar) welcome, seats on flower-filled sea-view terrace, 16 bedrooms and heated swimming pool, open all day in summer (all day Sun in winter, but closed Mon, Tues lunchtime and Weds). *(Bernard Stradling, R J Herd)*

Cumbria

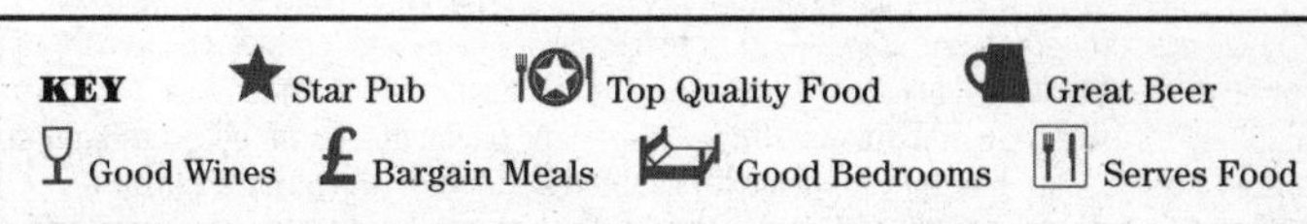

AMBLESIDE NY3704 Map 9

Golden Rule

(015394) 32257 – www.goldenrule-ambleside.co.uk

Smithy Brow; follow Kirkstone Pass signpost from A591 on N side of town; LA22 9AS

Simple town tavern with a cosy, relaxed atmosphere, and real ales

Thankfully, nothing changes here and it remains an unspoilt and unfussy town local. The bar area has built-in wall seats around cast-iron-framed tables (one with a local map set into its top), horsebrasses on black beams, assorted pictures on the walls, a welcoming winter fire and a relaxed atmosphere. Robinsons Cumbria Way, Dizzy Blonde, Double Hop, Trooper and Wizard on handpump and Weston's cider; they also offer various teas and good coffee all day. A brass measuring rule hangs above the bar (hence the pub's name). There's also a back room with TV (not much used), a room on the left with darts and a games machine, and another room, down a couple of steps on the right, with lots of seating. The backyard has benches and a covered heated area, and the window boxes are especially colourful. There's no car park.

The scotch eggs and pies (if they have them) run out fast, so don't assume you will get something to eat.

Robinsons ~ Tenant John Lockley ~ Real ale ~ Open 11am-midnight ~ Children welcome away from bar before 9pm ~ Dogs welcome ~ Wi-fi *Recommended by Nick Sharpe, Mike Benton, Arthur and Sarah Hedgcock, Abigail Slater*

AMBLESIDE NY3703 Map 9

Wateredge Inn

(015394) 32332 – www.wateredgehotel.co.uk

Borrans Road, off A591; LA22 0EP

Lakeside inn with plenty of room both inside and out, six ales on handpump and enjoyable all-day food; good bedrooms

'It's a real pleasure to stay here,' say readers who tend to return to this family-run inn on a regular basis. Bedrooms are stylish, comfortable and warm and have fine lake views, and staff are welcoming and attentive; the inn has its own moorings. The modernised bar has fine views through big windows over the sizeable garden that runs down to Lake Windermere. There's a wide mix of customers, a relaxed atmosphere, leather tub chairs around wooden tables on flagstones and several different areas leading off with similar furniture, exposed-stone or wood-panelled walls and interesting old photographs and paintings. A cosy and much favoured room has beams and timbering, sofas, armchairs and an open fire. The real ales on handpump include Jennings Cocker Hoop, Cumberland Ale and Sneck Lifter, Tirril Grasmere Gold and Wychwood Dirty Tackle and Hobgoblin and they offer nine wines by the glass, ten gins, several malt whiskies and quite a choice of coffees. Background music and board games. In warm weather, the picnic-sets close to the water get snapped up pretty quickly.

All-day food is of high quality: sandwiches and wraps, chicken liver parfait with orange, cinnamon and thyme butter, fish chowder, five-bean chilli with cheese, sour cream and lime, sea bream with mussel and dill risotto, steak and kidney pie, corn-fed chicken with a sage and onion stuffing ball, crispy bacon and caramelised red onion and red wine jus, lamb hotpot topped with sautéed potatoes with red cabbage, and puddings such as gooseberry and apple crumble with vanilla sauce. *Benchmark main dish: beer-battered fish and chips £13.25. Two-course evening meal £20.00.*

Free house ~ Licensee Derek Cowap ~ Real ale ~ Open 11-11 ~ Bar food 12-8.30 ~ Children welcome ~ Dogs allowed in bar ~ Wi-fi ~ Live music Fri, Sat ~ Bedrooms: £75/£140
Recommended by Max Simons, Heather and Richard Jones, John and Sylvia Harrop, Kerry and Guy Trooper, Edward Edmonton

BASSENTHWAITE LAKE NY1930 Map 9

Pheasant ★

(017687) 76234 – www.the-pheasant.co.uk

Follow Pheasant Inn sign at N end of dual carriageway stretch of A66 by Bassenthwaite Lake; CA13 9YE

Delightful, old-fashioned bar in smart hotel, with enjoyable bar food and a fine range of drinks; bedrooms

Of course, most customers are here to stay in the comfortable bedrooms and enjoy the particularly good food, but it's the surprisingly pubby and old-fashioned bar that many of our readers enjoy so much. This has mellow polished walls, cushioned oak settles, rush-seat chairs and library seats, and hunting prints and photographs. Coniston Bluebird Bitter, Cumbrian Legendary Loweswater Gold and Hawkshead Bitter on handpump, 16 good wines by the glass from a fine list, 80 malt whiskies and ten gins and ten vodkas all served by friendly, knowledgeable staff. There's a bistro at the front, a formal restaurant at the back overlooking the garden, and several comfortable lounges with log fires, beautiful flower arrangements, fine parquet flooring, antiques and plants. The garden has seats and tables and is surrounded by attractive woodland. Bedrooms are well equipped, comfortable and pretty, and two of them are pet-friendly. There are plenty of walks in all directions.

Very good food can be eaten in the bar, bistro or lounges at lunchtime, and in the bistro and restaurant only in the evening: sandwiches (until 4.30pm), haggis scotch egg with whisky and herb sauce, prawn cocktail, chicken caesar salad, cumberland sausages with creamy mash and onion gravy, venison burger with toppings and tomato and gin ketchup, ricotta tortellini with spinach and tomato sauce, sea bass fillet with parmentier potatoes and chive and cockle cream, and puddings such as chocolate and orange mousse and rhubarb and custard tart with meringue shards; they also offer a two- and three-course set lunch and early bird menu (6-7pm). *Benchmark main dish: shepherd's pie £14.50. Two-course evening meal £20.00.*

Free house ~ Licensee Matthew Wylie ~ Real ale ~ Open 11.30-11; 12-11 Sat ~ Bar food 12-2.30, 6-9 ~ Restaurant ~ Children welcome but must be over 8 in bedrooms ~ Dogs allowed in bar and bedrooms ~ Wi-fi ~ Bedrooms: £105/£120 *Recommended by Martin Day, Ian Herdman, Gordon and Margaret Ormondroyd, Patricia and Gordon Thompson, Dr D J & Mrs S C Walker*

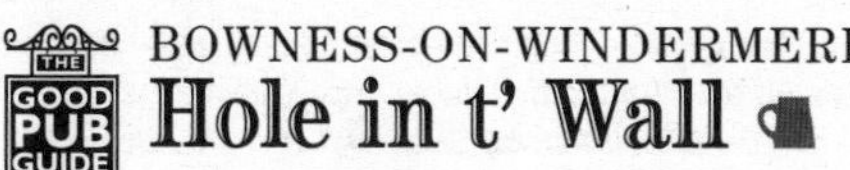

BOWNESS-ON-WINDERMERE SD4096 Map 9

Hole in t' Wall

(015394) 43488 – www.newhallinn.robinsonsbrewery.com

Fallbarrow Road, off St Martins Parade; LA23 3DH

Lively and unchanging town local with popular ales and friendly staff

An interesting stone tavern (and the oldest in town) with convivial licensees who welcome a wide mix of cheerful customers. There's a lot to look at in the character bar, and the split-level rooms have beams, stripped stone and flagstones, lots of country knick-knacks and old pictures, and a splendid log fire beneath a vast slate mantelpiece; the upper room has some noteworthy plasterwork. Robinsons Dizzy Blonde, Hartleys XB and Unicorn plus a couple of guest beers on handpump, 23 malt whiskies, a dozen gins and 11 vodkas; juke box in the bottom bar. The small flagstoned front courtyard has sheltered picnic-sets and outdoor heaters.

Bar food includes pâté of the day, scampi and chips, steak in ale or fish pies, a daily curry, steaks with trimmings, and puddings such as chocolate sponge and sticky toffee pudding. *Benchmark main dish: lamb henry £11.95. Two-course evening meal £19.00.*

Robinsons ~ Tenant Susan Burnet ~ Real ale ~ Open 11-11; 11am-11.30pm Fri, Sat; 12-11 Sun ~ Bar food 12-2.30, 6-8.30; 12-8 Fri, Sat; 12-5 Sun ~ Children welcome ~ Live music Fri and every other Sun Easter-Christmas *Recommended by Emma Scofield, Sandra Morgan, Darrell Barton, Mick Allen*

BRIGSTEER SD4889 Map 9

Wheatsheaf

(015395) 68938 – www.thewheatsheafbrigsteer.co.uk

Off Brigsteer Brow; LA8 8AN

Bustling pub with interestingly furnished and decorated rooms, a good choice of food and drink, and seats outside; luxury bunkhouse bedrooms

The various rooms here have plenty of easy-going character and we always receive positive reports from our readers. Well run and friendly, the bar has a two-way log fire, carved wooden stools against the counter and Bowness Bay Swan Blonde, Hawkshead Bitter, Marstons Wainwright and a guest beer such as Eden Fuggle on handpump, 16 wines by the glass and eight malt whiskies. There's an appealing variety of cushioned dining chairs, carved and boxed settles and window seats set around an array of tables on either flagstones or floorboards, walls with pale-painted woodwork or wallpaper hung with animal and bird sketches, cartoons or interesting clock faces, and lighting that is both old-fashioned and contemporary. Outside there are seats and tables along the front of the building and picnic-sets on raised terracing. Their luxury bunkhouse (half a mile up the road) has five ensuite rooms and fine country views; breakfasts are hearty.

Well regarded, generously served food includes sandwiches, twice-baked lancashire cheese soufflé with creamy leeks, salt and pepper squid with miso mayonnaise and lime, sharing boards, pizza and flatbreads with various toppings, a pie of the day, butternut squash and sage ravioli with roasted squash, basil pesto, pine nuts and pumpkin seeds, beer-battered fresh haddock and chips, 12-hour braised beef brisket, and puddings such as ruby grapefruit, pink peppercorn and thyme posset with mixed berries and sticky toffee pudding with toffee sauce and ice-cream. *Benchmark main dish: fish pie £12.95. Two-course evening meal £23.00.*

Individual Inns ~ Managers Nicki and Tom Roberts ~ Real ale ~ Open 10am-11pm ~ Bar food 12-2.30, 5.30-9; 12-7.30 Sun ~ Restaurant ~ Children welcome ~ Dogs allowed in bar ~ Wi-fi ~ Bedrooms: /£100 *Recommended by David and Charlotte Green, Matt and Hayley Jacob, David Appleyard, Susan and Tim Boyle, Liz and Mike Newton, Peter Andrews*

BROUGHTON MILLS SD2190 Map 9

Blacksmiths Arms

(01229) 716824 – www.theblacksmithsarms.com

Off A593 N of Broughton-in-Furness; LA20 6AX

Friendly small pub with rewarding food, local beers and open fires

As a charming little pub with a lot of character, this is just the place to head for after a walk. The four small rooms have a relaxed, friendly atmosphere and are simply but attractively decorated; three have original beams, slate floors and warm log fires. Three real ales such as Barngates Cracker, Chadwicks Kirkland Blonde and Cumberland Corby Ale on handpump, nine wines by the glass, 11 malt whiskies and summer farm cider; darts, board games and dominoes. The hanging baskets and tubs of flowers in front of the building are very pretty in summer, and there are seats and tables under parasols on the front terrace. The surrounding countryside is lovely and walks are peaceful.

Much liked food includes lunchtime sandwiches, pigeon salad with black pudding and pancetta and balsamic reduction, mushrooms sautéed in garlic and parsley butter on sourdough toast, gammon steak with pineapple and free-range eggs, chargrilled chicken with wild mushroom sauce and dauphinoise potatoes, slow-roasted pork belly with rösti potato, pickled red cabbage and mulled cider reduction, salmon fillet with cucumber, tomato, rocket and dill salad with lemon syrup, and puddings such as dark chocolate torte with peppered strawberries and chantilly cream and sticky toffee pudding with warm butterscotch sauce and vanilla ice-cream; they also offer a two- and three-course set lunch. *Benchmark main dish: slow-braised minted lamb shoulder with roasted root vegetables and dauphinoise potatoes £15.50. Two-course evening meal £20.00.*

Free house ~ Licensees Mike and Sophie Lane ~ Real ale ~ Open 12-2.30, 5-11; 12-11 Sat; 12-10.30 Sun; closed Mon except bank holidays ~ Bar food 12-2, 6-9 ~ Restaurant ~ Children welcome ~ Dogs welcome ~ Wi-fi *Recommended by Tina and David Woods-Taylor, Elise and Charles Mackinlay, Nicola and Nigel Matthews, Helene Grygar*

CARLETON NY5329 Map 9

Cross Keys

(01768) 865588 – www.thecrosskeyspenrith.co.uk

A686, off A66 roundabout at Penrith; CA11 8TP

Friendly refurbished pub with several connected seating areas, real ales and popular food

Lunchtime is when this pub is as its busiest with walkers, cyclists and so forth all hoping for a hearty meal. The beamed main bar has a friendly feel, pubby tables and chairs on light wooden floorboards, modern metal wall lights and pictures on bare stone walls, and Tirril 1823 and a guest such as Eden Best on handpump. Steps lead down to a small area with high bar stools around a high drinking table and then upstairs to the restaurant: a light, airy room with big windows, large wrought-iron candelabras hanging from the vaulted ceiling, solid pale wooden tables and chairs, and doors leading to a verandah. At the far end of the main bar are yet another couple of small connected bar rooms with darts, games machine, pool, juke box and dominoes; TV and background music. There are views of the fells from the garden. This is under the same ownership as the Highland Drove in Great Salkeld.

As well as interesting specials, the seasonally changing food includes sandwiches, chicken liver pâté with chutney, prawn cocktail, sharing platters, gammon with eggs and pineapple, beer-battered haddock and chips, local cumberland sausages with mash and gravy, chicken with bacon and cheddar croquette, stilton, broccoli and cranberry en croûte with provençale sauce, lamb, pepper and mushroom skewer with garlic and yoghurt dip and straw fries, salmon en papillote with pak choi, lemongrass and chilli, and puddings such as sticky toffee pudding with butterscotch sauce and crème brûlée. *Benchmark main dish: steak in ale pie £12.50. Two-course evening meal £19.00.*

Free house ~ Licensee Paul Newton ~ Real ale ~ Open 12-2.30, 5pm-1am; 12pm-2am Sat; 12pm-1am Sun ~ Bar food 12-2.30, 6-9 (8.30 Sun); 12-2.30, 5.30-9 Fri, Sat ~ Restaurant ~ Children welcome ~ Dogs allowed in bar ~ Wi-fi *Recommended by John Watson, Sarah Roberts, Frances Parsons, Jacqui and Alan Swan, Caroline and Peter Bryant*

CARTMEL FELL SD4189 Map 9

Masons Arms

(015395) 68486 – www.masonsarmsstrawberrybank.co.uk

Strawberry Bank, a few miles S of Windermere between A592 and A5074; perhaps the simplest way to find the pub is to go uphill W from Bowland Bridge (which is signposted off A5074) towards Newby Bridge and keep right, then left at the staggered crossroads – it's then on your right, below Gummer's How; OS Sheet 97 map reference 413895; LA11 6NW

Wonderful views, beamed bar with plenty of character, interesting food and a good choice of ales and wines; self-catering cottages and apartments

As always, we've had warmly enthusiastic reports on this very well run Lakeland pub; you'll have to arrive early to grab a seat with stunning views over the Winster Valley to the woods below Whitbarrow Scar. The main bar has plenty of character, with low black beams in the bowed ceiling, and country chairs and plain wooden tables on polished flagstones. A small lounge has oak tables and settles to match its fine Jacobean panelling. There's also a plain little room beyond the serving counter with pictures and a fire in an open range, a family room with the atmosphere of an old parlour, and an upstairs dining room; background music and board games. Bowness Bay Swan Blonde, Cumbrian Legenday Loweswater Gold, Hawkshead Bitter and Marstons Wainwright on handpump, quite a few foreign bottled beers, 14 wines by the glass, nine malt whiskies, 16 gins and farm cider; service is friendly and helpful. You can sit at rustic benches and tables on the heated and covered terrace, and the self-catering cottages and apartments are stylish and comfortable and share the same fine outlook.

Generous helpings of reliably good food includes hot and cold lunchtime sandwiches (until 6pm weekends), crab pot with avocado and cream, baked whole camembert topped with fig and walnut jam, smoked white bean, kale and pearl barley hotpot with herb dumplings, smoked haddock and saffron risotto with crispy chorizo and roasted red peppers, slow-roasted lamb shoulder with mustard and mint mash, chicken breast with pork and sage stuffing with honey and brandy glazed pancetta, and puddings such as pecan, blueberry and maple syrup bread and butter pudding and damson gin crème brûlée; they also serve breakfast (9.30-11am). *Benchmark main dish: pie of the day £13.95. Two-course evening meal £22.00.*

Individual Inns ~ Managers John and Diane Taylor ~ Real ale ~ Open 11.30-11; 12-10.30 Sun ~ Bar food 12-2.30, 6-9; 12-9 weekends ~ Restaurant ~ Children welcome ~ Dogs allowed in bedrooms ~ Wi-fi *Recommended by Hugh Roberts, Charles and Maddie Bishop, Liz and Martin Eldon, Mr and Mrs Richard Osborne, John Evans, Christian Mole*

CLIFTON NY5326 Map 9

George & Dragon

(01768) 865381 – www.georgeanddragonclifton.co.uk

A6; near M6 junction 40; CA10 2ER

Former coaching inn with attractive bars and sizeable restaurant, local ales, well chosen wines, smashing food and seats outside; smart bedrooms

For a civilised break from the M6, head for this 18th-c Lowther Estate inn. The relaxed reception room has bright rugs on flagstones, leather chairs around a low table in front of an open fire, and a table in a private nook to one side of the reception desk. The main bar area, through wrought-iron gates, has more cheerful rugs, assorted wooden farmhouse chairs and tables, grey panelling topped with yellow-painted walls, photographs of the Estate and of the family with hunting dogs, various sheep and fell pictures and some high bar stools by the bar counter. Eden Gold, Hawkshead Bitter and a changing guest beer on handpump, 20 wines by the glass from a well chosen list and interesting local liqueurs; background music and TV. The sizeable restaurant to the left of the entrance consists of four open-plan rooms: there are plenty of old pews and church chairs around tables set for dining, a woodburning stove and a contemporary open kitchen. Outside, tables and chairs are set in a decoratively paved front area and in a high-walled enclosed courtyard. The bedrooms are stylish and comfortable and breakfasts highly recommended.

Impressive food using produce grown at their garden at the Estate's Askham Hall includes sandwiches, twice-baked cheese and spring onion soufflé with chive cream, butter-poached smoked haddock with pickled fennel, a poached egg and gribiche dressing, chicken and chorizo hotpot with wild garlic dumplings, grilled salt cod with shellfish chowder, spicy goat burger with cucumber yoghurt and chilli, coleslaw and chips, truffle-infused cauliflower steak with puy lentil casserole, a poached duck egg and charred broccoli soldiers, lamb ragoût and grilled cutlets with sheep curd gnocchi and smoked caponata, and puddings such as honey, malt and mead trifle and dark chocolate and orange tart with orange tonka bean crème fraîche; they also offer breakfast (8-9.30am). *Benchmark main dish: slow-cooked rare-breed beef £16.50. Two-course evening meal £22.00.*

Free house ~ Licensee Charles Lowther ~ Real ale ~ Open 12-11 ~ Bar food 12-2.30, 6-9 ~ Restaurant ~ Children welcome ~ Dogs allowed in bar and bedrooms ~ Wi-fi ~ Bedrooms: £85/£100 *Recommended by Comus and Sarah Elliott, Rupert and Sandy Newton, Glen and Patricia Fuller, P and J Shapley, Simon and Sue Lamb, Sophie and James Collier*

CONISTON SD3098 Map 9

Sun

(015394) 41248 – www.thesunconiston.com

Signed left off A593 at the bridge; LA21 8HQ

Extended old pub with a lively bar, plenty of dining space, a fine choice of real ales, well liked food and seats outside; comfortable bedrooms

This is a fine spot and the dramatic mountain views are shared by seats and tables on the terrace and in the big tree-sheltered garden, and by the quiet and comfortable bedrooms. The cheerful bar has up to eight real ales on handpump: Barngates Cracker, Red Bull Terrier and Tag Lag, Coniston Bluebird, Cumbrian Legendary Loweswater Gold and frequent guests from other local brewers including Fell, Hardknott, Hawkshead and Ulverston. Also, ten wines by the glass, 20 malt whiskies, several gins and farm cider; service is friendly. There are beams and timbers, exposed stone walls, flagstones and a Victorian-style range – as well as cask seats, old settles and cast-iron-framed tables, quite a few Donald Campbell photographs (this was his HQ during his final attempt on the world water-speed record) and a good mix of customers (often with their dogs). Above the bar is another room with extra seating, more pictures, pool, darts and a TV for sport, and beyond that is a sizeable lounge. A big dining conservatory houses a day-time café.

Pleasing food includes lunchtime rolls and flatbreads, honey and coriander chicken kebab with lemon syrup, haggis and black pudding fritters with kashmiri mayonnaise, burger of the day with skinny fries and onion rings, mediterranean vegetable and pesto tarte tatin with crème fraîche, slow-braised lamb with a mint marinade and red wine and rosemary gravy, sea bass on a prawn, pea, parmesan and parsley risotto, and puddings such as a crumble of the day and chocolate brownie; they also serve breakfast (8.30-9.30am). *Benchmark main dish: a mix of three tapas £20.00. Two-course evening meal £20.00.*

Free house ~ Licensee Alan Piper ~ Real ale ~ Open 11-11 ~ Bar food 12-3, 5.30-8.30 ~ Restaurant ~ Children welcome ~ Dogs allowed in bar and bedrooms ~ Wi-fi ~ Bedrooms: £65/£95 *Recommended by Maria and Henry Lazenby, Scott and Charlotte Havers, Andrew Vincent*

CROSTHWAITE SD4491 Map 9

Punch Bowl

(015395) 68237 – www.the-punchbowl.co.uk

Village signed off A5074 SE of Windermere; LA8 8HR

Cumbria Dining Pub of the Year

Smart dining pub with a proper bar and other elegant rooms, a fine wine list, impressive food and friendly staff; stylish bedrooms

Head for the church to find this civilised dining pub, which has been here since the 16th c. Of course, many customers are here for the excellent food but there's a proper public bar too, and plenty of chatty locals. This bar has rafters, a couple of eye-catching rugs on flagstones, bar stools by the slate-topped counter, Barngates Tag Lag, Bowness Bay Swan Blonde and Marstons Wainwright on handpump, 15 wines (including champagne and prosecco) by the glass, 15 malt whiskies and local damson gin. To the right are two linked carpeted and beamed rooms with well spaced country pine furniture of varying sizes (including a big refectory table), and walls that are painted in restrained neutral tones with an attractive assortment of prints; winter log fire, woodburning stove, lots of fresh flowers and daily papers. On the left, the wooden-floored, light and airy restaurant area has comfortable high-backed leather dining chairs; background music. Tables and seats on a terrace are stepped into the hillside and overlook the pretty Lyth Valley. Bedrooms are lovely and well equipped and breakfasts first class.

Faultless food includes lunchtime sandwiches, black pudding with a poached egg, rhubarb ketchup and mustard seed vinaigrette, local beef carpaccio with salt-baked celeriac, roasted hazelnuts and cheese, tunworth cheese and rigatoni gratin with truffle, pork tenderloin and cheek with swede, mustard, cabbage and apple caramel jus, cod loin with roasted cauliflower, morecambe bay shrimps and sea vegetables, fillet steak and braised cheek with red wine jus and horseradish vinegar, and puddings such as banana soufflé with toffee and lime sauce and caramelised white chocolate mousse with rhubarb and stem ginger. *Benchmark main dish: duo of local lamb £24.50. Two-course evening meal £30.00.*

Free house ~ Licensee Richard Rose ~ Real ale ~ Open 11-11 ~ Bar food 12-4, 6-9 ~ Restaurant ~ Children welcome ~ Dogs allowed in bar ~ Wi-fi ~ Bedrooms: £95/£135 *Recommended by Colin McLachlan, Hugh Roberts, Mr and Mrs Richard Osborne, Christian Mole, Peter and Caroline Waites, Audrey and Andrew Nichols*

ELTERWATER NY3204 Map 9

Britannia

(015394) 37210 – www.thebritanniainn.com

Off B5343; LA22 9HP

Much loved inn surrounded by wonderful walks and scenery, with up to seven real ales and well liked food; bedrooms

Even when this particularly well run pub is packed out, the friendly, efficient staff still find time to make you feel welcome. A long-standing favourite with our readers, it remains unpretentious and rather special. The small front bar has beams and a couple of window seats that look across to Elterwater through the trees, while the small back bar is traditionally furnished: thick slate walls, winter coal fires, oak benches, settles, windsor chairs and a big old rocking chair. A couple of beers are named for the pub – Britannia Special (from Coniston) and Britannia Gold (from Eden) – plus Coniston Bluebird Bitter, Cumberland Corby Ale and guests such as Dent Golden Fleece and Jennings Neddy Boggle and Sneck Lifter on handpump, and 12 malt whiskies. The lounge is comfortable, and there's also a hall and dining room. Plenty of seats outside, and visiting dancers (morris and step and garland) in summer. Bedrooms are warm and charming. The surrounding scenery is spectacular and there are walks of every gradient that begin right from the front door.

Usefully served all day, the reliably good food includes lunchtime sandwiches, mackerel, salmon and trout fishcakes with garlic mayonnaise, grilled haggis with plum jam, cumberland sausage and mash with onion gravy, burgers with toppings and chips, chicken, ham and leek pie, wild and button mushroom stroganoff, sea bass fillet with crab mayonnaise and radish and avocado salad with lemon dressing, and puddings such as profiteroles with warm dark chocolate sauce and brûlée of the day. *Benchmark main dish: braised lamb shoulder in mint with red wine gravy £15.95. Two-course evening meal £20.50.*

Free house ~ Licensee Andrew Parker ~ Real ale ~ Open 10.30am-11pm ~ Bar food 12-5, 6-9 ~ Restaurant ~ Children welcome ~ Dogs allowed in bar and bedrooms ~ Wi-fi ~ Bedrooms: £95/£105 *Recommended by Peter Meister, Mr and Mrs Richard Osborne, Alan and Linda Blackmore, Heather and Richard Jones, Tina and David Woods-Taylor, Margaret and Peter Staples, John and Sylvia Harrop*

GREAT SALKELD NY5536 Map 10

Highland Drove

(01768) 898349 – www.highlanddroveinnpenrith.co.uk

B6412, off A686 NE of Penrith; CA11 9NA

Bustling place with cheerful customers, good food and fair choice of drinks, and fine views from the upstairs verandah; bedrooms

Donald Newton has been running this smashing all-rounder for some 20 years (he's helped by his son too) and it's a favourite with our readers. The spotlessly kept chatty main bar has sandstone flooring, stone walls, cushioned wheelback chairs around a mix of tables and an open fire in a raised stone fireplace. The downstairs eating area has more cushioned dining chairs around wooden tables on pale wooden floorboards, stone walls and ceiling joists, and a two-way fire in a raised stone fireplace that separates this room from the coffee lounge with its comfortable leather chairs and sofas. It's best to book to be sure of a table in the upstairs restaurant. Theakstons Black Bull and a guest such as Banks's Sunbeam on handpump, a dozen wines by the glass and 28 malt whiskies; background music, darts, pool and dominoes. The lovely views over the Eden Valley and the Pennines are best enjoyed from seats on the upstairs verandah; there are also seats on the back terrace. Bedrooms are clean and comfortable and breakfasts are hearty. This is under the same ownership as the Cross Keys in Carleton.

High standards of generously served food includes sandwiches, pigeon breast on stir-fried vegetables with crème de cassis dressing, grilled goats cheese crostini with roast pepper and beetroot salad, sharing platters, vegetable curry, cumberland sausage with wholegrain mustard mash and onion gravy, herb-crusted turkey escalope on cranberry and smoked bacon mash with turkey sauce, gammon steak with eggs and pineapple, beer-battered haddock and chips, and puddings. *Benchmark main dish: steak in ale pie £12.50. Two-course evening meal £19.00.*

Free house ~ Licensees Donald and Paul Newton ~ Real ale ~ Open 12-3, 6-1am; 12-1am Sat; 12-1am Sun; closed Mon lunchtime ~ Bar food 12-2, 6-9; 12-2, 6-8.30 Sun ~ Restaurant ~ Children welcome ~ Dogs allowed in bar ~ Wi-fi ~ Bedrooms: £60/£90 *Recommended by Mr and Mrs Richard Osborne, Shona and Jimmy McDuff, Trish and Karl Soloman, John Evans, Ian Herdman, Andrew Lawson*

HAWKSHEAD NY3501 Map 9

Drunken Duck

(015394) 36347 – www.drunkenduckinn.co.uk

Barngates; the pub is signposted from B5286 Hawkshead–Ambleside, opposite the Outgate Inn and from north first right after the wooded caravan site; LA22 0NG

Stylish little bar, several restaurant areas, own-brewed beers and bar meals as well as innovative restaurant choices; stunning views and lovely bedrooms

Of course, many customers are here to stay in the beautifully furnished bedrooms or enjoy a delicious meal in the restaurant, but at lunchtime it's the smart little bar that walkers head for. The star attraction then are their own-brewed ales on handpump from the Barngates brewery, including Brathay Gold, Cat Nap, Cracker Ale, Goodhews Dry Stout, Pale, Red Bull Terrier and Tag Lag, plus their own weiss beer. They also offer 16 wines by the glass (including pudding wines) from a fine list, 25 malt whiskies and 17 gins (including ones to which they add their own botanicals). There are leather bar stools by the slate-topped counter, leather club chairs, beams and oak floorboards, and old Lake District photographs on the walls. The three restaurant areas are elegant; there are plans to open a coffee lounge. Sit at the wooden tables and benches on grass opposite the building for spectacular views across the fells, and if you come in spring or summer the flowering bulbs are lovely. Please note: dogs are allowed in the bar only.

At lunchtime the menu is limited to sandwiches with chips, soup, a meze board to share and four 'bowls'. The evening food is excellent: treacle-glazed ox cheek with padron pepper and sourdough crumb, sea bream with confit lemon and jerusalem artichokes, roasted celeriac and hispi cabbage with mushrooms, truffle and hazelnuts, spiced lamb shoulder and rump with pearl barley and broccoli, skate wing with haricot beans, spätzle (a type of soft egg noodle) and rock samphire, and puddings such as doughnut with poached rhubarb and cinder toffee and plum bakewell with vanilla ice-cream. *Benchmark main dish: chicken with smoked mash, truffle, bacon and peas £22.00. Two-course evening meal £30.00.*

Own brew ~ Licensee Steph Barton ~ Real ale ~ Open 11.30-11; 12-10.30 Sun ~ Bar food 12-2.30, 5.30-9; 12-4, 6-9 Sun ~ Restaurant ~ Children welcome ~ Dogs allowed in bar ~ Wi-fi ~ Bedrooms: £78.75/£105 *Recommended by Peter Meister, Gordon and Margaret Ormondroyd, Sally Melling, Martin and Joanne Sharp, Colin McLachlan, Elspeth Macdonald, Dan and Belinda Smallbone*

INGS SD4498 Map 9

Watermill

(01539) 821309 – www.watermillinn.co.uk

Just off A591 E of Windermere; LA8 9PY

Bustling, cleverly converted pub with fantastic range of real ales including own brews; bedrooms

For real ale lovers this busy place is just the ticket. The 11 changing beers on handpump include their own brews Watermill A Bit'er Ruff, Collie Wobbles, Dogth Vader, Isle of Dogs, Windermere Blonde, Ruff Justice and W'ruff Night and guests such as Coniston Bluebird, Cumbrian Legendary Loweswater Gold and Theakstons Old Peculier. Also, a choice of foreign bottled beers and quite a few malt whiskies. The chatty bar has beams, black leather, wheelback and kitchen or mate's dining chairs around solid tables on tartan carpet, plus a woodburning stove in a stone fireplace. Another room has lots of old posters on rough plastered walls, and the interconnected dining rooms, similarly furnished, have flagstones and exposed and painted stone walls; several open fires, darts and board games. There are seats in the gardens and lots to do nearby.

Pubby food is served all day: hot and cold sandwiches, mini fish platter, chicken liver pâté with red onion marmalade, a full breakfast, game casserole, mixed vegetable and five-bean chilli, mustard chicken with chive mash and rosemary and black pepper sauce, lamb hotpot, fish pie, chilli con carne, and puddings such as dark chocolate and orange crème brûlée and sticky toffee pudding with toffee sauce. *Benchmark main dish: beef in ale pie £12.50. Two-course evening meal £18.50.*

Own brew ~ Licensee Brian Coulthwaite ~ Real ale ~ Open 11.15-11; 11.15-10.30 Sun ~ Bar food 12-9 ~ Children welcome ~ Dog allowed in bar and bedrooms ~ Wi-fi ~ Bedrooms: £49/£89 *Recommended by Tina and David Woods-Taylor, Gordon and Margaret Ormondroyd, Denis and Margaret Kilner, Sam Cole*

KIRKBY LONSDALE SD6178 Map 7

Sun

(015242) 71965 – www.sun-inn.info

Market Street (B6254); LA6 2AU

White-painted stone inn on cobbled alley with character bar, local ales and good wines and excellent food; lovely bedrooms

In a pretty village and backing on to the churchyard, this 17th-c inn strikes a good balance between a pub and a restaurant. The rambling beamed bar has flagstones and stripped oak boards, pews, armchairs and cosy window seats, paintings on cream walls and a woodburning stove. Hawkshead Bitter,

Marstons Wainwright and a guest beer on handpump served by helpful, friendly staff. There are a couple of dining rooms (one is red-walled) with a two-way woodburning stove and leather banquettes; background music. Bedrooms are attractive, comfortable and warm and several are dog-friendly; dogs get a welcome pack and they offer dog walking and sitting too. Turner stayed here in 1818 when painting the picture known as 'Ruskin's view'. Thursday is market day.

Using local, seasonal produce the first class food at lunchtime includes lamb kidneys with haggis, carrot purée and whisky sauce, bubble and squeak with a crispy egg and mustard sauce, wild mushroom risotto with truffle oil, moules frites and lamb hotpot, with imaginative restaurant choices such as confit duck leg with braised baby gem and blood orange purée, ham hock with quail scotch egg and blue cheese dressing, haunch of fallow deer with smoked potato purée and bourguignon garnish, chalk-stream trout with anchovy mayonnaise and green lentil salsa, and puddings such as buttermilk and rose pannacotta and dark chocolate and cherry délice. *Benchmark main dish: beer-battered fish and chips £10.95. Two-course evening meal £23.00.*

Free house ~ Licensees Jenny and Iain Black ~ Real ale ~ Open 10.30am-11pm; 11-11 Sun; opens 4pm Mon ~ Bar food 12-3, 6.30-9; snacks all day ~ Restaurant ~ Children welcome ~ Dogs allowed in bar and bedrooms ~ Bedrooms: £97.50/£115 *Recommended by Margaret McDonald, Jeremy Snow, Christopher May, Richard and Tessa Ibbot*

LANGDALE NY2806 Map 9

Old Dungeon Ghyll £

(015394) 37272 – www.odg.co.uk

B5343; LA22 9JY

Straightforward place in lovely position with real ales, traditional food and fine surrounding walks; bedrooms

At the heart of the Great Langdale Valley and surrounded by fells including the Langdale Pikes flanking the Dungeon Ghyll Force waterfall, this straightforward and friendly local is the perfect place for damp walkers and climbers after a busy day outdoors. There's no need to remove boots or muddy trousers in the straightforward bar; you can sit on seats in old cattle stalls by the big warming fire and enjoy the fine choice of six real ales on handpump: Cumbrian Legendary Esthwaite Bitter, Hawkshead Bitter and Windermere Pale, Theakston Old Peculier and Yates Best Bitter and Solway Gold. Also, farm cider and several malt whiskies. It's a good place to stay, with warm bedrooms, a plush residents' lounge and highly rated breakfasts. It may get lively on a Saturday night (there's a popular National Trust campsite opposite).

Tasty, honest food includes their own bread and cakes, lunchtime sandwiches, home-made soup, vegetable lasagne, chilli con carne, a changing curry, gammon and free-range eggs, cumberland sausage with mash and onion gravy, and puddings. *Benchmark main dish: pie of the day £7.95. Two-course evening meal £18.00.*

Free house ~ Licensee Neil Walmsley ~ Real ale ~ Open 11-11 (10.30 Sun) ~ Bar food 12-2, 6-9 ~ Restaurant ~ Children welcome ~ Dogs allowed in bar and bedrooms ~ Wi-fi ~ Bedrooms: £68/£136 *Recommended by Peter Meister, Mr and Mrs D Hammond, Charles Fraser, Lenny and Ruth Walters*

Cribbage is a card game using a block of wood with holes for matchsticks or special pins to score with; regulars in cribbage pubs are usually happy to teach strangers how to play.

LEVENS SD4987 Map 9

Strickland Arms

(015395) 61010 – www.thestricklandarms.com

4 miles from M6 junction 36, via A590; just off A590, by Sizergh Castle gates; LA8 8DZ

Friendly, open-plan pub with popular food, local ales and a fine setting; seats outside

This is a well run and gently civilised place with efficient, friendly and smartly dressed staff and plenty of customers; it's probably a good idea to book a table in advance at peak times. The bar on the right has oriental rugs on flagstones, a log fire, Bowness Bay Raven Red and Swan Blonde, Hawkshead Bitter, Marstons Lancaster Bomber and Old School Hopscotch on handpump, several malt whiskies and nine wines by the glass. On the left are polished boards and another log fire, and throughout there's a nice mix of sturdy country furniture, candles on tables, hunting scenes and other old prints on the walls, curtain in heavy fabric and some staffordshire china ornaments. Two of the dining rooms are upstairs; background music and board games. The flagstoned front terrace has plenty of tables and chairs and picnic-sets are arranged on a grassy area; disabled access and facilities. Sizergh Castle (owned by the National Trust) is opposite. The pub is part of the Ainscoughs group.

Highly thought-of food includes sandwiches and pub favourites plus deep-fried brie with plum sauce, potted morecambe shrimps, greek-style feta cheese salad, cumberland sausage and mash with onion rings and gravy, lancashire hotpot, sea bass fillets with garlic and citrus butter, gammon steak with black pudding and an egg, and puddings such as white chocolate and raspberry cheesecake and eton mess. *Benchmark main dish: pie of the day £13.00. Two-course evening meal £20.50.*

Free house ~ Licensee Michael Redmond ~ Real ale ~ Open 12-11 (10.30 Sun) ~ Bar food 12-9 ~ Children welcome ~ Dogs welcome ~ Wi-fi *Recommended by Hugh Roberts, Donald Allsopp, Sally and David Champion, Steve Whalley, Daniel King*

LITTLE LANGDALE NY3103 Map 9

Three Shires

(015394) 37215 – www.threeshiresinn.co.uk

From A593 3 miles W of Ambleside take small road signposted The Langdales, Wrynose Pass; then bear left at first fork; LA22 9NZ

Fine valley views from seats on the terrace, local ales, quite a choice of food and good service; comfortable bedrooms

As ever, we've had warm reports from our readers on this reliably well run and welcoming inn. The comfortably extended back bar has stripped timbers and a stripped beam-and-joist ceiling, green Lakeland stone and William Morris patterned wallpaper, antique oak carved settles, country kitchen chairs and stools on big dark slate flagstones and cumbrian photographs. Five real ales on handpump include Bowness Bay Swan Blonde, Coniston Old Man Ale, Cumbrian Legendary Langdale, Hawkshead Bitter and a changing guest, and they also have over 50 malt whiskies, a wide choice of gins including local ones and a decent wine list. The front restaurant is furnished with chunky leather dining chairs around solid tables on wood flooring, and a snug leads off here; the residents' lounge has leather sofas and an open fire. Background music, TV and board games. The view from seats on the terrace down over the valley to the partly wooded hills below is stunning; there are more seats on a neat lawn behind the car park, backed by a small oak wood, and award-winning summer hanging baskets. The pretty bedrooms have fine views and they also offer two self-catering cottages. The three shires of the pub's name are the historical counties of Cumberland, Westmorland and Lancashire, which converge at the top of nearby Wrynose Pass.

Enjoyable food includes lunchtime sandwiches and platters, pub favourites and dishes such as king prawns and mussels in garlic butter, sliced smoked venison loin with an apple and sultana chutney, spinach, sweet potato and chickpea jalfrezi with steamed rice, mango chutney and naan, braised local beef short rib with truffle potatoes, roasted honey and red wine jus, confit of duck leg with braised red cabbage, curly kale and creamed potatoes, monkfish and king prawn thai green curry with jasmine coconut rice, tomato and coriander relish and prawn crackers, and puddings such as apple and blackberry crumble with ice-cream and vanilla crème brûlée with fruit compote. *Benchmark main dish: beef in ale pie £13.95. Two-course evening meal £23.50.*

Free house ~ Licensee Ian Stephenson ~ Real ale ~ Open 10.30-10 (10.30 Sat); 11-10 Sun; check website for opening hours in winter ~ Bar food 12-2, 6-8.45 ~ Restaurant ~ Children welcome ~ Dogs allowed in bar ~ Wi-fi ~ Bedrooms: /£118 *Recommended by Tina and David Woods-Taylor, Mr and Mrs Richard Osborne, Margaret and Peter Staples, Jamie and Lizzie McEwan, Charlie and Mark Todd*

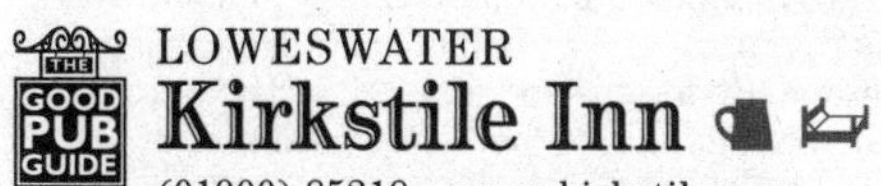

LOWESWATER NY1421 Map 9

Kirkstile Inn

(01900) 85219 – www.kirkstile.com

From B5289 follow signs to Loweswater Lake; OS Sheet 89 map reference 140210; CA13 0RU

Fine location for this well run, popular inn with busy bar, own-brewed beers, good food and friendly welcome; bedrooms

Even when really busy (which they deservedly usually are), the hard-working staff remain efficient, kind and welcoming. It's a 16th-c inn with stunning surrounding walks, so lunchtime space is at a premium. The main bar has a cosy atmosphere thanks to a roaring log fire, plus low beams and carpeting, comfortably cushioned small settles and pews, partly stripped stone walls, board games and a slate shove-ha'penny board. As well as their own-brewed Cumbrian Legendary Esthwaite Bitter, Langdale, Loweswater Gold, Vanilla Oatmeal Stout and a seasonal guest such as Buttermere Beauty on handpump, they keep nine wines by the glass and 20 malt whiskies. The stunning views of the peaks can be enjoyed from picnic-sets on the lawn, from the very attractive covered verandah in front of the building and from the windows in one of the rooms off the bar. Bedrooms are comfortable and breakfasts are especially good. Dogs are allowed only in the bar and not during evening food service.

Fair priced, pleasing food includes lunchtime sandwiches and pub classics plus breaded brie wedge with apricot and cranberry chutney, smoked haddock and parmesan omelette, cumberland sausage with spring onion mash and cumberland mustard and brandy cream, wild mushroom and quinoa patties with red pepper and mango salsa, slow-roasted lamb with redcurrant and rosemary jus, coley with an ale-battered prawn, samphire, parsley and white wine cream sauce, and puddings such as raspberry and vanilla bakewell tart with almond pannacotta and double jersey ice-cream and sticky toffee pudding with butterscotch sauce. *Benchmark main dish: steak in ale pie £13.00. Two-course evening meal £21.00.*

Own brew ~ Licensee Roger Humphreys ~ Real ale ~ Open 11-11 ~ Bar food 12-2, 6-9; light meals and tea in afternoon ~ Restaurant ~ Children welcome ~ Dogs allowed in bar ~ Bedrooms: £63.50/£117 *Recommended by Ian and Rose Lock, Margaret and Peter Staples, Sally and Colin Allen, Caroline and Peter Bryant*

LUPTON SO5581 Map 7

Plough

(015395) 67700 – www.theploughatlupton.co.uk

A65, near M6 junction 36; LA6 1PJ

Smart inn with open-plan smart rooms, a good choice of drinks, interesting food and seats outside; fine bedrooms

The perfect break from the M6 where you can be sure of a genuine welcome and some particularly good food, this stylish place is popular with our readers. There are spreading open-plan bars with beams, a nice mix of antique dining chairs and tables, comfortable leather sofas and armchairs in front of large woodburning stoves, prints on pink- and grey-painted walls, rugs on wooden floors, fresh flowers and daily papers; background music and board games. High bar stools sit beside the counter where neatly dressed, friendly staff serve Kirkby Lonsdale Monumental and Tiffin Gold, Marstons Wainwright and Tirril Ullswater Blonde on handpump, 13 wines by the glass, ten gins and local vodka; background music and board games. Outside, rustic wooden tables and chairs under parasols are set behind a granite-topped wall, with more in the back garden. Bedrooms are cosy, attractive and comfortable and much used by those exploring the Lake District.

Top quality food includes sandwiches (until 5pm) and pub classics plus imaginative choices such as potted rabbit rillette with pickled carrot and carrot top and dandelion salad, salmon gravadlax tartare with burnt lemon and celery and hazelnut salad, butternut squash and taleggio risotto with soy-glazed seeds and pumpkin oil, chicken alla milanese with gremolata and fries, confit duck leg with haricot bean and pancetta cassoulet, slow-cooked pork belly with caramelised apple and braised lentils, himalayan salt chamber aged rib-eye steak with a choice of sauces, and puddings such as prune and ginger pudding with toffee sauce and dark chocolate délice with double jersey ice-cream. *Benchmark main dish: beer-battered fish and chips £12.50. Two-course evening meal £22.00.*

Free house ~ Licensee Paul Spencer ~ Real ale ~ Open 11-11; 11-10.30 Sun ~ Bar food 12-9 ~ Restaurant ~ Children welcome ~ Dogs allowed in bar and bedrooms ~ Wi-fi ~ Bedrooms: £85/£120 *Recommended by Gordon and Margaret Ormondroyd, Amy and Luke Buchanan, Nick and Meriel Cox, Andrea and Philip Crispin, Mark and Mary Setting*

NEAR SAWREY SD3795 Map 9

Tower Bank Arms

(015394) 36334 – www.towerbankarms.com

B5285 towards the Windermere ferry; LA22 0LF

Well run pub with several real ales, well regarded bar food and a friendly welcome; nice bedrooms

As this inn features in Beatrix Potter's book *The Tale of Jemima Puddle-Duck* it's very popular with families. The low-beamed main bar has plenty of rustic charm with a rough slate floor, game and fowl pictures, a grandfather clock, a log fire and fresh flowers; there's also a separate restaurant. Barngates Cracker Ale and Tag Lag, Cumbrian Legendary Loweswater Gold and Hawkshead Bitter, Brodies Prime and Windermere Pale on handpump, nine wines by the glass, ten malt whiskies and four farm ciders; board games, dominoes and cribbage. There are pleasant views of the wooded Claife Heights from seats in the extended garden. The pretty bedrooms have a country outlook; breakfasts are good.

Well regarded food includes lunchtime sandwiches, potted chicken liver and pistachio pâté with cumberland sauce, crayfish cocktail, scotch egg with black pudding and pancetta salad, cumberland sausage with apple and sage mash and caramelised red onion gravy, gnocchi with wilted spinach and mushrooms in creamy tarragon sauce, pork medallions with brandy, green peppercorn and sage cream with bubble and squeak, and puddings such as sticky toffee pudding with caramel fudge and honeycomb ice-cream and raspberry eton mess. *Benchmark main dish: beef in ale stew £13.50. Two-course evening meal £19.00.*

Free house ~ Licensee Anthony Hutton ~ Real ale ~ Open 12-11; 12-10.30 Sun; closed Mon Nov-early Feb, one week early Dec, one week Jan ~ Bar food 12-2, 6-8 ~ Restaurant ~ Children welcome ~ Dogs allowed in bar and bedrooms ~ Wi-fi ~ Bedrooms: /£98
Recommended by Charles Welch, Sandra Hollies, Sophia and Hamish Greenfield, Selwyn Jones, Adam Jones

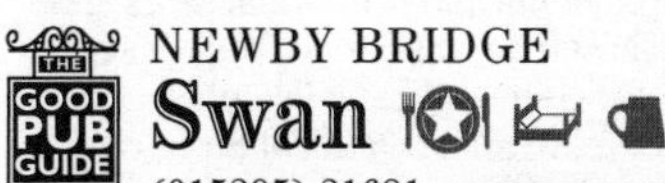

NEWBY BRIDGE SD3686 Map 9

Swan

(015395) 31681 – www.swanhotel.com
Just off A590; LA12 8NB

Bustling bar in riverside hotel, a fine choice of drinks, bold fabrics and décor and seats on a waterside terrace; lovely bedrooms

The 17th-c heart of this extended coaching inn remains the bustling bar, where you'll find a happy mix of locals, hotel guests and boating folk all mingling happily. There are low ceilings, cheerful floral print upholstered dining and church chairs around scrubbed tables on bare floorboards, window seats, decorative plates around a log fire in a little iron fireplace, and stools at the long bar counter. Jennings Cumberland, Cumbrian Legendary Loweswater Gold, Marstons Wainwright and a changing guest from Cumbrian Legendary on handpump, served by smart, friendly staff; background music. Towards the back is another log fire with a sofa and upholstered pouffes around a low table, and an additional, similarly furnished room; the front snug is cosy. Original features mix well with the bold fabrics and wallpaper, fresh flowers, nice old pieces of china and modern artwork – it's all been done with a great deal of thought and care. In the main hotel off to the left is a sizeable restaurant. Plenty of pretty iron-work tables and chairs line the terrace beside the River Leven. The comfortably contemporary bedrooms are well equipped and beautifully furnished and they also offer luxury cottages in the grounds.

A wide choice of tempting food includes sandwiches, ham hock terrine with piccalilli, soft shell crab with mango, chilli and lime, vegetable tagine with almond and apricot couscous and harissa, salmon with crushed potatoes, peas, mint and watercress mayonnaise, garlic and herb rotisserie chicken with apple, bacon and avocado salad, burger with toppings, sweetcorn relish and fries, lamb koftas with flatbread, hummus and tzatziki, spicy fishcakes with cucumber salad and sweet chilli, and puddings such as Malteser cheesecake and cookie dough sundae. *Benchmark main dish: burger with toppings, sweetcorn relish and fries £16.50. Two-course evening meal £20.00.*

Free house ~ Licensee Sarah Gibbs ~ Real ale ~ Open 10am-11pm ~ Bar food 10am-9.30pm ~ Restaurant ~ Children welcome until 7pm ~ Dogs allowed in bar ~ Wi-fi ~ Bedrooms: /£152 *Recommended by Gordon and Margaret Ormondroyd, Mr and Mrs D Hammond, John Evans, Cecily and Steven Evans*

PENRITH NY5130 Map 9

Dockray Hall

(01768) 210676 – www.dockrayhall.com

Great Dockray/Cornmarket; CA11 7DE

Historic inn with interesting bar and dining areas, local ales and good wines, first class food and seats outside

The renovations at this establishment (an inn since 1719) have been thoughtfully and carefully carried out to preserve its ancient character, and there are plenty of bars and dining rooms to choose from. The main bar has an inglenook fireplace, built-in wall seats and settles with scatter cushions and all manner of wooden or leather chairs around dark tables on big flagstones and daily papers on a beer barrel; steps lead up to another dining area with original oak panelling, a stone fireplace and a pretty bow window. Steps also lead down to a 14th-c bar with an original open fireplace, solid furnishings on parquet flooring and plush little bar stools; the Stables Bar has horse tack and other farming implements and traditional seats and tables on stripped wooden floorboards. Knowledgeable, friendly staff serve their own Cumbrian Legendary Loweswater Gold and Langdale plus a couple of seasonal beers such as Esthwaite Bitter and Vanilla Oatmeal Stout on handpump, nine good wines by the glass and ten malt whiskies. There's also a snug with comfortable upholstered wing and bucket chairs. Outside in front, walled off from the road, are picnic-sets. Richard III once owned this historic 15th-c building.

Local, seasonal produce is at the heart of the creative modern food: lunchtime sandwiches and pub favourites plus twice-baked caramelised onion and cheese soufflé, smoked haddock and leek risotto with a crispy egg and herb oil, thai green vegetable with coconut rice, poached chicken with potato dumplings, black garlic and mushroom and tarragon cream, local venison oil with venison ragoût, salsify and jus, sole with lemon, parsley and brown shrimp butter, and puddings such as chocolate malt mousse with passion-fruit syrup and passion-fruit sorbet and spiced pineapple cake with lime and cardamom ice-cream; they also offer a two- and three-course set menu. *Benchmark main dish: confit duck leg with smoked sausage and garlic cassoulet £13.50. Two-course evening meal £21.00.*

Free house ~ Licensee Roger Humphreys ~ Real ale ~ Open 11-11 Mon-Thurs; 11am-midnight Fri, Sat; 12-10.30 Sun ~ Bar food 12-2.30, 5.30-9; 12-3, 6-9 Fri-Sun; coffee and cake available all day ~ Children welcome ~ Dogs allowed in bar ~ Wi-fi *Recommended by Alexandra and Richard Clay, Robert and Diana Myers, Melanie and David Lawson, Neil Allen, Graham and Elizabeth Hargreaves, Jane and Philip Saunders*

RAVENSTONEDALE NY7203 Map 10

Black Swan

(015396) 23204 – www.blackswanhotel.com

Just off A685 SW of Kirkby Stephen; CA17 4NG

Bustling hotel with thriving bar, several real ales, enjoyable food and good surrounding walks; comfortable bedrooms

If you stay in this neatly kept Victorian hotel, the bedrooms are well appointed and very comfortable (some have disabled access, others are dog-friendly) and breakfasts are excellent. The popular U-shaped bar has hops on the gantry, quite a few original period features, stripped-stone walls, high wooden stools by the counter, a comfortable tweed banquette, various dining chairs and little stools around a mix of tables and fresh flowers; the cosy small lounge has armchairs and an open fire. You can eat in the bar or in two separate restaurants. Friendly, helpful staff serve Black Sheep Bitter, Timothy Taylors Boltmaker and a guest from Kirkby Lonsdale on handpump, 11 wines by the glass, more than 30 malt whiskies, 25 gins and a good choice of fruit juices and pressés; background music, TV, darts, board games, newspapers and magazines. The tree-sheltered streamside garden across the road has picnic-sets, and there are walks from the door (they have leaflets describing some routes).

From a seasonal menu, the interesting food includes lunchtime sandwiches, scallops with white chocolate and truffle risotto, cauliflower cheese soufflé with sweetcorn cream, celeriac rösti with creamed cabbage, a poached egg, apple and stilton, chicken breast and leg with roasted onions, pearl barley and black truffle sauce, sea bream with leeks, almonds, dill and mussel and chive broth, duck with slow-cooked breast, leg boulangère, plums and fennel, and puddings such as rhubarb, ginger cheesecake, yoghurt and popcorn, and chocolate with passion fruit, crème fraîche and rum and raisin ice-cream. *Benchmark main dish: lamb rump and braised shoulder with lentil dhal, mint yoghurt and pomegranate £19.00. Two-course evening meal £22.00.*

Free house ~ Licensee Louise Dinnes ~ Real ale ~ Open 11am-midnight (1am Sat) ~ Bar food 12-3 (4 Sun), 5-9; snacks throughout the afternoon ~ Restaurant ~ Children welcome ~ Dogs allowed in bar and bedrooms ~ Wi-fi ~ Bedrooms: £85/£110 *Recommended by Sophia and Hamish Greenfield, Neil and Angela Huxter, Jacqui and Alan Swan, Margo and Derek Peters*

STAVELEY SD4798 Map 10

Beer Hall at Hawkshead Brewery

(01539) 825260 – www.hawksheadbrewery.co.uk
Staveley Mill Yard, Back Lane; LA8 9LR

Hawkshead Brewery showcase plus a huge choice of bottled beers, brewery memorabilia and tasty food

The full range of Hawkshead Brewery ales are served by knowledgeable, friendly staff from 14 handpumps: these might include Bitter, Brodies Prime, Dry Stone Stout, Lakeland Gold, Lakeland Lager, Red, Windermere Pale and seasonal beers; regular beer festivals. Also, 40 bottled beers, 25 gins and 50 whiskies with an emphasis on independent producers. It's a spacious and modern glass-fronted building and the main bar is on two levels with the lower level dominated by the stainless-steel fermenting vessels. There are high-backed chairs around light wooden tables, benches beside long tables and nice dark leather sofas around low tables (all on oak floorboards); a couple of walls are almost entirely covered with artistic photos of barley, hops and the brewing process. You can buy T-shirts, branded glasses and polypins and there are brewery tours. Parking can be tricky at peak times.

A changing choice of up to 14 different tapas-style dishes plays a big part here (duck and chilli sausages, sticky barbecue baby back ribs, sweetcorn and coriander fritters, scotch egg and piccalilli), plus big, filled yorkshire puddings, whole dressed crab, twice-baked cheese soufflé with creamy leek sauce, beer-battered haddock and chips, venison burger with toppings and damson chutney, and puddings such as cherry bakewell tart and sticky toffee pudding with caramel sauce. *Benchmark main dish: brewer's lunch platter £16.00. Two-course evening meal £21.00.*

Own brew ~ Licensee Chris Ramwell ~ Real ale ~ Open 12-7 Mon-Thurs; 12-11 Fri, Sat; 12-8 Sun ~ Bar food 12-3 Mon-Thurs; 12-8.30 Fri, Sat; 12-6 Sun; hours may be extended during school holidays ~ Children welcome ~ Dogs allowed in bar ~ Wi-fi *Recommended by Nick Higgins, Penny and David Shepherd, John and Delia Franks, Colin and Daniel Gibbs*

STAVELEY SD4797 Map 9

Eagle & Child £

(01539) 821320 – www.eaglechildinn.co.uk

Kendal Road; just off A591 Windermere–Kendal; LA8 9LP

Friendly inn with a good range of local beers and enjoyable food; bedrooms

Even on a dreary Monday evening you'll find plenty of regulars here creating a chatty and cheerful atmosphere. The bar has plenty of separate parts furnished with pews, banquettes, bow window seats and high-backed dining chairs around polished dark tables, and there's a log fire beneath an impressive mantelbeam in the L-shaped flagstoned main area. Also, police truncheons and walking sticks, some nice photographs and interesting prints, a delft shelf of bric-a-brac, a few farm tools and another log fire. Five regularly changing ales come from breweries such as Bowness Bay, Coniston, Cumbrian Legendary, Hawkshead and Jennings on handpump, several wines by the glass, 30 malt whiskies, 30 gins and farm cider; background music. A barn-themed dining room upstairs has its own bar for functions. Bedrooms are comfortable and the breakfasts very generous. The sheltered garden by the River Kent has picnic-sets under parasols, with more on a good-sized back terrace and a second garden behind. This is a lovely spot with walks that fan out from the recreation ground just across the road.

Popular food includes sandwiches, mexican-spiced smoked salmon fishcakes with salsa, a tapas platter, sweet potato, cashew nut and spinach coconut curry, fish pie topped with cheddar mash, gammon with eggs and pineapple, chicken wrapped in smoked bacon in a rich barbecue sauce topped with cheese, steak in ale pie, and puddings such as apple crumble and hot chocolate fudge cake. *Benchmark main dish: moroccan-style lamb £11.95. Two-course evening meal £17.50.*

Free house ~ Licensees Richard and Denise Coleman ~ Real ale ~ Open 11.30-11 (11.30 Sat); 12-10.30 Sun ~ Bar food 12-2.30, 6-9; 12-9 weekends ~ Restaurant ~ Children welcome ~ Dogs allowed in bar ~ Wi-fi ~ Bedrooms: £75/£85 *Recommended by Chris Stevenson, Tina and David Woods-Taylor, Dave Braisted, John and Mary Warner, George and Alison Bishop*

STONETHWAITE NY2513 Map 9

Langstrath

(017687) 77239 – www.thelangstrath.com

Off B5289 S of Derwentwater; CA12 5XG

Nice little place in a lovely spot, popular food with a modern twist, real ales and good wines, and seats outside; bedrooms

In a tiny village surrounded by the steep fells above Borrowdale, this is a friendly and civilised small inn. The neat, simple bar – at its pubbiest at lunchtime – has a welcoming log fire in a big stone fireplace, rustic tables, plain chairs and cushioned wall seats, and walking cartoons and attractive Lakeland mountain photographs on its textured white walls. Jennings Cocker Hoop, Keswick Gold and KSB and Marstons Wainwright on handpump, 30 malt whiskies and several wines by the glass; background music and board games. The restaurant has fine views and there's a cosy residents' lounge too (in what was the original 16th-c cottage). The comfortable, warm bedrooms are just right as a base for a walking holiday and both the Cumbrian Way and the Coast to Coast path are close by. Outside, a big sycamore shelters several picnic-sets that look up to Eagle Crag.

Reliably good food includes lunchtime sandwiches, a vegetarian tart of the day, steak in ale pie, turkey, chorizo and mushroom suet pudding in a leek and white wine sauce, baked sea trout with spring onion and cheddar crushed potatoes and pesto dressing, pork medallions with wholegrain mustard sautéed potatoes and calvados and pancetta jus, rump steak with shallot and brandy cream sauce and thick chips, and puddings such as chocolate brownie and a crumble of the day. *Benchmark main dish: lamb with mint and rosemary gravy and buttered mash £18.95. Two-course evening meal £21.00.*

Free house ~ Licensees Guy and Jacqui Frazer-Hollins ~ Real ale ~ Open 12-10.30; closed Mon, all Dec, Jan ~ Bar food 12-4.30, 6-9 ~ Restaurant ~ Children welcome but must be over 12 in bedrooms ~ Dogs allowed in bar ~ Wi-fi ~ Bedrooms: /£124 *Recommended by Martin Day, Gwendoline and Ralph Mason, Mark and Mary Setting, Claire Adams*

TALKIN NY5457 Map 10

Blacksmiths Arms

(016977) 3452 – www.blacksmithstalkin.co.uk

Village signposted from B6413 S of Brampton; CA8 1LE

Neatly kept and welcoming with tasty bar food, several real ales and fine nearby walks; bedrooms

On a chilly day you'll find a friendly welcome and warm fires here. It's extended from an 18th-c former blacksmiths and the several neatly kept, traditionally furnished bars include a lounge on the right with upholstered banquettes and wheelback chairs around dark wooden tables on patterned red carpeting, with country prints and other pictures on the walls. The restaurant is to the left and there's also a long lounge opposite the bar, with a step up to another room at the back. Black Sheep, Cumbrian Legendary Loweswater Gold and Hawkshead Bitter and Windermere Pale on handpump, 20 wines by the glass, 20 malt whiskies and ten gins; background music, darts and board games. A couple of picnic-sets are placed outside the front door with more in the back garden. The cottagey bedrooms are comfortable, and the attractive surrounding countryside has good walks.

Pleasing food includes sandwiches, deep-fried black pudding bonbons with peppercorn dipping sauce, prawn cocktail, three-cheese macaroni, pork in cider and apple gravy, chicken topped with bacon, cheese and barbecue sauce, steak and kidney pie, salmon fillet with a white wine, cream and lemon sauce, beef stroganoff, and puddings. *Benchmark main dish: beer-battered haddock and chips £8.95. Two-course evening meal £15.00.*

Free house ~ Licensees Donald and Anne Jackson ~ Real ale ~ Open 12-midnight ~ Bar food 12-2, 6-9 ~ Restaurant ~ Children welcome ~ Wi-fi ~ Bedrooms: £60/£80 *Recommended by Scott and Charlotte Havers, Daniel King, John and Sylvia Harrop, Philip J Alderton, Robert and Diana Myers*

TIRRIL NY5026 Map 10

Queens Head

(01768) 863219 – www.queensheadinn.co.uk

B5320, not far from M6 junction 40; CA10 2JF

Dating from 1719 with two bars, real ales, speciality pies and seats outside; bedrooms

The oldest parts of the main bar here have original flagstones and floorboards, low beams and black panelling, and there are nice little tables and chairs on either side of the inglenook fireplace (always lit in winter). Another bar to the right of the entrance has pews and chairs around sizeable tables on a wooden floor, and candles in the fireplace, while the back locals' bar has heavy beams and a pool table; there are three dining rooms too. Robinsons Cumbria Way, Dizzy Blonde and Unicorn on handpump and several wines by the glass. Outside there are picnic-sets at the front, and modern chairs and tables under cover on the back terrace. The hard-working licensees also run the Pie Mill (you can eat their pies here) and the village shop. The pub is very close to several interesting places including Dalemain House and Garden at Dacre, and Ullswater is just a couple of miles away.

Food includes up to eight pies, plus sandwiches, creamy garlic mushrooms, vegetable lasagne, honey-roast ham and egg, a curry of the day, slow-roast lamb shoulder in redcurrant jelly, steaks with trimmings and chips, and puddings such as sticky toffee pudding and a fruit pie of the day. *Benchmark main dish: pie of the day £11.00. Two-course evening meal £17.00.*

Robinsons ~ Tenants Margaret and Jim Hodge ~ Real ale ~ Open 11-11; 11am-11.30pm Sat; 12-10 Sun ~ Bar food 12-2.30, 5-8.30 ~ Restaurant ~ Children welcome ~ Dogs allowed in bar and bedrooms ~ Wi-fi ~ Bedrooms: £50/£80 *Recommended by Neil and Angela Huxter, Shaun Mahoney, Tina and David Woods-Taylor, Pauline and Mark Evans, Paul Faraday*

ULVERSTON SD3177 Map 7

Bay Horse

(01229) 583972 – www.thebayhorsehotel.co.uk

Canal Foot signposted off A590, then wend your way past the huge Glaxo factory; LA12 9EL

Civilised waterside hotel with lunchtime bar food, three real ales and a fine choice of wines; smart bedrooms

All receive a warm welcome here and staff are kind and helpful. Lunchtime is when the bar is at its most informal, and there's a relaxed atmosphere despite its smart furnishings: cushioned teak dining chairs, paisley-patterned built-in wall banquettes, glossy hardwood traditional tables, a huge stone horse's head, black beams and props, and lots of horsebrasses. Magazines are dotted about, there's an open fire in the handsomely marbled, grey slate fireplace and decently reproduced background music; board games. Jennings Cumberland and Wychwood Hobgoblin on handpump, 16 wines by the glass (including champagne and prosecco) from a carefully chosen, interesting list and 15 malt whiskies. The conservatory restaurant has lovely views over Morecambe Bay and the terrace has plenty of seats and tables. This is a fine place to stay and bedrooms have french windows that open out to a panoramic view of the Leven estuary (the bird life is wonderful); breakfasts are excellent.

Local, seasonal produce is at the heart of the popular food: hot and cold sandwiches, baked potatoes with interesting fillings, duck liver pâté with quince and red chilli jelly, chicken, ham and pistachio nut terrine with gooseberry and juniper purée, bobotie (a spicy south african lamb dish), hazelnut pancakes filled with wild mushrooms in a garlic and chive cream sauce, cod fillet with local brown shrimps and caper, lemon and herb butter, venison medallions on mushroom and onion pâté with red wine, juniper and thyme sauce, highly rated sirloin or fillet steaks with a choice of sauce, and puddings. *Benchmark main dish: crab and salmon fishcakes with a creamy white wine sauce £19.95. Two-course evening meal £30.00.*

Free house ~ Licensee Robert Lyons ~ Real ale ~ Open 11-11; 11-10.30 Sun ~ Bar food 12-2, 7-8.15; light bar meals 6.30-8.30 ~ Restaurant ~ Children welcome at lunchtime, must be over 9 in bedrooms ~ Dogs allowed in bar and bedrooms ~ Wi-fi ~ Bedrooms: £95/£120 *Recommended by Tina and David Woods-Taylor, Denis and Margaret Kilner, Sally and Brian Turner, Barry and Daphne Gregson, Mike Benton, W K Wood*

WINSTER SD4193 Map 9

Brown Horse

(015394) 43443 – www.thebrownhorseinn.co.uk

A5074 S of Windermere; LA23 3NR

Traditional coaching inn with character bar and dining room, own-brewed ales, tasty varied food and seats outside; bedrooms

You'll find a fine choice of drinks here, including a couple of their own-brews from a list that includes Winster Valley Best Bitter, Cartmel Chaser, Dark Horse, Hurdler, Lakes Blonde and Old School, plus a guest such as Ringwood Boondoggle. Also, several wines by the glass, quite a few malt whiskies and an extraordinary list of 175 gins from all over the world with 13 different tonics to mix with them. The chatty beamed and flagstoned bar has church pews, a lovely tall settle and mate's chairs around a mix of tables, while the candlelit dining room has a medley of painted and antique chairs and tables, old skis, carpet beaters, hunting horns and antlers. The gents' is upstairs. There are seats outside among flowering tubs, with more on a raised terrace. The bedrooms are thoughtfully furnished and they also have three self-catering properties. This is a pretty valley with enjoyable surrounding walks.

An interesting choice of food includes lunchtime sandwiches, game terrine with cumberland sauce, smoked mackerel pâté with pickled cucumber and sourdough crisps, spinach and ricotta ravioli with confit tomatoes, crispy courgettes and a tomato butter sauce, corn-fed chicken breast with black pudding bonbon, parmentier potatoes, butternut squash and feta, cod with lentil dhal and onion bhaji in a light curry sauce, local pheasant with fondant potato, parsnips, spinach and mushrooms, and puddings such as chocolate and hazelnut sundae and damson gin crème brûlée with damson ice-cream. *Benchmark main dish: beer-battered haddock and chips £13.95. Two-course evening meal £21.00.*

Free house ~ Licensees Karen and Steve Edmondson ~ Real ale ~ Open 11-11 ~ Bar food 12-3, 6-9 ~ Restaurant ~ Children welcome ~ Dogs allowed in bar ~ Wi-fi ~ Bedrooms: /£115

Recommended by Tina and David Woods-Taylor, Gordon and Margaret Ormondroyd, Michael Butler, Mr and Mrs Richard Osborne, Barry, Alexandra and Richard Clay, Tim and Sarah Smythe-Brown

WITHERSLACK SD4482 Map 10

Derby Arms

(015395) 52207 – www.thederbyarms.co.uk

Just off A590; LA11 6RH

Bustling country inn with half a dozen ales, good food and wine and a genuine welcome; bedrooms

A cheerful new manager had taken over this busy pub just as we went to press and the fine range of drinks continues. On handpump they offer up to six real ales including Ashover Milk Stout, Bowness Bay Swan Blonde, Cumbrian Legendary Grasmoor Dark Ale, Ennerdale English Pride and Handsome Top Knot; also, 11 wines by the glass and 22 malt whiskies. The main bar has sporting prints on pale grey walls, elegant old dining chairs and tables on large rugs over floorboards, and an open fire. A larger room to

If we don't specify bar meal times for a featured entry, these are normally 12-2 and 7-9; we do show times if they are markedly different.

the right is similarly furnished (with the addition of some cushioned pews) and has local prints, another open fire, and alcoves in the back wall full of bristol blue glass, ornate plates and staffordshire dogs and figurines. Large windows lighten the rooms, helped at night by candles in brass candlesticks; background music, TV and pool. There are two additional rooms; one has dark red walls, a red velvet sofa, sporting prints and a handsome mirror over the fireplace. Bedrooms are fairly priced and there's plenty to do nearby – Sizergh Castle (National Trust), Levens Hall and good walks around the Southern Lakes and Dales. This is part of the Ainscoughs group.

Food includes sandwiches, ham hock terrine with piccalilli, crispy whitebait with tartare sauce, beef or chicken burger with relish and chips, sea bass fillets with citrus butter, cumberland sausage and mash with gravy, gnocchi with blue cheese, broccoli and candied walnuts, rib-eye steak with peppercorn sauce and chips and puddings. *Benchmark main dish: steak in ale pie £13.95. Two-course evening meal £19.50.*

Free house ~ Licensee Jamie King ~ Real ale ~ Open 12-11 (midnight Sat) ~ Bar food 12-2, 6-9; 12-9 Sat; 12-8 Sun ~ Children welcome ~ Dogs allowed in bar and bedrooms ~ Wi-fi ~ Live music twice a month Sat evening ~ Bedrooms: /£70 *Recommended by Sally Harrison, Len and Lilly Dowson, Nicholas and Lucy Sage, Alan and Alice Morgan*

YANWATH NY5128 Map 9

Gate Inn

(01768) 862386 – www.yanwathgateinn.uk

2.25 miles from M6 junction 40; A66 towards Brough, then right on A6, right on B5320, then follow village signpost; CA10 2LF

Cosy pub with welcoming staff, local beers and tasty food

Civilised and immaculately kept, this 17th-c pub is a popular place for both food and drink. The cosy bar of charming antiquity has country pine and dark wood furniture, lots of brasses on beams, candles on all tables and a woodburning stove in the attractive stone inglenook; background music and board games. Real ales on handpump come from breweries such as Barngates, Eden and Hesket Newmarket and there are good wines by the glass and Weston's cider; staff are courteous and helpful. The restaurant has oak flooring, works by local artists on the panelled walls, candlelight and a woodburning stove. There are seats and tables under parasols on the terrace and in the garden.

As we went to press, the new licensee had not yet made firm decisions on his menu, but food will include open sandwiches, cumberland sausages with mash and gravy, burgers with toppings and frites, hot smoked chicken caesar salad, fell-bred spring lamb, a pie of the day and interesting daily specials. *Benchmark main dish: beer-battered fish and chips £12.50. Two-course evening meal £25.00.*

Free house ~ Licensee Dave Edwards ~ Real ale ~ Open 12-10 (11 Sat) ~ Bar food 12-2, 5.30-9 ~ Restaurant ~ Children welcome ~ Dogs allowed in bar ~ Wi-fi *Recommended by Serena and Adam Furber, Freddie and Sarah Banks, Mark and Sian Edwards, Graham and Elizabeth Hargreaves, Simon and Sue Lamb*

'Children welcome' means the pub says it lets children inside without any special restriction. If it allows them in, but to restricted areas such as an eating area or family room, we specify this. Places with separate restaurants often let children use them, and hotels usually let children into public areas such as lounges. Some pubs impose an evening time limit – let us know if you find one earlier than 9pm.

Also Worth a Visit in Cumbria

Besides the fully inspected pubs, you might like to try these pubs that have been recommended to us and described by readers. Do tell us what you think of them: feedback@goodguides.com

ALLITHWAITE SD3876

Pheasant (015395) 32239
B5277; LA11 7RQ Welcoming family-run pub on village outskirts; enjoyable freshly cooked traditional food including blackboard specials and good Sun roasts, smaller appetites and special diets catered for, Thwaites Original and four guests, friendly efficient service, traditional bar with log fire, two dining areas off; Thurs quiz; children welcome (not in conservatory), dogs in bar, outside tables on deck with Humphrey Head and Morecambe Bay views, open (and food) all day. *(James Tilley)*

ALSTON NY7146

Angel (01434) 381363
Front Street; CA9 3HU Simple 17th-c inn on steep cobbled street of this charming small Pennine market town; mainly local ales and generously served food including daily specials, reasonable prices, timbers, traditional furnishings and open fires, friendly atmosphere; children and dogs welcome, tables in sheltered back garden, four bedrooms. *(Comus and Sarah Elliott)*

AMBLESIDE NY4008

★**Kirkstone Pass Inn** (015394) 33888
A592 N of Troutbeck; LA22 9LQ Historic inn (Lakeland's highest pub) set in wonderful rugged scenery; flagstones, stripped stone and dark beams, lots of old photographs and bric-a-brac, open fires, enjoyable good value pubby food and well kept changing cumbrian ales, hot drinks, friendly efficient service; soft background music, daily newspapers; well behaved children and dogs welcome, tables outside with stunning views to Windermere, bedrooms, bunkhouse and camping field, open all day in summer (till 6pm Sun), phone for winter hours. *(Geoff Owen, Denis and Margaret Kilner)*

APPLEBY NY6819

★**Royal Oak** (01768) 351463
B6542/Bongate; CA16 6UN Attractive old beamed and timbered coaching inn on edge of town; popular generously served food including early-bird and OAP deals, some themed nights, well kept Black Sheep and one or two local guests, friendly efficient young staff, log fire in panelled bar, lounge with easy chairs and carved settle, traditional snug and restaurant; background music, TV; children and dogs welcome (menus for both), terrace tables, 11 bedrooms and self-catering cottage, good breakfast, open all day from 8am. *(J H Bell, Margaret and Peter Staples)*

ASKHAM NY5123

Punch Bowl (01931) 712443
4.5 miles from M6 junction 40; CA10 2PF Attractive 18th-c village pub on edge of green opposite Askham Hall; spacious beamed main bar, locals' bar, snug lounge and dining room, open fires, well kept Hawkshead and guests, decent choice of enjoyable food (all day weekends) from pub standards up, friendly staff; children and dogs welcome, picnic-sets out in front and on small raised terrace, six bedrooms, open all day. *(Martin Day)*

BAMPTON GRANGE NY5218

★**Crown & Mitre** (01931) 713225
Opposite church; CA10 2QR Old inn set in attractive country hamlet (*Withnail and I* was filmed around here); opened-up bar with comfortable modern décor and nice log fire, separate dining room, popular good quality home-made evening food from pub favourites up, three well kept changing local ales (two in winter), friendly staff; children and dogs welcome, good walks from the door, eight bedrooms, shut lunchtimes (open from 5pm), winter hours may vary. *(Sally and Colin Allen)*

BARBON SD6282

Barbon Inn (015242) 76233
Off A683 Kirkby Lonsdale–Sedbergh; LA6 2LJ Charmingly set 17th-c fell-foot village inn; comfortable old world interior, log fires (one in range), some sofas, armchairs and antique carved settles, a couple of local ales and nice selection of wines, good food from bar meals up, restaurant, friendly staff and regulars; children and dogs welcome, wheelchair access (ladies' loo is upstairs), sheltered pretty garden and terrace, good walks, ten bedrooms, open (and food) all day weekends. *(John Evans)*

BASSENTHWAITE NY2332

Sun (017687) 76439
Off A591 N of Keswick; CA12 4QP White-rendered 17th-c village pub; rambling bar with low black beams and blazing winter fires in two stone fireplaces, built-in wall seats and heavy wooden tables, two Jennings ales and a guest, generous food served by friendly staff, cosy dining room; children and dogs welcome, terrace with views of the fells and Skiddaw, open all day Sun, from 4pm other days. *(Mick Allen)*

BEETHAM SD4979

Wheatsheaf (015395) 64652
Village (and inn) signed off A6 S of Milnthorpe; LA7 7AL This striking

old building with its fine black and white timbered cornerpiece has been refurbished under new owners; opened-up interior with wood floors, stained-glass windows and back open fire, three well kept changing local ales, 20 wines by the glass and good range of whiskies and other spirits, enjoyable food including daily specials, friendly helpful service; background music, quiz first Thurs of month; children and dogs welcome, plenty of surrounding walks, pretty 14th-c church opposite, four bedrooms, open (and food) all day. *(Alan and Alice Morgan)*

BOOT NY1701

Boot Inn (019467) 23711
Aka Burnmoor; signed just off the Wrynose/Hardknott Pass road; CA19 1TG Beamed country inn with Robinsons ales, decent wines and enjoyable home-made food including daily specials, friendly helpful staff, blazing log fire in bare-boards bar, conservatory; children and dogs welcome, garden with play area, lovely surroundings and walks, nine bedrooms, open (and food) all day. *(Kerry and Guy Setting)*

BOOT NY1701

★**Brook House** (019467) 23288
From Ambleside, W of Hardknott Pass; CA19 1TG Lovely views and walks from this friendly family-run country inn, good sensibly priced food from sandwiches to specials, half a dozen well kept ales such as Barngates, Cumbrian Legendary, Hawkshead and Yates, Weston's cider/perry, decent wines and over 180 whiskies, relaxed comfortable raftered bar with log fire and stuffed animals, smaller plush snug, peaceful separate restaurant; children and dogs welcome, tables on flagstoned terrace, eight reasonably priced bedrooms, good breakfast (for nearby campers too), mountain weather reports, excellent drying room, handy for Eskdale miniature railway terminus, open all day. *(Tina and David Woods-Taylor)*

BOOT NY1901

Woolpack (019467) 23230
Bleabeck, midway between Boot and Hardknott Pass; CA19 1TH Last pub before the Hardknott Pass; warm welcoming atmosphere in main walkers' bar and more contemporary café-bar, also an evening restaurant (Fri, Sat), good home-made food including wood-fired pizzas, pies, steaks and daily specials, up to eight well kept ales, real cider and vast range of vodkas and gins; regular events including live music, Apr sausage and cider festival and June beer festival, pool room, big-screen sports TV; children and dogs welcome, mountain-view garden with play area, eight bedrooms, open (and food) all day. *(Tina and David Woods-Taylor)*

BOUTH SD3285

★**White Hart** (01229) 861229
Village signed off A590 near Haverthwaite; LA12 8JB Cheerful bustling old inn with popular generously served food, six well kept mainly local ales and 25 malt whiskies, friendly service, sloping ceilings and floors, old local photographs, farm tools and stuffed animals, collection of long-stemmed clay pipes, two woodburners; background music; children and dogs (in one part of bar) welcome, seats outside and fine surrounding walks, playground opposite, five comfortable bedrooms, adjoining self-catering cottage, open all day, food all day Sun. *(Jamie and Lizzie McEwan)*

BOWLAND BRIDGE SD4189

★**Hare & Hounds** (015395) 68333
Signed from A5074; LA11 6NN Fine valley views from this quietly placed 17th-c inn; little bar with log fire, well kept ales including a house beer from Tirril (Hare of the Dog), local farm cider and a dozen wines by the glass, good sensibly priced food from sandwiches and pubby choices up, other attractively furnished rooms with mix of tables and chairs on black slate or old pine boards, numerous hunting prints on painted or stripped-stone walls; background music, board games, daily papers and free wi-fi; children and dogs (in bar) welcome, front terrace with teak furniture under parasols, more seats in spacious side garden, comfortable bedrooms, open all day, food all day weekends. *(Gerry and Pam Pollard, Robin and Anne Triggs, Gail and Frank Hackett, P and J Shapley, Helene Grygar)*

BOWNESS-ON-WINDERMERE SD4096

Royal Oak (015394) 43970
Brantfell Road; LA23 3EG Family-run inn handy for the steamer pier; interconnecting bar, dining room and big games room, old photographs and bric-a-brac, open fire, well kept ales such as Coniston, Jennings, Sharps, Timothy Taylors and Tetleys, generous reasonably priced pub food from baguettes to specials, friendly efficient service; pool, darts and TV; children welcome, tables out in front, eight bedrooms, open (and food) all day. *(George and Alison Bishop)*

BRAITHWAITE NY2324

Middle Ruddings (017687) 78436
Middle Ruddings, road running parallel with A66; CA12 5RY Welcoming family-run country inn; good food in bar or carpeted dining conservatory with fine Skiddaw views,

We include some hotels with a good bar that offers facilities comparable to those of a pub.

friendly attentive service, three well kept changing local ales and plenty of bottled beers, several ciders too and interesting range of malt whiskies, afternoon teas; children and dogs (in bar) welcome, garden with terrace picnic-sets, 14 bedrooms, good breakfast, open all day but no food weekday lunchtimes. *(Mike Benton)*

BRAITHWAITE NY2323

Royal Oak (017687) 78533
B5292 at top of village; CA12 5SY Recently refurbished village pub with warm welcoming atmosphere; four well kept Jennings ales and hearty helpings of good value traditional food (smaller servings available), efficient service, beamed bar and restaurant; background music, TV, board games; children welcome, no dogs at mealtimes, ten bedrooms, open all day. *(Daniel King)*

BROUGHTON-IN-FURNESS SD2187

Manor Arms (01229) 716286
The Square; LA20 6HY End-of-terrace drinkers' pub on quiet sloping square; up to eight well priced changing ales and good choice of ciders, flagstoned front bar with nice bow-window seat, coal fire in big stone fireplace, old photographs and chiming clocks, limited food such as toasties; pool, free wi-fi; children and dogs allowed, bedrooms, open all day. *(Jane and Philip Saunders)*

BUTTERMERE NY1716

Bridge Hotel (017687) 70252
Just off B5289 SW of Keswick; CA13 9UZ Welcoming and popular with walkers, hotel-like in feel but with two traditional comfortable beamed bars (dogs allowed in one), four well kept cumbrian ales and good food, more upmarket menu in evening dining room; free wi-fi; children welcome, fell views from flagstoned terrace, 21 bedrooms and six self-catering apartments, open (and food) all day. *(Caroline and Peter Bryant)*

CARLISLE NY4056

Kings Head (01228) 533797
Fisher Street (pedestrianised); CA3 8RF 17th-c split-level pub with lots of beams (some painted), wood or stone floors and friendly bustling atmosphere, well kept Yates Bitter and guests, low-priced pubby lunchtime food from sandwiches and baked potatoes up, cheerful quick service, upstairs dining room; background and summer live music (in courtyard), TV; no children or dogs, historical plaque outside explaining why Carlisle is not in the Domesday Book, open all day. *(Charles Fraser)*

CARTMEL SD3778

Cavendish Arms (015395) 36240
Cavendish Street, off the Square; LA11 6QA Former coaching inn with simply furnished open-plan beamed bar, roaring log fire (even on cooler summer evenings), three or four ales featuring a house beer from Cumberland, several wines by the glass and good range of gins, decent coffee, friendly staff, enjoyable fairly traditional food from lunchtime ciabattas up, restaurant; children welcome, dogs in bar, tables out in front and behind by stream (must pay in advance if you eat out here), nice village with notable priory church, racecourse and good walks, ten bedrooms – three more above their shop in the square, open (and food) all day. *(P and J Shapley)*

CARTMEL SD3778

Kings Arms (015395) 33246
The Square; LA11 6QB Bustling 18th-c pub close to the priory; cosy beamed rooms with flagstones and bare boards, log fires, nice mix of furniture including comfortable sofas, Hawkshead ales and a guest, food from sandwiches to daily specials, friendly service; live weekend bands (pub open till 1am then), free wi-fi; children and dogs welcome, seats outside facing the lovely square, open (and food) all day. *(Gordon and Margaret Ormondroyd)*

CARTMEL SD3778

★**Royal Oak** (015395) 36259
The Square; LA11 6QB Low-beamed flagstoned inn under same management as the Kings Arms next door; long rustic tables, settles, leather easy chairs and big log fire, cosy nooks, good value food including pub favourites, home-made pizzas, pasta and grills, well kept local ales such as Cumbrian Legendary, Hawkshead and Unsworths Yard, good choice of wines, welcoming helpful staff; background and weekend live music, two sports TVs, free wi-fi; children and dogs welcome, some seats out in square, nice big riverside garden behind with heated terrace, four neat bedrooms, open (and food) all day. *(Andrew Lawson)*

CASTERTON SD6379

★**Pheasant** (015242) 71230
A683; LA6 2RX Welcoming 18th-c family-run inn with neatly furnished beamed rooms; highly regarded attractively presented food from imaginative menu, well kept ales including a house beer brewed by Tirril, nice wines and several malt whiskies, friendly helpful staff, arched and panelled restaurant; background music, free wi-fi; children and dogs welcome, a few roadside seats, more in pleasant garden with Vale of Lune views, near church with notable Pre-Raphaelite stained glass and paintings, ten bedrooms, closed Mon lunchtime, otherwise open all day. *(Michael Doswell, Derek Stafford)*

CASTLE CARROCK NY5455

Duke of Cumberland
(01228) 670341 *Geltsdale Road; CA8 9LU* Popular and welcoming stone-built village-

green pub under newish management; freshly updated interior with upholstered wall benches and mix of pubby furniture on stone floor, open fire, dining area with old farmhouse tables and chairs, a couple of local ales and good food often including some asian choices; children and dogs (theirs is Poppy) welcome, picnic-sets out at front, accommodation planned, open all day weekends, closed Mon, Tues (and lunchtimes Weds-Fri in winter). *(Marcus Byron)*

CHAPEL STILE NY3205

Wainwrights (015394) 38088

B5343; LA22 9JH Popular white-rendered former farmhouse; half a dozen ales including Jennings and plenty of wines by the glass, enjoyable well priced pubby food from good sandwiches up, friendly helpful service (may slow when busy), roomy bar with slate floor and good log fire, other spreading carpeted areas with beams, some half-panelling, cushioned settles and mix of dining chairs around wooden tables, old kitchen range; background music, TV and games machines, Tues quiz; children welcome, dogs and boots in bar, terrace picnic-sets, fine views, open (and food) all day. *(Pauline and Mark Evans)*

COCKERMOUTH NY1230

Castle Bar (01900) 829904

Market Place; CA13 9NQ Busy 16th-c pub on three floors, beams, timbers and other original features mixing with modern furnishings, five well kept local beers such as Cumbrian Legendary and Jennings (cheaper 3-7pm Mon-Fri, all day Sun), Weston's cider, enjoyable home-made food including good value Sun roasts in upstairs dining room or in any of the three ground-floor areas, efficient service from friendly young staff; sports TV; children welcome, dogs downstairs, seats on sunny back tiered terrace, open all day. *(Edward Edmonton)*

CONISTON SD3097

Black Bull (015394) 41335/41668

Yewdale Road (A593); LA21 8DU Bustling 17th-c beamed inn brewing its own good Coniston beers; back area (liked by walkers and their dogs) with slate floor, more comfortable carpeted front part with log fire and Donald Campbell memorabilia, enjoyable food including daily specials, friendly helpful staff, lounge with Old Man of Coniston big toe (large piece of stone in the wall), restaurant; they may ask for a credit card if you run a tab; children welcome, plenty of seats in former coachyard, 15 bedrooms, open (and food) all day from 10am, parking not easy at peak times. *(Lorna and Jack Musgrave)*

CROOK SD4695

Sun (01539) 821351

B5284 Kendal–Bowness; LA8 8LA End-of-terrace roadside country pub under welcoming licensees; low-beamed bar with dining areas off, stone, wood and carpeted floors, log fires, enjoyable food from sandwiches up including weekday set lunch and themed evenings, two or three changing ales; occasional live music; children welcome (games for them), dogs and muddy boots in some parts, seats out at front by road, open (and food) all day. *(Daniel King)*

DENT SD7086

George & Dragon (015396) 25256

Main Street; LA10 5QL Two-bar corner pub acting as tap for Dent Brewery; their full range kept well plus real cider and perry, old panelling, partitioned tables and open fires, enjoyable food from snacks up, friendly engaging young staff, steps down to restaurant, games room with pool and juke box; sports TV, free wi-fi; children, walkers and dogs welcome, ten bedrooms, lovely village, open all day. *(1suzinorman)*

DUFTON NY6825

Stag (017683) 51608

Village signed from A66 at Appleby; CA16 6DB Traditional little 18th-c pub by pretty village's green; friendly licensees and regulars, good reasonably priced home-made food and interesting range of well kept changing beers, two log fires, one in splendid early Victorian kitchen range in main bar, room off to the left, dining room; quiz every other Thurs, darts; children, walkers and dogs welcome, tables out at front and in back garden with lovely hill views, handy for Pennine Way, self-catering cottage, open all day weekends, closed weekday lunchtimes. *(Mike Benton)*

ENNERDALE BRIDGE NY0716

Fox & Hounds (01946) 861373

High Street; CA23 3AR Popular community-owned village pub; beamed interior with bare boards and quarry tiles, upholstered wall benches and wheelback chairs around pubby tables, woodburners, up to five well kept cumbrian ales including local Ennerdale, tasty reasonably priced home-made food (Thurs steak night), friendly staff; Sun quiz, some live music, free wi-fi; children and dogs welcome, picnic-sets in streamside garden, three spacious bedrooms, handy for walkers on Coast to Coast path, open all day in summer. *(Selwyn Jones)*

ENNERDALE BRIDGE NY0615

Shepherds Arms (01946) 861249

Off A5086 E of Egremont; CA23 3AR Friendly well placed walkers' inn by car-free dale; bar with log fire and woodburner, up to five local beers and good generously served home-made food, can provide packed lunches, panelled dining room and conservatory; free wi-fi; children welcome, seats outside by beck, eight bedrooms, good breakfast. *(Martin Day)*

ESKDALE GREEN NY1200
Bower House (019467) 23244
0.5 miles W of Eskdale Green; CA19 1TD Comfortably modernised 17th-c stone inn extended around beamed core; four regional ales and enjoyable hearty food (all day weekends) in bar or biggish restaurant, log fires, friendly atmosphere; Sun quiz, free wi-fi; children and dogs welcome, sheltered garden with play area, charming spot by cricket field with great view of Muncaster Fell, good walks, 20 bedrooms (some in converted barn), open all day. *(Nicholas and Lucy Sage)*

ESKDALE GREEN NY1400
King George IV (019467) 23470
E of village; CA19 1TS Whitewashed country pub with cheerful beamed and flagstoned bar, log fire in stone fireplace, interesting range of local well kept ales and over 100 malt whiskies, ample helpings of sensibly priced pubby food from sandwiches up, friendly service, restaurant, games room with pool; free wi-fi; children, walkers and dogs welcome, disabled access/loos, nice views from outside tables (road nearby), lots of good walks, bedrooms and self-catering, open (and food) all day. *(Tina and David Woods-Taylor)*

FAR SAWREY SD3795
Cuckoo Brow (015394) 43425
B5285 N of village; LA22 0LQ Renovated 300-year-old coaching house in lovely setting; opened-up bar with wood floors and central woodburner, steps down to former stables with tables in stalls, harnesses on rough white walls, even water troughs and mangers, four well kept changing local ales and good hearty food served by friendly helpful staff; background music, free wi-fi; children, walkers and dogs welcome, seats on nice front lawn, 14 bedrooms, open (and food) all day. *(Kerry and Guy Trooper)*

FAUGH NY5054
String of Horses (01228) 670297
S of village, on left as you go downhill; CA8 9EG Welcoming 17th-c coaching inn with cosy communicating beamed rooms; log fires, oak panelling and some interesting carved furniture, tasty traditional food alongside latin american/mexican dishes, well kept local beers and nice house wines, restaurant; background music, sports TV, free wi-fi; children welcome, no dogs, a few picnic-sets out in front, 11 comfortable bedrooms, good breakfast, closed lunchtimes and all day Mon. *(Pauline and Mark Evans)*

FOXFIELD SD2085
★**Prince of Wales** (01229) 716238
Opposite station; LA20 6BX Popular and cheery bare-boards pub; half a dozen good changing ales including some bargains brewed here and at their associated Tigertops Brewery, bottled imports and real cider too, huge helpings of enjoyable home-made food (lots of unusual pasties), character landlord and good friendly service, hot coal fire; live music second/fourth Weds of month, pub games including bar billiards, daily papers and beer-related reading matter; children and dogs welcome, four reasonably priced bedrooms, open all day Fri-Sun, from 2.45pm Wed and Thurs, closed Mon, Tues. *(Mike Benton)*

GLENRIDDING NY3816
Travellers Rest (017684) 82298
Back of main car park, at the top of the road; CA11 0QQ Friendly low-beamed and panelled two-bar pub, good straightforward food and well kept ales such as Hesket Newmarket and Jennings, simple yet comfortable pubby décor, old local photographs, real fire; Ullswater views from terrace picnic-sets, children, walkers and dogs welcome (nearest pub to Helvellyn), open (and food) all day in summer. *(Tina and David Woods-Taylor)*

GOSFORTH NY0703
Gosforth Hall (019467) 25322
Off A595 and unclassified road to Wasdale; CA20 1AZ Friendly well run Jacobean inn with interesting history; beamed and carpeted bar (popular with locals), fine plaster coat of arms above woodburner, lounge/reception area with huge fireplace, ales such as Hawkshead, Keswick and Yates, enjoyable home-made food including good range of pies, restaurant; children and dogs welcome, nice big side garden, 22 bedrooms (some in new extension), open all day. *(Darren Ogden)*

GRASMERE NY3406
Travellers Rest (015394) 35604
A591 just N; LA22 9RR Welcoming 16th-c roadside coaching inn with attractive creeper-clad exterior; traditional linked rooms, settles, padded benches and other pubby furniture on flagstone or wood floors, old local photographs and open fires, well kept Jennings ales, good selection of wines and enjoyable reasonably priced food including steak menu and specials, friendly helpful service; background music, pool, steps up to gents'; children and dogs welcome, seats outside with fell views, ten bedrooms, open (and food) all day. *(Ian and Rose Lock)*

GRASMERE NY3307
Tweedies (015394) 35300
Part of Dale Lodge Hotel; LA22 9SW Lively properly pubby atmosphere in big square hotel bar; wide choice of beers on tap and in bottles, proper cider/perry and plenty of wines by the glass too, good service, traditional décor with hundreds of beer mats on display, log fire, sturdy furnishings in adjoining flagstoned dining room serving

good hearty food including children's choices, also separate restaurant; weekend live music, Sept beer/music festival; walkers and dogs welcome, picnic-sets out in large pleasant garden, comfortable well equipped bedrooms, open (and food) all day. *(Mr and Mrs Richard Osborne)*

GREYSTOKE NY4430

Boot & Shoe (017684) 83343

By village green, off B5288; CA11 0TP Cosy 17th-c two-bar pub in pretty 'Tarzan' village; low ceilings, exposed brickwork and dark woodwork, good generously served traditional food including blackboard specials, well kept Black Sheep and local microbrews, bustling friendly atmosphere; Thurs quiz, live music; children (until 8pm) and dogs (in bar) welcome, seats out at front and in back garden, on national cycle route, four bedrooms, open all day. *(Selwyn Jones)*

HARTSOP NY4013

Brotherswater Inn (017684) 82239

On Kirkstone Pass Road, S of Patterdale; CA11 0NZ Cosy well run walkers' and campers' pub in magnificent setting at the bottom of Kirkstone Pass; good local ales and enjoyable sensibly priced food served by friendly helpful staff, beautiful fell views across the lake from picture windows and terrace tables; children and dogs welcome, six bedrooms, bunkhouse and campsite, open all day (from 8am for breakfast). *(Tina and David Woods-Taylor)*

HAWESWATER NY4914

Haweswater (01931) 713235

Lakeside Road; CA10 2RP Remote 1930s hotel in commanding position overlooking reservoir; plenty of art deco detail in refurbished bar/bistro and separate evening restaurant, open fires, enjoyable food from pub favourites up, friendly efficient service; children and dogs (in bar) welcome, attractive gardens with red squirrels and wonderful views, on Wainwright's Coast to Coast path, 17 bedrooms, open (and food) all day. *(Stuart Doughty, Hugh Roberts)*

HAWKSHEAD SD3598

Kings Arms (015394) 36372

The Square; LA22 0NZ Old inn with low ceilings, traditional pubby furnishings and log fire, well stocked bar serving local ales such as Cumbrian Legendary and Hawkshead, good variety of enjoyable food from lunchtime sandwiches to daily specials, quick service, side dining area; background music, free wi-fi; children and dogs (in bar) welcome, terrace overlooking central square of this lovely Elizabethan village, bedrooms, self-catering cottages nearby, free fishing permits for residents, open all day till midnight. *(Adam Jones)*

HAWKSHEAD SD3598

Queens Head (015394) 36271

Main Street; LA22 0NS Black and white timbered pub in this charming village; low-ceilinged bar with heavy bowed black beams, red plush wall seats and stools around hefty traditional tables, decorative plates on panelled walls, open fire, snug little room off and several eating areas, Robinsons ales, a guest beer and good range of wines and whiskies, enjoyable bar food plus more elaborate evening meals, friendly helpful staff; background and occasional live music, TV, darts; children and dogs welcome, seats outside and pretty window boxes, 13 bedrooms, self-catering cottage, open all day. *(Andrew Lawson)*

HAWKSHEAD SD3598

Red Lion (015394) 36213

Main Street; LA22 0NS Cheerful old inn with well kept local ales including Hawkshead and enjoyable traditional home-made food, original panelling and good log fire; quiz Sun evening, sports TV, darts; dogs very welcome (menu for them), eight bedrooms (some sloping floors), open all day. *(Mick Allen)*

HAWKSHEAD SD3598

Sun (015394) 36236

Main Street; LA22 0NT Steps up to welcoming 17th-c beamed inn; Hawkshead, Jennings and a couple of guests, decent wines and extensive range of gins, popular fairly priced food from lunchtime sandwiches up, sizeable restaurant; live music, TV; children and dogs (in bar) welcome, tables out in small front courtyard, eight bedrooms, open all day, food all day Sun. *(Sue Parry Davies)*

HESKET NEWMARKET NY3438

Old Crown (016974) 78288

Village signed off B5299 in Caldbeck; CA7 8JG Straightforward cooperative-owned local in attractive village; small bar with bric-a-brac, mountaineering kit and pictures, woodburner, good Hesket Newmarket beers brewed in barn behind (can book tours), hearty home-made food (not Mon), reasonable prices and friendly service, dining room and garden room; folk night Mon, juke box, pool, darts and board games; children and dogs welcome, lovely walking country away from Lake District crowds (near Cumbria Way), open all day Fri-Sun, closed lunchtimes other days. *(Dr Geoff Butts)*

KENDAL SD5192

Riflemans Arms (01539) 241470

Greenside; LA9 4LD Old-fashioned local in village-green setting on edge of town, friendly regulars and staff, Greene King Abbot and guests, no food; Thurs folk night, Sun quiz, pool and darts (regular matches);

children and dogs welcome, closed weekday lunchtimes, open all day weekends. *(Hugh Roberts)*

KESWICK NY2623

Dog & Gun (017687) 73463

Lake Road; off top end of Market Square; CA12 5BT Smartly furnished beamed town pub; button-back leather banquettes, stools and small round tables on light wood flooring, collection of striking mountain photographs, reasonably priced hearty food including signature goulash (served in two sizes), friendly helpful staff, half a dozen or so well kept ales including Keswick and a house beer (Woof & Bang), log fire; occasional quiz nights, poker Weds; children till 9.30pm and dogs welcome, open (and food) all day, can get very busy in season. *(Mark and Mary Setting)*

KESWICK NY2623

George (017687) 72076

St Johns Street; CA12 5AZ Handsome 17th-c coaching inn with open-plan main bar and attractive dark-panelled side room; old-fashioned settles and modern banquettes under black beams, log fires, four Jennings ales and a couple of guests kept well, ten wines by the glass, generous home-made food including signature cow pie and gluten-free dishes, friendly helpful service, restaurant; background music, daily papers; children welcome in eating areas, dogs in bar, 12 bedrooms, open all day. *(Mick Allen)*

KESWICK NY2624

Inn on the Square 0800 840 1247

Market Square; CA12 5JF Hotel with contemporary scandinavian-influenced décor; enjoyable food in front and back bars or steakhouse restaurant, good choice of wines and cocktails, well kept ales such as Keswick, efficient friendly service; children and dogs (in bar areas) welcome, 34 bedrooms, open all day. *(Comus and Sarah Elliott)*

KESWICK NY2624

Pheasant (017687) 72219

Crosthwaite Road (A66, 1 mile out); CA12 5PP Small 17th-c beamed roadside local, generous helpings of popular home-made food at reasonable prices, well kept Jennings and guests, good friendly service, open fire, dining room; children (if eating) and dogs (in bar) welcome, a few picnic-sets out at front, beer garden up steps behind, bedrooms, near ancient church of St Kentigern, open all day. *(Richard Elliott, Nick and Meriel Cox)*

KESWICK NY2623

Royal Oak (017687) 74584

Main Street; CA12 5HZ Recently refurbished 18th-c coaching house, Thwaites ales, decent wines and good choice of popular food, friendly service; children and dogs welcome, comfortable redecorated bedrooms, open (and food) all day. *(Comus and Sarah Elliott)*

KESWICK NY2421

Swinside Inn (017687) 78253

Newlands Valley, just SW; CA12 5UE Refurbished 17th-c pub in peaceful valley setting; two bars and various dining areas, open fires, well kept ales including a couple named for them, good reasonably priced pubby food from lunchtime sandwiches up, friendly helpful staff; background music, free wi-fi; children and dogs (in some parts) welcome, tables in garden and on upper and lower terraces with fine views across to the high crags and fells around Rosedale Pike, six bedrooms, big breakfast, open all day. *(Mr and Mrs Richard Osborne, Tina and David Woods-Taylor)*

KIRKBY LONSDALE SD6178

Orange Tree (01524) 271716

Fairbank (B6254); LA6 2BD Family-run inn acting as tap for Kirkby Lonsdale brewery, well kept guest ales too, a real cider and good choice of wines and bottled belgian beers, carpeted beamed bar with central wooden servery, sporting cartoons and old range, enjoyable reasonably priced home-made food in back dining room, efficient young staff; background music, pool and darts; children and dogs welcome, comfortable bedrooms (some in building next door), open all day. *(Steve Whalley)*

KIRKOSWALD NY5641

Fetherston Arms (01768) 898284

The Square; CA10 1DQ Busy old stone inn with cosy bar and various dining areas; enjoyable food at reasonable prices including good home-made pies, interesting range of well kept changing beers, friendly helpful staff; bedrooms, nice Eden Valley village. *(Selwyn Jones)*

LANGDALE NY2906

Sticklebarn (015394) 37356

By car park for Stickle Ghyll; LA22 9JU Glorious views from this roomy and busy Langdale Valley walkers'/climbers' bar owned and run by the NT; up to five well kept changing ales and a real cider, shortish choice of enjoyable home-made food (some meat from next-door farm), mountaineering photographs, two woodburners; background music (live Sat in season), films shown Tues in upstairs function room, quiz Sun; children, dogs and boots welcome, big terrace with inner verandah, outside pizza oven and fire pit, open (and food) all day, shuts in winter at 6pm (9pm weekends). *(Peter Meister)*

LEVENS SD4885

Hare & Hounds (015395) 60004

Off A590; LA8 8PN Welcoming old village pub handy for Sizergh Castle (NT); five well kept changing local ales and good home-made pub food including burgers and pizzas, partly panelled low-beamed lounge bar, front tap room with open fire and further seating down steps, also a barn dining room; Weds winter quiz; children, walkers and dogs welcome, disabled loo, good views from front terrace, four bedrooms, open (and food) all day. *(Mr and Mrs Richard Osborne)*

LORTON NY1526

★**Wheatsheaf** (01900) 85199
B5289 Buttermere–Cockermouth; CA13 9UW Good local atmosphere in neatly furnished bar with two log fires and vibrant purple walls, Jennings ales, regularly changing guests and several good value wines, popular home-made food (all day Sun) from sandwiches up, smallish restaurant (best to book), affable hard-working landlord and friendly staff; children and dogs welcome, tables out behind and campsite, open all day weekends, closed lunchtimes Tues, Weds (Mon-Thurs lunchtimes in winter). *(Dan and Belinda Smallbone)*

LOW HESKET NY4646

Rose & Crown (01697) 473346
A6 Carlisle–Penrith; CA4 0HG Welcoming 18th-c coaching inn with split-level interior; enjoyable home-made food including vegetarian menu, Jennings Bitter and guests, good service, pitched-roof dining room with railway memorabilia and central oak tree; background music, TV; children welcome, closed Mon and lunchtimes apart from Sun. *(Jane and Philip Saunders)*

LOWICK GREEN SD3084

Farmers Arms (01229) 861853
Just off A5092 SE of village; LA12 8DT Stable bar with heavy black beams, huge slate flagstones and log fire, cosy corners, some interesting furniture and pictures in plusher hotel lounge/dining area, tasty generously served pubby food (all day weekends), Theakstons ales and decent wines from shortish list, good friendly service; background music, TV, pool and darts, free wi-fi; children and dogs welcome, ten comfortable bedrooms, ample breakfast, open all day. *(Dr K Nesbitt)*

MUNGRISDALE NY3630

Mill Inn (017687) 79632
Off A66 Penrith–Keswick, 1 mile W of A5091 Ullswater turn-off; CA11 0XR Part 17th-c pub in fine setting below fells with wonderful surrounding walks; neatly kept bar with old millstone built into counter, traditional dark wood furnishings, hunting pictures and woodburner in stone fireplace, Robinsons ales and good range of malt whiskies, traditional food from lunchtime sandwiches and baked potatoes up, friendly staff, separate dining room; darts and dominoes, pool in winter; children and dogs welcome, wheelchair access, seats in garden by river, six bedrooms, open (and food) all day. *(Daniel King)*

NETHER WASDALE NY1204

★**Strands** (01946) 726237
SW of Wast Water; CA20 1ET Lovely spot below the remote high fells around Wast Water; own-brew beers and popular good value food from changing menu, well cared-for high-beamed main bar with woodburner, smaller public bar with pool and table football, separate dining room, pleasant staff and relaxed friendly atmosphere; background and occasional live music; children and dogs welcome, neat garden with terrace and belvedere, 14 bedrooms, good breakfast, open all day. *(Kerry and Guy Trooper)*

NEWBIGGIN NY5649

Blue Bell (01768) 896615
B6413; CA8 9DH Small L-shaped village pub, friendly and unpretentious, with a changing local ale and enjoyable pubby food cooked by landlady, fireplace on right with woodburner; darts and pool; children welcome, good Eden Valley walks, closed weekday lunchtimes. *(Mick Allen)*

PAPCASTLE NY1131

Spotted Pig (01900) 823518
Belle Vue; CA13 0NT Revamped beamed corner pub on two levels, popular well presented food (all day Sun till 7pm) from lunchtime sandwiches to daily specials, local ales and nice range of gins and cocktails, friendly helpful service; background music; children welcome. *(Alan Eaves)*

PATTERDALE NY3915

White Lion (017684) 82214
A592 opposite village shop; CA11 0NW Tall narrow roadside inn with ready market of walkers and climbers (can get very busy especially in season), large helpings of enjoyable pub food and well kept beers such as Marstons and Theakstons, friendly hard-working staff, traditional flagstoned bar, open fires; children and dogs welcome, seven bedrooms (five ensuite), open (and food) all day. *(Tina and David Woods-Taylor)*

POOLEY BRIDGE NY4724

Sun (017684) 86205
Centre of village (B5320); CA10 2NN Friendly roadside local in row of whitewashed cottages, well kept Jennings and guests, decent choice of enjoyable fairly traditional food including hot and cold sandwiches, two bars with steps between (dogs allowed in lower one), restaurant; children welcome, picnic-sets in garden with play fort, nine reasonably priced comfortable bedrooms (three are dog-friendly). *(P and J Shapley)*

RAVENSTONEDALE NY7401

Fat Lamb (015396) 23242
Crossbank; A683 Sedbergh–Kirkby Stephen; CA17 4LL Isolated inn surrounded by great scenery and lovely

walks; comfortable old-fashioned feel, pews in beamed bar with fire in traditional black range, interesting local photographs and bird plates, propeller from 1930s biplane over servery, good choice of enjoyable food from sharing boards to daily specials, can eat in bar or separate dining room (less character), well kept Black Sheep or Pennine, decent wines and around 60 malt whiskies, friendly helpful staff; background music; children and dogs welcome, disabled facilities, tables out by nature reserve pastures, 12 bedrooms, open all day, food all day weekends. *(Graham and Carol Parker)*

RAVENSTONEDALE NY7204

★ **Kings Head** (015396) 23050

Pub visible from A685 W of Kirkby Stephen; CA17 4NH Sizeable riverside inn with opened-up beamed rooms, rugs on big flagstones and attractive array of wooden chairs and cushioned settles, prints on grey-painted walls, double-sided woodburner and another log fire in raised fireplace, similarly furnished dining room, Theakstons Best, a couple of guests and eight wines by the glass, popular interesting food, friendly staff, games room with darts and local photographs; background music; children and dogs (in bar) welcome, picnic-sets by the river in fenced-off area, comfortable clean bedrooms, good surrounding walks, open (and food) all day. *(Graeme and Sally Mendham, Ben and Jenny Settle, Tom and Lorna Harding, Mr and Mrs P R Thomas)*

ROSTHWAITE NY2514

Scafell (017687) 77208

B5289 S of Keswick; CA12 5XB 19th-c hotel's big tile-floored back bar useful for walkers, weather forecast board and blazing log fire, up to five well kept local ales in season, 60 malt whiskies and enjoyable food from sandwiches up, afternoon teas, also cocktail bar/sun lounge and dining room, friendly helpful staff; background music, pool; children and dogs welcome, tables out overlooking beck, 23 smart contemporary bedrooms, open all day. *(Brian and Anna Marsden)*

RULEHOLME NY5060

Golden Fleece (01228) 573686

Signed off A689; CA6 4NF Hospitable whitewashed inn with series of softly lit linked rooms; well liked interesting food (all day Sat), a couple of local ales and good range of wines by the glass, friendly attentive service; children welcome, handy for Hadrian's Wall and Carlisle Airport, seven comfortable well equipped bedrooms, hearty breakfast, open all day weekends, closed Mon and lunchtimes Tues-Fri. *(Edward Edmonton)*

RYDAL NY3606

Glen Rothay Hotel (015394) 34500

A591 Ambleside–Grasmere; LA22 9LR Small 17th-c roadside hotel with cosy back Badger Bar, copper-topped tables, stools and benches, lots of interesting local prints, up to five well kept changing ales and varied choice of locally sourced food from good sandwiches up, nice coffee, beamed and panelled dining lounge with open fire, restaurant, friendly efficient service; unusual loos cut into the rock; children, walkers and dogs welcome, tables in pretty garden (resident badgers are fed at dusk), eight comfortable bedrooms, good breakfast, handy for William Wordsworth's house, open all day. *(John and Sylvia Harrop)*

SANDFORD NY7316

Sandford Arms (01768) 351121

Village and pub signposted just off A66 W of Brough; CA16 6NR Neatly modernised former 18th-c farmhouse in peaceful village; quite a choice of good food (all day weekends Apr-Oct) from chef-landlord, friendly helpful service, L-shaped part-carpeted main bar with stripped beams and stonework, well kept ales including Black Sheep, comfortable raised and balustraded eating area, more formal dining room and second flagstoned bar, woodburner; background music; children and dogs welcome, seats in front garden and covered courtyard, five bedrooms, closed Tues and lunchtime Weds. *(George and Alison Bishop)*

SANTON BRIDGE NY1101

Bridge Inn (019467) 26221

Off A595 at Holmrook or Gosforth; CA19 1UX Old inn set in charming riverside spot with fell views; bustling beamed and timbered bar, some booths around stripped-pine tables, log fire, half a dozen well kept ales such as Jennings, enjoyable food (booking advised) including blackboard specials and Sun carvery, friendly helpful staff, separate dining room and small reception hall with open fire and daily papers; background music, free wi-fi, World's Biggest Liar competition (Nov); children and dogs (in bar) welcome, seats outside by quiet road, plenty of walks, 16 bedrooms, open (and food) all day, breakfast for non-residents. *(Sally and Colin Allen)*

SATTERTHWAITE SD3392

Eagles Head (01229) 860237

S edge of village; LA12 8LN Nice little pub prettily placed on edge of beautiful Grizedale Forest (visitor centre nearby); low black beams and comfortable furnishings, antlers, horsebrasses, decorative plates and other odds and ends, old tiled floor, woodburner, four real ales such as Barngates, Coniston, Cumbrian Legendary and Hawkshead, popular pubby food from shortish menu including good home-made pies, friendly welcoming staff; occasional live music, local artwork for sale; children, dogs and muddy boots welcome, picnic-sets in attractive tree-shaded courtyard garden, open all day summer, closed Mon in winter, food all day weekends. *(Andrew Lawson)*

SCALES NY3426

White Horse (017687) 79883

A66 W of Penrith; CA12 4SY Traditional Lakeland pub in lovely setting below Blencathra; log fire in flagstoned beamed bar, little snug and another room with black range, three real ales such as Cross Bay, Cumberland and Tirril, good pubby food (all day weekends); board games, free wi-fi; children and dogs welcome, picnic-sets out in front, bunkhouse, open all day. *(Charles Fraser)*

SEATHWAITE SD2295

Newfield Inn (01229) 716208

Duddon Valley, near Ulpha (not Seathwaite in Borrowdale); LA20 6ED Friendly 16th-c whitewashed stone cottage in quiet country setting; bar with unusual slate floor and interesting pictures, woodburner, four well kept changing local beers and good reasonably priced home-made food from sandwiches up; children and dogs welcome, tables in nice garden with hill views and play area, good walks, open (and food) all day. *(Mrs Edna Jones)*

SEDBERGH SD6592

Red Lion (015396) 20433

Finkle Street (A683); LA10 5BZ New management for this little beamed local opposite the church, down to earth and comfortable, with good value home-made food including Thurs pie night, well kept Jennings and other Marstons-related beers, open fire; free wi-fi; children and dogs welcome, gets very busy weekends, closed Mon. *(Adam Jones)*

THRELKELD NY3225

★**Horse & Farrier** (017687) 79688

A66 Penrith–Keswick; CA12 4SQ This popular 17th-c Lakeland pub was undergoing major refurbishment as we went to press – reports please; linked rooms with beams and open fires, Jennings ales and guests, well liked food from lunchtime sandwiches up in bar or partly stripped-stone restaurant, efficient friendly service; background music, TV and board games; children and dogs welcome, disabled facilities, fine views towards the Helvellyn range from outside tables and comfortable bedrooms, self-catering cottage, good walks, open (and food) all day including breakfast from 8am. *(Tina and David Woods-Taylor, Dr Peter Crawshaw, George Sanderson, Miles Green, Margaret and Peter Staples, Denise Courtney)*

TORVER SD2894

Church House (015394) 49159

A593/A5084 S of Coniston; LA21 8AZ Friendly 14th-c coaching house; pubby bar with heavy beams (some painted), straightforward tables and chairs on slate floors, Lakeland bric-a-brac and big log fire in sizeable stone fireplace, enjoyable home-made food (all day weekends) from sandwiches and sharing plates up, four changing ales and seven wines by the glass from barrel-fronted counter, comfortable lounge and separate dining room; occasional live music; children and dogs (in bar) welcome, lawned garden, four bedrooms and two bunk rooms, standing for five caravans/motor homes, good nearby walks to Lake Coniston, open all day. *(Lorna and Jack Musgrave)*

TORVER SD2894

Wilson Arms (015394) 41237

A593; LA21 8BB Old family-run roadside inn with adjoining deli; beams, nice log fire and one or two modern touches, well kept cumbrian ales and good locally sourced food cooked to order in bar or dining room, friendly service; free wi-fi; children and dogs welcome, hill views (including Old Man of Coniston) from tables in large garden, area with pigs, goats and ducks, seven bedrooms and three holiday cottages, open (and food) all day. *(Charles Fraser)*

TROUTBECK NY4103

Mortal Man (015394) 33193

A592 N of Windermere; Upper Road; LA23 1PL Beamed and partly panelled bar with cosy room off, log fires, well kept local ales including a house beer from Hawkshead, several wines by the glass and well liked food in bar and picture-window restaurant; folk night Sun, open mike Tues, quiz Weds, storytelling Thurs, free wi-fi; children and dogs welcome, great views from sunny garden, lovely village and surrounding walks, bedrooms, open (and food) all day. *(Alan and Alice Morgan)*

TROUTBECK NY4103

★**Queens Head** (015394) 32404

A592 N of Windermere; LA23 1PW Popular 17th-c beamed coaching inn well restored after devastating fire; some original features remain such as the four-poster bar and stone fireplaces, but generally an airier feel with good quality oak furniture on wood and flagstoned floors, enjoyable sensibly priced food from hot or cold sandwiches and pub favourites up, well kept Robinsons ales, a dozen wines by the glass and good selection of whiskies/gins, friendly efficient service; background music; children, walkers and dogs welcome, seats outside with fine views across to Applethwaite Moors, ten comfortably refurbished bedrooms (some in barn opposite), open (and food) all day, kitchen shuts 7pm Sun. *(Hugh Roberts, Margaret and Peter Staples, Christian Mole, Graham and Elizabeth Hargreaves)*

TROUTBECK NY3827

Troutbeck Inn (017684) 83635

A5091/A66; CA11 0SJ Former railway hotel with small bar, lounge and log-fire restaurant, a couple of Jennings ales and good food cooked by landlord-chef, efficient friendly service; children and dogs (in bar) welcome, seven bedrooms plus three self-catering cottages in converted stables, open all day in season. *(Mike Benton)*

ULDALE NY2436

Snooty Fox (016973) 71479

Village signed off B5299 W of Caldbeck; CA7 1HA Comfortable and welcoming two-bar village inn; ample helpings of good quality home-cooked food (not Weds) using local ingredients, up to four well kept changing ales including a summer brew named for the pub, decent selection of whiskies, friendly attentive staff, fox hunting memorabilia; winter pool table, free wi-fi; children welcome in dining areas, dogs in snug, nice location with garden at back, three bedrooms, closed lunchtimes. *(Mick Allen)*

ULVERSTON SD2878

★**Farmers Arms** (01229) 584469

Market Place; LA12 7BA Convivial recently refurbished town pub; front bar with comfortable leather armchairs and sofas, original fireplace, Cumberland Legendary Loweswater Gold and three quickly changing guests, a dozen wines by the glass, good varied choice of popular fair-priced food from sandwiches and deli boards up, cocktail bar leading to big raftered dining area with seating booths on either side (children here only); background music, Thurs quiz; colourful hanging baskets and tubs on front terrace warmed by fire pit, Thurs and Sat market days (pub very busy then), self-catering apartments/cottages nearby, open all day from 9am. *(Andrew Lawson)*

ULVERSTON SD2878

Mill (01229) 581384

Mill Street; LA12 7EB Converted 19th-c flour mill on three floors; ground-floor bar with huge waterwheel behind glass, mix of furniture including leather armchairs and sofas on wood floor, warming logburners, around ten real ales including Lancaster (brewery owns the pub), good wines and fine array of whiskies, gins and brandies, spiral stairs up to restaurant and second bar with terrace, very good well presented food from sandwiches and snacks up, evening cocktail lounge on top floor (Fri, Sat), friendly efficient young staff; live music and quiz nights; children welcome, open all day. *(Chris Taylor)*

UNDERBARROW SD4692

Black Labrador (015395) 68234

From centre of Kendal at town hall, turn left into Beast Banks signed for Underbarrow, then follow Underbarrow Road; LA8 8HQ Small friendly village local with open-plan beamed bar, mix of furniture including leather sofas on stone floor, woodburner, Hawkshead and a couple of local guests, good choice of enjoyable freshly prepared food, mezzanine restaurant; free wi-fi; children and dogs (in bar) welcome, picnic-sets and covered balcony outside, handy for walkers, open all day Fri-Sun and Weds, closed Tues. *(Selwyn Jones)*

WASDALE HEAD NY1807

Wasdale Head Inn (019467) 26229

NE of Wast Water; CA20 1EX Mountain hotel worth knowing for its stunning fellside setting; roomy walkers' bar with welcoming fire, several local ales and good choice of wines, ample helpings of enjoyable home-made food; residents' bar, lounge and panelled restaurant; children and dogs welcome, nine bedrooms, self-catering apartments in converted barn and camping, open all day. *(Jane and Philip Saunders)*

WETHERAL NY4654

Wheatsheaf (01228) 560686

Handy for M6 junctions 42/43; CA4 8HD Popular 19th-c pub in pretty village; three well kept changing ales and enjoyable home-made food including daily specials, good friendly service; Tues quiz, sports TV; children and dogs welcome, picnic-sets in small garden, open all day, no food Mon, Tues. *(Andrew Lawson)*

WINDERMERE SD4198

Crafty Baa (015394) 88002

Victoria Street, beside the Queens; LA23 1AB Small atmospheric bar with great selection of craft beers on tap and in bottles (listed on blackboards), good range of other drinks too including decent coffee, enjoyable food from snacks to more substantial cheese and charcuterie combinations served on slates, friendly knowledgeable staff, rustic décor with bare boards, exposed stone walls and log fire, some quirky touches, more room upstairs; background music; dogs welcome (theirs is Henry), a few seats out at front, open (and food) all day; being extended as we went to press so will be changes. *(Robert and Diana Myers)*

WREAY NY4349

Plough (016974) 75770

Village signed from A6 N of Low Hesket; CA4 0RL Welcoming 18th-c beamed pub in pretty village; modernised split-level interior with pine tables and chairs on wood or flagstone floors, some exposed stonework, woodburner, good choice of enjoyable freshly prepared food (not Mon) including specials, well kept Cumberland, Hawkshead and a guest from brick-fronted canopied bar, efficient friendly service; quiz Mon, live music (see website); children welcome, closed Mon lunchtime and Tues. *(Caroline and Peter Bryant)*

Derbyshire

BRADWELL SK1782 Map 7

Samuel Fox

(01433) 621562 – www.samuelfox.co.uk

B6049; S33 9JT

Friendly pub in the Hope Valley with real ales and fine food, good service and neat bar; comfortable bedrooms

As well as fine food cooked by the landlord, you'll find plenty of customers dropping in for a pint and a chat. The open-plan bar and interlinked dining room have red and dogtooth upholstered tub chairs grouped around tables on striped carpet or wooden flooring, country scenes hang on papered walls above a grey dado, curtains are neatly swagged and there are several open brick fireplaces. Intrepid Blonde and Pennine Best Bitter on handpump, 15 wines by the glass from a good list, and a farm cider served by helpful, courteous staff. The neat restaurant is similarly furnished but with red plush dining chairs. At the front of the building, cream metal seats are arranged around small ornamental trees and there are some wooden seats too. If you want to make the most of the surrounding Peak District National Park, do stay in the comfortable, quiet bedrooms. No dogs inside. Wheelchair access.

Modern british food is cooked by the chef-landlord (everything is made in-house) and includes ham hock and pheasant terrine with beetroot and cumin pickle, cured sea trout with orange and fennel, gnocchi with butternut squash, kale, sage and blue cheese, sea bream with pearl barley and mussel risotto, charred lettuce and aioli, venison bolognese with orzo, celeriac and spinach, slow-roasted pork belly with cannelloni, parsnip, braised cabbage and cider sauce, and puddings such as bitter sweet chocolate tart with mandarins, pistachios and chocolate sorbet and coconut pannacotta with mango and passion fruit. *Benchmark main dish: two-course set menu £23.00.*

Free house ~ Licensee James Duckett ~ Real ale ~ Open 6-11 Weds-Sat; 1-5.30 Sun; closed Mon, Tues (except for residents); lunchtimes (except Sun); first two weeks Jan ~ Bar food 6-9 Weds-Sat; 1-4 Sun ~ Restaurant ~ Children welcome ~ Wi-fi ~ Bedrooms: /£130
Recommended by Geoff and Ann Marston, Alexandra and Richard Clay, Diana and Bertie Farr, Alan and Linda Blackmore, Molly and Stewart Lindsay

BRETTON SK2078 Map 7

Barrel

(01433) 630856 – www.thebarrelinn.co.uk

Signposted from Foolow, which itself is signposted from A623 just E of junction with B6465 to Bakewell; can also be reached from either the B6049 at Great Hucklow, or the B6001 via Abney, from Leadmill just S of Hathersage; S32 5QD

Remote dining pub with traditional décor, popular food and friendly staff; bedrooms

Notably welcoming and with enjoyable, honest food, this pub is just right after a hike in the lovely surrounding countryside. Stubs of massive knocked-through stone walls divide the place into several spic and span areas. The cosy dark oak-beamed bar is charmingly traditional with gleaming copper and brass, a warming fire, patterned carpet, low doorways and stools lined up at the counter. Marstons Pedigree and EPA and Wychwood Hobgoblin on handpump, 28 malt whiskies, a farm cider and wines by the glass, all served by friendly, smartly dressed staff; maybe background radio. The outdoor seats on the front terrace by the road and in a courtyard garden are nicely sheltered from the inevitable breeze at this height, and on a clear day you can see five counties. Bedrooms are clean and comfortable.

Traditional food includes lunchtime hot and cold sandwiches, deep-fried brie wedges with tomato and red onion chutney, prawn cocktail, liver, bacon and onions, mediterranean vegetable pasta with pesto and parmesan, gammon and free-range eggs, beer-battered fish and chips, toad in the hole with onion gravy, breaded scampi with chips, half a roast chicken with stuffing and gravy, and puddings. *Benchmark main dish: steak in ale pie £12.95. Two-course evening meal £19.00.*

Free house ~ Licensee Philip Cone ~ Real ale ~ Open 11-3, 6-11; may open longer in summer; 11-11 Sat, Sun ~ Bar food 12-2, 6-9; 12-9 Sat, Sun ~ Well behaved children welcome ~ Wi-fi ~ Bedrooms: /£90 *Recommended by Sue Parry Davies, Pieter and Janet Vrancken, Beverley and Andy Butcher, Andrew Wall, Ann and Tony Bennett-Hughes, Brian and Anna Marsden*

CHELMORTON SK1170 Map 7

Church Inn £

(01298) 85319 – www.thechurchinn.co.uk

Village signposted off A5270, between A6 and A515 SE of Buxton; keep on up through village towards church; SK17 9SL

Cosy, convivial, traditional inn beautifully set in High Peak walking country, with good value food and well kept ales

Our readers love this warmly friendly old inn and the long-serving, professional licensees take great care of their customers. The chatty, low-ceilinged bar has an open fire and is traditionally furnished with built-in cushioned benches and simple chairs around polished cast-iron-framed tables (a couple still with their squeaky sewing treadles). Shelves of books, Tiffany-style lamps and house plants in the curtained windows, atmospheric Dales photographs and prints, and a coal-effect stove in the stripped-stone end wall all add a cosy feel. Abbeydale Moonshine, Marstons Pedigree, Thwaites Original and a couple of guests from Thornbridge and Wincle on handpump and nine wines by the glass; darts in a tile-floored games area on the left and board games. The inn is opposite a mainly 18th-c church and is prettily tucked into woodland with fine views over the village and hills beyond from good teak tables on a two-level terrace.

Fair value, pubby food includes sandwiches, black pudding fritters with spicy chutney, creamy mushrooms on garlic toast, lasagne, vegetable wellington with cheese sauce, gammon with egg and pineapple, chicken curry, salmon fillet with prawn and white wine sauce, steaks with onion rings and chips, daily specials, and puddings. *Benchmark main dish: steak and kidney pie £10.75. Two-course evening meal £18.00.*

Free house ~ Licensees Julie and Justin Satur ~ Real ale ~ Open 12-3, 6-10.30; 12-10.30 Sat, Sun ~ Bar food 12-2.30, 6-8.30; 12-8.30 weekends ~ Restaurant ~ Children welcome ~ Dogs allowed in bar ~ Wi-fi *Recommended by Kathleen I'Anson, Malcolm and Pauline Pellatt, Jane Rigby, Jane and Philip Saunders, Rob Yates, Jim King, Charles Welch*

CHINLEY SK0382 Map 7

Old Hall ★

(01663) 750529 – www.old-hall-inn.co.uk

Village signposted off A6 (very sharp turn) E of New Mills; also off A624 N of Chapel-en-le-Frith; Whitehough Head Lane, off B6062; SK23 6EJ

Fine range of ales and ciders in splendid building with lots to look at and good country food; comfortable bedrooms

This 16th-c stone-built inn, nestling prettily in a steep hamlet huddled below the moors, has so much going for it. The warm bar (basically four small friendly rooms opened into a single area tucked behind a massive central chimney) contains open fires, broad flagstones, red patterned carpet, sturdy country tables and a couple of long pews and various other seats. Marstons Wainwright and guests from breweries such as Howard Town, Kelham Island, Marble, Peak, Phoenix, Storm, Thornbridge and Whim on handpump, as well as some interesting lagers on tap, 20 malt whiskies, eight cask ciders, a rare range of bottled ciders and around 50 bottled (mostly belgian) beers. They hold a beer festival with music in September. Also, around a dozen new world wines by the glass and friendly, helpful service. The dining room is surprisingly grand with a great stone chimney soaring into high eaves, refectory tables on a parquet floor, lovely old mullioned windows and a splendid minstrels' gallery. The pretty walled garden has picnic-sets under sycamore trees. Some of the attractive bedrooms look over the garden and there are also a couple of self-catering cottages.

Well regarded food includes sandwiches, smoked haddock risotto topped with a quail egg, chicken liver, bacon and caper pâté, cheese, leek and apple pie, bourbon-glazed beef or jerk chicken burgers with coleslaw and triple-cooked chips, seared salmon with tarragon mash and crayfish butter, slow-braised ox cheek with salt-baked beetroot, dauphinoise potatoes, red wine jus and red pickled cabbage, honey-glazed duck breast with rhubarb, celeriac and parmentier potatoes, and puddings such as mascarpone crème brûlée with a walnut crumble topping and apple and blueberry compote and treacle tart with salted caramel ice-cream; they also offer an early bird menu 12-2 (not Sunday), 5-6.30 (not weekends). *Benchmark main dish: steak in ale pudding £13.50. Two-course evening meal £19.00.*

Free house ~ Licensee Daniel Capper ~ Real ale ~ Open 12-11 (midnight Sat) ~ Bar food 12-2, 5-9 (9.30 Fri, Sat); 12-7.30 Sun ~ Restaurant ~ Children welcome ~ Dogs allowed in bar ~ Wi-fi ~ Bedrooms: £79/£110 *Recommended by Martine and Lawrence Sanders, Ross Balaam, Lindy Andrews, David and Doreen Beattie, Gordon and Patricia Gorringe, Lorna and Jeff Mason*

FENNY BENTLEY SK1750 Map 7

Coach & Horses

(01335) 350246 – www.coachandhorsesfennybentley.co.uk

A515 N of Ashbourne; DE6 1LB

Cosy inn with pretty country furnishings, roaring open fires and food all day

It's a short walk from the Tissington Trail, a popular cycling/walking path along a former railway line (best joined at the nearby picture-book village of Tissington) to reach this 17th-c rendered stone house. The traditional interior has all the trappings you'd expect of a country pub, from roaring log fires, exposed brick hearths and flagstone floors to black beams hung with pewter mugs, and hand-made pine furniture that includes wall settles with floral-print cushions. There's also a conservatory dining room and a cosy front dining room. Marstons Pedigree and a changing guest such as Falstaff 3 Faze on handpump, a couple of farm ciders and seven wines by the glass; the landlord is knowledgeable about malt whiskies and he stocks around two dozen; quiet background music. A side garden by an elder tree (with views across fields) has seats and tables, and there are modern tables and chairs under cocktail parasols on a front roadside terrace. No dogs allowed inside.

Tasty all-day food includes sandwiches, smoked mackerel pâté with horseradish crème fraîche, deep-fried panko-coated ham hock with red onion chutney, sweet potato, butternut squash and chickpea curry, chicken breast stuffed with chorizo and wrapped in bacon with a tomato and thyme sauce, pork steak topped with garlic mushrooms and melted cheese, sea bass on tagliatelle with mixed seafood white wine sauce, and puddings. *Benchmark main dish: 10oz gammon steak with egg or pineapple £11.50. Two-course evening meal £25.00.*

Free house ~ Licensees John and Matthew Dawson ~ Real ale ~ Open 11-11; 12-10.30 Sun ~ Bar food 12-9 ~ Restaurant ~ Children welcome ~ Wi-fi *Recommended by Frances Parsons, Jim King, David and Leone Lawson, Frank and Marcia Pelling*

GREAT LONGSTONE SK1971 Map 7

Crispin

(01629) 640237 – www.thecrispingreatlongstone.co.uk

Main Street; village signed from A6020, N of Ashford in the Water; DE45 1TZ

Spotless, traditional pub with emphasis on good, fair-priced food

There's always quite a collection of customers here including walkers, cyclists and families who've been enjoying the beautiful surrounding countryside; the pub is helpfully open all day. Décor throughout is traditional: brass or copper implements, decorative plates, horsebrasses on beams in the red ceiling, cushioned built-in wall benches and upholstered chairs and stools around polished tables on red carpet – and a warming fire. A corner area (with a woodburning stove) is snugly partitioned off and there's a separate, more formal dining room on the right; darts, board games and maybe faint background music. Robinsons Beer Baracus, Dizzy Blonde, Trooper and Unicorn on handpump, Weston's Old Rosie cider and quite a choice of wines and whiskies. In warm weather there are seats in the garden and picnic-sets out in front (one under a heated canopy) set well back above the quiet lane.

As well as a two- and three-course lunchtime deal, the pubby choices include sandwiches, omelettes, seafood salad, curries, home-made pies and burgers, beer-battered fish and chips, chilli con carne, steaks from the local butcher, and puddings. *Benchmark main dish: steak, stilton and Guinness pie £12.95. Two-course evening meal £18.00.*

Robinsons ~ Tenant Paul Rowlinson ~ Real ale ~ Open 12-3, 6-11; 12-midnight Sat; 12-10.30 Sun ~ Bar food 12-2.30, 6-9 ~ Restaurant ~ Children welcome ~ Dogs welcome ~ Wi-fi *Recommended by Jo Garnett, Daniel King, Heather and Richard Jones, Andrew Wall, Toby Jones*

A star after the name of a pub shows exceptional quality. It means most people (after reading the report to see just why the star has been won) would think a special trip worthwhile.

HASSOP SK2272 Map 7

Old Eyre Arms

(01629) 640390 – www.eyrearms.com

B6001 N of Bakewell; DE45 1NS

Comfortable old farmhouse with long-serving owners, decent food and beer, and pretty views from the garden

At the centre of the Peak District, this 17th-c former coaching inn always has plenty of customers keen for refreshment. The low-ceilinged beamed rooms are snug and cosy with log fires and traditional furnishings that include cushioned oak settles, comfortable plush chairs, a longcase clock, old pictures and lots of brass and copper. The tap room, snug and lounge are similarly decorated with cushioned oak benches, old pictures and an impressive collection of brass and copper; the tap room also has a fine collection of teapots. Brunswick The Usual, Peak Swift Nick and guests such as Bradfield Farmers Blonde and Howard Town Super Fortress on handpump, 18 wines by the glass, ten gins, 20 malt whiskies and farm cider; darts and dominoes. Above the stone fireplace in the lounge is a painting of the Eyre coat of arms. The delightful garden (with its gurgling fountain) looks straight out to fine Peak District countryside and the summer hanging baskets are lovely. Chatsworth House and Haddon Hall are both close by, as is the Monsal Trail cycling/walking path.

As well as sandwiches and toasties, pub favourites include prawn cocktail, breaded mushrooms with garlic mayonnaise, aubergine and mushroom lasagne, chicken stuffed with leeks and stilton in a creamy sauce, rack of lamb with fennel and rosemary crust, venison steak with cranberry, port and orange sauce, lemon sole topped with parsley butter, and puddings such as plum crumble and bakewell pudding. *Benchmark main dish: rabbit pie £17.95. Two-course evening meal £19.95.*

Free house ~ Licensees Nick and Lynne Smith ~ Real ale ~ Open 12-3, 6-11; 12-10.30 Sun; closed Mon evening; first two weeks Jan ~ Bar food 12-2 (2.30 Sat), 6-9; 12-8 Sun ~ Children welcome ~ Dogs allowed in bar ~ Wi-fi *Recommended by Donald Allsopp, John and Delia Franks, Alan and Linda Blackmore, Ann and Tony Bennett-Hughes, Colin and Daniel Gibbs, Caroline Prescott*

HATHERSAGE SK2380 Map 7

Plough

(01433) 650319 – www.theploughinn-hathersage.co.uk

Leadmill; B6001 towards Bakewell; S32 1BA

Derbyshire Dining Pub of the Year

Comfortable dining pub with well presented food, beer and wine and seats in a waterside garden; bedrooms

There's no doubt that the emphasis in this neatly kept dining pub is on the highly enjoyable food, but they have a thoughtful choice of drinks too. The cosily furnished rooms have bright tartan and oriental patterned carpets, rows of dark wooden chairs and tables plus a very long banquette, three woodburning stoves and terracotta walls hung with decorative plates. The neat dining room is slightly more formal. A good wine list includes 21 by the glass and they keep 20 malt whiskies plus Abbeydale Moonshine, Bradfield Yorkshire Farmer and Timothy Taylors Landlord on handpump; quiet background music. The seats on the terrace have wonderful valley views and the nine-acre grounds are on the banks of the River Derwent where the pretty garden slopes down to the water. Well equipped bedrooms are in a barn conversion.

Interesting modern food includes sandwiches (until 5.30pm), seared scallops with curried parsnip purée, parsnip crisps and pomegranate, rabbit, pistachio and bacon terrine with spiced piccalilli, linguine with king prawns in lemon, garlic and chilli and parsley butter, smoked tofu with shiitake mushrooms, cashew nuts, coconut rice and a hot and sour broth, halibut with citrus tomatoes, straw potatoes and sage beurre noisette, liver and bacon with champ potato and onion gravy, moroccan-style corn-fed chicken with butternut squash and chickpea tagine, apricot and coriander couscous, rosewater and poppy seed yoghurt, and puddings such as chocolate marquise with blood orange and cinnamon ice-cream and ginger pudding with pineapple and mango compote with ginger beer syrup and mango ice-cream. *Benchmark main dish: steak and kidney pudding £14.00. Two-course evening meal £21.00.*

Free house ~ Licensees Bob, Cynthia and Elliott Emery ~ Real ale ~ Open 11-11; 12-10.30 Sun ~ Bar food 11.30-9.30; 12-8.30 Sun ~ Restaurant ~ Children welcome ~ Dogs welcome ~ Wi-fi ~ Bedrooms: £85/£130 *Recommended by Sue and Martin Neville, Patricia and Anton Larkham, Audrey and Paul Summers, Penny and David Shepherd*

HAYFIELD — SK0387 Map 7

Royal

(01663) 742721 – www.theroyalathayfield.com

Market Street; SK22 2EP

Big, bustling inn with fine panelled rooms, friendly service and thoughtful choice of drinks and food; bedrooms

Bedrooms here are well appointed and comfortable and make an excellent base for exploring the Peak District; breakfasts are good too. The inn is the centre of local life and the oak-panelled bar and lounge areas have open fires, a fine collection of seats from long settles with pretty scatter cushions through elegant upholstered dining chairs to tub chairs and chesterfields, around an assortment of solid tables on rugs and flagstones; house plants and daily papers. Howard Town Twenty Trees, Jennings Cumberland, Marstons Lancaster Bomber, Peak Bakewell Best Bitter and Thwaites Original on handpump, 11 wines by the glass, nine malt whiskies and two farm ciders; background music, TV and board games. This is an attractive village to wander around.

High quality food includes hot and cold sandwiches, black pudding, onions, bacon and a poached egg on hollandaise, chicken liver pâté with onion marmalade, vegetarian or cajun chicken burgers with coleslaw and chips, a curry of the day, sausages with wholegrain mustard mash with onion rings, braised beef cheeks with horseradish mash, slow-roasted lamb shank with rosemary and mint gravy, and puddings such as a cheesecake of the day and bakewell tart. *Benchmark main dish: pies with mash or chips £11.50. Two-course evening meal £18.00.*

Free house ~ Licensees Mark and Lisa Miller ~ Real ale ~ Open 11-11 (11.30 Sat); 11-10.30 Sun ~ Bar food 12-8.30 (9 Sat); 12-7 Sun ~ Children welcome ~ Dogs allowed in bar and bedrooms ~ Wi-fi ~ Bedrooms: £65/£85 *Recommended by Hilary and Neil Christopher, Carol and Barry Craddock, Ruth May, David and Doreen Beattie, Monica and Steph Evans, Max and Steph Warren*

HURDLOW — SK1265 Map 7

Royal Oak

(01298) 83288 – www.peakpub.co.uk

Monyash–Longnor Road, just off A515 S of Buxton; SK17 9QJ

Bustling, carefully renovated pub in rural spot with beamed rooms, friendly staff and tasty, all-day food

Food is usefully offered all day at this convivial pub – which is just what the many walkers and cyclists are hoping for. It's a two-roomed beamed bar with an open fire in a stone fireplace, lots of copper kettles, bed warming pans, horsebrasses and country pictures, cushioned wheelback chairs and wall settles around dark tables, and stools against the counter. Friendly staff serve Peak Bakewell Best Bitter, Sharps Doom Bar, Whim Hartington Bitter and Wincle Sir Philip on handpump, seven wines by the glass and two farm ciders; background music. The attractive dining room has country dining chairs, wheelback chairs, a cushioned pine settle in one corner on bare floorboards, pretty curtains and another open fire. For large groups, there's also a flagstoned cellar room with benches on either side of long tables. The terraced garden has plenty of seats and picnic-sets arranged on the grass. The self-catering barn with bunk bedrooms and the campsite are both very popular.

Quite a choice of food includes sandwiches, fried black pudding and chorizo with a balsamic glaze, crispy salt and pepper squid with sweet chilli mayonnaise, cauliflower rice stir-fry with peppers, red onion, spinach and mushrooms, chicken combo with breast, buffalo wings, thai green skewers and stilton dressing, slow-cooked pork belly with black pudding mash and cider gravy, blackened cajun salmon with lemon oil dressing and chips, local butcher's steaks with trimmings and onion rings, and puddings such as apple and mixed berry crumble with custard and white chocolate cheesecake. *Benchmark main dish: beef and stilton pie £13.95. Two-course evening meal £19.00.*

Free house ~ Licensee Paul White ~ Real ale ~ Open 10am-11pm; 8.30am-midnight Sat; 8.30am-11pm Sun ~ Bar food 10-9 ~ Children welcome ~ Dogs welcome ~ Wi-fi
Recommended by Emma Scofield, Buster May, William and Sophia Renton, Alf and Sally Garner, John McKenzie, Peter and Alison Steadman, Camilla and Jose Ferrera

KIRK IRETON SK2650 Map 7

Barley Mow

(01335) 370306
Village signed off B5023 S of Wirksworth; DE6 3JP

Welcoming old inn that focuses on real ale and conversation; bedrooms

This unchanging rural gem has been welcoming travellers since 1750 and has been run by the same kindly landlady for over 40 years. The small main bar is relaxed and pubby with chatty locals, a roaring coal fire, antique settles on tiles or built into panelling, four slate-topped tables and shuttered mullioned windows. Another room has built-in cushioned pews on oak parquet and a small woodburning stove; a third has more pews, low beams and big landscape prints. In casks behind a modest wooden counter are five well kept ales including Whim Hartington IPA and four guests from breweries such as Abbeydale, Blue Monkey, Burton Bridge, Peak, Shardlow, Storm and Thornbridge; french wines and farm cider too. There are two pub dogs; the newfoundland is confined but does not like other dogs on her patch. Outside you'll find a good-sized garden, a couple of benches at the front and a shop in what used to be the stable. Bedrooms are comfortable, and readers enjoy the good breakfasts served in the stone-flagged kitchen. Dogs may be allowed in bedrooms if they are clean, but not at breakfast; they must be kept on a lead at all times. This hilltop village is very pretty and within walking distance of Carsington Water.

Very inexpensive filled rolls – at lunchtime only – are the only food.

Free house ~ Licensee Mary Short ~ Real ale ~ No credit cards ~ Open 12-2, 7-11 (10.30 Sun) ~ Bar food lunchtime rolls only ~ Well behaved, supervised children lunchtime only ~ Dogs allowed in bar ~ Bedrooms: £45/£65 *Recommended by Luke Morgan, Maddie Purvis, Belinda and Neil Garth, Chris and Sophie Baxter*

OLD BRAMPTON SK3171 Map 7

Fox & Goose

(01246) 566335 – www.thefoxandgooseinn.com

Off A619 Chesterfield–Baslow at Wadshelf; S42 7JJ

Fine panoramic views for bustling pub with a restful bar, inventive food in light and airy restaurant, helpful staff and seats outside

The name Fox & Goose was derived from the ancient Viking board game, fox and geese, which the monks used to play here. The building was presented to the monks of Beauchief Abbey in a licence granted by Richard II in 1392. The character beamed bar has a woodburning stove in a big stone fireplace, mate's chairs and button-back wall seating surrounding a mix of wooden tables on large flagstones, Black Sheep, Bradwell Farmers Blonde, Peak Bakewell Best Bitter and Chatsworth Gold and a couple of guest beers on handpump and a dozen wines by the glass served by friendly staff. A small snug leads off with heavy beams, button-back wall seats, beige carpeting and a small fireplace, and there's also a dining room with double-sided plush banquette seating. If eating, most customers head for the airy Orangery restaurant with its contemporary high-backed plush chairs around polished tables and lovely panoramic views through big picture windows. Outside, there are plenty of seats and tables under parasols on a terrace and decked area, and picnic-sets arranged on gravel.

Well thought-of food using local produce includes sandwiches, tempura cod cheek satay with lime and red slaw, duck, chicken, cherry and tarragon terrine with star anise plum sauce, caesar salad (you can add various toppings), water buffalo burger with toppings, smoked onion mayonnaise and chips, thai green seafood curry with coconut wild rice, rabbit breast wrapped in pancetta with gnocchi, braised pears, toasted almonds, asparagus and tarragon, hand-dived scallops with charred pickled cauliflower with pulled pork cubes, pomegranate and lemon dressing, and puddings such as crème brûlée of the day and sticky toffee pudding with toffee sauce and vanilla ice-cream. *Benchmark main dish: 32-day-aged rump steak with trimmings and chips £16.95. Two-course evening meal £20.00.*

Free house ~ Licensee Craig Lynch ~ Real ale ~ Open 12-midnight; 12-6 Sun; closed Mon-Thurs ~ Bar food 12-9 (9.30 Sat); 12-7 Sun ~ Restaurant ~ Children welcome ~ Dogs allowed in bar ~ Wi-fi ~ Regular wine tasting evenings *Recommended by John Harris, Millie and Peter Downing, Lucy and Giles Gibbon, Brian and Susan Wylie, Diane Abbot*

OVER HADDON SK2066 Map 7

Lathkil

(01629) 812501 – www.lathkil.co.uk

Village and inn signposted from B5055 just SW of Bakewell; DE45 1JE

Traditional pub with long-serving owners (they've been here 37 years), super views, a good range of beers and well liked food; bedrooms

Our readers have been coming here for many years and enjoy all aspects of the place. The airy room on the right as you enter has a nice fire in an attractively carved fireplace, old-fashioned settles with upholstered cushions, chairs, black beams, a delft shelf of blue and white plates and some original prints and photographs. On the left, the sunny spacious dining area doubles as an evening restaurant and there's a woodburning stove. Peak Swift Nick and Whim Hartington Bitter with guests such as Bradfield Farmers Blonde, Kelham Island Easy Rider and Raw Brown Cow Bitter on handpump, a reasonable range of wines (including mulled wine and prosecco), 40 gins and a decent selection of malt whiskies; they hold a beer, cider and gin festival in September. Background music, darts, TV and board games. Dogs are welcome, but muddy boots must be left in the lobby. The views are spectacular and can be enjoyed from seats in the walled garden and from windows in the bar. The inn is right at the heart of the Peak District National Park and popular with walkers and cyclists who use the warm, comfortable bedrooms as a base; breakfasts are hearty.

Pleasing food includes sandwiches, mini whole camembert with pear and wine chutney, crab cakes with sweet chilli sauce, courgette, brie and potato crumble, steak and kidney pie, salmon fillet with asparagus and hollandaise sauce, venison and blackberry casserole, lamb chops with mint sauce, sirloin steak with mushrooms, onions and sherry peppered sauce, and puddings such as bakewell pudding and chocolate brownie with chocolate sauce with honeycomb ice-cream. *Benchmark main dish: chicken breast in stilton sauce with crispy prosciutto £12.95. Two-course evening meal £19.50.*

Free house ~ Licensee Alice Grigor-Taylor ~ Real ale ~ Open 11-11; 12-10.30 Sun ~ Bar food 12-2 (2.30 weekends), 6.30-8.30 ~ Restaurant ~ Children welcome but over-10s only in the bar ~ Dogs allowed in bar and bedrooms ~ Wi-fi ~ Bedrooms: £70/£85 *Recommended by Mike and Wena Stevenson, Geoff Rayner, Miranda and Jeff Davidson, Peter and Emma Kelly, Ann and Tony Bennett-Hughes, John Arnold*

STANTON IN PEAK — SK2364 Map 7

Flying Childers £

(01629) 636333 – www.flyingchilders.com

Village signposted from B6056 S of Bakewell; Main Road; DE4 2LW

Top notch beer and inexpensive simple bar lunches in a warm-hearted, unspoilt pub; a delight

Happily, little changes here and the friendly landlord still keeps Wells Bombardier and a couple of guests such as Storm PGA and Thornbridge Jaipur IPA on handpump, and several wines by the glass. The best room in which to enjoy your drinks is the snug little right-hand bar, virtually built for chat with its dark beam-and-plank ceiling, dark wall settles, single pew, plain tables, a hot coal and log fire, a few team photographs, dominoes and cribbage; background music. There's a bigger, equally unpretentious bar on the left. As well as seats out in front, there are picnic-sets in the well tended back garden. The surrounding walks are marvellous and both walkers and their dogs are warmly welcomed; they keep doggie treats behind the bar. In a beautiful steep stone village, this cottagey pub is named after an unbeatable racehorse of the early 18th c. Now that there's no longer a village shop the pub does sell some produce.

Cooked by the landlady, the simple lunchtime-only food includes filled rolls and toasties, home-made soups and weekend dishes such as rabbit casserole, home-made vegeterian burger, local sausages, and home-made cake and bakewell pudding. *Benchmark main dish: large bowl of soup £4.60.*

Free house ~ Licensees Stuart and Mandy Redfern ~ Real ale ~ No credit cards ~ Open 12-2 (3 weekends), 7-11; closed Mon and Tues lunchtimes ~ Bar food 12-2 ~ Children in lounge bar only ~ Dogs allowed in bar ~ Bi-monthly games evening *Recommended by Geoff Rayner, Lorna and Jack Mulgrave, Mrs Julie Thomas, Barry and Daphne Gregson, Brian and Anna Marsden, Ann and Tony Bennett-Hughes*

WOOLLEY MOOR SK3661 Map 7

White Horse

(01246) 590319 – www.thewhitehorsewoolleymoor.co.uk

Badger Lane, off B6014 Matlock–Clay Cross; DE55 6FG

Attractive old dining pub in pretty countryside with good food and drinks; bedrooms

The contemporary, well equipped bedroom suites each have a private balcony and floor-to-ceiling windows that give splendid views over the Amber Valley. The pub is neat and uncluttered; the bar, snug and dining room have wooden dining chairs and tables, stools and leather sofas on flagstoned or wooden floors, a woodburning stove (in the bar), an open fire (in the dining room) and boldly patterned curtains and blinds. Peak Bakewell Best Bitter and Chatsworth Gold and a guest such as Dancing Duck Ay Up on handpump, nine gins and 13 wines by the glass. In the front garden you'll find picnic-sets under parasols on gravel and boules. Ogston Reservoir is just a couple of minutes' drive away.

Rewarding food using seasonal, local produce includes korean fried chicken with asian slaw, scallop, black pudding and home-cured bacon with cauliflower purée, middle eastern-style bean cassoulet with baba ganoush and flatbread, chicken breast with boulangère potatoes, charred onions and chicken jus, salmon with soba noodles, pak choi and a ginger and coriander dressing, venison steak with parmentier potatoes, spinach, parsnip purée and red wine sauce, and puddings such as mango parfait with coconut sorbet and caramelised lemon curd with toasted oats, meringue and lemon ice-cream. *Benchmark main dish: crisp pork belly with spring onion mash and smoked bacon sauce £14.95. Two-course evening meal £19.00.*

Free house ~ Licensees David and Melanie Boulby ~ Real ale ~ Open 12-3, 6-11; 12-4 Sun; closed first three weeks Jan ~ Bar food 12-1.45, 6-8.45; 12-4 Sun ~ Restaurant ~ Children welcome ~ Wi-fi ~ Bedrooms: £139/£149 *Recommended by Michael Butler, Alistair Forsyth, Dr Simon Innes, Jo Garnett, Malcolm Phillips, Chris Cook, Derek and Sylvia Stephenson*

Also Worth a Visit in Derbyshire

Besides the fully inspected pubs, you might like to try these pubs that have been recommended to us and described by readers. Do tell us what you think of them: feedback@goodguides.com

ASHBOURNE SK1846

Smiths Tavern (01335) 300809

St John Street, bottom of marketplace; DE6 1GH Traditional little pub stretching back from heavily black-beamed bar through lounge to light and airy end room, up to seven well kept Marstons-related ales plus a weekend guest (tasting glasses available) and over 30 whiskies, friendly knowledgeable staff, good pork pies; darts; children (until 9pm) and dogs welcome, open all day. *(Belinda and Neil Garth)*

ASHFORD IN THE WATER SK1969

Ashford Arms (01629) 812725

Off A6 NW of Bakewell; Church Street (B6465, off A6020); DE45 1QB Attractive 18th-c inn set in pretty village; decent reasonably priced food including OAP weekday lunch and Weds steak night, well kept Black Sheep and two local guests, nice wines, restaurant and dining conservatory; free wi-fi; children and dogs welcome, plenty of tables outside, eight comfortable bedrooms, open all day Sun (food till 4.30pm). *(Jim King)*

ASHFORD IN THE WATER SK1969

★**Bulls Head** (01629) 812931

Off A6 NW of Bakewell; Church Street (B6465, off A6020); DE45 1QB Traditional 17th-c pub in attractive unspoilt village run by same family since 1953; cosy two-room beamed and carpeted bar with fires, one or two character gothic seats, spindleback and wheelback chairs around cast-iron-framed tables, local photographs and country prints on cream walls, four Robinsons ales and good choice of traditional food (not Tues evening), friendly efficient service; background music, daily papers;

children and dogs welcome, overshoes for walkers, hardwood tables and benches in front and in good-sized garden behind with boules and Jenga, open all day weekends in summer. *(Jim King)*

ASHOVER SK3462

★ **Old Poets Corner** (01246) 590888
Butts Road (B6036, off A632 Matlock–Chesterfield); S45 0EW Friendly unpretentious local in character village; easy-going bar with mix of chairs and pews, open fire, small room off and french door to tiny balcony, own-brewed Ashover ales and guests (beer festivals Mar and Oct), belgian beers, 12 ciders and good range of fruit wines and malt whiskies, straightforward food at fair prices, dining room; background music; acoustic folk/blues sessions Tues, and Sun, quiz Weds, poetry readings; children (away from bar) and dogs welcome, attractive bedrooms, holiday cottage sleeping up to eight, open all day, food all day Sat. *(Charlie Stevens, Amanda Shipley, John Harris)*

ASTON-UPON-TRENT SK4129

Malt (01332) 799116
M1 junction 24A on to A50, village signed left near Shardlow; The Green (one-way street); DE72 2AA Comfortably modernised village pub with enjoyable good value food (not Sun evening, less choice Mon, Tues), well kept Bass, Marstons Pedigree, Sharps Doom Bar and three guests, friendly atmosphere; some live music, TV; children and dogs welcome, back terrace, open all day. *(Lucy and Giles Gibbon)*

BAMFORD SK2083

Anglers Rest (01433) 659317
A6013/Taggs Knoll; S33 0BQ Friendly community-owned pub with five good local beers and tasty home-made food, Tues pizzas, Weds pie night and Fri evening fish and chips, also has a café and post office; some live music, quiz Weds, free wi-fi; children, walkers and dogs welcome, open all day, no pub food Mon or lunchtimes Tues and Weds. *(Dr J Barrie Jones, David H Bennett)*

BASLOW SK2572

Devonshire Arms (01246) 582551
A619; DE45 1SR Modernised village inn with opened-up bar and dining areas; a couple of Peak ales and a guest, good wines by the glass and well liked imaginative food together with more traditional choices, friendly staff; rooms fan out from central bar with partitioning and swagged curtains creating cosy niches, notable circular dining room, range of seating including tub chairs, chesterfields and button-back leather wall banquettes, flagstones, tiles and carpeting, woodburner, coffee shop; background music, TV, free wi-fi; children and dogs welcome, 11 comfortable bedrooms, free parking but must provide your registration at the bar to avoid a fine, open all day (food all day weekends). *(Scott and Charlotte Havers)*

BASLOW SK2572

Wheatsheaf (01246) 582240
Nether End; DE45 1SR Cheerful Marstons inn (former coaching house) with comfortable carpeted interior, popular reasonably priced pub food including good children's menu, four well kept ales, prompt friendly service; free wi-fi; plenty of seats outside and play area, bedrooms, handy for Chatsworth House, open all day. *(Mrs Edna Jones)*

BEELEY SK2667

★ **Devonshire Arms** (01629) 733259
B6012, off A6 Matlock–Bakewell; DE4 2NR Lovely 18th-c stone coaching inn in attractive Peak District village near Chatsworth House; original part with black beams, flagstones, stripped stone and cheerful log fires, contrasting ultra-modern bistro/conservatory, up to five well kept changing ales, several wines by the glass and nice range of malt whiskies, good imaginative food (not cheap) using local ingredients; background music; children welcome, dogs in bar and some of the 18 bedrooms, open all day. *(John and Penny Wildon)*

BIRCHOVER SK2362

★ **Druid** (01629) 653836
Off B5056; Main Street; DE4 2BL Welcoming 17th-c stone pub at edge of village; traditional quarry-tiled bar with open fire, dining areas either side plus more modern downstairs restaurant with wood-strip floor, good varied menu changing regularly and catering for special diets, up to six very well kept ales (tasters offered), Hogan's cider; background music and some live including jazz; children and dogs welcome, tables out in front on two levels, good area for walks, Nine Ladies stone circle nearby, closed Mon and Tues, otherwise open (and food) all day, kitchen shuts 5pm Sun. *(Brian and Anna Marsden)*

BIRCHOVER SK2362

Red Lion (01629) 650363
Main Street; DE4 2BN Welcoming early 18th-c stone-built pub with wholesome good value food including some italian influences (landlord is from Sardinia), also make their own cheese and have a deli next door, Sun carvery, Birchover ales (brewed here) and four ciders, glass-covered well inside, woodburners; acoustic music sessions and quiz nights; children and dogs welcome, nice rural views from outside seats, open all day weekends, closed Mon, Tues and lunchtimes Weds-Fri. *(Brian and Anna Marsden)*

BONSALL SK2758

★ **Barley Mow** (01629) 825685
Off A5012 W of Cromford; The Dale; DE4 2AY Basic one-room stone-built local

with friendly buoyant atmosphere; beams, pubby furnishings and woodburner, pictures and plenty of bric-a-brac, well kept local ales and real ciders, hearty helpings of good value popular food from short daily changing menu (be prepared to share a table); live music Fri and Sat, outside loos; children and dogs welcome, nice little front terrace, events such as hen racing and world record-breaking day, walks from the pub, camping, open all day weekends, closed Mon and lunchtimes Tues-Fri. *(Brian and Susan Wylie)*

BONSALL SK2758

Kings Head (01629) 822703

Yeoman Street; DE4 2AA Welcoming 17th-c stone-built village local with two cosy beamed rooms; pubby furniture including cushioned wall benches on carpet or tiles, various knick-knacks and china, woodburners, three Batemans ales and enjoyable good value home-made food, restaurant; live music, darts; children and dogs welcome (pub dog is Barney), seats out at front and in back courtyard, handy for Limestone Way and other walks, open all day weekends, closed Mon and Tues lunchtimes. *(Audrey and Paul Summers)*

BRACKENFIELD SK3658

Plough (01629) 534437

A615 Matlock–Alfreton, about a mile NW of Wessington; DE55 6DD Modernised 16th-c former farmhouse in lovely setting; three-level beamed bar with cheerful log-effect gas fire, well kept local ales and plenty of wines by the glass, good popular food including weekday lunchtime set deal and blackboard specials, appealing lower-level restaurant extension, friendly attentive staff and nice pub cat called Frank; background music; children welcome, large neatly kept gardens with terrace, closed Mon, otherwise open all day (food till 5.30pm Sun). *(Paul and Sonia Broadgate, M and GR)*

BRADWELL SK1781

Bowling Green (01433) 620450

Smalldale, off B6049 at Gore Lane/ Townend; S33 9JQ Popular and welcoming 16th-c village local with bar, dining room and garden room extension, good choice of reasonably priced pubby food (not Sun evening) including signature Desperate Dan steak pie and Sun carvery, well kept Sharps, Tetleys and a couple of guests, log fires; children and dogs (in bar) welcome, lovely views from garden, six bedrooms in separate building, open all day Fri-Sun, from 3pm other days. *(Ann and Tony Bennett-Hughes)*

BRASSINGTON SK2354

★**Olde Gate** (01629) 540448

Village signed off B5056 and B5035 NE of Ashbourne; DE4 4HJ Wonderfully unspoilt place – like stepping back in time; mullioned windows, 17th-c kitchen range with copper pots, old wall clock, rush-seated chairs and antique settles, beams hung with pewter mugs and shelves lined with embossed Doulton stoneware flagons, also a panelled Georgian room and, to the left of a small hatch-served lobby, a cosy beamed room with stripped settles, scrubbed tables and an open fire under a huge mantelbeam, Marstons, Thwaites and a guest, decent fair value food; cribbage and dominoes; well behaved children welcome, dogs in bar, benches in small front yard, garden with tables looking out over pastures, open all day Fri-Sun, closed Mon lunchtime. *(Julie and Andrew Blanchett, Patricia and Gordon Thompson, Cliff and Monica Swan)*

BUXTON SK0573

Gilberts (01298) 214071

High Street, on edge of Market Place; SK17 6ET Relaxed bar in former shop, solid rustic tables and chairs and some red leather chesterfields on bare boards, modern artwork and pendant lighting, woodburner, tractor-seat stools at corrugated-iron-fronted counter serving two or three well kept ales and a traditional cider, generous helpings of good freshly made food from sandwiches and sharing boards up, reasonable prices, friendly helpful staff; background and live music, free wi-fi; children and dogs (theirs is Bruce) welcome, enclosed back terrace, open all day from 9am for breakfast. *(David H Bennett)*

BUXTON SK0573

Old Sun (01298) 937986

High Street; SK17 6HA 17th-c coaching inn with several cosy linked areas; six well kept Marstons-related ales and good choice of wines by the glass, generous helpings of straightforward home-made food (not Sun evening, Mon-Thurs lunchtimes), low beams, panelling, bare boards and flagstones, soft lighting, old local photographs, open fire; background music, Weds quiz; children till 7pm, no dogs inside, roadside terrace, open all day. *(Barry Collett)*

BUXTON SK0573

Tap House (01298) 214085

Old Court House, George Street; SK17 6AT Buxton brewery tap with their cask and craft range plus guests, also good selection of bottled beers, wines and spirits, tasty well priced food including some cooked in smoker, various interesting teas and coffees, friendly knowledgeable staff; daily newspapers; children welcome, a few seats outside, open all day (till 1am Fri, Sat). *(Paul Moore)*

BUXWORTH SK0282

Navigation (01663) 732072

S of village towards Silkhill, off B6062; SK23 7NE Inn by restored Bugsworth canal basin; half a dozen ales including Marstons and Timothy Taylors, good value pubby food from sandwiches up, linked low-ceilinged rooms, canalia, brassware and old photographs, open fires, games room with pool and darts; background and live music, free wi-fi; children (away from main bar), walkers and dogs welcome, disabled access, tables on sunken flagstoned terrace, six bedrooms, open (and food) all day. *(David and Doreen Beattie)*

CALVER SK2374

Derwentwater Arms (01433) 639211
In centre, bear left from Main Street into Folds Head; Low Side; S32 3XQ Elevated stone-built village pub with big windows looking over to cricket pitch; good fairly priced food (all day Sun) from pies, pizzas and pub favourites to daily specials, three well kept ales including Bass and Bradfield, friendly helpful service; children, walkers and dogs (in bar) welcome, terraces on slopes below (disabled access from back car park), next-door holiday cottage, open all day. *(Diane Abbot)*

CASTLETON SK1583

Olde Cheshire Cheese
(01433) 620330 *How Lane; S33 8WJ*
Cosy 17th-c inn with two linked beamed and carpeted areas; six interesting ales such as Acorn, Bradfield and Peak, good range of popular reasonably priced wholesome food and decent house wines, quick friendly service, two gas woodburners, lots of photographs, toby jugs, plates and brassware, back dining room where children welcome; background and some live music, free wi-fi; dogs allowed in bar, ten bedrooms, parking across road, open (and food) all day. *(Selwyn Jones)*

CASTLETON SK1582

★**Olde Nags Head** (01433) 620248
Cross Street (A6187); S33 8WH Small solidly built hotel dating from the 17th c, interesting antique oak furniture and coal fire in civilised beamed and flagstoned bar, adjoining snug with leather sofas, steps down to restaurant, well kept Black Sheep, Sharps Doom Bar and guests, nice coffee and good generously served food from well filled sandwiches up, friendly helpful staff; live music Sat; children and dogs (in bar) welcome, nine comfortable bedrooms, good breakfast, open all day. *(Martin Day, David Hunt, Paul Humphreys)*

CHESTERFIELD SK3670

Rose & Crown (01246) 563750
Old Road; S40 2QT Popular Brampton Brewery pub with their full range plus Everards and two changing guests, enjoyable home-made food (not weekend evenings) from baguettes up, hands-on landlord and helpful staff, spacious traditional refurbishment with leather banquettes, panelling, wood or carpeted floors, brewery memorabilia and cast-iron Victorian fireplace, cosy snug area; Tues quiz, trad jazz first Sun of month, free wi-fi; tables outside, open all day. *(Andrew Wall)*

CHINLEY SK0482

Paper Mill (01663) 750529
Whitehough Head Lane; SK23 6EJ
Under same management as next door Old Hall (see Main Entries); good selection of ales and craft kegs, plenty of bottled belgian beers and couple of ciders, simple bar snacks including cheeseboards, mini ploughman's and home-made pizzas (Thurs-Sun), also a raclette room (must book in advance – minimum eight people), good choice of teas and coffees, friendly helpful staff, flagstones, woodburners and open fire, local artwork for sale; TV for major sports; children and dogs welcome, seats out at front and on split-level back terrace, plenty of good local walks, four bedrooms, open all day Sun, closed weekday lunchtimes and till 3pm Sat. *(Max and Steph Warren)*

CLIFTON SK1645

Cock (01335) 342654
Cross Side, opposite church; DE6 2GJ
Unpretentious beamed village local, comfortable and friendly, with two bars and separate dining room, enjoyable reasonably priced home-made pub food from baguettes and pies up, well kept Marstons Pedigree, Timothy Taylors Landlord and a couple of guests, decent choice of wines by the glass; quiz first Tues of month, darts; children, walkers and dogs welcome, garden with play equipment, closed Mon lunchtime. *(Molly and Stewart Lindsay)*

CLOWNE SK4975

Heist 07486 051317
Mill Street; S43 4JN Craft beer bar in former Victorian schoolhouse; split-level interior with pitched roof, brick walls and simple furnishings, half a dozen changing beers with plenty more in bottles/cans (they have a shop and recently installed a microbrewery), real ciders, decent wines and good range of gins, friendly knowledgeable service, some food such as pizzas; seats out in front, open all day till 8pm Mon-Thurs, 10pm Fri, Sat, 6pm Sun. *(Jim King)*

COMBS SK0378

Beehive (01298) 812758
Village signposted off B5470 W of Chapel-en-le-Frith; SK23 9UT Popular pub tucked away from main road by lovely valley; comfortable and roomy with log fire, heavy beams and copperware, emphasis on good freshly made food (all day Sun) from baguettes to steaks and interesting specials, also very good value weekday set menu and Tues grill night, ales including Marstons

Pedigree and a house beer from Wychwood, good choice of wines by the glass, friendly efficient service; background music, TV, Tues quiz; children and dogs welcome, wheelchair access (no disabled loo), plenty of tables out in front, good walks, one-bed holiday cottage next door, open all day. *(Penny and David Shepherd)*

CRICH SK3454

Cliff (01773) 852444
Cromford Road, Town End; DE4 5DP Unpretentious little two-room roadside pub; well kept ales such as Blue Monkey, Buxton, Dancing Duck and Sharps, generous helpings of good value straightforward food (not weekend evenings or Mon), friendly staff and regulars, two woodburners; quiz first Thurs of the month, folk night Sun, free wi-fi; children and dogs welcome, great views and walks, handy for National Tramway Museum, open all day weekends, closed weekday lunchtimes. *(Toby Jones)*

CROWDECOTE SK1065

Packhorse (01298) 83618
B5055 W of Bakewell; SK17 0DB Small three-room 16th-c pub in lovely setting, welcoming landlord and staff, good reasonably priced home-made food from weekday light bites and sandwiches up, four well kept changing ales, split-level interior with brick or carpeted floors, stripped-stone walls, open fire and two woodburners; Thurs quiz, pool and darts; children and dogs welcome, tables out behind, beautiful views and a popular walking route, closed Mon, Tues. *(Audrey and Paul Summers)*

DERBY SK3538

Abbey Inn (01332) 558297
Darley Street; DE22 1DX Former abbey gatehouse opposite park (pleasant riverside walk from centre); massive 15th-c or older stonework remnants, brick floor, studded oak doors, coal fire in big inglenook, stone spiral staircase to upper bar (not always staffed) with oak rafters and tapestries, bargain Sam Smiths and reasonably priced bar food; the loos with their beams, stonework and tiles are worth a look too; children welcome, dogs downstairs, open all day. *(Richard Tingle)*

DERBY SK3635

Alexandra (01332) 293993
Siddals Road; DE1 2QE Imposing Victorian pub with two simple rooms; traditional furnishings on bare boards or carpet, railway prints and memorabilia, well kept Castle Rock and several quickly changing microbrewery guests, lots of continental bottled beers with more on tap, snack food such as pork pies and cobs; background music; children and dogs welcome, nicely planted backyard, 1960s locomotive cab in car park, four bedrooms, open all day. *(Selwyn Jones)*

DERBY SK3535

Babington Arms (01332) 383647
Babington Lane; DE1 1TA Large open-plan Wetherspoons (former furniture showroom) with 17 real ales and up to six ciders, fast efficient service, usual well priced food, comfortable seating with steps up to back area where children allowed; TVs, free wi-fi; seats out at front by pavement, open all day from 8am for breakfast. *(Richard Tingle)*

DERBY SK3536

Brewery Tap (01332) 366283
Derwent Street/Exeter Place; DE1 2ED 19th-c Derby Brewing Co pub (aka Royal Standard) with unusual bowed end; ten real ales including five of their own from curved brick counter, lots of bottled imports, knowledgeable staff, decent good value food all day (till 5pm Sun) from sandwiches up (menu changing as we went to press), open-plan bare-boards interior with two high-ceilinged drinking areas, small upstairs room and roof terrace overlooking the Derwent; live music Tues; open all day (till 1am Fri, Sat). *(Selwyn Jones)*

DERBY SK3635

Brunswick (01332) 290677
Railway Terrace; close to Derby Midland Station; DE1 2RU One of Britain's oldest railwaymen's pubs, up to 16 ales including Everards and selection from own microbrewery, craft kegs, real ciders and good choice of bottled beers too, bargain food from generous sandwiches and snacks up, high-ceilinged panelled bar, snug with coal fire, chatty front parlour, interesting old train photographs and prints; live jazz upstairs first Thurs of month, darts, TV, games machine, free wi-fi; dogs welcome, walled beer garden behind, open all day, kitchen closed Sun evening, Mon, Tues evening and on Derby County home match days. *(Dr J Barrie Jones)*

DERBY SK3435

Exeter Arms (01332) 605323
Exeter Place; DE1 2EU Victorian survivor amid 1930s apartment blocks and car parks; extended into next-door cottage, but keeping its traditional character including tiled-floor snug with curved wall benches and polished open range, friendly staff, well kept Dancing Duck, Marstons and two guests, good all-day food (till 6pm Sun) from snacks and pubby choices up; quiz Mon, summer live music Sat in small garden with outside bar (beer festivals), children and dogs welcome, open all day (till midnight Fri, Sat). *(Selwyn Jones)*

DERBY SK3534

Falstaff (01332) 342902
Silver Hill Road, off Normanton Road; DE23 6UJ Big Victorian red-brick corner pub (aka the Folly) brewing its own good value ales, two friendly bars with interesting collection of memorabilia including

brewerania, games room; children (till 6pm) and dogs welcome, outside seating area, open all day. *(Selwyn Jones)*

DERBY SK3436

Five Lamps (01332) 348730
Duffield Road; DE1 3BH Corner pub with opened-up but well divided interior around central servery, wood-strip or carpeted floors, panelling, leather button-back bench seats and small balustraded raised section, a dozen well kept ales such as Everards, Oakham, Peak and Whim along with a house beer from Derby, real ciders, decent good value pubby food (not Sun evening); background music, TV; a few picnic-sets outside, open all day (till midnight Fri, Sat). *(Richard Tingle)*

DERBY SK3536

Olde Dolphin (01332) 267711
Queen Street; DE1 3DL Quaint 16th-c timber-framed pub just below cathedral; four small dark unpretentious rooms including appealing snug, big bowed black beams, shiny panelling, opaque leaded windows, lantern lights and coal fires, half a dozen well kept predominantly mainstream ales, reasonably priced bar food and upstairs evening restaurant (Thurs-Sat); quiz and live music nights; children welcome if eating, dogs in bar, sizeable outside area for drinkers/smokers, open all day. *(Richard Tingle)*

DERBY SK3335

Rowditch (01332) 343123
Uttoxeter New Road (A516); DE22 3LL Popular character local with own microbrewery (well kept Marstons Pedigree and guests too), friendly landlord, two bars and attractive little snug on right, coal fire; no children, dogs welcome at weekends, pleasant back garden, closed weekday lunchtimes. *(Selwyn Jones)*

DERBY SK3536

Silk Mill (01332) 349160
Full Street; DE1 3AF 1920s pub with central bar, lounge and skylit dining area, plush banquettes, cushioned stools and cast-iron-framed tables on wood floors, open fires, one or two quirky touches such as fish wallpaper, a stuffed crocodile and antler chandelier, good choice of real ales and ciders, several wines by the glass, enjoyable food (all day weekdays, till 8pm Sun) from sandwiches and sharing boards up, friendly service; daily newspapers and free wi-fi; open all day. *(Richard Tingle)*

DUFFIELD SK3543

Pattern Makers Arms
(01332) 842844 *Crown Street, off King Street; DE56 4EY* Welcoming Edwardian backstreet local with pubby furniture on wood or carpeted floors, upholstered banquettes and some stained-glass/etched windows, well kept Bass (from the jug), Marstons, Timothy Taylors and guests, bargain lunchtime food; background music, TV, darts, pool and other games, Sun quiz; dogs welcome, beer garden behind, open all day Fri-Sun. *(Diane Abbot)*

EARL STERNDALE SK0966

★**Quiet Woman** (01298) 83211
Village signed off B5053 S of Buxton; SK17 0BU Old-fashioned unchanging country local in lovely Peak District countryside; simple beamed interior with plain furniture on quarry tiles, china ornaments and coal fire, well kept Marstons Bitter and guests, own-label bottled beers (available in gift packs), good pork pies; family room with pool, skittles and darts; no dogs inside, picnic-sets out in front along with budgies, hens, ducks and donkeys, you can buy free-range eggs, local poetry books and even hay, good hikes across nearby Dove Valley towards Longnor and Hollinsclough, small campsite next door with caravan for hire. *(Toby Jones)*

EDALE SK1285

Old Nags Head (01433) 670291
Off A625 E of Chapel-en-le-Frith; Grindsbrook Booth; S33 7ZD Relaxed well used traditional pub at start of Pennine Way; good value food from sandwiches up including carvery (Sat evening, Sun lunchtime), a beer named for them plus three other well kept local ales, log fire, flagstoned area for booted walkers, airy back family room; background music, TV, pool and darts; dogs welcome, front terrace and garden, Sept beer barrel race, two self-catering cottages, open (and food) all day in summer, closed Mon and Tues in winter, can get very busy weekends. *(Lucy and Giles Gibbon)*

EDLASTON SK1842

Shire Horse (01335) 342714
Off A515 S of Ashbourne, just beside Wyaston; DE6 2DQ Timbered pub with good mix of drinkers and diners in large bar with open fire and separate restaurant/conservatory, friendly helpful staff, popular fairly priced food (not Sun evening) including specials board, well kept local ales and good house wines; children and dogs (in bar) welcome, tables out in front and in back garden with terrace, peaceful spot and nice views, open all day Sun. *(Andrew Wall)*

ELMTON SK5073

★**Elm Tree** (01909) 721261
Off B6417 S of Clowne; S80 4LS Popular competently run country pub with landlord-chef's good fairly traditional food including weekday set lunch and afternoon teas, well kept Black Sheep and a guest, several ciders and wide range of wines, friendly obliging service even when busy, stripped stone and panelling, log fire, back barn restaurant (mainly for functions); children

and dogs (in bar) welcome, garden tables, play area, closed Tues, otherwise open (and food) all day, till 6pm Sun. *(Derek and Sylvia Stephenson)*

EYAM SK2276

Miners Arms (01433) 630853

Off A632 Chesterfield to Chapel-en-le-Frith; Water Lane; S32 5RG Three-roomed 17th-c beamed inn with enjoyable food (not Sun evening) from sandwiches up, Greene King and Theakstons ales, friendly efficient service; TV, background music, free wi-fi; children, walkers and dogs welcome, picnic-sets out at front and in back garden, nice walks nearby especially below Froggatt Edge, seven bedrooms, open all day. *(Paul Humphreys)*

FOOLOW SK1976

★**Bulls Head** (01433) 630873

Village signposted off A623 Baslow–Tideswell; S32 5QR Friendly pub in pretty upland village by green; simply furnished flagstoned bar with interesting collection of photographs including some saucy Edwardian ones, Black Sheep, Peak and two guests, over 30 malts, good food (all day Sun) with more elaborate choices Sat evening, OAP weekday lunch deal, step down to former stables with high ceiling joists, stripped stone and woodburner, sedate partly panelled dining room with plates on delft shelves; background music; children, walkers and dogs welcome, side picnic-sets with nice views, paths from here out over rolling pasture enclosed by dry-stone walls, three bedrooms, closed Mon. *(Scott and Charlotte Havers)*

FROGGATT EDGE SK2476

★**Chequers** (01433) 630231

A625, off A623 N of Bakewell; S32 3ZJ Roadside dining pub surrounded by lovely countryside; opened-up bar and eating areas, cushioned settles, farmhouse and captain's chairs around mix of tables, antique prints, longcase clock and woodburner, good interesting food (all day weekends) along with more traditional choices, home-made chutneys and preserves for sale, Bradfield, Peak and a guest ale, several wines by the glass, friendly helpful staff; background music; children welcome, no dogs inside, garden with Froggatt Edge escarpment up through woods behind, six comfortable clean bedrooms, good breakfast, open all day. *(Mike and Wena Stevenson, Graham and Elizabeth Hargreaves)*

GLOSSOP SK0394

Star (01457) 853072

Howard Street; SK13 7DD Unpretentious corner alehouse opposite the station; four well kept changing ales along with Weston's Old Rosie cider, no food, traditional layout including flagstoned tap room with hatch service, old local photographs; dogs welcome, open all day from 4pm (2pm Fri, noon Sat, Sun). *(Jim King)*

GRINDLEFORD SK2378

Sir William (01433) 630303

B6001, opposite war memorial; S32 2HS Popular refurbished pub-hotel under welcoming management; good food from sandwiches up, Greene King ales and guests, friendly helpful service, restaurant; Sun quiz, free wi-fi; children, walkers and dogs (in a couple of areas) welcome, splendid view especially from terrace, eight comfortable bedrooms, open all day. *(Brian and Susan Wylie)*

HARDWICK HALL SK4663

★**Hardwick Inn** (01246) 850245

Quite handy for M1 junction 29; S44 5QJ Popular golden-stone pub dating from the 15th c at south park gate of Hardwick Hall (NT); several endearingly old-fashioned linked rooms including proper bar, open fires, fine range of some 220 malt whiskies and plenty of wines by the glass, well kept Black Sheep, Peak, Theakstons and a house beer (Bess of Hardwick) from Brampton, wide range of good reasonably priced bar food plus carvery restaurant, long-serving licensees (in same family for three generations), efficient friendly staff; unobtrusive background music; children allowed away from bar areas, dogs in one part, tables out at front and in pleasant back garden, open (and food) all day. *(Derek and Sylvia Stephenson, Stuart Doughty, Ian Herdman)*

HARTINGTON SK1260

Charles Cotton (01298) 84229

Market Place; SK17 0AL Popular stone-built hotel in attractive village centre; large comfortable bar-bistro with beams and open fire, enjoyable food from lunchtime sandwiches up (more restauranty evening choice), Weds steak night, ales including Jennings, Whim and a beer badged for them from Wincle, nice wines and italian coffee, friendly helpful service, restaurant and summer tearoom; background and some live music; children, walkers and dogs (in bar) welcome, seats out at front and in small back garden, 17 bedrooms, open all day. *(Lucy and Giles Gibbon)*

HARTINGTON SK1260

Devonshire Arms (01298) 84232

Market Place; SK17 0AL Unpretentious and unchanging two-bar pub in attractive village, welcoming and cheerful, with generous helpings of enjoyable food (smaller

Half pints: by law, a pub should not charge more for half a pint than half the price of a full pint, unless it shows that half-pint price on its price list.

servings available), a couple of mainstream ales along with a local guest, log fires; maybe background music; children and dogs welcome, tables out in front facing duck pond, more in small garden, good walks, open (and food) all day weekends. *(Martyn Hooper, Brian and Anna Marsden)*

HARTSHORNE SK3220

Bulls Head (01283) 215299

Woodville Road; DE11 7ET Popular red-brick local dating in part from 1600; big helpings of good value freshly cooked food including daily specials and meal deals, well kept Marstons Pedigree and a guest, several wines by the glass, cheery helpful staff; background music, free wi-fi; children welcome, clean comfortable bedrooms. *(Mike and Wena Stevenson)*

HATHERSAGE SK2381

★**Scotsmans Pack** (01433) 650253

School Lane, off A6187; S32 1BZ Bustling inn equally popular with drinkers and diners; dark panelled rooms with lots of interesting knick-knacks, upholstered stools and dining chairs, cushioned wall seats and assortment of tables, woodburner, five well kept Marstons-related ales and enjoyable food including daily specials, cream teas; background and some live music, quiz and bingo night Thurs, TV, darts; picnic-sets on terrace overlooking trout stream, plenty of surrounding walks, five bedrooms, open all day. *(Andrew Wall)*

HAYFIELD SK0388

Lantern Pike (01663) 747590

Glossop Road (A624 N) at Little Hayfield, just N of Hayfield; SK22 2NG This popular roadside pub still has its traditional red plush bar, warm fire and a few photos of the original *Coronation Street* cast (many were regulars along with series creator Tony Warren who based his characters on the locals); Abbeydale Moonshine, Timothy Taylors Landlord and a guest, decent pubby food; background music, live music, TV and free wi-fi; children welcome, dogs may be allowed, tables on stone-walled terrace looking over towards Lantern Pike, plenty of surrounding walks on windswept moors, five bedrooms, closed Mon lunchtime, open all day weekends. *(Julie and Andrew Blanchett, Donald Allsopp)*

HAYFIELD SK0387

Pack Horse (01663) 749126

Off A624 Glossop to Chapel-en-le-Frith; Market Street; SK22 2EP Modernised stone-built pub under welcoming licensees; good reasonably priced food from landlord-chef using local suppliers, four well kept ales and decent choice of wines, opened-up interior with some cosy areas, local artwork for sale, woodburners; background music; children, walkers and dogs welcome, a few seats out in front, open all day. *(Liz)*

HEAGE SK3750

Black Boy (01773) 856799

Old Road (B6013); DE56 2BN Modernised village pub-restaurant with popular good value food including fish specials in bar and upstairs dining room, well kept changing mainly local ales and real cider, friendly staff, open fire; live music and quiz nights; children welcome, no dogs, small outside seating area, open all day. *(Alan and Linda Blackmore)*

HOGNASTON SK2350

★**Red Lion** (01335) 370396

Off B5035 Ashbourne–Wirksworth; DE6 1PR Traditional 17th-c village inn with open-plan beamed bar; attractive mix of old tables, curved settles and other seats on ancient flagstones, three fires, Marstons Pedigree and guests, nice wines by the glass and good well presented home-made food from shortish menu, friendly service, dining conservatory; children and dogs welcome, picnic-sets in field behind, boules, handy for Carsington Water, three good bedrooms, big breakfast. *(Selwyn Jones)*

HOLBROOK SK3645

★**Dead Poets** (01332) 780301

Chapel Street; village signed off A6 S of Belper; DE56 0TQ Friendly drinkers' local with up to nine real ales (some served from jugs), traditional ciders and good range of other drinks, helpful knowledgeable landlord, filled cobs and other good value lunchtime bar food, simple cottagey décor with beams, stripped-stone walls and broad flagstones, high-backed settles forming booths, big log fire, plenty of tucked-away corners, woodburner in snug, well behaved children allowed in back conservatory till 8pm; quiet background music, no credit cards; dogs welcome, seats out at back, open all day Fri-Sun. *(Audrey and Paul Summers)*

HOPE SK1783

★**Cheshire Cheese** (01433) 620381

Off A6187, towards Edale; S33 6ZF 16th-c traditional stone inn with snug oak-beamed rooms on different levels; open fires, red carpets or stone floors, straightforward furnishings and gleaming brasses, up to five ales such as Abbeydale, Bradfield and Peak, 12 malt whiskies and enjoyable food from sandwiches and pub favourites up, friendly service; Weds quiz, folk night first and third Thurs of month; children and dogs welcome, good local walks in the summits of Lose Hill and Win Hill or the cave district around Castleton, four bedrooms, limited parking, open all day weekends in summer, closed Mon. *(Diane Abbot)*

HORSLEY WOODHOUSE SK3944

Old Oak (01332) 881299

Main Street (A609 Belper–Ilkeston); DE7 6AW Busy roadside local linked to nearby Bottle Brook and Leadmill microbreweries, their ales and guests plus weekend back bar with another eight well priced beers tapped from the cask, farm ciders too, basic snacks (can also bring your own food), beamed rooms with blazing coal fires; occasional live music; children and dogs welcome, hatch service to covered courtyard tables, nice views, open all day weekends, closed weekday lunchtimes till 4pm. *(Belinda and Neil Garth)*

ILKESTON SK4742

Dewdrop (0115) 932 9684

Station Street, Ilkeston junction, off A6096; DE7 5TE Large Victorian red-brick corner local in old industrial area, not strong on bar comfort but popular for its well kept beers (up to eight) such as Acorn, Blue Monkey, Bobs and Oakham, simple bar snacks, back lounge with fire and piano, connecting lobby to front public bar with pool, darts and TV, some Barnes Wallis memorabilia; children and dogs welcome, sheltered outside seating at back, walks by former Nottingham Canal, open all day weekends, closed weekday lunchtimes. *(Lorna and Jeff Mason)*

ILKESTON SK4641

Spanish Bar (0115) 930 8666

South Street; DE7 5QJ Busy bar with half a dozen well kept/priced ales, traditional ciders and bottled belgian beers, friendly efficient staff, evening overspill room; Tues quiz, free wi-fi; dogs welcome, small back garden and skittle alley, open all day. *(Molly and Stewart Lindsey)*

INGLEBY SK3427

John Thompson (01332) 862469

NW of Melbourne; turn off A514 at Swarkestone Bridge or in Stanton by Bridge; can also be reached from Ticknall (or from Repton on B5008); DE73 7HW Own beers from the longest established microbrewery in the UK; comfortable neatly kept lounge with beams, old settles, button-back leather seats and sturdy oak tables, antique prints and paintings, log-effect gas fire, a couple of smaller cosier rooms off, simple good value lunchtime food including carvery, piano, TV and games in conservatory; background music, free wi-fi; children welcome till 9pm, dogs in bar and conservatory, seats on lawns or partly covered terrace, pretty surrounding countryside, self-catering chalets, open all day weekends, closed Mon. *(David Eberlin)*

KING'S NEWTON SK3826

Hardinge Arms (01332) 863808

Not far from M1 junction 23A, via A453 to Isley, then off Melbourne/Wilson Road; Main Street; DE73 8BX Bright spacious old pub with enjoyable bar and evening restaurant food (not Mon), well kept local ales and good range of wines, quick friendly service, chunky low beams, brick, wood and flagstone floors, woodburner; children welcome in eating areas, handy for Donington Park and East Midlands Airport, bedrooms in converted stables, open all day (from 3pm Mon), no food Sun evening. *(Andrew Wall)*

LADYBOWER RESERVOIR SK1986

Ladybower Inn (01433) 651241

A57 Sheffield–Glossop, just E of junction with A6013; S33 0AX Batemans pub handy for the huge nearby reservoir; their ales and a couple of guests, enjoyable pubby food from sandwiches up, friendly service, various traditionally furnished carpeted areas with cast-iron fireplaces, Lancaster Bomber pictures recalling the Dambusters' practice runs on the reservoir; background music, darts, free wi-fi; children and dogs (in bar) welcome, picnic-sets out at front, annexe bedrooms, open (and food) all day. *(Martin Day, David H Bennett)*

LADYBOWER RESERVOIR SK2084

★Yorkshire Bridge (01433) 651361

A6013 N of Bamford; S33 0AZ Busy inn a short stroll from Ladybower dam and close to Derwent and Howden reservoirs; bar with woodburner, tankards hanging from beams, horsebrasses and copper items, lots of china plates, photographs and paintings on red walls, plush dining chairs around mix of tables on red patterned carpet, various other areas including airy garden room with fine valley views, ales such as Acorn, Bradfield, Howard Town and Peak, nine wines by the glass, generous helpings of popular pub food, friendly service; background music, free wi-fi; children welcome, no dogs at mealtimes, comfortable bedrooms, lovely surrounding walks, open all day, food all day weekends. *(Caroline Prescott, Nick Sharpe, David H Bennett, Jill and Dick Archer)*

LANGLEY MILL SK4248

Thorn Tree (01773) 768675

Woodlinkin, Nottingham Road; NG16 4HG Refurbished roadside restaurant/pub (part of the George's Tradition group) with great views over rolling country, good choice of enjoyable reasonably priced food including signature fish and chips and grills, three local ales, attentive friendly service, conservatory and deck taking in the view; children and dogs welcome, beer garden, open (and food) all day. *(Penny and David Shepherd)*

LITTLE LONGSTONE SK1971

Packhorse (01629) 640471

Off A6 NW of Bakewell via Monsal Dale; DE45 1NN Long low building with three comfortable linked beamed rooms, pine tables on flagstones, open fires, well kept ales including Black Sheep and Thornbridge, popular generously served home-made food from daily changing blackboard including good Sun lunch, affordably priced wine list, friendly accommodating service; Thurs quiz; children, dogs and hikers welcome (on Monsal Trail), terrace in steep little back garden, open (and food) all day weekends. *(Ann and Tony Bennett-Hughes, Frances Gibbs)*

LITTON SK1675

Red Lion (01298) 871458

Village signposted off A623, between B6465 and B6049 junctions; also signposted off B6049; SK17 8QU Welcoming traditional village pub, two linked front rooms with low beams, panelling and open fires, bigger stripped-stone back room, three well kept ales and enjoyable home-made food from sandwiches to daily specials; dogs allowed, seats and tables in front with more on village green, good walks in nearby dales, open (and food) all day. *(Mike and Wena Stevenson, Ann and Tony Bennett-Hughes)*

LULLINGTON SK2513

Colvile Arms (01827) 373212

Off A444 S of Burton; Main Street; DE12 8EG Popular 18th-c village pub under newish licensees; high-backed settles in simple panelled bar, cosy comfortable beamed lounge, well kept Bass, Marstons Pedigree and two guests, over 30 gins, no food except cobs, pleasant friendly atmosphere; background music, free wi-fi; children welcome till 7.30, dogs in bar, picnic-sets on small sheltered back lawn, closed lunchtimes apart from Sun, open all day weekends in summer. *(Lucy and Giles Gibbon)*

MAKENEY SK3544

★ Holly Bush (01332) 841729

From A6 heading N after Duffield, take first right after crossing River Derwent, then first left; DE56 0RX Unspoilt 17th-c two-bar village pub (former farmhouse); beams and black panelling, tiled and flagstone floors, three blazing fires, one in old-fashioned range by snug's curved high-backed settle, well kept changing ales (some served from jugs), craft beers and real cider, enjoyable lunchtime food from rolls and pork pies up, lobby with hatch service; beer festivals and occasional live music; children, walkers and dogs welcome, picnic-sets outside, open all day. *(Toby Jones)*

MARSTON MONTGOMERY SK1338

Crown (01889) 591430

On corner of Thurvaston Road and Barway; DE6 2FF Red-brick beamed village pub, clean and bright, with popular good value food, three real ales including Marstons Pedigree and several wines by the glass, friendly helpful staff, restaurant; some live music; children and dogs welcome, disabled access, terrace tables, seven good bedrooms, open all day, food till 7pm Sun. *(Selwyn Jones)*

MATLOCK SK2960

Moca (01629) 583973

Dale Road; DE4 3LT Light café-style bar with half a dozen or so well kept local beers and snacky lunchtime food, friendly knowledgeable staff, chunky pine furniture on bare boards, black and white photographs of musicians/bands; can fill up as not large; dogs welcome, back terrace, open all day. *(Jeremy King)*

MATLOCK SK2960

Thorn Tree (01629) 580295

Jackson Road, Matlock Bank; DE4 3JQ Superb valley views to Riber Castle from this homely 19th-c stone-built local; Bass, Greene King, Nottingham, Timothy Taylors and guests, simple well cooked food (Tues-Fri lunchtimes, Sun 5-6.30pm, Weds pie night), friendly staff and regulars; free wi-fi; children and dogs welcome, closed Mon lunchtime, open all day Fri-Sun. *(Andrew Wall)*

MAYFIELD SK1444

★ Rose & Crown (01335) 342498

Main Road (B5032 off A52 W of Ashbourne); DE6 2JT Welcoming dining pub with good attractively presented food cooked by owner-chef, reasonable prices, well kept Marstons Pedigree and nice range of good value wines, efficient friendly service, woodburner in beamed bar, restaurant; children welcome, no dogs inside, terrace tables under parasols, local walks, three bedrooms, closed Sun evening, Mon, food served 12-1.30pm, 6.30-8.30pm. *(Diane Abbot)*

MILLERS DALE SK1473

Anglers Rest (01298) 871323

Just down Litton Lane; pub is PH on OS Sheet 119 map reference 142734; SK17 8SN Newish owners for this creeper-clad pub in lovely quiet riverside setting; two bars and dining room, log fires, Bradfield, Kelham Island and a couple of guests, enjoyable simple food at reasonable prices, cheery helpful service; darts and pool; children welcome, muddy boots and dogs in public bar, wonderful gorge views and river walks (on the Monsal Trail), self-catering apartment, open all day, food all day Sat, till 8pm Sun. *(Lorna and Jeff Mason)*

MILLTOWN SK3561

Miners Arms (01246) 590218

Off B6036 SE of Ashover; Oakstedge Lane; S45 0HA Spotless stone dining pub with good freshly made food from well priced

Post Office address codings confusingly give the impression that a few pubs are in Derbyshire, when they're really in Cheshire (which is where we list them).

blackboard menu (booking advised), nice wines and one changing real ale, friendly staff, log fires; children welcome, no dogs inside, attractive country walks from the door, closed Mon-Weds (open Weds in Dec). *(Audrey and Paul Summers)*

MONSAL HEAD SK1871

★ **Monsal Head Hotel** (01629) 640250 *B6465; DE45 1NL* Outstanding hilltop location for this friendly inn; cosy stables bar with stripped timber horse-stalls, harness and brassware, cushioned oak pews, farmhouse chairs and benches on flagstones, big open fire, good selection of mainly local ales including one badged for them from Pennine, german bottled beers and plenty of wines by the glass, enjoyable locally sourced food from lunchtime sandwiches up (they may ask to keep a credit card while you eat), elegant restaurant; children (over 3), muddy walkers and well behaved dogs welcome, big garden, stunning views of Monsal Dale with its huge viaduct, seven comfortable bedrooms, open (and food) all day. *(Toby Jones)*

MONYASH SK1566

★ **Bulls Head** (01629) 812372 *B5055 W of Bakewell; DE45 1JH* Rambling stone pub with high-ceilinged rooms, straightforward traditional furnishings including plush stools lined along bar, horse pictures and a shelf of china, log fire, four real ales such as Black Sheep and Peak, restaurant with high-backed dining chairs on heated stone floor, popular traditional food (all day weekends) from sandwiches and baked potatoes up, friendly service, small back room with darts, board games and pool; background music; children and dogs welcome, plenty of picnic-sets under parasols in big garden, gate leading to well equipped public play area, good surrounding walks, open all day in high summer, all day Fri-Sun other times. *(Lucy and Giles Gibbon)*

MOORWOOD MOOR SK3656

White Hart (01629) 534888 *Inns Lane; village signed from South Wingfield; DE55 7NU* Cleanly updated country inn with good seasonal food in bar and restaurant, helpful attentive staff, well kept Sharps Doom Bar, Timothy Taylors Landlord and a couple of local guests; children and dogs welcome, tables on attractive heated terrace, ten modern bedrooms, open (and food) all day, kitchen closes 6.45pm Sun. *(Jim King)*

NEW MILLS SJ9886

Fox (0161) 427 1634 *Brook Bottom Road; SK22 3AY* Tucked-away old-fashioned country local in good walking area at end of single-track road, Robinsons ales and good value pub food (no credit cards), log fire; darts and pool; children and dogs welcome, lots of tables outside, open all day Fri-Sun. *(Brian and Susan Wylie)*

NEW MILLS SK0086

Pack Horse (01663) 742365 *Mellor Road; SK22 4QQ* Popular and friendly stone-built country inn with lovely views across broad Sett Valley to Kinder Scout; Tetleys and three guests kept well, good quality food in traditional log-fire bar and restaurant; children welcome, no dogs inside, terrace and garden on different levels, 12 well equipped clean bedrooms, open (and food) all day. *(Peter Sutton)*

NEWTON SOLNEY SK2825

Brickmakers Arms 07525 220103 *Main Street (B5008 NE of Burton); DE15 0SJ* Friendly end-of-terrace beamed pub owned by Burton Bridge Brewery; four of their well kept ales and a couple of guests including Timothy Taylors Landlord, real ciders and plenty of bottled beers, no food apart from Sun lunchtime cheeseboard, two rooms off bar, one with original panelling and delft shelf displaying jugs and plates, pubby furniture, built-in wall seats and coal fires, area with books; Mon quiz, Tues bingo, Thurs poker, free wi-fi; dogs welcome, tables on terrace, open all day weekends, closed lunchtimes during the week. *(Andrew Wall)*

OCKBROOK SK4236

Royal Oak (01332) 662378 *Off B6096 just outside Spondon; Green Lane; DE72 3SE* 18th-c village local run by same friendly family since 1953; good value honest food (not Sun evening) from good lunchtime cobs to steaks, well kept Bass and three interesting guest beers, tile-floored tap room, carpeted snug, inner bar with Victorian prints, larger and lighter side room, nice old settle in entrance corridor, open fires; darts and dominoes, some live music; children welcome, dogs in the evening, disabled access, sheltered cottage garden and cobbled front courtyard, separate play area, open all day weekends. *(Scott and Charlotte Havers)*

OSMASTON SK1943

Shoulder of Mutton (01335) 342371 *Off A52 SE of Ashbourne; DE6 1LW* Beamed red-brick pub incorporating post office/shop; Marstons Pedigree and a guest or two, generous helpings of enjoyable home-made food (all day weekends) from sandwiches up, good friendly service; free wi-fi; children welcome, no dogs inside, picnic-sets in attractive garden (farmland views), peaceful pretty village with thatched cottages, duck pond and good walks, open all day. *(Martin Day)*

PARWICH SK1854

Sycamore (01335) 390212 *By church; DE6 1QL* Welcoming old country pub freshened up under present management; flagstoned bar with mix of furniture including upholstered wall benches and some painted tables, woodburner, Robinsons ales and good reasonably priced home-made food including Tues steak night, efficient friendly service, a couple of back dining rooms, pub also houses the village shop; darts, free wi-fi; children and dogs welcome, picnic-sets in small front courtyard, more on side grass, good walks, open all day weekends. *(R L Borthwick)*

PENTRICH SK3852

Dog (01773) 513360
Main Road (B6016 N of Ripley); DE5 3RE Extended old stone pub with good variety of enjoyable bar and restaurant food, well kept Bass and a couple of guests from carved church-look counter, nice wines by the glass, friendly helpful staff, comfortable seating by bar's woodburner, big smartly presented dining room; background music, free wi-fi; well behaved children (not evenings in restaurant) and dogs (in bar) welcome, extensive garden behind, nice views and good walks, open all day Weds-Sun, no food Sun evening. *(David Hunt)*

PILSLEY SK2371

★**Devonshire Arms** (01246) 565405
Village signposted off A619 W of Baslow, and pub just below B6048; High Street; DE45 1UL Civilised little country inn on the Chatsworth Estate; gentle contemporary slant with flagstoned bar and several fairly compact areas off (each with own character – some steps), log fires in stone fireplaces, comfortable seating and big modern paintings, three well kept Peak ales, a cider such as Lilley's Strawberry and several wines by the glass, food from lunchtime sandwiches up using Estate produce, friendly staff; children and dogs welcome, a few picnic-sets out at front, Chatsworth farm shop at the top of lane, bedrooms, open all day. *(Brian and Susan Wylie)*

REPTON SK3027

Boot (01283) 346047
Boot Hill; DE65 6FT Restored 17th-c beamed inn (sister to the Dragon at Willington); own good microbrews (tasting notes provided) and very well liked interesting food (booking advised, particularly at weekends), friendly efficient young staff, modernised L-shaped interior; children and dogs (in bar area) welcome, split-level walled garden, nine bedrooms, open all day. *(Toby Jones)*

REPTON SK3026

Bulls Head (01283) 704422
High Street; DE65 6GF Lively village pub with interesting décor in various interconnecting bars; beams and pillars, mix of wooden dining chairs, settles, built-in wall seats and squashy sofas on bare boards or flagstones, driftwood sculptures, animal hides and an arty bull's head, log fires, ales from Marstons, Purity and Shardlow, lots of bottled beers and ciders, 15 wines by the glass and 20 malt whiskies, popular food including wood-fired pizzas and range of grilled yakitori sticks, cheerful staff, upstairs restaurant; background music, free wi-fi; children and dogs (in bar) welcome, sizeable heated terrace with neatly set tables and chairs under big parasols, open (and food) all day. *(Toby Jones)*

RIPLEY SK3950

Talbot Taphouse (01773) 742382
Butterley Hill; DE5 3LT Traditional pub with full range of local Amber ales and changing guests, also traditional ciders, draught belgian and bottled beers, friendly knowledgeable staff, long narrow panelled room with comfy chairs, open fire in brick fireplace; bar billiards and table skittles; open from 5pm Mon-Thurs, 3pm Fri, 2pm weekends. *(Max and Steph Warren)*

ROWSLEY SK2565

★**Peacock** (01629) 733518
Bakewell Road; DE4 2EB Small civilised 17th-c country hotel; comfortable seating in spacious modern lounge, inner bar with log fire, bare stone walls and some Robert 'Mouseman' Thompson furniture, very good if not cheap food from lunchtime sandwiches to restaurant meals, Peak ales, nice wines and well served coffee, pleasant helpful staff; attractive riverside gardens, trout fishing, 15 good bedrooms. *(Jim King)*

SHARDLOW SK4430

Malt Shovel (01332) 792066
3.5 miles from M1 junction 24, via A6 towards Derby; The Wharf; DE72 2HG Welcoming canalside pub in late 18th-c former maltings; interesting odd-angled layout with cosy corners and steps down to snug, Marstons Pedigree and a beer badged for the pub, very good value tasty food from sandwiches and baked potatoes up including popular breakfasts, evening meals Thurs only (thai/english menu), quick friendly service, beams, panelling and central open fire; live music Sun, free wi-fi; children and dogs welcome, lots of terrace tables by Trent & Mersey Canal, pretty hanging baskets, open all day. *(Belinda and Neil Garth)*

SHARDLOW SK4429

Old Crown (01332) 792392
Off A50 just W of M1 junction 24; Cavendish Bridge, E of village; DE72 2HL Good value pub with half a dozen well kept Marstons-related ales and decent choice of malt whiskies, traditional food (all day Sat, not Sun evening, Mon) from sandwiches and baguettes up, beams with masses of jugs and mugs, walls covered with other bric-a-brac and breweriana, big inglenook; quiz Mon, fortnightly live music Tues; children and dogs welcome, garden with play area, open all day. *(Andrew Wall)*

SHELDON SK1768

★**Cock & Pullet** (01629) 814292
Village signed off A6 just W of Ashford; DE45 1QS Charming no-frills village pub with low beams, exposed stonework, flagstones and open fire, cheerful mismatch of furnishings, large collection of clocks and various representations of poultry (some stuffed), well kept Sharps Doom Bar, Timothy Taylors Landlord and a guest such as Peak, tasty pub food from shortish menu including popular Sun roasts (best to book), reasonable prices and friendly efficient service; quiet background music, pool and TV in plainer public bar; children and dogs welcome, seats and water feature on pleasant back terrace, pretty village just off the Limestone Way and popular all year with walkers, clean bedrooms, open all day. *(Audrey and Paul Summers)*

SHIRLEY SK2141

Saracens Head (01335) 360330
Church Lane; DE6 3AS Modernised late 18th-c dining pub in attractive village; good range of well presented blackboard food from pubby choices to more expensive restaurant-style dishes, four Greene King ales, decent wines and speciality coffees, simple country-style dining furniture and two pretty working art nouveau fireplaces; background music; children and dogs (in bar area) welcome, picnic-sets out in front and on back terrace, open all day Sun. *(Jim King)*

SOUTH WINGFIELD SK3755

Old Yew Tree (01773) 833626
B5035 W of Alfreton; Manor Road; DE55 7NH Friendly 16th-c village pub with good reasonably priced home-made food (not Sun evening) including lunchtime/early evening deal, Bass, a local guest (two at weekends) and a proper cider, log fire, beams and carved panelling, separate restaurant area; Sat music, Weds quiz, TV, free wi-fi; children, walkers and dogs welcome, some rattan-style furniture out at the side, open all day Fri-Sun, closed Mon and Tues lunchtimes. *(Brian and Susan Wylie)*

STONEDGE SK3367

Red Lion (01246) 566142
Darley Road (B5057); S45 0LW Revamped bar-bistro (former 17th-c coaching inn) on edge of the Peak District; good attractively presented food (pricey for the area) from sandwiches up using local ingredients including own vegetables, real ales such as Peak and good choice of wines, bare stone walls, flagstones and wood floors, some substantial timbers, lounge area with comfortable seating and open fire; picnic-sets out under parasols at back, 27 bedrooms in adjacent modern hotel, open all day. *(Diane Abbot)*

SUDBURY SK1632

Vernon Arms (01283) 585329
Off A50/A515; Main Road; DE6 5HS Rambling 17th-c brick pub with three main rooms (stairs to bar), enjoyable reasonably priced food including good Sun roasts, four Marstons-related ales, log fires; background music, Sun quiz twice a month; children and dogs welcome, nice big garden, handy for Sudbury Hall (NT), open all day. *(Max and Steph Warren)*

SUTTON CUM DUCKMANTON SK4371

Arkwright Arms (01246) 232053
A632 Bolsover–Chesterfield; S44 5JG Friendly mock-Tudor pub with bar, pool room (dogs allowed here) and dining room, all with real fires, good choice of well priced food (not Sun evening), up to 16 changing ales, ten real ciders and four perries (beer/cider festivals Easter/Aug bank holidays); TV, games machine; children welcome, seats out at front and on side terrace, open all day. *(Jim King)*

THORPE SK1650

Old Dog (01335) 350990
Spend Lane/Wintercroft Lane; DE6 2AT Refurbished bistro-style village pub (former 18th-c coaching inn), lively and friendly, with popular food from sensibly short menu including good burgers, four well kept changing ales, friendly attentive service, candlelit tables on flagstones, woodburners; background music; children, walkers and dogs welcome, covered eating area outside, handy for Dovedale and Tissington Trail, closed Mon, otherwise open all day, food all weekends (till 7pm Sun). *(Belinda and Neil Garth)*

TICKNALL SK3523

★**Wheel** (01332) 864488
Main Street (A514); DE73 7JZ Stylish contemporary décor in bar and upstairs restaurant, enjoyable interesting home-made food (all day weekends) including daily specials, friendly efficient staff, well kept Marstons Pedigree and a guest; children welcome, no dogs inside, nice outside area with café tables on raised deck, near entrance to Calke Abbey (NT). *(R L Borthwick)*

TIDESWELL SK1575

Anchor (01298) 871371
A623 NE; SK17 8RB Comfortable smartened-up old beamed pub, good food from sandwiches and usual favourites up including signature rum-glazed steaks, well kept Robinsons ales and interesting selection of rums, friendly obliging service, log fires; children and dogs welcome, picnic-sets on grass, open (and food) all day. *(Ann and Tony Bennett-Hughes)*

TIDESWELL SK1575

Horse & Jockey (01298) 872211

Queen Street; SK17 8JZ Friendly and relaxed family-run local; beams, flagstones, cushioned wall benches and coal fire in small public bar's traditional open range, bare-boards lounge with button-back banquettes and woodburner, well kept Sharps Doom Bar and a couple of local guests, decent reasonably priced food (all day Sun), stripped-stone dining room; free wi-fi; children and dogs welcome, six comfortable bedrooms, good walks, open all day. *(Ann and Tony Bennett-Hughes)*

TIDESWELL SK1575

Star (01298) 872725

High Street; SK17 8LD Friendly little village pub with three well kept Marstons-related ales, enjoyable traditional food and reasonably priced wine list, quick cheerful service, four compact rooms including lounge with woodburner and dining room; Thurs quiz, darts and dominoes; children welcome, dogs in front bar, bedrooms planned, closed lunchtime apart from Sun, no food Mon. *(David Hunt)*

UPPER LANGWITH SK5169

Devonshire (01623) 747777

Rectory Road; NG20 9RF Popular dining pub with several cosy areas; highly rated food from lunchtime sandwiches up including good fish dishes (best to book), well kept Sharps Doom Bar and three guests such as local Priors Well, decent wines, friendly attentive service; children and dogs (in bar) welcome, easy disabled access, a few picnic-sets out at front, open all day (till 7pm Sun). *(Derek and Sylvia Stephenson)*

WARDLOW SK1875

★Three Stags Heads (01298) 872268

Wardlow Mires; A623/B6465; SK17 8RW Basic unchanging pub (17th-c longhouse) of great individuality; old country furniture on flagstones, heating from cast-iron kitchen ranges, old photographs, long-serving plain-talking landlord, locals in favourite corners, well kept Abbeydale ales including a strong house beer (Black Lurcher), proper cider and lots of bottled beers, simple food on home-made plates (licensees are potters and have a small gallery), may be free roast chestnuts or cheese on the bar, folk music Sun afternoon; no credit cards or mobile phones; well behaved children and dogs welcome (resident lurchers), hill views from front terrace, good walking country, only open Fri evening and all day weekends. *(Ann and Tony Bennett-Hughes)*

WHITTINGTON MOOR SK3873

Derby Tup (01246) 269835

Sheffield Road; B6057 just S of A61 roundabout; S41 8LS Popular Castle Rock local with their ales along with Pigeon Fishers (landlord owns the brewery) and several guests, also craft beers, up to seven ciders and good range of other drinks; coal fire, simple furniture and lots of standing room, two side snugs; live music including jam session last Mon of month; dogs welcome, seats out on small back deck, open all day Fri-Sun (can get very busy weekend evenings and match days), closed Mon-Thurs lunchtimes. *(Selwyn Jones)*

WILLINGTON SK2928

Dragon (01283) 704795

The Green; DE65 6BP Renovated and extended pub backing on to Trent & Mersey Canal; enjoyable well cooked food from sandwiches and sharing boards to pub favourites and grills, a couple of microbrews from sister pub the Boot at Repton and local guests; weekend live music, sports TV, free wi-fi; children and dogs (not in restaurant) welcome, picnic-sets out overlooking canal, moorings, open (and food) all day. *(Penny and David Shepherd)*

WINSTER SK2460

★Bowling Green (01629) 650219

East Bank, by Market House (NT); DE4 2DS Traditional old stone pub with good chatty atmosphere, character landlord and welcoming staff, enjoyable generously served food including popular pies, at least three well kept changing local ales and good selection of whiskies, end log fire, dining area and family conservatory (dogs allowed here too); nice village with good surrounding walks, closed Mon, Tues and lunchtimes apart from Sun. *(Brian and Anna Marsden)*

WINSTER SK2360

Miners Standard (01629) 650279

Bank Top (B5056 above village); DE4 2DR Simply furnished 17th-c stone local, friendly and relaxed, with bar, snug and restaurant, well kept ales such as Greene King, Marstons and Wychwood, good value honest pub food (not Sun evening), big woodburner, lead mining photographs and minerals, lots of brass, a backwards clock and ancient well; background music; children (away from bar) and dogs welcome, attractive view from garden, campsite next door, interesting stone-built village below, open all day. *(Andrew Wall)*

Virtually all pubs in this book sell wine by the glass. We mention wines if they are a cut above the average.

Devon

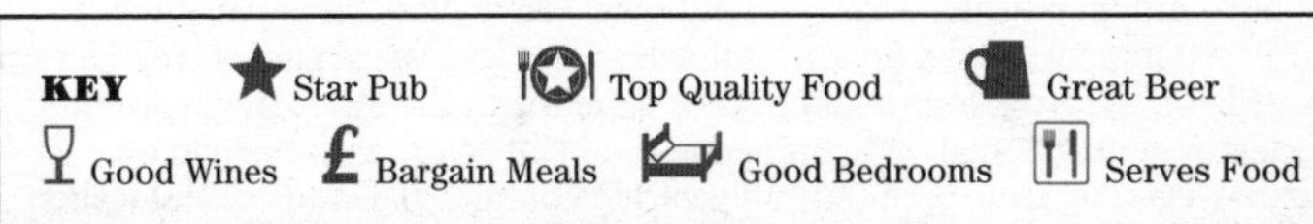

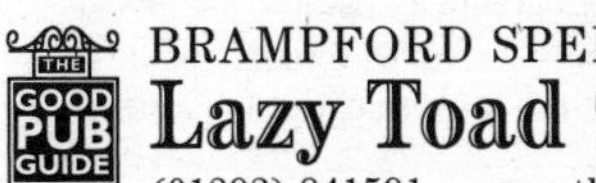

BRAMPFORD SPEKE SX9298 Map 1

Lazy Toad

(01392) 841591 – www.thelazytoad.co.uk

Off A377 N of Exeter; EX5 5DP

Well run dining pub in pretty village with popular food, real ales, friendly service and pretty garden

Before or after a drink or a meal here, do wander around this charming village of thatched cottages; there are also fine walks beside the River Exe and on the Exe Valley Way and Devonshire Heartland Way. The interconnected bar rooms have beams, standing timbers and slate floors, a comfortable sofa by an open log fire and cushioned wall settles and high-backed wooden dining chairs around a mix of tables; the cream-painted brick walls are hung with lots of pictures. Exeter County Best and Hanlons Yellowhammer on handpump and several wines by the glass are served by attentive staff; the irish terrier is called Rufus. The courtyard (once used by the local farrier and wheelwright) has oak benches and tables, with more in the walled garden.

Good, enjoyable food includes a roast of the day or toasted open sandwiches, baked field mushroom filled with spinach and goats cheese, pressed terrine of pork, chicken and game, roasted squash and cheddar or steak in ale pies, gammon and egg, corn-fed chicken breast with chicken cream sauce and crushed new potatoes, confit neck fillet of lamb with cabbage and bacon, sea bass fillets with bubble and squeak cake, creamed leeks and mushroom duxelles, and puddings such as chocolate brownie with hot chocolate sauce and a seasonal crumble with vanilla bean ice-cream. *Benchmark main dish: beer-battered fish and chips £13.95. Two-course evening meal £22.00.*

Free house ~ Licensees Harriet and Mike Daly ~ Real ale ~ Open 12-3, 6-10; 12-4 Sun; closed Sun evening, Mon ~ Bar food 12-2 (2.30 Sun), 6.30-9 ~ Children welcome ~ Dogs allowed in bar ~ Wi-fi *Recommended by Katherine and Hugh Markham, Amy Ledbetter, Rupert and Sandy Newton, Rosie and Marcus Heatherley*

BRANSCOMBE SY1888 Map 1

Fountain Head

(01297) 680359 – www.fountainheadinn.com

Upper village; W of Branscombe at Street; EX12 3BG

Friendly, unspoilt pub with local beers and tasty, well priced food

Looking down a lane lined by thatched cottages, with the steep pastures of the combe beyond, this medieval tiled stone house remains nicely old-fashioned and unchanging. The room on the left was once a smithy and has forge tools and horseshoes on high oak beams, cushioned pews and mate's chairs, and a log fire in the original raised hearth with its tall central chimney. There's Branscombe Vale Branoc, Golden Fiddle and Summa That on handpump, two local ciders and eight wines by the glass. On the right, an irregularly shaped snug room has another log fire, a white-painted plank ceiling with an unusual carved ceiling rose, brown-varnished panelling, a flagstone floor and local artwork for sale; darts and board games. You can sit outside on the front loggia and terrace listening to the little stream gurgling beneath the flagstoned path; barbecues and spit roasts may be held on Sunday evening from 6pm (end July-early September). Good coastal walks.

As well as sandwiches and toasties and a few well priced lunchtime staples, the pleasing food includes mixed fish and prawn salad with caviar dressing, cheesy garlic cod cakes with sweet chilli dip, roasted red peppers stuffed with ratatouille and wild mushrooms with a sweet red wine dressing, a fresh fish dish of the day, venison and red wine pie, 10oz rump steak with chips and puddings. *Benchmark main dish: beer-battered fish and chips £12.00. Two-course evening meal £18.00.*

Free house ~ Licensee Jon Woodley ~ Real ale ~ Open 11-3, 6-11; 12-10.30 Sun ~ Bar food 12-2, 6.30 (7 Sun in winter)-9 ~ Restaurant ~ Children welcome away from main bar area ~ Dogs welcome *Recommended by Roger and Donna Huggins, Alfie Bayliss, Diane Abbot, Lucy and Giles Gibbon, Thomas Green, Peter Pilbeam*

BUCKLAND MONACHORUM SX4968 Map 1

Drake Manor £

(01822) 853892 – www.drakemanorinn.co.uk

Off A386 via Crapstone, just S of Yelverton roundabout; PL20 7NA

Nice little village pub with snug rooms, popular food, quite a choice of drinks and pretty back garden; bedrooms

This charming little pub was originally built to house workers constructing the nearby church. It's much enjoyed by our readers and is run by a friendly, long-serving landlady who offers good, very reasonably priced food and comfortable bedrooms. The heavily beamed public bar on the left has a chatty, easy-going feel, brocade-cushioned wall seats, prints of the village from 1905 onwards, horse tack and a few ship badges and a woodburning stove in a very big stone fireplace; a small door leads to a low-beamed cubbyhole. The snug Drakes Bar has beams hung with tiny cups and big brass keys, a woodburning stove in another stone fireplace, horsebrasses and stirrups, and a mix of seats and tables (note the fine high-backed stripped-pine settle with hood). On the right is a small beamed dining room with settles and tables on flagstones. Darts and board games. Dartmoor Jail Ale, Sharps Doom Bar and Wychwood Dirty Tackle on handpump, ten wines by the glass, a dozen malt whiskies, 15 gins and three farm ciders. There are picnic-sets in the prettily planted and sheltered back garden and the front floral displays are much admired; morris men perform regularly in summer. They also offer an attractive self-catering apartment. Buckland Abbey (National Trust) is close by.

Good value food using home-reared pork and honey from their own bees includes lunchtime baguettes and ploughman's, smoked mackerel pâté with pickled fennel, caramelised feta, beetroot and pecan salad with curry oil, a burger of the day with chips, gammon with free-range eggs, spiced cajun chicken with sweet potato fries, corn on the cob and crème fraîche, steaks with a choice of sauce, specials such as seafood pancake and local venison, and puddings such as lemon posset and sticky toffee pudding with caramel sauce. *Benchmark main dish: pie of the day £10.50. Two-course evening meal £16.00.*

Punch ~ Lease Mandy Robinson ~ Real ale ~ Open 11.30-2.30, 6-11; 11.30-11.30 Fri, Sat; 12-11 Sun ~ Bar food 12-2, 6.30 (6 Fri)-9.30; 12-2.30, 6-9.30 Sat; 12-2.30, 6.30-9.30 Sun ~ Restaurant ~ Children welcome ~ Dogs allowed in bar ~ Wi-fi ~ Bedrooms: £80/£100
Recommended by Alison and Michael Harper, Donald Allsopp, Glen and Patricia Fuller, Freddie and Sarah Banks, Camilla and Jose Ferrera, John Evans

CHAGFORD SX7087 Map 1

Three Crowns

(01647) 433444 – www.threecrowns-chagford.co.uk
High Street; TQ13 8AJ

Stylishly refurbished bar and lounges in ancient inn, conservatory restaurant and good food and drinks; smart bedrooms

Spendidly renovated just over three years ago, this is a part-thatched 13th-c former manor house where ancient and modern features blend very well together. There are massive beams and standing timbers, huge fireplaces with wood fires (lit all year), exposed stone walls, flagstones and mullioned windows, and a contemporary, glazed atrium dining room. The bar areas have leather armchairs and stools, built-in panelled wall seats and a few leather tub chairs. St Austell Proper Job and Tribute on handpump, 20 wines by the glass and 21 gins served by friendly, efficient staff. Throughout the building are antique prints, photographs and polished copper kettles, pots and warming pans; background music and board games. Sturdy tables and chairs are placed among box topiary in the south-facing courtyard garden. Bedrooms are stylish and well appointed and blend character with modern design. Parking is limited to superior rooms only but there's also a nearby pay-and-display car park. Muddy boots and dogs are welcome.

Quite a choice of good food includes lunchtime sandwiches and sharing platters, beetroot and gin-cured salmon with celeriac rémoulade, goats cheese pannacotta with smoked cherry tomatoes, aioli and pine nuts, kansas-style pulled pork burger with red onion marmalade and coleslaw, moules frites, root vegetable cassoulet with blue cheese dumplings, hake fillet with cockles, samphire and saffron broth, asian smoked duck breast with confit duck leg croquette and spiced beetroot purée, and puddings such as chocolate and orange cheesecake with orange sorbet and orange truffle and spiced black treacle cake with honey-glazed plums and stem ginger ice-cream. *Benchmark main dish: lamb rump with dauphinoise potatoes and redcurrant jus £15.50. Two-course evening meal £21.00.*

St Austell ~ Managers John Milan and Steve Bellman ~ Real ale ~ Open 10am-11pm; 10am-midnight Fri, Sat ~ Bar food 12-9 (9.30 Sat); 8-10am breakfast, 10am-midday snacks; 2.30-6 sandwiches and cream teas ~ Restaurant ~ Children welcome ~ Dogs allowed in bar ~ Wi-fi ~ Bedrooms: £90/£110 *Recommended by Dr A E and Mrs Forbes, Dr A McCormick, Professor James Burke, Amy and Luke Buchanan, Catherine and Daniel King, Charlie and Mark Todd*

COCKWOOD SX9780 Map 1

Anchor

(01626) 890203 – www.anchorinncockwood.com
Off, but visible from, A379 Exeter–Torbay, after Starcross; EX6 8RA

Busy dining pub specialising in seafood (other choices available), with up to six real ales

You must arrive early to get a table (and even a parking space) at this popular place. Of course, its position is quite a draw: the much prized tables on the sheltered front terrace look over the small harbour with its bobbing boats, swans and ducks. There are several small, low-ceilinged, rambling rooms with black panelling and good-sized tables in various nooks, a snug with a cheerful winter coal fire, and an extension made up of mainly reclaimed timber and decorated with over 300 ship emblems, brass and copper lamps and nautical knick-knacks. Six real ales on handpump include Dartmoor Jail Ale, Otter Ale and St Austell Tribute with guests such as Beerd Monterey and South Hams Wild Blonde (they hold beer festivals at Easter and Halloween), eight wines by the glass, 13 gins and 40 malt whiskies; background music, darts, cards and board games.

Popular food majoring on fish and shellfish (non-fishy choices too) includes sandwiches, lightly spiced local crab gratin, baked camembert with orange and cranberry sauce, vegetarian sausages, scallops in spiced rum, double cream, orange and dill, steak and kidney or fish pies, shared shellfish selection, surf and turf (fillet steak in garlic with king prawns and scallops), gumbo pot (duo of fish and shellfish in a hot spicy tomato sauce), slow-roasted pork belly with cranberry stuffing, sherry and thyme-infused gravy and pigs in blankets, and puddings such as lemon tart and white chocolate mud pie. *Benchmark main dish: mussels with a choice of 18 different sauces £14.95. Two-course evening meal £21.00.*

Heavitree ~ Lease Malcolm and Katherine Protheroe, Scott Hellier ~ Real ale ~ Open 11-11; 11.30-10.30 Sun ~ Bar food 12-9 (9.30 Fri, Sat) ~ Restaurant ~ Children welcome if seated and away from bar ~ Dogs allowed in bar *Recommended by Dr and Mrs A K Clarke, Graeme and Sally Mendham, Nick Higgins, Lauren and Dan Frazer, Richard and Tessa Ibbot*

COLEFORD SS7701 Map 1

New Inn

(01363) 84242 – www.thenewinncoleford.co.uk

Just off A377 Crediton–Barnstaple; EX17 5BZ

Ancient thatched inn with welcoming licensees, good food and real ales; bedrooms

This must be one of the oldest 'new' inns around as it dates from the 13th c. It's warm and friendly and set between Exmoor and Dartmoor, so there are always plenty of customers. The U-shaped building has the servery in the 'angle' with interestingly furnished areas leading off it: ancient and modern settles, cushioned stone wall seats, some character tables (a pheasant worked into the grain of one) and carved dressers and chests. Also, paraffin lamps, antique prints on the white walls, landscape-decorated plates on one beam and pewter tankards on another. Captain, the chatty parrot, may greet you with a 'hello' or even a 'goodbye'. Otter Ale and Sharps Doom Bar with a guest such as the local Hunters Half Bore or Shepherd Neame Spitfire on handpump, local cider, 16 wines by the glass and a dozen malt whiskies; background music, darts and board games. There are chairs and tables on decking beneath a pruned willow tree by the babbling stream, and more in a covered dining area. Bedrooms are well equipped and comfortable and the breakfasts are very good indeed.

Popular food includes pub classics plus goats cheese salad on apple and walnut with orange vinaigrette and red onion marmalade, cod and salmon fishcakes with dill mayonnaise, sweet potato and aubergine moussaka, hake fillet with a pink prawn, cream and white wine sauce and vegetable medley, pulled pork in a brioche bun, confit free-range duck leg with cider sauce and boulangère and thyme potatoes, and puddings such as chocolate brownie and ice-cream and meringue fingers topped with cream, blueberries, pecan nuts, honey and raspberry coulis. *Benchmark main dish: steak in ale pie £12.95. Two-course evening meal £19.50.*

Free house ~ Licensees Carole and George Cowie ~ Real ale ~ Open 12-3, 6-11 (10.30 Sun) ~ Bar food 12-2, 6.30-9 ~ Restaurant ~ Children welcome ~ Dogs allowed in bar ~ Wi-fi ~ Quiz mid-month Sun evening; hog roasts May, July, Oct ~ Bedrooms: £72/£95
Recommended by Cliff and Monica Swan, Emma Scofield, Mike Benton, Chris and Angela Buckell, John Ledbury

DALWOOD ST2400 Map 1

Tuckers Arms

(01404) 881342 – www.thetuckersarms.co.uk
Village signposted off A35 Axminster–Honiton; keep on past village; EX13 7EG

13th-c thatched inn with friendly, hard-working licensees, real ales and interesting bar food

With enjoyable food, good-humoured staff and a genuine welcome it's not surprising our readers remain so enthusiastic about their visits to this thatched medieval longhouse. The flagstoned bar is kept warm by a big inglenook log fireplace, and there are heavy beams, traditional furnishings including assorted dining chairs, window seats and wall settles, numerous horsebrasses and a cheerful, bustling atmosphere. The back bar has an enormous collection of miniature bottles and there's also a more formal dining room; lots of copper implements and platters. Branscombe Vale Branoc, Exeter Avocet and Otter Bitter on handpump, several wines by the glass and up to 20 malt whiskies; background music and a double skittle alley. There are seats in the garden. The colourful summer window boxes, hanging baskets and tubs are really pretty and the pub is surrounded by narrow high-hedged lanes and hilly pasture countryside. Apart from the church, this is the oldest building in the parish.

Generous helpings of top quality food include lunchtime sandwiches, potted crab, puff pastry pork belly with apricot, cider and raisin chutney, pumpkin and sage ravioli, local moules marinière, an antipasti platter, steak in ale pie, smoked haddock florentine, lamb rump with redcurrant and rosemary gravy and bubble and squeak, and puddings such as butterscotch and ginger pudding with salted caramel ice-cream and lemon meringue slice. *Benchmark main dish: fisherman's platter £10.25. Two-course evening meal £19.00.*

Free house ~ Licensee Tracey McGowan ~ Real ale ~ Open 11.30-3, 6.30-11.30 ~ Bar food 12-2, 6.30-9 ~ Restaurant ~ Well behaved children in restaurant ~ Dogs allowed in bar ~ Wi-fi ~ Bedrooms: £45/£69.50 *Recommended by Ewan and Sue Hewitt, Andreas, Chris Stevenson, Jack Trussler, Diana and Bertie Farr, Alexandra and Richard Clay*

DARTMOUTH SX8751 Map 1

Royal Castle Hotel

(01803) 833033 – www.royalcastle.co.uk
The Quay; TQ6 9PS

350-year-old hotel by the harbour with a genuine mix of customers, real ales and good food; comfortable bedrooms

This is a most enjoyable place to stay (breakfasts are excellent) and some of the stylish bedrooms overlook the water; dogs, welcome in all rooms, get treats and a toy. They also have their own secure parking. The whole place has a great deal of character and many original features – some of the beams are said to have come from the wreckage of the Spanish Armada. The two ground-floor bars are quite different. The oak beamed Galleon bar (on the right) has a log fire in a Tudor fireplace, some fine antiques and maritime pieces and plenty of chatty locals. The Harbour Bar (to the left of the flagstoned entrance hall) is contemporary in style and rather smart, with a big-screen TV and live acoustic music on Thursday evenings. The Grill Room restaurant looks over the river; background music. Dartmoor Jail Ale, Otter Amber, Sharps Doom Bar and a weekly guest on handpump and 28 wines by the glass; service is helpful and friendly. This is a fine spot overlooking the inner harbour and beyond to the bigger boats in the main harbour.

Food is interesting and includes lunchtime sandwiches, sticky chicken wings with coleslaw, salt and pepper calamari, sharing platters, a pie of the week, gnocchi with wild mushrooms, spinach, butternut squash, courgette ribbons and lemon cream, chicken schnitzel burger with harissa mayonnaise and toppings, lobster and white fish curry with lime pickle, coriander and yoghurt, steaks with skinny fries and a choice of sauce, and puddings such as chocolate brownie mousse with meringue and honeycomb and vanilla pannacotta with jellied berries. *Benchmark main dish: beer-battered fish and chips £14.95. Two-course evening meal £25.00.*

Free house ~ Licensees Nigel and Anne Way ~ Real ale ~ Open 8am-11pm (10.30pm Sun) ~ Bar food 8am-10pm ~ Restaurant ~ Children welcome away from Harbour Bar ~ Dogs allowed in bar and bedrooms ~ Wi-fi ~ Live music Thurs evening ~ Bedrooms: £130/£180
Recommended by Tony Scott, Scott and Charlotte Havers, Elisabeth and Bill Humphries, Charles Welch

EXETER SX9192 Map 1

Fat Pig

(01392) 437217 – www.fatpig-exeter.co.uk
John Street; EX1 1BL

Enthusiastically run pub with own-brew beers, home-distilled spirits, big-flavoured food and a buoyant atmosphere

An excellent choice of drinks in this lively, cheerful pub includes their own-brewed Fat Pig Ham 69 and Phat Nancys IPA and a changing guest on handpump, good wines by the glass, around 100 malt whiskies and their own Exeter Distillery gins (they have three), vodka and apple pie moonshine. The big-windowed bar is simply furnished: elegant stools against a mahogany counter, more stools and long cushioned pews by sturdy pale wooden tables on bare boards, an open fire in a pretty fireplace, blackboards listing food choices and lots of mirrors. There's also a red-painted and red quarry-tiled conservatory with a happy jumble of hops and house plants, books and old stone bottles on shelves, more mirrors and long benches and settles with scatter cushions around rustic tables.

The high quality, robust food uses rare-breed meat from nearby farms, local game and home-made sausages, black pudding and dry-cured ham: pork and pigeon terrine with pickled rhubarb and watercress, baked mackerel with spring onions and horseradish vinaigrette, slow-smoked pulled chipotle beef with cheddar and pickles, fried potato gnocchi with wild mushrooms, courgettes and toasted almonds and cream, rosemary-fried breaded pork chop with creamed cabbage and bacon, salmon fillet and crushed potato with roast fennel and curry sauce, and puddings such as blood orange ice with fruit salad and mint and chocolate pudding. *Benchmark main dish: sausage and mash £16.00. Two-course evening meal £22.00.*

Free house ~ Licensee Paul Timewell ~ Real ale ~ Open 5-11pm; 4-midnight Fri; 12-midnight Sat; 12-5 Sun ~ Bar food 5-9; 12-9 Sat; 12-3 Sun ~ Restaurant ~ Children allowed Sun lunchtime only ~ Dogs welcome ~ Wi-fi *Recommended by Jamie and Sue May, Sophia and Hamish Greenfield, Adam Jones, Roger and Donna Huggins, Philip J Alderton, Sophie and James Collier*

FROGMORE SX7742 Map 1

Globe

(01548) 531351 – www.theglobeinn.co.uk

A379 E of Kingsbridge; TQ7 2NR

Extended and neatly refurbished inn with bar and several dining areas, real ales, popular food and seats outside; warm bedrooms

Our readers enjoy staying in the well equipped, comfortable bedrooms here and breakfasts are generous. The neatly kept bar has a double-sided woodburner with horsebrass-decorated stone pillars on either side, another fireplace filled with logs, cushioned settles, chunky farmhouse chairs and built-in wall seats around a mix of tables on wooden flooring, and a copper diving helmet. Attentive staff serve Otter Ale, Skinners Betty Stogs and South Hams Eddystone on handpump and several wines by the glass. The slate-floored games room has a pool table and darts. There's also a comfortable lounge with an open fire, cushioned dining chairs and tables on red carpeting, a big leather sofa, a model yacht and a large yacht painting – spot the clever mural of a log pile. Teak tables and chairs sit on the back terrace, with steps leading up to another level with picnic-sets; the summer window boxes are very pretty. This is a lovely area to explore and the surrounding South Hams countryside is very pretty.

Well liked food includes lunchtime sandwiches and baguettes, smoked haddock and salmon fishcakes with dill, lemon and horseradish dressing, baked goats cheese with roasted hazelnuts and balsamic onions, pizzas with lots of toppings, crab, squid and prawn linguine with lime, chilli and coriander, burger with toppings, onion rings and chips, curry of the day, steak in ale pie, 10oz rib-eye steak with a choice of home-made butters, and puddings such as white chocolate cheesecake with fruit compote and treacle tart with clotted cream. *Benchmark main dish: seafood pancake £13.95. Two-course evening meal £22.00.*

Free house ~ Licensees John and Lynda Horsley ~ Real ale ~ Open 12-11 (10.30 Sun); 15 Sept-30 June: 12-2.30, 6-11 (6.30-10.30 Sun in winter); closed Mon lunchtime in winter ~ Bar food 12-2, 6-9 ~ Restaurant ~ Children welcome ~ Dogs allowed in bar and bedrooms ~ Wi-fi ~ Folk evenings first Tues and third Thurs of month ~ Bedrooms: £75/£90

Recommended by Bob and Margaret Holder, B and F A Hannam, Paul Farraday, Jane Rigby, Freddie and Sarah Banks, Geoff and Ann Marston

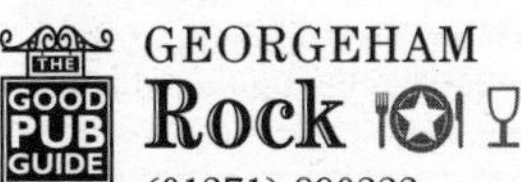

GEORGEHAM SS4639 Map 1

Rock

(01271) 890322 – www.therockinn.biz

Rock Hill, above village; EX33 1JW

Beamed pub with smashing food, five real ales, plenty of room inside and out and a relaxed atmosphere

The big bustling bar is the heart of this friendly 17th-c pub and is divided in two by a step. The pubby top part has half-planked walls, an open woodburning stove in a stone fireplace and captain's and farmhouse chairs around wooden tables on quarry tiles; the lower area has panelled wall seats, some built-in settles forming a cosy booth, old local photographs and ancient flat irons. Leading off here is a red-carpeted dining room with attractive black and white photographs of North Devon folk. Friendly young staff serve Exmoor Gold, Fullers London Pride, St Austell Tribute, Sharps Doom Bar and Timothy Taylors Landlord on handpump and more than a dozen wines by the glass; background music and board games. The light and airy back dining conservatory has high-backed wooden or modern dining chairs around tables under a vine, with a little terrace beyond. There are picnic-sets at the front beside pretty hanging baskets and tubs; wheelchair access.

Particularly good food includes lunchtime sandwiches, sharing platters, whole baked camembert with garlic and thyme and chutney, black pudding and sage scotch egg with home-made brown sauce and pickles, thai green vegetable curry, spaghetti vongole (clams and king prawns with chilli, garlic, white wine and parsley), a pie of the week, rack of barbecue hickory ribs with coleslaw and chips, stuffed fajitas with king prawns, chicken or vegetables, fillet of bass with crab and lobster bisque, mussels, clams, samphire and roasted fennel, and puddings such as chocolate fondant and apple and rhubarb crumble. *Benchmark main dish: loin of venison wellington with butternut purée, creamed savoy cabbage and redcurrant jus £19.95. Two-course evening meal £22.00.*

Star Pubs & Bars ~ Lease Daniel Craddock ~ Real ale ~ Open 11am-11.30pm (midnight Sat); 12-11.30 Sun ~ Bar food 12-2.30, 6-9; 12-8.30 Sun ~ Restaurant ~ Children welcome ~ Dogs allowed in bar ~ Wi-fi *Recommended by Bob and Margaret Holder, Mike Benton, Andrew and Michele Revell, John Wilson, Vibekke Böhl, Cecily and Steven Evans*

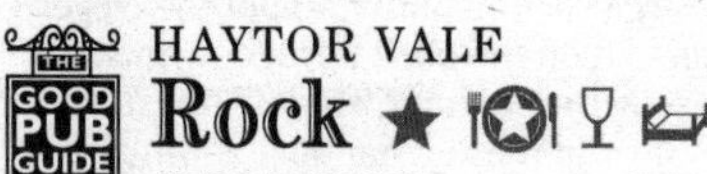

HAYTOR VALE
Rock

SX7777 Map 1

(01364) 661305 – www.rock-inn.co.uk

Haytor signposted off B3387 just W of Bovey Tracey, on good moorland road to Widecombe; TQ13 9XP

Smart Dartmoor inn with lovely food, real ales and seats in pretty garden; comfortable bedrooms

On the edge of Dartmoor National Park, this is a gently civilised place that's at its most informal at lunchtime. The two neatly kept, linked, partly panelled bar rooms have lots of dark wood and red plush, polished antique tables with candles and fresh flowers, old-fashioned prints and decorative plates, and warming winter log fires (the main fireplace has a fine Stuart fireback). Dartmoor Jail Ale and a guest from Otter on handpump, 15 wines (plus champagne and sparkling rosé) by the glass and 20 malt whiskies. There's also a light and spacious dining room in the lower part of the inn and a residents' lounge. The large, pretty garden opposite has some seats, with more on the little terrace next to the pub. Beamed bedrooms are smart (with either garden or moor views) and are highly regarded by our readers, and breakfasts are excellent. You can park at the back of the building. Dogs are allowed in the conservatory area and also in some bedrooms.

Food is excellent and includes pressed ham hock with baked apple purée and beer-pickled onions, citrus-cured salmon with passion fruit, cucumber and yuzu pearls, wild garlic risotto with goats cheese and puffed wild rice, cajun chicken burger with celeriac and pineapple slaw, hake fillet with chive and butter bean cassoulet and lovage oil, honey-roasted duck breast with duck croquette, wild garlic purée and red wine jus, halibut with chive crushed potatoes, samphire, asparagus and beurre noisette, and puddings such as raspberry parfait with white chocolate, olive oil cake and raspberry gel and sticky toffee pudding with caramel sauce and clotted cream. *Benchmark main dish: braised ox cheek with honey-roasted carrots and ale jus £14.95. Two-course evening meal £22.00.*

Free house ~ Licensee Christopher Graves ~ Real ale ~ Open 11am-10.30pm (11pm Sat); 12-10.30 Sun ~ Bar food 12-2, 7-9 (8.30 Sun) ~ Restaurant ~ Children welcome away from main bar ~ Dogs allowed in bedrooms ~ Wi-fi ~ Bedrooms: £80/£110 *Recommended by Dr and Mrs F McGinn, Maggie and Matthew Lyons, Robin and Anne Triggs, James and Becky Plath*

HORNDON SX5280 Map 1

Elephants Nest £

(01822) 810273 – www.elephantsnest.co.uk

If coming from Okehampton on A386, turn left at Mary Tavy Inn, then left after about 0.5 miles; pub signposted beside Mary Tavy Inn, then Horndon signposted; on OS Sheet it's named as the New Inn; PL19 9NQ

Isolated old inn with some interesting original features, real ales and changing food; good bedrooms

The attractively furnished and deeply comfortable bedrooms in what were three miners' cottages make a fine base for exploring the area, and breakfasts are especially good. It's a friendly place and the main bar has lots of beer pump clips on the beams, high bar chairs by the bar counter, Dartmoor Jail Ale, Palmers IPA and St Austell Proper Job on handpump, a couple of farm ciders, ten wines by the glass and 15 malt whiskies. Two other rooms have an assortment of wooden dining chairs around a mix of tables, and throughout there are bare stone walls, flagstones, horsebrasses and three woodburning stoves. When the weather is warm, the spreading, pretty garden (with an area reserved only for adults) really comes into its own, with picnic-sets under parasols and views across dry-stone walls to pastures and rougher moorland above.

Well regarded food includes lunchtime baguettes and pub favourites, seared king scallops with bisque, bacon and rosemary oil, pea, asparagus and broad bean risotto with herb sauce and whipped lemon cream, spicy mustard and garlic poussin with dauphinoise potatoes and celeriac purée, goats cheese and honey filo pastry pie, smoked haddock fillet topped with welsh rarebit on creamy mash and spinach, slow-roasted duck ragoût with fried breast and pasta, greek-style lamb shank with lemon and coriander-infused potatoes, and puddings such as lemon tart with clotted cream and cardamom and orange chocolate mousse cake with coffee ice-cream. *Benchmark main dish: steak and kidney pudding £16.95. Two-course evening meal £23.00.*

Free house ~ Licensee Hugh Cook ~ Real ale ~ Open 12-3, 6.30-11 (10.30 Sun) ~ Bar food 12-2.15 (3 Sun), 6.30-9 ~ Restaurant ~ Children welcome away from bar ~ Dogs welcome ~ Wi-fi ~ Bedrooms: £100/£120 *Recommended by Alexandra and Richard Clay, Louise and Oliver Redman*

IDDESLEIGH SS5608 Map 1

Duke of York

(01837) 810253 – www.dukeofyorkdevon.co.uk

B3217 Exbourne–Dolton; EX19 8BG

15th-c thatched local with tasty food and a fair choice of drinks; bedrooms

As an unfussy and lived-in old place with simple furnishings, this may not be to everyone's taste, but many of our readers enjoy its homely atmosphere and character. The unspoilt bar has plenty of chatty locals, rocking chairs, cushioned benches built into the wall's black-painted wooden dado, stripped tables and other simple country furnishings, banknotes pinned to beams, and a large open fireplace. Bays Topsail, Otter Bitter and a guest ale tapped from the cask, several wines by the glass and three farm ciders. It can get pretty cramped at peak times. The dining room has a huge inglenook fireplace. Through a small coach arch is a little back garden with some picnic-sets. Bedrooms are clean but old-fashioned (and some may have no lock on the door); three are in the pub, with three more just a minute's walk away. Michael Morpurgo, author of *War Horse*, got the inspiration to write the novel after talking to World War I veteran Wilfred Ellis in front of the fire here almost 30 years ago.

Bar food includes sandwiches, salt and pepper squid with sweet chilli dip, chicken liver pâté with toast, vegetable chilli with rice, home-cooked ham and eggs, beer-battered cod and chips, chicken fajitas with sour cream and salsa, slow-roasted pork belly with apple and cider sauce, and rump steak with battered onion rings. *Benchmark main dish: steak and kidney pudding £12.95. Two-course evening meal £15.00.*

Free house ~ Licensee John Pittam ~ Real ale ~ Open 11-midnight; 11-11 Sun ~ Bar food 12-9 ~ Restaurant ~ Children welcome ~ Dogs allowed in bar and bedrooms ~ Wi-fi ~ Bedrooms: £60/£80 *Recommended by Lindy Andrews, Frank and Marcia Pelling, Peter Pilbeam, Len and Lilly Dowson*

KINGSBRIDGE SX7344 Map 1

Dodbrooke Inn £

(01548) 852068

Church Street, Dodbrooke (parking some way off); TQ7 1DB

Bustling local with friendly licensees, chatty locals and well regarded food and drink

Whether you're a local or a visitor, the long-serving and friendly licensees (who've now been here for 28 years) will ensure you get a genuine welcome in this small terraced pub in a quiet residential area. The traditional bar has built-in cushioned stall seats and plush cushioned stools around pubby tables, some horse harness, local photographs and china jugs, a log fire and an easy-going atmosphere. Bass, Sharps Doom Bar, Youngs Bitter and a guest ale on handpump, local cider and eight wines by the glass. You can sit in the covered courtyard, which might be candlelit in warm weather.

Fair value food includes sandwiches, deep-fried whitebait with tartare sauce, scallops with crispy bacon, ham and egg, beef stroganoff, sausage in a basket, minted lamb shank, popular steaks and puddings. *Benchmark main dish: beer-battered fish and chips £9.75. Two-course evening meal £16.00.*

Free house ~ Licensees Michael and Jill Dyson ~ Real ale ~ Open 12-2, 5-11; 12-2.30, 7-10.30 Sun; closed Mon-Weds lunchtimes ~ Bar food 12-1.30, 5.30-8.30 ~ Children welcome if over 5 ~ Wi-fi *Recommended by Peter Brix, Edward May, Alf and Sally Garner, Charlie Stevens*

POSTBRIDGE SX6780 Map 1

Warren House

(01822) 880208 – www.warrenhouseinn.co.uk

B3212 0.75 miles NE of Postbridge; PL20 6TA

Isolated 18th-c pub, relaxing for a drink or meal after a Dartmoor ramble

An invaluable refuge for walkers and at the heart of Darmoor, this is a pub with local character that once served the tin mining community. The cosy bar is straightforward, with simple furnishings such as easy chairs and settles beneath the beamed ochre ceiling, old pictures of the inn on partly panelled stone walls and dim lighting (powered by the pub's own generator); one of the open fires is said to have been kept alight since 1845. There's also a family room. There's Otter Ale plus guests such as Black Tor Pride of Dartmoor and Summerskills Start Point on handpump, local farm cider and malt whiskies. The picnic-sets on both sides of the road have moorland views.

Bar food includes lunchtime ploughman's and baked potatoes, pasties, breaded king prawns with garlic dip, steak in ale pie, ricotta and spinach cannelloni, ham and chips, spanish-style lamb in sherry, cajun chicken with a dip and fries, smoked haddock and spring onion fishcakes, steaks with trimmings, and puddings. *Benchmark main dish: rabbit pie £13.50. Two-course evening meal £22.00.*

Free house ~ Licensee Peter Parsons ~ Real ale ~ Open 11-10; 12-10 Sun; 11-3 Mon, Tues in winter ~ Bar food 12-9; 12-8.30 Sun; 12-2.30 Mon, Tues in winter ~ Restaurant ~ Children in family room only ~ Dogs allowed in bar *Recommended by Robert Watt, Scott and Charlotte Havers, Peter and Alison Steadman, Edward May, Anne Taylor, Colin and Daniel Gibbs*

RATTERY SX7461 Map 1

Church House

(01364) 642220 – www.thechurchhouseinn.co.uk

Village signposted from A385 W of Totnes, and A38 S of Buckfastleigh; TQ10 9LD

Ancient place with friendly licensees, a good range of drinks, popular bar food and seats in the garden

Parts of the original building here, dating from around 1030, still survive – look out for the spiral stone steps behind a little stone doorway on the left. The rooms have a lot of character: massive oak beams and standing timbers in the open-plan bar, large fireplaces (one with a cosy nook partitioned around it), traditional pubby chairs and tables, some window seats, and prints and horsebrasses on plain white walls. There's also a dining room, a lounge and a separate restaurant with a courtyard garden that's equipped with smart seats and tables under big parasols. Dartmoor Jail Ale, Exeter Avocet and Otter Bitter on handpump, 19 malt whiskies and a dozen wines by the glass. There are picnic-sets at the front of the building with more on a large hedged-in lawn; the summer hanging baskets are pretty.

Seasonal menus and local produce are at the heart of the well liked food: lunchtime sandwiches, sharing boards, potted rabbit with curried carrot and apple relish, smoked haddock, leek and crème fraîche tart, spinach and ricotta ravioli with pesto and parmesan, free-range chicken and wild mushroom pie with red wine jus, salmon fillet with fondant potatoes, olive and peppers and sauce vierge, beer-battered fish of the day with chips, duck breast with lentils, pancetta, baby corn and jus, 28-day-aged rare-breed steaks with peppercorn sauce, and puddings. *Benchmark main dish: slow-roasted free-range pork belly with Devon cider cream sauce and mustard mash £13.50. Two-course evening meal £20.00.*

Free house ~ Licensees John and William Edwards ~ Real ale ~ Open 11.45-11; closed Mon Oct-Apr ~ Bar food 12-2.30, 6-9 ~ Restaurant ~ Children welcome ~ Dogs allowed in bar ~ Wi-fi *Recommended by M J Daly, Charles and Maddie Bishop, Matt and Hayley Jacob, John Evans, Andrew Low, Stuart and Natalie Granville, George and Alison Bishop*

SANDFORD SS8202 Map 1

Lamb

(01363) 773676 – www.lambinnsandford.co.uk

The Square; EX17 4LW

16th-c inn with several real ales and decent wines by the glass, very good food and seats in garden; well equipped bedrooms

We get many enthusiastic reports from our readers on this well run and charming little pub in the village centre. A good mix of locals and visitors gather in the linked, beamed bar and dining areas and the atmosphere is chatty and friendly. The bar has red leather sofas beside a log fire, cushioned window seats, a settle and various dining chairs round a few tables on patterned carpet. Dartmoor Jail Ale, Otter Bitter, St Austell Proper Job and South Hams Eddystone on handpump, ten wines by the glass, four farm ciders, ten gins (some are local) and 20 malt whiskies. The dining area has a woodburning stove, a cushioned wall pew, all manner of nice old wooden dining chairs and tables and quite a few mirrors. There's also a simpler public bar with board games and a skittle alley. The cobbled, three-level garden has fairy lights and rustic seats and tables, and beyond the hedge are some picnic-sets on grass. Bedrooms are comfortable, modern and well equipped. Nearby parking is at a premium, but the village car park is just a few minutes' walk up the small lane to the right.

A sensibly short choice of imaginative food includes lunchtime ciabattas and pub classics, scallops with chorizo, breaded goats cheese mousse with apple purée and spiced beetroot purée, herbed gnocchi with chestnut mushrooms, romanesco, mushrooms, pesto and spinach, chicken breast with dauphinoise potatoes, mushroom sauce, roasted leeks and cavolo nero, lemon sole with caper and herb hollandaise, fondant potatoes and pickles, pork belly and crackling with a pork fritter, kale and cider jus, and puddings. *Benchmark main dish: rack of lamb with pressed shoulder, fondant potatoes, kale and jus £16.95. Two-course evening meal £24.00.*

Free house ~ Licensee Nick Silk ~ Real ale ~ Open 9am-11pm (midnight Sat); 9am-10.30pm Sun ~ Bar food 12-2.15, 6.30 (6 Fri, Sat)-9; 12-3, 6-8.30 Sun ~ Restaurant ~ Children welcome ~ Dogs welcome ~ Wi-fi ~ Open mike Fri evening; live bands last Fri of month ~ Bedrooms: £69/£95 *Recommended by Dr A McCormick, Douglas Power, Richard and Penny Gibbs, Belinda Stamp, Edward May, Abigail Slater*

SIDBURY SY1496 Map 1

Hare & Hounds

(01404) 41760 – www.hareandhounds-devon.co.uk

3 miles N of Sidbury, at Putts Corner; A375 towards Honiton, crossroads with B3174; EX10 0QQ

Large, roadside pub with log fires, beams and attractive layout, popular daily carvery and a big garden

Although plenty of customers do drop in for a pint and a chat, most are here to enjoy the exceptionally highly thought-of carvery; you'll need to book a table in advance at lunchtime. The spreading rooms have two log fires (and rather unusual wood-framed leather sofas complete with pouffes), heavy beams, fresh flowers and red plush cushioned dining chairs, window seats and leather sofas around plenty of tables on carpeting or bare boards. Otter Ale and Bitter and St Austell Tribute tapped from the cask and eight wines by the glass. The newer dining extension, with its central open fire, leads out to a decked area; the seats here, and the picnic-sets in the big garden, have marvellous views down the Sid Valley to the sea at Sidmouth.

As well as the highly regarded carvery using the best local meat, they also offer a wide choice of dishes such as sandwiches and paninis, prawn and crayfish cocktail, mushrooms in cream, garlic and sherry, roasted vegetable tart with sweet potato fries, sweet and sour pork, chilli con carne, steak and kidney pudding, a fish dish of the day, mexican chicken burrito, sirloin steak with trimmings and a choice of sauce and puddings. *Benchmark main dish: daily carvery £11.25. Two-course evening meal £19.00.*

Heartstone Inns ~ Managers Graham Cole and Lindsey Chun ~ Real ale ~ Open 10am-11pm ~ Bar food 12-9 ~ Children welcome but no under-12s in bar ~ Dogs allowed in bar ~ Wi-fi *Recommended by Dylan, Jill and Dick Archer, Martine and Fabio Lockley, Joe and Belinda Smart, Ivy and George Goodwill*

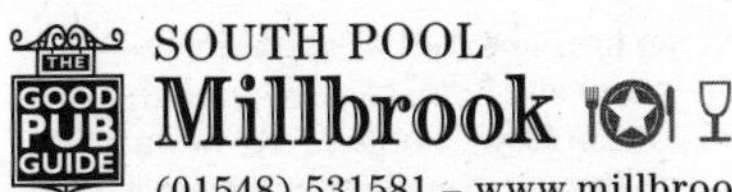

SOUTH POOL SX7740 Map 1

Millbrook

(01548) 531581 – www.millbrookinnsouthpool.co.uk

Off A379 E of Kingsbridge; TQ7 2RW

Devon Dining Pub of the Year

Delightful village local by the Salcombe estuary with local ales, very good food and a warm welcome for all

There's always a cheerful crowd of both locals and visitors in this charming, tiny pub, particularly at weekends. Among the little beamed bars, the main one has a log fire in an inglenook fireplace, a couple of settles and a blanket box on turkey rugs, and stools against the counter where they keep St Austell Trelawny, Salcombe Devon Amber, South Hams Wild Blonde and a seasonal guest from Otter on handpump, 21 wines by the glass, ten malt whiskies and a couple of local farm ciders; daily papers, darts and board games. The dining area to the right has a woodburning stove, settles and wheelback chairs around scrubbed wooden tables, and stone and cream walls decorated with maps. This leads to another small dining area and there's also a simply furnished Top Bar. Seats on the outside terrace overlook the water. They also offer an apartment (which can be on a self-catering basis). A Land Rover Defender can pick up customers from the nearby ferry and you can moor your boat on the village pontoon.

Imaginative food includes sandwiches, duck liver parfait with plum and red onion chutney, snails and wild mushrooms flambéed in cognac with a garlic butter sauce, beetroot and kale pearl barley risotto with parmesan, guinea fowl and smoked sausage on a traditional french vegetable stew, roasted loin and pulled pork with cauliflower mash, braised red cabbage and tarragon jus, gilt-head bream fillet with mussels and paella rice, shellfish sauce and chorizo, and puddings of the day. *Benchmark main dish: bouillabaisse with rouille, gruyère and croutons £20.00. Two-course evening meal £23.00.*

Free house ~ Licensees Charlie and Tess Baker ~ Real ale ~ Open 12-11; 12-9 Sun ~ Bar food 12-2, 7 (5 in summer)-9; 12-5, 7-9 Sun; not Sun evening in winter ~ Restaurant ~ Children welcome ~ Dogs allowed in bar ~ Wi-fi ~ Bedrooms: £135/£150 *Recommended by R L Borthwick, Megan and William Stapley, Sophie and James Collier, Barry and Daphne Gregson*

THE GOOD PUB GUIDE

SOUTH ZEAL SX6593 Map 1

Oxenham Arms

(01837) 840244 – www.theoxenhamarms.com

Off A30/A382; EX20 2JT

Wonderful 15th-c inn with lots of history, character bars, real ales, enjoyable food and big garden; bedrooms

They've been offering refreshment to customers here since 1477, though the building was constructed to combat the pagan power of the Neolithic standing stone that still forms part of the wall in the room behind the bar (there's actually 20 feet of stone below the floor). The heavily beamed and partly panelled front bar has elegant mullioned windows and Stuart fireplaces, all sorts of chairs and built-in wall seats with scatter cushions around low oak tables on bare floorboards, and bar stools against the counter where friendly staff serve Dartmoor Jail Ale and Merry Monk, a Red Rock beer named for the pub and Teignworthy Gun Dog on handpump; also, seven wines by the glass, 70 malt whiskies, 25 ports, local mead and three farm ciders. A small room has beams, wheelback chairs around polished tables, decorative plates and another open fire. The four-acre garden is reached up imposing curved stone steps and has plenty of seats and fine views – plus more tables under parasols out in front. Some of the bedrooms have four-poster beds; Charles Dickens, snowed up one winter, wrote a lot of *The Pickwick Papers* here. You can walk straight from the door on to the moor and they provide details of walking tours.

Good food includes sharing boards, chicken caesar salad, mussels with potato gnocchi, samphire and lemon butter sauce, nduja scotch egg with apple chutney, sweet and sour lamb curry, beer-battered fresh fish and chips, stilton, walnut and leek pie, venison with butternut squash and dauphinoise potatoes and juniper jus, duck breast with chicory, celeriac, toasted hazelnuts and pear, rib-eye steak with triple-cooked chips and blue cheese or peppercorn sauce, and puddings such as vanilla crème brûlée and an assiette of dark chocolate with salted almond caramel. *Benchmark main dish: pie of the day £11.95. Two-course evening meal £19.00.*

Free house ~ Licensees Simon and Lyn Powell ~ Real ale ~ Open 11-11 ~ Bar food 12-3, 6-9; cream teas in afternoon ~ Restaurant ~ Children welcome ~ Dogs allowed in bar ~ Wi-fi ~ Bedrooms: /£125 *Recommended by M J Daly, Serena and Adam Furber, Lenny and Ruth Walters, Gerry and Pam Pollard, Liz and Mike Newton*

SPREYTON SX6996 Map 1

Tom Cobley

(01647) 231314 – www.tomcobleytavern.co.uk

Dragdown Hill; W out of village; EX17 5AL

Huge range of quickly changing real ales and ciders, and wide choice of food in friendly, busy village pub

While the fantastic range of ales is a huge draw, our readers also heap warm praise on the food here. The comfortable bar has traditional furnishings, an open fire and local photographs and country scenes on the walls, and you can be sure of a genuine welcome from the hospitable landlord and his cheerful staff. Up to 14 real ales – well kept on handpump or tapped from the cask – change quickly and include Dartmoor IPA and Jail Ale, Holsworthy Tamar Black, Otter Ale, St Austell Tribute and Teignworthy Gun Dog; also, up to 14 farm ciders and perries. A large back dining room has beams and similar décor. There are picnic-sets in the garden and more out in front by the quiet street. Several of the comfortable bedrooms have views of Dartmoor.

Popular and of good quality, the traditional food includes lunchtime sandwiches and ciabattas, pasties, ploughman's and omelettes; evening choices might be prawn cocktail, breaded mushrooms with garlic mayonnaise, burgers with toppings, coleslaw and chips, vegetable chilli, thai cod and prawn fishcakes, a full rack of barbecue ribs, lambs liver in onion gravy with bacon, duck and cherry pie, mixed grill, steaks with trimmings and a choice of sauce, and puddings. *Benchmark main dish: steak and kidney pie £9.95. Two-course evening meal £18.00.*

Free house ~ Licensees Roger and Carol Cudlip ~ Real ale ~ Open 12-3, 6-11 (midnight Fri, Sat); 12-4, 7-11 Sun; closed Mon lunchtime ~ Bar food 12-2, 7-9; set Sunday roast 1pm, 7-9pm ~ Restaurant ~ Children welcome ~ Dogs allowed in bar ~ Bedrooms: £50/£100 *Recommended by Ian Herdman, David and Leone Lawson, Colin and Daniel Gibbs, Steve Watson, Selwyn Jones, Audrey and Andrew Nichols*

The symbol shows pubs that keep their beer unusually well, have a particularly good range or brew their own.

STAVERTON SX7964 Map 1

Sea Trout

(01803) 762274 – www.theseatroutinn.co.uk

Village signposted from A384 NW of Totnes; TQ9 6PA

Bustling old inn not far from the river with real ales, tasty food, helpful staff and back garden; bedrooms

This was known as the Church House for several hundred years until a previous landlord caught a sea trout in the River Dart and renamed it; you can still get daily fishing permits. The neatly kept beamed lounge has fishing flies and stuffed fish on the walls, and traditional tables and chairs on the part-carpeted and part-wood floor. The simpler locals' bar has wooden wall and other seats, a stag's head, guns and horsebrasses, a huge stuffed pike, a woodburning stove and a cheerful mix of regulars and visitors. Palmers Copper, Dorset Gold and 200 on handpump, 11 wines by the glass and several malt whiskies; background music and board games. There's also a smart, panelled restaurant and a conservatory. The attractive back garden has seats and tables, which some of the comfortable bedrooms look over; the breakfasts are good.

Pleasing food includes bar snacks, lunchtime sandwiches, salmon and spring onion fishcake with chilli jam, spicy biltong pâté with melba toast, chicken caesar salad, vegetarian moussaka, lamb and mint burger with toppings and fries, hake loin on crushed new potatoes with a cream, white wine and prawn sauce, lambs liver and bacon with red onion gravy, slow-braised beef and thyme casserole with a rosemary cobbler, and puddings such as chocolate brownie with chocolate sauce and malva pudding (a south african dessert similar to sticky toffee pudding) with butterscotch sauce and stem ginger ice-cream. *Benchmark main dish: beer-battered fish and chips £13.00. Two-course evening meal £20.00.*

Palmers ~ Tenants Nigel and Simon Newhouse ~ Real ale ~ Open 11-10.30 (11 Sat) ~ Bar food 12-2, 6-9; 12-2, 6-9.30 Fri; 12-2.30, 6-9.30 Sat; 12-3, 6.30-9 Sun ~ Restaurant ~ Children welcome ~ Dogs allowed in bar and bedrooms ~ Wi-fi ~ Bedrooms: £90/£110

Recommended by Dr A McCormick, Sara Fulton, Roger Baker, Gordon and Patricia Gorringe, Abigail Slater, Mike and Mary Carter

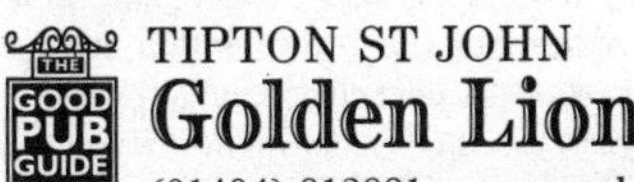

TIPTON ST JOHN SY0991 Map 1

Golden Lion

(01404) 812881 – www.goldenliontipton.co.uk

Pub signed off B3176 Sidmouth–Ottery St Mary; EX10 0AA

Busy village pub with three real ales, well liked food and plenty of seats in the attractive garden

With good food cooked by Mr Teissier, this bustling, neat pub attracts a good mix of villagers as well as diners from further afield. The main bar, split into two, has a comfortable, relaxed atmosphere, as does the back snug. Throughout are paintings by west country artists, art deco prints, Tiffany lamps and copper pots and kettles. A few tables are kept for those just wanting a pint and a chat. Otter Ale and Bitter and Sharps Doom Bar on handpump, 12 wines by the glass and several gins; background music. There are seats on the terracotta-walled terrace with outside heaters and grapevines and more seats on the grass edged by pretty flowering borders. Dog walkers may use a verandah.

The chef-landlord cooks the reliably enjoyable food which includes lunchtime sandwiches, prawns in filo with chilli jam, breaded whitebait, home-cooked ham and egg, vegetable lasagne, beer-battered cod and chips, moules frites, steak and kidney pudding, duck breast with oriental sauce, slow-cooked lamb shank, plaice in garlic butter, chargrilled steak with a choice of three sauces, and puddings such as crème brûlée and boozy chocolate pot. *Benchmark main dish: fish and shellfish soup £13.00. Two-course evening meal £25.00.*

Heavitree ~ Tenants François and Michelle Teissier ~ Real ale ~ Open 12-2.30, 6-10; 12-2.30 Sun ~ Bar food 12-2, 6-8; not Sun evening ~ Children welcome *Recommended by Revd Michael Vockins, Susan and Callum Slade, Mark Hamill, Claire Adams, Rosie and John Moore*

TOTNES SX8060 Map 1

Royal Seven Stars

(01803) 862125 – www.royalsevenstars.co.uk

Fore Street, The Plains; TQ9 5DD

Handsome hotel just across the road from the river with an easy-going bar, several dining rooms and seats outside; bedrooms

The lovely bedrooms in this civilised and well run hotel are individually styled and well equipped and breakfasts are very good. The companionable bar is to the left of the interesting entrance hall (which has an imposing staircase, antlers and stags' heads and big flagstones lined with leafy plant pots). The bar is friendly and easy-going with an open fire, button-back banquettes and cushioned wooden chairs around circular tables, and stools against the bar where they keep New Lion Pandit IPA (the brewery is in the town), Dartmoor Jail Ale, Sharps Doom Bar and a guest ale on handpump, carefully chosen wines, interesting gins and farm cider. The dining rooms have both antique and modern high-backed chairs, sofas, more banquettes, big gilt-edged mirrors, books on shelves, copper kettles, measuring jugs and warming pans, large paintings and stone jars; background music and TV. There are covered and heated seats and tables among box-planted troughs at the front of the building and the River Dart is just across the main road.

Accomplished cooking includes lunchtime sandwiches, local moules marinière, home-made ox faggot with roasted celeriac mash and shallot jus, goats cheese salad with roasted beetroot and mustard and herb dressing, slow-cooked pork belly with roasted root vegetables and rich gravy, a fish pie of the day, bavette steak with triple-cooked chips, daily specials, and puddings such as steamed stem ginger pudding with butterscotch sauce and rhubarb syllabub. *Benchmark main dish: beer-battered fish and chips £14.50. Two-course evening meal £20.00.*

Free house ~ Licensees Anne and Nigel Way ~ Real ale ~ Open 8am-11pm (11.30pm Sat) ~ Bar food 8am-9.30pm ~ Children welcome ~ Dogs allowed in bar and bedrooms ~ Wi-fi ~ Live music Fri evening ~ Bedrooms: £95/£130 *Recommended by Alan and Linda Blackmore, Maria and Henry Lazenby, George Sanderson, Sophie and James Collier*

TOTNES SX8059 Map 1

Steam Packet

(01803) 863880 – www.steampacketinn.co.uk

St Peters Quay, on W bank (ie not on Steam Packet Quay); TQ9 5EW

Quayside pub with an attractive layout, plenty of room for dining and drinking, friendly staff, good food and seats overlooking the water

Seats under big parasols on the terrace in front of this popular pub overlook the River Dart and get quickly snapped up in warm weather – when it's best to arrive early. Inside, there are three distinct bar areas with polished floorboards, bare stone and brick walls, half-panelling and delft shelving and open fires. There are built-in wall seats, dark wooden chairs and leather-topped stools around traditional tables and a comfortable sofa with scatter cushions beside shelves of books. The friendly, efficient staff, who cope well at peak times, serve Hunters Denbury Dreamer and Sharps Doom Bar on handpump, several wines by the glass and farm cider; background music and TV. There's also a conservatory restaurant. The four bedrooms are light, airy and comfortable with spotless, up-to-date bathrooms.

As well as breakfast (8-10.30am weekdays; 8.30-10.30am weekends), the popular food includes sandwiches (until 6pm), salt and pepper crispy squid with coriander and lime mayonnaise, wild mushrooms in brandy and cream on toasted ciabatta, sausages with bubble and squeak and onion gravy, chimichurri chicken breast burger with fries and mayonnaise, macaroni cheese with spinach and mushrooms, slow-roasted pork belly with black pudding mash and cider gravy, beef bourguignon, 28-day-aged steaks with trimmings and puddings. *Benchmark main dish: steak burger with toppings and fries £13.00. Two-course evening meal £22.00.*

Buccaneer Holdings ~ Manager Ian Durrant ~ Real ale ~ Open 8am-11pm ~ Bar food 12-9 (8 Sun) ~ Restaurant ~ Children welcome ~ Dogs allowed in bar ~ Wi-fi ~ Bedrooms: £120/£175 *Recommended by Peter and Alison Steadman, Max and Steph Warren, Mike Swan*

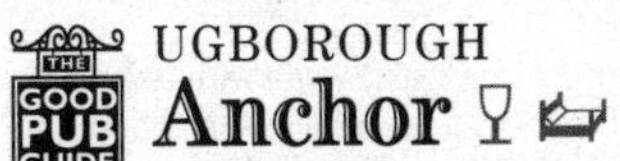

UGBOROUGH SX6755 Map 1

Anchor

(01752) 690388 – www.anchorinnugborough.co.uk

Off A3121; PL21 0NG

A wide mix of customers for 17th-c inn with beamed rooms, good food and drink and seats outside; bedrooms

The décor here is pleasing and contemporary and the atmosphere gently civilised and friendly. The beamed bar has an open fire, comfortable armchairs and dining chairs around a mix of tables on wooden flooring, and stools against the planked bar counter where they keep Sharps Doom Bar and a guest such as Salcombe Seahorse on handpump, eight wines by the glass and summer cider; background music, TV and board games. The two-level beamed restaurant has elegant rattan dining chairs and wooden tables on flagstones in one part and more traditional dark wooden furniture in the lower area; there's a woodburning stove in a big fireplace and modern art on pale-painted walls. If you want to explore nearby Dartmoor National Park, you can stay in the comfortable, attractive and individually furnished bedrooms – six are in the main inn and four in courtyard cabins.

As well as breakfast (8-10am), the rewarding food includes sandwiches, local mussels in cider, bacon, leeks and cream, confit duck leg and foie gras terrine with red onion jam, pumpkin and sage ravioli with pumpkin purée, blue cheese and truffle honey, steak in ale pie, herb-crusted cod with chorizo, red pepper and basil ragoût, roast rump of lamb with goats cheese gratin, aubergine caviar, olives and tomatoes with red wine sauce and pesto, and puddings such as profiteroles filled with honey cream with a dark and white chocolate sauce and lemon cheesecake with raspberry sorbet. *Benchmark main dish: cider-braised pork belly with a barbecue-pulled fritter, sausage and both apple and red wine sauces £14.00. Two-course evening meal £20.00.*

Free house ~ Licensee Sarah Cuming ~ Real ale ~ Open 11-11 ~ Bar food 12-2.30, 6.30-9; 12-2.30, 6-9 Fri, Sat; 12-3, 6-8 Sun ~ Restaurant ~ Children welcome ~ Dogs allowed in bar and bedrooms ~ Wi-fi ~ Live music second Sat evening of month ~ Bedrooms: £90/£99 *Recommended by Rosie and Marcus Heatherley, Jeff Davies, M J Winterton, Julie and Andrew Blanchett, Charles Todd*

WIDECOMBE SX7276 Map 1

Rugglestone

(01364) 621327 – www.rugglestoneinn.co.uk

Village at end of B3387; pub just S – turn left at church and NT church house, OS Sheet 191 map reference 720765; TQ13 7TF

Charming local with a couple of bars, cheerful customers, friendly staff, four real ales and traditional pub food

A world away from the busy tourist village just down the road, this remains a tucked-away gem. The unspoilt bar has just four tables, a few window and wall seats, a one-person pew built into the corner beside a nice old stone fireplace (with a woodburner) and a good mix of customers. The rudimentary bar counter dispenses Bays Gold, Dartmoor Legend, a beer named for the pub (from Teignworthy) and a changing guest tapped from the cask; local farm cider and a decent small wine list. The room on the right is slightly bigger and lighter in feel, with beams, another stone fireplace, stripped-pine tables and a built-in wall bench; there's also a small dining room. To reach the picnic-sets in the garden you have to cross a bridge over a little moorland stream. They have a holiday cottage to rent. There are good Dartmoor walks all around.

Honest food includes baguettes, chicken liver pâté, deep-fried brie with redcurrant jelly, home-cooked ham and eggs, spicy meatballs in tomato sauce with potato wedges, stilton and mushroom quiche with coleslaw, fish or chicken pies, lasagne, and puddings. *Benchmark main dish: steak and stilton pie £11.00. Two-course evening meal £16.00.*

Free house ~ Licensees Richard and Vicki Palmer ~ Real ale ~ Open 11.30-3, 6-11; 11.30-3, 5-11.30 Fri; 11.30am-midnight Sat; 12-11 Sun ~ Bar food 12-2, 6.30-9 ~ Restaurant ~ Children allowed away from bar area ~ Dogs welcome *Recommended by Anne and Ben Smith, Joe and Belinda Smart, Roger and Donna Huggins, Melanie and David Lawson, Moira and Jon Weller*

Also Worth a Visit in Devon

Besides the fully inspected pubs, you might like to try these pubs that have been recommended to us and described by readers. Do tell us what you think of them: feedback@goodguides.com

ABBOTSKERSWELL SX8568

Court Farm (01626) 361866

Wilton Way; look for the church tower; TQ12 5NY Attractive neatly extended 17th-c longhouse tucked away in picturesque hamlet; various rooms off long beamed and paved main bar, good mix of furnishings, woodburners, well priced popular food (worth booking) including weekday lunchtime bargains, friendly helpful service, Bass, Otter and other beers, farm cider and decent wines; background music, pool and darts; children welcome, picnic-sets in pretty lawned garden, open all day, food all day Thurs-Sun. *(Abigail Slater)*

APPLEDORE SS4630

Beaver (01237) 474822

Irsha Street; EX39 1RY Relaxed, well run harbourside pub with lovely estuary view from popular raised dining area; enjoyable reasonably priced food especially fresh local fish, prompt friendly service, good choice of west country ales, farm cider, decent house wines and great range of whiskies; background and some live music, quiz Weds, pool in smaller games room, TV; children and dogs (in bar) welcome, disabled access (but no nearby parking), tables on small sheltered water-view terrace. *(Liz and Mike Newton)*

APPLEDORE SS4630

Seagate (01237) 472589

The Quay; EX39 1QS Well run 17th-c quayside inn with four real ales, a couple of ciders and ten wines by the glass, good food from lunchtime sandwiches to fresh fish specials, smaller appetites catered for, friendly helpful service; children and dogs welcome, terrace seating front and back, ten bedrooms (some with estuary view), seven more in nearby sail loft, open all day from 8am. *(Glen and Patricia Fuller)*

ASHILL ST0811

Ashill Inn (01884) 840506

M5 junction 27, follow signs to Willand, then left to Uffculme and Craddock on B3440; Ashill signed to left; pub in centre of village; EX15 3NL Popular 19th-c village pub, cosy and friendly, with well kept local ales and highly rated home-cooked food including daily specials (booking advised), reasonable prices, black beams, woodburner in stone fireplace, modern dining extension overlooking small garden; some live music, darts and skittles, TV; children welcome, closed Mon lunchtime, no food Sun evening. *(Timothy)*

ASHPRINGTON SX8157

Durant Arms (01803) 732240

Off A381 S of Totnes; TQ9 7UP Traditional 18th-c village inn with enjoyable home-cooked food and three well kept ales including Noss Beer Works, good friendly service, slate-floored bar with stag's head above woodburner, china on delft shelf, other connecting rooms; children, walkers and dogs welcome, three bedrooms, open all day weekends, may close Mon in winter. *(Ian Gilpin)*

ASHPRINGTON SX8056

Watermans Arms (01803) 732214

Bow Bridge, on Tuckenhay Road; TQ9 7EG Whitewashed 17th-c creekside inn; beamed and quarry-tiled main bar area, built-in cushioned wall seats and wheelbacks around stripped tables, log fire, dining room with fishing-related décor, comfortable lounge area down steps, four Palmers ales and several wines by the glass, good traditional food from lunchtime baguettes up, friendly helpful service; background music; children and dogs (in bar) welcome, seats out by the water (maybe kingfishers) and in garden, 15 bedrooms (some in purpose-built annexe), car park across road, open all day. *(I D Barnett)*

AVONWICK SX6958

★Turtley Corn Mill (01364) 646100

0.5 miles off A38 roundabout at SW end of South Brent bypass; TQ10 9ES Converted watermill with series of linked areas; mix of wooden dining chairs and chunky tables on oriental rugs or dark flagstones, fat church candles, various prints and some framed 78rpm discs, woodburners, big windows looking out over grounds, Hanlons, Otter, St Austell and Summerskills, nine wines by the glass and 30 malt whiskies, wide choice of brasserie-style food, friendly service; free wi-fi; children and dogs (in bar) welcome, extensive garden with well spaced picnic-sets, giant chess set and small lake, six bedrooms, open (and food) all day from 9am for breakfast. *(Camille and Jose Ferrera)*

AXMOUTH SY2591

Harbour Inn (01297) 20371

B3172 Seaton–Axminster; EX12 4AF Ancient thatched pub by estuary; updated heavily beamed bar rooms with bare boards, flagstones and some stripped-stone walls, huge inglenook, lots of model boats, old pictures, photographs and accounts of shipwrecks, other partitioned dining/seating areas including carpeted part with armchairs by woodburner, Badger ales and several wines by the glass, enjoyable food from sharing boards up, steak night Fri; background music, Weds quiz; children and dogs (in bar) welcome, modern furniture on terrace, picnic-sets on grass, open (and food) all day from 9am. *(Colin and Daniel Gibbs)*

AYLESBEARE SY0490

Halfway (01395) 232273

A3052 Exeter–Sidmouth, junction with B3180; EX5 2JP Modernised roadside dining pub (same owners as the Bowd in Sidmouth), well cooked food from fairly priced pub favourites up including home-made american-style burgers, good fresh fish/seafood and Sun carvery, well kept Otter Bitter and Greene King Abbot, efficient friendly service, Dartmoor views from restaurant and raised outside seating area; children and dogs (in bar) welcome, open (and food) all day Sun. *(Joy Griffiths)*

BAMPTON SS9522

★Swan (01398) 332248

Station Road; EX16 9NG Popular, well run beamed village inn with spacious bare-boards bar, woodburners in two inglenooks, three changing west country beers, nice wines and fine choice of gins, very good food from interesting varied menu (both licensees are chefs), efficient friendly service; children and dogs welcome, well appointed bedrooms, big breakfast, closed Mon lunchtime otherwise open all day, no food Mon or third Sun evening of month. *(Jerry Russell)*

BANTHAM SX6643

★Sloop (01548) 560489

Off A379/B3197 NW of Kingsbridge; TQ7 3AJ Welcoming 14th-c split-level pub close to fine beach and walks, popular and relaxed, with good mix of customers in black-beamed stripped-stone bar, country tables and chairs on flagstones, blazing woodburner, well kept St Austell Tribute, Proper Job and a guest, several wines by the glass and very nice food from sandwiches to good fresh fish, courteous helpful service, restaurant; background music; children and dogs (in bar) welcome, seats out at back, five bedrooms (a couple with sea views), open all day in summer. *(Jane Durrant)*

BEER ST2289

Anchor (01297) 20386

Fore Street; EX12 3ET Sea-view inn with good choice of enjoyable food including local fish, Greene King, Otter and good value wines, open-plan interior with large eating area, friendly staff; background music, sports TV, fruit machine, free wi-fi; children well looked after, lots of tables in clifftop garden over road, six reasonably priced bedrooms, open (and food) all day. *(George and Alison Bishop)*

BEESANDS SX8140

★Cricket (01548) 580215

About 3 miles S of A379, from Chillington; in village turn right along foreshore road; TQ7 2EN Popular pub-restaurant with pebbly Start Bay beach just over the sea wall; light airy new england-style décor with dark wood or leather chairs around chunky tables, stripped-wood flooring by the bar, carpet in the restaurant, some nautical bits and pieces including model boats, relaxed chatty atmosphere with a few tables kept for drinkers, Otter and St Austell ales, local cider and 14 wines by the glass, very good food with emphasis on fish/seafood; background music, TVs, free wi-fi; children and dogs (in bar) welcome, wheelchair access/loo, picnic-sets by sea wall, seven attractive bedrooms (some overlooking the sea), South West Coast Path runs through the village, open all day, food all day in high summer. *(Simon King, R L Borthwick)*

BELSTONE SX61293

Tors (01837) 840689

A mile off A30; EX20 1QZ Popular small Victorian granite pub-hotel in peaceful Dartmoor-edge village, family-run and welcoming, with long carpeted bar divided by settles, well kept ales such as Dartmoor and Sharps, over 60 malt whiskies and good choice of wines, enjoyable food from baguettes to specials, cheerful prompt service, restaurant; children welcome and dogs (they have their own), disabled access, seats out on nearby grassy area overlooking valley, good walks, bedrooms, open all day weekends. *(Rosie and John Moore)*

BISHOP'S TAWTON SS5629

★Chichester Arms (01271) 343945

Signed off A377 outside Barnstaple; East Street; EX32 0DQ Friendly 15th-c cob and thatch pub serving generous helpings of good well priced food from sandwiches/baguettes to fresh local fish, quick obliging service even when crowded, St Austell Tribute, Charles Wells Bombardier and a guest, decent wines, heavy low beams, large stone fireplace, restaurant; free wi-fi; children and dogs welcome, awkward disabled access but staff very helpful, picnic-sets on front terrace and in back garden, open all day. *(Liz and Mike Newton)*

BOVEY TRACEY SX8178

Cromwell Arms (01626) 833473

Fore Street; TQ13 9AE Welcoming 17th-c beamed inn with several areas including separate restaurant, popular good value food and up to five St Austell ales; quiz Tues and Sun evenings, games machines, free wi-fi; children and dogs (in bar) welcome, disabled access/facilities, small garden with decking and pergola, 14 bedrooms, open all day. *(Melanie and David Lawson)*

BRANSCOMBE SY2088

★Masons Arms (01297) 680300

Main Street; signed off A3052 Sidmouth–Seaton, then bear left into village; EX12 3DJ Popular old pub near the sea in pretty village; rambling bar with ancient ships' beams, comfortable seats on slate floors and log fire in massive hearth, St Austell Proper Job, Tribute and guests, ten wines by the glass, enjoyable fairly traditional food including some vegetarian options and daily specials, afternoon cream teas, second bar with two-way woodburner and stripped pine, two smartly furnished dining rooms; free wi-fi; children and dogs (in bars) welcome, quiet flower-filled front terrace with thatched-roof tables, side garden, neat comfortable bedrooms (some in converted cottages), open all day and can get very busy at peak times. *(Ewan and Sue Hewitt, James and Sylvia Hewitt, John and Claire Masters, Joy Griffiths, Dr A J and Mrs B A Tompsett)*

BRATTON CLOVELLY SX4691

Clovelly (01837) 871447

From S (A30), turn left at church, pub is on the right; EX20 4JZ Friendly 18th-c village pub with cosy bar and two dining rooms, generous helpings of popular reasonably priced traditional food including specials, well kept Dartmoor, St Austell and a guest, cheerful staff, games room; may be live jazz second Mon of month; children and dogs welcome, 17th-c wall paintings in Norman church, open all day weekends. *(Lauren and Dan Frazer)*

BRAYFORD SS7235

★Poltimore Arms 07969 356278

Yarde Down; 3 miles towards Simonsbath; EX36 3HA Ivy-clad 17th-c beamed pub – so remote it generates its own electricity, and water is from a spring; good home-made evening food Thurs-Sat, also Sun lunchtime (best to book), two or three changing ales tapped from the cask, friendly helpful staff, traditional furnishings, woodburner in inglenook, two attractive restaurant areas separated by another woodburner, good country views; free wi-fi; children and dogs (in bar) welcome, picnic-sets in side garden, shop and gallery, open all day. *(Abigail Slater)*

BRENDON SS7547

★**Rockford Inn** (01598) 741214
Rockford; Lynton–Simonsbath Road, off B3223; EX35 6PT Homely and welcoming little 17th-c beamed inn surrounded by fine walks and scenery (sister to the Manor House at Ditcheat, Somerset); neatly linked rooms with cushioned settles, wall seats and other straightforward furniture, country prints and horse tack, open fires, good helpings of enjoyable well priced pubby food (not Mon lunchtime), a couple of well kept changing ales (often Cotleigh) tapped from the cask, Adlestone's and Thatcher's ciders, decent wines by the glass, lots of pump clips and toby jugs behind counter; background music, board games; children and dogs (in bar) welcome, seats across the road overlooking East Lyn river, well appointed bedrooms, open all day. *(Bob and Margaret Holder)*

BRENDON SS7648

Staghunters (01598) 741222
Leedford Lane; EX35 6PS Idyllically set family-run hotel with gardens by East Lyn river, can get packed, though quiet out of season; good choice of enjoyable reasonably priced food, up to six well kept ales such as Exmoor and Otter, real cider, friendly efficient staff, bar with woodburner, restaurant; children, walkers and dogs welcome, riverside tables, 14 good value bedrooms, open all day weekends (and weekdays if busy). *(Bob and Margaret Holder)*

BRIXHAM SX9256

★**Maritime** (01803) 853535
King Street (up steps from harbour – nearby parking virtually non-existent); TQ5 9TH Single bar packed with bric-a-brac; chamber-pots hanging from beams, hundreds of key fobs, cigarette cards, pre-war ensigns, toby jugs, mannequins, astronomical charts, even a binnacle by the door, Hunters Half Bore and Pheasant Plucker, over 80 malt whiskies, no food or credit cards, long-serving landlady, lively terrier called George and Mr Tibbs the parrot; background music, small TV, darts and board games; well behaved children and dogs allowed, fine views over harbour, six bedrooms (not ensuite), closed lunchtime. *(Tony Scott)*

BRIXHAM SX9256

New Quay (01803) 883290
King Street; TQ5 9TW Early 18th-c pub tucked down side street; well kept changing west country beers and ciders from board-fronted servery, good range of wines by the glass and gins, friendly helpful staff, beam and plank ceiling, spindleback chairs and mix of old tables on slate tiles, warming woodburner, fairly traditional menu using fresh local produce, upstairs restaurant with another woodburner and old town views; no children under 10, dogs welcome in bar, open all day Sun in summer, closed Mon-Weds and till 5.30pm Thurs-Sat. *(Timothy)*

BROADCLYST SX9997

New Inn (01392) 461312
Wimple Road; EX5 3BX Friendly former 17th-c farmhouse with stripped brickwork, boarded ceiling, low doorways and log fires, well cooked reasonably priced pubby food, Dartmoor, Hanlons, Otter and Sharps, good attentive service, small restaurant; skittle alley; children and dogs welcome, garden with play area, open all day. *(Ian Gilpin)*

BROADCLYST SX9897

Red Lion (01392) 461271
B3121, by church; EX5 3EL 16th-c pub under same owners as the Hunters at Newton Tracey; heavy beams, flagstones and log fires, well kept west country ales and enjoyable reasonably priced traditional food (special diets catered for) in bar and restaurant, good cheerful service; children and dogs welcome, picnic-sets out in front below wisteria, more in small enclosed garden across quiet lane, nice village and 15th-c church, not far from Killerton (NT), open all day weekends when can be busy. *(Nick and Meriel Cox)*

BROADHEMBURY ST1004

Drewe Arms (01404) 841267
Off A373 Cullompton–Honiton; EX14 3NF Extended partly thatched pub dating from the 15th c; carved beams and handsome stone-mullioned windows, woodburner and open fire, modernised bar area, five well kept local ales and seven wines by the glass, enjoyable pubby food (all day weekends), friendly helpful service, skittle alley; children and dogs welcome, terrace seats, more up steps on tree-shaded lawn, nice setting near church in pretty village, open all day. *(Roger and Donna Huggins)*

BROADHEMPSTON SX8066

Monks Retreat (01803) 812203
The Square; TQ9 6BN Old pub next to the village school; black beams, wood floors and woodburner in huge stone fireplace, cheerful welcoming staff, Dartmoor ales and enjoyable sensibly priced home-made food including daily specials, OAP lunch Tues and fish and chips Weds evening, steps to sizeable dining area, also new oak-framed dining extension; dogs welcome, two bedrooms, closed Mon lunchtime, no food Sun evening or Mon. *(Stuart and Natalie Granville)*

BUCKFAST SX7467

Abbey Inn (01364) 642343
Buckfast Road, off B3380; TQ11 0EA Lovely position perched on bank of River Dart; partly panelled bar with woodburner, three St Austell ales and Healey's cider, enjoyable reasonably priced pubby food from sandwiches and baguettes up, Sun carvery, big dining room with more panelling and river views; background music, free wi-fi; well

behaved children and dogs (in bar) welcome, terrace and bedrooms overlooking the water, open all day. *(John Evans)*

BUCKLAND BREWER SS4220

★**Coach & Horses** (01237) 451395

Village signposted off A388 S of Monkleigh; OS Sheet 190 map reference 423206; EX39 5LU Friendly 13th-c thatched pub with heavily beamed bar (mind your head), comfortable seats, handsome antique settle and inglenook woodburner, smaller lounge with log fire in another inglenook, Exmoor Gold, Otter Ale and Sharps Doom Bar, local ciders and several wines by the glass, decent food including home-made curries, small back games room (darts and pool) and skittle alley/function room; background music, games machine, occasional sports TV, free wi-fi; children and dogs (in bar) welcome, picnic-sets on front terrace and in side garden, holiday cottage next door. *(Bob and Margaret Holder)*

BUDLEIGH SALTERTON SY0681

Salterton Arms (01395) 445002

Chapel Street; EX9 6LX Welcoming pub off east end of the high street; clean comfortable bar with four well kept ales and good range of other drinks including cocktails, enjoyable competitively priced food (all day Fri, Sat, till 6pm Sun), weekday set menu, roomy upstairs gallery restaurant; live music Sat, quiz Thurs, sports TV, fruit machine; children and dogs welcome, open all day. *(Theocsbrian)*

BUTTERLEIGH SS9708

Butterleigh Inn (01884) 855433

Off A396 in Bickleigh; EX15 1PN Traditional heavy-beamed country pub, friendly and relaxed with good mix of customers, enjoyable reasonably priced pubby food (not Mon) including Sun carvery, four well kept ales such as Cotleigh and Otter, real ciders and good choice of wines, unspoilt lived-in interior with two big fireplaces, back dining room; free wi-fi; children and dogs welcome, picnic-sets in large garden, four comfortable bedrooms, closed Sun evening, Mon lunchtime. *(Melanie and David Lawson)*

CADELEIGH SS9107

★**Cadeleigh Arms** (01884) 855238

Village signed off A3072 W of junction with A396 Tiverton–Exeter at Bickleigh; EX16 8HP Attractive and friendly old pub owned by the local community; well kept Exeter Avocet, Hanlons Yellowhammer and a guest, Sandford Orchards cider, good locally sourced food (not Sun evening) from regularly changing menu, carpeted room on left with bay-window seat and ornamental stove, flagstoned room to the right with high-backed settles and log fire in big fireplace, valley views from airy dining room down a couple of steps; background music, skittle alley; children and dogs welcome, tables on sunny terrace and gently sloping lawn, closed Mon lunchtime. *(Jerry Russell)*

CALIFORNIA CROSS SX7053

California (01548) 821449

Brown sign to pub off A3121 S of A38 junction; PL21 0SG Neatly kept 18th-c or older beamed dining pub; red carpets, panelling and stripped stone, plates on delft shelving and other bits and pieces, log fire, good choice of enjoyable food from baguettes to steaks in bar and family area, popular Sun lunch (best to book), separate evening restaurant (Weds-Sun) and small snug, St Austell Tribute, Sharps Doom Bar and a local guest, traditional cider and decent wines by the glass, good friendly service; background music, free wi-fi; dogs welcome, attractive garden and back terrace, open all day. *(Glen and Patricia Fuller)*

CHAGFORD SX6987

Chagford (01647) 433109

Mill Street; TQ13 8AW Former coaching inn just off market square; main bar/dining room with understated modern décor; blue-painted half-panelling, mix of furniture including pine settles forming booths, local artwork, fresh flowers and woodburner, good food from changing menu featuring locally farmed Dexter beef, ales such as Butcombe, Dartmoor and Otter, Symonds's and Thatcher's ciders, good wines and proper coffee, friendly helpful staff; background music; children and dogs welcome, walled courtyard garden behind, three comfortable annexe bedrooms; for sale last we heard, so may be changes. *(Michael Longman)*

CHAGFORD SX7087

Ring o' Bells (01647) 432466

Off A382; TQ13 8AH Welcoming old shuttered pub with good mix of locals and visitors; beamed and panelled bar, four well kept ales including Dartmoor and enjoyable home-made food at fair prices, friendly attentive service, woodburner in big fireplace; some live music, free wi-fi; well behaved children and dogs welcome, sunny walled garden behind, nearby moorland walks, four comfortable spotless bedrooms, good breakfast, open all day. *(Ian Gilpin)*

CHALLACOMBE SS6941

Black Venus (01598) 763251

B3358 Blackmoor Gate–Simonsbath; EX31 4TT Low-beamed 16th-c pub with two or three well kept changing ales, Thatcher's cider and decent wines by the glass, well liked fairly priced food from sandwiches to popular Sun lunch, friendly helpful staff, pews and comfortable chairs, woodburner and big fireplace, roomy attractive dining area, games room with pool and darts; free wi-fi; children and dogs welcome, garden play area, lovely countryside and good walks from the door, open all day in summer. *(Sean Wilson)*

CHERITON BISHOP SX7792

★**Old Thatch Inn** (01647) 24204
Off A30; EX6 6JH Attractive thatched village pub with welcoming relaxed atmosphere; rambling beamed bar separated by big stone fireplace, Otter, Dartmoor and a couple of guests, ciders such as Sandfords, good freshly prepared food including range of burgers, efficient friendly service, restaurant; free wi-fi; children and dogs welcome, nice sheltered garden, open all day, no food Sun evening, Mon, Tues. *(Diana and Bertie Farr)*

CHERITON FITZPAINE SS8706

★**Ring of Bells** (01363) 860111
Off Barton Close, signed to village centre; EX17 4JG Refurbished 14th-c thatched and beamed country pub; very good food cooked by landlord-chef including set menus (popular Tues auberge night), ales such as Branscombe Vale, Exe Valley and Teignworthy, local cider, friendly efficient service; children and dogs welcome (pub dog is Ruben), self-catering cottage, closed Mon, no food Sun evening. *(Mike and Lynne Steane, Nick Borst-Smith)*

CHILLINGTON SX7942

Bear & Blacksmiths (01548) 581171
A379 E of Kingsbridge; TQ7 2LD Old refurbished pub (former Open Arms) with clean modern interior; landlord-chef's good food using local produce including some from own farm, three well kept ales, friendly helpful staff; children welcome, tables on back terrace. *(Timothy)*

CHITTLEHAMHOLT SS6420

Exeter Inn (01769) 540281
Off A377 Barnstaple–Crediton, and B3226 SW of South Molton; EX37 9NS 16th-c thatched coaching inn with enjoyable food from sandwiches and traditional choices up, well kept ales such as Exmoor and Otter (some tapped from the cask), local ciders and good wine choice, friendly staff, barrel seats by open stove in huge fireplace, beams dotted with hundreds of matchboxes, shelves of old bottles, traditional games, lounge with comfortable seating and woodburner, dining room and barn-style conservatory; background music; children and dogs welcome, gravel terrace, three bedrooms and four self-catering units. *(Gerry and Pam Pollard)*

CHITTLEHAMPTON SS6325

Bell (01769) 540368
Signed off B3227 S Molton–Umberleigh; EX37 9QL Family-run village inn on edge of square opposite historic church; decoratively tiled entrance to high-ceilinged bar with half-panelling and magnolia walls, lots of old photographs, animal heads and antlers, wooden pubby furniture, tasty good value home-made food from sandwiches and pub favourites up, ales such as Cotleigh and Exmoor, real ciders including local Winkleigh's, outstanding range of whiskies and over 50 gins, cheerful hard-working young staff; children (away from bar) and dogs welcome, ramp for wheelchairs, disabled loos, shaded circular picnic-sets on front cobbles, nice sunny garden behind, three bedrooms, open all day Fri-Sun. *(Chris and Angela Buckell)*

CHRISTOW SX8385

★**Teign House** (01647) 252286
Teign Valley Road (B3193); EX6 7PL Former farmhouse in country setting; very good freshly made food from pub favourites up, also an asian menu, up to five well kept local ales, own Brimblecombe's cider and nice wines, friendly helpful staff, open fire in beamed bar, dining room; some live music; well behaved children and dogs welcome, garden and camping field, open all day. *(Colin and Daniel Gibbs)*

CHUDLEIGH SX8679

Bishop Lacey (01626) 854585
Fore Street, just off A38; TQ13 0HY Old low-beamed former church house; three well kept west country beers and enjoyable reasonably priced home-made food, cheerful obliging staff, two bars, log fire; children and dogs welcome, open all day. *(Abigail Slater)*

CHULMLEIGH SS6814

Red Lion (01769) 580384
East Street; EX18 7DD Nicely updated 17th-c coaching inn with beams and open fires, enjoyable fairly priced food including range of burgers and pizzas, St Austell, Sharps and a guest, friendly helpful service; background music (live every other Sat), darts; children welcome, five bedrooms, open all day Fri-Sun, closed Mon lunchtime. *(Sophie and James Collier)*

CLAYHIDON ST1615

Half Moon (01823) 680291
On main road through village; EX15 3TJ Attractive old village pub with warm friendly atmosphere, wide choice of popular home-made food from sharing boards up, well kept Otter and a couple of guests, Healey's Cornish Rattler cider, good wine list, comfortable bar with inglenook log fire; some live music; children and dogs welcome, picnic-sets in tiered garden over road, lovely valley views, closed Sun evening, Mon. *(Guy Vowles, Bob and Margaret Holder)*

CLOVELLY SS3124

Red Lion (01237) 431237
The Quay; EX39 5TF Rambling 18th-c building in lovely position on curving quay below spectacular cliffs; beams, flagstones, log fire and interesting local photographs in character back bar (dogs allowed here), well kept Country Life and Sharps, enjoyable food including good value set lunch, efficient

service, upstairs restaurant; occasional live music; 11 attractive bedrooms (six more in Sail Loft annexe), own car park for residents and diners, open all day. *(Moira and Jon Weller)*

CLYST HYDON ST0201

Five Bells (01884) 277288
W of village, just off B3176 not far from M5 junction 28; EX15 2NT Thatched and beamed dining pub (former 16th-c farmhouse) under new ownership; smartly updated interior with several different areas including raised dining part, assorted tables and chairs on wood or slate floors, woodburner in large stone fireplace, good food from pub favourites up, efficient friendly service, beers such as Hanlons, Otter and Powderkeg, Sandford Orchards cider and a dozen wines by the glass; children welcome, dogs in bar, disabled access/loo, cottagey garden with country views, closed Sun evening, Mon. *(Gordon and Patricia Gorringe)*

CLYST ST GEORGE SX9888

St George & Dragon (01392) 876121
Topsham Road/A376, at roundabout; EX3 0QJ Spaciously extended open-plan Vintage Inn; low beams and some secluded corners, log fires, St Austell Tribute, Sharps Doom Bar and good choice of wines by the glass, popular reasonably priced food, good service; children and dogs welcome, bedrooms in adjoining Innkeepers Lodge, open all day. *(Roger and Donna Huggins)*

CLYST ST MARY SX9791

Half Moon (01392) 873515
Under a mile from M5 junction 30 via A376; EX5 1BR Popular old beamed pub near disused 12th-c bridge over the River Clyst; good home-made food at reasonable prices including daily specials (best to book), many dishes available in smaller helpings, well kept ales such as Otter and decent choice of wines by the glass, friendly helpful staff, bar and separate lounge/dining area, stone floors, some red plush seating and log fire; quiz or bingo night Sun; children and dogs welcome, disabled access, open all day Fri-Sun. *(Roger and Donna Huggins)*

COCKWOOD SX9780

★**Ship** (01626) 890373
Off A379 N of Dawlish; EX6 8NU Comfortable traditional 17th-c pub set back from the estuary and harbour – gets very busy in season; good food including some fish specials, five ales such as Dartmoor and St Austell, friendly staff and locals, partitioned beamed bar with big log fire and ancient oven, decorative plates and seafaring memorabilia, small restaurant; background music; children and dogs welcome, nice steep-sided garden, open all day, food all day Sun. *(Rosie and John Moore)*

COMBE MARTIN SS5846

Pack o' Cards (01271) 882300
High Street; EX34 0ET Unusual 'house of cards' building constructed in the late 17th c to celebrate a substantial gambling win – four floors, 13 rooms and 52 windows; snug bar area and various side rooms, three real ales such as Exmoor, St Austell and Wickwar, decent wines by the glass and good range of well liked food including children's choices and all-day Sun carvery, cream teas, friendly helpful service even at busy times, restaurant; dogs welcome, pretty riverside garden with play area, six comfortable bedrooms, generous breakfast, open all day. *(Roy and Gill Payne)*

COMBEINTEIGNHEAD SX9071

Wild Goose (01626) 872241
Off unclassified coast road Newton Abbot–Shaldon, uphill in village; TQ12 4RA Friendly 17th-c family-run pub; spacious back lounge with beams and agricultural bits and pieces on the walls, five west country ales and good freshly made food including daily specials, big fireplace in front bar, more beams, standing timbers and some flagstones, step down to area with another large fireplace, further cosy room with tub chairs; background and fortnightly live music, Sun quiz, TV projector for major sports; children and dogs welcome, nice country views from back garden, closed Mon. *(Timothy)*

COUNTISBURY SS7449

Blue Ball (01598) 741263
A39, E of Lynton; EX35 6NE Welcoming heavy-beamed roadside pub in lovely rural setting; good range of generous local food in bar and restaurant, three or four real ales including Exmoor and one badged for them, decent wines and proper ciders, log fires; background music, TV, free wi-fi; children, walkers and dogs welcome, views from terrace tables, good nearby cliff walks (pub provides details of circular routes), comfortable bedrooms, open all day, food all day in summer. *(Chris Pelham)*

CREDITON SS8300

Crediton Inn (01363) 772882
Mill Street (follow Tiverton sign); EX17 1EZ Small friendly local (the 'Kirton') under long-serving landlady; well kept Hanlons Yellowhammer and up to nine quickly changing guests (Nov beer festival), cheap well prepared weekend food, home-made scotch eggs at other times, back games

If you report on a pub that's not a featured entry, please tell us any lunchtimes or evenings when it doesn't serve bar food.

room/skittle alley; free wi-fi; open all day Mon-Sat. *(Ian Gilpin)*

CROYDE SS4439

Manor House Inn (01271) 890241

St Marys Road, off B3231 NW of Braunton; EX33 1PG Friendly family pub with three well kept west country ales and good choice of enjoyable food from lunchtime sandwiches to blackboard specials, Sun carvery, cream teas, cheerful efficient service, spacious bar, restaurant and dining conservatory; background and live music, sports TV, games end with pool and darts, skittle alley; free wi-fi; dogs welcome in bar, disabled facilities, attractive terraced garden with big play area, open all day. *(Neil and Brenda Skidmore)*

CROYDE SS4439

Thatch (01271) 890349

B3231 NW of Braunton; Hobbs Hill; EX33 1LZ Lively thatched pub near great surfing beaches (can get packed in summer); rambling and roomy with beams and open fire, settles and other good seating, enjoyable pubby food from sandwiches and baked potatoes up, well kept changing local ales, morning coffee, teas, cheerful young staff, smart restaurant with dressers and lots of china; background and live music; children in eating areas, dogs in bar, flower-filled suntrap terraces and large gardens shared with neighbouring Billy Budds, good play area, simple clean bedrooms above the pub and nearby, self-catering cottage, open (and food) all day. *(Neil and Brenda Skidmore)*

CULMSTOCK ST1013

Culm Valley (01884) 840354

B3391, off A38 E of M5 junction 27; EX15 3JJ Friendly 18th-c pub with good choice of food from varied menu, four real ales including Otter, local cider and plenty of wines by the glass, country-style décor with hotchpotch of furniture, rugs on wood floors and some interesting bits and pieces, small front conservatory; free wi-fi; children and dogs (in bar) welcome, totem pole outside, tables on raised grassed area (former railway platform) overlooking old stone bridge over River Culm, open all day Fri-Sun. *(Moira and Jon Weller)*

DARTINGTON SX7861

★**Cott** (01803) 863777

Cott signed off A385 W of Totnes, opposite A384 turn-off; TQ9 6HE Long 14th-c thatched pub with heavy beams, flagstones, nice mix of old furniture and two inglenooks (one with big woodburner), good locally sourced home-made food from traditional choices up in bar and restaurant, three well kept ales including local Hunters and Greene King, Ashridge's cider, nice wines by the glass, friendly efficient service; live music Sun; children and dogs welcome, wheelchair access (with help to restaurant), picnic-sets in garden and on pretty terrace, five comfortable bedrooms, open all day. *(John Evans, Mike and Mary Carter)*

DARTMOUTH SX8751

★**Cherub** (01803) 832571

Higher Street; walk along riverfront, right into Hauley Road and up steps at end; TQ6 9RB Ancient building (Dartmouth's oldest) with two heavily timbered upper floors jettying over the street, many original features including oak beams, leaded lights and big stone fireplace, bustling bar serving up to six well kept ales such as Exeter, South Hams and a house beer from St Austell, enjoyable food from pub favourites to blackboard specials, efficient friendly service, low-ceilinged upstairs restaurant; background music; children welcome (no pushchairs), dogs in bar, open all day. *(Tony Scott)*

DARTMOUTH SX8751

Floating Bridge (01803) 832354

Opposite Upper Ferry; Coombe Road (A379); TQ6 9PQ Popular pub in lovely quayside spot; bar with lots of stools by windows making most of waterside view, black and white photographs of local boating scenes, St Austell Tribute, Sharps Doom Bar and guests, several wines by the glass, enjoyable pubby food including daily specials, bare-boards dining room with leather-backed chairs around wooden tables; children and dogs (in bar) welcome, pretty window boxes, seats out by the river looking at busy ferry crossing, more on sizeable roof terrace, open (and food) all day. *(I D Barnett)*

DITTISHAM SX8654

★**Ferry Boat** (01803) 722368

Manor Street; best to park in village car park and walk down (quite steep); TQ6 0EX Cheerful riverside pub with lively mix of customers; beamed bar with log fires and straightforward pubby furniture, lots of boating bits and pieces, tide times chalked on wall, flags on ceiling, picture-window view of the Dart, at least three real ales such as Otter and Sharps, a dozen wines by the glass and good range of tasty home-made food including pie of the day and various curries, efficient service; background and some live music, quiz night Thurs; children and dogs welcome, moorings for visiting boats on adjacent pontoon and bell to summon ferry, good walks, open (and food) all day. *(Camille and Jose Ferrera)*

DITTISHAM SX8654

Red Lion (01803) 722235

The Level; TQ6 0ES Welcoming pub in lovely location looking down over attractive village and River Dart; enjoyable food including daily specials, Dartmoor, Palmers and a summer guest, carpeted bar and restaurant, open fires; also incorporates village store, tiny post office, library and craft shop; children and dogs welcome, eight bedrooms (some with river view), open from 8.30am summer, 9am winter, may shut Weds and weekend afternoons in winter. *(Daphne and Barry Gregson)*

DODDISCOMBSLEIGH SX8586

★ **Nobody Inn** (01647) 252394
Off B3193; EX6 7PS Atmospheric old country inn (same owners as Spoken in Exmouth); beamed lounge with handsomely carved antique settles, windsor and wheelback chairs around all sorts of wooden tables, guns and hunting prints in snug area by one of the big inglenooks, a beer named for the pub from Branscombe Vale and a couple of guests, three real ciders, 30 wines by the glass from extensive list and 270 malt whiskies, good food from shortish changing menu, friendly service, more formal restaurant; children welcome away from main bar (no under-5s in restaurant), dogs allowed in bar, pretty garden with rural views, local church worth a visit for its fine medieval stained glass, bedrooms, open all day. *(S G N Bennett, Dr and Mrs J D Abell, Nicola and Holly Lyons, Beth Aldridge, Katherine and Hugh Markham)*

DREWSTEIGNTON SX7390

Drewe Arms (01647) 281409
Off A30 NW of Moretonhampstead; EX6 6QN Pretty thatched village pub under welcoming licensees; unspoilt room on left with basic wooden wall benches, stools and tables, original serving hatch, ales such as Dartmoor and Otter from tap room casks, local cider, enjoyable sensibly priced pubby food including daily specials, two dining areas, one with Rayburn and history of Britain's longest serving landlady (Mabel Mudge), another with woodburner, darts and board games, some live music in back Long Room; free wi-fi; children and dogs welcome, good local walks and handy for Castle Drogo (NT), open all day Sun (no evening food then). *(Sean Wilson)*

DUNSFORD SX8189

Royal Oak (01647) 252256
Signed from Moretonhampstead; EX6 7DA Friendly comfortably worn-in village pub, generous helpings of traditional home-made food at reasonable prices, well kept ales such as Otter and Sharps, local cider, airy lounge with woodburner and view from sunny dining bay, simple dining room, steps down to pool room; background and some live music; children and dogs (on leads) welcome, sheltered tiered garden with play area, various animals including donkeys, miniature ponies and alpacas, good value bedrooms in converted barn. *(Mr and Mrs P R Thomas)*

EAST ALLINGTON SX7648

Fortescue Arms (01548) 521215
Village signed off A381 Totnes–Kingsbridge, S of A3122 junction; TQ9 7RA Pretty 19th-c wisteria-clad village pub; two-room bar with mix of tables and chairs on black slate floor, half-panelling and open fire, St Austell and Dartmoor ales, eight wines by the glass, spacious restaurant with high-backed dining chairs around pine tables and another fire in stone fireplace, enjoyable well priced traditional food cooked by landlord-chef including separate vegetarian/vegan evening menu, warm friendly service; background and occasional live music, free wi-fi; children welcome, dogs in bar (food for them), wheelchair access, tables out at front with more on sheltered terrace, closed Mon and lunchtime Tues. *(Simon King)*

EAST BUDLEIGH SY0684

Sir Walter Raleigh (01395) 442510
High Street; EX9 7ED Friendly little 16th-c low-beamed village local, well kept changing west country beers and good traditional food, restaurant down step; children and dogs welcome, parking some way off, wonderful medieval bench carvings in nearby church, handy too for Bicton Park Botanical Gardens. *(Chris Pelham)*

EAST DOWN SS5941

Pyne Arms (01271) 850055
Off A39 Barnstaple–Lynton near Arlington; EX31 4LX Welcoming old pub tucked away in small hamlet; cosy carpeted bar with lots of alcoves, woodburner, good well presented food from traditional choices up, Exmoor, St Austell and a guest, nice choice of wines, flagstoned area with sofas, conservatory; background music, free wi-fi; children and dogs welcome, small enclosed garden, good walks and handy for Arlington Court (NT), three comfortable bedrooms, open all day weekends, closed Mon lunchtime. *(Roy and Gill Payne)*

EAST PRAWLE SX7836

Pigs Nose (01548) 511209
Prawle Green; TQ7 2BY Quirky 16th-c three-room pub, lots of interesting bric-a-brac and pictures, mix of old furniture with jars of wild flowers and candles on tables, low beams, flagstones and open fire, local ales tapped from the cask, farm ciders and enjoyable simple pubby food, small family area with unusual toys, pool and darts; unobtrusive background music, hall for live bands (landlord was 1960s tour manager); friendly pub dogs (others welcome and menu for them), tables outside, pleasant spot on village green, closed Sun evening in winter. *(Billy)*

EXETER SX9390

Double Locks (01392) 256947
Canal Banks, Alphington, via Marsh Barton Industrial Estate; EX2 6LT Unsmart, individual and remotely located by ship canal; Wells, Youngs and guests, farm cider in summer, bar food (not Sun

evening); background and some live music; children and dogs welcome, seats out on grass or decking with distant view to city and cathedral (nice towpath walk out), big play area, camping, open all day. *(Rosie and John Moore)*

EXETER SX9292

Georges Meeting House
(01392) 454250 *South Street; EX1 1ED* Interesting Wetherspoons in grand former 18th-c chapel; bare-boards interior with three-sided gallery, stained glass and tall pulpit at one end, eight real ales from long counter, their usual good value food; children welcome, tables in attractive side garden under parasols, open all day from 8am. *(Roger and Donna Huggins)*

EXETER SX9292

★**Hour Glass** (01392) 258722
Melbourne Street; off B3015 Topsham Road; EX2 4AU Old-fashioned bow-cornered pub tucked away in surviving Georgian part above the quay; good inventive food including vegetarian choices from shortish regularly changing menu, up to five well kept local ales (usually one from Otter) and extensive range of wines and spirits, friendly relaxed atmosphere, beams, bare boards and mix of furnishings, assorted pictures on dark red walls and various odds and ends including a stuffed badger, open fire in small brick fireplace; background and live music; children (away from bar) and dogs welcome (resident cats), open all day weekends, closed Mon lunchtime. *(Roger and Donna Huggins)*

EXETER SX9193

Imperial (01392) 434050
New North Road (above St David's Station); EX4 4AH Impressive 19th-c mansion in own six-acre hillside park with sweeping drive; various different areas including two clubby little side bars, fine old ballroom with elaborate plasterwork and gilding and light airy former orangery on two levels, interesting pictures, up to 14 real ales, standard good value Wetherspoons menu; popular with students and can get very busy; plenty of seating in grounds and attractive cobbled courtyard, open all day. *(Roger and Donna Huggins, Dr and Mrs A K Clarke)*

EXETER SX9192

Mill on the Exe (01392) 214464
Bonhay Road (A377); EX4 3AB Former paper mill in good spot by pedestrian bridge over weir; spacious opened-up interior on two floors (each with bar), bare boards, old bricks, beams and timbers, four well kept ales including St Austell, good house wines and popular food from snacks and sharing boards up, Sun carvery, large airy conservatory with feature raised fire, friendly atmosphere; children and dogs welcome, river views from balcony tables, spiral stairs down to waterside garden (summer barbecues), 11 bedrooms in attached hotel side, open (and food) all day. *(Roger and Donna Huggins, Nick and Meriel Cox)*

EXETER SX9292

Old Fire House (01392) 277279
New North Road; EX4 4EP Relaxed city-centre pub in Georgian building behind high arched wrought-iron gates; arranged over three floors with dimly lit beamed rooms and simple furniture, up to ten real ales from casks behind bar, several ciders and good choice of bottled beers and wines, bargain food including late-night pizzas, friendly efficient staff; background music, live weekends and popular with young crowd (modest admission charge Fri, Sat night), Mon quiz; picnic-sets in front courtyard, open all day till late (3am Thurs-Sat). *(Roger and Donna Huggins)*

EXETER SX9292

Ship (01392) 272040
Martins Lane, near cathedral; EX1 1EY Historic heavy-beamed pub down alleyway; Greene King ales and guests, real cider, several wines by the glass and cocktails, decent reasonably priced food, steep narrow stairs up to comfortable quieter area with old easy chairs and sofas; background and live music, quiz nights, TV, machines; children and dogs welcome, open (and food) all day. *(IAA, HMW, Maria Sansoni)*

EXETER SX9292

White Hart (01392) 279897
South Street; EX1 1EE Rambling 15th-c inn close to the cathedral; various bars with heavy beams, oak flooring and some nice furnishings, inner cobbled courtyard, Marstons-related ales and good choice of reasonably priced food including deals, Sun carvery, friendly helpful staff; background music; children welcome, 65 bedrooms (40 in back extension), open all day. *(Richard Tilbrook)*

EXMINSTER SX9686

★**Turf Hotel** (01392) 833128
From A379 S of village, follow the signs to the Swans Nest, then continue to end of track, by gates; park and walk right along canal towpath – nearly a mile; EX6 8EE Remote but popular waterside pub reached by 20-minute towpath walk, cycle ride or 60-seater boat from Topsham quay (15-minute trip); several little rooms – end one with slate floor, pine walls, built-in seats and woodburner, simple room along corridor serves ales such as Branscombe, Exeter, Otter and Hanlons, local cider/juices and ten wines by the glass, interesting locally sourced food, friendly staff; background music, board games; children and dogs welcome, big garden with picnic-sets and summer barbecues, arrive early for a seat in fine weather, bedrooms and a yurt for hire,

good breakfast, open all day in summer (best to check other times). *(D W Stokes)*

EXMOUTH SY0080

Bicton Inn (01395) 272589

Bicton Street; EX8 2RU Traditional 19th-c backstreet corner local with friendly buoyant atmosphere, up to eight well kept ales and a proper cider, no food; regular live music including folk nights, pool, darts and other pub games; children and dogs welcome, open all day. *(Gerry and Pam Pollard)*

EXMOUTH SX9980

Grapevine (01395) 222208

Victoria Road; EX8 1DL Popular red-brick corner pub (calls itself a pub-bistro) on fringe of town centre, light and spacious with mix of wooden tables and seating, rugs on bare boards, modern local artwork, own Crossed Anchors beers plus changing west country guests, plenty of bottled imports and nice choice of wines by the glass, tasty well presented food including daily special, friendly service and relaxed atmosphere; background music, live bands Fri and Sat, free wi-fi; children and dogs welcome, open all day. *(Theocsbrian)*

EXMOUTH SY9980

Grove (01395) 272101

Esplanade; EX8 1BJ Roomy high-gabled Victorian pub set back from the beach; enjoyable affordably priced pubby food including local fish/seafood specials, well kept Youngs ales, guest beers and good range of wines by the glass, traditional furnishings, local prints and caricatures, attractive fireplace at back, sea views from appealing upstairs dining room and balcony; background music, quiz Thurs; children welcome, picnic-sets in front garden, open all day, food all day weekends. *(PL, Richard Tilbrook)*

EXMOUTH SY0080

Spoken (01395) 265228

Strand; EX8 1AL Corner bar under same ownership as the Nobody Inn at Doddiscombsleigh; quirky interior with eclectic mix of tables and chairs on wood floor, over 1,000 spirits including own gin, good selection of other drinks and popular food from breakfast on, knowledgeable staff, friendly relaxed atmosphere; pavement seats, children welcome, open all day from 10am. *(Sean Wilson)*

EXTON SX9886

Puffing Billy (01392) 877888

Station Road/Exton Lane; EX3 0PR Attractively opened-up dining pub with light spacious interior; pitched ceiling bar area with flagstones and woodburner, restaurant part with wood-strip flooring and second woodburner in two-way fireplace, some painted tables and chairs and upholstered wall benches, good food from sharing plates and pub favourites up, beers such as Bath, Bays and Otter, good selection of wines and gins, friendly attentive service; background music, quiz first Mon of month; children welcome, tables out at front by road and on paved side terrace, handy for Exe Estuary cycle trail, open all day. *(Giles and Annie Francis)*

GEORGEHAM SS4639

Kings Arms (01271) 890240

B3231 (Chapel Street) Croyde–Woolacombe; EX33 1JJ Welcoming comfortably modernised village pub with red walls, slate floors and leather sofas by big woodburner, good freshly cooked food using local ingredients, efficient friendly service, St Austell Tribute and a couple of local guests, good choice of wines, upstairs dining area with tables out on sunny balcony, some traditional pub games; background and live music; children and dogs welcome, small front terrace screened from road, open all day. *(Sophie and James Collier)*

HARBERTON SX7758

★**Church House** (01803) 863707

Off A381 S of Totnes; next to church; TQ9 7SF Ancient village inn (dates to the 13th c) with unusually long bar; blackened beams, medieval latticed glass and oak panelling, attractive 17th- and 18th-c pews and settles, woodburner in big inglenook, well kept ales including Salcombe and a house beer from Hunters, local cider and ten wines by the glass, good fairly priced food (just pizzas Sun evening), friendly efficient service, separate dining room; quiz and live music nights; children and dogs welcome, sunny walled back garden, comfortable bedrooms, open all day Sun till 9pm, closed Mon and Tues lunchtimes. *(Richard and Tessa Ibbot)*

HATHERLEIGH SS5404

Tally Ho (01837) 810306

Market Street (A386); EX20 3JN Friendly and relaxed old pub with own beers from back brewery plus a couple of guests; attractive heavy-beamed and timbered linked rooms, sturdy furnishings, big log fire and woodburner, good food from ciabattas up, restaurant, busy Tues market day (beer slightly cheaper then); background music, open mike night third Weds of month, darts; children and dogs welcome, tables in nice sheltered garden, three good value bedrooms, open all day. *(Jerry Russell)*

HEMYOCK ST1313

Catherine Wheel (01823) 680224

Cornhill; EX15 3RQ Popular and friendly village pub with bar, lounge and restaurant; Otter and Sharps Doom Bar, Thatcher's cider and plenty of wines by the glass, good food (not Sun evening, Mon) from varied menu, fresh flowers on tables, leather sofas by woodburner, efficient service; Sun quiz, darts, pool and skittle alley, free wi-fi; children and dogs welcome, closed Mon lunchtime. *(Guy Vowles)*

HOLSWORTHY SS3304

Rydon Inn (01409) 259444
Rydon (A3072 W); EX22 7HU Comfortably extended family-run dining pub, clean and tidy, with enjoyable food and well kept local ales, good service, raftered bar with thatched servery, woodburner in stone fireplace; background music; free wi-fi; well behaved children and dogs welcome, disabled facilities, views over lake from conservatory and deck, well tended garden, open all day. *(Chris Pelham)*

HONITON ST1599

Heathfield (01404) 45321
Walnut Road; EX14 2UG Ancient thatched and beamed pub in contrasting residential area; well run and spacious, with a couple of Greene King ales and good value food from comprehensive menu including the Heathfield Whopper (20oz rump steak), Sun lunchtime carvery, cheerful prompt service; skittle alley; children and dogs (in bar) welcome, seven bedrooms, open all day Fri-Sun. *(Bob and Margaret Holder)*

HONITON SY1198

★**Holt** (01404) 47707
High Street, W end; EX14 1LA Charming bustling little pub run by two brothers, relaxed and informal, with just one room downstairs, chunky tables and chairs on slate flooring, shelves of books and coal-effect woodburner, full range of Otter beers (the family founded the brewery), bigger brighter upstairs dining room with similar furniture on pale floorboards, very good 'tapas' and other inventive food, well chosen wine list, friendly efficient service; cookery classes and quarterly music festivals; well behaved children welcome, dogs in bar, closed Sun, Mon. *(Revd R P Tickle)*

HOPE COVE SX6740

Hope & Anchor (01548) 561294
Tucked away by car park; TQ7 3HQ Seaside inn on two floors; open kitchen serving decent choice of popular food from sharing plates to local fish, St Austell ales and a west country guest, several wines by the glass, helpful amiable young staff, flagstones and bare boards, two woodburners, dining room views to Burgh Island; background music, free wi-fi; children and dogs welcome, sea-view tables out on decked balcony and terrace, 11 bedrooms, open (and food) all day from 8am for breakfast. *(Helen and Brian Edgeley)*

HORNS CROSS SS3823

★**Hoops** (01237) 451222
A39 Clovelly–Bideford, W of village; EX39 5DL Pretty thatched and beamed inn dating from the 13th c, friendly and relaxed, with traditionally furnished bar, log fires in sizeable fireplaces and some standing timbers and partitioning, more formal restaurant with attractive mix of tables and chairs, some panelling, exposed stone and another open fire, St Austell Tribute and a guest such as Clearwater, over a dozen wines by the glass, enjoyable fairly straightforward food using local suppliers, cream teas, welcoming helpful staff; may be background music; children and dogs allowed, picnic-sets under parasols in enclosed courtyard, more seats on terrace and in two acres of gardens, 13 well equipped bedrooms, open (and food) all day. *(Bob and Margaret Holder)*

HORSEBRIDGE SX4074

★**Royal** (01822) 870214
Off A384 Tavistock–Launceston; PL19 8PJ Ancient dimly lit local with dark half-panelling, scrubbed tables on slate floors, log fires and interesting bric-a-brac, well kept Dartmoor, St Austell and Skinners direct from the cask, real cider and good reasonably priced food, friendly service; no children in the evening, dogs welcome, picnic-sets on front and side terraces and in big garden, quiet rustic spot by lovely old Tamar bridge, popular with walkers and cyclists. *(Lauren and Dan Frazer)*

IDE SX9090

Huntsman (01392) 272779
High Street; EX2 9RN Welcoming thatched and beamed family-run country pub; enjoyable sensibly priced home-made food including good Sun roasts, Butcombe, St Austell and Sharps, friendly attentive service; children welcome, picnic-sets in pleasant garden. *(Colin and Daniel Gibbs)*

IDE SX8990

Poachers (01392) 273847
3 miles from M5 junction 31, via A30; High Street; EX2 9RW Cosy beamed pub in quaint village; Branscombe Vale Branoc and five changing west country guests from ornate curved wooden bar, enjoyable home-made food, mismatched old chairs and sofas, various pictures and odds and ends, big log fire, restaurant; free wi-fi; dogs welcome (they have a boxer), tables in pleasant garden with barbecue, three comfortable bedrooms, open (and food) all day, till late Fri, Sat. *(Ian Gilpin)*

IDEFORD SX8977

★**Royal Oak** (01626) 852274
2 miles off A380; TQ13 0AY Unpretentious little 16th-c thatched and flagstoned village pub; a couple of changing local ales and generous helpings of tasty well priced pubby food, navy theme including interesting Nelson and Churchill memorabilia, beams, panelling and big open fireplace; children and dogs welcome, tables out at front and by car park over road, closed Mon. *(Richard and Tessa Ibbot)*

ILFRACOMBE SS5247

George & Dragon (01271) 863851

Fore Street; EX34 9ED One of the oldest pubs here (14th c) and handy for the harbour; clean and comfortable with friendly local atmosphere, ales such as Exmoor and Sharps, decent wines and traditional food including local fish, black beams, stripped stone and open fireplaces, lots of ornaments, china etc; background and some live music, Tues quiz, no mobile phones; children and dogs welcome, open all day and can get very busy weekends. *(Diana and Bertie Farr)*

ILFRACOMBE SS5247

Ship & Pilot (01271) 316085

Broad Street, off harbour; EX34 9EE Recently refurbished blue-painted pub near harbour attracting friendly mix of regulars and visitors; four well kept beers from Bath Ales and St Austell, real cider and several gins, enjoyable home-cooked food, good service; sports TV; children and dogs welcome, some tables outside, two bedrooms, open all day. *(Stuart and Natalie Granville)*

ILSINGTON SX7876

★Carpenters Arms (01364) 661629

Old Town Hill; TQ13 9RG Newish enthusiastic licensees for this welcoming little 18th-c pub next to the village church; smartly redecorated L-shaped room with painted beams and hefty flagstones, comfortable seats by woodburner in large stone fireplace, country-style tables and chairs, very good attractively presented food from shortish but varied menu including stone-baked pizzas, three well kept west country ales tapped from the cask, decent wine choice; children, walkers and dogs welcome, tables on pretty front terrace, good surrounding walks, closed Mon and Tues, no food Sun evening. *(Philip Crawford)*

INSTOW SS4730

Boat House (01271) 861292

Marine Parade; EX39 4JJ This well liked pub across from huge tidal beach was shut for major refurbishment as we went to press – news please.

KENN SX9285

Ley Arms (01392) 832341

Signed off A380 just S of Exeter; EX6 7UW Rambling old thatched dining pub in quiet spot near the church, good range of popular well presented/priced food using local produce including blackboard specials, smaller appetites and special diets catered for, well kept west country ales and decent range of wines, friendly helpful staff, beams, exposed stonework and polished granite flagstones, log fires, restaurant and garden room; children and dogs (theirs is Reggie) welcome, terrace tables under parasols, open all day, food all day weekends. *(Graham and Carol Parker, M J Winterton)*

KENNFORD SX9186

Seven Stars (01392) 834887

Centre of village; EX6 7TR Updated little village pub with three west country beers and good food including pies and takeaway pizzas, friendly atmosphere; quiz last Tues of month, open mike night first Fri of month, pool, darts and sports TV; children and dogs welcome, closed Mon, otherwise open all day. *(Melanie and David Lawson)*

KILMINGTON SY2698

New Inn (01297) 33376

Signed off Gammons Hill; EX13 7SF Traditional thatched local (originally three 14th-c cottages), friendly and welcoming, with good reasonably priced food including popular Sun roasts, well kept Palmers ales; skittle alley and boules court, monthly quiz; children and dogs welcome, disabled access/loo, picnic-sets in large garden with tree-shaded areas, closed Mon lunchtime, no food Sun evening, Mon. *(Sean Wilson)*

KILMINGTON SY2798

★Old Inn (01297) 32096

A35; EX13 7RB Bustling 16th-c thatched and beamed pub, well kept Branscombe Vale, Otter and a guest, decent choice of wines and enjoyable pubby food including daily specials, welcoming attentive service, small character front bar with traditional games (there's also a skittle alley), back lounge with inglenook log fire, small restaurant; children and dogs welcome, wheelchair access, terrace and lawned area, closed Sun evening. *(Phil and Jane Villiers, Tony and Jill Radnor)*

KING'S NYMPTON SS6819

★Grove (01769) 580406

Off B3226 SW of South Molton; EX37 9ST Welcoming 17th-c thatched pub in remote conservation village; beamed bar with lots of bookmarks hanging from the ceiling, simple pubby furnishings on flagstones, bare stone walls and a log fire, four well kept west country ales (maybe July beer festival), half a dozen ciders, over 30 wines (including champagne) by the glass and some 65 malt whiskies, very good home-cooked food (not Sun evening), restaurant; darts and board games, free wi-fi; well behaved children and dogs welcome, self-catering cottage, nice surrounding walks, closed Mon. *(Guy Vowles, Barbara Brown, Alan and Alice Morgan, Penny and David Shepherd, John Ledbury)*

KINGSKERSWELL SX8666

★Bickley Mill (01803) 873201

Bickley Road, follow Maddacombe Road from village, under new ring road, W of Kingskerswell; TQ12 5LN Restored 13th-c mill tucked way in lovely countryside; rambling beamed rooms with open fires and rugs on wood floors, variety of seating from rustic chairs and settles to sofas piled with cushions, modern art and black and white photos on stone walls, good well presented food including pub favourites from sensibly priced menu, a couple of Bays ales and 14 wines by the glass, cheerful helpful service; monthly jazz Sun lunchtime, free wi-fi; children and dogs (in bar) welcome, seats on big terrace, also a subtropical hillside garden, well appointed modern bedrooms, good breakfast, open all day. *(Mike and Mary Carter)*

KINGSTON SX6347

Dolphin (01548) 810314

Off B3392 S of Modbury (can also be reached from A379 W of Modbury); TQ7 4QE Peaceful and friendly 16th-c inn with knocked-through beamed rooms; traditional furniture on red carpeting, open fire, woodburner in inglenook fireplace, Otter, St Austell, Sharps and Timothy Taylors, a farm cider, straightforward food; children and dogs welcome, seats in garden, pretty tubs and summer window boxes, quiet village with several tracks leading down to the sea, three bedrooms in building across road, closed some Sun evenings in winter. *(Ian Gilpin)*

KINGSWEAR SX8851

★Ship (01803) 752348

Higher Street; TQ6 0AG Attractive old beamed local by church; well kept Otter, St Austell, Sharps and guests from horseshoe bar, Addlestone's cider and decent wines, popular food including local fish (good river views from restaurant up steps), nautical bric-a-brac and local photographs, two log fires; occasional live music, sports TV; children and dogs welcome, a couple of river-view tables outside, open all day in summer. *(Liz and Mike Newton)*

LAKE SX5288

Bearslake (01837) 861334

A386 just S of Sourton; EX20 4HQ New owners for this rambling thatch and stone pub (former longhouse dating from the 13th c); leather sofas on crazy-paved slate floor at one end, other beamed rooms with stripped stone walls, woodburners, toby jugs, farm tools and traps, ales such as Otter and Teignworthy, decent wines and enjoyable food from separate bar and restaurant menus; quiz nights; children welcome, large sheltered streamside garden, Dartmoor walks, six comfortable bedrooms, closed Sun evening, otherwise open all day. *(Timothy)*

LANDSCOVE SX7766

Live & Let Live (01803) 762663

SE end of village by Methodist chapel; TQ13 7LZ Friendly open-plan village local refurbished under new owners; good food and well kept ales such as Bays and Dartmoor, beams, exposed stonework and log fire; children and dogs welcome, tables on small front terrace and in little orchard across lane, good walks, closed Mon (and maybe Sun evening in winter). *(Ian Gilpin)*

LIFTON SX3885

★Arundell Arms (01566) 784666

Fore Street; PL16 0AA Good imaginative food in substantial country-house fishing hotel including set lunch, warmly welcoming and individual, with professional service, good choice of wines by the glass, morning coffee and afternoon tea; also adjacent Courthouse bar, complete with original cells, serving good fairly priced pubby food (not Sun evening, Mon) including children's meals, well kept Dartmoor Jail Ale and St Austell Tribute, darts and some live music; 25 bedrooms, useful A30 stop. *(Daphne and Barry Gregson)*

LOWER ASHTON SX8484

Manor Inn (01647) 252304

Ashton signposted off B3193 N of Chudleigh; EX6 7QL Friendly well run country pub with good quality sensibly priced food including lunchtime set menu, well kept ales such as Dartmoor, Otter and St Austell, good choice of wines, Sun afternoon cream teas, open fires in both bars, back restaurant in converted smithy; children and dogs welcome, disabled access, garden picnic-sets with nice rural outlook, open all day Sun, closed Mon. *(Jerry Russell)*

LUPPITT ST1606

★Luppitt Inn (01404) 891613

Back roads N of Honiton; EX14 4RT Unspoilt basic farmhouse pub tucked away in lovely countryside, an amazing survivor, with chatty long-serving landlady; tiny room with corner bar and a table, another not much bigger with fireplace, cheap Otter tapped from the cask, intriguing metal puzzles made by a neighbour, no food or music, lavatories across the yard; closed lunchtimes and all day Sun. *(Abigail Slater)*

LUSTLEIGH SX7881

★Cleave (01647) 277223

Off A382 Bovey Tracey–Moretonhampstead; TQ13 9TJ Busy thatched pub in lovely Dartmoor National Park village; low-ceilinged beamed bar with granite walls and log fire, attractive antique high-backed settles, cushioned wall seats and wheelbacks on red patterned carpet, Dartmoor, Otter and a guest, good variety of enjoyable home-cooked food, efficient friendly service, back room (formerly the old station waiting room) converted to light

We include some hotels with a good bar that offers facilities comparable to those of a pub.

airy bistro with pale wooden furniture on wood-strip floor, doors to outside eating area; children and dogs (in bar) welcome, more seats in sheltered garden, good circular walks, shuts around 7.30pm Sun, otherwise open (and food) all day, but best to check no functions planned. *(George and Alison Bishop)*

LUTON SX9076

★**Elizabethan** (01626) 775425
Haldon Moor; TQ13 0BL Popular tucked-away low-beamed dining pub (once owned by Elizabeth I, but much altered); wide choice of good well presented food including daily specials, three well kept ales and several reasonably priced wines by the glass, friendly attentive service; children welcome, pretty front garden, open all day Sun. *(Moira and Jon Weller)*

LYDFORD SX5184

★**Castle Inn** (01822) 820241
Off A386 Okehampton–Tavistock; EX20 4BH Pink-painted Tudor inn next to the castle and church, traditional twin bars with big slate flagstones, bowed low beams and granite walls, high-backed settles and four inglenook log fires, notable stained-glass door and plenty of bits and pieces to look at, hearty helpings of popular well priced food, St Austell ales and good wine selection, friendly helpful service, restaurant; free wi-fi; children and dogs welcome in certain areas, wheelchair access, seats out at front and in sheltered back garden, lovely NT river gorge nearby, eight bedrooms, open all day. *(Chris and Angela Buckell)*

LYDFORD SX5285

Dartmoor Inn (01822) 820221
Downton, A386; EX20 4AY Gently civilised inn, more restaurant-with-rooms and at its most informal at lunchtime with walkers from Dartmoor National Park; cheerful small bar with log fire, Otter Ale, St Austell Tribute and nice wines by the glass, good interesting food in several linked dining rooms with stylish contemporary décor; children and dogs (in bar) welcome, three well equipped pretty bedrooms (each with its own sitting area), closed evenings Sun and Mon; for sale as we went to press. *(Beverley and Andy Butcher, Sally and Lance Oldham, Holly and Tim Waite)*

LYMPSTONE SX9984

Redwing (01395) 222156
Church Road; EX8 5JT Modernised dining pub not far from the church; comfortable seating on oak or black slate floors, well kept local beers such as Hanlons and St Austell, wide range of wines by the glass and good freshly made food from ciabattas and pub favourites up, friendly attentive service, converted loft restaurant; children and dogs (in bar) welcome, terrace tables, attractive unspoilt village. *(Giles and Annie Francis, Peter L Harrison)*

LYMPSTONE SX9884

Swan (01395) 272644
The Strand, by station entrance; EX8 5ET Old beamed pub with enjoyable home-made food including local fish and bargain weekday set lunch, split-level dining area with big log fire, Hanlons Yellowhammer and four other west country ales, short but well chosen wine list; occasional live music, pool, free wi-fi; children welcome, picnic-sets out at front, popular with cyclists (bike racks provided), shore walks, open all day. *(Melanie and David Lawson)*

LYNMOUTH SS7249

Rising Sun (01598) 753223
Harbourside; EX35 6EG Nice old pub in wonderful position overlooking harbour; beamed and stripped-stone bar bustling with locals and tourists, good fire, three Exmoor ales and a guest, popular food from comprehensive menu (emphasis on fish), upmarket hotel side with attractive restaurant; background music; well behaved children (till 7.30pm) and dogs welcome, gardens behind, bedrooms in cottagey old thatched building, parking expensive during the day and sparse at night, open all day. *(Sean Wilson)*

LYNTON SS7248

Beggars Roost (01598) 753645
Manor Hotel; EX35 6LD
Stone-built country pub with friendly relaxed atmosphere; enjoyable freshly made food and well kept ales including Exmoor and a house beer brewed by Marstons, helpful cheerful staff; children and dogs welcome, good bedrooms in hotel side, also camping next door, open all day. *(Paul Walker)*

LYNTON SS6548

Hunters (01598) 763230
Pub well signed off A39 W of Lynton; EX31 4PY Large Edwardian country inn set in four-acre grounds (roaming peacocks), superb Heddon Valley position by NT information centre down very steep hill, great walks including to the sea; two bars one with woodburner, up to six ales including Exmoor and Heddon Valley (brewed for them locally), good range of other drinks and enjoyable well priced food from fairly pubby menu, efficient friendly service, dining room overlooking back garden; quiz and music nights, pool, board games, free wi-fi; children and dogs welcome, ten bedrooms, open all day. *(Timothy)*

MAIDENCOMBE SX9268

Thatched Tavern (01803) 329155
Steep Hill; TQ1 4TS Extended three-level thatched and beamed pub in attractive little village above small beach; traditional bar and airy back eating area, woodburners, Badger ales and several wines by the glass, good choice of well liked home-made food from

sandwiches to blackboard specials, friendly efficient service; children and dogs welcome, pretty garden with picnic-sets and fun nooks and crannies, good coastal walks, two bedrooms, open all day (till 6pm Sun). *(Lewis Canning)*

MARLDON SX8663

★**Church House** (01803) 558279
Off A380 NW of Paignton; TQ3 1SL Pleasant village pub dating from the 15th c; spreading bar with woodburner, unusual windows and some beams, dark pine and other dining chairs around solid tables, four real ales such as Dartmoor and Teignworthy, local cider, 16 wines by the glass and ten malt whiskies, other rooms including two restaurants (one in old barn), interesting much liked food, good service; background music, board games, free wi-fi; children and dogs (in bar) welcome, picnic-sets on three carefully maintained grassy terraces behind. *(Jane and Philip Saunders, Louise and Oliver Redman, Ben and Jenny Settle, Mike and Mary Carter)*

MARSH ST2510

Flintlock (01460) 234403
Pub signed just off A303 Ilminster–Honiton; EX14 9AJ Comfortable neatly maintained dining pub popular for its good value blackboard food including Sun lunches, well kept Butcombe and Otter, decent choice of wines, friendly accommodating service, woodburner in stone inglenook, beams and mainly stripped stone walls, copper and brass; background music, free wi-fi; children welcome, dogs in garden only, closed Mon. *(Mike and Mary Carter)*

MEAVY SX5467

★**Royal Oak** (01822) 852944
Off B3212 E of Yelverton; PL20 6PJ Partly 15th-c pub taking its name from the 800-year-old oak on green opposite; heavy beamed L-shaped bar with pews, red plush banquettes, old agricultural prints and church pictures, smaller locals' bar with flagstones and big open-hearth fireplace, separate dining room, good reasonably priced food served by friendly staff, four well kept ales including Dartmoor, farm ciders, a dozen wines by the glass and several malt whiskies; background music, board games; children and dogs (in bar) welcome, picnic-sets out in front and on the green, pretty Dartmoor-edge village, open all day. *(Gerry and Pam Pollard)*

MEETH SS5408

★**Bull & Dragon** (01837) 811742
A386 Hatherleigh–Torrington; EX20 3EP Welcoming 15th-c beamed and thatched village pub with large open bar, inglenook woodburner, well kept ales such as Exmoor and Otter, good reasonably priced home-made food from shortish menu plus some blackboard specials (booking advised), charming helpful staff; children and dogs welcome, at end of Tarka Trail cycle route, closed Sun evening and Weds. *(Jamie and Sue May)*

MOLLAND SS8028

London (01769) 550269
Village signed off B3227 E of South Molton; EX36 3NG Proper Exmoor inn at its busiest in the shooting season; two small linked rooms by old-fashioned central servery, local stag-hunting pictures, cushioned benches and plain chairs around rough stripped trestle tables, Exmoor Ale, attractive beamed room on left with famous stag story on the wall, panelled dining room on right with big curved settle by fireplace (good hunting and gamebird prints), enjoyable home-made food using fresh local produce including seasonal game (not Sun evening, no credit cards), small hall with stuffed animals; fine Victorian lavatories; children and dogs welcome, picnic-sets in cottagey garden, untouched early 18th-c box pews in church next door, two bedrooms, closed Mon lunchtime. *(Glen and Patricia Fuller)*

MONKLEIGH SS4520

Bell (01805) 938285
A388; EX39 5JS Welcoming thatched and beamed 17th-c village pub with carpeted bar and small restaurant; well kept Dartmoor and a couple of guests, enjoyable reasonably priced food including daily specials, themed evenings and Sun carvery, friendly staff; background music, quiz nights, darts; children (till 9pm) and dogs (treats for good ones) welcome, wheelchair access, garden with raised deck, views and good walks, closed Mon. *(Richard and Tessa Ibbot)*

MORCHARD BISHOP SS7607

London Inn (01363) 877222
Signed off A377 Crediton–Barnstaple; EX17 6NW Prettily placed 16th-c village coaching inn run by mother and daughter team, thriving local atmosphere, good generous home-made food (best to book weekends), Fullers London Pride and a local guest, helpful friendly service, low-beamed open-plan carpeted bar with woodburner in large fireplace, small dining room; pool, darts and skittles; children and dogs welcome, closed Mon lunchtime. *(Sophie and James Collier)*

MORELEIGH SX7652

New Inn (01548) 821326
B3207, off A381 Kingsbridge–Totnes in Stanborough; TQ9 7JH Cosy old-fashioned

We say if we know a pub allows dogs.

country local with friendly landlady (same family has run it for several decades); large helpings of enjoyable home-made food at reasonable prices including good steaks, Timothy Taylors Landlord tapped from the cask and a weekend guest, character old furniture, nice pictures and good inglenook log fire; only open from 6.30pm (12-2.30, 7-10.30 Sun). *(Abigail Slater)*

MORETONHAMPSTEAD SX7586

Horse (01647) 440242
George Street; TQ13 8NF Interesting place where there's always something going on from live bands to art shows; bar with leather chesterfields and deep armchairs by woodburner, all sorts of wooden chairs, settles and tables on carpet or bare boards, rustic tools, horse tack and military/hunting prints on the walls, a dresser with home-made cakes and local produce for sale, Dartmoor Legend, Otter Amber and a guest, two real ciders, a dozen wines by the glass and ten malt whiskies, excellent food cooked by landlord (pizzas only Sun evening), good friendly service, barn-like back dining room; free wi-fi; children and dogs (in bar) welcome, metal tables and chairs in sheltered inner courtyard, closed Mon lunchtime. *(Graham and Carol Parker, Caroline and Peter Bryant, Margo and Derek Peters)*

NEWTON ABBOT SX8671

Olde Cider Bar (01626) 354221
East Street; TQ12 2LD Basic old-fashioned cider house with plenty of atmosphere; around 30 interesting reasonably priced ciders (some very strong), a couple of perries, more in bottles, good country wines from the cask too, baguettes, pasties etc, friendly staff, stools made from cask staves, barrel seats and wall benches, flagstones and bare boards; regular live folk music, small back games room with bar billiards; dogs welcome, terrace tables, open all day. *(Gerry and Pam Pollard)*

NEWTON ABBOT SX8468

Two Mile Oak (01803) 812411
A381 2 miles S, at Denbury/Kingskerswell crossroads; TQ12 6DF Appealing two-bar beamed coaching inn; black panelling, traditional furnishings and candlelit alcoves, inglenook and woodburners, well kept Bass, Dartmoor and Otter tapped from the cask, nine wines by the glass, enjoyable well priced pubby food from sandwiches and baked potatoes up (special diets catered for), decent coffee, cheerful staff; background music; quiz last Tues of month; children and dogs welcome, round picnic-sets on terrace and lawn, open all day. *(Gerry and Pam Pollard)*

NEWTON FERRERS SX5447

Dolphin (01752) 872007
Riverside Road East: Newton Hill off Church Park (B3186) then left; PL8 1AE Shuttered 18th-c pub in attractive setting; L-shaped bar with a few low black beams, pews and benches on slate floors and some white plank panelling, open fire, up to four well kept ales including St Austell, decent wines by the glass and good helpings of enjoyable traditional food, friendly staff; children and dogs (in bar) welcome, terraces over lane looking down on River Yealm and yachts, open all day in summer when can get packed, parking limited. *(Sean Wilson)*

NEWTON ST CYRES SX8798

Beer Engine (01392) 851282
Off A377 towards Thorverton; EX5 5AX Former 19th-c railway hotel brewing its own beers since the 1980s; good home-made food including specials and popular Sun lunch, log fire in bar; children welcome, seats on decked verandah, steps down to garden, open all day, food all day Sun. *(Roger and Donna Huggins)*

NEWTON TRACEY SS5226

Hunters (01271) 858339
B3232 Barnstaple–Torrington; EX31 3PL Extended 15th-c pub with massive low beams and two inglenooks, popular reasonably priced food from pub standards up including choices for smaller appetites, well kept St Austell Tribute and Sharps Doom Bar, decent wines, friendly service, skittle alley/overflow dining area; soft background music; children and dogs welcome, disabled access using ramp, tables on small terrace behind, open all day weekends. *(Jerry Russell)*

NOMANSLAND SS8313

Mount Pleasant (01884) 860271
B3137 Tiverton–South Molton; EX16 8NN Informal country local with good mix of customers; huge fireplaces in long low-beamed main bar, happy mismatch of simple well worn furniture, candles on tables, country pictures, well kept ales such as Cotleigh, Exmoor and Sharps, several wines by the glass, Weston's cider, good range of enjoyable freshly cooked food (special diets catered for), friendly attentive service, cosy dining room in former smithy with original forge, darts in public bar; background music; well behaved children and dogs welcome, back garden with play area, open (and food) all day. *(Gordon and Patricia Gorringe)*

NOSS MAYO SX5447

★**Ship** (01752) 872387
Off A379 via B3186, E of Plymouth; PL8 1EW Charming setting overlooking inlet and visiting boats (can get crowded in good weather); thick-walled bars with bare boards and log fires, four well kept local ales such as Summerskills, good choice of wines and malt whiskies, popular food from varied menu, friendly efficient service, lots of local pictures and charts, books, newspapers and board games, restaurant upstairs; children

and dogs (downstairs) welcome, plenty of seats on heated waterside terrace, parking restricted at high tide, open (and food) all day. *(Chris Pelham)*

OKEHAMPTON SX5895

Fountain (01837) 53532

Fore Street (just off A30); EX20 1AP Well run and welcoming former coaching inn, good food from snacks to daily specials, Sun carvery, three or four well kept ales including Dartmoor, cocktails (happy hour Fri from 6.30pm), two bars and a restaurant; skittle alley; children and dogs welcome, seats out on recently added deck, six bedrooms, open all day. *(Jamie and Sue May)*

OTTERTON SY0885

Kings Arms (01395) 568416

Fore Street; EX9 7HB Big modernised village pub handy for families from extensive nearby caravan park; popular food from sandwiches and sharing plates through pub favourites to good fresh fish, Sun carvery, up to six well kept ales including Otter, decent wines, friendly helpful staff; quiz first Weds of the month, some live music, darts, free wi-fi; dogs very welcome (menu for them), attractive back garden with play area, also a covered terrace, 15 bedrooms (two with four-posters), open all day. *(Dr A J and Mrs B A Tompsett, PL, Peter and Anne Hollindale)*

OTTERY ST MARY SY0995

Volunteer (01404) 814060

Broad Street; EX11 1BZ Welcoming early 19th-c pub; traditional front bar with darts and open fire, more contemporary restaurant behind, four real ales tapped from the cask including Otter, good reasonably priced home-made food (not Sun evening), friendly service; upstairs loos; open all day. *(Joe and Belinda Smart)*

PARRACOMBE SS6644

★**Fox & Goose** (01598) 763239

Off A39 Blackmoor Gate–Lynton; EX31 4PE Popular rambling Victorian pub, hunting and farming memorabilia and interesting old photographs, well kept Cotleigh, Bath and a guest, Winkleigh's cider and several wines by the glass, good variety of well cooked generously served food from blackboard menus including local fish and game, also takeaway pizzas, friendly helpful staff, log fire, separate dining room; children and dogs welcome, wheelchair access with help, small front verandah, riverside terrace and garden room, four bedrooms, open all day in summer. *(Roy and Gill Payne, Chris and Angela Buckell)*

PAYHEMBURY ST0801

Six Bells (01404) 841261

Village signed from A373; leave A30 at Honiton; EX14 3HR Welcoming 17th-c village local under new licensees; good range of well kept beers such as Dartmoor and Otter, generous helpings of reasonably priced home-made food from sandwiches to specials, friendly helpful service, restaurant; skittle alley, pool; children and dogs welcome, open all day Fri-Sun, closed Mon lunchtime, no food Sun evening, Mon. *(Colin Bateman)*

PETER TAVY SX5177

★**Peter Tavy Inn** (01822) 810348

Off A386 near Mary Tavy, N of Tavistock; PL19 9NN Old stone village inn tucked away at end of small lane; bustling low-beamed bar with high-backed settles on black flagstones, mullioned windows, good log fire in big stone fireplace, snug dining area with carved wooden chairs, hops on beams and various pictures, up to five well kept west country ales, Winkleigh's cider and good wine/whisky choice, well liked food from varied menu including OAP lunch (not Sun) and early evening deal, friendly attentive service, separate restaurant; children, walkers and dogs welcome, picnic-sets in pretty garden, peaceful moorland views, open all day weekends. *(Phil and Jane Villiers, Helen and Brian Edgeley)*

PLYMOUTH SX4953

Bridge (01752) 403888

Shaw Way, Mount Batten; PL9 9XH Modern two-storey bar-restaurant with terrace and balcony overlooking busy Yacht Haven Marina; enjoyable food from sandwiches and pub favourites up, St Austell Tribute, Sharps Doom Bar and nice range of wines by the glass, impressive fish tank upstairs; children welcome, well behaved dogs downstairs, open all day from 9am for breakfast. *(Jerry Russell)*

PLYMOUTH SX4854

Dolphin (01752) 660876

Barbican; PL1 2LS Unpretentious drinkers' pub with buoyant chatty atmosphere, good range of well kept cask-tapped ales including Bass and St Austell, open fire, Beryl Cook paintings (even one of the friendly landlord), no food but can bring your own; dogs welcome, open all day. *(Gavin and Helle May)*

PLYMOUTH SX4755

Fortescue (01752) 660673

Mutley Plain; PL4 6JQ Traditional Victorian corner local with nine well kept mostly changing ales and good range of traditional ciders, no food apart from Sun lunch, cellar bar/function room; Sun quiz, TV, fruit machine; dogs welcome, seats on raised back terrace, open all day. *(Natasha Rodriguez)*

PLYMOUTH SX4854

Ship (01752) 667604

Quay Road, Barbican; PL1 2JZ Waterside corner pub with opened-up bare-boards interior; St Austell ales and quite a choice of enjoyable food, harbour views from upstairs restaurant, friendly attentive service; children and dogs (in bar) welcome, full wheelchair access, seats outside under umbrellas, open all day. *(Jerry Russell)*

PLYMPTON SX5455

Brook (01752) 297604

Longbrook Street; PL7 1ND Popular community pub with enjoyable sensibly priced home-made food and well kept local beers, good friendly service, separate coffee lounge; regular live music and other events, pool; children (till 9pm) and dogs welcome, garden picnic-sets, open all day till 9.30pm (10.30pm weekends), bar snacks only Sun evening. *(David Gibson, John Evans)*

PLYMTREE ST0502

Blacksmiths Arms (01884) 277474

Near church; EX15 2JU Well run, friendly 19th-c beamed and carpeted village pub with good reasonably priced food cooked by landlord, three well kept changing local ales and decent choice of wines by the glass; pool room and skittle alley; children welcome, dogs on leads (their leonberger is called Jagermeister), garden with boules and play area, open all day Sat, till 4pm Sun, closed Mon, lunchtimes Tues-Fri. *(Colin Bateman)*

PUSEHILL SS4228

Pig on the Hill (01237) 459222

Off B3226 near Westward Ho!; EX39 5AH Extensively revamped restauranty pub (originally a cowshed); good choice of highly enjoyable, well presented food (must book ahead), friendly helpful service, Country Life and local guests, games room with skittle alley; background music; children and dogs (in bar) welcome, disabled facilities, good views from terrace tables and picnic-sets on grass, play area, boules, three self-catering cabins, open all day. *(Joe and Belinda Smart)*

RINGMORE SX6545

Journeys End (01548) 810205

Signed off B3392 at Pickwick Inn, St Anns Chapel, near Bigbury; best to park opposite church; TQ7 4HL Ancient village inn (dates from the 13th c) with friendly chatty licensees; character panelled lounge and other linked rooms, Sharps Doom Bar and local guests tapped from the cask, farm cider, seven wines by the glass, well executed/presented food including some thai dishes from good shortish menu (not Sun evening, best to book in summer), log fires, family dining conservatory with board games; dogs welcome throughout, garden with picnic-sets on gravel, old-fashioned street lights and decked area, attractive setting near thatched cottages and not far from the sea, open all day weekends, closed Mon. *(Moira and Jon Weller)*

ROBOROUGH SS5717

New Inn (01805) 603247

Off B3217 N of Winkleigh; EX19 8SY Tucked-away 16th-c thatched village pub, cheerful and busy, with well kept local ales, great range of ciders, several wines by the glass and 40 gins, enjoyable fairly priced food from varied menu including takeaway pizzas, beamed bar with woodburner, tiny back room leading up to restaurant, friendly helpful staff; children and dogs welcome, seats on sunny front terrace, open all day Fri-Sun, closed lunchtimes Mon, Tues. *(Melánie and David Lawson)*

ROCKBEARE SY0195

★**Jack in the Green** (01404) 822240

Signed from A30 bypass E of Exeter; EX5 2EE Neat welcoming dining pub (most customers here to eat) run well by long-serving owner; flagstoned lounge bar with comfortable sofas, ales such as Butcombe, Otter and Sharps, local cider, a dozen wines by the glass (over 100 by the bottle), first class food from interesting menu including excellent puddings, good friendly service, carpeted dining rooms with old hunting/shooting photographs and high-backed leather chairs around dark tables, big woodburner, also airy restaurant and club-like ante-room with two-way stove; background music; well behaved children welcome, no dogs inside, disabled facilities, plenty of seats in courtyard, open all day Sun, closed 25 Dec-5 Jan, quite handy for M5. *(John Evans)*

SALCOMBE SX7439

Fortescue (01548) 842868

Union Street, end of Fore Street; TQ8 8BZ Linked rooms with painted beams and half-panelling, rugs and pine furniture on quarry tiles, old local photographs and some stuffed fish, woodburners, decent pubby food and well kept ales such as Otter, Salcombe and Sharps, public bar with parquet floor, booth seating, games, TVs and machines; children welcome, courtyard picnic-sets, three bedrooms, open (and food) all day. *(Richard and Tessa Ibbot)*

SALCOMBE SX7439

★**Victoria** (01548) 842604

Fore Street; TQ8 8BU Bustling town centre pub with traditionally furnished beamed bar, huge flagstones and open fire in big stone fireplace, two well kept St Austell ales, a beer named for the pub and a guest, several wines including champagne by the glass, a prosecco menu and around 25 gins, enjoyable food from good crab sandwiches up, other dining/drinking areas have stripped floorboards and nautical décor, more room upstairs; free wi-fi; children and dogs (in bar) welcome, pretty summer window boxes and large tiered back garden with play area, chickens and budgies, quirky but comfortable Hobbit House bedrooms, no breakfasts (cafés and restaurants nearby), open (and food) all day. *(Rosie and John Moore, Alice Wright, Roger and Donna Huggins)*

SAMPFORD COURTENAY SS6300

New Inn (01837) 82247
B3072 Crediton–Holsworthy; EX20 2TB Attractive 16th-c thatched pub-restaurant in picturesque village; good interesting food from landlord-chef at fair prices including weekday set lunch, also tasting menus and themed evenings, local ales tapped from the cask, proper cider and good range of wines and gins, relaxed friendly atmosphere with candlelit tables, beams and log fires; quiz last Weds of month; children and dogs (in bar) welcome, garden picnic-sets, closed Mon. *(Jerry Russell)*

SANDY PARK SX7189

Sandy Park Inn (01647) 432114
A382 Whiddon Down–Moretonhampstead; TQ13 8JW Hospitable little 17th-c thatched and beamed inn refurbished under present management; cosy bar with wall settles and open fire, small dining room on left and inner snug, well kept Exeter Avocet, Dartmoor IPA and Otter Bitter, food Sun lunchtime and evenings Mon-Sat; some acoustic live music; children and dogs welcome, nice back garden with country views, bedrooms planned, open all day weekends, otherwise closed till 4pm. *(Sean Wilson)*

SHALDON SX9372

Clifford Arms (01626) 872311
Fore Street; TQ14 0DE Attractive 18th-c open-plan pub on two levels; clean and bright, with good range of blackboard food including Weds-Sat evening set menu, up to four mainly local ales, lots of wines by the glass and cocktails, low beams and stone walls, wood or carpeted floors, log fire; regular live jazz; children over 5 welcome, café-style seating on front terrace, decked area behind with palms, pleasant seaside village, closed Sun and Mon evenings, otherwise open all day. *(Gerry and Pam Pollard)*

SHALDON SX9371

Ness House (01626) 873480
Ness Drive; TQ14 0HP Georgian hotel on Ness headland overlooking Teign estuary and well worth knowing for its position; comfortable nautical-theme bar with mixed furniture on bare boards, log fire, Badger ales and decent wines by the glass, popular food in beamed restaurant or small conservatory, afternoon teas; free wi-fi; children welcome, no dogs, disabled facilities, terrace with lovely views, picnic-sets in back garden, nine bedrooms, open all day. *(Chris Pelham)*

SHEBBEAR SS4309

Devils Stone Inn (01409) 281210
Off A3072 or A388 NE of Holsworthy; EX21 5RU Neatly kept 17th-c beamed village pub reputed to be one of England's most haunted; seats in front of open woodburner, long L-shaped pew and second smaller one, flagstone floors, St Austell Tribute and a couple of local guests, decent wines and enjoyable food in dining room across corridor, plain back games room with pool and darts; children and dogs welcome (they have a rottweiler), picnic-sets on front terrace and in garden behind, next to actual Devil's Stone (turned by villagers on 5 Nov to keep the devil at bay), eight bedrooms (steep stairs to some), open all day Sun, closed Weds lunchtime. *(Sophie and James Collier)*

SHEEPWASH SS4806

Half Moon (01409) 231376
Off A3072 Holsworthy–Hatherleigh at Highampton; EX21 5NE Ancient inn loved by anglers for its 7 miles of River Torridge fishing (salmon, sea and brown trout; simply furnished main bar, lots of beams, log fire in big fireplace, well kept ales such as Otter, St Austell and Sharps, several wines by the glass and tasty food from shortish menu, friendly service, separate extended dining room; children and dogs welcome, 11 bedrooms (four in converted stables), tiny Dartmoor village off the beaten track, open all day. *(Abigail Slater)*

SIDFORD SY1389

★**Blue Ball** (01395) 514062
A3052 just N of Sidmouth; EX10 9QL Handsome thatched pub in same friendly family for over 100 years; central bar with three main areas each with log fire, pale beams, nice mix of wooden dining chairs around circular tables on patterned carpet, prints, horsebrasses and plenty of bric-a-brac, well kept Bass, Otter, St Austell and Sharps, popular bar food, pleasant attentive service, chatty public bar, board games, darts and skittle alley; background music and games machine; children and dogs welcome, flower-filled garden, terrace and smokers' gazebo, coastal walks close by, bedrooms, open all day from 8am for good breakfasts. *(Roger and Donna Huggins)*

SIDMOUTH ST1287

Anchor (01395) 514129
Old Fore Street; EX10 8LP Welcoming family-run pub popular for its fresh fish and other good value food, well kept Caledonian ales including one named for them, decent choice of wines, good friendly service, large carpeted L-shaped room with nautical pictures and aquarium, steps down to restaurant; darts; tables out in front, more in back beer garden with stage for live acts, open (and food) all day. *(Roger and Donna Huggins)*

SIDMOUTH SY1090

Bowd (01395) 513328
Junction B3176/A3052; EX10 0ND Popular thatched and beamed dining pub with enjoyable sensibly priced food (all day Sun) including daily carvery, a couple of

Otter ales and Sharps Doom Bar, friendly helpful staff, spacious flagstoned interior with standing timbers and alcoves; children welcome, plenty of seats in big garden, play area, open all day. *(Roger and Donna Huggins)*

SIDMOUTH SY1287

Dukes (01395) 513320

Esplanade; EX10 8AR More brasserie than pub, but long bar on left serves Branscombe Vale and a couple of guests, good food all day specialising in local fish (best to book in the evening), friendly efficient young staff, linked areas including conservatory and flagstoned eating area (once a chapel), smart contemporary décor; big-screen TV, daily papers; children welcome, disabled facilities, prom-view terrace tables, bedrooms in adjoining Elizabeth Hotel, open all day (may be summer queues). *(Roger and Donna Huggins)*

SIDMOUTH SY1287

★**Swan** (01395) 512849

York Street; EX10 8BY Cheerful old-fashioned town-centre local, well kept Youngs ales and enjoyable good value blackboard food from sandwiches up, friendly helpful staff, lounge bar with interesting pictures and memorabilia, darts and woodburner in bigger light and airy public bar with boarded walls and ceilings, daily newspapers, separate carpeted dining area; no under-14s, dogs welcome (maybe treats for them), flower-filled garden with smokers' area, open all day. *(Roger and Donna Huggins)*

SILVERTON SS9503

Lamb (01392) 860272

Fore Street; EX5 4HZ Flagstoned local run well by friendly landlord; Exe Valley, Otter and a local guest tapped from stillage casks, inexpensive home-made pubby food including specials, separate eating area; quiz nights and other events, skittle alley, free wi-fi; children and dogs welcome, handy for Killerton (NT), open all day weekends. *(Chris Pelham)*

SLAPTON SX8245

Queens Arms (01548) 580800

Junction Sands Road and Prospect Hill; TQ7 2PN Smartly kept one-room village local with friendly staff and regulars, good value well balanced menu cooked by landlord, four real ales including Dartmoor and Otter, snug comfortable corners, roaring log fire, fascinating World War II photos and scrapbooks; children and dogs welcome, lots of tables in lovely suntrap stepped garden, parking can be tricky at weekends. *(Nick and Meriel Cox)*

SLAPTON SX8245

★**Tower** (01548) 580216

Church Road off Prospect Hill; TQ7 2PN Close to some fine beaches and backed by Slapton Ley nature reserve, this old inn has a low-beamed bar with settles, armchairs and scrubbed oak tables on flagstones or bare boards, log fires, three or four well kept west country ales including one badged for them from St Austell, local cider and decent wines by the glass, good interesting food cooked by french chef from lunchtime sandwiches up, friendly accommodating service; free wi-fi; children and dogs (in bar) welcome, wheelchair access to dining area (but not to lavatories), picnic-sets in pretty back garden overlooked by ivy-covered ruins of 14th-c chantry, comfortable bedrooms reached by external stone staircase, good breakfast, lane up to the pub is very narrow and parking can be tricky particularly at peak times, closed Sun evening and first two weeks of Jan. *(Simon King, B and F A Hannam)*

SOURTON SX5390

★**Highwayman** (01837) 861243

A386, S of junction with A30; EX20 4HN Unique place – a quirky fantasy of dimly lit stonework and flagstone-floored burrows and alcoves, all sorts of things to look at, one room a make-believe galleon; a couple of well kept local ales, proper cider and maybe organic wines, lunchtime sandwiches, home-made pasties and platters (evening food mainly for residents), friendly chatty service; nostalgic background music, open mike nights, poetry evenings; children allowed in certain areas, outside fairy-tale pumpkin house and an old-lady-who-lived-in-a-shoe, period bedrooms with four-posters and half-testers. *(Joe and Belinda Smart)*

SOUTH TAWTON SX6594

Seven Stars (01837) 840868

Off A30 at Whiddon Down or Okehampton, then signed from Sticklepath; EX20 2LW Recently refurbished 19th-c stone-built local in attractive village, friendly and welcoming, with good food in bar and restaurant, three well kept west country ales, log fire; children and dogs (theirs is Winnie) welcome, good walks (on the Tarka Trail), closed Mon lunchtime, otherwise open all day, best to check winter hours. *(Timothy)*

SPARKWELL SX5857

★**Treby Arms** (01752) 837363

Off A38 at Smithaleigh, W of Ivybridge, Sparkwell signed from village; PL7 5DD Stylishly presented innovative food (at a price) in this 17th-c village dining pub; little bar area with simple tables and chairs, woodburner in stone fireplace, St Austell Proper Job and Tribute, good wines by the glass and some 20 malt whiskies, another woodburner in dining room to the right with wheelback and captain's chairs around rustic tables, upstairs restaurant; children and dogs (in bar) welcome, sunny front terrace, open all day Fri-Sun, closed Mon, Tues. *(Buster and Helena Hastings, Charles Todd)*

STICKLEPATH SX6494

★**Devonshire** (01837) 840626

Off A30 at Whiddon Down or Okehampton; EX20 2NW Welcoming old-fashioned 16th-c thatched village local next to Finch Foundry museum (NT); low-beamed slate-floor bar with big log fire, longcase clock and easy-going old furnishings, stuffed animal heads, key collection, sofa in small snug, well kept low-priced ales tapped from the cask, farm cider, good value sandwiches, soup and home-made pasties from the Aga, games room, lively folk night first Sun of month; £1 fine for using mobile phone; dogs welcome), wheelchair access from car park, good walks, bedrooms, open all day Fri, Sat, closed Sun evening. *(Camille and Jose Ferrera)*

STOKE FLEMING SX8648

Green Dragon (01803) 770238

Church Street; TQ6 0PX Popular village local under friendly new management; beamed and flagstoned interior with open fire, well kept ales such as Otter and St Austell, nice wines by the glass and enjoyable home-made food; children welcome, tables out on partly covered terrace, lovely garden with play area, handy for coast path. *(Chris Pelham)*

STOKE GABRIEL SX8457

Church House (01803) 782384

Off A385 just W of junction with A3022; Church Walk; TQ9 6SD Popular and welcoming early 14th-c pub; lounge bar with fine medieval beam-and-plank ceiling, black oak partition wall, window seats cut into thick butter-coloured walls, woodburner in huge fireplace, look out for the ancient mummified cat, well kept Bass, Sharps Doom Bar and a guest, enjoyable good value food, also little locals' bar; background music, Sun quiz; well behaved children and dogs welcome, picnic-sets on small front terrace, old stocks (pub used to incorporate village courthouse), limited parking, open all day. *(Glen and Patricia Fuller)*

STOKENHAM SX8042

Church House (01548) 580253

N of A379 towards Torcross; TQ7 2SZ Extended old pub now under same owners as the Cricket at Beesands; three open-plan areas with low beams and flagstones, Otter ales and a guest, well liked food including Josper grills and good value weekday set menu, dining conservatory; live music Tues; children and dogs (in bar) welcome, picnic-sets on lawn with play area, village green behind, interesting church next door. *(Richard and Tessa Ibbot)*

STOKENHAM SX8042

Tradesmans Arms (01548) 580996

Just off A379 Dartmouth–Kingsbridge; TQ7 2SZ Picturesque partly thatched 14th-c pub; traditional low-beamed cottagey interior with log fire, well kept west country beers and decent wine list (usually one from Devon), good locally sourced food from lunchtime sandwiches to blackboard specials (booking advised), friendly attentive service, restaurant; children and dogs welcome, seats over lane on raised area looking down on village green, four nice bedrooms (they also have a self-catering apartment nearby), good breakfast. *(Hazel Hyde)*

TAVISTOCK SX4874

★**Cornish Arms** (01822) 612145

West Street; PL19 8AN Chef-owner's highly rated upscale pub food is a real draw here, can eat in bar or elegant dining room, comfortable seating and real fires, four well kept St Austell ales, good friendly service; daily newspapers, sports TV; children and dogs welcome, tables on split-level terrace, open all day. *(Phil and Jane Villiers, Keith Smith)*

TEIGNMOUTH SX9372

Olde Jolly Sailor (01626) 772864

Set back from Northumberland Place; TQ14 8DE Town's oldest pub (said to date from the 12th c), comfortable low-ceilinged interior with stripped-stone walls, various nooks and crannies, well kept Otter Ale, Sharps Doom Bar and a couple of guests, tasty pub food (all day weekends) including good sandwiches; live jazz Mon, sports TV, free wi-fi; children and dogs welcome, seats in front courtyard, more behind with estuary views, open all day. *(Gordon and Patricia Gorringe)*

THORVERTON SS9202

Thorverton Arms (01392) 860205

Village signed off A396 Exeter–Tiverton; EX5 5NS Spacious former coaching inn with five adjoining areas including log-fire bar and restaurant, uncomplicated well cooked food at affordable prices (good fish and chips), Otter and a couple of other beers, friendly helpful staff; quiz second Wed of month, live music, pool; children and dogs (in bar) welcome, wisteria-draped terrace and sunny garden, pleasant village, six comfortable bedrooms, good breakfast, open all day (till 5pm Sun in winter). *(Chris Hoyer Millar)*

THURLESTONE SX6743

Village Inn (01548) 563525

Part of Thurlestone Hotel; TQ7 3NN Updated 16th-c pub attached to smart family-run hotel; wide choice of well liked food from open sandwiches and other snacks up including good fish and chips, local beers and plenty of wines by the glass, friendly attentive service; background music, quiz Tues, free wi-fi; children and dogs welcome, picnic-sets out at front, handy for coast path, open all day weekends and in high season. *(Helen and Brian Edgeley)*

TOPSHAM SX9688

★ **Bridge Inn** (01392) 873862

2.5 miles from M5 junction 30: Topsham signposted from exit roundabout; in Topsham follow signpost (A376) Exmouth, on the Elmgrove Road, into Bridge Hill; EX3 0QQ Very special old drinkers' pub (former 16th-c maltings painted a distinctive pink), in landlady's family for five generations and quite unchanging and unspoilt; small characterful rooms and snugs, traditional furniture including a nice high-backed settle, woodburner, the 'bar' is landlady's front parlour (as notice on the door politely reminds customers), up to nine well kept ales tapped from the cask, simple food including good ploughman's, friendly staff and locals; live folk and blues, but no background music, mobile phones or credit cards; children and dogs welcome, picnic-sets overlooking weir. *(Chris Pelham)*

TOPSHAM SX9687

★ **Globe** (01392) 873471

Fore Street; 2 miles from M5 junction 30; EX3 0HR Handsome carefully renovated former coaching inn blending original features with up-to-date touches; red-painted panelling in beamed bar hung with old prints, armchairs in a corner and suede tub and pubby chairs around dark tables on bare boards, small brick fireplace, second tartan-carpeted bar has pale panelling, traditional furniture and woodburner, St Austell ales and several wines by the glass, good choice of enjoyable food from breakfast on, another log fire and huge candlesticks in elegant dining room; free wi-fi; children and dogs (in bar) welcome, large terrace with parasol-shaded tables, individually decorated modern bedrooms, open (and food) all day. *(Adrian Johnson, Roger and Donna Huggins, Dr and Mrs A K Clarke)*

TOPSHAM SX9688

Passage House (01392) 873653

Ferry Road, off main street; EX3 0JN Relaxed 18th-c pub just back from the estuary shore; traditional black-beamed bar and slate-floored lower dining area, very good food (booking advised) from ciabattas to local fish, several well kept west country ales, decent wines and some interesting gins, friendly service; Tues quiz night, free wi-fi; children and dogs welcome, picnic-sets on terrace looking over moorings and river to nature reserve beyond (lovely at sunset), open (and food) all day. *(Richard Tilbrook, Roger and Donna Huggins, The Rogue)*

TORBRYAN SX8266

★ **Old Church House** (01803) 812372

Pub signed off A381; TQ12 5UR Character 13th-c former farmhouse with attractive bar (popular with locals), benches built into fine panelling, settle and other seats by big log fire, Hunters, Skinners, St Austell and a guest, proper cider, several wines by the glass and around 35 malt whiskies, good variety of well liked wholesome food from baguettes up, cheerful helpful staff, discreetly lit lounges, one with a splendid deep Tudor inglenook; background and occasional live music; free wi-fi; children and dogs (in bar) welcome, refurbished bedrooms, good breakfast; closed Mon lunchtime, otherwise open all day. *(Nick and Meriel Cox)*

TORCROSS SX8242

Start Bay (01548) 580553

A379 S of Dartmouth; TQ7 2TQ More fish and chip restaurant than pub, but does sell Otter and St Austell, local wine and cider; very much set out for eating and exceptionally busy at peak times, staff cope well and food is generous and sensibly priced; wheelback chairs around dark tables, country pictures, some photographs of storms buffeting the building, winter coal fire, small drinking area by counter, large family room; no dogs during meal times, seats outside (highly prized) looking over pebble beach and wildlife lagoon, open all day. *(Timothy)*

TORQUAY SX9265

★ **Cary Arms** (01803) 327110

Beach Road: off B3199 Babbacombe Road, via Babbacombe Downs Road; turn steeply down near Babbacombe Theatre; TQ1 3LX Charming higgledy-piggledy hotel reached down a tortuously steep lane; small, glass-enclosed entrance room with large ship lanterns and cleats, beamed grotto-effect bar overlooking the sea, rough pink granite walls, alcoves, hobbit-style leather chairs around carved wooden tables, slate or bare-board floors, woodburner, Bays, Hanlons and Otter, two local ciders and nine good wines by the glass, enjoyable if not particularly cheap food; free wi-fi; children and dogs (in bar) welcome, plenty of outside seating on various terraces, outside bar, barbecue and pizza oven, steps down to quay with six mooring spaces, boutique-style bedrooms, self-catering cottages (glorious views) and chic beach huts and shore suites, open all day. *(Roger and Donna Huggins, Dr and Mrs A K Clarke)*

TORQUAY SX9166

Crown & Sceptre (01803) 328290

Petitor Road, St Marychurch; TQ1 4QA Friendly two-bar local (in same family for over 40 years) with eight well kept ales such as Butcombe, Courage, Dartmoor, Hanlons, Harveys and Otter, three proper ciders and basic good value lunchtime food (not Mon, Tues), interesting naval memorabilia and chamber-pot collection; regular live music including jazz Tues, folk Fri; children and dogs welcome, sunny deck and garden. *(Rosie and John Moore)*

TORQUAY SX9163

Hole in the Wall (01803) 200755

Park Lane, opposite clock tower; TQ1 2AU Ancient two-bar local tucked away near harbour; enjoyable reasonably priced pubby food including good fresh fish, seven well kept ales such as St Austell, Butcombe, Otter and Sharps, real cider, good friendly service, smooth cobbled floors, low beams and alcoves, lots of nautical brassware, ship models and old local photographs, restaurant/function room; live music; children and dogs welcome, some seats in alley out at front, open all day and can get very busy at weekends. *(Roger and Donna Huggins, Tony Scott)*

TORRINGTON SS4919

Black Horse (01805) 622121

High Street; EX38 8HN Popular twin-gabled former coaching inn; beams hung with stirrups in smallish bar with solid furniture and woodburner, lounge with striking ancient oak partition wall, back restaurant, five well kept ales including Courage and St Austell, generous helpings of tasty home-made food served by friendly staff; background music, darts and shove-ha'penny; children and dogs welcome, disabled access, three bedrooms, open all day. *(Liz and Mike Newton)*

TOTNES SX8060

Albert (01803) 863214

Bridgetown; TQ9 5AD Unpretentious slate-hung pub near the river, small bar and two other rooms, low beams, flagstones, panelling, some old settles and lots of knick-knacks, friendly landlord brewing his own good Bridgetown ales, real cider and plenty of whiskies, honest reasonably priced pub food, friendly local atmosphere; quiz and music nights, darts, free wi-fi; dogs welcome, paved beer garden behind. *(Ian Gilpin)*

TOTNES SX7960

Bay Horse (01803) 862088

Cistern Street; TQ9 5SP Welcoming traditional two-bar inn dating from the 15th c; half a dozen well kept ales including New Lion, ciders such as Sandford Orchards, simple lunchtime food; background and regular live music including good Sun jazz; children and dogs welcome, nice garden behind, three bedrooms, good breakfast, open all day. *(Ian Gilpin)*

TUCKENHAY SX8156

Maltsters Arms (01803) 732350

Ashprington Road, off A381 from Totnes; TQ9 7EQ Popular old pub (once owned by celebrity chef Keith Floyd) in lovely quiet spot by wooded Bow Creek; good food from bar snacks to fresh fish specials, well kept Bays and three west country guests, local ciders and great range of wines by the glass, friendly service, creek-view restaurant; background and some live music, free wi-fi; children and dogs welcome, waterside terrace with open-air bar, pontoon for visiting boats, six bedrooms (three with river views), open all day, food all day Fri-Sun during summer school holidays. *(Sean Wilson)*

UGBOROUGH SX6755

Ship (01752) 892565

Off A3121 SE of Ivybridge; PL21 0NS Friendly dining pub extended from cosy 16th-c flagstoned core; well divided open-plan eating areas a step down from neat bar with woodburner, popular food from bar meals up including blackboard specials (plenty of fish), well kept Palmers, St Austell and a local guest, nice house wines, cheerful chatty staff; background music; children and dogs (in bar) welcome, tables out in front, shuts Mon afternoon, otherwise open all day. *(Andrew Low)*

WEARE GIFFARD SS4722

Cyder Press (01237) 425517

Tavern Gardens; EX39 4QR Welcoming village local with impressive range of ciders, four real ales including a house beer from Clearwater and some interesting gins, enjoyable fairly priced home-made food Weds-Sat and Sun lunchtime, black beams and timbers, inglenook woodburner; Tues folk night, Fri darts; children (till 8.30pm) and dogs welcome, seats outside, beautiful countryside and handy for Tarka Trail, bedrooms, closed Mon and Tues lunchtimes, otherwise open all day (shuts Weds-Fri afternoons in winter). *(Joe and Belinda Smart)*

WELCOMBE SS2317

Old Smithy (01288) 331305

Signed off A39 S of Hartland; EX39 6HG Cosy thatched and low-beamed country pub; open-plan bar with mix of wooden chairs at scrubbed pine tables, quirky 1960/70s retro decor; fairy lights and open fires, well kept local ales, traditional ciders and popular pubby food, good friendly service, more room upstairs; background and live music including Mon folk night, quiz and pizza Thurs, various games, free wi-fi; children and dogs welcome, lovely garden and setting by narrow lane leading eventually to attractive rocky cove, bunkhouse, closed winter Sun evening and Mon lunchtime. *(Malcolm and Madeline Ashton)*

WEMBURY SX5349

Odd Wheel (01752) 863052

Knighton Road; PL9 0JD Popular modernised village pub with five well kept west country ales and good fairly traditional food from sandwiches/ciabattas up, reasonable prices including set lunch Mon-Fri, friendly helpful service, back restaurant; pool, darts, sports TV, free wi-fi; children and dogs (in bar) welcome, seats out on decking, fenced play area, open (and food) all day weekends. *(Hugh Roberts)*

WEMBWORTHY SS6609

Lymington Arms (01837) 83572

Lama Cross; EX18 7SA Large early 19th-c beamed dining pub in pleasant country setting, wide choice of enjoyable food including some interesting specials, character landlady and friendly staff, well kept Sharps Doom Bar and a west country guest, Winkleigh's farm cider, good wine list, comfortably plush seating and red tablecloths in partly stripped-stone bar, big back restaurant; children and dogs (in bar) welcome, picnic-sets outside, closed Sun evening, Mon and Tues (and may shut early if quiet). *(Chris and Angela Buckell)*

WESTON ST1400

Otter (01404) 42594

Off A373, or A30 at W end of Honiton bypass; EX14 3NZ Big busy family pub with heavy low beams; good choice of enjoyable reasonably priced food (best to book) including smaller appetites menu and two-for-one deals, carvery Thurs and Sun lunchtimes, cheerful helpful staff, well kept Otter ales and a guest, carpeted opened-up interior with good log fire; background music, pool; dogs allowed in one area, disabled access, picnic-sets on big lawn leading to River Otter, open (and food) all day. *(Bob and Margaret Holder)*

WHIMPLE SY0497

New Fountain (01404) 822350

Off A30 Exeter–Honiton; Church Road; EX5 2TA Two-bar beamed village pub with friendly local atmosphere, enjoyable home-made food (not Mon) using local ingredients, well kept Teignworthy and a guest, woodburner; children and well behaved dogs welcome, some outside seating, local heritage centre in car park (open Weds, Sat), pub closes Sun evening, Mon lunchtime. *(Lauren and Dan Frazer)*

WIDECOMBE SX7176

Old Inn (01364) 621207

B3387 W of Bovey Tracey; TQ13 7TA Busy dining pub with spacious beamed interior including side conservatory with large central woodburner, enjoyable fairly standard food at reasonable prices, afternoon cream teas, well kept Badger, Dartmoor and a guest; Weston's cider, good friendly service, free wi-fi; children and dogs (in bar) welcome, nice garden with water features and pleasant terrace, wandering ducks and chickens, great walks from this pretty moorland village, Widecombe Fair second Tues of Sept, open (and food) all day, kitchen closes 5.30pm Sun. *(Dave Statham)*

WONSON SX6789

★**Northmore Arms** (01647) 231428

Between Throwleigh and Gidleigh; EX20 2JA Proper traditional old pub set in beautiful remote walking country; two simple old-fashioned rooms, log fire and woodburner, low beams and stripped stone, well kept ales such as Dartmoor tapped from the cask, farm cider and decent house wines, good reasonably priced food cooked by landlord including popular Sun lunch; walkers and dogs welcome, tables in garden, open all day Sat, till 9pm Sun, closed Mon and lunchtime Tues. *(Chris Pelham)*

WOODBURY SALTERTON SY0189

Diggers Rest (01395) 232375

3.5 miles from M5 junction 30: A3052 towards Sidmouth, village signposted on right about 0.5 miles after Clyst St Mary; also signposted from B3179 SE of Exeter; EX5 1PQ New management as we went to press for this 500-year-old thatched and beamed village pub; main bar with antique furniture and open fire, two Otter ales, a local guest and several wines by the glass, tasty pub food (not Sun evening) including Tues steak night, modern extension opening on to garden; background music (live last Fri of month); children and dogs welcome, ramp provided for wheelchair access, pretty window boxes and flowering baskets, fine walks around Woodbury Common and in surrounding Otter Valley, open all day weekends. *(Glen and Patricia Fuller)*

YEALMPTON SX5851

Rose & Crown (01752) 686175

A379 Kingsbridge–Plymouth; PL8 2EB Central bar counter, all dark wood and heavy brass, leather-seated stools and mix of furnishings on stripped-wood floors, comfy sofa by woodburner, emphasis on popular bar and restaurant food including lunchtime/early evening set menu (not Sun), friendly attentive service, three St Austell ales, a dozen wines by the glass and decent coffee; children and dogs (bar area) welcome, tables in walled garden with pond, also a lawned area, eight well appointed bedrooms in separate building, open (and food) all day. *(Keith Smith)*

LUNDY SS1344

★**Marisco** (01271) 870870

Get there by ferry (Bideford and Ilfracombe) or helicopter (Hartland Point); EX39 2LY One of England's most isolated pubs, yet surprisingly busy most nights; great setting, steep trudge up from landing stage, galleried interior with lifebelts and shipwreck salvage, open fire, two St Austell ales named for the island and its spring water on tap, Weston's cider and reasonably priced house wines, good basic food using Lundy produce, friendly staff, books and games; no mobile phones; children welcome, tables outside, souvenir shop doubling as general store for the island's few residents, open (and food) all day from breakfast on. *(Timothy, Chris Pelham)*

Dorset

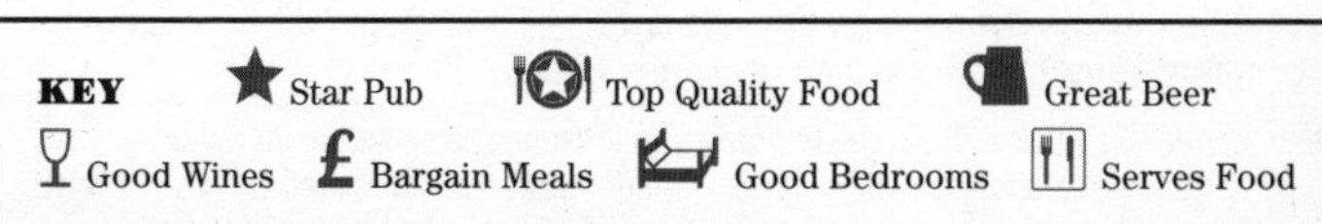

BOURTON

ST7731 Map 2

White Lion

(01747) 840866 – www.whitelionbourton.co.uk

High Street, off old A303 E of Wincanton; SP8 5AT

Stone inn built in 1723, with beamed bar and dining room, pleasing food and ales and seats in the garden; bedrooms

This is a handsome coaching inn with convivial landlords, a traditionally furnished bar and a two-level dining room with nice old wooden chairs around a medley of tables. Throughout there are beams, bare boards, fine flagstones, stripped stone and half-panelling, bow window seats, church candles and a log fire in an inglenook fireplace. Otter Amber and a couple of guest beers such as Keystone Bedrock and Wriggle Valley Copper Hoppa on handpump and several wines by the glass; background music. The back terrace and raised lawn have picnic-sets. Bedrooms are comfortable and breakfasts good. Stourhead (National Trust) is nearby.

Tasty food includes sandwiches, creamy garlic bake, pâté with chutney and toast, burger with pickles, toppings and chips, wild mushroom tortelloni with mushroom sauce, melted goats cheese and garlic doughballs, local venison faggots with mash and rosemary and redcurrant gravy, creamy chicken and chorizo gratin topped with cheddar, pork, mushroom and brandy stroganoff, seafood salad of prawns in marie rose sauce, scottish smoked salmon and large prawns, and puddings. *Benchmark main dish: steak and kidney pie £13.50. Two-course evening meal £19.50.*

Free house ~ Licensees William Smith and Stuart Knowles ~ Real ale ~ Open 12-11 ~ Bar food 12-2 (3 Sat), 6-9; 12-3, 7-9 Sun ~ Restaurant ~ Children welcome ~ Dogs welcome ~ Wi-fi ~ Live music Fri evening; opera every few months ~ Bedrooms: /£80

Recommended by Miranda and Jeff Davidson, David and Charlotte Green, M G Hart

BURTON BRADSTOCK

SY4889 Map 1

Three Horseshoes

(01308) 897259 – www.threehorseshoesburtonbradstock.co.uk

Mill Street; DT6 4QZ

Well placed and thatched village inn just a few minutes from the coast; traditional furnishings, a friendly welcome and popular food and drink

A dutch chef and his wife have taken over this welcoming thatched pub and reports from our readers are warm and enthusiastic. The bar has sofas in bow windows, a nice mix of old dining chairs around wooden tables on floor slates, built-in cushioned wall seats, button-back armchairs by the woodburning stove, some high, mustard-coloured chairs around equally high tables and stools against the stone bar counter. Walls and beams are decorated with bird prints, horsebrasses, mirrors and some farming implements, and there's also a dining room that's similarly furnished. Well kept Palmers Copper, Dorset Gold, IPA, Tally Ho, 200 and seasonal guests on handpump and a dozen wines (including prosecco) by the glass; background music and board games. At the front of the building are some rustic tables and chairs, while the back garden has a terrace and plenty of picnic-sets. Just a few minutes away is a lovely sandy beach.

Cooked by the landlord, the rewarding food from a seasonal menu includes lunchtime sandwiches and baguettes, beef tataki (lightly seared fillet steak with onion ponzu sauce, japanese mayonnaise, pickled beetroot and coriander), baked camembert with cornichon, celery, confit garlic and toasted sourdough, local pork sausages with spring onion mash, braised red cabbage and shallot and ale jus, butternut squash, beetroot and goats cheese tart with pomegranate and pear salad and apple balsamic reduction, indonesian seafood coconut curry, free-range duck breast with beetroot purée, pink fir potatoes and red wine jus, and puddings such as chocolate and peanut butter fondant and caramel ice-cream and crème brûlée. *Benchmark main dish: local lamb rump with sautéed potatoes, braised fennel and mint jus £16.00. Two-course evening meal £22.00.*

Palmers ~ Tenants Jaap and Hannah Schep ~ Real ale ~ Open 12-11 (10 Sun); 12-3, 5-11 weekdays in winter ~ Bar food 12-9; 12-3 Sun; 12-2, 6-9 weekdays in winter ~ Restaurant ~ Children welcome ~ Dogs allowed in bar ~ Wi-fi *Recommended by A W Johns, Nick Buckland, Pete and Sarah, Darrell Barton, Charlotte and William Mason, Gwendoline and Ralph Mason*

CERNE ABBAS ST6601 Map 2

New Inn

(01300) 341274 – www.thenewinncerneabbas.co.uk

Long Street; DT2 7JF

Carefully refurbished former coaching inn with character bar and two dining rooms, friendly licensees, local ales and inventive food; fine bedrooms

As a lovely pub in a chocolate-box pretty village, this place gets a lot of custom from our readers. It was built as a guest house for the nearby Benedictine abbey and there's plenty of history and original features that include mullioned windows, heavy oak beams and a pump and mounting block in the former coachyard. The bar has a solid oak counter, an attractive mix of old dining tables and chairs on slate or polished wooden floors, settles built into various nooks and crannies and a woodburner in the opened-up Yorkstone fireplace. Palmers Copper, Dorset Gold, IPA and 200 on handpump, ten wines by the glass, several malt whiskies and local cider. The dining room is furnished in a similar style; background music. There are seats on the terrace and picnic-sets beneath mature fruit trees or parasols in the back garden. Bedrooms are smart and well equipped and located in either the charming 16th-c main building or a converted stable block. You can walk from the attractive stone-built village to the prehistoric Cerne Abbas Giant chalk carving and on to other villages.

Attractively presented food includes wild boar kofta with spiced apple purée, local mussels with black garlic and cider cream, smoked pulled pork with fennel and poppyseed bap, pickles, fries and apple or barbecue sauce, roast sweet potato with toasted almonds and spiced tabbouleh, cod loin with confit leeks, salt-baked fir potatoes, local mussels and gremolata, and puddings such as baked rhubarb rice pudding with rhubarb compote and rhubarb ice-cream and steamed ale cake with beer ice-cream and muscavado sauce. *Benchmark main dish: barbecue lamb breast with smoked neck, salt-baked root vegetables, crispy kidney and jus £17.00. Two-course evening meal £22.00.*

Palmers ~ Tenant Julian Dove ~ Real ale ~ Open 12-11 (10 Sun) ~ Bar food 12-2.30, 7-9; 12-2.30, 6.30-9 Fri, Sat; 12-3, 7-8.30 Sun ~ Restaurant ~ Children welcome ~ Dogs allowed in bar and bedrooms ~ Wi-fi ~ Occasional live music Sun afternoons in courtyard ~ Bedrooms: £90/£120 *Recommended by S G N Bennett, Mike Kavaney, Richard Cole, Matthew and Elisabeth Reeves, Frances and Hamish Porter, Tracey and Stephen Groves, Christopher Mannings*

CHETNOLE ST6008 Map 2

Chetnole Inn

(01935) 872337 – www.thechetnoleinn.co.uk

Village signed off A37 S of Yeovil; DT9 6NU

Attractive country pub with beams and huge flagstones, real ales, popular food and seats in the back garden; bedrooms

Beside an old church in lovely countryside stands this well run beamed pub. The friendly bar has a relaxed country kitchen feel with wheelback chairs and pine tables on huge flagstones and a woodburning stove. Butcombe Rare Breed, Courage Directors and Wriggle Valley Ryme Nomad on handpump and around ten wines by the glass. Popular with locals, the snug has a leather sofa near another woodburner and stools against the counter; dogs are allowed in here. The airy dining room has more wheelback chairs around pale wooden tables on stripped floorboards and a small open fire. At the back, a delightful garden has picnic-sets and a view over fields. The comfortable bedrooms overlook the church.

Tempting food includes lunchtime sandwiches, ciabattas and platters, duck terrine with pear chutney, thai-spiced fishcakes with lime and chilli dip, southern fried chicken burger with cajun mayonnaise and fries, gypsy eggs (spicy mushrooms and peppers in a tomato sauce topped with quail eggs on toast), a pie of the day, slow-cooked pork belly with black pudding, glazed apple, creamy mash and pork jus, fried fish dish of the day with sautéed leeks and mussels, and puddings such as crème brûlée of the day and warm chocolate and nut brownie with dark chocolate sauce, popping candy and salted caramel ice-cream. *Benchmark main dish: fillet steak cooked at your table on a granite slab with skin-on chips £23.00. Two-course evening meal £19.00.*

Free house ~ Licensees Simon and Maria Hudson ~ Real ale ~ Open 11-3, 6-11; 11-11 Sat; 12-4 Sun ~ Bar food 12-2, 6.30-9; not Sun evening ~ Restaurant ~ Children welcome ~ Dogs allowed in bar ~ Wi-fi ~ Bedrooms: £80/£105 *Recommended by Alan and Linda Blackmore, Martin and Sue Neville, Holly and Tim Waite, Nick and Meriel Cox, Philip J Alderton, Selwyn Jones, Frank and Marcia Pelling*

CHIDEOCK SY4191 Map 1

Anchor

(01297) 489215 – www.theanchorinnseatown.co.uk

Off A35 from Chideock; DT6 6JU

Stunning spot for carefully renovated inn, lots of character, well kept ales and popular food and seats on front terrace; light, airy bedrooms

The splendid position here, just by the beach, is loved by customers in warm weather and the seats and tables on the spacious front terrace are much prized. Inside, plenty of original character has been kept in the three smallish, light rooms: padded wall seating, nice old wooden chairs and stools around scrubbed tables on bare boards, a couple of woodburning stoves (one under a huge bressumer beam), tilley lamps, model ships and lots of historic photographs of the pub, the area and locals. From the wood-panelled bar they serve Palmers Copper, Dorset Gold, IPA and 200 on handpump, seven wines by the glass, 25 gins, over 35 rums and cocktails; background music. The attractive, airy bedrooms overlook the sea and are decorated with nautical touches using driftwood and ropework. The inn nearly straddles the South West Coast Path, so the surrounding walks are lovely. You can park for free in front of the pub or across the road for £4 (refundable against a spend of £20 or more in the pub).

Rewarding food includes filled rolls, gurnard and mackerel tartare with sesame, pink ginger, chilli, soy, dill and capers, pressed lamb terrine with mint pea purée, broad beans and sorrel, chicken breast with chorizo and haricot bean cassoulet, cauliflower macaroni cheese with shredded spring vegetable salad, confit duck leg with sesame-dressed bulgar wheat salad, orange, pak choi and hoisin dressing, and puddings such as rhubarb and custard panacotta with gingerbread crumb and stem ginger ice-cream and white chocolate and cardamom brownie with peanut butter cream. *Benchmark main dish: malt vinegar and sea herb-battered fish and chips £14.00. Two-course evening meal £21.00.*

Palmers ~ Tenant Paul Wiscombe ~ Real ale ~ Open 10am-11pm ~ Bar food 12-9 ~ Children welcome ~ Dogs allowed in bar ~ Wi-fi ~ Bedrooms: £155/£170 *Recommended by A W Johns, Heather and Richard Jones, Nicola and Stuart Parsons, Kerry and Guy Trooper, Lyn and Freddie Roberts, Ian Duncan*

CHURCH KNOWLE SY9381 Map 2

New Inn

(01929) 480357 – www.newinn-churchknowle.co.uk

Village signed off A351 N of Corfe Castle; BH20 5NQ

Cheerful pub with plenty of seating in various rooms, open fires, a thoughtful choice of drinks, good food and a friendly landlord

Dating from the 16th c and partly thatched, this former farmhouse is popular with walkers using the nearby Dorset Coast Path. The linked character bar rooms are full of interest: brass and copper measuring jugs, bed warmers, venerable board games and books, stone jars, china plates, a glass cabinet filled with household items from years ago, tilley lamps, a coastguard flag and an old diver's helmet. The main bar has an open fire in a stone fireplace, high-backed black leather dining chairs and cushioned wall settles around heavy rustic tables on red patterned carpet and quite a few stools against the counter. Butcombe Bitter, Dorset Jurassic, Sharps Doom Bar and a summer guest on handpump, six wines by the glass and farm cider; there's a wineshack from which you can choose your own wines, and also a wide choice of teas, coffees and local soft drinks. The similarly furnished dining room leads off here. There are picnic-sets on the lawn and a campsite. Corfe Castle ruins (National Trust) are close by.

Much liked food from a seasonal menu includes daily fresh fish and shellfish such as mussels, hand-dived scallops, plaice, lemon and dover sole, turbot, brill and cracked crab and lobster; non-fishy choices include a sharing board, twice-baked cheese soufflé, chicken pâté with red onion marmalade, lambs liver and bacon with creamy mash and red onion reduction, steak in ale pie, slow-roasted pork belly on black pudding with apple sauce and jus, and puddings such as crème brûlée with gooseberry and elderflower ice-cream and spotted dick and custard; they also offer takeaway fish and chips and two-pint containers of beer. *Benchmark main dish: a roast of the day £11.00. Two-course evening meal £17.50.*

Punch ~ Tenants Maurice and Matthew Estop ~ Real ale ~ Open 10-3, 6 (5 in summer)-11 (10 in winter); 12-3, 6-10 Sun ~ Bar food 12-2.15, 6-9; 12-3, 5-9.15 Sun in summer ~

Restaurant ~ Children welcome ~ Wi-fi *Recommended by A W Johns, Mike Kavaney, Ian Wilson, Revd Carol Avery, Karl and Frieda Bujeya, Sally and Colin Allen, Charlie and Mark Todd*

CRANBORNE SU0513 Map 2

Inn at Cranborne

(01725) 551249 – www.theinnatcranborne.co.uk

Wimborne Street (B3078 N of Wimborne); BH21 5PP

Neatly refurbished 16th-c inn with a friendly atmosphere, good choice of drinks, highly rated food and seats outside; comfortable bedrooms

This is a nice place to stay in comfortable, well-equipped bedrooms that are clean and bright; the breakfasts are very good too. The main bar area, divided into two by a partition, is a favourite place to sit: grey-planked and tartan-cushioned built-in wall seats and assorted chairs (farmhouse, wheelback, ladder-back) on parquet flooring, flagstones or rugs, candles on each table and a woodburner in an inglenook fireplace. The rambling bars have heavy beams, open doorways, the odd standing timber and a chatty, relaxed atmosphere. Badger Best Bitter and a guest from Badger on handpump, ten wines by the glass, a dozen malt whiskies, 25 gins and local cider (and cider brandy) served by friendly, helpful staff; background music, TV, darts and board games. The dining areas spread back from here, with similar furnishings and a little brick fireplace. There's also a second bar with white-painted or wooden furniture and another woodburning stove; also, plenty of coaching prints on grey walls above a darker grey dado, and church candles. Outside you'll find benches, seats and tables on neat gravel and a lawn. Thomas Hardy was a regular visitor.

The interesting food uses produce from within a 30-mile radius: lunchtime sandwiches, duck terrine with baby artichokes and madeira jelly, local cock crab on toast with tarragon, pasta with cauliflower and manchego, smoked haddock and salmon fishcake with a poached egg and chive butter sauce, braised lamb shoulder with parsley crumbs, white beans in cream and rosemary jus, chicken with peas, broad beans, trompette mushrooms, parisienne potatoes and sauce royale, aged sirloin with triple-cooked chips and peppercorn sauce, and puddings such as lemon posset with raspberry sorbet and chocolate and orange croissant bread and butter pudding with vanilla ice-cream. *Benchmark main dish: pork belly with bubble and squeak and apple sauce £17.95. Two-course evening meal £22.00.*

Free house ~ Licensee Jane Gould ~ Real ale ~ Open 8am (8.30am Sat)-11pm; 8.30am-10pm Sun; closes 10pm Sun-Thurs in winter ~ Bar food 12-2.30, 6-9.30 (9 Sun) ~ Restaurant evenings only ~ Children welcome ~ Dogs welcome ~ Wi-fi ~ Bedrooms: £85/£130 *Recommended by Sophie Ellison, Paddy and Sian O'Leary, Alison and Michael Harper, Mr and Mrs P R Thomas, David and Judy Robison, Barbara and Phil Bowie*

EVERSHOT ST5704 Map 2

Acorn

(01935) 83228 – www.acorn-inn.co.uk

Off A37 S of Yeovil; DT2 0JW

Dorset Dining Pub of the Year

400-year-old inn in a pretty village with character rooms, log fires and knick-knacks and friendly licensees; bedrooms

You can be sure of a genuinely friendly welcome here and our readers are consistent in their praise on all aspects. The public bar, popular locally, has a log fire, lots of beer mats on beams, big flagstones and high chairs against the counter where they serve Dorset Jurassic and a guest beer on handpump, 31 wines by the glass, 25 gins (including a gin of the month) and over 100 malt whiskies. Dogs are looked after with a bowl of water and maybe a biscuit. A second bar has comfortable beige leather wall banquettes and little stools around tables set with fresh flowers, and a turkish rug on nice old quarry tiles. This leads to a bistro-style dining room with ladder-back chairs around oak tables; the slightly more formal restaurant is similarly furnished. There's also a comfortable lounge with armchairs, board games and shelves of books and a skittle alley. Throughout are open fires, wood panelling, pretty knick-knacks, all manner of copper and brass items, water jugs, wall prints and photographs; background music, TV, board games and darts. The walled garden has picnic-sets under a fine beech tree. Each of the attractive bedrooms is individually decorated and has a Thomas Hardy theme; the inn is immortalised as the Sow & Acorn in Thomas Hardy's *Tess of the D'Urbervilles*. Breakfasts are first class and guests can use the spa facilities at the nearby Summer Lodge hotel. Numerous nearby walks.

Enjoyable, stylish food includes sandwiches, twice-baked crab and yarg soufflé on pickled samphire with saffron and dill velouté, ham hock terrine with pesto crostini and piccalilli, burger with toppings, coleslaw and triple-cooked chips, local duck breast with ballotine of confit duck leg, boulangère potatoes, spiced carrot purée and berry jus, crispy buffalo mozzarella-stuffed arancini with mediterranean vegetables, spinach and wild garlic velouté and roasted cherry tomatoes, honey and ginger free-range chicken suprême on wild mushroom risotto with wilted pak choi and red wine jus, and puddings such as custard tart with poached rhubarb, coconut crumble, yoghurt ice-cream and rhubarb crisp and sticky toffee pudding with vanilla-infused pear, walnut crumble and vanilla ice-cream. *Benchmark main dish: beer-battered fish and chips £14.50. Two-course evening meal £22.00.*

Free house ~ Licensee Natalie Read ~ Real ale ~ Open 11-11; 12-11 Sun ~ Bar food 12-2, 7-9 ~ Restaurant ~ Children welcome ~ Dogs welcome ~ Wi-fi ~ Bedrooms: £94.50/£105

Recommended by Ian Malone, Nick Sharpe, Charlie May, Clive and Fran Dutson, Tracey and Stephen Groves, S G N Bennett, Isobel Mackinlay

FARNHAM ST9515 Map 2

Museum

(01725) 516261 – www.museuminn.co.uk

Village signposted off A354 Blandford Forum–Salisbury; DT11 8DE

Partly thatched smart inn with appealing rooms, brasserie-style food, real ales and fine wines, and seats outside; comfortable bedrooms

Good, modern food and a fine choice of drinks are just two attributes our readers enjoy in this civilised inn. There's a proper small bar with beams, flagstones, a big inglenook fireplace and quite an assortment of dining chairs around plain or painted wooden tables. Stools line the counter where friendly staff serve Flack Manor Double Drop, Ringwood Fortyniner and Waylands Sixpenny 6D Best on handpump, ten wines by the glass, 20 malt whiskies, 30 gins and local spirits and ciders. Leading off here is a simply but attractively furnished dining room with cushioned window seats, a long dark leather button-back wall seat, similar chairs and tables on bare floorboards and quite a few photographs on patterned wallpaper. There's also a quiet lounge with armchairs around a low table in front of an open fire, books on shelves and board games. A terrace has cushioned seats and tables under parasols. Four of the attractive bedrooms are in the main building, the remaining four in the converted stables; they also have a large thatched self-catering cottage.

High quality, up-to-date food includes sandwiches and pub classics plus local crab with dill and crème fraîche tortellini, watercress velouté and herb croutons, twice-baked cheese soufflé with candied walnuts, oriental hot and sour stew with mushroom and ginger dumplings and pak choi, pollack with confit chicken wing, samphire, saffron potatoes and red wine and caper butter, lamb rump with chargrilled ratte potatoes, olives, confit cherry tomatoes and wild garlic, guinea fowl breast with leek and tarragon croquettes, baby leeks and sautéed carrots, and puddings such as treacle tart with clotted cream, lemon curd and a brandy snap and vanilla and plum cheesecake with blackcurrant sorbet and star anise syrup. *Benchmark main dish: slow-roasted pork belly with glazed pig cheek, fondant potatoes and pickled beetroot £18.95. Two-course evening meal £25.00.*

Free house ~ Licensee Lee Hart ~ Real ale ~ Open 12-11 (10.30 Sun) ~ Bar food 12-2.30, 6-9.30; 12-9.30 Sat; 12-8 Sun ~ Restaurant Fri and Sat evenings, Sun lunch ~ Children welcome ~ Dogs allowed in bar and bedrooms ~ Wi-fi ~ Bedrooms: /£100 *Recommended by Joe and Belinda Smart, Philip J Alderton*

KINGSTON SY9579 Map 2

Scott Arms

(01929) 480270 – www.thescottarms.com

West Street (B3069); BH20 5LH

Magnificent views from a large garden, rambling character rooms, real ales and interesting food and an easy-going atmosphere; bedrooms

As well as rustic-style seating and an outside summer kitchen with a jerk shack for caribbean food (the landlady is Jamaican), there are wonderful views from the big, attractive garden over Corfe Castle (National Trust) and the Purbeck Hills. Inside, the bar areas and dining room are on several levels with stripped stone and brickwork, flagstones and bare boards, beams and high rafters, seats ranging from sofas and easy chairs through all manner of wooden chairs around tables of varying sizes, and open fires; stairs lead up from the bar to a small minstrels' gallery-like area with sofas facing one another across a table. Dorset Durdle Door and Jurassic and a guest from Waylands Sixpenny on handpump, 11 wines by the glass and local cider; background music and board games. The four bedrooms are attractively decorated, and the surrounding area has many good walks.

From a varied menu the food includes sandwiches, a sharing board, mushrooms on toast with tarragon and truffle, local clam chowder with hake, smoked mackerel, brown crab, potatoes, lemon and dill, moroccan vegetable stew in a spicy sauce with apricots, almonds, preserved lemon, harissa yoghurt and couscous, pork tenderloin wrapped in serrano ham with cider and sage jus and dauphinoise potatoes, free-range chicken in creamy wild mushroom sauce, and puddings such as chocolate torte and apple and cinammon crumble. *Benchmark main dish: Sunday roast £14.95. Two-course evening meal £22.00.*

Greene King ~ Lease Ian, Simon and Cynthia Coppack ~ Real ale ~ Open 11-10 (11 Sat) ~ Bar food 12-2.30, 6-8.30; 12-8.30 weekends ~ Children welcome ~ Dogs allowed in bar ~ Wi-fi ~ Bedrooms: £110/£120 *Recommended by Tony Scott, Usha and Terri Patel, M G Hart, Nick Sharpe, John Harris*

'Children welcome' means the pub says it lets children inside without any special restriction. If it allows them in, but to restricted areas such as an eating area or family room, we specify this. Some pubs may impose an evening time limit. We do not mention limits after 9pm as we assume children are home by then.

MIDDLEMARSH ST6607 Map 2

Hunters Moon

(01963) 210966 – www.hunters-moon.org.uk

A352 Sherborne–Dorchester; DT9 5QN

Plenty of bric-a-brac in several linked areas, reasonably priced food and quite a choice of drinks; comfortable bedrooms

Customers with dogs are warmly welcomed here and dogs are allowed in the bedrooms too (for a small charge). Our readers return to this traditional, neatly kept inn on a regular basis and the convivial, hands-on licensees work hard to create an easy-going, cheerful atmosphere. The beamed bar rooms are filled with a great variety of tables and chairs on red patterned carpet, an array of ornaments from horsebrasses and horse tack to pretty little tea cups hanging from beams, and lighting in the form of converted oil lamps; the atmosphere is properly pubby. Booths are formed by some attractively cushioned settles, walls are of exposed brick, stone and some panelling and there are three log fires (one in a capacious inglenook); background music, children's books and toys and board games. Butcombe Bitter, Ringwood Best and a local guest on handpump, farm cider and 16 wines by the glass. A neat lawn has picnic-sets, including some circular ones.

Fair-priced food includes sandwiches, chicken liver pâté with onion chutney, breaded calamari with paprika mayonnaise, a pie and a curry of the day, cumberland sausage with mash and gravy, vegetable lasagne, pork steak in cider and thyme gravy, beer-battered cod and chips, steaks with a choice of sauce and chips, and puddings such as lime and lemon posset with chantilly cream and dark chocolate and amaretto brownie with salted caramel ice-cream. *Benchmark main dish: chicken in cream, white wine and garlic sauce £14.00. Two-course evening meal £20.00.*

Enterprise ~ Lease Dean and Emma Mortimer ~ Real ale ~ Open 10.30-2.30, 6 (5 Fri)-11; 10.30am-11pm Sat, Sun ~ Bar food 12-2, 6-9; all day weekends ~ Children welcome ~ Dogs welcome ~ Wi-fi ~ Bedrooms: £65/£75 *Recommended by Guy Vowles, Dr Simon Innes, Justine and Neil Bonnett, RBC, Sandra and Neil White, Sally and Lance Oldham*

NETTLECOMBE SY5195 Map 2

Marquis of Lorne

(01308) 485236 – www.themarquisoflorne.co.uk

Off A3066 Bridport–Beaminster, via West Milton; DT6 3SY

Attractive country pub with enjoyable food and drink, friendly licensees and seats in big garden; bedrooms

The surrounding countryside here is particularly beautiful and Eggardon Hill, one of Dorset's most spectacular Iron Age hill forts with views over the coast and surrounding countryside, is within walking distance of the pub. The comfortable, bustling main bar has a log fire, mahogany panelling, old prints and photographs and neatly matching chairs and tables. Two dining areas lead off, the smaller of which has another log fire. The wooden-floored snug (liked by locals) has board games, table skittles and background music, and they keep Palmers Copper, Dorset Gold and IPA on handpump, with ten wines by the glass from a decent list. The big mature garden really comes into its own in warm weather with its pretty herbaceous borders, picnic-sets under apple trees and rustic-style play area.

Well regarded food includes sandwiches, creamed local goose egg with smoked salmon, game terrine with home-made beetroot and walnut bread, roasted aubergine with tomato, spinach, onion and goats cheese, rose veal and horseradish burger with toppings, slaw and fries, local pheasant breast and sausage with chorizo, butter beans and onion sauce, half lamb shoulder with honey, mint and garlic confit, traceable, aged steaks with pink peppercorn cream and fries, and puddings such as warm chocolate fudge brownie with vanilla ice-cream and waffle topped with bananas, toffee sauce and ice-cream. *Benchmark main dish: sea bass fillets with crushed new potatoes and a cream prawn velouté £16.50. Two-course evening meal £22.00.*

Palmers ~ Tenants Stephen and Tracey Brady ~ Real ale ~ Open 12-2.30, 6-11 ~ Bar food 12-2, 6-9 ~ Restaurant ~ Children welcome ~ Dogs allowed in bar ~ Wi-fi ~ Bedrooms: £85/£95 *Recommended by Ian Wilson, Jill and Hugh Bennett, Martine and Fabio Lockley, Jason Caulkin, Scott and Charlotte Havers*

PLUSH ST7102 Map 2

Brace of Pheasants

(01300) 348357 – www.braceofpheasants.co.uk

Village signposted from B3143 N of Dorchester at Piddletrenthide; DT2 7RQ

16th-c thatched pub with friendly service, popular food and pleasant garden; comfortable bedrooms

Once two cottages and the village smithy, this 16th-c thatched country pub has an easy-going atmosphere. The beamed bar has windsor chairs around good solid tables on patterned carpeting, a few standing timbers, a huge heavy-beamed inglenook at one end with cosy seating inside, and a good warming log fire at the other. Piddle Piddle, Ringwood Best and maybe a guest such as Flack Manor Double Drop are tapped from the cask and they offer a fine choice of wines with 20 by the glass and two proper farm ciders. A decent-sized garden includes a terrace and a lawn sloping up towards a rockery. Bedrooms are attractively fitted out and comfortable and each has a little outdoor terrace; they make an excellent base for walking and there's a bridleway behind the building that leads to the left of the woods and over to Church Hill.

Generously served food includes sandwiches, crab, caramelised leek and saffron tartlet, marinated thai beef spring rolls with crunchy coriander salad and sweet chilli sauce, warm marinated goats cheese salad with croutons, beetroot, walnuts and baby potatoes, lambs liver and bacon with creamy mash and onion gravy, beer-battered fish of the day with chips, duck breast with caramelised orange and madeira sauce and potato rösti, garlic and herb marinated venison steak with port and redcurrant sauce and confit garlic mash, and puddings such as malva pudding with a brandy glaze and stem ginger crème anglaise and flourless chocolate praline cake with chocolate sauce. *Benchmark main dish: venison burger with toppings and chips £12.95. Two-course evening meal £20.00.*

Free house ~ Licensees Phil and Carol Bennett ~ Real ale ~ Open 12-3, 7-11 (10.30 Sun) ~ Bar food 12-2.30, 7-9 ~ Children welcome ~ Dogs allowed in bar ~ Wi-fi ~ Bedrooms: £89/£99 *Recommended by Marianne and Peter Stevens, Richard Cole, Elisabeth and Bill Humphries, Scott and Charlotte Havers, Colin and Pat Honey, Alan Johnson, Sandra and Neil White*

SHAFTESBURY ST8622 Map 2

Grosvenor Arms

(01747) 850580 – www.thegrosvenorarms.co.uk

High Street; SP7 8JA

Relaxed hotel with a cheerful bar, several dining areas, enjoyable food and local ales, and seats in a courtyard; bedrooms

On our recent visit, we very much enjoyed the civilised bar at the back of this town-centre hotel. There are cheerful cushions on sofas and armchairs, cushioned settles, a woodburning stove, antlers on partly panelled walls, a coir and wood floor, and a few high chairs against the counter where they serve Otter Bitter and guests from Otter and Piddle on handpump and 20 wines by the glass; service is friendly and helpful. A conservatory area (looking over a central courtyard with a fountain surrounded by metal and wood-slat chairs and tables) links this bar with several spreading dining rooms. There's a bistro-like area, a restaurant with brown leather dining chairs and tables on a wood floor, a small end room with bookcase wallpaper and another little dining room at the front. Bedrooms are comfortable and up to date.

Interesting food using local, seasonal produce includes ciabatta sandwiches, bream ceviche with citrus and chilli dressing, goats cheese arancini with walnut mayonnaise and beetroot dressing, wood-fired pizzas, spiced lamb burger with raita and spicy slaw, venison and pork ragoût with salsa verde and tagliatelle, wild mushroom and red wine risotto with crispy shallots and oregano, rare-breed pork belly with wild garlic, apple and bubble and squeak, roast hake fillet with anchovies, cauliflower purée, lentils, chorizo and spring onions, and puddings such as salted caramel and chocolate tart with honeycomb and lemon posset with poached rhubarb and almond crumble. *Benchmark main dish: flat-iron chicken with spicy slaw £16.50. Two-course evening meal £24.00.*

Free house ~ Licensee Natalie Zvonek-Little ~ Real ale ~ Open 9am-11pm; 9am-10.30pm Sun ~ Bar food 9am-10pm; no food 3-5pm Mon~ Restaurant ~ Children welcome ~ Dogs allowed in bar and bedrooms ~ Wi-fi ~ Bedrooms: /£80 *Recommended by Dan and Nicki Barton, Andy and Louise Ramwell, Sally and Lance Oldham, Justine and Neil Bonnett, Ivy and George Goodwill*

SHERBORNE ST6316 Map 2

Digby Tap £

(01935) 813148

Cooks Lane; park in Digby Road and walk round corner; DT9 3NS

Regularly changing ales in simple alehouse, open all day with very inexpensive beer and food

Just a stroll away from the beautiful, golden-stone Sherborne Abbey, this unpretentious, down-to-earth tavern still draws in customers for its fine ales and amazingly cheap food. The atmosphere, as ever, is lively, chatty and warmly welcoming and the straightforward flagstoned bar with its cosy corners is full of understated character. The small games room has a pool table and a quiz machine, and there's also a TV room; mobile phones are banned. The splendid choice of beers on handpump includes Cerne Abbas Ale, Otter Bitter and Teignworthy Neap Tide. Also, several wines by the glass and a choice of malt whiskies.

Generous helpings of extraordinarily good value straightforward lunchtime food includes sandwiches and toasties, three-egg omelettes, sausages with free-range eggs, beef chilli, burgers and specials such as fish pie, sausage casserole and a mixed grill. *Benchmark main dish: liver and bacon £6.00.*

Free house ~ Licensees Oliver Wilson and Nick Whigham ~ Real ale ~ No credit cards ~ Open 11-11; 12-11 Sun ~ Bar food 12-2; not Sun ~ Children welcome until 6pm ~ Dogs allowed in bar ~ Wi-fi *Recommended by Patricia and Anton Larkham, Charlie Stevens, Lenny and Ruth Walters, Simon and Sue Lamb, Chloe and Michael Swettenham*

Please let us know what you think of a pub's bedrooms: feedback@goodguides.com or (no stamp needed) The Good Pub Guide, FREEPOST RTXY–ZCBC–BBAZ, Stream Lane, Sedlescombe, Battle TN33 0PB.

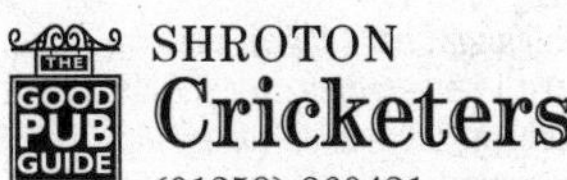

SHROTON ST8512 Map 2

Cricketers

(01258) 860421 – www.thecricketersshroton.co.uk

Off A350 N of Blandford (village also called Iwerne Courtney); follow signs; DT11 8QD

Country pub with real ales, well liked food and pretty garden; nice views and walks nearby

This red-brick country pub sits on the Wessex Ridgeway and is overlooked by the formidable grassy Iron Age ramparts of Hambledon Hill, which gradually descends to become the village cricket pitch in front of the pub. The bright, divided bar has a woodburning stove in a stone fireplace, cushioned high-backed windsor and ladder-back chairs in one area and black leather ones in another, all sorts of tables, a settle with scatter cushions, and red and cream walls decorated with cricket bats and photos of cricket teams. There's also a cosy alcove and a spreading dining area towards the back. Butcombe Bitter, Otter Amber and Sharps Doom Bar on handpump (they may hold a beer festival on the early May Bank Holiday weekend) and several wines by the glass; background music. The back garden is secluded and pretty with seats on a terrace and lawn, and there are also picnic-sets at the front. Walkers are requested to leave muddy boots outside and dogs are not allowed inside.

From a varied menu, the good food includes lunchtime croque monsieur, a quiche of the day and a ciabatta of the day plus twice-baked cheddar and stilton soufflé, baked crab pots with crispy onions, broccoli, courgettes and red onion puff pastry slice with roquefort and pesto, chicken, chorizo and butter bean casserole with saffron, peppers and garlic, a roasted whole fish of the day, lambs liver and bacon with mash and sage and onion gravy, and puddings such as steamed ginger pudding with ginger ice-cream and treacle tart with lemon crème fraîche. *Benchmark main dish: proper pie of the day £11.00. Two-course evening meal £19.00.*

Heartstone Inns ~ Licensees Joe and Sally Grieves ~ Real ale ~ Open 12-3, 6-11; 12-10.30 Sun ~ Bar food 12-2.30, 6.30-9; no food Sun evening Sept-May ~ Children welcome ~ Wi-fi

Recommended by Nick Higgins, Julie Swift, Usha and Terri Patel, Selwyn Jones, Abigail Slater, Sam Cole

WEST BAY SY4690 Map 1

West Bay

(01308) 422157 – www.thewestbayhotel.co.uk

Station Road; DT6 4EW

Relaxed inn looking out to sea with emphasis on seafood; bedrooms

Most customers are here to enjoy the daily fresh fish which is landed at the busy little harbour just a stroll away; you'll need to book a table in advance. The fairly simple front part of the building, with bare boards, a coal-effect gas fire and a mix of sea and nostalgic prints, is separated by an island servery from the cosier carpeted dining area, which has more of a country kitchen feel; background music and board games. Palmers Best, Copper, Dorset Gold and 200 and a seasonal guest are served on handpump alongside good house wines (including eight by the glass), cocktails and several malt whiskies. The pub's 100-year-old skittle alley does get used. There are tables in a small side garden and more in the large main garden, and bedrooms are quiet and comfortable. Two unspoilt beaches on either side of the small thriving harbour are much visited since the three *Broadchurch* TV series were filmed here.

Fresh fish and shellfish daily specials are the highlight but they also offer lunchtime sandwiches, smoked salmon blinis with horseradish crème fraîche, game terrine with sourdough toast, wild mushroom and spinach wellington with leek fondue and roasted root vegetables, burger with toppings and chips, venison steak with baked potato and bacon and damson jus, slow-cooked pork belly with wholegrain mustard sauce, sirloin steak topped with local scallops in garlic butter, and puddings. *Benchmark main dish: fresh fish dish of the day £18.00. Two-course evening meal £23.00.*

Palmers ~ Tenant Samuel Good ~ Real ale ~ Open 12-11 (midnight Sat); 12-3, 6-11 Nov-Mar ~ Bar food 12-2.30 (3 weekends), 6-9 ~ Children welcome until 8pm ~ Dogs allowed in bar ~ Wi-fi ~ Bedrooms: £102/£120 *Recommended by A W Johns, Pete and Sarah, Julie and Andrew Blanchett, David Appleyard, Dr and Mrs J D Abell, Roger and Donna Huggins, Andrew Low*

WEST STOUR — Ship

ST7822 Map 2

(01747) 838640 – www.shipinn-dorset.com

A30 W of Shaftesbury; SP8 5RP

Civilised and pleasantly updated roadside dining inn offering a wide range of food and ales; bedrooms

A cheerful, friendly landlord runs this deservedly busy, smart and comfortable inn and our readers enjoy their visits very much. The neatly kept rooms include a smallish but airy bar on the left with cream décor, a mix of chunky farmhouse furniture on dark boards and big sash windows that look beyond the road and car park to rolling pastures. The smaller flagstoned public bar has a good log fire and low ceilings. Bass, Butcombe Original and Otter Bitter on handpump, 13 wines by the glass, 19 gins, a dozen malt whiskies and five farm ciders. During their summer beer festival they showcase a dozen beers and ten ciders, all from the west country. On the right, two carpeted dining rooms with stripped pine dado, stone walls and shutters are similarly furnished in a pleasantly informal style, and have some attractive contemporary cow prints; TV, numerous board games and background music. The bedlington terriers are called Douglas and Elliot. The garden behind the pub is lovely, and the bedrooms are attractive and comfortable with pastoral views; breakfasts are particularly good. Rewarding surrounding walks.

Extremely good food includes lunchtime sandwiches, pigeon breast with olive and thyme hash brown, spinach, beetroot hummus and red wine jus, smoked haddock potato cake with a soft poached egg and hollandaise, cider-battered halloumi with pickled quail eggs, pea purée, bloody mary cherry tomatoes and fries, home-baked honey-cured ham with eggs, chips and gooseberry and coriander chutney, roasted lamb rump with slow-braised mutton shoulder, basil mash, white onion purée and rosemary jus, plaice fillets with citrus velouté, potato and garlic dumpling and wild garlic oil, and puddings such as white chocolate and passion-fruit crème brûlée and maple and pecan sponge pudding with clotted cream ice-cream. *Benchmark main dish: scallop, tiger prawns, salmon, smoked haddock and caper fish pie £14.95. Two-course evening meal £19.00.*

Free house ~ Licensee Gavin Griggs ~ Real ale ~ Open 12-3, 6-11.30; 12-10.30 Sat, Sun ~ Bar food 12-2.30, 6-9; not Sun evening ~ Restaurant ~ Children welcome ~ Dogs allowed in bar ~ Wi-fi ~ Bedrooms: £60/£90 *Recommended by Allan Bentley, M G Hart, Robert Watt, Mike and Sarah Abbot, Martin and Joanne Sharp, Edward Mirzoeff, Simon and Alex Knight*

The details at the end of each featured entry start by saying whether the pub is a free house, or if it belongs to a brewery or pub group (which we name).

WEYMOUTH SY6878 Map 2

Red Lion £

(01305) 786940 – www.theredlionweymouth.co.uk

Hope Square; DT4 8TR

Bustling place with sunny terrace, a smashing range of drinks, tasty food and lots to look at

For rum lovers particularly, the collection here is fantastic: they keep over 100 and have a rum 'bible' to explain them. Other drinks choices, served by friendly, efficient staff, include Dorset Jurassic, Lifeboat Bitter (named for the pub with 10p per pint going towards the RNLI), Skinners Betty Stogs, St Austell Tribute and a changing guest on handpump and 12 wines by the glass. The pub is known as the lifeboatmen's pub and features numerous pictures and artefacts relating to the lifeboat crews and their boats. The refurbished bare-boards interior, kept cosy with candles, has a cheerful, lively atmosphere, all manner of wooden chairs and tables, cushioned wall seats, some unusual maroon-cushioned high benches beside equally high tables, the odd armchair here and there, and plenty of bric-a-brac on stripped-brick walls. Some nice contemporary touches include the woven timber wall and loads of mirrors wittily overlapped; daily papers, board games and background music. Plenty of seats outside stay warmed by the sun well into the evening. The pub is owned by Tim Bird and Mary McLaughlin of Cheshire Cat Pubs & Bars.

Pleasing food includes lunchtime sandwiches, sharing plates and boards, mussels in white wine, shallots and cream, fried prawns in chilli and garlic, vegetarian pie with sweet potato mash, grilled free-range chicken burger with cheddar and sweet-cured bacon, local sausages with onion gravy, beer-battered haddock and chips, fresh fish pie, slow-cooked pork belly with mustard mash, spiced red cabbage and calvados sauce, and puddings such as warm chocolate brownie with vanilla ice-cream and sticky toffee pudding with rum and raisin ice-cream. *Benchmark main dish: steak in ale pie £13.25. Two-course evening meal £20.00.*

Free house ~ Licensee Brian McLaughlin ~ Real ale ~ Open 12-11 (10.30 Sun) ~ Bar food 12-9; may not serve food afternoons in winter ~ Children welcome until 7pm ~ Wi-fi ~ Live music outside Sun 2pm in summer *Recommended by Richard Cole, Jess and George Cowley, William and Sophia Renton, Glen and Patricia Fuller, David Bird, Alf and Sally Garner*

WIMBORNE MINSTER SZ0199 Map 2

Green Man £

(01202) 881021 – www.greenmanwimborne.com

Victoria Road, at junction with West Street (B3082/B3073); BH21 1EN

Cosy, warm-hearted town tavern with well liked food and Wadworths ales

As this cheerful town pub is open all day, customers are always popping in and out. The small linked areas have some timbering, tartan banquettes, wheelback and farmhouse chairs around pubby tables on parquet flooring or carpet, some William Morris-style wallpaper, horsebrasses and a high shelf of stone bottles. The bar features a woodburning stove and high chairs line the counter where friendly staff keep Wadworths 6X, IPA and Swordfish on handpump and a farm cider. Darts, a silenced games machine and juke box; the Barn houses a pool table. In summer, the award-winning flowering tubs, hanging baskets and window boxes are quite amazing and there are more on the heated back terrace.

Lunchtime-only food (they offer popular breakfasts too) includes sandwiches, baked potatoes, ham and free-range eggs, burgers with toppings and chips and daily specials such as faggots and mash, weekday roasts and beef curry; they also do steak and curry evenings on the last Wednesday of the month. *Benchmark main dish: beer-battered fish and chips £8.50.*

Wadworths ~ Tenants Katherine Twinn and Scott Valenti ~ Real ale ~ Open 10am-11pm (11-11 Mon); 10am-midnight Fri, Sat; 10am-10.30pm Sun ~ Bar food 11-4 Mon; 10-4 Tues-Sun ~ Restaurant ~ Children welcome until 8pm ~ Dogs allowed in bar ~ Wi-fi ~ Quiz Thurs; live music weekends *Recommended by Dr and Mrs A K Clarke, Andrew Wall, Lee and Jill Stafford, Thomas Green, Freddie and Sarah Banks*

WORTH MATRAVERS — SY9777 Map 2

Square & Compass ★

(01929) 439229 – www.squareandcompasspub.co.uk

At fork of both roads signposted to village from B3069; BH19 3LF

Unchanging country tavern with masses of character, in the same family for many years; lovely sea views and fine nearby walks

In the 100 years that the charming Newman family have run this quite unspoilt country gem, almost nothing has changed. A couple of simple rooms have straightforward furniture on flagstones and wooden benches around the walls, a woodburning stove, a stuffed albino badger and a loyal crowd of chatty locals. Cerne Abbas Tiger Tom Ruby Mild, Gower Gold and Hattie Browns HBA and Moonlite tapped from the cask, and home-produced and ten other farm ciders are passed through the two serving hatches to customers in the drinking corridor; also, 20 malt whiskies. From the local stone benches out in front there's a fantastic view over the village rooftops down to the sea. There may be free-roaming chickens and other birds clucking around and the small (free) museum exhibits fossils and artefacts from the surrounding area, mostly collected by the current landlord and his father. Wonderful walks lead to some exciting switchback sections of the coast path above St Aldhelm's Head and Chapman's Pool – you'll need to park in the public car park (£2 honesty box) 100 metres along the Corfe Castle road.

Bar food consists of home-made pasties and pies.

Free house ~ Licensees Charlie Newman and Kevin Hunt ~ Real ale ~ No credit cards ~ Open 12-11; 12-3, 6-11 Mon-Thurs in winter ~ Bar food all day ~ Children welcome ~ Dogs welcome ~ Live music weekend evenings *Recommended by Tony Scott, Robert Watt, Bob and Melissa Wyatt, Greta and Gavin Craddock, S G N Bennett, Sally and Brian Turner*

Please tell us if any pub deserves to be upgraded to a featured entry – and why: feedback@goodguides.com, or (no stamp needed) The Good Pub Guide, FREEPOST RTXY–ZCBC–BBAZ, Stream Lane, Sedlescombe, Battle TN33 0PB.

Also Worth a Visit in Dorset

Besides the fully inspected pubs, you might like to try these pubs that have been recommended to us and described by readers. Do tell us what you think of them: feedback@goodguides.com

ASKERSWELL SY5393

★**Spyway** (01308) 485250
Off A35 Bridport–Dorchester; DT2 9EP This welcoming country local was for sale as we went to press, so there may be changes; unspoilt little rooms cosily filled with cushioned wall and window seats and some tub chairs, old pub photos and rustic scenes, jugs hanging from beams, a warming Rayburn, two Otter beers, traditional cider and several wines by the glass, well regarded food, dining area with old oak beams and posts, red-cushioned chairs around dark tables on patterned carpet, horse tack and horsebrasses on the walls, woodburning stove, two other smaller rooms lead off; children welcome, wonderful downs and coast views from back terrace and large garden, play area, comfortable bedrooms overlooking grounds, good breakfasts. *(S G N Bennett, Pete and Sarah, John and Delia Franks, Rob Anderson)*

BISHOP'S CAUNDLE ST6913

White Hart (01963) 23301
A3030 SE of Sherborne; DT9 5ND Smallish 17th-c roadside pub with modernised carpeted interior; dark beams, panelling, stripped stone and log fire, good well presented food from varied fair-priced menu including daily specials, Sharps Doom Bar and local guests, friendly service, restaurant; skittle alley; children and dogs welcome, country views from garden, closed Sun evening, Mon. *(Barbara and Phil Bowie)*

BLANDFORD FORUM ST8806

Crown (01258) 456626
West Street; DT11 7AJ Civilised brick-built Georgian hotel on edge of town, spacious well patronised bar/dining area including snug with leather armchairs and roaring fire, full range of Badger ales from nearby brewery, numerous wines by the glass, cocktails, teas and coffee, enjoyable food from sandwiches and small plates up, separate restaurant; children welcome, dogs in bar, tables on big terrace with formal garden beyond, 27 recently refurbished bedrooms, open (and food) all day. *(Mr and Mrs Richard Osborne, David and Sally Cullen)*

BOURNEMOUTH SZ1092

Cricketers Arms (01202) 551589
Windham Road; BH1 4RN Well preserved Victorian pub near the station; separate public and lounge bars, tiled fireplaces and lots of dark wood, etched windows and stained glass, Fullers London Pride and two quickly changing guests, food weekend lunchtimes only from limited menu; folk night second and fourth Mon of the month, free wi-fi; children and dogs welcome, picnic-sets out in front, open all day. *(Dr and Mrs A K Clarke)*

BOURNEMOUTH SZ0891

Goat & Tricycle (01202) 314220
West Hill Road; BH2 5PF Interesting Edwardian local (two former pubs knocked together) with rambling split-level interior; Wadworths ales and guests from pillared bar's impressive rank of ten handpumps, real cider, reasonably priced pubby food, friendly staff; background music, Sun quiz, free wi-fi; no under-18s, dogs welcome, good disabled access, part-covered yard, open (and food) all day. *(Dr and Mrs A K Clarke, Ian Herdman)*

BRIDPORT SY4692

George (01308) 423187
South Street; DT6 3NQ Relaxed and welcoming old town pub; good food from open kitchen cooked by landlord-chef including daily specials, well kept Palmers and decent wines by the glass, attentive friendly service; children and dogs (in bar) welcome, disabled facilities, open all day (from 10am for brunch on Sat market day). *(Sandra and Miles Spencer)*

BRIDPORT SY4692

Ropemakers (01308) 421255
West Street; DT6 3QP Long rambling town-centre pub with lots of pictures and memorabilia, well kept Palmers ales and enjoyable home-made food from sandwiches up, good friendly service; regular weekend live music, Tues quiz, free wi-fi; children and dogs welcome, tables in back courtyard, open all day except Sun evening. *(Ian Duncan)*

BRIDPORT SY4692

★**Stable** (01308) 459922
At the back of the Bull Hotel; DT6 3LF Not a pub in any sense, but this lively cider/pizza bar is great fun and popular with customers of all ages; lofty barn-like room with rough planked walls and ceiling, big steel columns, two long rows of pale wooden tables flanked by wide benches, steps up to raised end area with cushioned red wall benches, over 80 ciders, St Austell Proper Job and six wines by the glass, good hand-made pizzas and other food such as pies, upstairs room (not always open); background music, free wi-fi; children and dogs welcome, open (and food) all day weekends, from 5pm weekdays (all day during school holidays). *(Sandra and Miles Spencer)*

BRIDPORT SY4692

Tiger (01308) 427543
Barrack Street, off South Street; DT6 3LY Cheerful and attractive open-plan Victorian beamed pub with Sharps Doom Bar and five quickly changing guests, real ciders, no food except breakfast for residents; skittle alley, darts, sports TV, free wi-fi; dogs welcome, seats in heated courtyard, six bedrooms, open all day. *(Isobel Mackinlay)*

BUCKHORN WESTON ST7524

★ **Stapleton Arms** (01963) 370396
Church Hill; off A30 Shaftesbury–Sherborne via Kington Magna; SP8 5HS Handsome Georgian inn with large civilised bar, sofas in front of fine stone fireplace, mix of other seating on flagstones or bare boards including farmhouse and chapel chairs around scrubbed tables, modern artwork on dark red walls, ales from Butcombe, Keystone and Plain, proper cider, 32 wines by the glass and 16 malt whiskies, good interesting food along with more traditional choices, separate elegantly furnished restaurant; some live music, free wi-fi; children and dogs (in bar) welcome, seats out at front and in charming back garden, good nearby walks, comfortable well equipped bedrooms, open all day weekends. *(Abigail Slater)*

BURTON BRADSTOCK SY4889

Anchor (01308) 897228
B3157 SE of Bridport; DT6 4QF Friendly helpful staff in pricey but good seafood restaurant, other local food including nice steaks, village pub part too with blackboard choices from baguettes up, ales such as Dorset, St Austell and Sharps, decent wines by the glass and several malt whiskies; live music second Sun of month, games including table skittles; children and dogs (in bar) welcome, two bedrooms, open all day. *(Mr and Mrs N D Buckland, Helene Grygar)*

CERNE ABBAS ST6601

Royal Oak (01300) 341797
Long Street; DT2 7JG Creeper-clad 16th-c thatched village-centre pub; low black beams, flagstones and rustic memorabilia, nice log fire, well kept ales including local Cerne Abbas, good home-made food from lunchtime sandwiches to daily specials, friendly helpful service; some live music; children and dogs welcome, small back garden, open all day Fri-Sun, may close Tues in winter. *(Nick and Meriel Cox)*

CHEDINGTON ST4805

Winyards Gap (01935) 891244
A356 Dorchester–Crewkerne; DT8 3HY Attractive dining pub surrounded by NT land with spectacular view over Parrett Valley into Somerset; enjoyable food including Sun carvery, four well kept changing ales, local ciders, friendly helpful service, bar with woodburner, steps down to restaurant, skittle alley/dining room; children and dogs welcome, tables on front lawn under parasols, good walks, comfortable bedrooms, open all day weekends, closed Mon in winter. *(Alf and Sally Garner)*

CHIDEOCK SY4292

★ **George** (01297) 489419
A35 Bridport–Lyme Regis; DT6 6JD Traditional thatched local with cosy low-ceilinged carpeted bar, well kept Palmers ales and a guest, real cider and six wines by the glass, popular straightforward food including good crab sandwiches, friendly attentive service, pewter tankards and brassware hanging from dark beams, old tools on cream walls, high shelves with bottles, plates and mugs, pews and long built-in banquettes, warm log fires, garden room; background music, TV, bar billiards, darts and board games; children and dogs welcome, pretty walled garden with terrace and much used wood-fired oven. *(Peter Brix, Sabina and Gerald Grimshaw, Shona and Jimmy McDuff, Colin and Pat Honey)*

CHILD OKEFORD ST8213

Saxon (01258) 860310
Signed off A350 Blandford–Shaftesbury and A357 Blandford–Sherborne; Gold Hill; DT11 8HD Welcoming 17th-c village pub; snug bar with log fire and two dining rooms, Butcombe, Otter and guests, nice choice of wines and enjoyable reasonably priced home-made food from changing blackboard menu, efficient friendly service; children and dogs (in bar) welcome, attractive back garden, good walks on Neolithic Hambledon Hill, four comfortable bedrooms. *(Ivy and George Goodwill)*

CHRISTCHURCH SZ1593

Rising Sun (01202) 486122
Purewell; BH23 1EJ Comfortably modernised old pub specialising in good authentic thai food, L-shaped bar serving Flack Manor Double Drop, Sharps Doom Bar and good choice of wines by the glass, pleasant helpful young staff; terrace with palms and black rattan furniture under large umbrellas, open all day. *(Frank and Marcia Pelling)*

CORFE CASTLE SY9681

Castle Inn (01929) 480208
East Street; BH20 5EE Welcoming little two-room pub mentioned in Hardy's *The Hand of Ethelberta*; up to three real ales and popular generously served food including Fri fish night, accommodating friendly service, heavy black beams with fairy lights, exposed stone walls, flagstones and woodburner; background music; children welcome, no dogs inside, back terrace and big sunny garden with mature trees, steam train views, open all day. *(Sally and Colin Allen)*

CORFE CASTLE SY9682

Greyhound (01929) 480205

A351; The Square; BH20 5EZ Bustling picturesque old pub in centre of this tourist village; three small low-ceilinged panelled rooms, steps and corridors, well kept ales such as Palmers, Ringwood and Sharps, local cider and good range of other drinks, nice food from ciabattas, light dishes and pizzas up, friendly staff coping well at busy times, traditional games including Purbeck longboard shove-ha'penny, family room; background and weekend live music; dogs welcome, garden with large decked area, great views of castle and countryside, pretty courtyard opening on to castle bridge, open (and food) all day, best to book in summer. *(Tony Scott, Peter and Anne Hollindale)*

DEWLISH SY7798

Oak (01258) 837352

Off A354 Dorchester–Blandford Forum; DT2 7ND Welcoming red-brick village pub; two or three well kept local ales and enjoyable good value food including specials and popular Sun lunch, friendly helpful service, woodburner and open fire in bar, small dining room; winter quiz; children welcome, good-sized garden behind, two bedrooms and self-catering cottage. *(Ian Duncan)*

DORCHESTER SY6990

Blue Raddle (01305) 267762

Church Street, near central short-stay car park; DT1 1JN Cheery pubby atmosphere in long carpeted and partly panelled bar, well kept ales such as Castle Rock, Dartmoor, Otter and St Austell, local ciders, good wines and coffee, enjoyable simple home-made lunchtime food (not Sun, Mon, Tues), evenings Thurs-Sat, efficient friendly service (they don't accept credit/debit cards), coal-effect gas fires; background and live folk music (Weds fortnightly), darts and crib teams; no under-14s, dogs welcome, good disabled access apart from one step, closed Mon lunchtime. *(David and Doreen Beattie, Clive and Fran Dutson)*

EAST CHALDON SY7983

Sailors Return (01305) 854441

Village signposted from A352 Wareham–Dorchester; from village green, follow Dorchester, Weymouth signpost; note that the village is also known as Chaldon Herring; OS Sheet 194 map reference 790834; DT2 8DN Thatched village pub with five well kept ales such as Palmers, Otter and Ringwood, Thatcher's Gold cider and good food from short fairly pubby menu plus daily specials, Weds pie night, friendly attentive service, flagstoned bar and various dining areas; Tues quiz in winter; children welcome, dogs in bar (no food in bar Fri evening), picnic-sets out at front and in side garden, useful for coast path, open all day weekends, closed Mon. *(S Holder)*

EAST MORDEN SY9194

★**Cock & Bottle** (01929) 459238

B3075 W of Poole; BH20 7DL Popular extended dining pub with wide choice of good food including specials (best to book), separate traditional bar with open fire, well kept Badger ales and nice selection of wines by the glass, efficient cheerful service; children and dogs allowed in certain areas, outside seating and pleasant pastoral outlook, closed Sun evening. *(Mike Kavaney)*

EAST STOUR ST8123

Kings Arms (01747) 838325

A30, 2 miles E of village; The Common; SP8 5NB Extended dining pub with popular generously served food from scottish landlord-chef including bargain lunch menu and all-day Sun carvery (best to book), St Austell Tribute, Sharps Doom Bar and a guest, decent wines and good selection of malt whiskies, friendly efficient staff, open fire in bar, airy dining area with light wood furniture, scottish pictures and Burns quotes; gentle background music; children and dogs (in bar) welcome, good disabled access, picnic-sets in big garden, bluebell walks nearby, three bedrooms, open all day Sun. *(R C Hastings, Roy Hoing)*

FIDDLEFORD ST8013

Fiddleford Inn (01258) 472886

A357 Sturminster Newton–Blandford Forum; DT10 2BX Beamed roadside pub with three linked areas; modern charcoal paintwork blending with traditional furnishings, old flagstones, carpets and some exposed stone and brick, two-way woodburner, well kept ales including one badged for the pub, good traditional food from shortish menu, friendly young staff; children and dogs welcome, big fenced garden, four bedrooms, open (and food) all day, kitchen closes 6.30pm Sun. *(Isobel Mackinlay)*

FONTMELL MAGNA ST8616

Fontmell (01747) 811441

A350 S of Shaftesbury; SP7 0PA Imposing dining pub with rooms, much emphasis on the enterprising modern cooking, but also some more straightforward cheaper dishes (own rare breed pork), good wine list, a house beer (Sibeth) from Keystone and two west country guests, small bar area with

Post Office address codings confusingly give the impression that some pubs are in Dorset, when they're really in Somerset (which is where we list them).

comfy sofas and easy chairs, restaurant overlooking fast-flowing stream that runs under the building; garden across road with two wood-fired pizza ovens, six comfortable well appointed bedrooms, open all day from 9am (10am Sun). *(Michael Doswell, Michael Hill, Edward Mirzoeff)*

GILLINGHAM ST7926

Buffalo (01747) 823759
Off B3081 at Wyke 1 mile NW of Gillingham, pub 100 metres on left; SP8 4NJ Welcoming family-run Badger local, two linked bars and restaurant serving generous helpings of good well priced italian food (best to book), friendly attentive service; background and some live music; children welcome, back terrace by car park. *(Edward Mirzoeff)*

HINTON ST MARY ST7816

White Horse (01258) 472723
Just off B3092 a mile N of Sturminster; DT10 1NA Welcoming traditional little village pub dating from the early 17th c; good varied choice of food from changing menu cooked by south african landlord-chef (best to book), own-brew beers and decent house wines, unusual inglenook fireplace in cheerful bar, extended dining room; children, walkers and dogs welcome (pub dog is Pepper), picnic-sets in small well maintained garden, attractive setting, closed Sun evening, Mon. *(Abigail Slater)*

HOLT SU0304

Old Inn (01202) 883029
Holt Lane; beside the church; BH21 7DJ Refurbished red-brick Badger dining pub, their ales kept well and good range of wines and gins, tasty food including wood-fired pizzas and Mon steak night, quick friendly service, mix of pubby furniture on wood-strip floors, beams and log fire; children and dogs welcome, picnic-sets on front terrace, more in part-covered back garden, open all day weekends. *(Councillor Stephen Chappell, David and Sally Cullen)*

HURN SZ1397

Avon Causeway (01202) 482714
Village signed off A338, then follow Avon, Sopley, Matchams sign; BH23 6AS Comfortable and roomy hotel/dining pub with enjoyable food from sandwiches and pub favourites up, well kept Wadworths ales, helpful staff, interesting railway decorations and coach restaurant (used for functions) by former 1870s station platform; children and dogs welcome, disabled access, nice garden (some road noise) with play area, 12 good value bedrooms, near Bournemouth Airport (2 weeks free parking if you stay before or after you fly), open all day, food all day Sun. *(Simon and Sue Lamb)*

IBBERTON ST7807

Ibberton (01258) 817956
Village W of Blandford Forum; DT11 0EN 16th-c village pub refurbished under present welcoming owners; bar with flagstones and inglenook woodburner, two dining areas (one carpeted, the other where dogs allowed), three local beers and Dorset Orchards' cider from brick-faced servery, popular good value food from traditional choices up, friendly helpful staff; children welcome, picnic-sets in front/side garden with stream, beautiful spot under Bulbarrow Hill with good walks, closed Mon, Tues and Sun evening. *(Darrell Barton)*

LANGTON MATRAVERS SY9978

Kings Arms (01929) 422979
High Street; BH19 3HA Friendly old-fashioned village local; ancient flagstoned corridor to bar, simple rooms off, one with a fine fireplace made from local marble, beers including Ringwood and enjoyable good value pubby food, cheerful helpful staff, splendid antique Purbeck longboard shove-ha'penny; children and dogs welcome, sunny picnic-sets outside, good walks including to Dancing Ledge, open all day. *(Alf and Sally Garner)*

LYME REGIS SY3492

Cellar 59 (01297) 445086
Broad Street; DT7 3QF Two-room flagstoned bar down steps, up to 14 real ales/craft kegs chalked on blackboard including their own Gyle 59 unfined beers, tasting trays available, friendly knowledgeable staff, tapas-style platters (vegetarians and vegans catered for), shop above selling wide range of bottled beers; outside seating area, open all day (may shut Mon, Tues in winter). *(Roger and Donna Huggins)*

LYME REGIS SY3391

Cobb Arms (01297) 443242
Marine Parade, Monmouth Beach; DT7 3JF Spacious place with well kept Palmers ales, decent wines and good choice of reasonably priced freshly cooked food (gluten-free options available), cream teas, quick service, a couple of sofas, ship pictures and marine fish tank, open fire; pool, juke box, TVs; children and dogs welcome, disabled access (one step up from road), tables on small back terrace, well located next to harbour, beach and coastal walk, three bedrooms, open all day. *(Tony Scott, Alan Johnson, Karl Lehmann)*

Anyone claiming to arrange, or prevent, inclusion of a pub in the *Guide* is a fraud. Pubs are included only if recommended by readers and if our own anonymous inspection confirms that they are suitable.

LYME REGIS SY3391

Harbour Inn (01297) 442299
Marine Parade; DT7 3JF More eating than pubby with thriving family atmosphere, generally very well liked food from lunchtime sandwiches to local fish/seafood (not particularly cheap, booking advised in season), Otter and St Austell ales, good choice of wines by the glass, tea and coffee, friendly service, clean-cut modern décor keeping some original flagstones and stone walls (lively acoustic), paintings for sale, sea views from front windows; background and occasional live music; dogs welcome, disabled access from street, tables on verandah and beachside terrace, open all day except Sun evening in winter. *(Mike Kavaney, Guy Vowles)*

LYME REGIS SY3492

Pilot Boat (01297) 443157
Bridge Street; DT7 3QA This popular bow-fronted Palmers pub near the waterfront was reopening after extensive restoration as we went to press – reports please.

LYME REGIS SY3492

Volunteer (01297) 442214
Top of Broad Street (A3052 towards Exeter); DT7 3QE Cosy old-fashioned pub with long low-ceilinged bar, nice mix of customers (can get crowded), a well kept house beer from Branscombe Vale tapped from the cask and west country guests, enjoyable modestly priced food in dining lounge (children allowed here), friendly young staff, roaring fires; dogs welcome, open all day. *(Roger and Donna Huggins)*

MARNHULL ST7818

Crown (01258) 820224
About 3 miles N of Sturminster Newton; Crown Road; DT10 1LN Part-thatched inn dating from the 16th c (the Pure Drop in Hardy's *Tess of the D'Urbervilles*); linked rooms with oak beams, huge flagstones or bare boards, log fire in big stone hearth in oldest part, more modern furnishings and carpet elsewhere, Badger ales, plenty of wines by the glass and enjoyable generously served food including Sun carvery, good friendly service, restaurant; children welcome, peaceful enclosed garden, six bedrooms, open all day. *(Justine and Neil Bonnett)*

MARTINSTOWN SY6488

Brewers Arms (01305) 889361
Burnside (B3159); DT2 9LB Friendly family-run village pub (former 19th-c school) with attractively updated interior; good reasonably priced home-made food from lunchtime baguettes to specials, popular Tues curry night, well kept Palmers and Sharps, restaurant; Weds quiz and some live music; children and dogs welcome, picnic-sets out at front and in courtyard, historic sheepwash pool nearby (start of the annual plastic duck race), good local walks, two bedrooms, closed Sun evening, Mon. *(Marianne and Peter Stevens)*

MELPLASH SY4897

Half Moon (01308) 488321
A3066 Bridport–Beaminster; DT6 3UD Welcoming 17th-c thatch and stone roadside pub under new family management; beams and log fire, good choice of well liked food from sandwiches and pub favourites up (two of the owners are chefs), Palmers ales, real ciders and decent choice of wines by the glass; children and dogs welcome, a few picnic-sets out in front, more in back garden, good nearby walks, closed Sun evening, Mon. *(Charlie and Mark Todd)*

MILTON ABBAS ST8001

Hambro Arms (01258) 880233
Signed off A354 SW of Blandford; DT11 0BP Nicely updated beamed pub under new ownership in beautiful late 18th-c thatched village; bar, lounge and restaurant, well kept local ales and decent choice of wines, good restauranty food including one or two pub favourites, efficient friendly service; children welcome, dogs in bar, tables on front terrace, four bedrooms, open (and food) all day. *(Alf and Sally Garner)*

MOTCOMBE ST8426

Coppleridge (01747) 851980
Signed from The Street, follow to Mere/Gillingham; SP7 9HW Welcoming country inn (former 18th-c farmhouse) with traditional bar and various dining rooms, good home-made food from ciabattas and pub favourites up including some imaginative choices, Thurs steak night, ales such as Butcombe and decent wines by the glass, friendly helpful staff; children welcome, dogs in bar and garden room, ten spacious courtyard bedrooms, barn function room (popular wedding venue), 15-acre grounds with play area and two tennis courts, lovely views over Dorset countryside, open all day. *(Michael Doswell)*

NORDEN HEATH SY94834

Halfway (01929) 480402
A351 Wareham–Corfe Castle; BH20 5DU Cosily laid-out partly thatched 16th-c beamed pub; Badger beers, nice wines by the glass and enjoyable freshly cooked food including children's and vegetarian choices, good service, front rooms with flagstones, stripped stone and woodburners, snug little side area, pitched-ceiling back room; dogs welcome, picnic-sets on paved terrace and lawn, good nearby walks, open all day, food all day during school holidays. *(David Bird)*

OSMINGTON MILLS SY7381

Smugglers (01305) 833125
Off A353 NE of Weymouth; DT3 6HF Old partly thatched family-oriented inn set

down from the road; well extended, with cosy dimly lit timber-divided areas, woodburners, old local pictures, Badger ales, guest beers and several wines by the glass, food generally good, service friendly and helpful; dogs welcome, picnic-sets on crazy paving by little stream, thatched summer bar, play area, lovely sea views from car park (parking charge refunded at bar), useful for coast path, four bedrooms, open (and food) all day. *(D W Stokes, Matthew)*

PAMPHILL ST9900

★**Vine** (01202) 882259
Off B3082 on NW edge of Wimborne: turn on to Cowgrove Hill at Cowgrove sign, then left up Vine Hill; BH21 4EE Simple old-fashioned place run by same family for three generations and part of Kingston Lacy Estate (NT); two tiny bars with coal-effect gas fire, handful of tables and seats on lino, local photographs and notices on painted panelling, narrow wooden stairs up to room with darts, a couple of real ales, local cider and foreign bottled beers, lunchtime bar snacks; quiet background music, no credit cards, outside lavatories; children (away from bar) and dogs welcome, verandah with grapevine, sheltered gravel terrace and grassy area, Sept pumpkin and conkers festival. *(Sandra and Miles Spencer)*

POOLE SZ0391

Bermuda Triangle (01202) 748087
Parr Street, Lower Parkstone (just off A35 at Ashley Cross); BH14 0JY Quirky 19th-c bare-boards local on different levels; four well kept changing ales, two or three good continental lagers and many other beers from around the world, friendly staff, no food, dark panelling, snug old corners and lots of nautical and other bric-a-brac; background and some live music; no children and a bit too steppy for disabled access, new decked seating area outside, open all day Fri-Sun. *(Barbara and Phil Bowie)*

POOLE SZ0190

Poole Arms (01202) 673450
Town Quay; BH15 1HJ Friendly 17th-c waterfront pub looking over harbour to Brownsea Island; one comfortably old-fashioned room with boarded ceiling and nautical prints, popular much enjoyed food (predominantly fresh fish/seafood) at fair prices, four well kept ales such as Ringwood and St Austell, good service; outside gents'; no children, picnic-sets in front of the handsome green-tiled façade, almost next door to the Portsmouth Hoy, open all day. *(Simon King)*

POOLE SZ0090

Portsmouth Hoy (01202) 673517
The Quay; BH15 1HJ Harbourside pub with views to Brownsea Island; old-world atmosphere with dark wood, beams and bare boards, well kept Badger ales and decent food including fresh fish, friendly service; children and dogs welcome, outside tables shared with the Poole Arms, open all day. *(Frank and Marcia Pelling)*

POOLE SZ0090

Rope & Anchor (01202) 675677
Sarum Street; BH15 1JW Split-level Wadworths pub next to Poole Museum; good food including fresh fish, well kept beers and some nice wines by the glass, friendly accommodating staff; background music (live Fri), daily papers, free wi-fi; children and dogs welcome, seats on back terrace, open (and food) all day. *(Ian Duncan)*

PORTESHAM SY6085

Kings Arms (01305) 871342
Front Street; DT3 4ET Large modernised and extended pub in pretty village; ales such as Otter, St Austell and Sharps, good seasonal food from light meals and sharing plates to specials and carve-your-own Sun roasts, friendly helpful service, candles and open fires, coffee lounge with daily papers; regular live music, quiz last Thurs of month; children welcome, picnic-sets in sizeable garden with stream and summer pizza oven, three ground-floor annexe bedrooms, good breakfast in farm shop/café, open all day, food all day in summer. *(Jason Caulkin, Ian Malone)*

PORTLAND SY6873

Cove House (01305) 820895
Follow Chiswell signposts – pub is at NW corner of Portland; DT5 1AW Low-beamed traditional 18th-c pub in superb position, effectively built into sea defences just above the end of Chesil Beach, great views from three-room bar's bay windows; Sharps Doom Bar and other well kept beers, good freshly cooked food including blackboard fish specials (booking advised), friendly efficient service, steep steps down to gents'; background music, folk night Thurs; children and dogs welcome, tables out by seawall, open all day, no food Sun evening. *(David and Doreen Beattie)*

POWERSTOCK SY5196

Three Horseshoes (01308) 485328
Off A3066 Beaminster–Bridport via West Milton; DT6 3TF Tucked-away Edwardian pub under welcoming newish owners; cheerful cosy bar with stripped panelling, windsor and mate's chairs around assorted tables on bare boards, Palmers ales and several wines by the glass, good freshly made food including specials; children and dogs welcome, picnic-sets on back terrace with garden and country views, good surrounding walks, two comfortable bedrooms, closed Sun evening, Mon and Tues in winter, best to check summer hours. *(Darrell Barton)*

PUDDLETOWN SY7594

Blue Vinny (01305) 848228
The Moor; DT2 8TE Large modernised

village pub with beamed oak-floor bar and restaurant, good choice of highly regarded well presented food from lunchtime baguettes up (booking advised), well kept Sharps Doom Bar and a couple of guests, friendly helpful young staff; children welcome, dogs in one part, terrace overlooking garden with play area, open all day Fri-Sun, no food Sun evening. *(Marianne and Peter Stevens, Roger White)*

PUNCKNOWLE SY5388

Crown (01308) 897711
Off B3157 Bridport–Abbotsbury; DT2 9BN Very welcoming 16th-c thatched inn run by two brothers; enjoyable food from sandwiches and pub favourites up (smaller appetites catered for), Palmers ales and good choice of wines by the glass, beams and inglenook log fires, small shop selling local produce; board games; children and dogs (in bar) welcome, disabled facilities, valley views from peaceful pretty back garden, good walks, two bedrooms, open all day Sat, till 7pm Sun. *(Helene Grygar)*

SANDFORD ORCAS ST6220

★**Mitre** (01963) 220271
Off B3148 and B3145 N of Sherborne; DT9 4RU Thriving tucked-away country local with welcoming long-serving licensees; three well kept changing ales and proper ciders, wholesome home-made food (not Mon) from good soup and sandwiches up, flagstones, log fires and fresh flowers, small bar and larger pleasantly homely dining area; occasional open mike nights, games including shove-ha'penny and dominoes; children and dogs welcome, pretty back garden with terrace, good local walks (on Macmillan Way and Monarch's Way), closed Mon lunchtime. *(Abigail Slater)*

SHAPWICK ST9301

Anchor (01258) 857269
Off A350 Blandford–Poole; West Street; DT11 9LB Welcoming red-brick Victorian pub owned by village consortium; popular freshly made food (booking advised) including blackboard specials, Sharps Doom Bar and a couple of guests, real cider, good friendly service, scrubbed pine tables on wood floors, pastel walls and open fires; children and dogs welcome, tables out in front, more in attractive back garden with terrace, handy for Kingston Lacy (NT), closed Sun evening, Mon, otherwise open all day. *(Isobel Mackinlay)*

SPETISBURY ST9102

Woodpecker (01258) 452658
A350 SE of Blandford; High Street; DT11 9DJ Popular 1930s village pub with comfortable open-plan interior, enjoyable affordably priced home-made food (not Sun evening), four well kept changing ales, good range of ciders/perries and several wines by the glass, friendly helpful staff; background music, quiz first Tues of the month, bar billiards; children and dogs welcome, wheelchair access, tables in narrow roadside garden, open all day weekends, closed Mon. *(Justine and Neil Bonnett)*

STOBOROUGH SY9286

Kings Arms (01929) 552705
B3075 S of Wareham; Corfe Road opposite petrol station; BH20 5AB Popular part-thatched 17th-c village pub, well kept Isle of Purbeck, Ringwood and up to three guests, good fairly priced food in bar and restaurant from snacks and pub favourites up including some interesting specials, cheerful efficient staff; children and dogs welcome, disabled access/loos, flower-decked terrace and garden with play area, views over marshes to River Frome, open all day during summer school holidays (all day Fri-Sun at other times). *(Spencer Barratt, Kristin Warry)*

STOKE ABBOTT ST4500

★**New Inn** (01308) 868333
Off B3162 and B3163 2 miles W of Beaminster; DT8 3JW Welcoming 17th-c pub in unspoilt thatched village with nice surrounding walks; well kept Palmers ales and good home-cooked food including daily specials, woodburner in big inglenook, beams, brasses and copper, some handsome panelling, flagstoned dining room; children and dogs (in bar) welcome, wheelchair access, two attractive gardens, street fair third Sat in July, closed Sun evening, all Mon and Tues lunchtime. *(Sally and Colin Allen)*

STOURPAINE ST8609

White Horse (01258) 453535
Shaston Road; A350 NW of Blandford; DT11 8TA Traditional country local extended from early 18th-c core (originally two cottages); popular food from landlord-chef including OAP deal, well kept Badger ales and sensible wine list, good friendly service, open-plan layout with scrubbed pine tables on bare boards, woodburners, games part with pool; post office and shop; well behaved children welcome, dogs in bar, seats out at front and on back deck, open (and food) all day. *(Abigail Slater)*

STOURTON CAUNDLE ST7115

Trooper (01963) 362405
Village signed off A30 E of Milborne Port; DT10 2JW Pretty little stone-built pub in lovely village setting (Enid Blyton's house opposite); friendly staff and atmosphere, well kept changing beers (their microbrewery is currently closed), real ciders and good range of gins, simple home-made lunchtime food (not Sun), evening meals Weds, Fri (fish and chips) and Sat, tiny low-ceilinged bar, stripped-stone dining room, darts, dominoes and shove-ha'penny, skittle alley; background and some live music (folk and jazz), sports TV, outside gents'; children,

walkers and dogs welcome, a few picnic-sets out in front, pleasant side garden with play area, bunkhouse and camping, closed Mon. *(Charlie and Mark Todd)*

STRATTON SY6593

Saxon Arms (01305) 260020

Off A37 NW of Dorchester; The Square; DT2 9WG Traditional (though recently built) flint-and-thatch local; spacious open-plan interior with light oak tables and comfortable settles on flagstones or carpet, log fire, well kept Butcombe, Timothy Taylors Landlord and two guests, good value wines, tasty generous food including deli boards and good choice of specials, pleasant efficient service, large comfortable dining section on right; background music, traditional games; children and dogs welcome, terrace tables overlooking village green, open (and food) all day Fri-Sun. *(Marianne and Peter Stevens)*

STUDLAND SZ0382

Bankes Arms (01929) 450225

Off B3351, Isle of Purbeck; Manor Road; BH19 3AU Creeper-clad stone pub in very popular spot above fine beach, outstanding country, sea and cliff views from huge garden over road with lots of seating; comfortably basic big bar with raised drinking area, beams, flagstones and good log fire, several real ales including own Isle of Purbeck (Aug beer festival), local cider, decent wines by the glass and generally well liked blackboard food from sandwiches up, darts and pool in side area; background music, machines, sports TV; over-8s and dogs welcome, just off coast path near to Old Harry Rocks, can get very busy on summer weekends and parking complicated (NT car park), good-sized comfortable bedrooms, open (and food) all day. *(S Holder)*

STURMINSTER MARSHALL **SY9499**

Golden Fox (01258) 857217

A350; BH21 4AQ Roadside country pub with popular good value food and up to three real ales such as Dartmoor, Hop Back and Sixpenny, friendly helpful service, long comfortable beamed and panelled bar with log fire; games machines; children and dogs (in bar) welcome, terrace seating, open all day Fri-Sun, closed Tues. *(Frank and Marcia Pelling)*

STURMINSTER MARSHALL **SY9500**

Red Lion (01258) 857319

Opposite church; off A350 Blandford–Poole; BH21 4BU Attractive village pub opposite handsome church; bustling local atmosphere, wide variety of enjoyable food including good value set menu (Tues-Thurs, Sun evening), special diets catered for, Badger ales and nice wines, roomy U-shaped bar with log fire, good-sized dining room in former skittle alley; background music; children and dogs welcome, disabled access, back garden with wicker furniture and picnic-sets, open all day Sun, closed Mon. *(Ivy and George Goodwill)*

STURMINSTER NEWTON ST7813

Bull (01258) 472435

A357, S of centre; DT10 2BS Cosy thatched and beamed 15th-c pub, well kept Badger ales and enjoyable good value home-made food, friendly helpful staff, log fires; children and dogs welcome, roadside picnic-sets, more in small back garden, closed Sun evening, Mon, otherwise open all day. *(Sandra and Neil White)*

SWANAGE SZ0278

Red Lion (01929) 423533

High Street; BH19 2LY Popular and unpretentious low-beamed local with great choice of ciders and up to six well kept ales such as Otter, Ringwood, Sharps and Timothy Taylors, good value food including curry night (Weds) and steak night (Fri), quick friendly service, brasses around log fire, restaurant; background and some live music, pool, darts and fruit machine; children welcome till 9pm, picnic-sets in garden with part-covered terrace, bedrooms in former back coach house, open all day. *(David Lamb)*

SYDLING ST NICHOLAS SY6399

Greyhound (01300) 341303

Off A37 N of Dorchester; High Street; DT2 9PD Former coaching inn with beamed and flagstoned serving area, woodburner in brick fireplace, hops above counter, three well kept changing ales and a couple of proper ciders, carpeted bar with Portland stone fireplace, painted panelling and exposed stonework, popular food including good value set lunch, friendly welcoming staff, covered well in cosy dining room, flagstoned conservatory; children and dogs (in bar) welcome, picnic-sets in little front garden, six comfortable bedrooms, open all day Sun. *(Marianne and Peter Stevens)*

TARRANT MONKTON ST9408

★**Langton Arms** (01258) 830225

Village signposted from A354, then head for church; DT11 8RX Bustling thatched pub in picturesque spot next to 15th-c church; high-backed dining chairs around wooden tables on flagstones, a cushioned window seat and a few high chairs against light oak counter, Flack Manor Double Drop and guests, real cider and decent choice of wines and whiskies, popular food using meat from own farm, two connecting beamed dining rooms with cushioned wooden chairs around white-clothed tables, airy conservatory; background music, board games, skittle alley; children and dogs (in bar) welcome, seats out at front and in back garden with play area, six bedrooms in brick buildings around courtyard and in neighbouring cottage, open all day, food all day weekends. *(Dr and Mrs A K Clarke, Mr and Mrs Richard Osborne)*

TOLPUDDLE SY7994

Martyrs (01305) 848249

Former A35 W of Bere Regis; DT2 7ES 1920s village dining pub with enjoyable home-made food including Mon curry, Fri fish and chips and Sun carvery, two or three Badger ales, friendly accommodating staff, opened-up bare-boards interior; background music; children welcome, good disabled access, small front terrace and garden behind, open (and food) all day. *(Ivy and George Goodwill)*

TRENT SY5818

★**Rose & Crown** (01935) 850776

Opposite the church; DT9 4SL Partly thatched pub opposite lovely church; cosy little right-hand bar with sofas in front of open fire, bigger bar opposite has old wooden tables and chairs on quarry tiles, Wadworths ales, a guest beer and 20 wines by the glass, good food from sandwiches and pub favourites to well presented restaurant dishes, attentive friendly service, two other interconnected rooms with pews, grandfather clock and more fireplaces, simply furnished back dining room; quiz last Sun of month, board games, free wi-fi; children and dogs welcome, parasol-shaded tables in back garden with fine views (and sunsets), pretty bedrooms in converted byre, excellent breakfast, open all day. *(Guy Vowles, Michael Hill, Thomas Coke-Smyth)*

UPLODERS SY5093

Crown (01308) 485356

Signed off A35 E of Bridport; DT6 4NU Attractive stone-built village pub; log fires, dark low beams, flagstones and mix of old furniture including stripped pine, grandfather clock, good fairly traditional home-made food using local suppliers, three Palmers ales; background music; children and dogs (in bar) welcome, tables in pretty two-tier garden, closed Mon. *(Lyn and Freddie Roberts)*

WAREHAM SY9287

Kings Arms (01929) 552503

North Street (A351, N end of town); BH20 4AD Traditional thatched town local, five well kept changing ales, real cider and decent good value pubby food (till 6pm Sun), friendly staff, back serving counter and two bars off flagstoned central corridor, beams and inglenook log fire, carpeted dining room to the right, another at the back; some live music, free wi-fi; children and dogs welcome, steps up to rear garden with round picnic-sets and smokers' shelter, open all day. *(Shentonashenton)*

WAREHAM SY9287

Old Granary (01929) 552010

The Quay; BH20 4LP Fine old brick building (recently refurbished) in good riverside position – can get very busy; beamed snug by entrance opening into main bar with brick walls and new oak standing timbers, well kept Badger ales and good wines by the glass, enjoyable fairly standard food at reasonable prices, friendly young staff, restaurant area with connecting rooms, also upstairs river-view dining room; quiet background music; children and dogs (in bar) welcome, seats out overlooking the water and on covered roof terrace, boats for hire over bridge, limited nearby parking, open all day from 9am (10am Sun), food served from brunch on. *(Barbara and Phil Bowie)*

WAREHAM SY9287

Quay Inn (01929) 552735

The Quay; BH20 4LP Comfortable 18th-c pub in great waterside position; enjoyable food including pubby favourites and cook-your-own meat on a hot stone, well kept Isle of Purbeck, Ringwood and Timothy Taylors, friendly attentive service, two open fires (one gas); weekend live music; children and dogs welcome, terrace area and picnic-sets out on quay (boat trips), market day Sat, three bedrooms, parking nearby can be difficult, open all day. *(Robert Watt)*

WAREHAM FOREST SY9089

Silent Woman (01929) 552909

Wareham–Bere Regis; Bere Road; BH20 7PA Long neatly kept dining pub divided by doorways and standing timbers, good choice of enjoyable food including daily specials, Badger ales kept well and plenty of wines by the glass, friendly helpful young staff, traditional furnishings, farm tools and stripped masonry; background music; no children inside, dogs welcome, wheelchair access, plenty of picnic-sets outside including a covered area, walks nearby, opening times vary during the year and it's a popular wedding venue, so best to check it's open. *(S Holder)*

WAYTOWN SY4797

Hare & Hounds (01308) 488203

Between B3162 and A3066 N of Bridport; DT6 5LQ Attractive 18th-c country local up and down steps; friendly staff and regulars, well kept Palmers tapped from the cask, local cider, and generous helpings of enjoyable good value food (not Sun evening) including popular Sun lunch, open fire, two small cottagey rooms and pretty dining room; children and dogs welcome, lovely Brit Valley views from sizeable well maintained garden with play area. *(Abigail Slater)*

WEST BEXINGTON SY5386

Manor Hotel (01308) 897660

Off B3157 SE of Bridport; Beach Road; DT2 9DF Relaxing quietly set hotel with long history and fine sea views; good choice of enjoyable food (highish prices) in beamed cellar bar, flagstoned restaurant or Victorian-style conservatory, well kept Otter, Thatcher's cider and several wines by the glass; children welcome, dogs on leads (not in restaurant), charming well kept garden, close to Chesil Beach, 13 bedrooms. *(Ian Duncan)*

WEST KNIGHTON SY7387

New Inn (01305) 852349

Off A352 E of Dorchester; DT2 8PE Extended country pub with carpeted bar and restaurant, good home-made food using local produce including daily specials and Sun carvery, a couple of real ales such as Palmers, friendly efficient staff; skittle alley, pool, free wi-fi; children welcome, dogs in bar, pleasant setting on edge of quiet village with farmland views, eight bedrooms, good breakfast, open all day Sun. *(Mrs Sheila Davies)*

WEST LULWORTH SY8280

Castle Inn (01929) 400311

B3070 SW of Wareham; BH20 5RN Comfortably refurbished 16th-c thatched pub in lovely spot near Lulworth Cove, good walks and lots of summer visitors; beamed and flagstoned bar with some booth seating and button-back wall benches, Butcombe ales, real cider and plenty of wines by the glass, good food from pub favourites up, small connecting bar sharing fireplace with restaurant; background music; children and dogs welcome, tables out at front, attractive tiered garden behind, 12 bedrooms, open (and food) all day. *(Jake Myers)*

WEYMOUTH SY6778

Boot 07809 440772

High West Street; DT4 8JH Friendly unspoilt old local near the harbour; beams, bare boards, panelling, hooded stone-mullioned windows and coal fires, cosy gently sloping snug, ten well kept ales including Ringwood and other Marstons-related beers (tasting trays available), real cider and good selection of malt whiskies, no food apart from pork pies and pickled eggs (regulars bring own food on Sun to share); live music Tues, quiz Weds; free wi-fi; disabled access, pavement tables, open all day. *(Ted Bayliss)*

WEYMOUTH SY6779

Handmade Pie & Ale House (01305) 459342

Queen Street; DT4 7HZ Friendly and relaxed place opposite the station; wide range of good home-made pies plus other food, six well kept changing ales and plenty of ciders, more dining space in upstairs raftered room; children welcome, open (and food) all day. *(Ted Bayliss)*

WEYMOUTH SY6878

Nothe Tavern (01305) 787300

Barrack Road; DT4 8TZ Updated 19th-c red-brick pub a short walk from the busy harbour area; enjoyable food from lunchtime sandwiches and bar snacks up including daily specials, some vegan choices and weekend breakfasts, Brakspears, Ringwood and a dozen wines by the glass, friendly efficient service, restaurant with harbour and more distant sea views; children and dogs (in bar) welcome, more views from terrace, near Nothe Fort, open all day, food all day Sun till 7pm. *(Tony Scott, David and Doreen Beattie)*

WIMBORNE MINSTER SZ0199

Minster Arms (01202) 840700

West Street; BH21 1JS Updated candlelit corner pub with log fires, leather sofas and an assortment of tables and chairs on wood floors, three real ales and extensive choice of wines by the glass, well liked food from varied menu, friendly service; live music Thurs; children and dogs welcome, courtyard area with heaters, comfortable modern bedrooms, open (and food) all day. *(Maggie Cullock)*

WIMBORNE MINSTER SU0100

Olive Branch (01202) 884686

East Borough, just off Hanham Road (B3073, just E of its junction with B3078); BH21 1PF Handsome townhouse with various opened-up dining areas, one with beams and view into kitchen, another more canteen-like with long tables and padded benches, popular food from range of small plates through burgers up, relaxed atmosphere, Badger beers in comfortable panelled bar with woodburner, also a coffee bar; mediterranean-style garden, open all day from 8am for breakfast. *(Timothy)*

WINTERBORNE WHITECHURCH ST8300

Milton Arms (01258) 880431

A354 Blandford–Dorchester; DT11 0HW Good variety of well liked sensibly priced food in this modernised village pub, local ciders and three well kept beers, friendly helpful staff; children and dogs welcome, closed Sun evening, otherwise open all day. *(Darrell Barton)*

Real ale to us means beer that has matured naturally in its cask – not pressurised or filtered. We name all real ales stocked.

Essex

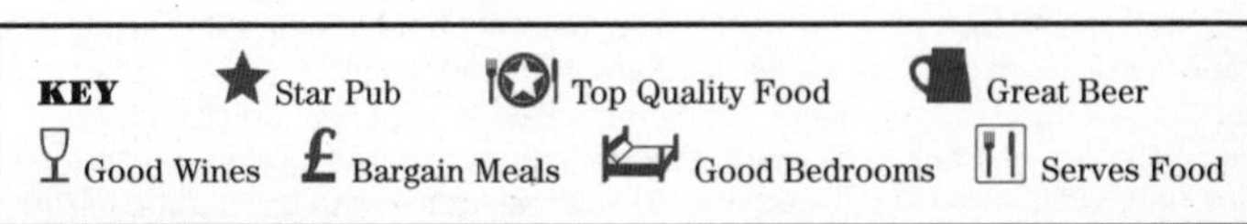

CHRISHALL TL4439 Map 5

Red Cow

(01763) 838792 – www.theredcow.com

High Street; off B1039 Wendens Ambo–Great Chishill; SG8 8RN

Bustling, well run local with beamed rooms, four real ales, well liked food and seats in attractive garden

There's a warm welcome for all in this thatched 16th-c pub from the hands-on landlord and his helpful staff. The neat bar is bustling and atmospheric and both it and the dining room are heavily beamed and timbered, with a woodburning stove and an open fire, all sorts of wooden dining chairs around tables of every size on bare floorboards, and a comfortable sofa and armchairs. Adnams Southwold and Woodfordes Wherry plus two guest beers such as Adnams Ghost Ship and Sharps Doom Bar on handpump, eight wines by the glass, Aspall's cider and cocktails; they hold a music and beer festival in May. Terraces have picnic-sets and the garden is pretty. The pub is well located for the Icknield Way.

Tasty food includes prawn and smoked trout fishcake with cucumber and sour cream, creamy garlic mushrooms on toast with parmesan, sharing boards, cumberland sausages with herb mash and gravy, roast butternut squash stuffed with celeriac and spinach with creamed leeks and roast tomatoes, a risotto of the day, steak burger with toppings, home-made pickled onions and onion rings, confit duck leg with roasted root vegetables and cider gravy, rib-eye steak with a choice of three sauces, and puddings such as warm chocolate brownie with mixed berries and rum chocolate sauce and sticky toffee pudding with butterscotch sauce and vanilla ice-cream. *Benchmark main dish: pie of the day £13.25. Two-course evening meal £20.00.*

Free house ~ Licensees Toby and Alexis Didier Serre ~ Real ale ~ Open 12-3, 6 (5.30 Fri)-midnight; 12-midnight Sat; 12-10.30 Sun; closed Mon ~ Bar food 12-2, 6-9; 12-2.30, 6-9.30 Sat; 12-3.30 Sun ~ Restaurant ~ Children welcome ~ Dogs allowed in bar ~ Wi-fi ~ Live music monthly Fri *Recommended by Mrs Margo Finlay, Jörg Kasprowski, Paul Farraday, Greta and Gavin Craddock, Bob and Melissa Wyatt, David Jackman, Serena and Adam Furber*

FEERING TL8720 Map 5

Sun

(01376) 570442 – www.suninnfeering.co.uk

Just off A12 Kelvedon bypass; Feering Hill (B1024 just W of Feering proper); CO5 9NH

Striking 16th-c pub with six real ales, well liked food and pleasant garden

The food here is well regarded, but with half a dozen real ales there are plenty of chatty customers propping up the bar for a pint and a chat. The busy slate-floored bar has an easy-going feel and two big woodburning stoves (one in the huge central inglenook fireplace, another by an antique winged settle on the left). Throughout there are handsomely carved black beams and timbers galore, and attractive wildflower murals in a frieze above the central timber divider. The beers on handpump include Shepherd Neame Bishops Finger, Master Brew, Spitfire Gold and Whitstable Bay Pale plus a guest such as Hercules Yardsman IPA, and they hold summer and winter beer festivals; also, 13 wines by the glass, ten malt whiskies and 21 gins served by cheerful staff. A brick-paved back courtyard has tables, heaters and a shelter, and tall trees shade green picnic-sets in the garden beyond. The pub has its own small car park through an archway in the middle of the adjoining terraced houses.

Enjoyable food includes lunchtime sandwiches, slow-roasted pork belly and scallops with apple purée and shaved fennel, salt-beef hash cake with tomato chutney and a fried quail egg, chestnut mushroom and halloumi fritters with a warm charred vegetable salad and sweet potato fries, wild boar and apple sausages with grain mustard mash and onion gravy, chicken breast with chive potato dumplings, braised leeks and white wine and spinach sauce, cod loin with smoked chorizo, patatas bravas, prosciutto crisp and lemon oil, and puddings such as white chocolate and passion-fruit roulade with vanilla bean ice-cream and rocky road cheesecake with double chocolate chip ice-cream. *Benchmark main dish: beef and stilton pie £12.95. Two-course evening meal £19.00.*

Shepherd Neame ~ Tenant Andy Howard ~ Real ale ~ Open 12-11; 12-midnight Fri, Sat; 12-10.30 Sun ~ Bar food 12-2.30, 6-9 (9.30 Fri, Sat); 12-8 Sun ~ Well behaved children welcome ~ Dogs welcome ~ Wi-fi *Recommended by David Fowler, Mrs Margo Finlay, Jörg Kasprowski, Frank and Marcia Pelling, Carolb, David Twitchett, Trevor and Michele Street*

FULLER STREET TL7416 Map 5

Square & Compasses

(01245) 361477 – www.thesquareandcompasses.co.uk
Back road Great Leighs–Hatfield Peverel; CM3 2BB

Neatly kept country pub with two woodburning stoves, three ales and enjoyable food

Handy for the Essex Way long-distance footpath and in attractive countryside, this 17th-c pub has a small extension for walkers and dogs. The L-shaped beamed bar has two woodburning stoves in inglenook fireplaces, and friendly staff serve Crouch Vale Brewers Gold and Essex Boys Best Bitter and Mighty Oak Captain Bob tapped from the cask, 23 wines by the glass, three farm ciders and home-made elderflower and lemon cordial; background jazz. The carpeted dining room features shelves of bottles and decanters against timbered walls, and an appealing variety of dining chairs around dark wooden tables set with linen napkins. Tables out in front on decking offer gentle country views.

The good, traditional food is seasonal and includes lunchtime sandwiches, garlic and rosemary baked mini camembert with red onion jam, pigeon breast with black pudding and plum and red wine sauce, chicken caesar salad, local pork sausages with spring onion mash and onion gravy, home-cooked ham and free-range eggs, a vegetarian dish and a fish dish of the day, burgers with toppings and chips, 28-day-aged rib-eye steak with trimmings, and puddings such as rhubarb and vanilla crème brûlée and chocolate brownie sundae with chocolate sauce. *Benchmark main dish: steak in ale pie £13.95. Two-course evening meal £21.00.*

Free house ~ Licensee Victor Roome ~ Real ale ~ Open 11.30-11; 12-11.30 Sat; 12-11 Sun ~ Bar food 12-2 (2.30 Sat), 6.30-9.30; 12-5.45 Sun ~ Restaurant ~ Well behaved children welcome ~ Dogs allowed in bar *Recommended by Rob Anderson, Ian Wilson, Patricia Healey, Andrew and Ruth Simmonds*

FYFIELD TL5706 Map 5

Queens Head

(01277) 899231 – www.queensheadfyfield.co.uk

Corner of B184 and Queen Street; CM5 0RY

Friendly old pub with seats in riverside garden, a good choice of drinks and highly regarded food

At weekends when this place is usefully open all day, customers tend to arrive early in warm weather in order to bag a seat in the prettily planted back garden that runs down to the sleepy River Roding. The compact, low-beamed, L-shaped bar has exposed timbers, pretty lamps on nice sturdy elm tables and comfortable seating from wall banquettes to attractive, unusual high-backed chairs, some in a snug little side booth. In summer, two facing fireplaces have church candles instead of a fire; background music. Adnams Broadside and Southwold and a guest such as St Austell Cousin Jack on handpump and seven good wines by the glass. The upstairs restaurant is more formal.

Enterprising food includes sandwiches, crab risotto with brown butter crumb, lemon crème fraîche and dill, ox cheek ragoût with linguine, parmesan and herbs, a pie of the day, mushroom, garlic and shallot pithivier with lemon and thyme mushrooms, celeriac and salsify, sea bass fillet with pork and prawn dumplings, sesame pak choi and shellfish and lemongrass consommé, chicken kiev with potato and thyme gallette, charred sweetcorn, cauliflower cheese and roasting juices, and puddings such as chocolate soufflé with chocolate sauce and pistachio ice-cream and blood orange sponge pudding with warm syrup and vanilla custard; they also offer a two- and three-course set lunch (not Sunday). *Benchmark main dish: cod bourguignon with charred pearl onions, smoked pancetta, parsnip purée and jus £19.00. Two-course evening meal £26.00.*

Free house ~ Licensee Daniel Lamprecht ~ Real ale ~ Open 11-3, 6-11; 11-11 Sat; 12-7 Sun; closed Mon (except bank holidays when open 12-7); Tues after bank holiday ~ Bar food 12-2.30 (4 Sat), 6.30-9.30; 12-6 Sun ~ Restaurant ~ Children welcome away from bar ~ Wi-fi *Recommended by Mrs Margo Finlay, Jörg Kasprowski, Nicholas and Maddy Trainer, Rosie and John Moore, Claire Adams, David and Leone Lawson*

GOLDHANGER TL9008 Map 5

Chequers

(01621) 788203 – www.thechequersgoldhanger.co.uk

Church Street; off B1026 E of Heybridge; CM9 8AS

Cheerful and neatly kept pub with six real ales, traditional furnishings, friendly staff and tasty food

'A cracking little pub,' says one happy reader who comes here on a regular basis. It's a friendly place, with a nice old corridor with red and black floor tiles leading to six rambling rooms. These include a spacious lounge with dark beams, black panelling and a huge sash window overlooking the graveyard, a traditional dining room with bare boards and carpeting and a games room with bar billiards; woodburning stove, open fires, TV and background music. Adnams Ghost Ship, Butcombe Original, Dark Star Hophead, Ringwood Old Thumper, Sharps Atlantic and Woodfordes Wherry on handpump, and they hold spring and autumn beer festivals. Also, 16 wines by the glass, ten malt whiskies and several farm ciders. There are picnic-sets under umbrellas in the courtyard with its grapevine. Do take a look at the fine old church next door.

The popular food includes sandwiches, duck, orange and cognac pâté with cumberland sauce, baked creamy stilton mushrooms, macaroni cheese and spinach bake, chicken curry, lamb and mint pudding with red wine gravy, smoked haddock and spring onion fishcakes with horseradish dip, steak and stout pie, jamaican jerk sirloin steak with thai battered prawns and chilli mayonnaise, and puddings such as lemon meringue pie and chocolate pot. *Benchmark main dish: chilli beef with sour cream and cheese £11.25. Two-course evening meal £17.00.*

Punch ~ Lease Philip Glover and Dominic Davies ~ Real ale ~ Open 11-11; 12-11 Sun ~ Bar food 12-3, 6.30-9; not Sun evening or Mon bank holiday evening ~ Restaurant ~ Children welcome except in tap room ~ Dogs allowed in bar ~ Wi-fi *Recommended by John and Mary Warner, Rupert and Sandy Newton, Amy Ledbetter, Dan and Belinda Smallbone*

HATFIELD BROAD OAK TL5416 Map 5

Dukes Head

(01279) 718598 – www.thedukeshead.co.uk

B183 Hatfield Heath–Takeley; High Street; CM22 7HH

Relaxed, well run dining pub with enjoyable food in an attractive layout of nicely linked separate areas

In warm weather, head for the back garden here with its sheltered terrace and chairs around teak tables under parasols; there are also picnic-sets at the front corner of the building which has some nice pargeting. Rambling around the central woodburner and side servery are various cosy seating areas: good solid wooden dining chairs around a variety of chunky stripped tables with a comfortable group of armchairs and a sofa at one end, and a slightly more formal area at the back on the right. Cheerful prints on the wall and some magenta panels in the mostly cream décor make for a buoyant mood. Greene King IPA, Sharps Doom Bar and Timothy Taylors Landlord on handpump and 20 wines by the glass from a good list, served by cheerful staff; background music and board games. Sam and Zac the pub dogs welcome other canines and there are always dog biscuits on offer.

Reliably good food includes crispy salmon and crab fishcakes with cauliflower purée, french-style peas and tomato butter sauce, oak-smoked bacon, free-range poached egg and hollandaise sauce, local sausages with creamy mash and shallot and thyme gravy, wild mushroom macaroni cheese with crispy halloumi, beer-battered fish and chips, free-range chicken with basil mash, brie and tomato and basil sauce, steak in ale pie, and puddings such as Cointreau crème brûlée and a crumble of the day with custard. *Benchmark main dish: king prawn spaghetti £13.25. Two-course evening meal £22.00.*

Enterprise ~ Lease Liz Flodman ~ Real ale ~ Open 11.30-11; 11.30-9 Sun ~ Bar food 12-2.30, 6-9; 12-9 Sat; 12-6 Sun ~ Restaurant ~ Children welcome ~ Dogs allowed in bar ~ Wi-fi *Recommended by Isobel Mackinlay, Shona and Jimmy McDuff, Paddy and Sian O'Leary*

Please tell us if any pub deserves to be upgraded to a featured entry – and why: feedback@goodguides.com, or (no stamp needed) The Good Pub Guide, FREEPOST RTXY–ZCBC–BBAZ, Stream Lane, Sedlescombe, Battle TN33 0PB.

HORNDON-ON-THE-HILL TQ6783 Map 3

Bell

(01375) 642463 – www.bell-inn.co.uk

M25 junction 30 into A13, then left after 7 miles on to B1007, village signposted from here; SS17 8LD

Essex Dining Pub of the Year

Lovely historic pub with fine food and a very good range of drinks; lovely bedrooms

Our readers love all aspects of this fine old place, and many return regularly. It's been run by the same friendly family for more than 80 years, and they treat it and their customers with great care and respect. The heavily beamed, panelled bar maintains a strongly pubby appearance with high-backed antique settles and benches, rugs on flagstones and highly polished oak floorboards, and an open log fire. Look out for the curious collection of ossified hot-cross buns hanging along a beam in the saloon bar – the first was put there in 1906 to mark the day (a Good Friday) that Jack Turnell became licensee. The timbered restaurant has numerous old copper pots and pans hanging from beams. An impressive range of drinks includes Crouch Vale Brewers Gold, Greene King IPA and London Glory, Morlands Old Hoppy Hen, Sharps Doom Bar and Shepherd Neame Hog Island and Spitfire Gold on handpump, 20 gins and over 114 well chosen wines (16 by the glass). Two giant umbrellas cover the courtyard, which has very pretty hanging baskets in summer. Centuries ago, many important medieval dignitaries would have stayed here as it was the last inn before travellers heading south could ford the Thames at Highams Causeway. Today, it remains a special place to stay with individually styled, thoughtfully equipped bedrooms of all sizes, from large and grand to small and cosy.

Excellent, imaginative food includes sandwiches, smoked haddock and crayfish ballotine with curried risotto ball, wild garlic mayonnaise and a poached quail egg, confit beef and white pudding spring roll with celeriac rémoulade and rocket pesto, leek and goats cheese ravioli with sautéed peas, warm lentil dressing and wild garlic velouté, herb-roasted lamb chump on cumin aubergine purée, piquillo and courgette couscous and mint yoghurt, chicken escalope with a fried egg, sea bass with carrot and courgette spaghetti, dill and cockles and seaweed rice crackers, venison escalope with venison spring roll, beetroot emulsion, pickled chestnut mushroom and jus, and puddings such as milk chocolate torte with salted caramel sauce and peanut butter ice-cream and mango cheesecake with lemon anglaise, poached kumquats and an orange crisp. *Benchmark main dish: local suckling pig £19.95. Two-course evening meal £27.50.*

Free house ~ Licensee John Vereker ~ Real ale ~ Open 11-11; 12-10.30 Sun ~ Bar food 12-2, 6.30 (6 Sun)-10 ~ Restaurant ~ Children welcome ~ Dogs allowed in bar and bedrooms ~ Wi-fi ~ Bedrooms: /£90 *Recommended by Patricia and Gordon Thompson, Matt and Hayley Jacob, Charles Todd, Gwendoline and Ralph Mason, Christopher May*

HOWE STREET TL6914 Map 5

Green Man

(01245) 408820 – www.galvingreenman.com

Just off A130 N of Chelmsford; CM3 1BG

Sizeable pub with up-to-date extensions, plenty of natural light, three real ales, first-class food, friendly staff and big garden

Cleverly extended to include a central conservatory area, this country place is owned by the Galvin brothers, both exceptional chefs – therefore the food plays a major role here. But for those wanting a chat and a drink after a walk with their dog, there is a cosy, timber-framed bar with proper character: flagstones or bare boards, an open fire, leather-topped stools, a button-back brown leather chesterfield, nice old wooden chairs around circular tables, a cushioned window seat and photos and prints on ochre walls. Also, Adnams Ghost Ship, Bishop Nick Heresy and Trumans Runner in handpump, good wines by the glass, several malt whiskies, organic cider and a non-alcoholic juice of the day. Staff are attentive, friendly and helpful. The high-raftered dining rooms are divided by a two-way woodburning stove in a large brick fireplace. Big windows and glass doors provide plenty of natural light and the contemporary furnishings include modern lighting, and dark painted cushioned dining chairs and long button-back leather banquettes on either pale floorboards or flagstones; background music and TV. The 1.5 acres of garden, with the River Chelmer running along the bottom, has black metal furniture on a terrace and picnic-sets on grass.

Excellent food includes baguettes, charred mackerel with guacamole, wasabi and apple blossom, whipped duck liver parfait with shallot marmalade, roasted aubergine with red pepper piperade and yoghurt sauce, lamb, rosemary and apricot pie, a fish dish of the day such as monkfish with chorizo and bean stew with samphire, caramelised duck breast with seville orange jus, sirloin steak with dauphinoise potatoes and shallot and red wine jus, and puddings such as apple tarte tatin with crème fraîche and hot Valrhona chocolate fondant with blood orange sorbet; they also offer a daily 'host a roast' where you share a roast and a pudding with friends or family. *Benchmark main dish: burger with tomato fondue, bacon and smoked cheese £15.50. Two-course evening meal £22.00.*

Galvin Pub Company ~ Licensee Chris and Jeff Galvin ~ Real ale ~ Open 12-11; 11am-11.30pm Sat; 11-9.30 Sun ~ Bar food 12-9.30; 11.30-10.30 Fri, Sat; 11.30-6 Sun ~ Restaurant ~ Children welcome ~ Dogs allowed in bar ~ Wi-fi *Recommended by Gilly Cooch, Mrs Margo Finlay, Jörg Kasprowski*

HULLBRIDGE TQ8195 Map 5

Anchor

(01702) 230777 – www.theanchorhullbridge.co.uk
Ferry Road; SS5 6ND

Big riverside pub with seats by the water, orangery-style restaurant, a good selection of drinks, up-to-date décor and modern british food

This pub's position by the River Crouch is lovely, and circular picnic-sets under parasols on grass and chrome and wicker seats on terraces look over the water. Inside, the décor and furnishings are contemporary but the bar is friendly (as are the efficient staff) and relaxed and they keep Fullers London Pride, Leigh on Sea Six Little Ships and a guest ale on handpump, good wines by the glass and plenty of cocktails; background music. There are sofas, curved banquettes and black leather wall seats on wooden floorboards and high chairs by the counter used by chatty locals. The main focus is probably on the restaurant with its floor-to-ceiling windows, pale leather dining chairs around wooden tables on more wooden floors and very tall button-back banquettes; the open kitchen keeps things lively.

Skilfully cooked, the highly popular bistro-style food includes sandwiches (until 5pm), garlic and chilli king prawns with white wine and tomato sauce, chicken and smoked ham croquette with red onion marmalade, build-your-own salads with a lengthy choice of toppings, cauliflower cheese and grain mustard suet pudding, slow-roasted pork belly in ale and mustard with apple purée and crackling, Josper oven-cooked steaks with peppercorn or béarnaise sauce, and puddings such as white chocolate cheesecake with honeycomb ice-cream and passion-fruit and lemon curd meringue mess with lemon sorbet. *Benchmark main dish: burgers with toppings, pickles and fries £13.00. Two-course evening meal £24.00.*

Oakman Inns & Restaurants ~ Manager Charlotte Claxton ~ Real ale ~ Open 11-11 (midnight Sat); 11-10.30 Sun ~ Bar food 11am-10pm (9pm Sun) ~ Restaurant ~ Dogs allowed in bar ~ Wi-fi *Recommended by David and Charlotte Green, David and Leone Lawson, John and Delia Franks*

LITTLE WALDEN TL5441 Map 5

Crown £

(01799) 522475 – www.thecrownlittlewalden.co.uk

B1052 N of Saffron Walden; CB10 1XA

Bustling old pub with a warming log fire, hearty food and bedrooms

This 18th-c cottage is very much the hub of the local community, but the hands-on landlord and his family always ensure that visitors feel just as welcome. The low-ceilinged rooms have a cosy, chatty atmosphere and traditional furnishings, with book-room-red walls, floral curtains, bare boards, navy carpeting, cosy warm fires and an unusual walk-through fireplace. A higgledy-piggledy mix of chairs ranges from high-backed pews to little cushioned armchairs spaced around a good variety of closely arranged tables, mostly big, some stripped. The small red-tiled room on the right has two small tables. Three changing beers, such as Adnams Broadside, Greene King Abbot and Woodfordes Wherry, and a guest ale are tapped straight from casks racked up behind the bar; TV. Tables on the terrace have views over the tranquil surrounding countryside. Our readers love staying overnight here and the breakfasts are excellent. Disabled access.

Well liked food includes lunchtime sandwiches and baguettes, crayfish cocktail, creamy garlic mushrooms, four-cheese ravioli, beer-battered fish and chips, honey-roast ham and eggs, moussaka, pork fillets in cajun sauce, caribbean king prawn curry, daily specials, and puddings such as spicy apple crumble and chocolate sponge with chocolate sauce. *Benchmark main dish: steak and mushroom pie £10.95. Two-course evening meal £17.00.*

Free house ~ Licensee Colin Hayling ~ Real ale ~ Open 11.30-2.30, 6-11; 12-11 Sun ~ Bar food 12-2, 7-9; 12-4 Sun ~ Restaurant ~ Children welcome ~ Dogs welcome ~ Wi-fi ~ Jazz Weds evening ~ Bedrooms: /£80 *Recommended by Sara Fulton, Roger Baker, Guy Henderson, Colin and Daniel Gibbs, Elisabeth and Bill Humphries, David Twitchett*

LITTLEY GREEN TL6917 Map 5

Compasses

(01245) 362308 – www.compasseslittleygreen.co.uk

Village signposted off B1417 Felsted road in Hartoft End (opposite former Ridleys Brewery), about a mile N of junction with B1008 (former A130); CM3 1BU

Charming brick tavern – a prime example of what is now an all too rare breed; bedrooms

The companionable bar here keeps a fine range of ales such as Bishop Nick Ridleys Rite (brewed in Felsted by the landlord's brother) as well as guests from Adnams, Crouch Vale, Green Jack, Mighty Oak, Red Fox, Skinners, Tyne Bank and two weekend guest ales, all tapped from casks in a back cellar. In summer and at Christmas they hold beer festivals featuring dozens of beers, alongside events that may include vintage ploughing in the field opposite. Also, constantly changing ciders from Biddenden, Carter's,

Millwhites, Orchard Pig and so forth, and eight wines by the glass. The bar has very traditional brown-painted panelling and wall benches, plain chairs and tables on quarry tiles, and chat and laughter rather than piped music as the backdrop. There's a piano, darts and board games in one side room, and decorative mugs hanging from beams in another. Picnic-sets sit out on the sheltered side grass and the garden behind, with a couple of long tables on the front cobbles by the quiet lane. Bedrooms are in a small newish block.

A big blackboard shows the day's range of huffers: big rolls with a hearty range of hot or cold fillings. They also serve ploughman's, baked potatoes and a few sensibly priced dishes such as chicken liver pâté, a changing curry, gammon and egg, and rib-eye steak. *Benchmark main dish: beer-battered cod and chips £10.00. Two-course evening meal £17.00.*

Free house ~ Licensee Jocelyn Ridley ~ Real ale ~ Open 12-3, 5.30-11.30; 12-11.30 Thurs-Sun ~ Bar food 12-2.30, 6.30-9.30; 12-2.30, 6-9.30 Fri; 12-4, 6-9.30 Sat; 12-8.30 Sun ~ Children welcome ~ Dogs welcome ~ Wi-fi ~ Live folk music every third Mon ~ Bedrooms: /£85
Recommended by Harvey Brown, Alf Wright, Donald Allsopp, David Jackman, David Twitchett, Alf and Sally Garner, Glen and Patricia Fuller

MARGARETTING TYE TL6801 Map 5

White Hart £

(01277) 840478 – www.thewhitehart.uk.com

From B1002 (just S of A12/A414 junction) follow Maldon Road for 1.3 miles, then turn right immediately after river bridge, into Swan Lane, keeping on for 0.7 miles; The Tye; CM4 9JX

Cheery pub with a fine choice of ales, good food, plenty of customers and a family garden; bedrooms

This ticks all the boxes for a well run country pub. The open-plan but cottagey rooms have walls and wainscoting painted in chalky traditional colours that match well with the dark timbers, and a mix of old wooden chairs and tables; a stuffed deer head is mounted on the chimney breast above a woodburning stove. Tapped straight from the cask, the range of ales includes Adnams Broadside and Southwold, Mighty Oak Maldon Gold and Mauldons Silver Adder, and they hold an annual beer festival in July. Also, a summer german wheat beer, interesting bottled beers, 14 wines by the glass, eight malt whiskies, 30 gins and winter mulled wine. The neat carpeted back conservatory is similar in style to the other rooms, and the front lobby has a bookcase of charity paperbacks. Darts, board games and background music. There are plenty of picnic-sets out on grass and terracing around the pub, with a fenced duck pond and views across the fields – the sunsets are lovely.

Reliably good cooking includes sandwiches, baked camembert parcel with figs, prawn, crayfish and avocado tian, leek, pear and blue cheese pie, beer-battered haddock with chips, herb-crusted lamb rump with celeriac dauphinoise, carrot purée and rosemary jus, rare-breed burger with toppings, coleslaw and onion rings, guinea fowl breast and confit leg with pancetta and shallot mash and wild mushroom jus, thai sea bass fillet with green curry sauce and pak choi, and puddings such as sticky fig and ginger pudding with toffee sauce and vanilla ice-cream and hot chocolate fondant. *Benchmark main dish: steak in ale pie £13.95. Two-course evening meal £22.00.*

Free house ~ Licensee Saran Duffy ~ Real ale ~ Open 11.30-3.30, 6-11; 11.30-midnight Sat; 11.30-11 Sun; closed Mon evening (closed all day in winter) ~ Bar food 12-2.30, 6-9; 12-2.30, 6-9.30 Fri; 12-3, 6-9.30 Sat; 12-7 Sun ~ Restaurant ~ Well behaved children welcome ~ Dogs allowed in bar and bedrooms ~ Wi-fi ~ Bedrooms: /£80 *Recommended by Sylvia and Phillip Spencer, Louise and Oliver Redman, David Twitchett*

SOUTH HANNINGFIELD TQ7497 Map 5

Old Windmill

(01268) 712280 – www.brunningandprice.co.uk/oldwindmill

Off A130 S of Chelmsford; CM3 8HT

Extensive, invitingly converted pub with interesting food and a good range of drinks

Cosy, rambling areas are created by a forest of stripped standing timbers and open doorways here, and there's an agreeable mix of highly polished old tables and chairs spread throughout, as well as frame-to-frame pictures on cream walls, woodburning stoves and big pot plants. Deep green or dark red dados and a few old rugs dotted on the polished wood floors provide splashes of colour; other areas are more subdued, with beige carpeting. Attentive young staff serve Phoenix Brunning & Price Original and Crouch Vale Brewers Gold with guests such as Brentwood Gold, Mighty Oak Captain Bob and Nethergate Five Rifles Red on handpump, a dozen wines by the glass, 70 malt whiskies and a good range of spirits; background music. A back terrace has tables and chairs under parasols and there are picnic-sets on the lawn and a few more seats out in front.

Up-to-date food includes sandwiches, seared scallops with shrimp fritters and pea purée, tempura vegetables with a lime and sweet chilli sauce, a charcuterie or meze board, spinach and ricotta filled pasta with tarragon crème fraîche sauce and toasted pine nuts, slow-roasted lamb shoulder with dauphinoise potatoes and minted gravy, fish pie, rump steak with watercress and horseradish butter and chips, and puddings such as lemon cheesecake with crushed meringue and sticky toffee pudding with toffee sauce and vanilla ice-cream. *Benchmark main dish: steak in ale pie £13.95. Two-course evening meal £21.00.*

Brunning & Price ~ Manager Nick Clark ~ Real ale ~ Open 11.30-11; 12-10.30 Sun ~ Bar food 12-10; 12-9.30 Sun ~ Restaurant ~ Children welcome ~ Dogs allowed in bar ~ Wi-fi

Recommended by Celia and Geoff Clay, Millie and Peter Downing, John and Abigail Prescott, Neil Allen, John Saville, David Twitchett, Heather and Richard Jones

STOCK TQ6999 Map 5

Hoop

(01277) 841137 – www.thehoop.co.uk

B1007; from A12 Chelmsford bypass take Galleywood, Billericay turn-off; CM4 9BD

Cheerful weatherboarded pub with interesting beers, nice food and a large garden

The good range of well kept real ales changes regularly but might include Adnams Bitter and guests such as Adnams Broadside, Pheasantry American Red Ale, Pitchfork GoldBine and Youngs Special on handpump; they also hold a beer festival at the end of May featuring 100 real ales, 80 ciders, a hog roast and a barbecue. The open-plan bar has a cheerful mix of customers and an upbeat atmosphere, beams and standing timbers (hinting at the original layout when it was once three weavers' cottages) and pubby tables and chairs. The dining room up in the timbered eaves is a fine space with an open fire in a big brick-walled fireplace, napery and elegant high-backed wooden chairs on bare boards. A large sheltered back garden, prettily bordered with flowers, has picnic-sets and a covered seating area. Parking is limited, so it's worth arriving early.

Pleasing pub food includes lunchtime sandwiches (until 5pm Sat), crab and prawn cocktail, whipped chicken liver parfait with burnt orange purée, a pie

and a vegetarian dish of the day, calves liver with crispy bacon, creamy potato, home-cooked onion rings and gravy, and ham with a mustard and honey glaze, duck eggs and chips; restaurant choices include whole grilled skate wing with cocotte potatoes, cucumber, brown shrimp and parsley, and roast pork belly with orange and fennel, caramelised chicory and squid croquette; puddings include treacle tart with clotted cream and white chocolate and vanilla bavarois with strawberry jelly and pistachio ice-cream. *Benchmark main dish: toad in the hole £12.95. Two-course evening meal £22.00.*

Free house ~ Licensee Michelle Corrigan ~ Real ale ~ Open 11.30-11; 12-10.30 Sun ~ Bar food 12-2.30, 6-9 (9.30 Fri); 12-9.30 Sat; 12-5 Sun ~ Restaurant ~ Children welcome on left-hand side of bar ~ Dogs allowed in bar ~ Wi-fi *Recommended by Patrick and Emma Stephenson, Patti and James Davidson, Lauren and Dan Frazer, Simon and Sue Lamb, Adam and Natalie Davis*

Also Worth a Visit in Essex

Besides the fully inspected pubs, you might like to try these pubs that have been recommended to us and described by readers. Do tell us what you think of them: feedback@goodguides.com

ARDLEIGH TM0429

★**Wooden Fender** (01206) 230466
A137 towards Colchester; CO7 7PA Extended old pub (former 17th-c staging post) with beams and log fires; good freshly made food from sharing plates through grills to daily specials, Greene King and guests, decent wines, friendly attentive service; children welcome in large dining area, dogs in bar, good-sized garden with play area, open all day Fri and Sat, till 9pm Sun, breakfast 7.30-11am Weds-Sun. *(Christopher May)*

AYTHORPE RODING TL5915

Axe & Compasses (01279) 876648
B184 S of Dunmow; CM6 1PP Attractive weatherboarded and part-thatched roadside pub, neatly kept and cosy, with beams, stripped brickwork and pale wood floors, modern furnishings, original part (on the left) has a two-way fireplace marking off a snug raftered dining area, popular food from light lunches up including deals, four real ales such as Adnams and Fullers, Weston's ciders and 13 wines by the glass; background and some live music, monthly quiz, board games; small back garden with stylish modern furniture, views across fields to windmill, open (and food) all day from 9am for breakfast. *(Serena and Adam Furber)*

BELCHAMP ST PAUL TL7942

Half Moon (01787) 277402
Cole Green; CO10 7DP Quaint 16th-c thatched and beamed pub overlooking village green, good reasonably priced home-made food (not Sun evening, Mon) from varied menu, well kept Greene King IPA and guests, decent wines by the glass, friendly helpful staff, snug carpeted interior with woodburner, restaurant; Aug beer/music festival; children welcome, no dogs inside, tables out in front and in back garden, open all day weekends. *(John and Delia Franks)*

BIRCHANGER TL5122

★**Three Willows** (01279) 815913
Under a mile from M11 junction 8: A120 towards Bishop's Stortford, then almost immediately right to Birchanger Village; don't be waylaid earlier by the Birchanger Services signpost; CM23 5QR Welcoming dining pub feeling nicely tucked away; spacious carpeted bar with lots of cricketing memorabilia, well furnished smaller lounge, Greene King ales and good range of popular fairly traditional food including plenty of fresh fish, efficient friendly service; children welcome, dogs allowed in bar area, picnic-sets out in front and on lawn behind (some motorway and Stansted Airport noise), good play area, closed Sun evening. *(Claire Adams)*

BISHOPS GREEN TL6317

Spotted Dog (01245) 231598
High Easter Road; CM6 1NF Pretty 18th-c thatched pub-restaurant in quiet rural hamlet; very good food cooked by landlord-chef including more affordable set menu (not Fri, Sat evenings or Sun lunchtime), friendly attentive staff, Greene King IPA and a guest, contemporary beamed interior with high-backed leather chairs at well spaced tables; background music; children welcome, rattan-style furniture out behind picket fence, closed Sun evening, Mon. *(Christopher May)*

BOREHAM TL7409

Lion (01245) 394900
Main Road; CM3 3JA Stylish bistro-bar with rooms, popular affordably priced food from snacks to daily specials, no bookings so may have to queue at busy times, several wines by the glass, bottled beers and up

to six well kept changing ales, efficient friendly staff, conservatory; monthly comedy club; children welcome, no dogs inside, 23 comfortable bedrooms, open all day. *(Tina and David Woods-Taylor)*

BOREHAM TL7509

Six Bells (01245) 467232
Main Road (B1137); CM3 3JE
Family dining pub with several linked areas including inglenook bar, good affordably priced home-cooked food (smaller appetites catered for), well kept Greene King ales and a guest, polite helpful staff; no dogs inside, play area in good-sized garden, open (and food) all day weekends. *(Tina and David Woods-Taylor)*

BRAINTREE TL7421

King William IV (01376) 567755
London Road; CM77 7PU Small friendly drinkers' local with two simple bars, up to five real ales tapped from the cask including own Moody Goose brews, also proper ciders/perries and some unusual lagers, no food apart from snacks; folk night third Sun of month; dogs welcome (theirs is Narla), picnic-sets in big garden, open all day Fri-Sun, from 3pm other days. *(Mark Crossley)*

BRENTWOOD TQ6195

Rose (01277) 218809
Chelmsford Road (A1023), Shenfield; CM15 8RN Updated beamed and timbered dining pub serving good fairly priced food all day (booking advised), a couple of real ales including one badged for them and plenty of wines by the glass, friendly attentive young staff, cosy interior with woodburners and separate restaurant; children welcome, no dogs inside, terrace tables (some under cover), open all day from 8am (midday Sun). *(Mrs Margo Finlay, Jörg Kasprowski)*

BULMER TYE TL8438

★**Bulmer Fox** (01787) 312277
A131 S of Sudbury; CO10 7EB Popular refurbished pub-bistro with good fairly priced food from varied menu, mix of tables and chairs on bare boards including some booth seating, forms to write your order (can also order at the bar), Adnams and Greene King IPA, friendly staff, quieter side room and intimate central snug, lots of colourful artwork, home-made chutneys, preserves etc for sale; children welcome, sheltered back terrace with arbour. *(Andrew and Ruth Simmonds)*

BURNHAM-ON-CROUCH TQ9596

Ship (01621) 785057
High Street; CM0 8AA Refurbished 18th-c dining pub with good fairly priced food from imaginative snacks up, local beers plus guests such as Harveys, decent wines and cocktails, friendly helpful staff, bare-boards bar with blue-painted panelling and woodburner, restaurant; background music; children welcome, some pavement seating, three comfortable boutique-style bedrooms, open (and food) all day. *(Martin Day)*

BURNHAM-ON-CROUCH TQ9495

★**White Harte** (01621) 782106
The Quay; CM0 8AS Cosy old-fashioned 17th-c hotel on water's edge overlooking yacht-filled River Crouch; partly carpeted bars with down-to-earth charm, assorted nautical bric-a-brac and hardware, other traditionally furnished high-ceilinged rooms with sea pictures on brown panelled or stripped brick walls, cushioned seats around oak tables, enormous winter log fire, good range of enjoyable well priced food including daily specials, beers from Adnams and Crouch Vale, friendly fast service; children and dogs welcome, outside seating jettied over the water, 19 bedrooms (eight with river view), good breakfast, open all day. *(Alf and Sally Garner)*

BURTON END TL5323

Ash (01279) 814841
Just N of Stansted Airport; CM24 8UQ Thatched 17th-c country pub; Greene King IPA and Abbott plus a beer badged for them, decent range of wines by the glass and enjoyable generously served food from lunchtime sandwiches/baguettes and pubby choices up, friendly staff, black beams and timbers, quarry tiled floors, woodburner, pitched-roof dining extension; sports TV, free wi-fi; children welcome, tables out on deck and grass, open (and food) all day. *(Mrs Margo Finlay, Jörg Kasprowski)*

CASTLE HEDINGHAM TL7835

Bell (01787) 460350
St James Street B1058; CO9 3EJ Beamed and timbered three-bar pub dating from the 15th c, unpretentious, unspoilt and run by the same family since the late 1960s; Adnams, Mighty Oak and guests tapped from the cask (July beer festival), popular pubby food along with turkish specials, good friendly service; background and live music including lunchtime jazz last Sun of month, quiz Sun evening; dogs welcome, children away from public bar, garden with hops and covered area, handy for Hedingham Castle, open all day Fri-Sun. *(Heather and Richard Jones)*

CHATHAM GREEN TL7115

Windmill (01245) 910910
Chatham Green, pub signed from A131; CM3 3LE Beamed and timbered country dining pub with well liked attractively presented food from chef-landlord, good wine list, cocktails and ales such as Bishop Nick Ridleys Rite and Greene King IPA, friendly helpful staff, cushioned wooden chairs around sturdy tables on bare boards or tartan carpet, some rustic bric-a-brac, log fires; dogs and children welcome (they eat free on Sun – one child per adult), tables out at

front, plans for bedrooms in adjacent stub of former windmill, open all day Fri and Sat, till 9pm Sun, closed Mon, Tues and lunchtimes Weds, Thurs. *(Pat Reed)*

CHELMSFORD TL7006

Orange Tree (01245) 262664

Lower Anchor Street; CM2 0AS Bargain lunchtime bar food (also steak and curry night Thurs) in two-room brick local, eight well kept ales such as Dark Star, Mighty Oak, Plain and Skinners (some tapped from the cask), efficient service; Tues charity quiz, sports TV; dogs welcome in public bar, back terrace, handy for county cricket ground and can get very busy on match days, open all day. *(Iain Bush)*

CHIGWELL ROW TQ4693

Two Brewers (020) 8501 1313

Lambourne Road; IG7 6ET Spacious Home Counties pub with welcoming relaxed atmosphere; assortment of tables and chairs and wall banquettes on flagstones or bare boards, heavy draped curtains, lots of pictures, photos and gilt-edged mirrors, two-way fireplace, good choice of real ales and wines by the glass, popular food from varied menu, friendly attentive young staff; children and dogs welcome, nice three-mile circular walk from the door, open (and food) all day. *(Andrew and Ruth Simmonds)*

CLAVERING TL4832

★**Cricketers** (01799) 550442

B1038 Newport–Buntingford; CB11 4QT Busy dining pub with plenty of old-fashioned charm, inventive food and signed cookbooks by Jamie Oliver (his parents own it); main area with very low beams and big open fireplace, bays of deep purple button-backed banquettes and padded leather dining chairs on dark floorboards, split-level back part with carpeted dining areas and some big copper and brass pans on dark beams and timbers, three Adnams beers and 19 wines by the glass; background music, free wi-fi; children welcome, attractive front terrace with rattan-style chairs around teak tables, bedrooms, handy for Stansted Airport, open all day from 7am, food all day Sun. *(Pat Reed)*

COLCHESTER TL9924

Fat Cat (01206) 577990

Butt Road/Alexandra Road; CO3 3BZ Small sister pub to the Ipswich and Norwich Fat Cats; eight well kept ales (including their own) and wide range of other beers all marked up on blackboard, enjoyable inexpensive food (not Mon-Weds), friendly helpful staff; beer festivals, Sun quiz, sports TV; children (until 5pm weekends only) and dogs welcome, open all day from 2pm (noon Fri and Sun, 11.30am Sat). *(Claire Adams)*

COLNE ENGAINE TL8530

Five Bells (01787) 224166

Signed off A1124 (was A604) in Earls Colne; Mill Lane; CO6 2HY Updated village pub with list of landlords back to 1579; half a dozen well kept changing ales including Adnams, popular home-made food from sandwiches and pub classics up, friendly if not always speedy service, bare boards or carpeted floors, painted beams, woodburners, old photographs, high-raftered dining area (former slaughterhouse), public bar with table football and darts; some live music, free wi-fi; children, walkers and dogs welcome, disabled facilities, attractive front terrace with gentle Colne Valley views, open all day, food all day weekends. *(Mrs Margo Finlay, Jörg Kasprowski)*

DANBURY TL7805

Bakers Arms (01245) 227300

Maldon Road; CM3 4QH Pink-painted roadside pub with pleasant informal atmosphere, well kept ales such as Adnams and Sharps, enjoyable food (not Sun evening) including pizzas and four sizes of fish and chips, welcoming cheerful staff; children and dogs allowed (they have a mastiff and great dane), picnic-sets in back garden, open all day (till 8pm Sun). *(Tina and David Woods-Taylor)*

DEBDEN TL5533

Plough (01799) 541899

High Street; CB11 3LE Welcoming village pub doing well under hard-working licensees; good freshly made food from landlord-chef including daily specials, up to four well kept local ales and decent wines, cheerful helpful service, restaurant, log fire; children and dogs (in bar) welcome, fair-sized garden behind, open all day Fri-Sun, closed Mon and lunchtime Tues. *(Brian Farley)*

DEDHAM TM0533

Sun (01206) 323351

High Street (B2109); CO7 6DF Tudor coaching inn opposite church; popular food with some italian influences (should book at peak times), impressive wine selection with many by the glass/carafe, well kept Adnams, Crouch Vale and two guests, Aspall's cider, afternoon teas, historic panelled interior with high carved beams, handsome furnishings and splendid fireplaces, split-level dining room; background music, TV; children and dogs (in bar) welcome, picnic-sets on quiet back lawn with mature trees and view of church, characterful panelled bedrooms, good Flatford Mill walk, open all day. *(Glen and Patricia Fuller)*

DUNMOW TL6222

★**Angel & Harp** (01371) 859259

Church Road, Church End; B1057 signposted to Finchingfield/The Bardfields, off B184 N of town; CM6 2AD Comfortable old place with linked rooms rambling around through standing timbers and doorways, mix of seating including armchairs, sofas and banquettes, stools each side of free-standing zinc 'counter' serving Adnams, Nethergate, a guest beer and 11 wines by the glass, good range of popular food (booking advised), friendly obliging service, substantial brick fireplace and some fine old floor tiles in low-ceilinged main area, steps up to interesting raftered room with one huge table, also attractive extension with glass wall overlooking flagstoned courtyard and grassed area beyond; background music, quiz last Weds of month, free wi-fi; children and dogs (in bar) welcome, open (and food) all day from 9am. *(David Jackman, David Twitchett)*

DUTON HILL TL6026

Three Horseshoes (01371) 870681

Off B184 Dunmow–Thaxted, 3 miles N of Dunmow; CM6 2DX Friendly traditional village local; well kept Mighty Oak and a couple of guests (late May Bank Holiday beer festival), central fire in main bar, aged armchairs by another fireplace in homely left-hand parlour, lots of interesting memorabilia, small public bar with darts and pool, no food; dogs welcome, old enamel signs out at front, garden with pond and views, closed lunchtimes Mon-Thurs. *(Christopher May)*

EARLS COLNE TL8528

Lion (01787) 226823

High Street; CO6 2PA Restored village pub dating from the 15th c and under same ownership as the Five Bells at Colne Engaine; popular food from ciabattas and wood-fired pizzas up, well kept Adnams, Colchester and a guest, interesting wines (choose a bottle from their small shop to drink in or take away), friendly service; children and dogs welcome, courtyard tables, open (and food) all day from 9am (10.30am Sun) for breakfast. *(J B and M E Benson)*

EPPING FOREST TL4501

Forest Gate (01992) 572312

Bell Common; CM16 4DZ Friendly open-plan pub dating from the 17th c and run by the same family for over 50 years; beams, flagstones and panelling, big woodburner, well kept Adnams and guests from brick-faced bar, inexpensive pubby food (they also have a smart upmarket restaurant next door); darts; children and dogs welcome, tables on front lawn popular with walkers, four bedrooms in separate building. *(Iain Bush)*

FINCHINGFIELD TL6832

Fox (01371) 810151

The Green; CM7 4JX Pargeted 16th-c building overlooking village duck pond; spacious beamed bar with exposed brickwork and central fireplace, flowers on tables, up to four changing local ales and good choice of wines by the glass, popular pubby food (not Sun evening) including lunchtime sandwiches, afternoon teas (must be pre-booked, not Sun), friendly helpful staff; background and some live music; children and dogs welcome, hanging baskets and picnic-sets in front, open all day. *(Mrs Margo Finlay, Jörg Kasprowski)*

FINGRINGHOE TM0220

Whalebone (01206) 729307

Off A134 just S of Colchester centre, or B1025; CO5 7BG Old village pub geared for dining; airy country-chic rooms with cream-painted tables on oak floors, fresh flowers and log fire, good varied choice of food from sandwiches/wraps up, four well kept beers including Adnams, friendly helpful staff, barn function room; background music; children and dogs welcome, charming back garden with peaceful valley view, front terrace, convenient for Fingringhoe Wick nature reserve, open all day Sat, till 6pm Sun. *(Trevor and Michele Street)*

GESTINGTHORPE TL8138

★Pheasant (01787) 461196

Off B1058; CO9 3AU Civilised country pub with old-fashioned character in small opened-up beamed rooms, settles and mix of other furniture on bare boards, books and china platters on shelves, woodburners in nice brick fireplaces, Adnams Southwold, a house beer from Woodfordes and an occasional guest, nine wines by the glass, good food using local and some home-grown produce including daily specials; children and dogs (in bar) welcome, seats outside under parasols with views over fields, five stylish bedrooms, closed Mon, lunchtimes Tues-Thurs and they also take days off Jan-May – so best to phone or check website. *(Claire Adams)*

GREAT BARDFIELD TL6730

Vine (01371) 811822

Vine Street; CM7 4SR Red-brick Victorian dining pub with highly rated well presented food from pub staples to monthly tasting menus, real ales such as Greene King, extensive wine list and some unusual gins, friendly helpful service, light airy décor with roaring log fire; children welcome, picnic-sets in good-sized garden (Aug beer festival), interesting village with links to notable artists, open all day. *(Stuart Doughty)*

GREAT BROMLEY TM0824

Court House (01206) 250322

Harwich Road/Frating Road; CO7 7JG Popular modernised roadside pub (a former courthouse), carpeted bar with white-painted beams, good reasonably priced pubby food from lunchtime sandwiches up, Shepherd Neame ales, friendly efficient service, restaurant and tea room; children welcome, bedrooms (some in motel-style building), closed Sun and Mon evenings, otherwise open all day. *(Mrs Margo Finlay, Jörg Kasprowski)*

GREAT BROMLEY TM0627

Cross (01206) 721772
Ardleigh Road, just off A120 Colchester–Harwich; CO7 7TL Welcoming community-owned country pub on crossroads; a couple of well kept ales such as Bishop Nick and Colchester, various gins and cocktails, low-priced food served Fri evening and on their regular events nights (live music, quizzes and so forth); post office and coffee shop, open Sun 12-3pm, closed Mon-Weds and lunchtimes Thurs-Sat. *(Lesley Broadbent)*

GREAT CHESTERFORD TL5142

Crown & Thistle (01799) 530278
1.5 miles from M11 junction 9A; pub signposted off B184, in High Street; CB10 1PL Substantial old building refurbished under present management; decorative plasterwork inside and out, particularly around the early 16th-c inglenook, low-ceilinged area by bar serving ales such as Fullers, Oakham and Woodfordes, enjoyable food from sandwiches and wraps through burgers and stone-baked pizzas up, long handsomely proportioned dining room; children, walkers and dogs (in bar) welcome, suntrap back courtyard, closed Sun evening. *(David and Leone Lawson)*

GREAT CHESTERFORD TL5142

Plough (01799) 531651
Off M11/A11 via B184; High Street; CB10 1PL Updated and extended 18th-c pub in peaceful village; popular fairly traditional food from sandwiches up including Fri steak night, Greene King ales and good range of other drinks, friendly attentive service, timbered pitch-roof bar and other connecting areas; background music; children and dogs welcome, attractive well maintained garden, open all day Fri-Sun, food all day Sat, till 6pm Sun. *(Mrs Margo Finlay, Jörg Kasprowski)*

GREAT EASTON TL6126

Green Man (01371) 852285
Mill End Green; pub signed 2 miles N of Dunmow, off B184 towards Lindsell; CM6 2DN Popular well looked-after country dining pub down long winding lane; linked beamed rooms including bar with log fire, good food (best to book weekends) from pub favourites and tapas up, real ales, decent wines by the glass and cocktails, friendly helpful service; background music; children welcome, dogs in bar, good-sized garden with terrace and play area, open all day Sat, closed Sun evening, Mon. *(Dan and Belinda Smallbone)*

GREAT HENNY TL8738

Henny Swan (01787) 267953
Henny Street; CO10 7LS Welcoming dining pub in great location on River Stour, well kept Adnams, Woodfordes and a couple of guests, proper cider and plenty of wines by the glass, good food from separate bar and restaurant menus, friendly efficient service; background music; children in restaurant until 8pm, dogs in bar and lounge, disabled loos, terrace and waterside garden, may offer summer boat trips, open all day. *(Heather and Richard Jones)*

GREAT WARLEY STREET TQ5890

Thatchers Arms (01277) 233535
Warley Road; CM13 3HU Old pub across from small village green; popular generously served food from sandwiches and baked potatoes up, real ales including one badged for them, friendly young staff, red-carpeted black-beamed interior; may be background music; children, walkers and dogs welcome, picnic-sets outside, open all day (till midnight Fri, Sat), food all day Sat, till 6pm Sun, not Mon evening. *(Eddie Edwards)*

HARLOW TL4411

Dusty Miller (01279) 424180
Junction Eastwick Road and Burnt Mill Lane; CM20 2QS Cream-painted brick and shuttered pub on rural outskirts; good food from varied menu including weekday lunch deal, McMullens ales, efficient service, simple interior with traditional wooden tables and chairs on bare boards, open fires; children welcome, garden with play area, open all day Sat, closed Sun evening, Mon. *(Mrs Margo Finlay, Jörg Kasprowski)*

HARWICH TM2632

Alma (01255) 318681
Kings Head Street; CO12 3EE Popular old seafarers' local just back from the quayside; highly rated food (best to book) from sharing plates up including good fresh fish/seafood, well kept Adnams and good range of other beers, proper ciders and decent wines, friendly service; live music Fri, maybe a shanty group first Mon of month, quiz every other Tues; children and dogs welcome, cosy back courtyard, six bedrooms, open (and food) all day. *(Clem Luxford)*

HASTINGWOOD TL4807

★**Rainbow & Dove** (01279) 415419
0.5 miles from M11 junction 7; CM17 9JX Pleasantly traditional low-beamed country pub (originally a small farmhouse) with three cosy rooms; built-in cushioned wall seats and mate's chairs around pubby tables, some stripped stonework, woodburner in original fireplace, three or four well kept changing ales, good choice of wines by the glass and enjoyable fairly priced food from sandwiches to popular Sun roasts, breakfast from 9am Sat, friendly helpful staff, barn function room; background music; children and dogs welcome, tables out under parasols, smallholding with rare-breed pigs, goats and chickens (own sausages and eggs), closed Sun and Mon evenings. *(Adam and Serena Furber)*

HATFIELD HEATH TL5115

Thatchers (01279) 730270
Stortford Road (A1005); CM22 7DU Thatched and weatherboarded 16th-c dining pub at end of large green; good food from short but varied menu, well kept Greene King IPA, St Austell Tribute and two guests from long counter, several wines by the glass, friendly attentive service, inglenook woodburner, beams, some copper and brass and old local photographs; background music; children in back dining area, no dogs inside, tables out in front behind picket fence, open (and food) all day, till 9pm (6pm) Sun. *(Christopher May)*

HENHAM TL5428

Cock (01279) 850347
Church End; CM22 6AN Old timbered building striking good balance between community local and dining pub; enjoyable well priced home-made food from fairly pubby menu, Greene King IPA, a beer from Saffron (brewed in the village) and Sharps Doom Bar, decent wines, good open fires, restaurant with leather-backed chairs on wood floor; quiz first Mon of month, sports TV in snug; children and dogs welcome, seats out at front and in tree-shaded garden behind, open all day Fri and Sat, till 7pm Sun. *(Pat Reed)*

HOWLETT END TL5834

White Hart (01799) 599030
Thaxted Road (B184 SE of Saffron Walden); CB10 2UZ Comfortable and well run pub-restaurant; two smartly set modern dining rooms either side of small bar, good generously served food from sandwiches and pubby choices up, a real ale such as Nethergate and nice choice of wines, friendly helpful service; children welcome, terrace and big garden, closed Sun evening, Mon (open bank holiday lunchtime). *(Iain Bush)*

KIRBY LE SOKEN TM2221

Ship (01255) 679149
B1034 Thorpe–Walton; CO13 0DT Refurbished 17th-c beamed pub with wide choice of enjoyable good value bar and restaurant food (all day Sat, till 5pm Sun), six real ales and a dozen ciders, friendly helpful service; children and dogs (in bar) welcome, disabled facilities, picnic-sets and flowers on fenced front terrace, garden and covered area behind, open all day. *(Adrian Johnson)*

LANGHAM TM0232

Shepherd (01206) 272711
Moor Road/High Street; CO4 5NR Roomy 1920s village pub on crossroads; L-shaped bar with areas off, wood floors and painted half-panelling, large OS map covering one wall, comfortable sofas, woodburner, two Adnams beers and a guest, plenty of wines by the glass and good selection of other drinks, enjoyable food from sharing plates up including good value set menu (Mon-Sat), efficient friendly service; quiz first Tues of month, live music second Sat; children and dogs (in bar) welcome, side garden, open all day, food all day Sat, till 5pm Sun. *(David and Charlotte Green)*

LEIGH-ON-SEA TQ8385

★ **Crooked Billet** (01702) 480289
High Street; SS9 2EP Steps up to homely old pub with waterfront views from big bay windows, packed on busy summer days when queues likely, Nicholsons, Sharps and changing guests including seasonals, enjoyable standard Nicholsons menu, log fires, beams, panelled dado and bare boards, local fishing pictures and bric-a-brac; background music; children welcome, dogs outside only, side garden and terrace, seawall seating over road shared with Osborne's good shellfish stall (plastic glasses for outside), pay-and-display parking by flyover, open (and food) all day. *(John and Enid Morris)*

LITTLE BRAXTED TL8413

Green Man (01621) 891659
Kelvedon Road; signed off B1389; OS Sheet 168 map reference 848133; CM8 3LB Compact cream-painted village pub opposite tiny green; modern décor with old beams and log fires, enjoyable reasonably priced traditional food from sandwiches and baked potatoes up, OAP set menu and other deals, Greene King ales and a guest, Aspall's cider, friendly helpful staff; children, walkers and dogs welcome, picnic-sets out at front and in pleasant sheltered garden, open all day Sat, till 7pm Sun, closed Mon evening. *(John and Delia Franks)*

LITTLE BROMLEY TM1028

Haywain (01206) 390004
Bentley Road; CO11 2PL Popular 18th-c pub freshened-up under present owners; carpeted/flagstoned interior with various cosy areas leading off main bar, beams, exposed brickwork, painted wainscoting and open fires, well kept Adnams and a couple of guests, enjoyable food from snacks to grills, friendly helpful service; children, walkers and dogs welcome, small side garden, closed Sun evening to Tues, otherwise open (and food) all day, breakfast from 9.30am Fri-Sat. *(Gwendoline and Ralph Mason)*

LITTLE TOTHAM TL8811

Swan (01621) 331713
School Road; CM9 8LB Welcoming little village local with half a dozen well kept ales tapped from the cask, farm ciders/perry and good straightforward lunchtime food; low 17th-c beams and log fire, back dining area, games bar with darts; live music and quiz nights, June beer festival; children, walkers and dogs welcome, disabled access, front lawned garden and small terrace, open all day. *(John and Delia Franks)*

LITTLE WALTHAM TL7013

White Hart (01245) 360205
The Street; CM3 3NY Handsome village pub with contemporary open-plan rooms; wood, slate and tartan-carpeted floors, seating from woven cane chairs through wall banquettes and cushioned window seats to upholstered armchairs, fireplaces (some piled high with logs), metal deer heads, antler chandeliers and candles in tall glass lanterns, Adnams, Nethergate and guests, Weston's cider and good wines by the glass, popular reasonably priced food from sandwiches and snacks up including deals, efficient friendly service; free wi-fi; children and dogs (in bar) welcome, garden with cheerfully coloured metal chairs and parasols along with rattan-style seating and picnic-sets, open (and food) all day from 9am breakfast on. *(Pat Reed)*

LOUGHTON TQ4296

Victoria (020) 8508 1779
Smarts Lane; IG10 4BP Chatty and welcoming flower-decked Victorian local; panelled bare-boards bar with small raised end dining area, five real ales including Sharps Doom Bar and Timothy Taylors Landlord, decent range of whiskies and good helpings of enjoyable home-made food from blackboard menu; children and dogs welcome, pleasant neatly kept front garden, Epping Forest walks nearby, open all day weekends. *(Claire Adams)*

MATCHING GREEN TL5310

Chequers (01279) 731276
Off Downhall Road; CM17 0PZ Red-brick Victorian pub-restaurant in picturesque village; good traditional and mediterranean-style food from lunchtime ciabattas and sharing plates up, also more affordable fixed-price weekday lunch, friendly helpful staff dressed in black, nice wines from comprehensive list, cocktails and three well kept ales including Greene King and Woodfordes; background music and occasional cabaret/tribute nights; disabled facilities, quiet spot overlooking large green, good local walks, open all day Fri-Sun, closed Mon except bank holidays. *(Heather and Richard Jones)*

MATCHING TYE TL5111

Fox (01279) 731335
The Green; CM17 0QS Long 18th-c village pub opposite tiny green; decent range of popular well priced food, Greene King IPA, Shepherd Neame Spitfire and a guest, welcoming service, various areas including beamed restaurant and raftered barn room, comfortable dark wood furniture, brasses, woodburners; regular live music and quiz nights, TV; children welcome, 12 bedrooms. *(Iain Bush)*

MESSING TL8919

★**Old Crown** (01621) 815575
Signed off B1022 and B1023; Lodge Road; CO5 9TU Bustling late 17th-c village pub near fine church; convivial carpeted bar with wheelback and farmhouse chairs around part-painted tables, open fire, ales such as Adnams and Crouch Vale, a dozen wines by the glass including champagne, highly regarded interesting food (not Sun evening), cheerful helpful service, two-room restaurant with white-painted chairs and rustic tables on bare boards, boating pictures on canary yellow or modern papered walls, another open fire; children and dogs (in bar) welcome, picnic-sets under parasols in back garden, more seats in front, deli behind the pub selling good local produce, open all day (till 8.30pm Sun). *(P Beardsell, Paddy and Sian O'Leary, Jacqui and Alan Swan, Max Simons, David Twitchett, Noel Privett)*

MILL GREEN TL6401

Viper (01277) 352010
The Common; from Fryerning (which is signposted off N-bound A12 Ingatestone bypass) follow Writtle signposts; CM4 0PT Unpretentious country local tucked away in wooded area; cosy unchanging rooms with spindleback and country kitchen chairs around neat little tables, tapestried wall seats and log fire, the fairly basic tap room is even simpler with parquet floor and coal fire, beyond is another room with sensibly placed darts; two beers named for the pub plus guests, Weston's cider/perry, straightforward lunchtime food; Easter and Aug beer/music festivals; children (at one end of bar) and dogs welcome, pretty garden (mass of summer colour) and lots of hanging baskets and window boxes, some seats on lawn, open all day weekends (busy with walkers and cyclists then). *(Christopher May)*

MISTLEY TM1131

★**Thorn** (01206) 392821
High Street (B1352 E of Manningtree); CO11 1HE Popular for American chef-landlady's excellent food (especially seafood), but there's also a friendly welcome if you just want a drink or coffee; high black beams give a clue to the building's age (Matthew Hopkins, the notorious 17th-c witchfinder general, based himself here), décor, though, is crisply up to date – bentwood chairs and mixed dining tables on terracotta tiles around central bar, cream walls above blue dado, colourful modern artwork, end brick fireplace with woodburner; newspapers and magazines, cookery classes; front pavement tables looking across to Robert Adam's swan fountain, interesting waterside village, 12 well appointed comfortable bedrooms (some in separate building), open all day. *(Comus and Sarah Elliott, Dr K Nesbitt)*

MOUNT BURES TL9031

★ **Thatchers Arms** (01787) 227460
Off B1508, Hall Road; CO8 5AT
Modernised well run country pub; good local food cooked to order from lunchtime hoagies up, four well kept ales including Adnams and Crouch Vale, cheerful efficient staff; background music, film and quiz nights, bar billiards; children and dogs welcome, picnic-sets out behind with peaceful Stour Valley views, closed Mon, otherwise open all day (till 9pm Sun). *(Andrew and Ruth Simmonds)*

NEWPORT TL5234

Coach & Horses (01799) 540292
Cambridge Road (B1383); CB11 3TR
Welcoming beamed village pub with good freshly made food including specials and Fri steak night, friendly prompt service, well kept Adnams, Fullers, Woodfordes and a guest; background music, free wi-fi; children welcome, garden with play boat, open all day Fri and Sat, till 6pm Sun. *(Pat Reed)*

NORTH SHOEBURY TQ9286

Angel (01702) 589600
Parsons Corner; SS3 8UD Timbered and partly thatched pub by busy roundabout; Greene King, Woodfordes and a couple of guests, popular food including daily specials, small quarry-tiled entrance bar flanked by tartan-carpeted dining rooms, step up to back bar with wood floor and some old local pictures, woodburner; background music, free wi-fi; children and dogs allowed in certain areas, disabled facilities, seats out at front, open all day weekends. *(Christopher May)*

PAGLESHAM TQ9492

Plough & Sail (01702) 258242
East End; SS4 2EQ Relaxed 17th-c weatherboarded dining pub in pretty country spot; popular fairly traditional food at affordable prices, well kept local ales and decent house wines, friendly service, low black beams and big log fires, pine tables, lots of brasses and pictures; background music; children welcome, front picnic-sets and attractive side garden, open all day Sun. *(Heather and Richard Jones)*

PELDON TL9916

Plough (01206) 735808
Lower Road; CO5 7QR Welcoming little weatherboarded village pub with a couple of real ales such as Adnams and Greene King, decent wines by the glass and good choice of enjoyable food, cheerful service, beams and woodburners, cosy restaurant; children and dogs welcome (their friendly victorian bulldog is Ponto), picnic-sets in back garden, shuts around 8pm Mon and Sun, also closed Mon lunchtime. *(Christopher May)*

PELDON TM0015

Rose (01206) 735373
B1025 Colchester–Mersea (do not turn left to Peldon village); CO5 7QJ Popular and friendly old inn with dark bowed beams, standing timbers and little leaded-light windows, some antique mahogany and padded leather wall banquettes, arched brick fireplace, a couple of Adnams ales along with Sharps Doom Bar, several wines by glass and well liked home-made food (not Sun evening), cosy restaurant plus contrasting airy garden room; children (away from bar) and dogs welcome, plenty of seats in spacious garden with pretty pond, comfortable country-style bedrooms, open all day but may shut Sun around 8.30pm if quiet. *(M G Hart)*

PLESHEY TL6614

Leather Bottle (01245) 237291
The Street; CM3 1HG Quaint little two-room local in nice village with good walks nearby; ales such as Greene King, Harveys, Sharps and Skinners, enjoyable home-made food, friendly helpful staff, low ceilings and log fires; children and dogs welcome, garden with play area, open all day. *(Eddie Edwards)*

PURLEIGH TL8401

Bell (01621) 828348
Off B1010 E of Danbury, by church at top of hill; CM3 6QJ Cosy rambling beamed and timbered pub with fine views over the marshes and Blackwater estuary; bare boards, hops and brasses, inglenook log fire, well kept ales such as Adnams and Mighty Oak, plenty of wines by the glass (some local), good sensibly priced home-made food including specials, friendly staff; cinema and local art exhibitions in adjoining barn; children welcome, picnic-sets on side grass, good walks (St Peter's Way), closed Sun evening, Mon (except bank holidays). *(Gwendoline and Ralph Mason)*

RIDGEWELL TL7340

White Horse (01440) 785532
Mill Road (A1017 Haverhill–Halstead); CO9 4SG Comfortable beamed village pub with up to four well kept changing ales (some tapped from the cask), real ciders and decent wines by the glass, good generous food including lunchtime set menu (Tues-Sat), friendly service; background music, free wi-fi; well behaved children welcome, no dogs, tables out on terrace, modern bedroom block with good disabled access, closed Mon lunchtime, otherwise open all day, no food Sun evening. *(Trevor and Michele Street)*

Half pints: by law, a pub should not charge more for half a pint than half the price of a full pint, unless it shows that half-pint price on its price list.

SAFFRON WALDEN TL5338

★**Eight Bells** (01799) 522790
Bridge Street; B184 towards Cambridge; CB10 1BU Handsome Tudor pub with open-plan beamed bar, leather armchairs, chesterfield sofas and old wooden settles on bare boards, coal-effect gas fire in brick fireplace, interesting old photographs, three real ales including Woodfordes Wherry, ten wines by the glass and several malt whiskies, good inventive food (they add a service charge), splendidly raftered and timbered back dining barn with dark modern furniture and upholstered wall banquettes, woodburner; background music, free wi-fi; children and dogs (in bar) welcome, garden with raised deck, nice walks nearby and handy for Audley End (EH), open (and food) all day, kitchen close 6pm Sun. *(Andrew Stone, Nicholas and Maddy Trainer, Bridget and Peter Gregson, Sandra King, Michael Sargent)*

SAFFRON WALDEN TL5438

Old English Gentleman
(01799) 523595 *Gold Street; CB10 1EJ* Busy 19th-c red-brick pub in centre of town; bare boards, panelling and log fires, plenty of inviting nooks and crannies, well kept Adnams Southwold, Woodfordes Wherry and a couple of guests, plenty of wines by the glass and good choice of enjoyable lunchtime only food from sandwiches and deli boards up, friendly staff; background music, TV; children welcome, part-covered heated terrace with modern furniture, open all day (till 1am Fri, Sat). *(David and Charlotte Green)*

SOUTHEND TQ8885

Pipe of Port (01702) 614606
Tylers Avenue, off High Street; SS1 1JN Cellar bar (not strictly a pub) with plenty of atmosphere, sawdust and candlelight, well liked food including signature pies and good value set menu, excellent range of affordably priced wines and other drinks from craft beers to cocktails, friendly knowledgeable staff; wine tasting evenings; closed Sun and bank holidays. *(Pat Green)*

SOUTHMINSTER TQ9699

Station Arms (01621) 772225
Station Road; CM0 7EW Popular little weatherboarded local; unpretentious L-shaped bar with bare boards and panelling, well kept Adnams Southwold and several guests, Weston's cider, friendly chatty atmosphere; live blues and folk nights, darts; back courtyard with barn, open all day weekends (from 2pm Sat). *(Alf and Sally Garner)*

STANSTED TL5125

Dog & Duck (01279) 812047
Lower Street; CM24 8LR Welcoming weatherboarded village pub; traditional beamed and carpeted bar serving Greene King ales, generous helpings of enjoyable reasonably priced pub food from baguettes up, also two-course OAP menu; live music and quiz nights, sports TV; children and dogs (in public bar) welcome, seats out on small front deck and in back garden, open (and food) all day, kitchen shuts 5pm Sun. *(Mrs Margo Finlay, Jörg Kasprowski)*

STAPLEFORD TAWNEY TL5001

Mole Trap (01992) 522394
Tawney Common; signed off A113 N of M25 overpass – keep on; OS Sheet 167 map reference 500013; CM16 7PU Tucked-away, yet popular, little country pub with unpretentious carpeted beamed bar (mind your head as you go in), brocaded wall seats and plain pub tables, steps down to similar area, log fires, well kept Fullers London Pride and guests, reasonably priced down-to-earth food (not Sun and Mon evenings); no credit cards, maybe quiet background radio; well behaved children welcome away from bar, dogs allowed at landlord's discretion, garden with rural views. *(Pat Reed)*

STEEPLE BUMPSTEAD TL6841

Fox & Hounds (01440) 731810
Chapel Street; CB9 7DQ New owners for this welcoming 15th-c beamed village pub; three eating areas serving popular home-made food (booking advised) from shortish menu, well kept Greene King IPA, three changing guests and several wines by the glass, friendly service, log fire in bar; some seats out in front behind picket fence, more on little terrace behind, open all day Fri-Sun (no food Sun evening). *(Mrs Margo Finlay, Jörg Kasprowski)*

STOCK TQ6998

Bakers Arms (01277) 840423
Common Road, just off B1007 Chelmsford–Billericay; CM4 9NF Popular open-plan beamed pub with good home-made food including some mediterranean influences, friendly attentive service, ales such as Adnams, Crouch Vale and Greene King, airy dining room with french windows to enclosed terrace, more seats out at front and in side garden; children welcome, open all day (food all day Fri-Sun). *(John and Enid Morris, Deborah Lammiman)*

STOW MARIES TQ8399

★**Prince of Wales** (01621) 828971
B1012 between South Woodham Ferrers and Cold Norton Posters; CM3 6SA Friendly atmosphere in this traditional weatherboarded pub; several little unspoilt low-ceilinged rooms, bare boards and log fires, conservatory dining area, half a dozen widely sourced ales, bottled/draught belgian beers including fruit ones and a couple of ciders, enjoyable food (all day Sun) with some interesting specials and home-smoked dishes, Thurs pizzas; live jazz (third Fri of

month); children in family room, terrace and garden tables, maybe summer barbecues, four good bedrooms in converted stable, open all day. *(Heather and Richard Jones)*

THEYDON BOIS TQ4598

Bull (01992) 812145
Station Approach; CM16 7HR Cosy beamed pub dating from the 17th c; polished wood and carpeted floors, log fire, three well kept ales including Wells Bombardier, several wines by the glass and good home-made food from sandwiches to blackboard specials (booking advised, especially weekends), friendly staff; sports TV; children and dogs (in bar) welcome, paved beer garden, open all day, food all day Thurs-Sat, kitchen closed Sun evening. *(David and Charlotte Green)*

UPSHIRE TL4100

Horseshoes (01992) 712745
Horseshoe Hill, E of Waltham Abbey; EN9 3SN Welcoming Victorian village pub with small bar area and dining room; good food cooked by chef-landlord with some emphasis on fish, well kept McMullens beers, friendly helpful staff; children and dogs (in bar) welcome, garden overlooking Lea Valley, more tables out in front, good walks, open all day, no evening food Sun or Mon. *(Iain Bush)*

WENDENS AMBO TL5136

★**Bell** (01799) 540382
B1039 W of village; CB11 4JY Cottagey local with cheery bustle in low-ceilinged bars; brasses on ancient timbers, wheelback chairs at neat tables, winter log fire, Adnams, Oakham and Woodfordes and a couple of guests, real ciders and several wines by the glass, well liked food (not Sun evening), pizza van Thurs evening; background music, free wi-fi; children and dogs welcome, three-acre garden with seats under parasols on paved terrace, pond leading to River Uttle, woodland walk and timber play area, camping (glamping pods planned), open all day. *(Sarah Fox)*

WICKHAM ST PAUL TL8336

★**Victory** (01787) 269364
SW of Sudbury; The Green; CO9 2PT Old village dining pub by cricket green, attractive and spacious, with varied choice of well liked food including OAP weekday lunch deal, friendly efficient service, Adnams and guests from brick-faced counter, beams and timbers, leather sofas and armchairs, inglenook woodburner; background music, pool and darts; children welcome, dogs in public bar, picnic-sets in neat front garden, open all day Fri-Sun, closed Mon, no food Sun evening. *(Sam Pearce)*

WIDDINGTON TL5331

★**Fleur de Lys** (01799) 543280
Signed off B1383 N of Stansted; CB11 3SG Welcoming unpretentious low-beamed and timbered village pub; enjoyable locally sourced food (not Sun evening, Mon, Tues) in bar and dining room from sandwiches to very good (if pricey) steaks, OAP set lunch Weds and Thurs, well kept Adnams, Woodfordes and a couple of guests chosen by the regulars, decent wines, dim lighting, tiled and wood floors, inglenook log fire; pool and other games in back bar; children and dogs welcome, picnic-sets in pretty garden, open all day Fri-Sun, closed Mon and Tues lunchtimes. *(Pat Reed)*

WIVENHOE TM0321

Black Buoy (01206) 822425
Off A133; CO7 9BS Village pub owned by local consortium; open-plan partly timbered bare-boards bar, well kept ales such as Colchester, Mighty Oak and Red Fox, a craft keg, Aspall's cider and several wines by the glass, good sensibly priced home-made food (not Sun evening) from lunchtime sandwiches to daily specials, cheerful service, open fires, upper dining area glimpsing river over roofs; well behaved children and dogs allowed in certain areas, seats out on brick terrace, two smart bedrooms up steep staircase, open all day. *(Christopher May)*

WOODHAM MORTIMER TL8104

Hurdlemakers Arms
(01245) 225169 *Post Office Road; CM9 6ST* Small quietly placed traditional country local with low ceilings and timbered walls, five well kept changing ales, good choice of ciders and generous helpings of enjoyable food from varied menu (special diets catered for), friendly service; children and dogs welcome, large garden with picnic-sets among trees and shrubs, play area and summer barbecues, open all day (till 9pm Sun), food all day weekends (till 7.30pm Sun). *(Steve Harding)*

A star symbol before the name of a pub shows exceptional character and appeal. It doesn't mean extra comfort. Even quite a basic pub can win a star, if it's individual enough.

Gloucestershire

BARNSLEY

SP0705 Map 4

Village Pub

(01285) 740421 – www.thevillagepub.co.uk

B4425 Cirencester–Burford; GL7 5EF

Bustling pub with top class food, a good choice of drinks and seats in the back courtyard; bedrooms

Drawing in customers from far and wide for the first class food, this still manages to remain a haven for the cheerful crowd of locals who've come for a pint and a chat; the friendly, attentive staff welcome all. Low-ceilinged bar rooms are smart and contemporary with pale paintwork, flagstones and oak floorboards, heavy swagged curtains, plush chairs, stools and window settles around polished candlelit tables, three open fireplaces and country magazines and newspapers. Flying Monk Elmers, North Cotswold Windrush Ale and Wye Valley Butty Bach and HPA on handpump, an extensive wine list with a dozen by the glass and up to six farm ciders in summer; background music. The sheltered back courtyard has solid wooden furniture under parasols, outdoor heaters and its own servery. Bedrooms are individually decorated and extremely comfortable and breakfasts are particularly recommended.

Appetising food includes twice-baked cheddar soufflé, venison tartare with charcoal mayonnaise, cured egg yolk, mushroom ketchup and crispy shallots, mushroom, spinach and gnocchi gratin with pine nut pesto, sticky spare ribs with new potato and watercress salad, roasted hake fillet with beetroot, macadamia nuts, mussels and crab bisque, garlic, lemon and paprika half chicken with slaw and chips, lamb leg with fondant potatoes, grelot onions, broad beans, anchovy and soft herb dressing, and puddings such as espresso and chocolate mousse and spotted dick and custard. *Benchmark main dish: smoked haddock and pea fishcakes with butter sauce and a boiled egg £16.50. Two-course evening meal £24.00.*

Free house ~ Licensee Michael Mella ~ Real ale ~ Open 11-11; 11-10.30 Sun ~ Bar food 12-2.30, 6-9.30 (10 Fri); 12-3, 6-10 Sat; 12-9 Sun ~ Children welcome ~ Dogs allowed in bar ~ Wi-fi ~ Bedrooms: /£109 *Recommended by Anne Taylor, Susan Eccleston, Andrew Lawson, Caroline and Peter Bryant, Sabina and Gerald Grimshaw, Mrs Zara Elliott, Guy Vowles*

'Children welcome' means the pub says it lets children inside without any special restriction. If it allows them in, but to restricted areas such as an eating area or family room, we specify this. Some pubs may impose an evening time limit. We do not mention limits after 9pm as we assume children are home by then.

BLEDINGTON SP2422 Map 4

Kings Head

(01608) 658365 – www.kingsheadinn.net

B4450 The Green; OX7 6XQ

16th-c inn with atmospheric furnishings, super wines by the glass, real ales and delicious food; smart bedrooms

This is a first class all-rounder and our readers enjoy it very much. It's a gently civilised old place with excellent food and lovely bedrooms but at its heart is a lively and friendly main bar with plenty of chatty locals. There are ancient beams and other atmospheric furnishings (high-backed wooden settles, gate-leg or pedestal tables), a warming log fire in a stone inglenook, ancient flagstones and sporting memorabilia relating to rugby, racing, cricket and hunting. To the left, a drinking area has built-in wall benches, stools and dining chairs around wooden tables, rugs on bare boards and a woodburning stove. Attentive, welcoming staff serve Hook Norton Hooky and guests such as Coach House Coachmans Best Bitter, Froth Blowers Bar-King Mad and Prescott Hill Climb on handpump, a super wine list with ten by the glass, 20 malt whiskies and an extensive gin collection; background music, board games and cards. There are seats out in front and rattan-style armchairs around tables in the pretty back courtyard garden with a pagoda; maybe free-ranging bantams and ducks. If you stay here they offer cosy rooms above the inn and more spacious ones in the courtyard, and the setting (opposite the green in a tranquil village) is most attractive. The same professional licensees also run the Swan at Swinbrook (in Oxfordshire).

The imaginative menu using free-range and organic local produce includes lunchtime open sandwiches, chilli and lime crab cakes with soy and cucumber, devilled lambs kidneys on toast, buffalo mozzarella, peas, grilled spring onions, pink grapefruit, pomegranate and parma ham salad with sweet basil dressing, wild garlic leaf, mint, pea and spinach risotto with white truffle oil and parmesan, corn-fed chicken breast with charred leek and black garlic purée, asparagus, peas, cep mushrooms and jus, sea bass fillet with a salad of piquillo peppers, tomatoes, ciabatta croutons, rocket and prawns with harissa dressing, and puddings such as rhubarb and custard roulade with poached rhubarb and an orange sorbet and chocolate brownie with raspberry and lavender marshmallow, mixed berries and blackberry sorbet. *Benchmark main dish: steak in Guinness pie £14.50. Two-course evening meal £21.00.*

Free house ~ Licensees Nicola and Archie Orr-Ewing ~ Real ale ~ Open 11-11 ~ Bar food 12-2, 6.30-9; 12-2.30, 6-9.30 Fri, Sat; 12-3, 6.30-9 Sun ~ Restaurant ~ Children welcome ~ Dogs allowed in bar ~ Wi-fi ~ Bedrooms: £90/£110 *Recommended by Keith Perry, Richard Tilbrook, Clive and Fran Dutson, Bob and Melissa Wyatt, Margo and Derek Peters, Alun and Jennifer Evans, Guy Vowles, Tracey and Stephen Groves*

BOURTON-ON-THE-HILL SP1732 Map 4

Horse & Groom

(01386) 700413 – www.horseandgroom.info

A44 W of Moreton-in-Marsh; GL56 9AQ

Georgian inn with quite a choice of drinks and lovely views from seats outside; bedrooms

In warm weather, head for the large garden behind this handsome old place that has plenty of seats under parasols and fine countryside views. Inside, the pubby bar is light, airy and simply furnished with a pleasing mix of farmhouse and other wooden chairs, settles, cushioned wall and window seats and tables on bare boards and a woodburning stove in a stone fireplace.

Ringwood Razorback and Wye Valley Butty Bach on handpump, good wines by the glass, maybe a local farm cider and local gin. There are plenty of original features throughout; background music. Dining areas spread off from here, again with an attractive variety of dining chairs and rustic tables, rugs, snug little corners, an open fire and pale-painted or exposed stone walls. Bedrooms are individually styled. It's best to arrive early to be sure of a space in the smallish car park. Batsford Arboretum is not far away.

Food from a seasonal menu includes lunchtime sandwiches, ham hock rillettes with piccalilli, seared pigeon breast with beetroot salad and balsamic dressing, celeriac, spinach and cheese tart with celeriac purée, corn-fed chicken breast with sorrel and mushroom sauce, burger with toppings, aioli and skinny fries, beer-battered haddock and triple-cooked chips, and puddings such as pistachio crème brûlée with shortbread biscuits and lemon and pomegranate tart with rhubarb sorbet. *Benchmark main dish: lample (lamb and apple) pie with dauphinoise potatoes £15.00. Two-course evening meal £23.00.*

Free house ~ Licensee Abbie Davies ~ Real ale ~ Open 12-11 ~ Bar food 12-3, 6.30-9 (8.30 Sun) ~ Restaurant ~ Children welcome ~ Dogs allowed in bar and bedrooms ~ Wi-fi ~ Bedrooms: /£120 *Recommended by Philip Chesington, Patricia and Gordon Tucker, Martine and Lawrence Sanders, Paul Faraday*

BROCKHAMPTON SP0322 Map 4

Craven Arms

(01242) 820410 – www.thecravenarms.co.uk

Village signposted off A436 Andoversford–Naunton – look out for inn sign at head of lane in village; can also be reached from A40 Andoversford–Cheltenham via Whittington and Syreford; GL54 5XQ

Friendly village pub with tasty bar food, real ales and seats in a big garden; bedrooms

This is a relaxing and enjoyable country pub, and our readers come here on a regular basis. The character bars have a chatty atmosphere, low beams, roughly coursed thick stone walls and some tiled flooring; although it's largely been opened out to give a sizeable eating area off the smaller bar servery, there's a feeling of several communicating rooms. The furniture is mainly pine, with comfortable leather sofas, wall settles and tub chairs; also, gin traps, various stuffed animal trophies and a woodburning stove. Served by attentive staff, drinks include Bristol Beer Factory Fortitude, Cotswold Lion Golden Fleece and Stroud Maltzart on handpump, eight wines by the glass and a farm cider; board games. The large garden has plenty of seats and the views are lovely. The two bedrooms are comfortable. You can walk around the surrounding fields and beyond.

Quite a choice of tasty food includes good baguettes, baked blue brie with fig chutney, mussels with white wine, cream, chilli and garlic, wild mushroom, leek and goats cheese loaf, salmon and dill fishcake with sweet chilli mayonnaise, duck breast with fondant potatoes, pickled chard and red wine jus, monkfish and chorizo with samphire and beetroot, interesting barbecue-style 'hot rock' meat and fish choices with all sorts of sauces and dips, and puddings such as salted caramel cheesecake and white chocolate eton mess parfait. *Benchmark main dish: chicken in a basket with fries and chipotle sauce £12.00. Two-course evening meal £19.00.*

Free house ~ Licensee Barbara Price ~ Real ale ~ Open 12-3, 6-11; 12-11 Sat; 12-5 Sun; closed Sun evening, Mon ~ Bar food 12-2 (2.30 Sat), 6.30-9; 12-3 Sun ~ Restaurant ~ Children welcome ~ Dogs allowed in bar ~ Wi-fi ~ Bedrooms: /£90 *Recommended by Richard Tilbrook, Peter Young, Dr A J and Mrs B A Tompsett, Helene Grygar, Guy Vowles*

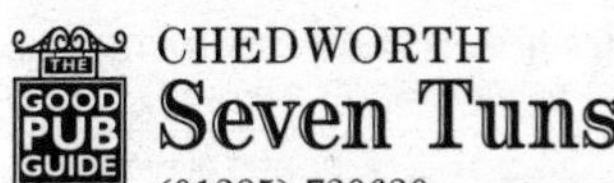

CHEDWORTH SP0512 Map 4

Seven Tuns

(01285) 720630 – www.seventuns.co.uk

Village signposted off A429 NE of Cirencester; then take second signposted right turn and bear left towards church; GL54 4AE

Bustling, enjoyable little pub with good food and wine, several real ales and seats outside

If you're visiting the nearby Roman villa it makes sense to visit this refurbished 17th-c village pub, which we've had good, positive reports on recently. Linked characterful rooms have flagstone and wooden floors, restored furniture along with newer comfortable seating, some curious artwork, embroideries and other bits and pieces, and woodburning stoves. Goffs Winter Ale, Hook Norton Hooky, Otter Bitter and a guest from Old Dairy on handpump, several wines by the glass and farm cider served by friendly, helpful staff. You can sit outside at the front and back of the building; good walks.

Popular food includes lunchtime sandwiches, bacon, black pudding and potato salad, smoked mackerel pâté, tomato, feta and olive gnocchi, chilli and garlic prawn linguine, home-cooked ham and eggs, sausages with broccoli gratin, pulled pork with pitta bread and slaw, and puddings such as sticky toffee pudding and vanilla cheesecake with prosecco berries; they also offer takeaway pizzas, steak supper is on Wednesday and fish and chips special is on Friday lunchtime and evening. *Benchmark main dish: steak in ale pie £14.00. Two-course evening meal £20.00.*

Youngs ~ Tenant Liz Henty ~ Real ale ~ Open 12-3, 6-11; 12-11 Sat, Sun ~ Bar food 12-2.30 (3 Sun), 6-8.30 ~ Restaurant ~ Children welcome ~ Dogs allowed in bar ~ Open mike last Tues of month *Recommended by Richard Tilbrook, Tom and Noelle Straiton, Sam Cole, Naomi and Andrew Randall*

CHELTENHAM SO9422 Map 4

Old Courthouse

(01242) 500930 – www.brunningandprice.co.uk/oldcourthouse

County Court Road; GL50 1HB

Stunning conversion of a former courthouse on two levels with a fine choice of drinks and food and a genuine welcome

Brunning & Price have cleverly converted this rather grand, Italianate-style former courthouse into a lovely two-storey pub. On the ground floor, what was the waiting room is now a big bar with cushioned wooden dining chairs around dark tables on rugs or parquet flooring, a central group of high chairs around equally high tables, a long, green leather button-back banquette stretching down one wall, lots of paintings and armchairs in front of open fires; background music and board games. Friendly young staff serve Phoenix Brunning & Price Original, Cotswold Lion Best in Show, Gloucester Session IPA, Hillside Over The Hill, Timothy Taylors Landlord and Wye Valley Butty Bach on handpump, good wines by the glass, 60 malt whiskies and over 90 gins. Leading off here are two small dining rooms with more open fires: one with blue décor and tartan-upholstered chairs and the other with lots of horse-racing prints and a dark red button-back leather wall banquette. At the top of the stairs, pass under a huge chandelier to reach the handsome main courtroom. The raised, panelled seating area, largely unaltered, is surrounded by paintings of judges and looks down on a dining room with elegant marble pillars, leather chairs and wall seats, more paintings, an open fire and a second bar counter. Throughout the building you'll find the group's trademark bookshelves, house plants and church candles. Outside, a few tables and chairs line the front pavement.

Good, interesting food includes sandwiches, scallops with cauliflower purée, black pudding fritters and apple dressing, slow-roasted duck leg with bubble and squeak and clementine jus, smoked haddock and salmon fishcake with a poached egg and a white wine and chive sauce, sweet potato, aubergine and spinach malaysian curry with coconut rice, chicken breast with fondant potatoes, celeriac purée, wild mushrooms and sherry jus, beef bourguignon with horseradish mash, and puddings such as lemon meringue roulade with raspberry sorbet and crème brûlée. *Benchmark main dish: slow-braised lamb shoulder with dauphinoise potatoes and rosemary gravy £17.95. Two-course evening meal £22.00.*

Brunning & Price ~ Manager Tom Foster ~ Real ale ~ Open 10.30am-11pm; 10.30am-midnight Fri, Sat; 10.30-10.30 Sun ~ Bar food 12-9.30; 12-10 Fri, Sat; 12-9 Sun ~ Children welcome ~ Dogs allowed in bar ~ Wi-fi *Recommended by Alister and Margery Bacon, Lorna and Jeff Mason, Ben and Jenny Settle*

CHELTENHAM SO9624 Map 4

Royal Oak

(01242) 522344 – www.royal-oak-prestbury.co.uk

Off B4348 just N; The Burgage, Prestbury; GL52 3DL

Bustling pub with popular food, several real ales and wine by the glass, and seats in the sheltered garden

Now owned by Butcombe, this remains a cheerful pub that our readers enjoy a lot. The congenial low-beamed bar has polished brasses, a comfortable mix of seating including chapel chairs on parquet flooring, some interesting pictures on the ochre walls and a woodburning stove in a stone fireplace. Helpful staff keep Butcombe Adam Hensons Rare Breed and Original plus two changing guest beers on handpump and seven wines by the glass; background music. Dining room tables are well spaced so that you don't feel crowded, and the skittle alley doubles as a function room. There are picnic-sets under parasols on the terrace and in a sheltered garden.

Well liked food includes pigeon breast with parsnip purée, yorkshire pudding and port and game reduction, chicken liver pâté with chutney, spicy chickpea burger with toppings, tzatziki and skin-on fries, toad in the hole with ale sausages, champ mash and onion gravy, confit chicken thighs with chorizo risotto and parmesan, rainbow trout fillet with asian vegetable broth, coconut milk, mussels and noodles, slow-roast pork belly with apricot and sausage meat stuffing, bubble and squeak and roast onion gravy, and puddings. *Benchmark main dish: lamb chump with a mustard and rosemary crust, black pudding, dauphinoise potatoes and red wine gravy £15.95. Two-course evening meal £21.00.*

Butcombe ~ Manager Thomas Wright ~ Real ale ~ Open 11-11; 12-10.30 Sun ~ Bar food 12-2, 6-9; 12-9 Fri, Sat; 12-8 Sun ~ Restaurant ~ Children welcome ~ Dogs allowed in bar ~ Wi-fi *Recommended by Peter Young, Ian Herdman, Alf and Sally Garner, Charlie Stevens, Dr and Mrs H J Field, Nick and Meriel Cox, Dr and Mrs A K Clarke*

COOMBE HILL SO8926 Map 4

Gloucester Old Spot ★

(01242) 680321 – www.thegloucesteroldspot.co.uk

Exit M5 junction 11 and use satnav GL51 9SY; access from junction 10 is restricted; GL51 9SY

Interestingly furnished country pub with much character, good ales and likeable food

This friendly, bustling place has been sympathetically refurnished recently but still retains the feel of a proper country local, despite being just outside Cheltenham. The quarry-tiled beamed bar has chapel chairs and other seats around assorted tables (including one in a bow-windowed alcove) and opens into a lighter, partly panelled area with cushioned settles and stripped kitchen tables. Purity Mad Goose, Tiny Rebel Cwtch and Wye Valley Bitter on handpump, eight decent wines by the glass and four farm ciders are served by young, friendly staff. Decoration is in unobtrusive good taste, with winter log fires. A handsome baronial-style separate dining room (once a hunting lodge to nearby Boddington Manor) has similar country furniture, high stripped-brick walls, dark flagstones and candlelight; background music. Outside, there are chunky benches and tables under parasols on a terrace, with some oak barrel tables on brickwork and pretty flowers in vintage buckets and baskets; heaters for cooler weather. It can get pretty packed on race days.

Reliably good food includes lunchtime cobs, crab and salmon fishcake with olive tapenade and romesco and almond sauce, spiced venison koftas with pickled cucumber and red onion salad and minted yoghurt, steak burger with toppings, celeriac slaw and chips, twice-baked cheese soufflé with creamed spinach, pheasant, smoked pork belly and leek pie with calvados jus, hake fillet with sautéed squid and chorizo with hummus and spiced aubergine, duck breast with merguez sausage, ratatouille and red wine reduction, and puddings such as iced chocolate and honeycomb parfait with mango and orange salsa and warm cinnamon doughnuts with caramel and banana sauce. *Benchmark main dish: rare-breed pork £15.00. Two-course evening meal £23.00.*

Free house ~ Licensees Simon and Kate Daws ~ Real ale ~ Open 10.30-10 (11 Fri, Sat) ~ Bar food 12-2, 6-9; 12-8 Sun ~ Restaurant ~ Children welcome ~ Dogs allowed in bar ~ Wi-fi *Recommended by Mike and Mary Carter, Dave Braisted, Chloe and Tim Hodge, M G Hart, John Copple*

COWLEY — SO9714 Map 4

Green Dragon

(01242) 870271 – www.green-dragon-inn.co.uk

Off A435 S of Cheltenham at Elkstone, Cockleford sign; OS Sheet 163 map reference 970142; GL53 9NW

Inn dating from 1643 with character bars, separate restaurant, popular food, real ales and seats on terraces; bedrooms

There are plenty of good walks surrounding this 17th-c inn and high quality food and drink to enjoy afterwards. The two beamed bars have a mix of both locals and visitors, plenty of character and a cosy, nicely old-fashioned feel; big flagstones, wooden floorboards, candlelit tables and winter log fires in two stone fireplaces. The furniture and the bar itself in the upper Mouse Bar were made by Robert 'Mouseman' Thompson craftsmen and have little mice running over the hand-carved tables, chairs and mantelpiece; there's also a small upstairs restaurant. Friendly staff keep a good range of drinks such as Hook Norton Old Hooky, Sharps Doom Bar and a guest such as Butcombe Bitter on handpump, ten wines by the glass, ten gins and ten malt whiskies; background music and a separate skittle alley. The bedrooms were refurbished in 2018 and breakfasts are generous. The outside terraces have lots of seats and tables.

Pleasing food includes lunchtime sandwiches (not Sunday), crispy duck leg confit with white radish, cucumber and sesame seeds and chicken liver pâté wrapped in bacon with home-made chutney, spinach and ricotta tortellini with basil pesto sauce, rare-breed sausages with bubble and squeak and gravy, steak and kidney suet pudding, grilled salmon fillet wrapped in serrano ham with a chive cream sauce, pheasant breast with an oregano and bacon cream sauce, duck breast with a mango and ginger sauce, and puddings such as four-layer chocolate fudge cake with vanilla ice-cream and crème brûlée. *Benchmark main dish: venison with juniper berries and wild mushroom sauce £15.95. Two-course evening meal £23.00.*

Buccaneer Holdings ~ Managers Simon and Nicky Haly ~ Real ale ~ Open 11-11; 12-10.30 Sun ~ Bar food 12-2.30 (3 Sat), 6-10; 12-3.30, 6-9 Sun ~ Restaurant ~ Children welcome ~ Dogs allowed in bar ~ Wi-fi ~ Bedrooms: £80/£105 *Recommended by Guy Vowles, Peter Young, Dr A J and Mrs B A Tompsett, Shona and Jimmy McDuff, Richard Tilbrook, Dr and Mrs A K Clarke, Andrea and Philip Crispin*

DIDMARTON ST8187 Map 2

Kings Arms

(01454) 238245 – www.kingsarmsdidmarton.co.uk

A433 Tetbury road; GL9 1DT

Bustling pub with enjoyable food, a good choice of drinks, and pleasant back garden; bedrooms

Bedrooms in this 17th-c former coaching inn are individually furnished and comfortable and they also have self-catering cottages in a converted barn and stable block. Several knocked-through beamed bar rooms work their way around a big central counter (where there are high chairs and stools against the counter), with grey-painted half-panelling, armchairs by a log fire in a stone fireplace, settles and window seats with scatter cushions, bare boards here and flagstones and rugs there, and a mix of farmhouse chairs and benches around wooden tables of all shapes and sizes. Church candles on shelves or in lanterns, antlers, prints and fresh flowers create interest; the jack russell is called Spoof. There's also a restaurant with another open fire. Bath Gem, Flying Monk Elmers, Otter Amber and Wychwood Hobgoblin on handpump, and good wines by the glass; darts. There are plenty of seats and picnic-sets in the pleasant back garden. The pub is handy for Westonbirt Arboretum. Disabled access.

Well presented food using local game includes lunchtime sandwiches, double-baked cheese soufflé, sweet and sour squid, charcuterie platter (to share), wild mushroom arancini with parsley pesto, burger with onion marmalade and skinny fries, duck breast with spiced plums and jerusalem artichokes, braised shoulder and roast cutlet of lamb with squash purée and red wine jus, halibut with chorizo cassoulet, and puddings such as white chocolate mousse with mango, passion-fruit and mint salad and orange sorbet and lemon brûlée with berry compote. *Benchmark main dish: duo of pork with spiced apple purée and cider jus £16.95. Two-course evening meal £26.00.*

Free house ~ Licensee Mark Birchall ~ Real ale ~ Open 11-11; 11-10 Sun ~ Bar food 12-2.30, 6-9; 12-3, 6-8 Sun ~ Restaurant ~ Children welcome ~ Dogs allowed in bar and bedrooms ~ Wi-fi ~ Bedrooms: £70/£140 *Recommended by Guy Vowles, Trish and Karl Soloman, Jill and Hugh Bennett, Dan and Belinda Smallbone, Julian Richardson*

DURSLEY ST7598 Map 4

Old Spot

(01453) 542870 – www.oldspotinn.co.uk

Hill Road; by bus station; GL11 4JQ

Unassuming and cheery town pub with a fine range of ales, regular beer festivals and good value lunchtime food

Tucked away behind a car park and bus station, it's easy to miss this white rendered old farmhouse with its lively mix of customers. The front door opens into a deep-pink small room with stools on shiny quarry tiles beside a pine-boarded bar counter and old enamel beer signs on the walls and ceiling. A little room leads off on the left towards the garden and a room to the right has lots of wooden benches and tables, with plenty of porcine paraphernalia throughout. Cheerful, enthusiastic staff keep a fine range of drinks that includes seven real ales on handpump such as Uley Old Ric, with guests such as Bath Gem, Flying Monk Elmers, Great Oakley Egret, Otter Bitter and Palmers Dorset Gold; they also hold two annual beer festivals and there are 20 malt whiskies, 40 gins, three farm ciders, half a dozen wines by the glass and artisan spirits. The heated and covered garden has benches and parasols. Wheelchair access but no disabled loos.

Lunchtime-only food is fair value: sandwiches (the soup and sandwich deal is popular), chicken liver parfait with green tomato chutney, creamy garlic mushrooms with griddled bread, grazing boards, scampi and chips, honey and mustard-glazed ham and free-range eggs, cauliflower, chickpea and red lentil curry, chicken breast wrapped in smoked bacon with cheese and barbecue sauce and sweet potato chips, steak in ale pie and puddings. *Benchmark main dish: sausages in maple syrup with root vegetables, mash and cider and mustard sauce £10.00.*

Free house ~ Licensee Ellie Sainty ~ Real ale ~ Open 12-11 (midnight Sat) ~ Bar food 12-3; 12-4 Sun ~ Children in family room ~ Dogs allowed in bar ~ Wi-fi ~ Quiz last Sun of month; live band monthly *Recommended by Monty Green, Angela and Steve Heard, Elisabeth and Bill Humphries, Maria and Henry Lazenby, Kerry and Guy Trooper*

EASTINGTON SO7705 Map 4

Old Badger

(01453) 822892 – www.oldbadgerinn.co.uk

Alkerton Road, a mile from M5 junction 13; GL10 3AT

Friendly, traditionally furnished pub with plenty to look at, five real ales, tasty food and seats in attractive garden

Our readers continue to send us enthusiastic reports on the food and drink here as it's a busy, old-fashioned and friendly pub. The split-level connected rooms have an informal, easy-going feel and feature two open fires and traditional furnishings such as built-in planked and cushioned wall seats, settles and farmhouse chairs around all sorts of tables, quarry tiles and floorboards. There are stone bottles, bookshelves, breweriana on red or cream walls and even a stuffed badger. Castles White Knight, Flying Monk Elmers, Milton Sparta, Moles Jailers Daughter and Wickwar Cotswold Way on handpump alongside ten wines by the glass, a dozen malt whiskies and farm cider; they hold beer and cider festivals with local musicians and also brewery trips. The nicely landscaped garden has benches and picnic-sets on a terrace and a lawn and under a covered gazebo; the flowering tubs and window boxes are pretty. Wheelchair access to the top bar/dining area only; disabled loos are shared with baby-changing facilities.

Old favourites and new choices include lunchtime baguettes, a range of tapas, wild mushroom or king prawn and crab linguine, barbecue chicken with sweet potato wedges and sweetcorn, spring onion and chilli salsa, beer-battered fish and chips, rib-eye steak with onion rings and peppercorn sauce, duck noodle curry, baked cod rarebit in a chive sauce, daily specials, and puddings such as sticky pear and ginger pudding with butterscotch sauce and tiramisu. *Benchmark main dish: burger with toppings, coleslaw and chips £13.00. Two-course evening meal £19.00.*

Free house ~ Manager Julie Gilborson ~ Real ale ~ Open 12-11.30 ~ Bar food 12-2.30, 6-9; 12-3 Sun ~ Children welcome away from bar area ~ Dogs welcome ~ Wi-fi ~ Live music monthly Fri or Sat *Recommended by Mike and Mary Carter, Guy Vowles, Trish and Karl Soloman, Chris and Angela Buckell, Charlie and Mark Todd*

EASTLEACH TURVILLE — SP1905 Map 4

Victoria

(01367) 850277 – www.thevictoriainneastleach.co.uk

Off A361 S of Burford; GL7 3NQ

Traditional stone pub in village with simply furnished bars, Arkells ales and decent food

We've been getting keen reports here since the newish licensees took over. A traditional old stone building dating from the early 18th c, it only became a pub in 1856. The open-plan low-ceilinged rooms cluster around the central servery, with cushioned window seats, leather armchairs and wheelbacks in the bar and more wheelbacks and cushioned settles in the dining room where there's a log fire. Well kept Arkells 3B and a changing guest and seven wines by the glass are served by friendly staff; background music and board games. Seats and tables under parasols and picnic-sets at the front overlook the picturesque village (which is famous for its spring daffodils), with more seats in the back garden. There are enjoyable surrounding walks.

Fair-priced pubby food cooked by the landlord includes sandwiches, game rillettes with onion marmalade, smoked haddock, cheese and hollandaise gratin, confit celeriac risotto with sage, parmesan and hazelnuts, chicken and leek pie, breaded pheasant with red cabbage slaw and fries, venison stew with dauphinoise potatoes and red cabbage, organic pork chop with pancetta, kale and apple sauce, and puddings such as chocolate pot and bread and butter pudding with clotted cream ice-cream. *Benchmark main dish: beer-battered haddock and chips £12.50. Two-course evening meal £20.00.*

Arkells ~ Tenants Tom and Maya Gabbitas ~ Real ale ~ Open 11-11; 11-3, 5-11 Mon-Thurs in winter ~ Bar food 12-2 (3 Sat), 6.30-9; no food Sun or Mon evenings ~ Restaurant ~ Children welcome ~ Dogs allowed in bar ~ Wi-fi ~ Live music (check website)

Recommended by Helene Grygar, Donald Allsopp, Susan and Callum Slade, Lorna and Jack Musgrave, R K Phillips

EBRINGTON — SP1839 Map 4

Ebrington Arms

(01386) 593223 – www.theebringtonarms.co.uk

Off B4035 E of Chipping Campden or A429 N of Moreton-in-Marsh; GL55 6NH

Gloucestershire Dining Pub of the Year

Nice old pub in attractive village with own-brewed ales, thoughtful choice of food and seats in garden; bedrooms

If you're visiting either Hidcote (National Trust) or Kiftsgate Court Gardens (both of which are nearby), why not come here for lunch? The character bar and dining room have beams, a log fire in a fine inglenook fireplace, a woodburning stove in a second fireplace (the ironwork is original) with armchairs beside it, an airy bow-window seat, ladder-back and farmhouse chairs and cushioned settles on old flagstones or bare boards, and fresh flowers and church candles. They keep three own-brewed Yubberton ales (Yubby Bitter, Yubby Goldie and the seasonal Yawnie Bitter) on handpump alongside local guests such as North Cotswold Moreton Mild, Otter Bitter and Wye Valley Dorothy Goodbodys Wholesome Stout, good wines from a thoughtful list (with notes), nine gins, farm cider and winter mulled wine. Board games, bagatelle, shut the box and dominoes. An arched stone wall shelters seats and tables under parasols on the terrace and picnic-sets line the lawn. The well equipped, country-style bedrooms are very comfortable and breakfasts are good. The three venerable oak trees after which this old stone pub was once named still stand outside by the village green. This is sister pub to the Killingworth Castle in Wootton (in Oxfordshire).

Imaginative food includes kofta-stuffed lamb belly with onion couscous, roast shallots and samphire, citrus-cured salmon with lemon gel, dill mayonnaise, pickled kohlrabi and fennel, bubble and squeak with jerusalem artichokes, purple sprouting broccoli and herb sauce, glazed ham with a duck egg, baked pineapple and chips, steak in ale pie, chicken breast with stuffed leg, pancetta and charred leek and potato terrine, hake fillet with tarka dhal, roasted cauliflower and bhaji, and puddings such as white chocolate and rhubarb cheesecake and blood orange pannacotta with passion-fruit mousse and almond crumble. *Benchmark main dish: beer-battered fish and chips £14.50. Two-course evening meal £21.00.*

Free house ~ Licensees Claire and Jim Alexander ~ Real ale ~ Open 9am-11pm ~ Bar food 12-2, 6-9 (9.30 Fri); 12-3.30, 6-9.30 (8 Sun) Sat ~ Restaurant ~ Children welcome ~ Dogs allowed in bar ~ Wi-fi ~ Folk night first Mon of month ~ Bedrooms: /£140

Recommended by Grace Ford, Mike and Sarah Abbot, Celia and Geoff Clay, Nicholas and Maddy Trainer, Frances Parsons, Ian Herdman, Martin and Sue Neville

GLOUCESTER SO8318 Map 4

Café René

(01452) 309340 – www.caferene.co.uk

Southgate Street; best to park in Blackfriars car park (Ladybellegate Street) and walk through passageway – pub entrance is just across road; GL1 1TP

Interestingly placed bar with fair value food all day, and good choice of drinks

This is certainly different and not a pub in the proper sense, but our readers like it. It has a very subterranean feel with black beams, dim lighting and no windows, plus stripped brick and timbering and an internal floodlit well with water trickling down into its depths. The long bar counter is made of dozens of big casks, and they keep four changing real ales tapped from the cask, such as Blue Monkey Evolution, Farr Brew The Best Bitter, Wickwar Falling Star and Wychwood Hobgoblin, plus farm ciders and a good choice of wines by the glass (decoration consists mainly of great banks of empty wine bottles). Service remains friendly and efficient even when really pushed. One antique panelled high-backed settle joins the usual pub tables and wheelback chairs on carpet, and there's a sizeable dining area on the right. Well reproduced background music, a silenced games machine and big-screen TV (for rugby only). They have regular live music and hold a popular rhythm and blues festival at the end of July. There are plenty of picnic-sets under parasols out by the churchyard. To get here you walk down a flagstoned passageway alongside the partly Norman church of St Mary de Crypt.

Served all day, food includes lunchtime sandwiches and wraps, sautéed mushrooms in white wine and cream sauce, prawn cocktail, linguine with tomato, basil and olive sauce topped with parmesan, fish or steak in ale pies, caribbean-style lamb curry with pea rice and cucumber raita, chargrilled rack of baby ribs in barbecue sauce, steaks and mixed grill, and puddings such as cheesecake of the week and chocolate fudge cake with cream. *Benchmark main dish: burger with toppings and salsa £10.95. Two-course evening meal £15.00.*

Free house ~ Licensee Paul Soden ~ Real ale ~ Open 11am-midnight (later Fri, Sat) ~ Bar food 12-10 ~ Restaurant ~ Wi-fi ~ Live music Weds and Fri evenings

Recommended by Julian Richardson, Mark Morgan, Trevor and Michele Street

KILCOT SO6925 Map 4

Kilcot Inn

(01989) 720707 – www.kilcotinn.com

2.3 miles from M50 junction 3; B4221 towards Newent; GL18 1NG

Attractively reworked small country inn, kind staff, enjoyable local food and drink; bedrooms

Happily, readers report that little changes here and it remains a friendly, popular place for a drink or a meal. The open-plan bar and dining areas have stripped beams, bare boards and dark flagstones, sunny bay-window seats, homely armchairs by one of the two warm woodburning stoves, tables with padded dining chairs and daily papers. Stools line the brick counter where the hard-working landlord and his staff serve Marstons EPA and Wye Valley Butty Bach on handpump, four draught ciders and perry (with more by the bottle), 20 malt whiskies, local wine and organic fruit juice; TV and maybe background music. The outside dining area has tables and chunky benches under thatched parasols next to a rose garden and there's also a children's play area; at the front are picnic-sets under cocktail-style parasols. Bedrooms are light, airy and comfortable and the breakfasts are praiseworthy. There's a smart shed for bicycle storage.

As well as breakfasts (for non-residents 9-11am; 9-10.30am weekends) and lunchtime sandwiches, the tasty food (they keep bees and grow their own herbs) includes salmon and smoked haddock fishcake with creamed leeks, seared pigeon and wild mushrooms with apple purée and fried sourdough crumbs, seared beef with sesame, beets, noodles, ginger and chilli, braised root vegetable, chickpea and spinach stew spiced with star anise, cumin and cinnamon and served with almond and pomegranate couscous, breast of lamb stuffed with apricots, hazelnuts, rosemary and leeks with dauphinoise potatoes and cabbage cooked with bacon, pollack with crab and parsley risotto and a crab fritter, and puddings such as chocolate mousse cake with vanilla ice-cream and vanilla pannacotta; Tuesday is steak night. *Benchmark main dish: cider-battered fish of the day with triple-cooked chips £13.25. Two-course evening meal £20.00.*

Free house ~ Licensee Mark Lawrence ~ Real ale ~ Open 9am-11pm ~ Bar food 12-2.30, 6-9 ~ Restaurant ~ Children welcome ~ Dogs allowed in bar ~ Wi-fi ~ Live music monthly (see website) ~ Bedrooms: £85/£95 *Recommended by Dave Braisted, Mike and Mary Carter, C Smith, Bridget and Peter Gregson, S Holder, Len and Lilly Dowson*

LOWER SLAUGHTER SP1622 Map 4

Slaughters Country Inn

(01451) 822143 – www.theslaughtersinn.co.uk

Village signposted off A429 Bourton-on-the-Water to Stow-on-the-Wold; GL54 2HS

Comfortable streamside inn with enticing food, real ales, attractive dining bar and fine grounds; smart bedrooms

In warm weather in particular this handsome stone building is lovely: it's set on the River Eye and the spacious grounds have tables and chairs under parasols on terraces and lawns that sweep down to the water. The spreading bar has a good mix of locals and visitors in several low-beamed linked rooms, plus well spaced tables on polished flagstones and a variety of seats from simple chairs to soft sofas. Log fires, mullioned windows, shelves of board games, a few carefully placed landscape pictures or stuffed fish on cream or puce walls create an air of understated refinement – and what really sets the style of the place is the thoroughly professional and efficient service. Brakspears Bitter and Wychwood Hobgoblin on handpump, and a dozen good wines by the glass. The smart evening restaurant looks over the lawn and the sheep pasture beyond. Bedrooms are comfortable and stylish and make a good base for exploring the area; some are in the main house, some across the courtyard.

Food is delicious and beautifully presented: lunchtime sandwiches, braised pig cheek with mash, apple, black pudding and radish, fish terrine with dill crème fraîche and seafood toast, butternut squash ravioli with silver-skin onions and chestnuts, cajun chicken with aioli, corn on the cob, mesclun salad and fries, blade of beef with horseradish mash, king brown mushrooms and smoked bacon, gilt-head bream with samphire and crab bisque, and puddings such as mango and banana baked alaska with mandarin brandy syrup and chocolate and coffee cheesecake with Baileys ice-cream. *Benchmark main dish: beer-battered fish and chips £15.50. Two-course evening meal £28.00.*

Free house ~ Licensee Stuart Hodges ~ Real ale ~ Open 10am-11pm ~ Bar food 12-3, 6.30-9; afternoon tea 3-5.30 ~ Restaurant ~ Children welcome ~ Dogs allowed in bar and bedrooms ~ Wi-fi ~ Bedrooms: /£190 *Recommended by Bernard Stradling, Tracey and Stephen Groves, Martin and Sue Neville, Robin and Anne Triggs, Monica and Steph Evans, Nick and Meriel Cox, Richard Tilbrook*

MEYSEY HAMPTON SU1199 Map 4

Masons Arms

(01285) 850164 – www.masonsarmsmeyseyhampton.com

Just off A417 Cirencester–Lechlade; High Street; GL7 5JT

Lovely old village pub, carefully renovated with old and new features blending well and enjoyable drinks and food; comfortable bedrooms

Once discovered, our readers find this beautifully refurbished 17th-c village inn becomes a firm favourite. The bar has heavy old beams, an open fire, country paintings and a collection of clock faces on contemporary paintwork, a cushioned window seat and church chairs around scrubbed tables, and stools against the counter. The interconnected dining areas are furnished with more church chairs plus high-backed wooden ones and built-in cushioned seats on bare floorboards, modern artwork on Cotswold stone or painted walls, and a woodburning stove. Welcoming and helpful staff serve Arkells 3B and Wiltshire Gold on handpump, 15 gins and good wines by the glass; background music, darts and board games. There are seats outside on the village green. The spotless bedrooms are stylish, up to date and well appointed and overlook the village, farm or manor house.

Good, enjoyable food includes sandwiches, squid and chorizo salad with chimichurri dressing and tomato concasse, sweet and sticky chicken wings with slaw, red lentil dhal with spinach, spring onions and coriander and coriander flatbread, mussel and fresh fish chowder, lamb cutlets with crispy lamb croquette, quinoa and pomegranate salad and spiced yoghurt, steak frites with garlic butter and fries, and puddings such as chocolate brownie with chocolate ice-cream and vanilla poached rhubarb with spiced beignets and micro mint. *Benchmark main dish: burger with toppings and chips £12.00. Two-course evening meal £20.00.*

Arkells ~ Licensee Paul Fallows ~ Real ale ~ Open 8.30-3, 5-11; 12-11 Sat; 12-10 Sun ~ Bar food 12-2, 6-9; 12-8 Sun ~ Restaurant ~ Children welcome ~ Dogs allowed in bar and bedrooms ~ Wi-fi ~ Bedrooms: £70/£90 *Recommended by Sara Fulton, Roger Baker, Sandra and Miles Spencer, Alexander and Trish Cutter*

The star-on-a-plate award, , distinguishes pubs where the food is of exceptional quality. The knife-and-fork symbol just means the pub serves food.

NAILSWORTH

ST8699 Map 4

Weighbridge

(01453) 832520 – www.weighbridgeinn.co.uk

B4014 towards Tetbury; GL6 9AL

Bustling pub with cosy old-fashioned bar rooms, a fine choice of drinks and food, friendly service and sheltered garden

You'll get a warm welcome here, a good choice of drinks and, of course, their famous two-in-one pies. The relaxed bar has three cosily old-fashioned rooms with open fires, stripped-stone walls and antique settles, country chairs and window seats. The black-beamed ceiling of the lounge bar is thickly festooned with black ironware – sheep shears, gin traps, lamps and a large collection of keys, many from the old Longfords Mill opposite the pub. Upstairs is a raftered hayloft with an engaging mix of rustic tables. No noisy games machines or background music. Wadworths 6X and guest beers such as Bath Gem, Stroud Budding and Uley Old Spot Prize Strong Ale on handpump, 18 wines (and champagne and prosecco) by the glass, farm cider, 12 malt whiskies and 20 gins. A sheltered landscaped garden at the back has picnic-sets under umbrellas. Good disabled access and facilities.

The renowned two-in-one pies (also available for home baking) come in a divided bowl – one half contains the filling of your choice (perhaps steak, kidney and stout, salmon in cream sauce, or root vegetables with beans and pulses in tomato sauce) with a pastry topping, the other half with home-made cauliflower cheese (or broccoli mornay or root vegetables). Also, lunchtime paninis, toasties and filled crêpes, moules marinière, panko-breaded prawns with sweet chilli dip, vegetable moussaka, lambs liver with bacon, mash and onion gravy, battered fresh fish and chips, and puddings such as fruit crumble and custard and a changing pannacotta with berry compote. *Benchmark main dish: two-in-pies £12.40. Two-course evening meal £19.00.*

Free house ~ Licensee Mary Parsons ~ Real ale ~ Open 12-10.30 (11 Fri, Sat); closes 10pm Mon-Thurs in winter ~ Bar food 12-8.30 (9 Fri, Sat) ~ Restaurant ~ Children welcome in upstairs dining room ~ Dogs welcome *Recommended by Jim and Sue James, Tom and Ruth Rees, Julia and Fiona Barnes, Lauren and Dan Frazer*

NETHER WESTCOTE

SP2220 Map 4

Feathered Nest ★

(01993) 833030 – www.thefeatherednestinn.co.uk

Off A424 Burford to Stow-on-the-Wold; OX7 6SD

Attractive surroundings, exceptional food and drink; lovely bedrooms

For many customers, it's the beautifully presented food that remains the biggest draw here, though it would be a shame to miss out on the companionable bar. This is cosy and friendly with Purity Mad Goose and Pure UBU on handpump and 24 wines by the glass from an impressive list; service is exemplary. Softly lit, the largely stripped-stone bar has real saddles as bar stools (some of the country's best racehorse trainers live locally), a carved settle among other carefully chosen seats, dark flagstones and low beams. This opens into a high-raftered room with ochre walls and deeply comfortable sofas by a vast log fire; background music and TV. A couple of attractively decorated dining rooms, both on two levels, have a pleasing mix of antique tables in varying sizes, and a lively, up-to-date atmosphere. A flagstoned terrace and heated shelter have teak tables and wicker armchairs, and a spreading lawn bounded by floodlit trees is set with groups of rustic seats, with the Evenlode Valley beyond. This is a special place to stay with individually decorated, well equipped rooms and delicious breakfasts.

Delicious food includes quail tortellini with salami and consommé, salmon with beetroot, black garlic and dill, cod with squid, noodles and nasturtium, sika deer with salsify, crosnes (chinese artichokes) and bilberries, ibérico pork with quince, sour slaw and potatoes, dover sole with monks beard and bouillabaisse, beef with foie gras, morels and madeira, turbot with purple sprouting broccoli and mace butter, and puddings such as Valrhona chocolate with peanut butter and goats milk and rhubarb with blood orange and meringue. *Benchmark main dish: wild boar £35.00. Two-course evening meal £38.00.*

Free house ~ Licensee Amanda Timmer ~ Real ale ~ Open 11-11; 11-9 Sun; closed Mon-Weds; two weeks Feb, two weeks July, one week Oct ~ Bar food 12-2.30, 6.30-9.30 ~ Restaurant ~ Children welcome ~ Dogs allowed in bar ~ Wi-fi ~ Bedrooms: £235/£285 *Recommended by Clive and Fran Dutson, Victoria and James Sargeant, David and Leone Lawson, Bernard Stradling, Jacqui and Alan Swan, Louise and Oliver Redman*

NEWLAND — SO5509 Map 4

Ostrich

(01594) 833260 – www.theostrichinn.com

Off B4228 in Coleford; or can be reached from the A466 in Redbrook, by turn-off at the England–Wales border – keep bearing right; GL16 8NP

Super range of beers in welcoming country pub, with spacious bar, open fire and good interesting food

If you're after a fine choice of ales at the end of a walk, do come here. The charming, warmly friendly landlady and her helpful staff keep up to eight on handpump such as Butcombe Gold, Fat Cat Wild Cat, Otter Bitter, RCH Pitchfork, Untapped Sundown and Wye Valley Butty Bach and HPA; also, several wines by the glass, a couple of farm ciders and a good range of soft drinks. The pub is mostly 16th-c and the low-ceilinged bar is spacious but cosily traditional, with a chatty, relaxed atmosphere, a roaring log fire, creaky floors, window shutters, candles in bottles on the tables, miners' lamps on uneven walls, and comfortable furnishings that include cushioned window seats, wall settles and rod-backed country kitchen chairs. Newspapers to read, perhaps quiet background jazz and board games. The walled garden has seats and tables, with more out in front. The church opposite, known as the Cathedral of the Forest for its unusual size, is worth a visit.

Rewarding food includes smoked duck breast and leg with cherry chutney, oak-smoked salmon tart with dill mustard sauce, pork ribs in a tangy sauce with garlic bread, butternut squash, buffalo mozzarella and fennel duxelles in puff pastry with sage cream sauce, smoked haddock in cream, eggs and horseradish topped with dauphinoise potatoes and mozzarella, wild boar sausages with red onion and wine gravy, monkfish and tiger prawns in white wine and chive cream sauce with gruyère mash and asparagus, beef wellington with port and thyme jus, and puddings. *Benchmark main dish: rack of welsh lamb with minted pea cream and crispy diced potatoes £19.00. Two-course evening meal £23.00.*

Free house ~ Licensee Kathryn Horton ~ Real ale ~ Open 12-3, 6.30-11.30; 12-3.30, 6-midnight Sat; 12-4, 6.30-11.30 Sun ~ Bar food 12-2.30, 6.30 (6 Sat)-9.30 ~ Restaurant ~ Children welcome ~ Dogs allowed in bar *Recommended by Dr A J and Mrs B A Tompsett, Sean Cornforth, Chrissi Gower-Smith, Clive and Fran Dutson, Andrew and Michele Revell, David and Leone Lawson*

Real ale may be served from handpumps, electric pumps (not just the on-off switches used for keg beer) or – common in Scotland – tall taps called founts (pronounced 'fonts') where a separate pump pushes the beer up under air pressure.

NORTH CERNEY SP0208 Map 4

Bathurst Arms

(01285) 832150 – www.bathurstarms.co.uk

A435 Cirencester–Cheltenham; GL7 7BZ

Bustling inn with beamed bar, open fires, real ales and wines by the glass and tasty food; bedrooms

Our readers enjoy their visits here, especially after a walk in the pretty surrounding countryside. The heart of the place is the original beamed and panelled bar with its convivial atmosphere, flagstones, attractive medley of old tables and chairs, old-fashioned window seats and a fireplace at each end – one is huge and houses an open woodburner; there's also an oak-floored room leading off here and a restaurant with another woodburning stove. Butcombe Bitter, St Austell Tribute and a changing guest ale on handpump and good wines by the glass. The attractively landscaped garden has the River Chun running through it and plenty of seats; boules. Bedrooms are comfortable and well appointed and the hearty breakfasts are served in the bar. Cerney House Gardens are worth a visit, and do have a look at the lovely church opposite.

Popular food includes lunchtime sandwiches and sharing platters, baked brie with onion jam, venison meatballs with wild mushrooms and plums on toasted ciabatta, vegetable curry, battered fish of the day with chips, grilled chicken breast wrapped in smoked bacon and topped with chorizo cream sauce, pesto-crusted cod with citrus mash and crème fraîche and chive sauce, duck breast with root vegetable cake, red cabbage and port jus, and puddings such as vanilla cheesecake and treacle tart. *Benchmark main dish: pie of the day £13.25. Two-course evening meal £20.50.*

Free house ~ Licensee Sian Clarke ~ Real ale ~ Open 11-11; 12-10.30 (8 in winter) Sun ~ Bar food 12-2.30, 6-9; 12-4, 6-9 Sat; 12-3, 6-9 Sun ~ Restaurant ~ Children welcome ~ Dogs allowed in bar and bedrooms ~ Wi-fi ~ Bedrooms: /£80 *Recommended by Giles and Annie Francis, James and Sylvia Hewitt, John and Claire Masters, Lyn and Freddie Roberts, Alexander and Trish Cutter*

NORTHLEACH SP1114 Map 4

Wheatsheaf

(01451) 860244 – www.cotswoldswheatsheaf.com

West End; the inn is on your left as you come in following the sign off A429, just SW of the junction with A40; GL54 3EZ

Attractive stone inn with contemporary food, real ales and a relaxed atmosphere; stylish bedrooms

This is a smart little place in a lovely small town. The airy, big-windowed linked rooms have high ceilings, antique and contemporary artwork, an attractive mix of dining chairs, big leather button-back settles and stools around wooden tables, flagstones in the central bar and wooden floors laid with turkish rugs in the dining rooms; also, three open fires. Butcombe Bitter, Stroud Budding and two guest ales on handpump, a dozen wines by the glass from a fantastic list of around 300 and local cider; background music and TV. There are seats in the pretty back garden. Bedrooms are comfortable and individually styled and breakfasts are much enjoyed. Dogs are genuinely welcomed and they even keep a jar of pigs' ears behind the bar for them.

Some sort of good food is served all day from breakfast onwards: twice-baked cheddar soufflé with spinach and grain mustard, duck and foie gras terrine with celeriac rémoulade, mussels with chorizo, sea vegetables and cider, courgette parmigiana with basil and mozzarella, venison pie, calves liver with bacon, mash, sage and onions, fillet of sea bream with olive tapenade, local goat saddle with wild garlic and green sauce, lobster tagliatelle with chilli, tomato and white wine, and puddings such as crème brûlée and sticky date pudding with salted caramel sauce. *Benchmark main dish: rare-breed pork chop with buttered kale and caramelised apple £18.00. Two-course evening meal £24.00.*

Free house ~ Licensee Chris Connor ~ Real ale ~ Open 8am-11pm ~ Bar food 12-3, 6-10.30; 12-3.45, 6-9.30 Sun ~ Restaurant ~ Children welcome ~ Dogs welcome ~ Wi-fi ~ Bedrooms: /£95 *Recommended by Peter Young, Kevin, Cliff and Monica Swan, Simon Day, Canon Michael Bourdeaux, Mark Mullins, Guy Vowles*

OAKRIDGE LYNCH SO9103 Map 4

Butchers Arms

(01285) 760371 – www.butchersarmsoakridge.com

Off Eastcombe–Bisley Road E of Stroud; GL6 7NZ

Bustling country pub with nice old bars and dining room, real ales, tasty food and seats in a big garden

On a sunny day, the big garden here has plenty of customers using the picnic-sets and other seats to enjoy the valley views; good surrounding walks in pretty countryside. The beamed bar has a relaxed feel, an open fire in a big stone fireplace with large copper pans to each side, an attractive mix of chapel and other country chairs around tables of various sizes on wooden floorboards, and modern art on exposed stone walls. Stools line the central counter where they keep Wadworths 6X, IPA and Horizon on handpump and several wines by the glass. The dining room is similarly furnished, with hunting prints and old photos on pale walls above a grey dado, a longcase clock and stone bottles on windowsills. They have a self-catering cottage next to the pub.

Popular food includes deep-fried brie with cajun-spiced ale chutney, fishcake with sweet chilli mayonnaise, pizzas, goats cheese and mushroom burger with relish, gherkins and fries, ham and egg, salmon fillet with creamy dill sauce and daupinoise potatoes, roast pork loin with cheese mash and wholegrain mustard and red wine gravy, steaks with blue cheese or peppercorn sauce, and puddings such as crème brûlée with fruit compote and chocolate brownie with vanilla ice-cream. *Benchmark main dish: lamb, apricot and rosemary sausages with creamy mash and caramelised onion gravy £10.95. Two-course evening meal £19.00.*

Wadworths ~ Tenant James Jones ~ Real ale ~ Open 11-11; 3-11 Tues; 12-10.30 Sun ~ Bar food 12-9; 3-9 Tues; 12-4 Sun ~ Restaurant ~ Children welcome ~ Dogs welcome ~ Wi-fi *Recommended by Andrew Stone, Rob Anderson, Charles and Maddie Bishop, Chloe and Tim Hodge, Mrs Zara Elliott*

OLDBURY-ON-SEVERN ST6092 Map 2

Anchor £

(01454) 413331 – www.anchorinn-oldbury.co.uk

Village signposted from B4061; BS35 1QA

Friendly country pub with tasty bar food, a thoughtful range of drinks and a pretty garden with hanging baskets

Hard-working, attentive staff serve a wide choice of drinks here, including Bass, Butcombe Bitter and St Austell Tribute on handpump, a dozen wines by the glass, three farm ciders, 30 gins and around 65 malt whiskies with helpful tasting notes. The neat lounge has black beams and stonework, cushioned window seats and a range of other wooden chairs, gate-leg tables, oil paintings of local scenes and a big log fire. The Village Bar has old and farming photographs on the walls, and there's a contemporary dining room towards the back of the building. The attractive garden is a real bonus with summer hanging baskets and window boxes, and seats beneath parasols or trees. You can walk from the pub to the River Severn and then along numerous footpaths and bridleways. There's wheelchair access to the dining room and a disabled lavatory. Nearby St Arilda's Church is interesting, set on an odd little knoll.

Well regarded food includes sandwiches, crayfish mayonnaise, warm goats cheese and chorizo salad, aubergine and mushroom lasagne, goan-style fish curry, chicken breast with parmentier potatoes and mushroom and brandy sauce, duck breast with dauphinoise potatoes and port and plum sauce, teriyaki salmon with noodles and stir-fried vegetables, 28-day-aged sirloin steak with fries, and puddings such as chocolate crunch with custard and crème caramel; they also offer a two- and three-course set menu (not Friday evening, Saturday or lunchtime Sunday). *Benchmark main dish: pork and bacon pie £12.95. Two-course evening meal £18.00.*

Free house ~ Licensees Michael Dowdeswell and Mark Sorrell ~ Real ale ~ Open 11.30-3, 6-10.30; 11.30-11 Fri, Sat; 12-10 Sun ~ Bar food 12-2 (2.30 Sat), 6-9; 12-3, 6-8 Sun ~ Restaurant ~ Children welcome but no under-12s in bar or lounge ~ Dogs allowed in bar ~ Bedrooms: £60/£85 *Recommended by Donald Allsopp, Margaret McDonald, Miranda and Jeff Davidson, Ian Wilson, Chris and Angela Buckell, Chloe and Michael Swettenham*

SELSLEY — SO8303 Map 4

Bell

(01453) 753801 – www.thebellinnselsley.com

Bell Lane; GL5 5JY

Tasty food and a good drinks choice in golden-stone inn with friendly service and seats overlooking valley

There are fine walks along the Cotswold Way and on Selsley Common, and this attractively updated 16th-c village dining pub is just the place for lunch. The three interconnected rooms have beams, a woodburning stove and an open fire, all manner of chairs and tables on wood-strip floors and Bath Prophecy, Stroud Tom Long and a beer named for the pub on handpump, several wines by the glass including champagne, 18 malt whiskies and 92 gins; service is friendly and helpful. The pub dog is called Bacchus. There's a garden room dining extension with retractable glass doors on to the terrace where picnic-sets enjoy spreading views of the valley. The two bedrooms are comfortable.

Well presented food cooked by the landlord includes lunchtime sandwiches, chicory marmalade tart with goats cheese bonbons and pear and walnut oil dressing, pressed ham hock and wild mushroom terrine with roast shallot and puy lentil salad, spinach and roquefort risotto with roasted artichokes, burger with toppings, coleslaw and triple-cooked chips, rump of local veal with garlic butter and roasted red onions, skate wing with caper noisette, cherry tomatoes and potatoes, overnight-cooked beef with horseradish mash, and puddings such as salted caramel pannacotta and pineapple tatin with thai ice-cream and passion fruit. *Benchmark main dish: beer-battered fish and chips £14.00. Two-course evening meal £23.00.*

Free house ~ Licensees Mark and Sarah Payne ~ Real ale ~ Open 11-11; 11-6 Sun; 11-3, 5-11 Mon-Thurs in winter; closed Sun evening ~ Bar food 12-2.30, 6-9; 12-3 Sun ~ Restaurant ~ Children welcome ~ Dogs welcome ~ Wi-fi ~ Bedrooms: /£95 *Recommended by Ruth Kelham, M Free, Tom and Ruth Rees, David and Charlotte Green, Charles Welch*

SHEEPSCOMBE SO8910 Map 4

Butchers Arms £

(01452) 812113 – www.butchers-arms.co.uk

Village signed off B4070 NE of Stroud; or A46 N of Painswick (but narrow lanes); GL6 7RH

Cheerful pub with open fire and woodburner, plenty to look at, several real ales and enjoyable food; fine views

A welcoming landlord and a bustling atmosphere make this country pub a happy place. The bar has farmhouse chairs and stools around scrubbed tables, two big bay windows with cushioned seats, low beams clad with horsebrasses, and flooring that's half parquet and half old quarry tiles. Also, delft shelves lined with china, brass and copper cups, lamps and blow torches (there's even a pitchfork) and walls decorated with hunting prints and photos of the village and surrounding area. Leading off here is a high-ceilinged room with exposed-stone walls hung with maps of local walks (there are many) and wheelback and mate's chairs around tables on bare boards. The cosy snug area is carpeted and has cushioned window seats, a long settle and a high-backed porter's seat, historic photos of the village and the area, and an open log fire. Prescott Hill Climb, Unity Brew House Pekin Pale Ale and a changing guest such as St Austell Proper Job on handpump, 12 wines by the glass and farm ciders; daily papers, chess, cribbage and Jenga. The view over the lovely steep beechwood valley is terrific, and the seats outside make the most of it. The area was apparently once a hunting ground for Henry VIII.

Quite a choice of food includes sandwiches and paninis, chicken liver pâté with port, herbs and spiced plum chutney, thai cod, salmon, lemon and coriander fishcake with a tomato and mixed pepper salsa, mediterranean vegetable gratin, roasted ham and eggs, a pie of the week, lambs liver with bacon and onion gravy and bubble and squeak, butterflied chicken breast topped with bacon, spinach, mustard, melting cheese and mushrooms, sea bass fillets with butternut squash, pak choi and a white wine, coriander and lemon cream sauce, and puddings. *Benchmark main dish: burger with toppings, coleslaw and rustic chips £11.50. Two-course evening meal £18.00.*

Free house ~ Licensees Mark and Sharon Tallents ~ Real ale ~ Open 11.30-3, 6.30-11; 11.30-11.30 Sat; 12-10.30 Sun ~ Bar food 12-2.30, 6.30-9.30; all day Sat; 12-8 (6 in winter) Sun ~ Restaurant ~ Children welcome ~ Dogs allowed in bar ~ Wi-fi *Recommended by Stan Abrahams, Richard Tilbrook, Mike and Sarah Abbot, Amy and Luke Buchanan, Bridget and Peter Gregson, Revd Michael Vockins, Dr and Mrs A K Clarke, Guy Vowles*

SOUTHROP SP2003 Map 4

Swan 

(01367) 850205 – www.thyme.co.uk

Off A361 Lechlade–Burford; GL7 3NU

Creeper-covered pub with a proper village bar, soft seating and simple tables, delicious food and a fine choice of drinks; seats in walled garden

A gently civilised all-rounder in a handsome creeper-clad building, this 17th-c pub is part of the Thyme company on the Southrop Manor Estate. A chatty, bustling bar has friendly locals (and maybe a dog or two), simple tables and chairs on flagstones, an open fire, stools against the counter, Cotswold Lion Shepherds Delight, Hillside Over The Hill, North Cotswold Shagweaver and Stroud Budding on handpump, up to 15 wines by the glass from a well chosen list, and helpful staff; background music, TV, skittle alley and board games. The two low-ceilinged dining rooms have tweed-upholstered chairs around a nice mix of tables, cushions on settles, rugs on flagstones, open fires and fresh flowers and candles. There are elegant metal chairs and tables on gravel in several sheltered walled garden areas and picnic-sets at the front; good surrounding walks.

Impressive food uses produce grown or raised on the Estate: sandwiches, crab toasts with cucumber and dill, pork and veal terrine with cornichons and preserves, polenta with globe artichokes, nettles, ricotta and herb salad, chicken, bacon and wild garlic pie (for two people), rack of pork with braised beans, greens and herbs, hake with parsley and wild garlic mash, sirloin steak with smoked garlic and thyme butter or horseradish cream, and puddings such as rhubarb, sherry and almond trifle and buttermilk pudding with raspberry preserve. *Benchmark main dish: steak, salad and hand-cut chips £23.00. Two-course evening meal £28.00.*

Free house ~ Licensee Dominic Abbott ~ Real ale ~ Open 11.30-11 ~ Bar food 12-2.30 (3 weekends), 6-9.30 (10pm Fri, Sat) ~ Restaurant ~ Children welcome but must be over 12 in bedrooms ~ Dogs welcome ~ Wi-fi ~ Bedrooms: /£285 *Recommended by Jane and Philip Saunders, Louise and Oliver Redman, Graeme and Sally Mendham, Cecily and Steven Evans*

STOW-ON-THE-WOLD SP1925 Map 4

Porch House

(01451) 870048 – www.porch-house.co.uk

Digbeth Street; GL54 1BN

Fine old character inn with carefully refurbished bars and dining areas, and imaginative food; comfortable bedrooms

There's plenty of space for both drinking and dining in this carefully restored, mainly 16th-c pub. The bar areas have beams (some hop-draped), big flagstones or bare floorboards, exposed stone walls and open fireplaces; background music and board games. Also, all sorts of cushioned wooden and upholstered chairs, little stools and settles with scatter cushions around myriad tables, church candles and lanterns, books on shelves, stone bottles on windowsills and a woodburning stove. The cosy snug is similarly furnished but also has sofas and armchairs. A beer named for the pub (from Brakspears) plus Brakspears Bitter and Oxford Gold on handpump and good wines by the glass and ten gins. There's a dining room with upholstered, high-backed chairs (some with striking blue cushions), and also a conservatory. A raised terrace has rattan chairs and cushioned wall benches around rustic tables intermingled with more contemporary seats. Bedrooms are individually designed and stylish and breakfasts particularly good. This is a lovely small town to visit.

Extremely good food includes lunchtime sandwiches and pub favourites plus twice-baked cheddar soufflé, roasted scallops with cauliflower textures and pancetta, squash and sage risotto with chestnuts and spinach, calves liver with pressed brisket and potato terrine, slow-roasted shallots and bourguignon jus, lemon and garlic chicken with spiced chickpea purée, chorizo and grilled courgettes, a fresh fish dish of the day, dry-aged fillet steak rossini with foie gras and bone marrow jus, and puddings such as chocolate orange fondant with rum and raisin ice-cream and sticky toffee pudding with butterscotch sauce. *Benchmark main dish: eight-hour-cooked pork belly with burnt toffee apple, parsnip rösti and cider jus £15.50. Two-course evening meal £22.00.*

Free house ~ Licensee Duncan Craig ~ Real ale ~ Open 8am-11pm (10.30pm Sun) ~ Bar food 12-3, 6-9.30; 12-9.30 Sat; 12-8.30 Sun ~ Restaurant ~ Children welcome ~ Dogs allowed in bar and bedrooms ~ Wi-fi ~ Bedrooms: /£99 *Recommended by NAJB, Patricia and Gordon Thompson, Joe and Belinda Smart, Helene Grygar, Mike and Mary Carter, Abigail Slater, John and Lorna Chew*

TETBURY ST8494 Map 4

Gumstool

(01666) 890391 – www.calcotmanor.co.uk

Part of Calcot Manor Hotel; A4135 W of town, just E of junction with A46; GL8 8YJ

Civilised bar with relaxed atmosphere, super choice of drinks and enjoyable food; bedrooms

Although attached to the very smart Calcot Manor Hotel, this well run bar-brasserie is a special place in its own right. The thoughtfully divided, stylish layout gives your table the feeling of having a snug area more or less to itself, without losing the friendly atmosphere of plenty going on around you. There are flagstones, elegant wooden dining chairs and tables, well chosen pictures and drawings and wooden 'stag's head and antlers' on mushroom-coloured walls, leather tub armchairs and stools and a neat row of copper cooking pans above the blazing log fire. From the long counter lined with modern chairs, they keep St Austell Tribute and Wickwar BOB on handpump, two dozen interesting wines by the glass and several malt whiskies; background music. The slightly sunken front courtyard has a few picnic-sets. Westonbirt Arboretum is not far away.

Delicious food (they also have a fireside grill) includes smoked trout and fennel jam mini pie with shallot salad and hollandaise, local duck in beer with kohlrabi and celeriac rémoulade and beer barbecue sauce, fireside grilled organic, rare-breed burger with bacon jam, toppings, onion mayonnaise and chips, lightly spiced salmon and haddock fishcakes with spinach, a poached egg and lemon butter sauce, truffled chicken kiev with wild mushrooms and parsley mash, cornish cod with aubergine caponata, black cabbage, anchovy and fennel butter, and puddings such as warm treacle tart with crème fraîche and lemon posset with crisp meringue. *Benchmark main dish: fireside grilled rump steak with smoked onion rings, a choice of sauce and chips £20.00. Two-course evening meal £30.00.*

Free house ~ Licensees Paul Sadler and Richard Ball ~ Real ale ~ Open 12-11 ~ Bar food 12-2 (2.30 Sat), 6-9.30; 12-4, 6-9 Sun ~ Children welcome ~ Wi-fi ~ Bedrooms: £184/£209

Recommended by Bernard Stradling, Buster and Helena Hastings, David Appleyard, IAA, HMW, Maria Sansoni, Stuart and Natalie Granville, Moira and Jon Weller

WESTON SUBEDGE SP1241 Map 4

Seagrave Arms

(01386) 840192 – www.seagravearms.com

B4632; GL55 6QH

Golden-stone inn with friendly staff and enjoyable food; contemporary bedrooms

There's a lot of character in this handsome old place, especially in the cosy little bar: ancient flagstones, half-panelled walls, an open fire, padded window seats and a chatty, informal atmosphere. Prescott Hill Climb and a guest from North Cotswold on handpump and 14 wines (plus prosecco and champagne) by the glass, served by helpful, friendly staff; background music, TV and board games. The two dining rooms have an appealing mix of wooden chairs and tables on floorboards. Outside, there are wicker chairs and tables on neat gravel at the front of the building and more seats in the back garden. Most of the well equipped, modern bedrooms are in the main house, with others in the converted stables; breakfasts are good and hearty. The Cotswold Way is nearby, so the pub is popular with walkers.

Tasty, up-to-date food includes sandwiches, chicken and sage terrine with wholegrain mustard, sea bass with charred fennel and chervil, chicken caesar salad, butternut squash risotto with puffed rice, goats curd and smoked almonds, roast salmon with crushed new potatoes, samphire, tarragon and shallot relish, pigeon breast with cauliflower cheese, blackberries and boulangère potatoes, flat-iron steak with slow-cooked tomatoes, king oyster mushroom and chips, and puddings such as peanut butter crème brûlée with peanut and banana crumb and brown sugar cheesecake with pomegranate jelly and frosted hazelnuts. *Benchmark main dish: burger with toppings and fries £12.95. Two-course evening meal £23.00.*

Free house ~ Licensee Magdalena Wojciechowska ~ Real ale ~ Open 12-11; 12-9 Sun ~ Bar food 12-2.30, 6-9.30; 12-8 Sun ~ Restaurant ~ Children welcome ~ Dogs allowed in bar and bedrooms ~ Wi-fi ~ Bedrooms: /£150 *Recommended by Bernard Stradling, Margo and Derek Peters, Lee and Jill Stafford, Jennifer and Nicholas Thompson*

WINCHCOMBE SP0228 Map 4

Lion

(01242) 603300 – www.thelionwinchcombe.co.uk

North Street; GL54 5PS

Historic inn in fine town with drinking and dining spaces in character rooms, fresh flowers and candlelight and seats on pretty terraces; warm, TV-free bedrooms

---

You'll find a wide mix of customers here and as the place is open all day, they tend to pop in and out all the time which creates a cheerful, bustling atmosphere. It's all very stylish with rustic-chic furnishings, exposed golden-stone walls, portraits and gilt-edged mirrors on pale paintwork, flagstones, armchairs, scatter cushions on wall seats, stools and elegant wooden dining chairs around all shapes and sizes of table, jugs of fresh flowers and plenty of big stubby candles. Marstons EPA, Prescott Hill Climb, Wye Valley Butty Bach and a changing guest on handpump, ten good wines by the glass, ten malt whiskies and 20 gins served by smiling, courteous staff; daily papers, board games, TV and background music. Wood and metal seats and tables sit on various terraced areas among shrubs and climbers and there are more seats on grass. Bedrooms are individually decorated in a country style; two have their own staircases and one is in a converted hayloft. Sudeley Castle is within walking distance and Cheltenham Racecourse is nearby.

Enticing food includes sandwiches, tandoori salmon with coconut cabbage and mango and coriander yoghurt, chicken leg and duck liver terrine with apricot ketchup, celeriac and black truffle risotto with pickled celeriac and puffed potato, pie of the day, butter-poached cod with cauliflower, smoked almonds and confit egg yolk, miso-glazed lamb rump with wild garlic, courgette and tomato, and puddings such as warm chocolate mousse with griottine cherries and passion-fruit sorbet and caramelised banana bread with praline crémeux and yoghurt sorbet; they also offer a two- and three-course set menu. *Benchmark main dish: beer-battered fish and chips £14.50. Two-course evening meal £21.00.*

Free house ~ Licensee Luke Buckle ~ Real ale ~ Open 10.30am-11pm ~ Bar food 12-3, 6-9 ~ Restaurant ~ Children welcome ~ Dogs allowed in bar and bedrooms ~ Wi-fi ~ Live music monthly ~ Bedrooms: £110/£190 *Recommended by Jo Rees, Richard Tilbrook, Mrs Julie Thomas, Mike and Mary Carter, Joe and Belinda Smart, Liz and Martin Eldon*

Post Office address codings confusingly give the impression that some pubs are in Gloucestershire, when they're really in Warwickshire (which is where we list them).

Also Worth a Visit in Gloucestershire

Besides the fully inspected pubs, you might like to try these pubs that have been recommended to us and described by readers. Do tell us what you think of them: feedback@goodguides.com

ALDSWORTH SP1510

Sherborne Arms (01451) 844346

B4425 Burford–Cirencester; GL54 3RB Rural pub (former 17th-c stone farmhouse) set down from the road and run by same family since 1984; enjoyable good value home-made food including signature lamb and apricot casserole, often a weekday meal deal, two or three changing ales and proper cider, friendly service, beams, stripped stone and log fire, smallish bar and big dining area, conservatory, games/function room; background music, film night first Mon of month; children and dogs welcome, disabled access, pleasant front garden with smokers' shelter, closed Sun evening, Mon (except bank holidays). *(Donald Allsopp)*

AMBERLEY SO8401

Amberley Inn (01453) 872565

Steeply off A46 Stroud–Nailsworth – gentler approach from N Nailsworth; GL5 5AF Popular well located old stone inn with beautiful views and good local walks; two comfortable bars, snug and a more formal restaurant, well kept Stroud ales, nice wines and enjoyable locally sourced food from bar snacks up (special diets catered for), friendly helpful staff; children and dogs (in bar) welcome, side terrace and back garden, 11 bedrooms. *(John and Lorna Chew)*

AMBERLEY SO8401

Black Horse (01453) 872556

Off A46 Stroud–Nailsworth to Amberley; left after Amberley Inn, left at war memorial; Littleworth; best to park by war memorial and walk down; GL5 5AL Two-bar pub with spectacular valley views from small conservatory and terraced garden; mix of pine furniture on wood and slate floors, exposed stone walls, modern artwork and two woodburners, up to five real ales such as Sharps, Stroud and Wickwar, Weston's cider and good range of whiskies and gins, enjoyable reasonably priced fairly traditional food (not Sun evening) from sandwiches up, nice staff; children, walkers and dogs welcome, wheelchair access (highish step by gate), outside gents', picnic-sets on front grass, more in split-level back garden, parking can be tricky, open all day. *(Lee and Jill Stafford)*

AMPNEY CRUCIS SP0701

Crown of Crucis (01285) 851806

A417 E of Cirencester; GL7 5RS Modernised roadside inn with spacious split-level bar, beams and log fires, good choice of enjoyable food including competitively priced dish of the day (weekday lunchtimes), Sharps Doom Bar, a guest beer and decent choice of wines, friendly helpful service; children and dogs welcome, disabled facilities, tables out by Ampney Brook with wooden bridge over to cricket pitch, handy for Palladian Way walkers, quiet modern courtyard bedrooms, good breakfast, open (and food) all day. *(Guy Vowles, Dr A J and Mrs B A Tompsett)*

ANDOVERSFORD SP0219

Royal Oak (01242) 821426

Signed just off A40; Gloucester Road; GL54 4HR Cosy 17th-c beamed village pub, lots of stripped stone, galleried raised dining room beyond big central open fire, well kept ales including Otter and over a dozen wines by the glass, good sensibly priced food from sandwiches and various burgers up, friendly welcoming staff; games end with pool and darts; children and dogs welcome, tables on back terrace, open all day. *(Tim Senn)*

APPERLEY SO8627

Farmers Arms (01452) 780307

Lower Apperley (B4213); GL19 4DR Extended country pub under new management; beams, big open fire and spacious split-level carpeted dining area, up to four Wadworths ales and a dozen wines by the glass, enjoyable food from traditional choices up, pleasant helpful staff; live music including Aug bank holiday festival; children and dogs welcome, picnic-sets on terrace and in garden overlooking fields, closed Sun evening. *(Peter Young, Theocsbrian, Katharine Cowherd)*

ARLINGHAM SO7110

Red Lion (01452) 740700

High Street; GL2 7JH Old village corner pub owned by the local community; good food from lunchtime sandwiches and pub favourites up, Uley Bitter and guests, friendly staff, updated interior with wood and carpeted floors, some beams and two woodburners; children and dogs welcome, picnic-sets out by the road, good circular walks (not far from the River Severn), closed Mon lunchtime, otherwise open all day (food all day Sat, till 6pm Sun, not Mon). *(Peter Young)*

ASHLEWORTH QUAY SO8125

Boat (01452) 700272

Ashleworth signposted off A417 N of Gloucester; quay signed from village; GL19 4HZ Tiny unpretentious old pub in lovely spot on the banks of the Severn; front parlour with mats on flagstones, built-in settle by scrubbed deal table, elderly chairs next to old-fashioned kitchen range, cribbage and dominoes, back quarry-tiled dining room with fireplace and a cosy snug, up to ten mostly local ales and good range of ciders, enjoyable food from baguettes to speciality burgers; live music and beer/cider festivals; children, dogs and muddy boots welcome, tricky for wheelchairs (friendly staff will help), sunny crazy-paved front courtyard, more seats to the side and on grass by river, moorings, near interesting 15th-c tithe barn (NT), open all day in summer (all day Fri-Sun, closed Mon and lunchtime Weds in winter). *(Mike and Mary Carter)*

AYLBURTON SO6101

Cross (01594) 842823
High Street; GL15 6DE Popular village pub with enjoyable well priced traditional food from sandwiches and baked potatoes up, ales such as Bath, Butcombe and Wye Valley, several wines by the glass and a dozen whiskies, welcoming helpful staff, open-plan split-level flagstoned bar, beams, modern furniture alongside high-backed settles, old local photographs, woodburners in large stone fireplaces, high-raftered dining room; free wi-fi; children and dogs welcome, wheelchair access from car park, pleasant garden with play area, open all day Fri-Sun. *(Julian Richardson)*

BIBURY SP1006

★**Catherine Wheel** (01285) 740250
Arlington; B4425 NE of Cirencester; GL7 5ND Attractive old dining pub in beautiful Cotswold village; enjoyable freshly made food (best to book weekends) from sandwiches and pizzas up including good local trout, well kept Hook Norton Hooky and a couple of guests, cheerful attentive young staff, open-plan main bar and smaller back rooms, low beams, stripped stone and log fires, raftered dining room; children and dogs welcome, picnic-sets in front and in good-sized garden, handy for country and riverside walks, four bedrooms in separate building, open (and food) all day. *(R K Phillips, Peter Young, Guy Vowles)*

BISHOP'S NORTON SO8425

Red Lion (01452) 730935
Wainlode Lane; GL2 9LW Isolated red-brick pub on picturesque bend of the River Severn (prone to flooding); ales such as Butcombe and Wye Valley, proper cider and decent range of wines, gins and whiskies, enjoyable food from sandwiches and sharing boards up including some interesting choices, bar to the left of entrance, two snugs to the right, stripped-wood floors, blue/grey dados and woodburners in brick fireplaces, pubby furniture including pews, old photos and agricultural posters; background music (turned down/off on request), TV, free wi-fi; children welcome, wheelchair access using portable ramp (friendly staff will help), picnic-sets on cobbled frontage, riverside garden across narrow road, adjacent campsite, good walks, open all day Fri-Sun, no food Sun evening. *(Chris and Angela Buckell)*

BISLEY SO9006

Bear (01452) 770265
Village signed off A419 E of Stroud; GL6 7BD Interesting 17th-c colonnaded inn (originally a courthouse); L-shaped bar with low ceiling, old oak settles, brass and copper implements around extremely wide stone fireplace, five well kept ales including Butcombe and Wells Bombardier, popular pubby food, friendly staff, separate stripped-stone family area; outside gents', ladies' upstairs; dogs welcome, small flagstoned courtyard, stone mounting blocks in garden across quiet road, one bedroom, open all day weekends. *(Julian and Fiona Barnes)*

BLAISDON SO7016

Red Hart (01452) 830477
Village signposted off A4136 just SW of junction with A40 W of Gloucester; OS Sheet 162 map reference 703169; GL17 0AH Bustling village pub with plenty to look at in flagstoned main bar and attractive carpeted restaurant: woodworking and farming tools on magnolia walls and hanging from beams, old photographs of prize farm stock, a framed inventory of the pub in 1903 and lots of books, pot plants and some interesting prints, candles on traditional tables, cushioned wall and window seats, well kept Otter and three guests, real cider and ten wines by the glass, popular food from sandwiches and traditional choices up; background music, board games, free wi-fi; children welcome (family dining part), dogs in bar, wheelchair access, picnic-sets on terrace and in garden with play area, pretty summer window boxes, little church nearby worth a visit. *(Mike and Mary Carter, Dr A J and Mrs B A Tompsett, Clive and Fran Dutson)*

BLOCKLEY SP1635

Great Western Arms
(01386) 700362 *Station Road (B4479); GL56 9DT* Simple little beamed pub with well kept Hook Norton ales, decent wines by the glass and tasty reasonably priced home-made food including Thurs steak night and Fri moules frites, friendly efficient service, comfortable bar where dogs allowed, dining room; children welcome, paved terrace with lovely valley view, attractive village, open all day Fri-Sun, closed Mon lunchtime. *(Maria Birch)*

BRIMPSFIELD SO9413

★**Golden Heart** (01242) 870261
Nettleton Bottom (not shown on road maps, so instead we list the pub under the name of the nearby village); on A417 N of the Brimpsfield turning northbound; GL4 8LA Traditional old roadside inn with low-ceilinged bar

divided into five cosy areas; log fire in huge inglenook, exposed stone walls and wood panelling, well worn built-in settles and other old-fashioned furnishings, brass items, typewriters and banknotes, parlour on right with decorative fireplace leading into further room, well kept Brakspears with guests such as Jennings, Stroud and Wychwood, several wines by the glass, popular sensibly priced food from extensive blackboard menu including several vegetarian/vegan options, friendly staff; children and dogs welcome, seats and tables on suntrap terrace with pleasant valley views, nearby walks, open all day. *(Guy Vowles)*

BROAD CAMPDEN SP1537

★**Bakers Arms** (01386) 840515
Village signed from B4081 in Chipping Campden; GL55 6UR Beamed 17th-c stone pub with tiny character bar, stripped-stone walls and inglenook woodburner, half a dozen well kept ales such as North Cotswold, Stanway, Wickwar and Wye Valley, simply furnished dining room serving popular pubby food (not Sun evening, Mon) plus blackboard specials; folk night last Weds of month, darts and board games; children (away from bar) and dogs (in bar) welcome, picnic-sets on terraces and in back garden, delightful Cotswold village and good nearby walks, open all day weekends, closed Mon lunchtime. *(Theocsbrian, Guy Vowles)*

BROADWELL SP2027

Fox (01451) 870909
Off A429, 2 miles N of Stow-on-the-Wold; GL56 0UF New management for this golden-stone pub set above broad village green; traditional furnishings in beamed bar with flagstones, stripped-stone walls and log fire, well kept/priced Donnington BB and SBA, hearty home-cooked food from shortish reasonably priced menu, friendly attentive staff, opened-up dining area; background music, darts and dominoes; children and dogs (in bar) welcome, picnic-sets on gravel in sizeable back garden, aunt sally, paddock for camping (ring for details), open all day weekends, no food Sun evening. *(Lauren and Dan Frazer)*

BROCKWEIR SO5301

Brockweir Inn (01291) 689548
Signed just off A466 Chepstow–Monmouth; NP16 7NG Welcoming country local near the River Wye; beams and stripped stonework, quarry tiles, sturdy settles and woodburner, nice snug with parquet floor and open fire, four well kept ales, three ciders and enjoyable food (not Sun evening) including OAP lunch deal (Tues, Thurs), small back dining area and room upstairs 'Devil's Pulpit' (games and books); live music first Tues of month; children and dogs welcome, little walled garden with clay oven, good walks, open all day weekends. *(Lyn and Freddie Roberts)*

BUSSAGE SO8804

Ram (01453) 883163
At Eastcombe, take The Ridgeway and first right The Ridge; pub is 500 metres on left; GL6 8BB Tucked-away Cotswold-stone local with roomy opened-up interior; good pub food (not Sun evening) from lunchtime sandwiches to daily specials, well kept Bath, Butcombe, Greene King and St Austell, varied choice of wines, friendly helpful staff; soft background music, free wi-fi; children welcome, dogs in bar (theirs is Bella), a few picnic-sets outside, good nearby walks, open all day Fri, Sat, till 8pm Sun. *(Mark Morgan)*

CAMP SO9111

★**Fostons Ash** (01452) 863262
B4070 Birdlip–Stroud, junction with Calf Way; GL6 7ES Open-plan dining pub (part of the small Cotswold Food Club group), light and airy, with good fairly priced food from sharing plates up, three well kept ales such as Bespoke, Sharps and Stroud, nice range of wines by the glass, welcoming helpful staff, one end with easy chairs and woodburner; background music, daily papers; children and dogs welcome, rustic tables in attractive garden with part-covered terrace and play area, good walks, open all day (food all day Sun). *(Guy Vowles)*

CHARLTON KINGS SO9620

Royal (01242) 228937
Horsefair, opposite church; GL53 8JH Large 19th-c pub with clean modern décor; good food (all day weekends) in bar or dining conservatory, several well kept ales (tasting trays available) and decent wines, prompt friendly service; Sun quiz, some live music; children and dogs welcome, picnic-sets in garden overlooking church, open all day. *(Peter Young, Guy Vowles)*

CHELTENHAM SO9421

Jolly Brewmaster (01242) 772261
Painswick Road; GL50 2EZ Popular convivial local with open-plan linked areas around big semicircular counter, fine range of changing ales and ciders, friendly obliging young staff, newspapers, log fire; quiz last Weds of month; dogs welcome, coachyard tables, open from 2.30pm (midday Sat, Sun). *(Andrea and Philip Crispin)*

CHELTENHAM SO9522

Old Restoration (01242) 522792
High Street; GL50 1DX Recently refurbished 17th-c beamed pub; extensive range of real ales and craft beers including Butcombe, enjoyable fair-priced food from sandwiches to good Sun roasts, friendly helpful staff, open fires, games room with darts, table football and retro video games; children (away from bar) and dogs welcome, open (and food) all day. *(Andrea and Philip Crispin)*

CHELTENHAM SO9624

Plough (01242) 361506

Mill Street, Prestbury; GL52 3BG
Convivial thatched and beamed village local tucked away behind church; comfortable little front lounge with brick fireplace, upholstered wall benches in flagstoned back tap room, old local photographs and a grandfather clock by big log fire, corridor hatch serving two or three changing ales from stillage casks and proper ciders, enjoyable good value food including range of Pieminister pies, friendly service; may be live folk music Thurs; children and dogs welcome, picnic-sets in big back garden with own bar, play area and boules, open all day, no food Sun evening. *(Mark Morgan)*

CHELTENHAM SO9321

Royal Union (01242) 519098

Hatherley Street; GL50 2TT Backstreet corner local with large bar and cosy snug up steps, around eight well kept local ales including Tivoli (brewed for the pub by TAP) plus craft kegs, reasonably priced wines and good range of whiskies/gins, enjoyable food (Weds-Sat evenings, Sun lunchtime), can also pre-book sharing dishes for up to ten people, informal restaurant in former skittle alley; Thurs quiz; well behaved children allowed (but no under-5s), dogs on leads, courtyard behind, bedrooms, open all day Sun, from 5pm other days. *(Andrea and Philip Crispin)*

CHELTENHAM SO9522

Sandford Park (01242) 571022

High Street; GL50 1DZ Former nightclub converted to a popular pub, three bar areas and upstairs function room, up to nine well kept changing ales along with craft and continental beers, several ciders and good value home-cooked food from short menu (not Sun evening, Mon lunchtime), friendly staff; Sun quiz, bar billiards; large back garden, open all day. *(Giles and Annie Francis)*

CHELTENHAM SO9522

Wild Beer at Jessop House

(01242) 534000 *Cambray Place; GL50 1JX* Relaxed and individual bar in Georgian town house owned by the Wild Beer Co; 20 craft beers on tap (mainly theirs) plus many more in bottles, decent wines and some well chosen gins, interesting food from various small plates up (dishes paired with beer), good friendly service, more room upstairs; background music; dogs welcome, tables in courtyard garden, open all day (till 7pm Sun). *(Kerry and Guy Trooper)*

CHIPPING CAMPDEN SP1539

★**Eight Bells** (01386) 840371

Church Street (one-way – entrance off B4035); GL55 6JG Lovely historic inn with cheerful bustling atmosphere; candlelit bar areas with massive timbers and beams, stripped-stone walls and log fires, cushioned pews, sofas and solid dark wood furniture on broad flagstones, ales such as Hook Norton, Goffs, Purity and Wye Valley from fine oak counter, also a couple of real ciders and seven wines by the glass, good food including lunchtime doorstep sandwiches, glass panel in dining room reveals church passage used by Catholic priests escaping the Roundheads; background music, board games, free wi-fi; well behaved children (not in bar after 7pm) and dogs (in bar) welcome, large terraced garden with striking views of almshouses and church, attractive comfortable bedrooms, good breakfast, open all day. *(Victoria and James Sargeant, Ivy and George Goodwill, Lorna and Jack Mulgrave, Michael Sargent)*

CHIPPING CAMPDEN SP1539

Kings (01386) 840256

High Street; GL55 6AW Eclectic décor in 18th-c hotel's bar-brasserie and separate restaurant, good food from lunchtime sandwiches and pubby dishes to more upmarket choices, friendly attentive service, well kept Hook Norton Hooky and good choice of wines by the glass (can be pricey), afternoon teas, daily papers and nice log fire; secluded back garden with picnic-sets and terrace tables, 12 comfortable bedrooms, open all day. *(Mark Morgan)*

CHIPPING CAMPDEN SP1539

Noel Arms (01386) 840317

High Street; GL55 6AT Handsome 16th-c inn with beamed and stripped-stone bar, nice food from sandwiches to steaks, some good curries too from sri lankan chef (curry night last Thurs of month), well kept Hook Norton, local guests and good choice of wines by the glass, friendly efficient staff, coffee bar (from 9am), conservatory and separate restaurant; lunchtime jazz first Sun of month; children and dogs welcome, sunny courtyard tables, 28 well appointed bedrooms, good breakfast, open all day. *(Dave Braisted)*

CHIPPING SODBURY ST7282

Horseshoe 07780 505563

High Street; BS37 6AP Welcoming unpretentious little pub in former stationers' making most of the space; seven well kept ales and six ciders, low priced pubby lunchtime food (not Sun, Mon), curry night Weds, otherwise rolls at the bar, comfortable sofas and settles, another intimate room upstairs; occasional live music, sports TV; dogs welcome, small pretty garden behind, open all day (till midnight weekends). *(Roger and Donna Huggins)*

CIRENCESTER SP0202

Corinium (01285) 659711

Dollar Street/Gloucester Street; GL7 2DG Civilised and comfortable Georgian-fronted hotel (originally a 16th-c wool merchant's house); bar with good mix of tables on wood or flagstone floors, leather bucket seats by woodburner in stone fireplace, enjoyable fairly priced food from sandwiches to daily specials, three well kept local ales and decent wines, cheerful helpful young staff, restaurant; entrance through charming courtyard, wheelchair access with help, picnic-sets in attractive walled garden, 15 bedrooms. *(Theocsbrian)*

CIRENCESTER SP0103

Drillmans Arms (01285) 653892

Gloucester Road, Stratton; GL7 2JY Unpretentious two-room roadside local with welcoming long-serving landlady, well kept Sharps Doom Bar and three quickly changing guests, basic lunchtime food (not Tues), low beams and woodburner; skittle alley, darts and pool; dogs welcome, tables out by small front car park, open all day Sat. *(Richard Tilbrook)*

CIRENCESTER SP0202

Fleece (01285) 658507

Market Place; GL7 2NZ Carefully renovated old inn with various bars, lounges and airy dining areas; bare boards, contemporary pale paintwork, plenty of prints and fresh flowers, Thwaites ales and guests such as Cotswold Lion and Flying Monk, several wines by the glass and good selection of coffees and teas, well liked food from sandwiches up served by efficient courteous staff; children and dogs (in bar) welcome, terrace with white metal tables and chairs under parasols, attractive well equipped bedrooms, hearty breakfast, open (and food) all day. *(Guy Vowles, Martin and Joanne Sharp, Patricia Healey, Michael Sargent, Roger and Donna Huggins)*

CIRENCESTER SP0202

Golden Cross (01285) 652137

Black Jack Street, between church and Corinium Museum; GL7 2AA Bustling backstreet coaching inn with long thin bar, snug and skylit restaurant, enjoyable food at sensible prices including Sat brunch, well kept Arkells and good range of wines and whiskies, friendly service; live music last Fri of month, sports TV; children and dogs welcome, rattan-style furniture in sunny courtyard garden, bedrooms, open all day (Sun till 9.30pm). *(Donald Allsopp)*

CIRENCESTER SP0201

Marlborough Arms (01285) 651474

Sheep Street; GL7 1QW Busy bare-boards drinkers' pub with eight well kept ales including Box Steam and North Cotswold, also proper ciders and continental draught/bottled beers, friendly staff and good mix of customers, brewery memorabilia, pump clips and shelves of bottles, open fire; live music and quiz nights, sports TV; enclosed back courtyard, open all day. *(Alexander and Trish Cutter)*

COATES SO9600

Tunnel House (01285) 770702

Follow Tarlton signs (right then left) from village, pub up rough track on right after railway bridge; OS Sheet 163 map reference 965005; GL7 6PW New management for this bow-fronted stone house by entrance to derelict canal tunnel; rambling character rooms with beams, exposed stonework and flagstones, good mix of furnishings and plenty to look at including old enamel signs, railway lamps, stuffed animals, even an upside-down card table fixed to the ceiling (complete with cards and drinks), sofas by log fire, Box Steam, Bristol Beer Factory, Butcombe and Timothy Taylors, a couple of Thatcher's ciders and nine wines by the glass, happy hour 4-7pm Mon-Fri, enjoyable pubby food (not Sun evening) including daily specials, good friendly service, more conventional dining extension and back conservatory; background music, free wi-fi; children and dogs welcome, disabled access/loos, impressive views from front terrace, big garden down to the canal, good nearby walks, open all day. *(Kim Adams)*

COLESBOURNE SO9913

Colesbourne Inn (01242) 870376

A435 Cirencester–Cheltenham; GL53 9NP Civilised 19th-c gabled coaching inn; decent choice of popular food from ciabattas and deli boards up, smaller appetites and gluten-free diets catered for, well kept Wadworths ales and plenty of wines by the glass, friendly service, linked partly panelled rooms, log fires, comfortable mix of settles, softly padded seats and leather sofas, candlelit back dining room; background music, TV; dogs welcome, views from attractive back garden and terrace, nine bedrooms in converted stable block, good breakfast (for non-residents too), open (and food) all day. *(Peter Young, Richard Tilbrook, Christian Mole)*

COMPTON ABDALE SP0717

★**Garniche at the Puesdown**

(01451) 860262 *A40 outside village; GL54 4DN* Spacious series of modernised linked bars and eating areas; mainly stripped-stone walls, rafter-effect or beamed ceilings, rugs on bare boards, chesterfield sofas and armchairs, high-backed dining chairs around mix of tables, log fire and two-way woodburner, a couple of Hook Norton ales and maybe a guest, good freshly made food from fairly pubby menu, morning coffee and afternoon tea, friendly helpful staff; background music, gift shop; children and dogs (in bar) welcome, tables in pretty back garden, three comfortable ground-floor bedrooms, closed Sun evening, Mon, otherwise open (and food) all day. *(Peter Young)*

Pubs close to motorway junctions are listed at the back of the book.

CROMHALL ST6990

Royal Oak (01454) 430993

Tortworth Road; GL12 8AD Spacious old country pub under helpful friendly licensees; good popular food from varied reasonably priced menu including set lunch, Butcombe and a couple of guests such as Bristol Beer Factory and Wickwar, good wine list, interesting split-level interior with log fires (one in inglenook), table built around illuminated medieval well in restaurant; children and dogs (in bar) welcome, wheelchair access to most areas, picnic-sets on paved terrace and grass, open all day. *(Ian Herdman)*

DYMOCK SO6931

Beauchamp Arms (01531) 890266

B4215; GL18 2AQ Friendly parish-owned village pub with well kept changing ales, local ciders and good value traditional food, cheerful helpful staff, three smallish rooms, log fire; children and dogs welcome, pleasant little garden with pond, nearby walks among daffodils and bluebells, church with corner devoted to the Dymock Poets, closed Mon, no food Sun evening. *(Lee and Jill Stafford)*

ELKSTONE SO9610

Highwayman (01285) 821221

Beechpike; A417 6 miles N of Cirencester; GL53 9PL Interesting 16th-c building with rambling interior, low beams, stripped stone and log fires, cosy alcoves, antique settles among more modern furnishings, generous helpings of enjoyable food (gluten-free options) from lunchtime sandwiches up, Arkells beers and good house wines, friendly service; free wi-fi; children and dogs welcome, disabled access, outside play area, bedrooms, closed Sun evening, Mon. *(Peter Young)*

EWEN SU0097

Wild Duck (01285) 770310

Off A429 S of Cirencester; GL7 6BY Character 16th-c village inn (former cottages and barns for Ewen Manor) now owned by the Lucky Onion group; old stone path to entrance with unusual duck clock up on right, dimly lit interior with appealing nooks and crannies, dark hop-strung beams, scrubbed pine tables on wood floors, crimson walls and antique furnishings, open fires including one in handsome Elizabethan fireplace, good if not particularly cheap food from varied changing menu (service charge added), six real ales including Butcombe, Sharps and Stroud, good selection of wines by the glass from extensive list; children and dogs welcome, currently no wheelchair access, tables under parasols in heated courtyard and garden, Thames Path not far away, bedrooms planned, open all day. *(Dave Snowden, Taff Thomas)*

FAIRFORD SP1501

★Bull (01285) 712535

Market Place; GL7 4AA Well renovated former coaching inn; beams and timbering blending with bold paintwork, old and new seating, huge mirrors and reclaimed floorboards; entrance to left-hand sitting area with sofa and armchairs by stone fireplace, two bar rooms opposite with chapel chairs and settles around wooden tables, gigantic bull's head over log fire, steps up to a further light and airy room, Arkells ales, a guest beer and 17 wines by the glass, good food from bar meals and pizzas to more restauranty choices, two dining rooms, one with walls made from old horseboxes; background music, TV; children and dogs (in bar) welcome, no garden or car park, 21 well equipped stylish bedrooms, church also worth a visit (has Britain's only intact set of medieval stained-glass windows), open all day. *(Liz Bell, Jill and Dick Archer, Chris Stevenson, Caroline and Peter Bryant, Hilary Gardiner)*

FORD SP0829

★Plough (01386) 584215

B4077 Stow–Alderton; GL54 5RU 16th-c pub opposite famous stables and popular with the local horse-racing fraternity; beamed and stripped-stone bar with racing prints and photos, old settles and benches around big tables on uneven flagstones, oak tables in snug alcove, open fires and woodburners, Donnington BB and SBA, eight wines by the glass and a dozen malt whiskies, generous helpings of good reasonably priced food; background music, TV (for the races), free wi-fi, darts; children and dogs (in bar) welcome, picnic-sets and pretty hanging baskets in front, large garden behind with play fort, comfortable clean bedrooms (some with views of the gallops), Cotswold Farm Park nearby, open all day from 9am, food all day Fri-Sun, gets packed on race days. *(Tracey and Stephen Groves, Peter Young, Dr A J and Mrs B A Tompsett, Richard Tilbrook, Helene Grygar, Dave Braisted)*

FORTHAMPTON SO8731

Lower Lode Inn (01684) 293224

At the end of Bishop's Walk by river; GL19 4RE Brick-built 15th-c coaching inn with River Severn moorings and plenty of waterside tables (prone to winter flooding); beams, flagstones and traditional seating, woodburners, enjoyable reasonably priced pubby food including summer Sun carvery, half a dozen well kept interesting beers, friendly helpful staff, restaurant, back pool room; children and dogs welcome, disabled facilities, four bedrooms and campsite, summer ferry from Lower Lode Lane, open (and food) all day in season, closed lunchtimes Mon-Thurs in winter. *(Theocsbrian)*

FOSSEBRIDGE SP0711

Fossebridge Inn (01285) 720721
A429 Cirencester to Stow-on-the-Wold; GL54 3JS 17th-c coaching inn set in four acres of attractive lawned riverside gardens; two original bar rooms with log fires, beams, stripped-stone walls and flagstones, copper implements and all sorts of chairs, stools and tables, well kept ales such as Butcombe, Cotswold Lion, Hook Norton, North Cotswold and Wadworths, several wines by the glass, popular sensibly priced traditional food, also afternoon cream teas, two other rather grand dining rooms; background music, TV; children, walkers and dogs welcome, bedrooms and self-catering cottages, Chedworth Roman Villa (NT) nearby, open (and food) all day. *(Guy Vowles, Giles and Annie Francis)*

FRAMPTON COTTERELL ST6681

Globe (01454) 778286
Church Road; BS36 2AB Popular white-painted pub next to church; large knocked-through bar-dining area with black beams and some stripped stone, usual furniture on parquet or carpet, woodburner in old fireplace, five well kept ales including Butcombe, Fullers and St Austell, Thatcher's ciders and well chosen wine list, enjoyable fairly priced pubby food from ciabattas up, attentive friendly staff; background music, Tues quiz; children and dogs welcome, wheelchair access via side door, disabled/ baby changing facilities, big grassy garden with play area and smokers' gazebo, on Frome Valley Walkway, open all day. *(Dr and Mrs A K Clarke)*

FRAMPTON MANSELL SO9202

★**Crown** (01285) 760601
Brown sign to pub off A491 Cirencester–Stroud; GL6 8JG Welcoming 17th-c country pub (former cider house) with pretty outlook; enjoyable food including daily specials, Butcombe, Sharps, Stroud, Uley and a guest, three ciders and good choice of wines, friendly helpful young staff, stripped stone and heavy beams, rugs on bare boards, two log fires and a woodburner, restaurant; various events including notable bonfire-night fireworks; children and dogs welcome, disabled access, picnic-sets in sunny front garden, 12 bedrooms in separate block, open all day from midday, food all day Sun. *(Donald Allsopp)*

FRAMPTON ON SEVERN SO7407

Three Horseshoes (01452) 742100
The Green (B4071, handy for M5 junction 13, via A38); GL2 7DY Cheerfully unpretentious 18th-c pub by splendid green; welcoming staff and locals, well kept Sharps, Timothy Taylors and Uley from small counter, proper ciders/perry too, good value home-made food including speciality pies, lived-in interior with parquet flooring, cushioned wall seats and open fire in large brick fireplace, quieter back lounge/ dining room; folk nights, darts; children, walkers and dogs welcome, wheelchair access, picnic-sets out in front, garden behind with two boules pitches, views over River Severn to Forest of Dean, parking can be tricky (narrow road), open all day weekends. *(Sandra and Neil White)*

FROCESTER SO7831

Frocester George (01453) 828683
Peter Street; GL10 3TQ Large refurbished Quality Inns pub on crossroads, bare-boards bar with modern furniture, light wood dados and big bay windows, some repro animal prints and oil-lamp fittings on off-white walls, warm woodburner in old fireplace, ales such as Brains, Moles, Otter and Quantock, decent choice of ciders and extensive range of gins, good food from bar snacks and pub favourites to restaurant dishes, pleasant prompt service, can eat in bar, back annexe or restaurant; children and dogs welcome, wheelchair access via back door, part-covered courtyard, ten well equipped comfortable bedrooms, open (and food) all day. *(Chris and Angela Buckell)*

GLASSHOUSE SO7121

★**Glasshouse Inn** (01452) 830529
Off A40 just W of A4136; GL17 0NN Much extended beamed red-brick pub with series of small linked rooms; tiled or flagstoned floors, ochre walls and boarded ceilings, appealing old-fashioned and antique furnishings, hunting pictures and taxidermy, cavernous black hearth with old iron pots etc, well kept ales including cask-tapped Butcombe and Sharps, Weston's cider, good reasonably priced wines, some interesting malt whiskies and a couple of decent gins, enjoyable home-made food from sandwiches and basket meals up (no bookings except Sun lunch), good friendly service, large flagstoned dining conservatory; background music; no under-14s (in bars) or dogs, good wheelchair access but no disabled loo, rustic furniture in neat garden with interesting topiary, flower-decked cider presses and lovely hanging baskets, nearby paths up wooded May Hill (NT), three self-catering lodges, closed Sun evening. *(Mike and Mary Carter, Christopher Mobbs, Chris and Angela Buckell)*

GLOUCESTER SO8318

Fountain (01452) 522562
Westgate Street; GL1 2NW Tucked-away 17th-c pub off pedestrianised street; well kept ales such as Bristol Beer Factory, Butcombe, Dartmoor, St Austell and Thwaites, a couple of craft beers, Thatcher's and Weston's ciders and a modestly priced wine list, good value pubby food from sandwiches and basket meals up, friendly chatty staff, open-plan carpeted bar with woodburner in handsome stone fireplace, some black beams and dark varnished dados,

pubby furniture and built-in wall benches; background music; children and dogs welcome, disabled access/loos, flower-filled courtyard with big gates to Berkeley Street, handy for cathedral, open all day (food all day Fri and Sat, till 5pm Sun). *(Chris and Angela Buckell, Alan Bird)*

GLOUCESTER SO8218

Lord High Constable of England

(01452) 302890 *Llanthony Warehouse, Llanthony Road; GL1 2EH* Busy Wetherspoons on east side of the docks; spacious and comfortable with high raftered ceiling, good range of real ales and craft beers, their usual well priced food, efficient service; TVs, free wi-fi; children welcome, outside area overlooking canal, open all day from 8am. *(Mike and Mary Carter)*

GLOUCESTER SO8318

New Inn (01452) 522177

Northgate Street; GL1 1SF Lovely beamed medieval building with galleried courtyard; Butcombe, Sharps and up to eight guests including smaller local breweries, decent wines, bargain daily lunchtime carvery and other good value food (all day Fri, Sat), friendly efficient service, restaurant and coffee shop; soft background music (live Fri, disco/karaoke Sat), sports TV, free wi-fi; children welcome, no dogs, wheelchair access to restaurant only, 33 affordably priced bedrooms, handy for cathedral, open all day. *(Mark Morgan)*

GREAT RISSINGTON SP1917

★Lamb (01451) 820388

Turn off A40 W of Burford to the Barringtons; keep straight on past Great Barrington until Great Rissington is signed on left; GL54 2LP Cotswold-stone village inn dating from the 18th c, bar with pubby furnishings including padded wall benches and sewing-machine tables on strip-wood floor, woodburner, leather chairs against counter serving well kept Brakspears, Wychwood Hobgoblin and a beer badged for the pub, decent wines by the glass and good choice of gins/malt whiskies, second woodburner in restaurant with collection of old agricultural tools, well liked interesting food along with sandwiches and a few pub standards, Weds steak day, friendly prompt service; background music, TV, free wi-fi; children and dogs (in bar) welcome, seats in sheltered hillside garden where Wellington bomber crashed in 1943 (see plaque and memorabilia), attractive circular walk, 13 bedrooms (four in converted outbuildings), open all day. *(Richard Tilbrook, Maria Birch)*

GRETTON SP0130

Royal Oak (01242) 604999

Off B4077 E of Tewkesbury; GL54 5EP Golden-stone pub under same ownership as the Wesley House hotel/restaurant in Winchcombe; bar with painted kitchen chairs, leather tub seats and pale wooden tables on bare boards or flagstones, open fires, airy dining room and conservatory, candelabras, antlers and big central woodburner, ales such as Goffs, Purity, Ringwood, St Austell and Wye Valley, plenty of wines by the glass, popular food from pub favourites to specials; background music; children and dogs (in bar) welcome, wheelchair access but not to raised dining room, seats on back terrace with views over village to Dumbleton Hills and Malverns, play area and bookable tennis court, GWR steam trains run along bottom of garden in summer, open all day, food till 7.30pm Sun. *(Ian Herdman, Dr A J and Mrs B A Tompsett, Guy Vowles)*

GUITING POWER SP0924

★Farmers Arms (01451) 850358

Fosseway (A429); GL54 5TZ Nicely old-fashioned with stripped stone, flagstones, lots of pictures and woodburner, well kept/priced Donnington BB and SBA, wide blackboard choice of good honest food cooked by landlord including notable rabbit pie and reasonably priced Sun roasts, welcoming prompt service, carpeted back dining part; games area with darts, dominoes, cribbage and pool, skittle alley; children welcome, garden with quoits, lovely village, good walks, bedrooms. *(Richard Tilbrook)*

GUITING POWER SP0924

★Hollow Bottom (01451) 850392

Village signposted off B4068 SW of Stow-on-the-Wold (still called A436 on many maps); GL54 5UX Cosy old cottage popular with the racing fraternity; opened-up beamed bar with wooden flooring, horse-racing pictures and woodburner in unusual pillared stone fireplace, Greene ales, several wines by the glass and 15 malt whiskies, enjoyable food from wraps, sharing boards and pizzas up, pleasant attentive service, flagstoned dining areas with exposed stone walls, built-in cushioned wall seats and medley of tables; background music, TVs for racing, free wi-fi; children and dogs (in bar) welcome, back garden has a decked area, heaters, fire pit and own thatched bar, views towards sloping fields and good nearby walks, five comfortable bedrooms (two in annexe), open (and food) all day from 9am. *(Richard Tilbrook, Michael Sargent, R K Phillips)*

HAM ST6898

Salutation (01453) 810284

On main road through village; GL13 9QH Welcoming unpretentious three-room country local; brasses on beams, horse and hunt pictures on Artex walls, high-backed settles, bench seats and other pubby furniture, six well kept local ales including own-brewed Tileys, nine real ciders/perries and good range of bottled beers, limited choice of simple low-priced lunchtime food such as ham, egg and chips (own pigs, hens and potatoes); folk night first Thurs of month and other live music, traditional games including shove-ha'penny, skittle alley, free wi-fi; wheelchair access, beer garden with views over deer park, handy for Berkeley Castle, open all day weekends, closed lunchtimes Mon-Thurs. *(Emma Scofield)*

HARTPURY SO7924

Royal Exchange (01452) 700273
A417 Gloucester–Ledbury; GL19 3BW Comfortable 19th-c country pub under same ownership as the Red Lion at Bishop's Norton and Swan in Staunton; modernised opened-up interior, flagstones, bare boards and carpet, two-way woodburner, popular reasonably priced food (not Sun evening) from sandwiches and sharing plates to chargrills and specials, Weds curry night, Wye Valley ales and guests, local cider/perry; quiz first Mon of month, sports TV; children and dogs (in bar) welcome, fine views from garden with terrace and covered deck, open all day Fri-Sun. *(Theocsbrian)*

HAWKESBURY UPTON ST7786

★**Beaufort Arms** (01454) 238217
High Street; GL9 1AU Unpretentious 17th-c pub in historic village; welcoming landlord and friendly chatty atmosphere, up to five well kept changing local ales and good range of ciders, popular no-nonsense food (all available to take away), extended dining lounge on right, darts in stripped-brick bare-boards bar, interesting local and brewery memorabilia; skittle alley, free wi-fi; well behaved children allowed, dogs in bar, disabled access throughout and facilities, picnic-sets in smallish enclosed garden, on Cotswold Way and handy for Badminton Horse Trials, open all day. *(Lee and Jill Stafford)*

HILLESLEY ST7689

Fleece (01453) 520003
Hawkesbury Road/Chapel Lane; GL12 7RD Comfortably updated old stone-roofed pub owned by the local community; up to seven well kept mainly local ales, good wines by the glass and decent range of gins, happy hour (4.30-6pm Mon-Fri), enjoyable good value food including specials, friendly chatty staff and locals, bar with mix of pubby furniture, cushioned benches and wall seats, woodburner, steps down to dining room and snug; quiz first Sun of month, acoustic music second Sun, darts, free wi-fi; children, walkers and dogs welcome (leave muddy boots in porch), wheelchair access to bar only, back garden with play area and smokers' shelter, small village in lovely countryside near Cotswold Way, closed till 4.30pm Mon, Tues, otherwise open all day. *(Andrew and Philip Crispin)*

HINTON DYRHAM ST7376

★**Bull** (0117) 937 2332
2.4 miles from M4 junction 18; A46 towards Bath, then first right (opposite the Crown); SN14 8HG Welcoming 17th-c stone pub in nice setting; main bar with two huge fireplaces, low beams, oak settles and pews on ancient flagstones, stripped-stone back area and simply furnished carpeted restaurant, good food from pub standards to specials (pork from own pigs), well kept Wadworths ales; background music; children and dogs welcome, difficult wheelchair access (steps at front, but staff willing to help), seats on front balcony and in sizeable sheltered upper garden with play equipment, handy for Dyrham Park (NT), open all day weekends (food till 6pm Sun), closed Mon. *(Mrs Zara Elliott, Dr and Mrs A K Clarke)*

IRON ACTON ST6883

Lamb (01454) 228265
B4058/9 Bristol–Chipping Sodbury; BS37 9UZ Welcoming 17th-c former coaching house: well stocked bar serving ales such as Flying Monk and Wickwar, competitively priced wines and interesting gins, enjoyable good value food including lunchtime/early evening BOGOF deal, prompt pleasant service, low-ceilinged carpeted bar with dark varnished dados, rough-plastered cream walls and pubby furniture, woodburners in huge stone fireplaces; unobtrusive background music, Mon quiz, pool and darts; children and dogs welcome, wheelchair access, picnic-sets on front terrace and in large grassy garden behind, open all day. *(Chris and Angela Buckell)*

KEMBLE ST9899

Thames Head (01285) 770259
A433 Cirencester–Tetbury; GL7 6NZ Roadside pub with opened-up modernised interior around central servery; faux black beams, stripped-stone walls and some rough-boarded dados/wall seats, fairly rustic furniture on tartan carpet, shelves of books, stoneware jugs and a bust of Old Father Thames, intriguing little front alcove, two open fires, enjoyable reasonably priced food, well kept Arkells and good value wines, friendly chatty staff; background music, free wi-fi, skittle alley; children and dogs (in bar area) welcome, wheelchair access using ramp, disabled loo, tables outside, four simple barn-conversion bedrooms, good breakfast, walk (crossing railway line) to nearby Thames source, open (and food) all day. *(Peter Young, Stuart Doughty)*

KILKENNY SP0118

Kilkeney Inn (01242) 820341
A436, 1 mile W of Andoversford; GL54 4LN Spaciously refurbished beamed pub (originally five stone cottages); stripped-stone and some plank-clad walls, wheelback, tub and leather dining chairs around tables on slate, wood or carpeted floors, open fire and woodburner, conservatory, Wells and Youngs ales, Symonds's cider and decent wines by the glass, well liked food from owner-chef including signature 'slow-cooked'

dishes, good friendly service and buzzy atmosphere; background music; children welcome, wheelchair access from car park, lovely Cotswold views from tables out at front, more seating in back garden, one well appointed bedroom, closed Sun evening, Mon. *(Richard Tilbrook, Peter Young)*

KINETON SP0926

Halfway House (01451) 850344
Signed from B4068 and B4077 W of Stow-on-the-Wold; GL54 5UG Welcoming 17th-c beamed village inn with enjoyable food including good burgers, well kept Donnington BB and SBA, Addlestone's cider and decent wines, separate dining area, log fire; pool and darts; children and dogs welcome, picnic-sets in sheltered back garden with pergola, good walks, bedrooms, open (and some food) all day. *(Lauren and Dan Frazer)*

KNOCKDOWN ST8388

Holford Arms (01454) 238669
A433; GL8 8QY Welcoming 16th-c beamed pub; bare-stone walls, flagstone or wood floors, leather sofas, armchairs and cushioned wall/window seats, candles on old dining tables, two woodburners (one in huge stone fireplace), six cask-tapped ales such as Cotswold Lion, Flying Monk and Stroud, own Sherston's cider and apple juice, good wine list, enjoyable food from sandwiches up including good value Sun lunch (own rare-breed pork), Mon steak night, Weds thai, pleasant helpful service; background and live music (bluegrass Fri), skittle alley; children and dogs welcome, wheelchair access (no disabled loos), picnic sets in side and back gardens, outside summer bar, six bedrooms, camping/glamping, handy for Westonbirt Arboretum, Highgrove and Badminton Horse Trials, open all day weekends, from 4pm weekdays. *(Michael Doswell)*

LEIGHTERTON ST8290

Royal Oak (01666) 890250
Village signposted off A46 S of Nailsworth; GL8 8UN Handsome early 18th-c mullion-windowed village pub under newish ownership; rambling beamed bar with two log fires, stripped stonework and pastel paintwork, mix of furniture including country pine, candles on tables, ales such as Flying Monk, Uley and Wye Valley, traditional cider and several wines by the glass, good food from interesting varied menu including some pub favourites and popular Sun lunch, helpful friendly service; children and dogs welcome, disabled access, sheltered side courtyard with teak and metal furniture, surrounding walks (on Monarch's Way) and handy for Westonbirt Arboretum, closed Sun evening, Mon. *(Maggie and Matthew Lyons)*

LITTLE BARRINGTON SP2012

Inn For All Seasons (01451) 844324
A40 3 miles W of Burford; OX18 4TN Handsome 16th-c creeper-clad coaching inn under new ownership; comfortable lounge bar with low beams, stripped stone, flagstones and log fire, a couple of ales such as St Austell Tribute and Wye Valley Butty Bach, nine wines by the glass, much liked food with some emphasis on fish, good friendly service, restaurant and conservatory; children and dogs welcome, picnic-sets in garden with aunt sally, walks from the door, ten bedrooms, open (and food) all day. *(R K Phillips, Peter Young)*

LITTLETON-UPON-SEVERN ST5989

★**White Hart** (01454) 412275
3.5 miles from M48 junction 1; BS35 1NR Sympathetically updated 17th-c farmhouse with three main rooms; nice mix of country furnishings, flagstones at front, huge tiles at the back, log fires (loveseat in inglenook), well kept Youngs ales and guests, good range of other drinks including their own cider, popular food cooked by landlord from bar snacks and traditional choices to more adventurous specials, efficient service (may ask for a credit card before you eat); children and dogs welcome, wheelchair access, tables on front lawn, more behind by orchard and vegetable patch, walks from the door, open all day, food all day weekends. *(Chris and Angela Buckell, R G Marshall)*

LONGBOROUGH SP1729

Coach & Horses (01451) 830325
Ganborough Road; GL56 0QU Traditional little 17th-c stone local with up to three well kept/priced Donnington ales, Thatcher's cider and enjoyable good value pub food including basket meals, friendly landlord and staff, leather armchairs on flagstones, inglenook woodburner, darts, dominoes and cribbage; background music, quiz last Sun of month; children and dogs welcome, tables out at front looking down on stone cross and pretty village, two simple clean bedrooms, handy for Sezincote house and gardens, open all day Fri-Sun. *(Helene Grygar)*

LOWER ODDINGTON SP2326

★**Fox** (01451) 870555
Signed off A436; GL56 0UR Attractively presented 16th-c creeper-clad inn with emphasis on their excellent food (must book) including good value weekday set lunch, top notch service too, Hook Norton and a couple of guests, Robinson's cider and well chosen wines, series of relaxed country-style flagstoned rooms with assorted chairs around pine tables, candles and fresh flowers, log fires including inglenook woodburner; background music; children and dogs (in bar) welcome, tables under parasols at front, enclosed cottagey back garden and heated terrace, pretty village, six comfortable bedrooms (three in adjoining building). *(Martin Constable, Richard Tilbrook, Alun and Jennifer Evans)*

LOWER SWELL SP1725

Golden Ball (01451) 833886
B4068 W of Stow-on-the-Wold; GL54 1LF Unassuming 17th-c stone-built village local surrounded by good walks; well kept Donnington ales (the attractive brewery is nearby), Addlestone's cider and well prepared/priced pubby food cooked by landlord-chef including charolais beef from the family farm, good friendly service, neatly kept beamed interior with some cosy nooks, woodburner; background music, sports TV, darts; children and dogs welcome, small garden and raised deck/balcony, aunt sally, open all day weekends, no food Sun evening. *(Richard Tilbrook, Clive and Fran Dutson)*

MARSHFIELD ST7773

★ **Catherine Wheel** (01225) 892220
High Street; signed off A420 Bristol–Chippenham; SN14 8LR Attractive Georgian-fronted building in unspoilt village; high-ceilinged bare-stone front part with medley of settles, chairs and stripped tables, charming dining room with impressive open fireplace, cottagey beamed back area warmed by woodburners, well kept Butcombe, Fullers London Pride and a local guest, interesting wines and other drinks, enjoyable sensibly priced food from pub favourites up; darts and dominoes, live music last Thurs of month, free wi-fi; well behaved children and dogs welcome, wheelchair access with help, flower-decked backyard, three bedrooms, open all day. *(Dr and Mrs A K Clarke)*

MAYSHILL ST6882

New Inn (01454) 773161
Badminton Road (A432 Frampton Cotterell–Yate); BS36 2NT Popular largely 17th-c coaching inn with two comfortably carpeted bar rooms leading to restaurant, good choice of enjoyable generously served pub food at fair prices, friendly staff, three well kept changing ales, Weston's cider and decent wines by the glass, log fire; children and dogs welcome, garden with play area, open all day Fri-Sun, food all day weekends. *(Roger and Donna Huggins, Neil Hammacott)*

MICKLETON SP1543

★ **Kings Arms** (01386) 438257
B4632 (ex A46); GL55 6RT 18th-c honey-stone pub with good imaginative food from lunchtime sandwiches to daily specials, real ales such as Greene King and Charles Wells, proper cider and several wines by the glass from interesting list, friendly helpful staff, atmospheric open-plan beamed lounge with nice mix of comfortable chairs, soft lighting and good log fire, lots of things to look at (some for sale), small locals' bar with darts, dominoes and cribbage; background music, free wi-fi; children and dogs welcome, circular picnic-sets under thatched parasols in courtyard, more tables in sizeable garden, attractive village, handy for Hidcote (NT) and Kiftsgate Court Gardens, open all day. *(Michael Doswell)*

MINCHINHAMPTON SO8500

Old Lodge (01453) 832047
Nailsworth–Brimscombe – on common, fork left at pub's sign; OS Sheet 162 map reference 853008; GL6 9AQ Welcoming dining pub (part of the Cotswold Food Club group) with civilised modern bistro feel, wood floors and stripped-stone walls, good food from pub favourites up, decent wines by the glass and four well kept changing beers; children and dogs (in bar) welcome, tables on neat lawn looking over NT common with grazing cows and horses, six bedrooms, open all day (food all day weekends). *(Mark Morgan)*

MINCHINHAMPTON SO8801

Ragged Cot (01453) 884643
Cirencester Road; NE of town; GL6 8PE Attractively updated 17th-c Cotswold stone inn; front bar with open fire one end woodburner the other, cushioned window seats and painted pine tables on wood-strip floor, connecting rooms including airy pitched-ceiling restaurant overlooking the garden, emphasis on good (if not especially cheap) food from one or two pub favourites up, three real ales including Ringwood Razorback and one badged for the pub, decent range of wines, good friendly service; children and dogs welcome, outside café called 'the Shed', nine well appointed bedrooms. *(Julian Richardson)*

MISERDEN SO9308

Carpenters Arms (01285) 821283
Off B4070 NE of Stroud; GL6 7JA Welcoming traditional 17th-c country pub (used in the 2015 BBC adaptation of *Cider with Rosie*) with opened-up low-beamed bar; stripped-stone walls, log fire and woodburner, some interesting old photographs, Wye Valley Butty Bach, HPA and a guest, fine range of ciders and decent wines, ample helpings of enjoyable reasonably priced food cooked by landlady using local/home-grown produce including good vegetarian choices, friendly helpful staff; Weds folk night, quiz Thurs; children and dogs welcome, seats out in front and to the side, popular with walkers and handy for Miserden Park, open (and food) all day, kitchen closes 6pm Sun. *(Giles and Annie Francis, Richard Tilbrook)*

MORETON-IN-MARSH SP2032

Black Bear (01608) 652992
High Street; GL56 0AX Friendly beamed and stripped-stone corner pub; wood-floor bar with sports TVs and a couple of carved bears either side of log fire, Donnington ales, decent wines by the glass and tasty good value home-made food including some weekday lunchtime bargains, woodburner

and light wood furniture in airy dining room; children welcome, open (and food) all day, kitchen closes 4pm Sun. *(Richard Tilbrook)*

MORETON-IN-MARSH SP2032

Inn on the Marsh (01608) 650709
Stow Road, next to duck pond; GL56 0DW Stone-built roadside pub with comfortable beamed bar; inglenook woodburner and some dutch influences to the décor, chef-landlady is dutch and cooks good value national dishes alongside pub favourites, well kept Marstons-related beers and guests, cheerful welcoming staff, modern conservatory restaurant; background music from vintage vinyl or maybe landlord playing his guitar; children and dogs welcome, seats at front and in back garden, closed Mon lunchtime. *(Julian and Fiona Barnes)*

MORETON-IN-MARSH SP2032

Redesdale Arms (01608) 650308
High Street; GL56 0AW Relaxed 17th-c hotel (former coaching inn); alcoves and big stone fireplace in comfortable solidly furnished panelled bar on right, darts in flagstoned public bar, three well kept ales, decent wines and coffee, enjoyable food from breakfast on served by courteous helpful staff, spacious child-friendly back brasserie and dining conservatory; background music, TVs, games machine; heated floodlit courtyard, 34 comfortable bedrooms (newer ones in mews), open all day from 8am. *(Dr and Mrs A K Clarke)*

MORETON-IN-MARSH SP2032

White Hart Royal (01608) 650731
High Street; GL56 0BA Substantial 17th-c coaching inn with Charles I connection; cosy beamed quarry-tiled bar with fine inglenook and nice old furniture, adjacent smarter panelled room with Georgian feel, separate lounge and restaurant, Hook Norton and a guest ale, good choice of wines, well liked food from sandwiches and pub favourites up including children's choices, friendly service; background music; courtyard tables, 28 bedrooms, good breakfast, open all day. *(Dr and Mrs A K Clarke)*

NAILSWORTH ST8499

Britannia (01453) 832501
Cossack Square; GL6 0DG Large open-plan pub (part of the small Cotswold Food Club chain) in former manor house; popular bistro food including stone-baked pizzas (best to book evenings), friendly helpful service, well kept Hook Norton, Wadworths and guests, good choice of wines by the glass, big log fire; children welcome, picnic-sets in front garden, open all day (food all day weekends). *(Julia Hanmer, Tom and Ruth Rees)*

NAILSWORTH ST8499

Egypt Mill (01453) 833449
Off A46; heading N towards Stroud, first right after roundabout, then left; GL6 0AE Converted 16th-c mill with working waterwheels; split-level brick and stone floor bar, stripped beams and some hefty ironwork in comfortable carpeted lounge, seating ranging from elegant dining chairs to cushioned wall seats and sofas, well kept ales, a dozen wines by the glass and generally well liked reasonably priced food including vegetarian/vegan options, good friendly service; background music; children welcome, plenty of tables in floodlit garden overlooking millpond, nicely equipped bedrooms (some with fine beams and timbering), open (and food) all day. *(Tom and Ruth Rees)*

NAUNTON SP1123

★**Black Horse** (01451) 850565
Off B4068 W of Stow-on-the-Wold; GL54 3AD Welcoming locals' pub with well kept/priced Donnington BB and SBA, Weston's cider and popular home-made food from traditional favourites to daily specials such as seasonal game, bargain set menu Mon evening (must book), friendly efficient service, black beams, stripped stone, flagstones and log fire, dining room; background music, darts and dominoes; children and dogs welcome, small seating area outside, charming village and fine Cotswold walks (walking groups asked to pre-order food), open all day Fri-Sun. *(Richard Tilbrook, Dr A J and Mrs B A Tompsett, Peter Young)*

NIBLEY ST6982

Swan (01454) 312290
Badminton Road; BS37 5JF Part of small local pub group, friendly and relaxed, with good food from snacks to daily specials, Bath, Butcombe and Cotswold Spring, real cider and over a dozen wines by the glass, good service, modernised interior with fireside leather sofas one side, dining tables the other, separate restaurant; background music; children and dogs (in bar) welcome, garden picnic-sets, open all day. *(Louise and Oliver Redman)*

NORTH NIBLEY ST7596

New Inn (01453) 543659
E of village itself; Waterley Bottom; GL11 6EF Former cider house in secluded rural setting popular with walkers; well kept Moles, Wickwar and a weekend guest from antique pumps, fine range of ciders and perries (more in bottles), enjoyable food cooked by landlord from lunchtime sandwiches and good ploughman's up, lounge bar with cushioned windsor chairs and high-backed settles, partly stripped-stone walls, simple cosy public bar with darts (no children here after 6pm), cider festivals and other events (maybe local mummers); no credit cards; dogs welcome, hitching rail and trough for horses, picnic-sets and swings on lawn, covered decked area with pool table, two bedrooms, open all day weekends,

closed Mon lunchtime (evening also in winter). *(Sandra and Neil White)*

OLD DOWN ST6187

★**Fox** (01454) 412507

3.9 miles from M5 junction 15/16; A38 towards Gloucester, then Old Down signposted; turn left into Inner Down; BS32 4PR Tucked-away yet popular family-owned country pub; six well kept ales such as Bath, Butcombe, Flying Monk and Sharps, Thatcher's cider and several wines by the glass, good reasonably priced traditional food (not Sun evening) from baguettes up, friendly staff and warm local atmosphere, low beams, carpeted, wood or flagstone floors, log fire, plain modern wooden furniture, dark green faux leather wall seats in bar, snug family room; live music first Sat of month; dogs welcome, good disabled access (no loos), front and back gardens, long verandah with grapevine, play area, open all day Sun. *(Chris and Angela Buckell, Roger and Donna Huggins)*

OLD SODBURY ST7581

Dog (01454) 312006

3 miles from M4 junction 18, via A46 and A432; The Hill (a busy road); BS37 6LZ Welcoming old pub with popular two-level carpeted bar, low beams, stripped stone and open fire, good reasonably priced food from sandwiches and baked potatoes to fresh fish and steaks, Sharps Doom Bar and three Wickwar ales kept well, friendly attentive young staff; children and dogs welcome, handy for Cotswold Way walkers, nice big garden with paved terrace, four annexe bedrooms, open all day. *(Tom and Ruth Rees, Giles and Annie Francis, Dr and Mrs A K Clarke, Guy Vowles)*

PAINSWICK SO8609

Falcon (01452) 814222

New Street; GL6 6UN Handsome stone-built inn dating from the 16th c; sympathetically updated open-plan layout with bar and two dining areas, good, popular food including daily specials, four well kept beers and good choice of fairly priced wines by the glass, friendly young staff; occasional live music; children and dogs welcome, 12 comfortable bedrooms, opposite churchyard famous for its 99 yews. *(Peter Young, Dr J Barrie Jones)*

PARKEND SO6107

Fountain (01594) 562189

Just off B4234; GL15 4JD Unpretentious 18th-c village inn by terminus of restored Dean Forest Railway; well kept ales such as Hillside, Greene King and Wye Valley, Weston's cider, wines in glass-sized bottles, enjoyable home-made traditional food including Sun carvery and OAP weekday lunch menu, welcoming helpful staff, assorted chairs and settles in two linked rooms, old tools, bric-a-brac, photographs and framed local history information, coal fire; quiz and live music nights; children, walkers and dogs welcome, wheelchair access, side garden, eight bedrooms and bunkhouse, open all day Sat. *(Julian Richardson)*

PARKEND SO6308

Rising Sun (01594) 562008

Off B4431; GL15 4HN Perched on wooded hillside and approached by roughish single-track drive – popular with walkers and cyclists; open-plan carpeted bar with modern pub furniture, Wickwar BOB and several guests, real ciders and well priced straightforward food from sandwiches and baked potatoes up, friendly service, lounge/games area with pool and machines; children and dogs welcome (pub dog is Willow), wheelchair access with help, views from balcony and terrace tables under umbrellas, big woodside garden with play area and duck pond, self-catering accommodation, open (and food) all day. *(Kerry and Guy Trooper)*

PAXFORD SP1837

Churchill Arms (01386) 593159

B4479, SE of Chipping Campden; GL55 6XH 17th-c village dining pub with popular well cooked/presented food from chef-owner including cheaper lunchtime set menu, a house beer (Winston) brewed by North Cotswold and two regional guests, several wines by the glass from good list, friendly helpful service from busy staff, attractively updated open-plan interior with flagstone and wood floors, some low painted beams and inglenook woodburner; children and dogs welcome, picnic-sets on small front terrace and gravelled back area, four bedrooms, limited street parking, closed Sun evening and Mon, otherwise open all day. *(Ian Herdman)*

PILNING ST5684

Plough (01454) 632556

Handy for M5 junction 17 via B4055 and Station Road; Pilning Street; BS35 4JJ Fairly remote but thriving roadside local much extended over the years; Wadworths ales and Thatcher's ciders, good value pubby food including children's and OAP's menus, cheerful efficient young staff, flagstone floors in the oldest part, polished wood and carpet elsewhere, dados and some old advertising pictures, log fires; live music and karaoke nights, pool and darts; dogs welcome (pub labrador is Bruiser), wheelchair access/loos, picnic-sets out at front and in large paddock with stage and play area, open all day, no food Sun evening. *(Chris and Angela Buckell)*

POULTON SP1001

Falcon (01285) 850878

London Road; GL7 5HN Popular bistro-feel village dining pub with highly regarded food from chef-owner including good value set lunch, well kept Hook Norton Old Hooky, a local guest beer and nice wines by the glass, friendly attentive service, neat modern interior with some old black beams, relaxed easy-going atmosphere; background music; well behaved children welcome, closed Sun evening, Mon. *(Giles and Annie Francis)*

QUENINGTON SP1404

Keepers Arms (01285) 750349
Church Road; GL7 5BL Community local in pretty Cotswold village; cosy and comfortable, with stripped stone, low beams and log fires, friendly helpful landlord and staff, good fairly priced food in bar and restaurant from changing menu including daily specials, three well kept beers, a dozen wines by the glass and interesting range of gins; quiz first Thurs of month; dogs welcome (their border collies are Denzil and Doris), picnic-sets out in front, three bedrooms, closed Mon and Tues lunchtimes, no food Sun evening. *(Lyn and Freddie Roberts)*

SALFORD HILL SP2629

Greedy Goose (01608) 646551
Junction A44/A436, near Chastleton; GL56 0SP Old roadside country dining pub with contemporary interior; enjoyable food from sandwiches and stone-baked pizzas up, three North Cotswold ales, friendly staff; children and dogs welcome, seats out at front and in back decked/gravelled area, campsite including wooden pods, open all day. *(Alexander and Trish Cutter)*

SAPPERTON SO9403

★**Bell** (01285) 760298
Village signposted from A419 Stroud–Cirencester; OS Sheet 163 map reference 948033; GL7 6LE Welcoming 250-year-old pub-restaurant with cosy connecting rooms around central bar, beams and exposed stonework, flagstone, wood and quarry-tiled floors, log fires, four well kept ales including a house beer from St Austell, plenty of wines by the glass and good choice of other drinks, well liked food (not Sun evening) from sandwiches, sharing boards and pub favourites to more ambitious choices, good friendly service; children and dogs welcome, seats out in front and in back courtyard garden, tethering for horses, plenty of surrounding walks, open all day (till 9pm Sun). *(Alisongrindrod, Helene Grygar, Tom and Ruth Rees, Tim Senn)*

SAPPERTON SO9303

Daneway Inn (01285) 760297
Daneway; off A419 Stroud–Cirencester; GL7 6LN Quietly tucked-away 18th-c whitewashed pub continuing well under present owners; three sympathetically refurbished linked rooms with bare boards or carpet, woodburner in amazing floor-to-ceiling carved oak dutch fireplace, also an inglenook, up to four Wadworths ales including a summer elderflower beer (Rare Find, named for the Large Blue butterfly found here), traditional cider/perry and enjoyable home-made food at fair prices, friendly staff, traditional games such as shove-ha'penny and ring the bull; quiz last Mon of month; children and dogs welcome, tricky wheelchair access (there are disabled loos), terrace tables and lovely sloping lawn, good walks by disused canal with tunnel to Coates, surrounding nature reserves, campsite with shepherd's hut, open (and food) all day except Sun when kitchen is closed 4-6pm. *(S Holder)*

SHIPTON MOYNE ST8989

Cat & Custard Pot (01666) 880249
Off B4040 Malmesbury–Bristol; The Street; GL8 8PN Popular early 18th-c pub (some recent expansion) in picturesque village; at least three real ales such as Flying Monk, Hook Norton and Wickwar, Weston's cider, some local gins and eight wines by the glass, enjoyable freshly made pubby food (not Sun evening), deceptively spacious inside with several dining areas, beams and bric-a-brac, hunting prints, cosy back snug, woodburner; sports TV; children, walkers and dogs welcome, wheelchair access to bar only, tables out on front lawn, handy for Beaufort Polo Club, Highgrove and Westonbirt Arboretum, five comfortable bedrooms, open all day weekends. *(Chris and Angela Buckell)*

SHURDINGTON SO8318

Bell (01242) 862245
A46 just S of Cheltenham; GL3 4PB Friendly early 19th-c pub with well liked fairly traditional food (some mediterranean influences) from lunchtime sandwiches up, Weds steak night, several local ales and good wines by the glass, attentive helpful staff, conservatory looking over cricket field; live music last Sat of month; children and dogs welcome, adjacent playground, open all day, no food Sun evening. *(Dr A J and Mrs B A Tompsett)*

SLAD SO8707

Woolpack (01452) 813429
B4070 Stroud–Birdlip; GL6 7QA Popular early 19th-c hillside village pub with lovely valley views; four unspoilt little connecting rooms, interesting photographs including some of Laurie Lee who was a regular (his books for sale), log fire, good imaginative food along with pub favourites, kitchen closes Sun evening and possibly Mon and Tues (although pizzas served Mon night), well kept Uley ales and guests, local farm cider/perry and decent wines by the glass, friendly prompt service; some live music; children, walkers and dogs welcome, nice garden taking in the view, open all day. *(Roger and Anne Mallard)*

SLIMBRIDGE SO7204

★**Tudor Arms** (01453) 890306
Shepherds Patch; off A38 towards Slimbridge Wetlands Centre; GL2 7BP

Much extended red-brick roadside pub just back from canal swing bridge; welcoming and popular with six mainly local ales, at least nine ciders/perries and good wines by the glass, also some interesting whiskies and gins such as Silent Pool and welsh Penderyn, enjoyable well priced pubby food including basket meals, daily specials and weekday two-course lunch deal, prompt friendly service, linked areas with wood, flagstone or carpeted floors, some leather chairs and settles, comfortable dining room, conservatory; darts, pool and skittle alley; children and dogs (in back bar) welcome, disabled access/loos, tables on part-shaded terrace, boat trips, 16 annexe bedrooms, caravan site off car park, open (and food) all day from 7.30am for breakfast. *(Chris and Angela Buckell, Peter Young, B A Congreve, Dr A J and Mrs B A Tompsett)*

SNOWSHILL SP0933

Snowshill Arms (01386) 852653

Opposite village green; WR12 7JU Unpretentious country pub in honeypot village – so no shortage of customers; well kept Donnington ales and reasonably priced straightforward (but tasty) food from sandwiches up, prompt friendly service, beams, log fire, stripped stone and neat array of tables, charming village views from bow windows, local photographs; skittle alley; children and dogs welcome, big back garden with stream and play area, handy for Snowshill Manor (NT), lavender farm and Cotswold Way walks. *(Mr and Mrs Richard Osborne)*

SOMERFORD KEYNES SU0195

Bakers Arms (01285) 861298

On main street through village; GL7 6DN Pretty little 17th-c stone-built pub with catslide roof; four well kept ales including Butcombe, Sharps and Stroud, Addlestone's cider, good house wines and generous helpings of tasty traditional food, quick friendly service, lots of pine tables in two linked areas, fire in big stone fireplace; children and dogs welcome, nice garden with play area, lovely village, handy for Cotswold Water Park, open (and food) all day except Sun when shuts at 6pm; for sale as we went to press, so could be changes. *(Lee and Jill Stafford)*

STANTON SP0634

★ Mount (01386) 584316

Village signposted off B4632 SW of Broadway; keep on past village on no-through road up hill, bear left; WR12 7NE Popular 17th-c pub with lovely views over village towards the welsh mountains; heavy beams in low ceilings, flagstones and inglenook log fire, well kept Donnington ales, good wines by the glass and much enjoyed food from baguettes to daily specials, prompt friendly service despite the crowds, picture-window restaurant taking in the view; darts and board games, free wi-fi; well behaved children and dogs welcome, seats on terrace and in quiet garden, good walks (Cotswold Way and Wyche Way nearby), closed Sun evening, plus Mon in winter. *(S Holder, Mrs Julie Thomas, Dr A J and Mrs B A Tompsett, Mr and Mrs Richard Osborne, Guy Vowles)*

STAUNTON SO7829

Swan (01452) 840323

Ledbury Road (A417), on mini roundabout; GL19 3QA Village pub owned by local farming family (they also have the Red Lion at Bishop's Norton and Royal Exchange in Hartpury); enjoyable well priced food from sandwiches up including set lunch Weds-Sat, ales such as Butcombe and Wye Valley, Weston's cider, bar with sofas and woodburner, spacious restaurant and modern conservatory, attached barn for functions; occasional quiz nights, free wi-fi; children and dogs welcome, pretty garden, open all day Fri-Sun, closed Mon and Tues lunchtimes, no evening food Sun-Tues. *(Donald Allsopp)*

STAUNTON SO5412

White Horse (01594) 834001

A4136; GL16 8PA Village pub on edge of Forest of Dean close to welsh border, welcoming and relaxed, with good freshly prepared food in bar or restaurant including popular Sun lunch, well kept local ales and ciders, friendly helpful service; small shop; children and dogs welcome, disabled access, picnic-sets in good-sized garden with glamping pods, open all day Sat, till 7.30pm Sun, closed Mon. *(John and Lorna Chew)*

STAVERTON SO9024

House in the Tree (01242) 680241

Haydon (B4063 W of Cheltenham); GL51 0TQ Friendly old beamed and partly thatched pub, five real ales including Dartmoor, Otter and Sharps, traditional cider and decent wine list, well liked generously served food from baguettes to daily specials, good helpful service, rambling linked areas, open fires; children and dogs welcome, plenty of tables in garden with good play area and pets corner, handy for M5 (junction 10), open all day, food all day Sat, till 6pm Sun. *(David Shaw)*

STOW-ON-THE-WOLD SP1925

Kings Arms (01451) 830364

The Square; GL54 1AF Revamped 16th-c coaching inn; black-beamed bar with wood floor, stripped stone and painted panelling,

> Ring the bull is an ancient pub game – you try to lob a ring on a piece of string over a hook (occasionally a bull's horn) on a wall or ceiling.

woodburner, Greene King ales (including one badged for the pub) and a guest, good up-to-date food here or in upstairs Chophouse restaurant with saggy oak floor, leopard-skin bar stools and ink-spot tables, prompt friendly service; children and dogs welcome, ten bedrooms including three courtyard 'cottages', open all day. *(I D Barnett, Guy Vowles)*

STOW-ON-THE-WOLD SP1925

Queens Head (01451) 830563

The Square; GL54 1AB Old traditional Donnington pub overlooking the market square; their well kept/priced beers along with good pubby food, friendly staff, stripped-stone front lounge, heavily beamed and flagstoned back bar with high-backed settles, coal-effect fire; background music; children (not in front bar) and dogs welcome, tables in attractive sunny back courtyard, open all day. *(Richard Tilbrook)*

STOW-ON-THE-WOLD SP1925

Talbot (01451) 870934

The Square; GL54 1BQ Relaxed one-bar pub in good position on market square; light airy décor with wood-clad walls and easy chairs by log fire, well liked food from sandwiches to grills, Wadworths ales, real cider and several wines by the glass, upstairs function room (and lavatories); background and live (Fri) music, free wi-fi; children and dogs welcome, a few courtyard tables, open all day (till 6pm Sun); some refurbishment planned as we went to press. *(Lauren and Dan Frazer)*

STROUD SO8505

Ale House (01453) 755447

John Street; GL5 2HA Fine range of well kept beers and ciders/perries (third-of-a-pint tasting glasses available), enjoyable food including signature curries and good value Sun lunch, main high-ceilinged part with sofa by big open fire, other rooms off; live music and quiz nights; well behaved children and dogs welcome, small side courtyard with café-style tables and chairs, farmers' market Sat, open all day Fri-Sun. *(Mark Morgan)*

SWINEFORD ST6969

Swan (0117) 932 3101

A431, right on the Somerset border; BS30 6LN Popular 19th-c roadside pub, well kept Bath and St Austell ales, local ciders, decent wines and good range of whiskies and gins including Penderyn welsh whisky, enjoyable food from lunchtime sandwiches up, efficient friendly staff, updated interior with quarry tiles and light wood floors, pastel paintwork and bluey-green panelling, raised back dining area, open fire; children and dogs welcome, wheelchair access to main bar, picnic-sets out at front and in large grassy garden with play area, open all day, food all day weekends. *(Chris and Angela Buckell, Ian and Rose Lock, Tom and Ruth Rees)*

TETBURY ST8893

Close (01666) 502272

Long Street; GL8 8AQ Old stone hotel's contemporary bar, comfortable and stylish with blazing log fire, enjoyable food from sandwiches up, also brasserie and more formal dining room, coffee and afternoon teas, charming staff; children welcome, tables in attractive garden behind, open all day. *(Lorna and Jeff Mason)*

TETBURY ST8993

★**Royal Oak** (01666) 500021

Cirencester Road; GL8 8EY Carefully renovated golden-stone inn; rambling open-plan bar with several snug areas and roaring log fire, variety of chairs around dark tables on wide floorboards, built-in green leather wall seats and a few elbow tables, ales such as Butcombe, Otter, Stroud and Wickwar from handsome carved counter, also traditional cider, ten wines by the glass and interesting spirits, upstairs dining room with fine raftered ceiling, dark polished furniture on more wide floorboards, fresh flowers and candles, good food (not Sun evening) including vegan menu, efficient cheerful service; background music (live Sun), free wi-fi; children welcome till 8pm (unless in restaurant), dogs in bar, disabled access/loos, tables under parasols on terraces and lawn, Airstream trailer for mexican street food in summer, good boutique bedrooms across cobbled courtyard (book well ahead), woodland walks from the door, open all day. *(Chris and Angela Buckell, Ivy and George Goodwill, Andrew and Ruth Simmonds, Nicky Michaels)*

TETBURY ST8993

Snooty Fox (01666) 502436

Market Place; GL8 8DD High-ceilinged stripped-stone hotel lounge serving four well kept local ales, a real cider and good house wines, enjoyable all-day bar food from sandwiches up, leather sofas and elegant fireplace, nice side room and anteroom, restaurant; background music; children and dogs welcome, a few sheltered tables out in front, 12 bedrooms. *(Jacqui and Alan Swan)*

TEWKESBURY SO8932

Nottingham Arms (01684) 276346

High Street; GL20 5JU Popular old black and white-fronted bare-boards local, timbered bar with well kept St Austell, Sharps and Wye Valley, Weston's cider,

> Cribbage is a card game using a block of wood with holes for matchsticks or special pins to score with; regulars in cribbage pubs are usually happy to teach strangers how to play.

enjoyable home-made food at reasonable prices including good Sun lunch, well priced wines too, friendly efficient service, back dining room; music and quiz nights; children and dogs welcome, open all day. *(Dr J Barrie Jones)*

TEWKESBURY SO8932

Royal Hop Pole (01684) 274039
Church Street; GL20 5RT Wetherspoons conversion of old inn (some parts dating from the 15th c), their usual value-minded all-day food and drink, good speedy service; free wi-fi; terrace seating and lovely garden leading down to river, 28 bedrooms, open from 7am. *(Theocsbrian, Dr J Barrie Jones)*

TEWKESBURY SO8932

Theoc House (01684) 296562
Barton Street; GL20 5PY Old pub now more like a café/wine bar but with local ales, good range of reasonably priced food including tapas and vegetarian choices, enthusiastic young staff, spacious split-level interior, books and board games; live jazz second and last Weds of month, free wi-fi; children and dogs welcome, open (and food) all day from 8.30am breakfast. *(Guy Vowles)*

TODDINGTON SP0432

Pheasant (01242) 621271
A46 Broadway–Winchcombe, junction with A438 and B4077; GL54 5DT Large stone-built roadside pub with modern open-plan interior, tartan carpets, blue panelled dados and log fire, Donnington ales and enjoyable good value food, friendly attentive staff; children and dogs (in bar area) welcome, picnic-sets outside, handy for preserved Gloucestershire Warwickshire Steam Railway station, open all day. *(Lyn and Freddie Roberts)*

TOLLDOWN ST7577

Crown (01225) 891166
1 mile from M4 junction 18 – A46 towards Bath; SN14 8HZ Cosy heavy-beamed stone pub on crossroads; most here for the good food (all day Sun) from sandwiches and pub favourites to more upmarket choices, efficient welcoming staff, Wadworths ales, Thatcher's cider, plenty of wines by the glass and some decent gins, warm log fires, candles on pine tables, wood, coir and quarry-tiled floors, animal prints on green rough plaster walls, some bare stonework; children and dogs (in bar) welcome, disabled access/loos, sunny beer garden, nine bedrooms in building behind, handy for Dyrham Park (NT), open all day. *(Dr and Mrs A K Clarke, Tom and Ruth Rees, Chris and Angela Buckell)*

ULEY ST7998

Old Crown (01453) 860502
The Green; GL11 5SN Unspoilt 17th-c pub prettily set by village green just off Cotswold Way; long narrow room with settles and pews on bare boards, step up to partitioned-off lounge, six well kept local ales including Uley, decent wines by the glass and small choice of well liked pubby food from baguettes up, friendly service, open fire; children and dogs welcome, a few picnic-sets in front and attractive garden behind, four bedrooms, open all day. *(Kerry and Guy Trooper)*

UPPER ODDINGTON SP2225

Horse & Groom (01451) 830584
Village signposted from A436 E of Stow-on-the-Wold; GL56 0XH 16th-c inn refurbished under present management; beamed bar with pale polished flagstones, stripped-stone walls and inglenook log fire, three real ales including Brakspears and Wye Valley, local cider and plenty of wines by the glass, enjoyable food from pub favourites up in bar, comfortable lounge or restaurant; background music, free wi-fi; children and dogs welcome, tables under parasols on terrace and in garden, bedrooms in main house and 'cottage', open all day. *(Bernard Stradling)*

WESTONBIRT ST8690

★**Hare & Hounds** (01666) 881000
A433 SW of Tetbury; GL8 8QL Substantial roadside hotel with separate entrance to pub; much liked food from snacks and sharing boards up, well kept regional ales such as Wickwar, interesting ciders, lots of wines by the glass and good gin/whisky/rum selection (some locally distilled), coffee and afternoon teas, prompt polite service from uniformed staff, two bar areas and series of interconnecting rooms with polished wood floors, various pictures (including hares and hounds) and woodburner in two-way fireplace, more formal restaurant; background music; children welcome, muddy boots and dogs (there's a menu for them) in bar, disabled access/loos/parking, shaded wicker tables on front paved terrace, pleasant gardens, 42 bedrooms (some in outbuildings), handy for the Arboretum, open all day and gets very busy (especially weekend lunchtimes). *(Chris and Angela Buckell, IAA, HMW, Maria Sansoni)*

WHITECROFT SO6005

Miners Arms (01594) 562483
B4234 N of Lydney; GL15 4PE Popular local with up to five changing ales, traditional ciders/perries and enjoyable sensibly priced food from lunchtime ciabattas up including some greek dishes (landlord is cypriot), attentive helpful service, rooms on either side of bar, slate and parquet floors, pastel walls with old photographs, conservatory; background and some live music, skittle alley; children and dogs welcome, disabled access/loos, nice gardens front and back, one with stream, good local walks and handy for Dean Forest Railway, self-catering cottage, open all day; for sale so may be changes. *(Chris and Angela Buckell)*

WILLERSEY SP1039

Bell (01386) 858405

B4632 Cheltenham–Stratford, near Broadway; WR12 7PJ Imposing neatly modernised 17th-c stone pub overlooking village green and duck pond; popular home-made food from sandwiches and bar meals up, Purity UBU and Mad Goose, prompt friendly service; children welcome, dogs in bar, lots of tables in big garden, good local walks (Cotswold Way), five bedrooms in outbuildings, open all day weekends. *(Maggie and Matthew Lyons)*

WINCHCOMBE SP0228

Corner Cupboard (01242) 602303

Gloucester Street; GL54 5LX Attractive old golden-stone pub with enjoyable food (all day weekends) including range of curries in back dining room, four well kept ales such as Fullers, Sharps, Wickwar and Wye Valley, decent wines by the glass, comfortable stripped-stone lounge bar with heavy-beamed Tudor core, traditional hatch-service lobby, small side room with woodburner in massive stone fireplace; sports TV; children and dogs welcome, tables in back garden, handy for Gloucestershire Warwickshire Steam Railway, open all day, food all day weekends. *(Dr A J and Mrs B A Tompsett)*

WINCHCOMBE SP0228

White Hart (01242) 602359

High Street (B4632); GL54 5LJ 16th-c inn with big windows looking out over village street, mix of chairs and small settles around pine tables on bare boards, well kept ales such as Goffs, Otter and Sharps, wine shop at back (corkage added if you buy to drink on premises), also good choice by the glass, generally well liked food including specials, afternoon teas, good friendly service, separate restaurant; children and dogs (in bar and bedrooms) welcome, open all day from 8am (9am weekends) for breakfast. *(Sandra and Neil White)*

WITHINGTON SP0315

Mill Inn (01242) 890204

Off A436 or A40; GL54 4BE Idyllic streamside setting for this mossy-roofed old stone inn, plenty of character with nice nooks and corners, beams, wood or flagstone floors, two inglenook log fires and woodburner, well kept/priced Sam Smiths tapped from the cask and ample helpings of traditional food including basket meals, four dining rooms, cheerful staff; children and dogs welcome, picnic-sets in big garden, splendid walks, open all day Fri-Sun in summer (all day Sat, closed Sun evening in winter), shut Mon lunchtime. *(Richard Tilbrook, Peter Young)*

WOOLASTON COMMON SO5900

Rising Sun (01594) 529282

Village signed off A48 Lydney–Chepstow; GL15 6NU New owners for this traditional 17th-c stone village pub on fringe of Forest of Dean; generous helpings of good home-made food, well kept Marstons Pedigree, Wye Valley Bitter and a guest, friendly service; quiz Weds; children and dogs welcome, seats out at front and in large back garden, open all day during summer school holidays, otherwise all day Fri-Sun, closed Mon lunchtime. *(Louise and Oliver Redman)*

Hampshire

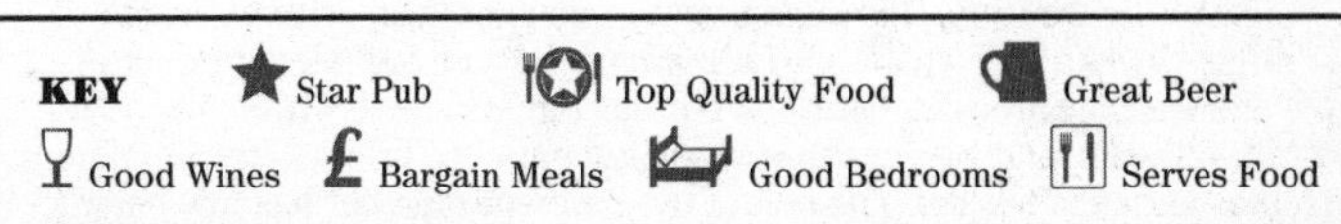

AMPORT SU2944 Map 2

Hawk Inn

(01264) 710371 – www.hawkinnamport.co.uk

Off A303 at Thruxton interchange; at Andover end of village just before Monxton; SP11 8AE

Relaxed rambling pub with contemporary furnishings, helpful staff and well thought-of food; bedrooms

With the famous Hawk Conservancy Trust just down the road, it makes sense to come here for lunch. The comfortable front bar is open-plan and modern, with brown leather armchairs and plush grey sofas by a low table, sisal matting on bare boards and a log fire in a brick fireplace. To the left, a tucked-away snug room has horse-racing photographs, shelves of books and a TV. Two dining areas have smart window blinds, black leather cushioned wall seating and elegant wooden chairs (some carved) around pale tables, big oil paintings on pale walls above a grey dado, and a woodburning stove; background music and board games. Black-topped stools line the counter, where courteous staff serve Upham Punter and Tipster and a couple of guests such as Nethergate Priory Mild and Upham Silver Blaze on handpump and quite a few wines by the glass. The sunny sandstone front terrace has picnic-sets looking across the lane to more seating on grass that leads down to Pill Hill Brook. The bedrooms have been recently refurbished and upgraded.

Starting with breakfast (7.30-10.30am; 8.30-10.30am weekends), the good food includes lunchtime sandwiches, sharing boards, devilled duck liver with wild mushrooms and toasted sourdough, crab and dill fishcake with pickled courgettes and ginger and saffron mayonnaise, baked root vegetable strudel with tomato sauce, sausages of the day with horseradish mash and crispy shallots, beer-battered haddock and triple-cooked chips, rib-eye steak with garlic butter and chips, and puddings such as chocolate parfait and praline cheesecake. *Benchmark main dish: burger with toppings, coleslaw and fries £14.50. Two-course evening meal £21.00.*

Free house ~ Licensee Becky Anderson ~ Real ale ~ Open 7.30am-11pm; 8.30am-11pm Sat; 8.30am-10.30pm Sun ~ Bar food 12-2.30 (3 Sun), 6-9 ~ Children welcome ~ Dogs welcome ~ Wi-fi ~ Bedrooms: /£100 *Recommended by Emma Scofield, Simon Sharpe, Andrew Lawson, Liz and Martin Eldon, Chloe and Michael Swettenham, Mick Allen*

Bedroom prices are for high summer. Even then you may get reductions for more than one night, or (outside tourist areas) weekends. Winter special rates are common, and many inns reduce bedroom prices if you have a full evening meal.

BANK SU2806 Map 2

Oak

(023) 8028 2350 – www.oakinnlyndhurst.co.uk

Signposted just off A35 SW of Lyndhurst; SO43 7FD

New Forest pub with a good mix of customers, popular food and interesting décor

Consistently well run, this tucked-away pub is popular with walkers, horse-riders and cyclists; staff remain friendly and efficient no matter how pushed they are. The L-shaped bar has bay windows with built-in red-cushioned seats, and two or three little pine-panelled booths with small built-in tables and bench seats. The rest of the bare-boarded bar has low beams and joists, candles in brass holders on a row of stripped old and newer blond tables set against the wall and all manner of bric-a-brac: fishing rods, spears, a boomerang, old ski poles, brass platters, heavy knives and guns. There are cushioned milk churns along the bar counter and little red lanterns among hop bines above the bar. Fullers London Pride, HSB and Seafarers and a local guest on handpump and 14 wines by the glass; background music. A pleasant side garden has picnic-sets and long tables and benches by big yew trees.

Pleasing food includes sandwiches, devilled mushrooms with a duck egg and brioche, seared pigeon with pearl barley, ale black pudding and watercress salad with raspberry dressing, grazing boards, moroccan-style vegetable tagine with feta and herb couscous, a pie of the day, chicken kiev with bacon, oyster mushrooms, spinach and mash, herb-crusted hake with braised leeks and parsley sauce, and puddings such as lemon posset and pineapple upside-down cake with rum drizzle and yoghurt ice-cream; they also offer a two- and three-course set menu (Monday-Thursday). *Benchmark main dish: beer-battered fish and chips £13.50. Two-course evening meal £20.00.*

Fullers ~ Manager Martin Barrett ~ Real ale ~ Open 11.30-11; 12-10.30 Sun ~ Bar food 12-2.30, 6-9; 12-5, 6-9 Sat; 12-5, 6-8 Sun ~ Children welcome until 6pm; over-10s only after 6pm; no under-5s evening restaurant in school holidays ~ Dogs allowed in bar ~ Wi-fi *Recommended by Dave Braisted, Katharine Cowherd, Darren and Jane Staniforth, Phil and Jane Villiers, John Evans*

BAUGHURST SU5860 Map 2

Wellington Arms

(0118) 982 0110 – www.thewellingtonarms.com

Baughurst Road, S of village; RG26 5LP

Hampshire Dining Pub of the Year

Delightful little country pub-with-rooms, exceptional cooking and a friendly welcome; character bedrooms

As ever, reports from our readers are full of enthusiasm for all aspects of this charming little inn, and it remains beautifully kept inside and out by the hands-on, hard-working owners and their courteous staff. Most customers are, of course, here for the excellent food but they do keep a couple of ales such as Longdog Bunny Chaser and West Berkshire Good Old Boy on handpump, ten wines by the glass from a smashing list, farm ciders, good aperitifs and home-made elderflower cordial; background music. The dining room is attractively decorated with an assortment of cushioned oak dining chairs around a mix of polished tables on terracotta tiles, pretty blinds, brass candlesticks, flowers and windowsills stacked with cookery books. The garden has lovely herbaceous borders, teak tables and chairs under parasols and some picnic-sets. The four bedrooms are charming and very well equipped and breakfasts are first class.

Cooked by the landlord, the food (using their own vegetables, home-reared livestock, honey from their bees and other very carefully sourced produce) is inspired: terrine of wild vension, pork and pistachio with spiced apple chutney, scallops wrapped in pancetta on pea purée with mint and brown butter, baked potato gnocchi in garlic butter with roast butternut squash, walnuts, sage and parmesan, fishcake of smoked haddock, cod and salmon fishcake on sautéed samphire with tartare sauce, potpie and mash (roe deer and root vegetables braised with red wine topped with flaky pastry), roast partridge stuffed with herbs with sticky red cabbage, mash and parsnip crisps, rack of home-reared jacob lamb with bashed carrot, parsnip and butternut squash and mint sauce, and puddings such as chocolate squidgy pudding with stem ginger ice-cream and caramel custard with oranges in cinnamon syrup. *Benchmark main dish: twice-baked cheese soufflé £10.00. Two-course evening meal £28.00.*

Free house ~ Licensees Simon Page and Jason King ~ Real ale ~ Open 9-3, 6-11; 9-5 Sun~ Bar food 12-1.30, 6.30-8.30; 12-1.30, 6-9 Fri, Sat; 12-3 Sun ~ Children welcome ~ Dogs welcome ~ Wi-fi ~ Bedrooms: /£110 *Recommended by Andrew and Ruth Simmonds, Nicholas and Maddy Trainer, John and Penny Wildon, Mrs P Sumner, Alexandra and Richard Clay, Melanie and David Lawson*

BEAULIEU SU3902 Map 2

Montagu Arms

(01590) 614986 – www.montaguarmshotel.co.uk

Almost opposite Palace House; SO42 7ZL

Separate Monty's Bar, open for both drinks and food

Although attached to the solidly built and civilised Montagu Arms hotel, Monty's Bar does have its own entrance and is usefully open all day. This simply furnished bar has panelling, bare floorboards, bay windows and a mix of pale tables surrounded by tartan-cushioned dining chairs; winter log fire. Stools line the bar counter where they keep Ringwood Best and Fortyniner and a seasonal guest on handpump and several wines by the glass, served by cheerful, helpful bar staff. Across the entrance hall is a smarter panelled dining room. Do visit the hotel's tucked-away back garden – it's quite charming in warm weather.

A sensibly smallish choice of food includes lunchtime sandwiches and ploughman's (until 5pm weekends), pigs cheek and smoked ham hock terrine with pickled vegetables, crispy crab cake with aioli, risotto and a vegetarian dish of the day, chicken caesar salad, fish pie topped with cheese, roasted lamb rump with chargrilled mediterranean vegetables, feta and potato croquette and tomato and anchovy purée, and puddings such as dark chocolate tart with brandy cream and chocolate sauce and seville orange soufflé with milk chocolate and szechuan pepper ice-cream. *Benchmark main dish: roasted barbary duck breast £16.95. Two-course evening meal £24.00.*

Free house ~ Licensee Andrew Nightingale ~ Real ale ~ Open 11-3, 6-11 (11.30 Sat); 11-3, 6-10.30 Sun ~ Bar food 12-2.30 (3 weekends), 6.30-9.30 ~ Restaurant ~ Children welcome ~ Dogs allowed in bar ~ Wi-fi ~ Bedrooms: £174/£229 *Recommended by Isobel Mackinlay, Usha and Terri Patel, Karl and Frieda Bujeya, Maggie and Matthew Lyons, Susan and Tim Boyle*

BRANSGORE SZ1997 Map 2

Three Tuns

(01425) 672232 – www.threetunsinn.com

Village signposted off A35 and off B3347 N of Christchurch; Ringwood Road, opposite church; BH23 8JH

Pretty thatched pub with proper old-fashioned bar and good beers, a civilised main dining area and inventive food

With a fine choice of drinks and creative food, it's not surprising that our readers enjoy their visits to this 17th-c pub so much. On the right is a separate traditional regulars' bar that seems almost taller than it is wide, with an impressive log-effect stove in a stripped-brick hearth, some shiny black panelling and individualistic pubby furnishings. The friendly, helpful licensees keep Otter Amber, Ringwood Best Bitter and Fortyniner and two or three quickly changing guests on handpump (they also hold a beer festival in September) plus a farm cider and a dozen wines by the glass. The roomy, low-ceilinged and carpeted main area has a fireside 'codgers' corner', as well as a good mix of comfortably cushioned low chairs around a variety of dining tables. The hanging baskets are lovely in summer and there are picnic-sets on an attractive, extensive, shrub-sheltered terrace with more tables on the grass looking over pony paddocks; pétanque. The Grade II listed barn is popular for parties – and they hold a civil ceremonies licence; disabled loo.

Enterprising food includes sandwiches, soy and spiced cured salmon with white radish, wasabi, pickled cucumber and ginger, smoked duck with caramelised onion ice-cream, baby orange and port jelly, chicken caesar salad, sausages with haricot beans in tomato sauce, pea and pepper risotto with carrot fluff and slow-roasted balsamic tomatoes, calves liver with bacon, mash and onion jus, slow-roasted local pork with compressed apple and dijonnaise sauce, cuttlefish stew with prawn ravioli, cod brandade and crispy pak choi, and puddings such as mango pavlova with stem ginger and apple doughballs with caramel sauce and custard. *Benchmark main dish: venison bonbons with root vegetable ribbons, purple potato purée and rhubarb and orange sauce £15.95. Two-course evening meal £22.00.*

Enterprise ~ Lease Nigel Glenister ~ Real ale ~ Open 11-11; 11.30-10.30 Sun ~ Bar food 12-2.15, 6-9.15; 12-9.15 weekends and bank holidays ~ Restaurant ~ Children welcome ~ Dogs allowed in bar ~ Wi-fi *Recommended by S Holder, Roy Shutz, Katharine Cowherd, Maria and Henry Lazenby, Jane and Philip Saunders, Phil and Jane Villiers, Dr Martin Owton*

CADNAM SU2913 Map 2

White Hart

(023) 8081 2277 – www.brunningandprice.co.uk/whitehartcadnam

Old Romsey Road, handy for M27 junction 1; SO40 2NP

New Forest pub with busy bar and dining rooms, a warm welcome, good choice of drinks and tasty food

The brasserie-style food and fine choice of drinks continue to draw plenty of customers into this bustling, carefully extended pub. It's a smart place and the bar, with its long curved counter, has an open fire, stools and tables on parquet flooring, Phoenix Brunning & Price Original, Flack Manor Double Drop and Hedge Hop, Hop Back Crop Circle and Minstrel and Itchen Valley Watercress Best on handpump, farm ciders, good wines by the glass and cocktails served by helpful, friendly staff. There's also a cosy area with a woodburning stove in a nice old brick fireplace, rugs and comfortable leather armchairs; background music and board games. Various dining rooms lead off with more rugs on carpet or tiles, all manner of cushioned dining chairs and wooden tables, frame-to-frame country pictures and photographs on pale walls above painted wooden dados, house plants on windowsills, mirrors and elegant metal chandeliers. The back terrace and garden have plenty of chairs and tables and there's a children's play area with a painted tractor.

Popular food includes sandwiches (until 5pm), juniper-cured pigeon with radicchio and clementine salad, baked garlic and rosemary camembert with walnut and apple salad, cheese, potato and onion pie with creamy leek sauce, king prawn linguine with chorizo and sunblush tomatoes, spicy jerk chicken with red beans and a sweet potato fritter, malaysian fish stew with sticky coconut rice, braised shoulder of lamb with dauphinoise potatoes and red wine and rosemary sauce, and puddings such as chocolate brownie with dark chocolate sauce and blackberry and sticky apple sponge with cinnamon custard. *Benchmark main dish: honey-roast ham, egg and chips £11.65. Two-course evening meal £21.00.*

Brunning & Price ~ Manager Steve Butt ~ Real ale ~ Open 10.30am-11.00pm (10.30pm Sun) ~ Bar food 12-9.30; 12-10 Fri, Sat; 12-9.30 Sun ~ Restaurant ~ Children welcome ~ Dogs allowed in bar ~ Wi-fi *Recommended by Victoria and James Sargeant, Rosie and John Moore, Tim and Mary Thomson, Mick Allen*

DROXFORD SU6018 Map 2

Bakers Arms

(01489) 877533 – www.thebakersarmsdroxford.com

High Street; A32 5 miles N of Wickham; SO32 3PA

Welcoming, opened-up and friendly pub with good beers, interesting cooking and cosy corners

This is a friendly pub with an easy-going atmosphere. It's attractively laid out with the central bar as the main focus: Bowman Swift One and Wallops Wood (the brewery is only a mile away) and a guest such as Ringwood Old Thumper on handpump, local cider and ten wines by the glass from a short, carefully chosen list. Well spaced tables on carpet or neat bare boards are spread around the airy, L-shaped, open-plan bar, with low leather chesterfields and an assortment of comfortably cushioned chairs at one end; a dark panelled dado, dark beams and joists and a modicum of country oddments emphasise the freshness of the crisp white paintwork. A good log fire and board games. To one side, with a separate entrance, is the village post office. There are picnic-sets outside. The walks along and around the nearby River Meon are lovely.

Rewarding food includes lunchtime baguettes (not Sunday), sharing boards, crispy crab cakes with tomato and coriander salsa and a poached egg, sautéed mixed mushrooms with truffled parmesan cream and polenta chips, sweet potato and spring onion fritter with warm quinoa, pomegranate and baby spinach salad, feta and pine nuts, faggots with mash and onion gravy, local chalk-stream trout with parmentier potatoes and caper and parsley brown butter, chicken breast with braised gem lettuce, pancetta and rösti potato, local steaks with dripping chips and a choice of sauce, and puddings such as lemon posset with toffee apple and ginger crumb and orange pannacotta with salted caramel and almond brittle. *Benchmark main dish: crab thermidor with fries and slaw £18.00. Two-course evening meal £22.00.*

Free house ~ Licensees Adam and Anna Cordery ~ Real ale ~ Open 12-3, 6-11; 12-6 Sun ~ Bar food 12-2, 6-9; 12-2.30, 6-9.30 Fri, Sat; 12-5 Sun ~ Well behaved children welcome ~ Dogs allowed in bar ~ Wi-fi *Recommended by David Gunn, Martine and Fabio Lockley, Phil and Jane Villiers, Sandra and Neil White, Nicola and Stuart Parsons*

FACCOMBE SU3958 Map 2

Jack Russell

(01264) 737315 – www.thejackrussellinn.com

Signed from A343 Newbury–Andover; SP11 0DS

Spacious, brick-built pub, recently renovated, with contemporary and old-style furnishings in bar and dining rooms, up-to-date food, friendly service and seats outside; bedrooms

Reopened after a major refurbishment, this sizeable, tucked-away country pub has hit the ground running – feedback from our readers has been enthusiastic. The main door leads to a small entrance room with armchairs and an open fire and this leads into the bar. Here, there's an informal, almost club-like feel with leather button-back wall seats, panelled walls inlaid with A-Z cartoon characters, and kitchen chairs and stools on black and white floor tiles. Friendly young staff serve Ramsbury Gold, Ringwood Razorback and West Berkshire Good Old Boy on handpump; background music, TV and board games. The grey-panelled dining area, split up by blue-painted wooden partitions, is furnished with mustard-coloured leather banquettes and chunky wooden chairs around a mix of tables on parquet flooring, and has another open fire, bunches of dried flowers and contemporary ceiling lights; a bigger back restaurant has pale button-back sofas and white-painted chairs around wooden tables on carpet. Throughout, there are china plates and dogs plus books and board games on delft shelving. The garden has plenty of seats and tables and a pond. Bedrooms (in a separate building) are comfortable, bathrooms are modern and breakfasts are good. There are plenty of surrounding walks.

Good, modern food includes sandwiches, rabbit spring roll with julienne vegetables and soy and sesame dressing, grilled goats cheese, apple, walnut, grape and celery salad with croutons, seared fillet of hake with kale and brown shrimp beurre blanc, roasted king oyster mushrooms with spinach, mash and mushroom ketchup, beef or venison burger with toppings and fries, sirloin steak with triple-cooked chips, slow-roast tomato and peppercorn sauce, and puddings. *Benchmark main dish: game pie £14.00. Two-course evening meal £25.00.*

Free house ~ Licensee Ross Nicol ~ Real ale ~ Open 11-11; 11-10.30 Sun ~ Bar food 12-3, 6-9.30 (10 Fri, Sat); 12-7 Sun ~ Children welcome ~ Dogs allowed in bar ~ Wi-fi ~ Bedrooms: £120/£160 *Recommended by Ian Herdman, Chloe and Michael Swettenham, Belinda Stamp*

FREEFOLK SU4848 Map 2

Watership Down

(01256) 892254 – www.watershipdowninn.com

Freefolk Priors, N of B3400 Whitchurch–Overton; brown sign to pub; RG28 7NJ

Cosy bar and open-plan dining rooms in refurbished country inn with five real ales, good food and pretty garden; bedrooms

Thoughtfully and attractively refurbished, this is a 200-year-old brick inn at the foot of the North Wessex Downs. The wood-floored bar has stools by the pale oak counter, high stools next to an elbow shelf and five real ales on handpump from within a 30-mile radius, such as Bowman Swift One, Flowerpots Bitter, Itchen Valley Hampshire Rose, Stonehenge Sign of Spring and West Berkshire Good Old Boy; several good wines by the glass. Leading off here are two connected dining rooms with mate's chairs and cushioned settles (some draped with animal skins) around chunky tables on more bare boards or old brickwork, and a woodburning stove in a raised fireplace; throughout, plants line windowsills and modern art and photos are hung on pale paintwork above a grey-green dado. A conservatory with high-backed, cushioned wicker chairs around solid tables on floor tiles leads to a two-tiered terrace with seats and tables under big parasols. A large area of lawn has plenty of picnic-sets and views over the River Test Valley. Three bedrooms (named after characters from the novel *Watership Down*) are airy and pretty and have country views.

Nicely presented, well regarded food includes flatbread sandwiches, seared scallops with roasted garlic and shallot purée, black pudding soil and sunblush tomatoes, chinese-infused shredded confit duck leg bonbon coated in sesame and black onion seeds with honey-roasted butternut squash purée, wild mushroom risotto with parmesan, rolled pork belly stuffed with sage and sausage meat with crushed mustard skin-on potatoes, sea bass fillets on sweet chilli and honey-glazed stir-fried vegetables with rice noodles, 28-day-aged rib-eye steak with brandy and peppercorn sauce and double-cooked chips, and puddings such as lemon and lime tart with raspberry sorbet and sticky toffee pudding with cinnamon ice-cream. ***Benchmark main dish:** beer-battered fresh haddock and chips £13.50. Two-course evening meal £22.00.*

Free house ~ Licensee Philip Denée ~ Real ale ~ Open 12-3, 6-11; 12-11.30 Fri-Sun ~ Bar food 12-2.30, 6.30-9; not Sun or Mon evenings ~ Restaurant ~ Children welcome ~ Dogs allowed in bar ~ Wi-fi ~ Bedrooms: /£90 *Recommended by Martin and Sue Neville, Rupert and Sandy Newton, Andy and Louise Ramwell, Jess and George Cowley, Sally and Brian Turner, Alf and Sally Garner*

FRITHAM SU2314 Map 2

Royal Oak

(023) 8081 2606 – www.royaloakfritham.co.uk

Village signed from M27 junction 1; SO43 7HJ

Rural New Forest spot with traditional rooms, log fires, seven real ales and simple lunchtime food

Quite unchanging and a favourite with our readers, this charming thatched pub is in a lovely spot right in the middle of the New Forest. It's part of a working farm, so there are ponies and pigs out on the green and plenty of livestock nearby. The three neatly kept, black-beamed rooms are straightforward but full of proper traditional character, with prints and pictures involving local characters on the white walls, restored panelling, antique wheelback, spindleback and other old chairs and stools with colourful seats around solid tables on oak floors, and two roaring log fires. The back bar has several books; darts and board games. Up to seven real ales are tapped from the cask including one named for the pub (from Bowman), Branscombe Vale Branoc, Dorset Flashmans Clout, Flack Manor Double Drop, Hop Back Entire Stout, Piddle Speak Easy and Ringwood Best. Also, nine wines by the glass (mulled wine in winter), 14 country wines, local cider and a September beer festival; service remains friendly and efficient even when the pub is packed (which it often is). Summer barbecues may be held in the neatly kept big garden, which has a marquee for poor weather and a pétanque pitch. They have three shepherd's huts to rent for overnight stays. Dogs are welcome but must be on a lead.

Good value, limited food – served at lunchtime only – consists of wholesome winter soup, a particularly good pork pie, quiche and sausages. ***Benchmark main dish:** home-made quiche £8.50.*

Free house ~ Licensees Neil and Pauline McCulloch ~ Real ale ~ Open 11-11; 12-10.30 Sun; 11-3, 5.30-11 weekdays in winter ~ Bar food 12-2.30 (3 weekends) ~ Children welcome ~ Dogs welcome *Recommended by Ann and Colin Hunt, Philip Pascall, Patrick and Emma Stephenson, Buster and Helena Hastings, Peter Meister, David and Judy Robison, Gerry and Pam Pollard, Holly and Tim Waite*

HIGHCLERE SU4358 Map 2

Yew Tree

(01635) 253360 – www.theyewtree.co.uk

Hollington Cross; RG20 9SE

Friendly country inn with character rooms, a good choice of drinks, enjoyable food and seats in garden; bedrooms

Downton Abbey fans visit this busy, 17th-c pub in their droves (Highclere Castle is close by) so it can get pretty packed at peak times. The main door opens into a heavy-beamed character bar with leather tub chairs and a leather sofa in front of a two-way fireplace housing a chiminea stove, and stools and high chairs against the counter (church candles in chunky candlesticks to either side). Loddon Hoppit, Ringwood Razorback and a changing guest on handpump and good wines by the glass, served by friendly, helpful staff. Leading off to the left is a room with antlers and stuffed squirrels on the mantelpiece above an inglenook fireplace, books piled on shelves, a pale button-back leather window seat, a mix of wooden and painted dining chairs around nice old tables on red and black tiles or carpet and, at one end, a tartan and leather wall banquette; background music and board games. Dining rooms to the left of the bar, divided by hefty timbers, have high-backed tartan seating creating booths and more wooden or painted chairs around a mix of tables on flagstones or sisal carpet. Doors lead to the garden where there's an outside bar and a variety of elegant metal and teak seats and tables either on gravel or raised decking. Well equipped and comfortable bedrooms (two on the ground floor) are named after trees; breakfasts are enjoyable.

Interesting food includes lunchtime sandwiches, garlic and chilli prawns with saffron aioli, black pudding scotch egg with celeriac rémoulade, sharing boards, chicken caesar salad, roast aubergine with tomatoes, peppers, courgettes and halloumi with a balsamic dressing, burger with toppings and skinny fries, duck breast with crispy cabbage, crushed new potatoes and cherry jus, lemon sole with samphire, spring onions and lemon caper butter, and puddings such as chocolate fondant with salted caramel ice-cream and blood orange pannacotta with orange syrup and ginger crumb. *Benchmark main dish: slow-roast pork belly with fondant potato, black pudding, burnt apple purée and jus £18.00. Two-course evening meal £23.00.*

Free house ~ Licensee Oliver Callaghan ~ Real ale ~ Open 8am-11pm ~ Bar food 12-2.30, 6-9 ~ Children welcome ~ Dogs welcome ~ Wi-fi ~ Bedrooms: /£120 *Recommended by Caroline Prescott, Emma Scofield, Andrew Wall, Susan and Tim Boyle, Richard Kennell, Darren and Jane Staniforth, David and Judy Robison*

HOOK SU7153 Map 2

Hogget

(01256) 763009 – www.thehogget.co.uk

1.1 miles from M3 junction 5; A287 N, at junction with A30 (car park just before traffic lights); RG27 9JJ

Well run and accommodating pub giving all-round good value

Locals and visitors enjoy the comfortable, welcoming atmosphere in this chatty pub, and it's certainly handy for the nearby M3. The various rooms ramble around the central servery so there's plenty of space for all; the wallpaper, lighting and carpet pattern, plus high-backed stools and bar tables on the right at the back, give an easy-going and homely feel – as does the way the layout provides several smallish distinct areas. Ringwood Fortyniner and Razorback and Youngs London Gold on handpump, 14 wines by the glass plus prosecco and plenty of neatly dressed staff; daily papers, background music and books (often cookbooks) on shelves. A sizeable terrace has sturdy tables and chairs, including some in a heated covered area.

Good food includes lunchtime sandwiches (not Sunday), moules frites, salt and pepper chicken wings with sweet chilli dipping sauce, kale spaghetti with roasted squash, beer-battered cod and chips, hot and sticky barbecue pork spare ribs, liver and bacon with mash and onion gravy, asian crispy noodles with a choice of topping, smoked fish pie with cider and bacon, and puddings such as vanilla crème brûlée and warm chocolate brownie with raspberry sorbet and clotted cream; they also offer a two- and three-course set lunch. *Benchmark main dish: steak burger with toppings and triple-cooked chips £12.50. Two-course evening meal £19.00.*

Marstons ~ Lease Tom and Laura Faulkner ~ Real ale ~ Open 12-3, 6-11; 12-11 Sat; 12-6 Sun ~ Bar food 12-2.30, 6.30-9; 12-9 Sat; 12-6 Sun ~ Restaurant ~ Children welcome but not after 7pm Fri, Sat ~ Dogs allowed in bar ~ Wi-fi *Recommended by Roger and Donna Huggins, Mike Swan, Jo Garnett, Mary and Douglas McDowell, Kerry and Guy Trooper*

HURSLEY SU4225 Map 2

Kings Head

(01962) 775208 – www.kingsheadhursley.co.uk

A3090 Winchester–Romsey; SO21 2JW

Creeper-covered pub with an easy, friendly atmosphere, interestingly furnished rooms, well kept ales, good wines and enjoyable food; lovely bedrooms

To find this well run and popular pub head for the ancient village church. Inside, the bar to the left has shutters by a cushioned window seat, high-backed plush green chairs and chunky leather stools around scrubbed tables on black floor slates, one high table with equally high chairs, and a raised fireplace with church candles on the mantelpiece above. Stools line the S-shaped, grey-painted counter where they serve Flack Manor Double Drop, Ringwood Best, Sharps Doom Bar and a beer named for the pub on handpump, 21 wines by the glass, 40 gins and ten malt whiskies; background music, daily papers and board games. A character lower room has a fine end brick wall, a woodburning stove and wall banquettes with leather and tartan upholstery, and cushioned settles on floorboards. You can hire out the atmospheric downstairs skittle alley. The smart courtyard garden has wooden or metal seats and tables on brickwork or gravel, parasols and heaters. Bedrooms (named after previous owners of the Hursley Estate) are thoughtfully equipped and comfortable with original fireplaces and antiques.

Rewarding food includes lunchtime sandwiches, flatbreads with toppings and sharing platters, twice-baked aged cheddar cheese soufflé, local crab cake with pineapple and sweet chilli jam and caramelised lime, wild mushroom and leek risotto with a pea fritter, pork sausages with bubble and squeak and an egg, roasted veal with mushroom duxelles, parmentier potatoes, ratatouille and brandy velouté, duck breast with wild garlic gnocchi and orange and caramel jus, and puddings such as peanut butter parfait with praline and butterscotch and chocolate délice with coffee and Kahlúa ice-cream. *Benchmark main dish: fresh fish of the day £16.00. Two-course evening meal £22.00.*

Free house ~ Licensees Mark and Penny Thornhill ~ Real ale ~ Open 11-11; 12-10.30 Sun ~ Bar food 12-3, 6-9 (9.30 Fri); 12-5, 6-9.30 Sat; 12-5, 6-9 Sun~ Restaurant ~ Children welcome ~ Dogs allowed in bar ~ Wi-fi ~ Bedrooms: £75/£110 *Recommended by Liz and Martin Eldon, Andrew Vincent, Andrew Lawson, Donald Allsopp, Toby Jones*

HURSTBOURNE TARRANT SU3853 Map 2

George & Dragon

(01264) 736277 – www.georgeanddragon.com

The Square (A343); SP11 0AA

Carefully renovated inn with plenty of original features, local ales, particularly good food and wine, and seats on a terrace; bedrooms

The beamed bar at the heart of this 15th-c coaching inn has a leather chesterfield and a couple of large upholstered pouffes on quarry tiles in front of a woodburning stove and stools against the counter. Here, helpful, convivial staff keep Betteridges HBT (named for the pub – the brewery is just a few yards away) and West Berkshire Mr Swifts Pale Ale on handpump and 16 wines by the glass (also served by the carafe) from a carefully chosen list; it's all very relaxed and friendly. Carpeted dining areas have mate's chairs and wheelbacks, cushioned banquettes line cosy window alcoves and a second woodburner is fronted by button-back armchairs. There are seats and tables on a small secluded terrace, and eight comfortable, quiet bedrooms. This is a pretty village surrounding by walking country.

As well as breakfasts (8-10am), the high quality, seasonal food includes local cured chalk-stream trout with pickled red cabbage and horseradish crème fraîche, loin of local organic hogget with dukkah and sweet and sour pickled carrot, wild boar and apple sausages with mash and red wine jus, chargrilled vegetables with chermoula, couscous, baba ganoush and flatbreads, pie of the day, red wine-poached brill with linguine, cockles, clams and samphire, duck breast with spiced pigs cheek croquette, stir-fried vegetables and ponzu, and puddings such as caramelised banana, dark chocolate and peanut crumble with peanut butter iced parfait and almond blancmange with kirsch cherries and almond granola. *Benchmark main dish: burger with toppings and fries £11.95. Two-course evening meal £22.00.*

Free house ~ Licensee Patrick Vaughan-Fowler ~ Real ale ~ Open 8am-11pm ~ Bar food 12-2.30, 6-9.30; 12-3.30, 6-8.30 Sun ~ Children welcome ~ Dogs allowed in bar ~ Wi-fi ~ Bedrooms: /£85 *Recommended by Bridget and Peter Gregson, Professor James Burke, Val and Malcolm Travers, Freddie and Sarah Banks, Alexandra and Richard Clay*

LITTLETON SU4532 Map 2

Running Horse

(01962) 880218 – www.runninghorseinn.co.uk
Main Road; village signed off B3049 NW of Winchester; SO22 6QS

Carefully renovated country pub with several dining areas, woodburning stove in the bar, enjoyable food and cabana in garden; pretty bedrooms

Once found, customers tend to come back to this well run pub on a regular basis. The spreading dining areas are attractively furnished with an appealing variety of chairs and tables on big flagstones or bare boards and the atmosphere is relaxed and friendly. Also, button-backed banquettes in a panelled alcove, an unusual wine-bottle ceiling light, old books on rustic bookshelves and big mirrors. A brick fireplace holds a woodburning stove, and leather-topped stools line the bar counter where they keep Upham Punter and Tipster and a changing guest from Weighbridge on handpump, 14 wines by the glass and a farm cider. The front and back terraces have seats and tables and there are picnic-sets on the back grass by a spreading sycamore, and a popular cabana with cushioned seats. The bedrooms are attractive and breakfasts are good.

Food is reliably good and includes breakfasts (7.30-9.30am; 8-10am weekends) and pub favourites plus sandwiches, tapas-style dishes, cured halibut with smoked horseradish emulsion, blinis and cucumber, crispy duck salad with chilli, spring onions and sesame dressing, roast cauliflower with cauliflower purée, curried romanesco, bhaji and herb oil, walnut, parsley and parmesan crust cod loin with pea risotto and crispy capers, chicken breast with dauphinoise potatoes, charred leeks and jus, duck breast with boulangère potatoes, wild mushrooms, braised red cabbage and truffle jus, and puddings such as rice pudding with berry compote and chocolate fondant with yoghurt ice-cream. *Benchmark main dish: calves liver with mash, crispy parma ham and onion gravy £13.50. Two-course evening meal £21.00.*

Upham ~ Licensee Anita Peel ~ Real ale ~ Open 11-11 (10.30 Sun) ~ Bar food 12-2.30, 6-9 (9.30 Fri, Sat); 12-8 Sun ~ Restaurant ~ Children welcome ~ Dogs allowed in bar and bedrooms ~ Wi-fi ~ Bedrooms: /£95 *Recommended by Ian Wilson, Mike Swan, Isobel Mackinlay, Amy and Luke Buchanan, James and Sylvia Hewitt, Lyn and Freddie Roberts, Frances and Hamish Potter*

LONGSTOCK SU3537 Map 2

Peat Spade

(01264) 810612 – www.peatspadeinn.co.uk

Off A30 on W edge of Stockbridge; SO20 6DR

Former coaching inn with imaginative food, real ales and some sporting décor; bedrooms

Keen fishermen enjoy this pub in particular as the River Test (just 100 metres away) is world famous for its fly fishing. But many other non-fishing customers (especially those walking the Test Way) are here to enjoy the highly regarded food in attractive surroundings; it's best to book a table in advance in the evening. The bars have plenty of hunting and fishing pictures and prints and the odd stuffed fish on green walls and several old wine bottles dotted here and there. Both the bar and dining room have pretty windows, an interesting mix of dining chairs around miscellaneous tables on bare boards and candlelight. Upham Punter and Stakes and a guest ale on handpump, 12 wines by the glass, 19 gins and 28 malt whiskies; background music, TV and board games. Seating on the terrace or in the garden ranges from modern rattan-style through traditional wooden chairs and tables to a sunken area with wall seats around a fire pit. This is a pretty village.

As well as offering breakfasts (7.30-9.30am; 8-10am weekends), the pleasing modern food includes lunchtime sandwiches and sharing platters, pressed duck leg and foie gras terrine with fig chutney, hot and cold smoked salmon with a panko-coated egg, beetroot, chicory and a honey and mustard dressing, salad of ricotta, roasted butternut squash, figs and pecans, dry-aged beef burger with toppings, truffle mayonnaise and fries, cod with pink fir potatoes, baby onions, mushrooms, pancetta and salsa verde, rib-eye steak with thyme and garlic butter and chips, and puddings such as crème brûlée and dark chocolate délice and milk ice-cream and almond praline; they also offer a two- and three-course set menu. *Benchmark main dish: herb-crusted lamb rump with dauphinoise potatoes and lamb sauce £22.00. Two-course evening meal £24.00.*

Upham ~ Manager Shelly Dias ~ Real ale ~ Open 8am-11pm; 9am-11pm Sat; 9am-10.30pm Sun ~ Bar food 12-2.30, 6.30-9; 12-2.30, 6-9 Fri, Sat; 12-8 Sun ~ Restaurant ~ Children welcome ~ Dogs allowed in bar and bedrooms ~ Wi-fi ~ Bedrooms: /£124 *Recommended by Jim King, John and Delia Franks, Martine and Lawrence Sanders, Miss B D Picton, Cecily and Steven Evans, Sally and Brian Turner*

LOWER FROYLE SU7643 Map 2

Anchor

(01420) 23261 – www.anchorinnatlowerfroyle.co.uk

Village signposted N of A31 W of Bentley; GU34 4NA

Plenty to look at in smart country pub, real ales and good wines; bedrooms

Throughout this tucked-away pub are all sorts of interesting knick-knacks, books, copper items, horsebrasses and lots of pictures and prints on contemporary paintwork. Also, log fires, candlelight, low beams and standing timbers, flagstones in the bar itself and stripped wood floors elsewhere, sofas and armchairs dotted here and there, and a mix of attractive tables and dining chairs. High bar chairs line the counter where they keep Courage Best, Triple fff Altons Pride and West Berkshire Good Old Boy on handpump, nice wines by the glass and a growing gin collection. This is a comfortable place to stay overnight. Chawton Cottage (Jane Austen's house) is a ten-minute drive away.

Good, contemporary food includes lunchtime sandwiches, blue cheese and pumpkin soufflé with apple slaw and blue cheese dressing, crispy pork shoulder with cumin aioli, cherry tomatoes and frozen pear, butternut squash and chestnut cannelloni with crispy leeks and beetroot, venison sausages with smoked mash and confit onion jus, monkfish with parma ham, squid ink linguine, scampi, caper salsa and hazelnuts, rib-eye steak with slow-roast tomatoes, béarnaise sauce and triple-cooked chips, and puddings such as sticky toffee pudding with toffee sauce and honeycomb and chocolate brownie with vanilla ice-cream and chocolate crumb; they also offer a two- and three-course set menu (not Friday evening or weekends). *Benchmark main dish: steak in ale pie £15.00. Two-course evening meal £23.00.*

Free house ~ Licensee Daisy May-Turney ~ Real ale ~ Open 11-11 (midnight Sat); 12-10.30 Sun ~ Bar food 12-2.30, 6.30-9 Mon-Thurs; 12-2.30, 6.30-9.30 Fri; 12-3, 6.30-9.30 Sat; 12-3.30, 6-8 Sun ~ Restaurant ~ Children welcome ~ Dogs allowed in bar and bedrooms ~ Wi-fi ~ Bedrooms: £110/£200 *Recommended by Usha and Terri Patel, Lorna and Jeff Mason, John and Delia Franks, Isobel Mackinlay*

LOWER WIELD SU6339 Map 2

Yew Tree ★ 🍷 £

(01256) 389224 – www.the-yewtree.org.uk

Turn off A339 NW of Alton at 'Medstead, Bentworth 1' signpost, then follow village signposts; or off B3046 S of Basingstoke, signposted from Preston Candover; SO24 9RX

Bustling country pub with a delightful, hard-working landlord, relaxed atmosphere and super choice of wines and food; sizeable garden

'Fantastic' and 'our favourite' are just two enthusiastic comments from readers on this particularly well run pub. The charming, hands-on landlord creates a special atmosphere and offers highly popular and very fairly priced food and ale. A small flagstoned bar area on the left has pictures above a stripped-brick dado, a ticking clock and a log fire. There's carpet around to the right of the serving counter (with a couple of stylish wrought-iron bar chairs), and miscellaneous chairs and mixed tables are spread throughout. Drinks include 13 wines by the glass from a well chosen list (with summer rosé and Louis Jadot burgundies), a beer named for the pub (from Bowman) and Longdog Golden Poacher on handpump, local Silverback gin and a locally made lager from Andwell. Outside, the front terrace has solid tables and chunky seats, a sizeable side garden has picnic-sets and there are pleasant views; the cricket field is across the quiet lane and there are walks nearby.

Fair-priced, enjoyable food includes sandwiches, smoked duck and kumquat pâté with spicy chutney, chorizo, red onion and black pudding warm salad, field mushroom, pepper and spiced halloumi burger with chips, lasagne, guinea fowl au vin with smoked bacon, baby onions and mash, half lamb shoulder with dauphinoise potatoes and red wine and rosemary jus, chicken breast wrapped in parma ham, stuffed with spicy smoked cheddar and spring onions in tomato sauce, cod fillet with lemon and ginger dressing on salami and fennel lentils, and puddings such as rhubarb, apple and berry crumble and layered chocolate, orange and pineapple biscuit fridge cake. *Benchmark main dish: goan chicken, pepper and potato curry £10.50. Two-course evening meal £18.50.*

Free house ~ Licensee Tim Gray ~ Real ale ~ Open 11-3, 6-11; 12-10.30 Sun; closed Mon; first two weeks Jan ~ Bar food 12-2, 6.30-9 (8.30 Sun) ~ Children welcome ~ Dogs allowed in bar ~ Wi-fi *Recommended by B and M Kendall, Ann and Colin Hunt, Gill Waller, Tony and Jill Radnor, Sandra and Neil White, John and Lorna Chew*

LYMINGTON SZ3394 Map 2

Mayflower

(01590) 672160 – www.themayflowerlymington.co.uk

Kings Saltern Road; SO41 3QD

Renovated inn with nautical décor, plenty of drinking and dining space, good food and drink and seats in garden; bedrooms

Right by Lymington Marina (there's a pleasant walk along the marina path) you'll find a popular place full of cheerful customers. The high-ceilinged front rooms have patterned wallpaper or turquoise paintwork, built-in wall seats and leather-seated dining chairs around dark wooden tables, candles and fresh flowers, and logs piled neatly into the fireplace. Mayflower Bitter (named for the pub from Marstons) and a guest such as Flack Manor Double Drop on handpump and several wines by the glass served by cheerful, efficient young staff. At the back, two rooms have similar seats and tables, model yachts and big modern lanterns, yachting photographs on planked walls, books and a raised woodburning stove; background music and TV. You can walk from here out on to the covered terrace and then down steps to the lawn with its heavy rustic tables and benches. The refurbished, airy bedrooms have nautical touches and some overlook the coast.

Well liked food includes sandwiches, aromatic duck salad with asian slaw and chilli coriander and ginger dressing, potted local crab with prawns and avocado, sweet pepper and chilli scones and dill butter, chicken caesar salad, pie of the day, chicken with crushed new potatoes and spinach, honey and mustard dressing, moules marinière, steak frites, sea bass with fennel salad and citrus salsa, and puddings such as warm treacle tart with rum and raisin ice-cream and apple and cinnamon crumble with salted caramel ice-cream. *Benchmark main dish: slow-roast pork belly with apple purée £16.95. Two-course evening meal £22.50.*

Free house ~ Licensee Gary Grant ~ Real ale ~ Open 12-11 (midnight Sat); 12-10 Sun ~ Bar food 12-3, 6-9 ; 12-9 Sat; 12-8 Sun ~ Restaurant ~ Children welcome ~ Dogs allowed in bar and bedrooms ~ Wi-fi ~ Bedrooms: /£200 *Recommended by Graham Smart, Edward Edmonton, Jeremy Snow, John Harris, Gavin and Helle May, Anne Taylor, Edward Nile*

THE GOOD PUB GUIDE

NORTH WARNBOROUGH SU7352 Map 2

Mill House

(01256) 702953 – www.brunningandprice.co.uk/millhouse

A mile from M3 junction 5: A287 towards Farnham, then right (brown sign to pub) on to B3349 Hook Road; RG29 1ET

Converted mill with an attractive layout, modern food, good choice of drinks and lovely waterside terraces

The sizeable raftered mill building here has several linked areas on the main upper floor with heavy beams, plenty of well spaced tables in a variety of sizes and styles, rugs on polished boards or beige carpet, coal-effect gas fires in pretty fireplaces and a profusion of often interesting pictures. A section of floor is glazed to reveal the rushing water and mill wheel below, and a galleried section on the left looks down into a dining room, given a more formal feel by panelling. Phoenix Brunning & Price Original, Andwell King John, Hogs Back TEA, Oakham Citra and West Berkshire Mr Chubbs Lunchtime Bitter on handpump, a fine range of 40 malt whiskies, 20 wines by the glass, 100 gins and local farm cider; background music and board games. At the back is an extensive garden with lots of solid tables and chairs on terraces, picnic-sets on grass and attractive landscaping around the sizeable millpond; a couple of swings too.

Brasserie-style food includes sandwiches, rabbit, ham hock and tarragon croquettes with piccalilli, potted mackerel and sea trout with shrimp and paprika butter and cucumber salad, sweet potato, cauliflower and butter bean tagine with apricot and date couscous, chicken, ham and leek pie, beer-battered cod and chips, braised lamb shoulder with dauphinoise potatoes and red wine and rosemary sauce, warm crispy beef salad with cashew nuts and sweet chilli dressing, and puddings such as black forest trifle with cherries, kirsch and dark chocolate and millionaire's cheesecake with raspberry sorbet. *Benchmark main dish: steak burger with toppings, coleslaw and chips £12.95. Two-course evening meal £21.50.*

Brunning & Price ~ Lease Ellie Moore ~ Real ale ~ Open 11-11; 11.30-10.30 Sun ~ Bar food 12-9.30; 12-10 Fri, Sat; 12-8 Sun ~ Restaurant ~ Children welcome ~ Dogs allowed in bar ~ Wi-fi *Recommended by Edward Mirzoeff, Mrs P Sumner, Susan Eccleston, Heather and Richard Jones, Ian Wilson*

PETERSFIELD SU7227 Map 2

Trooper

(01730) 827293 – www.trooperinn.com

From A32 (look for staggered crossroads) take turning to Froxfield and Steep; pub 3 miles down on left in big dip; GU32 1BD

Courteous landlord, popular food, decent drinks, persian knick-knacks and local artists' work; attractive bedrooms

With plenty to do and see nearby and some lovely surrounding walks, it makes sense to stay overnight in the neatly kept bedrooms here; the breakfasts are very good. The friendly bar has a log fire in a stone fireplace, all sorts of cushioned dining chairs around dark wooden tables, old film star photos, paintings by local artists (for sale), little persian knick-knacks, several ogival mirrors, lit candles and fresh flowers. The charming landlord and his friendly staff keep Bowman Swift One, Ringwood Best and Thwaites Wainwright on handpump, good wines by the glass and several gins. There's also a sun room with lovely downland views, carefully chosen background music, board games, newspapers and magazines. The attractive raftered restaurant has french windows to a paved terrace with views across the open countryside, and there are lots of picnic-sets on an upper lawn. The horse rail in the car park is reserved 'for horses, camels and local livestock'.

Highly enjoyable food includes sandwiches, country pâté with fig and apple chutney, beetroot, halloumi and rocket salad with balsamic drizzle, burgers with beer-battered onion rings, home-made relish and fries, aubergine and courgette bake with creamy tomato sauce, and cashew nut and butternut squash topping, salmon fillet with shallots, white wine and cream, duck breast with seville orange and Grand Marnier sauce, and puddings such as squidgy chocolate brownie with warm chocolate sauce and a choice of sorbets. *Benchmark main dish: rump of lamb with port and redcurrant sauce £17.50. Two-course evening meal £24.00.*

Free house ~ Licensee Hassan Matini ~ Real ale ~ Open 12-3, 6-11; 12-4 Sun; closed Sun evening, Mon-Weds lunchtimes (except bank holidays when open Mon lunchtime but closed evening) ~ Bar food 12-2, 6-9; 12-2.30 Sun ~ Restaurant ~ Children welcome ~ Dogs allowed in bar ~ Wi-fi ~ Bedrooms: £69/£99 *Recommended by Trevor and Michele Street, Ivy and George Goodwill, Alison and Tony Livesley, Christopher and Elise Way, Edward Nile, Julian Richardson*

ROCKBOURNE SU1118 Map 2

Rose & Thistle

(01725) 518236 – www.roseandthistle.co.uk

Signed off B3078 Fordingbridge–Cranborne; SP6 3NL

Homely cottage with hands-on landlord and friendly staff, informal bars, real ales and good food, and seats in garden

This is just the place to come for lunch after visiting the nearby Roman Villa. It's a cosy, thatched 16th-c building with nice old features including beams, timbers and flagstones. The bar has homely dining chairs, stools and benches around a mix of old pubby tables, Butcombe Gold, Sharps Doom Bar and a changing local ale such as Flack Manor Double Drop on handpump, eight wines by the glass and Black Rat cider; background music and board games. The restaurant has a log fire in each of its two rooms (one in a big brick inglenook), old engravings and cricket prints and an informal and relaxed atmosphere; background music. There are benches and tables under lovely hanging baskets at the front of the building, with picnic-sets under parasols on grass; good nearby walks. This is a pretty village on the edge of the New Forest.

Food is good and popular and includes lunchtime sandwiches, chicken liver pâté with piccalilli, twice-baked mature cheddar soufflé, open-top butternut squash and roasted shallot pie topped with feta, beef burger with toppings and chips, duck breast on wilted spinach with port jus, confit rare-breed pork belly with parsnip and honey purée and cider jus, salmon on crushed potatoes with clam and dill butter, and puddings such as pear and chocolate tart with custard and greek yoghurt and cranberry pannacotta with honey; they also offer a two- and three-course set menu. *Benchmark main dish: steak and kidney suet pudding £15.50. Two-course evening meal £22.00.*

Free house ~ Licensee Chris Chester-Sterne ~ Real ale ~ Open 11-3, 5-10.30; 11-10.30 Sat; 12-8 Sun ~ Bar food 12-2.15, 7-9.15; 12-2.15 Sun ~ Restaurant ~ Children welcome ~ Dogs allowed in bar ~ Wi-fi *Recommended by Robert and Diana Myers, Jill and Dick Archer, Patricia and Gordon Thompson, Mike and Sarah Abbot*

ST MARY BOURNE SU4250 Map 2

Bourne Valley

(01264) 738361 – www.bournevalleyinn.com

Upper Link (B3048); SP11 6BT

Bustling country inn with plenty of space, an easy-going atmosphere and enjoyable food and drink; good bedrooms

There are all sorts of different areas to choose from here; even a deli counter that provides coffee and cake, afternoon tea and picnic hampers. The bar areas have sofas, all manner of wooden dining chairs and tables on coir or bare boards, empty wine bottles lining shelves and windowsills, and a warm log fire. Flack Manor Double Drop, Ringwood Fortyniner, Sharps Juniper Rising and Upham Punter on handpump and lots of wines by the glass served by helpful, friendly staff; background music, board games and TV. A large barn extension, complete with rafters and beams, rustic partitioning and movable shelves made from crates, has big tables surrounded by leather, cushioned and upholstered chairs, more coir carpeting, a second open fire and doors that lead out to a terrace with picnic-sets and other seating. The comfortable, contemporary bedrooms are named after local lakes, brooks and rivers. Good nearby walks.

Starting with breakfasts (8.30-10.30am), the up-to-date food includes sandwiches, potted mackerel with pickled cucumber and horseradish cream, ham hock and root vegetable terrine with piccalilli, beetroot risotto with blue cheese beignet, shaved parmesan and sherry dressing, crispy chicken with cucumber and vegetable salad and chips, roasted lamb chump of lamb with pea and marjoram purée, sweet potato fondant and black olive and tomato jus, fillet of bream with fennel, citrus, brown shrimp and caper sauce, and puddings such as warm chocolate mousse and sticky toffee pudding with toffee sauce. *Benchmark main dish: burger with toppings and chips £13.50. Two-course evening meal £20.00.*

Free house ~ Licensee Ryan Stacey ~ Real ale ~ Open 11-11 ~ Bar food 12-2.30, 6-9; 12-3, 6-9.30 Fri, Sat; 12-3.30, 6-9 Sun ~ Children welcome ~ Dogs welcome ~ Wi-fi ~ Bedrooms: /£95 *Recommended by Lauren and Dan Frazer, Deborah and Duncan Walliams, Sandra Hollies, Nicholas and Maddy Trainer, Millie and Peter Downing*

STEEP SU7525 Map 2

Harrow £

(01730) 262685 – www.harrow-inn.co.uk

Take Midhurst exit from Petersfield bypass, at exit roundabout take first left towards Midhurst, then first turning on left opposite garage, and left again at Sheet church; follow over dual-carriageway bridge to pub; GU32 2DA

Unchanging, simple place with long-serving landladies, beers tapped from the cask, unfussy food and cottage garden; no children inside

'The perfect unchanging pub' is how several of our readers describe this delightful little place. It's been run by the same family for 86 years and remains quite unspoilt with no pandering to modern methods – no credit cards, no waitress service, no restaurant, no music and the rose-covered loos are outside. Everything revolves around village chat and the friendly locals are likely to involve you in light-hearted conversation. Adverts for logs sit next to calendars of local views (on sale in support of local charities) and news of various quirky competitions. The small public bar has hops and dried flowers (replaced every year) hanging from the beams, built-in wall benches on the tiled floor, stripped-pine wallboards, a good log fire in the big inglenook and wild flowers on scrubbed deal tables; dominoes. Bowman Swift One, Dark Star Hophead, Flack Manor Double Drop, Hop Back GFB, Langham Hip Hop and Ringwood Best are tapped straight from casks behind the counter, and they have local wine and apple juice; staff are polite and friendly, even when under pressure. The big garden has seats on paved areas surrounded by cottage garden flowers and fruit trees. The Petersfield bypass doesn't intrude much on this idyll, though you'll need to follow the directions above to find the pub. No children inside and dogs must be on leads. They sell honesty-box flowers outside for Macmillan nurses.

Honest food includes sandwiches, hot scotch egg, hearty soup, quiches, and puddings such as lemon crunch cheesecake and winter treacle tart. *Benchmark main dish: ploughman's £11.50. Two-course evening meal £17.00.*

Free house ~ Licensees Claire and Denise McCutcheon ~ Real ale ~ No credit cards ~ Open 12-2.30, 6-11; 11-3, 6-11 Sat; 12-3, 7-10.30 Sun; closed Sun evening in winter ~ Bar food 12-2, 7-9; not Sun evening ~ Dogs allowed in bar *Recommended by Tony and Jill Radnor, Lyn and Freddie Roberts, Andy and Rosemary Taylor, Serena and Adam Furber, Ian Wilson, Ann and Colin Hunt*

We say if we know a pub has background music.

TOTFORD SU5737 Map 2

Woolpack

(01962) 734184 – www.thewoolpackinn.co.uk

B3046 Basingstoke–Alresford; SO24 9TJ

Charming flint and brick pub with carefully refurbished rooms, plenty of character, first class food and drink and seats outside; lovely bedrooms

With interesting food, a thoughtful mix of contemporary and old-fashioned décor and a good drinks choice, this pub is a winner with those who know it. The bar has an easy-going atmosphere, leather button-back armchairs, little stools and wooden chairs around a mix of tables on wide floorboards, and high chairs against the counter where they offer Andwell Gold Muddler, Triple fff Altons Pride and Palmers Copper Ale on handpump, 15 wines by the glass and a rather special bloody mary. Leading off here is a dining room with flagstones and carpet, a raised fireplace with guns, bellows and other country knick-knacks above it and chunky tables and chairs. Throughout the other rooms are rugs on flagstones, exposed brick and stone work, a few bits of timbering and beamery, church candles, lots of photographs, some cosy booth seating and high-back upholstered dining chairs and leather wall seats around a mix of tables. The pool table converts into a dining table when they're really busy; background music, TV and board games. Outside, on the terrace, on gravel and on grass are teak tables and chairs and picnic-sets under parasols, and distant views. The bedrooms, named after game birds, are extremely comfortable and well equipped. Plenty of surrounding walks in the Candover Valley.

As well as lunchtime sandwiches (not Sunday), the modern british food includes sandwiches, guinea fowl spring roll with pomegranate salsa and lime and cardamom yoghurt, natural smoked haddock gratin with seafood cream sauce, wild mushroom and lemon thyme risotto with local watercress and parmesan salad, rabbit pie with smoked bacon, cabbage, mash and gravy, lambs liver with mash, crispy bacon, onion rings and red wine gravy, gurnard fillet with king prawns, clams, mussel and lobster broth, and puddings such as hot chocolate pudding with honeycomb ice-cream and prosecco, orange and rhubarb trifle. *Benchmark main dish: local venison loin with dorset snails, potato rösti and red wine sauce £22.50. Two-course evening meal £25.00.*

Free house ~ Licensee Andrew Cooper ~ Real ale ~ Open 11-11; 12-10.30 Sun ~ Bar food 12-2.30 (3 Sat), 6.30-9; 12-3.30, 5.30-8.30 Sun ~ Restaurant ~ Children welcome ~ Dogs welcome ~ Wi-fi ~ Bedrooms: £80/£200 *Recommended by Hilary and Neil Christopher, Jacqui and Alan Swan, Tony and Jill Radnor, Amy and Luke Buchanan, Matthew and Elisabeth Reeves*

WINCHESTER SU4829 Map 2

Wykeham Arms

(01962) 853834 – www.wykehamarmswinchester.co.uk

Kingsgate Street (Kingsgate Arch and College Street are now closed to traffic; there is access via Canon Street); SO23 9PE

Tucked-away pub with lots to look at, several real ales, many wines by the glass and highly thought-of food; pretty bedrooms

If you're coming to this fine old town, a visit here is a must. The series of bustling rooms have all sorts of interesting collections and three log fires – as well as 19th-c oak desks retired from Winchester College, kitchen chairs, deal tables with candles and big windows with swagged curtains. A snug room at the back, known as the Jameson Room (after the late landlord,

Graeme Jameson), is decorated with a set of Ronald Searle 'Winespeak' prints. A second room is panelled. Fullers HSB, London Pride and Spring Sprinter, Gales Seafarers and a guest such as Flowerpots Goodens Gold on handpump, 25 wines by the glass, 29 malt whiskies, a couple of farm ciders and quite a few ports and sherries; the tea list is pretty special. There are tables on a covered back terrace and in a small courtyard. The lovely bedrooms have been refurbished this year; some have four-posters and the two-level suite has its own sitting room.

First-class food includes lunchtime sandwiches, devilled mushrooms with a duck egg and brioche, smoked salmon with kohlrabi slaw and soft herbs, sweet potato with chickpeas, spinach, quinoa, pomegranate and tahini, beer-battered haddock with triple-cooked chips, torched cod suprême with salsify, cockles and parsley, lamb rump with braised shoulder, heritage carrots and flageolet beans, and puddings such as poached rhubarb with balsamic jelly, granola and coconut milk yoghurt and dark chocolate brownie with chocolate brûlée and apple sorbet; they also offer a two- and three-course set menu (not weekends). *Benchmark main dish: duck breast with carrot gnocchi, feta and mint and red wine jus £19.50. Two-course evening meal £24.00.*

Fullers ~ Manager Jon Howard ~ Real ale ~ Open 11-11 (10.30 Sun) ~ Bar food 12-3, 6-9.30; 12-3.30, 6.30-9 Sun ~ Restaurant ~ Children over 8 allowed at lunchtime ~ Dogs allowed in bar and bedrooms ~ Wi-fi ~ Bedrooms: £120/£176 *Recommended by Tony Scott, Mark Morgan, Richard Tilbrook, Ann and Colin Hunt, Phil and Jane Villiers, Christopher and Elise Way, Philip J Alderton*

Also Worth a Visit in Hampshire

Besides the fully inspected pubs, you might like to try these pubs that have been recommended to us and described by readers. Do tell us what you think of them: feedback@goodguides.com

ALRESFORD SU5832

Bell (01962) 732429

West Street; SO24 9AT Comfortable Georgian coaching inn with popular food including weekday fixed-price menu, up to five well kept changing ales and extensive choice of wines by the glass, bare-boards interior with scrubbed tables and log fire, hops and trophy heads (including a moose) in bar, separate smallish dining room; children and dogs welcome (resident spaniels Freddie and Teddy), attractive sunny back courtyard, six bedrooms, open all day (till 6pm Sun). *(D J and P M Taylor, Tony and Jill Radnor)*

ALRESFORD SU5831

Cricketers (01962) 732463

Jacklyns Lane; SO24 9LW Large welcoming pebble-dashed corner pub under newish management; cleanly updated inside, with good sensibly priced food (all day weekends) including two-course lunchtime/early evening deal, well kept beers and decent choice of wines by the glass, pleasant attentive staff, cricketing memorabilia and woodburner, separate dining area; monthly live music; children and dogs (in bar) welcome, sizeable garden with covered terrace, pizza oven and play area, open all day. *(Helen and Brian Edgeley)*

ALRESFORD SU5832

Horse & Groom (01962) 734809

Broad Street; town signed off A31 bypass; SO24 9AQ Comfortable attractively updated Fullers pub with roomy well divided interior; their well kept ales and a local guest, enjoyable food from fairly compact but varied menu, friendly young staff, pale beams (some supported by iron pillars), exposed brickwork and log fires, bow window seats and a few stepped levels, back restaurant area; fortnightly quiz, background music, some live music, daily newspapers and free wi-fi; children and well behaved dogs welcome, small enclosed back terrace, open all day, food all day Sun till 7pm. *(Ann and Colin Hunt)*

ALRESFORD SU5832

Swan (01962) 732302

West Street; SO24 9AD Long narrow bar in 18th-c hotel (former coaching inn); painted panelling and some rustic stall seating, well kept ales such as Itchen Valley, Sharps and Triple fff, decent wines, tea and coffee, popular reasonably priced food including breakfast (until 11am) and Sun roasts, efficient friendly service, two dining rooms (one more formal); children welcome, café-style table on terrace, 22 bedrooms, open all day. *(Edward Nile)*

ALTON SU7139

Ivy House (01420) 549011
Draymans Way; GU34 1SS Substantial centrally placed Wetherspoons linking 17th-c building with converted modern office block; Greene King, Sharps and several guests, good range of other drinks and extensive choice of inexpensive food from breakfast on, cheerful young staff coping well at busy times; TVs, free wi-fi; children welcome, plenty of outside seating, open all day from 8am (till 1am Fri, Sat). *(Minda and Stanley Alexander)*

AMPFIELD SU4023

★**White Horse** (01794) 368356
A3090 Winchester–Romsey; SO51 9BQ Snug low-beamed front bar with candles and soft lighting, inglenook log fire and comfortable country furnishings, spreading beamed dining area behind, well kept Greene King, guest ales and several wines by the glass, good food including all-day snacks, efficient service, locals' bar with another inglenook; background music; children and dogs welcome, pergola-covered terrace and high-hedged garden with plenty of picnic-sets, cricket green beyond, good walks in Ampfield Woods and handy for Hillier Gardens, open all day. *(Joy Griffiths)*

ARFORD SU8236

Crown (01428) 712150
Off B3002 W of Hindhead; GU35 8BT Low-beamed pub with log fires in several areas including local-feel bar and cosy upper dining room, well kept changing ales, decent wines by the glass and good food from pub favourites up (shortish menu, kitchen shut Sun evening, Mon), friendly staff; children welcome in eating areas, picnic-sets in peaceful dell by stream across road, closed Mon lunchtime. *(Patricia and Gordon Thompson)*

BARTON STACEY SU4341

Swan (01962) 760470
Village signed off A303; SO21 3RL Refurbished beamed coaching inn with good affordably priced pubby food (not Sun evening, Mon) from lunchtime sandwiches up, three real ales such as Alfreds Saxon Bronze and Sharps Doom Bar, very friendly owners and helpful young staff, bar with brick and timber walls, light wood flooring and inglenook log fire, back restaurant; board games, free wi-fi; children and dogs welcome, picnic-sets on front gravel and lawn, open all day Sat, till 6pm Sun, closed Mon. *(Nigel James, Edward Mirzoeff)*

BASING SU6653

Bartons Mill (Millstone)
(01256) 331153 *Bartons Lane, Old Basing; follow brown signs to Basing House; RG24 8AE* Busy converted watermill in tucked-away spot – lots of tables out by River Loddon looking across to viaduct through scrubland; Wadworths range kept well and a guest, real cider and several wines by the glass, enjoyable food (all day weekends) from sandwiches and sharing plates up, friendly staff, softly lit beamed and flagstoned interior; may be background music, Thurs quiz and other events, free wi-fi; children and dogs welcome, handy for Basing House ruins, open all day. *(Andrew Lawson)*

BATTRAMSLEY SZ3098

Hobler (01590) 623944
Southampton Road (A337 S of Brockenhurst); SO41 8PT Old roadside pub with several rooms; modern décor and furnishings alongside ancient heavy beams, wood and stone floors, log fire, tasty food from sandwiches and sharing plates up using fresh local ingredients, weekday set menu till 6pm, well kept Ringwood, Timothy Taylors and plenty of wines by the glass, friendly efficient service; children and dogs welcome (pub dogs are Hector and Sexby), nice garden with some tables under cover, good New Forest walks, open (and food) all day. *(Anne Taylor)*

BEAUWORTH SU5624

Milbury's (01962) 771248
Off A272 Winchester-Petersfield; SO24 0PB Traditional 17th-c tile-hung country pub; beams, panelling and stripped stone, inglenook log fire (even on cooler summer days), massive 17th-c treadmill for much older incredibly deep well, galleried area, three changing ales and enjoyable reasonably priced simple food such as pies and puddings; skittle alley; children (in eating areas) and dogs welcome, garden with fine downland views, good walks, regular classic car meetings including TVR, two bedrooms, closed Sun and Mon evenings. *(Ann and Colin Hunt, Richard Tilbrook)*

BENTLEY SU7844

Star (01420) 23184
Centre of village on old A31; GU10 5LW Welcoming little early 19th-c village pub; good reasonably priced food (smaller helpings available) cooked by landlady, Sharps Doom Bar, Triple fff Moondance and a guest, eight wines by the glass from decent list, good service, open fire in brick fireplace, restaurant; quiz first Mon of the

If you stay overnight in an inn or hotel, they are allowed to serve you an alcoholic drink at any hour of the day or night.

month, newspapers, free wi-fi; children and dogs welcome, garden with thatched gazebos, open all day, food all day Sun till 7pm. *(Charles Plumb)*

BENTWORTH SU6740

Sun (01420) 562338

Well Lane, off Station Road; signed Shaldon/Alton; GU34 5JT Creeper-clad 16th-c country tavern; unspoilt little beamed rooms with scrubbed deal tables, high-backed settles, pews and wheelback chairs on bare boards or brick floor, candles in bottles, various pictures and knick-knacks, three log fires, good range of local real ales and enjoyable attractively presented food from shortish menu, friendly service; children and dogs welcome, seats out at front and in back garden, open (and food) all day Sun. *(Mrs Zara Elliott, Tony and Jill Radnor)*

BISHOP'S WALTHAM SU5517

Barleycorn (01489) 892712

Lower Basingwell Street; SO32 1AJ Traditional 18th-c two-bar village local; popular generously served pub food at reasonable prices, good friendly service, well kept Greene King ales, a guest beer and decent wines, beams and some low ceiling panelling, open fires; well behaved children and dogs welcome, large garden and back smokers' area, open all day. *(Ann and Colin Hunt)*

BISHOP'S WALTHAM SU5517

★**Bunch of Grapes** (01489) 892935

St Peter's Street – near entrance to central car park; SO32 1AD Neat civilised little pub in quiet medieval street, smartly furnished keeping individuality and unspoilt feel (same family ownership for over a century), good chatty landlord and friendly regulars, a couple of ales such as Flack Manor and Flowerpots tapped from the cask, own wines from nearby vineyard, no food; charming walled garden behind, opening times may vary. *(Phil and Jane Villiers)*

BISHOP'S WALTHAM SU5517

Crown (01489) 893350

The Square; SO32 1AF Spacious 16th-c beamed coaching inn attractively updated by Fullers; their ales including Gales and popular fairly priced food from sandwiches to daily specials, cheerful helpful staff, bar area on the left with bare boards, comfortable seating and log fire, split-level dining room to the right with three further fireplaces; background music, free wi-fi; children and dogs welcome, courtyard tables, opposite entrance to palace ruins, eight good bedrooms, open all day from 8.30am, food all day Fri-Sun. *(Ann and Colin Hunt)*

BOLDRE SZ3198

★**Red Lion** (01590) 673177

Off A337 N of Lymington; SO41 8NE Relaxed New Forest-edge dining pub with five black-beamed rooms and three log fires; pews, sturdy cushioned dining chairs and tapestried stools, rural landscapes on rough-cast walls, other rustic bits and pieces including copper and brass pans, a heavy horse harness and some ferocious-looking traps, old cooking range in cosy bar, well kept Ringwood and guests, very good home-made food from varied menu (worth booking), friendly service; dogs welcome, opposite village green with seats out among flowering tubs and hanging baskets, more tables in back garden, self-catering apartment, open all day Sun. *(Phil and Jane Villiers, Malcolm Phillips)*

BRAISHFIELD SU3724

Wheatsheaf (01794) 368652

Village signposted off A3090 on NW edge of Romsey; SO51 0QE Friendly bay-windowed pub with four well kept beers and tasty home-cooked food, beams and cosy log fire; background music (live Thurs), sports TV, pool; children and dogs welcome, garden with play area and nice views, woodland walks nearby, close to Hillier Gardens, open all day. *(Alf and Sally Garner)*

BRAMBRIDGE SU4721

Dog & Crook (01962) 712129

Near M3 junction 12, via B3335; Church Lane; SO50 6HZ Bustling 18th-c pub with beamed bar and cosy dining room; enjoyable home-made food including separate gluten-free menu, Weds steak night, Wadworths 6X, a couple of local guests and several wines by the glass, friendly service; background music, TV, fortnightly quiz Thurs; children and dogs welcome, disabled access/facilities, garden with covered deck, Itchen Way walks nearby, open all day Fri-Sun. *(John and Lorna Chew)*

BRAMDEAN SU6127

Fox (01962) 771363

A272 Winchester–Petersfield; SO24 0LP Popular and welcoming 17th-c part-weatherboarded roadside pub; open-plan bar with black beams and log fires, well kept Sharps Doom Bar and guests, farmhouse ciders and several wines by the glass, ample helpings of good fairly traditional home-made food including fresh fish (delivered daily), cheerful helpful staff; children and dogs welcome, walled-in terraced area and spacious lawn under fruit trees, three shepherd's huts, good surrounding walks, open (and food) all day Fri-Sun, kitchen closes 6pm Sun. *(Richard Tilbrook)*

BREAMORE SU1517

Bat & Ball (01725) 512252

Salisbury Road; SP6 2EA Dutch-gabled, red-brick roadside pub with two linked bar areas and restaurant; well kept Ringwood ales and enjoyable reasonably priced food including some south african influences, friendly service; Thurs quiz/steak night, occasional live music; children and dogs welcome, pleasant side garden (summer barbecues), Avon fishing and walks (lovely ones up by church and stately Breamore House), open (and food) all day. *(Nicholas and Maddy Trainer)*

BROCKENHURST SU3002

Huntsman (01590) 622225
Lyndhurst Road (A337); SO42 7RH Large revamped roadside inn; popular food from sandwiches and sharing plates up including wood-fired pizzas and chargrilled steaks, three or four real ales such as Ringwood, cocktails and plenty of wines by the glass, coffee bar; skittle alley; children and dogs (in bar) welcome, decent-sized garden with covered terrace, 13 well appointed bedrooms, open (and food) all day. *(Phil and Jane Villiers)*

BROOK SU2714

Bell (023) 8081 2214
B3079/B3078, handy for M27 junction 1; SO43 7HE Really a hotel with golf club, but has neat flagstoned bar with lovely 18th-c inglenook fire, well kept ales such as Flack Manor, Ringwood and Wychwood, good cider, plenty of wines by the glass and extensive range of gins, nice food too from snacks up, afternoon teas (perhaps with a glass of house champagne), helpful friendly uniformed staff, attractive restaurant; children and dogs (in bar) welcome, picnic-sets in big garden, delightful village, 28 comfortable bedrooms, open all day. *(David and Sally Frost)*

BROOK SU2713

★**Green Dragon** (023) 8081 3359
B3078 NW of Cadnam, just off M27 junction 1; SO43 7HE Thatched New Forest dining pub dating from the 15th c; popular food from pubby favourites to blackboard specials, well kept Wadworths ales and good range of wines by the glass, friendly helpful staff, linked areas with beams, log fires and traditional furnishings, lots of pictures and other bits and pieces including some old leather 'bends' showing brand marks of forest graziers; children and dogs (not in restaurant) welcome, disabled access from car park, attractive small terrace, garden with play area and paddocks beyond, picturesque village, open all day. *(David and Sally Frost, PL, Phil and Jane Villiers)*

BROUGHTON SU3032

Tally Ho (01794) 301280
High Street, opposite church; signed off A30 Stockbridge–Salisbury; SO20 8AA Welcoming village pub with light airy bar and separate eating area, well kept ales such as Ringwood, Sharps and Timothy Taylors, good food from pub favourites up (more elaborate evening choice), Thurs evening pizzas, friendly service; children welcome, charming secluded back garden, good walks, open all day (food all day Fri-Sun). *(Ann and Colin Hunt, Margaret Merritt)*

BUCKLERS HARD SU4000

Master Builders House
(01590) 616253 *M27 junction 2 follow signs to Beaulieu, turn left on to B3056, then left to Bucklers Hard; SO42 7XB* Sizeable red-brick hotel in lovely spot overlooking river; character main bar with heavy beams, log fire and simple furnishings, rugs on wood floor, mullioned windows, interesting list of shipbuilders dating from 18th c, ales such as Ringwood Best and Sharps Doom Bar, decent wine list, stairs down to room with fireplace at each end, enjoyable bar and restaurant food from sandwiches and pizzas up, afternoon teas, prompt friendly service; children and dogs welcome, picnic-sets on stepped terrace, small gate at bottom of garden for waterside walks, summer barbecues, 26 bedrooms, open (and food) all day. *(Tony Scott, Ian Phillips)*

BURGHCLERE SU4660

Carpenters Arms (01635) 278251
Harts Lane, off A34; RG20 9JY Friendly little village pub with enjoyable reasonably priced food (not Sun evening) and well kept Arkells beers, good country views (Watership Down) from conservatory and terrace, log fire; background music; children, walkers and dogs welcome, tricky wheelchair access, handy for Sandham Memorial Chapel (NT) with its Stanley Spencer murals and Highclere Castle, eight comfortable annexe bedrooms, open all day. *(Ian Herdman)*

BURITON SU7320

Five Bells (01730) 263584
Off A3 S of Petersfield; GU31 5RX Low-beamed 17th-c pub with big log fire and some ancient stripped masonry, popular good value food (not Sun evening) from sandwiches to daily specials, Weds steak night, well kept Badger ales and good wines by the glass, friendly if not always speedy service; background music, darts; children and dogs welcome, nice garden and sheltered terraces, pretty village with good local walks, self-catering in converted stables, open all day. *(Ann and Colin Hunt)*

BURLEY SU2103

Queens Head (01425) 403423
The Cross; back road Ringwood–Lymington; BH24 4AB Large brick and tile pub dating partly from the 17th c; several updated rambling rooms, open fire, enjoyable reasonably priced food (order at bar) including vegetarian/vegan choices, Greene King and local guests, helpful friendly staff; children and dogs (in one area) welcome,

There are report forms at the back of the book.

plenty of space outside including at front overlooking busy road, car parking fee refunded at bar, pub and New Forest village can get packed in summer, open all day. *(Tony Scott)*

BURLEY SU2202

White Buck (01425) 402264
Bisterne Close; 0.7 miles E, OS Sheet 195 map reference 223028; BH24 4AZ Lovely New Forest setting for this well run 19th-c mock-Tudor hotel; Fullers ales in long bar with two-way log fire at either end, seats in big bow window, comfortable part-panelled shooting-theme snug and spacious well divided dining area on different levels, good attractively presented food (some prices on the high side) and nice wines, helpful personable staff; background music, free wi-fi; children and dogs welcome, terraces and spacious lawn, excellent walks towards Burley itself and over Mill Lawn, good bedrooms, open all day. *(David and Sally Frost, Mr and Mrs D J Nash)*

BURSLEDON SU4909

Jolly Sailor (023) 8040 5557
Off A27 towards Bursledon Station, Lands End Road; handy for M27 junction 8; SO31 8DN Steps down to brick-built Badger dining pub, worth knowing for its prime location overlooking yachting inlet; their ales (tasting trays available) and decent wine choice, enjoyable food from shortish menu (also daily specials), beams, bare boards and stone floors, some maritime bric-a-brac, log fires; dogs welcome, no wheelchair access and limited nearby parking, nice outside seating area, pontoon for tidal mooring, open (and food) all day. *(Phil and Jane Villiers)*

CADNAM SU3114

Compass (023) 8081 2237
Winsor Road, off Totton–Cadnam road at Bartley crossroads; OS Sheet 195 map reference 317143; SO40 2HE Tucked-away (though popular) 16th-c flower-decked pub, friendly and chatty, with well kept ales and generous helpings of tasty gluten-free food, beams and brasses, pubby furniture on bare boards, woodburner in brick fireplace; dogs very welcome (food for them – their characterful jack russell is Boris), side garden with decorative arbour, charity shop, open all day, food all day weekends. *(Millie and Peter Downing)*

CHALTON SU7316

Red Lion (023) 9259 2246
Off A3 Petersfield–Horndean; PO8 0BG Largely extended timber and thatch dining pub, interesting old core around inglenook (dates to the 12th c and has been a pub since the 1400s); well kept Fullers/Gales beers and popular food (all day weekends) from sandwiches and pub favourites up, friendly helpful service, back restaurant; children and dogs welcome, disabled access and facilities, nice views from neat rows of picnic-sets on rectangular lawn by large car park, good walks, handy for Queen Elizabeth Country Park, open all day. *(Tony and Wendy Hobden, John and Enid Morris, Ann and Colin Hunt)*

CHAWTON SU7037

Greyfriar (01420) 83841
Off A31/A32 S of Alton; Winchester Road; GU34 1SB Newish management and some refurbishment for this tile-hung beamed dining pub opposite Jane Austen's House Museum; enjoyable food (not Sun evening) from lunchtime sandwiches and bar snacks up, Fullers ales, guest beers and good selection of gins, welcoming relaxed atmosphere with comfortable seating and sturdy pine tables in neat linked areas, open fire in restaurant end; children and dogs welcome, small garden with terrace, good nearby walks, open all day. *(Ann and Colin Hunt, Tony and Jill Radnor)*

CHERITON SU5828

★**Flower Pots** (01962) 771318
Off B3046 towards Beauworth and Winchester; OS Sheet 185 map reference 581282; SO24 0QQ Unspoilt 19th-c red-brick country local in same family since 1968; three or four very good value cask-tapped ales from back brewery, enjoyable reasonably priced home-made food including generous baps, range of casseroles and popular Weds curry night, cheerful welcoming staff, extended public bar with painted brick walls, tiled floor, open fire and glass-covered well, another straightforward but homely room with country pictures and small log fire; no credit cards or children; dogs welcome, seats on pretty front and back lawns (some under apple trees), vintage motorcycles Weds lunchtime, no evening food Sun and bank holidays, and possible restrictions during busy times. *(Tony and Jill Radnor, Ann and Colin Hunt, David and Judy Robison)*

CHILBOLTON SU3939

Abbots Mitre (01264) 860348
Off A3051 S of Andover; SO20 6BA Traditional 19th-c brick-built village pub; five well kept local ales and decent wines by the glass, popular food from sandwiches and pubby choices up including daily specials, friendly service; children and dogs (in bar) welcome, wheelchair access, picnic-sets outside, River Test and other walks (circular one from the pub), open (and food) all day. *(Joe Tilford)*

CHILWORTH SU4118

Chilworth Arms (023) 8076 6247
Chilworth Road (A27 Southampton–Romsey); SO16 7JZ Modernised Mitchells & Butlers dining pub; good choice of popular food from sharing plates and home-made pizzas up, Sharps Doom Bar and a guest, lots of wines by the glass including champagne,

cocktails, comfortable bar with log fires, conservatory-style restaurant; background music; children and dogs (in bar) welcome, disabled access/loos, large neatly kept garden with terrace, open (and food) all day. *(Joy Griffiths)*

COLDEN COMMON SU4722

Rising Sun (01962) 711954
Spring Lane; SO21 1SB Refurbished 19th-c pub in residential street; reasonably priced tasty food including children's choices and OAP lunchtime menu (Mon-Thurs), four real ales, good friendly service, bare boards, half-panelling and painted ceiling joists, leather sofas by open fire; background and live music, Wed quiz, big-screen sports TV; children and dogs welcome, a few picnic-sets in front behind picket fence, more in garden beyond car park, open all day, food all day Sat, till 6pm Sun. *(Ann and Colin Hunt)*

CRONDALL SU7948

Plume of Feathers (01252) 850245
The Borough; GU10 5NT Attractive 15th-c brick and timber pub in picturesque village; good range of popular generously served food from standards up, friendly helpful staff, well kept Greene King, some unusual guest beers and nice wines by the glass, beams and dark wood, red carpet, prints on cream walls, restaurant with log fire in big brick fireplace; soft background music, free wi-fi; children welcome, picnic-sets in back terrace garden (bookable barbecues), three bedrooms, open all day Sun. *(Mike and Sarah Abbot)*

CROOKHAM SU7952

Exchequer (01252) 615336
Crondall Road; GU51 5SU Welcoming smartly presented dining pub (part of the Red Mist group – Royal Exchange at Lindford, Wheatsheaf in Farnham, Surrey, etc); popular home-made food from sandwiches and sharing boards to blackboard specials in bar and restaurant, four well kept local ales and good choice of wines by the glass including champagne, interesting range of gins and cocktails, also cider and lager from local Hogs Back, pleasant hard-working young staff, cosy woodburner, daily newspapers; children and dogs welcome, rattan-style furniture on split-level terrace, near Basingstoke Canal, open all day Fri-Sun, food all day Sun. *(Hugh Roberts, Roger)*

DENMEAD SU6211

Horse & Jockey (023) 9263 2728
Hipley; W on Southwick Road, right into Forest Road; PO7 4QY Lots of tables laid for their popular generously served food, but still plenty of room for drinkers, three or four well kept ales such as Ringwood, good cheerful service, beams and knick-knacks, open fire in bar area, central woodburner in restaurant; occasional jazz nights; children welcome, terrace and streamside garden with play area, open all day. *(Ann and Colin Hunt)*

DUMMER SU5846

Queen (01256) 397367
Under a mile from M3 junction 7; take Dummer slip road; RG25 2AD Comfortable well divided beamed pub with lots of softly lit alcoves; Andwell, Otter and Sharps, decent choice of wines by the glass and popular food from lunchtime sandwiches and light dishes up, friendly service, big log fire, pictures of the Queen and some steeplechase prints; background music, free wi-fi; children welcome in restaurant, picnic-sets under parasols on terrace and in back garden, attractive village with ancient church. *(Sandra and Neil White)*

DUNBRIDGE SU3126

Mill Arms (01794) 340355
Barley Hill (B3084); SO51 0LF Much extended 18th-c coaching inn opposite station; welcoming informal atmosphere in spacious high-ceilinged rooms, scrubbed pine tables, farmhouse chairs and several sofas on oak or flagstone floors, two log fires, local ales such as Flack Manor and enjoyable food, dining conservatory; darts and two skittle alleys; children and dogs (in bar) welcome, big garden, plenty of walks in surrounding Test Valley, six comfortable bedrooms, open all day (till 6pm Sun). *(Edward Nile)*

DUNDRIDGE SU5718

★ **Hampshire Bowman**
(01489) 892940 *Off B3035 towards Droxford, Swanmore, then right at Bishop's Waltham signpost; SO32 1GD* Chatty mix of customers at this homely relaxed country pub, five well kept local ales tapped from the cask (beer festival last weekend in July), summer farm cider and good value food (all day Fri-Sun) from generous sandwiches and hearty pub dishes to specials using local produce, good cheerful service, stable bar and cosy unassuming original one; mobile phones discouraged; children and dogs welcome, tables on terrace and peaceful lawn, play equipment, hitching post for horses, popular with walkers and cyclists, open all day. *(Ann and Colin Hunt)*

DURLEY SU5116

Farmers Home (01489) 860457
B3354 and B2177; Heathen Street/ Curdridge Road; SO32 2BT Comfortable red-brick beamed country pub, spacious but cosy, with two-bay dining area and restaurant, enjoyable food including good steaks and popular Sun lunch, friendly service, room for drinkers too with decent wines by the glass and three well kept ales including Gales HSB and Ringwood, woodburner; children and dogs (in bar) welcome, big garden with pergola and play area, nice walks, open (and food) all day. *(Phil and Jane Villiers)*

DURLEY SU5217

★**Robin Hood** (01489) 860229
Durley Street, just off B2177 Bishop's Waltham–Winchester – brown signs to pub; SO32 2AA Quirky open-plan beamed pub with well prepared food from varied blackboard menu (order at bar), a house beer from Greene King and a couple of guests, nice wines, good informed service from accommodating staff, log fire and leather sofas in bare-boards bar, dining area with stone floors and mix of old pine tables and chairs, bookcase door to loos; background music; children and dogs welcome, disabled facilities, decked terrace (barbecues) and garden with play area, country views, open all day Sun. *(Phil and Jane Villiers)*

EAST BOLDRE SU3700

Turf Cutters Arms (01590) 612331
Main Road; SO42 7WL Small dimly lit 18th-c New Forest local behind white picket fence; lots of beams and pictures, nicely worn-in furnishings on bare boards and flagstones, log fire, enjoyable home-made food from ciabattas up (worth booking evenings/weekends), well kept Ringwood ales and a guest, good friendly service and chatty relaxed atmosphere; children and dogs welcome, picnic-sets in large back garden, good heathland walks, bedrooms in nearby converted barn, open all day. *(Dave T, Martyn Stringer)*

EAST END SZ3696

★**East End Arms** (01590) 626223
Back road Lymington–Beaulieu, parallel to B3054; SO41 5SY Simple friendly pub (owned by former Dire Straits bass guitarist); unfussy bar with chatty locals and log fire, Ringwood Best or Fortyniner and several wines by the glass, enjoyable freshly made food (not Sun evening) served by cheerful helpful staff, attractive dining room; occasional live music, free wi-fi; children and dogs (in bar) welcome, picnic-sets in terraced garden, pretty cottagey bedrooms, open all day July-Sept (all day Fri-Sun other times). *(Phil and Jane Villiers)*

EAST MEON SU6822

Olde George (01730) 823481
Church Street; signed off A272 W of Petersfield, and off A32 in West Meon; GU32 1NH Atmospheric heavy-beamed village inn with well liked food from sandwiches and light lunches to more restauranty choices, Badger ales and decent selection of wines by the glass, cosy areas around central brick counter, inglenook log fires; children and dogs welcome, nice back terrace, five bedrooms, good breakfast, pretty village with fine church and surrounding walks, open all day Sun. *(Gerry and Pam Pollard)*

EAST STRATTON SU5339

★**Northbrook Arms** (01962) 774150
Brown sign to pub off A33 4 miles S of A303 junction; SO21 3DU Brick-built village pub, part of the Northbrook Estate; traditional tiled-floor bar on right with beams and standing timbers, ales such as Andwell, Bowman, Butcombe, Sharps and Triple fff, several wines by the glass and around 15 gins, slightly more formal left-hand bar ending in a dining room beyond little central hall, quite a choice of tasty food (all day Sat, till 6pm Sun), friendly helpful service; background music, skittle alley in former stables; children and dogs welcome, seats in pretty country garden to the side or on green opposite, good nearby walks, open all day. *(Ted and Mary Bates, Sandra and Michael Smith, Darren and Jane Staniforth, Tony and Jill Radnor)*

EASTON SU5132

Chestnut Horse (01962) 779257
3.6 miles from M3 junction 9: A33 towards Kings Worthy, then B3047 towards Itchen Abbas; Easton then signposted on right – bear left in village; SO21 1EG Comfortable 16th-c pub in pretty village of thatched cottages; open-plan interior but with a series of cosy separate areas, log fires, black beams and joists hung with jugs, mugs and chamber-pots, three Badger ales, plenty of wines by the glass and good selection of whiskies and gins, generally well liked food and attentive service from hands-on landlord and friendly staff; background music; children and dogs (in bar) welcome, seats and tables on smallish sheltered decked area, summer tubs and baskets, picnic-sets at the front; walks in Itchen Valley, open all day Fri-Sun, food all day Sun. *(Katharine Cowherd, David and Judy Robison)*

ECCHINSWELL SU4959

Royal Oak (01635) 297355
Ecchinswell Road; RG20 4UH Cosy and welcoming whitewashed village pub; bar with open fire, window seats and plush-topped stools around tables on wood floor, second room with another fire and airy dining room with country kitchen chairs and mix of tables on light boards, three well kept ales and enjoyable fair value food, good friendly service; children welcome, picnic-sets on front terrace behind picket fence, more in large back garden running down to stream. *(Kerry and Guy Trooper)*

EMERY DOWN SU2808

★**New Forest** (023) 8028 4690
Village signed off A35 just W of Lyndhurst; SO43 7DY Well run 18th-c weatherboarded village pub in one of the best parts of the New Forest for walking; good sensibly priced home-made food including vegetarian choices, daily specials

and popular Sun roasts (should book), friendly helpful uniformed staff, Ringwood and guests, real cider and several wines by the glass, coffee and tea; attractive softly lit separate areas on varying levels, each with own character, old pine and oak furniture, milk churn stools by bar, hunting prints and two log fires; background music; children and dogs welcome, covered terrace and nice little three-level garden, four good value simple bedrooms, open (and food) all day, can get very busy weekends. *(Sara Fulton, Roger Baker)*

EMSWORTH SU7405

Blue Bell (01243) 373394

South Street; PO10 7EG Friendly and relaxed little 1940s red-brick pub close to the quay; old-fashioned lived-in interior with nautical and other memorabilia, good choice of popular reasonably priced home-made food with emphasis on local produce including fresh fish (best to book), bar nibbles Sun lunchtime, well kept Sharps Doom Bar and a couple of guests such as Emsworth from brick and timber servery; TV, daily newspapers; dogs welcome, seats on small front and side terraces, Sun market in adjacent car park, open all day. *(Ken Board, Ann and Colin Hunt, Dom Escott, Tony Hobden)*

EMSWORTH SU7405

Coal Exchange (01243) 375866

Ships Quay, South Street; PO10 7EG Friendly little L-shaped Victorian local near harbour; well kept Fullers/Gales beers and guests, good value home-made lunchtime food (evenings Tues-Thurs including Weds pizza night), simple low-ceilinged bar with fire at each end; live music, free wi-fi; children and dogs welcome, tables outside and smokers' shelter, handy for Wayfarers Walk and Solent Way, open all day Fri-Sun. *(Ann and Colin Hunt, Tony Hobden)*

EMSWORTH SU7505

Lord Raglan (01243) 372587

Queen Street; PO10 7BJ Traditional 18th-c flint pub with wide choice of enjoyable home-made food from daily changing menu, well kept Fullers/Gales beers, good friendly service, log fire, restaurant; live music Sun evening, free wi-fi; dogs welcome, pleasant waterside garden behind, open all day weekends. *(Isobel Mackinlay)*

EVERSLEY SU7762

Tally Ho (0118) 973 2134

Fleet Hill; RG27 0RR Home Counties group pub in extended old brick farmhouse; four real ales, lots of wines by the glass and enjoyable bistro-style food, beams and wood floors, built-in wall seats and cushioned dining chairs around wooden tables, friendly chatty atmosphere; children welcome, dogs in bar, tables on terrace and lawn with swings and play tractor, open (and food) all day. *(Mo Dobson)*

EVERSLEY CROSS SU7861

Chequers (0118) 402 7065

Chequers Lane; RG27 0NS Stylish Peach dining pub dating in part from the 14th c; good seasonal food from deli boards to daily specials, well kept Hogs Back and local guests, carefully chosen wines and gins, cocktails, friendly helpful staff, linked beamed rooms including restaurant; children welcome, tables out at front under parasols, open all day from 9.30am for breakfast. *(Patric Curwen)*

EVERTON SZ2994

Crown (01590) 642655

Old Christchurch Road; pub signed just off A337 W of Lymington; SO41 0JJ Quietly set restaurant-pub on edge of New Forest; highly thought-of food cooked by landlord-chef including daily specials, friendly service, Greene King and Ringwood ales, decent wines, two attractive dining rooms off tiled-floor bar, log fires; children welcome, wheelchair access, picnic-sets on front terrace behind picket fence and in garden behind, closed Mon. *(Jackie Skinner)*

EXTON SU6120

★**Shoe** (01489) 877526

Village signposted from A32 NE of Bishop's Waltham; SO32 3NT Popular brick-built country dining pub on South Downs Way; three linked rooms with log fires, good well presented food (best to book) from traditional favourites to more imaginative restaurant-style dishes including fresh fish and seasonal game, home-baked bread (also for sale), well kept Wadworths ales and a guest, several wines by the glass including local sparkling, good service from friendly young staff; children and dogs welcome, disabled facilities, seats under parasols at front, more in garden across lane overlooking River Meon (ice-cream shack summer weekends), open all day weekends. *(David and Judy Robison)*

FAREHAM SU5705

Castle in the Air (01329) 280320

Old Gosport Road; PO16 0XH Open-plan Greene King pub by tidal Fareham Creek; their beers and guests kept well, enjoyable reasonably priced food including deals, friendly staff, flagstones and bare boards, big brick fireplace; live music and quiz nights; children and dogs welcome, terrace seating, open (and food) all day. *(Ann and Colin Hunt)*

FAREHAM SU5806

Cob & Pen (01329) 221624

Wallington Shore Road, not far from M27 junction 11; PO16 8SL Cheerful old corner local near Wallington River; four well kept ales including Hop Back, St Austell and Sharps, enjoyable well priced home-made food from sandwiches to specials, log fire; some live music, TV, darts; children and dogs welcome, large garden with play area and summer barbecues, open all day, no food Sun evening and winter Mon. *(Sally and Brian Turner)*

FARNBOROUGH SU8756

★**Prince of Wales** (01252) 545578
Rectory Road, near station; GU14 8AL
Ten well kept ales including five quickly changing guests at this friendly Victorian local, three small linked areas with exposed brickwork, carpet or wood floors, open fire and some antiquey touches, generous lunchtime pubby food at reasonable prices, also Mon curry night and Fri evening fish, good friendly service; quiz first Sun of month, some live music; well behaved children and dogs welcome, a few picnic-sets on front pavement, more seating on back terrace with smokers' gazebo, open all day Fri-Sun. *(Tony Hobden)*

FAWLEY SU4603

Jolly Sailor (023) 8089 1305
Ashlett Creek, off B3053; SO45 1DT
Cottagey waterside pub near small boatyard and sailing club; good value straightforward bar food, Ringwood Best and a guest, cheerful service, mixed pubby furnishings on bare boards, raised log fire, second bar with darts and pool; children and dogs welcome, tables outside looking past creek's yachts and boats to busy shipping channel, good shore walks, handy for Rothschild rhododendron gardens at Exbury, open all day, no food Sun evening, Mon. *(Edward Nile)*

FROGHAM SU1712

Foresters Arms (01425) 652294
Abbotswell Road; SP6 2JA Updated New Forest pub (part of the Little Pub Group); enjoyable good value food from lunchtime baguettes up, Wadworths ales and a guest, good friendly service, cosy rustic-chic interior with rugs on wood or flagstone floors, woodburners in brick fireplaces, pale green panelling, mix of old and new furniture including settles and pews, antlers and grandfather clock; monthly quiz; children, walkers and dogs (in bar) welcome, picnic-sets out at front under pergola and on lawn, maybe donkeys, open all day weekends. *(Neil Weddell)*

GOODWORTH CLATFORD SU3642

Royal Oak (01264) 324105
Longstock Road; SP11 7QY Comfortably modern L-shaped bar with ales such as Flack Manor and Ringwood, nice wines by the glass and good pubby food from sandwiches up, friendly efficient staff; children welcome, picnic-sets in pretty dell-like garden, attractive Test Valley village and good River Anton walks, closed Sun evening. *(Mike and Mary Carter, David and Judy Robison)*

GOSPORT SZ6198

Fighting Cocks (023) 9252 9885
Clayhall Road, Alverstoke; PO12 2AJ
Welcoming modernised local in residential area; Wadworths ales and good choice of enjoyable pubby food at sensible prices including Sat breakfast from 9.30am, friendly helpful service, bar with some booth seating and upholstered wall benches, skylit dining room; Sun quiz, darts, TV, fruit machine; children and dogs in bar (welcome), big garden with play equipment, handy for Stokes Bay beaches, open all day, no food Sun evening. *(Ann and Colin Hunt)*

GOSPORT SZ6100

Queens 07974 031671
Queens Road; PO12 1LG Classic bare-boards corner local with six real ales such as Fallen Acorn, Ringwood and Youngs kept in top condition by long-serving no-nonsense landlady, popular Oct beer festival, three areas off bar, good log fire in interesting carved fireplace, sensibly placed darts, TV for major sports; no children or dogs, open all day Sat, closed lunchtimes Mon-Thurs. *(Ann and Colin Hunt)*

GRAYSHOTT SU8735

Fox & Pelican (01428) 604757
Headley Road; GU26 6LG Large village pub with enjoyable food (all day Fri and Sat, till 6pm Sun) from sandwiches and light dishes up including weekday set lunch, Fullers/Gales beers and a guest, good friendly service, linked areas with comfortable seating on wood or carpeted floors, open fire in large fireplace, dining conservatory; background and some live music, quiz Thurs, darts, sports TV, games machines; children and dogs welcome, wheelchair access, tables on paved terrace and lawn, fenced play area, open all day. *(John and Bernadette Elliott)*

GREYWELL SU7151

Fox & Goose (01256) 702062
Near M3 junction 5; A287 towards Odiham, then first right to village; RG29 1BY Welcoming two-bar village pub popular with locals and walkers; traditional interior with country kitchen furniture and open fire, enjoyable home-made pubby food from good lunchtime sandwiches up, three well kept ales including Sharps Doom Bar; open mike night third Mon of month; children and dogs welcome, good-sized back garden and camping field, River Whitewater and Basingstoke Canal walks, open all day. *(D J and P M Taylor)*

GRIGGS GREEN SU8231

Deers Hut (01428) 724406
Off A3 S of Hindhead; GU30 7PD
Popular old country pub with horseshoe bar

It's very helpful if you let us know up-to-date food prices when you report on pubs.

and several rustically furnished dining areas; good if slightly pricey food (service charge added) from baguettes and pub staples to daily specials, Sharps Doom Bar, Youngs Bitter and a couple of guests, good choice of other drinks, friendly young staff; children welcome, attractive woodland setting with picnic-sets on front terrace and green, handy for Shipwrights Way walkers, classic car event (Father's Day), open all day. *(Tony and Jill Radnor, Jonathan Powell)*

HAMBLE SU4806

Bugle (023) 8045 3000
3 miles from M27 junction 8; SO31 4HA Bustling little 16th-c village pub just back from the River Hamble; beamed and timbered rooms with flagstones and polished boards, woodburner in fine brick fireplace, bar stools along herringbone-brick and timber counter, a beer named for the pub from Itchen Valley plus a couple of guests (often Flack Manor), popular food (all day Sun); background music, TV; children and dogs (in bar) welcome, picnic-sets on small raised front terrace with boat views, open all day. *(Joe Tilford)*

HAMBLE SU4806

King & Queen (023) 8045 4247
3 miles from M27 junction 8; High Street; SO31 4HA Popular with locals and visiting yachtsmen, this cheerful bustling pub has a simply furnished bar with log fire at one end, steps down to two small dining rooms, three changing ales, good wines, cocktails and some 30 different rums, generous helpings of enjoyable food from sandwiches and pizzas up, friendly young staff; children and dogs welcome, planked tables and picnic-sets in sunny front garden, open all day. *(Andrew Lawson)*

HAMBLE SU4806

Victory (023) 8045 3105
High Street; SO31 4HA Split-level 18th-c red-brick pub with four well kept ales and enjoyable reasonably priced bar food including popular Sun lunch, cheerful welcoming staff, nautical theme including Battle of Trafalgar mural (find the hidden faces), beams and half-panelling, wood, flagstone and carpeted floors; live music, darts, sports TV; children and dogs welcome, terrace picnic-sets, open all day. *(Mary and Douglas McDowell)*

HAMBLEDON SU6716

★**Bat & Ball** (023) 9263 2692
Broadhalfpenny Down; about 2 miles E towards Clanfield; PO8 0UB Extended dining pub opposite historic cricket pitch; log fires and comfortable modern furnishings in three linked rooms, lots of cricketing memorabilia (the game's rules are said to have been written here), Fullers ales and enjoyable food from well priced snacks up, panelled restaurant; free wi-fi; children and dogs welcome, tables on front terrace, garden behind with lovely downs views, good walks, open all day. *(Ann and Colin Hunt)*

HAVANT SU7106

Old House At Home
(023) 9248 3464 *South Street; PO9 1DA* Black and white Tudor pub next to church; modernised two-bar interior with low beams and nice rambling alcovey feel, enjoyable sensibly priced food from sandwiches and bar snacks up, good value set menu Mon-Fri, Fullers/Gales beers including seasonals, friendly service; juke box (some live music), sports TV, fruit machine, darts and board games; children (in smaller bar) and dogs welcome, pretty jettied frontage with hanging baskets, tables and smokers' shelter in back garden, open (and food) all day, kitchen closes 5pm Sun. *(Ann and Colin Hunt, Tony and Wendy Hobden)*

HAVANT SU7106

Robin Hood (023) 9248 2779
Homewell; PO9 1EE Traditional 18th-c pub tucked away opposite church, opened-up bar with beams and log fires, well kept Fullers/Gales ales tapped from the cask, tasty simple lunchtime food, friendly service; Tues quiz, sports TV; dogs welcome, seats in small back garden, open all day. *(Ann and Colin Hunt, Brian Lintern)*

HAVANT SU7206

Wheelwrights Arms (023) 9247 6502
Emsworth Road; PO9 2SN Sizeable stylishly decorated Victorian pub, five well kept beers including Upham, decent wine list and enjoyable pubby food from snacks and sharing plates up, OAP lunch deal Mon-Thurs, friendly service; background music, quiz night (Havant a Clue) first and third Weds of month; children and dogs welcome, shaded tables out at front and in courtyard garden behind, open all day, food all day Sun. *(Dr and Mrs J D Abell)*

HAWKLEY SU7429

Hawkley Inn (01730) 827205
Off B3006 near A3 junction; Pococks Lane; GU33 6NE Traditional tile-hung village pub with seven well kept mainly local ales from central bar, popular often interesting home-made food (not Sun evening), friendly staff, open fires (large moose head above one), rugs on flagstones, old pine tables and assorted chairs; children and dogs welcome, covered seating area at front, picnic-sets in big back garden, useful for walkers on Hangers Way, six comfortable bedrooms, open all day weekends. *(Mo Dobson)*

HAYLING ISLAND SU7201

Maypole (023) 9246 3670
Havant Road; PO11 0PS Sizeable two-bar 1930s roadside local, well run and friendly, with good reasonably priced home-made

pub food including Fri fish night, Fullers/Gales beers kept well, parquet floors and polished panelling, plenty of good seating, open fires; Thurs quiz, darts; children and dogs welcome, garden picnic-sets and play equipment, closed Sun evening. *(John and Delia Franks)*

HAZELEY SU7459

Shoulder of Mutton (0118) 932 6272
Red Hill; pub signed from B3011; RG27 8NB 18th-c dining pub with good range of food including some pasta dishes and summer pizzas, real ales such as Sharps Doom Bar from brick and timbered servery, friendly helpful staff, log fires; children welcome, terrace and garden with attractive views across meadows, closes 7pm Sun. *(Tony and Jill Radnor)*

HECKFIELD SU7260

New Inn (0118) 932 6374
B3349 Hook–Reading (former A32); RG27 0LE Rambling open-plan dining pub with good reasonably priced food (all day weekends) from sandwiches and baked potatoes up, well kept Badger ales and good choice of wines and whiskies, efficient friendly service, attractive layout with some traditional furniture in original core, two log fires, restaurant; quiz last Thurs of month; children welcome, good-sized heated terrace, 16 comfortable bedrooms in extension, open all day. *(Darren and Jane Staniforth)*

HERRIARD SS6744

Fur & Feathers (01256) 510510
Pub signed just off A339 Basingstoke–Alton; RG25 2PN Light and airy Victorian country pub with highly regarded food from sharing plates and a burger menu up, four well kept changing ales and good choice of wines and gins, selection of cuban cigars too, friendly efficient staff, smallish bar with dining areas either side, pine furniture on stripped-wood flooring, painted half-panelling, two woodburners; background music; children welcome, garden behind with paved terrace, closed Mon, otherwise open all day (till 6pm Sun). *(Jackie Skinner)*

HORDLE SZ2996

★**Mill at Gordleton** (01590) 682219
Silver Street; SO41 6DJ Charming tucked-away country inn; small panelled bar to the right with leather armchairs and Victorian-style mahogany dining chairs on parquet flooring, pretty corner china cupboard and electric woodburner, two Upham ales and a guest, 16 good wines by the glass and 15 malt whiskies, also cosy lounge with open fire, spacious second bar and sizeable beamed restaurant extension, food can be good including more affordable set menus (Mon-Thurs), afternoon teas; background music, free wi-fi; children and dogs (in front bar) welcome, lovely gardens with extensive series of interestingly planted areas, sculptures and several ponds, plenty of places to sit including main waterside terrace, good nearby walks, 12 comfortable individually furnished bedrooms, open all day. *(Alison Chalu, I D Barnett, Darren and Jane Staniforth, Mr and Mrs D J Nash, Christopher and Elise Way)*

HORNDEAN SU7013

Ship & Bell (023) 9307 9301
London Road; PO8 0BZ Comfortable traditionally refurbished 17th-c inn by former Gales brewery; well kept Fullers beers, decent range of wines and several gins paired with Fever Tree tonics, enjoyable good value food from sharing boards up, bar with deep well, steps up to dining room, open fires; Sun quiz, pool, fruit machine; children and dogs welcome, a few pavement tables, more in enclosed back garden, bedrooms, nice walk to Catherington church, open all day. *(Ann and Colin Hunt, Brian Lintern)*

HORSEBRIDGE SU3430

John O'Gaunt (01794) 388644
Off A3057 Romsey–Andover, just SW of Kings Somborne; SO20 6PU Neatly refurbished River Test village pub; L-shaped bar with mix of furniture including armchairs on bare boards, light wood dados, book wallpaper either side of woodburner, popular good value home-made food from baguettes up, Ringwood Razorback and three guests, a couple of Purbeck ciders and good choice of gins, friendly helpful service; children, walkers and dogs welcome, seats outside, open all day, food all day weekends. *(Mrs Julie Thomas, Ann and Colin Hunt)*

HOUGHTON SU3432

★**Boot** (01794) 388310
Village signposted off A30 in Stockbridge; SO20 6LH Well maintained country pub with cheery log-fire bar and more formal dining room; well kept ales such as Flack Manor, Otter and Ringwood, Weston's and Thatcher's ciders and a dozen wines by the glass, good bar and restaurant food (not Sun or Mon evening) from baguettes to blackboard specials, friendly helpful staff; children and dogs welcome, picnic-sets out in front and in spacious tranquil garden by lovely (unfenced) stretch of River Test, outside summer grill, opposite Test Way walking/cycling path. *(Charles and Maddie Bishop)*

KEYHAVEN SZ3091

★**Gun** (01590) 642391
Keyhaven Road; SO41 0TP Busy rambling 17th-c pub looking over boatyard and sea to Isle of Wight; low-beamed bar with nautical bric-a-brac and plenty of character (less in family rooms and conservatory), good fairly standard food including nice crab sandwiches, well kept Ringwood, Sharps, Timothy Taylors and Wells tapped from the cask, Weston's cider, lots of malt whiskies,

prompt service from helpful young staff; bar billiards; tables out in front and in big back garden with swings and fish pond, you can stroll down to small harbour and walk to Hurst Castle, open all day Sat, closed Sun evening. *(Alison Chalu, M J Daly, David and Judy Robison)*

KINGSCLERE SU5258

Bel & Dragon (01635) 299342
Swan Street; RG20 5PP Attractively updated 15th-c beamed village inn, emphasis on dining with well liked bar and restaurant food including Josper grills, weekend brunch, three real ales, cocktails and good selection of wines by the glass including champagne, friendly helpful staff; children welcome, nine bedrooms, good surrounding walks, open all day, food all day Sun. *(Anne Taylor)*

LANGSTONE SU7104

★**Royal Oak** (023) 9248 3125
Off A3023 just before Hayling Island bridge; Langstone High Street; PO9 1RY Charmingly placed waterside dining pub overlooking tidal inlet and ancient wadeway to Hayling Island – boats at high tide, wading birds when it goes out; four Greene King ales and good choice of wines by the glass, reasonably priced pubby food from sandwiches up, spacious flagstoned bar and linked dining areas, log fire; children welcome in restaurant, dogs in bar, nice garden with pond, good coast paths nearby, open (and food) all day from 10am. *(Tony Scott, Suzy Miller)*

LINDFORD SU8036

Royal Exchange (01420) 488118
Liphook Road; GU35 0NX Red Mist pub with spacious bar and light modern dining room, enjoyable food from sandwiches and sharing boards to good specials, four real ales including a house beer from Tilford, craft beers, plenty of wines by the glass and interesting selection of gins, efficient friendly service; children and dogs welcome, seats outside, open all day Fri-Sun, food all day Sun. *(Mike and Sarah Abbot)*

LINWOOD SU1910

High Corner (01425) 473973
Signed from A338 via Moyles Court, and from A31; BH24 3QY Big rambling pub in splendid New Forest position at end of track (beware of potholes); popular and welcoming with some character in original upper log-fire bar, big back extensions for the summer crowds, nicely partitioned restaurant, verandah lounge and other rooms, good helpings of enjoyable home-made food, well kept Wadworths ales and Weston's cider, friendly staff; children and dogs welcome, horses too (stables and paddock available), extensive wooded garden with play area, seven comfortable bedrooms, open all day in summer (all day weekends other times). *(Phil and Jane Villiers)*

LIPHOOK SU8330

Links Tavern (01428) 723773
Portsmouth Road; GU30 7EF Spacious Fullers pub with comfortably modernised interior, plenty of connecting rooms and intimate spaces, four of their ales and wide choice of wines by the glass, enjoyable food from sandwiches and sharing boards up, friendly service; some live music, free wi-fi; children welcome, picnic-sets on surrounding terraces and lawn, smokers' gazebo, pleasant woodland and lakeside walks at Foley Manor, open all day, food all day weekends. *(John and Bernadette Elliott)*

LISS SU7826

Jolly Drover (01730) 893137
London Road, Hill Brow; B2070 S of town, near B3006 junction; GU33 7QL Traditional 19th-c pub under long-serving licensees; neat carpeted beamed bar with a couple of chesterfields in front of brick inglenook, Sharps Doom Bar, Timothy Taylors Landlord and a dozen wines by the glass, generous helpings of enjoyable fairly priced food (puddings particularly good), friendly helpful service, two back dining sections; free wi-fi; children welcome, teak furniture on terrace, picnic-sets on lawn, six barn-conversion bedrooms, closed Sun evening. *(Mark Morgan, Andrew Vincent, Katherine Matthews, Tony and Wendy Hobden)*

LITTLE LONDON SU6259

Plough (01256) 850628
Silchester Road, off A340 N of Basingstoke; RG26 5EP Tucked-away local, cosy and unspoilt, with log fires, low beams and mixed furnishings on brick or tiled floors (watch the step), well kept Otter, Ringwood and interesting guests tapped from the cask, good value baguettes, no credit cards; bar billiards and darts; dogs welcome, attractive garden, handy for Pamber Forest and Calleva Roman remains. *(Edward Nile)*

LONG SUTTON SU7447

Four Horseshoes (01256) 862488
Signed off B3349 S of Hook; RG29 1TA Welcoming unpretentious country pub with loyal band of regulars; open plan with black beams and two log fires, long-serving landlord cooking uncomplicated bargain food such as lancashire hotpot and fish and chips, friendly landlady serving Palmers and maybe a guest ale; monthly quiz and jazz nights; children and dogs welcome, disabled access, small glazed-in front verandah, picnic-sets and play area on grass over road, pétanque, bedrooms with country views, closed Mon and Tues lunchtimes. *(Tony and Jill Radnor)*

LONGPARISH SU4344

Cricketers (01264) 720335
B3048, off A303 just E of Andover; SP11 6PZ Cheerful village local under newish management; connecting rooms

and cosy corners, beams, bare boards and flagstones, two woodburners (one two-way), some cricketing and other sporting memorabilia, enjoyable fairly priced food (not Sun or Mon evenings) from baguettes and stone-baked pizzas up, four Wadworths ales, ciders from Symonds and Westons; quiz and live music nights; children and dogs welcome, back garden with terrace, summer Sun barbecues, open all day. *(Edward Mirzoeff)*

LYMINGTON SZ3295

Angel & Blue Pig (01590) 672050

High Street; SO41 9AP Busy town-centre Georgian inn; cosy right-hand room with comfortable sofas and armchairs, rugs on bare boards and an open fire, flagstoned area and two beamed rooms to the left of the entrance with old range in brick fireplace, large boar's head and lots of books, throughout are numerous hunting prints and porcine paraphernalia, back bar has some nice old leather armchairs by woodburner, four real ales including a house beer from Ringwood, 16 wines by the glass and cocktails, enjoyable brasserie-style food; live music every second Fri, children and dogs (in bar) welcome, terrace with seats under blue parasols, 14 stylish modern bedrooms, open (and food) all day. *(Greta and Gavin Craddock, Anne and Ben Smith, Phil and Jane Villiers)*

LYMINGTON SZ3293

Chequers (01590) 673415

Ridgeway Lane, Lower Woodside – dead end just S of A337 roundabout W of Lymington, by White Hart; SO41 8AH Old beamed pub with enjoyable food from traditional favourites up (smaller helpings available), Ringwood ales and good wines by the glass, bare boards and quarry tiles, mix of furniture including spindleback chairs, wall pews and country pine tables, yacht-racing pictures, woodburner; well behaved children and dogs welcome, tables and summer marquee in neat walled back garden, good walks and handy for bird-watching on Pennington Marshes, open all day, food all day weekends. *(Darren and Jane Staniforth, Phil and Jane Villiers)*

LYMINGTON SZ3295

Kings Head (01590) 672709

Quay Hill; SO41 3AR Friendly dimly lit old pub in steep cobbled lane of smart small shops; well kept Fullers, Ringwood, Timothy Taylors and a couple of guests, several wines by the glass and enjoyable uncomplicated food from sandwiches up, pleasant helpful staff, nice mix of old-fashioned furnishings in rambling beamed rooms, log fire and woodburner; background music, daily papers; children and dogs welcome, sunny little courtyard behind, open all day and can get very busy (food all day weekends). *(Darren and Jane Staniforth)*

LYMINGTON SZ3295

Monkey House (01590) 676754

Southampton Road (A337); SO41 9HA Updated beamed dining pub with good variety of well liked sensibly priced food from open sandwiches up, well kept ales including local Dancing Cows Pony and a dozen wines by the glass, pleasant helpful staff, two rooms divided by a couple of steps, lower one with high pitched ceiling, log fires; background and Sun live music, TV; children and dogs welcome, tables on paved terrace and grass, two bedrooms, open all day, food all day Sun. *(Mr and Mrs D J Nash)*

LYNDHURST SU2908

Fox & Hounds (023) 8028 2098

High Street; SO43 7BG Big busy low-beamed pub, comfortable and much modernised/extended; good food including weekday set lunch and Tues burger night, well kept Fullers/Gales beers and a guest, plenty of wines by the glass, cheerful efficient service, rambling interior with exposed brick and standing timbers, rugs on wood floors, log fires; regular live music, Mon quiz, free wi-fi; children and dogs welcome, disabled facilities, tables in paved courtyard garden with murals, open all day, food all day weekends. *(John Beeken)*

LYNDHURST SU2908

Waterloo Arms (023) 8028 2113

Pikes Hill, just off A337 N; SO43 7AS Thatched 17th-c New Forest pub with low beams, stripped-brick walls and log fire, two Ringwood beers and Sharps Doom Bar, enjoyable well priced pubby food including blackboard specials, friendly staff, comfortable bar and roomy back dining area; live music Sun; children and dogs welcome, terrace and nice big garden, open (and food) all day. *(Mrs P Sumner)*

MAPLEDURWELL SU6851

★**Gamekeepers** (01256) 322038

Off A30, not far from M3 junction 6; RG25 2LU Dark-beamed dining pub with good upmarket food (not cheap and they add a service charge) from regularly changing blackboard menu, also some pubby choices and lunchtime baguettes, welcoming helpful landlord and friendly efficient staff, three well kept local ales including Andwell, good coffee, a few sofas in flagstoned and panelled core, well spaced tables in large dining room; background music, TV; children and dogs (in bar) welcome, terrace and garden, lovely thatched village with duck pond, good walks, open all day weekends. *(Jackie Skinner)*

MARCHWOOD SU3809

Pilgrim (023) 8086 7752

Hythe Road, off A326 at Twiggs Lane; SO40 4WU Picturesque thatched pub (originally three 18th-c cottages) with enjoyable sensibly priced food from lunchtime sandwiches up, well kept Fullers ales and decent wines, friendly helpful staff, open fires; children and dogs welcome, tree-lined garden with circular picnic-sets, 14 stylish bedrooms in building across car park, open all day. *(Phil and Jane Villiers)*

MATTINGLEY SU7357

Leather Bottle (0118) 932 6371
3 miles from M3 junction 5; in Hook, turn right-and-left on to B3349 Reading Road (former A32); RG27 8JU Old red-brick pub (Home Counties group) converted from three cottages; three local ales including Andwell, plenty of wines by the glass and popular varied choice of food, friendly efficient service, well spaced tables in linked areas, black beams, flagstones and bare boards, inglenook log fire, extension opening on to covered terrace; background music; children and dogs (in bar) welcome, disabled access/facilities, two garden areas, open (and food) all day. *(John and Delia Franks)*

MEONSTOKE SU6120

Bucks Head (01489) 877313
Village signed just off A32 N of Droxford; SO32 3NA Opened-up tile-hung pub in lovely village setting with ducks on pretty little River Meon; stone floors and log fires, popular food from sandwiches to blackboard specials, three well kept ales including Greene King, good friendly service; children and dogs welcome, small walled gardens either side, one overlooking river, good walks, five bedrooms, open all day in summer (till 9.30pm Sun). *(Ann and Colin Hunt, Patric Curwen)*

MILFORD-ON-SEA SZ2891

Beach House (01590) 643044
Park Lane; SO41 0PT Civilised well placed Victorian hotel-dining pub owned by Hall & Woodhouse; restored oak-panelled interior, entrance hall bar with Badger First Gold, Tanglefoot and a guest, nice wines by the glass and enjoyable sensibly priced food from lunchtime sandwiches and sharing boards to specials, friendly helpful service, magnificent views from dining room and terrace; children welcome, dogs in bar, grounds down to the Solent looking out to the Needles, 15 bedrooms, open (and food) all day. *(David and Sally Frost, Alison Chalu, Katharine Cowherd)*

MINLEY MANOR SU8357

Crown & Cushion (01252) 545253
A327, just N of M3 junction 4A; GU17 9UA Recently refurbished and extended pub dating from 1512; three well kept Shepherd Neame ales, a dozen wines by the glass and decent selection of gins, good fairly priced food from ciabattas and sharing plates up including signature barbecue ribs, prompt cheerful service, Sun carvery in big separate 'meade hall' with rafters, flagstones and huge log fire, new airy dining extension; children welcome, no dogs inside, revamped outside area overlooking cricket pitch, open (and food) all day. *(KC)*

MINSTEAD SU2810

★**Trusty Servant** (023) 8081 2137
Just off A31, not far from M27 junction 1; SO43 7FY Attractive 19th-c red-brick dining pub in pretty New Forest hamlet with wandering cattle and ponies and plenty of easy walks; two-room bare-boards bar and big dining room, local pictures and hunting-themed prints, open fires, well kept ales such as Flack Manor, Ringwood, Sharps and Upham, several wines by the glass, good popular food from doorstep sandwiches and pub favourites to local game, friendly helpful staff; children and dogs welcome, terrace and big sloping garden, interesting church where Sir Arthur Conan Doyle is buried, five bedrooms, open (and food) all day. *(Tony Scott, Phil and Jane Villiers, Peter Meister)*

NEW CHERITON SU5827

★**Hinton Arms** (01962) 771252
A272 near B3046 junction; SO24 0NH Popular neatly kept country pub with cheerful accommodating landlord and friendly staff, three or four real ales including Bowman Wallops Wood and a house beer brewed by Hampshire, decent wines by the glass, large helpings of enjoyable pub food from sandwiches to daily specials, sporting pictures and memorabilia; TV lounge; well behaved children and dogs welcome, terrace and big garden, lots of colourful tubs and hanging baskets, very handy for Hinton Ampner House (NT). *(Ann and Colin Hunt, M and GR)*

NORTH WALTHAM SU5645

★**Fox** (01256) 397288
3 miles from M3 junction 7: A30 southwards, then turn right at second North Waltham turn, just after Wheatsheaf; pub also signed from village centre; RG25 2BE Well run traditional flint pub with low-ceilinged bar; Andwell, Brakspears, West Berkshire and a guest, Aspall's cider (many more in bottles) and good range of wines and whiskies, padded country kitchen chairs on parquet floor, poultry prints above dark dado, big woodburner, good food from sandwiches/baguettes to daily specials, larger separate dining room with high-backed leather chairs and blue tartan carpet; free wi-fi; children and dogs (in bar) welcome, picnic-sets under parasols in colourful garden with pergola walkway, pretty window boxes and hanging baskets, nice walks including one to Jane Austen's church at Steventon,

We accept no free drinks or meals and inspections are anonymous.

open all day. *(Miranda and Jeff Davidson, Michael and Margaret Cross)*

OVERTON SU5149

★**White Hart** (01256) 771431
London Road; RG25 3NW Handsome 500-year-old beamed inn with some contemporary touches; cosy bar with open fire, carved counter serving Upham ales, 12 wines by the glass and cocktails, two-level dining room has a central woodburner and there's another room with cushioned wall seating, interesting up-to-date food from lunchtime sandwiches up; live music first Fri of month, free wi-fi; children and dogs (in bar) welcome, suntrap garden (heated awning for cooler days), comfortable bedrooms in converted stable block, handy for Laverstoke Mill (home to Bombay Sapphire distillery), open all day. *(Lenny and Ruth Watson, Mark and Mary Setting, Freddie and Sarah Banks)*

OVINGTON SU5631

Bush (01962) 732764
Off A31 W of Alresford; SO24 0RE Popular 17th-c country pub in charming spot with streamside garden (lots of picnic-sets); low-ceilinged bar, high-backed settles, pews and lots of old pictures, log fire, well kept Wadworths ales and good choice of wines by the glass, enjoyable food from sandwiches and sharing boards up, friendly service; free wi-fi; children and dogs welcome, good local walks, open all day weekends, food all day Sun. *(Phil and Jane Villiers)*

OWER SU3216

Mortimer Arms (023) 8081 4379
Romsey Road, by M27 junction 2; SO51 6AF Under same ownership as the New Forest Inn at Emery Down; cosy informal bar with tables around three-sided servery, more formal restaurant, well kept ales such as Ringwood, a dozen wines by the glass and some decent gins, good food from bar snacks and sharing plates to specials, welcoming helpful service; events such as themed food weeks, quiz nights and ukulele band every other Tues; children (till 7pm in bar) and dogs welcome, picnic-sets in enclosed garden, handy for Paultons theme park, 14 bedrooms, good breakfast, open (and food) all day. *(Sara Fulton, Roger Baker)*

PETERSFIELD SU7423

Old Drum (01730) 300208
Chapel Street; GU32 3DP Renovated town-centre pub dating from the 18th c; airy L-shaped bar with antique-style dining chairs and tables on bare boards, comfortable seating by open fire, stools at counter serving Bowman Wallops Wood, Dark Star Hophead and guests, traditional cider/perry, 16 wines by the glass and ten malt whiskies, beamed dining room with more stripped boards and papered walls, food and service can be good; background music, free wi-fi; children welcome till 8pm, dogs in bar, seats in back courtyard garden with plants in raised beds, comfortable stylish bedrooms, open all day (till midnight Fri, Sat, 8pm Sun, Mon). *(Len and Lilly Dowson, Patricia Healey, Jim and Sue James)*

PETERSFIELD SU7423

Square Brewery (01730) 264291
The Square; GU32 3HJ Friendly town-centre pub in modern-rustic style; three well kept Fullers ales and a guest, decent choice of wines and enjoyable sensibly priced food including good lunchtime sandwiches, wood floors, painted panelling and central woodburner; background music (live bands Sat), monthly quiz first Thurs of month, free wi-fi; children and dogs welcome, seats out in front and in covered courtyard behind, open all day, no food Sat evening or after 7pm Sun. *(Ann and Colin Hunt)*

PETERSFIELD SU7129

★**White Horse** (01420) 588387
Up on an old downs road about halfway between Steep and East Tisted, near Priors Dean – OS Sheet 186 or 197 map reference 715290; GU32 1DA New tenants about to take over this much-loved place as we went to press, so no current news; unspoilt country pub (aka the Pub With No Name) with two charming parlour rooms, open fires, oak settles and a mix of dark wooden dining chairs around nice old tables, various pictures, farm tools and a longcase clock, a couple of fireside rocking chairs, smarter beamed dining room with lots of pictures on the white or pink walls, has served up to ten real ales, farm ciders, several wines by the glass (including country ones) and 20 malt whiskies; some rustic seats outside and camping facilities; reports please. *(Ann and Colin Hunt, Phil and Jane Villiers, Dr Martin Owton)*

PHOENIX GREEN SU7555

Phoenix (01252) 842484
London Road, A30 W of Hartley Wintney; RG27 8RT Beamed 18th-c pub with timber dividers, rugs on bare boards and big end inglenook, good freshly made food from varied daily changing menu including speciality steaks, four well kept ales, two good ciders and 16 wines by the glass, friendly prompt service, back dining room; children and dogs (in bar) welcome, pleasant outlook from sunny garden (hats provided). *(Charles and Maddie Trainer)*

PILLEY SZ3298

★**Fleur de Lys** (01590) 672158
Off A337 Brockenhurst–Lymington; Pilley Street; SO41 5QG Attractive thatched and beamed village pub with 11th-c origins; highly regarded restauranty food from shortish menu (booking advised), Courage Directors, Sharps Doom Bar and a guest, good wines, friendly helpful service, inglenook log fires; well behaved children

and dogs welcome, pretty garden with old well, good forest and heathland walks, open all day Sat, till 6pm Sun, closed Mon. *(Dr and Mrs F McGinn, Mr and Mrs D J Nash)*

PORTSMOUTH SU6400

Brewhouse & Kitchen

(023) 9289 1340 *Guildhall Walk next to Theatre Royal; PO1 2DD* Popular mock-Tudor pub (former White Swan) visibly brewing its own good beers, also decent choice of well priced food from sandwiches and small plates up, friendly helpful staff; children welcome, open (and food) all day. *(Ann and Colin Hunt)*

PORTSMOUTH SZ6399

Bridge Tavern (023) 9275 2992

East Street, Camber Dock; PO1 2JJ Flagstones, bare boards and lots of dark wood, comfortable furnishings, maritime theme with good harbour views, Fullers ales and a dozen wines by the glass, generous helpings of good sensibly priced food including plenty of fish dishes, upstairs dining rooms (more modern and airy); children welcome, painted picnic-sets on waterside terrace, open all day and busy with diners at weekends (kitchen closes 6pm Sun). *(Ann and Colin Hunt, Jess and George Cowley)*

PORTSMOUTH SU6501

George (023) 9275 3885

Queen Street, near dockyard entrance; PO1 3HU Spotless old inn (Grade I listed) with two rooms (one set for dining), log fire, glass-covered well and maritime pictures, well kept Greene King Abbot, Sharps Atlantic and Doom Bar, well priced food (not Sun evening, Mon lunchtime) from sandwiches up, friendly staff; eight bedrooms, handy for dockyard and HMS *Victory*, open all day. *(Ann and Colin Hunt)*

PORTSMOUTH SU6706

George (023) 9222 1079

Portsdown Hill Road, Widley; PO6 1BE Comfortable one-bar Georgian pub with friendly local feel (despite being surrounded by busy roads); seven well kept ales and good range of gins, popular pubby food including good ploughman's, helpful pleasant staff; live music Tues, quiz every other Sun; dogs welcome, picnic-sets on side terrace, views of Hayling Island, Portsmouth and Isle of Wight, hill walks across the road, open all day. *(Isobel Mackinlay)*

PORTSMOUTH SZ6399

★**Old Customs House**

(023) 9283 2333 *Vernon Buildings, Gunwharf Quays; follow brown signs to Gunwharf Quays car park; PO1 3TY* Well converted 18th-c former customs house (Grade I listed) in prime waterfront development; big-windowed, high-ceilinged rooms with nautical prints and photographs, coal-effect gas fires, well padded chairs around sturdy tables on bare boards, broad stairs up to carpeted restaurant, enjoyable food from 9am breakfast on, Fullers/Gales beers and a couple of guests, decent range of wines by the glass, coffees and teas, efficient staff; background music, silenced games machines, free wi-fi; children and dogs (in bar) welcome, downstairs disabled access and facilities, handy for the Spinnaker Tower, open all day. *(Tony Scott, Miss A E Dare)*

PORTSMOUTH SZ6399

Pembroke (023) 9282 3961

Pembroke Road; PO1 2NR Traditional well run corner local with good buoyant atmosphere, comfortable and unspoilt under long-serving licensees, Bass, Fullers London Pride and Greene King Abbot from L-shaped bar, simple cheap food including fresh rolls, coal-effect gas fire; monthly live music, darts; dogs welcome, open all day (break 5-7pm every other Sun when there's a quiz night). *(Ann and Colin Hunt)*

PORTSMOUTH SU6300

Ship Anson (023) 9282 4152

Victory Road, The Hard (opposite Esplanade Station, Portsea); PO1 3DT No-frills mock-Tudor pub close to dockyard entrance, spacious and comfortable, with well kept Greene King ales and a guest, generous pub food at bargain prices, also coffee and cakes, buoyant local atmosphere; fruit machines, sports TVs; children welcome, seats outside overlooking ferry port, very handy for HMS *Victory*, open (and food) all day. *(Jess and George Cowley, Ann and Colin Hunt)*

PORTSMOUTH SZ6299

Still & West (023) 9282 1567

Bath Square, Old Portsmouth; PO1 2JL Great location with superb views of narrow harbour mouth and across to Isle of Wight, especially from glazed-in panoramic upper family area and waterfront terrace; nautical bar with fireside sofas, Fullers ales and good choice of wines by the glass, enjoyable all-day food from sandwiches and sharing plates to good fish dishes; background music, free wi-fi; dogs welcome in bar, handy for Historic Dockyard, nearby pay-and-display parking, open from 10am (11.30am Sun). *(Ann and Colin Hunt, Colin Gooch)*

RINGWOOD SU1504

Railway (01425) 473701

Hightown Road; BH24 1NQ Traditional two-bar Victorian local with up to four well kept changing ales (usually one from nearby Ringwood), enjoyable home-made food including range of burgers, also vegan/vegetarian menu, friendly service; Thurs quiz, darts; children and dogs welcome, nice enclosed garden with play area, vegetable patch, ducks and chickens, open all day. *(Joe Tilford)*

ROMSEY SU3521

Old House at Home (01794) 513175
Love Lane; SO51 8DE Attractive 17th-c thatched pub surrounded by new development; friendly and bustling, with comfortable low-beamed interior, wide choice of freshly made sensibly priced bar food including popular Sun lunch, well kept Fullers/Gales beers and a guest, cheerful service; regular folk sessions; children and dogs (in bar) welcome, split-level back terrace, open all day (no food Sun evening). *(Tony and Wendy Hobden)*

ROMSEY SU3520

Three Tuns (01794) 512639
Middlebridge Street (but car park signed straight off A27 bypass); SO51 8HL Good well presented food is the star at this old village pub but they do keep four beers including Flack Manor, local cider and 11 wines by the glass; bar with cushioned bow-window seat, dark wooden tables on flagstones, beer mats pinned to the walls and church candles in fireplace, dining areas either side, one with a huge stuffed fish over another fireplace, the other with prints on yellow walls above a black dado, a few rugs scattered around, heavy beams and antler chandeliers; background music, board games, free wi-fi; children and dogs welcome, back terrace with picnic-sets under parasols, more seats in front by the tiny street, open all day. *(R K Phillips, Phil and Jane Villiers)*

ROTHERWICK SU7156

Coach & Horses (01256) 768976
Signed from B3349 N of Hook; also quite handy for M3 junction 5; RG27 9BG Friendly 17th-c pub with traditional beamed front rooms, well kept Badger ales and good choice of popular reasonably priced pubby food including specials, cheerful accommodating staff, log fire and woodburners, newer back dining area; open mike night first Weds of month, quiz fourth Tues; children, dogs and muddy boots welcome, tables out at front behind picket fence and on back terrace overlooking fields, pretty flower tubs and hanging baskets, good walks, open all day Sat, till 6pm Sun, closed Mon (except bank holidays). *(Tony and Jill Radnor, Darren and Jane Staniforth)*

ROTHERWICK SU7156

Falcon (01256) 765422
Off B3349 N of Hook, not far from M3 junction 5; RG27 9BL Welcoming open-plan country pub (some recent refurbishment); good freshly made food, well kept ales and decent selection of wines and gins, friendly efficient service, rustic tables and comfy sofas in bare-boards bar, flagstoned dining area, log fires; quiz and live music nights, free wi-fi; children and dogs welcome (resident black labrador), disabled access, tables out in front and in back garden, open all day, food all day Sun. *(John and Delia Franks)*

ROWLAND'S CASTLE SU7310

Castle Inn (023) 9241 2494
Off B2148/B2149 N of Havant; Finchdean Road; PO9 6DA Comfortable little country local with public bar one side and larger dining bar the other, good choice of Fullers/Gales ales and enjoyable reasonably priced pubby food (not Sun evening), friendly service, log fire; children and dogs welcome, good-sized garden, nice local walks, open all day. *(Ann and Colin Hunt)*

SELBORNE SU7433

Selborne Arms (01420) 511247
High Street; GU34 3JR Old-fashioned 17th-c beamed village pub; character tables, pews and deep settles made from casks on antique boards, good range of local ales and popular food from lunchtime baguettes up, big log fire, carpeted dining room with local photographs; quiz and live music nights; children welcome, no dogs inside, garden with arbour and terrace heated by logburner, orchard and play area, zigzag path up the Hanger, handy for Gilbert White's House, open all day weekends. *(Ann and Colin Hunt)*

SHALDEN SU7043

Golden Pot (01420) 80655
B3349 Odiham Road N of Alton; GU34 4DJ Airy light décor with timbered walls, bare boards and log fires, decent food from baguettes up including themed nights, friendly service, a couple of ales such as Sharps Doom Bar and Triple fff Altons Pride, local artwork for sale in smallish restaurant; background music, skittle alley; children and dogs welcome, benches out in covered area at front, garden with play area, open all day. *(Mary and Douglas McDowell)*

SHEDFIELD SU5613

Samuels Rest (01329) 832213
Upper Church Road (signed off B2177); SO32 2JB Cosy and welcoming village local overlooking cricket pitch; well kept Wadworths ales and generous helpings of enjoyable sensibly priced home-made food, nice eating area away from bar, conservatory; some live music including folk night third Weds of month, pool and darts, free wi-fi; children and dogs (in bar) welcome, aviary with parrots, good sized garden, lovely church nearby, open all day, food all day weekends (till about 7pm Sun). *(Ann and Colin Hunt)*

SHEDFIELD SU5513

Wheatsheaf (01329) 833024
A334 Wickham–Botley; SO32 2JG Friendly recently extended/spruced-up traditional local, well kept/priced Flowerpots and guests tapped from the cask, proper cider, short sensible choice of enjoyable

bargain lunches (evening food Tues and Weds), good service; live music Sat, darts; dogs welcome, garden, handy for Wickham Vineyard, open all day. *(Ann and Colin Hunt)*

SHERFIELD ENGLISH SU3022

Hatchet (01794) 322487

Romsey Road; SO51 6FP Beamed and panelled 18th-c pub with good choice of popular fairly priced food including two-for-one steak deal (Tues, Thurs evenings) and OAP lunch (Mon-Thurs), four well kept ales such as Dartmoor, St Austell, Sharps and Timothy Taylors, good wine choice, friendly hard-working staff, long bar with cosy area down steps, woodburner, more steps up to second bar with darts, TV and juke box; monthly quiz; children and dogs (on leads) welcome, outside seating on two levels, play area, open all day weekends. *(Jackie Skinner)*

SHIPTON BELLINGER SU2345

Boot (01980) 842279

High Street; SP9 7UF Village pub with vast range of enjoyable reasonably priced food including chinese, thai, italian and mexican alongside traditional english dishes, friendly staff; background music; children welcome, garden behind with decked area, open all day Sun. *(Charles and Maddie Bishop)*

SOBERTON SU6116

White Lion (01489) 877346

School Hill; signed off A32 S of Droxford; SO32 3PF Attractive unchanging 17th-c pub in nice spot opposite raised village green; enjoyable home-made food from baguettes up, four real ales including Bowman and Sharps, good range of wines by the glass, friendly efficient service, low-ceilinged bar with built-in wall seats and open fire, separate small restaurant; children and dogs welcome, sheltered garden and suntrap terrace, good walks nearby, stable-conversion bedrooms, open all day, food all day Sun. *(Ann and Colin Hunt)*

SOPLEY SZ1596

Woolpack (01425) 672252

B3347 N of Christchurch; BH23 7AX Pretty 17th-c thatched dining pub with rambling open-plan low-beamed bar, enjoyable traditional food plus daily specials and range of sandwiches and wraps, well kept Ringwood Razorback, Sharps Doom Bar and a guest, Thatcher's cider and good choice of wines by the glass, modern dining conservatory overlooking weir; children and dogs (menu for them) welcome, terrace and charming garden with weeping willows, duck stream and footbridges, open (and food) all day. *(Edward Nile)*

SOUTHAMPTON SU4314

Butchers Hook (023) 8178 2280

Manor Farm Road; SO18 1NN One-room micro-pub in former Bitterne Park butchers (some original features remain including tiling), changing cask and keg beers from scaffold stillage (no bar), good bottled range too and real cider, friendly helpful service, no food (can bring your own); board games; well behaved dogs welcome, a few bench seats out in front, closed Mon, Tues and lunchtimes Weds-Fri, open all day Sat from 1pm, Sun from 2pm, gets packed at busy times. *(Dr Martin Owton)*

SOUTHAMPTON SU4111

Dancing Man (023) 8083 6666

Bugle Street/Town Quay; SO14 2AR Ancient listed building with plenty of atmosphere and character; up to 12 interesting beers including eight from on-site brewery (tours available), enjoyable food with creole/cajun influences and good choice for vegans, friendly efficient service, sweeping staircase to upper dining area with own bar and fine raftered ceiling; children and dogs welcome (menus for both), disabled access and lift, open all day. *(Phil and Jane Villiers)*

SOUTHAMPTON SU4111

★**Duke of Wellington**

(023) 8033 9222 *Bugle Street (or walk along city wall from Bar Gate); SO14 2AH* Striking timber-framed building dating from the 14th c (cellars even older); heavy beams and fine log fire, up to nine well kept Wadworths ales (tasting trays available), plenty of wines by the glass and good fairly priced food (not Sun evening), friendly helpful service; background music (live jazz Fri), free wi-fi; children welcome, sunny streetside picnic-sets, handy for Tudor House & Garden, open all day. *(Phil and Jane Villiers)*

SOUTHAMPTON SU4213

Rockstone (023) 8063 7256

Onslow Road; SO14 0JL Popular relaxed place with well liked generous food from signature burgers to asian street food (booking advised), good variety of real ales, craft beers and ciders from well stocked bar, friendly hard-working staff; some live music; children welcome, seats out at front, open (and food) all day (till 1am Fri, Sat). *(Mo Dobson)*

SOUTHAMPTON SU4213

White Star (023) 8082 1990

Oxford Street; SO14 3DJ Modernised opened-up bar with crescent-shaped banquettes, panelling and open fires, wood or stone floors, comfortable sofas and armchairs in secluded alcoves by south-facing windows, bistro-style dining area serving good up-to-date food along with pub favourites, Fullers ales and nice choice of wines by the glass, efficient attentive staff; background music; sunny pavement tables on pedestrianised street, 13 boutique bedrooms, open all day from 7am (8.30am weekends) for breakfast. *(Mo Dobson)*

SOUTHSEA SZ6699

Artillery Arms (023) 9273 3610

Hester Road; PO4 8HB Traditional two-bar Victorian backstreet local, half a dozen well kept ales including Triple fff, no food apart from rolls on match days (near Fratton Park), friendly atmosphere; Mon quiz, sports TV, pool and darts; children and dogs welcome, garden with play equipment, open all day. *(Tony Scott)*

SOUTHSEA SZ6498

Belle Isle (023) 9282 0515

Osbourne Road; PO5 3LR Popular café-bar-restaurant in former shop, friendly and relaxed, with interesting continental-feel décor, three real ales, international bottled beers, cocktails and eclectic blackboard menu, decent coffee too; background music; children welcome, a few seats out at front under awning, open all day. *(Millie and Peter Downing)*

SOUTHSEA SZ6698

Eastney Tavern (023) 9282 6246

Cromwell Road; PO4 9PN Bow-fronted corner pub just off the seafront, spacious and comfortable, with various eating areas (plenty of room for drinkers too), popular good value food including Weds steak night and Thurs curry (reduced menu Mon), Sharps Doom Bar and a couple of local guests, decent choice of wines by the glass, good cheerful service; Tues quiz, live music last Fri of the month, sports TV; children and dogs welcome, seats in courtyard garden, nearby parking difficult, closed Mon lunchtime, otherwise open all day. *(Ann and Colin Hunt)*

SOUTHSEA SZ6499

★Hole in the Wall (023) 9229 8085

Great Southsea Street; PO5 3BY Friendly unspoilt little local in old part of town, six interesting well kept/priced ales including Flowerpots Goodens Gold, four craft kegs and good range of bottled beers, real cider/perry, speciality local sausages and other simple good value food (evenings Tues-Sat, lunchtime Fri), nicely worn boards, dark pews and panelling, old photographs and prints, hundreds of pump clips on ceiling, little snug behind the bar and sweet shop; Oct beer festival; dogs welcome, small outside area at front with benches, side garden, open all day from 4pm (noon Fri, 2pm Sat and Sun). *(Phil and Jane Villiers, Ann and Colin Hunt)*

SOUTHSEA SZ6499

King Street Tavern (023) 9307 3568

King Street; PO5 4EH Refurbished corner pub with fine Victorian tiled façade in attractive conservation area; four well kept Wadworths ales and a couple of guests, craft kegs and two proper ciders, enjoyable good value food from smokehouse/barbecue menu, friendly atmosphere; live music including irish folk session every other Thurs, big-screen sports TV; children welcome, courtyard tables, open all day Fri and Sat, till 7pm Sun, closed lunchtimes Mon, Tues (and Weds in winter). *(Anne Taylor)*

SOUTHSEA SZ6498

Meat & Barrel (023) 9217 6291

Palmerston Road; PO5 3PT Sizeable bar-restaurant under same ownership as Southsea's Belle Isle; fine range of real ales and craft beers, tasters offered by friendly knowledgeable staff, enjoyable food including range of burgers and various sausage and mash combinations; children welcome, open all day. *(Anne Taylor)*

SOUTHSEA SZ6499

Wine Vaults (023) 9286 4712

Albert Road, opposite King's Theatre; PO5 2SF Bustling Fullers pub with several chatty rooms on different floors; main panelled bar with long plain counter and pubby furniture on bare boards, seven well kept ales and decent choice of food including pizzas and range of burgers, good service, separate restaurant; background music, live jazz or folk every other Tues, sports TV, table football; children welcome, dogs in bar, smokers' roof terrace, open (and food) all day. *(Anne Taylor)*

SOUTHWICK SU6208

Golden Lion (023) 9221 0437

High Street; just off B2177 on Portsdown Hill; PO17 6EB Spotless two-bar 16th-c beamed pub (where Eisenhower and Montgomery came before D-Day) under welcoming ebullient landlord; up to seven well kept local ales including two from Suthwyk using barley from surrounding fields, four ciders and a dozen wines by the glass, good locally sourced home-made food (not Sun or Mon evenings) from snacks up in bar and dining room, cosy lounge with sofas and log fire, live music including Tues jazz; good outside loos; children and dogs welcome, picnic-sets on side grass, picturesque Estate village with scenic walks, next to Southwick Brewhouse shop/museum (over 250 bottled beers), open all day Sat, till 7pm Sun. *(Suzy Miller, Ann and Colin Hunt, Penny and Peter Keevil, Paula Allen)*

STOCKBRIDGE SU3535

Greyhound (01264) 810833

High Street; SO20 6EY Substantial inn reworked as civilised pub-restaurant; log fires each end of bow-windowed bar (restaurant to the right), scrubbed old tables on woodstrip floor, dark low beams, highly regarded food from interesting varied menu (not cheap), three real ales including a house beer from Ringwood, good wine and whisky choice, friendly efficient staff (service charge added); children and dogs allowed, tables in charming Test-side garden behind, ten bedrooms, good walks and fly fishing, open all day. *(Andrew Lawson)*

STOCKBRIDGE SU3535

Three Cups (01264) 810527
High Street; SO20 6HB Lovely low-beamed building dating from 1500, spruced up and added to yet keeping country inn feel, some emphasis on dining with lots of smartly set tables, but also high-backed settles and rustic bric-a-brac, four well kept interesting ales and nice wines by the glass, generally well liked food from shortish menu including one or two pub favourites, friendly if not always prompt service, back 'orangery' restaurant extension; children and dogs welcome, charming streamside garden with vine-covered terrace, eight bedrooms (back ones quieter), open all day. *(Edward Mirzoeff)*

STOCKBRIDGE SU3535

White Hart (01264) 810663
High Street; A272/A3057 roundabout; SO20 6HF Spacious village-edge pub with pleasantly busy divided beamed bar, attractive décor with antique prints, oak pews and other seats around pine tables, decent choice of enjoyable food from bar snacks to daily specials, well kept Fullers/Gales beers, good friendly service, comfortable restaurant with open fire (children allowed); dogs in bar, terrace tables and nice garden, 14 bedrooms (more planned), open all day. *(Edward Mirzoeff, Ann and Colin Hunt, David and Judy Robison)*

SWANMORE SU5716

Brickmakers (01489) 890954
Church Road; SO32 2PA Large restyled 1920s pub in centre of village, friendly and relaxed, with four well kept ales (Bowman Wallops Wood always on), decent wines and good food cooked by landlord-chef including popular Sun roasts and OAP weekday lunch deal, cheerful efficient service, leather sofas by log fire, pitched-roof dining area with local artwork; Tues quiz, some live music; children and dogs welcome (pub dog is Rosie), garden with raised deck, nearby walks, open (and food) all day, except Sun when kitchen closes at 5.30pm. *(Ann and Colin Hunt)*

SWANMORE SU5815

Rising Sun (01489) 896663
Droxford Road; signed off A32 N of Wickham and B2177 S of Bishop's Waltham, at Hillpound E of village centre; SO32 2PS Welcoming 17th-c brick coaching inn; low-beamed carpeted bar, comfortable seating by log fire, pleasant roomier dining area with brick barrel vaulting in one part, a house beer from Flack Manor along with Flowerpots Goodens Gold and a local guest, good range of wines by the glass and enjoyable reasonably priced home-cooked food including daily specials, friendly speedy service; children and dogs (in bar) welcome, picnic-sets on side grass with play area, King's Way long-distance path nearby, closed Sun evening, Mon lunchtime. *(Shesh Bazzar, Ann and Colin Hunt)*

SWAY SZ2898

Hare & Hounds (01590) 682404
Durns Town, just off B3055 SW of Brockenhurst; SO41 6AL Comfortable New Forest family dining pub with hearty helpings of home-cooked food including daily specials, well kept ales such as Itchen Valley, Ringwood, St Austell and Timothy Taylors, good friendly service, some low beams and central log fire; background music, Sun quiz; children and dogs welcome, picnic-sets and play frame in neatly kept garden, open all day. *(Joe Tilford)*

THRUXTON SU2945

White Horse (01264) 772401
Mullens Pond, just off A303 eastbound; SP11 8EE Attractive old thatched pub (tucked below A303 embankment) with emphasis on enjoyable freshly made food, good friendly service, plenty of wines by the glass and well kept ales such as Greene King, spacious comfortably modernised interior with very low beams, woodburner and separate dining area; regular live music and other events; good-sized garden and terrace, summer barbecues, four bedrooms, open all day (Sun till 6pm). *(Mrs Zara Elliott)*

TICHBORNE SU5730

★**Tichborne Arms** (01962) 733760
Signed off B3047; SO24 0NA Welcoming old-fashioned thatched pub (rebuilt in the 1930s) at the edge of this quiet little village; half-panelled bare-boards bar with interesting pictures and other odds and ends, candlelit pine tables and raised woodburner, Palmers and local guests tapped from cooled casks, real cider, good fairly traditional home-made food (not Sun or Mon evenings, booking advised), friendly attentive service, locals' bar with piano, darts and open fire; children and dogs welcome, sheltered terrace and large peaceful garden with water meadow views, close to Wayfarers Walk and Itchen Way, open all day Sat, till 7.30pm Sun. *(Tony and Jill Radnor, David and Judy Robison)*

TITCHFIELD SU5305

Queens Head (01329) 842154
High Street; off A27 near Fareham; PO14 4AQ Welcoming early 17th-c family-run pub with enjoyable home-made food and four well kept changing ales; cosy bar with old local pictures, window seats and warm winter fire in central brick fireplace, small dining room; Sun quiz, function room for nostalgic dinner-dance and theatre nights; children welcome, picnic-sets in prettily planted backyard, pleasant conservation village near nature reserve and walks to coast, open all day. *(Jackie Skinner)*

TITCHFIELD SU5405

Wheatsheaf (01329) 842965
East Street; off A27 near Fareham; PO14 4AD Welcoming old pub with small bow-windowed front bar and large back restaurant extension, good food including small-plates menu, Tues steak night and popular Sun roasts, five well kept ales such as Flowerpots and Palmers, log fires; background music; terrace tables behind, open all day, food all day Sat, till 6.45pm Sun. *(Ann and Colin Hunt)*

TWYFORD SU4824

★**Bugle** (01962) 714888
B3355/Park Lane; SO21 1QT Modern dining pub with good enterprising food (highish prices) from daily changing menu, also lunchtime sandwiches/snacks and Mon evening set deal, well kept ales such as Bowman, Flowerpots and Upham, nice wines by the glass, attentive friendly young staff; background music; seats on attractive verandah, good walks nearby, three country-style bedrooms, open all day, no food Sun evening. *(Lorna and Jeff Mason)*

TWYFORD SU4824

Phoenix (01962) 713322
High Street (B3335); SO21 1RF Cheerful open-plan local with raised dining area and big inglenook log fire, jovial long-serving landlord and friendly attentive staff, eight well kept ales including Greene King, good value wines and large helpings of enjoyable traditional food from reasonably priced menu; background music, sports TV, quiz nights, skittle alley; children welcome, side terraces, open all day in summer. *(Ann and Colin Hunt)*

UPHAM SU5320

Brushmakers Arms (01489) 860231
Shoe Lane; village signed from Winchester–Bishop's Waltham downs road, and from B2177; SO32 1JJ Welcoming low-beamed village pub; L-shaped bar divided by central woodburner, cushioned settles and chairs around mix of tables, various brushes (once made here) and related paraphernalia, little back snug, enjoyable locally sourced home-made food, Bowman, Flack Manor, Flowerpots and a guest, good choice of wines; quiz first Weds of month, folk session third Sun (from 5pm); children and dogs welcome (there's a pub dog), big garden with picnic-sets on sheltered terrace and tree-shaded lawn, good nearby walks, open all day weekends, no food Sun evening in winter. *(Ann and Colin Hunt)*

UPPER CLATFORD SU3543

Crook & Shears (01264) 361543
Off A343 S of Andover, via Foundry Road; SP11 7QL Cosy and welcoming 17th-c thatched pub; well kept Otter and Ringwood ales, Thatcher's cider and reasonably priced traditional food (not Sun evening, Mon) from good baguettes to enjoyable Sun roasts, also Tues steak night, friendly attentive service, open fires and woodburner, small dining room, back skittle alley with own bar; children and dogs welcome, pleasant secluded garden behind, closed Mon lunchtime. *(Sandra and Neil White)*

UPPER FARRINGDON SU7135

Rose & Crown (01420) 587001
Off A32 S of Alton; Crows Lane – follow Church, Selborne, Liss signpost; GU34 3ED Early 19th-c tile-hung village pub freshened up under welcoming new management; L-shaped bar with bare boards and log fire, local ales, plenty of wines by the glass and nice range of gins, good food (not Sun evening) from pub favourites up including Mon steak night, friendly helpful service, back dining room; children and dogs welcome wide views from attractive garden, open all day Sat, till 9pm Sun. *(Guy Vowles, Tony and Jill Radnor)*

UPTON SU3555

Crown (01264) 736044
N of Hurstbourne Tarrant, off A343; SP11 0JS Popular old country pub refurbished under present licensees; good imaginative food from bar snacks up, two or three changing regional ales and well chosen wines by the glass including english sparkling, friendly helpful service, nice log fire, coffee lounge, restaurant and conservatory, also recently added farm shop; children and dogs (in bar) welcome, small garden and terrace, closed Mon and Tues, otherwise open all day, weekend brunch from 10am. *(Sally and Brian Turner)*

UPTON GREY SU6948

Hoddington Arms (01256) 862371
Signed off B3349 S of Hook; Bidden Road; RG25 2RL Nicely updated 18th-c beamed pub; good food from varied menu (not Sun evening), Flowerpots, Ringwood and a local guest, ten wines by the glass, friendly staff; events including live music, movie nights and beer/cider festivals; children and dogs welcome, big enclosed garden with terrace, quiet pretty village with interesting Gertrude Jekyll garden, good walking/cycling, open all day Fri-Sun. *(Nicholas and Maddy Trainer)*

VERNHAM DEAN SU3456

George (01264) 737279
Centre of village; SP11 0JY Rambling open-plan 17th-c beamed and timbered pub with notable eyebrow windows, some exposed brick and flint, inglenook log fire, well kept Flack Manor, Greene King, Hop Back and a guest, popular home-made pubby food (not Sun evening), good friendly service; variety of events including Aug beer festival; children and dogs welcome, pretty garden behind,

lovely thatched village and fine walks, open all day (Sun till 6pm). *(David and Judy Robison)*

WALHAMPTON SZ3396

Walhampton Arms (01590) 673113
B3054 NE of Lymington; aka Walhampton Inn; SO41 5RE Large comfortable Georgian-style family roadhouse handy for Isle of Wight ferry; popular well priced food including daily carvery in raftered former stables and two adjoining areas, pleasant lounge, Ringwood and Flack Manor ales and traditional cider, cheerful helpful staff; quiz nights; attractive courtyard, good walks, open (and food) all day. *(Anne Taylor)*

WALTHAM CHASE SU5614

Black Dog (01329) 832316
Winchester Road; SO32 2LX Old brick-built country pub with low-ceilinged carpeted front bar, three well kept Greene King ales and a guest, over a dozen wines by the glass and enjoyable well priced food (all day Sun) from basket meals up including weekday offers, cheerful helpful service, log fires, extended back restaurant; some live music, sports TV; children and dogs welcome, tables under parasols in good-sized neatly kept garden with deck, play area and colourful hanging baskets, open all day weekends. *(Ann and Colin Hunt, Joy Griffiths)*

WELL SU7646

★**Chequers** (01256) 862605
Off A287 via Crondall, or A31 via Froyle and Lower Froyle; RG29 1TL Appealing low-beamed country dining pub; very good restaurant-style food (some quite pricey) including fresh fish/seafood, also brasserie menu and lunchtime sandwiches, Badger ales kept well and good choice of wines, wood floors, panelling and log fires; free wi-fi; bench seating on vine-covered front terrace, spacious back garden overlooking fields, open (and food) all day. *(Jackie Skinner)*

WEST MEON SU6424

★**Thomas Lord** (01730) 829244
High Street; GU32 1LN Named after founder of Lord's Cricket Ground, so lots of cricketing memorabilia – even stuffed squirrels playing the game in cabinet above counter; bar has leather chesterfield and armchairs by log fire, animal-hide stools, wooden chairs and corner settles on parquet, Upham ales and guests, a dozen wines by the glass and good quality food using local produce (own vegetables and eggs), small similarly furnished room off with antlers above fireplace, slightly more formal restaurant and snug with big photo mural of local countryside; background music, board games, free wi-fi; children and dogs (in bar) welcome, picnic-sets in sizeable garden with pizza oven and barbecue, open all day. *(Peter Brix, Lindy Andrews, Holly and Tim Waite)*

WEST TYTHERLEY SU2730

Black Horse (01794) 340308
North Lane; SP5 1NF Compact unspoilt village local with welcoming chatty atmosphere; traditional beamed bar with a couple of long tables, woodburner in big fireplace, four mainly local ales and a real cider, nicely set dining area serving enjoyable reasonably priced food including Thurs steak night and good Sun roasts; quiz last Thurs of month, skittle alley; children, walkers and dogs welcome, open all day Sun till 7pm, closed Mon and lunchtime Tues. *(Gerry and Pam Pollard)*

WHERWELL SU3839

Mayfly (01264) 860283
Testcombe (over by Fullerton, not in Wherwell itself); A3057 SE of Andover, between B3420 turn-off and Leckford where road crosses River Test; OS Sheet 185 map reference 382390; SO20 6AX Busy red-brick pub in lovely position overlooking fast-flowing River Test; spacious beamed and carpeted bar with fishing paraphernalia, rustic pub furnishings and woodburner, Fullers ales and extensive range of wines by the glass, generally well liked food (must book for a good table), conservatory; background music; well behaved children and dogs welcome, plenty of riverside picnic-sets on terrace and grass, open (and food) all day. *(Martin Day)*

WHERWELL SU3840

White Lion (01264) 860317
B3420; SP11 7JF Early 17th-c multi-level beamed village inn, popular and friendly, with good choice of enjoyable food including speciality pies, well kept Sharps, Timothy Taylors and a local guest, ciders such as Orchard Pig and several wines by the glass, cheery helpful staff, open fire, comfy leather sofas and armchairs, dining rooms either side of bar; background music; well behaved children welcome, dogs on leads, teak furniture in sunny courtyard, Test Way walks, three bedrooms, open all day Sat, till 9pm Sun, closed Mon (apart from bank holidays). *(Martin Day, Edward Mirzoeff)*

WICKHAM SU5711

Greens (01329) 833197
The Square, at junction with A334; PO17 5JQ Civilised restauranty place with clean-cut modern décor, small bar with leather sofa and armchairs on light wood floor, extensive wine choice and a couple of real ales, obliging young staff, step down to split-level balustraded dining areas with good imaginative food along with more traditional choices and lunchtime set menu; background music; children welcome if eating, pleasant lawn overlooking water meadows, closed Sun evening, Mon. *(Sally and Brian Turner)*

WINCHESTER SU4829

Bishop on the Bridge
(01962) 855111 *High Street/Bridge Street; SO23 9JX* Popular 19th-c red-brick Fullers pub by the River Itchen; their well kept beers (not cheap) and enjoyable food from sandwiches to daily specials, good friendly service, opened up traditional bare-boards interior; free wi-fi; children and dogs welcome, nice back terrace overlooking the river, open all day. *(Edward Nile)*

WINCHESTER SU4828

★**Black Boy** (01962) 861754
B3403 off M3 junction 10 towards city, then left into Wharf Hill; no nearby daytime parking – 220 metres from car park on B3403; SO23 9NQ Wonderfully eccentric décor at this chatty old-fashioned pub, floor-to-ceiling books, lots of big clocks, mobiles made of wine bottles or spectacles, variety of stuffed animals including a baboon, donkey and dachshund, two open fires, orange-painted room with big oriental rugs on red floorboards, also a barn room with open hayloft, five well kept local ales, real cider and decent straightforward home-made food (not Sun evening, Mon) from sandwiches up, friendly service; table football and board games; supervised children and dogs welcome, slate tables out in front and seats on attractive secluded terrace, ten bedrooms in adjoining building, open all day. *(Ann and Colin Hunt, Phil and Jane Villiers)*

WINCHESTER SU4829

Eclipse (01962) 865676
The Square, between High Street and cathedral; SO23 9EX Picturesque unspoilt 16th-c local with massive beams and timbers in two small rooms, up to four real ales (can be pricey) such as Sharps Timothy Taylors and Youngs, proper ciders and decent choice of wines by the glass, traditional lunchtime food including Sun roasts, oak settles and open fire; children in back area, seats outside, handy for the cathedral, open all day. *(Edward Nile)*

WINCHESTER SU4830

Hyde Tavern (01962) 862592
Hyde Street (B3047); SO23 7DY Cosy 15th-c gabled pub with friendly chatty atmosphere in two wonderfully old-fashioned bars, well kept ales and a couple of proper ciders, no food (can bring your own), open fire; regular live music including folk nights, storytelling and writers' workshops, quiz first Sun of month, Father's Day beer festival; steps down to cellar bar and secluded garden, open all day weekends, shut weekdays till 5pm. *(Ann and Colin Hunt)*

WINCHESTER SU4829

★**Old Vine** (01962) 854616
Great Minster Street; SO23 9HA Popular big-windowed town bar with four well kept ales including local Alfreds, plenty of wines by the glass and decent range of whiskies, high beams and worn oak boards, larger dining side and modern conservatory (young children here only), good variety of food from sandwiches and pub staples up, efficient friendly service even though busy; background music; dogs welcome in bar, wheelchair accessible using ramp (no access to lavatories), by cathedral with a few pavement seats, more tables in partly covered back terrace, charming bedrooms, open all day. *(Richard Tilbrook)*

WINCHESTER SU4728

Queen (01962) 890542
Kingsgate Road; SO23 9PG Cottagey twin-gabled pub in attractive setting opposite College cricket ground; cosy interior with bare boards and log fire, up to ten well kept ales including own brews (tasting trays available), enjoyable sensibly priced home-made food from sandwiches, bar snacks and sharing plates up, good friendly service, step to restaurant; May beer/cider/music festival; children and dogs (in bar) welcome, paved front terrace and big garden behind, open all day (till late Fri, Sat). *(Tony and Jill Radnor)*

WINCHESTER SU4729

St James (01962) 861288
Romsey Road; SO22 5BE Smallish corner pub (Little Pub Group) with attractively refurbished split-level interior; bare boards and flagstones, pews and wheelback chairs by scrubbed pine tables, some leather armchairs, painted panelling and a Victorian fireplace, plenty of pictures and other odds and ends, Wadworths ales, craft beers and good selection of wines by the glass, enjoyable food from sharing plates up including Mon burger night and Weds pie night, gluten-free diets catered for, good friendly service; background and some live music, Tues quiz; children and dogs welcome, pleasant little terrace behind, open all day. *(Phil and Jane Villiers)*

WINCHESTER SU4829

Willow Tree (01962) 877255
Durngate Terrace; no adjacent weekday daytime parking, but Durngate car park is around corner in North Walls; a mile from M3 junction 9, by Easton Lane into city; SO23 8QX Popular 19th-c riverside pub; cosy pubby bar to the left with open fire, larger smarter restaurant to the right, well liked food from sandwiches and snacks up including good value weekday set lunch, up to four changing ales, well priced cocktails and several wines by the glass, friendly staff; Weds quiz, Thurs live music; children and dogs welcome, lovely waterside garden (summer wood-fired pizzas), Winnall Moors nature reserve over the road, closed Sun evening, Mon, otherwise open all day. *(Ann and Colin Hunt)*

Herefordshire

CAREY SO5631 Map 4

Cottage of Content

(01432) 840242 – www.cottageofcontent.co.uk

Village signposted from good back road betweeen Ross-on-Wye and Hereford E of A49, through Hoarwithy; HR2 6NG

Country furnishings in a friendly rustic cottage with interesting food, real ales and seats on terraces; bedrooms

Once this was three tucked-away labourers' cottages with its own integral cider and ale parlour. The inn has much character and there's a friendly welcome, a multitude of beams and country furnishings such as stripped-pine kitchen chairs, long pews beside one big table and various old-fashioned tables on flagstones or bare boards. Hobsons Best and Wye Valley Butty Bach on handpump, seven wines by the glass, a gin list and local cider and perry during the summer. You can make the most of the tranquil position by bagging one of the picnic-sets, either on the flower-filled front terrace or in the rural-feeling garden at the back. Bedrooms are quiet and the breakfasts are good.

Tasty food includes sandwiches, twice-baked cheese soufflé with mustard and ale sauce, pulled pork rillettes with roast pepper and chilli jam, aubergine and carrot pancakes with ratatouille, spiced feta, hummus and harissa dressing, tea-smoked duck breast with garlic mash, roasted root vegetables and fig chutney, steak in ale pie, fish dish of the day, griddled pork and chorizo cassoulet with black pudding and apple and roast celeriac, and puddings such as pink peppercorn meringue with clotted cream ice-cream and blackcurrant sundae and whisky marmalade pudding with custard; they also have a Friday tapas evening (5.30-7pm). *Benchmark main dish: braised lamb shoulder with rosemary crust, carrot purée and dauphinoise potatoes £17.50. Two-course evening meal £25.00.*

Free house ~ Licensees Richard and Helen Moore ~ Real ale ~ Open 12-2.30, 6.30 (6 Weds, Sat, 5.30 Fri)-10.30 (11 Fri, Sat); 12-3 Sun; closed Sun evening, Mon, winter Tues; one week Feb, one week Oct ~ Bar food 12-2, 6.30-9; 12-2 Sun ~ Restaurant ~ Children welcome ~ Dogs allowed in bar ~ Bedrooms: £65/£85 *Recommended by P and J Shapley, Philip J Alderton, Barry Collett, Mike and Mary Carter, Andrew Lawson, Anne Taylor*

EARDISLEY SO3149 Map 6

Tram £

(01544) 327251 – www.thetraminn.co.uk

Corner of A4111 and Woodseaves Road; HR3 6PG

Character pub with a lively mix of customers and good food and beer

This handsome old pub is most enjoyable and you're guaranteed a warm welcome. The beamed bar on the left has local character, especially in the cosy back section behind sturdy standing timbers. Here, regulars congregate on the bare boards by the counter, which serves Hobsons Best, Wye Valley Butty Bach and a guest such as Ludlow Blonde on handpump and three local organic ciders. Elsewhere there are antique red and ochre floor tiles, a handful of nicely worn tables and chairs, a pair of long cushioned pews enclosing one much longer table, a high-backed settle, old country pictures, interesting tram prints and a couple of pictorial Wye maps. There's a small dining room on the right, a games room (with pool and darts) in a converted brewhouse and a covered terrace; background music. The outside gents' is extremely stylish. A sizeable, neatly planted garden has picnic-sets on the lawn; pétanque. The famous black and white village is a big draw too. Wheelchair access to the restaurant but no disabled loos.

Good quality food includes lunchtime baguettes, quenelles of smoked mackerel pâté with cucumber and dill dressing, chicken, pork and apricot pâté with apple and apricot chutney, pasta with spinach, portobello and wild mushroom cream sauce and garlic bread, honey-roasted cold ham and free-range eggs, steak burger with toppings, coleslaw and chips, beer-battered hake and chips, duck breast with oriental stir-fried vegetables and noodles, 28-day-aged sirloin steak with onion rings and blue cheese or peppercorn sauce, and puddings such as warm chocolate brownie with chocolate sauce and coffee and walnut cheesecake with coffee syrup. *Benchmark main dish: steak and mushroom in ale pie £9.75. Two-course evening meal £20.00.*

Free house ~ Licensee James Wood ~ Real ale ~ Open 12-3, 6-midnight; 12-4, 7-10.30 Sun; closed Mon except bank holidays ~ Bar food 12-3, 6-9; 12-3 Sun; not Sun evening or Mon ~ Restaurant ~ Well behaved children welcome ~ Dogs allowed in bar ~ Wi-fi

Recommended by P and J Shapley, David Edwards, John and Jennifer Spinks, Alan and Linda Blackmore, Jill and Hugh Bennett, Guy Vowles, Susan and Callum Slade

KILPECK SO4430 Map 6

Kilpeck Inn

(01981) 570464 – www.kilpeckinn.com

Village and church signposted off A465 SW of Hereford; HR2 9DN

Imaginatively extended country inn in fascinating and peaceful village; bedrooms

If you stay overnight at this neat little country inn, you can make the most of the interesting nearby Kilpeck castle ruins and the unique Romanesque church; there are also plenty of good surrounding walks including on the Offa's Dyke Path. The beamed bar with dark slate flagstones rambles happily around to provide several tempting corners, with an antique high-backed settle in one and high stools around a matching chest-high table in another. This opens into two cosily linked dining rooms on the left, with high panelled wainscoting. Swan Ruffled Feathers and Wye Valley Butty Bach on handpump, seven wines by the glass, a gin list (including local ones) and farm cider; background music. The neat back grass has picnic-sets. Green values matter a lot here: they have high-spec insulation, underfloor heating run by a wood pellet boiler, solar heating panels and a rainwater recycling system.

Cooked by the landlord using local produce, the well regarded food includes sandwiches, pigeon breast with puy lentils, crispy kale and red wine jus, mussels and bacon in sage and cider, ricotta and parmesan gnudi (gnocchi-like dumplings) with roast vegetables and sage butter, burger with toppings, fennel and apple coleslaw and rosemary-salted chips, fillet of gilt-head bream with local asparagus, crushed potatoes and wild garlic salsa verde, local venison loin with beetroot dauphinoise and redcurrant jus, and puddings such as espresso crème brûlée and chocolate custard profiteroles with lime syrup. *Benchmark main dish: slow-roast pork belly, stuffed tenderloin, red cabbage, apple mash and cider gravy £16.00. Two-course evening meal £21.00.*

Free house ~ Licensee Ross Williams ~ Real ale ~ Open 12-3, 5.30-11; 12-11 Sat; 12-5 Sun; closed Sun evening, Mon lunchtime ~ Bar food 12-2 (2.30 Sat), 6.30-9; 12-3.30 Sun ~ Restaurant ~ Children welcome ~ Dogs allowed in bar ~ Wi-fi ~ Bedrooms: /£95

Recommended by P and J Shapley, Caroline and Steve Archer, Caroline and Peter Bryant, Colin and Daniel Gibbs, Charles Welch

LEDBURY SO7137 Map 4

Feathers

(01531) 635266 – www.feathers-ledbury.co.uk

High Street (A417); HR8 1DS

Handsome old hotel with chatty relaxed bar, more decorous lounge, good food and friendly staff; comfortable bedrooms

Of course, this elegantly striking Tudor place is a hotel rather than a pub but it's in the centre of town and the convivial bar-brasserie is always full of both chatty drinkers and diners; our readers enjoy their visits very much. Those wanting a pint and a chat congregate at one end: long beams covered in a mass of hop bines, prints and antique sale notices on stripped panelling, and stools lining the counter where they keep Fullers London Pride and a couple of guests such as Ledbury Bitter and Ludlow Gold on handpump, good wines by the glass and 40 malt whiskies. Staff are first class. In the main section, full of contented diners, there are cosy leather easy chairs and sofas by the fire, flowers and oil lamps on stripped kitchen and other tables, and comfortable bays of banquettes and other seats. The sedate lounge is just right for afternoon tea, with high-sided armchairs and sofas in front of a big log fire, and daily papers. In summer, a sheltered back terrace has seats and tables under parasols and abundant plant pots and hanging baskets. Bedrooms are individually furnished and stylish.

Interesting food attractively presented includes sandwiches, lambs kidneys with dijon mustard and parsley sauce, prawn, anchovy and squid ink linguine with salsa verde, gruyère, baby leek and spinach tartlet with celeriac purée and wild garlic pesto, beef and thyme burger with spicy tomato salsa and toppings, corn-fed chicken breast with serrano ham-wrapped tenderstem broccoli and grain mustard beurre blanc, hake fillet with crayfish thermidor, basil and pine nut mash, courgettes and broad beans, local steaks with beer-battered onion rings and a choice of sauce, and puddings such as cappuccino and white chocolate pannacotta and cinnamon madeleines and lime and coconut rice pudding with mango jelly and fresh mango and chilli salsa. *Benchmark main dish: beer-battered fish and chips £13.50. Two-course evening meal £22.00.*

Free house ~ Licensee Edward Elliston ~ Real ale ~ Open 10am-11pm (10.30pm Sun) ~ Bar food 12-2, 6.30-9.30; 12-2.30, 6.30-10 Fri, Sat; 12-2.30, 6.30-9 Sun ~ Restaurant ~ Children welcome ~ Dogs allowed in bar and bedrooms ~ Wi-fi ~ Bedrooms: £99/£150

Recommended by John and Claire Masters, Julia and Fiona Barnes, Simon Glover, Diana and Bertie Farr

LITTLE COWARNE SO6050 Map 4

Three Horseshoes

(01885) 400276 – www.threehorseshoes.co.uk

Pub signposted off A465 SW of Bromyard; towards Ullingswick; HR7 4RQ

Long-serving licensees and friendly staff in bustling country pub with good food using home-grown produce; bedrooms

This is very much a family concern and the kindly Mr and Mrs Whittall have now been at the helm for around 30 years. The L-shaped, quarry-tiled middle bar has upholstered settles, wooden chairs and tables, old local photographs above a woodburning stove, hop-draped beams and local guidebooks. Opening off one side is the garden room with wicker armchairs around tables, and views over an outdoor seating area; leading off the other side is the games room, with pool, darts, juke box, games machine and cribbage. Wye Valley Bitter, Butty Bach and HPA on handpump, local Oliver's cider and perry, ten wines by the glass and home-made elderflower cordial. A popular Sunday lunchtime carvery is offered in the stripped-stone, raftered and spacious restaurant extension. There are well sited tables and chairs on the terrace and in the neat, prettily planted garden. Bedrooms are reached by outside stairs. Disabled access.

From a varied menu, using some home-grown produce and making all their own chutneys, pickles and jams, the food includes lunchtime sandwiches, devilled lambs kidneys on toast, crab and lime fishcake with sweet chilli sauce, tomato and goats cheese tarte tatin, sea bass fillets with chive and white wine sauce, slow-braised lamb shoulder with red wine and mint gravy, fresh crab salad, chicken breast with cider and mushroom sauce, sirloin steak with mushrooms and pepper sauce, and puddings such as damson gin crème brûlée and stem ginger cheesecake. *Benchmark main dish: steak in ale pie £13.50. Two-course evening meal £20.00.*

Free house ~ Licensees Norman and Janet Whittall ~ Real ale ~ Open 11-3, 6.30-11; 11-3, 6-11.30 Sat; 12-4 Sun; closed Sun evening, Tues ~ Bar food 12-2, 6.30-9.30; 12-2.30 Sun ~ Restaurant ~ Children welcome ~ Wi-fi ~ Bedrooms: £40/£70 *Recommended by Revd Michael Vockins, Francis and Mandy Robertson, Dr and Mrs H J Field, Geoff and Ann Marston, Alf and Sally Garner*

MICHAELCHURCH ESCLEY — SO3133 Map 6

Bridge Inn

(01981) 510646 – www.thebridgeinnmichaelchurch.co.uk

Off back road SE of Hay-on-Wye, along Escley Brook valley; HR2 0JW

Character riverside inn with warm, simply furnished bar and dining rooms, local drinks, hearty food and seats by the water; bedrooms

Tucked away in an attractive valley beside a peaceful river and with stunning walks nearby, this well run pub is a good find. The simply furnished bar is homely and easy-going, with hops on dark beams, pine pews and dining chairs around rustic tables, a big woodburning stove and Wye Valley Butty Bach and HPA on handpump, good wines by the glass, local cider and their own gin served by the friendly landlord. Background music. Two dining areas, with contemporary paintwork, have prints on the walls. The bedrooms in the 17th-c farmhouse (one minute's walk away) are warm and comfortable and there's a cosy sitting room too; they also have two yurts available for hire and a riverside campsite with hard-standing sites and electric hook-ups.

Interesting food includes sandwiches, north african-spiced lamb with za'atar potatoes and steamed vegetables, burger in a home-made bun with toppings, onion rings and chips, steamed salmon with sushi ginger and lemon, chicken wrapped in serrano ham in a creamy garlic sauce, steak frites, and puddings such as chocolate fudge brownie with chocolate sauce and banoffi lova (a mix between banoffi pie and pavlova). *Benchmark main dish: beef and bacon in ale pie £14.75. Two-course evening meal £19.00.*

Free house ~ Licensee Glyn Bufton ~ Real ale ~ Open 12-3, 5-11; 6.30-11 Mon; 12-11 Sat, Sun; closed Mon and Tues lunchtimes ~ Bar food 12-2.30, 5.30 (6.30 Mon)-8.30; 12-3,

5.30-9.30 Fri, Sat; 12-3, 5.30-8.30 Sun ~ Restaurant ~ Children welcome ~ Dogs allowed in bar ~ Wi-fi ~ Live bands monthly (see website) ~ Bedrooms: /£100 *Recommended by Daniel King, Lauren and Dan Frazer, Philip J Alderton, Martine and Lawrence Sanders, Trevor and Michele Street*

ROSS-ON-WYE SO5924 Map 6

Kings Head

(01989) 763174 – www.kingshead.co.uk

High Street (B4260); HR9 5HL

Welcoming bar in well run market-town hotel with real ales and tasty food; good bedrooms

Handy for the centre of town and dating back in part to the 14th c, you'll find plenty of reason to linger a while here. The little beamed and panelled bar on the right has traditional pub furnishings, including comfortably padded bar seats and an antique cushioned box settle, stripped floorboards and a couple of black leather armchairs by a log-effect fire. Wye Valley Bitter and Butty Bach and a guest beer such as Purity Mad Goose on handpump, three farm ciders, 16 gins, 15 malt whiskies and several wines by the glass at sensible prices. The beamed lounge bar on the left, also with bare boards, has some timbering, soft leather armchairs, padded bucket seats and shelves of books, and there's also a big carpeted dining room; background music, TV and board games. A sheltered back courtyard has plenty of contemporary tables and chairs for warm weather. The comfortable bedrooms have a lot of character with beams and wonky floors, as well as good bathrooms and excellent breakfasts.

Enjoyable food includes lunchtime sandwiches on home-made bread, devilled crab on sourdough toast, game terrine with ale chutney, sharing boards, sweet potato and rosemary filo parcel with spiced peppers and chickpeas, beer-battered fish and triple-cooked chips, herb-crusted lamb rump with sweet potato purée, caramelised shallots and red wine and rosemary jus, slow-roast pressed pork belly with honey-roasted carrots, fondant potatoes and dijon mustard cream sauce, baked salmon fillet with crayfish bisque, samphire and linguine, and puddings such as white chocolate and raspberry bread and butter pudding with vanilla ice-cream and lemon and cardamom posset with coconut crunch. *Benchmark main dish: pie of the day £12.25. Two-course evening meal £18.00.*

Free house ~ Licensee James Vidler ~ Real ale ~ Open 11-11; 12-10.30 Sun ~ Bar food 12-2, 5.30-9 ~ Restaurant ~ Children welcome ~ Dogs allowed in bar and bedrooms ~ Wi-fi ~ Bedrooms: £60/£85 *Recommended by Steve Whalley, Monty Green, Martine and Lawrence Sanders, Richard and Tessa Ibbot, Peter and Emma Kelly*

SYMONDS YAT SO5616 Map 4

Saracens Head

(01600) 890435 – www.saracensheadinn.co.uk

Symonds Yat E; HR9 6JL

Lovely riverside spot with seats on waterside terraces, a fine range of drinks and interesting food; comfortable bedrooms

Lovers of the outdoors in particular are keen on this lively old place as there are walks in the nearby Forest of Dean. The flagstoned bar has plenty of chatty customers creating a buoyant atmosphere plus Sharps Doom Bar, Wye Valley Butty Bach and HPA and guests such as Bespoke Saved by the Bell, Kingstone Llandogo Trow and Wadworths 6X on handpump, 13 wines by the glass, 20 malt whiskies and several ciders; TV, background music. A cosy lounge and a modernised bare-boards dining room have fine old photos of the area and fresh flowers in jugs. There are lots of seats on terraces beside the River Wye; best to get here early in warm weather to bag one. Bedrooms in the main building have views over the water, while a boathouse annexe has two more contemporary rooms. One way to reach the inn is via the little hand-ferry (pulled by one of the staff). Disabled access to the bar and terrace.

Popular food includes lunchtime sandwiches and baguettes, tempura soft shell crab with sweet chilli jam, hot pork terrine with apple mustard sauce, vegetable keralan curry, beer-battered haddock and chips, confit duck leg with potato cake and blackberry jus, sea trout with mussels, saffron potatoes and shellfish bisque, beef fillet with watercress purée, potato terrine and bordelaise sabayon, and puddings such as treacle tart with milk ice-cream and orange blossom pannacotta with almond and polenta cake and blood orange sorbet. *Benchmark main dish: rare-breed beef burger with toppings, gherkins and chips £14.95. Two-course evening meal £23.00.*

Free house ~ Licensees P K and C J Rollinson ~ Real ale ~ Open 11-11; 11-10.30 Sun ~ Bar food 12-2.30, 6.30-9 ~ Restaurant ~ Children welcome but not in bedrooms ~ Dogs allowed in bar ~ Wi-fi ~ Bedrooms: £65/£90 *Recommended by Mike and Mary Carter, Christine and Tony Garrett, Liz and Martin Eldon, Mr and Mrs D J Nash, Lauren and Dan Frazer, Robert and Diana Myers*

TILLINGTON SO4645 Map 6

Bell

(01432) 760395 – www.thebelltillington.com

Off A4110 NW of Hereford; HR4 8LE

Relaxed and friendly pub with a snug character bar opening into civilised dining areas – good value

The friendly, hard-working and hands-on landlord keeps everything running smoothly here even when the pub is (deservedly) busy. The snug parquet-floored bar on the left has assorted bucket armchairs around low, chunky, mahogany-coloured tables, brightly cushioned wall benches, team photographs and shelves of books; the black beams are strung with dried hops. There's Fullers London Pride, Wye Valley Bitter and a weekly changing guest ale on handpump, cider made on site, several wines by the glass and locally produced spirits from Chase, all served by notably cheerful staff; daily papers, background music and board games. The bar opens into a comfortable bare-boards dining lounge with stripy plush banquettes and a coal fire. Beyond that is a pitched-ceiling restaurant area with more banquettes and big country prints; through slatted blinds you can see a sunken terrace with contemporary tables, and a garden with teak tables, picnic-sets and a play area.

High quality food includes sandwiches, bourbon-glazed belly pork with sour cream and chives, cream cheese-stuffed jalapeños with plum and soy dip, steak, mushroom and ale pie, chickpea and mushroom burger with blue cheese and red onion melt and coleslaw, goat and spinach curry with ginger rice, beer-battered fish and chips, duck breast with dauphinoise potatoes, crunchy vegetables and blackberry sauce, seafood pasta in parsley and lemon white wine sauce, and puddings such as Mars Bar cheesecake and butterscotch and banana tart. *Benchmark main dish: lamb rump with dauphinoise potatoes and lamb jus £16.50. Two-course evening meal £21.00.*

Free house ~ Licensee Glenn Williams ~ Real ale ~ Open 11-11 (midnight Sat); 12-10.30 Sun ~ Bar food 12-2.15, 6-9; all day Fri, Sat; 12-3 Sun ~ Restaurant ~ Children welcome ~ Dogs allowed in bar ~ Wi-fi *Recommended by John and Jennifer Spinks, Lindy Andrews, Nicholas and Maddy Trainer, Belinda Stamp, Sandra and Miles Spencer, Belinda and Neil Garth*

TITLEY SO3359 Map 6

Stagg

(01544) 230221 – www.thestagg.co.uk

B4355 N of Kington; HR5 3RL

Herefordshire Dining Pub of the Year

Wonderful food in three dining rooms, real ales and a fine choice of other drinks, and seats in the two-acre garden; comfortable bedrooms

This is a special place that our readers love, and while the emphasis is on the delicious food, there is a pubby and convivial little bar with friendly, chatty locals and a good choice of drinks. As well as a gently civilised atmosphere, furnishings are deliberately simple: high-backed elegant wooden or leather dining chairs around a medley of tables on bare boards, candlelight and (in the bar) 200 jugs hanging from the ceiling. Courteous, warmly welcoming staff serve Wye Valley Butty Bach and HPA on handpump, 18 house wines by the glass (plus a carefully chosen bin list), interesting soft drinks, a long list of cocktails, local cider and perry, 11 local gins and several whiskies. The two-acre garden has seats on a terrace and a croquet lawn. Bedrooms are either above the pub or in a Georgian vicarage four minutes' walk away; super breakfasts. The inn is surrounded by good walking country and is handy for the Offa's Dyke Path.

Immaculately presented, creative food using their own eggs and home-grown vegetables and fruit (when available) includes sandwiches on home-made ciabatta bread, salmon cured with local vodka and beetroot with smoked beetroot and horseradish, pigeon with pearl barley, bacon and crispy kale, pork sausages with onion rings and mash, chicken breast with leeks, mushrooms and white truffle oil, crispy duck leg with carrot and orange purée and fondant potatoes, vegetable wellington with red wine and shallots, venison loin and slow-cooked shoulder with celeriac, chestnuts and kalettes, cod fillet with lemon, garlic and herb crumb, mussels, samphire and parmentier potatoes, and puddings such as roast pineapple, coconut sorbet, coconut meringue and passion-fruit jelly and chocolate brownie with white chocolate mousse, dark chocolate sorbet and poached pear. *Benchmark main dish: local rump steak with béarnaise sauce and chips £17.90. Two-course evening meal £28.00.*

Free house ~ Licensees Steve and Nicola Reynolds ~ Real ale ~ Open 12-3, 6.30-11; 12-3.30, 6.30-10.30 Sun; closed Mon, Tues; one week Feb, one week June, two weeks Nov ~ Bar food 12-2, 6.30-9 (9.30 Sat); 12-3, 7-8.30 Sun ~ Restaurant ~ Children welcome ~ Dogs allowed in bar and bedrooms ~ Wi-fi ~ Bedrooms: £90/£110 *Recommended by P and J Shapley, Caroline and Oliver Sterling, Max and Steph Warren, Rosie and Marcus Heatherley*

UPPER COLWALL SO7643 Map 4

Chase

(01684) 540276 – www.thechaseinnmalvern.co.uk

Chase Road, brown sign to pub off B4218 Malvern–Colwall, first left after hilltop on bend going W; WR13 6DJ

Gorgeous sunset views from nicely old-fashioned tavern's garden, good drinks and traditional food

On a warm day, the seats and tables on the steep series of small, pretty back terraces make the best of the view across Herefordshire and even as far as the Black Mountains and the Brecon Beacons. This is a cheerful country pub with a chatty and companionable atmosphere. There's a great variety of seats (from a wooden-legged tractor seat to a carved pew) and tables, an old black kitchen range and plenty of decorations – china mugs, blue-glass flasks, lots of small pictures. Four well kept ales are tapped from the cask, such as Bathams Best, Courage Directors, Hobsons Best and Purity Bunny Hop, and friendly staff also serve six wines by the glass, 15 gins, six malt whiskies and a farm cider; board games. Plenty of good surrounding walks.

Pubby food includes lunchtime sandwiches, potted salmon mousse, red onion and rosemary scotch egg with piccalilli, cranberry, walnut and apple tart with stilton and new potato salad, honey and mustard roast ham with eggs, curried chicken skewer and kachumber salad (tomato, cucumber and onion indian-style), breaded scampi and beer-battered fish, both with chips; they offer takeaway fish and chips too (6.30-9pm). *Benchmark main dish: pie of the day £12.50. Two-course evening meal £19.00.*

Free house ~ Licensee Duncan Ironmonger ~ Real ale ~ Open 12-3, 5-11; 12-11 Sat; 12-10.30 Sun ~ Bar food 12-2 (2.30 weekends), 6.30-9 ~ Children welcome ~ Dogs allowed in bar ~ Wi-fi *Recommended by Emily and Toby Archer, Mike Benton, Patricia and Gordon Thompson, Nicholas and Maddy Trainer*

WALFORD — SO5820 Map 4

Mill Race

(01989) 562891 – www.millrace.info

B4234 Ross-on-Wye to Lydney; HR9 5QS

Contemporary furnishings in uncluttered rooms, good quality food, real ales served by attentive staff, and terrace tables

It's very civilised and stylish here and the hospitable landlord gives all his customers a genuine welcome. There's a row of strikingly high arched windows, comfortable leather armchairs and sofas on flagstones, and smaller chairs around broad pedestal tables. Photographs of the local countryside hang on the mainly cream or red walls, and one wall, stripped back to the stonework, contains a woodburning stove that's open to the comfortable, compact dining area on the other side; background music. From the granite-topped modern bar counter, friendly staff serve Wye Valley Bitter, Butty Bach and HPA on handpump, farm cider and 22 fairly priced wines by the glass. There are seats on the terrace with views towards Goodrich Castle (English Heritage), and more seats and tables in the garden. Good nearby walks and the pub has leaflets describing pleasant ones in the area.

Much of the produce comes from their nearby 1,000-acre farm and woodlands (cattle, rare-breed pigs, turkeys, geese, pheasant and ducks) and they list other local suppliers on their website: lunchtime sandwiches, sautéed chicken livers with mushrooms, bacon, shallots and red wine jus, crab bonbons with citrus sweet chilli and pickled fennel, herby ricotta dumplings with asparagus, watercress, spinach and vegetable broth, roast saddle of rabbit with parma ham, artichokes, morel mushrooms and fava bean ragoût, smoked haddock risotto with a soft poached egg, seared lamb rump with sweet potato gnocchi and pea and mint butter, and puddings such as cherry bakewell tart and custard and double chocolate parfait with chocolate soil and blood orange sauce. *Benchmark main dish: local steaks with a choice of sauce and chips £19.00. Two-course evening meal £21.00.*

Free house ~ Licensee Luke Freeman ~ Real ale ~ Open 12-3, 5-10; 12-10 Sat; 12-9 Sun; closed Mon (except bank holidays) ~ Bar food 12-2.30 (3 Sat), 6-9; 12-3 Sun ~ Restaurant ~ Children welcome ~ Dogs allowed in bar ~ Wi-fi *Recommended by Claire Scott, Mike and Mary Carter, Lee and Jill Stafford, Andrew Wall, Sarah and David Gibbs, Chris and Sophie Baxter*

If we know a featured-entry pub does sandwiches, we always say so – if they're not mentioned, you'll have to assume you can't get one.

WOOLHOPE SO6135 Map 4

Butchers Arms

(01432) 860281 – www.butchersarmswoolhope.com

Off B4224 in Fownhope; HR1 4RF

Pleasant half-timbered inn in peaceful setting, with an inviting garden, interesting food and a fine choice of real ales

They brew their own Butchers Arms Henry Hodges in this country pub and also have guests such as Ledbury Gold and Wye Valley Butty Bach on handpump, six wines by the glass from a good list, 14 malt whiskies and a couple of farm ciders. The bar has very low beams, built-in cushioned wall seats, farmhouse chairs and stools around a mix of old tables (some set for dining) on carpet, paintings by local artists on cream walls and a woodburning stove in a big fireplace; there's also a little beamed dining room, similarly furnished. The parrot is called Max. There are picnic-sets in a pretty, streamside garden. To really appreciate the surroundings, turn left as you come out of the pub and take the tiny left-hand road at the end of the car park; this turns into a track and then a path, and the view from the top of the hill is quite something (if you ask, the pub will provide a map).

The landlord cooks the well regarded food using local produce: sandwiches, crispy haggis fritters with beetroot relish, twice-baked cheese soufflé, vegetable and nut roast with roasted tomato, basil and red pepper sauce, lambs liver with mash, crispy onion rings, bacon and gravy, confit five-spice duck leg with stir-fried vegetables, red mullet fillets with cherry tomato and basil sauce and dauphinoise potatoes, partridge breasts with a creamy, brandy sauce and parmentier potatoes, and puddings such as raspberry bakewell tart with chantilly cream and white chocolate cheesecake with caramel sauce. *Benchmark main dish: pigeon with black pudding and bacon £15.95. Two-course evening meal £20.00.*

Free house ~ Licensee Philip Vincent ~ Real ale ~ Open 11-3, 6-11; 11-4 Sun; closed Sun evening, Mon (except bank holidays) ~ Bar food 12-2.30, 6-9; 12-3 Sun ~ Restaurant ~ Children welcome until 8pm ~ Dogs allowed in bar ~ Wi-fi *Recommended by Harvey Brown, Ian Duncan, David and Charlotte Green, Glen and Patricia Fuller, Peter and Alison Steadman, Amy Ledbetter*

WOOLHOPE SO6135 Map 4

Crown

(01432) 860468 – www.crowninnwoolhope.co.uk

Village signposted off B4224 in Fownhope; HR1 4QP

Chatty village local with fine range of local ciders and perries, and popular food

A cheerful, honest pub that's popular for its tasty food and fine choice of drinks. The bar has painted farmhouse and other wooden chairs, upholstered settles and rustic tables on wooden flooring, an open fire and a woodburning stove, some standing timbers and stools against the bar counter; background music, darts and board games. The landlord makes four farm ciders (and keeps a couple of guest ciders) and serves around two dozen bottled ciders and perrys from within a 15-mile radius; they also hold a May Day Bank Holiday festival with live music, beer, cider and perry. Also, Ledbury Bitter and Wye Valley Butty Bach and HPA on handpump and several wines by the glass. In summer, there's a bar in the lovely big garden, which has a fire pit and a particularly comfortable smokers' shelter with cushions and darts; marvellous views. Disabled access.

Enjoyable food includes lunchtime sandwiches, twice-baked cheese soufflé with creamy garlic mushrooms, crispy chilli beef with coriander and cucumber salad, risotto verde wellington with garlic cream, pheasant, leek and bacon open pie with coriander purée and onion bhaji, a pie of the day, beer-battered cod and chips, venison burger with toppings, french fries and chilli ketchup, chicken rogan josh with pilau rice and poppadum, and puddings such as chocolate brownie with chocolate sauce and crème brûlée. *Benchmark main dish: sirloin steak with beef-dripping chips and a choice of flavoured butters £21.00. Two-course evening meal £22.00.*

Free house ~ Licensees Matt and Annalisa Slocombe ~ Real ale ~ Open 12-3, 6-11; 12-11.30 Sat; 12-10 Sun ~ Bar food 12-2, 6-9 (9.30 Fri); 12-2.30, 6-9.30 Sat; 12-3.30, 6-9 Sun ~ Restaurant ~ Children welcome ~ Dogs allowed in bar ~ Wi-fi *Recommended by Martin Day, Mike Swan, David and Stella Martin, Audrey and Paul Summers, Robert and Diana Ringstone, Charlotte and William Mason*

Also Worth a Visit in Herefordshire

Besides the fully inspected pubs, you might like to try these pubs that have been recommended to us and described by readers. Do tell us what you think of them: feedback@goodguides.com

ALMELEY SO3351

Bells (01544) 327216

Off A480, A4111 or A4112 S of Kington; HR3 6LF Welcoming old country local with original jug-and-bottle entry lobby and carpeted beamed bar with woodburner, second bar has been converted to village shop/deli; a couple of well kept changing ales, traditional cider/perry and good honest home-made food (not evenings) from sandwiches up; children and dogs welcome, garden with decked area and boules, on Wyche Way long distance path, open all day. *(Chris)*

AYMESTREY SO4265

★ **Riverside Inn** (01568) 708440

A4110, at N end of village, W of Leominster; HR6 9ST Black and white inn with terrace and tree-sheltered garden making most of lovely waterside spot by ancient stone bridge over the Lugg; cosy rambling beamed interior with some antique furniture alongside stripped country kitchen tables, warm fires, well kept Hobsons, Wye Valley and a guest, local ciders, very good imaginative food from chef-patron using local rare-breed meat and own fruit and vegetables (bar snacks only Sun evening), friendly helpful staff; quiet background music; children welcome, dogs in bar, lovely circular walks, six bedrooms (more planned), fly fishing for residents, good breakfast, closed Mon lunchtime, otherwise open all day. *(John and Jennifer Spinks, Dr and Mrs H J Field)*

BISHOPS FROME SO6648

Green Dragon (01885) 490607

Just off B4214 Bromyard–Ledbury; WR6 5BP Welcoming early 17th-c village pub; four linked room with unspoilt rustic feel, beams, flagstones and log fires (one in fine inglenook), half a dozen ales including Otter, Timothy Taylors and Wye Valley, real ciders and enjoyable traditional food (Tues-Sat evenings and Sun lunchtime); children and dogs welcome, tiered garden with smokers' shelter, on Herefordshire Trail, closed weekday lunchtimes, open all day Sat. *(Charles Welch)*

BODENHAM SO5454

Englands Gate (01568) 797286

On A417 at Bodenham turn-off, about 6 miles S of Leominster; HR1 3HU Attractive black and white 16th-c coaching inn; rambling interior with beams and joists in low ceilings around a vast central stone chimneypiece, sturdy timber props, exposed stonework and well worn flagstones (one or two steps), Hobsons, Wye Valley and a guest, local cider and generally well liked food from lunchtime sandwiches up, friendly staff; background and occasional live music, July beer/cider/sausage festival; children welcome, dogs in bar, tables under parasols on terrace and in pleasant garden, modern bedrooms in converted coach house next door, open all day. *(Trevor and Michele Street)*

BOSBURY SO6943

Bell (01531) 640285

B4220 N of Ledbury; HR8 1PX Timbered village pub opposite the church; log fires in both bars, Otter, Wye Valley and a guest, three ciders and good choice of wines by the glass, dining area serving popular sensibly priced traditional food (not Sun evening, Mon, Tues) including Sun carvery, friendly staff; quiz night every other Mon, pool and darts; children and dogs welcome, large garden with covered terrace and play equipment, open all day Sun till 9pm, closed lunchtimes Mon-Thurs. *(Robert and Diana Ringstone)*

BRINGSTY COMMON SO6954

Live & Let Live (01886) 821462
Off A44 Knightwick–Bromyard 1.5 miles W of Whitbourne turn; take track southwards at Black Cat inn sign, bearing right at fork; WR6 5UW Bustling 17th-c timber and thatch cottage (former cider house); cosy flagstoned bar with log fire in cavernous stone fireplace, earthenware jugs hanging from low beams, old casks built into hop-strung counter serving three well kept ales including Wye Valley Butty Bach, local ciders/apple juice and decent wines by the glass, enjoyable fairly traditional food served by friendly staff, Thurs steak night, two dining rooms upstairs under steep rafters; children and dogs welcome, glass-topped well and big wooden hogshead used as terrace tables, peaceful country views from picnic-sets and rustic benches in former orchard, handy for Brockhampton Estate (NT), closed Mon, otherwise open all day (best to check winter hours). *(Charlotte and William Mason)*

BROMYARD DOWNS SO6755

★ **Royal Oak** (01885) 482585
Just NE of Bromyard; pub signed off A44; HR7 4QP Beautifully placed low-beamed 18th-c pub with wide views; open-plan carpeted and flagstoned bar, log fire and woodburner, dining room with huge bay window, well kept Malvern Hills, Purity and Woods, real cider, enjoyable food (special diets catered for) including daily specials, friendly helpful service; background music, pool and darts; children, walkers and dogs welcome, nice garden with front terrace and play area, closed Sun evening, Mon (open all day bank holiday weekends). *(Andrew Lawson)*

CANON PYON SO4648

Nags Head (01432) 830725
A4110; HR4 8NY Welcoming 17th-c timbered roadside pub; beamed bar with log fire, flagstoned restaurant and tearoom, three well kept changing ales and popular good value food from bar snacks up, pleasant attentive service; darts; children and dogs (in bar) welcome, extensive garden with play area, open all day Sat, till 5pm Sun, closed Mon and lunchtime Tues. *(Glen and Patricia Fuller)*

CLIFFORD SO2445

Castlefields (01497) 831554
B4350 N of Hay-on-Wye; HR3 5HB Rebuilt and enlarged family pub retaining some old features including a glass-covered well, generous helpings of popular good value food and a couple of changing ales, friendly helpful staff, wood or carpeted floors, two-way stone fireplace with woodburner, restaurant; pool, darts and various community-based events; lovely country views, camping, open all day weekends, closed Mon (winter hours may differ). *(Robert and Diana Myers)*

CLODOCK SO3227

Cornewall Arms (01873) 860677
N of Walterstone; HR2 0PD Wonderfully old-fashioned survivor in remote hamlet by historic church facing the Black Mountains; friendly stable-door bar with log fire each end, a few mats and comfortable armchairs on stone floor, lots of ornaments and knick-knacks, photos of past village events and other pictures, books for sale, games including darts and devil among the tailors, bottled Wye Valley and cider, no food or credit cards; dogs welcome, open all day weekends, closed weekday lunchtimes. *(Barry Collett)*

COLWALL SO7440

★ **Wellington** (01684) 540269
A449 Malvern–Ledbury; WR13 6HW Welcoming pub with highly thought-of food from bar snacks and standards to imaginative restaurant dishes (special diets catered for), well kept Goffs Tournament, a couple of guest ales and nice wines by the glass, friendly helpful landlord and staff, comfortably lived-in two-level beamed bar with red patterned carpet and quarry tiles, some built-in settles including unusual high-backed one framing a window, woodburner and open fire, spacious relaxed back dining area; occasional live music, daily newspapers; children and dogs welcome, picnic-sets on neat grass above car park, good local walks, closed evenings Sun and bank holiday Mon (shut all day Aug Bank Holiday Mon). *(Richard Kennell, Richard C Morgan)*

DORSTONE SO3141

★ **Pandy** (01981) 550273
Pub signed off B4348 E of Hay-on-Wye; HR3 6AN Ancient inn (12th-c origins) by village green; traditional rooms with low beams, stout timbers and worn flagstones, various alcoves and vast fireplace, several woodburners, four real ales including Three Tuns and Wye Valley, local cider and enjoyable reasonably priced food (not Sun evening) from changing blackboard menu; children and dogs (in bar) welcome, side garden with picnic-sets and play area, four good bedrooms in purpose-built timber lodge (now run independently, but breakfast in the pub), closed Mon lunchtime, otherwise open all day (till 9.30pm Sun), in winter closed lunchtime Mon-Thurs. *(Andrew Lawson)*

EWYAS HAROLD SO3828

Temple Bar (01981) 240423
Village centre signed from B4347; HR2 0EU Popular creeper-clad Georgian inn run by welcoming family; good freshly made food from bar meals to interesting evening restaurant dishes (weekly changing menu), Wye Valley Butty Bach and a couple of guests, local cider, modernised interior

keeping original oak beams, flagstones and log fire; children and dogs (in bar) welcome, disabled access, three comfortable bedrooms, hearty breakfast, open all day weekends, no evening food Sun, Mon or Tues. *(Peter and Jane Emmerson)*

GARWAY SO4622

Garway Moon (01600) 750270

Centre of village, opposite the green; HR2 8RQ Attractive 18th-c pub in pretty location overlooking common; good freshly made food (not Mon) served by friendly staff, well kept ales such as Butcombe, Kingstone and Wye Valley, proper ciders, beams and exposed stonework, woodburner in inglenook, restaurant; children, dogs and muddy boots welcome, garden with terrace and play area, three bedrooms, open all day weekends, closed lunchtimes Mon and Tues. *(Andy and Rosemary Taylor)*

GORSLEY SO6726

Roadmaker (01989) 720352

0.5 miles from M50 junction 3; village signposted from exit – B4221; HR9 7SW Popular 19th-c village pub run by group of retired gurkhas; large carpeted lounge bar with central log fire, good nepalese food here and in evening restaurant, also Sun roasts and other english choices, well kept ales such as Butcombe, efficient courteous service; quiz first Sun of month; children welcome, no dogs, terrace with water feature, open all day. *(Charles Welch)*

HAMPTON BISHOP SO5538

Bunch of Carrots (01432) 870237

B4224; HR1 4JR Spacious beamed country pub by River Wye, good daily carvery and choice of other pubby food (all day weekends), cheerful efficient service, well kept Wye Valley Butty Bach, Sharps Doom Bar and a couple of guests, local cider and several wines by the glass, traditional dimly lit bar area with wood and flagstone floors, woodburner, airy restaurant; children and dogs welcome, disabled access/loo, garden with play area, open all day. *(Charlotte and William Mason)*

HAREWOOD END SO5227

Harewood End Inn (01989) 730637

A49 Hereford to Ross-on-Wye; HR2 8JT Roadside pub in two connecting buildings; compact bar and a couple of bare-boards dining rooms, high-backed chairs around scrubbed-top tables, interesting collection of enamel signs on panelled walls, open fire, good choice of enjoyable home-made food from lunchtime sandwiches to grills including signature Harewood burger, three well kept ales and decent choice of wines, welcoming attentive staff; quiz last Sun of month, pool, darts and TV, free wi-fi; children and dogs welcome, nice garden and local walks, five bedrooms, closed Mon. *(Gary and Marie Miller)*

HEREFORD SO5139

Barrels (01432) 274968

St Owen Street; HR1 2JQ Friendly 18th-c coaching inn popular with good mix of customers; former home to the Wye Valley brewery and up to seven of their very well kept/priced ales from barrel-built counter (beer/music festival end Aug), Thatcher's cider, cheerful efficient staff, no food; live jazz first Mon of month, Thurs quiz, juke box, sports TV, pool and darts; dogs welcome, partly covered courtyard behind, open all day. *(Andy and Rosemary Taylor)*

HEREFORD SO5039

★Lichfield Vaults (01432) 266821

Church Street; HR1 2LR Popular place, a pub since the 18th c, in picturesque pedestrianised area near cathedral; dark panelling, some stripped brick and exposed joists, impressive plasterwork in large-windowed front room, traditionally furnished with dark pews, cushioned pub chairs and a couple of heavily padded benches, hot coal stove, charming greek landlord and friendly staff, five well kept ales such as Adnams, Caledonian and Sharps, enjoyable food from sandwiches up including greek dishes and good Sun roasts; faint background music, live blues/rock last Sun afternoon of month, TV projector for sports (particularly rugby), games machines, daily papers; children and dogs welcome, picnic-sets in pleasant back courtyard, open all day. *(Geoff and Anne Marston)*

HOARWITHY SO5429

New Harp (01432) 840900

Off A49 Hereford to Ross-on-Wye; HR2 6QH Open-plan village dining pub with cheerful bustling atmosphere; good well presented local food from chef-landlord, friendly helpful service, ales such as Wye Valley, Ledbury and Otter, Weston's cider (maybe their own organic cider in summer), pine tables on slate tiles, bay-window seats and half-panelling, screened-off dining area with light wood furniture, a couple of woodburners; background and some live music, sports TV; children, walkers and dogs welcome (pub labradors are Fudge and Jake), pretty tree-sheltered garden with stream, picnic-sets and decked area, little shop and Mon morning post office, unusual italianate Victorian church nearby, open all day. *(Barry Collett)*

KINGSLAND SO4461

★Corners (01568) 708385

B4360 NW of Leominster, corner of Lugg Green Road; HR6 9RY Comfortably updated, partly black and white 16th-c village inn with snug nooks and corners; log fires, low beams, dark red plasterwork and some stripped brickwork, bow-window seat and leather armchairs in softly lit carpeted bar, well kept Hobsons, Wye Valley and decent selection of wines, big side dining room in converted hay loft with rafters and huge window, enjoyable reasonably priced food from pubby choices up, cheerful attentive service; children welcome, no garden, comfortable bedrooms in modern block behind. *(Andrew Lawson)*

KINGTON SO3056

★**Olde Tavern** (01544) 231945
Victoria Road, just off A44 opposite B4355 – follow sign to Town Centre, Hospital, Cattle Market; pub on right opposite Elizabeth Road, no inn sign but Estd 1767 notice; HR5 3BX Gloriously old-fashioned with hatch-served side room opening off small plain parlour and public bar, plenty of dark brown woodwork, big windows, settles and other antique furniture on bare floors, gas fire, old local pictures, china, pewter and curios, four well kept local ales such as Hobsons and Ludlow, Weston's cider, generous helpings of enjoyable home-made food (Thurs-Sun), friendly atmosphere; children and dogs welcome, little yard at back, open all day weekends, closed weekday lunchtimes. *(Gary and Marie Miller)*

KINGTON SO2956

Oxford Arms (01544) 230322
Duke Street; HR5 3DR Traditional old-fashioned beamed inn; woodburners in main bar on left and dining area to the right, smaller lounge with sofas and armchairs, real ales such as Hobsons and Woods, good reasonably priced home-made food including Weds curry and Thurs steak nights, good friendly service; some live music, summer beer festivals, pool and darts; children and dogs welcome, terrace picnic-sets, clean comfortable bedrooms, open all day Fri-Sun, closed Mon and lunchtimes Tues-Thurs. *(Robert and Diana Myers)*

KINGTON SO2956

Royal Oak (01544) 230484
Church Street; HR5 3BE Welcoming 17th-c pub with enjoyable home-cooked evening food (Mon-Sat, not Tues) plus Sun lunchtime carvery, well kept ales such as Ringwood and Wye Valley and a proper cider, two little open fires, darts and sports TV in public bar; children and dogs (not in restaurant) welcome, garden with terrace, handy for Offa's Dyke Path walkers, three neat simple bedrooms, open all day Fri-Sun, closed Mon and Tues lunchtimes. *(Alister and Margery Bacon)*

LEDBURY SO7137

★**Prince of Wales** (01531) 632250
Church Lane; narrow passage from Town Hall; HR8 1DL Friendly old black and white local prettily tucked away down narrow cobbled alley; seven well kept ales, foreign draught/bottled beers and real cider, knowledgeable staff, decent uncomplicated low-priced food from sandwiches up, beams, nooks and crannies and shelves of books, long back room; background music, live blues Thurs night and Sun afternoon, folk session Weds evening; dogs welcome, a couple of tables in flower-filled backyard, open all day. *(Dr J Barrie Jones, David Dore)*

LEDBURY SO7137

Seven Stars (01531) 635800
Homend (High Street); HR8 1BN 16th-c beamed and timbered pub with good fairly straightforward food (all day weekends) using produce from own farm, also a vegan menu, three well kept ales including Shepherd Neame, friendly helpful staff, bar area with comfortable seating and cosy open fire, dining room behind; free wi-fi; children and dogs welcome, disabled access, walled back terrace, three bedrooms, open all day. *(Dr J Barrie Jones)*

LEDBURY SO7137

Talbot (01531) 632963
New Street; HR8 2DX Comfortable 16th-c black and white fronted coaching inn; log-fire bar with Wadworths ales and guests, plenty of wines by the glass and good fairly traditional food from sharing boards and lunchtime sandwiches up, regular deals, friendly efficient service, oak-panelled dining room; courtyard tables, 13 bedrooms (six in converted stables), good breakfast, open all day. *(Andy and Rosemary Taylor)*

LEINTWARDINE SO4073

Lion (01547) 540203
High Street; SY7 0JZ Restored inn beautifully situated by packhorse bridge over River Teme; helpful efficient staff and friendly atmosphere, good well presented food from varied menu including some imaginative choices (can be pricey), Tues steak night, restaurant and two separate bars (both with woodburners), well kept beers such as Ludlow and Wye Valley, afternoon teas; children welcome, safely fenced riverside garden with play area, eight attractive bedrooms, can arrange fishing trips, open all day (may shut early Sun in winter). *(Andrew Lawson)*

LEINTWARDINE SO4073

★**Sun** (01547) 540705
Rosemary Lane, just off A4113; SY7 0LP Fascinating 19th-c time warp: benches and farmhouse tables by coal fire in wallpapered brick-floored front bar (dogs welcome here), three well kept ales including Hobsons tapped from the cask (Aug beer festival), another fire in snug carpeted parlour, pork pies and perhaps a lunchtime ploughman's (can bring food from adjacent fish and chip shop), friendly staff and cheery locals; open mike night last Fri of month; new pavilion-style extension at back with bar and garden room, open all day. *(Glen and Patricia Fuller)*

LEOMINSTER SO4959

★**Grape Vaults** (01568) 611404
Broad Street; HR6 8BS Compact two-room character pub, popular and friendly, with five well kept ales including Ludlow, tasty good value traditional food (not Sun evening, no credit cards – ATM opposite), good cheerful service, two coal fires, beams and stripped woodwork, original dark high-backed settles and round copper-topped tables on bare boards, old local prints and posters, bottle collection, shelves of books in snug; live music Sun afternoon, occasional quiz nights, free wi-fi; dogs welcome, open all day. *(Roy and Gill Payne, Guy Vowles)*

LINTON SO6525

Alma (01989) 720355
On main road through village; HR9 7RY Cheerful village local with up to five well kept ales, Weston's cider and several wines by the glass, enjoyable pub food (not Sun, Mon) including specials, friendly service, front bar with open fire, restaurant, pool in small back room; live music (mainly acoustic) including open mike first Thurs of month, also June festival, quiz last Sun of month; children and dogs welcome, good-sized garden behind with nice views, closed Mon lunchtime. *(Richard and Tessa Ibbot)*

LUGWARDINE SO5441

Crown & Anchor (01432) 850630
Just off A438 E of Hereford; Cotts Lane; HR1 4AB Cottagey timbered pub dating from the 18th c; ample helpings of enjoyable reasonably priced food from traditional favourites up, well kept Wye Valley and a guest, decent wines, good friendly service, various smallish opened-up rooms, inglenook log fire; children and dogs (in bar) welcome, seats in front and back gardens, open all day. *(Charles Welch)*

MUCH DEWCHURCH SO4831

Black Swan (01981) 540295
B4348 Ross-on-Wye to Hay-on-Wye; HR2 8DJ Roomy and attractive beamed local (partly 14th-c) with welcoming long-serving landlady; well kept Timothy Taylors Landlord and local guests, Weston's cider, decent wines and enjoyable straightforward home-made food using local produce, log fires in cosy well worn bar and lounge/eating area, pool room with darts, TV and juke box; Thurs folk night; children and dogs welcome, seats on front terrace, open all day Sun. *(Robert and Diana Ringstone)*

MUCH MARCLE SO6634

Royal Oak (01531) 660300
On A449 Ross-on-Wye to Ledbury; HR8 2ND Roadside country dining pub with lovely views; good reasonably priced food (all day Sun) using meat from local farms, lunchtime deals, grill night Mon, prompt friendly service, well kept Brakspears and Marstons Pedigree, Weston's cider and several wines by the glass, smallish bare-boards bar area, various dining sections including library room and large back function room; skittle alley; children and dogs welcome, garden and terrace seating, two bedrooms. *(Dr A J and Mrs B A Tompsett)*

PEMBRIDGE SO3958

New Inn (01544) 388427
Market Square (A44); HR6 9DZ Timeless ancient inn overlooking small black and white town's church, unpretentious three-room bar with antique settles, beams, worn flagstones and impressive inglenook log fire, well kept changing ales, farm cider and generous helpings of popular good value food including notable cheese platter, friendly service, quiet little family dining room; traditional games, downstairs loos; no dogs, simple bedrooms and a couple of resident ghosts. *(Dave Braisted)*

PETERSTOW SO5524

Red Lion (01989)730546
A49 W of Ross-on-Wye; HR9 6LH Roadside country pub with much enjoyed food cooked by landlord-chef, sensible prices and smaller appetites catered for, good range of well kept ales and ciders, friendly staff, open-plan with large dining area and modern conservatory, log fires; quiz first Mon of month; children and dogs welcome, back play area, camping, open all day, except 3-6pm Sun. *(Matthew and Elisabeth Reeves)*

PRESTON SO3841

Yew Tree (01981) 500359
Village W of Hereford; HR2 9JT Small tucked-away pub handy for River Wye; simple and welcoming, with a changing ale tapped from the cask and real cider, good value home-made food including Fri steak night, beams and woodburner; some live music, pool, free wi-fi; children and dogs welcome, bunkhouse, open all day weekends. *(Geoff and Anne Marston)*

ROSS-ON-WYE SO5924

Mail Rooms (01989) 760920
Gloucester Road; HR9 5BS Open-plan Wetherspoons conversion of former post office; up to five real ales including Greene King, Weston's cider and good choice of wines, enjoyable well priced food, quick friendly service; silent TV, free wi-fi; children welcome till 8pm, decked back terrace, open all day from 8am. *(Dr J Barrie Jones)*

ROSS-ON-WYE SO6024

White Lion (01989) 562785
Wilton Lane; HR9 6AQ Friendly riverside pub dating from 1650; well kept Wye Valley and a couple of guests, enjoyable traditional food at reasonable prices, good service, big fireplace in carpeted bar, stone-walled gaol restaurant (building once a police station); free wi-fi; children and dogs welcome, lots of

tables in garden and on terrace overlooking the Wye and historic bridge, bedrooms and camping, open all day. *(Trevor and Michele Street)*

SELLACK SO5526

★**Lough Pool** (01989) 730888
Off A49; HR9 6LX Cottagey black and white country pub – some refurbishment but keeping character; bars with beams and standing timbers, rustic furniture on flagstones, open fire and woodburner, well kept Wye Valley ales and a guest, local farm ciders/perries and several wines by the glass, landlord-chef's good attractively presented food from interesting menu including daily specials, back restaurant, friendly attentive service; well behaved children and dogs (in bar) allowed, garden tables under parasols, good nearby walks, closed Sun evening, Mon. *(Martin Hartog)*

STAPLOW SO6941

Oak (01531) 640954
Bromyard Road (B4214); HR8 1NP Popular roadside village pub with two snug bar areas, beams, flagstones and woodburners, four real ales and good choice of wines, open-kitchen restaurant serving good food from lunchtime sandwiches/ ciabattas up, cheerful quick service; occasional live music; children and dogs welcome, garden picnic-sets, four comfortable bedrooms, open all day. *(Clive and Fran Dutson)*

STAUNTON ON WYE SO3844

Portway (01981) 500474
A438 Hereford to Hay-on-Wye, by Monnington turn; HR4 7NH Comfortable 16th-c beamed inn with good well priced food including Fri pie night and OAP lunch deal Tues and Thurs, Ludlow Gold, Sharps Doom Bar and Wye Valley, log-fire bar, lounge and restaurant; background music, TV, pool; children and dogs (in bar) welcome, picnic-sets in sizeable garden among fruit trees, nine bedrooms, open all day. *(Andy and Rosemary Taylor)*

STOCKTON CROSS SO5161

Stockton Cross Inn (01568) 612509
Kimbolton; A4112, off A49 just N of Leominster; HR6 0HD Renovated half-timbered 16th-c drovers' inn under new management; heavily beamed interior with inglenook woodburner, Wye Valley ales and guests, good choice of wines/gins and enjoyable food (not Sun evening) from sandwiches and pub favourites up; quiz third Tues of month; children and dogs welcome, picnic-sets in front garden and on gravel back terrace, handy for Berrington Hall (NT), closed Mon, otherwise open all day. *(R T and J C Moggridge, Mike and Mary Carter)*

SUTTON ST NICHOLAS SO5345

Golden Cross (01432) 880274
Corner of Ridgeway Road; HR1 3AZ Popular modernised pub with enjoyable good value food from ciabattas up, OAP lunch deal Mon-Fri, Wye Valley Butty Bach and two regularly changing guests from stone-fronted counter, good friendly service, clean décor, some breweriana, relaxed upstairs restaurant; live music Fri, juke box, pool and darts; children and dogs welcome, disabled facilities, no-smoking garden behind, pretty village and good surrounding walks, open all day Fri-Sun. *(Andrew Lawson)*

SYMONDS YAT SO5515

Old Ferrie (01600) 890232
Ferrie Lane, Symonds Yat West; HR9 6BL Unpretentious old pub set in picturesque spot by River Wye (own hand-pulled ferry); decent choice of enjoyable food including lunchtime sharing boards and various ploughman's, Wye Valley ales and local cider, friendly helpful staff, lived-in interior with log fires; background music, games room; children and dogs (in bar) welcome, waterside terrace, boat hire and good walks, bedrooms including two bunkhouses, open all day. *(Belinda and Neil Garth)*

TRUMPET SO6639

Trumpet Inn (01531) 670277
Corner A413 and A438; HR8 2RA Modernised black and white timbered pub dating from the 15th c; well kept Wadworths ales and plenty of wines by the glass, enjoyable food from sandwiches up (some mains available in smaller helpings), efficient service, carpeted interior with beams, stripped brickwork and log fires, restaurant; free wi-fi; children and dogs (in bar) welcome, tables in big garden behind, campsite with hard standings, open all day, food all day Sat, till 5pm Sun. *(Gary and Marie Miller)*

UPPER SAPEY SO6863

Baiting House (01886) 853201
B4203 Bromyard–Great Witley; WR6 6XT Refurbished 19th-c country inn; two bars with flagstone and wood-strip flooring, woodburners, very good food from lunchtime sandwiches up (more adventurous/pricey evening menu), five well kept ales including Hobsons and Wye Valley, local ciders, several wines by the glass and good selection of gins, friendly attentive service, restaurant; separate room for pool, darts and sports TV; children welcome, dogs in one bar and snug, disabled access, picnic-sets on brick terrace (summer pizza oven) and raised lawn, six comfortable well appointed bedrooms, open all day, no food Sun evening, Mon. *(Anne Cheston)*

You can send reports directly to us at feedback@goodguides.com

UPTON BISHOP SO6326

★**Moody Cow** (01989) 780470
B4221 E of Ross-on-Wye; HR9 7TT Popular tucked-away dining pub with modern rustic décor; L-shaped bar with sandstone walls, slate floor and woodburner, biggish raftered restaurant and second more intimate eating area, highly regarded freshly made food (can be pricey, some dishes available in smaller helpings), well kept ales and decent wines including some local ones, friendly efficient service; children, dogs and boots welcome, garden growing own fruit/vegetables, courtyard bedroom up spiral staircase, closed Sun evening, Mon and Tues. *(Mike and Mary Carter)*

WALTERSTONE SO3424

★**Carpenters Arms** (01873) 890353
Follow Walterstone signs off A465; HR2 0DX Charming unspoilt stone cottage with unchanging traditional rooms (known locally as the Gluepot – once you're in you don't want to leave); beams, broad polished flagstones, a roaring fire in gleaming black range warming ancient settles against stripped-stone walls, Wadworths 6X and a guest tapped from the cask, enjoyable straightforward food in snug main dining room with mahogany tables and oak corner cupboards, another little dining area with old oak tables and church pews on more flagstones; no credit cards, outside loos are cold but in character; children welcome, open all day Sat. *(Robert and Diana Ringstone)*

WELLINGTON HEATH SO7140

Farmers Arms (01531) 634776
Off B4214 just N of Ledbury – pub signed right, from top of village; Horse Road; HR8 1LS Roomy open-plan beamed pub with enjoyable food (booking advised) including daily specials and various themed nights, Otter, Wye Valley Butty Bach and a guest, friendly staff; free wi-fi; children and dogs welcome, picnic-sets on paved terrace, good walking country, open all day weekends, closed Mon (except bank holidays 12-4pm) and Tues lunchtime. *(Andrew Lawson)*

WEOBLEY SO4051

Salutation (01544) 318443
Off A4112 SW of Leominster; HR4 8SJ Old beamed and timbered inn at top of delightful village green, enjoyable food cooked by chef-landlord from bar snacks up including set lunch/early evening deal, well kept Hobsons, Wye Valley and a local guest, Robinson's cider, friendly helpful service, bar and various dining areas, inglenook log fires; quiz/curry night first Weds of month; children welcome, sheltered back terrace, three bedrooms, good breakfast, open all day. *(Charles Welch)*

WESTON-UNDER-PENYARD SO6323

Weston Cross Inn (01989) 562759
A40 E of Ross; HR9 7NU Creeper-clad roadside pub with good choice of enjoyable well priced food in bar or restaurant, Bass, Otter and a guest, Stowford Press cider, friendly helpful staff; children, walkers and dogs welcome, good-sized garden with plenty of picnic-sets and play area, open all day Sat, limited menu Sun evening. *(Guy Vowles)*

WHITBOURNE SO7156

Live & Let Live (01886) 822276
Off A44 Bromyard–Worcester at Wheatsheaf; WR6 5SP Welcoming pub on southern edge of the village; good freshly made food (not Sun evening) from blackboard menu including interesting specials, well kept ales such as Ludlow and Wye Valley, friendly helpful staff, beams and nice log fire, big-windowed restaurant; quiz second Sun of month; children welcome, garden with country views, open all day weekends, closed Mon lunchtime. *(Glen and Patricia Fuller)*

WIGMORE SO4168

Oak (01568) 770424
Ford Street; HR6 9UJ Restored 16th-c coaching inn mixing original features with contemporary décor; highly regarded imaginative food (not Sun evening), Hobsons and guests, real cider and nice wines by the glass, good friendly service; children and dogs (in one part) welcome, two bedrooms, open all day Sun till 8pm, closed Mon and lunchtime Tues. *(Andy and Rosemary Taylor)*

WINFORTON SO2946

Sun (01544) 327677
A438; HR3 6EA Friendly village pub under newish ownership; enjoyable freshly cooked food (not Sun evening) including a couple of specials, Wye Valley beers and Robinson's cider, country-style beamed areas either side of central servery, stripped stone and woodburners; children and dogs welcome, garden picnic-sets, open all day weekends, closed Mon. *(Glen and Patricia Fuller)*

Post Office address codings confusingly give the impression that a few pubs are in Herefordshire when they're really in Gloucestershire or even Wales (which is where we list them).

Hertfordshire

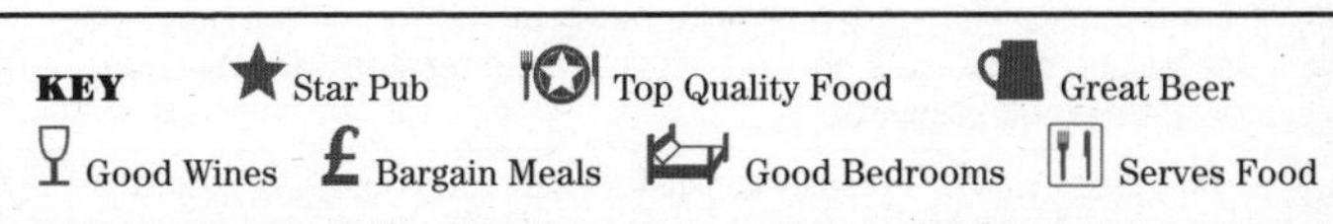

ARDELEY TL3027 Map 5

Jolly Waggoner

(01438) 861350 – www.jollywaggoner.co.uk

Off B1037 NE of Stevenage; SG2 7AH

Extended cottage in pretty village, homely bar and smarter restaurant, good food and well kept ales and seats in garden

Once farm workers' cottages, this is a 16th-c pub now owned by Church Farm opposite. It's beamed and traditionally furnished with lots of nooks and corners, horsebrasses along the bressumer beam above the log fire, some tartan-upholstered armchairs and high chairs against the counter; darts and background music. Friendly staff serve Fullers London Pride, Greene King IPA and a couple of guest beers on handpump, several wines by the glass and their own Old Vodka distilled on site at the farm. The restaurant, extended into the cottage next door, has high-backed dark leather dining chairs around white-clothed tables and modern prints on dark green walls. There are picnic-sets on gravel and in the lawned garden. This is a pretty, tucked-away village with thatched cottages around the green.

Using their own farm produce, the well liked food includes chicken liver pâté with plum chutney, omelette arnold bennett, pumpkin gnocchi with walnut, cheese, watercress and sage pesto, bubble and squeak with bacon, a poached egg and hollandaise, sausages and mash with caramelised onion gravy, free-range chicken kiev with sweetcorn and bacon fritter and ketchup dressing, slow-cooked parcel of lamb with parsnip purée, rainbow chard and cooking juices, rare-breed steaks with chips and a choice of sauce, and puddings such as apple and walnut crumble with vanilla custard and chocolate fondant with salted caramel ice-cream. *Benchmark main dish: loin of local lamb £19.50. Two-course evening meal £18.00.*

Free house ~ Licensee Tim Waygood ~ Real ale ~ Open 12-11 ~ Bar food 12-2.30, 6-9; 12-9 Sat; 12-6 Sun ~ Restaurant ~ Children welcome ~ Dogs allowed in bar ~ Wi-fi

Recommended by Rosie and John Moore, David Appleyard, Victoria and James Sargeant

BARNET TQ2599 Map 5

Duke of York

(020) 8449 0297 – www.brunningandprice.co.uk/dukeofyork

Barnet Road (A1000); EN5 4SG

Big place with reasonably priced bistro-style food and nice garden

Served from an impressive counter by friendly staff, the fine range of drinks here includes Phoenix Brunning & Price Original plus guests such as

Leighton Buzzard Bedfordshire Best, Sambrooks Session, Tring Side Pocket for a Toad, Trumans Swift and Weltons Sussex Pride on handpump, 20 wines by the glass, 30 gins and a large choice of whiskies. It's a rather grand building and open doorways and stairs cleverly divide up the spreading rooms, while big windows and mirrors keep everything light and airy. There's a relaxed atmosphere and an eclectic mix of furniture on tiled or wooden flooring, hundreds of prints and photos on cream walls, fireplaces and thoughtful touches such as table lamps, books, rugs, fresh flowers and pot plants; background music. The garden is particularly attractive, with a range of seats, tables and picnic-sets on a tree-surrounded terrace and lawn, and a tractor in the good play area.

An interesting choice of good food includes sandwiches (until 6pm), smoked mackerel with samphire, horseradish cream and beetroot jelly, tempura fried vegetables with sweet chilli sauce, thai steamed mussels with lemongrass, coconut milk and chilli, cauliflower and sweet potato biryani with lentil curry, lime pickle and red onion bhaji, steak and kidney pie with mash, king prawn, chorizo and squid salad with roasted mediterranean vegtables and gazpacho dressing, and puddings such as hot waffle with glazed banana, toffee sauce and honeycomb ice-cream and triple chocolate brownie with chocolate sauce. *Benchmark main dish: chicken breast with fondant potatoes, cavolo nero, smoked bacon and sherry sauce £14.50. Two-course evening meal £21.00.*

Brunning & Price ~ Manager John Johnston ~ Real ale ~ Open 11-11 (10.30 Sun) ~ Bar food 12-9 (9.30 Thurs-Sat) ~ Restaurant ~ Children welcome until 8pm ~ Dogs allowed in bar ~ Wi-fi *Recommended by Melanie and David Lawson, Peter and Emma Kelly, Usha and Terri Patel, Greta and Gavin Craddock, Justine and Neil Bonnett, Rob Anderson*

COTTERED
Bull

TL3229 Map 5

(01763) 281243 – www.thebullcottered.co.uk
A507 W of Buntingford; SG9 9QP

Busy dining pub in nice village, attractive bar rooms with an easy-going feel, several ales, interesting food and seats in sizeable garden

We get plenty of warm, enthusiastic reports from our readers on this well run pub in a pretty village. The interconnected bar and dining rooms have bare boards, contemporary paintwork, a woodburning stove and a log-effect gas fire, all sorts of upholstered or cushioned dining chairs around dark wooden tables, tartan armchairs and button-back banquettes; also, fresh flowers, candles in big white lanterns, country prints above wooden dados and stone bottles and carpentry planes. Greene King IPA and Abbot on handpump and nine decent wines served by helpful staff. Seats outside at the front of the building look across to charming thatched cottages and the large, attractive back garden has seats and tables under fine old trees.

Well thought-of food includes lunchtime sandwiches, fried brie with cranberry sauce, smoked salmon and prawn parcel, omelette arnold bennett, chicken or salmon caesar salad, wild mushroom and parmesan risotto, a pie of the day, burgers with toppings and chips, calves liver, smoked bacon and sage, pork fillet stuffed with mozzarella and parma ham and coated in herb breadcrumbs, sirloin steak with a choice of sauce, and puddings. *Benchmark main dish: sea bass fillet with ginger, garlic, soy sauce and chilli £18.95. Two-course evening meal £22.00.*

Greene King ~ Tenant Darren Perkins ~ Real ale ~ Open 12-3, 6.15-11; 12-10.30 Sun ~ Bar food 12-2, 6.30-9.30; 12-3.30, 6-8.30 Sun ~ Restaurant ~ Children welcome but no highchairs or changing facilities ~ Wi-fi ~ Dinner dance monthly *Recommended by Mrs Margo Finlay, Jörg Kasprowski, Alan and Angela Scouller, John and Delia Franks, Michael Sargent, Nik and Gloria Clarke*

FLAUNDEN TL0101 Map 5

Bricklayers Arms

(01442) 833322 – www.bricklayersarms.com

4 miles from M25 junction 18; village signposted off A41 – from village centre follow Boxmoor, Bovingdon road and turn right at Belsize, Watford signpost into Hogpits Bottom; HP3 0PH

Cosy country restaurant with fairly elaborate food; very good wine list

With great attention to detail and first class food served by helpful, attentive staff, this civilised old dining pub is a winner. It's mainly open-plan with stubs of knocked-through oak-timbered walls indicating the original room layout, and the well refurbished low-beamed bar is snug and comfortable, with a roaring log fire in winter. Stools line the brick counter where they keep Mad Squirrel Mister Squirrel, Paradigm Touch Point and Tring Side Pocket for a Toad on handpump, an extensive wine list with 20 by the glass and a good choice of spirits; background music. In summer, the terrace and beautifully kept old-fashioned garden have seats and tables. Just up the Belsize road, a path on the left leads through delightful woods to a forested area around Hollow Hedge. The pub is just 15 minutes by car from the Warner Bros Studios where the Harry Potter films were made; you can tour the studios but must book in advance.

Impressive food includes white crab meat, home-smoked salmon with chive cream and blinis, chicken and apricot terrine with an onion and walnut muffin and cucumber and yoghurt cream, mushroom feuilletée with calvados cream mushrooms and julienned vegetables, wild boar and apple sausages with chive mash and red wine onion gravy, lamb pie with root vegetables and a mash top, chicken ballotine cooked with honey carrots, a thyme crust and madeira jus, pork cheeks cooked with butter beans, silver skin onions and cider, lemon sole fillet with pea and purple basil mousse and tomato cream, and puddings such as bourbon vanilla crème brûlée and lemon tart with panacotta and raspberry ice-cream. *Benchmark main dish: duo of duck (breast and confit leg) with black fig jus £19.95. Two-course evening meal £25.00.*

Free house ~ Licensee Alvin Michaels ~ Real ale ~ Open 12-11.30 (midnight Sat); 12-8.30 Sun ~ Bar food 12-2.30, 6.15-9.30; 12-7 Sun and bank holidays ~ Restaurant ~ Children welcome ~ Dogs allowed in bar ~ Wi-fi *Recommended by Renrag, Moira and Jon Weller, Daniel King, Karl and Frieda Bujeya, Andrea Shorey, Peter and Jan Humphreys, Andy and Rosemary Taylor, Matthew and Elisabeth Reeves*

FRITHSDEN TL0109 Map 5

Alford Arms

(01442) 864480 – www.alfordarmsfrithsden.co.uk

A4146 from Hemel Hempstead to Water End, then second left (after Red Lion) signed Frithsden, then left at T junction, then right after 0.25 miles; HP1 3DD

Hertfordshire Dining Pub of the Year

Thriving dining pub with a chic interior, good food from imaginative menu and a thoughtful wine list

This pretty Victorian pub is always deservedly busy, so to be sure of a table it's best to book in advance. The elegant, understated interior has simple prints on pale cream walls, with blocks picked out in rich heritage colours, and an appealing mix of antique furniture from Georgian chairs to old commode stands on bare boards and patterned quarry tiles. A good mix of both drinkers and diners creates a cheerful atmosphere, and helpful staff serve Sharps Doom Bar and guest ales such as Chiltern Beechwood Bitter, Tring Side Pocket for a Toad and a changing guest on handpump, 31 wines by the glass (including two sparkling ones), 20 gins and 24 whiskies and bourbons; background jazz and darts. There are plenty of tables outside, and the pub is surrounded by lovely National Trust woodland.

Enterprising modern food includes local chicken and crème fraîche tian with chilli jam and chicken skin salt, brie and caramelised onion tartlet with ale-pickled baby onions, baked free-range eggs on moroccan-spiced vegetable stew with labneh and chickpea salad, free-range sausages of the day, sea bream with quinoa, spring onion and sprouting broccoli with cucumber and lemon salsa, lamb breast with champ, imam bayildi and red wine jus, maple-cured pork fillet with braised barley, heritage carrots and crispy shallots, and puddings such as lemon cheesecake with sichuan pepper meringue and poached rhubarb and dark chocolate brownie with orange and mascarpone ice-cream and orange syrup. *Benchmark main dish: bubble and squeak with oak-smoked bacon, free-range poached egg and hollandaise £13.75. Two-course evening meal £22.00.*

Salisbury Pubs ~ Lease Darren Johnston ~ Real ale ~ Open 11-11; 12-11 Sun ~ Bar food 12-2.30, 6.30-9.30; 12-3, 6-10 Fri, Sat; 12-9 Sun ~ Restaurant ~ Children welcome ~ Dogs allowed in bar ~ Wi-fi *Recommended by Ian Duncan, Patricia and Gordon Thompson, Professor James Burke, Margo and Derek Peters, Tracey and Stephen Groves, Peter and Jan Humphreys, Audrey and Andrew Nichols*

HERTFORD HEATH — TL3510 Map 5

College Arms

(01992) 558856 – www.thecollegearmshertfordheath.com

London Road; B1197; SG13 7PW

Light and airy rooms with contemporary furnishings, friendly service, good, interesting food and real ales; seats outside

The tasty, modern british food draws a good mix of customers to this civilised, well run place. The bar has long cushioned wall seats and pale leather dining chairs around tables on rugs or wooden floorboards, and a modern bar counter where attentive staff serve quickly changing ales such as Leeds Calypso and Oakham Citra on handpump and 20 wines by the glass; background music. Another area has more long wall seats and an open fireplace piled with logs, and there's also a charming little room with brown leather armchairs, a couple of cushioned pews, a woodburning stove in an old brick fireplace, hunting-themed wallpaper and another rug on floorboards. The elegant, partly carpeted dining room contains a real mix of antique-style dining chairs and tables. On the back terrace are tables, seats and a long wooden bench among flowering pots.

From seasonal menus the particularly good food is a mix of modern british and traditional pub classics and includes sandwiches and sharing platters, salt and pepper squid with chilli sauce, chicken liver parfait with pickles, honey-baked ham with duck egg and piccalilli, wild mushroom millefeuille with cornish yarg and cherry tomatoes, chicken with leeks, mushrooms, sautéed potatoes and pancetta jus, salmon and crab fishcake with caper butter and fries, rib-eye steak with garlic butter and chips, and puddings such as warm chocolate brownie with praline and vanilla ice-cream and lemon posset with mixed berries; they also open for weekend breakfasts (9.30-11am) and offer takeaway fish and chips early on Friday evening (5.30-7pm). *Benchmark main dish: beer-battered fish and chips £13.00. Two-course evening meal £23.00.*

Punch ~ Lease Andy Lilley ~ Real ale ~ Open 12-11; 12-midnight Fri, Sat; 12-8 Sun ~ Bar food 12-3 (5 Sat), 6-9; 12-6 Sun ~ Restaurant ~ Children welcome ~ Dogs allowed in bar ~ Wi-fi *Recommended by David Hunt, Lorna and Jack Musgrave, Chantelle and Tony Redman*

POTTERS CROUCH TL1105 Map 5

Holly Bush £

(01727) 851792 – www.thehollybushpub.co.uk

2.25 miles from M25 junction 21A: A405 towards St Albans, then first left, then after a mile turn left (ie away from Chiswell Green), then at T junction turn right into Blunts Lane; can also be reached fairly quickly, with a good map, from M1 junctions 6 and 8; AL2 3NN

Neat pub with gleaming furniture, well kept Fullers beers, good value food and an attractive garden

Although just a few minutes' drive from St Albans, this spotlessly kept cottage has a quiet and even remote feel. The long, stepped bar has particularly well kept Fullers ESB, London Pride, Seafarers and a Fullers seasonal beer on handpump and several wines by the glass. There are quite a few antique dressers (several filled with plates), a number of comfortably cushioned settles, a fox's mask, some antlers, a fine old clock with a lovely chime, daily papers and (on the right as you enter) a big fireplace. In the evening, neatly placed candles cast glimmering light over darkly varnished tables, all sporting fresh flowers. The fenced-off back garden has plenty of sturdy picnic-sets on a lawn surrounded by handsome trees.

Tasty food includes sandwiches, brussels pâté with apple and ale chutney, smoked salmon with lemon crème fraîche, flatbread pizzas, greek meze sharing plate, chilli con carne with sour cream and tortillas, wild mushroom and asparagus in creamy white wine or steak and kidney pies, lamb koftas with feta cheese, tzatziki and pitta bread, smoked haddock fishcakes with spinach and roasted vine tomatoes, and sticky toffee pudding with custard and cherry and almond tart. *Benchmark main dish: burger with toppings, coleslaw and chips £10.00. Two-course evening meal £20.00.*

Fullers ~ Tenants Steven and Vanessa Williams ~ Real ale ~ Open 12-2.30, 6-11; 12-3, 7-10 Sun ~ Bar food 12-2 (2.30 Sun), 6-9; not Sun-Tues evenings ~ Children welcome
Recommended by Max and Steph Warren, Peter and Emma Kelly, Paul Farraday, Stuart Doughty, Charles Todd, Jane Rigby

PRESTON TL1824 Map 5

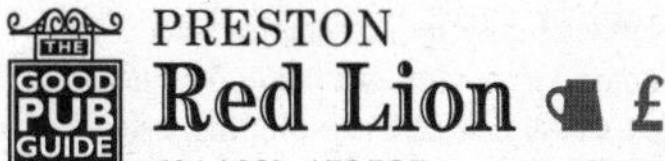

Red Lion £

(01462) 459585 – www.theredlionpreston.co.uk

Village signposted off B656 S of Hitchin; The Green; SG4 7UD

Homely village local with changing beers, fair-priced food and neat colourful garden

This bustling and cheerful village pub has been owned by the local community since 1982; it was the first in the country to do this and is a huge success. The main room on the left, with grey wainscoting, has sturdy, well varnished furniture including padded country kitchen chairs and cast-iron-framed tables on patterned carpet, a generous window seat, fox hunting prints and a log fire in a brick fireplace. The somewhat smaller room on the right has steeplechase prints, varnished plank panelling and brocaded bar stools on flagstones around the servery; background music, darts and dominoes. Fullers London Pride and Tring Side Pocket for a Toad with guests such as Cotleigh Tawny Owl and Oakham Citra on handpump, four farm ciders, ten wines by the glass (including an english house wine), a perry and winter mulled wine. A few picnic-sets on grass at the front face lime trees on the peaceful village green opposite, while the pergola-covered back terrace and good-sized sheltered garden with its colourful herbaceous border have seats and picnic-sets (some shade is provided by a tall ash tree).

Honest food includes smoked mackerel pâté with toast, prawns in garlic and chilli, wild mushroom, stilton and broccoli bake, chilli con carne, lamb moussaka, local rabbit ragoût with pasta, steak in red wine pie, moules frites, chicken malaysian curry, and puddings such as chocolate fudge cake and crème brûlée. *Benchmark main dish: fresh fish pie £12.50. Two-course evening meal £20.00.*

Free house ~ Licensee Raymond Lambe ~ Real ale ~ Open 12-2.30, 5.30-11; 12-3.30, 5.30-midnight Sat; 12-3.30, 7-10.30 Sun ~ Bar food 12-2, 6.30-8.30; not Sun evening, Mon ~ Children welcome ~ Dogs welcome ~ Wi-fi *Recommended by Karum, William Pace, Charles Welch, Lindy Andrews, Alan and Angela Scouller, Tracey and Stephen Groves, Miranda and Jeff Davidson*

REDBOURN TL1011 Map 5

Cricketers

(01582) 620612 – www.thecricketersofredbourn.co.uk

3.2 miles from M1 junction 9; A5183 signed Redbourn/St Albans, at second roundabout follow B487 for Hemel Hempstead, first right into Chequer Lane, then third right into East Common; AL3 7ND

Good food and beer in attractively updated pub with a bar and two restaurants

The relaxed front bar here is decorated in country style: comfortable tub chairs, cushioned bench seating and high-backed bar stools on pale brown carpet, and a woodburning stove. Four quickly changing ales on handpump include St Austell Tribute and Tring Side Pocket for a Toad with guests such as Sharps Doom Bar and Tring Drop Bar Pale Ale, 16 wines by the glass, farm cider, 18 gins and ten malt whiskies; background music. This bar leads back into an attractive, comfortably refurbished and unusually shaped modern restaurant; there's also an upstairs contemporary restaurant for private parties or functions. A side garden has plenty of seating and summer barbecues. Redbourn Common is opposite and many other walking and cycling opportunites surround this popular village pub. They can help with information on the Redbourn village museum next door.

Pleasing food includes sandwiches (not Sunday lunchtime), gin-cured sea trout with beetroot and apple salsa and pink peppercorn syrup, salt beef croquettes with sweet potato purée, creamy leek, asparagus and artichoke crumble with wild garlic crust, pizzas, calves liver with bubble and squeak, bacon and onion gravy, slow-cooked ox cheeks with charred baby gem, sautéed jersey royals and carrot salad, bouillabaisse with seaweed dust and herbed oil, corn-fed chicken breast with broccoli purée, almond poached celeriac and grated tenderstem broccoli, and puddings such as honey pannacotta with poached pear and roasted hazelnuts and marbled chocolate cheesecake with fresh berries. *Benchmark main dish: burger with toppings, tomato salsa and chips £12.95. Two-course evening meal £20.00.*

Free house ~ Licensees Colin and Debbie Baxter ~ Real ale ~ Open 12-11 (midnight Sat); 12-10.30 Sun ~ Bar food 12-3, 6-9; 12-4 Sun ~ Restaurant ~ Children welcome ~ Dogs allowed in bar ~ Wi-fi *Recommended by Lorna and Jack Mulgrave, Patrick and Emma Stephenson, John and Claire Masters, Richard Kennell, Rosie and John Moore, Rob Anderson*

SARRATT TQ0499 Map 5

Cricketers

(01923) 270877 – www.brunningandprice.co.uk/cricketers

The Green; WD3 6AS

Plenty to look at in rambling rooms, up to six real ales, nice wines, enjoyable food and friendly staff; seats outside

In a pleasant village setting overlooking the green and duck pond, this is a cleverly refurbished pub with a fine choice of drinks and interesting food. It's really worth wandering before you decide where you want to sit as the interlinked rooms have numerous little snugs and alcoves – perfect for a quiet drink. There are all manner of antique dining chairs and tables on rugs or stripped floorboards, comfortable armchairs or tub seats, cushioned pews, wall seats and two open fires in raised fireplaces; decoration includes cricketing memorabilia, fresh flowers, large plants and church candles. Phoenix Brunning & Price Original plus guests such as Malt Missenden Pale, Paradigm Best Practice (brewed in the village) and Tring Bring Me Sunshine on handpump, good wines by the glass, 30 gins and 50 malt whiskies; background music and board games. Several sets of french windows open on to the back terrace where there are tables and chairs, with picnic-sets on grass next to a colourfully painted tractor.

Brasserie-style food includes sandwiches, scallops with bean purée and chorizo fritters, harissa-spiced chicken thighs, apricot, pomegranate and mint salad and lemon yoghurt, mussels with bacon, leeks, cider and cream, cheese and potato pie with watercress and pea purée and lemon thyme dressing, venison, rabbit and pheasant pudding, braised lamb shoulder with dauphinoise potatoes and rosemary gravy, salmon and smoked haddock fishcake with a poached egg and chive and caper sauce, 10oz rib-eye steak with peppercorn sauce and portobello mushrooms, and puddings such as glazed lemon tart with raspberry sorbet and sticky toffee pudding with toffee sauce. *Benchmark main dish: steak burger with toppings, coleslaw and chips £13.45. Two-course evening meal £21.00.*

Brunning & Price ~ Licensee Simon Walsh ~ Real ale ~ Open 10am-11pm (10.30pm Sun) ~ Bar food 12-9.30; 12-9 Sun ~ Restaurant ~ Children welcome ~ Dogs allowed in bar ~ Wi-fi

Recommended by Geoff and Ann Marston, Tracey and Stephen Groves, Glen and Patricia Fuller, Max and Steph Warren, Daniel King

ST ALBANS TL1308 Map 5

Prae Wood Arms

(01727) 229090 – www.brunningandprice.co.uk/praewoodarms

Garden House Lane; AL3 6JZ

Spreading manor house in extensive grounds, with interestingly furnished rooms with plenty to look at, a fine range of drinks and modern food

This is a large and rather gracious pub with lovely surrounding grounds and a wide mix of cheerful customers. The various interconnected bar and dining areas have five open fires (one with button-back leather armchairs to each side) and a chatty atmosphere, though there are more intimate crannies too. Throughout, antique-style dining chairs and tables of every size and shape sit on bare boards, parquet and carpet, pale-painted walls are hung with portraits, prints and huge mirrors, elegant metal or glass chandeliers hang from high ceilings and the Brunning & Price trademark bookshelves, house plants and stone and glass bottles are much in evidence. Wooden stools line the counter where friendly, courteous young staff serve Phoenix Brunning & Price Original with guests such as 3 Brewers Golden English Ale, Hepworth Hiver IPA, Mighty Oak Oscar Wilde, Oakham JHB and Tring Side Pocket for a Toad on handpump, 18 wines by the glass and 54 gins; background music and board games. The loos are upstairs. There's a partly covered large stone terrace with plenty of good quality tables and chairs under green parasols, picnic-sets on grass and lawns that slope down to the River Ver at the bottom.

Enterprising food includes sandwiches, prawn cocktail, shredded ham hock with pickled vegetables, smoked haddock fishcake with a poached egg, feta burger with guacamole, beetroot relish and fries, slow-cooked pork belly with sweet potato mash, cauliflower purée, mixed cabbage cider and apple jus, hoisin beef brisket with crunchy asian salad, 10oz rib-eye steak with dijon mustard and tarragon butter, portobello mushrooms and chips, and puddings such as hot waffle with glazed bananas and banoffi ice-cream and crème brûlée. *Benchmark main dish: steak in ale pie £13.95. Two-course evening meal £21.00.*

Brunning & Price ~ Manager Rebecca Hall ~ Real ale ~ Open 11.30-11.30; 11.30-10.30 Sun ~ Bar food 12-9.30; 12-10 Fri, Sat; 12-9 Sun ~ Children welcome ~ Dogs allowed in bar ~ Wi-fi
Recommended by Audrey and Paul Summers, Alice Wright, Sandra Morgan, Nick Higgins, Cliff and Monica Swan, Sylvia and Phillip Spencer

ST ALBANS TL1407 Map 5

Verulam Arms

(01727) 836004 – www.the-foragers.com
Lower Dagnall Street; AL3 4QE

Quirky, enjoyable pub with foraged ingredients for both food and drink

If you're looking for a different kind of pub, you'll very much enjoy this place. It's run by a team of hunters and gatherers who use wild game, fruit and fungi for their interesting food, and brew their own ale with wild ingredients; they also make their own liqueurs and cocktails such as woodruff and apple vodka or a martini that uses sloe gin, vermouth and douglas fir syrup (a sort of christmas-tree-with-grapefruit taste). The beers include their own Foragers Saint Cloak Stout and Slingshot and a quickly changing guest on handpump; also, ales from around the world, tapped from the cask and in bottles, and cider. Furnishings and décor are simple: scrubbed tables surrounded by all manner of old dining chairs on floorboards, fireplaces with big gilt-edged mirrors above, a few prints on sage green paintwork, large blackboards with daily specials listed, frosted windows and candles. The gravelled garden has brightly painted picnic-sets and a heated awning where they grow hops and grapes. You can also buy tickets to join them on their foraging walks.

Innovative, seasonal food includes home-smoked mackerel and wood sorrel cacik (turkish tzatziki), slow-cooked, shredded muntjac with blue cheese and risotto rice balls, ramson (wild garlic) mayonnaise and hedgerow berry sauce, vegetarian burger (chestnuts, crab apples, windfall apples and mixed vegetables), slow-roasted pork belly with sweet apple sauce, mash, greens and crackling, scottish mussels with carrots, shallots, celeriac cooked in their own ale plus cream, dill, parsley and pickled sea purslane, venison in red wine stew with prunes and mushrooms, smoked haddock, hake and egg pie with herb alexander stems and purple sprouting broccoli, and puddings such as parsnip syllabub with rhubarb and a lavender shortbread and dark chocolate and local wild walnut cake with boozy blackberries from their own blackberry brandy. *Benchmark main dish: pork belly with jack-by-the-hedge (a herb) mash and elderberry gravy £14.50. Two-course evening meal £18.00.*

Free house ~ Licensee George Fredenham ~ Real ale ~ Open 12-11 (midnight Fri, Sat); 12-9 Sun ~ Bar food 12-3, 6.30-9; 12-5 Sun ~ Restaurant ~ Well behaved children welcome ~ Dogs welcome ~ Wi-fi *Recommended by Paul Humphreys, James and Becky Plath, Andrea and Philip Crispin, Bridget and Peter Gregson, Peter and Emma Kelly, Gary and Marie Miller, Gail and Arthur Roberts*

If we know a pub has an outdoor play area for children, we mention it.

WATTON-AT-STONE TL3019 Map 5

Bull

(01920) 831032 – www.thebullwatton.co.uk

High Street; SG14 3SB

Bustling old pub with beamed rooms, candlelight and fresh flowers, real ales served by friendly staff and enjoyable food

Wander around the pretty village and come to this charming 15th-c pub for lunch. The main bar has a relaxed atmosphere created by friendly staff, fresh flowers, contemporary paintwork, a leather button-back chesterfield and armchairs, solid dark wooden dining chairs and plush-topped stools around tables on bare boards and a leather banquette beside a landscape-patterned wall; the huge inglenook fireplace in the middle is a magnet for customers on chilly evenings. Adnams Ghost Ship and Sharps Atlantic and Doom Bar on handpump, 15 gins, good wines by the glass and a cocktail list; background music and TV. Near the entrance are some high bar chairs along counters by the windows; from here, it's a step up to a cosy room with just four tables, decorative logs in a fireplace, books on shelves, board games and an old typewriter. At the other end of the building is an elegantly furnished dining room (part-carpeted and part-slate floored). Outside, a covered terrace has seats and tables, there are picnic-sets on grass plus a small well equipped play area.

Well regarded food includes lunchtime sandwiches, prawn cocktail, duck liver parfait with red onion marmalade, sharing plates, three-bean chilli with wild rice, nachos, yoghurt and chives, a pie of the week, wild boar sausages with herb mash and beer-braised onions, slow-braised barbecue pork ribs with coleslaw and fries, whole grilled fish of the day with samphire and capers, slow-roast pork belly with cherry apples, bubble and squeak and spiced crackling, and puddings such as fudge and salted caramel pavlova with chantilly cream and blackcurrant crumble cake with rhubarb and yoghurt. *Benchmark main dish: burger with toppings, coleslaw and straw fries £13.95. Two-course evening meal £24.00.*

Star Pubs & Bars ~ Lease Alastair and Anna Bramley ~ Real ale ~ Open 9.30am-11pm; 12-6 Sun; closed Sun evening ~ Bar food 12-3 (4 Sat), 6-9; 12-4 Sun ~ Restaurant ~ Children welcome ~ Dogs allowed in bar ~ Wi-fi *Recommended by Adam Jones, Amy Ledbetter, Nik and Gloria Clarke, Ron and June Buckler, Rosie and John Moore, Sylvia and Phillip Spencer*

Also Worth a Visit in Hertfordshire

Besides the fully inspected pubs, you might like to try these pubs that have been recommended to us and described by readers. Do tell us what you think of them: feedback@goodguides.com

ALDBURY SP9612

Greyhound (01442) 851228

Stocks Road; village signed from A4251 Tring–Berkhamsted, and from B4506; HP23 5RT Picturesque village pub with some signs of real age inside; inglenook in cosy traditional beamed bar, more contemporary area with leather chairs, airy oak-floored back restaurant with wicker seats at big tables, Badger ales and a dozen wines by the glass, generally well liked food from lunchtime sandwiches, sharing plates and pubby choices up, set menu Mon-Thurs; children welcome, dogs in bar, front benches facing green with whipping post, stocks and duck pond, suntrap gravel courtyard, eight bedrooms (some in newer building behind), open all day, food all day weekends (till 7.30pm Sun). *(Rob Anderson)*

ALDBURY SP9612

★**Valiant Trooper** (01442) 851203

Trooper Road (towards Aldbury Common); off B4506 N of Berkhamsted; HP23 5RW Cheery traditional 17th-c village pub; appealing beamed bar with red and black floor tiles, built-in wall benches, a pew and small dining chairs around country tables, two further rooms (one with inglenook) and back barn restaurant, enjoyable generously served food (all day Sat, not Sun or Mon evenings), Chiltern, Tring and three guests, five ciders and plenty of wines by the glass, friendly helpful staff; background music, free wi-fi; children and dogs (in bar) welcome, enclosed garden with wooden adventure playground, well placed for Ashridge Estate beechwoods, open all day. *(Rosie & John Moore)*

ALDENHAM TQ1498

Round Bush (01923) 855532
Roundbush Lane; WD25 8BG Cheery and bustling traditional village pub with plenty of atmosphere; two front rooms and back restaurant, popular generously served food at fair prices, well kept Wells ales and a guest such as St Austell, friendly efficient staff; quiz first Weds of month, occasional live music, darts; children, walkers and dogs welcome, big enclosed garden with play area, open (and food) all day. *(Sylvia and Phillip Spencer)*

ALLENS GREEN TL4517

Queens Head (01279) 723393
Village signed from West Road, Sawbridgeworth; CM21 0LS Friendly semi-detached village drinkers' pub owned by the local community; four well kept beers (many more third weekend of the month and on bank holiday beer festivals), also good range of ciders/perries, straightforward reasonably priced food; live music; dogs welcome, large garden, open all day weekends, closed lunchtimes Mon and Tues. *(Kevin Bilton, Nigel Lusby)*

ASHWELL TL2639

★**Bushel & Strike** (01462) 742394
Off A507 just E of A1(M) junction 10, N of Baldock, via Newnham; Mill Street opposite church, via Gardiners Lane (car park down Swan Lane); SG7 5LY Smartly modernised 19th-c village dining pub (originally a brewery); highly regarded attractively presented food (Sun till 6pm) from chef-landlord's interesting menus including set choices and occasional themed nights, Charles Wells ales and nice selection of wines by the glass, friendly helpful service from young aproned staff; children and dogs (in bar) welcome, wheelchair access, picnic-sets on lawn and small terrace with view of church, closed Mon, otherwise open all day (till 10pm Sun). *(Graham and Carol Parker, John Walker)*

AYOT ST LAWRENCE TL1916

Brocket Arms (01438) 820250
Off B651 N of St Albans; AL6 9BT Attractive 14th-c country inn with low beams and inglenook log fires, good traditional food (special diets catered for) in bar and restaurant, friendly helpful staff, six real ales such as Greene King, Nethergate and Sharps, wide choice of wines by the glass; live music including jazz and open mike nights, quiz second Sun of the month; children welcome, dogs in bar, nice suntrap walled garden with play area, handy for George Bernard Shaw's house (Shaw's Corner – NT), six comfortable bedrooms, open all day, no food Sun evening. *(Sophie Ellison)*

BALDOCK TL2433

Orange Tree (01462) 892341
Norton Road; SG7 5AW Unpretentious old two-bar pub with up to 13 well kept ales including Greene King, four real ciders and large selection of whiskies, good value locally sourced home-made food (all day Sat, till 6pm Sun) including range of pies and blackboard specials, friendly helpful young staff, games room with bar billiards; quiz Tues, folk club Weds; children welcome and dogs (theirs is Arthur), garden with play area and maybe chickens, open all day Thurs-Sun. *(M G Hart)*

BARKWAY TL3834

Tally Ho (01763) 848071
London Road (B1368); SG8 8EX Little village-edge pub with clean modern décor; mix of wooden furniture on light boarded floor, log fire in central brick fireplace, four changing ales and good range of other drinks (happy hour 4-7pm Fri, Sat), limited menu of sandwiches, soup and bar snacks (may be fish and chip van or pop-up restaurants), friendly efficient staff; quiz second Weds of month; children welcome, decked seating area at front, picnic-sets and weeping willow in garden beyond car park, open all day (till 7pm Sun). *(Max and Steph Warren)*

BENINGTON TL3023

Bell (01438) 869827
Town Lane; just past Post Office, towards Stevenage; SG2 7LA Traditional 16th-c pub in very pretty village; local beers such as Buntingford and enjoyable caribbean food (licensees are from Trinidad), low beams, sloping walls and big inglenook; occasional folk nights and other events; big garden with country views, handy for Benington Lordship Gardens, open all day Sun (food till 6pm), closed Mon, Tues and Wed lunchtimes. *(Gary and Marie Miller)*

BERKHAMSTED SP9907

Boat (01422) 877152
Gravel Path, by bridge; HP4 2EF Cheerfully refurbished open-plan Fullers dining pub in attractive canalside setting (can get packed in fine weather); their ales kept well and guests, good choice of wines by the glass, cocktails, popular food from weekday lunchtime sandwiches and small plates to daily specials, mix of seating including padded stools and leather chesterfields on mainly parquet flooring, painted panelling and contemporary artwork, a couple of Victorian fireplaces; background

music, live jazz Sun afternoon; children and dogs welcome, french windows to paved terrace overlooking towpath and canal, moorings, open (and food) all day. *(Richard Kennell)*

BERKHAMSTED SP9807

Highwayman (01442) 285480

High Street; HP4 1AQ Bustling town pub with plenty of room for both drinkers and diners; relaxed bar with big windows overlooking the street, upholstered and leather chairs around all sorts of tables, lots of church candles in stubby holders, Sharps, Timothy Taylors and a guest, over 20 wines by the glass and well liked modern food from interesting menu, cheerful helpful young staff, bare-boards dining room has dark green leather wall seats and cushioned chairs at barley-twist tables, more seating in mezzanine above; monthly live music, free wi-fi; children and dogs (in bar) welcome, back terraced garden, open (and food) all day. *(Julian Thorpe, Peter and Jan Humphreys)*

BERKHAMSTED SP9907

Old Mill (01442) 879590

London Road/Bank Mill Lane (A4251); HP4 2NB Sizeable brick dining pub with attractive rambling layout, good choice of enjoyable food from deli boards up including weekday set lunch, well kept Greene King IPA, Tring Side Pocket for a Toad and a couple of guests, plenty of wines by the glass, interesting gins and cocktails, friendly service, two good fires; children and dogs (in bar) welcome, tables outside by mill race, some overlooking unspectacular stretch of Grand Union Canal, open (and food) all day, breakfast from 9.30am. *(Ross Balaam)*

BERKHAMSTED SP9907

Rising Sun (01442) 864913

George Street; HP4 2EG Victorian canalside pub known locally as the Riser; five well kept ales including one badged for them from Tring, up to 30 ciders/perries (four beer/cider festivals a year) and interesting range of spirits, two very small traditional rooms with a few basic chairs and tables, coal fire, snuff and cigars for sale, no food apart from substantial ploughman's, friendly service; background music, Thurs quiz; children and dogs welcome, chairs out by canal and well worn seating in covered side beer garden, colourful hanging baskets, open all day. *(Richard Kennell)*

BRAUGHING TL3925

Axe & Compass (01920) 821610

Just off B1368; The Street; SG11 2QR Nice country pub in pretty village with ford; enjoyable freshly prepared food (all day Sat, till 5.30pm Sun) from varied menu, own-baked bread, well kept ales including Harveys and several wines by the glass, friendly uniformed staff, mix of furnishings on wood floors in two roomy bars, lots of old local photographs, log fires, restaurant with little shop selling home-made chutney and relish; well behaved children and dogs welcome, garden overlooking playing field, outside bar, open all day. *(Sophie Ellison)*

BRAUGHING TL3925

Brown Bear (01920) 822157

Just off B1368; The Street; SG11 2QF Steps up to traditional little low-beamed pub with inglenook log fire in bar, up to four well kept changing ales and enjoyable home-cooked pubby food (not Tues) from ciabattas to good fish and chips, friendly staff, dining room with another good fire; Thurs quiz, occasional live music, games including darts, dominoes and shove-ha'penny; tricky disabled access, picnic-sets in garden behind with pizza oven, barbecue and pétanque, attractive village, closed Mon, otherwise open all day (till 6pm Sun). *(Rob Anderson)*

BRAUGHING TL3925

Golden Fleece (01920) 823555

Green End (B1368); SG11 2PE 17th-c dining pub with good food (special diets catered for) from chef-landlady including some imaginative choices, popular tapas night last Weds of the month and curry evenings, Adnams Southwold and guests, plenty of wines by the glass, cheerful service, bare-boards bar and two dining rooms, beams and timbers, good log fire; summer beer festival; children welcome, circular picnic-sets out at front, back garden with metal furniture on split-level paved terrace, play area, open all day weekends (food till 6pm Sun). *(Jane Rigby)*

BRICKET WOOD TL1302

Gate (01923) 678944

Station Road/Smug Oak Lane; AL2 3PW Popular family pub with good sensibly priced home-cooked food including british tapas, Wells and Youngs beers, friendly service, bar with log fire and side dining area; quiz Mon, free wi-fi; dogs welcome, garden (summer barbecues), open all day. *(David Appleyard)*

BUSHEY TQ1394

Horse & Chains (020) 8421 9907

High Street; WD23 1BL Comfortably modernised dining pub with woodburner in big inglenook; good choice of wines by the glass, real ales and enjoyable bar food from sandwiches and sharing plates up, also separate restaurant menu, themed nights and Sun brunch, kitchen view from compact dining room, good friendly service; children and dogs welcome (pub dog is Lizzie), open (and food) all day. *(Rob Anderson)*

CHAPMORE END TL3216

Woodman (01920) 463339

Off B158 Wadesmill–Bengeo; pub signed 300 metres W of A602 roundabout; OS Sheet 166 map reference 328164; SG12 0HF Early Victorian local in peaceful country hamlet; plain seats around stripped pub tables, floor tiles or broad bare boards, working period fireplaces, two well kept Greene King ales and guests poured from the cask, thai and tapas menus Weds-Sat evenings and Sun lunchtime, friendly staff, conservatory; children and dogs welcome, picnic-sets out in front under a couple of walnut trees, bigger back garden with fenced play area and boules, maybe summer Sun barbecues, closed Mon lunchtime, otherwise open all day. *(Victoria and James Sargeant)*

CHIPPERFIELD TL0400

Cart & Horses (01923) 263763
Quickmoor Lane/Common Wood; WD4 9BA Smallish 18th-c wisteria-clad pub popular for its enjoyable generously served food including bargain specials, two or three well kept changing ales and good choice of wines by the glass, friendly staff; children and dogs welcome, picnic-sets in big garden with marquee and play area, nice surrounding countryside and walks, open all day weekends, food all day Sun. *(Alice Wright)*

CHORLEYWOOD TQ0395

★**Black Horse** (01923) 282252
Dog Kennel Lane, The Common; WD3 5EG Welcoming 18th-c country pub popular for its good value generous food (smaller helpings available) from sandwiches to daily specials, five well kept ales including Adnams, Wadworths, Wells and Youngs, decent wines, tea and coffee, good cheery service even when busy, low dark beams and two log fires in thoroughly traditional rambling bar; daily papers and free wi-fi, open mike night second Sun of month; children, walkers and dogs welcome, disabled access, picnic-sets overlooking common, parking can be difficult, open all day, food all day Sun till 7pm. *(Roy Hoing)*

CHORLEYWOOD TQ0294

Land of Liberty, Peace & Plenty
(01923) 282226 *Long Lane, Heronsgate, just off M25 junction 17; WD3 5BS* Traditional 19th-c drinkers' pub in leafy outskirts; half a dozen well kept interesting ales and good choice of ciders/perries, snacky food such as pasties, simple layout, skittles, darts and board games; background jazz, TV (on request), no mobile phones or children inside; dogs welcome, garden with pavilion, open all day. *(Glen and Patricia Fuller)*

CHORLEYWOOD TQ0295

Stag (01923) 282090
Long Lane, Heronsgate, just off M25 junction 17; WD3 5BT Open-plan Edwardian dining pub with good varied choice of food from sandwiches and tapas up, well kept McMullens ales and several wines by the glass, friendly attentive service, bar and eating areas extending into conservatory, woodburner in raised hearth; daily papers, free wi-fi; children and dogs welcome, tables on back lawn, open all day, food all day Weds-Sun. *(Richard Kennell)*

CHORLEYWOOD TQ0396

White Horse (01923) 283033
A404 just off M25 junction 18; WD3 5SD Black-beamed roadside pub under good newish management, food such as pizzas, tapas and panini, Greene King ales, helpful staff, big log fire; children and dogs (in bar) welcome, small back terrace, open all day. *(Sophie Ellison)*

COLNEY HEATH TL2007

Plough (01727) 823720
Sleapshyde; handy for A1(M) junction 3; A414 towards St Albans, double back at first roundabout then turn left; AL4 0SE This cosy 18th-c thatched pub was closed for refurbishment as we went to press – reports please.

ESSENDON TL2608

Candlestick (01707) 261322
West End Lane; AL9 6BA Peacefully located country pub run by father and son team; emphasis on dining but also three well kept beers and several wines by the glass, relaxed friendly atmosphere, good value freshly prepared bar and restaurant food, comfortable clean interior with faux black timbers, log fires; quiz nights; children and dogs welcome, plenty of seats outside, good walks, closed Mon and Tues, otherwise open (and food) all day, Sun till 8pm (food 5pm). *(Julie and Andrew Blanchett)*

FLAUNDEN TL0100

Green Dragon (01442) 832269
Flaunden Hill; HP3 0PP Comfortable and chatty 17th-c beamed pub; partly panelled extended lounge, back restaurant and traditional little tap bar, log fire, popular good value food (not Mon), Fullers, St Austell and Youngs, friendly helpful service; background music, darts and other pub games; children and dogs welcome, hitching rail for horses, well kept garden with smokers' shelter, pretty village, only a short diversion from Chess Valley Walk, closed Sun evening and Mon lunchtime, otherwise open all day. *(Sophie Ellison)*

GILSTON TL4313

Plume of Feathers (01279) 424154
Pye Corner; CM20 2RD Old beamed corner pub with decent choice of well priced food (all day Fri and Sat, till 7pm Sun) including cook-your-own meat on a volcanic rock, Courage Best, Adnams Broadside and local guests, Weston's cider and maybe a mulled winter one, good choice of wines by the glass, friendly if not always speedy service, carpeted interior with brass-hooded log fire; background music, free wi-fi; children welcome, seats

on terrace and fenced grassy area with children's play equipment. *(Jane Rigby)*

GOSMORE TL1827

Bull (01462) 440035

High Street; SG4 7QG Popular 17th-c village pub with good often imaginative food (not Mon) cooked by landlord-chef, Fullers, Sharps and a guest, friendly welcoming service, beams and open fires, small back dining area; no under-14s in bar after 6pm or on Sun lunchtime, terrace tables, closed Sun evening, Mon lunchtime. *(Chantelle and Tony Redman)*

GREAT AMWELL TL3712

George IV (01920) 870039

St Johns Lane; SG12 9SW Pleasant 19th-c brick pub in pretty spot by church, good well presented food cooked by owner-chef from interesting snacks and pub staples up, can eat in log-fire bar or back restaurant, well kept changing beers and good choice of wines and gins, friendly helpful staff, flowers and candles on tables; quiz last Tues of month; attractive outside seating areas front and back, River Lea nearby, open all day Sat, till 6pm Sun, closed Mon (except 12-6 bank holidays). *(Mrs Margo Finlay, Jörg Kasprowski)*

GREAT HORMEAD TL4030

Three Tuns (01763) 289405

B1038/Horseshoe Hill; SG9 0NT Old thatched and timbered country pub-restaurant in lovely surroundings; enjoyable home-made food including blackboard specials, Buntingford Twitchell and a couple of guests, good choice of wines by the glass and local gin, small linked areas, huge inglenook with another great hearth behind, back conservatory extension; monthly quiz (Thurs), free wi-fi; children, walkers and dogs welcome, nice secure garden, open all day Sun till 7pm, closed Mon. *(Jane Rigby)*

HAILEY TL3610

Galley Hall (01992) 462906

Hailey Lane; SG13 7NY Traditional country pub with three bars; log fires, jugs hanging from beams, locals propping up the bar with their dogs, four well kept ales such as Greene King and Fullers, good choice of enjoyable food including specials, friendly staff; regular live music; children and dogs welcome, good outside space with play area, open all day and can get very busy. *(Mrs Margo Finlay, Jörg Kasprowski)*

HALLS GREEN TL2728

Rising Sun (01462) 790487

NW of Stevenage; from A1(M) junction 9 follow Weston signs off B197, then left in village, right by duck pond; SG4 7DR Welcoming 18th-c beamed and carpeted country pub; enjoyable good value traditional food (not Sun evening) in bar or conservatory restaurant, well kept McMullens ales, friendly helpful service, woodburner and open fire; children and dogs (in bar) welcome, disabled access, big garden with terrace, boules and plenty for kids including swings and playhouse, closed Mon, otherwise open all day. *(Rob Anderson)*

HARPENDEN TL1312

★**White Horse** (01582) 469290

Redbourn Lane, Hatching Green (B487 just W of A1081 roundabout); AL5 2JP Smart up-to-date Peach group dining pub; chatty split-level bar (one side a former stables), prints on painted panelling, stools by round tables, old parquet flooring and flagstones, some timbers and inglenook log fire, Sharps Doom Bar and a couple of guests, plenty of wines by the glass and interesting range of gins, airy dining room with tartan-upholstered chairs, pews and cushioned wall seats around pale wooden tables on stripped boards, enjoyable food including weekday fixed-price lunch; background music, board games, free wi-fi; children and dogs (in bar) welcome, contemporary tables and chairs under parasols on large flagstoned terrace, open (and food) all day from 9.30am breakfast on. *(Isobel Mackinlay)*

HATFIELD TL2308

Eight Bells (01707) 272477

Park Street, Old Hatfield; AL9 5AX Attractive old beamed pub (two buildings knocked together) with Charles Dickens association; small rooms on different levels, wood floors and open fire, three well kept ales including Sharps and Wells, good value lunchtime food; background music (live Tues, Sat), games machine, free wi-fi; children and dogs welcome, tables in backyard, open all day Fri-Sun, closed Mon. *(Edward May)*

HATFIELD TL2108

Harpsfield Hall (01707) 265840

Parkhouse Court, off Comet Way (A1001); AL10 9RQ Newly built aviation-theme Wetherspoons with large hangar-like interior; interesting décor using some old aircraft parts including a seating booth made from a jet engine housing, good range of beers and other drinks from long servery with time-zoned clocks in aeroplane windows, their usual good value food, friendly staff; TVs, free wi-fi; children welcome, disabled access, tables on paved terrace, open all day from 8am. *(Edward May)*

HATFIELD TL2308

Horse & Groom (01707) 264765

Park Street, Old Hatfield; AL9 5AT Friendly old town local with up to half a dozen well kept ales (beer festivals) and good value pubby lunchtime food, also Fri thai night and Tues and Sat suppers (free if you buy a pint), dark beams and good winter fire, old local photographs, darts and dominoes; quiz Thurs, sports TV; dogs welcome, a few tables out behind, handy for Hatfield House, open all day. *(Edward May)*

HEMEL HEMPSTEAD TL0411

Crown & Sceptre (01442) 234660
Bridens Camp; leaving on A4146, right at Flamstead/Markyate sign opposite Red Lion; HP2 6EY Traditional rambling pub, welcoming and relaxed, with well kept Greene King ales and up to six guests, generous helpings of good reasonably priced pubby food including Tues pie night, cheerful efficient staff, dining room with woodburner; children allowed, dogs in outside bar/games room, picnic-sets at front and in pleasant garden, good walks, open all day weekends, no food Sun evening. *(Peter and Jan Humphreys)*

HEMEL HEMPSTEAD TL0604

Paper Mill (01442) 288800
Stationers Place, Apsley; HP3 9RH Recently built canalside pub on site of former paper mill; roomy open-plan interior with upstairs restaurant, Fullers ales and a couple of guests (usually local), food from sandwiches and sharing plates up, friendly staff, log fire; Mon quiz and live music nights, free wi-fi; children welcome, tables out on balcony and by the water, open (and food) all day. *(Victoria and James Sargeant)*

HERTFORD TL3212

Old Barge (01992) 581871
The Folly; SG14 1QD Red-brick bay-windowed pub by River Lee Navigation canal; clean quaint interior arranged around central bar, wood and flagstone floors, some black beams and log fire, well kept Marstons-related beers, real ciders/perry and enjoyable reasonably priced food (not Sun evening) from sandwiches up, friendly staff; background music, Sun quiz, games machines; children and dogs (in one part of bar) welcome, a few tables out in front, more to the side, open all day. *(Jane Rigby)*

HERTFORD TL3212

Old Cross Tavern (01992) 583133
St Andrew Street; SG14 1JA Chatty old red-brick pub popular for its half a dozen particularly well kept changing ales including own microbrews, also bottled belgian beers and Aspall's cider, some snacky food such as pork pies, friendly staff and cosy relaxed atmosphere, open fires; May and Oct beer festivals; dogs welcome, small back terrace, open all day weekends, from 4.30pm other days. *(Max and Steph Warren)*

HERTFORD TL3212

Salisbury Arms (01992) 583091
Fore Street; SG14 1BZ Rambling 18th-c pub-hotel with three bars and smart restaurant, well kept McMullens ales and good fairly priced food from deli boards up, afternoon teas, efficient cheerful service, splendid Jacobean staircase to bedrooms; children welcome, open all day. *(Richard Tilbrook)*

HERTFORD HEATH TL3511

Goat (01992) 535788
Vicarage Causeway; SG13 7RT Popular 16th-c low-beamed pub facing village green; generous helpings of enjoyable fair-priced food, OAP set lunch Tues-Fri, Greene King IPA and a couple of guests, Aspall's cider, friendly helpful staff, restaurant; children and dogs (in lower bar) welcome, picnic-sets out at front, classic car meeting first Sun of month, open all day, no food Sun evening. *(J B and M E Benson)*

HIGH WYCH TL4614

Rising Sun (01279) 724099
Signed off A1184 Harlow–Sawbridgeworth; CM21 0HZ Opened-up 19th-c red-brick village local, up to five well kept ales such as Courage, Mighty Oak and Oakham tapped from the cask, friendly staff and regulars, woodburner, no food; live music and monthly quiz nights, darts; walkers and dogs welcome, small side garden, closed lunchtimes Tues and Thurs. *(Sophie Ellison)*

HITCHIN TL1828

Half Moon (01462) 453010
Queen Street; SG4 9TZ Tucked-away local freshened up under friendly new licensees; up to ten well kept ales (beer festivals Apr and Oct) and good value pubby food from sandwiches up; quiz first Tues of month, some live music; children (till 8pm) and dogs welcome, back garden with terrace, open all day (till 1am Fri, Sat), kitchen closed Sun evening, Mon. *(Rob Anderson)*

HITCHIN TL5122

Victoria (01462) 432682
Ickleford Road, at roundabout; SG5 1TJ Popular wedge-shaped Victorian corner local; Greene King ales and a couple of guests, enjoyable reasonably priced lunchtime food (also Mon and Fri evenings); events including live music, comedy and quiz nights, barn function room; children welcome, seats in sunny beer garden, open all day. *(Rob Anderson)*

HUNSDON TL4114

Fox & Hounds (01279) 843999
High Street; SG12 8NJ Village dining pub with good enterprising food from chef-landlord, not cheap but there is a weekday set menu, friendly efficient service, Adnams Southwold, a local guest beer and wide choice of wines by the glass, beams, panelling and fireside leather sofas, more formal restaurant with period furniture, bookcase door to lavatories; children welcome, dogs in bar, heated covered terrace, closed Sun evening, Mon. *(Rosie and John Moore)*

LEY GREEN TL1624

Plough (01438) 871394
Plough Lane, Kings Walden; SG4 8LA

Small brick-built rural local, plain and old-fashioned, with chatty regulars, two well kept Greene King ales and a guest, simple low-priced food; live music including Tues folk session, free wi-fi; children and dogs welcome, big informal garden with peaceful views, good walks nearby, camping, closed lunchtimes Mon and Tues, otherwise open all day. *(Glen and Patricia Fuller)*

LITTLE HADHAM TL4322

Nags Head (01279) 771555

Hadham Ford, towards Much Hadham; SG11 2AX Popular and welcoming 16th-c country dining pub with small linked heavily black-beamed rooms; enjoyable food from snacks to daily specials including good Sun roasts, close-set tables in small bar with Greene King ales and decent wines, restaurant down a couple of steps; occasional quiz nights; children welcome in eating areas, no dogs inside, tables out at front and in pleasant garden behind, open all day Sun till around 9pm. *(Max and Steph Warren)*

LONG MARSTON SP8915

Queens Head (01296) 668368

Tring Road; HP23 4QL Welcoming beamed village local with well kept Fullers beers and enjoyable good value food from pub favourites up (not Sun evening), helpful friendly service, open fire; children welcome, seats on terrace, good walks nearby, two bedrooms in annexe, open all day. *(Sylvia and Phillip Spencer)*

MARSWORTH SP9114

Anglers Retreat (01442) 822250

Startops End; HP23 4LJ Homely unpretentious pub near Tring Reservoirs and Grand Union Canal; smallish L-shaped angler-theme bar with stuffed fish and live parrot (Rosie), four well kept ales including Tring Side Pocket for a Toad, wide choice of good value food from baguettes up, Mon pizza night, friendly welcoming staff; regular live music, outside gents'; children, walkers and dogs welcome, side garden with tables under parasols, duck pond, aviary and an old tractor, bedrooms (some in separate building), open all day. *(Roy Hoing)*

MUCH HADHAM TL4219

Bull (01279) 841100

High Street; SG10 6BU Old village dining pub under new management; enjoyable food and well kept beers including Brakspears, friendly efficient service, inglenook log fire in bar, roomy dining lounge and back restaurant; children welcome, good-sized garden, Henry Moore Foundation nearby, open (and food) all day weekends, closed Mon lunchtime. *(Julie and Andrew Blanchett)*

NUTHAMPSTEAD TL4134

★**Woodman** (01763) 848328

Off B1368 S of Barkway; SG8 8NB Tucked-away thatched and weatherboarded village pub under long-serving family; 17th-c low beams/timbers and inglenook log fire, dining extension, enjoyable home-made food (not Sun evening) from traditional choices up, Buntingford, Greene King and Woodfordes tapped from the cask, friendly service, interesting USAF memorabilia and outside memorial (near World War II airfield); children in family room with play area, dogs in bar, benches out overlooking tranquil lane, two comfortable bedrooms, closed Mon, otherwise open all day (till 7pm Sun). *(Alice Wright)*

POTTEN END TL0108

Martins Pond (01442) 864318

The Green; HP4 2QQ New licensees for this 1920s brick dining pub facing the village green and pond; popular freshly prepared food from sandwiches up (Sat brunch from 10am), well kept Vale beers and several wines by the glass, friendly staff, conservatory; children and dogs (in bar) welcome, smallish paved garden, circular walks from the door, open all day, food all day weekends. *(Lewis Canning)*

REDBOURN TL1011

Hollybush (01582) 792423

Church End; AL3 7DU Picturesque pub dating from the 16th c run by father and son team; black-beamed lounge with big brick fireplace and heavy wooden doors, larger area with some built-in settles, ales such as Brakspears, Ringwood and Wychwood, enjoyable reasonably priced pubby food (not Sun evening) from sandwiches and basket meals up, friendly accommodating service; some live music, darts; children and dogs (in bar) welcome, picnic-sets in pleasant sunny garden (distant M1 noise), pretty spot near medieval church, open all day. *(Steve Lumb)*

REDCOATS GREEN TL2026

Farmhouse (01438) 729500

Stevenage Road; SG4 7JR Latest addition to the Anglian Country Inns group – including the Fox at Willian (this chapter) and White Horse at Brancaster Staithe (Norfolk); large 15th-c tile-faced building set in four-acre grounds, good food from shortish but varied menu (can be pricey), also fixed-price lunch and afternoon teas, plenty of wines by the glass including champagne, Adnams Southwold, friendly helpful staff, conservatory restaurant; children and dogs (in bar) welcome, 30 bedrooms (most in converted outbuildings), open all day, no food Sun evening. *(Edward May)*

RICKMANSWORTH TQ0594

Feathers (01923) 770081

Church Street; WD3 1DJ Old pub quietly set off the high street next to St Mary's Church; beams, panelling and soft lighting, well kept Fullers London Pride, Tring and two guests, good wine list, varied choice of freshly prepared food from sandwiches up including lunchtime deal and themed evenings, friendly young staff coping well at busy times; children allowed till 8pm, dogs in one side of the bar, picnic-sets out behind, open (and food) all day. *(Rob Anderson)*

RICKMANSWORTH TQ0592

Rose & Crown (01923) 773826
Woodcock Hill/Harefield Road, off A404 E of Rickmansworth at Batchworth; WD3 1PP Wisteria-clad low-beamed country pub under newish owners; well kept ales including Fullers London Pride, enjoyable traditional home-cooked food from sandwiches up, friendly young staff, airy dining room and conservatory, open fires; children and dogs welcome, large peaceful garden with views and goats, open all day. *(Brian Glozier, David Lamb)*

RIDGE TL2100

Old Guinea (01707) 660894
Crossoaks Lane; EN6 3LH Welcoming modernised country pub with good pizzeria alongside traditional bar; St Austell Tribute, nice italian wines and proper italian coffee, open fire; children and dogs (in bar) welcome, large garden with far-reaching views, open all day (food till 10pm). *(Sophie Ellison)*

ROYSTON TL3540

Old Bull (01763) 242003
High Street; SG8 9AW Coaching inn dating from the 16th c with bow-fronted Georgian façade; roomy high-beamed bar, exposed timbers and handsome fireplaces, plenty of tables and some easy chairs on wood floor, dining area with wall-sized photographs of old Royston, enjoyable pubby food including good value Sun carvery, Greene King ales, a guest beer and several wines by the glass, helpful pleasant service; background music, live folk second and last Fri of month, daily newspapers; children and dogs (in bar) welcome, suntrap courtyard, 11 bedrooms, open all day from 8am (till 1am Fri, Sat). *(Gail and Arthur Roberts)*

RUSHDEN TL3031

Moon & Stars (01763) 288330
Mill End; off A507 about a mile W of Cottered; SG9 0TA Cottagey low-beamed pub in peaceful country setting, good well priced home-made food in bar or small dining room, Adnams Southwold and a guest, friendly service; children and dogs (in bar) welcome, large back garden, closed Sun evening, Mon; management changing as we went to press. *(David Appleyard)*

SARRATT TQ0499

★**Boot** (01923) 262247
The Green; WD3 6BL Early 18th-c dining pub with good food (all day Sat, not Sun evening) from lunchtime sandwiches and sharing plates up, weekend breakfast (9.30-11.30am), also tapas and pizzas Fri and Sat evening, three well kept ales and good choice of wines by the glass, friendly young staff, rambling bar with unusual inglenook, restaurant extension; children and (in some parts) dogs welcome, good-sized garden with polytunnel growing own produce, pleasant spot facing green, handy for Chess Valley walks, open all day. *(Gary and Marie Miller)*

SARRATT TQ0498

Cock (01923) 282908
Church End: a very pretty approach is via North Hill, a lane N off A404, just under a mile W of A405; WD3 6HH Comfortably traditional 17th-c pub; latched back door opening directly into homely tiled snug with cluster of bar stools, vaulted ceiling and original bread oven, archway through to partly oak-panelled lounge with lovely inglenook log fire, red plush chairs at oak tables, lots of interesting artefacts and several namesake pictures of cockerels, Badger ales and decent choice of enjoyable food (not Sun evening) including OAP deal, carpeted restaurant in converted barn; background and live music, free wi-fi; children and dogs (in bar) welcome, picnic-sets out at front looking over quiet lane towards churchyard, more on sheltered lawn and terrace with open country views, play area, open all day. *(Jane Rigby)*

ST ALBANS TL1406

Garibaldi (01727) 894745
Albert Street; left turn down Holywell Hill past White Hart – car park left at end; AL1 1RT Busy little Victorian backstreet local with well kept Fullers/Gales beers and a guest, good wines by the glass and reasonably priced food (weekends only until 5pm), friendly staff; live music, sports TV, free wi-fi; children and dogs welcome, picnic-sets on enclosed terrace, lots of window boxes and flowering tubs, open all day (from 2.30pm Mon, 1pm Tues-Fri, noon weekends). *(Edward May)*

ST ALBANS TL1506

Great Northern (01727) 730867
London Road; AL1 1PQ Welcoming nicely updated roadside pub; good stylishly presented food from sensibly short regularly changing menus including early evening set deal (useful for next-door cinema), four well kept beers, good selection of wines and gins, efficient friendly service; terrace tables, open all day Fri-Sun, closed lunchtimes other days, no food Sun evening, Mon. *(Tom Savory)*

ST ALBANS TL1507

Mermaid (01727) 568912
Hatfield Road; AL1 3RL Bay-windowed pub with several seating areas (including window seats) arranged around central servery, half a dozen well kept ales, a dozen ciders/perries and good selection of bottled beers, friendly knowledgeable staff, small menu serving Pieminister pies and selection

of curries; background and live music, sports TV, darts; beer garden behind, open all day. *(Edward May)*

ST ALBANS TL1307

Six Bells (01727) 856945

St Michaels Street; AL3 4SH Rambling old pub with five well kept beers including Oakham, Timothy Taylors and Tring, reasonably priced home-made pubby food (not Sun evening) from good lunchtime sandwiches up, cheerful helpful staff, low beams and timbers, log fire, quieter panelled dining room; weekly live music, quiz nights; children and dogs welcome, small back garden, handy for Verulamium Museum, open all day. *(Paul Humphreys)*

ST ALBANS TL1406

White Hart Tap (01727) 860974

Keyfield, round corner from Garibaldi; AL1 1QJ Friendly 19th-c corner local with half a dozen well kept ales (beer festivals), decent choice of wines by the glass and reasonably priced home-made food (all day Sat, not Sun evening) including good fish and chips Fri; some live music, Weds quiz, daily newspapers; children and dogs welcome, tables outside, open all day. *(Edward May)*

THERFIELD TL3337

Fox & Duck (01763) 287246

Signed off A10 S of Royston; The Green; SG8 9PN Open-plan 19th-c bay-windowed pub in peaceful village setting with picnic-sets on small front green; good food (not Sun evening) from pub favourites up, Greene King and a couple of guests, friendly helpful staff, country chairs and sturdy stripped-top tables on stone flooring, smaller boarded area on left with darts, carpeted back restaurant; children and dogs welcome, garden behind with gate to park (play equipment), pleasant walks nearby, open all day weekends, closed Mon. *(Victoria and James Sargeant)*

TRING SP9211

Kings Arms (01442) 823318

King Street; by junction with Queen Street (which is off B4635 Western Road – continuation of High Street); HP23 6BE Cheerful backstreet pub built in the 1830s; five well kept ales including Tring, real cider and decent choice of malt whiskies and gins, good value food (not Sun evening) from pub favourites up including daily specials, stools around cast-iron tables, cushioned pews, some pine panelling and two warm coal fires (unusually below windows), separate courtyard restaurant (Fri-Sun); darts, free wi-fi; children till 8.30pm, no dogs inside, open all day weekends from 10am for breakfast. *(Tracey and Stephen Groves)*

TRING SP9211

Robin Hood (01442) 824912

Brook Street (B486); HP23 5ED Welcoming traditional local with four Fullers/Gales beers and a couple of guests kept well, good value pubby food (all day Sat), pop-up thai restaurant Sun evening, friendly service, several well cared-for smallish linked areas, main bar with banquettes and traditional tables and chairs on bare boards or carpet, conservatory with woodburner; background music, Weds quiz, free wi-fi; children welcome, dogs in bar, small back terrace, public car park nearby, open all day. *(Sophie Ellison)*

WESTMILL TL3626

Sword Inn Hand (01763) 271356

Village signed off A10 S of Buntingford; SG9 9LQ Beamed 14th-c colour-washed pub in pretty village next to church; good food in bar and pitched-ceiling dining room from snacks to evening specials, cheerful attentive service, Greene King IPA and a guest from brick-faced counter, pine tables on bare boards or tiles, log fires; children and dogs (in one part of bar) welcome, attractive outside seating area, four comfortable bedrooms in outbuilding, open all day Fri, Sat, closed Sun evening. *(Chantelle and Tony Redman)*

WHEATHAMPSTEAD TL1716

Cross Keys (01582) 832165

Off B651 at Gustard Wood 1.5 miles N; AL4 8LA Friendly 17th-c brick pub attractively placed in rolling wooded countryside; enjoyable reasonably priced pubby food (not Sun-Tues evenings) in bar and beamed restaurant including good Sun roasts, four well kept ales such as Adnams and Greene King, inglenook log fire; quiz second Mon of month; children, walkers and dogs welcome, picnic-sets in large garden with play area, three bedrooms, open all day weekends. *(Gary and Marie Miller)*

WIGGINTON SP9310

Greyhound (01442) 824631

Just S of Tring; HP23 6EH Friendly village pub under new management; good sensibly priced home-made food from fairly pubby menu including grills and daily specials, five changing ales and decent choice of wines, warm efficient service, woodburner in bare-boards bar, restaurant with well spaced tables on tartan carpet; monthly quiz, TV, free wi-fi; children and dogs (in bar) welcome, back garden with fenced play area, handy for Ridgeway walks,

Post Office address codings confusingly give the impression that some pubs are in Hertfordshire, when they're really in Bedfordshire, Buckinghamshire or Cambridgeshire (which is where we list them).

three bedrooms, open (and food) all day apart from Sun when kitchen closes at 5pm. *(Peter and Jan Humphreys, Malcolm and Sue Scott, Mrs P Sumner)*

WILDHILL TL2606

Woodman (01707) 642618

Off B158 Brookmans Park–Essendon; AL9 6EA Simple tucked-away country local with friendly staff and regulars, two well kept Greene King ales and four guests, real cider, open-plan bar with log fire, two smaller back rooms (one with TV), straightforward weekday bar lunches (not Sun); darts, free wi-fi; children and dogs welcome, plenty of seating in big garden. *(David Appleyard)*

WILLIAN TL2230

★**Fox** (01462) 480233

A1(M) junction 9; A6141 W towards Letchworth then first left; SG6 2AE Civilised contemporary dining pub (in the Anglian Country Inns group); pale wood tables and chairs on stripped boards or big ceramic tiles, paintings by local artists, good inventive food along with more traditional choices including sandwiches, Adnams, Fullers and three guests, good wine list (14 by the glass), attentive friendly young staff; background music, summer beer festival, TV; children and dogs (in bar) welcome, side terrace with smart tables under parasols, picnic-sets in good-sized back garden below handsome 14th-c church tower, open all day. *(John Gibbon, M G Hart)*

WILSTONE SP9014

Half Moon (01442) 826410

Tring Road, off B489; HP23 4PD Popular old village pub, clean and comfortable, with good value pubby food from sandwiches/panini up (best to book), well kept ales including Malt, Tring and XT, friendly efficient staff, big log fire, low beams, old local pictures and lots of brasses; may be background radio, games including Scrabble, dominoes and darts, free wi-fi; children and dogs welcome, some seats out in front and in good-sized back garden, handy for Grand Union Canal walks, open all day, no evening food Sun or Mon. *(Roy Hoing)*

WINKWELL TL0206

Three Horseshoes (01442) 862585

Just off A4251 Hemel–Berkhamsted; Pouchers End Lane, just over canal swing bridge; HP1 2RZ 16th-c pub worth knowing for its charming setting by unusual swing bridge over Grand Union Canal; low-beamed three-room core with inglenooks, traditional furniture including settles, a few sofas, ales such as Courage Directors and Wells Bombardier, good selection of wines by the glass, food from british tapas to burgers (they may ask to keep a credit card while you eat), bay-windowed extension overlooking canal; background music, comedy and quiz nights; children welcome, picnic-sets out by the water, open (and food) all day. *(Rosie and John Moore)*

Virtually all pubs in this book sell wine by the glass. We mention wines if they are a cut above the average.

Isle of Wight

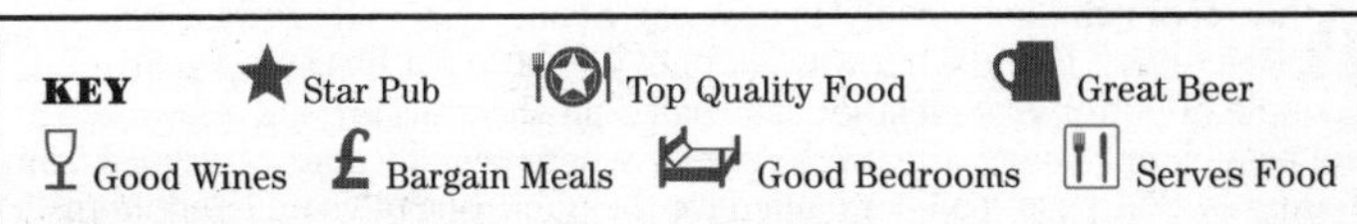

FISHBOURNE SZ5592 Map 2

Fishbourne Inn

(01983) 882823 – www.thefishbourne.co.uk

From Portsmouth car ferry turn left into Fishbourne Lane (no-through road); PO33 4EU

Attractively furnished pub with a contemporary feel, real ales, plenty of wines by the glass and all-day food; bedrooms

If you're out and about the exploring the island, this bustling half-timbered pub helpfully offers some sort of food all day. The open-plan bar has tartan-upholstered built-in wall seats and wooden chairs on slate flooring, a woodburning stove with a huge mirror above it and stools against the counter where friendly staff serve Fullers Seafarer, Timothy Taylors Landlord and a guest from Goddards on handpump and a dozen wines by the glass; leading off here is a comfortable, beamed lounge area with leather sofas, large pouffes, a couple of button-back armchairs and a flatscreen TV. There's also a bare-boards room with several clocks and a smart, airy dining room with high-backed black leather chairs around all sorts of tables, chandeliers and house plants. The outside seating areas have picnic-sets and contemporary tables and chairs. Bedrooms are comfortable and breakfasts are good. The inn is handy for the Wightlink ferry terminal. This is sister pub to the Boathouse in Seaview.

A wide choice of food includes lunchtime sandwiches, pâté of the day with onion chutney, shell-on prawns in garlic butter, wild mushroom and green bean tagliatelle in creamy parmesan sauce and truffle oil, pie of the day, trio of local sausages with mash and gravy, gammon and eggs, hake and mussels in a lemon, white wine and pink peppercorn sauce, chicken suprême in creamy mushroom sauce with sautéed potatoes, 10oz rump steak with a choice of sauces, corn on the cob, battered onion rings and chips, and puddings such as warm chocolate brownie with chocolate sauce and salted caramel ice-cream and lemon and stem ginger posset. *Benchmark main dish: whole fish of the day £13.95. Two-course evening meal £17.00.*

Inns of Distinction ~ Lease Martin Bullock ~ Real ale ~ Open 9am-11pm (10.30pm Sun) ~ Bar food 9am-9.30pm ~ Restaurant ~ Children welcome ~ Dogs allowed in bar ~ Wi-fi ~ Live music summer evenings and Sun lunchtime ~ Bedrooms: £85/£125

Recommended by D J and P M Taylor, John and Enid Morris, Isobel Mackinlay, Claire Adams, Sally and Brian Turner, Lenny and Ruth Walters

Please let us know what you think of a pub's bedrooms: feedback@goodguides.com or (no stamp needed) The Good Pub Guide, FREEPOST RTXY–ZCBC–BBAZ, Stream Lane, Sedlescombe, Battle TN33 0PB.

GODSHILL SZ5281 Map 2

Taverners

(01983) 840707 – www.thetavernersgodshill.co.uk

High Street (A3020); PO38 3HZ

Well run, friendly country pub with local ales, food cooked by the landlord, a relaxed atmosphere and seats in garden

'A haven of calm and civility' is how one of our readers describes this welcoming 17th-c whitewashed pub. The little bar has an open fire, a couple of button-back leather armchairs, plush stools around a few tables and high chairs against the brick counter where friendly staff serve ales from Goddards, Sharps and a beer named for the pub from Yates on handpump, ten wines by the glass and interesting home-made liqueurs. The dining areas have a two-way open fire as well as a woodburning stove, chapel, mate's and wheelback chairs around scrubbed country kitchen tables on flagstones, bare boards and nice old bricks. Mirrors and old local photographs hang on walls and wine decanters and horsebrasses sit on mantelpieces. The garden has seats and tables on a terrace and on grass, there's a children's play area and vegetable patches. A shop sells home-made and local produce. The pub is handy for the Model Village.

The chef-patron cooks the good food using home-grown and other local produce and daily baked bread and pastries: sandwiches, chicken liver pâté with onion marmalade, potted shrimps on toast, sharing plates, triple-cheese macaroni with garlic bread, pork sausages with bubble and squeak and onion gravy, beef in ale pie, moroccan-style lamb heart tagine with saffron couscous and yoghurt, black bream fillet with lemon, caper and tomato butter and spinach, salt-roasted pig cheeks with home-made pork faggot, celeriac purée and red cabbage, and puddings such as warm gingerbread with butterscotch sauce and pear and almond tart with clotted cream. *Benchmark main dish: beer-battered fresh fish and chips £12.50. Two-course evening meal £19.00.*

Free house ~ Licensee Roger Sergent ~ Real ale ~ Open 11-11; 11-5 Sun ~ Bar food 12-2.45, 6-8.45 (9.15 Fri, Sat); no food Sun evening ~ Restaurant ~ Children welcome ~ Dogs allowed in bar *Recommended by Steve Whalley, Martine and Lawrence Sanders, Paul Faraday*

SEAVIEW SZ5992 Map 2

Boathouse

(01983) 810616 – www.theboathouseiow.co.uk

On B3330 Ryde–Seaview; PO34 5AW

Isle of Wight Dining Pub of the Year

Contemporary décor in well run pub with real ales, quite a choice of food, a friendly welcome and seats outside; bedrooms

As the beach is just across the road, you'll find plenty of cheery customers in this extended blue-painted Victorian pub. The appealing interior has a bar with built-in wall seats, armchairs and leather pouffes, a large model yacht on the mantelpiece above a woodburning stove with a huge neat stack of logs beside it, and Fullers Seafarers, Sharps Doom Bar and a guest from Goddards on handpump, several gins and 11 wines by the glass; background music. The dining rooms have elegant wooden and high-backed black leather dining chairs, portraits on pale blue walls and an ornate mirror over an open fire; one of these rooms has a dinghy (complete with oars) leaning against the wall. Throughout, the paintwork is light and fresh and there's a mix of polished bare boards, flagstones and carpet. Some of the airy bedrooms have a view of the sea, as do picnic-sets and other seats under parasols on the terrace. This is sister pub to the Fishbourne Inn at Fishbourne.

Popular food includes sandwiches, pressed ham hock and parsley terrine with red onion chutney, mussels with bacon, cider and cream, honey and mustard glazed ham with local eggs, smoked cod fillet with quinoa, avocado and green beans salad, leek and tomato macaroni cheese gratin, chicken breast with wild mushroom and garlic tagliatelle, asian-spiced slow-cooked duck leg with garlic, ginger and spring onion noodles and sour cherry dressing, surf and turf (12oz rib-eye steak topped with garlic king prawns), and puddings such as citrus tart with lemon and lime syrup glaze and dark chocolate and raspberry bavarois. *Benchmark main dish: sea bass fillet with asparagus and salsa verde £14.95. Two-course evening meal £17.00.*

Inns of Distinction ~ Lease Martin Bullock ~ Real ale ~ Open 9am-11pm (10.30pm Sun) ~ Bar food 9am-9.30pm ~ Restaurant ~ Children welcome ~ Dogs allowed in bar ~ Wi-fi ~ Bedrooms: /£95 *Recommended by D J and P M Taylor, Stephen Funnell, Christopher May, Dave Chapman, Sandra and Michael Smith, Monty Green*

SHALFLEET SZ4089 Map 2

New Inn

(01983) 531314 – www.thenew-inn.co.uk

A3054 Newport–Yarmouth; PO30 4NS

Bustling pub with cheerful bar, local ales and popular food

This is an 18th-c former fishermen's haunt near the quay and still popular with visiting sailors. The rambling rooms have plenty of character with log fires, boarded ceilings and scrubbed pine tables on flagstone or carpeted floors. Friendly staff keep Ringwood Razorback, St Austell Proper Job and guests from local island breweries such as Goddards, Island and Yates on handpump and several wines by the glass; background music.

Well liked food includes lunchtime sandwiches, scallops with black pudding and pulled pork bonbons and pea purée, crab ramekin, pea, pine nut and pesto linguine, beer-battered fish and chips, lambs liver with bacon, mash and red wine and shallot gravy, corn-fed chicken with wild mushrooms, bacon and tarragon sauce and rosemary, hake fillet with ratatouille and sautéed potatoes, and puddings such as toffee apple cheesecake and golden syrup sponge with vanilla ice-cream; they also offer a two- and three-course lunch menu. *Benchmark main dish: fresh local crab salad £16.00. Two-course evening meal £21.00.*

Enterprise ~ Lease Dan and Kate Witherwick ~ Real ale ~ Open 11-11 ~ Bar food 12-3, 6-9; 12-9 weekends ~ Children welcome ~ Dogs allowed in bar ~ Wi-fi *Recommended by John and Enid Morris, Mike and Sarah Abbot, Patricia and Gordon Thompson*

Also Worth a Visit on the Isle of Wight

Besides the fully inspected pubs, you might like to try these pubs that have been recommended to us and described by readers. Do tell us what you think of them: feedback@goodguides.com

ARRETON SZ5386

White Lion (01983) 528479

A3056 Newport–Sandown; PO30 3AA

Former coaching inn under new management; beamed bar with stripped-wood floor and comfortable seats by log fire, Sharps Doom Bar, Timothy Taylors Landlord and a guest, several wines by the glass, good choice of well liked food, friendly attentive staff, restaurant; children and dogs welcome, pleasant terrace with view up to ancient church, nice walks, open all day. *(Paul Faraday)*

BEMBRIDGE SZ6587

Crab & Lobster (01983) 872244

Foreland Fields Road, off Howgate Road (which is off B3395 via Hillway Road);

PO35 5TR Clifftop pub with wonderful view from coastal bluff over the Solent; interior decorated in a parlour-like style, with lots of yachting memorabilia, old local photographs and a blazing winter fire, a house beer (Coastguard) from Yates along with Goddards and Sharps, ten wines by the glass, 16 malt whiskies and good food with fresh fish/seafood the highlight; children and dogs (in bar) welcome, sea views from terrace and two of the light and airy bedrooms, shore is just a stroll away, open (and food) all day. *(Holly and Tim Waite, Thomas Green, Colin and Daniel Gibbs, Charles Todd)*

BEMBRIDGE SZ6488

Pilot Boat (01983) 872077
Station Road/Kings Road; PO35 5NN Harbourside pub shaped like a boat – even has portholes; good food from sandwiches to local seafood, well kept Goddards and guests, friendly staff, restaurant area with woodburner and local artwork for sale; sports TV, darts; children and dogs welcome, disabled access, tables out overlooking the water or in two pleasant courtyards behind, well placed for coast walks, five redecorated bedrooms (overnight cycle storage), open all day. *(William Pace)*

BEMBRIDGE SZ6487

Spinnaker (01983) 873572
Steyne Road; PO35 5UH Attractively refurbished Edwardian inn (sister to the island's Boathouse at Seaview and Fishbourne Inn in Fishbourne – see Main Entries); interesting mix of dining chairs and tables on wooden floors, some bold paintwork, photos and nautical memorabilia, sofas beside an open fire and a woodburner, ales such as Goddards Fuggle-Dee-Dum, several wines by the glass and good imaginative food using island produce, afternoon teas; seats outside, 14 comfortable bedrooms, open all day from 9am for breakfast. *(William Pace)*

BONCHURCH SZ5778

★**Bonchurch Inn** (01983) 852611
Bonchurch Shute; from A3055 E of Ventnor turn down to Old Bonchurch; opposite Leconfield Hotel; PO38 1NU Quirky former stables with restaurant run by welcoming italian family (here since 1984); congenial bar with narrow-planked ship's decking and old-fashioned steamer-style seats, a couple of ales such as Courage and Wells tapped from the cask, decent wine list, bar food and good italian dishes, charming helpful service; background music, darts, shove-ha'penny and other games; children and dogs welcome, delightful continental-feel courtyard (parking here can be tricky), holiday flat. *(Patricia and Gordon Thompson)*

CARISBROOKE SZ4687

★**Blacksmiths** (01983) 529263
B3401 1.5 miles W; PO30 5SS Hillside pub refurbished under same owners as the Pointer at Newchurch; airy bare-boards dining extension with superb Solent views, popular food from sandwiches and pub favourites up, scrubbed tables in neat beamed and flagstoned front bar serving Yates, a couple of guests and good choice of wines by the glass; children, dogs and walkers welcome (Tennyson Trail nearby), more views from terrace and garden down steps, play equipment, open (and food) all day. *(Paul Faraday)*

COWES SZ4995

Duke of York (01983) 295171
Mill Hill Road; PO31 7BT Welcoming inn with good choice of popular generously served pub food and well kept ales such as Goddards, Dartmoor and Sharps, real cider, lots of nautical bits and pieces; free wi-fi; children and dogs welcome, well situated near high street and ferry, bedrooms, open all day. *(Moira and Jon Weller)*

COWES SZ4996

Globe (01983) 506053
The Parade; PO31 7QJ Modernised bar-restaurant worth knowing for its waterfront location, great Solent views from balcony and roof terrace with own bar; Goddards Island Pride, Ringwood Fortyniner and maybe Adnams Lighthouse from well stocked downstairs bar with big-screen sports TV and pool, popular smokehouse menu from sandwiches and wraps up, also weekend brunch and Sun carvery, efficient friendly service, upstairs dining room; children welcome (not on roof terrace), open all day, food all day weekends. *(Richard Tilbrook)*

CULVER DOWN SZ6385

Culver Haven (01983) 406107
Seaward end, near Yarborough Monument; PO36 8QT Superb Channel views from this isolated clifftop pub, clean and modern, with popular fairly priced home-made food, well kept changing ales such as Goddards, Timothy Taylors and Wadworths, several wines by the glass and decent coffee, friendly service, big restaurant; children and dogs welcome, small terrace, good walks. *(Dave Chapman)*

FRESHWATER SZ3487

★**Red Lion** (01983) 754925
Church Place; from A3055 at E end of village by Freshwater Garage mini roundabout follow Yarmouth signpost, then take first real right turn signed to

We say if we know a pub allows dogs.

Parish Church; PO40 9BP Bay-windowed red-brick pub on quiet village street; well kept St Austell Proper Job, three guest beers and several wines by the glass, popular well priced food from changing blackboard menu (booking advised), efficient friendly young staff, open-plan bar with country-style furnishings on flagstones or bare boards, woodburner; well behaved children and dogs welcome, a couple of picnic-sets out at front with view of church, more tables in back garden, good walking on nearby Freshwater Way, open all day. *(Charles Todd)*

GURNARD SZ4796

Woodvale (01983) 292037

Princes Esplanade; PO31 8LE Large 1930s inn with splendid picture-window views of the Solent (great sunsets); good choice of food from sandwiches and baguettes to daily specials, Fullers London Pride, Ringwood Fortyniner and a couple of guests, plenty of wines by the glass, friendly staff; weekend live music, Mon quiz; children and dogs welcome, garden with terrace and summer barbecues, five bedrooms, open all day, food all day weekends. *(Kim Stevens)*

HAVENSTREET SZ5590

White Hart (01983) 883485

Off A3054 Newport–Ryde; Main Road; PO33 4DP Old brick and stone village pub with good choice of popular food (all day Sun, special diets catered for) from sandwiches up, Ringwood and Goddards ales, friendly efficient service, cosy log-fire bar and carpeted dining area; children and dogs welcome, tables in secluded garden behind, open all day. *(Paul Faraday)*

HULVERSTONE SZ3984

★**Sun** (01983) 741124

B3399; PO30 4EH Lovely sea views from this pretty thatched pub; low-ceilinged bar with character furniture (including a fine old settle) on flagstones or bare boards, brick and stone walls, horsebrasses and ironwork around woodburner, ales such as Courage, Hancocks, Sharps and Wells, ten wines by the glass, and enjoyable pubby food, traditionally furnished dining room with big windows taking in the view; children and dogs welcome, picnic-sets in split-level cottagey garden, open (and food) all day. *(Glen and Patricia Fuller, Nicola and Holly Lyons)*

NEWCHURCH SZ5685

★**Pointer** (01983) 865202

High Street; PO36 0NN Well run old two-room pub by Norman church, generous helpings of good fairly priced local food including blackboard specials (booking advised in season), well kept Fullers ales and a guest, friendly attentive service; children and dogs welcome, views from pleasant back garden, boules, open (and food) all day. *(S Holder)*

NEWPORT SZ5089

Bargemans Rest (01983) 525828

Little London; PO30 5BS Quayside pub with spreading bare-boards interior packed with nautical memorabilia; good choice of generous reasonably priced pubby food including vegetarian and gluten-free options, Goddards, Ringwood and four guests; frequent live music, free wi-fi; children (away from bar) and dogs welcome, part-covered terrace overlooking River Medina, handy for Quay Arts Centre, open (and food) all day. *(Alf and Sally Garner)*

NEWPORT SZ4989

Newport Ale House 07791 514668

Holyrood Street; PO30 5AZ Steps up to intimate one-room pub with friendly chatty atmosphere, stools and leatherette bucket chairs on bare boards, half-panelling and some striking wallpaper, five well kept changing ales tapped from the cask by knowledgeable landlord, pies, rolls and sandwiches; regular live music, darts; dogs welcome, open all day. *(Alf and Sally Garner)*

NINGWOOD SZ3989

★**Horse & Groom** (01983) 760672

A3054 Newport–Yarmouth, a mile W of Shalfleet; PO30 4NW Roomy carefully extended pub liked by families; comfortable leather sofas grouped around low tables on flagstones, sturdy tables and chairs well spaced for relaxed dining, winter log fire, Ringwood Best, a couple of guest beers and a dozen wines by the glass, popular freshly made food served by friendly staff (smaller appetites catered for); background music, games machine, board games, free wi-fi; dogs allowed in bar, garden with well equipped play area including bouncy castle and crazy golf, nearby walks, open all day from 9am for breakfast. *(Penny and Peter Keevil)*

NITON SZ5075

★**Buddle** (01983) 730243

St Catherine's Road, Undercliff; off A3055 just S of village, towards St Catherine's Point; PO38 2NE 16th-c former smugglers' haunt with character traditional bar rooms; heavy black beams, captain's chairs, wheelbacks and cushioned wall seats around solid wooden tables, big flagstones or carpeted floors, open fire in a broad stone fireplace with a massive black oak mantelbeam, a beer named for the pub plus Fullers London Pride, Goddards Fuggle-Dee-Dum and Sharps Atlantic, 11 wines by the glass and a couple of farm ciders, enjoyable food including good fresh fish; background music, free wi-fi; children and dogs welcome, picnic-sets on two stone terraces and in neatly kept sloping garden looking down to the sea, coast path nearby, open (and food) all day. *(Heather and Richard Jones, Dave Chapman, Sophie and James Collier)*

NORTHWOOD SZ4983

Travellers Joy (01983) 298024
Off B3325 S of Cowes; PO31 8LS Friendly pub with simple contemporary interior; up to eight well kept ales (tasters offered), enjoyable reasonably priced food from sandwiches and pubby choices to daily specials, long bar with log fire, dining conservatory, pool room; Sun quiz and some live music; children, walkers and dogs welcome, garden with pétanque and play area, open all day. *(Edward May)*

SEAVIEW SZ6291

Seaview Hotel (01983) 612711
High Street; off B3330 Ryde–Bembridge; PO34 5EX Small civilised but relaxed Victorian hotel; traditional wood furnishings, seafaring paraphernalia and log fire in pubby bare-boards bar, comfortable more refined front bar (like a naval wardroom), three well kept ales including Goddards, eight wines by the glass from good list and well executed pub food, also first class upscale set menu in separate restaurant, pleasant helpful staff; background music; children welcome, dogs in bar, sea glimpses from tables on tiny front terrace, 13 bedrooms (some with sea views, seven in modern back annexe), self-catering cottage, good breakfast, open all day. *(Charles Todd)*

SHANKLIN SZ5881

★**Fishermans Cottage**
(01983) 863882 *Bottom of Shanklin Chine; PO37 6BN* Early 19th-c thatched cottage in terrific setting tucked into the cliffs on Appley beach, steep zigzag walk down beautiful chine; two cosy little rooms with low beams, flagstones and stripped-stone walls, old local pictures, fireplace with two-tier mantelpiece, Fullers London Pride and a couple of Island beers, good value pub food including plenty of fish, friendly staff; background and some live music; children and dogs welcome, sun-soaked terrace overlooking sea, lovely walk to Luccombe, open all day in summer, but may shut early in bad weather, also closed much of winter (best to check times). *(Steve Whalley, Stephen Funnell, Dave Chapman)*

SHANKLIN SZ5881

Steamer (01983) 862641
Esplanade; PO37 6BS Busy nautical-theme beachfront bar, fun for holiday families, with good choice of enjoyable well priced food from snacks to daily specials, ales such as Goddards, Ringwood and Yates, friendly hard-working staff, mix of seating including cushioned pews and leather sofas on quarry tiles; live music most weekends; fine sea views from part-covered two-tier terrace, eight bedrooms, open all day. *(Steve Whalley, Dave Chapman)*

SHORWELL SZ4582

Crown (01983) 740293
B3323 SW of Newport; PO30 3JZ Popular pub in attractive rural setting; four opened-up rooms around central bar, Fullers London Pride, Sharps Doom Bar and a local guest, proper cider and 11 wines by the glass, good choice of enjoyable food, knocked-through beamed lounge with china on carved dresser, country prints on stripped-stone walls and winter log fire; background music (live Fri evening, Sun lunchtime), free wi-fi; children and dogs welcome, streamside garden with small trout-filled pool and play area, open (and food) all day. *(Thomas Green, Neil Allen, Dave Chapman)*

ST HELENS SZ6289

Vine (01983) 872337
Upper Green Road; PO33 1UJ Victorian red-brick local overlooking large village green; enjoyable home-cooked food (all day Sat, Sun) including stone-baked pizzas, ales such as Island, Ringwood and Sharps, cheerful helpful staff; weekend live music, Weds quiz, pool and darts, free wi-fi; children and dogs welcome, some seats out in front, play area across road, open all day. *(A N Bance)*

VENTNOR SZ5677

Perks (01983) 857446
High Street; PO38 1LT Popular little bar packed with interesting memorabilia behind shop-window front, well kept ales including Bass and good range of wines, enjoyable well priced home-made food from sandwiches and baked potatoes up, bargain OAP two-course lunch, fast friendly service; dogs welcome, open all day. *(Edward May)*

VENTNOR SZ5677

★**Spyglass** (01983) 855338
Esplanade, SW end; road down is very steep and twisty, and parking nearby can be difficult – best to use pay-and-display (free in winter) about 100 metres up the road; PO38 1JX Perched above the beach with a fascinating jumble of seafaring memorabilia in snug quarry-tiled interior, Ringwood ales and guests, good choice of wines and popular food including fish/seafood dishes (good crab sandwiches), friendly helpful service; background music, live daily in summer; children welcome, dogs and muddy boots in bar, sea-wall terrace with lovely views, coast walk towards the

'Children welcome' means the pub says it lets children inside without any special restriction; some may impose an evening time limit earlier than 9pm – please tell us if you find this.

Botanic Garden, heftier hikes on to St Boniface Down and towards the eerie shell of Appuldurcombe House, four sea-view bedrooms, open (and food) all day. *(D J and P M Taylor, Dave Chapman)*

VENTNOR SZ5677

Volunteer (01983) 852537

Victoria Street; PO38 1ES Welcoming one-room local now under same management as nearby Perks; five well kept changing ales (always one from an Isle of Wight brewery) and a real cider, renovated interior with bare boards and carpet, upholstered pews, farmhouse chairs and cast-iron-framed tables, some military and Ventnor brewery memorabilia, Victorian tiled fireplace (electric fire); simple home-made food including sandwiches; background music, darts and the local game of rings; dogs welcome, no children, open all day. *(Kevin Upton)*

WHITWELL SZ5277

White Horse (01983) 730375

High Street; PO38 2PY Extended 15th-c pub with popular good value food from pub staples to daily specials (booking advised), well kept ales such as Goddards and Yates, good friendly service, carpeted beamed bar with exposed stonework, restaurant; Mon quiz, darts and pool; children and dogs welcome, picnic-sets among fruit trees in big garden with play area, open all day (food all day weekends). *(Paul Faraday)*

YARMOUTH SZ3589

Bugle (01983) 760272

The Square; PO41 0NS Old coaching house with long frontage and several linked rooms, chesterfields by open fire in low-ceilinged panelled lounge, farmhouse-style furniture in dining areas, books on shelves (and book wallpaper), restaurant with high-backed leather chairs around a mix of tables on bare boards or carpet, generous helpings of enjoyable pub food including daily fresh fish, quick cheerful service, traditionally furnished bar with five real ales such as Courage and Sharps, conservatory; background music; children and dogs welcome, picnic-sets and lots of hanging baskets in large courtyard garden, seven bedrooms, handy for ferry, open (and food) all day. *(Martine and Lawrence Sanders)*

YARMOUTH SZ3589

Wheatsheaf (01983) 760456

Bridge Road, near ferry; PO41 0PH Opened-up and modernised Victorian pub with generous well priced food including good burgers and daily specials, cheerful service, Goddards, Ringwood and a guest; winter pool table; children and dogs welcome, outside seating, open (and food) all day. *(Charles Todd)*

Kent

BIDDENDEN TQ8238 Map 3

Three Chimneys

(01580) 291472 – www.thethreechimneys.co.uk

Off A262 at pub sign, a mile W of village; TN27 8LW

Kent Dining Pub of the Year

Pubby beamed rooms of considerable individuality, log fires, imaginative food and big, pretty garden; comfortable bedrooms

As ever, our readers are full of praise for all aspects of this lovely old inn. The five bedrooms, each with their own terrace, are proving extremely popular, and breakfast are very good. The small, low-beamed bar and dining rooms are civilised but informal with plenty of character. They're simply done out with plain wooden furniture and old settles on flagstones and coir matting, some harness and sporting prints on the stripped-brick walls and good log fires. Served by well trained staff, drinks include Adnams Southwold, Harveys Best and a changing weekly guest beer tapped from the cask, 14 wines plus sparkling wine and champagne by the glass from a good list, local Biddenden's cider and nine malt whiskies; background music in the restaurant and cards. A candlelit bare-boards restaurant has rustic décor and french windows that open into a newly extended conservatory looking over seats in the pretty garden, where raised beds contain herbs and other produce for the kitchen. At the front of the building is an extended and enclosed open-air dining courtyard. They've just opened a holiday cottage for rent. The gardens at Sissinghurst (National Trust) are nearby.

Impressive food includes ploughman's, baked field mushrooms topped with caramelised red onion and grilled goats cheese, salmon and smoked haddock fishcakes with home-made tartare sauce, duck and bacon hash on wild rocket topped with a fried egg, three-cheese and onion croquettes on creamed leeks, wilted spinach and mushroom fricassée, duck breast with roasted carrots and swede, braised savoy cabbage, parmentier potatoes and rich jus, smoked haddock on creamed leeks and crushed new potatoes with chives, bacon and spring onions and chive velouté, and puddings such as dark chocolate délice on a praline biscuit base with pistachio ice-cream and apple and plum crumble with cream. *Benchmark main dish: rack of lamb with dauphinoise potatoes, butternut squash and rich jus £19.95. Two-course evening meal £24.00.*

Free house ~ Licensee Craig Smith ~ Real ale ~ Open 11.30-11 (11.30 Sat); 12-11 Sun ~ Bar food 12-2.30, 6.30-9 (9.30 Fri, Sat); bar menu also 2-6pm ~ Restaurant ~ Children welcome ~ Dogs allowed in bar ~ Wi-fi ~ Bedrooms: £90/£130 *Recommended by Hunter and Christine Wright, Alexandra and Richard Clay, Serena and Richard Furber, Julia and Fiona Barnes, Alan Cowell*

CHIDDINGSTONE CAUSEWAY TQ5146 Map 3

Little Brown Jug

(01892) 870318 – www.thelittlebrownjug.co.uk

B2027; TN11 8JJ

Bustling pub with interconnected bar and dining rooms, open fires, four real ales and enjoyable food; seats outside

Even when really busy, which this well run place often is, the efficient, helpful staff keep things running smoothly. The beamed front bar has rugs on bare boards or tiled floors, a roaring log fire, leather chesterfield sofas and chunky stools in one corner and high chairs against the carved counter where they keep Greene King Ale Fresco and Old Speckled Hen, Larkins Traditional and Westerham Summer Perle on handpump and 22 wines by the glass; background music and board games. Throughout, various dining areas merge together with open doorways and timbering, and there's all manner of cushioned wooden dining chairs, wall seats and settles with scatter cushions around polished dark wood or rustic tables, and more open fires. Also, hundreds of prints, framed old cigarette cards, maps and photos on painted walls, books on shelves, house plants, old stone bottles and candles on windowsills and big mirrors. A terrace has seats and tables, there are picnic-sets on grass and a children's play area; you can hire the 'dining huts' for £25, but you must book in advance.

As well as breakfast (9-11am Friday-Sunday), the wide choice of good food includes sandwiches (until 6pm), squid, prawn and chorizo stew, baked garlic and rosemary camembert with onion jam, burger with toppings, aioli and skinny fries, cod, leek and dill fishcake with lemon mayonnaise and tomato and red onion salad, mustard-glazed lamb shoulder with dauphinoise potatoes and lamb sauce, duck breast with potato terrine, carrot and ginger purée, and orange and pomegranate sauce, dry-rub spiced pork chop salad with yoghurt dressing and baby cucumber and radish, and puddings such as chocolate brownie with chocolate sauce and rice pudding with strawberry jam. *Benchmark main dish: beer-battered cod and chips £14.95. Two-course evening meal £20.00.*

Whiting & Hammond ~ Lease Paulo de Silva ~ Real ale ~ Open 10am-11pm; 9am-11pm Sat; 9am-11pm Sun ~ Bar food 12-9.30; 12-9 Sun ~ Restaurant ~ Children welcome ~ Dogs allowed in bar ~ Wi-fi *Recommended by Tony Scott, Christian Mole, Neil Allen, Nik and Gloria Clarke, Miles Green*

CHIPSTEAD TQ5056 Map 3

George & Dragon

(01732) 779019 – www.georgeanddragonchipstead.com

Near M25 junction 5; 39 High Street; TN13 2RW

Excellent food in popular village dining pub with three real ales, friendly, efficient service and seats in garden

'This pub delivers on all counts,' says one of our readers who comes here regularly, and others readily agree. The opened-up bar has heavy black beams and standing timbers, grey-green panelling, framed articles about their suppliers on the walls, and an easy-going, friendly atmosphere; background music. In the centre, a comfortable sofa and table sit in front of a log fire, with a tiny alcove to one side housing a built-in wall seat and just one table and chair. Westerham George's Marvellous Medicine (named for the pub) and Grasshopper on handpump and 21 wines by the glass served by courteous, helpful staff. Up a step to each side are two small dining areas with more panelling, an attractive assortment of nice old chairs around various tables on bare floorboards and two more (unused) fireplaces. Upstairs there's a sizeable timbered dining room with similar furnishings and a cosy room that's just right for a private party. The back garden has benches, modern chrome and wicker chairs and tables under parasols, and raised beds for flowers, herbs and vegetables. Wheelchair access to the garden only.

Attractively presented and particularly good, the food includes sandwiches, 'bang bang' smoked chicken salad with crunchy bean sprouts, pak choi and carrots, poached sea trout with pickled spring vegetables and broad bean pesto, wild garlic risotto with toasted pine nuts and parmesan crisp, a roast of the day, duck breast with orange blossom and carrot purée, fondant potatoes and charred leeks, baked cod with baby potato fricassée, smoked pancetta, baby peas and chervil, lamb rump with dauphinoise potatoes, wild garlic pesto and black olive tapenade, and puddings such as chocolate and amaretti torte with coffee chantilly cream and raspberry and coconut tart. *Benchmark main dish: wild boar and chorizo burger with toppings and chips £15.50. Two-course evening meal £21.00.*

Free house ~ Licensee Ben James ~ Real ale ~ Open 12-11 (10.30 Sun) ~ Bar food 12-3 (4 Sat), 6-9.30; 12-4, 6-8.30 Sun ~ Restaurant ~ Children welcome ~ Dogs allowed in bar ~ Wi-fi *Recommended by Michael Breeze, Richard Cole, Colin McLachlan*

GOUDHURST TQ7037 Map 3

Green Cross

(01580) 211200 – www.greencrossinn.co.uk

East off A21 on to A262 (Station Road); TN17 1HA

Down-to-earth bar with real ales and more formal back restaurant

Most customers are here to enjoy the first class fish and shellfish, but the properly pubby little two-roomed front bar is chatty and relaxed and they do keep Harveys Best and half a dozen wines by the glass. There are stripped floorboards, dark wooden furnishings, wine bottles on windowsills, hop-draped beams, brass jugs on a mantelshelf above the fire and a few plush bar stools by the counter; background music. Attractive in an old-fashioned sort of way, the back dining room has flowers on tables, dark beams in cream walls and country paintings for sale. You can sit out on a small terrace along the side of the pub.

Majoring on fish and shellfish, the menu includes baguettes, avocado and crab bake, wild mushrooms with wholegrain mustard, wine and cream on toast, spaghetti with lobster, cherry tomatoes, garlic and parsley, rack of barbecue pork ribs, moules frites, huge cornish cock crab salad, seared loin of swordfish with smoked paprika, lemon juice, olive oil and parsley, king scallops coquilles st jacques, seafood paella, fillet steak with crushed peppercorns, brandy and cream sauce, and puddings such as mulberry crème brûlée and zabaglione. *Benchmark main dish: local skate wing with black butter and capers £19.85. Two-course evening meal £24.00.*

Free house ~ Licensee Lou Lizzi ~ Real ale ~ Open 12-3, 6-11; closed Sun evening ~ Bar food 12-2.30, 7-9 ~ Restaurant ~ Children welcome ~ Dogs allowed in bar ~ Wi-fi *Recommended by Robin Waters, Harvey Brown, Emma Scofield, Sabina and Gerald Grimshaw, Professor James Burke, Emily and Toby Archer*

ICKHAM TR2258 Map 3

Duke William

(01227) 721308 – www.thedukewilliamickham.com

Off A257 E of Canterbury; The Street; CT3 1QP

Friendly pub with character rooms, good food and ales and seats in pretty garden; bedrooms

This is a pretty village just ten minutes' drive from Canterbury and the pub is gently civilised and well run. The spreading bar has huge oak beams and stripped joists, seats that range from country kitchen to cushioned settles with animal skin throws, all manner of tables on stripped wooden floors and a log fire with a low barrel table in front of it. Seats line the bar where friendly staff serve Fullers London Pride, McCanns Harry Hop and Timothy Taylors Landlord on handpump, eight wines by the glass and a good choice of gins and whiskies. The low-ceilinged dining room is similarly furnished and a conservatory looks over the garden and fields beyond. Throughout, paintwork is contemporary, tables are set with fresh flowers and candles in stone bottles and there are interesting paintings, prints and china plates on the walls; background music and board games. Modern seats and tables are set under parasols on the partly covered terrace, with picnic-sets and a children's play area on grass. Bedrooms (named after the owner's culinary heroes) are attractively and simply furnished and breakfasts are generous.

As well as offering a weekend brunch menu (11-3), the well regarded food includes sandwiches, potted shrimps on toast, salmon fishcake with tartare hollandaise, bubble and squeak with a fried egg, plaice with sea vegetables and crushed new potatoes, burger with toppings, pickles, bourbon sauce and fries, slow-cooked pork belly with chorizo and cannellini beans, roast lamb rump with whipped peas, lovage and creamy mash, roasted huss with spinach, wild garlic and horseradish new potato salad, and puddings such as banoffi pie with caramelised banana and passion fruit and Valrhona chocolate pot with honeycomb ice-cream. *Benchmark main dish: fish pie £14.00. Two-course evening meal £20.00.*

Free house ~ Licensee Mark Sargeant ~ Real ale ~ Open 12-11; 11-midnight Sat; 11-10.30 Sun ~ Bar food 12-3, 6-9; 12-3, 6.30-9.30 Sat; 12-5 Sun ~ Restaurant ~ Live music monthly (check website) ~ Dogs allowed in bar ~ Wi-fi ~ Bedrooms: /£120 *Recommended by Sarah Ridout, V Brogden, Peter and Emma Kelly, Deborah and Duncan Walliams, Heather and Richard Jones, Gerry and Pam Pollard, Alison and Tony Livesley*

LANGTON GREEN TQ5439 Map 3

Hare

(01892) 862419 – www.brunningandprice.co.uk/hare

A264 W of Tunbridge Wells; TN3 0JA

Interestingly decorated Edwardian pub with a fine choice of drinks and imaginative food

Cheerfully efficient young staff keep an interesting range of drinks here, including Greene King IPA and guests such as Hogs Back TEA, St Austell Tribute and Tonbridge Coppernob on handpump, 30 wines by the glass, 75 malt whiskies, 25 gins and a farm cider. Chatty regulars gather at stools around the counter. The high-ceilinged rooms are light and airy with rugs on bare boards, built-in wall seats, stools and old-style wooden tables and chairs, dark dados below pale-painted walls covered in old photographs and prints, romantic pastels and a huge collection of chamber-pots hanging from beams; background radio and board games. French windows open on to a big terrace with pleasant views of the tree-ringed village green. Parking in front of the pub is limited, but you can park in the lane to one side.

Well executed food from an up-to-date menu includes sandwiches, sticky sesame pork belly with ginger and orange dressing, scallops with ham fritters, pea purée and lemon dressing, thai green curry with sweet potato, aubergine, baby corn, cashew nuts and coconut rice, pork and leek sausages with mash and onion gravy, salmon and smoked haddock fishcake with a poached egg and chive and caper sauce, rosemary and garlic chicken breast with wild mushrooms, bacon and spinach on pasta, braised beef with horseradish dumplings and root vegetables, fish pie, and puddings such as crème brûlée and chocolate brownie with chocolate sauce. *Benchmark main dish: lamb shoulder with dauphinoise potatoes and thyme and rosemary gravy £17.25. Two-course evening meal £20.00.*

Brunning & Price ~ Manager Rebecca Bowen ~ Real ale ~ Open 11-11; 11-midnight Sat, Sun ~ Bar food 12-9.30; 12-10 Fri, Sat; 12-9 Sun ~ Restaurant ~ Children welcome ~ Dogs allowed in bar ~ Wi-fi *Recommended by Richard and Penny Gibbs, Monica and Steph Evans, Emily and Toby Archer, Gerry and Rosemary Dobson, Pauline and Mark Evans, Rob Anderson*

MEOPHAM TQ6364 Map 3

Cricketers

(01474) 812163 – www.thecricketersinn.co.uk

Wrotham Road (A227); DA13 0QA

Busy village pub with friendly staff, plenty to look at, several real ales, good wines and well thought-of food

At weekends in particular you'll find a wide mix of customers keen to enjoy the tasty food here; those wanting just a drink and a chat head for the front bar. This has cushioned wall settles, a mix of old-style wooden dining chairs and tables, a raised fireplace, newspapers to read and Caledonian Deuchars IPA and guests such as Bexley Session Golden Ale, Fullers London Pride and Tonbridge Coppernob and Countryman on handpump and around a dozen wines by the glass; staff are hard-working and helpful. Glass partitioning separates an end room which has bookshelves either side of another fireplace, rugs on bare floorboards and big house plants. Down steps to one side of the bar is a sizeable dining room with another raised fireplace and similar chairs and tables on more rugs and boards. Throughout there are frame-to-frame photos, prints and paintings, and church candles on each table; background music. Doors in the end family room open to sizeable outdoor seating areas (overlooking the windmill) with contemporary black rattan-style seats under parasols; there are a few seats out in front too. The village green is opposite.

As well as weekend breakfasts (9-11am), the wide choice of pleasing food includes sandwiches, chicken liver parfait with red onion jam, whitebait with tartare sauce, macaroni cheese with garlic bread, beer-battered cod and chips, pork and leek sausages with mash and red wine and onion gravy, a pie of the day, sea bass with chilli and ginger pak choi and honey and soy dressing, lamb shank with creamy mash, sticky red cabbage and red wine gravy, half a rack of barbecue ribs with coleslaw and chips, and puddings such as sticky toffee pudding with toffee sauce and chocolate fudge and sea salt brownie with chocolate sauce. *Benchmark main dish: chargrilled steak burger with toppings, burger sauce and skinny chips £11.95. Two-course evening meal £20.00.*

Whiting & Hammond ~ Manager Joel Dos Santos ~ Real ale ~ Open 9am-11pm; 9am-midnight Fri, Sat ~ Bar food 12-9.30 (9 Sun) ~ Restaurant ~ Children welcome ~ Dogs allowed in bar ~ Wi-fi *Recommended by Tina and David Woods-Taylor, Daniel King, Bridget and Peter Gregson, Martin Day, Mick Allen, Louise and Simon Peters*

PENSHURST TQ5142 Map 3

Bottle House

(01892) 870306 – www.thebottlehouseinnpenshurst.co.uk

Coldharbour Lane; leaving Penshurst SW on B2188 turn right at Smarts Hill signpost, then bear right towards Chiddingstone and Cowden; keep straight on; TN11 8ET

Country pub with friendly service, a good choice of drinks, tasty food and sunny terrace; nearby walks

At lunchtime, this cottagey pub is especially popular with walkers; it's in a lovely rural setting. The bars have all sorts of joists and beams (a couple of particularly low ones are leather-padded) and the open-plan rooms are split into cosy areas by numerous standing timbers. Pine wall boards and bar stools are ranged along the timber-clad copper-topped counter where they keep Larkins Traditional and Tonbridge Coppernob on handpump, 20 wines by the glass from a good list and local gin. There's also a hotchpotch of wooden tables (with fresh flowers and candles), fairly closely spaced chairs on dark boards or coir, a woodburning stove and photographs of the pub and local scenes; background music. Some walls are of stripped stone. The sunny, brick-paved terrace has teak chairs and tables under parasols, and olive trees in white pots. Parking is limited.

High quality food includes baked pecan and apricot-crusted baby camembert with sticky onions, smoked haddock and roasted cod fishcake with tomato and basil salsa and herb dressing, wild garlic and pea risotto with parmesan, home-roasted ham and eggs, beef in ale stew with horseradish dumplings, roasted lamb rump with champ mash and mint jus, cod loin with mussels and parsley cream sauce, 28-day-aged rump steak with a choice of sauce and chips, and puddings such as treacle tart with vanilla ice-cream and rhubarb and stem ginger trifle. *Benchmark main dish: slow-roasted pork belly with creamed cabbage and bacon, dauphinoise potatoes and apple and cider jus £15.95. Two-course evening meal £20.00.*

Free house ~ Licensee Paul Hammond ~ Real ale ~ Open 11-11; 11-10.30 Sun ~ Bar food 12-10 (9 Sun) ~ Restaurant ~ Children welcome ~ Dogs allowed in bar ~ Wi-fi

Recommended by Bob and Margaret Holder, Barry Collett, Andy and Rosemary Taylor, Trevor and Michele Street, Buster and Helena Hastings

PLUCKLEY — TQ9243 Map 3

Dering Arms

(01233) 840371 – www.deringarms.com

Pluckley station, which is signposted from B2077; or follow Station Road (left turn off Smarden Road in centre of Pluckley) for about 1.3 miles S, through Pluckley Thorne; TN27 0RR

Handsome building with stylish main bar, carefully chosen wines, three ales and good fresh fish dishes; comfortable bedrooms

Our readers remain consistently enthusiastic about their visits to this well run and interesting place. It has an imposing frontage, mullioned arched windows and dutch gables and was originally built as a hunting lodge on the Dering Estate. The high-ceilinged, stylishly plain main bar has a solid country feel with a variety of wooden furniture on flagstones, a roaring log fire in a big fireplace, country prints and some fishing rods. The smaller half-panelled back bar has similar dark wood furnishings, plus an extension with a woodburning stove, comfortable armchairs, sofas and a grand piano; board games. A beer named for the pub from Goachers and Goachers Gold Star Ale on handpump, 11 good wines by the glass from a fine list, local cider, 30 malt whiskies and 20 cognacs. This is a comfortable place to stay overnight and the breakfasts are highly regarded. Classic car meetings (the long-serving landlord James has a couple of classic motors) are held here on the second Sunday of the month.

First class fish and shellfish are the stars here, though they do offer non-fishy choices too. There's a new tapas menu plus chicken livers sautéed with onions, bacon and mushrooms and brandy cream sauce, provençale fish soup with rouille and croutons, skate wing with caper butter, lamb rump with spring onion mash and minted stilton sauce, hake fillet with crayfish beurre noisette and braised gem lettuce, confit of duck with bubble and squeak potato cake and black cherry and ginger sauce, and puddings such as oranges in caramel with Grand Marnier and cream and apple, sultana and calvados tart with vanilla ice-cream. *Benchmark main dish: sea bass fillet with leeks, bacon and saffron sauce £14.95. Two-course evening meal £24.00.*

Free house ~ Licensee James Buss ~ Real ale ~ Open 11.30-3.30, 6-11; 12-4 Sun; closed Sun evening, Mon ~ Bar food 12-2.30, 6.30-9; 12-3 Sun ~ Restaurant ~ Children welcome ~ Dogs allowed in bar ~ Bedrooms: £85/£95 *Recommended by Richard Kennell, Pieter and Janet Vrancken, Robert and Diana Myers, Elisabeth and Bill Humphries, Belinda and Neil Garth, Susie and Spencer Gray*

SEVENOAKS TQ5055 Map 3

Kings Head ♀

(01732) 452081 – www.kingsheadbesselsgreen.co.uk

Bessels Green; A25 W, just off A21; TN13 2QA

Bustling pub with open-plan character rooms, quite a choice of ales, good food and seats in garden

With a choice of up to six real ales on handpump (from breweries such as Caledonian, Dark Star, Gun, Old Dairy, Tonbridge and Whitstable) and a dozen wines by the glass, the little bar here is always full of chatty locals. A dog-friendly and attractive small room with a two-way open fire leads off. Spreading dining areas have a wide mix of cushioned dining chairs, button-back wall seats and settles with scatter cushions around rustic or dark wooden tables on bare-board or tile floors. Also, open fires, frame-to-frame prints, old photos and maps on painted walls, house plants, church candles and old bottles on windowsills, and bookshelves; background music. Outside there are teak tables and chairs on a terrace, picnic-sets on grass and one or two circular 'dining huts' (bookable in advance for £25).

As well as breakfast (9-11.30am Friday-Sunday), a wide choice of pleasing food includes sandwiches, chicken liver parfait with onion chutney, grilled sardines with tomato salsa, sharing boards, honey-glazed ham and free-range eggs, burger with toppings, skinny chips and smoked sweet mustard mayonnaise, chicken, ham and leek pie, seafood linguine, vegetarian chilli, rack of free-range barbecue pork ribs with slaw and corn on the cob, double chocolate brownie with dark chocolate sauce and sticky toffee pudding with toffee sauce and honeycomb ice-cream. *Benchmark main dish: beer-battered fish and chips £10.95. Two-course evening meal £20.00.*

Whiting & Hammond ~ Manager Jamie Owen ~ Real ale ~ Open 10am-11pm; 10am-midnight Sat; 11-10.30 Sun ~ Bar food 12-9.30 (9 Sun) ~ Children welcome ~ Dogs allowed in bar ~ Wi-fi *Recommended by Dave Braisted, William and Sophia Renton, Beverley and Andy Butcher, Gene and Kitty Rankin, Sylvia and Phillip Spencer, Joe and Belinda Smart*

SEVENOAKS TQ5352 Map 3

White Hart ♀

(01732) 452022 – www.brunningandprice.co.uk/whitehart

Tonbridge Road (A225 S, past Knole); TN13 1SG

Well run coaching inn with lots to look at in character rooms, rewarding food and friendly, helpful staff

Gently civilised and with a thoughtful choice of food and drink, this carefully renovated old place keeps customers coming back on a regular basis. There's much to look at in the many atmospheric rooms (connected by open doorways and steps): open fires and woodburners, antique-style chairs and tables, rugs and bare floorboards and hundreds of prints and old photographs of local scenes or schools on cream-painted walls. Fresh flowers, house plants and candles too. There's Phoenix Brunning & Price Original and Old Dairy Blue Top plus guests from breweries such as Empire, Harveys, Timothy Taylors, Tonbridge and Westerham on handpump, 20 good wines by the glass, 50 malt whiskies and a farm cider; daily papers, board games. At the front of the building are picnic-sets under parasols, with wooden benches and chairs around tables under more parasols on the back terrace.

Cooked with flair, the modern food includes sandwiches, pigeon kiev with baby leeks, red cabbage purée and wild mushrooms, scallops with crab fritters, pea purée and lemon dressing, salmon and smoked haddock fishcake with a poached egg and tomato salad, thai green vegetable curry with butternut squash, aubergine, sticky coconut rice and tempura okra, warm crispy beef salad with sweet chilli dressing and roasted cashew nuts, venison rump with venison shepherd's pie and blackberry jus, and puddings such as hot waffle with glazed bananas and honeycomb ice-cream and triple chocolate brownie with chocolate sauce and vanilla-ice cream. *Benchmark main dish: steak burger with toppings, coleslaw and chips £13.45. Two-course evening meal £21.00.*

Brunning & Price ~ Manager Tom McGloin ~ Real ale ~ Open 11.30-11; 12-11 Sun ~ Bar food 12-9.30 (10 Fri, Sat, 9 Sun) ~ Children welcome away from bar until 7pm ~ Dogs allowed in bar ~ Wi-fi *Recommended by Jean P & Myriam Alderson, Martin Day, Adam Jones, Tony R, Mike Buckingham, Julie and Andrew Blanchett*

SHIPBOURNE TQ5952 Map 3

Chaser

(01732) 810360 – www.thechaser.co.uk
Stumble Hill (A227 N of Tonbridge); TN11 9PE

Busy country pub with rambling rooms and interesting décor, log fires, good choice of drinks, enjoyable food and seats outside

At weekends particularly, it's essential to book a table in advance as this easy-going, friendly pub is always deservedly busy. The comfortably opened-up bar and dining areas have an eclectic mix of solid wood tables (each set with a church candle) surrounded by prettily cushioned dining chairs, stripped wooden floors and several roaring log fires. Frame-to-frame pictures, maps and old photos line the walls above pine wainscoting, house plants and antique glass bottles are placed on windowsills, and rows of books sit on shelves. Courteous staff serve Greene King Old Speckled Hen, Larkins Traditional, Timothy Taylors Landlord and Tonbridge Coppernob on handpump, good wines by the glass, 20 malt whiskies and two farm ciders; background music. A striking, school chapel-like room at the back has wooden panelling and a high, timber-vaulted ceiling. French windows open on to an enclosed central courtyard with wicker-style tables and chairs on large flagstones and plants in wall pots; this has a retractable awning and a woodburning stove and creates extra family dining space. A side garden with hedges and shrubs has picnic-sets and is overlooked by the church. You can use the small back car park or park in the lane opposite by the green-cum-common; local walks.

Interesting food includes sandwiches, garlic and rosemary camembert with cranberry sauce, seafood platter, honey and mustard roast ham and free-range eggs, cod, leek and dill fishcake with tomato and red onion salad, bubble and squeak cake with sautéed spinach, carrot purée, fried egg and parsley oil, steak burger with toppings, garlic mayonnaise and skinny chips, minced beef and onion pie, duck breast with pea purée, pickled apple, sour cherries and cherry sauce, local sirloin steak with peppercorn sauce and chips, and puddings such as eton mess and triple chocolate pannacotta with genoise sponge and chocolate soil. *Benchmark main dish: herb and mustard-crusted lamb shoulder with dauphinoise potatoes and redcurrant mint gravy £20.95. Two-course evening meal £22.50.*

Whiting & Hammond ~ Manager Duke Chidgey ~ Real ale ~ Open 10am-11pm; 9am-11pm Thurs, Sat; 9am-10.30pm Sun ~ Bar food 12-9.30; 9am-9.30pm Thurs-Sat; 9-9 Sun ~ Children welcome ~ Dogs allowed in bar ~ Wi-fi *Recommended by Martin Day, Angela and Steve Heard, Paddy and Sian O'Leary, Ian Phillips, Gene and Kitty Rankin, Mark Hamill, Buster and Helena Hastings*

STALISFIELD GREEN TQ9552 Map 3

Plough

(01795) 890256 – www.theploughinnstalisfield.co.uk

Off A252 in Charing; ME13 0HY

Ancient country pub with rambling rooms, open fires, interesting local ales and smashing food

Those in the know are drawn to this pub, set on its own amid downland farmland, by the excellent food cooked by the landlord. But drinkers are just as welcome and the atmosphere is relaxed and cheerful. The hop-draped rooms ramble around, up and down, with open fires in brick fireplaces, interesting pictures, books on shelves, farmhouse and other nice old dining chairs around a mix of pine or dark wood tables on bare boards, and the odd milk churn dotted about; background music. Fullers London Pride, Musket Fife & Drum, Old Dairy Red Top and Westerham Spirit of Kent plus a guest beer on handpump, 15 wines by the glass, 11 malt whiskies, five local ciders, 12 rums and 21 gins. There are picnic-sets on a simple terrace overlooking the village green below. As we went to press they were adding six bedrooms in a barn-style building.

Enticing food cooked by the landlord includes lunchtime sandwiches and rolls, thyme and honey-baked camembert with home-made tomato relish, smoked haddock and spring onion fishcake with samphire and beetroot ketchup, a pie of the day, local beer-battered fish and chips, confit duck leg with braised red cabbage, stone bass with crushed potatoes and purple sprouting broccoli, lamb rump with champ and carrot purée, 28-day-aged steaks with triple-cooked chips, confit cherry tomatoes and a choice of sauce, and puddings such as poached pear and ginger parkin with butterscotch sauce and chocolate délice with chocolate crémeux and mint ice-cream. *Benchmark main dish: slow-cooked pork belly with chorizo croquette and spiced pears £16.00. Two-course evening meal £23.50.*

Free house ~ Licensees Richard and Marianne Baker ~ Real ale ~ Open 12-3, 5-11; 12-11 Sat; 12-6 Sun; closed Sun evening, Mon (open in high season); first week Jan ~ Bar food 12-1.45, 7-9; not Sun evening ~ Restaurant ~ Children welcome ~ Dogs allowed in bar ~ Live entertainment (see website) *Recommended by Barry and Daphne Gregson, Patricia and Gordon Thompson, Ivy and George Goodwill, Mike and Sarah Abbot*

STONE IN OXNEY TQ9428 Map 3

Ferry

(01233) 758246 – www.oxneyferry.com

Appledore Road; N of Stone-cum-Ebony; TN30 7JY

Bustling small pub with character rooms, candlelight, open fires, real ales and popular food

The chatty main bar in this former smugglers' haunt has hop-draped painted beams, a green dado and stools against the counter where they serve a beer named for the pub (from Goachers), Harveys Best, Sharps

Doom Bar and a guest such as Tonbridge Golden Rule on handpump, ten wines by the glass, farm ciders and quite a few gins. To the right is a cosy eating area with wheelback chairs and a banquette around a few long tables, and a log fire in an inglenook with candles in wall sconces on either side. To the left of the main door is a dining area with big blackboards on red walls, a woodburning stove beneath a large bressumer beam and high-backed, light wooden dining chairs around assorted tables; up a couple of steps, a smarter dining area has modern chandeliers. Throughout there are wooden floors, all sorts of pictures and framed maps, a stuffed fish, beer flagons, an old musket and various brasses. Background music, TV, darts and pool in the games room. In warm weather, the tables and benches on the front terrace and seats in the back garden are much sought after; a river runs along the bottom and the sunsets can be lovely. Disabled access in the bar and on the terrace.

Much enjoyed food includes rosemary-infused baked baby camembert with onion marmalade, prawn cocktail, tagliatelle with tomato, mushroom and pepper sauce, duck breast with port and black cherry jus and herbed rösti potatoes, steak and kidney pudding, parmesan-coated guinea fowl with dauphinoise potatoes and red pepper and smoked paprika sauce, bacon steak with local eggs and wholegrain mustard sauce, local brill with prawn and lobster bisque, and puddings such as plum and cinnamon tart and whisky bread and butter pudding with custard. *Benchmark main dish: beer-battered local fish and chips £13.45. Two-course evening meal £20.00.*

Free house ~ Licensee Paul Withers Green ~ Real ale ~ Open 11-11 (midnight Sat); 12-10.30 Sun ~ Bar food 12-3, 6-9; 12-9 Sat; 12-8 Sun ~ Restaurant ~ Children welcome ~ Dogs allowed in bar ~ Wi-fi *Recommended by V Brogden, Celia and Geoff Clay, Jane and Philip Saunders, Karl and Frieda Bujeya, Helene Grygar, Miranda and Jeff Davidson, David Appleyard*

TUNBRIDGE WELLS TQ5839 Map 3

Sankeys

(01892) 511422 – www.sankeys.co.uk

Mount Ephraim (A26 just N of junction with A267); TN4 8AA

Pubby bar, real ales, decent food and cheerful feel; downstairs brasserie (wonderful fish and shellfish) and seats on sunny back terrace

Always bustling and cheerful, this street-level bar has a good mix of customers keen to enjoy the wide choice of drinks. Served by helpful staff there might be Harveys Best, Larkins Traditional and Tonbridge Golden Rule on handpump, a constantly changing range of craft beers, fruit beers, lagers and ciders, 16 wines by the glass and an extensive range of spirits. There are comfortably worn leather sofas and pews around all sorts of tables on bare boards, a fine collection of rare enamel signs and antique brewery mirrors, and old prints, framed cigarette cards and lots of old wine bottles and soda siphons; a big flatscreen TV (for rugby only) and background music. Downstairs is a sizeable new function room with french windows that lead out to an inviting suntrap deck.

Pubby food includes sandwiches, wraps and baguettes, halloumi, chicken, beef and lamb burgers with a choice of seven toppings, smokie fish pie, paella, and puddings such as sticky toffee pudding with butterscotch sauce and dark chocolate brownie with honeycomb ice-cream. *Benchmark main dish: beer-battered fish and chips £13.50. Two-course evening meal £19.00.*

Free house ~ Licensee Matthew Sankey ~ Real ale ~ Open 12pm-1am; 12-11 Sun ~ Bar food 12-3, 6-10; 12-10 Sat; 12-6 Sun ~ Restaurant ~ Children welcome ~ Dogs allowed in bar ~ Wi-fi *Recommended by Monty Green, Buster and Helena Hastings, Bob and Melissa Wyatt*

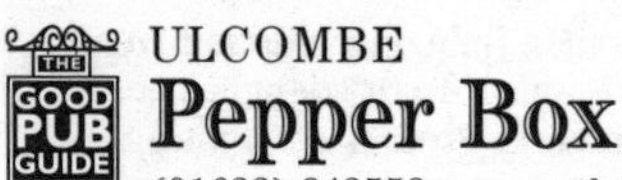

ULCOMBE TQ8550 Map 3

Pepper Box

(01622) 842558 – www.thepepperboxinn.co.uk

Fairbourne Heath; signposted from A20 in Harrietsham, or follow Ulcombe signpost from A20, then turn left at crossroads with sign to pub, then right at next minor crossroads; ME17 1LP

Friendly country pub with a fine log fire, well liked food, fair choice of drinks and seats in a pretty garden

A favourite with many, this is lovely and quiet outside (the pub overlooks a great plateau of rolling arable farmland) and inside as well (no background music, TV or games machines). It remains well run by attentive and convivial licensees and the homely bar has standing timbers and a few low beams (some hung with hops), copper kettles and pans on windowsills, and nice horsebrasses on the fireplace's bressumer beam; two leather sofas are set beside the splendid inglenook fireplace with its lovely log fire. A side area, furnished more functionally for eating, extends into the opened-up beamed dining room with a range in another inglenook and more horsebrasses. Shepherd Neame Master Brew and guests such as Shepherd Neame Spitfire and Whitstable Bay Pale Ale on handpump and 15 wines by the glass; background music. In summer, the hop-covered terrace and shrub-filled garden is just the place to relax after a walk along the nearby Greensand Way footpath. The village church is worth a look.

Good, popular food includes lunchtime sandwiches, goats cheese fritters with smoky tomato sauce, tiger prawns in garlic, chilli, ginger and coriander butter, wild mushroom, lentil and red wine ragoût with pasta, basil and parmesan, sizzle platter of chicken, mushrooms, pak choi and peppers with sweet chilli and soy sauce, pie of the day, hake fillet with steamed clams, samphire, garlic, white wine and cream, peppered lamb rump with beetroot and watercress salad and crème fraîche and mint dressing, steaks with a choice of sauce, and puddings such as crème brûlée of the day and pear, plum and apple crumble with custard. *Benchmark main dish: fresh fish dish of the day £15.50. Two-course evening meal £21.00.*

Shepherd Neame ~ Tenant Sarah Pemble ~ Real ale ~ Open 11-3, 6-11; 12-5 Sun ~ Bar food 12-2.15, 6.30-9.30; 12-3 Sun ~ Restaurant ~ Children over 10 only ~ Dogs allowed in bar ~ Wi-fi *Recommended by Michael Breeze, Nick Higgins, Justine and Neil Bonnett, Jill and Hugh Bennett, Martin Day, Sophie Ellison, Victoria and James Sargeant*

WHITSTABLE TR1066 Map 3

Pearsons Arms

(01227) 773133 – www.pearsonsarmswhitstable.co.uk

Sea Wall off Oxford Street after road splits into one-way system; public parking on left as road divides; CT5 1BT

Seaside pub with an emphasis on imaginative food, several local ales and good mix of customers

There's something to please everyone in this beachside pub, from local ales, 14 good wines by the glass and an extensive list of cocktails to attractively presented, interesting food and regular evening live music. There are two front bars divided by a central chimney: cushioned settles, captain's chairs and leather armchairs on a stripped-wood floor, driftwood walls and big flower arrangements on the bar counter. Courteous staff serve Pearsons Arms (named for them from Adnams), Fullers Olivers Island, Gadds Seasider and St Austell Tribute on handpump; background music. A cosy lower room has a bookcase mural and a couple of big chesterfields and dining chairs around plain tables on a stone floor. Up a couple of flights of stairs, the restaurant (overlooking the water) has mushroom-coloured paintwork, contemporary wallpaper, more driftwood and church chairs and pine tables on nice wide floorboards.

As well as offering weekend breakfasts (8.30-11am), the highly regarded food includes tapas-style snacks, rabbit and foie gras ballotine with crisp chorizo and shaved fennel and red chicory salad, crab tian with avocado purée and radish, cauliflower and truffle couscous with a poached egg, roasted cauliflower and shaved truffle, burger with toppings, coleslaw, burger sauce and chips, chicken and ham pie, fillet of sea bream with roasted salsify purée and mussel and saffron broth, chargrilled rose veal loin with peas, asparagus, morels and truffle and maderia cream, and puddings such as lemon tart with white chocolate snow and raspberry sorbet and sticky toffee pudding with glazed bananas and banana ice-cream; they also offer a two- and three-course set menu (not weekends). *Benchmark main dish: beer-battered fish and chips £16.00. Two-course evening meal £21.50.*

Enterprise ~ Lease Jake Alder ~ Real ale ~ Open 12-midnight (11 Sun) ~ Bar food 12-2.30, 6.30-9.30; 12-7 ~ Restaurant ~ Children welcome ~ Dogs allowed in bar ~ Wi-fi ~ Live music evenings Sun and Tues; resident DJ Fri evening *Recommended by Richard Kennell, Serena and Richard Furber, Max and Steph Warren, Richard Tilbrook, Lee and Jill Stafford, JJ, Jacqui and Alan Swan, Graeme and Sally Mendham*

WINGHAM TR2457 Map 3

Dog

(01227) 720339 – www.thedog.co.uk

Canterbury Road (A257); CT3 1BB

Carefully refurbished old inn with plenty of room for eating and drinking, first class food, local ales, friendly staff and seats on terrace; bedrooms

The hands-on, hard-working licensees have refurbished this medieval inn with care and thought, blending contemporary touches with heavy beams and old brickwork. The carpeted bar has a woodburning stove in an inglenook fireplace with armchairs grouped in front of it, more armchairs against the walls, a cushioned window seat, dog motifs on the back of leather chairs and a white-painted piano; dotted around are fabric dogs, dog cartoons and prints on grey paintwork, pub games and daily papers. Swivelling wooden stools line the counter where they keep Harveys Best and Shepherd Neame Master Brew and Whitstable Bay Pale Ale on handpump and nice wines by the glass; background music. One part of the dining room has metal and animal-hide chairs and upholstered wall banquettes around wooden tables on wide floorboards, a few animal-hide stools by the bar and an open fire. The airy second dining area has a woodburning stove, high-backed tartan or leather chairs around more tables on flagstones and plants on windowsills. Outside on the terrace are grey or white up-to-date chairs and tables and a gazebo. They have eight stylish, well equipped and individually styled bedrooms and breakfasts are particularly good.

Attractively presented, interesting modern food includes sandwiches, warm saddle of rabbit with crispy leg rissole and carrot emulsion, citrus-cured salmon with grapefruit, lime jelly and keta (cured salmon roe), cheese dumplings with roast squash, asparagus and sage crisps, honey-glazed duck breast with polenta fries and celeriac, seared bream with potato gnocchi, samphire and shellfish beignet, fillet of beef with oxtail, mushroom purée, shallot marmalade and anna potatoes, and puddings such as sticky ginger syrup sponge with roast pineapple and apple and calvados crème brûlée. *Benchmark main dish: lamb rump with garlic risotto and pancetta £23.00. Two-course evening meal £30.00.*

Free house ~ Licensee Marc Brigden ~ Real ale ~ Open 11-11; 11-9 Sun ~ Bar food 12-2.30, 6-9; 12-5 Sun ~ Restaurant ~ Children welcome ~ Dogs welcome ~ Wi-fi ~ Bedrooms: £80/£90 *Recommended by Katharine Cowherd, Belinda and Neil Garth, Charlotte and William Mason, Diana and Bertie Farr*

WYE TR0546 Map 3

Kings Head

(01233) 812418 – www.kingsheadwye.com

Church Street; TN25 5BN

Busy high-street pub with good food, ales and wines by the glass – and bright bedrooms

This is part of the handsome high street and is an interesting place with an informal, chatty atmosphere. The bare-boards bar is divided by a two-way log fire, with a long brown button-back wall banquette in one part and armchairs beside the fire on the other side by a glass-topped trunk table. Other furnishings include comfortable chairs around all sorts of tables and pale-painted high chairs beside the counter where they keep Shepherd Neame Whitstable Bay Pale Ale plus a seasonal guest on handpump and 13 good wines by the glass, plus an array of olives, cakes, home-made pork crackling and so forth; a dresser is lined with jams and flavoured olive oils for sale. The dining room has one long wall banquette and painted kitchen chairs around pine tables, with an open fire at one end. Throughout there are rustic boarded walls, church candles, photographs of the local area, daily papers and background jazz. A small courtyard has a few tables and chairs, and the bedrooms are airy and simply furnished.

Enjoyable food includes breakfast (8-11am), lunchtime sandwiches and omelettes, duck scotch egg with cranberry relish, guinea fowl terrine with pickled red cabbage, pie of the day, spiced chickpea casserole with peppers, courgettes, red onions and aubergine, pancetta-wrapped monkfish with roasted red pepper and tomato sauce, lemon and herb-crusted local lamb with pea purée, spring greens and lamb jus, wild boar hotpot, and puddings such as spotted dick with crème anglaise and buttermilk pannacotta with rhubarb compote and orange sorbet. *Benchmark main dish: burger with toppings, coleslaw, chipotle mayonnaise and a choice of chips £14.00. Two-course evening meal £21.00.*

Shepherd Neame ~ Tenant Scott Richardson ~ Real ale ~ Open 8am-11pm Weds-Sat; 8am-10pm Sun-Tues ~ Bar food 12-3, 6-9; all day weekends (till 5pm Sun) ~ Restaurant ~ Children welcome ~ Dogs welcome ~ Wi-fi ~ Bedrooms: /£95 *Recommended by Peter Pilbeam, Richard Kennell, Frances Parsons, Celia and Geoff Clay, Matt and Hayley Jacob*

Also Worth a Visit in Kent

Besides the fully inspected pubs, you might like to try these pubs that have been recommended to us and described by readers. Do tell us what you think of them: feedback@goodguides.com

APPLEDORE TQ9529

Black Lion (01233) 758206

The Street; TN26 2BU Bustling and enjoyable 1930s village pub with good generously served food (all day Fri-Sun), lamb from Romney Marsh and local fish, four or five well kept ales including Goachers, Biddenden cider, welcoming helpful staff, partitioned back eating area, log fire; background music, events such as bank holiday hog roasts; children welcome, tables out on green, attractive village and good Military Canal walks, open all day. *(Mick Allen)*

BARHAM TR2050

Duke of Cumberland

(01227) 831396 *The Street; CT4 6NY* Open-plan pub close to village green, enjoyable home cooking including good

Sun roasts, well kept Harveys, Greene King, Timothy Taylors and a guest, friendly staff, plain tables and chairs on bare boards or flagstones, hops and log fire; quiz second Tues of month, board games and darts; children welcome, dogs in bar, garden with boules and play area, three bedrooms, handy for A2, open all day, food all day weekends. *(Trevor and Michele Street)*

BEARSTED TQ8055

Oak on the Green (01622) 737976

The Street; ME14 4EJ Well run pub with friendly bustling atmosphere (sister to the Old Mill at Kennington); two hop-festooned bar areas with bare boards and half-panelling, wide choice of home-made food including some mexican dishes, Harveys Best and three guests, restaurant (they also own the smaller fish restaurant next door, closed Mon); children and dogs (in bar) welcome, disabled access, seats out at front under big umbrellas, open (and food) all day. *(Matt and Hayley Jacob)*

BENENDEN TQ8032

★**Bull** (01580) 240054

The Street; by village green; TN17 4DE Relaxed informal atmosphere in bare-boards or dark terracotta-tiled rooms, pleasing mix of furniture, church candles on tables, log fire in brick inglenook, ales such as Dark Star, Harveys, Larkins and Old Dairy from carved wooden counter, Biddenden cider, more formal dining room, tasty generously served food (not Sun evening) including speciality pies and popular Sun carvery, friendly helpful staff; background music (live Sun afternoon); children and dogs (in bar) welcome, picnic-sets out in front behind white picket fence, back garden, open all day. *(V Brogden)*

BETHERSDEN TQ9240

George (01233) 820235

The Street; TN26 3AG Tile-hung village local with good buoyant atmosphere; well kept Brakspears, Harveys, Greene King and a guest, generous sensibly priced food including good value carvery (Sun, Weds), large public bar with open fire, smaller lounge next to dining area; pool, free wi-fi; children and dogs welcome, open all day, no food Sun evening, Mon lunchtime. *(Sylvia and Phillip Spencer)*

BIDBOROUGH TQ5643

★**Kentish Hare** (01892) 525709

Bidborough Ridge; TN3 0XB Good imaginative food at this popular dining pub including set menus; leather armchairs around open fire in main bar, unusual stools made of corks, bookcase wallpaper, a house beer from Tonbridge along with Harveys and a guest, 30 wines by the glass and good choice of other drinks, modern two-way woodburner in cosy middle room, second bar with seating booths and airy back restaurant with view into the kitchen; background music, free wi-fi; children welcome (under-5s eat free), dogs allowed in some areas, contemporary tables and chairs on deck overlooking lower terrace, open all day Sat, closed Sun evening, Mon. *(Charlie Stevens, Audrey and Paul Summers)*

BODSHAM TR1045

Timber Batts (01233) 750083

Following Bodsham, Wye sign off B2068 keep right at unsigned fork after about 1.5 miles; TN25 5JQ Eccentric old rural pub under family ownership; traditional beamed bar with inglenook log fire, eclectic mix of furniture, lots of taxidermy and other quirky bits and pieces, three kentish ales and four ciders, some evening food (Thurs-Sat) including Fri pizzas; live music and DJ nights, bar billiards, pinball, board games; children and dogs welcome, lovely views over wide-spreading valley from garden with wandering chickens, camping, working forge next door (landlord is a blacksmith), closed Mon-Weds, open from 4pm Thurs, all day Fri and Sat, till 7pm Sun. *(Edward May)*

BOUGH BEECH TQ4846

Wheatsheaf (01732) 700100

B2027, S of reservoir; TN8 7NU Attractive 14th-c pub with emphasis on food including children's meals, three Westerham ales along with Harveys and good choice of wines, beams and timbering, bare boards and log fires (one in a huge fireplace), high ceilinged dining room, more tables upstairs; dogs welcome, nice outside seating area and good walks including circular one around Bough Beech Reservoir, open all day (till 9pm Sun). *(Martin Day)*

BOXLEY TQ7758

Kings Arms (01622) 755177

1.75 miles from M20 junction 7; opposite church; ME14 3DR Cosy dining pub in pretty village at foot of the downs, largely 16th/17th-c, with good choice of popular food from lunchtime baguettes to weekly specials, four well kept ales including Fullers and Harveys, welcoming helpful service, low black beams, red chesterfields by big brick fireplace; background music, monthly quiz; children and dogs welcome, picnic-sets and play area in nice garden, good local walks, open (and food) all day. *(Dave Braisted)*

BOYDEN GATE TR2265

Gate Inn (01227) 860498

Off A299 Herne Bay–Ramsgate signed for Hillboro', Reculver, then left to Chislet; Chislet also signed off A28 Canterbury–Margate at Upstreet – keep right on to Boyden; CT3 4EB Rustic beamed pub with unpretentious quarry-tiled bar rooms, cushioned pews around character tables, attractively etched windows, old local photographs and double-aspect log fire, Shepherd Neame and occasional guests from tap room casks, popular sensibly priced home-made food from doorstep sandwiches to specials (must book weekends), bare-boards restaurant in former bakery, woodburner; Weds quiz and some live folk nights; children and dogs (in bar) welcome, sheltered garden bounded by two streams, ducks and chickens, open all day weekends, no food Sun evening. *(Gerry and Pam Pollard)*

BRABOURNE TR1041

★**Five Bells** (01303) 813334

East Brabourne; TN25 5LP Popular 16th-c inn at foot of North Downs (same owners as the Globe in Rye (Sussex) and Woolpack at Warehorne); opened-up interior with hop-strung beams, standing timbers and ancient brick walls, all manner of dining chairs and tables on stripped boards, wall seats here and there, two log fires, quirky decorations including candles in upturned bottles on the walls and a garland-draped mermaid figurehead, four well kept changing local ales, Biddenden cider and selection of kentish wines, well liked food from varied menu, friendly service, shop selling local produce, monthly arts and crafts market; some live music, unisex loos; children and dogs welcome, tables out at front under pergola, comfortable if eccentric bedrooms, open all day from 9am for breakfast. *(Peter Meister, Richard Kennell)*

BRASTED TQ4654

Stanhope Arms (01959) 561970

Church Road; TN16 1HZ Welcoming old village pub next to the church; six real ales including Greene King and well liked pubby food (not Sun evening, Mon, limited choice Tues), good service, cosy traditional bar with darts, bright cheerful restaurant with white tablecloths and napkins; children and dogs welcome (resident labradors), summer barbecues and bat and trap in back garden, closed Mon lunchtime, otherwise open all day. *(Martin Day)*

BRENCHLEY TQ6841

★**Halfway House** (01892) 722526

Horsmonden Road; TN12 7AX Beamed 18th-c inn with attractive mix of rustic and traditional furnishings on bare boards, old farm tools and other bric-a-brac, two log fires, cheerful staff and particularly friendly landlord, up to a dozen well kept changing ales tapped from the cask (bank holiday beer/cider festivals end of May, Aug), enjoyable traditional home-made food including popular Sun roasts, two eating areas; quiz every other Weds; children and dogs welcome, picnic-sets and play area in big garden, summer barbecues, two bedrooms, open all day, no food Sun evening. *(Sophie Ellison)*

BROADSTAIRS TR3868

Four Candles 07947 062063

Sowell Street; CT10 2AT Quirky, much enjoyed one-room micropub in former shop; good selection of local beers chalked on blackboard including own brews, kentish ciders and wines, high tables and stools on sawdust floor, bucket lightshades and various odds and ends including pitchfork handles (the famous *Two Ronnies* sketch was inspired by a Broadstairs ironmonger), local cheese and pork pies, friendly chatty atmosphere; closed weekday lunchtimes, open all day Sat. *(Peter Meister)*

BROADSTAIRS TR3967

Tartar Frigate (01843) 862013

Harbour Street, by quay; CT10 1EU Flint-faced harbourside pub dating from the 18th c; pleasantly old-fashioned bar with interesting local photographs and fishing memorabilia, hanging pots and brasses, log fire, well kept ales such as Ramsgate, lunchtime bar food (Mon-Sat) and good fish/seafood in popular upstairs restaurant with fine Viking Bay views, also good value four-course Sun lunch with two sittings 12.30pm and 3.30pm, friendly hospitable staff; background and weekly live music including Weds folk session; open all day, no food Sun evening. *(John Wooll)*

BURMARSH TR1032

Shepherd & Crook (01303) 872336

Shear Way, next to church; TN29 0JJ Traditional 16th-c marshside village local with smuggling history; well kept ales such as Hop Fuzz along with Weston's Rosie's Pig cider, good straightforward home-made food at reasonable prices including deals and gluten-free options, friendly service, interesting photographs and blow lamp collection, open fire; bar games such as ring the bull; children and dogs welcome, seats on side terrace, closed Mon (except bank holidays), otherwise open all day (Sun till 6pm). *(Nik and Gloria Clarke)*

CANTERBURY TR1458

Dolphin (01227) 455963

St Radigunds Street; CT1 2AA Busy modernised dining pub with plenty of tables in light spacious bar; enjoyable fairly traditional home-made food from baguettes to popular Sun roast, Sharps Doom Bar, Timothy Taylors Landlord and guests, nice wines including country ones, friendly staff, bric-a-brac on delft shelf, board games, flagstoned conservatory; free wi-fi; children

A star symbol before the name of a pub shows exceptional character and appeal. It doesn't mean extra comfort. Even quite a basic pub can win a star, if it's individual enough.

welcome, dogs at management's discretion, disabled access, picnic-sets in good-sized back garden, open all day (food all day Sat). *(Ivy and George Goodwill)*

CANTERBURY TR1457

Foundry (01227) 455899

White Horse Lane; CT1 2RU Backstreet pub in former 19th-c iron foundry, light and airy interior on two floors, Canterbury Brewers beers from visible microbrewery plus local guests, craft lagers and kentish cider, they also distil their own gin and vodka, pubby food (till 6pm Sun, Mon) from sandwiches and sharing plates up including range of home-made pies, helpful cheerful staff; children welcome, disabled access/loo, small courtyard area, open all day (till late Fri, Sat). *(Stuart Doughty)*

CANTERBURY TR1557

Lady Luck (01227) 763298

St Peters Street; CT1 2BQ Quirky rock 'n roll bar with music-themed decor; real ales, craft beers and good selection of other drinks including a rum menu, enjoyable home-cooked food with plenty for vegetarians/vegans, good friendly service; regular live bands and DJs, juke box, pool, daily newspaper and board games; a couple of pavement tables, more seats in beer garden behind, open all day (till 2am Fri, Sat), food served till 7pm (3pm Sun). *(Eddie Edwards)*

CANTERBURY TR1558

New Inn (01227) 464584

Havelock Street; CT1 1NP Friendly little Victorian terraced local not far from the city centre; seven well kept changing ales (tasters offered), a proper cider and good range of whiskies, bare-boards bar with woodburner, modern back conservatory, no food; juke box and various games; dogs welcome, seats in garden behind, nearby parking can be difficult, open all day Fri-Sun. *(Edward May)*

CANTERBURY TR1457

Parrot (01227) 454170

Church Lane – the one off St Radigunds Street, 100 metres E of St Radigunds car park; CT1 2AG Ancient heavy-beamed pub with wood and flagstone floors, stripped masonry, dark panelling and three open fires, up to six ales such as Shepherd Neame and Sharps, well liked food including pre-theatre menu, extensive wine list, friendly service, upstairs vaulted restaurant; some live music in bar, free wi-fi; nicely laid out courtyard with central barbecue, open (and food) all day. *(Edward May)*

CANTERBURY TR1457

White Hart (01227) 765091

Worthgate Place, opposite tree-shaded square off Castle Street; CT1 2QX Friendly little pub popular under new owners; Shepherd Neame ales and enjoyable well priced food cooked by landlady including some italian dishes, opened up bare-boards interior with woodburner in side room; quiz nights; children and dogs welcome, large garden behind (one of very few in the city), open (and food) all day. *(Edward May)*

CAPEL TQ6444

Dovecote (01892) 835966

Alders Road; SE of Tonbridge; TN12 6SU Cosy pub in nice country surroundings with open fire, beams and some stripped brickwork, up to six cask-tapped ales including Harveys, enjoyable well priced food (not Sun evening, Mon) from pitched-ceiling dining end, friendly helpful staff; live acoustic music Mon, quiz every other Weds; well behaved children allowed, dogs in bar (not at food times), lots of picnic-sets in back garden with terrace and play area, bat and trap, open all day Sun, closed Mon lunchtime. *(Frances Parsons)*

CHARING TQ9551

Bowl (01233) 712256

Egg Hill Road; TN27 0HG Popular 16th-c pub high on the downs (near Pilgrims Way) run by father and daughter; beamed bare-boards bar with inglenook log fire, tusky boar's head behind dark-panelled counter serving good kentish beers, carpeted dining area, enjoyable fairly priced food (all day Sat, till 5pm Sun) from lunchtime sandwiches/baguettes up including range of burgers, friendly helpful service; July beer/cider/cocktail festival with live music; children and dogs welcome, chunky picnic-sets on heated front terrace, more tables in big lawned garden, good local walks, six bedrooms, open all day. *(Joe and Belinda Smart)*

CHARTHAM TR1054

Artichoke (01227) 738316

Rottington Street; CT4 7JQ Attractive timbered pub (dates from the 15th c) under new licensee; generous helpings of enjoyable reasonably priced pub food (till 5pm Sun) from sandwiches and baked potatoes up, well kept Shepherd Neame ales, good service, carpeted log-fire bar, dining area with light wood tables (one built around a glass-topped well); quiz last Thurs of month, darts and bat and trap; children welcome, picnic-sets in back garden, closed Mon lunchtime, otherwise open all day. *(Mick Allen)*

CHIDDINGSTONE CAUSEWAY TQ5247

Greyhound (01892) 870275

Charcott, off back road to Weald; TN11 8LG Red-brick village pub refurbished under friendly newish licensees; well kept Larkins and a couple of guests, Dudda's Tun's cider and good range of gins, enjoyable home-made food at reasonable prices (some produce from own farm), log fire; children, walkers and dogs welcome, picnic-sets out in front and in side garden, closed Mon, otherwise open all day (till 9pm Sun), no food Sun evening. *(Martin Day)*

CHIDDINGSTONE HOATH TQ4943

★**Rock** (01892) 870296

Hoath Corner on back road Chiddingstone–Cowden; OS Sheet 188 map reference 497431; TN8 7BS Welcoming little tile-hung cottage with undulating brick floor, simple furnishings and woodburner in fine brick inglenook, local Larkins (brewed close by) and good home-made food (not Sun evening) from varied menu including specials, large stuffed bull's head for ring the bull, up a step to smaller room with long wooden settle by nice table; walkers and dogs welcome, picnic-sets out in front and on back lawn, open all day (Sun till 8pm). *(Tony Scott, Martin Day, Peter Carr)*

CHILHAM TR0653

★**White Horse** (01227) 730355

The Square; CT4 8BY 15th-c pub in picturesque village square; handsome ceiling beams and massive fireplace with lancastrian rose carved in the mantel beam, chunky light oak furniture on pale wood flooring and more traditional pubby furniture on quarry tiles, three well kept ales, Aug beer/cider festival, enjoyable varied food (all day Sat, not Sun evening), amiable helpful service; live music and quiz nights, free wi-fi; children welcome, dogs in bar, handy for the castle, open all day. *(Jacqui and Alan Swan)*

CHILLENDEN TR2653

★**Griffins Head** (01304) 840325

SE end of village; 2 miles E of Aylesham; CT3 1PS Attractive 14th-c beamed and timbered pub surrounded by appealing countryside; gently upscale local atmosphere in two bars and flagstoned back dining room, big log fire, full range of Shepherd Neame ales, good wine list and decent choice of popular home-made food, attentive friendly service; no under-8s, dogs welcome, summer weekend barbecues in pretty garden, vintage car meetings first Sun of the month, shuts 4pm Sun and 5pm Mon, otherwise open all day. *(Edward May)*

CHIPSTEAD TQ4956

★**Bricklayers Arms** (01732) 743424

Chevening Road; TN13 2RZ Attractive flower-decked pub (originally three cottages) overlooking lake and green, relaxed chatty atmosphere, well kept Harveys from casks behind long counter, good choice of popular fairly priced food (not Sun evening) from baguettes up including Mon steak night and Fri fish, cheerful helpful service, heavily beamed flagstoned bar with open fire and fine racehorse painting, larger back restaurant; Tues quiz and monthly live music; children and dogs welcome, disabled access/loo, seats out in front, open all day. *(Martin Day, Tony Scott, Alan Cowell)*

CONYER QUAY TQ9664

Ship (01795) 520881

Conyer Road; ME9 9HR Renovated and extended 18th-c creekside pub owned by adjacent Swale Marina; bare boards and open fires, enjoyable home-cooked food (not Sun evening) including weekend breakfast from 10am, Adnams, Shepherd Neame and guests; live folk first and third Tues of month, jazz/blues dinner third Thurs; children and dogs welcome, useful for boaters, walkers (on Saxon Shore Way) and birders, seats out at front, open all day weekends (till 9.30pm Sun). *(Mick Allen)*

COWDEN TQ4640

Fountain (01342) 850528

Off A264 and B2026; High Street; TN8 7JG Good fairly priced food from sandwiches up in attractive tile-hung village pub; steep steps up to bar with well kept Harveys and decent wines by the glass, friendly helpful staff, beams, half-panelling and old photographs, good log fire, mix of tables in adjoining room, woodburner in small back dining area, conservatory; background music, quiz first Thurs of month; children, walkers and dogs welcome, picnic-sets on small terrace and lawn, pretty village, open all day Sun but no evening food. *(Barry Collett, Martin Day)*

COWDEN TQ4642

★**Queens Arms** (01342) 850598

Cowden Pound; junction B2026 with Markbeech Road; TN8 5NP Friendly little Victorian time warp known as Elsie's after former long-serving landlady – present local owner has thankfully kept things much the same; two simple unpretentious rooms with open fires, a well kept/priced ale from Larkins, no food, darts, shove-ha'penny and other traditional games, piano; folk music (second and third Tues of month and some Sats), morris dancers and Christmas mummers; dogs welcome, open 5-10.30pm Mon, Tue, 5-7.30pm Weds, Thurs, 5-9pm Fri, 5-7.30pm Sat (longer if music), 12-3pm Sun. *(Tony Scott)*

DARGATE TR0761

Dove (01227) 751360

Village signposted from A299; ME13 9HB Tucked-away 19th-c restauranty pub with rambling rooms; good food from sandwiches and sharing plates up including evening pizzas and set lunch (Weds-Fri), Shepherd Neame ales, guest beers and nice wines by the glass, efficient pleasant service, plenty of stripped-wood tables on bare boards, some old pictures of the pub, woodburner in brick and stone fireplace; children, walkers and dogs welcome, sheltered garden with bat and trap, summer classic car meetings, open all day in summer (all day Fri-Sun, closed Mon and Tues in winter). *(Mike and Sarah Abbot)*

DARTFORD TQ5272

Horse & Groom (01322) 290056

Leyton Cross Road; DA2 7AP Refurbished pub next to Dartford Heath with large bar and restaurant extension; five mainly local ales, a dozen wines by the glass and good food from regularly changing menu including some pub favourites, friendly service; free wi-fi, children welcome, open all day, food all day Fri-Sun. *(Dave and Jan Pilgrim)*

DARTFORD TQ5473

Malt Shovel (01322) 224381

Darenth Road; DA1 1LP Cheerful 17th-c waney-boarded pub with two bars and conservatory; well kept Youngs, St Austell and a guest, several wines by the glass and good reasonably priced food (not Sun evening, Mon or Tues) from sandwiches and sharing plates up, friendly helpful staff; Mon quiz, some live music including folk night second Sun of month, free wi-fi; children and dogs welcome, tables on paved part-covered terrace, closed Mon lunchtime, otherwise open all day. *(Mick Allen)*

DEAL TR3751

Berry (01304) 362411

Canada Road; CT14 7EQ Small no-frills local opposite old Royal Marine barracks; welcoming enthusiastic landlord serving up to 11 well kept ales including Dark Star and Harveys (tasting notes on slates, regular beer festivals), kentish farm cider and perry, no food, L-shaped carpeted bar with coal fire; quiz second Fri of month, darts teams, pool and some live music; dogs welcome, small vine-covered back terrace, open all day (from 3pm Tues). *(Frances Parsons)*

DEAL TR3752

Bohemian (01304) 361939

Beach Street opposite pier; CT14 6HY Seafront bar with five real ales and good choice of bottled beers, extensive range of spirits too including 170 gins, popular traditional home-made food, friendly helpful staff, L-shaped room with mismatched furniture (some découpage tables), polished wood floor, lots of pictures, mirrors, signs and other odds and ends (customers encouraged to donate items), sofas and weekend papers, similar décor in upstairs cocktail bar with good sea views; background music; children and dogs welcome, sunny split-level deck behind and heated smokers' gazebo, open all day and can get very busy (particularly weekends). *(Frances Parsons)*

DEAL TR3752

Just Reproach 07432 413226

King Street; CT14 6HX Popular and genuinely welcoming micropub in former corner shop; simple drinking room with sturdy tables on bare boards, stools and cushioned benches, friendly knowledgeable service from father and daughter team, three or four changing small brewery ales tapped from the cask, also real ciders and some organic wines, locally made cheese, friendly chatty atmosphere; no mobile phones (fine for using them); dogs welcome, closed Sun evening. *(Kyle Brown)*

DEAL TR3753

Prince Albert (01304) 375425

Middle Street; CT14 6LW Compact 19th-c corner pub in conservation area; bowed entrance doors, etched-glass windows and fairly ornate interior with assorted bric-a-brac, three changing local ales, popular food (Weds-Sat evenings) and Sun carvery in back dining area, friendly staff; dogs welcome, small garden behind, bedrooms, closed lunchtimes except Sun. *(Kyle Brown)*

DEAL TR3752

Royal (01304) 375555

Beach Street; CT14 6JD Popular early 18th-c hotel right on the seafront; light and comfortable with plenty of casual drinkers in pubby bar, Shepherd Neame ales and good choice of enjoyable well priced food from sandwiches to fresh fish, friendly uniformed staff, restaurant; children and dogs (in bar) welcome, terrace overlooking the beach, 18 bedrooms (some with sea-view balconies), open (and food) all day from 8am for brunch. *(John Wooll)*

DEAL TR3753

Ship (01304) 372222

Middle Street; CT14 6JZ Traditional dimly lit two-room local in historic maritime quarter; five well kept/priced ales including Dark Star and Ramsgate served by friendly staff, no food, bare boards and lots of dark woodwork, stripped brick and local ship and wreck pictures, evening candles, cosy panelled back bar, open fire and woodburner; dogs welcome, small pretty walled garden, open all day. *(Tony Scott, Kyle Brown)*

DOVER TR3241

Blakes (01304) 202194

Castle Street; CT16 1PJ Small flagstoned cellar bar down steep steps; brick and flint walls, dim lighting, woodburner, Adnams and six changing guests, farm ciders/perries, several wines by the glass and over 50 malt whiskies, good bar food from sandwiches up, panelled carpeted upstairs restaurant, friendly staff; well behaved children welcome, dogs in bar, side garden and suntrap back terrace, four bedrooms, open (and food) all day. *(Sophie Ellison)*

DUNGENESS TR0916

Pilot (01797) 320314

Battery Road; TN29 9NJ Single-storey, mid 20th-c seaside café-bar by shingle beach; well kept Adnams, Courage, Harveys and a guest, decent choice of good value food from nice sandwiches to fish and chips, friendly efficient service (even when packed), open-plan interior divided into three areas, dark plank panelling (including the slightly curved ceiling), lighter front part overlooking beach, prints and local memorabilia, books for sale (proceeds to RNLI); background music, free wi-fi; children welcome, picnic-sets in side garden, open all day till 10pm (9pm Sun). *(Professor James Burke)*

DUNKS GREEN TQ6152

★**Kentish Rifleman** (01732) 810727
Dunks Green Road; TN11 9RU Relaxing Tudor country pub with bare-boards bar and two carpeted dining areas; various rifles and guns on low beams, cosy log fire, well kept ales such as Harveys, Tonbridge, Westerham and Whitstable, enjoyable reasonably priced food from light meals to popular Sun roasts, Tues pie and pint deal, friendly efficient staff; children and dogs welcome, tables in pretty garden with well, good walks from the door, one bedroom, open all day Fri-Sun, no food Sun or Mon evenings. *(Bob and Margaret Holder, B and M Kendall)*

EAST PECKHAM TQ6548

Man of Kent (01622) 871345
Tonbridge Road; TN12 5LA Traditional tile-hung pub dating from the 16th c; low black beams, mix of pubby furniture on carpet or slate tiles, fresh flowers, big two-way woodburner in central fireplace, ales such as Harveys, Sharps, Timothy Taylors and Tonbridge, enjoyable well priced home-made food (all day Sat, not Sun evening); children welcome, terrace seating by River Bourne, nearby walks, open all day. *(Mick Allen)*

EASTLING TQ9656

Carpenters Arms (01795) 890234
Off A251 S of M2 junction 6, via Painters Forstal; The Street; ME13 0AZ Partly 14th-c red-brick pub revived under new licensees; well kept Shepherd Neame ales and good reasonably priced pubby food from sandwiches and various ploughman's to daily specials, friendly attentive service, big log fires front and back, oak beams and mix of old and new furniture on brick or bare-boards floors, vintage photographs of the pub and surroundings; some live music; children welcome, paved terrace with rattan-style furniture, open all day Sat. *(David Harries, John Hunter Wright)*

EGERTON TQ9047

Barrow House (01233) 756599
The Street; TN27 9DJ Stylishly refurbished 16th-c weatherboarded pub under same ownership as the Milk House at Sissinghurst; back bar with high beams and light stone floor, inglenook log fire (plastered canopy has signatures of World War II airmen), main bar with more beams and timber partitions, attractive wooden counter serving well kept ales such as Dark Star and Harveys and good choice of wines, enjoyable food from snacks and sharing plates up, two-room restaurant with bare boards, painted tables and antler chandeliers, friendly staff; background and live music including folk/blues night last Tues of month; children, walkers and dogs welcome, disabled access via garden, three comfortable bedrooms, open all day from 9am. *(Joe and Belinda Smart)*

FAVERSHAM TR0161

Bear (01795) 532668
Market Place; ME13 7AG Traditional late Victorian Shepherd Neame pub (back part dates from the 16th c); their ales kept well and occasional guests, pubby lunchtime food (evenings Tues-Thurs) including popular Sunday roasts, friendly relaxed atmosphere, locals' front bar, snug and back dining lounge (all off side corridor); quiz last Mon of month, darts, free wi-fi; a couple of pavement tables, open all day. *(Alexander and Trish Cutter)*

FAVERSHAM TR0160

Elephant (01795) 590157
The Mall; ME13 8JN Traditional town ale house, friendly and chatty, with four or five good changing ales mainly from smaller kent brewers, maybe a local cider too, no food (can bring your own), single bare-boards bar with central log fire and cosy seating areas, dim lighting; juke box and some live music; children and dogs welcome, peaceful suntrap back garden with pond, open all day Sat, till 7pm Sun, from 3pm weekdays, closed Mon. *(Ivy and George Goodwill)*

FAVERSHAM TR0161

Sun (01795) 535098
West Street; ME13 7JE Rambling 15th-c pub in pedestrianised street; unpretentious feel in small low-ceilinged partly panelled rooms, scrubbed tables and big inglenook, well kept Shepherd Neame ales and enjoyable bar food, smart restaurant attached; background and some live music (Fri), free wi-fi; wheelchair access negotiating small step, pleasant back courtyard, eight bedrooms, open all day. *(Mick Allen)*

FAVERSHAM TR0161

Vaults (01795) 591817
Preston Street; ME13 8PA Centrally placed old pub (more spacious than it looks) with half a dozen well kept ales (at least one local) and a couple of real ciders, cheerful helpful staff, enjoyable good value food (all day Fri and Sat, till 4pm Sun) including nice steaks and carve-your-own Sun roasts; quiz and curry first Mon of the month, traditional games; children and dogs welcome, big back garden, open all day. *(Jacqui and Alan Swan)*

FINGLESHAM TR3353

★**Crown** (01304) 612555
Just off A258 Sandwich–Deal; The Street; CT14 0NA Neatly kept low-beamed country local dating from the 16th c; good

value generous home-made food from usual pub dishes to interesting specials, afternoon cream teas (not Sun), friendly helpful service, four well kept local ales such as Ramsgate, Biddenden cider, softly lit split-level carpeted bar with stripped stone and inglenook log fire, two attractive dining rooms; children and dogs welcome, lovely big garden with play area and bat and trap, campsite with five hook-ups, open all day Fri-Sun. *(Trevor and Michele Street)*

FOLKESTONE TR2336

British Lion (01303) 251478

The Bayle, near churchyard; CT20 1SQ Popular 18th-c flower-decked pub nestling behind parish church; comfortable and cosy, with four well kept ales and a couple of real ciders, big helpings of good value traditional food, friendly helpful service; children welcome, tables out in small yard, open all day Sun. *(Mick Allen)*

FORDCOMBE TQ5240

Chafford Arms (01892) 740267

B2188, off A264 W of Langton Green; TN3 0SA Picturesque 19th-c tile-hung pub; good selection of wines and enjoyable food from sandwiches and baguettes to imaginative specials, helpful friendly staff, lounge bar with comfy leather armchairs, dining room and locals' bar where dogs allowed (their black lab is Charlie), three woodburners; free wi-fi; children welcome (menu for them), picnic-sets on front terrace and in attractive sheltered back garden with Weald views, 1930s telephone box in car park, closed Sun evening, Mon, otherwise open (and food) all day. *(Nigel and Jean Eames)*

FORDWICH TR1859

★ **Fordwich Arms** (01227) 710444

Off A28 in Sturry; CT2 0DB Interesting 1930s red-brick building by the River Stour (the much older pub burnt down); most customers here for young chef-landlord's excellent modern food (not Sun evening, Mon), but still drinkers in the long parquet-floored bar where they serve four real ales and good wines by the glass, courteous friendly staff, simply furnished panelled back dining room with open fire; background music; children and dogs welcome, tables on side lawn and riverside terrace, the town hall opposite is thought to be England's oldest, closed Mon, otherwise open all day. *(Edward May)*

FORDWICH TR1759

George & Dragon (01227) 710661

Off A28 at Sturry; CT2 0BX Handsome old Home Counties group pub on the banks of the River Stour in Britain's smallest town; spreading character rooms with beams and timbers, rugs on polished boards or flagstones, assortment of nice old chairs and tables (one a giant bellows), armchairs either side of open fire, Phoenix Brunning & Price, Shepherd Neame and guests, good wines by the glass and well liked brasserie-style food, friendly helpful staff; children and dogs welcome, disabled access/facilities, picnic-sets and a play tractor in garden, handy for Howletts Wild Animal Park, open (and food) all day. *(Alexander and Trish Cutter)*

FRITTENDEN TQ8141

Bell & Jorrocks (01580) 852415

Corner of Biddenden Road/The Street; TN17 2EJ Simple 18th-c tile-hung village local; well kept Harveys, Woodfordes Wherry and a couple of guests (Easter weekend beer festival), Weston's and Thatcher's ciders, good home-made food (not Sun evening, Mon, Tues), friendly welcoming atmosphere, beamed interior with propeller from german bomber above fireplace; regular live music and other events, sports TV, kentish darts; children and dogs welcome, closed Mon and Tues lunchtimes till 3pm, otherwise open all day. *(Edward May)*

GOODNESTONE TR2554

Fitzwalter Arms (01304) 840303

The Street; NB this is in E Kent not the other Goodnestone; CT3 1PJ Old lattice-windowed beamed village pub under newish management; rustic bar with wood floor and open fire, Shepherd Neame ales, enjoyable reasonably priced pubby food (beer and burger Weds, steak night Sat), friendly service, carpeted dining room with another fire; bar billiards and darts; well behaved children and dogs welcome, terrace with steps up to peaceful garden, lovely church next door and close to Goodnestone Park Gardens, three bedrooms, open all day, no evening food Sun or Mon. *(Frances Parsons)*

GOUDHURST TQ7237

Star & Eagle (01580) 211512

High Street; TN17 1AL Steps up to striking medieval inn next to the church; settles and Jacobean-style seats in old-fashioned carpeted areas on different levels, beams and log fires, good choice of enjoyable food including some spanish influences, well kept ales such as Brakspears and Harveys, afternoon teas, friendly service, restaurant; children welcome, no dogs inside, tables out at back with lovely views, attractive village, 11 character bedrooms, good breakfast, open all day. *(Mick Allen)*

GOUDHURST TQ7037

Vine (01580) 211105

High Street; TN17 1AG White-painted 17th-c tile-hung village pub; four refurbished linked rooms (steps down to two on left), mix of old wooden tables and chairs on bare boards, some half-panelling and exposed timbers, various pictures, old photographs and a large boar's head, woodburner in brick fireplace, Harveys Best, three changing guests and several wines by the glass including english sparkling, decent choice of enjoyable mid-priced food from pub favourites to interesting specials, upstairs grill room (not Sun evening, Tues) and cocktail lounge; background music, free wi-fi; children and dogs (in bar) welcome, picnic-sets out at front around olive tree, enclosed gravel terrace behind, closed Mon, otherwise open all day (till 9pm Sun). *(V Brogden)*

GROOMBRIDGE TQ5337

★**Crown** (01892) 864742

B2110; TN3 9QH Charming tile-hung wealden inn with snug low-beamed bar; old tables on worn flagstones, panelling, bric-a-brac, fire in sizeable brick inglenook, well kept Harveys, Larkins and a guest, enjoyable pubby food (all day Sat, till 5pm Sun) from lunchtime sandwiches up including plenty of gluten-free options, good friendly service, refurbished two-room restaurant with smaller inglenook; background music, free wi-fi; children and dogs (in bar) welcome, tables on narrow brick terrace overlooking steep green, more seats in garden behind, four bedrooms, handy for Groombridge Place gardens, open all day Sat, till 9pm Sun. *(Hunter and Christine Wright, Martin Day)*

HAWKHURST TQ7531

★**Great House** (01580) 753119

Gills Green; pub signed off A229 N; TN18 5EJ Stylish white-weatherboarded restauranty pub (part of the Elite Pubs group); good variety of well liked if not always cheap food, ales such as Harveys, Old Dairy and Sharps from marble counter, polite efficient service, sofas, armchairs and bright scatter cushions in chatty bar, stools against counter used by locals, dark wood dining tables and smartly upholstered chairs on slate floor beside log fire, steps down to airy dining room with Aga (they do cook on it) and doors out to terrace; background music, jazz afternoons and other events; children and dogs (in bar) welcome, open all day (food all day weekends). *(Nicky Menzies)*

HAWKHURST TQ7630

Queens (01580) 754233

Rye Road (A268 E); TN18 4EY Fine Georgian-fronted inn (building actually dates from the 16th c) set back from the road; revamped main bar with heavy beams and bare boards, some high modern chairs and barrel tables, armchairs either side of inglenook woodburner, dining area and cosy snug, well liked food from bar meals up, ales such as Old Dairy, Rockin' Robin and Sharps, decent wines by the glass, good friendly service, separate restaurant to left of entrance with another inglenook; background music; children welcome, tables out in front, seven bedrooms including family rooms, open all day, breakfast for non-residents. *(Joe and Belinda Smart)*

HEAVERHAM TQ5758

Chequers (01732) 670266

Watery Lane; TN15 6NP Attractive 16th-c beamed country pub under new management; well kept Shepherd Neame ales, decent wines by the glass and enjoyable fairly traditional food at sensible prices, friendly helpful service, public bar with open fire, inglenook woodburner in dining area, old timbered barn for functions; children and dogs welcome, big garden, good North Downs walks, closed Mon, otherwise open all day, no food Sun evening. *(Martin Day)*

HERNE TR1865

Butchers Arms (01227) 371000

Herne Street (A291); CT6 7HL The UK's first micropub (converted from a butchers in 2005); up to half a dozen well kept changing ales (mainly local) tapped from backroom casks, tasters offered by friendly former motorbike-racing landlord, just a couple of benches and butcher's-block tables (seats about ten), lots of bric-a-brac; dogs welcome, disabled access, tables out under awning, open 12-1.30pm, 6-9pm, closed Sun evening. *(Edward May)*

HERNHILL TR0660

Red Lion (01227) 751207

Off A299 via Dargate, or A2 via Boughton Street and Staple Street; ME13 9JR Pretty Tudor pub by church and attractive village green, some refurbishmentt but keeping character; densely beamed with antique-style tables and chairs on flagstones or parquet, log fires, fairly traditional food from sharing boards up, well kept ales such as Sharps and Shepherd Neame, decent wines, friendly helpful staff, upstairs restaurant; background and some live music; children and dogs welcome, seats in front and in big garden, open all day. *(Gerry and Pam Pollard)*

HEVER TQ4743

Greyhound (01732) 862221

Uckfield Lane; TN8 7LJ Fully restored 19th-c country pub with good popular food from sandwiches up, three well kept ales including Harveys, friendly efficient service, restaurant; handy for Hever Castle, five comfortable bedrooms, closed Mon lunchtime in Nov, no food Sun evening in winter. *(Justine Young)*

HEVER TQ4744

Henry VIII (01732) 862457

By gates of Hever Castle; TN8 7NH Predominantly 17th-c with some fine oak

All *Guide* inspections are anonymous. Anyone claiming to be a *Good Pub Guide* inspector is a fraud. Please let us know.

panelling, wide floorboards and heavy beams, inglenook fireplace, Henry VIII touches to décor, emphasis on enjoyable fairly priced food from pubby choices up, well kept Shepherd Neame ales, friendly efficient staff, restaurant; children and dogs welcome, outside covered area with a couple of leather sofas, steps down to deck and pondside lawn, open all day, food all day weekends (till 7pm Sun). *(Martin Day, R and S Bentley, Tony Scott, Tina and David Woods-Taylor)*

HODSOLL STREET TQ6263

Green Man (01732) 823575

Signed off A227 S of Meopham; turn right in village; TN15 7LE Friendly family-run village pub with traditional furnishings in neat mainly carpeted rooms around central bar; painted half-panelling, old framed photographs and woodburner in standalone fireplace, Harveys, Sharps, Timothy Taylors and a guest, wide choice of enjoyable blackboard food from sandwiches/baguettes up including popular two-course weekday lunch deal; background music (live Sun), quiz Mon, free wi-fi; children and dogs welcome, picnic-sets in front overlooking small green, more tables and climbing frame on back lawn, open (and food) all day Fri-Sun. *(Michael Breeze)*

HOLLINGBOURNE TQ8455

Dirty Habit (01622) 880880

B2163, off A20; ME17 1UW Ancient dimly lit beamed pub in same group as the Great House in Hawkhurst, Gun at Gun Hill (Sussex) etc; ales such as Harveys and Shepherd Neame, several wines by the glass and popular food including seasonal offers, armchairs and stools on slate floor in main bar area, panelled end room with mix of tables and chairs, low beamed dining room and a further raftered eating area with brick floor and woodburner; children welcome, good outside shelter with armchairs and sofas, on North Downs Way (leaflets for walkers) and handy for Leeds Castle, open all day. *(Mick Allen)*

HOLLINGBOURNE TQ8354

★**Windmill** (01622) 889000

M20 junction 8, A20 towards Lenham then left on to B2163 – Eyhorne Street; ME17 1TR Most people here for the impressive food but there's a small back bar serving local Musket, Sharps, a guest beer and up to 15 wines by the glass; light and airy main room with white-painted beams, animal skins on bare boards and log fire in low inglenook, mix of furniture including armchairs, heavy settles with scatter cushions, red leather banquette and dark wood dining tables and chairs, two further dining rooms (steps up to one), candles and fresh flowers; background music (live Weds), free wi-fi; children and dogs (in bar) welcome, back terrace, summer barbecues, open all day. *(Dave Braisted, Miss A E Dare)*

IDE HILL TQ4851

Cock (01732) 750310

Off B2042 SW of Sevenoaks; TN14 6JN Pretty village-green local dating from the 15th c, chatty and friendly, with two bars (steps between), well kept Greene King ales and a beer badged for them, enjoyable good value traditional food including notable steak and kidney pudding, decent affordably priced wine list, cosy in winter with inglenook log fire; children and dogs welcome, picnic-sets out at front, handy for Chartwell and Emmetts Garden (both NT), nice walks nearby, open all day. *(Ian Phillips)*

IGHTHAM TQ5956

George & Dragon (01732) 882440

The Street, A227; TN15 9HH Ancient half-timbered pub with spacious modernised interior, enjoyable fairly pubby food from sandwiches/baguettes up including weekday set lunch, well kept Shepherd Neame ales and decent wines, friendly staff, sofas among other furnishings in long main bar, heavy-beamed end room, woodburner and open fires, restaurant; children and dogs welcome, back terrace by car park, handy for Ightham Mote (NT), good walks, open all day from 10am for breakfast, no food Sun evening. *(Kyle Brown)*

IGHTHAM COMMON TQ5855

★**Harrow** (01732) 885912

Signposted off A25 just W of Ightham; pub sign may be hard to spot; TN15 9EB Smart and comfortable with emphasis on good food from daily changing menu, also some traditional choices and Sunday roasts, relaxed cheerful bar area to the right with candles and fresh flowers, dining chairs on herringbone wood floor, winter fire, charming little antiquated conservatory and more formal dining room, well kept Loddon and nice wines by the glass; background music; children welcome (not in dining room Sat evening), pretty little pergola-enclosed back terrace, handy for Ightham Mote (NT), closed Mon-Weds and Sun evening. *(Edward May)*

IGHTHAM COMMON TQ5955

Old House (01732) 886077

Redwell, S of village; OS Sheet 188 map reference 591559; TN15 9EE Basic unchanging two-room country local tucked down narrow lane (no inn sign); beams, bare bricks and big inglenook log fire, half a dozen interesting changing ales from tap room casks, good selection of whiskies and gins, no food; darts; dogs welcome, closed weekday lunchtimes (opens 7pm) and may shut early if quiet. *(Martin Day)*

KENNINGTON TR0245

Old Mill (01223) 661000

Mill Lane; TN25 4DZ Updated and much extended early 19th-c dining pub (same owners as the Oak on the Green at Bearsted);

good choice of popular food from sandwiches and snacks up, well kept ales and nice selection of wines, friendly helpful service; children welcome, plenty of terrace and garden seating, open (and food) all day. *(Paul Humphreys)*

KINGSDOWN TR3748

Kings Head (01304) 373915
Upper Street; CT14 8BJ Tucked-away split-level local with two cosy bars and L-shaped extension; black timbers, lots of old photographs on faded cream walls, woodburner, three real ales and popular reasonably priced food including blackboard specials and children's menu, friendly landlord and staff; background music, a few vintage amusement machines and darts, occasional live music and other events; dogs welcome, small side garden, skittle alley, open all day Sun, closed weekdays till 5pm. *(Diana and Bertie Farr)*

KINGSTON TR2051

Black Robin (01227) 830230
Elham Valley Road, off A2 S of Canterbury at Barham signpost; CT4 6HS 18th-c pub named after a notorious highwayman who was hanged nearby; kentish ales and good helpings of enjoyable home-made food from shortish menu (can eat in bar or back restaurant extension), stone-baked pizzas to take away, friendly staff; background and live music including some established folk artists, sports TV, free wi-fi; children and dogs welcome, disabled access, seats out on decking, open all day (till 8pm Sun). *(Kyle Brown)*

LADDINGFORD TQ6848

Chequers (01622) 871266
The Street; ME18 6BP Friendly old beamed and weatherboarded village pub; good sensibly priced food from sandwiches and sharing boards up, some themed nights, well kept Adnams Southwold and three guests; events including ale and cheese festival Apr/May; children and dogs welcome, big garden with play area, shetland ponies in paddock, Medway walks nearby, one bedroom, open all day weekends. *(Sylvia and Phillip Spencer)*

LEIGH TQ5646

Plough (01732) 832149
Powder Mill Lane/Leigh Road, off B2027 NW of Tonbridge; TN11 9AJ Attractive opened-up Tudor country pub; lattice windows, hop-strung beams and parquet flooring, some cushioned pews and farmhouse chairs, massive grate in two-way inglenook, well kept Tonbridge Coppernob and up to three local guests, popular home-cooked food, friendly helpful staff, small flagstoned room behind servery with old mangle and darts; quiz third Thurs of month; children and dogs welcome, picnic-sets in garden with play area, old barn for weddings and other functions, open all day Sun till 9pm, closed Mon-Weds. *(Tony Scott)*

LINTON TQ7550

Bull (01622) 743612
Linton Hill (A229 S of Maidstone); ME17 4AW Comfortably modernised 17th-c dining pub; good choice of food from sandwiches and light dishes to pub favourites and grills, popular Sun carvery, fine fireplace in nice old beamed bar, carpeted restaurant, well kept Shepherd Neame ales, friendly efficient service; children and dogs (in bar) welcome, side garden overlooking church, splendid far-reaching views from back decking, two gazebos, open all day. *(Ivy and George Goodwill)*

LITTLE CHART TQ9446

Swan (01233) 840011
The Street; TN27 0QB Attractive 15th-c village pub with notable arched Dering windows, open fires and clean fresh décor in unspoilt front bar and good-sized dining area, flowers on tables, enjoyable home-made food (not Sun evening), well kept beers such as Old Dairy and decent wines by the glass, friendly staff; Sun quiz; children and dogs (in bar) welcome, nice riverside garden, closed Mon, otherwise open all day. *(Mike and Sarah Abbot)*

LOWER HARDRES TR1453

Granville (01227) 700402
Faussett Hill, Street End; B2068 S of Canterbury; CT4 7AL Spacious pub with contemporary furnishings in several linked areas, one with unusual central fire under large conical hood, also a proper public bar with farmhouse chairs, settles and woodburner, generally well liked food from baguettes and pub favourites to more restauranty dishes, good value set lunch and other deals, up to three Shepherd Neame ales including Master Brew, 13 wines by the glass; background music, artwork for sale; children and dogs welcome, seats on small sunny terrace and in garden under large spreading tree, open all day. *(Frances Parsons)*

LUDDESDOWNE TQ6667

★**Cock** (01474) 814208
Henley Street, N of village – OS Sheet 177 map reference 664672; off A227 in Meopham, or A228 in Cuxton; DA13 0XB Early 18th-c country pub under long-serving no-nonsense landlord; at least seven well kept ales such as Adnams, Goachers, Harveys and St Austell, also some good german beers, snacky bar food, rugs on bare boards in bay-windowed lounge, beams and panelling, quarry-tiled locals' bar, woodburners, settles, cask tables and other pubby furnishings, aircraft pictures, beer mats and bric-a-brac from stuffed animals to model cars, back dining conservatory; music quiz fourth Mon of month, bar billiards and darts; no children inside or on part-covered

heated back terrace, dogs welcome, big secure garden, good walks, open all day Fri-Sun, from 4pm other days. *(Tony R)*

LYNSTED TQ9460

Black Lion (01795) 521229

The Street; ME9 0RJ Welcoming early 17th-c village pub; well kept Goachers and good freshly made pubby food (all day Sat, not Sun evening) including blackboard specials, settles and old tables on bare boards, log fires; some live music, pool; children and dogs welcome, well tended garden with play area, open all day. *(Kyle Brown)*

MARDEN TQ7547

Stile Bridge (01622) 831236

Staplehurst Road (A229); TN12 9BH Friendly roadside pub with five well kept ales including Dark Star and Goachers, also lots of bottled beers, real ciders and extensive range of gins, good traditional food (not Sun evening); events including beer festivals, live music and comedy nights; dogs welcome in bar, back garden and terrace, open all day. *(Jan Stevens)*

MARKBEECH TQ4742

Kentish Horse (01342) 850493

Off B2026 Hartfield–Edenbridge; TN8 5NT Attractive village pub (originally three cottages) next to the church, friendly and welcoming, with three well kept ales including Harveys and Larkins from brick counter, good value traditional food (not Sun or Mon evenings), friendly helpful staff, long carpeted bar with black beams and log fire, restaurant with woodburner in large brick fireplace, french windows to terrace; folk night second Sun of month; children welcome, picnic-sets and fenced play area in big garden, nice views, open all day. *(Edward May)*

MARTIN TR3347

Lantern (01304) 852276

Off A258 Dover–Deal; The Street; CT15 5JL Pretty 17th-c brick pub (originally two farmworker's cottages) in lovely setting; small refurbished bar with low beams, stripped brick and cosy corners, extensive range of craft beers and real ales from copper-topped counter, decent wines by the glass including prosecco on tap, cocktails, enjoyable food from traditional choices up, friendly helpful service, soft lighting, log fires; background and some acoustic live music, other events such as book club and wine tasting, shop selling home-made and local produce; children and dogs welcome, some tables out at front, more in good-sized back garden with big play house, open all day in summer, all day Fri-Sun winter. *(Diana and Bertie Farr)*

MATFIELD TQ6642

Poet at Matfield (01892) 722416

Maidstone Road; TN12 7JH 17th-c beamed pub-restaurant named for Siegfried Sassoon who was born nearby; highly regarded modern cooking from south african chef-patron including good value weekday set menu, ales such as Harveys and Westerham, well chosen wines and some interesting gins, friendly efficient staff; closed Sun evening and Mon, otherwise open all day. *(Nick Taylor)*

MATFIELD TQ6541

Star (01892) 725458

Maidstone Road (B2160); TN12 7JR Creeper-clad pub close to the village duck pond; beamed and bare-boards front bar with real ales such as Harveys, enjoyable food (not Sun evening) including signature home-made pies, friendly service, restaurant in older back part with inglenook woodburner; quiz third Thurs of month, occasional live music; picnic-sets on gravel terrace, open all day. *(Gene and Kitty Rankin)*

MERSHAM TR0438

Farriers Arms (01233) 720444

The Forstal/Flood Street; TN25 6NU Large early 17th-c pub owned by the local community; beers from on-site microbrewery including seasonal ales, decent choice of wines and enjoyable home-made food from bar snacks to daily specials, friendly staff, opened-up interior with beams and log fires, restaurant; July beer festival; children and dogs welcome, pretty streamside garden behind with pleasant country views, open all day. *(Jacqui and Alan Swan)*

NEWENDEN TQ8327

White Hart (01797) 252166

Rye Road (A268); TN18 5PN Popular 16th-c weatherboarded local; long low-beamed bar with big stone fireplace, dining areas off serving enjoyable reasonably priced pub food including good Sun roasts, well kept Harveys, Rother Valley and guests (July beer/cider festival), friendly helpful young staff, back games area with pool; background music, quiz nights, sports TV; children and dogs welcome, boules in large garden, near river (boat trips to NT's Bodiam Castle), six bedrooms, open all day. *(Edward May)*

NORTHBOURNE TR3352

Hare & Hounds (01304) 369188

Off A256 or A258 near Dover; The Street; CT14 0LG Welcoming 17th-c

We mention bottled beers and spirits only if there is something unusual about them – imported belgian real ales, say, or dozens of malt whiskies; so do please let us know about them in your reports.

village pub with two or three well kept ales and good choice of wines from brick-faced servery, decent pubby food, bare-boards and flagstoned bar separated by a couple of archways, nice log fire; children and dogs welcome, paved terrace and garden with play area, open all day Weds-Sun. *(Mick Allen)*

OARE TR0163

★ **Shipwrights Arms** (01795) 590088
S shore of Oare Creek, E of village; signed from Oare Road/Ham Road junction in Faversham; ME13 7TU Remote marshland tavern with plenty of character; three dark simple little bars separated by standing timbers, wood partitions and narrow door arches, medley of seats from tapestry-cushioned stools to black panelled built-in settles forming booths, flags and boating pennants on ceiling, wind gauge above main door (takes reading from chimney), up to six kentish beers tapped from the cask (pewter tankards over counter), simple home-cooked food lunchtime only; children (away from bar area) and dogs welcome, large garden with bat and trap, path along Oare Creek to Swale estuary, lots of surrounding birdlife, closed Mon. *(Sophie Ellison)*

OARE TR0063

Three Mariners (01795) 533633
Church Road; ME13 0QA Comfortable simply restored 18th-c pub with good food including fresh fish and evening set menu, Shepherd Neame ales and plenty of wines by the glass, beams, bare boards and log fire; children and dogs (in bar) welcome, attractive garden overlooking Faversham Creek, good walks, open all day (till 9pm Sun). *(Sophie Ellison)*

PAINTERS FORSTAL TQ9958

Alma (01795) 533835
Signed off A2 at Ospringe; ME13 0DU Welcoming weatherboarded and timbered village local, homely and tidy, with well kept Shepherd Neame ales, decent wines and good value home cooking including notable steak and kidney pudding (no food Sun evening), Tues lunchtime set deal, helpful service; darts; children and dogs (in bar) welcome, picnic-sets in small enclosed garden, play area over the road, campsite nearby. *(Joe and Belinda Smart)*

PEMBURY TQ6240

Camden Arms (01892) 822012
High Street (The Green); TN2 4PH Substantial tile-hung inn opposite village green; good generously served food from extensive reasonably priced menu, Sun carvery, well kept ales such as Harveys and decent choice of other beers and wines, friendly welcoming staff, large opened-up central bar with smaller dining rooms off, beams, bare boards and flagstones, various bits and pieces including landlord's remarkable collection of Dinky Toys; children and dogs (in bar) welcome, tables on covered terrace, picnic-sets on lawn, 15 bedrooms some with four-posters, open (and food) all day. *(Gerry and Rosemary Dobson, Nigel and Jean Eames)*

PETT BOTTOM TR1652

Duck (01227) 830354
Off B2068 S of Canterbury, via Lower Hardres; CT4 5PB New management for this popular tile-hung pub in attractive downland spot; long bare-boards bar with scrubbed tables, pine-panelling and two log fires, good food cooked by landlord-chef including weekday set lunch, friendly attentive service, two or three well kept beers and good wine choice; children and dogs welcome, seats and old well out in front, garden behind where Ian Fleming used to make notes for his James Bond books (see blue plaque), camping nearby, closed Mon. *(Charlotte and William Mason)*

PETTERIDGE TQ6640

Hopbine (01892) 722561
Petteridge Lane; NE of village; TN12 7NE Unspoilt tiled and weatherboarded cottage in quiet hamlet; two small rooms with open fire between, traditional pubby furniture, hops and horsebrasses, well kept Tonbridge, Long Man and a guest, proper cider and enjoyable good value home-made food including wood-fired pizzas (two-for-one deal Weds), friendly staff, steps up to simple back part with brick fireplace; dogs welcome, outside gents'; terrace seating, open all day Fri-Sun, no food Mon, Tues. *(Gene and Kitty Rankin)*

PLUCKLEY TQ9144

Rose & Crown (01233) 840048
Mundy Bois – spelled Monday Boys on some maps – off Smarden Road SW of village centre; TN27 0ST Popular 17th-c tile-hung pub with good food (all day Sat and Sun) from french chef, three well kept beers such as Adnams, Harveys and Shepherd Neame, friendly attentive service, main bar with massive inglenook, small snug and restaurant; background music, beer festival Aug; children and dogs (in bar) welcome, pretty garden and terrace with views, play area, open all day. *(Miss A E Dare)*

RAMSGATE TR3764

Artillery Arms (01843) 853202
West Cliff Road; CT11 9JS Old-fashioned little corner local on two levels, chatty and welcoming, with half a dozen well kept interesting beers and enjoyable food (all day weekends), artillery prints/memorabilia and

There are report forms at the back of the book.

fine listed windows depicting Napoleonic scenes; dogs welcome, wheelchair access, open all day. *(Gerry and Pam Pollard)*

RAMSGATE TR3764

Conqueror 07890 203282
Grange Road/St Mildreds Road; CT11 9LR Cosy single-room micropub in former corner shop; welcoming enthusiastic landlord serving three changing ales direct from the cask, also local cider and apple juice, friendly chatty atmosphere, large windows and old photos of eponymous cross-channel paddle steamer; dogs welcome, closed Sun evening, Mon. *(Mick Allen)*

RAMSGATE TR3765

Great Tree (01843) 590708
Margate Road; CT11 7SP Quirky relaxed place with unusual café-bar décor; four real ales and 20 proper ciders, also interesting teas and good coffee, local artwork on show plus regular events such as jazz, folk, film and poetry evenings; children (away from bar) and dogs welcome, open Tues-Sun from 1pm, closed Mon lunchtime. *(Mick Allen)*

ROCHESTER TQ7468

Coopers Arms (01634) 404298
St Margarets Street; ME1 1TL Ancient jettied building behind the cathedral; cosily unpretentious with two comfortable beamed bars, low-priced pub food and good range of well kept beers, list of landlords back to 1543 and ghostly tales of a walled-up monk (mannequin marks the spot); live music (Sun) and quiz nights; tables in attractive courtyard, open all day. *(Tony Scott)*

ROLVENDEN TQ8431

Bull (01580) 241212
Regent Street; TN17 4PB Welcoming tile-hung cottage with woodburner in fine brick inglenook, high-backed dining chairs around rustic tables on stripped boards, built-in panelled wall seats, well kept Harveys and Old Dairy, enjoyable food (not Sun evening in winter) from pub favourites and pizzas up, pale oak tables in dining room; background music; children and dogs (in bar) welcome, picnic-sets behind picket fence at front and side, more seats in sizeable back garden, open all day. *(Gerry and Pam Pollard)*

SANDGATE TR2035

Ship (01303) 248525
High Street; CT20 3AH Long narrow corner pub with traditional nautical-theme bar and dining area at front and modern conservatory restaurant behind overlooking the sea, half a dozen cask-tapped ales including Dark Star, Hop Back and Greene King, real cider, decent wines and good range of gins, popular food with emphasis on local fish/seafood, affable long-serving landlord and friendly efficient staff; more good sea views from roof terrace and bedrooms, open all day. *(Richard Kennell)*

SANDWICH TR3358

George & Dragon (01304) 613106
Fisher Street; CT13 9EJ 15th-c backstreet dining pub under new ownership; shortish choice of enjoyable food cooked in open kitchen including some lunchtime pub favourites, a dozen wines by the glass from decent list (can also bring your own – corkage charged), three well kept changing ales, good friendly service, open-plan beamed interior with three-way log fire, skylit dining extension opening on to paved terrace; children and dogs (in bar) welcome, closed Sun evening, otherwise open all day. *(Professor James Burke)*

SARRE TR2564

Crown (01843) 847808
Ramsgate Road (A253) off A28; CT7 0LF Historic 15th-c inn (Grade I listed) sandwiched between two main roads; front bar and other rambling rooms including restaurant, beams and log fires, well kept Shepherd Neame ales and decent fairly priced wines, own cherry brandy (pub known locally as the Cherry Brandy House), generous helpings of enjoyable locally sourced food from sandwiches up, good friendly service; children welcome, side garden (traffic noise), comfortable surprisingly quiet bedrooms, open all day. *(Edward May)*

SEASALTER TR0864

★**Sportsman** (01227) 273370
Faversham Road, off B2040; CT5 4BP Restauranty pub just inside seawall – rather unprepossessing from outside but surprisingly light and airy; imaginative contemporary cooking using plenty of seafood (not Sun evening, Mon, must book and not cheap), good wine choice including english and a couple of well kept Shepherd Neame ales, knowledgeable landlord and friendly staff; two plain linked rooms and long conservatory, scrubbed pine tables, wheelback and basket-weave dining chairs on wood floor, local artwork; children welcome, plastic glasses for outside, wide views over marshland with grazing sheep and (from seawall) across to Sheppey, small caravan park one side, wood chalets the other, open all day Sun till 10pm. *(Charlotte and William Mason, Frances Parsons)*

SEVENOAKS TQ5555

★**Bucks Head** (01732) 761330
Godden Green, just E; TN15 0JJ Welcoming and relaxed old flower-decked pub with neatly kept bar and restaurant area, good freshly cooked blackboard food from baguettes to Sun roasts, well kept Shepherd Neame and a guest, beams, panelling and splendid inglenooks; children and dogs welcome, front terrace overlooking informal green and duck pond, pretty back garden with mature trees, pergola and views over

quiet country behind Knole (NT), popular with walkers, closed Mon except bank holidays. *(Trevor and Michele Street)*

SEVENOAKS TQ5355

Halfway House (01732) 463667

2.5 miles from M25 junction 5; TN13 2JD Nicely updated old roadside pub with friendly staff and regulars, good competitively priced food from sensibly short blackboard menu, three changing ales, local wines and some interesting flavoured vodkas, upper bar with record deck and LPs (can bring your own), some live music too; handy for the station, parking can be tricky, open all day. *(Kyle Brown)*

SHADOXHURST TQ9737

Kings Head (01233) 732243

Woodchurch Road; TN26 1LQ Old family-run pub with clean updated interior, good value enjoyable food in bar and separate restaurant including blackboard specials, well kept Shepherd Neame and guests, friendly efficient staff, stripped pine tables on bare boards or quarry tiles, various bits and pieces including china, copper and brass, vintage photos and old horse tack, log fires; games area with pool, quiz last Sun of month; children and dogs welcome, tables on front terrace and in garden behind with play area, closed Sun evening, Mon. *(Joe and Belinda Smart)*

SHOREHAM TQ5161

Kings Arms (01959) 523100

Church Street; TN14 7SJ Part-weather-boarded 16th-c pub in quaint unspoilt village close to the River Darent; cosy and unpretentious, with generous helpings of good honest food including Fri fish and chips, two or three well kept beers such as Greene King, Harveys and Sharps, friendly helpful staff, log fire, plates and brasses, small restaurant area; children welcome, no dogs, picnic-sets outside (some under cover), note the ostler's box (compete with mannequin) at the front, good local walks, open all day, no evening food Sun-Tues. *(Mrs Margo Finlay, Jörg Kasprowski, Mike Buckingham)*

SHOREHAM TQ5261

Olde George (01959) 522017

Church Street; TN14 7RY Traditional 16th-c pub opposite the church; low beams, uneven floors and a cosy fire, two or three well kept changing ales and enjoyable pubby food including bargain OAP lunch (Thurs), friendly attentive service, carpeted dining area to one side; children, walkers and dogs welcome, picnic-sets by road, open all day. *(B and M Kendall)*

SHOREHAM TQ5161

Two Brewers (01959) 522800

High Street; TN14 7TD Busy rather smart family-run pub with two stylishly modernised beamed rooms, back part more restauranty, good freshly made food from varied menu, can be pricey but they also do a set lunch, well kept kentish ales and nice wines from carefully chosen list, afternoon teas, friendly attentive staff, snug areas with comfortable seating, two woodburners; children welcome, trees in planters and a couple of benches out in front behind picket fence, café-style tables on small Astroturf deck, near the Shoreham Cross and good walks, closed Sun evening, Mon and Tues. *(Martin Day, B and M Kendall)*

SISSINGHURST TQ7937

★ Milk House (01580) 720200

The Street; TN17 2JG Bustling village inn near Sissinghurst Castle Garden (NT); bar on right with grey-painted beams and handsome Tudor fireplace fronted by plush sofas, wicker-fronted counter serving Dark Star, Harveys and a local guest, real cider, 14 wines by the glass and good range of gins and whiskies, restaurant to the left with small room off (perfect for a private party), good popular food including pizzas from outside oven; background music, daily papers, free wi-fi; children and dogs (in bar) welcome, large side terrace with sturdy furniture under green parasols, garden picnic-sets and children's play hut by fenced-in pond, comfortable well equipped bedrooms, open all day from 9am. *(David Jackman)*

SMARDEN TQ8642

Bell (01233) 770283

From Smarden follow Water Lane (between church and Chequers), then left at T junction; or from A274 take unsignposted turn E a mile N of B2077 to Smarden; TN27 8PW Old brick and tile country pub with series of cosy beamed rooms, enjoyable food from traditional choices up, Shepherd Neame ales and decent range of wines, good friendly service; picnic-sets in garden with own bar, closed Mon, otherwise open all day. *(Sophie Ellison)*

SNARGATE TQ9928

★ Red Lion (01797) 344648

B2080 Appledore–Brenzett; TN29 9UQ Unchanging 16th-c pub in same family for over 100 years; simple old-fashioned charm in three timeless little rooms with original cream wall panelling, heavy beams in sagging ceilings, dark pine Victorian farmhouse chairs on bare boards, an old piano and coal fire, local cider and four or five ales including Goachers tapped from casks behind unusual free-standing marble-topped counter, no food, traditional games like toad in the hole, nine men's morris and table skittles, friendly staff; children in family room, dogs in bar, outdoor lavatories, cottage garden, closed Mon evening. *(Kyle Brown)*

SPELDHURST TQ5541

★ George & Dragon (01892) 863125

Village signed from A264 W of Tunbridge Wells; TN3 0NN Handsome pub based around a 13th-c manorial hall (lovely original features); entrance lobby with half-panelled room to the right, wheelback and other dining chairs, cushioned wall pew, small pictures and horsebrasses, doorway to another dining room with similar furnishings and second inglenook, bar to left of entrance has woodburner in small fireplace, high-winged cushioned settles and other wooden furniture on stripped-wood floor, good range of well liked food from baguettes up, obliging friendly service, Harveys, Larkins and a guest, several wines by the glass, upstairs restaurant; background music, free wi-fi; children and dogs (in bar) welcome, teak furniture on front gravel terrace, covered back area and lower terrace with 200-year-old olive tree, open all day, no food Sun evening. *(Adrian Johnson, Mrs J Ekins-Daukes)*

ST MARY IN THE MARSH TR0627

Star (01797) 362139
Opposite church; TN29 0BX Remote down-to-earth pub with Tudor origins; popular, straightforward food (not Sun, Mon or evenings Tues-Thurs), well kept ales including Youngs from brick-faced counter, friendly service, inglenook woodburner; bar billiards and darts, free wi-fi; children and dogs welcome, tables in nice garden, good value beamed bedrooms with Romney Marsh views, lovely setting opposite ancient church (Edith Nesbit, author of *The Railway Children*, buried here), popular with walkers and cyclists, open all day. *(Graeme and Sally Mendham)*

STAPLEHURST TQ7846

Lord Raglan (01622) 843747
About 1.5 miles from town centre towards Maidstone, turn right off A229 into Chart Hill Road opposite Chart Cars; OS Sheet 188 map reference 785472; TN12 0DE Country pub with cosy chatty area around narrow counter, hop-strung low beams, big log fire and woodburner, mix of comfortably worn dark wood furniture, Goachers, Harveys and a guest, farm cider and perry, well liked reasonably priced home-cooked food, good wine list; children and dogs welcome, wheelchair access, tables on terrace and in the side orchard, Aug bank holiday onion festival, closed Sun. *(Mike and Sarah Abbot)*

STODMARSH TR2160

★**Red Lion** (01227) 721339
High Street; off A257 just E of Canterbury; CT3 4BA Tucked-away pub close to Stodmarsh National Nature Reserve; bar rooms with country kitchen tables and chairs, plenty of candles and fresh flowers, books on shelves and windowsills, tankards hanging from beams, big log fire, Greene King IPA and a guest tapped from the cask, real cider and eight wines by the glass, decent pubby food; background music, free wi-fi; children and dogs (in bar) welcome, tables in back garden, bedrooms, open all day. *(Troy Tranah, Pieter and Janet Vrancken)*

SUNDRIDGE TQ4855

White Horse (01959) 562837
Main Road; TN14 6EH Refurbished open-plan village pub on crossroads, decent range of well liked food (some choices available in smaller helpings at lunchtime), Adnams Southwold, St Austell Tribute and maybe a guest, several wines by the glass, good friendly service, log fires and low beams; children welcome, dogs in bar areas, picnic-sets under parasols on fenced lawn, open all day, no food Sun or Mon evenings. *(Edward May)*

SUTTON VALENCE TQ8050

Plough (01622) 842555
Sutton Road (A274), Langley; ME17 3LX Refurbished roadside dining pub; main bar painted in shades of grey with mix of wooden and copper-topped tables, side bar and candlelit dining extension behind with view into kitchen, well kept Harveys, local Rockin' Robin and Sharps Doom Bar, several wines by the glass, happy hours Mon-Fri, enjoyable food from sandwiches and bar snacks to restauranty choices, friendly relaxed atmosphere; some live music; children and dogs welcome, tables and vintage plough out at front behind picket fence, open all day (Sun till 10pm). *(Peter Meister)*

TENTERDEN TQ8833

White Lion (01580) 765077
High Street; TN30 6BD Comfortably updated beamed and timbered 16th-c inn behind Georgian façade; popular food including Josper grills and pizzas from open kitchen, mainly local ales such as Old Dairy and a beer badged for them, good choice of other drinks, big log fire, friendly helpful staff; background music, free wi-fi; heated terrace overlooking street, comfortable well equipped bedrooms, open (and food) all day. *(Richard Tilbrook)*

TOYS HILL TQ4752

★**Fox & Hounds** (01732) 750328
Off A25 in Brasted, via Brasted Chart and The Chart; TN16 1QG Welcoming traditional country pub under newish management; bar area separated by two-way woodburner, plain tables and chairs on bare boards or stone floor, grey-painted half-panelling, modern carpeted dining extension with big windows overlooking tree-sheltered garden, well prepared/presented food (not Sun evening) from lunchtime ciabattas and pub favourites up, two Greene King ales and guest such as Westerham, nice wines by the glass, cheerful helpful staff; children and dogs (in bar) welcome, roadside verandah used by smokers, good (if steep) local walks and views, handy for Chartwell and Emmetts Garden (both NT), open all day. *(Ian Phillips, B and M Kendall)*

TUDELEY TQ6145

Poacher & Partridge
(01732) 358934 *Hartlake Road; TN11 0PH* Renovated in smart country style by Elite Pubs (Great House in Hawkhurst, Dirty Habit at Hollingbourne etc); light interior with feature pizza oven, wide range of enjoyable food including daily specials, Tues steak night, ales such as Sharps Doom Bar and Timothy Taylors Landlord, good choice of wines by the glass, friendly attentive staff; live music including some afternoon jazz; children and dogs welcome, outside bar and grill, play area, nearby interesting church with Chagall stained glass (note roof paintings at pub's entrance), circular local walks (leaflets provided), open (and food) all day. *(Nicky Menzies)*

TUNBRIDGE WELLS TQ5839

Black Pig (01892) 523030
Grove Hill Road; TN1 1RZ Under new management and refurbishment planned as we went to press; long narrow bare-boards bar with leather sofas each side of woodburner, bookshelves, unusual cow wallpaper and a large antelope's head, overflow room up steps, Harveys Best and good wines by the glass, food from open kitchen has been interesting and popular, character dining room with contemporary wallpaper, panelling and oriental paintings, button-back wall banquettes and assortment of wooden tables and chairs; children and dogs (in bar) welcome, back gravel terrace, handy for the station, has opened all day. *(Professor James Burke)*

TUNBRIDGE WELLS TQ5837

Bull (01892) 263489
Frant Road; TN2 5LH Friendly 19th-c pub towards the southern outskirts of town; two modernised linked areas with one or two quirky touches, chunky pine tables and kitchen chairs on stripped-wood floor, a couple of leather sofas by open fire, well kept Shepherd Neame and good food cooked by chef-landlord from shortish menu (not Sun evening, Mon); children (till 8.30pm) and dogs welcome, seats out on fenced roadside terrace, closed Mon lunchtime, otherwise open all day. *(Professor James Burke)*

UNDERRIVER TQ5552

★**White Rock** (01732) 833112
SE of Sevenoaks, off B245; TN15 0SB Attractive village pub with good food from pubby choices up (all day weekends, best to book), friendly helpful service, well kept Harveys, Tonbridge and a beer badged for the pub, decent wines, beams, bare boards and stripped brickwork in cosy original part with adjacent dining area, another bar in modern extension with woodburner; background and some live music, darts, pool; children welcome, dogs may be allowed but ask first, small front garden, back terrace and large lawn with boules and bat and trap, pretty churchyard and walks nearby, open all day in summer, all day weekends winter. *(Martin Day, Gordon and Margaret Ormondroyd, Ian Phillips)*

UPNOR TQ7671

Ship (01634) 290553
Upnor Road, Lower Upnor; ME2 4UY Smallish mock-Tudor pub overlooking the Medway and boats; good home cooking including fish specials, ales such as Sharps, Shepherd Neame and Charles Wells, friendly staff, carpeted interior with marine knick-knacks; children and dogs welcome, picnic-sets out at front and in garden behind, open all day. *(Mick Allen)*

UPPER UPNOR TQ7570

Tudor Rose (01634) 714175
Off A228 N of Strood; High Street; ME2 4XG 16th-c pub down narrow cobbled street just back from the river and next to Upnor Castle (best to use village car park at top); cosy beamed rooms with mix of old furniture and some nautical bits and pieces, Shepherd Neame ales and an occasional guest, popular pubby food (not Sun evening) from baguettes up, good friendly service; free wi-fi; children welcome, seats out at front made from an old boat, large enclosed garden behind with arbour, open all day. *(Frances Parsons)*

WAREHORNE TQ9832

★**Woolpack** (01233) 732900
Off B2067 near Hamstreet; TN26 2LL Part-weatherboarded 16th-c dining pub under same ownership as the Five Bells at Brabourne and the Globe in Rye (Sussex); interesting interior with various connecting areas, beams, inglenook fire and woodburner, brick and quarry-tiled floors, walls (some boarded) hung with prints, old photographs, hops and ornate mirrors, lots of other bits and pieces including farming implements, fishing rods, oars and a boar's head, candles on tables, four well kept regional ales direct from the cask, local cider and good wines by the glass, much liked food including daily specials (no bookings so best to arrive early), helpful service and friendly easy-going atmosphere; background jazz; children and dogs welcome, rows of outside seating overlooking quiet lane and 15th-c church, five comfortable quirky bedrooms, open all day. *(Peter Meister)*

WEALD TQ5250

★**Windmill** (01732) 463330
Windmill Road; TN14 6PN Popular and friendly village pub with six well kept ales including Goachers and Larkins, local ciders and good fair-priced food (not Sun evening, Mon) from interestingly varied menu, attentive helpful service, traditional hop-strung interior with etched windows and two fires, mix of seating including old pews and carved settles by candlelit tables, jugs

and bottles on delft shelves, snug dining area; live music, darts; children and dogs welcome, easy wheelchair access, nice quiet back garden, closed Mon lunchtime, otherwise open all day. *(Martin Day, Chris Billington, Jason Caulkin)*

WEST MALLING TQ6757

Sacred Cow (01732) 840408

Offham Road; ME19 6RB Cosy brick-built pub with good mexican food along with pizzas and more traditional choices, well kept Adnams ales, friendly helpful service; background and some live music; children welcome, nice back garden, open all day Sun. *(Malcolm and Jane Levitt)*

WEST PECKHAM TQ6452

Swan on the Green (01622) 812271

Off A26/B2016 W of Maidstone; ME18 5JW Attractively placed brick and weatherboarded pub facing village cricket green; own-brewed Swan beers in relaxed open-plan beamed bar, stripped brickwork, bare boards and mixed furnishings, two-way log fire, enjoyable freshly made food (not Sun evening) from varied menu, friendly efficient service; children and dogs welcome, next to interesting part-Saxon church, good walks including Greensand Way, open all day Sun till 9pm. *(Susan and Neil McLean)*

WESTBERE TR1862

Old Yew Tree (01227) 710501

Just off A18 Canterbury–Margate; CT2 0HH Heavily beamed 14th-c pub in pretty village; simply furnished bare-boards bar with inglenook log fire, good reasonably priced food from varied menu including Thurs pie and pint deal, Shepherd Neame Master Brew and a guest, friendly helpful staff; quiz first Weds of the month, open mike last Weds; picnic-sets in garden behind, open all day weekends, closed Mon. *(Sophie Ellison)*

WESTERHAM TQ4454

Grasshopper on the Green

(01959) 562926 *The Green; TN16 1AS* Old black-beamed pub (small former coaching house) facing village green; three linked bar areas with log fire at back, well kept ales including Westerham, popular pubby food from sandwiches up, helpful pleasant service, restaurant upstairs; sports TV, free wi-fi; children and dogs welcome, seating out at front and in back garden with play area, open all day. *(Martin Day)*

WESTGATE-ON-SEA TR3270

Bake & Alehouse 07913 368787

Off St Mildreds Road down alley by cinema; CT8 8RE Friendly micropub in former bakery; simple little bare-boards room with a few tables (expect to share when busy), five well kept interesting ales tapped from the cask, real ciders (maybe a warm winter one – Monks Delight), kentish wines, local cheese, sausage rolls and pork pies, friendly chatty atmosphere; closed Sun evening, shuts around 9pm other days. *(Nik and Gloria Clarke)*

WHITSTABLE TR1066

Black Dog

High Street; CT5 1BB Quirky micropub (former deli) with five changing ales and several artisan ciders tapped from back room, friendly staff may offer tasters, snacky food, narrow dimly lit Victorian-feel bar with high tables and benches along two sides, intriguing mix of pictures and other bits and pieces on green walls, prominent chandelier suspended from red ceiling; eclectic background music and occasional folk sessions; open all day. *(Kyle Brown)*

WHITSTABLE TR1066

Old Neptune (01227) 272262

Marine Terrace; CT5 1EJ Great view over Swale estuary from this popular unpretentious weatherboarded pub set right on the beach (rebuilt after being washed away in 1897 storm); Harveys, Shepherd Neame and a guest, reasonably priced lunchtime food from shortish menu including decent fish and chips, friendly young staff; weekend live music; children and dogs welcome, picnic-sets on the shingle (plastic glasses out here and occasional barbecues), fine sunsets, can get very busy in summer, open all day. *(Shane A Still)*

WHITSTABLE TR1066

Smack Inn (01227) 772910

Middle Wall next to Baptist church; CT5 1BJ Small Victorian backstreet local away from the tourist trail; three Shepherd Neame ales and shortish choice of enjoyable low-priced food including burgers and fish and chips, cheerful helpful staff, cosy interior arranged around central servery, panelling, stripped brickwork and log fire; regular live music, often in beach-theme back garden (barbecues); children and dogs welcome, open all day. *(Adam Bellinger)*

WICKHAMBREAUX TR2258

Rose (01227) 721763

The Green; CT3 1RQ Attractive 16th-c and partly older pub in nice spot across green from church and watermill; enjoyable home-made food, Greene King IPA and three guests (May/Aug beer festivals), local ciders on rotation, friendly helpful staff, small bare-boards bar with log fire in big fireplace, dining area beyond standing timbers with woodburner, hop-strung beams, panelling and stripped brick; quiz second Weds of month;

If you report on a pub that's not a featured entry, please tell us any lunchtimes or evenings when it doesn't serve bar food.

children and dogs welcome, enclosed side garden and small courtyard, open (and food) all day, kitchen closes 4pm Sun. *(Matt and Hayley Jacob)*

WILLESBOROUGH STREET TR0341

Blacksmiths Arms (01233) 623975
The Street; TN24 0NA Well run, beamed village pub dating in part from the 17th c; Fullers London Pride and a couple of guests, good traditional home-cooked food using local produce from sandwiches and snacks up, daily blackboard specials, friendly service, open fires including inglenook; children and dogs welcome, picnic-sets in good-sized garden with play area, handy for M20 (junction 10), open all day, no food Sun evening. *(Graeme and Sally Mendham)*

WROTHAM TQ6159

Bull (01732) 789800
1.7 miles from M20, junction 2 – Wrotham signed; TN15 7RF Restored 14th-c coaching inn with large beamed bar and separate restaurant, matching tables and chairs throughout, enjoyable food (can be pricey) from pubby dishes up including a smokehouse/barbecue menu, real ales such as Dark Star, craft kegs and good wine list, friendly efficient service; Fri live music; children welcome, 11 comfortable bedrooms, open all day, food all day weekends. *(Gordon and Margaret Ormondroyd, Mike Buckingham)*

WYE TR0546

New Flying Horse (01233) 812297
Upper Bridge Street; TN25 5AN 17th-c Shepherd Neame inn with beams and inglenook; enjoyable food including fixed-price menu in bar and restaurant, friendly accommodating staff; Sun quiz, occasional live music, free wi-fi; children welcome, good-sized pretty garden with play area and miniature thatched pub (a former Chelsea Flower Show exhibit), nine bedrooms (some in converted stables), open (and food) all day, breakfast from 8am for non-residents. *(Edward May)*

WYE TR0446

Tickled Trout (01233) 812227
Signed off A28 NE of Ashford; TN25 5EB Popular summer family pub by River Stour; rustic-style carpeted bar with beams, stripped brickwork, stained-glass partitions and open fire, spacious conservatory/restaurant, good choice of food, ales such as Canterbury, Old Dairy and Sharps, kentish ciders and several wines by the glass, friendly helpful staff; live music Sun evening, quiz first Weds of month, free wi-fi; children and dogs welcome, tables on terrace and riverside lawn, open (and food) all day. *(Edward May)*

YALDING TQ6950

★**Walnut Tree** (01622) 814266
B2010 SW of Maidstone; ME18 6JB Timbered village pub with split-level main bar; fine old settles, a long cushioned mahogany bench and mix of dining chairs on brick or carpeted floors, church candles on chunky wooden tables, interesting old photographs, big inglenook log fire, well kept Black Sheep, Harveys and Skinners, good bar food and more inventive restaurant menu, attractive raftered dining room; background and occasional live music, TV; a few picnic-sets out by road, open all day, no food Sun evening. *(Nigel and Jean Eames)*

Please keep sending us reports. We rely on readers for news of new discoveries, and particularly for news of changes – however slight – at the fully described pubs: feedback@goodguides.com, or (no stamp needed) The Good Pub Guide, FREEPOST RTXY–ZCBC–BBAZ, Stream Lane, Sedlescombe, Battle TN33 0PB.

Lancashire

with Greater Manchester, Merseyside and Wirral

BASHALL EAVES SD6943 Map 7

Red Pump

(01254) 826227 – www.theredpumpinn.co.uk

NW of Clitheroe, off B6478 or B6243; BB7 3DA

Beautifully placed country inn with a cosy bar and first class food in contemporary, inviting dining rooms; bedrooms

'It's such a shame this lovely pub is so far from our home as I'd be here regularly,' says one reader. There are two inviting dining rooms and a cosy, traditional central bar with bookshelves, cushioned settles and wheelbacks on flagstones, and log fires, and the convivial licensees create a cheerful, friendly atmosphere. Three regional beers on handpump change weekly and might include a beer named for the pub, Bowland Hen Harrier and Lytham Blonde, plus eight wines by the glass and several malt whiskies; background music and board games. The views from seats on the terrace in front of the pub are splendid. You can stay in individually decorated and comfortable bedrooms or in the glamping yurts surrounded by lovely Forest of Bowland countryside; breakfasts are good and generous and residents can go fishing in the nearby river.

Extremely good food specialises in slowly matured steaks from grass-fed cattle but also includes gin-cured salmon with pickled cucumber and beetroot ketchup, chicken liver and whiskey parfait with apple and vanilla chutney, tagliatelle with roast mediterranean vegetables and tomato, black olive and garlic sauce, salmon niçoise salad, moroccan-style chicken with couscous and ras el hanout yoghurt, beef bourguignon, a fresh fish dish of the day, slow-grilled lamb rump with a choice of chips or potatoes, and puddings such as amaretto baba and sticky toffee pudding. *Benchmark main dish: chargrilled 40-day dry-aged sirloin steak with a choice of butters and sauces £23.00. Two-course evening meal £26.00.*

Free house ~ Licensees Frances and Jonathan Gledhill ~ Real ale ~ Open 12-10; 12-11 Fri, Sat; 12-8 Sun; closed Mon, Tues; first two weeks Jan ~ Bar food 12-2, 6-8.30 (9 Fri, Sat); 12-5.30 Sun ~ Restaurant ~ Children welcome ~ Dogs allowed in bar and bedrooms ~ Wi-fi ~ Bedrooms: £102/£120 *Recommended by Caroline and Steve Archer, Lyn and Freddie Roberts, James and Sylvia Hewitt, Frances and Hamish Porter, Mr and Mrs P R Thomas, Patricia and Gordon Thompson, Nicholas and Maddy Trainer*

Real ale to us means beer that has matured naturally in its cask – not pressurised or filtered. We name all real ales stocked.

BAY HORSE SD4952 Map 7

Bay Horse

(01524) 791204 – www.bayhorseinn.com

1.2 miles from M6 junction 33: A6 southwards, then off on left; LA2 0HR

18th-c former coaching inn with log fires, comfortable bar and restaurant, well regarded food, local ales and friendly staff

Handy for the M6, this family-owned and gently civilised inn is the perfect place for lunch. There's a series of small, rambling linked rooms and the cosily pubby beamed bar has cushioned wall banquettes in bay windows, lamps on windowsills and a good log fire. Black Sheep, Moorhouses Pendle Witches Brew and maybe a guest beer on handpump, ten wines by the glass, ten malt whiskies and 20 gins served by friendly, efficient staff. The dining room has a woodburning stove and lovely views over the garden – where there are plenty of seats and tables.

The same rewarding food is served in both the bar and dining room and includes open sandwiches, home-cured treacle salmon with beetroot and burnt orange and dill oil, pork, apricot, bacon and pistachio terrine with celeriac and mustard and brown sauce, black kale, crispy egg, celeriac purée, mushrooms, parsley oil and truffle dressing, chicken breast with mushrooms, bacon and creamy leek sauce with black truffle and cep powder, silver hake fillet with puy lentils braised in cider, dry-aged local beef with creamy peppercorn sauce and chips, and puddings such as lemon tart with rhubarb and warm orange and almond sponge with vanilla ice-cream; they also offer a two- and three-course set menu (Wednesday-Friday). *Benchmark main dish: slow-cooked maize-fed duck legs with red wine figs, puy lentils and duck gravy £18.75. Two-course evening meal £25.00.*

Free house ~ Licensee Craig Wilkinson ~ Real ale ~ Open 12-3, 6-10 (11 Sat); 12-4, 6-10 Sun; closed Mon, Tues ~ Bar food 12-2 (2.30 Sat), 6-9; 12-3, 6-8 Sun ~ Restaurant ~ Children welcome ~ Dogs allowed in bar *Recommended by Bob and Melissa Wyatt, Graeme and Sally Mendham, Amy and Luke Buchanan, Jim and Sue James, Andrew and Ruth Simmonds*

BISPHAM GREEN SD4813 Map 7

Eagle & Child

(01257) 462297 – www.eagleandchildbispham.co.uk

Maltkiln Lane (Parbold–Croston road, off B5246); L40 3SG

Civilised pub with antiques, enterprising food, an interesting range of beers and appealing rustic garden

We get consistently positive reports on all aspects of this well run pub. The largely open-plan bar is carefully furnished with several handsomely carved antique oak settles (the finest made in part, it seems, from a 16th-c wedding bedhead), a mix of small old oak chairs, an attractive oak coffer, old hunting prints and engravings and hop-draped low beams. Also, red walls, coir matting, oriental rugs on ancient flagstones in front of a fine old stone fireplace and counter; the pub dogs are called Beryl, Betty, Brenda and Rolo. Friendly young staff serve Bowland Hen Harrier, Hawkshead Windermere Pale, Marstons Wainwright, Moorhouses White Witch and Thwaites Original on handpump, farm cider, ten wines by the glass, 25 gins and around 30 malt whiskies. A popular beer festival is usually held on the early May Bank Holiday weekend. The spacious garden has a well tended but unconventional bowling green; beyond is a wild area that's home to crested newts and moorhens. A handsome side barn houses a shop selling interesting wines and pottery, plus a proper butcher and a deli. This is part of the Ainscoughs group.

Rewarding food includes sandwiches, breaded pheasant goujons with mustard mayonnaise, seared scallops with cauliflower purée, pancetta and black pudding, cheese and onion pie with tomato and onion salad, burger with toppings, onion rings, bacon jam and chips, confit pork belly with caramelised apple and cider jus, chicken breast with black olive mash and truffle jus, rack of lamb with minted red wine jus, hake fillet with pesto on tagliatelle, and puddings such as sticky toffee pudding sundae and lemon curd tart with chantilly cream and mixed berries. *Benchmark main dish: steak and mushroom pie £12.75. Two-course evening meal £20.00.*

Free house ~ Licensee Peter Robinson ~ Real ale ~ Open 12-11; 12-10.30 Sun ~ Bar food 12-2, 5.30-8.30 (9 Fri); 12-9 Sat; 12-8 Sun ~ Children welcome ~ Dogs welcome ~ Wi-fi ~ Live music last Fri evening of month *Recommended by Alistair Forsyth, Patricia Healey, Steve Whalley, Angela and Steve Heard, Katherine Matthews*

DOWNHAM SD7844 Map 7

Assheton Arms

(01200) 441227 – www.asshetonarms.com

Off A59 NE of Clitheroe, via Chatburn; BB7 4BJ

Lancashire Dining Pub of the Year

Fine old inn with plenty of dining and drinking space, a friendly welcome, several real ales and creative food; bedrooms

This traditional country inn takes its name from the family of Lord Clitheroe, who bought the village in 1558; the setting at the top of a steep hill is very pretty. A small front bar, with a hatch to the kitchen, has tweed-upholstered armchairs and stools on big flagstones around a single table, a woodburning stove surrounded by logs, and drawings of dogs and hunting prints on grey-green walls. Off to the right, a wood-panelled partition creates a cosy area where there are similarly cushioned pews and nice old chairs around various tables on a rug-covered wooden floor, and a couple of window chairs. The main bar, up a couple of steps, has old photographs of the pub and the village on pale walls and a marble bar counter where they serve Marstons Wainwright, Moorhouses White Witch and Timothy Taylors Boltmaker on handpump, a dozen wines by the glass and farm cider. Background music and board games. Staff are helpful and attentive. A two-level restaurant has carpet or wooden flooring, two fireplaces (one with a woodburning stove and the other with a lovely old kitchen range) and hunting prints. Picnic-sets and tables and chairs enjoy far-reaching views. The attractive, comfortable bedrooms (once a post office and two cottages) make a fine base for exploring the area. Do note the charming church opposite. This is part of the Seafood Pub Company.

Delicious food includes sandwiches, devilled crab, salmon and shrimp pâté with sea salt croûtes, veal kidneys on toasted brioche with brandy cream and crispy pancetta, aromatic tuna with asian shredded salad and soy and citrus dressing, imam bayildi (slow-roasted aubergine, fragrant spices, roast almonds, citrus couscous and fattoush salad), goan monkfish and prawn curry with coconut rice and grilled flatbread, persian-spiced chicken with jewelled rice, rose petal harissa and yoghurt dressing, pork belly, chorizo and pork sausage with crispy rosemary potatoes, daily fresh scallops, langoustines, skate wing, brill and turbot, and puddings such as praline profiteroles with chocolate and caramel sauce and crêpes suzette. *Benchmark main dish: chicken pot pie with ham hock and leeks £13.95. Two-course evening meal £23.00.*

Free house ~ Licensee Jocelyn Neve ~ Real ale ~ Open 12-11; 12-midnight Sat; 12-10.30 Sun ~ Bar food 12-9; 12-Fri, Sat; 12-8 Sun ~ Restaurant ~ Children welcome ~ Dogs allowed in bar ~ Wi-fi *Recommended by Gary Baldwin, Martin and Joanne Sharp, Jim and Sue James, Emily and Toby Archer, W K Wood, Nicola and Stuart Parsons, Maggie and Matthew Lyons*

FORMBY SD3109 Map 7

Sparrowhawk

(01704) 882350 – www.brunningandprice.co.uk/sparrowhawk

Southport Old Road; brown sign to pub just off A565 Formby bypass, S edge of Ainsdale; L37 0AB

Light and airy pub with interesting décor, good food and drinks choices and wooded grounds

All are warmly welcomed at this sizeable country house, including dogs who get special biscuits and a bowl of water. The various open-plan rooms, spreading out from the central bar, have plenty of interest: attractive prints on pastel walls, church candles, flowers, snug leather fireside armchairs in library corners and seats and tables with rugs on dark boards by big bow windows. There's also a comfortably carpeted conservatory dining room; background music. Helpful young staff serve 21 wines by the glass, 89 malt whiskies, 49 gins and Phoenix Brunning & Price Original, Salopian Oracle, Titanic Plum Porter and guests such as Heritage St Modwen Golden Ale and Ossett Silver King and Yorkshire Blonde on handpump. Five acres of woods and parkland surround the pub and a flagstoned side terrace has sturdy tables, with picnic-table sets on lawns by a set of swings and an old Fergie tractor. A walk from the pub to coastal nature reserves might just yield red squirrels, still hanging on in this area.

Brasserie-style food includes sandwiches, five-spice duck leg with spring onion, cucumber, hoisin sauce and pancakes, hot smoked salmon with beetroot pannacotta and horseradish crème fraîche, aubergine, potato and courgette massaman curry with coriander and lime rice, fish pie, chicken breast with mushroom risotto, rocket and truffle oil, rustic sausages with mash and onion gravy, pork tenderloin with sage prosciutto, colcannon potatoes and gooseberry purée, and puddings such as crème brûlée and chocolate brownie with chocolate sauce. *Benchmark main dish: crispy beef salad with sweet chilli dressing and cashew nuts £14.95. Two-course evening meal £21.50.*

Brunning & Price ~ Manager Iain Hendry ~ Real ale ~ Open 10am-11pm; 9am-11pm Sat; 9am-10.30pm Sun ~ Bar food 10am (9am Sat)-9.30pm; 9-9 Sun ~ Children welcome ~ Dogs allowed in bar ~ Wi-fi *Recommended by Greta and Gavin Craddock, Margo and Derek Peters, Mrs S Wilson-Sproat, Darrell Barton, George and Alison Bishop*

GREAT MITTON SD7138 Map 7

Aspinall Arms

(01254) 826555 – www.brunningandprice.co.uk/aspinallarms

B6246 NW of Whalley; BB7 9PQ

Cleverly refurbished and extended riverside pub with cheerful helpful service and a fine choice of drinks and food

You can make the most of the riverside position here in kind weather as there are seats and tables on a terrace and picnic-sets on grass overlooking the water. The various rambling rooms have seating that ranges from attractively cushioned old-style dining chairs through brass-studded leather ones to big armchairs and sofas around an assortment of dark tables. Floors are flagstoned, carpeted or wooden and topped with rugs, while the pale-painted or bare stone walls are hung with an extensive collection of prints and local photographs. Dotted about are large mirrors, house plants, stone bottles and bookshelves and there are both open fires and a woodburning stove. From the central servery, knowledgeable staff serve Phoenix Brunning & Price Original and Moorhouses Aspinall Witch (named for the pub) with guests such as Goose Eye Chinook Blonde, Moorhouses Black Cat, Saltaire Blonde and Timothy Taylors Golden Best on handpump, 15 wines by the glass, 50 gins, an amazing 150 malt whiskies and a farm cider; background music and board games.

Attractively presented modern food includes sandwiches, chicken liver pâté with plum and ginger chutney, scallops with squash purée, crispy pancetta, toasted pumpkin seeds and lemon and sage butter, massaman curry of aubergine, potato and okra with coriander and lime rice, steak in ale pudding, moroccan-spiced cod with sweet potato tagine and tempura okra, braised lamb shoulder with dauphinoise potatoes and lamb jus, and puddings such as coconut pannacotta with roasted pineapple, chilli and honey and crème brûlée. *Benchmark main dish: tandoori chicken breast with onion bhaji, sag aloo and chapatis £14.50. Two-course evening meal £21.00.*

Brunning & Price ~ Manager Sus Engelmann ~ Real ale ~ Open 10.30am-11pm; 10.30-10.30 Sun ~ Bar food 12-9.30 (9 Sun) ~ Restaurant ~ Children welcome ~ Dogs allowed in bar ~ Wi-fi *Recommended by Alf and Sally Garner, Francis and Mandy Robertson, James and Sylvia Hewitt, W K Wood, John and Sylvia Harrop*

GREAT MITTON SD7139 Map 7

Three Fishes

(01254) 826888 – www.thethreefishes.com

Mitton Road (B6246, off A59 NW of Whalley); BB7 9PQ

Stylish pub with tremendous attention to detail, excellent regional food given a modern touch and interesting drinks

---

Imaginatively converted, this place has been cleverly laid out to include plenty of cosy corners. The areas closest to the bar are elegantly traditional with a couple of big stone fireplaces, rugs on polished floors and upholstered stools. Then there's a series of individually furnished and painted rooms with exposed stone walls, careful spotlighting, contemporary seats, tables and long button-back wall banquettes and wooden slatted blinds, ending with another impressive fireplace. Staff are young and friendly and there's a good chatty atmosphere: Black Sheep, Bowland Pheasant Plucker, Moorhouses White Witch and Timothy Taylors Landlord on handpump, ten wines by the glass, 12 gins and 15 malt whiskies; background music and TV. Seats and tables on the terrace and in the garden have delightful views over the Ribble Valley.

Enjoyable food includes sandwiches (until 6pm, not Sunday), devilled crab and tarragon tart with grapefruit and radish salad, twice-baked blue cheese soufflé with chicory, pear and walnut salad, seafood platter, cheese and onion pie with baked potato and sour cream, burger with toppings and dripping chips, sea bream with mussels, roasted fennel and bisque, lancashire hotpot with pickled red cabbage, rare-breed pork belly with braised cheek, black pudding chipolatas, bacon, scorched onions and gravy, and puddings such as warm chocolate brownie with spiced chocolate ganache and cherry compote and kaffir lime pannacotta with roasted pineapple, mango and toasted coconut. *Benchmark main dish: fish pie £13.75. Two-course evening meal £19.50.*

Ribble Valley Inns ~ Manager Daniel McCarthy ~ Real ale ~ Open 12-11; 12-10.30 Sun ~ Bar food 12-9; 12-9.30 Fri, Sat; 12-8 Sun ~ Children welcome ~ Dogs allowed in bar ~ Wi-fi *Recommended by William and Sophia Renton, David Appleyard, Colin and Daniel Gibbs, Simon and Alex Knight, Martin and Joanne Sharp, Louise and Simon Peters*

We checked prices with the pubs as we went to press in summer 2018.
They should hold until around spring 2019.

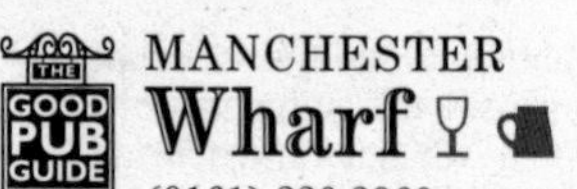

MANCHESTER

SJ8297 Map 7

Wharf

(0161) 220 2960 – www.brunningandprice.co.uk/thewharf

Blantyre Street/Slate Wharf; M15 4SW

Big wharf-like pub with large terrace overlooking the water and a fine range of drinks and food

Living up to its name, this huge pub is open-plan and on several levels but has enough cosy nooks and alcoves to keep some sense of cosiness. Downstairs is more pubby and informal with groups of high tables and chairs, while the restaurant upstairs has table service. Throughout there's an appealing variety of pre-war-style dining chairs around quite a choice of dark wooden tables on rugs and shiny floorboards, hundreds of interesting prints and posters on bare brick or painted walls, old stone bottles, church candles, house plants and fresh flowers on windowsills and tables, bookshelves and armchairs here and there, and large mirrors over open fires. Efficient, hard-working staff serve Phoenix Brunning & Price Original and Weetwood Cheshire Cat plus up to seven quickly changing guest ales on handpump, such as Castle Rock Harvest Pale, Moorhouses Black Cat, Poynton Hoppy Daze, Rudgate Valkyrie APA, Titanic Lifeboat and Wishbone Ruby Weapon, as well as farm cider, 19 wines by the glass, 60 gins and over 50 malt whiskies. The large front terrace has plenty of wood and chrome tables and chairs around a fountain, and picnic-sets overlooking the canal basin.

Enterprising food includes sandwiches, fried scallops with crab fritters, pea purée and lemon dressing, pork and black pudding scotch egg with pickled vegetable salad, cheese, potato and onion pie with carrot purée and red wine jus, lamb tikka salad with spiced potatoes, papaya, toasted almonds, coriander and mint yoghurt, chicken breast with cauliflower and squash biryani and red onion bhaji, hake with serrano ham and butter bean and spinach cassoulet, soy and honey-roasted duck breast with sautéed asian vegetables and egg noodles, and puddings such as rhubarb and ginger trifle with pistachio granola and triple chocolate brownie with chocolate sauce. *Benchmark main dish: steak burger with toppings, coleslaw and chips £13.45. Two-course evening meal £21.00.*

Brunning & Price ~ Manager Siobhan Youngs ~ Real ale ~ Open 10am-11pm; 10am-midnight Fri, Sat; 10am-10.30pm Sun ~ Bar food 12-9.30; 12-10 Fri, Sat; 12-9 Sun ~ Restaurant ~ Children welcome ~ Dogs allowed in bar ~ Wi-fi ~ Live music Fri evening *Recommended by Mike and Wena Stevenson, David and Charlotte Green, Shona and Jimmy McDuff, Brian and Anna Marsden, William Pace, Lenny and Ruth Walters*

MELLOR

SD6530 Map 7

Millstone

(01254) 813333 – www.millstonehotel.co.uk

The Mellor near Blackburn; Mellor Lane; BB2 7JR

Smart, popular dining pub with rewarding food, real ales and seats outside; bedrooms

We've had warm praise from readers since this handsome and neatly kept 18th-c stone coaching inn was refurbished recently. The extensive panelling on both sides of the central bar has remained, and both here and in the dining rooms there are elegant painted wooden and attractively upholstered modern dining chairs and button-back wall seats around polished tables on carpet or parquet flooring. Also, several log fires, books on shelves, mirrors, flowers on tables and attractive prints on pale paintwork. Thwaites Original and guests such as Marstons Wainwright and Thwaites

Limited Edition IPA and Mildly Moreish on handpump served by friendly staff and a dozen wines by the glass; background music. A side terrace has seats and tables under parasols. Bedrooms are well equipped and comfortable (some are in a separate block across the car park) and breakfasts are good.

From a seasonal menu the pleasing food includes duck spring rolls with sticky plum sauce, ham hock terrine with pickled baby vegetables and apple gel, sharing platters, roasted tomato tart with tapenade, mozzarella and balsamic drizzle, steak and kidney in ale pudding, burger with toppings, coleslaw and chips, roasted hake fillet and breaded monkfish cheek with chorizo, squid and sea vegetable broth, duck breast with crispy leg and black cherry and kirsch jus, and puddings such as lemon meringue pie with poached oranges and basil sorbet and chocolate fondant and délice with chocolate ice-cream. *Benchmark main dish: chicken tandoori £15.00. Two-course evening meal £19.00.*

Thwaites ~ Manager Tim Parker ~ Real ale ~ Open 9am-11pm; 9am-midnight Fri, Sat; 9am-10.30pm Sun ~ Bar food 12-9.30 (9 Sun) ~ Restaurant ~ Children welcome ~ Dogs allowed in bar ~ Wi-fi ~ Bedrooms: /£89 *Recommended by Dr A McCormick, Beverley and Andy Butcher, Dr D J & Mrs S C Walker, Martine and Fabio Lockley, Edward Edmonton*

NETHER BURROW SD6175 Map 7

Highwayman

(01524) 273338 – www.highwaymaninn.co.uk

A683 S of Kirkby Lonsdale; LA6 2RJ

Large and skilfully refurbished old stone house with country interior and serving carefully sourced food; attractive gardens

They seem to have got everything just right in this substantial 17th-c stone pub. There's a bustling atmosphere and a friendly mix of customers and both the food and drink are highly regarded. Even though it's a sizeable place, the stylishly simple flagstoned interior is nicely divided into intimate corners, with a couple of large log fires, wooden, leather-seated or tartan chairs around dark tables, and button-back or leather wall banquettes. There are some big photos on the walls and interesting modern lighting. Thwaites 1816 and Original and Marstons Wainwright on handpump, ten wines by the glass, 12 gins and 15 malt whiskies served by friendly, efficient staff; background music amd TV. French windows open out to a big terrace and lovely gardens with smart rattan-style furniture. The surrounding Lune Valley countryside is very pretty.

From seasonal menus using local produce, the well regarded food includes sandwiches, pulled ham hock terrine with piccalilli, salmon and dill fishcake with hollandaise sauce, cheese and onion pie with beetroot salad, beer-battered haddock with dripping chips, avocado salad with prawns, slow-roast pork belly with black pudding potato cake, apple fritter and sticky cider sauce, confit duck leg with pickled red cabbage and red wine sauce, lancashire hotpot, 28-day-aged rib-eye steak with a choice of sauces and chips, and puddings such as toffee apple crumble and white chocolate and raspberry cheesecake with raspberry ripple ice-cream. *Benchmark main dish: steak in ale pie £13.50. Two-course evening meal £19.50.*

Ribble Valley Inns ~ Manager Laura Bromwell ~ Real ale ~ Open 12-11; 12-10.30 Sun ~ Bar food 12-9; 12-9.30 Fri, Sat; 12-8 Sun; no food 2-5pm Mon-Thurs in winter ~ Restaurant ~ Children welcome ~ Dogs allowed in bar ~ Wi-fi *Recommended by Charlie May, Margaret McDonald, Sandra and Michael Smith, Audrey and Paul Summers, Sandra and Neil White, Catherine and Daniel King*

If you know a pub is ever open all day, please tell us.

PLEASINGTON SD6528 Map 7

Clog & Billycock

(01254) 201163 – www.theclogandbillycock.com

Village signposted off A677 Preston New Road on W edge of Blackburn; Billinge End Road; BB2 6QB

Carefully sourced local food in extremely appealing and well run stone-built village pub

This has the feel of an upmarket barn conversion and is light and airy with flagstoned floors, high ceilings with beams and joists and pale grey walls above a grey dado. Several rooms run together with leather seated or plush cushioned dining chairs and tartan wall banquettes around light wooden tables, big photographs, lamps in various niches and an open fire. Friendly, hard-working licensees serve Thwaites 1865 and guests such as Bowland Pheasant Plucker and Marstons Wainwright on handpump, ten wines by the glass, 15 malt whiskies and 30 gins; background music and TV. The small garden has an awning-covered terrace with benches, seats and tables.

Pleasing food includes sandwiches, wild mushroom risotto, cod fishcake with creamed leeks, egg and chives, cheese and onion pie, boneless and breadcrumbed chicken leg with coleslaw and skin-on fries, gammon and poached eggs with onion rings, fish pie, cumberland sausage with mash and onion gravy, burger with toppings, pickles and fries, sirloin steak with battered onion rings, and puddings such as black cherry eton mess with kirsch and chocolate and lemon curd cheesecake with candied lemons and cream. *Benchmark main dish: lancashire hotpot £13.50. Two-course evening meal £19.50.*

Ribble Valley Inns ~ Manager Rob Broadbent ~ Real ale ~ Open 12-11; 12-10.30 Sun ~ Bar food 12-9; 12-9.30 Fri, Sat; 12-8 Sun ~ Children welcome ~ Dogs allowed in bar ~ Wi-fi
Recommended by Mark and Sian Edwards, Geoff and Ann Marston, Robert and Diana Myers, Monica and Steph Evans, Serena and Adam Furber

PRESTON SD5634 Map 7

Haighton Manor

(01772) 706350 – www.brunningandprice.co.uk/haightonmanor

Haighton Green Lane, Haighton; PR2 5SQ

Rather grand stone building surrounded by lawns and countryside with interesting furnishings in interconnected rooms, thoughtful drinks and food choice, and seats outside

At the heart of this rather lovely 17th-c place (a former hospital) is a big bustling bar with an open fire, wooden chairs around a large farmhouse kitchen table, elegant metal chandeliers and stools against the counter where cheerful staff serve Phoenix Brunning & Price Original plus guests such as Lancaster Blonde, Mobberley Maori, Phoenix Arizona, Salopian Spiral and Timothy Taylors Landlord on handpump, 120 malt whiskies, 100 gins and six farm ciders; board games. Various open-plan rooms lead off here with rugs on wooden floors, wall-to-wall prints, photographs and mirrors on pale walls above painted dados, more open fires, antique-style cushioned dining chairs around dark tables, and house plants and candles. One cosy character room has armchairs and chesterfield sofas on flagstones and exposed stone walls, and there's a big, carpeted conservatory dining extension. Good quality chairs, benches and tables under parasols are set out on a terrace surrounded by lawns (on which there's a trademark tractor for children); pleasant country views.

Brasserie-style modern food includes sandwiches, cider-braised pig cheeks with sour apple, crispy black pudding and celeriac purée, goats cheese pannacotta with semi-dried grapes, walnut and celery salad, red pepper and sunblush tomato quiche, crispy beef salad with chillis and cashew nuts, south indian fish curry with king prawns and sea bass, fragrant rice and stir-fried vegetables, chicken breast with jersey royal potato cake, black garlic and madeira sauce, braised lamb shoulder with dauphinoise potatoes, carrot mash and rosemary gravy, and puddings such as crème brûlée and chocolate torte with peanut butter ice-cream and honeycomb. *Benchmark main dish: steak sandwich £10.95. Two-course evening meal £20.00.*

Brunning & Price ~ Licensee Chris Humphries ~ Real ale ~ Open 11-11; 12-10.30 Sun ~ Bar food 12-9.30; 12-10 Fri, Sat ~ Children welcome ~ Dogs allowed in bar ~ Wi-fi
Recommended by Nicola and Holly Lyons, Rosie and Marcus Heatherley, Amanda Shipley, Steve Whalley, W K Wood, John Perry, Gwendoline and Ralph Mason

THE GOOD PUB GUIDE

SAWLEY SD7746 Map 7

Spread Eagle

(01200) 441202 – www.spreadeaglesawley.co.uk
Village signed just off A59 NE of Clitheroe; BB7 4NH

Nicely refurbished pub with quite a choice of food, riverside restaurant and four real ales; bedrooms

A fine place for lunch after visiting the substantial ruins of the nearby 12th-c cistercian abbey or after an exhilarating walk in the Forest of Bowland, this well run, attractive old coaching inn is popular with our readers. The bar rooms have a pleasing mix of nice old and quirky modern furniture (anything from an old settle and pine tables to up-to-date low chairs upholstered in animal print fabric), all set off well by the grey rustic stone floor. Low ceilings, cosy sectioning, a warming fire and cottagey windows keep it feeling intimate. The dining areas are more formal, with modern stripes and a bookshelf mural; background music and board games. Young, efficient and friendly staff serve Bowland Sawley Duck, Dark Horse Hetton Pale Ale, Marstons Wainwright and Moorhouses White Witch on handpump and several wines by the glass. Bedrooms are individually furnished and comfortable and breakfasts are good.

A wide choice of pleasing food includes sandwiches, grilled bacon with a herb crumpet, fruity brown sauce and poached egg, rillette of salmon with pickled beetroot and grain mustard, sharing platters, spiced tagine of chickpea and cauliflower with pearl couscous and dried fruit, a pie of the day, mussels cooked in cider cream with frites, daube of beef with potato purée and red wine sauce, chicken breast with squash ravioli, sage and butternut squash sauce, and puddings such as vanilla pannacotta with warm gingerbead, apple purée and spiced syrup and bread and butter ice-cream terrine with apricot sorbet, custard and apricot sauce. *Benchmark main dish: rib-eye steak with onion rings, chips and peppercorn sauce £19.95. Two-course evening meal £20.00.*

Individual Inns ~ Managers Greig and Natalie Barns ~ Real ale ~ Open 12-11; 12-9 Sun ~ Bar food 12-2, 5.30-9; 12-2, 6-9.30 Sat; 12-7 Sun ~ Restaurant ~ Children welcome ~ Dogs allowed in bar and bedrooms ~ Wi-fi ~ Jazz first Sun of month ~ Bedrooms: £92/£120
Recommended by Muriel and Spencer Harrop, Moira and John Wheeler, Adam Jones, Louise and Anton Parsons, Andy Dawson, Sue and Paul Green, John and Sylvia Harrop

Post Office address codings confusingly give the impression that some pubs are in Lancashire when they're really in Cumbria or Yorkshire (which is where we list them).

THORNTON HOUGH SJ2979 Map 7

Red Fox

(0151) 353 2920 – www.brunningandprice.co.uk/redfox

Liverpool Road; CH64 7TL

Sizeable spreading pub with a fine choice of beers, wines, gins and whiskies, courteous staff serving enjoyable food and large back garden

To reach this substantial brick and sandstone pub you follow a driveway surrounded by lawns and pleasant country views. There are stairs from the entrance up to the spacious main bar: large central pillars divide the room into smaller areas with high stools and tables in the middle, dark wooden tables and chairs to each side and deep leather armchairs and fender seats next to the big fireplace. This leads into a long, airy, carpeted dining room with two rows of painted iron supports, hefty leather and wood chairs around highly polished tables and a raised firepit; doors from here lead out to a terrace. Two additional dining rooms are similarly furnished, one with an elegant chandelier hanging from a fine moulded ceiling. Throughout there are photographs, prints and pictures covering the walls, big plants, stone bottles and shelves of books. Friendly, cheerful staff serve Phoenix Brunning & Price Original and Facers Sunlight Blonde with guests from breweries such as Brightside, Conwy, Liverpool Craft, Tatton and Ticketybrew on handpump, 20 wines by the glass, 180 malt whiskies, 160 gins and ten farm ciders; background music and board games. At the back are terraces with good quality wooden chairs and tables under parasols, and steps down to picnic-sets around a fountain.

Interesting food includes sandwiches, spicy satay king prawns with asian rice noodle salad and peanut dip, haggis and black pudding hash cake with a poached egg and grain mustard sauce, sweet potato and three-bean chilli with guacamole and tortilla chips, venison, pheasant and rabbit pudding with mash, lamb hotpot with pickled red cabbage, steak burger with toppings, coleslaw and chips, a trio of duck (breast, faggot and confit leg) with dauphinoise potatoes and port and cherry sauce, and puddings such as glazed lemon tart with raspberry sorbet and raspberry compote and bread and butter pudding with apricot sauce. *Benchmark main dish: braised lamb shoulder with dauphinoise potatoes, carrot mash and mint gravy £17.25. Two-course evening meal £22.00.*

Brunning & Price ~ Manager David Green ~ Real ale ~ Open 10-11; 10-10.30 Sun ~ Bar food 12-9.30; 12-10 Fri, Sat; 12-9 Sun ~ Restaurant ~ Children welcome ~ Dogs allowed in bar ~ Wi-fi *Recommended by Edward May, Isobel Mackinlay, Matthew and Elisabeth Reeves, Christopher May, Christine and Tony Garrett, Frances and Hamish Potter*

UPPERMILL SD0006 Map 7

Church Inn £

(01457) 820902 – www.churchinnsaddleworth.co.uk

From the main street (A607), look out for the sign for Saddleworth Church, and turn off up this steep narrow lane – keep on up; OL3 6LW

Community pub with big range of own-brew beers at unbeatable bargain prices and tasty food; children very welcome

Even though this ancient pub is all alone by an isolated church on a steep moorland slope, it's always deservedly packed full of happy customers keen to enjoy the fantastic own-brewed beers and amazing value food. The big, unspoilt, L-shaped main bar has a cheerful, friendly atmosphere, high beams and some stripped stone, settles, pews, a good individual mix of chairs, lots of attractive prints, staffordshire and other china on a high delft shelf, jugs, brasses and so forth. They keep up to 11 of their own Saddleworth beers – though if the water levels from the spring aren't high enough for brewing, they bring in guests such as Black Sheep and Copper Dragon. Some of their own seasonal ales are named after the licensee's children, only appearing around their birthdays; two home-brewed lagers on tap too. TV (for sporting events) and unobtrusive background music. A conservatory opens on to the terrace. The local bellringers arrive on Wednesdays to practise with a set of handbells kept here, and anyone can join the morris dancing on Thursdays. Children enjoy the numerous animals, including rabbits, chickens, dogs, ducks, geese, alpacas, horses, 14 peacocks in the next-door field and some cats that live in an adjacent barn; dogs are made to feel very welcome.

Traditional, incredible value food includes sandwiches, mushrooms in creamy garlic sauce, breaded king prawns with sweet chilli or barbecue sauce, deep-fried cod and chips, full english breakfast, chilli beef, vegetable fajita sizzler served with two wraps, sour cream, salsa and guacamole, a roast of the day, lamb shank in minted gravy, mixed grill, and puddings such as hot chocolate fudge cake and cheesecake of the day. *Benchmark main dish: steak and kidney pudding £9.95. Two-course evening meal £15.00.*

Own brew ~ Licensee Christine Taylor ~ Real ale ~ Open 12-midnight (1am Sat) ~ Bar food 12-3, 5-9; 12-9.30 Fri-Sun and bank holidays ~ Restaurant ~ Children welcome ~ Dogs allowed in bar ~ Wi-fi *Recommended by Buster May, Steve Whalley, Jim and Sue James, Buster and Helena Hastings, Chloe and Michael Swettenham, Amy and Luke Buchanan*

WHITEWELL SD6546 Map 7

Inn at Whitewell ★

(01200) 448222 – www.innatwhitewell.com

Most easily reached by B6246 from Whalley; road through Dunsop Bridge from B6478 is also good; BB7 3AT

Fine manor house with smartly pubby atmosphere, top quality food, exceptional wine list, real ales and professional, friendly service; luxury bedrooms

A very special place and much loved by our readers over many years. It's an elegant manor house hotel high on the banks of the River Hodder with spectacular views down the valley into the heart of the Forest of Bowland. The riverside bar and adjacent terrace make the most of these views. The civilised bar rooms have handsome old wood furnishings, including antique settles, oak gate-leg tables and sonorous clocks, set off beautifully against powder blue walls neatly hung with big appealing prints. The pubby main bar has roaring log fires in attractive stone fireplaces and heavy curtains on sturdy wooden rails; one area has a selection of newspapers and magazines, local maps and guidebooks. There's a piano for anyone who wants to play, and board games. Early evening sees a cheerful bustle that later settles to a more tranquil and relaxing atmosphere. Drinks include a marvellous wine list of around 230 wines with 17 by the glass (reception has a good wine shop), 24 whiskies, eight gins, organic ginger beer, lemonade, fruit juices and Black Sheep, Moorhouses Blond Witch, Timothy Taylors Landlord and Tirril Kirkstone Gold on handpump. The bedrooms are lovely (several have open fires), and there's also a self-catering holiday house. They own several miles of trout, salmon and sea trout fishing on the River Hodder; picnic hamper on request.

From seasonal menus using local produce the excellent food includes sandwiches, potted cornish crab with avocado purée and cucumber pickle, rustic pork terrine wrapped in pancetta with home-made pickles and chutney, cheese and onion pie with crushed root vegetables and home-made brown sauce, cumberland sausages with champ and caramelised onion jus, confit lamb shoulder with roast garlic purée, white beans and minted jus, seared fillet of cajun-spiced salmon with roast pepper salsa, pickled fennel and gnocchi potatoes, and puddings such as chocolate and hazelnut brownie with chocolate sauce and sticky toffee pudding with butterscotch sauce. *Benchmark main dish: fish pie with haddock and prawns in creamy sauce £12.00. Two-course evening meal £22.00.*

Free house ~ Licensee Charles Bowman ~ Real ale ~ Open 11am-midnight ~ Bar food 12-2, 7.30-9.30 ~ Restaurant ~ Children welcome ~ Dogs allowed in bar and bedrooms ~ Wi-fi ~ Bedrooms: £97/£134 *Recommended by Muriel and Spencer Harrop, Peter and Alison Steadman, Peter and Emma Kelly, Professor James Burke, Maria and Henry Lazenby, John and Sylvia Harrop, Bill Braithwaite, Alan and Alice Morgan*

THE GOOD PUB GUIDE

WORSLEY SD7401 Map 7

Worsley Old Hall

(0161) 703 8706 – www.brunningandprice.co.uk/worsleyoldhall

A mile from M60 junction 13: A575 Walkden Road, then after roundabout take first left into Worsley Park; M28 2QT

Very handsomely converted landmark building, now a welcoming pub scoring high on all counts

There's a real sense of grandeur here and some lovely original architectural features that include a gracefully arched inglenook and matching window alcove, a handsome staircase, heavy beams and glowing mahogany panelling. The relaxed and chatty main area spreads generously around the feature central bar, where well trained staff serve 17 good wines by the glass, more than 100 malt whiskies and 38 gins. Also, Phoenix Brunning & Price Original and Timothy Taylors Landlord with guests such as Cross Bay Sunset Blonde, Digfield Barnwell Bitter and Pennine Hair of the Dog on handpump. There's also the usual abundance of well chosen prints, fireside armchairs and a wide collection of cushioned dining chairs and wooden tables, and rugs on oak parquet; board games and background music. On a sunny day, the seats and tables on the big flagstoned terrace behind are quickly snapped up; there's also a barbecue area, a neat lawn beyond the fountain with picnic-table sets and views over the golf course. The Worsley Bridgewater Canal heritage area is a ten-minute walk away.

Creative food includes sandwiches, smoked mackerel with samphire, horseradish cream and beetroot jelly, tempura vegetables with sweet chilli sauce, sweet potato, aubergine and chickpea tagine with almond and lemon couscous and minted yoghurt, steak in ale pudding, cumberland sausages with mash and onion gravy, seared salmon with thai green stir-fried noodle broth and pak choi, warm, crispy beef salad with sweet chilli sauce and cashew nuts, braised lamb shoulder with dauphinoise potatoes, carrot mash and rosemary gravy, and puddings such as hot waffle with caramelised banana, butterscotch sauce and vanilla ice-cream and steamed apple and treacle sponge with custard. *Benchmark main dish: spiced chicken breast with roast sweet potatoes and tzatziki £14.50. Two-course evening meal £22.00.*

Brunning & Price ~ Manager Ryan Maguire ~ Real ale ~ Open 10am-11pm; 10am-10.30pm Sun ~ Bar food 10-10; 10-9.30 Sun ~ Restaurant ~ Children welcome ~ Dogs allowed in bar ~ Wi-fi *Recommended by Michael Butler, Amy Ledbetter, Donald Allsopp, Barry and Daphne Gregson, Scott and Charlotte Havers*

Also Worth a Visit in Lancashire

Besides the fully inspected pubs, you might like to try these pubs that have been recommended to us and described by readers. Do tell us what you think of them: feedback@goodguides.com

ASTLEY SJ6899

Archer (01942) 665459
Manchester Road; M29 7EJ Comfortably refurbished dining pub (former Manchester Road Inn); enjoyable food from lunchtime sandwiches and pub favourites up including good value set lunch, three real ales from well stocked bar, good friendly service; maybe live music Sat; children and dogs welcome, wheelchair access, seats out at front and in beer garden behind, open all day. *(Christine and Tony Garrett)*

BARLEY SD8240

★**Barley Mow** (01282) 690868
Barley Lane; BB12 9JX Bars and dining rooms reminiscent of a hunting lodge; animal hide chairs and cushions, antlers and stuffed animals including a big boar's head, exposed-stone, cream-coloured or planked walls, woodburners (one in a raised two-sided fireplace), mix of furniture including long rustic wall seats on carpet, bare boards or flagstones, Moorhouses, Thwaites and Timothy Taylors, eight wines by the glass and well liked hearty food; background music, TV, board games, free wi-fi; children and dogs (in bar) welcome, comfortable bedrooms, open (and food) all day. *(Edward Edmonton)*

BARLEY SD8240

Pendle (01282) 614808
Barley Lane; BB12 9JX Friendly 1930s stone pub in shadow of Pendle Hill; three cosy rooms, two log fires and six well kept regional ales including Moorhouses, popular good value pubby food (all day weekends) using local produce including lamb from family farm, conservatory; fortnightly quiz, free wi-fi; children and dogs welcome, picnic-sets on strip of lawn at front, small fenced play area across road by stream, lovely village and good walking country, bedrooms, open all day Fri-Sun. *(Nicola and Stuart Parsons)*

BARNSTON SJ2783

★**Fox & Hounds** (0151) 648 7685
3 miles from M53 junction 3: A552 towards Woodchurch, then left on A551; CH61 1BW Early 20th-c pub under new management; local Brimstage, Theakstons and guests, over 70 malt whiskies, 25 gins and decent choice of wines by the glass, good traditional home-made food (all day Fri-Sun, not Mon evening) including popular Sun lunch, roomy carpeted bay-windowed lounge with built-in banquettes and plush-cushioned captain's chairs around solid tables, old local prints and collection of police and other headgear, charming quarry-tiled corner with antique range, copper kettles and earthenware, also small traditional locals' bar and snug where dogs allowed; free wi-fi; children welcome, beer garden behind with teak furniture, open all day; refurbishment and new conservatory planned as we went to press. *(Paul Humphreys)*

BARTON SD5137

Sparling (01772) 860830
A6 N of Broughton; PR3 5AA Contemporary dining pub with decent food including set deals, roomy bar with comfortable sofas and other seats, plenty of tables in linked areas off, wood and flagstone floors, modern fireplaces, real ales such as Marstons Wainwright and good choice of wines by the glass, friendly efficient young staff; free wi-fi; children welcome, handy for M6. *(Millie and Peter Downing)*

BLACKBURN SD6525

Oyster & Otter (01254) 203200
1.8 miles from M65 junction 3: A674 towards Blackburn, turn right at Feniscowles mini roundabout, signposted to Darwen and Tockholes, into Livesey Branch Road; BB2 5DQ Distinctive clapboard and stone building in modern new england style; open-plan interior with cushioned dining booths by big windows on one side, other cosy seating areas divided by shoulder-high walls and large central hearth, end part with comfy sofas, good food including signature fish/seafood from open kitchen, Marstons Wainwright, a guest ale and a dozen wines by the glass, helpful young staff in aprons; background music, free wi-fi; children welcome, seats on decking above road, open (and food) all day. *(John Watson)*

BOLTON SD7112

Brewery Tap (01204) 302837
Belmont Road; BL1 7AN Two-room corner tap for Bank Top, their full range kept well and a guest, knowledgeable friendly staff, no food; quiet background music, free wi-fi; children (until 7pm) and dogs welcome, disabled access, seats outside, open all day. *(Beverley and Andy Furber)*

BRINDLE SD5924

★**Cavendish Arms** (01254) 852912
3 miles from M6 junction 29, via A6 and B5256 (Sandy Lane); PR6 8NG Traditional village pub (dates from the 15th c) on corner adjacent to church; beams, cosy snugs with open fires, stained-glass windows depicting the battle of Brunanburh, carpets throughout, four Marstons-related

ales and good inexpensive home-made food including Thurs specials and Fri fish, friendly helpful service, back dining room; Tues quiz; children and dogs (in tap room) welcome, heated canopied terrace with water feature, more tables in side garden, good walks, open (and food) all day weekends, closed lunchtimes Mon and Tues (no food those days or lunchtimes Weds-Fri). *(Steve Whalley)*

BROUGHTON SD4838

Plough at Eaves (01772) 690233
A6 N through Broughton, first left into Station Lane under a mile after traffic lights, then left after 1.5 miles, Eaves Lane; PR4 0BJ Pleasantly unpretentious old country tavern with two homely beamed bars; well kept Thwaites and good choice of enjoyable reasonably priced food, friendly accommodating service, lattice windows and traditional furnishings, old guns over woodburner in one room, log fire in dining bar with conservatory; background music; children welcome, front terrace and spacious side/back garden, well equipped play area, open all day Fri-Sun. *(Edward Edmonton)*

BURY SD8008

Swan & Cemetery (0161) 764 1508
Manchester Road; BL9 9NS Renovated Thwaites pub with two bars and connecting restaurant, their ales and sensibly priced food from extensive menu including children's choices, friendly staff; Weds quiz night, fruit machine; seats out on south-facing back deck, open all day. *(Clive and Fran Dutson)*

BURY SD8313

Trackside (0161) 764 6461
East Lancashire Railway station, Bolton Street; BL9 0EY Welcoming busy station bar by East Lancs steam railway; bright, airy and clean with ten real ales including a house beer from local Outstanding, also bottled imports, real ciders and great range of whiskies, enjoyable home-made food (Sat and Sun only); folk night last Thurs of month; children (till 7pm) and dogs welcome, platform tables under canopy, open all day. *(P A Lord)*

CARNFORTH SD5173

Longlands (01524) 781256
Tewitfield, about 2 miles N; A6070, off A6; LA6 1JH Popular family-run village inn; good food in bar and airy restaurant from pub favourites and pizzas up, four local beers, helpful friendly staff; live music; children and dogs welcome, bedrooms and self-catering cottages, Lancaster Canal and M6 nearby, open all day. *(Sandra and Neil White)*

CHATBURN SD7644

Brown Cow (01200) 440736
Bridge Road; BB7 4AW Welcoming village pub refurbished under new management; opened-up interior with separate dining room, enjoyable well priced home-made food including weekly specials, Marstons Wainwright and three guests, friendly helpful service; children and dogs (in bar area) welcome, wheelchair access (ramp provided) and disabled loo (others upstairs), back garden with flagstone terrace, closed Mon, otherwise open all day, food all day weekends. *(Darrell Barton)*

CHEADLE SJ8588

James Watts (0161) 428 3361
High Street (A560); SK8 1AX Newly refurbished mock-Tudor pub owned by Hydes; fine range of cask and craft beers plus 100 more in bottles (all marked on little blackboard panels), good choice of wines and other drinks too, food from snacks to various sharing combinations served on slates, friendly helpful staff; live acoustic music Mon and Thurs; back terrace, open all day (till midnight Fri, Sat). *(Christine and Tony Garrett)*

CHEADLE HULME SJ8785

Church Inn (0161) 485 1897
Ravenoak Road (A5149 SE); SK8 7EG Popular old family-run pub with good food from varied menu including set deals, well kept Robinsons beers and nice selection of wines by the glass, gleaming brass on panelled walls, warming coal fire, pleasant staff and locals, back restaurant; live music most Sun evenings; children welcome, seats outside (some under cover), car park across road, open all day. *(Mike and Wena Stevenson, Michael Butler)*

CLAUGHTON SD5666

★**Fenwick Arms** (01524) 221157
A683 Kirkby Lonsdale–Lancaster; LA2 9LA Civilised 250-year-old black and white pub in Lune Valley, mainly popular for its food including good fish/seafood; smartly updated with white-painted beams in wonky ceilings, open fires (one in a black range) and painted panelling, upholstered and antique-style dining chairs around all shapes of table on carpet or bare boards, window seats with scatter cushions, Marstons Wainwright, Timothy Taylors Landlord and a guest, 18 wines by the glass and a good choice of spirits, efficient friendly staff; background music, free wi-fi; children and dogs (in bar) welcome, picnic-sets on front terrace, nine comfortable modern bedrooms, open (and food) all day. *(Michael Butler, John and Sylvia Harrop)*

CLITHEROE SD7441

Holmes Mill (01200) 401035
Greenacre Street; BB7 1EB Conversion of town's last working cotton mill; cavernous industrial interior keeping some of the old machinery (giant flywheel in the engine room), lovely flagged floor and plenty of recycled fixtures and fittings, walls fitted with leather benches and scrubbed plank

tables, sturdy canteen chairs and high-backed stools elsewhere, vast U-shaped counter serving 24 real ales including six from Bowland (brewery visible behind glass partitions), good selection of enjoyable food including grills, also has a café and boutique hotel; prominent background music and some live; picnic-sets outside along with covered seating in shipping containers, open (and food) all day, till 8pm Sun. *(Steve Whalley)*

CLITHEROE SD7441

New Inn (01200) 423312

Parson Lane; BB7 2JN Traditional old-fashioned local with ten or more well kept ales including Coach House and Moorhouses from central bar, knowledgeable staff, cosy rooms with log fires; fortnightly irish session (Sun afternoon) and other live music; dogs welcome, seats out at front and back, camping, open all day. *(Martin and Joanne Sharp)*

COLNE SD8940

Black Lane Ends (01282) 863070

Skipton Old Road, Foulridge; BB8 7EP Country pub tucked away in quiet lane; generous helpings of good sensibly priced food, three well kept real ales including Timothy Taylors Landlord and decent wine choice, cheerful attentive staff, long bar with spindleback chairs, padded wall benches and scrubbed tables, large fireplace partially separating small dining room with cast-iron range; children welcome, play area in back garden, nice views towards Wycoller from terrace, handy for canal and reservoir walks. *(Michael Breeze, Steve Whalley)*

DELPH SD9809

Royal Oak (01457) 874460

Off A6052 about 100 metres W of White Lion, turn up steep Lodge Lane and keep on up into Broad Lane; OL3 5TX Welcoming traditional 18th-c pub opposite old moorland church in steep narrow winding lane, great views of surrounding valleys; real fires in three small rooms, comfortable solid furniture, four well kept ales including Millstone and Moorhouses, no food; closed Mon and lunchtimes apart from Sun when open 12-6pm. *(Frances and Hamish Potter)*

DENSHAW SD9710

Printers Arms (01457) 874248

Oldham Road; OL3 5SN Above Oldham in shadow of Saddleworth Moor, modernised interior with small log-fire bar and three other rooms, popular good value food including bargain set menu (till 6.30pm, 4pm Sat, not Sun), Black Sheep and Timothy Taylors Golden Best, several wines by the glass, friendly staff; children welcome, lovely views from two-tier beer garden, open (and food) all day. *(Serena and Adam Furber)*

DENSHAW SD9711

Rams Head (01457) 874802

2 miles from M62 junction 22; A672 towards Oldham, pub N of village; OL3 5UN Sweeping moorland views from this roadside dining pub (don't be put off by the rather austere exterior); good food (all day weekends) including seasonal game and seafood, ales such as Marstons and Timothy Taylors kept well, friendly service, four thick-walled little rooms, beam-and-plank ceilings, panelling, oak settles and built-in benches, log fires, coffee shop and adjacent delicatessen selling local produce; soft background music; children welcome (not Sat evening), closed Mon and Tues. *(Christine and Tony Garrett)*

DENTON SJ9395

Lowes Arms (0161) 336 3064

Hyde Road (A57); M34 3FF Thriving 19th-c pub with own Westwood beers and local guests such as Crossbay and Torrside, jovial community-spirited landlord and helpful friendly staff, reasonably priced food including daily specials, bar with pool and darts, restaurant; children and dogs welcome, tables outside, smokers' shelter, open all day. *(Darrell Barton)*

DIGGLE SE0007

Diggle (01457) 872741

Village signed off A670 just N of Dobcross; OL3 5JZ Sturdy four-square hillside pub in quiet spot just below the moors overlooking Standedge Canal tunnel; good value food (till 7pm Sun, not Mon) from snacks up, well kept ales such as Black Sheep, Millstone and Timothy Taylors, helpful staff; free wi-fi; children and dogs welcome, disabled access, picnic-sets out among trees, four bedrooms, open all day. *(Millie and Peter Downing)*

DOLPHINHOLME SD5153

Fleece (01524) 791233

A couple of miles from M6 junction 33; W of village; Chipping Lane/Anyon Road; LA2 9AQ Extensively renovated old stone inn (parts date from the 16th c); various rooms including black beamed bar with rugs on flagstones and log fire with unusual copper canopy, four well kept regularly changing ales and decent wines by the glass, popular sensibly priced food (not Mon), friendly efficient service, dining lounge with some modern booth seating and sofas in front of woodburner, little shop selling local produce; children and dogs welcome, modern

Real ale to us means beer that has matured naturally in its cask – not pressurised or filtered. We name all real ales stocked.

rattan-style furniture on terrace with Trough of Bowland views, nine comfortable well appointed bedrooms, excellent breakfast, closed Mon lunchtime, otherwise open all day. *(Serena and Adam Furber)*

DUNHAM TOWN SJ7488
Axe & Cleaver (0161) 928 3391
School Lane; WA14 4SE Big 19th-c country house converted into spacious open-plan Chef & Brewer; good value popular food from light lunchtime choices and sharing plates up (best to book Sun lunch), three well kept ales, friendly service; children welcome, garden picnic-sets, handy for nearby Dunham Massey (NT), open (and food) all day. *(Mike and Wena Stevenson)*

DUNHAM TOWN SJ7288
Vine (0161) 928 3275
Barns Lane, Dunham Massey; WA14 5RU Tucked-away (but busy) old-fashioned little village local with friendly staff and regulars, well kept/priced Sam Smiths and several ciders, enjoyable generously served food (not Sun evening, Mon), cosy bar and other smallish rooms, coal fires in brick fireplaces; children and dogs welcome, picnic-sets in good-sized garden, handy for Dunham Massey (NT), open all day. *(Steve Whalley)*

EDENFIELD SD7919
Coach (01706) 825000
Market Street; BL0 0HJ Updated and extended 19th-c dining pub under new management; good food from lunchtime sandwiches up, three real ales, over a dozen wines by the glass and good range of gins, friendly young staff; free wi-fi; children welcome, disabled access/facilities, a few tables on front pavement, open (and food) all day, except Mon when kitchen closed. *(Angela and Steve Heard)*

FENCE SD8237
Fence Gate (01282) 618101
2.6 miles from M65 junction 13; Wheatley Lane Road, just off A6068 W; BB12 9EE Imposing 18th-c dining inn with good choice of enjoyable food, five real ales and several wines by the glass, friendly but not always speedy service, panelled bar with pewter counter and woodburner in large stone fireplace, contemporary brasserie plus various function rooms, look out for their display of over 600 gins; background and regular live music; children welcome, rattan-style furniture out at front, 24 bedrooms, open all day. *(Martin and Joanne Sharp)*

FENCE SD8237
★**White Swan** (01282) 611773
Wheatley Lane; BB12 9QA Whitewashed village dining pub with comfortably renovated Victorian-style interior, highly regarded imaginative food (not cheap) from short daily changing menu, good friendly service, four well kept Timothy Taylors ales from curved polished wood servery, nice wines, own infused spirits and good coffee, old pictures of the pub, some antlers and stuffed animal heads, wall lights and chandeliers, fireplace at each end; children welcome, outside seating on two levels with chunky wooden tables, open all day, food till 6pm Sun, kitchen closed Mon. *(Steve Whalley, W K Wood)*

GISBURN SD8248
White Bull (01200) 415805
Main Street (A59); BB7 4HE Refurbished roadside pub with opened-up dining areas either side of entrance, more room further back to right of bar; taupe-painted walls and stone-effect wallpaper, nice mix of dark furniture on polished wood or flagstone floors, some beams and whitewashed standing timbers, good attractively presented food cooked by chef-owner from pub standards up, four well kept ales (including a Holts beer named for the pub) from semi-circular counter with cherry wood top, friendly service; children and dogs (in one section) welcome, narrow access to large back car park, open all day. *(Simon Granville)*

GOOSNARGH SD5738
Horns (01772) 865230
On junction of Horns Lane and Inglewhite Road; pub signed off B5269, towards Chipping; PR3 2FJ Early 18th-c inn (same family ownership since 1952) with neatly kept carpeted rooms including a rare 'parlour' behind the servery; enjoyable home cooking from pub standards to local duck and game, own Goosnargh ales and an occasional microbrewery guest, plenty of wines by the glass and good choice of malts, log fires; background music, free wi-fi; children welcome, dogs in garden only, six bedrooms in converted stone barn (some with road noise), caravan park, not far from M6, open (and food) all day Sun, closed Mon lunchtime. *(W K Wood)*

GOOSNARGH SD5636
Stags Head (01772) 446185
Whittingham Lane (B5269); PR3 2AU Old roadside dining pub extensively refurbished under present owners; good range of popular freshly made food at fair prices, daily specials and deals such as Weds grill night, friendly helpful service, ales such as Caledonian Deuchars IPA and Theakstons Best, lots of separate areas including pitched-roof restaurant, open fires; Weds quiz, board games, TV; children, walkers and dogs welcome, tables out in pleasant garden with fenced play area, open (and food) all day. *(Frances and Hamish Potter)*

GREAT ECCLESTON SD4240
★**Farmers Arms** (01995) 672018
Halsall Square (just off A586); PR3 0YE Popular attractively refurbished country pub not far from Fylde Coast and Blackpool;

smart dining areas, on two floors, with painted panelled walls and eclectic collection of seating including cushioned settles on carpet or polished boards, woodburners in stone fireplaces, ales such as Marstons Wainwright and Timothy Taylors Boltmaker, good choice of wines/gins and highly regarded food with emphasis on fish/seafood and grills, cheerful attentive service; free wi-fi; children and dogs (in bar) welcome, teak furniture on sheltered terrace, open (and food) all day. *(Gordon and Margaret Ormondroyd, Frank and Joan Carruthers)*

GREAT HARWOOD SD7332

Royal (01254) 876237
Station Road; BB6 7BA Popular Victorian local with half a dozen well kept changing ales and generous helpings of enjoyable pub food, friendly staff; some live music, pool and darts; children welcome, partly covered terrace, open all day. *(Simon Granville)*

GREENFIELD SD9904

King William IV (01457) 873933
Chew Valley Road (A669); OL3 7DD Welcoming 19th-c village local with half a dozen well kept ales including local Greenfield and Millstone, enjoyable home-made food (not Mon, Tues or lunchtimes Weds, Thurs), helpful, friendly staff; Mon quiz, sports TV, free wi-fi; children and dogs welcome, tables on walled front terrace, open all day. *(Gilly Todd)*

GREENFIELD SD9904

Railway Hotel (01457) 872307
Shaw Hall Bank Road, opposite station; OL3 7JZ Friendly four-room stone pub with half a dozen well kept mainly local ales, no food, old local photographs and open fire; live music Thurs, Fri and Sun, sports TV, upstairs, games bar with darts and pool; children and dogs welcome, disabled access, beer garden with good views, open all day. *(Alan and Alice Morgan)*

HEST BANK SD4766

★**Hest Bank Inn** (01524) 824339
Hest Bank Lane; off A6 just N of Lancaster; LA2 6DN Picturesque stone coaching house in nice setting close to Morecambe Bay; good choice of well liked food from snacks and pub favourites up, reasonable prices, well kept ales such as Black Sheep, Theakstons and Thwaites, decent wines, friendly helpful young staff, separate restaurant area; children and dogs welcome, plenty of tables out by Lancaster Canal, open all day, food all day weekends. *(Roy and Gill Payne)*

HESWALL SJ2782

Jug & Bottle (0151) 342 5535
Mount Avenue; CH60 4RH Nicely updated Victorian building with views through trees of the Dee estuary and welsh mountains beyond; good-sized bar with wood and flagstone floors, open fire, dining rooms off, half a dozen well kept ales including Brains, Brimstage and a house beer from Coach House, lots of wines by the glass, good choice of popular fairly priced food from sandwiches and sharing plates up, friendly attentive staff; children and dogs welcome, teak furniture on front deck and surrounding garden, six bedrooms, open (and food) all day. *(Iain Bignold)*

HURST GREEN SD6837

★**Shireburn Arms** (01254) 826678
Whalley Road (B6243 Clitheroe–Goosnargh); BB7 9QJ Welcoming 17th-c hotel with peaceful Ribble Valley views from big airy restaurant and neatly kept garden, food from sandwiches and traditional dishes to daily specials (all day weekends), leather armchairs, sofas and log fire in beamed and flagstoned lounge bar with linked dining area, two well kept ales such as Lancaster and Thwaites, several wines by the glass; occasional live music, daily papers; children and dogs welcome, pretty Tolkien walk from here, 22 comfortable bedrooms, open all day from 8am for coffee. *(Edward Edmonton)*

HYDE SJ9595

Sportsman (0161) 368 5000
Mottram Road; SK14 2NN Welcoming Victorian local with Rossendale ales and lots of changing guests (frequent beer festivals), bargain bar food and popular upstairs cuban restaurant, bare boards and open fires, pub games; children and dogs welcome, back terrace with heated smokers' shelter, open all day. *(Louise and Simon Peters)*

INGLETON SD6972

Masons Arms (01524) 242040
New Road (A65); LA6 3HL Welcoming roadside village inn refurbished by present owners; stools and upholstered chairs around mix of pubby tables on wood-strip flooring, tartan-carpeted dining end with woodburner, generous helpings of tasty straightforward food from lunchtime hot or cold sandwiches up (more evening choice), well kept ales such as Black Sheep and Sharps, decent wine list with half a dozen by the glass, good friendly service; children and dogs welcome, three bedrooms, open (and some food) all day. *(John and Sylvia Harrop)*

IRBY SJ2586

★**Irby Mill** (0151) 604 0194
Mill Lane, off Greasby Road; CH49 3NT Converted miller's sandstone cottage (original windmill demolished 1898); friendly and welcoming, with eight well kept ales including Caledonian Deuchars IPA, good choice of wines by the glass and ample helpings of popular reasonably priced food from sandwiches up, efficient service, two low-beamed traditional flagstoned rooms and extended carpeted dining area, log fire, interesting old photographs and history;

tables on terraces and revamped side area, good local walks, open (and food) all day, gets crowded evenings/weekends when parking limited. *(Paul Humphreys)*

LANCASTER SD4761

Borough (01524) 64170

Dalton Square; LA1 1PP Popular city-centre pub, stylish and civilised, with chandeliers, dark leather sofas and armchairs, lamps on antique tables, high stools and elbow tables, eight real ales including some from on-site microbrewery, lots of bottled beers too, big dining room with booths along one side, decent food including daily specials and deals, jams and local produce for sale; upstairs comedy night Sun; children and dogs welcome, lovely tree-sheltered garden, bedrooms, open (and food) all day from 8am. *(Angela and Steve Heard)*

LANCASTER SD4761

Sun (01524) 66006

Church Street; LA1 1ET Hotel bar with ten well kept ales including five from Lancaster, plenty of continental beers and good choice of wines by the glass too, popular food from sandwiches, sharing boards and pub staples up, exposed stonework, panelling and several fireplaces, conservatory; background music, TV; children welcome away from servery, tables on walled and paved terrace, 16 comfortable bedrooms, open all day (till 1am Fri, Sat). *(Chris Taylor)*

LANCASTER SD4761

Water Witch (01524) 63828

Parking in Aldcliffe Road behind Royal Lancaster Infirmary, off A6; LA1 1SU Attractive conversion of 18th-c canalside stables; flagstones, stripped stone, rafters and pitch-pine panelling, half a dozen well kept changing ales, extensive choice of fairly traditional food from sandwiches and deli boards up including weekday lunch deal, upstairs restaurant; Weds open mike night, Thurs quiz, free wi-fi; children in eating areas, picnic-sets out by water, moorings, open (and food) all day. *(Simon Granville)*

LANESHAW BRIDGE SD9141

Alma (01282) 857830

Emmott Lane, off A6068 E of Colne; BB8 7EG Attractively renovated 18th-c inn with popular food, several wines by the glass and three real ales including Moorhouses Pride of Pendle and Marstons Wainwright, friendly helpful staff, flagstoned bar and part-panelled lounge with rugs on bare boards, open fires, large garden room extension; background music; well behaved children and dogs welcome, nine comfortable well appointed bedrooms, open (and food) all day, breakfast for non-residents. *(John and Eleanor Holdsworth)*

LITTLE ECCLESTON SD4240

★**Cartford** (01995) 670166

Cartford Lane, off A586 Garstang–Blackpool, by toll bridge; PR3 0YP Riverside coaching inn with unusual four-level layout combining traditional and contemporary elements, four real ales including a house beer (Giddy Kipper) from Moorhouses, speciality bottled beers, 18 wines by the glass and interesting range of gins and whiskies, highly regarded imaginative food plus some pub favourites, restaurant, on-site shop and delicatessen; children welcome (no under-10s after 8pm), garden tables looking out over tidal River Wyre (crossed by toll bridge), individually decorated bedrooms and two new studio cabins, closed Mon lunchtime, otherwise open all day, food all day Sun. *(Camilla and Jose Ferrera, Andy and Rosemary Taylor, Trish and Karl Soloman, John and Claire Masters)*

LITTLEBOROUGH SD9517

Moorcock (01706) 378156

Halifax Road (A58); OL15 0LD Long roadside inn high on the moors with far-reaching views; wide range of food (all day Fri-Sun) from sandwiches and pub favourites up in flagstoned bar or restaurant, four well kept beers; sports TV; terrace tables taking in the view, seven comfortable reasonably priced bedrooms, open all day. *(Millie and Peter Downing)*

LIVERPOOL SJ3489

Baltic Fleet (0151) 709 3116

Wapping, near Albert Dock; L1 8DQ Unusual bow-fronted pub with six interesting beers including Wapping (brewed in the cellar), real ciders and several wines by the glass, simple well cooked/priced lunchtime food such as traditional scouse, bare boards, big arched windows, simple mix of furnishings and some nautical paraphernalia, fires in parlour and snug; background music, TV; children welcome in eating areas, dogs in bar, back terrace, open all day. *(David H Bennett, Anthony Barnes)*

LIVERPOOL SJ3589

Belvedere (0151) 709 0303

Sugnall Street; L7 7EB Unspoilt small 19th-c two-room pub with friendly chatty atmosphere, original features including etched glass and coal fires, four well kept changing ales such as Melwood and Salopian, good selection of bottled beers, real cider and fine choice of gins; dogs welcome, open all day. *(Gilly Todd)*

Half pints: by law, a pub should not charge more for half a pint than half the price of a full pint, unless it shows that half-pint price on its price list.

LIVERPOOL SJ3589

Cracke (0151) 709 4171
Rice Street; L1 9BB Friendly unchanging local with five well kept ales including Phoenix and Thwaites, traditional cider, no food, small unspoilt bar with bare boards and bench seats, snug and a bigger back room with unusual Beatles diorama, local artwork and some photos of John Lennon who used to drink here; juke box, sports TV; picnic-sets in sizeable tree-shaded back garden, open all day and popular with tourists. *(Gilly Todd)*

LIVERPOOL SJ3590

Crown (0151) 707 6027
Lime Street; L1 1JQ Well preserved art nouveau showpiece; fine tiled fireplace and copper bar front, dark leather banquettes, panelling and splendid ceiling, smaller back room with another good fireplace, impressive staircase sweeping up under cupola to handsome area with ornate windows, eight real ales including Greene King, Peerless and Timothy Taylors, good choice of bottled beers, wide range of good value food; sports TV; very handy for the station, open all day from 8am for breakfast. *(Gilly Todd, Edward Edmonton)*

LIVERPOOL SJ3490

Dead Crafty Beer 07977 228918
Dale Street opposite the old magistrates' court; L2 5TF New craft beer bar with 20 on tap and over 150 in bottles, tasters offered by friendly knowledgeable staff, compact fairly basic interior with bare boards and exposed brickwork, bar made from flight cases; unisex loos downstairs; dogs allowed, open all day Fri-Sun, closed Mon and lunchtimes Tues-Thurs. *(Edward Edmonton)*

LIVERPOOL SJ3589

Dispensary (0151) 709 2160
Renshaw Street; L1 2SP Small busy central pub worth knowing for its very well kept beers (up to ten), good choice of bottled imports too, no food, bare boards and polished panelling, wonderful etched windows, comfortable raised back bar with fireplace (not used), some Victorian medical artefacts; background music, silent TVs, notices on house rules; open all day (till midnight Fri, Sat). *(Simon Granville)*

LIVERPOOL SJ3589

Fly in the Loaf (0151) 708 0817
Hardman Street; L1 9AS Former bakery with smart gleaming bar serving Okells, guest ales and several foreign beers, enjoyable home-made food at low prices including bar snacks such as pigs in blankets, efficient, friendly service, long refurbished room with panelling and some raised sections; background music, sports TV, upstairs loos; open all day, till midnight Fri, Sat, no food Sun evening. *(Dave Braisted)*

LIVERPOOL SJ3490

Hole In Ye Wall (0151) 227 3809
Off Dale Street; L2 2AW Character 18th-c pub (the city's oldest) with thriving local atmosphere in high-beamed panelled bar, half a dozen changing ales fed by gravity from upstairs (no cellar as pub is on Quaker burial site), extensive gin range, baguettes, pies, burgers and so forth, friendly staff, plenty of woodwork, stained glass and old Liverpool photographs, coal-effect gas fire in unusual brass-canopied fireplace; live music evenings Mon, Fri and Sat, traditional sing-along Sun, sports TV, fruit machine; children allowed till 5pm, no dogs, open all day. *(Simon Granville, Edward Edmonton)*

LIVERPOOL SJ3490

Lion Tavern (0151) 236 1734
Moorfields, off Tithebarn Street; L2 2BP Beautifully preserved ornate Victorian corner pub; sparkling etched glass, big mirrors, panelling and tilework, serving hatches in central bar, two small back lounges one with fine glass dome, eight changing beers and extensive range of whiskies, simple reasonably priced lunchtime food including good pork pies, friendly staff; sports TV, free wi-fi; open all day. *(Simon Granville)*

LIVERPOOL SJ3590

Ma Egerton's Stage Door
(0151) 345 3525 *Pudsey Street, opposite side entrance to Lime Street station; L1 1JA* Victorian pub behind the Empire Theatre and named after a former long-serving landlady/theatrical agent; refurbished but keeping old-fashioned character with green leather button-back banquettes (note the bell pushes), swagged curtains, wood floors, panelling and small period fireplace, lots of celebrity pictures and other memorabilia, a couple of changing ales and enjoyable food including sharing plates and popular pizzas, friendly staff; Mon quiz, Fri sing-along, bingo last Thurs of the month; open all day. *(Gilly Todd)*

LIVERPOOL SJ3589

Peter Kavanaghs (0151) 709 3443
Egerton Street, off Catherine Street; L8 7LY Character Victorian pub popular with locals and students; interesting décor in several small rooms, old-world murals, stained glass and all kinds of bric-a-brac (lots hanging from ceiling), piano, wooden settles and real fires, well kept Greene King Abbot and guests, friendly licensees; free wi-fi; open all day (till 1am Fri, Sat). *(David H Bennett)*

LIVERPOOL SJ3589

Philharmonic Dining Rooms
(0151) 707 2837 *36 Hope Street; corner of Hardman Street; L1 9BX* Beautifully preserved Victorian pub with wonderful period detail; centrepiece mosaic-faced counter, heavily carved and

polished mahogany partitions radiating out under intricate plasterwork ceiling, main hall with stained glass of Boer War heroes Baden-Powell and Lord Roberts, rich panelling, mosaic floor and copper panels of musicians above fireplace, other areas including two side rooms called Brahms and Liszt, the original Adamant gents' is also worth a look, ten real ales, several wines by the glass and decent choice of malt whiskies, fair-priced food; background music and machines; children welcome till 7pm, open (and food) all day. *(Mike and Wena Stevenson, David H Bennett, Anthony Barnes)*

LIVERPOOL SJ3589

Roscoe Head (0151) 709 4365
Roscoe Street; L1 2SX Unassuming old local with cosy bar, snug and two other spotless unspoilt little rooms, friendly long-serving landlady, well kept Jennings, Tetleys and five guests, inexpensive home-made lunches (not weekends), interesting memorabilia; Tues quiz and traditional games such as crib, free wi-fi; open all day. *(Gilly Todd)*

LIVERPOOL SJ3490

Ship & Mitre (0151) 236 0859
Dale Street; L2 2JH Friendly local with fine art deco exterior and ship-like interior; up to a dozen unusual changing ales (many beer festivals), real ciders and over 70 bottled beers, decent choice of good value food (all day Fri-Sun) such as wraps, burgers and all-day breakfast, upstairs function room with original 1930s décor; well behaved children (till 7pm) and dogs welcome, open all day. *(David H Bennett)*

LIVERPOOL SJ3490

★**Thomas Rigbys** (0151) 236 3269
Dale Street; L2 2EZ Spacious three-room Victorian pub; main bare-boards bar with iron pillars supporting sturdy beams, panelling and stained glass, Okells ales and guests from long counter, also good range of imported draught/bottled beers and several gins, back Nelson Room with impressive fireplace and an oak-panelled dining parlour where children allowed, enjoyable reasonably priced pubby food till early evening, attentive staff; sports TV; disabled access (although some steps and downstairs lavatories), seats in big courtyard, open all day. *(David H Bennett)*

LONGRIDGE SD6137

Corporation Arms (01772) 782644
Lower Road (B6243); PR3 2YJ Updated 18th-c roadside inn next to reservoir; good range of popular home-cooked food generously served and reasonably priced, four well kept changing ales, plenty of wines by the glass, cheerful service and good welcoming atmosphere in three small linked rooms and restaurant; quiz second and fourth Tues of month, children allowed, five comfortable bedrooms, open (and food) all day. *(Sandra and Neil White)*

LONGRIDGE SD6038

★**Derby Arms** (01772) 782370
Chipping Road, Thornley; 1.5 miles N of Longridge on back road to Chipping; PR3 2NB Creeper-clad village pub with attractively refurbished bar and connecting dining rooms, wide floorboards or grey carpet, woodburner and open fire, assorted seating including high-backed chairs, settles with scatter cushions, wall banquettes and leather-topped stools, Copper Dragon, Thwaites and Timothy Taylors from stylish oak-planked servery, nice selection of wines by the glass too, good food including chargrills and daily fish specials, cheerful helpful service; free wi-fi; children and dogs (in bar) welcome, good quality furniture on front terrace behind picket fence, comfortable airy bedrooms, open (and food) all day, breakfast for non-residents. *(David Fowler, Bryan)*

LONGRIDGE SD6037

New Drop (01254) 878338
Higher Road, Longridge Fell, parallel to B6243 Longridge–Clitheroe; PR3 2YX Pleasant modernised dining pub in lovely moors-edge country overlooking Ribble Valley; good choice of reasonably priced food, decent wines and three well kept ales such as Black Sheep, friendly service; children welcome, open all day Sun, closed Mon. *(Beverley and Andy Butcher)*

LYDGATE SD9704

★**White Hart** (01457) 872566
Stockport Road; Lydgate not marked on some maps and not the one near Todmorden; take A669 Oldham–Saddleworth, right at brow of hill to A6050 after almost 2.5 miles; OL4 4JJ Smart up-to-date dining pub overlooking Pennine moors; mix of locals (in bar or simpler end rooms) and diners in elegant brasserie with smartly dressed staff, highly regarded if not cheap food, Lees, Timothy Taylors and a guest beer, 16 wines by the glass, old beams and exposed stonework contrasting with deep red or purple walls and modern artwork, open fires; children welcome, dogs in bar, picnic-sets on back lawn making most of position, 12 bedrooms, open all day. *(Serena and Adam Furber)*

LYTHAM SD3627

★**Taps** (01253) 736226
A584 S of Blackpool; Henry Street – in centre, one street in from West Beach; FY8 5LE Popular town pub just a couple of minutes from the beach; ten well kept ales including Greene King and a couple of proper ciders, simple good value lunchtime food (not Sun), friendly efficient staff, open-plan bar with wood or tiled floor, stripped brickwork

and open fires, dining area leading through to sunny terrace; quiz Mon, TV for major sports, darts, fruit machine; children allowed till 7.30pm, parking nearby difficult (best to use West Beach car park on seafront, free Sun), open all day. *(Michael Butler, Steve Whalley)*

MANCHESTER SJ8498

Angel (0161) 833 4786
Angel Street, off Rochdale Road; M4 4BR Friendly place on edge of the Northern Quarter; good value home-made food, ten well kept ales including one badged for them, bottled beers and a couple of ciders/perries, piano in bare-boards bar, smaller upstairs restaurant with two log fires and local artwork; free wi-fi; children and dogs welcome, back beer garden, open all day. *(Larry King)*

MANCHESTER SJ8398

Ape & Apple (0161) 839 9624
John Dalton Street; M2 6HQ Large open-plan pub with five well kept/priced Holts beers plus guests, hearty traditional bar food including deals, comfortable seating, bare boards, carpet and tiles, lots of old prints and posters, upstairs restaurant/function room, friendly atmosphere; Mon salsa dancing and Weds comedy night, juke box, games machines, free wi-fi; children and dogs welcome, disabled access, central courtyard and roof terrace, open all day (till 9pm Sun). *(Dr and Mrs A K Clarke)*

MANCHESTER SJ8397

★**Britons Protection** (0161) 236 5895
Great Bridgewater Street, corner of Lower Mosley Street; M1 5LE Lively unpretentious pub with rambling rooms and notable tiled murals of 1819 Peterloo Massacre which took place nearby; plush little front bar with tiled floor, glossy brown and russet wall tiles, solid woodwork and ornate red and gold ceiling, two cosy inner lounges, both served by hatch, with attractive brass wall lamps and solidly comfortable furnishings, coal-effect gas fire in simple art nouveau fireplace, five ales including Jennings, Robinsons and a Thwaites beer named for the pub from massive counter with heated footrail, also over 300 malt whiskies, straightforward lunchtime food Mon-Fri; occasional storytelling and live music, free wi-fi; children till 5pm, tables in enclosed back garden, handy for Bridgewater Hall concerts, open all day (very busy lunchtime and weekends). *(Dr and Mrs A K Clarke)*

MANCHESTER SJ8498

Castle (0161) 237 9485
Oldham Street, about 200 metres from Piccadilly, on right; M4 1LE Restored 18th-c pub run well by former *Coronation Street* actor; simple traditional front bar, small snug, Robinsons ales and guests from fine bank of handpumps, Weston's Old Rosie cider; juke box, back room for regular live music and other events, overspill space upstairs; nice tilework outside, open all day till late. *(Dr and Mrs A K Clarke)*

MANCHESTER SJ8497

Circus Tavern (0161) 236 5818
Portland Street; M1 4GX Traditional little two-room local; friendly staff serving well kept Robinsons and Tetleys from tiny corridor bar (or may be table service), leatherette wall benches and panelling, back room with football memorabilia and period fireplace; sports TV; open all day and can get crowded. *(Larry King)*

MANCHESTER SJ8398

City Arms (0161) 236 4610
Kennedy Street, off St Peters Square; M2 4BQ Friendly old-fashioned two-bar local sandwiched between two other pubs; eight well kept quickly changing ales, belgian bottled beers and decent range of whiskies and gins, simple weekday lunchtime food, bare boards, panelling and button-back banquettes, coal fires; background music, sports TV, darts and dominoes; wheelchair access but steps down to back lounge, open all day (till 8pm Sun). *(Larry King)*

MANCHESTER SJ8397

Dukes 92 (0161) 839 8642
Castle Street, below the bottom end of Deansgate; M3 4LZ Friendly informal atmosphere in refurbished former stables overlooking canal basin, modern furnishings on light tiled floor, exposed brickwork, stairs up to stylish gallery bar leading to roof terrace, a couple of local ales such as Seven Bro7hers, decent wines and wide range of spirits (happy-hour cocktails Mon-Thurs), good food choice from bar snacks and pizzas up; background music, DJs Fri and Sat, live music Sun; children welcome, no dogs inside, waterside tables on big terrace with outside bar/kitchen, open all day (till 1am Fri, Sat). *(Dr and Mrs A K Clarke)*

MANCHESTER SJ8194

Font (0161) 871 2022
Manchester Road, Chorlton; M21 9PG Relaxed split-level bar with eight changing ales, 16 craft kegs and extensive range of bottled beers, also traditional ciders and fair-priced cocktails, enjoyable food from sandwiches and wraps to burgers and burritos; weekend DJs, free wi-fi; children and dogs welcome, seats out at front behind railings, open (and food) all day (till 1am Fri, Sat), popular with students. *(Larry King)*

MANCHESTER SJ8397

Knott Bar (0161) 839 9229
Deansgate; M3 4LY Modern glass-fronted café-bar under railway arch by Castlefield heritage site; eight well kept changing ales, also lots of craft beers and continental imports, pizza-based menu; background

music; upstairs balcony overlooking Rochdale Canal, open (and food) all day. *(Dr and Mrs A K Clarke)*

MANCHESTER SJ8497

Lass o' Gowrie (0161) 273 5822
36 Charles Street; off Oxford Road; M1 7DB Traditional tile-fronted side-street local refurbished a few years ago but keeping Victorian character; big-windowed bar with cosy room off, wood floors and stripped brickwork, pendant lighting, various pictures including black and white photos of old Manchester, three well kept Greene King ales plus local guests, simple bargain food such as home-made pies, friendly service; Thurs quiz, some live music; balcony overlooking River Medlock, open all day. *(Chris Parker)*

MANCHESTER SJ8499

★**Marble Arch** (0161) 832 5914
Rochdale Road (A664), Ancoats; centre of Gould Street, just E of Victoria station; M4 4HY Cheery pub with fine listed Victorian interior; long narrow bar with high ceiling, extensive glazed brickwork, marble and tiling, sloping mosaic floor and frieze advertising various drinks, old stone bottles on shelves, real ales including their own Marble beers (brewery visible from windows in back dining room – tours by arrangement), well liked home-made food including separate cheese menu; background music; children welcome, small garden, open (and food) all day. *(Larry King)*

MANCHESTER SJ8398

★**Mr Thomas's Chop House**
(0161) 832 2245 *Cross Street; M2 7AR* Interesting late 19th-c pub with well preserved original features; generously served food including signature corned beef hash, ales such as Holts and Black Sheep, decent wines by the glass, front bar with panelling, old gas lamp fittings and framed cartoons, stools at wall and window shelves, back green-tiled eating areas have rows of tables on black and white Victorian tiles, archways and high ceilings; seats out at back, open (and food) all day. *(Edward Edmonton)*

MANCHESTER SJ8298

New Oxford (0161) 832 7082
Bexley Square, Salford; M3 6DB Red-brick Victorian corner pub with up to 18 well kept changing ales (chalked on blackboard), plus extensive range of draught and bottled continental beers, real ciders too, light airy feel in small front bar and back room, coal fire, low-priced basic food till 6pm; open mike and quiz nights, monthly beer festivals, juke box, free wi-fi; café-style seating out in square, open all day. *(Larry King)*

MANCHESTER SJ8398

★**Oast House** (0161) 829 3830
Crown Square, Springfields; M3 3AY Quirky mock-up of a kentish oast house surrounded by modern high-rises; lofty rustic interior with bare boards, timbers and plenty of tables, good selection of draught and bottled beers, wines and cocktails, enjoyable fairly priced food from deli boards to barbecues and rotisserie grills, friendly helpful young staff, busy cheerful atmosphere; background and nightly live music; children welcome, spacious outside seating area, open all day (till 2am Fri, Sat). *(Chris Parker)*

MANCHESTER SJ8397

★**Peveril of the Peak**
(0161) 236 6364 *Great Bridgewater Street; M1 5JQ* Vivid art nouveau external tilework and three sturdily furnished old-fashioned bare-boards rooms, interesting pictures, lots of mahogany, mirrors and stained or frosted glass, log fire, four ales such as Brightside, Seven Bro7hers, Skinners and Timothy Taylors from central servery, cheap basic lunchtime food; background music, TV, table football and pool; children and dogs welcome, pavement tables, open all day. *(Dr and Mrs A K Clarke)*

MANCHESTER SJ8498

Port Street Beer House
(0161) 237 9949 *Port Street; M1 2EQ* Fantastic range of draught and bottled craft beers along with well kept changing ales, knowledgeable staff, no food, can get very busy but more room upstairs; events such as 'meet the brewer' and 'tap takeovers'; open all day weekends, from 2pm Fri, 4pm other days. *(Angela and Steve Heard)*

MANCHESTER SJ8397

Rain Bar (0161) 235 6500
Great Bridgewater Street; M1 5JG Bare boards and lots of woodwork in former umbrella works, Lees ales and plenty of wines by the glass, good choice of enjoyable fair value food from sandwiches to grills, friendly relaxed atmosphere, nooks and corners, coal fire in small snug, large upstairs bar/function room; background music; good back terrace overlooking Rochdale Canal, handy for Bridgewater Hall, open (and food) all day, Sun till 8pm. *(Dr and Mrs A K Clarke)*

MANCHESTER SJ8398

Sams Chop House (0161) 834 3210
Back Pool Fold, Chapel Walks; M2 1HN Downstairs dining pub (offshoot from Mr Thomas's Chop House) with original Victorian décor, enjoyable british food served by formal waiters, such as steak and kidney pudding, corned beef hash and various grills, weekend brunch, well kept beers and good wine choice, a former haunt of LS Lowry (a bronze statue of him sits contemplatively at the bar), back restaurant with black and white tiled floor; background music, sports TV; children welcome, some pavement tables, open all day. *(Larry King)*

MANCHESTER SJ8498

Smithfield (0161) 819 2767

Swan Street; M4 5JZ Simply presented pub on edge of the Northern Quarter owned by Blackjack brewery, their ales and guests from six handpumps, also a dozen craft kegs, real cider and good selection of spirits, straightforward food such as sausages and pies, three main areas with vintage mismatched furniture on wood floors; occasional live music, traditional games including darts, shove-ha'penny and table skittles; dogs welcome, open all day weekends, from 4pm Mon, 2pm Tues-Fri. *(Edward Edmonton)*

MARPLE SJ9389

Hare & Hounds (0161) 427 0293

Dooley Lane (A627 W); SK6 7EJ Well run dining pub above River Goyt with modern layout and décor; big helpings of tasty traditional food at reasonable prices from sandwiches up, Hydes ales and a guest, friendly service; background music; well behaved children welcome, outside seating, open (and food) all day. *(Michael Butler)*

MARPLE SJ9588

Ring o' Bells (0161) 427 2300

Church Lane; by Macclesfield Canal, bridge 2; SK6 7AY Popular old-fashioned canalside local with assorted memorabilia in four linked rooms; well kept Robinsons ales and good reasonably priced food (all day weekends); quiz nights and some live music including brass bands in the waterside garden; children welcome, dogs at licensees' discretion, own narrowboat, one bedroom, open all day. *(Scott and Charlotte Havers)*

MARPLE BRIDGE SJ9889

Hare & Hounds (0161) 427 4042

Mill Brow; from end of Town Street in centre turn left up Hollins Lane and keep on uphill; SK6 5LW Comfortable, civilised and well run stone-built country pub in lovely spot; good modern cooking including a grazing menu and popular Sun lunch, well kept Robinsons ales and nice wines, quite small inside (can get crowded), log fires; children and dogs (in bar) welcome, garden behind, open all day weekends (food till 7pm Sun), closed lunchtimes Mon-Thurs. *(Sandra and Neil White)*

MORECAMBE SD4264

Midland Grand Plaza

(01524) 424000 *Marine Road W; LA4 4BZ* Classic art deco hotel in splendid seafront position; comfortable if unorthodox contemporary furnishings in spacious sea-view Rotunda Bar, rather pricey but enjoyable food from interesting lancashire tapas to restaurant meals (popular and very good afternoon tea), good service; 1930s vintage festival Sept, free wi-fi; children welcome, 44 bedrooms, open all day. *(Darrell Barton)*

NEWTON SD6950

★ **Parkers Arms** (01200) 446236

B6478 7 miles N of Clitheroe; BB7 3DY Welcoming arch-windowed pub on edge of village, good locally sourced seasonal food from lunchtime sandwiches (home-baked bread) to imaginative specials, can eat in bar or restaurant, three real ales including Bowland, nice range of wines and decent coffee, pale green and cream walls, old oak boards or flagstones, upholstered window seats, open fires; children and well behaved dogs welcome, disabled access, lovely views from picnic-sets on front lawn, two bedrooms, closed Mon, Tues. *(Steve Whalley)*

PARBOLD SD4911

Windmill (01257) 462935

Mill Lane; WN8 7NW Modernised and opened-up beamed pub next to village windmill and facing Leeds & Liverpool Canal; mix of furniture on flagstone or oak floors including settles and some interesting carved chairs, candles on tables, animal prints on the walls, good open fire, five well kept ales (some from own microbrewery), several wines by the glass and generally well liked food from pub favourites up, friendly young staff; Tues quiz; children and dogs (in snug) welcome, too many steps for wheelchairs, seats out in front behind railing and on back paved terrace, good local walks, open all day, food all day weekends. *(Mike and Wena Stevenson, Steve Whalley)*

PRESTON SD5329

Black Horse (01772) 204855

Friargate; PR1 2EJ Listed Victorian pub in pedestrianised street; splendid ornate curved and mosaic-tiled main bar serving eight well kept ales (Robinsons and guests), friendly helpful staff, panelling, stained glass and old local photographs, open fires, two quiet cosy snugs, mirrored back area and upstairs function room; no food (snacks available) or children; open all day from 10.30am (midday Sun). *(Christine and Tony Garrett)*

RABY SJ3179

★ **Wheatsheaf** (0151) 336 3416

Raby Mere Road, The Green; from A540 heading S from Heswall, turn left into Upper Raby Road, village about a mile further; CH63 4JH Up to nine well kept ales in pretty 17th-c black and white thatched pub, simply furnished rambling rooms with homely feel, cosy central bar

We include some hotels with a good bar that offers facilities comparable to those of a pub.

and nice snug formed by antique settles around fine old fireplace, small coal fire in more spacious room, well liked reasonably priced bar food including good range of sandwiches/toasties, à la carte menu in large former cowshed restaurant, good friendly service, conservatory; children welcome, dogs in bar, picnic-sets on terrace and in pleasant back garden, open all day and gets very busy at weekends, no food Sun or Mon evenings. *(Shaun Mahoney, Steve Whalley)*

RAMSBOTTOM SD8016

Eagle & Child (01706) 557181
Whalley Road (A56); BL0 0DL Friendly refurbished roadside pub; generally well liked food from fairly ambitious menu using locally sourced produce including own vegetables, well kept Thwaites ales, real cider and decent choice of wines by the glass, good service; children welcome, orangery dining extension and interesting garden with valley views over roof tops to Holcombe Moor and Peel Tower, five owl-themed bedrooms (two with balconies), open all day Fri and Sat, till 7pm Sun. *(Robin Harris)*

RAMSBOTTOM SD8017

★**Fishermans Retreat** (01706) 825314
Twine Valley Park/Fishery signed off A56 N of Bury at Shuttleworth; Bye Road; BL0 0HH Remote yet busy pub-restaurant with highly regarded food (can be pricey) using produce from surrounding Estate and trout lakes (they can arrange fishing), also have own land where they raise cattle; mountain lodge-feel bar with beams and bare stone walls, five well kept ales including Copper Dragon, Moorhouses, Timothy Taylors and Thwaites, over 300 malt whiskies and good wine list, small family dining room and restaurant/function room extension, helpful friendly staff; a few picnic-sets with lovely valley views, closed Mon, otherwise open (and food) all day. *(Alan and Alice Morgan)*

RAMSBOTTOM SD7816

Major (01706) 826777
Bolton Street; BL0 9JA Whitewashed end-of-terrace stone local with two carpeted bars, banquettes and other pubby furniture, old local pictures, two-way woodburner; Bank Top Flat Cap, St Austell Tribute and three guests, enjoyable inexpensive home-made food with some choices available in smaller helpings, friendly helpful staff; maybe Tues quiz, sports TVs, pool, fruit machine; dogs welcome, beer garden behind, open all day, food all day Sat, till 6pm Sun. *(Louise and Simon Peters)*

RAWTENSTALL SD8213

Buffer Stops (0161) 764 7790
Bury Road; in East Lancashire Railway station; BB4 6EH Platform bar at Rawtenstall heritage station; five well kept ales including Outstanding Piston Broke, real cider/perry and selection of bottled beers, snacky food and pies, popular with locals and railway enthusiasts, good friendly service; quiz night first and third Weds of month; children (in former waiting room) and dogs welcome, platform tables, open all day (till 9pm Mon, Tues). *(P A Lord)*

RILEY GREEN SD6225

★**Royal Oak** (01254) 201445
A675/A6061; PR5 0SL Cosy low-beamed four-room pub (former coaching inn) extended by present owners; popular freshly made food (all day Sat and Sun) served by friendly efficient staff, Thwaites ales and maybe a guest from long back bar, ancient stripped stone, open fires and lots of nooks and crannies, impressive woodwork and some bric-a-brac, seats from high-backed settles to plush armchairs on carpet, comfortable dining rooms; children and dogs welcome, picnic-sets at front and in side beer garden, short walk from Leeds & Liverpool Canal, footpath to Hoghton Tower, open all day. *(Simon Granville)*

ROCHDALE SD8913

Baum (01706) 352186
Toad Lane (off Hunters Lane) next to the Rochdale Pioneers (Co-op) Museum; OL12 0NU Welcoming pub with plenty of old-fashioned charm in surviving cobbled street; seven well kept changing ales and lots of international bottled beers, good value food all day (Sun till 6pm) from sandwiches and tapas up including daily roast, cheerful young staff, bare boards, old advertising signs, conservatory; free wi-fi; children and dogs welcome, garden with pétanque, open all day (till midnight Fri, Sat). *(Frank Blanchard)*

ROMILEY SJ9390

Platform 1 (0161) 406 8686
Stockport Road next to station; SK6 4BN Red-brick Victorian pub with airy opened-up interior; six mostly local ales including a well priced house beer, good value pubby food from sandwiches up, carpeted upstairs restaurant called Platform 2; occasional live music; children welcome, small decked seating area outside, open (and food) all day, kitchen closes 7pm Sun. *(Martin and Joanne Sharp)*

SALESBURY SD6732

Bonny Inn (01254) 248467
B6245 Ribchester–Wilpshire; BB1 9HQ Cleanly refurbished and opened up with light airy bar and split-level carpeted dining room, popular freshly made food including blackboard specials, Thwaites ales and several wines by the glass, good service, back conservatory with fine Ribble Valley views; children and dogs (in bar) welcome, sturdy picnic-sets out in front under awning, more seats and views on terrace behind, open all day, food all day Sun. *(Gilly Todd)*

SCARISBRICK SD4011

Heatons Bridge Inn (01704) 840549
Heatons Bridge Road; L40 8JG Pretty 19th-c pub by bridge over Leeds & Liverpool Canal (popular with boaters); good value home-made food (not Sun evening, Mon, Tues), well kept Black Cat and two guests, friendly welcoming staff, four traditional cosy areas and dining room; free wi-fi; children and dogs welcome, pretty hanging baskets, garden with play area and World War II pillbox (pub hosts two vintage military vehicle events during the year), open all day. *(Christine and Tony Garrett)*

SILVERDALE SD4675

Royal (01524) 702608
Emesgate Lane; LA5 0RA Cleanly refurbished village-centre pub with smallish parquet-floored bar, three local ales from light wood counter, sofa and armchairs by woodburner in stone fireplace, good reasonably priced food including breakfast from 10am, friendly helpful service, small front conservatory and upstairs dining room; daily newspapers, sports TV, free wi-fi; children welcome, no dogs inside, picnic-sets on terrace, two self-catering cottages, open all day, food all day weekends. *(David Coupe)*

STALYBRIDGE SJ9598

Station Buffet (0161) 303 0007
The Station, Rassbottom Street; SK15 1RF Charming little Victorian buffet bar; period advertisements, old photographs of the station and other railway memorabilia on wood-panelled and red walls, fire below etched-glass mirror, Millstone, Timothy Taylors and six quickly rotating guests, two proper ciders, seven wines by glass and ten malt whiskies, straightforward low-priced food, newish conservatory and extension into what was the ladies' waiting room and part of the stationmaster's quarters with original ornate ceilings; free wi-fi; children and dogs welcome, open (and food) all day. *(Alan and Alice Morgan)*

STOCKPORT SJ8990

★**Arden Arms** (0161) 480 2185
Millgate Street/Corporation Street, opposite pay car park; SK1 2LX Cheerful Victorian pub in handsome dark-brick building; several well preserved high-ceilinged rooms off island bar (one tiny old-fashioned snug accessed through servery), tiling, panelling and two coal fires, sensibly priced lunchtime food from sandwiches to specials (also Thurs-Sat evenings), half a dozen well kept Robinsons ales, friendly efficient service; background and live music including Mon jazz, Tues quiz, free wi-fi; children and dogs welcome, tables in sheltered courtyard with smokers' shelter, open all day. *(John Wooll)*

STOCKPORT SJ8990

Crown (0161) 429 6948
Heaton Lane, Heaton Norris; SK4 1AR Busy but welcoming partly open-plan Victorian pub popular for its well kept changing ales (up to 16), also bottled beers and real cider, three cosy lounge areas off bar, bargain lunchtime food; frequent live music, pool and darts; dogs welcome, tables in cobbled courtyard, huge viaduct soaring above, open all day. *(Louise and Simon Peters)*

STOCKPORT SJ8890

Magnet (0161) 429 6287
Wellington Road North; SK4 1HJ Busy pub with 14 cask ales including own Watts beers from on-site brewery, real cider, pizza van Fri evenings; pool, darts and juke box; children (till 8pm) and dogs welcome, revamped beer garden with two raised terraces, open all day Fri-Sun, from 4pm other days. *(Darrell Barton)*

STOCKPORT SJ8990

Swan With Two Necks
(0161) 480 2341 *Princes Street; SK1 1RY* Traditional narrow pub with welcoming local atmosphere; front panelled bar, room behind with button-back wall benches, stone fireplace and skylight, drinking corridor, well kept Robinsons ales and decent lunchtime food (not Sun, Mon) from sandwiches up; dogs and children welcome, small outside area, open all day. *(Serena and Adam Furber)*

STRINES SJ9686

Sportsmans Arms (0161) 427 2888
B6101 Marple–New Mills; SK6 7GE Comfortable roadside local with panoramic Goyt Valley view from picture-window lounge bar; good changing ale range and enjoyable well priced honest food including specials and steak night (last Weds of month), small separate bar, log fires; folk night first Weds of month, darts, sports TV; children and dogs welcome, tables out on narrow side decking with steps down to paved terrace and smokers' shelter, open all day weekends. *(Angela and Steve Heard)*

TATHAM SD6169

Tatham Bridge Inn (01524) 221326
B6480, off A683 Lancaster–Kirkby Lonsdale; LA2 8NL Popular 17th-c pub with cosy low-beamed bar; well kept ales such as Tetleys, good range of enjoyable fairly priced home-cooked food, friendly helpful staff, restaurant with woodburner; children and well behaved dogs welcome, large garden, camping, open all day except Weds and Thurs when closed 2-5pm. *(Darrell Barton)*

TOCKHOLES SD6623

Black Bull (01254) 581381
Between Tockholes and Blackburn; BB3 0LL Welcoming 19th-c country pub on crossroads high above Blackburn; home to

the Three B's Brewery with their good beers including Black Bull Bitter from brick-fronted counter (tasting trays available), no food, opened-up neat interior with dark blue patterned carpet and leaf wallpaper, cushioned wall seats and high-backed chairs, woodburner, snug to left of entrance with another fire; background music; seats outside (some under cover – including summerhouse), good views, open all day weekends, otherwise from 4pm, closed Mon, Tues. *(Simon Granville)*

TOCKHOLES SD6621

Royal (01254) 705373

Signed off A6062 S of Blackburn, and off A675; Tockholes Road; BB3 0PA Friendly old pub with unpretentious little rooms and big open fires, four well kept ales such as local Three B's from tiny back servery, well priced pubby food including some blackboard specials (good steak night Weds); some live music, free wi-fi; children, walkers and dogs welcome, big garden with views from sheltered terrace, good walks including to Darwen Tower, closed Mon, otherwise open all day. *(Beverley and Andy Butcher)*

TODMORDEN SD9324

The Pub (01706) 812145

Lower part of Brook Street; OL14 5AJ New micropub/gin bar with cosy rustic décor, half a dozen well kept interesting ales from plank-faced servery and around 25 gins, helpful chatty staff, stools and window seats by small round tables, more room and loos upstairs; open all day till 9pm (10pm Fri, Sat). *(Jennifer Fairbanks)*

TUNSTALL SD6073

★**Lunesdale Arms** (01524) 236191

A683 S of Kirkby Lonsdale; LA6 2QN New owners and stylish refurbishment for this attractive 17th-c stone-built dining pub; opened-up interior with bar, split-level restaurant and snooker room, lots of modern artwork, Marstons Wainwright and Timothy Taylors Landlord, good range of wines and gins, highly regarded mediterranean-influenced food (best to book), friendly efficient service; children and dogs (in bar) welcome, pretty Lune Valley village, church has Brontë associations, open all day, food all day weekends. *(Christine and Tony Garrett)*

WADDINGTON SD7243

Higher Buck (01200) 423226

The Square; BB7 3HZ Welcoming pub in picturesque village; smartly modernised open-plan interior with airy new england feel and nice mix of seating, good food including pub favourites (all day Sun till 8pm), well kept Thwaites from pine servery, good friendly service; background music; children welcome, tables out on front cobbles and in small back courtyard, seven attractively refurbished bedrooms, open all day. *(Simon Granville)*

WADDINGTON SD7243

★**Lower Buck** (01200) 423342

Edisford Road; BB7 3HU Old stone village pub tucked away behind the church; four smartly presented little rooms, each with a warming coal fire, thriving front bar with scrubbed tables, large rug on bare boards and some stained glass panelling, five well kept real ales including Bowland, Moorhouses and Timothy Taylors, several wines by the glass and enjoyable reasonably priced food from sandwiches up, friendly helpful service; daily newspapers; children and dogs welcome, picnic-sets out on front cobbles and in the sunny back garden, good Ribble Valley walks nearby, open all day. *(Freddie and Sarah Banks, Steve Whalley)*

WADDINGTON SD7243

★**Waddington Arms** (01200) 423262

Clitheroe Road (B6478 N of Clitheroe); BB7 3HP Character inn with four linked bars, left one snuggest with blazing woodburner in huge fireplace, other low-beamed rooms have fine oak settles, chunky stripped-pine tables and lots to look at including antique and modern prints and vintage motor-racing posters, tasty food, well kept Moorhouses and four guests, good choice of wines by the glass and a dozen malt whiskies; children and dogs welcome, seats out at front looking over to village church, also two-level back terrace and neat tree-sheltered lawn, comfortable bedrooms, good walks in nearby Forest of Bowland, open all day. *(Angela and Steve Heard)*

WALLASEY SJ3094

Queens Royal (0151) 691 0101

Marine Promenade opposite the lake; CH45 2JT Imposing double-fronted Victorian seafront hotel with airy modernised bar; mix of furniture including comfy leather sofas and high tables on wood floor, interesting old photographs of New Brighton, six regional ales and good range of ciders from marble-topped island servery, enjoyable food from sandwiches to popular Sun carvery, afternoon teas, good friendly service, restaurant; free wi-fi; children welcome, front terrace with striking sea views, comfortable bedrooms, handy for Floral Pavilion theatre, open (and food) all day. *(Chloe and Michael Swettenham)*

WEST BRADFORD SD7444

Three Millstones (01200) 443339

Waddington Road; BB7 4SX Attractive old building, but more restaurant than pub, with all tables laid for owner-chef's highly praised good value food including set menu choices, four comfortable linked areas, beams, timbers and warming fires in two grand fireplaces, ales such as Bowland and Moorhouses, good choice of wines, friendly efficient service; five bedrooms in new

block, closed Sun evening, Mon, Tues.
(John and Eleanor Holdsworth)

WEST KIRBY SJ2186

White Lion (0151) 625 9037
Grange Road (A540); CH48 4EE
Friendly proper pub in interesting 18th-c sandstone building; several small beamed areas on different levels, Black Sheep, Courage and a couple of quickly changing guests, good value simple bar lunches (not Sun), coal stove; no children, steep steps up to attractive secluded back garden with fish pond, parking in residential side streets, open all day. *(Larry King)*

WHALLEY SD7336

★**Swan** (01254) 822195
King Street; BB7 9SN Modernised 17th-c former coaching inn with friendly staff and good mix of customers in spacious bar; a couple of Bowland ales plus Timothy Taylors Landlord, enjoyable food from fairly standard menu, further room with leather sofas and armchairs on bare boards; background music; children and dogs welcome, picnic-sets on back terrace and on grass strips by car park, six bedrooms, open (and food) all day.
(Gilly Todd)

WHEATLEY LANE SD8338

★**Sparrowhawk** (01282) 603034
Wheatley Lane Road; towards E end of village road, which runs N of and parallel to A6068; one way to reach it is to follow Fence signpost, then turn off at Barrowford signpost; BB12 9QG
Comfortably civilised 1930s feel in imposing black and white pub; oak panelling, parquet flooring and leather tub chairs, domed stained-glass skylight, six well kept ales including Reedley Hallows from cushioned leatherette counter, nice wines by the glass and good food from sandwiches and light lunches up, friendly young staff; background and live music; children and dogs (in bar) welcome, heavy wooden tables on spacious front terrace with good views to the moors beyond Nelson and Colne, open all day.
(Sandra and Neil White)

WISWELL SD7437

★**Freemasons Arms** (01254) 822218
Village signposted off A671 and A59 NE of Whalley; pub on Vicarage Fold, a gravelled pedestrian passage between Pendleton Road and Old Back Lane in village centre (don't expect to park very close); BB7 9DF Civilised dining pub with three linked rooms; antique sporting prints on cream or pastel walls, rugs on polished flagstones, carved oak settles and variety of chairs around handsome stripped or salvaged tables, candles and log fires, ales such as Bowland and Reedley Hallows, well chosen wines and highly praised imaginative food (all day Sun till 6pm), efficient friendly service from uniformed staff, more rooms upstairs; children and dogs (in bar) welcome, flagstoned front terrace with heaters and awning, open all day weekends, closed Mon, Tues and maybe first two weeks of Jan.
(Dr Peter Crawshaw)

WOODFORD SJ8882

Davenport Arms (0161) 439 2435
A5102 Wilmslow–Poynton; SK7 1PS
Popular red-brick country local (aka the Thief's Neck) run by same family since 1932; well kept Robinsons ales and enjoyable lunchtime food from snacks up (evening menu Fri and Sat), friendly service, refurbished snug rooms, log fires; sports TV; children and dogs welcome, tables on front terrace and in nice back garden with play area, open all day. *(Darrell Barton)*

WRIGHTINGTON SD5011

Rigbye Arms (01257) 462354
3 miles from M6 junction 27; off A5209 via Robin Hood Lane and left into High Moor Lane; WN6 9QB 17th-c dining pub in attractive moorland setting, welcoming and relaxed, with wide choice of good sensibly priced food including game menu and Thurs steak night, hot and cold sandwiches too, well kept Timothy Taylors and two guests, decent wines, several carpeted rooms including cosy tap room, open fires, separate evening restaurant (Weds-Sat, booking required); free wi-fi; children welcome, garden and bowling green, regular car club meetings, open (and food) all day Sun.
(Scott and Charlotte Havers)

WRIGHTINGTON BAR SD5313

Corner House (01257) 451400
B5250, N of M6 junction 27; WN6 9SE
Opened-up 19th-c corner pub-restaurant; good food (all day weekends) from traditional to more upscale choices, meal deals and daily specials, a couple of local ales and good quality wines, plenty of tables in different modernised areas; children and dogs welcome, seats outside, open all day.
(Millie and Peter Downing)

Leicestershire

and Rutland

BREEDON ON THE HILL SK4022 Map 7

Three Horseshoes

(01332) 695129 – www.thehorseshoes.com

Main Street (A453); DE73 8AN

Comfortable pub with friendly licensees and emphasis on popular food

Both the food and drink here are commendable and served by chatty, helpful staff; our readers enjoy their visits very much. Well run and nicely restored, it's an 18th-c dining pub with a stylishly simple feel in the clean-cut bar plus heavy worn flagstones, green walls and ceilings, a log fire, pubby tables and a dark wood counter. Marstons Pedigree and maybe a guest beer such as Shardlow Narrow Boat on handpump and decent house wines. Beyond the bar is a dining room with maroon walls, dark pews and tables, while a two-room dining area on the right has a comfortably civilised and chatty feel with big antique tables set quite closely together on coir matting, and colourful modern country prints and antique engravings on canary yellow walls. Even at lunchtime there are lit candles in elegant modern holders. The farm shop sells their own and other local produce: eggs, jams, meat, smoked foods and chocolates. Look out for the quaint conical village lock-up opposite. The hillside church is interesting to visit and can be seen for miles around.

Highly regarded food includes sandwiches, fish and spinach pancake with cheese, smoked salmon with dill mayonnaise, roast vegetable casserole, beef hotpot with yorkshire pudding, local sausages with mash and onion gravy, lamb shank with mustard mash, blackened salmon with crème fraîche, chicken in stilton sauce with garlic mash, duck breast with sweet potatoes, rib-eye steak with tarragon butter, and puddings such as treacle tart and chocolate whisky trifle. *Benchmark main dish: beer-battered fish and chips £12.50. Two-course evening meal £25.00.*

Free house ~ Licensees Ian Davison, Jennie Ison, Stuart Marson ~ Real ale ~ Open 11.30-2, 5.30-10.30; 12-3.30 Sun; closed Sun evening, Mon ~ Bar food 12-2, 5.30-9; 12-3.30 Sun ~ Restaurant ~ Children welcome ~ Dogs allowed in bar ~ Wi-fi *Recommended by Brian and Anna Marsden, Claire and Emma Braithwaite, Alison and Graeme Spicer, Clive and Fran Dutson, Malcolm Phillips, Usha and Terri Patel*

Please tell us if the décor, atmosphere, food or drink at a pub is different from our description. We rely on readers' reports to keep us up to date: feedback@goodguides.com, or (no stamp needed) The Good Pub Guide, FREEPOST RTXY–ZCBC–BBAZ, Stream Lane, Sedlescombe, Battle TN33 0PB.

CLIPSHAM SK9716 Map 8

Olive Branch

(01780) 410355 – www.theolivebranchpub.com

Take B668/Stretton exit off A1 N of Stamford; Clipsham signposted E from exit roundabout; LE15 7SH

Leicestershire Dining Pub of the Year

A special place for a drink, a meal or an overnight stay; bedrooms

Of course, the excellent food and carefully chosen range of drinks come in for top praise, but it's also true that this gently civilised inn remains so appealingly and remarkably unstuffy. Once labourers' cottages, the various small and attractive bar rooms have a country feel, with dark joists and beams, rustic furniture, an interesting mix of pictures (some by local artists), candles on tables and a cosy log fire in a stone inglenook fireplace; background music, bar billiards and board games. There's a beer named for the pub, Timothy Taylors Landlord and guests from Grainstore or Oakham on handpump, an enticing wine list (with at least 25 by the glass or carafe), a thoughtful choice of spirits and cocktails (they make their own using seasonal ingredients) and several british and continental bottled beers. Service is efficient and genuinely friendly. Outside, there are tables, chairs and big plant pots on a pretty little terrace, with seating on the neat lawn, sheltered in the crook of the two low buildings. A renovated Georgian property across the road from the main pub houses the individually decorated, restful bedrooms, and breakfasts are delicious. The wine shop also sells their own jams and chutneys, you can order individual dishes to take away and they can even organise food for a dinner party at home.

Exceptionally good food cooked by the chef-landlord includes monkfish tail wrapped in prosciutto with griddled baby leeks and romanesco sauce, seared pigeon breast with puffed wild rice, beetroot relish and asian pear, smoked garlic gnocchi with wild mushroom florentine, confit shallots and parmesan, grilled brill fillet with champ mash, asparagus, palourde clams and lime butter, corn-fed chicken breast with butternut squash and parsley risotto, slow-braised lamb shoulder with garlic potato terrine, braised red cabbage and herb crust, and puddings such as sticky parsnip pudding with crème anglaise and lemon thyme ice-cream and white chocolate crémeux with berries, balsamic ripple ice-cream and szechuan pepper brittle; they also offer a two- and three-course set lunch. *Benchmark main dish: spiced honey-glazed pork belly with pickled apple tatin, shallot purée and crushed chestnuts £19.95. Two-course evening meal £26.00.*

Free house ~ Licensees Sean Hope and Ben Jones ~ Real ale ~ Open 12-11; 12-10.30 Sun ~ Bar food 12-2 (2.15 Sat), 6.30-9.30; 12-2.45, 7-9 Sun ~ Restaurant ~ Children welcome ~ Dogs allowed in bar and bedrooms ~ Wi-fi ~ Bedrooms: £117.50/£135 *Recommended by Comus and Sarah Elliott, Ian Wilson, R L Borthwick, Sophie and James Collier, Abigail Slater, Naomi and Andrew Randall, Louise and Simon Peters*

GREETHAM SK9314 Map 7

Wheatsheaf

(01572) 812325 – www.wheatsheaf-greetham.co.uk

B668 Stretton–Cottesmore; LE15 7NP

Warmly friendly stone pub with interesting food, real ales, a dozen wines and seats in front and back gardens

There's always a happy, friendly atmosphere in this particularly well run pub, all helped along by the hands-on and hard-working licensees and their staff. The linked L-shaped rooms have both a log fire and a blazing open stove, traditional settles and cushioned captain's chairs around tables of varying sizes, and Brewsters Hophead, Grainstore Ten Fifty and Greene King IPA on handpump, a dozen wines by the glass, 30 gins and home-made cordials; you must book a table in advance for the restaurant. A games room has TV, darts, pool, board games and background music. The pub dogs are a dachshund and a labradoodle, and visiting dogs are welcome in the bar. There are chunky picnic-sets on the front lawn and more seats on a back terrace by a pretty stream with a duck house; pétanque. They sell their own pickles, chutneys and chocolates. There's a ramp for wheelchairs.

Cooked by the landlady (who bakes bread daily), the particularly good food includes lunchtime sandwiches, deep-fried rabbit and bacon fritters with sweet chilli sauce, thai red curry, steamed mussels, wild mushroom tortellini with morels, spinach and truffle oil, tiger prawns with garlic, parsley, lemon and home-made chips, gressingham duck breast with pickled pear, crispy cured ham, sage potatoes dauphinoise and red wine sauce, crispy pork belly with rösti potato and mustard sauce, and puddings such as salted chocolate brownie with banana and caramel ice-cream and orange and cardamom crème brûlée. *Benchmark main dish: chargrilled bavette steak with green peppercorn and tarragon butter and chips £17.50. Two-course evening meal £22.00.*

Punch ~ Lease Scott and Carol Craddock ~ Real ale ~ Open 12-3, 6-11; 12-11 Fri, Sat; 12-10.30 Sun; closed Mon (except bank holidays); first two weeks Jan ~ Bar food 12-2 (2.15 Sat), 6.30-9; 12-2.45 Sun ~ Restaurant ~ Children welcome ~ Dogs allowed in bar ~ Wi-fi *Recommended by Michael and Jenny Back, Geoff and Ann Marston, Melanie and David Lawson, Glen and Patricia Fuller, Peter and Alison Steadman*

LYDDINGTON SP8797 Map 4

Marquess of Exeter

(01572) 822477 – www.marquessexeter.co.uk

Main Street; LE15 9LT

Stone inn with contemporary décor, real ales and excellent food; bedrooms

There's something for everyone here. Good drinks, highly rated food, a relaxed, friendly atmosphere and comfortable bedrooms. The spacious open-plan areas have understated but stylish furnishings plus fine flagstone or wooden floors, thick walls, beams and exposed stonework. There's a mix of old tables and chairs, smart fabrics, leather sofas, pine chests and old barrels, and several open fires (one a quite striking piece in dark iron). A beer named for the pub (from Marstons) and Ringwood Boondoggle on handpump and around a dozen wines by the glass. Outside, a terrace has seats and picnic-sets, with more in the tree-sheltered gardens that seem to merge with the countryside beyond. Bedrooms are comfortable and attractive. The pub is named after the Burghley family, which has long owned this charming village (Burghley House is about 15 miles away).

As well as breakfast (7-9am Monday-Friday; 8-10am Saturday, Sunday), the impressive food cooked by the landlord includes sandwiches (until 6pm), saké-marinated salmon with asian salad, pickled ginger and wasabi mayonnaise, chicken liver parfait with home-made piccalilli, tandoori sea bass fillet with bombay potatoes, onion bhaji and ginger and yoghurt dressing, superseed and avocado salad with chicken, roasted butternut squash with pomegranate, mint salad and gorgonzola crostini, roasted lamb rump with chickpea ratatouille and mint, garlic and artichoke salsa verde, and puddings such as crème brûlée and white chocolate and apricot tiramisu. *Benchmark main dish: sharing plates £15.00. Two-course evening meal £21.00.*

Marstons ~ Lease Brian Baker ~ Real ale ~ Open 11-11 (midnight Sat); 12-10.30 Sun ~ Bar food 12-2.30, 6.30-9.30; 12-3, 6.30-9 Sun ~ Restaurant ~ Children welcome ~ Dogs allowed in bar and bedrooms ~ Wi-fi ~ Bedrooms: £79.50/£99 *Recommended by Heather and Richard Jones, Beth Aldridge, Mark Morgan, Ted and Mary Bates, Richard Kennell, Louise and Oliver Redman, Karl and Frieda Bujeya*

OAKHAM SK8509 Map 4

Grainstore £

(01572) 770065 – www.grainstorebrewery.com

Station Road, off A606; LE15 6RE

Super own-brewed beers in a former Victorian grain store, cheerful customers and pubby food

'A wonderful place' and 'you must combine a visit to this excellent pub with a brewery tour' are just two enthusiastic reports from readers. The rather special Grainstore brewery is housed in a converted railway grain warehouse and the ten own-brews are served traditionally on handpump at the left end of the bar counter and through swan necks with sparklers on the right. Following the traditional tower system of production, the beer is brewed on the upper floors of the building directly above the down-to-earth bar; during working hours, you'll hear the busy noises of the brewery rumbling overhead. They offer Cooking, Rutland Osprey, Rutland Panther, Ten Fifty, Triple B and a seasonal ale plus beer takeaways, and hold a beer festival (with over 80 real ales and live music) on the August Bank Holiday weekend. There's also a farm cider, several wines by the glass and 15 malt whiskies. Décor is plain and functional, with well worn wide floorboards, bare ceiling boards above massive joists supported by red metal pillars, a long brick-built bar counter with cast-iron stools, tall cask tables and simple elm chairs; games machine, darts, board games, giant Jenga and bottle-walking. In summer, the huge glass doors are pulled back, opening on to a terrace with picnic-sets. Brewery tours are available (though not on Friday or Saturday evenings) and you can book online. Disabled access.

As well as weekend breakfasts (9-11.30am), the popular food includes sandwiches, honey-glazed whole camembert with onion jam, barbecue-glazed chicken wings with coleslaw, sharing platters, stilton and garlic-stuffed mushrooms with fries, steak in ale pie, sausage, egg and chips, slow-cooked lamb shank with minted mash, beer-battered fish and chips, rump steak with onion rings, roasted tomatoes and mushrooms, and puddings such as chocolate brownie with chocolate sauce and lemon cheesecake. *Benchmark main dish: burger with toppings, coleslaw and skinny fries £11.95. Two-course evening meal £17.50.*

Own brew ~ Licensee Peter Atkinson ~ Real ale ~ Open 11-11; 9am-midnight Sat; 9am-11pm Sun ~ Bar food 12-3, 6-9; 9-9 Sat; 9-4 Sun ~ Children welcome ~ Dogs welcome ~ Wi-fi ~ Live music once monthly, quiz first Weds of month, comedy last Thurs of month *Recommended by Beth Aldridge, Anne and Ben Smith, Guy Henderson, Matt and Hayley Jacob, Barry Collett, Richard Tilbrook*

OAKHAM SK8608 Map 4

Lord Nelson ★

(01572) 868340 – www.kneadpubs.co.uk/the-lord-nelson

Market Place; LE15 6DT

Splendidly restored and full of interest, usefully open all day, real ales and ciders and enjoyable food

This is an interesting place with half a dozen rooms spread over two floors and you can choose from cushioned church pews, leather elbow chairs, long oak settles, sofas, armchairs or, to watch the passing scene, a big bow-window seat; carpet, bare boards and ancient red and black tiles, plus fresh new paintwork and William Morris wallpaper. There's plenty to look at too, from intriguing antique *Police News* and other prints (plenty of Nelson, of course) to the collections of mullers, copper kettles and other homely bric-a-brac in the heavy-beamed former kitchen with its Aga. You'll find a choice of London Pride and Oakham JHB with guest ales such as Black Sheep, Hopshackle Jaramillo and Sadlers Peaky Blinder on handpump; also 15 gins with half a dozen tonics, four farm ciders and 16 wines by the glass. Background music, TV and board games.

Rewarding food includes nibbles such as yorkshire pudding with dipping gravy, pigs in blankets with mustard mayonnaise, baked camembert with tomato chutney, hummus with toasted red peppers and flatbread, plus lentil and chickpea cassoulet with salted rosemary potatoes, local sausages with creamy mash and red wine and onion gravy, superfood salad with grilled chicken or smoked salmon, game hotpot with herb dumplings, pulled pork with garlic and herb crumb, cheddar, parmesan and garlic and rosemary bread, steak in stout pie, and puddings such as apple and blackberry crumble with vanilla custard and chocolate and clementine brownie with blood orange sorbet. *Benchmark main dish: pizzas – build your own £8.00. Two-course evening meal £14.00.*

Knead Pubs ~ Manager Lee Jones ~ Real ale ~ Open 9am-11pm ~ Bar food 12-2.30, 6-9; 9-9 Sat; 9-8 Sun ~ Children welcome ~ Dogs allowed in bar ~ Wi-fi *Recommended by Trevor and Michele Street, Barry Collett, Rosie and Marcus Heatherley, James and Becky Plath, Michael Butler, Gail and Arthur Roberts, Robin and Anne Triggs*

PEGGS GREEN SK4117 Map 7

New Inn £

(01530) 222293 – www.thenewinnpeggsgreen.co.uk

Signposted off A512 Ashby–Shepshed at roundabout, then turn immediately left down Zion Hill towards Newbold; pub is 100 metres on the right, with car park on opposite side of road; LE67 8JE

Intriguing bric-a-brac in unspoilt pub, friendly welcome, well liked food at fair prices and real ales; cottagey garden

For 40 years the kindly licensees here have created a homely and cheerful atmosphere and collected an extraordinary amount of bric-a-brac that covers almost every inch of the walls and ceilings in the two cosy tiled front rooms. The little room on the left, a bit like an old kitchen parlour (called the Cabin), has china on the mantelpiece, lots of prints and photographs, three old cast-iron tables, wooden stools and a small stripped kitchen table. The room to the right has attractive stripped panelling and more appealing bric-a-brac. The small back 'Best' room is good for private meetings and doubles as a gift shop selling pottery, glass and cards plus home-made gifts (which sell for charity). Bass, Marstons Pedigree and a quickly changing guest beer on handpump; background music and board games. There are plenty of seats in front of the pub, with more in the peaceful back garden. Do check the unusual opening and food service times carefully.

There's a visiting fish and chip van on Monday evening and a pizza van on Wednesday evening (you can eat both in the pub); Tuesday is pie night; chips and toppings are on offer on Friday nights, and filled rolls on Friday and Saturday lunchtimes; Sunday brunch (10-3) is for open toasties. Filled cobs are always available.

Enterprise ~ Lease Maria Christina Kell ~ Real ale ~ Open 5.30-11 Mon-Thurs; 12-2.30, 5.30-11 Fri; 12-3, 6.30-11 Sat; 10-3, 7-10.30 Sun ~ Bar food 5.30-9 Mon; 6-8 Tues; 6-9 Weds; 5.30-9.30

Thurs; 7-10, 12-2 Fri, Sat; 10-2 Sun toast menu ~ Well behaved children welcome ~ Dogs welcome ~ Wi-fi ~ Live folk club and quiz evenings (check website) *Recommended by Anne and Ben Smith, Brian and Sally Wakeham, Shona and Jimmy McDuff, Colin and Daniel Gibbs, Andrew Wall, Rob Anderson*

SILEBY SK6015 Map 7

White Swan

(01509) 814832 – www.whiteswansileby.co.uk

Off A6 or A607 N of Leicester; in centre turn into King Street (opposite church), then after mini roundabout turn right at Post Office signpost into Swan Street; LE12 7NW

Exemplary town local, a boon to its chatty regulars, with tasty home cooking and a friendly welcome

This has all the touches that mark the best of between-the-wars estate pub design, such as an art deco-tiled lobby, polychrome-tiled fireplaces, a shiny red Anaglypta ceiling and a comfortable layout of linked but separate areas including a small restaurant (lined with books). Packed with bric-a-brac from bizarre hats to decorative plates and lots of prints, it quickly draws you in thanks to the genuinely bright and cheerful welcome from the long-serving Mrs Miller. Fullers London Pride and maybe a guest beer on handpump and six wines by the glass. Mrs Miller also runs a highly successful outside catering business for domestic and business meals. The pub is particularly popular with walkers from Cossington Meadows and those moored at Sileby Marine.

Fair value food includes sandwiches, crispy-coated brie with cranberry sauce, smoked haddock mini fishcakes with tartare sauce, stilton and mushroom pie, chicken breast in parmesan cheese sauce topped with parma ham, moroccan-style lamb with couscous, spicy prawn linguine with tomato, garlic and chilli sauce, steak casserole in red wine gravy, rump steak with sausage and black pudding, and puddings such as chocolate brownie and apple pie; they also offer a one-, two- and three-course daily menu. *Benchmark main dish: beef cobbler topped with a stilton scone £11.75. Two-course evening meal £16.25.*

Free house ~ Licensee Theresa Miller ~ Real ale ~ Open 6-10 Tues-Sat; 6-11 Sat; 12-3.30 Sun; closed Sun evening, all day Mon, lunchtimes Tues-Sat ~ Bar food 6-8.30 Tues-Sat; 12-1.30 Sun ~ Restaurant ~ Children welcome ~ Dogs allowed in bar ~ Wi-fi

Recommended by John Harris, Neil Allen, Jack Trussler, Simon and Alex Knight, Julia and Fiona Barnes, Mark Morgan

SUTTON CHENEY SK4100 Map 4

Hercules Revived

(01455) 699336 – www.herculesrevived.co.uk

Off A447 3 miles S of Market Bosworth; CV13 0AG

Attractively furnished bar and upstairs dining rooms, highly regarded food, real ales and helpful staff

There's plenty of space here (and a warm welcome) for drinkers or diners and the atmosphere is relaxed and chatty. The long bar has brown leather wall seating with attractive scatter cushions, upholstered brown and white checked or plain wooden church chairs around various tables, rugs on wooden flooring, fresh flowers, prints and ornamental plates on creamy yellow walls and a big open fire; background music. There are high leather chairs against the rough hewn counter, where they serve Church End What the Foxs Hat and Sharps Doom Bar on handpump and ten wines by the glass. Upstairs, each of the interlinked, grey-carpeted dining rooms has its own colour scheme and tartan dining chairs around dark wooden tables; one wall is a giant map of the area. There are picnic-sets with parasols on the little back terrace, with views across a meadow to the church. Dogs are allowed in the downstairs area.

Quite a choice of much enjoyed food includes salmon, crab and prawn tian with tomato and spring onion salsa, marinated chilli chicken with crispy tortilla spaghetti and sour cream and guacamole, falafel and field mushroom burger with chilli jam and chips, a curry of the day, slow-braised beef stew with smoked bacon, baby mushrooms and onion with cheddar mash, duck breast and confit duck with potato croquette, parsnip purée and raspberry and redcurrant jus, sea bass with leek-crushed potatoes and lemon beurre blanc, and puddings such as chocolate and hazelnut brownie with orange jelly and chocolate custard and vanilla cheesecake with braised rhubarb, ginger syrup and rhubarb ice-cream. *Benchmark main dish: trio of pork (loin, pulled pork, wild boar sausage) with chive mash and gravy £16.95. Two-course evening meal £23.00.*

Free house ~ Licensee Oliver Warner ~ Real ale ~ Open 12-3.30, 6-11; 12-11 Sat; 12-6 Sun ~ Bar food 12-2.30, 6-9; 12-4 Sun ~ Restaurant ~ Children welcome ~ Dogs allowed in bar *Recommended by Lindy Andrews, Alison and Michael Harper, Charles and Maddie Bishop, Celia Caulkin, David and Charlotte Green, John and Delia Franks*

SWITHLAND SK5512 Map 7

Griffin

(01509) 890535 – www.griffininnswithland.co.uk

Main Street; between A6 and B5330, between Loughborough and Leicester; LE12 8TJ

A good mix of cheerful customers and well liked food in a well run, busy pub

The three beamed communicating rooms in this attractive stone-built pub are cosy and traditional with some panelling, leather armchairs and sofas, cushioned wall seating, a woodburner, a nice mix of wooden tables and chairs and lots of bird prints. Stools line the counter where Everards Original, Sunchaser and Tiger and a couple of changing guests such as Bath Gem and Everards Tubby are well kept on handpump plus a couple of farm ciders, several malt whiskies and wines by the glass from a good list; background music. The terrace, screened by plants, has wicker seats and there are more seats in the streamside garden overlooking open fields, as well as painted picnic-sets outside the Old Stables. They also have a café/deli selling local produce and artisan products. This is a tucked-away village with walks in nearby Swithland Wood or Bradgate Park. Good wheelchair access and disabled facilities.

Pleasing food includes baguettes, spiced turkish lamb kofta with mint yoghurt, moules marinière, thai green vegetable curry, beef or tandoori chicken burgers with toppings, coleslaw and fries, beer-battered fresh fish and chips, lambs liver with mash and onion gravy, chicken parmigiano with genovese (potatoes, green beans, pesto and parmesan) pasta, hake fillets with fennel and parmentier potatoes and chilli and tomato salsa, and puddings such as peanut butter and white chocolate cheesecake and ginger, rhubarb and granola fool. *Benchmark main dish: paella (chicken, chorizo, squid, king prawns and mussels) £13.95. Two-course evening meal £20.00.*

Everards ~ Tenant John Cooledge ~ Real ale ~ Open 12-11 (10.30 Sun) ~ Bar food 12-2.30, 5.30-9 (9.30 Fri); 12-9.30 Sat; 12-8 Sun ~ Restaurant ~ Children welcome ~ Dogs allowed in bar ~ Wi-fi *Recommended by Susan Eccleston, Peter Pilbeam, Dr and Mrs A K Clarke, Justine and Neil Bonnett, Audrey and Andrew Nichols, Nicholas and Lucy Sage, Peter and Emma Kelly*

It's very helpful if you let us know up-to-date food prices when you report on pubs.

WING SK8902 Map 4

Kings Arms

(01572) 737634 – www.thekingsarms-wing.co.uk

Village signposted off A6003 S of Oakham; Top Street; LE15 8SE

Former farmhouse with big log fires, super choice of wines by the glass and good modern cooking; bedrooms

If you stay here you can choose between the Old Bake House (the village's former bakery) or Orchard House (just up the pub's private drive); both have well equipped, pretty rooms, and breakfasts are particularly good. You'll find a medieval turf maze just up the road and it's only a couple of miles to one of England's two osprey hotspots. The neatly kept and inviting long main bar has two large log fires (one in a copper-canopied central hearth), various nooks and crannies, nice old low beams and stripped stone, and flagstone or wood-strip floors. Friendly, helpful staff serve almost three dozen wines by the glass, as well as Black Sheep and Grainstore Cooking and a guest ale such as Black Sheep Holy Grail on handpump, 30 wines by the glass, 12 gins, 14 malt whiskies and 12 home-made hedgerow liqueurs; dominoes and cards. There are seats out in front, and more in the sunny yew-sheltered garden; the car park has plenty of space.

High quality food uses produce from their own smokehouse, home-baked bread and home-made pickles, chutneys, preserves and so forth: big rolls, button mushrooms in stilton cream sauce, ham hock and smoked pheasant terrine with apricot, cranberry and red onion jam, ham with their own eggs and beef-dripping chips, squirrel crépinette and smoked partridge crown with bacon cabbage, mustard mayonnaise and parmentier potatoes, paneer or chicken korma, fallow deer saddle with dauphinoise potatoes, beetroot purée and red wine glaze, and puddings such as vanilla crème brûlée wih berry compote and vanilla and pistachio cookies and cherry and chocolate panettone pudding with warm cherry sauce; they also offer a weekly changing, good value two- and three-course set lunch. *Benchmark main dish: pie with mash and chips £15.50. Two-course evening meal £22.00.*

Free house ~ Licensee David Goss ~ Real ale ~ Open 12-3, 6.30-11; 12-3, 5-11 Fri; 12-11 Sat; 12-3 Sun; 12-3, 5-11 Sat in winter; closed Sun evening, Mon lunchtime ~ Bar food 12-2, 6.30-8.30 (9 Fri, Sat); 12-2 Sun ~ Restaurant ~ Children welcome but must be seated and eating ~ Dogs allowed in bar and bedrooms ~ Wi-fi ~ Bedrooms: £75/£100 *Recommended by Colin Chambers, Martin and Clare Warne, S Holder, Kate Roberts, Martin and Sue Neville, Millie and Peter Downing, Peter Andrews, Martin Day*

WYMONDHAM SK8518 Map 7

Berkeley Arms

(01572) 787587 – www.theberkeleyarms.co.uk

Main Street; LE14 2AG

Well run village pub with interesting food, interlinked beamed rooms, a relaxed atmosphere and sunny terrace

With the landlord cooking the extremely good food and the landlady making all her customers feel genuinely welcomed, this golden-stone inn is a lovely pub. The atmosphere is easy-going with knick-knacks, magazines, table lamps and cushions, and at one end (in front of a log fire), two wing chairs on patterned carpet beside a low coffee table. The red-tiled or wood-floored dining areas, dense with stripped beams and standing timbers, are furnished in a kitchen style with light wood tables and red-cushioned chunky chairs. Batemans XB, Castle Rock Harvest Pale and a guest from Grainstore on handpump, 11 wines by the glass and local cider.

Outside, on small terraces to either side of the front entrance, picnic-sets get the sun nearly all day long. Good surrounding walks.

Imaginative food cooked by Mr Hitchen includes sea trout gravadlax with pickled cucumbers and toasted sourdough, beef bresaola with rocket, parmesan and truffle salad, warm gratin of macaroni, courgettes, sun-dried tomatoes and olives, local maple-cured gammon with pineapple and free-range local egg, chicken breast with girolle mushrooms and pea risotto, honey-glazed duck breast with turnips, radish, greens and red wine sauce, roasted plaice with samphire, brown shrimps and jersey royals, and puddings such as local gooseberry trio (crumble, jelly and posset) and warm chocolate pudding with raspberry compote and raspberry sorbet; they also offer a two- and three-course lunch menu (January-March) and a two- and three-course set evening menu. *Benchmark main dish: local lamb rump with potato and chorizo gratin, ratatouille and rosemary gravy £18.00. Two-course evening meal £24.00.*

Free house ~ Licensee Louise Hitchen ~ Real ale ~ Open 12-3, 6-11; 12-5 Sun; closed Sun evening, Mon; first two weeks Jan, two weeks summer ~ Bar food 12-1.45, 6.30-9; 12-3 Sun ~ Restaurant ~ Children welcome ~ Dogs allowed in bar *Recommended by R L Borthwick, Rosie and John Moore, David Appleyard, Michael Butler, Barry Collett, David and Leone Lawson, Elise and Charles Mackinlay*

Also Worth a Visit in Leicestershire

Besides the fully inspected pubs, you might like to try these pubs that have been recommended to us and described by readers. Do tell us what you think of them: feedback@goodguides.com

AB KETTLEBY SK7519

Sugar Loaf (01664) 822473

Nottingham Road (A606 NW of Melton); LE14 3JB Beamed roadside pub with modern open-plan bar; wooden tables and chairs on tartan carpet, old prints and photographs, wood-strip end with coal-effect gas fire, airy dining conservatory, enjoyable reasonably priced pubby food from baguettes and light lunches to daily specials, Sharps Doom Bar and three guests, welcoming attentive service; background and occasional live music, TV, free wi-fi, darts; children welcome, no dogs inside, seats on small side terrace and grass, open (and food) all day. *(Johnston and Maureen Anderson, John and Sylvia Harrop)*

ASHBY-DE-LA-ZOUCH SK3516

Tap at No 76 No phone

Market Street; LE65 1AP High-street micropub in former tea rooms; fine range of ales and craft beers including Tollgate (tasting trays available), proper ciders and several wines by the glass, friendly helpful staff, cosy interior with scatter-cushion wall benches and high tables on light wood floor, pendant lighting and good woodburner, some old beams and a back skylit area, snacky food such as pork pies; open all day weekends, closed Mon and lunchtimes. *(Hannah Barlow)*

BARROWDEN SK9400

Exeter Arms (01572) 747365

Main Street, just off A47 Uppingham–Peterborough; LE15 8EQ Former coaching inn refurbished by current welcoming family; open-plan bar with beams, stripped stone and woodburner, Black Sheep, Grainstore, Greene King and Sharps from long central counter, enjoyable food from pubby choices up including two-course lunch deal Weds-Fri and steak night Weds, friendly helpful service; quiz first Thurs of the month, open mike third Thurs; children and dogs welcome, picnic sets on narrow front terrace with lovely views over village green and Welland Valley, more tables and boules in large garden behind, good local walks, three bedrooms, closed Sun evening, Mon and lunchtime Tues. *(Mike and Margaret Banks)*

BELMESTHORPE TF0410

Blue Bell (01780) 763859

Village signposted off A16 just E of Stamford; PE9 4JG Cottagey 17th-c stone pub in attractive remote hamlet; good keenly priced home-made food and decent range of well kept ales such as Grainstore and Oakham, friendly welcoming staff, comfortable dining areas either side of central bar, beams and huge inglenook; children and dogs welcome, seats in garden, open all day weekends, closed Mon lunchtime. *(Barry Collett)*

BRANSTON SK8129

Wheel (01476) 870376

Main Street near the church; NG32 1RU Beamed 18th-c stone-built village pub with enjoyable food from sandwiches up including set lunch/early evening deal, three well kept changing ales such as Brewsters from central servery (May beer festival), proper cider and good choice of wines, friendly staff, woodburner and open fires; background and occasional live music, skittle alley; children welcome, dogs in bar, attractive garden, splendid countryside near Belvoir Castle, open all day (till 8pm Sun). *(Sophie and James Collier)*

BRAUNSTON SK8306

Blue Ball (01572) 722135

Off A606 in Oakham; Cedar Street opposite church; LE15 8QS Pretty 17th-c thatched and beamed dining pub with good food (not Sun evening) from light lunches up, well kept ales including Marstons EPA and one badged for them, decent choice of wines, happy hour 5-7pm Fri and Sun, friendly welcoming staff, log fires, leather furniture and country pine in linked rooms, small conservatory; monthly jazz Sun lunchtime, free wi-fi; children and dogs (in bar) welcome, painted furniture on decking, attractive village, open all day Sat, till 8pm Sun, closed Mon. *(Barry Collett)*

BRAUNSTON SK8306

Old Plough (01572) 722714

Off A606 in Oakham; Church Street; LE15 8QT Comfortably opened-up black-beamed village local; four well kept changing ales, craft beers and good range of gins, food (not Sun evening) from ciabattas to grills including good value weekday lunch deal, log fire, back dining conservatory; free wi-fi; children, dogs and muddy boots welcome, tables in sheltered back garden with pétanque, five bedrooms, open all day. *(Barry Collett)*

BRUNTINGTHORPE SP6089

★**Joiners Arms** (0116) 247 8258

Off A5199 S of Leicester: Church Walk/ Cross Street; LE17 5QH More restaurant than pub with most of the two beamed rooms set for eating, drinkers have area by small light oak bar with open fire; civilised relaxed atmosphere, candles on tables, elegant dining chairs and big flower arrangements, first class imaginative food served by efficient friendly staff, cheaper set menu option Mon-Sat lunchtimes/Tues evening, plenty of wines by the glass including champagne, one mainstream ale such as Greene King or Sharps; picnic-sets in front, closed Sun evening, Mon. *(Audrey and Andrew Nichols)*

BUCKMINSTER SK8822

★**Tollemache Arms** (01476) 860477

B676 Colsterworth–Melton Mowbray; Main Street; NG33 5SA 19th-c country dining inn with good food from pub favourites up in bar or restaurant, OAP lunch Thurs and other deals; boarded floors in linked areas with mix of wooden furniture including some small hand-made pews, armchairs by open fire in bar, leather sofas in library room off restaurant, Grainstore, Oakham and a guest such as Adnams, good choice of wines by the glass and several malt whiskies, friendly attentive service; background music, TV, free wi-fi; children and dogs (in bar) welcome, plenty of teak tables and chairs in sizeable garden, comfortable well equipped bedrooms, good breakfast, lovely village and handy for A1, open (and food) all day Sat, till 5pm Sun, closed Mon. *(Lauren and Dan Frazer, Deborah and Duncan Walliams)*

BURBAGE SP4492

Anchor (01455) 636107

Church Street; LE10 2DA Popular nautically themed pub (locals call it the Yacht Club), opened-up interior with beams, woodburners and some red plush, well kept Marstons-related ales, friendly staff, no food (maybe cobs on the bar); weekly live music, Sun winter quiz, sports TV; dogs welcome, circular picnic-sets in sunken garden behind, pleasant village, open all day. *(Matt Francis)*

BURROUGH ON THE HILL SK7510

Grants (01664) 452141

Off B6047 S of Melton Mowbray; Main Street; LE14 2JQ Cosy old pub with own Parish ales (brewed next door) including the fearsomely strong Baz's Bonce Blower, well liked food served by helpful staff, open fires, restaurant and games room; occasional live music, sports TV, free wi-fi; children and dogs welcome, tables in garden, good walk to nearby Iron Age fort, open all day weekends, closed Mon. *(John and Delia Franks)*

BURTON OVERY SP6797

Bell (0116) 259 2365

Main Street; LE8 9DL This popular 1930s pub was for sale as we went to press, so may be changes; open-plan L-shaped bar with comfortable sofas and log fire, ales such as Langton and Timothy Taylors, good choice of well liked/priced blackboard food (not Mon) from lunchtime sandwiches up; friendly service, separate dining room used mainly for larger parties; children welcome, nice garden and lovely village, open all day weekends, closed lunchtimes Mon and Tues. *(R King)*

CALDECOTT SP8693

Plough (01536) 770284

Main Street; LE16 8RS Welcoming pub in attractive ironstone village; carpeted bar with banquettes and small tables leading to spacious eating area, log fires, four well kept changing beers, real ciders and wide range of popular inexpensive food including blackboard specials, prompt service; children and dogs welcome, good-sized garden at back, bedrooms and self-catering apartments, closed weekday lunchtimes. *(Robin and Anne Triggs)*

COLEORTON SK4016

Angel (01530) 834742

The Moor; LE67 8GB Friendly and homely with good range of enjoyable reasonably priced food (all day Sun) including carvery, well kept beers such as Marstons Pedigree, hospitable attentive staff, beams and open fire; children welcome, tables outside, open all day Sun. *(Dave Sibury)*

COLEORTON SK4117

★**George** (01530) 834639
Loughborough Road (A512 E); LE67 8HF Traditional and homely with well divided beamed bar, scatter-cushioned pews and wall seats, church candles on tables, dark panelled dado with local photographs above, shelves of books, leather sofa and tartan-upholstered tub chairs by woodburner, ales such as Leatherbritches, Marstons and Tollgate, several wines by the glass and popular fair value food, friendly young staff, bigger room on left with another woodburner and plenty to look at; background music, free wi-fi; well behaved children welcome, dogs in bar, spreading back garden with sturdy furniture and country views, open all day Fri, Sat, till 9pm Sun; new management as we went to press, so may be changes. *(Mark Morgan, Jeremy Snow, Malcolm and Pauline Pellatt)*

CROXTON KERRIAL SK8329

Geese & Fountain (01476) 870350
A607 SW of Grantham; NG32 1QR Modernised 17th-c coaching inn with five real ales such as Brewsters, Grainstore and Oakham, several craft beers and extensive bottled range, also organic wines and some interesting spirits, wide choice of food from sandwiches and pizzas up, big open-plan beamed bar with log fire, dining room and garden room; occasional live music, darts; children, walkers and dogs welcome, secure bike racks for cyclists, picnic-sets in inner courtyard and sloping garden with views, seven good bedrooms in separate block, open all day summer, best to check winter hours. *(Ian Herdman)*

DADLINGTON SP4097

Dog & Hedgehog (01455) 213151
The Green, opposite church; CV13 6JB Popular red-brick village dining pub with good choice of food including well liked Sun lunch, friendly staff and hands-on character landlord, rebadged ales from brewers such as Quartz and Tunnel, nice wines, restaurant; children and dogs welcome, garden looking down to Ashby-de-la-Zouch Canal, closed Sun evening, otherwise open all day. *(Glen and Patricia Fuller)*

DISEWORTH SK4524

Plough (01332) 810333
Near East Midlands Airport and M1 junction 23A; DE74 2QJ Extended 16th-c beamed pub with well kept ales such as Bass, Marstons and Timothy Taylors, low-priced traditional food (not Sun evening), friendly staff, bar and spacious well divided restaurant, log fires; children and dogs welcome, large paved terrace with steps up to lawn, handy for Donington Park race track, open all day. *(Frank Hacking)*

EXTON SK9211

Fox & Hounds (01572) 812403
The Green; signed off A606 Stamford–Oakham; LE15 8AP Handsome 17th-c inn facing small village green; high-ceilinged candlelit lounge with comfortable seating and big stone fireplace, well cooked/presented food here or in more formal restaurant, Grainstore, Greene King and a guest, nice wines by the glass, attentive service; soft background music; children welcome, dogs in bar, sheltered walled garden overlooking pretty paddocks, three bedrooms, handy for Rutland Water and the gardens at Barnsdale, open all day in summer. *(Mrs D A Thatcher)*

FOXTON SP6989

★**Foxton Locks** (0116) 279 1515
Foxton Locks, off A6 3 miles NW of Market Harborough (park by bridge 60/62 and walk); LE16 7RA Busy place in great canalside setting at foot of spectacular flight of locks; large comfortably reworked L-shaped bar, popular pubby food including Sun carvery, converted boathouse (not always open) for snacks, friendly service, well kept ales including Theakstons and one named for the pub; some live music, free wi-fi; children and dogs welcome, glassed-in dining 'terrace' overlooking the water, steps down to fenced waterside lawn, good walks, open (and food) all day. *(Gerry and Rosemary Dobson, Mike and Margaret Banks)*

GADDESBY SK6813

Cheney Arms (01664) 840260
Rearsby Lane; LE7 4XE Friendly red-brick country pub set back from the road; bar with bare-boards and terracotta-tiled floor, well kept Everards and a guest from brick-faced servery, open fires including inglenook in more formal dining room, big helpings of reasonably priced food (not Sun evening, Mon) from good lunchtime baguettes up, Weds pie night, Thurs steaks; sports TV, free wi-fi; children welcome, disabled access, walled back garden with smokers' shelter, lovely medieval church nearby, four bedrooms, closed Mon lunchtime. *(Nicholas and Lucy Sage)*

GILMORTON SP5787

Grey Goose (01455) 552555
Lutterworth Road; LE17 5PN Popular bar-restaurant with good range of enjoyable freshly made food including lunchtime/early evening weekday set menu and Sun carvery, ales such as Sharps Doom Bar and several wines by the glass, good friendly staff coping well at busy times, light contemporary décor, stylish wood and metal bar stools mixing with comfortable sofas and armchairs, woodburner in stripped-brick fireplace;

modern furniture on terrace, closed Sun evening, otherwise open all day. *(Mike and Margaret Banks)*

GLASTON SK8900

Old Pheasant (01572) 822326

A47 Leicester–Peterborough, E of Uppingham; LE15 9BP Attractive much-extended stone inn; beamed bar with inglenook log fire and some comfortable leather armchairs, well kept Grainstore from central brick servery, good range of generously served food including Weds steak night, steps up to restaurant; bar billiards; children and dogs (in bar) welcome, picnic-sets on sheltered terrace, good value bedrooms, open all day. *(Mike and Margaret Banks)*

GREETHAM SK9214

Plough (01572) 813613

B668 Stretton–Cottesmore; LE15 7NJ Traditional village pub, comfortable and welcoming, with good home-made food including weekday deals, breakfast Sat from 9.30am, can eat in cosy lounge or fire-divided restaurant, Grainstore, Timothy Taylors and guests, helpful friendly service; children and dogs welcome, garden behind, good local walks and not far from Rutland Water, closed Tues lunchtime, otherwise open all day. *(Abigail Slater)*

GRIMSTON SK6821

Black Horse (01664) 812358

Off A6006 W of Melton Mowbray; Main Street; LE14 3BZ Steps up to popular old village-green pub on two levels; welcoming licensees and friendly locals, well kept Adnams, Marstons and a couple of guests, decent wines, fairly priced traditional food from baguettes to blackboard specials, open fire; darts; children welcome, pétanque in back garden, attractive village with stocks and 13th-c church, closed Sun evening. *(John and Delia Franks)*

GUMLEY SP6890

Bell (0116) 279 0126

NW of Market Harborough; Main Street; LE16 7RU Friendly beamed village local; L-shaped bar with hunting prints and two open fires, Timothy Taylors Landlord, Woodfordes Wherry and guests, fair-priced home-cooked food including blackboard specials, weekday lunch deal and steak nights (Mon, Weds); live music, sports TV; children and dogs welcome, terrace garden with pond, local walks and cycle routes, open all day weekends. *(Isobel Mackinlay)*

HALLATON SP7896

Bewicke Arms (01858) 555734

On Eastgate, opposite village sign; LE16 8UB Attractive 18th-c thatched dining pub; good interesting food from sensibly short menu using local ingredients, ales such as Grainstore and Timothy Taylors, proper cider and well chosen wines, bar dining areas and restaurant, log fires and woodburners, memorabilia from ancient inter-village bottle-kicking match (still held on Easter Mon); children and dogs welcome, disabled facilities, big terrace overlooking paddock, play area, three bedrooms in converted stables, café and shop, closed Mon, otherwise open all day. *(Abigail Slater)*

HARBY SK7531

Nags Head (01949) 869629

Main Street; LE14 4BN Popular old beamed pub with four comfortably refurbished linked rooms; good pubby food including burger menu and Tues evening deal, Jennings Cumberland, Marstons Wainwright and a guest, friendly service, real fires; live music first Fri of month and bank holidays, quiz last Thurs, sports TV, free wi-fi; picnic-sets in large garden, interesting Vale of Belvoir village, open all day Fri-Sun, closed Mon lunchtime. *(Robin and Anna Triggs)*

HINCKLEY SP4293

Railway (01455) 612399

Station Road; LE10 1AP Friendly chatty pub owned by Steamin' Billy, their ales and guests from seven pumps, also draught continentals and real cider, sensibly priced food including Weds pie and Thurs steak nights, friendly young staff, open fires; Sun night quiz, darts; dogs welcome, beer garden behind, handy for the station, open all day. *(David Seward)*

HOBY SK6717

Blue Bell (01664) 434247

Main Street; LE14 3DT Attractive well run thatched pub with good range of popular realistically priced food (smaller appetites catered for), friendly attentive uniformed staff, four well kept Everards ales and two guests, lots of wines by the glass, teas/coffees, open-plan and airy with beams, comfortable traditional furniture, old local photographs; background music, skittle alley and darts; children, walkers and dogs welcome, picnic-sets in valley-view garden with boules, open all day, food all day weekends. *(Audrey and Andrew Nichols)*

HOUGHTON ON THE HILL SK6703

Old Black Horse (0116) 241 3486

Main Street (just off A47 Leicester–Uppingham); LE7 9GD Welcoming village pub with enjoyable home-made food (not Sun evening, Mon) including Thurs pie night, well kept Everards and a guest (July beer festival), decent wines by the glass, opened up inside into distinct areas, mix of bare boards, tiles and carpet, some panelling; background and live music, regular quiz nights, sports TV, darts; children and dogs welcome, attractive big garden with boules, open all day Fri and Sun, closed Mon lunchtime. *(Mike and Margaret Banks)*

HUNGARTON SK6907

Black Boy (0116) 259 5410
Main Street; LE7 9JR Large partly divided restauranty bar with open fire; well priced food cooked to order by landlord-chef (weekend booking advised) including various themed nights, changing ales such as Greene King, Fullers and Wells, cheerful staff; background music; children welcome, picnic-sets on decking, closed Sun evening, Mon. *(Julian and Fiona Barnes)*

ILLSTON ON THE HILL SP7099

★**Fox & Goose** (0116) 259 6340
Main Street, off B6047 Market Harborough–Melton Mowbray; LE7 9EG Refurbished little village pub under same owners as the Foxton Locks at Foxton; two rooms keeping traditional feel with hunting pictures and assorted oddments including some stuffed animals, woodburner and open fire, well kept Everards, a guest beer and decent choice of other drinks, popular good quality home-made food (not Sun evening, Mon, Tues) from lunchtime huffers up, cheerful helpful staff; children, walkers and dogs (in bar) welcome, disabled access, outside seating at front and side, Sept onion growing competition, open all day Weds-Sat, till 9pm Sun, closed Mon lunchtime. *(R L Borthwick)*

KNIPTON SK8231

Manners Arms (01476) 879222
Signed off A607 Grantham–Melton Mowbray; Croxton Road; NG32 1RH Handsome Georgian hunting lodge reworked as comfortable country inn; bare-boards bar with log fire, four well kept ales such as Batemans and Fullers, nice choice of wines by the glass and good reasonably priced food, friendly helpful staff, sizeable restaurant with attractive conservatory; background music; children and dogs welcome, terrace with ornamental pool, lovely views over pretty village, ten comfortable individually furnished bedrooms, open all day. *(Abigail Slater)*

KNOSSINGTON SK8008

Fox & Hounds (01664) 452129
Off A606 W of Oakham; Somerby Road; LE15 8LY Attractive 18th-c ivy-clad village dining pub, beamed bar with log fire and cosy eating areas, well liked food (best to book) from traditional choices to blackboard specials, Fullers London Pride, attentive friendly service; children (over 8) and dogs welcome, big back garden, closed Sun evening, Mon and lunchtimes Tues-Thurs. *(John and Delia Franks)*

LANGHAM SK8411

Wheatsheaf (01572) 869105
Burley Road/Bridge Street; LE15 7HY Popular and relaxed village pub; central bar flanked by eating areas, four real ales including Fullers London Pride and Greene King Abbot, fine range of gins (150 and rising), good generously served home-made food including a vegetarian/vegan menu, friendly helpful staff; children and dogs welcome, seats on pleasant flower-decked terrace, closed lunchtimes Mon and Tues, otherwise open all day, food all day Sun. *(Barry Collett)*

LEICESTER SK5804

Ale Wagon (0116) 262 3330
Rutland Street/Charles Street; LE1 1RE Basic 1930s two-room corner local; nine well kept ales including own Hoskins Brothers beers, traditional cider, no food apart from baps, coal fire, upstairs function room; background music; handy for Curve Theatre and the station, open all day, closed Sun lunchtime. *(Frank Hacking)*

LEICESTER SK5804

Criterion (0116) 262 5418
Millstone Lane; LE1 5JN 1960s building with dark wood and carpeted main room; up to a dozen well kept ales and extensive range of bottled beers, real ciders too, good value stone-baked pizzas plus some other snacky food, room on left with games and old-fashioned juke box; regular live music and quiz nights, annual comedy festival Feb; picnic-sets outside, open all day and popular on Leicester Tigers match days. *(Frank Hacking)*

LEICESTER SK5804

Globe (0116) 253 9492
Silver Street; LE1 5EU Original character and lots of woodwork in partitioned areas off central bar; bare boards and some Victorian mosaic flooring, mirrors and working gas lamps, four Everards ales, three guests and a couple of real ciders, over a dozen wines by the glass, friendly staff, well priced food from bar snacks up including deals, function room upstairs; background music (not in snug); children and dogs welcome, metal café-style tables out in front, open all day. *(Frank Hacking)*

LEICESTER SK5804

King Richard III (0116) 262 6833
Highcross Street; LE1 4NN Nicely restored Victorian pub with chef-landlord's good interesting food from 'grazing boards' up using locally sourced ingredients, attentive friendly service, Everards and a couple of local guests, carefully selected wines and good coffee, back restaurant; walled beer garden, open all day Fri-Sun, closed Mon and lunchtimes Tues-Thurs, no food Sun evening. *(Frank Hacking, Ed Jennings)*

LEICESTER SK5804

★**Rutland & Derby Arms**
(0116) 262 3299 *Millstone Lane; nearby metered parking; LE1 5JN* Neatly kept

modern town bar with open-plan interior; long counter serving Everards and guests, 20 wines by the glass and good range of malt whiskies and other drinks, well liked food including pizzas and some german-influenced dishes; background and regular live music, Mon quiz, annual St Patrick's Day Guinness and oyster festival, free wi-fi; children welcome, sunny courtyard with tables under parasols, more seats on upper terrace, closed Sun, otherwise open (and food) all day (till 1am Fri, Sat). *(Ed Jennings)*

LEICESTER SK5804

Salmon (0116) 253 2301
Butt Close Lane, near bus station; LE1 4QA Small tucked-away Victorian corner pub with U-shaped bar, well kept Black Country ales, guest beers and a couple of ciders from 12 handpumps, simple food including bargain Sun lunch, friendly staff; sports TV; open all day. *(John Salter)*

LITTLE BOWDEN SP7386

Cherry Tree (01858) 463525
Kettering Road; edge of Market Harborough, near supermarket roundabout; LE16 8AE Traditional thatched and beamed pub with two bars, dining room and games room (darts, skittles and sports TV), well kept Everards, guest ales and enjoyable low-priced food from baguettes and basket meals up, cheerful efficient service; children and dogs welcome, two gardens, one with play area, the other for adults only, near 12th-c church, open all day Fri-Sun, no food Sun or Mon evenings. *(John Salter)*

LONG WHATTON SK4823

★**Royal Oak** (01509) 843694
The Green; LE12 5DB Compact smartly updated village dining pub with good well presented modern food along with pub favourites, set menu choices and Sun pie night, well kept ales such as Charnwood and St Austell, nice wines by the glass from extensive list, friendly efficient staff; comfortable spotless bedrooms in separate building, good breakfast, handy for East Midlands Airport, open all day. *(Michael Doswell)*

LYDDINGTON SP8796

★**Old White Hart** (01572) 821703
Village signed off A6003 N of Corby; LE15 9LR Popular and welcoming 17th-c inn across from small green; two cosy linked bars with log fires and heavy beams, cushioned wall benches and simple wooden furniture on tiled floors, some fine hunting prints, Greene King IPA and a guest, good food (not Sun evening in winter) including own sausages and cured meats (long-serving landlord is a butcher), half-price offer Mon-Thurs, efficient obliging service, attractive restaurant and small conservatory with rugs on strip-wood floors; children welcome, seats by heaters in pretty walled garden (dogs welcome here), eight floodlit boules pitches, handy for Bede House (EH) and good nearby walks, 14 bedrooms, open all day (may be a break Sun afternoon). *(Mike and Margaret Banks, Peter Andrews, Mr and Mrs D J Nash)*

MANTON SK8704

Horse & Jockey (01572) 737335
St Marys Road; LE15 8SU Welcoming early 19th-c pub under same ownership as the Fox at North Luffenham; updated low-beamed interior, modern furniture on wood or stone floors, woodburner, well kept ales such as Grainstore and Greene King plus a house beer (Fall at the First), decent fairly priced food from baguettes to blackboard specials, cheery service; background music; children and dogs welcome, colourful tubs and hanging baskets, terrace picnic-sets (they may ask for a card if you eat out here), nice location, on Rutland Water cycle route (racks provided), open all day in summer (all day Fri, Sat, till 7pm Sun in winter). *(Barry Collett, Mike and Margaret Banks)*

MARKET HARBOROUGH SP7387

Beerhouse (01858) 465317
St Marys Road; LE16 7DX Micropub conversion tucked away behind fish and chip shop; a dozen real ales tapped from stillage, plenty of craft kegs and a couple of real ciders, friendly knowledgeable staff, no food (can bring your own), simple interior with connecting rooms; Mon quiz and some live music, free wi-fi; dogs welcome, a few picnic-sets outside, closed lunchtimes Mon and Weds, all day Tues, otherwise open all day. *(John Salter)*

MARKET OVERTON SK8816

Black Bull (01572) 767677
Opposite the church; LE15 7PW Attractive low-beamed thatch and stone pub dating from the 17th c; good home-made food (booking advised) from pub staples up in long carpeted bar and two separate dining areas, woodburner, banquettes and sofas, well kept Black Sheep and a couple of guests, friendly welcoming staff; background and some live music, free wi-fi; children and dogs welcome, tables out in front by small carp pool, pretty village well placed for Rutland Water, two bedrooms, open till 6pm Sun, closed Mon. *(Barry Collett)*

MEDBOURNE SP7992

★**Nevill Arms** (01858) 565288
B664 Market Harborough–Uppingham; LE16 8EE Handsome stone-built Victorian inn facing stream and little footbridge; good bar and restaurant food served by friendly helpful staff, well kept ales such as Adnams, St Austell and Wells, craft kegs and good choice of wines by the glass including champagne, carpeted bar with beams and mullion windows, two woodburners (one in stone inglenook), modernised restaurant

with banquettes and light wood furniture on white tiles; children and dogs (in bar) welcome, streamside picnic-sets, back terrace and stable-conversion café (9am-5pm), ten bedrooms, open all day. *(Barry Collett)*

MELTON MOWBRAY SK7519

Anne of Cleves (01664) 481336

Burton Street, by St Mary's church; LE13 1AE Monks' chantry dating from the 14th c and gifted to Anne of Cleves by Henry VIII; heavy beams, flagstones and mullioned windows, tapestries on burnt orange walls, chunky tables, character chairs and settles, log fire, well kept Everards and guests, decent wines and generously served food, small end dining room; background music, free wi-fi; children and dogs welcome, tables in pretty little walled garden. *(Dr and Mrs A K Clarke)*

MELTON MOWBRAY SK7518

Boat (01664) 500969

Burton Street; LE13 1AF Chatty and welcoming local with well kept Adnams, Bass, Wells Bombardier and a guest, over 40 malt whiskies, no food, bar with panelling and open fire in range, another fire (not often used) in snug; live music, darts; dogs welcome, handy for the station, open all day Thurs-Sun (Fri from 2pm), closed lunchtimes Mon and Weds. *(Phil and Jane Hodson)*

MOUNTSORREL SK5715

Swan (0116) 230 2340

Loughborough Road, off A6; LE12 7AT Former coaching inn with split-level interior; log fires, old flagstones and stripped-stone walls, good well priced often interesting food from baguettes up (best to book evenings), monthly themed nights such as malaysian, greek and moroccan, friendly efficient staff, Black Sheep and other well kept ales, good choice of wines, neat dining area and restaurant; dogs welcome in bar, pretty walled back garden down to canalised River Soar, open all day weekends. *(Colin and Daniel Gibbs)*

MOWSLEY SP6488

Staff of Life (0116) 240 2359

Village signposted off A5199 S of Leicester; Main Street; LE17 6NT Gabled village pub with roomy fairly traditional bar, high-backed settles on flagstones, wicker chairs on shiny wood floor and stools around unusual circular counter, woodburner, ales such as Black Sheep, Exmoor and Wadworths, a dozen wines by the glass and decent whisky choice, well liked food from interesting mid-priced menu, also set evening deal Weds-Fri; background music; well behaved children welcome (no under-12s Fri and Sat nights), no dogs, seats out in front and on nice leaf-shaded deck, open Sun till 7pm, closed Mon (including bank holidays) and weekday lunchtimes. *(Mike and Margaret Banks)*

NORTH LUFFENHAM SK9303

★**Fox** (01780) 720991

Pinfold Lane; LE15 8LE Refurbished sister pub to the Horse & Jockey at Manton; flagstoned bar with woodburner, four well kept ales and several wines by the glass from light wood servery, lounge with comfortable seating on wood floor, exposed stone walls and another woodburner, good quality food including pub favourites, spacious modern dining room, friendly prompt service; darts and TV upstairs; children and dogs welcome, large planters and picnic-sets under parasols on paved terrace, pretty village, open all day weekends, closed Mon lunchtime. *(Barry Collett)*

OADBY SK6202

★**Cow & Plough** (0116) 272 0852

Gartree Road (B667 N of centre); LE2 2FB Converted farm buildings with extraordinary collection of brewery memorabilia in two dark back rooms – enamel signs and mirrors advertising long-forgotten beers, an aged brass cash register, furnishings and fittings salvaged from pubs and churches (there's some splendid stained glass behind the counter), own Steamin' Billy beers and several guests, two real ciders and a dozen malt whiskies, good generously served pubby food plus some interesting specials (booking essential weekends), long front extension and conservatory; background music, live jazz Weds lunchtime, TV, darts and board games, free wi-fi; children and dogs (in bars and garden) welcome, picnic-sets in the old yard, open all day, no food Sun evening. *(O K Smyth, Barry Collett, Mike and Margaret Banks)*

OAKHAM SK8508

Admiral Hornblower

(01572) 723004 *High Street; LE15 6AS* Attractive pub-hotel in former 17th-c farmhouse with several differently decorated areas, good imaginative food at sensible prices from interesting sandwiches and sharing boards up, also some pub favourites (with a twist) and good value set menus, three well kept ales, efficient friendly service; children and dogs welcome, seats out at front behind railings and in terrace garden, ten refurbished bedrooms, substantial breakfast, open all day, food all day Sun, weekend brunch from 9am. *(Richard Tilbrook, Michael Butler)*

OAKHAM SK8508

Wheatsheaf (01572) 723458

Northgate; Church Street end; LE15 6QS Attractive and popular 17th-c local near church; well kept Everards and guests, good selection of wines by the glass and generous pubby food including specials, cheerful comfortable bar with open fires, quieter lounge, back conservatory; some live music; pretty suntrap courtyard, open all day Fri-Sun. *(Barry Collett)*

OLD DALBY SK6723

★**Crown** (01664) 820320
Debdale Hill; LE14 3LF Extended and cleverly revamped 17th-c creeper-clad pub; cosy rustic rooms in original part, plenty of reclaimed wood, nice old floorboards, flagstones and eclectic collection of old and new furniture, shelves of books, advertising mirrors, even a stuffed hare holding a shotgun; Charnwood Vixen and guests, three ciders, 14 wines by the glass and cocktails, popular interesting food along with more traditional choices and good value set menu; background and some live music, quiz last Tues of month, darts and board games; children welcome, dogs in bar, partly covered garden room leading to sunny terrace and lawn, open all day weekends, closed Mon lunchtime, food till 6pm Sun. *(Phil and Jane Hodson, Christopher May, Emily and Toby Archer)*

REDMILE SK7935

★**Windmill** (01949) 842281
Off A52 Grantham–Nottingham; Main Street; NG13 0GA Old village pub under new management; snug low-beamed bar with sofas, easy chairs and log fire in large raised hearth, comfortable roomier dining areas with woodburners, wide choice of good generously served food including daily specials, well kept ales such as Adnams Ghost Ship and good choice of wines by the glass, efficient friendly young staff, pictures of 1980s TV series *Auf Wiedersehen, Pet* being filmed at the pub ; children, walkers and dogs welcome (resident labrador is Buster), sizeable front terrace, open all day Sat, till around 8pm Sun (no evening food), closed Mon and Tues. *(Phil and Jane Hodson)*

ROTHLEY SK5812

Woodmans Stroke (0116) 230 2785
Church Street; LE7 7PD Family-run 18th-c thatched pub with good value weekday lunchtime food from sandwiches up (order at the bar), well kept changing ales and nice wines by the glass, friendly staff, beams and settles in front rooms, open fire, old local photographs and rugby/cricket memorabilia; sports TV; pretty front hanging baskets, attractive garden with heated terrace and pétanque, open all day Sat. *(Barry Collett)*

RYHALL TF0310

Wicked Witch (01780) 763649
Bridge Street; PE9 4HH Village dining pub with highly regarded upmarket food cooked by chef-owner from weekly changing set menu, also occasional themed evenings, two dining areas and comfortable bar serving Banks's Mansfield and maybe a guest, nice wines, good friendly service; children welcome till 7pm, tables in back garden, closed Sun evening, Mon. *(Julian and Fiona Barnes)*

SADDINGTON SP6591

Queens Head (0116) 240 2536
S of Leicester between A5199 (ex A50) and A6; Main Street; LE8 0QH Welcoming village pub with well kept Everards, nice wines and good attractively presented food (all day Sat, till 6pm Sun) including Fri grill night, clean interior on different levels, country and reservoir views from dining conservatory and sloping terrace; free wi-fi; children welcome, garden play area, farm shop (9am-2pm), open all day Weds-Sun (closed 2.30-5.30pm Mon and Tues). *(David and Charlotte Green)*

SEATON SP9098

★**George & Dragon** (01572) 747418
Main Street; LE15 9HU New management and refurbishment for this cosy 17th-c stone pub; split-level interior with bar (former bakery) and separate restaurant, Bass, Grainstore and a beer badged for them, highly praised food from interesting varied menu including good Sun lunch, attentive friendly service; children and dogs (in bar) welcome, rattan-style tables and chairs on paved terrace, unspoilt hilltop village with good views of Harringworth Viaduct, three bedrooms, open all day Fri and Sat, till 9pm Sun, closed Mon-Thurs lunchtimes. *(Barry Collett)*

SHARNFORD SP4891

Bricklayers (01455) 271799
Leicester Road; LE10 3PP Welcoming 18th-c beamed and timbered village pub; big main bar, side lounge with woodburner and dining room in newer extension, beers such as Bass, Fullers and Greene King, decent choice of enjoyable reasonably priced pub food including Weds burger night, Thurs tapas/pizza night and popular Sun lunch (should book), friendly efficient staff; children welcome, garden, handy for Fosse Meadows nature park, open all day Fri-Sun. *(R L Borthwick)*

SHAWELL SP5480

White Swan (01788) 860357
Main Street; village signed down declassified road (ex A427) off A5/A426 roundabout – turn right in village; not far from M6 junction 1; LE17 6AG Attractive little 17th-c beamed dining pub with clean contemporary interior; good interesting food from landlord-chef along with some pub staples, local Dow Bridge ales and guests, lots of wines by the glass (wine tasting evenings), champagne breakfast Sat; children welcome, closed Sun evening and Mon, otherwise open all day. *(Isobel Mackinlay)*

SHEARSBY SP6290

Chandlers Arms (0116) 247 8384
Fenny Lane, off A50 Leicester–Northampton; LE17 6PL Comfortable

old creeper-clad pub in attractive village; seven well kept ales including Dow Bridge (tasting trays, June beer festival), a summer cider and good value pubby food including range of 'sizzling' dishes; background music, table skittles; children welcome, secluded raised garden overlooking green, open Sun till 7pm, closed Mon and lunchtimes Tues-Thurs. *(Abigail Slater)*

SOMERBY SK7710

★**Stilton Cheese** (01664) 454394
High Street; off A606 Oakham–Melton Mowbray, via Cold Overton, or Leesthorpe and Pickwell; LE14 2QB Friendly old ironstone pub with beamed bar/lounge, comfortable furnishings on red patterned carpets, country prints, plates and copper pots, stuffed badger and pike, open fire, Grainstore, Marstons and three guests, 30 malt whiskies, good reasonably priced pubby food along with daily specials, restaurant; children welcome, seats on terrace, peaceful setting on edge of pretty village. *(Mike and Margaret Banks)*

SOUTH LUFFENHAM SK9401

★**Coach House** (01780) 720166
Stamford Road (A6121); LE15 8NT Old roadside inn under new mother and son team (he cooks); stripped-stone and flagstoned bar, scatter cushions on short pews, log fire, four real ales including Greene King and Sharps, plenty of wines by the glass and much liked food from lunchtime sandwiches and pub favourites to upscale restaurant choices, friendly efficient service, separate snug with neat built-in seating, smarter more modern dining room; children and dogs (in bar) welcome, small back deck, seven bedrooms, open all day Sat, till 9pm Sun, closed Mon lunchtime. *(Sophie and James Collier)*

SPROXTON SK8524

Crown (01476) 861608
Coston Road; LE14 4QB Friendly fairly compact 19th-c stone-built inn; good reasonably priced food cooked by landlady, three well kept changing ales, good wines and coffee, light airy bar with woodburner, lounge area and restaurant; children and dogs (in bar) welcome, sunny courtyard, attractive village and good local walks, three bedrooms, open all day Fri-Sun, closed lunchtimes Mon-Thurs. *(Frank Hacking)*

STRETTON SK9415

★**Jackson Stops** (01780) 410237
Rookery Lane; a mile or less off A1, at B668 (Oakham) exit; follow village sign, turning off Clipsham Road into Manor Road, pub on left; LE15 7RA Attractive thatched former farmhouse with plenty of character; meandering rooms filled with period features, black-beamed country bar with wall timbering, coal fires and elderly settle on worn tile and brick floor, a couple of Grainstore ales, eight wines by the glass and ten malt whiskies, smarter airy room on right with mix of ancient and modern tables on dark blue carpet, corner fire, two dining rooms, one with stripped-stone walls and old open cooking range, much liked food including deals, warm friendly service; rare nurdling bench (a game involving old pennies), background music; children and dogs (in bar) welcome, closed Sun evening, Mon. *(Barry Collett, Ian Prince)*

THORNTON SK4607

Reservoir (01530) 382433
Main Street; LE67 1AJ Busy pub with pleasant modern décor, decent home-made food from varied menu (not Sun evening) including good value set lunch, Weds burger night and Tues/Thurs pie and wine evenings, Charnwood and Steamin' Billy ales, friendly efficient service, restaurant; children welcome, muddy boots and dogs in bar, good circular walk around Thornton Reservoir, open all day Sat, closed Mon. *(Dave Sibury)*

THORPE LANGTON SP7492

★**Bakers Arms** (01858) 545201
Off B6047 N of Market Harborough; LE16 7TS Civilised thatched restauranty pub with small bar; very good imaginative food (must book) from regularly changing menu including several fish/seafood dishes, cottagey beamed linked areas and stylishly simple country décor, a well kept ale from Langton (brewed in the village) and good choice of wines by the glass, friendly licensees and efficient service, maybe a pianist; no under-12s or dogs, picnic-sets in back garden with country views, closed Sun evening, Mon and weekday lunchtimes. *(R L Borthwick, Gerry and Rosemary Dobson)*

THRUSSINGTON SK6415

Star (01664) 424220
Village signposted off A46 N of Syston; The Green; LE7 4UH Neatly modernised 18th-c village inn; L-shaped bar with low stripped beams, broad floorboards and inglenook woodburner, unusual double-sided high-backed settle, Belvoir Star Bitter, a couple of guests and 14 wines by the glass, steps up to skylit dining room with banquettes and high-backed chairs, popular all-day food including Mon pie night and Tues fish and chips; background music, Sun quiz, TV, free wi-fi; children and dogs (in bar)

Post Office address codings confusingly give the impression that some pubs are in Leicestershire, when they're really in Cambridgeshire (which is where we list them).

welcome, side garden and flagstoned terrace, nine bedrooms, open all day from 8am for breakfast. *(Glen and Patricia Fuller)*

TILTON ON THE HILL SK7405

Rose & Crown (0116) 259 7234
Main Street (B6047); LE7 9LF Friendly old beamed pub opposite village church; three knocked-together rooms, one with inglenook log fire, a couple of Greene King ales and generous helpings of inexpensive pub food; dogs welcome in bar, beer garden behind, closed Mon. *(Barry Collett)*

TUGBY SK7600

Fox & Hounds (0116) 259 8188
A47 6 miles W of Uppingham; LE7 9WB Attractively modernised village-green dining pub serving good well priced food (all day Sat, till 6pm Sun) from bar snacks to daily specials, efficient welcoming staff, ales such as Courage, Grainstore and Sharps, compact open-plan interior with stripped beams and quarry tiles, dining part with light-wood furniture and woodburner; background music, TV; fenced terrace by car park, open all day weekends. *(Mike and Margaret Banks, Barry Collett)*

UPPER HAMBLETON SK8907

Finchs Arms (01572) 756575
Off A606; Oakham Road; LE15 8TL 17th-c stone inn on Rutland Water peninsula; beamed and flagstoned bar with log fires and old settles, five real ales such as Grainstore, Oakham and Timothy Taylors, good selection of wines by the glass including champagne, modern back restaurant opening on to spacious hillside terrace with lovely views over the water, well liked food from ciabattas and sharing boards up, also set menus and afternoon teas; children and dogs (in bar) welcome, good surrounding walks, ten bedrooms (four with reservoir views), open all day, food all day Sun. *(Martin Day)*

UPPINGHAM SP8699

Falcon (01572) 823535
High Street East; LE15 9PY Quietly refined old coaching inn, welcoming and relaxed, with oak-panelled bar, spacious nicely furnished lounge and restaurant, roaring fire and big windows overlooking market square, good food (not Sun evening) from bar snacks up, three Grainstore ales, efficient friendly service; live music; children welcome, dogs in bar, back garden with terrace, bedrooms (some in converted stable block), open all day. *(Barry Collett, Martin Day)*

UPPINGHAM SP8699

Vaults (01572) 823259
Market Place next to church; LE15 9QH Attractive old pub with compact modernised interior; popular reasonably priced traditional food along with pizzas, two Greene King ales, Marstons Pedigree, Theakstons Lightfoot and a house beer from Grainstore, several wines by the glass, friendly service, two pleasant little upstairs dining rooms; background music, sports TVs; children and dogs welcome, tables out overlooking picturesque square, four bedrooms (booking from nearby Falcon Hotel), open all day. *(Barry Collett)*

WALTHAM ON THE WOLDS SK8024

Royal Horseshoes (01664) 464346
Melton Road (A607); LE14 4AJ Attractive sympathetically restored stone and thatch pub in centre of village; good varied choice of generous affordably priced blackboard food, well kept Castle Rock, Marstons, Sharps and three guests, interesting wine list and some 30 gins, two main rooms with beams and open fires; darts; children welcome, no dogs inside, courtyard tables, good value comfortable bedrooms in annexe, hearty breakfast, open all day weekends. *(Abigail Slater)*

WELHAM SP7692

Old Red Lion (01858) 565253
Off B664 Market Harborough–Uppingham; Main Street; LE16 7UJ Popular comfortably updated corner dining pub (part of the King Henry's Taverns group); beamed rooms, some on different levels, including unusual barrel-vaulted back area, leather sofas by log fire, Fullers London Pride and Greene King IPA, nice selection of wines, decent coffee and extensive choice of enjoyable fairly conventional food including good steaks and Sun carvery, efficient friendly staff; children and walkers welcome (ramblers menu), no dogs, open (and food) all day. *(Mike and Margaret Banks)*

WHITWICK SK4316

Three Horseshoes (01530) 837311
Leicester Road; LE67 5GN Unpretentious and unchanging local with long quarry-tiled bar; old wooden benches and open fires, tiny snug to the right, well kept Bass and Marstons Pedigree, no food; piano, darts, dominoes and cards, outside loos; no proper pub sign so easy to miss, known locally as Polly's. *(Frank Hacking)*

WOODHOUSE EAVES SK5214

★**Curzon Arms** (01509) 890377
Maplewell Road; LE12 8QZ Cheerful old beamed pub in pretty Charnwood Forest village (sister to the Crown at Old Dalby); popular food (not Sun evening) from lunchtime sandwiches and pub favourites up, also Weds steak night and weekday lunchtime/early evening set menu, Sharps Doom Bar, Timothy Taylors Landlord and a couple of guests, several wines by the glass and range of cocktails, good friendly service, attractive up-to-date décor in linked areas; background music, Tues quiz, TV, free wi-fi; children, walkers and dogs welcome, ramp

for wheelchairs, good-sized front lawn and terrace, open all day Fri-Sun. *(R L Borthwick)*

WOODHOUSE EAVES SK5313

Wheatsheaf (01509) 890320

Brand Hill; turn right into Main Street, off B591 S of Loughborough; LE12 8SS Brick and stone wisteria-clad country pub with pretty window boxes and tubs; traditionally furnished beamed bar areas with open fires, some black and white motor-racing photographs, dining rooms with wheelback or high-back chairs around country pine tables, ales such as Adnams, Charnwood, Fullers and Timothy Taylors, several wines by the glass and generally well liked food, friendly service; children and dogs (in bar) welcome, seats outside in courtyard under parasols, open all day Sat, closed Sun evening. *(Phil and Jane Villiers)*

WYMESWOLD SK6023

Windmill (01509) 881313

Brook Street; LE12 6TT Bustling side-street village pub with enjoyable good value home-made food (not Sun evening) from lunchtime snacks up, Tues steak night, three well kept rotating ales, good cheerful service even though busy; quiz last Sun of month; children welcome, dogs in bar, back garden with decked area, open all day Fri and Sat, till 9pm Sun. *(Mike and Margaret Banks)*

Lincolnshire

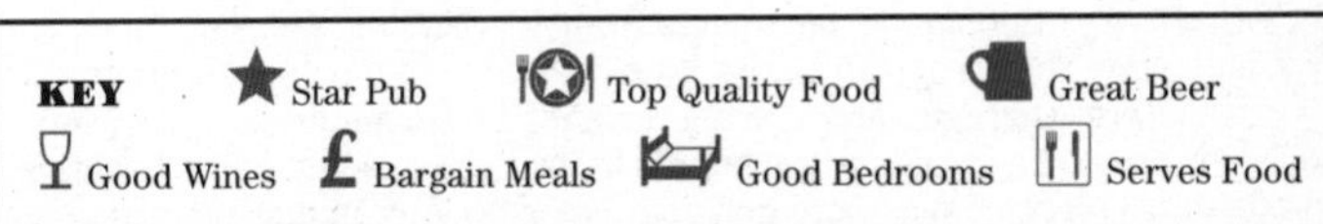

BARNOLDBY LE BECK TA2303 Map 8

Ship

(01472) 822308 – www.the-shipinn.com

Village signposted off A18 Louth–Grimsby; DN37 0BG

Tranquil refined dining pub with plenty to look at

Lucky locals to have this well run pub on their doorstep. Many customers are here for the good, interesting food but the Edwardian and Victorian collection of bric-a-brac is really worth examining too. There are stand-up telephones, violins, a horn gramophone, a bowler and top hats, old racquets, riding crops and hockey sticks. Heavy dark-ringed drapes swathe the windows and the furnishings fit in well, with pretty cushions on comfortable Lloyd Loom-style chairs, heavily stuffed gold plush Victorian-looking chairs on a new rust-coloured carpet and a warming winter coal fire. Axhome Cleethorpes Pale Ale, Batemans XB and Black Sheep on handpump, eight malt whiskies and good wines by the glass; background music. A fenced-off sunny area behind has hanging baskets and a few picnic-sets under parasols. This is a charming village to visit.

Distinctive food includes sandwiches, cod cheeks with confit tomato and black pudding crumb, lobster tail with coriander butter and soy, ginger and chilli noodles, goats cheese and red onion filo tart with couscous, steak burger with toppings and sweet potato chips, seared tuna niçoise with baby gem, beans, sunblush tomatoes, olives, a soft boiled egg and sauce verte, pulled and rolled lamb shoulder with golden beetroot purée, roasted red beetroot and honey and sherry reduction, whole lemon sole with samphire, clam and shallot butter and lemon-scented new potatoes, and puddings such as vanilla crème brûlée with fresh fruit and chocolate brownie with vanilla ice-cream. *Benchmark main dish: daily fresh fish dishes £16.00. Two-course evening meal £20.00.*

Free house ~ Licensee Michele Robinson ~ Real ale ~ Open 12-3, 6-11; 12-5 Sun; closed Sun evening, Mon ~ Bar food 12-2, 6-9; 12-4 Sun ~ Restaurant ~ Children welcome ~ Wi-fi
Recommended by Daniel King, Lorna and Jack Mulgrave, Mike and Sarah Abbot, Peter and Anne Hollindale, Lindy Andrews, Susan Eccleston

'Children welcome' means the pub says it lets children inside without any special restriction. If it allows them in, but to restricted areas such as an eating area or family room, we specify this. Places with separate restaurants often let children use them, and hotels usually let children into public areas such as lounges. Some pubs impose an evening time limit – let us know if you find one earlier than 9pm.

BASTON TF1113 Map 8

White Horse

(01778) 560923 – www.thewhitehorsebaston.co.uk

Church Street; PE6 9PE

Refurbished village pub with four real ales, friendly staff and good, popular food

With a lively atmosphere, customers from near and far, pleasing food and a fine choice of drinks, this blue-painted 18th-c pub is a winner. It's been interestingly renovated using reclaimed farm materials that include the bricks in the bay window, the boards in the ceiling, some of the beams and the huge piece of sycamore that acts as the counter in the snug bar. The main bar has built-in wall seats with scatter cushions, windsor and farmhouse chairs and stools around all sorts of tables on wooden flooring, a woodburning stove in a brick fireplace (with big logs piled into another) and horse-related items on pale paintwork; background music, TV and board games. The dining area is similarly furnished. Stools line the blue-painted counter where they keep Adnams Southwold, Grainstore Spring Time and Oakham JHB with a changing guest on handpump, 28 wines by the glass, 16 gins and 14 malt whiskies; the resident springer spaniel is called Audrey. There are seats and tables on a side terrace.

As well as weekend breakfasts (9.30-11.30am), the impressive food includes sandwiches, crab churros with aioli, smoked pigeon bao bun with pickled red cabbage and miso mayonnaise, chicken caesar salad, mushroom and wild garlic arancini with rocket, pine nut and parmesan salad, beer-battered haddock and chips, lamb rump with caponata, white beans and salsa verde, rolled pork belly with smoked bacon roly-poly, white onions and cider-glazed carrots, and puddings such as banoffi pie with salted caramel, roast banana pudding and buttermilk mousse and bay leaf pannacotta with almond and fennel seed-coated rhubarb. *Benchmark main dish: burger with toppings and chilli jam £13.50. Two-course evening meal £20.00.*

Free house ~ Licensees Ben and Germaine Larter ~ Real ale ~ Open 4-11 Mon, Tues; 12-11 Wed-Fri; 9.30am-midnight Sat; 9.30am-10.30pm Sun ~ Bar food 5.30-9 Tues; 12-2.30, 5.30-9 Wed-Sat; 12-6 Sun; no food Mon ~ Restaurant ~ Children welcome until 9pm ~ Dogs allowed in bar ~ Wi-fi *Recommended by Lenny and Ruth Walters, Charles and Maddie Bishop, Martin and Joanne Sharp, Miranda and Jeff Davidson, Colin and Angela Boocock, Alison and Dan Richardson*

BOURNE TF0920 Map 8

Smiths

(01778) 426819 – www.kneadpubs.co.uk/smiths-of-bourne

North Street; PE10 9AE

Former grocery store with intriguing bric-a-brac in many rooms, well kept ales, popular food and seats in garden

It's great fun wandering around this cleverly thought-out pub. Arranged over three floors, the place has been interestingly converted from an old grocery store (with its lovely original frontage). From the panelled front bar, there's a warren of interconnected rooms – a cook's pantry, one with hop-hung rafters, kitchenware on a big dresser and painted wooden settles, others with orange button-back banquettes set in semicircles and chunky leather dining chairs, benches and an eclectic mix of pubby chairs, and floors made up of nice old boards, flagstones and crazy-paved stone. The 'stables' is split into stalls with saddlery and horse tack, troughs and tin buckets, and even a horse cart. There are woodburning stoves and open fires, the bare-brick walls are hung with vintage enamelled advertising signs and mirrors, and assorted items include tilley lamps and a sizeable butterchurn, pots, pans and cauldrons and an old-fashioned butcher's bike. Fullers London Pride, Oakham JHB and guests such as Great Heck Black Jesus, Left Hand Warrior IPA, Menace Pragmatic Pale and Milestone Shine On on handpump, good wines by the glass and 11 gins; background music, TV and games machine. The partly covered, enclosed courtyard has metal seats and tables and the garden has picnic-sets on grass and a children's play area.

As well as serving breakfasts at weekends (8.30-11am), the changing food includes sandwiches and baguettes, nibbles and starters such as yorkshire pudding with dipping gravy, beer-battered prawns with sweet chilli sauce and garlic and rosemary baked camembert with fig jelly plus pizzas with a huge choice of toppings, pumpkin and ricotta cannelloni, chicken caesar salad, 14-hour braised beef in ale pie, moroccan-style lamb meatballs with apricot and chickpea tagine, salmon fillet with lemon, pea and mint risotto and roasted pepper coulis, and puddings such as chocolate belgian waffle topped with honeycomb ice-cream, marshmallows, popping candy and chocolate sauce and lemon curd tart with rapsberry sorbet. *Benchmark main dish: beer-battered fish and chips £13.95. Two-course evening meal £20.50.*

Knead Pubs ~ Manager Hayley Taylor ~ Real ale ~ Open 10am-11pm (midnight Fri); 8.30am-midnight Sat; 8.30am-11pm Sun ~ Children welcome ~ Dogs welcome ~ Wi-fi
Recommended by Jim and Sue James, Trevor and Michele Street, Colin and Daniel Gibbs, Martine and Fabio Lockley, Heather and Richard Jones

GREAT LIMBER TA1308 Map 8

New Inn

(01469) 569998 – www.thenewinngreatlimber.co.uk
High Street; DN37 8JL

Rather grand with an easy-going atmosphere, marvellous food, fine wines and large back garden; bedrooms

The proper working bar here is popular with locals who drop in for a pint and a chat, quiz evenings or a game of darts. Of course, many are here for the impressive food. There are windsor chairs, red button-back wall seats, some upholstered tub chairs and oak tables on pale floorboards, neatly stacked logs to either side of one fireplace and shelves of books by another, and chairs against the counter where efficient, friendly staff serve Batemans XXXB, Tom Woods Old Codger and a guest from Axeholme on handpump and a dozen wines by the glass. A snug little corner has a curved high-backed wall seat just right for a small group. The dining room is split into two, with cushioned wooden chairs in one part and comfortable red chairs and long wall seats with pretty scatter cushions in another. Throughout, the walls are hung with modern art, black and white photos and big mirrors; background music, darts and TV. The landscaped back garden has both picnic-sets and tables and chairs. Bedrooms are quiet and comfortable and breakfasts highly regarded.

Using produce from the Brocklesby Estate (to which this pub belongs), the interesting food includes sandwiches, chicken liver parfait with red onion marmalade, beetroot risotto with peas and melting goats cheese, hot smoked salmon niçoise, spicy tomato and basil linguine with ricotta and chives, beer-battered fish and chips, chicken breast with mozzarella and sunblush tomatoes and blue cheese mash, loin of cod with mussel and tiger prawn broth, duo of lamb cutlets and traditional hotpot with sweet potato mash, wilted greens and puy lentils, and puddings such as double chocolate brownie and sticky toffee pudding with vanilla custard. *Benchmark main dish: sausages (leek and stilton, venison, black pudding) with creamy mash £13.00. Two-course evening meal £18.00.*

Free house ~ Licensee Lolita Brizga ~ Real ale ~ Open 12-11.30 (4.30-10 Mon); 11.30-11 Sat; 11.30-10 Sun; closed Mon lunchtime (except bank holidays) ~ Bar food 12-2.30, 6.30-9; 12-3.30 Sun; not Sun evening, Mon lunchtime ~ Restaurant ~ Children welcome ~ Dogs allowed in bar and bedrooms ~ Wi-fi ~ Bedrooms: £89/£99 *Recommended by Lucy and Giles Gibbon, Sally and Lance Oldham, Dr and Mrs A K Clarke, Philip J Alderton, Susan and Tim Boyle, Celia and Rupert Lemming*

HEIGHINGTON TF0369 Map 8

Butcher & Beast

(01522) 790386 – www.butcherandbeast.co.uk

High Street; LN4 1JS

Traditional village pub with terrific choice of drinks, pubby food and a pretty garden by a stream

With a thriving atmosphere created by the hands-on and hard-working licensees, this popular pub is enjoyed by our readers. The thoughtful range of drinks includes half a dozen real ales such as Batemans XB, XXXB and Dark Mild, Timothy Taylors Landlord and Oakham Green Devil IPA on handpump, two farm ciders, eight wines by the glass, 30 gins and 20 malt whiskies. The simply decorated bar has button-back wall banquettes, pubby furnishings and stools along the counter, while the Snug has red-cushioned wall settles and high-backed wooden dining chairs. The beamed and extended dining room is neatly set with an attractive medley of wooden or painted chairs around chunky tables on floorboards, and there's a woodburning stove; throughout, the cream or yellow walls are hung with old village photos and country pictures. The award-winning hanging baskets and tubs make quite a show in summer, and for warmer weather there are picnic-sets on a lawn that runs down to a stream.

Well regarded food includes lunchtime sandwiches, halloumi fries with sweet chilli dip, meatballs in spicy tomato sauce with garlic bread, a vegetarian curry, a weekly fresh fish dish, steak in ale pie, scampi and chips, beef stroganoff, chicken with apricot and stilton, and puddings such as sticky toffee pudding with toffee sauce and seasonal crumble. *Benchmark main dish: sirloin steak £15.95. Two-course evening meal £21.00.*

Batemans ~ Tenants Mal and Diane Gray ~ Real ale ~ Open 12-11 (10.30 Sun) ~ Bar food 12-2, 5-8; 10-2, 5-9 Fri, Sat; 12-8 Sun ~ Restaurant ~ Children welcome away from bar ~ Dogs allowed in bar ~ Wi-fi *Recommended by Mark and Mary Setting, Caroline and Steve Archer, James and Sylvia Hewitt, Neil Allen, Usha and Terri Patel*

HOUGH-ON-THE-HILL SK9246 Map 8

Brownlow Arms

(01400) 250234 – www.thebrownlowarms.com

High Road; NG32 2AZ

Lincolnshire Dining Pub of the Year

Refined country house with beamed bar, real ales, imaginative food and graceful terrace; bedrooms

The delicious food is at the heart of things here. The comfortable and warmly welcoming bar has beams, plenty of panelling, some exposed brickwork, local prints and scenes, a large mirror, and a pile of logs beside a big fireplace. Seating includes elegant, stylishly mismatched upholstered armchairs, and the carefully arranged furnishings give the impression of several separate and cosy areas. Served by impeccably polite staff, the ales on handpump are Black Sheep and Timothy Taylors Landlord, there are ten wines by the glass and 15 malt whiskies; background music. Bedrooms are well equipped and comfortable and the breakfasts are very good.

Imaginative food using the best local produce includes lunchtime sandwiches, beer-battered tiger prawns with chilli, lime and ginger dipping sauce, smoked duck, orange, pear, radish and pine nut salad with celeriac rémoulade, truffled wild mushroom and parmesan tagliatelle, chicken suprême stuffed with mushroom and tarragon duxelles, wrapped in pancetta, with crushed root vegetables, confit potatoes and red wine jus, roast cod with roasted beetroot and beetroot purée, celeriac, cauliflower and hazelnuts with apple crisp, crème fraîche and hazelnut oil, slow-braised local venison with mash, sautéed balsamic shallots, griottine cherries, parsnip purée and redcurrant rosemary jus, and puddings such as espresso pannacotta, dulce de leche doughnut with mocha sauce and rhubarb and ginger soufflé with rhubarb sorbet, gingerbread and poached rhubarb. *Benchmark main dish: rolled plaice fillets stuffed with crabmeat with beurre blanc sauce, samphire and crushed new potatoes £19.95. Two-course evening meal £27.00.*

Free house ~ Licensee Paul L Willoughby ~ Real ale ~ Open 12-3, 6-11; 12-3.30 Sun; closed Sun evening, Mon, Tues lunchtime ~ Bar food 12-2, 6.30-9; 12-2.30 Sun ~ Restaurant ~ Children welcome but must be over 8 in evening ~ Wi-fi ~ Bedrooms: £75/£120
Recommended by Ian Wilson, Mrs Julie Thomas, Jim King, Dr K Nesbitt, Ian Herdman, Melanie and David Lawson, Emily and Toby Archer

INGHAM SK9483 Map 8

Inn on the Green

(01522) 730354 – www.innonthegreeningham.co.uk
The Green; LN1 2XT

Nicely modernised place serving thoughtfully prepared food and with a chatty atmosphere

If you just want a chat and a pint, head for the locals' bar. This is informal and pubby with a log fire, and caring staff who serve a beer named for the pub plus Ferry Ales Just Jane Bitter, Sharps Doom Bar and Welbeck Abbey Henrietta on handpump, 12 wines by the glass, 18 malt whiskies, 35 gins and home-made cordials; several tables may also be occupied by those enjoying the tasty food. The beamed and timbered dining room is spread over two floors, with lots of exposed brickwork, local prints and a warm winter fire; do book ahead to be sure of a table. The lounge between these rooms has leather sofas and background music, and a bar counter where you can buy home-made jams, marmalade and chutney. There are attractive views across the village green. Dogs are allowed in the bar outside of food service times.

Appetising food includes baguettes (until 6pm), prawn cocktail, chinese-style crispy beef with sweet chilli jam and carrot and cumin salad, vegetable tikka masala, hunters chicken (cheese and barbecue sauce) with coleslaw and fries, roast lamb rump with brussels sprouts, potato rösti, smoked bacon and baby onion jus, lemon sole fillet with onion bhaji and curried crayfish sauce, pork fillet with chorizo meatballs, roasted garlic mash and vegetable jus, and puddings such as chocolate and pistachio brownie with chocolate ripple ice-cream and sticky toffee pudding with caramel sauce; they also offer a breakfast menu on the last Saturday of the month, a hamper and preserves list and a takeaway dinner party menu. *Benchmark main dish: pie of the day £10.50. Two-course evening meal £19.00.*

Free house ~ Licensees Andrew Cafferkey and Sarah Sharpe ~ Real ale ~ Open 12-11; 12-10.30 Sun; closed Mon ~ Bar food 12-8.30; 3-8 Tues (pies only); 12-7 Sun ~ Restaurant ~ Children welcome ~ Wi-fi *Recommended by Peter Meister, Jeff Davies, Anne and Ben Smith, Jill and Hugh Bennett, Sabine and Gerald Grimshaw*

KIRKBY LA THORPE TF0945 Map 8

Queens Head £

(01529) 305743 – www.thequeensheadinn.com

Village and pub signposted off A17, just E of Sleaford, then turn right into Boston Road cul-de-sac; NG34 9NU

Reliable dining pub very popular for its good food and helpful, efficient service

Customers are drawn back to this gently traditional and neatly comfortable place on a regular basis to enjoy the particularly good food. There are open fires, elaborate flower arrangements and plenty of courteous dark-waistcoated staff, and the carpeted bar has stools along the counter, button-back banquettes, sofas and captain's chairs around shiny dark tables. The smart, beamed restaurant has high-backed, orange-upholstered dining chairs around linen-set tables on carpet, heavy curtains and a woodburning stove; there's also a popular dining conservatory. Nice decorative touches take in thoughtful lighting, big prints, china plates on delft shelves and handsome longcase clocks (it's quite something when they all chime at midday). Batemans XB and guests such as 8 Sail Windmill Bitter and Sharps Doom Bar on handpump; background music. Easy disabled access.

Cooked by the landlord, the enticing food includes lunchtime sandwiches and omelettes, pigeon breast with black pudding fritters and walnut dressing, smoked salmon and eggs benedict with chive oil, butternut squash and spinach curry, dark sugar and mustard roast ham with free-range eggs and chips, chicken breast with pea risotto and parmesan galette, loin of venison with truffle mash, butternut squash purée, cripsy shallots and red wine sauce, lambs liver with onions, bacon and mash, sea bass with red pepper mash, chorizo and saffron shallots, and puddings such as sticky ginger and date pudding with clotted cream and vanilla custard and rich chocolate torte with white chocolate brûlée; they also offer a fish night on Friday and a set menu (6-9.30pm Monday-Wednesday). *Benchmark main dish: steak in ale pie £11.95. Two-course evening meal £16.95.*

Free house ~ Licensee John Clark ~ Real ale ~ Open 12-3, 6-11; 12-10.30 Sun ~ Bar food 12-2.30, 6-9.30; 12-8.30 Sun ~ Restaurant ~ Children welcome ~ Dogs allowed in bar

Recommended by Phoebe Peacock, Andrew Stone, Miranda and Jeff Davidson, Pauline and Mark Evans, Peter and Emma Kelly, Christopher Mannings

STAMFORD TF0306 Map 8

George of Stamford

(01780) 750750 – www.georgehotelofstamford.com

High Street, St Martins (B1081 S of centre, not the quite different central pedestrianised High Street); PE9 2LB

Lovely coaching inn with traditional bar, several dining areas and lounges, excellent staff and top class food and drink; bedrooms

It would stretch the imagination to call this handsome and rather special old place a straightforward pub, but our readers still very much enjoy the properly pubby little York Bar at the front. It offers Adnams Broadside, Black Sheep and Grainstore Triple B on handpump alongside 20 wines from an exceptional list and 30 malt whiskies; food here is simple. The atmosphere throughout remains gently civilised and yet informal, and service is first class. The various areas are furnished with all manner of seats from leather, cane and antique wicker to soft sofas and easy chairs, and there's a room to suit every occasion. The central lounge is particularly striking with sturdy timbers, broad flagstones, heavy beams and massive stonework. Service is professional yet friendly. There's an amazing oak-panelled restaurant (jacket required) and a less formal Garden Room restaurant, which has well spaced furniture on herringbone glazed bricks around a central tropical planting. Seats in the charming cobbled courtyard are highly prized and the immaculately kept walled garden is beautifully planted; there are also sunken lawns and croquet. Bedrooms are individually and thoughtfully decorated and breakfasts are splendid.

The simplest food option is the York Bar snack menu with sandwiches (their toasties are especially good), a proper ploughman's and a plate of smoked salmon with capers. Excellent food in the restaurants includes moules marinière, crab and prawn fishcake with roasted red pepper mayonnaise, penne pasta with tomato and basil sauce and crème fraîche, crispy battered fresh haddock and chips, calves liver with parsley mash and red onion marmalade, slow-cooked pork belly with pak choi and five-spice jus, lobster benedict with toasted muffin, avocado, poached egg and hollandaise, and puddings from their famous trolley such as baked alaska and dark chocolate tart with orange sorbet. *Benchmark main dish: roast sirloin of english beef £27.85. Two-course evening meal £45.00.*

Free house ~ Licensee Paul Reseigh ~ Real ale ~ Open 11-11 ~ Bar food 12-2.30, 7-9; York Bar opens 11am ~ Restaurants ~ Dogs allowed in bar and bedrooms ~ Wi-fi ~ Bedrooms: £130/£215 *Recommended by William and Sophia Renton, James and Becky Plath, Michael Sargent, Sally Harrison, Stuart Doughty, Martin Day, Brian and Sally Wakeham*

STAMFORD TF0307 Map 8

Tobie Norris

(01780) 753800 – www.kneadpubs.co.uk/the-tobie-norris

St Pauls Street; PE9 2BE

A warren of ancient rooms, a good period atmosphere, a fine choice of drinks, enjoyable food and seats outside

The best has been made of this building's great age and the charming series of characterful little rooms have worn flagstones, meticulously stripped stonework, a huge hearth for the woodburning stove in one room, and steeply pitched rafters in one of the two upstairs room – it's been beautifully restored. There's a wide variety of furnishings from pews and wall settles to comfortable armchairs, and a handsomely panelled shrine to Nelson and the Battle of Trafalgar. Attentive, friendly staff serve Fullers London Pride, Oakham JHB and guests such as Framework Brewery Summit Pale Ale, Grainstore Ten Fifty and St Austell Tribute on handpump, farm cider and 19 wines by the glass; board games and TV. A snug end conservatory opens out to a narrow but sunny two-level courtyard with seats and tables.

Interesting food includes sandwiches, nibbles and starters such as yorkshire pudding with dipping gravy, pigs in blankets with mustard mayonnaise, garlic and rosemary baked camembert with fig jelly, sharing boards, beetroot and goats cheese tortellini with basil pesto, lamb kofta kebabs with aubergine, herbed roasted cauliflower and crumbled feta and home-made hummus, piri-piri poussin with pickled red cabbage and coriander yoghurt, beer-battered fish and triple-cooked chips, 14-hour braised beef in ale pie, slow-cooked pork belly with apple and fennel croquette, sage and onion mash and cider jus, and puddings such as chocolate tart with white chocolate ice-cream and lemon posset and strawberry ice-cream. *Benchmark main dish: stone-baked pizzas £11.95. Two-course evening meal £20.00.*

Knead Pubs ~ Licensee Matthew Williamson ~ Real ale ~ Open 10am-11pm (midnight Sat); 11am-midnight Sun ~ Bar food 12-2.30, 6-9; 12-9.30 Fri, Sat; 12-8 Sun ~ Children welcome until 8pm ~ Dogs welcome ~ Wi-fi *Recommended by Mike and Sarah Abbot, Jane Rigby, Alice Wright, Ted and Mary Bates, Stuart Doughty, John Saville, Elizabeth and Andrew Harvey, Anna and Mark Evans*

WOOLSTHORPE SK8334 Map 8

Chequers

(01476) 870701 – www.chequersinn.net

Woolsthorpe near Belvoir, signposted off A52 or A607 W of Grantham; NG32 1LU

Interesting food in comfortably relaxed inn with good drinks and appealing castle views from outside tables; bedrooms

There's a lot of history surrounding this former coaching inn and the heavily beamed main bar has two big tables (one a massive oak construction), a comfortable mix of seating including some handsome leather chairs and banquettes, and a huge boar's head above a good log fire in the big brick fireplace. Among cartoons on the wall are some of the illustrated claret bottle labels from the series commissioned from famous artists. There are more leather seats in a dining area on the left and a corridor leads off to the light and airy extended main restaurant and then to another bar; background music. Gloucester Cascade, Greene King Abbot and Ruddles County and Pheasantry Single Hop on handpump, 30 wines by the glass, 50 malt whiskies, around 20 gins, a seasonal cocktail list and a farm cider. There are good quality teak tables, chairs and benches outside and, beyond these, some picnic-sets on the edge of the pub's cricket field, with views of Belvoir Castle. If you want to explore the delightful Vale of Belvoir, it makes sense to stay in the comfortable bedrooms in the converted stables next door.

First class food includes thai-style mussels with chilli, coriander and garlic, queenie scallops with garlic butter, breadcrumbs and gruyère, an antipasti sharing board, chickpea curry with basmati rice, onion bhaji and raita, a pie of the day, burger with toppings, horseradish and beetroot relish and chips, free-range chicken with tarragon and garlic ballotine and dauphinoise potatoes, grilled fresh fish of the day with herb butter, 22oz côte du boeuf (for two) with onion rings, garlic mushrooms and chips, and puddings such as chocolate fondant with raspberry marshmallow and cherry baked alaska. *Benchmark main dish: house salad (chicken, bacon, new potatoes, poached egg, hollandaise) £13.00. Two-course evening meal £20.50.*

Free house ~ Licensee Justin Chad ~ Real ale ~ Open 12-11; 12-midnight Sat; 12-10.30 Sun ~ Bar food 12-2.30, 6-9.30; 12-4, 6-8.30 Sun ~ Restaurant ~ Children welcome ~ Dogs allowed in bar and bedrooms ~ Wi-fi ~ Bedrooms: £60/£80 *Recommended by Martin and Clare Warne, Dr and Mrs F McGinn, Malcolm Phillips, Jacqui and Alan Swan, Elisabeth and Bill Humphries, Alison and Michael Harper*

Also Worth a Visit in Lincolnshire

Besides the fully inspected pubs, you might like to try these pubs that have been recommended to us and described by readers. Do tell us what you think of them: feedback@goodguides.com

ALLINGTON SK8540

★**Welby Arms** (01400) 281361

The Green; off A1 at N end of Grantham bypass; NG32 2EA Welcoming, well run and well liked village inn; large simply furnished bar divided by stone archway, beams and joists, log fires (one in attractive arched brick fireplace), comfortable plush wall banquettes and stools, up to six changing ales, over 20 wines by the glass and plenty of malt whiskies, good popular food including blackboard specials, reasonable prices, can eat in bar or back dining lounge; background music; children welcome, tables in walled courtyard with pretty flower baskets, picnic-sets on front lawn, comfortable bedrooms, open all day weekends. *(Gordon and Margaret Ormondroyd, Johnston and Maureen Anderson, Mike and Margaret Banks)*

ASLACKBY TF0830

Robin Hood & Little John

(01778) 440681 *A15 Bourne–Sleaford; NG34 0HL* Old mansard-roofed roadside country pub; split-level bar with beams, flagstones and woodburners, popular traditional food including vegetarian choices, gluten-free and daily specials (two-course deal Mon-Thurs), Greene King Abbot and guests, friendly staff, separate more modern oak-floored restaurant; children and dogs (in bar) welcome, tricky wheelchair access, three-level terrace, open (and food) all day weekends. *(Lindy Andrews)*

BARHOLM TF0810

Five Horseshoes (01778) 560238
W of Market Deeping; village signed from A15 Langtoft; PE9 4RA Welcoming old-fashioned village local, cosy and comfortable, with beams, rustic bric-a-brac and log fire, well kept Adnams, Oakham and four guests, good range of wines, Fri and Sat pizza van, occasional Sun barbecues; pool room with TV, some live music; children and dogs welcome, garden and shady arbour, play area, open all day weekends, closed weekday lunchtimes. *(Ian Tanner)*

BASSINGHAM SK9160

Five Bells (01522) 788269
High Street; LN5 9JZ Cheerful old red-brick pub with well liked food including good value lunchtime set menu (Mon-Thurs) and steak nights (Weds, Thurs), Greene King ales and good range of brandies, efficient friendly service, bare-boards interior with hop-draped beams, country furniture and cosy log fires, lots of brass and bric-a-brac, an old well in one part; well behaved children and dogs welcome, a few tables out in front fenced from the road, open all day (food till 7pm Sun). *(Tony and Maggie Harwood)*

BELCHFORD TF2975

★**Blue Bell** (01507) 533602
Village signed off A153 Horncastle–Louth; LN9 6LQ Popular 18th-c dining pub with cosy comfortable bar, Batemans XB and guests, Thatcher's cider, good traditional and modern food (best to book), efficient friendly service, restaurant; children and dogs welcome, picnic-sets in terraced back garden, useful base for Wolds walks and Viking Way (remove muddy boots), open all day Sun, closed Mon; for sale last we heard. *(Anne and Ben Smith)*

BICKER TF2237

Red Lion (01775) 821200
A52 NE of Donnington; PE20 3EF Nicely decorated 17th-c village pub; enjoyable home-made food including set lunch and popular Sun carvery, also a 'Lincolnshire tapas' menu, friendly helpful service, Courage Directors and a guest, bowed beams (some painted), exposed brickwork and half panelling, wood and flagstone floors, woodburners, part-raftered restaurant; quiz first Weds of month; children welcome, no dogs inside, rattan-style furniture on brick terrace with pergola, lawned garden, open all day Sun till 7pm, closed Mon, Tues. *(Martine and Fabio Lockley)*

BILLINGBOROUGH TF1134

★**Fortescue Arms** (01529) 240228
B1177, off A52 Grantham–Boston; NG34 0QB Beamed village pub with old stonework, exposed brick, panelling and big see-through fireplace in carpeted rooms, tables in bay windows overlooking high street, well kept Greene King ales and a guest, enjoyable home-made food including some decent vegetarian options, good friendly service even at busy times, Victorian prints, brass and copper, a stuffed badger and pheasant, dining rooms at each end; Thurs quiz, free wi-fi; children and dogs welcome, picnic-sets and rattan-style furniture in sheltered courtyard with flowering tubs, useful big car park, open all day weekends. *(Anne and Mark Evans)*

BOSTON TF3244

Mill (01205) 352874
Spilsby Road (A16); PE21 9QN Roadside pub run by friendly italian landlord, reasonably priced food (not Tues) including some italian choices and blackboard specials, Batemans XB and a guest; children welcome, tables out in front, open all day. *(Susan Eccleston)*

BURTON COGGLES SK9725

Cholmeley Arms (01476) 550225
Village Street; NG33 4JS Well kept ales such as Fullers, Grainstore and Greene King in small beamed pubby bar with warm fire, generous helpings of good reasonably priced home-made food (not Sun evening), friendly accommodating staff, restaurant; children welcome in bar till 8pm, dogs at licensees' discretion, farm shop, four comfortable modern bedrooms in separate building overlooking garden, handy for A1, open all day weekends, closed lunchtimes Mon, Tues. *(Michael Butler)*

CASTLE BYTHAM SK9818

Castle Inn (01780) 411223
Off A1 Stamford–Grantham, or B1176; NG33 4RZ Beamed 17th-c village pub under friendly new management; enjoyable pubby food and three well kept changing ales, fire in inglenook range (some food cooked here); events including quiz and karaoke nights; children and dogs welcome, disabled access, tables on back terrace, open all day. *(Heather and Richard Jones)*

CAYTHORPE SK9348

Red Lion (01400) 272632
Signed just off A607 N of Grantham; High Street; NG32 3DN Popular 17th-c village pub; good fairly traditional home-made food (not Sun evening) including lunchtime deals (Weds-Fri) and Tues fish and chips night, friendly helpful staff, well kept Adnams and Everards, good sensibly

priced wines, bare-boards bar with light wood counter, black beams and roaring fire, modern restaurant; back terrace by car park, open all day Sun. *(Peter and Emma Kelly)*

CHAPEL ST LEONARDS TF5672

Admiral Benbow (01754) 871847

The Promenade; PE24 5BQ Small bare-boards beach bar in former shelter; ales including Black Sheep, foreign bottled beers and decent range of other drinks, sandwiches and snacks, friendly staff, cushioned bench seats, stools and barrel tables, lots of bric-a-brac and nautical memorabilia on planked walls and ceiling; free wi-fi; children and dogs welcome, picnic-sets out on mock-up galleon, great sea views, open when the flag is flying, usually all day summer (all Fri-Sun winter). *(Christopher Mannings)*

CLAYPOLE SK8449

Five Bells (01636) 626561

Main Street; NG23 5BJ Friendly brick-built village pub with good-sized beamed bar and smaller dining area beyond servery, well kept Greene King IPA and mainly local guests, a couple of ciders, enjoyable reasonably priced home-made food including range of burgers and daily specials; pool and darts; children welcome, dogs in bar, grassy back garden with play area, four bedrooms, closed lunchtimes Mon and Tues, otherwise open all day. *(Celia and Rupert Lemming)*

CLEETHORPES TA3009

No 2 Refreshment Room

07905 375587 *Station Approach beneath the clock tower; DN35 8AX* Small comfortable station bar with well kept Hancocks HB, Rudgate Ruby Mild, Sharps Doom Bar and guests, real cider too, friendly staff, interesting old pictures of the station, historical books on trains and the local area, no food apart from free Sun evening buffet; tables out under heaters, open all day from 7.30am (9am Sun). *(Christopher Mannings)*

CLEETHORPES TA3008

Nottingham House (01472) 505150

Sea View Street; DN35 8EU Seafront pub with lively main bar, lounge and snug, seven well kept ales including Tetley Mild, Timothy Taylors Landlord and Oakham Citra, Weston's ciders, good reasonably priced food (not Mon, Tues) from sandwiches and pub favourites up in bar or upstairs restaurant, helpful friendly staff; regular live music, annual winter beer festival; children and dogs (in bar) welcome, bedrooms, good breakfast, open all day. *(Christopher Mannings)*

CLEETHORPES TA3108

★**Willys** (01472) 602145

Highcliff Road; south promenade; DN35 8RQ Popular mock-Tudor seafront pub enjoying panoramic Humber views; open-plan interior with tiled floor and painted brick walls, own good ales from visible microbrewery, also changing guests and belgian beers, enjoyable home-made bar lunches at bargain prices, good mix of customers; children welcome, no dogs at food times, a few tables out on the prom, open all day (till 2am Fri, Sat). *(Christopher Mannings)*

COLEBY SK9760

Bell (01522) 813778

Village signed off A607 S of Lincoln, turn right and right into Far Lane at church; LN5 0AH Restauranty pub with very good food from owner-chef including early bird menu (Weds-Fri), welcoming staff, well kept Timothy Taylors and several wines by the glass (not cheap), bar and three dining areas; children over 8 welcome, terrace tables, village on Viking Way with lovely fenland views, three bedrooms, open evenings Weds-Sat and lunchtime Sun. *(Susan Eccleston)*

CONINGSBY TF2458

Leagate Inn (01526) 342370

Leagate Road (B1192 southwards, off A153 E); LN4 4RS Heavy-beamed 16th-c fenland pub run by same family for over 25 years; three cosy linked rooms, medley of furnishings including high-backed settles around the biggest of three log fires, ancient oak panelling, dim lighting, attractive dining room, even a priest hole; reasonably priced food from extensive menu, Batemans (including one badged for them) and Timothy Taylors Landlord; free wi-fi; children welcome (they eat for free 6-7pm Mon-Fri), dogs in bar, pleasant garden with play area, site of old gallows at front, eight motel bedrooms, open all day Sun. *(Lee Smith)*

DONINGTON ON BAIN TF2382

Black Horse (01507) 343640

Main Road; between A153 and A157, SW of Louth; LN11 9TJ Welcoming roadside village inn with two carpeted bars (back one with low beams) and restaurant; good locally sourced food cooked by landlord-chef including daily specials, well kept John Smiths and guests, proper cider, open fires and woodburner, games room with pool, darts and dominoes; free wi-fi; children and dogs (in bars) welcome, picnic-sets in back garden, eight motel-style bedrooms, on Viking Way and convenient for Cadwell Park race circuit, closed Mon and Tues lunchtimes. *(Colin Goodman)*

DRY DODDINGTON SK8546

Wheatsheaf (01400) 281458

Main Street; 1.5 miles off A1 N of Grantham; NG23 5HU Welcoming and well cared-for 16th-c village pub; front bar (basically two rooms) with woodburner, variety of built-in wall seats, settles and little wooden stools, windows looking out to green and lovely 14th-c church with its crooked tower, Greene King Abbot and IPA, several wines by the glass and good range of gins, generally well liked food from varied menu including lunchtime/early evening set menu and some themed nights, friendly if not always speedy service, light slope down to comfortable extended dining room (once a cow byre perhaps dating from the 13th c); background music, free wi-fi; children and dogs (in bar) welcome, side disabled access, neat tables under parasols on front terrace, closed Mon. *(John Saville)*

FOSDYKE TF3132

Ship (01205) 260764
Moulton Washway; A17; PE12 6LH Useful roadside pub with popular reasonably priced food from varied menu, Sun carvery, two Adnams beers and Batemans XB, friendly staff, simple pine and quarry tile décor, woodburner; quiz every other Mon; children and dogs welcome, garden tables, open all day. *(Celia and Rupert Lemming)*

FULBECK SK9450

Hare & Hounds (01400) 272322
The Green (A607 Leadenham–Grantham); NG32 3JJ Converted 17th-c maltings overlooking attractive village green; modernised linked areas, easy chairs by bar's woodburner, highly regarded food from pub favourites up including 'hot rock' menu, friendly attentive service, four well kept ales and an affordable wine list, raftered upstairs function room; no dogs inside, terrace seating, eight good bedrooms in adjacent barn conversion, generous breakfast, open all day Sun till 8pm (food till 7pm). *(Anne and Ben Smith)*

GAINSBOROUGH SK8189

Eight Jolly Brewers (01427) 611022
Ship Court, Silver Street; DN21 2DW Small drinkers' pub in former warehouse; eight interesting real ales such as Dukeries, traditional cider and plenty of bottled beers, friendly staff and locals, beams and bare brick, more room upstairs; live music Thurs; seats outside, open all day. *(Martine and Fabio Lockley)*

GREAT GONERBY SK8938

Recruiting Sargeant
(01476) 562238 *High Street; NG31 8JP* Friendly village pub with popular good value food cooked to order from lunchtime baguettes up, well kept Everards ales, comfortable back restaurant (separate menu); Tues quiz, TV; children and dogs (in bar) welcome, disabled access/loo, open all day Fri-Sun, no evening food Sun-Tues, handy for A1. *(Mike and Margaret Banks)*

KIRMINGTON TA1011

Marrowbone & Cleaver
(01652) 688335 *High Street; DN39 6YZ* Friendly 19th-c local owned by British motorbike racer/presenter Guy Martin and his sister; enjoyable good value home-made food (all day Sun) from sandwiches to blackboard specials, three well kept ales including a house beer from Batemans and Sharps Doom Bar, carpeted bar with log fire, flying and racing memorabilia, snug, dining conservatory; live music last Sat of month, TV and darts; children welcome, picnic-sets on side lawn, open all day. *(Jill and Hugh Bennett)*

KIRKBY ON BAIN TF2462

★**Ebrington Arms** (01526) 354560
Main Street; LN10 6YT Popular village pub with good value traditional food (not Mon, booking advised) and half a dozen well kept ales such as Adnams, Timothy Taylors and Sharps, friendly staff, beer mats on low 16th-c beams, carpets and banquettes, open fire, restaurant behind; background music, darts; children and dogs welcome, wheelchair access, tables out in front by road, lawn to the side with play equipment, campsite next door, closed Mon lunchtime. *(David Jackman)*

LEADENHAM SK9552

George (01400) 272251
Off A17 Newark–Sleaford; High Street; LN5 0PN Former coaching inn with comfortable old-fashioned two-room bar; well kept ales, several wines by the glass and remarkable range of over 700 whiskies, good choice of enjoyable food from fairly pubby menu, Sun carvery, friendly helpful service, restaurant; events including live music and comedy nights; children and dogs welcome, outside seating, six annexe bedrooms, open all day. *(Tony and Maggie Harwood)*

LINCOLN SK9871

Dog & Bone (01522) 522403
John Street; LN2 5BH Comfortable and welcoming backstreet local with well kept Batemans, several guest beers and real cider, log fires, various things to look at including collection of valve radios, local artwork and exchange-library of recent fiction; background and live music, beer festivals; dogs welcome, picnic-sets on back terrace, open all day Fri-Sun, from 4.30pm other days. *(Heather and Richard Jones)*

LINCOLN SK9771

Jolly Brewer (01522) 528583
Broadgate; LN2 5AQ Popular no-frills pub with unusual art deco interior; half a dozen well kept ales such as Idle, Tom Woods and Welbeck Abbey, real cider and decent range of other drinks, friendly staff, no food; regular live music including Weds open mike night; back courtyard with covered area, open all day (till 8pm Sun). *(Tony and Maggie Harwood)*

LINCOLN TF0854

Red Lion (01526) 321686
North Street; LN4 3LY Welcoming family-run village pub; comfortable beamed front bar, restaurant and a couple of other snug dining areas, good reasonably priced food

cooked by chef-landlady including some vegetarian/vegan options, Weds steak night, four changing ales, helpful friendly service; Sun quiz, pool and darts; children welcome, closed Mon and lunchtime Tues, no food Sun evening. *(Heather and Richard Jones)*

LINCOLN SK9771

Strugglers (01522) 535023
Westgate; LN1 3BG Cosily worn-in beer lovers' haunt tucked beneath the castle walls, built in 1841 and once run by the local hangman (note the pub sign); half a dozen or more well kept ales including Greene King and Timothy Taylors, bare boards throughout with lots of knick-knacks and pump clips, two open fires (one in back snug); some live acoustic music; no children inside, dogs welcome, steps down to sunny back courtyard with heated canopy, open all day (till 1am Fri, Sat). *(Lee Smith)*

LINCOLN SK9771

Victoria (01522) 541000
Union Road; LN1 3BJ Old-fashioned local just outside the castle gates, half a dozen well kept ales including Batemans and Castle Rock, foreign draught and bottled beers and real cider, simply furnished tiled front lounge with pictures of Queen Victoria, coal fire, basic lunchtime food, friendly knowledgeable staff and good mix of customers (gets especially busy at lunchtime and later in the evening); live music Sat; children and dogs welcome, seats on heated terrace, play area, good castle views, open all day till midnight (1am Fri, Sat). *(David Hunt)*

LINCOLN SK9771

Widow Cullens Well (01522) 523020
Steep Hill; just below cathedral; LN2 1LU Ancient reworked building on two floors (upstairs open to the rafters), well kept/priced Sam Smiths beers and good value pubby food including children's choices, chatty mix of customers (busy evenings and weekends), friendly service, beams, stone walls and log fire, back extension with namesake well; dogs welcome, terrace seating, open all day. *(Tracey and Stephen Groves)*

LINCOLN SK9771

★**Wig & Mitre** (01522) 535190
Steep Hill; just below cathedral; LN2 1LU Civilised café-style dining pub with attractive period features and plenty of character; big-windowed downstairs bar, beams and exposed stone walls, pews and Gothic furniture on oak boards, comfortable sofas in carpeted back area, quieter upstairs dining room with views of castle walls and cathedral, antique prints and caricatures of lawyers/clerics, well liked food from breakfast on including good value set menus, extensive choice of wines by the glass from good list, Everards Tiger and guests such as Oakham, friendly service; children and dogs welcome, open 8.30am-midnight. *(Brian and Anna Marsden, Richard Tilbrook)*

LONG BENNINGTON SK8344

Reindeer (01400) 281382
Just off A1 N of Grantham – S end of village, opposite school; NG23 5DJ Cleanly refurbished 17th-c roadside pub; enjoyable fair value food (not Sun evening) from snacks and pub favourites to daily specials, three real ales including Timothy Taylors Landlord, friendly staff, low painted beams, log fire in stone fireplace; background music; children and dogs welcome, white picnic-sets on fenced front terrace, open all day Fri, Sat, till 8pm Sun, closed Mon. *(Sabine and Gerald Grimshaw)*

LONG BENNINGTON SK8344

Royal Oak (01400) 281332
Main Road; just off A1 N of Grantham; NG23 5DJ Popular local with spacious open-plan bar serving Marstons ales, several wines by the glass and good sensibly priced home-made food including specials and popular Sun roasts, friendly helpful staff; children welcome, seats out in front and in big back garden with play area, path for customers to river, open all day. *(Susan Eccleston)*

MAREHAM LE FEN TF2861

Royal Oak (01507) 568920
A115; PE22 7RL Partly thatched 15th-c pub reopened by local family after long closure; comfortably renovated black-beamed interior with bar and two dining areas, well kept Batemans and guests from barrel-faced counter, enjoyable good value food including blackboard specials, friendly service; quiz second Sun of month, some live folk music, sports TV, pool and darts; children and dogs (in bar) welcome, disabled access/loo, picnic-sets in lawned garden, closed Mon lunchtime and all day Tues, otherwise open all day. *(Lee Smith)*

MARKET DEEPING TF1310

Bull (01778) 343320
Market Place; PE6 8EA Refurbished and under new management; reworked bar and extended restaurant, the heavy-beamed medieval Dugout Bar remains, flagstone and oak floors, woodburner in original stone fireplace, well kept Everards Tiger and Original plus guests, generous helpings of

Anyone claiming to arrange, or prevent, inclusion of a pub in the *Guide* is a fraud. Pubs are included only if recommended by readers and if our own anonymous inspection confirms that they are suitable.

enjoyable reasonably priced food served promptly by friendly staff; children welcome, beer garden with own bar in converted stable, play area, open all day from 8am for breakfast. *(Elisabeth and Bill Humphries)*

MARKET RASEN TF1089

Aston Arms (01673) 842313
Market Place; LN8 3HL Popular market-square pub serving generous helpings of inexpensive food, Theakstons, John Smiths and a guest, friendly staff, beamed bar, lounge and games area; children and well behaved dogs welcome, side terrace, open all day. *(Susan Eccleston)*

NORTON DISNEY SK8859

Green Man (01522) 789804
Main Street, off A46 Newark–Lincoln; LN6 9JU Old beamed village pub-restaurant; enjoyable popular food from chef-landlord (booking advised) including pub standards and daily specials, good Sun roasts, Black Sheep, Brains Rev James and a guest, friendly, helpful staff, opened-up modernised interior; children welcome, tables out in front and in spacious back garden, closed Sun evening, Mon lunchtime. *(Colin Goodman)*

PINCHBECK TF2326

Ship (01775) 711746
Northgate; PE11 3SE Popular thatched and beamed riverside pub refurbished under present licensees; cosy split-level bar with warm woodburner, four real ales and enjoyable generously served food, friendly helpful staff, restaurant; traditional games such as shove-ha'penny; children and dogs welcome, tables out on decking, open all day Sat, closed Sun evening, Mon. *(Peter and Emma Kelly)*

REVESBY TF2961

Red Lion (01507) 568665
A155 Mareham–Spilsby; PE22 7NU Former 19th-c red-brick coaching inn set back from the road; ample helpings of enjoyable home-made food from reasonably priced pubby menu, Sun carvery, can eat in comfortable lounge bar with open fire or separate dining room, well kept Batemans ales, friendly staff; games area with pool; children welcome, tables out at front and on large side lawn, four bedrooms, open all day. *(Brian Root)*

SCAMPTON SK9579

Dambusters (01522) 731333
High Street; LN1 2SD Welcoming pub with several beamed rooms around central bar; masses of interesting Dambusters and other RAF memorabilia, generous helpings of reasonably priced straightforward food (not Sun evening) from shortish menu, also home-made chutneys, pâté and biscuits for sale, six interesting ales including own microbrews (ceiling covered in beer mats), short list of well chosen wines, pews and chairs around tables on wood floor, log fire in big two-way brick fireplace, more formal seating at back; children and dogs welcome (their black labrador is Bomber), very near Red Arrows runway viewpoint, closed Mon, otherwise open all day (till 7.30pm Sun). *(Lindy Andrews)*

SKENDLEBY TF4369

Blacksmiths Arms (01754) 890662
Off A158 about 10 miles NW of Skegness; PE23 4QE Cottagey-fronted 17th-c pub with cosy old-fashioned two-room bar, low beams and log fire, view into the cellar from servery, well kept Batemans XB, a house beer from Horncastle and guest, good home-made food served by friendly staff, back dining extension with deep well; children and dogs welcome, unsuitable for wheelchairs, wolds views from back garden, closed Sun evening, Mon lunchtime. *(Christopher Mannings)*

SKILLINGTON SK8925

Cross Swords (01476) 861132
The Square; NG33 5HB Unassuming 19th-c stone pub on crossroads in delightful village, welcoming and homely, with very good food (not Sun evening) cooked by long-serving landlord-chef, up to three changing ales; background music; no under-10s or dogs, three annexe bedrooms, closed Sun evening and Mon lunchtime. *(Sally Anne and Peter Goodale)*

SOUTH FERRIBY SE9921

Hope & Anchor (01652) 635334
Sluice Road (A1077); DN18 6JQ Refurbished nautical theme-pub; bar, snug and back dining area with wide views over confluence of Rivers Ancholme and Humber (plenty for bird-watchers), popular locally sourced food (all day Fri, Sat, not Sun evening) from pub standards to more restauranty choices including 40-day-aged steaks (not cheap), Theakstons, Tom Woods and a guest, several wines by the glass including champagne, good friendly service; children and dogs welcome, disabled access/facilities, outside tables, closed Mon, otherwise open all day. *(Heather and Richard Jones)*

SOUTH RAUCEBY TF0245

Bustard (01529) 488250
Main Street; NG34 8QG Modernised 19th-c stone-built pub with good food from shortish but varied menu (can be pricey, early evening discount on some dishes), well kept Batemans, Loxley and a house beer Cheeky Bustard (actually Batemans XB), plenty of wines by the glass, friendly efficient staff, flagstoned bar with log fire, steps up to bare-stone restaurant (former stables); live jazz third Weds of month; children welcome, no dogs inside, attractive sheltered garden, open all day Sat, closed Sun evening, Mon. *(Usha and Terri Patel)*

SOUTH WITHAM SK9219

Angel (01572) 768302
Church Street; NG33 5PJ Welcoming old stone pub next to the village church; good value pubby food cooked by co-owner/chef including Mon burger night, OAP lunch (Tues, Thurs) and popular Sun carvery, well kept Black Sheep, Wells Bombardier and a guest; sports TV; dogs welcome, open all day and handy for A1. *(Thomas Allen)*

SPALDING TF2422

Priors Oven 07972 192750
Sheep Market; PE11 1BH Friendly well run micropub in ancient building (former bakery); small octagonal room with vaulted ceiling, island bar serving up to six well kept changing ales and local cider, no food apart from jars of nuts, spiral staircase up to loos and comfortable lounge with period fireplace; open all day. *(Dr J Barrie Jones)*

STAMFORD TF0207

All Saints Brewery – Melbourn Brothers (01780) 7521865
All Saints Street; PE9 2PA Well reworked old building (core is a medieval hall) with warren of rooms on three floors; upstairs bar serving bottled fruit beers from adjacent early 19th-c brewery and low-priced Sam Smiths on handpump, food from pub favourites up including set deals and good vegetarian options, ground-floor dining area with log fire and woodburner, top floor with leather sofas and wing chairs; children and dogs welcome, picnic-sets in cobbled courtyard, brewery tours, open all day. *(Lee Smith)*

STAMFORD TF0306

★ **Bull & Swan** (01780) 766412
High Street, St Martins; PE9 2LJ Handsome former staging post with three traditional linked rooms; low beams, rugs on floorboards, portraits on bare stone or painted walls, several open fires and good mix of seating including high-backed settles, leather banquettes and bow-window seats, Adnams Southwold, Sharps Doom Bar and guests, 20 wines by the glass and 30 malt whiskies, well liked food from panini and sharing boards up, helpful staff; background music, free wi-fi; children and dogs welcome, tables in back coachyard, character bedrooms named after animals, open all day. *(Lee Smith)*

STAMFORD TF0207

Crown (01780) 763136
All Saints Place; PE9 2AG Substantial well modernised stone-built hotel in same small group as the Tobie Norris (also in Stamford, see Main Entries); good choice of popular food using local produce (some from their own farm), prompt friendly service, well kept ales such as Fullers, Oakham and Timothy Taylors (can be pricey), lots of wines by the glass and cocktails, decent coffee and afternoon teas, spacious main bar with long leather-cushioned counter, substantial pillars, step up to more traditional flagstoned area with stripped stone and armchairs, restaurant; background music, free wi-fi; well behaved children and dogs allowed, seats in back courtyard, 28 comfortable bedrooms (some in separate townhouse), good breakfast, open (and food) all day. *(Gerry and Rosemary Dobson)*

STAMFORD TF0207

Jolly Brewer (01780) 755141
Foundry Road; PE9 2PP Welcoming unpretentious 19th-c stone pub; six well kept ales including own Bakers Dozen, traditional cider and wide range of interesting whiskies (some from India and Japan), low-priced simple food (weekday lunchtimes and Fri evenings), open fire in brick fireplace; regular beer festivals and fortnightly Sun quiz, sports TV, pool, darts and other games; dogs welcome, picnic-sets out at front, open all day. *(Lee Smith)*

SURFLEET TF2528

Mermaid (01775) 680275
B1356 (Gosberton Road), just off A16 N of Spalding; PE11 4AB Two high-ceilinged carpeted rooms, huge sash windows, banquettes, captain's chairs and spindlebacks, Adnams and a couple of guests, good choice of fairly standard food including monthly themed night, restaurant; background music; children welcome, pretty terraced garden with summer bar and seats under thatched parasols, play area walled from River Glen, moorings, four bedrooms, closed Sun evening, Mon. *(Susan Eccleston)*

TATTERSHALL THORPE TF2159

Blue Bell (01526) 342206
Thorpe Road; B1192 Coningsby–Woodhall Spa; LN4 4PE Ancient low-beamed pub (said to date from the 13th c) with friendly cosy atmosphere; RAF memorabilia including airmen's signatures on the ceiling (pub was used by the Dambusters), big open fire, three well kept ales such as local Horncastle and Tom Woods Bomber County, nice wines and enjoyable well priced pubby food, small dining room; some live music; garden tables, bedrooms, closed Sun evening, Mon. *(Colin Goodman)*

TETFORD TF3374

White Hart (01507) 533255
East Road, off A158 E of Horncastle; LN9 6QQ Friendly bay-windowed village pub dating from the 16th c; Brains Rev James and a couple of guests, good value generous pubby food, pleasant inglenook bar with curved-back settles and slabby elm tables on red tiles, other areas including pool room; regular live music; children and dogs welcome, sheltered back lawn with guinea pigs,

rabbits and chickens, pretty countryside, bedrooms. *(Jill and Hugh Bennett)*

THEDDLETHORPE ALL SAINTS TF4787

★**Kings Head** (01507) 339798
Pub signposted off A1031 N of Maplethorpe; Mill Road; LN12 1PB Welcoming 16th-c thatched pub; carpeted two-room front lounge with very low ceiling, brass platters on timbered walls, antique dining chairs and tables, easy chairs by log fire, central bar (more low beams) serving well kept ales such as Batemans and a local cider, coal fire with side oven, shelves of books, stuffed owls and country pictures, long dining room, good local food from sandwiches and sharing plates to steaks and fresh Grimsby fish, popular Sun roasts; children and dogs welcome, one or two picnic-sets in front area, more on lawn, self-catering apartment, open all day weekends, closed Mon and lunchtime Tues (all day Tues winter). *(Peter and Emma Kelly)*

THREEKINGHAM TF0836

Three Kings (01529) 240249
Just off A52 12 miles E of Grantham; Saltersway; NG34 0AU Former coaching inn with big entrance hall, fire and pubby furniture in comfortable beamed lounge, also a panelled restaurant and bigger dining/function room, good choice of home-made food including Thurs steak night, Bass, Timothy Taylors Landlord and guests; Weds quiz; children and dogs (in bar) welcome, sunny paved terrace and small lawned area, various car club meetings, closed Mon. *(Martine and Fabio Lockley)*

WAINFLEET TF5058

★**Batemans Brewery**
(01754) 880317 *Mill Lane, off A52 via B1195; PE24 4JE* Circular bar in brewery's ivy-covered windmill tower; Batemans ales in top condition, czech and belgian beers on tap too, ground-floor dining area with cheap food including baguettes and a few pubby dishes, popular Sun carvery, old pub games (more outside), lots of brewery memorabilia and plenty for families to enjoy; no dogs inside, entertaining brewery tours and shop, tables on terrace and grass, bar open 11.30am-4pm, bistro 12-2pm, seasonal hours for brewery tours and shop. *(Lindy Andrews)*

WASHINGBOROUGH TF0170

Ferry Boat (01522) 790794
High Street; LN4 1AZ Friendly old village pub with enjoyable traditional food including good value two-course weekday lunch, a couple of ales such as Sharps and Wells; high-raftered central bar with low-beamed areas off including restaurant, bare-stone and stripped-brick walls, mix of furniture on wood floors, open fire; background and some live music, Weds quiz, games part with pool, darts and TV; children welcome, dogs in bar (maybe a treat), beer garden, good river walks nearby, open all day. *(Lee Smith)*

WEST DEEPING TF1009

Red Lion (01778) 347190
King Street; PE6 9HP Stone-built pub with long low-beamed bar, four well kept ales including Fullers London Pride and often local Hopshackle, popular freshly made food from baguettes up including weekday evening deal, back dining extension; occasional live music, free wi-fi; children welcome, no dogs inside, tables in back garden with terrace and fenced play area, vintage car/motorcycle meetings, open till 4pm Sun, closed Mon. *(Colin Goodman)*

WILSFORD TF0043

Plough (01400) 230304
Main Street; NG32 3NS Traditional old two-bar village pub next to church; beams and open fires, a couple of real ales, nice range of wines and good choice of well presented bar food (till 7.45pm Sun), pleasant friendly service, dining conservatory; pool and other games in adjoining room; children welcome, small walled back garden, good local walks, open all day Fri and Sun. *(Jill and Hugh Bennett)*

WITHAM ON THE HILL TF0516

Six Bells (01778) 590360
Village signed from A6121, SW of Bourne; PE10 0JH Well restored Edwardian stone inn with smart comfortable bar, popular food including wood-fired pizzas and weekday set lunch, well kept Bass and guests, good friendly service; children and dogs welcome, rattan-style furniture on front terrace, nice village, three well appointed bedrooms, good breakfast. *(Anna and Mark Evans)*

WOODHALL SPA TF1963

Village Limits (01526) 353312
Stixwould Road; LN10 6UJ Modernised country pub-restaurant on village outskirts; good locally sourced food cooked by landlord-chef from pub standards up, well kept Batemans and a beer badged for the pub from local Horncastle, friendly service, banquettes in smallish beamed bar, dining room with light wood furniture on wood-strip floor; children welcome, eight courtyard bedrooms, good views from garden, closed Mon lunchtime. *(Susan Eccleston)*

Post Office address codings confusingly give the impression that a few pubs are in Lincolnshire, when they're really in Cambridgeshire (which is where we list them).

Norfolk

BAWBURGH

TG1508 Map 5

Kings Head

(01603) 744977 – www.kingshead-bawburgh.co.uk

Harts Lane; A47 just W of Norwich then B1108; NR9 3LS

Norfolk Dining Pub of the Year

Busy, small-roomed pub with five real ales, good wines by the glass, interesting food and friendly service

A regular favourite with many of our readers who call the place 'a little gem'. Dating from the 17th c, it has much character and the helpful, friendly staff will quickly make you feel at home. The small rooms have plenty of low beams and standing timbers, leather sofas and an attractive assortment of old dining chairs and tables on wood-strip floors; also, a knocked-through open fire and a couple of woodburning stoves in the restaurant areas. There's Adnams Ghost Ship and Lighthouse and a couple of changing guests on handpump, 11 wines by the glass and eight malt whiskies, and service is friendly and helpful; background music. There are seats in the garden and the pub is opposite a little green. The six bedrooms (in a separate building) are comfortable and pretty, and they now also offer two self-catering apartments.

Impressive food includes sandwiches, game terrine with sticky fig and apple and ale chutney, seared scallops with cauliflower cheese purée, chorizo, popcorn cockles and apple and watercress salad, gnocchi with blue cheese sauce and baby spinach with toasted hazelnuts, chicken breast with leg kiev, truffled polenta and tomato and roasted pepper purée, hake with celeriac and apple couscous with hot tartare sauce and crispy cod cheek, beef stroganoff with chargrilled pak choi, seafood platter, and puddings such as sticky jamaican gingerbead with poached pear, salted caramel and rum and raisin ice-cream and lemon parfait with lemon curd, meringue and basil sorbet. *Benchmark main dish: steak burger with toppings, beetroot and apple slaw and chips £13.00. Two-course evening meal £22.00.*

Free house ~ Licensee Anton Wimmer ~ Real ale ~ Open 11-11; 12-9 Sun ~ Bar food 12-2, 5.30-9; 12-3, 5.30-8 Sun ~ Children welcome ~ Wi-fi ~ Bedrooms: £90/£110 *Recommended by Glenn and Julia Smithers, Patti and James Davidson, Amanda Shipley, Charles Fraser, Chloe and Michael Swettenham, John Evans, John and Mary Warner, Molly and Stewart Lindsay*

'Children welcome' means the pub says it lets children inside without any special restriction; some may impose an evening time limit earlier than 9pm – please tell us if you find this.

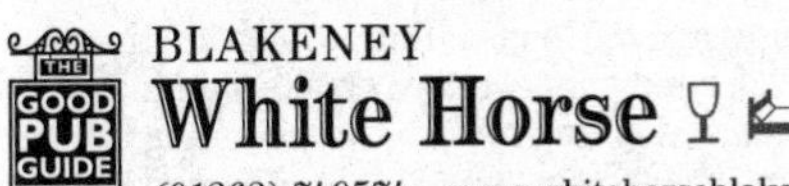

BLAKENEY TG0243 Map 8

White Horse

(01263) 740574 – www.whitehorseblakeney.co.uk
Off A149 W of Sheringham; High Street; NR25 7AL

Friendly inn popular with both locals and holidaymakers, bars and airy conservatory, local ales, well liked food and seats outside; charming bedrooms

In a lovely spot just up from Blakeney Quay, this refurbished inn has plenty of space for both drinking and dining. The long, split-level bar has chatty locals on high chairs by the counter, button-back seats along the walls, simple dining chairs and tartan-upholstered armchairs around pine-topped tables and drinks served by friendly staff that take in Adnams Broadside, Ghost Ship and Southwold and a guest beer on handpump, a dozen wines by the glass and six malt whiskies; background music and board games. The airy dining conservatory has modern art on planked walls, white rattan armchairs with colourful scatter cushions around pale-topped tables on floor tiles and big ceiling lanterns. The breakfast room is similarly furnished to the bar and there's a cosy lounge with sofas and armchairs in front of a little woodburning stove. A suntrap walled side terrace has black rattan-style furniture under big parasols. Some of the contemporary, attractive and comfortable bedrooms have views of the coastal marshes; breakfasts are highly rated. The coastal path is nearby.

As well as breakfasts (8.30-10am), the wide choice of good food includes sandwiches, home-made scotch egg with brown sauce, mini game pie with celeriac purée, sweet potato and chickpea harissa stew with courgette fritter and tzatziki, smoked haddock, salmon and hake fish pie, steak burger with toppings and triple-cooked chips, seared duck breast with dauphinoise potatoes, kirsch cherry and red wine jus, beef in stout pudding, and puddings such as chocolate brownie with sea salt caramel sauce and griottine cherries and fig and almond frangipane tart with rosemary ice-cream. *Benchmark main dish: mussels with shallots, cream and parsley £14.00. Two-course evening meal £25.00.*

Free house ~ Licensee Nick Attfield ~ Real ale ~ Open 11-11; 11-10.30 Sun ~ Bar food 12-2.30, 6-9; 12-2.30, 6-8.30 Sun ~ Restaurant ~ Children welcome ~ Dogs allowed in bar and bedrooms ~ Wi-fi ~ Bedrooms: £84/£114 *Recommended by Cliff and Monica Swan, Andrew Vincent, Samuel and Melissa Turnbull*

BURSTON TM1383 Map 5

Crown

(01379) 741257 – www.burstoncrown.com
Village signposted off A140 N of Scole; Mill Road; IP22 5TW

Friendly, relaxed village pub usefully open all day, with a warm welcome, real ales and well liked bar food

Locals tend to gather in an area by the bar counter, where they serve Adnams Broadside and Southwold and guests such as Oakham Hawse Buckler, Old Pie Factory Pie in the Sky, Station 119 Heartbreaker and Three Blind Mice Nothing Rhymes with Orange on handpump or tapped from the cask, ten wines by the glass and seven malt whiskies. On a chilly day, the best place to sit in this heavily beamed, quarry-tiled bar room is on the comfortably cushioned sofas in front of a woodburning stove in a huge brick fireplace; there are also stools by a low chunky wooden table, and newspapers and magazines. The public bar on the left has a nice long table and panelled settle on an old brick floor in one alcove, a pool table, and more tables and chairs towards the back near a dartboard. Both rooms are hung with paintings by local artists; background music, board games, dominoes and cards. The simply furnished, beamed dining room has another big brick fireplace. Outside, there's a smokers' shelter, seats and tables on a terrace and in the secluded garden, and a play area for children.

The landlord cooks the popular food, which includes sandwiches, chicken and blue cheese mousse with bacon jam, caramelised shallot purée and pickled shallots, hot smoked local salmon with grilled asparagus, citrus and dill crème fraîche and lemon gel, spinach and ricotta dumplings with rosemary polenta, tomato ragoût and parmesan, honey-roasted gressingham duck breast with smashed sweet potatoes and blueberry and port jus, chicken breast stuffed with brie and sunblush tomatoes, wrapped in serrano ham, with potato terrine and salsa verde, whiting fillet with sautéed potatoes, wilted spinach and warm tartare sauce, and puddings such as chocolate pot with raspberry coulis and crème caramel with glazed pears. *Benchmark main dish: fresh beer-battered fish and chips £12.50. Two-course evening meal £21.00.*

Free house ~ Licensees Bev and Steve Kembery ~ Real ale ~ Open 12-11; 12-10.30 Sun ~ Bar food 12-2, 6.30-9; 12-4 Sun; no food Sun evening, Mon ~ Restaurant ~ Children welcome ~ Dogs allowed in bar ~ Wi-fi ~ Live music Fri 8.30pm, every second Sun from 5pm; plays and art festival (see website) *Recommended by Ruth May, Melanie and David Lawson, Lucy and Giles Gibbon, Heather and Richard Jones, Graeme and Sally Mendham*

CASTLE ACRE TF8115 Map 8

Ostrich

(01760) 755398 – www.ostrichcastleacre.com
Stocks Green; PE32 2AE

Friendly old village pub with original features, fine old fireplaces, real ales and tasty food; bedrooms

If you're walking the ancient Peddars Way, why not stop here for refreshment? The L-shaped, low-ceilinged front bar (on two levels) has a woodburning stove in a huge old fireplace, lots of wheelback chairs and cushioned pews around pubby tables on a wood-strip floor and gold patterned wallpaper; there's a step up to an area in front of the bar counter where there are similar seats and tables and a log fire in a brick fireplace. Do look out for the original masonry, beams and trusses. Friendly, helpful staff serve Greene King Abbot, IPA, Old Speckled Hen and a beer named for the pub on handpump, around a dozen wines by the glass and several malt whiskies; background music, darts and board games. There's a separate dining room with another brick fireplace. The sheltered garden has picnic-sets under parasols and the inn faces the tree-lined village green; nearby are the remains of a Norman castle and a cluniac priory (English Heritage). Bedrooms are warm and comfortable.

Nicely presented food includes sandwiches and ciabattas, sharing platters, nine different pizzas, peppered squid with sweet chilli tartare, seared scallops and garlic green-lipped mussels, roasted baby pumpkin stuffed with spiced vegetables, spiced chicken shawarma with greek yoghurt, garlic mayonnaise, hummus and flatbread, chargrilled suprême of salmon with red onion marmalade, sea bream with seafood broth, honey-roasted pork belly with sweet potato mash, raisin purée and daikon, and puddings such as chocolate brownie with chocolate sauce and apple and blackberry frangipane. *Benchmark main dish: burger with toppings and chips £13.95. Two-course evening meal £20.00.*

Greene King ~ Tenant Tiffany Turner ~ Real ale ~ Open 10am-10.30pm; 10am-11.30pm Sat, Sun ~ Bar food 12-3, 6-9; 12-3 Sun; no food Sun evening ~ Restaurant ~ Children welcome ~

Dogs allowed in bar ~ Wi-fi ~ Bedrooms: £75/£85 *Recommended by Andrea and Philip Crispin, Thomas Green, Mr and Mrs Richard Osborne, Paddy and Sian O'Leary, Bruce white, Elisabeth and Bill Humphries*

EAST RUDHAM TF8228 Map 8

Crown

(01485) 528530 – www.crowninnnorfolk.co.uk

A148 W of Fakenham; The Green; PE31 8RD

Smart and attractive open-plan seating areas, cosy back sitting room, good food, real ales and friendly atmosphere; bedrooms

Drop in for an enjoyable meal and you'll find a cosy corner or two to sit in, alongside friendly staff and locals. It's a civilised place and at the end of the main room a log fire is flanked by a grandfather clock on one side and bookshelves on the other, with wooden and brown leather dining chairs around a mix of tables and rugs on stripped floorboards. The other end is slightly more informal, with another bookshelf beside a second fireplace, a pubby part with white-painted, cushioned built-in seats, and high chairs against the handsome slate-topped counter where they keep Adnams Broadside, Black Sheep, Woodfordes Wherry and a changing guest on handpump and 20 wines by the glass. There's also a snug lower area to the back of the building with comfortable leather sofas and armchairs and a flatscreen TV; an upstairs dining room has a high-pitched ceiling and a woodburning stove. The gravelled terrace at the front has seats under parasols. Bedrooms are comfortable.

Quite a choice of food includes sandwiches, crayfish and avocado cocktail, duck liver parfait with pepper and orange butter and fig chutney, pea and fresh mint risotto with parmesan, roast monkfish with bombay-style potatoes, spinach and coconut milk, chicken breast with gnocchi, chestnut mushrooms and cherry tomatoes, steak burger with toppings, onion rings and skinny fries, herbed lamb loin with parmesan polenta, olives, sun-dried tomatoes and red wine sauce, king prawn linguine, and puddings such as white chocolate and pistachio brûlée and passion-fruit mousse with mango salsa. *Benchmark main dish: lemon and peppered monkfish with spinach and tagliatelle £17.40. Two-course evening meal £22.00.*

Free house ~ Licensee Tristram McEwen ~ Real ale ~ Open 11-11; 11am-midnight Sat ~ Bar food 12-2.30, 6-9; 12-8 Sun ~ Children welcome ~ Dogs welcome ~ Wi-fi ~ Bedrooms: /£110 *Recommended by Tony Scott, Freddie and Sarah Banks, Monica and Steph Evans, Barbara Brown, Jill and Dick Archer*

GREAT MASSINGHAM TF7922 Map 8

Dabbling Duck

(01485) 520827 – www.thedabblingduck.co.uk

Off A148 King's Lynn–Fakenham; Abbey Road; PE32 2HN

Unassuming from the outside but with character bars, real ales and interesting food; comfortable bedrooms

In dreary weather, the three woodburning stoves are most welcome, as are the friendly staff and easy-going atmosphere; our readers enjoy their visits here. The cosy bars have leather sofas and armchairs, a mix of antique wooden dining tables and chairs on flagstones or stripped wooden floors, a very high-backed settle, 18th- and 19th-c quirky prints and cartoons, and plenty of beams and standing timbers. At the back of the pub is the Blenheim room, just right for a private group, and there's also a candlelit dining room. Adnams Broadside and Ghost Ship, Grain Oak and Woodfordes Wherry on handpump and a dozen wines by the glass, served from a bar counter made of great slabs of polished tree trunk; background music, TV, darts and board games. Tables and chairs on the pub's front terrace take in the pleasant setting (the village green and big duck ponds are opposite) and there are more seats and a play area in the enclosed back garden. The nine bedrooms are named after famous local sportsmen and airmen from the World War II air base in Massingham. Wheelchair access.

As well as breakfasts (8-10am), the highly regarded food includes fried pigeon with vanilla carrots and black garlic aioli, goats cheese doughnut with beetroot jam, candied beetroot and smoked candy floss, smoked aubergine and feta salad with grains, roasted red peppers and walnut and mint pesto, cod with cauliflower purée, smoked dauphinoise potatoes and raisin purée, goan curry with chicken or prawn, 16oz rib-eye steak with chimichurri dressing, a choice of sauce and chips, and puddings such as banoffi pudding with banana ice-cream and salted caramel sauce and peanut butter parfait with pineapple jelly and coconut foam; they also serve garden pizzas (you can take them away too). *Benchmark main dish: rare-breed local burger with toppings and dripping fries £13.50. Two-course evening meal £20.50.*

Free house ~ Licensee Dominic Symington ~ Real ale ~ Open 12-11 (10.30 Sun) ~ Bar food 12-9 ~ Restaurant ~ Children welcome ~ Dogs allowed in bar and bedrooms ~ Wi-fi ~ Bedrooms: /£110 *Recommended by Peter and Alison Steadman, Elise and Charles Mackinlay, Tracey and Stephen Groves, William Pace, Camilla and Jose Ferrera*

HOLKHAM TF8943 Map 8

Victoria

(01328) 711008 – www.victoriaatholkham.co.uk

A149 near Holkham Hall; NR23 1RG

Smart, handsome inn with pubby bar, plenty of character dining space, thoughtful choice of drinks, friendly staff and enjoyable food; bedrooms

You'll find plenty of space both inside and outside here and the atmosphere is gently upmarket yet informal and friendly. There's a proper bare-boards bar to the left of the main door that's popular with locals, where efficient, polite staff serve Adnams Southwold, Marstons Pedigree and Woodfordes Wherry on handpump and 20 wines by the glass; background music, TV, darts and board games. A spreading dining and sitting area has an appealing variety of antique-style dining chairs and tables on rugs and stripped floorboards, antlers and antique guns, and sofas by a big log fire. A small drawing room (for hotel guests only) has homely furniture, an open fire and an honesty bar. The airy conservatory dining room, decorated in pale beige, leads out to a back terrace with green-painted furniture; in summer the outside bar and seafood shack is very popular. Some of the stylish bedrooms have views of the sea and breakfasts are good and generous; dogs are allowed in some rooms. Holkham Beach with its vast stretches of sand backed by pine woods is across the road.

Using Holkham Estate and other local produce, the well regarded food includes breakfast (8-10am), ploughman's, duck liver pâté with sticky red cabbage, brie, pear and hazelnut strudel with apricot and orange compote, cheese burger with fries, lemon and thyme chicken with garlic potatoes and mushroom fricassée, hake suprême with salt and vinegar mash and tartare cream, cannon of pork with fondant potatoes and calvados sauce, half a lobster with garlic butter and french fries, and puddings such as stem ginger pannacotta and chocolate and orange brownie with salted caramel ice-cream. *Benchmark main dish: Holkham Estate beef with french fries and béarnaise sauce £18.30. Two-course evening meal £20.00.*

Free house ~ Licensee Lord Coke ~ Real ale ~ Open 11-11; 12-10.30 Sun ~ Bar food 12-2.30, 6-9; bar snacks 12-5 ~ Restaurant ~ Children welcome ~ Dogs welcome ~ Wi-fi ~ Bedrooms: £135/£195 *Recommended by William and Sophia Renton, Peter and Emma Kelly, Tracey and Stephen Groves, Mr and Mrs Richard Osborne, Michael Sargent, David Jackman, Tim and Mary Thomson*

ITTERINGHAM TG1430 Map 8

Walpole Arms

(01263) 587258 – www.thewalpolearms.co.uk

Village signposted off B1354 NW of Aylsham; NR11 7AR

Owned by a local farming family and with plenty of character in beamed rooms, contemporary food, local ales and seats in garden

If you're visiting nearby Blickling Hall (National Trust), why not come to this 18th-c country pub for some excellent modern british food? The sizeable open-plan bar is beamed and timbered with a woodburning stove, stripped-brick wall and cushioned wooden dining chairs around dark tables on red carpet. Friendly staff serve Adnams Southwold, Grain ThreeOneSix, Norfolk Moon Gazer Ruby Ale and a guest from Woodfordes on handpump, several wines by the glass and quite a few gins; background music. The light restaurant garden room, also with beams and timbers, has pale oak tables and chairs on floorboards and old photos on painted walls, and leads into an area with leather armchairs in front of a contemporary, glass-fronted woodburner. Doors from here open on to a vine-covered terrace and the two-acre landscaped garden has picnic-sets under parasols.

Using produce from their own farm, the imaginative food includes sandwiches, battered king prawns with Jack Daniels marie rose sauce and blow-torched baby gem lettuce, broccoli and goats cheese millefeuille with broccoli stalk and caper dressing, pickled pear and blue cheese risotto, roast hake with fennel marmalade, dauphinoise potatoes, tomato and caper concasse, crispy capers and pak choi, slow-cooked ox cheek with horseradish mash, shallot purée, roast beetroot, kale and puffed rice, and puddings such as custard pannacotta with passion-fruit broth, poached rhubarb, fennel crumble and rhubarb powder and tiramisu with cappuccino semifreddo, espresso syrup, chocolate coffee beans and amaretti crumb. *Benchmark main dish: free-range confit duck leg, roast celeriac, fondant potatoes and orange gel £16.50. Two-course evening meal £22.00.*

Free house ~ Licensee Oliver Harrold ~ Real ale ~ Open 12-3, 6-11; 12-11 Sat; 12-5 Sun; closed Sun evening ~ Bar food 12-2.30, 6.30-9; 12-3 Sun ~ Restaurant ~ Children welcome ~ Dogs allowed in bar ~ Wi-fi ~ Jazz some summer evenings (see website) *Recommended by Alan and Angela Scouller, David Twitchett, Patricia and Gordon Tucker, Alan and Linda Blackmore*

KING'S LYNN TF6119 Map 8

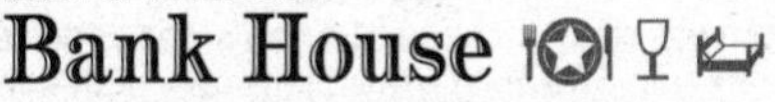

Bank House

(01553) 660492 – www.thebankhouse.co.uk

Kings Staithe Square via Boat Street and along the quay in one-way system; PE30 1RD

Georgian bar-brasserie with plenty of history and character, airy rooms, real ales and imaginative food from breakfast onwards; bedrooms

Our readers enjoy every aspect of this particularly well run town inn (it was the first site in 1780 for what became Barclays Bank), which is helpfully open and serves some kind of food all day. The various stylish rooms include the elegant bar (once the bank manager's office) with sofas and armchairs, a log fire with fender seating, Adnams Southwold, Woodfordes Wherry and Wychwood Dirty Tackle on handpump, 14 wines by the glass, 74 gins (including local ones – they also make their own tonic waters), seven whiskies, interesting vodkas, cocktails and a farm cider; background music. The restaurant has antique chairs and tables on bare boards, an airy brasserie has sofas and armchairs around low tables and a big brick fireplace, and two other areas (one with fine panelling, the other with a half-size billiards table) have more open fires. The atmosphere throughout is gently civilised but easy-going and service is helpful and courteous. An outside area, flanked by magnificent wrought-iron gates, has fire pits for warmth on chillier evenings, and the riverside terrace (fine sunsets) has an open-air bar. Most of the lovely bedrooms overlook the river and breakfasts are first class. This is a splendid quayside spot and the Corn Exchange theatre and arts centre is just five minutes away. Sister pub is the Rose & Crown in Snettisham.

As well as breakfasts (7-11am), the excellent food includes sandwiches, scallops with crushed avocado and bacon, black pudding pancake roll with apple and crispy shallot salad, sharing platters, puy lentil, spinach, sugar snap, edamame bean and pea shoot salad, steak burger with toppings, barbecue sauce and french fries, salmon fillet wrapped in parma ham with sautéed potatoes, brussels sprouts and walnut pesto, guinea fowl suprême with chorizo lentil casserole and purple sprouting broccoli, braised lamb shank tagine with cauliflower couscous, and puddings such as tonka bean crème brûlée with apricot sorbet and pineapple tarte tatin with mojito granita and mango salsa. *Benchmark main dish: seafood platter (crayfish, potted shrimps, anchovies, rollmop herring, smoked salmon, whitebait) £18.50. Two-course evening meal £24.00.*

Free house ~ Licensee Anthony Goodrich ~ Real ale ~ Open 8am-11pm; 8am-10.30pm Sun ~ Bar food 12-9.30 (8.30 Sun) ~ Restaurant ~ Children welcome ~ Dogs allowed in bar and bedrooms ~ Wi-fi ~ Bedrooms: £95/£125 *Recommended by Revd Michael Vockins, Ian Herdman, John Wooll, Dr J Barrie Jones, James Tilley, Scott and Charlotte Havers, Alison and Michael Harper*

LARLING — TL9889 Map 5

Angel

(01953) 717963 – www.angel-larling.co.uk

From A11 Thetford–Attleborough, take B1111 turn-off and follow pub signs; NR16 2QU

Good-natured, chatty atmosphere in busy pub with several real ales and tasty bar food; bedrooms

The same friendly family have run this bustling pub since 1913 and they still have the original visitors' books from 1897 to 1909. The comfortable 1930s-style lounge on the right has squared panelling, cushioned wheelback chairs, a nice long cushioned panelled corner settle and some good solid tables for eating; also, a collection of whisky-water jugs on a delft shelf over the big brick fireplace, a woodburning stove, a couple of copper kettles and some hunting prints. Adnams Southwold and four guests from breweries such as Crouch Vale, Grainstore, Oakham, Orkney and Swannay on handpump, 100 malt whiskies, ten wines by the glass, 40 gins and a farm cider; they hold an August beer festival with more than 100 real ales and ciders, live music and a barbecue. The quarry-tiled, black-beamed public bar has a good local feel, with a juke box, games machine, board games and background music. There's a neat grass area behind the car park with picnic-sets around a big fairy-lit apple tree and a fenced play area. The five bedrooms are attractive and comfortable. Their four-acre meadow is used as a caravan and camping site from March to October. Good surrounding walks.

Pubby food includes sandwiches, prawn and crayfish salad, creamy and garlic mushroom pot, a pie of the day, sweet pepper lasagne, beer-battered fish of the day, chicken and bacon caesar salad, sausages with egg and chips, burger with toppings, coleslaw and chips, salmon and prawn pasta with creamy white wine and dill sauce, a mixed grill, and puddings such as alabama chocolate cake and italian ice-creams and sorbets. *Benchmark main dish: steak and kidney pie £12.00. Two-course evening meal £17.00.*

Free house ~ Licensee Andrew Stammers ~ Real ale ~ Open 10am-11pm ~ Bar food 12-9.30 (10 Fri, Sat) ~ Restaurant ~ Children welcome ~ Wi-fi ~ Bedrooms: £60/£90
Recommended by Hilary and Neil Christopher, Andrew Stone, Ruth May, Cliff and Monica Swan, Colin and Daniel Gibbs

MORSTON TG0043 Map 8

Anchor

(01263) 741392 – www.morstonanchor.co.uk
A149 Salthouse–Stiffkey; The Street; NR25 7AA

Quite a choice of rooms filled with bric-a-brac and prints, real ales and pleasing food

A most enjoyable pub run well by hands-on licensees and set in a small seaside village, this spot has plenty of customers. Three traditional rooms on the right offer a friendly atmosphere and have straightforward seats and tables on original wooden floors, coal fires, local 1950s beach photographs and lots of prints and bric-a-brac. Adnams Ghost Ship, local Winters Golden and Woodfordes Wherry on handpump, 20 wines by the glass and 13 gins; background music, darts and board games. The contemporary airy extension on the left, with comfortable benches and tables, leads into the more formal restaurant where local art is displayed on the walls. You can sit outside at the front of the building. If parking is tricky at the pub, there's an off-road overflow around the corner and a National Trust car park five minutes' walk away. The surrounding area is wonderful for bird-watching and walking, and you can book seal-spotting trips here.

Well executed food includes lunchtime sandwiches, twice-baked cheese soufflé, smoked salmon fishcakes with curried sauce and crispy kale, spelt and goats cheese gnocchi with butternut squash, pine nuts and sage, chicken breast with local mussels, garlic, parsley and duck fat potatoes, pheasant and venison ragoût with parmesan, wholegrain mustard and pasta, burger with toppings, burger sauce and fries, fish stew, and puddings such as crème brûlée with honeycomb ice-cream and sticky toffee pudding with salted caramel sauce and banoffi ice-cream. *Benchmark main dish: crab linguine £16.00. Two-course evening meal £21.00.*

Free house ~ Licensees Harry Farrow and Rowan Glennie ~ Real ale ~ Open 9am-11pm (10.30pm Sun) ~ Bar food 12-3, 6-9 ~ Restaurant ~ Children welcome ~ Dogs allowed in bar ~ Wi-fi *Recommended by Victoria and James Sargeant, Monty Green, Phil and Jane Villiers, Caroline and Peter Bryant, David Eberlin, D and NF, Tracey and Stephen Groves*

NORTH CREAKE TF8538 Map 8

Jolly Farmers

(01328) 738185 – www.jollyfarmersnorfolk.co.uk
Burnham Road; NR21 9JW

Friendly village local with three cosy rooms, open fires and woodburners, well liked food and several real ales

A friendly new landlord took over this former coaching inn as we went to press. There are three cosy and relaxed rooms, including the main bar with a large open fire in a brick fireplace, a mix of pine farmhouse and high-backed leather dining chairs around scrubbed pine tables on quarry tiles and pale yellow walls. Beside the wooden bar counter are some high bar chairs, and they keep Adnams Broadside, Woodfordes Wherry and a guest or two on handpump, 11 wines by the glass and a dozen malt whiskies; service is helpful and friendly. A smaller bar has pews and a woodburning stove, while the dining room has similar furniture to the bar and another woodburner. The terrace outside has plenty of seats and tables.

The menu had not been finalised as we went to press, but will include sandwiches, soups, haddock smokies and traditional pub choices. *Benchmark main dish: beer-battered fish and chips £13.00. Two-course evening meal £20.00.*

Free house ~ Licensee Christopher Dimblebee ~ Real ale ~ Open 12-2, 5-10; 12-3 Sun; closed Sun evening, Mon ~ Bar food 12-2, 5-9; 12-3 Sun ~ Children welcome ~ Dogs allowed in bar ~ Wi-fi *Recommended by Paul Faraday, Guy Henderson, Peter and Emma Kelly, Bridget and Peter Gregson, Paddy and Sian O'Leary*

NORWICH TG2109 Map 5

Fat Cat

(01603) 624364 – www.fatcatpub.co.uk

West End Street; on foot from city centre (1 mile) turn R down Nelson Street off Dereham Road; NR2 4NA

A place of pilgrimage for beer lovers and open all day; lunchtime rolls and pies

A classic town pub with a quite extraordinary range of up to 32 quickly changing ales kept perfectly by the landlord and his helpful staff who can guide you through the choices. On handpump or tapped from the cask in a stillroom behind the bar – big windows reveal all – are their own beers (Fat Cat Bitter, Honey Ale, IPA, Marmalade Cat and Wild Cat), as well as guests such as Adnams Southwold, Crouch Vale Yakima Gold, Dark Star American Pale Ale, Fullers ESB, Greene King Abbot, Oakham Green Devil IPA and Inferno and Timothy Taylors Landlord – and many more choices from across the country. You'll also find imported draught beers and lagers, over 50 bottled beers from around the world, ten malt whiskies, ten rums and 20 ciders and perries. The no-nonsense furnishings include plain scrubbed pine tables and simple solid seats, lots of brewery memorabilia, bric-a-brac and stained glass; board games. There are tables outside.

Bar food consists of rolls and good pies at lunchtime (not Sunday).

Own brew ~ Licensee Colin Keatley ~ Real ale ~ No credit cards ~ Open 12-11; 11-midnight Sat ~ Bar food Filled rolls available until sold out; not Sun ~ Children allowed until 6pm ~ Dogs welcome ~ Wi-fi *Recommended by Edward May, Mike Swan, Mark Morgan, Dr J Barrie Jones*

RINGSTEAD TF7040 Map 8

Gin Trap

(01485) 525264 – www.thegintrapinn.co.uk

Village signed off A149 near Hunstanton; OS Sheet 132 map reference 707403; PE36 5JU

Bustling country pub with plenty of room in character bars for both eating and drinking and seats outside; bedrooms

There's an amazing 130 gins here (including one named for the pub) and they hold gin festivals in June and September. The original beamed bar has a woodburning stove, farmhouse and mate's chairs around solid pine tables on bare boards, yellow tartan window seats, pub photos on walls and horse tack and coach lamps. Adnams Ghost Ship, Greene King Abbot, Ale Fresco and IPA and Woodfordes Wherry on handpump and several wines by the glass. A step leads up to quarry-tiled room with a conservatory beyond and there's a character back snug with red painted walls and nice old floor tiles. The back garden has picnic-sets and a play area and there are more seats out in front. Bedrooms are comfortable and well equipped. The Peddars Way is close by.

A decent choice of popular food includes local crab with tarragon mayonnaise, onion bhaji scotch egg with cucumber raita, vegan burger with toppings and triple-cooked chips, honey-roast gammon and egg with pineapple salsa, smoked haddock, chive and mozzarella fishcakes with parsley cream sauce, lamb in ale pie, steak of the day, szechuan beef with egg noodles, chilli, lime, pak choi and peanuts, a steak of the day, and puddings such as dark chocolate and pistachio brownie with coconut sorbet and a sundae of the day. *Benchmark main dish: beer-battered fish and chips £12.50. Two-course evening meal £20.00.*

Free house ~ Licensees Dave Wann and Annelli Taylor ~ Real ale ~ Open 11.30-11 ~ Bar food 12-2, 6-8.30; 12-2.30, 6-9 Fri, Sat; 12-3, 6-8 Sun ~ Restaurant ~ Children welcome ~ Dogs allowed in bar and bedrooms ~ Wi-fi ~ Bedrooms: /£99 *Recommended by Lisa Walker, Tracey and Stephen Groves, Katherine and Hugh Markham, Sandra Morgan, Paul Scofield*

SALTHOUSE TG0743 Map 8

Dun Cow

(01263) 740467 – www.salthouseduncow.com

A149 Blakeney–Sheringham (Purdy Street, junction with Bard Hill); NR25 7XA

Cheerful village pub, a good all-rounder with enterprising food

In warm weather, the picnic-sets on the front grass looking out towards the sea are quickly snapped up; there are more seats in a sheltered back courtyard and an orchard garden beyond. The flint-walled bar consists of a pair of high-raftered rooms opened up into one area, with stone tiles round the counter where regulars congregate, and a carpeted seating area with a fireplace at each end. Also, scrubbed tables, one very high-backed settle, country kitchen chairs and elegant little red-padded dining chairs, with big sailing ship and other prints. Adnams Broadside, Norfolk Moon Gazer Golden Ale, Woodfordes Reedlighter and Wherry on handpump, 19 wines by the glass and 14 malt whiskies. Bedrooms are self-catering.

Rewarding food (with quite an emphasis on fresh fish) includes sandwiches (until 5pm), salt and pepper squid with chilli and garlic dip, curried potted crab, sharing platters, shakshuka (pepper, chickpea and tomato stew with baked eggs, cumin and chilli), crispy buttermilk chicken burger with toppings, fries and coleslaw, steak in ale pie, sticky baby back ribs with slaw, local crab linguine with chilli, mint and lime, rare tuna niçoise, and puddings such as treacle tart and custard and flourless orange and almond cake with clotted cream. *Benchmark main dish: keralan fish curry £15.00. Two-course evening meal £21.00.*

Punch ~ Lease Daniel Goff ~ Real ale ~ Open 11.30-11 ~ Bar food 12-9 ~ Children welcome ~ Dogs welcome ~ Wi-fi *Recommended by Claire Adams, Camilla and Jose Ferrera, Alison and Graeme Spicer, Alison and Dan Richardson, Lee and Jill Stafford, D and NF, Roy Hoing*

You can send reports directly to us at feedback@goodguides.com

SHOULDHAM — Kings Arms

TF6708 Map 8

(01366) 347410 – www.kingsarmsshouldham.co.uk

The Green; PE33 0BY

Bustling pub by the village green with local ales, interesting food and a buoyant atmosphere

A cheerful place with good food, this is Norfolk's first co-operative pub. The bar rooms have beams, flagstones, exposed-stone or red-painted walls hung with prints, a homely mix of assorted dining chairs and tables, a leather button-back sofa and a woodburning stove in an inglenook fireplace. The three real ales tapped from the cask might be Adnams Ghost Ship, Beeston Worth the Wait and Grain Oak, there are ten wines by the glass, 14 malt whiskies, 17 gins and local cider; background music. There's also a café staffed by volunteers selling village-baked cakes and scones. The garden has painted picnic-sets on grass. They hold an annual beer, cider and music festival (check the website for dates) and there are classic car or motorcyle meetings on the first Sunday of the month.

Highly rated food includes lunchtime sandwiches and baked potatoes, garlic and rosemary-infused baked camembert, king prawns on roasted fennel, chorizo and baby spinach salad, sweet potato, balsamic onion and goats cheese tart, steak burger with toppings, slaw, chipotle mayonnaise and chips, venison casserole, black bream fillet with harissa-crushed potatoes, tomato, roasted vegetable and preserved lemon tagine and tapenade, pork loin steak with cider-braised cabbage, garlic and rosemary roasted baby potatoes and gravy, and puddings. *Benchmark main dish: steak in ale pie £11.95. Two-course evening meal £20.00.*

Free house ~ Licensee Ian Skinner ~ Real ale ~ Open 5-10.30 Mon; 12-11; 12-10.30 Sun; closed Mon lunchtime ~ Bar food 12-2 (2.30 Fri, Sat), 6-9; 12-4 Sun; not Sun evening or Mon ~ Restaurant ~ Children welcome ~ Dogs allowed in bar ~ Wi-fi ~ Live music throughout the year (see website) *Recommended by Sylvia and Phillip Spencer, Mike and Sarah Abbot, Daniel King, Amy Ledbetter, Elise and Charles Mackinlay*

SNETTISHAM — Rose & Crown

TF6834 Map 8

(01485) 541382 – www.roseandcrownsnettisham.co.uk

Village signposted from A149 King's Lynn–Hunstanton just N of Sandringham; coming in on the B1440 from the roundabout just N of village, take first left into Old Church Road; PE31 7LX

Particularly well run inn with log fires and interesting furnishings, imaginative food, a fine range of drinks and stylish seating on heated terrace; well equipped bedrooms

Once again, there's plenty of high praise for all aspects of this particularly well run inn – our readers love it. The two main bars have distinct character and simple charm, with an open fire and woodburning stove, old quarry tiles or coir flooring, cushioned wall seating and wooden tables and chairs, candles on mantelpieces and daily papers. There are stools against the bar where locals enjoy Adnams Broadside, Ghost Ship and Southwold, Marstons Pedigree, Ringwood Boondoggle and Thwaites Lancaster Bomber on handpump; also, 13 wines by the glass, eight malt whiskies, 30 gins (including local ones), seasonal cocktails and jugs of sangria, local cider and fresh fruit juices. Staff are well trained and interested. A small wood-floored back room has old sports equipment, the landlord's sporting trophies and photos of the pub's cricket team. The civilised little restaurant (decorated in soft greys) has cushions and picture mounts with splashes of bright green and flowers in old galvanised watering cans sitting on windowsills. At the back of the building, two rooms make up the bustling Garden Room, with sofas, wooden farmhouse and white-painted dining chairs around a mix of tables, church candles in large lanterns, attractive striped blinds and doors that lead to the pretty walled garden. Here there are plenty of contemporary seats and tables underneath cream parasols, outdoor heaters, colourful herbaceous borders and a wooden galleon-shaped climbing structure for children. Bedrooms are spacious and well appointed and breakfasts very good. Disabled lavatories and wheelchair ramp. This is sister pub to the Bank House in King's Lynn.

Championing local produce, the top quality food includes breakfasts (7.30-11am), plus sandwiches, crispy ham hock and black pudding bonbons with caramelised apple purée, tempura red mullet with tartare sauce and black garlic aioli, lunchtime ham and egg, wild mushroom and kale spelt risotto with leeks, scampi basket with lemon mayonnaise and fries, whole quail with potato purée, grilled chicory, turnips and shallot and pancetta dressing, chargrilled veal chop with peppercorn sauce, beef stroganoff, and puddings such as chocolate torte with vanilla ice-cream and chocolate soil and mango brûlée with brown sugar shortbread. *Benchmark main dish: slow-cooked venison with pearl barley, root vegetables and sweet dumplings £16.00. Two-course evening meal £24.00.*

Free house ~ Licensee Anthony Goodrich ~ Real ale ~ Open 11-11; 12-10.30 Sun ~ Bar food 12-9; 12-9.30 Fri, Sat; 12-8.30 Sun ~ Restaurant ~ Children welcome ~ Dogs welcome ~ Wi-fi ~ Bedrooms: £100/£120 *Recommended by Katherine and Hugh Markham, Mark and Mary Setting, Muriel and Spencer Harrop, Dr K Nesbitt, D and NF, John Wooll, Roy Hoing*

THORNHAM TF7343 Map 8

Lifeboat

(01485) 512236 – www.lifeboatinnthornham.com

A149 by Orange Tree, then first left; PE36 6LT

Lots of character in traditional inn, plenty of space for eating and dining, real ales and super surrounding walks; bedrooms

If it's just a drink and a chat you want, head for the character main bar with its beams, horse tack and farming implements, big lamps, brass and copper jugs and pans, cushioned window seats, chairs and settles around dark sturdy tables on quarry tiles and woodburning stove; the antique penny-in-the-hole game is hidden under a bench cushion. A second bar, favoured by locals, is smaller, with some fine carving around the counter. Adnams Broadside and Ghost Ship, Woodfordes Mardlers Mild and Wherry and a guest ale such as Norfolk Moon Gazer Ruby Ale on handpump, good wines by the glass and nine gins; background music. The formal entrance hall has sofas and fender seats by a big open fire, there's another room with more sofas and a cylindrical woodburner and also a simply furnished dining room. A quarry-tiled conservatory (used for eating) has fairy lights and steps that lead up to the back garden with grey-painted picnic-sets and a couple of cabanas; there are more picnic-sets at the front of the building. Bedrooms are warm and comfortable and you can walk from here to the salt marshes about a mile away.

Well regarded food includes crispy squid rings with crayfish and apple salad and sweet chilli dressing, chicken liver pâté with ale chutney, sharing platters, goats cheese, slow-cooked tomato and onion chutney tart with sweet potato fries, local sausages with onion rings, gravy and mash, fish pie with cheesy mash, chicken wrapped in bacon and stuffed with smoked cheese, with barbecue glaze and fondant potatoes, lambs liver with bacon, onion rings, creamy mash and roasted baby onion jus, and puddings such as triple chocolate brownie with salted caramel ice-cream and maple treacle tart with custard. *Benchmark main dish: beer-battered fresh fish and chips £14.50. Two-course evening meal £20.00.*

Punch ~ Tenant Keith Barnes ~ Real ale ~ Open 11-11; 12-11 Sun ~ Bar food 12-9 ~ Restaurant ~ Children welcome ~ Dogs allowed in bar and bedrooms ~ Wi-fi ~ Bedrooms: £140/£160 *Recommended by Tracey and Stephen Groves, John Wooll, Patricia and Gordon Thompson, Monty Green, David Brown, Andrew Clark, Melanie and David Lawson*

THORNHAM TF7343 Map 8

Orange Tree

(01485) 512213 – www.theorangetreethornham.co.uk

Church Street/A149; PE36 6LY

Nice combination of friendly bar and contemporary dining, plus suntrap garden; bedrooms

At peak times and in warm weather, you'll need to arrive here early to be sure of a table – even if it's just a drink and a chat that you want. The sizeable pubby bar has a good mix of cheerful customers, white-painted beams, red leather chesterfields in front of a log fire, and flowery upholstered or leather and wooden dining chairs and plush wall seats around a mix of tables on wood or quarry-tiled floors. Adnams Ghost Ship, Woodfordes Wherry and a guest beer on handpump, 37 wines by the glass, 19 gins and a farm cider are served by courteous, hard-working staff. Background music and flatscreen TV. A little dining room leads off here with silver décor, buddha heads and candles, and the two-part restaurant is simple and contemporary in style. The front garden is pretty with lavender beds and climbing roses, lots of picnic-sets under parasols, outdoor heaters and a small smart corner pavilion. At the back of the building is a second outdoor area with children's play equipment. The bedrooms (our readers particularly recommend those in the Old Bakery) make a good base for this lovely stretch of the north Norfolk coast; breakfasts are good. They're kind to dogs and have a doggie menu plus snacks.

Interesting food includes sandwiches, crispy fried chicken with asian miso coleslaw, mango yoghurt, satay, nuts and seeds, hot smoked mackerel with smoked mackerel hummus, pickled candy beetroot, beetroot meringue and beetroot purée, goats cheese and fig brûlée with oyster mushroom, freekeh, baby fennel, herb gnocchi and tarragon oil, rare-breed burger with toppings, creamy thyme and mustard coleslaw and chips, red swimming crab claw and clam linguine with lemon crème fraîche, dill and chilli oil, king prawn, free-range chicken or vegetable balti, and puddings such as Baileys profiteroles with chocolate sauce and banana sticky toffee pudding with banoffi ice-cream and toffee sauce. *Benchmark main dish: free-range chicken, ham and wild mushroom pie £16.95. Two-course evening meal £24.00.*

Punch ~ Lease Mark Goode ~ Real ale ~ Open 8am-11pm; 8am-10.30pm Sun ~ Bar food 12-9 ~ Restaurant ~ Children welcome ~ Dogs allowed in bar and bedrooms ~ Wi-fi ~ Bedrooms: £80/£89 *Recommended by Tracey and Stephen Groves, John and Abigail Prescott, Patti and James Davidson, W K Wood, Gail and Arthur Roberts, Jamie and Lizzie McEwan*

THORPE MARKET TG2434 Map 8

Gunton Arms

(01263) 832010 – www.theguntonarms.co.uk

Cromer Road; NR11 8TZ

Impressive place with an easy-going atmosphere, open fires and antiques, real ales, interesting food and friendly staff; bedrooms

A rather grand country house surrounded by a 1,000-acre deer park, this is certainly rather individual and different, and the large entrance hall sets the scene. The simply furnished bar has dark pubby chairs and tables on a wooden floor, a log fire, a long settle beside a pool table, and high stools against the mahogany counter where they serve Adnams Broadside and Southwold, Woodfordes Wherry and a guest beer on handpump, 13 wines by the glass, 16 malt whiskies and two ciders; staff are chatty and helpful. Heavy curtains line an open doorway into a dining room, where vast antlers hang above a big log fire (they often cook over this) and there are straightforward chairs around scrubbed tables on stone tiles. A lounge, with comfortable old leather armchairs and a sofa on a fine rug in front of yet another log fire, has genuine antiques and standard lamps. The restaurant is more formal with candles and napery, and there are also two homely sitting rooms for hotel residents. Many of the walls are painted dark red and hung with assorted artwork and big mirrors; background music, darts, TV and board games. The bedrooms have many original fittings, but no TV.

Robust food using Estate produce includes sandwiches (until 5pm), all-day nibbles such as spicy wild boar sausages with chilli jam, rare-breed meatballs with tomato and basil sauce, and lamb kofta with tzatziki and red onion salad plus stuffed saddle of rabbit with pickles and crab apple jelly, home-smoked salmon with irish soda bread, chicken, bacon and leek pie, pork and leek sausages with mash and onion gravy, cod fillet with air-dried tuna and vegetable noodles, crab pasta with chilli and coriander, and puddings such as chocolate truffle torte with griottine cherries and honey cheesecake with stem ginger ice-cream. *Benchmark main dish: sirloin steak cooked over the open fire with goose fat roast potatoes and béarnaise sauce £25.00. Two-course evening meal £24.00.*

Free house ~ Licensee Simone Baker ~ Real ale ~ Open 12-11; 12-10.30 Sun ~ Bar food 12-3, 6-10 (9 Sun) ~ Restaurant ~ Children welcome ~ Dogs allowed in bar and bedrooms ~ Wi-fi ~ Bedrooms: /£165 *Recommended by Mark and Mary Setting, Alison and Graeme Spicer, David Twitchett, Bob and Melissa Wyatt, Ben and Jenny Settle*

WARHAM TF9441 Map 8

Three Horseshoes

(01328) 710547 – www.warhamhorseshoes.co.uk

Warham All Saints; village signed from A149 Wells-next-the-Sea to Blakeney, and from B1105 S of Wells; NR23 1NL

Renovated old pub with straightforward furnishings, gaslight in some rooms, friendly service, tasty food and seats in garden; bedrooms

Although this old-fashioned pub has been refurbished and gently smartened up, it has been done so without losing its charm or unspoilt feel. The little rooms (some are gaslit) have quarry tiles, padded leather or upholstered wall seats and kitchen chairs around rustic pine tables, some panelling and painted roughcast walls hung with china plates and royalist photographs, and several Victorian fireplaces. Adnams Ghost Ship and guests such as Beeston Drink to Remember and Norfolk Moon Gazer Golden Ale on handpump and 12 wines by the glass served through a hatch by friendly staff; darts, dominoes, shove-ha'penny, cards and board games. There's a courtyard garden with flower tubs, a terrace with metal chairs and tables and lawns with picnic-sets. Four stylish bedrooms have been opened up in what was the post office next door.

As well as their popular pies, the traditional food includes lunchtime sandwiches, game terrine with plum chutney, cheese and parsley croquettes with chilli jam, vegetarian risotto, burger with toppings and relish, beer-battered fish and chips, local mussels with ale and blue cheese, suet pudding filled with sausage meat, bacon, onion and sage, and puddings such as a cheesecake of the day and rhubarb and pomegranate gin jelly with lemon sorbet. *Benchmark main dish: pie of the day £10.00. Two-course evening meal £17.00.*

Free house ~ Licensees Victoria and James Hadley ~ Real ale ~ Open 11-11; 12-10.30 Sun ~ Bar food 12-2.30, 6-9; 12-9 Sat; 12-8 Sun ~ Children welcome ~ Dogs welcome ~ Wi-fi ~ Bedrooms: £120/£140 *Recommended by John Utley, Alison and Dan Richardson, Amanda Shipley, Sally and Lance Oldham*

WELLS-NEXT-THE-SEA TF9143 Map 8

Crown

(01328) 710209 – www.crownhotelnorfolk.co.uk

The Buttlands; NR23 1EX

Handsome white-painted inn with a friendly informal bar, local ales, good modern food and elegant restaurant; comfortable bedrooms

This is a smart old coaching inn overlooking a tree-lined green and run by the chef-owner. There's a good mix of drinkers and diners and plenty of different rooms to choose from. The rambling bar is on several levels with beams and standing timbers, grey-painted planked wall seats and leather dining chairs on stripped floorboards, with Adnams Fat Sprat and Mosaic and a beer named for the pub on handpump and good wines by the glass. There's an airy dining room and more formal restaurant, rugs on more floorboards, armchairs and sofas, painted farmhouse and other chairs, lots of books on shelves, boating paintings and large horns on pale-painted walls, and several woodburning stoves. There are seats and tables outside. Bedrooms are smart, comfortable and well equipped. This is part of Flying Kiwi Inns.

Imaginative food cooked by the owner includes lunchtime sandwiches, crayfish caesar salad, pork, pistachio and apricot terrine with parsnip and chilli chutney, gammon steak with sautéed new potatoes, a poached egg and english mustard sauce, halloumi fritters with roast mediterranean vegetables and lemon couscous, fish of the day in a thai watermelon curry with coriander yoghurt and fragrant rice, chicken breast with tagliatelle in bacon and mushroom cream sauce, rack of lamb with crispy lamb croquette and mustard spring cabbage, and puddings such as double chocolate parfait on chocolate crumb with salt caramel and toasted marshmallow and lemon posset shot with lemon drizzle cake, crushed meringue and rapsberries. *Benchmark main dish: cod with clams and sweetcorn chowder £21.95. Two-course evening meal £28.00.*

Flying Kiwi Inns ~ Licensee Chris Coubrough ~ Real ale ~ Open 11-11; 11-10 Sun ~ Bar food 12-2.30, 6-9; 12-9 Sun ~ Restaurant ~ Children welcome ~ Dogs allowed in bar and bedrooms ~ Bedrooms: £140/£230 *Recommended by Thomas Green, Charlie Stevens, Freddie and Sarah Banks*

WIVETON TG0442 Map 8

Wiveton Bell

(01263) 740101 – www.wivetonbell.co.uk

Blakeney Road; NR25 7TL

Busy dining pub where drinkers are welcomed too, local beers, consistently enjoyable food and seats outside; bedrooms

With a good mix of customers and a bustling atmosphere, our readers enjoy their visits here. The mainly open-plan rooms have some fine old beams, an attractive mix of dining chairs around wooden tables on a stripped-wood floor, a log fire and prints on yellow walls. The sizeable conservatory has smart beige dining chairs around wooden tables on coir flooring. Friendly, attentive staff serve only local ales such as Norfolk Moon Gazer Golden Ale, Woodfordes Wherry and Yetmans Red on handpump, and a dozen wines by the glass; complimentary sausage rolls and nibbles are on offer early on Friday evening. Picnic-sets on the front grass look across to the church; at the back, stylish wicker tables and chairs on several decked areas are set among decorative box hedging; there's a new front terrace with similar furniture. This is a nice place to stay and the character bedrooms are comfortable and well equipped (three have their own small terrace); a continental breakfast hamper is delivered to your room each morning. There's also a self-catering cottage to rent.

Inventive food includes lunchtime sandwiches, half dressed local crab salad with honey-soused vegetables, chicken liver pâté with dill and cucumber, chicken caesar salad, roast hispi cabbage with morel mushrooms, shallot confit, compressed apple and onion broth, salt marsh-grazed beef burger with candied bacon, rarebit, red cabbage slaw and chips, monkfish with cauliflower purée, caper and raisin dressing and red onion fritters, lamb rump with potato terrine, peas, gem lettuce and bacon, and puddings such as whisky and white chocolate bread and butter pudding with marmalade ice-cream and millionaire's shortbread with pear sorbet; they also offer a Monday-Thursday deal in winter that includes a glass of wine or a real ale. *Benchmark main dish: halibut with crab-crushed potatoes, asparagus and crab butter sauce £22.00. Two-course evening meal £24.00.*

Free house ~ Licensee Berni Morritt ~ Real ale ~ Open 12-11 (10.30 Sun) ~ Bar food 12-2.15, 6-9; 12-8 Sun ~ Children welcome ~ Dogs allowed in bar ~ Wi-fi ~ Bedrooms: /£120
Recommended by Dr Tony Whitehead, Revd Michael Vockins, Ian Herdman, Mr and Mrs Richard Osborne, Michael Sargent, Dr K Nesbitt, Roy Hoing

WOLTERTON TG1732 Map 8

Saracens Head

(01263) 768909 - www.saracenshead-norfolk.co.uk
Wolterton; Erpingham signed off A140 N of Aylsham, on through Calthorpe; NR11 7LZ

Remote inn with stylish bars and dining room and seats in courtyard; good bedrooms

Once found, customers tend to return to this tucked-away Georgian inn on a regular basis. The two-room bar is simple but stylish with high ceilings, light terracotta walls and tall windows with cream and gold curtains – all lending a feeling of space, though it's not large. There's a mix of seats from built-in wall settles to wicker fireside chairs, as well as log fires and flowers. Friendly staff serve Woodfordes Wherry and a changing guest such as Panther Red Panther on handpump and several wines by the glass. The windows look on to a charming old-fashioned gravel stableyard with plenty of chairs, benches and tables. A pretty six-table parlour on the right has another big log fire. Bedrooms are comfortable and up to date.

Distinctive food includes pigeon breast with apple and black pudding salad, local mussels with white wine, shallots, garlic and cream, roasted cauliflower with grilled halloumi, tahini and harissa dressing and preserved lemon, pheasant breast wrapped in parma ham with chestnuts and dauphinoise potatoes, halibut with leek, mussel and potato broth, lamb steak with crispy fried potatoes, crushed peas and red wine jus, local sirloin steak with pink peppercorn sauce, and puddings such as vanilla pannacotta with raspberry sorbet and boozy cherries and chocolate nemesis with pistachio ice-cream. *Benchmark main dish: slow-roast pork belly with chickpea, chorizo and tomato stew £15.50. Two-course evening meal £21.50.*

Free house ~ Licensees Tim and Janie Elwes ~ Real ale ~ Open 11-3, 6-10.30; closed Sun evening in winter ~ Bar food 12-2, 6 (6.30 Mon)-8.30; 12.30-2.30, 6.30-8 Sun ~ Restaurant ~

Children welcome ~ Dogs allowed in bar and bedrooms ~ Wi-fi ~ Bedrooms: £75/£110
Recommended by Dr Tony Whitehead, John and Penny Wildon, Karl and Frieda Bujeya, Chloe and Tim Hodge, Brian and Sally Wakeham, Alison and Graeme Spicer

WOODBASTWICK TG3214 Map 8

Fur & Feather

(01603) 720003 – www.thefurandfeather.co.uk
Off B1140 E of Norwich; NR13 6HQ

Full range of first class Woodfordes brewery ales, friendly service and popular bar food

Carefully converted from a row of thatched cottage buildings, this is a charming pub in a lovely Estate village. It's next door to Woodfordes brewery, so the perfectly kept ales tapped from the cask include Bure Gold, Nelsons Revenge, Norfolk Nog, Reedlighter and Wherry, plus two guests. Efficient, helpful staff also serve a dozen wines by the glass and 12 malt whiskies. The style and atmosphere are not what you'd expect of a brewery tap as it's set out more like a comfortable and roomy dining pub with wooden chairs and tables on tiles or carpeting, plus sofas and armchairs; background music. There are seats and tables in the pleasant garden where they keep chickens. You can also visit the brewery shop (and if you eat here, you get a ten per cent discount voucher for the shop).

Enjoyable food includes sandwiches, local crab cake with pea purée, braised pig cheeks with spring onion rémoulade, goats cheese risotto, beef, pork and lamb burgers with toppings, slaw and fries, chicken caesar salad, venison pie, sea bass with horseradish mash and camomile tea sauce, pork chops in a honey glaze with bubble and squeak, minute steak with peppercorn sauce and chips, and puddings such as bakewell tart with lemon curd ice-cream and fudge brownie with salted caramel ice-cream. *Benchmark main dish: steak and kidney pudding £13.95. Two-course evening meal £20.00.*

Woodfordes ~ Tenant Nicholas Dolan ~ Real ale ~ Open 11-11 (midnight Sat) ~ Bar food 12-9; 12-7 Sun ~ Restaurant ~ Children welcome ~ Dogs welcome ~ Wi-fi
Recommended by Beth Aldridge, Elise and Charles Mackinlay, Mark Morgan, Dave & Sue, Matthew and Elisabeth Reeves, Christopher May

Also Worth a Visit in Norfolk

Besides the fully inspected pubs, you might like to try these pubs that have been recommended to us and described by readers. Do tell us what you think of them: feedback@goodguides.com

AYLMERTON TG1840

Roman Camp (01263) 838291
Holt Road (A148); NR11 8QD Large 19th-c mock-Tudor roadside inn; comfortable panelled bar, cosy sitting room off with warm fire and light airy dining room, decent choice of enjoyable sensibly priced food from sandwiches up, well kept Adnams, Greene King and a guest, friendly helpful service from uniformed staff; free wi-fi; children welcome, attractive sheltered garden behind with sunny terraces and pond, 16 bedrooms. *(Andrew Vincent)*

AYLSHAM TG1926

★**Black Boys** (01263) 732122
Market Place; off B1145; NR11 6EH Small friendly hotel with imposing Georgian façade; informal open-plan beamed bar with comfortable seating and plenty of tables on carpet or bare boards, popular generously served food from snacks up including meal deals and good Sun roasts, Adnams, guest ales and decent wines, helpful young uniformed staff coping well at busy times; children and dogs welcome, seats in front by marketplace, more behind, bedrooms, big cooked breakfast from 8am, open (and food) all day. *(Mrs Margo Finlay, Jörg Kasprowski)*

BANNINGHAM TG2129

★**Crown** (01263) 733534
Colby Road; opposite church by village green; NR11 7DY Welcoming 17th-c beamed pub in same family for 27 years; good choice of popular food (they're helpful with gluten-free diets), well kept Greene King, local guest ales and decent wines, friendly efficient service, log fires and woodburners; events including Aug music festival and winter quiz nights (last Tues of month), TV, free wi-fi; children and dogs welcome, disabled access, open (and food) all day weekends. *(David Twitchett)*

BARTON BENDISH TF7105

Berney Arms (01366) 347995
Off A1122 W of Swaffham; Church Road; PE33 9GF Attractive dining pub in quiet village; good freshly made food from pub favourites to more inventive dishes including good value set lunch, welcoming helpful staff, Adnams beers and several wines by the glass, afternoon teas, restaurant; children and dogs (in bar) welcome, nice garden with gazebos and unusual church tower slide, good bedrooms in converted stables and forge (also two in main building), open all day, food all day Sun. *(Alison and Michael Harper)*

BINHAM TF9839

Chequers (01328) 830297
B1388 SW of Blakeney; NR21 0AL Long low-beamed 17th-c local away from the bustle of the coastal pubs; comfortable bar with coal fires at each end, Adnams Southwold, Norfolk Moon Gazer Golden and guests, enjoyable pub food at reasonable prices, friendly staff; various games; children and dogs welcome, picnic-sets in front and on back grass, interesting village with huge priory church, open all day weekends. *(Sandra Morgan)*

BLAKENEY TG0243

Kings Arms (01263) 740341
West Gate Street; NR25 7NQ A stroll from the harbour to this chatty 18th-c pub; three simple low-ceilinged connecting rooms and airy garden room, Adnams, Greene King and guests, generous wholesome food from breakfast on; children and dogs welcome, big garden, seven bedrooms, open (and food) all day from 9.30am (midday Sun). *(Ben and Jenny Settle)*

BLICKLING TG1728

Bucks Arms (01263) 732133
B1354 NW of Aylsham; NR11 6NF Handsome Jacobean inn well placed by gates to Blickling Hall (NT); small proper bar, dining lounge with woodburner and smarter more formal restaurant with another fire, Adnams and a guest, several wines by the glass and substantial helpings of enjoyable pub food, good friendly service; background music; children and dogs welcome, tables out on lawn, lovely walks nearby, three bedrooms, open all day (food all day Sun). *(Ian Herdman, David Twitchett)*

BODHAM STREET TG1240

Red Hart (01263) 588270
The Street; NR25 6AD Old family-run village pub with well liked fairly traditional home-cooked food from lunchtime ciabattas up, ales such as Woodfordes Wherry, friendly helpful service; pool, sports TV, free wi-fi; children and dogs welcome (menus for both), garden picnic-sets, open all day. *(Sally and Lance Oldham)*

BRANCASTER TF7743

Ship (01485) 210333
London Street (A149); PE31 8AP Popular roadside inn, part of the small Flying Kiwi group; compact bar with built-in cushioned and planked wall seats, four well kept local ales and nice wines by the glass from oak counter, several dining areas with woodburner in one and log-piled fireplace in another, food and service can be good, contemporary paintwork throughout, pale settles and nice mix of other furniture on rugs and bare boards, bookcases, shipping memorabilia and lots of prints; background music, TV, daily papers; children and dogs (biscuits on the bar) welcome, gravelled seating area with circular picnic-sets out by car park, nine attractive well equipped bedrooms, open all day, food all day Sun. *(Tracey and Stephen Groves)*

BRANCASTER STAITHE TF7944

★**Jolly Sailors** (01485) 210314
Main Road (A149); PE31 8BJ Unpretentious pub set in prime bird-watching area on edge of NT dunes and salt flats; chatty mix of locals and visitors in simply furnished bars, wheelbacks, settles and cushioned benches around mix of tables on quarry tiles, photographs and local maps on the walls, woodburner, their own Brancaster ales (brewery not on site) and guests, several wines by the glass, sizeable back dining room with popular food including pizzas (price reasonable for the area); children and dogs welcome, plenty of picnic-sets and play equipment in peaceful back garden, ice-cream hut in summer, vine-covered terrace, open all day (food all day in season). *(John Wooll)*

BRANCASTER STAITHE TF8044

★**White Horse** (01485) 210262
A149 E of Hunstanton; PE31 8BY Popular restauranty place, but does have proper informal front bar serving own Brancaster beers (also in bottles), guest ales, lots of wines by the glass (including a local rosé) and good range of gins, log fire, pine furniture, historical photographs and bar billiards, middle part with comfortable sofas and newspapers, splendid views over tidal marshes from airy dining conservatory and

raised lounge, good bar and restaurant food including tapas and plenty of fish, efficient attentive staff (may ask for a credit card if you run a tab); children welcome, dogs in bar, seats on sun deck enjoying the view, more under cover on heated front terrace, 15 nice bedrooms, coast path at bottom of garden, open (and bar food) all day, from 9am for breakfast. *(Tracey and Stephen Groves, W K Wood, Roy Hoing)*

BRISLEY TF9521

Brisley Bell (01362) 705024
B1145; The Green; NR20 5DW Refurbished 17th-c pub in good spot on edge of sheep-grazed common (one of England's biggest); friendly atmosphere, various areas ranging from cosy beamed snug with large open fire to airy garden room, well liked interesting food (not Sun evening) including set lunch, Adnams and local guests, nice wines and decent range of other drinks (norfolk whisky/gin), friendly efficient service; events such as live music, book club and charity auction; children and dogs welcome, terrace and good-sized garden, new bedrooms in converted outbuildings (glamping also planned), closed Mon, otherwise open all day. *(Gina Foster)*

BROCKDISH TM2179

Old Kings Head (01379) 668843
The Street; IP21 4JY Light and airy old pub at centre of village; several well kept changing ales, decent wines by the glass and over 100 gins, enjoyable food with Italian slant including good pizzas, friendly helpful staff, L-shaped beamed bar with comfortable leather sofa, tub chairs, pews and scrubbed wooden tables on bare boards, log fire, steps up to smaller seating area, café serving good coffee and cakes, local artwork for sale; live music nights; popular with Angles Way walkers, dogs welcome in bar, a few tables out at the side, closed Mon, otherwise open (and food) all day, shuts 9pm Sun. *(Bob and Melissa Wyatt)*

BROOKE TM2899

Kings Head (01508) 550335
Norwich Road (B1332); NR15 1AB Welcoming 17th-c village pub with enjoyable food from traditional choices up including regular themed evenings, four real ales and excellent choice of wines by the glass, maybe a Norfolk whisky, light and airy bare-boards bar with log fire, eating area up a step; occasional quiz and live music, free wi-fi; children and dogs welcome, tables in sheltered garden, open all day (from 9.30am weekends for breakfast). *(Mat)*

BROOME TM3591

Artichoke (01986) 893325
Yarmouth Road; NR35 2NZ Unpretentious split-level roadside pub with up to ten well kept ales (some from tap room casks) including Adnams, belgian fruit beers and excellent selection of whiskies, good traditional home-made food in bar or dining room, friendly helpful staff, wood and flagstone floors, log fire in big fireplace; dogs welcome, garden picnic-sets, smokers' shelter, good walks nearby, closed Mon otherwise open all day. *(Charlie Stevens)*

BURNHAM MARKET TF8342

Hoste (01328) 738777
The Green (B1155); PE31 8HD Stylish hotel's character front bar with informal chatty atmosphere, leather dining chairs, settles and armchairs (note the glass-topped suitcase table), wood-effect flooring, farming implements and cartoons on the walls, woodburner, Greene King and Woodfordes, 25 wines by the glass from extensive carefully chosen list and several malt whiskies, good if not cheap food including lunchtime sandwiches, afternoon teas, elegant dining areas, bustling conservatory and smart airy back restaurant, art gallery upstairs; children and dogs (in bar) welcome, attractive garden, luxurious bedrooms, open all day from 9am. *(David Jackman, D and NF)*

BURNHAM MARKET TF8342

Nelson (01328) 738321
Creake Road; PE31 8EN Dining pub with nice food from sandwiches and pub favourites to more ambitious dishes in bar and restaurant, pleasant efficient staff, well kept Adnams Ghost Ship, Woodfordes Wherry and guests from pale wood servery, extensive wine list, L-shaped bar with leather sofas and armchairs, local artwork for sale; children and dogs welcome, terrace picnic-sets under parasols, seven bedrooms (two in converted outbuilding), open all day. *(Tony Scott)*

BURNHAM OVERY STAITHE TF8444

★**Hero** (01328) 738334
Wells Road (A149); PE31 8JE Spacious refurbished roadside pub (sister to the Anchor at Morston – see Main Entries); good choice of well liked often inventive food from sandwiches and snacks up (booking advised), three real ales such as Adnams and Grain, decent wines and interesting range of gins, friendly young staff, large bar and separate pitched-ceiling restaurant, woodburners; children and dogs welcome, terrace seating front and back, bedrooms, open all day from 9am. *(David Stewart, Roy Hoing)*

CHEDGRAVE TM3699

White Horse (01508) 520250
Norwich Road; NR14 6ND Welcoming pub with five well kept ales such as Adnams and Timothy Taylors, decent wines by the glass and good choice of popular sensibly priced food (all day Sun) including a 'healthy options' menu and themed nights, friendly attentive staff, log fire and sofas in bar, restaurant; monthly quiz, some live

music, pool and darts; children and dogs welcome, garden picnic-sets, open all day. *(Max Simons)*

COCKLEY CLEY TF7904

Twenty Churchwardens (01760) 721439 *Off A1065 S of Swaffham; PE37 8AN* Informal pub in converted school next to church; three linked beamed rooms, good open fire, decent well-priced food including nice home-made pies, well kept Adnams Southwold; newspapers, second-hand books for sale, no credit cards; children and dogs (particularly) welcome, tiny unspoilt village. *(Molly and Stewart Lindsay)*

COLTISHALL TG2719

Kings Head (01603) 737426 *Wroxham Road (B1354); NR12 7EA* Dining pub close to River Bure and moorings; imaginative food from owner-chef (especially fish/seafood), also bar snacks, lunchtime set menu and children's choices, well kept Adnams and good wines by the glass, open fire, fishing nets and stuffed fish including a monster pike; background music; seats outside (noisy road), four bedrooms, open (and food) all day Sun. *(Patricia and Gordon Tucker)*

CONGHAM TF7123

Anvil (01485) 600625 *St Andrews Lane; PE32 1DU* Tucked-away modern country pub with welcoming licensees; wide choice of generously served home-made food (smaller helpings available) including good value Sun carvery, quick friendly service, three or more well kept ales (at least one local); live music and quiz nights; children welcome, no dogs inside, picnic-sets in small walled front garden, campsite, closed Mon, otherwise open all day. *(Christopher May)*

CROMER TG2242

Red Lion (01263) 514964 *Off A149; Tucker Street/Brook Street; NR27 9HD* Substantial Victorian hotel with elevated sea views; original features including panelling and open fires, up to six well kept local ales and a couple of ciders in bare-boards flint-walled bar, good reasonably priced food from sandwiches and sharing plates up including daily specials, efficient friendly service, spacious restaurant and conservatory; background music; children and dogs welcome, disabled access/facilities, tables in back courtyard, 14 comfortable bedrooms, open all day. *(Tina and David Woods-Taylor, Revd R P Tickle, Dr J Barrie Jones)*

DEREHAM TF9813

George (01362) 696801 *Swaffham Road; NR19 2AZ* Welcoming 18th-c inn/restaurant; enjoyable generously served food at fair prices including popular Fri steak night and some themed evenings, Adnams and Woodfordes ales, friendly helpful staff, panelled interior with decent sized bar, dining room and conservatory; children and dogs welcome, heated terrace, seven bedrooms (two in annexe), open all day. *(Tony and Wendy Hobden)*

DERSINGHAM TF6930

Coach & Horses (01485) 540391 *Manor Road; PE31 6LN* Friendly local with well kept Woodfordes Wherry and a couple of guests, enjoyable food including daily specials and Weds steak night, cheerful efficient service, bar and back dining room; Thurs quiz, some live music, free wi-fi; children and dogs (in bar) welcome, painted picnic-sets in garden with play area and pétanque, three bedrooms, open all day, no food Sun evening out of season. *(Tracey and Stephen Groves)*

DERSINGHAM TF6930

Feathers (01485) 540768 *B1440 towards Sandringham; Manor Road; PE31 6LN* Jacobean carrstone inn (once part of the Sandringham Estate); two adjoining bars (main one with big open fire), well kept Adnams, Woodfordes and a guest, enjoyable good value food including OAP lunch deal Mon-Fri, welcoming helpful service, back dining room; background music; children and dogs welcome, large garden with play area, function room in converted stables, six bedrooms, open all day, food all day weekends. *(John Wooll, Tracey and Stephen Groves)*

EAST WINCH TF6916

Carpenters Arms (01553) 841228 *A47 Lynn Road; PE32 1NP* Useful roadside pub with good value home-made food including daily specials in bar or separate restaurant, several beers and ciders; quiz night third Thurs of month, free wi-fi; children welcome, no dogs inside, open (and food) all day. *(Paddy and Sian O'Leary)*

EDGEFIELD TG0934

Pigs (01263) 587634 *Norwich Road; B1149 S of Holt; NR24 2RL* Popular country pub with rooms; Adnams, Greene King, Woodfordes and a house beer brewed by Wolf tapped from casks in tiled-floor bar, dining areas either side, one split into stalls by standing timbers and low brick walls, the other light and airy with white-painted floorboards, good variety of well liked food (all day Sun) including Norfolk tapas, games room with pool and table football, also children's playroom; background music; dogs allowed in bar, good wheelchair access, rustic furniture on big covered front terrace, adventure playground, boules, ten bedrooms (seven with spa facilities including sauna and outside bath), open all day from 8am (breakfast for non-residents). *(Alan McQuilan)*

ELSING TG0516

Mermaid (01362) 637640
Church Road; NR20 3EA Welcoming 17th-c pub in quiet little village; L-shaped carpeted bar with woodburner, well kept Adnams, Woodfordes and guests tapped from the cask, enjoyable home-made food including range of pies and suet puddings (signature steak and kidney roly-poly), indian and thai curries also available, friendly helpful service; pool and other games such as dominoes and shut the box, free wi-fi; children and dogs welcome, handy for walkers on Wensum Way, nice garden, 14th-c church opposite with interesting brasses, closed Mon lunchtime. *(Andrew Bebbington)*

GAYTON TF7219

Crown (01553) 636252
Lynn Road (B1145/B1153); opposite church; PE32 1PA Low-beamed village pub with plenty of character; three main areas and a charming snug, reasonable value food including generous buffet lunch (Mon-Sat) and carvery (Tues-Fri evenings, all day Sun), well kept Greene King ales, sofas and good log fire, games room, free wi-fi; children welcome in restaurant, dogs in bar, disabled access, picnic-sets in attractive sheltered garden, four bedrooms, open (and food) all day. *(David Jackman)*

GREAT BIRCHAM TF7632

Kings Head (01485) 578265
B1155, S end of village (called and signed Bircham locally); PE31 6RJ Handsome Edwardian hotel with cheerful little bar, comfortable sofas, tub chairs and log fire, four well kept local ales such as Norfolk and Woodfordes, good range of wines, whiskies and over 80 gins, lounge areas and airy modern restaurant with varied choice of much liked food, friendly helpful staff; background music, free wi-fi; children and dogs welcome, tables out at front and in back garden with nice country views, 12 comfortable bedrooms, open all day, food all day during summer school holidays. *(David Jackman)*

GREAT CRESSINGHAM TF8401

★**Windmill** (01760) 756232
Village signed off A1065 S of Swaffham; Water End; IP25 6NN Shuttered red-brick pub with interesting pictures and bric-a-brac in warren of rambling linked rooms, plenty of cosy corners, wide range of tasty food from sandwiches to chargrills, a house beer (Windy Miller) brewed by Purity along with Adnams, Greene King and two guests, good choice of wines by the glass and extensive range of whiskies/gins, friendly efficient staff, games room with pool and other pub games; background music, big sports TV in side snug; children and dogs welcome, large garden with picnic-sets and good play area, caravan parking, bedrooms, open all day from 7.30am for breakfast. *(Brian Glozier)*

GREAT HOCKHAM TL9592

Eagle (01953) 498893
Harling Road; IP24 1NP Friendly 19th-c red-brick corner local; half a dozen well kept ales including Adnams, Greene King and Woodfordes, pubby food all day Fri, Sat and till 6pm Sun, just lunchtime snacks other days; fortnightly quiz Weds, pool, darts, free wi-fi; children and dogs welcome, open all day weekends. *(Freddie and Sarah Banks)*

HARPLEY TF7825

Rose & Crown (01485) 521807
Off A148 Fakenham–Kings Lynn; Nethergate Street; PE31 6TW Friendly old village pub competently run by welcoming licensees, good generously served home-made food including popular Sun roasts, well kept Woodfordes Wherry and guests, Aspall's cider, modernised interior with open fires; free wi-fi; children and dogs welcome, picnic-sets in garden, open (and food) all day. *(David Jackman)*

HEYDON TG1127

★**Earle Arms** (01263) 587376
Off B1149; NR11 6AD Popular old dutch-gabled pub overlooking green and church in delightfully unspoilt Estate village; well kept Adnams, Woodfordes and a guest, food from varied if not extensive menu using local fish and meat (gluten-free choices marked), decent wine list, racing prints, some stuffed animals and good log fire in old-fashioned candlelit bar, more formal dining room; free wi-fi; children and dogs welcome, picnic-sets in small cottagey back garden, open all day Sun (no evening food then), closed Mon. *(John Rooney)*

HICKLING TG4123

Greyhound (01692) 598306
The Green; NR12 0YA Popular little village pub with welcoming long-serving landlord; good choice of enjoyable pubby food in bar and neat restaurant, three or four well kept ales including Adnams and Sharps, local cider, nice open fire; sports TV; well behaved children and dogs welcome, seats out at front and in pretty back garden with covered terrace, handy for nature reserve, open all day but may shut early if quiet. *(Roy Hoing)*

HILBOROUGH TF8200

Swan (01760) 756380
Brandon Road (A1065); IP26 5BW Welcoming early 18th-c pub with good quality food including interesting blackboard specials and Sun carvery, also a gluten-free menu, up to four well kept beers and good value wine list, pleasant helpful staff, small back restaurant; free wi-fi; children and dogs (in bar) welcome, picnic-sets on sheltered lawn, eight bedrooms, open all day, food all day Fri-Sun. *(Guy Smith)*

HINGHAM TG0202

White Hart (01953) 850214
Market Place, just off B1108 W of Norwich; NR9 4AF Georgian-fronted coaching inn with character rooms arranged over two floors; beams and standing timbers, stripped floorboards with oriental rugs, mix of furniture including comfortable sofas in quiet corners, lots of prints and photographs, woodburners, galleried long room up steps from main bar with egyptian frieze, upstairs dining/function room, good choice of enjoyable food including british tapas, four real ales, lots of wines by the glass and cocktails; background music, bar billiards; children welcome, dogs downstairs, modern benches and seats in gravelled courtyard, pretty village with huge 14th-c church, five refurbished bedrooms, open all day, food all day Sat and Sun. *(Charlie Stevens)*

HOLME-NEXT-THE-SEA TF7043

White Horse (01485) 525512
Kirkgate Street; PE36 6LH Attractive old-fashioned place with warm log fires and lots of nooks and crannies, ample choice of enjoyable inexpensive food including local fish, friendly efficient service, Adnams, Greene King and decent wines, side extension; children and dogs welcome, small back garden, more seats out in front and on lawn opposite, play area, open all day. *(John Wooll)*

HOLT TG0738

Feathers (01263) 712318
Market Place; NR25 6BW Relaxed hotel with popular locals' bar comfortably extended around original panelled area, open fire, antiques in attractive entrance/reception area, good choice of enjoyable fairly priced food including blackboard specials, Wed thai and Thurs curry nights, friendly accommodating service, Greene King ales and decent wines, good coffee, restaurant and dining conservatory; background music; children and dogs (in bar) welcome, 14 comfortable bedrooms, open all day. *(John Evans)*

HONINGHAM TG1011

Honingham Buck (01603) 880393
Just off A47 W of Norwich; The Street; NR9 5BL Picturesque and smartly renovated 16th-c pub; beamed and timbered bar with flagstones and inglenook woodburner, Lacons beers and plenty of wines by the glass including champagne, very good imaginative food from unusual snacks up, friendly attentive service, comfortable restaurant with upholstered chairs and banquettes; children welcome, seats on sheltered lawn, eight clean modern bedrooms in converted outbuildings, open all day, food all day Sun till 7pm. *(Chris and Diana Aylott, Dr Peter Crawshaw)*

HORSEY TG4622

★**Nelson Head** (01493) 393378
Off B1159; The Street; NR29 4AD Red-brick country pub, nicely tucked away and unspoilt, with impressive range of beers (some tapped from the cask), proper ciders and good sensibly priced bar food (not Sun evening in winter) from sandwiches and snacks to daily specials, friendly chatty staff, log fire and lots of interesting bric-a-brac including various guns, small side dining room; quiet background music; children welcome, well behaved dogs in bar, outside seating (some in field opposite), good coast walks (seals), open all day. *(Amy Ledbetter)*

HORSTEAD TG2619

Recruiting Sergeant (01603) 737077
B1150 just S of Coltishall; NR12 7EE Light, airy and spacious roadside pub; enjoyable generously served food from wraps and jacket potatoes up including good fish choice (booking recommended), efficient friendly service, up to half a dozen changing ales such as Adnams, Greene King, Timothy Taylors and Woodfordes, plenty of wines by the glass, big open fire; children and dogs welcome, terrace and garden tables, variety of local walks, bedrooms, open all day, breakfasts from 8am Mon-Fri. *(Charlie Stevens)*

HUNWORTH TG0735

Bell (01263) 711151
Signed off B roads S of Holt; NR24 2AA Renovated 18th-c beamed pub (known locally as the Hunny Bell) under same ownership as the Duck at Stanhoe; neat bar with country chairs around wooden tables, stone floor and woodburner, cosy snug and high-raftered restaurant, good food from sandwiches and pubby choices to more restauranty dishes cooked by landlord-chef, five real ales such as Greene King, Woodfordes and Yetmans, friendly helpful service; children and dogs welcome, wheelchair access, tables on terrace overlooking village green, more seats in garden among fruit trees, open all day, food all day Sun. *(Molly and Stewart Lindsay)*

KENNINGHALL TM0485

Red Lion (01953) 887849
B1113 S of Norwich; East Church Street; NR16 2EP Beamed 16th-c pub with stripped beams, bare boards and old floor tiles; well kept Greene King IPA, Woodfordes Wherry and guests, decent home-made food from baguettes and baked potatoes up including Fri fish and Sun brunch, friendly helpful staff, bar with woodburner, cosy panelled snug and back restaurant; regular live music and quiz nights, free wi-fi; children (not in bar) and dogs welcome, tables out by back bowling green, bedrooms in former stable block, open all day. *(Peter and Emma Kelly)*

KING'S LYNN TF6120

Crown & Mitre (01553) 774669
Ferry Street; PE30 1LJ Old-fashioned unchanging pub in great riverside spot; lots of interesting naval and nautical memorabilia, up to six well kept ales and good value straightforward home-made food, river-view back conservatory; no credit cards; well behaved children and dogs allowed, quayside tables; for sale as we went to press. *(John Wooll)*

KING'S LYNN TF6119

Marriotts Warehouse (01553) 818500 *South Quay; PE30 5DT* Bar-restaurant-café in converted 16th-c brick and stone warehouse; well priced food from lunchtime sandwiches and light dishes up (greater evening choice), good range of wines, beers such as Sharps Doom Bar and Woodfordes Wherry, cocktails, small upstairs bar with river views; children welcome, quayside tables, open all day from 10am. *(Dr J Barrie Jones)*

LESSINGHAM TG3928

Star (01692) 580510
School Road; NR12 0DN Popular little pub on outskirts of village; low ceilings and inglenook woodburner, local ales and ample helpings of enjoyable reasonably priced food, warm friendly service, small back restaurant; children and dogs welcome, good-sized garden, two bedrooms in building behind, closed Mon, no food Sun evening. *(Roy Hoing)*

LETHERINGSETT TG0638

Kings Head (01263) 712691
A148 (Holt Road) W of Holt; NR25 7AR Country house-style dining inn under same ownership as the Jolly Sailors in Brancaster; rugs on quarry tiles, hunting/coaching prints and open fires, own Brancaster beer along with Norfolk Moon Gazer and Woodfordes, food from good sandwiches and pubby choices up, skylit bare-boards dining room with built-in wall seating, farm tools on cream-painted flint and cob walls, back area under partly pitched ceiling with painted rafters; background music, sports TV, free wi-fi; children and dogs welcome, picnic-sets out at front and in big garden with play area, four bedrooms, open (and food) all day. *(Denis and Margaret Kilner, M and GR, James Tilley)*

LYNG TG0617

Fox (01603) 872316
The Street; NR9 5AL Old beamed village pub with several linked areas and separate restaurant; ample helpings of good inexpensive home-made food including Mon street-food menu, Tues steak night and midweek two-course lunch deal, ales such as Adnams and Woodfordes, friendly staff; pool and giant chessboard in one part; children and dogs (in front bar) welcome, enclosed garden with view of church, open all day in summer apart from Mon lunchtime. *(Christopher May)*

MARSHAM TG1924

Plough (01263) 735000
Old Norwich Road; NR10 5PS Welcoming 18th-c inn with open-plan split-level bar; enjoyable food using local produce (special diets catered for) including good value set lunch, Adnams Southwold and a couple of guests, friendly helpful staff; free wi-fi; children welcome, dogs in garden only, comfortable bedrooms, lock-up for bicycles, open all day. *(Sally and Lance Oldham)*

MUNDFORD TL8093

Crown (01842) 878233
Off A1065 Thetford–Swaffham; Crown Road; IP26 5HQ Unassuming 17th-c pub with heavy beams, huge fireplace and interesting local memorabilia, Courage Directors and one or two guests, over 50 malt whiskies, enjoyable generously served food at sensible prices, friendly staff, spiral iron stairs to two restaurant areas (larger one has separate entrance accessible to wheelchairs), locals' bar with sports TV; children and dogs welcome, back terrace and garden with wishing well, Harley-Davidson meeting first Sun of month, bedrooms (some in adjoining building), also self-catering accommodation, open all day. *(Amanda Shipley)*

NEW BUCKENHAM TM0890

Inn on the Green (01953) 860172
Chapel Street; NR16 2BB Modern renovation of late Victorian red-brick pub by little green close to the Kings Head; emphasis on good freshly prepared food from pub favourites to more restauranty dishes including blackboard specials, Adnams, Woodfordes and good selection of wines, pleasant efficient staff; children (away from bar) and dogs (in bar) welcome, terrace tables, handy for Banham Zoo, closed Mon. *(Ben and Jenny Settle)*

NEW BUCKENHAM TM0890

Kings Head (01953) 861247
Market Place; NR16 2AN Family-run 17th-c pub by small green opposite medieval market cross, ales such as Adnams Southwold and generous helpings of popular reasonably priced pubby food (booking advised), helpful service, modern open-plan bar with beams and inglenook, big back dining area; pool, free wi-fi; five bedrooms, open all day. *(Andrew Vincent)*

NORTH TUDDENHAM TG0413

Lodge (01362) 638466
Off A47; NR20 3DJ Modernised dining pub with good sensibly priced food from traditional choices up including burger menu and daily specials, local beers (just one in winter) such as Woodfordes Reedlighter,

friendly attentive service; Weds steak night, monthly quiz; children and dogs (in bar) welcome, tables outside (some on deck), closed Sun evening and Mon, otherwise open (and food) all day. *(Tony and Wendy Hobden)*

NORTHREPPS TG2439

Foundry Arms (01263) 579256

Church Street; NR27 0AA Welcoming village pub with good reasonably priced traditional food (not Sun evening) from generous sandwiches up, well kept Woodfordes Wherry and a couple of guests, decent choice of wines, good friendly service, woodburner, smallish comfortable restaurant; pool and darts in separate area; children and dogs welcome (pub dog is Freddie), picnic-sets in back garden, open all day. *(Peter and Anne Hollindale, Tina and David Woods-Taylor)*

NORWICH TG2309

Adam & Eve (01603) 667423

Bishopgate; follow Palace Street from Tombland, N of cathedral; NR3 1RZ Ancient pub dating from at least 1240 when used by workmen building the cathedral, has a Saxon well beneath the lower bar floor and striking dutch gables (added in 14th and 15th c); old-fashioned small bars with tiled or parquet floors, cushioned benches built into partly panelled walls and some antique high-backed settles, three real ales including Adnams and Theakstons, Aspall's cider and around 40 malt whiskies, traditional pubby food (not Sun evening), friendly service; background music; children allowed in snug till 7pm, no dogs inside, picnic-sets out among pretty tubs and hanging baskets, open all day, closed 25, 26 Dec, 1 Jan. *(Sandra Morgan)*

NORWICH TG2408

Coach & Horses (01603) 477077

Thorpe Road; NR1 1BA Light and airy tap for Chalk Hill brewery (tours available), friendly staff, standard food from baguettes and panini up, lunch deals and Sat brunch, L-shaped bare-boards bar with open fire, six Chalk Hill ales, pleasant back dining area; sports TVs, gets very busy on home match days; disabled access possible (not to lavatories), front terrace, open all day. *(Charlie Stevens)*

NORWICH TG2210

Duke of Wellington (01603) 441182

Waterloo Road; NR3 1EG Rambling corner local with huge range of well kept quickly changing ales including Fullers, Oakham and Wolf, many served from tap room casks, foreign bottled beers too, no food apart from sausage rolls and pies (can bring your own) and weekend summer barbecue, real fire; live music and quiz nights, Aug and Oct beer festivals, traditional games, free wi-fi; well behaved dogs welcome, nice back terrace, open all day. *(Sandra Morgan)*

NORWICH TG2308

Edith Cavell (01603) 765813

Tombland/Princes Street; NR3 1HF Corner pub-restaurant named after the gallant World War I Norfolk nurse; popular fairly priced food from sandwiches to good steaks cooked on hot rocks, three real ales including a house beer from Wolf, friendly helpful service, smallish bar, upstairs restaurant (and loos); diagonally across from Erpingham Gate leading into cathedral green, open all day (till 1am Fri, Sat). *(Amy Ledbetter)*

NORWICH TG2310

Fat Cat Tap (01603) 413153

Lawson Road; NR3 4LF This 1970s shed-like building is home to the Fat Cat brewery and sister pub to the Fat Cat (see Main Entries) and Fat Cat & Canary; good buzzy atmosphere, their ales and up to 12 guests along with draught continentals, lots of bottled beers and eight or more local ciders/perries, no food apart from chips (with or without toppings) and cheeseboards, can also bring your own; regular live music and quiz nights; dogs welcome, children till 6pm, seats out front and back, open all day. *(McClennan Jamie)*

NORWICH TG2309

★ **Kings Head** (01603) 620468

Magdalen Street; NR3 1JE Traditional Victorian local with good friendly atmosphere in two simply furnished bare-boards bars (front one is tiny), a dozen very well kept changing regional ales, good choice of imported beers and a local cider, no food except pork pies; bar billiards in back bar, free wi-fi; dogs welcome, open all day. *(Sandra Morgan, Christopher May)*

NORWICH TG2208

Plough (01603) 661384

St Benedicts Street; NR2 4AR Little city-centre pub owned by Grain, their ales and guests kept well, good wines and cocktails, food limited to sausage pie, cheeseboards and summer barbecues, simply updated split-level interior with bare boards and open fire; background music; good spacious beer garden behind, open all day. *(Amy Ledbetter)*

NORWICH TG2308

Ribs of Beef (01603) 619517

Wensum Street, S side of Fye Bridge; NR3 1HY Comfortable and welcoming riverside pub; nine real ales including Oakham, four traditional ciders and good wine choice, deep leather sofas and small tables upstairs, attractive smaller downstairs room with river view, generous well priced lunchtime food (till 5pm weekends), quick cheerful service; Sun live music; children welcome, seats out on narrow waterside terrace (maybe summer barbecue), open all day. *(John Wooll)*

NORWICH TG2308

St Andrews Brew House (01603) 305995 *St Andrews Street; NR2 4TP* Interesting place visibly brewing its own good beers (can tour the brewery), also plenty of guest ales, craft kegs and bottled beers, utilitarian bare-boards interior with exposed ducting, rough masonry walls and eclectic mix of seating including some button-back booths, popular sensibly priced food from british tapas and sharing boards up, Thurs steak night, busy efficient staff, upstairs function room; background music, sports TV, Tues quiz and occasional comedy nights; children and dogs welcome, pavement tables, open all day. *(Tracey and Stephen Groves)*

NORWICH TG2309

Wig & Pen (01603) 625891 *St Martins Palace Plain; NR3 1RN* Popular 17th-c beamed pub opposite cathedral close; good value food from sandwiches up, prompt friendly service, six ales including Adnams, Humpty Dumpty and Woodfordes, well priced wines; background music, sports TVs, spring beer festival; metal café-style furniture out at front, open all day (till 6.30pm Sun). *(Max Simons)*

OLD HUNSTANTON TF6842

Lodge (01485) 532896 *Old Hunstanton Road (A149); PE36 6HX* Old red-brick roadside pub with clean contemporary décor; popular food in bar or restaurant from pizzas and pub favourites up, well kept local beers such as Woodfordes Wherry and good choice of wines by the glass, friendly helpful staff, plenty of seating on wood floors including booths and sofas by woodburner; sports TV, occasional live music; children and dogs (in bar) welcome, tables on covered terrace and small lawn, 16 good bedrooms, open all day. *(Paul Scofield)*

OVERSTRAND TG2440

Sea Marge (01263) 579579 *High Street; NR27 0AB* Substantial half-timbered sea-view hotel (former Edwardian country house) with separate entrance to spacious bar; enjoyable food from ciabattas to local seafood including weekday deal (till 6pm) on some main courses, real ales and decent wines by the glass, panelled restaurant (more upmarket menu); children welcome, dogs in some areas, five-acre grounds with terraced lawns down to clifftop and steep steps to coast path and beach, 26 comfortable bedrooms, open (and bar food) all day. *(Paddy and Sian O'Leary)*

OVERSTRAND TG2440

White Horse (01263) 579237 *High Street; NR27 0AB* Comfortably modernised red-brick pub with good choice of well liked food in bar, dining room or barn restaurant (also used for functions), up to five well kept regional ales, friendly attentive staff; background music, silent sports TV, pool; children and dogs welcome, picnic-sets out in front, more in garden behind with play equipment (may be bouncy castle), short walk to beach, eight bedrooms, open all day from 8am. *(Christopher May)*

OXBOROUGH TF7401

★**Bedingfeld Arms** (01366) 328300 *Near church; PE33 9PS* Attractively furnished Georgian inn peacefully set opposite Oxburgh Hall (NT); wood-floored bar with green leather chesterfields, tub chairs and window seats, open fire in marble fireplace with gilt mirror above, fresh flowers and candles, long counter serving Adnams Broadside, Woodfordes Wherry and a guest, ten wines by the glass, airy dining room has high-backed chairs around antique tables, wall seats with scatter cushions and bird prints on pale grey walls, good food from lunchtime sandwiches up; background music, TV for major sports, free wi-fi; well behaved children welcome, dogs in bar, covered verandah extension, more seats in garden with view of church, nine bedrooms (five in coach-house annexe), good breakfasts, open all day, food all day Sun. *(John Harris, Lyn and Freddie Roberts, Alexandra and Richard Clay, Max and Steph Warren)*

ROYDON TF7022

Three Horseshoes (01485) 600666 *The one near King's Lynn; Lynn Road; PE32 1AQ* Updated brick and stone village pub under same ownership as nearby Congham Hall Hotel; pleasant pastel décor with simple wood furniture, stone-floor bar and split-level part-carpeted restaurant, woodburner in each, generous helpings of well liked uncomplicated food (all day Sun) from reasonably priced blackboard menu, smaller helpings available for some dishes, three real ales including Greene King IPA, friendly helpful staff; children and dogs (in bar) welcome, tables outside, closed Mon, Tues, otherwise open all day. *(John Wooll)*

SCULTHORPE TF8930

★**Sculthorpe Mill** (01328) 856161 *Inn signed off A148 W of Fakenham, opposite village; NR21 9QG* Welcoming dining pub in rebuilt 18th-c mill, appealing

Post Office address codings confusingly give the impression that a few pubs are in Norfolk, when they're really in Cambridgeshire or Suffolk (which is where we list them).

riverside setting with seats out under weeping willows and in attractive garden behind; light, airy and relaxed with leather sofas and sturdy tables in bar/dining area, good reasonably priced food from sandwiches to daily specials, attentive service, Greene King ales and good house wines, upstairs restaurant; background music, free wi-fi; six comfortable bedrooms, open all day in summer (all day weekends in winter). *(John Wooll)*

SEDGEFORD TF7036

King William IV (01485) 571765
B1454, off A149 King's Lynn–Hunstanton; PE36 5LU Homely inn handy for beaches and bird-watching; bar and dining areas decorated with paintings of north Norfolk coast and migrating birds, high-backed dark leather dining chairs around pine tables on slate tiles, log fires, Adnams, Greene King and Woodfordes, ten wines by the glass, straightforward food; magazines and daily papers; children welcome (no under-4s in main restaurant after 6.30pm), dogs allowed in bar and a couple of the bedrooms, seats on terrace and under parasols on grass, also an attractive covered dining area surrounded by flowering tubs, closed Mon lunchtime, otherwise open all day. *(Tracey and Stephen Groves)*

SHERINGHAM TG1543

Lobster (01263) 822716
High Street; NR26 8JP Almost on seafront and popular with locals and tourists; friendly panelled bar with log fire and seafaring décor, wide range of ales including Adnams, Greene King and Woodfordes, two or three ciders and decent wines by the glass, generous reasonably priced bar food from good sandwiches up, restaurant with seasonal seafood including lobster and crab; some live music; children and dogs welcome, bedrooms, open all day. *(Dr J Barrie Jones)*

SMALLBURGH TG3324

Crown (01692) 536314
A149 Yarmouth Road; NR12 9AD Character thatched and beamed village inn dating from the 15th c; well kept Adnams, Fullers, Lacons, Timothy Taylors and a guest, enjoyable home-made food including blackboard specials and regular african themed nights (friendly landlady is from the Ivory Coast), can eat in log-fire bar or small dining room; monthly quiz, occasional live music, darts; children and dogs welcome, picnic-sets in pretty back garden, Aug anglo-african festival, two bedrooms, open all day. *(Peter and Emma Kelly)*

SOUTH LOPHAM TM0481

White Horse (01379) 688579
A1066 Diss–Thetford; The Street; IP22 2LH Popular beamed village pub with well kept Adnams, Woodfordes and an occasional guest, enjoyable home-made food including vegetarian options and blackboard specials, log fires; live music, TV; children welcome, big garden with play area, handy for Bressingham Gardens, open all day. *(Charlie Stevens)*

SOUTHREPPS TG2536

★**Vernon Arms** (01263) 833355
Church Street; NR11 8NP Popular old-fashioned brick and cobble village pub, welcoming and relaxed, with good home-made food (booking advised), friendly helpful staff, well kept Adnams, Greene King, Woodfordes and a guest, good choice of wines and malt whiskies, big log fire; darts and pool, occasional live music; tables outside, children, dogs and muddy boots welcome, open all day, no evening food Sun or Mon. *(Dr Tony Whitehead)*

STANHOE TF8037

★**Duck** (01485) 518330
B1155 Docking–Burnham Market; PE31 8QD Smart pub under same ownership as the Bell at Hunworth with emphasis on good imaginative food; little entrance bar with cushioned Edwardian-style chairs around wooden tables on dark slate floor, stools against fine slab-topped counter serving Adnams, Elgoods and a dozen wines by the glass, woodburner in small area off, two dining rooms with scatter-cushion wall seats, scrubbed tables and local seascapes; free wi-fi; children and dogs (in bar) welcome, disabled access/loo, tables out on front gravel and under fruit tree in small garden, there's also a garden room with fairy lights and candles, comfortable well appointed bedrooms, good breakfast, open all day, food all day Sun. *(Gail and Frank Hackett, Roy Hoing)*

STIFFKEY TF9643

Red Lion (01328) 830552
A149 Wells–Blakeney; NR23 1AJ Popular old village pub; main bar with tiled floor and inglenook woodburner, cushioned pews and other pubby seats, Woodfordes ales, a dozen wines by the glass and some local gins, well liked food (all day weekends) from pubby choices to local fish/shellfish, friendly service, two back dining rooms, one a flint-walled conservatory; children and dogs welcome, big partly covered gravelled courtyard, more tables on covered deck, ten bedrooms in modern block with own balconies or terraces, nearby coastal walks, open all day. *(Tracey and Stephen Groves)*

STOW BARDOLPH TF6205

Hare Arms (01366) 382229
Just off A10 N of Downham Market; PE34 3HT Popular modernised village pub; bare-boards bar with traditional pub furnishings and log fire, Greene King ales and a couple of well kept guests, ten wines by the glass, generous helpings of enjoyable good value food (all day Sun) from

sandwiches up, three dining areas including converted coach house; children welcome in some parts, no dogs inside, plenty of seats in front and back gardens, maybe wandering peacocks, Church Farm Rare Breeds Centre nearby, open (and food) all day weekends. *(Tracey and Stephen Groves)*

SURLINGHAM TG3107

Ferry House (01508) 538659

Ferry Road: far end by river; NR14 7AR Welcoming unpretentious pub by River Yare; well kept regional ales and hearty helpings of good inexpensive home-made food from baguettes up, helpful accommodating service, central woodburner in brick fireplace; some live music; children and dogs welcome, very busy with boats and visitors in summer (free mooring), picnic-sets on waterside lawn, handy for RSPB reserve, open (and food) all day. *(Denis and Margaret Kilner)*

THOMPSON TL9296

Chequers (01953) 483360

Griston Road, off A1075 S of Watton; IP24 1PX Picturesque 16th-c thatched dining pub tucked away in attractive setting; enjoyable food including bargain weekday lunch offer and regular themed nights, ales such as Greene King and Woodfordes, friendly atmosphere, series of quaint rooms with low beams, inglenooks and some stripped brickwork; children and dogs (in bar) welcome, seats out in front and in back garden with swing, bedroom block, open (and food) all day Sun. *(Camilla and Jose Ferrera)*

THORNHAM TF7343

Chequers (01485) 512229

High Street (A149); PE36 6LY Updated 16th-c roadside inn under same owners as the nearby Lifeboat (see Main Entries); two front bar rooms with pale-painted beams, wooden chairs or cube seats around mix of wooden tables on carpet or painted floorboards, some local photographs, open fire, a few stools at counter serving two local ales and decent wines by the glass, well liked food from norfolk tapas and pizzas up, cosy room off with sofas, armchairs and woodburner, modern back dining room; children welcome, painted picnic-sets out at front, more seating in back courtyard garden with a couple of cabanas, 11 comfortable modern bedrooms, open all day. *(Tracey and Stephen Groves)*

WALSINGHAM TF9336

Black Lion (01328) 820235

Friday Market Place; NR22 6DB Attractively renovated beamed village inn dating from the 15th c; nice mix of old furniture on flagstones or quarry tiles, shelves of books, farming tools and other bits and pieces including a tandem on one wall, woodburners and open fire, tractor-seat stools by counter serving Adnams, Woodfordes, a guest ale and a dozen wines by the glass, good traditional home-made food, friendly service; background and some live music; children and dogs welcome, a few tables out at front, more on little terrace with old well, six comfortable bedrooms, open all day. *(Denis and Margaret Kilner)*

WALSINGHAM TF9336

Bull (01328) 820333

Common Place/Shire Hall Plain; NR22 6BP Quirky pub in pilgrimage village; lived-in bar with shelves of curious knick-knacks, pictures of archbishops and clerical visiting cards, a half-size statue of Charlie Chaplin, even a mirror ball in one part, three well kept changing ales and tasty reasonably priced food (not weekend evenings), welcoming friendly service, roaring fire, typewriter in snug, old-fashioned cash register in the gents'; TV, free wi-fi; children welcome, courtyard and attractive flowery terrace by village square, dovecote stuffed with plastic lobsters and crabs, outside games room, nice snowdrop walk in nearby abbey garden, bedrooms, open all day. *(Dr J Barrie Jones)*

WEASENHAM ST PETER TF8522

Fox & Hounds (01328) 838868

A1065 Fakenham–Swaffham; The Green; PE32 2TD Traditional 18th-c beamed local well run by friendly family; bar and two dining areas (one with inglenook woodburner), three changing ales and good reasonably priced home-made food (not Sun evening), pubby furniture and carpets throughout, brasses and lots of military prints; children welcome, big well maintained garden and terrace, closed Mon. *(Charlie Stevens)*

WELLS-NEXT-THE-SEA TF9143

Albatros 07979 087228

The Quay; NR23 1AT Bar on 1899 quayside clipper, charts and other nautical memorabilia, Woodfordes ales served from the cask, dutch food including speciality pancakes, seats on deck with good views of harbour and tidal marshes; regular live music; children welcome, no good for disabled visitors, cabin accommodation with shared showers, open all day. *(Dr J Barrie Jones)*

WELLS-NEXT-THE-SEA TF9143

Bowling Green (01328) 710100

Church Street; NR23 1JB Welcoming 17th-c pub in quiet spot on outskirts; Greene King, Woodfordes and a guest, generous helpings of reasonably priced traditional food including bargain OAP lunch Tues, L-shaped bar with corner settles, flagstone and brick floor, two woodburners, raised dining end; children and dogs welcome, sunny back terrace, two bedrooms in converted barn, also self-catering accommodation. *(Paul Scofield)*

WELLS-NEXT-THE-SEA TF9143

Edinburgh (01328) 710120
Station Road/Church Street; NR23 1AE Traditional 19th-c pub near main shopping area; good home-made food including blackboard specials, three well kept ales such as Woodfordes, open fire, sizeable restaurant, also 'lifeboat' dining room decorated in RNLI colours; background music, free wi-fi; children and dogs welcome, disabled access, courtyard with heated smokers' shelter, three bedrooms, open all day. *(Dr J Barrie Jones)*

WELLS-NEXT-THE-SEA TF9143

★**Globe** (01328) 710206
The Buttlands; NR23 1EU Handsome Georgian inn on elegant square, a short walk from the quay; plenty of space and nice atmosphere in opened-up contemporary rooms, tables on oak boards, big bow windows, well kept Adnams beers, thoughtful wine choice and enjoyable food including Weds steak night, good efficient service; background and some live music; children and dogs welcome, attractive courtyard with pale flagstones, more seats at front overlooking green, 18 bedrooms (some in courtyard annexe) and nearby holiday house, open all day. *(Phil and Jane Villiers, Tracey and Stephen Groves)*

WEST ACRE TF7815

Stag (01760) 755395
Low Road; PE32 1TR Small family-run local with three or more well kept changing ales in appealing unpretentious bar, good value home-made food including set Sun lunch, efficient friendly service, neat dining room; quiz third Sun of month; attractive spot in peaceful village, closed Mon. *(Sandra Morgan)*

WEYBOURNE TG1143

Ship (01263) 588721
A149 W of Sheringham; The Street; NR25 7SZ Popular traditional 19th-c village pub; well kept Woodfordes Wherry, two local guests and decent wine choice, big bar with pubby furniture and woodburner, two dining rooms, good reasonably priced home-made food (should book weekends) from lunchtime sandwiches through pub favourites to local fish/seafood, efficient friendly young staff; background music, monthly quiz, free wi-fi; well behaved children welcome, dogs in bar, seats out at front and in nice side garden handy for Muckleburgh military vehicle museum, open all day in season, no food Sun evening. *(Mr and Mrs Richard Osborne, Roy Hoing)*

WYMONDHAM TG1001

★**Green Dragon** (01953) 607907
Church Street; NR18 0PH Picturesque heavily timbered medieval pub with plenty of character; small beamed bar and snug, bigger dining area, interesting pictures, log fire under Tudor mantelpiece, three well kept changing ales (beer/cider festival May) and over 50 whiskies, generous helpings of popular good value food including daily specials (best to book), friendly helpful staff, upstairs function room; quiz Thurs, open mike night third Sun of month, ukulele group third Tues; children and dogs welcome, garden behind with raised deck, near glorious 12th-c abbey church, open all day (food all day Fri-Sun). *(Alan McQuilan)*

Northamptonshire

ASHBY ST LEDGERS SP5768 Map 4

Olde Coach House

(01788) 890349 – www.oldecoachhouse.co.uk

Main Street; 4 miles from M1 junction 18; A5 S to Kilsby, then A361 S towards Daventry; village also signed off A5 N of Weedon; CV23 8UN

Much character in ex-farmhouse with real ales, good wines, well liked food and plenty of outside seating; bedrooms

In a little village of thatched houses, this is a handsome creeper-clad inn with rewarding food and drink. The opened-up bar on the right, full of original charm, has stools against the counter where friendly staff serve Marstons Pedigree, Wells Bombardier and a monthly guest on handpump and 16 wines by the glass. Several informal dining areas take in paintwork ranging from white and light beige to purple, and flooring that includes stripped wooden boards, original red and white tiles and beige carpeting. All manner of pale wooden tables are surrounded by assorted church chairs, high-backed leather dining chairs and armchairs, with comfortable squashy leather sofas and pouffes in front of a log fire. There are hunting pictures, large mirrors, an original old stove and fresh flowers; background music and TV. The back garden has picnic-sets among shrubs and trees, modern tables and chairs out in front under pretty hanging baskets, and a dining courtyard. Eleven of the well equipped, contemporary bedrooms are located in the converted stables and breakfasts are good. The church is of interest and the nearby manor house was once owned by one of the gunpowder plotters.

Interesting food includes sandwiches, scallops with pork belly, pigeon with pancetta, mushrooms and sorrel purée, thai beef salad with noodles and peanuts, sausages with dijon mash and caramelised onion gravy, stone-baked pizzas, vegetable risotto with parmesan crisps, burgers with toppings, aioli and chips, free-range chicken with minted peas and asparagus, jersey royals and crispy skin, sea bass with clams, pancetta and samphire, twice-cooked pork belly with fondant potato, brown onion purée and pork quaver, and puddings such as dark chocolate pot with boozy cherries and crème brûlée. *Benchmark main dish: steak in ale pie £12.95. Two-course evening meal £20.00.*

Quicksilver Management ~ Lease Mark Butler ~ Real ale ~ Open 12-11 (10 Sun) ~ Bar food 12-2, 6-9.30; 12-8 Sun ~ Restaurant ~ Children welcome ~ Dogs allowed in bar ~ Wi-fi ~ Bedrooms: /£95 *Recommended by Robert Wivell, Greta and Gavin Craddock, Charles Fraser, Stuart Doughty, Pauline and Mark Evans, Sylvia and Phillip Spencer*

If we know a pub has an outdoor play area for children, we mention it.

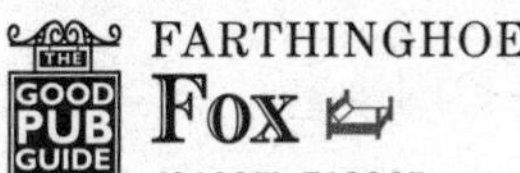

FARTHINGHOE SP5339 Map 4

Fox

(01295) 713965 – www.foxfarthinghoe.co.uk

Just off A422 Brackley–Banbury; Baker Street; NN13 5PH

Bustling stone inn with a neat bar and dining rooms, tasty food, helpful service and seats in the garden; bedrooms

The hands-on landlord runs this stylish golden-stone pub with efficiency and friendliness. The dark beamed bar has stools and a log fire in a stripped-stone fireplace, and the dining areas have seats ranging from leather tub chairs to banquettes, cushioned wall seats with scatter cushions and quite a range of wooden dining chairs, all arranged around rustic wooden tables; pastel walls are hung with mirrors and country prints. Courage Directors, Youngs Bitter and a guest beer on handpump, nine wines by the glass and a good choice of gins; background music. The terrace and lawn have picnic-sets under a giant parasol. Bedrooms in an adjoining barn conversion are peaceful and comfortable; one is suitable for disabled customers.

Well regarded food includes sandwiches, smoked salmon and spinach mousse with capers and marinated cucumber, ham and leek terrine with pickled red cabbage, mushroom and spinach enchilada with tomato and chilli sauce, seared mackerel with pepperonata and grilled potatoes, pie of the day, barbecue brisket with sweet potato mash, bacon macaroni, jalapeno and cornbread, chicken with pesto potato cake and tomato and basil dressing, steak of the day, and puddings such as chocolate and raspberry roulade and treacle tart with custard. *Benchmark main dish: beer-battered fish and chips £12.00. Two-course evening meal £20.00.*

Charles Wells ~ Lease Neil Bellingham ~ Real ale ~ Open 12-10; 12-11 Sat; 12-10.30 Sun ~ Bar food 12-2.30, 6-9; 12-9 Sat; 12-8 Sun ~ Restaurant ~ Children welcome ~ Dogs allowed in bar ~ Wi-fi ~ Bedrooms: /£75 *Recommended by Julia and Fiona Barnes, Frances and Hamish Porter, Gerry and Rosemary Dobson, Julie Swift, John and Claire Masters*

FARTHINGSTONE SP6155 Map 4

Kings Arms £

(01327) 361604

Off A5 SE of Daventry; village signed from Litchborough; NN12 8EZ

Individual place with cosy traditional interior, carefully prepared food and lovely garden

'Charming' is how many of our readers describe this little 18th-c pub. Plenty of chatty customers create a cheerful, relaxed atmosphere and the cosy flagstoned bar has a huge log fire, comfortable homely sofas and armchairs near the entrance, whisky-water jugs hanging from oak beams, and lots of pictures and decorative plates on the walls. A games room at the far end has darts, dominoes, cribbage, table skittles and board games. The ever-changing beers are kept in top condition and might include Butcombe Bitter, Harveys Best, St Austell Trelawny and Woodfordes Wherry on handpump; also Weston's Old Rosie cider and a short but decent wine list. Look out for the interesting newspaper-influenced décor in the outside gents'. The handsome gargoyled stone exterior is nicely weathered and very pretty in summer when the hanging baskets are at their best. There are seats on a tranquil terrace among plant-filled, painted tractor tyres and recycled art, and they've recorded over 200 species of moth and 20 different butterflies. This is a picturesque village and good walks nearby include the Knightley Way. It's worth ringing ahead to check the opening and food times.

The popular food – served at weekend lunchtimes only – includes sandwiches, yorkshire puddings with fillings, cassoulets, casseroles, and puddings such as gingerbread pudding and meringues. *Benchmark main dish: sharing platters £12.00.*

Free house ~ Licensees Paul and Denise Egerton ~ Real ale ~ Open 7-11 Tues-Thurs; 6.30-11.30 Fri; 12-11.30 Sat; 12-5, 9-11 Sun; closed Mon, weekday lunchtimes ~ Bar food 12-2.15 or so weekends; maybe evening snacks ~ Children welcome ~ Dogs allowed in bar ~ Wi-fi ~ Live music occasional Sat *Recommended by Victoria and James Sargeant, Justine and Neil Bonnett, Mark and Mary Setting, Colin Humphreys*

FOTHERINGHAY TL0593 Map 5

Falcon

(01832) 226254 – www.thefalcon-inn.co.uk

Village signposted off A605 on Peterborough side of Oundle; PE8 5HZ

Upmarket dining pub with a good range of drinks and modern british food, and attractive garden

Our readers enjoy their visits to this stylish pub and you're sure to get a genuine welcome from the hands-on landlady. The atmosphere is gently civilised and there are winter log fires in stone fireplaces, fresh flowers, cushioned slatback armchairs, bucket chairs and comfortably cushioned window seats and bare floorboards. The Orangery restaurant opens on to a charming lavender-surrounded terrace with delightful views of the huge church behind and of the attractively planted garden; plenty of seats under parasols. The thriving little locals' tap bar has a fine choice of drinks including Fullers London Pride, Greene King IPA and a guest from local breweries such as Digfield, Kings Cliffe, Nobbys and Oakham on handpump, 16 good wines by the glass and eight malt whiskies; darts team and board games. This is a lovely village (Richard III was born here) with plenty of moorings on the River Nene; the ruins of Fotheringhay Castle, where Mary, Queen of Scots was executed, is nearby.

A fine choice of popular food includes sandwiches, home-cured gravadlax with lemon and dill mayonnaise, prawn cocktail, sweet potato, chickpea and spinach korma, calves liver with bacon, onions, mash and gravy, pie of the day, confit chicken with bean and chorizo cassoulet, halibut fillet with potato purée, baby vegetables and red wine sauce, cannon of lamb with minted pea purée, fondant potatoes and rosemary jus, and puddings such as banoffi mess with caramel sauce and chocolate crumb and lightly spiced pineapple carpaccio with chilli and ginger and mango sorbet. *Benchmark main dish: salmon, crab and dill fishcakes £13.50. Two-course evening meal £16.00.*

Free house ~ Licensee Sally Facer ~ Real ale ~ Open 12-11; 12-10.30 Sun (12-4 in winter) ~ Bar food 12-2, 6-9; 12-3 Sun (12-3, 5-8 May-Sept) ~ Restaurant ~ Children welcome ~ Dogs allowed in bar ~ Wi-fi *Recommended by Michael Sargent, Stuart Doughty, Ian Herdman, Peter Andrews, Emily and Toby Archer, Deborah and Duncan Walliams*

GREAT BRINGTON SP6664 Map 4

Althorp Coaching Inn

(01604) 770651 – www.althorp-coaching-inn.co.uk

Off A428 NW of Northampton, near Althorp Hall; until recently known as the Fox & Hounds; NN7 4JA

Northamptonshire Dining Pub of the Year

Friendly golden-stone thatched pub with some fine architectural features, tasty popular food, well kept real ales and sheltered garden

'The epitome of what a country pub should be' is how one reader describes this well run 16th-c place. The ancient bar has all the traditional features you'd wish for, from a dog or two sprawled by the huge log fire, to old beams, sagging joists and an appealing mix of country chairs and tables (set with fresh flowers) on broad flagstones and bare boards; background music. There are snug alcoves, nooks and crannies with some stripped-pine shutters and panelling, two fine log fires and an eclectic medley of bric-a-brac from farming implements to an old clocking-in machine and country pictures. Greene King Abbot and IPA, Phipps India Pale Ale, St Austell Tribute and Sharps Doom Bar on handpump; also, eight wines by the glass, a dozen malt whiskies and farm cider. A function room is located in a converted stable block next to the lovely cobbled and paved courtyard (also accessible by the old coaching entrance) with sheltered tables and tubs of flowers; more seating is available in the charming garden.

A thoughtful menu offers sandwiches, venison and black pudding scotch egg with celeriac rémoulade, smoked salmon mousse with crayfish and cucumber salsa, feta and chestnut mushroom fritters with roasted vegetable salsa and sweet potato fries, chicken breast with tomato, olive and basil sauce with wild rice, moroccan-spiced leg of lamb steak on pomegranate and mint couscous, sea bass fillet with bacon, tomatoes and basil oil and parmentier potatoes, 10oz sirloin steak with mushrooms, tomatoes and chips, and puddings such as baked vanilla cheesecake with blackcurrant sorbet and chocolate brownie with chocolate sauce. *Benchmark main dish: slow-braised blade of beef with wild mushrooms and mash £12.95. Two-course evening meal £19.00.*

Free house ~ Licensee Michael Krempels ~ Real ale ~ Open 12-11; 12-midnight Sat; 12-10 Sun ~ Bar food 12-3, 6-9; 12-9 Sat; 12-7 Sun ~ Restaurant ~ Children welcome ~ Dogs allowed in bar ~ Wi-fi *Recommended by David Appleyard, Alice Wright, Stuart Doughty, Alistair Forsyth, Peter Andrews, Francis and Mandy Robertson, Patti and James Davidson*

NORTHAMPTON SP7559 Map 4

Malt Shovel £

(01604) 234212 – www.maltshoveltavern.com

Bridge Street (approach road from M1 junction 15); no parking in nearby street, best to park in Morrisons central car park, far end – passage past Europcar straight to back entrance; NN1 1QF

Friendly, well run real ale pub with bargain lunches and over a dozen varied beers

There's a fantastic range of drinks on offer in this excellent city tavern, starting with up to 13 real ales served by knowledgeable, enthusiastic staff. From a battery of handpumps lined up on the long counter, regulars might include Fullers London Pride, Hook Norton Old Hooky, Oakham Bishops Farewell and JHB and Phipps NBC India Pale Ale, with seven quickly changing guests. They also stock belgian draught and bottled beers, 50 malt whiskies, 17 rums, 17 vodkas, 17 gins and Cheddar Valley farm cider; regular beer festivals. The pub is also home to quite an extensive collection of carefully chosen brewing memorabilia – look out for the rare Northampton Brewery Company star, displayed outside the pub, and some high-mounted ancient beer engines; darts, daily papers and background music. The secluded back yard is furnished with tables and chairs and a smokers' shelter; disabled facilities.

Lunchtime-only food includes baguettes and wraps, sharing platters, sweet potato, spinach and lentil curry, lamb kofta kebabs, chicken and bacon salad with honey and mustard dressing, shepherd's pie, gammon and egg, and lambs liver and bacon casserole. *Benchmark main dish: burger with toppings, coleslaw and chips £7.00.*

Free house ~ Licensee Scott Whyment ~ Real ale ~ Open 11.30-11; 12-10.30 Sun ~ Bar food 12-3; 12-4 weekends ~ Well behaved children welcome in bar ~ Dogs allowed in bar ~ Wi-fi ~ Blues music Weds evening *Recommended by Tony Hobden, Dr J Barrie Jones, Sabine and Gerald Grimshaw, Bob and Melissa Wyatt, Stuart Doughty*

Also Worth a Visit in Northamptonshire

Besides the fully inspected pubs, you might like to try these pubs that have been recommended to us and described by readers. Do tell us what you think of them: feedback@goodguides.com

ABTHORPE SP6446

★**New Inn** (01327) 857306
Signed from A43 at first roundabout S of A5; Silver Street; NN12 8QR Traditional partly thatched country local run by cheery farming family; fairly basic rambling bar with dining area down a couple of steps, four well kept Hook Norton beers and Weston's cider, good pubby food (not Sun evening, Mon) using local produce including own meat, blackboard specials, beams, stripped stone and inglenook woodburner, darts and table skittles; open mike night second Sun of month, quiz last Sun, free wi-fi; children, dogs and muddy boots welcome, garden tables, bedrooms in converted barn (short walk across fields), open all day Fri-Sun, closed lunchtimes Mon and Tues. *(Neil Allen)*

ARTHINGWORTH SP7581

Bulls Head (01858) 525637
Kelmarsh Road, just above A14 by A508 junction; pub signed from A14; LE16 8JZ Steps up to much extended black-beamed pub with various seating areas in L-shaped bar, pubby furniture and upholstered banquettes on patterned carpet, woodburner, enjoyable good value food including Weds steak deal, well kept Adnams and a couple of guests (May beer festival), efficient cheery service, restaurant; background music, TV, darts and skittles, free wi-fi; disabled access (from back) and facilities, terrace picnic-sets, eight bedrooms in separate block, handy for Kelmarsh Hall, open all day weekends (food till 7.30pm Sun). *(Sylvia and Phillip Spencer)*

ASHTON TL0588

Chequered Skipper (01832) 273494
The Ashton NE of Oundle, signed from A427/A605 roundabout; PE8 5LD Handsomely rebuilt thatched pub on chestnut-tree green of elegant Estate village; well kept changing local ales and good home-made food from snacks and stone-baked pizzas up (gluten-free diets catered for), helpful friendly young staff, spacious open-plan layout with dining areas either side; free wi-fi; children welcome, well behaved dogs in bar area, good 4-mile circular walk, open all day, closed Mon. *(Kyle Brown)*

AYNHO SP5133

Cartwright (01869) 811885
Croughton Road (B4100); handy for M40 junction 10; OX17 3BE Welcoming 16th-c coaching inn with linked areas; contemporary furniture on wood or tiled floors, some exposed stone walls, leather sofas by big log fire in small bar, ales such as Adnams and Butcombe, nice wines and good coffee, popular well presented food including set deals, friendly helpful uniformed staff; background music, TV, daily papers and free wi-fi; children welcome, a few seats in pretty corner of part-cobbled coachyard, 21 bedrooms, good breakfast, pleasant village with apricot trees growing against old cottage walls, open all day. *(Jan Stevens)*

AYNHO SP4932

★**Great Western Arms**
(01869) 338288 *On B4031 1.5 miles E of Deddington, 0.75 miles W of Aynho, adjacent to Oxford Canal and Old Aynho station; OX17 3BP* Attractive old pub with series of cosy linked rooms; fine solid country tables on broad flagstones, golden stripped-stone walls and some deep red plasterwork, log fires, well kept Hook Norton and guests, good wines by the glass and enjoyable food cooked by landlord-chef from pubby choices up (separate gluten-free menu), friendly attentive young staff, elegant dining area on right, extensive GWR collection including steam locomotive photographs; background music; children and dogs welcome, white cast-iron furniture in back former stable courtyard, moorings on Oxford Canal and nearby marina, four bedrooms, open all day, food all day Sun. *(Michael Sargent, Robert Watt)*

BADBY SP5558

Windmill (01327) 311070
Village signposted off A361 Daventry–Banbury; NN11 3AN Attractive 17th-c thatched and beamed village pub under newish owners; flagstoned bar with tiled fireplace in huge inglenook, another log fire in adjoining snug, three mainstream ales and a regional guest, good food from interesting varied menu including daily specials, welcoming helpful staff, back restaurant extension; background music, free wi-fi; children and dogs welcome, picnic-sets out at front by small green, nice walks (Badby

bluebell woods close by), eight bedrooms, open all day in summer, all day weekends winter. *(Martin Watson)*

BARNWELL TL0584

Montagu Arms (01832) 273726

Off A605 S of Oundle, then fork right at Thurning/Hemington sign; PE8 5PH Attractive old stone-built pub in pleasant streamside village; well kept Adnams, Digfield (brewed close by) and guests, real ciders, good helpings of enjoyable home-cooked food (not Sun evening, Mon) including Weds evening set deal, cheerful staff, log fire, low beams, flagstones or tile and brick floors, back dining room and conservatory; children and dogs welcome, big garden with play area, nice local walks, open all day weekends, closed Mon lunchtime. *(Pauline and Mark Evans)*

BRAUNSTON SP5465

Admiral Nelson (01788) 891900

Dark Lane, Little Braunston, overlooking Lock 3 just N of Grand Union Canal tunnel; NN11 7HJ 18th-c ex-farmhouse in peaceful setting by canal and hump bridge; good freshly made food (not Sun evening, Mon, Tues) from sandwiches/baguettes and traditional favourites up, well kept ales including one brewed for them by local Merrimen, efficient service; L-shaped bar with log fire and two seating areas to the right (sofas at low tables), a couple of steps down to cosy dining alcove, brick-partitioned restaurant extension to the left with sturdy tables and high-backed leather chairs; some live music including Aug festival, hood skittles and darts, free wi-fi; well behaved children and dogs welcome, wheelchair access, lots of waterside picnic-sets, closed Mon lunchtime in winter, otherwise open all day. *(Gerry and Rosemary Dobson)*

BRAYBROOKE SP7684

Swan (01858) 462754

Griffin Road; LE16 8LH Nicely kept thatched pub with Everards ales and good choice of other drinks, popular sensibly priced food (not Sun evening) from sandwiches and pub favourites up, friendly attentive staff, fireside sofas, soft lighting, beams and some exposed brickwork, restaurant; quiet background music, quiz second Tues of month; children and dogs welcome, disabled facilities, pretty hedged garden with covered terrace, open all day Sat, closed Mon. *(Mr and Mrs D J Nash)*

BRIXWORTH SP7470

Coach & Horses (01604) 880329

Harborough Road, just off A508 N of Northampton; NN6 9BX Welcoming early 18th-c thatched and beamed pub; enjoyable food from fairly straightforward menu plus more adventurous specials including seasonal game, lunchtime and early evening set deals, well kept Marstons-related ales, prompt friendly service, log-fire bar with small dining area off, back lounge; tables on gravelled terrace behind, bedrooms in converted outbuildings, charming village with famous Saxon church, open (and food) all day Sun; still for sale so could be changes. *(Gerry and Rosemary Dobson)*

CHACOMBE SP4943

George & Dragon (01295) 711500

Handy for M40 junction 11, via A361; Silver Street; OX17 2JR Welcoming 17th-c pub with beams, flagstones, panelling and bare stone walls, two inglenook woodburners and deep glass-covered well, good popular food (not Sun evening) in three dining areas including various deals, Everards ales and a guest from brass-topped counter, several wines by the glass; background and maybe some live music, charity quiz first Sun of month; children and dogs (in bar) welcome, picnic-sets on suntrap terrace, pretty village with interesting church, open all day. *(Kyle Brown)*

CHAPEL BRAMPTON SP7366

★**Brampton Halt** (01604) 842676

Pitsford Road, off A5199 N of Northampton; NN6 8BA Popular well laid out McManus pub on Northampton & Lamport Railway (which is open some weekends) in much-extended former station master's house; railway memorabilia and train theme throughout, wide choice of enjoyable food from sandwiches to blackboard specials, meal deal Mon-Thurs, half a dozen well kept ales including Fullers and Timothy Taylors (beer festivals), plenty of wines by the glass and good range of other drinks, cheerful attentive service even when very busy, large restaurant; background music, TV in bar; children welcome, no dogs inside, lots of tables in big garden with awnings and heaters, summer barbecues and marquee, pretty views over small lake, Nene Way walks, open (and food) all day. *(Gerry and Rosemary Dobson, Adrian Johnson, Mike and Margaret Banks, Revd R P Tickle)*

CHARLTON SP5235

Rose & Crown (01295) 811317

Main Street; OX17 3DP Cosy 17th-c thatched village pub under welcoming family management; enjoyable reasonably priced home-made food, ales such as Greene King and Timothy Taylors, good friendly service, beams and stripped stone, nice log fire; children, walkers and dogs welcome, back garden with picnic-sets and wisteria arbour, Cherwell Valley views, open all day Fri, Sat, till 6pm Sun, closed Mon. *(Martin Watson)*

CLIPSTON SP7181

Bulls Head (01858) 525268

B4036 S of Market Harborough; LE16 9RT Welcoming village pub with popular good value food (not Mon) served in bar and restaurant, Everards ales and up to five guests, log fire and heavy beams (coins inserted by World War II airmen); background music, Tues quiz, TV; children and dogs welcome, terrace tables, three comfortable bedrooms, open all day weekends, closed Mon lunchtime. *(Mike and Margaret Banks)*

COGENHOE SP8360

Royal Oak (01604) 890922
Whiston Road; NN7 1NJ Modernised beamed village pub with very good food (best to book) from varied menu including summer wood-fired pizzas, three real ales such as Hook Norton Hooky and St Austell Tribute, friendly helpful staff, open fire in bar, smallish restaurant; children welcome, picnic-sets on part-covered deck, steps down to garden with play area, open all day Fri and Sat, till 7.30pm Sun, closed Mon. *(Alan Sutton)*

COLLINGTREE SP7555

Wooden Walls of Old England (01604) 760641 *1.2 miles from M1 junction 15; High Street; NN4 0NE* Cosy thatch and stone village pub dating from the 15th c and named as a tribute to the navy; four well kept Marstons-related ales and good choice of wines by the glass, generous helpings of home-made food (smaller appetites also catered for), weekday early bird deal (6-7pm), friendly staff, beams and open fire, northamptonshire skittles in one room; background music, sports TV, free wi-fi; big back garden with part-covered terrace, open all day Fri-Sun, closed Mon and till 4pm Tues-Thurs, no food Sun evening. *(John and Claire Masters)*

COLLYWESTON SK9902

★**Collyweston Slater** (01780) 444288
The Drove (A43); PE9 3PQ Roomy 17th-c main road inn with good popular pub food, well kept Everards ales and decent selection of wines, friendly service, contemporary interior with brown leather sofas and easy chairs, smart modern two-part dining room plus some more informal areas, one with raised woodburner in dividing wall, beams, stripped stone and mix of dark flagstones, bare boards and carpeting; background music, TV, darts; children welcome, dogs in bar areas, teak furniture on flagstoned terrace, boules, three bedrooms, open all day, no food Sun evening, Mon. *(Colin McLachlan)*

COSGROVE SP7942

Barley Mow (01908) 562957
The Stocks; MK19 7JD Friendly old village pub close to Grand Union Canal; well kept Everards ales and a guest, decent range of wines and enjoyable reasonably priced home-made food, beamed interior with various connecting areas, dark furniture on carpet or light stone floors, some half-panelling, two-way woodburner in stone fireplace; occasional live music, TV, free wi-fi; children and dogs welcome, tables on terrace and lawn down to the canal, open all day, food all day weekends. *(Kyle Brown)*

CRICK SP5872

★**Red Lion** (01788) 822342
1 mile from M1 junction 18; in centre of village off A428; NN6 7TX Nicely worn-in stone and thatch coaching inn run by same family since 1979; charming traditional low-ceilinged bar with lots of old horsebrasses (some rare) and tiny log stove in big inglenook, straightforward low-priced lunchtime food, more elaborate evening menu (not Sun) including popular steaks, plenty for vegetarians too, Adnams Southwold, Wells Bombardier and a guest, good friendly service; quiz last Sun of month, free wi-fi; children (under-12s lunchtime only) and dogs welcome, picnic-sets on terrace and in Perspex-covered coachyard with pretty hanging baskets. *(Stuart Doughty)*

DUDDINGTON SK9800

Royal Oak (01780) 444267
High Street, just off A43; PE9 3QE Stone-built inn on edge of pretty village; modern bar area with leather sofas and chairs on flagstones, panelling and log fire, three Grainstore ales from brick servery, restaurant with stone walls, wood floor and light oak furniture, enjoyable food from pub favourites up including weekday set lunch; background music; children welcome, disabled facilities, tables on small grassy area at front, six bedrooms, open (and food) all day Fri-Sun. *(Pauline and Mark Evans)*

EAST HADDON SP6668

Red Lion (01604) 770223
High Street; village signposted off A428 (turn right in village) and off A50 N of Northampton; NN6 8BU Substantial and elegant golden-stone thatched hotel with sizeable dining room, log-fire lounge and bar, emphasis on their well presented fairly priced food from pub favourites to more restauranty choices, most tables set for dining, but they do keep Wells Bombardier, Youngs Bitter and offer over a dozen wines by the glass, efficient friendly service; background music, cookery school; children welcome, attractive grounds including walled side garden, seven comfortable bedrooms and two-bed cottage, good breakfast, open all day. *(Michael Butler, Gerry and Rosemary Dobson)*

EASTON ON THE HILL TF0104

Blue Bell (01780) 763003
High Street; PE9 3LR Stone-built village pub with good italian food (not Sun evening, Mon), three or four changing ales including Grainstore and plenty of wines by the glass, friendly italian licensees and staff, restaurant; some live music, pool and TV in games area, May beer festival; children

and dogs welcome, picnic-sets in sheltered garden behind, open all day Sun, closed Mon lunchtime. *(Colin McLachlan)*

EASTON ON THE HILL TF0104

★**Exeter Arms** (01780) 756321
Stamford Road (A43); PE9 3NS Carefully renovated 18th-c pub with friendly easy-going atmosphere; country-feel bar with cushioned captain's chairs, wall/window seats and copper pans above woodburner, tractor seats by counter serving several wines by the glass and ales such as Shepherd Neame and local Stoney Ford, good food (not Sun evening) from varied menu, pizzas in summer, restaurant and airy orangery opening on to sunken terrace; free wi-fi; children and dogs (in bar) welcome, picnic-sets on lawn, light comfortable bedrooms, open all day, no food Sun evening. *(R L Borthwick, Pieter and Janet Vrancken)*

EYDON SP5450

★**Royal Oak** (01327) 263167
Lime Avenue; village signed off A361 Daventry–Banbury, and from B4525; NN11 3PG Interestingly laid-out 300-year-old ironstone dining pub, some lovely period features including fine flagstone floors and leaded windows, cosy snug on right with cushioned benches built into alcoves, seats in bow window, inglenook log fire, long corridor-like central bar linking three other small characterful rooms, very good well presented food from owner-chef (not Sun evening, Mon, Tues), friendly attentive staff; children and dogs welcome, terrace seating (some under cover), open all day Thurs-Sun. *(Jan Stevens)*

FLORE SP6460

White Hart (01327) 341748
A45 W of M1 junction 16; NN7 4LW Welcoming pub with good range of enjoyable affordably priced food from lunchtime baguettes up, three real ales including Sharps Doom Bar, modernised interior (some contemporary touches) with several linked areas around central bar including restaurant; TV, free wi-fi; tables on back deck by car park, open (and food) all day, till 9pm (6pm) Sun. *(Richard Kennell)*

GRAFTON REGIS SP7546

★**White Hart** (01908) 542123
A508 S of Northampton; NN12 7SR Thatched roadside dining pub with several linked rooms; good pubby food (not Sun evening) including range of home-made soups and popular Sun roasts (best to book), Greene King Abbot and IPA, Aspall's cider and nice wines by the glass, friendly helpful staff coping well when busy, restaurant with open fire; background music; children and dogs welcome (they have a couple of boxers and a parrot), terrace tables and gazebo in good-sized garden, self-catering cottage, closed Mon. *(Neil Allen)*

GREAT BILLING SP8162

Elwes Arms (01604) 407521
High Street; NN3 9DT Thatched and low-beamed 16th-c village pub with two bars (steps between); wide choice of good value tasty food including weekday lunch deal, Black Sheep, Wadworths 6X and Shepherd Neame Spitfire, friendly service, pleasant dining room where children allowed; background music, open mike night first Weds of month, quiz Thurs and Sun, sports TV, darts, free wi-fi; no dogs, garden tables and nice covered decked terrace, play area, open all day, food all day Sat, till 5pm Sun. *(Sylvia and Phillip Spencer)*

GREAT OXENDON SP7383

★**George** (01858) 452286
A508 S of Market Harborough; LE16 8NA Refurbished pub under same owners as the Joiners Arms at Bruntingthorpe (Leicestershire); small back bar with two Langton ales and a craft beer, all other areas for dining/pre-dining with bistro-style décor, very good well presented food from shortish but varied menu including a few specials, higher than average prices, friendly well turned out staff; children welcome, no dogs inside, terrace overlooking garden, eight bedrooms (four in annexe), open (and food) all day. *(Gerry and Rosemary Dobson, Mike and Margaret Banks)*

HACKLETON SP8054

White Hart (01604) 870271
B526 SE of Northampton; NN7 2AD Comfortably traditional 18th-c country pub; wide choice of enjoyable food from sandwiches and baked potatoes up, curry night Tues, friendly helpful staff, Fullers London Pride, Greene King IPA and a guest, decent choice of wines and other drinks, flagstoned bar with log fire, dining area up steps, beams, stripped stone and brickwork, illuminated well; background music, TV, pool and hood skittles; supervised children and dogs welcome, disabled access, picnic-sets in sunny garden, open all day, no food Sun evening. *(Jimmy)*

HARRINGTON SP7780

Tollemache Arms (01536) 711770
High Street; off A508 S of Market Harborough; NN6 9NU Pretty thatched and beamed Tudor pub under same ownership as the Red Lion at East Haddon; enjoyable food including sharing boards, pizzas and burgers, three well kept ales from Wells and Youngs plus a guest, good choice of wines by the glass, cocktails and a local artisan gin, friendly attentive staff; children and dogs (in bar) welcome, back garden with country views and play area, lovely quiet ironstone village, handy for Carpetbagger Aviation Museum, open all day weekends (till 9pm Sun). *(Gerry and Rosemary Dobson, Sophie Marple, Alan Sutton)*

HARRINGWORTH SP9197

White Swan (01572) 747035

Seaton Road; village SE of Uppingham, signed from A6003, A47 and A43; NN17 3AF Handsome 16th-c coaching inn refurbished under present management; large stone fireplace dividing flagstoned bar and dining area with high-backed leather chairs, woodstrip floor and painted beams, three changing ales, Weston's cider and enjoyable fairly traditional food including Fri fish and chips; free wi-fi; children and dogs (in bar) welcome, tables on paved terrace with pretty hanging baskets, not far from magnificent 82-arch viaduct spanning the Welland, five bedrooms, open all day weekends, closed Mon, Tues. *(M and GR)*

HIGHAM FERRERS SP9668

Griffin (01933) 312612

High Street; NN10 8BW Welcoming 17th-c pub-restaurant (bigger than it looks) with enjoyable food including fresh fish and popular Sun carvery (till 5pm), five well kept rotating ales and good selection of wines and malt whiskies, comfortable front bar with log fire, large back restaurant and smart dining conservatory, friendly relaxed atmosphere; free wi-fi; tables on heated terrace, open all day Fri-Sun. *(Stuart Doughty, Revd R P Tickle)*

HINTON-IN-THE-HEDGES SP5536

Crewe Arms (01280) 705801

Off A43 W of Brackley; NN13 5NF Updated 17th-c stone-built village pub; well kept ales including Hook Norton and enjoyable home-made food (not Sun evening) from bar snacks to specials, good friendly service, log fire; background music, free wi-fi; children and dogs welcome, picnic-sets in garden, two comfortable bothy bedrooms, open all day, from 3pm Mon. *(Neil Allen)*

KETTERING SP8778

Alexandra Arms (01536) 522730

Victoria Street; NN16 0BU Backstreet pub with up to 15 quickly changing ales kept well by knowledgeable landlord; basic opened-up bar with pump clips covering walls and ceiling, some snacky food, darts, hood skittles and TV in back games room; quiz night Weds; dogs welcome, a couple of picnic-sets out in front, small beer garden with benches behind, open all day (from 2pm Mon-Thurs). *(Martin Watson)*

KILSBY SP5671

★**George** (01788) 822229

2.5 miles from M1 junction 18: A428 towards Daventry, left on to A5 – pub off on right at roundabout; CV23 8YE Welcoming pub handy for the motorway; proper old-fashioned public bar, wood-panelled lounge with plush banquettes and coal-effect gas stove opening into smarter comfortably furnished area, well kept Adnams, Fullers, Timothy Taylors and a guest, fine range of malt whiskies, enjoyable good value home-made food including daily specials and themed evenings; Sun quiz, free-play pool tables, darts, TV, free wi-fi; children welcome if eating, dogs in bar, garden picnic-sets, six bedrooms, open Sun till 6pm. *(Pauline and Mark Evans)*

KINGS SUTTON SP4936

White Horse (01295) 812440

The Square; OX17 3RF Attractively updated Cotswold-stone pub; low beams, flagstone and wood floors, open fire, highly rated creative cooking from chef-landlord along with some more pubby choices and good value set lunch, well kept Brakspears and Jennings, 16 wines by the glass, gin bar with over 30 varieties and cocktails, good friendly service; children and dogs (in bar) welcome, wheelchair access, front picnic-sets looking over village green to striking church, open all day, food all day Sun, kitchen shut Mon, Tues. *(Martin Watson)*

KISLINGBURY SP6959

Cromwell Cottage (01604) 830288

High Street; NN7 4AG Sizeable dining pub tucked away near River Nene; comfortable modernised bar/lounge with some beams and open fire, civil war themed pictures, maps and a large mural on one wall, smart dining room, popular food (booking advised) from snacks to specials including weekend brunch from 9am, well kept changing ales and nice wines, friendly neat staff; no dogs, plenty of seats on paved terrace, open (and food) all day. *(Mike and Margaret Banks)*

KISLINGBURY SP6959

Sun (01604) 833571

Off A45 W of Northampton; Mill Road; NN7 4BB Welcoming thatch and ironstone village pub; Greene King IPA, St Austell Tribute and a guest, enjoyable fairly traditional food from sandwiches and sharing plates up including Tues pie night, L-shaped bar/lounge and small separate dining area; quiz last Sun of month and occasional live music, sports TV, free wi-fi; children welcome, no dogs inside, disabled access, a few picnic-sets out in front, open all day weekends, no food Sun evening, Mon or lunchtime Tues. *(John and Claire Masters)*

LITCHBOROUGH SP6353

Old Red Lion (01327) 830064

Banbury Road, just off former B4525 Banbury–Northampton; opposite church; NN12 8JF Attractive beamed pub owned by local farming family and doubling as village shop; four rooms including cosy flagstoned bar with woodburner in big inglenook, three real ales such as Great Oakley and Merrimen, shortish choice of enjoyable food (not Mon) using own produce, friendly relaxed atmosphere, barn-conversion restaurant at back; table skittles, darts; children and dogs welcome, popular with walkers, terrace seating, closed Sun evening, Mon lunchtime. *(Dan Clayton)*

LITTLE BRINGTON SP6663

★**Saracens Head** (01604) 770640
4.5 miles from M1 junction 16, first right off A45 to Daventry; also signed off A428; Main Street; NN7 4HS Friendly old village pub with enjoyable fairly priced food (not Sun evening, Mon) from lunchtime sandwiches up, well kept Greene King IPA, Timothy Taylors Landlord and a guest, several wines by the glass, roomy U-shaped beamed lounge with woodburner, flagstones, bare boards and tiled floors, chesterfields and lots of old prints, book-lined dining room; gentle background music; plenty of tables out on gravel/paved area with country views, walks nearby and handy for Althorp House and Holdenby House. *(Mike and Margaret Banks)*

LITTLE HARROWDEN SP8671

Lamb (01933) 673300
Orlingbury Road/Kings Lane – off A509 or A43 S of Kettering; NN9 5BH Popular 17th-c pub in delightful village; split-level carpeted lounge bar with log fire and brasses on beams, dining area, good promptly served food including Thurs steak night, Wells Eagle and a couple of guests, short sensibly priced wine list; games bar with darts, hood skittles and machines; background music, Fri quiz, free wi-fi; children welcome, small raised terrace and garden, open all day weekends. *(Jan Stevens)*

LITTLE HOUGHTON SP8059

Four Pears (01604) 890900
Bedford Road, off A428 E of Northampton; NN7 1AB Popular modernised pub owned by four local couples (hence the name); well kept mainly local ales, several wines by the glass and decent coffee, enjoyable food (not Sun evening) from light dishes to daily specials, friendly service, good-sized bar, comfortable lounge with woodburner and separate restaurant; children and dogs welcome, spacious outside area, parking can be tricky (no car park, narrow village street), open all day from noon. *(Gerry and Rosemary Dobson)*

LODDINGTON SP8178

Hare (01536) 710337
Main Street; NN14 1LA Welcoming 17th-c stone-built dining pub with modernised interior; good fairly priced home-made food from baguettes up, five well kept ales such as Greene King, Gun Dog and Wells; background music, TV, Sun quiz; children and dogs welcome, picnic-sets on front lawn, open all day weekends, closed Mon. *(Mike and Margaret Banks)*

LOWICK SP9780

Snooty Fox (01832) 733434
Off A6116 Corby–Raunds; NN14 3BH Solidly built 17th-c village pub with spacious lounge bar, woodburner in sizeable fireplace, stripped stone and handsomely moulded dark oak beams, leather sofas, bucket chairs and stools on big terracotta tiles, formidable carved counter serving two changing ales, a real cider and lots of wines by the glass, more formal dining rooms with chunky tables on pale wood floor, food can be good and some choices expensive; background music, free wi-fi; children and dogs (in bar) welcome, picnic-sets under parasols on front grass, play area, open all day weekends, closed Mon. *(Peter Andrews)*

MAIDWELL SP7477

Stag (01604) 686700
Harborough Road (A508 N of Northampton); a mile from A14 junction 2; NN6 9JA Beamed dining pub (some sprucing-up) with woodburner in pubby part by bar, extensive eating areas, good value traditional food served by friendly staff, well kept often local ales and good choice of other drinks; background music, sports TV, free wi-fi; children and dogs (in bar) welcome, disabled facilities, picnic-sets on back terrace, good-sized sloping garden beyond, five bedrooms, not far from splendid Palladian Kelmarsh Hall and park, open all day Fri and Sun. *(Mike and Margaret Banks, Gerry and Rosemary Dobson)*

MOULTON SP7866

Telegraph (01604) 648228
West Street; NN3 7SB Welcoming old village pub with good popular food (not Sun evening) from sandwiches and pizzas up, well kept Fullers, Sharps and a couple of guests, maybe an interesting craft keg, log fire in bar, back restaurant extension; children welcome, open (and food) all day Fri and Sat. *(Kyle Brown)*

NETHER HEYFORD SP6658

Olde Sun (01327) 340164
1.75 miles from M1 junction 16; village signposted left off A45 westbound; Middle Street; NN7 3LL Popular quirky place with small atmospheric linked rooms, bric-a-brac packed into nooks and crannies and hanging from the ceilings including brassware, 1930s cigarette cards, railway memorabilia, advertising signs and World War II posters, nice old cash till on one of the two counters serving Banks's, Greene King, Wychwood and a guest, well priced food including Sun carvery, beams and low ceilings, partly glazed dividing panels, rugs

A star symbol before the name of a pub shows exceptional character and appeal. It doesn't mean extra comfort. Even quite a basic pub can win a star, if it's individual enough.

on parquet, red tiles or flagstones (steps between some areas), big inglenook log fire, games room with hood skittles and darts; background music, quiz night second Sun of month; children and dogs welcome, lots of old farm equipment outside, open all day, no food Sun evening. *(Neil Allen)*

NORTHAMPTON SP7560

Albion Brewery Bar (01604) 946606
Kingswell Street; NN1 1PR Tap for the revived 19th-c Albion Brewery (visible through glass partition, tours available); half a dozen Phipps/Hoggleys ales in top condition plus a guest and local cider, also their own Kingswell gin, bar snacks available Tues-Sat, friendly staff, pitched-ceiling bar with big windows and reclaimed fittings (many from closed Phipps pubs), traditional games including northamptonshire skittles and bar billiards; live music (upstairs concert venue planned for autumn 2018); children and dogs welcome, disabled access/loo, open all day Fri, Sat, closed Sun evening and Mon lunchtime. *(Stuart Doughty)*

NORTHAMPTON SP7560

Lamplighter (01604) 631125
Overstone Road; NN1 3JS Welcoming Victorian corner pub in the Mounts area attracting good mix of customers; wide choice of draught and bottled beers, well priced generously served food including range of burgers, good vegetarian options and popular Sun roasts; regular live music (open mike Mon), quiz Weds; children welcome if eating, picnic-sets in heated courtyard, open (and food) all day. *(Michael Domeney)*

NORTHAMPTON SP7661

Olde England 07981 043285
Kettering Road, near the racecourse; NN1 4BP Quirky conversion of Victorian corner shop over three floors (steepish stairs to upper level and down to cellar bar), ground-floor room with assorted tables and chairs on bare boards, 20 well kept changing ales and similar number of ciders served from hatch on stairs, lots of pictures with medieval or Arthurian themes, plus the odd banner, flag and suit of armour, cheap food with more extensive choice weekends when pub at its busiest, friendly staff and broad mix of customers; cards and board games; children and dogs welcome, closed Mon-Fri lunchtimes, otherwise open all day. *(Jan Stevens)*

NORTHAMPTON SP7660

Princess Alexandra (01604) 245485
Alexandra Road; NN1 5QP Refurbished backstreet pub (near the town centre) calling itself a Craft Beer & Alehouse; spacious relaxed bars with pleasing modern décor, recycled timber, exposed brickwork and woodburner, wide range of changing beers and some interesting ciders, tasters offered by friendly knowledgeable staff, shortish menu including snacks and pizzas (discounts for NHS workers); children and dogs welcome, small garden behind, parking nearby can be difficult, closed Mon-Weds lunchtime, otherwise open all day (till 1am Fri, Sat). *(Stuart Doughty, Jan Stevens)*

NORTHAMPTON SP7560

Wig & Pen (01604) 622178
St Giles Street; NN1 1JA Long L-shaped beamed room with bar running most of its length, up to a dozen well kept ales (tasters offered) including Adnams, Fullers and Greene King, traditional ciders and good choice of bottled beers, whiskies and gins, generous servings of nicely presented food (not weekend evenings) from sandwiches, tapas and deli boards up, brunch from 10am, friendly young staff; Tues jazz and other live music, sports TVs; split-level walled garden, handy for Guildhall and Derngate Theatre, open all day (till 1.30am Fri, Sat) and busy on Saints rugby days. *(Michael Domeney, Dr J Barrie Jones)*

OLD SP7873

White Horse (01604) 781297
Walgrave Road, N of Northampton between A43 and A508; NN6 9QX Popular and welcoming village pub with good sensibly priced food (booking advised) from shortish menu supplemented by some interesting daily specials, three well kept ales, craft beers, proper ciders and decent wines by the glass, friendly efficient staff, additional dining area upstairs; quiz night first Thurs of month, live music last Fri, free wi-fi; well behaved children and dogs welcome, garden and deck overlooking 13th-c church, outside pizza oven, open all day Fri and Sat, till 7pm Sun, closed Mon. *(Gerry and Rosemary Dobson, Pete Newton, Mike and Margaret Banks)*

OUNDLE TL0388

Ship (01832) 273918
West Street; PE8 4EF Bustling down-to-earth pub run by two brothers; heavily beamed lounge to left of central corridor, cosy areas with mix of leather and other seats, sturdy tables and log fire in stone inglenook, well kept Brewsters, Nene Valley, Sharps and Timothy Taylors, eight wines by the glass and fair value pubby food (not Sun evening), charming panelled snug at one end, also a wood-floored public bar and terrace bar with pool, darts and TV; background music, poker night Weds, free wi-fi; children and dogs welcome, series of small covered terraces (lit at night), bedrooms, open all day. *(Amy and Luke Buchanan, Heather and Richard Jones, Mike Benton)*

OUNDLE TL0388

Talbot (01832) 273621
New Street; PE8 4EA Hotel in handsome former merchant's house; various rooms including comfortably modernised bar,

a couple of real ales like Digfield and Mad Hatter, enjoyable food from sandwiches and sharing plates up, good helpful service, restaurant; children welcome, seats in courtyard and garden, 40 bedrooms, open (and food) all day, breakfast from 7am. *(Martin Watson)*

PITSFORD SP7567

Griffin (01604) 880346

Off A508 N of Northampton; High Street; NN6 9AD Friendly pub in pretty village near Brixworth Country Park and Pitsford Water; cosy beamed bar, back lounge with steps up to small eating area and pleasant restaurant extension, Potbelly, St Austell and a guest, well liked reasonably priced home-made food including good steaks and set deal; Sun quiz and occasional live music; children welcome, dogs in front bar, a few picnic-sets outside, open all Fri-Sun, closed Mon. *(John and Claire Masters)*

RUSHDEN SP9566

Station Bar (01933) 318988

Station Approach; NN10 0AW Not a pub but part of station HQ of Rushden Historical Transport Society (non-members can sign in for £1); bar in former ladies' waiting room with gas lighting, enamel signs and railway memorabilia, seven ales including Dark Star and Phipps, tea and coffee, filled rolls and perhaps some hot food, friendly staff; also museum and summer train rides, table skittles in a Royal Mail carriage; outside benches, open all day weekends, closed weekday lunchtimes. *(Neil Allen)*

RUSHTON SP8483

Thornhill Arms (01536) 710251

Station Road; NN14 1RL Busy family-run dining pub (booking advised) opposite lovely village's cricket green; enjoyable food including keenly priced set menu (weekday evenings, Sat lunchtime) and carvery (Sun, Mon evening), gluten-free menu too, up to four well kept ales such as Black Sheep and Sharps, smart high-beamed back restaurant and several other neatly laid-out dining areas, open fire; children welcome, garden with decked area, open (and food) all day Sun. *(Neil Allen)*

SHUTLANGER SP7249

Plough (01604) 864644

Main Road, off A43 N of Towcester; NN12 7RU Revamped dining pub with excellent food presented with real flair (booking advised), three real ales including St Austell Tribute, good choice of wines by the glass, cocktails (weekday happy hour 5-7pm), efficient friendly service; painted picnic-sets on gravel terrace, nearby walks (dogs allowed in the bar), closed Mon and Tues, otherwise open all day (Sun till 9pm, food till 4.30pm). *(Alan Sutton)*

SPRATTON SP7170

Kings Head (01604) 847351

Brixworth Road, off A5199 N of Northampton; NN6 8HH Combination of brasserie, bar and coffee shop; pale flagstones and ancient stripped stonework mixing well with handsome new wood flooring and up-to-date décor, leather chesterfields, an antique settle and café chairs around stripped tables, woodburner in brick fireplace, Shepherd Neame Spitfire, a changing beer from Grainstore and eight wines by the glass, decent range of gins and cocktails, good popular food from light lunches up; background music, free wi-fi; children and dogs (in bar) welcome, back courtyard with modern tables and chairs, open all day, no food Sun evening, coffee shop from 8.30am, breakfast till 5pm (closed Sun). *(Pauline and Mark Evans)*

STANWICK SP9871

Duke of Wellington (01933) 622452

Church Street; NN9 6PS Welcoming 19th-c stone pub next to the church; fresh contemporary décor in split level interior, good well presented food (not Sun evening) from lunchtime sandwiches and pub favourites up, real ales such as Greene King Abbot and IPA; background and occasional live music; children welcome, picnic-sets out at front under parasols, more behind, closed Mon, otherwise open all day (till 10pm Tues-Thurs, 9pm Sun). *(Steve Sanford)*

STAVERTON SP5461

Countryman (01327) 311815

Daventry Road (A425); NN11 6JH Beamed and carpeted dining pub with popular food from smallish menu including some interesting vegetarian options, Phipps IPA, Wells Bombardier and a guest, bar divided by brick pillars, restaurant; background music; children and dogs (in bar) welcome, disabled access, some tables out at front and in small garden behind, open (and food) all day Sun. *(Jimmy)*

STOKE BRUERNE SP7449

Boat (01604) 862428

3.5 miles from M1 junction 15 – A508 towards Stony Stratford, then signed on right; Bridge Road; NN12 7SB Long thatched pub (run by the same family since 1887) in picturesque canalside spot; traditional flagstoned bar with open fire, half a dozen well kept Marstons-related ales and maybe a local guest, Thatcher's cider, enjoyable fairly standard food at reasonable

All *Guide* inspections are anonymous. Anyone claiming to be a *Good Pub Guide* inspector is a fraud. Please let us know.

prices from baguettes up, friendly service, more modern central-pillared back bar and bistro, comfortable upstairs bookable restaurant with separate menu (closed Mon, Sun evening); background music, northamptonshire skittles; children and dogs welcome, disabled facilities, tables out by towpath opposite canal museum, shop for boaters and trips on own narrowboat, open all day and can get very busy in summer, especially weekends when parking nearby is difficult, open all day from 9am for breakfast. *(Mike and Margaret Banks, Revd R P Tickle)*

STOKE DOYLE TL0286

★**Shuckburgh Arms** (01832) 272339
Village signed (down Stoke Hill) from SW edge of Oundle; PE8 5TG Relaxed 17th-c pub in quiet hamlet; four traditional rooms with some modern touches, low black beams in bowed ceilings, pictures on pastel walls, lots of pale tables on wood or carpeted floors, stylish art deco seats and elegant dining chairs, inglenook woodburner, ales such as Nene Valley and Black Sheep from granite-top bar, well selected wines and popular food including Thurs steak night, helpful attentive staff; soft background music; children welcome, garden with decked area and play frame, bedrooms in separate modern block, closed Sun evening, Mon. *(Sylvia and Phillip Spencer)*

SUDBOROUGH SP9682

Vane Arms (01832) 730033
Off A6116; Main Street; NN14 3BX Old thatched pub in pretty village; low beams, stripped stonework and inglenook fires, well kept Everards Tiger and guests, enjoyable freshly cooked food served by friendly staff, restaurant; free wi-fi; children and well behaved dogs (in bar) welcome, disabled loo, terrace tables, three bedrooms in nearby building, closed Sun evening. *(Jan Stevens)*

SULGRAVE SP5545

★**Star** (01295) 760389
Manor Road; E of Banbury, signed off B4525; OX17 2SA Handsome creeper-clad inn again under new management; woodburner in fine inglenook, working shutters, old doors and flagstones, moss or plum-coloured walls, mix of antique, vintage and retro furniture, polished copper and brass, Hook Norton ales, several wines by the glass and enjoyable fairly standard food, friendly service, dining room with working range, snug in former farmhouse kitchen; children and dogs welcome, back garden with vine-covered trellis, aunt sally, short walk to Sulgrave Manor (George Washington's ancestral home), four bedrooms, closed Sun evening, Mon. *(Neil Allen)*

THORNBY SP6675

★**Red Lion** (01604) 740238
Welford Road; A5199 Northampton–Leicester; NN6 8SJ Popular old village pub with interesting range of well kept/priced changing ales, very good home-cooked food (not Sun evening, Mon) from standards up including notable steak and stilton pie, smaller helpings available for some lunchtime dishes, prompt friendly service, beams and log fire, lots of old local photographs, back dining area; children and dogs welcome, garden with picnic-sets, accommodation in converted barn, open all day Fri-Sun when can get very busy (booking advised), closed Mon lunchtime. *(Gerry and Rosemary Dobson, Mike and Margaret Banks)*

THORPE MANDEVILLE SP5344

★**Three Conies** (01295) 711025
Off B4525 E of Banbury; OX17 2EX Attractive and welcoming 17th-c ironstone pub; well kept Hook Norton ales and good choice of enjoyable locally sourced food (not Sun evening, Mon), beamed bar with some stripped stone, mix of old tables and comfortable seating on bare boards, log fires, large dining room; background music (live Fri), TV, hood skittles; children and dogs welcome, disabled facilities, tables out in front, more behind on decking and lawn, closed Mon lunchtime, otherwise open all day. *(Gerry and Rosemary Dobson)*

TOWCESTER SP7047

Folly (01327) 354031
A5 S, opposite racecourse; NN12 6LB Early 18th-c thatched and beamed dining pub with highly rated food (booking advised) including set lunch menu, good selection of wines and a couple of well kept local beers, friendly efficient staff, small bar with steps up to dining area; children (till 8pm) and dogs (in bar) welcome, tables out at back, open all day Sun till 9pm, closed Mon. *(Gerry and Rosemary Dobson)*

TOWCESTER SP6948

Towcester Mill (01327) 437060
Chantry Lane; NN12 6YY Old mill tucked away behind market square surrounded by redevelopment; nice little bare-boards bar acting as tap for on-site brewery (tours available – book ahead), seven ales including a couple of guests, also good range of ciders and country wines, friendly knowledgeable staff; live music, comedy and quiz nights in upstairs room; walkers and dogs welcome, garden behind with seats by mill race and pond, closes 9pm Sun and Mon (and winter lunchtimes Mon-Thurs), otherwise open all day. *(Andy Brown)*

TURWESTON SP6037

Stratton Arms (01280) 704956
E of crossroads in village; pub itself just inside Buckinghamshire; NN13 5JX Friendly chatty local in picturesque village; five well kept ales including Otter and good choice of other drinks, enjoyable

reasonably priced traditional food (Weds-Sun lunchtimes, Fri and Sat evenings), low ceilings and two log fires, small restaurant; background music, sports TV; children and dogs welcome, large pleasant garden by Great Ouse with barbecue and play area, camping, open all day Weds, Fri and Sat, till 8pm other days, closed Tues. *(Jimmy)*

TWYWELL SP9578

Old Friar (01832) 732625

Lower Street, off A14 W of Thrapston; NN14 3AH Welcoming pub with enjoyable food including set lunch menu and carvery (Thurs-Sat evenings, all day Sun), Tues pie and Weds grill nights, Greene King and a couple of guests, modernised split-level interior with beams and some exposed stonework; children and dogs (in bar) welcome, garden with good play area, open (and food) all day weekends. *(Mike and Margaret Banks)*

UPPER BODDINGTON SP4853

Plough (01327) 260364

Warwick Road; NN11 6DH 18th-c thatched village inn keeping much of its original character; small beamed and flagstoned bar, lobby with old local photos, Greene King IPA, Shepherd Neame Spitfire and a guest, good value fairly traditional food in restaurant, snug or intimate 'Doll's Parlour' named after former veteran landlady, friendly efficient service, woodburners; quiz first Sun of month, occasional live music and beer festivals, free wi-fi; children and dogs welcome, five bedrooms (some sharing bathroom), usually closed weekday lunchtimes, open all day weekends, no food Sun evening, Mon. *(Jan Stevens)*

WADENHOE TL0183

★ Kings Head (01832) 720024

Church Street; village signposted (in small print) off A605 S of Oundle; PE8 5ST Beautifully placed 17th-c country pub with picnic-sets on sun terrace and among trees on grassy stretch by River Nene (moorings); uncluttered partly stripped-stone bar with woodburner in fine inglenook, pale pine furniture and a couple of cushioned wall seats, simple bare-boards public bar and attractive little beamed dining room with more pine furniture, good well presented food (booking advised), three well kept changing ales and several wines by the glass, friendly efficient service; games room with darts, dominoes and table skittles; children and dogs (in bar) welcome, good nearby walks, closed Sun evening, Mon. *(Nigel Cowdery)*

WALGRAVE SP8072

Royal Oak (01604) 781248

Zion Hill, off A43 Northampton–Kettering; NN6 9PN Welcoming old stone-built village local; generous helpings of good fairly priced food from changing menu (best to book) including specials and popular two-for-one Tues evening deal on main courses, well kept Adnams, Greene King and three guests, decent wines, friendly prompt service, long three-part carpeted beamed bar, small lounge and back restaurant extension; quiz nights, sports TV; children welcome, no dogs inside, small garden with play area, open all day Sun; for sale as we went to press. *(Gerry and Rosemary Dobson, Mike and Margaret Banks)*

WELFORD SP6480

Wharf Inn (01858) 575075

Pub just over Leicestershire border; NN6 6JQ Spacious castellated Georgian folly in delightful setting by two Grand Union Canal marinas; six well kept ales such as Grainstore, Marstons and Oakham in unpretentious bar, popular reasonably priced food (all day Sun) including good steak and kidney pudding and daily specials, helpful friendly service, pleasant dining section; children and dogs welcome, wheelchair access using portable ramps (disabled loo), big waterside garden and good local walks, four bedrooms, open all day. *(Stuart Doughty, R T and J C Moggridge, Mike and Margaret Banks)*

WELLINGBOROUGH SP8867

Coach & Horses (01933) 441848

Oxford Street; NN8 4HY L-shaped bar adorned with breweriana including hundreds of pump clips fixed to beams, 12 well kept changing ales, 15 ciders and around 40 gins, good value pubby food including speciality pies, Weds fish and chips and Thurs curry, friendly staff, comfortable cosy atmosphere with open fire; children and dogs welcome, disabled access, beer garden, open all day (till 6pm Sun, 9pm Mon), no food Sun evening to Tues. *(Tony and Wendy Hobden)*

WELTON SP5866

White Horse (01327) 702820

Off A361/B4036 N of Daventry; behind church, High Street; NN11 2JP Beamed 17th-c village pub on different levels; well kept Adnams, Purity, Oakham and a guest, local cider and nice house wines, reasonably priced food (not Sun evening, Mon, Tues) including good value steak deal Weds-Sat, roasts only on Sun, woodburners, separate games bar with darts and skittles, small dining room; fortnightly Sun quiz; children and dogs welcome in one part, attractive garden and terrace, open all day Fri-Sun, closed Mon and Tues lunchtimes. *(Kyle Brown)*

WESTON SP5846

Crown (01295) 760310

The Weston N of Brackley; Helmdon Road; NN12 8PX Handsome 16th-c stone-built inn (ex-farmhouse); updated interior with log fires, painted beams and exposed stone walls, Hook Norton Hooky, Sharps Doom Bar and Towcester Mill Race, well liked food from sandwiches and good value pubby dishes to more restauranty choices, Weds fish night, good friendly service; children and dogs welcome, five bedrooms, attractive village handy for Canons Ashby (NT) and Sulgrave Manor, closed Sun evening and lunchtimes Mon, Tues. *(Pauline and Mark Evans)*

WHITTLEBURY SP6943

Fox & Hounds (01327) 858048
High Street; NN12 8XJ Double-fronted 19th-c village bar-restaurant; modern interior with wood flooring and comfy stylish seating, four well kept ales including local Gun Dog, nice selection of wines and good well presented food from thick-cut sandwiches and sharing boards up (separate bar and restaurant menus), friendly helpful service; children and dogs welcome, picnic-sets on suntrap gravel terrace, handy for Silverstone, open all day weekends, closed Mon. *(Brian Glozier)*

YARDLEY HASTINGS SP8656

★**Rose & Crown** (01604) 696276
Just off A428 Bedford–Northampton; NN7 1EX Spacious and popular 18th-c dining pub in pretty village; flagstones, beams, stripped stonework and quiet corners, step up to big comfortable dining room, flowers on tables, good well presented food from interesting changing menu along with bar snacks and pubby choices, efficient friendly young staff, six well kept ales including a house beer from local Hart Family, four ciders and decent range of wines; background and occasional live music, daily newspapers; children welcome till 9pm, dogs in bar, tables under parasols in split-level garden, boules, open all day (from 5pm Mon). *(S Holder, Stuart Doughty)*

Northumbria

(County Durham, Northumberland and Tyneside)

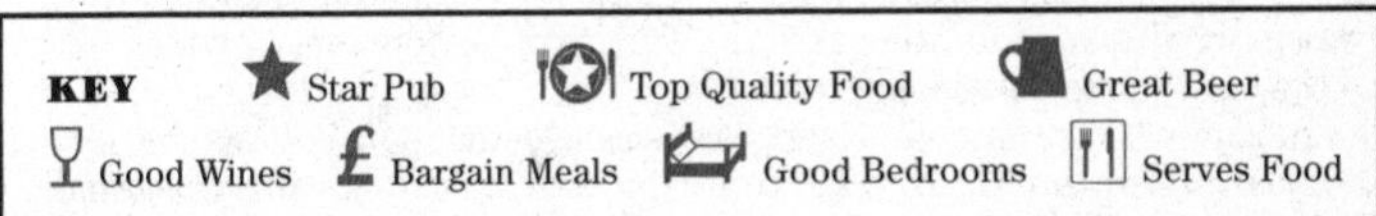

BARRASFORD NY9173 Map 10

Barrasford Arms

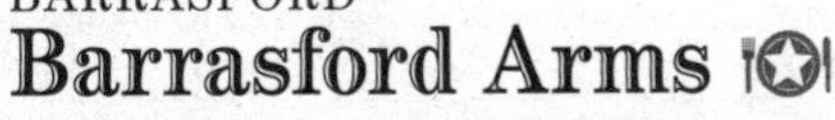

(01434) 681237 – www.barrasfordarms.co.uk

Village signposted off A6079 N of Hexham; NE48 4AA

Good local atmosphere in friendly bar, smarter dining rooms, rewarding food and drinks and seats outside; bedrooms

The warm, comfortable bedrooms in this bustling sandstone inn make a fine base for visiting nearby Hadrian's Wall; breakfasts are highly rated. There's a genuine welcome from the hands-on licensees, and the traditional bar has a log fire, old photos and bric-a-brac and an ale such as Allendale Golden Plover on handpump, seven wines by the glass, local gins and five malt whiskies. Two dining rooms have either upholstered and striped or leather high-backed chairs around wooden tables; one has wall seating at the end of the room and the other has a stone chimneybreast hung with guns and copper pans; background music, TV, darts and board games. Good fishing can be found on the North Tyne River just 100 metres away.

Cooked by the landlord, the well regarded food includes sandwiches, twice-baked cheese soufflé, smoked salmon mousse with cucumber and chives, wild black trumpet risotto with garlic crisps and parmesan, hake and salmon fishcake with spinach, poached egg and creamy grain mustard sauce, chicken breast with roast peanut crust, boulangère potatoes and red cabbage, lambs liver with a trio of onions, duchess potatoes and onion-infused jus, and puddings such as rhubarb pannacotta with poached rhubarb and hazelnut crumble topping and warm chocolate brownie with mint chocolate ice-cream; they also offer a two- and three-course set lunch. *Benchmark main dish: rib-eye steak with peppercorn sauce, onion rings and chips £22.00. Two-course evening meal £21.00.*

Free house ~ Licensees Mr and Mrs Eames ~ Real ale ~ Open 12-midnight; closed Mon ~ Bar food 12-2, 6-8.30; 12-3 ~ Restaurant ~ Children welcome ~ Wi-fi ~ Live music first Tues of month ~ Bedrooms: £65/£85 *Recommended by Michael Doswell, Richard and Tessa Ibbot, Robert and Diana Myers, Julia and Fiona Barnes*

BLANCHLAND NY9650 Map 10

Lord Crewe Arms

(01434) 675469 – www.lordcrewearmsblanchland.co.uk

B6306 S of Hexham; DH8 9SP

Wonderful historic building, with unique Crypt bar, cosy dining rooms and spacious restaurant; comfortable, well equipped bedrooms

'Exceptional', 'superb' and 'just wonderful'. These are just a few comments from our readers who have loved their visits here, and it is indeed a special place. It was built as a guest house in 1235 for the neighbouring Premonstratensian monastery and the architecture is remarkable. The unique Crypt bar is a medieval vaulted room sculpted by thick stone walls, lit by candlelight and with family crests on the ceiling. There are high wooden stools by wall shelves and against the armour-plated counter, cushioned settles and plush stools around a few little tables, with Hadrian Border Tyneside Blonde, Wylam Red Kite and Lord Crewe Brew (named for the pub from Wylam) on handpump, 14 wines by the glass, ten malt whiskies and a farm cider; background music and board games. One character sitting area has a leather sofa and two big tartan armchairs on flagstones in front of a large open fire, while the grand yet informal restaurant features a fine old wooden floor, cushioned wall seating and leather-cushioned dining chairs around oak-topped tables, fresh flowers, antlers on the walls and a large central candelabra. It's a real treat to stay here in bedrooms that range from cosy to luxury suites. Derwent Reservoir is nearby.

Delicious food includes sandwiches, fried duck egg with Morecambe Bay shrimps and wild garlic, home-cured smoked salmon with dill potato salad, baked goats cheese crottin with beetroot, sweet-cured bacon chop with frizzy herb salad and chips, mutton sausages with lamb chop and whipped potatoes, baked scottish salmon in puff pastry with spinach, rice and an egg, salt-aged flat-iron steak with chophouse sauce, local veal rump with grilled sprouting broccoli and lemon, and puddings such as chocolate mousse with roasted apricots and crème catalan; there is also afternoon tea. *Benchmark main dish: crispy skin chicken sharing platter with barbecue sauce, chicory salad and fries £32.00. Two-course evening meal £22.00.*

Free house ~ Licensee Tommy Mark ~ Real ale ~ Open 7am-midnight ~ Bar food 12-2.30, 6-9; 12-3, 6-9 Sat; 12-3.30, 6.30-8.30 Sun ~ Restaurant ~ Children welcome ~ Dogs allowed in bar and bedrooms ~ Wi-fi ~ Bedrooms: /£119 *Recommended by Elise and Charles Mackinlay, Mark and Mary Setting, Stuart Doughty, Peter Meister, Bill Braithwaite, Andrew and Michele Revell, Buster and Helena Hastings*

CARTERWAY HEADS NZ0452 Map 10

Manor House Inn

(01207) 255268 – www.themanorhouseinn.com

A68 just N of B6278, near Derwent Reservoir; DH8 9LX

Handy for the A68 and nearby walks, with recently refurbished bar and lounge, four real ales and highly regarded food; bedrooms

From picnic-sets on the terrace there are stunning views over the Derwent Valley and Reservoir; the comfortable bedrooms share the same lovely outlook. Inside, the locals' bar has an original boarded ceiling, pine tables, chairs and stools, old oak pews and a mahogany counter. The lounge bar (warmed by a woodburning stove) and restaurant are comfortably pubby with wheelback chairs, stripped-stone walls and picture windows that make the most of the fine setting. Greene King Old Speckled Hen and a couple of guests such as Allendale Pennine Pale and Consett Ale Works Steel Town Bitter on handpump, alongside 12 wines by the glass, 20 malt whiskies and Weston's Old Rosie cider; board games and background music.

Using seasonal local produce, the enjoyable food includes lunchtime sandwiches, grain mustard pannacotta with goats cheese and carrot crisps, king prawns with prosciutto, pomegranate and watercress, butternut squash and sage ravioli with potato purée and brown butter, pork sausages with gravy, creamy mash and gravy, roasted chicken breast with cauliflower purée, roast cauliflower and red wine jus, hake fillet with lemon and herb cream sauce, and puddings such as apple fritter with poached rhubarb and white chocolate sauce and sticky toffee pudding with butterscotch sauce. *Benchmark main dish: steak burger on home-made brioche with purple slaw and chips £12.00. Two-course evening meal £18.50.*

Enterprise ~ Lease Chris Baxter ~ Real ale ~ Open 12-11 (10 Sun); may close early in winter if weather is appalling ~ Bar food 12-3, 5-9; 12-9 Sat; 12-7 Sun ~ Restaurant ~ Children welcome ~ Dogs allowed in bar and bedrooms ~ Wi-fi ~ Bedrooms: £75/£90
Recommended by Deborah and Duncan Walliams, Claire Adams, Charlie Stevens, Mark Hamill, Katherine Matthews, Jim and Sue James

COTHERSTONE NZ0119 Map 10

Fox & Hounds

(01833) 650241 – www.cotherstonefox.co.uk
B6277; DL12 9PF

Bustling inn with cheerful beamed bar, good food and quite a few wines by the glass; bedrooms

There's a cheerful, simply furnished beamed bar in this Georgian country inn with a partly wooden floor (elsewhere it's carpeted), a good winter log fire, thickly cushioned wall seats and local photographs and country pictures in various alcoves and recesses. McColls Golden Ale and a couple of guests such as Black Sheep Ram Tackle and Tirril 1823 on handpump, alongside eight wines by the glass and over 20 gins and malt whiskies. There are seats outside on a terrace and quoits. The bright, clean and comfortable bedrooms make a good base for exploring the area; fine surrounding walks.

Popular food using fresh fish delivered daily includes ploughman's, pot of prawns, leeks, mushrooms and cheese with a herb crust, smoked salmon, melon and prawn platter, beer-battered haddock and chips, ratatouille gratin, a pie of the day, lambs liver with crispy bacon, mustard mash and roast gravy, pork platter (gammon, black pudding and sausage) with egg and chips, and puddings such as chocolate cream crunch and sticky toffee pudding. *Benchmark main dish: cheese-filled chicken with bacon and creamy leek sauce £11.95. Two-course evening meal £21.00.*

Free house ~ Licensee Nichola Swinburn ~ Real ale ~ Open 12-3, 6-11 (10.30 Sun); closed Mon-Weds lunchtimes Nov-Easter ~ Bar food 12-2, 6-8.30; 12-2, 6-9 Fri, Sat ~ Restaurant ~ Children welcome ~ Dogs allowed in bar and bedrooms ~ Wi-fi ~ Bedrooms: £50/£90
Recommended by David Milton, S G N Bennett, Julie and Andrew Blanchett, Buster and Helena Hastings, Trevor and Michele Street

CRASTER NU2519 Map 10

Jolly Fisherman

(01665) 576461 – www.thejollyfishermancraster.co.uk
Off B1339, NE of Alnwick; NE66 3TR

Stunning views, very good food and plenty of seasonal visitors

A fine base for walkers – the route from here along the cliff to Dunstanburgh Castle (English Heritage) is popular – this unpretentious local is at its best on a clear day when you can enjoy the lovely position overlooking the harbour and out to sea. The friendly, bustling bar has a cheerful atmosphere, a warming winter fire, leather button-back wall banquettes and upholstered and wooden dining chairs around hefty tables on bare boards, a few stools scattered here and there, and photographs and paintings in gilt-edged frames; background music. There's Black Sheep, Mordue Workie Ticket and Northumbrian Blonde and Timothy Taylors Landlord on handpump, served by friendly staff. From big windows in the upstairs dining room you look down on the water. Seats and tables in the garden have the same outlook and get snapped up pretty quickly. They have a couple of fishermen's cottages and an apartment for rent as well as a café and gift shop opposite the pub.

Well regarded food includes lunchtime sandwiches, their famous crab soup, scottish mussels in white wine and cream, omelette Arnold Bennett, burger with toppings and dripping chips, asian-spiced hake with cauliflower purée, piccalilli bhaji and bombay potatoes, grilled squid with chickpeas, pancetta and herb salad, rib-eye or venison steaks with beef dripping chips, and puddings such as lemon posset and double chocolate cheesecake. *Benchmark main dish: fresh fish board £17.00. Two-course evening meal £21.50.*

Punch ~ Lease David Whitehead ~ Real ale ~ Open 11-11; 12-10.30 Sun ~ Bar food 11-3, 5.30-8.30; 12-4, 5-8.30 Sun; closed Mon evening in winter ~ Restaurant ~ Children welcome ~ Dogs allowed in bar ~ Wi-fi *Recommended by John and Sylvia Harrop, Roger and Donna Huggins, Martinthehills, Barry Collett, Margaret and Peter Staples, Darren and Jane Staniforth, Tracey and Stephen Groves*

DIPTONMILL NY9261 Map 10

Dipton Mill Inn £

(01434) 606577 – www.diptonmill.co.uk

S of Hexham; off B6306 at Slaley; NE46 1YA

Own-brew beers from on-site microbrewery, good value bar food and waterside terrace

A favourite with both regulars and visitors, this is a quaint little country pub with own-brewed ales and remarkable value food. The neatly kept snug bar has genuine character, dark ply panelling, low ceilings, red furnishings, a dark red carpet and two welcoming open fires. Six beers from the family-owned Hexhamshire Brewery are well kept on handpump: Blackhall English Stout, Devils Elbow, Devils Water, Shire Bitter and Whapweasel. Also, 11 wines by the glass, 18 malt whiskies and a guest cider. The garden is peaceful and pretty with attractive planting and seats on grass by a restored mill stream. Hexham Racecourse is not far away and there are also woodland walks nearby.

Tasty, fair-priced food includes sandwiches, chicken liver pâté, smoked salmon and prawns, tagliatelle with parmesan and basil, chicken breast with sherry sauce, lambs liver and sausages, haddock baked with tomato and basil, steak and kidney pie, and puddings such as syrup sponge and custard and creamy lemon tart. *Benchmark main dish: mince and dumplings £7.50. Two-course evening meal £14.00.*

Own brew ~ Licensee Mark Brooker ~ Real ale ~ No credit cards ~ Open 12-2.30, 6-11; 12-3 Sun; closed Sun evening ~ Bar food 12-2, 6-8.30; 12-2 Sun ~ Children welcome ~ Wi-fi *Recommended by Celia and Rupert Lemming, Colin and Daniel Gibbs, Martinthehills, Martine and Colin Fresher, Sally and Brian Turner*

DURHAM NZ2742 Map 10

Victoria

(0191) 386 5269 – www.victoriainn-durhamcity.co.uk

Hallgarth Street (A177, near Dunelm House); DH1 3AS

Unchanging and neatly kept Victorian pub with royal memorabilia, cheerful locals and well kept regional ales; bedrooms

The long-serving owners have been running this charmingly unspoilt and immaculately kept inn for over 40 years, and it still has the original

Victorian decor. Three small rooms, leading off a central bar, have mahogany, etched and cut glass and mirrors, colourful William Morris wallpaper over a high panelled dado, some maroon plush seats in little booths, leatherette wall seats and long narrow drinkers' tables. Also, coal fires in handsome iron and tile fireplaces, photographs and articles showing a real pride in the pub, lots of period prints and engravings of Queen Victoria, and staffordshire figurines of her and the Prince Consort. Big Lamp Lamp Light Bitter, Durham White Stout, Fyne Jarl, Saltaire Blonde and Wylam Gold Tankard on handpump, over 35 irish whiskeys, 60 scottish malts and cheap house wines; dominoes. Attractive bedrooms, hearty breakfasts and free off-street parking make this little gem perfect for exploring the city's castle and cathedral. Credit cards are accepted only for accommodation. No food.

Free house ~ Licensee Michael Webster ~ Real ale ~ No credit cards ~ Open 12-11; 12-10.30 Sun ~ Children welcome ~ Dogs welcome ~ Bedrooms: £65/£85 *Recommended by Martinthehills, Edward May*

ELLINGHAM NU1625 Map 10

Pack Horse

(01665) 589292 – www.packhorseinn-ellingham.co.uk

Signed off A1 N of Alnwick; NE67 5HA

Stone-built inn with good food, friendly staff and pretty garden; attractive bedrooms

Our readers enjoy this charming small pub very much. The flagstoned bar has masses of jugs hanging from beams, a long settle and upholstered stools around pubby tables, a log fire and tall stools against the counter where friendly staff serve Black Sheep and Timothy Taylors Landlord with a guest from the local Rigg & Furrow brewery on handpump; background music. The snug has a woodburning stove in a large stone fireplace with a stag's head above and captain's chairs and other seats on bare floorboards. The restaurant is divided into two, with high-backed chairs around pale tables on tartan carpet. As well as picnic-sets in the enclosed garden, there's an area where they grow their own vegetables and they may have jams or marmalade for sale in aid of local charities. The pretty bedrooms make a good base for exploring the lovely coastline and nearby castles.

Good food (using their own dexter and highland cows and the landlord's rare-breed pigs) includes sandwiches, salt and chilli squid with coriander and roast chilli salad, pheasant goujons with garlic aioli, red lentil curry with cucumber and mint yoghurt and chargrilled broccoli, beer-battered cod and chips, steak in ale pie, short rib of beef with rosemary and redcurrant jus and black pepper mash, pork chop with mint and redcurrant jus and mustard mash, beef bourguignon, lamb moussaka, and puddings such as warm dark chocolate brownie with strawberry coulis and rhubarb and ginger crumble with custard. *Benchmark main dish: rare-breed burger with toppings, red slaw and fries £11.90. Two-course evening meal £18.00.*

Free house ~ Licensee Oliver Simpson ~ Real ale ~ Open 12-11; 12-2, 6-11 in winter ~ Bar food 12-2, 6-9; 12-3 Sun ~ Restaurant ~ Children welcome ~ Dogs allowed in bar and bedrooms ~ Wi-fi ~ Open mike last Sun evening of month ~ Bedrooms: £72/£85 *Recommended by Michael Doswell, Andrew Lawson, Patrick and Emma Stephenson, GSB, Sophia and Hamish Greenfield*

Please tell us if the décor, atmosphere, food or drink at a pub is different from our description. We rely on readers' reports to keep us up to date: feedback@goodguides.com, or (no stamp needed) The Good Pub Guide, FREEPOST RTXY–ZCBC–BBAZ, Stream Lane, Sedlescombe, Battle TN33 0PB.

GILSLAND NY6366 Map 10

Samson

(016977) 47880 – www.thesamson.co.uk

B6318, E end of village; CA8 7DR

Friendly village pub in wonderful countryside, with cheerful atmosphere in cosy bar, local ales and enjoyable food; bedrooms

This small pub is just 30 metres from the Hadrian's Wall Path and on Hadrian's Cycleway, so it gets pretty busy, especially at lunchtime. The cosy bar has a chatty feel, red patterned carpeting, swagged curtains, woodburning stoves, cushioned settles, traditional chairs and stools around sewing machine-treadle and other pubby tables, and plush stools at the carved wooden counter. Allendale Pennine Pale, Silverstone Pitstop Bitter and a guest from Muckles on handpump and several wines by the glass served by friendly staff; throughout the year they hold quiz nights, themed evenings and live music events. In the dining room are beige tartan-upholstered chairs around white-clothed tables on wide floorboards and prints on red or yellow walls. There are picnic-sets on the back lawn. Bedrooms are warm and attractive and make a good base for exploring the area. They also run Willowford Farm B&B just outside the village.

Well liked food using produce from their own farms includes lunchtime sandwiches, chicken liver, orange and smoked bacon pâté with chilli jam, creamy mushroom soufflé with buttery roasted chestnuts, curried leek risotto with leek pakora, shepherd's pie, chicken, ham and cheese pie, pork sausages on creamy mash with caramelised onion gravy, slow-cooked beef with roasted carrots, parsnips and gravy, cod fillet with crispy bacon, bubble and squeak pattie and butter sauce, and puddings such as pear, blackberry and hazelnut crumble with custard and sticky toffee pudding with toffee sauce and ice-cream. *Benchmark main dish: rare-breed beef burger with toppings and fries £9.50. Two-course evening meal £19.00.*

Free house ~ Licensees Liam McNulty and Lauren Harrison ~ Real ale ~ Open 12-10.30 ~ Bar food 12-2.30, 6-8.30 ~ Children welcome ~ Dogs allowed in bar ~ Wi-fi ~ Acoustic night second Sun of month ~ Bedrooms: £65/£85 *Recommended by Alan McQuilan, Carol and Barry Craddock, Caroline Prescott, Serena and Adam Furber, Geoff and Ann Marston*

HEDLEY ON THE HILL NZ0759 Map 10

Feathers

(01661) 843607 – www.thefeathers.net

Village signposted from New Ridley, which is signposted from B6309 N of Consett; OS Sheet 88 map reference 078592; NE43 7SW

Northumbria Dining Pub of the Year

Imaginative food, interesting beers from small breweries and friendly welcome in quaint tavern

Tiny but very well run and welcoming, this 200-year-old hilltop tavern is much enjoyed by our readers. It's run by hard-working, hands-on licensees who keep everything just right and the pub is the heart of the local community. The two neat, homely bars are properly pubby, with open fires, tankard-hung beams, stripped stonework, solid furniture including settles, and old black and white photographs of local places and farm and country workers. Allendale Wagtail Best Bitter, Mordue Workie Ticket and a guest beer on handpump, as well as a wide range of farm ciders, 30 wines by the glass, 30 malt whiskies, home-flavoured gins and home-produced cordials. They regularly hold wine and beer evenings, festivals and other events (see the website for details); dominoes and board games. The picnic-sets at the front are a nice place to sit and watch the world drift by. They've launched a cookery school led by the landlord.

Using only the best, carefully sourced local produce from artisan producers and farmers, the fine british food includes crispy duck egg with smoked celeriac purée and herb dressing, a plate of home-made charcuterie, spiced roast cauliflower steak with roasted tomato and pepper sauce and warm cracked wheat, mutton and beef shepherd's pie, their own sausages with mash and ale gravy, halibut with samphire, pink fir apple potatoes and white wine sauce, slow-cooked lamb with braised spelt, leeks, carrots and mint, and puddings such as almond and orange sponge with vanilla custard and rhubarb and almond tart with clotted cream. *Benchmark main dish: local roe deer wellington with wild mushrooms, dauphinoise potatoes and port and redcurrant jelly sauce £21.00. Two-course evening meal £20.00.*

Free house ~ Licensees Rhian Cradock and Helen Greer ~ Real ale ~ Open 12-11 (6-10.30 Mon, Weds); 12-10.30 Sun; closed Mon and Weds lunchtimes, all day Tues ~ Bar food 6-8.30 Weds; 12-2, 6-8.30 Thurs, Fri; 12-2.30, 6-8.30 Sat; 12-4.30 Sun ~ Children welcome ~ Wi-fi
Recommended by Lucy and Giles Gibbon, John and Abigail Prescott, Chris and Sophie Baxter, Martine and Colin Fresher

NEWTON NZ0364 Map 10

Duke of Wellington

(01661) 844446 – www.thedukeofwellingtoninn.co.uk
Off A69 E of Corbridge; NE43 7UL

Big stone pub with modern and traditional furnishings, well kept ales, good wines by the glass and highly thought-of food; bedrooms

The comfortable and well equipped bedrooms here (two are dog-friendly) are popular with those exploring the area; breakfasts are hearty. The bustling bar has leather chesterfields, built-in cushioned wall seats, farmhouse chairs and tables on honey-coloured flagstones, a woodburning stove with a shelf of books to one side, and rustic stools against the counter. Here they keep Greene King Abbot, Firebrick Pagan Queen and a guest ale on handpump, a dozen wines by the glass and 12 malt whiskies; TV, darts, dominoes and daily papers. The L-shaped restaurant has elegant tartan-upholstered and wood dining chairs around pale tables on bare boards, modern art on exposed stone walls, and french windows that lead out to the terrace. Paintwork throughout is contemporary. In fine weather, the seats on the back terrace have lovely views across the Tyne Valley.

As well as breakfasts (8-10am), the distinctive food includes twice-baked cheese soufflé with parmesan cream, smoked duck breast with pistachio, allium, granola and truffle powder, mushroom-filled ravioli with chilli pesto, artichoke, spinach and whipped goats cheese, beer-battered cod and chips, spiced lamb kofta with pitta bread, a pie of the day, pork loin with honey-roast pear, cider and sage fondant and sage jus, stone bass with greens, cauliflower purée, cannellini beans, prawns, cucumber and oyster, and puddings such as cherry and white chocolate cannelloni with sour cherry sorbet and milk chocolate mousse. *Benchmark main dish: steak burger with toppings, slaw and fries £11.95. Two-course evening meal £19.00.*

Free house ~ Licensee Rob Harris ~ Real ale ~ Open 11-11 ~ Bar food 12-9; 12-5 Sun ~ Restaurant ~ Children welcome ~ Dogs allowed in bar ~ Wi-fi ~ Bedrooms: £95/£120
Recommended by Andy and Louise Ramwell, Claire and Emma Braithwaite, Katherine and Hugh Markham, John Harris

We accept no free drinks or meals and inspections are anonymous.

NEWTON-BY-THE-SEA NU2424 Map 10

Ship

(01665) 576262 – www.shipinnnewton.co.uk

Low Newton-by-the-Sea, signed off B1339 N of Alnwick; NE66 3EL

In a charming square with good simple food and own-brew beers; best to check winter opening times

Tables outside this row of converted fishermen's cottages look across the sloping village green and down to the sea, and you can walk from here along the massive stretch of empty, beautiful beach with views all the way to Dunstanburgh Castle (English Heritage). The plainly furnished but cosy bare-boards bar on the right has nautical charts on dark pink walls, while another simple room on the left has beams, hop bines, some bright modern pictures on stripped-stone walls and a woodburning stove in a stone fireplace. They brew their own beers and usually have four on handpump at any one time from a choice of 26 – maybe Ship Inn Dolly Daydream, Indian Summer, Squid Ink and a guest beer such as Sandcastles at Dawn; also 14 malt whiskies and half a dozen wines by the glass. There's darts and dominoes. It can get extremely busy at peak times, so it's best to book in advance, and there might be a queue for the bar. There's no nearby parking from May to September, but there is a car park up the hill.

Good tasty food includes sandwiches, kipper pâté and toast, grilled halloumi cheese with peppers, tomatoes and basil, hand-picked local crab with salad, pasta with pesto, roasted cherry tomatoes and cheese, lamb cutlets with hot fennel salsa and crushed potatoes, hake fillet with chilli, soy and spring onion dressing, rib-eye steak with onion marmalade, and puddings such as orange and almond cake with lime mascarpone and apple and berry crumble. *Benchmark main dish: ploughman's £8.50. Two-course evening meal £20.00.*

Own brew ~ Licensee Christine Forsyth ~ Real ale ~ Open 11-11; 12-10 Sun; 11-5 Mon-Weds, 12-5 Sun in winter ~ Bar food 12-2.30, 7-8; not Sun-Tues evenings ~ Well behaved children welcome ~ Dogs welcome ~ Wi-fi ~ Live music (check website) *Recommended by James and Becky Plath, Serena and Richard Furber, Freddie and Sarah Banks, Martinthehills, Tracey and Stephen Groves*

NORTH SHIELDS NZ3668 Map 10

Staith House

(0191) 270 8441 – www.thestaithhouse.co.uk

Fish Quay/Union Road; NE30 1JA

Smashing food and real ales in refurbished dining pub with friendly staff and seats outside

Many customers are here to enjoy the creative food cooked by a former *MasterChef* finalist. But the enthusiastic staff also offer Caledonian Deuchars IPA, Robinsons Dizzy Blonde and Theakstons Lightfoot Bitter on handpump and ten wines by the glass. The attractive interior blends stripped wood, brickwork and stone with upholstered armchairs and dining chairs, captain's chairs and tartan wall seating, a medley of wooden tables and slate flooring and bare boards; to one end are some high bar chairs around equally high tables. Above the white woodburning stove are candles on a big mantelbeam and a large, rustic mirror, while the walls have ships' lamps and old photographs of the River Tyne. Picnic-sets and solid benches and tables sit on side terraces and the hanging baskets look pretty set against the blue-painted pub walls.

Cooked by the landlord, the inventive food includes local crab on toast with chervil and radish, mussels in garlic and cider, seared mackerel fillets with samphire and new potato and red onion salad, pork belly with sweetheart cabbage, mash, crackling and gravy, lamb rump with creamy polenta and basil and tomato fondue, smoked haddock with vegetable broth, aged sirloin steak with peppercorn sauce, onion rings and chips, and puddings such as caramel chocolate mousse with boozy cherries and honeycomb and frangipane with vanilla pannacotta and blueberries. *Benchmark main dish: grilled lemon sole with asparagus and anchovy butter £16.00. Two-course evening meal £21.50.*

Free house ~ Licensee John Calton ~ Real ale ~ Open 11-11; 12-11 Sun ~ Bar food 12-3, 6-9; 12-3.30, 6-9.30 Sat; 12-4.30 Sun ~ Children welcome until 7.30pm ~ Dogs allowed in bar ~ Wi-fi ~ Live music Sun 3pm *Recommended by John Stephenson, Alf and Sally Garner, Glen and Patricia Fuller, John and Claire Masters, Chloe and Tim Hodge, Neil Allen*

ROMALDKIRK NY9922 Map 10

Rose & Crown

(01833) 650213 – www.rose-and-crown.co.uk

Just off B6277; DL12 9EB

18th-c coaching inn with accomplished cooking, attentive service and a fine choice of drinks; bedrooms

If you stay in the comfortable bedrooms here (in the main building, the courtyard or Monk's Cottage), the owners provide an in-house guide for days out in the area, and a *Walking in Teesdale* book. The beamed bar area has lots of brass and copper, old-fashioned seats facing a warming log fire, a Jacobean oak settle, a grandfather clock and old farm tools and black and white pictures of Romaldkirk on the walls. Black Sheep and Marstons Wainwright with maybe a well kept seasonal guest such as Village Brewer White Boar on handpump, seven wines by the glass from a good list, 22 malt whiskies and several gins. The hall has wine maps and other interesting prints, a cosy little snug has sofas and armchairs by a woodburning stove and there's an oak-panelled restaurant; background music. Picnic-sets line the front terrace. This is a lovely Teesdale village and the handsome old inn faces the green where you can still see the original stocks and water pump. The village church is interesting and the exceptional Bowes Museum and High Force waterfall are nearby.

Imaginative food includes lunchtime sandwiches, pressed terrine of ham hock and mustard with burnt apple purée, textures of pork pie, parma ham and watercress, smoked eel fishcake with puy lentils, beetroot and gherkins, sharing platters, sweet potato, wild mushroom and spinach wellington with red wine sauce, beef bourguignon pie with rösti potato, loin of lamb with crispy belly, celeriac, mint pesto and lamb jus, salmon fillet with salmon and brown shrimp fishcake, sautéed potatoes and hollandaise, and puddings such as dark chocolate crémeux with kendal mint cake ice-cream and vanilla rice pudding with roasted pear purée and medlar jam. *Benchmark main dish: venison pie £14.00. Two-course evening meal £22.00.*

Free house ~ Licensee Cheryl Robinson ~ Real ale ~ Open 11-10 (11 Sat) ~ Bar food 12-2.30, 6-8.30; not Mon lunchtime ~ Restaurant ~ Children welcome but under-8s must leave by 8pm ~ Dogs allowed in bar and bedrooms ~ Wi-fi ~ Bedrooms: £130/£140 *Recommended by Gail and Frank Hackett, Camilla and Jose Ferrera, Muriel and Spencer Harrop, Ruby and Simon Swettenham, Ian Herdman, Caroline and Steve Archer*

A star after the name of a pub shows exceptional quality. It means most people (after reading the report to see just why the star has been won) would think a special trip worthwhile.

SEAHOUSES NU2232 Map 10

Olde Ship ★ £

(01665) 720200 – www.seahouses.co.uk

Just off B1340, towards harbour; NE68 7RD

Lots of atmosphere and maritime memorabilia in busy little inn, with views across harbour to Farne Islands; bedrooms

Our readers enjoy their regular visits here. The old-fashioned and unchanging bar has a cheerful, bustling atmosphere and a rich assemblage of nautical bits and pieces (even the floor is made of scrubbed ships' decking): lots of shiny brass fittings, ships' instruments and equipment, a knotted anchor made by local fishermen, sea pictures and model ships (including fine ones of the North Sunderland lifeboat and the Seahouses' *Grace Darling* lifeboat). There's also a model of the *Forfarshire*, the paddle steamer that local heroine Grace Darling went to rescue in 1838 (you can read more of the story in the pub), and even the ship's nameboard. An anemometer takes wind-speed readings from the top of the chimney. It's all gently lit by stained-glass sea-picture windows, lantern lights and a winter open fire. Simple furnishings include built-in leatherette pews around one end, stools and cast-iron tables. Black Sheep, Courage Directors, Greene King Old Speckled Hen and Ruddles County, Hadrian Border Farne Island Pale Ale and Theakstons Best Bitter on handpump (summer guests too), eight wines by the glass from a good wine list, 30 gins and 55 malt whiskies; background music and TV. The battlemented side terrace (you'll also find fishing memorabilia out here) and one window in the sun lounge look across the harbour to the Farne Islands (as do some bedrooms). If you find yourself here as dusk falls, the light of the Longstones lighthouse shining across the fading evening sky is a charming sight. The pub is not really suitable for children, though there is a little family room, and children are welcome on the terrace (as are walkers). You can book boat trips to the Farne Islands at the harbour, and there are bracing coastal walks, notably to Bamburgh, the birthplace of Grace Darling.

The sensibly short menu includes a wide choice of hot and cold sandwiches, duck and orange pâté, tempura prawns with marie rose sauce, vegetable lasagne, steak in ale pie, smoked fish chowder, barbecue spare ribs with chips, fresh crab salad, beef bourguignon, rib-eye steak with peppercorn sauce and onion rings, and puddings such as raspberry pavlova and apricot bread and butter pudding. *Benchmark main dish: beer-battered fish and chips £9.25. Two-course evening meal £18.00.*

Free house ~ Licensees Judith Glen and David Swan ~ Real ale ~ Open 11-11; 12-11 Sun ~ Bar food 12-2.30, 7-8.30 ~ Restaurant ~ Children allowed in lounge and dining room if eating, but must be over 10 in bedrooms ~ Wi-fi ~ Bedrooms: £50/£100 *Recommended by Pieter and Janet Vrancken, Martinthehills, Margaret and Peter Staples, Tracey and Stephen Groves, Monica and Steph Evans, Mark and Mary Setting*

STANNERSBURN NY7286 Map 10

Pheasant £

(01434) 240382 – www.thepheasantinn.com

Kielder Water road signposted off B6320 in Bellingham; NE48 1DD

Friendly village inn with quite a mix of customers, homely bar food and streamside garden; bedrooms

This is a nice family-run inn surrounded by lovely walks. The low-beamed lounge has ranks of old local photographs on stripped stone and panelling, brightly polished surfaces, shiny brasses, dark wooden pubby tables and chairs and upholstered stools ranged along the counter; there are several open fires. The separate public bar is simpler and opens into another snug seating area with beams and panelling. The friendly licensees and courteous staff serve Timothy Taylors Landlord and a couple of guests such as Mordue Northumbrian Blonde and Wylam 007 Vic Secret on handpump, several wines by the glass, 40 malt whiskies and a couple of farm ciders. There are picnic-sets in the streamside garden, plus a pony paddock. Staying overnight in the comfortable bedrooms gives you time to explore the beautiful surrounding countryside (Kielder Water is nearby), and they have a self-catering cottage as well.

Good, popular food includes sandwiches, twice-baked cheese soufflé, hot-smoked salmon with warm new potatoes, fennel and french bean salad and horseradish dressing, a vegetarian dish of the day, chicken breast filled with cream cheese and sun-dried tomatoes and wrapped in parma ham, moroccan-style cod with roasted vegetable couscous, local dressed crab salad, game and mushroom pie, sirloin steak with garlic butter or green peppercorn sauce, and puddings such as lime and lemon cheesecake and warm chocolate pudding. *Benchmark main dish: slow-roast shoulder of local lamb with rosemary and redcurrant £14.50. Two-course evening meal £21.00.*

Free house ~ Licensees Walter and Robin Kershaw ~ Real ale ~ Open 12-3 (2.30 Sun); closed Mon and Tues Nov-Feb ~ Bar food 12-2.30, 6-8.30 ~ Restaurant ~ Children welcome ~ Dogs allowed in bedrooms ~ Wi-fi ~ Bedrooms: £80/£110 *Recommended by Dr Peter Crawshaw, Simon and Alex Knight, Jill and Hugh Bennett, Elise and Charles Mackinlay, Alfie Bayliss*

WARK NY8676 Map 10

Battlesteads

(01434) 230209 – www.battlesteads.com

B6320 N of Hexham; NE48 3LS

Eco pub with good local ales, fair value interesting food and a relaxed atmosphere; comfortable bedrooms

The owners here are extremely conscientious about the environment and gently weave their beliefs into every aspect of the business; they grow their own produce, have a charging point in the car park for electric cars and use a biomass boiler. The nicely restored, low-beamed, carpeted bar has a woodburning stove with a traditional oak surround, comfortable seats including some deep leather sofas and easy chairs, and old *Punch* country life cartoons on the terracotta walls above a dark dado. As well as 13 wines by the glass, 20 malt whiskies, 35 gins and a farm cider, they keep four good changing local ales such as Durham Magus, Fyne Jarl and Hadrian Border Secret Kingdom and Tyneside Blonde on handpump at the heavily carved dark oak bar counter; service is excellent. Background music and TV. There's also a restaurant, a spacious conservatory and tables on the terrace, and they're licensed to hold civil marriages. Some of the bedrooms on the ground floor have disabled access.

They put their kitchen garden to good use for the well liked food: sandwiches, crispy sea bass with marinated vegetables and thai cashew dressing, fishcake with goats cheese and green chilli jam, deli boards, grilled halloumi with wild mushrooms, pink ginger and sautéed potatoes, moroccan-style hogget with couscous, harissa and coriander, beer-battered hake with pea purée and chips, local pheasant with prunes, black pudding and champ, braised beef cheek with mash, and puddings such as warm chocolate brownie with chocolate sauce and lemon posset with blackcurrant sorbet. *Benchmark main dish: cajun chicken with cream, prawns, bacon and sautéed potatoes £13.95. Two-course evening meal £20.50.*

Free house ~ Licensees Richard and Dee Slade ~ Real ale ~ Open 11-11 ~ Bar food 12-3, 6.30-9 ~ Restaurant ~ Children welcome ~ Dogs allowed in bar and bedrooms ~ Wi-fi ~ Bedrooms: £70/£120 *Recommended by R L Borthwick, Caroline and Steve Archer, Charlie Stevens, Martinthehills, Peter Smith and Judith Brown, Michael and Sarah Lockley, Rosie and Marcus Heatherley*

Also Worth a Visit in Northumbria

Besides the fully inspected pubs, you might like to try these pubs that have been recommended to us and described by readers. Do tell us what you think of them: feedback@goodguides.com

ACOMB NY9366

Miners Arms (01434) 603909
Main Street; NE46 4PW Friendly little 18th-c village pub with good value traditional food (not Sun evening, Mon) including weekday set menu and popular Sun roasts, Wylam, Yates and guests, comfortable settles in carpeted bar, huge fire in stone fireplace, back dining area; quiz last Thurs of month; children and dogs welcome, a couple of tables out in front, more in back courtyard, open all day weekends, closed weekday lunchtimes. *(Chris and Sophie Baxter)*

ALLENDALE NY8355

Golden Lion (01434) 683225
Market Place; NE47 9BD Friendly 18th-c two-room pub with enjoyable good value traditional food, well kept Timothy Taylors, Wylam and guests alongside beers from on-site microbrewery, games area with pool and darts, upstairs weekend restaurant; regular live music; children and dogs welcome, Allendale Fair first weekend of June, New Year's Eve flaming barrel procession, open all day (till late Fri, Sat). *(Peter Meister)*

ALNMOUTH NU2410

★**Red Lion** (01665) 830584
Northumberland Street; NE66 2RJ Friendly 18th-c coaching inn with peaceful sheltered garden and raised deck giving wide views over the Aln estuary; pleasant relaxed bar with heavy black beams, classic leather wall banquettes and window seats, old local photographs on dark mahogany brown panelling, cheerful fires, well kept ales such as Black Sheep, Roosters, Tempest and Wylam (Oct beer festival), half a dozen wines by the glass, popular fairly pubby food from sandwiches up, stripped-brick restaurant with flagstones and woodburner; background and monthly live music, Tues quiz, free wi-fi; children and dogs (in bar) welcome, comfortable well equipped bedrooms, open all day. *(Louise and Simon Peters)*

ALNWICK NU1813

John Bull (01665) 602055
Howick Street; NE66 1UY Popular chatty drinkers' pub – essentially the front room of an early 19th-c terraced house; good selection of well kept changing ales, real cider and lots of bottled belgian beers, also over 100 malt whiskies; fortnightly live music Mon, darts and dominoes; small beer garden, closed weekday lunchtimes. *(JimmyB)*

ALNWICK NU1913

Market Tavern (01665) 602759
Fenkle Street; NE66 1HW Refurbished split-level pub in central position; popular fairly priced food including good steaks, well kept ales such as Black Sheep and Marstons, Weston's cider and decent wines by the glass, friendly helpful service; background and occasional live music, TV, free wi-fi; children and dogs welcome, six bedrooms, open all day. *(Jim Trood)*

ALNWICK NU1813

Plough (01665) 602395
Bondgate Without; NE66 1PN Smart contemporary pub-boutique hotel in Victorian stone building (under same management as the Jolly Fisherman at Craster – see Main Entries); well kept Timothy Taylors Landlord and a guest, several wines by the glass and extensive range of gins, good food (not Sun evening) in bar, bistro or upstairs restaurant, friendly helpful staff; children and dogs welcome, pleasant streetside raised terrace, seven bedrooms, open all day. *(John Harris)*

ALNWICK NU1813

Tanners Arms (01665) 602553
Hotspur Place; NE66 1QF Welcoming little drinkers' pub with three well kept local ales and a decent glass of wine; flagstones and stripped stone, warm woodburner, plush stools and wall benches, small tree in the centre of the room; juke box and some live acoustic music, TV; dogs welcome, open all day weekends, closed weekday lunchtimes. *(John Harris)*

ANICK NY9565

★**Rat** (01434) 602814
Village signposted NE of A69/A695 Hexham junction; NE46 4LN Popular country pub with cosy traditional bar; coal fire in kitchen range, cottagey knick-knacks such as floral chamber-pots hanging from

beams, china and glassware on a delft shelf, six well kept ales such as Hexhamshire, Timothy Taylors and Wylam, farm cider, a dozen wines by the glass (including champagne) and a local gin, good well presented interesting food (not Sun evening), efficient service, conservatory; background music, free wi-fi; children welcome, charming garden with dovecote, statues and lovely North Tyne Valley views, limited parking (you can park around the village green), open all day. *(Comus and Sarah Elliott)*

AYCLIFFE NZ2822

★**County** (01325) 312273

The Green, Aycliffe; just off A1(M) junction 59, off A167 at West Terrace and then right to village green; DL5 6LX Smart inn with comfortable open-plan rooms, seating from cushioned dining chairs to tartan banquettes, stripy carpets, painted ceiling joists and log fires, highly regarded imaginative food in minimalist wood-floored restaurant, Marstons Lancaster Bomber, two guest ales, a craft beer and 11 wines by the glass, friendly service; free wi-fi; children welcome, no dogs inside, metal tables and chairs out at front facing green, seven attractive bedrooms, open all day, food all day Sun till 7pm. *(Alistair Forsyth)*

BAMBURGH NU1834

Castle (01668) 214616

Front Street; NE69 7BW Clean comfortably old-fashioned pub with generous helpings of reasonably priced food from good crab sandwiches to daily specials, friendly efficient service, well kept local ales such as Alnwick and decent house wines, cheery part-panelled bar and expanded dining area to cope with summer visitors, local artwork for sale, open fires (one in old range); free wi-fi; children welcome, no dogs inside, circular picnic-sets in nice beer garden, open (and food) all day. *(Margaret and Peter Staples, Revd Michael Vockins, Tracey and Stephen Groves)*

BAMBURGH NU1834

Lord Crewe Arms (01668) 214243

Front Street; NE69 7BL Small early 17th-c hotel prettily set in charming coastal village dominated by Norman castle; bar and restaurant (Wynding Inn) with painted joists and panelling, bare stone walls and light wood floor, warm woodburner, a couple of local ales such as Anarchy and a craft beer, good varied menu from lunchtime sandwiches up, friendly helpful staff; children and dogs (in one area) welcome, sheltered garden with castle view, short walk from splendid sandy beach, seven comfortable bedrooms, open all day. *(William and Ann Reid, Barry Collett)*

BARDON MILL NY7566

Twice Brewed (01434) 344534

Military Road (B6318 NE of Hexham); NE47 7AN Large busy inn well placed for fell-walkers and major Hadrian's Wall sites; up to half a dozen ales including some from own microbrewery, craft beers and good value home-cooked food (shortish menu), winter steak nights Tues and Thurs, cheerful helpful service, freshened-up interior with warm woodburners, artwork for sale; children and dogs welcome, disabled access, picnic-sets in back garden, 18 bedrooms, open (and food) all day. *(John and Sylvia Harrop, Peter Meister)*

BEADNELL NU2229

Beadnell Towers (01665) 721211

The Wynding, off B1340; NE67 5AY This popular pub-hotel was closed for refurbishment as we went to press, but should have reopened by the time you read this – reports please.

BEAMISH NZ2154

Beamish Hall (01207) 233733

NE of Stanley, off A6076; DH9 0YB Converted stone-built stables in courtyard at back of hotel; popular and family-friendly (can get crowded), with five or six beers from own microbrewery (tours available), decent wines and enjoyable food from light lunches up, uniformed staff; regular events such as live music, barbecues and a summer festival; plenty of seats outside, big play area, open (and food) all day. *(Peter Smith and Judith Brown)*

BEAMISH NZ2055

Black Horse (01207) 232569

Red Row (off Beamishburn Road NW, near A6076); OS Sheet 88, map reference 205541; DH9 0RW Late 17th-c country dining pub with contemporary/rustic interior; heritage colours blending with beams, flagstones and some exposed stonework, enjoyable fairly traditional food (not Sun evening) from hot or cold sandwiches up, half a dozen well kept changing beers and decent wines by the glass, friendly attentive staff, cosy fire-warmed front room extending to light spacious dining area with central bar, another dining room upstairs, airy conservatory; children welcome, dogs in bar, restful views from big paved terrace, more tables on grass, open all day. *(Peter Smith and Judith Brown)*

BERWICK-UPON-TWEED NT9952

Barrels (01289) 308013

Bridge Street; TD15 1ES Small friendly pub with interesting collection of pop memorabilia and other bric-a-brac, some

We checked prices with the pubs as we went to press in summer 2018.
They should hold until around spring 2019.

eccentric furniture too including a barber's chair in bare-boards front bar, well kept Anarchy Blonde Star, four guests and range of foreign bottled beers, snacky food, red banquettes in back room; regular live acoustic sessions (often in basement bar) and good quality background music; children and dogs welcome, open all day. *(John and Lorna Chew)*

CATTON NY8257

★**Crown** (01434) 618351

B6295, off A686 S of Haydon Bridge; NE47 9QS Welcoming 18th-c village pub in good walking country; inner bar with stripped-stone and bare boards, dark tables, mate's chairs and a traditional settle, good log fire, well kept Allendale beers and enjoyable home-cooked blackboard food, efficient staff, extension with folding glass doors opening on to small garden, lovely Allen Valley views; folk night Thurs, quiz every other Tues, bar billiards; children and dogs welcome, open (and food) all day weekends, closed till 5pm weekdays. *(Sophia and Hamish Greenfield)*

CHATTON NU0528

Percy Arms (01668) 215244

B6348 E of Wooler; NE66 5PS Sympathetically refurbished stone-built country inn (same owners as the Northumberland Arms at Felton); good well presented food from standard dishes up in flagstoned log-fire bar or light panelled dining room (booking advised), six well kept ales including a house beer from local Hetton Law, good whisky and gin choice, friendly helpful staff, open fire and woodburner; May beer festival, darts; children and dogs (in bar) welcome, picnic-sets on small front lawn, five well appointed bedrooms, good breakfast, quiet village with sweeping views of the Cheviot Hills, open (and food) all day. *(John and Sylvia Harrop, Tracey and Stephen Groves)*

CONSETT NZ1150

Travellers Rest (01207) 507555

Forster Street; DH8 7JU Renovated brick-built pub on two floors; bare-boards bar with farmhouse furniture, woodburner in big fireplace, good pubby food including blackboard specials and Weds burger deal, three changing ales, friendly attentive staff, upstairs galleried dining area; jukebox and TV, free wi-fi; children welcome, paved beer garden behind, open all day. *(Mathew Cartmell)*

CORBRIDGE NY9964

★**Angel** (01434) 632119

Main Street; NE45 5LA Imposing coaching inn at end of broad street in this attractive old town; best sense of building's age in separate lounge with oak panelling and a big stone fireplace, also look out for the fine 17th-c arched doorway in left-hand porch; airy modern bar serving six local ales including a Wylam house beer, Weston's cider; a dozen wines by the glass and 30 malt whiskies, good food from varied menu, raftered back restaurant; background music, daily newspapers; children welcome, heated tables out at front under parasols; comfortable bedrooms and hearty breakfasts, open (and food) all day. *(Comus and Sarah Elliott, Robert Wivell, Moira and Jon Weller, Andrea and Philip Crispin, Stuart Doughty)*

CORBRIDGE NY9864

★**Black Bull** (01434) 632261

Middle Street; NE45 5AT Rambling 18th-c beamed pub with four linked rooms, mix of traditional pub furniture including leather banquettes, wood, flagstone or carpeted floors, log fires (one in open hearth with gleaming copper canopy), ceramic collection in front room and information about Hadrian's Wall, enjoyable reasonably priced pubby food, three Greene King ales, a guest beer and good choice of wines by the glass, efficient cheery service; children welcome, no dogs, seats out on two-level terrace, open all day. *(Comus and Sarah Elliott)*

CORBRIDGE NY9868

★**Errington Arms** (01434) 672250

About 3 miles N of town; B6318, on A68 roundabout; NE45 5QB Busy 18th-c stone-built pub by Hadrian's Wall attracting good mix of diners and walkers; beamed bars with pine panelling, stone and burgundy walls, farmhouse and other chairs around pine tables on strip-wood flooring, log fire and woodburner, good choice of popular fresh food from interesting sandwiches up, several wines by the glass and well kept ales such as Jennings and Wylam, friendly helpful staff; background music; children welcome, a few picnic-sets out in front, closed Sun evening, Mon, Tues. *(Martin Day, Peter Smith and Judith Brown)*

CORNHILL-ON-TWEED NT8539

Collingwood Arms (01890) 882424

Main Street; TD12 4UH Restored and comfortably updated Georgian stone hotel; nice little bar with decent wines, around 25 malt whiskies and a well kept local ale such as Alnwick, good reasonably priced food in adjoining dining room or more pricey restaurant, friendly helpful staff, open fires; free wi-fi; children and dogs (in bar) welcome, tables out in lovely grounds, local fishing and shooting, 15 well appointed bedrooms (named after ships from the Battle of Trafalgar), good breakfast, open all day. *(Richard and Diana Ibbot)*

CROOKHAM NT9138

Blue Bell (01890) 820252

Pallinsburn; A697 Wooler–Cornhill; TD12 4SH Welcoming 18th-c roadside country pub; enjoyable freshly prepared food, well kept ales such as Fyne and Greene King and good selection of gins, friendly attentive service; dogs welcome in bar, comfortable clean bedrooms, good breakfast, open (and food) all day weekends. *(Robert and Diana Myers)*

DARLINGTON NZ2814

Number Twenty 2 (01325) 354590
Coniscliffe Road; DL3 7RG Popular long Victorian pub with high ceiling, wood and carpeted floors, exposed brickwork and striking red and gold wallpaper, up to 13 quickly changing ales (tasters offered) including own Village Brewer range, draught continentals and decent wine selection, snacky food till 7pm in back part, good friendly service; closed Sun, otherwise open all day. *(John Harris)*

DINNINGTON NZ2073

White Swan (01661) 872869
Prestwick Road; NE13 7AG Large open-plan pub-restaurant popular for its wide range of good value food including gluten-free menu, reasonably priced wines and a well kept changing ale, efficient friendly service even at busy times; background music; family area (children's menu till 5.30pm), no dogs inside, disabled facilities, orangery and attractive garden with pond, handy for Newcastle Airport, open all day Sun till 6pm. *(Gerry and Rosemary Dobson)*

DUNSTAN NU2419

Cottage (01665) 576658
Off B1339 Alnmouth–Embleton; NE66 3SZ Comfortable single-storey beamed inn; enjoyable reasonably priced food (smaller helpings available) from fairly standard menu, three well kept ales, restaurant and conservatory; live music, quiz nights, free wi-fi; children and dogs welcome, attractive garden with terrace and play area, ten bedrooms, open all day. *(Monica and Steph Evans)*

DURHAM NZ2742

Dun Cow (0191) 386 9219
Old Elvet; DH1 3HN Unchanging backstreet pub in pretty 16th-c black and white timbered cottage; tiny chatty front bar with wall benches, corridor to long narrow back lounge, well kept ales such as Black Sheep and Camerons, good value simple food, friendly staff; background and occasional live music, Mon quiz, free wi-fi; children and dogs welcome, open all day. *(Alfie Bayliss)*

DURHAM NZ2742

Head of Steam (0191) 383 2173
Reform Place, North Road; DH1 4RZ Hidden-away pub close to the river; modern open-plan interior on two floors, good range of well kept changing ales, real ciders and plenty of bottled continental beers, competitively priced food till early evening (4pm Sun) including burgers and pizzas; background music (live upstairs); dogs welcome, outside tables, open all day. *(Peter Smith and Judith Brown)*

DURHAM NZ2642

Old Elm Tree (0191) 386 4621
Crossgate; DH1 4PS Comfortable friendly old pub on steep hill across from the castle; two-room main bar and small lounge up steps, half a dozen well kept interesting beers including Wychwood Hobgoblin (occasional beer festivals), reasonably priced home-made food, open fires, folk and quiz nights; dogs welcome, small back terrace, open all day. *(Alfie Bayliss)*

DURHAM NZ2742

Shakespeare (0191) 340 9438
Saddler Street; DH1 3NU Friendly 19th-c brick pub (bigger inside than it looks); fairly compact front bar incorporating former snug, larger back lounge, well kept Caledonian Deuchars IPA, Fullers London Pride and two guests, pubby lunchtime food; Weds folk night; children (till 5pm) and dogs welcome, convenient for castle, cathedral and river, can get crowded (particularly weekends), open all day. *(Paul Humphreys, Alfie Bayliss)*

DURHAM NZ2742

Swan & Three Cygnets
(0191) 384 0242 *Elvet Bridge; DH1 3AG* Victorian pub in good bridge-end spot high above the river, city views from big windows and terrace; bargain lunchtime food and Sam Smiths ales, helpful friendly young staff, popular with locals and students; open all day. *(Mark Hamill)*

EACHWICK NZ1069

Plough (01661) 853555
Stamfordham Road (extension of B6324), S of village; NE18 0BG Large refurbished stone inn tucked away in remote countryside; open-plan split-level lounge with comfortable furniture including sofas, tub and wing chairs on wood or carpeted floors, good choice of enjoyable food from snacks to specials, also evening chinese menu, well kept Caledonian Deuchars IPA, a couple of guests and fairly priced wines, efficient courteous service, separate restaurant; outside seating, three bedrooms, open all day Fri and Sat, closed Mon. *(Michael Doswell)*

EARSDON NZ3273

★**Beehive** (0191) 252 9352
Hartley Lane; NE25 0SZ Popular well run 18th-c country pub with cosy linked rooms; low painted beams, soft lighting, woodburners and one or two quirky touches, three well kept hatch-served ales (tasting trays available), good fairly priced home-made food (best to book weekends) from sandwiches, light dishes and sharing boards up, friendly service; background and some live music, TVs; children welcome, dogs in one area, picnic-sets out overlooking fields,

summer bar and separate family garden with play area, open (and food) all day, kitchen shuts 6pm Sun. *(Martinthehills)*

EDMUNDBYERS NZ0150

Punch Bowl (01207) 255545
B6278; DH8 9NL Small village's community local; well kept ales and good choice of reasonably priced food including daily specials, friendly service; TV, free wi-fi; children and dogs (in bar) welcome, fishing on nearby Derwent Reservoir (permits from the pub), six updated bedrooms, good breakfast, open (and food) all day. *(Katherine Matthews)*

EGLINGHAM NU1019

★**Tankerville Arms** (01665) 578444
B6346 Alnwick–Wooler; NE66 2TX Traditional 19th-c stone pub with contemporary touches and cosy friendly atmosphere; beams, bare boards and some stripped stone, banquettes and warm fires, well kept Hadrian Border and a guest, good wines, enjoyable nicely presented food from shortish menu, raftered split-level restaurant; free wi-fi; children, walkers and dogs welcome, lovely country views from back garden, attractive village, three bedrooms, closed lunchtimes Mon, Tues, otherwise open (and food) all day. *(Buster and Helena Hastings)*

EMBLETON NU2322

Dunstanburgh Castle Hotel
(01665) 576111 *B1339; NE66 3UN* Comfortable hotel in attractive spot near magnificent coastline; good choice of enjoyable bar and restaurant food using local meat and fish, good vegetarian options too, efficient friendly service, local ales and decent wines, two lounges for coffee with open fires; children welcome, seats in nice garden, good for Embleton Bay and Dunstanburgh Castle (EH), bedrooms and self-catering cottages, open all day. *(Caroline and Steve Archer)*

EMBLETON NU2322

Greys (01665) 576983
Stanley Terrace off WT Stead Road, turn at the Blue Bell; NE66 3UY Welcoming pub with carpeted bar and cottagey back dining room; well priced home-made food (wider evening choice) including good crab sandwiches and local fish, interesting range of well kept regional beers such as Hadrian Border and Wylam; juke box, sports TV; children and dogs welcome, small walled back garden with village views from raised deck, open all day. *(Mark and Mary Setting)*

ESH NZ1944

Cross Keys (0191) 373 1279
Front Street; DH7 9QR Friendly 18th-c village local; hearty helpings of good well priced food (not Sun evening) including blackboard specials, half a dozen ales such as Big Lamp and Black Sheep, afternoon teas; children welcome, colourful hanging baskets out at front, good country views from behind, closed Mon, otherwise open all day, but may close if quiet. *(Lynn Davies)*

FELTON NU1800

Northumberland Arms (01670) 787370 *West Thirston; B6345, off A1 N of Morpeth; NE65 9EE* Stylish 19th-c inn across road from River Coquet; roomy open-plan lounge bar with beams, exposed stone/brickwork and nice mix of furnishings including big sofas on flagstones, woodburner, bare-boards restaurant with mix of light wood tables, good sensibly priced food from bar snacks and standard dishes up (best to book), bread from their own bakery, three or four well kept mainly local beers and nice wines by the glass (short well chosen list); children welcome, dogs in bar, six good bedrooms, open (and food) all day. *(Monica and Steph Evans)*

FROSTERLEY NZ0236

★**Black Bull** (01388) 527784
Just off A689 W of centre; DL13 2SL Unique in having its own peal of bells (licensee is a campanologist); great atmosphere in three interesting traditional beamed and flagstoned rooms with coal fires (one in old range), landlord's own good photographs and three grandfather clocks, four well kept local ales, traditional cider/perry and carefully chosen wines, good range of malt whiskies too, highly rated food using local and organic ingredients (best to book evenings and Sun lunch), friendly helpful staff; some acoustic live music; well behaved children and dogs welcome, attractive no-smoking terrace with wood-fired bread oven and old railway furnishings (opposite steam line station), closed Sun evening to Weds, otherwise open all day. *(John Saville)*

GATESHEAD NZ2563

Central (0191) 478 2543
Half Moon Lane; NE8 2AN Unusual 19th-c wedge-shaped pub (Grade II listed) restored by the Head of Steam group; well preserved features including notable buffet bar, great choice of changing local ales, real ciders and lots of bottled beers, low-priced food such as burgers from short menu, upstairs function rooms and roof terrace; some live music; dogs welcome, open all day (till 12am Fri, Sat). *(Patti and James Davidson)*

GREAT WHITTINGTON NZ0070

Queens Head (01434) 672516
Village signed off A68 and B6018 N of Corbridge; NE19 2HP Handsome golden-stone village pub; dark leather chairs around sturdy tables, some stripped-stone walls and soft lighting, nice hunting mural above old fireplace in long narrow bar, ales such as Firebrick and High House Farm, friendly helpful service, popular chinese restaurant

at back; background music, quiz nights, pool; children and dogs (in bar) welcome, picnic-sets under parasols on little front lawn, closed lunchtimes (all day Mon Oct-Apr). *(Martinthehills)*

GRETA BRIDGE NZ0813

★**Morritt** (01833) 627232
Hotel signposted off A66 W of Scotch Corner; DL12 9SE Striking 17th-c country house hotel popular for weddings and the like; pubby bar with big windsor armchairs and sturdy oak settles around traditional cast-iron-framed tables, open fires and remarkable 1946 mural of Dickensian characters by JTY Gilroy (known for Guinness advertisements), big windows looking on to extensive lawn, Thwaites Major Morritt (named for them) and Timothy Taylors Landlord, 19 wines by the glass from extensive list, bar and restauarant food, afternoon teas, friendly staff; background music; children and dogs (in bar and bedrooms) welcome, attractively laid-out split-level garden with teak tables and play area, open all day. *(WAH, Barry Collett)*

HALTWHISTLE NY7166

Milecastle Inn (01434) 321372
Military Road; B6318 NE – OS Sheet 86 map reference 715660; NE49 9NN Sturdy stone-built pub on remote moorland road running alongside Hadrian's Wall; small rooms off beamed bar, brasses, horsey and local landscape prints, two log fires, well kept ales such as Big Lamp and a few wines by the glass, popular traditional food (best to book weekends), small comfortable restaurant; children welcome, no dogs inside, tables and benches in big sheltered garden with dovecote and stunning views, self-catering cottage next door. *(Peter Hacker, Peter Lowe, Peter Meister)*

HART NZ4634

White Hart (01429) 265468
Just off A179 W of Hartlepool; Front Street; TS27 3AW End of terrace pub with ship's figurehead outside, fires in both bars (one in old range), enjoyable fairly traditional food (not Sun evening), two changing ales; children welcome, no dogs inside, open all day. *(Geoff and Anne Marston)*

HAYDON BRIDGE NY8364

★**General Havelock** (01434) 684376
Off A69 Corbridge–Haltwhistle; B6319 (Ratcliffe Road); NE47 6ER Old darkly painted pub, a short stroll upstream from Haydon Bridge itself; L-shaped bar with open fire and some Philip Larkin memorabilia, well kept Great North Eastern Rivet Catcher and a guest, decent choice of wines by the glass and highly rated generously served food (not Sun evening, Mon) cooked by owner-chef, elegant stripped-stone barn dining room and terrace with fine South Tyne river views; children and dogs (in bar) welcome, closed Mon lunchtime. *(Michael Doswell)*

HEXHAM NY9464

Heart of Northumberland (01434) 608013 *Market Street; NE46 3NS* Renovated old local with Timothy Taylors Landlord and four guests kept well, also craft beers, proper ciders and plenty of wines by the glass, well cooked reasonably priced food from pub favourites up, good cheerful service, traditional furniture on bare boards, some blue-painted panelling and exposed stonework, woodburner in big fireplace; live music Tues; children and dogs welcome, small outside seating area behind, open (and food) all day including brunch from 11am. *(Comus and Sarah Elliott, GSB)*

HIGH HESLEDEN NZ4538

Ship (01429) 836453
Off A19 via B1281; TS27 4QD Popular Victorian inn with seven well kept changing ales and good food cooked by landlady (some interesting specials), sailing ship models including big one hanging with lanterns from boarded ceiling, log fire; sea views over farmland from garden, six bedrooms in modern block, open all day Sun till 8pm, closed Mon and lunchtimes Tues-Fri. *(John Harris)*

HOLWICK NY9126

Strathmore Arms (01833) 640362
Back road up Teesdale from Middleton; DL12 0NJ Attractive and welcoming old stone-built country pub in beautiful scenery just off Pennine Way; four well kept ales including a house beer (Strathmore Gold) brewed by Mithril and several real ciders, good low-priced traditional food, beams, flagstones and open fire; live music Fri, quiz first Weds of month, pool, free wi-fi; well behaved dogs welcome, popular with walkers, four bedrooms, closed Tues, otherwise open all day. *(Caroline and Steve Archer)*

HOLY ISLAND NU1241

Crown & Anchor (01289) 389215
Causeway passable only at low tide, check times (01289) 330733; TD15 2RX New owners for this comfortably unpretentious pub-restaurant by the priory; three well kept Hadrian Border ales including gluten-free Grainger, enjoyable food cooked by landlord-chef from pub favourites up (maybe local crab), cosy bar with open fire, more roomy modern back dining room; children and dogs (in bar) welcome, disabled access/loo, garden with lovely views, four bedrooms, open all day, food till 6pm Sun. *(Simon Richardson)*

HOLY ISLAND NU1241

Ship (01289) 389311
Marygate; TD15 2SJ Well positioned and busy in season; beamed bar with wood floors, stone walls and maritime memorabilia, big

stove, steps down to carpeted lounge/dining area, popular pubby menu including fish/seafood (good crab sandwiches), Holy Island Blessed Bitter badged for them by Hadrian Border plus one or two guests, also 30 malt whiskies and their own gin; background music; children welcome and usually dogs (but do ask first), sheltered sunny garden, four bedrooms, may close at quiet times. *(Tracey and Stephen Groves, Roger and Donna Huggins)*

HURWORTH-ON-TEES NZ2814

★**Bay Horse** (01325) 720663
Church Row; DL2 2AQ Popular dining pub (best to book, particularly weekends) with very good imaginative food, quite pricey but they do offer a fixed-price alternative (lunchtimes Mon-Sat, evenings Mon-Thurs), also vegetarian menu and children's meals, three well kept changing ales, extensive wine list, efficient friendly young staff, sizeable bar with good open fire, restaurant, and another dining room upstairs; seats on back terrace and in well tended walled garden, charming village by River Tees, open all day. *(Richard Cole)*

HURWORTH-ON-TEES NZ3110

Otter & Fish (01325) 720019
Off A167 S of Darlington; Strait Lane; DL2 2AH Pleasant village setting across road from the Tees; up-to-date open-plan layout with flagstones and stripped wood, open fires and church candles, nice mix of dining furniture, comfortable armchairs and sofas by bar, popular well presented local food including set deals and decent vegetarian and children's choices (best to book especially weekends), friendly helpful staff, ales such as Black Sheep and several wines by the glass; closed Sun evening. *(Louise and Simon Peters)*

KNARSDALE NY6754

Kirkstyle (01434) 381559
Signed off A689; CA8 7PB Welcoming 18th-c country pub in lovely spot looking over South Tyne Valley to hills beyond; enjoyable reasonably priced food including range of sausages and some interesting specials, well kept Yates and a summer guest, dining room; games area with darts and pool; children and dogs welcome, handy for Pennine Way, South Tyne Trail and South Tynedale Railway (Lintley terminus), closed Sun evening, Tues and may shut around 9pm if quiet, no food Mon. *(Richard and Tessa Ibbot)*

LANGDON BECK NY8531

Langdon Beck Hotel
(01833) 622267 *B6277 Middleton–Alston; DL12 0XP* Isolated unpretentious inn with two cosy bars and spacious lounge; good choice of enjoyable generous food using local Teesdale beef and lamb, Black Sheep and Ringwood, friendly helpful staff, interesting rock collection in 'geology room'; events such as Easter 'egg jarping', late May beer festival; children and dogs welcome, wonderful fell views from garden, well placed for walks including Pennine Way; seven bedrooms (some sharing bathrooms), open all day, closed Mon in winter. *(Alfie Bayliss)*

LANGLEY ON TYNE NY8160

Carts Bog Inn (01434) 684338
A686 S, junction B6305; NE47 5NW Isolated 18th-c moorside pub with heavy beams and stripped-stone walls, old photographs, spindleback chairs around mix of tables on red carpet, nice open fire, enjoyable generously served food from sandwiches up including signature Bog Pie (steak and mushroom suet pudding) and popular Sun lunch (best to book), two or three well kept local ales, friendly efficient young staff, games room with pool and darts; children and dogs welcome, picnic-sets in big garden with views, quoits, open all day weekends, closed Mon, Tues. *(Martinthehills)*

LESBURY NU2311

★**Coach** (01665) 830865
B1339; NE66 3PP Picturesque stone pub at heart of pretty village; low-beamed rooms with pubby furniture on tartan carpet, dark leather stools by counter serving well kept Timothy Taylors Landlord and a guest, snug off to left with sofas and armchairs, small dining room and restaurant both with woodburners, popular good value home-made food including daily specials, friendly staff; background music; children and dogs (not in restaurant) welcome, picnic-sets on front terrace and in back garden, lovely flowering tubs and baskets, handy for Alnwick Castle, open (and food) all day in summer, closed afternoons in winter and no food Sun evening. *(Dr Nick Wright)*

LONG NEWTON NZ3716

Vane (01642) 580401
Darlington Road; TS21 1DB Revamped 19th-c pub popular for landlord-chef's good food from pub favourites to imaginative restaurant dishes, lunchtime/early evening set menu, Black Sheep and a couple of guests, warm friendly service, pale green walls contrasting solid dark dining tables and chairs, upholstered banquettes, cosy bar with log fire; background music, Sun quiz; children and dogs (in bar) welcome, picnic-sets in garden with far-reaching views across fields, three bedrooms, open all day Sun, closed Mon and lunchtime Tues, no food Sun evening. *(Michael Doswell)*

LONGFRAMLINGTON NU1301

Granby (01665) 570228
Front Street; NE65 8DP Welcoming old coaching inn run by same family for three generations; highly regarded food cooked by chef-landlord from well executed pub favourites to creative restaurant dishes, also

good value set lunch and afternoon teas, a real ale such as Sharps Doom Bar kept well and several malt whiskies, comfortable traditional beamed interior with bar, lounge and small restaurant; children welcome, no dogs, five bedrooms, open (and food) all day. *(Michael Doswell)*

LONGFRAMLINGTON NU1301

Village Inn (01665) 570268
Just off A697; Front Street; NE65 8AD Friendly 18th-c stone inn arranged into three distinct areas; tasty freshly prepared pub food including good Sun carvery, own-brewed VIP beers along with local guests; comfortable bedrooms and self-catering cabins (just outside village), open all day. *(Francis and Many Robertson)*

LONGHORSLEY NZ1494

Shoulder of Mutton (01670) 788236
East Road; A697 N of Morpeth; NE65 8SY Comfortable bar and restaurant with welcoming staff, good choice of enjoyable reasonably priced food from lunchtime baguettes up, weekday deals and popular Sun carvery till 6pm (must book), Courage Directors, Caledonian Deuchars IPA and a guest, good selection of other drinks; background music, TV, fruit machine; children and dogs (in bar) welcome, picnic-sets in back garden, two bedrooms, open all day, food all day Thurs-Sun. *(Buster and Helena Hastings)*

MAIDEN LAW NZ1749

Three Horseshoes (01207) 520900
A6067 N of Lanchester; DH7 0QT Spacious whitewashed roadside dining pub, family-run, with enjoyable good value food from varied menu including several vegetarian options, also bargain weekday two-course lunch deal and afternoon teas, neatly kept open-plan interior with central beamed and quarry-tiled bar, mix of high-backed cane chairs, leatherette sofas and tub chairs, two-way woodburner, conservatory; children welcome, disabled parking and wheelchair access, garden with play area, open all day Sat, till 5pm Sun, closed Mon. *(Michael Doswell)*

MICKLETON NY9724

★**Crown** (01833) 640381
B6277; DL12 0JZ Bustling pub under friendly hands-on licensees; simply furnished bars and dining areas, cushioned settles, upholstered leather and wooden dining chairs around all sorts of tables on polished boards, country prints and photographs, woodburner flanked by two leather armchairs, Jennings, Banks's and local guests, several wines by the glass and good quality food; children and dogs welcome, rustic picnic-sets in garden with fine country views, two self-catering properties and campsite, open (and food) all day, till 9pm (6pm) Sun. *(Alison and Dan Richardson, GSB)*

MIDDLETON NZ0685

Ox (01670) 772634
Village signed off B6343, W of Hartburn; NE61 4QZ Welcoming unpretentious Georgian country pub in small tucked-away village; a couple of local ales and tasty straightforward home-made food including good Sun lunch; children and dogs welcome, seats outside, handy for Wallington (NT), open all day weekends, closed weekday lunchtimes, no food Sun evening. *(Caroline and Steve Archer)*

MILFIELD NT9333

Red Lion (01668) 216224
Main Road (A697 Wooler–Cornhill); NE71 6JD Comfortable 18th-c coaching inn with good fairly priced food from chef-owner including Sun carvery, smaller appetites catered for, well kept ales such as Black Sheep and Thwaites, a dozen wines by the glass and decent coffee, friendly efficient service; Weds quiz; children welcome, pretty garden by car park at back, six bedrooms, good breakfast, open all day. *(Alfie Bayliss)*

MORPETH NZ1986

Tap & Spile (01670) 513894
Manchester Street; NE61 1BH Cosy two-room pub with up to eight well kept ales including Everards, Greene King and Timothy Taylors, Weston's cider, fruit wines and short choice of good value lunchtime food, friendly staff, traditional pub furniture and interesting old photographs, quieter back lounge (children allowed here) with coal-effect gas fire, board and other games; background and live acoustic music Sun afternoon, sports TV; dogs welcome in front bar, open all day Fri-Sun. *(Edward May)*

NETHERTON NT9807

Star (01669) 630238
Off B6341 at Thropton, or A697 via Whittingham; NE65 7HD Simple unchanging village local run by charming long-serving landlady (licence has been in her family since 1917); large high-ceilinged room with wall benches and many original features, friendly regulars, range of bottled beers, no food, music, children or dogs; quiz first Weds of the month; open evenings only from 7.30pm, closed Mon, Thurs and possibly other days (best to ring ahead). *(Katherine Matthews)*

NEW YORK NZ3269

Shiremoor Farm (0191) 257 6302
Middle Engine Lane; at W end of New York A191 bypass turn S into Norham Road, then first right (pub signed); NE29 8DZ Busy Sir John Fitzgerald dining pub cleverly converted from former derelict farm building, spacious well divided interior with beams and joists (the conical rafters of a former gin-gan in one part), broad flag-stones, several kilims and mix of unusual

furniture, farm tools, shields, swords and country pictures, popular fair-priced food, quieter bar with well kept mainly local ales and several wines by the glass, hard-working uniformed staff; children welcome, seats outside on covered heated terrace, open all day. *(GSB)*

NEWBROUGH NY8768

Red Lion (01283) 576182
Stanegate Road; NE47 5AR Former coaching inn with light airy feel; log fire, flagstones and half-panelling, old local photographs and some large paintings, good sensibly priced food in bar and two dining areas from well filled baguettes up (more elaborate evening menu), a couple of well kept local ales, friendly efficient service, games room with pool and darts, little shop selling local art/craftwork; children and dogs (not at food times) welcome, garden behind with decking, good walks and on NCN cycle route 72, six bedrooms, open all day. *(Chris and Sophie Baxter)*

NEWCASTLE UPON TYNE NZ2464

★**Bacchus** (0191) 261 1008
High Bridge E, between Pilgrim Street and Grey Street; NE1 6BX Smart, spacious and comfortable Fitzgerald pub with ocean liner look; two-level interior with lots of varnished wood, pillars, ship and shipbuilding photographs, nine very well kept changing ales (beer festivals), plenty of bottled imports, farm cider and splendid range of whiskies, decent coffee too, friendly helpful staff, no food; background music; disabled facilities, handy for Theatre Royal, open all day and can get very busy. *(Peter Smith and Judith Brown)*

NEWCASTLE UPON TYNE NZ2464

Bodega (0191) 221 1552
Westgate Road; NE1 4AG Majestic Edwardian drinking hall next to Tyne Theatre; eight real ales and good range of bottled beers, friendly service, snug front cubicles, spacious back area with two magnificent stained-glass cupolas; background music, Thurs quiz, big-screen TVs (very busy on match days), darts, free wi-fi; open all day. *(John Harris)*

NEWCASTLE UPON TYNE NZ2563

★**Bridge Hotel** (0191) 232 6400
Castle Square, next to high-level bridge; NE1 1RQ Spacious 19th-c Sir John Fitzgerald pub with well divided bar; high-ceiling, stained-glass windows, replica slatted snob screens and magnificent fireplace, well kept Anarchy Blonde Star, Sharps Doom Bar and eight quickly changing guests, real cider, friendly helpful staff, bargain lunchtime food, great river and bridge views from raised back area, live music upstairs including long-standing Mon folk club; background music, sports TV, games machines; flagstoned terrace overlooking part of old town wall, open all day. *(Roger and Donna Huggins)*

NEWCASTLE UPON TYNE NZ2563

Bridge Tavern (0191) 261 9966
Under the Tyne Bridge; NE1 3UF Bustling place under same ownership as the Town Wall; airy interior with brick walls and lots of wood, industrial-style ceiling, view into back microbrewery (joint venture with Wylam), a dozen or so beers including local guests (tasting trays available), generous helpings of well liked often unusual food (all day, till 7pm Fri-Sun) from snacks and sharing boards up, friendly helpful staff; background music; well behaved children and dogs allowed before 7pm, upstairs bar and good roof terrace, open all day (till 1am Fri, Sat). *(David Thorpe, Comus and Sarah Elliott, Peter Smith and Judith Brown)*

NEWCASTLE UPON TYNE NZ2563

Broad Chare (0191) 211 2144
Broad Chare, just off quayside opposite law courts; NE1 3DQ Traditional feel although only recently converted to a pub; popular british-leaning food from bar snacks such as crispy pigs ears and Lindisfarne oysters to hearty main courses, four real ales including a house beer from Wylam (Writer's Block), good choice of bottled beers, wines and whiskies, bare-boards bar and snug, old local photographs, upstairs dining room; background music; children welcome till 7pm (later upstairs), no dogs, next door to the Live Theatre, open all day (no food Sun evening). *(John Harris)*

NEWCASTLE UPON TYNE NZ2464

Centurion (0191) 261 6611
Central Station, Neville Street; NE1 5HL Glorious high-ceilinged Victorian décor with tilework and columns in former first-class waiting room, well restored with comfortable leather seats giving club-like feel, half a dozen ales including Black Sheep and Caledonian, good value food till early evening; background music, big-screen sports TV; useful café-deli next door, open all day. *(Paul Humphreys, Susan and John Douglas)*

NEWCASTLE UPON TYNE NZ2464

City Tavern (0191) 232 1308
Northumberland Road; NE1 8JF Revamped half-timbered city-centre pub on different levels; ten real ales including a couple badged for them, decent wine list and some 60 gins, enjoyable food from reasonably priced varied menu (plenty for vegetarians), friendly staff; children and dogs (theirs are Alfie, Hector and Dillon) welcome with menu for both, open (and food) all day, kitchen closes 7pm Sun. *(John Harris)*

NEWCASTLE UPON TYNE NZ2664

Cluny (0191) 230 4474
Lime Street; NE1 2PQ Bar-café-music venue in interesting 19th-c mill/warehouse (part of the Head of Steam group); low-priced home-made food including various burgers

and hot dogs, Sun brunch, up to eight well kept ales, good selection of other beers, ciders and some exotic rums, efficient friendly service, sofas in comfortable raised area with daily papers and art magazines, back gallery featuring local artists; background music and regular live bands (also in Cluny 2 next door); children (till 7pm) and dogs allowed, picnic-sets out on green, striking setting below Metro bridge, parking nearby can be difficult, open (and food) all day. *(Paul Humphreys)*

NEWCASTLE UPON TYNE NZ2365

Cosy Dove (0191) 260 2895

Hunters Road, Spital Tongues; NE2 4NA Refurbished pub on city fringe; opened-up interior blending contemporary and traditional features, exposed stonework and quirky colour scheme, leather sofas and rugs on wood floor, bookcases and open fire, good fairly priced food from open kitchen including range of burgers and some clay oven dishes, well kept Batemans, Deuchars, Theakstons and a beer badged for the pub, good range of wines and gins, friendly welcoming staff; background music, quiz nights and sports TV; tables out behind planters, open all day, no food Sun evening. *(John Harris)*

NEWCASTLE UPON TYNE NZ2563

★**Crown Posada** (0191) 232 1269

The Side; off Dean Street, between and below the two high central bridges (A6125 and A6127); NE1 3JE City's oldest pub, just a few minutes' stroll from the castle; long narrow room with elaborate coffered ceiling, stained-glass counter screens and fine mirrors with tulip lamps on curly brass mounts (matching the great ceiling candelabra), long green built-in leather wall seat flanked by narrow tables, old photos of Newcastle and plenty of caricatures, Allendale, Hadrian Border, Highland, Titanic and Wylam, may do sandwiches, heating from fat low-level pipes, music from vintage record player; no credit cards; well behaved children in front snug till 6pm, open all day (midnight Fri, Sat) and can get packed at peak times. *(Paul Humphreys, Roger and Donna Huggins, Peter Smith and Judith Brown)*

NEWCASTLE UPON TYNE NZ2664

Cumberland Arms (0191) 265 1725

James Place Street; NE6 1LD Unspoilt traditional 19th-c pub with half a dozen well kept mainly local ales along with good range of craft beers and ciders, two annual beer festivals, limited choice of reasonably priced snacky food, friendly obliging staff, bare boards and open fires; events most nights including regular folk sessions, film and quiz evenings; dogs welcome, tables out overlooking Ouseburn Valley, four bedrooms, open all day weekends, from 5pm Mon-Weds, 3pm Thurs, Fri. *(John Harris)*

NEWCASTLE UPON TYNE NZ2664

Free Trade (0191) 265 5764

St Lawrence Road, off Walker Road (A186); NE6 1AP Splendidly basic and unpretentious with outstanding views up river from big windows, terrace tables and seats on grass; up to seven real ales, traditional ciders and plenty of bottled beers and whiskies, good sandwiches/pasties and regular pizza nights, warm friendly atmosphere, original Formica tables and coal fire, free juke box, steps down to back room and loos; open all day. *(Roger and Donna Huggins)*

NEWCASTLE UPON TYNE NZ2266

Old George (0191) 260 3035

Cloth Market, down alley past Pumphreys; NE1 1EZ Attractive 16th-c pub (former coaching inn) in cobbled yard; painted beams and panelling, comfortable armchairs by open fire, half a dozen well kept/priced ales including Bass, plenty of wines by the glass and cocktails, good value food including deals, friendly staff; background music at one end, open mike Thurs and Sun, DJs Fri and Sat, sports TV, free wi-fi; children welcome, open all day (till 2am Fri, Sat). *(John Harris)*

NEWCASTLE UPON TYNE NZ2463

Split Chimp

Arch 7, Westgate Road; NE1 1SA Two-floor micropub built into a railway arch; ground-floor bar with cask tables, stools, pews and leather sofas, six well kept ales, five craft beers (more in bottles), real cider and some wines by the glass, snacky food, upstairs skittle alley; live music; open all day Fri and Sat, from 3pm other days, closed Sun. *(Roger and Donna Huggins)*

NEWCASTLE UPON TYNE NZ2463

Town Wall (0191) 232 3000

Pink Lane; across from Central Station; NE1 5HX Newish pub in handsome listed building; spacious bare-boards interior with dark walls, button-back banquettes and mix of well spaced tables and chairs, pictures in heavy gilt frames, up to a dozen ales (one badged for them), good choice of bottled beers and several wines by the glass, well priced food including sharing boards, burgers and pub favourites, basement overspill/function room; background music, free wi-fi; well behaved children and dogs allowed, open all day (till 1am Fri, Sat), food till 7pm Fri-Sun. *(Peter Smith and Judith Brown, John Harris)*

NEWTON-BY-THE-SEA NU2325

★**Joiners Arms** (01665) 576112

High Newton-by-the-Sea, by turning to Linkhouse; NE66 3EA Updated open-plan village pub-restaurant; flagstoned bar with big front windows and open fire, wood-clad dining area behind, good well presented food from interesting sandwiches (stotties) and sharing plates up, four local ales including Anarchy, carefully chosen wines; background music; children and dogs (in bar) welcome, picnic-sets out at front and back, good coastal walks, five stylish bedrooms, open all day. *(Geoff and Anne Marston)*

NEWTON-ON-THE-MOOR NU1705

Cook & Barker Arms (01665) 575234 *Village signed from A1 Alnwick–Felton; NE65 9JY* Traditional stone-built country inn; rustic beamed bar with partly panelled walls, upholstered wall benches by scrubbed pine tables, bottles and bric-a-brac on delft shelf, fire in old range one end, woodburner the other, Black Sheep, a couple of guests and several wines by the glass from extensive list, popular food including lots of fish options, weekday set lunch and early bird deal Weds and Thurs, friendly efficient staff, separate restaurant with exposed stonework and raftered ceiling; background music; children welcome, dogs in snug and lounge, small outside seating area, 16 bedrooms, Boxing Day hunt starts here, open (and food) all day. *(Johnston and Maureen Anderson, Darren and Jane Staniforth)*

NORTH SHIELDS NZ3668

Salty Sea Dog

Union Quay; NE30 1HJ Quirky little bar in the Fish Quay district; local ales, craft beers and great selection of gins and other spirits, friendly helpful staff; dogs welcome, some pavement seating, open all day (till 1am Fri, Sat). *(Darren Liddle)*

OTTERBURN NY8992

William de Percy (01830) 520261

Jedburgh Road; NE19 1NR Refurbished former coaching inn with french-inspired shabby-chic décor, good food from sharing plates up including range of crêpes, a couple of ales from Alnwick, continental beers and decent choice of wines and cocktails; background music; children and dogs welcome, lovely mediterranean-style gardens with palms and fountain, eight stylish bedrooms, more in adjoining Petit Chateau (popular wedding venue), open (and food) all day. *(Monica and Steph Evans)*

PIERCEBRIDGE NZ2115

Fox Hole (01325) 374286

B6275 N of village, or off A67; DL2 3SJ Reworked 19th-c roadside pub with well liked interesting food from lunchtime sandwiches and sharing plates up, Theakstons beers, decent wine choice and extensive range of spirits, contemporary opened-up interior, woodburners, dining room with kitchen view; TV for major sports; children welcome (under-7s till 7.30pm), dogs in bar, tables on terrace and small lawn, open all day, food till 4pm Sun. *(Elaine Taylor, Rod Lambert)*

PONTELAND NZ1773

Blackbird (01661) 822684

North Road opposite church; NE20 9UH Imposing ancient stone pub with opened-up interior; mix of furniture including several high tables and button-back banquettes, wood, slate and tartan-carpeted floors, striking old map of Northumberland and etching of Battle of Otterburn either side of fireplace, larger Tudor stone fireplace in unusual Tunnel Room, good popular food from bar snacks to restauranty dishes, six well kept ales including one badged for them and over 50 gins, friendly service; background music, sports TV, free wi-fi; children and dogs welcome, picnic-sets out at front, more tables on back lawn, open all day, food till 5pm Sun. *(Gerry and Rosemary Dobson)*

RENNINGTON NU2118

★**Horseshoes** (01665) 577665

B1340; NE66 3RS Comfortable and welcoming family-run pub with nice local feel (may be horses in car park); a couple of well kept ales including Hadrian Border Farne Island, decent wines by the glass and ample helpings of enjoyable locally sourced food, friendly efficient service, simple neat bar with flagstones and woodburner, carpeted restaurant; darts, free wi-fi; children welcome, picnic-sets out on small front lawn, attractive quiet village near coast, Aug scarecrow competition, closed Mon. *(Edward May)*

ROCHESTER NY8497

Redesdale Arms (01830) 520668

A68 3 miles W of Otterburn; NE19 1TA Isolated old roadside inn (aka the First & Last) surrounded by unspoilt countryside, warm and cosy, with enjoyable food cooked by landlord including daily specials, Allendale ales, friendly attentive staff; ten bedrooms, open (and food) all day. *(John and Lorna Chew)*

SEATON SLUICE NZ3477

Kings Arms (0191) 237 0275

West Terrace; NE26 4RD Friendly busy old pub in pleasant seaside location perched above tidal Seaton Sluice Harbour; good range of beers and enjoyable pubby food (not Sun evening) including gluten-free choices and blackboard specials, beamed and carpeted bar with old photographs and woodburner at each end, restaurant; children welcome, a few picnic-sets on sunny front grass, more seats in enclosed beer garden behind, open all day. *(Martine and Colin Fresher)*

SEDGEFIELD NZ3528

Dun Cow (01740) 620894

Front Street; TS21 3AT Popular 18th-c village inn with low-beamed bar, back tap room and restaurant, extensive choice of enjoyable reasonably priced food including good Sun roast, cheerful efficient staff, four well kept ales such as Black Sheep and Theakstons; children welcome, six comfortable bedrooms, open (and food) all day weekends. *(D M and B K Moores)*

SHINCLIFFE NZ2940

Seven Stars (0191) 384 8454
High Street N (A177 S of Durham); DH1 2NU Comfortable and welcoming 18th-c village inn; good generously served food from pub favourites up including weekday set menu and other deals, three well kept changing ales, coal-effect gas fire in lounge bar, panelled dining room; children welcome in eating areas, dogs in bar, some picnic-sets outside, eight bedrooms, closed Mon, otherwise open all day. *(Robert and Diana Myers)*

SLALEY NY9757

Rose & Crown (01434) 673996
Church Close; NE47 0AA Welcoming 17th-c pub owned by the village; enjoyable good value pubby food from sandwiches/baguettes up (not Sun evening), Thurs steak night, local ales such as Allendale, beams and log fires; Sun quiz; children and dogs welcome, garden with long country views, two bedrooms, open all day in summer. *(Patti and James Davidson)*

SLALEY NY9658

Travellers Rest (01434) 673231
B6306 S of Hexham (and N of village); NE46 1TT Attractive stone-built country pub, spaciously opened up, with farmhouse-style décor, beams, flagstones and polished wood floors, huge fireplace, comfortable high-backed settles forming discrete areas, friendly welcoming staff, enjoyable food (not Sun evening, Mon) in bar or quieter dining room, real ales such as Black Sheep and Caledonian; children and dogs welcome, tables outside and well equipped adventure play area, three good value bedrooms, open all day. *(Chris and Sophie Baxter)*

SOUTH SHIELDS NZ3567

Alum Ale House (0191) 427 7245
Ferry Street (B1344); NE33 1JR Welcoming 18th-c bow-windowed pub adjacent to North Shields ferry; open-plan bare-boards bar with fire in old range, a dozen well kept Marstons-related ales; music and quiz nights; no children, seats on front deck overlooking the river, handy for marketplace, open all day. *(Francis and Mandy Robertson)*

SOUTH SHIELDS NZ3566

Steamboat (0191) 454 0134
Mill Dam/Coronation Street; NE33 1EQ Friendly 19th-c corner pub with nine well kept changing ales, lots of nautical bric-a-brac, bar ceiling covered in flags, raised seating area and separate lounge; near river and marketplace, open all day. *(Francis and Mandy Robertson)*

STANNINGTON NZ2179

★**Ridley Arms** (01670) 789216
Village signed off A1 S of Morpeth; NE61 6EL Extended Fitzgerald pub with several separate areas; open fire and cushioned settles in proper front bar, stools along counter serving up to seven local ales such as Alnwick and Hadrian Border, a dozen wines by the glass and good coffee, decent choice of enjoyable reasonably priced food, pleasant helpful staff, several dining areas with upholstered bucket chairs around dark tables on bare boards or carpet, cartoons and portraits on cream, panelled or stripped-stone walls; background music, Tues quiz, free wi-fi; children welcome, good disabled access, picnic-sets out at front and on back terrace, open (and food) all day, handy for A1. *(Comus and Sarah Elliott, Martinthehills)*

SUNDERLAND NZ4057

Ivy House (0191) 567 3399
Worcester Terrace; SR2 7AW Friendly Victorian corner pub off the beaten track; five well kept changing ales, interesting bottled beers and good range of spirits, popular reasonably priced food from open kitchen including burgers and pizzas; background and live music, quiz Weds (and sometimes Sun), sports TV; open (and food) all day. *(John Harris)*

THROPTON NU0202

Three Wheat Heads (01669) 620262
B6341; NE65 7LR Popular 18th-c village inn with good generously served food including Sun carvery, well kept local ales and decent choice of wines, busy but friendly service, open fires (one in fine tall stone fireplace), lovely country views from dining room's big windows; children and dogs (in bar) welcome, disabled access, garden with play area, comfortable bedrooms and good breakfast, handy for Cragside (NT), open (and food) all day. *(Mark and Mary Setting)*

TYNEMOUTH NZ3669

Hugos at the Coast (0191) 257 8956
Front Street; NE30 4DZ Recently refurbished Sir John Fitzgerald pub with open-plan split-level interior, four changing ales, decent choice of wines by the glass and cocktails, reasonably priced food from shortish menu including sandwiches, friendly service; Weds quiz, sports TV; children welcome, some pavement seating, open all day, food till 4pm. *(Katherine Matthews)*

Please tell us if any pub deserves to be upgraded to a featured entry – and why: feedback@goodguides.com, or (no stamp needed) The Good Pub Guide, FREEPOST RTXY–ZCBC–BBAZ, Stream Lane, Sedlescombe, Battle TN33 0PB.

TYNEMOUTH NZ3668

Turks Head (0191) 257 6547
Front Street; NE30 4DZ Friendly drinkers' pub with eight changing ales and three craft kegs, no food, steps between two comfortable small bars, ancient stuffed border collie called Willie and accompanying sad story (pub known locally as the Stuffed Dog); background music, sports TVs, darts; open all day. *(Roger and Donna Huggins)*

WARDEN NY9166

Boatside (01434) 602233
Village signed N of A69; NE46 4SQ Old stone pub in attractive spot by Tyne bridge; modern décor (but still cosy), enjoyable fairly priced food from varied menu, a couple of local ales and decent selection of new world wines, good friendly service; sports TV; children welcome, small neat enclosed garden, bedrooms in adjoining cottages (some self-catering), open (and food) all day. *(Robert and Diana Myers)*

WARENFORD NU1429

White Swan (01668) 213453
Off A1 S of Belford; NE70 7HY Friendly bar with ales such as Alnwick, Greene King and Rigg & Furrow, steps down to cosy restaurant serving good well presented imaginative food along with more traditional choices, cheerful efficient service, warm fires; children and dogs (in bar) welcome, bedrooms, open all day. *(William and Ann Reid, Darren and Jane Staniforth)*

WARKWORTH NU2406

Hermitage (01665) 711258
Castle Street; NE65 0UL Rambling former coaching inn with good choice of popular home-made food including Sun carvery, Jennings, Marstons and guests, decent range of wines, friendly staff, quaint décor with fire in old range, small upstairs restaurant; background and some live music; children and dogs welcome in bar, benches and hanging baskets out at front, attractive setting, bedrooms, open (and food) all day. *(Caroline and Steve Archer)*

WELDON BRIDGE NZ1398

★**Anglers Arms** (01665) 570271
B6344, just off A697; village signposted with Rothbury off A1 N of Morpeth; NE65 8AX Traditional coaching inn nicely located by bridge over River Coquet; two-part bar with cream walls or oak panelling, shiny black beams hung with copper pans, profusion of fishing memorabilia, taxidermy and a grandfather clock, some low tables with matching chairs, sofa by coal fire, three changing ales, around 40 malt whiskies and decent wines by the glass, well liked generously served food, friendly helpful staff; background music, Thurs quiz; children and dogs (in bar) welcome, attractive garden with good play area, fishing rights, comfortable bedrooms, open (and food) all day. *(Martinthehills)*

WEST BOLDON NZ3460

Red Lion (0191) 536 4197
Redcar Terrace; NE36 0PZ Bow-windowed, flower-decked pub with various cosy linked areas; beamed bar with open fire, three real ales including Black Sheep and Mordue from ornate wood counter, separate snug and conservatory dining room, good choice of popular well priced food, friendly relaxed atmosphere; seats out on back decking, open all day. *(Roger and Donna Huggins)*

WEST WOODBURN NY8986

Bay Horse (01434) 270218
A68; NE48 2RX Modernised 18th-c roadside inn with horse-themed décor; Belhaven and other Greene King ales, decent wines and good range of reasonably priced food including Sun carvery, friendly service, can eat in carpeted log fire bar or separate restaurant; background music; children and dogs welcome, riverside garden, bedrooms. *(John Harris)*

WHITFIELD NY7857

Elks Head (01434) 345282
Off A686 SW of Haydon Bridge; NE47 8HD Extended old stone pub attractively set in steep wooded valley: light and spacious, with bar and two dining areas, good value tasty food, Fullers London Pride and a couple of local guests, several wines by the glass, friendly helpful service; children and dogs (in bar) welcome, picnic-sets in small pretty front garden by little river, scenic area with good walks, ten bedrooms (some in adjacent cottage), open all day in summer. *(JimmyB)*

WHITLEY BAY NZ3742

Left Luggage Room
Metro Station, Northam Road; NE26 3NR Quirky micropub in former station room; high vaulted ceiling and brick walls left in original rough condition adding to the character, mismatched wooden furniture on boarded floor, artwork for sale, old suitcases and trunks stacked below bar counter, changing craft beers, ales, ciders and good range of other drinks including several whiskies and gins (all listed on blackboards), no food apart from bar snacks, friendly knowledgeable staff and vibrant chatty atmosphere; live music some evenings; dogs welcome, tables out on platform, open all day. *(Martinthehills)*

WHORLTON NZ1014

Fernavilles Rest (01833) 627341
High Stakes, N of village green; DL12 8XD Old stone pub on pretty village's green; log-fire bar and well

divided half-panelled restaurant, popular reasonably priced food, a house beer from local Mithril and two guests kept well, friendly young staff; children, walkers and dogs welcome, three good value comfortable bedrooms, near historic narrow suspension bridge over the Tees and handy for Bowes Museum, open all day till around 9pm (10pm weekends). *(Louise and Simon Peters)*

WINSTON NZ1416

Bridgewater Arms (01325) 730302

B6274, just off A67 Darlington–Barnard Castle; DL2 3RN This converted Victorian school house was up for sale as we went to press, so may be changes; high-ceilinged bar with log fire, cushioned settles and chairs, a wall lined with bookcases, Brakspears, Rudgate and a guest, a dozen wines by the glass and several malt whiskies, two restaurant rooms with high-backed leather chairs around clothed tables, food has been very good with emphasis on fresh fish/seafood; well behaved children welcome, picnic-sets out at front, the fine old bridge across the River Tees is also worth a look, closed Sun, Mon. *(Max and Steph Warren)*

WYLAM NZ1164

★**Boathouse** (01661) 853431

Station Road, handy for Newcastle–Carlisle railway; across Tyne from village (and George Stephenson's Birthplace – NT); NE41 8HR Convivial two-room pub with a dozen real ales, traditional ciders and good choice of malt whiskies, thai menu and some snacky food, friendly knowledgeable staff, light interior with one or two low beams and woodburner; fortnightly buskers night (Tues), juke box, sports TV; children and dogs welcome, seats outside, close to station and river, open all day (evenings can be very busy). *(Roger and Donna Huggins)*

WYLAM NZ1164

Ship (01661) 854538

Main Road; NE41 8AQ Genuine warm welcome at this sizeable open-plan dining pub; good individual cooking from owner-chef including Sat steak night and Sun set lunch, a house beer from Theakstons and well chosen wine list; Thurs quiz, free wi-fi, children and dogs welcome, picnic-sets in beer garden, bedrooms, handy for George Stephenson's cottage (NT), closed Mon, otherwise open all day (till 6pm Sun). *(Michael Doswell)*

Nottinghamshire

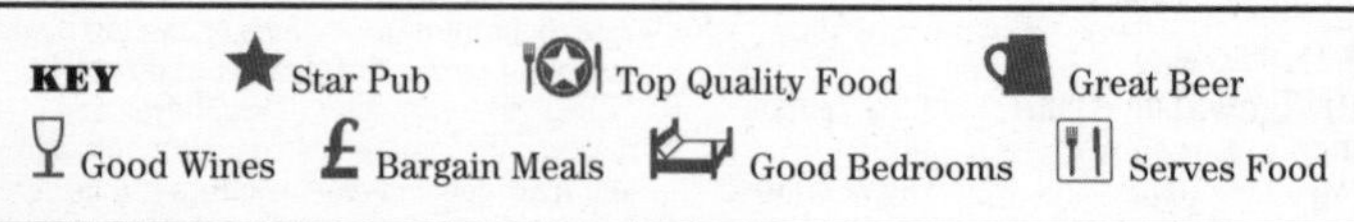

CAYTHORPE SK6845 Map 7

Black Horse

(0115) 966 3520 – www.caythorpebrewery.co.uk

Turn off A6097 0.25 miles SE of roundabout junction with A612, NE of Nottingham; into Gunthorpe Road, then right into Caythorpe Road and keep on; NG14 7ED

Quaintly old-fashioned little pub brewing its own beer, with simple interior and enjoyable homely food; no children, no credit cards

Little changes in this old country local. It's been run by three generations of the same friendly family and the good value food and own-brewed ales continue to draw in customers. The homely, uncluttered, carpeted bar has just five tables, along with brocaded wall banquettes and settles, decorative plates on a delft shelf, a few horsebrasses attached to the ceiling joists, and a coal fire. Cheerful regulars might occupy the few bar stools to enjoy Caythorpe Bitter and Dover Beck brewed in outbuildings here and served alongside a couple of guests such as Bass and Greene King Abbot on handpump; seven wines by the glass and half a dozen whiskies too. Off the front corridor is an inner room, partly panelled with a wall bench running all the way round three unusual, long, copper-topped tables; there are several old local photographs, darts and board games. Down on the left, an end room has just one huge round table. There are seats outside. The pub is close to the River Trent where there are waterside walks. No children.

Good value home-cooked food (you'll need to book a table in advance) includes sandwiches, prawn cocktail, mushrooms on toast, three-egg omelettes, lamb chops with creamed potatoes, gammon and eggs, fish in parsley sauce, and puddings such as sticky toffee pudding and treacle sponge with custard. *Benchmark main dish: beer-battered fish and chips £12.00. Two-course evening meal £17.00.*

Own brew ~ Licensee Sharron Andrews ~ Real ale ~ No credit cards ~ Open 12-2.30, 5.30-11; 12-5, 8-11 Sun; closed Mon except bank holidays ~ Bar food 11.45-1.45, 6-8.30; not Sat evening; all day Sun ~ Dogs allowed in bar ~ Wi-fi *Recommended by Anne and Ben Smith, Maddie Purvis, Thomas Green, Peter Pilbeam*

COLSTON BASSETT SK6933 Map 7

Martins Arms

(01949) 81361 – www.themartinsarms.co.uk

Village signposted off A46 E of Nottingham; School Lane, near market cross in village centre; NG12 3FD

Nottinghamshire Dining Pub of the Year

Smart dining pub with impressive food, good range of drinks including seven real ales and attractive grounds

With creative food and a first class choice of drinks, this 16th-c former farmhouse is a special place. Our readers love their visits here. There's a civilised and comfortably relaxed atmosphere, warm log fires in Jacobean fireplaces, fresh flowers and candlelight, and the smart décor includes period fabrics and colours, antique furniture and hunting prints; dominoes and cards. The main dining room is painted in a warm red with gold silk curtains. Neatly uniformed staff serve a beer named for the pub, Bass, Greene King Ruddles County, Marstons Wainwright and Timothy Taylors Landlord on handpump, 22 wines by the glass or carafe (including prosecco, champagne and sweet wines) and a fair choice of whiskies and Armagnacs. The lawned garden (with summer croquet and barbecues) backs on to National Trust parkland. Do visit the church opposite and Colston Bassett Dairy (just outside the village) which produces and sells its own stilton cheese.

Inspired cooking includes lunchtime sandwiches, crispy ox cheek with pickled plum purée and home-made kimchi, locally shot, tea-smoked pigeon breast with beetroot and goats cheese mousse, a home-made pie of the day (in the bar), beer-braised jacobs ladder with potato purée, roasted shallots and coffee and malt glaze, lemon sole with charred cabbage, celeriac, potato, samphire and mussel cream, and puddings such as sticky ginger pudding with ginger wine sauce and ice-cream and lemon curd with shortbread, caramelised white chocolate and fennel meringue. *Benchmark main dish: miso-glazed pork rib-eye with pulled pork, potato terrine, pak choi and pineapple purée and jus £22.00. Two-course evening meal £26.00.*

Free house ~ Licensees Lynne Strafford Bryan and Salvatore Inguanta ~ Real ale ~ Open 12-3, 6-11; 12-5, 7-10.30 Sun ~ Bar food 12-2, 6-9; 12-2.30 Sun; not Sun evening ~ Restaurant ~ Children welcome ~ Wi-fi *Recommended by Jacqui and Alan Swan, Adam Jones, Rosie and John Moore, Matt and Hayley Jacob, Patrick and Emma Stephenson*

NEWARK SK7953 Map 7

Prince Rupert

(01636) 918121 – www.kneadpubs.co.uk/the-prince-rupert

Stodman Street, off Castle Gate; NG24 1AW

Thoughtfully restored historic pub with fine original features, interestingly furnished small bars, local ales and tasty food

A lively timber-framed 15th-c pub, this has regular events and plenty of chatty locals, though the convivial staff welcome visitors just as warmly. The cosy, carefully renovated rooms have a lot of character with some very fine high-backed settles, cushioned wall seats, pubby chairs around polished antique tables, advertising mirrors and old enamelled wall signs, hops, open fires and floors of terracotta tiles, bare floorboards and some carpet. A light and airy conservatory has tricycles hanging from the ceiling, and doors that lead out to the terraced garden. Ales served on handpump from the ornately carved counter include Brains Rev James and Oakham JHB and guests from breweries such as Beermats, Blue Monkey, Ilkley, Pheasantry and Thornbridge and they also offer 22 wines by the glass; background music and TV. The pub is close to the market square in the town centre.

Rewarding food includes pigs in blankets with brown sauce, baked camembert with chutney, quite a choice of stone-baked pizzas, cheese and spinach pie, beer-battered fish and chips, moroccan-style lamb meatballs with lemon couscous and flatbread, corn-fed chicken with wild mushroom and tarragon sauce, smoked salmon and dill tagliatelle, 14-hour braised beef in ale with bubble and squeak and redcurrant jelly, and puddings such as chocolate brownie with clotted cream ice-cream and banana sticky toffee pudding with caramel sauce. *Benchmark main dish: burger with toppings and twice-cooked chips £13.95. Two-course evening meal £19.00.*

Knead Pubs ~ Managers Sam Johnson and Nikki Booth ~ Real ale ~ Open 11-11 (1am Sat) ~ Bar food 12-2.30, 6-9; 12-9 Sat; 12-8 Sun ~ Children welcome ~ Dogs welcome ~ Wi-fi
Recommended by David Hunt, Tony and Maggie Harwood, Professor James Burke, Mary Joyce, Max Simons

Also Worth a Visit in Nottinghamshire

Besides the fully inspected pubs, you might like to try these pubs that have been recommended to us and described by readers. Do tell us what you think of them: feedback@goodguides.com

AWSWORTH SK4844

Gate (0115) 932 9821
Main Street, via A6096 off A610 Nuthall–Eastwood bypass; NG16 2RN Renovated Victorian free house near site of once-famous railway viaduct; seven well kept changing ales and some snacky food, bar with woodburner, coal fire in lounge, friendly welcoming atmosphere; occasional live music and comedy nights, skittle alley; dogs welcome, disabled access/loo, back courtyard and roof terrace, open all day. *(Thomas Green)*

BAGTHORPE SK4751

Dixies Arms (01773) 810505
A608 towards Eastwood off M1 junction 27, right on B600 via Sandhill Road, left into School Road; Lower Bagthorpe; NG16 5HF Friendly unspoilt 18th-c brick local with DH Lawrence connections; beams and tiled floors, well kept Greene King Abbot, Theakstons Best and a guest, no food, entrance bar with tiny snug, good fire in small part-panelled parlour's fine fireplace, longer narrow room with toby jugs, darts and dominoes; live music Sat, beer/folk festival June, free wi-fi; children and dogs (on leads) welcome, picnic-sets out at front, big garden and play area behind, open all day. *(Dawson Clay)*

BEESTON SK5236

Crown (0115) 925 4738
Church Street; NG9 1FY Everards pub with 14 well kept ales, real ciders/perry and good choice of other drinks, friendly knowledgeable staff, no hot food but fresh cobs and snacks; front snug and bar with slate and quarry-tiled floors, carpeted parlour with padded wall seats, Victorian décor and new polished bar in lounge, beams, panelling and bric-a-brac including an old red telephone box; weekend live music, regular quiz nights and beer festivals; dogs welcome, terrace tables (some under cover), open all day. *(Johnston and Maureen Anderson, David Hunt)*

BEESTON SK5336

Star (0115) 854 5320
Middle Street; NG9 1FX Refurbished three-room inn with fine range of well kept changing ales and extensive choice of whiskies, friendly knowledgeable staff, good keenly priced pub food along with freshly baked pizzas; live music and quiz nights, separate games room with pool, darts and sports TV; children and dogs welcome, permanent marquee leading through to heated terrace and large grassy garden with play equipment, eight good value bedrooms, open all day. *(Johnston and Maureen Anderson, David Hunt)*

BEESTON SK5336

★**Victoria** (0115) 925 4049
Dovecote Lane, backing on to the station; NG9 1JG Genuine down-to-earth all-rounder (red-brick former station hotel) attracting good mix of customers; up to 16 real ales (regular beer festivals), two farm ciders, 120 malt whiskies and 30 wines by the glass, good sensibly priced food (order at bar) from varied blackboard menu including plenty for vegetarians, efficient friendly service, three fairly simple unfussy rooms with original long narrow layout (last one for diners only), solid furnishings, bare boards and stripped woodwork, stained-glass windows, some brewerania, open fires; live music and other events including July VicFest, newspapers and board games; children welcome till 8pm, dogs in bar, seats out on covered heated area overlooking platform (trains pass just a few feet away), limited parking, open (and food) all day. *(Johnston and Maureen Anderson, David Hunt)*

BINGHAM SK7039

Horse & Plough (01949) 839313
Off A52; Long Acre; NG13 8AF Castle Rock pub in 1818 Methodist chapel; low beams, flagstones and stripped brickwork, comfortable open-plan seating including pews, prints and old brewery memorabilia,

If you report on a pub that's not a featured entry, please tell us any lunchtimes or evenings when it doesn't serve bar food.

good selection of beers including their own (tasters offered), real cider and decent wine choice, enjoyable reasonably priced bar food and popular upstairs grill room with open kitchen, Thurs curry night, good friendly service; background music; children and dogs welcome, disabled facilities, open all day. *(Matt and Hayley Jacob)*

BLYTH SK6287

White Swan (01909) 591222
High Street; S81 8EQ Old whitewashed pub opposite the village green; beams, flagstones and exposed brickwork, mix of dining chairs and padded banquettes around assorted tables on flagstones or carpet, Black Sheep, Sharps Doom Bar and Timothy Taylors Landlord, enjoyable pubby food including Sun carvery, friendly service; Sun quiz, TV; children welcome, no dogs inside, tables out in front and in small back garden, open all day. *(Martin Day, Malcolm Phillips, John Saville)*

BUNNY SK5829

Rancliffe Arms (0115) 984 4727
Loughborough Road (A60 S of Nottingham); NG11 6QT Substantial old coaching inn with linked dining areas, emphasis on good food including popular carvery (Mon evening, Weds, Sat and Sun) with excellent range of fresh vegetables, friendly welcoming staff, chunky country chairs around mixed tables on flagstones or carpet, well kept changing range of Marstons-related beers in comfortable log-fire bar with sofas and armchairs; background music; children welcome, decking outside, open all day Fri-Sun. *(Johnston and Maureen Anderson, Gerry and Rosemary Dobson)*

CAR COLSTON SK7242

Royal Oak (01949) 20247
The Green, off Tenman Lane (off A46 not far from A6097 junction); NG13 8JE Good well priced traditional food (not Sun evening) in biggish 19th-c pub opposite one of England's largest village greens; four well kept Marstons-related ales and decent choice of wines by the glass, woodburner in lounge bar with tables set for eating, public bar with unusual barrel-vaulted brick ceiling; skittle alley, free wi-fi; children and dogs welcome, picnic-sets on spacious back lawn, heated smokers' den, camping, open all day Fri-Sun. *(Chrissy Proctor)*

CAUNTON SK7459

★**Caunton Beck** (01636) 636793
Newark Road; NG23 6AE Reconstructed low-beamed dining pub (on site of 16th-c tavern) made to look old using original timbers and reclaimed oak; scrubbed pine tables and country kitchen chairs, open fire, Oakham JHB and a couple of beers from sister pub's microbrewery (see Bottle & Glass at Harby), over two dozen wines by the glass, well presented popular food from breakfast on, cheerful obliging staff and relaxed atmosphere; daily newspapers, free wi-fi; children and dogs (in bar) welcome, seats on flowery terrace, handy for A1, open (and food) all day from 8.30am. *(Malcolm Phillips)*

CAYTHORPE SK6846

Old Volunteer (0115) 966 5822
Caythorpe Road; NG14 7EB Refurbished village dining pub with good food, decent wines and four well kept ales including Timothy Taylors and Theakstons, friendly helpful service, upstairs dining room with view over fields; children and dogs (in bar) welcome, seats out at front and on back deck, open (and food) all day, but may close early if quiet. *(Philip Turton)*

CLAYWORTH SK7288

★**Blacksmiths** (01777) 818171
Town Street; DN22 9AD Stylishly refurbished pub with very good inventive food (not Sun evening) along with more traditional choices, contemporary dining areas with dramatic flower arrangements and candles in large glass jars, bar has leather chesterfields, armchairs and upholstered cube by woodburner; Timothy Taylors Landlord, a guest beer and several wines by the glass, well trained friendly staff, upstairs private dining area with balcony; children welcome, dogs in bar till 5.30pm, seats in sunny walled garden, local church worth a look (Phoebe Anna Traquair murals), Chesterfield Canal walks, four bedrooms, open all day Sun till 8pm, closed Mon (except bank holidays when shuts Tues instead). *(Paul Sherfield, Stephen Woad, Dr and Mrs A K Clarke, Ian Prince)*

CUCKNEY SK5671

Greendale Oak (01623) 844441
A616, E of A60; NG20 9NQ Updated country pub with good all-day food (till 7pm Sun) from sandwiches and pizzas to chargrilled steaks, fresh fish Thurs, eight real ales including Everards, friendly helpful service, restaurant; background music, quiz Weds; children welcome, no dogs inside, sturdy bench seating on front terrace, garden behind, open all day (till 1am Fri, Sat). *(Jeff Grant)*

EDWINSTOWE SK6266

Forest Lodge (01623) 824443
Church Street; NG21 9QA Friendly 18th-c inn with enjoyable home-made food in pubby bar or restaurant, good service, five well kept ales including Wells Bombardier and a house beer from Welbeck Abbey, beams and log fire; children welcome, 13 bedrooms, handy for Sherwood Forest. *(Patrick and Emma Stephenson)*

EPPERSTONE SK6548

Cross Keys (0115) 966 9430
Main Street; NG14 6AD Refurbished dining pub with chef-proprietor's good, well presented/priced food from regularly

changing menu, three real ales including Nottingham and nice wines by the glass, friendly efficient service, woodburner separating lounge bar and restaurant; quiz Sun; children welcome, muddy walkers and dogs in boot room, a few picnic-sets out at front, more in back garden with raised deck, pretty village and surrounding countryside, open (and food) all day, apart from Sun when kitchen closes at 6pm. *(Gerry and Rosemary Dobson)*

FARNDON SK7652

Boathouse (01636) 676578
Off A46 SW of Newark; keep on towards river – pub off Wyke Lane, just past the Riverside pub; NG24 3SX Big-windowed contemporary bar-restaurant overlooking the Trent, emphasis on food but they do serve a couple of changing ales, good choice of wines and some interesting cocktails; main area with high ceiling trusses supporting bare ducting, simple modern tables and upholstered chairs, shallow step up to second similarly furnished dining area, good variety of food including early bird deal; background and Sun live music, July garden party with live bands, free wi-fi; children welcome, wicker chairs around teak tables on heated terrace, own moorings, open all day, food all day Sun. *(Tim Cranston)*

FISKERTON SK7351

Bromley Arms (01636) 830789
Main Street; NG25 0UL Popular Trentside pub with modernised opened-up interior; fairly compact bar area with upholstered stools and leather armchairs/sofas, two-way fireplace, three well kept Greene King ales and a beer badged for them, decent range of wines by the glass, river-view dining part with upholstered chairs on patterned carpet (some matching wallpaper), enjoyable fairly priced food including weekday set menu till 6pm, friendly helpful service; background music, live acoustic session Thurs; children welcome, rattan-style furniture on narrow walled terrace, picnic-sets by edge of wharf giving best views, open (and food) all day and can get very busy in summer. *(Gerry and Rosemary Dobson)*

GRANBY SK7436

★**Marquis of Granby** (01949) 859517 *Off A52 E of Nottingham; Dragon Street; NG13 9PN* Friendly 18th-c pub in attractive Vale of Belvoir village; tap for Brewsters with their well kept ales and interesting guests from chunky yew counter, no food, two small comfortable rooms, broad flagstones, some low beams and striking wallpaper, open fire; children and dogs welcome, open all day weekends, from 4pm Mon-Fri. *(Thomas Green)*

HARBY SK8870

Bottle & Glass (01522) 703438
High Street; village signed off A57 W of Lincoln; NG23 7EB 19th-c pub with pair of bay-windowed front bars and restaurant extension; enjoyable food including set menu and blackboard specials, a couple of beers from on-site microbrewery along with a guest such as Black Sheep, good choice of wines, friendly service, open fire and woodburners; shop selling their bottled beers, general provisions and gifts; children welcome, dogs in bar, modern wrought-iron furniture on back terrace, picnic-sets on grass beyond and out at front, open (and food) all day, except Sun when kitchen closes 6pm, breakfast from 10am (9am weekends). *(Matt and Hayley Jacob)*

HOCKERTON SK7156

Spread Eagle (01636) 813322
Caunton Road; A617 Newark–Mansfield; NG25 0PL Refurbished village corner pub; compact interior with linked beamed rooms, a couple of woodburners, smallish bar area serving Black Sheep, a guest beer and decent choice of wines, generous helpings of good freshly made food from baguettes to daily specials, friendly accommodating staff; children welcome, dogs in one area, beer garden and separate deck, closed Mon, otherwise open (and food) all day, till 8pm (7pm) Sun. *(Jeff Grant)*

KIMBERLEY SK4944

★**Nelson & Railway** (0115) 938 2177
Station Road; handy for M1 junction 26 via A610; NG16 2NR Cheery Victorian beamed pub in same family for over 40 years, popular and comfortable, with decent inexpensive home-made food from snacks to blackboard specials, well kept Greene King ales and guests, mix of Edwardian-looking furniture, brewery prints (was tap for defunct Hardys & Hansons Brewery) and railway signs, dining extension; juke box, games machine, darts, free wi-fi; children and dogs allowed, disabled access, nice front and back gardens, 11 good value bedrooms, proper breakfast, open all day, food all day Sat, till 6pm Sun. *(Stuart Doughty)*

KIMBERLEY SK5044

Stag 07934 043755
Nottingham Road; NG16 2NB Traditional 18th-c local under new management; two cosy rooms, small central counter and corridor, low beams, dark panelling and settles, some old Shipstones Brewery photographs, up to eight well kept ales including Adnams, Bass, Oakham and Timothy Taylors (beer festival first weekend Aug), no food apart from weekend rolls; some

> Post Office address codings confusingly give the impression that a few pubs are in Nottinghamshire, when they're really in Derbyshire (which is where we list them).

live music, sports TV, darts and dominoes, free wi-fi; children and dogs welcome, wheelchair access from behind, new front decking and attractive back garden with play area and summer barbecues, open all day Sat and Sun, from 4pm other days. *(Tim Cranston)*

LAXTON SK7266

★ **Dovecote** (01777) 871586
Off A6075 E of Ollerton; NG22 0NU Red-brick pub doing well under hard-working owners; cosy country atmosphere in three traditionally furnished dining areas, popular home-made food from sandwiches and light lunches to daily specials, also a children's menu, three well kept changing ales, proper cider and several wines by the glass, friendly helpful staff; background music, free wi-fi, no dogs inside, disabled access, small front terrace and sloping garden with views towards church, interesting village still using the medieval 'strip farming' system, two bedrooms, open all day Sat, Sun till 9pm (food till 6.30pm); handy for A1. *(Derek and Sylvia Stephenson)*

LOWDHAM SK6745

Railway (0115) 966 3222
Longmoor Avenue, near the station; NG14 7DU Revamped 19th-c village pub with clean modern décor, five real ales such as Castle Rock and Theakstons, 20 wines by the glass and plenty of gins, shortish but varied choice of well liked/presented food cooked in open kitchen including good value set menu (lunchtime, early evening), friendly helpful staff; children and dogs welcome, chunky picnic-sets outside and play area, more seats on elevated back terrace, open all day, no food Sun evening. *(Mary Joyce)*

MANSFIELD SK5363

Railway Inn (01623) 623086
Station Street; best approached by viaduct from near Market Place; NG18 1EF Friendly traditional local under long-serving landlady; four changing ales, real cider and good bargain home-made food (till 5pm Sun), two little front rooms leading to main bar, another cosy room at back, laminate flooring throughout; some live music; children and dogs welcome, small courtyard and beer garden, handy for Robin Hood Line station and the newish bus station, open all day. *(David Hunt)*

MAPLEBECK SK7160

Beehive
Signed down pretty country lanes from A616 Newark–Ollerton and from A617 Newark–Mansfield; NG22 0BS Tiny beamed country tavern in nice spot, unpretentious and welcoming, with cosy front bar and slightly bigger side room, traditional furnishings and open fire, a couple of well kept changing ales, no food; children and dogs welcome, tables on small front terrace and grassy bank running down to stream, play area, may be closed weekday lunchtimes, busy weekends and bank holidays. *(Thomas Green)*

MORTON SK7251

Full Moon (01636) 830251
Pub and village signed off Bleasby–Fiskerton back road, SE of Southwell; NG25 0UT Attractive old brick pub tucked away in remote hamlet close to River Trent; modernised pale-beamed bar with two roaring fires, comfortable armchairs, eclectic mix of tables and other simple furnishings, Castle Rock, Sharps, Timothy Taylors and a couple of guests, nine wines by the glass and cocktails (two-for-one Fri 5-7pm), enjoyable sensibly priced food from ciabattas up including good value lunchtime/early evening set menu, separate carpeted restaurant; background and some live music, board games, free wi-fi; children and dogs (in bar) welcome, picnic-sets out at front, more on peaceful back terrace and sizeable lawn with sturdy play equipment, open all day Fri-Sun, no food Sun evening. *(Derek and Sylvia Stephenson)*

NEWARK SK8054

Castle Barge (01636) 677320
Town Wharf next to Trent Bridge; NG24 1EU Old grain barge moored near the castle; top deck has enclosed dining area, below is cosy bar, lots of changing local beers (cheaper Thurs and Sun evenings) and proper cider, cocktail happy hour 5-8pm, good value straightforward food including pizzas, friendly service; Weds quiz, free wi-fi; children (not in bar) and dogs welcome, picnic-sets out on wharf, open all day. *(David Hunt, Tony and Maggie Harwood)*

NEWARK SK7953

Just Beer (01636) 312047
Swan & Salmon Yard, off Castle Gate (B6166); NG24 1BG Welcoming one-room micropub tucked down alley; four or five interesting quickly changing beers from brick counter, real cider/perry, limited range of other drinks, bright airy minimalist décor with some brewery memorabilia, half a dozen tables on stone floor, good mix of customers; darts, dominoes and board games; dogs welcome, open all day (from 1pm weekdays). *(David Hunt, Nikki Squires)*

NORMANTON ON THE WOLDS SK6232

Plough (0115) 937 2401
Off A606 5 miles S of Nottingham; NG12 5NN Welcoming ivy-clad pub on edge of village; good food from extensive menu including nice steaks, popular Sun lunch (booking advised) and set deal (Tues-Thurs 5.30-6.30pm), Black Sheep, Timothy Taylors and a couple of guests, friendly uniformed staff, fires in bar and extended restaurant; soft background music; children welcome,

big garden with play area and summer barbecues, open all day, no food Sun evening. *(Tim Cranston)*

NOTTINGHAM SK5739

★**Bell** (0115) 947 5241

Angel Row; off Market Square; NG1 6HL Deceptively large pub with late Georgian frontage concealing two much older timber-framed buildings; front Tudor Bar with glass panels protecting patches of 300-year-old wallpaper, larger low-beamed Elizabethan Bar with half-panelled walls and maple parquet flooring, more heavy panelling and a 15th-c crown post in upstairs Belfry; up to a dozen real ales including Greene King and Nottingham from remarkable deep sandstone cellar (can arrange tours), ten wines by the glass, reasonably priced straightforward bar food; background and regular live music including trad jazz, TV, silent fruit machine; children welcome in some parts, pavement tables, open all day (till 1am Sat). *(Jeff Grant)*

NOTTINGHAM SK5843

Bread & Bitter (0115) 960 7541

Woodthorpe Drive; NG3 5JL Welcoming pub in former suburban bakery (ovens remain); three bright and airy bare-boards rooms with brewery memorabilia, around a dozen well kept ales including Castle Rock, good range of bottled beers, traditional cider and decent choice of wines, reasonably priced pubby food from cobs to specials, friendly staff; well behaved children and dogs welcome, open (and food) all day, kitchen closes 7pm Sun. *(Jeff Grant)*

NOTTINGHAM SK5739

Canalhouse (0115) 955 5060

Canal Street; NG1 7EH Converted wharf building with bridge over indoors canal spur (complete with narrowboat), lots of bare brick and varnished wood, huge joists on steel beams, long bar serving Castle Rock and three guests, well over 100 bottled beers and good choice of wines, sensibly priced food from snacks up including range of burgers; background music; masses of tables out on attractive waterside terrace, open all day (till 1am Fri, Sat), food till 7pm Sun. *(Jess and George Cowley)*

NOTTINGHAM SK5739

Cock & Hoop (0115) 948 4414

High Pavement opposite Galleries of Justice; NG1 1HF Pub attached to the Lace Market Hotel; cosy panelled front bar with fireside armchairs and characterful décor, Castle Rock and several local guests, enjoyable fairly priced food from sandwiches to good Sun roasts, more room downstairs; children and dogs welcome, covered outside seating area, 42 bedrooms (ones by the street can be noisy at weekends), open (and food) all day. *(Jeff Grant)*

NOTTINGHAM SK5739

★**Cross Keys** (0115) 941 7898

Byard Lane; NG1 2GJ Victorian city-centre pub on two levels; lower carpeted part with leather banquettes, panelling and chandeliers, upper area with old wooden tables and chairs and some bucket seats on bare boards, interesting pictures/prints, well kept Navigation beers and a couple of guests, good reasonably priced food from breakfast on, friendly service, upstairs function/dining room; sports TV; seats outside, open all day from 9am. *(Jeff Grant)*

NOTTINGHAM SK5739

Fellows Morton & Clayton

(0115) 988 1957 *Canal Street (part of inner ring road); NG1 7EH* Flower-decked former canal warehouse under new management, but no major changes; up to eight well kept ales including Adnams, Black Sheep, Nottingham, Sharps and Timothy Taylors, four real ciders, enjoyable pubby food (not evenings Sun-Thurs), friendly uniformed staff, softly lit downstairs bar with alcove seating, wood floors and lots of exposed brickwork, pictures of old Nottingham, two raised areas and upstairs restaurant/function room; background music, sports TVs, free wi-fi; children and dogs welcome, tables outside, open all day (till 12.30am Fri, Sat). *(Dave Braisted, Dr J Barrie Jones)*

NOTTINGHAM SK5542

Fox & Crown (0115) 942 2002

Church Street/Lincoln Street, Old Basford; NG6 0GA Range of Shipstones beers from the Little Star brewery behind this tucked-away open-plan pub, also guest ales, continentals and good choice of wines, restaurant area serving reasonably priced authentic thai food (not Sun); events including Mon quiz, live music and card nights, sports TV, games machines, pool and darts; disabled access/loo, tables on revamped back terrace, open all day, till 1am Fri, Sat. *(David Hunt, Jeff Grant)*

NOTTINGHAM SK5642

Gladstone (0115) 912 9994

Loscoe Road, Carrington; NG5 2AW Welcoming mid-terrace backstreet local, half a dozen well kept ales such as Castle Rock, Fullers, Oakham and Timothy Taylors, good range of malt whiskies, comfortable lounge with collection of books, basic bar with old

We mention bottled beers and spirits only if there is something unusual about them – imported belgian real ales, say, or dozens of malt whiskies; so do please let us know about them in your reports.

sports memorabilia and darts, upstairs folk club Weds, quiz Thurs; background music, sports TV, free wi-fi; tables in small back garden among colourful tubs and hanging baskets, open all day weekends, closed weekday lunchtimes. *(David Hunt)*

NOTTINGHAM SK5640

Hand & Heart (0115) 958 2456

Derby Road; NG1 5BA Unexceptional exterior but unusual inside with bar and dining areas cut deep into back sandstone; a house beer from Dancing Duck, Maypole and guests, two real ciders and good wine and whisky choice, enjoyable fairly priced traditional food from sandwiches and snacks up, set lunch deal Mon-Sat, friendly helpful service, glassed-in upstairs room overlooking street; background and interesting live music Thurs; children welcome till 7pm if eating, dogs in bar, open all day (till midnight Fri, Sat), breakfasts from 8am. *(Jess and George Cowley)*

NOTTINGHAM SK5739

★Kean's Head (0115) 947 4052

St Marys Gate; NG1 1QA Cheery pub in attractive Lace Market area; fairly functional single room with big windows overlooking the street, simple wooden café furnishings on wood-strip floor, some exposed brickwork, red tiling and small fireplace, six real ales including Castle Rock, ten craft kegs, draught belgian beers and extensive bottled range, also 20 wines by the glass, over 60 malt whiskies and similar number of gins, teas/coffees, popular fairly traditional food (not Sun evening), friendly service; background music, daily papers and free wi-fi; children welcome till 7pm, church next door worth a look, open all day. *(Jeff Grant)*

NOTTINGHAM SK5539

King William IV (0115) 958 9864

Manvers Street/Eyre Street, Sneinton; NG2 4PB Victorian corner local with plenty of character (aka the King Billy); well kept Black Iris, Oakham and six guests from circular bar, also craft beers and real cider, good fresh cobs and sausage rolls, friendly staff; irish folk session Thurs, monthly quiz, silent sports TV, pool upstairs, free wi-fi; dogs welcome, seats on roof terrace, handy for cricket, football and rugby grounds, open all day (from 2pm Mon). *(Steve Garner)*

NOTTINGHAM SK5740

★Lincolnshire Poacher

(0115) 941 1584 *Mansfield Road; up hill from Victoria Centre; NG1 3FR* Impressive range of drinks at this popular down-to-earth pub (attracts younger evening crowd), 13 well kept ales including Castle Rock, lots of continental draught/bottled beers, half a dozen ciders and over 70 malt whiskies, shortish choice of reasonably priced uncomplicated food; big simple traditional front bar with wall settles, wooden tables and breweriana, plain but lively room on left and corridor to chatty panelled back snug with newspapers and board games, conservatory overlooking tables on large heated back area; live music Weds and Sun, free wi-fi; children (till 8pm) and dogs welcome, open all day (till midnight Thurs-Sat). *(David Hunt)*

NOTTINGHAM SK5541

★Lion (0115) 970 3506

Lower Mosley Street, New Basford; NG7 7FQ Around ten real ales (tasters available) including Bass and Castle Rock from one of the city's deepest cellars (glass viewing panel – can be visited at quiet times), also plenty of craft beers and proper ciders, good well priced burger/hot dog menu (all day weekends); big open-plan room with feel of separate areas, bare bricks and dark oak boards, old brewery pictures and posters, open fires; regular live music including popular Sun lunchtime jazz, Weds quiz; children welcome till 6pm, no dogs, disabled facilities, garden with terrace and smokers' shelter, open all day. *(Jeff Grant)*

NOTTINGHAM SK5739

Malt Cross (0115) 941 1048

St James's Street; NG1 6FG Former Victorian music hall with high vaulted glass roof and gallery overlooking bar area; ornate iron pillars, chesterfield sofas and button-back seating booths on bare boards, good selection of drinks including some interesting real ales, decent well priced food from shortish menu, teas/coffees and daily newspapers; regular live music on small stage, Mon quiz; cellars converted into art gallery and workshops, ancient caves (tours available); open all day (till 9pm Sun). *(Steve Garner)*

NOTTINGHAM SK5739

Newshouse (0115) 952 3061

Canal Street; NG1 7HB Friendly two-room 1950s Castle Rock pub with blue tiled exterior; their ales and half a dozen changing guests, belgian and czech imports, decent lunchtime food, mix of bare boards and carpet, local newspaper/radio memorabilia, beer bottles on shelves, darts, table skittles and bar billiards; background music, big-screen sports TV; a few tables out in front, walking distance from both football grounds (busy on match days), open all day. *(Jeff Grant)*

NOTTINGHAM SK6141

Old Volunteer (0115) 987 2299

Burton Road, Carlton; NG4 3DQ Imposing 19th-c community pub acting as tap for Flipside; five of their well kept ales and several guests, good range of whiskies, friendly helpful staff, some food including burgers; live music and beer festivals; dogs welcome, picnic-sets on side terrace, open all day. *(Jeff Grant, Steve Garner)*

NOTTINGHAM SK5739

Olde Salutation (0115) 947 6580
Hounds Gate/Maid Marian Way; NG1 7AA Low beams, flagstones, ochre walls and cosy corners including two small quiet rooms in ancient lower back part, plusher modern front lounge, up to eight real ales and good choice of draught/bottled ciders, quickly served food till 8pm (6pm Sun, not Mon), helpful friendly staff (ask them to show you the haunted caves below the pub); background music, weekend live bands/DJs upstairs; open all day (till 3am Fri, Sat). *(Steve Garner)*

NOTTINGHAM SK5739

★**Olde Trip to Jerusalem**
(0115) 947 3171 *Brewhouse Yard; from inner ring road follow 'The North, A6005 Long Eaton' signpost until in Castle Boulevard, then right into Castle Road; pub is on left; NG1 6AD* Unusual rambling pub seemingly clinging to sandstone rock face, largely 17th-c and a former brewhouse for the hilltop castle; downstairs bar carved into the stone with some rocky alcoves, dark panelling and simple built-in seats, tables on flagstones, Greene King IPA and Hardys & Hansons Olde Trip plus guests (tasting trays available), good value food all day, efficient staff dealing well with busy mix of customers; popular little tourist shop with panelled walls soaring into dark cavernous heights; children welcome, seats and ring the bull in snug courtyard, open all day (till midnight Fri, Sat). *(Richard Tilbrook, Jess and George Cowley)*

NOTTINGHAM SK5640

Organ Grinder (0115) 970 0630
Alfreton Road; NG7 3JE Tap for Blue Monkey with up to nine well kept ales including guests, a couple of ciders and a perry, good local pork pies, open-plan bare-boards interior with woodburner; sports TV; well behaved dogs welcome, seats out behind, open all day. *(Jeff Grant)*

NOTTINGHAM SK5739

Pitcher & Piano (0115) 958 6081
High Pavement; NG1 1HN Remarkable lofty-roofed conversion of 19th-c church; enjoyable all-day food including popular weekday lunch deal, good range of drinks from craft beers to cocktails; some live music; outside bar and terrace, open all day (till late Thurs-Sat). *(Jess and George Cowley)*

NOTTINGHAM SK5540

Plough (0115) 970 2615
St Peters Street, Radford; NG7 3EN Friendly 1930s local with own good value Nottingham ales brewed behind, also guest beers and traditional cider, two bars (one carpeted, the other with terrazzo flooring), banquettes, old tables and chairs, bottles on delft shelving, coal fires; Thurs quiz, TV, traditional games including outside skittle alley; dogs welcome, beer garden with covered smokers' area, open all day. *(Jeff Garner)*

NOTTINGHAM SK5344

Roebuck (0115) 979 3400
St James's Street (pedestrianised) off Old Market Square; NG1 6FH Light airy Wetherspoons conversion of 18th-c red-brick town house, high ceilings and some original features, extensive choice of well kept ales (tasting paddles available), ciders/perry and good wine choice, their usual reasonably priced food from toasties up, friendly staff, upper galleried area and enclosed roof terrace; muted TV; children welcome, disabled facilities, open all day from 8am. *(David Hunt)*

NOTTINGHAM SK5349

Station (0115) 963 2588
Station Terrace, Hucknall; NG15 7TQ Comfortably refurbished red-brick Victorian pub with four spacious rooms, fine range of well kept ales including four from Lincoln Green, also extensive choice of whiskies and gins, decent pubby food along with freshly made pizzas, friendly helpful staff; some live music; children and dogs welcome, simple bedrooms (shared bathroom), open all day, no food Sun evening. *(David Hunt)*

NOTTINGHAM SK5838

Trent Navigation (0115) 986 5658
Meadow Lane; NG2 3HS Welcoming tile-fronted Victorian pub close to canal and home to the Navigation Brewery; their beers and guests from half a dozen pumps along with ciders/perries, popular pubby food including daily deals; Sun quiz, regular live music, sports TVs (pub is next to Notts County FC); children welcome, brewery shop at back, open all day, food all day Thurs-Sun. *(Steve Garner)*

NOTTINGHAM SK5739

★**Vat & Fiddle** (0115) 985 0611
Queensbridge Road; alongside Sheriffs Way (near multi-storey car park); NG2 1NB Open-plan 1930s brick pub – tap for next-door Castle Rock Brewery; varnished pine tables, bentwood chairs and stools on parquet or terrazzo flooring, some brewery memorabilia and interesting photographs of demolished local pubs, up to 13 real ales, bottled continentals, traditional ciders and over 30 malt whiskies, decent pubby food (not Sun evening) including Tues curry night, modern dining extension, visitors' centre

Pubs close to motorway junctions are listed at the back of the book.

with own bar; some live music, free wi-fi; children and dogs welcome, picnic-sets out at front by road, open all day (till midnight Fri-Sat). *(Jeff Grant)*

RADCLIFFE ON TRENT SK6439

Horse Chestnut (0115) 933 1994
Main Road; NG12 2BE Smart pub with plenty of Victorian/Edwardian features; well kept Fullers, Oakham, St Austell and four guests, craft beers and decent wines by the glass, sensibly priced home-made food (not Sun evening) including some italian choices (good pizzas) and deal nights such as Tues curry and Thurs steak, friendly service, two-level main bar, parquet and mosaic floor, panelling, big mirrors and impressive lamps, handsome leather wall benches and period fireplaces; some live music; children and dogs welcome, disabled access, terrace seating, open all day. *(Chrissy Proctor)*

RAMPTON SK7978

Eyre Arms (01777) 248771
Main Street; DN22 0HR Shuttered red-brick village pub with enjoyable good value food from chef-owner including extensive specials menu and weekday lunchtime bargains, well kept changing ales, friendly helpful service, dining area overlooking pleasant garden, locals bar with pool; open all day. *(Tim Cranston)*

RUDDINGTON SK5733

Three Crowns (0115) 846 9613
Easthorpe Street; NG11 6LB Open-plan pub known locally as the Top House; well kept Fullers, Blue Monkey and three guests (beer festivals), very good indian food in back Three Spices evening restaurant; open all day weekends, closed lunchtimes Mon and Tues. *(Thomas Green)*

SCAFTWORTH SK6692

King William (01302) 710292
A631 Bawtry–Everton; DN10 6BL Popular red-brick country pub with friendly relaxed atmosphere; good well presented home-made food (best to book Sun lunch), Theakstons Best, a couple of regional guests and good choice of wines by the glass, bar, snug and two dining rooms with old high-backed settles, plain tables and chairs and log fires; background music; children and dogs welcome, seats on terrace and in big back garden running down to River Idle, swings, open all day, food till 7.30pm Sun. *(Mary Joyce)*

SELSTON SK4553

★**Horse & Jockey** (01773) 781012
Handy for M1 junctions 27/28; Church Lane; NG16 6FB Interesting pub on different levels dating from the 17th c; low heavy beams, dark flagstones, individual furnishings and good log fire in cast-iron range, friendly staff, Greene King Abbot and Timothy Taylors Landlord poured from the jug and up to four guests, real cider, no food, games area with darts and pool; folk night Weds, quiz Sun; dogs welcome, terrace and smokers' shelter, pleasant rolling countryside. *(Dawson Clay)*

SOUTHWELL SK7054

★**Final Whistle** (01636) 814953
Station Road; NG25 0ET Popular railway-themed pub commemorating the long defunct Southwell line; ten well kept ales including Brewsters and Salopian (beer festivals), real ciders/perries, foreign bottled beers and good range of wines, snacky food such as pork pies; traditional opened-up bar with tiled or wood floor, settles and armchairs in quieter carpeted room, corridor drinking area, two open fires, panelling, lots of railway memorabilia and other odds and ends; quiz and live music nights (folk club third Thurs of month); children (till 9pm) and dogs welcome, back garden with wonderful mock-up of 1920s platform complete with track and buffers, on Robin Hood Way and Southwell Trail, open all day. *(Patrick and Emma Stephenson)*

SOUTHWELL SK7053

Hearty Goodfellow (01636) 919176
Church Street (A612); NG25 0HQ Welcoming open-plan mock-Tudor pub; Everards Tiger and Sunchaser, guest beers, traditional ciders and good range of house wines, popular fairly straightforward food (not Sun evening) at reasonable prices, also takeaway fish and chips and pop-up fish/seafood restaurant (Sept-Mar) in converted outbuilding, cheerful young staff, lots of polished wood, beams and two brick fireplaces; background and some live music, sports TVs; children and dogs welcome, covered terrace and nice big tree-shaded garden beyond car park, play area, handy for Southwell Workhouse (NT) and Minster, open all day Fri-Sun. *(Michael Butler)*

STAUNTON IN THE VALE SK8043

Staunton Arms (01400) 281218
High Street, N of church on crossroads; NG13 9PE Attractive early 19th-c brick-built country inn; good well presented food from pub standards to more imaginative modern dishes, also lighter lunchtime choices and brunch from 10am Mon-Sat, Bass, Castle Rock and a guest, good range of wines and other drinks, efficient friendly service, L-shaped beamed bar with bare boards and open fire, steps up to dining area; free wi-fi; children and dogs welcome, rattan-style furniture on front terrace, eight good bedrooms, open (and food) all day. *(Michael and Lucy Archer)*

TUXFORD SK7471

Fountain (01777) 872854
Lincoln Road on edge of village near East Coast railway line; NG22 0JQ Comfortably updated family dining pub with

welcoming atmosphere; enjoyable affordably priced food (not Sun evening, Mon) from pub favourites and grills to daily specials, local ales and ciders such as Welbeck Abbey and Scrumpy Wasp, friendly service; free wi-fi; picnic-sets out in fenced area, open all day Fri-Sun, closed lunchtimes Mon and Tues. *(Mary Joyce)*

UPTON SK7354

★**Cross Keys** (01636) 813269
Main Street (A612); NG23 5SY 17th-c pub with rambling heavy-beamed bar, log fire in brick fireplace, own Mallard ales (brewed in Maythorne) and good home-made food from lunchtime sandwiches to specials, friendly staff, back extension; seats on decked terrace, handy for the Museum of Timekeeping (British Horological Institute), open all day Fri-Sun, closed lunchtimes Mon and Tues, no food Sun evening. *(Chrissy Proctor)*

WEST BRIDGFORD SK5838

Larwood & Voce (0115) 981 9960
Fox Road; NG2 6AJ Well run open-plan dining pub (part of the small Moleface group); good locally sourced home-made food in bar and restaurant area including some imaginative choices, plenty of wines by the glass, cocktail menu and three well kept ales, attentive cheerful staff; sports TV; children welcome away from bar, seats out on raised deck with heaters, on edge of the cricket ground and handy for Nottingham Forest FC, open all day, from 10am weekends for breakfast. *(David Hunt)*

WEST BRIDGFORD SK5938

Poppy & Pint (0115) 981 9995
Pierrepont Road; NG2 5DX Converted former British Legion Club backing on to bowling green and tennis courts; large bar with raised section and family area, around a dozen real ales including Castle Rock and a couple of ciders, decent food from breakfast on, friendly atmosphere; monthly folk night and other events, free wi-fi; dogs welcome in bar, open all day from 9.30am (10am Sun). *(David Hunt)*

WEST BRIDGFORD SK5837

★**Stratford Haven** (0115) 982 5981
Stratford Road, Trent Bridge; NG2 6BA Good traditional Castle Rock pub; bare-boards front bar leading to linked areas including airy skylit back part with relaxed local atmosphere, up to 14 well kept ales, interesting bottled beers, proper ciders and good wine and whisky choice, wide range of reasonably priced home-made food including themed nights, fast friendly service; Sun quiz, live music and regular beer events; children (during the day) and dogs welcome, tables outside, handy for cricket ground and Nottingham Forest FC (busy on match days), open (and food) all day. *(Dawson Clay)*

WEST STOCKWITH SK7994

White Hart (01427) 892672
Main Street; DN10 4EY Small country pub at junction of Chesterfield Canal and River Trent; own good Idle beers from next-door brewery plus guests, enjoyable well priced traditional food (not Sun evening) including blackboard specials and regular evening deals, friendly atmosphere; live music Fri, pool and sports TV; children and dogs welcome, garden overlooking the water, open all day. *(Geoffrey King)*

WYSALL SK6027

Plough (01509) 880339
Keyworth Road; off A60 at Costock, or A6006 at Wymeswold; NG12 5QQ Attractive 17th-c beamed village local; popular good value lunchtime food from shortish menu, cheerful staff, Bass, Greene King Abbot, Sharps Doom Bar, Timothy Taylors Landlord and three guests, rooms either side of bar with nice mix of furnishings, big log fire; Tues quiz, pool; children welcome, dogs after 2.30pm, french doors to pretty terrace, open all day. *(Matt and Hayley Jacob)*

Oxfordshire

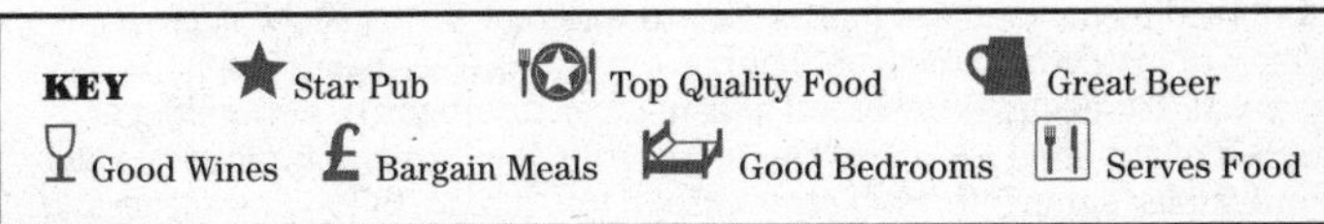

ASTHALL SP2811 Map 4

Maytime

(01993) 822068 – www.themaytime.com

Off A40 at W end of Witney bypass, then first left; OX18 4HW

17th-c former coaching inn with individually furnished bar and dining rooms, good food and seats outside; smart bedrooms

This is a lovely place on a warm day, with seats and tables under parasols on the back terrace and more in the extended garden overlooking the River Windrush; boules. Inside, the lofty, character bar has a lively atmosphere, exposed roof trusses, flagstones, leather sofas, cushioned wall seats and stools against the counter where friendly staff serve two quickly changing ales such as Bluestone Bedrock Blonde and Otter Bitter on handpump, 30 good wines by the glass from a fine list, over 100 gins and cocktails; background music and board games. Several white-painted beamed rooms lead off on different levels with cushioned window seats, a mix of tartan upholstered and traditional wooden chairs around tables of varying size on black slates or bare boards, and pictures on painted or stone walls; one room has a glass ceiling. The pub's springer is called Alfie. Our readers enjoy staying here in the stylish and well equipped bedrooms, and breakfasts are highly rated. Good walks from the door.

Rewarding food using local produce includes lunchtime sandwiches, ham hock terrine with scotch quail egg and piccalilli purée, salt and pepper squid with pickled red onion and wasabi mayonnaise, sharing boards, home-baked honey and mustard ham with free-range eggs, ricotta-filled arancini rice balls with courgette, chilli and pine nuts, buttermilk-fried chicken with potato salad, red cabbage slaw, jalapeno mayonnaise and hot sauce, seared tuna with borlotti and cannellini beans tossed with fennel, chilli and coriander with a lime and soy dressing, lamb rump with parmesan risotto, spinach, roasted shallots and wild mushrooms, and puddings such as lemon posset with white chocolate and lavender and tiramisu. *Benchmark main dish: wild boar burger with comté cheese, chilli jam, onion rings and skinny chips £14.00. Two-course evening meal £20.00.*

Free house ~ Licensee Dominic Wood ~ Real ale ~ Open 11-11 ~ Bar food 12-2.30 (3 Sun), 6-9.30 ~ Restaurant ~ Children welcome but not in bedrooms ~ Dogs allowed in bar ~ Wi-fi ~ Live music 3-5pm every other Sun in summer ~ Bedrooms: £85/£95 *Recommended by Tracey and Stephen Groves, M G Hart, Helene Grygar, Katharine Cowherd, John and Sharon Hancock, Guy Vowles, William and Sophia Renton*

It's very helpful if you let us know up-to-date food prices when you report on pubs.

BANBURY SP4540 Map 4

Olde Reindeer

(01295) 270972 – www.yeoldereindeer.co.uk

Parsons Street, off Market Place; OX16 5NA

Fine town pub with a friendly welcome, real ales and decent food

There's usually a cheerful crowd of regulars in this splendid old inn but the convivial landlord makes sure to welcome visitors too. There's plenty of history and the front bar has a good, easy-going atmosphere, heavy 16th-c beams, very broad polished oak floorboards, a magnificent carved overmantel for one of the two roaring log fires and traditional solid furnishings; some interesting breweriana too. It's worth looking at the handsomely proportioned Globe Room used by Oliver Cromwell as his base during the Civil War. Quite a sight, it still has some very fine 17th-c carved dark oak panelling. Attentive staff serve Hook Norton Hooky, Old Hooky, Hooky Mild and a couple of seasonal guest beers on handpump, three craft beers from Hook Norton, 12 wines by the glass, eight gins, fruit wines and several malt whiskies. The little back courtyard has tables and benches under parasols, aunt sally and pretty flowering baskets.

Fair value, honest food includes sandwiches, baked camembert with rosemary and garlic and red onion chutney, grilled sweet chilli halloumi skewers, ham and free-range eggs, mushroom and chickpea curry with onion bhaji and naan, scampi with chips, slow-cooked beef in barbecue and ale sauce with coleslaw and corn on the cob, 6oz rump steak with peppercorn sauce and chips, and puddings such as plum and apple crumble and custard and vanilla cheesecake with raspberry sorbet; Saturday is steak night (from 6pm). *Benchmark main dish: venison burger with toppings, coleslaw and chips £14.00. Two-course evening meal £18.00.*

Hook Norton ~ Tenant Anthony Murray ~ Real ale ~ Open 11-11; 11-midnight Fri, Sat; 12-10.30 Sun ~ Bar food 12-3, 6-9; 12-9 Fri, Sat; 12-6 Sun ~ Restaurant ~ Children welcome ~ Dogs welcome ~ Blues/jazz first Sun of month, live music last Sat of month

Recommended by Ian Herdman, Cliff and Monica Swan, Maria and Henry Lazenby, Camilla and Jose Ferrera, Charlie Stevens

BESSELS LEIGH SP4501 Map 4

Greyhound

(01865) 862110 – www.brunningandprice.co.uk/greyhound

A420 Faringdon–Botley; OX13 5PX

Cotswold-stone inn with rambling rooms, a fine range of real ales, lots of wines by the glass and enjoyable food

A handsome old pub that's strikingly well run, with a welcome for both diners and drinkers. The knocked-through rooms have plenty of character and interest: all manner of old photographs and pictures cover the half-panelled walls, individually chosen cushioned dining chairs, leather-topped stools and dark wooden tables are grouped on carpeting or rug-covered floorboards, and there are books on shelves, glass and stone bottles on windowsills, big gilt mirrors, three fireplaces (one housing a woodburning stove) and sizeable pot plants. Wooden bar stools line the counter where efficient, friendly staff serve Phoenix Brunning & Price Original and Timothy Taylors Landlord with guests such as Adnams Ghost Ship, Little Ox Goldilox, Loose Cannon Abington Bridge, Hook Norton Cotswold Pale and Vale Black Beauty Porter on handpump, 19 wines by the glass, around 70 gins, 30 rums and up to 70 malt whiskies; board games. By the back dining extension is a white picket fence-enclosed garden with picnic-sets under green parasols; the summer window boxes and hanging baskets are very pretty.

Bistro-style food includes sandwiches, a trio of smoked fish (salmon, trout and mackerel) with caper salad and horseradish crème fraîche, baked garlic and rosemary camembert with walnut and apple salad and chutney, vegetarian cottage pie with sweet potato mash, korean chicken thighs with kimchi salad and sriracha (hot chilli) sauce, steak and kidney pudding, venison and juniper meatballs with pasta and red wine sauce, smoked haddock fishcakes with tomato and spring onion salad, and puddings such as crème brûlée and hot waffle with caramelised banana, toffee sauce and vanilla ice-cream. *Benchmark main dish: slow-braised lamb shoulder with dauphinoise potatoes and rosemary gravy £17.95. Two-course evening meal £21.00.*

Brunning & Price ~ Manager Damien Mann ~ Real ale ~ Open 10am-11pm; 10-10 Sun ~ Bar food 12-9.30; 12-10 Fri, Sat; 12-9 Sun; coffee and pastries from 10am ~ Well behaved children welcome ~ Dogs allowed in bar ~ Wi-fi *Recommended by Emily and Toby Archer, Charles Fraser, Neil and Angela Huxter, Cliff and Monica Swan, Simon Day*

BRIGHTWELL BALDWIN SU6594 Map 4

Nelson

(01491) 612497 – www.thenelsonbrightwell.co.uk

Off B480 Chalgrove–Watlington, or B4009 Benson–Watlington; OX49 5NP

Attractive inn with several character bars, real ales, good wines by the glass and enjoyable well regarded food; bedrooms

To find this 300-year-old inn, just head for the church. As well as 18th-c gable ends and an attractive arched verandah, there's a bar with candles and fresh flowers, wine bottles on windowsills, horsebrasses on standing timbers, lots of paintings on white or red walls, wheelback and other dining chairs around assorted dark tables and a big brick inglenook fireplace. One cosy room has cushions on comfortable sofas, little lamps on dark furniture, ornate mirrors and portraits in gilt frames; background music. Rebellion IPA and a changing guest on handpump, 20 wines (including champagne) by the glass, a dozen malt whiskies and winter mulled wine. There are seats and tables on the back terrace and in the willow-draped garden.

Good food from a seasonally changing menu includes duck liver parfait with chilli jam, pigeon breast with smoked bacon, black pudding and red wine sauce, creamy risotto with leeks, kale and parmesan, steak burger with toppings, coleslaw and fries, rabbit casserole with wholegrain mustard sauce and mash, half a roast duck with orange sauce and greens, smoked haddock on colcannon topped with a poached egg, rack of lamb with rosemary and red wine sauce and dauphinoise potatoes, and puddings such as tipsy bread and butter pudding with cream and crêpe filled with banana and ice-cream and sticky toffee sauce. *Benchmark main dish: individual beef wellington with red wine jus and dauphinoise potatoes £24.00. Two-course evening meal £24.00.*

Free house ~ Licensees Roger and Carole Shippey ~ Real ale ~ Open 12-3, 6-11; 12-5 Sun ~ Bar food 12-2.15, 6-10; 12-4 Sun ~ Restaurant ~ Children welcome ~ Dogs allowed in bar ~ Wi-fi ~ Bedrooms: £75/£100 *Recommended by Caroline and Peter Bryant, Trish and Karl Soloman, Gerald and Brenda Culliford, Roy Hoing, Max and Steph Warren, Lenny and Ruth Walters*

BURFORD SP2512 Map 4

Highway

(01993) 823661 – www.thehighwayinn.co.uk

High Street (A361); OX18 4RG

Comfortable old inn with a good choice of wines, well liked bar food and seats outside; comfortable bedrooms

Customers drop in and out of this cheerful pub as it's usefully set at the centre of the village and open all day. There are all sorts of interesting touches in the bars, but the main feature is the pair of large windows overlooking the bustle of the pretty High Street; each consists of several dozen panes of old float glass and has a long cushioned window seat. Do notice the stag candlesticks for the rather close-set tables on well worn floorboards, the neat, modern, dark leather chairs, the nice old station clock above the big log fire in a pleasingly simple stone fireplace and the careful balance of ancient stripped stone with black and pale blue filigree wallpaper. A small corner counter has Hook Norton Hooky and Hooky Gold on handpump, 20 wines (including champagne) by the glass and 13 malt whiskies; they hold a beer festival and barbecue in the second week of June; background music and board games. On the right, a second bar room, with another big window seat, is carpeted but otherwise similar in style. A few picnic-sets stand above the pavement at the front and the high-walled courtyard garden has painted chairs and picnic-sets under parasols. The bedrooms are individually decorated in a country house style and breakfasts are good.

Interesting food includes lunchtime sandwiches and omelettes, ham hock and black pudding terrine with apple compote and balsamic onions, seared king scallops with pea purée and crispy prosciutto, moroccan-spiced nut roast with mint yoghurt, lemon sole with samphire and burnt citrus butter, duck breast with dauphinoise potatoes, braised chicory and port and redcurrant sauce, braised lamb shank with chorizo, butter bean and root vegetable cassoulet, and puddings such as Baileys pannacotta and lemon curd meringue roulade. *Benchmark main dish: beer-battered fish and chips £13.00. Two-course evening meal £23.00.*

Free house ~ Licensee Scott Williamson ~ Real ale ~ Open 12-11 (midnight Sat); 12-10.30 Sun ~ Bar food 12-3, 6-9.30; 12-4.30, 6-8.30 Sun ~ Restaurant ~ Children welcome ~ Dogs allowed in bar and bedrooms ~ Wi-fi ~ Bedrooms: £90/£130 *Recommended by Audrey and Paul Summers, Margo and Derek Peters, Caroline Prescott, Celia and Geoff Clay, Ivy and George Goodwill*

BURFORD SP2412 Map 4

Lamb

(01993) 823155 – www.cotswold-inns-hotels.co.uk/lamb

Village signposted off A40 W of Oxford; Sheep Street (B4425, off A361); OX18 4LR

Lovely 500-year-old inn with a bustling bar, real ales and an extensive wine list, interesting bar and restaurant food, and pretty gardens; bedrooms

A steady old place where the bars are always packed with cheerful customers. The atmosphere is one of old-fashioned dignity and character and the cosy bar has armchairs on rugs and flagstones in front of log fires, china plates on shelves, Hook Norton Hooky and Wickwar Cotswold Way on handpump, an extensive wine list with 17 by the glass and 26 malt whiskies. The roomy beamed main lounge is charmingly traditional with distinguished old chairs, oak tables, seats built into stone-mullioned windows, polished floorboards, fresh flowers and antiques and other fine decorations; background music in the restaurant. A pretty terrace with teak furniture leads down to neatly kept lawns surrounded by flowers, shrubs and small trees. The garden, enclosed by the warm stone of the surrounding buildings, is a real suntrap. They're kind to dogs and even have a special menu for them.

Impressive food includes sandwiches, vodka and beetroot-cured salmon with candied beetroot and horseradish, duck liver parfait with hazelnuts and red onion jam, butternut squash risotto with blue cheese and truffle oil, chicken caesar salad, burger with toppings and skinny chips, duck breast with braised red cabbage and confit leg croquettes, lamb rack with dauphinoise potatoes and crab apple jelly, grilled Torbay sole with brown shrimps, herb and lemon butter and fennel salad, and puddings such as earl grey sponge with blood orange sorbet and chocolate crumble and coffee, orange and hazelnut ganache with hazelnut ice-cream. *Benchmark main dish: sharing charcuterie or fish boards for two people £21.00. Two-course evening meal £21.00.*

Cotswold Inns & Hotels ~ Manager Jess Pawley ~ Real ale ~ Open 11-11 ~ Bar food 12-9 ~ Restaurant ~ Children welcome ~ Dogs allowed in bar and bedrooms ~ Wi-fi ~ Bedrooms: /£220 *Recommended by R K Phillips, M G Hart, Val and Malcolm Travers, Sarah Roberts, Peter and Jan Humphreys, Sandra and Michael Smith*

CHARLBURY SP3519 Map 4

Bull

(01608) 810689 – www.bullinn-charlbury.com

Sheep Street; OX7 3RR

Interesting refurbishment of handsome old inn, a civilised but informal atmosphere throughout, imaginative food and seats on terrace; lovely bedrooms

This is a stylishly refurbished 16th-c inn with an informal, relaxed atmosphere and a welcome for both locals and visitors. They've cleverly mixed original features with shabby-chic décor in both the bar and dining rooms: exposed stone and grey-painted panelled walls hung with colourful modern artwork, linen-cushioned seats with bright scatter cushions, painted wooden and upholstered dining chairs around simple tables on rugs or wooden floors and both a woodburning stove and an inglenook log fire. Fullers London Pride, Hook Norton Hooky and Wye Valley HPA on handpump from a bar made from an apothecary's chest painted peacock blue, plus good wines by the glass and 14 whiskies served by friendly, helpful staff; background music and daily papers. The attractive and sunny back terrace has a vine-covered pergola. Bedrooms are individually styled and comfortable, with four in a converted barn. This is sister pub to the Swan at Ascott under Wychwood (see Also Worth a Visit).

As well as breakfasts for non-residents (8-11am daily), the modern british food includes scallops with pea purée, charred cauliflower, pancetta and truffle oil, twice-baked goats cheese soufflé with beetroot purée, raspberries and hazelnuts, sharing boards, buffalo mozzarella, pea, mint, sugar snap, tomatoes, watercress and pumpkin salad with lemon dressing, a pie of the day, root vegetable rösti with a poached egg and chive hollandaise, a fish dish of the day, 21-day-aged 10oz rib-eye steak with béarnaise sauce and fries, and puddings such as chocolate and orange mousse with brownie, vanilla ice-cream and peanut brittle and crème brûlée with seasonal fruit. *Benchmark main dish: burger with toppings and fries £17.00. Two-course evening meal £23.00.*

Free house ~ Licensees Charlie and Willow Crossley ~ Real ale ~ Open 8am-11pm (midnight) ~ Bar food 12-9 (9.30 Sat) ~ Restaurant ~ Children welcome ~ Dogs welcome ~ Wi-fi ~ Bedrooms: /£100 *Recommended by Liz Bell, Rosie and Marcus Heatherley, Jennifer and Nicholas Thompson*

EAST HENDRED SU4588 Map 2

Eyston Arms

(01235) 833320 – www.eystonarms.co.uk

Village signposted off A417 E of Wantage; High Street; OX12 8JY

Attractive bar areas with low beams, flagstones, log fires and candles, imaginative food and courteous service

The hands-on landlord and his attentive staff here are genuinely welcoming and helpful. Although many customers come to enjoy the particularly good food, plenty of locals also pop in for a drink and a chat which keeps the atmosphere bustling and easy-going. There are seats at the bar and they keep a few tables free for drinkers keen to try the Hook Norton Hooky, Sharps Doom Bar and Wadworths 6X on handpump, ten wines by the glass, 14 gins and ten malt whiskies. Several separate-seeming candlelit areas have contemporary paintwork and modern country-style furnishings, low ceilings and beams, stripped timbers and the odd standing upright, nice tables and chairs on flagstones, some cushioned wall seats and an inglenook fireplace; background music and TV. Picnic-sets outside overlook the pretty lane and there are seats in the back courtyard garden.

Top class food includes lunchtime sandwiches, tom yum soup with thai crackers and pickled chillis, potted duck with foie gras butter and gooseberry jam, chargrilled miso chicken salad with roast cashews, crispy shallots, carrot, chinese cabbage, pickled pears, edamame beans and a hot and sour dressing, black bean burger with avocado, onion marmalade, blue cheese and string chips, king prawn spaghetti with cherry tomatoes, saffron, shellfish stock and crispy squid, chargrilled steaks with garlic butter or béarnaise sauce, and puddings such as rhubarb and pistachio millefeuille with vanilla-poached blueberries and sticky toffee pudding with cream. *Benchmark main dish: crispy duck lyonnaise with a duck egg and toulouse sausage £16.95. Two-course evening meal £21.00.*

Free house ~ Licensees George Dailey and Daisy Barton ~ Real ale ~ Open 11-11; 11-9 Sun ~ Bar food 12-2, 6-9; 12-3.30, 6-8 Sun ~ Restaurant ~ Well behaved children allowed at lunchtime ~ Dogs allowed in bar ~ Wi-fi *Recommended by Sandra and Michael Smith, Paul Farraday, Alistair Forsyth, Neil and Angela Huxter, Rob Anderson, Mark Hamill*

FILKINS SP2304 Map 4

Five Alls

(01367) 860875 – www.thefiveallsfilkins.co.uk

Signed off A361 Lechlade–Burford; GL7 3JQ

Thoughtfully refurbished inn with creative food, quite a range of drinks, a friendly welcome and seats outside; bedrooms

Popular locally, the beamed bar in this stone pub has a cosy area with three leather chesterfields grouped around a table by an open fire, an informal dining space with farmhouse chairs and cushioned pews around tables on bare boards and a nice little window seat for two. Stools line the bar where friendly staff serve a beer named for the pub (from Brakspears) plus Brakspears Oxford Gold, Otter Amber and Wychwood Dirty Tackle on handpump, 16 wines by the glass and six malt whiskies. Décor in the dining room includes some unusual postage-stamp wallpaper, an attractive mix of chairs and tables on rugs, floorboards and flagstones, plus chandeliers, church candles, fresh flowers and modern artwork on pale painted walls; background music and TV. The back terrace has chunky tables and chairs under parasols and there are a few picnic-sets at the front. Bedrooms are comfortable and attractively refurbished and make a good base for exploring the area. Sister pub is the Plough at Kelmscott.

The landlord cooks the interesting food, which includes sandwiches, sesame-seared tuna with asian slaw and hoisin salad, chicken liver and foie gras parfait with plum and apple chutney, beetroot, thyme, red onion, goats cheese and horseradish tart, salmon, prawn and mussel thai laksa with glass noodles, coriander, chilli and mangetout, chargrilled calves liver and bacon with bubble and squeak, beetroot relish and mint, chicken milanese with griddled vegetables and salsa verde, flat-iron steak with chimichurri and triple-cooked truffled wedges, and puddings such as Grand Marnier chocolate mousse and baked alaska. *Benchmark main dish: pork with white bean and sage cassoulet, caramelised apples and crackling £18.00. Two-course evening meal £19.00.*

Free house ~ Licensee Sebastian Snow ~ Real ale ~ Open 12-11; 12-9 Sun ~ Bar food 12-2.30, 6-9.30; 12-3 Sun ~ Restaurant ~ Children welcome ~ Dogs allowed in bar ~ Wi-fi ~ Jazz last Fri of month ~ Bedrooms: £95/£120 *Recommended by Bernard Stradling, Keith Perry, Nicholas and Maddy Trainer, P and J Shapley, Beverley and Andy Butcher, Liz and Mike Newton*

GORING SU5980 Map 2

Miller of Mansfield

(01491) 872829 – www.millerofmansfield.com

High Street; RG8 9AW

First class food and drink in handsome inn with easy-going bars and dining rooms; comfortable bedrooms

This is a handsome 18th-c former coaching inn with excellent food cooked by the chef-patron. But it's not a straightforward dining pub, it's a relaxed inn with a friendly atmosphere and a carefully chosen range of drinks. Décor in the beamed bars is simple and unfussy with armchairs around open fires or in bay windows, plain wooden tables, bare floorboards, exposed stone and brick walls and a few prints and gilt-edged mirrors. Sharps Cornish Coaster and West Berkshire Good Old Boy on handpump, ten wines by the glass from a thoughtful list and a large choice of gins, rums and malt whiskies; service is courteous and helpful. The dining rooms have antique-style or contemporary dining chairs on more boards; background music. The multi-level terraced garden has solid furniture under parasols among flowering tubs. The bedrooms are individually decorated and well equipped. Woodland walks are a few minutes' away.

Excellent food includes local fallow deer tartare with mushrooms, horseradish and sourdough crouton, cock crab fritter with sweetcorn, pickled seaweed and hot pepper mayonnaise, jerusalem artichoke gnocchi with apple chutney, crispy skins and cheese, poached cod with crab toast, braised chicory, golden beetroot and crab sauce, duck with cavolo nero, potato cake and orange and spiced duck sauce, lamb cannon with broad beans, sheeps yoghurt and burnt rosemary, and puddings such as rum-soaked sponge with peanut butter mousse and lime and banana ice-cream and chocolate mousse with cocoa nibs, aged balsamic vinegar and coffee ice-cream; they also offer afternoon tea. *Benchmark main dish: smoked rare-breed steak with beef-glazed carrots, roscoff onions and shallot red wine sauce £27.00. Two-course evening meal £30.00.*

Enterprise ~ Lease Mary and Nick Galer ~ Real ale ~ Open 11-11; 11-9 Sun ~ Bar food 12-2, 6-9; 12-2.30, 5-7 Sun ~ Restaurant ~ Children welcome ~ Dogs allowed in bar and bedrooms ~ Wi-fi ~ Bedrooms: £80/£120 *Recommended by Charles and Maddie Bishop, Ted and Mary Bates, Andrew and Ruth Simmonds, Alexandra and Tim Fledgling*

HEADINGTON SP5407 Map 4

Black Boy

(01865) 741137 – www.theblackboy.uk.com

Old High Street/St Andrews Road; off A420 at traffic lights opposite B4495; OX3 9HT

Enterprising dining pub with good, enjoyable food and useful summer garden

Our readers enjoy eating here and it's a stylish place with black leather seats on dark parquet, big mirrors, silvery patterned wallpaper, nightlights in fat opaque cylinders and glittering bottles behind the long bar counter. The feel is light and airy, particularly at the two tables in the big bay window; just to the side are lower, softer seats beside an open fire. Crisp white tablecloths and bold black and white wallpaper lend the area on the left a touch of formality. Everards Midland Red, Burton Bridge Stairway to Heaven and a changing guest on handpump, 20 wines by the glass, ten malt whiskies and several coffees and teas. Behind the building is an appealing terrace with picnic-sets under alternating black and white parasols on smart pale stone chippings, and a central seat encircling an ash tree. The four bedrooms are well equipped and up to date.

As well as breakfast (7.30-9.30am; 8.30-9.30am weekends), there are sandwiches (until 5.30) and tapas-style dishes plus rewarding choices such as crayfish and broad bean risotto with dill and parmesan, chicken skewers with peanuts, lime and chilli, vegetable thai green curry, spaghetti carbonara, a salad bowl with a choice of toppings, pizzas, sausages with thyme mash and beer onion jus, bavette steak with chimichurri and chips, and puddings such as dark chocolate brownie with mint ice-cream and vanilla pannacotta with blackcurrant coulis and honey ice-cream. *Benchmark main dish: burger with toppings and chips £11.95. Two-course evening meal £20.00.*

Greene King ~ Lease Abi Rose and Chris Bentham ~ Real ale ~ Open 12-11; 12-10.30 Sun ~ Bar food 12-2.45, 6-9.15 ~ Restaurant ~ Children welcome ~ Wi-fi ~ Bedrooms: /£125
Recommended by Ruby and Simon Swettenham, Bridget and Peter Gregson, Frank and Marcia Pelling, Lorna and Jack Musgrave, Jim King

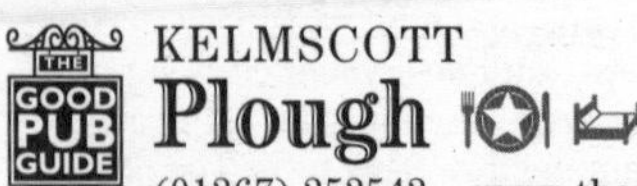

KELMSCOTT — SU2499 Map 4

Plough

(01367) 253543 – www.theploughinnkelmscott.com
NW of Faringdon, off B4449 between A417 and A4095; GL7 3HG

Lovely spot for tranquil pub with character bar and dining rooms, attractive furnishings and friendly owners; bedrooms

This is a lovely spot in a peaceful hamlet by the upper Thames and the pub is run by welcoming, hard-working licensees. The small, traditional, beamed front bar has ancient flagstones and stripped-stone walls along with a good log fire and the relaxed, chatty feel of a real village pub. Arkells Wiltshire Gold, Flying Monk Elmers and Sharps Doom Bar on handpump, good wines by the glass and maybe farm cider. The dining room has elegant wooden or painted dining chairs around all sorts of tables, striped and cushioned wall seats, cartoons on exposed stone walls, rugs on the floor and plants on the windowsills. Outside in the garden are seats and tables (some under cover). Bedrooms are comfortable and breakfasts good. The Oxfordshire Cycleway runs close by and the inn is handy for Kelmscott Manor (open Wednesdays and Saturdays April-October). This is sister pub to the Five Alls at Filkins.

Interesting food cooked by the landlord includes sandwiches, white dressed crab on toast with avocado, pigeon breast with plum, poached pear and toasted almonds, puy lentil hotpot with root vegetable mash, roasted partridge with savoy cabbage, sweet potatoes and cranberry sauce, hake fillet with saffron potato, spinach and crayfish sauce, slow-cooked crispy duck leg with sautéed potato, sprouts and rosemary sauce, calves liver with spinach, mash, crispy sage, shallot and port sauce, and puddings such as Baileys bread and butter pudding and apple and pear crumble with vanilla custard. *Benchmark main dish: pork tenderloin with spring greens, caramelised root vegetables and jus £18.50. Two-course evening meal £22.00.*

Free house ~ Licensee Sebastian Snow ~ Real ale ~ Open 12-11 (4-8 Mon); closed Mon lunchtime ~ Bar food 12-2.30, 6-9.30; 12-3, 6-10 Sat; 12-6 Sun; not Mon ~ Restaurant ~

Children welcome ~ Dogs allowed in bar ~ Wi-fi ~ Bedrooms: £80/£110 *Recommended by Sally and John Quinlan, Bernard Stradling, Dr Simon Barley, R K Phillips, Martine and Lawrence Sanders, Victoria and James Sargeant*

KINGHAM SP2624 Map 4

Plough

(01608) 658327 – www.thekinghamplough.co.uk

Village signposted off B4450 E of Bledington; or turn S off A436 at staggered crossroads a mile SW of A44 junction – or take signed Daylesford turn off A436 and keep on; The Green; OX7 6YD

Oxfordshire Dining Pub of the Year

Friendly dining pub combining an informal pub atmosphere with creative food; bedrooms

Lucky regulars to have this Cotswold-stone inn as their local. Of course, it's the delicious food cooked by Emily Watkins that customers are here for, but this remains a proper pub with cheerful staff and an informal feel. The little bar, looking over the village green, has an interesting choice of drinks, some nice old high-backed settles and brightly cushioned chapel chairs on broad dark boards, candles on stripped tables and cheerful farmyard animal and country prints; at one end is a big log fire, at the other a woodburning stove. A snug one-table area is opposite the servery where they keep Hook Norton Hooky and a guest such as Donnington On the Nose on handpump, ten wines by the glass including three sparkling ones, 14 malt whiskies, several gins and local cider; background music. The fairly spacious and raftered two-part dining room is up a few steps. The bedrooms are comfortable and pretty and the breakfasts very good.

Exceptional food cooked by the landlady includes sandwiches, cock crab with kohlrabi, apple and fennel, tartare of beef with pear, celeriac, hazelnuts and tarragon, ricotta dumplings with vegetables, wild garlic pesto and cheese, line-caught hake with cauliflower, garlic and brown shrimp butter, roast duck with leg pie, hispi cabbage, parsnip and garlic, hanger steak with bone marrow butter, onions and triple-cooked chips, and puddings such as chocolate mousse with blood orange sorbet and ginger pannacotta with poached rhubarb and rhubarb sorbet. *Benchmark main dish: venison wellington £24.00. Two-course evening meal £30.00.*

Free house ~ Licensees Emily Watkins and Miles Lampson ~ Real ale ~ Open 12-11 ~ Bar food 12-2.30, 6-9; 11.30-3 Sun ~ Children welcome ~ Dogs allowed in bar and bedrooms ~ Wi-fi ~ Bedrooms: £110/£145 *Recommended by Terry Davis, Professor James Burke, John and Claire Masters, Alun and Jennifer Evans, Neil and Angela Huxter, Audrey and Andrew Nichols, Jamie and Lizzie McEwan*

KIRTLINGTON SP4919 Map 4

Oxford Arms

(01869) 350208 – www.oxford-arms.co.uk

Troy Lane, junction with A4095 W of Bicester; OX5 3HA

Civilised and friendly stripped-stone pub with enjoyable food using local produce and good wine choice

Much enjoyed by our readers, this is an appealing stone-built pub in a lovely village. The long line of linked rooms is divided by a central stone hearth with a great circular stove, and by the servery itself – where you'll find Black Sheep Holy Grail and Hook Norton Hooky on handpump, an interesting range of 13 wines by the glass, eight malt whiskies, farm cider and organic soft drinks. Past the bar area with its cushioned wall pews, creaky beamed ceiling and age-darkened floor tiles, dining tables on parquet have neat high-backed chairs; beyond that, leather sofas cluster round a log fire at the end. Also, church candles, fresh flowers and plenty of stripped stone. A sheltered back terrace (upgraded in 2018) has teak tables under giant parasols with heaters, as well as white metal furniture and picnic-sets on neat gravel. The geranium-filled window boxes are pretty. Dogs must be kept on a lead. No children under 12.

Cooked by the chef-patron and using some produce from their organic kitchen garden, the enticing food includes natural smoked haddock and leek tart, bang bang chicken, saffron, broad bean and pea risotto, a charcuterie board (for two), grilled tuna steak on warm caponata, venison burger with triple-cooked chips, salmon and prawn fishcakes with sweet chilli sauce, confit duck leg with toulouse sausage and butter bean broth, and puddings such as rhubarb crème brûlée and cognac prunes with vanilla ice-cream; they also offer themed food evenings (see website). *Benchmark main dish: sea bass fillet with lemon oil and green beans £18.50. Two-course evening meal £25.00.*

Star Pubs & Bars ~ Lease Bryn Jones ~ Real ale ~ Open 12-3, 6-11; 12-4 Sun ~ Bar food 12-2, 6.30-8.45; 12-2.30 Sun ~ Restaurant ~ No children under 12 ~ Dogs welcome

Recommended by Dave Braisted, Anya Van Gulck, Louise and Oliver Redman, Camilla and Jose Ferrera, John and Lorna Chew, Tim and Mary Thomson

LETCOMBE REGIS — SU3886 Map 2

Greyhound

(01235) 771969 – www.thegreyhoundletcombe.co.uk

Main Street; OX12 9JL

Refurbished pub with original windows and fireplaces, plenty of eating and dining space and seats outside; bedrooms

We've been getting warm and enthusiastic reports on this lovely red-brick village pub, and we can see why. The welcome is genuine, the food is excellent and the light bedrooms are well equipped and up to date (dogs are allowed in two of them). The bar is just the place for a drink by the log fire, and simple furnishings include pubby chairs and plush stools around a mix of tables on wide floorboards, with more stools against the counter. There's four ales from breweries such as Butts, Dark Star, Little Ox, North Cotswold, Ramsbury and West Berkshire on handpump, 20 wines by the glass, seven gins and seven malt whiskies; background music, TV, darts and board games. The main dining room has lots of prints on pale walls, cushioned wooden dining chairs and settles with scatter cushions around solid tables and rugs on more bare boards; one red-walled room has similar furnishings on quarry tiles and a woodburning stove. At the back, picnic-sets sit under parasols on a grass area. There are good surrounding walks and the chalk horse at Uffington is nearby.

From a seasonal menu, the high quality food includes lunchtime sandwiches (not Sunday), truffled confit rabbit ravioli with celeriac, hazelnut and truffle pesto, twice-baked cheddar soufflé with smoked haddock chowder, cumin-roasted carrot, lentil and barley with shallots, orange, crispy sage and sour cream, steak burger with bacon jam, walnut slaw and chips, guinea fowl suprême with truffle-stuffed thigh, artichoke purée, king oyster mushrooms and port sauce, cod fillet with fricassée of leeks, salsify, samphire and mussels, and puddings such as chocolate fondant with salted caramel ice-cream and treacle tart with blood orange and whisky marmalade ice-cream. *Benchmark main dish: beer-battered fish and chips £13.00. Two-course evening meal £19.50.*

Free house ~ Licensee Catriona Galbraith ~ Real ale ~ Open 10am-11pm; 3.30-10 Mon; 10am-11.30pm Sat; 11-10 Sun; closed Mon lunchtime; 1 week Jan ~ Bar food 12-2.30, 6-9 (9.30 Fri, Sat); 12-3.30, 6-8.30 Sun ~ Children welcome ~ Dogs allowed in bar and bedrooms ~ Wi-fi ~ Live music some Sun afternoons ~ Bedrooms: £75/£90 *Recommended by Neil and Angela Huxter, Gail and Arthur Roberts, Sophie and James Collier, Martine and Colin Fresher*

MILTON UNDER WYCHWOOD SP2618 Map 4

Hare

(01993) 835763 – www.themiltonhare.co.uk

High Street; OX7 6LA

Renovated stone inn with linked bar and dining rooms, attractive contemporary furnishings, real ales, good food and seats in the garden

The refurbishments carried out here a couple of years ago were done with care and thought, and customers – both regulars and visitors – enjoy it very much. There's a bar and a couple of little drinking areas warmed by a woodburning stove, with various dining areas leading off: wooden floors, dark grey-painted or exposed-stone walls, painted beams, big gilt-edged mirrors and seating that includes stools, wooden or leather dining chairs, long button-back wall seats and cushioned settles around tables of every size – each set with a little glass oil lamp. Splashes of bright colour here and there brighten things considerably. Throughout you'll find all manner of hare paraphernalia, including photos, paintings, statues, a large glass case with stuffed boxing hares, motifs on scatter cushions and so forth. Stools line the counter, where friendly, well trained staff serve beers from Hook Norton and North Cotswold plus a local guest on handpump and good wines by the glass; on Fridays at 5pm it's champagne happy hour. The garden has tables, benches and chairs on a terrace and on a lawn.

First class fish and seafood fresh from Cornwall is the speciality here, but they also offer lunchtime sandwiches, potted duck with red onion and thyme chutney, ham hock and parsley scotch egg with mustard mayonnaise, chicken caesar salad, twice-baked goats cheese soufflé with roast sweet potato and beetroot and cheese sauce, minted lamb burger with feta, red cabbage slaw, tzatziki and skinny fries, chicken kiev with wild garlic butter, creamed leeks and sautéed parsley potatoes, and puddings such as glazed lemon tart with mascarpone cream and orange compote and espresso crème brûlée with vanilla doughnuts and cappuccino ice-cream. *Benchmark main dish: fresh fish specials £17.50. Two-course evening meal £22.00.*

Free house ~ Licensees Sue and Rachel Hawkins ~ Real ale ~ Open 12-3, 5.30-11; 12-11 Sat; 11-11 Sun ~ Bar food 12-2.30, 6-9 (9.30 Fri, Sat); 12-8 Sun; light snacks available 2.30-6 ~ Restaurant ~ Children welcome but over-12s only after 5pm ~ Dogs allowed in bar ~ Wi-fi *Recommended by Liz Bell, Barry Collett, Len and Lilly Dowson, Richard Tilbrook, Susan Eccleston, John and Delia Franks*

MINSTER LOVELL SP3211 Map 4

Old Swan & Minster Mill

(01993) 774441 – www.oldswanandminstermill.co.uk

Just N of B4047 Witney–Burford; OX29 0RN

Ancient inn with old-fashioned bar, real ales, a fine wine list, excellent food and acres of gardens and grounds; exceptional bedrooms

The beating heart of this rather lovely 15th-c building (more of a hotel and restaurant than a pub) remains the unchanging and tranquil little bar.

Here, you'll find stools at the wooden counter, Brakspears Oxford Gold and Wychwood Hobgoblin on handpump, good wines by the glass from a fine list, 30 malt whiskies and quite a choice of teas and coffees. Leading off are several attractive low-beamed rooms with big log fires in huge fireplaces, comfortable armchairs, sofas, dining chairs and antique tables, rugs on bare boards or ancient flagstones, antiques, prints, lots of horsebrasses, bed-warming pans, swords, hunting horns and even a suit of armour; also, fresh flowers and board games. Seats are dotted around the 65 acres of grounds (the white metal ones beside the water are much prized) and they have fishing rights to a mile of the River Windrush, as well as tennis courts, boules and croquet. The bedrooms have plenty of character, and some are positively luxurious.

Imaginative, seasonal food includes lunchtime sandwiches, air-dried ham with baked figs and marinated cottage cheese, chicken liver parfait with pickled vegetables, ham hock and eggs with triple-cooked chips, red onion marmalade and hollandaise, spiced baked aubergine with chickpea and pulse ragoût and confit cherry tomatoes, a pie of the day with smoked bacon and cabbage and chive potato purée, slow-roast pork belly with duck fat bubble and squeak, gilt-head bream with saffron new potatoes, brown shrimps and herb butter, sirloin steak with brandy cream sauce and chips, and puddings such as strawberry eton mess and peanut butter cheesecake; they also offer full afternoon tea (1-5pm). *Benchmark main dish: marinated pork tenderloin with apple and sage mash and stout-battered onion rings £18.50. Two-course evening meal £24.00.*

Free house ~ Licensee Oscar Garcia ~ Real ale ~ Open 10am-midnight ~ Bar food 12.30-9 ~ Restaurant ~ Children welcome ~ Dogs allowed in bar ~ Wi-fi ~ Bedrooms: £165/£175

Recommended by Guy Vowles, Gail and Frank Hackett, Patti and James Davidson, Rosie and Marcus Heatherley, Alison and Tony Livesley

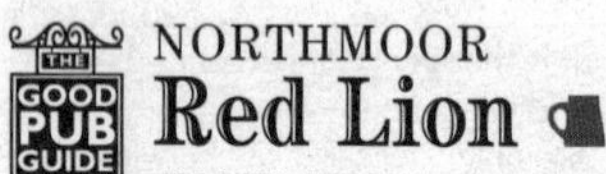

NORTHMOOR — SP4202 Map 4

Red Lion

(01865) 300301 – www.theredlionnorthmoor.com

B4449 SE of Stanton Harcourt; OX29 5SX

Community pub in pretty village with cheerful staff, good food and drink, and seats outside

---

The local community own this renovated 15th-c village pub and it's run by the convivial team of Ian and Lisa Neale. There's a cosy atmosphere with heavy beams and bare stone walls, built-in wall seats and painted chairs around scrubbed tables on bare boards, books on shelves, and an open fire at one end (with a piano beside it) and a woodburning stove at the other. Up to four real ales on handpump include Brakspears Bitter, Hop Kettle Liquid Highway, Loose Cannon Abingdon Bridge and maybe a guest from Two Cocks, and there are plenty of wines by the glass, all served by friendly young staff. At the front of the pub are a couple of picnic-sets, with more seats in the garden. Good nearby walks.

Cooked by the landlord using home-grown produce, the sensibly short choice of tasty food includes sandwiches, potted local trout, pork and chorizo terrine with chutney and pickles, gnocchi with beetroot purée and goats cheese, rare-breed burger with toppings and chunky chips, pork and sage sausages with onion gravy and risotto gravy, cider-roasted ham with free-range eggs and triple-cooked chips, brill fillet with sweetcorn purée, girolle mushrooms and pancetta, roast partridge with fondant potatoes and celeriac purée, and puddings such as crème brûlée and chocolate fondant with salt butter caramel, honeycomb ice-cream and chocolate sauce. *Benchmark main dish: beer-battered fish and chips £12.50. Two-course evening meal £20.00.*

Free house ~ Licensees Ian and Lisa Neale ~ Real ale ~ Open 11-3, 5.30-11; 11-11 Sat; 12-6 Sun; closed Sun evening, Mon ~ Bar food 12-2.30, 6-9.30; 12-3 Sun ~ Restaurant ~ Children welcome ~ Dogs allowed in bar ~ Wi-fi ~ Open mike nights (see website) *Recommended by Franklyn Roberts, Darrell Barton, Sam Cole, Charlie and Mark Todd, Martine and Colin Fresher*

OXFORD SP5106 Map 4

Bear

(01865) 728164 – www.bearoxford.co.uk

Alfred Street/Wheatsheaf Alley; OX1 4EH

Delightful pub with friendly staff, two cosy rooms, six real ales and well liked bar food

As the oldest drinking house in the city (and dating from 1242), this charming small backstreet local attracts a good mix of customers. The two small rooms are beamed, partly panelled and have a chatty, bustling atmosphere (in term time it's often packed with students), winter coal fires, thousands of vintage ties on the walls and up to six real ales from handpumps on the fine pewter bar counter: Fullers ESB, HSB, London Pride and Olivers Island and a changing guest. Staff are friendly and helpful; board games. There are seats under parasols in the large terraced back garden where summer barbecues are held.

Bar food includes sandwiches, seared tiger prawns with chilli, coriander and aioli, wild mushrooms on toast with tarragon cream sauce, moroccan-style vegetable and feta tagine with herb couscous, ham, egg and triple-cooked chips, beer-battered fish and chips, shepherd's pie, burgers with toppings and chips, and puddings such as chocolate brownie with vanilla ice-cream and sticky toffee pudding with toffee sauce and salted caramel ice-cream. *Benchmark main dish: pie of the day £13.50. Two-course evening meal £19.00.*

Fullers ~ Manager James Vernede ~ Real ale ~ Open 11-11 (midnight Fri, Sat); 11.30-10.30 Sun ~ Bar food 12-4, 5-9; 12-9 Fri, Sat; 12-6 Sun (barbecue 6-9 in summer) ~ Children welcome but no pushchairs inside ~ Dogs welcome ~ Wi-fi *Recommended by Charles Fraser, Paddy and Sian O'Leary, Richard Tilbrook, Revd R P Tickle, Nicola and Holly Lyons, Mary and Douglas McDowell*

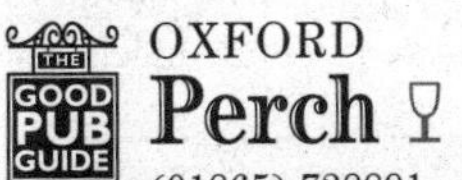

OXFORD SP4907 Map 4

Perch

(01865) 728891 – www.the-perch.co.uk

Binsey Lane, on right after river bridge leaving city on A420; OX2 0NG

A fine mix of customers for beautifully set inn with riverside gardens, local ales, popular food and friendly service

With helpful staff offering a genuinely warm welcome to thirsty students, muddy walkers and their dogs and those aiming for a good meal, this thatched 17th-c limestone pub is a special place. The heavily beamed bar has a huge, curved red leather chesterfield in front of a woodburning stove, a very high-backed settle, little stools around tables and fine old flagstones. Hook Norton Hooky and guests such as Prescott Hill Climb and XT Eight on handpump and plenty of wines by the glass; background music and board games. Leading off here are the dining areas with bare floorboards, scatter cushions on built-in wall seats, wheelbacks and other chairs around light tables, a second woodburner with logs piled to the ceiling next to it and a fine brass chandelier. They hold an annual beer and cider festival, outdoor film evenings in summer and a folk festival. A partly covered terrace has seats and tables, there are picnic-sets on the lawn (which runs down to the

Thames Path where there are moorings), a summer bar and an attractively furnished marquee. It's said that this might be one of the first places that Lewis Carroll gave public readings of *Alice in Wonderland*.

Good, enjoyable food includes duck croquette with carrot purée, beetroot relish and crispy fried kale, smoked mackerel pâté with pickled apple and celery, sharing boards, vegetable wellington with wild garlic pesto and cauliflower purée, burger with toppings and triple-cooked chips, free-range chicken, leek and ham pie, mussels in cider, lovage and cream, rare-breed pork belly with rosemary mash, apple purée and mustard jus, whole roast free-range chicken (to share) with smoked bacon, jersey royals and herb-buttered peas, and puddings such as dark chocolate and orange fondant with honeycomb and vanilla ice-cream and toffee, prune and walnut pudding with butterscotch sauce. ***Benchmark main dish: braised ox cheeks with cauliflower champ and braised cabbage £17.95. Two-course evening meal £23.00.***

Free house ~ Licensee Jon Ellse ~ Real ale ~ Open 10.30am-11pm; 10am-11pm Sun ~ Bar food 12-9.30 ~ Restaurant ~ Children welcome ~ Dogs allowed in bar

Recommended by Laura Moore, Melanie and David Lawson, Angela, Neil and Angela Huxter, Beth Aldridge, David and Charlotte Green, Susan and Callum Slade

OXFORD

Pint Shop

SP5106 Map 4

(01865) 251194 – www.pintshop.co.uk

George Street; OX1 2AU

Lively, cheerful bar-restaurant with a fine choice of drinks and hearty food

Like its sister place in Cambridge, this is great fun. Perhaps not somewhere for a quiet tête-à-tête, the atmosphere is busy and chatty with customers of all ages keen to enjoy the huge range of beers and robust food. There's a street-level bar and downstairs restaurant. Furnishings are simple: long cushioned wall seats and wooden chairs around plain wooden tables on parquet or bare boards, high stools around equally high tables, modern, industrial-style ceiling lamps and contemporary artwork on pale-painted walls. Leather-topped stools line the wood-planked counter where they serve Adnams Fat Sprat, Clouded Minds Simcoe and XT Thirteen on handpump, 16 wines by the glass, over 100 gins, and 50 malt whiskies; staff are efficient and helpful. The New Theatre is opposite.

All-day food includes sandwiches, hot bites such as duck tacos with plum sauce, crispy pork balls with brown sauce, and trout pancakes with horseradish cream plus english and vegetarian breakfasts, coal-baked flatbreads with pickled cabbage, mint yoghurt, chilli sauce and toppings such as lentil falafel with tahini sauce and dukkah and chopped chicken with spiced potato crisps, burgers with toppings and chips, beef massaman curry, cornflake fried chicken with slaw and chilli mayonnaise, smoked pork ribs with corn, potato salad and pickled red onions, and steaks with a choice of five sauces. ***Benchmark main dish: devilled lamb shoulder kebab £12.00. Two-course evening meal £25.00.***

Free house ~ Licensee Jack Etherington ~ Real ale ~ Open 11-11; 11am-midnight Fri, Sat ~ Bar food 12-10; 10am-10.30pm Fri; 11-10.30 Sat; 11-9 Sun ~ Restaurant ~ Children welcome ~ Dogs welcome ~ Wi-fi *Recommended by Susie and Spencer Gray, Barbara and Phil Bowie, Louise and Simon Peters*

Please let us know what you think of a pub's bedrooms: feedback@goodguides.com or (no stamp needed) The Good Pub Guide, FREEPOST RTXY–ZCBC–BBAZ, Stream Lane, Sedlescombe, Battle TN33 0PB.

OXFORD SP5005 Map 4

Punter

(01865) 248832 – www.thepunteroxford.com

South Street, Osney (off A420 Botley Road via Bridge Street); OX2 0BE

Easy-going atmosphere in bustling pub overlooking the water with plenty of character and enjoyable food

There's almost a boathouse feel to this Thames-side place that's run by an enthusiastic landlord and his friendly staff. The lower part has attractive rugs on flagstones and an open fire, while the upper room has more rugs on bare boards and a single big table surrounded by oil paintings (just right for a private group). Throughout are all manner of nice old dining chairs around an interesting mix of tables, art for sale on whitewashed walls and a rather fine stained-glass window. Greene King Morlands Original and Old Golden Hen and a changing guest beer on handpump from the tiled counter and several wines by the glass; board games.

As well as their £7 lunch special, the well regarded food includes spider crab and saffron croquettes with kohlrabi escabeche, baked camembert with plum chutney (to share), huevos rancheros (mexican-style baked eggs with a flour tortilla, guacamole and sour cream), fillet of sea bass and crayfish risotto with crispy leeks, slow-cooked wild boar and sausage casserole, calves liver, bacon and onions with mash and gravy, panko-crumbed fish and chips, and puddings. *Benchmark main dish: venison burger with toppings £13.00. Two-course evening meal £18.00.*

Greene King ~ Lease Tom Rainey ~ Real ale ~ Open 12-midnight; 12-11.30 Sun ~ Bar food 12-3, 6-10; 12-10 Sat; 12-9 Sun ~ Children welcome ~ Dogs welcome ~ Wi-fi

Recommended by Richard Tilbrook, Harvey Brown, Phoebe Peacock, John Harris, Diane Abbot, Amanda Shipley

OXFORD SP5107 Map 4

Rose & Crown

(01865) 510551 – www.roseandcrownoxford.com

North Parade Avenue; very narrow, so best to park in a nearby street; OX2 6LX

Lively friendly local with a fine choice of drinks and proper home cooking

What could be a fairly ordinary neighbourhood pub is given a great deal of atmosphere and individuality by its long-serving licensees who have now been here 35 years. The front door opens into a passage with a small counter and shelves of reference books for crossword buffs. This leads to two rooms: a cosy one at the front overlooking the street, and a panelled back room housing the main bar and traditional pub furnishings. A good mix of customers of all ages enjoy well kept Adnams Southwold, Hook Norton Old Hooky, Loddon Ferrymans Gold and Shotover Scholar on handpump, around 30 malt whiskies and 20 wines by the glass (including champagne and sparkling wine). The pleasant walled and heated back courtyard can be covered with a huge awning; at the far end is a 12-seater dining/meeting room. Please note, no dogs or children.

Fair value, honest food includes sandwiches and baguettes, potted shrimps and potted crab, dips with hot pitta bread, a choice of omelettes, niçoise or greek salads, english breakfast, very good chips with scampi, burger and four varieties of pie, locally sourced sirloin steak with garlic butter or peppercorn sauce, and puddings such as apple pie or a hot pudding. *Benchmark main dish: pint of sausages with chips £13.00. Two-course evening meal £17.00.*

Free house ~ Licensees Andrew, Debbie and Adam Hall ~ Real ale ~ Open 11-11; 11-2.30, 4.30-11 Aug, early Sept ~ Bar food 12-2.15 (3 Sun), 6-9 ~ Wi-fi ~ Live jazz Sun evening (check website) *Recommended by Nick Higgins, Gus Swan, Peter Brix, Toby Jones, Susan Eccleston*

RAMSDEN SP3515 Map 4

Royal Oak

(01993) 868213 – www.royaloakramsden.com

Village signposted off B4022 Witney–Charlbury; OX7 3AU

Busy pub with long-serving licensees, large helpings of varied food, carefully chosen wines and seats outside; bedrooms

Mr Oldham has been running this country inn for 33 years now and it's a favourite with our readers. The unpretentious bar rooms are relaxed and friendly with old settles and tables and old-fashioned pub fittings; open fires. Gales HSB, Loose Cannon Abingdon Bridge, Wye Valley Bitter and changing guests from Cotswold Lion and Ramsbury on handpump, 40 wines by the glass from a carefully chosen list and three farm ciders. Folding doors from the dining room give easy access to the back terrace, and there are some tables and chairs out in front. Bedrooms in the converted coach house and stable block are comfortable and the surrounding countryside is lovely. The village church is opposite.

Food is well liked and includes smoked duck and wheatberry with rocket and horseradish cream, devilled whitebait with tartare sauce, asian noodle salad topped with roasted cashews and chilli, lime and ginger dressing, pearl barley and vegetable risotto topped with rocket and shaved cheese, burger with toppings and fries, beer-battered cod with triple-cooked chips, half a roast chicken in lemon and garlic marinade with rosemary fries, sausages with spring onion mash, crispy onions and red wine jus, and puddings such as black forest eton mess and sticky toffee pudding with vanilla ice-cream. *Benchmark main dish: steak and kidney pudding £16.00. Two-course evening meal £22.00.*

Free house ~ Licensee Jon Oldham ~ Real ale ~ Open 11.30-3.30, 6.30-11; 11.30-11 Sat; 12-6 Sun ~ Bar food 12-2.30, 7-10 ~ Restaurant ~ Children welcome ~ Dogs allowed in bar ~ Wi-fi ~ Bedrooms: £65/£85 *Recommended by Keith Perry, Steve Whalley, Pieter and Janet Vrancken, Harvey Brown, DHV, Helene Grygar*

SHILTON SP2608 Map 4

Rose & Crown

(01993) 842280 – www.shiltonroseandcrown.com

Just off B4020 SE of Burford; OX18 4AB

Simple and appealing small pub with particularly good food, real ales and fine wines

There's always a good crowd of both regulars and visitors here, all keen to enjoy the tasty food and genuine welcome. It's a pretty little place and very much the focus of this lovely village. The chatty, bustling small front bar has an unassuming but civilised feel, low beams and timbers, exposed stone walls, a log fire in a big fireplace and half a dozen or so farmhouse chairs and tables on the red-tiled floor. There are usually a few locals at the planked counter where they serve Hook Norton Old Hooky, Loose Cannon Recoil and Youngs Bitter on handpump, along with ten wines by the glass, seven malt whiskies and farm cider. A second room, similar but bigger, is used mainly for eating, and has another fireplace. An attractive side garden has picnic-sets.

Cooked by the chef-patron, the rewarding food includes ciabatta sandwiches, pigeon terrine with gherkins, gravadlax with dill and mustard sauce, aubergine parmigiana with mozzarella, pressed lamb shoulder with greens, carrots and mash, smoked haddock, salmon and prawn fish pie, lambs liver and bacon, sirloin steak with garlic butter and chips, and puddings such as chocolate torte with salted caramel sauce and vanilla ice-cream and rhubarb and ginger steamed sponge. *Benchmark main dish: steak in ale pie £14.00. Two-course evening meal £20.50.*

Free house ~ Licensee Martin Coldicott ~ Real ale ~ Open 11.30-3, 6-10; 11.30-10.30 Sat; 12-9 Sun; closed Sun from 7pm, all Mon in Jan, Feb ~ Bar food 12-2 (2.45 weekends and bank holidays), 7-9 ~ Restaurant ~ Children welcome lunchtime only ~ Dogs allowed in bar ~ Wi-fi *Recommended by R K Phillips, Helene Grygar, Gwendoline and Ralph Mason, Sally and Brian Turner, Selwyn Jones*

SHIPLAKE SU7779 Map 2

Baskerville

(0118) 940 3332 – www.thebaskerville.com

Station Road, Lower Shiplake (off A4155 just S of Henley); RG9 3NY

Emphasis on imaginative food but a proper bar too, interesting sporting memorabilia and a pretty garden; cosy, comfortable bedrooms

The hands-on family work very hard at all aspects of this first-class pub, and it shows. As well as a gently civilised atmosphere, the bar has a few beams, leather tub chairs and dining chairs around pine tables on oak floors or patterned carpet, plush red banquettes by the windows and a couple of log fires in brick fireplaces. Flowers and large house plants are dotted about, and the pale walls are hung with a fair amount of signed rugby shirts and rowing memorabilia, oars, pictures and river maps (Henley is a 35-minute walk away via the Thames Path or a four-minute train journey); TV. Bar chairs line the light, modern counter where they keep Loddon Ferrymans Gold and Hoppit and Rebellion IPA and Smuggler on handpump, 13 wines by the glass from a thoughtfully chosen list, 40 malt whiskies and farm cider, all served by friendly, enthusiastic staff. They support WaterAid by charging 75p for a jug of iced water and at the time of writing have raised £9,200. The separate restaurant plays background music when it's quiet. The pretty garden has a covered barbecue area, teak furniture and picnic-sets under parasols. Bedrooms are well equipped and comfortable and the breakfasts are excellent. Wheelchair access using ramp; no disabled loos.

Interesting food from a thoughtful menu includes open sandwiches, king scallops with black pudding, crispy pancetta, pea purée and truffle oil, chicken liver parfait with red onion marmalade, aubergine lasagne, steak, mushroom and Guinness pie, 30-day dry-aged steak burger with toppings and french fries, coq au vin, lamb rack with couscous, spring roll and cured rhubarb, lemon sole with sautéed potatoes and romesco sauce, confit duck leg with boulangère potatoes and red wine jus, and puddings such as vanilla crème brûlée and profiteroles with chantilly cream and chocolate sauce. *Benchmark main dish: beer-battered fish and chips £14.50. Two-course evening meal £25.00.*

Free house ~ Licensee Allan Hannah ~ Real ale ~ Open 11-11; 12-10.30 Sun ~ Bar food 12-2.30, 6-9; 12-3 Sun; food times vary with the season so do check website ~ Restaurant ~ Children welcome but not in restaurant after 7pm Fri, Sat ~ Dogs allowed in bar and bedrooms ~ Wi-fi ~ Bedrooms: £100/£110 *Recommended by Holly and Tim Waite, Alison and Dan Richardson, John Pritchard, Matt and Hayley Jacob, Miranda and Jeff Davidson*

STANFORD IN THE VALE SU3393 Map 4

Horse & Jockey

(01367) 710302 – www.horseandjockey.org

A417 Faringdon–Wantage; Faringdon Road; SN7 8NN

Bustling, traditional village local with real character, highly regarded and fair value food and well chosen wines; bedrooms

This is a charming pub with plenty of chatty customers and since it's surrounded by racehorse-training country, the walls are hung with big Alfred Munnings racecourse prints, card collections of Grand National winners and other horse and jockey pictures. The convivial, hands-on licensees are warmly friendly to all. The place is split into two sections: a contemporary dining area and an older part with flagstones, wood flooring, low beams and raftered ceilings. There are old high-backed settles and leather armchairs, a woodburning stove in a big fireplace and an easy-going atmosphere. A beer named for the pub (from Greene King), Belhaven IPA and Ruddles Best on handpump, carefully chosen wines by the glass, 16 gins and a dozen malt whiskies; background music and board games. As well as tables under a heated courtyard canopy, there's a separate enclosed informal garden. Bedrooms, housed in another building, are quiet and comfortable.

Well liked food uses some home-grown produce and includes lunchtime sandwiches, home-smoked, landlord-caught trout pâté, garlic and rosemary camembert with red onion marmalade (for two), stone-baked pizzas, wild mushroom tagliatelle, ham and eggs, beer-battered haddock with chips, breadcrumbed chicken breasts with barbecue baked beans, coleslaw, cajun potato wedges and onion rings, 8oz sirloin steak with a choice of sauces, and puddings such as mango cheesecake with home-made passion-fruit ice-cream and a seasonal crumble with vanilla custard. *Benchmark main dish: 7oz steak burger with toppings and fries £11.95. Two-course evening meal £19.50.*

Greene King ~ Lease Charles and Anna Gaunt ~ Real ale ~ Open 11-3, 5-midnight; 11am-12.30am Sat; 12-11 Sun ~ Bar food 12-2.30, 6.30-9 (9.30 Fri, Sat) ~ Restaurant ~ Children welcome but not in bedrooms ~ Dogs allowed in bar ~ Wi-fi ~ Open mike first Weds of month ~ Bedrooms: £65/£80 *Recommended by Shona and Jimmy McDuff, R K Phillips, Gwendoline and Ralph Mason, Sally and Brian Turner*

STONESFIELD SP3917 Map 4

White Horse

(01993) 891063 – www.whitehorsestonesfield.com

Village signposted off B4437 Charlbury–Woodstock; Stonesfield Riding; OX29 8EA

Neatly kept little pub with a relaxed atmosphere and enjoyable food and beer

Weekends tend to be when this attractively upgraded small country pub is at its busiest, especially at lunchtime when walkers on the Oxfordshire Way long-distance footpath need refreshment. There's a friendly, uncluttered feel – just a few pieces of contemporary artwork on green and cream paintwork – and the cosy bar has a woodburning stove, country-style chairs and plush or leather stools around solid tables on bare boards, Little Ox Goldilox and XT Thirteen and Fifteen on handpump and six wines by the glass; background music. The dining room has similar but more elegant furnishings. Doors open on to a neat walled garden with picnic-sets and there are more seats in the courtyard. It's handy for the Roman Villa at nearby North Leigh (English Heritage), but do note the pub's restricted opening hours.

Food uses some home-grown produce and includes sandwiches, barbecue chicken goujons, creamy garlic mushrooms, a full english breakfast, burger with toppings and chips, nasi goreng with chicken or prawns, beer-battered fish and chips, gammon with eggs, 10oz sirloin steak with stilton or peppercorn sauce, and puddings such as rhubarb crumble and sticky toffee pudding; they hold a popular annual micro beer fest (see website) and regular summer barbecues. *Benchmark main dish: steak frites £13.95. Two-course evening meal £18.00.*

Free house ~ Licensee Marina Barnes ~ Real ale ~ Open 5-11 Tues-Fri; 12-3, 5-11 Fri; 12-3, 6-11 Sat; 12-3 Sun; closed Sun evening, Mon, lunchtimes Tues-Thurs ~ Bar food 6-9 Tues-Fri; 12-2, 6-9 Fri, Sat; 12-3 Sun ~ Restaurant ~ Children welcome ~ Dogs allowed in bar ~ Wi-fi *Recommended by Isobel Mackinlay, Edward May, Emma Scofield, Amanda Shipley, Gerry and Pam Pollard, Maggie and Matthew Lyons*

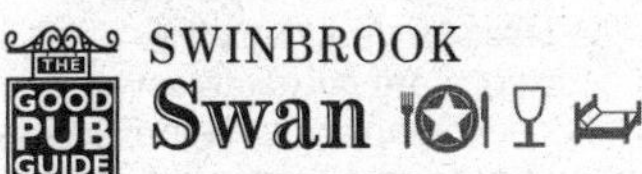

SWINBROOK SP2812 Map 4

Swan

(01993) 823339 – www.theswanswinbrook.co.uk

Back road a mile N of A40, 2 miles E of Burford; OX18 4DY

Smart old pub with handsome oak garden rooms, antiques-filled bars, local beers and contemporary food; bedrooms

The elegant, comfortable and warm bedrooms in this civilised, 400-year-old pub are in a smartly converted stone barn and five are beside the River Windrush. The little bar has simple antique furnishings, settles and benches, an open fire and (in an alcove) a stuffed swan; locals do drop in for a pint and a chat. As the inn is owned by the Devonshire Estate, there are plenty of interesting Mitford family photographs blown up on the walls. A small dining room leads off from the bar to the right of the entrance, and there are also two garden rooms with high-backed beige and green dining chairs around pale wood tables and views across the garden and orchard. Battledown Amber Ale, Butcombe Rare Breed and Hook Norton Hooky on handpump, nine wines by the glass, farm ciders and local draught lager; staff are first class. Background music, board games and TV. The outdoor seats and circular picnic-sets make the best of the position by a bridge over the river. The Kings Head in Bledington (Gloucestershire) is run by the same first class licensees.

Superb modern food includes lunchtime sandwiches, rabbit and pork terrine with piccalilli, prawns with cherry tomatoes, avocado purée, cashew nuts, crispy shallots, garlic and red chilli lime dressing, asparagus, butternut squash, leek, spinach, fig and goats cheese tart with sun-dried tomatoes, herb oil and pumpkin seeds, confit duck leg with roasted sweet potatoes, green beans, ginger, lime and sultanas, lemon sole with purple sprouting broccoli, jersey royals, anchovies and herb butter, rare-breed dry-aged sirloin steak with peppercorn sauce and triple-cooked chips, and puddings such as apple crumble with cinnamon ice-cream and chocolate fondant with salted caramel, honeycomb and pecan nuts and vanilla ice-cream. *Benchmark main dish: hake with fennel, broad beans, peas, samphire and white wine sauce £17.50. Two-course evening meal £23.00.*

Free house ~ Licensees Archie and Nicola Orr-Ewing ~ Real ale ~ Open 11-11 ~ Bar food 12-2, 6.30-9; 12-2, 6.30-9.30 Fri, Sat ~ Restaurant ~ Children welcome ~ Dogs allowed in bar ~ Wi-fi ~ Bedrooms: /£150 *Recommended by Julia and Fiona Barnes, Chloe and Tim Hodge, Guy Vowles, Neil and Angela Huxter, William and Sophia Renton, Moira and Jon Weller*

We mention bottled beers and spirits only if there is something unusual about them – imported belgian real ales, say, or dozens of malt whiskies; so do please let us know about them in your reports.

TADPOLE BRIDGE SP3200 Map 4

Trout

(01367) 870382 – www.trout-inn.co.uk

Back road Bampton–Buckland, 4 miles NE of Faringdon; SN7 8RF

Busy country inn with waterside gardens, civilised bar and dining rooms and a fine choice of drinks and food; bedrooms

In warm weather, the pretty garden by this 17th-c inn on the banks of the Thames really comes into its own; there are plenty of seats and tables under parasols and moorings for six boats. The smart bar has exposed stone walls, beams and standing timbers, a woodburning stove with logs neatly piled to one side, leather armchairs and stools, scatter cushions on window seats, a large stuffed trout and bare boards and flagstones. Upholstered stools line the blue-painted counter where courteous, friendly staff serve a beer named for the pub (from Ramsbury), Loose Cannon Abingdon Bridge, Marstons EPA and White Horse Village Idiot on handpump, 15 wines by the glass from a wide-ranging, carefully chosen list, 12 malt whiskies and two farm ciders. Dining rooms have green-and-brown-checked chairs around a mix of nice wooden tables, fresh flowers and candlelight; the pale wood or blue-painted tongue-and-groove walls are hung with trout and stag prints, oars and mirrors. Background music. Six bedrooms (three open on to a small courtyard and four are suitable for dogs) are attractive and comfortable.

Interesting food includes sandwiches, smoked chalk-stream trout with beetroot and avocado, black pudding hash with a poached duck egg, chorizo and peas, creamy polenta with mushrooms, goats cheese bonbons and spinach, old spot pork belly with celeriac rémoulade, cider tempura oyster and lovage, gilt-head bream with brown shrimp beurre noisette, confit leeks and tapenade, longhorn rump steak with stilton, roasted onions and chips, and puddings such as double chocolate and salted caramel tart with whipped whisky cream and candy pistachio and chilled coconut rice pudding with mango curd, pineapple compote and coconut ice-cream. *Benchmark main dish: beer-battered haddock and triple-cooked chips £14.50. Two-course evening meal £25.00.*

Free house ~ Licensee Simon Young ~ Real ale ~ Open 12-11; 12-10.30 Sun ~ Bar food 12-3, 6.30-9 (8.30 Sun) ~ Restaurant ~ Children welcome ~ Dogs allowed in bar and bedrooms ~ Wi-fi ~ Bedrooms: /£130 *Recommended by Mrs Zara Elliott, Chloe and Michael Swettenham, Ben and Jenny Settle, Colin McLachlan, Alan and Linda Blackmore, Max Simons*

WOLVERCOTE SP4809 Map 4

Jacobs Inn

(01865) 514333 – www.jacobs-inn.com

Godstow Road; OX2 8PG

Enjoyable pub with enthusiastic staff, simple furnishings, inventive cooking and seats in the garden

The slightly quirky décor and bustling and easy-going atmosphere here appeal to our readers. The simply furnished bar has leather armchairs and chesterfields, some plain tables and benches, wide floorboards, a small open fire and high chairs at the counter where they keep Banks's Sunbeam, Brakspears Bitter, Wells Bombardier and Wychwood Hobgoblin on handpump, 13 wines by the glass, a good choice of spirits and lots of teas and coffees; background music. You can eat at plain wooden tables in a grey panelled area with an open fire or in the smarter knocked-through dining room. This has standing timbers in the middle, a fire at each end and shiny, dark wooden chairs and tables on floorboards; there are standard lamps, stags' heads, a reel-to-reel tape recorder, quite a few mirrors and various deli items for sale. Several seating areas outside have good quality tables and chairs under parasols, picnic-sets on decking and deckchairs and more picnic-sets on grass. This is sister pub to the Woodstock Arms in Woodstock.

Interesting, hearty food using home-reared pigs, free-range eggs and other local produce includes crispy duck salad with honey and sesame dressing, pork rillette with pickled vegetables, smoked haddock and tarragon fishcakes with beurre blanc sauce, pearl barley and pumpkin salad with wild mushrooms, mint yoghurt and hazelnut oil, braised beef shortrib with horseradish mash, baby onions, bacon and bourguignon sauce, sea trout fillet with caper and pea purée, roast beetroot, samphire and lemon dressing, and puddings such as millionaire's cheesecake and spiced plum and apple crumble with vanilla ice-cream. *Benchmark main dish: chicken and bacon pie £14.50. Two-course evening meal £20.50.*

Marstons ~ Lease Damion Farah and Johnny Pugsley ~ Real ale ~ Open 9am-11pm ~ Bar food 9am-10pm ~ Restaurant ~ Children welcome ~ Dogs allowed in bar ~ Wi-fi
Recommended by Rosie and John Moore, Richard Tilbrook, Alison and Tony Livesley, Nicola and Holly Lyons

WOODSTOCK SP4416 Map 4

Woodstock Arms

(01993) 811251 – www.woodstockarms.co.uk
Market Street; OX20 1SX

Cheerful town pub with enjoyable food and drink, back courtyard and knowledgeable staff; bedrooms

Set in the Estate town to stunning Blenheim Palace, this is a pretty stone inn with three comfortable, contemporary and compact bedrooms upstairs and plenty of welcoming space for drinking and dining downstairs. The bar has a few leather winged chairs, wooden tables and chairs on patterned floor tiles or large rugs, hops on beams, bare stone walls, a log fire beneath a large copper hood and high chairs by the green-painted counter. A beer named for the pub, Greene King IPA and Old Speckled Hen and a guest such as Black Sheep on handpump and good wines by the glass, served by cheerful staff. The hop-strung, dark beamed dining room has chunky tables and dark wooden chairs on parquet flooring, scatter cushions or animal hides on wall seating and a woodburning stove. It's all very easy-going and friendly. The back courtyard has rustic benches and chairs and tables on flagstones, and there are a few seats out in front too. This is sister pub to the Jacobs Inn at Wolvercote.

As well as breakfasts (7.30am-noon; 8-11.30am Sat; 8-11am Sun), good food from a thoughtful menu includes sandwiches (until 4pm), smoked haddock scotch egg with mayonnaise, chicken terrine with chutney, pork and leek sausages with creamy mash, gammon with egg and pineapple, beer-battered haddock and chips, venison chilli, barnsley chops with sautéed potatoes and sauce vierge, lobster and crayfish spaghetti with clams and shellfish sauce, and puddings such as eton mess cheesecake and sticky toffee pudding with ice-cream. *Benchmark main dish: chicken and bacon pie £14.50. Two-course evening meal £20.00.*

Greene King ~ Lease Damion Farah and Johnny Pugsley ~ Real ale ~ Open 8am-11pm ~ Bar food 8am-10pm ~ Restaurant ~ Children welcome ~ Dogs allowed in bar ~ Wi-fi ~ Bedrooms: /£100 *Recommended by Louise and Anton Parsons, Katherine and Hugh Markham, Paul Dunleavy, Robin and Anne Triggs, John Pritchard*

The star-on-a-plate award, , distinguishes pubs where the food is of exceptional quality. The knife-and-fork symbol just means the pub serves food.

WOOTTON SP4320 Map 4

Killingworth Castle

(01993) 811401 – www.thekillingworthcastle.com

Glympton Road; B4027 N of Woodstock; OX20 1EJ

Handsome 17th-c stone inn with simply furnished bar and dining rooms, own-brews and good wines, highly regarded food and pretty back garden; lovely bedrooms

You'll find a good range of drinks in this striking, three-storey coaching inn from their own-brewed Yubberton Goldie, Yawnie and Yubby ales on handpump and guests such as North Cotswold Windrush Ale and Stroud Budding to local cider, a thoughtful wine list and a good range of gin and whisky. The bare-boards bar has a woodburning stove at one end, benches and wall seats around wooden tables and plush-topped stools at the counter; staff are friendly. The simply furnished and candlelit dining rooms have built-in wall seats plus chapel and other chairs around rustic tables on more floorboards and there's an open log fire. As well as seats out in front of the inn, there's a back garden with picnic-sets under parasols. Boutique-style bedrooms, some on the ground floor, some on the first, are well equipped and most appealing. This is sister pub to the Ebrington Arms in Ebrington (Gloucestershire).

From a seasonal menu and using local produce, the pleasing food includes grilled mackerel with seaweed linguine and salsa verde, rosemary and garlic pork belly with apple, sage and watercress, beer-battered haddock and chips, glazed ham with a duck egg and pineapple, curried cauliflower, spinach and sautéed potatoes with sultanas and almonds, chicken breast and thigh with sweet potato and swede hash and tarragon sauce, langoustine broth with mussels, gurnard and ling, crab fritters, saffron potatoes and roast fennel, and puddings such as chocolate and Guinness sponge with brown sugar custard and caramelised white chocolate with rhubarb and basil. *Benchmark main dish: pie of the day £15.00. Two-course evening meal £21.00.*

Free house ~ Licensees Claire and Jim Alexander ~ Real ale ~ Open 9am-11pm ~ Bar food 12-2, 6-9; 12-3.30, 6-9.30 Sat; 12-3.30, 6-8.30 Sun ~ Restaurant ~ Children welcome ~ Dogs allowed in bar ~ Wi-fi ~ Bedrooms: /£120 *Recommended by Paul Scofield, Scott and Charlotte Havers, Christine and Tony Garrett, Peter and Alison Steadman, William and Sophia Renton*

Also Worth a Visit in Oxfordshire

Besides the fully inspected pubs, you might like to try these pubs that have been recommended to us and described by readers. Do tell us what you think of them: feedback@goodguides.com

ABINGDON SU4997

Brewery Tap (01235) 521655
Ock Street; OX14 5BZ Former tap for defunct Morland Brewery but still serving Original along with changing guests (autumn beer festival), proper ciders and good choice of wines, enjoyable well priced food (not Sun evening) from bar snacks to popular Sun roasts, stone floors and panelled walls, two log fires; background and weekend live music, darts, free wi-fi; children and dogs welcome, enclosed courtyard where aunt sally is played, three bedrooms, open all day (till 1am Fri, Sat). *(Susie and Spencer Gray)*

ADDERBURY SP4735

★**Red Lion** (01295) 810269
The Green; off A4260 S of Banbury; OX17 3NG Attractive 17th-c stone coaching inn with good choice of enjoyable well priced food (all day weekends) including deals, helpful friendly staff, Greene King ales and decent range of wines, linked bar rooms with high stripped beams, panelling and stonework, big inglenook log fire, old books and Victorian/ Edwardian pictures, more modern restaurant extension; background music, games area; children and dogs welcome, picnic-sets out on roadside terrace, 13 character bedrooms, good breakfast, open (and food) all day. *(Terry Davis)*

ALVESCOT SP2704

Plough (01993) 842281
B4020 Carterton–Clanfield, SW of Witney; OX18 2PU Popular brightened-up stone-built village pub; Wadworths ales and enjoyable food from sandwiches and pub standards up including good home-made pies, some choices available in smaller servings, friendly helpful staff; children and dogs (in bar) welcome, back terrace and garden with play area, open (and food) all day. *(R K Phillips)*

ARDINGTON SU4388

Boars Head (01235) 835466
Signed off A417 Didcot–Wantage; OX12 8QA Modernised 17th-c timber-framed pub with good value popular food from daily changing menu (more evening choice), friendly attentive staff, well kept ales including Loose Cannon, Fullers London Pride and one badged for them, low beams and log fires; background music (maybe live piano); children and dogs (in one area) welcome, terrace seating, peaceful attractive village. *(Keith Perry)*

ARDLEY SP5427

Fox & Hounds (01869) 346883
B430 (old A43), just SW of M40 junction 10; OX27 7PE Roadside pub dating from the early 19th c with later additions; long opened-up low-beamed dining lounge with big fireplace at each end, enjoyable home-made food from lunchtime snacks to daily specials, two changing ales and good wine choice, helpful friendly staff, another open fire in cosy carpeted bar; sports TV; children welcome, no dogs inside, attractive beer garden, bedrooms, open all day Sat. *(Darrell Barton)*

ASCOTT UNDER WYCHWOOD **SP2918**

Swan (01993) 832332
Shipton Road; OX7 6AY Renovated 16th-c coaching inn under same ownership as the Bull at Charlbury (see Main Entries); stylish interior with blue panelling, wood floors, limed beams and shuttered windows, easy chairs by inglenook, Hook Norton ales plus a beer named for the pub, well chosen wines and good range of spirits, enjoyable food from pub standards up including various sharing plates, restaurant with seagrass flooring, striking wallpaper and woodburner; children and dogs welcome, back courtyard garden, handy for Oxfordshire Way and Wychwood Way, eight individually styled bedrooms (two in outbuilding), closed Mon and Tues in winter, otherwise open all day. *(Liz Bell)*

ASHBURY SU2685

Rose & Crown (01793) 710222
B4507/B4000; High Street; SN6 8NA Friendly 16th-c coaching inn with roomy open-plan beamed bar; three well kept Arkells beers and decent range of wines by the glass, generously served good food from 'grazing platters' and pub favourites to specials, polished woodwork, traditional pictures, chesterfields and pews, a raised section with oak tables and chairs, separate restaurant and games room (table tennis, pool and darts); background and occasional live music, quiz nights, sports TV; children and dogs welcome, disabled facilities, tables out at front and in garden behind, lovely view down pretty village street of thatched cottages, handy for Ridgeway walks, eight bedrooms, closed Mon lunchtime. *(R K Phillips)*

ASTON TIRROLD SU5586

Sweet Olive (01235) 851272
Aka Chequers; Fullers Road; village signed off A417 Streatley–Wantage; OX11 9EN Newish owners for this rustic dining pub; main room with wall settles, mate's chairs and sturdy tables on quarry tiles or slate floor, small brick fireplace, well liked food from pub favourites to more pricey restaurant dishes, Sharps Doom Bar and West Berkshire Mr Chubbs, nice wines by the glass, friendly service; background music; children and dogs (in bar area) welcome, tables in small cottagey garden, closed Sun evening. *(Gail and Arthur Roberts)*

BANBURY SP4540

Three Pigeons (01295) 275220
Southam Road; OX16 2ED Renovated 17th-c coaching inn (handy for town centre) with several small rooms surrounding bar; beams, flagstones, bare boards and gas woodburners (no logs because of part-thatched roof), good friendly atmosphere, well prepared food (all day weekends) from sandwiches to restaurant dishes, also set menu, three changing ales, decent selection of wines by the glass and over 30 malt whiskies; children welcome, tables under parasols on paved terrace, well equipped up-to-date bedrooms, useful but limited parking, open all day. *(Charlie and Mark Todd)*

BECKLEY SP5611

★**Abingdon Arms** (01865) 655667
Signed off B4027; High Street; OX3 9UU Old community-owned dining pub in lovely unspoilt village; sympathetically refurbished beamed rooms including pitched-roof dining area, country furniture on bare boards, open fires, four regional ales such as Shotover and XT, over a dozen wines by the glass and good range of gins, well regarded food from shortish but varied menu, friendly accommodating service; background and some live music, quiz first Weds of month; children and dogs welcome, big garden dropping away from decked terraces, superb views over RSPB Otmoor reserve and good walks, closed Mon, otherwise open all day (till 9pm Sun). *(Sam Cole)*

BEGBROKE SP4713

Royal Sun (01865) 374718

A44 Oxford–Woodstock; OX5 1RZ Welcoming old stone-built pub with modernised bare-boards interior; good choice of enjoyable food from lunchtime sandwiches and pub favourites up, well kept Hook Norton, a guest, beer and several wines by the glass, good friendly service; may be background music, free wi-fi; children welcome, no dogs inside, tables on terrace and in small garden, open all day Fri and Sat, till 6pm Sun. *(Louise and Simon Peters)*

BICESTER SP5822

Jacobs Plough (01869) 388101

North Street; OX26 6NB Stone-built village pub with open-plan bar and dining rooms; leather chesterfields by open fire (woodburner as well), button-back wall seating, painted and wooden dining chairs around simple tables on bare boards and flagstones, antlers and various stuffed animals, Greene King, Hook Norton and Timothy Taylors, good choice of wines by the glass and wide range of spirits, enjoyable food including popular roasts, grills and weekday set lunch, friendly helpful staff; seats outside in courtyard; comfortable cosy bedrooms, open (and food) all day. *(Cliff and Monica Swan)*

BLEWBURY SU5385

Red Lion (01235) 850403

Nottingham Fee – narrow turning N from A417; OX11 9PQ Attractive red-brick downland village pub dating from the early 17th c; emphasis on owner-chef's highly regarded food from interesting varied menu including set lunch and daily specials, well kept Brakspears and good choice of wines from brick-faced counter, efficient service, dark beams, quarry-tiled floor and big log fire, separate dining area; free wi-fi; children and dogs (in bar) welcome, wheelchair access, peaceful enclosed back garden, three bedrooms, good breakfast, closed Sun evening and Tues, otherwise open all day. *(Alan and Linda Blackmore)*

BRIGHTWELL SU5890

Red Lion (01491) 837373

Signed off A4130 2 miles W of Wallingford; OX10 0RT Busy but welcoming 16th-c thatched village pub; four or five well kept ales such as Loddon and West Berkshire, decent wines and enjoyable good value home-made food including popular pies, friendly efficient staff, two-part bar with snug seating by log fire, dining extension to the right; live music Sun, quiz last Mon of the month, free wi-fi; children and dogs welcome, tables out at front and in back garden, open (and food) all day weekends. *(Mike Kavaney, John Pritchard)*

BRITWELL SALOME SU6793

Red Lion (01491) 613140

B4009 Watlington–Benson; OX49 5LG Brick and flint pub with freshly modernised bar and dining room in pastel greys, assorted tables and chairs on wood or carpeted floors, open fires, ales such as West Berkshire and XT, real cider and good choice of wines by the glass, well liked food from short but varied menu, friendly efficient service; children welcome, seats in courtyard garden, closed Sun evening, no food Mon, Tues. *(Max Simon)*

BROUGHTON SP4238

★**Saye & Sele Arms** (01295) 263348

B4035 SW of Banbury; OX15 5ED Attractive old stone house, part of the Broughton Estate (castle just five minutes away); sizeable bar with polished flagstones, cushioned window seats and dark wooden furnishings, Sharps Doom Bar, a couple of guest beers and nine wines by the glass, good food cooked by landlord including Weds steak night (free pudding), friendly service, two carpeted dining rooms with exposed stone walls, open fires, over 240 ornate water jugs hanging from beams; monthly quiz; children welcome, no dogs inside, picnic-sets and hanging baskets on terrace, neat lawn with tables under parasols, pergola and smokers' shelter, aunt sally, closed Sun evening. *(Paul Scofield)*

BUCKLAND SU3497

★**Lamb** (01367) 870484

Off A420 NE of Faringdon; SN7 8QN Well run 18th-c stone-built dining pub in lovely Estate village; highly praised interesting food cooked by chef-owner, can eat in low-beamed bar with log fire or restaurant, a couple of changing local ales and good choice of wines by the glass, also local gin and vodka, friendly helpful staff; well behaved children and dogs welcome, seats in courtyard and pleasant tree-shaded garden, good walks (close to Thames Path), three comfortable well equipped bedrooms, closed Sun evening, Mon. *(Keith Perry)*

BUCKNELL SP5525

Trigger Pond (01869) 252817

Handy for M40 junction 10; Bicester Road; OX27 7NE Cotswold-stone beamed pub opposite pond; small bar with dining areas either side, inglenook woodburner, conservatory, Wadworths ales and good choice of enjoyable food from sandwiches, pizzas and pub favourites up, helpful cheery

We include some hotels with a good bar that offers facilities comparable to those of a pub.

staff, lots of humorous signs and notices; children and dogs welcome, tables out on colourful terraces, steps up to back lawn with more picnic-sets, closed Mon, otherwise open all day (till 7pm Sun). *(Philippa Ward)*

BURFORD SP2512

Angel (01993) 822714

Witney Street; OX18 4SN Long heavy-beamed dining pub in interesting 16th-c building, warmly welcoming with roaring log fire, good popular food from sandwiches and pub favourites up, Hook Norton ales and well chosen wines; Aug beer festival, TV; children and dogs welcome, large secluded garden, three comfortable bedrooms, open (and food) all day. *(Max and Steph Warren)*

BURFORD SP2512

Mermaid (01993) 822193

High Street; OX18 4QF Handsome 16th-c beamed dining pub with flagstones, stripped stone and good log fire, enjoyable food (all day weekends) at sensible prices including gluten-free menu, friendly service, well kept Greene King ales and a guest, bay window seating at front, further airy back dining room and upstairs restaurant, afternoon cream teas; background music (live Fri); children and dogs welcome, tables out at front and in courtyard behind, open all day. *(Robert Lester, M J Winterton)*

CAULCOTT SP5024

★**Horse & Groom** (01869) 343257

Lower Heyford Road (B4030); OX25 4ND Pretty 16th-c roadside thatched cottage; L-shaped red-carpeted room with log fire in big inglenook (brassware under its long bressumer), plush-cushioned settles, chairs and stools around a few dark tables at low-ceilinged bar end, Black Sheep and a couple of guests (July beer festival), decent house wines, popular food (not Sun evening, booking essential) cooked by french owner-chef, also O'Hagans sausage menu, dining room at far end with jugs hanging on black joists, decorative plates, watercolours and original drawings, small side sun lounge; shove-ha'penny and board games; well behaved over-5s welcome, awkward for disabled customers (some steps and no car park), picnic-sets in nice little front garden, closed Mon. *(Richard Heath)*

CHADLINGTON SP3222

Tite (01608) 676910

Off A361 S of Chipping Norton; Mill End; OX7 3NY Friendly 17th-c country pub; bar with eating areas either side, beams and stripped stone, pubby furniture including spindleback chairs and settles, flagstones and bare boards, woodburner in large fireplace, well kept Sharps Doom Bar and a couple of guests, Weston's cider and a dozen wines by the glass, enjoyable fairly traditional home-cooked food (not Sun evening), good service; occasional live music, winter quiz nights; well behaved children and dogs welcome, lovely shrub-filled garden with split-level terrace, good walks nearby, open all day. *(Bernard Stradling, Keith Perry)*

CHALGROVE SU6397

Red Lion (01865) 890625

High Street (B480 Watlington–Stadhampton); OX44 7SS Attractive beamed village pub owned by local church trust since 1637; good variety of freshly made food (not Sun evening) from sandwiches to blackboard specials, popular pudding evening second Tues of the month, well kept Butcombe, Fullers, Rebellion and two guests, friendly helpful staff, quarry-tiled bar with big open fire, separate carpeted restaurant; children and dogs welcome, nice gardens (front one borders stream), public car park across the road, open all day Sun (and Sat if busy). *(David Lamb)*

CHARLTON-ON-OTMOOR SP5615

Crown (01865) 331850

Signed off B4027 in Islip; High Street, opposite church; OX5 2UQ Refurbished 17th-c village local with welcoming relaxed atmosphere in bar and separate restaurant, well kept Brakspears and a guest, decent wines and popular often interesting food from landlord-chef including pub favourites and pizzas; darts; children and dogs welcome, open all day Sat, till 7pm Sun, closed Mon and till 4pm Tues-Fri. *(William and Sophie Renton)*

CHARNEY BASSETT SU3794

Chequers (01235) 868642

Chapel Lane off Main Street; OX12 0EX Welcoming 18th-c village-green pub with spacious modernised interior, Marstons-related ales and enjoyable fairly priced food from lunchtime sandwiches/baguettes to steaks (booking advised), log fire; free wi-fi; children and dogs (in bar) welcome, picnic-sets in small garden, three bedrooms. *(Charlie Stevens)*

CHAZEY HEATH SU6979

Packhorse (0118) 9722140

Off A4074 Reading–Wallingford by B4526; RG4 7UG Attractive 17th-c beamed village dining pub skilfully enlarged and modernised (part of Home Counties group); good choice of food from sandwiches and light dishes up, Loddon, West Berkshire and three guests, plenty of wines by the glass and some interesting gins, friendly staff, polished tables on wood and rug floors, built-in leatherette banquettes, shelves of books and lots of framed pictures, big log fire in raised hearth; background music; children and dogs (in main bar) welcome, disabled facilities, parasol-shaded tables in back garden with play area, handy for Mapledurham house and watermill, open (and food) all day. *(Darren and Jane Staniforth)*

CHECKENDON SU6684

★**Black Horse** (01491) 680418
Village signed off A4074 Reading–Wallingford; RG8 0TE Charmingly old-fashioned country tavern (run by the same family since the 1900s) tucked into woodland away from the main village; relaxing and unchanging series of rooms, back one with West Berkshire and Rebellion tapped from the cask, one with bar counter has tent pegs above the fireplace (they used to be made here), there's also a homely side lounge and another room beyond that, some snacky food such as baguettes and pickled eggs; no credit cards; children allowed but must be well behaved, dogs outside only, seats on verandah and in garden, popular with walkers and cyclists, closed Sun evening in winter and may shut early if quiet. *(Amanda Shipley)*

CHIPPING NORTON SP3127

Blue Boar (01608) 643108
High Street/Goddards Lane; OX7 5NP Spacious refurbished former coaching inn (first licensed in 1683); four well kept Youngs ales and popular well priced food, friendly helpful staff, woodburner in big stone fireplace, raftered back restaurant and airy flagstoned garden room; background and weekend live music, Weds quiz, darts, sports TV, free wi-fi; children and dogs welcome, open (and food) all day. *(Liz and Mike Newton)*

CHIPPING NORTON SP3127

Chequers (01608) 644717
Goddards Lane; OX7 5NP Bustling traditional town pub (recent change of management and some refurbishment planned); three softly lit beamed rooms, no frills but comfortable and full of character, flagstones, low ochre ceilings and log fire, up to eight mainly Fullers ales, 15 wines by the glass and enjoyable food (not Sun evening) from shortish menu, friendly staff, airy conservatory restaurant behind; TV, free wi-fi; children and dogs (in bar) welcome, theatre next door, open all day. *(Beverley and Andy Butcher)*

CHISELHAMPTON SU5998

Coach & Horses (01865) 890255
B480 Oxford–Watlington, opposite B4015 to Abingdon; OX44 7UX Extended 16th-c coaching inn with two homely and civilised beamed bars; big log fire, sizeable restaurant with polished oak tables and wall banquettes, good choice of popular reasonably priced food (not Sun evening), friendly obliging service, three well kept ales usually including Hook Norton; background music; neat terraced gardens overlooking fields by River Thame, some tables out in front, nine bedrooms in courtyard block, closed 3.30-7pm Sun, otherwise open all day. *(Roy Hoing)*

CHOLSEY SU5886

Red Lion (01491) 651295
Cholsey–Wallingford road; OX10 9LG Old village pub under consortium of three local families; decent choice of enjoyable food (not Sun evening, Mon) including burgers and pizzas, friendly helpful staff, Brakspears, guest ales and good range of gins; children and dogs welcome, picnic-sets out at front behind picket fence, more tables in back garden, open all day weekends, closed Mon lunchtime. *(Jeremy Charnaud)*

CHRISTMAS COMMON SU7193

Fox & Hounds (01491) 612599
Off B480/B481; OX49 5HL Old Chilterns pub in lovely countryside; spacious front barn restaurant serving enjoyable home-made food from open kitchen, Brakspears, a guest beer and decent wines in two cosy beamed bar rooms, simply but comfortably furnished with bow windows, red and black floor tiles and big inglenook, snug little back room too; board games; children, walkers and dogs (in bar) welcome, rustic benches and tables outside, open all day (till 7pm Sun). *(Rosie and John Moore)*

CHURCH ENSTONE SP3725

★**Crown** (01608) 677262
Mill Lane; from A44 take B4030 turn-off at Enstone; OX7 4NN Popular 17th-c beamed country pub (for sale so may be changes); pleasant bar with straightforward furniture, old local photographs on stone walls and log fire in large fireplace, well kept Hook Norton and guests, good fairly priced food cooked by landlord from pub favourites up, friendly service, carpeted dining room with red walls, slate-floored conservatory; children welcome, dogs in bar, white metal furniture on front terrace overlooking lane, picnic-sets in sheltered back garden, closed Sun evening. *(Hunter and Christine Wright, Barry Collett, Helene Grygar)*

CHURCH HANBOROUGH SP4212

Hand & Shears (01993) 881392
Opposite church; signed off A4095 at Long Hanborough, or off A40 at Eynsham roundabout; OX29 8AB Cotswold-stone village pub with opened-up interior on different levels; L-shaped bare-boards bar, exposed stonework, some rustic half-panelling and a couple of cushioned window seats, sofa by log fire, two Wells ales and a guest from stone-faced counter, steps down to spacious part-raftered dining area divided by balustrades, enjoyable fairly pubby food, attentive friendly service; children welcome. *(Keith Perry)*

We say if we know a pub allows dogs.

CHURCHILL SP2824

★**Chequers** (01608) 659393
Church Road; B4450 Chipping Norton to Stow-on-the-Wold (and village signed off A361 Chipping Norton–Burford); OX7 6NJ Golden-stone pub in pretty village opposite impressive church; relaxed bare-boards bar with mix of seating around nice old tables, some exposed stonework and inglenook log fire, stag's head over counter serving six real ales such as Butcombe, Hook Norton and Wye Valley, real cider, plenty of wines by the glass (several champagnes) and a dozen malt whiskies, good interesting food including some pub favourites, large high-raftered back extension with big lantern lights and long button-back leather banquettes, more dining space upstairs; background music, darts, free wi-fi; children and dogs welcome, wheelchair access, flagstoned back terrace, open all day. *(Liz Bell, Richard Tilbrook, Brian Glozier, Guy Vowles, Frances and Hamish Porter, P and J Shapley)*

CLANFIELD SP2802

Clanfield Tavern (01367) 810117
Bampton Road (A4095 S of Witney); OX18 2RG Pleasantly extended 17th-c stone pub (former coaching inn) adjacent to the Plough; opened-up beamed interior keeping feel of separate areas, mostly carpeted with mix of pubby furniture including some old settles (built-in one by log fire), smallish bar with comfortable seating and woodburner in snug flagstoned area, Marstons-related ales and enjoyable sensibly priced food including some specials, cheerful friendly service, more contemporary dining conservatory; background music, quiz last Weds of month, free wi-fi; children welcome, dogs in bar, picnic-sets on small flower-bordered lawn looking across to village green, closed Mon, otherwise open all day. *(R K Phillips)*

CLANFIELD SP2802

★**Plough** (01367) 810222
Bourton Road; OX18 2RB Substantial old stone inn with lovely Elizabethan façade, civilised atmosphere and plenty of character, log fires in comfortable beamed lounge bar, various dining areas, good food, particularly fish and seasonal game, well kept Hook Norton Hooky and a guest, over two dozen wines by the glass and more than 180 gins (can organise tasting sessions), friendly attentive service; children and dogs welcome, attractive gardens with teak tables on sunny front terrace, 12 bedrooms, open all day. *(R K Phillips, Ian Phillips)*

CLIFTON SP4931

Duke of Clifton (01869) 226334
B4031 Deddington–Aynho; OX15 0PE Attractively refurbished thatch and stone pub; low beams and flagstones, log fire in vast fireplace, enjoyable food (not Mon) including good value set lunch and daily specials, well kept Hook Norton and guests, friendly helpful service; children and dogs welcome, nice back garden, ten-minute walk from canal, five comfortable bedrooms and on-site camping, closed Mon lunchtime, otherwise open all day. *(Toby Jones)*

COLESHILL SU2393

Radnor Arms (01793) 861575
B4019; village signposted from Faringdon and Highworth; SN6 7PR Pub and village owned by NT; small quarry-tiled bar with cushioned settle, upholstered carver chairs and woodburner, more seating in back alcove, steps down to main dining area, once a blacksmith's forge with lofty beamed ceiling, log fire and some old tools on the walls, Old Forge ales brewed on site (tasters offered), proper ciders and enjoyable well priced home-made food including specials, friendly staff; children, walkers and dogs welcome, picnic-sets on narrow side terrace, garden beyond car park with some unusual tree-trunk furniture, play area, open all day. *(Keith Perry)*

CRAWLEY SP3412

Lamb (01993) 708792
Steep Hill; just NW of Witney; OX29 9TW 18th-c stone-built dining pub under new management; polished boards and lovely inglenook log fire, Brakspears and Wychwood ales, various dining areas with cushioned settles, high-backed chairs and built-in wall seats, exposed stone walls throughout; live music; dogs welcome in bar, views from tables on back terrace and lawn, pretty village, good walks (on Palladian Way). *(Bernard Stradling)*

CROWELL SU7499

Shepherds Crook (01844) 355266
B4009, 2 miles from M40 junction 6; OX39 4RR Welcoming old village pub with good varied choice of freshly made food (not Sun evening) including daily specials, up to six real ales such as Adnams, Rebellion, St Austell and Timothy Taylors, extensive wine list (ten by the glass) and 30 or so whiskies, beamed bar with stripped brick and flagstones, woodburner, high-raftered dining area; monthly live music; children and dogs welcome, tables out on front terrace and small green, nice walks, open all day in summer. *(Susie and Spencer Gray)*

CROWMARSH GIFFORD SU6189

Queens Head (01491) 839857
The Street (A4130); OX10 8ER Ancient village pub with four well kept Fullers/Gales beers and good selection of wines, enjoyable food from fairly compact menu plus some blackboard specials, good friendly service, oak-beamed bar and medieval dining hall; children and dogs welcome (their rhodesian ridgeback is called Treacle), tables in large garden, open all day, food all day weekends. *(John Pritchard)*

CUDDESDON SP5902

Bat & Ball (01865) 874379

S of Wheatley; High Street; OX44 9HJ Old coaching inn with low beams (mostly painted), flagstones and wood floors, exposed stone/brickwork and lots of cricketing memorabilia, three well kept Marstons-related ales, decent wines and cocktails, enjoyable pubby food from ciabattas and panini up including weekday set lunch, helpful friendly young staff, tables laid for dining throughout (feels more pubby at the front); background music; children and dogs (in bar area) welcome, sunny back terrace, seven bedrooms (some quite small), open all day. *(Richard Kennell, David Smith)*

CUMNOR SP4503

Bear & Ragged Staff (01865) 862329 *Signed from A420; Appleton Road; OX2 9QH* Extensive pub-restaurant dating from the 16th c and recently refurbished by Peach; contemporary décor in linked rooms with wood or flagstone floors, painted beams, exposed stonework and log fires, well liked food (something available all day) including good value set lunch, five real ales such as Greene King, Hook Norton and Purity, 15 wines by the glass, cocktails, airy garden room; background music, free wi-fi; children and dogs (in bar) welcome, tables on sunny terrace, nine bedrooms (four in converted cottages), open all day from 7am, (7.30am weekends) for breakfast. *(Charlie and Mark Todd)*

CURBRIDGE SP3208

Lord Kitchener (01993) 772613

Lew Road (A4095 towards Bampton); OX29 7PD Modernised and extended roadside pub with wide range of food including gluten-free choices and signature pies, many dishes available in smaller helpings, Greene King Old Speckled Hen and a beer badged for the pub, several wines by the glass, good friendly service; live music Sat; children and dogs welcome, wheelchair access, closed Sun evening, Mon. *(R K Phillips)*

CUXHAM SU6695

Half Moon (01491) 612165

4 miles from M40 junction 6; S on B4009, then right on B480 at Watlington; OX49 5NF 16th-c thatched and beamed pub in sleepy village surrounded by fine countryside; sensibly priced italian-leaning food including popular pizzas, Rebellion IPA and Smuggler and several wines by the glass, good italian coffee, friendly accommodating staff; free wi-fi; children and dogs welcome, nice garden behind, open (and food) all day. *(Paul Scofield)*

DENCHWORTH SU3891

Fox (01235) 868258

Off A338 or A417 N of Wantage; Hyde Road; OX12 0DX Comfortable 17th-c thatched and beamed pub in pretty village; good sensibly priced food from extensive menu including Sun carvery (best to book) and OAP lunchtime deal Mon-Thurs, friendly efficient staff, a couple of well kept changing ales and good choice of reasonably priced wines, plush seats in low-ceilinged connecting areas, two log fires, old prints and paintings, airy dining extension; children and dogs welcome, tables under umbrellas in pleasant sheltered garden with heated terrace, play area and aunt sally. *(Liz and Mike Newton)*

DORCHESTER-ON-THAMES SU5794

Fleur de Lys (01865) 340502

Just off A4074 Maidenhead–Oxford; High Street; OX10 7HH Traditional 16th-c coaching inn opposite abbey; knocked-through split-level bar/dining area with open fire and woodburner, plain wooden tables and some interesting old photographs of the pub, fairly limited lunchtime food but more evening choice including good restauranty set menu, two or three changing ales, friendly efficient service; children (away from bar) and dogs welcome, picnic-sets on front terrace, more in back garden with play area and aunt sally, five bedrooms, closed Sun evening, Mon lunchtime (no food Mon evening); for sale, so could be changes. *(Bridget Barker, Sally and John Quinlan, John Pritchard)*

DORCHESTER-ON-THAMES SU5794

George (01865) 340404

Just off A4074 Maidenhead–Oxford; High Street; OX10 7HH Handsome 15th-c timbered hotel in lovely village (both used for TV's *Midsomer Murders*); inglenook log fire in comfortably furnished beamed bar, good choice of enjoyable well presented food from baguettes up, three or four real ales such as Brakspears, Butcombe and Wadworths, cheerful efficient uniformed staff, high-raftered restaurant; background music; children welcome, 17 bedrooms, open all day. *(John Saville)*

DUCKLINGTON SP3507

Bell (01993) 700341

Off A415, a mile SE of Witney; Standlake Road; OX29 7UP Pretty thatched and beamed village local; good value home-made food including Sun carvery, Greene King ales, friendly service, big stripped-stone bar with scrubbed tables on flagstones, log fires and glass-covered well, old local photographs

If you know a pub is ever open all day, please tell us.

and farm tools, hatch-served public bar and roomy restaurant; background music, sports TV, pool, free wi-fi; children welcome, seats outside and play area, five bedrooms, open all day (till 9.30pm Sun), no food Sun evening. *(Darrell Barton)*

DUNS TEW SP4528

White Horse (01869) 340272
Off A4260 N of Kidlington; OX25 6JS 16th-c beamed pub in attractive village; stripped brick and stonework, rugs on flagstones or wood floors, oak timbers and panelling, inglenook woodburners, three well kept ales including Greene King, over a dozen wines by the glass and enjoyable food from shortish menu, two dining rooms; children and dogs welcome, disabled access, teak tables on paved terrace, bedrooms in former stables, open all day. *(Cliff and Monica Swan)*

EATON SP4403

Eight Bells (01865) 862261
Signed off B4017 SW of Oxford; OX13 5PR Popular old low-beamed pub with welcoming landlord and relaxed local atmosphere; two small knocked-through bars with open fires and a dining area, five well kept ales including Loose Cannon, good authentic thai food plus traditional choices, friendly helpful staff; children and dogs welcome, pleasant garden with aunt sally, nice walks, open (and food) all day weekends, closed Mon, no food weekday lunchtimes. *(The Rogue)*

EPWELL SP3540

★**Chandlers Arms** (01295) 780153
Sibford Road, off B4035; OX15 6LH Warmly welcoming little 16th-c stone pub with very good freshly made food (booking advised) from sandwiches and bar meals up, well kept Fullers London Pride and Hook Norton, proper coffee, bar with country-style furniture, two dining areas, good attentive service; free wi-fi; children welcome, no dogs, pleasant garden with aunt sally and summer entertainment, attractive out-of-the-way village near Macmillan Way long-distance path, open all day. *(Bernard Stradling)*

EWELME SU6491

Shepherds Hut (01491) 836636
Off B4009 about 6 miles SW of M40 junction 6; High Street; OX10 6HQ Popular extended bay-windowed village pub with beams, bare boards and woodburner; good home-made food (not Sun evening) from baguettes and snacks up including OAP set menu, four mainly Greene King ales and good range of wines by the glass, friendly efficient staff, back dining area; children, walkers and dogs welcome, terrace picnic-sets with steps up to lawn and play area, car park over the road, open all day. *(John Pritchard, David Lamb)*

EXLADE STREET SU6582

★**Highwayman** (01491) 682020
Just off A4074 Reading–Wallingford; RG8 0UA Whitewashed brick building with two beamed bar rooms, mainly 17th-c (parts older), with interesting rambling layout and mix of furniture, two-way woodburner, good freshly cooked food from landlord-chef including weekday set lunch, three well kept beers and plenty of wines by the glass, friendly efficient service, airy conservatory dining room; soft background music; children and dogs welcome, terrace and garden with fine views, closed Sun evening, Mon. *(Tracey G, David Lamb)*

FERNHAM SU2991

★**Woodman** (01367) 820643
A420 SW of Oxford, then left into B4508 after about 11 miles; village another 6 miles on; SN7 7NX 17th-c country dining pub with heavily beamed character main rooms, candlelit tables and a big open fire, also some newer areas, up to four changing ales, several gins/malt whiskies and decent choice of wines by the glass, good generously served food from pub standards up including Tues steak night (free minibus for eight or more local diners), friendly helpful service; background and some live music; children and dogs welcome, disabled access/loos, seats on small front lawn and heated back terrace, good walks below the downs, open all day Sun till 9pm, closed Mon. *(Keith Perry, R K Phillips)*

FINSTOCK SP3616

★**Plough** (01993) 868333
Just off B4022 N of Witney; High Street; OX7 3BY Thatched and low-beamed village pub with long rambling bar; leather sofas by massive stone inglenook, pictures of local scenes and some historical documents, two or three well kept ales including Adnams, traditional cider, several wines by the glass and decent choice of whiskies, friendly landlord and staff, popular home-made pubby food (best to book) including deals, roomy dining room with candles on stripped-pine tables; soft background music, bar billiards; children and dogs (in bar) welcome, seats in neatly kept garden with aunt sally, woodland and River Evenlode walks, open all day Sat, closed Sun evening, Mon lunchtime. *(Sam Cole)*

FRINGFORD SP6028

Butchers Arms (01869) 277363
Off A421 N of Bicester; Main Street; OX27 8EB Welcoming partly thatched creeper-clad local in Flora Thompson's 'Candleford' village; traditional food including good Sun roasts (three sittings, must book), well kept Black Sheep, Hook Norton and Sharps (June beer festival), charming efficient service, unpretentious interior with L-shaped bar and back dining

room, good log fire; children and dogs welcome, picnic-sets out at front beside cricket green, open all day. *(Louise and Simon Peters)*

FYFIELD SU4298

★**White Hart** (01865) 390585
Main Road; off A420 8 miles SW of Oxford; OX13 5LW Grand medieval hall with soaring eaves, huge stone-flanked window embrasures and minstrels' gallery, contrasting cosy low-beamed side bar with woodburner in large inglenook, fresh flowers and evening candles, civilised friendly atmosphere and full of history; good imaginative modern food (not Sun evening, best to book) cooked by licensee-chef using home-grown produce, Loose Cannon and a couple of guests, around 12 wines by the glass and several malt whiskies, cocktails too (Fri happy hour from 5.30pm); background music; well behaved children welcome, elegant furniture under umbrellas on spacious heated terrace, lovely gardens, good walks by Thames, open all day weekends, closed Mon. *(S F Parrinder)*

GALLOWSTREE COMMON SU6980

Reformation (0118) 972 3126
Horsepond Road; RG4 9BP Welcoming beamed village local; enjoyable varied choice of home-made food including blackboard specials, Brakspears and a couple of Marstons-related guests, plenty of wines by the glass, open fires, conservatory; some live music and other events such as tractor runs and log-splitting competitions; children and dogs welcome, garden with 'shipwreck' play area, closed Sun evening, Mon, Tues. *(Max Simon)*

GODSTOW SP4809

★**Trout** (01865) 510930
Off A40/A44 roundabout via Wolvercote; OX2 8PN Pretty 17th-c Mitchells & Butlers dining pub in lovely riverside location (gets packed in fine weather); good choice of food from varied menu including weekday set deal till 6pm (booking essential at busy times), four beamed linked rooms with contemporary furnishings, flagstones and bare boards, log fires in three huge hearths, Brakspears, Sharps and a guest, several wines by the glass, cocktails, friendly helpful staff; background music; children and dogs (in bar) welcome, plenty of terrace seats under big parasols, footbridge to island (may be closed), abbey ruins opposite, car park fee refunded at bar, open (and food) all day. *(Robert Wivell, Richard Tilbrook, B and F A Hannam)*

GORING SU5980

★**Catherine Wheel** (01491) 872379
Station Road; RG8 9HB Friendly 18th-c village pub with two cosily traditional bar areas, especially the more individual lower room with its dark beams and inglenook log fire; popular home-made food (not Sun evening) from seasonal menu, well kept Brakspears and other Marstons-related ales, Aspall's cider and a dozen wines by the glass, back restaurant, notable doors to lavatories; background and some live music, monthly quiz, TV, free wi-fi; children and dogs welcome, sunny garden with gravel terrace and summer pizza oven, handy for Thames Path, open all day. *(Amanda Shipley)*

GORING SU5980

John Barleycorn (01491) 872509
Manor Road; RG8 9DP Friendly low-beamed cottagey local with cosy unpretentious lounge bar and adjoining dining room; Brakspears, Ringwood and a guest, seven wines by the glass and popular good value pubby food (not Sun evening) from lunchtime sandwiches up, efficient cheerful service, public bar with log fire and bar billiards; children welcome, enclosed beer garden, short walk to the Thames, three bedrooms, open all day. *(Alan and Linda Blackmore)*

GREAT TEW SP3929

★**Falkland Arms** (01608) 683653
The Green; off B4022 about 5 miles E of Chipping Norton; OX7 4DB Part-thatched 16th-c golden-stone pub in lovely village; unspoilt partly panelled bar with high-backed settles, stools and plain tables on flagstones or bare boards, lots of mugs and jugs hanging from beam-and-plank ceiling, interesting brewerania and dim converted oil lamps, shutters for mullioned lattice windows, log fire in fine inglenook, Wadworths and guests, Weston's cider, country wines and some 30 malt whiskies, snuff for sale, locally sourced freshly made food, friendly service, separate dining room; folk night Sun; children and dogs welcome, tables out at front and under parasols in back garden, six bedrooms and cottage, open all day from 8am (breakfast for non-residents). *(Keith Perry, Guy Vowles, Peter Meister, Helene Grygar)*

HAILEY SP3414

Bird in Hand (01993) 868321
Whiteoak Green; B4022 Witney–Charlbury; OX29 9XP Attractive 17th-c extended stone inn under new ownership; good food from fairly pubby menu (highish prices), well kept ales such as Hook Norton and several wines by the glass, helpful friendly service, beams, timbers and stripped stone, comfortable armchairs on polished boards, large log fire, cosy corners in carpeted restaurant, lovely Cotswold views; parasol-shaded terrace tables, 16 bedrooms in modern block around grass quadrangle, open all day. *(John and Penny Wildon)*

HAILEY SU6485

★**King William IV** (01491) 681845
The Hailey near Ipsden, off A4074 or A4130 SE of Wallingford; OX10 6AD

Popular fine old pub in lovely countryside; beamed bar with good sturdy furniture on tiles in front of big log fire, three other cosy seating areas opening off, enjoyable freshly made food (not Sun evening) from baguettes to specials, Brakspears and guests tapped from the cask, helpful friendly staff; children and dogs welcome, terrace and large garden enjoying peaceful far-reaching views, good walking (Chiltern Way and Ridgeway), leave muddy boots in porch, open all day weekends in summer (closed Sun evening winter). *(Colin McLachlan)*

HAILEY SP3512

Lamb & Flag (01993) 702849

B4022 a mile N of Witney; Middletown; OX29 9UB Rambling 17th-c stone-built village pub with plenty of character; beams, some ancient flagstones and inglenook woodburner, freshly made food at affordable prices including good Sun lunch, friendly attentive staff, well kept changing beers and good choice of wines by the glass; pool and darts; children welcome, lovely garden, open all day weekends, closed Mon and lunchtimes Tues-Thurs. *(Paul Scofield)*

HAMPTON POYLE SP5015

Bell (01865) 376242

From A34 S, take Kidlington turn and village signed from roundabout; from A34 N, take Kidlington turn, then A4260 to roundabout, third turning signed for Superstore (Bicester Road); village signed from roundabout; OX5 2QD Extended old stone-built country inn; front bar with three snug rooms, lots of big black and white photoprints, sturdy simple furnishings, scatter cushions and window seats, a stove flanked by bookshelves one end, large fireplace the other, open kitchen (feature pizza oven) in biggish inner room, spreading restaurant with plenty of tables on pale limestone floor, inventive well liked food including cheaper weekday set menu, good choice of wines by the glass, ales such as Hook Norton and Sharps, friendly service and cheerful buzzy atmosphere; background music; children and dogs (in bar) welcome, modern seats on sunny front terrace by quiet village lane, nine good bedrooms, open all day. *(Liz and Mike Newton)*

HANWELL SP4343

Moon & Sixpence (01295) 730544

Main Street; OX17 1HW Refurbished stone-built pub in attractive village setting; good food cooked by owner-chef from pub favourites up including set menu choices, comfortable bar and dining areas with view into kitchen, well kept Wells and Youngs beers and several wines by the glass from carefully chosen list; children welcome, disabled access, seats on back terrace, open till 6pm Sun. *(Gail and Arthur Roberts)*

HEADINGTON SP5406

Butchers Arms (01865) 742470

Wilberforce Street; OX3 7AN Welcoming backstreet local attracting good mix of customers; bare-boards interior with roaring fire, well kept Fullers beers and good value tasty food including ciabattas, pub favourites and stone-baked pizzas; Sun quiz, live jazz first Mon of month, darts, free wi-fi; children and dogs welcome, disabled access, heated terrace with smokers' shelter, open all day Fri-Sun. *(Toby Jones)*

HEADINGTON SP5407

White Hart (01865) 761737

St Andrews Road, Old Town; OX3 9DL Traditional split-level 18th-c stone pub facing the church; well kept Everards and changing guests, real cider, reasonably priced wines and enjoyable pubby food including range of pies, friendly staff; children welcome, delightful sunny back garden (May beer festival), open and food all day, kitchen closes 5pm Sun. *(Alex Mentzer)*

HENLEY SU7682

Angel on the Bridge (01491) 410678

Thames-side, by the bridge; RG9 1BH 17th-c and worth knowing for its prime Thames-side position (packed during the regatta); small front bar with log fire, downstairs back bar and adjacent restaurant, beams, uneven floors and dim lighting, Brakspears ales and maybe a guest such as Ringwood, good choice of wines by the glass, enjoyable food from sandwiches and pubby choices up, cheerful efficient service; tables under parasols on popular waterside deck with own bar (plastic glasses here), moorings for two boats, open all day at least in summer. *(Richard Kennell, Simon Collett-Jones)*

HENLEY SU7582

Argyll (01491) 573400

Market Place; RG9 2AA Comfortable traditional pub with panelled walls, wood flooring and suit of armour by bar, well kept Greene King ales, a house beer called Midsomer Murders (the pub has featured in the TV series) and decent wines by the glass, enjoyable reasonably priced pubby food from good sandwiches up, efficient friendly service; background music, TV; nice terrace garden behind and useful parking, open (and food) all day. *(Martin Day)*

HIGHMOOR SU6984

★Rising Sun (01491) 640856

Witheridge Hill, signposted off B481; OS Sheet 175 map reference 697841; RG9 5PF Welcoming 17th-c pub in small Chilterns village; cosy beamed bar with red and black quarry-tiled floor, comfortable sofa by inglenook woodburner, Brakspears Bitter and a couple of Marstons-related guests, a dozen wines by the glass, three linked eating areas with rugs and pubby furniture on bare boards, pictures on dark red walls, log fire, well liked food from baguettes up; background music, free wi-fi; children and dogs (in bar) welcome, picnic-sets and white metal tables and chairs in pleasant back garden, good surrounding walks, open all day Sat, till 9pm Sun, no food Sun evening. *(M A Borthwick, Gene and Kitty Rankin)*

HOOK NORTON SP3534

★Gate Hangs High (01608) 737387

N towards Sibford, at Banbury–Rollright crossroads; OX15 5DF Tucked-away old stone pub; cosy low-ceilinged bar with attractive inglenook and traditional furniture on bare boards, good reasonably priced home-made food from snacks to daily specials, well kept Hook Norton ales and a guest, decent wines, friendly helpful service, side dining extension; background music; children and dogs (in bar) welcome, pretty courtyard and country garden, four bedrooms, camping, quite near Rollright Stones (EH), open all day. *(Peter Meister)*

HORNTON SP3945

Dun Cow (01295) 670524

West End; OX15 6DA Traditional 17th-c thatch and ironstone village pub, friendly and relaxed, with sensibly short seasonal choice of good fresh food from lunchtime sandwiches up (must book by Fri for Sun lunch), Hook Norton and Purity, a dozen wines by the glass; charity quiz first Weds of the month; children and dogs welcome, appealing small garden behind, open all day weekends, closed lunchtimes Mon-Thurs, no evening food Sun, Mon or Tues. *(Paul Scofield)*

ISLIP SP5214

Red Lion (01865) 375367

High Street (B4027); OX5 2RX Part of small local group including the Jacobs Inn at Wolvercote and Woodstock Arms in Woodstock (for both, see Main Entries); spreading bar and dining areas with cushioned wooden chairs, upholstered benches and wall seats around simple tables on bare boards, carpet or flagstones, some leather sofas and armchairs, two woodburners (one in a sizeable inglenook), Black Sheep, Sharps and a guest, good choice of wines by the glass and enjoyable food from pub classics up including set lunch, friendly helpful staff; children welcome, tables and chairs outside in roped-off area, picnic-sets on lawn, open (and food) all day from 9am for breakfast. *(William and Sophie Renton)*

KIDMORE END SU6979

New Inn (0118) 972 3115

Chalkhouse Green Road; signed from B481 in Sonning Common; RG4 9AU Extended black and white pub by village church; beams and big log fire, enjoyable freshly made food, well kept Brakspears ales and decent wines by the glass, pleasant restaurant; children welcome, tables in large sheltered garden with pond, six bedrooms, open all day Thurs-Sat, till 8pm Sun, shuts 3-6pm Mon-Weds. *(Charlie Stevens)*

LANGFORD SP2402

Bell (01367) 860249

Village signposted off A361 N of Lechlade, then pub signed; GL7 3LF New owners and some refurbishment for this 17th-c pub set in charming village; cosy flagstoned bar with Hook Norton Hooky, Sharps Doom Bar and a guest, several wines by the glass from good list, two heavily beamed dining rooms with traditional furniture on more flagstones, log fires, well liked varied choice of food from snacks and wood-fired pizzas up (best to book), pleasant helpful staff; children and dogs welcome, tables out at front and to the side, eight renovated bedrooms, open all day. *(R K Phillips)*

LAUNTON SP6022

Bull (01869) 248158

Just E of Bicester; Bicester Road; OX26 5DQ Cleanly modernised, part-thatched 17th-c village pub; enjoyable good value food including OAP lunch deal (Mon-Fri) and Tues steak night, Greene King IPA and a couple of guests, friendly staff; background music, Sun quiz; children and dogs welcome, wheelchair access from car park, garden with terrace, open all day, no food Tues. *(Beverley and Andy Butcher)*

LEWKNOR SU7197

★Olde Leathern Bottel

(01844) 351482 *Under a mile from M40 junction 6; off B4009 towards Watlington; OX49 5TW* Popular old village pub with two heavy-beamed bars; understated décor and rustic furnishings, woodburners (one in brick inglenook), well kept Brakspears, Marstons Pedigree and a guest, several wines by the glass and tasty pub food including specials, good friendly service, family room separated by standing timbers; dogs welcome, nice garden with lots of picnic-sets under parasols, play area, boules and aunt sally, handy for walks on Chiltern escarpment. *(R K Phillips, David Reed)*

LITTLE MILTON SP6100

Lamb (01844) 279527

3 miles from M40 junction 7: A329 Thame–Wallingford; OX44 7PU Attractive little 16th-c thatched pub with dark beams, stripped stone and low windows, lots of tables on two levels, woodburner, good choice of enjoyable food (not Sun evening) from lunchtime sandwiches/baguettes up, three well kept ales including Brakspears and decent range of wines, friendly helpful service; background music; children and dogs welcome, tables on back terrace and in pretty garden, open all day Sun. *(John Pritchard)*

LONG HANBOROUGH SP4214

★**George & Dragon** (01993) 881362
A4095 Bladon–Witney; Main Road; OX29 8JX Substantial pub with original two-room bar (17th c or older); low beams, stripped stone and two woodburners, Wells and Youngs ales and decent range of wines, roomy thatched restaurant extension with comfortably padded dining chairs around sturdy tables, wide choice of good food from sandwiches and snacks up, Thurs pie night, prompt friendly service; background music; children and dogs (in bar) welcome, large back garden with picnic-sets among shrubs, tables beneath canopy on separate sheltered terrace, summer barbecues, open (and food) all day. *(Charlie and Mark Todd)*

LONG WITTENHAM SU5493

Plough (01865) 407738
High Street; OX14 4QH Welcoming 17th-c two-bar local with low beams, inglenook fires and lots of brass, two or three well kept ales including Butcombe, good reasonably priced home-cooked food (not Sun evening) from sandwiches and traditional choices to interesting specials, efficient service, dining room, games in public bar; children and dogs welcome, two bedrooms, Thames moorings at bottom of long garden, play area, June music festival, open all day. *(David Lamb)*

LONGWORTH SU3899

★**Blue Boar** (01865) 820494
Tucks Lane; OX13 5ET This traditional country pub was for sale as we went to press, so things may change; three low-beamed characterful little rooms, brasses, hops and assorted bits and pieces on walls and ceilings, scrubbed wooden tables, benches and faded rugs on floor tiles, open fires (one by the bar is noteworthy), Brakspears and Otter, good range of whiskies/gins and a dozen wines by the glass, food has been well liked, main eating area is room at end, there's also a quieter restaurant extension; children and dogs (in bar) welcome, tables on front and back terraces, open all day, food all day weekends (till 7.30pm Sun). *(R K Phillips, Keith Perry, Jill and Hugh Bennett)*

MAIDENSGROVE SU7288

Five Horseshoes (01491) 641282
Off B480 and B481, W of village; RG9 6EX Character 16th-c dining pub set high in the Chilterns; rambling bar with low ceiling and log fire, well liked food from changing menu including seasonal game, set lunch Tues-Fri, friendly service, well kept Brakspears and good choice of wines by the glass, airy conservatory restaurant; regular jazz evenings; children and dogs (in bar) welcome, plenty of tables in suntrap garden with rolling countryside views, good walks, open all day Sat, closed Mon and evenings Tues, Sun. *(Louise and Simon Peters)*

MARSH BALDON SU5699

Seven Stars (01865) 343337
The Baldons signed off A4074 N of Dorchester; OX44 9LP Competently run, community-owned beamed pub on edge of village green; good food (all day Weds-Sat) including plenty of gluten-free and vegetarian choices, well kept Fullers London Pride and three mainly local guests, helpful friendly young staff coping well at busy times, modernised bar areas, seats by corner fire, raftered barn restaurant; monthly quiz and occasional live music; children, dogs and muddy boots welcome, seats outside overlooking fields and horses, open all day (till midnight Fri, Sat), closes 7pm Sun in winter. *(Neil and Angela Huxter, Katharine Cowherd, Mike Kavaney, John Pritchard, Baz Manning)*

MILCOMBE SP4034

Horse & Groom (01295) 722142
Off A361 SW of Banbury; OX15 4RS Stone-built 17th-c pub at western edge of the village; generous servings of good fresh food from lunchtime sandwiches up, three changing ales and a dozen wines by the glass, friendly helpful service, inglenook woodburner in appealing low-beamed and flagstoned bar, back restaurant; children and dogs (in bar) welcome, picnic-sets out in front, four bedrooms, good breakfast, handy for Wigginton Heath waterfowl and animal centre, closed Sun evening. *(Amanda Shipley)*

MILTON COMMON SP6503

Three Pigeons (01844) 277183
A40, by M40 junction 7; OX9 2JN Unusual pub-restaurant (part of Lassco's architectural reclamation centre, so lots of interesting bits and pieces for sale); rugs on bare boards, two open fires, a couple of Shotover beers and nine wines by the glass, good imaginative food from changing menu, teas, coffees and cakes, nice friendly staff; eclectic background music, live jazz Thurs; well behaved children and dogs welcome, open all day Thurs-Sat, till 5pm Sun-Weds, breakfast from 9.30am (not Sun). *(Sally Anne and Peter Goodale)*

MURCOTT SP5815

★**Nut Tree** (01865) 331253
Off B4027 NE of Oxford, via Islip and Charlton-on-Otmoor; OX5 2RE Despite its Michelin star, this 15th-c beamed and thatched place manages to keep a relaxed pubby atmosphere; first-rate imaginative cooking using own produce including home-reared pigs (they also do sandwiches and cheaper bar food), good attentive but not intrusive service from friendly staff, well spaced tables with crisp white cloths, leather chesterfields in bar area, Vale, two guest beers and carefully chosen wines; background music; children and dogs (in bar) welcome, terrace and pretty garden,

unusual gargoyles on front wall (modelled loosely on local characters), closed Sun evening, otherwise open all day. *(Michael Lamb)*

NORTH HINKSEY SP4905

Fishes (01865) 249796

Off A420 just E of A34 ring road; N Hinksey Lane, then turn left opposite church into cul-de-sac signed to rugby club; OX2 0NA Popular brick and tile Victorian pub (part of the Peach group) set in three acres of wooded grounds; extended open-plan interior with conservatory, good choice of food from sandwiches and deli boards up including weekday set menu till 6pm, well kept Greene King ales and a guest, plenty of wines by the glass and nice selection of gins, friendly helpful staff; children welcome, dogs in bar and snug, tables out at front, on back deck and in streamside garden with summer barbecues and tipi, open (and food) all day from 9.30am for breakfast. *(Toby Jones)*

NORTH MORETON SU5689

Bear at Home (01235) 811311

Off A4130 Didcot–Wallingford; High Street; OX11 9AT Village pub dating from the 16th c run by friendly father and daughter team; traditional bar, cosy fireside areas and dining part with stripped-pine furniture, lots of beams, carpeted floors, pictures on rough walls, enjoyable sensibly priced food from pub staples up including daily specials, Timothy Taylors, a house beer from West Berkshire and a couple of local guests, Weston's cider and a dozen wines by the glass; regular quiz nights; children and dogs welcome, nice back garden overlooking cricket pitch (July beer and cricket festival), pretty village, open all day Sat, closed Sun evening. *(John Pritchard)*

OXFORD SP5106

Anchor (01865) 510282

Hayfield Road; OX2 6TT 1930s red-brick dining pub; wood-floored bar with padded wall benches and stools around light wood tables, log fire in small carved stone fireplace, a couple of well kept Wadworths ales and a guest from oak-panelled servery, good range of wines, bistro-feel dining room with black and white tiles and another fireplace (woodburner), nice food including daily specials and some good vegetarian options, efficient service; children welcome, café-style tables and chairs on paved terrace, open all day, weekend brunch from 10am. *(Clive and Fran Dutson)*

OXFORD SP5106

Chequers (01865) 727463

Off High Street; OX1 4DH Narrow 16th-c pub tucked away in courtyard down small alleyway; several areas on three floors with interesting architectural features, beams, panelling and stained glass, eight or so well kept ales and enjoyable good value Nicholsons menu, afternoon tea, friendly service; background music; walled garden, open (and food) all day. *(Tony and Wendy Hobden)*

OXFORD SP5106

Eagle & Child (01865) 302925

St Giles; OX1 3LU Long narrow Nicholsons pub dating from the 16th c; two charmingly old-fashioned panelled front rooms with Tolkien and C S Lewis connections (the Inklings writers' group used to meet here and referred to it as the Bird & Baby), ales including Brakspears and Hook Norton, enjoyable pubby food in stripped-brick dining extension and conservatory, can get busy but service remains good; children allowed in back till 8pm, open all day. *(Philip J Alderton, Richard Tilbrook, Revd R P Tickle)*

OXFORD SP5203

Isis Farmhouse (01865) 243854

Off Donnington Bridge Road; no car access; OX4 4EL Early 19th-c former farmhouse in charming waterside spot (accessible only to walkers/cyclists/boaters); relaxed lived-in interior with two woodburners, short choice of tasty home-made food at sensible prices, a couple of beers from local Shotover and decent wines, afternoon teas with freshly baked cakes, friendly staff; background and weekend live music including Sun afternoon jazz, folk club second Fri of month; children and dogs welcome, terrace and garden picnic-sets, short walk to Iffley Lock and nearby lavishly decorated early Norman church, closed Mon-Weds in summer, only open weekends and alternate Fri evenings in winter, may close in bad weather. *(Max and Steph Warren)*

OXFORD SP5006

Old Bookbinders (01865) 553549

Victor Street; OX2 6BT Dark and mellow family-run local tucked away in the Jericho area; friendly and unpretentious, with old fittings and lots of interesting bric-a-brac, Greene King ales and three guests, decent choice of whiskies and other spirits, enjoyable french-leaning food including speciality crêpes and good value lunchtime/early evening set menu; shove-ha'penny and board games, quiz Tues, open mike night Sun; children, dogs and students welcome, some entertaining features such as multiple door handles to the gents', tables out on pavement, closed Mon otherwise open all day. *(Richard Tilbrook)*

OXFORD SP5105

Royal Blenheim (01865) 242355

Ebbes Street; OX1 1PT Popular corner pub opened by Queen Victoria during her Golden Jubilee and now jointly owned by Everards, Titanic and White Horse; their well kept beers and guests, good value well presented pub food (till 5pm weekends) including some decent vegetarian/vegan options, friendly chatty staff, single airy room (recently refurbished) with raised perimeter seating; Weds quiz, TV projector for major sports; open all day (till midnight Fri, Sat). *(Max and Steph Warren)*

OXFORD SP5106

Turf Tavern (01865) 243235
Bath Place; via St Helens Passage, between Holywell Street and New College Lane; OX1 3SU Interesting characterful pub hidden away behind high walls; small dark-beamed bars with lots of snug areas, up to a dozen constantly changing ales including Greene King, Weston's cider and maybe winter mulled wine, popular reasonably priced food from sandwiches up, pleasant helpful service; newspapers and free wi-fi; children and dogs welcome, three walled-in courtyards (one with own bar), open (and food) all day. *(Max and Steph Warren)*

PISHILL SU7190

★**Crown** (01491) 638364
B480 Nettlebed–Watlington; RG9 6HH 15th-c inn at heart of the Chilterns; beamed bars with old local photographs, prints and maps, some panelling and nice mix of wooden tables and chairs, well kept Brakspears and Rebellion ales, seven wines by the glass and a dozen malt whiskies, tasty generously served food, good service, knocked-through back area with standing timbers and three log fires (not always lit); priest hole is thought to be one of the largest in the country; well behaved children welcome, dogs in bar, seats in pretty garden with thatched barn for functions, lots of nearby walks, self-catering cottage, closed Sun evening. *(David and Judy Robison)*

PLAY HATCH SU7477

Shoulder of Mutton (0118) 947 3908
W of Henley Road (A4155) roundabout; RG4 9QU Dining pub with low-ceilinged log-fire bar and large back conservatory restaurant, good food from landlord-chef including signature mutton dishes, well kept Greene King and a guest such as nearby Loddon, reasonably priced house wines, friendly service (can slow at busy times); children welcome, picnic-sets in carefully tended walled garden with well, closed Sun evening, Mon and maybe Tues evening (not summer). *(John Pritchard)*

ROKE SU6293

Home Sweet Home (01491) 838249
Off B4009 Benson–Watlington; OX10 6JD Wadworths country dining pub with several linked rooms; two smallish bars, heavy stripped beams, big central log fire and traditional furniture, carpeted room on right leading to restaurant area, good popular food including weekday set menu, friendly staff; background music, Rokefest music/beer festival late May Bank Holiday; children and dogs welcome, attractive low-walled front garden, open all day Sat, till 5pm Sun (food till 3.30pm), closed Mon. *(David Lamb, John Pritchard)*

ROTHERFIELD GREYS SU7282

★**Maltsters Arms** (01491) 628400
Can be reached off A4155 in Henley, via Greys Road passing Southfields long-stay car park; or follow Greys Court signpost off B481 N of Sonning Common; RG9 4QD Chilterns country pub with black-beamed front bar, comfortable wall banquettes and woodburner, Brakspears and other Marstons-related beers, Aspall's cider and eight wines by the glass, linked lounge and restaurant, good sensibly priced food from fairly pubby menu plus several blackboard specials, service friendly but may slow at busy times; background music; children and dogs (in bar) welcome, terrace tables under big heated canopy, picnic-sets on grass looking over paddocks and rolling countryside, good walks nearby and handy for Greys Court (NT), open all day Sun. *(Alan and Linda Blackmore)*

ROTHERFIELD PEPPARD SU7081

Unicorn (01491) 628674
Colmore Lane; RG9 5LX Attractive little country pub under new management; bustling bare-boards bar with open fire, Brakspears Bitter and a couple of guests, enjoyable food including daily specials and deals, friendly service, separate dining room; Weds quiz and some live music, TV for major sports; children, walkers and dogs welcome, seats in back garden, open all day, no food Sun evening. *(Darrell Barton)*

SHENINGTON SP3742

Bell (01295) 670274
Off A422 NW of Banbury; OX15 6NQ Early 18th-c two-room pub in charming quiet village; good popular food cooked by landlord-chef, well kept Hook Norton Hooky, a guest beer and good range of wines by the glass, friendly service, heavy beams, some flagstones, stripped stone and pine panelling, two woodburners; children welcome in eating areas, dogs in bar, picnic-sets out at front, good surrounding walks, closed Sun evening to lunchtime Weds, open all day Sat. *(Cliff and Monica Swan)*

SHIPTON-UNDER-WYCHWOOD SP2717

Wychwood Inn (01993) 831185
High Street; OX7 6BA Refurbished former coaching inn run by mother and son; contemporary décor in recently extended open-plan bar/dining area, more period character in flagstoned public bar with black beams and inglenook, Greene King IPA and three guests, plenty of wines by the glass and enjoyable food from lunchtime wraps to grills, Thurs evening fish specials, friendly

young staff, private dining room in glassed-in coach entrance; TV for major sporting events; children and dogs welcome, picnic-sets on small terrace, five bedrooms, open all day. *(Bernard Stradling)*

SIBFORD GOWER SP3537

Wykham Arms (01295) 788808

Signed off B4035 Banbury to Shipston-on-Stour; Temple Mill Road; OX15 5RX Cottagey 17th-c thatched and flagstoned dining pub; good food (not Sun evening) from light dishes up, friendly attentive staff, two well kept changing ales and over 20 wines by the glass, comfortable open-plan interior with low beams and stripped stone, glass-covered well, inglenook; children and dogs welcome, country views from big garden, lovely manor house opposite and good walks nearby, open all day Sun, closed Mon. *(Susie and Spencer Gray)*

SOULDERN SP5231

Fox (01869) 345284

Off B4100; Fox Lane; OX27 7JW Early 19th-c pub set in delightful village; open-plan beamed interior with woodburner in two-way fireplace, well kept ales such as Hook Norton, Otter and Timothy Taylors, several wines by the glass and good fairly priced food from shortish menu, friendly attentive service; regular quiz nights; terrace and walled garden, aunt sally, four bedrooms, open all day Sat, till 5pm Sun. *(Gail and Arthur Roberts)*

SOUTH LEIGH SP3908

Hanburys Mason Arms (01993) 656220 *3 miles S of A40 Witney–Eynsham; Station Road; OX29 6XN* 16th-c thatched country inn-restaurant refurbished under new owners; good imaginative food from daily changing menu (can be pricey), Hook Norton Hooky and a guest, craft beers, cocktails and plenty of wines by the glass, efficient friendly service, individual décor including some quirky touches such as prison doors to the loos; children and dogs welcome, garden with shepherd's hut, seven stylish bedrooms (two in converted outbuildings), open all day. *(S F Parrinder)*

SOUTH NEWINGTON SP4033

Duck on the Pond (01295) 721166

A361; OX15 4JE Roadside dining pub with small flagstoned bar and linked carpeted eating areas up a step; very well liked food (till 6pm Sun) from lunchtime baguettes up including some good vegetarian choices and popular Sun lunch, Hook Norton Hooky and a couple of guests, cheery pleasant staff, lots of duck-related items, woodburner; children welcome, no dogs inside, spacious grounds with tables on deck and lawn, pond with waterfowl and little River Swere winding down beyond, open all day weekends. *(Sam Cole)*

SPARSHOLT SU3487

Star (01235) 751873

Watery Lane; OX12 9PL Modernised 16th-c dining pub with easy-going relaxed atmosphere; highly regarded up-to-date food along with more traditional choices, lunchtime set menu and Sun evening grill, charming efficient service, dining rooms with pale farmhouse chairs around chunky tables on floorboards or big flagstones, hop-strung beams, open fire, ales such as Hook Norton and Sharps in simply furnished bar; background music, board games; children and dogs welcome (pub dogs are Minnie and Ella), seats in back garden, pretty village – snowdrops fill the churchyard in spring, eight comfortable barn conversion bedrooms, open all day. *(R K Phillips, Neil and Angela Huxter)*

STANTON ST JOHN SP5709

Talk House (01865) 351654

Middle Road/Wheatley Road (B4027 just outside village); OX33 1EX Attractive part-thatched dining pub; older part on left with steeply pitched rafters soaring above stripped-stone walls, mix of old dining chairs and big stripped tables, large rugs on flagstones; rest of building converted more recently but in similar style with massive beams, flagstones or stoneware tiles, and log fires below low mantelbeams, good food from lunchtime sandwiches up, three Fullers ales and over 20 wines by the glass; children welcome, inner courtyard with teak tables and chairs, a few picnic-sets on side grass, four bedrooms, open all day except Sun evening, brunch from 10.15am. *(Amanda Shipley)*

STEEPLE ASTON SP4725

★**Red Lion** (01869) 340225

Off A4260 12 miles N of Oxford; OX25 4RY Cheerful village pub with neatly kept beamed and partly panelled bar, antique settle and other good furnishings, well kept Hook Norton ales and decent wines by the glass, enjoyable food from shortish menu including pizzas, obliging young staff, back timber-framed dining extension; Mon quiz; well behaved children till 7pm, dogs in bar, suntrap front garden with lovely flowers and shrubs, parking can be be tricky, open all day Sat, till 5pm Sun. *(David Lamb)*

STEVENTON SU4691

North Star

Stocks Lane, The Causeway, central westward turn off B4017; OX13 6SG Very traditional little village pub through yew tree gateway; tiled entrance corridor, main area with ancient high-backed settles forming booth in front of brick fireplace, three well kept ales from side tap room, hatch service to another room with plain seating, a couple of tables and coal fire, simple lunchtime food, friendly staff; children and dogs welcome, tables on front grass, aunt sally, open all day weekends, closed weekday lunchtimes. *(Charlie and Mark Todd)*

STOKE LYNE SP5628

Peyton Arms 07546 066160
From minor road off B4110 N of Bicester fork left into village; OX27 8SD Beautifully situated and largely unspoilt one-room stone alehouse; character landlord (Mick the Hat) and loyal regulars, very well kept Hook Norton ales from casks behind small corner bar, no food apart from filled rolls, inglenook fire, tiled floor and lots of memorabilia, games area (darts and pool); no children or dogs; pleasant garden with aunt sally, open all day weekends till 7pm, closed weekday lunchtimes, and may shut early if quiet. *(Sam Cole)*

STOKE ROW SU6884

Cherry Tree (01491) 680430
Off B481 at Highmoor; RG9 5QA Sympathetically updated 18th-c pub-restaurant (originally three cottages); enjoyable often interesting food from sharing plates to daily specials, Brakspears ales and good range of wines by the glass, helpful friendly staff, small linked rooms mainly set for dining, heavy low beams, stripped boards and flagstones; background music, TV in bar; well behaved children and dogs welcome, lots of tables in attractive garden, nearby walks, four good bedrooms in converted barn, open all day, no food Sun evening. *(Bob and Margaret Holder)*

STOKE ROW SU6884

★**Crooked Billet** (01491) 681048
Nottwood Lane, off B491 N of Reading – OS Sheet 175 map reference 684844; RG9 5PU Nice place, but more restaurant than pub; charming rustic layout with heavy beams, flagstones, antique pubby furnishings and fine inglenook log fire, crimson Victorian-style dining room, very good interesting food cooked by owner-chef using local and home-grown ingredients, cheaper set lunches Mon-Fri, helpful friendly staff, Brakspears Oxford Gold tapped from the cask (no counter), good wines, relaxed homely atmosphere; weekly live music often including established artists; children very welcome, big garden by Chilterns beechwoods, open all day, food all day weekends. *(Colin McLachlan)*

STRATTON AUDLEY SP6026

Red Lion (01869) 277225
Off A421 NE of Bicester; Church Street; OX27 9AG Traditional thatched pub in pretty village; L-shaped bar with stripped stone, low beams and woodburner in big inglenook, enjoyable fairly pubby food (not Sun evening) from lunchtime baguettes up, Hook Norton Hooky, Timothy Taylors Landlord and a guest, friendly helpful service; live music and quiz nights; children welcome, dogs until 7pm (4pm to close Sun), pavement tables, more in colourful back courtyard garden, open all day. *(Chris Sallnow)*

SUNNINGWELL SP4900

Flowing Well (01865) 735846
Just N of Abingdon; OX13 6RB Refurbished timbered pub in former 19th-c rectory; good food including british tapas, range of burgers and gluten-free menu, a couple of Greene King ales and a guest, good choice of wines; free wi-fi; children welcome, dogs in bar, big heated raised terrace, more seats in garden with small well, open (and food) all day. *(Toby Jones)*

SUTTON COURTENAY SU5094

Swan (01235) 847446
The Green; OX14 4AE Red-brick restauranty pub (calls itself a foodhouse and bar) overlooking green; unfussy décor with grey-painted woodwork and white walls, plain modern wooden tables on quarry tiles, log fire, good well presented food including tapas, blackboard specials and Fri evening fish, stools at bar serving a couple of real ales such as Timothy Taylors Landlord, friendly staff; background music; children welcome, picnic-sets out at front and in enclosed back garden with play area, open all day Sat, till 6pm Sun, closed Mon. *(John Pritchard)*

SWERFORD SP3830

★**Boxing Hare** (01608) 683212
A361 Banbury–Chipping Norton; OX7 4AP Old stone dining pub (former Masons Arms) under good new ownership; highly regarded interesting food, including signature dry-aged steaks, lunchtime set menu (Weds-Fri) and daily specials, friendly attentive service, well kept Hook Norton and Timothy Taylors, good wines by the glass and several whiskies/gins such as local Cotswold, attractive split-level interior with rugs on bare boards, white-painted beams and log fires; children welcome, lovely country views from neat garden, closed Sun evening to Tues lunchtime. *(Peter Meister, Chris and Pauline Sexton, Monty Green, Patricia Healey, M J Winterton, Philippa Ward)*

SWINFORD SP4308

Talbot (01865) 881348
B4044 just S of Eynsham; OX29 4BT Roomy and comfortable 17th-c beamed pub; well kept Arkells tapped from cooled casks and good choice of wines, enjoyable well priced pubby food from sandwiches and basket meals up including weekday deals, Sun carvery, friendly staff, long attractive flagstoned bar with some stripped

There are report forms at the back of the book.

stone, cheerful log-effect gas fire; charity quiz second Mon of month; children and dogs welcome, garden with decked area overlooking Wharf Stream, nice walk along lovely stretch of the Thames towpath, moorings quite nearby, 11 bedrooms, open all day. *(Brian Glozier, Richard Tilbrook)*

THAME SP7105

Cross Keys (01844) 218202
Park Street/East Street; OX9 3HP Friendly one-bar 19th-c corner local; eight well kept ales including own Thame beers (not always available) and half a dozen ciders, no food apart from scotch eggs and occasional cheese and wine nights but can bring your own; Weds quiz and regular comedy nights; courtyard garden, open all day Sun. *(Cliff and Monica Swan)*

THAME SP7005

James Figg (01844) 260166
Cornmarket; OX9 2BL Friendly coaching inn with four well kept ales such as Hook Norton, Purity and Sharps, Aspall's cider and ten wines by the glass, enjoyable good value food including pizzas and burgers, two-for-one deals Mon-Weds, log fire in brick fireplace with moose's head above, portrait of eponymous James Figg (local 18th-c boxer) and photos of more recent sporting champions, converted stables with own bar for music/functions; gets busier and noisier in the evening; children and dogs welcome, back beer garden, open (and food) all day, kitchen closes 6pm Sun. *(John Saville)*

THAME SP7006

★**Thatch** (01844) 214340
Lower High Street; OX9 2AA Characterful timbered and thatched 16th-c dining pub (Peach group); good interesting food from deli boards to daily specials, well kept ales, nice wines and some interesting gins, friendly service, cosy bar and appealing collection of little higgledy-piggledy rooms, heavy beams, old quarry tiles, flagstones and double-sided inglenook, smart contemporary furnishings and bold paintwork; children welcome, prettily planted terraced garden with tables under parasols, open (and food) all day. *(Andrew Chetty)*

TOOT BALDON SP5600

★**Mole** (01865) 340001
Between A4074 and B480 SE of Oxford; OX44 9NG Light open-plan restauranty pub with very good if not cheap food (booking advised) including light lunch and weekly changing set menus, friendly attentive service, nice wines by the glass and a couple of well kept ales such as Hook Norton Hooky, leather sofas by bar, neat country furniture or more formal leather dining chairs in linked eating areas including conservatory, stripped 18th-c beams and big open fire; background music; children welcome, no dogs inside, lovely gardens, open all day. *(M A Borthwick)*

UFFINGTON SU3089

Fox & Hounds (01367) 820680)
High Street; SN7 7RP Traditional beamed village pub; three changing ales and good reasonably priced home-made food from shortish menu including one or two specials, friendly helpful staff, garden room extension with view of White Horse Hill; live music and quiz nights, sports TV, free wi-fi; children and dogs welcome, picnic-sets outside (maybe summer pizzas on Sun), handy for Tom Brown's School Museum, four ground-floor bedrooms, open all day, kitchen closed Sun evening, Mon. *(R K Phillips)*

WALLINGFORD SU6089

Partridge (01491) 839305
St Marys Street; OX10 0ET Pub-restaurant refurbished under new owners; bar with comfortable furnishings including leather sofas and armchairs on bare boards, adjoining dining area, Greene King IPA, a guest beer and over a dozen wines by the glass, good well presented food from pub favourites up, friendly helpful staff; children and dogs welcome, steps up to back garden, open all day Sat, till 6pm Sun, closed Mon and lunchtimes Tues-Fri. *(Colin McLachlan)*

WARBOROUGH SU6093

Six Bells (01865) 858265
The Green S; just E of A329, 4 miles N of Wallingford; OX10 7DN Thatched 16th-c pub opposite village cricket green; a couple of well kept Brakspears ales and good pubby food (not Sun or Mon evenings) from sandwiches and sharing boards to popular Sun roasts, friendly accommodating staff, low beams and attractive country furnishings in small linked areas off bar, bare boards, stripped stone and big log fire; tables out in front and in pleasant orchard garden behind where aunt sally is played, open all day weekends and often very busy. *(Keith Perry, Colin McLachlan, Barry Collett, Paul Humphreys, John Pritchard)*

WARDINGTON SP4946

Hare & Hounds (01295) 750645
A361 Banbury–Daventry; OX17 1SH Comfortable and welcoming traditional village local, well kept Hook Norton ales and enjoyable home-made food including bargain OAP lunch, low-ceilinged bar leading to dining area, woodburner; quiz nights, darts and dominoes; children and dogs welcome, garden with play area and aunt sally, open all day Fri, Sat, till 8pm Sun. *(Beverley and Andy Butcher)*

WATLINGTON SU6994

Fat Fox (01491) 613040
Shireburn Street; OX49 5BU Centrally placed 17th-c inn; beamed and bare-boards bar with open fire, separate restaurant, good food from changing menu using local

produce, four real ales including Brakspears and good choice of wines by the glass, friendly helpful staff; free wi-fi; children and dogs (in bar) welcome, Ridgeway walks, nine bedrooms (seven in converted back barn), good breakfast, handy for M40 (junction 3), open all day. *(Toby Jones)*

WEST HANNEY SU4092

Plough (01235) 868987

Just off A338 N of Wantage; Church Street; OX12 0LN Community-owned thatched and beamed village pub with light modern décor; four well kept ales including Greene King IPA, generous helpings of popular home-made food (not Sun evening, Tues), friendly service; free wi-fi; children and dogs welcome, nice walled garden behind, aunt sally, good walks from the door, open all day weekends, closed Mon. *(Paul Scofield)*

WESTON-ON-THE-GREEN SP5318

Chequers (01869) 351743

Handy for M40 junction 9, via A34; Northampton Road (B430); OX25 3QH Extended thatched and beamed village pub with three areas off main bar; well kept Fullers ales, a dozen wines by the glass and 14 gins from semicircular servery, good fairly priced food including sandwiches and snacks, chargrills and popular Sun carvery, breakfast from 10am, friendly attentive service, mix of traditional furniture on flagstone or parquet floors, some painted panelling; background music, children and dogs welcome, terrace and garden tables, open all day Sat, till 6pm Sun. *(Louise and Simon Peters)*

WHITCHURCH SU6377

Ferry Boat (0118) 984 2161

High Street, near toll bridge; RG8 7DB Welcoming comfortably updated 18th-c pub; airy bar with log fire and separate restaurant, good variety of home-made food including stone-baked pizzas, real ales such as Black Sheep and Timothy Taylors, several wines by the glass; background music, free wi-fi; well behaved children and dogs (in bar) welcome, café-style seating in courtyard garden, closed Sun evening, Mon. *(Amanda Shipley)*

WHITCHURCH SU6377

Greyhound (0118) 343 3016

High Street, just over toll bridge from Pangbourne; RG8 7EL Attractive former ferryman's cottage with small knocked-together low-beamed rooms; three changing ales and good value pubby food, friendly efficient staff; monthly live music; children and dogs welcome, small sheltered back garden, attractive village on Thames Path, open all day Sat, till 6pm Sun, closed Mon and lunchtime Tues. *(Gail and Arthur Roberts)*

WITNEY SP3509

Angel (01993) 703238

Market Square; OX28 6AL Unpretentious 17th-c town local with wide choice of enjoyable well priced food from sandwiches up, Marstons-related ales including a house beer from Wychwood and an occasional guest, efficient friendly service even when packed, beams and open fire; background music (live weekends), sports TVs; lovely hanging baskets, back terrace with smokers' shelter, parking nearby can be difficult, open (and food) all day. *(Darrell Barton)*

WITNEY SP3509

Fleece (01993) 892270

Church Green; OX28 4AZ Smartly presented town pub (part of the Peach group), popular for its wide choice of good often imaginative food from sandwiches and deli boards up, fixed-price menu too (Mon-Fri 12-6), Greene King and a couple of guests, decent coffee, leather armchairs on wood floors, restaurant; background and occasional live music, daily papers; children welcome, café-style tables out at front overlooking green, ten comfortable affordable bedrooms, good breakfast, open (and food) all day from 9am. *(R K Phillips)*

WITNEY SP3509

Hollybush (01993) 708073

Corn Street; OX28 6BT Popular modernised 18th-c pub under same ownership as the Horseshoes across the road; front bar with woodburner in big fireplace, settles and window seats, various dining areas off, good food from sandwiches and deli boards up, weekday lunchtime set menu and other offers, three well kept ales including a house beer from Greene King and nice selection of wines, efficient friendly staff; background music, free wi-fi; children and dogs welcome, open (and food) all day. *(Darrell Barton)*

WITNEY SP3510

Horseshoes (01993) 703086

Corn Street, junction with Holloway Road; OX28 6BS Attractive 16th-c stone pub with good freshly made food (all day weekends) from pub favourites up including gluten-free choices, deli counter and weekday set lunch deal, three changing ales and decent wines by the glass, heavy beams, stripped-stone walls, oak floors and log fires, separate back dining room; children and dogs welcome, a few seats out at front, tables on sunny paved terrace behind, open all day. *(Steve Whalley)*

WOLVERCOTE SP4909

Plough (01865) 556969

First Turn/Wolvercote Green; OX2 8AH Two connecting buildings with comfortably worn-in pubby rooms; armchairs and Victorian-style carpeted bays in main lounge, a well kept Greene King beer such as Hardys & Hansons and a couple of guests, traditional cider and decent wines by the glass, enjoyable good value usual food in flagstoned stables dining room and library (children allowed here), bargain OAP lunchtime menu, traditional snug, woodburner; dogs welcome in bar, disabled access/facilities, picnic-sets on part-decked terrace looking over rough meadow to canal and woods, open all day Sun. *(Tony and Jill Radnor)*

WOODSTOCK SP4417

Black Prince (01993) 811530
Manor Road (A44 N); OX20 1XJ
Old pub with single low-ceilinged bar; timbers, stripped stone and log fire, suit of armour, good value home-made food (not Sun evening) from sandwiches to specials, well kept St Austell and guests, friendly service; some live music, outside lavatories; children, walkers and dogs welcome, tables in pretty garden by small River Glyme, nearby right of way into Blenheim parkland, open all day. *(Max Simon)*

WOODSTOCK SP4416

★**Kings Arms** (01993) 813636
Market Street/Park Lane (A44); OX20 1SU Bustling town-centre hotel with unfussy bar attracting good mix of customers; appealing variety of old and new furnishings on stripped-wood floor, some black and white photographs and a modern woodburning stove, neat restaurant with high-backed leather chairs around mix of tables on black and white tiles, logs stacked either side of another woodburner, Fullers ales, a dozen wines by the glass and 35 malt whiskies, good food from varied menu; background music, free wi-fi; children and dogs (in bar) welcome, café-style pavement tables, 15 bedrooms, open all day from 7am. *(Phil and Helen Holt, Bob and Melissa Wyatt, David and Judy Robison)*

WOOLSTONE SU2987

White Horse (01367) 820726
Off B4507; SN7 7QL Appealing partly thatched black and white pub with prominent gables and latticed windows; stone flooring and two open fires in spacious beamed bar, Arkells ales and enjoyable food from regularly changing menus, wood-fired pizzas (Weds-Sat), restaurant; well behaved children and dogs allowed, plenty of seats in front and back gardens, secluded interesting village handy for White Horse and Ridgeway (good circular walk), six bedrooms, open all day. *(Ian Phillips)*

WYTHAM SP4708

White Hart (01865) 244372
Off A34 Oxford ring road; OX2 8QA
Renovated 16th-c country dining pub in unspoilt preserved village; several areas with log fires including converted stables, some settles, handsome panelling and uneven flagstones, good food (not Sun evening) from lunchtime sandwiches to blackboard specials, also vegetarian/vegan choices, cosy bar with well kept Wadworths ales and lots of wines by the glass, conservatory; children and dogs welcome, courtyard tables, evening barbecues Fri and Sat (weather permitting), open all day (till 8pm Sun). *(S F Parrinder)*

Post Office address codings confusingly give the impression that some pubs are in Oxfordshire, when they're really in Berkshire, Buckinghamshire, Gloucestershire or Warwickshire (which is where we list them).

Shropshire

BASCHURCH SJ4221 Map 7

New Inn

(01939) 260335 – www.newinnbaschurch.com

Church Road; SY4 2EF

A good mix of customers for bustling village pub with several beers and highly popular food; seats in attractive garden

Once they've found this handsome whitewashed pub, our readers return on a regular basis – there's a good range of ales, appealing food and the attractively refurbished interlinked rooms have an easy-going atmosphere. At one end, the bar has a woodburning stove, a leather sofa and armchairs, traditional wooden chairs and stools around tables on quarry tiles and bare boards, and lots of wall prints. Friendly, cheerful staff serve Hobsons Best Bitter, Salopian Shropshire Gold, Stonehouse Station Bitter and Three Tuns Solstice on handpump, 13 wines by the glass and ten gins. The two heavily beamed dining rooms have logs piled into brick fireplaces, high-backed leather-seated chairs around more light tables and candles in glass jars and lanterns; the table flowers are pretty. There are seats outside on decking.

Enticing food includes sandwiches, crab arancini with saffron aioli, pulled pork scotch duck egg with home-made brown sauce, sharing platters, steak burger with bacon jam, toppings and parmesan and truffle fries, mushroom, courgette, spinach and goats cheese wellington with watercress cream, pheasant breast with confit leg pithivier, parsnip purée and wild mushrooms, venison loin with broccoli and blue cheese purée, baked pear and red wine jus, seared sea trout with mussels and crayfish, samphire, white wine cream and sautéed potatoes, and puddings such as green apple mousse with cinnamon shortbread and bread and butter pudding with custard. *Benchmark main dish: steak in ale pie £12.50. Two-course evening meal £18.00.*

Free house ~ Licensees Graham and Clare Jenkins ~ Real ale ~ Open 12-3, 6-11; 12-11 Sat; 12-7 Sun; closed Mon except bank holidays ~ Bar food 12-2, 6-9; 12-5 Sun ~ Restaurant ~ Children welcome ~ Dogs allowed in bar ~ Wi-fi *Recommended by Jacqui and Alan Swan, Caroline and Peter Bryant, Nick Higgins, Charles Welch, Julian Richardson, Colin and Daniel Gibbs*

BRIDGNORTH SO7192 Map 4

Old Castle £

(01746) 711420 – www.oldcastlebridgnorth.co.uk

West Castle Street; WV16 4AB

Cheerful town pub, relaxed and friendly, with generous helpings of good value pubby food, well kept ales and good-sized suntrap terrace

A real plus for the town, this busy pub has an open-plan, low-beamed bar of proper character: you'll find tiles and bare boards, cushioned wall banquettes and settles around cast-iron-framed tables, and bar stools arranged along the counter where the friendly landlord and his staff serve Hobsons Town Crier, Sharps Doom Bar and Wye Valley Butty Bach and HPA on handpump. A back conservatory extension has darts, pool and a games machine; background music and big-screen TV for sports events. A big plus here is the sunny back terrace with picnic-sets, lovely hanging baskets, big pots of flowers, shrub borders and decking at the far end that gives an elevated view over the west side of town; children's playthings. Do walk up the street to see the ruined castle – its 20-metre Norman tower tilts at such an extraordinary angle that it makes the Leaning Tower of Pisa look like a model of rectitude.

Reasonably priced traditional food includes sandwiches and baguettes, devilled whitebait, chicken dippers with barbecue sauce, vegetable chilli, lasagne, steak and stilton or fish and shellfish pie with creamy sherry sauce topped with cheesy mash, gammon with egg or pineapple, burgers with toppings and chips, mixed grill, and puddings. *Benchmark main dish: lamb shank with mash and lamb gravy £10.95. Two-course evening meal £19.00.*

Punch ~ Tenant Bryn Charles Masterman ~ Real ale ~ Open 11.30-11; 11.30-10.30 Sun ~ Bar food 12-3, 6.30-8.30 ~ Children welcome ~ Dogs welcome ~ Wi-fi *Recommended by Julian Richardson, Rona Mackinlay, Dave Braisted, John Harris, David and Leone Lawson*

CARDINGTON SO5095 Map 4

Royal Oak

(01694) 771266 – www.at-the-oak.com

Village signposted off B4371 Church Stretton–Much Wenlock, pub behind church; also reached via narrow lanes from A49; SY6 7JZ

Heaps of character in well run and friendly rural pub with seasonal bar food and real ales

Tucked away in the country, little changes here. Which is just how the chatty locals like it. The rambling, low-beamed traditional bar has a roaring winter log fire, a cauldron, black kettle and pewter jugs in a vast inglenook fireplace, aged standing timbers from a knocked-through wall, and red and green tapestry seats solidly capped in elm; board games and dominoes (they have two pub teams). Ludlow Best and Sharps Doom Bar with guests such as Purple Moose Elderflower Ale and Three Tuns XXX on handpump, eight wines by the glass, ten gins, several malt whiskies and farm cider. A comfortable dining area has exposed old beams and studwork. This is a glorious spot for walks, such as the one to the summit of Caer Caradoc, a couple of miles to the west (ask for directions at the pub), and the front courtyard makes the most of its beautiful position.

Using local producers and preparing the meat, game and fish in-house, the tasty seasonal food includes lunchtime baguettes, smoked mackerel pâté, bacon and black pudding salad with wholegrain mustard dressing, macaroni cheese with butternut squash and chilli, steak and mushroom pie, salmon tagliatelle with garlic bread, southern fried chicken and barbecue ribs with coleslaw, corn on the cob and chips, sirloin steak with a choice of sauces, and puddings. *Benchmark main dish: fidget pie £12.50. Two-course evening meal £18.00.*

Free house ~ Licensees Steve and Eira Oldham ~ Real ale ~ Open 12-2.30, 6-11; 12-11 Sat; 12-9 Sun (12-4 in winter); closed Mon except bank holiday lunchtime ~ Bar food 12-2.30, 6-9 ~ Restaurant ~ Children welcome ~ Dogs allowed in bar ~ Wi-fi *Recommended by Michael Butler, Paddy and Sian O'Leary, Barbara Brown, M G Hart, Celia and Andrew King, Valerie and Gordon Wauton*

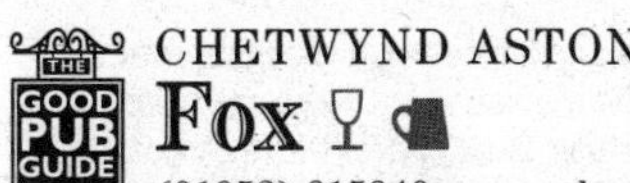

CHETWYND ASTON SJ7517 Map 7

Fox

(01952) 815940 – www.brunningandprice.co.uk/fox

Village signposted off A41 and A518 just S of Newport; TF10 9LQ

Civilised dining pub with generous helpings of well liked food and a fine array of drinks served by ever attentive staff

Although the interior here is large and spreading, there are cosy corners too. The linked rooms (one with a broad arched ceiling) has plenty of tables of varying shapes and sizes, some quite elegant, and a loosely matching diversity of comfortable chairs on parquet, polished boards or attractive floor tiles. Masses of prints and photographs line the walls, there are three open fires and big windows and careful lighting contribute to the relaxed atmosphere; board games. Bar stools line the long bar counter where courteous, efficient staff keep some 20 wines by the glass, 50 rums, 120 gins, 80 malt whiskies, two farm ciders and Phoenix Brunning & Price Original, Weetwood Cheshire Cat, Woods Shropshire Lad and three quickly changing guests such as Big Hand Appaloosa, Froth Blowers Piffle Snonker and New Plassey Dragons Breath on handpump. The large garden behind the pub is quite lovely, with a sunny terrace, picnic-sets tucked into the shade of mature trees and extensive views across quiet country fields; there's a play tractor for children. Good disabled access.

Distinctive food includes sandwiches, smoked mackerel with samphire, horseradish cream and beetroot jelly, cured smoked mutton with pea and mint polenta, pickled capers and spring onion aioli, crispy polenta with braised fennel, roast tomatoes and white bean cassoulet, warm crispy beef salad with spiced cashews and sweet chilli dressing, steak in ale pudding, fish pie with salmon, smoked haddock, prawns and egg, braised lamb shoulder with dauphinoise potatoes, chicken with parmesan gnocchi, edamame bean fricassée and tomato concasse, and puddings such as pistachio pannacotta with raspberry sorbet and hot waffle with caramelised banana and banana ice-cream. *Benchmark main dish: beer-battered cod and chips £13.75. Two-course evening meal £20.00.*

Brunning & Price ~ Manager Samantha Forrest ~ Real ale ~ Open 11-11; 11-10.30 Sun ~ Bar food 12-9.30; 12-10 Fri, Sat; 12-9 Sun ~ Children welcome ~ Dogs allowed in bar ~ Wi-fi

Recommended by Andrew Lawson, Angela and Steve Heard, Trevor and Michele Street, Monty Green

CLUN SO3080 Map 6

White Horse £

(01588) 418139 – www.whi-clun.co.uk

The Square; SY7 8JA

Bustling local with own-brewed and guest ales and good value traditional food; bedrooms

There's always a friendly mix of both regulars and visitors here, all keen to try the own-brewed beers. The low-beamed front bar is cosy and friendly and warmed in winter by an inglenook woodburning stove; from here, a door leads into a separate little dining room with a rare plank and muntin screen. Attentive staff serve well kept Clun Citadel, Loophole, Pale Ale and Solar, with guests such as Hobsons Best Bitter and Wye Valley Butty Bach on handpump. Also, five wines by the glass, half a dozen malt whiskies and two farm ciders. In the games room at the back you'll find a TV, games machine, darts, pool, juke box and board games. There's also a small garden. The bedrooms are quiet and comfortable.

Tasty food at fair prices includes sandwiches and baguettes, a changing pâté, mushroom stroganoff, chicken korma, beef bourguignon, local sausages with mash and gravy, burger with toppings, onion rings and chips, lamb cutlets with new potatoes, 28-day-aged steaks with a choice of sauces, and puddings such as syrup sponge and rice pudding. *Benchmark main dish: steak in ale pudding £12.95. Two-course evening meal £20.00.*

Own brew ~ Licensee Jack Limond ~ Real ale ~ Open 11-11 (midnight Sat) ~ Bar food 12-3, 6-9 ~ Restaurant ~ Children welcome ~ Dogs allowed in bar and bedrooms ~ Wi-fi ~ Live music every second Mon, occasionally Fri ~ Bedrooms: £50/£70 *Recommended by John Watson, John and Sharon Hancock, Peter Pilbeam, Thomas Green, Daniel King*

COALPORT SJ7002 Map 4

Woodbridge

(01952) 882054 – www.brunningandprice.co.uk/woodbridge

Village signposted off A442 1.5 miles S of A4169 Telford roundabout; down in valley, turn left across narrow bridge into Coalport Road, pub immediately left; TF8 7JF

Superb Ironbridge Gorge site for extensive, handsomely reworked pub, an all-round success

In a lovely spot, this 18th-c pub is highly regarded for the fine choice of drinks served by quick, friendly staff: Phoenix Brunning & Price Original and guests such as Battlefield Saxon Gold, Gorgeous Beer Company Ruby Porter, Hobsons Town Crier, Holdens Black Country Bitter and Woods Shropshire Lass on handpump, ten wines by the glass, 50 malt whiskies and 20 gins. The spreading series of linked rooms are comfortable and civilised with log fires and Coalport-style stoves, rugs on broad boards as well as tiles or carpet, black beams in the central part and plenty of polished tables and cosy armchair corners. A mass of mainly 18th- and 19th-c prints, often of local scenes, line the walls and are well worth a look; background music and board games. Named after the wooden bridge that once connected the pub to the village, the place is on the banks of the River Severn, with tables and chairs on a big deck looking over the water and picnic-sets on grass and a play tractor.

Interesting food includes sandwiches, scallops with butternut squash purée, crispy bacon and caper and lemon dressing, wild mushroom tortellini with spinach and leek purée, tempura king prawns with pak choi and watermelon salad with chilli dressing, cauliflower, sweet potato and chickpea tagine with apricot couscous and crispy courgettes, honey, soy and ginger duck breast with spicy cashew nuts, pork and leek sausages with mash and onion gravy, sea bass fillets with crab and chervil risotto and crispy mussels, and puddings such as cherry and amaretti cheesecake with Cointreau ice-cream and triple chocolate brownie with chocolate sauce and vanilla ice-cream. *Benchmark main dish: braised lamb shoulder with dauphinoise potatoes £17.95. Two-course evening meal £23.00.*

Brunning & Price ~ Manager Vrata Krist ~ Real ale ~ Open 11.30-11; 11.30-midnight Sat; 11.30-10.30 Sun ~ Bar food 12-9.30; 12-10 Fri, Sat; 12-9 Sun ~ Restaurant ~ Children welcome ~ Dogs allowed in bar ~ Wi-fi *Recommended by Richard and Tessa Ibbot, Michael Sargent, Alfie Bayliss, Celia and Rupert Lemming, Dan and Nicki Barton*

IRONBRIDGE SJ6703 Map 4

Golden Ball

(01952) 432179 – www.goldenballironbridge.co.uk

Brown sign to pub off Madeley Road (B4373) above village centre – pub behind Horse & Jockey, car park beyond on left; TF8 7BA

Low-beamed, partly Elizabethan pub with popular food and drink; bedrooms

This friendly inn is tucked away in a little hamlet of other ancient buildings; you can walk down to the River Severn, and beyond, but it's pretty steep getting back up. The bar has worn floorboards, red-cushioned pews, one or two black beams and a woodburning stove. Butcombe Original, Hobsons Town Crier, Purity Pure UBU and Wye Valley HPA on handpump, quite a few belgian bottled ales, nine wines by the glass and several gins and whiskies; background music and TV. A pretty fairy-lit pergola path leads to the door and a sheltered side courtyard has tables under parasols. If you stay overnight, the bedrooms are comfortable and breakfasts are good.

Good food listed on blackboards includes lunchtime sandwiches and baguettes, camembert with home-made chutney, confit duck leg with orange salad, moroccan-style mushrooms and apricot couscous, lime and chicken coconut with sweet potato wedges, hake on fried greens with caper butter, sirloin steak with brandy and cracked peppercorn sauce, and puddings such as fruit cheesecake and honey and rhubarb pannacotta. *Benchmark main dish: home-made pies £10.00. Two-course evening meal £16.00.*

Enterprise ~ Lease Jessica Janke ~ Real ale ~ Open 12-11; 12-11.30 Sat (10 in winter ~ Bar food 12-9 (8 in winter); 12-7 (6 in winter) Sun ~ Restaurant ~ Children welcome ~ Dogs allowed in bar and bedrooms ~ Wi-fi ~ Open mike second Sun of month; live band monthly; quiz every two weeks ~ Bedrooms: £60/£65 *Recommended by Ben and Jenny Settle, Alexander and Trish Gendall, Ian Herdman, John and Lorna Chew, Alexandra and Tim Fledgling*

LUDLOW SO5174 Map 6

Charlton Arms

(01584) 872813 – www.thecharltonarms.co.uk

Ludford Bridge, B4361 Overton Road; SY8 1PJ

Fine position for bustling pub near town centre, plenty of space for both drinking and dining and extensive terraces looking over the river; bedrooms

In warm weather, arrive early to bag a seat on one of the two balconies which overlook the River Teme and the massive medieval bridge. The character bar has proper pubby tables and chairs on tiled and bricked floors, gluggle jugs along the gantry, a double-sided woodburner, and stools against the hop-hung counter where friendly staff serve Hobsons Best Bitter, Ludlow Gold and Stairway and Wye Valley Butty Bach and HPA on handpump, 15 wines by the glass and a farm cider. The two rooms of the lounge (sharing a two-way woodburning stove) are comfortable and chatty with tub chairs, armchairs and high-backed black leather seats on pale wooden floors. The dining room looks over the fine bridge; background music and board games. Bedrooms are well equipped and cosy and have views of the water.

Pleasing food includes sandwiches, fish soup with rouille and croutons, duck and pork terrine, coconut quinoa and lentil curry with lime and mango, dressed crab with lemon mayonnaise, burger with burger sauce and skinny fries, pork tenderloin with black pudding mousse, dauphinoise potatoes and cepe mushroom sauce, lemon sole with brown shrimp butter, lamb shank with creamy mash and roasted root vegetables, and puddings such as vanilla crème brûlée and chocolate fondant with cherry ice-cream. *Benchmark main dish: beer-battered fish and chips £12.95. Two-course evening meal £19.50.*

Free house ~ Licensee Cedric Bosi ~ Real ale ~ Open 11-11 (midnight Sat); 12-10.30 Sun ~ Bar food 12-2.30, 6-9 (8.30 Sun) ~ Restaurant ~ Children welcome ~ Dogs allowed in bar ~ Wi-fi ~ Bedrooms: £95/£100 *Recommended by Michael Butler, Graeme and Sally Mendham, Katherine and Hugh Markham, Alison and Dan Richardson*

LUDLOW SO5174 Map 4

Church Inn

(01584) 874034 – www.thechurchinn.com

Church Street, behind Butter Cross; SY8 1AW

Splendid range of real ales in character town-centre pub

This is right at the centre of a charming hilltop town. The ground floor is divided into three appealingly decorated areas, with hops hanging from heavy beams and comfortable banquettes in cosy alcoves; the pulpit and pews come from a local church. A long central area has a fine stone fireplace, a chess table and board games, while, upstairs, the civilised lounge bar has vaulted ceilings and gives good views of St Laurence's church and the surrounding countryside. A fine range of ales served by friendly staff includes Hobsons Best Bitter, Ludlow Black Knight, Gold and Stairway, Salopian Darwins Origin and a rotating guest on handpump, 14 wines by the glass, 25 gins and a farm cider. There are picnic-sets in the back garden (which they share with the church).

High quality food includes lunchtime sandwiches (not Sunday), baked camembert (for two to share) with wild mushroom fricassée, smoked mackerel with pickled cucumber, beetroot and horseradish cream, nut roast with white wine sauce and sautéed potatoes, local faggots with onion gravy, chicken and ham hock pie, bavette steak with peppercorn sauce and onion rings, and puddings such as bread and butter pudding with marmalade ice-cream and warm chocolate fondant with mint ice-cream. *Benchmark main dish: beer-battered haddock and chips £11.00. Two-course evening meal £19.00.*

Free house ~ Licensee Matt Tommey ~ Real ale ~ Open 11-11; 11-midnight Fri, Sat; 12-10.30 Sun ~ Bar food 12-3, 6-9 (8.30 Sun) ~ Restaurant ~ Children welcome ~ Dogs allowed in bar ~ Wi-fi *Recommended by Roy and Gill Payne, Shona and Jimmy McDuff, Christopher May, Susie and Spencer Gray, Adam and Natalie Davis*

MAESBURY MARSH SJ3125 Map 6

Navigation

(01691) 672958 – www.thenavigation.co.uk

Follow Maesbury Road off A483 S of Oswestry; by canal bridge; SY10 8JB

Friendly canalside pub with cosy bar and local seasonal produce in a choice of dining areas

As well as running this traditional pub, the hands-on licensees also run a book exchange, a shop where you can buy fresh local produce (including fish and shellfish) and offer a two-pint takeaway service. The place has a community feel and the old-fashioned, quarry-tiled bar on the left has squishy brown leather sofas by an old-style black range, upholstered cask seats around three small tables, and dozens of wrist- and pocket-watches hanging from the beams. A couple of steps lead up beyond a balustrade to a carpeted area, with armchairs and sofas around low tables, and a piano (that does get used); off to the left is a dining area with paintings by local artists. The main beamed dining room, with some stripped stone, is beyond another small bar with a coal-effect gas fire, and an amazing row of cushioned carved choir stalls complete with misericord seats. Joules Slumbering Monk and Stonehouse Cambrian Gold and Station Bitter on handpump, 11 wines by the glass, nine malt whiskies (including one from Wales) and a farm cider (in summer); quiet background music and board games. There are picnic-sets beside the Montgomery Canal and the windows in the dining room share the same view.

Cooked by Brent Ellis (one of the owners) and using carefully sourced free-range produce, the good food includes sandwiches (lunchtime Wednesday to Saturday), duck rillettes with gherkins and pickles, prawn cocktail, a trio of free-range pork sausages with braised red cabbage and gravy, free-range chicken breast wrapped in bacon with crushed new potatoes, sautéed leeks and mushrooms and a choice of sauce (white wine, peppercorn or blue cheese), lamb steak with carrot and swede mash, braised shallots and lamb jus, duck breast with crushed new potatoes, crispy kale and orange and maple syrup sauce, and puddings such as crème caramel with dark chocolate mousse and marmalade and Drambuie bread and butter pudding with custard; Friday is fish and chips day. *Benchmark main dish: crispy pork belly with creamed spinach, black pudding mash and apple purée £14.95. Two-course evening meal £20.50.*

Free house ~ Licensees Brent Ellis and Mark Baggett ~ Real ale ~ Open 12-2, 6-11; 12-6 Sun; closed Sun evening, all day Mon, lunchtime Tue; first two weeks Jan ~ Bar food 12-2, 6-8.30; 12-2 Sun ~ Restaurant ~ Children welcome ~ Dogs allowed in bar ~ Wi-fi *Recommended by Sally Harrison, Jeff Davies, Gordon and Patricia Gorringe, Catherine and Daniel King*

NEENTON **Pheasant**

SO6387 Map 4

(01746) 787955 – www.pheasantatneenton.co.uk

B4364 Bridgnorth–Ludlow; WV16 6RJ

Renovated village pub owned by locals with a traditionally furnished bar and dining room, local ales and good food; seats in orchard garden

Although this is owned by and run for the community, there's a genuine welcome for visitors too. The cosy front bar has leather sofas and armchairs by a woodburning stove, rugs on tiles and stools by the counter where they serve Hobsons Town Crier and Twisted Spire, Wye Valley HPA and a guest from Hop & Stagger on handpump, 14 wines by the glass, quite a few gins and farm cider; background music, darts and board games. Staff are friendly and helpful. The airy dining room is in an oak-framed extension at the back with a homely medley of cushioned chairs and wooden tables on bare boards. There are picnic-sets on the lawn and under trees in the orchard and a children's play area; boules. The three bedrooms are comfortable and breakfasts are good. There are good nearby walks in the attractive Shropshire hills.

Enjoyable food includes sandwiches, smoked mackerel pâté with cucumber and shallot relish, wild mushroom with garlic, white wine and herb tagliatelle, steak in ale pie, butternut squash, roast red pepper and pea risotto with ricotta, crispy shallots and herb oil, burger with toppings, onion rings and skin-on chips, beer-battered haddock and chips, gammon with a fried egg and french fries, chicken breast with fondant potatoes, pancetta and red wine jus, and puddings such as lemon posset with chantilly cream and sticky toffee pudding with toffee sauce and honeycomb ice-cream. *Benchmark main dish: seared cod loin with spinach, confit tomatoes, crispy poached egg and mustard sauce £16.95. Two-course evening meal £22.00.*

Free house ~ Licensees Mark Harris and Sarah Cowley ~ Real ale ~ Open 12-3, 6-11; 12-11 Sat; 12-9 Sun ~ Bar food 12-2.30, 6-9; 12-4.30 Sun ~ Restaurant ~ Children welcome ~ Dogs allowed in bar and bedrooms ~ Wi-fi ~ Bedrooms: /£90 *Recommended by Amy and Luke Buchanan, Emily and Toby Archer, George Sanderson, Alun Jones, Celia and Andrew King, Alexandra and Tim Fledgling*

If we know a featured-entry pub does sandwiches, we always say so – if they're not mentioned, you'll have to assume you can't get one.

NORTON SJ7200 Map 4

Hundred House

(01952) 730353 – www.hundredhouse.co.uk

A442 Telford–Bridgnorth; TF11 9EE

Family-run inn with rambling rooms, open fires, a very good choice of drinks and rewarding food; large, comfortable bedrooms

Very much a family concern, this is a carefully run inn that our readers have enjoyed greatly over many years. The rambling bar rooms have log fires in handsome fireplaces (one has a large Jacobean arch with fine old black cooking pots) and a variety of interesting chairs and settles with long colourful patchwork leather cushions around sewing machine tables. Hops and huge bunches of dried flowers and herbs hang from beams, and bunches of fresh flowers brighten the tables and counter in the neatly kept bar. Steps lead up past a little balustrade to a partly panelled eating area, where the stripped brickwork looks older than it does elsewhere. Enville Ale, Heritage Victoria Pale Ale, Hobsons Mild, Sadlers Peaky Blinder and Wells St Georges Thirstslayer on handpump, 18 wines by the glass, a dozen malt whiskies, a growing choice of gins and a farm cider; background music and TV. The lovely garden at the back has old-fashioned roses, herbaceous plants and a big working herb garden (with around 50 varieties); they've also got a rescue donkey too. Bedrooms feature antique four-posters or half-testers, Victorian-style baths and rain showers, and their trademark velvet-cushioned swing.

Appetising food includes roast beetroot with goats cheese mousse and apple chutney, meze platter, butternut squash, thyme and ricotta tart with sun-dried tomatoes and grilled courgettes, chicken breast and mini garlic kiev with smoked bacon and potato terrine and kale, crispy salmon fillet, king prawn and crab salad with asparagus and parmesan chips, hake with jerusalem artichoke purée with charred gem, brown shrimps, rosemary and brown almond butter, and puddings such as treacle tart with custard and rhubarb cheesecake with cinnamon syrup. *Benchmark main dish: smoked duck breast with duck croquette and blueberry port wine sauce £18.95. Two-course evening meal £24.00.*

Free house ~ Licensees Henry, Stuart and David Phillips ~ Real ale ~ Open 11-11; 11-10 Sun ~ Bar food 12-2.30, 6-9; 12-8 Sun ~ Restaurant ~ Children welcome ~ Dogs allowed in bar and bedrooms ~ Wi-fi ~ Bedrooms: £89/£99 *Recommended by Peter and Emma Kelly, Chloe and Tim Hodge, Frank and Marcia Pelling, Jill and Hugh Bennett*

SHIPLEY SO8095 Map 4

Inn at Shipley

(01902) 701639 – www.brunningandprice.co.uk/innatshipley

Bridgnorth Road; A454 W of Wolverhampton; WV6 7EQ

Light and airy country pub – a good all-rounder

A fine range of drinks and interesting food draw plenty of customers into this handsome old pub. The rambling rooms have a chatty, informal atmosphere and several woodburning stoves and log fires that surround the central bar: one in a big inglenook in a cosy, traditionally tiled black-beamed end room and another by a welcoming set of wing and other leather armchairs. All sorts of dining chairs are grouped around a variety of well buffed tables in the rambling rooms, rugs are set on polished boards, attractive pictures are hung frame to frame and big windows let in plenty of daylight; church candles, careful spotlighting and chandeliers add atmosphere. The various areas are interconnected but manage to also feel distinct and individual; upstairs is a separate private dining room. Phoenix Brunning & Price Original, Enville Ale and Wye Valley Butty Bach plus three rotating guests on handpump, 17 wines by the glass, 80 malt whiskies, 70 gins and two farm ciders; good, neatly dressed staff, background music and board games. There are plenty of sturdy tables outside, some on a sizeable terrace with a side awning, others by weeping willows on the main lawn behind the car park, more on smaller lawns around the building.

From a modern menu and attractively presented, the food includes sandwiches, seared scallops with pea and chervil purée and crisp parma ham, home-made black pudding with crispy poached egg, wild mushroom risotto with tarragon, rocket and truffle oil, caramelised red onion sausages with mash and onion gravy, steak burger with toppings, coleslaw and chips, lamb rump with confit new potatoes, roasted salsify and artichoke purée, fish pie with french-style peas, and puddings such as lemon meringue pie and raspberry sorbet and dark chocolate and pecan brownie with chocolate sauce and white chocolate ice-cream. *Benchmark main dish: braised lamb shoulder with dauphinoise potatoes, carrot purée and rosemary gravy £17.45. Two-course evening meal £21.00.*

Brunning & Price ~ Manager Oliver Parrish ~ Real ale ~ Open 10.30am-11pm (10.30pm Sun) ~ Bar food 12-9.30 (10 Thurs-Sat) ~ Restaurant ~ Children welcome ~ Dogs allowed in bar ~ Wi-fi *Recommended by Sandra and Michael Smith, Patricia Healey, Alexandra and Tim Fledgling, David and Leone Lawson, Mark Hamill*

SHREWSBURY — SJ4812 Map 6

Armoury

(01743) 340525 – www.brunningandprice.co.uk/armoury

Victoria Quay, Victoria Avenue; SY1 1HH

Vibrant atmosphere in interestingly converted riverside warehouse with tempting all-day food

The spacious open-plan interior here, with its long runs of big arched windows and views across the broad river at the back, makes quite an impression when you first arrive. But despite its size the pub has a personal feel, helped by the eclectic décor, furniture layout and cheerful bustle. A mix of wood tables and chairs are grouped on stripped-wood floors, the huge brick walls display floor-to-ceiling books or masses of old prints mounted edge to edge, and there's a grand stone fireplace at one end. Colonial-style fans whirr away on the ceilings, which are supported by green-painted columns, and small wall-mounted glass cabinets display smokers' pipes. Phoenix Brunning & Price Original, Salopian Oracle and Woods Shropshire Lad with guest beers such as Ambridge Citra and Mosaic, Skinners Cornish Knocker and Three Tuns XXX on handpump, 17 wines by the glass, 100 malt whiskies, 84 gins, lots of rums and vodkas, a variety of brandies and a farm cider. The hanging baskets are quite a sight in summer. The pub doesn't have its own car park, but there are plenty of parking places nearby.

Brasserie-style food includes sandwiches, smoked trout fillet with pickled vegetables and chive crème fraîche, slow-cooked crispy duck with toasted hazelnut and orange salad, thai green vegetable curry with coconut steamed rice and pak choi, honey roasted ham and eggs, pork and leek sausages with mash and onion gravy, cod loin with black pudding crumb, fondant potatoes and salsa verde, chicken breast with tomato, spinach and chorizo risotto and parmesan, crispy beef and rice noodle salad with peanuts, red peppers and mango, and puddings such as waffle with cherries, chocolate sauce and cherry crumble ice-cream and blueberry meringue with white chocolate pannacotta and blueberry compote. *Benchmark main dish: steak burger with toppings, coleslaw and chips £12.95. Two-course evening meal £23.00.*

Brunning & Price ~ Manager Emily Periam ~ Real ale ~ Open 10am-11.30pm (midnight Sat); 10am-10.30pm Sun ~ Bar food ~ Children welcome ~ Dogs allowed in bar ~ Wi-fi
Recommended by Michael Butler, Usha and Terri Patel, Gill and Hugh Bennett, Christine and Tony Garrett, Ian Duncan

SHREWSBURY SJ4912 Map 6

Lion & Pheasant

(01743) 770345 – www.lionandpheasant.co.uk
Follow City Centre signposts across the English Bridge; SY1 1XJ

Shropshire Dining Pub of the Year

Civilised bar and upstairs restaurant in comfortable, neatly updated and well placed inn; bedrooms

Our readers enjoy their visits to this carefully run pub – a first class all-rounder. It's a 16th-c inn where original features blend seamlessly with more contemporary touches, making the décor throughout extremely appealing. The big-windowed bar consists of three linked levels, the lowest of which has armchairs on dark flagstones by a big inglenook; elsewhere, there's a cushioned settee or two, but most of the seats are at sturdy stripped tables on dark floorboards. A few modern paintings, plentiful flowers and church candles brighten up the restrained cream and grey décor, as do the friendly staff and background music. Hobsons Old Prickly, Salopian Shropshire Gold and Wye Valley Butty Bach on handpump, 14 wines by the glass and farm cider. Off quite a warren of corridors, the restaurant is in the older back part of the building with beams and timbering (you can eat from the restaurant menu in the bar too). Outside, there are seats and tables under parasols with olive trees and flowering pots dotted about. A lovely place to stay, the bedrooms are comfortable and breakfasts are good; some rooms give glimpses of the River Severn below the nearby English Bridge.

Excellent food includes sandwiches, tuna sashimi with avocado, cucumber, yuzu, puffed rice and wasabi, duck ravioli with squash, sage, parmesan and brown butter, soy-glazed aubergine with tempura vegetables, tomato relish, oyster mushrooms and coriander, steak burger with toppings and chips, stone bass with seaweed arancini, charred leeks, mandarin and sea herbs, braised lamb shoulder with potato purée, grelot onions, shallots and wild garlic, and puddings such as chocolate tart with glazed banana, caramel popcorn and banana and mascarpone ice-cream and baked alaska with lemon curd parfait, sorrel sorbet and lemon marmalade. *Benchmark main dish: rib-eye steak with parmesan and truffle salad, chips and a choice of sauce £25.00. Two-course evening meal £30.00.*

Free house ~ Licensee Jim Littler ~ Real ale ~ Open 10am-1am ~ Bar food 12-3, 6-9; 12-9.30 Sat; 12-4, 6-8 Sun ~ Restaurant ~ Children welcome ~ Wi-fi ~ Bedrooms: £99/£115
Recommended by Isobel Mackinlay, Edward May, Julia and Fiona Barnes, Miranda and Jeff Davidson, Justine and Neil Bonnett

'Children welcome' means the pub says it lets children inside without any special restriction. If it allows them in, but to restricted areas such as an eating area or family room, we specify this. Places with separate restaurants often let children use them, and hotels usually let children into public areas such as lounges. Some pubs impose an evening time limit – let us know if you find one earlier than 9pm.

Also Worth a Visit in Shropshire

Besides the fully inspected pubs, you might like to try these pubs that have been recommended to us and described by readers. Do tell us what you think of them: feedback@goodguides.com

ADMASTON SJ6313

Pheasant (01952) 251989
Shawbirch Road; TF5 0AD Modernised 19th-c red-brick pub fronting the road; enjoyable generously served home-made food (all day Sat, till 7pm Sun), three or four well kept ales including Salopian and Wye Valley, decent range of wines, helpful service; background music, free wi-fi; children welcome, no dogs during food times, garden with picnic-sets and play area, open all day. *(Cecily and Steven Evans)*

BISHOP'S CASTLE SO3288

★**Castle Hotel** (01588) 638403
Market Square, just off B4385; SY9 5BN Substantial coaching inn at top of lovely market town; clubby little beamed and panelled bar with log fire, larger rooms off with another fire, well kept ales such as Hobsons, Six Bells and Three Tuns, local cider, ten wines by the glass and 30 or so malt whiskies, popular food served by friendly staff, handsome panelled dining room; background music; children and dogs welcome, pretty hanging baskets at front, garden behind with terrace seating and pergolas, good views and surrounding walks, 13 spacious bedrooms, useful big car park, open all day. *(Justine and Neil Bonnett)*

BISHOP'S CASTLE SO3288

Six Bells (01588) 630144
Church Street; SY9 5AA Friendly 17th-c pub brewing its own good beers in back microbrewery (tours available); simple little bar with inglenook woodburner, old local photographs and prints, bigger room with mix of furniture on bare boards and another woodburner, sandwiches only lunchtimes Mon-Sat, good value meals Fri and Sat evenings, roasts Sun; July beer/cider festival; well behaved children and dogs welcome, café in brewery, open all day. *(Alfie Bayliss)*

BISHOP'S CASTLE SO3288

★**Three Tuns** (01588) 638797
Salop Street; SY9 5BW Extended old pub adjacent to unique four-storey Victorian brewhouse (a brewery is said to have existed here since 1642); busy chatty atmosphere in public, lounge and snug bars, Three Tuns beers (including 1642) from old-fashioned handpumps (cheaper 5-7pm Fri), several wines by the glass, tasty good value food (not Sun evening) from sandwiches up, friendly young staff, modernised dining room done out in smart oak and glass; lots going on including film club, music nights, fortnightly open mike (Tues) and summer beer festival; children and dogs welcome, open all day. *(Michael Butler)*

BOULDON SO5485

Tally Ho (01584) 841811
W end of village, set back from road; SY7 9DP Welcoming tucked-away pub owned by group of villagers; good local beers such as Hobsons and Salopian, enjoyable fairly priced food (not Mon) from sandwiches and light meals up, rugs on quarry tiles, woodburner in big stone fireplace, various pictures and other memorabilia; darts; children and dogs welcome, country views from nice garden, open all day weekends, closed Mon lunchtime. *(Michael Butler)*

BRIDGES SO3996

★**Bridges** (01588) 650260
Pub signed from Pulverbatch–Wentnor road, W of Ratlinghope; SY5 0ST Old renovated beamed country pub owned by Three Tuns with their full range in excellent condition; bare-boards bar to right, large dining room to left, enjoyable fairly traditional home-made food including daily specials, helpful friendly staff; occasional live music; children and well behaved dogs welcome, tables out by little River Onny (some on raised deck), bedrooms in separate buildings, also camping and youth hostel nearby, great walking country, open (and food) all day, breakfast from 9.30am. *(Ian Duncan)*

BRIDGNORTH SO6890

★**Down** (01746) 789539
The Down; B4364 Ludlow Road 3 miles S; WV16 6UA Good value roadside dining pub overlooking rolling countryside; enjoyable food (all day weekends) including popular daily carvery, efficient friendly service, ales such as Hobsons and Salopian; background music; children welcome, no dogs, nine comfortable bedrooms, open all day. *(Christine and Tony Garrett)*

BRIDGNORTH SO7193

Kings Head (01746) 762141
Whitburn Street; WV16 4QN 16th-c timbered coaching inn with high-raftered back stable bar and restaurant; Hobsons, Wye Valley and a couple of guests, decent choice of wines and good popular food served by friendly helpful staff, log fires, beams and

We say if we know a pub has background music.

flagstones, pretty leaded windows; children and dogs welcome, courtyard tables, open all day, food all day Sun. *(Charles Welch)*

BRIDGNORTH SO7192

★ **Railwaymans Arms** (01746) 760920 *Severn Valley Railway station, Hollybush Road (off A458 towards Stourbridge); WV16 5DT* Bathams, Hobsons and plenty of other well kept ales in chatty old-fashioned converted waiting room at Severn Valley steam railway terminus, bustling on summer days; old station signs and train nameplates, superb mirror over fireplace; snacky food such as pork pies; children and dogs welcome, wheelchair access with help, tables out on platform – the train to Kidderminster (station bar there too) has an all-day bar and bookable Sun lunches, open all day. *(David and Leone Lawson)*

BRIDGNORTH SO7192

White Lion (01746) 763962 *West Castle Street; WV16 4AB* Fairly compact 18th-c two-bar pub with seven well kept ales including own Hop & Stagger brews, traditional cider and reasonably priced bar food such as home-made scotch eggs and butcher-made pies, friendly helpful staff, comfortable carpeted lounge with open fire; regular events including folk club (first Tues of month), storytelling (second Tues) and charity quiz (last Tues); children and dogs welcome, lawned garden with terrace, four good value clean bedrooms (no breakfast), open all day. *(David and Leone Lawson)*

BRIDGNORTH SO7093

Woodberry (01746) 762950 *Victoria Road/Sydney Cottage Drive; WV16 4LF* Welcoming dining inn with good choice of enjoyable locally sourced food, ales such as Battlefield and Hobsons, friendly efficient service; background music, free wi-fi; children welcome, large garden with benches, comfortable bedrooms, good breakfast, closed Sun evening, otherwise open (and food) all day. *(Jack S)*

BROMFIELD SO4877

★ **Clive** (01584) 856565 *A49, 2 miles NW of Ludlow; SY8 2JR* Civilised bar-restaurant-hotel named after Clive of India who once lived here; much emphasis on their popular well presented food but also Hobsons and Ludlow ales, several wines by the glass and good bar snacks, friendly service; dining room with light wood tables and chairs on wood-strip floor, door to bar and step down to raftered room with woodburner in huge fireplace; background music, free wi-fi; children welcome, tables under parasols on secluded terrace, garden with fish pond, 15 bedrooms in separate building, Ludlow Food Centre next door, open all day. *(Mike and Mary Carter)*

BUCKNELL SO3574

★ **Baron** (01547) 530549 *Chapel Lawn Road; just off B4367 Knighton Road; SY7 0AH* Modernised family-owned country inn, friendly and efficiently run, with enjoyable sensibly priced food cooked to order from pub favourites and pizzas up, a couple of well kept ales such as Ludlow and Wye Valley, woodburner in carpeted bar opening into conservatory, pitched-roof dining room with small gallery, old cider press and grindstone, further Stable Bar with pool and TV where dogs allowed; children welcome, peaceful setting with lovely views from big garden, good walks from the door, eight bedrooms including three chalets with hot tubs, open all day Sat, till 6pm Sun, closed lunchtimes Mon-Thurs. *(Brian and Jacky Wilson)*

BURLTON SJ4526

Burlton Inn (01939) 270284 *A528 Shrewsbury–Ellesmere, near B4397 junction; SY4 5TB* Welcoming attractively updated 18th-c inn; enjoyable pubby food and well kept Robinsons ales (maybe a guest), friendly helpful staff, beams, timbers and log fires, comfortable snug, restaurant with garden room; Fri jazz, Sun quiz; children and dogs (in bar) welcome, disabled access/facilities, teak furniture on pleasant terrace, six comfortable well equipped bedrooms, open all day Sun (food till 7pm). *(Phil and Margaret Walker)*

BURWARTON SO6185

★ **Boyne Arms** (01746) 787214 *B4364 Bridgnorth–Ludlow; WV16 6QH* Handsome Georgian coaching inn under welcoming newish management; enjoyable home-made food (not Sun evening, Mon, Tues) including Fri steak night, two Wye Valley ales, Robinson's and Thatcher's ciders, friendly helpful service, separate restaurant and public bar (dogs allowed here); children welcome, play area in pretty garden, open all day weekends, closed Mon lunchtime. *(Dan and Nicki Barton)*

CHURCH STRETTON SO4593

Housmans (01694) 724441 *High Street; SY6 6BX* Buzzing and welcoming restaurant-bar with good wine and cocktail lists plus a couple of well kept ales from Three Tuns, nice range of food including tapas-style sharing plates and specials (Mon fish), local artwork on display, occasional live jazz and other acoustic music; children welcome, open all day weekends. *(Valerie and Gordon Wauton)*

CLAVERLEY SO8095

Woodman (01746) 710553 *B4176/Danford Lane; WV5 7DG* Rural 19th-c red-brick dining pub; contemporary beamed interior arranged around central bar, good popular food (must book) using local produce including some from farm opposite, well kept Black Sheep and Enville, lots of wines by the glass and interesting range of gins, efficient service; terrace and garden tables, closed Sun evening, Mon. *(Jill and Hugh Bennett)*

CLUN SO3080

Sun (01588) 640559
High Street; SY7 8JB Beamed and timbered 15th-c pub in peaceful village surrounded by lovely rolling countryside; traditional flagstoned public bar with inglenook woodburner, larger carpeted lounge with fragment of 17th-c wallpaper and set of fine old beer pumps, six well kept Three Tuns beers and enjoyable home-made food from lunchtime sandwiches up, friendly helpful staff; children (in lounge), walkers and dogs (in bar) welcome, paved back terrace, four bedrooms (two in converted outbuildings), open all day, food all day weekends. *(Christine and Tony Garrett)*

CLUNTON SO3381

Crown (01588) 660265
B4368; SY7 0HU Welcoming community-owned country local under friendly new tenants; up to four well kept ales including Hobsons and Ludlow, traditional ciders, food currently limited to fish and chips Weds evening, curry Thurs and roasts Sun lunchtime, also a themed night first Sat of month, log fire in cosy flagstoned bar, carpeted dining room and separate games room with pool and darts; children welcome in restaurant, dogs in bar, a few seats out at front with more in small back garden, open all day weekends, closed Mon and lunchtimes Tues-Fri. *(Charles Welch)*

COALPORT SJ6902

Shakespeare (01952) 580675
High Street; TF8 7HT Welcoming early 19th-c inn by pretty Severn gorge; timbering, bare stone walls and tiled floors, well kept Everards, Hobsons, Ludlow and a guest, good value generously served food from sandwiches through pub standards to international dishes; children welcome, picnic-sets in tiered garden with play area, handy for Coalport China Museum, four bedrooms, open all day weekends, closed weekdays till 5pm. *(Ian Duncan)*

CORFTON SO4985

Sun (01584) 861239
B4368 Much Wenlock–Craven Arms; SY7 9DF Lived-in unchanging three-room country local with own good Corvedale ales (including an unfined beer), friendly long-serving landlord often busy in the back brewery, decent pubby food from baguettes to steaks, lots of breweriana, basic quarry-tiled public bar with darts, pool and juke box, quieter carpeted lounge, dining room with covered well; children and dogs (in bar) welcome, good wheelchair access throughout and disabled loos, tables on terrace and in large garden with play area, open all day. *(Jill and Hugh Bennett)*

ELLERDINE HEATH SJ6122

Royal Oak (01939) 250300
Hazles Road; TF6 6RL Friendly little country pub known locally as the Tiddly (Wink); half a dozen well kept ales and good value straightforward food (not Mon, Tues), open fires; children and dogs welcome, good sized garden, open all day. *(Alfie Bayliss)*

GOLDSTONE SJ7128

Wharf (01630) 661226
Off A529 S of Market Drayton, at Hinstock; keep on towards Cheswardine; TF9 2LP Clean and tidy pub by Shropshire Union Canal (Bridge 55); Exmoor Gold, Joules Pale Ale, Sharps Doom Bar and a guest served from central bar, generous helpings of popular pub food (should book), good friendly service, winter fire; children welcome, no dogs inside, plenty of seats out by canal, caravan park, open all day. *(Tony Hobden)*

GRINDLEY BROOK SJ5242

Horse & Jockey (01948) 662723
A41; SY13 4QJ Extended 19th-c roadside pub with enjoyable good value food from varied menu, eight well kept ales including a house beer from Woods named after resident chocolate labrador Blaze, teas and coffees, friendly helpful service, well divided open-plan interior with mix of furniture on wood or carpeted floors, woodburners and some interesting bits and pieces; sports TV, pool; children, dogs and muddy boots welcome, play area on side lawn, handy for Sandstone Trail and Llangollen Canal, open (and food) all day. *(Mike and Wena Stevenson, Ed McKeegan)*

HIGHLEY SO7483

Ship (01746) 861219
Severnside; WV16 6NU Modernised 18th-c inn set in lovely riverside location; good pubby food including popular Sun carvery, five real ales such as Banks's and Hobsons; children welcome, disabled access and facilities, tables on raised front deck, handy for Severn Way walks (and Severn Valley Railway), fishing rights, bedrooms and nearby camping, open all day. *(Dave Braisted)*

HODNET SJ6128

★**Bear** (01630) 685214
Drayton Road (A53); TF9 3NH Black and white timbered inn with rambling open-plan main room; heavy 16th-c beams and timbers creating separate areas, wooden tables and chairs on rugs or flagstones, woodburner in large stone fireplace (there are three other woodburners), view into former bear pit through glass floor panel; smaller beamed and quarry-tiled bar with

ales such as Salopian, Three Tuns and Timothy Taylors, 13 wines by the glass, 20 malt whiskies and around 30 gins, well liked food served by friendly helpful staff; children and dogs (in bar) welcome, picnic-sets and play area in garden, comfortable well equipped bedrooms, Hodnet Hall Gardens opposite and handy for Hawkstone Park, open all day Fri and Sat, till 7pm Sun, closed lunchtimes other days. *(Neil and Brenda Skidmore)*

HOPE SJ3401

Stables (01743) 891344
Just off A488 3 miles S of Minsterley; SY5 0EP Hidden-away little 17th-c beamed country pub (former drovers' inn), friendly and welcoming, with good home-made food and a couple of well kept ales such as Three Tuns, log fires; dogs welcome, fine views from garden, two bedrooms and shepherd's hut, open all day weekends, closed weekday lunchtimes. *(Jill and Hugh Bennett)*

KNOCKIN SJ3322

Bradford Arms (01691) 682358
B4396 NW of Shrewsbury; SY10 8HJ Sizeable neatly kept village local with notable three-faced roof clock; popular good value pubby food (best to book) and well kept Marstons-related beers, friendly welcoming staff, games rooms; TV, free wi-fi; children and dogs welcome, garden behind by car park, open (and food) all day. *(Susie and Spencer Gray)*

LEEBOTWOOD SO4798

Pound (01694) 751477
A49 Church Stretton–Shrewsbury; SY6 6ND Thatched cruck-framed building (dates from 1458) under new management; opened-up, extended and much modernised interior, core keeping hefty beams and woodburner in big fireplace, enjoyable reasonably priced pubby food from sandwiches to daily specials, real ales such as Hobsons and Wye Valley, friendly helpful service; children and dogs (in bar) welcome, seats on flagstoned terrace, open (and food) all day. *(David and Leone Lawson)*

LEIGHTON SJ6105

Kynnersley Arms (01952) 510233
B4380; SY5 6RN Victorian building built on remains of ancient corn mill; coal fire and woodburner in main opened-up area, armchairs and sofas in back part with stairs to lower level containing mill machinery (there's also a 17th-c blast furnace), five well kept mainly local ales including Salopian and Three Tuns, traditional food along with pizzas and pasta dishes, Sun carvery, friendly helpful staff; background and occasional live music, regular quiz nights, sports TV, pool, free wi-fi; children and dogs welcome, good walks nearby, open all day. *(Celia and Andrew King)*

LEINTWARDINE SO4175

★**Jolly Frog** (01547) 540298
A4113 Ludlow–Knighton, E edge of village; The Toddings; SY7 0LX Cheerful well run place (more bar-bistro than pub) in glorious countryside; front bar with just a few tables on light oak boards, check tablecloths and red leatherette dining chairs, woodburner at each end and frenchified décor (kepis and other hats hanging from stripped beams, Paris street signs and a map of the Métro), similarly furnished dining room up a few steps, ales such as Otter and Three Tuns, nice wines by the glass and good food from wood-fired pizzas to fresh fish/seafood, friendly professional staff; background music, free wi-fi; children welcome, inner courtyard with tables under sail canopy, more seating on upper deck with wide pastoral views, closed Mon. *(Michael Butler, Frank Price)*

LITTLE STRETTON SO4491

★**Green Dragon** (01694) 722925
Village well signed off A49 S of Church Stretton; Ludlow Road; SY6 6RE Popular village pub at the foot of the Long Mynd; wide choice of good reasonably priced food from sandwiches and sharing boards up in bar or small adjacent dining area (well behaved children allowed here), well kept Bass, Hobsons, Ludlow, Salopian, Wye Valley and a guest, proper cider, friendly helpful staff, cosy beamed interior with warm woodburner, area for muddy paws and boots; tables outside and play area, handy for Carding Mill Valley (NT), open (and food) all day, best to book evenings. *(John Watson, Brian Glozier, Don Beattie, Ian Wilson, David and Doreen Beattie)*

LITTLE STRETTON SO4492

★**Ragleth** (01694) 722711
Village well signed off A49 S of Church Stretton; Ludlow Road; SY6 6RB Characterful 17th-c wisteria-clad dining pub; light and airy bay-windowed front bar with eclectic mix of old tables and chairs, some exposed brick and timber work, huge inglenook in heavily beamed brick and tile-floored public bar, four real ales such as Hobsons, Ludlow, Three Tuns and Wye Valley, good food including several fish dishes, cheerful attentive service; background music, TV, darts and board games; children welcome, dogs in bar, lovely garden with tulip tree-shaded lawn and good play area, thatched and timbered church and fine hill walks nearby, open all day Sat (summer) and Sun. *(Bernard Stradling, David and Doreen Beattie)*

LITTLE WENLOCK SJ6507

Huntsman (01952) 503300
Wellington Road; TF6 5BH Welcoming modernised village pub; enjoyable food from sandwiches/snacks and pub standards up, four well kept/priced changing ales

and good selection of wines, black beamed bar with stone floor and central log fire, restaurant has high-backed upholstered chairs at light wood tables and woodburner in big fireplace; occasional live music; children and dogs (in bar) welcome, terrace seating, bedrooms and self-catering cottage, handy for Wrekin walks, open (and food) all day, kitchen shuts 7pm Sun. *(Charles Welch)*

LOPPINGTON SJ4729

Dickin Arms (01939) 233471

B4397; SY4 5SR Welcoming recently refurbished pub in pretty village; split-level interior with up-to-date country-style décor, beams, flagstones, some painted panelling and big woodburner in two-way brick fireplace, good freshly made food (not Sun evening, Mon) including range of tapas-style starters/snacks, four well kept local ales and good range of other drinks, attentive friendly service; children welcome, dogs and muddy boots in bar, open all day Sat, till 9pm Sun, closed Mon lunchtime. *(Christine and Tony Garrett)*

LUDLOW SO5174

Blue Boar (01584) 878989

Mill Street; SY8 1BB Recently renovated former coaching inn with lots of linked areas, well kept ales such as Black Sheep, Hobsons and Three Tuns, good choice of wines by the glass and enjoyable well priced home-made food (not Sun evening), friendly staff; upstairs live music, quiz third Thurs; children and dogs welcome, back suntrap courtyard, bedrooms, open all day. *(Ian Duncan)*

LUDLOW SO5174

Queens (01584) 879177

Lower Galdeford; SY8 1RU Welcoming and popular 19th-c family-run pub; good reasonably priced food with emphasis on fresh local produce (booking advised, particularly Sun lunchtime), four well kept ales including Hobsons, Ludlow and Wye Valley, helpful friendly service, long narrow oak-floor bar, steps down to dining area with vaulted-ceiling; some live music; children welcome (not in bar after 6pm), dogs allowed in one area, modern seating on enclosed deck, courtyard bedrooms, open all day. *(Alfie Bayliss)*

LUDLOW SO5175

Unicorn (01584) 873555

Corve Street, bottom end; SY8 1DU Small half-timbered 17th-c coaching inn under welcoming newish management; character bare boards bar with beams and part panelled walls, log fire, well kept ales such as Ludlow and Wye Valley, good wine list and much liked food cooked by landlady-chef, friendly helpful service, back dining room; background music; children and dogs welcome (there are resident cockapoos), terrace among willows by river. *(Roy and Gill Payne, Roger Yates)*

LUDLOW SO5174

Wheatsheaf (01584) 872980

Lower Broad Street; SY8 1PQ Traditional 17th-c pub spectacularly built into medieval town gate; good reasonably priced food including daily specials and popular Sun lunch, three Marstons-related ales, welcoming helpful staff, dark beams, exposed stonework and open fire; children and dogs welcome, a few seats out in front, five refurbished bedrooms, hearty breakfast, open all day, food all day weekends. *(Roy and Gill Payne)*

MAESBURY SJ3026

Original Ball (01691) 587360

Maesbury Road; SY10 8HB Old renovated brick-built country pub under new management (restaurant side run separately); hefty beams and woodburner in bar's central fireplace, Marstons Pedigree, Stonehouse Station Bitter and a guest, decent wines, enjoyable fairly traditional food using local and organic ingredients, monthly themed nights, friendly helpful staff; background music, sports TV; children and dogs (in bar) welcome, disabled access, seats outside (some under cover), open all day weekends, closed Mon and lunchtimes Tues-Fri. *(Justine and Neil Bonnett)*

MARKET DRAYTON SJ6734

Red Lion (01630) 652602

Great Hales Street; TF9 1JP Extended 17th-c coaching inn acting as tap for Joules Brewery; back entrance into attractive modern bar with light wood floor and substantial oak timbers, traditional dark-beamed part to the right, updated but keeping original features, with pubby furniture on flagstones, brewery mirrors and signs, woodburner, more breweriana in dining/function room to left featuring 'Mousey' Thompson carved oak panelling and fireplace; Joules Blonde, Green Monkey, Pale Ale, Slumbering Monk and a couple of seasonal beers (tasting trays available), good selection of wines, fairly standard home-made food including Sun carvery till 4pm; some live music; picnic-sets outside, brewery tours first Weds of month (must pre-book), open (and food) all day. *(Tony Hobden)*

MARTON SJ2802

★**Sun** (01938) 561211

B4386 NE of Chirbury; SY21 8JP Welcoming family-run dining pub, clean and neatly kept, with high standard of cooking including seasonal game and good fresh fish, light and airy black-beamed bar with comfortable sofa and traditional furnishings, stove in big stone fireplace, Hobsons Best and several wines by the glass, chunky pale tables and ladder-back chairs in restaurant; children welcome, dogs in bar (but do ask first), front terrace, closed Sun evening to Weds lunchtime. *(Celia and Andrew King)*

MUCH WENLOCK SO6299

Gaskell Arms (01952) 727212
High Street (A458); TF13 6AQ Substantial 17th-c coaching inn with comfortable old-fashioned lounge divided by two-way fireplace, brassware and prints, well kept Wye Valley Butty Bach and a couple of local guests such as Bewdley and Hobsons, enjoyable straightforward food served by friendly attentive staff, civilised beamed restaurant and separate locals' bar; background music, free wi-fi; well behaved children allowed, no dogs inside, disabled facilities, spacious walled garden behind with terrace, 14 bedrooms (four in mews building), open all day; for sale, so could be changes. *(Ian Duncan)*

MUCH WENLOCK SO6299

★**George & Dragon** (01952) 727009
High Street (A458); TF13 6AA Busy town pub filled with fascinating collection of pub paraphernalia – old brewery and cigarette advertisements, bottle labels, beer trays and George and the Dragon pictures, also 200 jugs hanging from beams; main quarry-tiled room with antique settles and open fires in two attractive Victorian fireplaces, timbered back dining room, Greene King, Hobsons, St Austell and guest, big helpings of well priced food (not Weds or Sun evenings), good friendly service; background and some live music: children and dogs (in bar) welcome, pay-and-display car park behind, open all day. *(Mike and Wena Stevenson)*

MUNSLOW SO5287

★**Crown** (01584) 841205
B4368 Much Wenlock–Craven Arms; SY7 9ET Former courthouse with imposing exterior and pretty back façade showing Tudor origins; lots of nooks and crannies, split-level lounge bar with old-fashioned mix of furnishings on broad flagstones, bread oven by log fire, another fire in traditional snug, eating area with more beams, flagstones and stripped stone, also upstairs restaurant (weekends only), good food from sandwiches and sharing boards through pub standards to restauranty dishes, popular Sun lunch, steak nights Tues and Weds, ales such as Otter, Three Tuns and Wye Valley, local bottled cider and nice wines, helpful efficient staff, friendly bustling atmosphere; background music; children welcome, level wheelchair access to bar only where dogs allowed, bedrooms, closed Sun evening, Mon. *(Christine and Tony Garrett)*

NEWPORT SJ7419

New Inn (01952) 812295
Stafford Road; TF10 7LX Modernised and extended Joules pub on crossroads; their beers and a guest from five handpumps, over 50 gins and good uncomplicated food (not Sun evening) served by friendly staff, opened-up interior with some cosy corners, log fire and woodburner; live music Sun, beer and gin festivals; children and dogs welcome, picnic-sets under parasols on terrace and lawn, open all day. *(Alfie Bayliss)*

PICKLESCOTT SO4399

Bottle & Glass (01694) 751252
Off A49 N of Church Stretton; SY6 6NR Remote 17th-c country pub with plenty of character in quarry-tiled bar and lounge/dining areas; low black beams, oak panelling and log fires, assortment of old tables and chairs, good traditional home-made food from baps to daily specials, will cater for special diets, well kept ales such as Hobsons and Three Tuns, friendly helpful service; TV; children welcome, dogs in bar, seats out on raised front area, good walks, three bedrooms, open till 7pm Sun, closed Mon lunchtime (and evening winter). *(Susie and Spencer Gray)*

ROWTON SJ3612

Windmill (01743) 884234
A458; SY5 9EJ Popular and welcoming 18th-c pub in same family for nearly a century; refurbished beamed bar with inglenook and a couple of dining areas off, good interesting food at sensible prices along with pub favourites, well kept ales such as Hobsons, Salopian and Wye Valley, nice choice of wines; children and dogs (in bar) welcome, lovely country views from garden, open all day Sat, till 8pm Sun. *(Tony and Jill Radnor)*

SHAWBURY SJ5621

Fox & Hounds (01939) 250600
Wytheford Road; SY4 4JG Light and spacious 1960s pub; various opened-up areas including book-lined dining room with woodburner, rugs and assorted dark furniture on wood floors, cream-painted dados and lots of pictures, good fairly priced food from light lunches and sharing boards to daily specials, Weds pie night, four or five well kept ales such as Greene King and Rowton, good choice of wines, efficient helpful service; free wi-fi; children welcome, picnic-sets on terrace and lawn, open (and food) all day. *(Valerie and Gordon Wauton)*

SHIFNAL SJ74508

White Hart (01952) 461161
High Street; TF11 8BH Nine well kept ales in this chatty 17th-c timbered pub, quaint and old-fashioned with separate bar and lounge, good home-made lunchtime food (not Sun) at reasonable prices, several wines by the glass and a proper cider, friendly welcoming staff; no credit cards; children and dogs (in bar) welcome, couple of steep steps at front door, back terrace and beer garden, open all day. *(Cecily and Steven Evans)*

SHREWSBURY SJ4912

Admiral Benbow (01743) 244423
Swan Hill; SY1 1NF Great choice of regional ales, also ciders and bottled foreign beers, friendly staff; darts, free wi-fi; no

children, beer garden behind, closed lunchtimes except Sat. *(Ian Duncan)*

SHREWSBURY SJ4812

Bricklayers Arms (01743) 359999
Copthorne Road/Hafren Road; SY3 8NL Spotless 1930s suburban pub (walkable from the town centre) owned by Joules; their well kept beers and generous helpings of popular traditional food including good Sun lunch, cheerful efficient service, bare boards, panelling and open fire, screens and gleaming stained glass, one wall with examples of different bricklaying patterns; children and dogs welcome, picnic-sets out in front, open (and food) all day Fri-Sun, from 4pm other days. *(Ian Duncan)*

SHREWSBURY SO4912

Coach & Horses (01743) 365661
Swan Hill/Cross Hill; SY1 1NF Relaxed beamed corner local off the beaten track; chatty panelled bar, cosy little side room and back dining lounge, well kept Salopian, Stonehouse and guests, real cider, happy hour (5-7.30pm Mon-Fri), enjoyable freshly made food including popular Sun carvery; background music, free wi-fi; children allowed in dining room, dogs in bar, open all day. *(Michael Butler, Robert W Buckle)*

SHREWSBURY SJ4913

Dolphin (01743) 247005
A49 0.5 mile N of station; SY1 2EZ Traditionally renovated 19th-c pub with friendly welcoming atmosphere; well kept Joules ales and guests, good interesting snacks and other reasonably priced food from short blackboard menu, compact bare-boards interior keeping original gas lighting and open fires; music and quiz nights, darts, free wi-fi; dogs welcome; seats on sunny back deck, open all day Fri-Sun, from 2pm other days. *(Ian Duncan, Jack S)*

SHREWSBURY SJ4912

Loggerheads (01743) 362398
Church Street; SY1 1UG Chatty old-fashioned local with panelled back room, flagstones, scrubbed-top tables, high-backed settles and coal fire, three other little rooms with lots of prints, bare boards and more flagstones, quaint linking corridor and hatch service for the half dozen well kept Marstons-related beers, no food, friendly service; weekly folk session, TV for major sports; dogs welcome (in some areas), open all day. *(Jack S)*

SHREWSBURY SJ4912

Nags Head (01743) 362455
Wyle Cop; SY1 1XB Attractive old two-room pub near English Bridge, small, unpretentious and welcoming, with good range of well kept ales such as Hobsons, Timothy Taylors Landlord and Wye Valley, no food; TV, juke box; dogs welcome, remains of ancient timbered building (used as a smokers' shelter) and garden behind, open all day (till 1am Fri). *(Ian Duncan)*

SHREWSBURY SJ4812

Shrewsbury Hotel (01743) 236203
Mardol/Mardol Quay; SY1 1PU Partly open-plan Wetherspoons (former coaching inn) opposite the river; seven well kept/priced ales and their usual good value food, helpful friendly service; TVs for subtitled news, free wi-fi; children welcome, tables out in front, 22 bedrooms (residents' car park), open all day from 7am. *(Jack S)*

SHREWSBURY SJ4912

★**Three Fishes** (01743) 344793
Fish Street; SY1 1UR Timbered and heavily beamed 16th-c pub in quiet cobbled street; small tables on flagstones around three sides of central bar, old pictures, up to six well kept mainly local beers, good value wines and enjoyable fairly priced food (not Sun) from baguettes to blackboard specials, good friendly service even when busy; Mon quiz, free wi-fi; dogs welcome, open all day Fri-Sun. *(Ian Duncan)*

STIPERSTONES SJ3600

★**Stiperstones Inn** (01743) 791327
Village signed off A488 S of Minsterley; SY5 0LZ Cosy traditional pub in fine walking country – some stunning hikes on the Long Mynd or up dramatic quartzite ridge of the Stiperstones; small carpeted lounge with comfortable leatherette wall banquettes and lots of brassware on ply-panelled walls, plainer public bar with darts, TV and fruit machine, open fires, a couple of real ales such as Six Bells and Stonehouse, various home-infused gins such as rose petal and whinberry, good value bar food usefully served all day, also afternoon teas with freshly baked cakes and home-made jams, friendly helpful service; background music; children and dogs (in bar and garden) welcome, two comfortable bedrooms, also self-catering in nearby converted chapel, open all day. *(Charles Welch)*

STOTTESDON SO6782

Fighting Cocks (01746) 718270
High Street; DY14 8TZ Welcoming old half-timbered community pub in unspoilt countryside; carpeted split-level interior with low ceilings and log fire, five well kept mainly local ales, real ciders and decent gin selection, good reasonably priced home-made food including range of pies, more dining space upstairs; regular live music; children and dogs welcome, garden with play area and rural views, good walks, small shop behind, open all day weekends, closed Mon. *(Don Beattie)*

UPTON MAGNA SJ5512

Haughmond (01743) 709918
Pelham Road; SY4 4TZ Welcoming restyled 17th-c village inn; bar with painted

beams, oak-strip flooring/carpet and log fire, a house beer (Antler) brewed by Marstons and two local guests from brick servery, good food in brasserie (shuts Sun evening, Mon) including tasting menus, village shop/café; children and dogs (in bar) welcome, great view to the Wrekin from attractive back garden, handy for Haughmond Hill walks and Attingham Park (NT), five bedrooms named after deer, open all day weekends, closed Mon lunchtime. *(R T and J C Moggridge)*

WALL UNDER HEYWOOD SO5092

Plough (01694) 771833
B4371; SY6 7DS Welcoming country pub with good generously served food including Sun carvery, five well kept ales such as Hobsons, Ludlow and Wye Valley, log fire and various odds and ends in small front bar, snug with darts, comfortable 'piano' lounge and dining conservatory; some live music (maybe Sun lunchtime jazz); children and dogs welcome, tables in back garden, good local walks, open all day. *(Celia and Andrew King)*

WELLINGTON SJ6511

Cock (01952) 244954
Holyhead Road (B5061 – former A5); TF1 2DL Welcoming 18th-c coaching inn with well kept Hobsons and five changing guests usually from small breweries, handpulled cider and extensive range of bottled beers too, friendly helpful staff, some food such as pies, big fireplace; free wi-fi; dogs welcome, beer garden with covered area, bedrooms, closed lunchtime Mon-Weds, otherwise open all day. *(Alfie Bayliss)*

WELLINGTON SJ6411

Pheasant (01952) 260683
Market Street; TF1 1DT Town-centre pub with one long room, seven well kept ales including Everards Tiger and up to three from own Rowton brewery, two real ciders and enjoyable good value lunchtime food served till 4pm (not Sun), friendly helpful staff; children and dogs welcome, disabled access and facilities, beer garden behind, open all day. *(Cecily and Steven Evans)*

WELSHAMPTON SJ4335

Sun (01948) 710847
A495 Ellesmere–Whitchurch; SY12 0PH Extended roadside village pub; good choice of enjoyable reasonably priced food, Stonehouse Station Bitter and three guests, friendly helpful service; live music and quiz nights; children and dogs welcome, tables in fenced back garden, 15-minute walk to Llangollen/ Shropshire Union Canal, three bedrooms, open (and food) all day. *(Charles Welch)*

WHITCHURCH SJ5441

Black Bear (01948) 663800
High Street/Bargates; SY13 1AZ Black and white building opposite church (a pub since 1667); half a dozen interesting well kept beers including Stonehouse, enjoyable home-made food from open sandwiches up, characterful interior and good atmosphere; regular live music; children and dogs (in bar) welcome, beer garden behind, open all day weekends. *(Christine and Tony Garrett)*

WHITCHURCH SJ5441

Old Town Hall Vaults (01948) 664682 *St Marys Street; SY13 1QU* Red-brick 19th-c Joules local (birthplace of composer Sir Edward German) under friendly newish management; four of their ales and a guest, enjoyable good value food from snacks up, main room divided into distinct areas with bar in one corner, oak panelling, stained glass, mirrors and signs, sturdy furniture including bench seating and cast-iron-framed tables, log fires, further room with glazed ceiling; outside listed gents'; dogs welcome, partly covered yard with barrel tables, open all day, food all day till 6.30pm apart from Tues when kitchen closed. *(Christine and Tony Garrett)*

WHITCHURCH SJ5345

Willey Moor Lock (01948) 663274
Tarporley Road; signed off A49 just under 2 miles N; SY13 4HF Large opened-up pub in picturesque spot by Llangollen Canal; two log fires, low beams and countless teapots and toby jugs, cheerful chatty atmosphere, half a dozen changing local ales and 30 or so malt whiskies, good value pub food from sandwiches up; background music, games machine; children welcome away from bar, well behaved dogs in some areas, terrace tables, secure garden with big play area. *(Mike and Wena Stevenson)*

WISTANSTOW SO4385

Plough (01588) 673251
Off A49 and A489 N of Craven Arms; SY7 8DG Welcoming village pub adjoining the Woods brewery; their beers in peak condition and enjoyable home-made food including daily specials, friendly efficient service, smallish bar, airy high-ceilinged modern restaurant and games part with darts, dominoes and pool; background music, sports TV, free wi-fi; children and dogs (in bar) welcome, some tables outside, open all day, food all day Sun till 7pm. *(Celia and Andrew King)*

Somerset

with Bristol

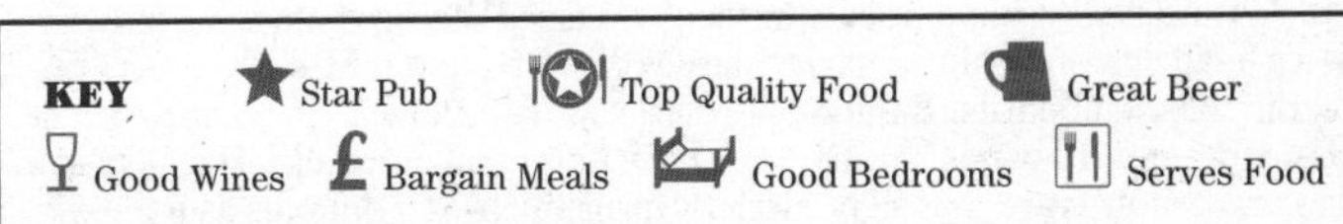

ASHCOTT ST4337 Map 1

Ring O'Bells

(01458) 210232 – www.ringobells.com

High Street; pub well signed off A39 W of Street; TA7 9PZ

Friendly village pub with homely décor in several bars, separate restaurant, tasty bar food and changing local ales

Just the place for lunch after bird-watching at the nearby RSPB Ham Wall reserve, this reliably well run pub has been owned by the same family for many years. Loyal locals account for many of the customers, but visitors will receive just as warm a welcome. The three main bars, on different levels, are all comfortable, with maroon plush-topped stools, cushioned mate's chairs and dark wooden pubby tables on patterned carpet, horsebrasses along the bressumer beam above a big stone fireplace and a growing collection of hand bells; background music and board games. Changing local ales include Cheddar Gorge Best and Pitchfork Ales Pitchfork on handpump, eight wines by the glass and local farm cider. There's also a separate restaurant, a skittle alley/function room, and plenty of picnic-sets out on the terrace and in the garden.

Tasty country cooking includes fresh grilled sardines, spinach and feta cheese filo parcels with onion relish, red kidney bean and mushroom bordelaise in red wine sauce, home-cooked ham and free-range eggs, a pie of the day, keralan beef curry with coconut and fenugreek, chicken breast with sun-dried tomato stuffing and red wine and tomato sauce, whole grilled lemon sole with lime and parsley butter, crispy pork belly with cider and apple sauce, and puddings such as apricot cheesecake and spicy bread and butter pudding. *Benchmark main dish: smoked chicken and mushrooms au gratin £12.75. Two-course evening meal £18.00.*

Free house ~ Licensees John and Elaine Foreman and John Sharman ~ Real ale ~ Open 12-3, 7-11; 12-3, 7-10.30 Sun ~ Bar food 12-2, 7-10 ~ Restaurant ~ Children welcome ~ Dogs allowed in bar ~ Wi-fi ~ Folk music first Sat of month *Recommended by Mr and Mrs J Watkins, Frank Willy, Dr A J and Mrs B A Tompsett, M G Hart, Marianne White, Camilla and Jose Ferrera*

BABCARY ST5628 Map 2

Red Lion

(01458) 223230 – www.redlionbabcary.co.uk

Off A37 S of Shepton Mallett; 2 miles or so N of roundabout where A37 meets A303 and A372; TA11 7ED

Thatched pub with comfortable rambling rooms, interesting food and local beers and seats outside; bedrooms

There's plenty of room for both drinkers and diners in this handsome thatched inn, where several distinct areas work their way around the bar counter. To the left is a longish room with dark red walls, a squashy leather sofa and two winged armchairs around a low table by a woodburning stove – plus a few well spaced tables and captain's chairs. There are elegant rustic wall-lights, clay pipes in a display cabinet, daily papers, magazines and board games. A more dimly lit public bar with lovely dark flagstones has a high-backed old settle and other more straightforward chairs; table skittles and background music. In the good-sized dining room a big stone lion's head sits on a plinth above a large open fire, and tables and chairs are set on polished boards. Exmoor Ale, Otter Amber and a local rotating guest on handpump, 18 wines by the glass, farm cider and cocktails. The Den, set in a pretty courtyard, has light modern furnishings and doubles as a party, wedding and conference venue. The long informal garden has a play area and plenty of seats. Bedrooms are comfortable and well equipped and the pub is handy for the Fleet Air Museum at Yeovilton, the Haynes Motor Museum in Sparkford and for shopping at Clarks Village in Street. Wheelchair access.

A wide choice of food includes a spring/late summer outside pizza area plus sandwiches, home-cured smoked salmon with dill crème fraîche, fishcakes with sautéed spinach and hollandaise, halloumi, courgette and mint cakes with romesco sauce and toasted almonds, chicken breast with black garlic, fondant potatoes, asparagus and chicken jus, a pie of the day, lamb cutlets with lamb fritter, crushed new potatoes and lamb jus, sea bass with brown crab mayonnaise and avocado purée, 30-day-aged sirloin steak with caramelised shallots, a choice of sauce and chips, and puddings such as chocolate and walnut brownie with chocolate sauce and lemon posset with lemon curd. *Benchmark main dish: steak burger with toppings, pickles and frites £12.95. Two-course evening meal £20.00.*

Free house ~ Licensee Charles Garrard ~ Real ale ~ Open 11-3, 6-11; 11am-midnight Fri-Sun ~ Bar food 12-2.30, 6.30-9; 12-3, 6.30-9.30 weekends ~ Restaurant ~ Children welcome ~ Dogs allowed in bar ~ Wi-fi ~ Bedrooms: £95/£115 *Recommended by Bob and Margaret Holder, Ewan and Sue Hewitt, Ian and Rose Lock, Adam Jones, Charlie Stevens*

BATH ST7564 Map 2

Old Green Tree

(01225) 448259

Green Street; BA1 2JZ

Tiny, unspoilt local with up to six real ales and lots of cheerful customers

In a time warp of its own and much loved by our readers, this charming little 18th-c tavern simply doesn't change – and thank heavens for that. There's oak panelling and low ceilings of wood and plaster, and just three small rooms. These include a comfortable lounge on the left as you go in – its walls decorated with wartime aircraft pictures (in winter) and local artists' work (in spring and summer) – and a back bar. The big skylight lightens things attractively. Half a dozen beers on handpump might include Green Tree Bitter (named for the pub by Blindmans Brewery) and Butcombe Bitter with guests such as Exmoor Gold, Nethergate Marys Ruby Mild and Pitchfork Ales Pitchfork; also, seven wines by the glass from a nice little list with helpful tasting notes, 36 malt whiskies and a farm cider. The gents' is basic and down steep steps. No children and no dogs.

Lunchtime-only food includes doorstep sandwiches, soup, pâté, fish and chips, vegetable curry, burger with toppings and chips, and lambs liver with bacon and roast garlic mash. *Benchmark main dish: sausage and mash £9.95.*

Free house ~ Licensee Tim Bethune ~ Real ale ~ No credit cards ~ Open 11-11; 12-4.30 Sun; 12-6.30 Sun in winter ~ Bar food 12-2.30 (3 Sat); not evenings or Sun (though they do Sunday roasts in winter) *Recommended by Roger and Donna Huggins, Dr and Mrs A K Clarke, Taff Thomas, Stuart Doughty*

BATH — ST7565 Map 2

Star

(01225) 425072 – www.abbeyales.co.uk

Vineyards; The Paragon (A4), junction with Guinea Lane; BA1 5NA

Quietly chatty and unchanging old town local, the brewery tap for Abbey Ales

Since this pub is just five minutes' walk from the city centre, it can get pretty busy at peak times. The four small linked rooms have a lively atmosphere and a good mix of customers, plus many original features such as traditional wall benches (one is known as Death Row), panelling, dim lighting and open fires. Abbey Bellringer and Bass plus guests such as Castle [illegible] Pale and Robinsons Trooper tapped from the cask, several [illegible] Valley cider; darts, shove-[illegible] helf the full length of the pub, [illegible] p and quickly changing, the [illegible] as Bath

Food consists of filled rolls.

Star Pubs & Bars ~ Lease Paul Waters and Alan Morgan ~ Real ale ~ Open 12-2.30, 5.30-midnight; noon-1am Fri, Sat; 12-midnight Sun ~ Children welcome ~ Dogs welcome ~ Wi-fi ~ Irish folk Fri evening, quiz first Sun of month *Recommended by Taff Thomas, Stuart Doughty, Glen and Patricia Fuller, Alf and Sally Garner*

BISHOPSWOOD — ST2512 Map 1

Candlelight

(01460) 234476 – www.candlelight-inn.co.uk

Off A303/B3170 S of Taunton; TA20 3RS

Neat dining pub with a good choice of drinks, enjoyable food and seats in the garden; handy for A303

The neatly kept interconnected dining rooms here (separated into different areas by standing stone pillars and open doorways) have wooden and painted country kitchen chairs around solid tables on polished floorboards, a few settles, books on shelves and exposed stone walls. The beamed bar has high chairs by the counter where they serve Batemans XXXB, Brains Rev James, Otter Bitter and Ringwood Old Thumper tapped from the cask, good wines by the glass and maybe a farm cider. Also, captain's chairs, pews and cushioned window seats, and there's both an open fire and a woodburning stove; background music. Outside, there are picnic-sets on decking and a neatly landscaped garden.

Highly regarded food includes smoked salmon with dill crème fraîche, chicken liver parfait with chutney, vegetable, green lentil and coconut tarka dhal with pilau rice, pigeon breasts with roasted vegetables, pearl barley and sweetcorn purée, bouillabaisse, burger with toppings, pickles and fries, chicken, ham hock and leek pie, pheasant breast with mushroom sauce, fresh fish dish of the day, and puddings such as chocolate and cherry sponge and crème caramel with mixed berries; they also offer a two- and three-course set lunch. *Benchmark main dish: fish and chips with pea purée £13.00. Two-course evening meal £20.00.*

Free house ~ Licensee Mike Rose ~ Real ale ~ Open 12-3, 6 (5 Fri)-11; 12-11 Sat, Sun; closed Mon in winter ~ Bar food 12-2, 7-9; 12-2.30, 6.30-9.30 Fri, Sat; 12-2, 6.30-9 Sun ~ Children welcome ~ Dogs welcome ~ Wi-fi *Recommended by John Watson, Margo and Derek Peters, Julia and Fiona Barnes, Bob and Margaret Holder, Pauline and Mark Evans, Ivy and George Goodwill*

BRISTOL ST5873 Map 2

Highbury Vaults £

(0117) 973 3203 – www.highburyvaults.co.uk

St Michaels Hill, Cotham; BS2 8DE

Cheerful town pub with up to eight real ales, good reasonably priced food and friendly atmosphere

Its location near the university and excellent choice of changing ales mean a steady stream of cheerful customers for this unpretentious pub. The little front bar, with a corridor beside it, leads through to a series of small rooms: wooden floors, green and cream paintwork and old-fashioned furniture and prints (including plenty of royal family period engravings and lithographs in the front room). A model railway runs on a s[illegible] with tunnels through the walls. On handpum[illegible] ales might include Youngs Bitter and London Gold plus guests such as Bath Gem, Bristol Beer Factory Subtropic, Great Western Old Higby and St Austell Tribute; also, six wines by the glass and ten malt whiskies. They offer hot sausage rolls from the oven on Thursday and Friday evenings at 10pm; bar billiards, TV and board games. The attractive back terrace has tables built into a partly covered flowery arbour, and there's disabled access to the main bar (but not to the lavatories).

Basic, good value food includes filled rolls, ploughman's, baked potatoes, burgers with toppings and coleslaw, beef in ale or fish pie, lasagne, sweet potato and chickpea curry, slow-braised lamb shepherd's pie, wild boar sausages with chorizo and butter bean stew, and puddings such as sticky toffee pudding with custard. *Benchmark main dish: chilli con carne £7.95. Two-course evening meal £14.00.*

Youngs ~ Manager Bradd Francis ~ Real ale ~ Open 12-midnight; 12-11 Sun ~ Bar food 12-2 (2.30 Sat), 5.30-8.30; 12-4 Sun ~ Children welcome ~ Wi-fi *Recommended by Peter Myers, Sally and Colin Allen, Darrell Barton, Thomas Green, Camilla and Jose Ferrera*

CHARLTON HORETHORNE ST6623 Map 2

Kings Arms

(01963) 220281 – www.thekingsarms.co.uk

B3145 Wincanton–Sherborne; DT9 4NL

Bustling inn with relaxed bars and more formal restaurant, good ales and wines and enjoyable food; bedrooms

With a good mix of customers, appealing food and thoughtful choice of drinks, this rather smart inn is a popular place. The main bar has a pleasing assortment of local art (all for sale) on dark mulberry or cream walls, nice old carved wooden dining chairs and pine pews around a mix of tables, a slate floor and a woodburning stove. Leading off is a cosy room with sofas and newspapers on low tables. Butcombe Bitter and a couple of guests such as Butcombe Original, Otter Ale and Timothy Taylors Landlord on handpump are served from the rather fine granite bar counter; they also keep 16 wines by the glass, nine malt whiskies, 12 gins and local farm cider. To the left of the main door is an informal dining room with Jacobean-style chairs and tables on a pale wooden floor and more local artwork. The back restaurant (past the open kitchen which is fun to peek into) has decorative wood and glass mirrors, wicker or black leather high-backed dining chairs around chunky, polished, pale wooden tables on coir carpeting, and handsome striped curtains. The attractive courtyard at the back of the inn has chrome and wicker chairs around teak tables under green parasols; a smokers' shelter overlooks a croquet lawn. Bedrooms are contemporary, comfortable and well equipped.

With everything made in-house, the appetising food includes ciabatta sandwiches, ham hock and apple terrine with pickled apples and black pudding crumb, braised blade of beer with pea purée, pickled beetroot and horseradish crème fraîche, butternut squash and sweet potato tagine with almond, red pepper and honey bulgar wheat and yoghurt with mint and cucumber, smoked haddock and cheddar fishcakes with leek and tarragon cream sauce and tomato dressing, plaice with caper butter, bacon lardons, peas, samphire and spinach, 28-day-aged rib-eye steak with peppercorn sauce, and puddings such as dark chocolate tart with blood orange sorbet and elderflower cheesecake with blueberry compote. *Benchmark main dish: lamb rump with aubergine, courgettes, roast tomato and olive sauce and lamb jus £21.00. Two-course evening meal £25.00.*

Free house ~ Licensee Tony Lethbridge ~ Real ale ~ Open 11-11 ~ Bar food 12-2.30, 7-9.30 (10 Fri, Sat) ~ Restaurant ~ Children welcome ~ Dogs allowed in bar ~ Wi-fi ~ Bedrooms: /£145 *Recommended by Trish and Karl Soloman, Simon and Alex Knight, Mrs Zara Elliott, Sarah and David Gibbs, Robert and Diana Ringstone*

CHURCHILL ST4459 Map 1

Crown £

(01934) 852995

The Batch; in village, turn off A368 into Skinners Lane at Nelson Arms; BS25 5PP

Unchanging small cottage with friendly customers and staff, super range of real ales and homely lunchtime food

'Loads of charm and character' and 'what more could you ask for in a pub' are two enthusiastic reports from our readers on this smashing little tavern. The interior is completely untouched (it's perhaps not the place for those keen on more modern comforts), the locals are chatty and friendly and they keep a fine choice of seven real ales too. Tapped from the cask, these include Bath Gem, Butcombe Bitter, Palmers IPA, Otter Bitter, St Austell Tribute and a quickly changing guest such as Batch Terriers Bitter; also several wines by the glass and five local ciders. The small and rather local-feeling room on the right, with a stone floor and cross beams, has a big log fire in a large stone fireplace and steps that lead up to another seating area. The left-hand room – with a slate floor, window seats and a log burner – leads through to the Snug. There's no noise from music or games (except perhaps dominoes). The outside lavatories are basic. There are garden tables at the front, more seats arranged on the back lawn from which there are hill views; the Mendip morris men visit in summer and some of the best walking on the Mendips is nearby. There isn't a pub sign outside, but no one seems to have a problem finding the place.

Traditional, lunchtime-only food includes sandwiches (the rare roast beef is popular), beef casserole, cauliflower cheese, lasagne, and puddings. *Benchmark main dish: rare roast beef sandwich £6.25.*

Free house ~ Licensee Brian Clements ~ Real ale ~ No credit cards ~ Open 11-11; 12-10.30 Sun ~ Bar food 12-2.30 ~ Children must be well behaved ~ Dogs allowed in bar ~ Wi-fi *Recommended by Tracey and Stephen Groves, Peter Myers, Dr and Mrs A K Clarke, Taff Thomas, Hugh Roberts*

CLAPTON-IN-GORDANO

ST4773 Map 1

Black Horse £

(01275) 842105 – www.thekicker.co.uk

4 miles from M5 junction 19; A369 towards Portishead, then B3124 towards Clevedon; in North Weston opposite school, turn left signposted Clapton, then in village take second right, may be signed 'Clevedon, Clapton Wick'; BS20 7RH

Unpretentious 14th-c pub with lots of cheerful customers, friendly service, real ales, cider and simple lunchtime food; pretty garden

This is very much a country pub, with walkers (and their dogs), cyclists, farmers and other regular customers all mixing happily together. The partly flagstoned, partly red-tiled main room has winged settles and built-in wall benches around narrow, dark wooden tables, window seats, a big log fire with stirrups and bits on the mantelbeam, and amusing cartoons and photographs of the pub. A window in an inner snug retains metal bars from the days when this room was the petty sessions gaol; also, high-backed settles – one with a marvellous carved and canopied creature, another with an art nouveau copper insert reading 'East, West, Hame's Best' – lots of mugs hanging from black beams and numerous small prints and photographs. A simply furnished room is the only place where families are allowed; background music. Bath Gem, Butcombe Bitter, Otter Bitter and St Austell Tribute on handpump or tapped from the cask, six wines by the glass and three farm ciders. The garden has rustic tables and benches, with more to one side of the car park. Paths from the pub lead up Naish Hill or to Cadbury Camp (National Trust) and there's access to local cycle routes. Wheelchair access but no disabled loos.

Honest lunchtime-only food includes baguettes and baps with lots of hot and cold fillings and daily specials such as soup, creamy mushroom stroganoff, corned beef hash topped with a fried egg, shepherd's pie, chilli con carne, and pork and cider casserole. *Benchmark main dish: beef in red wine £9.50.*

Enterprise ~ Lease Nicholas Evans ~ Real ale ~ Open 11-11; 12-9.30 Sun ~ Bar food 12-2.30; not evenings or Sun ~ Children in family room only ~ Dogs welcome ~ Wi-fi

Recommended by Chris and Angela Buckell, Taff Thomas, Donald Allsopp, Anne Taylor

COMBE HAY

ST7359 Map 2

Wheatsheaf

(01225) 833504 – www.wheatsheafcombehay.co.uk

Village signposted off A367 or B3110 S of Bath; BA2 7EG

Smart country dining pub with first class food and drink; attractive bedrooms

As befits a pub so highly rated for its food, much of the space here is devoted to dining. Walkers with their dogs and those just wanting a drink and a chat can sit in a central area by a big fireplace where there are sofas on dark flagstones and daily papers and current issues of *The Field* and *Country Life* on a low table. Friendly staff serve Butcombe Bitter and Gold and Otter Bright on handpump, 16 wines by the glass from a very good list, 18 malt whiskies and a farm cider. Other civilised but informally friendly areas have stylish, high-backed, grey wicker dining chairs around chunky modern dining tables, on parquet or coir matting. It's all fresh and bright, with block-mounted photoprints, contemporary artwork and mirrors with colourful ceramic mosaic frames (many for sale) on white-painted stonework or robin's-egg-blue plaster walls. The sills of the many shuttered windows house anything from old soda siphons to a stuffed kingfisher and a Great Lakes model tugboat. Glinting glass wall chandeliers and nightlights in entertaining holders supplement the ceiling spotlights; background music. The two-level front garden has picnic-sets and a fine view over the church and valley; there are enjoyable surrounding walks. Bedrooms are quiet, spacious and comfortable.

Imaginative food includes ham hock terrine with pickled onions and cider jelly, seared foie gras and creamed wild mushrooms on toast, beer-battered cod and chips, pigeon with hogs pudding and onion and smoked bacon gnocchi, hot smoked salmon wellington with creamed leeks and brown crab sauce, braised blade of beef with wild garlic mash and blue cheese croquette, duck breast with orange potato rösti, roast carrots and spiced duck leg sauce, and puddings such as warm treacle tart with Guinness ice-cream and white chocolate cheesecake with raspberry sorbet and crushed meringue; pizzas on Wednesday evenings in warm weather and steak night is Tuesday. *Benchmark main dish: burger with toppings and skinny chips £15.00. Two-course evening meal £22.00.*

Free house ~ Licensee Ian Barton ~ Real ale ~ Open 10.30-3, 6-11; 10.30-3 Sun; closed Sun evening, Mon except bank holidays ~ Bar food 12-2.30, 6.30-9 ~ Restaurant ~ Children welcome ~ Dogs welcome ~ Wi-fi ~ Bedrooms: /£120 *Recommended by Dr and Mrs A K Clarke, Lindy Andrews, Daniel King, Patricia and Gordon Thompson, Jane Rigby*

CORTON DENHAM ST6322 Map 2

Queens Arms

(01963) 220317 – www.thequeensarms.com

Village signposted off B3145 N of Sherborne; DT9 4LR

Handsome 18th-c inn with super choice of drinks, interesting food and a sunny garden; comfortable, stylish bedrooms

In glorious countryside and well worth leaving the often traffic-laden A303 for, you'll find this a gently civilised place with a proper community spirit and plenty going on. The bustling, high-beamed bar has rugs on flagstones and two big armchairs in front of an open fire, some old pews, barrel seats and a sofa, church candles and big bowls of flowers. There's also a couple of separate restaurants, one of which has cushioned wall seats and chunky leather chairs around dark wooden tables, mirrors down one side and a drop-down cinema screen (screenings are held twice a month). They keep Gyle 59 The Queens Legless Liz plus ales from breweries such as Exmoor, Otter and Plain Ales on handpump, 22 wines (including champagne) by the glass from a carefully chosen list, 57 malt whiskies, 26 gins, unusual bottled beers from Belgium, Germany and the US, and four local ciders and apple juices. A south-facing back terrace has teak tables and chairs under parasols (or heaters, if the weather is cool) and colourful flower tubs. Comfortable bedrooms have lovely country views and breakfasts are particularly good. Cadbury Castle hill fort is not far away and there are fine nearby walks.

As well as offering breakfasts to non-residents (7.30-9.30am; 8.30-9.30am weekends) and using their own farm produce and other home-grown and local ingredients, the rewarding food includes lunchtime sandwiches and sharing platters, salmon confit with beetroot, apple and shallots, a trio of home-made sausages with creamy mash, duck confit with roasted fig and salad, charred cauliflower with raisins, curry spice and parsley, hake with shallots, celeriac purée and purple potatoes, chicken with cumin leeks, poached tomatoes, chives and onion purée, and puddings such as dark chocolate mousse with salted caramel and honeycomb ice-cream and lemon tart with raspberry sorbet. *Benchmark main dish: pork belly with roast broccoli, spiced almonds, potato terrine and jus £18.50. Two-course evening meal £22.50.*

Free house ~ Licensees Jeanette and Gordon Reid ~ Real ale ~ Open 8am-11pm; 8am-midnight Sat; 8am-10.30pm Sun ~ Bar food 12-3, 6-9.30; 12-9.30 Sat; 12-8 Sun ~ Restaurant ~ Children welcome ~ Dogs allowed in bar and bedrooms ~ Wi-fi ~ Bedrooms: £95/£125
Recommended by Marianne and Peter Stevens, Ian Herdman, Julian Thorpe, Christopher and Elise Way, Tracey and Stephen Groves, Dan and Belinda Smallbone

DULVERTON

SS9127 Map 1

Woods ★

(01398) 324007 – www.woodsdulverton.co.uk
Bank Square; TA22 9BU

Smartly informal place with exceptional wines, real ales, first rate food and a good mix of customers

'A real diamond' is how one of our readers describes this excellent pub, and once visited, who could disagree? There are satisfied diners to the right and happy drinkers enjoying a drink and a chat to the left. The pub is on the edge of Exmoor, so there are plenty of good sporting prints on salmon pink walls, antlers and other hunting trophies, stuffed birds and a couple of salmon rods. By the bar counter are bare boards, daily papers, tables partly separated by stable-style timbering and masonry dividers, and (on the right) a carpeted area with a woodburning stove in a big fireplace; maybe unobjectionable background music. The marvellous drinks choice includes Hop Back Crop Circle and St Austell Cornish Best and HSD tapped from the cask, farm cider, many sherries and some unusual spirits – but it's the stunning wine list that draws the most attention. Mr Groves reckons he could put 1,000 different wines up on the bar and will open any of them (with a value of up to £100) for just a glass. He is there every night and will happily chat to tables of restaurant customers about any wines they might be interested in. Big windows look on to the quiet town centre (there are also a couple of metal tables on the pavement) and a small suntrap courtyard at the back has a few picnic-sets.

Excellent food using produce from their own farm includes sandwiches, beef bresaola and smoked venison with sunblush tomatoes, marinated artichoke, parmesan and truffle oil, smoked eel and gravadlax with avruga caviar, quail egg and lemon oil, wild mushroom linguine with creamed white wine sauce, beer-battered fish and chips, confit lamb shoulder and loin with black pudding, ratatouille, fondant potato and red wine sauce, grey mullet fillet with tiger prawns, caper nut brown butter and herb salad, and puddings such as vanilla pannacotta with poached rhubarb, stem ginger ice-cream and apple purée and white chocolate cheesecake with pistachio ice-cream. *Benchmark main dish: seared steak and bacon salad £13.58. Two-course evening meal £20.00.*

Free house ~ Licensee Patrick Groves ~ Real ale ~ Open 12-3.30, 6-11; 12-3, 7-11 Sun ~ Bar food 12-2, 6-9.30; 12-2, 7-9 Sun ~ Restaurant ~ Children welcome ~ Dogs welcome ~ Wi-fi
Recommended by Hugh Roberts, Charles and Maddie Bishop, Graham Smart, Valerie and Gordon Wauton, Alison and Michael Harper, Elisabeth and Bill Humphries

DUNSTER

SS9943 Map 1

Luttrell Arms

(01643) 821555 – www.luttrellarms.co.uk
High Street; A396; TA24 6SG

Character bars and dining areas in lovely hotel, a thoughtful choice of drinks, enjoyable food and seats in courtyard and garden; luxurious bedrooms

This civilised hotel is on the site of three ancient houses mentioned in records in 1443 and has some lovely medieval features. The Old Kitchen Bar retains the workings of the former kitchen with meat hooks on the beamed ceiling and a large log fire and bread oven. The main bar is popular locally and has swords and guns on the wall above a huge fireplace, cushions on antique chairs, horsebrasses, copper kettles, plates and warming pans, animal furs dotted here and there, a stag's head and an antler chandelier, and various country knick-knacks. Exmoor Ale, Otter Amber and a guest from Cotleigh on handpump, 25 good wines by the glass, a dozen malt whiskies and three farm ciders; staff are courteous and helpful. There's also the Boot Bar with a lovely panelled wall seat and rugs on quarry tiles, a small snug and a deeply comfortable sitting room with one beautiful panelled wall, a woodburning stove and lots of armchairs, sofas and window seats; board games. The lovely garden is on several levels with seats on lawns or terraces and haunting castle views; a little galleried courtyard has metalwork chairs and tables. Some bedrooms are opulent with four-posters, antiques and carved fireplaces; breakfasts are first class.

Beautifully presented, seasonal food includes sandwiches, hand-picked crab and prawn salad with candied lemon and lime dressing, smoked chicken and pepper terrine with red pepper reduction, pepper confetti and tarragon toast, ravioli with burnt pear, blue cheese and walnuts with pickled pear purée and charred cauliflower, burger with toppings and buttermilk dressing, chicken kiev with carrot and courgette spaghetti and chicken velouté, cod, spring onion and coriander fishcakes with chilli jam and crème fraîche, and puddings such as chocolate devil cake with mint chocolate chip ice-cream and peppermint macaroon, and banana and popcorn iced parfait with caramel cashews and chocolate; they also offer afternoon tea (3-5.30pm). *Benchmark main dish: beer-battered fish and chips £13.00. Two-course evening meal £20.00.*

Free house ~ Licensee Tim Waldren ~ Real ale ~ Open 10am-11pm; 12-11 Sun ~ Bar food 9.30am-9.30pm ~ Restaurant ~ Children welcome ~ Dogs allowed in bar and bedrooms ~ Wi-fi ~ Bedrooms: £105/£150 *Recommended by Peter Myers, Gerry and Rosemary Dobson, Mr and Mrs D J Nash, Joe and Belinda Smart, Victoria and James Sargeant*

EXFORD SS8538 Map 1

Crown

(01643) 831554 – www.crownhotelexmoor.co.uk

The Green (B3224); TA24 7PP

17th-c coaching inn in pretty moorland village, character bar with real ales and enjoyable food, and big back garden; comfortable bedrooms

There's so much to see and do around this area that it makes sense to stay a few days in the warm and comfortable bedrooms here. The easy-going, two-room bar has a log fire in a big stone fireplace, plenty of stuffed animal heads and hunting prints on grey walls, some hunting-themed plates and old photographs of the area, cushioned benches and other traditional pubby tables and chairs on bare boards. There are stools against the counter where they serve Bath Gem and Exmoor Ale and Gold on handpump, 13 wines by the glass, ten malt whiskies, 12 gins and two farm ciders; TV. The dining room is rather smart. At the front of the building are some tables and chairs with more on a back terrace; a stream also threads its way past gently sloping lawns in the three-acre garden. They're very dog-friendly and can arrange riding, fishing, shooting, hunting, wildlife-watching, cycling and trekking.

Well regarded food includes baguettes and sandwiches, seared foie gras with caramelised apples and port syrup, game terrine wrapped in bacon with plum chutney, beer-battered cod and chips, wild boar and apple sausages with wholegrain mustard creamed potatoes and caramelised onion sauce, slow-cooked ox cheek and braised oxtail with fondant potatoes and ox jus, chicken breast stuffed with chorizo mousse and wrapped in bacon with creamed mushrooms, dauphinoise potatoes and peppercorn sauce, sea bream with pak choi, olives, fennel and lemon beurre blanc, 28-day-aged sirloin steak with a choice of sauce and chips, and puddings such as dark chocolate mousse with sour cherry sorbet and treacle tart with blackberry ice-cream. *Benchmark main dish: beef in ale pie £14.95. Two-course evening meal £22.50.*

Free house ~ Licensee Sara Whittaker ~ Real ale ~ Open 12-11; 4-11pm Mon-Thurs in winter ~ Bar food 12-2.30, 6-9.30; 6-9.30 Mon-Thurs in winter ~ Restaurant ~ Children welcome ~ Dogs allowed in bar and bedrooms ~ Wi-fi ~ Bedrooms: £82.50/£139
Recommended by Sandra and Michael Smith, Sophie Ellison, Buster and Helena Hastings, Patricia Healey

FROME — ST7747 Map 2

Archangel

(01373) 456111 – www.archangelfrome.com
King Street; BA11 1BH

Ancient place with contemporary design, several eating and drinking areas, a bustling atmosphere, rewarding food and drink and courtyard seats; bedrooms

They've managed to blend the ancient and the modern here cleverly and effectively. The old beams and walls remain but there's contemporary artwork and touches of glass, steel, slate and leather throughout. The bar is bustling and convivial with a good mix and age range of customers sitting on wall banquettes or at high tables and chairs dotted around the room; brick walls are painted white and there's a strip of blue neon lighting at ground level. They have a beer named for them (from Milk Street), Box Steam Piston Broke and Ringwood Old Thumper on handpump, good wines by the glass and a large cocktail list. Stairs lead up to the restaurant with its rather dramatic glass-enclosed mezzanine cube, there are mustard yellow and pale green leather chairs around a mix of tables on big floorboards, high rafters lined with electric candles and a large carved angel on a plinth; background music. A long slate-floored passageway links this main part to a two-roomed snug area with large leather sofas and armchairs and an open fire, and a small, rather cosy dining room. The central courtyard has colourful tables and chairs and a mediterranean feel.

Popular food includes sandwiches, thai-style mussels, blue cheese ravioli, chicken ballotine with smoked mash and pak choi, a fresh fish dish of the day, burger with toppings and fries, duck breast with red onion purée and braised little gem lettuce, beer-battered fish and chips, and puddings such as passion-fruit fool and rhubarb pudding with sorbet. *Benchmark main dish: pesto linguine £14.00. Two-course evening meal £20.00.*

Free house ~ Real ale ~ Open 11-11 ~ Bar food 12-9.30; 12-8 Sun ~ Restaurant ~ Children welcome ~ Dogs allowed in bar and bedrooms ~ Wi-fi ~ Live music last Sun of month ~ Bedrooms: £70/£80 *Recommended by Edward Mirzoeff, Andrew Lawson, Ivy and George Goodwill, Sylvia and Phillip Spencer*

Please keep sending us reports. We rely on readers for news of new discoveries, and particularly for news of changes – however slight – at the fully described pubs: feedback@goodguides.com, or (no stamp needed) The Good Pub Guide, FREEPOST RTXY–ZCBC–BBAZ, Stream Lane, Sedlescombe, Battle TN33 0PB.

HINTON ST GEORGE ST4212 Map 1

Lord Poulett Arms

(01460) 73149 – www.lordpoulettarms.com

Off A30 W of Crewkerne and off Merriott road (declassified – former A356, off B3165) N of Crewkerne; TA17 8SE

Somerset Dining Pub of the Year

Thatched 17th-c stone inn with top class food, good choice of drinks and pretty garden; attractive bedrooms

Walk around the peaceful and appealing village or enjoy one of the nearby walks, then come here for lunch. It's a civilised old place and the several attractive and cosy linked bar areas have hop-draped beams, walls made of honey-coloured stone or painted in bold Farrow & Ball colours and rugs on bare boards or flagstones; also, open fires (one in an inglenook, another in a raised fireplace that separates two rooms), antique brass candelabra, fresh flowers and candles, and some lovely old farmhouse, windsor and ladderback chairs around fine oak or elm tables. Butcombe Bitter, Otter Ale and St Austell Trelawny on handpump, 14 wines by the glass, home-made cordial, some interesting spirits and local bottled cider; background music, board games and table skittles. The pub cat is called Honey. Outside, beneath a wisteria-clad pergola, are white metalwork tables and chairs in a mediterranean-style, lavender-edged gravelled area, and picnic-sets in a wildflower garden; boules. Bedrooms are pretty and breakfasts splendid.

Food is excellent and includes sandwiches, devilled duck eggs with chipotle mayonnaise and crispy bacon and shallots, cured pigeon with roast figs, grilled cauliflower with blue cheese bread and butter pudding and balsamic onions, burger with toppings, chutney and chips, chicken breast with bubble and squeak fritter, black pudding and morel sauce, cod fillet with pea and wild garlic succotash, grilled lettuce and carrots, tandoori-dusted beef cheek with dhal, poppadum and mango chutney, and puddings such as stem ginger crème brûlée with poached rhubarb and mango and dark brown sugar bavarois with rum syrup; they also offer a two- and three-course set menu. *Benchmark main dish: cider-battered fish and chips £15.00. Two-course evening meal £25.00.*

Free house ~ Licensees Steve Hill and Michelle Paynton ~ Real ale ~ Open 12-11 ~ Bar food 12-2.30, 6.30-9.15; 12-3, 7-9.15 Sun ~ Children welcome ~ Dogs allowed in bar ~ Wi-fi ~ Bedrooms: £65/£90 *Recommended by Tim and Sarah Smythe-Brown, Charles Todd, Sylvia and Phillip Spencer, Patricia and Anton Larkham, Sally and Brian Turner, Sam Cole*

HOLCOMBE ST6649 Map 2

Holcombe Inn

(01761) 232478 – www.holcombeinn.co.uk

Off A367; Stratton Road; BA3 5EB

Charming inn with far-reaching views, cosy bars, a wide choice of drinks and good food; lovely bedrooms

Plenty of space for both eating and drinking include the cosy room to the right of the main entrance, which has sofas around a central table and an open woodburning stove. To the left is the bar: fine old flagstones, window seats and chunky captain's chairs around pine-topped tables, and a carved wooden counter where they serve Bath Gem, Butcombe Bitter and Otter Ale on handpump, 21 wines and champagne by the glass, 25 malt whiskies, cocktails and a thoughtful choice of local drinks (cider, vodka, sloe gin, various juices); board games and background music. A two-way woodburning stove also warms the dining room, which is partly carpeted and partly flagstoned and has partitioning creating snug seating areas, and a mix of high-backed patterned or leather and brass-studded dining chairs around all sorts of tables; daily newspapers. Just off here is a little sitting area serving specialist teas and coffees. There are picnic-sets on a terrace and side lawn, and the sunsets can be stunning. Dogs are welcome everywhere (except the restaurant) and in two of the lodges by prior arrangement. The well equipped bedrooms make a good base for exploring the area and some have views over peaceful farmland to Downside Abbey's school.

Pleasing food includes lunchtime sandwiches, grilled quail with onion purée, diced celeriac, caramelised apple and meat juices, salt and pepper whitebait with lemon mayonnaise, rare-breed burger with toppings and smoked garlic mayonnaise, rack of lamb with pistachio and parmesan crust and dauphinoise potatoes, maple-glazed pork belly with butter beans, broccoli and crispy skin, duck leg confit with mash, sweet pickled red cabbage and madeira cream sauce, cod with ratte potatoes, spinach, beetroot and horseradish purée and orange and chardonnay buerre blanc, and puddings such as rhubarb and orange jelly with poached rhubarb and chocolate marquise with blood orange, honeycomb and crème fraîche. *Benchmark main dish: pie of the day £14.50. Two-course evening meal £23.00.*

Free house ~ Licensee Julie Berry ~ Real ale ~ Open 12-11 ~ Bar food 12-2.30, 6-9; 12-9 Sat, Sun ~ Restaurant ~ Children welcome ~ Dogs allowed in bar and bedrooms ~ Wi-fi ~ Bedrooms: £75/£120 *Recommended by Taff Thomas, Toni, Christopher May, Ben and Jenny Settle, Roger and Anne Mallard, Lenny and Ruth Walters, Claire Adams*

HUISH EPISCOPI ST4326 Map 1

Rose & Crown £

(01458) 250494

Off A372 E of Langport; TA10 9QT

17th-c pub with local cider and real ales, simple food and a friendly welcome from long-serving licensees

The same family have been running this unspoilt thatched inn (known locally as 'Eli's' after the licensees' grandfather) for more than 158 years. There's no bar as such, just a central flagstoned still room where drinks are served: Teignworthy Reel Ale and a couple of guests such as Butcombe Rare Breed and Hop Back Crop Circle, local farm cider and Somerset cider brandy. The casual little front parlours, with their unusual pointed arch windows, have family photographs, books, cribbage, dominoes, shove-ha'penny and bagatelle and attract a good mix of both locals and visitors. A much more orthodox big back extension has pool, a games machine and a juke box. There are plenty of seats and tables in the extensive outdoor area and two lawns – one is enclosed and has a children's play area. Pub customers can camp (by arrangement) on the adjoining paddock. There's also a separate skittle alley, a large car park, morris men (in summer) and fine nearby river walks; they hold a Friday evening organic produce co-op in one of their rooms (4.30-7pm). The Civil War site of the Battle of Langport (1645) is not far away.

Fair-priced, home-made food includes sandwiches, good soups, cottage pie, a vegetarian tart, pork, apple and cider cobbler, chicken in tarragon sauce, and puddings such as sticky toffee pudding and apple crumble. *Benchmark main dish: steak in ale pie £8.95. Two-course evening meal £13.00.*

Free house ~ Licensees Maureen Pittard, Stephen Pittard and Patricia O'Malley ~ Real ale ~ No credit cards ~ Open 11.30-2.30, 5.15-11; 11.30-11.30 Fri, Sat; 12-10.30 Sun ~ Bar food 12-2, 5.30-7.30; not Sun evening or Mon ~ Children welcome ~ Dogs welcome ~ Wi-fi ~

Irish music last Thurs of month, folk singaround third Sat of month except June-Sept
Recommended by Lindy Andrews, Edward May, Isobel Mackinlay, Valerie and Gordon Wauton, Lorna and Jeff Mason

KINGSDON ST5126 Map 2

Kingsdon Inn

(01935) 840543 – www.kingsdoninn.co.uk
At Podimore roundabout on A303, follow sign to Langport (A372) then right on B3151; TA11 7LG

Charming old thatched pub with low-ceilinged rooms, west country beers, friendly staff and well thought-of food; bedrooms

This is a pretty little thatched cottage and very popular with our readers. The main bar has a woodburning stove, built-in wooden and cushioned wall seats with pretty scatter cushions, farmhouse and wheelback chairs around scrubbed kitchen tables set with candles and fresh flowers, and red quarry tiles on the floor; background classical music and TV. Some steps lead up to a carpeted dining area with a few low sagging beams, half-panelled walls and similar furnishings; one table is snugly set into a former inglenook fireplace. The stools on pale tiles against the counter are popular, and courteous, helpful staff serve Butcombe Bitter and Teignworthy Neap Tide with a guest such as Otter Bright on handpump, 14 wines by the glass and local farm cider. There's a second dining area plus an attractive separate restaurant with another woodburning stove. The garden has picnic-sets on grass, a herb garden and a small cottagey path leading to the front door. Bedrooms are cosy and breakfasts are good. The pub is handy for the Fleet Air Arm Museum.

Cooked by the landlord, the imaginative food includes hand-dived scallops with caramelised cauliflower risotto, katsuobushi (dried bonito) butter and black sesame, confit rabbit terrine with a spiced samosa, moroccan-style tagine with spiced pepper, apricot, dates and a red pepper and sherry purée, chicken suprême with dauphinoise potatoes, butternut squash purée, spinach and red wine jus, venison and red wine suet pudding with creamed savoy cabbage, 10oz 28-day-aged sirloin steak with roasted cherry vine tomatoes, peppercorn sauce and chips, and puddings such as ginger pannacotta with roast plums and plum sorbet and banana parfait with honeycomb ice-cream and caramelised banana; they also offer a two- and three-course set lunch on Monday. *Benchmark main dish: cider-braised pork belly with apple and vanilla purée, creamed potatoes and crackling £16.00. Two-course evening meal £26.00.*

Game Bird Inns ~ Managers Adam Cain and Cinzia Iezzi ~ Real ale ~ Open 12-3 (4 Sat), 6-11; 12-5 Sun; closed Sun evening; first week Jan ~ Bar food 12-2, 6.30-9; 12-3 Sun ~ Children welcome ~ Dogs allowed in bar and bedrooms ~ Wi-fi ~ Bedrooms: £70/£95
Recommended by Ewan and Sue Hewitt, David and Sally Cullen, Sandra and Miles Spencer, Barbara and Phil Bowie, Hugh Roberts

LUXBOROUGH SS9837 Map 1

Royal Oak

(01984) 641498 – www.theroyaloakinnluxborough.co.uk
Kingsbridge; S of Dunster on minor roads into Brendon Hills; TA23 0SH

Smashing place in wonderful countryside with local beers and ciders and popular food; comfortable bedrooms

This is an atmospheric inn deep in Exmoor National Park, with fine surrounding walks. The compact beamed bar has the most character, a good mix of chatty locals (often with their dogs) and an informal and cheerful feel: ancient flagstones, several rather fine settles, scrubbed kitchen tables and a huge brick fireplace with a warm log fire; a simpler back room has a very old cobbled floor, some quarry tiles and a stone fireplace. A room just off the bar is set for dining, with attractive pine furniture, and there are two dining rooms as well. Butcombe Union, Exmoor Ale and Otter Amber on handpump, several wines by the glass and farm cider; they have a record player for customers to use. There are some seats out in the charming back courtyard. Our readers enjoy staying here; the Coleridge Way is nearby.

Tasty food includes lunchtime sandwiches, chicken liver pâté with chutney, beer-battered prawns with aioli, aubergine parmigiana, ham and free-range eggs, lambs liver and bacon, herb-crusted hake with tomato, olive and chorizo tapenade and white wine butter, pork fillet stuffed with apple, black pudding and sage with cider sauce and sautéed potatoes, rib-eye steak with peppercorn sauce and chips, and puddings such as crème brûlée and chocolate profiteroles. *Benchmark main dish: pie of the day £12.50. Two-course evening meal £20.00.*

Free house ~ Licensee Douglas Yiend ~ Real ale ~ Open 12-11; closed Mon ~ Bar food 12-2, 6.30-9 ~ Restaurant ~ Children welcome ~ Dogs allowed in bar and bedrooms ~ Bedrooms: /£100 *Recommended by Pauline and Mark Evans, Jane Rigby, Sarah Roberts, David Appleyard*

MELLS — Talbot

ST7249 Map 2

(01373) 812254 – www.talbotinn.com

W of Frome, off A362 or A361; BA11 3PN

Interesting old coaching inn with real ales and good wines, inventive food and seats in courtyard; lovely bedrooms

A tucked-away, handsome old inn, this has a nicely informal, candlelit bar with various wooden tables and chairs on big quarry tiles, a woodburning stove in a stone fireplace, and stools (much used by locals) against the counter where friendly, helpful staff serve a beer named for the pub (from Keystone), Butcombe Bitter and a guest on handpump, 14 good wines by the glass and a farm cider. Two interconnected dining rooms have brass-studded leather chairs around wooden tables, a log fire with candles in fine clay cups on the mantelpiece above and lots of coaching prints on the walls; quiet background music and board games. Outside, the courtyard has pale green metalwork chairs and tables. Off here, in separate buildings, are the rustic-feeling sitting room with sofas, chairs and tables, a huge mural and vast glass bottles, and the grill room, where food is cooked simply on a big open fire overlooked by 18th-c portraits. Bedrooms are smart and stylish and breakfasts are good. Do visit the lovely church where the poet Siegfried Sassoon is buried; the walled gardens opposite the inn are very pretty. This is sister pub to the Beckford Arms at Fonthill Gifford (Wiltshire).

Good, seasonal food includes sandwiches, crispy lamb sweetbreads with pickled beetroot, broad beans and garlic pesto, salmon and haddock chowder with fennel, bacon, sweetcorn and sea herbs, beer-battered fish and chips, chicken caesar salad, roasted cauliflower with fregola, hazelnut brown butter, pumpkin seeds and honey granola, lamb brisket with a potato cake, feta, cumin yoghurt and tomatoes, hake with quinoa, grilled fennel, picked white crab meat, spinach and squid ink vinaigrette, and puddings such as rhubarb parfait with crème pâtissière, gingerbread crumb and rhubarb sorbet. *Benchmark main dish: burger with toppings, coleslaw and chips £13.50. Two-course evening meal £20.00.*

Free house ~ Licensee Matt Greenlees ~ Real ale ~ Open 8am-11pm; 8am-10.30pm Sun ~ Bar food 12-3, 6-9.30 ~ Restaurant ~ Children welcome ~ Dogs welcome ~ Wi-fi ~

Bedrooms: /£100 *Recommended by Taff Thomas, Matthew and Elisabeth Reeves, R L Borthwick, S G N Bennett, Roy Hoing, Sandra and Miles Spencer, Jamie and Lizzie McEwan*

MILVERTON ST1225 Map 1

Globe

(01823) 400534 – www.theglobemilverton.co.uk

Fore Street; TA4 1JX

Handsome coaching inn with good ales, quite a choice of tasty food and seats outside; bedrooms

You'll get a friendly welcome from the helpful staff here and there's a cheerful mix of locals and visitors. The opened-up rooms have solid rustic tables surrounded by an attractive mix of wooden or high-backed black leather chairs, artwork on pale-painted walls above a red dado, and a big gilt-edged mirror above a woodburning stove in an ornate fireplace; background music. Bar chairs line the counter where they keep three beers from Exmoor, Otter and Quantock on handpump, ten wines by the glass and local farm cider. The sheltered outside terrace has raffia-style chairs and tables and cushioned wall seating under parasols. The two bedrooms are comfortable and breakfasts are continental.

Quite a choice of seasonal food includes sandwiches, tempura tiger prawns with sweet chilli sauce, slow-roasted oxtail croquettes with parsnip purée and carrot crisps, roasted vegetable and tomato risotto, burger with toppings and chips, slow-roasted lamb shoulder with apricot and thyme stuffing and redcurrant sauce, fish and leek pie topped with cheddar mash, free-range chicken breast wrapped in prosciutto with tarragon cream sauce and sautéed potatoes, and puddings such as chocolate cheesecake with a white chocolate mocha sauce and sticky toffee pudding with toffee sauce and clotted cream. *Benchmark main dish: pork belly glazed with honey with potatoes of the day £16.95. Two-course evening meal £22.00.*

Free house ~ Licensees Mark and Adele Tarry ~ Real ale ~ Open 12-3, 6-11 (11.30 Sat); 12-3 Sun; closed Sunday evening, Mon lunchtime ~ Bar food 12-2, 6.30-9 ~ Restaurant ~ Children welcome ~ Dogs allowed in bar ~ Wi-fi ~ Bedrooms: £65/£70 *Recommended by Valerie Sayer, Colin and Dañiel Gibbs, Bob and Margaret Holder, Alexandra and Tim Fledgling, Belinda and Neil Garth*

MONKTON COMBE ST7761 Map 2

Wheelwrights Arms

(01225) 722287 – www.wheelwrightsarms.co.uk

Just off A36 S of Bath; Church Cottages; BA2 7HB

18th-c stone pub with cheerful staff, helpful landlord and staff, good food and seats outside; comfortable bedrooms

Our readers enjoy their visits here – it's a thoroughly nice place. The bar-dining room has an open fire in a raised fireplace at one end, cushioned and wood-planked built-in wall seats, rush-seated or cushioned high-backed dining chairs around tables (each set with a small lamp), parquet flooring or carpet, and old photographs and oil paintings (the one above the fireplace of a dog is particularly nice). The middle room has some pretty frieze work, a high shelf of wooden wader birds and stools against the green-painted counter where they keep Butcombe Bitter and Otter Bitter on handpump, 12 wines by the glass, several gins and farm cider; background jazz and board games. A small end room is just right for a group. Gravelled terraces have wood and metal tables and chairs and picnic-sets. Bedrooms, in a restored annexe, are quiet, well equipped and comfortable. The peaceful village is surrounded by picturesque hills and valleys.

The choice of interesting food includes lunchtime flatbreads with toppings, mussels in cider cream with parsley, mixed game terrine with plum and port jelly and apricot and almond cake, sweet potato and chickpea curry with feta and mint spring roll and sumac yoghurt, lamb and red wine ragoût on pasta with salsa verde, chicken breast with wild garlic mash, roast celeriac and puy lentil sauce, roast venison haunch with butternut squash purée, roast squash wedge and chocolate and raspberry jus, and puddings such as chocolate brownie with toffee popcorn and salted caramel ice-cream and apple and blackberry crumble. *Benchmark main dish: beer-battered fish and triple-cooked chips £14.00. Two-course evening meal £22.00.*

Free house ~ Licensee David Munn ~ Real ale ~ Open 8am-11pm ~ Bar food 12-2 (3 weekends), 6-9.30 ~ Children welcome ~ Wi-fi ~ Bedrooms: £85/£155
Recommended by John and Abigail Prescott, Holly and Tim Waite, Rosie and John Moore, Dr and Mrs A K Clarke, Peter and Emma Kelly

NORTON ST PHILIP — ST7755 Map 2

George

(01373) 834224 – www.georgeinnnsp.co.uk
A366; BA2 7LH

Wonderful ancient building full of history and interest with well liked food, real ales and decent wines by the glass; character bedrooms

---

It's worth visiting this exceptional building to take in the fine surroundings of a traditional inn that has been offering hospitality to travellers for more than 700 years. The main room, which serves as the bar, has heavy beams, an oak-panelled settle and old church chairs on the wooden floor, various illustrations on the walls (as well as an early 18th-c clock) and an open fire with an old iron fireback in the handsome stone fireplace. Wadworth 6X, Horizon, Studs Up and Swordfish on hand pump and several wines by the glass. As you enter the building from the car park, there's a room on the right with high dark beams, squared dark half-panelling, a broad carved stone fireplace and a big mullioned window. The dining room has a wonderful pitched ceiling with trusses and timbering, a fine tapestry on the walls, a big old stone fireplace, high-backed cushioned dining chairs on floorboards and an oak dresser. Bedrooms are full of character: some, with four-posters, are reached up a Norman stone stair-turret, while others are across the cobbled courtyard in a fine half-timbered upper gallery. Opposite the inn is the 500-year-old Plaine B&B (part of the same business), where the rooms are more contemporary in design. To the side of the inn, an alley leads to the village green and the attractive churchyard around the medieval church whose bells struck Pepys (who passed through on 12 June 1668) as 'mighty tuneable'. The terraced garden has a beautiful view of the church and the village cricket pitch.

Decent quality food includes sandwiches, smoked haddock and creamed leek tart with a poached egg and hollandaise, garlic king prawns with tomato, basil and parmesan, sharing boards, home-cooked honey-glazed ham and free-range eggs, beetroot and goats cheese tortellini in spinach, tomato and mascarpone sauce, burger with toppings, onion rings and chips, confit duck leg with peas in garlic and thyme and creamy mash, a pie of the day, fresh fish of the day in beer batter with pea purée, 28-day-aged sirloin steak with a choice of sauce, and puddings. *Benchmark main dish: calves liver with bacon, garlic mash and roasted shallot jus £16.50. Two-course evening meal £22.00.*

Wadworths ~ Manager Jenny Searle ~ Real ale ~ Open 11-10.30; 12-10 Sun ~ Bar food 12-2.30, 5.45-9; 12-8 Sun ~ Restaurant ~ Children welcome until 8pm ~ Dogs allowed in bar and bedrooms ~ Wi-fi ~ Bedrooms: /£100 *Recommended by Lucy and Giles Gibbon, Elise and Charles Mackinlay, Katherine and Hugh Markham, Nicola and Nigel Matthews*

ODCOMBE ST5015 Map 2

Masons Arms

(01935) 862591 – www.masonsarmsodcombe.co.uk

Off A3088 or A30 just W of Yeovil; Lower Odcombe; BA22 8TX

Own-brew beers and tasty food in pretty thatched cottage; bedrooms

Both the own-brewed ales and the food here are praiseworthy. The simple little bar has joists and a couple of standing timbers, a mix of cushioned dining chairs around all sorts of tables on cream and blue patterned carpet, and a couple of tub chairs and a table in the former inglenook fireplace. Up a step is a similar area, while more steps lead down to a dining room with a squashy brown sofa and a couple of cushioned dining chairs in front of a woodburning stove; the sandstone walls are hung with black and white local photographs and country prints. Their own ales are Odcombe No.1, Roly Poly and seasonal beers on handpump, they make their own sloe and elderflower cordials, have 11 wines by the glass and serve farm cider. There's a thatched smokers' shelter and picnic-sets in the garden, plus a vegetable patch, chicken coop and a campsite. Bedrooms are well equipped and comfortable and the breakfasts are good and hearty.

Using home-grown and other local produce, the well regarded food includes sandwiches and paninis, seared scallops with minted pea purée and pancetta crisp, lamb koftas with spiced moroccan couscous and mint and cumin yoghurt, butternut squash, goats cheese and spinach lasagne, pulled pork hash with chorizo oil and a poached egg, chicken breast with creamy mushroom and pancetta tagliatelle, steak and kidney pudding with horseradish mash and gravy, baby back barbecue ribs with sweet potato and parsnip slaw and crispy onions, and puddings such as toffee apple cheesecake with cinnamon ice-cream and peanut butter crème brûlée. *Benchmark main dish: burger with toppings, burger sauce and chips £13.00. Two-course evening meal £20.00.*

Own brew ~ Licensees Drew Read and Paula Tennyson ~ Real ale ~ Open 8am-3pm, 6-midnight; 8am-midnight Sun ~ Bar food 12-2, 6.30-9.30 ~ Children welcome ~ Dogs welcome ~ Wi-fi ~ Bedrooms: £63/£93 *Recommended by Paddy and Sian O'Leary, Richard and Tessa Ibbot, Mrs Zara Elliott, Peter Pilbeam, Andy and Louise Ramwell*

PITNEY ST4527 Map 1

Halfway House £

(01458) 252513 – www.thehalfwayhouse.co.uk

Just off B3153 W of Somerton; TA10 9AB

Bustling, friendly local with a fine choice of real ales, local ciders and good simple food

The perfect example of an unpretentious village local with excellent beers to boot. The atmosphere is chatty and easy-going and the cheerful mix of customers gather in the three old-fashioned rooms: communal tables, roaring log fires and a homely feel underlined by a profusion of books, maps and newspapers. Tapped from the cask, the ales might include Butcombe Haka, Cheddar Seismic Shift, Hop Back Summer Lightning, Liberation Pale Ale, Oakham Citra, Otter Bright, Quantock Sunraker, Teignworthy Reel Ale and Titanic Plum Porter; also, four farm ciders, a dozen malt whiskies and several wines by the glass; board games. There are tables outside.

Simple, fair-priced food includes sandwiches, faggots with mash and onion gravy, pork steak with scrumpy sauce and mash, ham, eggs and chips, vegetable tagine, fish casserole, chicken breast wrapped in bacon and stuffed with mozzarella and creamy sun-dried tomato sauce, a pie of the day, and beef chilli. *Benchmark main dish: beer-battered fish and chips £10.50. Two-course evening meal £16.00.*

Free house ~ Licensee Mark Phillips ~ Real ale ~ Open 11.30-3, 4-11; 11.30-11 Sat; 12-11 Sun ~ Bar food 12-2.30, 7-9.30; 1-4, 6.30-8.30 Sun ~ Children welcome ~ Dogs welcome ~ Wi-fi *Recommended by Bob and Margaret Holder, S G N Bennett, Edward May, Julie and Andrew Blanchett, Rob Anderson*

PRIDDY ST5250 Map 2

Queen Victoria £

(01749) 676385 – www.thequeenvicpriddy.co.uk

Village signed off B3135; Pelting Drove; BA5 3BA

Stone-built country pub with a friendly atmosphere, real ales and honest food; seats outside

Fine countryside surrounds this popular pub and customers usually include walkers with their dogs and cyclists. The various rooms and alcoves have a lot of character and plenty of original features, and there's both an open fire in a large grate (with a huge cauldron to one side) and a woodburning stove in a back bar. There are flagstoned or slate floors, bare stone walls (the smarter dining room is half panelled and half painted), horse tack, farm tools and photos of Queen Victoria. Furniture is traditional: cushioned wall settles, farmhouse and other solid chairs around all manner of wooden tables, a nice old pew beside a screen settle making a cosy alcove, and high chairs next to the bar counter where they serve Butcombe Bitter and Rare Breed and a guest such as Bristol Beer Factory No 7 on handpump, two farm ciders, nine malt whiskies, nine gins and nine wines by the glass. There are plenty of seats in the front courtyard, with more across the lane where there's also a children's playground; the smokers' shelter is a converted dray wagon. Wheelchair access.

Fair value, traditional food includes baguettes, deep-fried brie wedges with plum sauce, smoked salmon and prawn cocktail, tomato, garlic and roasted peppers tagliatelle, ham and eggs, beef chilli with rice, beer-battered cod and chips, chicken curry, fish pie, and puddings such as warm chocolate fudge cake and treacle sponge. *Benchmark main dish: beef and mushroom in ale pie £9.95. Two-course evening meal £13.00.*

Butcombe ~ Tenant Mark Walton ~ Real ale ~ Open 11-11; 1-10.30 Sun ~ Bar food 12-3, 5-9; 12-8 Sun ~ Children welcome ~ Dogs welcome ~ Wi-fi ~ Live music monthly in summer *Recommended by Dave Sutton, Sophie Ellison, Chris and Angela Buckell, M G Hart, Peter Myers, Ivy and George Goodwill*

SOMERTON ST4828 Map 2

White Hart

(01458) 272273 – www.whitehartsomerton.com

Market Place; TA11 7LX

Attractive old place with several bars, open fires, spacious dining room and enjoyable food; bedrooms

Have a wander around this lovely village before heading here. You'll find it a good all-rounder with a lively atmosphere, a fine drinks choice and interesting food. The main bar has long wall seats with attractive scatter cushions, stools around small tables, big wall mirrors and Bath Gem, Cheddar Potholer, Otter Amber and a guest from the local Brotherhood Brewery on handpump, 22 wines by the glass and local cider; staff are helpful and friendly. A doorway leads to a cosy room with a leather sofa, armchairs, a chest table and an open fire; another snug bar is similarly furnished, while a simpler room has straightforward wooden dining chairs and tables, a little brick fireplace and some stained glass. Throughout there are rugs on parquet flooring (some plain bare boards too), church candles, contemporary paintwork and interesting lighting – look out for the antler chandelier with its pretty hanging lampshades; background music and board games. Outside, the flower-filled terrace has tables and chairs under parasols, with more on grass. Some of the airy, well equipped and comfortable bedrooms overlook the square and church.

A wide choice of smashing food includes breakfasts (7.30-11am), lunchtime ciabattas, bream ceviche with citrus and chilli dressing, goats cheese arancini with walnut mayonnaise and beetroot dressing, wild mushroom and wine risotto with pearled spelt, crispy shallots and oregano, spiced lamb burger with raita, spicy slaw, gherkins and chips with smoked paprika salt, flat-iron chicken with crispy potato wedges and chimichurri, local venison and pork ragoût with tagliatelle and salsa verde, hake fillet with anchovies, cauliflower purée, lentils, chorizo and spring onion, and puddings such as salted caramel and chocolate tart with cream and honeycomb and lemon posset with poached rhubarb and apple crumble. *Benchmark main dish: wood-fired pizzas £12.00. Two-course evening meal £19.00.*

Free house ~ Licensee Abbie Windust ~ Real ale ~ Open 9am-11pm ~ Bar food 9am-9.45pm ~ Restaurant ~ Children welcome ~ Dogs allowed in bar and bedrooms ~ Wi-fi ~ Bedrooms: /£85 *Recommended by Peter and Emma Kelly, Richard Tilbrook, Charles Todd, Mark Hamill, Miranda and Jeff Davidson, Edward Mirzoeff, Trevor and Michele Street*

STANTON WICK — ST6162 Map 2

Carpenters Arms

(01761) 490202 – www.the-carpenters-arms.co.uk

Village signposted off A368, just W of junction with A37 S of Bristol; BS39 4BX

Bustling, friendly dining pub on country lane with pleasing food, helpful staff and fine choice of drinks; nice bedrooms

Our readers enjoy staying in the comfortable and quiet bedrooms here and breakfasts are very good. It's neatly run by friendly licensees and the Coopers Parlour on the right has a couple of beams, seats around heavy tables on a tartan carpet and attractive curtains; in the angle between here and the bar area is a wide woodburning stove in an opened-through fireplace. The bar has wall settles with cushions, stripped-stone walls and a big log fire in an inglenook. There's also a snug inner room (brightened by mirrors in arched recesses) and a restaurant with leather sofas, easy chairs and a lounge area at one end. Butcombe Bitter and Sharps Cornish Coaster and Doom Bar on handpump, ten wines by the glass (and some interesting bin ends) and several malt whiskies; TV in the snug. The front terrace has picnic-sets and there are pretty flower beds, hanging baskets and tubs. Good walks in the peaceful surrounding countryside.

A thoughtful choice of good food includes sandwiches, confit duck with orange marmalade and pickled vegetables, twice-baked cheese soufflé, sharing boards, mushroom and ricotta cannelloni in rich tomato sauce, burger with toppings and fries, monkfish, mussels and prawns in bouillabaisse, maple-glazed pork belly with parsnip mash and roasted vegetables, sirloin steak with a choice of sauce and straw fries, and puddings such as rhubarb and grenadine crème brûlée and white chocolate parfait. *Benchmark main dish: poppadum-crusted chicken with curry cream sauce £15.50. Two-course evening meal £22.00.*

Buccaneer Holdings ~ Manager Simon Pledge ~ Real ale ~ Open 11-11; 12-10.30 Sun ~ Bar food 12-2.30, 6-9.30 (10 Fri, Sat); 12-9.30 Sun ~ Restaurant ~ Children welcome ~

Dogs allowed in bar ~ Wi-fi ~ Bedrooms: £80/£120 *Recommended by Mr and Mrs P R Thomas, Phil and Helen Holt, Mr and Mrs J Watkins, Dr and Mrs A K Clarke, Trish and Karl Soloman, Michael Doswell, Chris Pocock*

WATERROW ST0525 Map 1

Rock

(01984) 623293 – www.rockinnwaterrow.co.uk

B3227 Wiveliscombe–Bampton; TA4 2AX

Handsome inn with local ales, interesting food and a nice mix of customers; comfortable bedrooms

Of course, there's quite an emphasis on the imaginative food and attractive cottagey bedrooms in this striking timbered inn, but locals do drop in regularly for a pint and a chat, which keeps the atmosphere relaxed and informal. The bar area has wheelback chairs and cushioned window seats around scrubbed kitchen tables on pale floorboards, sympathetic lighting and a woodburning stove in a stone fireplace. High black leather bar chairs line the copper-topped bar counter where they serve Otter Bitter and Amber and a guest beer on handpump, ten wines by the glass, a dozen malt whiskies and local farm cider; TV, darts and board games. The elegant restaurant is up some steps with pale grey-painted panelled walls, a large wicker stag's head and high-backed wooden chairs around chunky kitchen tables on more pale floorboards; there's also a snug with sofas and leather armchairs. In front of the building are seats under umbrellas, and although parking by the inn is limited, there's more on the far side of the main road over the bridge. Bedrooms are decorated in a country style and are warm and comfortable.

Cooked by the landlord using the best local produce, the impressive food includes sandwiches, soufflé omelette with smoked haddock and cheese, pigeon breast with black pudding and truffle-dressed salad, sweet potato-flavoured gnocchi with spinach, red onions, grilled artichokes and parmesan, guinea fowl with tartiflette potatoes, creamed brussels sprouts with smoked bacon and truffle sauce, free-range duck with creamed onion purée and dauphinoise potatoes, 28-day-aged 10oz sirloin steak with a choice of sauce, and puddings. *Benchmark main dish: 14-hour-cooked aberdeen angus beef in black garlic and black treacle with cheddar cheese mash £17.00. Two-course evening meal £23.00.*

Free house ~ Licensees Daren and Ruth Barclay ~ Real ale ~ Open 12-3, 6-11; 12-3 Sun; closed Sun evening, all day Mon, Tues lunchtime (all day in winter) ~ Bar food 12-2, 6.30-9; 12-3 Sun ~ Restaurant ~ Children welcome ~ Dogs welcome ~ Wi-fi ~ Bedrooms: £75/£85 *Recommended by Gary Wilkinson, Kate and Mark Foskett, Audrey and Andrew Nichols, Gwendoline and Ralph Mason*

WEDMORE ST4348 Map 1

Swan

(01934) 710337 – www.theswanwedmore.com

Cheddar Road, opposite Church Street; BS28 4EQ

Lively place with a friendly, informal atmosphere, lots of customers, efficient service and tasty food; bedrooms

In the centre of the village and with good parking, this is a handsome place with customers bustling in and out all day. Mirrors dotted around give the open-plan layout a feeling of even more space. The main bar has all sorts of wooden tables and chairs on floorboards, a wall seat with attractive scatter cushions, a woodburning stove, suede stools against the panelled counter and a rustic central table with daily papers; background music. Cheddar

Potholer, Otter Amber and Bitter and a guest beer on handpump, 20 wines by the glass and two farm ciders are served by quick, friendly staff. At one end of the room, a step leads down to an area with rugs on huge flagstones, a leather chesterfield, armchairs and brass-studded leather chairs, then down another step to more sofas and armchairs. The airy dining room has attractive high-backed chairs, tables set with candles in glass jars and another woodburner. There are plenty of seats and tables on the terrace and lawn, and the metal furniture among flowering tubs at the front of the building gives a continental feel. Bedrooms are pretty (some are generously proportioned) and breakfasts are good.

Good, modern food includes sandwiches, bream ceviche with citrus and chilli dressing and radicchio and radish salad, crab cakes with harissa, aioli and dill, sharing platters, wild mushroom and red wine risotto with pearled spelt, crispy shallots and oregano, hake fillet with anchovies, herbs, capers, cauliflower purée, lentils and chorizo, venison and pork ragoût with salsa verde and pangritata (breadcrumbs and herbs crisped in oil), spiced lamb burger with raita, spicy slaw and chips with smoked paprika salt, and puddings such as salted caramel and chocolate tart with cream and honeycomb and lemon posset with poached rhubarb and almond crumble. *Benchmark main dish: flat-iron chicken with spicy slaw £16.50. Two-course evening meal £24.00.*

Free house ~ Licensee Kirsty Schmidt ~ Real ale ~ Open 9am-11pm (10.30pm Sun) ~ Bar food 9am-10pm ~ Restaurant ~ Children welcome ~ Dogs allowed in bar and bedrooms ~ Wi-fi ~ Bedrooms: /£85 *Recommended by Bob and Melissa Wyatt, S Holder, Sylvia and Phillip Spencer, Millie and Peter Downing*

WRAXALL ST4971 Map 2

Battleaxes

(01275) 857473 – www.flatcappers.co.uk

Bristol Road B3130, E of Nailsea; BS48 1LQ

Bustling pub with relaxed dining and drinking areas, helpful staff and good food; big bedrooms with contemporary bathrooms

---

Handy for nearby Tyntesfield (National Trust), this Victorian pub is popular for its all-day food. The spacious interior is split into separate areas with an easy-going atmosphere throughout: polished floorboards or flagstones, portraits and pictures on walls above painted and panelled dados, mirrors on boldly patterned wallpaper, fresh flowers and house plants, books on windowsills and church candles. The bar has leather-topped stools against the counter where they keep a beer named for the pub (from Three Castles) and a couple of guests such as Bristol Beer Factory Optimist and Castles White Knight on handpump and several wines by the glass; background music. You'll find long pews with scatter cushions, church chairs and a medley of other wooden dining chairs around chunky tables and groups of leather armchairs. There are picnic-sets outside and some of the spacious bedrooms have country views. Wheelchair access using ramps.

Starting with breakfasts (8-11am), the wide choice of food includes nibbles such as sticky soy-pulled pork with crispy noodles, hummus with cashew nuts, lemon, parsley oil and chargrilled flatbread, and salt and pepper squid with aioli and lime, plus teriyaki tofu stir-fry with jasmine rice, summer beans and brassicas with chilli and coriander, beer-battered haddock and triple-cooked chips, lemon and thyme roasted half chicken with hasselback potatoes, pickled red cabbage, flatbread, harissa and garlic yoghurt, duck confit with sautéed heirloom potatoes, wilted gem lettuce, peas, pancetta and café au lait sauce, and puddings such as triple chocolate brownie with salted caramel sauce and vanilla ice-cream and queen of puddings (baked custard sponge, rhubarb jam and meringue). *Benchmark main dish: 16-hour braised pork belly with fondant potatoes, crackling and jus £14.50. Two-course evening meal £20.50.*

Flatcappers ~ Manager Kate Foskett ~ Real ale ~ Open 8am-11pm ~ Bar food 8am-9pm (10pm Fri, Sat) ~ Children welcome ~ Dogs allowed in bar ~ Wi-fi ~ Bedrooms: /£100
Recommended by Dr and Mrs A K Clarke, Celia and Andrew King, Sandra and Neil White, Martine and Colin Fresher

WRINGTON ST4762 Map 2

Plough

(01934) 862871 – www.theploughatwrington.co.uk
2.5 miles off A370 Bristol–Weston, from bottom of Rhodiate Hill; BS40 5QA

Welcoming pub with bustling bar and two dining rooms, good food, well kept beer and seats outside

This well run, neatly kept pub is handy for both Cheddar Gorge and Bristol Airport, so it's best to book a table in advance. The bar is chatty and convivial with locals perched on stools against the counter where they keep Butcombe Bitter (the brewery is in the village), St Austell Tribute and Youngs Bitter on handpump and 18 wines by the glass, served by friendly and efficient staff. Two dining rooms (the one at the back has plenty of big windows overlooking the gazebo and garden) have open doorways and throughout you'll find (three) winter fires, slate or wooden floors, beams and standing timbers, plenty of pictures on the planked, red or yellow walls and all manner of high-backed leather, wooden dining or farmhouse chairs around tables of many sizes. Also, fresh flowers, table skittles and a chest containing games. There are picnic-sets at the front and on the back grass; boules. They hold a farmers' market on the second Friday of the month. This is sister pub to the Rattlebone at Sherston (Wiltshire). Disabled access and lavatories.

Well regarded food includes open sandwiches and ciabattas, pigeon breast with roasted beetroot, fresh blackberries and blackberry emulsion, crispy calamari with garlic mayonnaise and chilli, sharing boards, gnocchi with wild mushrooms, sage, spinach and blue cheese sauce, burgers with lots of toppings, coleslaw and skinny fries, sea bream fillet with saffron and pea risotto and chilli oil, lamb duo (braised neck and rump) with pea purée, almond croquette and jus, and puddings such as chocolate délice with salted caramel, white chocolate snow and toasted cashews and lemon tart with mulled fruits and raspberry sorbet; steak night is Wednesday. *Benchmark main dish: smoked haddock with spinach in a cream sauce £12.95. Two-course evening meal £20.00.*

Youngs ~ Tenant Jason Read ~ Real ale ~ Open 12-3, 5-11 Mon, Tues; 12-11 Weds, Thurs, Sun; 12-midnight Fri, Sat ~ Bar food 12-2.30, 6-9.30; 12-4, 7-9 Sun ~ Restaurant ~ Children welcome ~ Dogs welcome ~ Wi-fi *Recommended by Bob and Margaret Holder, Dr and Mrs A K Clarke, Peter Myers, Dr A J and Mrs B A Tompsett, Mark Morgan, Katherine Matthews*

'Children welcome' means the pub says it lets children inside without any special restriction. If it allows them in, but to restricted areas such as an eating area or family room, we specify this. Some pubs may impose an evening time limit. We do not mention limits after 9pm as we assume children are home by then.

Also Worth a Visit in Somerset

Besides the fully inspected pubs, you might like to try these pubs that have been recommended to us and described by readers. Do tell us what you think of them: feedback@goodguides.com

AXBRIDGE ST4354

Lamb (01934) 732253
The Square; off A371 Cheddar–Winscombe; BS26 2AP Big rambling carpeted pub with heavy 15th-c beams and timbers, stone and roughcast walls, old settles and large stone fireplaces, unusual bar front with bottles set in plaster, Butcombe beers, well chosen wines and good coffee, enjoyable food (all day weekends) from sandwiches up; board games, table skittles and skittle alley, sports TV, free wi-fi; children and dogs allowed, seats out at front and in small sheltered back garden, medieval King John's Hunting Lodge (NT) opposite, open all day. *(Peter Myers)*

BACKWELL ST4969

George (01275) 462770
Farleigh Road; A370 W of Bristol; BS48 3PG Modernised and extended roadside dining pub (former coaching inn); enjoyable food in bar and restaurant from ciabattas to daily specials, also a gluten-free menu, well kept Bath, Butcombe, St Austell and a guest, good choice of wines; background music in some areas; children and dogs welcome, gravel terrace and lawn behind, seven bedrooms, open (and food) all day. *(Sarah and David Gibbs)*

BARRINGTON ST3918

Barrington Boar (01460) 259281
Opposite church; TA19 0JB Old stone-built dining pub in pretty village; good variety of well liked food (not Sun evening, Mon) from lunchtime sandwiches and light meals up, friendly helpful service, Exmoor, St Austell and a beer badged for them, Thatcher's cider, updated interior with solid furnishings, wood and stone floors, woodburners (boar's head above one); children and dogs welcome, picnic-sets out in front and in pleasant beer garden behind, four bedrooms, handy for Barrington Court (NT), open all day Sun till 9pm, closed Mon lunchtime. *(Alan and Angela Scouller)*

BATCOMBE ST6839

★**Three Horseshoes** (01749) 850359
Village signposted off A359 Bruton–Frome; BA4 6HE Handsome honey-stone inn with long narrow main room, beams, local pictures, built-in cushioned window seats and nice mix of tables, woodburner one end, open fire the other, Butcombe and guests, local ciders, around a dozen wines by the glass and several malt whiskies, well liked food (best to book, especially weekends), helpful friendly service, attractive stripped-stone dining room; children, walkers and dogs welcome, three simple but pretty bedrooms, lovely church next door, open all day weekends. *(Pete and Sarah)*

BATH ST7464

Bath Brew House (01225) 805609
James Street West; BA1 2BX Interesting spaciously converted pub visibly brewing its own James Street beers (brewery tours available), also guest ales and craft kegs, food from open kitchen including spit-roasts, various events such as comedy nights and live music in upstairs room with own bar and sports TV; well behaved children and dogs allowed in some areas, sizeable split-level beer garden with covered eating area, summer barbecues, open (and food) all day. *(Dr and Mrs A K Clarke)*

BATH ST7565

Bell (01225) 460426
Walcot Street; BA1 5BW Long narrow split-level pub owned by the local community; nine real ales, traditional ciders and some basic good value food, lots of pump clips and gig notices, a couple of fires (one gas), bar billiards, table football and board games; packed and lively in the evening with regular live music and DJs; canopied garden, even has its own laundrette, open all day. *(Dr and Mrs A K Clarke)*

BATH ST7465

Chequers (01225) 360017
Rivers Street; BA1 2QA Busy 19th-c city-centre pub with good interesting food (can be pricey) along with more standard choices, Bath Gem, Butcombe Bitter and several wines by the glass, friendly service, parquet-floored bar with wedgwood-blue paintwork and some fine plasterwork, cushioned wall pews, chapel, farmhouse and kitchen chairs around mix of flower-topped tables, coal-effect gas fire, attractive little candlelit restaurant upstairs with view into kitchen; children and dogs (in bar) welcome, pavement picnic-sets under awning, open all day. *(Dr and Mrs A K Clarke)*

BATH ST7564

★**Coeur de Lion** (01225) 463568
Northumberland Place, off High Street; BA1 5AR Tiny stained-glass-fronted single-room pub, simple, cosy and friendly, with candles and log-effect gas fire, well kept Abbey ales and guests, good well priced traditional food from snacks and baguettes up (vegetarian options), Christmas mulled wine, more room and loos upstairs; may be

background music; tables out in charming flower-filled flagstoned pedestrian alley, open all day, food till 6pm. *(Dr and Mrs A K Clarke, Stuart Doughty)*

BATH ST7564

★**Crystal Palace** (01225) 482666
Abbey Green; BA1 1NW Spacious two-room Fullers pub; rugs on wood floors and comfortable mix of seating, panelled walls and groups of pictures, popular sensibly priced food from lunchtime sandwiches up including set deal and Somerset cheese and port menu, speedy friendly service, four well kept ales from plank-faced bar, log fire, garden room opening on to nice sheltered courtyard; background music, sports TV, free wi-fi; children and dogs welcome, handy for Roman Baths and main shopping areas, open (and food) all day. *(Michael Sargent, Dr and Mrs A K Clarke)*

BATH ST7464

Garricks Head (01225) 318368
St Johns Place/Westgate, beside Theatre Royal; BA1 1ET Civilised and relaxed dining pub with good food including pre-theatre menu; bar with tall windows, wheelback and other chairs around wooden tables on bare boards, candles and a couple of sizeable brass chandeliers, gas-effect coal fire with fine silver meat domes on wall above, four interesting regional ales, real ciders and decent wines by the glass, proper cocktails, separate smartly set dining room; may be soft background jazz; children and dogs (in bar) welcome, pavement tables, open all day. *(Dr and Mrs A K Clarke)*

BATH ST7564

Graze (01225) 429392
Behind Bath Spa station; BA1 1SX Spacious and popular Bath/St Austell bar-restaurant (part of the city's Vaults development) arranged over upper floor and served by lift; modern steel and glass construction with leather chairs and benches on wood-strip flooring, slatted ceiling with exposed ducting and pendant lighting, good selection of beers (some from on-site microbrewery, can be pricey), extensive range of wines and spirits and very good coffee, highly regarded food cooked in open kitchen from light dishes and sharing boards (good fish one) to Josper grills, helpful friendly young staff; background music; children welcome, disabled facilities, two sizeable terraces overlooking Bath one side, the station the other, life-size models of cows, pigs and chickens, open all day. *(Chris and Angela Buckell, Dr and Mrs A K Clarke)*

BATH ST7464

Griffin (01225) 420919
Monmouth Street; BA1 2AP Cleanly refurbished little corner pub with fine range of well kept ales, craft beers and ciders, enjoyable freshly made food from shortish menu including good Sun roasts, friendly staff; comfortable bedrooms, open (and food) all day, kitchen closes 3pm Sun. *(Kate Ritcher, Dr and Mrs A K Clarke)*

BATH ST7465

Hall & Woodhouse (01225) 469259
Old King Street; BA1 2JW Conversion of stone-fronted warehouse/auction rooms; big open-plan interior on two floors, steel girders and glass, palms and chandeliers, mix of modern and traditional furniture including old-fashioned iron-framed tables with large candles and some simple bench seating, parquet and slate floors, Badger ales from full-length servery on the right, sweeping stairs up to another bar and eating area (disabled access via lift), roof terrace, decent choice of food from pub favourites to specials, helpful chatty staff; gets very busy with after-work drinkers when standing room only, open (and food) all day from 9am for breakfast. *(Dr and Mrs A K Clarke)*

BATH ST7467

★**Hare & Hounds** (01225) 482682
Lansdown Road, Lansdown Hill; BA1 5TJ Wonderful far-reaching views over villages and fields from inside and out; long single bar with easy-going feel, chapel chairs and cushioned wall settles around pale wood-topped tables on bare boards, minimal decoration on pale walls above blue-grey dado, Bath, Butcombe and a beer badged for the pub from attractively carved counter, several wines by the glass, good food from breakfasts on, log fire with bronze hare and hound above, small slate-floored conservatory; background music, free wi-fi; children and dogs welcome, decked terrace, more seats and tables down steps, open all day from 8.30am. *(Dr and Mrs A K Clarke)*

BATH ST7465

★**Hop Pole** (01225) 446327
Albion Buildings, Upper Bristol Road; BA1 3AR Bustling family-friendly Bath/St Austell pub, their beers and guests kept well, decent wines by the glass and good choice of whiskies and other spirits, nice food (all day Fri-Sun) from sandwiches and traditional favourites up in bar and former skittle alley restaurant, friendly helpful staff, settles and other pub furniture on bare boards in four linked areas, lots of dark woodwork, ochre walls and some bric-a-brac; background music, discreet sports TV; wheelchair access to main bar area only, pleasant two-level back courtyard with boules, fairy-lit vine arbour and heated summerhouses, opposite Royal Victoria Park (great kids' play area), open all day. *(Dr and Mrs A K Clarke, Chris and Angela Buckell)*

BATH ST7565

King William (01225) 428096
Thomas Street/A4 London Road; BA1 5NN Cosy corner dining pub with well

cooked food from short daily changing menu, four local ales and good choice of wines by the glass, chunky old tables on bare boards, steep stairs up to restaurant (a little more formal); background music; children and dogs welcome, open all day weekends. *(Jane Jones, Dr and Mrs A K Clarke, Stuart Doughty)*

BATH ST7465

★ **Marlborough** (01225) 423731
35 Marlborough Buildings/Weston Road; BA1 2LY Busy pub centrally placed and usefully open all day from 8am (9am weekends); U-shaped bare-boards bar with candles in sizeable jars on windowsills and above the fireplace, seating ranging from thick button-back wall seats to chapel, kitchen and high-backed dining chairs, flowers on tables, Butcombe and Box Steam ales, traditional cider and lots of wines by the glass including champagne, well liked food from pub favourites up, cheerful staff; background music, free wi-fi; children and dogs welcome, suntrap courtyard garden. *(Dr and Mrs A K Clarke)*

BATH ST7565

Pig & Fiddle (01225) 460868
Saracen Street; BA1 5BR Lively place (particularly weekends) with five well kept ales including Butcombe and fairly simple affordably priced food, friendly staff, bare-boards interior with two big open fires and collection of sporting memorabilia, steps up to bustling servery and little dining area, games part (darts and table football); live music and DJ nights, several TVs for sport; picnic-sets on big heated terrace, open all day, food till early evening. *(Dr and Mrs A K Clarke)*

BATH ST7565

Pulteney Arms (01225) 463923
Daniel Street/Sutton Street; BA2 6ND Cosy, cheerful and largely unspoilt 18th-c pub; Box Steam Piston Broke, Fullers London Pride, Timothy Taylors Landlord and guests, Thatcher's cider, enjoyable freshly made food at sensible prices, traditional furniture on wooden floors, old gas lamps, woodburner and lots of Bath RFC memorabilia; background music, sports TV, darts, Mon quiz; children (until 9pm) and dogs welcome, pavement tables and small back terrace, handy for Sydney Gardens and Holburne Museum, open all day Fri-Sun, no food Sun evening. *(Dr and Mrs A K Clarke, Taff Thomas)*

BATH ST7464

Raven (01225) 425045
Queen Street; BA1 1HE Small buoyant 18th-c city-centre free house; two well kept house ales from Blindmans and four guests, craft beers and a changing cider, decent wines by the glass too, limited choice of food (good Pieminister pies), quick friendly service, bare boards, some stripped stone and an open fire, newspapers, quieter upstairs bar; monthly events including storytelling evenings and science/art discussion groups; no under-14s or dogs; open all day. *(Dr and Mrs A K Clarke)*

BATH ST7364

Royal Oak (01225) 481409
Lower Bristol Road; near Oldfield Park station; BA2 3BW Friendly roadside pub with its own Ralphs beers (named after the resident husky) along with five guests such as Butts and Downton, good range of ciders/perries and bottled beers, no food, two bare-boards bar areas with open fires; regular live music, Tues quiz; dogs welcome, side beer garden, open all day (from 2pm Mon-Thurs). *(Dr and Mrs A K Clarke)*

BATH ST7464

Salamander (01225) 428889
John Street; BA1 2JL Busy city local with full range of well kept Bath ales, St Austell Tribute and good choice of wines by the glass, bare boards, black woodwork and ochre walls, popular food from sandwiches up (more choice evenings/weekends), friendly helpful young staff, upstairs restaurant with open kitchen; background music, daily papers; children till 8pm, no dogs, open all day (till 1am Fri, Sat), gets packed on Bath RFC days. *(Dr and Mrs A K Clarke, Mike Gleave, Philip J Alderton, Taff Thomas)*

BATH ST7564

Sam Weller (01225) 474910
Upper Borough Walls; BA1 1RH Fairly simple busy pub with ales such as Abbey, St Austell, Sharps and Timothy Taylors, decent choice of wines by the glass and sensibly priced tasty food, friendly service, small and cosy with big window to watch the world go by; light background music; open all day (may shut early Sun if quiet). *(Mike Kavaney, Dr and Mrs A K Clarke)*

BATH ST7365

Victoria Pub & Kitchen (01225) 422563 *Upper Bristol Road; BA1 3AT* Opened-up and modernised gastropub opposite Royal Victoria Park (sister to the Duke of Cumberland at Holcombe); bar/kitchen area with a couple of easy chairs and small dining section, two further rooms (one down steps) with mix of furniture including some bench tables and old metal chairs, polished wood floors, pale grey walls and painted panelling, reclaimed floorboards used to clad one part, Butcombe, Sharps and a guest such as St Austell, Thatcher's ciders and good wines, much liked food at fair prices including lunchtime/early evening deal, happy helpful staff; background music; children and dogs welcome, partial wheelchair access, disabled loo, small decked terrace and raised beer garden, open all day, food all day Fri-Sun. *(Chris and Angela Buckell)*

BATH ST7564

Volunteer Riflemans Arms (01225) 425210 *New Bond Street Place; BA1 1BH* Friendly little city-centre pub with leather sofas and a few close-set tables, wartime/military posters, open fire, half a dozen well kept ales including a house beer from Moles, a couple of draught ciders and good value tasty lunchtime food, small upstairs dining room and roof terrace; background music; pavement tables, open all day. *(Dr and Mrs A K Clarke, Mike Kavaney)*

BATH ST7564

White Hart (01225) 338053 *Widcombe Hill; BA2 6AA* Bistro-style pub with scrubbed pine tables on bare boards, candles and fresh flowers, good imaginative if not cheap food, well kept Butcombe from traditional panelled counter, proper cider and plenty of wines by the glass, quick friendly service; background and occasional live music outside in summer; children and dogs welcome, pretty beer garden, four bedrooms (some sharing bathroom), open all day (Sun till 5pm). *(Dr and Mrs A K Clarke, Roger and Anne Mallard)*

BATHFORD ST7866

Crown (01225) 852426 *Bathford Hill, towards Bradford-on-Avon, by Batheaston roundabout and bridge; BA1 7SL* Bistro pub with good french-influnced blackboard food, ales such as Bath and Timothy Taylors, nice wines, friendly service; children and dogs welcome, tables out in front and in back garden with pétanque, open all day. *(Dr and Mrs A K Clarke)*

BICKNOLLER ST1139

Bicknoller Inn (01984) 656234 *Church Lane; TA4 4EW* Welcoming old thatched pub nestling below the Quantocks; traditional flagstoned front bar, side room and large back restaurant with open kitchen, popular food from pub favourites up, Sun carvery (booking advised), friendly helpful service, four well kept Palmers ales and a couple of real ciders, skittle alley, free wi-fi; children and dogs (in bar) welcome, courtyard and nice back garden, boules, attractive village, open all day weekends. *(Peter Pilbeam)*

BISHOPS LYDEARD ST1629

Lethbridge Arms (01823) 433467 *Off A358 Taunton–Watchet; Gore Square; TA4 3BW* Welcoming 16th-c beamed coaching inn with good well presented/priced traditional food from sandwiches and baked potatoes up, Sun carvery, well kept Quantock Wills Neck and Sharps Doom Bar, Thatcher's ciders, efficient smiling service; pool and darts, free wi-fi; children and dogs welcome, bedrooms, open all day weekends. *(Diana Hill and Brian Sturgess)*

BLAGDON HILL ST2118

Lamb & Flag (01823) 421893 *4 miles S of Taunton; TA3 7SL* Atmospheric beamed pub with traditional furniture including some slab-topped tables on bare boards or flagstones, woodburner in two-way fireplace, Exmoor, Quantock, St Austell and a guest, traditional ciders and decent wines by the glass, good reasonably priced home-made food (not Sun evening, Mon) from sandwiches up, helpful friendly service, galleried upstairs area, skittle alley; background and occasional live music; children and dogs welcome, picnic-sets in nice garden with Taunton Vale views, closed Mon lunchtime, otherwise open all day (till 9pm Sun). *(Peter Kirkman)*

BLEADON ST3457

Queens Arms (01934) 812080 *Just off A370 S of Weston; Celtic Way; BS24 0NF* Popular 16th-c beamed village pub under new licensees; generous reasonably priced food (not Sun evening) from lunchtime baguettes to steaks, themed nights, Butcombe, Timothy Taylor and other well kept ales (some tapped from the cask), friendly service, stripped-stone back bar with woodburner, winged settles and sturdy tables, flagstoned restaurant; children and dogs welcome, partial wheelchair access, picnic-sets on pretty terrace, open all day. *(Sally and Colin Allen)*

BRADFORD-ON-TONE ST1722

White Horse (01823) 461239 *Fairly near M5 junction 26, off A38 towards Taunton; TA4 1HF* Popular 17th-c family-run village pub across from the church; ample helpings of enjoyable good value food from fairly pubby menu including blackboard specials and weekday light lunch deal, friendly helpful staff, well kept ales such as Hanlons, Otter and St Austell, bare-boards bar with leather sofas and armchair by woodburner, linked dining areas; background and occasional live music, Mon quiz, skittle alley; children and dogs (in bar) welcome, picnic-sets in nice garden (maybe Percy the peacock), unusual glass pub sign, closed Sun evening, Mon lunchtime. *(Bob and Margaret Holder, Ian Herdman)*

BRISTOL ST5773

Albion (0117) 973 3522 *Boyces Avenue, Clifton; BS8 4AA* Popular former 17th-c coaching house tucked away in backstreet courtyard; refurbished interior on two floors (private dining upstairs), enjoyable food from sandwiches and sharing plates up including Mon steak night, well kept Bath and St Austell ales, lots of wines by the glass and good choice of other drinks, cheerful attentive service; background music; children and dogs welcome, tables and heaters out in front, open all day, food all day Fri and Sat, till 4pm Sun. *(Chris and Angela Buckell)*

BRISTOL ST5773

Alma (0117) 973 5171
Alma Vale Road, Clifton; BS8 2HY
Two-bar pub with west country beers, Aspall's and Thatcher's ciders and several wines by the glass, good range of whiskies too, well liked imaginative food along with more standard choices including pizzas and good Sun roasts, friendly hard-working staff, dark panelled traditionally furnished front bar with wood flooring, more contemporary back room with bright modern wallpaper and local artwork, thriving upstairs theatre (10% food discount for ticket holders); background music (live Sun), comedy nights, easy wheelchair access (no disabled loo), small paved terrace behind (closed late evening), open all day. *(Dan and Belinda Smallbone)*

BRISTOL ST5873

Bank (0117) 930 4691
John Street; BS1 2HR Small proper single-bar pub, centrally placed (but off the beaten track) and popular with office workers; four changing local ales (may include a porter), real ciders and enjoyable well priced food till 4pm including sandwiches, burgers and one or two unusual choices, good Sun lunch too, comfortable bench seats, newspapers, books on shelf above fireplace; background and regular live music, Tues quiz, free wi-fi; children and dogs welcome, wheelchair access, tables under umbrellas in paved courtyard, open all day (till 1am Thurs-Sat). *(Celia and Andrew King)*

BRISTOL ST5972

Barley Mow (0117) 930 4709
Barton Road; The Dings; BS2 0LF
Late 19th-c Bristol Beer Factory pub in old industrial area close to floating harbour; up to eight well kept changing ales, excellent selection of craft kegs and bottled beers, proper cider and decent choice of wines by the glass, enjoyable good value food (not Sun evening) from short menu catering for vegetarians, cheerful chatty staff, wood floors, off-white walls and blue half-panelling, cushioned wall seats and pubby furniture, various odds and ends dotted about, open fire in brick fireplace; free wi-fi; disabled access, open all day (till 10pm Sun). *(Valerie and Gordon Wauton)*

BRISTOL ST5872

Beer Emporium (0117) 379 0333
King Street opposite the Old Vic; BS1 4EF Unusual staircase down to bar-restaurant in vaulted cellars; long stone-faced counter under stained-glass skylight, 24 regularly changing ales/craft beers (tasters offered) plus over 150 in bottles from around the world, good selection of malt whiskies and other spirits, interesting wine list, coffees and teas, italian food including range of pizzas (vegetarians/vegans catered for), cheerful chatty staff; some live music; wheelchair access via lift, disabled loos, open (and food) all day (till 2am Mon-Sat), can get crowded; beer shop upstairs. *(Chris and Angela Buckell, Dr and Mrs A K Clarke)*

BRISTOL ST5872

BrewDog (0117) 927 9258
Baldwin Street, opposite church; BS1 1QW Corner bar serving own BrewDog beers and guests from other craft breweries (draught and bottled), tasters offered by knowledgeable young staff, limited but interesting selection of bar snacks and pizzas, starkly modern feel with exposed brick, stainless-steel furniture and granite surfaces, can get noisily busy; wheelchair access, open all day till midnight (1am Thurs-Sat). *(Alison and Michael Harper)*

BRISTOL ST5874

Chums 07757 681261
Chandos Road; BS6 6PF Micropub in former corner shop, mismatched furniture on boarded floor, painted half-panelling and lots of modern artwork for sale, six real ales (listed on blackboard) from pine-planked servery, real ciders/perries and range of bottled belgian beers, some decent malt whiskies and gins, snacky food; mobile phones discouraged; alternating live music/quiz night Weds; wheelchair access using ramp (staff will help), disabled loo, open all day weekends, from 4pm other days. *(Chris and Angela Buckell)*

BRISTOL ST5872

Commercial Rooms (0117) 927 9681
Corn Street; BS1 1HT Spacious colonnaded Wetherspoons (former early 19th-c merchants' club) in good location; main part with lofty stained-glass domed ceiling, large oval portraits of Bristol notables and gas lighting, comfortable quieter back room with ornate balcony, note the unusual wind gauge above horseshoe servery; good changing choice of real ales, local ciders and nice chatty bustle (busiest weekend evenings), their usual food and low prices; ladies' with chesterfields and open fire; children welcome, no dogs, side wheelchair access and disabled facilities, open all day from 8am and till late Fri-Sun. *(Dr and Mrs A K Clarke, Roger and Donna Huggins)*

BRISTOL ST5872

Cornubia (0117) 925 4415
Temple Street opposite fire station; BS1 6EN Tucked-away 18th-c real ale pub with fine selection including a good locally brewed house beer, also interesting bottled beers, farm ciders and perry, snacky food such as pasties and pork pies, friendly helpful service, walls and ceilings covered in pump clips, union jacks and other patriotic memorabilia, open fire and an aquarium for turtles; quiz Tues; dogs welcome, not suitable for wheelchairs, picnic-sets in secluded front beer garden (summer barbecues and jazz

Sun afternoons), boules pitch, closed Sun evening, otherwise open all day. *(Taff Thomas, Dr and Mrs A K Clarke)*

BRISTOL ST5976

Drapers Arms

Gloucester Road; BS7 8TZ Welcoming one-room micropub in former draper's shop; seven well kept local beers tapped from the cask, proper ciders and decent wines by the glass, no food apart from bar snacks; donation to charity box if you use a mobile phone; open from 5pm (midday Sat) till 9.30pm. *(Roger and Donna Huggins)*

BRISTOL ST5773

Eldon House (0117) 922 1271

Lower Clifton Hill, Clifton; BS8 1BT Extended terrace-end Clifton pub; mix of wooden tables and chairs on bare boards, circular stone-walled dining area with glazed roof, snug with original stained glass and half-door servery, well kept Bath, guest ales and several wines by the glass, food from lunchtime snacks to daily changing evening menu (pop-up kitchens), friendly staff; background and regular live music, Mon quiz and other events, free wi-fi; children welcome till 8pm, dogs in bar, open (and some food) all day. *(Charlie Stevens)*

BRISTOL ST5876

Gloucester Old Spot (0117) 924 7693

Kellaway Avenue; BS6 7YQ Popular opened-up and refurbished family-run pub; well kept ales such as Butcombe, Exmoor and Timothy Taylors from horseshoe servery, decent wines and good range of spirits, enjoyable reasonably priced food from sandwiches and sharing boards up, friendly prompt service, back bar and large parquet-floored dining lounge opening on to verandah and AstroTurf beer garden; Tues quiz, free wi-fi; children and dogs welcome, wheelchair access using portable ramp (staff will help, no disabled loos), play area with wendy house, open all day from 9am for breakfast. *(Chris and Angela Buckell)*

BRISTOL ST5872

Golden Guinea (0117) 987 2034

Guinea Street; BS1 6SX Steps up to cosy backstreet pub with well kept changing ales, interesting craft beers and proper ciders, simple bargain home-made food, friendly staff, pews, wing armchairs and farmhouse tables on bare boards, some flock wallpaper and contemporary street art; live music (including Tues folk), comedy and quiz nights, sports TV; dogs welcome, seats out in front and behind, closed till 4pm Mon-Weds, otherwise open all day from noon (1pm Sun). *(Chris and Angela Buckell, Charlie Stevens)*

BRISTOL ST5772

Grain Barge (0117) 929 9347

Hotwell Road; BS8 4RU Converted 100-ft barge owned by Bristol Beer Factory, their ales kept well and fair priced food (all day weekends) including good sandwiches, burgers and Sun roasts, steak night Thurs, great harbour views from seats out on top deck, tables and sofas in wood floor bar below, also a 'hold bar' for functions and Tues open mike night; children welcome, open all day. *(Taff Thomas, Chris and Angela Buckell)*

BRISTOL ST5873

Green Man (0117) 925 8062

Alfred Place, Kingsdown; BS2 8HD Cosy local with country pub feel; bare boards and dark woodwork, well kept Dawkins and guests, real cider, several wines by the glass and around 60 gins, food Weds-Fri evenings only including good burgers, also popular Sun roasts, friendly staff; background and regular live music, Weds quiz, free wi-fi; children and dogs welcome, wheelchair access with help, open all day from 4pm Mon-Thurs, 1pm Fri and Sat, midday Sun. *(Lindy Andrews)*

BRISTOL ST5873

Horts City Tavern (0117) 925 2520

Broad Street; BS1 2EJ Imposing 18th-c Youngs pub, their well kept beers along with Bath and St Austell, good fairly priced food (all day weekends) including sharing boards and burgers, spacious interior with big windows overlooking street, some raised sections and side rooms, old pictures of the city, 26-seat cinema at back (free film Weds evening); background music, Thurs quiz, sports TVs; tables in cobbled courtyard, open all day and at its busiest lunchtime/early evening. *(Chris and Angela Buckell)*

BRISTOL ST5977

Inn on the Green (0117) 952 1391

Filton Road (A38), Horfield; BS7 0PA Busy open-plan pub with up to 12 changing ales, half a dozen ciders/perries and good selection of whiskies/gins, enjoyable generously served food including daily deals, helpful friendly staff, wood or slate floors, lots of mirrors and old prints, modern pub furniture along with sofas and armchairs, more screened seating in former skittle alley dining area; bar billiards and darts; children and dogs welcome, disabled access/facilities, beer garden with sheltered pool table and summer table tennis, open (and food) all day. *(Chris and Angela Buckell)*

BRISTOL ST5774

Jersey Lily (0117) 973 8590

Whiteladies Road; BS8 2SB Compact corner pub with matt-black frontage; well kept Wickwar ales and guests, decent wines and good range of gins, enjoyable reasonably priced food from shortish menu including lunchtime ciabattas, sharing plates and range of burgers, busy but attentive service, painted dados and polished wood floors, some high tables and stools, step up to part with sofas and easy chairs; live acoustic music Thurs, Sun quiz, sports TV, free wi-fi; partial wheelchair access, pavement seats and awning, decked side area through arch, open all day. *(Chris and Angela Buckell)*

BRISTOL ST5874

Kensington Arms (0117) 944 6444
Stanley Road; BS6 6NP Dining pub (aka the Kenny) in centre of Redland; highly regarded food at fair prices from chef-patron including interesting snacks, well executed pub favourites and daily specials, well kept Bristol Beer Factory ales and guests, Thatcher's cider and plenty of wines by the glass from comprehensive list, friendly attentive staff; background music; children and dogs welcome, disabled facilities (no wheelchair access to dining room, but can eat in bar), heated front terrace, open all day. *(Charlie Stevens)*

BRISTOL ST5972

Kings Head (0117) 929 2338
Victoria Street; BS1 6DE Welcoming and relaxed little 17th-c pub; traditional bar with big front window and splendid mirrored bar-back, corridor to cosy panelled snug with serving hatch, toby jugs on joists, old-fashioned local prints and photographs, five well kept ales including Harveys and Sharps, range of pies; a few pavement tables, open all day except Sun. *(Dr and Mrs A K Clarke)*

BRISTOL ST5972

Knights Templar (0117) 930 8710
The Square; BS1 6DG Glass and steel Wetherspoons very handy for Temple Meads station; spacious carpeted room with raised area, great range of beers from well stocked bar, their usual good value food served from breakfast till late, helpful staff; lots of TVs, free wi-fi; children welcome, disabled access/loos, plenty of outside seating, open all day. *(Chris and Angela Buckell, Giles and Annie Francis)*

BRISTOL ST5276

Lamplighters (0117) 279 3754
End of Station Road, Shirehampton; BS11 9XA Popular 18th-c riverside pub; well kept Bath and a guest, Thatcher's ciders, teas and coffees, competitively priced traditional food (not Sun evening) including children's choices, OAP meal deals and themed nights, modern bar furniture on carpet or bare boards, some faux leather sofas and armchairs, pastel walls with darker greeny-blue dados, bold patterned wallpaper here and there, mezzanine dining area and cellar bar (not always open); occasional live music; disabled access/loos, picnic-sets on paved front terrace, limited parking nearby (beware of the high spring tides), riverside walks, open all day. *(Chris and Angela Buckell)*

BRISTOL ST5976

Lazy Dog (0117) 924 4809
Ashley Down Road; BS7 9JR Popular local with two bar areas (one upstairs), ales such as Bath, Bristol Beer Factory, Purity and Wye Valley, local ciders, some interesting wines and good range of spirits, well liked food from fairly extensive menu including some unusual dishes, helpful chatty staff, charcoal grey interior with wood panelled alcoves, white marble-effect bar counter, leather wall benches, sofas and armchairs on light wood floors, family room with metal furniture (children till 7pm); quiz and comedy nights; dogs welcome, disabled access/loos, seats out at front and in partly decked back garden, open all day. *(Chris and Angela Buckell)*

BRISTOL ST5673

Mall (0117) 974 5318
The Mall, Clifton; BS8 4JG Smartened-up corner pub with good selection of draught and bottled craft beers, lots of wines by the glass and interesting range of other drinks including cocktails, popular modern pub food, helpful friendly staff, mix of old and new furniture on wood floors, tall windows, some panelling and ornate ceilings, downstairs bar; free wi-fi; children (till 9pm) and dogs welcome, tiered garden behind (summer barbecues), open (and food) all day. *(Peter Myers)*

BRISTOL ST5772

Nova Scotia (0117) 929 7994
Baltic Wharf, Cumberland Basin; BS1 6XJ Welcoming old local on south side of floating harbour with views to Clifton and Avon Gorge; Caledonian ales and a guest such as Moles, Thatcher's ciders, generous helpings of enjoyable pub food (not Sun evening) from doorstep sandwiches to blackboard specials, four linked areas, snob screen, mahogany and mirrors, nautical charts as wallpaper, welcoming relaxed atmosphere; Mon folk night; wheelchair access with help through snug's door, no disabled loo, plenty of tables out by water, open all day. *(Dr and Mrs A K Clarke, Chris and Angela Buckell)*

BRISTOL ST5872

Old Duke (0117) 401 9661
King Street; BS1 4ER Corner pub in interesting cobbled area between docks and Bristol Old Vic; named after Duke Ellington and festooned with jazz posters, good bands nightly and Sun lunchtime, up to six real ales and a couple of ciders, simple food, usual pub furnishings; picnic-sets on cobbles outside, open all day (till 1am Fri, Sat), gets packed evenings. *(Peter Myers, Dr and Mrs A K Clarke, Taff Thomas, Chris and Angela Buckell)*

BRISTOL ST5872

Old Fish Market (0117) 921 1515
Baldwin Street; BS1 1QZ Fullers pub in imposing brick-built former fish market; their well kept ales, craft beers, a dozen wines by the glass and fine range of whiskies/gins

from handsome wooden counter, enjoyable food including pizzas and various chowders, friendly relaxed atmosphere; background music, Sun live jazz from 7pm, sports TVs, free wi-fi; children and dogs welcome, open all day (food all day weekends). *(Dr and Mrs A K Clarke)*

BRISTOL ST5772

Orchard (0117) 926 2678

Hanover Place, Spike Island; BS1 6XT Friendly unpretentious corner local with up to eight well kept stillaged ales and great range of ciders/perries listed on blackboard, food such as baguettes, pies and pasties; live music including Mon blues jam and Tues jazz, sports TV (pub gets very busy on match days); wheelchair access to most of bar, tables out in front, handy for SS *Great Britain*, open all day. *(Chris and Angela Buckell)*

BRISTOL ST5672

Portcullis (0117) 973 0270

Wellington Terrace; BS8 4LE Compact pub in Regency terrace close to Clifton Suspension Bridge; five well kept ales including three from Dawkins, traditional cider and good range of wines and spirits, low-priced pubby food (not Weds), friendly service, flame-effect gas fire, dark wood and usual pubby furniture, upstairs room leading to beer garden; occasional acoustic live music, board games, free wi-fi; dogs welcome, tricky wheelchair access, open all day Fri-Sun, closed lunchtimes Mon-Thurs (also Fri in winter). *(Taff Thomas, Peter Myers, Chris and Angela Buckell)*

BRISTOL ST5772

Pump House (0117) 927 2229

Merchants Road; BS8 4PZ Spacious well converted dockside building (former 19th-c pumping station); charcoal-grey brickwork, tiled floors and high ceilings, good locally sourced food in bar and smart candlelit mezzanine restaurant, Butcombe, Twisted Oak and guests, decent wines from comprehensive list and over 400 gins, good selection of rums and whiskies too, friendly staff and cheerful atmosphere; waterside tables, open all day. *(Chris and Angela Buckell)*

BRISTOL ST5872

Riverstation (0117) 914 4434

The Grove; opposite Hole in the Wall pub; BS1 4RB Modern harbourside bar-restaurant converted some years ago from a former police building; light and airy split-level bar/dining area with tiled and polished wood floors, mix of seating including sofas and squashy banquettes, good views from french windows opening on to waterside terrace, Youngs ales, Orchard Pig cider and several international bottled beers, good selection of wines, spirits and cocktails too, spacious upstairs restaurant with high curved ceiling and lots of glass, further terraces overlooking the water, well liked food from interesting varied menu including weekend brunch, helpful staff; background music; limited wheelchair access, open (and food) all day. *(Chris and Angela Buckell)*

BRISTOL ST5672

Rose of Denmark (0117) 329 0352

Dowry Place; BS8 4QL Early 19th-c pink-painted corner pub on busy junction; varied choice of enjoyable fair-priced food including evening deals (Weds curry, Thurs burgers, Fri steak), St Austell and Sharps ales from wood-faced counter, good range of gins, cheerful chatty staff, bare boards, some stripped brickwork and open fire, more dining space in cellar rooms; dogs allowed in bar, wheelchair access via side door, no disabled loos, tables out behind front railings, open (and food) all day, just ribs Sun evening. *(Chris and Angela Buckell, Charlie Stevens)*

BRISTOL ST5872

Royal Naval Volunteer

(0117) 316 9237 *King Street; BS1 4EF* 17th-c pub in cobbled street, wide range of draught and bottled british beers, ciders/perries and a dozen wines by the glass, friendly knowledgeable staff, good interesting food in back restaurant; weekend live music, sports TV; dogs welcome, terrace seating. *(Dr and Mrs A K Clarke)*

BRISTOL ST5972

Seven Stars (0117) 927 2845

Thomas Lane; BS1 6JG Unpretentious one-room real ale pub near harbour (and associated with Thomas Clarkson and slave trade abolition), popular with students and local office workers, up to eight well kept changing ales (20 from a featured county on first Mon-Thurs of the month), some interesting malts and bourbons, dark wood and bare boards, old local prints and photographs, no food – can bring in takeaways; weekend acoustic music, pool, games machine; dogs welcome, disabled access (but narrow alley with uneven cobbles and cast-iron kerbs), open all day. *(Alison and Michael Harper)*

BRISTOL ST5872

Small Bar

King Street; BS1 4DZ Bustling real ale/craft beer pub with over 30 choices including own Left Handed Giant, all served in smaller glasses (up to two-thirds of a pint), good range of bottled beers too, enjoyable food such as burgers and hotdogs along with vegetarian/vegan choices, bare boards and

All *Guide* inspections are anonymous. Anyone claiming to be a *Good Pub Guide* inspector is a fraud. Please let us know.

flagstones, roughly exposed brickwork here and there and wood plank walls, some barrel tables and a couple of old fireplaces, upstairs area with armchairs, sofas and shelves of books; background music; open all day (till 1am Fri, Sat). *(Dr and Mrs A K Clarke)*

BRISTOL ST6375

Snuffy Jacks Ale House

(0117) 965 5158 *Fishponds Road; BS16 3TE* New micropub in former stationers; up to eight cask-tapped ales, real ciders and some good quality gins from planked servery, friendly knowledgeable staff, mismatching furniture including old church pews on wood-strip floor, vibrant blue walls hung with local artwork, bare pendant lighting; no mobile phones, credit cards or food (maybe bar nibbles Sun); dogs welcome, wheelchair access, open all day Sat, till 4.30pm Sun and from 5pm weekdays. *(Chris and Angela Buckell)*

BRISTOL ST5872

Three Tuns (0117) 329 4310

St Georges Road; BS1 5UR Popular city-centre pub; seven real ales including local Arbor, four craft kegs and interesting selection of bottled beers, several ciders too, snacky food along with Sun roasts, pine tables on bare boards, a couple of small leather sofas in alcoves, open fire; regular events including Mon live music, art exhibitions and magic nights; covered and heated back terrace down steps, near cathedral, open all day (till midnight Fri, Sat). *(Alison and Michael Harper)*

BRISTOL ST5971

Victoria Park (0117) 330 6043

Raymend Road; BS3 4QW Brick-fronted family dining pub in hilly residential part of the city, welcoming and friendly, with large opened-up L-shaped interior, mix of furniture including long refectory tables and old pews on stripped-wood floors, dark-grey walls hung with local artwork, modern pendant lighting, white tiled back bar with folding glass doors to splendid tiered garden (rooftop views over to Dundry Hill), changing ales such as Butcombe, Ringwood and Wadworths, Thatcher's and Weston's ciders and good choice of other drinks, popular food from interesting blackboard menu (booking advised weekends), also sandwiches and pizzas; background music, quiz every other Tues; dogs welcome, tricky wheelchair access and no disabled loos, nearby parking at a premium, open all day. *(Luke Freeman, Chris and Angela Buckell)*

BRISTOL ST5973

Volunteer (0117) 955 8498

New Street, near Cabot Circus; BS2 9DX Tucked-away local with good choice of changing ales/craft beers, a couple of ciders and decent wines by the glass, well liked food such as pop-up mexican nights and popular Sun roasts, friendly relaxed atmosphere; live music and beer festivals; children and dogs welcome, walled garden behind, open all day. *(Taff Thomas)*

BRISTOL ST5976

Wellington (0117) 951 3022

Gloucester Road, Horfield (A38); BS7 8UR Updated and opened-up 1920s red-brick pub on edge of Horfield Common; well kept Bath and St Austell, craft beers, local cider and good choice of other drinks including range of gins, enjoyable reasonably priced food till 10pm, pleasant efficient service, separate dining area opening on to sunny paved terrace and grassy beer garden; Mon quiz; children welcome, wheelchair access from back door (or front using ramp), disabled loos, popular boutique bedrooms (best to book early), open all day (from 9am weekends for breakfast). *(Chris and Angela Buckell, Dr and Mrs A K Clarke)*

BRISTOL ST5872

Wild Beer (0117) 239 5693

Gaol Ferry Steps, Wapping Wharf, behind the M Shed Museum; BS1 5WE Busy bar in new development overlooking the old docks; over 20 craft beers (including Wild Beer) listed on blackboards and served in third, half and two-thirds of a pint glasses (tasters offered), interesting wines and good selection of whiskies/gins, reasonably priced food from snacks up, cheerful helpful staff, flagstones, pale green walls and floor-to-ceiling windows, exposed ducting and a large mural on one wall, a couple of steps up to dining area with open kitchen; background music; children welcome, disabled access/facilities, split-level terrace with deckchairs and picnic-sets, parking nearby difficult, open all day. *(Chris and Angela Buckell)*

BURROW BRIDGE ST3530

King Alfred (01823) 698379

Main Road, by the bridge; TA7 0RB Old-fashioned pub with relaxed friendly atmosphere in flagstoned bar, well kept ales such as Butcombe and Otter, local ciders and decent wines by the glass, landlord-chef's good reasonably priced food (not Sun evening) from pub standards up, comfortable dining room upstairs with view over River Parrett and Somerset Levels, roof terrace; live music and quiz/curry nights; children and dogs welcome, self-catering cottage, open all day (till 9pm Sun). *(Bob and Margaret Holder, Tessa Barton)*

BUTLEIGH ST5133

Rose & Portcullis (01458) 850287

Sub Road/Barton Road; BA6 8TQ Welcoming stone-built country pub with enjoyable good value home-made food (not Sun evening), five well kept ales and good range of local ciders, helpful friendly staff, bar and airy dining extension; sports

TV, free wi-fi; children and dogs welcome, tables outside, may close Mon lunchtime in winter. *(Glen and Patricia Fuller)*

CASTLE CARY ST6432

George (01963) 350761
Just off A371 Shepton Mallet–Wincanton; Market Place; BA7 7AH Old-fashioned thatched country-town hotel (former 15th-c coaching inn); popular front bar with big inglenook, bistro-bar and restaurant (evenings only), well liked food from sandwiches up, three changing real ales and decent wines by the glass, friendly staff; free wi-fi; children and dogs welcome, 17 bedrooms (some in courtyard), open all day. *(Peter and Emma Kelly)*

CATCOTT ST3939

Crown (01278) 722288
Off A39 W of Street; Nidon Lane, via Brook Lane; TA7 9HQ Roomy traditional old pub just outside the village; welcoming landlord and staff, enjoyable food including good Sun carvery (booking advised), real ales such as Otter and Sharps, decent wines by the glass, cosy area by log fire; skittle alley; children and dogs welcome, picnic-sets and play area out behind, closed Mon lunchtime. *(Roy Hoing)*

CHARLTON MUSGROVE ST7229

Smithy (01963) 824899
B3081, 5 miles SE of Bruton; about a mile off A303; BA9 8HG Restored 18th-c pub under friendly licensees; bar with stripped stone, heavy beams and inglenook woodburner, rugs on flagstone/concrete floor, mismatch of furniture (some tables made from old cheeseboards), Greene King ales and guests from plank-fronted servery, well liked uncomplicated food (not Sun evening), intimate dining area overlooking garden, restaurant in former skittle alley; background and monthly live music, quiz nights, TV for major sports; children and dogs welcome, bedrooms still planned, open all day. *(Katherine and Hugh Markham)*

CHEDDAR ST4653

White Hart (01934) 741261
The Bays; BS27 3QN Welcoming village local at the bottom of Cheddar Gorge; well kept beers, traditional cider and enjoyable fairly priced home-made food from good ploughman's to Sun carvery, log fire; live music and quiz nights, free wi-fi; children welcome, picnic-sets out at front and in back garden with play area, open (and food) all day. *(Tony Scott)*

CHEW MAGNA ST5861

★ **Pony & Trap** (01275) 332627
Knowle Hill, New Town; from B3130 in village, follow Bishop Sutton, Bath signpost; BS40 8TQ Michelin-starred dining pub in nice rural spot near Chew Valley Lake; first rate food from snacks and some lunchtime pubby choices through to beautifully presented expensive restaurant dishes (must book), professional friendly service, Butcombe ales and a guest, front bar with cushioned wall seats and built-in benches on parquet, old range in snug area on left, dark plank panelling and housekeeper's chair in corner, lovely pasture views from two-level back dining area with white tables on slate flagstones; children welcome, dogs in bar, modern furniture on back terrace, picnic-sets on grass with chickens in runs below, front smokers' shelter, good walks. *(Dr and Mrs A K Clarke, R L Borthwick, Mrs Zara Elliott)*

CHEWTON MENDIP ST5953

Waldegrave Arms (01761) 241384
High Street (A39); BA3 4LL Friendly village pub run by the same family for over 30 years; traditional food from sandwiches up including Sun roasts, well kept ales such as Butcombe, Cottage and Slaters; quiz nights and darts leagues; dogs welcome in bar, colourful window boxes and hanging baskets, flower-filled garden behind, open (and food) all day Sun. *(Andy and Louise Ranwell)*

CHISELBOROUGH ST4614

★ **Cat Head** (01935) 881231
Cat Street; leave A303 on A356 towards Crewkerne; take the third left (at 1.4 miles) signed Chiselborough, then left after 0.2 miles; TA14 6TT Character 15th-c hamstone pub refurbished under present licensees; bar and two dining areas, flagstones, mullioned windows and two permanently lit woodburners (one in fine inglenook), well executed fairly traditional food cooked by landlady, a couple of ales such as Sharps and Butcombe, friendly service; classical background music; children and dogs (in bar) welcome, picnic-sets in lovely back garden, closed Sun evening, Mon. *(Ewan and Sue Hewitt)*

CLEVEDON ST4071

Moon & Sixpence (01275) 872443
The Beach; BS21 7QU Substantial seafront Victorian family dining pub on three levels – ground-floor carpeted lounge, mezzanine bar and upstairs restaurant with balcony view of pier and estuary, reasonably priced food including some greek choices, Greene King ales, Weston's cider; children and dogs welcome, wheelchair access possible to lounge and bar using ramps (staff will help), terrace seating, small car park with disabled space, five bedrooms, open all day. *(Dave Braisted)*

COMPTON DANDO ST6464

Compton Inn (01761) 490321
Court Hill; BS39 4JZ Welcoming stone-built village pub in lovely setting; enjoyable home-made food (not Sun evening), well kept Butcombe, Sharps and a guest, wood-floored bar with dining area at each end (one down

a couple of steps), two-way woodburner in stone fireplace; charity quiz first Mon of month, TV; children, walkers and dogs welcome, picnic-sets out in front, garden behind with boules, open all day. *(Jane Rigby)*

CONGRESBURY ST4363

Old Inn (01934) 832270

Pauls Causeway, down Broad Street opposite The Cross; BS49 5DH Popular 16th-c low-beamed dimly lit local; deep-set windows, flagstones and huge fireplaces, one with stove opening to both bar and dining area, mix of old furniture including pews and upholstered benches, leather ceiling straps, good choice of enjoyable reasonably priced pubby food (not Sun evening, Mon), well kept Youngs and a couple of guests such as St Austell and Butcombe tapped from casks, Thatcher's cider and decent wines; children and dogs welcome, tables in back garden with pétanque, open all day. *(Bob and Margaret Holder)*

CONGRESBURY ST4363

★**Plough** (01934) 877402

High Street (B3133); BS49 5JA Popular old-fashioned character local – a pub since the 1800s; half a dozen well kept changing west country ales such as Butcombe, Cheddar and St Austell, ciders from Orchard Pig and Thatcher's, quick friendly service, generous helpings of well cooked food (not Sun evening) including daily specials, several small interconnecting rooms off flagstoned main bar, mix of old and new furniture, built-in pine wall benches, old prints, photos, farm tools and some morris dancing memorabilia, log fires; Sun quiz; no children inside, dogs welcome (theirs is Stanley), wheelchair access from car park, garden with rustic furniture and boules. *(Bob and Margaret Holder)*

CORFE ST2319

White Hart (01823) 421388

B3170 S of Taunton; TA3 7BU Friendly traditional 17th-c village pub; enjoyable sensibly priced pubby food (not Tues) including vegetarian options, curry night last Thurs of the month (booking advised), well kept ales such as Butcombe and Exmoor, beams, woodburner and open fire; bar billiards, skittle alley; dogs welcome, open all day Sat, closed Tues lunchtime. *(David Appleyard)*

CRANMORE ST6643

Strode Arms (01749) 880450

West Cranmore; signed with pub off A361 Frome–Shepton Mallet; BA4 4QJ Pretty stone dining pub (former 15th-c farmhouse) overlooking village duck pond, rambling beamed rooms with log fires in handsome fireplaces, carpeted or flagstone floors, country furnishings, enjoyable generously served food from snacks up, Wadworths ales and decent wines by the glass, good friendly service; children, walkers and dogs welcome, seats on front terrace, handy for East Somerset Railway (steam trains), open all day weekends. *(Pete and Sarah)*

CROSCOMBE ST5844

★**George** (01749) 342306

Long Street (A371 Wells–Shepton Mallet); BA5 3QH Former coaching inn run by friendly canadian family; main bar with stripped stone, dark wooden tables and chairs, a settle by one of the inglenooks and a grandfather clock, snug area with woodburner, Blindmans and three guests (some tapped from the cask), ten wines by the glass and up to four ciders, good food from varied menu, attractive dining room has more stripped stone, local artwork on burgundy walls and high-backed chairs around mix of tables, there's also a back bar, family room and skittle alley; darts, shove-ha'penny and a canadian table game called crokinole; dogs welcome in bar (pub dogs are Tessa and Pixy), attractive garden with seats on covered terrace, wood-fired pizza oven, chickens and swings, clean comfortable bedrooms, good breakfast, open (and food) all day weekends. *(Tim and Moira Hurst, Freddie and Sarah Banks, Dr Stuart Jenkins)*

CROSS ST4254

New Inn (01934) 732455

A38 Bristol–Bridgwater, junction A371; BS26 2EE Steps up to popular old roadside pub with well kept Otter and several interesting guests (Easter/Aug bank holiday beer festivals), good choice of enjoyable fairly traditional food from baguettes and baked potatoes up (booking advised), friendly service, more dining space upstairs; children and dogs welcome (their cocker spaniel is Guinness), views from nice hillside garden with play area, open (and food) all day. *(Tessa Barton, Hugh Roberts)*

CROWCOMBE ST1336

Carew Arms (01984) 618631

Just off A358 Taunton–Minehead; TA4 4AD Interesting 17th-c beamed country inn attracting good mix of customers; hunting trophies, huge flagstones and good inglenook log fire in small lived-in front bar, up to five well kept ales such as Exmoor, Otter and St Austell, real cider, enjoyable reasonably priced home-made food (not Sun evening in winter) including daily specials and takeaway fish and chips (6-7pm Fri), friendly service; children (in dining room), walkers and dogs welcome, tables in good-sized garden, outside skittle alley, six bedrooms, open all day in summer (all day Fri-Sun winter). *(S G N Bennett)*

CURRY RIVEL ST3925

Firehouse (01458) 887447

Church Street; TA10 0HE Stylishly renovated village pub; light beams, exposed stonework and log fires, cosy bar with tractor-seat stools at counter serving four real ales (always Butcombe), decent wines and cocktails, well liked fairly pubby food along with pizzas from feature oven, lunchtime/early evening deal (Mon-Fri), friendly helpful young staff, various dining areas including upstairs raftered room and cellar bar with fine 14th-c vaulted ceiling; live music and quiz nights; children welcome, circular picnic-sets on paved terrace, open all day. *(Stuart Reeves)*

DINNINGTON ST4013

Dinnington Docks (01460) 52397
NE of village; Fosse Way; TA17 8SX Good cheery atmosphere in large old-fashioned rural local, unspoilt and unfussy, with good choice of inexpensive home-made food, well kept Butcombe and guests, farm ciders, friendly attentive staff, memorabilia to bolster myth that there was once a railway line and dock here, log fire; children and dogs welcome, large garden behind, good walks, open all day Fri-Sun. *(Sally and Colin Allen)*

DITCHEAT ST6236

★**Manor House** (01749) 860276
Signed off A37 and A371 S of Shepton Mallet; BA4 6RB Pretty 17th-c red-brick village inn (sister to the Rockford Inn at Brendon, Devon), popular with jockeys from nearby stables; enjoyable food from short but varied menu, well kept ales such as Butcombe, Cotleigh and Prescott, friendly helpful staff, unusual arched doorways linking big flagstoned bar to comfortable lounge and restaurant, open fires; skittle alley; children welcome, tables on back grass, handy for Bath & West Showground, five bedrooms, good breakfast, open all day. *(Mr and Mrs P R Thomas, Hugh Roberts)*

DOWLISH WAKE ST3712

New Inn (01460) 52413
Off A3037 S of Ilminster, via Kingstone; TA19 0NZ Comfortable and welcoming dark-beamed village pub; enjoyable home-made food from sandwiches and pub favourites up including Mon steak night, well kept Butcombe and Otter, local cider, friendly helpful staff, woodburners in stone inglenooks, pleasant dining room; quiz first Sun of the month; dogs welcome, attractive garden and village, Perry's cider mill and shop nearby, four bedrooms in separate annexe. *(Ewan and Sue Hewitt)*

DULVERTON SS9127

Bridge Inn (01398) 324130
Bridge Street; TA22 9HJ Welcoming unpretentious little pub next to River Barle; reasonably priced locally sourced food from snacks and sandwiches up, four well kept ales including Exmoor, some unusual imported beers, comfortable sofas, woodburner; occasional live music and quiz nights, free wi-fi; children and dogs welcome, two terraces, open all day in summer. *(Donald Allsopp)*

DUNDRY ST5666

Carpenters (0117) 964 6423
Wells Road; BS41 8NE Welcoming village pub with well kept ales such as Bath and Butcombe, Thatcher's cider and enjoyable fairly priced traditional food including specials and Tues steak night, helpful friendly staff; quiz Weds, free wi-fi; children and dogs welcome, disabled access, picnic-sets on lawn, open all day Fri-Sat, till 6pm Sun. *(Sylvia and Phillip Spencer)*

DUNSTER SS9843

★**Stags Head** (01643) 821229
West Street (A396); TA24 6SN Friendly accommodating staff in unassuming 16th-c roadside inn; popular good value food including daily specials, Exmoor and a guest ale, beams, timbers and inglenook log fire, steps up to small back dining room; dogs welcome in bar area, comfortable simple bedrooms, good breakfast, open all day in summer, no food Weds; for sale as we went to press, so may be changes. *(R L Borthwick)*

EAST HARPTREE ST5453

Castle of Comfort (01761) 221321
B3134, SW on Old Bristol Road; BS40 6DD Former coaching inn set high in the Mendips (last stop before the gallows for some past visitors); hefty timbers and exposed stonework, cushioned settles and other pubby furniture on carpet, log fires, Butcombe, Sharps and a guest, ample helpings of reasonably priced traditional food including good steaks, friendly staff; children and dogs (in bar) welcome, wheelchair access, big garden with raised deck and play area, attractive walks nearby. *(Ivy and George Goodwill)*

EAST LAMBROOK ST4218

Rose & Crown (01460) 240433
Silver Street; TA13 5HF Old-fashioned stone-built dining pub spreading extensively from compact 17th-c core with inglenook log fire, friendly helpful staff and relaxed atmosphere, good choice of well liked freshly made food using local suppliers, steak night Weds, curry Thurs, fish and chips Fri, Palmers ales, Thatcher's cider and several wines by the glass, decent whisky selection too, restaurant extension with old glass-covered well, skittle alley; children and dogs (in bar) welcome, disabled access from the side, picnic-sets on neat lawn, opposite East Lambrook Manor Gardens, closed Sun evening, Mon. *(Ewan and Sue Hewitt, M J Winterton)*

EVERCREECH ST6336

Natterjack (01749) 860253
A371 Shepton Mallet–Castle Cary; BA4 6NA Welcoming former Victorian

station hotel (line closed 1966); good choice of generously served food at reasonable prices, cheerful service (may be a wait at busy times), Butcombe, Bath and a guest, real cider and nice range of wines, long bar with eating areas off; children and dogs welcome, lots of tables under parasols in big neatly kept garden, nine bedrooms, closed Sun evening. *(Mr and Mrs P R Thomas)*

EXFORD SS8538

★**Exmoor White Horse** (01643) 831229 *B3224; TA24 7PY* Popular and welcoming old creeper-clad inn; more or less open-plan bar with good log fire, high-backed antique settle among more conventional seats, scrubbed deal tables, hunting prints and local photographs, Exmoor ales, Thatcher's cider and over 200 malt whiskies, good locally sourced bar and restaurant food including Sun carvery; children and dogs welcome, tables outside by river, pretty village, Land Rover Exmoor safaris, 28 comfortable bedrooms, open (and food) all day. *(Patricia Healey)*

FAULKLAND ST7555

★**Tuckers Grave** (01373) 834230 *A366 E of village; BA3 5XF* Tiny totally unspoilt place named after Edward Tucker who hanged himself nearby in 1747 and was buried at the pub crossroads; new landlady but things kept the same; entrance opening into simple tap room with woodburner, casks of Butcombe and Thatcher's Cheddar Valley cider in alcove on left, lunchtime sandwiches on request and occasional evening meals, two high-backed settles facing each other across a single table in right, side room, snug lounge (Rose Room) with Victorian fireplace; shove-ha'penny, skittle alley, outside loos; well behaved children and dogs allowed, lots of tables and chairs on attractive back lawn with good views, plans for campsite, closed Mon lunchtime, may open all day weekends in summer. *(Dr and Mrs A K Clarke, Taff Thomas)*

FRESHFORD ST7960

★**Inn at Freshford** (01225) 722250 *Off A36 or B3108; BA2 7WG* Refurbished 16th-c village pub in lovely spot across from River Frome (same management as the Old Crown at Kelston (this chapter) and Cross Guns in Avoncliff (Wiltshire); well kept ales such as Box Steam, craft beers, a couple of local ciders and 24 wines by the glass, interesting whiskies and gins too, popular home-made food from varied menu (all day Sat, till 7pm Sun) including selection of small plates and lunchtime sandwiches, friendly efficient young staff; background music; children and dogs welcome, wheelchair access to bar area (steps to dining room), no disabled loo, attractive tiered hillside garden overlooking valley with outside bar and barbecue, good riverside walks, open all day. *(Dr and Mrs A K Clarke, Chris and Angela Buckell, Alistair Holdoway)*

FROME ST7748

Griffin (01373) 467766 *Milk Street; BA11 3DB* Unpretentious bare-boards bar with etched glass and open fires, long counter serving good Milk Street beers brewed here by friendly landlord, hot food Weds (usually a themed night) and Sun, easy-going mixed crowd; regular live music including Thurs open mike night, Mon quiz; small garden, open all day Sun till 9pm, otherwise from 5pm (Fri 4pm, Sat 3pm). *(Trevor and Michele Street)*

FROME ST7747

Three Swans (01373) 452009 *King Street; BA11 1BH* Appealing and quirky 17th-c beamed pub; well kept Abbey Bellringer, Butcombe and a local guest, nice wines by the glass, snacky food such as home-made pork pies and scotch eggs, also popular Sun roasts (must book), good friendly service, more space in small upstairs room; children welcome till 7pm, dogs in bar (not after 8pm Fri, Sat), part-covered beer garden, open all day Fri-Sun, closed other days till 4.30pm. *(Christopher Moss)*

HALLATROW ST6357

★**Old Station** (01761) 452228 *A39 S of Bristol; BS39 6EN* Former 1920s station hotel with extraordinary collection of bric-a-brac including railway memorabilia, musical instruments, china cows, postboxes, even half an old Citroën; wide mix of furnishings too, Brains Rev James, Butcombe Bitter and a guest, several wines by the glass and good choice of highly regarded food cooked by landlord-chef, Pullman carriage restaurant, cheerful helpful service; children and dogs (in bar) welcome, café-style furniture on decking, picnic-sets on grass, polytunnel growing own vegetables, five bedrooms in converted outbuilding (no breakfast), open all day Fri-Sun. *(M G Hart, Dr and Mrs A K Clarke)*

HASELBURY PLUCKNETT ST4711

★**White Horse** (01460) 78873 *North Street; TA18 7RJ* Popular open-plan village dining pub; good enterprising food cooked by chef-landlord from bar snacks up including set menu choices, west country ales tapped from the cask, local ciders and ten wines by the glass, friendly efficient service, candlelit tables on flagstones or bare boards, leather sofa by inglenook log fire; children and dogs welcome, pretty back terrace with roses and old well, closed Sun evening, Mon and Tues. *(Alistair Newton)*

HILLFARANCE ST1624

Anchor (01823) 461334 *Oake; pub signed off Bradford-on-Tone to Oake road; TA4 1AW* Comfortable village pub with dining area off attractive two-part bar; three local ales and good choice of enjoyable fairly priced food including home-made pies and Sun carvery, friendly atmosphere; children welcome, garden with play area, bedrooms, open all day Sun. *(Bob and Margaret Holder)*

HINTON BLEWETT ST5956

★**Ring o' Bells** (01761) 452239
Signed off A37 in Clutton; BS39 5AN Charming and welcoming low-beamed stone-built country local opposite village green; old-fashioned bar with solid furniture including pews, log fire, enjoyable good value home-cooked food catering for gluten-free diets, obliging service, well kept ales such as Butcombe, Fullers and Timothy Taylors, local cider and good wines by the glass, dining room; children, walkers and dogs welcome, nice view from tables in sheltered front courtyard, open all day Fri-Sun, no food Sun evening. *(M G Hart)*

HOLCOMBE ST6648

Duke of Cumberland
(01761) 233731 *Edford Hill; BA3 5HQ* Modernised riverside pub, sister to the Victoria Pub & Kitchen in Bath; enjoyable fairly priced food including home-made pizzas, Butcombe, Wadsworth and guests, Thatcher's cider, friendly helpful staff, flagstoned bar with easy chairs by log fire, comfortable cosy snug, skittle alley in the dining area; background and some live music, quiz nights, sports TV; children and dogs welcome, small waterside garden, open all day. *(Taff Thomas)*

HOLFORD ST1541

Plough (01278) 741652
A39; TA5 1RY Welcoming beamed village local with well kept ales such as Exmoor, decent wines and hearty helpings of enjoyable pubby food, friendly helpful staff, inglenook log fire; children and dogs welcome, attractive garden, wonderful Quantocks walks, open (and food) all day in summer, best to check winter hours. *(Buster and Helena Hastings)*

HORSINGTON ST7023

Half Moon (01963) 370140
Signed off A357 S of Wincanton; BA8 0EF Friendly 17th-c pub with light and airy knocked-through bars; beams, stripped stone and oak floors, inglenook log fires, decent sensibly priced pubby food, up to five well kept ales including Fullers and St Austell, decent wines and a dozen gins, evening restaurant; skittle alley, free wi-fi; children and dogs welcome, disabled access, attractive sloping front garden and big back one, good walks nearby, bedrooms in separate buildings behind, closed Sun evening, best to check winter hours. *(Sarah and David Gibbs)*

HORTON ST3214

★**Five Dials** (01460) 55359
Hanning Road; off A303; TA19 9QH Smartly updated village pub run by friendly helpful licensees; popular reasonably priced home-made food including good steaks and fish, Otter, Sharps Doom Bar and a guest, local ciders and well chosen wines by the glass, restaurant; children and dogs welcome, six comfortable bedrooms, open all day Fri-Sun, closed Mon. *(Sally and Colin Allen)*

KELSTON ST7067

Old Crown (01225) 423032
Bitton Road; A431 W of Bath; BA1 9AQ Nicely updated 15th-c pub in same small group as the Inn at Freshford (this chapter) and Cross Guns in Avoncliff (Wiltshire); four small rooms, beams and polished flagstones, carved settles and cask tables, logs burning in ancient open range, also woodburner and coal-effect gas fire, well kept Bass, Butcombe and guest, real cider, enjoyable good value food from shortish menu plus daily specials in bar or restaurant, sandwiches available till 6pm Mon-Fri; children and dogs welcome, wheelchair access with help, picnic-sets under apple trees in sheltered sunny back garden with covered deck, outside bar and barbecue, open (and food) all day, kitchen shuts 7pm Sun. *(Dr and Mrs A K Clarke)*

KEYNSHAM ST6669

★**Lock-Keeper** (0117) 986 2383
Keynsham Road (A4175 NE of town); BS31 2DD Welcoming riverside pub with relaxed worn-in feel and plenty of character; simple left-hand bar with big painted settle, cushioned wall benches, trophy cabinet and old local photographs, two more little rooms with assorted cushioned dining chairs, more photographs and rustic prints, Wells and Youngs ales plus guests, Thatcher's ciders and good range of wines, whiskies and gins, popular well priced bar food from ciabattas up served by cheerful helpful young staff, light modern conservatory (quite different in style); background and weekend live music; children welcome, dogs in bar, disabled access/facilities, teak furniture and giant parasols on big heated deck overlooking water, steps down to picnic-sets on grass, outside bar and barbecue, pétanque, open (and food) all day and can get very busy. *(Dr and Mrs A K Clarke, Chris and Angela Buckell, Taff Thomas)*

KILVE ST1442

Hood Arms (01278) 741114
A39 E of Williton; TA5 1EA Welcoming refurbished 17th-c village inn; well kept Bath, Exmoor and St Austell, good reasonably

If you stay overnight in an inn or hotel, they are allowed to serve you an alcoholic drink at any hour of the day or night.

priced food including popular Sun lunch (booking advised), friendly helpful service, warm woodburner in beamed bar, carpeted restaurant; children and dogs welcome, ramp for wheelchairs, disabled loo, tables in back garden, bedrooms, closed Sun evening, Mon. *(Bob and Margaret Holder, Richard and Penny Gibbs)*

KINGSTON ST MARY ST2229

Swan (01823) 451383
Lodes Lane, in centre of village; TA2 8HW Cosy 17th-c roadside village pub with long knocked-through panelled bar, modern furniture on carpets, black-painted beams and rough plastered walls with signed cricket bats (landlord a keen cricketer), big stone fireplaces, popular home-made pubby food (not Sun or Mon evening), well kept Dartmoor, Exmoor and Sharps, Thatcher's Cheddar Valley cider, cheerful helpful staff; background music; children welcome, no dogs inside, front wheelchair access, garden with play area, skittle alley, handy for Hestercombe Gardens. *(Bob and Margaret Holder, Mrs Zara Elliott, Martin Day)*

KNAPP ST3025

Rising Sun (01823) 491027
Village W of North Curry (pub signed from here); TA3 6BG Tucked-away 15th-c longhouse surrounded by lovely countryside; handsome beams, flagstones and two inglenooks with woodburners, Exmoor and Sharps Doom Bar, proper cider, good pubby food including popular Sun roasts, friendly helpful staff; children and dogs welcome, sunny little front terrace, open all day Sat, closed Sun evening (except first Sun of month when there's a quiz) and Mon. *(Dan and Belinda Smallbone)*

KNOLE ST4825

Lime Kiln (01458) 241242
A372 E of Langport; TA10 9JH Creeper-clad beamed 17th-c country pub set back from the road; good range of decent locally sourced food, some main courses available in smaller helpings, well kept Butcombe ales, Thatcher's Cheddar Valley cider, flagstoned bar and large carpeted dining room, inglenook log fire; free wi-fi; children and dogs (in bar) welcome, pleasant garden with southerly views, open (and food) all day weekends. *(Glen and Patricia Fuller)*

LANGFORD BUDVILLE ST1122

Martlet (01823) 400262
Off B3187 NW of Wellington; TA21 0QZ Cosy and comfortable 17th-c village pub with friendly landlady and staff; well kept/priced local ales including Exmoor and Otter, good generously served food (becomes more restauranty in the evening with fewer drinkers), beams and flagstones, central woodburner and inglenook, steps up to dining room, conservatory; children welcome, terrace picnic-sets, closed Sun evening, Mon and lunchtime Tues. *(Andy and Louise Ranwell)*

LANGPORT ST4625

★**Devonshire Arms** (01458) 241271
B3165 Somerton–Martock, off A372 E of Langport; TA10 9LP Handsome gabled inn (former hunting lodge) on village green; simple flagstoned back bar with high-backed chairs around dark tables, up to three west country ales tapped from the cask, several wines by the glass and local cider brandy, stylish main room with comfortable leather sofas and glass-topped log table by fire, scatter cushions on long wall bench, church candles, elegant dining room with wicker chairs and pale wood tables on broad boards, good interesting food from lunchtime sandwiches up (local suppliers listed), charming efficient service, maybe evening pianist; wheelchair access from car park, teak furniture out at front, pretty box-enclosed courtyard behind with water-ball feature, more seats on raised terraces, nine comfortable bedrooms, good breakfast. *(Hugh Roberts)*

LANSDOWN ST7268

Blathwayt Arms (01225) 421995
Next to Lansdown Golf Club and Bath Racecourse; BA1 9BT Hilltop stone pub with well prepared traditional food (not Sun evening) including themed nights, ales such as Butcombe and Otter from dark wood bar, also Weston's cider, decent wines and good range of gins, pleasant prompt service, mix of carpeted, wood and stone flooring, simple furniture, some raised areas in bar and conservatory, local photos and a map of the Battle of Lansdown (Civil War); background music; children welcome, wheelchair access to most areas, disabled loo, racecourse view from garden, play area, open all day. *(Chris and Angela Buckell)*

LITTON ST5954

★**Litton** (01761) 241554
B3114, NW of Chewton Mendip; BA3 4PW Extensively refurbished partly 15th-c stone pub; airy interior with wood and flagstone floors, main bar with long polished elm servery and mix of furniture including spindleback and bentwood chairs around scrubbed tables, some high cask tables, leather chesterfields and fur-draped settles, good varied choice of food from snacks, sharing plates and bar meals up, friendly helpful staff, local ales, craft beers and ciders, plenty of wines by the glass and good range of gins, separate whisky bar with copper-topped counter; background music; children and dogs welcome (menus for both), wheelchair access from back entrance, disabled loos, courtyard seating with steps up to lawned area, also terrace overlooking River Chew, good reservoir walks nearby, 12 individually styled bedrooms, open all day. *(Pete and Sarah, Chris and Angela Buckell)*

LONG ASHTON ST5370

Bird in Hand (01275) 395222

Weston Road; BS41 9LA Painted stone dining pub (sister to the Pump House in Bristol); good modern food from seasonal menu including popular Sun roasts, well kept Bath Gem, St Austell Tribute and two guests, Ashton Press cider, nice wines and some interesting gins, friendly young staff, spindleback chairs and blue-painted pine tables on wood floors, collection of old enamel signs, open fire and woodburner; children and dogs welcome, side terrace, parking can be difficult, open all day. *(David Appleyard)*

LONG ASHTON ST5370

Miners Rest (01275) 393449

Providence Lane; BS41 9DJ Welcoming three-room country pub, comfortable and unpretentious, with well kept Butcombe, Fullers and an occasional guest tapped from the cask, traditional ciders, generous helpings of simple inexpensive lunchtime food, cheerful prompt service, local mining memorabilia, log fire, darts; no credit cards; well behaved children and dogs welcome, wheelchair access possible with some heroics, vine-covered verandah and suntrap terrace, open all day. *(Sylvia and Phillip Spencer)*

LOWER GODNEY ST4742

★**Sheppey Inn** (01458) 831594

Tilleys Drove; BA5 1RZ Although rather unprepossessing from the outside, this quirky fun place is full of character and surprisingly popular for its remote setting; eclectic mix of furniture on bare boards including plastic chairs by chunky wooden tables, cushioned wall benches and some 1950s retro, various stuffed animals, old photographs, modern artwork and assorted kitsch, at least six ciders tapped from the barrel along with local ales and craft beers, imaginative choice of well liked food, some cooked in charcoal oven, friendly staff, black beams and log fire, long dining area with high pitched ceiling; background and regular live music; children and dogs welcome, seats on deck overlooking small River Sheppey, three individually styled bedrooms, open all day weekends. *(Stuart Reeves, Hugh Roberts)*

LYDFORD ON FOSSE ST5630

Cross Keys (01963) 240473

Just off A37; TA11 7HA Beamed and flagstoned pub with good traditional home-made food including generous ploughman's and award-winning pies, cheerful service, up to half a dozen well kept ales tapped from the cask such as Downton, proper ciders and nice wines by the glass, connecting rooms (main dining area at front), chunky rustic furniture and log fires in substantial old fireplaces; live music, quizzes and other events in function room; children and dogs welcome, disabled access/loos, seats on covered terrace and in sunny garden, six comfortable well equipped bedrooms, camping field, popular with Fosse Way walkers, open all day. *(Trevor and Michele Street)*

MIDDLEZOY ST3732

George (01823) 698215

Off A372 E of Bridgwater; TA7 0NN Steps up to friendly 17th-c beamed village pub; well kept St Austell Tribute and a couple of guests (Easter beer festival), proper ciders and eight wines by the glass, simple home-made lunchtime food, more evening choice including good steaks, attentive welcoming staff, bare stone walls, flagstones and two log fires; quiz, live music and bingo nights, pool, darts, skittle alley; children and dogs welcome, a few tables outside, open all day Sun till 7pm, closed Mon and lunchtime Tues, no food Sun or Tues. *(Patricia Healey)*

MIDFORD ST7660

★**Hope & Anchor** (01225) 832296

Bath Road (B3110); BA2 7DD 17th-c pub near Colliers Way and close to walks on the disused Somerset & Dorset railway; neatly kept open-plan interior with civilised bar, heavy-beamed flagstoned restaurant with mix of dark wooden furniture and woodburner, modern back conservatory liked by families, enjoyable good value food cooked by landlord including daily specials, Otter Amber, Sharps Doom Bar and a guest, traditional cider and plenty of wines by the glass, courteous staff; dogs welcome in bar, seats on two-tier back terrace, open all day weekends. *(Julian Richardson, Tim King, Dr and Mrs A K Clarke)*

MINEHEAD SS9746

Old Ship Aground (01643) 703516

Quay West next to lifeboat station; TA24 5UL Friendly flower-decked Edwardian quayside pub owned by local farming family; Marstons-related ales including Courage, Thatcher's cider and good selection of wines and spirits, enjoyable food using own meat and other local produce, Sun carvery, cheerful efficient service even when busy, faux black beams decorated with pump clips and nautical ropework, pubby furniture on carpeted or polished wood floors, window-seat views; background music (live Fri), free wi-fi; children and dogs welcome, wheelchair access via side door, disabled loo, picnic-sets out at front overlooking harbour, 12 bedrooms, open all day. *(Simon Boughey, Mr and Mrs D J Nash, Chris and Angela Buckell)*

MONKSILVER ST0737

Notley Arms (01984) 656095

B3188; TA4 4JB Bustling pub in lovely village on edge of Exmoor National Park; open-plan bar rooms with log fires and woodburners, cushioned window seats and settles, appealing collection of old dining chairs around mixed wooden tables on slate tiles or flagstones, paintings on cream or panelled walls, fresh flowers and church candles, tractor-seat stools by counter serving Exmoor, St Austell and a guest, proper cider, 30 wines by the glass and 20 malt whiskies, good food from pub classics (with a twist) to inventive restaurant dishes; background music; children and dogs welcome, neat garden with plenty of picnic-sets, heated pavilion and a clear-running stream at the bottom, attractive comfortable bedrooms in former coach house, open all day from 8am. *(Bob and Margaret Holder, Mrs Zara Elliott, Martin Day)*

MONTACUTE ST4917

Kings Arms (01935) 822255

Bishopston; TA15 6UU Extended 17th-c stone inn next to church; stripped-stone bar with comfortable seating and log fire, contemporary restaurant, three real ales including Timothy Taylors, nice house wines and well liked food from bar snacks to restaurant dishes, friendly courteous staff; background music; children welcome, pleasant garden behind, 15 bedrooms (most ensuite), handy for Montacute House (NT), open all day. *(Alan and Angela Scouller)*

NAILSEA ST4469

Blue Flame (01275) 856910

Netherton Wood Lane, West End; BS48 4DE Small friendly 19th-c farmers' local with two unchanging lived-in rooms; well kept ales from casks behind bar, traditional ciders and some snacky food such as fresh rolls and pies, coal fire, pub games; outside gents'; sizeable informal garden, limited parking (may be filled with Land Rovers and tractors); open all day Thurs-Sun, closed lunchtimes Mon, Tues. *(Peter Myers)*

OVER STRATTON ST4315

Royal Oak (01460) 240906

Off A303 via Ilminster turn at South Petherton roundabout; TA13 5LQ Attractive 17th-c thatched dining pub under enthusiastic newish owners; linked rooms with oak beams, flagstones and thick stone walls, scrubbed kitchen tables, pews and settles, log-effect gas fire, much enjoyed food cooked by landlord-chef from pub favourites up including set lunch, and daily specials, fair prices, well kept Badger ales and good wines, friendly attentive service; children and dogs (theirs is Alfie) welcome, wheelchair access, back garden with paved terrace, open (and food) all day weekends, closed Mon evening (although may open in summer). *(Ewan and Sue Hewitt, Jason Caulkin)*

PITMINSTER ST2219

Queens Arms (01823) 421529

Off B3170 S of Taunton (or reached direct); near church; TA3 7AZ Popular village pub-restaurant with good competitively priced food from varied set menus (best to book), well kept Sharps and other west country ales, Thatcher's ciders and decent range of wines, friendly helpful staff; downstairs skittle alley; children and dogs (in bar) welcome, picnic-sets out at back, closed Sun evening, Mon. *(Bob and Margaret Holder)*

PORLOCK SS8846

★**Ship** (01643) 862507

High Street; TA24 8QD Picturesque old thatched pub with beams, flagstones and big inglenook log fires, popular reasonably priced food from sandwiches up, well kept ales such as Exmoor, Otter and St Austell, friendly service, back dining room, small locals' front bar with games; children welcome, attractive split-level sunny garden with decking and play area, nearby nature trail to Dunkery Beacon, five bedrooms, open all day; known as the Top Ship to distinguish it from the Ship at Porlock Weir. *(Lindy Andrews)*

PORLOCK WEIR SS8846

★**Ship** (01643) 863288

Porlock Hill (A39); TA24 8PB Unpretentious thatched pub in wonderful spot by peaceful harbour – can get packed; long and narrow with dark low beams, flagstones and stripped stone, simple pub furniture, woodburner, west country ales like Exmoor and Otter, real ciders, a perry and good whisky and soft drinks choice, enjoyable pubby food served promptly by friendly staff, games rooms across small backyard, also a tea room; background and occasional live music, TV; children and dogs welcome, sturdy picnic-sets out at front and side, good coastal walks, three bedrooms, limited free parking but pay-and-display opposite; calls itself the Bottom Ship to avoid confusion with the Ship at Porlock. *(Mr and Mrs D J Nash)*

PORTISHEAD ST4576

★**Windmill** (01275) 818483

M5 junction 19; A369 into town, then follow Sea Front sign and into Nore Road; BS20 6JZ Busy dining pub perched on steep hillside with panoramic Severn estuary views; curving glass frontage rising two storeys (adjacent windmill remains untouched), contemporary furnishings, four Fullers ales and a couple of guests, Thatcher's cider and plenty of wines by the glass, decent range of enjoyable food from sandwiches and baked potatoes to chargrills and daily specials, early bird deal (3-7pm Mon-Fri), hard-working helpful staff; children welcome, dogs allowed in bar, disabled access/facilities including chairlift, metal furniture on tiered lantern-lit terraces and decking, open (and food) all day. *(Chris and Angela Buckell)*

PRIDDY ST5450

★**Hunters Lodge** (01749) 672275

From Wells on A39 pass hill with TV mast on left, then next left; BA5 3AR

Welcoming farmers', walkers' and potholers' pub above Ice Age cavern, unchanging and in same family for generations; well kept local beers tapped from casks behind bar, Thatcher's and Wilkin's ciders, simple cheap home-made food, log fires in huge fireplaces, low beams, flagstones and panelling, caving memorabilia and old lead mining photographs, Tues folk night; no mobiles or credit cards; children and dogs in family room, wheelchair access, garden picnic-sets. *(Taff Thomas)*

PRISTON ST6960

Ring o' Bells (01761) 471467
Village SW of Bath; BA2 9EE Unpretentious old stone pub with large knocked-through bar; good reasonably priced traditional food cooked by licensees using nearby farm produce, real ales from small local brewers including Butcombe, quick friendly service, flagstones, beams and good open fire; skittle alley, free wi-fi; children, dogs and boots welcome, benches out at front overlooking little village green (maypole here on May Day), good walks, closed Mon and lunchtimes Tue-Thurs, no food Sun evening. *(Taff Thomas)*

RIMPTON ST6021

White Post Inn (01935) 851525
Rimpton Hill, B3148; BA22 8AR Small modern dining pub straddling Dorset border (boundary actually runs through the bar); highly rated imaginative food from chef-owner including reworked pub favourites and tasting menus, local ales and ciders, a dozen wines by the glass and interesting list of spirits including a milk vodka, friendly helpful staff, cosy carpeted bar area with leather sofas and woodburner, fine country views from restaurant and back terrace; children welcome, three ensuite bedrooms, closed Sun evening, Mon. *(Peter and Emma Kelly)*

RODE ST8053

Cross Keys (01373) 830900
High Street; BA11 6NZ Popular pub in former brewery; two bars and restaurant, old well in one part, enjoyable freshly made food (not Sun evening, Mon) including good value Fri steak night, well kept Butcombe and a couple of guests, proper ciders and decent range of gins, good friendly service; monthly comedy night; children and dogs welcome, large enclosed garden and terrace, three bedrooms, open all day weekends, closed Mon lunchtime. *(Guy Vowles)*

SALTFORD ST6867

Bird in Hand (01225) 873335
High Street; BS31 3EJ Comfortable and friendly with busy L-shaped bar; four well kept ales such as Butcombe and Sharps, good choice of popular fairly priced food (all day weekends) from well filled rolls up, prompt cheerful service, pubby furniture including settles, carpets throughout, back conservatory dining area; Mon quiz, free wi-fi; wheelchair access at front (not from car park), picnic-sets down towards river, pétanque, handy for Bristol & Bath Railway Path. *(Dr and Mrs A K Clarke, Roger and Anne Mallard)*

SANDFORD ST4159

Railway (01934) 611518
Station Road; BS25 5RA Owned by Thatcher's and extensively modernised; their full range of ciders, real ales such as Butcombe and St Austell, plenty of wines by the glass and enjoyable food from shortish menu including good value set lunch, pleasant young staff, lofty flagstoned bar with long oak counter, comfortable bare-boards area off with exposed stone walls and open fire, attractive timber-framed dining extension; free wi-fi; children and dogs welcome, outside seating on two levels, open all day. *(M G Hart)*

SHEPTON MONTAGUE ST6731

★**Montague Inn** (01749) 813213
Village signed off A359 Bruton–Castle Cary; BA9 8JW Simply but tastefully furnished dining pub with welcoming licensees, popular for civilised meal or just a drink; stripped-wood tables and kitchen chairs, inglenook log fire, nicely presented often interesting food including range of burgers from shortish menu plus a few specials, well kept ales such as Bath, Cottage and Wadworths tapped from the cask, ciders such as Orchard Pig, good wine and whisky choice, helpful well informed young staff, bright spacious restaurant extension behind; children and dogs (in bar) welcome, disabled access, garden and big terrace with teak furniture, maybe Sun jazz in summer, peaceful farmland views, closed Sun evening. *(Edward Mirzoeff)*

SIMONSBATH SS7739

★**Exmoor Forest Inn** (01643) 831341 *B3223/B3358; TA24 7SH* Welcoming 19th-c inn beautifully placed in remote countryside; split-level bar with circular tables by counter, larger area with cushioned settles, upholstered stools and mate's chairs around mix of tables, hunting trophies, antlers and horse tack, woodburner, generously served good traditional food alongside more imaginative choices including local game, well kept ales such as Clearwater, Exmoor and Otter, Weston's cider, good range of wines and malt whiskies, airy dining room, residents' lounge; children

If we know a pub has an outdoor play area for children, we mention it.

and dogs welcome, seats in front garden, fine walks along River Barle, own trout and salmon fishing, comfortable bedrooms and self-catering cottage, open all day in high season. *(Bob and Margaret Holder, Ian Herdman)*

SOUTH CHERITON ST6924

White Horse (01963) 370394
A357 Wincanton–Blandford; BA8 0BL Renovated 17th-c roadside country pub under friendly family management; well kept ales, craft beers and decent range of wines by the glass, good locally sourced home-made food (not Sun evening) in bar or restaurant (separate menus), cheerful service; some live music, skittle alley; children and dogs welcome, picnic-sets in small back garden, open all day weekends. *(Stuart Reeves)*

SOUTH STOKE ST7461

Pack Horse (01225) 830300
Off B3110, S edge of Bath; BA2 7DU Historic pub saved from developers by the local community and recently reopened after long closure; two sympathetically restored rooms separated by servery, main one with heavy black beam-and-plank ceiling, stone-mullioned windows, quarry-tiled floor and log fire in handsome stone inglenook, room on left with another fire, changing local beers, traditional cider and enjoyable reasonably priced food from sandwiches/snacks and pub favourites up, good friendly service, two further rooms upstairs; quiz Weds, folk night last Sun of month; children and dogs (downstairs) welcome, picnic-sets in nice garden with lovely valley views, good walks (route sheets available from the bar), limited parking, best to park at top of village and walk down, open all day, no food Sun evening. *(Pete and Sarah)*

SPAXTON ST2336

Lamb (01278) 671350
Barford Road, Four Forks; TA5 1AD Welcoming simply furnished little pub at foot of the Quantocks; open-plan beamed bar with woodburner, well kept beers and enjoyable good value food (not Sun evening) including notable local steaks and blackboard specials, booking advised; quiz last Sun of month; tables on lawn behind, closed all day Mon and lunchtimes apart from Sun. *(Katherine and Hugh Markham)*

STANTON DREW ST5963

Druids Arms (01275) 332230
Off B3130; BS39 4EJ Refurbished pub in stone-circle village (there are some standing stones in the garden); linked flagstoned rooms with low black beams, bare stone walls and green dados, cushioned window seats and pubby furniture, candles here and there, open fires, tractor-seat stools by pale wood bar serving Butcombe and Sharps Doom Bar, Thatcher's cider and modest wine list, friendly service, enjoyable often creative food from bar snacks up (not Sun evening), Mon fish and chips, Tues OAP lunch deal; occasional live music, darts, free wi-fi; children and dogs welcome, front wheelchair access using portable ramp, picnic-sets out by lane and in garden backing on to 14th-c church, maybe summer bouncy castle, open all day. *(Michael Doswell)*

STAPLE FITZPAINE ST2618

Greyhound (01823) 480227
Off A358 or B3170 S of Taunton; TA3 5SP Rambling country pub with decent choice of popular home-made food (not Mon), well kept Badger ales and good wines by the glass, welcoming helpful staff, flagstones and inglenooks, nice mix of settles and chairs, old pictures, farm tools and so forth; children and dogs welcome, three bedrooms, good breakfast, closed Mon lunchtime, otherwise open all day. *(Bob and Margaret Holder, Guy Vowles)*

STOKE ST GREGORY ST3527

Rose & Crown (01823) 490296
Woodhill; follow North Curry signpost off A378 by junction with A358 – keep on to Stoke, bearing right in centre, passing church and follow lane for 0.5 miles; TA3 6EW Popular dining pub with good food (best to book) and two or three local ales, friendly helpful staff, more or less open-plan, with stools by curved brick and wood counter, long high-raftered flagstoned dining room and two further beamed eating areas, one with glass-covered well; background music; children welcome, seats on sheltered front terrace, one bedroom, closed Sun evening; application has been made for conversion to private house. *(Bob and Margaret Holder, Paul and Claudia Dickinson)*

STOKE SUB HAMDON ST4717

Prince of Wales (01935) 822848
Ham Hill; TA14 6RW Traditional stone pub at top of Ham Hill with superb views; changing ales tapped from the cask and good food from sandwiches and west country deli boards up, curry night Thurs, summer pizzas from outside oven, friendly staff; children, dogs and muddy boots welcome, open (and food) all day from 8.30am for breakfast. *(Andy and Louise Ranwell)*

TARR SS8632

★**Tarr Farm** (01643) 851507
Tarr Steps – narrow road off B3223 N of Dulverton; deep ford if you approach from the W (inn is on E bank); TA22 9PY Fine Exmoor position for this 16th-c inn above River Barle's medieval clapper bridge; compact unpretentious bar rooms with good views, leather chairs around slabby rustic tables, some stall and wall seating, game bird pictures on wood-clad walls, three woodburners, well kept Exmoor ales and several wines by the glass, good food using local produce, residents' end with

smart evening restaurant, friendly helpful service, log fire in pleasant lounge with dark leather armchairs and sofas; children and dogs welcome, slate-topped stone tables outside making most of setting, extensive grounds, good bedrooms (no under-10s) in separate modern building, open all day but may be closed early Feb. *(Bob and Margaret Holder, S G N Bennett, Peter L Harrison)*

TAUNTON ST2525

Hankridge Arms (01823) 444405
Hankridge Way, Deane Gate (near Sainsbury's); just off M5 junction 25 – A358 towards city, then right at roundabout, right at next roundabout; TA1 2LR Interesting well restored Badger dining pub based on 16th-c former farmhouse – quite a contrast to the modern shopping complex surrounding it; different-sized linked areas, beams, timbers and big log fire, popular food from lunchtime sandwiches through pubby choices up, well kept (if pricey) ales and decent wines by the glass, friendly efficient young staff; background music; dogs welcome, plenty of tables in pleasant outside area, open all day weekends. *(R T and J C Moggridge)*

TAUNTON ST2225

Plough (01823) 324404
Station Road; TA1 1PB Popular little pub with three or four local ales including Exeter Avocet and guests, racked ciders and seven wines by the glass, simple food including range of pies, bare boards, panelling, candles on tables, cosy nooks and open fire, hidden door to lavatories; background and live music (open mike Sun), weekly quiz; dogs welcome, handy for station, open (and food) all day. *(Donald Allsopp)*

TAUNTON ST2223

Vivary Arms (01823) 272563
Wilton Street; across Vivary Park from centre; TA1 3JR Popular low-beamed 18th-c local (Taunton's oldest pub); good value fresh food from light lunches up in snug plush lounge and small dining room, takeaway fish and chips, well kept ales including Butcombe and decent wines by the glass, friendly helpful young staff, interesting collection of drink-related items; pool and darts; lovely hanging baskets and flowers out at front, nice little garden behind. *(Bob and Margaret Holder)*

TEMPLE CLOUD ST6258

Temple (01761) 451145
Main Road; BS39 5DA Renovated 17th-c pub reopened after six-year closure (part of the Red Oak Taverns group); modern open-plan bar with popular food from sandwiches and pizzas up, four changing ales and a dozen wines by the glass, friendly service; Tues quiz and some live music; children and dogs welcome, ten bedrooms, open all day, food all day weekends. *(Pete and Sarah)*

TINTINHULL ST5019

★**Crown & Victoria** (01935) 823341
Farm Street, village signed off A303; BA22 8PZ Handsome golden-stone inn useful for the A303; carpeted bar with farmhouse furniture and big woodburner, high bar chairs at light oak counter serving four well kept ales including Butcombe and Sharps, good popular food using free range/organic ingredients, efficient friendly service, dining room with more pine tables and chairs, former skittle alley also used for eating, end conservatory; well behaved children welcome, dogs in bar, disabled facilities, big garden with play area, five bedrooms, handy for Tintinhull Garden (NT), closed Sun evening. *(Ewan and Sue Hewitt)*

TRULL ST2122

Winchester Arms (01823) 284723
Church Road; TA3 7LG Cosy streamside village pub with good value generous food served daily including blackboard specials and popular Sun lunch, curry night first Weds of the month, west country ales and local ciders, friendly helpful service, small dining room; Sun quiz, skittle alley, free wi-fi; dogs welcome, garden with decked area and summer barbecues, six cosy bedrooms, open all day. *(Alison and Michael Harper)*

TUNLEY ST6959

King William (01761) 470408
B3115 SW of Bath; BA2 0EB Updated family-run 17th-c coaching inn with good fairly priced pub food from baguettes to daily specials (smaller helpings available and plenty of gluten-free choices), well kept ales such as St Austell and decent wines, friendly efficient staff, bar popular with locals, other room set for dining; courtyard tables, three comfortable bedrooms, open all day Sat, till 6pm Sun, closed Mon. *(Ian and Rose Lock)*

UPTON ST0129

Lowtrow Cross Inn (01398) 371220
A3190 E of Upton; TA4 2DB Welcoming old pub with character low-beamed bar, bare boards and flagstones, open fire and woodburner, two country-kitchen dining areas, one with enormous inglenook, well kept ales such as Exmoor Gold, Thatcher's cider and popular reasonably priced home-made food including good steaks, fish and chips deal Weds and Thurs (also Tues in summer); children and dogs welcome, lovely surroundings, two bedrooms, camping next door, closed Sun evening, Mon and winter Tues. *(Valerie and Gordon Wauton)*

VOBSTER ST7049

Vobster Inn (01373) 812920
Lower Vobster; BA3 5RJ Spacious old stone-built dining pub; enjoyable reasonably priced home-made food (special diets catered for) including evening set menu,

Butcombe, Ashton Press cider and nice wines by the glass, three comfortable open-plan areas with antique furniture, plenty of room for just a drink; children and dogs (in bar) welcome, seats on lawn, boules, four bedrooms (also yurts and shepherd's huts), closed Sun evening, Mon and lunchtime Tues. *(Taff Thomas)*

WASHFORD ST0440

White Horse (01984) 640415
Abbey Road/Torre Rocks; TA23 0JZ Welcoming and popular old local, good selection of well kept ales and enjoyable reasonably priced pubby food including good traditional breakfast, specials and deals, can eat in bar or separate restaurant, log fires; pool; large smokers' pavilion over road next to trout stream, field with interesting collection of fowl and goats, handy for visits to Exmoor National Park, dog-friendly; seven bedrooms (three in newly built timber lodge), open all day. *(Richard and Penny Gibbs)*

WATCHET ST0743

Pebbles (01984) 634737
Market Street; TA23 0AN Popular, welcoming and relaxed little bar in former shop near Market House Museum and harbour; extensive range of regional ciders (tasters offered), also cask-tapped ales such as Exmoor, Moles and Otter and good choice of whiskies, cider brandies and other drinks, friendly helpful staff, no food but can bring your own (plates and cutlery supplied, fish and chip shop next door); regular live music (some impromptu) including folk and jazz, sea shanty and poetry evenings, free wi-fi; dogs on leads welcome, open all day. *(Richard and Penny Gibbs)*

WATCHET ST0643

Star (01984) 631367
Mill Lane (B3191); TA23 0BZ Late 18th-c beamed pub at end of lane just off Watchet harbour; main flagstoned bar with other low-ceilinged side rooms, some exposed stonework and rough wood partitioning, mix of traditional furniture including oak settles, window seats, woodburner in ornate fireplace, good selection of pubby food mostly sourced locally including fresh fish, half a dozen well kept west country ales such as Butcombe and Cotleigh, Sheppy's cider and a few malt whiskies, cheerful helpful staff; background music; children welcome and dogs (food for them), wheelchair access, picnic-sets out in front and in sloping beer garden behind, handy for marina and West Somerset Railway. *(Nigel Morton)*

WEDMORE ST4347

New Inn (01934) 712099
Combe Batch; BS28 4DU Welcoming unpretentious village pub popular with locals and visitors alike; well kept Butcombe and guests, real cider and big helpings of enjoyable sensibly priced home-made pubby food, comfortable dining area; skittle alley, darts, sports TV and lots of local events including penny chuffing, conker competitions and the Turnip Prize (for worst piece of local artwork); children and dogs welcome, open all day weekends, closed lunchtimes Mon and Tues. *(Gordon Harold)*

WELLOW ST7358

Fox & Badger (01225) 832293
Signed off A367 SW of Bath; BA2 8QG Popular opened-up village pub under same owners as the White Hart at Widcombe Hill (Bath); flagstones one end, bare boards the other, woodburner in massive hearth, some snug corners, Butcombe and a guest, real ciders and good range of well liked food (booking advised weekends), friendly service; children and dogs welcome, picnic-sets in covered courtyard, open all day Fri, Sat, closed Sun evening. *(S G N Bennett, Taff Thomas)*

WELLS ST5445

Crown (01749) 673457
Market Place; BA5 2RF Former 15th-c coaching inn close to the cathedral; various bustling areas with light wooden flooring, plenty of matching chairs and cushioned wall benches, Butcombe, Cotleigh, Palmers and Sharps, popular reasonably priced food (all day Sun) in bar and bistro including good value set menu (must book weekends), friendly efficient service; background music, TV, newspapers; children welcome till 8pm, dogs in bar, small heated back courtyard, 20 bedrooms, street market Weds and Sat, open all day. *(Richard Tilbrook, Ian Phillips, Mrs Zara Elliott)*

WELLS ST5546

★**Fountain** (01749) 672317
St Thomas Street; BA5 2UU Relaxed restauranty place with big comfortable bar, interesting décor and large open fire, quite a choice of popular food here or in upstairs dining room (booking advised weekends), Mon steak night, ales such as Bath, Butcombe and Fullers, several wines by the glass, chatty attentive staff; unobtrusive background music, newspapers; well behaved children and dogs (in one area) welcome, pretty in summer with window boxes and shutters, handy for cathedral and moated Bishop's Palace, closed Sun evening, Mon lunchtime. *(R K Phillips, Mark Kerrigan)*

WEST CHINNOCK ST4613

Muddled Man (01935) 881235
Lower Street; TA18 7PT Friendly unassuming family-run pub in attractive rustic village; single bar with three well kept changing west country ales, real cider and over 50 malt whiskies, enjoyable straightforward food using local produce; skittle alley; children and dogs welcome, small garden, two bedrooms, open all day Fri-Sun. *(Pete and Sarah)*

WEST HUNTSPILL ST3145

Crossways (01278) 783756

A38, between M5 junctions 22 and 23; TA9 3RA Rambling 17th-c tile-hung pub with split-level carpeted areas, beams and log fires, six well kept mostly local ales (tasting trays available, Aug beer festival), good choice of enjoyable generously served food at reasonable prices (booking recommended), cheerful efficient staff; skittle alley, pool, TV, free wi-fi; children and dogs (not weekend evenings in dining areas) welcome, disabled facilities, garden with play area and heated smokers' shelter, seven bedrooms, open all day. *(R K Phillips)*

WEST MONKTON ST2628

Monkton (01823) 412414

Blundells Lane; signed from A3259; TA2 8NP Popular village dining pub with good choice of freshly made food including some south african influences (best to book weekends), bare-boards bar with central woodburner and snug off, separate restaurant with strip-wood floor, well kept Exmoor, Otter and Sharps, Orchard Pig and Thatcher's ciders, nine wines by the glass, good service; children and dogs welcome, wheelchair access from the front, lots of tables in big garden bounded by stream, play area. *(Bob and Margaret Holder)*

WEST PENNARD ST5438

Red Lion (01458) 832941

A361 E of Glastonbury; Newtown; BA6 8NH Traditional 16th-c stone-built village inn; bar and dining areas off small flagstoned black-beamed core, enjoyable home-made food including pub favourites and popular Sun roasts, three changing ales, inglenook woodburner and open fires; background and some live music, free wi-fi; children and dogs welcome, tables on big forecourt, good nearby walks, skittle alley, bedrooms in converted side barn. *(Sandra and Neil White)*

WIDCOMBE ST2216

Holman Clavel (01823) 421070

Culmhead, on ridge road W of B3170, follow sign for Blagdon; 2 miles S of Corfe; TA3 7EA Country local dating from the 14th c, friendly and relaxed, with good interesting food from short but varied menu (vegetarian and gluten-free diets catered for), Butcombe Bitter and Gold, guest beers and good local cider including own Tricky, flagstoned bar with woodburner in big fireplace, room off has a long dining table (seats 24); some live music; children, dogs and muddy boots welcome, well placed for Blackdown Hills, open all day Fri-Sun, closed Tues. *(Guy Vowles)*

WINCANTON ST7028

Nog Inn (01963) 32998

South Street; BA9 9DL Welcoming old split-level pub with Sharps and St Austell and a couple of guests, real cider and continental beers, good reasonably priced traditional food including Sun carvery (not summer) and themed nights, bare boards, carpet and flagstones, pump clips on bar ceiling, log fires; background and some live music, occasional comedy and quiz nights, darts; well behaved children and dogs welcome, pleasant back garden with heated smokers' shelter, open (and food) all day. *(Sally and Colin Allen)*

WINFORD ST5262

Crown (01275) 472388

Crown Hill, off Regil Road; BS40 8AY Popular old pub set in deep countryside; linked beamed rooms with mix of pubby furniture including settles on flagstones or quarry tiles, old pictures and photographs on rough walls, copper and brass, leather sofas in front of big open fire, enjoyable generous home-made food (all day Sun) at very reasonable prices including Thurs evening deal, Butcombe, St Austell and a guest, good choice of wines by the glass, friendly landlord and staff; table skittles and skittle alley; children and dogs welcome, wheelchair access with help, tables out in front and in back garden, closed Mon-Weds lunchtime, otherwise open all day. *(Glen and Patricia Fuller)*

WINSFORD SS9034

★**Royal Oak** (01643) 851455

Off A396 about 10 miles S of Dunster; TA24 7JE Prettily placed thatched and beamed Exmoor inn; enjoyable often interesting home-made food (greater evening choice), Exmoor ales, west country ciders and decent wine list, friendly helpful staff, carpeted bar with woodburner in big stone fireplace, large bay window seat looking across to village green and foot and packhorse bridges over River Winn, restaurant and other lounge areas; children and dogs (in bar) welcome, disabled facilities, eight good bedrooms some with four-posters. *(Bob and Margaret Holder)*

WITHAM FRIARY ST7440

★**Seymour Arms** (01749) 850742

Signed from B3092 S of Frome; BA11 5HF Well worn-in unchanging flagstoned country tavern, in same friendly family since 1952; two simple rooms off 19th-c hatch-service lobby, panelled benches and open fires, well kept Cheddar Potholer and an occasional guest, Rich's local cider tapped

Virtually all pubs in this book sell wine by the glass. We mention wines if they are a cut above the average.

from back room, low prices, no food but can bring your own; bar billiards, darts and table skittles; children and dogs welcome, garden by main rail line, cricket pitch over the road, open all day. *(Taff Thomas)*

WITHYPOOL SS8435

Royal Oak (01643) 831506

Village signed off B3233; TA24 7QP Prettily placed old-fashioned country inn – where R D Blackmore stayed while writing *Lorna Doone*; lounge with raised working fireplace, comfortably cushioned wall seats and slat-backed chairs, sporting trophies, paintings and copper/brass ornaments, enjoyable food here and in restaurant, well kept Exmoor and a guest, real cider, character locals' bar; walkers and dogs welcome (leave muddy boots in porch), well behaved children in eating areas, wooden benches on terrace, attractive riverside village with lovely walks, grand views from Winsford Hill just up the road, eight bedrooms (twisting staircase to top floor). *(Peter Myers)*

WOOKEY ST5245

Burcott (01749) 673874

B3139 W of Wells; BA5 1NJ Beamed roadside pub with two simply furnished old-fashioned front bar rooms; flagstones, some exposed stonework and half-panelling, lantern wall lights, old prints, woodburner, a couple of ales such as Hop Back and a real cider, enjoyable food from snacks up in bar and restaurant, small games room; soft background music; children welcome in restaurant, no dogs inside, front window boxes and tubs, picnic-sets in sizeable garden with Mendip Hills views, four self-catering cottages in converted stables, closed Sun evening, Mon. *(Peter Pilbeam)*

WOOKEY HOLE ST5347

Wookey Hole Inn (01749) 676677

High Street; BA5 1BP Open-plan family dining pub usefully placed opposite the caves; welcoming and relaxed with unusual contemporary décor, wooden and tiled floors, tables with paper cloths for drawing on (crayons provided), two woodburners, decent food from pub favourites to daily specials, three changing local ales, several belgian beers, ciders and perry, efficient friendly staff; background music; dogs allowed, pleasant garden with various sculptures, five individually styled bedrooms, open all day apart from Sun evening. *(Katherine and Hugh Markham)*

YARLINGTON ST6529

Stags Head (01963) 440393

Pound Lane; BA9 8DG Under newish owners and some refurbishment for this old low-ceilinged pub tucked away by the church in tiny village; cosy bar serving well kept ales such as Exmoor, Otter and Wild Beer, traditional ciders, good food from sandwiches and pub favourites to more restauranty choices, efficient friendly service, wood-floored restaurant with big log fire, high-backed chairs and feature cider-press table; background music; well behaved children welcome, dogs in bar, small stream in sheltered back garden, good walks, closed Sun evening. *(Trevor and Michele Street)*

Staffordshire

BREWOOD SJ8708 Map 4

Oakley

(01902) 859800 – www.brunningandprice.co.uk/oakley

Kiddemore Green Road; ST19 9BQ

Substantial, cleverly extended pub with interesting food and drink and seats outside

There's a lot to see near this sizeable place, so it's a good choice for lunch. The open-plan rooms have been furnished with thought and care, and the many windows and pastel paintwork keep it all very light and airy. Partitioning and metal standing posts split larger areas into cosier drinking and dining spaces, and throughout there are plenty of house plants, mirrors above open fires (some in pretty Victorian fireplaces), books on shelves, elegant metal chandeliers, standard lamps, stubby candles and fresh flowers. Seating ranges from groups of leather armchairs to all manner of cushioned wooden dining chairs around character tables, the walls (some half-panelled) are hung with hundreds of prints, and flooring consists of rugs on big boards and, in the restaurant, carpet. From the long counter, friendly, helpful staff serve Phoenix Brunning & Price Original, Salopian Oracle and Wye Valley Butty Bach with guests such as Backyard Blonde, Rudgate Jorvik, Titanic Plum Porter and Woods Shropshire Lad on handpump, 16 wines by the glass, 100 whiskies, 120 gins and 80 rums; board games. The spreading back terrace has a number of seats and benches among flowering tubs and raised flower beds and overlooks a lake. There's a rack outside for cyclists. Disabled parking and lavatories.

Likeable food includes sandwiches, wild mushroom arancini with pea and mint purée and pickled shallots, king prawns with chilli and garlic, lentil, chickpea and vegetable shepherd's pie with sweet potato mash and thyme jus, chicken caesar salad, scampi and chips in a basket with tartare sauce, honey-roast ham and eggs, steak burger with toppings, coleslaw and chips, sticky pork belly with watermelon, pineapple, pickled ginger salad and chilli dressing, and puddings such as hot waffle with blueberry compote and clotted cream ice-cream and crème brûlée. *Benchmark main dish: slow-braised lamb shoulder with dauphinoise potatoes, carrot mash and rosemary gravy £17.25. Two-course evening meal £21.00.*

Brunning & Price ~ Manager John Duncan ~ Real ale ~ Open 10am-11pm; 10am-10.30pm Sun ~ Bar food 12-9.30; 12-10 Fri, Sat; 12-9 Sun ~ Restaurant ~ Children welcome ~ Dogs allowed in bar ~ Wi-fi *Recommended by Hilary and Neil Christopher, James Landor, Kate Moran, Tony Selinger, Andrew and Ruth Simmonds, Edward May, Claire Adams*

CAULDON SK0749 Map 7

Yew Tree ★★ £

(01538) 309876 – www.yewtreeinncauldon.co.uk

Village signposted from A523 and A52 about 8 miles W of Ashbourne; ST10 3EJ

A unique collection of curios in friendly pub with good value snacks and bargain beer – very eccentric

Don't be put off by the unassuming exterior of this unique place. Once inside, it's like a museum, filled with fascinating curiosities and antiques. The most impressive pieces are the working polyphons and symphonions which are 19th-c developments of the musical box, some taller than a person, each with quite a repertoire of tunes and elaborate sound-effects. There are also two pairs of Queen Victoria's stockings, an amazing collection of ceramics and pottery including a Grecian urn dating back almost 3,000 years, penny-farthing and boneshaker bicycles and the infamous Acme Dog Carrier. Seats include 18th-c settles, plenty of little wooden tables and a four-person oak church choir seat with carved heads that came from St Mary's church in Stafford. Look out for the array of musical instruments ranging from a one-string violin (phonofiddle) through pianos and a sousaphone to the aptly named serpent. Drinks are very fairly priced, so it's no wonder the place is popular with locals. Burton Bridge Bitter, Rudgate Ruby Mild and a guest from Dancing Duck on handpump, ten interesting malt whiskies, eight wines by the glass and farm cider; they hold a music and beer festival in July and a vintage vehicle rally in September. Darts and table skittles. There are seats outside the front door and in the cobbled stableyard, and they have a basic campsite for pub customers and a small caravan for hire. The pub is almost hidden by a towering yew tree.

The modest menu includes sandwiches, locally made pies, vegetable or beef chilli, beef stew with mash, and puddings. *Benchmark main dish: pie with mash and gravy £7.50. Two-course evening meal £20.00*

Free house ~ Licensee Dan Buckland ~ Real ale ~ Open 12-3, 6-11; 12-midnight Sat; 12-11 Sun ~ Bar food 12-9; 12-3 Mon, Thurs – evening food available if pre-booked ~ Children welcome away from bar area ~ Dogs welcome ~ Wi-fi ~ Quiz first Sat of month, open mike last Sun of month *Recommended by Alf Wright, Len and Lilly Dowson, Dan and Nicki Barton, Buster May, Charles Todd*

CHEADLE SK0342 Map 7

Queens at Freehay

(01538) 722383 – www.queensatfreehay.co.uk

A mile SE of Cheadle; take Rakeway Road off A522 (via Park Avenue or Mills Road), then after a mile turn into Counslow Road; ST10 1RF

Gently civilised dining pub with three real ales and attractive garden

Of course, many customers are here to enjoy the good food but some seating is set aside for those who want just a drink and a chat. The neat rooms have some cottagey touches that blend in well with the modern refurbishments. The comfortable lounge bar has pale wood tables on stripped-wood floors, small country pictures and curtains with matching cushions. It opens via an arch into a simple light and airy dining area with elegant chairs and tables on tartan carpeting. Helpful staff serve Lancaster Bomber, Marstons Pedigree and Wells Bombardier on handpump and ten wines by the glass. In warm weather, the attractive and immaculately kept little back garden is a pleasant place to sit, with picnic-sets among mature shrubs and flowering tubs.

A fine choice of food includes tiger prawn and mussel marinière, mushroom, black pudding and cheddar melt with creamy peppercorn sauce, pasta with sunblush tomato, basil, garlic and pine nut pesto with baby spinach and parmesan, burger with toppings, crispy onions and chips, moroccan harissa chicken with couscous, slow-roast lamb shank with real ale, rosemary and redcurrant jus, 34-day-aged rib-eye steak with a choice of four sauces, and puddings such as syrup sponge and custard and mini Aero cheesecake; posh fish supper is Tuesday and grill nights are Monday and Wednesday. *Benchmark main dish: beef in red wine pie £13.95. Two-course evening meal £20.00.*

Free house ~ Licensee Adrian Rock ~ Real ale ~ Open 12-3, 6-11; 12-4, 6.30-10.30 Sun ~ Bar food 12-2, 6-9.30; 12-2.30, 6.30-9.30 Sun ~ Restaurant ~ Children welcome ~ Wi-fi *Recommended by Frank and Marcia Pelling, George Sanderson, Alexander and Trish Cutter, Amy and Luke Buchanan*

ELLASTONE

SK1143 Map 7

Duncombe Arms

(01335) 324275 – www.duncombearms.co.uk

Main Road; DE6 2GZ

Staffordshire Dining Pub of the Year

Nooks and crannies, a thoughtful choice of drinks, friendly staff and lovely food; seats and tables in large garden

Whether you're out for a walk or to have a seriously good meal, there's a welcome for all in this stylishly refurbished village pub. There's somewhere interesting to sit whatever the occasion, and as well as beams, the rooms have bare-brick, exposed-stone and painted walls, open fires and woodburners, horse prints and photos, big bold paintings of pigs, sheep, cows and chickens, large clocks and fresh flowers, and stubby candles on mantelpieces, in big glass jars and on the tables. Flooring ranges from carpet to flagstones, bare floorboards and brick. Furnishings are just as eclectic: long leather button-back and cushioned wall seats, armchairs, all manner of wooden or upholstered dining chairs and tables made from mahogany, pine and even driftwood. They serve a beer named for the pub plus Marstons Pedigree and Rat White Rat on handpump, 50 wines by the glass from a fine list, 30 gins and over 25 malt whiskies; background music. An appealing terrace has wooden or rush seats around tables under parasols, braziers for cooler evenings and a view down over the garden to Worthy Island Wood.

Excellent food includes sandwiches, ham and parsley terrine with violet mustard and pickles, salmon rillettes with cucumber and radish, pea and wild garlic risotto with cheese, smoked haddock with colcannon, a soft poached egg and grain mustard, burger with toppings and skin-on fries, duck breast with cabbage and bacon, celeriac purée and duck fat chips, rare-breed pork chop with hispi cabbage, mash and apple sauce, and puddings such as green apple soufflé and cinnamon ice-cream and sticky toffee pudding with crystallised pecans and ginger ice-cream; they also offer a two- and three-course set menu (not Friday or Saturday evenings, or all Sunday). *Benchmark main dish: rib-eye steak with peppercorn sauce £25.00. Two-course evening meal £28.00.*

Free house ~ Licensees Johnny and Laura Greenall ~ Real ale ~ Open 12-11; 12-midnight Sat; 12-10 Sun; closed one week Jan ~ Bar food 12-2.30, 6-9; 12-5 Sun ~ Restaurant ~ Children welcome ~ Dogs allowed in bar ~ Wi-fi *Recommended by Millie and Peter Downing, Brian and Anna Marsden, Elise and Charles Mackinlay, Brian and Sally Wakeham*

Pubs close to motorway junctions are listed at the back of the book.

LONGDON GREEN SK0813 Map 7

Red Lion

(01543) 490410 – www.brunningandprice.co.uk/redlion

Hay Lane; WS15 4QF

Large, well run pub with interesting furnishings, a fine range of drinks, enjoyable food and spreading garden

In summer, it's relaxing to sit and watch cricket matches on the village green opposite this handsome pub; there's also a large garden with seats and tables on a suntrap terrace, picnic-sets on grass, a gazebo and swings and a play tractor for children. The interior has been extended and thoughtfully opened up but the bustling bar remains the heart of the place, with spreading rooms and nooks and crannies leading off. One dining room has skylights, rugs on nice old bricks, house plants lining the windowsill, an elegant metal chandelier and a miscellany of cushioned dining chairs around dark wooden tables. Similar furnishings fill the other rooms, and the walls are covered with old photos, pictures and prints relating to the local area and big gilt-edged mirrors; background music and board games. Open fires include a raised central fire pit. You'll find Phoenix Brunning & Price Original and guests such as Blythe Bagots Bitter, Palmers Poison and Staffie, Froth Blowers Piffle Snonker and Wye Valley Butty Bach on handpump, 20 wines by the glass, 50 malt whiskies, 30 gins and two farm ciders. Staff are friendly, courteous and helpful.

Appealing food includes sandwiches, crab mousse and smoked salmon with lemon and caper salad, beetroot polenta with celeriac and apple rémoulade and sweetcorn, smoked haddock and salmon fishcake with a poached egg and chive and caper sauce, sweet potato, courgette and aubergine thai red curry, chicken breast with creamed mushroom, spinach and tarragon pasta and parmesan, sea bass with spinach, samphire and a shallot and caper butter, duck breast with asian vegetable and egg noodle stir-fry and miso broth, and puddings such as lemon mousse with raspberries and crushed meringue and cherry and almond bakewell with cherry crumble ice-cream. *Benchmark main dish: beer-battered cod and chips £13.75. Two-course evening meal £20.00.*

Brunning & Price ~ Manager Paul Drain ~ Real ale ~ Open 10.30am-11pm; 10.30-10.30 Sun ~ Bar food 12-9.30 (9 Sun) ~ Restaurant ~ Children welcome ~ Dogs allowed in bar ~ Wi-fi

Recommended by Susan Jackman, Luke Morgan, Christine and Tony Garrett, Usha and Terri Patel, Serena and Adam Furber, Miranda and Jeff Davidson

SALT SJ9527 Map 7

Holly Bush £

(01889) 508234 – www.hollybushinn.co.uk

Village signposted off A51 S of Stone (and A518 NE of Stafford); ST18 0BX

Delightful medieval pub with all-day food

Decked with brightly coloured flowers in summer, this thatched pub is in a pretty village; it's worth arriving early in good weather as the back garden is beautifully tended and filled with flowers, and the rustic picnic-sets on a big lawn get quickly snapped up. From the standing-only serving section, several cosy areas spread out with high-backed cushioned pews, old tables and more conventional seats. The oldest part has a heavy-beamed and planked ceiling (some of the beams are attractively carved), a woodburning stove and a salt cupboard built into a big inglenook, with other nice old-fashioned touches including copper utensils, horsebrasses and an ancient pair of riding boots on the mantelpiece. A modern back extension, with beams, stripped brickwork and a small coal fire, blends in well. Adnams Southwold, Marstons Pedigree and a beer named for the pub (from Marstons) on handpump, alongside ten wines by the glass. They operate a secure locker system for credit cards, which they'll ask to keep if you run a tab.

Well regarded and fair-priced (the Value Award is for lunchtime choices) the food includes lunchtime sandwiches, baguettes and toasties, baked camembert with apricot preserve, prawn cocktail, goats cheese, field mushroom and basil wellington with sautéed potatoes and herby tomato sauce, honey- and mustard-glazed ham with poached eggs, salmon, lemon and dill fishcakes with parsley sauce, chilli con carne, slow-cooked venison casserole, free-range chicken breast with bacon, chorizo, salami, barbecue sauce and melted mozzarella, greek-style lamb shoulder with greek salad, fresh fish dish of the day, and puddings. *Benchmark main dish: steak and kidney pudding £13.45. Two-course evening meal £19.00.*

Admiral Taverns ~ Licensee Geoffrey Holland ~ Real ale ~ Open 12-11 (10.30 Sun) ~ Bar food 12-9.30 (9 Sun) ~ Children welcome ~ Wi-fi *Recommended by Dr D J and Mrs S C Walker, Alistair Forsyth, Belinda Stamp, Martine and Lawrence Sanders, Celia and Geoff Clay*

SWYNNERTON SJ8535 Map 7

Fitzherbert Arms

(01782) 796782 – www.fitzherbertarms.co.uk

Off A51 Stone–Nantwich; ST15 0RA

Thoughtfully renovated pub with character rooms, interesting décor, local ales and rewarding food; seats outside with country views

If you time the circular walk (mentioned on their website) from this charming, village-centre pub just right, you can arrive here ready for lunch; dogs are greeted with a biscuit and bowl of water. It's been thoughtfully refurbished and once through an impressive glass door, the bar sits to the right with a raised fireplace styled like a furnace along with blacksmith's tools and relics. Down a step to the left is the older part of the pub, with button-back leather armchairs beside a two-way fireplace, rugs on flagstones, hops and some fine old brickwork. Fitzherbert Best (from Weetwood) and Swynnerton Stout (from Titanic) on handpump with a couple of guests from breweries within a 35-mile radius; also, 16 good wines by the glass, 30 fantastic and carefully chosen ports with helpful notes (they hold port tasting evenings – phone for details), a dozen gins and a farm cider from the Apple County Cider Company. Staff are helpful and friendly. The beamed dining room is similarly furnished with a nice mix of old dining chairs and tables, plus window seats with scatter cushions, gilt-edged mirrors, black and white photographs and chandeliers; background music and board games. Do look out for the glass-topped giant bellows and anvil tables, door handles made of historic smithy irons, and candles in old port bottles. Outside, a covered, oak-timbered terrace has contemporary seats around rustic tables, heaters, fairy-lit shrubs in pots and country views; there are more seats in a small hedged garden. The pub is owned by Tim Bird and Mary McLaughlin of Cheshire Cat Pubs & Bars.

Highly enjoyable food includes sandwiches, sharing plates, braised pig cheeks with apple and balsamic glaze and crispy squid and apple salad, seared scallops with pickled courgette and samphire and lemon and brown shrimp butter, aubergine, chickpea and squash with pomegranate and apricots and cauliflower fritters, smoked fish pie with seasonal vegetables, crispy buttermilk chicken burger with black garlic mayonnaise, coleslaw and chips, pork chop with sage butter, spring onion mash and spring cabbage and bacon, and puddings such as lemon meringue cheesecake and sticky toffee pudding with vanilla ice-cream. *Benchmark main dish: steak in ale pie £13.95. Two-course evening meal £19.00.*

Free house ~ Licensee James Griffiths ~ Real ale ~ Open 12-11; 12-10.30 Sun ~ Bar food 12-9.15; 12-9.45 Sat; 12-8.30 Sun ~ Children welcome but no under-10s after 7pm ~ Dogs allowed in bar ~ Wi-fi ~ Live acoustic music Fri evening, jazz Sun lunchtime *Recommended by Diane Abbott, Martin and Joanne Sharp, Jane Rigby, Joe and Belinda Smart, Charlotte and William Mason, Naomi and Andrew Randall*

WRINEHILL SJ7547 Map 7

Hand & Trumpet

(01270) 820048 – www.brunningandprice.co.uk/hand

A531 Newcastle–Nantwich; CW3 9BJ

All-day food in big attractive dining pub with a good choice of ales and wines by the glass, served by courteous staff

With appealing food and an excellent choice of drinks, this substantial place is always full of chatty customers. The linked open-plan areas work their way around the long, solidly built counter, with a mix of dining chairs and sturdy tables on polished tiles or stripped oak boards with rugs. There are nicely lit prints and mirrors on cream walls between a mainly dark dado, lots of house plants, open fires and deep red ceilings. Original bow windows and a large skylight keep the place light and airy, and french windows open on to a spacious balustraded deck with teak tables and chairs, and a view down to ducks swimming on a big pond in the sizeable garden. Friendly attentive staff serve Phoenix Brunning & Price Original and Salopian Oracle with guests such as Facers North Star Porter, Hawkshead Windermere Pale, Timothy Taylors Landlord and Weetwood Eastgate on handpump, as well as 16 wines by the glass, 20 rums, 40 gins, 20 bourbons and about 70 whiskies; board games. Good disabled access and facilities.

Distinctive food includes sandwiches, garlic and rosemary baked camembert with fruit chutney, chicken liver pâté with carrot and apricot chutney, cauliflower, sweet potato and chickpea tagine with quinoa and toasted almonds, steak burger with toppings, coleslaw and chips, slow-roasted pork belly with black pudding boulangère, celeriac and pig cheek fritter and cider jus, braised lamb shoulder with roast potatoes and gravy, hake fillet wrapped in prosciutto ham with butter bean and spinach cassoulet and chorizo crisps, thai green chicken curry, and puddings such as triple chocolate brownie with chocolate sauce and glazed clementine tart with orange sorbet. *Benchmark main dish: crispy beef salad with sweet chilli, lemongrass and cashews £13.95. Two-course evening meal £21.00.*

Brunning & Price ~ Manager Ryan Platt ~ Real ale ~ Open 12-11 (10.30 Sun) ~ Bar food 12-9.30 (9 Sun) ~ Children welcome ~ Dogs allowed in bar ~ Wi-fi *Recommended by Laura Reid, Chris Stevenson, Sabine and Gerald Grimshaw, Caroline and Peter Bryant, Alexandra and Richard Clay, Mark and Mary Setting*

A star symbol after the name of a pub shows exceptional character and appeal. It doesn't mean extra comfort. And it's nothing to do with exceptional food quality, for which there's a separate star-on-a-plate symbol. Even quite a basic pub can win a star, if it's individual enough.

Also Worth a Visit in Staffordshire

Besides the fully inspected pubs, you might like to try these pubs that have been recommended to us and described by readers. Do tell us what you think of them: feedback@goodguides.com

ABBOTS BROMLEY SK0824

Coach & Horses (01283) 840256
High Street; WS15 3BN Well cared for 18th-c village pub with good choice of popular home-made food (not Sun evening) from baguettes and pizzas up, also good value weekday deals, Marstons Pedigree, St Austell Tribute and a guest, several wines by the glass; beamed bar with stone floor and button-back banquettes, dark wood pubby furniture in carpeted restaurant, log fire; children and dogs (in bar) welcome, pleasant garden with circular picnic-sets, open all day Sun. *(Charlotte and William Mason)*

ABBOTS BROMLEY SK0824

Goats Head (01283) 840254
Market Place; WS15 3BP Black and white 16th-c village pub under welcoming new management; well kept Jennings Cumberland, Marstons Pedigree and a guest, nice range of gins and enjoyable good value food including blackboard specials, opened-up beamed interior with oak floors, traditional furnishings and fire in large inglenook; children and dogs welcome, tables on deck and sheltered lawn looking up to church tower. *(Amy and Luke Buchanan)*

ALSAGERS BANK SJ8048

Gresley Arms (01782) 722469
High Street; ST7 8BQ At the top of Alsagers Bank with wonderful far-reaching views from the back, welcoming and popular, with eight or more interesting ales from smaller breweries and several real ciders, ample helpings of good value pubby food (not Mon-Weds lunchtimes or Sun evening) including bargain Thurs steak night (must book) and eat-for-£1 Mon if you buy a drink, traditional slate-floor bar with beams and open fire, comfortable lounge, picture-window dining room taking in the view, and a lower family room (children's menu); Mon quiz; walkers and dogs welcome, garden picnic-sets, Apedale Heritage Centre nearby, open all day Thurs-Sun, otherwise from 3pm. *(Nick)*

ALSTONEFIELD SK1355

★**George** (01335) 310205
Village signed from A515 Ashbourne–Buxton; DE6 2FX Simply furnished family-run pub in pretty village overlooking small green; chatty bar with low beams and quarry tiles, old Peak District photographs and pictures, log fire, Marstons-related ales and a dozen wines by the glass from copper-topped counter, really good imaginative food (can be pricey) using some home-grown produce, friendly efficient service, small snug and neat dining room with woodburner, simple farmhouse furniture, candlelight; free wi-fi, children and dogs (in bar) welcome, picnic-sets out at front, more seats in big sheltered stableyard behind, open all day Fri and Sat, till 9.30pm Sun. *(Clive and Fran Dutson, GSB, Maxine Carlier)*

ARMITAGE SK0716

Plum Pudding (01543) 490330
Rugeley Road (A513); WS15 4AZ Canalside pub and italian restaurant; good food in bar and dining room including selection of small plates (piattini) and daily specials, well kept Bass, Greene King Old Speckled Hen and a guest, friendly helpful staff; children welcome, no dogs inside, tables on waterside terrace and narrow canal bank, moorings, open (and food) all day. *(Robert W Buckle)*

BIDDULPH SJ8959

Talbot (01782) 512608
Grange Road (N, right off A527); ST8 7RY Family dining pub in 19th-c stone building (Vintage Inn); enjoyable freshly made food including weekday set menus, well kept ales such as Sharps, and decent choice of other drinks, raised two-way log fire in restaurant part, some secluded areas; background music; dogs allowed in tiled bar area, handy for Biddulph Grange (NT), open (and food) all day. *(Suzy Miller)*

BLACKBROOK SJ7638

Swan with Two Necks (01782) 680343 *Nantwich Road (A51); ST5 5EH* Country pub-restaurant with smart modern décor in open-plan split-level dining areas, good well presented food (booking advised) from sharing boards up, Timothy Taylors Landlord, three guest ales and plenty of wines by the glass including champagne; background music; children welcome, tables in garden and on parasol-shaded deck, open (and food) all day. *(Alexandra and Richard Clay)*

BREWOOD SJ8808

Swan (01902) 850330
Market Place; ST19 9BS Former coaching inn with two low-beamed bars and inglenook log fire; well kept Wye Valley HPA, Courage Directors and four guests such as Salopian and Burton Bridge, good selection of whiskies

We say if we know a pub allows dogs.

and gins, no food; upstairs skittle alley, Sun quiz; dogs allowed, open all day. *(Tony Hobden)*

BURTON UPON TRENT SK2523

★**Burton Bridge Inn** (01283) 536596
Bridge Street (A50); DE14 1SY Friendly down-to-earth local with good Burton Bridge ales from brewery across old-fashioned brick yard; simple little front area leading into adjacent bar, plain walls hung with notices, awards and brewery memorabilia, 16 malt whiskies and lots of country wines, small beamed and oak-panelled lounge with simple furniture and flame-effect fire, upstairs dining room and skittle alley, short choice of low-priced lunchtime food Thurs-Sat, steak night first Tues of month, fish night third Tues; no credit cards; children and dogs (in bar) welcome, open all day Fri, Sat, closed Mon lunchtime. *(Colin Gooch)*

BURTON UPON TRENT SK2423

★**Coopers Tavern** (01283) 532551
Cross Street; DE14 1EG Traditionally refurbished 19th-c backstreet local tied to Joules – was tap for the Bass brewery and still has some wonderful ephemera including mirrors and glazed adverts; homely and warm with coal fire, straightforward front parlour, back bar doubling as tap room with their beers, up to half a dozen guests (including Bass) and good selection of ciders/perries, cheese boards and pies only but can bring your own food (or take beer to next-door curry house); regular live music; children (till 8pm) and dogs welcome, small back garden, open all day Thurs-Sun, from 4pm other days. *(Dave Braisted)*

CHEDDLETON SJ9752

Black Lion (01538) 360620
Leek Road, by the church; ST13 7HP Convivial bustling atmosphere at this 19th-c village local; generous helpings of good traditional lunchtime food including popular Sun roasts, Fri night fish and chips, otherwise just snacks such as local pork pies in the evening, Bass, Timothy Taylors Landlord and a couple of guests, Weston's cider, friendly efficient staff; some live music, pool and darts; children and dogs welcome, seats out in front and in fenced back garden, open all day. *(Brian and Anna Marsden)*

CHEDDLETON SJ9751

Boat (01538) 360521
Basford Bridge Lane, off A520; ST13 7EQ Cheerful unpretentious canal-side local handy for Churnet Valley steam railway, flint mill and country park; long bar with low plank ceiling, well kept Marstons-related ales and enjoyable honest food from sandwiches to steaks, dining room behind; live music; children welcome, dogs in bar, seats out overlooking Caldon Canal, open all day. *(Tony Hobden)*

CODSALL SJ8603

Codsall Station (01902) 847061
Chapel Lane/Station Road; WV8 2EH Converted vintage waiting room and ticket office of working station, comfortable and welcoming with well kept Holdens ales and a couple of guests, good value pubby food (not Mon) including home-made pork pies and blackboard specials, just sandwiches and pies Sun, lots of railway memorabilia, open fire, conservatory, free wi-fi; children and dogs welcome, disabled access, terrace seating, open all day. *(Claire Adams)*

CONSALL SK0049

Black Lion (01782) 550294
Consall Forge, OS Sheet 118 map reference 000491; best approach from Nature Park, off A522, using car park 0.5 miles past Nature Centre; ST9 0AJ Traditional take-us-as-you-find-us place tucked away in rustic canalside spot by restored steam railway station; generous helpings of enjoyable pub food, up to five well kept ales including Black Hole and several ciders, flagstones and good coal fire; background music; children and dogs welcome, seats out overlooking canal, area for campers and shop for boaters, good walks, open all day and can get very busy weekend lunchtimes. *(Tony Hobden)*

COPMERE END SJ8029

Star (01785) 850279
W of Eccleshall; ST21 6EW Friendly two-room 19th-c country local with well kept Bass, Titanic Anchor, Wells Bombardier and a couple of guests, good choice of reasonably priced food from sandwiches up (not Sun evening), open fire and woodburner; occasional live music; children and dogs welcome, tables and play area in back garden overlooking mere, good walks, open all day weekends, closed Mon. *(Mark and Mary Setting)*

DENSTONE SK0940

Tavern (01889) 590847
College Road; ST14 5HR Welcoming 17th-c stone-built pub with good food (not Mon) including freshly made pizzas (Fri, Sat evenings) and Sun carvery, well kept Marstons ales and good range of wines by the glass, pleasant service, comfortable lounge with antiques, dining conservatory; darts, some live music, free wi-fi; children and dogs welcome, picnic-sets out at front among tubs and hanging baskets, village farm shop and lovely church, open all day Fri-Sun, closed Mon lunchtime. *(Celia and Geoff Hunt)*

DRAYCOTT IN THE MOORS SJ9840

Draycott Arms (01782) 911030
Junction of Uttoxeter Road and Cheadle Road; ST11 9RQ Welcoming modernised pub with good sensibly priced food including

selection of small tapas-style plates, Sharps Doom Bar and a guest, Aspall's cider, friendly attentive service, two-way woodburner separating bar and restaurant; darts; children and dogs (in bar) welcome, garden with covered area, open all day Sat, till 5pm Sun, closed Mon. *(Valerie Davis)*

DUSTON SP7262

Hopping Hare (01604) 580090

Hopping Hill Gardens; NN5 6PF Imposing red-brick former manor surrounded by housing; largish bar adjacent to entrance, log fires and lots of different dining areas, well kept Adnams, Black Sheep and a guest, good range of wines by the glass and highly rated attractively presented food, friendly efficient service; children welcome, dogs allowed outside, seats out on decking, 20 modern bedrooms, open (and food) all day. *(Gerry and Rosemary Dobson)*

ECCLESHALL SJ8329

Old Smithy (01785) 850564

Castle Street; ST21 6DF Comfortable pub-restaurant with clean modern décor; good freshly made food at fair prices including decent vegetarian options and some themed nights, four mainstream ales and good choice of other drinks, friendly efficient staff; children welcome, small external seating area for diners only, open (and food) all day. *(Amy and Luke Buchanan)*

ECCLESHALL SJ8329

Royal Oak (01785) 859065

High Street; ST21 6BW Restored beamed and colonnaded coaching inn with well kept Joules ales and enjoyable locally sourced food, friendly chatty staff; live music; children and dogs (in bar) welcome, beer garden, open (and food) all day, kitchen closes 4.30pm Sun. *(Claire Adams)*

FLASH SK0267

Travellers Rest/Knights Table

(01298) 236695 *A53 Buxton–Leek; SK17 0SN* Isolated main-road pub and one of the highest in Britain with views over the moors, clean and friendly, with good reasonably priced traditional food (not Sun evening), four well kept ales and good selection of wines, beams, bare stone walls and open fires, medieval knights theme; free wi-fi; children very welcome, no dogs inside, great Peak District views from back terrace, classic car meeting last Thurs of month, bedrooms, closed Mon and Tues, otherwise open all day. *(Nina Parker)*

FRADLEY SK1414

White Swan (01283) 790330

Fradley Junction; DE13 7DN Terrace-row pub (aka the Mucky Duck) in good canalside location at Trent & Mersey and Coventry junction; Everards ales and guests, enjoyable reasonably priced food including pizzas and popular Sun carvery, cheery traditional public bar with woodburner and open fire, quieter lounge and lower vaulted dining room (former stable); Thurs folk night, open mike Sun; children and dogs welcome, waterside tables, open all day. *(Jimmy)*

GNOSALL SJ8220

Boat (01785) 822208

Gnosall Heath, by Shropshire Union Canal Bridge 34; ST20 0DA Popular little canalside pub run by friendly family; comfortable first-floor bar with curved window seat overlooking narrowboats, Marstons-related ales and decent choice of reasonably priced pubby food including, steak night (second Tues of the month), open fire; darts and dominoes; children and dogs welcome, tables out by canal, moorings and nice walks, open all day weekends (no food Sun evening), closed Mon lunchtime. *(Claire Adams)*

GNOSALL SJ8220

George & Dragon 07779 327551

High Street; ST20 0EX Welcoming unpretentious little pub dating from 18th c; well kept Holdens Golden Glow, Woods Shropshire Lad and three guests, four proper ciders and decent range of other drinks, just snacky food such as cobs and home-made sausage rolls, simple interior with woodburner and some quirky tables made from old farming gear; dogs welcome, open all day weekends, from 4pm weekdays. *(Tony Hobden)*

HARTSHILL SJ8645

Jolly Potters 07875 586902

Hartshill Road (A52); ST4 7NH Welcoming traditional drinkers' pub with five rooms off central corridor; well kept Bass, Black Sheep and up to three guests, good selection of gins, no food apart from summer pizzas from outside oven; pool and darts; children and dogs welcome, garden with stage for live music, open from 3pm Mon-Fri (noon Sat, Sun). *(Celia and Geoff Hunt)*

HIGH OFFLEY SJ7725

Anchor (01785) 284569

Off A519 Eccleshall–Newport; towards High Lea, by Shropshire Union Canal Bridge 42; Peggs Lane; ST20 0NG Built around 1830 to serve the Shropshire Union Canal and little changed in the century or more this family has run it; two small simple front rooms, one with a couple of fine high-backed settles on quarry tiles, Wadworths 6X and Weston's cider, sandwiches on request, owners' sitting room behind bar; outbuilding with semi-open lavatories (swallows may fly through); no children inside, lovely garden with hanging baskets and notable topiary anchor, small shop, moorings (near Bridge 42), caravans/camping, closed Mon-Thurs in winter. *(Mark and Mary Setting)*

HIMLEY SO8990

★**Crooked House** (01384) 238583
Signed down long lane from B4176 Gornalwood–Himley, OS Sheet 139 map reference 896908; DY3 4DA Extraordinary sight, building thrown wildly out of kilter by mining subsidence, one side 4-ft lower than the other and slopes so weird that things appear to roll up them; public bar (dogs allowed here) with grandfather clock and hatch serving Banks's and other Marstons-related ales, lounge bar, good food from snacks and pub standards to more unusual choices, some local antiques in level extension, conservatory; children welcome in eating areas, big outside terrace, closed Mon, otherwise open all day (till 6pm Sun). *(Daniel King)*

HULME END SK1059

Manifold Inn (01298) 84537
B5054 Warslow–Hartington; SK17 0EX Fairly isolated stone coaching inn near River Manifold; enjoyable traditional home-made food at reasonable prices including Mon steak night, four well kept ales such as Cottage, Leatherbritches and Marstons, pleasant friendly staff, log fire in traditional carpeted bar, adjacent restaurant and conservatory; background music, TV; children and dogs (in some parts) welcome, disabled facilities, tables outside, 11 bedrooms (eight in converted barns), self-catering cottage, good walks including Manifold Trail, cycling routes nearby, open (and food) all day. *(Jimmy)*

KNIGHTON SJ7240

White Lion (01630) 647300
B5415 Woore–Market Drayton; TF9 4HJ Welcoming roadside country pub with good food from interestingly varied menu, up to 15 well kept local ales (including one badged for them) and extensive range of gins, friendly attentive service, beams and open fires, dining conservatory; some live music, darts; children and dogs welcome (pub dog is Ted), tables outside, closed lunchtimes Mon and Tues. *(Alexandra and Richard Clay)*

LEEK SJ9956

Earl Grey (01538) 372570
Ashbourne Road; ST13 5AT Traditional little red-brick corner pub with refurbished split-level interior; a house ale brewed by Whim plus several other interesting changing beers (tasters offered), real ciders and decent range of whiskies/gins, friendly knowledgeable staff and good mix of customers, no food; juke box, some live music and quiz nights; dogs welcome, open all day Fri-Sun, from 5pm Mon, 3pm other days. *(Tony Hobden)*

LEEK SJ9856

Wilkes Head 07976 592787
St Edward Street; ST13 5DS Friendly no-frills three-room local dating from the early 18th c (still has back coaching stables), owned by Whim with their ales and interesting guests, real ciders and good choice of whiskies, no food apart from rolls, lots of pump clips, pub games; juke box in back room and regular live music events including festivals organised by musician landlord; children allowed in one room (not really a family pub), dogs on leads (but do ask first as landlord has own dog), fair disabled access, garden with stage, open all day except Mon lunchtime. *(Nina Parker)*

LICHFIELD SK1109

Beerbohm (01543) 898252
Tamworth Street; WS13 6JP Increasingly popular continental style café-bar with enthusiastic friendly owners; four real ales including Salopian and a beer badged for them, plenty of international beers (draught and bottled) and good choice of other drinks, helpful knowledgeable staff, cosy bar with rug on wood floor, comfortable seating including armchairs and banquette by iron-framed tables, similar décor in upstairs lounge with prints, old beer advertising signs and large mirrors on plum or grey painted walls, no food but can bring your own (plates and cutlery supplied), tea and coffee; background music, free wi-fi; well behaved dogs welcome, closed Sun and Mon, otherwise open all day. *(Suzy Miller)*

LICHFIELD SK0705

Boat (01543) 361692
A461; from A5 at Muckley Corner, take A461 signed Walsall; continue over M6 Toll bridge and take next right (Hilton) to return on dual carriageway; WS14 0BU Refurbished beamed pub with emphasis on dining; view into kitchen from skylit entrance, split-level bar/eating areas with sturdy modern pine furniture on carpet or wooden floors, imaginative locally sourced food including all-day snacks and afternoon teas (not Sun), three changing ales and several wines by the glass, attentive friendly service; background music; children welcome, garden with seats on raised deck, closed Mon and Tues, otherwise open all day till 10pm. *(Daniel King)*

LICHFIELD SK1109

Duke of York (01543) 307313
Greenhill/Church Street; WS13 6DY Old beamed pub with split-level front bar, cosy carpeted lounge and converted back stables, inglenook woodburners, well kept Joules ales and guests, simple lunchtime food

If you report on a pub that's not a featured entry, please tell us any lunchtimes or evenings when it doesn't serve bar food.

(not Sun) served by pleasant staff; some live music, Apr beer festival; no children but dogs allowed, terrace picnic-sets behind and own bowling green, open all day. *(Charlotte and William Mason)*

LICHFIELD SK1308

Horse & Jockey (01543) 262924
Tamworth Road (A51 Lichfield–Tamworth); WS14 9JE Cosy old-fashioned pub with wide range of popular freshly prepared food including good home-made pies and fish specials (booking advised), ales such as Castle Rock, Marstons and Sharps, good friendly service, open fire; quiz nights, darts; children welcome if eating, no dogs, picnic sets and play area in back garden, open (and food) all day. *(Daniel King)*

LITTLE BRIDGEFORD SJ8727

Mill (01785) 282710
Worston Lane; near M6 junction 14; turn right off A5013 at Little Bridgeford; ST18 9QA Dining pub in attractive 1814 watermill; enjoyable sensibly priced food including Sun carvery, Greene King ales, good friendly service; Thurs quiz; children and dogs welcome, disabled access, nice grounds with adventure playground and nature trail (lakes, islands etc), open (and food) all day. *(Jimmy)*

LONGDON SK0814

Swan with Two Necks (01543) 491570 *Off A51 Lichfield–Rugeley; Brook Lane; WS15 4PN* Welcoming village pub with long low-beamed quarry-tiled bar, two-way woodburner and some leather wall benches, separate wood-floored lounge/restaurant with a couple of open fires, enjoyable fairly pubby food, Marston Pedigree, Sharps Doom Bar and two guests, good range of gins, friendly helpful service; children (away from bar) and dogs (in bar) welcome, garden with play area, open (and food) all day, kitchen shuts 7pm Sun. *(Mr and Mrs John Clifford)*

MARCHINGTON SK1330

Dog & Partridge (01283) 820394
Church Lane; ST14 8LJ Flower-decked 18th-c village pub with various beamed and tile-floored rooms; Bass and three changing guests (beer festivals), good food (not Sun evening) including themed nights and bargain two-course lunch, good value wines, attentive friendly staff, real fires and some interesting bits and pieces; background music (live Sun from 5pm), free wi-fi; children and dogs (in bar) welcome, tables under parasols in paved back terrace by car park, open all day. *(Amy and Luke Buchanan)*

MEERBROOK SJ9960

Lazy Trout (01538) 300385
Centre of village; ST13 8SN Popular country dining pub with good sensibly priced food from regularly changing menu including daily specials, friendly helpful staff, small bar area serving five well kept ales such as Greene King, Marstons and Wincle from curved stone counter, log fire in comfortable dining lounge on the right, another dining room to the left with quarry tiles, pine furniture and old cooking range; juke box; children welcome, dogs and muddy boots in some parts, seats out at front by quiet lane and in appealing garden behind (splendid views to the Roaches and Hen Cloud), good walks, open (and food) all day. *(Clive and Fran Dutson)*

NEWBOROUGH SK1325

Red Lion (01283) 576182
Duffield Lane; DE13 8SH Old pub facing church in quiet village; comfortable bar with open fire, Marstons-related ales including Pedigree and good choice of other drinks, enjoyable fair-priced food from snacks to pub classics, smallish dining room, friendly accommodating staff; children welcome, seats out at front, open (and food) all day, kitchen shuts 6pm Sun. *(Nina Parker)*

ONECOTE SK0455

★**Jervis Arms** (01538) 304206
B5053; ST13 7RU Cosy whitewashed country pub refurbished under welcoming new management; five well kept changing ales, Celtic Marches cider and good range of wines and gins, generous helpings of popular reasonably priced food including set menu (Tues and Weds) and good Sun roasts, friendly prompt service, woodburners in all three rooms, beams and some exposed stonework, settles and other country furniture on old quarry tiles or wood floors; occasional live music, darts; children and dogs welcome, streamside (River Hamps) garden with footbridge to car park, open (and food) all day in summer, closed weekday lunchtimes and all day Mon in winter. *(Claire Adams)*

PENKRIDGE SJ9214

Littleton Arms (01785) 716300
St Michaels Square/A449 – M6 detour between junctions 12 and 13; ST19 5AL Cheerfully busy dining pub-hotel (former coaching inn) with contemporary open-plan interior; good variety of enjoyable well presented food from sandwiches and sharing boards to popular Sun roasts, five well kept changing ales and appealing choice of wines/gins from island servery, afternoon teas,

Half pints: by law, a pub should not charge more for half a pint than half the price of a full pint, unless it shows that half-pint price on its price list.

friendly accommodating staff; background music (live last Fri of the month); children and dogs (in bar area) welcome, terrace seating under parasols, ten bedrooms, open all day (till midnight Fri, Sat), breakfast from 7am Mon-Fri (8am weekends). *(Richard Moore, Tony Hobden)*

RUGELEY SK0418

Yorkshireman (01889) 583977
Near railway station, junction Colton Road (B5013) and Blithbury Road; WS15 3HB Friendly pub with enjoyable bistro-style food from good value fixed-price menus, local Blythe and Freedom beers, a dozen wines by the glass including champagne, friendly staff, restaurant; children and dogs (in bar) welcome, tables in back garden, shuts 9.30pm (8pm Sun). *(Dan Dodd)*

SEIGHFORD SJ8725

Hollybush (01785) 281644
3 miles from M6 junction 14 via A5013/B5405; ST18 9PQ Modernised and extended beamed pub owned by the village; good value locally sourced pubby food (not Sun evening, Mon lunchtime) from sandwiches and light choices up, ales including Titanic and Everards; Sun quiz, portable skittle alley; children and dogs welcome, disabled access, beer garden, open all day Fri-Sun. *(Sandra Morgan)*

SHEEN SK1160

Staffordshire Knot (01298) 84329
Off B5054 at Hulme End; SK17 0ET Welcoming traditional 17th-c stone-built village pub; nice mix of old furniture on flagstones or red and black tiles, stag's head and hunting prints, two log fires in hefty stone fireplaces, good interesting food cooked by landlady (booking advised), well kept local Whim Hartington and reasonably priced wines, friendly helpful staff; closed Mon. *(Daniel King)*

SHENSTONE SK1004

Plough (01543) 481800
Pinfold Hill, off A5127; WS14 0JN Village dining pub with clean modern interior; enjoyable locally sourced food (not Sun evening) from sandwiches, sharing boards and pizzas up, ales such as Greene King and Holdens, good range of wines by the glass, friendly service; children welcome, dogs in bar, tables out on front terrace, open all day. *(Mark and Mary Setting)*

STAFFORD SJ9323

Swan (01785) 258142
Greengate Street; ST16 2JA Modernised 18th-c two-bar coaching inn; well kept Marstons-related ales and guests, cocktails and plenty of wines by the glass, good bar and brasserie food including lunchtime set menu and Weds steak night, vegetarians/vegans catered for too, coffee shop, friendly helpful staff; occasional live music in courtyard garden, 31 bedrooms, open (and food) all day, weekend brunch from 11am. *(Jimmy)*

STANLEY SJ9352

Travellers Rest (01782) 502580
Off A53 NE of Stoke; ST9 9LX Comfortable old stone village pub with large restaurant/bar area; beams and some exposed stonework, pubby tables and chairs on patterned carpet, button-back banquettes, brassware and knick-knacks, well kept Bass, Marstons Pedigree and guests from central servery, wide choice of reasonably priced popular food including deals (booking advised), friendly helpful service; children allowed away from bar, no dogs inside, tables out at front under parasols, self-catering cottages, open all day, food all day weekends. *(Tony Hobden)*

STOKE-ON-TRENT SJ8649

Bulls Head (01782) 834153
St Johns Square, Burslem; ST6 3AJ Old-fashioned two-room tap for Titanic with up to ten real ales (including guests) from horseshoe bar, also good selection of belgian beers, ciders and wines; well cared-for interior with varnished tables on wood or carpeted floors, coal fire; bar billiards and table skittles; drinking area outside (may be barbecue if Port Vale are at home), open all day Fri-Sun, closed till 3pm other days. *(Daniel King)*

STOKE-ON-TRENT SJ8745

Glebe (01782) 860670
35 Glebe Street, by the Civic Centre; ST4 1HG Well restored 19th-c Joules corner pub, their ales, Weston's cider and good reasonably priced wines from central mahogany counter, William Morris leaded windows, bare boards and panelling, some civic portraits and big fireplace with coat of arms above, wholesome bar food (not Sun, Mon evening) from good doorstep sandwiches up, friendly staff; quite handy for station, open all day. *(Dr J Barrie Jones)*

STOKE-ON-TRENT SJ8647

Holy Inadequate 07771 358238
Etruria Old Road; ST1 5PE Drinkers' pub with well kept Joules Pale Ale and several guest ales, craft kegs, german lagers and lots of bottled beers, snacky food such as pies and scotch eggs, friendly staff; dogs welcome, open all day Fri-Sun, from 4pm other days. *(Tony Hobden)*

STONE SJ9034

Royal Exchange (01785) 812685
Corner Radford Street (A520) and Northesk Street; ST15 8DA End-of-terrace pub owned by Titanic; their well kept ales and several guests including Everards, snacky lunchtime food (Fri and

Sat only), also Mon evening meal deal, friendly helpful staff, three seating areas (steps) and two fires; occasional acoustic music and quiz nights; dogs welcome, open all day (till midnight Fri, Sat).
(Tony Hobden)

STOWE SK0027

Bistro le Coq (01889) 270237

Off A518 Stafford–Uttoxeter; ST18 0LF Bistro-style conversion of old beamed pub opposite village church; well executed french food including good value set menus, split-level restaurant and small bar area serving real ale and seven wines by the glass from french list (mainly smaller producers), friendly efficient service; well behaved children welcome, country views from garden behind, closed Sun evening, Mon. *(Celia and Geoff Hunt)*

TAMWORTH SK2004

Market Vaults (01827) 66552

Market Street next to Town Hall; B79 7LU Popular and friendly traditional little pub with front bar and raised back lounge, dark oak, brass and original fireplaces, well kept Joules Pale Ale and seven guests, up to 16 real ciders, bargain lunchtime food (not Mon); regular live music, TV, free wi-fi; nice garden behind, open all day. *(Colin Gooch, Dave Braisted)*

TRYSULL SO8594

Bell (01902) 892871

Bell Road; WV5 7JB Extended 18th-c red-brick village pub next to church; cosy bar, inglenook lounge and large high-ceilinged back dining area, well kept Bathams, Holdens and guests, reasonably priced wines and decent food including Sun roasts; children and dogs (in bar) welcome, paved front terrace, open all day, no food Sun evening. *(Amy and Luke Buchanan)*

WATERFALL SK0851

Red Lion (01538) 308279

From A523 at Waterhouses, take Waterfall Lane; ST10 3HZ Welcoming stone-built pub in quiet Peak village; log fires in two linked rooms, three well kept ales and enjoyable traditional food (not Sun evening); darts; children and dogs welcome, tables outside with lovely country views, closed weekday lunchtimes, open all day weekends. *(Daniel King)*

WETTON SK1055

Royal Oak (01335) 310287

Village signed off Hulme End–Alstonefield road, between B5054 and A515; DE6 2AF Old stone pub in lovely NT countryside – a popular stop for walkers; traditional bar with white ceiling boards above black beams, small dining chairs around rustic tables and log fire in stone fireplace, carpeted sun lounge, four well kept ales such as Heritage, Storm, Whim and Wincle, good selection of malt whiskies, enjoyable fairly priced home-made food from sandwiches up, friendly helpful staff; children and dogs welcome, picnic-sets in shaded garden, camping, open all day Fri and Sat, till around 9pm Sun, closed Mon, Tues. *(Nina Parker)*

WHEATON ASTON SJ8512

Hartley Arms (01785) 840232

Long Street (canalside, Tavern Bridge); ST19 9NF Popular roomy pub in pleasant spot just above Shropshire Union Canal (Bridge 19); good affordably priced food from landlord-chef including OAP lunch deal (Mon-Fri), Thurs grill night and Sun carvery, well kept Banks's and other Marstons-related beers, efficient friendly service; children welcome, no dogs, picnic-sets outside, open all day.
(Sandra Morgan)

Suffolk

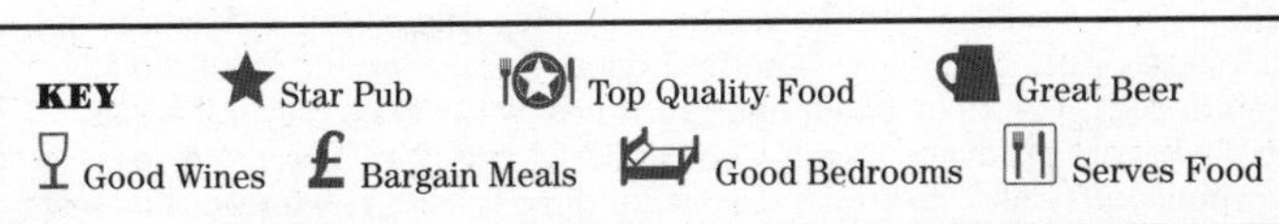

ALDEBURGH TM4656 Map 5

Cross Keys

(01728) 452637 – www.adnams.co.uk

Crabbe Street; IP15 5BN

16th-c pub with seats outside near the beach, chatty atmosphere, friendly licensee and local beers; bedrooms

The seafront position means this traditional old pub is much favoured in summer; the seats on the sheltered back terrace look across the promenade and shingle to the water. The low-ceilinged interconnecting bars come with a cheerful, bustling atmosphere and a warm welcome from the obliging landlord, as well as antique and other pubby furniture, miscellaneous paintings on the walls and log fires in two inglenook fireplaces. Adnams Broadside, Ghost Ship and Southwold on handpump, six decent wines by the glass and eight malt whiskies; background music and games machine. The bedrooms are attractively furnished.

Popular food includes home-made soup, ploughman's, salt and pepper squid, fresh fish dishes such as mussels, whole plaice, skate wing with brown butter and cromer crab, and puddings such as fruit crumble and sticky toffee pudding. *Benchmark main dish: beer-battered cod and chips £10.95. Two-course evening meal £17.00.*

Adnams ~ Tenants Mike and Janet Clement ~ Real ale ~ Open 11-11; 12-11 Sun ~ Bar food 12-2.30, 6.30-8.30 (9 Fri); 12-3, 6.30-9 Sat; 12-3 Sun ~ Children welcome away from bar ~ Dogs welcome ~ Wi-fi ~ Bedrooms: £75/£95 *Recommended by Comus and Sarah Elliott, Brian and Susan Wylie, Sandra Morgan, Tracey and Stephen Groves*

BARROW TL7663 Map 5

Weeping Willow

(01284) 771881 – www.theweepingwillow.co.uk

Off A45 W of Bury; IP29 5AB

Carefully refurbished old village pub with up-to-date colourful furnishings, first class food, kind service and prettily planted garden

Reopened after a three-year closure, this 16th-c village pub – recorded as one of the oldest buildings in the village – has been carefully and thoughtfully restored and refurbished, blending modern décor with some fine original features. Walk through the main door to an area with very high-backed floral as well as purple leather armchairs in front of an open fire; this leads into the bar with black leather stools against the counter (there are more by a couple of high tables), plush button-back bucket seats and candy-striped wall seats around a few tables on pale wood flooring and blue leather chesterfield sofas. The raftered dining room gives 90-degree views through huge glass windows of the garden and is furnished with colourful upholstered dining chairs, marble-topped tables and a long, high-backed banquette that separates this from a 'chef's table' area by the open kitchen; there's also a private dining room that seats up to 14 people. A small beamed room with stylish modern flower arrangements (one of the owners is a renowned florist) has blue, purple and pink plush stools and cushioned wall seating. A fine range of drinks includes Adnams Ghost Ship and Southwold, Nethergate Suffolk County, Timothy Taylors Boltmaker and Landlord and Woodfordes Wherry on handpump, 16 wines by the glass (several wines on the list are produced locally), cocktails, 21 gins, farm cider and early morning coffee and afternoon tea; background music. The terrace has seats under parasols and stools by long rustic tables; this spills into the beautifully planted garden with walkways, which in turn extends in a meadow with a safely fenced area for children to run around.

Imaginative food from seasonal menus includes nibbles and sandwiches, chicken liver parfait with fig and apple chutney, artichoke, brie and leek tart, butter and thyme roasted chicken with caesar salad and a soft poached egg, artichoke and olive pasta with salsa verde and feta, hake with chorizo and mussel broth, white beans, capers and dill, a trio of sausages with mash, crispy onions and red wine jus, chicken and wild mushroom pie, local lamb rump with pickled red cabbage and piccolo parsnips, 40-day-aged rump steak with béarnaise sauce, and puddings such as chocolate brownie with cinnamon ice-cream and sticky toffee pudding with butterscotch sauce. *Benchmark main dish: seasonal risotto £13.90. Two-course evening meal £21.00.*

Free house ~ Licensee Paula Pryke ~ Real ale ~ Open 11-11; 12-10 Sun ~ Bar food 12-2.30, 6-9; 12-5.30 Sun ~ Restaurant ~ Children welcome ~ Dogs allowed in bar ~ Wi-fi
Recommended by Alexandra and Tim Fledgling, Barbara and Phil Bowie, Jamie and Lizzie McEwan

BROMESWELL — TM3050 Map 5

Unruly Pig

(01394) 460310 – www.theunrulypig.co.uk
Orford Road, Bromeswell Heath; IP12 2PU

Refurbished dining pub with local ales, creative food, an informal feel, helpful, attentive staff and seats outside

There's always a good mix of customers here, from walkers and cyclists (there are cycle racks) to chatty locals and lovers of first class food, and the atmosphere throughou is friendly and relaxed. The bar has button-back leather wall seats, black leather dining chairs, simple tables, rugs on floorboards, woodburning stoves and contemporary seats against the counter where charming, courteous staff serve Adnams Southwold on handpump, 50 good wines by the glass, home-made cordials and interesting non-alcoholic drinks of particular appeal to drivers. The various linked dining rooms have beams and standing timbers, modern art and photos of well known pop stars on painted panelling, more up-to-date leather chairs and banquettes and rugs on bare boards; background music. There are seats and tables under cream parasols on the front terrace. The pub is just a few minutes' drive from Sutton Hoo (National Trust).

Excellent food using the best local, seasonal produce includes sandwiches, duck liver parfait with pistachios, octopus with nduja tortellini and burrata, taleggio with potato terrine, cauliflower and hazelnut, seared scallops with celeriac, sprouting broccoli and parma ham, pork rib-eye with spiced hollandaise, polenta and turnip, hare with chocolate, blackberry and parsley root, rib-eye steak with bone marrow, dripping potatoes and grelot onions, and puddings such as white chocolate tart with rhubarb and basil and rum baba with pineapple and vanilla; they also offer a two- and three-course set menu. *Benchmark main dish: burger with toppings and brioche £10.95. Two-course evening meal £25.00.*

Punch ~ Lease Brendan Padfield ~ Real ale ~ Open 12-3.30, 6-11; 12-4, 5-11 Sat; 12-10.30 Sun ~ Bar food 12-2.30, 6-9; 12-3, 5-9.30 Sat; 12-8 Sun ~ Restaurant ~ Children welcome ~ Dogs allowed in bar ~ Wi-fi *Recommended by Freddie and Sarah Banks, Muriel and Spencer Harrop, Camilla and Jose Ferrera, W K Wood, Alexander and Trish Cutter, Christopher Mannings*

CHELMONDISTON TM2037 Map 5

Butt & Oyster

(01473) 780764 – www.debeninns.co.uk/buttandoyster

Pin Mill – signposted from B1456 SE of Ipswich; continue to bottom of road; IP9 1JW

Chatty old riverside pub with pleasant views, good food and drink and seats on the terrace

Named for the flounders and oysters which used to be caught here, this remains a simple old bargeman's pub in a fine spot by the River Orwell – the seats on the terrace make the most of its setting. The half-panelled little smoke room is pleasantly worn and unfussy with high-backed and other old-fashioned settles on a tiled floor. There's also a two-level dining room with country kitchen furniture on bare boards, and pictures and boat-related artefacts on the walls above the dado. Adnams Mosaic and Southwold and a couple of guests tapped from the cask by friendly, efficient staff, several wines by the glass and local cider; board games. The annual Thames Barge Race (end June/early July) is fun. The car park can fill up pretty quickly.

The menu is strong on fish dishes such as seared scallops with cauliflower and vanilla purée and crispy bacon, king prawns in garlic butter, seared mackerel fillets, fritto misto and fish stew; non-fishy choices include superfood salad with chargrilled chicken breast or grilled halloumi, spinach and mushroom stew, burger with toppings, chutney and chips, ham steak with eggs and mustard mayonnaise, local sausages with mash and braised red cabbage, 10oz rib-eye steak with peppercorn sauce, and puddings. *Benchmark main dish: beer-battered fish and chips £12.95. Two-course evening meal £20.00.*

Deben Inns ~ Lease Steve Lomas ~ Real ale ~ Open 9am-11pm ~ Bar food 9am-9.30pm ~ Restaurant ~ Children welcome ~ Dogs allowed in bar ~ Wi-fi *Recommended by Dan and Nicki Barton, Patricia and Anton Larkham, Nicholas and Maddy Trainer, Sophie Ellison*

DUNWICH TM4770 Map 5

Ship

(01728) 648219 – www.shipatdunwich.co.uk

St James Street; IP17 3DT

Friendly, well run and pleasantly traditional pub in a coastal village, tasty bar food and local ales; bedrooms

Our readers enjoy staying in the comfortable bedrooms here and breakfasts are good and hearty. The pub was once the haunt of smugglers and seafarers, but now you'll find a cosy, cheerful feel and a traditionally furnished main bar with benches, pews, captain's chairs and wooden tables on a tiled floor, a woodburning stove (left open in cold weather) and lots of sea prints. Adnams Southwold, local Calvors Lodestar, Wolf Prairie Gold and Woodfordes Sundew are served from antique handpumps at the handsomely panelled bar counter, as well as several wines by the glass; background music in dining areas. A simple conservatory looks on to a back terrace, and the large garden is very pleasant, with well spaced picnic-sets, two large anchors and an enormous fig tree. The RSPB reserve at Minsmere and nearby Dunwich Museum are worth visiting and there are enjoyable walks in Dunwich Forest.

As well as breakfasts to non-residents (8-10am), the well regarded food includes smoked mackerel and horseradish pâté with beetroot relish, deep-fried brie with home-made chilli jam, slow-roasted vegetable tagine with lemon couscous and stone-baked pitta, rabbit and venison pie with red wine gravy, rump burger with toppings, coleslaw and chips, beer-battered cod or haddock and chips, slow-braised pork belly with lyonnaise potatoes, red cabbage and apple purée, and puddings such as bakewell tart with custard and chocolate brownie with honeycomb ice-cream and salted caramel sauce. *Benchmark main dish: home-made fish pie £13.95. Two-course evening meal £20.00.*

Free house ~ Licensee Gareth Clarke ~ Real ale ~ Open 8am-11pm ~ Bar food 12-3, 6-9; 12-9 weekends and school holidays ~ Restaurant evening only ~ Children welcome ~ Dogs allowed in bar and bedrooms ~ Wi-fi ~ Bedrooms: /£120 *Recommended by Comus and Sarah Elliott, S Holder, Julie Swift, Robin and Anne Triggs, Tracey and Stephen Groves, Dan and Anne Morgan, Chris Stevenson*

EASTBRIDGE TM4566 Map 5

Eels Foot

(01728) 830154 – www.theeelsfootinn.co.uk

Off B1122 N of Leiston; IP16 4SN

Country local with hospitable atmosphere, fair value food and Thursday evening folk sessions; bedrooms

At lunchtime in particular there are plenty of walkers and bird-watchers here, and as they don't take bookings you'll need to arrive early to get a seat. The upper and lower parts of the bar have light modern furnishings on stripped-wood floors, a warming fire, Adnams Broadside, Ghost Ship, Southwold and seasonal guests such as Fat Sprat and Freewheel on handpump, 11 wines by the glass, several malt whiskies and a farm cider; darts in a side area, board games, cribbage and a neat back dining room. The terrace has seats and tables and the lovely big back garden has benches around more tables. The comfortable, attractive and quiet bedrooms are in a separate building (one room has wheelchair access); breakfasts are tasty. This simple, friendly inn borders the freshwater marshes and RSPB Minsmere is nearby; a footpath leads directly to the sea. They are a certified Caravan Club site and can provide electric hook-ups.

Popular food includes lunchtime sandwiches (the welsh rarebit is popular), sticky barbecue spare ribs with sour cream dip, pâté of the day with granary toast, sharing boards, butternut squash, chickpea and spinach curry with rice, treacle and wholegrain mustard ham and eggs, lasagne, beer-battered cod and chips, rolled pork belly with colcannon and cider gravy, and puddings such as chocolate brownie and sticky toffee pudding. *Benchmark main dish: lemon and thyme chicken burger with toppings and chips £12.95. Two-course evening meal £19.50.*

Adnams ~ Tenant Julian Wallis ~ Real ale ~ Open 12-3, 6-11; 12-11 Fri; 11.30-11 Sat; 11.30-11.30 Sun ~ Bar food 12-2.30, 6-9; 12-9 Fri-Sun ~ Children welcome ~ Dogs welcome ~ Wi-fi ~ Live folk music Thurs and last Sun of month ~ Bedrooms: £85/£115

Recommended by Holly and Tim Waite, Alison and Dan Richardson

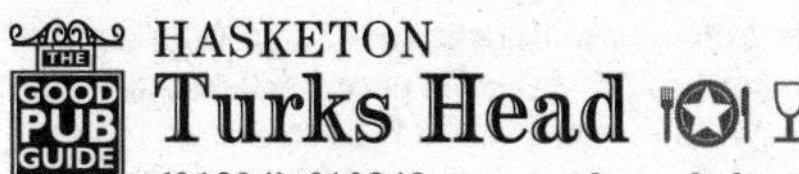

HASKETON TM2450 Map 5

Turks Head

(01394) 610343 – www.theturksheadhasketon.co.uk

Top Road; follow village signs taking B1079 from second Woodbridge roundabout; IP13 6JG

Neatly renovated pub with airy bar, snug and dining room, local ales, imaginative food, attentive service and seats outside

The fresh modern décor in this country dining pub is light and appealing and there's a genuine welcome for all. The bar has white-painted beams, traditional chairs, stools and cushioned wall seats around tables on big flagstones, a woodburning stove in a large fireplace, books on shelves and high chairs against the pale oak counter. Here, courteous staff serve Adnams Ghost Ship, Earl Soham Victoria Bitter, Fullers London Pride and a guest such as Captain Barlow (named for them from Greene King) on handpump, over 20 wines by the glass and 22 gins. A similarly furnished snug has a small woodburner (dogs are allowed in here) and the spreading, high-raftered, airy dining room has cushioned chairs and cream upholstered banquettes around dark tables on floorboards, animal sketches and butterfly prints on RAF-blue paintwork and doors out to the terrace; background music and board games. There are plenty of chairs and tables under large parasols on the terrace and picnic-sets on a lawn; three pétanque pistes.

First rate food includes a brunch menu (10am-2pm) with choices such as a full english breakfast, huevos rancheros (tortilla, avocado, fried egg, refried beans, cheddar cheese and hot chilli sauce) and american pancakes with caramelised banana, clotted cream and maple syrup, plus sticky pork belly with apple purée and crispy sage, crayfish and smoked salmon terrine with brown shrimp dressing, risotto with asparagus, peas, samphire and vegetarian parmesan, 28-day-aged burger with gherkin fritters and chips, free-range chicken with savoury bread and butter pudding, crispy pancetta and roast jus, local venison fillet wellington with organic carrots and red wine sauce, duck breast with potato hash, kimchi and oriental dressing, and puddings such as banoffi pie with caramelised banana and clotted cream and dark chocolate fondant with cherries in kirsch; they also offer a two- and three-course set lunch. *Benchmark main dish: monkfish curry £19.00. Two-course evening meal £24.00.*

Free house ~ Licensee Jemima Withey ~ Real ale ~ Open 11-11; 11-midnight Fri, Sat; 11-8 Sun ~ Bar food 12-3, 6-9; 12-3 Sun ~ Restaurant ~ Children welcome ~ Dogs allowed in bar ~ Wi-fi *Recommended by Gail and Frank Hackett, Mary Joyce, Patti and James Davidson, Freddie and Sarah Banks, Jim and Sue James*

IPSWICH TM1844 Map 5

Fat Cat

(01473) 726524 – www.fatcatipswich.co.uk

Spring Road, opposite junction with Nelson Road (best bet for parking is up there); IP4 5NL

Wonderful choice of changing real ales in a well run town pub; garden

With a huge range of up to 18 real ales from around the country on handpump or tapped from the cask, this cheerful pub is always packed. There might be Adnams Southwold, Crouch Vale Brewers Gold and Yakima Gold plus Fat Cat Honey Ale, Fullers London Pride, Hop Back Summer Lightning, Oakham Citra, Sharps Doom Bar, Skinners Porthleven, Woodfordes Wherry and so forth. They also stock quite a few belgian bottled beers, farm cider and seven wines by the glass. The bars have a mix of café chairs and stools, unpadded wall benches and cushioned seats around cast-iron and wooden pub tables, bare floorboards and lots of enamel brewery signs and posters; board games and shove-ha'penny. There's also a spacious back conservatory and several picnic-sets on the terrace and lawn. Very little nearby parking. Well behaved dogs are welcome but note that they must be kept on a lead.

They keep a supply of rolls, spicy scotch eggs and sausage rolls made in their small kitchen and are happy for you to bring in takeaway food (not Friday or Saturday).

Free house ~ Licensees John and Ann Keatley ~ Real ale ~ No credit cards ~ Open 12-11; 12-midnight Fri; 11.30am-midnight Sat; 12-11 Sun ~ Bar food all day while it lasts ~ Dogs welcome ~ Wi-fi ~ Occasional live music in summer (see website) and gin or wine tastings; quiz third Mon of month *Recommended by Mike Swan, Richard and Penny Gibbs, Edward May, Geoff and Ann Marston, Alexandra and Richard Clay*

LONG MELFORD TL8646 Map 5

Black Lion

(01787) 312356 – www.blacklionhotel.net

Church Walk; CO10 9DN

Carefully refurbished hotel with a relaxed atmosphere in bar and dining rooms, first class food and drinks choice and seats in pretty garden; stylish bedrooms

This carefully renovated and civilised hotel, with plenty of space for both drinking and dining, is in a handsome street opposite the village green. The back bar – liked by locals – has comfortable leather chairs, stools against the counter and an open fire, and friendly, efficient staff serve Adnams Southwold and Nethergate Stour Valley Gold on handpump and 20 well chosen wines by the glass. The two dining rooms have open fires, a mix of high-backed dark leather chairs and nice old wooden, cushioned and armed chairs round candlelit tables, portraits and gilt-edged mirrors on green-painted walls, and both window blinds and long curtains; background music. There's also a conservatory, which leads to the back garden, and a drawing room with sofas and another open fire. You'll find seats and tables in the charming Victorian walled garden with an archway to the street, and more seats on the front terrace looking across to the green. The comfortable, well equipped bedrooms have this same outlook or background views of the grand cathedral-like church (which is well worth a visit) and range from cosy to luxurious suites.

As well as breakfasts (7.30-9.30am; 8-10am weekends), the imaginative food includes sandwiches, scorched mackerel with rhubarb, blood orange vinaigrette and nasturtium, confit duck leg ballotine with onion jam, shallot crisp and potato bread, twice-baked goats cheese soufflé with braised celery, salt-baked beetroot, walnuts and granola, stone-baked pizzas, burger with toppings and fries, slow-braised pork belly with black pudding, fennel, potato croquette and jus, monkfish wrapped in smoked streaky bacon with haricot beans, shallots and aubergine caviar, and puddings such as salted caramel and pecan tart and lime and coconut baked alaska; they also offer a two- and three-course set lunch (not Sunday) and afternoon tea (2.30-5.30). *Benchmark main dish: slow-braised local pork with parmentier potatoes, fennel and pickled apple £17.00. Two-course evening meal £25.00.*

Chestnut Group ~ Manager Chris Poole ~ Real ale ~ Open 11-11 ~ Bar food 12-2.30, 6.15-9.30; 12-3.30, 6.15-8.30 Sun ~ Restaurant ~ Children welcome ~ Dogs allowed in bar and bedrooms ~ Wi-fi ~ Bedrooms: /£125 *Recommended by Lenny and Ruth Walters, Freddie and Sarah Banks, Susie and Spencer Gray, Rosie and Marcus Heatherley*

It's very helpful if you let us know up-to-date food prices when you report on pubs.

If you stay in the well equipped and comfortable bedrooms in this civilised inn, you can take time to explore the pretty village and walk the many well marked surrounding footpaths. The extensive open-plan dining bar is carefully laid out to give several distinct-feeling areas: a sofa and easy chairs on flagstones near the serving counter, a couple of armchairs under heavy beams by the big woodburning stove, one sizeable table tucked nicely into a three-sided built-in seat and a lower side room with more beams and cheerful floral wallpaper. Tables are mostly stripped veterans, with high-backed dining chairs, but there are more modern chunky pine tables at the back; also, contemporary artwork (mostly for sale) and daily papers. Friendly staff serve Adnams Ghost Ship, Crouch Vale Brewers Gold, Woodfordes Wherry and a changing guest such as Humpty Dumpty Broadland Sunrise on handpump and Aspall's cider. Wine is a key feature, with 30 by the glass and hundreds more from the glass-walled 'cellar shop' in one corner – you can buy wine there to take away too. The sheltered flagstoned back terrace has comfortable teak furniture, heaters, big terracotta-coloured parasols and a peaceful view over rolling, lightly wooded countryside. Good disabled access.

As well as breakfasts (7.30-10.30am Mon-Sat; 8-10.30am Sun), the first class food includes smoked duck with chicory, honey-roasted pecan and walnut crumb with blood orange gel, warm crab and spring onion salad with sardine dressing, shallot, wild mushroom and blue cheese tart with creamed leeks, beef and venison burger with toppings, garlic mayonnaise and cajun fries, calves liver with treacle-cured bacon, roast garlic and spring onion mash and wilted spinach, confit rabbit pappardelle with wild mushroom cream and tarragon and lemon mascarpone, cod fillet with chorizo and crayfish butter and roasted garlic mash, and puddings such as cappuccino crème brûlée and orange marmalade steamed sponge with cream; they also offer a two- and three-course set lunch. *Benchmark main dish: beer-battered haddock and chips £15.00. Two-course evening meal £25.00.*

Free house ~ Licensee Richard Sunderland ~ Real ale ~ Open 11-11; 11-10.30 Sun ~ Bar food 12-2.30, 6-9.30 (10 Fri, Sat); 12-9 Sun ~ Children welcome ~ Dogs allowed in bar ~ Wi-fi ~ Bedrooms: £100/£145 *Recommended by Andrea and Philip Crispin, Caroline and Steve Archer, Ted and Mary Bates, Mrs Margo Finlay, Jörg Kasprowski, Charlie and Mark Todd, Belinda and Neil Garth*

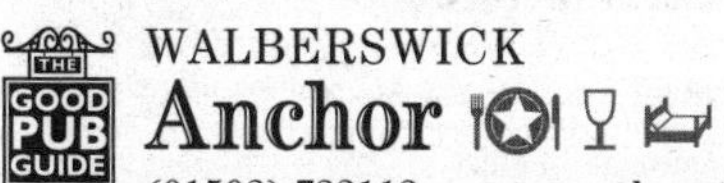

WALBERSWICK — TM4974 Map 5

Anchor

(01502) 722112 – www.anchoratwalberswick.com
The Street (B1387); village signed off A12; IP18 6UA

Friendly, bustling pub with good food and thoughtful choice of drinks; bedrooms and chalets

---

This is a first class all-rounder and our readers enjoy their visits here very much. The simply furnished front bar, divided into snug halves by a two-way open fire, has big windows, heavy stripped tables on original oak flooring, sturdy built-in green leather wall seats and nicely framed black and white photographs of fishermen that are displayed on colour-washed panelling; there's a woodburner too, as well as daily papers and board games. Helpful, friendly staff serve Adnams Ghost Ship, Mosaic and Southwold on handpump, 50 bottled beers and around 20 wines by the glass; they hold an oyster and beer festival in August. The extensive dining area stretches back from a small, more modern-feeling lounge. There are plenty of seats in the attractive garden, with an outdoor bar and wood-fired pizza oven serving the flagstoned terraces. The six spacious chalet-style rooms in the garden have views of either the water or beach huts and sand dunes, while from the bedrooms in the main house you can hear the sea just a few hundred metres away; dogs are allowed in some rooms. As well as the coast path, there's a pleasant walk to Southwold.

As well as breakfasts (8.30-10am), the excellent food uses the best local produce and includes fish soup with rouille and croutons, pork, rabbit and pistachio terrine with chutney, polenta, goats cheese, mushrooms and wood-roasted vegetables, beer-battered cod and chips with spicy tartare sauce, pork belly with mustard mash, choucroute (french sauerkraut) and bacon lentils, crab linguine with chilli and garlic, and puddings such as hazelnut nougat parfait with honeycomb cream and lemon meringue roulade; they also hold regular Friday curry nights and summer barbecues. *Benchmark main dish: home-made fishcake with creamed spinach £15.75. Two-course evening meal £21.00.*

Boudica Inns ~ Lease Mark and Sophie Dorber ~ Real ale ~ Open 8am-11pm ~ Bar food 12-3, 6-9 ~ Restaurant ~ Children welcome ~ Dogs allowed in bar and bedrooms ~ Wi-fi ~ Bedrooms: /£135 *Recommended by Tracey and Stephen Groves, Nicola and Holly Lyons, Louise and Anton Parsons, Liz and Martin Eldon, Andrew Vincent*

WALBERSWICK TM4974 Map 5

Bell

(01502) 723109 – www.bellinnwalberswick.co.uk

Just off B1387; IP18 6TN

Interesting and thriving 16th-c inn with good food and drinks choice, friendly atmosphere and nice garden; cosy bedrooms

Our readers enjoy their visits to this 600-year-old inn and there's a lot of original character in the various rooms. The charming, rambling bar has a chatty atmosphere, antique curved settles, cushioned pews and window seats, scrubbed tables, and two huge fireplaces. The fine old flooring encompasses sagging ancient bricks, broad boards, flagstones and black and red tiles. Friendly staff serve 12 wines by the glass and Adnams Ghost Ship, Southwold and a seasonal guest on handpump; darts. The Barn Café is open during the school holidays for light snacks, cakes, teas and so forth. A big, neatly planted sheltered garden behind has picnic-sets and the rolling sand dunes are a stroll away. The summer rowing-boat ferry to Southwold is nearby (there's a footbridge a bit further away). Bedrooms, some with sea or harbour views, are attractively decorated, and breakfasts are good.

Enjoyable food includes sandwiches, coronation chicken terrine with curried aioli, potted crab with lemon and coriander in sweet chilli butter, chickpea, tomato and spinach curry with apricot and ginger bhaji, home-baked honey and mustard glazed ham and free-range poached eggs, chargrilled chicken on sunblush tomato, chorizo, red pepper, olive, pearl barley and courgette ribbons, fish pie with cod, smoked haddock, salmon, prawns and grated egg, rump steak burger with toppings and chips, confit duck with cumberland sauce and crispy pancetta, and puddings such as rhubarb frangipane tart with ginger ice-cream and salted caramel pannacotta with popcorn crumble and caramelised popcorn. *Benchmark main dish: steak and mushroom in ale pie £13.00. Two-course evening meal £20.00.*

Adnams ~ Tenant Nick Attfield ~ Real ale ~ Open 11-11 ~ Bar food 12-2.30, 6-9 ~ Children welcome ~ Dogs allowed in bar and bedrooms ~ Wi-fi ~ Bedrooms: /£95
Recommended by Comus and Sarah Elliott, S Holder, Usha and Terri Patel, Greta and Gavin Craddock, Nik and Gloria Clarke

The symbol shows pubs that keep their beer unusually well, have a particularly good range or brew their own.

WALDRINGFIELD TM2844 Map 5

Maybush

(01473) 736215 – www.debeninns.co.uk/maybush

Off A12 S of Martlesham; The Quay, Cliff Road; IP12 4QL

Busy pub with tables outside by the riverbank; nautical décor and a fair choice of drinks and fair value food

Lots of picnic-sets on a terrace behind this family-friendly pub overlook the lovely River Deben, but they may get snapped up quickly in fine weather by bird-watchers and ramblers – so do arrive early. Some of the window tables inside also look over the water and the spacious knocked-through bar is divided into separate areas by fireplaces or steps. There's a nautical theme, with an elaborate ship's model in a glass case and a few more in a light, high-ceilinged extension, as well as lots of old lanterns, pistols and aerial photographs; background music and board games. Adnams Ghost Ship and Southwold and a guest beer on handpump and a fair choice of wines by the glass; board games. River cruises are available nearby, though you have to pre-book. There is a large pay-and-display car park (charges are refunded to pub customers).

Popular food includes sandwiches, baked brie with sun-dried tomatoes and caramelised onion chutney, prawn and crayfish cocktail, spicy five-bean chilli with guacamole, burgers with toppings, coleslaw and chips, gammon with free-range eggs, chargrilled tandoori chicken salad, pork tenderloin in stroganoff sauce, sea bass fillets with pesto, roasted vine tomatoes and herb-crushed new potatoes, sirloin steak topped with chilli prawns, and puddings such as banoffi pie and a changing fruit crumble. *Benchmark main dish: beer-battered cod and chips £11.95. Two-course evening meal £20.00.*

Deben Inns ~ Lease Steve and Louise Lomas ~ Real ale ~ Open 9am-11pm ~ Bar food 9am-9.30pm ~ Restaurant ~ Children welcome ~ Dogs allowed in bar ~ Wi-fi
Recommended by Lenny and Ruth Walters, Mark and Sian Edwards, Nik and Gloria Clarke, Dr Martin Owton, Adam Jones

WESTLETON TM4469 Map 5

Crown

(01728) 648777 – www.westletoncrown.co.uk

B1125 Blythburgh–Leiston; IP17 3AD

Bustling old inn with a cosy chatty bar, carefully chosen drinks and interesting food; bedrooms

At the heart of this stylish old coaching inn is an attractive little bar with a lovely log fire and plenty of original features. Locals drop in here for a pint and a chat, which keeps the atmosphere informal and relaxed, and they serve Adnams Southwold and Woodfordes Wherry on handpump, 26 wines by the glass from a thoughtful list and several malt whiskies; background music and board games. There's also a parlour, a dining room and a conservatory, with all manner of wooden dining chairs and tables and historic photographs on some fine old bare-brick walls. The charming terraced garden has plenty of seats and tables. Bedrooms are comfortable and spotlessly kept (some are in the main inn, others are in converted stables and cottages – ask for the larger ones); breakfasts are excellent.

Rewarding food includes lunchtime sandwiches and wraps, chicken liver pâté with piccalilli, tempura prawns with asian salad, wild mushroom, parmesan and herb risotto, chargrilled bacon steak with eggs, beer-battered fish and chips, slow-cooked pork belly with sautéed potatoes and cider sauce, sea bass fillets with ratatouille and basil pesto, 28-day-hung sirloin steak with garlic butter and chips, and puddings such as dark chocolate mousse with white chocolate dust and raspberries and mango parfait with charred pineapple, lime yoghurt and mint sugar; they also offer afternoon tea. *Benchmark main dish: roast chicken breast with fondant potatoes, roasted root vegetables and madeira cream sauce £17.50. Two-course evening meal £21.00.*

Free house ~ Licensee Gareth Clarke ~ Real ale ~ Open 7.15am-11pm ~ Bar food 12-2.30, 6.30-9.30 ~ Restaurant ~ Children welcome ~ Dogs allowed in bar and bedrooms ~ Wi-fi ~ Bedrooms: /£140 *Recommended by Tracey and Stephen Groves, Peter and Alison Steadman, Mark and Mary Setting, Mike Benton, Simon Day*

WHEPSTEAD TL8258 Map 5

White Horse

(01284) 735760 – www.whitehorsewhepstead.co.uk

Off B1066 S of Bury; Rede Road; IP29 4SS

Charming, partly 17th-c country pub with attractively furnished rooms and well liked food and drink

We get plenty of warm praise from our readers on this particularly well run pub for the genuine welcome and rewarding food and drink. The dark-beamed bar has a woodburning stove in a low fireplace, stools around pubby tables on floor tiles, and Woodfordes Bure Gold and Wherry and a guest such as Oakham Asylum on handpump, served from the copper-topped counter. Linked rooms have country kitchen tables and chairs, some rather fine old farmhouse chairs and traditional wall seats with pretty scatter cushions, antique floor tiles or carpet, and walls hung with artworks; background music. Tilly is the friendly pub dog. A sheltered back terrace has seats and tables under parasols and there are picnic-sets on grass and a children's play area with swings and a climbing frame. There are plenty of surrounding walks.

Interesting food includes sandwiches, corn-fed free-range teriyaki chicken satay and chilli and ginger peanut dip, breaded free-range sausage meat fritter with a poached egg and chive hollandaise, sharing boards, garlic, wild mushroom and spinach puff pastry parcels with creamed leeks and rosemary-roasted potatoes, steak burger with toppings, aioli and chips, sea bass fillet with mussel broth and caper-crushed new potatoes, roast saddle of venison with dauphinoise potatoes and red wine gravy, and puddings such as lemon curd cheesecake and Baileys bread and butter pudding with vanilla custard; they also offer a two- and three-course set weekday menu. *Benchmark main dish: beer-battered fish and chips £11.95. Two-course evening meal £20.00.*

Free house ~ Licensees Hana and Lee Saunders ~ Real ale ~ Open 11.30-3, 6-11; 11.30-4 Sun; closed Sun evening, Mon except bank holidays ~ Bar food 12-2, 6-9; 12-3 Sun ~ Restaurant ~ Children welcome ~ Dogs welcome ~ Wi-fi *Recommended by Brian and Sally Wakeham, Alf and Sally Garner, Charlie Stevens, Conrad Freezer, Marianne and Peter Stevens, Marianne and Michael Huggins*

'Children welcome' means the pub says it lets children inside without any special restriction. If it allows them in, but to restricted areas such as an eating area or family room, we specify this. Places with separate restaurants often let children use them, and hotels usually let children into public areas such as lounges. Some pubs impose an evening time limit – let us know if you find one earlier than 9pm.

Also Worth a Visit in Suffolk

Besides the fully inspected pubs, you might like to try these pubs that have been recommended to us and described by readers. Do tell us what you think of them: feedback@goodguides.com

ALDEBURGH TM4656

Mill (01728) 452563
Market Cross Place, opposite Moot Hall; IP15 5BJ Part-timbered, latticed-windowed seafront pub; split-level interior with cosy beamed areas, log fire and some RNLI memorabilia, enjoyable pubby food including good fresh fish and one or two smokehouse dishes, four Adnams ales and decent choice of wines by the glass; background and monthly live music; children (until 9pm) and dogs welcome, handy for the fishermen's huts, open all day. *(Eddie Edwards)*

ALDEBURGH TM4656

White Hart (01728) 453205
High Street; IP15 5AJ Friendly local in former reading room; high ceiling, stained-glass windows, panelling and open fire, Adnams ales and guests, decent wines by the glass, bar snacks, also summer pizzas in back courtyard; occasional live music, free wi-fi; no children inside, dogs welcome, open all day. *(Cecily and Steven Evans)*

ALDRINGHAM TM4461

Parrot & Punchbowl (01728) 830221 *B1122/B1353 S of Leiston; IP16 4PY* Welcoming 17th-c beamed country pub; good fairly priced traditional food catering for special diets, well kept Adnams Southwold and a couple of guests, two-level restaurant; occasional quiz nights; children and dogs (in bar) welcome, nice sheltered garden, also family garden with play area, closed Sun evening. *(Mike Benton)*

BADINGHAM TM3068

White Horse (01728) 638280
A1120 S of village; IP13 8JR Welcoming 15th-c low-beamed inn; generous helpings of good reasonably priced food including themed nights, summer wood-fired pizzas, Adnams and guests, Aspall's and Weston's ciders, inglenook log fire and a couple of woodburners; occasional live music and quiz nights; children, dogs and muddy boots welcome, disabled access, neat bowling green and nice rambling garden, three bedrooms with exposed beams, open all day Sun. *(Charlie and Mark Todd)*

BARHAM TM1251

Sorrel Horse (01473) 830327
Old Norwich Road; IP6 0PG Friendly open-plan beamed and timbered country inn with good log fire in central chimneybreast, well kept ales including Greene King, popular home-made pubby food (all day weekends); free wi-fi; children and dogs welcome, disabled facilities, picnic-sets on side grass with large play area, bedrooms in converted barn, open all day Weds-Sun. *(Patti and James Davidson)*

BILDESTON TL9949

★**Crown** (01449) 740510
B1115 SW of Stowmarket; IP7 7EB Picturesque 15th-c timbered country inn; smart beamed main bar with leather armchairs and inglenook log fire, contemporary artwork in back area, ales such as Adnams and Greene King along with good choice of wines, gins and cocktails, highly praised imaginative food from snacks and reworked pub favourites up including set lunch (Mon-Thurs) and tasting menus, afternoon teas (maybe with a glass of champagne), more formal dining room; children welcome, disabled access and parking, tables laid for eating in appealing central courtyard, more in large beautifully kept garden with decking, 13 bedrooms. *(Geoff and Anne Marston)*

BILDESTON TL9949

Kings Head (01449) 741434
High Street; IP7 7ED Small 16th-c beamed village pub with own good beers (brewery behind – can view by appointment) plus local guests, enjoyable well priced home-made food (Fri evening, Sat, Sun lunchtime only), pleasant chatty staff, wood floor bar with inglenook woodburner; games and live music evenings including Weds open mike, quiz last Thurs of month, May beer festival; children and dogs welcome, back garden with terrace and play equipment, open all day weekends, closed Mon, Tues and lunchtimes Weds-Fri. *(Guy Henderson)*

BLAXHALL TM3656

Ship (01728) 688316
Off B1069 S of Snape; can be reached from A12 via Little Glemham; IP12 2DY New management for this popular low-beamed 18th-c pub in charming country setting; enjoyable reasonably priced traditional food in bar or restaurant, well kept Adnams and guests; live music including folk session fourth Weds of month and Mon afternoon sing-around; children in eating areas, dogs in bar, eight chalet bedrooms, open all day. *(Sandra and Michael Smith)*

BRAMFIELD TM3973

Queens Head (01986) 784214
The Street; A144 S of Halesworth; IP19 9HT Smartly restored village pub next to interesting church; various rooms with heavy beams, timbering and tiled floors,

woodburner in impressive brick fireplace in high-raftered dining room, Adnams and guests, good food from fairly pubby menu including plenty of gluten-free choices, friendly service; children welcome, tiered garden, open (and food) all day, Sun till 6pm (4pm). *(Andrew Vincent)*

BRANDESTON TM2460

Queen (01728) 685307

The Street/Low Lane; IP13 7AD Red-brick pub set back from the road; simply decorated open-plan rooms with stripped boards or quarry tiles, settles, built-in wall seats and grey-painted dining chairs around rustic tables, open fire and woodburner, Adnams Ghost Ship, Southwold and a summer guest, decent wines by the glass and generally well liked food (not Sun evening) from shortish menu; background music, free wi-fi; children and dogs welcome, teak tables and chairs out among planters on front gravel, three shepherd's huts, open all day Fri-Sun, closed Mon (and Tues in winter), plus two weeks in Jan. *(Jim King, David Appleyard, Justine and Neil Bonnett)*

BRENT ELEIGH TL9348

★Cock (01787) 247371

A1141 SE of Lavenham; CO10 9PB Timeless thatched country pub; well kept Adnams and two guests, organic farm cider and enjoyable traditional food cooked by landlady, cosy ochre-walled snug and second small room, antique floor tiles, lovely coal fire, old photographs of village (church well worth a look); darts, shove-ha'penny and toad in the hole; well behaved children and dogs welcome, picnic-sets up on side grass with summer hatch service, one bedroom, open (and food) all day Fri-Sun. *(Monica and Steph Evans)*

BROCKLEY GREEN TL7247

Plough (01440) 786789

Hundon Road; CO10 8DT Neatly kept knocked-through bar with beams, timbers and stripped brick, scrubbed tables and open fire, generally well liked food from lunchtime sandwiches and deli boards up, Tues steak night, three changing ales, good choice of wines by the glass and several malt whiskies/gins, friendly helpful service, restaurant; quiz first Thurs of month; children and dogs welcome, attractive grounds with peaceful country views, comfortable bedrooms, open all day Sun. *(Rosie and Marcus Heatherley)*

BUNGAY TM3389

Castle (01986) 892283

Earsham Street; NR35 1AF Pleasantly informal 16th-c dining inn with good interesting food from chef-owner including themed nights; opened-up beamed interior with restaurant part at front, two open fires, Cliff Quay Sea Dog, Earl Soham Victoria and a couple of craft beers, Aspall's cider, nice choice of wines by the glass and several gins, afternoon teas, friendly efficient staff, french windows to pretty courtyard garden shaded by an indian bean tree; children welcome, dogs in bar area, four comfortable bedrooms, closed Sun evening, Mon (also Tues evening in winter), otherwise open all day. *(Frances Parsons)*

BUNGAY TM3491

Green Dragon (01986) 892681

Broad Street; NR35 1EF Unpretentious 1930s corner pub brewing its own good well priced beers, simple food (not Mon and Tues) including Weds curry night, friendly local atmosphere; maybe live music Sun afternoon; children and dogs welcome, tables on terrace, open all day (till 9pm Sun). *(Philip Saunders)*

BURY ST EDMUNDS TL8463

Dove (01284) 702787

Hospital Road; IP33 3JU Friendly 19th-c alehouse with rustic bare-boards bar and separate parlour, half a dozen well kept/priced mainly local beers and a couple of proper ciders; regular folk and other acoustic music; dogs welcome, some seats out at front, closed weekday lunchtimes. *(Guy Henderson)*

BURY ST EDMUNDS TL8564

★Nutshell (01284) 764867

The Traverse, central pedestrian link off Abbeygate Street; IP33 1BJ Tiny simple local with timeless interior (can be a crush at busy times); lots of interest including vintage bank notes, military and other badges, a wooden propeller and a great metal halberd, even a mummified cat (found walled up here) and companion rat, short wooden benches along shopfront windows and a cut-down sewing-machine table, Greene King ales, no food; background music, steep narrow stairs up to lavatories; children (till 7pm) and dogs welcome, open all day. *(Guy Henderson)*

BURY ST EDMUNDS TL8564

Old Cannon (01284) 768769

Cannon Street, just off A134/A1101 roundabout at N end of town; IP33 1JR Newish management for this early Victorian town house brewing its own beers in the bar (two huge gleaming stainless-steel vessels and views up to balustraded malt floor above the counter), Old Cannon Best, Gunner's Daughter and seasonal ales, also guests including Adnams Southwold and good range of other drinks, enjoyable food (not Sun evening) from pub favourites up, weekday set lunch, Mon pizza night and occasional themed evenings, assortment of old and new furniture on bare boards; well behaved children and dogs allowed, comfortable bedrooms in old brewhouse across courtyard, open all day. *(Adrian Johnson, Alison Nicholls)*

BURY ST EDMUNDS TL8564
One Bull (01284) 848220
Angel Hill; IP33 1UZ Contemporary pub with own Brewshed beers, local guests and extensive range of wines by the glass (some unusual choices), good food (all day Sat) from sandwiches and sharing boards up, friendly attentive service; free wi-fi; children till 6pm in bar (8pm restaurant), closed Sun evening, otherwise open all day and can get busy. *(D Hillaby)*

BURY ST EDMUNDS TL8563
★**Rose & Crown** (01284) 755934
Whiting Street; IP33 1NP Cheerful black-beamed corner local with long-serving affable licensees; bargain simple lunchtime home cooking (not Sun), particularly well kept Greene King ales (including XX Mild) and guests, pleasant lounge with lots of piggy pictures, good games-oriented public bar, rare separate off-sales hatch; background radio, no credit cards or under-14s; pretty back courtyard, open all day weekdays. *(John Harris)*

BUXHALL TM9957
★**Crown** (01449) 736521
Off B1115 W of Stowmarket; Mill Road; IP14 3DW A pub of two halves; steps down to cosy low-beamed bar on left with woodburner in brick inglenook, larger timbered dining area beyond with view of old windmill, well kept Adnams Broadside, Earl Soham Victoria and nice choice of wines by the glass; light airy dining room to the right with its own bar and another woodburner, very good if not particularly cheap food from interesting menu using local produce, friendly service; children and dogs welcome, plenty of tables on terrace with views over open country (ignore the pylons), herb garden, closed Sun evening, Mon. *(Jim and Sue James)*

CAMPSEA ASHE TM3356
Dog & Duck (01728) 746211
Station Road; IP13 0PT Refurbished roadside pub with good varied choice of popular food including set lunch menu, Adnams, a guest beer and several wines by the glass from copper-topped counter, friendly welcoming staff, bar with woodburner, restaurant; children and dogs welcome, wheelchair access, nice garden with gazebo, bedrooms, open all day, food till 4pm Sun. *(Andrew and Clare Reid)*

CAVENDISH TL8046
Bull (01787) 280245
A1092 Long Melford–Clare; CO10 8AX Traditional old pub with heavy beams, timbers and open fires, Greene King IPA and a couple of guests, real cider and enjoyable reasonably priced pub food including sandwiches and highly rated Sun roasts (till 4.30pm), good friendly service; charity quiz first Sun of month; children allowed in eating areas, dogs in bar (but best to ask first), paved back terrace with steps up to car park (useful in this picturesque honeypot village), closed Sun evening. *(Mrs Margo Finlay, Jörg Kasprowski)*

CAVENDISH TL8046
★**George** (01787) 280248
A1092; The Green; CO10 8BA Restauranty 16th-c inn with contemporary feel in two bow-windowed front areas; beams and timbers, big woodburner in stripped-brick fireplace, well liked food from short but varied menu including lunchtime sandwiches, also good value set deal, Nethergate and plenty of wines by the glass, Aspall's cider, back servery and further eating area, charming helpful staff; background music, daily newspapers; children and well behaved dogs welcome, stylish furniture on sheltered back terrace, tree-shaded garden with lovely village church behind, five bedrooms up rather steep staircase, good breakfast, closed Sun evening, otherwise open all day. *(Andrew Vincent)*

CHELSWORTH TL9848
Peacock (01449) 743952
B1115 Sudbury–Needham Market; IP7 7HU Prettily set 14th-c village dining pub in conservation village; cosy beamed bar with exposed brickwork, grandfather clock and inglenook woodburner, ales such as Adnams, Nethergate and Woodfords, separate timbered dining room, good sensibly priced food from sandwiches to seasonal game, friendly service; children and dogs welcome, five bedrooms, picnic-sets in small side garden, closed Sun evening. *(Cecily and Steven Evans)*

CHILLESFORD TM3852
★**Froize** (01394) 450282
B1084 E of Woodbridge; IP12 3PU More restaurant than pub and only open during mealtimes; very good if not cheap buffet-style food from owner-chef using carefully sourced local produce including seasonal game, nice wines by the glass and well kept Adnams, warmly welcoming service, little deli next to bar; occasional events including folk music; seats on terrace, no dogs inside, closed evenings Sun-Thurs, all day Mon. *(Guy Henderson)*

CREETING ST MARY TM1155
Highwayman (01449) 760369
A140, just N of junction with A14; IP6 8PD Attractively updated 17th-c pub with two bars and pleasant galleried barn extension; welcoming landlord and friendly relaxed atmosphere, popular freshly cooked food from landlady-chef, well kept Greene King IPA and guests, decent wines; unobtrusive background music; children welcome, no dogs inside, tables on gravel terrace and back lawn with pretty pond, closed Sun evening, Mon. *(David Twitchett)*

CRETINGHAM TM2260

Bell (01728) 685419

The Street; IP13 7BJ Attractive and welcoming old beamed and timbered pub; enjoyable traditional home-made food from sandwiches up, well kept ales such as Adnams and Earl Soham, nice wines by the glass, bare-boards bar, dining tables in tiled second room with woodburner in big fireplace; regular live music; children and dogs (in snug) welcome, garden picnic-sets. *(Alexandra and Richard Clay)*

EARL SOHAM TM2263

Victoria (01728) 685758

A1120 Yoxford–Stowmarket; IP13 7RL Simple two-bar pub popular with locals; well kept Earl Soham ales (used to be brewed here) and reasonably priced home-cooked food, friendly service, kitchen chairs, pews and scrubbed country tables on bare boards or tiled floors, panelling and open fire; outside gents'; children and dogs welcome, seats out in front and on raised back lawn, handy for working windmill at Saxtead (EH). *(Mike Benton)*

EASTON TM2858

White Horse (01728) 746456

N of Wickham Market on back road to Earl Soham and Framlingham; IP13 0ED Attractive 16th-c village dining pub refurbished under welcoming new management; much liked food from pub favourites up, three well kept ales including Adnams and good choice of wines, friendly attentive service; children and dogs welcome, a few tables out at front, more in enclosed back garden with play area, open all day Fri-Sun, closed Mon. *(Caroline Prescott)*

EDWARDSTONE TL9542

White Horse (01787) 211211

Mill Green, just E; village signed off A1071 in Boxford; CO10 5PX Unpretentious pub with a dozen well kept ales including Adnams, Crouch End and Timothy Taylors (beer/cider/music festivals), various sized bars with lots of beer mats, rustic prints and photos on the walls, second-hand tables and chairs including an old steamer bench and panelled settle on bare boards, woodburner and open fire, fairly pubby food including range of burgers; live music, bar billiards, darts, ring the bull and other games, free wi-fi; children and dogs welcome, end terrace with sturdy teak furniture, attractive smokers' shelter, makeshift picnic-sets on grass, two scandinavian-style self-catering chalets plus campsite with shower block, open all day. *(Jim and Sue James)*

EYE TM1473

Queens Head (01379) 870153

Cross Street; IP23 7AB Popular three-room beamed pub; Adnams and local guests such as Bullards tapped from the cask (July beer festival), 11 wines by the glass and good fairly priced food (not Sun evening) cooked by landlord including fish specials, friendly accommodating staff, interesting local artwork, woodburner; background music, monthly quiz and karaoke, free wi-fi; children and dogs (on leads, theirs is Franco) welcome, garden with play area, open all day (Sun till 9pm). *(Nik and Gloria Clarke)*

FELIXSTOWE TM3134

Fludyers Arms (01394) 691929

Undercliff Road E; IP11 7LU Restored and extended Edwardian pub-hotel on seafront; opened-up bare-boards bar and several dining areas including panelled restaurant, Adnams, Woodfordes and guests, good food from bar snacks to upmarket restauranty choices, weekday set menu, friendly attentive service; jazz and some other live music; children welcome, sea views from modern heated front terrace, 12 bedrooms (more views) and mews apartment, open (and food) all day. *(J B and M E Benson)*

FELIXSTOWE FERRY TM3237

Ferry Boat (01394) 284203

Off Ferry Road, on the green; IP11 9RZ Nautical-themed 17th-c pub tucked between golf links and dunes near harbour, martello tower and summer rowing-boat ferry; good fair value food including range of fish dishes and some vegetarian options, friendly efficient staff, well kept Adnams Southwold, Woodfordes Wherry and a guest, decent coffee, warm log fire; background music; children and dogs welcome, tables out in front, on green opposite and in fenced garden, good coast walks, open all day weekends and busy in summer. *(Monica and Steph Evans)*

FRAMLINGHAM TM2862

Station Hotel (01728) 723455

Station Road (B1116 S); IP13 9EE Simple high-ceilinged bar with big windows, scrubbed tables on bare boards, half-panelling and woodburner, well kept Earl Soham ales and good choice of house wines, popular freshly cooked food from interesting menu, also wood-fired pizzas Thurs-Sat evenings, friendly relaxed atmosphere, back snug with tiled floor; free wi-fi; children and dogs welcome, picnic-sets in pleasant garden. *(Jimmy)*

FRESSINGFIELD TM2677

★**Fox & Goose** (01379) 586247

Church Street; B1116 N of Framlingham; IP21 5PB Relaxed dining pub in beautifully timbered 16th-c former Guildhall next to church; highly regarded food from bar meals served in cosy informal heavy-beamed rooms to upscale fixed-price menus in upstairs restaurant, friendly efficient service, Adnams and a guest tapped from the cask and a dozen wines by the glass; soft background music; children welcome, downstairs disabled facilities, tables out by duck pond, closed Mon. *(John and Jennifer Spinks)*

FRISTON TM4160

Old Chequers (01728) 688039

Just off A1094 Aldeburgh–Snape; IP17 1NP Welcoming village pub modernised under present licensees; L-shaped bar with wood flooring and woodburner in brick fireplace, enjoyable home-made food including daily specials, well kept ale such as Adnams, Greene King and Woodfordes from brick-faced servery; well behaved children and dogs welcome (there's a resident scottie), sunny back terrace, nice circular walks to Aldeburgh and Snape, open all day Sun till 9pm, closed Mon, Tues. *(John Harris)*

GREAT BRICETT TM0450

Red Lion (01473) 657863

B1078, E of Bildeston; IP7 7DD Refurbished and extended old beamed pub; very good vegetarian and vegan food at competitive prices (nothing for meat eaters), children's menu and takeaways too, real ales such as Greene King; dogs welcome in bar, garden with deck and play equipment, closed Sun evening, Mon, Tues. *(Alexandra and Richard Clay)*

GREAT GLEMHAM TM3461

Crown (01728) 663693

Between A12 Wickham Market–Saxmundham and B1119 Saxmundham–Framlingham; IP17 2DA Traditionally restored early 19th-c red-brick village pub; four fireplaces and some nice old suffolk furniture on wood and quarry-tiled floors, mostly local beers from old brass handpumps, good interesting food (not Sun evening, Tues) along with pub favourites, back coffee lounge with freshly baked cakes, friendly helpful staff; some acoustic music and themed events, monthly quiz, darts, table skittles, free wi-fi; well behaved children and dogs welcome, disabled facilities, cast-iron furniture on back lawn, closed Mon evening and Tues lunchtime. *(Belinda and Neil Garth)*

GREAT WRATTING TL6848

Red Lion (01440) 783237

School Road; CB9 7HA Popular village pub with a couple of ancient whale bones flanking the entrance; log fire in bar and lots of copper and brass, well kept Adnams and generous helpings of enjoyable pubby food, friendly staff, restaurant; children and dogs welcome, big back garden with play equipment, open all day Sat. *(Frances Parsons)*

GRUNDISBURGH TM2250

Dog (01473) 735267

The Green; off A12 via B1079 from Woodbridge bypass; IP13 6TA Friendly pink-washed pub with villagey public bar, log fire, settles and dark wooden carvers around pubby tables on tiles, Adnams, Earl Soham, Woodfordes and a guest, half a dozen wines by the glass, good value food including daily specials, themed nights and set lunch (Tues-Sat), carpeted lounge linking to bare-boards dining room; free wi-fi; children and dogs welcome, picnic-sets out in front by flowering tubs, more seats in wicker-fenced mediterranean-feel back garden, play area, open all day, closed Mon. *(Alexander and Trish Cutter)*

HADLEIGH TM0242

Kings Head (01473) 828855

High Street; IP7 5EF Modernised Georgian-fronted pub (building is actually much older) with popular food from daily changing menu including some themed nights, well kept Adnams and guests, Aspall's cider, friendly helpful staff; Apr beer festival; children and dogs (in some areas) welcome, open all day from 9.30am (midday Sun). *(Guy Henderson)*

HADLEIGH TM0242

Ram (01473) 822880

Market Place; IP7 5DL Smartly updated bar-restaurant (sister to the Swan at Long Melford) facing Georgian corn exchange; good well presented food including themed nights, brunch from 10am, plenty of wines by the glass from extensive list, cocktails, interesting gins and a beer from Greene King, efficient service; children welcome, small courtyard garden behind, open all day (Sun till 6pm). *(Patti and James Davidson)*

HARTEST TL8352

Crown (01284) 830250

B1066 S of Bury St Edmunds; IP29 4DH Old pub by church behind pretty village green; good food (all day Sun) from sandwiches and sharing boards up, popular Weds pie and pint deal, own Brewshed beers plus a couple from Greene King, plenty of wines by the glass, friendly attentive uniformed staff, split-level beamed interior (note the coins left by departing World War I soldiers), good log fire in big fireplace; free wi-fi; children (not in bar after 8pm) and well behaved dogs welcome, tables on big back lawn and in sheltered side courtyard, good play area, open all day. *(John Harris)*

HAUGHLEY TM0262

Kings Arms (01449) 614462

Off A45/B1113 N of Stowmarket; Old Street; IP14 3NT Extended 16th-c village pub with good food (not Sun evening) cooked by owner-chef including set lunch deal Weds-Fri, Greene King beers (Abbot ale was named here by a landlord in 1950), also a guest and decent choice of wines, friendly service, spacious timbered interior with plenty of room for diners, woodburner in big brick fireplace; children and dogs (in bar) welcome, tables in back garden, closed Mon and Tues, otherwise open all day (till 9pm Sun). *(Jeremy King)*

HAWKEDON TL7953

Queens Head (01284) 789218
Off A143 at Wickham Street, NE of Haverhill; and off B1066; IP29 4NN Flint Tudor pub in pretty setting looking down broad peaceful green to interesting largely Norman village church; quarry-tiled bar with dark beams and ochre walls, plenty of pews and chapel chairs around scrubbed tables, elderly armchairs by antique woodburner in huge fireplace, cheerful helpful staff, Adnams, Woodfordes and guests, proper cider/perry and nice choice of wines, good food (not Mon, Tues) using home-reared meat, dining area stretching back with country prints and a couple of tusky boars' heads; some live music and occasional wine tastings and games nights; picnic-sets out in front, more on back terrace overlooking rolling country, little shop (Fri and Sat mornings) selling their own bacon, pies, casseroles etc, open all day Fri-Sun, closed lunchtimes Mon-Thurs. *(Geoff and Anne Marston)*

HORRINGER TL8261

Beehive (01284) 736737
A143; IP29 5SN Brick and flint village pub with cosy series of beamed rooms; ales such as Adnams, Humpty Dumpty, Oakham and Mauldons, good food from chef-manager including daily specials and lighter meals; some live music, pool; children and dogs welcome, back terrace and raised lawn, handy for Ickworth (NT), closed Sun evening, Mon and lunchtimes Tues-Thurs. *(Sally Anne and Peter Goodale)*

IPSWICH TM1644

Dove Street (01473) 211270
St Helens Street; IP4 2LA Drinkers' pub with over 20 well kept quickly changing ales including their own brews (regular beer festivals), farm ciders, bottled beers and good selection of whiskies, low priced simple pub food including substantial pork pies, bare-boards bar, carpeted snug and back conservatory; free wi-fi; children (till 7pm) and dogs welcome, disabled facilities, seats on heated covered terrace, two bedrooms over the road along with the brewery shop, open (and food) all day. *(Sandra and Michael Smith)*

IPSWICH TM1645

Greyhound (01473) 252862
Henley Road/Anglesea Road; IP1 3SE Popular 19th-c pub close to picturesque Christchurch Park; cosy front bar with corridor to larger lounge/dining area, five well kept Adnams ales and a couple of guests, good home cooking including bargain weekday lunch and daily specials, quick friendly service; occasional Sun quiz, sports TV, free wi-fi; children welcome, picnic-sets under parasols on back terrace, open (and food) all day weekends. *(Jimmy)*

IPSWICH TM1747

Railway Inn (01473) 252337
Westerfield Road close to the station; IP6 9AA Popular split-level roadside pub with reasonably priced food (all day weekends) including daily specials and set menus, three well kept Adnams ales and several wines by the glass; children and dogs (in bar) welcome, four bedrooms, outside tables and colourful hanging baskets, open all day. *(Sandra and Michael Smith)*

IPSWICH TM1744

Woolpack (01473) 215862
Tuddenham Road; IP4 2SH Welcoming traditional red-brick pub dating from the 1600s; Adnams and four other well kept beers, several wines by the glass and popular fairly pubby food at reasonable prices, helpful accommodating service, two bars, snug and back dining area, corner with piano and board games; live music including jazz last Weds of the month, quiz second Sun; children and dogs welcome, seats on heated front terrace, opposite Christchurch Park, open all day from 10am for breakfast. *(Sandra and Michael Smith)*

KERSEY TM0044

Bell (01473) 823229
Signed off A1141 N of Hadleigh; The Street; IP7 6DY Attractive 14th-c black and white pub in notably picturesque village with ford; popular good value home-made food (not Sun or Mon evenings) including good steak and kidney pudding, Adnams and a couple of guests, friendly service, low-beamed carpeted bar with log fire, restaurant; children and dogs welcome, hanging baskets out at front, split-level terrace and garden behind, open all day. *(Tina and David Woods-Taylor)*

KESGRAVE TM2346

Kesgrave Hall (01473) 333741
Hall Road; IP5 2PU Country hotel with comfortably modern bare-boards bar; Adnams and a couple of guests from granite-topped servery, several wines by the glass and cocktails, popular if pricey food cooked in brasserie's open kitchen (no booking so best to arrive early), afternoon teas, children and dogs welcome, attractive heated terrace with huge retractable awning, sweeping grounds, 23 stylish bedrooms, open (and food) all day. *(Mike Benton)*

LAVENHAM TL9149

★**Angel** (01787) 247388
Market Place; CO10 9QZ Handsome Tudor building in delightful small town; long bar with inglenook log fire and some fine 16th-c ceiling plasterwork, relaxed feel with chesterfield sofas and armchairs,

further dining areas and more heavy beams and panelling, popular food including pub favourites, pizzas and grills, well kept ales Adnams and a guest, Aspall's cider and good range of wines, friendly staff; children and dogs (in bar) welcome, sizeable back garden, eight bedrooms, open all day from 8am for breakfast. *(Jimmy)*

LAVENHAM TL9149

Swan (01787) 247477

High Street; CO10 9QA Smart hotel in series of handsome medieval buildings; appealing network of beamed and timbered rooms including tiled-floor inner bar, log fire and memorabilia from its days as a local for US pilots, well kept Adnams and a guest, lots of wines by the glass from extensive list and good range of other drinks, well thought-of innovative food, can eat in bar, informal brasserie or lavishly timbered restaurant, afternoon teas, efficient friendly young staff; children and dogs welcome, sheltered courtyard garden, 45 bedrooms, open all day. *(John Harris)*

LAXFIELD TM2972

★ **Kings Head** (01986) 798395

Gorams Mill Lane, behind church; IP13 8DW Unspoilt thatched pub with no bar counter – Adnams ales and a guest poured in tap room; interesting little chequer-tiled front room dominated by booth of high-backed settles next to range fire, two other rooms with pews, old seats and scrubbed deal tables, well liked food including good home-made pies; occasional live music; children and dogs welcome, neatly kept garden with arbour and small pavilion for cooler evenings, boules, three bedrooms, open all day, no food Sun evening and kitchen may close early other days if quiet. *(Dr Peter Crawshaw)*

LEVINGTON TM2339

Ship (01473) 659573

Gun Hill; from A14/A12 Bucklesham roundabout take A1156 exit, then first sharp left into Felixstowe Road, after nearly a mile, the village and pub are signed to right; IP10 0LQ Charming part-thatched 13th-c village pub beside little lime-washed church; beams, timber dividers and some nautical trappings, settles and built-in wall benches, inglenook woodburner, Adnams ales and good locally sourced food served by friendly attentive staff, restaurant; children and dogs welcome, views (if a little obscured) over River Orwell estuary, nice circular walk, open all day. *(Frances Parsons)*

LINDSEY TYE TL9846

Lindsey Rose (01449) 741424

Village signposted off A1141 NW of Hadleigh; IP7 6PP Newish owners and refurbishment for this old village pub; main bar with low beams, standing timbers and open fire, second similarly furnished room and another big fireplace, good fairly priced food from shortish but varied menu plus daily specials, Adnams ales and a guest, friendly helpful staff; children and dogs welcome, a few picnic-sets out on front gravel, more on back lawn with play area, open all day (till 6pm Sun). *(Martin Orton)*

LONG MELFORD TL8645

Swan (01787) 464545

Hall Street; CO10 9JQ Beamed dining pub in same group as the Ram at Hadleigh; good imaginative food (best to book) including brunch from 8am, well selected wines, interesting gins, cocktails and a couple of real ales, split-level interior with pastel décor and some unusual wallpaper, high-backed dining chairs and mix of tables on wood or carpeted floors, log fire, deli; unobtrusive background music; children welcome, tables out on terrace and lawn, seven bedrooms (four in next-door building), open all day. *(Monica and Steph Evans)*

MELTON TM2850

Olde Coach & Horses

(01394) 384851 *Melton Road; IP12 1PD* Attractively modernised beamed former staging inn; good choice of enjoyable fairly priced food from sandwiches, snacks and sharing plates up (special diets catered for), lunchtime meal deal Mon-Sat, ales including Adnams and Woodfordes, decent wines by the glass, good friendly service; free wi-fi; children welcome, dogs in wood-floored area, tables out under parasols among colourful hanging baskets and planters, open (and food) all day. *(Jim and Sue James)*

NAYLAND TL9734

★ **Anchor** (01206) 262313

Court Street; just off A134 – turn-off S of signposted B1087 main village turn; CO6 4JL Friendly pub by River Stour under same ownership as the Angel at Stoke-by-Nayland; bare-boards bar with assorted wooden dining chairs and tables, big gilt mirror on silvery wallpaper one end, another mirror above pretty fireplace the other, five changing ales and several wines by the glass (happy hour 9-10pm Fri, Sat), enjoyable seasonal food including some home-smoked dishes and flame grills, two other rooms behind and steep stairs up to cosy restaurant; children welcome, dogs in bar, terrace tables looking out over river, open all day, food till 6pm Sun. *(Andrew Vincent)*

NEWBOURNE TM2743

Fox (01473) 736307

Off A12 at roundabout 1.7 miles N of A14 junction; The Street; IP12 4NY Pink-washed 16th-c pub decked in summer flowers; low-beamed bar with slabby elm and other dark tables on quarry-tiled floor, stuffed fox in inglenook, comfortable carpeted dining room with various mirrors, Adnams Southwold, guest ales and decent wines by the glass, good choice of popular food including deals; background music, free wi-fi; children and dogs (in bar) welcome, wheelchair access, attractive grounds with rose garden and pond, open (and food) all day from 9am for breakfast. *(Cecily and Steven Evans)*

NEWTON TL9140

Saracens Head (01787) 379036
A134 4 miles E Sudbury; CO10 0QJ Old roadside pub with beamed and timbered interior; Adnams and Greene King beers, good choice of food including vegetarian options and generous Sun lunch, friendly attentive service; bar billiards; children and dogs welcome, garden overlooking pond and common/golf course, closed Mon, otherwise open all day, food till 6pm Sun. *(Giles and Annie Francis)*

ORFORD TM4249

★**Jolly Sailor** (01394) 450243
Quay Street; IP12 2NU Welcoming old pub under mother and daughter team; several snug rooms with exposed brickwork, boating pictures and other nautical memorabilia, four well kept Adnams beers and popular sensibly priced food from good lunchtime sandwiches up, efficient cheerful service, unusual spiral staircase in corner of flagstoned main bar by brick inglenook, horsebrasses and local photographs, two cushioned pews and long antique stripped-deal table; free wi-fi; children and dogs welcome, tables on back terrace and lawn with views over marshes, popular with walkers and bird-watchers, bedrooms, open all day weekends. *(Bob and Margaret Holder, JER, David Fowler)*

ORFORD TM4249

★**Kings Head** (01394) 450271
Front Street; IP12 2LW Friendly 13th-c village inn (plenty of authentic atmosphere) surrounded by fine walks and lovely coastline; snug main bar with heavy low beams, Adnams ales and several wines by the glass, good home-made food (not Sun evening) from sandwiches to daily specials with a focus on fish, popular Sun roast (must book), dining room has old stripped-brick walls and rugs on ancient boards, woodburners; occasional live music; children and dogs welcome, four bedrooms, open all day Fri-Sun. *(Barry Collett)*

POLSTEAD TL9938

Cock (01206) 263150
Signed off B1068 and A1071 E of Sudbury, then pub signed; Polstead Green; CO6 5AL 16th-c beamed and timbered village local; bar with woodburner, Greene King IPA and two guests, good choice of wines and enjoyable home-made food from lunchtime baguettes up, light and airy barn restaurant; background music; children and dogs welcome, disabled facilities, picnic-sets overlooking small green, closed Sun evening, Mon and Tues. *(Belinda and Neil Garth)*

RAMSHOLT TM3041

Ramsholt Arms (01394) 411209
Signed off B1083; Dock Road; IP12 3AB Lovely isolated spot overlooking River Deben; modernised open-plan bar with log fire, enjoyable good value food from lunchtime sandwiches up, Adnams, a couple of guest beers and decent choice of wines by the glass; children and dogs welcome, plenty of tables outside taking in the view, handy for bird walks and Sutton Hoo (NT), best to check opening times. *(Comus and Sarah Elliott)*

REDE TL8055

★**Plough** (01284) 789208
Village signposted off A143 Bury St Edmunds–Haverhill; IP29 4BE Quaint partly thatched pub at end of quiet green in tucked-away village; traditional low-beamed rooms kept spic and span, wheelback chairs and plush red wall banquettes around dark pubby tables, solid-fuel stove in a brick fireplace, changing ales such as Harveys, Ringwood and Timothy Taylors, several wines by the glass and well liked food (not Sun evening); background music, free wi-fi; children welcome till 8pm, picnic-sets out at front and in sheltered cottagey garden; licensees hoping to retire, so could be changes. *(Lucy and Giles Gibbon, Mark and Sian Edwards)*

REYDON TM4977

★**Randolph** (01502) 723603
Wangford Road (B1126 just NW of Southwold); IP18 6PZ Comfortable inn with quite an emphasis on dining and bedroom side; bar with high-backed leather dining chairs around chunky wooden tables on parquet floor, a couple of comfortable armchairs and sofa, prints of the pub from 1910 and photographs of Southwold beach, Adnams beers, more high-backed chairs in carpeted restaurant with pretty Victorian fireplace, popular food from short but varied menu including lunchtime sandwiches and snack baskets, weekday lunchtime deals, Sat afternoon tea (must book), pleasant staff; background music, TV; children welcome, dogs in small back bar, wheelchair access, picnic-sets on decked area and grass, summer barbecues, ten bedrooms and self-catering bungalow, good breakfast, open all day. *(Belinda and Neil Garth)*

ROUGHAM TL9063

Ravenwood Hall (01359) 270345
Off A14 E of Bury St Edmunds; IP30 9JA Country-house hotel set in seven acres of lovely grounds; two compact bar rooms, tall ceilings, patterned wallpaper and big heavily draped windows overlooking sweeping lawn with stately cedar, well kept Adnams, good choice of wines and malt whiskies, back area set for eating with upholstered settles and dining chairs, sporting prints and log fire,

generally well liked food served by pleasant staff, comfortable lounge area has horse pictures, a few moulded beams and early Tudor wall decoration above big inglenook, separate more formal restaurant; background music; children and dogs welcome, teak furniture in garden, swimming pool and croquet, big enclosures for geese, pygmy goats and shetland ponies, 14 bedrooms, open all day. *(Comus and Sarah Elliott)*

SHOTTISHAM TM3244

Sorrel Horse (01394) 411617

Hollesley Road; IP12 3HD Charming 15th-c thatched community-owned local; well kept Adnams, Earl Soham, Woodfordes and guests tapped from casks, decent choice of home-made traditional food, attentive friendly young staff, good log fire in tiled-floor bar with games area (bar billiards), woodburner in attractive dining room; live music Mon, quiz every other Weds, free wi-fi; children and dogs welcome, tables out on sloping front lawn and in small garden behind, open all day weekends. *(Annette Wilkins)*

SNAPE TM3958

★Crown (01728) 688324

Bridge Road (B1069); IP17 1SL Small well laid-out 15th-c beamed pub with brick floors, inglenook log fire and fine double suffolk settle, good reasonably priced food using local ingredients including own meat (reared behind the pub), steak night first Thurs of month, well kept Adnams ales, efficient friendly young staff; folk evening last Thurs of month, darts, free wi-fi; children and dogs welcome, garden, two bedrooms. *(Comus and Sarah Elliott)*

SNAPE TM4058

Golden Key (01728) 688510

Priory Lane; IP17 1SA Welcoming village pub now under same management as the nearby Plough & Sail; low-beamed lounge with old-fashioned settle and straightforward tables and chairs on stripped-wood or chequerboard tiled floor, woodburner, small snug and two cosy dining rooms, well kept Adnams ales, local cider and several wines by the glass, good well presented food from sandwiches to daily specials, fish and chips deal Fri, cheerful efficient young staff; children and dogs welcome, two terraces with pretty hanging baskets and seats under parasols, handy for the Maltings, two refurbished bedrooms, open all day weekends. *(Comus and Sarah Elliott)*

SNAPE TM3957

Plough & Sail (01728) 688413

The Maltings, Snape Bridge (B1069 S); IP17 1SR Part of the Maltings complex, this former smugglers' haunt is run by twin brothers (one is the chef); mostly open-plan with good blend of traditional and modern furnishings, the original 17th-c core has country pine tables and chairs on terracotta tiles and open fire, there's a second cosy room with leather chesterfields by woodburner, a simply furnished bar hall and spacious modern dining room with wood-strip floor and pitched ceiling, an additional restaurant is upstairs, Adnams and Greene King ales, several wines by the glass and good up-to-date food along with pub favourites; background music, free wi-fi; children and dogs (in bar) welcome, some picnic-sets out at front, more tables on flower-filled terrace, open all day. *(JER, Tracey and Stephen Groves, Comus and Sarah Elliott)*

SOUTH ELMHAM TM3385

St Peters Brewery (01986) 782288

St Peter South Elmham; off B1062 SW of Bungay; NR35 1NQ Beautifully but simply furnished manor dating from the 13th c (much extended in the 16th c) with own St Peters ales and bottled beers, bar and dining hall with dramatic high ceiling, elaborate woodwork and flagstoned floor, antique tapestries, woodburner in fine fireplace, two further rooms reached up steepish stairs, short choice of food including sandwiches, afternoon teas; children and dogs (in bar) welcome, outside tables overlooking original moat, open all day Sat, till 6pm Sun, 4pm Weds-Fri, closed Mon and Tues, winter hours may vary, they also hold weddings and other events, so best to check. *(Frances Parsons)*

SOUTHWOLD TM5076

★Lord Nelson (01502) 722079

East Street, off High Street (A1095); IP18 6EJ Busy local near seafront with partly panelled traditional bar and two small side rooms, coal fire, light wood furniture on tiles, lamps in nice nooks and corners, interesting Nelson memorabilia including attractive nautical prints and fine model of HMS Victory, five well kept Adnams ales, several wines by the glass and decent pubby food, good friendly service; board games, free wi-fi; children (away from the bar) and dogs welcome, wheelchair access possible, seats out in front with sidelong view of the sea, sheltered and heated back garden with Adnams brewery in sight, open all day. *(John Wooll)*

SOUTHWOLD TM5076

Red Lion (01502) 722385

South Green; IP18 6ET Under newish management and some redecoration; front bar with big windows looking over green towards the sea, sturdy wall benches and bar stools on wood floor, well kept Adnams including seasonals, back room with mate's chairs, pews and polished dark tables, lots of framed black and white photographs, good range of popular food served by friendly staff, three linked dining rooms; background music (live Fri evening and Sun afternoon); tables out in front (dogs welcome here) and in small sheltered back courtyard, next to the Adnams retail shop. *(John Wooll)*

SOUTHWOLD TM5076

Sole Bay (01502) 723736

East Green; IP18 6JN Busy single-room pub near Adnams Brewery; their full range kept well and good wine choice, cheerful efficient staff, enjoyable reasonably priced simple food including good fish and chips (no booking), airy contemporary interior with well spaced tables; sports TV; children and dogs welcome, disabled facilities, picnic-sets outside, moments from sea and lighthouse, open (and food) all day. *(Comus and Sarah Elliott)*

SOUTHWOLD TM5076

Swan (01502) 722186

Market Place; IP18 6EG Major refurbishment for this smart Adnams-owned hotel, their full range kept well plus bottled beers and good choice of wines, food and service can be good, afternoon teas in front lounge, nice garden, 42 bedrooms (some in separate block), open all day. *(Mike Benton)*

STANSFIELD TL7851

Compasses (01284) 789263

High Street; CO10 8LN Simple little country pub with good often interesting locally sourced food cooked by character landlord (some ingredients from next-door farm), own-brewed beers and local guests, beams, bare boards and large woodburner; monthly quiz and occasional live music; children, walkers and dogs welcome, outside tables with lovely rural views, open Thurs evening to Sun lunchtime. *(John Harris)*

STOKE ASH TM1170

White Horse (01379) 678222

A140/Workhouse Road; IP23 7ET Sizeable 17th-c gabled coaching inn on crossroads, beams and inglenook fireplaces, generous helpings of enjoyable reasonably priced pub food, well kept ales such as Adnams, Greene King and Woodfordes, Aspall's cider, efficient friendly service; free wi-fi; children welcome, bedrooms in modern annexe, open (and food) all day from 8am. *(Jim and Sue James)*

STOKE-BY-NAYLAND TL9836

★**Angel** (01206) 263245

B1068 Sudbury–East Bergholt; CO6 4SA Elegant 17th-c inn (same owners as the Anchor at Nayland); lounge with handsome beams, timbers and stripped brickwork, leather chesterfields and wing armchairs around low tables, more formal room featuring deep glass-covered well, chatty bar with straightforward furniture on red tiles, well kept Adnams and Woodfordes, several wines by the glass and good range of gins and cocktails, very well liked food including lunchtime set menu, afternoon teas (not Sun, booking required), efficient friendly service; children and dogs (in some parts) welcome, seats on sheltered terrace, six individually styled bedrooms, good breakfast, open all day from 10am. *(Sandra and Michael Smith)*

STOWUPLAND TM0759

Crown (01449) 490490

Church Road (A1120 just E of Stowmarket); IP14 4BQ Extended thatched pub set back from the road behind white picket fence; refurbished interior blending traditional and contemporary features, well liked sensibly priced food from pub favourites up including good stone-baked pizzas (visible oven), real ales and a dozen wines by the glass, friendly efficient service, bar with log fire, restaurant; children and dogs welcome, good-sized garden, open all day, just pizzas Sun evening. *(Mrs Margo Finlay, Jörg Kasprowski)*

STRATFORD ST MARY TM0434

★**Swan** (01206) 321244

Lower Street; CO7 6JR Big changes afoot for this 16th-c coaching inn (previous Main Entry) with forthcoming closure for restoration and extensions – news please; has offered fantastic choice of drinks and creative food in two beamed bars and timbered back restaurant; children and dogs have been allowed, seats on terrace and on big lawn across road, some tables under willows by River Stour, has closed Mon and Tues. *(Adam Jones, Andy and Rosemary Taylor, Paul Farraday)*

STUTTON TM1434

Gardeners Arms (01473) 328868

Manningtree Road, Upper Street (B1080); IP9 2TG Cottagey roadside pub on edge of small village; well kept Adnams Southwold and guests, good value home-made food including daily specials, friendly helpful service, cosy L-shaped bar with log fire, side dining room and larger area stretching to the back, lots of bric-a-brac, film posters and musical instruments; children and dogs welcome, two-tier back garden with pond, open all day Sun, closed Mon. *(Diana Abbot)*

SUDBURY TL8741

Brewery Tap (01787) 370876

East Street; CO10 2TP Corner tap for Mauldons brewery; their range and guests kept well, also belgian fruit beers and good range of malt whiskies, some snacky food (can bring your own, cutlery provided); comedy club first Weds of month, quiz and live music nights, darts, cribbage and bar billiards; dogs welcome, open all day. *(Rosie and Marcus Heatherley)*

SWEFFLING TM3464

White Horse (01728) 664178

B1119 Framlingham–Saxmundham; IP17 2BB Traditional little two-room country pub with woodburner in one room, range in the other, up to three well kept changing east anglian beers served from tap room door, real cider and some interesting local wines and spirits, simple food such as ploughman's and locally made winter pies, friendly service; some live acoustic music, bar billiards, darts and other traditional games; children and dogs welcome, small beer garden with rustic arbour, self-catering cottage and campsite including yurts, closed lunchtimes (apart from Sun), and evenings Tues-Thurs. *(Mike Benton)*

SWILLAND TM1852

Moon & Mushroom (01473) 785320

Off B1078; IP6 9LR Popular 16th-c country local serving four changing east anglian beers from racked casks behind long counter, old tables and chairs on quarry tiles, log fire, enjoyable good value home-made food sourced locally; quiz first Weds of month, occasional live music; children and dogs welcome, heated flower-filled terrace, closed Sun evening, Mon. *(Belinda and Neil Garth)*

THORNDON TM1469

Black Horse (01379) 678523

Off A140 or B1077, S of Eye; The Street; IP23 7JR Welcoming 17th-c village pub with enjoyable fairly traditional food including good lunchtime carvery, three well kept local ales such as Adnams, friendly helpful service, lots of timbering, stripped brick and big fireplaces; well behaved children and dogs (in bar) welcome, tables on lawn, country views behind, open all day Sun till 9pm, closed Tues. *(Cecily and Steven Evans)*

THORNHAM MAGNA TM1070

Four Horseshoes (01379) 678777

Off A140 S of Diss; Wickham Road; IP23 8HD Extensive thatched dining pub dating from the 12th c; well divided dimly lit carpeted bar, Greene King ales and good choice of wines and whiskies, enjoyable reasonably priced food with some main courses available in smaller helpings, popular Sun carvery, friendly helpful staff, very low heavy black beams, country pictures and brass, big log fireplace and an old illuminated well; background music; children and dogs (in bar) welcome, disabled access, picnic-sets on big sheltered lawn, handy for Thornham Walks and interesting thatched church, seven comfortable bedrooms, open all day. *(Geoff and Anne Marston)*

THORPENESS TM4759

★**Dolphin** (01728) 454994

Just off B1353; Old Homes Road; village signposted from Aldeburgh; IP16 4FE Extended and neatly kept dining pub in interesting seaside village (all built in the early 1900s); main bar with scandinavian feel, pale wooden tables and assortment of old chairs on broad modern quarry tiles, log fire, well kept Adnams, guest beers and several wines by the glass from good value list, more traditional public bar with pubby furniture on stripped-wood floor, built-in cushioned wall seats and old local photographs, airy dining room has country kitchen-style furniture and traditional panelling, enjoyable locally sourced food from shortish but interesting menu, friendly service; background music, TV, free wi-fi; children and dogs welcome, spacious garden, three refurbished bedrooms, open all day weekends, closed Mon in winter. *(Tracey and Stephen Groves)*

THURSTON TL9165

Fox & Hounds (01359) 232228

Barton Road; IP31 3QT Rather imposing former 19th-c station inn; well kept Adnams Broadside, Greene King IPA and four guests, traditional furnishings in carpeted lounge (back part set for dining), ceiling fans and lots of pump clips, generously served reasonably priced pubby food (not Sun evening, Mon lunchtime) including regular themed nights, friendly service, bare-boards public bar with pool, darts and machines; background and some live music, quiz and bingo nights; children and dogs welcome, picnic-sets on grassed area by car park and on small covered side terrace, pretty village, self-catering apartment, open all day. *(Mike Benton)*

TUDDENHAM TM1948

★**Fountain** (01473) 785377

The Street; village signed off B1077 N of Ipswich; IP6 9BT Popular dining pub in nice village; several linked café-style rooms with heavy beams and timbering, stripped floors, wooden dining chairs around light tables, open fire, lots of prints (some by cartoonist Giles who spent time here after World War II), wide choice of well cooked food (all day Sun till 7pm) including set menus and blackboard specials, Adnams Southwold and good selection of wines by the glass, decent coffee; background music; no under-10s in bar after 6.30pm, dogs welcome, wicker and metal chairs on covered heated terrace, rows of picnic-style tables under parasols on sizeable lawn. *(Patti and James Davidson)*

UFFORD TM2952

★**Crown** (01394) 461030

High Street; IP13 6EL Broad mix of customers at this popular family-run pub-restaurant; good food cooked by landlady's brother from interestingly varied menu, bar and dining areas with cushioned wooden dining chairs and leather banquettes around medley of dark tables, shelves of books, modern ceiling lights, open fires in brick fireplaces, stools against counter serving Adnams Southwold, Earl Soham Victoria Bitter and a dozen good wines by the glass, friendly service; free wi-fi; children and dogs (in bar) welcome, seats out at front, picnic-sets under parasols in back garden with play area, open all day weekends (till 8pm Sun), closed Tues. *(Liz and Martin Eldon, Sandra King, Christopher Mannings)*

UFFORD TM2952

White Lion (01394) 460770

Lower Street (off B1438, towards Eyke); IP13 6DW 16th-c village pub near quiet stretch of River Deben; home to the Uffa Brewery with their beers and guests tapped from the cask, enjoyable generously served home-made food (own pigs, free-range hens and bees), raised woodburner in large central fireplace, captain's chairs and spindlebacks around simple tables, shop/deli; nice views from outside tables, summer barbecues and wood-fired pizzas, closed Sun evening, Mon lunchtime. *(Alexandra and Richard Clay)*

WANGFORD TM4779

Plough (01502) 578239

Barnaby Green; A12 next to service station; NR34 8AY Useful roadside stop with enjoyable reasonably priced home-made food from sandwiches to daily specials, well kept Adnams and decent range of wines, friendly staff; children and dogs welcome, big garden with play area, five courtyard bedrooms and small campsite, open all day, no food Sun evening. *(Jim and Sue James)*

WENHASTON TM4274

Star (01502) 478240

Hall Road; IP19 9HF Friendly well run 19th-c country pub with three small rooms; Adnams Southwold, five guest beers and decent wines, wide range of enjoyable inexpensive home-made food; children, dogs and muddy boots welcome, sizeable lawn with boules, nice views, camping (must be pre-booked) open all day Sun. *(Andrew Vincent)*

WESTLETON TM4469

White Horse (01728) 648222

Darsham Road, off B1125 Blythburgh–Leiston; IP17 3AH Friendly and relaxed traditional pub; well liked home-cooked food from blackboard menu including daily specials, four well kept Adnams ales, high-ceilinged bar with central fire, steps down to stone-floored back dining room; quiz nights, darts, free wi-fi; children and dogs welcome, picnic-sets in cottagey garden, more out by village duck pond, bedrooms, good breakfast. *(Charlie and Mark Todd)*

WINGFIELD TM2276

De La Pole Arms (01379) 384983

Off B1118 N of Stradbroke; Church Road; IP21 5RA Timbered 16th-c pub revamped under present welcoming licensees; enjoyable food from sandwiches to daily specials, Sun carvery, well kept Adnams, St Peters and decent wines by the glass, good friendly service, beams, flagstones and quarry tiles, bar with log fire in big fireplace, raftered restaurant, deli/café; children and dogs (in bar) welcome, disabled access, tables under parasols on sunny terrace, closed Mon, otherwise open all day from 11am (till 7pm Sun). *(Guy Henderson)*

WOODBRIDGE TM2648

Cherry Tree (01394) 384627

Opposite Notcutts Nursery, off A12; Cumberland Street; IP12 4AG Opened-up 17th-c pub (bigger than it looks) with eight well kept ales including Adnams (beer festivals), good wines by the glass and generous helpings of tasty reasonably priced food, friendly service, beams and two log fires, mix of pine furniture, old local photographs; Thurs quiz; children and dogs (in bar) welcome, garden with play area, three bedrooms in converted barn, good breakfast (for non-residents too), open (and food) all day. *(John Harris)*

WOODBRIDGE TM2748

Crown (01394) 384242

Thoroughfare/Quay Street; IP12 1AD Stylish 17th-c dining inn; well kept ales such as Adnams from glass-roofed bar (boat suspended above counter), lots of wines by the glass and cocktails, good imaginative food from light meals up including set menu, steak night Thurs, afternoon teas (must book), pleasant young staff, various eating areas with contemporary furnishings; occasional live jazz; children and dogs (in bar) welcome, courtyard tables, ten well appointed bedrooms, open (and food) all day. *(Comus and Sarah Elliott)*

WOODBRIDGE TM2749

Olde Bell & Steelyard (01394) 382933 *New Street, off Market Square; IP12 1DZ* Ancient timber-framed pub with plenty of old world character (the listed steelyard still overhangs the street); two smallish beamed bars and cosy dining room, log fire, well kept Greene King ales and three changing guests from canopied servery, standard home-made food (not Sun evening); traditional games including bar billiards, sports TV, free wi-fi; children and dogs welcome, disabled access, pretty flower-filled back terrace, open all day Fri-Sun. *(John Harris, Mike Benton)*

WOOLPIT TL9762

Swan (01359) 240482

The Street; IP30 9QN Welcoming old coaching house pleasantly situated in village square; heavy beams and painted panelling, mixed tables and chairs on carpet, roaring log fire at one end, good seasonal food served by efficient friendly staff, well kept Adnams from slate-topped counter and lots of wines by the glass; maybe background music, quiz last Sun of month; walled garden behind, four bedrooms in converted stables, closed Sun evening, Mon. *(Geoff and Anne Marston)*

Surrey

BUCKLAND TQ2250 Map 3

Pheasant

(01737) 221355 – www.brunningandprice.co.uk/pheasant

Reigate Road (A25 W of Reigate); RH3 7BG

Busy roadside pub with a thoughtful range of drinks and food served by friendly staff, character rooms and seats on terrace and lawn

The various open-plan rooms in this attractive, carefully extended, weatherboarded pub are interconnected and split into cosier areas by timbering and painted standing pillars. A couple of dining rooms at one end, separated by a two-sided open fire, have captain's chairs and cushioned dining chairs around a mix of tables on bare boards or rugs – and throughout there are wall-to-wall prints and pictures, gilt-edged mirrors, house plants, old stone bottles and elegant metal chandeliers. The busy bar has a long high table with equally high chairs, another two-way fireplace with button-back leather armchairs and sofas in front of it and stools against the counter where they keep Brunning & Price Phoenix Original plus guests such as Dark Star Not Into Yoga, Harveys Olympia Golden Ale, Pilgrim Quench, Surrey Hills Gilt Complex and Windsor & Eton Knight of the Garter on handpump, 24 wines by the glass, 60 whiskies and 73 gins; background music and board games. One of the two other dining rooms has a big open fire pit in the middle. Out on the terrace is another open fire pit surrounded by built-in seats plus solid tables and chairs, while the lawn has plenty of picnic-sets and a play tractor for children.

Interesting food includes sandwiches, rabbit satay on thai vegetable noodle salad, crispy salt and pepper baby squid, wild mushroom and truffle pasta with wilted spinach, caramelised basil and parmesan shavings, cumberland sausages with mash and onion gravy, chicken, ham hock and leek pie with white wine sauce, fillet of sea trout with cauliflower purée, roast beetroot and crispy kale, guinea fowl on warm quinoa, green lentil and bacon salad with honey and mustard dressing, and puddings such as apple and blackberry crumble with vanilla custard and chocolate brownie with vanilla ice-cream. *Benchmark main dish: mint and lime harissa rump of lamb with cumin roasted new potatoes, tzatziki and watercress £19.95. Two-course evening meal £21.00.*

Brunning & Price ~ Manager Bethany Wells ~ Real ale ~ Open 10am-11pm; 9am-11pm Sat; 9am-10.30pm Sun ~ Bar food 12-9 (9.30 Sat); breakfast 9-10.45am weekends ~ Restaurant ~ Children welcome ~ Dogs allowed in bar ~ Wi-fi *Recommended by M G Hart, Chantelle and Tony Redman, Sarah and David Gibbs, Dave Chapman, Mike and Sarah Abbot, Patrick and Emma Stephenson*

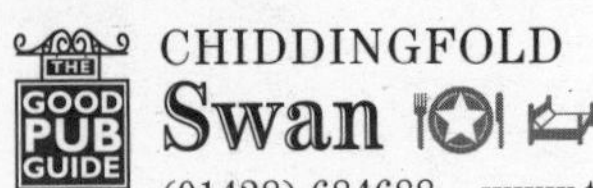

CHIDDINGFOLD SU9635 Map 3

Swan

(01428) 684688 – www.theswaninnchiddingfold.com

Petworth Road (A283 S); GU8 4TY

Open-plan, light and airy rooms in well run inn, with local ales, modern food and seats in terraced garden; bedrooms

This is a stylishly updated tile-hung inn on the edge of pretty countryside. The bar has an open fire in an inglenook fireplace with leather armchairs in front and antlers above, wooden tables and chairs and cushioned wall seats on pale floorboards and leather-topped stools against the counter where they keep Upham Punter, Tipster and a guest ale on handpump, 19 wines by the glass and a good choice of spirits. Staff are helpful and friendly. The dining room leads off here with modern chairs and chunky tables set with fresh flowers on more bare boards. Outside, a three-tiered terraced garden has plenty of seats and tables. The well equipped and comfortable bedrooms make a good base for exploring the area – there's plenty to do and see nearby.

As well as offering a buffet breakfast to non-residents (9-10.30am weekends), the enjoyable food includes hay-smoked venison loin with beetroot, carrots and watercress purée, seared foie gras with gooseberries and spiced apple purée, blue cheese and walnut pastilla with charred celery heart, oven-dried tomatoes and lovage dressing, burger with toppings and shoestring fries, corn-fed chicken breast with smoked leg croquette and broccoli and sweetcorn fricassée, cod in crab bisque with saffron potatoes, spaghetti vegetables and mussels, and puddings such as date sponge pudding with caramel sauce and espresso semifreddo with brioche doughnuts. *Benchmark main dish: calves liver with celery and potato hash, streaky bacon and onion jus £15.95. Two-course evening meal £22.00.*

Upham ~ Managers Zach and Sinead Leach ~ Real ale ~ Open 7am-11pm; 9am-11pm Sat; 9am-10.30pm Sun ~ Bar food 12-3, 6.30-9.30 (9 Sun); snacks 3-6.30 ~ Children welcome ~ Dogs allowed in bar ~ Wi-fi ~ Bedrooms: /£85 *Recommended by Helena and Trevor Fraser, Tim and Sarah Smythe-Brown, Sally and David Champion, Miss A E Dare, Bryce, Bridget and Peter Gregson, Alison and Dan Richardson*

CHIPSTEAD TQ2757 Map 3

White Hart

(01737) 554455 – www.brunningandprice.co.uk/whitehartchipstead

Hazelwood Lane; CR5 3QW

Airy open-plan rooms, a thoughtful choice of drinks, rewarding food and friendly staff

Surrounded by pretty countryside, this is a comfortable pub for an interesting drink or a meal. The raftered dining room to the right has elegant metal chandeliers, rough-plastered walls, an open fire in a brick fireplace and a couple of carved metal standing uprights. Helpful staff serve Phoenix Brunning & Price Original and Sambrooks Wandle with guests such as Adnams Ghost Ship, Fullers London Pride, Hogs Back TEA and Pilgrim Surrey Bitter on handpump, 20 wines by the glass, more than 35 gins and up to 60 malt whiskies; background music and board games. The long room to the left is light and airy, with wall panelling at one end, a woodburning stove and numerous windows overlooking the seats on the terrace. Throughout there's a fine mix of antique dining chairs and settles around all sorts of tables, rugs on bare boards, hundreds of interesting cartoons, country pictures, cricketing prints and rugby team photographs, large ornate mirrors and, on the windowsills and mantelpieces, old glass and stone bottles, clocks, books and plants.

Distinctive food includes sandwiches, seared scallops with roasted celeriac, pancetta and caramelised apple purée, ham hock hash with pea velouté, crispy hen egg and charred spring onion, sharing boards, cauliflower and butternut squash biryani with lentil dhal, lime pickle and red onion bhaji, crispy beef salad with sweet chilli sauce and roasted cashew nuts, fish pie (salmon, smoked haddock and prawns) with french-style peas, moroccan-spiced chicken thighs with lemon couscous, sweet potato falafel and apricot and pomegranate salad, duck breast with duck croquette, tenderstem broccoli and clementine jus, and puddings such as triple chocolate brownie with chocolate sauce and crème brûlée. *Benchmark main dish: braised lamb shoulder with dauphinoise potatoes and gravy £16.95. Two-course evening meal £21.00.*

Brunning & Price ~ Manager Ollie Simmonds ~ Real ale ~ Open 11.30-11 (10.30 Sun) ~ Bar food 12-9.30; 12-10 Fri, Sat; 12-9 Sun ~ Restaurant ~ Children welcome ~ Dogs allowed in bar ~ Wi-fi *Recommended by M G Hart, Robert and Diana Ringstone, Sally and Colin Allen, Martin and Joanne Sharp, Andrew and Ruth Simmonds*

CHOBHAM SU9761 Map 2

White Hart

(01276) 857580 – www.brunningandprice.co.uk/whitehartchobham

High Street; GU24 8AA

Brick-built village inn with cheerful customers and a thoughtful choice of food and drink

As ever, the fantastic choice of drinks and up-to-the-minute food draws plenty of cheerful customers to this handsome old place. The opened-up bar remains at its heart and has white-painted beams, standing pillars, rugs on parquet or wide boards, an assortment of dark wooden dining chairs and tables, and armchairs beside two fireplaces; background music and board games. High chairs line the counter where cheerful, well trained staff serve Phoenix Brunning & Price Original and guests such as Crafty Brewing Dunsfold Best, Reunion Opening Gambit, Surrey Hills Greensand IPA and Thurstons Horsell Gold on handpump, 20 wines by the glass, 40 gins and over 40 malt whiskies. An L-shaped dining room has a leather wall banquette and leather and brass-studded dining chairs around a mix of tables and lots of old photos and prints on exposed-brick or painted walls. There's also a comfortable dining room with similar furniture, carpeting and a large elegant metal chandelier. The little side garden has seats under parasols.

Good food includes sandwiches, chargrilled octopus with tomato chutney, korean chicken wings with kimchi salad, salmon and smoked haddock fishcake with a poached egg and chive and caper sauce, potato, cauliflower, okra and chickpea curry with coconut rice, cumberland sausages with mash and onion gravy, sage-roasted pork tenderloin with pigs cheek and celeriac croquette and prune and Armagnac gravy, chicken breast with marsala sauce, wild mushrooms and egg pappardelle, and puddings such as white chocolate cheesecake with blackcurrant sorbet and crème brûlée; they also offer weekend brunch (9-11am). *Benchmark main dish: braised lamb shoulder with dauphinoise potatoes and rosemary gravy £17.95. Two-course evening meal £20.00.*

Brunning & Price ~ Manager Stan Morgan ~ Real ale ~ Open 11-11; 9am-11pm Sat; 9am-10.30pm Sun ~ Bar food 12-9; 12-10 Fri; 9am-10pm Sat; 9-9 Sun ~ Restaurant ~ Children welcome away from the bar ~ Dogs allowed in bar ~ Wi-fi
Recommended by Jo Garnett, Liz and Martin Eldon, William and Sophia Renton, Francis and Mandy Robertson, Mark Hamill

ELSTEAD SU9044 Map 2

Mill at Elstead

(01252) 703333 – www.millelstead.co.uk

Farnham Road (B3001 just W of village, which is itself between Farnham and Milford); GU8 6LE

Fascinating building with big attractive waterside garden, Fullers beers and well liked food

A largely 18th-c watermill, this is in a special setting above the prettily banked River Wey; picnic-sets are dotted about by the water and there's a lovely millpond with swans and weeping willows. A series of rambling linked bar areas on the spacious ground floor have big windows that make the most of the view; there's an upstairs restaurant too. You'll find brown leather armchairs and antique engravings by a longcase clock, neat modern tables and dining chairs on bare boards, big country tables on broad ceramic tiles, iron pillars, stripped masonry and a log fire in a huge inglenook. Fullers ESB, London Pride, Olivers Island and a seasonal beer on handpump, 15 wines by the glass and several malt whiskies and gins; background music, board games and TV.

From a seasonal menu the food might include lunchtime sandwiches, chicken and black pudding terrine with piccalilli, sharing boards, burger of the day with toppings and fries, sautéed gnocchi with vine tomatoes, artichokes, basil and mozzarella, a pie of the day, beer-battered fish and chips, duck breast with feta and mint, poached salmon with lemon and herb dressing and roasted vegetables, sirloin steak with triple-cooked chips and béarnaise sauce, and puddings such as banoffi cheesecake with salted caramel sauce and lemon tart with raspberry sorbet. *Benchmark main dish: harissa chicken with middle eastern couscous £14.00. Two-course evening meal £19.00.*

Fullers ~ Manager Paul Stephens ~ Real ale ~ Open 11-11; 12-10.30 Sun ~ Bar food 12-9; 12-7 Sun ~ Restaurant ~ Children welcome ~ Dogs welcome ~ Wi-fi ~ Quiz every second Weds of month *Recommended by Geoff and Ann Marston, Edward and William Johnston, Heather and Richard Jones, Joe and Belinda Smart*

ENGLEFIELD GREEN SU9869 Map 2

Bailiwick

(01784) 477877 – www.brunningandprice.co.uk/bailiwick

Wick Road; TW20 0HN

Fine position by parkland for busy pub, with lots of interest in various bars and dining rooms, well liked food and drink and super staff

Before coming here for lunch, you could enjoy a circular walk that starts at the pub and follows the south-east corner of Windsor Great Park from where you can see the polo lawns, Virginia Water lake and the vast expanses of landscaped parkland. The busy open-plan bar area at the front (where dogs are allowed) has cushioned dining chairs around wooden tables on rugs and bare boards, and an attractive Victorian fireplace with a large mirror above. Stools line the counter where knowledgeable, warmly friendly staff serve Phoenix Brunning & Price Original, Ascot Gold Cup, Twickenham Naked Ladies and Windsor & Eton Guardsman on handpump, 21 good wines by the glass, 20 rums, 26 vodkas, 48 gins, 96 malt whiskies and farm cider. Steps lead down to a dining area and on again to a bigger room with caramel-coloured leather dining chairs, banquettes and tables of every size. Throughout there are elegant metal chandeliers, prints and black and white photographs, lots of house plants and windowsills full of old stone and glass bottles; background music and board games. A small front terrace has a few seats and tables. There's no car park but there are 20 free spaces in the long lay-by on Wick Road; if these are full there's a large pay-on-entry car park alongside.

As well as offering breafasts (10-12; 9-11am weekends), the interesting food includes sandwiches, rabbit spring roll with pickled carrot salad, a charcuterie sharing board, smoked haddock fishcake with a poached egg, tomato concasse and tartare sauce, crispy beef salad with sweet chilli dressing and cashew nuts, cauliflower, sweet potato and spinach curry, pork sausages with mash and onion gravy, salmon with clams, crushed new potatoes and beurre blanc sauce, braised lamb shoulder with dauphinoise potatoes, red cabbage and rosemary gravy, and puddings such as crème brûlée and sticky toffee pudding with toffee sauce. *Benchmark main dish: chicken, ham hock and leek pie £13.95. Two-course evening meal £21.00.*

Brunning & Price ~ Manager Claudette Thake ~ Real ale ~ Open 10am-11pm; 9am-11pm Sat; 9am-10pm Sun ~ Bar food 12-9 (9.30 Sat) ~ Children welcome ~ Dogs allowed in bar ~ Wi-fi *Recommended by Alexander and Trish Gendall, Nick and Meriel Cox, Maggie and Matthew Lyons, Martin and Sue Neville, Len and Lilly Dowson*

ESHER TQ1566 Map 3

Marneys

(020) 8398 4444 – www.marneys.co.uk

Alma Road (one-way), Weston Green; heading N on A309 from A307 roundabout; after half a mile turn left into Lime Tree Avenue (signposted to All Saints Parish Church), then left at T junction into Chestnut Avenue; KT10 8JN

Country-feeling pub with good value food and attractive garden

Turning off the busy trunk road, it's a real surprise to find this cottagey little pub in such a pleasant spot right on the edge of a well wooded common. The chatty low-beamed bar has a good mix of customers, Fullers London Pride, Sharps Doom Bar and Youngs Bitter on handpump, 16 wines by the glass, ten malt whiskies and perhaps horse-racing on the unobtrusive corner TV. To the left, past a little cast-iron woodburning stove, the dining area has big pine tables, pews, pale country kitchen chairs and cottagey blue-curtained windows; background music. There are seats and wooden tables on the front terrace, which has views over the common, village church and duck pond, and more seats on the decked area in the pleasantly planted sheltered garden. The pub is handy for Hampton Court Palace.

Well regarded food includes king scallops and chorizo with cauliflower purée, baked camembert with chutney, pear, walnut and roquefort salad, steak in ale pie, lamb burger with goats cheese and caramelised onions, cumberland sausage and mustard mash with onion gravy, scampi and chips, and puddings such as sticky toffee pudding and chocolate brownie with ice-cream. *Benchmark main dish: home-made thai fishcakes £12.95. Two-course evening meal £20.00.*

Free house ~ Licensee Thomas Duxberry ~ Real ale ~ Open 11-11; 12-10.30 Sun ~ Bar food 12-2.30, 6-9; 12-3.30 Sun; not Fri-Sun evenings ~ Restaurant ~ Children welcome away from bar ~ Dogs allowed in bar ~ Wi-fi *Recommended by Julie Braeburn, Tom and Ruth Rees, Dan and Nicki Barton, Chloe and Tim Hodge, Margo and Derek Stapley*

Please tell us if the décor, atmosphere, food or drink at a pub is different from our description. We rely on readers' reports to keep us up to date: feedback@goodguides.com, or (no stamp needed) The Good Pub Guide, FREEPOST RTXY–ZCBC–BBAZ, Stream Lane, Sedlescombe, Battle TN33 0PB.

MICKLEHAM TQ1753 Map 3

Running Horses

(01372) 372279 – www.therunninghorses.co.uk

Old London Road (B2209); RH5 6DU

Country pub with plenty of customers in bar and dining rooms, enjoyable food and drink and seats on big front terrace; bedrooms

The picnic-sets on the terrace in front of this smart, substantial, white-painted inn with its big sash windows and lovely flowering tubs and hanging baskets take in a peaceful view of the old church with its strange stubby steeple, just across the quiet lane. Inside, the stylish and spacious bar has cushioned wall settles and other dining chairs around straightforward tables on parquet flooring, racing cartoons and Hogarth prints on the walls, lots of race tickets hanging from a beam and a log fire in an inglenook fireplace; some wood-panelled booths have red leather banquettes. Stools line the counter where friendly, helpful staff serve Brakspears Bitter and Oxford Gold, Fullers London Pride and a guest beer such as Brakspears Honey Bee on handpump and around 20 wines by the glass; background music. The panelled restaurant is an attractive mix of upholstered and wooden dining chairs around a medley of tables on tartan carpet. Parking is in a narrow lane (you can also park on the main road).

As well as breakfasts for non-residents (8-10am), the tempting food includes lunchtime sandwiches, garlic king prawns with coriander, chicken, apricot and tarragon terrine with pickled beetroot and apple purée, sharing boards (the mixed seafood with taramasalata with flatbread is popular), harissa-spiced chickpeas with sweet potato cake, charred bean salsa and salsa verde, burger with toppings and triple-cooked chips, dressed crab with salad and truffled mayonnaise, lamb trio (roasted rump, sweetbread bonbon and belly) with potato terrine and port and rosemary jus, rabbit loin with confit leg pie, carrot purée, spinach and thyme jus, and puddings such as sticky toffee pudding with clotted cream ice-cream and lemon tart with raspberry sorbet. *Benchmark main dish: sea bass with sea vegetables and sweetcorn and sunblush tomato broth £16.50. Two-course evening meal £22.00.*

Brakspears ~ Manager Chris Holmes ~ Real ale ~ Open 11-11 (10.30 Sun) ~ Bar food 12-9; 12-10 Fri, Sat; 12-8 Sun ~ Restaurant ~ Children welcome ~ Dogs allowed in bar ~ Wi-fi ~ Bedrooms: /£125 *Recommended by Professor James Burke, Jennifer and Nicholas Thompson, Francis and Mandy Robertson*

MILFORD SU9542 Map 2

Refectory

(01483) 413820 – www.brunningandprice.co.uk/refectory

Portsmouth Road; GU8 5HJ

Beamed and timbered rooms of much character, six real ales and other thoughtful drinks and well liked food

Once an antiques shop and tea room (and before that a lowly cattle barn), this is now a stunning pub of golden stone and oak timbers. The L-shaped, mainly open-plan rooms are spacious and interesting with exposed-stone walls, stalling and standing timbers creating separate seating areas, strikingly heavy beams and a couple of large log fires in fine stone fireplaces. A two-tiered and balconied part at one end has a wall covered with huge brass platters; elsewhere there are nice old photographs and a variety of paintings. Dining chairs and dark wooden tables are grouped on wooden, quarry-tiled or carpeted floors, and there are bookshelves, big pot plants, stone bottles on windowsills and fresh flowers. High wooden bar stools line the long counter where they serve Phoenix Brunning &

Price Original, Hogs Back TEA, Dark Star Hophead and three quickly changing guests on handpump, a dozen wines by the glass, 60 gins, around 80 malt whiskies and two farm ciders. The back courtyard (adjacent to the characterful pigeonry) has teak tables and chairs. Wheelchair facilities and disabled parking.

High quality food includes sandwiches, blue cheese pannacotta with apple, celery, grapes, candied walnuts and mustard dressing, smoked trout with beetroot relish and horseradish cream, smoked haddock fishcake with a poached egg, tandoori halloumi salad with pineapple, lime and mint salad, chicken breast with wild mushroom croquette, celeriac purée and sherry jus, warm crispy beef salad with sweet chilli dressing and cashew nuts, baised shoulder of lamb with minted new potatoes, tenderstem broccoli and rosemary gravy, fish pie with salmon, smoked haddock and prawns, boiled egg and french-style peas, and hot waffle with toffee sauce and caramelised banana and crème brûlée. *Benchmark main dish: steak burger with toppings, coleslaw and chips £13.45. Two-course evening meal £21.00.*

Brunning & Price ~ Manager Damian W Hayden ~ Real ale ~ Open 11-11; 11-10.30 Sun ~ Bar food 12-9.30 (10 Fri, Sat) ~ Restaurant ~ Children welcome ~ Dogs allowed in bar ~ Wi-fi ~ Live music occasional Sun *Recommended by Brian and Susan Wylie, Jeff Davies, Edward May, R and M Thomas, Miss A E Dare, Christopher and Elise Way*

NORWOOD HILL TQ2342 Map 3

Fox Revived

(01293) 229270 – www.brunningandprice.co.uk/foxrevived

Leigh–Charlwood back road; RH6 0ET

Extended, well run pub with attractive, interesting bar and dining areas, super staff, interesting food and a fine range of drinks; seats outside

Life here centres around the bustling bar where courteous, helpful staff keep Phoenix Brunning & Price Original and Surrey Hills Shere Drop with guests such as Crafty Brewing Loxhill Biscuit, Crouch Vale Brewers Gold, Harveys Best and Old Dairy Gold Top on handpump, 18 wines by the glass, 17 rums, 40 gins and 20 whiskies all served by courteous, helpful staff; background music and board games. There are button-back armchairs and stools by open fires and the various dining areas and nooks are divided up by balustrading and standing timbers. Walls are hung with photos, prints and gilt-edged mirrors, big house plants are scattered here and there or sit on windowsills, elegant metal chandeliers hang from ceilings and antique-style and high-backed leather dining chairs are grouped around tables of varying sizes on rugs, bare boards and carpet; one area has scatter cushions on a long L-shaped settle and lots of books on shelves. Seats and tables on the stone terrace in the garden look over the hills beyond, and there's a five-mile walk straight from the door.

Creative food includes sandwiches, teriyaki salmon with edamame, noodle and sesame salad, baked garlic and rosemary camembert with walnut and apple salad, thai vegetable curry with basil and jasmine rice, chicken, ham hock and leek pie, sea bass with clams, creamed leeks and parsley potato cake, cajun pork rib-eye medallions with roasted sweet potato and spicy dressed salad, slow-cooked beef with horseradish mash, and puddings such as dark chocolate brownie with chocolate sauce and lemon roulade with lemon curd, berry coulis and raspberry sorbet. *Benchmark main dish: slow-cooked beef with horseradish mash £15.75. Two-course evening meal £21.00.*

Brunning & Price ~ Manager Alistair Craig ~ Real ale ~ Open 10.30am-11pm; 10.30-10.30 Sun ~ Bar food 12-9.30 (9 Sun) ~ Restaurant ~ Children welcome ~ Dogs allowed in bar ~ Wi-fi *Recommended by Gail and Frank Hackett, Lucy and Giles Gibbon, Andy and Louise Ramwell, Belinda Stamp, Dave Chapman, Anne Taylor*

OXTED TQ3951 Map 3

Haycutter

(01883) 776955 – www.brunningandprice.co.uk/haycutter

Tanhouse Road, Broadham Green; off High Street opposite Old Bell; RH8 9PE

Plenty of chatty dining rooms and bars, lots to look at, attentive staff serving a fine choice of drinks and food, and seats outside

From the road this looks like a little cottagey pub, but it's been cleverly extended at the back into a sizeable place with plenty of room for both diners and drinkers. The large main bar is split up into different areas by metal uprights and there's a medley of dining chairs around wooden tables on parquet flooring or large rugs, some high tables with equally high stools in one corner, masses of photos and pictures on pale grey-green walls and a long counter stretching along a back wall. Friendly young staff serve Phoenix Brunning & Price Original, Harveys Best, Pilgrim Quest, Surrey Hills Shere Drop, Timothy Taylors Landlord, Wantsum Hengist and Westerham Finchcocks on handpump, 19 wines by the glass, 58 gins and 78 whiskies. A quarry-tiled walkway leads down towards the original building from where a couple of small rooms lead off to each side: similar tables and chairs and leather armchairs on bare boards and more rugs, open fires, house plants, books on shelves, more photos and prints on bare brick walls, elegant metal chandeliers and candles. One area has a massive circular table surrounded by a dozen chairs and there's also a private dining room. Outside, a big paved area with raised flower beds has good quality tables and chairs under large parasols and there are picnic-sets on lawns. Dogs are welcomed with a bowl of water and a biscuit.

Brasserie-style food includes sandwiches, deep-fried brie with pineapple chutney, scallops with sunblush tomato and artichoke purée, crisp ham and lemon and caper dressing, asparagus mint and feta quiche with potato salad, steak and stilton pie, smoked haddock chowder with clams, prawns, white wine and cream, wild garlic and basil half chicken with lemon and pepper sauce, beetroot slaw and sweet potato fries, beef curry with wild and basmati rice, lime and chilli, and puddings such as clementine cheesecake with orange sorbet and dark chocolate ganache and banoffi tart with clotted cream. *Benchmark main dish: pork three-ways £14.95. Two-course evening meal £21.00.*

Brunning & Price ~ Manager Chris Little ~ Real ale ~ Open 11.30-11; 12-10.30 Sun ~ Bar food 12-10; 12-9 Sun ~ Restaurant ~ Children welcome away from the front area ~ Dogs welcome ~ Wi-fi *Recommended by Amy Ledbetter, William Pace, Camilla and Jose Ferrera, Peter and Alison Steadman*

RIPLEY TQ0556 Map 2

Anchor

(01483) 211866 – www.ripleyanchor.co.uk

High Street; GU23 6AE

Stylish dining pub with first class food, real ales, friendly service and sunny courtyard

Despite the emphasis on eating here, there's an easy-going atmosphere and those just wanting a drink and a chat are more than welcome. The several low-ceilinged rooms are interlinked and have heavy beams, slate floors and open fires and are decorated in a stylish, simple way that's immediately inviting. There are church chairs around polished tables in the bar, dark wooden chairs and cushioned wall seats in the dining areas, contemporary paintwork or exposed-brick walls and elegant flower arrangements. Timothy Taylors Landlord and a couple of guests such as Wadworths IPA and Wimbledon Common Pale Ale on handpump, 25 good wines by the glass, 16 gins and nine malt whiskies; background music. Outside, a sunny, decked back courtyard has cushioned wicker chairs and sofas.

Creative food includes sandwiches, duck ravioli with smoked beetroot and parmesan sauce, sea trout with fennel salad, apple and vanilla, pumpkin and goats cheese cannelloni with mushrooms and sage pesto, burger with red onion marmalade, toppings and skinny chips, gurnard with samphire and carrot and coconut sauce, slow-cooked pork belly with soy and honey glaze, carrot purée and charred cabbage, and puddings such as pineapple and camomile upside-down cake with honeycomb and mint and pineapple sorbet and milk chocolate and salted peanut parfait with lime and biscotti. *Benchmark main dish: loin of venison with beetroot, celeriac and black pudding purée £24.00. Two-course evening meal £24.00.*

Free house ~ Licensee Michael Wall-Palmer ~ Real ale ~ Open 12-11; 12-9 Sun; closed Mon ~ Bar food 12-2.30, 6-9.30; 12-9.30 Fri, Sat; 12-8 Sun ~ Restaurant ~ Children welcome before 7pm ~ Wi-fi *Recommended by Geoffrey Kemp, Robin Waters, Mary and Douglas McDowell, Andrew Wall, Ian Wilson, John Evans, Dan and Anne Morgan, Gordon and Patricia Gorringe*

SHAMLEY GREEN TQ0343 Map 3

Red Lion

(01483) 892202 – www.redlionshamleygreen.com

The Green; GU5 0UB

Pleasant dining pub with popular food and attractive gardens

In warm weather, there are plenty of hand-made rustic tables and benches at the front of this busy pub looking over the village green and cricket pitch; it's more secluded at the back, where you'll find more seats on a heated, covered terrace and grassed dining areas. Inside, the two interconnected bars are fairly traditional with a mix of new and old wooden tables, chairs and cushioned settles on bare boards and red carpet, stripped standing timbers, fresh white walls, deep red ceilings and open fires. Hogs Back TEA, Sharps Doom Bar and Youngs London Gold on handpump, 11 wines by the glass and several gins and malt whiskies; background music.

Popular food includes sandwiches, crispy duck salad with hoisin dressing, garlic king prawns, greek spinach and feta pie, honey-roasted ham and eggs, lambs liver and bacon with mash and red wine gravy, chicken breast stuffed with cheese, garlic, lemon, rosemary and sun-dried tomatoes with fries, salmon with crayfish and parsley butter sauce, lamb shank in redcurrant and rosemary sauce on mash, veal schnitzel in garlic and lemon butter and topped with a fried egg, and puddings such as ginger pudding with ginger wine and brandy sauce and peach and apricot crumble. *Benchmark main dish: steak in ale pie £12.95. Two-course evening meal £19.50.*

Punch ~ Lease Debbie Ersser ~ Real ale ~ Open 11.30-11; 12-10 Sun (12-8 in winter) ~ Bar food 12-2.30 (3 Sat), 6.30-9.30; 12-3, 6.30-8.30 Sun; no food Sun evening in winter ~ Restaurant ~ Children welcome ~ Dogs allowed in bar ~ Wi-fi *Recommended by Gerry and Pam Pollard, Margaret McDonald, Rosie and John Moore, Pauline and Mark Evans*

SUNBURY TQ1068 Map 3

Flower Pot

(01932) 780741 – www.theflowerpotsunbury.co.uk

1.6 miles from M3 junction 1; follow Lower Sunbury sign from exit roundabout, then at Thames Street turn right; pub on next corner, with Green Street; TW16 6AA

Former coaching inn with appealing, contemporary bar and dining room, real ales and all-day food; bedrooms

Although not actually on the river, this handsome place with its elegant wrought-iron balconies and pretty summer hanging baskets is in a villagey area with waterside walks nearby. The airy bar has leather tub chairs around copper-topped tables, high chairs upholstered in brown and beige tartan around equally high tables in pale wood, attractive flagstones, contemporary paintwork and stools against the counter; there's also a couple of comfortably plush burgundy armchairs. The bar leads into a dining area with pale blue-painted and dark wooden cushioned dining chairs around an assortment of partly painted tables on bare boards, artwork on papered walls and a large gilt-edged mirror over an open fireplace; candles in glass jars, fresh flowers, background music and newspapers. Brakspears Bitter and Honey Bee and Youngs Special on handpump and 15 wines by the glass. A side terrace has wood and metal tables and chairs. The bedrooms are smart and comfortable.

Well regarded food includes breakfast (7-11am) plus mackerel pâté with chutney, lemon and herb chicken skewers with sweet chilli sauce, sharing boards, stone-baked pizzas, feta and chargrilled vegetable pasta with basil oil, burger with toppings, coleslaw and chips, cod fillet and vegetable broth, slow-cooked baby back pork ribs in barbecue sauce with chips, a pie of the day, 28-day-aged rump steak with crispy onion rings and a choice of sauce, and puddings such as a seasonal crumble with custard and chocolate brownie with chocolate sauce and ice-cream. *Benchmark main dish: corn-fed chicken with dauphinoise potatoes and peppercorn sauce £13.95. Two-course evening meal £20.00.*

Authentic Inns ~ Tenant Simon Bailey ~ Real ale ~ Open 7am-11pm; 8am-11pm Sat, Sun ~ Bar food 12-3, 6-9; 12-9 weekends ~ Restaurant ~ Children welcome ~ Dogs allowed in bar ~ Wi-fi ~ Live music last Fri of month ~ Bedrooms: /£99 *Recommended by Edward Edmonton, Pauline and Mark Evans, Diana and Bertie Farr, Mary and Douglas McDowell, Kerry and Guy Trooper*

WALTON ON THE HILL TQ2255 Map 3

Blue Ball

(01737) 819003 – www.theblueball.co.uk

Not far from M25 junction 8; Deans Lane, off B2220 by pond; KT20 7UE

Popular pub with spreading drinking and dining areas, helpful staff, well liked food and drink and lots of outside seating

Opposite Banstead Heath, this sizeable pub is especially busy in warm weather as the outside terrace has lots of seats and tables plus a fire pit under a gazebo, and you can hire cabanas for a private group (you must book in advance as they're extremely popular). The entrance bar has a chatty atmosphere, colourful leather-topped stools at the counter plus rugs on bare boards, house plants on windowsills, all manner of old pictures and photographs on the walls, antique-style cushioned, farmhouse and high-backed kitchen chairs around tables of every size, and a large wine cage. There's a beer named for the pub plus Fullers London Pride, Timothy Taylors Landlord, Upham First Drop and Wadworths Epic Brew on handpump and good wines by the glass. Leading back from here, several dining rooms have multicoloured button-back leather banquettes, similar chairs and tables on more rugs and wooden floors, bookshelves, gilt-edged mirrors and a big central conical open fire; background music.

A wide choice of food includes sandwiches (until 6pm), crispy whitebait with sweet chilli sauce, baked rosemary and garlic camembert with onion jam (to share), halloumi burger with toppings and sweet potato fries, smoked chicken caesar salad, beer-battered cod and chips, lambs liver with mash, bacon and onion gravy, whole plaice with beurre noisette and crushed caper and herb new potatoes, sirloin steak with marrowbone butter or peppercorn sauce, and puddings such as lemon posset pot with drunken berries and sticky toffee pudding with toffee sauce and honeycomb ice-cream. *Benchmark main dish: breaded katsu chicken with curry sauce and sticky rice £12.95. Two-course evening meal £20.00.*

Whiting & Hammond ~ Manager Spencer Goddard ~ Real ale ~ Open 10am-11pm; 9am-11pm Sat; 9am-10.30pm Sun ~ Bar food 12-9.30; 9am-9.30pm Sat; 9-9 Sun ~ Restaurant ~ Children welcome ~ Dogs allowed in bar ~ Wi-fi *Recommended by Maggie and Matthew Lyons, Charles Fraser, Gene and Kitty Rankin, Kitty and Stuart Flint, Martine and Derek Cotton*

WEST END SU9461 Map 2

The Inn West End

(01276) 858652 – www.the-inn.co.uk

Just under 2.5 miles from M3 junction 3; A322 S, on right; GU24 9PW

Surrey Dining Pub of the Year

Plenty of dining and drinking space in carefully refurbished rooms, excellent wines and inventive food; bedrooms

Excellent wines, impressive food and a genuine welcome all add up to this pub being held in consistently high esteem by our readers. The relaxed, friendly bar has white-painted beams, slatted and cushioned wooden benches and elegant chairs around a mix of tables on bare floorboards, pretty curtains, a large central barrel and chairs against the counter where they keep Dark Star Hophead, Fullers London Pride and Thurstons Horsell Gold on handpump. Wine plays a big role, with 20 by the glass from a fantastic list of around 500 (Iberia is the speciality); they also have several sherries, sweet wines and port, 30 malt whiskies, 20 gins and six vodkas. Do ask about the unusual clock. There's an extended restaurant and a lounge area with books on shelves and daily papers; Sunny and Teddy are the pub dogs. The pretty garden and terrace have plenty of seats for warm weather. Children are only allowed if dining with adults. Bedrooms are comfortable (one is dog-friendly and one has wheelchair access) and breakfasts are first class.

As well as breakfast (7-10.30am; 8.30-11am weekends) and championing local game and other first class produce from the area, the enticing food includes sandwiches, ham hock terrine with piccalilli, home-smoked scottish salmon and tiger prawn cocktail, pumpkin tortellini with butternut squash purée, goats cheese and artichoke heart, beer-battered haddock and chips, chicken suprême with wild mushroom and parmesan pasta and pancetta crumb, sea bream with charred peppers, artichoke and coriander, 10oz rib-eye steak with béarnaise sauce and chips, and puddings such as apple and blackberry crumble with crème anglaise and vanilla crème brûlée. *Benchmark main dish: venison filo parcel with mash and red wine jus £18.00. Two-course evening meal £25.00.*

Free house ~ Licensees Gerry and Ann Price ~ Real ale ~ Open 7am-11pm; 8.30am-midnight Sat; 8.30am-10.30pm Sun ~ Bar food 12-2.30, 6-9.30; 12-3, 6-9 Sun ~ Restaurant ~ Children over 5 allowed if dining ~ Dogs allowed in bar and bedrooms ~ Wi-fi ~ Bedrooms: £97.50/£112.50 *Recommended by Susan and John Douglas, Peter and Alison Steadman, Alison and Dan Richardson, Derek Stafford, Christopher and Elise Way, Louise and Simon Peters, Jill and Dick Archer*

Bedroom prices are for high summer. Even then you may get reductions for more than one night, or (outside tourist areas) weekends. Winter special rates are common, and many inns reduce bedroom prices if you have a full evening meal.

Also Worth a Visit in Surrey

Besides the fully inspected pubs, you might like to try these pubs that have been recommended to us and described by readers. Do tell us what you think of them: feedback@goodguides.com

ALBURY TQ0447

Drummond Arms (01483) 202039

Off A248 SE of Guildford; The Street; GU5 9AG Modernised 19th-c pub in pretty village; four real ales such as Adnams, Courage and Hogs Back, good choice of wines and enjoyable food from sandwiches and sharing plates up, opened-up bar with leather chesterfields and log fire, parquet-floored dining room, conservatory; children welcome, pretty back garden by little River Tillingbourne, summer barbecues and hog roasts, pleasant walks nearby, 11 bedrooms, open all day, food all day weekends. *(Dan and Anne Morgan)*

ALFOLD TQ0435

Alfold Barn (01403) 752288

Horsham Road, A281; GU6 8JE Beautifully preserved 16th-c building with bar and restaurant; very good locally sourced home-made food from daily changing menu with some emphasis on fish/seafood (Sun booking esential), friendly attentive service, up to three well kept ales from nearby breweries, beams and rafters, mixed furniture on flagstones or carpet, log fires; children welcome, closed Sun evening, Mon, Tues. *(Thomas Green)*

ALFOLD TQ0334

Three Compasses (01483) 275729

Dunsfold Road; GU6 8HY Welcoming 450-year-old pub refurbished under present management; well kept Otter and a couple of guests, good fairly priced food (not Sun evening, Mon) in bar and restaurant areas, big log fire; children and dogs welcome, good-sized garden, on back lane to former Dunsfold Aerodrome (now Dunsfold Park with little museum), Wey & Arun Canal nearby, open all day (till 9pm Sun). *(Thomas Green)*

BATTS CORNER SU8140

Blue Bell (01252) 792801

Batts Corner; GU10 4EX Busy tucked-way country pub with linked stone-floor rooms, light fresh décor and mix of furniture including sofas by big log fire, well kept ales such as Frensham, Langham and Triple fff, good home-made food from sandwiches to popular Sun lunch (must book), also weekday set lunch, helpful friendly staff; children, walkers and dogs welcome, attractive spacious garden with rolling views, summer barbecues and good play area, handy for Alice Holt Forest, open all day Sat, till 8pm Sun. *(Gordon and Patricia Gorringe)*

BLETCHINGLEY TQ3250

Bletchingley Arms (01883) 743711

High Street (A25); RH1 4PE Spacious modernised Barons group pub with plenty of opened-up areas (some steps) including beamed part with flagstones and woodburner, good choice of well prepared sensibly priced food from snacks up, three real ales, plenty of wines by the glass and good range of gins, friendly staff; background music (live last Fri of month), newspapers, sports TV; children and dogs (in bar) welcome, outside seating areas with own bar, beach huts and good play area, open all day. *(Ian Phillips, Ian Wilson)*

BLETCHINGLEY TQ3250

Red Lion (01883) 743342

Castle Street (A25), Redhill side; RH1 4NU Modernised and well looked-after beamed village dining pub, decent range of good home-made food such as steak and kidney pudding and beef stroganoff, well kept Greene King ales and a dozen wines by the glass, friendly staff; quiz and live music nights; children welcome, heated part-covered terrace, secret garden, open (and food) all day. *(Dave Chapman)*

BRAMLEY TQ0044

★**Jolly Farmer** (01483) 893355

High Street; GU5 0HB Family-run village pub with traditional beamed interior packed with collections of plates and old bottles, enamel signs, sewing machines, antique tools and so forth, timbered semi-partitions and open fire, Crafty Brewing, Greene King and up to six guests, a couple of summer ciders and over a dozen wines by the glass, generous helpings of fairly traditional food including good Sun carvery (worth booking); background music, quiz every other Weds, board games, free wi-fi; children and dogs (in bar) welcome, tables out by car park, walks up St Martha's Hill and handy for Winkworth Arboretum (NT), bedrooms, open all day. *(Peter Hailey, Mrs Zara Elliott, Sarah and John Webb)*

Post Office address codings confusingly give the impression that some pubs are in Surrey when they're really in Hampshire or London (which is where we list them). And there's further confusion from the way the Post Office still talks about Middlesex – which disappeared in local government reorganisation nearly 50 years ago.

BROCKHAM TQ1949

Inn on the Green (01737) 845101

Brockham Green; RH3 7JS Restauranty pub facing village green (part of the small Grumpy Mole group); good food from traditional choices up including cook-your-own steaks on a hot stone, helpful friendly service, well kept Fullers London Pride and Surrey Hills Shere Drop, several wines by the glass, afternoon teas, conservatory; children welcome, picnic-sets out at front, garden behind, open all day, food all day weekends. *(Len and Lilly Dowson)*

BROCKHAM TQ1949

Royal Oak (01737) 843241

Brockham Green; RH3 7JS Nice spot on charming village green below the North Downs; bare-boards bar and light airy dining area, well kept Fullers, Sharps and Youngs, decent home-made pub food, newspapers and log fires; events such as quiz nights and live jazz; children and dogs allowed, tables out in front looking across to fine church, more seats in back garden, handy for Greensand Way, open all day. *(Anne Taylor)*

BROOK SU9238

Dog & Pheasant (01428) 682763

Haslemere Road (A286); GU8 5UJ Popular pub looking across busy road to cricket green; long beamed bar divided up by standing timbers, cushioned wall settles, open fire in brick fireplace, four well kept ales such as Sharps from linenfold counter, plenty of wines by the glass and decent range of gins, dining area on right, further room to left with big inglenook, generally well liked food including pie of the day and Weds grill night; children and dogs welcome, picnic-sets on back deck and grass, play equipment, open all day, food till 4pm Sun. *(Martine and Derek Cotton)*

BURROWHILL SU9763

Four Horseshoes (01276) 856257

B383 N of Chobham; GU24 8QP Busy pub attractively set by village green; updated interior with beams and log fires, up to four well kept ales including Fullers London Pride and a Caledonian house beer (Shoes), popular interesting food from sandwiches and sharing boards up (best to book weekends, kitchen shuts 4.30pm Sun), cheerful helpful staff, dining extension; children, dogs and muddy boots welcome, tables out at front (some under ancient yew), also back terrace and garden with picnic-sets and deck chairs, open all day (till 7pm Sun). *(Ian Phillips)*

CARSHALTON TQ2764

Hope (020) 8240 1255

West Street; SM5 2PR Chatty community-owned mock-Tudor local; Downton, Windsor & Eton and five guests, also craft kegs, real cider/perry and over 50 bottled beers, generous low-priced pubby food (limited evening choice); 1950s-feel U-shaped bar with open fire, lots of pump clips, larger back room with bar billiards; live acoustic music second Weds of month, regular beer and cider festivals, board games; dogs welcome, disabled access/loos, garden, open all day. *(Louise and Simon Peters)*

CATERHAM TQ3254

Harrow (01883) 343260

Stanstead Road, Whitehill; CR3 6AJ Simple 16th-c beamed pub high up in open country by North Downs Way; L-shaped bare-boards bar and carpeted back dining area, several real ales (sometimes tapped from the cask) such as Fullers and Ringwood, well-liked food including daily specials, friendly staff and good local atmosphere; children and dogs welcome, garden picnic-sets, popular with walkers and cyclists, open all day, no food Sun evening. *(Margo and Derek Stapley)*

CHARLESHILL SU8844

Donkey (01252) 702124

B3001 Milford–Farnham near Tilford; coming from Elstead, turn left as soon as you see pub sign; GU10 2AU Old-fashioned beamed dining pub with enjoyable home-made food including weekday deals, up to three well kept changing ales and good choice of wines by the glass, prompt friendly service, conservatory restaurant; children and dogs welcome, attractive garden with paddock for much-loved donkeys Pip and Dusty, good walks, open all day weekends. *(William and Sophie Renton)*

CHARLTON TQ0868

Harrow (01932) 783122

Charlton Road, Ashford Common; off B376 Laleham–Shepperton; TW17 0RJ Pretty little thatched pub thought to date from 1130; simple beamed and carpeted interior with inglenook, Greene King ales and well priced food from pubby choices to good authentic indian dishes (takeaways available), side dining extension, some signed celebrity photos (Shepperton film studios nearby; sports TV, free wi-fi; picnic-sets in flower-filled front area, more seats in bigger back garden, small car park across busy road, open all day. *(Susan and John Douglas)*

CHARLWOOD TQ2441

Half Moon (01293) 863414

The Street; RH6 0DS Old pub next to churchyard in attractive village; spacious L-shaped bar (front part open to original upstairs windows), well kept Sharps Doom Bar, St Austell Tribute and a guest, enjoyable sensibly priced traditional food from sandwiches up, friendly service, back dining room, occasional live music; children and dogs (in bar) welcome, picnic-sets in nice courtyard area, handy for Gatwick Airport, food all day weekends. *(Tony Scott)*

CHERTSEY TQ0466

Olde Swan (01932) 562129
Windsor Street; KT16 8AY Former coaching house run by McLean Inns; generous helpings of popular reasonably priced food including pizzas, burgers and good Sun lunch, four well kept ales such as Marstons Wainwright and Sharps Doom Bar from well stocked bar, friendly efficient young staff, opened-up split-level interior with rugs on bare boards, candles on tables, comfortable seating and lots of pictures, mirrors and other bits and pieces; weekend live music; children and dogs welcome, nice outside area, seven bedrooms, open all day, food till 6pm Sun. *(Hunter and Christine Wright)*

CHIDDINGFOLD SU9635

★**Crown** (01428) 682255
The Green (A283); GU8 4TX Lovely 700-year-old timbered building with strong sense of history; bar and linked dining rooms with massive beams (some over 2-ft thick), oak panelling, moulded plasterwork and fine stained-glass windows, magnificently carved fireplace, some nice antique tables along with cushioned wall seats, mate's and other pubby chairs, lots of portraits, simple split-level back public bar with open fire, up to five changing ales and several wines by the glass, enjoyable often interesting food (all day Fri-Sun); quiz first Thurs of month; children welcome, dogs in some areas, seats out looking across village green to interesting church, more tables in central sheltered courtyard, character creaky bedrooms, open all day Fri-Sun. *(Mark Hamill)*

CHILWORTH TQ0347

Percy Arms (01483) 561765
Dorking Road; GU4 8NP Extended stylishly decorated pub with two bustling bars; smaller one has logs neatly piled above woodburner, a long slate-topped table and L-shaped settle, flagstoned main room with tartan-cushioned chairs against counter serving Greene King ales (one named for the pub), a guest beer and 16 wines by the glass, interesting food including some south african specialities, courteous efficient service, restaurant rooms to left of entrance with upholstered tub and high-backed chairs on bare boards or rugs, further dining rooms down steps; TV, free wi-fi; children and dogs (in bar areas) welcome, two-part garden connected by bridge over little stream, play equipment, open all day till 10pm (11pm Sat), food all day weekends. *(Rosie and Marcus Heatherley, Elise and Charles Mackinlay)*

CHIPSTEAD TQ2555

Well House (01737) 830640
Chipstead signed with Mugswell off A217, N of M25 junction 8; CR5 3SQ Originally three 16th-c cottages (converted from tea rooms to pub in 1955); log fires in all three rooms, low beams and rustic décor, bric-a-brac and pewter tankards hanging from ceiling, well kept Fullers, Surrey Hills and a local guest, food from ciabattas up, friendly staff, small dining conservatory, resident ghost (Harry the Monk); Tues quiz, occasional live music, free wi-fi; children and dogs allowed (in bars, they have cats), large pleasing hillside garden with ancient well (mentioned in the Domesday Book), delightful country setting, open all day. *(Tony Scott, Dave Chapman)*

CHURT SU8538

Crossways (01428) 714323
Corner of A287 and Hale House Lane; GU10 2JE Friendly down-to-earth local attracting good mix of customers; quarry-tiled public bar and carpeted saloon with panelling and plush banquettes, good beer range (some served direct from the cellar) and four real ciders, enjoyable well priced pub lunches (not Sun) including home-made pies, evening food Weds only, cheerful staff; darts, TV, no credit cards; children under 10 in garden only, dogs welcome, open all day Fri, Sat. *(Camilla and Jose Ferrera)*

CLAYGATE TQ1563

Foley (01372) 462021
Hare Lane; KT10 0LZ Restored 19th-c Youngs inn; pubby part at front with wooden tables and chairs on bare boards, leather armchairs and sofas by Victorian fireplace, lots of interconnected sitting and dining areas leading off, well kept ales, plenty of wines by the glass and interesting range of spirits, good choice of coffees and teas, fairly standard food from open kitchen, some prices on the high side; background music, sports TV, daily papers and free wi-fi; children and dogs (in bar) welcome, seats on two-level terrace, modern bedrooms, open (and food) all day including breakfast from 7.30am (8.30am Sun). *(David and Sally Frost)*

CLAYGATE TQ1563

Hare & Hounds (01372) 465149
The Green; KT10 0JL Renovated 19th-c flower-decked village pub; good sensibly priced french food along with some pub favourites in bar or smaller restaurant, nice wines and well kept changing ales including local Brightwater, friendly caring service; regular live music, occasional Sun quiz, free wi-fi; children and dogs welcome, disabled access/loo, tables on attractive front terrace and in small back garden with play area, open (and food) all day, kitchen closes 7pm Sun and Mon afternoon. *(Geoffrey Kemp, Robin Waters)*

CLAYGATE TQ1563

Platform 3 (01372) 462334
The Parade, next to Claygate station; KT10 0PB Tiny pub in converted taxi office

acting as tap for the Brightwater brewery, a couple of their beers and often a guest, Claygate cider and good range of wines and soft drinks, no food apart from crisps and nuts; outside seating (there's no room inside), closed Mon-Weds, till 3pm other days, but weather/season dependent (best to check website/Twitter). *(Sean)*

COBHAM TQ1059

Plough (01932) 589790
3.2 miles from M25 junction 10; right off A3 on A245; in Cobham, right into Downside Bridge Road; Plough Lane; KT11 3LT Smartly updated beamed village pub, part of the small Rarebreed group (see Shurlock Inn, Shurlock Row, Berkshire); much liked food cooked in open kitchen from bar snacks to grills, real ales including a Caledonian house beer and St Austell Tribute, good wine list, interesting gins and cocktails, friendly helpful service, roaring log fire; background and live music; children and dogs (in more informal area) welcome, some outside seating, open (and food) all day, kitchen closes 6pm Sun. *(Ian Phillips)*

COBHAM TQ1159

Running Mare (01932) 862007
Tilt Road; KT11 3EZ Attractive old flower-decked pub overlooking green (can get very busy); well kept Fullers, Hogs Back and Youngs, good food including popular Sun lunch, efficient friendly service, two timbered bars and restaurant; regular live music; children very welcome, a few tables out at front and on rose-covered back terrace, open all day, no food Sun evening. *(Robin Waters)*

COLDHARBOUR TQ1544

Plough (01306) 711793
Village signposted in the network of small roads around Leith Hill; RH5 6HD Former 17th-c beamed coaching house under welcoming licensees – also incorporates the village shop; own-brew Leith Hill beers and guests, proper cider and a dozen wines by the glass, good popular food (not Sun evening) in bar or restaurant; background music, TV, free wi-fi, events in barn room such as live music, food fairs, bridge nights and french lessons; children, walkers and dogs welcome, seats out at front and on back terrace overlooking fields, six comfortable bedrooms, open all day (until 9pm Sun). *(Ian and Rose Lock)*

COMPTON SU9646

★**Withies** (01483) 421158
Withies Lane; pub signed from B3000; GU3 1JA Gently old-fashioned and civilised 16th-c pub on edge of Loseley Park; atmospheric low-beamed carpeted bar, some 17th-c carved panels between windows, splendid art nouveau settle among old sewing-machine tables, log fire in massive inglenook, well kept Adnams, Greene King, Hogs Back and Sharps, highly regarded food (restaurant choices can be pricey and they add a service charge), efficient staff in bow ties; children welcome, no dogs inside, seats on terrace, under apple trees and creeper-hung arbour, flower-edged neat front lawn, handy for Watts Gallery, closed Sun evening. *(Dr W I C Clark, Miss A E Dare, Helen and Brian Edgeley, Nick Hales)*

CRANLEIGH TQ0739

Park Hatch (01483) 274374
Bookhurst Road, Parkmead Estate – towards Shere; GU6 7DN Refurbished 17th-c brick and tile-hung dining pub; low beams, flagstones and big inglenook with woodburner, enjoyable food cooked by owner-chef including set lunch menu and themed nights, five well kept changing ales, good friendly service, new oak-framed dining extension; children and dogs (in some parts) welcome, garden picnic-sets, open all day (closed Mon). *(Thomas Green)*

CRANLEIGH TQ0539

Richard Onslow (01483) 274922
High Street; GU6 8AU Busy Peach group pub with cheerful small bar, leather tub chairs and built-in sofa, slate-floored drinking area, ales including Greene King and Surrey Hills, a proper cider and ten wines by the glass, food from deli plates up including weekday set menu, two dining rooms with open fires and sizeable restaurant with pale tables on wood floor, modern flowery wallpaper and big windows overlooking the street; background music, board games, free wi-fi; children and dogs (in bar) welcome, seats out at front and in terraced back garden, ten smart well equipped bedrooms, open (and food) all day from 7am (7.30am weekends) for breakfast. *(Mike Benton, Jim and Sue James)*

DORKING TQ1649

Cricketers (01306) 889938
South Street; RH4 2JU Chatty and relaxed little Fullers local with up to five well kept ales and simple weekday lunchtime food, friendly service, some cricketing memorabilia on stripped-brick walls; events including monthly quiz, beer festivals, Scalextric championship and onion-growing competition, darts, sports TV and free wi-fi; children allowed until early evening, nice split-level suntrap back terrace, open all day. *(Anne Taylor)*

DORKING TQ1649

Old House at Home (01306) 889664
West Street; RH4 1BY Bustling old Youngs pub with opened-up beamed interior; good food from bar snacks up (not Sun evening, Mon, Tues), friendly staff; dogs welcome, back terrace with heated beach huts, closed Mon lunchtime, otherwise open all day (till 8pm Sun). *(Anne Taylor)*

DORMANSLAND TQ4042

Old House at Home (01342) 836828
West Street; RH7 6QP Friendly refurbished 19th-c village pub; beamed bar with traditional furniture on parquet floor, two-way woodburner, Shepherd Neame ales and several wines by the glass from unusual barrel-fronted counter, good well priced traditional food (not Sun evening, Mon, Tues), restaurant with wood and stone floor, darts and TV in snug; some live music, free wi-fi; children and dogs (in bar) welcome, tables out in front, open all day Thurs-Sun. *(Pauline and Mark Evans)*

DORMANSLAND TQ4042

Plough (01342) 832933
Plough Road, off B2028 NE; RH7 6PS Friendly traditional old pub in quiet village; well kept Fullers, Harveys and Sharps, Weston's cider and decent wines, good choice of enjoyable lunchtime bar food including specials and popular Sun roast, thai restaurant (Mon evening-Sat), log fires and other original features; some live music; children welcome, disabled facilities, good-sized garden, open all day. *(Tony Scott, Martin Day)*

DUNSFOLD TQ0036

Sun (01483) 200242
Off B2130 S of Godalming; GU8 4LE Old double-fronted pub with four rooms (brighter at the front), beams and some exposed brickwork, scrubbed pine furniture, two massive log fires, ales such as Greene King, St Austell and Sharps, decent wines and enjoyable reasonably priced home-made food including curry evenings and popular Sun lunch (best to book), good friendly service; occasional quiz, darts, second-hand books for sale; children and dogs welcome, seats on terrace and common opposite, good walks. *(Tony and Wendy Hobden)*

EASHING SU9543

★**Stag on the River** (01483) 421568
Lower Eashing, just off A3 southbound; GU7 2QG Civilised, gently upmarket riverside inn with Georgian façade concealing much older interior; attractively opened-up rooms including charming old-fashioned locals' bar with armchairs on red and black quarry tiles, log-fire in cosy snug beyond, Hogs Back TEA, one or two Marstons-related ales and a house beer from Andwell, Hazy Hog cider, plenty of emphasis on food with several linked dining areas including river room up a couple of steps, attentive courteous staff; children welcome, dogs in bar, extensive terrace with wicker or wooden furniture under parasols (some by weir), picnic-sets on grass, seven bedrooms, open all day, food all day weekends. *(Mary and Douglas McDowell)*

EAST CLANDON TQ0551

★**Queens Head** (01483) 222332
Just off A246 Guildford–Leatherhead; The Street; GU4 7RY Busy attractively refurbished dining pub in same small group as Duke of Cambridge at Tilford, Stag at Eashing and Wheatsheaf in Farnham; well liked food (best to book) from light dishes to good daily specials, set lunch deal (Mon-Thurs), a beer badged for them, Surrey Hills and a couple of guests from fine elm-topped counter, also Hazy Hog cider and nice wines by the glass, efficient friendly service, comfortable linked rooms, woodburner in big inglenook; daily newspapers and free wi-fi, silent TV in bar; children welcome, tables out in front and on side terrace, handy for Hatchlands Park (NT), open (and food) all day Fri and Sat, closes 9pm Sun. *(John Evans, Ian Phillips)*

ELSTEAD SU9043

Woolpack (01252) 703106
B3001 Milford–Farnham; GU8 6HD Comfortably modernised tile-hung dining pub run by italian family; enjoyable home-cooked food including stone-baked pizzas and weekly themed nights, cask-tapped ales including Youngs and decent wines by the glass, friendly efficient service, long main bar, restaurant, open fires; children welcome, garden with picnic-sets, open all day Sun. *(Len and Lilly Dowson)*

EPSOM TQ1960

Jolly Coopers (01372) 723222
Wheelers Lane; KT18 7SD Refurbished 19th-c pub with own Fuzzchat beers from attached microbrewery, also guest ales, a dozen wines by the glass and 35 gins, good fairly priced food including some unusual choices such as goat curry, can eat in bar or restaurant, friendly efficient service; Tues quiz; seats on sunny paved terrace, open all day (till 8pm Sun). *(Simon King)*

ESHER TQ1364

Wheatsheaf (01372) 464014
The Green; KT10 8AG Refurbished early 19th-c dining pub with neat opened-up bar area; light wood flooring, blue-painted panelling and mix of furniture including sofas and easy chairs, lots of colourful artwork and a couple of Victorian fireplaces, four well kept beers including Surrey Hills and plenty of wines by the glass, good food from upscale bar snacks, sharing plates and traditional favourites to more enterprising restauranty dishes, friendly staff, high-ceilinged back dining extension with small outside eating area; background music, sports TV, daily newspapers and free wi-fi; well behaved children till 7.30pm, dogs in bar, teak tables under parasols on front paved terrace looking across to green, open (and food) all day. *(Rob Unsworth, Hunter and Christine Wright)*

FARNHAM SU8545

Spotted Cow (01252) 726541

Bourne Grove, Lower Bourne (towards Tilford); GU10 3QT Welcoming red-brick dining pub on edge of town in nice wooded setting (good walks nearby); highly regarded food from pub favourites and sharing boards up (booking advised), two or three changing local ales and decent range of wines, friendly helpful staff; children and dogs welcome, big garden, open all day weekends (food till 7pm Sun). *(Patric Curwen, Mr and Mrs J Watkins)*

FARNHAM SU8346

Wheatsheaf (01252) 717135

West Street; GU9 7DR Stylishly updated old pub in same group as the Queens Head at East Clandon, Stag at Eashing and Duke of Cambridge at Tilford; enjoyable food (all day Fri-Sun) from open kitchen including weekday set menu, gluten-free diets catered for, well kept local ales such as Hogs Back, craft beers and good choice of wines and whiskies, friendly helpful staff; free wi-fi; children welcome, no dogs inside, seats in back courtyard, open all day, no nearby parking. *(Martin and Sue Neville)*

FICKLESHOLE TQ3960

White Bear (01959) 573166

Featherbed Lane/Fairchildes Lane; off A2022 just S of A212 roundabout; CR6 9PH Long 16th-c country dining pub with lots of small rooms; beams, flagstones and open fires, tasty food from home-made classics up (order at the bar), Brakspears, Pilgrim and a couple of guests such as local Titsey; children and well behaved dogs welcome, picnic-sets and stone bear on front terrace, sizeable back garden with pond and summer weekend 'burger shack', open all day, food till 7pm Sun. *(Eric Shanes)*

FRIDAY STREET TQ1245

Stephan Langton (01306) 730775

Off B2126; RH5 6JR Refurbished 1930s pub prettily placed in tucked-away hamlet; good imaginative food from sandwiches up (all day Sat, till 4pm Sun), well kept local Tillingbourne beers and guests, nice wines and fine gin selection, afternoon teas (must book), efficient friendly service; children and dogs (in bar and snug) welcome, wooded setting with pond, good nearby walks, closed Mon (except bank holidays), otherwise open all day (till 7pm Sun). *(Glen Locke)*

GODALMING SU9643

Star (01483) 417717

Church Street; GU7 1EL Friendly 17th-c local in pedestrianised cobbled street; cosy low-beamed and panelled L-shaped bar, up to ten well kept ales (some tapped from the cask) including Hardys & Hansons, five real ciders/perries and simple lunchtime food from generous sandwiches up, evening bar snacks Mon-Thurs, more modern back room; Mon folk session from 9pm; no dogs, heated terrace behind, open all day. *(Robert Kennedy, Dave Chapman)*

GOMSHALL TQ0847

Gomshall Mill (01483) 203060

Station Road; GU5 9LB Attractive timber-framed and weatherboarded medieval mill with interesting multi-level interior, part of the Home Counties pub group and quite restauranty; good sensibly priced food from extensive menu including sandwiches and children's meals, four well kept local ales and several wines by the glass, friendly helpful staff; terrace with view of River Tillingbourne running under the pub, open all day. *(Calum Stewart, Dr Nick Fletcher, Ian Wilson, Dave Chapman)*

GRAYSWOOD SU9134

Wheatsheaf (01428) 644440

Grayswood Road (A286 NE of Haslemere); GU27 2DE Welcoming family-run dining pub with light airy décor; enjoyable freshly made food in bar or restaurant, good range of well kept beers, friendly helpful staff; occasional live music, quiz first Tues of month, free wi-fi; children and dogs welcome, disabled access, front verandah and side terrace, six bedrooms in extension, good breakfast, open all day Sun till 7pm. *(Kerry and Guy Trooper)*

GUILDFORD SU9949

White House (01483) 302006

High Street; GU2 4AJ Refurbished Fullers pub in pretty waterside setting; their ales and good range of wines, fair-priced food from small plates up, sizeable bar with conservatory, upstairs rooms and roof terrace; children welcome, a few picnic-sets out by River Wey, open (and food) all day. *(Joe and Belinda Smart)*

HASCOMBE TQ0039

White Horse (01483) 208258

B2130 S of Godalming; GU8 4JA Spacious renovated pub with 16th-c origins; four well kept ales including Otter, decent wines by the glass and good food (not Sun evening) from traditional choices up, friendly efficient staff, scrubbed tables and pews in beamed bar, some old black and white photographs and farming memorabilia, various other linked rooms including smart pitched ceiling restaurant (separate more upmarket menu); children and dogs welcome in some parts, small front terrace and attractive back garden, pretty village with duck pond, good walks and handy for Winkworth Arboretum (NT), open all day. *(Martin and Joanne Sharp)*

HEADLEY TQ2054

★**Cock** (01372) 377258

Church Lane; KT18 6LE Relaxed opened-up country pub in same group as the Queens Head at East Clandon and the

Duke of Cambridge at Tilford; light modern refurbishment (parts date from the 18th c) with open fires and comfortable seating, good but not cheap food (all day Fri-Sun) from lunchtime sandwiches and sharing plates up, set lunch Mon-Thurs, a house beer (Red Mist) and a couple of guests, interesting wines including champagne by the glass, extensive gin selection, friendly attentive service; free wi-fi; children welcome, dogs in one area, disabled access using lift from upper car park, terrace tables under parasols, attractive setting and good woodland walks, open all day. *(John Evans, Glen Locke)*

HOLMBURY ST MARY TQ1144

Kings Head (01306) 731112
Pitland Street; RH5 6NP This popular old pub, tucked away in a hillside village, was changing hands as we went to press with major refurbishment planned – news please.

HORSELL SU9959

★**Red Lion** (01483) 768497
High Street; GU21 4SS Large popular pub with airy split-level bar, comfortable sofas and easy chairs, clusters of pictures on cream-painted walls, Fullers London Pride, St Austell Tribute and a guest from long wooden servery, a dozen wines by the glass, back dining room with exposed brick walls, old pews and blackboards listing the good bistro-style food, friendly staff; free wi-fi; children allowed till 7pm, ivy-clad passage to garden and comfortable tree-sheltered terrace, good walks, open (and food) all day. *(Thomas Green)*

HORSELL COMMON TQ0160

Sands at Bleak House (01483) 756988 *Chertsey Road, The Anthonys; A320 Woking–Ottershaw; GU21 5NL* Smart contemporary pub-restaurant on edge of Horsell Common; grey sandstone floor (and bar front), brown leather sofas and cushioned stools, two dining rooms with dark wood furniture, woodburners, good well presented food (can be pricey), Hogs Back and Sharps, friendly attentive uniformed staff; background music, TV, free wi-fi; children welcome, dogs in courtyard only, good shortish walk to sandpits that inspired H G Wells's *The War of the Worlds*, seven bedrooms, open all day (till 6pm Sun). *(Gordon and Patricia Gorringe)*

LALEHAM TQ0568

★**Three Horseshoes** (01784) 455014
Shepperton Road (B376); TW18 1SE Bustling dining pub near pleasant stretch of the Thames with several interconnecting rooms; bar with white walls and contrasting deep blue woodwork, easy-going mix of tables and chairs on bare boards, log fire fronted by armchairs and squashy sofa, well kept Fullers/Gales beers and plenty of wines by the glass, wide choice of highly regarded reasonably priced food (booking advised) including blackboard specials, efficient friendly young staff, dining areas with assorted tables and chairs, pictures and mirrors on grey walls; soft background music, free wi-fi; children welcome till 8pm, attractive flagstoned terrace, picnic-sets on grass, open (and food) all day. *(Geoffrey Kemp, Hunter and Christine Wright, Simon Collett-Jones)*

LEIGH TQ2147

★**Seven Stars** (01306) 611254
Dawes Green, south of A25 Dorking–Reigate; RH2 8NP Attractive tile-hung country dining pub; comfortable beamed and flagstoned bar with traditional furnishings and inglenook, Fullers, Harveys, Sharps and Youngs from glowing copper counter, several wines by the glass and enjoyable sensibly priced food, plainer public bar and sympathetic restaurant extension where children allowed; dogs welcome in bar areas, plenty of outside seating, open all day, food all day Sat and till 6pm Sun. *(Caroline West, Dave Chapman)*

LIMPSFIELD CHART TQ4251

Carpenters Arms (01883) 722209
Tally Road; RH8 0TG Friendly open-plan pub owned by Westerham with their full range kept well (tasting trays available), good food (not Sun evening) from light lunches up, friendly efficient staff, garden room; quiz first Sun of month, free wi-fi; children and dogs welcome, tables on terrace and lawn, delightful setting by village common, lovely walks and handy for Chartwell (NT), open all day weekends. *(Ian Phillips)*

MICKLEHAM TQ1753

King William IV (01372) 372590
Just off A24 Leatherhead–Dorking; Byttom Hill; RH5 6EL Steps up to small pub tucked away from the main road; well kept Hogs Back TEA, Surrey Hills Shere Drop and a guest, enjoyable food from lunchtime sandwiches to blackboard specials, friendly attentive service, pleasant outlook from cosy plank-panelled front bar, carpeted dining area with grandfather clock and log fire; background music, live summer jazz outside (Sun 4.30-7.30pm); children and dogs welcome, plenty of tables in pretty terraced garden (some in open-sided timber shelters), lovely valley views, open (and food) all day. *(Dan and Anne Morgan)*

MOGADOR TQ2453

Sportsman (01737) 246655
From M25 up A217 past second roundabout, then Mogador signed; KT20 7ES Modernised and extended low-ceilinged pub on edge of Walton Heath (originally a 16th-c royal hunting lodge); well kept ales including Sharps and Youngs,

good food from interesting varied menu, restaurant with raised section; free wi-fi; children welcome (no pushchairs), dogs in bar, seats out on common, front verandah and back lawn, popular with walkers and riders, open (and food) all day. *(Martine and Derek Cotton)*

OCKLEY TQ1337

Punchbowl (01306) 627249
Oakwood Hill, signed off A29 S; RH5 5PU Attractive 16th-c tile-hung country pub with slabby Horsham stone roof; good value food (not Sun evening) including range of burgers and Weds steak night, three changing ales, central bar with flagstones and low beams, inglenook log fire decorated with horsebrasses, carpeted restaurant on the left, second bar to the right; children (until 9pm) and dogs welcome, picnic-sets in pretty garden, quiet spot with good walks including Sussex Border Path, open all day. *(Louise and Simon Peters)*

OUTWOOD TQ3246

★**Bell** (01342) 842989
Outwood Common, just E of village; off A23 S of Redhill; RH1 5PN Attractive 17th-c extended dining pub; smartly rustic beamed bar with oak and elm furniture (some Jacobean in style), soft lighting, low beams and vast stone inglenook, Fullers London Pride, ESB and a guest, 20 wines by the glass and wide range of spirits, popular food from pub standards to good fresh fish (best to book, especially evenings when drinking-only space limited); background music, free wi-fi; children and dogs (in bar) welcome, disabled access, well maintained garden looking out past pine trees to rolling fields, open all day, food all day weekends. *(Tony Scott)*

OUTWOOD TQ3146

Dog & Duck (01342) 844552
Prince of Wales Road; turn off A23 at station sign in Salfords, S of Redhill – OS Sheet 187 map reference 312460; RH1 5QU Relaxed beamed country pub with enjoyable fairly priced home-made food in bar or large two-part restaurant, four well kept Badger ales and good range of wines, friendly helpful service; children and dogs (in bar) welcome, sizeable garden with raised decking, fenced duck pond and play area (also circuit for motorised kids' jeeps), open all day (till 9pm Sun). *(Tony Scott)*

OXTED TQ4048

Grumpy Mole (01883) 722207
Caterfield Lane, Staffhurst Wood, S of town; RH8 0RR Refurbished country pub, popular and welcoming, with ales such as Godstone, Greene King and Westerham, lots of wines by the glass and good food from sandwiches and pub staples up including steak cooked on a hot stone, afternoon teas, friendly obliging service, well divided bar and dining areas, open fire; children and dogs welcome, rattan-style furniture on paved terrace, picnic-sets on lawn, lovely views across fields, open all day. *(Martin Day)*

PUTTENHAM SU9347

Good Intent (01483) 810387
Signed off B3000 just S of A31 junction; The Street/Seale Lane; GU3 1AR Convivial beamed village local with big log fire in cosy front bar, alcove seating, some old farming tools and photographs of the pub, Timothy Taylors, Hogs Back and guests, reasonably priced traditional food (not Sun evening, Mon) from sandwiches up, parquet-floored dining area; darts, free wi-fi; well behaved children and dogs welcome, small sunny garden, good walks, open all day weekends. *(Margo and Derek Stapley)*

REDHILL TQ2750

Garland (01737) 764612
Brighton Road; RH1 6PP Friendly 19th-c Harveys corner local with their full range kept well including seasonals, enjoyable traditional food (not Sun evening); live music Sat, bar billiards, darts, free wi-fi; children (till 9pm) and well behaved dogs welcome, picnic-sets in back garden, open all day. *(Tony Scott, Tony Hobden)*

REDHILL TQ2749

Plough (01737) 766686
Church Road, St Johns; RH1 6QE Popular early 17th-c beamed pub with warm friendly local atmosphere; lots of bits and pieces to look at including copper and brass hanging from the ceiling, nice open fire, Fullers, Youngs and a couple of guests, enjoyable sensibly priced blackboard food (not Sun evening), good helpful service; Weds quiz; no under-10s inside, dogs welcome, back garden and terrace (barbecues and spit roasts), open all day. *(Tony Scott)*

REIGATE HEATH TQ2349

★**Skimmington Castle** (01737) 243100 *Off A25 Reigate–Dorking via Flanchford Road and Bonny's Road; RH2 8RL* Nicely located small country pub with emphasis on good home-made food from baguettes up (can get very busy and best to book), well kept Harveys, St Austell and a couple of guests, a dozen wines by the glass, friendly efficient service, snug beamed and panelled rooms, log fires; children, dogs and muddy boots welcome, seats out on three sides (some heaters), open all day, food till 7.30pm Sun (9pm summer). *(Tony Scott, Dave Chapman)*

RIPLEY TQ0456

Seven Stars (01483) 225128
Newark Lane (B367); GU23 6DL Neat 1930s pub with snug areas; enjoyable food from varied menu, Greene King, Fullers, Sharps and Shepherd Neame, good wines

and coffee, red patterned carpet, gleaming brasses and open fire; quiet background music; picnic-sets and heated wooden booths in well tended garden, river and canalside walks, closed Sun evening. *(Chloe and Tim Hodge)*

ROWLEDGE SU8243

Hare & Hounds (01252) 792287
The Square; GU10 4AA Popular village pub with friendly welcoming atmosphere; good honest home cooking and four well kept ales including Greene King Ruddles County, smallish eating area; children and dogs welcome, garden with terrace and play area, open all day, no food Sun evening. *(Tony and Jill Radnor)*

SEND TQ0156

New Inn (01483) 762736
Send Road, Cartbridge; GU23 7EN Traditional old beamed pub by River Wey Navigation; long bar and dining room, log fires, Adnams, Fullers, Greene King, Sharps and a guest, good choice of generously served food (all day weekends) from ciabattas to blackboard specials, friendly helpful service; quiz first Weds of month; children and dogs welcome, large waterside garden with moorings, open all day and can get very busy in summer. *(John Pritchard)*

SHACKLEFORD SU9345

Cyder House (01483) 810360
Peper Harow Lane; GU8 6AN Refurbished 1920s village pub in pleasant leafy setting; Badger ales, proper ciders/perry and nice selection of wines by the glass, good home-made food from lunchtime sandwiches and baked potatoes up, popular burger night Mon, airy linked areas around central servery, wood floors, log fire; quiz night (every other Mon), free wi-fi; children and dogs welcome, back terrace with steps up to play area, good walks, closed Tues, otherwise open all day (till 8pm Sun). *(Margaret Hawkes)*

SHALFORD TQ0047

Queen Victoria (01483) 566959
Station Row; GU4 8BY Tile-hung, bay-windowed local with compact modernised interior around central bar, enjoyable reasonably priced food (not Sun evening) from lunchtime sandwiches up, Otter and guests (often St Austell and Sharps), woodburner; quiz first and third Thurs of month, some live music, TV; well behaved children and dogs welcome, seats out at front and on back terrace, open all day. *(Frances and Mandy Robertson)*

SHAMLEY GREEN TQ0343

Bricklayers Arms (01483) 898377
Guildford Road, S of the green; GU5 0UA Red-brick village pub with five well kept ales such as Exmoor, Fullers, Harveys and Surrey Hills, enjoyable pubby food (not Sun evening) including themed evenings, U-shaped layout (a couple of steps) with bare boards, carpets and flagstones, exposed brickwork and stripped wood, old local photographs, sofas by woodburner; quiz nights, pool, darts and TV; children and dogs welcome, a couple of picnic-sets out in front, more seats behind, open all day. *(William and Sophie Renton)*

SHEPPERTON TQ0866

Red Lion (01932) 244526
Russell Road; TW17 9HX In nice position across from the Thames; bistro-style renovation (oldest part a pub since the 18th c), good well presented food from varied regularly changing menu (can be pricey), Sat brunch and popular Sun lunch, Fullers, Theakstons and a guest, good range of other drinks, afternoon teas, friendly staff; children and dogs welcome, modern furniture on picket-fenced front terrace, more seats over road on riverside deck, open (and food) all day. *(Robin Waters)*

SHEPPERTON TQ0765

Thames Court (01932) 221957
Shepperton Lock, Ferry Lane; turn left off B375 towards Chertsey, 100 metres from Square; TW17 9LJ Spacious Vintage Inn dining pub in great Thames-side location (former private residence of the dutch ambassador); comfortably updated and opened up with many different areas (some up steps), log fires, their usual good choice of food from sandwiches and sharing plates up including weekday set menus, plenty of wines by the glass, decent gins and well kept ales such as St Austell, Sharps and Timothy Taylors, enthusiastic friendly young staff ; background and some live music; children welcome, modern furniture on large tree-shaded terrace with river views, open (and food) all day, can get very busy weekends. *(Minda and Stanley Alexander, Ian Phillips)*

SHERE TQ0747

White Horse (01483) 202518
Shere Lane; signed off A25 3 miles E of Guildford; GU5 9HS Splendid Chef & Brewer with several rooms off small bar; uneven floors, massive beams and timbers, Tudor stonework, oak wall seats and two log fires (one in huge inglenook), interesting range of enjoyable food including deals, Greene King IPA and a couple of guests, Weston's cider and plenty of wines by the glass, good, friendly service; children and dogs (in bar) welcome, seats out at front and in big garden behind, beautiful film-set village, open (and food) all day. *(John Evans, Ian Phillips)*

STAINES TQ0371

Bells (01784) 454240
Church Street; TW18 4ZB Comfortable and sociable Youngs pub in old part of town by St Mary's church; their well kept ales and a guest, decent choice of wines and good promptly served food (not Sun evening),

central fireplace; sports TV; dogs allowed in bar, disabled access, tables in nice back garden with heated terrace, limited roadside parking, open all day. *(Thomas Green)*

STOKE D'ABERNON TQ1259

★**Old Plough** (01932) 862244

Station Road, off A245; KT11 3BN Popular attractively updated 300-year-old pub; good freshly made food including daily specials, Fullers beers, a couple of guests and plenty of wines by the glass, competent friendly staff, restaurant with various knick-knacks; newspapers and free wi-fi; children (not in bar after 7pm) and dogs welcome, seats out under pergola and in pretty garden, open (and food) all day. *(Ron Corbett)*

TADWORTH TQ2355

★**Dukes Head** (01737) 812173

Dorking Road (B2032 opposite common and woods); KT20 5SL Welcoming 19th-c pub, roomy and comfortably modernised, with popular generously served food from varied menu (booking advised), five well kept ales including Fullers, Youngs and a Morlands house beer (KT20), Aspall's cider, good choice of wines by the glass, helpful friendly staff, three dining areas and two big inglenook log fires; background music, Weds quiz; children welcome (no highchairs), dogs in some areas, lots of hanging baskets and plenty of tables in well tended terraced garden, open (and food) all day, till 8pm (6.30pm) Sun. *(Camilla and Jose Ferrera)*

THAMES DITTON TQ1567

Albany (020) 8972 9163

Queens Road, signed off Summer Road; KT7 0QY Mitchells & Butlers bar-with-restaurant popular for its lovely Thames-side position, light airy modern feel, with variety of food from sharing plates and pizzas to more upscale dishes, also a vegan menu, good choice of wines by the glass, cocktails, craft beers and a couple of real ales such as Sharps Doom Bar, cheerful if not always quick service; background music; disabled access/loo, nice balconies and two-level heated deck overlooking river to Hampton Court Palace grounds, moorings, open (and food) all day. *(Lisa Walker, Tom and Ruth Rees)*

TILFORD SU8742

Duke of Cambridge (01252) 792236

Tilford Road; GU10 2DD Refurbished dining pub in same small group as the Queens Head at East Clandon, Stag at Eashing and Wheatsheaf at Farnham; nice food from varied menu including gluten-free and children's choices, good selection of wines and gins (some local), well kept ales such as Hogs Back and Surrey Hills along with a Tilford craft beer (brewed on-site), helpful service; May charity music festival; children and dogs welcome, terrace and garden with outside bar/grill, good play area, open all day, food all day Sun. *(John and Bernadette Elliott, Patric Curwen)*

VIRGINIA WATER SU9968

Rose & Olive Branch (01344) 843713 *Callow Hill; GU25 4LH* Cosy unpretentious red-brick pub with good choice of nicely presented food including speciality pies and several vegetarian and gluten-free options, two Greene King ales and a guest, decent wines, friendly busy staff; background music; children and dogs welcome, tables on front terrace and in garden behind, good walks, open (and food) all day weekends. *(Nick and Meriel Cox)*

WALLISWOOD TQ1138

Scarlett Arms (01306) 627243

Signed from Ewhurst–Rowhook back road, or off A29 S of Ockley; RH5 5RD Cottagey 16th-c village pub with low beams and flagstones, simple furniture and two log fires (one in big inglenook), well kept Badger ales and enjoyable reasonably priced food (not Sun evening), friendly prompt service, various smaller rooms off main bar; background music, darts; children and dogs welcome, tables out at front and in garden under parasols, play area, good walks, open all day. *(Gerry and Rosemary Dobson)*

WALTON-ON-THAMES TQ0966

Anglers (01932) 223996

Riverside, off Manor Road; KT12 2PF Roomy dining pub on Thames towpath; enjoyable food from varied menu (not overlong and can be pricey), real ales including a house beer from Caledonian, craft kegs and lots of wines by the glass, friendly efficient service, wooden tables and chairs on bare boards, log fire, more seating in upstairs river-view room with own copper-topped servery; background music; children welcome, solid tables and benches out by the water, open (and food) all day. *(Minda and Stanley Alexander, Peter Edwards)*

WARLINGHAM TQ3955

Botley Hill Farmhouse (01959) 577154 *S on Limpsfield Road (B269); CR6 9QH* Refurbished 16th-c country pub set high on the North Downs; low-ceilinged linked rooms up and down steps, fresh flowers and candles, popular locally sourced food from sandwiches and pub standards up (till 7pm Sun, booking advised), well kept ales including own Titsey beers from

A star symbol before the name of a pub shows exceptional character and appeal. It doesn't mean extra comfort. Even quite a basic pub can win a star, if it's individual enough.

on-site microbrewery as well as Pilgrim and Westerham tapped from the cask (tasters offered), a dozen wines by the glass, good friendly service, big log fire in one room, tea shop selling local produce; children and dogs welcome, disabled access, terrace and garden with fine views, good local walks, open all day, Sun breakfast from 9am. *(Richard Cole)*

WEST CLANDON TQ0451

★**Bulls Head** (01483) 222444
A247 SE of Woking; GU4 7ST Comfortably old-fashioned village pub based around 1540s timbered hall-house; enjoyable good value pubby food (not Sun evening) including proper home-made pies, friendly helpful staff, Youngs ales and guests, small lantern-lit beamed front bar with open fire, some stripped brickwork, old local prints and bric-a-brac, simple raised back inglenook dining area, games room (darts and pool); children and dogs welcome, disabled access from car park, play area in neat little garden, nice walks, open all day Sun. *(Mary and Douglas McDowell)*

WEST CLANDON TQ0452

★**Onslow Arms** (01483) 222447
A247 SE of Woking; GU4 7TE Busy modernised pub with heavily beamed rambling rooms leading away from central bar; wooden dining chairs and tables on wide floorboards, painted panelling, all sorts of copper implements, hunting horns and pictures, leather chesterfields in front of open fire, four real ales including Fullers, Surrey Hills and a house beer brewed by Greene King, good popular food from lunchtime sandwiches and traditional choices up, pleasant helpful service; live music first Weds of month, TV, daily papers and free wi-fi; children (till early evening) and dogs welcome, pretty courtyard garden with tables under parasols, open (and food) all day. *(Kirsty, Miss A E Dare, Robin Waters, Mrs P Sumner, Christopher and Elise Way)*

WEST HORSLEY TQ0853

Barley Mow (01483) 282693
Off A246 Leatherhead–Guildford at Bell & Colvill garage roundabout; The Street; KT24 6HR Welcoming beamed village pub with well kept ales such as Fullers and Surrey Hills, decent wines and good thai food along with more conventional lunchtime menu, log fires, barn function room; background music; children and dogs (in bar) welcome, spacious garden, open all day. *(Len and Lilly Dowson)*

WEST HORSLEY TQ0752

King William IV (01483) 282318
The Street; KT24 6BG Comfortable and welcoming early 19th-c village pub; low entrance door to front and side bars, beams, flagstones and log fire, back conservatory restaurant, good variety of food (not Sun evening) including gluten-free menu, four real ales such as Surrey Hills and Wells; background and occasional live music, quiz nights, free wi-fi; children and dogs welcome, disabled access, small sunny garden with deck and play area, good for walkers, open all day. *(Martin and Sue Neville)*

WEYBRIDGE TQ0765

Old Crown (01932) 842844
Thames Street; KT13 8LP Comfortably old-fashioned three-bar pub dating from the 16th c; good value traditional food (not Sun-Tues evenings) from sandwiches to fresh fish, Courage, Youngs and a guest kept well, good choice of wines by the glass, friendly efficient service, family lounge and conservatory; may be sports TV in back bar with Lions RFC photographs; children and dogs welcome, secluded terrace, steps down to suntrap garden overlooking Wey/Thames confluence, mooring for small boats, open all day. *(Kerry and Guy Trooper)*

WEYBRIDGE TQ0664

Queens Head (01932) 839820
Bridge Road; KT13 8XS 18th-c pub owned by Raymond Blanc's White Brasserie Company; good food from open kitchen including well priced lunchtime/early evening set menu (not Sun), also a proper bar serving real ales and plenty of wines by the glass, friendly staff; soft background music, newspapers; children welcome, tables out on small front terrace, open (and food) all day. *(Geoffrey Kemp)*

WINDLESHAM SU9264

Bee (01276) 479244
School Road; GU20 6PD Cosy village pub with good food from sandwiches and traditional favourites up including steaks cooked on a hot stone, four well kept ales and decent wines by the glass, friendly accommodating staff, bar area with painted panelling and open fire in small brick fireplace, back dining room; TV; children and dogs (in bar) welcome, picnic-sets on small front terrace and in garden behind with play area, open all day, no food Sun evening. *(Dr Martin Owton)*

WINDLESHAM SU9464

Brickmakers (01276) 472267
Chertsey Road (B386, W of B383 roundabout); GU20 6HT Airy country dining pub with updated linked areas in pastel shades or vibrant reds, light wood furniture on flagstone and wood floors, two-way woodburner, good freshly prepared food (all day Fri-Sun when best to book), well kept Courage Best, Fullers London Pride and Sharps Doom Bar, reasonable choice of wines by the glass and decent coffee, friendly service, conservatory; well behaved children allowed, appealing garden with pergola, open all day from 9am for breakfast. *(Ian Phillips, Ian Wilson)*

WITLEY SU9439

White Hart (01428) 683695
Petworth Road; GU8 5PH Picture-book beamed Tudor pub; well kept St Austell Tribute, Youngs Bitter and a guest, craft beers, plenty of wines by the glass and extensive range of whiskies, popular food including signature home-smoked/chargrilled dishes, friendly helpful staff, bar, restaurant and cosy panelled snug with inglenook (where George Eliot used to drink); children and dogs welcome, seats on cobbled terrace and in garden, nice walks nearby, open all day (till 6pm Sun). *(Anne Taylor)*

WOKING TQ0058

Herbert Wells (01483) 722818
Chertsey Road; GU21 5AJ Popular corner Wetherspoons named after H G Wells; fine selection of beers and ciders and their usual competitively priced all-day food, friendly helpful staff, lots of cosy areas and side snugs, old local pictures; free wi-fi and daily papers; children welcome, a few pavement tables, open from 8am. *(Pauline and Mark Evans)*

WONERSH TQ0145

Grantley Arms (01483) 893351
The Street; GU5 0PE Popular refurbished 16th-c village pub; opened-up beamed and timbered bar with mix of new and old furniture on light wood floor, a couple of steps up to long pitched-roof dining area, four real ales and interesting wine list, good well presented food from lunchtime sandwiches up including Mon steak night, cosy space in former bakery for private dining, friendly helpful staff; occasional live music and quiz nights, daily newspapers and free wi-fi; children (until 7.30pm) and dogs (in bar) welcome, ramp for wheelchairs, attractive paved terrace, open (and food) all day. *(Hunter and Christine Wright)*

WOOD STREET SU9550

Royal Oak (01483) 235137
Oak Hill; GU3 3DA 1920s village local with half a dozen well kept ales including Marstons (Aug beer festival), good value traditional home-cooked food, friendly staff; music and quiz nights, free wi-fi; children and dogs welcome, good-sized garden with play area, open all day Fri and Sat, till 8pm Sun, closed Mon lunchtime. *(Joe and Belinda Smart)*

WORPLESDON SU9854

Jolly Farmer (01483) 235897
Burdenshott Road, off A320 Guildford–Woking, not in village; GU3 3RN Old Fullers pub in pleasant country setting; their well kept ales in beamed and flagstoned bar with small log fire, enjoyable fairly traditional food from lunchtime sandwiches up, bare-boards dining extension under pitched roof; background music, free wi-fi; children and dogs welcome, garden with parasol-shaded tables and pergola, open all day. *(Mark Hamill)*

WRECCLESHAM SU8344

Bat & Ball (01252) 792108
Bat & Ball Lane, South Farnham; approach from Sandrock Hill and Upper Bourne Lane, then narrow steep lane to pub; GU10 4SA Fairly traditional pub tucked away in hidden valley; enjoyable food (all day weekends) from interestingly varied menu, special diets catered for, six well kept local ales and plenty of wines by the glass, friendly helpful staff; live music including open mike last Thurs of month and June beer/music festival, charity quiz Tues, free wi-fi; children and dogs welcome, disabled facilities, attractive terrace with vine arbour, more tables and substantial play fort in garden, open all day and can get very busy in summer. *(Tony and Jill Radnor)*

WRECCLESHAM SU8244

Royal Oak (01252) 728319
The Street; GU10 4QS 17th-c black-beamed village local; enjoyable good value home-made food (smaller helpings available for some main courses) including steak night Weds, burgers Thurs, three well kept Greene King ales, friendly helpful staff, log fire; Sun quiz, sports TV, darts; children and dogs welcome, big garden with play area, open all day. *(Tony and Jill Radnor)*

Sussex

ALFRISTON

TQ5203 Map 3

George

(01323) 870319 – www.thegeorge-alfriston.com

High Street; BN26 5SY

Venerable 14th-c timbered inn with comfortable, heavily beamed bars, good wines and several real ales; bedrooms

After a wander around this lovely village, come here for lunch. It has plenty of character throughout and the long bar, dominated by a huge stone inglenook fireplace with a winter log fire (or summer flower arrangement), has massive hop-hung low beams, settles and chairs around sturdy stripped tables, soft lighting and lots of copper and brass. Greene King Abbot and Old Speckled Hen, Dark Star Hophead and a guest beer such as Hardys & Hanson Olde Trip on handpump, 16 wines by the glass (including champagne and a pudding wine) and 25 gins served by friendly staff; background music and board games. The lounge has comfortable sofas, standing timbers and rugs on the wooden floor, and the restaurant is cosy and candlelit. There are seats in the spacious flint-walled garden, and the beamed bedrooms are comfortable. There's no car park but you can park a couple of minutes away. Two long-distance paths (the South Downs Way and Vanguard Way) cross here, and the quietly beautiful Cuckmere Haven beach is not far away.

All-day food is good and includes lunchtime sandwiches and toasties, grilled sardines with garlic and lemon, wild mushroom and asparagus risotto with cream and parmesan, sharing boards, lentil and vegetable cottage pie, chicken stuffed with chorizo, cream cheese and spinach and wrapped in bacon with madeira sauce, hake with parsley mash and prawn, mussel and wine sauce, pork belly with celeriac and pear mash, root vegetables and cider sauce, and puddings such as banoffi pie and chocolate mousse cake. *Benchmark main dish: king prawn, chorizo and mussel linguine £16.50. Two-course evening meal £23.50.*

Greene King ~ Lease Roland and Cate Couch ~ Real ale ~ Open 11-11; 12-11 Sat, Sun ~ Bar food 12-9 ~ Restaurant ~ Children welcome ~ Dogs welcome ~ Wi-fi ~ Bedrooms: £75/£100

Recommended by Chantelle and Tony Redman, Kerry and Guy Trooper, Tina and Steven Hobden, Adam and Betty Lawrence

Please keep sending us reports. We rely on readers for news of new discoveries, and particularly for news of changes – however slight – at the fully described pubs: feedback@goodguides.com, or (no stamp needed) The Good Pub Guide, FREEPOST RTXY–ZCBC–BBAZ, Stream Lane, Sedlescombe, Battle TN33 0PB.

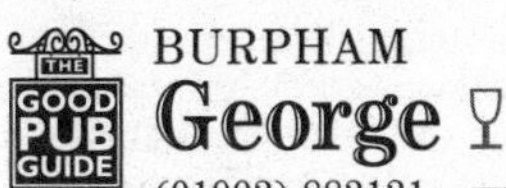

BURPHAM TQ0308 Map 3

George

(01903) 883131 – www.georgeatburpham.co.uk

Off A27 near Warningcamp; BN18 9RR

Well run, popular cottagey pub with good food and ales

Follow a long and winding lane to reach this community-owned pub, set at the end of the hilltop village between the partly Norman church (which has some unusual decoration) and the cricket ground; just a short walk away are splendid views down to Arundel Castle and the river. It's a busy 17th-c place with an attractively updated beamed interior, sofas by the woodburning stove in the bar and farmhouse and other dining chairs around wooden tables on bare boards in the interconnected eating areas (there's a second woodburner too); background music, darts and board games. There's Arundel Sussex Gold, Greyhound Amber Eyes and Hammerpot Red Hunter on handpump, 21 wines by the glass, nine gins and six vodkas. Picnic-sets are set under parasols at the front.

Quite a choice of food includes sandwiches, deep-fried whitebait, baked camembert with cranberry sauce, mushroom and spinach bread and butter pudding with stilton sauce, dressed crab salad, chipotle and sea salt pork sausages with bubble and squeak and onion jus, chicken kiev, burger with toppings and chips, duck breast with fondant potatoes and orange sauce, torbay sole with chive butter and crushed new potatoes, and puddings such as double chocolate brownie with vanilla ice-cream and forest fruits pannacotta with jelly topping and strawberry ice-cream. *Benchmark main dish: pie of the day £13.95. Two-course evening meal £22.00.*

Free house ~ Licensee Jason Lloyd ~ Real ale ~ Open 10.30-3, 6-11; 10.30am-11pm Sat; 12-11 Sun; closed Sun evening and Mon in winter ~ Bar food 12-2.30, 6-9; 12-3, 6-9.30 Sat; 12-4, 6-8 Sun ~ Restaurant ~ Children welcome ~ Dogs welcome ~ Wi-fi

Recommended by Ruth and Peter Bacon, Jocelyn and Helen Dalby, Victoria and Len Meadows

CHARLTON SU8812 Map 2

Fox Goes Free

(01243) 811461 – www.thefoxgoesfree.com

Village signposted off A286 Chichester–Midhurst in Singleton, also from Chichester–Petworth via East Dean; PO18 0HU

400-year-old pub with beamed bars, popular food and drink and big garden; bedrooms

Even when this well run pub is at its busiest (race days at nearby Goodwood are a prime example), staff remain friendly, efficient and helpful. The bar, the first of several cosy separate rooms, has old irish settles, tables and chapel chairs and an open fire. Standing timbers divide up a larger beamed bar with a huge brick fireplace and old local photographs on the walls. A dining area overlooks the garden. The family extension is a clever conversion from horse boxes and the stables where the 1926 Goodwood winner was once housed; darts, board games and background music. A beer named for the pub (from Arundel), Upham First Drop and Weltons English Pride on handpump, 15 wines by the glass, quite a few gins and Addlestone's cider. The attractive back garden has picnic-sets under apple trees and the South Downs as a backdrop, and there are rustic benches and tables on the gravelled front terrace too. Chrming, country-style bedrooms are comfortable. You can walk up to Levin Down nature reserve, or stroll around the Iron Age hill fort on the Trundle with huge views to the Isle of Wight; the Weald & Downland Living Museum and West Dean Gardens are nearby too.

Enjoyable food includes lunchtime sandwiches, moules marinière, tian of smoked salmon and avocado with horseradish cream and gazpacho sauce, sharing platters, wild mushroom stroganoff, gnocchi with parmesan, a risotto of the day, beer-battered fish and chips, rolled leg of lamb with dauphinoise potatoes and garlic and thyme jus, panko-crusted half roast chicken with spicy sauce and potato wedges, steaks with trimmings and a choice of sauce, and puddings such as blueberry pancakes with toffee sauce and ice-cream and chocolate mousse with coffee cream and fruit and nut chocolate. *Benchmark main dish: fish pie £14.50. Two-course evening meal £23.00.*

Free house ~ Licensee David Coxon ~ Real ale ~ Open 11-11 (11.30 Sat); 12-11 Sun ~ Bar food 12-2.30, 6.15-9.30; 12-10 Sat; 12-9.30 Sun ~ Restaurant ~ Children welcome ~ Dogs allowed in bar ~ Wi-fi ~ Bedrooms: £73/£98 *Recommended by Christian Mole, Suzy Miller, Susie and Spencer Gray, Simon Collett-Jones, Tim and Sue Mulligan, Tina and Steven Hobden*

CHILGROVE SU8214 Map 2

White Horse

(01243) 519444 – www.thewhitehorse.co.uk

B2141 Petersfield–Chichester; PO18 9HX

Handsome coaching inn with a thoughtful choice of drinks, first class food and plenty of outside seating; bedrooms

Our readers enjoy their visits to this civilised, whitewashed inn, especially after a walk. The bar area has an easy-going feel, leather armchairs in front of a woodburning stove and daily papers on the light oak counter where friendly staff serve Tipsy Horse (named for the pub from Ringwood) plus Dark Star Hophead and Marstons 61 Deep on handpump and 18 good wines by the glass. Just off here, a room with leather button-back wall seats and mate's and other dark wooden dining chairs has all sorts of country knick-knacks: stuffed animals, china plates, riding boots, flower paintings, dog drawings, stone bottles and books on shelves. The dining room to the other side of the bar has a huge painting of a galloping white horse, a long suede wall banquette, high-backed settles creating stalls, elegant chairs, lots of mirrors and big metal chandeliers. Throughout, there are fat candles in lanterns, flagstones and coir carpet, beams and timbering, and animal skin throws; background music and board games. A two-level terrace has dark grey rattan-style seats around glass-topped tables under parasols among pretty flowering tubs; an area up steps has rustic benches and tables and there are picnic-sets on grass at the front. Each of the comfortable, contemporary and light bedrooms has a little private courtyard (two have a hot tub). Good surrounding walks.

Good, modern british food includes fried chicken livers with crispy pancetta and caramelised onions, mussels with cider, spring onion and cream sauce, baked cauliflower with pearl barley, mushrooms and cheddar, corn-fed chicken breast with charred leeks, sautéed potatoes and wild garlic, local game pie, skate wing with cauliflower purée, pickled cauliflower, caper and citrus sauce, pork tenderloin with white bean and chorizo cassoulet, and puddings such as peanut and granola parfait and chocolate torte with white chocolate sorbet. *Benchmark main dish: cod fillet on crushed jersey potatoes with a poached egg and chive butter sauce £17.95. Two-course evening meal £23.00.*

Free house ~ Licensee Richard Miller ~ Real ale ~ Open 11-11 ~ Bar food 12-3, 6-9; 12-9.30 Sat; 12-8 Sun ~ Restaurant ~ Children welcome ~ Dogs allowed in bar and bedrooms ~ Wi-fi ~ Bedrooms: /£120 *Recommended by Malcolm and Sue Scott, Hunter and Christine Wright, Katherine Matthews, Celia and Geoff Clay, Miss A E Dare, Tracey and Stephen Groves, Peter L Harrison*

COPTHORNE TQ3240 Map 3

Old House

(01342) 718529 – www.theoldhouseinn.co.uk

B2037 NE of village; RH10 3JB

Charming old pub with plenty of character, real ales, enjoyable food and attentive staff; attractive bedrooms

Walking into the little entrance bar in this timbered higgledy-piggledy building, you'll feel immediately welcomed. There's a brown leather chesterfield sofa, armchairs and carved wooden chairs around all sorts of tables, a big sisal mat on flagstones, a decorative fireplace and nightlights. Courage Best, Ringwood Razorback and a guest beer on handpump, several good wines by the glass and a couple of huge glass flagons holding Sipsmith vodka and gin; staff are friendly and helpful. The nooks and crannies in the interconnected rooms leading off here are just as cosy. Off to the left is a charming small room with a woodburning stove in an inglenook fireplace and two leather armchairs in front, white-painted beams in a low ceiling (this is the oldest part, dating from the 16th c), cushioned settles and pre-war-style cushioned dining chairs around varying tables. A teeny back room, like something you'd find on an old galleon, has button-back wall seating up to the roof, a few chairs and heavy ropework. Dining rooms are beamed (some painted) and timbered with parquet, quarry tiles or sisal flooring, high-backed leather and other dining chairs, more wall seating and fresh flowers and candles; background music and board games. The terraced garden has heavy rustic tables and benches and a converted barn houses the smartly comfortable bedrooms.

Quite a choice of good food includes sandwiches, sausage and black pudding scotch egg with home-made brown sauce, chicken, shiitake and leek terrine with spring onions and golden raisin purée, thai green vegetable curry, cumberland sausages with mash and gravy, crayfish, chorizo and squid pasta with roasted tomatoes and chilli, duck breast with dauphinoise potatoes, madeira jus and pickled raspberries, pork tenderloin with potato rösti and mushroom sauce, corn-fed chicken with tomato and red pepper cassoulet and parma ham crisp, and puddings such as vanilla pannacotta with raspberry sorbet and sticky toffee pudding with toffee sauce. *Benchmark main dish: pie of the day £13.00. Two-course evening meal £22.00.*

Free house ~ Licensee Stephen Godsave ~ Real ale ~ Open 11-11; 11-10.30 Sun ~ Bar food 12-3, 6-9 (9.30 Fri, Sat); 12-3, 6-8 Sun ~ Restaurant ~ Children welcome ~ Dogs allowed in bar ~ Wi-fi ~ Bedrooms: /£130 *Recommended by Mrs Zara Elliott, Ian, Andrew and Michele Revell, R and M Thomas, Jonny and Andrew Haughton, Andrea and Laurie Grist*

DANEHILL TQ4128 Map 3

Coach & Horses

(01825) 740369 – www.coachandhorses.co

Off A275, via School Lane towards Chelwood Common; RH17 7JF

Well run dining pub with bustling bars, a welcoming landlord, very good food and ales and sizeable garden

In warm weather, the big garden here really comes into its own: there's an adults-only terrace beneath a huge maple, picnic-sets and a children's play area on lawns and views of the South Downs. Inside, the little bar to the right has half-panelled walls, simple furniture on polished floorboards, a woodburner in a brick fireplace and a big hatch to the bar counter: Harveys Best and Long Man Best Bitter on handpump, local Black Pig farmhouse cider and eight wines by the glass including prosecco and Bluebell sparkling wine from Sussex. A couple of steps lead down to a half-panelled area with a mix of dining chairs around characterful wooden tables (set with flowers and candles) on a fine brick floor, and changing artwork on the walls. Then another step down leads to a dining area with stone walls, beams, flagstones and a woodburning stove.

Highly regarded food includes sandwiches, crispy chilli beef salad, duck liver parfait with chicory and bacon relish, potato dumplings with provençale vegetables and basil and hazelnut pesto, local pork sausages with mash and caramelised onions, duck breast with cauliflower, fondant potatoes and cranberry jus, whole local plaice with cockle and mussel beurre blanc and paprika fries, sirloin steak with garlic butter and chips, stone bass with crushed brown butter parsnips, salsify, burnt apple purée and chestnuts, and puddings such as chocolate and salted caramel pavlova with candied hazelnuts and vanilla and rhubarb cheesecake with poached rhubarb. *Benchmark main dish: seared calves liver and bacon £15.00. Two-course evening meal £21.00.*

Free house ~ Licensee Ian Philpots ~ Real ale ~ Open 12-3, 5.30-11; 12-11.30 Sat; 12-10.30 Sun ~ Bar food 12-2, 6.30-9; 12-2.30, 6.30-9.30 Sat; 12-3 Sun ~ Restaurant ~ Children welcome ~ Dogs allowed in bar ~ Wi-fi *Recommended by John Preddy, Chris Bell, Tracey and Stephen Groves, Robert and Diana Ringstone, Kate and Mark Foskett, Abigail Slater*

DIAL POST
Crown

TQ1519 Map 3

(01403) 710902 – www.crown-inn-dialpost.co.uk

Worthing Road (off A24 S of Horsham); RH13 8NH

Tile-hung village pub with interesting food and a good mix of customers; bedrooms

You can be sure of a warm welcome from the friendly staff here, and there's always a good mix of both chatty drinkers and diners. The bustling, beamed bar has a couple of standing timbers, brown squashy sofas, pine tables and chairs on the stone floor and a small woodburning stove in a brick fireplace. Greyhound K-9, Hammerpot Red Hunter and Long Man Best Bitter on handpump are served from the attractive herringbone brick counter, alongside a local cider, eight wines by the glass plus prosecco, champagne and interesting soft drinks. To the right of the bar, the restaurant (with more beams) has an ornamental woodburner in a brick fireplace, a few photographs, chunky pine tables and chairs, a couple of cushioned pews and a shelf of books; steps lead down to an additional dining room; background music and board games. The pub dog is called Chops. A straightforwardly furnished dining conservatory, facing the village green, is light and airy, and there are picnic-sets in the back garden.

Good, up-to-date food includes lunchtime sandwiches, baby spinach, toasted walnuts, beetroot, orange and feta salad, terrine of local pork, chicken and pink peppercorns with red cabbage chutney, vegetable and nut wellington with rich tomato gravy, ham and free-range eggs, fillet of local salmon with prawn, pea and potato chowder, confit chicken with mixed bean ragoût, puy lentils and chorizo, king prawns with wild garlic, white wine and spaghetti topped with gremolata, local fillet steak with red wine jus and garlic butter, and puddings such as warm prune and Armagnac tart with orange caramel sauce and rhubarb and ginger crumble with custard. *Benchmark main dish: steak burger £12.00. Two-course evening meal £20.00.*

Free house ~ Licensees James and Penny Middleton-Burn ~ Real ale ~ Open 12-3, 6-11; 12-4 Sun; closed Sun evening ~ Bar food 12-2, 6-9 (9.30 Fri, Sat); 12-3 Sun ~ Restaurant ~ Children welcome ~ Dogs welcome ~ Wi-fi ~ Bedrooms: £51/£69 *Recommended by Elisabeth and Bill Humphries, Barbara and Phil Bowie, R and M Thomas, Martin Bailey, Martine and Derek Cotton*

DUNCTON SU9517 Map 3

Cricketers

(01798) 342473 – www.thecricketersduncton.co.uk
Set back from A285; GU28 0LB

Charming old coaching inn with real ales, popular food and suntrap back garden

This family-run pub makes the best of its position in the Goodwood Hills, and you'll need to book a table in advance on motor sport and horse-racing days; you can now make a weekend of it by staying in their new bedrooms in a converted barn. The traditional bar has a display of cricketing memorabilia, a few standing timbers, simple seating and an open woodburning stove in an inglenook fireplace. Steps lead down to a dining room with farmhouse chairs around wooden tables. Flowerpots Bitter, Langham Hip Hop and Triple fff Moondance on handpump, nine wines by the glass and three farm ciders; board games. There are picnic-sets out in front beneath the flowering window boxes and more on decked areas and under parasols on grass in the picturesque back garden. The pub got its present name from its 19th-c owner John Wisden, the cricketer who published the famous *Wisden Cricketers' Almanack*.

Tasty food includes lunchtime sandwiches, chicken liver parfait, moules marinière, butternut squash risotto topped with parmesan, a trio of sausages with mash and onion gravy, catalan fish stew, chicken breast stuffed with goats cheese and red peppers with parmentier potatoes, steak and stilton stroganoff, roasted partridge on mushrooms with game chips and madeira sauce, teriyaki rib-eye steak on oriental soba noodle salad, and puddings. *Benchmark main dish: steak and mushroom in ale pie £11.95. Two-course evening meal £19.00.*

Free house ~ Licensee Martin Boult ~ Real ale ~ Open 11-11; 12-10.30 Sun ~ Bar food 12-2.30, 6-9; 12-9 weekends; cream teas 2.30-6 ~ Children welcome ~ Dogs welcome ~ Wi-fi
Recommended by Simon Sharpe, Chris and Sophie Baxter, Alexander and Trish Cutter, Richard and Tessa Ibbot, Charles Fraser

EARTHAM SU9309 Map 2

George

(01243) 814340 – www.thegeorgeeartham.com
Signed off A285 Chichester–Petworth, from Fontwell off A27, from Slindon off A29; PO18 0LT

170-year-old pub in tucked-away village with country furnishings and contemporary touches, local ales and enjoyable food

The licensees here continue to work really hard to keep standards of food and service at tip top level and they're certainly succeeding – our readers love their visits. The light and prettily decorated bar was being refurbished as we went to press, but will still have dining chairs around wood-topped tables (each set with fresh flowers and candles) on parquet flooring, plus sofas, armchairs, a dresser with country knick-knacks, paintings on cream-painted walls above a grey-planked dado and stone bottles and books. The charming, beamed restaurant has high-backed grey tartan chairs and pale settles on pale floorboards; background music and board games. In cold weather, three open fires keep the pub warm. A beer named for the pub (from Otter) and guests from local breweries such as Arundel, Goldmark, Gun, Hepworth and Langham on handpump, 13 wines by the glass, up to 40 gins, 20 malt whiskies and farm cider; they also plan to offer eight locally sourced craft beers. The large garden has picnic-sets on grass and seats and tables under a gazebo. There are some lovely walks and cycle routes in the surrounding South Downs. Easy disabled access.

Using the best local produce the imaginative food includes sandwiches, breaded whitebait with rustic tartare, smoked salmon with pickled cucumber and horseradish crème fraîche, lambs liver and bacon with creamy mash and sweet onion gravy, steak burger with toppings, coleslaw and fries, mushroom, goats cheese and red onion marmalade wellington with truffle mash and mushroom sauce, sticky rib of beef with smoked bacon crumb, mac and cheese, confit tomatoes and watercress salad, lemon sole stuffed with smoked salmon, chicory, silverskin onions, bacon lardons and peas in a creamy white wine sauce, and puddings such as fruit crumble of the day with vanilla custard and warm chocolate brownie with chocolate sauce and ice-cream. *Benchmark main dish: pie of the day £12.95. Two-course evening meal £19.00.*

Free house ~ Licensees James and Anita Thompson ~ Real ale ~ Open 11.30-11; 12-6 Sun; closed Mon ~ Bar food 12-3, 6-9 (9.30 Fri, Sat); 12-4 Sun ~ Restaurant ~ Children welcome ~ Dogs allowed in bar ~ Wi-fi *Recommended by Tracey and Stephen Groves, Adam and Natalie Davis, Simon Collett-Jones, Colin and Daniel Gibbs, Beverley and Andy Butcher*

EAST LAVANT SU8608 Map 2

Royal Oak

(01243) 527434 – www.royaloakeastlavant.co.uk

Pook Lane, off A286; PO18 0AX

Bustling and friendly dining pub with proper drinking area, interesting food, a thoughtful wine list and seats outside; stylish bedrooms

This pretty little white house, handy for Goodwood and some pleasant walks, has a proper drinking area despite its emphasis on food. This area, to the left of the door, has an open fire, a high, button-back wall seat and wooden chairs around a few tables on stripped wooden boards and stools against the brick counter where helpful, friendly staff keep Marstons Pedigree and Ringwood Razorback on handpump, 11 wines by the glass, nine gins and nine malt whiskies; background music, board games and TV. The open-plan dining areas to the right have crooked beams and are furnished with upholstered armchairs, red button-back banquettes and cushioned wooden chairs around rustic tables on a fine old brick floor; also, hunting scenes and mirrors on the walls and a woodburning stove in one fireplace with a large lamp in another. An end room with green or black banquettes on floor tiles has a large wooden propeller from a World War I french fighter plane on a flint wall. There's a flagstoned front terrace with seats and tables under parasols and more seats on a stepped side terrace. Bedrooms, which are at the back of the cottage, are charming and up to date, and you can walk up a couple of steps to fields with a view of the church to the left. The car park is across the lane, where they also have a couple of self-catering rooms.

Rewarding food includes lunchtime open sandwiches, pigeon and venison terrine with chestnuts, bacon and caramelised apple, ravioli with celeriac, white truffle and baby spinach and dolcelatte cream, mushroom risotto with white truffle oil and parmesan crisp, king scallops with confit chicken wings, tamarind curry sauce and coconut rice, slow-cooked beef with wild mushroom gratin, confit potato and fresh horseradish gravy, herb-crusted rack of lamb with celeriac gratin, braised red cabbage and port and lamb jus, and puddings such as green apple pannacotta with apple sorbet and apple purée and chocolate fondant with peanut butter ice-cream. *Benchmark main dish: beer-battered fish and chips £16.00. Two-course evening meal £24.00.*

Free house ~ Licensee Szilard Szucs ~ Real ale ~ Open 9am-11pm; 9am-10.30pm Sun ~ Bar food 12-2.30, 6-9; 12-3, 6-8 Sun ~ Restaurant ~ Children welcome ~ Dogs allowed in bar ~ Wi-fi ~ Bedrooms: £85/£125 *Recommended by Andrea and Laurie Grist, Jonny and Andrew Haughton, Dan and Anne Morgan*

ERIDGE GREEN TQ5535 Map 3

Nevill Crest & Gun

(01892) 864209 – www.brunningandprice.co.uk/nevillcrestandgun

A26 Tunbridge Wells–Crowborough; TN3 9JR

Handsome old building with lots of character, plenty to look at, six real ales and enjoyable modern food

A farmhouse over 500 years ago, this has been meticulously renovated keeping many original features that blend cleverly with modern touches. The whole building has been opened up and extended with standing timbers and doorways keeping some sense of separate rooms. Throughout there are heavy beams (some carved), panelling, rugs on wooden floors and woodburning stoves and open fires in three fireplaces (the linenfold carved bressumer above one is worth seeking out). Also, all manner of individual dining chairs around dark wood or copper-topped tables, lots of pictures, maps and photographs relating to the local area, and windowsills crammed with toby jugs, stone and glass bottles and plants. Phoenix Brunning & Price Original plus Harveys Best, Holler Boys Cheat Mode, Long Man Best Bitter, Old Dairy Spring Top and Pig & Porter Skylarking on handpump, 15 wines by the glass and lots of gins and malt whiskies; board games and background music. At the front are some picnic-sets and out on a back terrace – beside the airy, raftered dining extension – there are also plenty of good quality wooden tables and chairs.

Enterprising modern food includes sandwiches, potted crab with mint apple salad, hot and spicy chicken wings with blue cheese dipping sauce, sweet potato, cauliflower and chickpea tagine with lemon and coriander couscous, a charcuterie board (to share), pork and leek sausages with mash and onion gravy, steak burger with toppings, coleslaw and chips, malaysian fish curry with sticky coconut rice, slow-roast pork belly with black pudding croquettes and cider and mustard gravy, and puddings such as Baileys cheesecake with coffee ice-cream and apple and rhubarb crumble with vanilla ice-cream. *Benchmark main dish: teriyaki sea bass with wasabi rice balls, pickled ginger, chilli, soy and sesame dressing £15.95. Two-course evening meal £21.50.*

Brunning & Price ~ Manager Edward Hoskins ~ Real ale ~ Open 11.30-11; 12-10 Sun ~ Bar food 12-10 (9 Sun) ~ Children welcome ~ Dogs allowed in bar ~ Wi-fi *Recommended by Paddy and Sian O'Leary, Nicola and Stuart Parsons, R and M Thomas, Belinda Stamp, Rosie and John Moore, Elise and Charles Mackinlay*

EWHURST GREEN TQ7924 Map 3

White Dog

(01580) 830264 – www.thewhitedogewhurst.co.uk

Turn off A21 to Bodiam at S end of Hurst Green, cross B2244, pass Bodiam Castle, cross river then bear left uphill at Ewhurst Green sign; TN32 5TD

Welcoming village pub with a nice little bar, several real ales and popular food; bedrooms

A father and daughter team are in charge here, and our readers enjoy their visits very much. The bustling bar has a roaring log fire in an inglenook fireplace, beams, wood panelling and a mix of chairs and tables on old brick or flagstoned floors. They keep a beer named for the pub (from Hardys &

Hansons), Harveys Best, Rother Valley Level Best and a guest from Tonbridge on handpump and 20 wines by the glass. A dining room has sturdy wooden tables and chairs on more flagstones, while the games room (which opens on to the front terrace) has darts and pool; background music. There can be few pubs with a view as stunning as the one over Bodiam Castle (National Trust) from the seats and tables in the back garden here, and one of the light and airy bedrooms shares this view; they also have tipis for hire.

Well thought-of seasonal food includes sandwiches, potted shrimps with toasted sourdough, seared pigeon breast marinated in juniper and thyme with rhubarb compote, gnocchi with fresh tomato and pesto sauce topped with cheese, chargrilled sea bass with salt and rosemary and chips, guinea fowl breast on tarragon sauce with roast butternut squash, glazed rack of local lamb, fondant potatoes and port wine sauce, cod fillet and mussel bouillabaisse with rouille, 28-day-aged rare-breed 10oz rib-eye steak with chips, and puddings such as chocolate fondant and blackberry and apple crumble. *Benchmark main dish: seafood linguine £12.95. Two-course evening meal £23.00.*

Free house ~ Licensees Harriet Bull and Dale Skinner ~ Real ale ~ Open 12-11 ~ Bar food 12-2 (2.30 Sat), 6.30-9; 12-3, 6.30-9 ~ Restaurant ~ Children welcome ~ Dogs allowed in bar and bedrooms ~ Wi-fi ~ Live music Sun afternoons ~ Bedrooms: /£95 *Recommended by David Jackman, Mr Frederick Peach, Mandy and Gary Redstone, Gene and Kitty Rankin, Marianne and Michael Huggins, Darrell Barton*

FLETCHING TQ4223 Map 3

Griffin

(01825) 722890 – www.thegriffininn.co.uk

Village signposted off A272 W of Uckfield; TN22 3SS

Sussex Dining Pub of the Year

Busy, gently upmarket inn with a fine wine list, real ales, bistro-style bar food and a big garden; pretty bedrooms

We get consistently high praise from our readers for all aspects of this civilised and notably well run inn. It's very much the focal point of this handsome village and the beamed and quaintly panelled bar rooms have blazing log fires, old photographs and hunting prints, straightforward close-set furniture including some captain's chairs, and china on a delft shelf. A small bare-boarded serving area is off to one side and there's another cosy bar with sofas and a TV; background music. The place gets pretty packed at weekends. Harveys Best, Long Man American Pale Ale and a couple of guests on handpump, plus 20 wines by the glass from a good list (including champagne, prosecco and sweet wine); they hold a monthly wine club with supper (on a Thursday evening). At the garden entrance there's an outside bar and wood oven, tables and chairs under parasols and a stunning view over Sheffield Park; there are more seats on a sandstone terrace. The bright and pretty bedrooms are comfortable and breakfasts good. There are ramps for wheelchairs.

Delicious food includes moules marinière, duck liver and peppercorn pâté with onion marmalade, wild mushroom pasta with spinach, parmesan, pesto cream and pine nuts, local venison sausages with herb mash, roasted onions and red wine jus, half a roast mallard with creamy mash, romanesco sauce and kirsch jus, sesame-crusted salmon fillet with stir-fried pak choi, peppers and bean sprouts and sweet chilli and soy, beef fillet en croûte with mushroom duxelles, crisp panacetta and sarladaises potatoes, and puddings such as chocolate chilli tart with crème fraîche and vanilla crème brûlée. *Benchmark main dish: beer-battered cod and chips with pea purée £14.50. Two-course evening meal £25.00.*

Free house ~ Licensees James Pullan and Samantha Barlow ~ Real ale ~ Open 11am-midnight (11pm Sun); 11am-1am Sat ~ Bar food 12-2.30 (3 Sat), 7-9.30; 12-3, 7-9 Sun ~ Restaurant ~ Children welcome ~ Dogs allowed in bar and bedrooms ~ Wi-fi ~ Live music Fri evening, Sun lunch ~ Bedrooms: £70/£110 *Recommended by Robin Waters, Amanda Shipley, Richard Cole, John Preddy, Peter Meister, Carol and Barry Craddock, Sam Cole*

FRIDAY STREET TV6203 Map 3

Farm at Friday Street

(01323) 766049 – www.farmfridaystreet.com

B2104, Langney; BN23 8AP

Handsome old place with lots to look at, efficient staff serving popular food and drink and seats outside

A farmhouse in the 17th c (houses have replaced the fields that used to surround it), this has had many extensions since then, but it's been done well and there are plenty of both drinking and dining areas. The open-plan rooms are split by brick pillars into cosier areas with sofas, stools and all manner of wooden dining chairs and tables on bare boards, creamy coloured flagstones, coir or carpet. Throughout, there are open fires, big house plants, stubby church candles, frame-to-frame prints and pictures and farming implements; the atmosphere is easy-going and friendly. Long Man Best Bitter, St Austell Tribute, Timothy Taylors Landlord and Wadworths 6X on handpump and 14 wines by the glass; background music. The dining room is on two levels with timbered walls, glass partitions, a raised conical roof and an open kitchen. The front lawn has plenty of picnic-sets.

Popular food includes sandwiches, prawn and crayfish cocktail, pork spring rolls with sweet and sour sauce, three-cheese macaroni with garlic bread, sausages and mash with onion gravy, beer-battered cod and chips, barbecue chicken board with coleslaw and chilli mayonnaise, seared tuna niçoise with anchovies and a poached egg, pork tenderloin wrapped in parma ham with mushroom duxelles, beetroot purée and jus, and puddings such as warm chocolate brownie with chocolate ice-cream and apple and mixed berry crumble with custard. *Benchmark main dish: half shoulder of lamb £21.95. Two-course evening meal £21.00.*

Whiting & Hammond ~ Manager Paul Worman ~ Real ale ~ Open 11-11; 9am-11pm Sat, Sun ~ Bar food 12-9.30; 9am-9.30pm Sat; 9-9 Sun ~ Restaurant ~ Children welcome ~ Dogs allowed in bar ~ Wi-fi *Recommended by Peter and Elizabeth May, Greta and Gavin Craddock, Chloe and Tim Hodge, Richard Cole, Sally and Brian Turner*

HASTINGS TQ8109 Map 3

Crown

(01424) 465100 – www.thecrownhastings.co.uk

All Saints Street, Old Town; TN34 3BN

Informal and friendly corner pub with high quality food, local ales and simple furnishings

With proper character, a genuine welcome and interesting food and drinks, this well run pub is a big hit with our readers. It's situated just back from the seafront in the Old Town, and the simply furnished bar has bare boards, plain chairs around tables inlaid with games and set with posies of flowers, a log fire and plenty of windows to keep everything light (despite the dark paintwork). A snug has leather armchairs in front of another open fire, a couple of tables, and books and house plants on a windowsill and mantelpiece; background music and board games. Stools line the counter where they keep four changing ales from breweries such as Cellar Head,

Gun, Holler Boys, Old Dairy and Three Legs on handpump, 14 good wines by the glass, 15 gins, 15 whiskies and local cider; service is friendly and helpful. There's a dining area at one end of the bar with scatter cushions on wall seats, mismatched chairs and some large tables. Local art (for sale) hangs on the walls and one window is hung with aprons and lined with shelves of local pottery, greetings cards and hand-made purses; daily papers and background music. Dogs and children receive a genuinely warm welcome. There are a few picnic-sets outside at the front.

Imaginative food includes sandwiches, partridge breast with spiced squash, barbecue onions, purple sprouting broccoli and green sauce, haggis croquette with bacon and cayenne sauce and a poached egg, jerusalem artichoke, cheese and onion hotpot with kale and a cheese scone, tandoori cod with mixed pulse dhal, labneh, cauliflower and mint pakora, chicken bourguignon with roast celeriac and cauliflower and kohlrabi salad, and puddings such as warm parkin cake with whisky mac syrup and blue cheese and pannacotta with roasted rhubarb and danish pastry. *Benchmark main dish: rare-breed ham and egg £10.00. Two-course evening meal £23.00.*

Free house ~ Licensees Tess Eaton and Andrew Swan ~ Real ale ~ Open 11-11 (10.30 Sun) ~ Bar food 12-5, 6-9.30; 11-5, 6-9.30 weekends ~ Children welcome ~ Dogs welcome ~ Wi-fi
Recommended by Peter Meister, Julie and Andrew Blanchett, Angela and Steve Heard, Adam and Natalie Davis, George and Alison Bishop

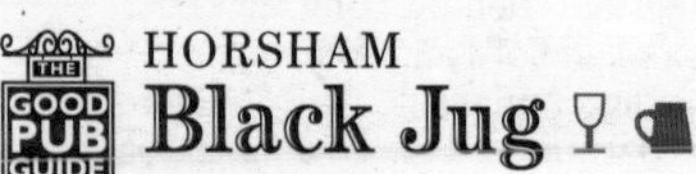

HORSHAM — TQ1730 Map 3

Black Jug

(01403) 253526 – www.brunningandprice.co.uk/blackjug
North Street; RH12 1RJ

Busy town pub with wide choice of drinks, attentive staff and rewarding food

A good mix of customers keeps the atmosphere lively and good natured, and staff cope with the crowds with efficiency and cheerfulness. The single, large, early 20th-c room has a long central bar, a nice collection of sizeable dark wood tables and comfortable chairs on a stripped-wood floor, bookcases and interesting old prints and photographs above a dark wood-panelled dado on cream walls; background music and board games. A spacious, bright conservatory has similar furniture and lots of hanging baskets. Harveys Best and Wychwood Hobgoblin Gold with guests such as Arundel Stronghold, Calvors Smooth Hoperator and Hook Norton Hooky on handpump, 16 wines by the glass, 150 malt whiskies, 50 gins, 30 rums, 30 bourbons and farm cider. The pretty, flower-filled back terrace has plenty of garden furniture; parking is in the council car park next door, as the small one by the pub is for staff and deliveries only.

Brasserie-style food includes sandwiches, smoked duck with celery, apple and pickled walnuts, goats cheese arancini with pea purée, broad beans and lemon dressing, a charcuterie sharing board, sweet potato, cauliflower and chickpea tagine with lemon couscous, steak burger with toppings, coleslaw and chips, monkfish wrapped in parma ham with basil gnocchi and pizzaiola sauce, lamb shoulder with dauphinoise potatoes and carrot purée, and puddings such as crème brûlée and hot waffle with caramelised banana, toffee sauce and vanilla ice-cream. *Benchmark main dish: honey-roasted ham and egg £11.45. Two-course evening meal £22.00.*

Brunning & Price ~ Tenant Ben Mannering ~ Real ale ~ Open 11.30am-11pm; 12-10.30 Sun ~ Bar food 12-10 (9.30 Sun) ~ Children welcome till 7pm ~ Dogs allowed in bar ~ Wi-fi
Recommended by Tony Scott, Gail and Arthur Roberts, Sarah and David Gibbs, Graeme and Sally Mendham, Bob and Melissa Wyatt

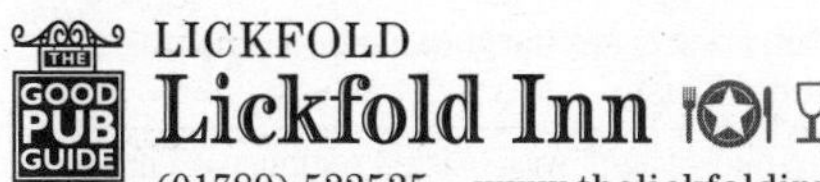

LICKFOLD SU9226 Map 2

Lickfold Inn

(01789) 532535 – www.thelickfoldinn.co.uk

NE of Midhurst, between A286 and A283; GU28 9EY

Tudor inn with impressive food in bars and upstairs restaurant, friendly staff, a thoughtful choice of drinks and attractive garden

There is a bar here that locals use for a pint and a chat, but of course most customers want to enjoy the excellent, innovative food. The two easy-going bar rooms have heavy Tudor beams, a fine herringbone brick floor, comfortable sofas to each side of a woodburning stove, chapel chairs, armchairs, Georgian settles and nice old tables (some with fine inlaid panels); it's fun watching the kitchen hard at work behind a big glass window. Langham Best Bitter and Upham Punter and Tipster on handpump, a dozen wines by the glass and a good choice of gins, rums and whiskies. Upstairs, the restaurant has more heavy beams, pale grey upholstered dining chairs around dark polished wood tables on bare boards, a few standing timbers and another woodburning stove. An outside terrace has plenty of seats and tables and there's also a garden across the drive on several levels with more seating.

Exceptionally good food includes enterprising bar nibbles such as barbecue salmon with dill and seaweed, their much loved scotch egg, confit duck leg, tempura cauliflower and salted lemon, chilli beef puff pie and wild garlic velouté with an egg; also, gin salmon with cucumber, dill and seaweed, aged beef tartare with garnishes, pork with spring onion and onion tart, cod with mussels, broccoli stem and herbs, côte de boeuf (for two), and puddings such as rose sorbet with chocolate and strawberry cheesecake; they also offer a two- and three-course set lunch. *Benchmark main dish: halibut with yeast, cauliflower and pickled sloes £29.00. Two-course evening meal £40.00.*

Free house ~ Licensee Tom Sellers ~ Real ale ~ Open 11.30-10; 11.30-11 Sat; 11.30-7 Sun; closed Mon, Tues; ten days Jan ~ Bar food 12-9.30 ~ Restaurant ~ Children welcome ~ Dogs allowed in bar ~ Wi-fi ~ Live music first Sun evening of month *Recommended by Jack Trussler, Andrew and Michele Revell, Brian and Sally Wakeham, Diana and Bertie Farr, Celia and Rupert Lemming, Miss A E Dare, Chantelle and Tony Redman*

LOWER BEEDING TQ2225 Map 3

Crabtree

(01403) 892666 – www.crabtreesussex.co.uk

Brighton Road; RH13 6PT

Airy bar and cosy dining rooms in bustling pub with excellent food, helpful service and pretty garden

In warm weather head for the lovely landscaped garden with its picnic-sets, wendy house and fine country views. Inside, behind the Victorian façade, there are Tudor beams and a huge inglenook dated 1537, and the airy, simply furnished front bar has a green leather chesterfield, plush stools around just three tables on parquet flooring, a warming woodburning stove, fresh flowers and nightlights and maybe background jazz. Badger Best and a seasonal guest on handpump and good wines (some organic) by the glass, served by knowledgeable staff. A garden room leads off with wicker chairs, leather wall banquettes and a dresser full of home-made jellies and chutney. Several dining rooms towards the back are interlinked and cosy with beams, brick floors, high-backed dining chairs around wooden-topped painted tables and country paintings (which are for sale);

a small room to the right of the entrance is similarly furnished. The pub is handy for visits to Nymans (National Trust).

Innovative food includes seared duck magret with toasted sesame pak choi and satay sauce, grilled mackerel with beetroot, horseradish, goats cheese curd and dill oil, parsley and garlic risotto with hazelnuts, fishcakes with celeriac rémoulade and crispy caper salad, sweet potato fondant with butternut squash, roast cauliflower, quinoa, coconut and coriander, burger with toppings and triple-cooked chips, a pie of the day, moules frites, moroccan-style lamb rump with chickpea salsa, harissa pearl couscous, almonds and apricot, salmon fillet with warm potato and green bean salad and a poached egg, 28-day-aged rib-eye steak with a sauce of the day and triple-cooked chips, and puddings such as warm orange bread and butter pudding with marmalade custard and lime leaf crème brûlée; they also offer a two- and three-course set weekday lunch. *Benchmark main dish: sea bass with saffron risotto, plums and basil oil £17.50. Two-course evening meal £22.00.*

Badger ~ Tenant Simon Hope ~ Real ale ~ Open 10am-midnight ~ Bar food 12-9.30; 12-5 Sun ~ Restaurant ~ Children welcome ~ Dogs allowed in bar ~ Wi-fi *Recommended by Edward Edmonton, Susan and Callum Slade, David and Leone Lawson, David and Charlotte Green, Martin Day, Jill and Dick Archer, Alison and Michael Harper*

LURGASHALL SU9327 Map 2

Noahs Ark

(01428) 707346 – www.noahsarkinn.co.uk

Off A283 N of Petworth; GU28 9ET

Busy old pub in nice spot with neatly kept bar and dining rooms, real ales and pleasing food using local produce

Walkers, diners and cricketers give this 16th-c pub a bustling, chatty atmosphere. The simple, traditional bar has stools by the counter where they serve Greene King IPA and Abbot and a guest such as Hogs Back TEA on handpump, 23 wines by the glass and a fine bloody mary. There are also beams, a mix of wooden chairs and tables, parquet flooring and an inglenook fireplace. Open to the top of the rafters, the dining room is spacious and airy with church candles and fresh flowers on light wood tables, and a couple of comfortable sofas facing each other in front of an open woodburning stove; background music and board games. The border terrier is called Gillie and visiting dogs may get a dog biscuit. There are tables in a large side garden and the village green and cricket pitch are opposite.

Popular food includes lunchtime sandwiches, lamb kofta with mint yoghurt, rocket and pine nut salad, venison carpaccio with pickled red cabbage, parmesan and olive oil and lemon dressing, cauliflower and walnut riosotto with cambozola bonbons, burger with toppings, coleslaw and chips, chicken suprême stuffed with parma ham, spinach and pine nuts, thai green monkfish and prawn curry with home-made flatbread, 10oz rib-eye steak with creamy mushroom sauce, and puddings such as damson bakewell tart with clotted cream and salted caramel and chocolate mousse. *Benchmark main dish: beer-battered fish and chips £14.50. Two-course evening meal £20.00.*

Greene King ~ Lease Henry Coghlan and Amy Whitmore ~ Real ale ~ Open 11am-11.30pm; 12-10 Sun (12-8 in winter) ~ Bar food 12-2.30, 7-9.30; 12-3.30 Sun ~ Restaurant ~ Children welcome ~ Dogs allowed in bar ~ Wi-fi *Recommended by Miss A E Dare, Jennifer and Nicholas Thompson, Liz and Mike Newton, Chantelle and Tony Redman, Gary and Marie Miller*

We mention bottled beers and spirits only if there is something unusual about them – imported belgian real ales, say, or dozens of malt whiskies; so do please let us know about them in your reports.

MARK CROSS TQ5831 Map 3

Mark Cross Inn

(01892) 852423 – www.themarkcross.co.uk

A267 N of Mayfield; TN6 3NP

Sizeable pub with interconnected rooms, real ales and popular food, and good views from seats in the garden

Usefully serving food and drinks all day, this big spreading pub is on several linked levels but kept cosy with church candles and open fires, shelves lined with books and stone bottles, gilt-edged mirrors, big clocks and large house plants. There's all manner of seating from farmhouse, mate's and cushioned dining chairs to settles and stools grouped around dark shiny tables on rugs and bare boards, and the walls are lined almost frame to frame with photographs, prints, paintings and old newspaper cuttings. Helpful staff serve Fullers London Pride, Long Man Best Bitter, Musket Trigger and Westerham Grasshopper Kentish Bitter on handpump and good wines by the glass; daily papers and background music. In warm weather, the benches and tables on the terrace and the picnic-sets on grass get snapped up quickly by customers keen to make the most of the far-reaching views; there's also a children's play fort.

Generous helpings of tasty food includes sandwiches, beef carpaccio with stilton mousse, baked garlic and rosemary camembert with crudités and chutney, beetroot risotto with goats cheese and rocket, smoked chicken caesar salad, burger with toppings, coleslaw and skinny fries, clams with red chillies, tomatoes and garlic on linguine, piri-piri chicken with sweetcorn purée, sweetcorn fritter, jalapenos and coriander, and puddings such as chocolate brownie with chocolate sauce and sticky toffee pudding with toffee sauce and honeycomb ice-cream. *Benchmark main dish: beer-battered fish and chips £14.95. Two-course evening meal £20.00.*

Whiting & Hammond ~ Manager Michelle Fairless ~ Real ale ~ Open 9am-11pm (midnight Fri, Sat); 9am-10.30pm Sun ~ Bar food 12-9.30 (9 Sun) ~ Restaurant ~ Children welcome ~ Dogs allowed in bar ~ Wi-fi *Recommended by Jo Garnett, Rob Anderson, Valerie and Gordon Wauton, Kitty and Stuart Flint, Peter Pilbeam*

OVING SU9005 Map 2

Gribble Inn

(01243) 786893 – www.gribbleinn.co.uk

Between A27 and A259 E of Chichester; PO20 2BP

Own-brewed beers in bustling village pub with popular bar food and pretty garden

The own-brewed ales here remain quite a draw. On handpump, these might include Fuzzy Duck, Lazy Buzzard, Pig's Ear, Plucking Pheasant, Reg's Tipple and seasonal ales such as Sussex Quad Hopper or strong Wobbler Ale; they also have 16 wines by the glass, 40 gins, 20 malt whiskies, 30 vodkas and unusual rums. It's a 16th-c thatched place and the chatty bar features a lot of heavy beams and timbering while the other various linked rooms have a cottagey feel with sofas round two roaring log fires; board games. The barn houses a venue for parties. There are seats outside in a covered area and more chairs and tables in the pretty garden with its apple and pear trees.

Well liked food includes duck liver pâté with chutney, queen scallop and chorizo risotto with basil oil, sharing platters, root vegetable tagine with lemon, chilli and coriander cauliflower couscous, steak burger with toppings and chips, slow-braised oxtail served off the bone with grain mustard mash and parsnip purée, beer-battered haddock and chips, 10oz rib-eye steak with a choice of sauce, and puddings such as white chocolate and vanilla rice pudding with sloe gin berry compote and rhubarb and Pernod cheesecake topped with rhubarb jelly with honey and ginger ice-cream. *Benchmark main dish: slow-roast pork belly with creamed cabbage and bacon £16.00. Two-course evening meal £20.00.*

Free house ~ Licensees Simon Wood and Nicola Tester ~ Real ale ~ Open 11-11; 12-11 Sun ~ Bar food 12-9; 12-4 Sun ~ Restaurant ~ Children welcome away from bar ~ Dogs allowed in bar ~ Wi-fi *Recommended by Ian and Barbara Rankin, Christian Mole, Tony Selinger, Phil and Jane Villiers, Philippa Ward, Sally and John Quinlan, Kitty and Stuart Flint*

PETWORTH SU9721 Map 2

Angel

(01798) 342153 – www.angelinnpetworth.co.uk

Angel Street; GU28 0BG

Medieval building with 18th-c façade, chatty atmosphere in beamed bars, friendly service and good, interesting food; bedrooms

If you wish to spend time in this pretty market town and explore the many antique shops, why not stay in the comfortable bedrooms here; breakfasts are good too. The interconnected rooms have the feel of a country inn and retain many of their original features. The front bar has beams, a log fire in an inglenook fireplace and an appealing variety of old wooden and cushioned dining chairs and tables on wide floorboards. It leads through to the main room with high chairs by the counter where they keep a beer named for the pub (from Langham), Arundel Sussex Gold and Langham Hip Hop on handpump, 22 wines by the glass from an extensive list and ten gins; board games. Staff are courteous and helpful. There are also high-backed brown leather and antique chairs and tables on pale wooden flooring, the odd milk churn and french windows to a three-level terrace garden. The cosy and popular back bar is similarly furnished, with a second log fire.

Highly rated food includes sandwiches, ham hock terrine with pickled quince and honey and mustard dressing, scallops with chestnut purée and maple smoked bacon, oyster mushroom and black cabbage gnocchi with cep cream, burger with toppings, french fries and smoky burger sauce, local venison haunch with red wine and balsamic jus and roast potatoes, sea bass fillet with roasted butternut squash, fondant potato and kale pesto, and puddings such as treacle tart with granola, honey and clotted cream and caramelised banana bread and butter pudding with chocolate sauce and white chocolate ice-cream. *Benchmark main dish: beer-battered fish and chips £14.00. Two-course evening meal £20.00.*

Free house ~ Licensee Will Morley ~ Real ale ~ Open 10.30am-11pm; 11.30-10.30 Sun ~ Bar food 12-2.30, 6.30-9 ~ Children welcome ~ Dogs welcome ~ Wi-fi ~ Bedrooms: £90/£160 *Recommended by Sally and John Quinlan, Belinda and Neil Garth, Simon Collett-Jones, Robin and Anne Triggs, Rupert and Sandy Newton*

PETWORTH SU9921 Map 2

Welldiggers Arms

(01798) 344288 – www.thewelldiggersarms.co.uk

Low Heath; A283 E; GU28 0HG

Civilised inn with character bar and airy dining room, four real ales and good wines, helpful service and seats on terrace; bedrooms

A civilised pub with a character bar, this has drawn warm praise from our readers since its refurbishment a couple of years ago. A warming woodburner has long wooden slab tables to either side (each set with candles in brass holders and a plant) and there are wall banquettes and settles with scatter cushions, wheelback chairs, white-painted beams and stools against the counter where cheerful, attentive staff serve Teds Tickle (named for them by Hepworth), Brakspears Oxford Gold, Langham Hip Hop and Ringwood Fortyniner on handpump and good wines by the glass; background music. An end room is just right for a small group with a wooden settle and chunky chairs around a single table, and horse and hunting pictures. The big, airy dining room at the back has spreading country views from large picture windows, wall settles and more wheelbacks and country kitchen chairs with pretty cushions around tables of all size on flagstones, and a busy open kitchen. Through french windows is the terrace, which is largely enclosed by a marquee and furnished with teak tables and chairs. The cottagey-style bedrooms (either in the pub or in a separate annexe and all with views) are comfortable.

High quality food includes duck hash with a fried egg and bacon crumb, pork nugget with poached rhubarb, caramelised onion and dressed dandelion leaves, roast cauliflower with cheese croquette, curry spices, seared baby gem and coriander, cod with white beans, chorizo, jerusalem artichokes and purple sprouting broccoli, sticky slow-braised beef with mash, pickled girolles and cabbage, beer-battered fish and chips, 30-day-aged rib-eye steak with a choice of sauce and roasted shallots, and puddings such as prune and almond tart with amaretto custard and hot chocolate pudding with chocolate sauce and salted caramel ice-cream. *Benchmark main dish: beef and bacon burger with cheese and fries £14.95. Two-course evening meal £23.00.*

Free house ~ Licensee Nicholas King ~ Real ale ~ Open 11-11; 11-10.30 Sun ~ Bar food 12-3, 6-9; 12-3 Sun ~ Restaurant ~ Children welcome ~ Dogs allowed in bar and bedrooms ~ Wi-fi ~ Live jazz Sun lunchtime ~ Bedrooms: /£100 *Recommended by Richard Tilbrook, Sandra and Miles Spencer, Belinda and Neil Garth, Tina and Steven Hobden, Ruth and Peter Bacon*

RINGMER — TQ4313 Map 3

Cock £

(01273) 812040 – www.cockpub.co.uk

Uckfield Road – blocked-off section of road off A26 N of village turn-off; BN8 5RX

Country pub with a wide choice of popular bar food, real ales in character bar, and plenty of seats in the garden

You can be sure of a warm welcome from one of the convivial licensees in this 16th-c former coaching inn. It's tucked well away from the main road and the unspoilt bar has traditional pubby furniture on flagstones, heavy beams, a log fire in an inglenook fireplace, Harveys Best and a couple of guests from local breweries such as Downlands, Gun, Hammerpot and Holler Boys on handpump, ten wines by the glass and a dozen malt whiskies. There are also three dining areas; background music. Outside, on the terrace and in the garden, are lots of picnic-sets with views across open fields to the South Downs; a new side terrace has now been opened. The owners' dogs are called Bailey and Tally, and visiting canines are offered a bowl of water and a chew. This is sister pub to the Highlands at Uckfield.

A wide choice of pleasing food includes sandwiches, deep-fried camembert with cranberry sauce, crayfish and avocado cocktail, home-cooked ham and free-range eggs, vegetable lasagne, chicken curry with rice and poppadum, local venison burger with toppings and chips, liver and bacon with mash and onion gravy, salmon fillet with creamy watercress sauce, pork fillet in cream and mustard sauce, and puddings such as fruit crumble with custard and banoffi pie with cream. *Benchmark main dish: steak in ale pie £11.95. Two-course evening meal £19.00.*

Free house ~ Licensees Ian, Val, Nick and Matt Ridley ~ Real ale ~ Open 11-3, 6-11.30; 11-9.30 Sun ~ Bar food 12-2.15 (2.30 Sat), 6-9.30; 12-8.30 Sun ~ Restaurant ~ Well behaved children welcome but no toddlers ~ Dogs allowed in bar ~ Wi-fi *Recommended by James and Sylvia Hewitt, Martine and Fabio Lockley, Liz and Martin Eldon, Katherine Matthews, Ted and Mary Bates*

ROBERTSBRIDGE TQ7323 Map 3

George

(01580) 880315 – www.thegeorgerobertsbridge.co.uk

High Street; TN32 5AW

Former coaching inn with good food and ales and seats in courtyard garden; bedrooms

At the heart of a bustling village and with hard-working, hands-on licensees, this handsome old place is popular with both locals and visitors. The right-hand bar area has a log fire in a brick inglenook with a leather sofa and a couple of armchairs in front – just the place for a quiet pint and a chat – plus high bar stools by the counter where they serve Harveys Best and Whitstable Pearl of Kent plus a couple of guests from breweries such as Pig & Porter and Romney Marsh on handpump, good wines by the glass and a farm cider. The dining area is opposite, with elegant high-backed beige-tartan or leather chairs around a mix of tables (each with fresh flowers and a tea-light) on stripped floorboards and more tea-lights in a small fireplace; background music. The back terrace has plenty of seats and tables. Bedrooms are comfortable and the breakfasts well regarded.

Enjoyable food includes lunchtime baguettes and ciabattas, pork and chorizo terrine with chutney, twice-baked goats cheese soufflé, sharing boards, chargrilled cheese or five-bean and sweet potato burgers with toppings and chips, chicken with lemon and thyme, sautéed potatoes and spinach, chargrilled garlic, red onion and rosemary lamb rump with blackberry jus, slow-cooked pork belly with cider gravy and pear compote, and puddings such as crème brûlée of the day and vanilla sponge topped with local plum and apple compote with custard. *Benchmark main dish: tempura fish £12.50. Two-course evening meal £19.50.*

Free house ~ Licensees John and Jane Turner ~ Real ale ~ Open 12-11; 12-9 Sun; closed Mon ~ Bar food 12-9; 12-7 Sun ~ Children welcome but must be accompanied by an adult at all times ~ Dogs allowed in bar ~ Wi-fi *Recommended by Robert Mitchell, Peter Meister, Heather and Richard Jones, Sheila and Sam Thorpe, Kate and Mark Foskett*

SALEHURST TQ7424 Map 3

Salehurst Halt £

(01580) 880620 – www.salehursthalt.co.uk

Village signposted from Robertsbridge bypass on A21 Tunbridge Wells–Battle; Church Lane; TN32 5PH

Bustling country local in quiet hamlet with easy-going atmosphere, real ales, well liked bar food and seats in pretty back garden

Always full of cheerful, chatty customers (especially when the local bellringers pile in on Wednesday evenings), this particularly well run pub is much enjoyed by our readers. To the right of the door is a small bare-boards area with a few tables and chairs, a woodburning stove and shelves of books. The main bar has hops on beams, farmhouse and wheelback chairs, a sofa, settles with scatter cushions and scrubbed tables on floorboards; background music and board games. Harveys Best and guests from breweries such as Burning Sky, Dark Star, Long Man, Old Dairy and

Shepherd Neame on handpump, farm cider, several malt whiskies and eight wines by the glass. The charming, cottagey back garden has views over the Rother Valley and there's a terrace with metal chairs and tiled tables under a vine-covered arbour; outdoor table tennis.

As well as the popular summer Wednesday evening pizzas from the wood-fired oven, the tasty food includes sandwiches, home-made pâté with apple and date chutney, pork rillettes with croûtes and pickles, chicken, pheasant and goat curries, various pies, sea trout niçoise, a hungarian dish of spicy pork and beef wrapped in cabbage leaves, burgers with toppings and chips, mediterranean fish stew, moroccan-style lamb, popular steaks, and puddings such as salted caramel chocolate tart and key lime pie. *Benchmark main dish: pea and pancetta tortellini with creamy white wine sauce £14.00. Two-course evening meal £20.00.*

Free house ~ Licensee Andrew Augarde ~ Real ale ~ Open 12-11; closed Mon except bank holidays ~ Bar food 12-3, 6.30-9; 12-4 Sun ~ Children welcome ~ Dogs welcome ~ Wi-fi ~ Live music on terrace in summer *Recommended by Robert Mitchell, Nigel and Jean Eames, Peter Meister, Adam and Betty Lawrence, Chris and Sophie Baxter*

TICEHURST

TQ6830 Map 3

Bell

(01580) 200300 – www.thebellinticehurst.com

High Street; TN5 7AS

Carefully restored inn with beamed rooms, real ales and good wines by the glass, popular food and seats in pretty courtyard garden; bedrooms

Everyone congregates in the heavily beamed, character bar here with its cheerful, lively atmosphere and good mix of customers. There's an inglenook fireplace, tables surrounded by cushioned wooden dining chairs on bare boards, quirky decorations such as a squirrel in a rocking chair, and stools by the counter where Harveys Best, Long Man Best Bitter and Cellar Head Sub Three are served on handpump alongside seven wines by the glass, local gin and a dozen malt whiskies. The dining room continues from the bar and is similarly furnished, with the addition of cushioned wall settles and an eclectic choice of paintings on the red walls; background music. A separate snug has comfortable sofas grouped around a low table in front of another open fire, interesting wallpaper, a large globe, an ancient typewriter and various books and pieces of china. What was the carriage room holds a long sunken table with benches on either side (perfect for an informal party) and there's an upstairs function room too. At the back is a courtyard garden with seats and tables and built-in cushioned seating up steps on a raised area. The bedrooms in the coaching inn are comfortable and very individually decorated and there are also separate lodges (each with their own little garden built around a fire pit).

Well thought-of food includes venison slider with pickled cabbage and smoked cheddar, salmon tartare with soy, sesame, onion and avocado purée, wild mushroom macaroni cheese, beer-battered cod and chips, aromatic pork belly with parsnips, pear and star anise, calves liver with chickpeas, mango and lime, chagrilled beef rump (to share), and puddings such as apple and rhubarb crumble and sticky toffee pudding with butterscotch sauce, *Benchmark main dish: steak burger with toppings and chips £13.50. Two-course evening meal £20.00.*

Free house ~ Licensee Howard Canning ~ Real ale ~ Open 7am-midnight ~ Bar food 12-3, 6-9.30 (9 Sun) ~ Restaurant ~ Children welcome ~ Dogs allowed in bar and bedrooms ~ Wi-fi ~ Bedrooms: /£95 *Recommended by John and Penny Wildon, Barbara and Phil Bowie, Belinda Stamp, Edward Nile, Elise and Charles Mackinlay, Nick Sharpe*

TILLINGTON SU9621 Map 2

Horse Guards

(01798) 342332 – www.thehorseguardsinn.co.uk

Off A272 Midhurst–Petworth; GU28 9AF

300-year-old inn with beams, panelling and open fires in rambling rooms, enjoyable food and charming garden; cottagey bedrooms

Gently civilised and well run, this is an 18th-c inn that our readers return to on a regular basis. The neatly kept, beamed front bar has country furniture on bare boards, a chesterfield in one corner and a fine view beyond the village to the Rother Valley from a seat in the big panelled bow window. High bar chairs line the counter where they keep Burning Sky Plateau, Firebird Citra and 81 Artisan Underway on handpump, 17 wines by the glass, home-made liqueurs and local farm juices. Other rambling beamed rooms have similar furniture on brick floors, rugs and original panelling and there are fresh flowers throughout; background music and board games. When the weather is fine the leafy, sheltered garden has picnic-sets, day beds, deckchairs and even a hammock, and there's also a charming terrace. Cosy country bedrooms are comfortable and breakfasts are good. Constable and Turner both painted the medieval church with its unusual spire; Petworth mansion and park (National Trust) is nearby.

Cooked to order from a small seasonal menu and using some home-grown and foraged produce, the interesting food includes sandwiches, deep-fried chickpea chips with smoked aubergine dip, local cuttlefish with peanut sambal, asian slaw and lime, pasta with tomatoes, chilli parmesan, walnuts and pumpkin seeds, bouillabaisse with rouille, pork shoulder blanquette with white wine, cocoa beans, sherry, cream, thyme and roasted root vegetables, 35-day-hung rib-eye steak with miso and mushroom butter, and puddings such as marmalade sponge with Drambuie custard and egyptian-style chilled rice pudding with cardamom, rose water, blood orange and salted peanuts. *Benchmark main dish: local venison haunch with sussex pudding, ragoût and red wine sauce £21.50. Two-course evening meal £25.00.*

Enterprise ~ Lease Sam Beard and Michaela Hofirkova ~ Real ale ~ Open 12-midnight ~ Bar food 12-2.30, 6.30-9 (9.30 Fri); 12-3, 6-9.30 Sat; 12-3.30, 6.30-9 Sun ~ Children welcome ~ Dogs welcome ~ Wi-fi ~ Bedrooms: £90/£110 *Recommended by John Evans, Miss A E Dare, Richard Tilbrook, Alison and Tony Livesley, Rosie and John Moore*

UCKFIELD TQ4720 Map 3

Highlands

(01825) 762989 – www.highlandsinn.co.uk

Eastbourne Road/Lewes Road; TN22 5SP

Busy, well run pub with plenty of space, real ales and well thought-of food; seats outside

Although this place is quite big, you can find cosy corners for a drink and a chat and our favourite spot is around the bar counter. There are high tartan benches, high leather chairs around equally high tables and armchairs, and Harveys Best and two quickly changing local guests on handpump, nine wines by the glass, a dozen malt whiskies and a cocktail menu. Service from friendly, helpful young staff is good. The large, spreading restaurant on the right is split into two by a dividing wall with bookcase wallpaper, and has painted rafters in high ceilings, big glass lamps and walls decorated with local photographs and animal pictures. Also, all manner of cushioned dining and painted farmhouse chairs, long chesterfield sofas, upholstered banquettes and scatter cushions on settles around wooden tables on the part carpeted, part wooden and part ceramic flooring; background music. There's also an end bar with more long chesterfields, a pool area, TV, games machine and an open fire. A big two-level terrace has been built at the front of the pub: the sunny top half is used for dining while the lower shaded, decked area has sofas and more tables and chairs. Sister pub is the Cock at Ringmer.

Popular food includes sandwiches, tiger prawns with garlic butter and sweet chilli, honey, garlic and rosemary baked camembert with chutney, sweet potato, spinach, cauliflower and chickpea curry, pork and herb sausages with mash and onion gravy, a pie of the day, chicken breast topped with bacon, smoked cheddar, barbecue cream sauce and fries, salmon fillet topped with pesto with sautéed potatoes and ratatouille, 10oz rib-eye steak with a choice of sauce and chips, and puddings such as treacle and ginger tart with custard and chocolate brownie with chocolate sauce. *Benchmark main dish: beef, chicken or halloumi burger with toppings, coleslaw and fries £11.50. Two-course evening meal £20.00.*

Ridley Inns ~ Managers Ian, Val, Nick and Matt Ridley ~ Real ale ~ Open 11-11; 11am-midnight Fri, Sat; 11-10.30 Sun ~ Bar food 12-2.30, 6-9.30; 12-9.30 Sat; 12-7.30 Sun ~ Restaurant ~ Children welcome ~ Dogs allowed in bar ~ Wi-fi *Recommended by Andrea and Philip Crispin, Charlie Stevens, Peter Brix, John and Delia Franks, Gus Swan*

WARNINGLID TQ2425 Map 3

Half Moon

(01444) 461227 – www.thehalfmoonwarninglid.co.uk

B2115 off A23 S of Handcross or off B2110 Handcross–Lower Beeding; RH17 5TR

Simply furnished pub with real ales, rewarding food, lots of wines by the glass and seats in sizeable garden; bedrooms

This is a family-owned 18th-c pub with a good mix of both drinkers and diners. The lively locals' bar has a proper pubby atmosphere, straightforward wooden furniture on bare boards and a small Victorian fireplace; a room just off here has oak beams and flagstones. A couple of steps lead down to the dining areas, which have a mix of wooden chairs, cushioned wall settles and nice old tables on floorboards, plank panelling and bare brick, and old village photographs; there's also another open fire and a glass-covered well. Hammerpot Summer and Harveys Best and Wild Hop on handpump, around 18 wines by the glass, several malt whiskies and a farm cider. The sizeable sheltered garden has picnic-sets on a lawn and a spectacular avenue of trees with uplighters that glow at night-time. Bedrooms are contemporary and comfortable and breakfasts highly rated.

Up-to-date food choices include goats cheese pannacotta with fig jelly and honey and walnut dressing, home-made black pudding scotch egg with celeriac rémoulade, tomato, lemon and pea risotto with halloumi and chermoula dressing, moroccan-style lamb burger with mint yoghurt, chilli and skinny fries, duck breast with marmite-glazed liver and celeriac rösti, roast haunch, braised shoulder and faggot of venison with parsnip purée, braised red cabbage and port and redcurrant jus, and puddings such as crème brûlée with a changing salsa and Grand Marnier marquis. *Benchmark main dish: sumac-crusted lamb with spicy kofta, falafel, samosa and romesco sauce £18.50. Two-course evening meal £22.00.*

Free house ~ Licensee James Amico ~ Real ale ~ Open 11.30-3, 5.30-11; 12-9 Sun ~ Bar food 12-2, 6-9.30; 12-3 Sun ~ Restaurant ~ Children welcome ~ Dogs allowed in bar ~ Wi-fi ~ Bedrooms: /£95 *Recommended by Belinda Stamp, Margo and Derek Peters, Serena and Adam Furber, Alexandra and Richard Clay*

There are report forms at the back of the book.

WEST HOATHLY TQ3632 Map 3

Cat

(01342) 810369 – www.catinn.co.uk

Village signposted from A22 and B2028 S of East Grinstead; North Lane; RH19 4PP

16th-c inn with old-fashioned bar, airy dining rooms, local real ales, tempting food and seats outside; lovely bedrooms

Our readers enjoy staying in the comfortable and well equipped bedrooms here and breakfasts are particularly good; there's plenty to see and do nearby. With a genuine welcome from the hands-on licensees, the lovely old bar has beams, pubby tables and chairs on an old wooden floor, and a fine log fire in an inglenook fireplace. Harveys Best and Old Ale and guests such as Firebird Parody Session IPA, Larkins Traditional and Long Man Copper Hop on handpump, as well as two local farm ciders, local apple juice, over 20 wines by the glass or carafe (plus six locally made sparkling wines) from a carefully chosen list, and a growing list of non-alcoholic choices. Look out for the glass cover over the 75-ft deep well. The light, airy dining rooms have a nice mix of wooden dining chairs and tables on pale wood-strip flooring, and throughout there are hops, china platters, brass and copper ornaments and a gently upmarket atmosphere. The contemporary-style garden room has glass doors that open on to a terrace with teak furniture. The cocker spaniel is called Harvey. Steam train enthusiasts can visit the Bluebell Railway, and the Priest House in the village is a fascinating museum in a cottage endowed with an extraordinary array of ancient anti-witch symbols. Parking is limited but there is a public car park 300 metres away.

Imaginative food using local, seasonal produce includes lunchtime sandwiches, chicken and ham hock terrine with piccalilli and tarragon emulsion, toulouse sausage scotch egg with dijon mustard mayonnaise, burger with toppings, onion jam and french fries, chicken with black pudding, hash browns and cauliflower, sea bream fillet with parmesan and sage gnocchi, mushrooms, butternut squash velouté and sage oil, haunch of venison with mushrooms, creamed spinach and red wine sauce, confit duck leg with pancetta and puy lentils and caramelised baby onions, and puddings such as caramelised lemon curd tart and salt-baked pineapple with lime curd, meringue and coconut sorbet. *Benchmark main dish: steak and mushroom in ale pie £14.75. Two-course evening meal £22.00.*

Free house ~ Licensee Andrew Russell ~ Real ale ~ Open 12-11; 12-10 Sun ~ Bar food 12-2, 6-9; 12-2.30, 6-9.30 Fri, Sat; 12-2.30, 6-8.30 Sun ~ Children over 7 welcome ~ Dogs allowed in bar and bedrooms ~ Wi-fi ~ Bedrooms: £95/£125 *Recommended by Peter Meister, Tony Scott, Robin Waters, Robert and Diana Ringstone, Sylvia and Phillip Spencer, Nicholas and Maddy Trainer*

WITHYHAM TQ4935 Map 3

Dorset Arms

(01892) 770278 – www.dorset-arms.co.uk

B2110; TN7 4BD

Friendly, bustling inn with beamed rooms, real ales and good wines, interesting food and seats in garden; bedrooms

This is part of the Buckhurst Estate (much produce used in the cooking is grown on the Estate) and the pub is named after the Earls and Dukes of Dorset. To the left of the front door is a friendly and informal beamed bar with fender seats around an open fire, scatter cushions on a built-in wall seat, a couple of armchairs, a few simple seats and tables, and darts. Harveys Best and a couple of guests such as Long Man Copper Hop and Shepherd Neame Spitfire on handpump, good wines by the glass and a growing collection of gins, served by friendly, courteous staff. The dining room has a cottagey feel with pretty curtains, bookshelves to either side of a small fireplace, horse pictures and paintings, rosettes and pieces of china, a long red leather wall seat and wheelback and farmhouse chairs around dark wooden tables. A small room leads off with high-backed red leather chairs round more dark tables, a big ornate gilt-edged mirror, antlers and a chandelier; a lower room with contemporary seats and tables has a retractable roof. Outside, there are seats on the front terrace and picnic-sets on grass, and steep steps lead up to a lawned garden with more picnic-sets. The six bedrooms are attractively decorated and comfortable.

Rewarding food includes sandwiches, crab cakes with horseradish cream, pork, chicken and green peppercorn terrine, pea, mint and asparagus risotto, venison burger with blue cheese and frites, calves liver with bacon, wholegrain mustard mash and balsamic jus, crab linguine with wild garlic, chilli, spring onions and lime, grilled flat-iron chicken with rocket salad and frites, duck breast with fondant potatoes and cassis jus, and puddings such as apple and rhubarb crumble and chocolate and hazelnut brownie with hot fudge sauce. *Benchmark main dish: lemon sole with samphire, brown shrimp butter and fries £18.00. Two-course evening meal £22.00.*

Free house ~ Licensee Simon Brazier ~ Real ale ~ Open 12-11 (10.30 Sun) ~ Bar food 12-2.30, 6-9; 12-9 Sat; 12-8 Sun ~ Restaurant ~ Children welcome ~ Dogs allowed in bar and bedrooms ~ Wi-fi ~ Bedrooms: /£115 *Recommended by R and S Bentley, Hunter and Christine Wright, Tim and Sue Mulligan, Victoria and Len Meadows*

Also Worth a Visit in Sussex

Besides the fully inspected pubs, you might like to try these pubs that have been recommended to us and described by readers. Do tell us what you think of them: feedback@goodguides.com

ALBOURNE TQ2514

Ginger Fox (01273) 857888
Take B2117 W from A23; pub at junction with A281; BN6 9EA Thatched country dining pub with simple rustic interior; highly regarded modern cooking, not cheap but they also do a good value two-course weekday lunch and popular Sun roasts (booking recommended), small bar area serving local ales such as Harveys and plenty of wines by the glass from good list, friendly professional service; children welcome, attractive garden with downs views, play area, open all day. *(Chris and Sophie Baxter)*

ALCISTON TQ5005

Rose Cottage (01323) 870377
Village signposted off A27 Polegate–Lewes; BN26 6UW Part tile-hung pub (originally two cottages) now freshened up; simple furnishings in bar and snug, beams, log fires and some old local pictures, good popular home-made food from pub favourites up, Burning Sky and Harveys, real cider and several wines by the glass, friendly helpful service; children and dogs welcome, tables on front terrace and in grassy garden overlooking fields, you can walk straight to the South Downs from here, one new bedroom and two self-catering apartments, closed Sun evening, Mon and Tues. *(Darrell Barton)*

ALFOLD BARS TQ0333

Sir Roger Tichborne
(01403) 751873 *B2133 N of Loxwood; RH14 0QS* Renovated and extended beamed country pub keeping original nooks and crannies; five well kept ales including local Firebird and Youngs from brick-faced servery, popular well presented food (all day Fri-Sun) from fairly priced varied menu, some themed evenings, friendly attentive service, flagstones and inglenook log fire, pitched-roof restaurant with french windows to garden; children welcome, dogs in bar, back terrace and large sloping lawn with lovely rural views, play area, good walks, open all day. *(Tony and Wendy Hobden, Tony Scott)*

ALFRISTON TQ5203

Olde Smugglers (01323) 870241
Waterloo Square; BN26 5UE Black-beamed 14th-c village inn; wood and brick floors, panelling and various nooks and crannies, sofas by big inglenook, Harveys, Long Man and a couple of guests, proper cider and half a dozen wines by the glass, reasonably priced traditional food from sandwiches to daily specials, conservatory; background music, quiz first Thurs of month; children and dogs welcome, tables on back suntrap terrace and lawn, four bedrooms (two sharing bathroom), open all day. *(Tony Scott)*

ALFRISTON TQ5203

★**Star** (01323) 870495
High Street; BN26 5TA Handsome 13th-c timbered inn decorated with fine medieval carvings, the striking red lion on the corner (known as Old Bill) was probably the figurehead from a wrecked dutch ship; heavy dark beams in character front bar, cushioned settles, stools and captain's chairs around pubby tables on bare boards, log fire in Tudor fireplace, tankards hanging over counter serving Harveys, Long Man and ten wines by the glass, steps down to big two-level bar (one level has lovely herringbone brick floor), rustic tables, chapel chairs, open fire and woodburner, further room with book wallpaper, plush burgundy armchairs/sofas and another woodburner, good locally sourced food served by friendly young staff; live music including folk night second Tues of month, TV; comfortable contemporary bedrooms, open all day, food all day Fri-Sun. *(John and Mary Warner, Gerald and Brenda Culliford, Robin Waters, Tracey and Stephen Groves, Richard Cole)*

AMBERLEY TQ0211

Bridge (01798) 831619
Houghton Bridge, off B2139; BN18 9LR Welcoming open-plan dining pub, comfortable and relaxed, with good mix of locals and visitors, pleasant bar and two-room dining area, candles on tables, log fire, wide range of popular reasonably priced food from good sandwiches up, well kept Harveys and two guests, cheerful efficient young staff; children and dogs welcome, seats out in front, more tables in enclosed side garden, handy for the station, open all day. *(Rod and Diana Pearce, Tony Scott, Suzy Miller)*

AMBERLEY TQ0313

Sportsmans (01798) 831787
Crossgates; Rackham Road, off B2139; BN18 9NR Popular 17th-c tile-hung pub with three rooms around central bar; well kept local Greyhound ales and fairly priced home-cooked food from good sandwiches up, friendly staff, great views over Amberley Wildbrooks nature reserve from back conservatory and decked terrace; children and dogs welcome, pretty little front garden, good walks, five bedrooms (three taking in the view), open all day Sat, till 6pm Sun. *(Johnny Beerling)*

ANGMERING TQ0604

Lamb (01903) 774300
The Square; BN16 4EQ Updated 18th-c village coaching inn; popular food (not Sun evening) from varied menu including good value two-course lunch, ales such as Harveys from light wood servery, good choice of wines by the glass, helpful friendly service, painted half-panelling and wood-strip floors, inglenook log fire in bar, woodburner on raised plinth in restaurant; children and dogs welcome, terrace seating, eight modernised bedrooms, open all day. *(Gary and Marie Miller)*

ANGMERING TQ0704

Spotted Cow (01903) 783919
High Street; BN16 4AW Up to six well kept ales including Harveys, Sharps and Timothy Taylors, decent wines by the glass and good choice of popular food from traditional choices up, efficient friendly service; smallish bar to the left, long dining extension with large conservatory on right, two fires; occasional live music, regular quiz nights, free wi-fi; children and dogs (in bar) welcome, disabled access (outside gents'), hedged garden with pretty flower borders and hanging baskets, also lower garden with country views, boules and play area, nice walk to Highdown Hill Iron Age fort, open all day Fri-Sun. *(Tony and Wendy Hobden)*

ARDINGLY TQ3430

★**Gardeners Arms** (01444) 892328
B2028 2 miles N; RH17 6TJ Cosy and relaxed 17th-c pub opposite South of England showground; well liked food (all day Sun) from sandwiches and pub favourites up, Badger ales, pleasant efficient service, linked rooms with standing timbers and inglenooks, scrubbed pine furniture on flagstones and broad boards, old local photographs, mural in back part, children and dogs welcome, disabled facilities, pretty terrace and side garden, handy for Borde Hill Garden and Wakehurst (NT), open all day. *(Victoria and Len Meadows)*

ARLINGTON TQ5507

Old Oak (01323) 482072
Caneheath; off A22 or A27 NW of Polegate; BN26 6SJ 17th-c former almshouse with open-plan L-shaped bar, beams, log fires and comfortable seating, well kept Harveys and Long Man, enjoyable traditional food from sandwiches to specials, afternoon teas; background music, old Sussex coin game toad in the hole played here; children and dogs welcome, circular picnic-sets out in front and in garden with play area, walks in nearby Abbots Wood, open all day (food all day weekends). *(Tina and Steven Hobden)*

ARLINGTON TQ5407

Yew Tree (01323) 870590
Off A22 near Hailsham, or A27 W of Polegate; BN26 6RX Neatly cared-for Victorian village pub under long-serving family; generous helpings of good home-made food (booking advised), well kept Harveys and Long Man, decent wines, prompt friendly service, log fires, hop-covered beams and old local photographs, darts in thriving bare-boards bar, bigger plush dining lounge and comfortable conservatory; children welcome, big garden with play area, good local walks, open (and food) all day Sun. *(Tony Scott, John Beeken, Fr Robert Marsh)*

ARUNDEL TQ0208

Black Rabbit (01903) 882638

Mill Road, Offham; keep on and don't give up; BN18 9PB Riverside pub in lovely spot near wildfowl reserve, popular with families and can get very busy; long bar with eating areas at either end, good choice of reasonably priced food from sandwiches and sharing boards up, well kept Badger ales and decent wines by the glass, friendly service, various bits and pieces including stuffed fish, fishing rods and a rowing boat used in the *Harry Potter and the Philosopher's Stone* film, log fires; dogs welcome, covered tables and pretty hanging baskets out at front, extensive terrace across road overlooking river, good walks, open (and food) all day. *(Ian Phillips, Darren and Clare Jones)*

ARUNDEL TQ0107

Swan (01903) 882314

High Street; BN18 9AG Georgian inn's comfortably relaxed L-shaped bar, well kept Fullers/Gales beers and occasional guests, popular fairly priced food including set lunch and other deals, friendly efficient young staff, wood flooring, sporting memorabilia and old photographs, local artwork for sale, open fire, connecting restaurant; children and dogs (in bar) welcome, 14 bedrooms, no car park (pay-and-display opposite), open all day, breakfast for non-residents. *(Tony and Wendy Hobden, Tony Scott, Ann and Colin Hunt)*

BALLS CROSS SU9826

★**Stag** (01403) 820241

Village signed off A283 at N edge of Petworth; GU28 9JP Cheery unspoilt 17th-c country pub; cosy flagstoned bar with log fire in huge inglenook, a few seats and bar stools, Badger beers, Weston's Old Rosie cider and several wines by the glass, second tiny room and appealing bare-boards cottagey restaurant, fishing rods, horse tack, country knick-knacks and old photographs, enjoyable pubby food (not Mon or Sun evenings), good service; bar skittles, darts and board games in separate room, outside loos; well behaved children allowed away from main bar, dogs welcome, seats out in front and in pretty back garden, open all day weekends. *(Julian Thorpe, Heather and Richard Jones, Susan Eccleston, Tony and Wendy Hobden)*

BARCOMBE TQ4416

Anchor (01273) 400414

Barcombe Mills; BN8 5BS Late 18th-c pub with lots of tables out by winding River Ouse (boat hire); well kept ales including Harveys and good reasonably priced pubby food, two beamed bars, restaurant and small front conservatory; well behaved children and dogs welcome, self-catering chalet, open all day and can get crowded summer weekends. *(Marianne and Michael Huggins)*

BARCOMBE CROSS TQ4212

Royal Oak (01273) 400418

Off A275 N of Lewes; BN8 5BA Village pub with good mix of locals and visitors, well kept Harveys ales, reasonably priced wines and 20 malt whiskies, generously served food from bar snacks up (kitchen closes Sun evening-Weds, pizza van Mon evening), long bar with restaurant attached, beams, bare boards and open fire; skittle alley; children and dogs welcome, a few tables out in front and in small tree-shaded garden, open all day. *(John Beeken)*

BARNS GREEN TQ1227

Queens Head (01403) 730436

Chapel Road; RH13 0PS Welcoming traditional tile-hung village pub; generous helpings of popular home-made food including daily specials, five well kept ales such as Fullers and Harveys, good range of wines by the glass; acoustic music first Weds of the month, quiz nights, classic car event Aug; children and dogs welcome, tables out at front and in back garden with play area, open all day, no food Sun evening. *(Sophie and James Collier)*

BERWICK TQ5105

★**Cricketers Arms** (01323) 870469

Lower Road, S of A27; BN26 6SP Charming brick and flint local with three small unpretentious bars, huge supporting beam in each low ceiling, simple country furnishings on quarry tiles, cricketing pictures and bats, two log fires, friendly staff, four Harveys ales tapped from the cask, country wines and good coffee, well cooked uncomplicated food at reasonable prices; old Sussex coin game toad in the hole; children (in family room) and dogs welcome, delightful cottagey front garden with picnic-sets among small brick paths, more seats behind, Bloomsbury Group wall paintings in nearby church and handy for Charleston, good South Downs walks, open (and food) all day Sat, shuts 8pm Sun. *(Tony Scott, Alan Cowell)*

BILLINGSHURST TQ0830

Blue Ship (01403) 822709

The Haven; hamlet signposted off A29 just N of junction with A264, then follow signpost left towards Garlands and Okehurst; RH14 9BS Unspoilt pub in quiet country spot; beamed front bar with wall benches and scrubbed tables on brick floor, inglenook woodburner, cask-tapped Badger ales served from hatch, good home-made food from pub favourites up, two small carpeted back rooms; bar billiards, darts, shove-ha'penny, cribbage and dominoes; children and dogs welcome, tables out at front and in side garden with play area, camping, closed Sun evening, Mon. *(Adam and Betty Lawrence)*

BILLINGSHURST TQ0725

Limeburners (01403) 782311

Lordings Road, Newbridge (B2133/ A272 W); RH14 9JA Friendly characterful local in converted row of cottages, three Fullers ales and generous helpings of enjoyable reasonably priced pubby food from snacks up, part-carpeted bar with horsebrasses on dark beams and inglenook at each end, chatty atmosphere; live music and quiz nights, bar billiards, TV; children and dogs welcome, picnic-sets in pleasant front garden with play area, campsite behind. *(Tony and Wendy Hobden)*

BILLINGSHURST TQ0825

Olde Six Bells (01403) 782124

High Street (A29); RH14 9QS Picturesque partly 14th-c timbered pub; updated interior with large bar and split-level restaurant, flagstone and wood floors, inglenook log fire, four well kept Badger ales, enjoyable reasonably priced pubby food (not Sun evening) from baguettes and baked potatoes up; occasional live music, games room, free wi-fi; children and dogs welcome, roadside garden and terrace, open all day. *(Andrea and Laurie Grist)*

BINSTED SU9806

Black Horse (01243) 553325

Binsted Lane; about 2 miles W of Arundel, turn S off A27 towards Binsted; BN18 0LP Modernised 17th-c dining pub with good varied choice of food from sandwiches up, ales such as Harveys and local Listers, wood-floored bar and separate dining room; regular live music; children and dogs welcome, plenty of outside seating on terrace with covered well, lawn and in open-fronted cart lodge, valley views over golf course, closed Sun evening, Mon. *(Tony and Wendy Hobden)*

BLACKBOYS TQ5220

★**Blackboys Inn** (01825) 890283

B2192, S edge of village; TN22 5LG Old weatherboarded inn set back from the road; main bar to the right with beams, timbers, dark wooden furniture and log fire, locals' bar to left with lots of bric-a-brac, Harveys ales including seasonals, several wines by the glass and wide choice of enjoyable food (all day Sat, till 8pm Sun), panelled dining areas; background and some live music including open mike nights; children and dogs (in bar) welcome, sizeable garden with seats under trees, on terrace and under cover by duck pond, good walks (Vanguard Way passes the pub, Wealdway close by), eight bedrooms in converted stables, open all day. *(Tim and Sue Milligan)*

BODIAM TQ7825

Castle Inn (01580) 830330

Village signed from B2244; opposite Bodiam Castle; TN32 5UB Bustling country pub very handy for Bodiam Castle (NT); Shepherd Neame ales and a couple of guests, good choice of wines, popular reasonably priced food from sandwiches up, friendly helpful service, plain tables and chairs in snug bar with log fire, back restaurant; occasional live music; picnic-sets on big sheltered terrace, open all day, food all day weekends. *(Peter Pilbeam)*

BOGNOR REGIS SZ9201

Royal Oak (01243) 821002

A259 Chichester Road, North Bersted; PO21 5JF Old-fashioned two-bar beamed local (aka the Pink Pub); well kept ales such as Wadworths and Shepherd Neame, shortish choice of popular reasonably priced food till 6.30pm (2.30pm Sun), friendly service; occasional live music and quiz nights, bar billiards, darts, sports TV, free wi-fi; children and dogs welcome, open all day. *(Ruth and Peter Bacon)*

BOLNEY TQ2623

Bolney Stage (01444) 881200

London Road, off old A23 just N of A272; RH17 5RL Sizeable 16th-c black and white country dining pub (part of the Home Counties group); good varied choice of popular food, four changing ales and good selection of wines by the glass, friendly prompt service, low beams and polished flagstones, nice mix of old furniture, woodburner and big two-way log fire; children and dogs (in main bar) welcome, disabled facilities, tables on terrace and lawn, play area, handy for Sheffield Park (NT), Bluebell Railway and a useful M23/A23 stop, open (and food) all day. *(Tony Scott)*

BOLNEY TQ2622

Eight Bells (01444) 881396

The Street; RH17 5QW Popular and welcoming family-run village pub; wide choice of good sensibly priced food from bar snacks up, breakfasts (7.30-11.30am), OAP lunch (Tues, Weds) and afternoon teas, efficient friendly young staff, well kept Harveys, a couple of guests and decent range of wines, brick-floored bar with eight handbells suspended above servery, second flagstoned bar and timbered dining extension, open fires; bar billiards, pool and darts, sports TV; children and dogs welcome, disabled facilities, tables out on deck under huge canopy, outside bar and play area, various events including Easter Mon pram race, three bedrooms in separate beamed cottage, open all day (till 1am Fri, Sat), no food Sun evening. *(Tony Scott, Gavin Dunbar)*

BOSHAM SU8003

★**Anchor Bleu** (01243) 573956

High Street; PO18 8LS Waterside inn overlooking Chichester Harbour; two simple bars with low ochre ceilings, worn flagstones and exposed timbered brickwork, lots of nautical bric-a-brac, robust furniture (some tables close together), up to six real ales and popular sensibly priced bar food, efficient friendly staff (they may ask for a credit card if you run a tab), upstairs dining room; children and dogs welcome, seats on front terrace and raised back one (access through massive wheel-operated bulkhead door), lovely views over sheltered inlet, can park by water but note tide times, church up lane depicted in Bayeux Tapestry, village and shore worth exploring, open all day in summer and can get very crowded. *(Miss A E Dare)*

BOSHAM SU8105

White Swan (01243) 696465

A259 roundabout; Station Road; PO18 8NG Spic and span 18th-c dining pub with sensibly priced blackboard food including daily specials, three well kept ales such as Dark Star, Hop Back and Upham, cheerful helpful service, good-sized flagstoned bar, restaurant beyond with old bread oven, darts in snug; fortnightly quiz Weds, sports TV; children and dogs welcome in certain areas, open all day, no food Sun evening. *(Ann and Colin Hunt, Tony and Wendy Hobden)*

BREDE TQ8218

Red Lion (01424) 882188

A28 opposite church; TN31 6EJ Popular 15th-c family-run village pub; beams, inglenook log fire and plain tables and chairs on bare boards, good competitively priced home-made food (should book) including local fish and Sun carvery, takeaway fish and chips Tues evenings, well kept Harveys, Sharps, Youngs and guests, good value wines from short list, friendly efficient service, back dining area decorated with sheet music and instruments (occasional live music); children and dogs welcome, garden behind with roaming chickens (may have eggs for sale), narrow entrance to car park, open all day Fri-Sun. *(V Brogden)*

BRIGHTON TQ3104

★ Basketmakers Arms

(01273) 689006 *Gloucester Road – the E end, near Cheltenham Place; off Marlborough Place (A23) via Gloucester Street; BN1 4AD* Cheerful bustling backstreet local run by long-serving landlord; eight pumps serving Fullers beers and guests, decent wines by the glass and over 100 malt whiskies (good range of other spirits), well liked reasonably priced bar food, two small low-ceilinged rooms, lots of interesting old tins, enamel signs, photographs and posters; background music; children (till 8pm) and dogs welcome, disabled access, a few pavement tables, open (and food) all day, shuts midnight Fri, Sat. *(Bob and Melissa Wyatt)*

BRIGHTON TQ3004

Brighton Beer Dispensary

(01273) 205797 *Dean Street; BN1 3EG* Popular little terraced pub now owned by Southey, their ales and guests, craft beers and an extensive bottled range, hand-pulled ciders too, friendly knowledgeable staff, interesting bar snacks provided by local company Dizzy Gull plus Sun roasts, small back conservatory; quiz nights; open all day and can get packed. *(Richard and Tessa Ibbot)*

BRIGHTON TQ3203

Bristol Bar (01273) 605687

Paston Place; BN2 1HA Kemptown pub overlooking the sea; well kept Harveys and plenty of wines by the glass, enjoyable fairly priced bistro-style food from open kitchen, friendly staff; children (at lunchtime) and dogs welcome, wheelchair access, open all day. *(Fr Robert Marsh)*

BRIGHTON TQ3005

Chimney House (01273) 556708

Upper Hamilton Road; BN1 5DF Red-brick corner pub in residential area; bare-boards interior arranged around central bar, one or two quirky touches such as antler chandeliers, good innovative food from open kitchen using local ingredients (some foraged), three real ales including Harveys, home-made jams, chutney and bread for sale; folk night Sun; children and dogs welcome, closed Mon, otherwise open all day, no food Sun evening. *(Alexander and Trish Cutter)*

BRIGHTON TQ3104

Colonnade (01273) 328728

New Road, off North Street; by Theatre Royal; BN1 1UF Small richly restored theatre bar with ornate frontage – note Willie the 19th-c automaton in small bay window; shining brass and mahogany, plush banquettes, velvet swags and gleaming mirrors, interesting pre-war playbills and signed theatrical photographs, three well kept ales including Fullers London Pride, good range of wines and interesting gins; downstairs loos; pavement seats overlooking Pavilion gardens, open all day. *(Alexander and Trish Cutter)*

BRIGHTON TQ3004

Craft Beer Company

(01273) 723736 *Upper North Street; BN1 3FG* Busy corner pub with fine selection of interesting draught and bottled beers, friendly knowledgeable staff, pubby snacks and tapas, simple L-shaped bar with raised back section; closed weekday lunchtimes, open all day weekends. *(Tony Scott)*

You can send reports directly to us at feedback@goodguides.com.

BRIGHTON TQ3004

Evening Star (01273) 328931

Surrey Street; BN1 3PB Chatty drinkers' pub near the Lanes attracting good mix of customers; simple pale wood furniture on bare boards, up to four well kept Dark Star ales (originally brewed here) and lots of changing guests, continental beers (in bottles too) and traditional ciders/perries, bar snacks, friendly staff coping well at busy times; background and some live music, free wi-fi; pavement tables, open all day. *(Peter Pilbeam)*

BRIGHTON TQ3203

Ginger Dog (01273) 620990

College Place, Kemptown; BN2 1HN Restauranty Kemptown pub in same small group as the Ginger Pig (Hove) and Ginger Fox (Albourne); well regarded modern food from changing menu (not especially cheap), good wines, cocktails and local beers, well informed friendly service, fairly traditional bare-boards interior; children and dogs (in bar) welcome, open all day. *(Peter Pilbeam)*

BRIGHTON TQ2804

★ **Ginger Pig** (01273) 736123

Hove Street; BN3 2TR Bustling place just a short walk from the beach; informal bare-boards bar area with plush stools and simple wooden dining chairs around mixed tables, armchairs and sofas here and there, Harveys Best and a guest, nice wines by the glass and interesting local spirits and soft drinks, raised restaurant part with long button-back wall seating and more wooden tables and chairs, enterprising modern food (highish prices) served by friendly attentive staff; background music; children welcome, 11 stylish ensuite bedrooms, open all day. *(Katherine Matthews)*

BRIGHTON TQ3103

Hand in Hand (01273) 699595

Upper St James Street, Kemptown; BN2 1JN It may be Brighton's smallest pub, but the canary yellow exterior makes it hard to miss; own-brewed ales along with well kept local guests, plenty of bottled beers and a real cider, dimly lit bar with a few tables and benches, tie collection and lots of newspaper cuttings on the walls, photographs including Victorian nudes on the ceiling, some snacky food, cheerful service and colourful mix of customers; interesting background music (live jazz Sun), veteran fruit machine; dogs welcome, open all day and can get crowded. *(Peter Pilbeam)*

BRIGHTON TQ3004

Lion & Lobster (01273) 327299

Sillwood Street; BN1 2PS Red-painted backstreet pub spread over three floors (three bars and restaurant); softly lit interior with lots of pictures, well kept ales such as Dark Star and Harveys, extensive choice of well presented enterprising food (booking advised) including daily specials and a late-night menu, friendly efficient young staff; regular jazz evenings, Mon quiz, sports TV; large terrace on two levels (can get very busy in summer), open (and food) all day, till 2am Fri and Sat. *(Tony Scott, John Beeken)*

BRIGHTON TQ3309

Stanmer House (01273) 680400

Stanmer Park; BN1 9QA Whiting & Hammond pub-restaurant in 18th-c parkland mansion; three impressive front rooms with button-back leather chesterfields on bare boards or marble, ornate fireplaces, gilt-edged mirrors and chandeliers, stone lions/metal sculptures in wall recesses, old local photographs and shelves of books, well kept Park Life (brewed for them by Turners), guest ales and 16 wines by the glass, enjoyable interesting food, popular afternoon teas, dining rooms (to left) with Victorian and Edwardian-style chairs around heavy dark tables, big portraits, church candles and opulent flower arrangements; children and dogs (in some parts) welcome, rustic furniture on terrace and around garden's pond, contemporary seats on front flagstones, open (and some food) all day from 10am. *(Guy Vowles, R and M Thomas)*

BROWNBREAD STREET TQ6714

Ash Tree (01424) 892104

Off A271 (was B2204) W of Battle; first northward road W of Ashburnham Place, then first fork left, then bear right into Brownbread Street; TN33 9NX Tranquil 17th-c country local tucked away in isolated hamlet; enjoyable affordably priced home-made food including specials, good choice of wines and well kept ales such as Harveys Best, cheerful service, cosy beamed bars with nice old settles and chairs, stripped brickwork, interesting dining areas with timbered dividers, good inglenook log fire; children (in eating area) and dogs welcome, pretty garden, closed Sun and Mon evenings, otherwise open all day. *(J H Bell)*

BURWASH TQ6724

Rose & Crown (01435) 882600

Inn sign on A265; TN19 7ER Welcoming old tile-hung local tucked down lane (parking can be tricky) in pretty village; well kept Harveys, decent wines and enjoyable food (not Sun or Mon evenings), friendly staff, very low ceilings with banknotes on beams near servery, pubby furniture on patterned carpet, inglenook log fire, restaurant to the left with another inglenook, glass-covered well just inside front door; occasional live music; children and dogs welcome, small side garden and pleasant back terrace, four bedrooms, handy for Batemans (NT), open all day. *(Rupert and Sandy Newton)*

BURY TQ0013

Squire & Horse (01798) 831343
Bury Common; A29 Fontwell–Pulborough; RH20 1NS 16th-c roadside dining pub with very good attractively presented food from australian chef, well kept Harveys, a guest ale and good choice of wines, several partly divided beamed areas, plush wall seats, hunting prints and ornaments, log fire; children welcome, no dogs inside, pleasant garden and pretty terrace (some road noise), open (and food) all day Sun. *(Robert Mitchell)*

BYWORTH SU9821

★**Black Horse** (01798) 342424
Off A283; GU28 0HL Popular chatty country pub with smart simply furnished bar, pews and scrubbed tables on bare boards, pictures and old photographs, open fires, four real ales such as Flowerpots and Fullers, Cornish Orchards cider, enjoyable food (not Sun evening) from light lunchtime dishes up, children's menu, back restaurant with nooks and crannies and old range, spiral staircase to heavily beamed function/dining room, games area (pool and darts); occasional live music and other events; dogs allowed in bar, attractive garden with tables on steep grassy terraces, lovely downs views, converted stable-block bedroom, open all day. *(Robin and Anna Triggs)*

CATSFIELD TQ7213

White Hart (01424) 892650
B2204, off A269; The Green; TN33 9DJ Friendly weatherboarded and beamed village pub, well kept Harveys and good range of malt whiskies, enjoyable reasonably priced traditional food including Mon curry night, warm log fire, raftered dining room with pubby furniture and woodburner; quiz first Tues of month, some live music; children, walkers and dogs welcome, fenced garden, two bedrooms, open all day. *(Gene and Kitty Rankin)*

CHAILEY TQ3919

Five Bells (01825) 722259
A275, 9 miles N of Lewes; BN8 4DA Attractive old roadside pub with good food (not Sun evening, Mon) cooked by landlord-chef from bar snacks and pub favourites up, four well kept ales including Harveys and decent choice of wines, friendly staff, different rooms and alcoves leading from low-beamed central bar, inglenook log fire, older-style furniture on bare boards or quarry tiles; board games; children and dogs welcome, pretty garden front and side, open all day (till 7pm Sun and Mon). *(Peter Meister)*

CHICHESTER SU8605

Chichester Inn (01243) 783185
West Street; PO19 1RP Georgian pub (quieter than the city-centre ones) with half a dozen local ales such as Dark Star, Harveys and Langham, good value pubby food from snacks up, smallish front lounge with plain wooden tables and chairs, sofas by open fire, larger back public bar; live music and other events such as comedy nights and beer festivals, sports TV, pool; courtyard garden with smokers' shelter, four bedrooms, open all day. *(Colin and Daniel Gibbs)*

CHICHESTER SU8504

Crate & Apple (01243) 539336
Westgate; PO19 3EU Refurbished dining pub under new management; enjoyable food from shortish but varied menu including some pub favourites, local ales such as Harveys and Long Man, good range of wines by the glass, cocktails, friendly helpful service, modern décor with simple tables and chairs on wood or stone floors, painted dados, leather sofas by woodburner; quiz nights; children welcome, sunny front terrace with umbrellas, more seats behind, closed Sun evening, otherwise open all day. *(Rosie and John Moore)*

CHICHESTER SU8604

Eastgate (01243) 774877
The Hornet (A286); PO19 7JG Welcoming town pub with light airy interior extending back; five ales including Fullers/Gales, well cooked affordably priced traditional food (not Sat or Sun evenings), cheerful prompt service, woodburner; background and weekend live music, darts, pool and cribbage; children and dogs welcome, small heated back terrace, open all day. *(Phil and Jane Villiers)*

CHICHESTER SU8605

Park Tavern (01243) 785057
Priory Road; PO19 1NS Friendly popular pub in pleasant spot opposite Priory Park; good choice of Fullers/Gales beers and enjoyable reasonably priced pubby food (all day Sat, not Sun or Mon evenings), smallish front bar, extensive back eating area; live music and quiz nights; children and dogs welcome, open all day. *(Tony and Wendy Hobden, Phil and Jane Villiers)*

CHIDDINGLY TQ5414

★**Six Bells** (01825) 872227
Village signed off A22 Uckfield–Hailsham; BN8 6HE Lively unpretentious village local run well by hard-working hands-on landlord; small linked bars with interesting bric-a-brac, local pictures and posters, old furniture, cushioned window seats and log fires, family extension giving much-needed extra space, well kept Courage, Harveys and a guest, decent wines by the glass and a proper cider, enjoyable low-priced food; regular live music including blues/folk night every other Tues, free wi-fi; dogs welcome in bar, seats out at back by big raised goldfish pond, boules, monthly vintage and kit-car meetings,

church opposite with interesting Jefferay Monument, open all day. *(Gene and Kitty Rankin)*

CHIDHAM SU7804

★ **Old House at Home**

(01243) 572477 *Off A259 at Barleycorn pub in Nutbourne; Cot Lane; PO18 8SU* Neat 18th-c red-brick pub in remote unspoilt farm hamlet; good choice of popular food from open sandwiches to fish specials, lunchtime set menu, several wines by the glass and at least four real ales including a Langham house beer, friendly service, low beams and timbering, log fire; children allowed in eating areas, tables on front terrace and in attractive back garden, Chichester Harbour walks nearby, open all day. *(J A Snell, Tony and Jill Radnor)*

CHILGROVE SU8116

Royal Oak (01243) 535257

Off B2141 Petersfield–Chichester, signed Hooksway; PO18 9JZ Unchanging country pub close to South Downs Way; two simple cosy bars with huge log fires, country kitchen furniture and cottagey knick-knacks, Bowman, Exmoor, Fullers and a guest, good honest food, homely dining room with woodburner, plainer family room; background and occasional live music, cribbage, dominoes and shut the box, free wi-fi; children and dogs (in bar) welcome, picnic-sets under parasols in pretty garden, closed Sun evening, Mon. *(Tony and Jill Radnor)*

CLAPHAM TQ1105

Coach & Horses (01903) 694721

Arundel Road (A27 Worthing–Arundel); BN13 3UA Friendly 18th-c former coaching inn beside dual carriageway; well liked food from sandwiches to blackboard specials including Mon deal, four changing ales, local gins and vodka, rugs on wood floor, open fire in brick fireplace, flagstoned dining area to left of bar; background music, quiz second and last Weds of month, TV; children and dogs welcome, some tables out at front under parasols, open all day, food all day Sat, till 7pm Sun; hotel part being built at the back as we went to press. *(Tony and Wendy Hobden)*

COCKING CAUSEWAY SU8819

Greyhound (01730) 814425

A286 Cocking–Midhurst; GU29 9QH Pretty 18th-c tile-hung pub set back from the road; four well kept changing ales and enjoyable good value home-made food (all day weekends – should book), friendly helpful staff, open-plan but cosy beamed and panelled bar with alcoves, log fire, pine furniture in big back dining conservatory; monthly quiz; children and dogs welcome, grassed area at front with picnic-sets and huge eucalyptus, sizeable garden and play area behind, open all day. *(John Beeken, Tony and Wendy Hobden)*

COLEMANS HATCH TQ4533

★ **Hatch** (01342) 822363

Signed off B2026, or off B2110 opposite church; TN7 4EJ Quaint and appealing little weatherboarded Ashdown Forest pub dating from 1430; big log fire in quickly filling beamed bar, small back dining room with another fire, popular freshly made food (not Sun evening) from varied menu, well kept Harveys, Larkins and one or two guests, friendly staff and good mix of customers including families and dogs; picnic-sets on front terrace and in beautifully kept big garden, not much parking so get there early. *(Tony Scott)*

COOLHAM TQ1423

★ **George & Dragon** (01403) 741320

Dragons Green, Dragons Lane; pub signed off A272; RH13 8GE Tile-hung cottage surrounded by fine countryside; cosy bar with massive unusually low beams (date cut into one is either 1577 or 1677), heavily timbered walls, traditional furniture and log fire in big inglenook, Dark Star Hophead, Harveys Best, Skinners Betty Stogs and a guest, decent wines by the glass and enjoyable food (not evenings Sun, Mon or Tues), dining room with pale farmhouse chairs around rustic tables on wood floor, quiz nights; children and dogs (in bar) welcome, pretty garden with seating area, two attractive double bedrooms in converted outbuilding, open all day Fri-Sun. *(Tony and Wendy Hobden)*

COUSLEY WOOD TQ6533

Old Vine (01892) 782271

B2100 Wadhurst–Lamberhurst; TN5 6ER New owners for this 16th-c weatherboarded pub; linked rooms with heavy beams and open timbering, inglenook log fire, ales such as Harveys and Timothy Taylors, several wines by the glass, enjoyable food including some latin american influences; children and dogs welcome, picnic-sets on front terrace, closed Mon, otherwise open (and food) all day. *(John and Delia Franks)*

COWFOLD TQ2122

Hare & Hounds (01403) 865354

Henfield Road (A281 S); RH13 8DR Small friendly village pub with popular good value pubby food and a couple of well kept ales including Harveys, beamed and flagstoned bar with log fire, little room off to the right, dining room to the left; children and dogs welcome, a couple of picnic-sets out in front, more seating on back terrace, open all day Fri-Sun, no food Sun evening. *(Tony and Wendy Hobden)*

CRAWLEY TQ2636

Brewery Shades (01293) 514105

High Street; RH10 1BA Popular old tile-hung pub in town centre; ten well kept beers including Greene King, several ciders and enjoyable all-day pubby food from sandwiches up, friendly helpful staff; sports TVs; seats outside in pedestrianised area, open till 1.30am Fri, Sat. *(Tony Scott)*

CUCKFIELD TQ3025

Rose & Crown (01444) 414217
London Road; RH17 5BS Former 17th-c coaching inn run by father and son team; good if pricey food from regularly changing menus (not Sun evening), well kept Harveys and a guest, local Hepworth lagers and good choice of wines; children and dogs welcome, tables out in front and in nice garden behind, open all day (Sun till 9pm). *(Sylvia and Phillip Spencer)*

DALLINGTON TQ6619

Swan (01424) 838242
Woods Corner, B2096 E; TN21 9LB Old tile-hung roadside local with cheerful chatty atmosphere; well kept Harveys and a guest, decent wines by the glass and good blackboard food including deals, efficient friendly service, bare-boards bar divided by standing timbers, old enamel signs (on walls and floor), mixed furniture including cushioned settle and high-backed pew, candles in bottles, swan ornaments, big woodburner, simple back restaurant with far-reaching views to the coast; occasional background music, board games; children and dogs welcome, steps down to loos and garden, may close early if quiet. *(Victoria and James Sargeant)*

DELL QUAY SU8302

Crown & Anchor (01243) 781712
Off A286 S of Chichester – look out for small sign; PO20 7EE 19th/20th-c beamed pub in splendid spot overlooking Chichester Harbour – best at high tide and quiet times (can get packed on sunny days and parking difficult); comfortable bow-windowed lounge and panelled public bar, two log fires, well kept Youngs and a couple of guests, lots of wines by the glass including champagne, enjoyable freshly made food from pub favourites to specials, friendly staff; children and dogs welcome, views from large waterside terrace with 'crab and burger shack', nice walks, open all day, food all day weekends. *(J A Snell, Suzy Miller)*

DITCHLING TQ3215

Bull (01273) 843147
High Street (B2112); BN6 8TA Sympathetically restored and extended 500-year-old inn; heavily beamed main bar with inglenook log fire, benches, settles and leather dining chairs around scrubbed wooden tables on bare boards, modern artwork and historic photos of the village, Bedlam, Timothy Taylors and a guest, 24 wines by the glass and good range of spirits, lots of teas and coffees, other rooms including contemporary dining room with pale grey chairs and cushioned wall seats against half-planked walls, big folding glass doors to terrace, generally well liked modern food, prices on the high side (for drinks too); quiz second Sun of month, free wi-fi; children and dogs (in bar) welcome, L-shaped garden with vegetable patch, pizza bar and play area, stylish well equipped bedrooms, open all day, food all day weekends. *(Tony Scott, Tracey and Stephen Groves)*

DONNINGTON SU8501

Blacksmiths (01243) 785578
B2201 S of Chichester; PO20 7PR Neatly kept little roadside pub; bar with pale wooden wall seats, plush-topped stools and metal-legged tables on wide floorboards, open fire, high wicker chairs against counter serving a couple of changing ales from Arundel or Langham, ten wines by the glass, popular food from sandwiches up, two dining rooms, one with another fire; maybe live music Sun evening in summer, free wi-fi; children and dogs (in bar) welcome, teak tables under parasols on terrace enclosed by glass panels, fire pit and country views, attractive comfortable bedrooms, open all day (till 6pm Sun). *(Alan and Alice Morgan)*

EAST ASHLING SU8207

Horse & Groom (01243) 575339
B2178; PO18 9AX Busy unpretentious country pub run by long-serving landlord; five well kept ales including Dark Star, Hop Back and Youngs, decent choice of wines by the glass and reasonably priced tasty food from open sandwiches and baguettes up, unchanging front drinkers' bar with old pale flagstones and inglenook range, scrubbed trestle tables in carpeted area, airy extension with solid country kitchen furniture; children and dogs allowed in some parts, garden picnic-sets under umbrellas, 11 neat bedrooms (some in barn conversion), open all day (closes 6pm Sun evening). *(Pieter and Janet Vrancken, Ann and Colin Hunt)*

EAST CHILTINGTON TQ3715

Jolly Sportsman (01273) 890400
2 miles N of B2116; Chapel Lane – follow sign to 13th-c church; BN7 3BA Civilised place with impressive modern cooking from landlord-chef including set lunch Tues-Sat and Fri fish night; small character log-fire bar for drinkers, local ales including Harveys, excellent range of malt whiskies, cognacs and Armagnacs and very good wine list, smart but cosy restaurant with contemporary light wood furniture and modern landscapes, garden room; free wi-fi; children and dogs (in bar) welcome, rustic tables under trees in front garden, more seats on big back lawn with views towards the South Downs, closed Sun evening, Mon. *(Tracey and Stephen Groves)*

EAST DEAN SU9012

Star & Garter (01243) 811318
Village signed with Charlton off A286 in Singleton; also signed off A285;

PO18 0JG Brick and flint dining pub in peaceful village setting; pleasant bar and restaurant with exposed brickwork, panelling and oak floors, furnishings from sturdy stripped tables and country kitchen chairs through chunky modern to antique carved settles, Arundel ales tapped from the cask and several wines by the glass, good food including local fish/seafood, friendly service; background music, free wi-fi; children and dogs (in bar) welcome, teak furniture on heated terrace, smokers' shelter, steps down to walled lawn with picnic-sets, near South Downs Way, bedrooms, open (and food) all day weekends. *(Katherine Matthews)*

EAST DEAN TV5597

★**Tiger** (01323) 423209

Off A259 Eastbourne–Seaford; BN20 0DA Attractive pub overlooking delightful cottage-lined sloping green; small beamed bar with window seat, long cushioned wall bench and other rustic tables and chairs, walls hung with fish prints and a stuffed tiger's head, open woodburner, own-brew Beachy Head and guests, proper cider, nine wines by the glass and local gin, step down to another little room with fine high-backed curved settle, separate dining room serving fairly traditional food; children and dogs (in bar) welcome, seats on flower-filled terrace (can also sit on the green), comfortable bedrooms, walks to the coast and along Seven Sisters clifftops, open all day. *(Trevor and Michele Street, Maggie and Matthew Lyons)*

EAST HOATHLY TQ5216

Kings Head (01825) 840238

High Street/Mill Lane; BN8 6DR Creeper-clad 17th-c pub on crossroads (was the village school), own 1648 ales (brewed next door) plus Harveys Best, long open-plan room with wood floor, brick walls and log fire, pubby furniture including upholstered settles, enjoyable reasonably priced traditional food, function room; occasional quiz nights, TV, free wi-fi; children and dogs welcome, steps up to walled back garden, open all day. *(Chris and Sophie Baxter)*

EASTBOURNE TV6098

Bibendum (01323) 735363

Grange Road/South Street opposite Town Hall; BN21 4EU Roomy 19th-c corner pub with wine bar feel; well kept ales such as Harveys and Long Man, several wines by the glass and interesting selection of gins, enjoyable varied choice of food from snacks up, friendly helpful staff, restaurant; quiz first Sun and third Tues of month; seats out in front under awning, open (and food) all day. *(Darrell Barton)*

EASTBOURNE TV6098

Dolphin (01323) 746622

South Street; BN21 4XF Traditional pub with bare boards, panelling and some stained glass, open fire in brick fireplace, Brakspears and guests such as Dark Star, Harveys and Long Man from horseshoe servery, enjoyable good value food including range of burgers, steak night Thurs, good friendly service, back parquet-floored dining room; Weds quiz, live jazz/blues Sun; children and dogs welcome, terrace tables, open all day (till midnight Fri, Sat), food all day weekends. *(Tony and Wendy Hobden)*

EASTBOURNE TV5999

Lamb (01323) 720545

High Street; BN21 1HH Ancient inn arranged around central servery, lounge bar with sturdy beams and substantial stone fireplace, latticed bow windows and antique furnishings, steps down to half-panelled bare-boards dining area with mix of old tables and chairs and another big fireplace, well kept Harveys ales, good choice of wines and enjoyable home-made food at fair prices, friendly efficient service, internal glass-covered well and historic cellars; upstairs folk club first and third Weds of month, also quiz and comedy nights, TV and darts in public bar; children and dogs welcome, by 12th-c church away from seafront, five bedrooms, open all day. *(Tony Scott, Darrell Barton)*

EASTBOURNE TV6199

Marine (01323) 720464

Seaside Road (A259); BN22 7NE Comfortable spacious pub under welcoming long-serving licensees, near the seafront and well known for its extravagant Christmas decorations; panelled bar, lounge with sofas and tub chairs, log fire, three well kept ales, good choice of wines and around 45 whiskies/brandies, generous helpings of good freshly made food including up to a dozen daily specials, back conservatory; children welcome, terrace and covered smokers' area, open (and food) all day Sun. *(Fr Robert Marsh, Alan Johnson)*

EASTBOURNE TV6097

Pilot (01323) 723440

Holywell Road, Meads; just off front below approach from Beachy Head; BN20 7RW Busy corner inn with good fairly priced home-cooked food from lunchtime sandwiches up, well kept ales such as Harveys and Sharps, good selection of wines by the glass, friendly staff; free wi-fi; children welcome, dogs in bar, seats out at front and in nice split-level beer garden behind, walks up to Beachy Head, bedrooms, open all day, no food Sun evening. *(Darrell Barton)*

EASTERGATE SU9405

Wilkes Head (01243) 543380

Just off A29 Fontwell–Bognor; Church Lane; PO20 3UT Small friendly red-brick local with two traditional bars and back dining extension; beams, flagstones and inglenook log fire, enjoyable reasonably priced blackboard food from sandwiches up, Adnams

Southwold, several guest ales and proper cider; occasional live music, beer festivals, darts; children welcome, tables in big garden with play area, open all day. *(Tony and Wendy Hobden)*

ELSTED SU8320

Elsted Inn (01730) 813662
Elsted Marsh; GU29 0JT Attractive and welcoming Victorian country pub; good interesting food from shortish regularly changing menu using local produce, three or four well kept ales and plenty of wines by the glass, friendly accommodating service, two log fires, nice country furniture on bare boards, old Goodwood racing photos (horses and cars), dining area at back; folk night first Sun of the month, classic car meeting second Weds; children and dogs (in bar) welcome, downs-view garden with large part-covered terrace, four comfortable bedrooms, open all day, restaurant closed Sun evening and Mon, but some snacky food available. *(Gary and Marie Miller)*

ELSTED SU8119

★**Three Horseshoes** (01730) 825746
Village signed from B2141 Chichester–Petersfield; from A272 about 2 miles W of Midhurst, turn left heading W; GU29 0JY Good mix of customers and a congenial bustle at this pretty white-painted old pub; beamed rooms, log fires and candlelight, ancient flooring, antique furnishings and interesting prints/photographs, up to five real ales tapped from the cask such as Bowman, Flowerpots, Langham and Youngs, summer cider, highly rated food from extensive blackboard menu, good friendly service; children allowed, dogs in bar, two delightful connecting gardens with plenty of seats, lovely roses and fine South Downs views, maybe wandering chickens, good surrounding walks. *(Miss A E Dare, John Beeken, S G N Bennett, Tony and Jill Radnor, Christopher and Elise Way, John Evans)*

ERIDGE STATION TQ5434

★**Huntsman** (01892) 864258
Signed off A26 S of Eridge Green; TN3 9LE 19th-c brick and tile country local; two cosy opened-up rooms with painted half-panelling and lots of old photographs and prints, mix of furniture on bare boards including scrubbed pine, sofa in front of log fire, three well kept Badger ales and several wines by the glass, good home-made food (not Sun evening) from baguettes up, friendly helpful service, downstairs function/overflow room; children and dogs welcome, tables on fenced front terrace, picnic-sets in garden set down behind, next to Eridge station with lots of cars parked on the road (pub has its own parking), closed Mon, otherwise open all day. *(Victoria and Len Meadows)*

FALMER TQ3508

Swan (01273) 681842
Middle Street (just off A27 bypass); BN1 9PD Long thin building with seating areas either side of small central bar, Palmers and local guests, straightforward sensibly priced lunchtime food (evenings Thurs and Fri), barn function room; some live music, sports TV, free wi-fi; dogs welcome, seats on little terrace, near Sussex University (student discounts), closed Mon evening, otherwise open all day, busy on Albion match days. *(Tina and Steven Hobden)*

FERNHURST SU9028

Red Lion (01428) 643112
The Green, off A286 via Church Lane; GU27 3HY Friendly 16th-c wisteria-clad pub tucked quietly away on edge of green and cricket pitch; heavy beams and timbers, attractive furnishings, inglenook woodburner, good food (not Sun evening) from sandwiches and snacks up, well kept Fullers/Gales beers and a guest, decent wines, restaurant; children and dogs welcome, seats out in front and in back garden with well, walks from the door, open all day. *(Marianne and Michael Huggins)*

FERRING TQ0903

Henty Arms (01903) 241254
Ferring Lane; BN12 6QY Popular 19th-c local with five well kept changing ales and a real cider, generous helpings of well priced food (can get busy so best to book), breakfast served 9am-midday Tues-Sat, friendly staff, opened-up lounge/dining area, log fire, separate bar with TV and games including bar billiards; children and dogs welcome, garden tables, play area, open (and food) all day. *(Tony and Wendy Hobden)*

FINDON TQ1208

Gun (01903) 873206
High Street; BN14 0TA Welcoming low-beamed pub with opened-up bar area and restaurant; very good food (not Sun evening) including burger night (Mon), french night (Tues) and popular Sun lunch, four well kept Marstons-related beers, friendly chatty staff, log fire; free wi-fi; children and dogs (in bar) welcome, sheltered garden, pretty village below Cissbury Ring (NT), open all day. *(Sally and John Quinlan)*

FIRLE TQ4607

★**Ram** (01273) 858222
Village signed off A27 Lewes–Polegate; BN8 6NS 500-year-old pub tucked beneath the downs (popular with walkers); main bar with log fire and dark pubby tables on bare boards/quarry tiles, gilt-edged paintings on dark brown walls, Harveys Best, guest ales and 21 wines by the glass, second cosy bar

If you know a pub is ever open all day, please tell us.

with another fire, built-in wall seats and more dark furniture on parquet flooring, throughout are ceramic rams' heads, black and white local photos and candles in hurricane jars, steps up to back dining room overlooking flint-walled garden, good food using produce from Firle Estate, friendly helpful service; live folk night first Mon of month, darts and coin game toad in the hole, daily papers, free wi-fi; children (away from bar) and dogs welcome, picnic-sets under parasols on front terrace, comfortable bedrooms, good breakfast, open (and food) all day from 9am. *(Tony Scott, PL, Matthew and Elisabeth Reeves)*

FISHBOURNE SU8304

Bulls Head (01243) 839895

Fishbourne Road (A259 Chichester–Emsworth); PO19 3JP Former 17th-c farmhouse with traditional interior, copper pans on black beams, some stripped brick and panelling, paintings of local scenes, good log fire, five well kept Fullers/Gales beers and good choice of enterprising reasonably priced food, friendly efficient service, intimate dining room; background music and daily newspapers; children welcome, dogs in bar, tables on small covered deck, four bedrooms in former skittle alley, handy for Fishbourne Roman Palace, open all day weekends. *(Christian Mole, Miss A E Dare, John Beeken)*

FITTLEWORTH TQ0118

Swan (01798) 865154

Lower Street (B2138, off A283 W of Pulborough); RH20 1EN Pretty tile-hung dining inn; beamed main bar with mix of furniture including windsor chairs, high-backed stools and banquettes on wood flooring, wall of pictures and old pub sign one end, big inglenook log fire the other, ales such as Harveys and Langham, several wines by the glass and traditional cider, good food from pubby choices up in bar and separate panelled restaurant, efficient friendly staff; background and occasional live music, quiz nights, free wi-fi; children and dogs (in bar) welcome, plenty of tables on big back lawn, good walks nearby, 16 well priced comfortable bedrooms, open all day. *(Sophie and James Collier)*

FRANT TQ5835

Abergavenny Arms (01892) 750233

A267 S of Tunbridge Wells; TN3 9DB Attractively refurbished beamed dining pub; good freshly cooked food from varied menu including themed evenings, six well kept local ales such as Harveys, Larkins, Long Man and Tonbridge (maybe bank holiday beer festivals), good choice of wines by the glass and several interesting gins, friendly efficient staff, leather sofas by big woodburner in brick inglenook, three separate dining areas; background music, daily papers; children welcome, terrace seating on different levels, front part looking over road to Eridge Park (good walks), open (and food) all day. *(Martin Day)*

FULKING TQ2411

Shepherd & Dog (01273) 857382

Off A281 N of Brighton, via Poynings; BN5 9LU 17th-c bay-windowed pub in beautiful spot below the South Downs; low beams, panelling and inglenook, fine range of real ales and craft beers including Downlands (brewed a couple of miles away), also bottled beers, ciders and plenty of wines by the glass, enjoyable food from light lunches up, friendly young staff; beer, cider and 'gin and jazz' festivals, free wi-fi; children and dogs welcome, terrace and pretty streamside garden with own bar, straightforward climb to Devil's Dyke, open all day. *(Adam and Betty Lawrence)*

FUNTINGTON SU7908

Fox & Hounds (01243) 575246

Common Road (B2146); PO18 9LL Bustling old bay-windowed pub with updated beamed rooms; enjoyable food from open sandwiches and snacks to daily specials, popular Sun carvery, well kept Timothy Taylors and guests, lots of wines by the glass and good coffee, friendly service, comfortable spacious dining extension; free wi-fi; children and dogs (in bar) welcome, tables out in front and in walled back garden, open (and food) all day, weekend breakfast from 9am. *(Andrea and Laurie Grist)*

GRAFFHAM SU9217

White Horse (01798) 867331

On road signed to Heyshott/Midhurst at W end of village; GU28 0NT Large refurbished dining pub under newish owners; highly rated restauranty food along with some more traditional choices, Sharps Doom Bar, three local guests and plenty of wines by the glass, welcoming attentive service, bar/dining room and conservatory restaurant with South Downs views; children and dogs (in bar) welcome, big back garden and terrace (maybe summer jazz), good local walks, six well appointed bedrooms in two courtyard blocks, closed Mon in winter, otherwise normally open all day (but best to check website). *(Tony and Wendy Hobden)*

GUN HILL TQ5614

Gun (01825) 872361

Off A22 NW of Hailsham, or off A267; TN21 0JU Big 15th-c country dining pub (part of the small Elite group) with enjoyable bistro-style food from sharing boards and pizzas up; large central bar with nice old brick floor, stools against counter, Aga in corner, small grey-panelled room off with rugs on bare boards, animal skins on cushioned wall benches and mix of scrubbed and dark tables, logs piled into tall fireplace, well kept ales such as Harveys and Timothy Taylors, decent wines by the glass, cocktails (happy hour 5-7pm Mon-Thurs), close-set tables in two-room cottagey restaurant, beams and open fires, old bottles and glasses along gantry, gun prints and country pictures; background music; children welcome, picnic-sets in garden and on lantern-lit front terrace, Wealdway walks, open (and food) all day. *(John Preddy)*

HALNAKER SU9008

★**Anglesey Arms** (01243) 773474
A285 Chichester–Petworth; PO18 0NQ Georgian pub belonging to the Goodwood Estate and very much a village local; bare boards, settles and other country furniture, log fire, four well kept ales such as Harveys and Youngs, decent wines, good food from varied if not particularly cheap menu including local organic produce and Selsey fish, friendly accommodating service, simple L-shaped dining room (children allowed) with woodburners, stripped pine and some flagstones; traditional games, occasional live music; dogs welcome in bar, tables in big tree-lined garden, good nearby walks, open all day Fri-Sat. *(Simon Collett-Jones)*

HAMMERPOT TQ0605

★**Woodman Arms** (01903) 871240
On N (eastbound) side of A27; BN16 4EU Pretty thatched pub with beams, timbers and inglenook woodburner, good choice of well liked food (smaller helpings available) including popular Sun lunch, three or four Fullers/Gales beers and decent wines by the glass, attentive friendly staff, comfortable bar with snug one side, restaurant the other; occasional live music, free wi-fi; children and dogs (in bar) welcome, nice garden, open all day Fri and Sat, till 5pm Sun. *(Ann and Colin Hunt)*

HANDCROSS TQ2629

Red Lion (01444) 400292
High Street; RH17 6BP Extensive stylishly renovated dining pub; beamed bar with wood and polished stone floor, armchairs and long thickly cushioned banquette facing circular copper-topped tables, Harveys and Sharps, plenty of wines by the glass and good range of other drinks including cocktails, side area has some ancient recycled timbers and stripped tables on nice oak boards, another part with lower white-painted plank ceiling, rather more contemporary furnishings and big two-way fireplace, good choice of popular well presented food from sandwiches, sharing plates and pizzas up, also a vegan menu, friendly service; background music; children and dogs (in bar) welcome, handy for Nymans (NT), open all day. *(IAA, HMW, Maria Sansoni)*

HANDCROSS TQ2529

Royal Oak (01444) 401406
Horsham Road (B2110), W of A23; RH17 6DJ Traditional tile-hung village pub under friendly canadian landlady; well kept Harveys and a couple of guests, Weston's cider, decent wines and nice coffee, good well presented food cooked to order including some canadian recipes such as barbecue ribs, happy hour 3-5pm weekdays; fortnightly quiz Tues, bar billiards and darts, daily newspapers, free wi-fi; children and dogs welcome, seats out at front and on small terrace overlooking fields and woods, handy for Nymans (NT), open all day. *(Peter Meister, Ian Phillips, Tony Scott)*

HARTFIELD TQ4634

Gallipot (01892) 770008
B2110 towards Forest Row; TN7 4AJ Traditional stone and weatherboarded country pub; long narrow beamed interior with central bar and fire at one end, good home-made food from pub classics up (not many tables so best to book), three well kept local beers including Harveys, friendly helpful staff; some live music; children and dogs welcome, pleasant sloping garden behind with good views, handy for Pooh Bear country, open all day. *(Tim and Sue Mulligan)*

HASTINGS TQ8109

Dolphin (01424) 431197
Rock-a-Nore, off A259 at seafront; TN34 3DW Friendly tile-hung pub facing the fishermen's huts; compact carpeted interior with masses of fishing/maritime paraphernalia, enjoyable pubby food including fresh local fish, well kept Dark Star, Harveys, Youngs and guests plus craft beers; background and regular live music, quiz Thurs; children (till 7pm) and dogs welcome, raised front terrace, open all day. *(Ruth and Peter Bacon)*

HASTINGS TQ8209

First In Last Out (01424) 425079
High Street, Old Town; TN34 3EY Congenial and chatty pub serving its own FILO beers (brewed close by) and a guest ale, good fairly priced food including some interesting vegetarian/vegan choices, evening tapas (Mon) and indian thali (Thurs), friendly helpful staff, open-plan carpeted bar with 1970s Artex walls, dark wood booths and feature central raised log fire, lighter back dining room; regular live music, quiz first Sun of month; open all day, no food Sun evening or Mon lunchtime. *(Erik Wilkinson)*

HEATHFIELD TQ5920

★**Star** (01435) 863570
Church Street, Old Heathfield, off A265/B2096 E; TN21 9AH Nice old country pub next to church; ancient heavy beams, built-in wall settles, window seats, panelling and inglenook log fire, doorway to similarly decorated room set up more for eating, upstairs dining room with striking barrel-vaulted ceiling, Harveys Best and guests, 11 wines by the glass and well liked food; background music, free wi-fi; children and dogs welcome, seats in pretty garden with

views of rolling pasture dotted with sheep and lined with oak trees, open all day. *(Gerald and Brenda Culliford)*

HENLEY SU8925

★ **Duke of Cumberland Arms** (01428) 652280 *Down steep narrow lanes off A286 S of Fernhurst; GU27 3HQ* Pretty country cottage with two small low-ceilinged rooms; big scrubbed oak tables on brick or flagstoned floors, rustic decorations and open fire, Harveys and a couple of guests tapped from the cask, several wines by the glass and much enjoyed food (not Sun or Mon evenings), more modern dining extension with sofas in front of woodburner; background music, board games, free wi-fi; well behaved children and dogs (in bar) welcome, seats and picnic-sets on decking and in big tiered garden with trout ponds, beautiful views, open all day. *(Miss A E Dare, Christopher and Elise Way, David Jackman)*

HERMITAGE SU7505

★ **Sussex Brewery** (01243) 371533 *A259 just W of Emsworth; PO10 8AU* Bustling little 18th-c pub on the West Sussex/Hampshire border; small bare-boards bar with good fire in brick inglenook, simple furniture, flagstoned snug, well kept Youngs ales and guests, ten wines by the glass and popular hearty food including speciality sausages (even vegetarian ones), small upstairs restaurant; children and dogs welcome, picnic-sets in back courtyard, open all day (food all day Sun till 7.30pm). *(Bob and Melissa Wyatt)*

HIGH HURSTWOOD TQ4925

★ **Hurstwood** (01825) 732257 *Hurstwood Road off A272; TN22 4AH* Although the main draw to this small country pub is their excellent inventive food (must book), they still attract some loyal local drinkers; open-plan U-shaped interior with beams and bare boards, high spindleback chairs against counter serving Harveys and Sharps, good wines by the glass and cocktails, friendly attentive young staff, area by tiled Victorian fireplace with sofas and armchairs, dining tables set with red gingham napkins, little plants and church candles, hunting prints and other artwork above painted dado, various lamps/lanterns and a piano (which gets played); children and dogs (in bar area) welcome, french windows on to deck with lawn beyond, open all day (till 5.30pm Sun). *(David Jackman)*

HOOE TQ6910

Red Lion (01424) 892371 *Denbigh Road; off B2095; TN33 9EW* Attractive old local behind screen of pollarded lime trees – originally a farmhouse but a pub since the 17th c; plenty of original features including hop-strung beams, flagstones and two big inglenooks, generous helpings of popular home-cooked food (worth booking), well kept Harveys, a guest and plenty of continental beers, good friendly service, main bar and back snug, overflow function room and further eating space upstairs; children and dogs welcome, wheelchair access, seats out at front and in garden behind, closed Mon evening, otherwise open all day. *(Simon King)*

HORSTED KEYNES TQ3828

Crown (01825) 791609 *The Green; RH17 7AW* 16th-c inn with emphasis on chef-owner's good contemporary cooking; spreading dining areas with rustic-style tables on red patterned carpet, beams, timbering and bare brick walls, also a proper bar with simple furniture on big flagstones and huge inglenook, Bedlam, Dark Star and Harveys, 20 wines by the glass; children and dogs (in bar) welcome, seats out at front and in terraced back garden overlooking village cricket green, four comfortable country-style bedrooms, open all day Sun till 9pm (food till 4pm), closed other days 3-5pm. *(Geoff and Ann Marston, Patricia and Anton Larkham, Lucy and Giles Gibbon)*

HOUGHTON TQ0111

★ **George & Dragon** (01798) 831559 *B2139 W of Storrington; BN18 9LW* 13th-c beams and timbers in attractive bar rambling up and down steps, note the elephant photograph above the fireplace, good Arun Valley views from back extension, well liked reasonably priced food, Marstons-related ales and decent wines by the glass, good friendly service; background music; children and dogs welcome, tables on decked terrace taking in the views (they may ask for a credit card if you eat out here), charming sloping garden, good walks, open all day Fri and Sat, till 9pm Sun. *(Tony Scott, Tony and Wendy Hobden, Darren and Clare Jones)*

HUNSTON SU8601

Spotted Cow (01243) 786718 *B2145 S of Chichester; PO20 1PD* Modernised slate-faced village pub with beams, flagstones and big log fires; good choice of food (not Sun evening, Mon lunchtime) including specials, Fullers/Gales beers, friendly helpful staff, small front bar, roomier side lounge with armchairs, sofas and low tables, airy high-ceilinged restaurant; maybe background music, darts; children (if eating) and dogs welcome, good disabled access, enclosed garden with play equipment, handy for towpath walkers, open all day. *(R and M Thomas)*

HURSTPIERPOINT TQ2816

New Inn (01273) 834608 *High Street; BN6 9RQ* Popular 16th-c beamed village pub; Harveys and a couple of guests, good wines by the glass and enjoyable food from pub favourites up, seafood specials

(Fri, Sat), themed evenings and summer wood-fired pizzas, friendly staff, linked areas including oak-panelled back bar with log fire and more formal restaurant; quiz nights, sports TV; children and dogs welcome, enclosed garden with terrace and play area, open all day, no food Sun evening. *(Alexander and Trish Cutter)*

ICKLESHAM TQ8716

★**Queens Head** (01424) 814552

Off A259 Rye–Hastings; TN36 4BL Friendly well run country pub, extremely popular locally (and at weekends with cyclists and walkers); open-plan areas around big counter, high timbered walls and vaulted roof, bottles on shelves and plenty of farming implements and animal traps, pubby furniture on patterned carpet, other areas with inglenooks and a back room with old bicycle memorabilia, up to eight well kept ales including Greene King and Harveys, local cider, several wines by the glass and good choice of reasonably priced pub food; background jazz and blues (live 4-6pm Sun), occasional pub quiz; well behaved children till 8.30pm, dogs welcome, picnic-sets, boules and play area in peaceful garden with fine Brede Valley views, you can walk to Winchelsea from here, open all day (food all day weekends). *(V Brogden, Tony Scott, Mike and Eleanor Anderson)*

ICKLESHAM TQ8716

★**Robin Hood** (01424) 814277

Main Road; TN36 4BD Friendly family-run beamed pub with buoyant local atmosphere; good value unpretentious home-made food (all day Sun) including blackboard specials, Mon steak night and Weds curry, well kept Greene King IPA, up to six guests and three proper ciders, hops overhead and lots of copper bric-a-brac, log fire, games part with pool, back dining conservatory; free wi-fi; children and dogs (in bar) welcome, play area and boules in big garden, lovely Brede Valley views, open all day Fri-Sun. *(Serena and Adam Furber)*

ISFIELD TQ4417

Laughing Fish (01825) 750349

Station Road; TN22 5XB Bustling opened-up Victorian local with affable landlord and cheerful efficient staff, enjoyable good value home-cooked food (not Sun evening) including daily specials and themed nights, well kept Greene King ales and three local guests (always one from Isfield), open fire; bar billiards and other traditional games, various events including entertaining beer race Easter Mon; children and dogs welcome, disabled access, small pleasantly shaded walled garden with enclosed play area, field for camping, right by Lavender Line railway (pub was station hotel), post office facilities Thurs morning, open all day. *(Ann and Colin Hunt, John Beeken, Tony and Wendy Hobden)*

JEVINGTON TQ5601

Eight Bells (01323) 484442

Jevington Road, N of East Dean; BN26 5QB Friendly village pub in good walking country; simple furnishings, heavy beams, panelling, parquet floor and inglenook, popular home-made food from sandwiches and good ploughman's up, well kept ales including Harveys; background music (live Mon), Tues quiz; children and dogs welcome, front terrace and secluded downs-view garden, adjacent cricket field, open all day. *(Gene and Kitty Rankin, Mrs J Ekins-Daukes)*

KINGSTON TQ3908

Juggs (01273) 472523

Village signed off A27 by roundabout W of Lewes; BN7 3NT Tile-hung village pub with heavy 15th-c beams and very low front door, lots of neatly stripped masonry, sturdy wooden furniture on bare boards and stone slabs, log fires, smaller eating areas including a family room, food from sandwiches and pub standards up, Harveys and Shepherd Neame, good wines and coffee; background music, quiz nights; children and dogs welcome, disabled access/facilities, lots of outside tables including covered area with heaters, tubs and hanging baskets, play area, nice South Downs walks, open (and food) all day. *(Peter Pilbeam)*

KIRDFORD TQ0126

★**Half Moon** (01403) 820223

Opposite church, off A272 Petworth–Billingshurst; RH14 0LT Attractive old tile-hung village pub newly opened/refurbished by celebrity model Jodie Kidd; beamed bar on right with cushioned window seat, barrel stools and armchairs by woodburner, some nice old photos and hunting wallpaper, a couple of local ales and plenty of wines by the glass from blue-painted counter, two restaurant rooms with rustic planked wall seats, painted or wooden chairs around simple tables and fine inglenook fireplace, good interesting food (not Sun evening) including weekday set lunch and tasting menus, friendly staff, background music; tables on terrace and lawn, kitchen garden to one side overlooked by church tower, closed Mon and Tues, otherwise open all day (till 8pm Sun). *(Katherine Matthews)*

Cribbage is a card game using a block of wood with holes for matchsticks or special pins to score with; regulars in cribbage pubs are usually happy to teach strangers how to play.

LEWES TQ4110

Black Horse (01273) 473653
Western Road; BN7 1RS Bow-windowed pub with knocked-through bar keeping traditional feel, two log fires, wood floor, panelling and lots of old pictures, seven well kept ales including Greene King, interesting gins, enjoyable home-made food, friendly service; occasional live music and quiz nights, sports TV, bar billiards and coin game toad in the hole; children welcome, beer garden, open all day. *(Tony Scott)*

LEWES TQ4210

Gardeners Arms (01273) 474808
Cliffe High Street; BN7 2AN Unpretentious little bare-boards local opposite Harveys brewery shop; lots of beer mats on gantry, homely stools, built-in wall seats and plain scrubbed tables around three narrow sides of bar, dog water bowl by blocked-up fireplace, Harveys and five interesting changing guests, real ciders, some lunchtime food including sandwiches, pasties and pies, photos of Lewes bonfire night; background music, TV, darts; no children, dogs welcome; open all day. *(Peter Pilbeam)*

LEWES TQ4210

★**John Harvey** (01273) 479880
Bear Yard, just off Cliffe High Street; BN7 2AN Bustling tap for nearby Harveys brewery, four of their beers including seasonals kept in top condition (some poured from the cask), small choice of enjoyable well priced traditional food (not Sun evening), friendly efficient young staff, beamed and flagstoned bar with woodburner, huge vat halved to make two snug seating areas, lighter room on left and upstairs restaurant/function room; live music first Sun of the month; children welcome in restaurant, dogs in bar, a few tables outside, open all day. *(Tony Scott, Fr Robert Marsh, Ann and Colin Hunt)*

LEWES TQ4110

★**Lewes Arms** (01273) 473152
Castle Ditch Lane/Mount Place – tucked behind castle ruins; BN7 1YH Cheerful unpretentious little local with five well kept Fullers ales and two guests, 30 malt whiskies and plenty of wines by the glass, generous helpings of enjoyable reasonably priced bar food including good Sun roasts; tiny front bar on right with stools along curved counter and bench window seats, two other simple rooms hung with photographs and information about the famous Lewes bonfire night, beer mats pinned over doorways; folk evenings and more obscure events such as pea throwing and dwyle flunking; children (away from front bar) and dogs welcome, picnic-sets on attractive split-level back terrace, open all day (till midnight Fri, Sat). *(Tony Scott)*

LEWES TQ4110

★**Pelham Arms** (01273) 476149
At top of High Street; BN7 1XL Popular 17th-c beamed pub with characterful rambling interior; good well presented food (not Mon, booking advised) including some interesting vegetarian choices and meat/fish from on-site smokehouse, friendly efficient service, own Abyss beers and guests; children and dogs (in bar) welcome, small courtyard garden, closed Mon lunchtime, otherwise open all day. *(Alan Johnson)*

LEWES TQ4110

Rights of Man (01273) 486894
High Street; BN7 1YE Harveys pub close to the Crown Court; five of their well kept ales and enjoyable food including tapas, Victorian-style décor with a series of booths, another bar at the back and roof terrace; background music, free wi-fi; open all day, food till 6pm Sun. *(Peter Pilbeam)*

LEWES TQ4210

★**Snowdrop** (01273) 471018
South Street; BN7 2BU Welcoming pub tucked below the chalk cliffs; narrowboat theme with brightly painted servery and colourful jugs, kettles, lanterns etc hanging from curved planked ceiling, wide mix of simple furniture on parquet floor, old sewing machines and huge stone jars, rather bohemian atmosphere; well kept local ales such as Bedlam, Gun and Harveys, a couple of ciders and enjoyable reasonably priced food from interestingly varied menu (some good vegetarian options), nice coffee, cheerful efficient staff (may ask for a card if running a tab), more tables in upstairs room (spiral stairs) with bar billiards and darts; background and frequent live music including Mon jazz; dogs very welcome (menu for them), outside seating on both sides, pretty hanging baskets, open (and food) all day, kitchen shuts 6pm Sun. *(John Beeken)*

LINDFIELD TQ3425

Bent Arms (01444) 483146
High Street; RH16 2HP Surprisingly spacious 16th-c village coaching inn with low black beams, timbers and some stained glass, most tables set for their popular affordably priced food including lunchtime sandwiches and ploughman's using own bread, good value evening set menu, three well kept Badger ales, friendly service; children welcome, sizeable back garden with covered area, nine bedrooms and cottage. *(Tony Scott, Mrs P R Sykes)*

LITLINGTON TQ5201

Plough & Harrow (01323) 870632
Between A27 Lewes–Polegate and A259 E of Seaford; BN26 5RE Neatly extended 17th-c flint village pub; large beamed and wood-floored bar with smaller rooms off, candles on tables, brewery mirrors and

old farming implements on the walls, snug with inglenook, half a dozen well kept ales including at least three from Long Man, decent wines by the glass and good choice of generously served food from lunchtime pub staples to more enterprising dishes using local produce, friendly helpful service; quiz second Weds of month, some live music, Aug beer festival; children and dogs welcome, attractive back garden, good walks (on South Downs Way), open all day. *(PL, John Beeken, Sue Parry-Davies)*

LITTLEHAMPTON TQ0202

★ **Arun View** (01903) 722335
Wharf Road; W towards Chichester; BN17 5DD Refurbished pub in lovely harbour spot with busy waterway directly below windows; popular good value food (all day Sun) from sandwiches/ciabattas to good fresh fish, well kept Fullers, guest beers and several wines by the glass, cheerful helpful staff, flagstoned and panelled back bar with banquettes and dark wood tables, large dining conservatory; background music, TVs, pool; children and dogs welcome, disabled facilities, flower-filled terrace, interesting waterside walkway to coast, four bedrooms, open all day. *(Rupert and Sandy Newton)*

LITTLEHAMPTON TQ0202

Steam Packet (01903) 715994
River Road; BN17 5BZ 19th-c corner pub just across from the Arun View; open-plan interior providing several separate seating areas, well kept local ales such as Bedlam, Cellar Head and Downlands, enjoyable reasonably priced food from tapas to daily specials; quiz Thurs, regular live jazz; seats out in small area facing river, raised back garden, three bedrooms, closed Mon, otherwise open all day, no food Sun evening. *(Tony Scott, Tony and Wendy Hobden)*

LITTLEWORTH TQ1921

Windmill (01403) 710308
Pub signed off B2135; village signed off A272 southbound, W of Cowfold; RH13 8EJ Refurbished brick and tile inn dating from the 17th c; two beamed and flagstoned bars, one with inglenook log fire, the other with woodburner, lots of old farming tools and so forth on walls and ceiling, enjoyable home-made food (all day weekends) from sandwiches and pub standards up, wood-fired pizzas in summer, well kept Harveys and a couple of guests, restaurant; quiz first Tues of month, occasional live music, bar billiards, darts, TV and free wi-fi; children and dogs welcome, picnic-sets in peaceful garden overlooking fields, bedrooms, open all day. *(Robin and Anna Triggs)*

LODSWORTH SU9321

Halfway Bridge Inn (01798) 861281
Just before village, on A272 Midhurst–Petworth; GU28 9BP Restauranty 17th-c coaching inn with characterful linked rooms; beams, wooden floors and log fires (one in polished kitchen range), good if not especially cheap food from interesting menu (also pub favourites and set lunch), ales such as Arundel, Langham and Sharps, wide range of wines by the glass, pleasant helpful staff; background music, newspapers and free wi-fi; children and dogs (in bar) welcome, small back terrace, six bedrooms in former stables, open all day, food all day weekends. *(Patric Curwen)*

LODSWORTH SU9223

Hollist Arms (01798) 861310
Off A272 Midhurst–Petworth; GU28 9BZ 18th-c pub (new management) in lovely spot by village green; small snug room on right with open fire, public bar on left serving local ales and several wines by the glass, enjoyable fairly traditional food (not Sun evening), L-shaped dining room with wood-strip floor, inglenook and comfortable seating area; quiz nights, free wi-fi; children and dogs welcome, steps up to cottagey back garden, picnic-sets on terrace or you can sit under a very large horse chestnut on the green, good walks nearby, open all day weekends. *(Colin and Daniel Gibbs)*

LYMINSTER TQ0204

Six Bells (01903) 713639
Lyminster Road (A284), Wick; BN17 7PS Unassuming 18th-c flint pub with opened-up bar and separate dining room; well kept Fullers London Pride and maybe a guest, decent house wines and enjoyable sensibly priced food (some dishes available in smaller helpings), friendly attentive staff, low black beams, wood floor and big inglenook with horsebrasses, pubby furnishings; background music, free wi-fi; children and dogs (in one area) welcome, terrace and garden seating. *(Tony and Wendy Hobden)*

MAREHILL TQ0618

White Horse (01798) 872189
Mare Hill Road (A283 E of Pulborough); RH20 2DY White-painted roadside country pub with several linked areas; enjoyable food including daily specials, well kept Fullers/Gales beers and several wines by the glass, friendly staff, two open fires, nice views from restaurant; some live music; children and dogs welcome, attractive garden behind, handy for RSPB Pulborough Brooks reserve, open all day. *(Richard Tilbrook)*

MAYFIELD TQ5826

Middle House (01435) 872146
High Street; TN20 6AB Handsome 16th-c timbered inn (Grade I listed); L-shaped beamed bar with massive fireplace, several well kept ales including Harveys, local cider and decent wines, quiet lounge area with leather chesterfields around log fire in ornate carved fireplace, good choice of enjoyable

food, friendly staff coping well at busy times, attractive panelled restaurant with modern glass extension; background music; children welcome, terraced back garden, lovely country views, bedrooms, open (and food) all day weekends. *(Tony Scott)*

MAYFIELD TQ5927

★**Rose & Crown** (01435) 872200
Fletching Street; TN20 6TE Pretty 16th-c weatherboarded pub set down lane from village centre; two cosy front character rooms with coins stuck to low ceiling boards, bench seats built into partly panelled walls and simple furniture on floorboards, inglenook log fire, tankards above bar serving Harveys, a guest beer and several wines by the glass, decent food including tapas night last Thurs of month, further small room behind servery and larger carpeted one down steps; regular live music including open mike night first Thurs of month, Tues quiz, free wi-fi; children (till 8.30pm) and dogs welcome, raised front terrace, decked back garden, open all day. *(Rosie and John Moore)*

MID LAVANT SU8508

Earl of March (01243) 533993
A286 Lavant Road; PO18 0BQ Updated and extended with emphasis on eating, but seats for drinkers in flagstoned log-fire bar, well kept Harveys, Timothy Taylors and a guest, nice wines by the glass including champagne and english fizz, good if pricey food (much sourced locally), plush dining area and conservatory with seafood bar, pleasant staff; free wi-fi; children and dogs welcome, delightful location and local walks, view up to Goodwood from neatly kept garden, open all day. *(Miss A E Dare, John Evans, Hunter and Christine Wright)*

MILLAND SU8328

Rising Sun (01428) 741347
Iping Road junction with main road through village; GU30 7NA Busy 20th-c red-brick Fullers pub; three of their ales and varied choice of fresh well presented food including specials and weekday lunchtime/early evening offers, friendly helpful staff, three linked rooms including cheery log-fire bar and bare-boards restaurant; quiz and curry night Thurs, live music Fri, free wi-fi; children and dogs welcome, extensive lawns attractively divided by tall yew hedge, canopied heated terrace and smokers' gazebo, good walking area, open all day (Fri-Sun). *(John Evans)*

NETHERFIELD TQ7118

Netherfield Arms (01424) 838282
Just off B2096 Heathfield–Battle; TN33 9QD Welcoming low-ceilinged 18th-c country dining pub; wide choice of enjoyable food including good specials and vegetarian/vegan dishes, friendly attentive service, decent wines and a well kept ale such as Long Man, inglenook log fire, cosy restaurant; picnic-sets in lovely back garden, far-reaching views from front, closed Sun evening, Mon. *(John and Delia Franks)*

NETHERFIELD TQ7118

White Hart (01424) 838382
Darwell Hill, B2096; TN33 9QH Smartened-up country pub with busy little front bar, cushions on built-in wall seats, log fire at one end, hops and country prints, stools by counter serving well kept Harveys and Shepherd Neame, lounge area with sofas and scatter cushions, huge stag's head and bookshelves, tasty food served by friendly, helpful staff, dining room has rush-seated chairs around dark tables on coir, some half-panelling and woodburner; children and dogs welcome, rattan chairs around tables out on gravel, fine far-reaching views, closed Sun evening, Mon. *(Sylvia and Phillip Spencer)*

NEWHAVEN TQ4500

Hope (01273) 515389
Follow West Beach signs from A259 westbound; BN9 9DN Big-windowed pub overlooking busy harbour entrance; long bar with raised area, nautical-themed décor, open fires and comfy sofas, upstairs dining conservatory and breezy balcony tables with even better view towards Seaford Head, well kept ales such as Dark Star and Harveys, good choice of generous well priced food (till 7pm Sun), friendly staff; regular live music, Weds quiz; tables on grassed waterside area, open all day. *(Peter Pilbeam)*

NUTBOURNE TQ0718

Rising Sun (01798) 812191
Off A283 E of Pulborough; The Street; RH20 2HE Unspoilt creeper-clad village pub dating partly from the 16th-c (same owner for 37 years); front bar with beams, exposed brickwork and woodburner, scrubbed tables on bare boards, some 1920s fashion and dance posters, Fullers London Pride, Hogs Back and a couple of guests, good well presented food from pub favourites up, friendly service, second bar leading through to quarry-tiled restaurant, cosy back family room; background and live music; dogs welcome, terrace with small pond and smokers' shelter, archway through to lawned area, closed Sun evening. *(Tony Scott)*

NUTHURST TQ1926

Black Horse (01403) 891272
Off A281 SE of Horsham; RH13 6LH Welcoming 17th-c country pub with plenty of character in its several small rooms; low black beams, flagstones/bare boards and inglenook log fire, enjoyable good value pubby food served by friendly attentive staff, four real ales including Harveys; popular charity quiz Weds; children and dogs welcome, pretty streamside back garden, more seats on front terrace, open all day weekends. *(Katherine Matthews)*

OFFHAM TQ3912

Blacksmiths Arms (01273) 472971

A275 N of Lewes; BN7 3QD Popular open-plan dining pub in rural village; good food (not Sun evening) from shortish menu, well kept ales such as Goldstone and Harveys, efficient friendly service, clean updated interior with a couple of woodburners, one in huge end inglenook; children and dogs (in bar) welcome, french windows to terrace, four bedrooms (steep stairs) open all day (till 8pm Sun). *(Chris and Sophie Baxter)*

PARTRIDGE GREEN TQ1819

★Green Man (01403) 710250

Off A24 just under a mile S of A272 junction – take B2135 at West Grinstead signpost; pub at Jolesfield, N of Partridge Green; RH13 8JT Relaxed gently upmarket dining pub with popular enterprising food cooked by chef-landlord, well chosen wines by the glass (including champagne), ales such as Hurst, Long Man and Palmers, good friendly service; unassuming front area by counter with bentwood bar seats, stools and library chairs around one or two low tables, old curved high-back settle, main eating area widening into back part with pretty enamelled stove, pitched ceiling area on left, more self-contained room on right; children and dogs (in bar) welcome, cast-iron seats and picnic-sets under parasols in neat back garden, closed Sun evening, Mon. *(Darrell Barton)*

PARTRIDGE GREEN TQ1819

Partridge (01403) 710391

Church Road/High Street; RH13 8JS Spacious 19th-c village pub (former station hotel) now tap for Dark Star; their full range and maybe a guest, real cider, enjoyable sensibly priced home-made food (not Sun evening) including blackboard specials and deals, friendly relaxed atmosphere; darts and pool, free wi-fi; children and dogs welcome, garden with large terrace and play equipment, open all day. *(Gary and Marie Miller)*

PATCHING TQ0705

Fox (01903) 871299

Arundel Road; signed off A27 eastbound just W of Worthing; BN13 3UJ Neatly kept pub with good generously served food including popular Sun roasts (best to book), quick friendly service even at busy times, two or three well kept local ales including Harveys, large dining area off roomy panelled bar, dark pubby furniture on patterned carpet, hunting pictures; quiet background music; children and dogs welcome, disabled access, colourful hanging baskets and good-sized tree-shaded garden with well laid-out seating, heaters and play area, open all day Sun till 9pm. *(Tony and Wendy Hobden)*

PEASMARSH TQ8822

Horse & Cart (01797) 230034

School Lane; TN31 6UW Refurbished village pub, light beams and wood floors, red leather sofa and armchair by open fire, back restaurant separated by gas woodburner in two-way brick fireplace, good mix of seating from pews to banquettes, a beer badged for the pub from Romney Marsh along with local Three Legs, extensive wine list (several by the glass and carafes of house wine), very good food from pub stables up (can be pricey), also takeaway pizzas and weekend breakfast from 8am, friendly helpful service; games including shove-ha'penny; children and dogs welcome, a couple of tables out at front with more on back terrace and lawn, pétanque, four bedrooms, closed Sun evening and Mon, otherwise open all day (winter hours may vary); for sale, so there may be changes. *(James Castro-Edwards, Sue Kinder, Peter Meister)*

PETT TQ8713

Royal Oak (01424) 812515

Pett Road; TN35 4HG Friendly brick and weatherboarded village pub; roomy main bar with big open fire, well kept Harveys and a couple of changing guests, popular home-made food including several fish dishes, two dining areas, efficient helpful service; occasional live music and quiz nights, traditional games; dogs welcome, small garden behind, open all day, no food Sun evening. *(Peter Meister)*

PETT TQ8613

Two Sawyers (01424) 812255

Pett Road, off A259; TN35 4HB Meandering low-beamed rooms including bare-boards bar with stripped tables, tiny snug and restaurant down sloping passageway, open fires, well kept Harveys, Sharps and guests, local cider/perry and wide range of wines, popular good value home-made food, friendly helpful service; background and some live music; children (in restaurant) and dogs (in bar) welcome, suntrap front courtyard, back garden with shady trees and well spaced tables, four bedrooms, open all day. *(Victoria and Len Meadows)*

PETWORTH SU9719

Badgers (01798) 342651

Station Road (A285 1.5 miles S); GU28 0JF Restauranty dining pub with good up-to-date food including seasonal game and locally sourced seafood, frequent Sun hog/lamb roasts, can eat in bar areas or restaurant, friendly accommodating staff, a couple of changing ales such as Sharps and Youngs, good choice of wines, cosy fireside area with sofas; free wi-fi; over-5s allowed in

We include some hotels with a good bar that offers facilities comparable to those of a pub.

bar's eating area, stylish tables and seats on terrace by water lily pool, summer barbecues, three well appointed bedrooms, good breakfast. *(Tina and Steven Hobden)*

PETWORTH SU9721

Star (01798) 342569

Market Square; GU28 0AH Opened-up and refurbished old pub with well kept Fullers/ Gales beers, decent wines and good choice of enjoyable food (all day Sat, not Sun evening), friendly helpful service, log fire; occasional live music, Fri disco, free wi-fi; children and dogs (in bar) welcome, a few seats on terrace looking out over market square, open all day from 9am. *(Darrell Barton)*

PETWORTH SU9722

Stonemasons (01798) 342510

North Street; GU28 9NL Attractive 17th-c low-beamed inn; enjoyable freshly made food from sandwiches up including blackboard specials, Otter, Skinners Betty Stogs and Wells Bombardier, helpful friendly staff, opened-up modernised areas in former adjoining cottages, inglenook log fires; TV; children and dogs welcome, picnic-sets in sheltered back garden, five bedrooms, opposite Petworth House (NT) so can get busy, open (and food) all day, kitchen shuts 6pm Sun. *(Ann and Colin Hunt)*

PLUMPTON TQ3613

Half Moon (01273) 890253

Ditchling Road (B2116); BN7 3AF Enlarged beamed and timbered roadside dining pub; good food from pub favourites up, local ales and plenty of wines by the glass, log fire with unusual flint chimneybreast; background music; children and dogs (in bar) welcome, tables in wisteria-clad front courtyard and on back terrace, big downs-view garden with picnic area, good walks, open all day (till 6pm Sun). *(Tim and Sue Milligan)*

POYNINGS TQ2611

Royal Oak (01273) 857389

The Street; BN45 7AQ Welcoming traditional 19th-c pub in rural setting; large beamed bar with smaller more intimate areas up steps, well kept Harveys and a guest from three-sided servery, enjoyable reasonably priced home-cooked food, friendly efficient service, traditional furnishing, hanging hops and old photographs, paintings for sale, woodburner; children and dogs welcome, big garden with country/downs views, play area and barbecue, good walks. *(Patric Curwen, John Beeken)*

RINGMER TQ4512

Green Man (01273) 812422

Lewes Road; BN8 5NA Welcoming 1930s roadside pub with busy mix of locals and visitors; six real ales from brick-faced counter including Greene King, wide range of generous good value food, efficient friendly service, long bar with log fire, large restaurant and conservatory; children and dogs welcome, terrace tables, more on lawn under trees, play area, open (and food) all day. *(John Beeken)*

RODMELL TQ4105

Abergavenny Arms (01273) 472416

Back road Lewes–Newhaven; BN7 3EZ Welcoming beamed and raftered ex-barn; large open-plan bar with wood and tiled floors, several recesses and log fire in big fireplace, good selection of enjoyable bar food (not Sun evening), steak night Thurs, well kept Harveys and one or more local guests, upstairs eating area, games room; occasional live music, free wi-fi; children welcome, large two-level back terrace, handy for Virginia Woolf's Monk's House (NT) and South Downs Way, open all day. *(Ruth and Peter Bacon)*

ROWHOOK TQ1234

★**Chequers** (01403) 790480

Off A29 NW of Horsham; RH12 3PY Attractive 15th-c country pub; beamed and flagstoned front bar with portraits and inglenook log fire, step up to low-ceilinged lounge, well kept Harveys and guests, decent wines by the glass and good food from chef-landlord using local ingredients including home-grown vegetables, efficient service from friendly chatty young staff, separate restaurant; background music; children and dogs welcome, tables out on front terraces and in pretty garden behind, good play area, closed Sun evening. *(Hunter and Christine Wright, Sally and John Quinlan, Christopher and Elise Way)*

RUSPER TQ2037

Star (01293) 871264

Off A264 S of Crawley; RH12 4RA Several linked rooms in cosy 15th-c beamed coaching inn; well kept ales and decent food (all day Sun) from sandwiches and light meals up including some greek dishes, wood floors, old tools on walls, fine brick inglenook; children and dogs welcome, small back terrace, open all day. *(Rosie and John Moore)*

RYE TQ9220

★**George** (01797) 222114

High Street; TN31 7JT Sizeable hotel with popular beamed bar, mix of furniture including settles on bare boards, log fire, local ales such as Dark Star, Harveys and Old Dairy, continental beers on tap too, friendly helpful service from neat young staff, interesting bistro-style food and good selection of wines including local vineyards

We say if we know a pub has background music.

such as Chapel Down, big spreading restaurant to right of main door; maybe background jazz; children and dogs welcome, seats on pleasant back terrace, attractive bedrooms, open all day. *(Nigel and Jean Eames, Mike Buckingham, Caroline Prescott)*

RYE TQ9220

★**Globe** (01797) 225220
Military Road; TN31 7NX Small weatherboarded pub under same owners as the Five Bells at Brabourne and Woolpack at Warehorne (both in Kent); quirky touches such as corrugated iron-clad walls, hanging lobster-pot lights and eclectic range of furniture from school chairs to a table made from part of an old fishing boat, even hay bale seats in one part, fresh flowers, candles and paraffin lamps, two log fires, good locally sourced food from open kitchen with wood-fired oven, interesting local ales and ciders (no bar counter), also some wines from nearby Chapel Down, shelves of home-made preserves for sale, quick cheerful service; unisex loos; children and dogs welcome, seats on side decking, Sat market, open all day. *(Peter Pilbeam)*

RYE TQ9220

★**Mermaid** (01797) 223065
Mermaid Street; TN31 7EY Fine old timbered inn on famous cobbled street (cellars date from 12th c, although pub was rebuilt in 1420); civilised antiques-filled bar, Victorian gothick carved chairs, older but plainer oak seats and huge working inglenook with massive bressumer (ask about the priest hole and secret passages), Harveys, Sharps and a guest, good selection of wines, gins and malt whiskies, bar food (not Sat evening) or more elaborate and expensive restaurant choices, efficient friendly service, reputedly haunted by five ghosts; background music; children welcome, seats on small back terrace, bedrooms (most with four-posters), open all day. *(Peter Pilbeam)*

RYE TQ9120

★**Standard** (01797) 225231
The Mint, High Street; TN31 7EN Ancient pub sympathetically opened up and renovated; moulded beams, exposed brickwork and panelling, brown leather and farmhouse chairs at rustic tables on quarry tiles, candles and log fires (stag's head above one), four well kept ales including nearby Three Legs, good fairly priced food using local ingredients (fish from the harbour), nice wines and decent coffee, friendly accommodating staff; outside gents'; well behaved children and dogs welcome, picnic sets on small back terrace, five well appointed character bedrooms (more in their recently opened café/bakery nearby), open all day. *(Mike and Eleanor Anderson, Paul and Karen Cornock)*

RYE TQ9220

Waterworks Micropub 07974 941393 *Tower Street/Rope Walk; TN31 7AT* Micropub in interesting old building (ex-waterworks); friendly hard-working landlord serving eight well kept local beers and three or four real ciders (all marked-up on blackboard), also wines by the glass and some snacky food, furniture and other bits and pieces for sale; dogs welcome, open all day weekends, otherwise from 2pm, handy for the station. *(Mike and Eleanor Anderson)*

RYE TQ9220

★**Ypres Castle** (01797) 223248
Gun Garden; steps up from A259, or down past Ypres Tower; TN31 7HH New management and some minor refurbishment for this traditional tucked-away 17th-c pub; main bar with wall banquettes, assorted tables and chairs on bare boards and open fire, half a dozen local beers and a couple of proper ciders, good food from pub favourites up, two dining rooms, friendly relaxed atmosphere; background and live music including open mike night first Tues of month; children and dogs welcome, lovely views from sheltered garden over the River Rother, open all day. *(Tony Scott, Richard Cole, Mike and Eleanor Anderson, Richard Tilbrook)*

RYE HARBOUR TQ9419

Inkerman Arms (01797) 222464
Rye Harbour Road; TN31 7TQ Welcoming 19th-c end-of-terrace pub near nature reserve; enjoyable food including good fish and chips, well kept ales such as Harveys; children and dogs welcome, picnic-sets in sheltered back terrace with pond, open all day Fri-Sun. *(Robin and Anna Triggs)*

RYE HARBOUR TQ9419

William the Conqueror
(01797) 223315 *Opposite lifeboat station, bottom of Harbour Road; TN31 7TU* Welcoming refurbished harbourside pub; three well kept Shepherd Neame ales and decent choice of wines by the glass, good reasonably priced food including local fish and some greek dishes, friendly helpful staff, three main areas (ramp down to lower dining part), nautical-themed décor with framed charts and old local pictures, some wooden booth seating and cushioned benches on bare boards, log fires; background and occasional live music, free wi-fi; children and dogs welcome, picnic-sets out in front, open all day (till 10pm Mon-Thurs, 6pm Sun). *(John Hills, Peter Meister)*

SEDLESCOMBE TQ7817

Queens Head (01424) 870228
The Green; TN33 0QA Attractive old tile-hung village green pub (watch out for the wandering geese); beamed central bar

with armchairs on bare boards, some window seats and a huge cartwheel, Harveys, Sharps Doom Bar and a guest such as Old Dairy, decent choice of wines by the glass, dining areas either side with open fires (one in large inglenook), good popular food from shortish menu (also blackboard specials), helpful friendly staff; maybe quiet background music; children and dogs welcome, picnic-sets in spacious side garden, open all day, food till 6.30pm Sun. *(Caroline Prescott)*

SHORTBRIDGE TQ4521

Peacock (01825) 762463

Piltdown; OS Sheet 198 map reference 450215; TN22 3XA Old country dining pub with two fine yew trees flanking entrance, civilised and welcoming, with dark beams, timbers and big inglenook, some nice old furniture on parquet floors, good food from ciabattas up, steak night Fri, two or three well kept ales and decent wines by the glass, friendly attentive staff, restaurant; children and dogs welcome, back garden and terrace, bedrooms, open all day Sun till 9pm (6pm winter). *(Tony Scott)*

SIDLESHAM SZ8697

★**Crab & Lobster** (01243) 641233

Mill Lane; off B2145 S of Chichester; PO20 7NB Restaurant-with-rooms rather than pub but does have a small flagstoned bar serving real ales, plenty of wines by the glass (including champagne) and light meals; stylish upmarket restaurant with good imaginative (and pricey) food including excellent local fish, competent friendly young staff; background music; children welcome, tables on back terrace overlooking marshes, smart bedrooms and self-catering cottage, open all day (food all day weekends). *(Richard Tilbrook, Guy Vowles, Philippa Ward)*

SINGLETON SU8713

Partridge (01243) 811251

Just off A286 Midhurst–Chichester; PO18 0EY Pretty 16th-c pub in attractive village setting; all sorts of light and dark wood tables and dining chairs on polished wood floors, flagstones or carpet, some country knick-knacks, open fires and woodburner, well kept Fullers London Pride, Harveys Best and a summer guest, several wines by the glass, tasty food (all day Sat, till 6pm Sun) from sandwiches and baked potatoes up, cream teas (must book), friendly welcoming service; background and live music, monthly quiz, daily papers and board games, free wi-fi; children and dogs welcome, plenty of seats under parasols on terrace and in walled garden (may ask for a credit card if you eat outside), handy for Weald & Downland Living Museum, open all day. *(John Evans, Simon Collett-Jones)*

SLINDON SU9708

Spur (01243) 814216

Slindon Common; A29 towards Bognor; BN18 0NE Roomy 17th-c pub with well kept ales and good choice of popular food from bar snacks up, friendly staff, pine tables and two big log fires, large panelled restaurant, games room with darts and pool, also a skittle alley; quiz fourth Weds of month, some live music; children welcome, dogs in bar, pretty garden (some traffic noise), good local walks, open all day Sun. *(Tony and Wendy Hobden)*

SMALL DOLE TQ2112

Fox (01273) 491196

Henfield Road; BN5 9XE Busy roadside village pub with good choice of well liked/priced home-made food including popular weekday set menu, quick friendly service even at busy times, well kept Harveys and one or two guests, large dining area off roomy panelled bar, dark pubby furniture on patterned carpet, hunting pictures; quiet background music; children and dogs welcome, disabled access, colourful hanging baskets and good-sized tree-shaded garden with play area, open all day weekends (food all day Sun till 8pm). *(Tony and Wendy Hobden)*

SOMPTING TQ1605

Marquis of Granby (01903) 231102

West Street; BN15 0AP Large 1930s pub with well kept ales including Sharps and good reasonably priced food from baguettes up, themed nights, friendly welcoming staff, part-flagstoned lounge with raised dining area; pool, darts, TV and fruit machine in sports bar; children and dogs welcome, garden with picnic-sets, play area and marquee, open all day, no food Sun evening. *(Nigel and Jean Eames)*

SOUTH HARTING SU7819

★**White Hart** (01730) 825124

B2146 SE of Petersfield; GU31 5QB Sympathetically renovated 16th-c village inn; bars and dining area with beams and standing timbers, a couple of woodburners and open fire, nice mix of furniture on bare boards or flagstones, candles and fresh flowers, well kept Upham ales and a guest, real cider, 17 wines by the glass (from Berry Brothers of London) and a dozen malt whiskies, good food including lunchtime set menu, pleasant service; live music and quiz nights; children and dogs (in bar) welcome, terrace and garden tables, handy for Uppark (NT), comfortable character bedrooms, open all day, breakfast for non-residents. *(Douglas*

All *Guide* inspections are anonymous. Anyone claiming to be a *Good Pub Guide* inspector is a fraud. Please let us know.

Power, Anne and Ben Smith, Daphne and Robert Staples, John Evans, Simon Collett-Jones)

SOUTHWATER TQ1528

Bax Castle (01403) 730369

Two Mile Ash, a mile or so NW; RH13 0LA Early 19th-c country pub with well liked/priced home-made food including wood-fired pizzas and Sun carvery, three Marstons-related ales, friendly staff, sofas next to big log fire, barn restaurant; background music; children and dogs welcome, pleasant garden with play area, near Downs Link path on former railway track, shuts 6pm Sun, otherwise open (and food) all day. *(John and Delia Franks)*

STAPLEFIELD TQ2728

Jolly Tanners (01444) 400335

Handcross Road, just off A23; RH17 6EF Split-level local by cricket green, welcoming landlord and pub dogs, two good log fires, padded settles and lots of china, brasses and old photographs, Harveys and guests (beer festivals), real cider, enjoyable pubby food including burgers and 'sizzling' dishes, friendly chatty atmosphere; background and some live music, Thurs quiz; children and dogs welcome, attractive suntrap garden, quite handy for Nymans (NT), open all day Fri-Sun, food till 7pm Sun. *(Tony Scott, Tony and Wendy Hobden)*

STAPLEFIELD TQ2728

Victory (01444) 400463

Warninglid Road; RH17 6EU Pretty little shuttered dining pub overlooking cricket green (and London to Brighton veteran car run, first Sun in Nov); friendly welcoming staff, good choice of popular home-made food (all day Sat, till 5pm Sun) with smaller helpings for children, well kept Harveys Best and a guest, local cider and decent wines from zinc-topped counter, beams and woodburner; dogs welcome in bar, nice tree-shaded garden with play area, closed Mon, otherwise open all day. *(Ian Phillips, Tony and Wendy Hobden)*

STEDHAM SU8522

Hamilton Arms (01730) 812555

School Lane (off A272); GU29 0NZ Village local run by friendly thai family; standard pub food as well as popular thai bar snacks and restaurant dishes (you can buy ingredients in their little shop), reasonably priced wines and four or more well kept ales; background and occasional live music; pretty hanging baskets on front terrace overlooking small green, nearby walks, open all day Thurs-Sun, closed Mon. *(Colin and Daniel Gibbs)*

STOPHAM TQ0318

White Hart (01798) 874903

Off A283 E of village, W of Pulborough; RH20 1DS Fine old beamed pub by medieval River Arun bridge; well kept Harveys, Sharps and a guest, generally well liked food from sandwiches, sharing plates and stone-baked pizzas up; some live music; children and dogs (in bar) welcome, waterside tables, open all day, no food Sun evening. *(Rupert and Sandy Newton)*

STOUGHTON SU8011

Hare & Hounds (023) 9263 1433

Signed off B2146 Petersfield–Emsworth; PO18 9JQ Airy pine-clad country dining pub with good reasonably priced food from sandwiches to Sun roasts, up to six well kept ales and Weston's cider, cheerful service, flagstones and big open fires, locals' bar with darts; quiz nights; children (in eating areas) and dogs welcome, tables on pretty front terrace and grass behind, lovely setting near Saxon church, good walks, open all day. *(Ann and Colin Hunt, Tony and Jill Radnor)*

THAKEHAM TQ1017

White Lion (01798) 813141

Off B2139 N of Storrington; The Street; RH20 3EP Steps up to 16th-c pub in pretty village; heavy beams, panelling, bare boards and traditional furnishings, four changing ales including Fullers and decent wines by the glass, well liked food (not Sun evening) including good selection of blackboard specials, efficient service, pleasant dining room with inglenook; children and dogs welcome, sunny terrace and small enclosed lawn, open all day. *(David Jackman)*

TICEHURST TQ6831

★**Bull** (01580) 200586

Three Leg Cross; off B2099 towards Wadhurst; TN5 7HH Attractive 14th-c country pub popular with good mix of customers; big log fires in two heavy-beamed old-fashioned bars, well kept Harveys and a couple of guests, contemporary furnishings in light airy dining extension serving good food, friendly service; children and dogs welcome, charming front garden (busy in summer), bigger back one with play area, good PYO fruit farm nearby, four bedrooms, open all day. *(P Beardsell)*

TURNERS HILL TQ3435

★**Red Lion** (01342) 715416

Lion Lane, just off B2028; RH10 4NU Old-fashioned, unpretentious and welcoming country local; snug parquet-floored bar with plush wall benches and small open fire, steps up to carpeted dining area with inglenook log fire, cushioned pews and settles, old photos and brewery memorabilia, well kept Harveys ales and good home-made food (lunchtime only – must book Sun); occasional live music including open mike nights, fortnightly quiz; children (away from bar) and dogs welcome, picnic-sets on side grass overlooking village, open all day weekends. *(Katherine Matthews)*

UDIMORE TQ8818

Plough (01797) 223381
Cock Marling (B2089 W of Rye); TN31 6AL Popular refurbished and extended 17th-c roadside pub; enjoyable freshly made food including tapas and good steaks, meal deals Weds and Thurs evenings, well kept Harveys, Long Man and Three Legs, good choice of wines by the glass, friendly welcoming staff, U-shaped bar with wood and quarry-tiled floors, fairy lights on beams, two woodburners; Fri happy hour (5.30-7pm) followed by live music; children and dogs welcome, tables on good-sized sunny back terrace, Brede Valley views, self-catering apartment, closed Sun evening. *(Mike and Eleanor Anderson)*

UPPER DICKER TQ5409

Plough (01323) 844859
Coldharbour Road; BN27 3QJ Extended 17th-c pub with small central beamed bar, seats by inglenook, two restaurant areas off to the left and step up to larger dining bar on right with raised section, well kept Harveys and Shepherd Neame, enjoyable food from pubby choices up, friendly young staff; background and occasional live music, free wi-fi; children and dogs welcome, spacious garden with play area, open all day. *(Nigel and Jean Eames)*

WALBERTON SU9705

Holly Tree (01243) 553110
The Street; BN18 0PH Grey-painted 19th-c village pub with fun quirky décor, enjoyable food from sandwiches up (not Sun evening), themed food nights and various deals, friendly young staff; live music and quiz nights; children and dogs welcome, café-style furniture and planters on front terrace, open all day. *(Suzy Miller)*

WALDERTON SU7910

Barley Mow (023) 9263 1321
Stoughton Road, just off B2146 Chichester–Petersfield; PO18 9ED Popular red-brick country pub with well liked food including Sun carvery, ales such as Adnams, Ringwood and Sharps, friendly welcoming staff, two log fires in U-shaped bar with roomy dining areas; skittle alley; children and dogs welcome, big streamside back garden, good walks (Kingley Vale nearby) and handy for Stansted Park, open all day weekends, food till 4pm Sun. *(Ann and Colin Hunt, Tony and Jill Radnor)*

WALDRON TQ5419

★**Star** (01435) 812495
Blackboys–Horam side road; TN21 0RA Pretty pub in quiet village across from the church; beamed main bar with settle next to good log fire in brick inglenook, wheelbacks around pubby tables on old quarry tiles, several built-in cushioned wall and window seats, old local pictures and photographs, high stools by central counter serving well kept Harveys, Sharps and a guest, maybe own apple juice, good food (not Sun evening) including bar snacks, pubby dishes and specials, dining areas with painted chairs around pine-topped tables on parquet or bare boards, bookshelf wallpaper, chatty local atmosphere and friendly staff; occasional quiz, live music and comedy nights; picnic-sets in pleasant back garden, small café and shop next door. *(PL)*

WARBLETON TQ6018

★**Black Duck** (01435) 830636
S of B2096 SE of Heathfield; TN21 9BD Friendly licensees at this small renovated pub tucked down from church; L-shaped main room with pale oak flooring, cushioned leather sofas in front of inglenook log fire, beams and walls hung with horsebrasses, tankards, musical instruments, farm tools, even an old typewriter, high-backed dining chairs around mix of tables, good pubby food including daily specials, bar area up a step with stools along counter, Harveys and a guest, nice wines by the glass, cabinet of books and board games; background and occasional live music; picnic-sets in back garden with sweeping valley views, more on front grass, open all day Fri-Sat, closed Mon. *(Robin and Anna Triggs)*

WARNHAM TQ1533

Greets (01403) 265047
Friday Street; RH12 3QY Welcoming 15th-c beamed pub with appealing simple décor, stripped pine tables on uneven flagstones, inglenook log fire, lots of nooks and corners, well kept Harveys and a dozen wines by the glass, good choice of fairly traditional food at sensible prices, friendly helpful staff, convivial locals' side bar with leather ceiling straps; children welcome, garden tables, open (and food) all day weekends. *(Mike and Marion Higgins)*

WARNHAM TQ1533

Sussex Oak (01403) 265028
Just off A24 Horsham–Dorking; Church Street; RH12 3QW Cheerfully busy country pub with heavy beams and timbers, mix of flagstones, tiles, wood and carpeting, big inglenook log fire, well kept Fullers, Harveys, Timothy Taylors and guests from carved servery, real cider and plenty of wines by the glass, enjoyable fairly traditional food (smaller helpings available); background music, Thurs quiz, darts, free wi-fi; children and dogs welcome, disabled facilities/parking, picnic-sets in large garden, good local walks, open all day, food all day weekends. *(Tony Scott, Tony and Wendy Hobden)*

WARTLING TQ6509

★**Lamb** (01323) 832116
Village signed with Herstmonceux Castle off A271 Herstmonceux–Battle;

BN27 1RY Popular family-owned country pub; small entrance bar with open fireplace, Harveys Best and a couple of local guests, several wines by the glass from good list, two-level beamed and timbered dining room to the left with inglenook woodburner, bigger back bar and restaurant, well liked food including blackboard specials, friendly service; children and dogs welcome, steps up to garden with chunky seats, five bedrooms, closed Sun evening, otherwise open all day. *(Edward Edmonton, Bob)*

WEST ASHLING SU8007

Richmond Arms (01243) 572046

Just off B2146; Mill Road; PO18 8EA Village dining pub in quiet pretty setting near big millpond with ducks and geese; highly regarded imaginative food (quite pricey, best to book) from bar snacks up, also wood-fired pizzas cooked in a vintage van (Fri, Sat evenings), well kept Harveys ales and good wines by the glass, competent friendly staff; children welcome, two nice bedrooms, closed Sun evening, Mon and Tues. *(Tracey and Stephen Groves)*

WEST MARDEN SU7713

Victoria (02392) 631330

B2146 2 miles S of Uppark; PO18 9EN Friendly village pub popular with downland walkers; good traditional food (not Sun evening) in beamed bar and small back restaurant, well kept Langham and guests (beer festivals), log fire; occasional live music; children and dogs welcome, attractive garden, open all day weekends, closed Mon (except bank holidays). *(Tony and Jill Radnor)*

WEST WITTERING SZ8099

Lamb (01243) 511105

Chichester Road; B2179/A286 towards Birdham; PO20 8QA Modernised 18th-c tile-hung country pub; three Badger ales and enjoyable home-cooked food including popular Sun roasts (booking advised), friendly capable staff, bar with painted beams and timbers, assorted furniture on wood floor including kitchen chairs and scrubbed pine tables, woodburner in brick fireplace, two bare-boards dining rooms with some interesting artwork; background music; children and dogs welcome, tables out in front and in small sheltered back garden with play area, open all day Fri-Sun, food all day Sun. *(Ben Wright)*

WESTFIELD TQ8115

New Inn (01424) 752800

Main Road; TN35 4QE Popular village pub with light open-plan interior, pubby furniture including wheelback and captain's chairs on pale wood floors, sparsely decorated white walls, conservatory, four or five mainly local ales including Harveys, enjoyable reasonably priced home-made food from weekly changing menu (till 7pm Sun, not Mon evening), cheerful helpful staff; free wi-fi; children and dogs welcome, disabled access, seats out on gravel terrace, open all day. *(Caroline Prescott)*

WILMINGTON TQ5404

Giants Rest (01323) 870207

Just off A27; BN26 5SQ Early 20th-c country pub under new management; long wood-floored bar with adjacent open areas, simple furniture, rural pictures and log fire, Long Man and a couple of local guests, South Downs cider (made in the village), enjoyable pubby food including good home-made pies, friendly service; wooden puzzles and games; children and dogs welcome, picnic-sets on front grass, surrounded by South Downs walks and village famous for chalk-carved Long Man, two bedrooms, open (and food) all day, kitchen may shut early Sun evening if quiet. *(John Beeken, Richard Kennell, Mrs J Ekins-Daukes)*

WINEHAM TQ2320

★**Royal Oak** (01444) 881252

Village signposted from A272 and B2116; BN5 9AY Splendidly old-fashioned local with log fire in big inglenook, Harveys Best and guests tapped from stillroom casks, enjoyable home-cooked food (not Sun evening), jugs and ancient corkscrews on very low beams, collection of cigarette boxes and old bottles, various stuffed animals including a stoat and crocodile, more bric-a-brac and old local photographs in back parlour with views of quiet countryside; occasional folk music and morris men; children away from bar and dogs welcome, picnic-sets out at front, closed evenings 25 and 26 Dec, 1 Jan. *(Tony Scott)*

WISBOROUGH GREEN TQ0626

Bat & Ball (01403) 700199

Newpound Lane; RH14 0EH Refurbished 18th-c red-brick Badger dining pub set in six-acre grounds; their ales and 20 wines by the glass including champagne from counter faced in wine boxes, short but varied choice of well liked food, afternoon teas, connecting beamed rooms with cosy corners and plenty of rustic charm including high-raftered restaurant, quiz nights; children and dogs (in bar) welcome, pretty garden with pond at front, camping and shepherd's huts, handy for Fishers Farm Park, open all day (till 8pm Sun). *(Sally and John Quinlan)*

WISBOROUGH GREEN TQ0526

Cricketers Arms (01403) 700369

Loxwood Road, just off A272 Billingshurst–Petworth; RH14 0DG Attractive old pub on edge of village green; well kept ales such as Harveys, St Austell and Sharps, good choice of fairly priced food (not Mon evening) including specials, gluten-free diets catered for, cheerful staff, open-plan with two big woodburners and pleasing mix of country furniture on parquet flooring, stripped-brick dining area on left; some live music; children welcome, tables out in front, annual lawn mower race on the green. *(Tony Scott, Tony and Wendy Hobden)*

WISBOROUGH GREEN TQ0525

Three Crowns (01403) 700239

Billingshurst Road (A272); RH14 0DX Family-run beamed village pub with rather quirky décor; enjoyable freshly made food (all day Sat) from open sandwiches, sharing boards and pub favourites up, prompt friendly service, well kept Harveys, Shepherd Neame and four guests, extensive choice of wines by the glass including champagne and good range of gins, afternoon teas; quiz first Weds of month; children and dogs welcome (pub dog is Ted), sizeable tree-shaded back garden, closed Tues, otherwise open all day (till 9pm Sun). *(Bob and Melissa Wyatt)*

WIVELSFIELD GREEN TQ3519

Cock (01444) 471668

North Common Road; RH17 7RH Pleasant red-brick village pub; good choice of enjoyable reasonably priced food including themed nights, Harveys and guests, helpful friendly staff, two bars and restaurant, log fire; monthly quiz night, darts, bar billiards, pool and sports TV; children, walkers and dogs welcome, seats out at front and in back garden, open all day, food all day Fri and Sat, till 8pm Sun. *(Ruth and Peter Bacon)*

WOODMANCOTE SU7707

Woodmancote (01243) 371019

The one near Emsworth; Woodmancote Lane; PO10 8RD Village pub with unusual contemporary décor – plenty of quirky touches; good popular food (best to book) from sandwiches and sharing boards up, weekly themed nights, three real ales including one badged for them and several wines by the glass, restaurant; regular quiz nights; children and dogs (in bar) welcome, seats out under cover, open (and food) all day from 9.30am for breakfast, kitchen shuts 7pm Sun. *(Peter Pilbeam)*

WORTHING TQ1502

Corner House (01903) 216463

High Street; BN11 1DJ Refurbished and extended pub with bright modern interior; comfortable seating including some sofas around three sides of central bar, four real ales, craft beers and good range of wines marked up on blackboard, enjoyable reasonably priced food, may ask for a credit card if you run a tab; quiz Mon; children and dogs welcome, paved and heated back terrace, open all day, no food Sun evening. *(Tony and Wendy Hobden)*

WORTHING TQ1402

Egremont (01903) 600064

Brighton Road; BN11 3ED Restored 19th-c pub near seafront; up to six real ales including Harveys and a couple from Goldmark badged for them, good range of interesting gins, enjoyable reasonably priced pubby food from ciabattas and sharing plates up, friendly helpful staff, split-level mainly bare-boards interior arranged around central bar, one part laid for dining, mix of furniture including button-back banquettes, stools, sofas and some high tables, original Kemptown Brewery stained glass, old enamel signs and other interesting bits and pieces; quiz and live music nights, TV for major sports; children and dogs welcome, pavement picnic-sets, open all day. *(Tony and Wendy Hobden)*

WORTHING TQ1502

Selden Arms (01903) 234854

Lyndhurst Road, between Waitrose and hospital; BN11 2DB Friendly unchanging 19th-c backstreet local opposite the gasworks; welcoming long-serving licensees, six well kept ales, craft kegs and extensive range of bottled belgian beers (Jan beer festival), bargain lunchtime food (not Sun) including doorstep sandwiches and various pies, regular curry nights, seafood Fri, comfortably worn interior with photographs of old Worthing pubs, pump clips on ceiling, log fire; occasional live music and quiz nights, darts; dogs welcome, open all day. *(Tony and Wendy Hobden)*

Warwickshire

with Birmingham and West Midlands

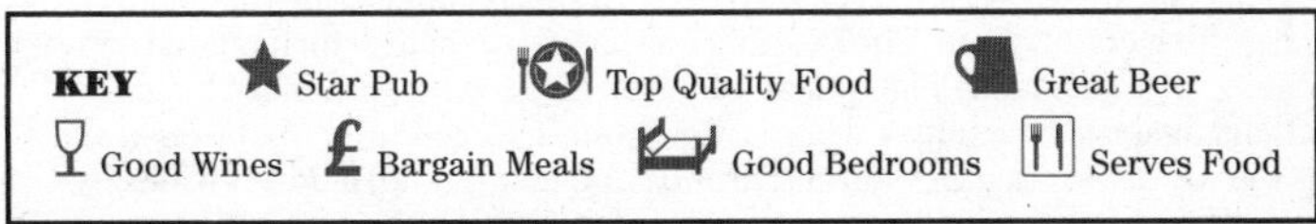

ALDERMINSTER SP2348 Map 4

Bell

(01789) 450414 – www.thebellald.co.uk

A3400 Oxford–Stratford; CV37 8NY

18th-c inn with sympathetically modernised character bars, a two-storey restaurant, excellent modern cooking and thoughtful choice of drinks; bedrooms

Just a few miles from Stratford, this is a civilised Georgian coaching inn in the middle of an attractive village surrounded by lovely countryside. The open-plan rooms cleverly manage to create a contemporary feel that fits in well with the many original features: beams, standing timbers, flagstoned or wooden floors and open fires. The bustling bar serves Alscot Ale (named for the pub from North Cotswold), North Cotswold Shagweaver and Purity Pure UBU on handpump, a dozen wines by the glass and cocktails. The bar is comfortably furnished with a mix of traditional wooden chairs and tables, upholstered sofas, armchairs in front of open fires, high bar chairs by the blue-painted counter and daily papers; background music. The two-storey restaurant is stylish and modern. The lower floor, with stunning chandeliers, is decorated in soft pastels and silvers and has folding doors leading directly to the terrace, while the upper floor has attractive chairs around polished copper tables on dark floorboards, seats on a balcony and panoramic views across the Stour Valley; there's also a private dining room with its own decked area and lawn. An appealing courtyard and gardens have seats and tables looking over water meadows and the lovely valley. The individually decorated, boutique-style bedrooms are well equipped and comfortable.

Appetising food includes lunchtime sandwiches and grazing boards, crispy beef with asian slaw and sticky soy dressing, crayfish and lobster cakes with guacamole and smoked chilli mayonnaise, stuffed pitta with bean and courgette fritters and tzatziki, beer-battered cod and chips, chicken suprême with crispy prosciutto, dauphinoise potatoes, chorizo mousse and red wine jus, hake fillet, mussel and sweetcorn chowder with pak choi, rib-eye steak with peppercorn sauce and chips or sweet potato fries, and puddings such as lemon drizzle cake with vanilla custard and rhubarb eton mess; they also offer a two- and three-course weekday menu. *Benchmark main dish: lamb cutlets and sweetbreads with hispi cabbage, parmentier potatoes and jus £21.50. Two-course evening meal £25.00.*

Free house ~ Licensee Emma Holman-West ~ Real ale ~ Open 9am-11pm ~ Bar food 12-2.30, 6.30-9 (9.30 Fri, Sat); 12-3, 6.30-8.30 Sun ~ Restaurant ~ Children welcome ~ Dogs allowed in bar ~ Wi-fi ~ Bedrooms: £75/£100 *Recommended by Dr and Mrs A K Clarke, William and Sophia Renton, Mitchell Cregor, Julie and Andrew Blanchett, Victoria and James Sargeant*

ARMSCOTE SP2444 Map 4

Fuzzy Duck

(01608) 682635 – www.fuzzyduckarmscote.com

Off A3400 Stratford–Shipston; CV37 8DD

Interestingly refurbished former coaching inn with real ales, a good wine list, inventive food and seats outside; bedrooms

This is a smart, gently civilised place in a pretty hamlet surrounded by rolling countryside. The bustling bar has an open fire, high chunky leather chairs around equally high metal tables on flagstones, with more leather chairs against the counter where friendly staff serve Purity Mad Goose and a weekly guest such as Church Farm IPA on handpump, a dozen wines by the glass, 12 malt whiskies and a farm cider; a wall of glass-faced boxes holds bottles of spirits belonging to regular customers. Three interconnected dining rooms have a mix of dark wooden tables surrounded by leather and other elegant chairs on pale floorboards, a sofa here and there and a two-way woodburning stove in an open fireplace. Throughout, cartoons and arty photographs hang on pale or dark grey walls and flowers are arranged in big vases; background music and board games. At the back, another dining room (also used for private parties) leads to a decked terrace with basket-weave armchairs, cushioned sofas and small modern metal chairs and tables under big parasols; there's also a small lawn with fruit trees. Bedrooms (each named after a species of duck) are extremely comfortable, well equipped and pretty and make a perfect base for exploring the area.

Impressive food from seasonal menus includes sandwiches, lobster and crab thermidor tart with avocado purée, scotch duck egg with smoked bacon, parsley and creamed peas, pasta with roasted red peppers, spinach, black olives and pesto, beer-battered cod and chips, free-range chicken breast kiev with warm potato salad and sweetcorn, sea bass fillet with crab cake, kohlrabi, pak choi, tahini and soy dressing, dry-aged local sirloin steak with truffle and parmesan chips and café de paris sauce, and puddings such as chocolate éclair with chocolate cream, dulce de leche and coffee ice-cream and lemon curd and meringue tart with pistachios and crème fraîche ice-cream. *Benchmark main dish: roast lamb rump with panko-breadcrumbed breast, dauphinoise potatoes and confit cherry tomatoes £20.00. Two-course evening meal £25.00.*

Free house ~ Licensee Annabelle Lyall ~ Real ale ~ Open 10am-11pm; 11-5 Sun; closed Sun evening, Mon ~ Bar food 12-2.30, 6.30-9; 12-3 Sun ~ Restaurant ~ Children welcome ~ Dogs welcome ~ Wi-fi ~ Bedrooms: /£140 *Recommended by Miles Green, Charles Welch, Patricia Hawkins, Michael Doswell, Dr and Mrs A K Clarke, Ian Herdman, Dave Braisted*

BARSTON SP1978 Map 4

Malt Shovel

(01675) 443223 – www.themaltshovelatbarston.com

3 miles from M42 junction 5; A4141 towards Knowle, then first left into Jacobean Lane/Barston Lane; B92 0JP

Well run country dining pub full of happy customers, with an attractive layout, good service and seats in sheltered garden

Everything here is just right and our readers love their visits. Those just wanting a drink and a chat should head for the light and airy bar that rambles extensively around the zinc-topped central counter, with big terracotta floor tiles neatly offset by dark grouting, and cream, tan and blue paintwork. Black Sheep, Marstons Wainwright, Sharps Doom Bar and Wells Bombardier on handpump, 16 wines by the glass and 17 malt whiskies;

service is exemplary. Furnishings are comfortable, with informal dining chairs and scatter-cushioned pews around stripped-top tables of varying types and sizes, there are cheerful fruit and vegetable paintings on the walls, and french café-style shutters. The barn restaurant to the side is partially panelled with distressed dark grey paintwork that is topped with rows of pewter plates; background music. The sheltered back garden has a weeping willow and picnic-sets, and the terrace and verandah are furnished with cushioned teak seats and tables.

First class food includes chicken and chorizo patties with guacamole, tortilla chips and sour cream, pigeon breast with jerusalem artichoke purée, grapes and tarragon crisp, thai vegetable curry, confit duck leg with potato gratin and cider and orange marmalade, calves liver with mash and maple-roasted onions, parmesan-crusted veal schnitzel with a fried egg, capers and potato salad, halibut with roast parsnips, kale crisps and béarnaise sauce, and puddings such as blackberry and apple tart, pecan crumble and caramelita ice-cream and chocolate slice with nougat and chocolate orange sauce. *Benchmark main dish: salmon fishcake with spinach, a poached egg and tarragon hollandaise £14.95. Two-course evening meal £23.00.*

Free house ~ Licensee Helen Somerfield ~ Real ale ~ Open 12-midnight; 12-7 Sun ~ Bar food 12-2.30, 6-9.30; 12-4 Sun ~ Restaurant ~ Children welcome away from restaurant ~ Dogs allowed in bar *Recommended by Susan and John Douglas, Alison and Graeme Spicer, Ian Herdman, John and Claire Masters, Julia and Fiona Barnes*

BIRMINGHAM SP0686 Map 4

Old Joint Stock £

(0121) 200 1892 – www.oldjointstocktheatre.co.uk

Temple Row West; B2 5NY

Big bustling Fullers pie-and-ale pub with impressive Victorian façade and interior, and a small back terrace; own theatre

To find this extraordinary place, just head for the cathedral as the pub is opposite. It's all impressively flamboyant: chandeliers hang from the soaring pink and gilt ceiling, gently illuminated busts line the top of the ornately plastered walls and there's a splendid cupola above the centre of the room. Photographs of the historic building's past line the walls; there's also a big dining balcony reached up a grand sweeping staircase. The place is packed to the gunnels at peak times, but efficient staff manage to remain friendly and helpful, serving Fullers ESB, HSB, London Pride, Olivers Island and a guest such as Fixed Wheel Mild Concussion on handpump, 17 wines by the glass and 36 gins; background music. The small and colourful back terrace has nicely quirky seats and tables and heaters. Most nights there's something on in the purpose-built, first-floor theatre and you can book a two-course pre-theatre meal in advance.

As well as breakfast (9-11.30am), the popular food includes sandwiches, tapas-style small plates such as vietnamese spicy chicken wings, mini steak in ale pie and black pudding croquettes with apple purée plus pasta with tomatoes, spinach, rosemary and chilli breadcrumbs, beer-battered fish and chips, chicken breast with parsley potatoes, spinach and chorizo butter, burgers with toppings and triple-cooked chips, smoked haddock fishcakes with gribiche sauce, and puddings such as bakewell tart and chocolate brownie. *Benchmark main dish: steak in ale pie £13.95. Two-course evening meal £18.00.*

Fullers ~ Manager Paul Bancroft ~ Real ale ~ Open 8am-11pm; 9am-11pm Sat; 9-6 Sun; closed Sun evening ~ Bar food 9am-10pm; 9-4 Sun ~ Restaurant ~ Children allowed until 6pm ~ Wi-fi ~ Regular live entertainment in theatre (check website) *Recommended by Alan Johnson, Susan and John Douglas, Colin Gooch, Sandra and Neil White, Martine and Derek Cotton*

BIRMINGHAM SP0585 Map 4

Physician

(0121) 272 5900 – www.brunningandprice.co.uk/physician

Harborne Road, Edgbaston; B15 3DH

Substantial, extended pub with plenty of drinking and dining space, fantastic range of drinks including eight ales, interesting food and friendly atmosphere; seats outside

There's a lot of historical grandeur here and Brunning & Price have used the 19th-c rooms with their high ceilings and big sash windows to great effect. The interlinked areas of all shape and size have leather armchairs in front of open fires, a medley of cushioned wooden dining chairs and mate's chairs around polished solid tables on bare boards, rugs or carpet, lots of old prints on pale-painted walls, large gilt-edged mirrors and big house plants, stone bottles and books on shelves and lighting that ranges from table lamps to elegant metal chandeliers. Friendly, well trained staff serve Phoenix Brunning & Price Original plus Backyard The Hoard, Sadlers Worcester Sorcerer, Titanic Plum Porter and Wye Valley HPA on handpump, over 20 wines by the glass, 100 gins, 50 rums, 90 malt whiskies and farm cider; background music. Terraces have good quality wooden seats and tables under green parasols among flowering tubs and flower beds. The building once housed the Sampson Gamgee Library for the History of Medicine.

Brasserie-style food includes sandwiches, seared scallops with crispy ham fritters and pea purée, chicken liver pâté with carrot and apricot chutney, pumpkin tortellini with sunblush tomato and butternut squash velouté, steak burger with toppings, coleslaw and chips, steak in ale pudding, massaman king prawn, salmon and mussel curry, honey and chilli-glazed pork belly with red cabbage, apple and carrot salad, and puddings such as spiced plum and almond bakewell with cinnamon ice-cream and hot waffle with caramelised banana and ice-cream. *Benchmark main dish: braised lamb shoulder with dauphinoise potatoes, carrot mash and rosemary gravy £17.25. Two-course evening meal £21.00.*

Brunning & Price ~ Manager Lisa Rogers ~ Real ale ~ Open 10am-11pm (10.30pm Sun) ~ Bar food 12-10 (9 Sun) ~ Children welcome ~ Dogs allowed in bar ~ Wi-fi *Recommended by Chris and Sophie Baxter, Mandy and Gary Redstone, Audrey and Paul Summers, Peter and Emma Kelly, Freddie and Sarah Banks*

GAYDON SP3654 Map 4

Malt Shovel

(01926) 641221 – www.maltshovelgaydon.co.uk

Under a mile from M40 junction 12; B4451 into village, then over roundabout and across B4100; Church Road; CV35 0ET

Bustling pub in a quiet village with a nice mix of pubby bar and smarter restaurant

Customers come from far and wide to enjoy the rewarding food in this cheerful village pub. Varnished mahogany floorboards through to bright carpeting link the entrance with the bar counter to the right and a woodburning stove on the left. The central area has a high-pitched ceiling, milk churns and earthenware containers in a loft above the bar and three steps that lead up to a space with comfortable sofas overlooked by a big stained-glass window; reproductions of classic posters line the walls. Fullers London Pride, Sharps Doom Bar and Timothy Taylors Landlord on handpump, with 11 wines by the glass and two farm ciders. A busy dining area has fresh flowers on a mix of kitchen, pub and dining tables; background music, darts. The pub's jack russell is called Mollie.

Cooked by the landlord, the well regarded food includes lunchtime sandwiches and baguettes, smoked haddock welsh rarebit, pâté with plum and apple chutney, omelettes, goats cheese and pesto cannelloni with cherry tomatoes and basil, battered haddock and chips, gammon and egg, beef casserole with horseradish and dijon mustard mash, 8oz sirloin steak with a choice of sauce and chips, and puddings such as lemon cheesecake and sticky toffee pudding with cream. *Benchmark main dish: pie of the day £12.95. Two-course evening meal £17.00.*

Enterprise ~ Lease Richard and Debi Morisot ~ Real ale ~ Open 11-3, 5-11; 11-11 Fri, Sat; 12-10.30 Sun ~ Bar food 12-2, 6-9 ~ Restaurant ~ Children welcome ~ Dogs allowed in bar ~ Wi-fi *Recommended by Tony Smaithe, John Watson, Frances and Hamish Porter, Frank and Marcia Pelling, John Evans, Rob Anderson*

HAMPTON-IN-ARDEN SP2080 Map 4

White Lion

(01675) 442833 – www.thewhitelioninn.com

High Street; handy for M42 junction 6; B92 0AA

Popular village local with a good choice of ales; bedrooms

Opposite a church mentioned in the Domesday Book, this former farmhouse has a good choice of real ales. On handpump there might be Banks's Sunbeam, Hobsons Best, M&B Brew XI, St Austell Proper Job, Sharps Doom Bar and Wye Valley HPA and they stock 12 wines by the glass and two farm ciders. The carpeted bar is nice and relaxed, with a mix of furniture tidily laid out, neatly curtained small windows, low-beamed ceilings and some local memorabilia on the cream-painted walls; background music, TV and board games. The modern dining areas are fresh and airy with light wood and cane chairs on stripped floorboards. Bedrooms are quiet and comfortable.

Traditional food includes lunchtime sandwiches, honey and mustard ham hock terrine with apple chutney, moules of the day, sharing boards, mushroom and pesto linguine with garlic bread, chicken with bacon, cheese and barbecue sauce, beer-battered cod and chips, beef bourguignon, slow-cooked lamb shank with mash and red wine gravy, and puddings such as chocolate brownie with vanilla ice-cream and sticky toffee pudding with custard. *Benchmark main dish: home-made pies £10.95. Two-course evening meal £17.00.*

Free house ~ Licensee Chris Roach ~ Real ale ~ Open 12-11 (10.30 Sun) ~ Bar food 12-2.30, 6-9; 12-4 Sun ~ Restaurant ~ Children welcome ~ Dogs welcome ~ Wi-fi ~ Bedrooms: £90/£100 *Recommended by Dr and Mrs A K Clarke, Andrew Wall, Gerry and Pam Pollard, Charlie Stevens, Moira and Jon Weller*

HUNNINGHAM SP3768 Map 4

Red Lion

(01926) 632715 – www.redlionhunningham.co.uk

Village signposted off B4453 Leamington–Rugby just E of Weston, and off B4455 Fosse Way 2.5 miles SW of A423 junction; CV33 9DY

Civilised and friendly place, with a good range of drinks and well liked food

Friendly and easy-going, the light, open-plan interior here has been cleverly divided up and appealingly furnished. There are pews with scatter cushions, an assortment of antique dining chairs and stools around nice polished tables on bare boards (with a few big rugs here and there) and contemporary paintwork. A cosy room has tub armchairs around an open coal fire. They keep a beer named for the pub, Purity Pure UBU, Stratford

Upon Avon Stratford Mosaic and Wye Valley Bitter on handpump, 17 wines by the glass and 40 malt whiskies; background music. Picnic-sets in the garden are much prized as they look across to the arched 14th-c bridge over the River Leam. There's a basket of rugs for customers to take outside and more picnic-sets are provided out at the front.

Quite a choice of popular food includes sandwiches (until 3pm), scallops of the day, fried foie gras with grenadine and rhubarb chutney, sharing platters, roast butternut squash and red bean chilli with sour cream, beer-battered fish and chips, burger with toppings and chips, whole lemon sole with samphire and lemon caper butter, beef bourguignon, confit duck leg with sweet potato fondant and red wine jus, steak frites, and puddings such as potted chocolate mousse with honeycomb and apple and rhubarb crumble with custard. *Benchmark main dish: cassoulet £13.50. Two-course evening meal £20.00.*

Free house ~ Licensee Richard Merand ~ Real ale ~ Open 11-11 (10.30 Sun) ~ Bar food 12-9 ~ Restaurant ~ Children welcome ~ Dogs allowed in bar ~ Wi-fi *Recommended by Jeremy Snaithe, Sandra King, Dr and Mrs A K Clarke, Belinda and Neil Garth, Buster May, Jane Rigby*

ILMINGTON SP2143 Map 4

Howard Arms

(01608) 682226 – www.howardarms.com

Village signed with Wimpstone off A3400 S of Stratford; CV36 4LT

Lovely mellow-toned interior, lots to look at and tasty food and drink; bedrooms

After enjoying one of the nearby hill walks, come to this golden-stone inn for refreshment. The various beamed and flagstoned rooms have a pleasing mix of furniture ranging from pews and rustic stools to leather dining chairs around all sorts of tables, rugs on bare boards, shelves of books, candles and a log fire in a big inglenook. Purity Mad Goose, Stratford Upon Avon Stratford Gold, Timothy Taylors Landlord and Wye Valley HPA on handpump, 14 wines by the glass, a fair choice of whiskies and brandies, and local cider; background music and board games. The big back garden has seats under parasols and a colourful herbaceous border. Bedrooms are well equipped and comfortable and the breakfasts highly regarded.

As well as lunchtime sandwiches (not Sunday), the likeable food includes trout gravadlax with potato salad, a quail egg and horseradish crème fraîche, ham hock terrine with plum chutney, asparagus risotto with parmesan and herb oil, duck breast with wild garlic potato cake, beetroot, mushrooms and jus, lamb leg steak with rosemary-crushed potatoes, cherry tomatoes and pak choi, fillet of salmon with butternut squash, creamy mash and sorrel velouté, and puddings such as pistachio crème brûlée and chocolate and ginger pot with ginger ice-cream. *Benchmark main dish: calves liver £15.00. Two-course evening meal £22.00.*

Free house ~ Licensee Pawel Sobiszek ~ Real ale ~ Open 10am-11pm (10pm Sun) ~ Bar food 12-2.30, 6-9.15; 12-7.30 Sun ~ Restaurant ~ Children welcome ~ Dogs allowed in bar ~ Wi-fi ~ Bedrooms: /£110 *Recommended by Geoff and Ann Marston, Alan and Alice Morgan, Chantelle and Tony Redman, Ian Herdman, Matt and Hayley Jacob*

'Children welcome' means the pub says it lets children inside without any special restriction. If it allows them in, but to restricted areas such as an eating area or family room, we specify this. Some pubs may impose an evening time limit. We do not mention limits after 9pm as we assume children are home by then.

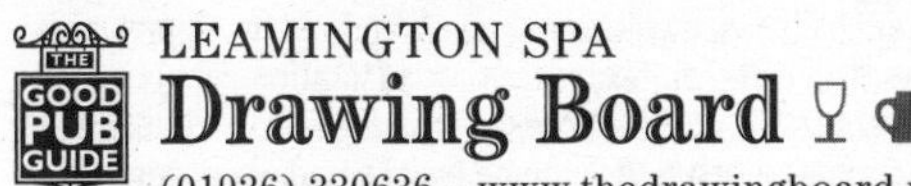

LEAMINGTON SPA SP3265 Map 4

Drawing Board

(01926) 330636 – www.thedrawingboard.pub

Newbold Street; CV32 4HN

Town-centre pub with interesting, quirky décor, a thoughtful choice of food and drinks; good fun

This place is at the centre of town, so there's a cheerful, bustling atmosphere helped along by a first class landlord. Set out over two floors, there are some intriguing design features plus rugs on bare boards, flagstones, leather sofas and chesterfields, mismatched dining chairs and rustic tables interspersed with contemporary furniture, large house plants, antlers, several woodburning stoves and even a bike. But it's the framed vintage comic books on the grey walls and shelves of old-fashioned boys' and girls' annuals that are really worth looking at, along with some pop art and neon lighting. Deya Just A Glimmer, Magic Rock Ringmaster, Old Pie Factory Elephant Wash and Purity Bunny Hop on handpump, several craft ales, 18 wines by the glass, 80 malt whiskies, 30 gins, 26 bourbons, 120 rums and farm cider, all served by friendly, young staff; background music, TV, a retro arcade games machine and board games.

Well executed and inventive, the food includes sandwiches (until 3pm), curry-cured salmon with saffron mooli, molasses emulsion and pomegranate, chicken liver mousse with spiced rambutan and lotus root chips, tomato, feta, olive and basil risotto, chargrilled rare-breed burger with toppings, onion dipping stew and french fries, roast cod with couscous, tataki sauce (ginger, spring onion, soy, sesame and lime) and maple butter, grass-fed short rib of beef with wild mushrooms, onions and red wine sauce, and puddings such as warm chocolate fondant tart with pistachio ice-cream and steam ginger crème brûlée and poached rhubarb. *Benchmark main dish: calves liver with pickled shallot mash, pancetta and crackling crumble £16.50. Two-course evening meal £21.00.*

Free house ~ Licensee Sam Cornwall Jones ~ Real ale ~ Open 11-11; 12-9.30 Sun ~ Bar food 12-3, 5.30-9.30; 12-9.30 Sat; 12-6 Sun ~ Restaurant ~ Children welcome ~ Dogs welcome ~ Wi-fi *Recommended by Chris and Sophie Baxter, Charlie and Mark Todd, Bridget and Peter Gregson, Philip J Alderton, Alf and Sally Garner*

LONG COMPTON SP2832 Map 4

Red Lion

(01608) 684221 – www.redlion-longcompton.co.uk

A3400 S of Shipston-on-Stour; CV36 5JS

Traditional character and contemporary touches in comfortably furnished coaching inn; bedrooms

As one of our readers put it: 'This is a lovely place where the original character has been enhanced rather than swept away.' The roomy, charmingly furnished lounge bar has some exposed stone and beams and nice rambling corners with cushioned settles among pleasantly assorted and comfortable seats and leather armchairs; there are tables on flagstones and carpets, animal prints on warm paintwork and both an open fire and a woodburning stove. Friendly, attentive staff serve Hook Norton Hooky and Wickwar Cotswold Way with a guest such as Brains Rev James on handpump, a dozen wines by the glass and summer farm cider. The chocolate labrador is called Cocoa. The simple public bar has darts, pool, a juke box and a TV; background music. There are tables out in the large back garden, with a play area. Bedrooms are spotlessly kept, quiet and pretty and breakfasts are particularly good.

Enjoyable food includes sandwiches, warm goats cheese and red onion tart with beetroot and watercress salad, cajun chicken caesar salad, stuffed peppers with wild mushrooms, spinach and toasted hazelnut couscous and tomato and tarragon sauce, chargrilled burger with toppings, horseradish crème fraîche and chips, teriyaki salmon with noodles, sautéed pak choi, chilli and prawns, bacon-wrapped chicken breast stuffed with spinach and blue cheese with creamed leeks, and puddings such as steamed spotted dick with apples, brandy and custard and baked vanilla cheesecake with poached blackcurrants; they also offer a two- and three-course weekday set menu (until 7pm). *Benchmark main dish: steak in ale pie £15.00. Two-course evening meal £22.00.*

Cropthorne Inns ~ Manager Lisa Phipps ~ Real ale ~ Open 10am-11pm ~ Bar food 12-2.30, 6-9; 12-9.30 Fri, Sat; 12-9 Sun ~ Children welcome ~ Dogs welcome ~ Wi-fi ~ Bedrooms: £65/£100 *Recommended by J A Snell, Michael Doswell, Tracey and Stephen Groves, Mitchell Cregor, Alun and Jennifer Evans, Steve Whalley, Trevor Crowther, Paul Faraday, Sarah Roberts*

SHIPSTON-ON-STOUR SP2540 Map 4

Black Horse

(01608) 238489 – www.blackhorseshipston.com

Station Road (off A3400); CV36 4BT

16th-c pub with simple country furnishings, well kept ales, an extensive choice of thai food and seats outside

This ancient and very pretty stone tavern has held a pub licence since 1540, and is the oldest building in the village. From a central entrance passage, low-beamed, character bars lead off with some fine old flagstones and floor tiles and two open fires (one in an inglenook). There are also wheelbacks, stools, rustic seats and tables and built-in wall benches, half-panelled or exposed-stone walls, and plenty of copper kettles, pans and bedwarmers, horse tack and toby jugs. Friendly staff serve Prescott Hill Climb, Sambrooks Junction and Wye Valley Butty Bach on handpump, eight wines by the glass, 18 gins and ten malt whiskies; background music, TV, darts and board games. The little dining room has pale wooden tables and chairs on bare boards. There are a couple of benches on the front cobbles, contemporary seats and tables on a partly covered, raised decked area at the back and picnic-sets on grass; in summer, the flowering baskets and tubs are lovely.

The popular food is thai: tom yum soups, steamed dumplings, chicken satay, spicy salads such as seafood, lots of curries, chicken, duck and pork in tamarind, sweet soy and plum sauces, stir-fries and a large choice of dishes with noodles and rice. *Benchmark main dish: thai green curry £8.00. Two-course evening meal £18.00.*

Free house ~ Licensee Gabe Saunders ~ Real ale ~ Open 12-11; 12-midnight Fri, Sat; closed Mon lunchtime ~ Bar food 12-2.30, 6-10; not Mon ~ Restaurant ~ Children welcome ~ Dogs allowed in bar ~ Wi-fi *Recommended by Jo Garnett, Charles Welch, Trevor and Michele Street, Buster May, Mark Hamill, Graham Smart*

SHIPSTON-ON-STOUR SP2540 Map 4

George

(01608) 661453 – www.thegeorgeshipston.co.uk

High Street; CV36 4AJ

Handsome town-centre inn with opened-up bars and dining areas, rewarding food and drink and seats in courtyard; bedrooms

Boasting a splendid Georgian façade and sitting in the centre of a pretty town, this refurbished inn is full of cheerful customers dropping in and out all day. The spacious interior has been opened ,with several updated areas linked by timbering and bare-stone or brick walls. The bar has high stools and chairs around equally high tables, cushioned wall seating and all sorts of armchairs and sofas. There are colourful rugs on wooden floors, wall prints, mirrors, modern ceiling lights and the atmosphere is friendly and easy-going. High-backed upholstered or wooden chairs around a medley of tables fill the various dining areas and fireplaces house two woodburning stoves. Friendly, helpful staff keep Brakspears Bitter and Oxford Gold and a guest from North Cotswold on handpump, 17 wines by the glass, ten gins and proper cocktails. The courtyard has quality tables and chairs with bright orange cushions under parasols. Bedrooms are contemporary and comfortable and breakfasts highly regarded.

As well as breakfast for non-residents (8-11am), the fine choice of good food includes sandwiches (until 5pm), salt and pepper squid with aioli, thai-spiced chicken croquette with chilli and lime dressing, spiced chickpea and potato cakes with sweetcorn and shallot salsa, a pie of the day, rare-breed burger with toppings and skin-on fries, chalk-stream trout with miso and teriyaki dressing, lamb rump with rosemary polenta, pea purée and rosemary jus, 30-day-aged rare-breed rump steak with triple-cooked chips, and puddings such as warm treacle tart with clotted cream and passion-fruit and lemon posset with almond crumble; pie night is Monday, burger evening is Wednesday and there are two-for-one cocktails on Thursday evenings. *Benchmark main dish: salmon and dill fishcake with spinach, poached egg and hollandaise £15.00. Two-course evening meal £25.00.*

Brakspears ~ Manager Pete Nicholas ~ Real ale ~ Open 8am-11pm; 8am-midnight Sat; 8am-10pm Sun ~ Bar food 11am-9.30pm; lighter meals in afternoon ~ Restaurant ~ Children welcome ~ Dogs allowed in bar and bedrooms ~ Wi-fi ~ Live jazz and fizz last Fri evening of month ~ Bedrooms: /£120 *Recommended by Martin and Joanne Sharp, Charles and Maddie Bishop, Angela and Steve Heard, Monty Green*

WARMINGTON SP4147 Map 4

Falcon

(01295) 692120 – www.brunningandprice.co.uk/falcon

B4100 towards Shotteswell; OX17 1JJ

Carefully extended roadside pub with spreading bar and dining rooms, a fine choice of drinks and food, and seats outside

This handsome and beautifully restored golden-stone inn has much character and plenty to look at in its interconnected bar and dining areas. There are beams, mirrors over several open fires, rugs on pale floorboards, elegant metal chandeliers, prints and photos covering pale-painted walls, bookshelves, house plants and stone bottles. Cushioned Edwardian-style chairs and leather armchairs are grouped around a wide mix of tables and the main dining room has a central fire pit. Friendly young staff serve Phoenix Brunning & Price Original and guests such as Black Sheep, Hook Norton Hooky, Oakham JHB, Gun Dog Chilly Dog and Timothy Taylors Landlord on handpump, 14 wines by the glass, 120 gins and numerous malt whiskies; background music and board games. The garden has good quality seats and tables under a gazebo. The pub was originally built to take advantage of what was a busy turnpike road.

Up-to-date food includes sandwiches, crayfish and crab spring roll with asian salad and coriander dressing, deep-fried brie with pickled cranberries and candied pecan salad, cauliflower and chickpea curry with coconut rice and onion bhaji, chicken breast with puy lentils, smoked bacon, caramelised cauliflower purée and red wine jus, beer-battered cod and chips, steak and kidney pudding, braised lamb shoulder with dauphinoise potatoes, red cabbage and gravy, and puddings such as triple chocolate brownie with chocolate sauce and crème brûlée. *Benchmark main dish: steak burger with toppings, coleslaw and chips £12.95. Two-course evening meal £21.00.*

Brunning & Price ~ Manager Peter Palfi ~ Real ale ~ Open 10am-11pm (10.30pm Sun) ~ Bar food 12-9.30 (9 Sun) ~ Children welcome ~ Dogs allowed in bar ~ Wi-fi *Recommended by Peter and Emma Kelly, Melanie and David Lawson, Jason Caulkin, Terry Davis, Peter and Caroline Waites, Dr and Mrs H J Field, Charles Todd*

WELFORD-ON-AVON SP1452 Map 4

Bell

(01789) 750353 – www.thebellwelford.co.uk

Off B439 W of Stratford; High Street; CV37 8EB

Warwickshire Dining Pub of the Year

Enjoyably civilised pub with appealing ancient interior, good carefully sourced food, a great range of drinks and an attractive garden with table service

Our readers have consistently enjoyed this very well run pub for many years, with comments such as 'the kind staff could not do enough for us and we felt very special and valued' and 'in ten years of visiting this lovely pub, we've only got top praise for every aspect of it'. The attractive interior has plenty of signs of the building's venerable age, and is divided into five comfortable areas, each with its own character. These range from the cosy terracotta-painted bar to a light and airy gallery room with antique wood panelling, solid oak floor and contemporary Lloyd Loom chairs. Flagstone floors, stripped or well polished antique or period-style furniture and three good fires (one in an inglenook) add warmth and cosiness. You'll find Hobsons Best and Postmans Knock, Hook Norton Old Hooky and Purity Pure Gold and Pure UBU on handpump and 16 wines (including prosecco, champagne and sweet wine) by the glass; background music. In summer, the virginia creeper-covered exterior is festooned with colourful hanging baskets. The lovely garden has solid teak furniture, a vine-covered terrace, water features and gentle lighting.

Local, seasonal produce is at the heart of the menu and options include sandwiches, crayfish, prawn and melon cocktail, baked fig and goats cheese wrapped in prosciutto on bruschetta, thai red vegetable curry, pork and smoked bacon sausages on cheese mash with wholegrain mustard gravy, piri-piri and mango chicken suprême on roasted red peppers with sour cream and potato wedges, 10oz gammon steak with fresh pineapple or a free-range egg, smoked haddock with a cheesy crust on creamed garlic potatoes, faggots with sage and onion gravy, and puddings such as toffee crunch cheesecake and pot au chocolat with home-made biscuits. *Benchmark main dish: steak pie £14.95. Two-course evening meal £22.00.*

Free house ~ Licensees Colin and Teresa Ombler ~ Real ale ~ Open 11.30-3, 6-11; 11.30-11.30 Sat; 11.45-11 Sun ~ Bar food 11.45-2.30, 6.15-9.30 (10 Fri); 11.45-10 Sat; 12-9.30 Sun ~ Children welcome ~ Wi-fi *Recommended by Mrs Sheila Lupton, Jamie Thompson, Steve Whalley, Douglas Powell, Alan Organ, Phil and Helen Holt, Clive and Fran Dutson, Peter Northover and Sheila Ward, R and P Irani, T M Parsons, P Gwilliam, Ian and Liz Lowe, John and Sharon Hancock, Frank and Anne Busby, Mr and Mrs Ted Hollingworth*

Please let us know what you think of a pub's bedrooms: feedback@goodguides.com or (no stamp needed) The Good Pub Guide, FREEPOST RTXY–ZCBC–BBAZ, Stream Lane, Sedlescombe, Battle TN33 0PB.

Also Worth a Visit in Warwickshire

Besides the fully inspected pubs, you might like to try these pubs that have been recommended to us and described by readers. Do tell us what you think of them: feedback@goodguides.com

ALCESTER SP0957

Holly Bush (01789) 507370

Henley Street (continuation of High Street towards B4089; not much nearby parking); B49 5QX Welcoming 17th-c Everards pub under new management; their beers and one or two guests kept well, real ciders and decent choice of wines by the glass, good value food from varied menu, six smallish rooms with simple furniture including pews and wall benches, bare boards, flagstones and carpet, two woodburners and an open fire; TV, free wi-fi; children and dogs welcome, seats in pretty back garden, open all day. *(Selwyn Jones)*

ALCESTER SP0857

Turks Head (01789) 765948

High Street, across from church; B49 5AD Updated old town pub with good friendly atmosphere; small front room and another off corridor, well kept Wye Valley and three guests, craft and continental beers, local cider and decent choice of wines and whiskies, enjoyable food from sharing plates and pizzas up including good fish and chips, Sat brunch from 10am; free wi-fi; children and dogs welcome, tables in walled garden behind, open all day, no food Sun evening. *(Dave Braisted)*

ALDRIDGE SK0500

Turtles Head (01922) 325635

Croft Parade; off High Street; WS9 8LY Friendly micropub in row of 1960s shops; simple drinking area with leather sofa and some tub chairs on light wood floor, four well kept/priced ales, proper ciders and decent choice of other drinks, snacky food such as rolls and pork pies, very popular with locals; closed Mon, otherwise open all day (till 9pm Sun). *(Suzy Miller)*

ALVESTON SP2356

Ferry (01789) 269883

Ferry Lane; end of village, off B4086 Stratford–Wellesbourne; CV37 7QX Comfortable beamed dining pub with enjoyable food and well kept ales such as Black Sheep and Wye Valley, friendly staff; quiz first Tues of month, occasional live music; children and dogs welcome, nice spot with seats out at front (some on raised deck), open all day weekends, closed Mon. *(Sandra and Neil White)*

ARDENS GRAFTON SP1153

Golden Cross (01789) 772420

Off A46 or B439 W of Stratford, corner of Wixford Road/Grafton Lane; B50 4LG Modernised 18th-c stone pub; beamed bar with dark flagstones, mix of furniture including chapel chairs and pews around kitchen tables, woodburner in big old fireplace, Wells Bombardier and a couple of guests, eight wines by the glass, tasty uncomplicated home-made food including deals and themed nights, friendly helpful service, attractive lounge with unusual coffered ceiling, big mullioned bay window and log fire; background music, free wi-fi; children and dogs (in bar) welcome, wheelchair access, back garden with sturdy rustic furniture on terrace and picnic-sets on lawn, nice views, open (and food) all day. *(Martine and Derek Cotton)*

ASTON CANTLOW SP1360

Kings Head (01789) 488242

Village signed off A3400 NW of Stratford; B95 6HY Black and white Tudor pub with low-beamed bar on right, old settles on flagstones and woodburner in big inglenook, quarry-tiled main room with window seats and big country tables, ales such as Greene King and Purity, real cider and several wines by the glass, enjoyable food from sandwiches and pub favourites up, friendly efficient service; background music, free wi-fi; children welcome, dogs in bar, garden with picnic-sets and big chestnut tree, open (and food) all day. *(Clive and Fran Dutson)*

BARSTON SP2078

★**Bulls Head** (01675) 442830

From M42 junction 5, A4141 towards Warwick, first left, then signed down Barston Lane; B92 0JU Unassuming and unspoilt partly Tudor village pub; well kept ales such as Adnams, Exmoor, Purity and Sharps, popular traditional home-made food (not Sun evening) from sandwiches to specials, cheerful helpful staff, log fires, comfortable lounge with pictures and plates, oak-beamed bar and separate dining room; monthly quiz; children and dogs allowed, good-sized secluded garden, open all day Fri-Sun. *(John and Claire Masters)*

BINLEY WOODS SP3977

Roseycombe (024) 7654 1022

Rugby Road; CV3 2AY Warm and friendly 1930s pub with wide choice of bargain home-made food (not Mon evening, Sun), Bass, Fullers London Pride and Greene King IPA; Weds quiz, some live music; children welcome, big garden, open all day Fri-Sun. *(Alan Johnson)*

BIRMINGHAM SP0788

★**Bartons Arms** (0121) 333 5988
High Street, Aston (A34); B6 4UP Magnificent listed Edwardian landmark standing alone among busy roads and modern development; impressive richly decorated linked rooms from the palatial to the snug, original tilework murals, stained glass and mahogany, decorative fireplaces, sweeping stairs to handsome upstairs rooms, well kept Oakham ales from ornate island bar with snob screens, interesting imported bottled beers and frequent mini beer festivals, well priced thai food (vegan options available), good service from friendly young staff; occasional live music; open all day. *(David Edwards)*

BIRMINGHAM SP0686

Brasshouse (0121) 633 3383
Broad Street; B1 2HP Spacious bank conversion with enjoyable good value food from tapas, burgers and pizzas up, various deals, well kept Marstons-related ales and guests, good range of other drinks including craft beers and cocktails, efficient friendly service; TV and games machines; children welcome in dining area till 6pm, seats out overlooking canal, handy for National Sea Life Centre, International Convention Centre and Symphony Hall, open all day from 8am (till 2am Fri, Sat). *(Richard Tingle)*

BIRMINGHAM SP0688

Lord Clifden (0121) 523 7515
Great Hampton Street (Jewellery Quarter); B18 6AA Fairly traditional pub with some contemporary touches; leather banquettes and padded stools around dimpled copper-top tables, interesting collection of urban street art including Banksy, bustling atmosphere, wide choice of good value generous food from sandwiches and burgers to daily specials, Wye Valley and guests plus draught continentals, prompt friendly service; darts in front bare-boards section, sports TVs (outside too), Thurs quiz and weekend DJs; children over 10 welcome for lunch, otherwise over-21s only, plenty of seats in enclosed part-covered beer garden with table tennis and table football, open all day (till late Fri, Sat). *(Dave Braisted)*

BIRMINGHAM SP0786

Old Contemptibles (0121) 200 3310
Edmund Street; B3 2HB Spacious Edwardian corner pub (Nicholsons) with lofty ceiling and lots of woodwork, good choice of real ales and enjoyable well priced food, friendly efficient young staff; upstairs lavatories; no children, handy central location and popular at lunchtime with office workers, open all day (till 6pm Sun). *(Alan Johnson)*

BIRMINGHAM SP0784

Old Moseley Arms (0121) 440 1954
Tindal Street; B12 9QU Tucked-away red-brick Victorian pub; five well kept ales such as Church End, Enville and Wye Valley (regular festivals), nice selection of gins and good value authentic indian food (evenings and all day Sun); sports TVs, darts; outside seating area, handy for Edgbaston cricket ground, open all day. *(Dave Braisted)*

BIRMINGHAM SP0384

Plough (0121) 427 3678
High Street, Harborne; B17 9NT Popular place with spacious modern interior (one or two steps); enjoyable food including stone-baked pizzas and chargrilled burgers, regular offers, well kept Purity, Wye Valley and guests, plenty of wines by the glass and 50 or so whiskies, good coffee, friendly staff; background music, TVs and various events such as wine/gin tasting; well behaved children welcome, paved garden with covered area, open (and food) all day from 8am (9am weekends) for breakfast. *(Selwyn Jones)*

BIRMINGHAM SP0686

Post Office Vaults (0121) 643 7354
New Street/Pinfold Street; B2 4BA Two entrances to this simple downstairs bar serving a dozen interesting ciders/perries, eight real ales including a house beer from Kinver (First Class Stamp) and over 300 international bottled beers, friendly knowledgeable staff, no food but can bring your own (plates and cutlery provided); bar billiards; handy for New Street station, open all day. *(Selwyn Jones)*

BIRMINGHAM SP0686

Purecraft Bar & Kitchen
(0121) 237 5666 *Waterloo Street; B2 5TJ* Industrial-chic bar with excellent range of cask and craft beers including several from Purity, interesting bottled range too along with Dunkerton's cider and a dozen wines by the glass, open kitchen serving good food all day (not Sun evening) from sandwiches and deli boards up (food and beer pairings), friendly helpful service; children welcome, open all day. *(Selwyn Jones)*

BIRMINGHAM SP0687

Rose Villa (0121) 236 7910
By clocktower in Jewellery Quarter (Warstone Lane/Vyse Street); B18 6JW Well preserved 1920s red-brick pub (Grade II listed); front saloon with impressive stained-glass windows leading through to splendid little skylit bar with floor-to-ceiling green tiles and massive tiled arch over fireplace, quirky touches here and there such as antler chandeliers and a red phone box, four or five well kept ales including Sharps Doom Bar,

craft beers and over 100 vodkas, reasonably priced food from american diner menu, also themed nights and deals; live music and DJs Fri, Sat night when can get very busy; children and dogs welcome, open all day, weekend brunch from 11am. *(Selwyn Jones)*

BIRMINGHAM SP0686

★**Wellington** (0121) 200 3115

Bennetts Hill; B2 5SN Traditionally renovated high-ceilinged pub with 16 well kept interesting ales (listed on TV screens) including three from Black Country, also real ciders, bottled beers and good range of gins/ whiskies, experienced landlord and friendly staff, no food but plates and cutlery provided if you bring your own, more room and roof terrace upstairs; regular beer festivals and quiz nights, darts; open all day and can get very busy. *(Alan Johnson)*

BRIERLEY HILL SO9286

★**Vine** (01384) 78293

B4172 between A461 and (nearer) A4100; immediately after the turn into Delph Road; DY5 2TN Popular black country pub (aka the Bull & Bladder) offering a true taste of the West Midlands; down-to-earth welcome and friendly chatty locals in meandering series of rooms, each different in character, traditional front bar with wall benches, comfortable extended snug has solidly built red plush seats and there's a tartan-decorated back bar, well kept/priced Bathams from next-door brewery, a couple of simple low-priced lunchtime dishes, cobs and snacks the rest of the day; quiz nights, TV, games machine, darts and dominoes; children and dogs welcome, tables in backyard, open all day. *(Peter and Emma Kelly)*

BROOM SP0853

★**Broom Tavern** (01789) 778199

High Street; off B439 in Bidford; B50 4HL Spacious 16th-c brick and timber village pub, relaxed and welcoming, with good interesting food from chef-owners including excellent Sun roasts, four well kept ales such as North Cotswold, Purity, Sharps and Wye Valley, well chosen wine list with several by the glass, good attentive (but not intrusive) service, main room divided into two parts, one with cottage-style tables and chairs, the other with oak furniture, black beams and log fire, also a snug perfect for a group of diners; Mon quiz; children welcome, dogs in lower bar area, tables out on grass either side, handy for Ragley Hall, open all day weekends, no food Sun evening. *(Freddie and Sarah Banks)*

CHERINGTON SP2836

Cherington Arms (01608) 685183

Off A3400; CV36 5HS Refurbished 17th-c stone-built village pub; popular food (not Mon) from french landlord-chef including open sandwiches, pub favourites, blackboard specials and Sun carvery, well kept Hook Norton and a couple of guests, welcoming efficient service, beamed bar with log fire, separate dining room; regular live music; children and dogs welcome, tables on terrace and in big garden bordering River Stour, good nearby walks, open all day Fri and Sat, till 6pm Sun, closed Mon lunchtime. *(Cameron Townsend, Clive and Fran Dutson)*

CLAVERDON SP2064

★**Red Lion** (01926) 842291

Station Road; B4095 towards Warwick; CV35 8PE Upmarket beamed Tudor dining pub with highly regarded food from sharing plates up including some mediterranean and middle eastern influences, well kept Hook Norton and several wines by the glass, friendly efficient staff, log fires in linked rooms, back area with country views over sheltered heated deck and gardens; children welcome, no dogs inside, open all day Sat, closed Sun evening. *(Phil and Helen Holt)*

COVENTRY SP3279

Old Windmill (024) 7625 1717

Spon Street; CV1 3BA Friendly 15th-c pub with lots of tiny rooms (known locally as Ma Brown's), exposed beams in uneven ceilings, inglenook woodburner, seven well kept ales including Sharps, Theakstons and Timothy Taylors, good local pork pies; live music, juke box, sports TV and games machines, darts; closed Mon lunchtime, otherwise open all day (till 1am Fri, Sat), busy at weekends. *(Dave Braisted, Alan Johnson)*

COVENTRY SP3379

Slug & Lettuce (024) 7622 2727

Bayley Lane; CV1 5RN Former courtroom in the cathedral quarter preserving judge's bench, witness box, dock and public gallery, also steps down to cells (now a dining area); three changing ales, decent choice of wines and cocktails, fairly extensive good value menu from sandwiches and sharing boards up, welcoming hard-working young staff; DJs Fri and Sat night, TVs, free wi-fi; children welcome, disabled loo, open (and food) all day from 10am for breakfast, shuts 2am Fri, Sat. *(Dave Braisted, Alan Johnson)*

COVENTRY SP3379

Town Wall (024) 7622 0963

Bond Street, among car parks behind Belgrade Theatre; CV1 4AH Busy Victorian city-centre local; half a dozen or more well kept ales including Adnams, Bass and Caledonian, Weston's cider, enjoyable good value pub food (not Sun evening, Mon) from lunchtime sandwiches up, unspoilt basic front bar and tiny snug, engraved windows, bigger back lounge with actor/ playwright photographs and pictures of old Coventry, open fires; big-screen sports TV, juke box; no children, open all day. *(Dave Braisted, Alan Johnson)*

EARLSWOOD SP1274

Blue Bell Cider House (01564) 702328 *Warings Green Road, not far from M42 junction 4; B94 6BP* Welcoming 19th-c red-brick pub by Stratford Canal; roomy lounge, cosy bar and conservatory, good value generous food including OAP weekday lunch and popular Sun carvery, own-brew organic beers plus guests, traditional ciders, friendly helpful staff; open mike nights and Weds quiz; children and dogs welcome, plenty of outside seating, moorings, open all day. *(Dave Braisted)*

EASENHALL SP4679

Golden Lion (01788) 833577 *Main Street; CV23 0JA* Bar in 16th-c part of busy hotel; white-painted beams, half-panelling and log fire, some original wattle and daub and fine 17th-c carved bench depicting the 12 apostles, a couple of real ales and good food including cook your own meat on a hot rock, prompt friendly service, more formal restaurant; background music; children and small dogs welcome, disabled access/loos, tables on side terrace and spacious lawn, 17 well equipped bedrooms (some with four-posters), attractive village, open (and food) all day. *(Buster May)*

EDGE HILL SP3747

★**Castle** (01295) 670255 *Off A422; OX15 6DJ* Crenellated octagonal tower built in 1742 as gothic folly (marks where Charles I raised his standard at the Battle of Edgehill); major renovation creating bar and four dining areas, plenty of original features including arched windows and doorways, beams and stone fireplaces, fantastic views (some floor-to-ceiling windows), good food (not Sun evening), also deli bar for sandwiches, coffee and afternoon teas (must book), well kept Hook Norton ales, friendly helpful young staff; downstairs lavatories; children welcome, seats in lovely big garden with more outstanding views, beautiful Compton Wynyates nearby, four bedrooms, parking can be tricky at busy times, open all day Sat, till 7pm Sun. *(Susan and John Douglas, Dr and Mrs H J Field)*

FARNBOROUGH SP4349

Kitchen (01295) 690615 *Off A423 N of Banbury; OX17 1DZ* Refurbished golden-stone dining pub in NT village; bar with painted beams, wood floor and cushioned window seats, red woodburner in big fireplace, saddle- and tractor-seat stools at blue-panelled counter serving Purity ales and nice wines by the glass, good seasonal food from interesting if not especially cheap menu, some produce from own kitchen garden, two-room dining area, friendly helpful staff; jazzy background music, free wi-fi; children and dogs (in bar) welcome, neat sloping garden with blue picnic-sets and pizza oven, local walks, open all day weekends, closed Tues, Weds and lunchtime Thurs. *(Jane Rigby)*

FENNY COMPTON SP4152

Merrie Lion (01295) 771134 *Brook Street; CV47 2YH* Spotless early 18th-c beamed village pub; three well kept beers including one badged for them, decent range of wines and good freshly made food from pubby choices up, friendly welcoming atmosphere; quiz nights and other events; dogs welcome, tables outside, handy for Burton Dassett Hills Country Park, open all day Fri-Sun. *(Matt and Hayley Jacob)*

FILLONGLEY SP2787

Cottage (01676) 540599 *Black Hall Lane; CV7 8EG* Popular country dining pub on village outskirts; good value fairly traditional food including OAP lunch, early evening deal and Thurs fish and chips, beers such as Bass, St Austell and Timothy Taylors, friendly service; back terrace and lawn overlooking fields, closes 6pm Sun evening. *(Charles Todd)*

FIVE WAYS SP2270

★**Case Is Altered** (01926) 484206 *Follow Rowington signs at junction roundabout off A4177/A4141 N of Warwick, then right into Case Lane; CV35 7JD* Convivial unspoilt old cottage licensed for over three centuries; Old Pie Factory, Wye Valley and three guests served by friendly long-serving landlady, no food, simple small main bar with fine old poster of Lucas Blackwell & Arkwright Brewery (now flats), clock with hours spelling out Thornleys Ale (another defunct brewery), and just a few sturdy old-fashioned tables and a couple of stout leather-covered settles facing each other over spotless tiles, modest little back room with old bar billiards table (takes sixpences); no children, dogs or mobile phones; full disabled access, stone table on little brick courtyard. *(Paul Faraday)*

FLECKNOE SP5163

Old Olive Bush (01788) 891134 *Off A425 W of Daventry; CV23 8AT* Unspoilt chatty little Edwardian pub in quiet photogenic village; enjoyable traditional food cooked by landlady (Weds-Sat evenings, Sun lunchtime), well kept changing ales and decent wines, open fire in bar with stripped-wood floor, steps up to games room (table skittles), small dining room with etched windows and another fire; Thurs quiz; children welcome, pretty garden, closed Sun evening, Mon and lunchtimes Tues-Fri. *(Angela and Steve Heard)*

FRANKTON SP4270

Friendly (01926) 632430 *Just over a mile S of B4453 Leamington Spa–Rugby; Main Street; CV23 9NY* Popular 16th-c village pub living up to its name; four well kept ales including Greene King IPA, good reasonably priced traditional home-made food (not Sun evening, Mon), two low-ceilinged rooms, open fire; dogs welcome, open all day weekends, closed Mon lunchtime. *(Mark Hamill)*

HALESOWEN SO9683

Waggon & Horses (0121) 550 4989

Stourbridge Road; B63 3TU Popular refurbished and extended 19th-c red-brick corner pub; Black Country ales along with plenty of interesting guests (tasting trays available) and four real ciders, friendly knowledgeable staff, snacky food such as cobs and pork pies, sloping floor in narrow main bar, open fire; dogs welcome in some parts, open all day. *(Selwyn Jones)*

HAMPTON LUCY SP2557

Boars Head (01789) 840533

Church Street, E of Stratford; CV35 8BE Welcoming unpretentious village pub with nicely decorated interior, beams and log fires, good range of changing local ales and reasonably priced wines, enjoyable modestly priced pubby food from baguettes up (all day Sat, not Sun evening), welcoming staff, deli counter selling sauces, spices, olives etc; children welcome, seats in enclosed back courtyard, near lovely church and handy for Charlecote Park (NT) and M40, open all day. *(Paul Humphreys)*

HARBOROUGH MAGNA SP4779

Old Lion (01788) 833238

3 miles from M6 junction 1; B4112 Pailton Road; CV23 0HQ Stylishly modernised village pub under welcoming new management; good food from pub favourites and pizzas to steaks, friendly attentive staff, well kept ales including one badged for them, nice choice of wines; some live music; children and dogs (in bar) welcome, terrace seating, open all day Sat, till 5pm Sun. *(Sandra and Neil White)*

HATTON SP2367

★**Falcon** (01926) 484281

Birmingham Road, Haseley (A4177, not far from M40 junction 15); CV35 7HA Modernised dining pub with relaxing rooms around island bar, lots of stripped brickwork and low beams, tiled and oak-planked floors, good moderately priced food from sandwiches, sharing boards and pub favourites up, lunchtime/early evening deal Mon-Fri, friendly service, nice choice of wines by the glass and well kept Marstons-related ales, barn-style back restaurant; children and dogs (in bar) welcome, disabled facilities, garden with heated covered terrace, eight bedrooms in converted barn, open (and food) all day. *(Ian Herdman)*

HENLEY-IN-ARDEN SP1566

Bluebell (01564) 793049

High Street (A3400, off M40 junction 16); B95 5AT Impressive timber-framed dining pub with fine coach entrance, rambling old beamed and flagstoned interior with contemporary furnishings creating stylish but relaxed atmosphere, big fireplace, well kept ales such as Church End and Purity, 20 wines by the glass, good variety of food served by friendly staff, coffee and afternoon teas, daily papers; occasional art exhibitions and live music, free wi-fi; children welcome if eating (till 8.30pm), dogs allowed, tables on back decking, open till 7.30pm Sun, closed Mon, otherwise open all day. *(Martine and Derek Cotton)*

KENILWORTH SP2872

Clarendon Arms (01926) 852017

Castle Hill; CV8 1NB Busy pub opposite castle and under same ownership as next-door Harringtons restaurant; several rooms off long bare-boards bustling bar, well kept ales, tasty reasonably priced pub food, cheerful staff, largish peaceful upstairs dining room; children and dogs (in bar) welcome, metal tables on small raised terrace, daytime car park fee deducted from food bill, open (and food) all day weekends. *(John and Claire Masters)*

KENILWORTH SP2872

Old Bakery (01926) 864111

High Street, off A452; CV8 1LZ Small hotel's cosy two-room bar (popular with older customers); four well kept ales including Wye Valley HPA and good choice of wines, whiskies and gins, food Mon evening only (till 7.30pm); no music, TVs or machines; disabled access from behind, 14 comfortable bedrooms, good english breakfast, opens from 5.30pm (5pm Fri-Sun) and can get very busy. *(Charles Todd)*

KENILWORTH SP2872

★**Virgins & Castle** (01926) 853737

High Street; CV8 1LY Small snugs by entrance corridor and maze of intimate rooms off inner servery; flagstones, heavy beams and lots of woodwork, coal fire, four well kept Everards ales and a couple of guests (beer festivals), good reasonably priced food including some filipino dishes and weekday set lunch, friendly service, games bar upstairs; children allowed in eating areas, dogs in some areas, disabled facilities, tables in sheltered garden, parking close by can be tricky, open all day, no food Sun evening. *(Charles Todd)*

LADBROKE SP4158

★**Bell** (01926) 811224

Signed off A423 S of Southam; CV47 2BY Refurbished beamed country pub set back from the road, smallish bar with tub chairs by log fire, snug off with library wallpaper and another fire in little brick fireplace, three well kept ales including Ringwood and plenty of wines by the glass, very good well presented food from pub favourites and grills up, also gluten-free choices and weekday set menu, airy candlelit restaurant with light oak flooring, friendly efficient young staff; background music, free wi-fi; children and dogs (in bar) welcome, a few picnic-sets out in front and on side grass, pleasant surroundings, closed Sun evening, Mon. *(Nigel and Sue Foster, Michael Doswell)*

LAPWORTH SP1871

★**Boot** (01564) 782464
Old Warwick Road; B4439 Hockley Heath–Warwick – 2.8 miles from M40 junction 1, but from southbound carriageway only, and return only to northbound; B94 6JU Popular upmarket dining pub near Stratford Canal; good range of food from interesting menu including weekday fixed-price offer, efficient cheerful young staff, upscale wines, well kept Purity Pure UBU and Sharps Doom Bar, stripped beams and dark panelling, big antique hunting prints, cushioned pews and bucket chairs on ancient quarry tiles and bare boards, warm fire, charming low-raftered upstairs dining room; background music; children and dogs welcome, tables on side terrace (some under extendable canopy), more seating on grass beyond with tipi, nice walks, open all day. *(Ian Herdman, Phil and Helen Holt)*

LAPWORTH SP1970

Navigation (01564) 783337
Old Warwick Road (B4439 SE); B94 6NA Modernised beamed pub by the Grand Union Canal; slate-floor bar with woodburner, bare-boards snug and restaurant, well kept ales such as Byatts, Purity, Timothy Taylors and Wadworths, unusually Guinness also on handpump, decent wines and enjoyable reasonably priced food (all day weekends) from sandwiches and other bar choices up, breakfast from 10am weekends, good Sun roasts, friendly efficient staff; children welcome, dogs in bar, covered terrace and waterside garden, handy for Packwood House and Baddesley Clinton (both NT), open all day. *(Chris Francis, Clive and Fran Dutson)*

LEAMINGTON SPA SP3165

Cricketers Arms (01926) 881293
Archery Road; CV31 3PT Friendly town local opposite bowling greens; fairly priced food using meat from good local butcher including popular Sun roasts (till 6pm), home-made sausage rolls and scotch eggs, well kept ales such as Timothy Taylors from central bar, Weston's cider, some panelling and cricketing memorabilia, comfortable banquettes, open fires; occasional live music, fortnightly quiz Mon, poker night Weds, sports TV, darts, free wi-fi; children and dogs welcome, heated back terrace, open all day. *(Jane Rigby)*

LEAMINGTON SPA SP3166

★**Star & Garter** (01926) 359960
Warwick Street; CV32 5LL Bustling open-plan town-centre pub (part of the Peach group); bare-boards bar with upholstered wall seats, blue leather banquettes, red leather armchairs and small wooden stools around mixed tables, Greene King ales (including one named for the pub), St Austell Tribute and lots of wines by the glass, good selection of gins/cocktails too, enjoyable food from deli boards up, well priced weekday set menu and weekend brunch from 9am, open-kitchen dining area with booths down one side, steps up to second bar area with tub seats, bright scatter cushions and some bold paintwork, friendly helpful staff; background music, free wi-fi; children and dogs (in bar) welcome, open all day. *(Matt and Hayley Jacob)*

LEEK WOOTTON SP2868

Anchor (01926) 853355
Warwick Road; CV35 7QX Neat and well run dining lounge popular for its good fresh food including range of burgers and daily specials, well kept ales such as Bass, Hook Norton and Purity, good selection of affordably priced wines and soft drinks, attentive friendly service, lots of close-set pine tables, smaller overflow dining area; background music, sports TV, free wi-fi; children welcome, no dogs inside, long garden behind with play area, open (and food) all day weekends. *(Alan Johnson)*

LIGHTHORNE SP3455

Antelope (01926) 651188
Old School Lane, Bishops Hill; a mile SW of B4100 N of Banbury; CV35 0AU Attractive early 18th-c stone-built pub in pretty village setting; two neatly kept comfortable bars and separate dining area, beams, flagstones, exposed stonework and big open fire, well kept Greene King IPA, Sharps Doom Bar and a couple of guests, enjoyable food from sandwiches up including a vegan menu, Weds burger night, friendly efficient service; children and dogs welcome, picnic-sets out by well and on small grassy area, open (and food) all day Fri-Sun. *(Gerald and Brenda Culliford)*

LITTLE COMPTON SP2530

★**Red Lion** (01608) 674397
Off A44 Moreton-in-Marsh to Chipping Norton; GL56 0RT Low-beamed 16th-c Cotswold-stone inn; well liked food (not Sun evening, Mon) cooked by landlord-chef from fairly traditional menu, Donnington ales and good choice of wines by the glass, friendly helpful service, snug alcoves, inglenook woodburner; darts and pool in public bar; some live music; well behaved children and

You can send reports directly to us at feedback@goodguides.com.

dogs welcome, white-painted metal furniture in pretty garden, comfortable bedrooms, open all day, but may shut afternoons if quiet. *(Martin Constable, Bernard Stradling)*

LONG ITCHINGTON SP4165

Duck on the Pond (01926) 815876

Just off A423 Coventry–Southam; The Green; CV47 9QJ Popular village pub with stylish modern interior (large bar and two main dining areas); good well presented food including set lunchtime/early evening menu, brunch from 10.30am, well kept Wells and Youngs ales, over a dozen wines by the glass, efficient cheerful service; children welcome, rattan-style furniture in fenced front garden, open all day, no food Sun evening. *(John and Mary Ling)*

LONG ITCHINGTON SP4164

Two Boats (01926) 812640

A423 N of Southam, by Grand Union Canal; CV47 9QZ Traditional brick-built pub with lovely canal views from window seats in long picture-filled main room, enjoyable generously served food from good value pubby menu, Wells, Youngs and guests, friendly helpful staff; TV and darts in side bar; children and dogs welcome, waterfront terrace and moorings, open all day, no food Sun evening. *(Mr and Mrs D Hammond)*

LONGFORD SP3684

Greyhound (024) 7636 3046

Sutton Stop, off Black Horse Road/ Grange Road; junction of Coventry and North Oxford canals; CV6 6DF Cosy 19th-c canalside pub with plenty of character; up to half a dozen well kept ales and range of enjoyable food including lunchtime sandwiches and baked potatoes, friendly helpful staff, coal-fired stove, unusual tiny snug; occasional live music; children and dogs (in bar) welcome, tables on attractive waterside terrace, nice spot (if you ignore the pylons), open all day. *(Paul Faraday)*

LOWER BRAILES SP3139

George (01608) 685788

B4035 Shipston–Banbury; OX15 5HN New licensees as we went to press for this handsome 14th-c pub – reports please; roomy front bar with dark oak tables on flagstones, inglenook log fire, beamed and panelled back bar, separate restaurant; has served Hook Norton ales and good food; sizeable sheltered back garden with terrace; also a few tables out at front, lovely village with interesting church, good nearby walks, comfortable bedrooms. *(Richard Tilbrook, Clive and Fran Dutson, Sally Harrison)*

LYE SO9284

★**Windsor Castle** (01384) 897809

Stourbridge Road (corner A458/A4036; car park in Pedmore Road just above traffic lights – don't be tempted to use the next-door restaurant's parking!); DY9 7DG Interesting range of well kept beers from impressive row of handpumps including own Sadlers ales (brewery tours available); central flagstoned part with bar stools by counter and window shelf overlooking road, several other rooms including 1920s-inspired gin bar, enjoyable home-cooked food (not Sun evening), burger night Tues, friendly service; free wi-fi; children and dogs (in bar) welcome, disabled facilities, terrace and verandah seating, four bedrooms, handy for Lye station, open all day (from 9am Sat for breakfast). *(Angela and Steve Heard)*

NAPTON SP4560

Folly (01926) 815185

Off A425 towards Priors Hardwick; Folly Lane, by locks; CV47 8NZ Beamed red-brick pub in lovely spot on Oxford Canal by Napton Locks and Folly Bridge (113); three bars on different levels, mix of furnishings and two big fireplaces (one with woodburner), lots of interesting bric-a-brac, pictures and old framed photographs, good straightforward home-made food (not Sun evening), well kept ales including Hook Norton; sports TV, free-wi-fi; children and dogs welcome, open all day. *(John and Claire Masters)*

NETHER WHITACRE SP2292

Gate (01675) 481292

Gate Lane; B46 2DS Welcoming traditional community pub with good honest food and seven well kept Marstons-related ales, log-fire bar, lounge and dining conservatory; games room with pool and darts; occasional quiz nights; children and dogs (in bar) welcome, garden picnic-sets and play area, open all day, food all day weekends (till 7pm Sun). *(Sarah Watkinson)*

NETHERTON SO9488

★**Old Swan** (01384) 253075

Halesowen Road (A459 just S of centre); DY2 9PY Victorian tavern full of traditional character and known in the area as Ma Pardoe's after former long-serving landlady; wonderfully unspoilt front bar with big swan centrepiece in patterned enamel ceiling, engraved mirrors, traditional furnishings and old-fashioned cylinder stove, other rooms including cosy back snug and more modern lounge, own well priced ales and enjoyable good value bar food (best to book/check times), upstairs restaurant (evenings only and Sun lunch); no under-16s, dogs allowed in bar, open all day. *(Jane Rigby)*

NORTON LINDSEY SP2263

New Inn (01926) 258411

Main Street; CV35 8JA Refurbished village pub owned by the local community; enjoyable reasonably priced food (not Sun evening, Mon) including blackboard specials and OAP weekday lunch deal, friendly accommodating staff, ales such as Church Farm, Greene King and Purity, good range of gins; monthly quiz; children and dogs welcome, back garden, closed Mon lunchtime, otherwise open all day. *(Mark Tomlinson)*

OFFCHURCH SP3665

★**Stag** (01926) 425801
N of Welsh Road, off A425 at Radford Semele; CV33 9AQ Popular 16th-c thatched and beamed village dining pub; oak-floored bar with log fires, ales such as Hook Norton, Purity and Wye Valley, a dozen wines by the glass and good food from interesting menu including excellent steaks, friendly efficient young staff, more formal cosy restaurant areas with bold wallpaper, striking fabrics, animal heads and big mirrors; children and dogs (in bar) welcome, nice garden with rattan-style furniture on terrace, open all day. *(Clive and Fran Dutson, Dr Matt Burleigh)*

OLD HILL SO9686

Waterfall (0121) 559 9198
Waterfall Lane; B64 6RG Unpretentious two-room local with tankards and jugs hanging from boarded ceiling, well kept Holdens and guests, good straightforward low-priced food, friendly atmosphere; dogs welcome, seats on small raised front area and in back garden, open all day. *(Charles Todd)*

OXHILL SP3149

★**Peacock** (01295) 688060
Off A422 Stratford–Banbury; CV35 0QU Popular stone-built pub in pretty village; good varied menu including blackboard specials, friendly attentive staff, ales such as Marstons, Sharps and Wells, good selection of wines by the glass, cosy beamed bar with big solid tables and woodburner, half-panelled bare-boards dining room; background music; children and dogs (in bar) welcome, nice back garden, closed Mon, otherwise open all day, no food Sun evening. *(Dr and Mrs H J Field)*

PRESTON BAGOT SP1765

Crabmill (01926) 843342
A4189 Henley-in-Arden to Warwick; B95 5EE Civilised and attractively revamped former cider mill; smart two-level lounge with rugs and comfortable seating on stripped wood floor, snug corners in flagstoned bar serving ales such as Purity and Sharps and 16 wines by the glass (weekday happy hour 4-7pm), generally well liked food including lunchtime/early evening set menu, elegant low-beamed dining area with leather banquettes, open fires; background music, free wi-fi; children and dogs (in bar) welcome, plenty of tables in attractive decked garden, open all day (till 7pm Sun). *(Jenni Owen, Laura Reid, Dr and Mrs A K Clarke, Ian Wilson, M G Hart)*

PRIORS MARSTON SP4857

Holly Bush (01327) 260934
Off A361 S of Daventry; Holly Bush Lane; CV47 7RW 16th-c village pub under newish management; rambling linked rooms with beams, flagstones and lots of stripped stonework, log fire and woodburners, two changing ales and enjoyable home-made food, friendly service; children and dogs (not in restaurant) welcome, terrace and sheltered garden, closed lunchtimes Mon and Tues, otherwise open all day, no food Sun evening. *(Mark Hamill)*

RATLEY SP3847

Rose & Crown (01295) 678148
Off A422 NW of Banbury; OX15 6DS Ancient golden-stone pub, charming and cosy, with five well kept changing ales (St Austell Tribute and Wells Bombardier feature regularly), blackboard list of wines, enjoyable good value food (not Sun evening, Mon) including daily specials, friendly efficient staff, carpeted black-beamed bar with woodburner each end, traditional furniture and window seats, cosy snug; background music, darts; children, walkers and dogs welcome, tables on sunny split-level terrace, aunt sally, near lovely church in sleepy village, handy for Upton House (NT), open all day Fri-Sun, closed Mon lunchtime. *(Peter and Emma Kelly)*

ROWINGTON SP1969

Tom o' the Wood (01564) 782252
Off B4439 N of Rowington, following Lowsonford sign; Finwood Road; CV35 7DH Spaciously modernised and extended canalside pub; good home-cooked food (not Sun evening) from sharing baskets and stone-baked pizzas up, themed evenings including Thurs pie night, well kept Greene King IPA and a guest, Weston's Rosie's Pig cider, friendly staff, conservatory; live music, free wi-fi; children and dogs (not in restaurant) welcome, tables on terrace and side lawn, open all day (till 8pm Sun). *(Freddie and Sarah Banks)*

RUGBY SP5075

Merchants (01788) 571119
Little Church Street; CV21 3AN Open-plan pub tucked away near main shopping area, cheerfully busy, with nine quickly changing ales, real ciders and huge selection of belgian and other bottled imports, regular beer/cider/gin festivals, low-priced lunchtime food including range of burgers, occasional curry nights, quite dark inside with beams, bare boards and flagstones, lots of pump clips and interesting breweriana; background

Virtually all pubs in this book sell wine by the glass. We mention wines if they are a cut above the average.

music (live Tues), quiz last Mon of month, sports TVs; open all day, till 1am Fri, Sat. *(Buster May)*

RUGBY SP5075

Seven Stars (01788) 535478

Albert Square; CV21 2SH Traditional 19th-c red-brick local with a dozen well kept ales such as Everards, Grainstore, Gun Dog and Oakham, friendly landlord and staff, main bar, lounge, snug and conservatory, rugby memorabilia, snacky food including home-made scotch eggs, pie and pint night Weds; sports TV, darts and board games; children (till 7pm) and dogs welcome, café-style seating in part-covered courtyard with murals, closed Mon lunchtime, otherwise open all day. *(Buster May)*

RUSHALL SK03001

Manor Arms 07428 521730

Park Road, off A461; WS4 1LG Interesting low-beamed 18th-c pub (on much older foundations) by Rushall Canal; three rooms in contrasting styles, one with big inglenook, well kept Banks's ales from pumps fixed to the wall (there's no counter), simple snacky food, friendly staff; no card payments; children, walkers and dogs welcome, waterside garden with moorings, next to Park Lime Pits nature reserve, open all day. *(Charles Todd)*

SEDGLEY SO9293

★ **Beacon** (01902) 883380

Bilston Street; A463, off A4123 Wolverhampton–Dudley; DY3 1JE Plain old brick pub with own good Sarah Hughes ales from traditional Victorian tower brewery behind; cheery locals in simple quarry-tiled drinking corridor, little snug on left with wall settles, imposing green-tiled marble fireplace and glazed serving hatch, old-fashioned furnishings such as velvet and net curtains, mahogany tables on patterned carpet, small landscape prints, sparse tap room on right with blackened range, dark-panelled lounge with sturdy red leather wall settles and big dramatic sea prints, plant-filled conservatory (no seats), little food apart from cobs; no credit cards; children allowed in some parts including garden with play area, dogs not allowed. *(Selwyn Jones)*

SHIPSTON-ON-STOUR SP2540

Horseshoe (01608) 662190

Church Street; CV36 4AP New management for this popular 17th-c timbered local; two-room carpeted bar with cushioned wall seats and wheelbacks around scrubbed tables, copper pans hanging from bressumer over open fire, Purity, Sharps and Wye Valley, Weston's Old Rosie cider, traditional food including Sun carvery, can eat in bar or end dining room; children and dogs welcome, café style tables and chairs on back terrace, open all day Fri-Sun. *(Julian Thorpe, Douglas Power, Des Mannion)*

SHUSTOKE SP2290

★ **Griffin** (01675) 481205

Church End, a mile E of village; 5 miles from M6 junction 4; A446 towards Tamworth, then right on to B4114 straight through Coleshill; B46 2LB Unpretentious country local with a dozen well kept changing ales including own Griffin (brewed in next-door barn), farm cider and country wines, standard lunchtime bar food (not Sun); cheery low-beamed L-shaped bar with log fires in two stone fireplaces (one a big inglenook), fairly simple décor including cushioned café seats, elm-topped sewing trestles and a nice old-fashioned settle, beer mats on ceiling, conservatory (children allowed here); dogs welcome, old-fashioned seats on back grass with distant views of Birmingham, large terrace, play area and summer marquee (live music), camping field, open all day Fri-Sun. *(Sandra and Neil White)*

SHUSTOKE SP2290

Plough (01675) 481557

B4114 Nuneaton–Coleshill; B46 2AN Old-fashioned feel with rooms arranged around central bar; well kept Bass and four guests, good choice of fairly straightforward food from sandwiches and baked potatoes up, some themed nights, friendly helpful staff, separate dining room, black beams, open fire and gleaming brassware; regular quiz nights (usually Mon), pool and darts, fruit machine, free wi-fi; children and dogs welcome, disabled facilities, seats out at back, open all day Fri-Sun. *(Buster May)*

STOCKTON SP4365

Boat (01926) 812657

A426 Southam–Rugby; CV23 8HQ Fairly traditionally updated canalside pub with open-plan split-level interior (raised part mainly for dining); dark wood furniture on pale stone or stripped boards, woodburner in brick fireplace, brewery mirrors and advertising signs, bottles and jugs on delft shelf, a house beer from Nethergate, three guest ales and several craft beers, popular reasonably priced pubby food (not Sun evening), friendly staff, little deli; children and dogs (in bar) welcome, waterside picnic-sets under pergola, garden behind with play area, moorings, open all day. *(Jane Rigby)*

STOCKTON SP4363

Crown (01926) 812255

High Street; CV47 8JZ Friendly village pub with well kept St Austell and local guests, generous helpings of popular straightforward food, restaurant in ancient barn, log fires; children and dogs welcome, garden with play area, open all day. *(Paul Faraday)*

STOURBRIDGE SO9084

Duke William (01384) 440202

Coventry Street; DY8 1EP Friendly and popular Edwardian corner pub in semi-pedestrianised area; own Craddocks beers from on-site microbrewery (tours available) plus guests and draught/bottled imports, good pie, mash and peas menu, traditional old black country feel with long corridor, open fire in bar and cosy snug; regular events including music, quiz and film nights (some in upstairs function room); no children, beer garden, open all day. *(Charles Todd)*

STOURBRIDGE SO8983

Plough & Harrow (01384) 397218

Worcester Street; DY8 1AX Friendly little end-of-terrace bay-windowed local (sister to the nearby Duke William); well kept Craddocks ales and several guests, snacky food (nothing hot), cosy horseshoe bar with log fires and piano; live music and quiz nights; dogs welcome, no children inside, partly covered beer garden with woodburner, close to Mary Stevens Park, open all day. *(Charles Todd)*

STRATFORD-UPON-AVON SP2054

Garrick (01789) 292186

High Street; CV37 6AU Ancient pub with fine timbered frontage, heavy beams in irregularly shaped rooms, simple furnishings on bare boards or flagstones, well kept Greene King ales and decent wines by the glass, fairly priced food from sandwiches and light dishes up, small back dining area; background music, TV, games machine; children welcome, open (and food) all day. *(Alan Johnson, Tony Selinger)*

STRATFORD-UPON-AVON SP1955

Old Thatch (01789) 295216

Rother Street/Greenhill Street; CV37 6LE Cosy and welcoming 15th-c thatched pub on corner of market square, well kept Fullers ales, nice wines and popular fairly priced food including Sun carvery, rustic décor, beams, slate or wood floors, sofas and log fire, back dining area; children and dogs welcome, covered tables outside, open all day. *(Alan Johnson)*

STRATFORD-UPON-AVON SP2055

One Elm (01789) 404919

Guild Street; CV37 6QZ Modernised Peach group pub on two floors; well liked food from sandwiches and pub standards up (smaller helpings for children), Purity, Sharps and guests, plenty of wines by the glass and good range of gins and cocktails, friendly efficient service; children and dogs welcome, seats out at front and in attractive paved courtyard behind, open (and food) all day, weekend breakfasts from 10am. *(Peter and Emma Kelly)*

STRATFORD-UPON-AVON SP1955

White Swan (01789) 297022

Rother Street; CV37 6NH Extensively renovated historic hotel (dates from 1450) with warren of connecting heavily beamed areas around central bar (one or two steps), good mix of seating including leather armchairs/sofas and antique settles, Shakespearean themed pictures and prints, oak-panelled dining room with two fine carved fireplaces and 16th-c wall painting of Tobias and the Angel, five Fullers/Gales beers, several wines by the glass and good choice of food to suit all tastes and occasions, quick friendly service; background music, daily newspapers, free wi-fi; children welcome, seats out at front overlooking market square and to the side, character bedrooms, open (and food) all day. *(Alan Johnson)*

STRATFORD-UPON-AVON SP1954

Windmill (01789) 297687

Church Street; CV37 6HB Near the striking Guild Chapel, this pub was first licensed in 1600 (there's a list of landlords back to 1720); updated interior with low beams and standing timbers, big fireplaces and wood and carpeted floors, Greene King, Purity UBU and guests, good choice of enjoyable fairly priced food including range of burgers, various deals, friendly efficient staff; background music, sports TV, games machine, free wi-fi; children welcome, courtyard tables, open (and food) all day. *(Peter and Emma Kelly)*

STRETTON-ON-FOSSE SP2238

★ Plough (01608) 661053

Just off A429; GL56 9QX Popular little 17th-c village local with welcoming landlady; central servery separating small bar and snug dining area, well kept Sharps Doom Bar and three guests, good home-cooked food (not Sun evening) including blackboard specials, low oak beams, stripped-brick/stone walls and some flagstones, inglenook log fire; dominoes and cribbage, free wi-fi; children welcome, no dogs, a few tables outside, open all day Fri-Sun, closed Mon. *(Matt and Hayley Jacob)*

SUTTON COLDFIELD SP1195

Brewhouse & Kitchen

(0121) 796 6838 *Birmingham Road; B72 1QD* Revamped mock-Tudor pub with own microbrewery (tours available), eight real ales (mainly theirs) plus good range of craft kegs and bottled beers, around a dozen wines by the glass and enjoyable reasonably priced food from snacks, burgers and ribs up (menu pairs beers to food), friendly helpful staff, spacious modern interior with plenty of different seating areas including boothed dining part; children welcome, open (and food) all day. *(Dave Braisted)*

TANWORTH-IN-ARDEN SP1071

Warwickshire Lad (01564) 742346

Broad Lane/Wood End Lane, Wood End; B94 5DP Beamed country pub with good choice of enjoyable food cooked by landlord-chef, well kept ales such as St Austell, Sharps, Silhill and Wye Valley, friendly service; children and dogs welcome, popular with walkers (bridleway opposite), seats outside, open all day, food all day Fri and Sat, till 7pm Sun, handy for M42 (junction 3). *(Freddie and Sarah Banks)*

TEMPLE GRAFTON SP1355

Blue Boar (01789) 750010
1 mile E, towards Binton; off A422 W of Stratford; B49 6NR Welcoming stone-built dining inn with good food from sandwiches and sharing platters up, well kept Banks's, Wychwood and a couple of guests, afternoon teas, beams, stripped stonework and log fires, glass-covered well with goldfish, smarter dining room up a couple of steps; occasional live music, sports TV, free wi-fi; children and dogs welcome, picnic-sets outside, bedrooms. *(Paul Faraday)*

TIDDINGTON SP2255

Crown (01789) 297010
Main Street; CV37 7AZ Family-friendly pub with good well priced home-made food (smaller helpings available), four well kept ales including Sharps Doom Bar, friendly staff; darts, pool and TV in side bar; monthly quiz night; dogs welcome, garden with play area, open all day Fri-Sun, no food Sun evening. *(Alan Johnson)*

TIPTON SO9492

Pie Factory (0121) 557 1402
Hurst Lane, Dudley Road towards Wednesbury; A457/A4037; DY4 9AB Eccentric décor and quirky food – mixed grill served on a shovel, and you're awarded a certificate if you finish their massive Desperate Dan Cow Pie, other good value food including Sun carvery, meal deals Mon-Weds, well kept Lump Hammer house beers (brewed by Enville) and guests; background and weekend live music, TV; children welcome, open (and food) all day. *(Martine and Derek Cotton)*

UFTON SP3762

White Hart (01926) 612976
Just off A425 Southam–Leamington; CV33 9PJ Friendly old pub in elevated roadside position next to church; modernised beamed bar with log fire, high-backed leather chairs and some booth seating, stripped-stone walls, a few steps here and there, well kept ales such as Greene King, St Austell and Slaughterhouse, several wines by the glass and enjoyable good value food, efficient service; children and dogs welcome, picnic-sets in hilltop garden with panoramic views, closed Sun evening, Mon. *(Sandra and Neil White)*

UPPER BRAILES SP3039

Gate (01608) 685212
B4035 Shipston-on-Stour to Banbury; OX15 5AX Traditional low-beamed village local; well kept Hook Norton and a guest, Weston's cider and enjoyable reasonably priced food from shortish menu including good fish and chips, efficient friendly service, coal fire; TV and darts; children welcome, play area and aunt sally in extensive back garden, pretty hillside spot with lovely walks, two comfortable bedrooms, good breakfast, closed weekday lunchtimes, no food Sun evening, Mon. *(Jane Rigby)*

UPPER GORNAL SO9292

★**Britannia** (01902) 883253
Kent Street (A459); DY3 1UX Popular old-fashioned 19th-c local with friendly chatty atmosphere (known locally as Sally's after former landlady); coal fires in front bar and time-trapped little back room with its wonderful wall-mounted handpumps, particularly well kept/priced Bathams, some bar snacks including good local pork pies; sports TV, occasional live music; dogs welcome, flower-filled back courtyard, open all day. *(Kevin)*

WALSALL SP0198

Black Country Arms
(01922) 640588 *High Street; WS1 1QW* Imposing 17th-c building with pillared frontage and big Georgian-style windows; recently refurbished high-ceilinged bar on different levels including mezzanine, Black Country ales and many guests from traditional wooden servery, also craft beers and real ciders, enjoyable home-made pubby food at bargain prices, good friendly service; background and live music, quiz nights, sports TV; dogs welcome (they have two), small side terrace, open all day (till midnight Fri, Sat), no food Sun evening, Mon. *(Liz and Brian Barnard)*

WARWICK SP2864

★**Rose & Crown** (01926) 411117
Market Place; CV34 4SH Friendly bustling Peach group inn with uncluttered modern décor, good choice of interesting sensibly priced food including fixed-price menu, well kept ales such as Church Farm and Purity, good wines, cocktails and coffee, cheerful efficient service; background music, newspapers; children and dogs (in front bar) welcome, tables out under parasols, 13 comfortable bedrooms, open (and food) all day from 8am for breakfast. *(Lesley and Brian Lynn, Ian Herdman, Alan Johnson)*

WEST BROMWICH SO9992

Sow & Pigs (0121) 553 1191
Hill Top, towards Wednesbury; B70 0PS Revamped by Two Crafty Brewers and Sadlers in contemporary style but keeping original features, well kept beers from both breweries and up to three guests, enjoyable

We say if we know a pub has background music.

good value food including burgers, pizzas and pies; live music; children and dogs welcome, open all day. *(Dave Braisted)*

WHICHFORD SP3134

Norman Knight (01608) 684621
Ascott Road, opposite village green; CV36 5PE Sympathetically extended beamed and flagstoned pub; own Stratford Upon Avon beers with guests such as Hook Norton, good food (not Mon) using local produce including organic meat from the family farm, helpful friendly service; quiz last Mon of month, occasional live music; children and dogs welcome, picnic-sets on front lawn facing lovely village green, aunt sally, three glamping pods and self-catering apartment, nice walks, open all day Fri, Sat, till 6pm Sun, closed Mon lunchtime. *(Guy Vowles, Clive and Fran Dutson)*

WILLEY SP4885

Barn (01788) 833810
Coalpit Lane; CV23 0SL New family management and refurbishment for this pub-restaurant in converted barn; own O'Neills beers (view into the brewery) plus Sharps Doom Bar and a guest, decent range of wines and gins, enjoyable reasonably priced food from sandwiches and sharing boards to burgers and grills, Sun carvery till 6pm, friendly helpful service, more room in upstairs galleried area; Sat live music; children and dogs, welcome, terrace with country views, open all day, food all day Fri and Sat. *(Alan Johnson)*

WILLEY SP4984

Sarah Mansfield (01455) 553133
Just off A5, N of A427 junction; Main Street; CV23 0SH Comfortable 17th-c beamed village pub; good choice of enjoyable well priced food served by friendly attentive staff, four real ales including Greene King and Sharps from stone-faced servery, open fire; pool and darts, free wi-fi; children welcome, a few tables outside, closed Mon lunchtime. *(Mike and Margaret Banks)*

WILLOUGHBY SP5267

Rose (01788) 891180
Just off A45 E of Dunchurch; Main Street; CV23 8BH Neatly decorated old thatched dining pub; low beam and plank ceiling, wood or tiled floors, some panelling and inglenook woodburner, good range of popular food cooked by chef-landlord including monthly tapas night, well kept ales and reasonably priced house wines, friendly attentive young staff; children and dogs welcome, disabled facilities, seating in side garden with gate to park and play area, closed Sun evening, Mon. *(Angela and Steve Heard)*

WOLVERHAMPTON SO9298

★**Great Western** (01902) 351090
Corn Hill/Sun Street, behind railway station; WV10 0DG Cheerful pub hidden away in cobbled lane down from mainline station; Holdens and guests kept well, real cider and bargain home-made food (not Sun, reduced choice after 3pm), helpful friendly staff, traditional front bar, other rooms including neat dining conservatory, open fires and interesting railway memorabilia; TV; children and dogs welcome, maybe summer barbecues in yard, open all day and busy with Wolves fans on match days. *(Alan C Curran)*

WOLVERHAMPTON SJ8901

Hail to the Ale 07846 562910
Pendeford Avenue/Blackburn Avenue; WV6 9JN One-room micropub in converted shop, four well kept/priced beers including Morton and several real ciders, simple food such as pork pies and sausage rolls, warm friendly atmosphere; dogs welcome, seats outside, open all day Sat, till 5pm Sun, closed Mon-Weds and lunchtimes Thurs, Fri. *(Philip Farmer)*

WOOTTON WAWEN SP1563

Bulls Head (01564) 795803
Stratford Road, just off A3400; B95 6BD Attractive black and white dining pub; Elizabethan beams and timbers, stone and quarry-tiled floors, log fires, decent choice of enjoyable fairly priced food from sandwiches up, deals for two on some main courses, Marstons, Ringwood and a guest, friendly staff; children welcome, dogs in bar, outside tables front and back, handy for one of England's finest churches and Stratford Canal walks, open all day (till 8pm Sun). *(Dave Braisted)*

Wiltshire

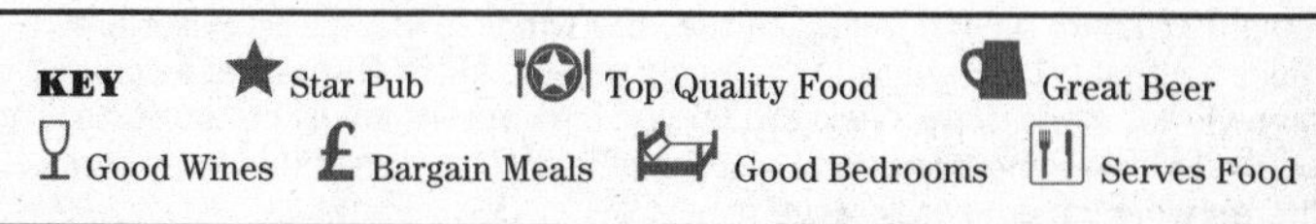

ALDBOURNE SU2675 Map 2

Blue Boar £

(01672) 540237 – www.theblueboarpub.co.uk

The Green (off B4192 in centre); SN8 2EN

Simple pubby furnishings in bar, cosy restaurant, decent food and seats outside

Picnic-sets at the front of this bustling local make the most of the charming location by the pretty village green, and the summer window boxes are lovely. The heavily beamed bar has a relaxed, chatty atmosphere helped along by cheerful staff and plenty of regulars. You'll find built-in wooden window seats, tall farmhouse and other red-cushioned pubby chairs on flagstones or bare boards, a woodburning stove in an inglenook fireplace with a stuffed boar's head and large clock above it, and horsebrasses on the bressumer beam; a noticeboard has news of beer festivals and live music events. Wadworths IPA, 6X and a guest beer on handpump, eight wines by the glass, 17 malt whiskies and a farm cider. The back restaurant is beamed and cottagey with standing timbers, dark wooden chairs and tables on floorboards and rugs, and plates on a dresser.

Traditional food at honest prices includes lunchtime sandwiches and baguettes, smoked mackerel pâté, crispy mushroom dippers with apricot and ginger chutney, home-cooked ham and free-range eggs, root vegetable nut roast with goats cheese, butterflied chicken breast with white wine and tarragon sauce, salmon with lemon and parsley butter and baby potatoes, 10oz sirloin steak with red wine sauce, and puddings such as banoffi pie and Baileys and dark chocolate cheesecake with whipped cream. *Benchmark main dish: steak and kidney pie £9.50. Two-course evening meal £18.00.*

Wadworths ~ Tenants Michael and Joanne Hehir ~ Real ale ~ Open 11.30-3, 5.30-11.30; 11.30am-midnight Fri, Sat; 12-11 Sun ~ Bar food 12-2 (2.30 Fri, Sat), 6.30-9; 12-4 Sun ~ Restaurant ~ Children welcome ~ Dogs allowed in bar ~ Wi-fi ~ Live music regularly (phone to check) *Recommended by Andrew Vincent, Simon Day, Dan and Anne Morgan, Celia and Andrew King*

BRADFORD-ON-AVON ST8261 Map 2

Castle

(01225) 865657 – www.flatcappers.co.uk

Mount Pleasant, by junction with A363, N edge of town; extremely limited pub parking but spaces in nearby streets; BA15 1SJ

Substantial stone inn with local ales, popular food, plenty of character and fine views; bedrooms

Once a toll house, this handsome stone building is much enjoyed by our readers. The unspoilt bar has a lot of individual character: a wide range of seats (church chairs, leather armchairs, cushioned wall seating, brass-studded leather dining chairs) around chunky pine tables on dark flagstones, church candles, fringed lamps and a good log fire; daily papers, background music and board games. A bare-boards snug on the right is similar in style. Cheerful staff serve a beer named for the pub (from Three Castles), Bristol Beer Factory Holler, Navigation Patriot, Three Castles Barbury Castle and Yeovil Hopkandi on handpump and several wines by the glass; a beer and music festival is held twice a year. Seats outside at the front offer sweeping town views, while in the back garden you look across lovely countryside. The boldly decorated bedrooms are comfortable and have spacious bathrooms. There's wheelchair access at the rear.

Highly regarded food includes breakfast (8.30-12), tapas-like choices such as maple pork belly squares, duck satay and smoked haddock croquettes plus fennel, pomegranate, orange, saffron and quinoa salad, cod and triple-cooked chips, ham hock and broad bean panzanella, sea bass and crab salad with crab mayonnaise, lamb belly with smoked aubergine, onions, garlic and jus, chicken and mushroom pie, 8oz rump steak with a choice of sauce, and puddings such as chocolate and hazelnut brownie with chocolate sauce and pumpkin meringue pie. *Benchmark main dish: burger with toppings, coleslaw and fries £9.95. Two-course evening meal £18.00.*

Free house ~ Licensee Tom Atkinson ~ Real ale ~ Open 8.30am-11pm ~ Bar food 8.30am-10pm (9.30pm Sun) ~ Children welcome but must be seated from 7.30pm ~ Dogs welcome ~ Wi-fi ~ Bedrooms: /£100 *Recommended by Max Simons, Jeff Davies, Rupert and Sandy Newton, Taff Thomas, Dr and Mrs A K Clarke, Jonny and Andrew Haughton*

BRADFORD-ON-AVON ST8260 Map 2

Timbrells Yard

(01225) 869492 – www.timbrellsyard.com

St Margarets Street; BA15 1DE

Town-centre pub next to the river, with interesting décor, a thoughtful choice of drinks and food, and cheerful staff; bedrooms

Given a clever makeover by blending original features with quirky, contemporary décor and furnishings, this is a bustling 18th-c inn right in the centre of town. The bar has stripped floorboards, walls of exposed stone, planking and grey paintwork, there are dining chairs, upholstered and modern ones, scatter-cushioned wall seats, cubed or leather-topped stools, wooden tables of every size and shape, mirrors, hanging lamps, a group of sofas and armchairs and both a woodburning stove and an open fire – it's all very entertaining, with a wide mix of customers and a chatty atmosphere. From the tiled counter, friendly, efficient staff serve Kettlesmith Faultline, Otter Bitter and a guest such as Three Daggers Blonde on handpump, 22 wines by the glass, local cider and perry and cocktails. The light and airy restaurant is similarly furnished, and the sunny front terrace has seats and tables. Stylish, up-to-date bedrooms (some with mezzanines) are deeply comfortable and well equipped.

Food is rewarding and includes breakfasts (8.30-11am) and all-day cakes and coffee plus lunchtime ciabattas and salads such as roasted squash, tahini, coriander, grapefruit, lentil and mint, bream ceviche with citrus and chilli dressing, radicchio and radish, goats cheese arancini with walnut mayonnaise and beetroot dressing, flat-iron chicken with spicy slaw, crispy potato wedges and chimichurri sauce, local venison and pork ragoût with pasta, salsa verde and pangritata, fresh fish of the day with capers and seaweed butter, potatoes and fennel, and puddings such as rocky road sundae with toffee sauce and vanilla ice-cream and lemon posset with poached rhubarb and almond crumble. *Benchmark main dish: slow-cooked pork belly with pepperonata £16.50. Two-course evening meal £22.00.*

Free house ~ Licensee Henry Gray ~ Real ale ~ Open 7.30am-11pm; 8am-10.30pm Sun ~ Bar food 12-3, 6-9.45 (9 Sun) ~ Restaurant ~ Children welcome ~ Dogs allowed in bar and bedrooms ~ Bedrooms: /£100 *Recommended by Chris and Sophie Baxter, Alexander and Trish Gendall, Ben and Jenny Settle, Dr and Mrs A K Clarke, Ruth and Peter Bacon*

CHILTON FOLIAT SU3270 Map 2

Wheatsheaf

(01488) 680936 – www.thewheatsheafchiltonfoliat.co.uk
B4192; RG17 0TE

Lots going on in bustling old pub with a good mix of customers, simple furnishings, local ales and smashing food

An enthusiastic young couple have sensitively restored this delightful, thatched 17th-c pub, but they've been careful not to lose its traditional character. He cooks the imaginative food (and was a *MasterChef* semi-finalist), she runs front of house and you can be sure of a genuine welcome from both of them. You'll find plenty going on including live music events, a regular pub quiz (every third Tuesday), cookery classes and an upstairs shop selling vintage furniture, clothes and shoes; darts, board games and background music. The beamed bar and dining room are furnished with wheelbacks and mate's chairs, built-in settles and bow-window seats around dark tables on patterned carpets, artwork on the walls (some painted by the landlord), a piano and woodburning stoves. Local ales include Ramsbury Gold and guests from breweries such as Butts and Two Cocks on handpump, plus 15 organic wines by the glass, home-made liqueurs, organic soft drinks and farm cider. Green values mean a lot here, as does using seasonal, local produce, free-range, organic or wild meat and responsibly sourced fish. There are a few picnic-sets at the front. Disabled access.

Using his father's rare-breed pigs, sheep and chickens and other local produce and describing his cooking as 'upmarket peasant food', the landlord offers lots of nibbles and starters such as pork terrine with crab apple purée, smoked salmon and truffle honey on bruschetta and chicken with aioli and popcorn; also, nettle soufflé with cheese and asparagus cream, mushroom pie with root vegetables, carbonara pasta with bacon, egg, cream, salami and parmesan, hake curry with mussels, squash, cauliflower and couscous, aged burger with beetroot jam and chips, chargrilled chicken and blue cheese with polenta and leeks, 40-day-aged steak with chips and tarragon aioli, and puddings such as orange jelly with pineapple and st clements treacle tart; they also serve breakfast on Saturday morning. *Benchmark main dish: wood-fired organic pizzas £14.00. Two-course evening meal £20.00.*

Free house ~ Licensees Ollie and Lauren ~ Real ale ~ Open 12-3, 5.30-11.30; 12-11.30 Fri; 9.30am-11.30pm Sat; 12-9.30 Sun ~ Bar food 12-2.15, 6-9.15 ~ Restaurant ~ Children welcome ~ Dogs welcome ~ Wi-fi ~ Live music and film showings (check website) *Recommended by Michael Doswell, Charlotte and William Mason, Sophie and James Collier, Selwyn Jones*

COMPTON BASSETT SU0372 Map 2

White Horse

(01249) 813118 – www.whitehorse-comptonbassett.co.uk
At N end of village; SN11 8RG

Bustling pub with three ales, good wines by the glass, interesting food and seats in big garden; pretty bedrooms

Head here for lunch after enjoying a walk in the lovely surrounding countryside. There's a friendly, bustling bar with cushioned window and wall seats and settles, chunky wood and leather dining chairs around assorted tables on parquet flooring, a woodburning stove, and bar stools against the counter where they keep Ramsbury Gold, Three Daggers Blonde and Wadworths 6X on handpump, 15 wines by the glass, 13 malt whiskies, a good range of spirits and farm cider. The dining room has dark red walls and tiles at one end and bare floorboards and pale paintwork at the other; throughout there are beams and joists and miscellaneous antique tables and chairs. Also, there's another woodburning stove, and background music and board games. The large, neatly kept garden has picnic-sets and other seats, while the paddock is home to pigs and geese. Bedrooms (in a separate building overlooking the grounds) are attractive and well equipped and breakfasts are good.

Making everything in-house and using local, seasonal produce, the creative food includes sandwiches, scallops with black pudding, cauliflower and raisin purée and shaved fennel, fishcake with herbs, a poached egg and hollandaise sauce, tagliatelle with porcini mushrooms and cheese, chorizo spiced pork and pulled pork burger with toppings, pickles and fries, pollack, mussels and squid with lobster bisque and saffron potatoes, corn-fed chicken with truffle mash, baby leeks and rosemary velouté, and puddings such as peanut butter parfait with banana ice-cream and sticky toffee pudding with toffee sauce; they also offer a two- and three-course weekday set lunch. *Benchmark main dish: lamb rump with creamy garlic potatoes, ratatouille and basil jus £23.50. Two-course evening meal £25.00.*

Free house ~ Licensee Kristian Goodwin ~ Real ale ~ Open 12-11; 12-9 Sun ~ Bar food 12-3, 6-9 (8 Sun) ~ Restaurant ~ Children welcome ~ Dogs allowed in bar ~ Wi-fi ~ Bedrooms: £75/£85 *Recommended by Sally and Lance Oldham, Andy and Louise Ramwell, Nicola and Nigel Matthews, Karl and Frieda Bujeya, Basil and Joyce Rampley, Victoria and Len Meadows*

CORSHAM — ST8670 Map 2

Methuen Arms

(01249) 717060 – www.themethuenarms.com

High Street; SN13 0HB

Charming hotel with refurbished character bar and dining rooms, friendly staff, imaginative food, good wines and ales, and seats outside; comfortable bedrooms

---

There's always a pleasing mix of drinkers and diners in this handsome Georgian inn and the atmosphere is civilised yet informal. The proper front bar has stools, simple dining chairs, built-in cushioned wall seats and a settle round a mix of tables on bare boards, a large gilt-edged mirror above the fireplace housing a woodburning stove, and fresh flowers, with Butcombe Bitter and Rare Breed and a couple of guest beers on handpump, 12 wines by the glass, ten malt whiskies and quite a few gins. Across the counter is a small dining room with cushioned wall seats, wooden chairs and a long, button-back bench by a medley of tables on floorboards, and a fireplace neatly piled with logs; background music. The attractively decorated main dining room has a long blue leather wall seat, blue leather and elegant wooden chairs around wooden tables on parquet flooring, and a large wall tapestry, while a second smaller, panelled room is similarly furnished but with big, bright, modern bird prints. The pretty garden has good quality seats and tables under parasols. Bedrooms are smart, comfortable and well equipped and breakfasts are highly regarded.

As well as breakfasts for non-residents (7-10.30am; from 8am weekends), the excellent food from a thoughtful menu includes pressed ham hock with parsley and pickles, seared scallops with smoked pork belly, black treacle, lime, cauliflower, apple and curry powder, pea and mint arancini with gorgonzola, sugar snap peas and tempura courgette, chicken in a basket (barbecue breast, sticky wing and kentucky leg) with baby corn, red cabbage slaw and chicken gravy, asian duck salad confit leg with stir-fried salad, sesame and kumquats, lamb rump with breast and sweetbreads, broccoli, blue cheese beignet and toasted almonds, and puddings such as chocolate fondant with beetroot, raspberry and yoghurt and lemon cheesecake with crème fraîche, rosemary and lemon turkish delight meringue. *Benchmark main dish: stone bass with prawn and crab cake, tempura prawn and crab bisque £23.00. Two-course evening meal £30.00.*

Butcombe ~ Managers Abi and Ashley Harlow ~ Real ale ~ Open 12-11 (10.30 Sun) ~ Bar food 12-2.30, 6-9.30; 12-3, 6-9 Sun ~ Restaurant ~ Children welcome ~ Dogs allowed in bar and bedrooms ~ Wi-fi ~ Bedrooms: £120/£140 *Recommended by Michael Doswell, Mike Gleave, Jacqui and Alan Swan, Colin McLachlan, Dr and Mrs A K Clarke, Valerie and Gordon Wauton, Diana and Bertie Farr*

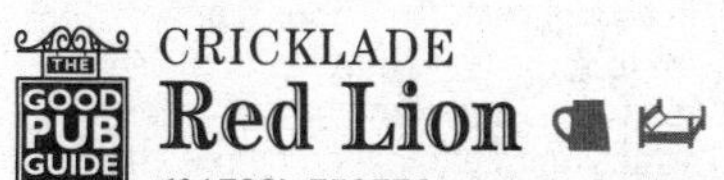

CRICKLADE SU1093 Map 4

Red Lion

(01793) 750776 – www.theredlioncricklade.co.uk

Off A419 Swindon–Cirencester; High Street; SN6 6DD

16th-c inn with well liked food in two dining rooms, ten real ales, friendly, relaxed atmosphere and big garden; bedrooms

They keep a fantastic range of drinks plus rewarding food here, and our readers also enjoy the community atmosphere and traditional décor. From their on-site Hop Kettle microbrewery, there might be Hop Kettle C.O.B., Element and North Wall and up to seven quickly changing guests. They also keep 60 bottled beers, six farm ciders, ten wines by the glass, ten malt whiskies and 15 gins (gin hour is 5.30-6.30pm). The bar has stools by the nice old counter, wheelbacks and other chairs around dark wooden tables on red patterned carpet, an open fire and all sorts of bric-a-brac on the stone walls including stuffed fish, animal heads and old street signs. You can eat here or in the slightly more formal dining room, furnished with pale wooden farmhouse chairs and tables, beige carpeting and a woodburning stove in a brick fireplace. There are plenty of picnic-sets in the big back garden. Bedrooms are comfortable and breakfasts good. You can walk along the nearby Thames Path or around the historic, pretty town.

Highly thought-of food includes lunchtime sandwiches (not Sun), potted crab with rapeseed mayonnaise, brown butter and pickled gherkins, goats cheese with chargrilled tenderstem broccoli, salt-baked beetroot and pickled walnut purée, sharing plates, spicy bean burger with cheese, home-made chilli jam and triple-cooked chips, mussels in cider and seaweed butter with skinny fries, ox tongue and cheek with baby turnips, red cabbage and braised ox sauce, 15-hour cider-braised pork belly with pork cheek ragoût, salt-baked celeriac, apple purée and red wine sauce, and puddings such as chocolate and salted caramel tart with honeycomb and clotted cream pannacotta with rhubarb purée, rose jelly, crushed cookie and popcorn powder. *Benchmark main dish: burger with toppings and chips £13.00. Two-course evening meal £20.00.*

Free house ~ Licensee Tom Gee ~ Real ale ~ Open 12-11; 12-midnight Sat; 12-10.30 Sun ~ Bar food 12-2.30, 6.30-9; 12-2.30, 6.30-9.30 Fri, Sat; 12-3, 6.30-9 Sun ~ Restaurant ~ Children welcome ~ Dogs welcome ~ Wi-fi ~ Bedrooms: /£90 *Recommended by Dr W I C Clark, Alison and Tony Livesley, Gerry and Pam Pollard, Catherine and Daniel King, John and Lorna Chew, Alison and Michael Harper*

Pubs close to motorway junctions are listed at the back of the book.

CRUDWELL — ST9592 Map 4

Potting Shed

(01666) 577833 – www.thepottingshedpub.com

A429 N of Malmesbury; The Street; SN16 9EW

Friendly dining pub with low-beamed rooms, an interesting range of drinks and food, and seats in the big garden

Appetising food, interesting drinks and charming, chatty staff continue to draw praise from our readers for this civilised place. Low-beamed rooms ramble around the bar with its bare stone walls, open fires and woodburning stoves (one in a big worn stone fireplace), mixed plain tables and chairs on pale flagstones, armchairs and a sofa in one corner and daily papers. Four steps lead up into a high-raftered area with wood flooring, and there's another separate, smaller room that's ideal for a lunch or dinner party. Also, lots of country prints and more modern pictures, fresh flowers, candles and some quirky, rustic decorations such as a garden-fork door handle, garden-spade beer pumps and so forth. Butcombe Gold and Original, Flying Monk Elmers, Oakham Citra, Prescott Hill Climb and Ramsbury Bitter on handpump, as well as carefully chosen wines and champagne by the glass, home-made seasonal cocktails and local fruit liqueurs; background music and board games and dogs may get treats. There are teak seats around cask tables among the weeping willows, as well as a boules piste. Sister business the Rectory Hotel is a stone's throw away. There's wheelchair access to the front door from the car park, and disabled loos.

Creative british cooking includes twice-baked cheese soufflé with spinach and grain mustard, smoked haddock croquette with creamed leeks, a soft boiled egg and curried mayonnaise, a pie of the day, wagyu beef burger with toppings and triple-cooked chips, lamb rump with wild garlic, radishes and asparagus, whole sole with miso and seaweed butter, local pork chop with roast fennel, nduja sausage and salsa verde, T-bone steak (for two) with a choice of sauce, and puddings such as a changing crème brûlée and crumble of the day. *Benchmark main dish: calves liver with pancetta, sage and greens £14.50. Two-course evening meal £21.00.*

Enterprise ~ Lease Alex Payne ~ Real ale ~ Open 11-11; 11-midnight Fri, Sat ~ Bar food 12-2.30, 6.30-9.30; 12-4, 6-10 Sat; 12-5, limited menu 6-8 Sun ~ Restaurant ~ Children welcome ~ Dogs welcome ~ Wi-fi *Recommended by Michael Sargent, Mrs Zara Elliott, Beverley and Andy Butcher, Holly and Tim Waite, Chris and Angela Buckell, Mr and Mrs P R Thomas*

EAST CHISENBURY — SU1352 Map 2

Red Lion

(01980) 671124 – www.redlionfreehouse.com

At S end of village; SN9 6AQ

Wiltshire Dining Pub of the Year

Country inn in peaceful village run by hard-working chef-owners, contemporary décor, an informal atmosphere and excellent food; fine bedrooms

'It's such a treat coming here and a very special place to stay overnight, too,' says one reader with enthusiasm; so many others agree. The wonderful food cooked by Mr and Mrs Manning (both are top chefs) draws customers from far and wide, but this is also a proper pub where locals congregate at high chairs by the bar for a pint and a chat: Flack Manor Union Flack on handpump, 30 wines by the glass, home-made cordial and quite a range of gins and malt whiskies. One long room is split into different areas by brick and green-planked uprights. A big woodburner sits in a brick inglenook fireplace at one end; at the other is a comfortable black leather sofa and armchairs, and in between are high-backed and farmhouse wooden dining chairs around various tables on bare boards or stone tiles, with pretty flowers and church candles dotted about. There's an additional dining area too and an upstairs private dining room; background music. Outside, the terrace and grassed area above it have picnic-sets and tables and chairs. The very well equipped, boutique-style bedrooms are in a separate building with private decks just a few metres from the River Avon; breakfasts are delicious and the bloody marys and bucks fizz are complimentary. They make their own dog treats and can organise a packed lunch for walkers.

They raise their own pigs, keep chickens and grow some produce for the inspired food: lunchtime sandwiches and smoked ham and eggs plus ceviche of scallops with burnt apple, jalapenos and dill, tagliatelle of mussels with saffron, Pernod and chives, mushroom and cheese pithivier with chestnuts, kalettes, cavolo nero, truffle nage and crispy parmesan, herb-roast guinea fowl breast with potato millefeuille, charred leek, black truffle and madeira velouté, roast turbot with saffron-braised potatoes, fennel, brown shrimps, monk's beard and sauce bourride, and puddings such as new york cheesecake with bay leaf, rhubarb and iced Hendricks and tonic and Valrhona chocolate torte with banana compote, coffee cream and hazelnut praline; they also offer a two- and three-course set menu. *Benchmark main dish: slow-cooked pork belly and tenderloin with crisp polenta, fresh morels, onions, crackling and jus £24.00. Two-course evening meal £32.00.*

Free house ~ Licensees Britt and Guy Manning ~ Real ale ~ Open 9am-11pm; 9am-3pm Sun; closed Sun evening, Mon, Tues ~ Bar food 12-2.30, 6-8.30; 12-2 Sun ~ Children welcome ~ Dogs allowed in bar and bedrooms ~ Wi-fi ~ Bedrooms: /£195 *Recommended by Penny and David Shepherd, Simon and Alex Knight, Rosie and Marcus Heatherley, Dan and Nicki Barton, Barbara and Phil Bowie*

EAST KNOYLE ST8731 Map 2

Fox & Hounds

(01747) 830573 – www.foxandhounds-eastknoyle.co.uk

Village signposted off A350 S of A303; The Green (named on some road atlases), a mile NW at OS Sheet 183 map reference 872313; or follow signpost off B3089, about 0.5 miles E of A303 junction near Little Chef; SP3 6BN

Pretty thatched village pub with splendid views, welcoming service, good beers and popular, enjoyable food

It's well worth the effort negotiating the little lanes to reach this ancient pub in a pretty spot by the village green. Three linked areas (on different levels around the central horseshoe-shaped server) have woodburning stoves, plentiful oak woodwork and flagstones, comfortably padded dining chairs around big scrubbed tables, and a couple of leather sofas; the furnishings are all very individual and uncluttered. There's also a small light-painted conservatory restaurant. Butcombe Bitter, Hop Back Summer Lightning and Three Daggers Blonde on handpump, a dozen wines by the glass and Thatcher's farm cider; board games and skittle alley. On a clear day you can enjoy remarkable views into Somerset and Dorset from the picnic-sets in front of this partly thatched old place. The nearby woods are good for a stroll and the Wiltshire Cycleway passes through the village.

Well regarded food includes lunchtime ploughman's (not Sunday), deep-fried rosemary and garlic-crusted brie wedges with cranberry sauce, japanese-style battered prawns with sweet chilli dipping sauce, pizzas, chickpea, spinach and butternut squash curry, a changing pie, chicken wrapped in bacon with creamy pesto sauce, beef casserole, duck breast with rösti potato and red wine sauce, flat-iron steak with peppercorn sauce and chips, and puddings such as stem ginger and syrup cheesecake and hazelnut and praline chocolate torte with ice-cream. *Benchmark main dish: beer-battered fish of the day and chips £12.00. Two-course evening meal £21.00.*

Free house ~ Licensee Murray Seator ~ Real ale ~ Open 11.30-3, 5-11 ~ Bar food 12-2.15, 6.30-9; 12-2, 6.30-8.30 Sun ~ Children welcome ~ Dogs welcome ~ Wi-fi *Recommended by John and Abigail Prescott, Glen and Patricia Fuller, Camilla and Jose Ferrera, Sally and Colin Allen, Edward Mirzoeff*

FONTHILL GIFFORD ST9231 Map 2

Beckford Arms

(01747) 870385 – www.beckfordarms.com

Hindon Lane; from Fonthill Bishop, bear left after tea rooms through Estate gate; from Hindon follow High Street signed for Tisbury; SP3 6PX

Handsome 18th-c inn with character bar and restaurant, unfailingly good food, thoughtful choice of drinks and an easy-going atmosphere; comfortable bedrooms

Always filled with happy drinkers and diners, this is a gently civilised Georgian country inn with a friendly and informal atmosphere. The main bar has various old wooden dining chairs and tables on parquet flooring, a huge fireplace and bar stools beside the counter where they keep an interesting range of drinks. This includes Butcombe Bitter, Keystone Phoenix (named for them) and Timothy Taylors Landlord on handpump, 15 wines by the glass, 20 malt whiskies, farm cider, winter mulled wine and cider, and cocktails such as a bellini using locally produced peach liqueur and a bloody mary using home-grown horseradish. The cosy sitting room is stylish with comfortable sofas facing one another across a low table with newspapers, an appealing built-in window seat among other chairs and tables, and an open fire in a stone fireplace with candles in brass candlesticks and fresh flowers on the mantelpiece. Also, a separate restaurant and private dining room. Much of the artwork on the walls is local. The mature rambling garden has seats on a brick terrace, hammocks under trees, games for children, a dog bath and boules. Bedrooms are individually decorated and breakfasts are good and generous; they also offer two self-catering lodges. The surrounding rolling parkland is lovely and there's plenty to do nearby.

Imaginative food from a seasonal menu (they grow some produce themselves) includes braised ox tongue with jerusalem artichokes, balsamic and pomegranate, chargrilled mackerel fillet with fermented cucumber, chilli and onion, burger with toppings, pickles and chips, butternut squash risotto with wild mushrooms, cheese, pine nuts and egg yolk, slow-braised cuttlefish with chorizo, red pepper, black-eyed peas and coriander, lamb leg steak with french-style peas and new potatoes, 10oz bavette steak with roquefort sauce, beetroot and chips, and puddings such as carrot cake with crème anglaise and salted popcorn praline and poached rhubarb, baked white chocolate, ginger and rhubarb sorbet. *Benchmark main dish: beer-battered fish and chips with pea purée £14.50. Two-course evening meal £22.00.*

Free house ~ Licensees Dan Brod and Charlie Luxton ~ Real ale ~ Open 8am-11pm ~ Bar food 12-3, 6-9.30 (9 Sun) ~ Children welcome ~ Dogs welcome ~ Wi-fi ~ Bedrooms: /£95 *Recommended by Edward Mirzoeff, S G N Bennett, Rosie and Marcus Heatherley, Lee and Jill Stafford, Frances and Hamish Porter, Ian Herdman, David and Sally Cullen, John and Hilary Murphy*

Children – if the details at the end of a featured entry don't mention them, you should assume that the pub does not allow them inside.

GREAT BEDWYN SU2764 Map 2

Three Tuns

(01672) 870280 – www.tunsfreehouse.com

Village signposted off A338 S of Hungerford, or off A4 W of Hungerford via Little Bedwyn; High Street; SN8 3NU

Friendly village pub with highly rated food and local ales; seats outside

The hands-on chef-owner and his wife work hard to keep standards consistently high in this carefully refurbished village pub. The beamed front bar is traditional and simply furnished with pubby stools and chairs on bare floorboards, and has an open fire, artwork by local artists on the walls and plenty of original features. They keep quickly changing ales including Butcombe Bitter, Flack Manor Union Flack and Otter Bitter on handpump, 12 wines by the glass, several malt whiskies, gins and vodkas and Sheppy's farm cider. French doors in the back dining room lead into the garden where there are tables and chairs, an outdoor grill and boules. The Kennet & Avon Canal runs through the village and the pub is on the edge of Savernake Forest, which has lovely walks and cycle routes. It's also handy for the station.

Cooked by the chef-patron who makes everything in-house, the excellent food includes ham hock and parsley terrine with pickled cucumber, cumberland sausage scotch egg with celeriac rémoulade, apple purée and crackling, asparagus and pea risotto with goats cheese, cola-cooked ham and eggs, beef burger with toppings, mustard slaw and chips, anchovy and chilli ragoût with parmesan and croutons, roast hake with tabbouleh, prune purée and labneh, rare bavette steak with bone marrow and mustard butter and chips, and puddings such as rhubarb, strawberry and mint nut crumble and chocolate mousse with Oreo cookies, Mars Bar sauce, honeycomb and toasted marshmallow. *Benchmark main dish: buttermilk fried chicken burger £13.00. Two-course evening meal £22.00.*

Free house ~ Licensees James and Ashley Wilsey ~ Real ale ~ Open 10-3, 6-11; 10am-11pm Sat; 12-6 Sun; closed Sun evening, Mon ~ Bar food 12-2.30, 6.30-9.30 ~ Restaurant ~ Children welcome ~ Dogs welcome ~ Wi-fi *Recommended by Alan and Alice Morgan, Edward and William Johnston, Buster and Helena Hastings, Belinda Stamp, Miss B D Picton, Trevor and Michele Street*

GRITTLETON ST8680 Map 2

Neeld Arms

(01249) 782470 – www.neeldarms.co.uk

From M4 junction 17, follow A429 to Cirencester and immediately left, signed Stanton St Quintin and Grittleton; SN14 6AP

Bustling village pub with popular food and drink and friendly staff; bedrooms

There are plenty of chatty locals (though visitors are made just as welcome) in this 17th-c pub and the atmosphere throughout is gently civilised but unstuffy and relaxed. The open-plan rooms have Cotswold-stone walls, contemporary colours on wood panelling and a pleasant mix of seating ranging from bar stools and traditional settles to window seats and pale wooden dining chairs around an assortment of tables – each set with fresh flowers. The little brick fireplace houses a woodburning stove and there's an inglenook fireplace on the right. Flying Monk Habit, St Austell Tribute, Wadworths 6X and a guest beer on handpump and decent wines are served from the blue-painted panelled and oak-topped bar counter. The back dining area has another inglenook with a big woodburning stove and white-painted chairs and settles around solid tables; even back here, you still feel thoroughly part of the action. Bedrooms are attractive, neatly looked after and comfortable. An outdoor terrace has a pergola and a few tables behind a low roadside wall at the front.

Food is good and includes ciabatta sandwiches at lunchtime, moules marinière, local wild boar salami and parma ham, goats cheese, tomato and basil pesto tart, local sausages and mash, calves liver with black pudding on a potato rösti, whole grilled sea bass with butter and parsley sauce, pork medallions with apple and calvados sauce, sirloin steak with all the trimmings, and puddings such as amaretto trifle and fresh mango crème brûlée. *Benchmark main dish: pie of the day £10.95. Two-course evening meal £20.00.*

Free house ~ Licensees Charlie and Boo West ~ Real ale ~ Open 12-3, 5.30-11.30; 12-midnight Sat; 12-11 Sun ~ Bar food 12-2, 6.30-9.30; 12-2.30, 7-9 Sun ~ Restaurant ~ Children welcome ~ Dogs welcome ~ Wi-fi ~ Bedrooms: £60/£80 *Recommended by Tom and Lorna Harding, Claire and Emma Braithwaite, Charlotte and William Mason, Roger and Anne Mallard, Patricia and Gordon Thompson, Sophie Ellison*

HOLT ST8561 Map 2

Toll Gate

(01225) 782326 – www.tollgateinn.co.uk

Ham Green; B3107 W of Melksham; BA14 6PX

Bustling pub with cheerful staff, woodburners, real ales and popular food; pretty bedrooms

Our readers greatly enjoy this friendly, 16th-c stone pub and tend to return on a regular basis. The relaxed bar has real character, with seats by one woodburner and a mix of tables and chairs on pale floorboards. Served by hard-working, helpful staff you'll find Box Steam Golden Bolt (the brewery is in the village), Butcombe Bitter and Rare Breed, Sharps Doom Bar and Tollgate Gold (named for them from Box Steam) on handpump, 18 wines by the glass from a good list (if you eat with them on Thursday evenings you can bring your own wine – no corkage), interesting gins and three farm ciders; background music and board games. The dining room leads off the bar with high-backed leather and other cushioned chairs and a second woodburner. Up a few steps, the high-raftered restaurant is similarly furnished with white deer heads on a dark blue wall and church windows (this used to be a workers' chapel). The suntrap paved back terrace has seats and tables; boules. Bedrooms, some of which are in their old farm shop, have open fires; there's also a holiday cottage for rent. Wheelchair access to main bar and dining area (but not to the loos).

Pleasing food includes lunchtime rolls, ham hock, wholegrain mustard and honey terrine with sauce gribiche, confit pheasant crispy parcels with hoisin, cucumber and spring onion, wild mushroom and brie risotto with pine nut crust and a crispy egg, calves liver with bacon, black pudding and apple mash with caremelised onion jus, venison, chocolate and apple pie, chicken breast with celeriac dauphinoise and wild mushroom café au lait, smoked haddock kedgeree with a poached egg and sautéed potatoes, and puddings such as crème brûlée and hazelnut praline iced parfait with butterscotch sauce and pineapple jelly. *Benchmark main dish: burger with toppings and chips £12.95. Two-course evening meal £19.00.*

Free house ~ Licensees Laura Boulton and Mark Hodges ~ Real ale ~ Open 8am-11.30pm; 8.30am-midnight Sat; 8.30am-4pm Sun; closed Sun evening ~ Bar food 12-2, 6.30-9; 12-9 Sat; 12-2.30 Sun ~ Restaurant ~ Children welcome ~ Wi-fi ~ Live music Fri evenings July, Aug ~ Bedrooms: £60/£80 *Recommended by Michael Doswell, Sophie Ellison, Guy Henderson, Dr and Mrs A K Clarke, Martin and Sue Neville, Chris and Angela Buckell, Gene and Kitty Rankin, Ian Herdman*

HORNINGSHAM

ST8041 Map 2

Bath Arms

(01985) 844308 – www.batharms.co.uk

By tradesmen's entrance to Longleat House; BA12 7LY

Bustling pub with plenty of space, rustic furnishings, interesting food and real ales; bedrooms

There's a proper country atmosphere in this handsome old stone-built inn and plenty of character in the several linked bar and dining areas. A simple end room has an open fire, paintings and photos of the village, and cushioned pews, wall seats and dining chairs around big tables on wide floorboards. You go through a smaller dining room into the main bar, where there's another open fire with a large mirror above it, rustic tables and chairs and a long cushioned settle on rugs and bare boards, candles in big wooden candlesticks and paintings of fancy-plumaged birds. They keep Butcombe Bitter, Three Daggers Blonde and Wessex Golden Apostle on handpump, Orchard Pig cider and a good choice of wines and other drinks, all promptly served by competent staff; background music, board games, juke box and skittle alley. The restaurant is similarly furnished, with chandeliers and a big painting of a sultan. An attractive back garden has a two-level terrace with circular picnic-sets and there are more at the front and on gravel under pollarded trees; views overlook woods to the Avon Valley. Bedrooms are attractive and comfortable. Wheelchair access to bars is via a side door; disabled loos.

Food is good and includes sandwiches, smoked pork and rabbit rillettes with apple and cranberry chutney, oak-smoked bacon with bubble and squeak, hollandaise and a poached free-range egg, butternut squash and wild mushroom fregola with roasted chestnut cream, a burger and a pie of the day, duck breast with red lentil cake, cauliflower purée and cassis jus, coffee and cardamom-crusted lamb loin with roasted pineapple purée, fondant potatoes and red wine jus, and puddings such as a crumble of the day with custard and dark chocolate and peanut butter fondant with yoghurt ice-cream. *Benchmark main dish: parmesan-crusted venison rump £19.50. Two-course evening meal £22.50.*

Free house ~ Licensee Des Jones ~ Real ale ~ Open 7.30am-11pm; 8.30am-11pm Sat, Sun ~ Bar food 12-2.45, 6-8.45 ~ Restaurant ~ Children welcome ~ Dogs allowed in bar and bedrooms ~ Wi-fi ~ Bedrooms: £95/£105 *Recommended by Chris and Angela Buckell, Elise and Charles Mackinlay, Jennifer and Nicholas Thompson, David and Charlotte Green, David and Leone Lawson*

LOWER CHUTE

SU3153 Map 2

Hatchet

(01264) 730229 – www.thehatchetinn.com

The Chutes well signposted via Appleshaw off A342, 2.5 miles W of Andover; SP11 9DX

Neatly kept 13th-c thatched inn with a friendly welcome for all, real ales and enjoyable food; comfortable bedrooms

'A remote rural delight' is how one reader describes this tucked-away country cottage and it is indeed quite charming. The beamed bar has a peaceful local feel, a splendid 16th-c fireback in a huge fireplace (and a roaring winter log fire) and various comfortable seats around oak tables; there's also an extensive restaurant. You'll get a warm welcome from the convivial landlord, and despite the remote setting, plenty of customers find their way here. Timothy Taylors Landlord and a couple of guests such as Hatchet (named for the pub from Greene King) and Otter Bitter on handpump, eight wines by the glass, 20 malt whiskies and several farm ciders; background music and board games. There are seats out on a terrace and the side grass, and a safe play area for children. The snug bedrooms make this an excellent place to stay (dogs are welcome in a couple of rooms) and breakfasts are hearty.

Country cooking includes baguettes, tempura prawns with sweet chilli sauce, creamy garlic mushrooms, spinach and red pepper lasagne, ham and eggs, pork medallions with grain mustard sauce and sautéed potatoes, beef bourguignon, chicken with leek, bacon and stilton sauce, fish pie, lamb rump in red wine, redcurrant and rosemary sauce, and puddings. *Benchmark main dish: steak in ale pie £11.95. Two-course evening meal £16.00.*

Free house ~ Licensee Jeremy McKay ~ Real ale ~ Open 11.30-3, 6-11; 11.30-11 Sat; 12-10.30 Sun ~ Bar food 12-2.15, 6-9.30; 12-3, 7-9 Sun ~ Restaurant ~ Children welcome ~ Dogs allowed in bar and bedrooms ~ Wi-fi ~ Open mike night first Fri of month; quiz Tues evening ~ Bedrooms: £75/£85 *Recommended by Pip White, Alison and Graeme Spicer, Serena and Adam Furber, Christopher Mannings, Mark Morgan*

MARSTON MEYSEY SU1297 Map 4

Old Spotted Cow

(01285) 810264 – www.theoldspottedcow.co.uk

Off A419 Swindon–Cirencester; SN6 6LQ

An easy-going atmosphere in cottagey bar rooms, friendly young staff, lots to look at, well kept ales and enjoyable food; bedrooms

With interesting food, fine ales and a genuine welcome, you can't go wrong at this charming little pub. You'll see many cows of all sorts around the bars, and some of them actually are spotted: paintings, drawings, postcards, all manner and colour of china objects and embroidery and toy ones too. The main bar has high-backed cushioned dining chairs around chunky pine tables on wooden floorboards or parquet, a few rugs here and there, an open fire at each end of the room (with comfortable sofas in front of one), fresh flowers and brass candlesticks with candles, and beer mats and banknotes pinned to beams. Otter Bitter, Ringwood Boondoggle and Skinners Betty Stogs on handpump, ten wines by the glass, summer farm cider and quite a few gins and malt whiskies; board games. A cottagey dining room leads off here with similar tables and chairs, a couple of long pews and a big bookshelf. There are seats and picnic-sets on the front grass and a children's play area beyond a big willow tree. A classic car show is held here on the late May Bank Holiday with live music and local beers.

Cooked by the landlady, the reliably good food includes sandwiches and burgers, a choice of tapas, lemon and mascarpone risotto with asparagus and parmesan, sesame crab cakes with warm salad of rice noodles, nam jim sauce and pak choi, four-egg omelettes, bubble and squeak with bacon, mustard cream sauce and a poached free-range egg, burger with toppings, chilli sauce and mustard mayonnaise, king prawns in beer batter with chips, rib-eye steak with garlic butter or a choice of sauce, and puddings such as banana and walnut bread and butter pudding and cappuccino cheesecake with chocolate ice-cream. *Benchmark main dish: spicy fish stew with coconut rice £14.00. Two-course evening meal £20.50.*

Free house ~ Licensee Anna Langley-Poole ~ Real ale ~ Open 11-11; 11-6.30 Sun ~ Bar food 12-2, 7-9; 12-3 Sun; no food Mon ~ Restaurant ~ Children welcome but must be over 8 in bar ~ Dogs allowed in bar ~ Wi-fi ~ Bedrooms: £65/£80 *Recommended by Ben and Diane Bowie, Keith Perry, Edward Mirzoeff, Adam Jones, Andrea and Philip Crispin, Patricia and Gordon Thompson*

MIDDLETON TM4267 Map 5

Bell

(01728) 648286

Off A12 in Yoxford via B1122 towards Leiston; also signposted off B1125 Leiston–Westleton; The Street; IP17 3NN

Low beamed bars, good beer and popular good value food – a peaceful spot

Part of this 16th-c pub is thatched and, together with the lovely hanging baskets in summer, it's picture-postcard pretty; there are picnic-sets out in front under parasols with more in the big back garden. Inside, on the left, the traditional bar has a log fire in a big hearth, old local photographs, a low plank-panelled ceiling, bar stools and pew seating. Helpful staff serve Adnams Broadside, Ghost Ship, Mosaic and Southwold tapped from the cask and nine wines by the glass. On the right, an informal two-room dining area has bare boards and a nice mix of cushioned dining chairs around polished dark tables under low black beams; there's also a room with a big table just right for a family by a large woodburning stove. Dogs are welcomed with treats and a bowl of water. The RSPB reserve at Minsmere is nearby, as are walks along the coast.

Well regarded food includes sandwiches, duo of salmon and dill terrine with pickles, hoisin duck thai salad, wild mushroom and tarragon tagliatelle, chicken caesar salad, beef and horseradish burger with toppings and chips, calves liver with bacon, onion rings and red wine gravy, cod loin with hasselback potatoes and bacon and chorizo jam, 10oz rib-eye steak with trimmings, and puddings such as a crumble of the day and chocolate brownie with chocolate sauce. *Benchmark main dish: beer-battered fish and chips £12.95. Two-course evening meal £19.00.*

Adnams ~ Tenants Amy and Julian ~ Real ale ~ Open 12-3, 6-11 (midnight Sat); 12-10 Sun ~ Bar food 12-2.30, 6-9; 12-5 Sun ~ Restaurant ~ Children welcome ~ Dogs welcome ~ Wi-fi
Recommended by Peter Pilbeam, Val and Malcolm Travers, Revd Carol Avery, Cecily and Steven Evans, Dan and Anne Morgan

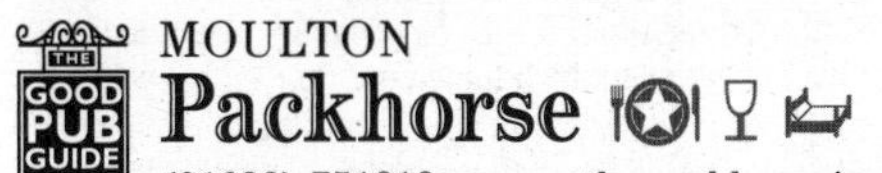

MOULTON TL6964 Map 5

Packhorse

(01638) 751818 – www.thepackhorseinn.com

Bridge Street; CB8 8SP

Smart, friendly inn with stylishly refurbished bar and dining rooms, a thoughtful choice of drinks, excellent food and seats on terrace; lovely bedrooms.

Attractively extended and refurbished, this civilised inn is at the heart of the local community. Adjacent is a delightful 15th-c bridge across the River Kennett, while Newmarket Racecourse, gallops and stables are close by. The dining rooms are open-plan but have cosy areas too: nice old-style cushioned wooden dining chairs and button-back wall seating around solid polished tables on rugs or bare floorboards, open fireplaces (one is two-way), candlelight and exotic flower arrangements, game bird and other prints on pale paintwork and some boldly patterned window blinds. The simply furnished bar area has armchairs with scatter cushions, wooden chairs and tables, antlers and a boar's head and stools against the counter where friendly staff serve Adnams Mosaic and Woodfordes Wherry on handpump and 20 good wines by the glass. There are seats and tables under parasols on the terrace and on a lawn. Bedrooms are stylish, up to date and well equipped and breakfasts are particularly good.

From seasonal menus, the first class food includes lunchtime sandwiches, roast quail with pumpkin and pickled walnut sauce, sardines on toast with garlic mayonnaise and lemon, burger with smoked garlic aioli, french fries and chestnut mushroom ketchup, hake with poached leeks, cauliflower and crab, local Estate venison with salt-baked turnip, barley and mushroom ragoût, slow-cooked lamb shoulder casserole, and puddings such as macerated strawberries with lime posset and sorrel ice-cream and dark chocolate mousse with milk ice-cream and pistachios; they also offer a two- and three-course set lunch (not Sunday). *Benchmark main dish: lamb with peas and jersey royal potatoes £21.00. Two-course evening meal £30.00.*

Chestnut Group ~ Manager Philip Turner ~ Real ale ~ Open 12-11.30; 11-midnight Sat; 11am-11.30pm Sun ~ Bar food 12-2.30, 7-9.30; 12-3.30, 7-8.30 Sun ~ Restaurant ~ Children welcome ~ Dogs welcome ~ Wi-fi ~ Bedrooms: /£125 *Recommended by Caroline and Steve Archer, Max and Steph Warren, Thomas Green, Patti and James Davidson*

PETTISTREE TM2954 Map 5

Greyhound

(01728) 746451 – www.greyhoundinnpettistree.co.uk

The Street; brown sign to pub off B1438 S of Wickham Market, 0.5 miles N of A12; IP13 0HP

Neatly kept village pub with enjoyable food and drink; seats outside

In a peaceful setting next to the church, this is a nice old place that our readers enjoy greatly. It's basically two smallish rooms with open fires, some rather low beams, chunky farmhouse chairs and cushioned settles around dark wooden tables on bare floorboards and candlelight. Earl Soham Victoria Bitter and guests such as Adnams Freewheel and Ghost Ship on handpump, several wines by the glass and quite a few malt whiskies; it's best to book in advance to be sure of a table. The well kept side garden has picnic-sets under parasols, with more beside the gravelled front car park.

The landlady cooks the enjoyable food: gin-cured salmon with tonic jelly, pickled cucumber, potato scone and horseradish cream, ham hock and parsley terrine with red onion jam and pickled vegetables, linguine with wild garlic and pine nut pesto, roasted peppers and soda bread croutons, dressed crab with bloody mary mayonnaise and chips, corn-fed chicken breast stuffed with sunblush tomatoes, charred baby gem and watercress dressing, cod, haddock and salmon fishcakes with confit and roasted fennel and tartare sauce, hanger steak marinated in rosemary and garlic with cracked pepper sauce, and puddings such as honey pannacotta with flapjack crumb and rhubarb and yoghurt fool with lemon curd. *Benchmark main dish: slow-cooked lamb shoulder with apricot and toasted almond bulgar wheat, date purée and minted yoghurt £17.00. Two-course evening meal £20.00.*

Free house ~ Licensees Stewart and Louise McKenzie ~ Real ale ~ Open 12-3, 6-11; 12-4 Sun; closed Sun evening, Mon; two weeks Jan ~ Bar food 12-2.30, 6-9; 12-3 Sun ~ Restaurant ~ Children welcome ~ Dogs allowed in bar ~ Wi-fi *Recommended by JER, Dr A E and Mrs Forbes, Sally and Lance Oldham, Jeff Davies, Sarah and David Gibbs, Diane Abbot, Neil Allen, Beth Aldridge*

SIBTON TM3570 Map 5

White Horse

(01728) 660337 – www.sibtonwhitehorseinn.co.uk

Halesworth Road/Hubbards Hill, N of Peasenhall; IP17 2JJ

Suffolk Dining Pub of the Year

Particularly well run inn with nicely old-fashioned bar, good mix of customers, real ales and imaginative food; bedrooms

The bedrooms, housed in a separate building next door, are warm, contemporary and well equipped and our readers enjoy staying here. This bustling village pub is run by hands-on licensees and their friendly staff and all are made welcome. The appealing bar has a roaring log fire in a large inglenook fireplace, horsebrasses and tack on the walls, vintage settles and pews, Adnams Southwold, Green Jack Trawlerboys Best Bitter and Woodfordes Nelsons Revenge on handpump, ten wines by the glass and 12 malt whiskies served from an old oak-panelled counter. A viewing panel reveals the working cellar and its ancient floor, and they hold a beer festival in July. Steps lead up past an old, partly knocked-through timbered wall into a carpeted gallery, and there's also a smart dining room and a secluded (and popular) dining terrace. The big garden has plenty of seats.

Using produce from their kitchen garden and local free-range meat, poultry and eggs, the accomplished food includes lunchtime sandwiches, beetroot-cured salmon gravadlax with whipped cream cheese, baby beetroot, lemon jelly and honey and mustard dressing, king scallops with crispy black pudding, cauliflower purée, apple and watercress, parmesan gnocchi with ricotta, butternut squash and wild garlic pesto, beer-battered cod and twice-cooked chips, chicken breast with thigh kiev, king oyster mushroom, sweet onion purée, bacon crisp and potato noodles, hazelnut-crusted pork tenderloin with glazed cheek, fondant potatoes, carrot purée and pickled mustard seeds, and puddings such as rhubarb and custard crumble tart with rhubarb sorbet and coconut pannacotta with mango and chilli salsa, burnt coconut and mango sorbet; they also offer a two- and three-course set lunch. *Benchmark main dish: duck breast with caramelised chicory, dauphinoise potatoes and red wine sauce £16.00. Two-course evening meal £21.00.*

Free house ~ Licensees Neil and Gill Mason ~ Real ale ~ Open 12-3, 6.30 (6 Sat)-11; 12-4, 7-10.30 Sun; closed Mon lunchtime ~ Bar food 12-2, 6.30-9; 12-2.30, 7-8.30 Sun ~ Restaurant ~ Well behaved children welcome but over-6s only in evening ~ Dogs allowed in bar ~ Wi-fi ~ Bedrooms: £90/£100 *Recommended by Elise and Charles Mackinlay, Holly and Tim Waite, Buster and Helena Hastings, Guy Henderson, John Harris*

SOUTHWOLD TM5076 Map 5

Crown

(01502) 722275 – www.thecrownsouthwold.co.uk

High Street; IP18 6DP

Graceful old coaching inn with plenty of room for both drinking and dining, local ales, good wines and seats outside; good bedrooms

This comfortable, civilised hotel makes an excellent lunch stop for those exploring the local shops and if you just continue along the High Street, you'll hit the beach; from here there are miles of coastline to explore. There's an elegant beamed front bar and dining room that are light and airy with a curved high-backed settle and other dark varnished settles, kitchen chairs and bar stools, a carefully restored and rather fine carved wooden fireplace; daily papers. Our readers are fond of the informal and chatty back bar with its oak panelling, bare floorboards and antique tables and chairs; dogs are welcome here. Adnams Bitter, Broadside, Fat Sprat and Ghost Ship on handpump, 12 wines by the glass and eight malt whiskies; background music and board games. There are seats on the sheltered side terrace or outside at the front by the High Street. Bedrooms are well equipped and individually furnished and breakfasts highly rated.

Using local, seasonal produce, the well regarded food includes sandwiches, mussels in cider and dill, chicken liver parfait with mango jelly, salt-baked beetroot with gnocchi, butternut squash purée and pickled shiitake mushrooms, chicken breast with apple boudin, clapshot (similar to neeps and tatties), pearl barley and chestnut crumb, sea trout with baked chervil root and shellfish broth, chargrilled hanger steak with sweet potato purée, a duck egg and crispy shallots, and puddings such as ginger and apple sponge with butterscotch sauce and warm rice pudding with bramble compote and pistachios. *Benchmark main dish: bacon chop with butternut purée, gnocchi and mushrooms £18.50. Two-course evening meal £25.00.*

Adnams ~ Manager Nick Attfield ~ Real ale ~ Open 11-11 ~ Bar food 12-3, 6-9 ~ Children welcome ~ Dogs allowed in bar ~ Wi-fi ~ Bedrooms: /£150 *Recommended by Brian and Sally Wakeham, John and Abigail Prescott, Tom and Lorna Harding, Sally Harrison, Frances Parsons, Ted and Mary Bates, Sandra and Michael Smith*

SOUTHWOLD TM4975 Map 5

Harbour Inn

(01502) 722381 – www.harbourinnsouthwold.co.uk

Blackshore, by the boats; from A1095, turn right at the Kings Head, and keep on past the golf course and water tower; IP18 6TA

Great spot down by the boats with lots of outside tables and interesting interior; popular food with emphasis on local seafood

There's plenty of charm in this old fishermen's pub. It's right on the water with picnic-sets on the terrace offering views of the boats on the estuary; more seats and tables behind the pub overlook the marshy commons to the town. Inside, the back bar is nicely nautical with dark panelling and built-in wall seats around scrubbed tables, and cheerful staff serve a dozen wines by the glass, along with Adnams Broadside, Ghost Ship, Southwold and a guest such as Arabella SB on handpump. The low ceiling is draped with ensigns, signal flags and pennants, and there's a quaint old stove, rope fancywork, local fishing photographs and even portholes with water bubbling behind them; they have their own weather station for walkers and sailors. The lower front bar, with a tiled floor and panelling, is broadly similar, while the large, elevated dining room has panoramic views of the harbour, lighthouse, brewery and churches beyond the marshes. You can walk from here along the Blyth estuary to Walberswick (where the Bell is under the same good management) via a footbridge and return by the one-man ferry.

There's quite an emphasis on locally caught fresh fish: smoked haddock chowder with pancetta and a poached egg, smoked trout with horseradish pâté, grilled sardines with tomato and basil salad and monkfish carbonara. Non-fishy choices include sandwiches, chickpea and sweet potato falafel with sun-dried tomato and herb couscous, tahini sauce and toasted pitta, steak in ale pie, thyme and garlic chicken schnitzel with apple chutney and dauphinoise potatoes, steak burger with toppings and chips, and puddings such as chocolate brownie with vanilla ice-cream and lemon curd and raspberry eton mess. *Benchmark main dish: beer-battered fish and chips £13.00. Two-course evening meal £19.00.*

Adnams ~ Tenant Nick Attfield ~ Real ale ~ Open 11-11 ~ Bar food 12-9 ~ Restaurant ~ Children welcome ~ Dogs allowed in bar ~ Folk music second Thurs and third Sun of month *Recommended by Bob and Margaret Holder, Rupert and Sandy Newton, Michael and Sarah Lockley, Celia and Andrew King, Mandy and Gary Redstone*

STOKE-BY-NAYLAND TL9836 Map 5

Crown ★

(01206) 262001 – www.crowninn.net

Park Street (B1068); CO6 4SE

Smart dining pub with attractive modern furnishings, imaginative food, real ales and a great wine choice; good bedrooms

NEWTON TONY SU2140 Map 2

Malet Arms

(01980) 629279

Village signposted off A338 Swindon–Salisbury; SP4 0HF

Smashing village pub with no pretensions, a good choice of local beers and highly regarded food

A favourite with many of our readers (and with us as well) this has genuine, unspoilt character and attracts a fine mix of customers. If you like your pubs neat and tidy, perhaps you might feel this is a little worn about the edges but that's exactly why so many people love it. The low-beamed interconnecting rooms have all sorts of tables of differing sizes with high-winged wall settles, carved pews, chapel and carver chairs, and lots of pictures of local scenes and from imperial days. The main front windows are said to be made from the stern of a ship, and there's a log and coal fire in a huge fireplace. The snug is noteworthy for its fantastic collection of photographs and prints celebrating the local aviation history of Boscombe Down, alongside archive photographs of Stonehenge festivals of the 1970s and '80s. At the back is a homely, red-painted dining room. Four real ales on handpump come from breweries such as Butcombe, Fullers, Hop Back, Itchen Valley, Palmers, Plain, Ramsbury, Stonehenge and Triple fff and they also keep over 30 malt whiskies, ten wines by the glass and farm cider; board games. There are seats on the small front terrace with more on grass and in the back garden. The road leading to the pub goes through a ford, and it may be best to use an alternative route in winter when the water can be quite deep. There's an all-weather cricket pitch on the village green.

Using seasonal game from local shoots (some bagged by the landlord), lamb raised in the surrounding fields and free-range local pork, the country cooking includes chicken liver pâté with onion marmalade, venison carpaccio with truffle oil and parmesan, mushroom and chestnut cottage pie with parsnip mash, pork, honey and watercress sausages with mash, fried onions and gravy, fresh plaice, mackerel, torbay and sole from Brixham, lamb shoulder with mash and minted pea purée, crispy roast pork belly with kale, sage and onion mash and scrumpy gravy, and puddings such as treacle tart and rocky road chocolate crunch. *Benchmark main dish: venison pie £13.75. Two-course evening meal £19.50.*

Free house ~ Licensees Noel and Annie Cardew ~ Real ale ~ Open 12-3, 6-11; 12-3, 6-10 Sun; closed Sun evening in winter ~ Bar food 12-2.15, 6.30-9.15 ~ Restaurant ~ Children allowed only in restaurant or snug ~ Dogs allowed in bar *Recommended by M J Daly, Roger and Donna Huggins, Ian Herdman, Edward Mirzoeff, Gordon and Patricia Gorringe, Ruth and Peter Bacon*

RAMSBURY SU2771 Map 2

Bell

(01672) 520230 – www.thebellramsbury.com

Off B4192 NW of Hungerford, or A4 W; SN8 2PE

300-year-old coaching inn with a civilised feel, character bar and dining rooms, and a thoughtful choice of both drinks and food; spotless bedrooms

With creative food, a gently civilised but informal atmosphere and a good choice of drinks, it's not surprising this handsome old inn is so busy – it's best to book a table in advance. The two rooms of the chatty bar have tartan-cushioned wall seats and pale wooden dining chairs around assorted tables, country and wildlife paintings, interesting stained-glass windows and a woodburning stove. Neat, efficient staff serve Ramsbury

Bitter, Gold and Mango Libation and a guest such as Navigation Splendor on handpump, a dozen wines by the glass and 20 malt whiskies. A cosy room between the bar and restaurant has armchairs and sofas before an open fire, a table of magazines and papers, a couple of portraits, stuffed birds and a squirrel, books on shelves and patterned wallpaper. Smart and relaxed, the restaurant is similarly furnished to the bar with white-clothed tables on bare boards or rugs, oil paintings and winter-scene photographs on beige walls; fresh flowers decorate each table. A nice surprise is the charming back café with white-painted farmhouse, tub and wicker chairs on floorboards, where they offer toasties, buns, cakes and so forth. The garden has picnic-sets on a lower terrace and raised lawn, with more on a little terrace near the front. The well equipped, restful bedrooms are named after game birds or fish.

First class food using some home-grown produce includes ham hock terrine with hay-baked celeriac and pickled berries, fir pine-cured and smoked salmon with capers, shallots and gherkins, buckwheat and mushroom pancakes with a crispy poached duck egg, celeriac, truffle and mushroom sauce, steak and kidney pie, duck breast with burnt cabbage, root vegetables and red wine sauce, rare-breed rib-eye steak with garlic butter or red wine sauce, and puddings such as poached pear tart with ginger syrup and vanilla ice-cream and baked white chocolate and Kahlúa cheesecake with blackberry sorbet. *Benchmark main dish: beer-battered haddock and triple-cooked chips £14.00. Two-course evening meal £21.00.*

Free house ~ Licensee Alistair Ewing ~ Real ale ~ Open 12-11 (10 Sun) ~ Bar food 12-2.30, 6-9; 12-3, 6-8 Sun ~ Restaurant ~ Children welcome ~ Dogs allowed in bar ~ Wi-fi ~ Bedrooms: /£130 *Recommended by David Phillips, V Brogden, Richard Tilbrook, Sally Harrison, Michael and Sarah Lockley, Sam Cole, Darrell Barton*

ROWDE ST9762 Map 2

George & Dragon

(01380) 723053 – www.thegeorgeanddragonrowde.co.uk

A342 Devizes–Chippenham; SN10 2PN

Gently upmarket inn with good food, west country ales and a relaxed atmosphere; bedrooms

This is a former coaching inn with a lot of character, and some excellent food too. The two low-ceilinged rooms have beams, large open fireplaces, wooden dining chairs (both straightforward and rather elegant) and wall seats with scatter cushions around candlelit tables, antique rugs and walls hung with old pictures and portraits; the atmosphere is pleasantly chatty. From the rustic bar counter, friendly staff serve Butcombe Bitter and guests from breweries such as Prescott and Kennet & Avon on handpump and several wines by the glass. There are tables and chairs in the pretty garden. Bedrooms are individually furnished and well equipped, and you can walk from here along the nearby Kennet & Avon Canal.

The highlight of the menu is the first class daily fresh fish from Cornwall for their special seafood platter, but they also offer double-baked cheese soufflé with parmesan cream, salmon tartare with avocado, lime and chilli, asparagus, pea and parmesan risotto with pesto oil, hake with prawn and whiskey chowder and rainbow chard, slow-roasted pork belly with borlotti beans and salsa verde, and puddings such as chocolate and espresso roulade with jersey cream and apple and plum crumble with vanilla ice-cream; they also offer a two- and three-course set menu (Monday-Thursday plus Friday lunch). *Benchmark main dish: crispy crumb dover sole with hollandaise sauce £25.00. Two-course evening meal £25.00.*

Free house ~ Licensee Christopher Day ~ Real ale ~ Open 12-3 (4 Sat), 6-11; 12-4 Sun; closed Sun evening ~ Bar food 12-3 (4 Sat), 6-10; 12-4 Sun ~ Restaurant ~ Children welcome ~ Dogs allowed in bar and bedrooms ~ Bedrooms: £75/£95 *Recommended by Pauline and Mark Evans, Rosie and John Moore, Sophia and Hamish Greenfield, Ian Herdman, Amanda Shipley, Susie and Spencer Gray, Barry Collett*

SHERSTON — ST8585 Map 2

Rattlebone

(01666) 840871 – www.therattlebone.co.uk

Church Street; B4040 Malmesbury–Chipping Sodbury; SN16 0LR

17th-c village pub with rambling rooms, real ales and good bar food using local and free-range produce; friendly staff

Of course, the interesting food in this 17th-c pub is a major draw but this is also a proper pub with chatty locals and a welcome for visitors, and we continue to get warm reports from our readers. The rambling, softly lit rooms have an easy-going atmosphere and in the public bar and long back dining room you'll find beams, standing timbers and flagstones, pews, settles and country kitchen chairs around an assortment of tables, and armchairs and sofas by roaring fires. Flying Monk Elmers, Marstons Pedigree, St Austell Tribute and Timothy Taylors Landlord on handpump, 20 wines by the glass from a thoughtful list, local cider and home-made lemonade; background music, darts, board games, TV and games machine. Outside is a skittle alley and three boules pitches, often in use by one of the many pub teams; a boules festival is held in July, in addition to mangold hurling (similar to boules, but using cattle-feed turnips) and other events. The two pretty gardens include an extended terrace where they hold barbecues and spit roasts. Wheelchair access.

Rewarding food includes lunchtime ciabattas and hot open sandwiches on rosemary focaccia, sharing platters, sizzling king prawns with garlic and chilli oil, chicken samosa with garlic mayonnaise, red pepper and pea arancini with smoked paprika aioli, cumberland sausage with creamy mash, crispy leeks and honey and dijon mustard sauce, cod loin with crab, chilli and tomato chowder, slow-cooked beef short ribs with caramelised onions and dauphinoise potatoes, and puddings such as apricot and white chocolate sponge with honeycomb ice-cream and four-way lemon cheesecake; gourmet burger night is Monday and steak evening is Wednesday. *Benchmark main dish: lamb rump with pea purée and red wine jus £17.50. Two-course evening meal £21.50.*

Youngs ~ Tenant Jason Read ~ Real ale ~ Open 12-3, 5-11; 12-midnight Fri, Sat; 12-11 Sun ~ Bar food 12-2.30, 6-9.30; 12-5 Sun (pizzas only 6-8.30) ~ Restaurant ~ Children welcome ~ Dogs allowed in bar ~ Wi-fi

Recommended by Chris and Angela Buckell, Freddie and Sarah Banks, Amy Ledbetter, Helene Grygar, Lorna and Jeff Mason, Andrea and Laurie Grist

SOUTH WRAXALL — ST8364 Map 2

Longs Arms

(01225) 864450 – www.thelongsarms.com

Upper S Wraxall, off B3109 N of Bradford-on-Avon; BA15 2SB

Friendly owners for well run and handsome old stone inn with plenty of character, real ales and first class food

Having an affable and enthusiastic landlord at the helm of a charming pub is all important, but when he also cooks the excellent food, it's a fantastic bonus. The bar has windsor and other pubby chairs round wooden tables on flagstones, a fireplace with a woodburning stove and high chairs by the counter where they keep Courage Directors, Kettlesmith Faultline and Robinsons Light Brigade on handpump, ten wines and prosecco and champagne by the glass, 12 gins and farm cider. Another room has cushioned and other dining chairs, a nice old settle and a wall banquette around a mix of tables on carpeting, fresh flowers and lots of prints and paintings; board games. There are tables and chairs in the pretty walled back garden, which also has raised beds and a greenhouse for salad leaves and herbs.

Inventive food includes sandwiches, hand-dived scallops with crackling, grapefruit, black garlic and hazelnuts, smoked salmon with keta (salmon roe), pickled cucumber and samphire, a pie of the day, mushrooms, potato terrine, purple sprouting broccoli and pine nuts, maple-cured ham and local eggs, pork belly with rhubarb, fondant potatoes and red cabbage, skate wing with smoked salmon, wild garlic mash and wild sea kale, and puddings such as dark chocolate tart with raspberry sorbet and gooseberry parfait with blueberries and honeycomb. *Benchmark main dish: lamb rump with local asparagus and hazelnuts £20.00. Two-course evening meal £22.00.*

Free house ~ Licensees Rob and Liz Allcock ~ Real ale ~ Open 12-3.30, 6-11.30; 12-5 Sun; closed Sun evening, Mon, Tues; three weeks Jan, two weeks Sept ~ Bar food 12-2.30, 6-9.30; 12-3 Sun ~ Children welcome ~ Dogs welcome ~ Wi-fi *Recommended by Taff Thomas, Michael Doswell, Sarah Le Fevre, Gerry and Pam Pollard, Robin and Anne Triggs, Dr and Mrs A K Clarke, Monica and Steph Evans, GSB*

SWALLOWCLIFFE ST9627 Map 2

Royal Oak

(01747) 870211 – www.royaloakswallowcliffe.com

Signed just off A30 Wilton–Shaftesbury; Common Lane; SP3 5PA

Thoughtfully restored inn with attractive décor, a well stocked bar, good seasonal food and seats in garden; bedrooms

It took a great deal of work and effort by a group of villagers to restore this pretty part-thatched building after a long closure. It's now a gently civilised and stylishly furnished inn with contemporary and locally made pale oak chairs, benches and tables on flagstones, light paintwork and chesterfield sofas facing each other in front of the inglenook fireplace. A row of stools line the planked counter where helpful staff serve a beer named for the pub (from Butcombe), Hop Back Admiral and a changing guest on handpump, 14 wines by the glass, ten gins, local cider and perry and a good choice of teas and coffee; board games. The conservatory dining room, beautifully beamed and timbered, is similarly furnished to the bar, with logs piled tightly into fireplaces and wall-to-wall windows. Doors open from here on to the terrace and garden, where there are rustic tables surrounded by chairs and benches. The six bedrooms are spotlessly clean, extremely comfortable and up to date; breakfasts are first class. There are plenty of surrounding walks and places to visit.

From a seasonal menu the carefully crafted food includes lunchtime sandwiches and salads, ham hock terrine with piccalilli, beetroot and vodka-cured salmon with oyster beignet and horseradish cream, spiced bean cassoulet with tomato, cumin and black wild rice, burger with toppings and skinny chips, chicken suprême with parsley root, pea purée, smoked bacon and sauce royale, braised lamb shoulder with rosemary, creamy white beans and griotte onions, sea bass fillet with apple and fennel salad, and puddings such as vanilla pannacotta and chocolate and orange croissant bread and butter pudding; they also offer Saturday brunch. *Benchmark main dish: slow-roast pork belly with bubble and squeak and apple and vanilla purée £16.95. Two-course evening meal £25.00.*

Free house ~ Licensee Steve Radford ~ Real ale ~ Open 11-11 ~ Bar food 12-2.30, 6-9 ~ Restaurant ~ Dogs allowed in bar and bedrooms ~ Wi-fi ~ Bedrooms: /£100

Recommended by Sally and Lance Oldham, Michael and Sarah Lockley, Rupert and Sandy Newton, Michael Doswell, Glen and Patricia Fuller

SWINDON SU1384 Map 2

Weighbridge Brewhouse

(01793) 881500 – www.weighbridgebrewhouse.co.uk

Penzance Drive; SN5 7JL

Stunning building with stylish modern décor, own microbrewery ales, a huge wine list, a big range of popular food and helpful staff

Even though this is a huge place, it does get packed out so you should book ahead to be sure of a table. The highly regarded food plays a big part, of course, but the fine choice of drinks is just as important and this includes their own-brews (you can peek through a glass viewing panel to see all the equipment) such as Best, Brinkworth Village, Dubbel, GWR 175 Special Mild, Pooleys Golden and a guest ale; also, 20 wines by the glass, 20 gins and a fine choice of malt whiskies and rums. The bar area has comfortable brown leather chesterfields and wood and leather armchairs around a few tables on dark flagstones, much-used blue bar chairs against the long dimpled and polished steel counter and a sizeable carved wooden eagle on a stand. The stylishly modern, open-plan dining room is the only place you can eat and you need to book in advance; this has a steel-tensioned high-raftered roof (the big central skylight adds even more light), attractive high-backed striped chairs and long wall banquettes, bare brick walls, candles in red glass jars on windowsills and a glass cabinet at the end displaying about 1,000 bottled beers from around the world. Metal stairs lead up to an area overlooking the dining room with big sofas and chairs beside a glass piano; another room on the same level is used for cosier dining occasions. There are seats on an outside terrace.

A good choice of enjoyable food includes lunchtime ploughman's, a charcuterie platter for two, mexican-style tagliatelle, faggots with onion gravy and dauphinoise potatoes, griddled pork chop on chorizo and cider cream sauce, crispy half duck with a sauce of redcurrant jelly, cherry wine and fresh strawberries, beef and black pudding stack with shiitake mushrooms and creamy marsala wine sauce, salmon, monkfish, mussels and prawns in a creamy Pernod sauce, thai-style crocodile, and puddings such as white chocolate and raspberry brûlée and lemon posset. *Benchmark main dish: rack of british lamb with rosemary and garlic breadcrumbs and mint, red wine and cream sauce £26.00. Two-course evening meal £30.00.*

Free house ~ Licensees Anthony and Allyson Windle ~ Real ale ~ Open 12-11; 12-midnight Sat; 12-10 Sun ~ Restaurant ~ Children welcome before 8pm ~ Dogs allowed in bar ~ Wi-fi ~ Live music Thurs-Sat evenings *Recommended by Edward Edmonton, Caroline and Steve Archer, Max and Steph Warren, Julie and Andrew Blanchett, Mike and Sarah Abbot*

TOLLARD ROYAL ST9317 Map 2

King John

(01725) 516207 – www.kingjohninn.co.uk

B3081 Shaftesbury–Sixpenny Handley; SP5 5PS

Pleasing contemporary furnishings in carefully opened-up pub, courteous, helpful service, good drinks and excellent food; pretty bedrooms

Regulars do drop into this friendly, civilised pub for a pint and a chat, but most customers come to enjoy the impressive food. The open-plan L-shaped bar has a log fire, nice little touches such as a pot of herbs and tiny metal buckets of salt and pepper on scrubbed kitchen tables, a screen made up of the sides of wine boxes, and candles in big glass jars. An attractive mix of seats takes in spindlebacks, captain's and chapel chairs (some built into the bay windows) plus the odd cushioned settle, and there are big terracotta floor tiles, lantern-style wall lights, hound, hunting and other photographs, and prints of early 19th-c scientists. A beer named for the pub (from Marstons), Gritchie Brewing Company English Lore and Waylands Sixpenny 6d Gold on handpump and wines from a good list. A second log fire has fender seats on each side and leather chesterfields in front, and there's also a stuffed heron and grouse; daily papers and background music. Outside at the front are seats and tables underneath parasols, with more reached by steps up to the raised garden where there's also an outdoor kitchen pavilion. Bedrooms are comfortable and pretty.

Creative food includes sandwiches, wild mushroom ravioli with celeriac velouté, portland crab on toast, burger with toppings and fries, braised octopus with lentils, chorizo and crispy sweetbread, confit lamb and lamb rump with salsa verde, côte du boeuf with béarnaise sauce and fries, megrim sole fillet with hollandaise sauce and poached egg, flat-iron steak with fries and béarnaise sauce, and puddings such as mango and passion-fruit cheesecake with coconut sorbet and apple doughnuts with toffee sauce and bay leaf ice-cream. *Benchmark main dish: twice-baked cheddar soufflé with fries £14.50. Two-course evening meal £20.00.*

Free house ~ Licensee Paolo Corgiolu ~ Real ale ~ Open 11-11; 11-10.30 Sun ~ Bar food 12-2.30, 6-9; 12-4, 6-8.30 Sun ~ Restaurant ~ Children welcome ~ Dogs welcome ~ Wi-fi ~ Bedrooms: /£90 *Recommended by Lyn and Freddie Roberts, Robert and Diana Myers, Sam Cole, Mr and Mrs P R Thomas, Tim and Sue Mulligan, Naomi and Andrew Randall*

Also Worth a Visit in Wiltshire

Besides the fully inspected pubs, you might like to try these pubs that have been recommended to us and described by readers. Do tell us what you think of them: feedback@goodguides.com

BADBURY SU1980

Plough (01793) 740342

A346 (Marlborough Road) just S of M4 junction 15; SN4 0EP Busy country pub with wide choice of fairly priced food, well kept Arkells beers and decent wines, friendly efficient service, large rambling bar with log fire, light airy dining room; background music; children and dogs welcome, far-reaching views from tree-shaded garden, open all day, food all day weekends, useful M4 stop. *(Sam Stainton)*

BARFORD ST MARTIN SU0531

Barford Inn (01722) 742242

B3089 W of Salisbury (Grovely Road), just off A30; SP3 4AB Welcoming 16th-c coaching inn; dark panelled front bar with big log fire, well kept Badger ales and decent wines by the glass, other connecting rooms including beamed bare-brick restaurant, wide choice of popular reasonably priced food (not Sun evening), prompt friendly service; children and dogs welcome, wheelchair access (not to bar), disabled loo, tables on terrace and in back garden, four annexe bedrooms, good walks, closed Mon, otherwise open all day. *(Mark Morgan)*

BECKHAMPTON SU0868

Waggon & Horses (01672) 539418

A4 Marlborough–Calne; SN8 1QJ Handsome stone and thatch former coaching inn; decent choice of enjoyable fairly priced food (not Sun evening) including gluten-free options in open-plan beamed bar or separate dining area, well kept Wadworths ales, friendly service; background music; children and dogs welcome, pleasant raised garden with play area, handy for Avebury (NT), open all day Fri-Sun. *(Celia and Andrew King)*

BERWICK ST JAMES SU0739

★**Boot** (01722) 790243

High Street (B3083); SP3 4TN Welcoming 18th-c flint and stone pub not far from Stonehenge; good locally sourced food (not Sun evening, Mon) from daily changing blackboard menu cooked by landlord-chef, friendly efficient staff, well kept Wadworths ales and a guest, huge log fire in inglenook at one end, sporting prints over brick fireplace the other, small back dining room with collection of celebrity boots; children and dogs welcome, sheltered side lawn, open 6-8pm Mon (12-3pm bank holiday Mon), otherwise regular hours. *(Michael Sargent)*

BERWICK ST JOHN ST9422

★**Talbot** (01747) 828222

Village signed from A30 E of Shaftesbury; SP7 0HA Unspoilt 17th-c pub in attractive village; simple furnishings and big inglenook in heavily beamed bar, Ringwood Best, Wadworths 6X and a guest, several wines by the glass, reasonable choice of popular home-made food including some vegetarian options, friendly service, restaurant; darts, free wi-fi; children and dogs (pub has its own) welcome, seats outside, good local walks, closed Sun evening, Mon. *(Lorna and Jeff Mason)*

BIDDESTONE ST8673

Biddestone Arms (01249) 714377

Off A420 W of Chippenham; The Green; SN14 7DG Spacious whitewashed stone pub mostly set out for dining; very popular food from standards up including signature home-made pies, Sun carvery, friendly efficient service despite being busy, well kept Sharps, Wadworths and guests, nice open fire; children and dogs (in front bar) welcome, pretty back garden, picturesque old village. *(Dr and Mrs A K Clarke)*

BIDDESTONE ST8673

White Horse (01249) 713305

The Green; SN14 7DG Prettily placed 16th-c three-room local near the village duck pond; a couple of real ales and enjoyable fairly pubby food (not Sun evening) including a few specials and menu for smaller appetites, friendly staff; children and dogs welcome, tables out at front and in back garden with clematis-covered pergola and play area, open all day Sun, closed Mon. *(Dr and Mrs A K Clarke)*

BISHOPSTONE SU2483

Royal Oak (01793) 790481

Cues Lane; near Swindon; at first exit roundabout from A419 N of M4 junction 15, follow sign for Wanborough then Bishopstone, at small sign on telegraph pole turn left; SN6 8PP Informal dining pub run by local farmers in pretty village below Ridgeway and White Horse; well liked seasonal food from daily changing menu including properly hung home-reared steaks, Arkells beers, organic wines, and good choice of whiskies and gins; mainly scrubbed-wood furnishings on bare boards or parquet, log fire on left and little maze of dark pews, refurbished upstairs dining area (same level as garden) with own bar and good disabled access/loos; children and dogs welcome, modern furniture on front deck, picnic-sets on grass and among trees, 12 bedrooms in separate recently converted building, open all day Sun. *(Richard Maccabee)*

BOX ST8168

Northey Arms (01225) 742333

A4, Bath side; SN13 8AE 19th-c stone-built dining pub with good interesting food from snacks up including children's menu, well kept Wadworths ales and plenty of wines by the glass, friendly young staff, fresh contemporary décor with chunky modern tables and high-backed rattan chairs, afternoon teas (not Sun); background music; tables and play area in garden behind, 11 well appointed bedrooms, open (and food) all day from 8am for breakfast. *(Dr and Mrs A K Clarke)*

BOX ST8369

★**Quarrymans Arms** (01225) 743569

Pub signed from A4 at Box Hill in both directions; SN13 8HN Enjoyable unpretentious pub with friendly staff and informal relaxed atmosphere; plenty of mining-related photographs and memorabilia (once a local for Bath-stone miners – you can hire a key to visit the extensive mines or take a guided tour), well kept Butcombe, Moles, Wadworths and guests, 60 malt whiskies and several wines by the glass, decent choice of fairly priced food (all day Sun) including daily specials; children and dogs welcome, picnic-sets on terrace with sweeping views, popular with walkers and potholers, four bedrooms, open all day. *(Taff Thomas, Dr and Mrs A K Clarke)*

BRADFORD-ON-AVON ST8261

Bunch of Grapes (01225) 938088

Silver Street; BA15 1JY Attractively renovated bar-restaurant with good french-influenced food including set menu choices, local ales such as Butcombe, craft beers and plenty of well chosen french wines, good coffee and cakes too, friendly efficient service, upstairs dining room; children welcome, open all day Fri-Sun, closed lunchtime Mon-Weds; for sale, so may be changes. *(Dan Rodeck)*

BRADFORD-ON-AVON ST8060

Cross Guns (01225) 862335

Avoncliff, 2 miles W of Bradford-on-Avon on Turleigh road, turn left for Avoncliff; park at dead end and walk across the bridge; BA15 2HB New owners and refurbishment for this popular 16th-c pub with its steeply terraced areas above the bridges, aqueduct and river; opened-up low-beamed interior, bare boards, stripped stone and inglenook log fire, four changing ales, local ciders and extensive range of spirits (over 100 gins), enjoyable food including 'bunny chow' (south african curry in hollowed-out bread), breakfast from 10am, friendly service; maybe sea shanties Tues evening, beer festivals Mar and Oct; children and dogs welcome, wheelchair access but no disabled loo, canal moorings nearby, open (and food) all day in summer. *(Jake Robinson)*

BRADFORD-ON-AVON ST8261

Dandy Lion (01225) 863433

Market Street; BA15 1LL Comfortably

modernised 18th-c pub; bar with stripped-wood floor and painted panelling, steps up to snug, more room in carpeted upstairs dining room, Wadworths ales, over a dozen wines by glass and good reasonably priced home-made food from fairly pubby menu, helpful friendly service; background music, board games, free wi-fi; children and dogs welcome, closed 3-6pm Mon and Tues, otherwise open (and food) all day. *(David and Stella Martin)*

BRADFORD-ON-AVON ST8161

Dog & Fox (01225) 862137
Ashley Road; BA15 1RT Welcoming unpretentious two-room local on country outskirts; beams and painted half-panelling, well kept Bath Gem, Courage Best and Sharps Doom Bar, four draught ciders, enjoyable affordably priced traditional food, right-hand part with little serving hatch and comfy seating by woodburner, carpeted dining area behind, small bare-boards bar to the left with darts; children and dogs welcome, picnic-sets and play area in lawned garden, open all day Fri-Sun. *(Taff Thomas, Dr and Mrs A K Clarke)*

BRADFORD-ON-AVON ST8261

★**George** (01225) 865650
Woolley Street; BA15 1AQ Neatly updated 18th-c stone dining pub with highly regarded food including good value set lunch and themed evenings (last Thurs of month – booking advised), also weekend breakfast (from 9.30am) and afternoon teas (Fri-Sun), efficient friendly service, a house beer from Butcombe and a couple of guests, good choice of wines and whiskies, two smallish rooms either side of entrance (one with open kitchen), mix of tables and chairs on wood floors, pictures for sale, cosy back lounge bar with sofas and wing chairs by log fire; children and dogs welcome, attractive split-level back garden, two self-catering apartments, open all day Fri and Sat, till 5pm Sun. *(Taff Thomas, Mr and Mrs P R Thomas, Michael Doswell)*

BRINKWORTH SU0184

Three Crowns (01666) 510366
The Street; B4042 Wootton Bassett–Malmesbury; SN15 5AF Old stone pub under new ownership; beamed bar with cushioned wall settles and sturdy mate's chairs around tables on patterned carpet, fireplace at each end, Butcombe Original and a couple of guests, Thatcher's and Weston's ciders, 15 wines by the glass, flagstoned conservatory restaurant and other spreading dining areas with shelves of bottles and a giant pair of bellows, good food from pub staples up including daily specials and weekend breakfasts, small shop; children welcome, dogs in bar (menu for them), tables under parasols on terrace, more seats in garden, open all day, no food Sun evening. *(Christopher Mannings)*

BROAD HINTON SU1176

Barbury (01793) 731510
On A4361 Swindon–Devizes, E of village; SN4 9PF Roadside sister pub to the Vine Tree in Norton; long bar with woodburner at each end, comfortable seating on bare boards, hunting and shooting prints, well kept ales such as Butcombe and lots of wines by the glass, steps up to carpeted dining room, good food from shortish interesting menu (not Sun evening, Mon); background music, TV, free wi-fi; children and dogs welcome, seats and tables on partly covered back terrace, closed Mon lunchtime, otherwise open all day. *(Basil and Joyce Rampley)*

BROKENBOROUGH ST9189

★**Horse Guards** (01666) 822302
Signed from Malmesbury on Tetbury road; SN16 0HZ Well run 18th-c village dining pub with fresh modern décor; beams and some bare stone walls in cosy bar, large two-way woodburner, lower plainer back part mainly for eating, good home-made food using local ingredients including seasonal game, well kept Uley and a guest, interesting wines from shortish list, welcoming owners and friendly staff; children and dogs allowed, two comfortable bedrooms, closed Mon lunchtime. *(Michael Doswell, Guy Vowles, Theocsbrian)*

BROMHAM ST9665

★**Greyhound** (01380) 850241
Off A342; High Street; SN15 2HA Popular old dining pub refurbished under present welcoming owners; bar with white-painted beams and light modern décor, snug area to the right, dining part to the left, wood and tartan-carpeted floors, woodburner, back restaurant with walk-across well, good reasonably priced food from landlord-chef including weekday lunch deal, efficient friendly service, well kept Wadworths ales and wide choice of wines, upstairs skittle alley/overflow restaurant; background music; children welcome, dogs in bar, circular picnic-sets in big enclosed garden with play equipment, ample parking in square opposite, closed Mon, otherwise open all day (till 7pm Sun). *(Barry Collett, Michael Doswell)*

BULKINGTON ST9458

Well (01380) 828287
High Street; SN10 1SJ Popular dining pub with modernised open-plan interior; good food from sandwiches and traditional favourites up, efficient friendly service, four real ales including Butcombe, Sharps and Timothy Taylors, well priced wines;

We say if we know a pub allows dogs.

background music, free wi-fi; children and dogs (in bar) welcome, wheelchair access, closed Mon. *(Taff Thomas)*

BURCOMBE SU0631

★**Ship** (01722) 744879
Burcombe Lane; brown sign to pub off A30 W of Salisbury, then turn right; SP2 0EJ Busy welcoming pub with most customers here for the good fairly traditional food from sandwiches to popular dry-aged steaks; section by entrance with log fire, beams and leather-cushioned wall and window seats on slate tiles, step up to spreading area of pale wood dining chairs around bleached tables, three changing ales, Symonds cider, nice wines by the glass and good range of gins/whiskies, friendly helpful staff; quiz last Thurs of month, free wi-fi; well supervised children welcome, dogs and muddy boots in bar, picnic-sets and pond in pretty back garden sloping down to willows by mill stream, open (and food) all day Sat, closed Mon. *(Ashley O'Connor)*

CASTLE COMBE ST8477

Castle Inn (01249) 783030
Off A420; SN14 7HN Handsome old inn under newish ownership; beamed bar with big stone fireplace, padded bar stools and fine old settle, some vintage french posters, ales such as Castle Combe and St Austell from oak servery, 18 wines by the glass including champagne, well liked traditional food served by friendly attentive staff, two snug lounges, formal dining rooms and big upstairs conservatory opening on to charming little terrace; children and dogs (in bar) welcome, tables out at front looking down idyllic main street of this remarkably preserved Cotswold village, fascinating medieval church clock, 12 bedrooms, car park shared with next-door hotel, open all day from 9.30am (food from midday). *(Tony Scott)*

CHICKSGROVE ST9729

★**Compasses** (01722) 714318
From A30 5.5 miles W of B3089 junction, take lane on N side signposted 'Sutton Mandeville, Sutton Row', then first left fork (small signs point the way to the pub in Lower Chicksgrove; look out for the car park); can also be reached off B3089 W of Dinton, passing the glorious spire of Teffont Evias church; SP3 6NB Popular 14th-c thatched inn with unchanging character bar; old bottles and jugs hanging from beams above the roughly timbered counter, farm tools and traps on stripped-stone walls, high-backed settles forming snug booths, flagstones and log fire, ales such as Bristol Beer Factory, Butcombe and Three Daggers, real cider and a dozen wines by the glass, good sensibly priced food (not Sun evening) from interesting menu; children and dogs welcome, quiet garden behind with terraces and courtyard, good surrounding walks, comfortable bedrooms and self-catering cottage, open all day in summer. *(Helene Grygar, Harriet Mitchell)*

CHILMARK ST9732

Black Dog (01722) 716344
B3089 Salisbury–Hindon; SP3 5AH Cosy 15th-c beamed village pub under welcoming new management; several linked areas, cushioned window seats, inglenook woodburner and interesting photographs from around the world, good food with emphasis on fish/seafood, three well kept Wadworths ales, friendly attentive service; children and dogs (in bar) welcome, disabled access, good-sized garden fenced from the road, open (and some food) all day, breakfast from 9am Sun. *(Gene and Kitty Rankin)*

CHIPPENHAM ST9173

Old Road Tavern (01249) 247080
Old Road, by N side of station; SN15 1JA Friendly old-fashioned town pub dating from the 19th c; public bar and two-part lounge, half a dozen well kept ales including Bath, Otter and Wye Valley, straightforward lunchtime food Thurs-Sat; live music and comedy nights in side barn, pool; nice secluded back garden, open all day. *(Dr and Mrs A K Clarke)*

CHOLDERTON SU2242

Crown (01980) 629247
A338 Tidworth–Salisbury roundabout, just off A303; SP4 0DW Thatched low-beamed cottage with nicely informal eating areas in L-shaped bar, a couple of well kept ales such as Fullers, good home-made food cooked by landlord-chef including regular themed evenings, separate restaurant; quiz first Weds of month, open mike nights, Sept beer festival; children and dogs welcome, picnic-sets out at front and in garden with play area, open (and food) all day Sun. *(Sam Stainton)*

CHRISTIAN MALFORD ST9678

Rising Sun (01249) 721571
Station Road; SN15 4BL Refurbished community-run village pub dating from the early 19th c; small beamed bar with wood floor, leather sofas by log fire, carpeted restaurant with high-backed dining chairs around modern wooden tables, enjoyable well presented food (not Sun evening, Mon, Tues), three well kept seasonally changing ales, ciders including Black Rat, good friendly service; children and dogs (in bar) welcome, disabled loo, a few picnic-sets out at front, garden behind with play area and boules, open all day weekends, closed Mon-Thurs lunchtimes. *(Alison and Michael Harper)*

COLERNE ST8171

Six Bells (01225) 742413
High Street; SN14 8DD 17th-c stone pub with good well presented food cooked by landlord-chef including generous Sun roasts,

efficient friendly service, well kept Butcombe Gold and Sharps Doom Bar, single room with bare boards or carpet, regimental badges and horsebrasses on black beams, boar's head, flag-draped mirror and assorted pictures on green walls, woodburner in stone fireplace; background and some live music, skittle alley; children and dogs welcome, open all day weekends (no food Sun evening), closed weekday lunchtimes. *(Michael Doswell, Dr and Mrs A K Clarke)*

COLLINGBOURNE DUCIS SU2453

Tipple Inn (01264) 850050

High Street; SN8 3EQ Comfortable 18th-c village pub well cared for by friendly landlord; three changing ales and enjoyable fairly standard home-cooked food (not Sun evening) from good baguettes up, woodburners in bar and smallish restaurant with light wood furniture and some vibrant artwork; quiz and live music nights, sports TV, pool, darts and free wi-fi; children, walkers and dogs welcome, small roadside terrace with pretty hanging baskets, grassy garden behind beyond car park, one bedroom, open all day weekends, closed Tues. *(Michael Doswell)*

CORTON ST9340

★**Dove** (01985) 850109

Off A36 at Upton Lovell, SE of Warminster; BA12 0SZ Modernised brick pub on edge of small Wylye Valley village not far from the A303; popular well prepared food from sandwiches and pub favourites to more enterprising dishes including generous fish boards, well kept Otter, Wadworths and local guests, Thatcher's cider and nice wines by the glass from good list, chatty helpful staff, opened-up rooms with flagstones and light oak boards, pale green dados and lots of animal pictures/figurines, flowers on good quality dining tables, log fires, sunny conservatory; children and dogs welcome, wheelchair access/loos, grassy beer garden sheltered by thatched cob wall, five comfortable bedrooms in courtyard annexe, self-catering cottage, open all day and can get very busy. *(Chris and Angela Buckell)*

CROCKERTON ST8642

★**Bath Arms** (01985) 212262

Off A350 Warminster–Blandford; BA12 8AJ Welcoming dining pub dating from the 17th c; beamed bar with plush banquettes and matching chairs, well spaced tables on parquet, woodburner, two Wessex ales and a weekend guest, Orchard Pig cider and several wines by the glass, owner-chef's good food including signature sticky beef from interesting changing menu (booking advised), helpful friendly staff, two restaurant areas and garden room; background music, free wi-fi; children and dogs (in bar) welcome, well divided garden with plenty of picnic-sets, good local walks, two bedrooms, open all day, till 9pm Sun (6pm in winter), gets crowded during school holidays (Longleat close by). *(Edward Mirzoeff)*

DEVIZES SU0061

Bear (01380) 722444

Market Place; SN10 1HS Ancient coaching inn with big carpeted main bar, log fires, winged wall settles and upholstered bucket chairs, well kept Wadworths, a couple of decent ciders and extensive choice of wines by the glass, steps down to Bear Grills bistro with painted panelling, large fireplace and open kitchen, good food from here and in more formal back restaurant, cellar bar for live music and comedy nights; children welcome, dogs in front bar, wheelchair access using ramp, modern tables and chairs in paved courtyard, 32 bedrooms, good breakfast, open all day. *(Ann and Colin Hunt)*

DEVIZES SU0061

Black Swan (01380) 727777

Market Place; SN10 1JQ Traditional 18th-c coaching inn with plenty of atmosphere; quirky bare-boards interior filled with antiques and interesting bits and pieces (lots for sale), candles and open fire, Wadworths ales and a guest, sensibly priced food (not Sun evening) from fairly pubby menu, friendly service; quiz Thurs; children and dogs welcome, nice courtyard garden with own bar (weekend live music and DJs), 12 bedrooms, open all day. *(Paul Humphreys, Ann and Colin Hunt)*

DEVIZES SU0061

British Lion (01380) 720665

A361 Swindon roundabout; SN10 1LQ Chatty little drinkers' pub with four well kept quickly changing ales and a proper cider, bare-boards bar with brewery mirrors and gas fire, back part with pool and darts, no food; free wi-fi; garden behind, open all day. *(Mike and Sarah Abbot)*

DEVIZES SU0061

Three Crowns (01380) 722331

Maryport Street; SN10 1AG Popular town-centre pub with good food and well kept range of Wadworths ales, cider from a couple of barrels behind the bar, efficient helpful staff; some live music; children and dogs welcome, lovely sunny courtyard garden, open all day. *(Richard Tilbrook)*

DONHEAD ST ANDREW ST9124

★**Forester** (01747) 828038

Village signposted off A30 E of Shaftesbury, just E of Ludwell; Lower Street; SP7 9EE Attractive 14th-c thatched restaurant-pub in charming village; nice relaxed bar with stripped tables on wood floors and inglenook log fire, sofa and magazines in alcove, Butcombe Bitter, a guest beer and good selection of wines by the glass including champagne, well regarded food (some emphasis on fresh fish/seafood), efficient friendly service, comfortable restaurant with well spaced country kitchen tables, second cosier dining room; children and dogs welcome, country views from good-sized terrace, can walk up White Sheet Hill and past the old and 'new' Wardour castles, closed Sun evening, Mon. *(John and Hilary Murphy)*

DOWNTON SU1721

Wooden Spoon (01725) 511899

High Street (A338 S of Salisbury); SP5 3PG Popular 18th-c red-brick pub with two bars; good reasonably priced food from blackboard menus cooked by landlady, well kept Ringwood and a guest, friendly efficient service, open fire, extensive banknote collection; children and dogs welcome, nice garden behind, closes 9pm Sun. *(Diana and Bertie Farr)*

EBBESBOURNE WAKE ST9924

★Horseshoe (01722) 780474

On A354 S of Salisbury, right at signpost at Coombe Bissett; village about 8 miles further; SP5 5JF Popular unspoilt village pub under welcoming long-serving landlord; Bowman, Otter, Palmers and guests tapped from the cask, farm cider, generous helpings of good traditional home-cooked food served by friendly staff, neatly kept and comfortable character bar with collection of farm tools and bric-a-brac on beams, conservatory and small restaurant; children (away from bar) and dogs welcome, seats in pretty little garden with views over Ebble Valley, play area, chickens and goat in paddock, good nearby walks, one bedroom, closed Sun evening, Mon. *(Michael Hill, Marianne and Peter Stevens, David and Judy Robison)*

EDINGTON ST9353

★Three Daggers (01380) 830940

Westbury Road (B3098); BA13 4PG Smart but relaxed pub brewing its own beers in farm shop opposite; open-plan beamed interior with leather sofas and armchairs at one end by woodburner, wide range of enjoyable food including two-course lunch menu, well chosen wines (plenty by the glass), helpful friendly service, candlelit restaurant with slate floor and two-way fireplace, stairs up to high raftered dining/function room, airy conservatory; background music, darts and board games, free wi-fi; children and dogs (in bar) welcome, picnic-sets on grass, fenced play area, nine good bedrooms (six in separate building), open all day. *(Beth Aldridge, Revd R T Tickle, Thomas Green, Hilary and Neil Christopher)*

ENFORD SU14351

★Swan (01980) 670338

Long Street, off A345; SN9 6DD Attractive and welcoming thatched village pub; opened-up beamed interior with log fire in large fireplace, five well kept changing ales and good locally sourced home-made food from lunchtime sandwiches and snacks up, prompt friendly service; darts and board games, beer/music festival Aug Bank Holiday; children, walkers and dogs welcome, seats out on small front terrace and in big landscaped back garden, gallows-style inn sign spanning the road, open all day Fri-Sun, closed Mon lunchtime. *(Mrs Zara Elliott, Michael Doswell)*

FORD ST8474

White Hart (01249) 782213

Off A420 Chippenham–Bristol; SN14 8RP Handsome 16th-c Marstons-managed country inn; beamed bars with bare boards or quarry tiles, dining and tub chairs, cushioned wall seats and button-back sofas, lots of prints on bold paintwork, open fire and woodburner, three real ales including Bath Gem and a beer badged for the pub, good range of other drinks (20 wines by the glass), popular food from sandwiches/baguettes to signature steaks cooked in charcoal oven, friendly efficient staff; free wi-fi; children and dogs (in bar) welcome, front courtyard and terrace, trout stream by small stone bridge, comfortable modern bedrooms, open (and food) all day. *(Dr and Mrs A K Clarke, Mr and Mrs D J Nash)*

FOXHAM ST9777

Foxham Inn (01249) 740665

NE of Chippenham; SN15 4NQ Small tucked-away country dining pub with simple traditional décor: enterprising food strong on local produce along with more straightforward bar meals and themed nights, well kept ales such as St Austell Tribute, nice choice of wines by the glass and good coffee, woodburner, more contemporary conservatory-style restaurant with kitchen view, own bread, chutneys, jams etc for sale; children and dogs welcome, disabled access and facilities, terrace with pergola, extensive views from front, two comfortable bedrooms, closed Mon. *(Mr and Mrs P R Thomas)*

FROXFIELD SU2968

Pelican (01488) 682479

Off A4, Bath Road; SN8 3JY Modernised and extended 17th-c coaching inn; enjoyable home-made food from sandwiches and panini up, helpful friendly young staff, local ales such as Wickwar, comfortable relaxed atmosphere; quiz first Fri of month; children and dogs welcome, pleasant streamside garden with terrace and duck pond, Kennet & Avon Canal walks (bridge 90), eight bedrooms, open all day, no food Sun evening. *(Penny and Peter Keevil)*

GASTARD ST8868

Harp & Crown (01249) 715697

Velley Hill; SN13 9PU Spacious village pub under newish management; bar with two-way fireplace into snug, well kept Wickwar and a local guest such as Ramsbury, enjoyable sensibly priced pubby food from shortish menu, friendly staff, flagstoned dining conservatory; area for darts; children and dogs welcome, picnic-sets out at front and in back garden, open all day weekends, closed Mon lunchtime. *(Michael Doswell)*

GREAT DURNFORD SU1337

Black Horse (01722) 782270

Follow Woodfords sign from A345 High Post traffic lights; SP4 6AY Popular 17th-c red-brick country pub under welcoming licensees; four cosy unpretentious rooms with lots of quirky bits and pieces, large inglenook woodburner in one, well kept ales including Ringwood Razorback, real cider and generous helpings of good straightforward home-made food; darts, table skittles; children and dogs welcome, big informal garden with play area, closed Sun evening, Mon. *(Christopher Mannings)*

HAMPTWORTH SU2419

Cuckoo (01794) 390302

Hamptworth Road; SP5 2DU Welcoming 17th-c thatched New Forest pub owned by the Hamptworth Estate; peaceful and unspoilt, with friendly mix of customers from farmers to families in four compact rooms around tiny servery, up to nine real ales such as Hop Back and Palmers tapped from the cask, real ciders/perry, simple food including sandwiches, ploughman's, pasties and pies, basic wooden furniture (some tables made using Estate trees), open fire and woodburner; shove-ha'penny, shut the box and other traditional games, occasional live music; children (till 9pm) and dogs welcome, big garden with view of golf course, two pétanque pitches, open all day Fri-Sun. *(Mark Morgan)*

HANNINGTON SU1793

Jolly Tar (01793) 762245

Off B4019 W of Highworth; Queens Road; SN6 7RP Old painted stone pub in pretty village; relaxing beamed bar with big log fire, steps up to flagstoned and stripped-stone dining area, good reasonably priced home-made food including popular Sun lunch (should book), well kept Arkells ales, friendly helpful service; free wi-fi; children and dogs (in bar) welcome, picnic-sets on front terrace and in big garden with play area, four comfortable bedrooms, good breakfast, closed Mon lunchtime, no food Sun evening. *(Sam Stainton)*

HEDDINGTON ST9966

Ivy (01380) 859652

Off A3102 S of Calne; SN11 0PL Picturesque thatched village local dating from the 15th c; L-shaped bar with heavy low beams, timbered walls and inglenook log fire, assorted furnishings on parquet floor, cask-tapped Wadworths ales, good wine choice and well cooked/priced pubby food, back dining room; children and dogs welcome, wheelchair access (no disabled loo), picnic-sets out at front and in small side garden, open all day in summer (till 8pm Sun), closed Mon, Tues and lunchtime Weds in winter. *(Mrs Zara Elliott)*

HINDON ST9132

Lamb (01747) 820573

B3089 Wilton–Mere; SP3 6DP Attractive refurbished old hotel; roomy log-fire bar, two flagstoned lower sections with very long polished table, high-backed pews and settles, steps up to third, bigger area, well kept Youngs, Wells Bombardier and a guest, several wines by the glass and around 25 malt whiskies, cocktails and cuban cigars, enjoyable bar and restaurant food (service charge added), friendly service, can get very busy; children and dogs welcome, tables on roadside terrace and in garden across road with boules, 19 bedrooms, open all day from 7.30am for breakfast. *(Roger and Donna Huggins, Gene and Kitty Rankin)*

KILMINGTON ST7835

Red Lion (01985) 844263

B3092 Mere–Frome, 2.5 miles S of Maiden Bradley; 3 miles from A303 Mere turn-off; BA12 6RP NT-owned country pub with low-beamed flagstoned bar, cushioned wall and window seats, curved high-backed settle, woodburner in big fireplace at either end, well kept ales such as Butcombe and Wessex, traditional ciders and enjoyable straightforward home-made food including lunchtime sandwiches, afternoon teas, newer big-windowed back dining area where children allowed; dogs welcome in bar, attractive big garden with fine views, White Sheet Hill (hang-gliding) and Stourhead gardens (NT) nearby, open till 6pm Sun, 8pm Mon and Tues, 9pm other days, evening food Weds-Sat. *(Edward Mirzoeff)*

KINGTON ST MICHAEL ST9077

Jolly Huntsman (01249) 750305

Handy for M4 junction 17; SN14 6JB Roomy 18th-c stone-built pub; Moles and a couple of guests, proper cider and good home-made food from pub standards up, friendly service, carpeted interior with some scrubbed tables, comfortable sofas and good log fire; children and dogs (in bar) welcome, bedrooms in separate block. *(Jonny and Andrew Haughton)*

LACOCK ST9268

Bell (01249) 730308

E of village; SN15 2PJ Extended cottagey pub with warm welcome; local ales including a house beer from Great Western (beer festivals), traditional ciders, well chosen/priced wines and good selection of malt whiskies and gins, enjoyable generously served food from lunchtime platters, pub favourites and grills up, friendly efficient young staff, linked rooms off bar including more formal restaurant and bright airy conservatory; children and dogs (in bar) welcome, disabled access (not to conservatory) from car park, well tended garden with play area and smokers' shelter (the Coughing Shed), long views across Avon Valley, open (and food) all day weekends. *(Dr and Mrs A K Clarke, Chris and Angela Buckell)*

LACOCK ST9168

George (01249) 730263

West Street; village signed off A350 S of Chippenham; SN15 2LH Rambling old inn at centre of busy NT tourist village; low-beamed bar with upright timbers creating cosy corners, some flagstones and stone-mullioned windows, dog treadwheel in outer breast of central fireplace, lots of pictures including photos of *Cranford* and *Harry Potter* being filmed in the village, six mainly Wadworths beers and Weston's cider, lots of wines by the glass, popular sensibly priced food from sandwiches up, friendly staff; background music; children and dogs welcome, tricky wheelchair access, nice courtyard with pillory and old well, picnic-sets on grass, open all day summer. *(Dr and Mrs A K Clarke, Ann and Colin Hunt)*

LACOCK ST9168

Red Lion (01249) 730456

High Street; SN15 2LQ Popular NT-owned Georgian inn; sizeable opened-up interior with log fire in big stone fireplace, bare boards and flagstones, roughly carved screens here and there and some cosy alcoves, well kept Wadworths ales, Thatcher's and Weston's ciders, enjoyable food from sandwiches and sharing plates up; background music, free wi-fi; children and dogs welcome, wheelchair access to main bar area only, picnic-sets out on gravel, four modern bedrooms, open (and food) all day. *(Dr and Mrs A K Clarke)*

LACOCK ST9367

Rising Sun (01249) 730363

Bewley Common, Bowden Hill – out towards Sandy Lane, up hill past abbey; OS Sheet 173 map reference 935679; SN15 2PP Old stone pub with three knocked-together simply furnished rooms, beams and log fires, Moles ales, real cider and enjoyable fairly traditional food (not Sun evening) from snacks and sharing boards up, friendly attentive service; background music (live every other Weds), free wi-fi; well behaved children welcome, dogs in bar, no wheelchair access, wonderful views across Avon Valley from conservatory and two-level terrace, closed Mon evening, otherwise open all day (till 9pm Sun), winter hours may vary. *(Dr and Mrs A K Clarke)*

LEA ST9586

Rose & Crown (01666) 822053

The Street; SN16 9PA Creeper-clad Victorian stone pub next to the village church; enjoyable good value home-made food from sandwiches up (puddings particularly good), Arkells and guests kept well, over 20 gins, friendly efficient service, compact interconnecting rooms with mix of furnishings, fires including two-way woodburner; daily newspapers, free wi-fi; children and dogs welcome, picnic-sets out at front and in large well maintained garden with paved terrace and play area, closed Mon, otherwise open (and food) all day, kitchen shuts 5pm Sun. *(Michael Doswell)*

LITTLE SOMERFORD ST9784

Somerford Arms (01666) 826535

Signed off B4042 Malmesbury–Brinkworth; SN15 5JP Modernised village pub under new management; opened-up interior with two-way woodburner, painted half-panelling and stone flooring, enjoyable food (not Sun evening) cooked by father and son team from pub classics up, three well kept changing ales and over a dozen wines by the glass, friendly helpful service; children and dogs welcome, open all day Sat, till 10pm Sun, closed Mon. *(Michael Doswell)*

LOCKERIDGE SU1467

Who'd A Thought It (01672) 861255

Signed off A4 Marlborough–Calne, just W of Fyfield; SN8 4EL Attractively revamped village pub-restaurant (sister to the Outside Chance at Manton); popular food from interestingly varied menu, well kept Wadworths beers and decent wines including champagne by the glass, friendly service; children and dogs welcome, pleasant back garden with play area, lovely bluebell walks nearby, open all day, no food Sun evening. *(Dave Snowden)*

LONGBRIDGE DEVERILL ST8640

George (01985) 840396

A350/B3095; BA12 7DG Popular updated and extended roadside inn owned by Upham; their beers kept well and generous helpings of enjoyable freshly made food including Sun carvery, friendly helpful service, conservatory; quiz nights; children and dogs (in bar) welcome, big riverside garden with play area, 12 bedrooms, handy for Longleat, open all day, breakfast for non-residents from 8am Mon-Sat. *(Edward Mirzoeff)*

LOWER WOODFORD SU1235

Wheatsheaf (01722) 782203

Signed off A360 just N of Salisbury; SP4 6NQ Updated and extended 18th-c dining pub, open airy feel, with decent choice of fairly priced food from sandwiches and sharing boards up, well kept Badger ales, good wines and coffee, beams, panelling and exposed brickwork, mix of old furniture, log fire and woodburner; background music, free wi-fi; well behaved children welcome in restaurant, muddy boots and dogs in bar, disabled loo and parking, tree-lined fenced garden with play area, pretty setting, open (and food) all day. *(I D Barnett)*

LUCKINGTON ST8384

Old Royal Ship (01666) 840222
Off B4040 SW of Malmesbury; SN14 6PA Friendly pub by village green; one long bar divided into three areas, ales such as Sharps and Wadworths from central servery, also traditional cider and several wines by the glass, good range of food including some vegetarian options, neat tables, spindleback chairs and small cushioned settles on dark boards, stripped masonry and small open fire, skittle alley; background music; children welcome, plenty of seats in garden (beyond car park) with boules and play area, Badminton House close by, open all day weekends. *(Mark Morgan)*

MANTON SU1768

★**Outside Chance** (01672) 512352
Village (and pub) signposted off A4 just W of Marlborough; High Street; SN8 4HW Popular country pub with three small linked rooms (sister pub to Who'd A Thought It in Lockeridge); hop-strung beams, flagstones or bare boards, plain pub furnishings such as chapel chairs and a long-cushioned pew, one room has more cosseted feel with comfortable banquette, décor (as name suggests) celebrates unlikely racing winners such as 100-1 shot Mr Spooner's Only Dreams, log fire in big main fireplace, wide choice of enjoyable food, Wadworths ales and eight wines by the glass; background music, board games; children and dogs welcome, suntrap side terrace with contemporary tables, more rustic furniture under ash trees in good-sized garden, private access to local playing fields and play area, open all day. *(Lenny and Ruth Walters, Val and Malcolm Travers, Neil Allen)*

MARDEN SU0857

★**Millstream** (01380) 848490
Village signposted off A342 SE of Devizes; SN10 3RH Rather smart red-brick dining pub in leafy setting at top end of this attractive village; highly regarded food cooked by landlady-chef including fish/seafood specials and good value Sun lunch (best to book), well kept Wadworths ales, friendly efficient young staff, appealing layout of linked cosy areas, beams and log fires, red-cushioned dark pews and small padded dining chairs around sturdy oak and other good tables, comfy sofas in one part; free wi-fi; children and dogs welcome (resident pointers are Sophie and Francesca), disabled access/loos, neat terrace by entrance and big lawned garden down to tree-lined stream, 12th-c church worth a visit, closed Sun and Mon evenings. *(Michael Doswell)*

MARKET LAVINGTON SU0154

Green Dragon (01380) 813235
High Street; SN10 4AG Rambling early 17th-c red-brick pub; four well kept Wadworths ales, good value wines and enjoyable reasonably priced food from sandwiches and baked potatoes up, friendly welcoming staff; collection of vintage wireless sets; darts, free wi-fi; children and dogs welcome, wheelchair access, large back garden with shelter, six refurbished bedrooms (four in converted outbuildings), hearty breakfast, open all day. *(Revd R P Tickle, Mrs Zara Elliott)*

MARLBOROUGH SU1869

★**Lamb** (01672) 512668
The Parade; SN8 1NE Bustling town local with good mix of customers, cheerful atmosphere in main bar, wall banquettes and wheelback chairs around wooden tables on parquet flooring, Cecil Aldin prints on red walls, two-way woodburner, generous helpings of traditional home-made food (not Fri-Sun evenings), Wadworths ales tapped from the cask, ten wines by the glass and 15 malt whiskies, friendly staff; juke box, games machine, darts and TV; tables in pleasant back courtyard, pretty summer window boxes, bedrooms, hearty breakfast, open all day. *(Mark Morgan, Thomas Green, Graham Wheeler, Dave Snowden)*

MONKTON FARLEIGH ST8065

Kings Arms (01225) 852300
Signed off A363 Bradford–Bath; BA15 2QH New friendly management for this imposing 17th-c stone pub in lovely village; beamed bar with wood-strip floor and inglenook, zinc-topped counter serving three local ales such as Box Steam and a traditional cider, enjoyable food from shortish but varied menu, parquet-floored restaurant; quiz nights; children welcome, seats in front courtyard and two-tier back garden with country views, bedrooms, closed Mon and Tues, otherwise open (and food) all day. *(Taff Thomas, Dr and Mrs A K Clarke)*

NESTON ST8668

Neston Country Inn (01225) 811694
Church Rise, Pool Green; SN13 9SN Welcoming unpretentious early 19th-c inn; good reasonably priced food cooked by landlord including some south african influences and themed nights, well kept Fullers London Pride and a couple of local guests, friendly helpful staff; quiz last Thurs of month, darts; children and dogs welcome, picnic-sets in back garden with gate to village playing field, four bedrooms, open all day weekends (till 9pm Sun), closed Mon lunchtime (Tues lunchtime after bank holiday). *(Mr and Mrs P R Thomas)*

NETHERHAMPTON SU1129

★**Victoria & Albert** (01722) 743174
Just off A3094 W of Salisbury; SP2 8PU Cosy black-beamed bar in simple 16th-c thatched cottage; old-fashioned cushioned wall settles on ancient floor tiles, log fire, three well kept changing ales, proper cider and decent wines, welcoming helpful staff,

popular home-made food from sandwiches up at sensible prices, restaurant; children and dogs welcome, hatch service for sizeable terrace and garden behind, handy for Wilton House and Nadder Valley walks, closed Sun evening. *(David and Laura Young)*

NOMANSLAND SU2517

Lamb (01794) 390246

Signed off B3078 and B3079, Forest Road; SP5 2BP Lovely New Forest village-green setting (the county border runs through the pub); family run and popular with locals, decent choice of enjoyable home-made food from lunchtime baguettes up, popular Sun roasts, four changing ales and sensibly priced wine list, friendly staff, log fire in traditional carpeted bar, small dining room, lots of bits and pieces to look at, games room with pool; TV; children and dogs welcome, tables on terrace, green (with grazing ponies) and in colourful back garden, open all day Fri-Sun. *(Ann and Colin Hunt)*

NORTON ST8884

Vine Tree (01666) 837654

4 miles from M4 junction 17; A429 towards Malmesbury, then left at Hullavington, Sherston signpost, then follow Norton signposts; in village turn right at Foxley signpost, which takes you into Honey Lane; SN16 0JP Civilised dining pub (sister to the Barbury in Broad Hinton); three neat small rooms, beams, old settles and unvarnished wooden tables on flagstones, sporting prints and church candles, large fireplace in central bar, ales such as St Austell and Butcombe, 40 wines by the glass, 35 gins and several malt whiskies, well liked food from sharing boards up, restaurant with woodburner; children and dogs welcome, hitching rail for horses, picnic-sets and play area in two-acre garden, suntrap terrace, closed Sun evening. *(Dr and Mrs A K Clarke)*

OGBOURNE ST ANDREW SU1871

Silks on the Downs (01672) 841229

A345 N of Marlborough; SN8 1RZ Popular and civilised restauranty pub with horse-racing theme; highly regarded food (best to book) from shortish but varied menu, Ramsbury Gold and a guest, proper cider and decent wines by the glass, helpful friendly service, stylish décor with mix of dining tables on polished wood floors, some good prints and photographs as well as framed racing silks; well behaved children allowed, no dogs inside, small decked area and garden, closed Sun evening. *(Michael Sargent)*

PEWSEY SU1561

Waterfront (01672) 564020

Pewsey Wharf (A345 just N); SN9 5NU Bar-bistro in converted wharf building next to canal; ample helpings of good reasonably priced food including daily specials, three well kept changing ales tapped from the cask in upstairs bar with views (can eat here too), good quality wines, efficient friendly staff; children and dogs (not downstairs) welcome, waterside picnic-sets, nice walks, parking fee to the Kennet & Avon Canal Trust, open all day Fri-Sun. *(Ian Herdman, Peter Meister)*

PITTON SU2131

Silver Plough (01722) 712266

Village signed from A30 E of Salisbury (follow brown signs); SP5 1DU Former 18th-c farmhouse under newish management; front bar with pewter and china tankards, copper kettles and toby jugs hanging from black beams, cushioned antique settles around rustic pine tables, counter made from carved Elizabethan overmantel serving Badger ales and good range of wines by the glass, enjoyable food from pub standards up, back locals' bar, a couple of woodburners; skittle alley, some live music; children and dogs welcome, south-facing lawn with tables under parasols, more seats on heated terrace, two bedrooms, good nearby walks including Clarendon Way, closed Sun evening, Mon lunchtime. *(Rod and Diana Pearce, Ian Duncan, Edward Mirzoeff)*

POULSHOT ST9760

★Raven (01380) 828271

Off A361; SN10 1RW Attractive half-timbered pub opposite village green; two cosy neatly kept black-beamed rooms with comfortable banquettes and other pubby furniture, open fire, Wadworths IPA and 6X plus a changing guest tapped from the cask, 13 wines by the glass, good popular food cooked by landlord, friendly efficient service; background music in dining room only, free wi-fi; children and dogs welcome, picnic-sets under parasols in walled back garden, nearby walks, closed Sun evening Oct-Easter, Mon end Oct-early May. *(Susan Eccleston, Taff Thomas, Mr and Mrs P R Thomas, Muriel and Spencer Harrop)*

REDLYNCH SU2021

Kings Head (01725) 510420

Off A338 via B3080; The Row; SP5 2JT Early 18th-c pub on edge of New Forest; three or four well kept ales such as Hop Back and Ringwood, decent house wines and coffee, good value home-made food from pub favourites up, beamed and flagstoned main bar with woodburner in large brick fireplace, small conservatory; free wi-fi; children, dogs and muddy boots welcome, picnic-sets out in front and in side garden, Pepperbox Hill (NT) walks nearby, open (and food) all day Sun, closed Mon lunchtime. *(Sam Stainton)*

SALISBURY SU1429

★Haunch of Venison (01722) 411313

Minster Street, opposite Market Cross; SP1 1TB Ancient jettied pub with small downstairs rooms dating from 1320, massive beams, stout oak benches built into timbered walls, log fires, tiny snug (the Horsebox) with pewter counter and rare set of antique taps for gravity-fed spirits, well kept Courage Best, Hop Back Summer Lightning and GFB plus a guest, enjoyable food including various venison dishes and weekday set lunch, friendly staff, steep stairs to restaurant, halfway up is panelled room with splendid fireplace and (behind glass) the mummified hand of an 18th-c card sharp said to haunt the pub; children and dogs (in bars) welcome, open all day. *(Mike Kavaney, Ann and Colin Hunt, Richard Tilbrook)*

SALISBURY SU1429

New Inn (01722) 326662

New Street; SP1 2PH Much-extended old building with massive beams and timbers; good choice of home-made food from pub staples up, well kept Badger ales and decent house wines, cheerful welcoming staff, flagstones, bare boards and carpet, quiet cosy alcoves, inglenook log fire; children welcome, pretty walled garden with striking view of nearby cathedral spire, three bedrooms, open all day. *(Richard Tilbrook)*

SALISBURY SU1430

Wyndham Arms (01722) 331026

Estcourt Road; SP1 3AS Friendly red-brick corner local with full Hop Back range (brewery was originally based here), also a guest ale, bottled beers and country wines, no food, small front and side rooms, longer main bar; darts and board games, quiz night Thurs; children and dogs welcome, open all day Thurs-Sun, from 4.30pm other days. *(Jake Richardson)*

SEEND ST9361

Barge (01380) 828230

Seend Cleeve; signed off A361 Devizes–Trowbridge; SN12 6QB Busy waterside pub with plenty of seats in garden making most of boating activity on Kennet & Avon Canal (moorings); rambling interior with log fires, some unusual seating in bar such as painted milk churns, Wadworths ales and extensive range of wines by the glass, decent choice of enjoyable well priced food including summer barbecues, efficient service; background music, free wi-fi; children and dogs welcome, open all day, food all day weekends. *(Dr and Mrs A K Clarke)*

SEMINGTON ST9259

Lamb (01380) 870263

The Strand; A361 Devizes–Trowbridge; BA14 6LL Modernised dining pub with various eating areas including bar with wood-strip floor and log fire, enjoyable food (not Sun evening) from sharing tapas plates through pub favourites to specials, a couple of Box Steam ales, friendly staff; background music; children and dogs welcome, pleasant garden with views to the Bowood Estate, play area, two self-catering cottages. *(Alison and Michael Harper)*

SEMINGTON ST8960

Somerset Arms (01380) 870067

Off A350 bypass 2 miles S of Melksham; BA14 6JR 16th-c coaching inn with long heavy-beamed bar and restaurant, four well kept local ales such as Box Steam and Otter, real ciders, enjoyable pubby food (not Sun evening) from baguettes up including plenty of gluten-free choices, friendly young staff; children and dogs welcome, picnic-sets in small garden behind, three bedrooms, short walk from Kennet & Avon Canal, open all day, breakfast from 9am. *(Edward Mirzoeff)*

SHALBOURNE SU3162

Plough (01672) 870295

Off A338; SN8 3QF Traditional low-beamed pub by small village green; good variety of enjoyable fairly priced food cooked by landlord including some vegetarian options, Butcombe and Wadworths ales, friendly landlady and staff, open fire in neat bar, separate carpeted restaurant with central woodburner; free wi-fi; children and dogs welcome, disabled access, play area in small garden, closed Mon, no food Sun evening. *(Lorna and Jeff Mason)*

SHERSTON ST8586

Carpenters Arms (01666) 840665

Easton Town (B4040); SN16 0NT Friendly whitewashed roadside pub doing well under present owners; ales such as Butcombe, Flying Monk and Sharps, Thatcher's ciders and decent reasonably priced wines, enjoyable food including weekday OAP lunch, Weds burger night and Sat steak/wine deal, small interconnecting rooms with low beams, stripped-stone or grey-painted walls, light-wood flooring, log fires, modern dining conservatory; background music, pool; children and dogs welcome, disabled access/loos, garden with play area, open all day. *(Chris and Angela Buckell)*

STEEPLE ASHTON ST9056

Longs Arms (01380) 870245

High Street; BA14 6EU Attractively presented 17th-c stone coaching inn with friendly local atmosphere; Sharps and Wadworths ales kept well, plenty of wines by the glass and very good locally sourced food from lunchtime sandwiches/ciabattas and home-made pizzas up, bar with lots of pictures and old photos, adjacent dining part, woodburner; free wi-fi; children and dogs welcome, play area and boules in big garden, self-catering cottage, delightful village, open all day weekends if busy. *(Richard Tilbrook)*

SUTTON VENY ST8941

Woolpack (01985) 840834

High Street; BA12 7AW Small well run 1920s village local; good food including some inventive dishes cooked by landlord-chef from reassuringly short blackboard menu (best to book), home-made chutneys, pickles etc for sale, a couple of real ales and sensibly priced wines by the glass, prompt friendly service, modernised interior with compact side dining area screened from bare-boards bar, woodburner; background music; closed Sun evening, Mon lunchtime. *(Mrs Zara Elliott, Edward Mirzoeff)*

TISBURY ST9429

Boot (01747) 870363
High Street; SP3 6PS Ancient unpretentious village local under welcoming long-serving licensees; three well kept changing ales tapped from the cask, cider/perry, enjoyable reasonably priced pubby food including range of pizzas, open fire; dogs welcome, tables in good-sized back garden, closed Sun evening and lunchtimes Mon, Tues. *(Gene and Kitty Rankin)*

UPAVON SU1355

Ship (01980) 630313
High Street; SN9 6EA Large thatched pub with good choice of enjoyable home-made food including wood-fired pizzas (Thurs-Sat evenings) and Weds steak night, well kept changing ales such as Butcombe and Wadworths, a couple of traditional ciders and decent range of wines and whiskies, some interesting nautical memorabilia; occasional live music; dogs and muddy boots welcome, picnic-sets in front and on small side terrace, parking can be tricky, open all day. *(Ruth and Peter Bacon)*

UPTON LOVELL ST9441

Prince Leopold (01985) 850460
Up Street, village signed from A36; BA12 0JP Prettily tucked-away Victorian country pub; simply furnished bar with light wood floor, ales such as Butcombe and plenty of wines by the glass from hand-crafted elm counter, cosy snug leading off with shelves either side of open fire and comfortable sofas, two other linked rooms and airy back restaurant overlooking River Wylye (as do some outdoor balcony tables), well liked food from sandwiches and pub favourites up, friendly service; children and dogs welcome, garden with own bar and waterside tables, bedrooms, open all day Sat, till 8pm Sun, closed Mon. *(Pete and Sarah)*

UPTON SCUDAMORE ST8647

★**Angel** (01985) 213225
Off A350 N of Warminster; BA12 0AG 16th-c inn well placed for Longleat; farmhouse tables and chairs and leather sofa in bare-boards bar, Butcombe Bitter and Sharps Doom Bar, good wines by the glass, well liked food from shortish menu plus a few specials, friendly service, a couple of steps up to informal dining room with some sizeable paintings, more steps to tartan-carpeted restaurant with elegant chairs around polished tables; children and dogs (in bar) welcome, modern tables and chairs under parasols in terraced back garden, well equipped comfortable bedrooms, closed Sun evening, Mon. *(Dave Sutton, Francis and Mandy Robertson, Edward Mirzoeff)*

URCHFONT SU0357

Lamb (01380) 848848
The Green; SN10 4QU Welcoming part-thatched village local; well kept Wadworths ales and enjoyable good value pubby food from baguettes up, homely feel with several rooms around bar; skittle alley, darts; free wi-fi; children and dogs welcome, picnic-sets on back lawn, pétanque, smokers' shelter, open all day Sun (food till 6pm), closed Mon lunchtime. *(Paul Humphreys)*

WARMINSTER ST8745

Organ (01985) 211777
High Street; BA12 9AQ Former 18th-c inn (reopened 2006 after 93 years as a shop); front bar, snug and traditional games room, welcoming owners and chatty regulars, four well kept regional beers including one badged for them (beer festivals), real ciders/perries, some snacky food, local artwork in upstairs gallery; quiz and live music nights, skittle alley, darts; no under-21s, dogs welcome, open all day Sat, from 4pm other days. *(Dan and Anne Morgan)*

WARMINSTER ST8744

Snooty Fox (01985) 846505
Fore Street/Brook Street; BA12 8DN Modernised restauranty pub on the outskirts, neat clean and comfortable, with good varied choice of popular food cooked by owner-chef, ales such as Bath and Wadworths from brick-faced counter, good friendly service; free wi-fi; seats out on terrace and small lawn, open all day Sun (till 4pm in winter), closed Mon, Tues. *(Jed Stevens)*

WARMINSTER ST8745

★**Weymouth Arms** (01985) 216995
Emwell Street; BA12 8JA Charming backstreet pub with snug panelled entrance bar, log fire in fine stone fireplace, ancient books on mantelpiece, leather tub chairs around walnut and satinwood table, more seats against the walls, daily newspapers, Butcombe, Wadworths 6X and half a dozen wines by the glass, second heavily panelled room with wide floorboards and smaller fireplace, candles in brass sticks, split-level dining room stretching back to open kitchen serving good food from snacks and pub favourites up, friendly helpful service; children and dogs (in bar) welcome, seats in flower-filled back courtyard, six well equipped comfortable bedrooms, open all day. *(Edward Mirzoeff, Jed Stevens)*

WEST OVERTON SU1368

Bell (01672) 861099
A4 Marlborough–Calne; SN8 1QD Early 19th-c coaching inn with good imaginative

cooking from owner-chef using fresh local ingredients, also lunchtime sandwiches and some pubby choices, well kept Moles and other local beers, attentive friendly uniformed staff, bar with woodburner, spacious restaurant beyond; background music; disabled access, nice secluded back garden with terrace and own bar, country views, good walks nearby, closed Sun evening, Mon. *(Mark Morgan)*

WESTWOOD ST8159

★**New Inn** (01225) 863123
Off B3109 S of Bradford-on-Avon; BA15 2AE Traditional 18th-c country pub with linked rooms; beams, stripped stonework and log fires, scrubbed tables on slate floor, lots of pictures, highly rated good value food cooked by chef-owner from pub staples to more imaginative choices, a couple of well kept Wadworths ales and a guest such as Bath Gem, good service and cheerful buzzy atmosphere; children and dogs welcome, sturdy furniture and gazebo in paved back garden, pretty village with good surrounding walks, Westwood Manor (NT) in road opposite, closed Sun evening. *(Taff Thomas, Robert Henderson, Mike Fountain)*

WHITLEY ST8866

Pear Tree (01225) 704966
Off B3353 S of Corsham; SN12 8QX Attractive stone dining pub (former 17th-c farmhouse); revamped beamed interior with lots of contemporary/rustic charm in front bar, restaurant and airy garden room, good food from varied if not particularly cheap menu, three regional ales including Bath Gem, interesting wine list (plenty by the glass) and good range of other drinks, friendly attentive service; comedy nights; children welcome, terrace and pretty garden, eight well equipped bedrooms (four in converted barn), open all day from 7.30am (8.30am Sun) for breakfast. *(Brian Wheeldon, Dr and Mrs A K Clarke)*

WILCOT SU1461

Golden Swan (01672) 562289
Signed off A345 N of Pewsey, and in Pewsey itself; SN9 5NN Steeply thatched country pub near Kennet & Avon Canal, friendly and welcoming, with well kept Wadworths ales and popular good value food cooked by landlady, small bar with log fire, snug and dining room, also games room with pool and darts; quiz first Sun of month; children and dogs welcome, metal furniture on front grass, more tables and wandering chickens behind, field for camping, three good value bedrooms (not ensuite), open all day weekends. *(Peter Meister)*

WILTON SU2661

★**Swan** (01672) 870274
The village S of Great Bedwyn; SN8 3SS Popular light and airy 1930s pub; good well presented seasonal food (not Sun evening) including daily specials and sharing boards, two Ramsbury ales and up to three local cask-tapped guests, real ciders and good value wines from extensive list, friendly efficient staff, stripped pine tables, high-backed settles and pews on bare boards, woodburner; children and dogs welcome, disabled access, picnic-sets in front garden, picturesque village with windmill, open all day weekends. *(Mrs Zara Elliott)*

WINGFIELD ST8256

Poplars (01225) 752426
B3109 S of Bradford-on-Avon (Shop Lane); BA14 9LN Appealing country pub with warm friendly atmosphere, beams and log fires, enjoyable sensibly priced food from pub staples to interesting specials, Wadworths ales (including seasonal) and Weston's cider, airy family dining extension; quiz first Sun of month; nice garden and own cricket pitch. *(Tim and Sue Mulligan)*

WINSLEY ST7960

★**Seven Stars** (01225) 722204
Off B3108 bypass W of Bradford-on-Avon; BA15 2LQ Handsome bustling village inn with low-beamed linked areas, pastel paintwork and stripped-stone walls, farmhouse chairs around candlelit tables on flagstones or carpet, woodburner, good attractively presented food from pub favourites up including highly rated Sun roasts, friendly attentive service, well kept Palmers IPA and west country guests, proper cider; background and live music, winter quiz; children and dogs (in bar) welcome, wheelchair access using ramp to most areas, disabled loo, tables on terrace and neat grassy surrounds, bowling green opposite, open (and food) all day Fri-Sun. *(Taff Thomas, Alistair Holdoway, Michael Doswell, Dr Matt Burleigh, Pete and Sarah, Chris and Angela Buckell)*

A star symbol before the name of a pub shows exceptional character and appeal. It doesn't mean extra comfort. Even quite a basic pub can win a star, if it's individual enough.

Worcestershire

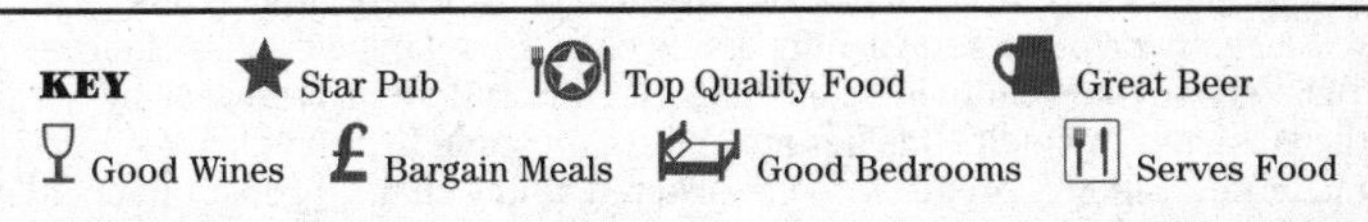

BAUGHTON SO8742 Map 4

Jockey

(01684) 592153 – www.thejockeyinn.co.uk

4 miles from M50 junction 1; A38 northwards, then right on to A4104 Upton–Pershore; WR8 9DQ

Smart bar and dining rooms in elegantly redesigned pub with a fine choice of drinks, rewarding food, courteous staff and seats outside

Stylishly refurbished and carefully extended, this enjoyable pub is just the place for both drinking and dining and the contemporary open-plan areas work well together. The smart dining rooms have high-backed upholstered chairs, long button-back wall seats, a mix of pale-topped tables and bare floorboards with décor that takes in an unusual woven-wicker wall, deer antler chandeliers, oil portraits, horse-racing photographs, bookshelves, stubby candles in glass lanterns, old jockey saddles and up-to-date paintwork. Stools on flagstones line the counter in the beamed bar, where friendly, attentive staff serve Butcombe Rare Breed, Sharps Doom Bar and Wye Valley Butty Bach and HPA on handpump, and 29 wines by the glass (including champagne and sweet wines) from the large glass walk-in wine cellar on display behind the bar; also, cocktails and 21 gins. There's background music. Big leather armchairs, sofas and pouffes are grouped together and there's an open fire and a neat, ceiling-high stack of logs beside a two-way woodburning stove. Outside, the attractive paved courtyard has glass-topped tables, dark wicker chairs and large heated parasols surrounded by bamboo and wild herbs in planters.

Highly rated food includes sandwiches, whole baked camembert with red onion marmalade and tomato and red pepper jam, scotch egg three-ways (pork with truffle mayonnaise, pork and chorizo with aioli, pork and black pudding with mustard mayonnaise), sharing boards, butternut squash, pine nut and gorgonzola risotto, a pie of the day, seared sea bream fillet with crab arancini, herb risotto, caramelised fennel and champagne velouté, confit pork belly with bubble and squeak and sticky cider reduction, 10oz rib-eye steak with a choice of sauce, and puddings such as miso crème brûlée with peanut butter ice-cream and chocolate mousse with vanilla-poached pear and honeycomb; they also offer a two- and three-course set lunch. *Benchmark main dish: burger with toppings, slaw and a choice of fries or chips £14.75. Two-course evening meal £21.00.*

Free house ~ Licensee Rebekah Seddon-Wickens ~ Real ale ~ Open 11.30am-11pm (11.30pm Sat); 12-6 Sun; closed Mon except bank holidays ~ Bar food 12-9; 12-9.30 Fri, Sat; 12-4 Sun ~ Restaurant ~ Children welcome ~ Dogs allowed in bar ~ Wi-fi

Recommended by Colin Humphreys, Chris and Angela Buckell, Bernard Stradling, Charles Welch, Mike and Mary Carter

BRANSFORD SO8052 Map 4

Bear & Ragged Staff ♀

(01886) 833399 – www.bearatbransford.co.uk

Off A4103 SW of Worcester; Station Road; WR6 5JH

Well run dining pub with pleasant places to sit both inside and out, and popular food and drink

In a hamlet in the Teme Valley and surrounded by lovely countryside, this is a gently civilised and friendly dining pub. The relaxing bar has Hobsons Twisted Spire and Unity Frizzle British IPA on handpump, ten wines by the glass, several malt whiskies and quite a few brandies and liqueurs. The restaurant is more formal, with upholstered dining chairs, proper tablecloths and linen napkins. These interconnecting rooms give fine views of attractive rolling country (as do the pretty garden and terrace). In winter, there's a warming open fire. Background music, board games and a pub cat called Princess. Good disabled access and facilities.

Baking bread daily and using some home-grown produce, the enjoyable food includes lunchtime sandwiches (not Sunday), chicken liver pâté with beetroot chutney, creamy garlic mushrooms with a herby breadcrumb topping, home-baked ham with free-range eggs, wild mushroom, spinach and blue cheese wellington, minted lamb burger with toppings and triple-cooked chips, a curry of the day, beer-battered fish and chips, rib-eye steak with a choice of sauce, and puddings such as rapsberry and lemongrass crème brûlée and sticky toffee pudding with butterscotch sauce and honeycomb ice-cream. *Benchmark main dish: beer-battered fish and chips £12.95. Two-course evening meal £20.50.*

Free house ~ Licensee Lynda Williams ~ Real ale ~ Open 12-2.30, 6-10.30 (11 Sat); 12-3 Sun; closed Sun evening; first week Jan ~ Bar food 12-2, 6-9 ~ Restaurant ~ Children welcome ~ Dogs allowed in bar ~ Wi-fi *Recommended by Jamie and Lizzie McEwan, Charles Welch, Gary and Marie Miller, Jonny and Andrew Haughton, Amy Ledbetter*

BRETFORTON SP0943 Map 4

Fleece ★ £

(01386) 831173 – www.thefleeceinn.co.uk

B4035 E of Evesham: turn S off this road into village; pub is in central square by church; there's a sizeable car park at one side of the church; WR11 7JE

Marvellously unspoilt medieval pub owned by the National Trust; bedrooms

If you've come to enjoy the famous historic interior here, it's best to visit during the week as it can get very busy at weekends. For 500 years, this lovely former farm was owned by the same family and many of the furnishings are original heirlooms; it was bequeathed to the National Trust in 1977. The fine country rooms include a great oak dresser holding a priceless 48-piece set of Stuart pewter, two grandfather clocks, ancient kitchen chairs, curved high-backed settles, a rocking chair and a rack of heavy pointed iron shafts, probably for spit roasting in one of the huge inglenook fireplaces; two other log fires. As well as massive beams and exposed timbers, there are worn and crazed flagstones (scored with marks to keep out demons) and plenty of oddities such as a great cheese press and set of cheese moulds and a rare dough-proving table; a leaflet details the more bizarre items. Uley Pigs Ear and Wye Valley Bitter with guests such as North Cotswold Moreton Mild and Purity Mad Goose on handpump, nine wines by the glass, a similar number of malt whiskies and four farm ciders; board games. They hold an asparagus auction at the end of May, as part of the Vale of

Evesham Asparagus Festival, and also host the village fête on August Bank Holiday Monday. The calendar of events includes morris dancing and the village silver band plays here regularly. The lawn, with fruit trees around a beautifully restored thatched and timbered barn, is a lovely place to sit, and there are more picnic-sets and a stone pump-trough in the front courtyard.

Bar food includes sandwiches, crab and asparagus terrine, soup of the day, halloumi, field mushroom and sun-dried tomato burger with twice-cooked chips, faggots or a trio of local sausages with mash and gravy, breaded chicken breast on roast vegetables with asparagus sauce, beer-battered cod and twice-cooked chips, herb-crusted lamb shank with new potatoes, sirloin steak with trimmings and a choice of sauce, and puddings such as chocolate brownie with chocolate sauce and a crumble of the day. *Benchmark main dish: pie of the day £11.95. Two-course evening meal £20.00.*

Free house ~ Licensee Nigel Smith ~ Real ale ~ Open 10.30am-11pm ~ Bar food 12-2.30, 6.30-9; 12-8.30 Sun ~ Children welcome ~ Dogs welcome ~ Wi-fi ~ Bedrooms: /£97.50
Recommended by John Saville, John and Abigail Prescott, Nigel and Sue Foster, Beth Aldridge, Caroline and Oliver Sterling, Mark and Mary Setting

BROADWAY SP0937 Map 4

Crown & Trumpet £

(01386) 853202 – www.crownandtrumpet.co.uk
Church Street; WR12 7AE

Honest local with good real ales and decent food; bedrooms

With a fine range of drinks and remarkable value food, this old-fashioned and unpretentious pub remains extremely popular. The bustling beamed and timbered bar has a cheerful, easy-going feel, antique high-backed dark settles, large solid tables and a blazing log fire. You'll find a beer named for the pub (from Stanway) plus Goffs Cheltenham Gold, Prescott Chequered Flag and Timothy Taylors Landlord on handpump alongside eight wines by the glass, nine malt whiskies and farm ciders. There's an assortment of pub games including darts, Jenga, shut the box, dominoes and ring the bull; TV and background music. The hardwood chairs and tables outside are set among flowers on a slightly raised front terrace and much used by walkers.

Exceptional value food includes lunchtime sandwiches, scrambled egg with salmon and chives, deep-fried brie with cranberry sauce, omelettes, duck and apricot sausages with plum gravy, lasagne, chilli con carne, battered haddock and chips, gammon and egg, sirloin steak with trimmings and a choice of sauce, and puddings such as apple and cinnamon crumble with custard and pancakes with vanilla ice-cream. *Benchmark main dish: home-made pies £9.95. Two-course evening meal £14.90.*

Laurel (Enterprise) ~ Lease Andrew Scott ~ Real ale ~ Open 10.30am-11pm; 10.30am-11.30pm Fri, Sat ~ Bar food 12-9.30; lighter choices 2.30-5.45 ~ Children welcome ~ Dogs allowed in bar ~ Wi-fi ~ Live music Thurs-Sat evenings ~ Bedrooms: £68/£78
Recommended by Guy Vowles, Naomi and Andrew Randall, Stuart and Natalie Granville, Charlie Stevens, Moira and Jon Weller

CHILDSWICKHAM SP0738 Map 4

Childswickham Inn

(01386) 852461 – www.childswickhaminn.co.uk
Off A44 NW of Broadway; WR12 7HP

Bustling dining pub with highly regarded food, good drinks choice, attentive staff and seats in neat garden

After a walk in the lovely surrounding countryside, customers head here for lunch. The chatty bar with leather sofas and armchairs is full of friendly regulars (often with their dogs) and there's Greene King Abbot, Timothy Taylors Landlord and Wells Bombardier Burning Gold on handpump, 12 wines by the glass (with Friday evening deals on champagne and prosecco), malt whiskies, a growing collection of gins and farm cider; background music. There are two dining areas, one with high-backed dark leather chairs on terracotta tiles, the other with country kitchen chairs on bare floorboards. Both have contemporary artwork on part-timbered walls painted cream or pale violet; an open fire and a woodburning stove. A new conservatory with folding doors on to the neat garden was added in 2018, and a decked area has rush-seated chairs and tables. Disabled facilities.

High quality food using local seasonal produce includes lunchtime sandwiches, sea bream fillet with sesame pak choi and noodles in szechuan sauce, blue cheese and spring onion croquettes and goats cheese on mushrooms with pepper and garlic coulis, sharing boards, roast vegetable moussaka with greek salad, ham and free-range eggs, tandoori lamb rack with curried fondant potatoes and spicy lamb kofta, mussels and clams in thai green broth, slow-roast pork belly with a cider-baked apple stuffed with maple-glazed pulled ham, creamy mustard leeks and dauphinoise potatoes, and puddings such as lime and cinnamon treacle tart with stem ginger ice-cream and banana and salted caramel chocolate fondant with banoffi ice-cream; steak night is Thursday. *Benchmark main dish: pie of the day £12.95. Two-course evening meal £20.00.*

Star Pubs & Bars ~ Lease Carol Marshall ~ Real ale ~ Open 11.30-11 (midnight Sat) ~ Bar food 12-9; 12-6 Sun ~ Restaurant closed Sun evening and Mon lunch ~ Children welcome ~ Dogs allowed in bar ~ Wi-fi *Recommended by Ian Duncan, Richard Kennell, Guy Vowles, Mike and Mary Carter, Miranda and Jeff Davidson, Sylvia and Phillip Spencer*

CLENT SO9279 Map 4

Fountain

(01562) 883286 – www.thefountainatclent.co.uk

Adams Hill/Odnall Lane; off A491 at Holy Cross/Clent exit roundabout, via Violet Lane, then right at T junction; DY9 9PU

Restauranty pub often packed to overflowing, with imaginative dishes and good choice of drinks

It's best to book a table in advance at this spotlessly kept, friendly pub as it's extremely popular, particularly at lunchtime. The long carpeted dining bar (consisting of three knocked-together areas) is fairly traditional, with teak chairs and pedestal tables and some comfortably cushioned brocaded wall seats. There are nicely framed local photographs on the rag-rolled pinkish walls above a dark panelled dado, pretty wall lights and candles on the tables (flowers in summer). The changing real ales on handpump include Courage Directors and Marstons EPA and Wainwright on handpump, farm cider and most of their wines are available by the glass; also farm cider, speciality teas and good coffees. Background music and skittle alley. There are tables outside on a decked area.

A wide choice of popular food includes sandwiches, nut-crusted goats cheese with beetroot and cranberry compote, prawn cocktail, vegetable lasagne, tandoori swordfish with tomato and onion salad and mint raita, oriental pork belly with soy and sweet chilli dressing, chicken and shallot tatin on a red wine and mushroom sauce, beef wellington, veal medallions with wild mushrooms and cream, steaks with a choice of sauce, and puddings such as cheesecake of the day and chocolate brownie with hot chocolate sauce and vanilla ice-cream; they also offer a two- and three-course set menu (not Friday or Saturday evenings or Sunday). *Benchmark main dish: lamb shoulder pot roast £17.95. Two-course evening meal £25.00.*

Marstons ~ Lease Richard and Jacque Macey ~ Real ale ~ Open 11-11; 12-8.30 Sun ~ Bar food 12-2, 6-9 (9.30 Fri, Sat); 12-6 Sun ~ Children welcome ~ Wi-fi *Recommended by Anne Taylor, Lionel Smith, Carol and Barry Craddock, Sarah and David Gibbs, Dr and Mrs H J Field, Jim King, Peter Brix*

CUTNALL GREEN SO8868 Map 4

Chequers

(01299) 851292 – www.chequerscutnallgreen.co.uk

Kidderminster Road; WR9 0PJ

Bustling roadside pub with plenty of drinking and dining space in interesting rooms, and rewarding food

Our readers enjoy their visits here, particularly for the interesting food. The pub was built on the site of an old coaching inn and is a clever mix of ancient and modern. There are red-painted walls between beams and timbering, broad floorboards and weathered quarry tiles, and warm winter fires. Also, leather sofas and tub chairs, high-backed purple and red or ladder-back dining chairs around all sorts of tables, plenty of mirrors giving the impression of even more space, brass plates and mugs, candles and fresh flowers. Ringwood Boondoggle, Sharps Doom Bar and Wye Valley HPA on handpump and 14 wines by the glass. One elegant but cosy room, known as the Players Lounge, has photographs of the landlord Mr Narbett, who is a former chef for the England football team. The pretty garden has three 'beach huts' for hire, chairs with barrel tables, sofas, heaters and parasols.

Food is very good and includes weekend breakfasts (9-11am) plus box-baked baby camembert with honey and thyme, spiced lamb kofta with watermelon, feta and pomegranate salad, tzatziki and flatbread, stone-baked pizzas, aubergine, mozzarella and spinach parcels with toasted pine nuts, a pie of the day, calves liver and bacon with mash and red onion jam jus, chicken milanese with tomato fondue and parmesan, a fresh fish dish of the day, sirloin steak with battered onion rings, chips and a choice of sauce, and puddings such as sticky toffee pudding with butterscotch sauce and millionaire's fudge shortbread sundae with toffee ice-cream. *Benchmark main dish: slow-braised lamb shoulder £16.95. Two-course evening meal £18.45.*

Free house ~ Licensees Roger and Jo Narbett ~ Real ale ~ Open 12-11 (10.30 Sun) ~ Bar food 12-9; 12-8.30 Sun ~ Restaurant ~ Children welcome ~ Dogs allowed in bar ~ Wi-fi *Recommended by Susan and John Douglas, Camilla and Jose Ferrera, Liz and Mike Newton, Graham Lovis, Gail and Frank Hackett, John and Abigail Prescott*

ELDERSFIELD SO8131 Map 4

Butchers Arms

(01452) 840381 – www.thebutchersarms.net

Pub and village signposted from B4211; Lime Street (coming from A417, fourth road on left), OS Sheet 150 map reference 815314; village also signposted from B4208 N of Staunton; GL19 4NX

16th-c pub with an unspoilt interior, local ales and carefully chosen wines, excellent food and seats in garden

The interior of this pretty cottage has been kept stylishly simple by the new licensees. Both the bar and the dining room have black beams, knocked-through walls and standing timbers, cream paintwork, plain but individual wooden chairs, pews and some high-backed settles on bare boards or tiles and rustic tables. Also, two woodburning stoves, hop bines and wall prints. Some high chairs line the counter where friendly staff serve Wye Valley Golden Ale tapped from the cask, 11 good wines by the glass including sparkling and pudding choices and farm cider. The good-sized garden has seats on lawns and looks out on to pasture; quoits.

Cooked by the landlord using the best local, seasonal produce, the first class food includes duck confit and ham hock terrine with piccalilli, salt cod scotch egg with chorizo and romesco sauce, pork faggots with onions, black pudding and mash, cornish pollock with mussels and saffron sauce, lamb shoulder with pearl barley and salsa verde and puddings such as chocolate fondant with caramel ice-cream and pistachios and buttermilk pannacotta with rhubarb, oat crumble and raspberry sorbet. *Benchmark main dish: rare-breed beef fillet with fondant potato and Armagnac jus £29.50. Two-course evening meal £32.00.*

Free house ~ Licensee Mark Block ~ Real ale ~ Open 7-11; 12-3, 7-11 Fri, Sat; 12-3 Sun; closed all Mon, Tues-Thurs lunchtimes, Sun evening; last two weeks Aug, two weeks over Christmas ~ Bar food 7-9pm Tues-Sat; 12-2 Fri-Sun ~ Restaurant ~ Children allowed if over 10 ~ Dogs allowed in bar ~ Wi-fi *Recommended by Dan and Belinda Smallbone, Alister and Margery Bacon, Robin and Anne Triggs*

KNIGHTWICK SO7355 Map 4

Talbot

(01886) 821235 – www.the-talbot.co.uk

Knightsford Bridge; B4197 just off A44 Worcester–Bromyard; WR6 5PH

Worcestershire Dining Pub of the Year

Interesting old coaching inn with good own-brewed beer, highly regarded food and riverside garden; bedrooms

With rewarding food, consistently helpful, friendly staff and own brews, this former coaching inn is a winner. The heavily beamed and extended lounge bar is traditionally furnished with a variety of seats from small carved or leatherette armchairs to winged settles by the windows, and there's both a warm log fire and a vast stove in a big central stone hearth. The bar opens into a light and airy garden room. From their own Teme Valley microbrewery (using locally grown hops) they produce Talbot Blonde, That, This, T'Other and a seasonal ale on handpump and hold regular beer festivals; also, a dozen wines by the glass and 16 malt whiskies. The back public bar has pool on a raised side area, a TV, darts, a juke box and cribbage; in contrast, the dining room is a stylish and sedate place for a quiet meal. In warm weather, it's lovely to use the tables on the lawn beside the River Teme (it's across the lane from the inn, but they serve out here too) or you can sit in front of the building on old-fashioned seats. The clean, warm bedrooms have a small decanter of their own damson gin and biscuits. A farmers' market takes place here on the second Sunday of the month. Wheelchair access and loo.

Food is distinctive, imaginative and uses some home-grown produce (they also make their own preserves, bread, raised pies and black pudding): rabbit and pork terrine wrapped in bacon with lime and chilli jam, local pike mousse, potato gnocchi dumplings with wild garlic pesto, sausage, egg and chips, chicken and leek pie, ham hock and wild goose with blanquette sauce and sautéed mushrooms, mutton tagine with orange, star anise and cinnamon and roasted vegetable couscous, 72-hour cooked beef with garlic and herb polenta and honey-glazed carrots, fish platter with celeriac and red onion coleslaw, and puddings such as cheesecake of the day and treacle hollygog (pastry rolled with golden syrup and baked in milk); they also offer breakfast to non-residents (8-11am). *Benchmark main dish: beer-battered fish and chips £16.00. Two-course evening meal £21.50.*

Own brew ~ Licensee Annie Clift ~ Real ale ~ Open 8am-11pm ~ Bar food 8am-9pm ~ Restaurant ~ Children welcome ~ Dogs welcome ~ Wi-fi ~ Bedrooms: £65/£110 *Recommended by Dr and Mrs Paul Cartwright, Ben and Diane Bowie, Nicola and Stuart Parsons, Lenny and Ruth Walters, Peter Harrison, Steve Whalley*

MALVERN SO7845 Map 4

Nags Head

(01684) 574373 – www.nagsheadmalvern.co.uk

Bottom end of Bank Street, steep turn down off A449; WR14 2JG

A delightfully eclectic layout and décor, remarkable choice of ales, tasty lunchtime bar food and warmly welcoming atmosphere

As ever, this is a favourite with our readers and is always packed with cheerful customers who wish to enjoy the fine range of ales in easy-going surroundings. A series of snug, individually decorated rooms, separated by a couple of steps and with two open fires, have leather armchairs, pews sometimes arranged as booths and a mix of tables (including sturdy ones stained different colours). There are bare boards here, flagstones there, carpet elsewhere, plenty of interesting pictures and homely touches such as house plants, shelves of well thumbed books and daily papers; board games. If you struggle to choose from the 15 or so beers on handpump, you'll be offered a taster by the professional, friendly staff: Banks's Bitter, Bathams Best Bitter, Ringwood Fortyniner, St Georges Dragons Blood, Dreamweaver and Friar Tuck and Woods Shropshire Lad, with guests such as Arbor Citra, Courage Best, Lakehouse Cherry-Chocolate Porter, Marstons 61 Deep, Purity Bunny Hop and Skinners Betty Stogs. Also, two farm ciders, 30 malt whiskies, 20 gins, ten bottled craft ales/lagers and ten wines by the glass including pudding ones. The front terrace and garden have picnic-sets, benches and rustic tables as well as parasols and heaters.

Popular lunchtime food includes rolls, ham and egg, omelettes, chargrilled chicken caesar salad, beef and mushroom in ale pie and cheeseburger with chips, with evening meals (served in the barn-extension dining room only) such as thai cod fishcakes, ham hock pakoras with aioli and a poached egg yolk, mushroom and salsify pie, sea bass fillet with bacon-wrapped asparagus, tomato sauce and sautéed potatoes, cajun-spiced chicken and pepper skewers with potato wedges and sweetcorn relish, sweet and sour crispy pork, king prawn, fennel and dill pie with a cheesy topping, and puddings. *Benchmark main dish: beer-battered fresh cod and chips £13.90. Two-course evening meal £20.50.*

Free house ~ Licensee Alex Whistance ~ Real ale ~ Open 11am-11.15pm; 11am-11.30pm Fri, Sat; 12-11 Sun ~ Bar food 12-2.30, 6.30-8.30; 12-2.30, 7-8.30 Sun ~ Restaurant ~ Children welcome ~ Dogs welcome ~ Wi-fi *Recommended by Katherine Matthews, Barry Collett, Patti and James Davidson, Lee and Jill Stafford, Mark Hamill, Clive and Fran Dutson, Andrew Lawson, Guy Henderson*

NEWLAND SO7948 Map 4

Swan

(01886) 832224 – www.theswaninnmalvern.co.uk

Worcester Road (set well back from A449 just NW of Malvern); WR13 5AY

Popular, interesting pub with well kept real ales and seats in the big garden

From the carved bar counter, friendly staff offer up to eight real ales on handpump: Purity Mad Goose, Ringwood Fortyniner and St Georges

Dragons Blood plus quickly changing guest ales; also, several wines by the glass, malt whiskies and four farm ciders. The dimly lit, dark-beamed bar is quite traditional, with a forest canopy of hops, whisky-water jugs, beakers and tankards. Several of the comfortable and clearly individually chosen seats are worth a close look for their carving, and the wall tapestries are interesting. On the right is a broadly similar red-carpeted dining room and beyond it, in complete contrast, an ultra-modern glass garden room; board games. The garden is as individual as the pub, with a cluster of huge casks topped with flowers, even a piano doing flower-tub duty and a set of stocks on the pretty front terrace.

Well thought-of food includes lunchtime sandwiches and baguettes, pressed ham hock terrine with pickles, crab croquettes with lemon and basil mayonnaise, goats cheese, pine nut, spinach and black olive tart with sautéed potatoes, thai-spiced pork belly curry with chilli and cucumber salad, honey-roasted chicken breast with pea and potato hash, polish smoked sausage with sauerkraut, roast hake with sweet potato, beans and lentil stew, and puddings. *Benchmark main dish: steak in ale pie £14.90. Two-course evening meal £21.00.*

Free house ~ Licensee Duncan Ironmonger ~ Real ale ~ Open 12-11.30 ~ Bar food 12-2.30, 6.30-9 ~ Restaurant ~ Children welcome ~ Dogs welcome ~ Wi-fi *Recommended by Jack Trussler, Alister and Margery Bacon, Chantelle and Tony Redman, Gail and Arthur Roberts, Chris Stevenson*

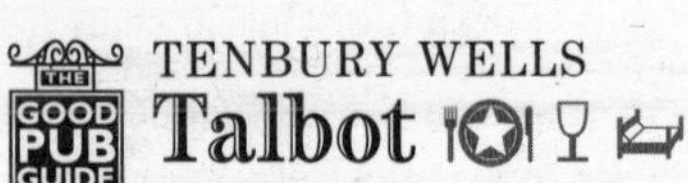

TENBURY WELLS SO6468 Map 4

Talbot

(01584) 781941 – www.talbotinnnewnhambridge.co.uk

Newnham Bridge; A456; WR15 8JF

Carefully refurbished coaching inn with character bar and dining rooms and highly rated food; bedrooms

Many customers are here to enjoy the imaginative food, but there's also a friendly, gently civilised atmosphere and welcoming staff. You'll find nice old red and black and original quarry tiles, bare floorboards, open fires, hops and candlelight; the bar and dining rooms are quite different in style. There's an assortment of dark pubby, high-backed painted wooden and comfortably upholstered dining chairs around a variety of tables, leather tub chairs and sofas, bookshelves, old photographs of the local area, table lights and standard lamps, and some elegant antiques. It gets pretty busy at the weekend, when you'll need to book a table in advance. Hobsons Town Crier and Wye Valley Bitter and HPA on handpump, local cider and good wines by the glass; background music, TV and board games. To make the most of the delightful Teme Valley countryside and surrounding towns, stay for a few days in the thoughtfully decorated and well equipped bedrooms; breakfasts are well regarded too.

Excellent, interesting food includes sandwiches, fishcake with coriander mayonnaise, pear, blue cheese and walnut salad, chicken breast with red onions, kale, cider fondant potatoes and sweetcorn chutney, sage gnocchi with pumpkin, red onion and spinach, plaice fillet with chicory, salsa verde, samphire and garlic potato purée, sea bass fillet with curried cauliflower, crispy egg and dauphinoise potatoes, duck breast with confit duck leg, turnip and beetroot dauphinoise, and puddings such as chocolate and malt cake with chocolate meringue and chocolate ice-cream and orange cheesecake with vanilla ice-cream. *Benchmark main dish: sirloin steak with wild garlic butter £18.00. Two-course evening meal £23.00.*

Free house ~ Licensee Barnaby Williams ~ Real ale ~ Open 12-11 (midnight Sat); 12-11.30 Sun; closed first two weeks Jan ~ Bar food 12-2.30, 6-9.30; 12-7.30 Sun ~

Restaurant ~ Children welcome ~ Dogs allowed in bar and bedrooms ~ Wi-fi ~ Bedrooms: £80/£90 *Recommended by Lance and Sarah Milligan, Kerry and Guy Trooper, Graham Smart, Isobel Mackinlay, Susan Eccleston*

THE GOOD PUB GUIDE

WELLAND — SO8039 Map 4

Inn at Welland

(01684) 592317 – www.theinnatwelland.co.uk

Just off A4104 W of Upton upon Severn, signed for Hook Bank; WR13 6LN

Stylish contemporary country dining bar with good food and wines and nice tables outside

Handy for the Three Counties Showground, this is a popular place for lunch. The rooms have a chatty, easy-going atmosphere, cool grey paintwork, a few carefully chosen modern prints and attractive seat fabrics, with beige flagstones in the central area, wood flooring to the sides and a woodburning stove at one end. Ledbury Gold and Wye Valley Butty Bach on handpump, 43 wines by the glass including champagne, sparkling and an unusually wide range of pudding wines, mocktails, cocktails and quite a few gins, all served by neatly dressed, efficient staff. The good-sized tidy garden, offering tranquil views of the Malvern Hills, has tables with comfortable teak or wicker chairs on a biggish sheltered deck or on individual separate terraces set into lawn.

First class food includes king scallops with smoked pancetta and pearl barley, celeriac purée and confit vegetables, ham hock with a truffle beignet, an egg and piccalilli, omelette arnold bennett, interesting sharing boards, a vegetarian risotto of the day, rare-breed beef burger with stilton rarebit and fries, guinea fowl breast with bubble and squeak and white beans and chorizo, hake with saffron potato and mussel bouillabaisse, venison loin with juniper-smoked jus, parsnip purée and roast turnip and mushroom pie, 8oz rib-eye steak with trimmings and triple-cooked chips, and puddings such as lemon drizzle cake with compressed pineapple and white chocolate ice-cream and dark chocolate délice with blood orange curd and crème fraîche ice-cream. *Benchmark main dish: pork belly with shallot purée, baked apple and cider reduction £16.90. Two-course evening meal £25.00.*

Free house ~ Licensees David and Gillian Pinchbeck ~ Real ale ~ Open 12-3, 5.30-11; 12-4 Sun; closed Sun evening, Mon ~ Bar food 12-2.30, 6-9.30; 12-2.30 Sun ~ Restaurant ~ Children welcome ~ Wi-fi *Recommended by Louise and Anton Parsons, Andy and Louise Ramwell, Val and Malcolm Travers, Phil and Helen Holt, Cecily and Steven Evans, Darrell Barton, Dan and Belinda Smallbone*

Also Worth a Visit in Worcestershire

Besides the fully inspected pubs, you might like to try these pubs that have been recommended to us and described by readers. Do tell us what you think of them: feedback@goodguides.com

ABBERLEY SO7567

Manor Arms (01299) 890300

Netherton Lane; WR6 6BN Modernised country inn tucked away in quiet village backwater opposite fine Norman church; changing local ales and ciders, 20 wines by the glass and highly praised well presented food from seasonal menu including snacks and pub favourites, afternoon tea, helpful friendly service; children and dogs welcome, two-level deck with lovely valley views, good walks (on Worcestershire Way), six bedrooms, open all day. *(Charlie Stevens)*

ALVECHURCH SP0172

Weighbridge (0121) 445 5111

Scarfield Wharf; B48 7SQ Little red-brick pub (former weighbridge office) by Worcester & Birmingham Canal marina; bar and a couple of other small rooms, half a dozen well kept ales including Kinver Bargee Bitter and Weatheroak Tillerman's Tipple (beer festivals), simple low-priced food (not Tues, Weds); tables outside. *(Dan and Belinda Smallbone)*

ASHTON UNDER HILL SO9938

Star (01386) 881325

Elmley Road; WR11 7SN Smallish pub perched above road in quiet village at foot of Bredon Hill; linked beamed rooms around bar, one with flagstones and log fire, steps up to pitch-roofed dining room with woodburner, well liked food (not Sun or Mon evenings) including meal deals Mon-Fri lunchtime and Tues evening, real ales such as Black Sheep and Greene King IPA, friendly welcoming staff; background music, TV and games machine; children and dogs welcome, picnic-sets in pleasant garden, good walks (Wyche Way passes nearby), open all day. *(Peter Young, Philip O'Connor)*

BECKFORD SO9835

Beckford Inn (01386) 881532

Cheltenham Road (A435); GL20 7AN Sizeable 18th-c roadside inn owned by Wadworths, their beers and good range of wines by the glass, enjoyable food (all day Fri-Sun) from traditional choices up; children and dogs welcome, wheelchair access, large garden, 12 comfortable bedrooms (some in renovated cottage), open all day from 8am. *(Dr A J and Mrs B A Tompsett)*

BELBROUGHTON SO9277

Olde Horse Shoe (01562) 731663

High Street; DY9 9ST Popular old beamed corner pub with smallish stone-floored bar and separate restaurant; usually three real ales including St Austell and Wye Valley, good range of well liked freshly made food (not Sun evening, Mon), afternoon teas, friendly service, open fires, may be paintings for sale; occasional live music including tribute acts; children and dogs welcome, big back garden, closed Mon till 4pm, otherwise open all day. *(Clifford Blakemore)*

BELBROUGHTON SO9177

Queens (01562) 730276

Queens Hill (B4188 E of Kidderminster); DY9 0DU Old red-brick pub by Belne Brook; several linked areas including beamed slate-floor bar, very good modern food alongside pub standards, three well kept beers such as Ringwood and Thwaites, nice selection of wines, friendly staff coping well at busy times; disabled facilities, small roadside terrace, pleasant village handy for M5 (junction 4), open all day, till 6pm Sun. *(Jonny and Andrew Haughton)*

BELBROUGHTON SO9277

Talbot (01562) 730249

Off A491, Hartle Lane; DY9 9TG Refurbished village pub with good food in bar and restaurant from sandwiches and tapas-style dishes up, three well kept Marstons-related ales including one badged for them, friendly helpful staff; children and dogs (in bar) welcome, garden with covered terrace, open all day. *(Dr and Mrs H J Field)*

BERROW SO7835

Duke of York (01684) 833449

Junction A438/B4208; WR13 6JQ Bustling old country pub with two linked rooms, beams, nooks and crannies and log fire, enjoyable generously served food including good seafood platter and OAP lunch deal, ales such as Otter, Sharps and Wye Valley, friendly service, restaurant; children and dogs welcome, big garden behind, handy for Malvern Hills. *(Amy Ledbetter)*

BEWDLEY SO7775

Hop Pole (01299) 401295

Hop Pole Lane; DY12 2QH Modernised 19th-c pub with good choice of popular food (booking advised) from pub favourites up including set menus and themed nights, three well kept Marstons-related ales and several wines by the glass, country-chic décor, cast-iron range in dining area; regular live music and other events, free wi-fi; children and dogs (in bar) welcome, seats on raised front terrace, vegetable garden to the side, back play area, open all day. *(Mark and Mary Setting)*

BEWDLEY SO7875

Little Pack Horse (01299) 403762

High Street; no nearby parking – best to use main car park, then cross B4190 (Cleobury Road), and keep walking on down narrowing High Street; DY12 2DH Town pub tucked away in side street; cosy old timbered rooms with bare boards and quarry tiles, some reclaimed oak panelling, woodburner, generous helpings of tasty food including good pies and suet puddings, a couple of Hobsons ales and a guest, bottled ciders/perries, good wine choice, cheerful helpful service, restaurant; background music, fortnightly quiz Sun; children and dogs (in bar) welcome, open all day weekends, closed weekday lunchtimes. *(John and Abigail Prescott)*

BEWDLEY SO7875

Mug House (01299) 402543

Severn Side North; DY12 2EE 18th-c bay-windowed pub in lovely spot by River Severn; good food from traditional choices up including set menus, can eat in bar or more upmarket evening restaurant with lobster tank, six well kept ales such as Bewdley, Purity, Timothy Taylors and Wye Valley (May beer festival), log fire; children (daytime only) and dogs welcome, disabled access, glass-covered terrace behind, seven river-view bedrooms, open all day, no food Sun evening. *(Susan Eccleston)*

BIRLINGHAM SO9343

Swan (01386) 750485
Church Street; off A4104 S of Pershore, via B4080 Eckington Road, turn off at sign to Birlingham with integral 'The Swan Inn' brown sign (not the 'Birlingham (village only)' road), then left; WR10 3AQ Pretty family-run thatched and timbered cottage; updated beamed quarry-tiled bar with woodburner in big stone fireplace, well kept ales such as Hook Norton and Purity, real cider, good food from reasonably priced varied menu including fresh fish specials, friendly efficient service, dining conservatory; nice back garden, handy for River Avon walks, open all day Sun till 7pm, closed Mon except bank holidays. *(Peter Young, Dr and Mrs H J Field, Guy Vowles)*

BREDON SO9236

★**Fox & Hounds** (01684) 772377
4.5 miles from M5 junction 9; A438 to Northway, left at B4079, in Bredon follow sign to church; GL20 7LA Cottagey 16th-c thatched pub with open-plan carpeted bar; low beams, stone pillars and stripped timbers, central woodburner, upholstered settles and variety of wheelback, tub and kitchen chairs around handsome mahogany and cast-iron-framed tables, elegant wall lamps, smaller side bar, ales such as Banks's, Butcombe, Wadworths, Wells and Wye Valley, nice wines by the glass and wide choice of enjoyable food including specials, fast friendly service; background music, quiz Sun evening (no food then); children welcome, dogs in bar, outside picnic-sets (some under cover) and pretty hanging baskets, closed Mon. *(R J Herd)*

BROADWAS-ON-TEME SO7555

Royal Oak (01886) 821353
A44; WR6 5NE Red-brick roadside pub with various areas including lofty dining hall; popular good value daily carvery and other enjoyable food, weekday set menus, well kept Marstons-related ales and decent wines by the glass, friendly helpful service; free wi-fi; children welcome, no dogs inside, disabled access, garden with play area, open (and food) all day. *(Jim King)*

BROADWAY SP0937

Swan (01386) 852278
The Green (B4362); WR12 7AA Sizeable Mitchells & Butlers dining pub with imaginative décor in several linked areas; popular sensibly priced food including good value fixed-price menu (till 6pm Mon-Fri), three well kept changing ales including Purity and Sharps, plenty of wines by the glass and good range of cocktails, polite friendly young staff; children welcome, tables under parasols on small front terrace looking over road to village green, open all day. *(Richard Kennell)*

CALLOW END SO8349

Blue Bell (01905) 830261
Upton Road; WR2 4TY Popular Marstons local with two bars and dining area, their well kept ales and wide variety of reasonably priced food including lots of specials (some good vegetarian choices), friendly welcoming staff, open fire; quiz last Thurs of the month, sports TV, pool and darts; children allowed, dogs in garden only, open all day weekends. *(Dr and Mrs H J Field)*

CALLOW END SO8349

Old Bush (01905) 830792
Off Upton Road (B4424); WR2 4TE Friendly black and white village local; well kept ales such as Butcombe and Hobsons and enjoyable home-cooked food, cosy small areas around central bar, beams, woodburner and various memorabilia, separate dining room; live music including Aug blues festival; children and dogs welcome, nice garden with play area, camping, open all day Fri-Sun. *(Dave Braisted)*

CALLOW HILL SP0164

Brook Inn (01527) 543209
Elcocks Brook, off B4504; B97 5UD Modernised country dining pub with well liked locally sourced food from lunchtime sandwiches up (not Mon), Marstons-related ales, friendly staff; tables out at front and in pleasant back beer garden, open all day. *(Peter Brix)*

CALLOW HILL SO7473

Royal Forester (01299) 266286
Near Wyre Forest visitor centre; DY14 9XW Dining pub dating in part from the 15th c; good food including regular themed evenings, friendly helpful service, well kept ales such as Timothy Taylors, Robinson's cider, relaxed lounge bar and restaurant; regular live music, quiz nights; children and dogs welcome, seats outside, seven contemporary bedrooms, open all day. *(Isobel Mackinlay)*

CAUNSALL SO8480

Anchor (01562) 850254
Caunsall Road, off A449; DY11 5YL Traditional unchanging two-room pub (in same family since 1927), popular and welcoming, with five well kept ales such as Hobsons, Three Tuns and Wye Valley, traditional ciders and good value generously filled cobs, friendly efficient service; children and dogs welcome, large outside seating area behind, near Staffordshire & Worcestershire Canal. *(Brian and Anna Marsden)*

CHADDESLEY CORBETT SO8973

Swan (01562) 777302
Off A448 Bromsgrove–Kidderminster; DY10 4SD Popular old local with friendly buoyant atmosphere; well kept Bathams and enjoyable good value pubby food from

sandwiches and pizzas up, various rooms including high-raftered lounge bar; Thurs jazz, open mike nights, TV, games machine; children and dogs welcome, picnic-sets in big lawned garden with play area and country views, Aug classic car show, handy for Harvington Hall, open all day, food all day Sat. *(Sylvia and Phillip Spencer)*

CLAINES SO8558

Mug House (01905) 456649
Claines Lane, off A449 3 miles W of M5 junction 3; WR3 7RN Fine views from this ancient country tavern in unique churchyard setting by fields below the Malvern Hills; several small rooms around central bar, low doorways and heavy oak beams, well kept Banks's and other Marstons-related ales, simple lunchtime pub food; no credit cards, outside lavatories; children (away from servery) and dogs welcome, open all day weekends. *(Miranda and Jeff Davidson)*

CROPTHORNE SO9944

Bell (01386) 861860
Main Road (B4084); WR10 3NE Isolated rather stark-looking roadside pub with contrasting brightly modernised interior; painted beams, bare boards and colourful carpet in L-shaped bar, well divided seating areas (one down a couple of steps), log fire, small back conservatory, emphasis on dining with popular freshly made food from good ploughman's up, children's choices, three changing ales, welcoming efficient service; background music; open all day Sat, till 8pm Sun, closed Mon, Tues. *(Darrell Barton)*

CROWLE SO9256

Chequers (01905) 381772
Crowle Green, not far from M5 junction 6; WR7 4AA Busy beamed dining pub (sister to the Forest at Feckenham); good food (some quite pricey) from sandwiches and one or two pubby choices up, well kept ales such as St Austell and Wye Valley, lots of wines by the glass and good range of other drinks, friendly attentive staff; children and dogs (in bar) welcome, open all day. *(Charlie Stevens)*

DEFFORD SO9042

★**Monkey House** (01386) 750234
A4104, after passing Oak pub on right, it's the last of a small group of cottages; WR8 9BW Tiny black and white thatched cider house, a wonderful time warp and in the same family for over 150 years; ciders and a perry tapped from barrels into pottery mugs and served by landlady from hatch, no other drinks or food (can bring your own); children welcome, no dogs, garden with caravans, sheds and small spartan outbuilding with a couple of plain tables, settle and fireplace, open Fri and Sun lunchtimes, Weds and Sat evenings. *(Amy Ledbetter)*

DEFFORD SO9042

Oak (01386) 750327
Woodmancote (A4104); WR8 9BW Modernised 17th-c beamed country pub with two front bars and back restaurant, well kept ales such as Sharps and Wye Valley, Thatcher's cider, good fairly priced food (all day Sat, till 7pm Sun), friendly staff; occasional live music; children and dogs (in bar) welcome, vine-covered front pergola, garden with orchard and chickens, open all day. *(Jim King)*

DODFORD SO9372

Dodford Inn (01527) 835825
Whinfield Road; B61 9BG Mid 19th-c red-brick country pub tucked away in six-acre grounds, fresh modern refurbishment, up to four well kept ales including Purity and Wye Valley, good home-made food (all day Sat, not Sun evening) from sandwiches up, friendly welcoming staff; children allowed, no dogs inside, nice views over wooded valley from terrace tables, good walks, open all day Fri and Sat, till 7pm Sun, closed Mon. *(Mrs B H Adams)*

DROITWICH SO8963

Gardeners Arms (01905) 772936
Vines Lane; WR9 8LU Individual place on the edge of town; cosy traditional bar to the right, bistro-style restaurant to the left with red gingham tablecloths and lots of pictures (mostly for sale), four Marstons-related ales, well priced food from varied menu including range of good local sausages; regular live music and quiz nights, also themed food evenings, whisky tastings and a cigar club; children and dogs welcome, outside seating areas on different levels below railway embankment with quirky mix of furniture, play area, camping, close to Droitwich Canal, open (and food) all day. *(Jonny and Andrew Haughton)*

DROITWICH SO9063

Hop Pole (01905) 770155
Friar Street; WR9 8ED Heavy-beamed local with panelled rooms on different levels, well kept Malvern Hills, Wye Valley and a guest, bargain home-made lunchtime food including doorstep sandwiches; dominoes, darts and pool, occasional live music; children welcome, partly canopied back garden, open all day. *(Peter Brix)*

DUNLEY SO7969

Dog (01299) 822833
A451 S of Stourport; DY13 0UE Attractive creeper-clad roadside dining pub; good choice of well priced enjoyable food

(not Sun evening) from bar meals up, well kept Wye Valley and guests, friendly staff; free wi-fi; children and dogs welcome, garden with play area and bowling green, three bedrooms, open all day Sun. *(Jim King)*

ECKINGTON SO9241

Bell (01386) 750033

Church Street (B4080); WR10 3AN Modernised village dining pub with much enjoyed food (special diets catered for) including good value two-course lunch, you can also cook your own on a hot stone, two well kept ales, efficient friendly service; quiz first Sun of month; children and dogs (in Farmers Bar) welcome, enclosed back garden, on Wyche Way long-distance path, four bedrooms, open (and food) all day weekends. *(Guy Vowles)*

EVESHAM SP0344

Old Red Horse (01386) 442784

Vine Street; WR11 4RE Attractive black and white 15th-c coaching inn, two bars with beams, bare boards and open fires, three real ales, traditional ciders and enjoyable reasonably priced pub food including lunchtime meal deal (Mon-Sat) and steak nights (Tues, Weds), good cheerful service; TV, darts and machines, free wi-fi; children and dogs welcome, nice covered inner courtyard with small pond, five bedrooms, open all day, no evening food weekends. *(Dr J Barrie Jones)*

FECKENHAM SP0061

Forest (01527) 894422

B4090 Droitwich–Alcester; B96 6JE Contemporary décor and good interesting food at this village dining pub (sister to the Chequers at Crowle), well kept Hook Norton and Timothy Taylors, efficient friendly service, oak-floored bar with light-wood stools at high tables and some other more comfortable seating, panels of bookshelf wallpaper dotted about, woodburner, adjoining restaurant with upholstered booth seats, conservatory; children welcome, disabled access/facilities, rattan furniture on block-paved terrace with big outdoor fireplace, more tables on raised lawn, closed Mon and Tues, otherwise open all day, food till 6pm Sun. *(Mike and Mary Carter)*

FLADBURY SO9946

Chequers (01386) 861854

Chequers Lane; WR10 2PZ Modernised old pub in peaceful village; long beamed bar with log fire in old-fashioned range, ales such as Timothy Taylors and Wye Valley, Aspall's and Weston's ciders, enjoyable sensibly priced home-made food including Mon grill night, timbered back restaurant with conservatory; background music, free wi-fi; children welcome, steps up to walled terrace, play area on lawn with country views, eight bedrooms in extension, open all day Fri-Sun, closed Mon lunchtime. *(Isobel Mackinlay)*

FLYFORD FLAVELL SO9754

Boot (01386) 462658

Off A422 Worcester–Alcester; Radford Road; WR7 4BS Popular food including two-course lunch deal, cook your own steak on a hot stone and blackboard specials, Fullers London Pride and Sharps Doom Bar, good friendly service, log fires in ancient heavily beamed and timbered core, modern conservatory, games room with pool and TV; background music; children, walkers and dogs (in bar) welcome, tables on split-level terrace and small lawned area, five bedrooms, open all day. *(Mike and Mary Carter)*

HADLEY SO8662

Bowling Green (01905) 620294

Hadley Heath; off A4133 Droitwich–Ombersley; WR9 0AR Popular refurbished 16th-c inn with beams and big log fire, well kept Wadworths ales and decent wines by the glass, good food (all day Sun) from sandwiches and deli boards up, comfortable back lounge and restaurant; children welcome, tables out overlooking own bowling green (UK's oldest), comfortable bedrooms, nice walks (footpath starts from car park), open all day. *(Peter Brix)*

HANLEY CASTLE SO8342

★**Three Kings** (01684) 592686

Church End, off B4211 N of Upton upon Severn; WR8 0BL Timeless, hospitable and by no means smart – in same family since 1911 and a favourite with those who put unspoilt character and individuality first; cheerful, homely tiled-floor tap room separated from entrance corridor by monumental built-in settle, equally vast inglenook fireplace, room on left with darts and board games, separate entrance to timbered lounge with second inglenook and blacked kitchen range, leatherette armchairs, spindleback chairs and antique winged settle, well kept Butcombe, Hobsons and three guests from smaller brewers, Weston's cider and around 75 malt whiskies, simple snacks including good sandwiches; live music; children and dogs welcome, old-fashioned wood and iron seats on front terrace looking across to great cedar shading tiny green, on Wyche Way long-distance path. *(Barry Collett, Dave Braisted)*

HANLEY SWAN SO8142

★**Swan** (01684) 311870

B4209 Malvern–Upton; WR8 0EA Contemporary/rustic décor and furnishings blending well with old low beams (some painted), bare boards and log fire, extended back part set for their good well presented food (all day Sat, not Sun evening) from sandwiches/baguettes and pub favourites to more restauranty dishes (booking advised), friendly helpful staff, St Austell Tribute, Sharps Doom Bar and Wye Valley HPA, seven wines by the glass, oak-framed conservatory; children and dogs welcome, disabled access/loos, seats out on paved terrace and grass, nice spot facing green and big duck pond, five comfortable good value bedrooms, open all day, weekend breakfast from 8am. *(Richard Kennell)*

HIMBLETON SO9458

Galton Arms (01905) 391672
Harrow Lane; WR9 7LQ Friendly old black and white bay-windowed country pub; good food (not Sun evening, Mon) including daily specials in split-level beamed bar or restaurant, well kept ales such as Banks's, Bathams and Wye Valley, woodburner; sports TV; children and dogs welcome, picnic-sets in small part-paved garden, local walks, open all day Sun, closed Mon lunchtime. *(Sylvia and Phillip Spencer)*

HOLT HEATH SO8063

Red Lion (01905) 620600
Witley Road (A443/A4133); WR6 6LX Modernised dining pub specialising in good value caribbean food, also traditional meals including early bird deal till 6pm; bar with white-painted beams, high-backed dining chairs around cheerfully clothed tables and some colourful artwork, three real ales and several rums, good friendly service, raftered restaurant; pool, sports TV, fruit machine; picnic-sets in lawned garden with decked area, open all day weekends. *(Dave Braisted)*

KEMERTON SO9437

Crown (01386) 725020
Back Road Bredon–Beckford; GL20 7HP Small 18th-c pub in pretty village; hospitable landlord and cheerful staff, good freshly made food (not Sun evening) from sandwiches up including sharing dishes and daily specials, ales such as Wye Valley, local cider, flagstoned bar with log fire, separate restaurant; children and dogs welcome, roadside tables and peaceful courtyard garden behind, good walks over Bredon Hill, four pleasant bedrooms, closed Mon lunchtime, otherwise open all day. *(Gerald Warner)*

LONGDON SO8434

Hunters Inn (01684) 833388
B4211 S, towards Tewkesbury; GL20 6AR Beamed and timbered country pub with flagstone floors, stripped brickwork and log fires, enjoyable locally sourced food including Sun carvery, real ales such as Donnington and Otter, local ciders and decent wines by the glass, friendly service, raftered dining area with linen-clothed tables, good views; some live music and quiz nights, darts; children welcome, extensive well tended garden, campsite, open all day weekends, closed Mon and lunchtime Tues. *(Dan and Belinda Smallbone)*

LOWER BROADHEATH SO8056

Dewdrop (01905) 640012
Bell Lane; WR2 6RR Refurbished rather upmarket dining pub; much enjoyed food from sandwiches and snacks up including some pub favourites and good value set menu (Mon-Sat lunch, Mon-Thurs evening), Wye Valley and a guest, ciders such as Robinson's and a dozen wines by the glass, afternoon teas, friendly attentive service; children welcome, dogs in bar and part of restaurant, tables out at front, nine bedrooms in separate buildings, handy for the Firs (NT) – Elgar's birthplace, open all day, food all day weekends. *(Theocsbrian, Dave Braisted)*

MALVERN SO7746

Foley Arms (01684) 573397
Worcester Road; WR14 4QS Substantial Georgian hotel (former coaching inn) owned by Wetherspoons, friendly staff and usual good value, splendid views from main bar, sunny terrace and back bedrooms; free wi-fi; children welcome, open all day from 7am. *(Dr J Barrie Jones)*

MALVERN SO7640

Malvern Hills Hotel (01684) 540690
Opposite British Camp car park, Wynds Point; junction A449/B4232 S; WR13 6DW Big comfortable lounge bar with oak panelling and woodburner, three well kept Wye Valley ales and a guest (two in summer), quite a few malt whiskies, enjoyable food here or in two more modern restaurants (one with lovely country views), good friendly service; background music; children and dogs (in bar) welcome, terrace seating under parasols, cosy bedrooms, open (and food) all day. *(John Evans, Clive and Fran Dutson)*

MALVERN SO7746

Red Lion (01684) 564787
St Anns Road; WR14 4RG Tucked up a narrow lane near town centre; enjoyable food (all day Sat) from sandwiches and baguettes up, also very good adjacent thai restaurant (evenings Tues-Sat), well kept Marstons-related ales such as Ringwood, cheerful prompt service, modern décor with stripped pine, bare boards, flagstones and pastel colours; background music, darts; attractive partly covered front terrace, well placed for hill walks, open (and food) all day Sat, closed Sun-Thurs lunchtimes. *(Susan Eccleston)*

MALVERN SO7643

Wyche (01684) 575396
Wyche Road; WR14 4EQ Comfortable busy pub near top of Malvern Hills, splendid views and popular with walkers; Wye Valley and guests, decent range of affordable pubby food from sandwiches up including themed nights, good service; pool and games machine in one bar; children and dogs welcome, four bedrooms plus self-catering apartments, open all day. *(Miranda and Jeff Davidson)*

OMBERSLEY SO8463

Cross Keys (01905) 620588
Just off A449; Main Road (A4133, Kidderminster end); WR9 0DS Refurbished 19th-c country pub; carpeted bar with fire, archways opening into several separate areas, beams, banquettes and brassware, Timothy Taylors Landlord and Wye Valley HPA, well liked food from sandwiches to daily specials, friendly helpful service, dining conservatory; background music; children and dogs welcome, terrace seating, open all day Sun (food till 7pm), closed Mon lunchtime. *(Darrell Barton)*

OMBERSLEY SO8463

Kings Arms (01905) 620142
Main Road (A4133); WR9 0EW Imposing beamed and timbered Tudor pub; low-ceilinged brick-floored bar with built-in panelled wall seat and woodburner in large fireplace, three dining areas, steps down to one, another with Charles II coat of arms decorating the ceiling, good food and service, well kept Marstons-related ales; background music; children and dogs welcome, seats on tree-sheltered courtyard, colourful hanging baskets and tubs, open all day Fri-Sun. *(John and Abigail Prescott)*

PENSAX SO7368

★**Bell** (01299) 896677
B4202 Abberley–Clows Top, Snead Common part of village; WR6 6AE Mock-Tudor roadside pub with good local atmosphere; seven well kept ales including Exmoor and Hobsons, real cider/perry and popular good value pub food (not Sun evening) from sandwiches up, L-shaped main bar with traditional décor, cushioned pews and pubby tables on bare boards, vintage beer ads and wartime front pages, two open fires and woodburner, dining room with french windows opening on to deck; children and dogs (in bar) welcome, country-view garden, closed Mon lunchtime. *(Dave Braisted)*

PEOPLETON SO9350

Crown (01905) 840222
Village and pub signed off A44 at Allens Hill; WR10 2EE Cosy village pub with friendly mix of drinkers and diners; beamed bar with big inglenook and well laid-out eating area, good food (must book) from sandwiches and pub favourites up including OAP deals and regular themed evenings, ales such as Fullers, Sharps and Wye Valley, nice wines by the glass, pleasant efficient service; children allowed till 9pm, dogs in bar, flower-filled back garden, open all day. *(Amy Ledbetter)*

PERSHORE SO9445

Pickled Plum (01386) 556645
High Street; WR10 1EQ Modernised old pub with good range of well kept ales and ciders, enjoyable generously served food at fair prices including lunchtime/early evening two-course deal and blackboard specials, quick friendly service, beams and log fires; Sun quiz, acoustic music session first Mon of month; children and dogs welcome, open all day, no food Sun evening. *(Denis and Margaret Kilner)*

SEVERN STOKE SO8544

Rose & Crown (01905) 371249
A38 S of Worcester; WR8 9JQ Attractive 16th-c black and white pub; low beams, good fire and various knick-knacks in character bar, some cushioned wall seats and high-backed settles among more modern pub furniture, tiled or carpeted floors, well kept Marstons-related ales, Weston's cider and decent choice of enjoyable sensibly priced food from sandwiches and sharing plates up, good friendly service, carpeted back restaurant; fortnightly quiz Weds, monthly folk night; children (away from bar) and dogs welcome, tricky wheelchair access but possible with help, picnic-sets in big garden with play area, Malvern Hills views and good walks, open (and food) all day. *(Dave Braisted, Chris and Angela Buckell)*

SHATTERFORD SO7981

Bellmans Cross (01299) 861322
Bridgnorth Road (A442); DY12 1RN Welcoming 19th-c mock-Tudor dining pub; good well presented food cooked by french chef-landlord including lunchtime set menu and weekday themed evenings, restaurant with kitchen view, Enville and a couple of guests from neat timber-effect bar, good choice of wines, teas and coffees; children welcome, picnic-sets outside, handy for Severn Woods walks, open (and food) all day weekends. *(Jim King)*

STOKE POUND SO9667

Queens Head (01527) 557007
Sugarbrook Lane, by Bridge 48, Worcester & Birmingham Canal; B60 3AU Smartly modernised by the small Lovely Pubs group; fairly large bar with comfortable seating area, dedicated dining part beyond, good choice of food including sharing plates, wood-fired pizzas and charcoal spit-roasts, early evening discount (Mon-Fri) and two-for-one pizzas (Mon-Thurs), well kept ales such as Purity, Sharps and Wye Valley, large selection of wines from glass-fronted store, helpful pleasant staff; occasional live music; children welcome, waterside garden with tipi, moorings, good walk up the 30 locks of Tardebigge Steps, quite handy for Avoncroft Museum, open (and food) all day. *(Peter Brix)*

STOKE WORKS SO9365

Boat & Railway (01527) 575597
Shaw Lane, by Bridge 42, Worcester & Birmingham Canal; B60 4EQ Neat and tidy canalside pub under welcoming

newish management; enjoyable good value home-cooked food including deals, Marstons-related ales, friendly helpful staff, large separate dining area overlooking the canal; children (till 9pm) and dogs (in bar) welcome, narrow covered waterside terrace, moorings, open (and food) all day, kitchen shuts 6pm Sun. *(Dave Braisted)*

STOKE WORKS SO9365

Bowling Green (01527) 861291

A mile from M5 junction 5, via Stoke Lane; handy for Worcester & Birmingham Canal; B60 4BH
Friendly comfortable pub with enjoyable straightforward food at bargain prices (particularly good faggots), well kept Banks's ales and a Marstons guest, wall chart showing cost of a pint over the years; children welcome, big garden with play area and well tended bowling green, camping, open all day, no food Sun. *(Dave Braisted)*

TENBURY WELLS SO5966

Fountain (01584) 810701

Oldwood, A4112 S; WR15 8TB Timbered 17th-c roadside pub with big black-beamed bar, good choice of well prepared/priced pubby food, ales from Hobsons and sometimes Wye Valley, friendly helpful service; children and dogs welcome, a few picnic-sets out at front, more in lawned garden with play equipment, ten bedrooms (separate block), open all day, food all day weekends. *(Theocsbrian)*

TENBURY WELLS SO5968

Pembroke House (01584) 810301

Cross Street; WR15 8EQ Striking timbered building (oldest in town) with pubby beamed bar and two dining rooms, good popular food (not Sun evening, Mon, best to book) including themed nights, friendly efficient staff, Hobsons Best and a guest, woodburner, games area with pool, darts and TV; background and some live music; children welcome, no dogs inside, smokers' shelter and pleasant garden, open all day Fri-Sun, closed Mon lunchtime. *(Mark and Mary Setting)*

UPHAMPTON SO8464

Fruiterers Arms (01905) 620305

Off A449 N of Ombersley; WR9 0JW
Friendly country local (looks like a private house, and has been in the same family since the mid 19th c); good value Cannon Royall ales brewed at the back and a couple of guests, farm cider and perry, simple rustic Jacobean panelled bar and lounge with comfortable armchairs, beams and log fire, lots of photographs and memorabilia, snacky food such as rolls and pork pies; children allowed till 9pm, dogs in one area, back terrace and some seats out in front, open all day. *(Jonny and Andrew Haughton)*

WEST MALVERN SO7645

Brewers Arms (01684) 575408

The Dingle, signed off B4232; WR14 4BQ
Attractive little two-bar beamed country local down steep path; well kept Malvern Hills, Wye Valley and up to five guests at busy times, good value pubby food, airy dining room; live music Fri, free wi-fi; children, walkers and dogs welcome, glorious view from small garden, open all day. *(Susan Eccleston)*

WILLERSEY SP1039

New Inn (01386) 853226

Main Street; WR12 7PJ Friendly old stone-built local in lovely village; generous helpings of good value pub food (not Sun evening) from sandwiches up, well kept Donnington ales, flagstoned bar with raised quarry-tiled end section, some black beams, games room (pool and darts) and separate skittle alley; background music, TV; rattan-style tables and chairs outside, good local walks, open all day. *(Peter Brix)*

WORCESTER SO8554

Cardinals Hat (01905) 724006

Friar Street; just off A44 near cathedral; WR1 2NA Dating from the 14th c with three small character rooms (one with fine oak panelling), five changing ales, real ciders and plenty of bottled beers, friendly well informed staff, good bar snacks and cheese/meat platters; free wi-fi; children welcome, pleasant little brick-paved terrace behind, four good bedrooms (continental breakfast), closed Mon lunchtime, otherwise open all day. *(Dave Braisted, Jim King)*

WORCESTER SO8455

Dragon (01905) 25845

The Tything (A38); WR1 1JT Refurbished Georgian alehouse run by friendly landlady; L-shaped carpeted bar with woodburner, six well kept Church End ales and a couple of guests, traditional cider and seven wines by the glass, snacky food such as pork pies and sausage rolls, more room (and loos) upstairs; no children inside, dogs welcome, partly covered back terrace, open all day Fri-Sun, from 4pm other days. *(Jim King)*

WORCESTER SO8454

Farriers Arms (01905) 27569

Fish Street; WR1 2HN Welcoming and relaxed old timbered pub off the High Street; compact interior with bar and dining areas wrapping around central bar, enjoyable inexpensive food, well kept ales such as Wells Bombardier and St Austell Tribute, decent house wines, good cheerful service; pool, darts, TV and machines; children welcome away from bar, beer garden, handy for cathedral, open all day and gets busy lunchtimes. *(Dave Braisted, Mrs J Ekins-Daukes)*

WORCESTER SO8554

King Charles II (01905) 726100

New Street; WR1 2DP Small jettied Tudor building; heavy beams, fine panelling and woodburners in carved fireplaces, settles and pews on bare boards, up to eight well kept ales from Craddocks and associated Bridgnorth and Two Thirsty Brewers, traditional ciders, enjoyable range of Pieminister pies served with peas and different types of mash (limited range of other food), friendly helpful staff (ask them about the skeleton under the floor), more seating upstairs; quiz night Tues; open all day (food all day weekends). *(Jim King)*

WORCESTER SO8455

Ounce (01905) 330460

The Tything (A38); some nearby parking; WR1 1JL Formerly called the Marwood and refurbished under new owners; long narrow series of small linked areas, dark flagstones and broad floorboards, stripped or cast-iron-framed tables, open fires, also an upstairs room, Sharps Doom Bar and a couple of Wye Valley beers, a dozen wines by the glass, cocktails, good food with emphasis on steaks (order by weight – £1 per ounce on Tues), friendly helpful staff; background music, live Sat; children and dogs (in bar) welcome, sunny flagstoned back courtyard, closed Mon, otherwise open all day (till 7pm Sun). *(Charlie Stevens)*

WORCESTER SO8555

Plough (01905) 21381

Fish Street; WR1 2HN Traditional corner pub with two simple rooms off entrance lobby, six well kept interesting beers including Hobsons and Malvern Hills, local cider/perry and good whisky choice, straightforward food available Fri, Sat lunchtimes plus rolls all day weekends and Sun roast; outside loos and small back terrace with cathedral view, open all day. *(Jim King)*

WYRE PIDDLE SO9647

Anchor (01386) 244590

Off A4538 NW of Evesham; WR10 2JB Great position by River Avon with moorings, decking on three levels, floodlit lawn and view from airy back dining room; recent and ongoing improvements by new management, really good food from sharing plates and pub favourites up, set lunch deal Tues-Sat, swift friendly service, beers such as Greene King, local Pershore and Wye Valley; children and dogs welcome, open (and food) all day, apart from Sun and Mon evenings when kitchen is closed. *(Richard Tilbrook)*

Post Office address codings confusingly give the impression that some pubs are in Worcestershire, when they're really in Gloucestershire, Herefordshire, Shropshire or Warwickshire (which is where we list them).

Yorkshire

BECK HOLE NZ8202 Map 10

Birch Hall

(01947) 896245 – www.beckhole.info/bhi.htm

Off A169 SW of Whitby, from top of Sleights Moor; YO22 5LE

Extraordinary place in lovely valley with friendly landlady, real ales and simple snacks

This is a resolutely unchanging and tiny pub-cum-village shop in stunning surroundings by a bridge over a river and close to Thomason Foss waterfall; many customers are walkers with their dogs. The two simple rooms have built-in cushioned wall seats, wooden tables (one embedded with 136 pennies), flagstones or composition flooring, unusual items such as a tube of toothpaste priced 1/-3d, and a model train running around a head-height shelf. Black Sheep, North Yorkshire Beckwatter and a guest such as Helmsley Striding the Riding on handpump, several malt whiskies and wines by the glass. The shop sells postcards, sweets and ice-creams. There are benches outside in a streamside garden and one of the wonderful nearby walks is along a disused railway. They have a self-catering cottage for hire.

Bar snacks only, such as local pork pie, butties, scones and their famous beer cake.

Free house ~ Licensee Glenys Crampton ~ Real ale ~ No credit cards ~ Open 11-11; 11-3, 7.30-11 Weds-Sun in winter ~ Bar food available during opening hours ~ Children in small family room ~ Dogs welcome *Recommended by Elizabeth and Peter May, Nigel Havers, Thomas Green, Sally and Colin Allen, Alexander and Trish Gendall, Nick Sharpe, Toby Jones*

BLAKEY RIDGE SE6799 Map 10

Lion

(01751) 417320 – www.lionblakey.co.uk

From A171 Guisborough–Whitby follow 'Castleton, Hutton-le-Hole' signposts; from A170 Kirkby Moorside–Pickering follow 'Keldholm, Hutton-le-Hole, Castleton' signposts; OS Sheet 100 map reference 679996; YO62 7LQ

Extended pub in fine scenery and open all day; popular food; bedrooms

Once again, we've had enthusiastic reports from readers staying at this isolated 16th-c inn, and breakfasts are first class. There are numerous surrounding hikes and the Coast to Coast path is nearby; the views over the valleys of Rosedale and Farndale are breathtaking. The low-beamed rambling bars have open fires, a few big high-backed rustic settles around cast-iron-framed tables, lots of small dining chairs, a nice leather sofa and stone walls hung with old engravings and photographs of the pub under snow (it can easily get cut off in winter – 40 days is the record so far). The fine choice of beers on handpump might include Black Sheep Best, Beer Monkey Brew Blonde Rogue, Great Yorkshire Yorkshire Golden, Marstons Wainwright and Theakstons Best and Old Peculier, as well as 13 wines by the glass and several malt whiskies; background music and games machine.

Hearty helpings of popular food includes sandwiches, prawn cocktail, giant yorkshire pudding with gravy, nut roast with port and cranberry sauce, ham with egg or pineapple, beef curry, home-made fishcakes with tartare sauce, chicken topped with creamy leek and bacon sauce, beer-battered cod and chips, duck breast in orange sauce, fillet steak medallions in stilton sauce, and puddings such as chocolate nut sundae and jam roly-poly with custard. *Benchmark main dish: steak and mushroom pie £12.50. Two-course evening meal £17.25.*

Free house ~ Licensees Barry, Diana, Paul and David Crossland ~ Real ale ~ Open 10am-11pm (midnight Sat) ~ Bar food 12-10 ~ Restaurant ~ Children welcome ~ Dogs allowed in bar ~ Wi-fi ~ Bedrooms: £42.50/£86 *Recommended by Dr J Barrie Jones, Martin and Joanne Sharp, Mike and Sarah Abbot, Camilla and Jose Ferrera, Alf and Sally Garner*

BOROUGHBRIDGE — Black Bull £

SE3966 Map 7

(01423) 322413

St James Square; B6265, just off A1(M); YO51 9AR

Bustling town pub with real ales, several wines by the glass and traditional bar food; bedrooms

For a good value lunch and a warm welcome, head for this ancient inn: it's been looking after customers travelling this very route between England and Scotland for hundreds of years. It's an attractive place with lots of separate drinking and eating areas, and plenty of cheerful regulars drop in and out at all times of the day for a pint and a chat. The main bar area has a big stone fireplace and comfortable seats and is served through an old-fashioned hatch; there's also a cosy snug with traditional wall settles, and a tap room, lounge bar and restaurant. John Smiths Bitter, Sambrooks Wandle and Timothy Taylors Boltmaker on handpump, six wines by the glass and 21 malt whiskies; dominoes and board games. The borzoi dog is called Spot and the two cats are Kia and Mershka. The hanging baskets are lovely.

Our Value Award is for the bar snacks menu, which includes pork sausages with mash and onion gravy, thai-style beef strips with egg noodles and stir-fried vegetables in hot and sour sauce, gammon and egg, and spicy chicken goujons with chips, but they also offer chicken liver pâté with cumberland sauce, crispy duck salad with hoisin and plum sauce, pork tenderloin with pink peppercorn and calvados sauce, chicken wrapped in parma ham with wild mushrooms in port and garlic sauce, sirloin steak with trimmings and chips, and puddings such as jam sponge and custard and dark chocolate truffle torte. *Benchmark main dish: pie of the day £9.95. Two-course evening meal £15.00.*

Free house ~ Licensee Anthony Burgess ~ Real ale ~ Open 11-11 (midnight Fri, Sat); 11.30-11 Sun ~ Bar food 12-2, 6-9 (9.30 Fri, Sat); 12-2.30, 6-9 Sun ~ Restaurant ~ Children welcome ~ Dogs welcome ~ Wi-fi ~ Bedrooms: £50/£75 *Recommended by Andrew and Michele Revell, Melanie and David Lawson, Michael Butler, Denis and Margaret Kilner, Angela and Steve Heard*

Real ale to us means beer that has matured naturally in its cask – not pressurised or filtered. We name all real ales stocked.

BRADFIELD SK2290 Map 7

Strines Inn £

(0114) 285 1247 – www.thestrinesinn.co.uk

From A57 heading E of junction with A6013 (Ladybower Reservoir) take first left turn (signposted with Bradfield) then bear left; with a map can also be reached more circuitously from Strines signpost on A616 at head of Underbank Reservoir, W of Stocksbridge; S6 6JE

Bustling inn in stunning scenery with hearty food and plenty of customers; bedrooms

Originally this was a 13th-c manor house (although most of the building dates from the 16th c) and its location in an isolated spot on the edge of the Peak District National Park means it's much loved by walkers. The main bar has black beams liberally decked with copper kettles and so forth, a coal fire in a rather grand stone fireplace, quite a menagerie of stuffed animals, and homely, red plush-cushioned traditional wooden wall benches and small chairs; background music. Two other rooms, to the right and left, are similarly furnished. Acorn Yorkshire Pride, Jennings Cocker Hoop and Marstons Pedigree on handpump, nine wines by the glass and eight malt whiskies. There are plenty of picnic-sets outside, as well as swings, a play area and peacocks and geese. The bedrooms have four-poster beds and a dining table (they serve breakfast in your room) and our readers enjoy staying here; the front room overlooks the Strines Reservoir.

Good, traditional food includes hot and cold sandwiches, garlic mushrooms, smoked mackerel with salad, giant yorkshire puddings filled with butter bean stew, chilli or sausage and gravy, burgers with chips, cajun chicken breast with chips, lasagne, a big mixed grill, gammon steak with egg or pineapple, and puddings such as chocolate fudge cake or caramel apple pie. *Benchmark main dish: steak in ale pie £10.25. Two-course evening meal £14.50.*

Free house ~ Licensee Bruce Howarth ~ Real ale ~ Open 10.30am-11pm ~ Bar food 12-9; 12-2.30, 5.30-8.30 weekdays in winter ~ Children welcome ~ Dogs welcome ~ Bedrooms: £70/£90 *Recommended by Dave Sutton, Edward and William Johnston, Julie Braeburn, Susan and Tim Boyle, Diana and Bertie Farr, Graham Smart*

BROUGHTON SD9450 Map 7

Bull

(01756) 792065 – www.thebullatbroughton.com

A59; BD23 3AE

Handsome, carefully refurbished inn with a fine choice of drinks and enjoyable bar food

The various carefully furnished rooms in this handsome stone inn make good use of contemporary paintwork and pale oak furniture and have handsome flagstones, open log fires, exposed stone walls, built-in wall seats, a mix of dining chairs around polished tables and photographs of local suppliers. Even when really busy (which it deservedly usually is), staff remain warmly friendly and helpful. Timothy Taylors Landlord and guests such as Black Sheep, Dark Horse Hetton Pale Ale and Naylors Pinnacle Blonde on handpump, 15 malt whiskies, ten wines by the glass and a dozen gins; background music and TV. In warm weather you can sit at the solid chairs and tables on the attractive terrace in front of the building. There's a lot to do and see nearby, including walking through Broughton Hall Estate's 3,000 acres of beautiful countryside and parkland.

The menu is a tempting combination of old favourites and up-to-date dishes: sandwiches (until 6pm; not Sunday), black pudding with onions, a poached free-range egg and brown sauce, ham hock croquette with home-made piccalilli, cauliflower and sweet potato curry, seafood platter, lancashire hotpot with pickled red cabbage, burgers with toppings and skin-on fries, chicken with barbecue sauce and scallop potatoes, rare-breed pork belly with apple fritter, crackling and sticky cider sauce, 30-day-aged rib-eye steak with battered onion rings and dripping chips, and puddings such as black forest chocolate brownie with chocolate sauce and apple crumble with custard. *Benchmark main dish: steak in ale pie £13.50. Two-course evening meal £20.00.*

Ribble Valley Inns ~ Manager Paul Morris ~ Real ale ~ Open 12-11 (10.30 Sun) ~ Bar food 12-9; 12-9.30 Fri, Sat; 12-8 Sun ~ Children welcome ~ Dogs allowed in bar ~ Wi-fi
Recommended by Michael Butler, Chloe and Michael Swettenham, Pat and Tony Martin, John and Sylvia Harrop, Giles and Suzie Nunn, Gwendoline and Ralph Mason

COLTON SE5444 Map 7

Old Sun

(01904) 744261 – www.yeoldsuninn.co.uk
Off A64 York–Tadcaster; LS24 8EP

Whitewashed inn in pretty village with five real ales, highly thought-of food, and seats and an outside bar in the garden

The hard-working licensees in this neat 18th-c place are very hands-on and draw in a good mix of both diners and drinkers. The simply furnished bar has stools and small tables on bare boards, built-in window seats and high chairs against the bar where they serve Black Sheep and guests such as Pennine Amber Necker, Stancill Barnsley Bitter, Timothy Taylors Landlord and Yorkshire Heart Hearty Bitter on handpump and 13 wines by the glass. In the corner of the bar is a little shop selling locally produced chutney, oils, chocolates and so forth. Dining areas fan out from here with solid wooden and tartan-upholstered chairs and cushioned wall seats around polished tables on carpet, terracotta and stripped wooden floors, there's some exposed old brickwork and both open fires and a woodburning stove; background music. Outside, they have a log cabin-style garden bar with a wood-fired pizza oven, plus seats on a sunny front terrace and in the rambling garden with country views. Their Old Barn studio can be booked on a bed and breakfast or self-catering basis.

Cooked by the landlord, the extremely good food includes ham hock terrine with orange marmalade, cured and torched mackerel fillet with horseradish cream and parsley oil, sharing boards, wild mushroom and chive macaroni with a cheese croquette and basil pesto, duck breast with pancetta, beetroot, savoy cabbage and raspberry jus, plaice fillet wrapped in smoked ham with local asparagus, a poached egg and hollandaise sauce, crispy beef fillet with egg noodles, hoisin sauce, asian vegetable salad, candied pineapple and wasabi peas, and puddings such as triple chocolate brownie with chocolate sauce and warm strawberry scone with green tea pannacotta, whipped cream and strawberry compote. *Benchmark main dish: beer-battered fish and chips £14.00. Two-course evening meal £20.00.*

Free house ~ Licensees Ashley and Kelly McCarthy ~ Real ale ~ Open 12-3, 6-11; 6-11 Tues; 12-11 Fri, Sat; 12-10.30 Sun; closed Mon, lunchtime Tues ~ Bar food 12-2, 6-9; 12-9 Fri; 12-9.30 Sat; 12-8 Sun ~ Restaurant ~ Children in eating area of bar ~ Dogs welcome ~ Wi-fi *Recommended by Chloe and Michael Swettenham, Amy and Luke Buchanan, Edward Nile, John and Delia Franks*

There are report forms at the back of the book.

CONSTABLE BURTON SE1690 Map 10

Wyvill Arms

(01677) 450581 – www.thewyvillarms.co.uk

A684 E of Leyburn; DL8 5LH

Well run, friendly dining pub with interesting food, a dozen wines by the glass, real ales and efficient helpful service; bedrooms

The comfortable bedrooms in this stylish former farmhouse make a lovely base for exploring the area and breakfasts are generous. The small bar area has a finely worked plaster ceiling with the Wyvill family's coat of arms, a mix of seating and an elaborate stone fireplace with a warm winter fire. The second bar has been refurbished but has kept the model train on a railway track running around the room. A reception area includes a huge leather sofa that can seat up to eight people, another carved stone fireplace and an old leaded stained-glass church window partition. Both rooms are hung with pictures of local scenes. Theakstons Best, Wensleydale Coverdale Gamekeeper and a guest beer on handpump, plus nine wines by the glass and nine malt whiskies; chess, backgammon and dominoes. There are several large wooden benches under sizeable white parasols for outdoor dining and picnic-sets by a well. Constable Burton Hall is opposite.

First rate food using home-grown herbs, local game and other seasonal produce includes smoked haddock, cod and salmon fishcake with a poached egg and hollandaise sauce, terrine of ham hock, chicken and wensleydale cheese with pear and apple chutney, spicy egyptian-style aubergine, courgette and red pepper stew topped with mozzarella, salmon on steamed leeks with a coarse-grain mustard sauce, steak and onion pie, breaded chicken suprême stuffed with mozzarella and bacon on creamed leeks with stilton sauce, moroccan-style lamb shank, half a crispy confit duck with black cherry sauce on cabbage and bacon, and puddings such as three-way brûlée (vanilla, blueberry and strawberry) and sticky toffee pudding with toffee sauce. *Benchmark main dish: aberdeen angus sirloin steak with a choice of sauce and trimmings £19.50. Two-course evening meal £21.00.*

Free house ~ Licensee Nigel Stevens ~ Real ale ~ Open 11-3, 5.30 (6 Sun)-11; closed all day Mon, Tues lunchtime ~ Bar food 12-2.15, 5.30-9 ~ Restaurant ~ Children welcome until 8.30 ~ Dogs allowed in bar ~ Wi-fi ~ Bedrooms: £65/£100 *Recommended by Millie and Peter Downing, Barbara Brown, Christine and Tony Garrett, Frances and Hamish Porter, Richard Cole, S Holder, Paul Faraday, Joe and Belinda Smart*

CRAY SD9479 Map 7

White Lion

(01756) 760262 – www.bestpubinthedales.co.uk

B6160 N of Kettlewell; BD23 5JB

Refurbished inn with open fires in bar and dining room, a fair choice of food and seats outside; bedrooms

To make the most of the lovely countryside high up on Buckden Pike, stay for a few days in the airy comfortable bedrooms in the pub or in the converted barn. There are lovely big flagstones and beams throughout the pub, and the bar has button-back leather chesterfield sofas and armchairs in front of a woodburning stove, a cushioned window seat, books on shelves and a brass chandelier; a simple little back room (good for wet dogs) has some tables and chairs. Black Sheep Best, Wharfedale Blonde and a guest ale on handpump and eight wines by the glass. An attractive dining room has antique-style dining chairs around chunky tables, an open fire, some exposed stone walling and bits and pieces of old farming equipment;

background music. In warm weather you can sit at picnic-sets above the quiet steep lane or on flat limestone slabs in the shallow stream which tumbles down opposite.

Well liked food includes lunchtime sandwiches, confit duck and chorizo salad with home-smoked duck breast and hoisin sauce, trio of salmon (home-cured gravadlax, oak-smoked salmon salad and beer-battered mini fillet and chips), mixed vegetable crumble with goats cheese and braised red cabbage, a pie of the day, haddock and salmon wellington with lovage and nettle potato cake and hollandaise sauce, lemon and thyme chicken with french-style peas and dauphinoise potatoes, lamb rump with creamed rosemary potatoes, salt-baked swede, celeriac purée and minted pea jus, and puddings. *Benchmark main dish: pork belly with champ mash, braised chicory and apple and mustard jus £21.00. Two-course evening meal £20.00.*

Free house ~ Licensee Dennis Peacock ~ Real ale ~ Open 12-10.30 ~ Bar food 12-2.30, 6-8.30 ~ Restaurant ~ Children welcome ~ Dogs allowed in bar ~ Wi-fi ~ Bedrooms: /$100 *Recommended by Peter and Emma Kelly, Susan and Callum Slade, Simon and Sue Lamb, Glen and Patricia Fuller, William and Sophia Renton*

CRAYKE — SE5670 Map 7

Durham Ox

(01347) 821506 – www.thedurhamox.com

Off B1363 at Brandsby, towards Easingwold; West Way; YO61 4TE

Friendly, well run inn, with interesting décor in old-fashioned rooms, fine drinks and smashing food; comfortable bedrooms

This is a civilised inn that appeals to both locals and visitors, who enjoy the pubby bar, excellent food and comfortable bedrooms. The old-fashioned lounge bar has venerable tables, antique seats and settles on flagstones, pictures and photographs on dark red walls, interesting satirical carvings in the panelling (Victorian copies of medieval pew ends), polished copper and brass and an enormous inglenook fireplace. In the bottom bar is a framed illustrated account of local history (some of it gruesome) dating from the 12th c, and a large framed print of the famous Durham Ox, which weighed 171 stone. The Burns Bar has a woodburning stove, exposed brickwork and large french windows that open on to a balcony. Black Sheep Best, Timothy Taylors Boltmaker, York Guzzler and a guest beer on handpump, 20 wines by the glass, a dozen malt whiskies and interesting spirits; background music and board games. In warm weather you can make the most of the seats in the courtyard garden, the bottom of which offers views on three sides over the Vale of York; on the fourth is a charming view to the medieval church on the hill – supposedly the very hill up which the Grand Old Duke of York marched his men. Bedrooms, in the main building or in renovated farm cottages (dogs allowed here), are well equipped, spacious and comfortable, and breakfasts are very good. The nearby A19 leads straight to a park & ride for York city centre.

Excellent food includes lunchtime sandwiches, beetroot-cured salmon gravadlax with horseradish crème fraîche, sticky spicy pork belly with chilli, honey and sesame asian salad, queenie scallops with garlic and parsley butter, gruyère and cheddar crust and frites, pea ravioli with cheese and rocket, chicken milanese with lemon and caper butter and skinny fries, lamb rump with dauphinoise potatoes and mint and redcurrant reduction, hake with shrimp butter and samphire, 10oz rib-eye steak with a choice of sauce, and puddings such as vanilla crème brûlée and dark chocolate pot with white chocolate ice-cream, nuts and salted caramel crumb; they also offer an early bird menu (5.30-6.45pm). *Benchmark main dish: seafood platter £24.00. Two-course evening meal £22.00.*

Free house ~ Licensee Michael Ibbotson ~ Real ale ~ Open 11-11 (midnight Sat) ~ Bar food 12-2.30, 5.30-9.30; 12-3, 5.30-8.30 Sun ~ Restaurant ~ Children welcome ~ Dogs allowed in bar and bedrooms ~ Wi-fi ~ Bedrooms: £100/£120 *Recommended by Dr Peter Crawshaw, Naomi and Andrew Randall, Alister and Margery Bacon, Jamie and Lizzie McEwan, Peter Pilbeam, Freddie and Sarah Banks*

EAST WITTON SE1486 Map 10

Blue Lion

(01969) 624273 – www.thebluelion.co.uk

A6108 Leyburn–Ripon; DL8 4SN

Civilised dining pub with a proper bar, real ales, highly enjoyable food and courteous service; comfortable bedrooms

A delightful Georgian inn with long-serving owners, this remains on top form. It's a lovely all-rounder, with walkers dropping in after a damp walk mixing easily with those out for a special meal or staying for a few days. The big squarish bar is civilised but informal with soft lighting, high-backed antique settles and old windsor chairs on turkish rugs and flagstones, ham hooks in the high ceiling decorated with dried wheat, teazles and so forth, a delft shelf full of bric-a-brac, plus several prints, sporting caricatures and other pictures; daily papers. Black Sheep Best and Holy Grail and Theakstons Best on handpump, an impressive wine list including 15 (plus champagne) by the glass and 20 malt whiskies. The candlelit, high-ceilinged and elegant dining room has another open fire. Picnic-sets on the gravel outside look beyond the stone houses on the far side of the village green to Witton Fell, and there's a big and attractive back garden. The comfortable bedrooms have pretty country furnishings, with some in the main house and others in converted stables across the courtyard (these are dog-friendly).

Accomplished food using the best seasonal produce includes seared foie gras with earl grey-soaked golden sultanas, quince jelly and orange syrup, confit chicken wing and roast hazelnut risotto with crispy winglet and shaved truffle, potato and thyme rösti with mushroom, garlic and leek fricassée, beef and ale pudding, slow-roasted honey-glazed duckling with apple gravy (evening only), salmon with braised fennel, confit beetroot and orange and brown shrimp dressing, veal loin with mushroom and thyme pithivier, confit shallots and red wine sauce, and puddings such as ginger and lemongrass carpaccio of pineapple with mascarpone sorbet and warm chocolate fondant with sweet date purée and walnut ice-cream; they also offer a two- and three-course set lunch (not Sunday). *Benchmark main dish: poached fillet of smoked haddock with mushroom and leek cream, soft poached egg and gruyère £19.50. Two-course evening meal £29.00.*

Free house ~ Licensee Paul Klein ~ Real ale ~ Open 11-11 ~ Bar food 12-2, 7-9.15; 12-9 Sun ~ Restaurant ~ Children welcome ~ Dogs allowed in bar and bedrooms ~ Wi-fi ~ Bedrooms: /£99 *Recommended by Clive and Fran Dutson, Neil and Angela Huxter, Richard Kennell, Tim and Sue Halstead, Alexandra and Richard Clay, Serena and Adam Furber*

ELSLACK SD9249 Map 7

Tempest Arms

(01282) 842450 – www.tempestarms.co.uk

Just off A56 Earby–Skipton; BD23 3AY

Busy inn with three log fires in stylish rooms, six real ales, good wines and well regarded food; bedrooms

'Best pub for miles around' and 'as smashing as ever' are just two comments from contented readers after visiting this stylish 18th-c stone inn. The bar and surrounding dining areas have much character plus a good mix of customers: cushioned armchairs, built-in wall seats with comfortable cushions, stools, plenty of tables and three log fires (one greets you at the entrance and divides the bar and restaurant). Also, quite a bit of exposed stonework, amusing prints on cream walls, half a dozen real ales such as Dark Horse Hetton Pale Ale, Greene King Old Speckled Hen, Theakstons Best and Thwaites Wainwright on handpump, 12 wines by the glass, 30 malt whiskies and 20 gins; background music and board games. The tables outside are largely screened from the road by a raised bank. The bedrooms are comfortable and well equipped and make a perfect base for exploring the area; the surrounding walks are lovely.

Food is particularly good and includes sandwiches and sharing boards, white crab cannelloni with mascarpone and a light bisque sauce, creamy french cheese baked in a box with garlic and basil topping, wild mushroom and sun-dried tomato risotto with pesto and parmesan, chicken tikka masala, steak burger with toppings, coleslaw and chips, venison, wild mushroom and chestnut casserole, lambs liver and bacon with creamy mash and onion gravy, red snapper with sweet potato wedges and tomato salad, and puddings such as sherry trifle and crème brûlée. *Benchmark main dish: steak, ale and mushroom pudding £12.95. Two-course evening meal £21.00.*

Individual Inns ~ Managers Martin and Veronica Clarkson ~ Real ale ~ Open 11-11; 12-10.30 Sun ~ Bar food 12-2.30, 6-9; 12-7.30 Sun ~ Restaurant ~ Children welcome ~ Dogs allowed in bar and bedrooms ~ Wi-fi ~ Bedrooms: £80/£105 *Recommended by Robert and Diana Ringstone, Steve Whalley, Philip J Alderton, John and Sylvia Harrop, David Heath, Richard Cole, Justine and Neil Bonnett*

FELIXKIRK — SE4684 Map 10

Carpenters Arms

(01845) 537369 – www.thecarpentersarmsfelixkirk.com
Village signed off A170 E of Thirsk; YO7 2DP

Stylishly refurbished village pub with spacious rooms, real ales and highly regarded food; lodge-style bedrooms

There's something for everyone here with a good choice of drinks, appetising food and well equipped, modern bedrooms. The opened-up bars are spacious and relaxed with dark beams and joists, candlelight and fresh flowers, a mix of chairs and tables on big flagstones or carpet, and stools against the panelled counter where they keep Black Sheep Best, Theakstons Best and York Guzzler on handpump, around 20 wines by the glass, 18 malt whiskies, quite a few gins and farm cider. A snug seating area has tartan armchairs in front of a double-sided woodburning stove. In the red-walled dining room you'll find a mix of antique and country kitchen chairs around scrubbed tables, and the walls throughout are hung with traditional prints, local pictures and maps; background music. On a raised decked terrace that overlooks the landscaped garden are lots of seats and tables, with picnic-sets at the front. The bedrooms come with a drying wardrobe for wet days and a log-effect gas fire, and they make a good base for both short walks and long-distance hikes (the Cleveland Way is in the locality); dogs are welcome. This is part of the Provenance Inns & Hotels group.

As well as breakfasts (8-10am), the thoughtful menu offers sandwiches, crab and ginger cakes with asian salad and brown crab and chilli mayonnaise, fried pigeon breast with cauliflower purée, girolles and sherry vinegar, tasting of cauliflower (couscous, tempura and charred) with spiced cauliflower cream, beer-battered fish and chips, chicken breast with peas, bacon and wild garlic and fondant potatoes, duo of lamb (roast rack and braised shoulder croquette) with leeks, broad beans and rosemary jus, and puddings such as chocolate and rhubarb fondant with blood orange sorbet and sticky toffee pudding with butterscotch sauce and cinder toffee ice-cream. *Benchmark main dish: 10oz 28-day-aged rib-eye steak £25.95. Two-course evening meal £20.00.*

Free house ~ Licensee Stephanie Plint ~ Real ale ~ Open 8am-11pm ~ Bar food 12-2.30, 5.30-9.30; 12-3, 5.30-8.30 Sun ~ Restaurant ~ Children welcome ~ Dogs allowed in bar and bedrooms ~ Wi-fi ~ Bedrooms: /£120 *Recommended by Jim and Sue James, Mike Benton, Dave Webster, Michael Doswell, Comus and Sarah Elliott, Janet and Peter Race*

GRANTLEY SE2369 Map 7

Grantley Arms

(01765) 620227 – www.grantleyarms.com

Village signposted off B6265 W of Ripon; HG4 3PJ

Relaxed and interesting dining pub with good food

After visiting nearby Fountains Abbey and Studley Royal Water Garden (National Trust), do come here for lunch. You'll get a warm welcome from the convivial, hands-on licensees and a reliably good meal. The front bar has an easy-going local atmosphere, beams, a huge fireplace built of massive stone blocks and housing a woodburning stove, traditional furnishings such as comfortable dining chairs and polished tables set with evening tea-lights and some of the landlady's own paintings of ponies and dogs. The back dining room has crisp linen tablecloths, decorative plates and more paintings, mainly landscapes. Theakstons Best and a guest ale on handpump, nine wines by the glass, eight malt whiskies, a local farm cider and attentive friendly service. Teak tables and chairs on the flagstoned front terrace have a pleasant outlook.

Enjoyable food includes lunchtime open sandwiches, prawns in lemon mayonnaise with avocado purée and lime and cucumber sorbet, chicken liver parfait with plum chutney, mushroom stroganoff, a pie of the week, lager-battered haddock and chips, confit rare-breed pork belly with crackling, apple purée and red wine sauce, a fresh fish dish of the day (anything from mackerel and brill to turbot or halibut), local rump steak with a choice of sauce, and puddings such as a trio of chocolate terrine and pear and ginger sponge with custard; they also offer a two- and three-course set lunch (not Sunday). *Benchmark main dish: fish pie £13.95. Two-course evening meal £20.00.*

Free house ~ Licensees Valerie Sails and Eric Broadwith ~ Real ale ~ Open 12-3, 5.30-10.30; 12-3, 5.30-11 Fri, Sat; 12-10.30 Sun; closed Mon except bank holidays ~ Bar food 12-2, 5.30-9 (9.30 Sat); 12-3.30, 5.30-8 Sun ~ Restaurant ~ Well behaved children welcome ~ Wi-fi *Recommended by Rosie and John Moore, Sophia and Hamish Greenfield, John Stephenson, Trish and Karl Soloman, Charles Todd, David Appleyard*

GRINTON SE0498 Map 10

Bridge Inn

(01748) 884224 – www.bridgeinn-grinton.co.uk

B6270 W of Richmond; DL11 6HH

Bustling pub with traditional, comfortable bars, log fires, real ales, malt whiskies and tasty bar food; neat bedrooms

This friendly old pub is in a pretty village opposite a lovely church known as the Cathedral of the Dales. There's a relaxing, comfortable atmosphere, bow-window seats and a pair of stripped traditional settles among more usual pub seats (all well cushioned), a good log fire and Jennings Cumberland and Marstons Wainwright with three changing guest ales on handpump; also, eight wines by the glass, 20 malt whiskies, ten gins and farm cider. On the right, a few steps lead down to a room with darts and ring the bull. On the left, past leather armchairs and a sofa next to a second log fire (and a glass chess set), is an extensive two-part dining room with décor in cream and shades of brown, and a modicum of fishing memorabilia. The bedrooms are neat, simple and comfortable, and breakfasts good. There are picnic-sets outside and fine surrounding walks.

Decent food includes lunchtime baguettes, deep-fried breaded brie with cranberry sauce, crayfish cocktail in spicy marie rose sauce, a risotto of the day, beer-battered cod and chips, beef burger with toppings, onion rings and chips, duck breast with garlic mash and star anise jus, gammon with egg or pineapple, 28-day-aged beef with trimmings, and puddings such as lemon and lime cheesecake and ginger sponge with toffee sauce. *Benchmark main dish: steak in ale pie £11.50. Two-course evening meal £18.00.*

Jennings (Marstons) ~ Lease Andrew Atkin ~ Real ale ~ Open 12-11 ~ Bar food 12-2.30, 6-9 (8 Tues); 12-3, 6-9 Sat; 12-3, 6-8 Sun ~ Restaurant ~ Children welcome ~ Dogs allowed in bar and bedrooms ~ Wi-fi ~ Live music Thurs evening ~ Bedrooms: £51/£82
Recommended by Sabine and Gerald Grimshaw, Margaret McDonald, Liz and Mike Newton, Trevor and Michele Street, Ivy and George Goodwill

HALIFAX SE1027 Map 7

Shibden Mill

(01422) 365840 – www.shibdenmillinn.com

Off A58 into Kell Lane at Stump Cross Inn, near A6036 junction; keep on, pub signposted from Kell Lane on left; HX3 7UL

Yorkshire Dining Pub of the Year

Interesting 300-year-old pub with a spreading bar, four real ales and inventive, top class bar food; luxury bedrooms

The rambling bar in this warmly friendly, restored 17th-c mill has a lot of character and is full of nooks and crannies, and its bustling atmosphere is helped along by a good mix of locals and visitors. Some cosy side areas have banquettes heaped with cushions and rugs, well spaced attractive old tables and chairs, and candles in elegant iron holders giving a feeling of real intimacy; also, old hunting prints, country landscapes and a couple of big log fires. A beer named for them (from Moorhouses) plus Black Sheep Best, Little Valley Withens Pale Ale and a changing guest on handpump, 27 wines by the glass from a wide list, 22 malt whiskies and 20 gins. There's also an upstairs restaurant; background music. Outside on the pleasant heated terrace are plenty of seats and tables, and the building is prettily floodlit at night. To make the most of the lovely surrounding countryside, our readers often stay in the stylish and well equipped bedrooms; breakfasts are enjoyable and hearty.

Creative food includes lunchtime sandwiches, pigeon breast with beetroot fondant, pear, nasturtium leaf and charred shallots, seared king scallops with cucumber, lime and cauliflower, tofu, fennel and lemongrass parcels with pak choi and gooseberry chutney, duo of wild rabbit with pistachio, sautéed chanterelle mushrooms and glazed carrots, sea bream fillet with peas, asparagus, fennel, mustard and tarragon velouté, lamb loin and pressed lamb shoulder with nettle purée and red wine jus, and puddings such as chocolate mousse with chocolate Aero, salted caramel and yoghurt sorbet and apricot frangipane tart with spiced apricot and cardamom cream; they also offer a two- and three-course weekday set menu (12-2, 5.30-7pm) and proper afternoon tea (3-5pm; not Sunday). *Benchmark main dish: slow-braised short rib of beef with parmentier potatoes, burnt onions, swiss chard £18.00. Two-course evening meal £24.00.*

Free house ~ Licensee Glen Pearson ~ Real ale ~ Open 12-11 (10.30 Sun) ~ Bar food 12-2, 5.30-9; 12-2.30, 5.30-9.30 Fri, Sat; 12-7.30 Sun ~ Restaurant ~ Children welcome ~ Dogs allowed in bar ~ Wi-fi ~ Bedrooms: £109/£135 *Recommended by Laura Reid, Celia and Geoff Clay, Mr and Mrs P R Thomas, Steve Whalley, Helene Grygar, Bob and Melissa Wyatt*

HELPERBY SE4370 Map 7

Oak Tree

(01423) 789189 – www.theoaktreehelperby.com

Raskelf Road; YO61 2PH

Attractive pub with real ales in friendly bar, fine food in cosy dining rooms and seats on terrace; comfortable bedrooms

There's a friendly, easy-going atmosphere in this handsome old inn and a good mix of customers. The informal bar has church chairs and elegant wooden dining chairs around a mix of wooden tables on old quarry tiles, flagstones and oak floorboards, prints and paintings on bold red walls and open fires; background music. Stools line the counter where they keep Black Sheep Best, John Smiths Bitter and Theakstons Best and a guest such as York Guzzler on handpump, 24 wines by the glass, good collections of malt whiskies and gin, and farm cider. The main dining room has a large woodburner in a huge brick fireplace, a big central flower arrangement, high-backed burgundy and graceful wooden chairs around nice old tables on oak flooring, ornate mirrors and some striking artwork on exposed brick walls. French windows lead out to the terrace where there are plenty of seats and tables for summer dining. Upstairs, a private dining room has a two-way woodburner, a sitting room and doors leading to a terrace. The modern bedrooms are comfortable and well equipped. This belongs to the Provenance Inns & Hotels group.

Using only local, seasonal produce the highly thought-of food includes lunchtime sandwiches and locally reared beef cooked in their wood-fired oven, as well as cumin and coriander spiced lamb kofta with cauliflower rice and raita, prawn cocktail, roast mediterranean vegetables with grilled polenta and basil oil, chicken breast with spring bean casserole, crispy greens and crème fraîche, lemon and ginger lamb shank with broad beans, sea bream fillets with carrot and courgette spaghetti and warm mint and citrus salsa, 10oz rib-eye steak with chips and a choice of sauce, and puddings such as chocolate fudge cake and mixed berry cheesecake; they also offer an early bird menu (5.30-6.30pm – not Saturday). *Benchmark main dish: steak in ale pie £13.95. Two-course evening meal £20.00.*

Free house ~ Licensee Lizzie Richards ~ Real ale ~ Open 12-3, 5-11; 12-11 Fri-Sun ~ Bar food 12-2.30, 5.30-9.30; 12-4, 5.30-9 Sun ~ Restaurant ~ Children welcome ~ Dogs allowed in bar and bedrooms ~ Wi-fi ~ Bedrooms: /£100 *Recommended by George and Alison Bishop, Louise and Simon Peters, Dan and Belinda Smallbone, Nick and Meriel Cox, Julian Richardson*

HETTON SD9658 Map 7

Angel

(01756) 730263 – www.angelhetton.co.uk

Off B6265 Skipton–Grassington; BD23 6LT

Creeper-covered inn with delicious food, real ales and an excellent wine list; lovely bedrooms

Of course, most customers are here to enjoy the excellent food but if it's just a drink you want after walking in the glorious surrounding countryside, you'll be made just as welcome. The informal bar-brasserie is a fine panelled and beamed room with standing timbers, a working Victorian farmhouse range set in a big stone fireplace, copper and brassware, the odd gun or two on cream-painted walls, and farmhouse and wheelback chairs around wooden tables. Black Sheep Best and Dark Horse Craven Bitter and Hetton Pale Ale on handpump, an award-winning wine list with 20 by the glass and a large choice of malt whiskies. The two formal restaurant rooms, also beamed and with some timbering, have smart high-backed dining chairs around a medley of tables and a gently civilised and relaxed atmosphere. Tables and chairs on the front terrace are under retractable awnings. The individually styled bedrooms and suites are in a converted barn or the more modern Sycamore Bank opposite; breakfasts are excellent.

Imaginative and beautifully presented food includes their famous 'moneybags' (queenies, prawns, salmon and smoked fish with a julienne of peppers and courgettes in crispy pastry with lobster sauce), bang bang chicken with chilli dipping sauce, spiced squash and spinach lasagne with mango and blood orange salad, guinea fowl ballotine with crispy skin, cheesy hasselback potatoes, morels, braised fennel and lemon cream sauce, kedgeree of smoked haddock, saffron risotto and quail egg, viennese-style pork tenderloin with stuffed sweetheart lettuce, candied pear and pear reduction jus, fish of the day en papillote with chanterelles, shallots and bacon, potato and dill fondue and parsley sauce, and puddings such as tropical summer pudding with coconut ice-cream and Baileys and chocolate fondant with vanilla ice-cream. *Benchmark main dish: tuscan lamb rump with confit peppers, chargrilled courgette, parmesan roasties and minted pesto £18.95. Two-course evening meal £25.00.*

Free house ~ Licensee Juliet Watkins ~ Real ale ~ Open 12-11 (11.30 Sat); 12-10.30 Sun ~ Bar food 12-8.30 (9 Sat) ~ Restaurant ~ Children welcome ~ Dogs allowed in bar ~ Wi-fi ~ Bedrooms: £135/£150 *Recommended by Nick Higgins, Hunter and Christine Wright, Len and Lilly Dowson, Beverley and Andy Butcher, Edward Edmonton*

ILKLEY SE1347 Map 7

Wheatley Arms

(01943) 816496 – www.wheatleyarms.co.uk

Wheatley Lane, Ben Rhydding; LS29 8PP

Smart stone inn with a cosy bar, restful dining rooms, professional service and good food and drink; comfortable bedrooms

---

As there are wonderful walks surrounding this substantial stone inn and it's near Ilkley Moor, the individually decorated, well equipped and comfortable bedrooms are much used by those exploring the area; some have a private roof terrace. The interconnected dining rooms have all manner of nice antique and upholstered chairs and stools and prettily cushioned wooden or rush-seated settles around assorted tables, rugs on bare boards, some bold wallpaper, various prints and two log fires; our readers like the smart garden room. One half of the locals' bar has tub armchairs and other comfortable seats, the other has tartan-cushioned wall seats and mate's chairs, with classic wooden stools against the counter where they keep BAD Love Over Gold, Brash Fake News, Ilkley Mary Jane and Thwaites Original on handpump. Also, 23 wines by the glass (including prosecco and champagne), a dozen malt whiskies and a farm cider; background music and TV. There are seats and tables on the terrace.

As well as breakfast (8-11am), the reliably good food includes sandwiches (until 5.30pm), hot smoked salmon and prawn rillettes with pickled vegetable stir-fry and crispy noodles, spinach and ricotta risotto, lamb breast stuffed with anchovies and lemon with ratatouille, grilled sea bream with crab, tomato and shallot salad and a crispy egg, burger with toppings, fries and slaw, barbecue-glazed chicken breast with beetroot and tomato couscous and herbed potato salad, slow-roast pork belly with grilled king prawns, potato terrine and pork sauce, and puddings. *Benchmark main dish: steak and mushroom in ale pie £15.00. Two-course evening meal £21.00.*

Individual Inns ~ Licensee Steve Benson ~ Real ale ~ Open 11-11; 11-midnight Fri, Sat; 11-10.30 Sun ~ Bar food 12-2, 5.30-9; 12-7 Sun ~ Restaurant ~ Children welcome ~ Dogs allowed in bar ~ Wi-fi ~ Live jazz first Sun lunchtime of month ~ Bedrooms: £80/£90 *Recommended by Caroline Sullivan, Gordon and Margaret Ormondroyd, Michael Butler, Dan and Nicki Barton, Martine and Fabio Lockley, Nicola and Holly Lyons*

KIRKBY FLEETHAM SE2894 Map 10

Black Horse

(01609) 749010 – www.blackhorseinnkirkbyfleetham.com

Village signposted off A1 S of Catterick; Lumley Lane; DL7 0SH

Attractively reworked country inn with well liked food, good drinks choice and cheerful atmosphere; comfortable bedrooms

Although this carefully run village inn is deservedly popular locally, you'll receive a genuine welcome as a visitor too. There's plenty of stylish character and the long, softly lit beamed bar on the right has flagstones, cushioned wall seats, some little settles and high-backed dining chairs by the log fire at one end, Black Sheep Best, Saltaire Blonde and Timothy Taylors Boltmaker on handpump and 11 wines by the glass. The cosy snug has darts. A dining room towards the back is light and open, with big bow windows on either side and a casual contemporary look thanks to loose-covered dining chairs or pastel garden settles with scatter cushions around tables painted pale green; background pop music. The neat sheltered back lawn and flagstoned side terrace have teak seats and tables and there are picnic-sets at the front; quoits. Bedrooms are attractive and comfortable with plenty of antique charm, and breakfasts are good.

Rewarding food includes twice-baked goats cheese soufflé with pressed pear and red chicory salad, gin and beetroot-cured salmon with blackberries, samphire and granola, sweet potato rösti with wild mushrooms, a crispy egg and hollandaise sauce, curried cod with spiced lentils, pak choi, pomelo and coconut and an onion bhaji, pork belly with braised pig cheek, quince, turnips and fondant potato, charred duck breast with pistachio, kohlrabi, confit potato and jasmine sauce, and puddings such as chocolate délice with toasted marshmallow and candied hazelnuts and lemon tart with raspberry gin granita and balsamic caramel; they also offer a two- and three-course set menu. *Benchmark main dish: steak and kidney suet pudding £13.95. Two-course evening meal £20.00.*

Free house ~ Licensee Steven Barker ~ Real ale ~ Open 12-11 ~ Bar food 12-2.30, 5-9; 12-8 Sun ~ Restaurant ~ Children welcome ~ Dogs allowed in bar and bedrooms ~ Wi-fi ~ Bedrooms: /£110 *Recommended by Chantelle and Tony Redman, Karl and Frieda Bujeya, Andrea and Philip Crispin, Alexandra and Tim Fledgling, Giles and Suzie Nunn*

LEDSHAM SE4529 Map 7

Chequers

(01977) 683135 – www.thechequersinn.com

1.5 miles from A1(M) junction 42: follow Leeds signs, then Ledsham signposted; Claypit Lane; LS25 5LP

Friendly pub with hands-on landlord, log fires in several beamed rooms, real ales and interesting food; pretty back terrace

Set in a charming village, this neatly kept, well run pub is handy for the A1 so it's especially popular at lunchtime – when it's best to book a table.

The several small, individually decorated rooms have plenty of character, with low beams, log fires, lots of cosy alcoves, toby jugs and all sorts of knick-knacks on the walls and ceilings (cricket fans will be interested to see a large photo in one room of four yorkshire heroes). From the little old-fashioned, panelled-in central servery they offer Brown Cow Sessions Pale Ale, Leeds Best, Theakstons Best, Timothy Taylors Landlord and a guest beer on handpump and eight wines by the glass. The lovely, sheltered two-level terrace at the back has lots of tables among roses, and the hanging baskets and flowers are very pretty. RSPB Fairburn Ings reserve is not far and the ancient village church is worth a visit.

High standards of good food includes sandwiches, Whitby crab brûlée, smoked chicken with curried mayonnaise, toasted almonds and apricot, corned beef hash layered with caramelised onions and potatoes, lamb noisettes with sweet potato and rosemary mash and redcurrant sauce, mushroom, spinach and butter bean crumble, monkfish with crayfish and saffron risotto and straw potatoes, gressingham duck breast with celeriac purée, fondant potatoes and five-spice jus, fillet steak with slow-roast tomatoes, mushroom and tarragon sauce and chips, and puddings such as chocolate brownie with ice-cream and lemon tart with meringue and lemon curd ice-cream. *Benchmark main dish: steak and mushroom pie £13.45. Two-course evening meal £21.00.*

Free house ~ Licensee Chris Wraith ~ Real ale ~ Open 11-11; 12-6 Sun; closed Sun evening ~ Bar food 12-9; 12-5 Sun ~ Restaurant ~ Children welcome ~ Dogs allowed in bar ~ Wi-fi

Recommended by Stephen Woad, John and Eleanor Holdsworth, Gerald Warner, Ian Wilson, Roger and Donna Huggins, Tony and Caroline Elwood

LEVISHAM SE8390 Map 10

Horseshoe

(01751) 460240 – www.horseshoelevisham.co.uk

Off A169 N of Pickering; YO18 7NL

Friendly village pub with super food, neat rooms, real ales and seats on the village green; bedrooms

As a focal point for a charming village, this is a particularly well run pub that our readers enjoy very much. The bustling bars have beams, blue banquettes, wheelback and captain's chairs around a variety of tables on polished wooden floors, vibrant landscapes by a local artist on the walls and a log fire in the stone fireplace; an adjoining snug has a woodburning stove, comfortable leather sofas and old photographs of the pub and the lovely village. Served by the courteous staff are Black Sheep Best and guests such as Cropton Yorkshire Moors and Timothy Taylors Golden Best on handpump, 14 wines by the glass and over a dozen malt whiskies. There are seats on the attractive green, with more in the back garden. The clean, comfortable bedrooms make a good base for exploring the North York Moors National Park; breakfasts are hearty. The historic church is worth a visit. This is sister pub to the Fox & Rabbit in Lockton.

One of the landlords cooks the carefully crafted food: sandwiches, crab and smoked salmon terrine, black pudding wrapped in bacon with sautéed potatoes and apple sauce, butternut squash, leek and pine nut risotto with parmesan, sausage and mash with onion gravy, chicken wrapped in bacon on creamed leeks, steak in ale pie, gammon with a fried egg and pineapple, braised lamb shank with rosemary mash and mint gravy, deep-fried Whitby haddock and chips, pork stroganoff with rice, sirloin steak with onion rings and peppercorn sauce, and puddings such as chocolate truffle torte and lime cheesecake. *Benchmark main dish: slow-roasted pork belly with thyme mash and cider gravy £14.50. Two-course evening meal £25.00.*

Free house ~ Licensees Toby and Charles Wood ~ Real ale ~ Open 11-11 (10 Sun) ~ Bar food 12-2, 6-8.30 ~ Children welcome ~ Dogs allowed in bar ~ Wi-fi ~ Bedrooms: /£90
Recommended by Dr and Mrs F McGinn, John Coatsworth, Stuart and Natalie Granville, Alex Macdonald, Dr K Nesbitt, Martin Day, Monica and Steph Evans, Geoff and Ann Marston

LEYBURN SE1190 Map 10

Sandpiper

(01969) 622206 – www.sandpiperinn.co.uk
Just off Market Place; DL8 5AT

Appealing food and cosy bar for drinkers in pretty inn, real ales and impressive choice of whisky; bedrooms

Set away from the main bustle of the town, this 17th-c stone cottage is extremely popular for its super food, and our readers like staying in the comfortable, well equipped bedrooms too. The cosy bar has a couple of black beams in the low ceiling, a log fire and wooden or cushioned built-in wall seats around a few tables. The back snug, up three steps, features lovely dales photographs – get here early if you want a seat. There are photographs and a woodburning stove in a stone fireplace by the linenfold panelled bar counter; to the left is the attractive restaurant, with dark wooden tables and chairs on bare boards and fresh flowers. Black Sheep Best and a couple of guests from the Wensleydale brewery on handpump, 100 malt whiskies, good wines by the glass and a growing number of gins; background music. In good weather, you can enjoy a drink on the front terrace among the pretty hanging baskets and flowering climbers.

Enjoyable food cooked by the chef-patron includes sandwiches, tempura squid and vegetables with wasabi mayonnaise, crispy pork belly and black pudding with spiced vegetable purée, double-baked cheese soufflé with wilted greens, rib burger with toppings and fries, chicken breast on mediterranean vegetable and chorizo risotto, moroccan-spiced lamb with jumbo couscous, lemon and coriander, cod fillet with mushy peas and chips, 36-day-aged beef with garlic and herb mushrooms, local venison with crispy smoked bacon, butternut squash and duck fat potatoes, and puddings such as vanilla crème brûlée and bread and butter pudding with rum and raisin ice-cream. *Benchmark main dish: crispy duck leg with braised red cabbage and sautéed potatoes £17.00. Two-course evening meal £25.00.*

Free house ~ Licensees Jonathan and Janine Harrison ~ Real ale ~ Open 12-3, 6-11; 11.30-3, 6-10 Sun; closed Mon; Tues in winter, two weeks Jan ~ Bar food 12-2.30, 6.30-8.30 (9 Fri); 12-2.30, 6-9.30 Sat; 12-2.30, 6-8 Sun ~ Restaurant ~ Children welcome ~ Dogs allowed in bar and bedrooms ~ Wi-fi ~ Bedrooms: £90/£100 *Recommended by Clive and Fran Dutson, Caroline and Steve Archer, Dan and Belinda Smallbone, Michael Butler, Sylvia and Phillip Spencer*

LINTON IN CRAVEN SD9962 Map 7

Fountaine

(01756) 752210 – www.fountaineinnatlinton.co.uk
Off B6265 Skipton–Grassington; BD23 5HJ

Neatly kept pub with attractive furnishings, open fires, five real ales and popular food; bedrooms

This civilised and friendly place has plenty of satisfied customers, many of whom come here after enjoying one of the fine nearby walks. The bars have beams and white-painted joists in low ceilings, log fires (one in a beautifully carved heavy wooden fireplace), attractive built-in cushioned wall benches and stools around a mix of copper-topped tables, little wall lamps and quite a few prints on the pale walls. John Smiths Bitter, Tetleys

Cask, Thwaites Original and guests such as Dark Horse Hetton Pale Ale and Wharfedale Blonde on handpump, 20 wines by the glass, ten gins and a dozen malt whiskies served by efficient staff; background music and ring the bull. The terrace, looking across the road to the duck pond, has teak benches and tables under green parasols, and the hanging baskets are most attractive. The well equipped bedrooms are in a converted barn behind the pub.

Pleasing food includes sandwiches, house-cured salmon with beetroot pannacotta, goats cheese and lemon oil, chicken liver pâté with ale chutney, various platters, roasted butternut squash, chestnut and broad bean risotto, guinea fowl with smoked cheese and bacon rösti and roasted baby vegetables, steak in ale pie, gammon and eggs, catalan fish stew, 10oz rump steak with peppercorn sauce and chips, and puddings such as chocolate fudge brownie and bakewell tart with ice-cream. *Benchmark main dish: lamb rump with roasted root vegetables and jus £16.00. Two-course evening meal £21.00.*

Individual Inns ~ Manager Christopher Gregson ~ Real ale ~ Open 11-11; 12-10.30 Sun ~ Bar food 12-9 ~ Restaurant ~ Children welcome ~ Dogs allowed in bar and bedrooms ~ Wi-fi ~ Bedrooms: £75/£99 *Recommended by Michael Breeze, Dr and Mrs F McGinn, Steve Whalley, Peter Smith and Judith Brown, B and M Kendall, Gus Swan*

LOCKTON SE8488 Map 10

Fox & Rabbit

(01751) 460213 – www.foxandrabbit.co.uk

A169 N of Pickering; YO18 7NQ

Neatly kept pub with fine views, a friendly atmosphere, real ales and highly regarded food

As host and chef, the two brothers running this bustling pub are committed to giving their customers their absolute best. The interconnected rooms have beams, panelling and some exposed stonework, wall settles and banquettes, dark pubby chairs and tables on tartan carpet, a log fire and an inviting atmosphere; fresh flowers, brasses, china plates, prints and old local photographs too. The locals' bar is busy and cheerful and there are panoramic views from the comfortable restaurant – it's worth arriving early to bag a window seat. Black Sheep Best, Cropton Yorkshire Moors and Timothy Taylors Golden Best on handpump, seven wines by the glass, 12 malt whiskies and home-made elderflower cordial; background music and pool. Outside are seats under parasols and some picnic-sets. The inn is in the North York Moors National Park, so there are plenty of surrounding walks. They have a caravan site. This is sister pub to the Horseshoe in Levisham.

Highly regarded food includes sandwiches, baguettes and wraps, pigeon breast with mixed peppers, chorizo and sautéed potatoes, chicken liver and brandy pâté with tomato chutney, wild mushroom and spinach cannelloni with garlic bread, Whitby haddock and chips, venison burger with toppings, onion rings and chips, pork tenderloin wrapped in bacon with black pudding, champ mash and brandy cream sauce, lambs liver with parsley mash, bacon and red onion gravy, butterflied and breadcrumbed chicken breast with tomato salsa and goats cheese, and puddings such as lemon tart and sticky toffee pudding with toffee sauce. *Benchmark main dish: steak in ale pie £11.95. Two-course evening meal £22.00.*

Free house ~ Licensees Toby and Charles Wood ~ Real ale ~ Open 11-11 (10 Sun) ~ Bar food 12-2, 5-8.30; light snacks 2-4pm ~ Restaurant ~ Children welcome ~ Dogs allowed in bar ~ Wi-fi *Recommended by Michael Butler, Joe and Belinda Smart, Mark Hamill, Rosie and John Moore, Millie and Peter Downing*

MALHAM SD9062 Map 7

Lister Arms

(01729) 830444 – www.listerarms.co.uk

Off A65 NW of Skipton; BD23 4DB

Friendly inn in fine countryside with cosy bars and dining room, enjoyable food and seats outside; comfortable bedrooms

With good, hearty breakfasts and attractive, warm and comfortable bedrooms (some in the pub, others in the next-door-cottage and more in the barn conversion), our readers stay here on a regular basis. It's a handsome, creeper-covered inn with views over the Yorkshire Dales National Park, and one bar has a medley of cushioned dining chairs and leather or upholstered armchairs around antique wooden tables on slate flooring, with a big deer's head above the inglenook fireplace. A second bar has a small brick fireplace with logs piled to each side, rustic slab tables, cushioned wheelback chairs and comfortable wall seats. Thwaites Lancaster Bomber, Nutty Black and Original Bitter on handpump, 20 wines by the glass and Weston's farm cider. A woodburning stove stands in the fireplace of the airy dining room where there are swagged curtains and smartly upholstered high-backed and pale wooden farmhouse chairs around rustic tables on bare floorboards. The flagstoned and gravelled courtyard has seats and benches around tables under parasols – some overlook the small green at the front.

Generously served, the tasty, popular food includes sandwiches, crispy duck spring roll with spring onions and hoisin dipping sauce, fritto misto (fried calamari, octopus, whitebait and mussels) with chilli aioli, twice-baked blue cheese soufflé with waldorf salad, local pork sausages with mash and onion gravy, a pie of the day, burger with toppings and skinny fries, cajun-spiced chicken with smoked corn on the cob, fries and blue cheese dip, 16oz T-bone steak with a choice of sauce, and puddings such as chocolate brownie with a vanilla shake and toasted coconut marshmallow and vanilla crème brûlée. *Benchmark main dish: beer-battered fish and chips £11.00. Two-course evening meal £17.00.*

Thwaites ~ Manager Darren Dunn ~ Real ale ~ Open 12-11 (10.30 Sun) ~ Bar food 12-9.30 ~ Restaurant ~ Children welcome ~ Dogs allowed in bar and bedrooms ~ Wi-fi ~ Bedrooms: /£105 *Recommended by Tim and Sue Halstead, Steve Whalley, Gary and Marie Miller, Celia Caulkin, Peter Smith and Judith Brown*

THE GOOD PUB GUIDE

MARTON-CUM-GRAFTON SE4263 Map 7

Punch Bowl

(01423) 322519 – www.thepunchbowlmartoncumgrafton.com

Signed off A1 3 miles N of A59; YO51 9QY

Refurbished old inn in lovely village, with character bar and dining rooms, real ales, interesting food and seats on terrace

There's plenty of room for both drinking and dining in this handsome old inn, and plenty of original features to seek out. The main bar is beamed and timbered with a built-in window seat at one end, lots of red leather-topped stools, and cushioned settles and church chairs around pubby tables on flagstones or bare floorboards. Black Sheep Best, Theakstons Best and York Guzzler on handpump, 24 wines by the glass and a good number of malt whiskies and gins; background music. Open doorways lead to five separate dining areas, each with an open fire, heavy beams and an attractive mix of cushioned wall seats and wooden or high-backed red-leather dining chairs around antique tables on oak floors; the red walls are covered with photographs of vintage car races and racing drivers, sporting-themed cartoons and old photographs of the pub and village. Up a spiral staircase is a coffee loft and a private dining room. There are seats and tables in the back courtyard where they hold summer barbecues. This is part of Provenance Inns & Hotels.

Good, seasonal food includes lunchtime sandwiches, turmeric and lime chicken skewers with cauliflower rice and sweet cucumber pickle, salmon and smoked haddock cake with a soft poached egg and parsley sauce, roast red pepper polenta cake with spicy bean cassoulet and basil oil, burger with toppings and fries, slow-roasted lamb shoulder with spelt, broad beans, carrot purée and wild garlic pesto, fish pie with king prawns, smoked haddock, salmon and lemon and dill velouté, 21-day-aged sirloin steak with a choice of sauce, and puddings such as spiced carrot cake with orange frosting, crushed meringue and candied walnuts and peach pannacotta with white chocolate and raspberry; they also offer an early bird menu (5.30-7pm). *Benchmark main dish: steak in ale pie £14.95. Two-course evening meal £20.00.*

Free house ~ Licensee Paulo Pinto ~ Real ale ~ Open 12-3, 5-11; 12-11 Fri, Sat; 12-10.30 Sun ~ Bar food 12-2.30, 5.30-9.30; 12-8 Sun ~ Children welcome ~ Dogs allowed in bar ~ Wi-fi *Recommended by Ian Duncan, Paul Scofield, Daphne and Robert Staples, Sue Parry Davies, Alison and Tony Livesley, Jacob Matt, Tracey and Stephen Groves, Kate and Mark Foskett, Colin and Daniel Gibbs*

MASHAM SE2281 Map 10

Black Sheep Brewery

(01765) 680100 – www.blacksheepbrewery.co.uk

Brewery signed off Leyburn Road (A6108); HG4 4EN

Lively place with friendly staff, unusual décor in big warehouse room, well kept beers and popular food

Not a straightforward pub, this is more akin to a bistro but there's a bar in the huge upper warehouse room where they keep their own-brewed Black Sheep Ale, Best, Golden Sheep and Riggwelter plus a couple of other changing Black Sheep beers such as BAA BAA and Shearer on handpump, several wines by the glass and a fair choice of soft drinks. The contemporary refurbishment is light and attractive with high wooden chairs around equally high tables on stripped floorboards and a good deal of bare woodwork, with cream-painted rough stonework and green-painted steel girders and pillars; background music, TV and friendly service. The tours of the sizeable brewery are popular and a glass wall lets you see into the brewing exhibition centre; a shop sells beers and beer-related items from pub games and T-shirts to pottery and fudge. There are picnic-sets out on the grass.

Tasty pubby food includes sandwiches, garlic and rosemary baked camembert with celery, apple and walnut salad, chicken liver parfait with chutney, sharing boards, vegetable, chickpea and lentil curry, slow-cooked rack of baby back pork ribs in smoked barbecue sauce, coleslaw, charred corn on the cob and skinny fries, pork and ale sausages with ale onion gravy and mash, beer-battered fresh haddock and chips, lamb casserole with apple and thyme dumplings, flat-iron steak with onion rings and a choice of sauce, and puddings such as cinnamon doughnuts with hot chocolate sauce and sticky toffee pudding with stout and toffee sauce. *Benchmark main dish: steak in ale pie £12.50. Two-course evening meal £20.00.*

Free house ~ Licensee Paul Casterton ~ Real ale ~ Open 10am-5pm Sun-Weds, 10am-11pm Thurs-Sat ~ Bar food 12-2.30 Sun-Weds; 12-2.30, 6-9 Thurs-Sat ~ Restaurant ~ Children welcome ~ Dogs allowed in bar ~ Wi-fi *Recommended by Jeremy Snow, Nigel Havers, Tony and Wendy Hobden, Barbara and Phil Bowie, Stuart and Natalie Granville, M and GR*

MINSKIP SE3965 Map 7

Wild Swan

(01423) 326334 – www.wildswan.pub

Main Street; YO51 9JF

Renovated country pub with stylish but relaxed bar and restaurant, well kept ales, excellent food and seats in charming garden

If you want a break from the busy A1, head just a minute down the road to this pretty little country pub in a farming village. It's been reopened and refurbished by one of our former Licensees of the Year, so we know our readers will love it. The heavily beamed bar is just the place for a cosy pint and a chat and has traditional dark wooden chairs, cushioned settles and stools on rugs or bare boards and a couple of armchairs by the two-way open fire; this opens up into an informal dining area with farmhouse chairs around scrubbed kitchen tables, pewter tankards on a delft shelf and a big stag's head. Friendly, helpful staff serve Black Sheep Best, Timothy Taylors Landlord and a guest such as Rudgate Yorvik on handpump, ten wines by the glass and ten local gins. The plusher, carpeted restaurant is furnished with high-backed, tartan-upholstered dining chairs around more stripped farmhouse tables (each set with a church candle and flowers), sage-green walls hung with mirrors, decorative wicker-work and oil paintings, and there's an open kitchen; this shares the open fire with the bar. The flower-filled garden has plenty of seating. They have plans to open studio bedrooms in a converted barn. Disabled access and loos.

Cooked by the chef-owner and making their own different flavoured focaccia daily, the first class food includes lunchtime sandwiches, black pudding scotch egg with home-made brown sauce, smoked haddock fishcake with a poached egg, peas, lettuce and bacon, thai green vegetable curry, daube of beef with a mini yorkshire pudding and red wine jus, seafood tagliatelle (king prawns, salmon, queen scallops and haddock) with salsa verde, slow-roasted lamb over charred aubergine, rosemary, lemon, capers and mint yoghurt, fresh Whitby crab salad, and puddings such as belgian chocolate brownie with ice-cream and rhubarb and vanilla pannacotta with praline; they also offer a two-course early bird menu (before 5.30pm). *Benchmark main dish: sea bass fillet on queen scallop risotto £16.75. Two-course evening meal £21.00.*

Free house ~ Licensee Karl Mainey ~ Real ale ~ Open 12-11 ~ Bar food 12-2.15, 5-9.15; 12-7 Sun ~ Restaurant ~ Children welcome ~ Dogs allowed in bar ~ Wi-fi *Recommended by Les and Sandra Brown, Lorna and Jack Musgrave, David and Leone Lawson, Susan and Callum Slade*

MOULTON NZ2303 Map 10

Black Bull

(01325) 377556 – www.theblackbullmoulton.com

Just E of A1, a mile E of Scotch Corner; DL10 6QJ

Character pub with a traditional bar, a large open restaurant, high quality food and courteous efficient service; bedrooms

The bar in this well run place has a convivial atmosphere, some original panelling, leather wall seating topped with scatter cushions and a fine range of drinks, including Black Sheep Best, Timothy Taylors Boltmaker and a guest such as Hambleton White Boar on handpump, 24 wines by the glass and over 20 malt whiskies. There's also a dining area with cushioned wooden chairs around a mix of tables on pale flagstones, a couple of leather armchairs in front of a woodburner in a brick fireplace, and horse tack, stone bottles, wooden pails and copper items on windowsills. The dining extension has high windows, a wooden floor, attractive brown-orange high-backed dining chairs or cushioned settles and a rather nice wire bull; background music. Doors from here lead out to a neat terrace with modern seats and tables set among pots of rosemary or tall bay trees. This is part of the Provenance Inns & Hotels group.

Excellent food includes lunchtime sandwiches, tea-smoked duck breast with poached apricot, endive and walnut oil, prawn cocktail, harissa-roasted vegetables with beetroot, carrots, chickpeas, ricotta and macadamia nuts, chicken breast with lemon and thyme rösti, maitake mushrooms and truffle, red mullet with roasted fennel, saffron fondant potatoes and shellfish bisque, lamb rump and shoulder with pea and mint fregola, baby courgettes and mint gel, and puddings such as strawberry and white chocolate crème brûlée with champagne sorbet and compressed strawberries and sticky toffee pudding with butterscotch sauce and cinder toffee ice-cream; they also offer a two- and three-course lunch menu (not Sunday) and an early bird menu (5.30-6.45pm, not Saturday). *Benchmark main dish: fish pie £16.95. Two-course evening meal £21.50.*

Free house ~ Licensee Richard Marsy ~ Real ale ~ Open 12-3, 5-11; 12-11 Fri-Sun ~ Bar food 12-2.30, 5.30-9.30; 12-3, 5.30-8.30 Sun ~ Restaurant evening ~ Children welcome ~ Dogs allowed in bar ~ Wi-fi *Recommended by Tony Selinger, Richard and Tessa Ibbot, Professor James Burke, Julia and Fiona Barnes, Victoria and Len Meadows*

NUN MONKTON SE5057 Map 7

Alice Hawthorn

(01423) 330303 – www.thealicehawthorn.com

Off A59 York–Harrogate; The Green; YO26 8EW

Carefully and attractively renovated pub with appealing décor, imaginative food and picturesque setting

Located next to one of the oldest working greens in Yorkshire (cattle roam about quite freely), this is a lovely village pub. There's a cosy bar (dogs and boots are welcome here), with comfortable seats and an open fire, Black Sheep Best, Timothy Taylors Landlord and Yorkshire Heart Hearty Bitter (brewed in the village) on handpump and a dozen wines by the glass served by friendly, helpful staff. The elegant dining rooms are divided by a two-way open fire and have button-back wall seating and beige plush and upholstered chairs around all manner of tables, plus candles in lanterns; a snug (the oldest part of the building) leads off here with big piles of logs to either side of another log fire. They grow their own fruit and vegetables in raised beds in the sunny garden which has plenty of seats and tables.

Creative food using local, seasonal produce includes queenie scallops with garlic butter, gruyère and panko crumbs, beetroot-cured salmon gravadlax with avocado and horseradish cream, jerusalem artichoke and truffle ravioli with king oyster mushrooms, basil pesto and parmesan, chicken breast with morels, peas and broad beans, wild garlic and dauphinoise potatoes, local venison haunch with celeriac purée, roast beetroot, chervil and parsley roots and blackberry and damson gin juices, crisp confit duck leg with fried duck egg and mustard and maple syrup glaze, cider-braised pig cheeks and chargrilled tenderloin with crushed sweet potatoes, and puddings. *Benchmark main dish: roast cod and prawns in a chive beurre blanc £15.50. Two-course evening meal £25.00.*

Free house ~ Licensee Claire Topham ~ Real ale ~ Open 12-11; 12-8 Sun; closed Mon, Tues ~ Bar food 12-2.30, 5.30-9; 12-3.30 Sun ~ Restaurant ~ Children welcome ~ Dogs allowed in bar ~ Wi-fi *Recommended by Sarah and David Gibbs, Ben and Jenny Settle, Janet and Peter Race, Margaret Merritt, Francis and Mandy Robertson, Caroline and Oliver Sterling*

RIPPONDEN SE0419 Map 7

Old Bridge

(01422) 822595 – www.theoldbridgeinn.co.uk

From A58, best approach is Elland Road (opposite the Golden Lion), park opposite the church in pub's car park and walk back over ancient hump-back bridge; HX6 4DF

Pleasant old pub run by a long-serving family with relaxed communicating rooms and well-liked food

Notably welcoming and in a lovely spot next to a beautiful medieval pack-horse bridge, this ancient place is run by the third generation of the same family. The three communicating rooms, each on a slightly different level, have oak settles built into window recesses in the thick stone walls, antique oak tables, rush-seated chairs and comfortably cushioned free-standing settles, a few well chosen pictures and prints on the panelled or painted walls and a big woodburning stove. Timothy Taylors Best, Golden Best, Landlord and Ram Tam, a couple of guests such as Salopian Oracle and Vocation Bread & Butter on handpump, quite a few foreign bottled beers, 15 wines by the glass, 15 gins, 30 malt whiskies and farm cider; quick, efficient service. Seats in the garden overlook the little River Ryburn. There's no traditional pub sign outside, so to find it, head for the church next door.

The ever-popular weekday lunchtime cold meat and salad buffet has been running since 1963 (they also offer soup and sandwiches at lunch). Evening and weekend choices include king prawns with chorizo in tomato and garlic sauce, black pudding and bacon salad with a poached egg and honey mustard dressing, a pie of the day, mixed bean, tomato, chilli and coriander wraps with cheese and crème fraîche, beef goulash, slow-roasted lamb shank in red wine and rosemary jus, 10oz sirloin steak with stilton or peppercorn sauce, and puddings such as a crumble of the day and ginger sponge with ginger sauce. *Benchmark main dish: smoked haddock and spinach pancakes £11.00. Two-course evening meal £20.00.*

Free house ~ Licensees Tim and Lindsay Eaton Walker ~ Real ale ~ Open 12-3, 5-11; 12-11 Sat; 12-10.30 Sun ~ Bar food 12-2, 5-9 (9.30 Fri, Sat); 12-4 Sun ~ Children allowed until 8pm but must be seated away from bar ~ Wi-fi *Recommended by Jill and Dick Archer, Maria and Henry Lazenby, Graeme and Sally Mendham, Buster and Helena Hastings, Jim and Sue James*

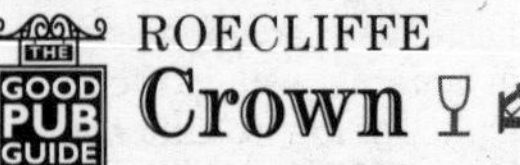

ROECLIFFE SE3765 Map 7

Crown

(01423) 322300 – www.crowninnroecliffe.com

Off A168 just W of Boroughbridge; handy for A1(M) junction 48; YO51 9LY

Attractively placed pub with some refurbishment under new licensees, rewarding food, local ales and seats outside; comfortable bedrooms

This bustling pub has seen a few changes under its new owners. The bar has a colour scheme of dark reds and off-whites with a polished flagstone floor and a winter log fire. The fireplace serves both this area and the restaurant which has been furnished with new dining tables and dark tables on a plaid carpet. You can choose between the cosy, olive-green dining room or the newly decorated restaurant with fresh cream paintwork. Black Sheep Best, Timothy Taylors Landlord and Wells Bombardier on handpump, good wines by the glass, several malt whiskies and quite a few local gins; background music. The garden has rattan sofas and tables set out on decking. The cosy bedrooms are decorated in a country style and breakfasts are good. The village green is opposite.

From a thoughtful menu, the interesting food includes sesame and soy pork belly with an asian salad, pak choi and lemongrass dressing, smoked mackerel salad with pomegranate and radish, sweet potato and chickpea tagine with carrot and beetroot salad, chicken wrapped in pancetta with crispy garlic and thyme potatoes and chicken stock velouté, cod loin fillet with courgette, lemon and mussel risotto and a crab beignet, cheek and fillet of pork with white pudding, sage dauphinoise potatoes, apple and carrot, salt-aged steaks with a choice of sauce, and puddings such as white chocolate and matcha tea cheesecake and orange and saffron tart with marshmallow and marmalade; they also offer a two- and three-course lunch menu. *Benchmark main dish: côte de boeuf for two people £49.90. Two-course evening meal £24.00.*

Free house ~ Licensee Joe Stuart ~ Real ale ~ Open 12-11; 12-10 Sun ~ Bar food 12-2.15, 6-9.30; 12-7 Sun ~ Restaurant ~ Children welcome ~ Dogs allowed in bar and bedrooms ~ Wi-fi ~ Bedrooms: /£110 *Recommended by Lindy Andrews, Jim King, Patrick and Emma Stephenson, Ivy and George Goodwill*

SANCTON SE9039 Map 7

Star

(01430) 827269 – www.thestaratsancton.co.uk

King Street (A1034 S of Market Weighton); YO43 4QP

Bustling bar with up to four real ales, more formal dining rooms with accomplished food, and a friendly, easy-going atmosphere

Of course, the excellent food cooked by the landlord is one of the main draws here, but this is a proper pub with a good mix of locals, walkers and cyclists (the pub is at the foot of the Yorkshire Wolds Railway) and the hands-on landlady offers a warm welcome to all. The bar has a woodburning stove, traditional red plush stools around a mix of tables, a cheerful atmosphere and ales from breweries such as Black Sheep, Broughs, Great Newsome and Wold Top on handpump from the brick counter, plus 19 wines by the glass or carafe including prosecco and champagne, 20 gins and over 20 malt whiskies. The more formal (though still relaxed) dining rooms have comfortable high-backed dark leather dining chairs around wooden tables on carpeting, and prints on red- or cream-painted walls; background music. There are picnic-sets outside at the back.

Food is inventive and modern and as well as honest pub fare includes sandwiches, seared mackerel with pickled fennel, poached apple, samphire and dill mayonnaise, pressed ham terrine with chutney and grain mustard dressing, cauliflower mac and cheese with a chive and cheese straw, cumberland sausage and mash with crispy bacon and shallot gravy, crispy duck breast with confit leg pie, spiced duck jus and rhubarb and juniper chutney, braised beef cheek with chestnut mushroom and tarragon gratin, crispy ox tongue fritter, red onion tarte tatin and red wine jus, monkfish with soya bean and wild mushroom fricassée, roast garlic purée and brown shrimps, and puddings such as liquorice pannacotta with vanilla and anise poached pear and ale and chocolate cake with caramel ice-cream; they also offer a two- and three-course set lunch. *Benchmark main dish: steak in ale pie £14.95. Two-course evening meal £25.00.*

Free house ~ Licensees Ben and Lindsey Cox ~ Real ale ~ Open 12-3, 6-11; 12-11 Sun; closed Mon; first week Jan ~ Bar food 12-2, 6-9.30; 12-3, 6-8 Sun ~ Restaurant ~ Children welcome *Recommended by Richard Cole, Alison and Graeme Spicer, Monica and Steph Evans, Adam Jones, Val and Malcolm Travers, Mark and Sian Edwards*

The symbol shows pubs that keep their beer unusually well, have a particularly good range or brew their own.

SANDHUTTON SE3882 Map 10

Kings Arms

(01845) 587887 – www.thekingsarmssandhutton.co.uk

A167, a mile N of A61 Thirsk–Ripon; YO7 4RW

Cheerful pub with friendly service, interesting food and beer, and comfortable furnishings; bedrooms

For 200 years this bustling inn has been the hub of the village, and the father and son team running it make sure it remains just the same today. The bar has an easy-going atmosphere, an unusual circular woodburner in one corner, a high central table with four equally high stools, modern ladder-back wooden dining chairs around light pine tables, a couple of cushioned wicker armchairs, some attractive modern bar stools and photographs of the pub in years gone by. Black Sheep Best and Village Brewer White Boar Bitter on handpump, 11 wines by the glass and efficient, friendly service. The two connecting dining rooms have similar furnishings to the bar (plus some high-backed brown leather dining chairs), arty flower photographs on cream walls and a small woodburning stove; background music, darts, board games and TV. There's a small beer garden and they have secure bike storage with air, puncture repair kits and a heated towel rail for drying wet kit. The pub does get pretty packed on race days at Thirsk Racecourse.

Enjoyable food includes lunchtime sandwiches, black pudding on toasted home-made sourdough with crispy parma ham and a poached egg, scallops with chorizo and gruyère, a pie of the day, falafel burger with salsa and avocado, battered scampi and chips, pasta with free-range chicken, sunblush tomatoes and pesto topped with parmesan, pulled pork burrito with cheese, sour cream, salsa and guacamole, chilli con carne, burger with toppings, onion rings and chips, 10oz fillet steak with a choice of sauce, and puddings such as a cheesecake and crème brûlée of the day. *Benchmark main dish: salmon, cod and prawn fishcake with sweet chilli sauce £11.95. Two-course evening meal £20.00.*

Free house ~ Licensees Raymond and Alexander Boynton ~ Real ale ~ Open 12-11; 12-10 Sun ~ Bar food 12-2.30, 6-9; 12-5 Sun ~ Restaurant ~ Children welcome ~ Dogs allowed in bar ~ Wi-fi ~ Bedrooms: £60/£90 *Recommended by Jeremy Snaithe, Helena and Trevor Fraser, Maggie and Matthew Lyons, Gail and Frank Hackett, Ted and Mary Bates, Sandra and Michael Smith*

SOUTH STAINLEY SE3163 Map 7

Inn at South Stainley

(01423) 779060 – www.innatstainley.co.uk

Ripon Road; HG3 3ND

Attractively renovated pub with bar and dining rooms, local ales, interesting food and seats in garden

After a considerable refurbishment, this now stylish country pub reopened at the end of 2017. There's plenty of space for both drinking and eating and our readers have been quick to voice their enthusiasm. The rooms are interlinked; the bar has button-back and tartan-upholstered dining chairs and wooden settles around a medley of tables on floorboards and high chairs lining the bar counter where friendly, helpful staff serve Black Sheep Best and Timothy Taylors Landlord on handpump, good wines by the glass and a growing number of gins and malt whiskies; background music. A two-way woodburning stove separates the bar from the dining rooms which have curved banquettes, long leather wall seats and dark wooden chairs on more bare boards and prints on painted, planked walls. A covered terrace outside has seats and tables under large parasols and there are more seats in the sizeable mature garden. Bedrooms are modern, airy and comfortable and breakfasts are hearty. This is part of the Seafood Pub Company.

Imaginative food includes sandwiches, devilled crab, salmon and shrimp pâté with sea salt croûtes, vietnamese beef summer rolls with rice wine dipping sauce, potato gnocchi with sunblush tomatoes, squash, rocket and blue cheese, pizzas, goan monkfish and prawn curry with coconut rice, chicken, ham and leek pie, venison haunch, with celeriac gratin, spring cabbage, baby carrots and blackberries, persian spiced chicken with jewelled rice, rose petal harissa and yoghurt dressing, fresh fish and shellfish daily specials with scallops, crab, halibut, hake and sea bass, and puddings such as praline profiteroles with chocolate and caramel sauce and rhubarb parfait with ginger biscotti and rhubarb compote. *Benchmark main dish: fish pie £12.95. Two-course evening meal £18.00.*

Free house ~ Licensee Claire Quinn ~ Real ale ~ Open 12-10; 12-11 Sat; 12-9.30 Sun ~ Bar food 12-9 (8 Sun) ~ Restaurant ~ Children welcome ~ Dogs allowed in bar and bedrooms ~ Wi-fi ~ Bedrooms: /£80 *Recommended by John Harris, David and Charlotte Green, Andrew and Michele Revell*

THORNTON WATLASS SE2385 Map 10

Buck

(01677) 422461 – www.buckwatlass.co.uk

Village signposted off B6268 Bedale–Masham; HG4 4AH

Honest village pub with up to five real ales, a traditional bar and function room, well liked food and popular Sunday jazz; bedrooms

Opposite the village green and part of a row of low stone cottages, this is a friendly place and very much the heart of the local community. The pleasantly traditional bar on the right has upholstered wall settles on carpet, a fine mahogany bar counter, local artwork on the walls and a brick fireplace; background music. A snug area overlooks the garden and has a woodburning stove. The Long Room (with views of the cricket green) has photos and trophies from Thornton Watlass cricket teams past and present, and is the venue for the Sunday afternoon jazz sessions. Black Sheep Best, Theakstons Best, Three Brothers Trilogy and Wensleydale Falconer on handpump, eight wines by the glass and nine malt whiskies. The sheltered garden has a well equipped children's play area. Bedrooms are well appointed and comfortable and breakfasts good. Wheelchair access with ramp.

Good quality food includes sandwiches, king prawns wrapped in parma ham, caramelised onion and goats cheese tart, arancini with spicy tomato sauce, lasagne, chicken curry, sea bass fillet with lemon and dill butter with sautéed potatoes, pork fillet stuffed with black pudding on wholegrain mustard mash and cider gravy, duck breast with rhubarb compote, 10oz rib-eye steak with chips and a choice of sauce, and puddings such as crème brûlée and chocolate and pistachio semi-freddo. *Benchmark main dish: steak in ale pie £11.95. Two-course evening meal £18.00.*

Free house ~ Licensees Victoria and Tony Jowett ~ Real ale ~ Open 12-11 (10.30 Sun) ~ Bar food 12-2, 6-9; 12-3, 6-8.30 Sun ~ Restaurant ~ Children welcome ~ Dogs allowed in bar and bedrooms ~ Wi-fi ~ Live trad jazz Sun lunchtime monthly (phone to check) ~ Bedrooms: £65/£95 *Recommended by Peter and Caroline Waites, Martine and Fabio Lockley, Martin and Joanne Sharp, Mark Morgan, Andrew Vincent*

Bedroom prices include full english breakfast, VAT and any inclusive service charge that we know of.

WELBURN SE7168 Map 7

Crown & Cushion

(01653) 618777 – www.thecrownandcushionwelburn.com

Off A64; YO60 7DZ

Plenty of dining and drinking space in well run inn with real ales and good food – and seats outside

After a visit to Castle Howard, this handsome inn is just the place for lunch. It's been carefully and attractively refurbished and the little tap room has rustic tables and chairs on wide floorboards, high stools around an equally high central table, beams and timbering, Black Sheep Best and Ram Tackle, Theakstons Best and York Guzzler on handpump, a good choice of malt whiskies and gins, 24 wines by the glass and farm cider. The other interconnecting rooms are for dining and on different levels: smart high-backed chairs mix with wooden ones and an assortment of cushioned settles and wall seats around various tables on flagstones or red and black floor tiles. There are open fires and a woodburning stove, old prints of the pub and local scenes on painted or exposed-stone walls and lots of horsebrasses, copper pans and kettles and old stone bottles; background music. The contemporary tables and chairs on the outdoor terrace and picnic-sets below, with long-reaching views across to the Howardian Hills, are popular in warm weather. This is part of Provenance Inns & Hotels.

Interesting food includes sandwiches, tempura king prawns with asian vegetable and coriander salad, ham hock terrine with pickled vegetables and mustard dressing, sweet potato, chickpea and spinach curry with coconut rice, salmon and haddock gratin with cheese and parsley crumb, chicken breast with roast chorizo and pea and broad bean pesto, beer-battered fish and chips, lamb rump with broccoli purée, wilted samphire and minted jus, game ragoût with pasta and pecorino, 10oz 21-day-aged rump steak with a choice of sauce, and puddings such as strawberry pannacotta and chocolate marquise with basil sorbet, coffee sponge and sweet basil syrup; they also offer an early bird menu (5.30-6.45pm). *Benchmark main dish: fish pie £13.95. Two-course evening meal £20.00.*

Free house ~ Licensee Guy Richardson ~ Real ale ~ Open 12-3, 5-11; 12-11 Fri-Sun ~ Bar food 12-2.30, 5.30-9.30; 12-8 Sun ~ Restaurant ~ Children welcome ~ Dogs allowed in bar ~ Wi-fi *Recommended by Mike Benton, Simon Sharpe, Jane and Philip Saunders, Caroline and Steve Archer, Elise and Charles Mackinlay, Dan and Belinda Smallbone*

WIDDOP SD9531 Map 7

Pack Horse £

(01422) 842803 – www.thepackhorseinn.pub

The Ridge; from A646 on W side of Hebden Bridge, turn off at Heptonstall signpost (as it's a sharp turn, coming out of Hebden Bridge the road signs direct you around a turning circle), then follow Slack and Widdop signposts; can also be reached from Nelson and Colne, on high, pretty road; OS Sheet 103 map reference 952317; HX7 7AT

Friendly pub up on the moors and liked by walkers for generous, tasty honest food, four real ales and plenty of malt whiskies

If you're a walker or cyclist on the Pennine Way and Pennine Bridleway, this isolated moorland pub is a cosy haven. The snug bar has winter fires, window seats cut into the partly panelled stripped-stone walls (from where you can take in the beautiful views), sturdy furnishings and horsey mementoes. Black Sheep Best and Marstons Wainwright plus a couple of changing guests on handpump, over 100 single malt whiskies plus some irish ones, and a dozen wines by the glass. There are seats outside in the cobblestoned beer garden and pretty summer hanging baskets.

Bar food uses local produce and includes sandwiches and soups, sausages and a pie of the day with mash and gravy, gammon and eggs, a vegetarian choice, thick roast beef with yorkshire pudding and vegetables, local game, rack of lamb, and puddings such as treacle sponge and chocolate fudge cake. *Benchmark main dish: lamb shank £13.95. Two-course evening meal £19.00.*

Free house ~ Licensee Sean Hogan ~ Real ale ~ Open 12-3, 5.30-11; 12-11 Sat; 12-7 Sun; closed Mon, Tues (open Tues lunchtime in summer) ~ Bar food 12-2, 6.30-9; 12-7 Sun ~ Children welcome ~ Dogs welcome *Recommended by Alan and Alice Morgan, Simon and Alex Knight, Diane Abbott, WAH, Professor James Burke*

YORK SE5951 Map 7

Judges Lodging

(01904) 639312 – www.judgeslodgingyork.co.uk

Lendal; YO1 8AQ

Lovely town house with a modern interior, character cellar bar, several dining rooms, well liked food and outside seating; stylish bedrooms

If you stay in the top bedroom in this fine Georgian house (all the bedrooms are comfortable, modern and well equipped) there are York Minster views across the rooftops. Although the building is old, the interior is interestingly refurbished and contemporary. The proper bar is in the cellar (and open for drinks and food all day) with fine vaulted ceilings, upholstered dining chairs and sofas on big flagstones, Marstons Lancaster Bomber and Wainwright, Spitting Feathers Empire IPA, Thwaites Original, Timothy Taylors Landlord and Treboom Yorkshire Sparkle on handpump and good wines by the glass; this leads through a dining room to a bright and airy garden room, both of which have green-painted farmhouse chairs around blond wooden tables on pale floorboards. On the first floor is what they call the Medicine Cabinet – a reception room for both the dining rooms and hotel – with quirky men's trouser-leg stools by the bar counter, a couple of grey button-back leather armchairs on either side of the fireplace and plaster judges' heads on Farrow & Ball paintwork. Leading off here, the two restaurants have leather chesterfields and more upholstered chairs around a mix of tables on bare boards, painted panelling, tall window shutters, chandeliers, gilt-edged mirrors and some unusual wire sculptures – it's all very smart and civilised. There are modern seats and tables at the front of the building between lavender pots, white metal furniture beside the garden room and traditional wooden chairs, tables and picnic-sets in the back courtyard.

Food is good and includes sandwiches (until 5pm), dill and orange marinated salmon with horseradish crème fraîche and chive blinis, mini lamb kofta with mango purée and minted yoghurt, platters, spiced sweet potato and squash burger with beetroot slaw and chipotle mayonnaise, chicken caesar salad, prosciutto-wrapped monkfish with spiced couscous, grilled courgettes, aubergine caviar and balsamic reduction, marinated lamb chump with crushed new potatoes and niçoise jus, chargrilled steaks with a choice of sauce, and puddings such as dark chocolate and ginger brownie with orange sorbet and lemon meringue tart with raspberry purée; they also offer a two- and three-course weekday menu (12-5pm). *Benchmark main dish: chicken and leek pie with cabbage and bacon £13.00. Two-course evening meal £19.50.*

Thwaites ~ Lease Rachel Guy ~ Real ale ~ Open 11-11 (10.30 Sun) ~ Bar food 12-10 ~ Restaurant ~ Children welcome ~ Dogs allowed in bar ~ Wi-fi ~ Bedrooms: £109/£115 *Recommended by Phil and Jane Villiers, Julian Thorpe, Alice Wright, Paul Baxter, Peter Smith and Judith Brown, Patricia Healey, Monty Green, Liz and Martin Eldon*

YORK SE5951 Map 7

Maltings £

(01904) 655387 – www.maltings.co.uk

Tanners Moat/Wellington Row, below Lendal Bridge; YO1 6HU

Bustling, friendly city pub with cheerful landlord, interesting real ales and other drinks plus good value standard food

As ever, the hard-working, convivial landlord welcomes all into his busy, cheerful pub. There's a fine range of interesting drinks that includes Black Sheep Best, Treboom Yorkshire Sparkle and York Guzzler on handpump with four quickly rotating guests, six continental beers on tap, four craft beers, lots of bottled beers, six farm ciders, 15 country wines and 25 whiskies from all over the world. The atmosphere is bustling and friendly and the tricksy décor is strong on salvaged, somewhat quirky junk: old doors for the bar front and much of the ceiling, a marvellous collection of railway signs and amusing notices, an old chocolate dispensing machine, cigarette and tobacco advertisements alongside cough and chest remedies, what looks like a suburban front door for the entrance to the ladies', partly stripped orange brick walls and even a lavatory pan in one corner; games machine. The day's papers are framed in the gents'. The pub is very handy for the National Railway Museum and the station; nearby parking is difficult. Please note that dogs are allowed only after food service has finished.

Exceptional value food includes sandwiches and toasties, baked potatoes with lots of fillings, ham and egg, sausage and chips, beef in ale pie, mushroom and spinach lasagne, chilli tacos, and burgers. *Benchmark main dish: chilli chips £4.95.*

Free house ~ Licensee Shaun Collinge ~ Real ale ~ No credit cards ~ Open 11am-11.30pm; 12-10.30 Sun ~ Bar food 12-2 weekdays; 12-4 weekends ~ Children allowed only during meal times ~ Wi-fi ~ Live music Mon and Tues evenings *Recommended by David Thorpe, Dr J Barrie Jones, Rob Anderson, Professor James Burke, Andrew and Ruth Simmonds, Graham Smart, Mark Hamill*

Also Worth a Visit in Yorkshire

Besides the fully inspected pubs, you might like to try these pubs that have been recommended to us and described by readers. Do tell us what you think of them: feedback@goodguides.com

ADDINGHAM SE0749

Fleece (01943) 830397

Main Street (B6160, off A65); LS29 0LY Old village pub attractively renovated by the Seafood Pub Company after fire damage; good food from well balanced menu including fresh fish/seafood, four real ales such as Black Sheep and Ilkley, lots of wines by the glass (comprehensive list), friendly helpful staff, low ceilings, flagstone and wood floors, log fires, upstairs gin and champagne bar (mainly for functions); children and dogs (in some areas) welcome, wheelchair access using ramp, seats under parasols on front terrace, open (and food) all day. *(Michael Butler)*

ADDINGHAM SE0749

Swan (01943) 430003

Main Street; LS29 0NS Popular local with linked rooms around central servery, flagstones and log fires (one in fine old range), six well kept changing ales and good food from sandwiches/baguettes to daily specials, Tues fish and chips, steak night Fri, friendly helpful service (may be a wait at busy times); live bands Sat, quiz nights; children and dogs welcome, tables out by pavement, open all day, food all day Sun till 7pm. *(Tina and David Woods-Taylor)*

AINDERBY STEEPLE SE3392

Wellington Heifer (01609) 775718

A684, 3 miles from A1; opposite church; DL7 9PU Modernised late 18th-c pub with four connecting rooms (some steps); flagstone and carpeted floors, comfortable scatter-cushion bench seating and sturdy tables, log fires, good range of beers and wines from carved counter, enjoyable food including good value lunchtime/early evening set menu, restaurant at end of corridor; quiz nights; children welcome, three well appointed bedrooms, open all day Sun (food till 7pm). *(Giles and Suzie Nunn)*

AINTHORPE NZ7007

Fox & Hounds (01287) 660218
Brook Lane; YO21 2LD Tranquil moorland setting with grazing sheep and wonderful views for this traditional 16th-c inn; comfortable beamed bar with open fire in unusual stone fireplace, well kept changing ales and good choice of wines by the glass, generous fairly priced food including daily specials, friendly staff, restaurant, games room; free wi-fi; dogs welcome (great walks from the door), seven bedrooms and attached self-catering cottage, open all day. *(Victoria and Len Meadows)*

AISLABY SE8508

Forge (01947) 811522
Main Road, off A171 W of Whitby; YO21 1SW Refurbished mellow-stone village pub with opened-up interior, light wood floor, upholstered wall benches and woodburner in brick fireplace, well kept ales such as Black Sheep from small central servery, good home-made food at sensible prices including popular Sun roasts served till 7pm, friendly accommodating staff; Tues quiz; children and dogs welcome, six bedrooms. *(Angela and Martin Kendall)*

ALDBOROUGH SE4166

Ship (01423) 322749
Off B6265 just S of Boroughbridge, close to A1; YO51 9ER Attractive 14th-c beamed village dining pub adjacent to medieval church; good food from sandwiches and pub standards up including early bird deal (not Mon lunchtime), cheerful helpful service, well kept Black Sheep and Theakstons, extensive affordably priced wine list, some old-fashioned seats around cast-iron-framed tables, lots of copper and brass, inglenook fire, candlelit back restaurant; children and dogs welcome, a few picnic-sets outside, handy for Roman remains and museum, open all day Fri-Sun (food till 6pm Sun). *(Stuart Lymath)*

ALLERSTON SE8783

Cayley Arms (01723) 859904
A170 Pickering–Scarborough; YO18 7PJ Recently refurbished under new owners; long knocked-through bar with light wood and stone floor, two woodburners, upholstered captain's chairs, leather cushioned wall benches and some comfortable button-back armchairs, antlers on bare stone walls, Theakstons, Wold Top and a guest such as Black Sheep, good freshly made food in bar or restaurant; well behaved children and dogs welcome, picnic-sets out at front and in back garden by brook, six well appointed bedrooms, open all day in summer, check website for other times. *(Sara Fulton, Roger Baker)*

APPLETON-LE-MOORS SE7388

★**Moors** (01751) 417435
N of A170, just under 1.5 miles E of Kirkby Moorside; YO62 6TF Traditional 17th-c stone-built village pub; beamed bar with built-in high-backed settle next to old kitchen fireplace, plenty of other seating, three changing regional ales and wide range of malt whiskies and gins, good sensibly priced food from sandwiches/ciabattas and pub favourites up including daily specials, dining room with leather chairs at polished tables, friendly helpful staff; background and occasional live music; children and dogs welcome, tables in lovely walled garden with quiet country views, walks to Rosedale Abbey and Hartoft End, eight good bedrooms, open all day. *(Luke Bruce)*

APPLETREEWICK SE0560

★**Craven Arms** (01756) 720270
Off B6160 Burnsall–Bolton Abbey; BD23 6DA Character creeper-clad 16th-c beamed pub; cushioned settles and rugs on flagstones, open fires (one in old range), gas lighting and lots of interesting pictures and bric-a-brac, up to eight well kept ales including cask-tapped Theakstons Old Peculier and a house beer from Dark Horse, real cider and several wines by the glass, enjoyable home-made food (not Mon or Tues lunchtimes) from hot or cold sandwiches up, friendly helpful service, small dining room and splendid thatched and raftered cruck barn with gallery; free wi-fi; children, dogs and muddy boots welcome (plenty of surrounding walks), wheelchair access, nice country views from front picnic-sets, more seats in back garden, shepherd's hut accommodation, open all day. *(Stuart Doughty)*

ARNCLIFFE SD9371

★**Falcon** (01756) 770205
Off B6160 N of Grassington; BD23 5QE Basic no-frills tavern in lovely setting on village green; coal fire in small bar with elderly furnishings, well kept Timothy Taylors Boltmaker and a guest either from handpump or poured from stoneware jugs in central hatch-style servery, inexpensive simple lunchtime food (non-residents must book evening meals), friendly service, attractive watercolours, sepia photographs and humorous sporting prints, back sun-room overlooking pleasant garden; quiz first Fri of month; children (till 9pm) and dogs welcome, four miles of trout fishing, walks in lovely surrounding countryside, six bedrooms (two with own bathroom), open all day. *(B and M Kendall, Helene Grygar)*

ASKRIGG SD9491

Crown (01969) 650387
Main Street; DL8 3HQ Friendly open-plan local in James Herriot village; three areas off main bar, open fires (one in old-fashioned

range), enjoyable simple pub food at reasonable prices including deals, ales such as Black Sheep and Theakstons; children, walkers and dogs welcome, tables outside, open all day. *(Kate and Mark Foskett)*

ASKRIGG SD9491

Kings Arms (01969) 650113
Signed from A684 Leyburn–Sedbergh in Bainbridge; DL8 3HQ Popular 18th-c coaching inn (the Drovers in TV's *All Creatures Great and Small*) freshened up under friendly new management; high-ceilinged main bar with flagstones, traditional furnishings and good log fire, a couple of well kept house beers from nearby Yorkshire Dales plus Black Sheep, Theakstons and a guest, several wines by the glass, enjoyable reasonably priced food including some evening offers, more modern restaurant with inglenook, games room in former barrel-vaulted beer cellar; background music, sports TV; children and dogs (in bar) welcome, side courtyard, bedrooms run separately as part of Holiday Property Bond complex behind, open (and food) all day. *(John and Enid Morris, Ian Wilson, John Beeken)*

AUSTWICK SD7668

★**Game Cock** (01524) 251226
Just off A65 Settle–Kirkby Lonsdale; LA2 8BB Quaint civilised place in pretty spot below Three Peaks; friendly old-fashioned beamed back bar with bare-boards and good log fire, well kept Thwaites and a guest, winter mulled wine and decent coffee, cheerful efficient staff, plenty of emphasis on french chef-owner's good fairly priced food including themed nights, two refurbished restaurant areas and small conservatory-style extension; children, walkers, cyclists and dogs welcome, garden with play equipment, five bedrooms, open all day. *(Steve Lumb)*

AYSGARTH SE0188

Aysgarth Falls (01969) 663775
A684; DL8 3SR Creeper-clad moorland hotel with good food and welcoming accommodating service; ales such as Black Sheep, Theakstons and Wensleydale in log-fire bar where dogs welcome, comfortable eating areas, some interesting ancient masonry at the back recalling its days as a pilgrims' inn; great scenery near broad waterfalls, 13 bedrooms, camping (adults only), open all day. *(Simon and Sue Lamb)*

AYSGARTH SE0088

★**George & Dragon** (01969) 663358
Just off A684; DL8 3AD Welcoming 17th-c posting inn with emphasis on good locally sourced food from sandwiches up, lunchtime set menu, two big dining areas and small beamed and panelled bar with log fire, well kept ales including Black Sheep, Theakstons and a house beer from Yorkshire Dales, good choice of wines by the glass, friendly helpful staff; may be background music, free wi-fi; children and dogs (in bar) welcome, nice paved garden, lovely scenery and walks, handy for Aysgarth Falls, bedrooms, open all day. *(Bob and Melissa Wyatt)*

BAILDON SE1538

Junction (01274) 582009
Baildon Road; BD17 6AB Friendly wedge-shaped local with three traditional linked rooms; seven well kept ales including own Junction brews (July festival), good value home-made food Fri lunchtime, games part with pool; live music Sun evening and Tues, Thurs quiz, sports TV; open all day. *(Monty Green)*

BARDSEY SE3642

Bingley Arms (01937) 572462
Church Lane; LS17 9DR Ancient pub with spacious lounge divided into separate areas, substantial beams and huge fireplace (priest holes in the chimney), well kept Sharps, Timothy Taylors, Tetleys and a beer named for them (Bingley 953), good range of home-cooked food, afternoon teas, friendly staff, smaller public bar, upstairs raftered restaurant; children welcome, attractive terraced garden behind, lovely Saxon church nearby, open all day. *(Nigel and Sue Foster, Michael Butler)*

BARKISLAND SE0419

★**Fleece** (01422) 820687
B6113 towards Ripponden; HX4 0DJ Large well renovated and extended 18th-c beamed moorland dining pub; very good popular food including weekday set menu, Timothy Taylors Boltmaker, a guest beer and plenty of wines by the glass, efficient friendly uniformed staff; background music; children welcome, no dogs, front disabled access, lovely Pennine views from first-floor terrace and garden, summer barbecues, five bedrooms, useful for M62, open all day from 8am for breakfast, food till 7pm Sun. *(Gordon and Margaret Ormondroyd, John and Eleanor Holdsworth)*

BARMBY-ON-THE-MARSH SE6828

Kings Head (01757) 630705
High Street; DN14 7HT Renovated and extended early 19th-c beamed village pub, good locally sourced food including yorkshire tapas and Sun lunchtime carvery, OAP lunch deal, four well kept local ales, bar, lounge, restaurant and deli (home-baked bread to order); children welcome, disabled access/facilities, open all day weekends, closed Mon and lunchtime Tues. *(Ted and Mary Bates)*

BARNSLEY SE3400

Cock (01226) 744227
Pilley Hill, Birdwell; S70 5UD Welcoming village local set down from the road; reasonably priced home-made food (not Sun evening, Mon) and several well kept

ales including Tetleys, cheerful helpful staff, main bar with beams, stone floor and open fire, lounge and back dining room; children and dogs welcome, open all day (from 4pm Mon). *(David H Bennett)*

BARNSLEY SE3203

Strafford Arms (01226) 287488
Near Northern College, about 2.5 miles NW of M1 junction 36; S75 3EW Pretty stone-built village pub (Fine & Country Inns) with opened-up contemporary interior; well liked food from lunchtime sandwiches and platters to Josper grills, local ales such as Bradfield and Timothy Taylors, good range of wines and cocktails, friendly service, log fires including one in big Yorkshire range; Tues quiz, free wi-fi; children welcome, no dogs inside, garden with play area, on Trans Pennine Trail and by entrance to Wentworth Castle, open (and food) all day. *(Peter Watts)*

BEDALE SE2688

Old Black Swan (01677) 422973
Market Place; DL8 1ED Popular old pub with attractive bay-windowed frontage; well kept ales including Theakstons and generous helpings of good value food, friendly efficient staff, log fire; darts, pool, sports TV; children and dogs welcome, disabled facilities, small covered back terrace, Tues market, open all day. *(Francis and Mandy Robertson)*

BEVERLEY TA0339

★**White Horse** (01482) 861973
Hengate, off North Bar; HU17 8BN Timeless place known locally as Nellie's; carefully preserved Victorian interior with basic little rooms huddled around central bar, brown leatherette seats (high-backed settles in one little snug) and plain chairs/benches on bare boards, antique cartoons and sentimental engravings, gas lighting including chandelier, coal fires, bargain Sam Smiths beers and guests, straightforward food, friendly staff, more space upstairs; charity quiz Tues, games room; children till 7pm, dogs welcome, courtyard picnic-sets, open all day. *(Steve and Alex Cardis)*

BEVERLEY TA0239

Woolpack (01482) 867095
Westwood Road, W of centre; HU17 8EN Nice little pub at end of 19th-c row of terrace cottages; new management and popular for its good traditional food including Mon curry, Tues pie-and-pint and Weds steak nights, also breakfast Sat from 9am, seven well kept Marstons-related beers and good range of gins, friendly service, open fires and simple furnishings, brasses, knick-knacks and prints, cosy snug where dogs allowed; Thurs quiz, some acoustic live music; children welcome, benches out at front, beer garden behind, closed Mon lunchtime and may shut in the afternoon if quiet. *(John Saville)*

BINGLEY SE1039

Brown Cow (01274) 564345
B6429 just W of junction with A650; BD16 2QX Open-plan pub in nice riverside spot; Timothy Taylors range and good choice of enjoyable generously served food, friendly staff; live music and quiz nights; children and dogs welcome, tables out on sheltered terrace, open all day. *(Caroline and Oliver Sterling)*

BINGLEY SE1242

Dick Hudsons (01274) 552121
Otley Road, High Eldwick; BD16 3BA Refurbished Vintage Inn dining pub named after a former landlord; their usual reasonably priced food including set menu choices, ales such as Black Sheep, Marstons and Timothy Taylors, lots of wines by the glass, efficient friendly staff; children welcome, tables outside with great views over Baildon Moor, open all day. *(David Appleyard)*

BIRSTALL SE2126

Black Bull (01274) 973203
Kirkgate, off A652; head down hill towards church; WF17 9HE Recently refurbished old stone-built pub opposite part-Saxon church; long row of small linked rooms, low beams, painted panelling and log fire, four real ales including Black Sheep and decent range of gins, low-priced food including burgers and pizzas, upstairs former courtroom (now a function room); children and dogs welcome, picnic-sets on gravel terrace, open all day, food served Weds-Sat evenings and Sun lunchtime. *(Michael Butler)*

BIRSTWITH SE2459

★**Station Hotel** (01423) 770254
Off B6165 W of Ripley; HG3 3AG Welcoming immaculately kept stone-built dales pub; bar, log-fire restaurant and garden room, very good home-made food from extensive menu including themed nights, four local ales and 14 wines by the glass, friendly efficient staff; Mon quiz and monthly open mike night; tables in landscaped garden with heated smokers' shelter, picturesque valley, bedrooms, open (and food) all day. *(John and Eleanor Holdsworth)*

BISHOPTHORPE SE5947

Woodman (01904) 706507
Village signed just off A64 York S bypass; Main Street; YO23 2RB Welcoming open-plan pub with good range of enjoyable food cooked by landlord-chef, four regional ales and decent choice of wines by the glass, friendly efficient service, woodburner; background music; children and dogs welcome, seats out in front and in large back garden with play equipment, handy for York Racecourse, open all day, food all day weekends (till 6pm Sun). *(Toby Jones)*

BOLTON ABBEY SE0754

Devonshire Arms (01756) 710441
B6160; BD23 6AJ Elegant and comfortable 18th-c hotel in wonderful position on edge of Bolton Abbey Estate; good if not cheap food from light meals up in bright modern brasserie-bar, contemporary paintings (some for sale) on roughcast walls, colourful armchairs around cast-iron-framed tables on pale wood floor, well kept ales and good wines by the glass, afternoon teas, more formal restaurant; tables in spacious courtyard with extensive views, Estate and Strid river-valley walks, bedrooms in old and new wings, open all day. *(Ivy and George Goodwill)*

BRADFIELD SK2692

Old Horns (0114) 285 1207
High Bradfield; S6 6LG Welcoming old Thwaites pub in hill village with stunning views; good hearty food including bargain themed days and Sun carvery, can eat in part-flagstoned bar or carpeted pitch-roofed dining room, half a dozen well kept beers, friendly helpful staff; background music, Tues quiz, TV; children welcome, raised terrace taking in the view, picnic-sets and play area in garden, next to interesting 14th-c church, good walks, open (and food) all day, kitchen shuts 7pm Sun. *(Martin Day)*

BRADFORD SE1533

Fighting Cock (01274) 726907
Preston Street (off B6145); BD7 1JE Traditional bare-boards alehouse by industrial estate; a dozen well kept changing ales, foreign draught/bottled beers and real ciders, friendly staff and lively atmosphere, all-day sandwiches plus good simple lunchtime hot dishes (not Sun), coal fires; beer festivals; dogs welcome, open all day. *(William and Sophie Renton)*

BRADFORD SE1533

New Beehive (01274) 721784
Westgate; BD1 3AA Robustly old-fashioned five-room Edwardian inn; plenty of period features including gas lighting, big mirrors, interesting paintings and coal fires, changing ales (mostly from smaller brewers) along with continental bottled beers, welcoming staff and friendly atmosphere (busy on BCFC match days), weekend live music in cellar bar; pool and bar billiards; children (until 8pm) and dogs welcome, back courtyard, 17 simple bedrooms, open all day from around 2pm Fri, Sat, otherwise open from 6pm. *(Geoff and Anne Marston)*

BRADFORD SE1633

Sparrow Bier Café (01274) 270772
North Parade; BD1 3HZ Refurbished bare-boards bar now owned by Kirkstall; their ales and guests along with good range of craft kegs and bottled beers, friendly knowledgeable staff, deli-style platters, more tables in cellar bar; background music; open all day. *(Adam Jones)*

BRAMHAM SE4242

Swan (01937) 843570
Just off A1 2 miles N of A64; LS23 6QA Unspoilt and unchanging little local up steep hill from village square (also known as the 'Top Pub'); friendly atmosphere and good mix of customers, well kept ales such as Black Sheep, Hambleton and Leeds, no food, two coal fires; open all day Sat, from 4pm weekdays. *(Les and Sandra Brown)*

BRANTINGHAM SE9329

Triton (01482) 667261
Ellerker Road; HU15 1QE Spacious comfortably refurbished and extended old stone pub; good choice of enjoyable home-made food in bar and restaurant, three local ales, swift friendly service; children, walkers and dogs welcome, tables out at front and in sheltered back garden, open all day weekends (food all day Sat, till 6.30pm Sun), closed Mon. *(Alf and Sally Garner)*

BREARTON SE3260

Malt Shovel (01423) 862929
Village signposted off A61 N of Harrogate; HG3 3BX Cosy 16th-c dining pub under new management; heavily beamed rooms with two open fires and woodburner, attractive mix of tables and chairs on wood or slate floors, some partitioning separating several eating areas, good food including weekday set lunch, Rudgate and Theakstons from linenfold oak counter, plenty of wines by the glass, airy conservatory; children welcome, no dogs inside, tables under parasols in garden, pretty hanging baskets, circular walks from the door, closed Sun evening, Mon. *(Michael Doswell)*

BRIDGE HEWICK SE3370

Black-a-moor (01765) 603511
Boroughbridge Road (B6265 E of Ripon); HG4 5AA Roomy family-run dining pub with good choice of popular home-cooked food including set menu, well kept local beers and decent wines, friendly young staff, sofas and woodburner in bar area; free wi-fi; children welcome, dogs in snug, five comfortable bedrooms, open (and food) all day, kitchen closes 7pm Sun. *(Monica and Steph Evans)*

BURN SE5928

Wheatsheaf (01757) 270614
Main Road (A19 Selby–Doncaster); YO8 8LJ Busy but friendly 19th-c roadside pub; comfortable seats in partly divided open-plan bar with lots to look at – air force wartime memorabilia, gleaming copper kettles, polished buffalo horns, cases of model vans and lorries, decorative mugs above one bow-window seat, a drying rack over the log fire, half a dozen well kept ales, 20 malt whiskies, straightforward good value food; background and live music, Sun

quiz, games machine, TV; children and dogs welcome, picnic-sets on terrace in small back garden, open all day, no evening food Sun, Mon or Tues. *(Freddie and Sarah Banks)*

BURNISTON TA0193

Three Jolly Sailors (01723) 871259
A171 N of Scarborough; High Street; YO13 0HJ Comfortable and welcoming village pub with wide range of enjoyable reasonably priced food from sandwiches up, OAP and children's menus, ales such as Timothy Taylors Landlord, main bar, restaurant and conservatory, open fires; dogs welcome, tables under parasols in small side garden, handy for Cleveland Way and coastal walks, open (and food) all day. *(D W Stokes)*

BURYTHORPE SE7964

★**Bay Horse** (01653) 658302
Off A64 8.5 miles NE of York ring road, via Kirkham and Westow; 5 miles S of Malton, by Welham Road; YO17 9LJ Welcoming old stone pub with plenty of authentic character; cosy linked rooms with warming fires, old brick and flagstone floors, traditional furniture with candles on tables, lots of bits and pieces on walls and hanging from beams, eight well kept ales including All Hallows (brewed at sister pub the Goodmanham Arms at Goodmanham), real ciders and generous helpings of good reasonably priced home-made food including some italian dishes, evening food (till 7.30pm) just Tues (steak night) and Fri (sharing platter or stew), friendly caring service; children and dogs welcome, flat disabled access from car park, nice wolds-edge village with fine surrounding walks, open all day. *(Camilla and Jose Ferrera)*

CARLTON SE0684

Foresters Arms (01969) 640272
Off A684 W of Leyburn; DL8 4BB Old stone pub owned by local co-operative; bar with dark low beams, flagstones and log fire, four well kept yorkshire-brewed ales and good range of popular affordably priced food (not Sun evening, Mon, Tues lunchtime), carpeted restaurant; events including fortnightly quiz and monthly live music; dogs welcome, disabled access/loos, a few picnic-sets out at front, pretty village in heart of Yorkshire Dales National Park, lovely views, three bedrooms, open all day Sat, closed Mon lunchtime (and Tues lunchtime in winter). *(John and Enid Morris)*

CARLTON HUSTHWAITE SE4976

Carlton Inn (01845) 501265
Butt Lane; YO7 2BW Cosy modernised beamed dining pub; good fairly priced food cooked by landlady including daily specials and lunchtime/early evening set menu, friendly helpful service, John Smiths and Theakstons, local cider, mix of country furniture including some old settles, open fire; children welcome, dogs in back bar area, garden picnic-sets, open all day Sun, closed Mon. *(Mark and Sian Edwards)*

CARPERBY SE0089

Wheatsheaf (01969) 663216
A mile NW of Aysgarth; DL8 4DF Friendly early 19th-c inn set in quiet dales village and popular with walkers; cosy traditional bar with warming fire, three or four well kept ales such as Black Sheep, Theakstons and Jennings, enjoyable good value home-cooked food, lounge and dining room; children and dogs welcome, 13 comfortable bedrooms (James Herriot had his honeymoon here in 1941), good breakfast, lovely walks including to Aysgarth Falls, open all day. *(Peter Smith and Judith Brown)*

CARTHORPE SE3083

★**Fox & Hounds** (01845) 567433
Village signed from A1 N of Ripon, via B6285; DL8 2LG Popular neatly kept pub run by same family since 1983 and emphasis on their very good well presented food; attractive high-raftered restaurant with lots of farm and smithy tools, Black Sheep and Worthington in L-shaped bar with two log fires, plush seating, plates on stripped beams and evocative Victorian photographs of Whitby, some theatrical memorabilia in corridors, good friendly service; background classical music; children welcome, handy for A1, closed Mon and maybe first week Jan. *(Janet and Peter Race)*

CATTAL SE4455

Victoria (01423) 330249
Station Road; YO26 8EB Bustling Victorian-themed dining pub with extensive choice of good attractively presented food, charming attentive service, well kept ales including one from local Rudgate named for the landlord, good value wines; children welcome, picnic-sets in gravelled back garden, open (and food) all day Sun, from 4pm Tues-Sat, shut Mon, handy for the station. *(Les and Sandra Brown)*

CHAPEL-LE-DALE SD7477

★**Old Hill Inn** (01524) 241256
B5655 Ingleton–Hawes, 3 miles N of Ingleton; LA6 3AR Welcoming former farmhouse with fantastic views to Ingleborough and Whernside; clean rustic interior, beams, log fires and bare-stone recesses, straightforward furniture on stripped-wood floors, pictures and some interesting local artefacts, Black Sheep, Dent and a guest, good wholesome food including lovely puddings (look out for the landlord's

We include some hotels with a good bar that offers facilities comparable to those of a pub.

sugar sculptures), separate dining room and sun lounge, relaxed chatty atmosphere; children welcome, dogs in bar, wonderful remote surrounding walks, two bedrooms and space for five caravans, open all day Sat, closed Mon. *(Val and Malcolm Travers)*

CLIFTON SE1622

Black Horse (01484) 713862
Westgate/Coalpit Lane; signed off Brighouse Road from M62 junction 25; HD6 4HJ Friendly 17th-c inn-restaurant at the heart of this pleasant village; good interesting food (can be pricey) in front dining rooms, also some pubby dishes and set menu choices, efficient uniformed staff, open fire in back bar with beam-and-plank ceiling, well kept ales such as Leeds and Timothy Taylors, good range of wines; children and dogs (in bar) welcome, nice courtyard, 22 comfortable bedrooms, open all day, food all day weekends. *(Michael Butler)*

CLOUGHTON SE9798

Falcon (01723) 870717
Pub signed just off A171 out towards Whitby; YO13 0DY Large 19th-c country inn set in five-acre grounds; well divided opened-up interior including log-fire lounge and dining conservatory, enjoyable pubby food from sandwiches to daily specials, beers such as Theakstons and good choice of wines, distant sea view from end windows; background music; children welcome, picnic-sets in neat walled garden, good walks (leave muddy boots by the door), eight bedrooms and glamping pods, closed Mon and Tues in winter. *(Alan McQuilan)*

CLOUGHTON NEWLANDS TA0195

Bryherstones (01723) 870744
Newlands Road, off A171 in Cloughton; YO13 0AR Popular traditional stone pub; several interconnecting rooms including dining room up on right and flagstoned stable-theme bar on left, very well liked food using local produce, Timothy Taylors and a few guests, good friendly service, games room (pool and darts); children and dogs welcome, picnic-sets and play area in sheltered back garden, closed lunchtimes Mon-Weds. *(Edward Edmonton)*

COLEY SE1226

Brown Horse (01422) 202112
Lane Ends, Denholme Gate Road (A644 Brighouse–Keighley, a mile N of Hipperholme); HX3 7SD Popular roadside pub (some renovations) with good reasonably priced home-made food (not Sun evening), well kept Brakspears, Saltaire, Timothy Taylors Landlord and a guest, cheerful attentive staff, open fires, small back conservatory overlooking beer garden; children welcome, no dogs inside, open all day. *(Gordon and Margaret Ormondroyd, John and Eleanor Holdsworth)*

CONEYTHORPE SE3958

★**Tiger** (01423) 863632
2.3 miles from A1(M) junction 47; A59 towards York, then village signposted (and brown sign to Tiger Inn); bear left at brown sign in Flaxby; HG5 0RY Spreading red-carpeted bar with hundreds of pewter tankards hanging from painted joists, padded wall seats, pews and settles around sturdy scrubbed tables, old prints, china figurines in one arched alcove, open fire, more formal back dining area, good sensibly priced food from pub favourites up including set deals, June lobster festival, well kept Black Sheep Bitter, Timothy Taylors Landlord and extensive range of wines, friendly helpful staff; background music; children welcome, picnic-sets on front gravel terrace and on small green opposite, open (and food) all day. *(John and Eleanor Holdsworth, Les and Sandra Brown)*

COXWOLD SE5377

Fauconberg Arms (01347) 868214
Off A170 Thirsk–Helmsley, via Kilburn or Wass; easily found off A19 too; YO61 4AD 17th-c village pub under new ownership; heavily beamed flagstoned bar, log fires in both linked areas (one in unusual arched fireplace in broad low inglenook), some attractive oak chairs made by local craftsmen alongside more usual pub furnishings, old local photographs and copper implements, Theakstons and a couple of guests, well liked traditional home-cooked food with some themed nights, friendly service, elegant dining room; monthly quiz night, live music some weekends, pool, free wi-fi; children welcome, dogs in bar, views from terrace over fields to Byland Abbey (EH), picnic-sets on front cobbles, eight comfortable bedrooms, open all day Fri-Sun. *(Richard Kennell)*

CROPTON SE7588

New Inn (01751) 417330
Village signposted off A170 W of Pickering; YO18 8HH Modernised village pub with own Great Yorkshire beers and guests (can tour brewery Weds-Sat lunchtime for £7.50 – includes a pint); public bar with plush seating, panelling and small fire, downstairs conservatory (doubles as visitor centre at busy times) and elegant restaurant with local artwork, fairly straightforward food from sandwiches up, friendly staff; background music, TV, games machine, darts and pool; well behaved children and dogs (in bar) welcome, garden and brewery shop, bedrooms, open all day. *(Nick and Meriel Cox)*

DACRE BANKS SE1961

★**Royal Oak** (01423) 780200
B6451 S of Pateley Bridge; HG3 4EN Popular 18th-c stone pub with lovely Nidderdale views from the back; good

traditional food (not Sun or Mon evenings) along with daily specials and some seafood events, attentive friendly staff, half a dozen well kept changing ales and good choice of wines and gins, beams and panelling, log-fire dining room, games room with darts, dominoes and pool; background music, TV, free wi-fi; children welcome in eating areas, no dogs, seats on front terrace and in back garden, three bedrooms, big breakfast, open all day. *(Max Simons)*

DANBY NZ7008

Duke of Wellington (01287) 660351

West Lane; YO21 2LY 18th-c creeper-clad inn overlooking village green; usually four well kept ales such as Daleside, enjoyable home-made food from shortish menu; children and dogs (in main bar) welcome, clean tidy bedrooms, closed Mon lunchtime, open all day Fri-Sun. *(Lindy Andrews)*

DARLEY SE1961

Wellington Inn (01423) 780362

B6451; Darley Head; HG3 2QQ Extended roadside stone inn with fine Nidderdale views; beams and big open fire in bar, modern restaurant with light wood floor and small conservatory, enjoyable freshly made food from sandwiches up, Sun set lunch, well kept Black Sheep, Timothy Taylors and Tetleys, helpful friendly staff; children and dogs (in bar) welcome, seats on large grassed area, 12 bedrooms, good breakfast, open all day. *(Simon Sharpe)*

DEWSBURY SE2622

Huntsman (01924) 275700

Walker Cottages, Chidswell Lane, Shaw Cross – pub signed; WF12 7SW Cosy low-beamed converted cottages alongside urban-fringe farm; original features including an old range in the snug, agricultural bric-a-brac, brassware, plates and bottles on delft shelving, blazing woodburner, small front extension, four local beers such as Bosuns, Partners, Spire and Timothy Taylors, well priced traditional home-made food (Thurs-Sat, till 4pm Sun), friendly staff and nice relaxed atmosphere; children welcome, no dogs inside, open all day Fri-Sun, closed Mon and lunchtimes Tues, Weds. *(Michael Butler)*

DEWSBURY SE2421

★**West Riding Licensed Refreshment Rooms** (01924) 459193

Station (Platform 2), Wellington Road; WF13 1HF Convivial three-room early Victorian station bar, nine well kept changing ales, foreign bottled beers and farm ciders, good value food such as burgers and pizzas, friendly staff, lots of railway memorabilia and pictures, coal fire; juke box and live music; children till 7pm in two end rooms, disabled access, on Transpennine Real Ale Trail, open all day. *(Rosie and John Moore)*

DONCASTER SE5702

Corner Pin (01302) 340670

St Sepulchre Gate West, Cleveland Street; DN1 3AH Traditional corner pub with plush beamed lounge and cheery public bar, six well kept ales and good value traditional home-made food (not Mon-Thurs) including popular Sun lunch; juke box, TV, Sun quiz; children welcome, seats on back decking, open all day. *(Gus Swan)*

DOWNHOLME SE1197

★**Bolton Arms** (01748) 823716

Village signposted just off A6108 Leyburn–Richmond; DL11 6AE Stone-built pub with wonderful Swaledale views from garden and dining conservatory; simply furnished carpeted bar down a few steps with two smallish linked areas, plush wall banquettes, collection of gleaming brass and few small country pictures, log fire in neat fireplace, ales such as Timothy Taylors and Wensleydale, ten wines by the glass and eight malt whiskies, good food from lunchtime baguettes up; background music, free wi-fi; children welcome, two bedrooms sharing bathroom, closed Tues lunchtime. *(Patricia Hawkins, Caroline Sullivan)*

EASINGWOLD SE5270

★**George** (01347) 821698

Market Place; YO61 3AD Neat market town hotel (former 18th-c coaching inn) with slightly old-fashioned feel and popular with older customers; well kept Black Sheep, Timothy Taylors and a guest, good food in bar and restaurant from sandwiches/panini to daily specials, smaller appetites catered for, helpful cheerful service; soft background music, free wi-fi; children welcome, no dogs, disabled access, pleasant bedrooms and good breakfast, open all day. *(Paul Faraday)*

EAST MARTON SD9050

Cross Keys (01282) 844326

A59 Gisburn–Skipton; BD23 3LP Spacious 17th-c pub behind small green looking down on Leeds & Liverpool Canal; black beams, bare boards and patterned carpet, woodburner in big stone fireplace, good generous food from hot and cold sandwiches, sharing plates and pub favourites up, well kept Copper Dragon and guests, friendly service, further dining area down steps; background music; children, walkers and dogs welcome, picnic-sets on front deck, near Pennine Way, closed Mon and Tues in winter, otherwise open all day till 9pm (9.30pm Sat, 6pm Sun). *(John and Eleanor Holdsworth)*

EAST MORTON SE0941

Busfeild Arms (01274) 563169

Main Road; BD20 5SP Attractive 19th-c stone-built village pub (originally a school); traditionally furnished beamed and flagstoned bar with woodburner, Saltaire,

Timothy Taylors, Tetleys and a guest, popular fairly priced food from sandwiches/ciabattas up including early bird deal (5.30-6.30pm), efficient cheerful service, restaurant; Thurs quiz, live music Sat, sports TV, free wi-fi; children welcome, picnic-sets on front terrace, three bedrooms, open all day, food till 6pm Sun. *(Gordon and Margaret Ormondroyd, John and Eleanor Holdsworth)*

EAST WITTON SE1487

★**Cover Bridge Inn** (01969) 623250
A6108 out towards Middleham; DL8 4SQ Cosy and welcoming 16th-c flagstoned country local; good choice of well kept yorkshire-brewed ales and enjoyable generously served pub food at sensible prices, small restaurant, roaring fires; children and dogs welcome, riverside garden with play area, three bedrooms, open all day. *(Patricia Healey)*

EGTON NZ8006

★**Wheatsheaf** (01947) 895271
Village centre; YO21 1TZ 19th-c village pub of real character; interesting pictures and collectables in small bare-boards bar with fire in old range, very good generously served food including daily specials, friendly service, Black Sheep, Timothy Taylors Landlord and a summer guest, several wines by the glass, restaurant; four bedrooms and adjacent cottage, open all day weekends (no food Sun evening), closed Mon. *(Nick Sharpe)*

EGTON BRIDGE NZ8005

Horseshoe (01947) 895245
Village signed off A171 W of Whitby; YO21 1XE Attractively placed 18th-c stone inn; open fires and woodburners, high-backed built-in winged settles, wall seats and spindleback chairs, various odds and ends including a big stuffed trout (caught nearby in 1913), Theakstons Best and three guests, popular food using their own eggs and vegetables and locally sourced meat; background and some live music, free wi-fi; children welcome, dogs in side bar during mealtimes, seats on quiet terrace in nice mature garden by small River Esk, good walks (on Coast to Coast path), six bedrooms, open all day, food all day Sun till 7pm. *(Freddie and Sarah Banks)*

EGTON BRIDGE NZ8005

★**Postgate** (01947) 895241
Village signed off A171 W of Whitby; YO21 1UX Moorland village pub next to railway station; good imaginative food at fair prices including fresh local fish (lots of blackboard menus), well kept Black Sheep and a guest, friendly staff, traditional quarry-tiled bar with beams, panelled dado and coal fire in antique range, elegant restaurant; children and dogs welcome, walled front garden with picnic-sets either side of brick path, three comfortable bedrooms. *(John Harris)*

EMBSAY SE0053

Elm Tree (01756) 790717
Elm Tree Square; BD23 6RB Popular open-plan beamed village pub; hearty helpings of good value food including blackboard specials, four well kept ales such as Tetleys and Timothy Taylors, cheerful young staff; comfortable bedrooms, handy for Embsay & Bolton Abbey Steam Railway, open all day weekends. *(Toby Jones)*

FACEBY NZ4903

Sutton Arms (01642) 700382
Mill Lane/Bank Lane; TS9 7BW Welcoming village dining pub at foot of Cleveland Hills, clean, comfortable and cosy, with low beamed central bar flanked by eating areas, highly regarded freshly made food (best to book) from pub favourites to more restauranty choices including excellent steaks, well kept ales and good selection of wines, friendly attentive service; tables on tiered front deck, simply furnished but well appointed bedrooms, good hearty breakfast, closed Sun evening, Mon, Tues and lunchtimes apart from Sun. *(Michael Doswell)*

FEARBY SE1980

Black Swan (01765) 689477
Keld Bank; HG4 4NF Refurbished and extended country pub; beamed bar with dining area to the right, woodburner in pale stone fireplace, Black Sheep, Theakstons and a couple of regional summer guests, several wines by the glass and good food from varied menu including daily specials (seafood and game festivals), friendly helpful service, lovely valley views from back restaurant (more rustic in style); children welcome till 7pm, dogs in bar, 14 modern bedrooms (12 in annexe), camping, open all day summer (from 3pm weekdays, all day weekends in winter). *(M and GR)*

FERRENSBY SE3660

★**General Tarleton** (01423) 340284
A655 N of Knaresborough; HG5 0PZ Carefully renovated 18th-c coaching inn, more restaurant-with-rooms than pub, but there's an informal bar with sofas and woodburner serving well kept Black Sheep, Timothy Taylors Landlord and a dozen wines by the glass; other open-plan rooms with low beams, exposed stonework and brick pillars creating alcoves, dark leather high-backed dining chairs around wooden tables; first

Half pints: by law, a pub should not charge more for half a pint than half the price of a full pint, unless it shows that half-pint price on its price list.

class modern cooking from owner-chef along with more traditional food and children's menu, friendly well trained staff; seats in covered courtyard and tree-lined garden, pretty country views, 13 stylish bedrooms, good breakfast. *(Peter and Anne Hollindale, Janet and Peter Race, WAH)*

FILEY TA1180

Bonhommes (01723) 515325
The Crescent; YO14 9JH Friendly old-fashioned bustling bar with up to five well kept ales and four ciders, good value food (not Sun evening) including home-made pizzas; live music, karaoke, bingo and quiz nights; children and dogs welcome, open all day. *(Graham Smart)*

FINGHALL SE1889

★**Queens Head** (01677) 450259
Off A684 E of Leyburn; DL8 5ND Welcoming dining pub dating from the 1700s; log fire either end of low-beamed carpeted bar divided by stone archway, settles making stalls around big tables, four real ales such as Theakstons and Wensleydale, good food from deli boards and traditional favourites up including lunchtime/evening set menus, efficient service, extended dining room with fine country views; children welcome, no dogs inside, disabled access/facilities, back garden with decking (same view), three bedrooms, may open all day on busy weekends. *(Clive and Fran Dutson, Peter Smith and Judith Brown)*

GARGRAVE SD9253

Masons Arms (01756) 749510
Church Street/Marton Road (off A65 NW of Skipton); BD23 3NL Traditional beamed pub with welcoming local atmosphere; opened-up interior divided into bar, lounge and restaurant, log fire, ample helpings of enjoyable home-made food at very fair prices, well kept ales such as Timothy Taylors and Tetleys from ornate counter, friendly efficient staff; live acoustic music first Fri of month in winter, quiz nights, darts; children and dogs welcome, tables out behind overlooking own bowling green, charming village on Pennine Way and not far from Leeds & Liverpool Canal, six barn conversion bedrooms, open (and food) all day. *(Ted and Mary Bates)*

GIGGLESWICK SD8164

Black Horse (01729) 822506
Church Street – take care with the car park; BD24 0BE Hospitable licensees at this 17th-c village pub prettily set by church; cosy bar with gleaming copper and brass, bric-a-brac and coal-effect fire, good value generously served food, well kept Settle ales and a beer badged for them, quick friendly service, intimate dining room; piano (often played), quiz nights; children welcome till 9pm, no dogs (the resident doberman is Trevor), heated back terrace and smokers' shelter, reasonably priced bedrooms, good breakfast, open all day weekends, closed Mon. *(Jim and Sue James)*

GIGGLESWICK SD8164

Harts Head (01729) 822086
Belle Hill; BD24 0BA Refurbished 18th-c village inn under same owners as the Plough at Lupton (see Cumbria Main Entries); bar/lounge and restaurant, up to half a dozen well kept ales including Black Sheep, good food from varied menu, friendly helpful staff; children and dogs (in bar) welcome, picnic-sets on sloping lawn, bedrooms, open (and food) all day. *(Julian Richardson)*

GILLAMOOR SE6890

★**Royal Oak** (01751) 431414
Off A170 in Kirkbymoorside; YO62 7HX 18th-c stone-built dining pub in attractive village; good food at sensible prices including vegetarian options and daily specials, two-course lunch deal Mon-Sat, friendly staff, ales such as Black Sheep and Copper Dragon, reasonably priced wines, roomy bar with heavy dark beams, log fires in two tall stone fireplaces (one with old kitchen range), overspill dining room where dogs allowed; children welcome, eight comfortable modern bedrooms, good breakfast, handy for Bransdale Moor walks, open all day. *(Giles and Suzie Nunn)*

GILLING EAST SE6176

★**Fairfax Arms** (01439) 788212
Main Street (B1363, off A170 via Oswaldkirk); YO62 4JH Smartly presented pub in pleasant village; beamed bar with woodburner, Black Sheep, Tetleys and a couple of local guests from handsome oak counter, interesting wines by the glass, two-part carpeted dining room, good modern food (can be pricey) along with sandwiches and pub favourites, neat attentive staff, orangery and outside seating area by floodlit roadside stream; well placed for Howardian Hills and North York Moors, comfortable up-to-date bedrooms, good breakfast, open all day, food till 7pm Sun. *(John Coatsworth)*

GILLING WEST NZ1805

White Swan (01748) 825122
High Street (B6274 just N of Richmond); DL10 5JG Welcoming 17th-c family-run village inn with open-plan bar and dining room, log fires, well kept ales including a house beer brewed by Mithril, enjoyable home-made food from yorkshire tapas, through burgers and fresh fish to steaks, Sat brunch, friendly accommodating staff; live music; children and dogs welcome, tables in courtyard, bedrooms, open all day. *(Victoria and Len Meadows)*

GOATHLAND NZ8200

Mallyan Spout Hotel (01947) 896486 *Opposite church; YO22 5AN* Late 19th-c creeper-clad stone hotel; two bars and three spacious lounges, open fires, popular fairly priced food from pub favourites up, Black Sheep and a guest such as Timothy Taylors, good choice of wines and malt whiskies, afternoon teas, friendly helpful staff, smart restaurant (separate menu); well behaved children welcome, dogs in one bar, lovely gardens and views, handy for namesake waterfall, 20 comfortable bedrooms, good breakfast, open all day. *(Angela and Martin Kendall)*

GOODMANHAM SE8943

Goodmanham Arms (01430) 873849
Main Street; YO43 3JA Unpretentious little red-brick country pub (not to everyone's taste) with three traditional linked areas; beam-and-plank ceilings, some red and black floor tiles, mix of new and old furniture and plenty of interesting odds and ends, even a Harley-Davidson, seven real ales – three from on-site All Hallows microbrewery, unfussy food from italian owner (no starters), maybe a winter casserole cooked over the open fire, evening meals served 5-7pm Mon (steak and pies) and Fri only; folk night first Thurs of month, jazz/blues third Thurs, quiz every other Weds; children welcome, no dogs during food times, good walks (on Wolds Way), open all day. *(Simon and Sue Lamb)*

GRANGE MOOR SE2215

Kaye Arms (01924) 840228
Wakefield Road (A642); WF4 4BG Smartly updated dining pub divided into three distinct areas; popular good value food including meal deal for two (not Sat evening, Sun), well kept ales such as Black Sheep and plenty of wines by the glass, efficient friendly service; children welcome, handy for National Coal Mining Museum, open all day weekends, food till 7pm Sun. *(Gordon and Margaret Ormondroyd)*

GRASSINGTON SE0064

Foresters Arms (01756) 752349
Main Street; BD23 5AA Comfortable opened-up coaching inn with friendly bustling atmosphere; six well kept regional ales such as Black Sheep and Tetleys, good hearty food (smaller appetites catered for too) including range of pizzas delivered by dumb waiter from upstairs kitchen, efficient cheerful service, log fires; popular Mon quiz, sports TV, darts and pool; children, walkers and dogs welcome, a few tables out at front, seven affordable bedrooms, good breakfast, open all day, food all day weekends. *(M J Winterton)*

GREAT AYTON NZ5610

Royal Oak (01642) 722361
Off A173 – follow village signs; High Green; TS9 6BW Popular early 18th-c village inn with good fairly priced food including blackboard specials, meal deals and themed nights, four well kept ales such as Timothy Taylors and Theakstons, bar with log fire, beam-and-plank ceiling and bulgy old partly panelled stone walls, traditional furnishings including antique settles, pleasant views of elegant green from bay windows, two linked dining rooms; Sun quiz and occasional live music; children welcome, dogs in bar, comfortable refurbished bedrooms, handy for Cleveland Way, open (and food) all day. *(Tony and Wendy Hobden)*

GREAT BROUGHTON NZ5405

Bay Horse (01642) 712319
High Street; TS9 7HA Big creeper-clad dining pub in attractive village; wide choice of food including blackboard specials and good value set lunch, friendly attentive service, real ales such as Camerons and Jennings, restaurant; children welcome (under-5s till 8pm), seats outside, open (and food) all day Sat. *(Bob and Melissa Wyatt)*

GREAT HABTON SE7576

★**Grapes** (01653) 669166
Corner of Habton Lane and Kirby Misperton Lane; YO17 6TU Popular and genuinely welcoming beamed dining pub in small village, homely and cosy, with good cooking including fresh local fish and game, Marstons-related ales, open fire, small public bar with darts and TV; background music; a few roadside picnic-sets, nice walks, open all day Sun, closed Mon and weekday lunchtimes. *(Francis and Mandy Robertson)*

HALIFAX SE0925

Mill (01422) 647494
Dean Clough; HX3 5AX Recently opened bar in former carpet mill; good choice of craft beers, wines and cocktails, enjoyable food from italian leaning menu including good pizzas, friendly efficient service; background music; handy for Northern Broadsides theatre, closed Sun and 2-5pm Mon and Tues, otherwise open all day. *(Caroline and Oliver Sterling)*

HALIFAX SE0924

Three Pigeons (01422) 347001
Sun Fold, South Parade; off Church Street; HX1 2LX Carefully restored, four-room 1930s pub (Grade II listed); art deco fittings, ceiling painting in octagonal main area, original flooring, panelling and tiled fireplaces, range of Ossett beers and guests including related Fernandes and Rat, good pies, friendly chatty staff; tables outside, handy for Eureka! museum and Shay Stadium (pub very busy on match days), open all day Fri-Sun, otherwise from 4pm. *(Toby Jones)*

HARDRAW SD8691

Green Dragon (01969) 667392
Village signed off A684; DL8 3LZ Traditional dales pub (under new management) dating from 13th c and full of character; stripped stone, antique settles and other old furniture on flagstones, lots of pictures and bric-a-brac, low-beamed snug with fire in old iron range, another in

big main bar, five well kept ales including Timothy Taylors, Theakstons and Yorkshire Dales, enjoyable pubby food, small restaurant; children and dogs welcome, tables in attractive courtyard, bedrooms, bunkhouse and self-catering, next to Hardraw Force (England's highest single-drop waterfall), open all day, but may shut early if quiet. *(D J and P M Taylor)*

HAROME SE6482

★**Star** (01439) 770397

High Street; village signed S of A170, E of Helmsley; YO62 5JE Pretty 14th-c thatched pub-restaurant; bar with bowed beam-and-plank ceiling, plenty of bric-a-brac and interesting furniture including Robert 'Mouseman' Thompson pieces, well polished tiled kitchen range, log fire, three changing ales and plenty of wines by the glass, smart restaurant for chef-owner's highly regarded inventive cooking (not cheap), also snacks in cocktail bar and a coffee loft in the eaves, well trained helpful staff; background music; children welcome, seats on sheltered front terrace, more in garden, nine bedrooms (some quirky touches) in building across road, very good breakfast, open all day Sun, closed Mon lunchtime. *(John and Penny Wildon)*

HARPHAM TA0961

St Quintin Arms (01262) 490329

Main Street; YO25 4QY Comfortable old village pub with enjoyable reasonably priced home-made food including good range of specials, well kept Theakston and Wold Top, efficient friendly service, bar and small dining room; sports TV, daily papers; children welcome, sheltered garden with pond, on National Cycle Route 1, three bedrooms, open all day Sun, closed lunchtimes Mon and Tues. *(Paul Faraday)*

HARROGATE SE3155

Coach & Horses (01423) 561802

West Park; HG1 1BJ Friendly bustling pub with up to eight good yorkshire-brewed ales, 80 malt whiskies and over 30 gins, enjoyable good value lunchtime food plus some themed evenings, comfortable interior arranged around central bar with booths and other cosy areas; regular Fri charity raffle, Sun quiz; no children or dogs, open all day. *(Rosie and John Moore)*

HARROGATE SE2955

★**Hales** (01423) 725570

Crescent Road; HG1 2RS Classic Victorian décor in 18th-c gas-lit local close to the Pump Rooms; leather seats in alcoves, lots of pictures and stuffed birds, comfortable saloon and tiny snug, half a dozen ales including a house beer from Daleside, simple good value lunchtime food (not Mon), friendly helpful staff; open all day (till 1am Thurs-Sat) and can get lively weekend evenings. *(Monty Green)*

HARROGATE SE2955

Old Bell (01423) 507930

Royal Parade; HG1 2SZ Refurbished Market Town Tavern with eight real ales, craft beers and good selection of wines and gins, friendly helpful staff, fairly traditional food from sandwiches up, mix of furniture including iron-framed tables and leather tub chairs on wood floors, Anaglypta dado, servery made from an old mahogany dresser, some vintage sweet shop ads, further seating upstairs; children (if eating) and dogs welcome, open (and food) all day. *(Steve Whalley)*

HAWES SD8789

White Hart (01969) 667214

Main Street; DL8 3QL Welcoming 16th-c coaching inn on cobbled street; emphasis on good fairly priced food, but also at least four well kept regional ales, friendly quick service, bar with fire in antique range, daily papers, restaurant; children and dogs welcome, bedrooms, open all day. *(WAH)*

HEADINGLEY SE2736

Arcadia (0113) 274 5599

Arndale Centre; LS6 2UE Glass-fronted Market Town Tavern in former bank; eight changing regional ales, a couple of craft kegs and over 100 bottled beers, good range of wines too, friendly knowledgeable staff, snacky food including good local cheese, stairs to mezzanine; no children; open all day. *(Peter Smith and Judith Brown)*

HEATH SE3520

Kings Arms (01924) 377527

Village signposted from A655 Wakefield–Normanton – or, more directly, turn off to the left opposite Horse & Groom; WF1 5SL Popular old-fashioned gas-lit pub of genuine character; fire in black range (long row of smoothing irons on the mantelpiece), plain elm stools, built-in oak settles and dark panelling, well kept Ossett beers (one named for the pub) and guests, standard food (all day Fri and Sat, till 7pm Sun), more comfortable extension preserving original style, two other small flagstoned rooms and a conservatory; summer folk events, Tues quiz, free wi-fi; children and dogs (in bar) welcome, benches out at front facing village green (surrounded by fine 19th-c stone merchants' houses), picnic-sets on side lawn and in nice walled garden, usually open all day (may shut early if quiet). *(Michael Butler)*

HEBDEN SE0263

Clarendon (01756) 752446

B6265; BD23 5DE Well cared-for modernised inn surrounded by wonderful moorland walking country; bar, snug and restaurant, open fire, well kept ales such as Black Sheep, Timothy Taylors and Wensleydale, good range of enjoyable food (till 7pm Sun) from pubby choices up including local game and blackboard specials, cheerful relaxed atmosphere; Sun quiz; children and dogs (in bar) welcome, farm shop, five bedrooms, open all day weekends. *(John and Eleanor Holdsworth, Hunter and Christine Wright, B and M Kendall)*

HEBDEN BRIDGE SD9922
Hinchcliffe Arms (01422) 883256
Off B6138; HX7 5TA Tucked-away stone-built pub in great walking country on the Calderdale Way and near Stoodley Pike; open-plan bar to the left, restaurant on right, well kept Lees and a couple of local guests, very good food from new chef-owner served by friendly staff; children, dogs (in bar) and walkers welcome, a few seats out at front, picturesque setting close to stream and Victorian church, open (and food) all day, Sun till 9pm (6pm). *(John and Eleanor Holdsworth)*

HEBDEN BRIDGE SD9927
Old Gate (01422) 843993
Oldgate; HX7 8JP Popular bar-restaurant with wide choice of good food served from 10am breakfast on, nine well kept ales, plenty of bottled beers and good range of wines by the glass including champagne, helpful friendly service, upstairs room for comedy club and live music; children welcome, tables outside, open (and food) all day. *(WAH)*

HEBDEN BRIDGE SD9827
Stubbing Wharf (01422) 844107
About a mile W; HX7 6LU Friendly well presented pub in good spot sandwiched between the Rochdale Canal and River Calder; popular good value food from sandwiches and light meals up, weekday two-course deal till 7pm, half a dozen regional ales such as Acorn, Kelham Island and Rudgate kept well, proper ciders, cheerful hard-working young staff; well behaved children and dogs welcome, adjacent moorings, open (and food) all day. *(Steve Whalley)*

HECKMONDWIKE SE2223
Old Hall (01924) 404774
New North Road (B6117); WF16 9DP Interesting largely 15th-c building, Grade I listed and childhood home of Joseph Priestley who discovered oxygen; lots of beams and timbers, mullioned windows and stripped masonry, snug low-ceilinged alcoves, upper gallery room, good value Sam Smiths beers and enjoyable inexpensive food (not Sun evening), friendly helpful service; children (till 7pm) and dogs welcome, open all day. *(Mark and Sian Edwards)*

HELMSLEY SE6183
Feathers (01439) 770275
Market Place; YO62 5BH Substantial old stone inn overlooking the market square; enjoyable food (all day Sat) from sandwiches to popular Sun carvery, well kept Black Sheep, Tetleys and a local guest, good friendly service, several rooms with comfortable seats, walnut and oak tables (some by Robert 'Mouseman' Thompson – as is the bar counter), flagstones or tartan carpet, heavy medieval beams and huge inglenook; children and dogs (in bar) welcome, terrace tables, 22 bedrooms, open all day. *(Tony and Wendy Hobden)*

HELWITH BRIDGE SD8169
Helwith Bridge Inn (01729) 860220
Off B6479 N of Stainforth; BD24 0EH Friendly unpretentious village local popular with walkers; five well kept ales in flagstoned bar, enjoyable reasonably priced pub food including Thurs steak night, dining room with light wood furniture on bare boards; free wi-fi; children and dogs welcome, camping and bunkhouse, by River Ribble and Settle–Carlisle railway, open all day, food all day weekends. *(Geoff and Anne Marston)*

HEPWORTH SE1606
Butchers Arms (01484) 687147
Village signposted off A616 SE of Holmfirth; Towngate; HD9 1TE Old country dining pub with french-influenced cooking including themed evenings, three well kept regional ales, decent wines by the glass and cocktails, flagstones by counter, bare boards elsewhere, log fire, low beams (handsomely carved in room on right); wine tasting evenings, live music and quiz nights; children, walkers and dogs welcome, enclosed garden with pizza oven, closed Mon, otherwise open (and food) all day (till 7pm Sun). *(Graham Smart)*

HIGH HOYLAND SE2710
Cherry Tree (01226) 382541
Bank End Lane; 3 miles W of M1 junction 38; S75 4BE Split-level whitewashed village pub; five well kept ales including Acorn Barnsley Bitter, Black Sheep Bitter and Bradfield Farmers Blonde, good range of enjoyable generously served food (not Sun evening), competitive prices and friendly young staff, beams and open fire, dining areas each end of bar and separate small restaurant; background music; children and dogs welcome, front roadside picnic-sets with lovely views over Cannon Hall Country Park, open all day. *(Ted and Mary Bates)*

HOLMBRIDGE SE1206
Bridge (01484) 687652
Woodhead Road; HD9 2NQ Modernised old Yorkstone pub with own beers from on-site microbrewery plus guests, good variety of well liked food (all day Sat, till 7.30pm Sun, not Mon evening) including vegetarian and gluten-free choices, Weds pie and pint night, Thurs steak and wine deal, good friendly service; Tues quiz, free wi-fi; children welcome, outside seating and

wendy house, car park over road, open all day (till 8.30pm Mon). *(Martin Day)*

HOLMFIRTH SD1408

Nook (01484) 681568

Victoria Square/South Lane; HD9 2DN Friendly tucked-away 18th-c stone local run by same family for two generations; own-brew beers and guests, low-priced home-made pubby food including good burgers, no-frills bar areas with flagstones and quarry tiles, big open fire; juke box, pool; heated streamside terrace, bedrooms, open (and food) all day. *(Jim and Sue James)*

HOPPERTON SE4256

Masons (01423) 330442

Hopperton Street; HG5 8NX Village dining pub with good food from standards up, a couple of real ales and excellent choice of gins, friendly helpful staff, snug pubby bar, extended restaurant with high-backed leather chairs around mix of tables on tiled floor, open fires; background music, free wi-fi; children and dogs (in bar) welcome, closed Mon and Tues, no food Sun evening. *(Julian Richardson)*

HORBURY SE2918

Boons (01924) 277267

Queen Street; WF4 6LP Comfortably unpretentious flagstoned local, chatty and relaxed, with Black Sheep, Clarks, Timothy Taylors and several quickly changing guests, pleasant young staff, no food or children, rugby league memorabilia, warm fire, back tap room with pool and TV; courtyard tables, open all day. *(Michael Butler)*

HORBURY SE2918

Cricketers (01924) 267032

Cluntergate; WF4 5AG Welcoming red-brick Edwardian pub; Bosuns Blonde, Timothy Taylors Landlord and six guests, also craft beers such as BrewDog, real cider and good selection of spirits, reasonably priced cheeseboards and meze platters; regular beer festivals and tap takeovers; open all day Fri-Sun, from 4pm other days. *(Monica and Steph Evans)*

HORSFORTH SE2438

Town Street Tavern (0113) 281 9996

Town Street; LS18 4RJ Market Town Tavern with eight well kept ales and lots of draught/bottled continental beers, good food in small bar or upstairs restaurant, friendly helpful service; children and dogs (downstairs) welcome, small terrace, open all day, food all day Fri, Sat, till 6pm Sun. *(Camilla and Jose Ferrera)*

HUBBERHOLME SD9278

★**George** (01756) 760223

Dubbs Lane; BD23 5JE Ancient little dales inn, beautifully placed and run by warmly welcoming licensees; heavy beams, flagstones and stripped stone, enjoyable fairly priced home-made food (booking advised) from lunchtime sandwiches (not Sun) up, Mon pie night, well kept Black Sheep and three guests, open fire, perpetual candle on bar; outside lavatories; children allowed in dining area, well-behaved dogs in bar (pub jack russell is George), terrace seating, River Wharfe fishing rights, six comfortable clean bedrooms (three in annexe), good breakfast, open all day Sat, till 5pm Sun, closed Mon lunchtime, Tues. *(Steve Lumb, Hunter and Christine Wright)*

HUDDERSFIELD SE1416

Grove (01484) 430113

Spring Grove Street; HD1 4BP Friendly two-bar pub with very wide selection of bottled beers (some gluten-free), 19 well kept/priced ales including Oakham and Thornbridge, 120 malt whiskies and 60 vodkas, also real cider, knowledgeable staff, no food but interesting choice of snacks; art gallery; children and dogs welcome, back terrace, open 12-11pm Fri-Sun, from 2pm other days. *(Max Simons)*

HUDDERSFIELD SE1416

Kings Head (01484) 511058

Station, St Georges Square; HD1 1JF Friendly well run pub in renovated neoclassical Victorian station building; spacious high-ceilinged main bar with original tiled floor, other rooms off, ten well kept beers including Magic Rock and Timothy Taylors, no food apart from sandwiches/cobs; regular live music, Jimi Hendrix pub sign; dogs welcome, disabled access via platform 1, open all day. *(Lindy Andrews)*

HUDDERSFIELD SE1416

Rat & Ratchet (01484) 542400

Chapel Hill; HD1 3EB Popular split-level pub with own-brew beers and several guests including Ossett, good range of ciders/perries too, pork pies and sausage rolls, friendly staff; quiz nights and live music; open all day Fri-Sun, from 3pm other days. *(Val and Malcolm Travers)*

HUDDERSFIELD SE1417

Slubbers Arms (01484) 429032

Halifax Old Road; HD1 6HW Friendly V-shaped traditional three-room pub; good range of beers including Timothy Taylors from horseshoe bar, pie-and-peas menu, black and white photographs and old wartime posters, warm fire, games room; well behaved dogs welcome, terrace for smokers, open from 4pm Mon-Thurs, 3pm Fri, Sat, 2pm Sun. *(Edward Edmonton)*

HUDDERSFIELD SE1417

Sportsman (01484) 421929

St Johns Road; HD1 5AY Same owners as the West Riding Licensed Refreshment Rooms at Dewsbury; restored 1930s interior with lounge and two cosy side rooms, eight real ales and plenty of craft beers, friendly knowledgeable staff, pie menu served Fri-Sun; live music; dogs welcome, handy for station, open all day. *(Edward Edmonton)*

HUDDERSFIELD SE1415

Star (01484) 545443
Albert Street, Lockwood; HD1 3PJ Friendly unpretentious local with excellent range of competitively priced ales kept well by enthusiastic landlady, continental beers and real cider too, beer festivals in back marquee, open fire; open all day weekends, closed Mon and lunchtimes Tues-Fri. *(Toby Jones)*

HUDSWELL NZ1400

George & Dragon (01748) 518373
Hudswell Lane; DL11 6BL Popular community-owned village pub run by welcoming landlord; enjoyable good value home-made food from short menu plus a few daily specials, five well kept local ales and various craft kegs, friendly atmosphere; small shop and library, free wi-fi; children and dogs welcome, panoramic Swaledale views from back terrace, open all day weekends, no food Sun evening. *(Colin and Daniel Gibbs)*

HULL TA1028

★**Olde White Harte** (01482) 326363
Passage off Silver Street; HU1 1JG Dating from the 16th c with Civil War history; carved heavy beams, attractive stained glass, oak panelling and two big inglenooks with frieze of delft tiles, well kept Caledonian, Theakstons and guests from copper-topped counter, 80 or so malt whiskies; old skull (found here in the 19th c and displayed in a Perspex case); children welcome, dogs in bar, heated courtyard, open all day. *(John and Delia Franks)*

HUNMANBY TA1077

Piebald (01723) 447577
Sands Lane; E of level crossing; YO14 0LT Comfortably renovated pub with well stocked bar and separate dining room, popular generously served food featuring more than 50 different pies, up to five real ales including a house beer from Greene King, friendly helpful staff; children welcome, picnic-sets on side terrace and lawn bordering railway line, camping, open (and food) all day. *(Stephen Woad)*

HUTTON-LE-HOLE SE7089

Crown (01751) 417343
The Green; YO62 6UA Friendly village local overlooking pretty green with wandering sheep in classic coach-trip country; Black Sheep, Tetleys and a guest, decent wines by the glass and enjoyable home-made pubby food (not Sun evening), cheerful efficient service, opened-up bar with varnished woodwork, dining area; quiz first Sun of month; children and clean dogs welcome, small site available for caravans behind, Ryedale Folk Museum next door and handy for Farndale walks, open all day (but may close Mon and Tues in winter). *(Nick and Meriel Cox)*

ILKLEY SE1147

Bar t'at (01943) 608888
Cunliffe Road; LS29 9DZ Extended and refurbished Market Town Tavern with eight well kept mainly local ales and good wine and bottled beer choice, enjoyable well priced pubby food from sandwiches and snacks up, friendly service, candlelit cellar dining area; upstairs loos; dogs welcome, back terrace with heated canopy, open (and food) all day, kitchen closes 6pm Sun. *(David and Leone Lawson)*

ILKLEY SE1147

Flying Duck (01943) 609587
Church Street; LS29 9DS Old stone pub with nine well kept beers including own Wharfedale ales brewed in barn behind, tasters offered by friendly knowledgeable staff, shortish choice of enjoyable good value food including selection of light dishes (perfect for sharing), beamed and flagstoned bar with woodburner in large stone fireplace; Tues quiz; children and dogs welcome, first-floor terrace, open all day (till late Thurs-Sat), no food weekend evenings or Mon. *(Michael Butler)*

KEIGHLEY SE0641

Boltmakers Arms (01535) 661936
East Parade; BD21 5HX Small open-plan split-level character local, friendly and bustling, with full Timothy Taylors range and a guest kept well, traditional cider and several malt whiskies, lots to look at including brewing pictures and celebrity photos, coal fire; Tues quiz, Weds live music, sports TV; small beer garden, short walk from Keighley & Worth Valley Railway, open all day. *(Mark and Sian Edwards)*

KETTLESING SE2257

★**Queens Head** (01423) 770263
Village signposted off A59 W of Harrogate; HG3 2LB Popular stone-built pub with very good well priced traditional food; L-shaped carpeted main bar, lots of close-set cushioned dining chairs and tables, open fires, little heraldic shields on the walls along with 19th-c song sheet covers and lithographs of Queen Victoria, delft shelf of blue and white china, smaller bar on left with built-in red banquettes and cricketing prints, life-size portrait of Elizabeth I in lobby, well kept Black Sheep, Roosters and Theakstons, efficient friendly service; background music, free wi-fi; children welcome, seats in neatly kept sunny back garden, benches in

If you know a pub is ever open all day, please tell us.

front by lane, eight bedrooms, open all day Sun. *(John and Eleanor Holdsworth, Helene Grygar)*

KETTLEWELL SD9672

Blue Bell (01756) 760230

Middle Lane; BD23 5QX Roomy knocked-through former coaching inn, popular and welcoming, with well kept Theakstons, Wharfedale and plenty of guest beers, generous helpings of enjoyable pubby food, friendly helpful service, low beams and simple furnishings, old country photographs, woodburner; Sun quiz, TV, free wi-fi; children, walkers and dogs welcome, shaded picnic-sets on cobbles facing bridge over River Wharfe, seven annexe bedrooms, open (and food) all day. *(Edward Mirzoeff)*

KETTLEWELL SD9772

★**Kings Head** (01756) 761600

The Green; BD23 5RD Welcoming old pub tucked away near church; flagstoned main bar with log fire in big arched inglenook, three well kept local ales such as Dark Horse and well chosen wines, very good affordably priced food (all day Sun till 7pm) cooked by chef-landlord from pub favourites to imaginative restaurant dishes, efficient friendly service; children allowed, no dogs inside, six bedrooms (some quite small) named after kings, attractive dales village with good surrounding walks, closed Mon (Oct-end Mar), otherwise open all day. *(Lewis Canning, Martin Day, Edward Mirzoeff, B and M Kendall)*

KETTLEWELL SD9672

Racehorses (01756) 760233

B6160 N of Skipton; BD23 5QZ Comfortable and friendly two-bar inn next to River Wharf (across from the Blue Bell); tasty sensibly priced home-made food and three well kept Timothy Taylors ales, log fires, separate dining areas; children and dogs (in some parts) welcome, front and back terrace seating, pretty village well placed for Wharfedale walks, parking can be difficult, 13 good bedrooms, open all day. *(Martin Day)*

KILBURN SE5179

Forresters Arms (01347) 868386

Between A170 and A19 SW of Thirsk; YO61 4AH Welcoming beamed village inn next to the Robert 'Mouseman' Thompson furniture workshops (early examples of his work in both bars); roaring fires, well kept local ales and good choice of home-made food, restaurant; background music; children welcome, dogs in some areas, suntrap seats out in front, smokers' shelter behind, ten bedrooms, open all day from 8am. *(Michael Butler)*

KILDWICK SE0145

White Lion (01535) 632265

Priest Bank Road; off A629 Keighley–Skipton; BD20 9BH Refurbished two-bar stone pub in attractive village next to ancient church; popular food (not Sun evening) from lunchtime sandwiches up, local ales such as Black Sheep, Goose Eye and Timothy Taylors, obliging service; open mike night first Sat of month; well behaved children and dogs welcome, sunny garden with Aire Valley views, good walks and near Leeds & Liverpool Canal, bedrooms, open all day. *(D W Stokes)*

KIRBY HILL NZ1406

Shoulder of Mutton (01748) 822772

Off A66 NW of Scotch Corner, via Ravensworth; DL11 7JH Traditional 18th-c ivy-clad village inn; four local beers and well liked food from pub favourites up, front bar areas linking to long back restaurant, log fires; quiz last Mon of month; children and dogs (in bar) welcome, fine Holmedale views from picnic-sets behind and bedrooms (you do hear the tuneful church bell), open all day Sun, from 5pm weekdays. *(William and Sophie Renton)*

KIRKBYMOORSIDE SE6986

George & Dragon (01751) 433334

Market Place; YO62 6AA Friendly 17th-c family-run coaching inn; front bar with beams and panelling, tub seats around wooden tables on carpet or stripped wood, log fire, well kept changing ales and several malt whiskies, wide choice of enjoyable generously served bar food, good service, also a snug, bistro and more formal restaurant; background music; children welcome, seats and heaters on front and back terraces, 20 bedrooms, Weds market, open all day. *(Bob and Melissa Wyatt)*

KNAYTON SE4388

Dog & Gun (01845) 537368

Moor Road, off A19; YO7 4AZ Well cared-for family-run pub, cosy and comfortable, with roaring fire at one end, tables laid for their popular traditional home-made food (till 6pm Sun, not Tues, best to book) including blackboard specials and deals, Black Sheep and Copper Dragon, good friendly service; late summer charity music festival; children and dogs welcome, heated outside seating area, open all day weekends, closed Mon and lunchtimes Tues-Fri. *(Tony and Wendy Hobden)*

LANGTHWAITE NY0002

★**Charles Bathurst** (01748) 884567

Arkengarthdale, a mile N towards Tan Hill; DL11 6EN Busy 18th-c country inn (sister to the Punch Bowl at Low Row); strong emphasis on dining and bedrooms, but pubby feel in long bar with scrubbed pine tables and country chairs on stripped floors, snug alcoves, open fire, Black Sheep, Caledonian Deuchars IPA and a local guest, several wines by the glass and good choice of popular interesting food, cheerful helpful staff, dining room with Robert 'Mousey'

Thompson furniture and views of Scar House, several other eating areas; background music, TV, pool and darts; children welcome, dogs in bar, lovely walks from the door and views over village and Arkengarthdale, 19 smart bedrooms (best not above dining room), open all day; worth checking there are no corporate events/weddings before you visit. *(John Harris)*

LANGTHWAITE NZ0002

★**Red Lion** (01748) 884218
Just off Arkengarthdale Road, Reeth–Brough; DL11 6RE Proper pub dating from 17th c in charming dales village with ancient bridge; long-serving character landlady and homely old-fashioned atmosphere, lunchtime sandwiches, pasties and sausage rolls, a couple of well kept Black Sheep ales, Thatcher's cider, country wines, tea and coffee, well behaved children allowed lunchtime in low-ceilinged side snug, newspapers and postcards; the ladies' is a genuine bathroom; no dogs inside, a few picnic-sets out at front, good walks including circular ones from the pub – maps and guides for sale. *(Caroline and Oliver Sterling)*

LASTINGHAM SE7290

★**Blacksmiths Arms** (01751) 417247
Off A170 W of Pickering; YO62 6TL 17th-c pub opposite beautiful Saxon church in charming village; small bar with log fire in open range, tankards hanging from beams, traditional furnishings, well kept Theakstons and other regional ales, several wines by the glass and good sensibly priced home-made food (not Sun evening) including vegetarian and gluten-free choices, prompt friendly service, two dining rooms; background music, darts and board games; children, walkers and dogs welcome, seats out at front and in back beer garden, three bedrooms, open all day. *(Nick and Meriel Cox)*

LEALHOLM NZ7607

★**Board** (01947) 897279
Off A171 W of Whitby; YO21 2AJ 18th-c pub in wonderful moorland village spot by wide pool of River Esk; homely bare-boards bar on right with squashy old sofa and armchairs by big black stove, three well kept changing ales, five ciders and dozens of whiskies, good seasonal food using meat from own farm and other local produce, friendly helpful landlady; children, dogs and muddy boots welcome, secluded waterside garden with decking, bedrooms (good breakfast) and self-catering cottage, open all day. *(Geoff and Anne Marston)*

LEAVENING SE7863

Jolly Farmers (01653) 658276
Main Street; YO17 9SA Friendly bustling village local with up to five regional ales and popular good value pub food (not Mon, Tues), front bar with eating area behind, separate dining room; some live music; children and dogs welcome, open all day weekends, closed weekday lunchtimes. *(Adam Jones)*

LEEDS SE3131

★**Garden Gate** (0113) 345 1234
Whitfield Place, Hunslet; LS10 2QB Impressive Edwardian pub (Grade II* listed) owned by Leeds Brewery; their well kept ales from rare curved ceramic counter, a wealth of other fine period features in rooms off central drinking corridor including intricate glass and woodwork, art nouveau tiling, moulded ceilings and mosaic floors; some live music; dogs welcome, tables out in front, open all day. *(Glen and Patricia Fuller)*

LEEDS SE2932

★**Grove** (0113) 243 9254
Back Row, Holbeck; LS11 5PL Unspoilt and lived-in 1930s-feel local overshadowed by towering office blocks, tables and stools in main bar with marble floor, panelling and original fireplace, large back room and snug off drinking corridor, eight well kept regional ales including Daleside and Theakstons, Weston's cider, lunchtime food (not Sat, Sun), friendly staff; regular live music including folk club; dogs welcome, open all day. *(Alf and Sally Garner)*

LEEDS SE3033

Kirkstall Bridge (0113) 278 4044
Bridge Road, Headingley–Kirkstall; LS5 3BW Welcoming traditionally renovated pub by bridge over River Aire; main bare-boards bar with lots of brewerania and other rescued items from closed pubs, well kept Kirkstall beers and several guests, generous helpings of popular reasonably priced food from deli boards and pizzas up, downstairs flagstoned bar (dogs welcome here) leading out to riverside garden; Weds quiz, some live music, free wi-fi; well placed for Kirkstall Abbey, open (and food) all day, kitchen closes 5pm Sun. *(Andrew Bosi)*

LEEDS SE2932

Midnight Bell (0113) 244 5044
Water Lane, Holbeck; LS11 5QN Leeds Brewery pub on two floors in Holbeck Urban Village; their ales and guests kept well, enjoyable home-made food, friendly staff, light contemporary décor mixing with original beams and stripped brickwork; children welcome, dogs in courtyard beer garden only, open (and food) all day, kitchen shuts 7pm Sun. *(Alf and Sally Garner)*

LEEDS SE3033

Scarbrough (0113) 243 4590
Bishopgate Street, opposite station; LS1 5DY Nicholsons pub with ornate tiled façade; eight well kept changing ales served by friendly knowledgeable staff, enjoyable food including speciality pies and breakfasts; sports TV; open all day and busy lunchtime, early evening. *(Peter Smith and Judith Brown)*

LEEDS SE3033

Victoria (0113) 245 1386

Great George Street; LS1 3DL
Opulent mid-Victorian city pub; long bar with chandeliers hanging from high ornate ceiling, grand cut and etched mirrors, leather-seat booths with snob screens, other smaller rooms off, up to eight real ales from majestic servery, friendly efficient service, fairly standard food; open all day. *(Monica and Steph Evans)*

LEEDS SE3033

★Whitelocks (0113) 245 3950

Turks Head Yard, off Briggate; LS1 6HB
Classic Victorian pub full of character (if a little worn around the edges); long narrow bar with fine tiled counter, grand mirrors, mahogany and glass screens, heavy copper-topped tables and red leather seating, coal fire, a dozen well kept ales and enjoyable food; children welcome, tables in narrow courtyard, open (and food) all day, can get crowded at lunchtime. *(Freddie and Sarah Banks)*

LINTHWAITE SE1014

★Sair (01484) 842370

Lane Top, Hoyle Ing, off A62; HD7 5SG
Old-fashioned four-room pub brewing its own good value Linfit beers; pews and chairs on rough flagstones or wood floors, log-burning ranges, dominoes, cribbage and shove-ha'penny, piano and vintage rock juke box; no food or credit cards; children (till 8pm) and dogs welcome, plenty of tables out in front with fine Colne Valley views, restored Huddersfield Narrow Canal nearby, open all day Fri-Sun, otherwise from 3pm. *(Camilla and Jose Ferrera)*

LITTON SD9074

Queens Arms (01756) 770096

Off B6160 N of Grassington; BD23 5QJ
Beautifully placed 17th-c whitewashed stone pub; main bar with slate floor and beam-and-plank ceiling, old photographs on rough stone walls, coal fire, plainer carpeted dining room with woodburner, three real ales including Wharfedale and one badged for the pub, enjoyable freshly made food, friendly staff; children and dogs welcome, plenty of seats in two-tier garden, country views and good surrounding walks, four bedrooms, open all day Fri-Sun, closed Mon except bank holidays. *(Christopher Acomb)*

LOFTHOUSE SE1073

Crown (01423) 755206

Pub signed from main road; Nidderdale; HG3 5RZ Prettily placed dales inn, friendly and relaxed, with hearty simple food from sandwiches up, well kept Black Sheep and Theakstons, small public bar, comfortable dining extension where children allowed, open fire; outside gents'; dogs welcome, nice garden and good walks from the door, bedrooms. *(Mark and Sian Edwards)*

LOW BRADFIELD SK2691

Plough (0114) 285 1280

Village signposted off B6077 and B6076 NW of Sheffield; New Road; S6 6HW
Comfortably modernised old pub ideally placed for some of South Yorkshire's finest scenery; L-shaped bar with stone walls, button-back banquettes and captain's chairs, log fire in big arched fireplace, well kept Bradfield and guests, good value food from sandwiches and baked potatoes up; background music, Weds quiz, sports TV and free wi-fi; children and dogs welcome, seats on back verandah, terrace and lawn, Damflask and Agden Reservoirs close by, open (and food) all day. *(Michael Butler)*

LOW CATTON SE7053

Gold Cup (01759) 371354

Village signposted with High Catton off A166 in Stamford Bridge or A1079 at Kexby Bridge; YO41 1EA Bustling village pub under long-serving owners; cheerful neatly kept bar, plenty of smart tables and chairs on stripped-wood floors, open fire at one end, John Smiths and Theakstons kept well, enjoyable fairly priced home-cooked food (smaller appetites catered for), spacious restaurant with solid pews and tables (said to be made from a single oak), pleasant views over surrounding fields; background music, pool, free wi-fi; children and dogs (in bar) welcome, pleasant garden, paddock with ponies, pub also has fishing rights on adjacent River Derwent, open (and food) all day weekends, closed Mon lunchtime. *(Gordon and Margaret Ormondroyd, John Saville, Mark and Sian Edwards)*

LOW ROW SD9898

Punch Bowl (01748) 886233

B6270 Reeth–Muker; DL11 6PF 17th-c country inn under same ownership as the Charles Bathurst at Langthwaite; long bare-boards bar with peaceful view over Swaledale, stripped kitchen tables and a variety of seats including armchairs and sofa by woodburner, enjoyable food (menu on huge mirror), nice wines by the glass, well kept Black Sheep ales and a guest, friendly staff, separate dining room similar in style; children and dogs (in bar) welcome, wide views from terrace set above road, comfortable bedrooms, good breakfast, open all day. *(WAH)*

LUND SE9748

★Wellington (01377) 217294

Off B1248 SW of Driffield; YO25 9TE
Smart busy pub with cosy Farmers' Bar overlooking village green; beams, well polished wooden banquettes and square tables, log fire in quirky fireplace, plainer side room with flagstones and wine-theme décor, Yorkstone walkway to further room with village's Britain in Bloom awards, well kept ales including Timothy Taylors and

Theakstons, good wine list and 25 malt whiskies, highly rated well presented food (not Sun evening, Mon, and not cheap) in restaurant or bistro dining area, friendly efficient staff; background music, TV; children welcome, dogs in some areas (but ask first), disabled access/loo, picnic-tables in pretty back courtyard, open all day Sun, closed Mon lunchtime. *(Colin and Angela Boocock)*

MALTBY NZ4613

Chadwicks (01642) 590300
High Lane; TS8 0BG Beamed 19th-c pub-restaurant; first rate food including some cheaper lunchtime/early evening pub favourites, set menus and Weds steak and wine night, good knowledgeable service, a changing local ale, several gins and cocktails; wine tasting evenings; wheelchair access, seats on front terrace, closed Mon lunchtime, otherwise open all day, no food Sun evening, Mon. *(Val and Malcolm Travers)*

MANFIELD NZ2213

Crown (01325) 374243
Vicars Lane; DL2 2RF Unpretentious two-bar village local, friendly and welcoming, with seven interesting ales including Bass and Village Brewer, proper ciders and enjoyable home-made food, open fires, games room with pool and darts; occasional live music; children and dogs welcome, picnic-sets and caravan in part-lawned garden, good walks nearby, closed lunchtimes Mon-Thurs, otherwise open all day. *(Edward Edmonton)*

MARSDEN SE0411

Riverhead Brewery Tap (01484) 841270 *Peel Street, next to Co-op; just off A62 Huddersfield–Oldham; HD7 6BR* Owned by Ossett with up to ten well kept ales including Riverhead range (microbrewery visible from bare-boards bar); friendly bustling atmosphere, airy upstairs beamed restaurant with stripped tables (moors view from some) and open kitchen, good choice of enjoyable food (till 7pm Sun, just sandwiches Mon and Tues); background and occasional live music, Tues quiz; children and dogs welcome, a few tables out by river, open all day. *(Max Simons)*

MASHAM SE2281

White Bear (01765) 689319
Wellgarth, Crosshills; signed off A6108 opposite turn into town; HG4 4EN Comfortably updated beamed inn; small public bar with full Theakstons range kept well and several wines by the glass, welcoming coal fire in larger lounge, decent choice of food, from sandwiches/baguettes up, afternoon teas, friendly efficient staff, restaurant extension; background music; children and dogs (in bar) welcome, terrace tables, 14 bedrooms, open all day. *(Lindy Andrews)*

MAUNBY SE3586

Buck (01845) 587777
Off A167 S of Northallerton; YO7 4HD Brick-built dining pub in quiet out-of-the-way village by River Swale; ales such as Theakstons and York, eight wines by the glass and good food from lunchtime sandwiches and traditional choices up (shortish menu), friendly helpful service, carpeted beamed bar with comfy leather sofa and inglenook fire, more contemporary restaurant and conservatory with one huge table; children welcome, dogs in bar, closed Sun evening. *(Simon Sharpe)*

MIDDLEHAM SE1288

Richard III (01969) 623240
Market Place; DL8 4NP Traditional 17th-c beamed inn with friendly landlady and locals, cosy front bar, Black Sheep, John Smiths and Theakstons, good range of generous food cooked by landlord, back bar and restaurant, lots of racehorse pictures; sports TV; tables out by square, six bedrooms, open all day, food all day Fri-Sun. *(Peter Smith and Judith Brown)*

MIDDLEHAM SE1287

★**White Swan** (01969) 622093
Market Place; DL8 4PE Extended coaching inn opposite cobbled market square; beamed and flagstoned entrance bar with log fire, well kept Theakstons ales, nice wines by the glass and several malt whiskies, good choice of enjoyable food (all day Sun) in modern brasserie with large fireplace or back dining room, afternoon teas, friendly efficient staff; background music; children welcome, 17 comfortable bedrooms, hearty breakfast. *(Gus Swan)*

MIDDLESMOOR SE0974

Crown (01423) 755204
Top of Nidderdale Road from Pateley Bridge; HG3 5ST Remote unpretentious family-run inn with beautiful view over stone-built hamlet high in upper Nidderdale; warmly welcoming character landlord and good local atmosphere, well kept Black Sheep and guests, several whiskies and simple wholesome food, blazing fires in cosy spotless rooms, old photographs and bric-a-brac, homely dining room; children and dogs welcome, small garden, seven good value bedrooms, self-catering cottage and camping, open all day weekends. *(Nick Sharpe)*

MIDDLETON TYAS NZ2205

Shoulder of Mutton (01325) 377271
Just E of A1 Scotch Corner roundabout; DL10 6QX Welcoming old pub under newish management; three softly lit low-ceilinged rooms on different levels, good freshly made food from sharing boards and pub classics up, Thurs steak night, Black Sheep Bitter, Marston 61 Deep and a guest, decent range of wines, whiskies and gins,

friendly helpful service; quiz last Weds of month; children and dogs (in bar) welcome, a useful A1/A66 stop, open (and food) all day Sun. *(Tony Selinger)*

MIDHOPESTONES SK2399

Mustard Pot (01226) 761155

Mortimer Road, S off A616; S36 4GW Cosy and welcoming 18th-c country pub; three small rooms, beams, flagstones and exposed stonework, assorted chairs, tables and settles, two log fires, well kept ales such as Black Sheep and Timothy Taylors, several wines by the glass and generous helpings of good home-made food (special diets catered for) including lunchtime tapas-style dishes, burger night Thurs, friendly helpful service, restaurant; background music; (maybe live Fri); children and dogs welcome, seats out front and back, play area, bedrooms, open (and food) all day, kitchen closes 7pm Sun. *(Graham Kelly)*

MILLINGTON SE8351

Gait (01759) 302045

Main Street; YO42 1TX Friendly 16th-c beamed local; five well kept regional ales (July beer festival) and enjoyable straightforward home-made food, nice mix of old and newer furnishings, large map of Yorkshire on the ceiling, big inglenook log fire; live music or quiz Weds; children and dogs welcome, garden picnic-sets, appealing village in good wolds walking country, closed Mon and lunchtimes Tues-Thurs. *(David and Charlotte Green)*

MIRFIELD SE2019

Flower Pot (01924) 496939

Calder Road; WF14 8NN Comfortably refurbished three-room Ossett pub with their well kept beers and four local guests, short but enjoyable lunchtime menu including good sandwiches and locally made pies, real fires; children and dogs welcome, flowering tubs in nice riverside garden, open all day. *(Pat and Tony Martin)*

MOORSHOLM NZ6912

Jolly Sailor (01287) 660270

A171 nearly a mile E; TS12 3LN Remotely placed dining pub with good variety of enjoyable food, well kept Black Sheep and a guest, friendly staff, long beamed and stripped-stone bar, restaurant; children and dogs welcome, outside tables with views of surrounding moors, open all day. *(Graham Smart)*

MUKER SD9097

★**Farmers Arms** (01748) 886297

B6270 W of Reeth; DL11 6QG Small down-to-earth pub in beautiful valley village popular with walkers and other visitors (can get very busy); warmly welcoming, with four well kept local ales such as Wensleydale and Yorkshire Dales, good choice of wines by the glass, teas and coffees, enjoyable good value home-made food (delivered by dumb waiter from upstairs kitchen), friendly helpful service, clean interior with warm fire, simple modern pine furniture, flagstones and panelling; darts and dominoes; children, dogs and muddy boots welcome, hill views from terrace tables, self-catering apartment opposite, open all day. *(Clive and Fran Dutson, Roy and Gill Payne)*

NEWTON-ON-OUSE SE5160

★**Dawnay Arms** (01347) 848345

Off A19 N of York; YO30 2BR 18th-c pub with two bars and airy river-view dining room; low beams and stripped masonry, chunky pine tables and old pews on bare boards or flagstones, fishing memorabilia, open fire and inglenook woodburner, highly regarded original food, also good lunchtime sandwiches (home-baked bread), set menu (not Sat evening), interesting vegetarian menu and children's choices, ales such as Tetleys and Timothy Taylors, good range of wines by the glass, friendly efficient service; terrace tables, lawn running down to Ouse moorings, handy for Beningbrough Hall (NT), closed Sun evening, Mon (except bank holidays) and winter Tues. *(Ted and Mary Bates)*

NORTH DALTON SE9352

Star (01377) 217688

B1246 Pocklington–Driffield; YO25 9UX Picturesque 18th-c red-brick inn next to village pond; good range of changing ales and well cooked pubby food (not Sun evening, Mon, Tues), open fire in pubby bar, restaurant; some live music including open mike nights; children and dogs welcome, open all day weekends, from 4pm weekdays. *(Jim and Sue James)*

NORTH RIGTON SE2749

Square & Compass (01423) 733031

Hall Green Lane/Rigton Hill; LS17 0DJ Substantial stone building with smart modern interior; beamed bar serving four real ales including Leeds Pale and Theakstons Best, good range of bottled beers and plenty of wines by the glass, well liked food from sandwiches, sharing boards and pizzas up, friendly efficient service by aproned staff, restaurant; children and dogs (in bar) welcome, tables out on tiered terrace, peaceful village, open (and food) all day. *(Michael Butler)*

OLDFIELD SE0138

Grouse (01535) 643073

Harehills; 2 miles towards Colne; BD22 0RX Comfortable old pub in undisturbed moorland hamlet; well kept Timothy Taylors ales and enjoyable food from light lunches to good steaks and daily specials, weekday deals, friendly attentive service; children and dogs (in snug) welcome, picnic-sets on terrace with lovely Pennine views, open (and food) all day. *(Gordon and Margaret Ormondroyd)*

OSMOTHERLEY SE4597

Three Tuns (01609) 883301
South End, off A19 N of Thirsk; DL6 3BN Small stylish pub-restaurant with décor inspired by Charles Rennie Mackintosh; very good freshly made food in bistro setting with pale oak furniture and panelling, friendly efficient service, flagstoned bar with built-in cushioned wall benches, stripped-pine tables and pale-stone fireplace, well kept ales such as Timothy Taylors, good friendly service; children welcome, dogs in bar, seats out at front and in charming terrace garden, good nearby walks, comfortable bedrooms. *(Julian Richardson)*

OSSETT SE2719

★**Brewers Pride** (01924) 273865
Low Mill Road/Healey Lane (long cul-de-sac by railway sidings, off B6128); WF5 8ND Friendly local with own Horbury ales (brewed at back of pub) along with Rudgate Ruby Mild and seven guests, cosy front rooms and flagstoned bar, brewery memorabilia, open fires, good well priced food (not Sun evening) including Tues evening tapas, modern back dining extension (Millers Restaurant); live music Sat, quiz and pie night Mon; well behaved children and dogs welcome, big back garden, near Calder & Hebble Navigation, open all day. *(Michael Butler)*

OSSETT SE2820

Old Vic (01924) 273516
Manor Road, just off Horbury Road; WF5 0AU Friendly four-room roadside pub; well kept Ossett ales and guests including Fullers London Pride, competitively priced home-cooked food (not Sun evening, Mon), traditional décor with old local photographs, shelves of bottles and antique range; pool room, darts; children and dogs welcome, open all day Fri-Sun, from 4pm other days. *(Michael Butler)*

OSSETT SE2719

Tap (01924) 272215
The Green; WF5 8JS Cosy tap for Ossett Brewery; simple traditional décor with flagstones, bare boards and woodburner, mix of seating including upholstered banquettes and padded stools, photos of other Ossett pubs, their well kept ales and guests plus competitively priced wines by the glass, friendly relaxed atmosphere; dogs on the lead welcome, small car park (other nearby parking can be difficult), open all day Thurs-Sun, from 3pm other days. *(Michael Butler)*

OTLEY SE2045

Old Cock (01943) 464424
Crossgate; LS21 1AA Traditional two-room drinkers' pub with nine mostly local ales and a couple of ciders, also foreign beers and some gluten-free choices, no cooked food but good pork pies and sandwiches, more room upstairs; no under-18s, dogs welcome, open all day. *(Jim King)*

OTLEY SE2047

★**Roebuck** (01943) 463063
Roebuck Terrace; LS21 2EY Smartly modernised 18th-c beamed pub; good food from sandwiches and sharing plates up including range of hearty pies, Black Sheep and five changing local beers, plenty of wines by the glass, friendly helpful service, log fire and woodburner, raftered restaurant with mix of old furniture including pews on wood floor; children and dogs (in bar) welcome, wheelchair access, tables out on terrace and small lawn, open all day (closed Mon in winter), food till 7pm Sun. *(John and Eleanor Holdsworth)*

OXENHOPE SE0335

Bay Horse (01535) 642921
Upper Town; BD22 9LN Bustling community pub run by friendly licensees, good value food cooked to order and half a dozen well kept local ales; free wi-fi; children, walkers and dogs welcome, seats outside, open all day. *(Toby Jones)*

OXENHOPE SE0434

★**Dog & Gun** (01535) 643159
Off B6141 towards Denholme; BD22 9SN Spacious beautifully placed 17th-c moorland pub, smartly extended and comfortable, with wide choice of good generously served food from sandwiches to daily specials, cheerful, welcoming staff, full Timothy Taylors range kept well and good selection of malt whiskies, beamery, copper, brasses, plates and jugs, big log fire each end, padded settles and stools, glass-covered well in one dining area, wonderful views; bedrooms in adjoining hotel, open all day weekends (food all day Sun). *(Gordon and Margaret Ormondroyd)*

PICKERING SE7983

Black Swan (01751) 798209
Birdgate; YO18 7AL Renovated 18th-c coaching inn with own Great British Breworks beers from on-site brewery, also plenty of guests, real ciders and good choice of wines/gins, enjoyable home-made food from pizzas up, friendly staff, recently refurbished beamed bar with log fire, restaurant and separate cocktail bar; background music, free wi-fi; children and dogs welcome, bedrooms, open all day. *(David and Leone Lawson)*

PICKERING SE7984

White Swan (01751) 472288
Market Place, just off A170; YO18 7AA Civilised and welcoming 16th-c coaching inn run by same family for 36 years; cosy properly pubby bar, sofas and a few tables, panelling and log fire, Black Sheep, Timothy Taylors Landlord and a dozen wines by the glass, second bare-boards room

with big bow window and handsome art nouveau iron fireplace, good food (everything made in-house, even ketchup), flagstoned restaurant and next-door deli, efficient friendly staff, residents' lounge in converted beamed barn; children and dogs (in bar) welcome, bedrooms, open all day from 7.30am. *(Michael Butler)*

POOL SE2445

★**White Hart** (0113) 203 7862
Just off A658 S of Harrogate, A659 E of Otley; LS21 1LH Popular light and airy Mitchells & Butlers dining pub (bigger inside than it looks); good food from sharing plates and pizzas to more restauranty dishes, also fixed-price menu, efficient friendly young staff, 25 wines by the glass including champagne, cocktails and three well kept ales, stylishly simple bistro eating areas, armchairs and sofas on bar's flagstones and bare boards, welcoming log fires and relaxing atmosphere; background music; children and dogs welcome, plenty of tables outside, open (and food) all day. *(Michael Butler, Derek Stafford)*

PUDSEY SE2037

Thornhill (0113) 256 5492
Town Gate – Blackett Street; LS28 5NF Updated 17th-c roadside pub with wide range of enjoyable food from meze sharing plates, mexican choices, burgers and hot dogs up, real ales such as Theakstons and plenty of wines by the glass, friendly efficient staff; free wi-fi; children and dogs welcome, seats outside, open (and food) all day. *(John and Eleanor Holdsworth)*

REDMIRE SE0491

Bolton Arms (01969) 624336
Hargill Lane; DL8 4EA Welcoming village dining pub (former 17th-c farmhouse) with enjoyable fairly traditional food at reasonable prices, well kept Black Sheep and guests, efficient friendly service, woodburner in comfortable carpeted bar, attractive dining room; free wi-fi; children and dogs (in bar) welcome, disabled facilities, picnic-sets in small part-paved garden, good walks and handy for Wensleydale Railway and Bolton Castle, five bedrooms (two with views from shared balcony, others in converted outbuilding), open all day. *(Clive and Fran Dutson)*

REETH SE0399

Black Bull (01748) 884213
B6270; W side of village green; DL11 6SZ Popular 17th-c village inn overlooking broad sloping green; Black Sheep and Theakstons ales, enjoyable reasonably priced food including good Sun carvery, friendly helpful staff, traditional dark beamed and flagstoned L-shaped front bar, open fires, lovely dales views from dining room; juke box and some live music, pool and darts; children and dogs (in bar) welcome, tables out at front, bedrooms (also with views), open all day. *(Roy and Gill Payne)*

REETH SE0499

Buck (01748) 884210
Arkengarthdale Road/Silver Street; DL11 6SW Friendly 18th-c coaching inn adjacent to village green; well kept ales such as Black Sheep, Ossett and Wensleydale, enjoyable fairly pubby food, part-carpeted beamed bar with open fire, steps up to dining area; some live music, July beer festival, free wi-fi; children welcome, dogs in bar (theirs is Marley), a few tables out in front, hidden walled garden with play equipment, good walking country, ten comfortable bedrooms, open all day. *(Denis and Margaret Kilner)*

RIPLEY SE2860

Boars Head (01423) 771888
Off A61 Harrogate–Ripon; HG3 3AY Informal and relaxed old hotel belonging to the Ripley Castle Estate; long bar-bistro with nice mix of dining chairs and tables, walls hung with golf clubs, cricket bats, some jolly cricketing/hunting drawings, a boar's head and interesting religious carving, local ales, 20 wines by the glass and several malt whiskies, good food using Estate produce, separate restaurant; children welcome, dogs in bar and bedrooms, pleasant little garden, open all day, food all day Sun. *(John and Delia Franks)*

RIPON SE3171

★**One-Eyed Rat** (01765) 607704
Allhallowgate; HG4 1LQ Small friendly drinkers' pub with seven well kept changing ales, draught continentals and traditional cider; roaring fire in long narrow bare-boards bar, back carpeted area with piano and TV projector for sports, no food; some live music and a couple of beer festivals; dogs welcome, outside seating area, open all day Fri-Sun, from 5pm other days. *(Colin and Daniel Gibbs)*

RIPON SE3171

Royal Oak (01765) 602284
Kirkgate; HG4 1PB Centrally placed 18th-c coaching inn on pedestrianised street; smart modern décor, Timothy Taylors ales and guests kept well, good choice of wines, split-level dining area serving good food from pub staples to more enterprising restauranty dishes, friendly service; background music; children and dogs (in bar) welcome, seats in courtyard with retractable awning, eight bedrooms, open (and food) all day. *(David Appleyard)*

If we know a pub has an outdoor play area for children, we mention it.

RISHWORTH SE0316

Booth Wood (01422) 825600
Oldham Road (A672); HX6 4QU Welcoming beamed and flagstoned country dining pub; good range of enjoyable well priced food from sandwiches to blackboard specials, lunchtime/early evening bargains, up to five well kept ales including Holts Bitter and Bradfield Farmers Blonde, friendly staff, some leather sofas and wing-back chairs, two blazing woodburners; regular live music including folk nights; children welcome, open (and food) all day weekends. *(Rosie and John Moore)*

ROBIN HOOD'S BAY NZ9505

★**Laurel** (01947) 880400
Bay Bank; village signed off A171 S of Whitby; YO22 4SE Charming little pub at bottom of row of fishermen's cottages in especially pretty and unspoilt village; beamed main bar with open fire, old local photographs, Victorian prints and brasses, Adnams and Theakstons ales, no food or credit cards; background music, darts and board games; children in snug bar only, dogs welcome, open all day in summer. *(Diane Abbott, Elizabeth and Peter May, Simon and Alex Knight)*

ROBIN HOOD'S BAY NZ9505

Victoria (01947) 880205
Station Road; YO22 4RL Clifftop Victorian hotel with great bay views; good choice of local beers from curved counter in traditional carpeted bar, enjoyable fresh-made food here or in restaurant (separate evening menu), Thurs curry night, also a coffee shop/tea room; children and dogs welcome, useful car park, play area and picnic-sets in big garden overlooking sea and village, comfortable bedrooms, good breakfast. *(Darren and Jane Staniforth)*

SANDAL SE3418

Star (01924) 229674
Standbridge Lane; WF2 7DY Friendly buzzy atmosphere at this comfortable 19th-c local; well kept ales including own good Morton Collins microbrews (not always available), simple well priced lunchtime food (evening sharing plates); Tues quiz and some live music; children and dogs welcome, a few seats out at front, more in back garden with decked area, open all day. *(Michael Butler)*

SAWLEY SE2467

Sawley Arms (01765) 620642
Village signposted off B6265 W of Ripon; HG4 3EQ Popular village dining pub with good variety of well liked food from sandwiches and hot ciabattas up, Timothy Taylors Landlord and Theakstons Best, a dozen wines by the glass, welcoming helpful staff, comfortable interior with log fire and conservatory; children welcome, seats on terrace and in attractive garden, close to Fountains Abbey (NT), open (and food) all day. *(Paul Faraday)*

SCARBOROUGH TA0588

Golden Ball (01723) 353899
Sandside, opposite harbour; YO11 1PG Tall mock-Tudor seafront pub with good harbour and bay views from highly prized window seats (busy in summer), panelled bar with good mix of visitors and locals, some nautical memorabilia and open fire, well kept low-priced Sam Smiths; family lounge upstairs, tables out in yard, open all day. *(Monty Green)*

SCARBOROUGH TA0388

Stumble Inn 07837 716774
Westborough; YO11 1TS Simple one-room micropub with friendly chatty atmosphere; half a dozen well kept changing ales and extensive range of ciders/perries, knowledgeable landlord happy to offer tasters, walls and ceiling adorned with hundreds of pump clips; no food or children; café-style tables out on pavement, open all day and handy for the station. *(Malcolm Carson)*

SCARBOROUGH TA0387

Valley (01723) 372593
Valley Road; YO11 2LX Family-run Victorian pub with basement bar, up to six well kept changing ales, eight ciders/perries and excellent choice of bottled belgian beers, friendly staff, no food, more seats and pool room upstairs; bedrooms, open all day. *(Max Simons)*

SCORTON NZ2500

Farmers Arms (01748) 812533
Northside; DL10 6DW Comfortably modernised little pub in terrace of old cottages overlooking green; well kept Sharps Doom Bar and guests such as Black Sheep, decent wines and good freshly made food including popular Sun lunch, friendly accommodating staff, bar with open fire, darts and dominoes, restaurant; background music, fortnightly quiz; children and dogs welcome, open all day weekends, closed Mon lunchtime. *(Tony and Wendy Hobden)*

SCOTTON SE3259

Guy Fawkes Arms (01423) 868400
Main Street; HG5 9HU Hospitable neatly refurbished pub run by two local families in village where Guy Fawkes lived; very popular food (must book) including plenty of fish and good value set lunch, well kept Black Sheep, Copper Dragon and three local guests, charming staff; Mon quiz, daily newspapers; children welcome (box of toys for them), no dogs at food times, open from 4pm Mon and Tues (no food those days), otherwise open all day, kitchen closes 7pm Sun; for sale, so may be changes. *(Brian and Anna Marsden)*

SETTLE SD8163

Lion (01729) 823459

B6480 (main road through town), off A65 bypass; BD24 9DU Market town inn with grand staircase sweeping down into baronial-style high-beamed bar, lovely log fire, second bar with bare boards and dark half-panelling, lots of old local photographs and another fire, well kept Thwaites, guest ales and decent wines by the glass, good value food from deli boards to specials, helpful friendly staff, recently refurbished restaurant; children and dogs welcome, courtyard tables, 14 bedrooms, open (and food) all day. *(Ivy and George Goodwill)*

SETTLE SD8263

Talbot Arms (01729) 823924

High Street; BD24 9EX Friendly place with six well kept ales including Theakstons and local brews such as Settle and Three Peaks, reasonably priced traditional food from sandwiches up including some evening deals, pubby furniture on carpet, woodburner in impressive stone fireplace, parquet-floored games area with pool and darts; live music Fri; children and dogs welcome, picnic-sets in two-level back garden, open (and food) all day. *(Tony Clarke, Brian and Anna Marsden)*

SHEFFIELD SK3487

Bath (0114) 249 5151

Victoria Street, off Glossop Road; S3 7QL Victorian corner pub with well restored 1930s interior, two rooms and a drinking corridor, well kept Thornbridge and guests, simple snacky food including weekend hot pork sandwiches, friendly staff; live jazz/blues/folk Weds, Thurs quiz; closed Sun and bank holiday Mon, otherwise open all day. *(Richard Tingle)*

SHEFFIELD SK3687

Fat Cat (0114) 249 4801

Alma Street; S3 8SA Cheerfully busy little Victorian pub with a dozen interesting beers on handpump including next-door Kelham Island, also draught/bottled continentals and traditional cider, friendly knowledgeable staff, straightforward bargain food (not Sun evening) catering for vegetarians/vegans; Mon quiz; seats in back courtyard, open all day. *(Richard Tingle)*

SHEFFIELD SK3588

Harlequin (0114) 275 8195

Nursery Street; S3 8GG Welcoming open-plan corner pub owned by nearby Exit 33, their well kept ales and great selection of changing guests, also bottled imports and real ciders/perries, straightforward cheap lunchtime food including Sun roasts; weekend live music plus jazz second Thurs of month, Weds quiz, beer festivals; children (till 7pm) and dogs welcome, outside seating, open all day. *(Patricia Healey)*

SHEFFIELD SK4086

Kelham Island Tavern

(0114) 272 2482 *Kelham Island; S3 8RY* New licensees as we went to press for this busy little pub; a dozen interesting ales and good range of other draft and bottled beers, two rooms with simple pubby furnishings, has served decent lunchtime food); Sun folk night; children (in back room) and dogs welcome, flower-filled back courtyard garden, open all day. *(WAH)*

SHEFFIELD SK3290

★**New Barrack** (0114) 232 4225

Penistone Road, Hillsborough; S6 2GA Friendly and lively with nine real ales including Castle Rock, lots of bottled belgian beers and good value traditional food; comfortable front lounge with log fire and upholstered seats on old pine floors, another fire in tap room, function room (own bar); live music and comedy nights, pool, darts, sports TV; children (till 9pm) and dogs welcome, attractive little walled garden, parking nearby can be difficult, closed lunchtimes Mon-Weds, otherwise open all day. *(Jim King)*

SHEFFIELD SK3186

Ranmoor (0114) 230 1325

Fulwood Road (across from church); S10 3GD Comfortable and friendly 19th-c local; open-plan interior with etched bay windows, big mirrors and period fireplaces, four well kept ales including Abbeydale and Bradfield, enjoyable food; two outside seating areas, open all day. *(John Harris)*

SHEFFIELD SK3487

Red Deer (0114) 272 2890

Pitt Street; S1 4DD Friendly traditional backstreet pub among university buildings; bigger inside than it looks with eight well kept ales and a real cider from central bar, good value food (all day weekends) from sandwiches and snacks up catering for vegetarians/vegans; Tues quiz, live music, board games; tables outside, open all day (till 1am Fri, Sat). *(Richard Tingle)*

SHEFFIELD SK3185

Rising Sun (0114) 230 3855

Fulwood Road; S10 3QA Extended community pub with a dozen ales (several from Abbeydale) and good selection of craft beers, tasty fairly priced food, friendly service; background music, quiz Weds and Sun; children welcome, a few tables out in front, more on back terrace, open all day. *(Ewan and Sue Hewitt)*

SHEFFIELD SK3586

Sheffield Tap (0114) 273 7558

Station, platform 1B; S1 2BP Busy station bar in restored Edwardian refreshment room, popular for its extensive range of international beers on draught and in bottles, also own Tapped ales from visible microbrewery and plenty of guests including Thornbridge, knowledgeable helpful staff, snacky food, spacious tiled interior with vaulted ceiling; open all day. *(Jim King)*

SHEFFIELD SK3687

Wellington (0114) 249 2295

Henry Street; by Shalesmoor tram stop; S3 7EQ Traditional little 19th-c corner pub; well kept Neepsend ales and guests from seven handpumps, friendly staff, coal fire in lounge, some photographs of old Sheffield; tables out behind, open all day Fri-Sun, from 3pm Mon-Thurs. *(Jim King)*

SHEFFIELD SK3584

White Lion (0114) 255 1500

London Road; S2 4HT Terrace-row pub dating from the late 18th c with various small lounges and snugs off central corridor, 12 well kept changing ales (marked on blackboard) and good selection of whiskies, friendly relaxed atmosphere; regular live music in back room, Weds quiz; open all day from 4pm (midday Sat, 2pm Sun). *(John Harris)*

SHELLEY SE2112

★**Three Acres** (01484) 602606

Roydhouse (not signed); from B6116 towards Skelmanthorpe, turn left in Shelley (signposted Flockton, Elmley, Elmley Moor), go up lane for 2 miles towards radio mast; HD8 8LR Civilised former coaching inn with emphasis on hotel and dining side; roomy lounge with leather chesterfields, old prints and so forth, tankards hanging from main beam, well kept ales such as Timothy Taylors, Tetleys and Yorkshire, 40 malt whiskies and up to 17 wines by the glass from serious (not cheap) list, several formal dining rooms, wide choice of good if expensive food from lunchtime sandwiches up, competent friendly service; conferences, weddings and events; children welcome, fine moorland setting and lovely views, smart well equipped bedrooms. *(Giles and Suzie Nunn)*

SHERIFF HUTTON SE6566

Highwayman (01347) 878328

The Square; YO60 6QZ Friendly comfortably refurbished family-run pub; hearty helpings of good value home-made food (not Sun evening, Mon) from sandwiches and baguettes up, a house beer from Pennine (Stand & Deliver), Theakstons Best and a guest kept well, cheerful helpful service, beamed interior with bar, restaurant and games room (pool and darts); Thurs quiz, TV; children and dogs welcome, picnic-sets in big garden, attractive village with castle ruins and 12th-c church, open all day weekends, closed Mon lunchtime. *(Pat and Tony Martin)*

SHIPLEY SE1437

Fannys Ale House (01274) 591419

Saltaire Road; BD18 3JN Bare-boards alehouse on two floors, cosy and friendly, with eight well kept beers including Timothy Taylors, bottled imports and traditional ciders, gas lighting, brewery memorabilia, log fire and woodburner, back extension and upstairs area; free wi-fi; dogs welcome, closed Mon lunchtime, otherwise open all day and can get crowded weekend evenings. *(Victoria and Len Meadows)*

SHIPLEY SE1337

Hop (01274) 582111

Bingley Road; BD18 4DH Cavernous glass-fronted tramshed conversion on edge of Saltaire World Heritage Site; high pitched ceilings with some rather grand chandeliers, raised seating areas and stairs up to gallery, well kept Ossett range and guests from central curved counter, good choice of enjoyable food including sandwiches, sharing boards and wood-fired pizzas, early bird weekday set menu (5-7pm), friendly helpful service; live music and quiz nights; no under-18s after 8pm, picnic-sets out at front among the old tram tracks, open all day, food all day Fri, Sat and till 7pm Sun. *(Steve Whalley)*

SICKLINGHALL SE3648

Scotts Arms (01937) 582100

Main Street; LS22 4BD Popular 17th-c roadside village pub; enjoyable generously served food (all day weekends) including blackboard specials, rambling interior with interesting nooks and crannies, low beams, old timbers and log fires (one in lovely fireplace), four well kept ales, good wine range, friendly efficient staff; free wi-fi; children and dogs welcome, wheelchair access from behind, disabled loos, big garden with teak furniture on paved terrace, open all day. *(Gordon and Margaret Ormondroyd)*

SINNINGTON SE7485

★**Fox & Hounds** (01751) 431577

Off A170 W of Pickering; YO62 6SQ Popular 18th-c coaching house in pretty village; carpeted beamed bar with two-way woodburner, comfortable seating, various pictures and old artefacts, well kept Black Sheep and a guest, several wines by the glass and some interesting whiskies, appealing attractively presented food including a light lunch/early evening menu, friendly helpful service, lounge and smart restaurant; background music, free wi-fi; children and

If you stay overnight in an inn or hotel, they are allowed to serve you an alcoholic drink at any hour of the day or night.

dogs welcome, picnic-sets out at front and in garden, ten good comfortable bedrooms; for sale, so may be changes. *(Michael Butler, Michael Doswell, Janet and Peter Race)*

SKIPTON SD9851

Beer Engine 07834 456134

Albert Street; BD23 1JD Popular micropub with interesting range of changing ales, bottled imports and real ciders, good choice of wines by the glass too, friendly knowledgeable staff; occasional live music; children and dogs welcome, closed Tues, otherwise open all day (till 8pm Mon). *(Christopher H)*

SKIPTON SD9851

Narrow Boat (01756) 797922

Victoria Street; pub signed down alley off Coach Street; BD23 1JE Popular pub down cobbled alley with eight real ales including Ilkley, Okells and Timothy Taylors, also fruit and wheat beers, traditional cider/perry, dining chairs, pews and stools around wooden tables on bare boards, upstairs galleried area with interesting canal mural, generous helpings of enjoyable food at fair prices; background music, folk night Mon, quiz Weds; children (if eating) and dogs welcome, picnic-sets under front colonnade, Leeds & Liverpool Canal nearby, open all day, food all day Sat, till 6pm Sun. *(Steve Whalley)*

SKIPTON SD9851

Woolly Sheep (01756) 700966

Sheep Street; BD23 1HY Bustling narrow pub just off the High Street; full Timothy Taylors range kept well, several wines by the glass and good range of gins, whiskies and cocktails, friendly service; two beamed bars off flagstoned passage, exposed brickwork, coal fire in stone fireplace, split-level dining area at the back with good choice of enjoyable well priced food; children welcome, wheelchair access with help, rattan furniture in covered back terrace, 12 bedrooms, good breakfast, open (and food) all day. *(Steve Whalley, Michael Butler)*

SLEDMERE SE9364

★**Triton** (01377) 236078

B1252/B1253 junction, NW of Great Driffield; YO25 3XQ Handsome old inn by Sledmere House; open-plan bar with old-fashioned atmosphere, dark wooden furniture on red patterned carpet, 15 clocks ranging from grandfather to cuckoo, lots of willow pattern plates, paintings and pictures, suit of armour in one part, open fire, Greene King, Timothy Taylors, Tetleys and Wold Top, 50 gins, big helpings of well liked freshly cooked food (only take bookings in separate restaurant), friendly helpful staff; children welcome till 8pm, wheelchair access to bar and restaurant, five good bedrooms, generous breakfast, open day Sun till 9pm (food till 6.30pm), closed Mon in winter. *(Michael Butler)*

SLINGSBY SE6975

Grapes (01653) 628076

Off B1257 Malton–Hovingham; Railway Street; YO62 4AL Busy 18th-c village pub with good sensibly priced food from traditional menu (not Sun evening), well kept ales such as Elland, Timothy Taylors, Theakstons and York, cheerful staff, bare boards, flagstones and painted beams, nice mix of old furniture and some interesting bits and pieces including a tusky boar's head above one of the woodburners, games area with bar billiards; dogs welcome, tables and pizza oven out behind, open all day Fri-Sun, closed Mon. *(Michael Heuck)*

SNAITH SE6422

Brewers Arms (01405) 862404

Pontefract Road; DN14 9JS Newly refurbished open-plan Georgian inn; local Old Mill ales and decent home-made food from sandwiches and panini up, friendly helpful staff; children welcome in eating areas, attractive well appointed bedrooms, open all day. *(Simon and Sue Lamb)*

SNAPE SE2684

★**Castle Arms** (01677) 470270

Off B6268 Masham–Bedale; DL8 2TB Welcoming homely pub in pretty village, flagstoned bar with straightforward pubby furniture, horsebrasses on beams and open fire, Marstons-related ales, enjoyable food from good sandwiches up, pleasant attentive service, dining room (also flagstoned) with dark tables and chairs and another fire; children and dogs welcome, picnic-sets out at front and in courtyard, fine walks in Yorkshire Dales and on North York Moors, nine good bedrooms in converted barn. *(Michael Butler)*

SOUTH DALTON SE9645

★**Pipe & Glass** (01430) 810246

West End; brown sign to pub off B1248 NW of Beverley; HU17 7PN Attractive tucked-away village pub with main emphasis on landlord-chef's excellent food; beamed and bow-windowed bar, copper pans hanging above woodburner in sizeable fireplace, cushioned window seats and high-backed wooden dining chairs around mix of tables, Black Sheep, a house beer (Two Chefs) from Great Yorkshire and a couple of guests, 15 wines by the glass and some 40 malt whiskies, friendly staff, contemporary area beyond with leather chesterfields and another woodburner leading to airy restaurant overlooking parkland; background music, free wi-fi; children welcome, tables on lawn and front terrace, stylish bedrooms including three luxury suites, charming village with 62-metre church spire, closed Mon, otherwise open (and food) all day, kitchen closes 4pm Sun. *(Chris Stevenson, Penny and David Shepherd, Tim and Sarah Smythe-Brown)*

SOUTH KILVINGTON SE4284

Old Oak Tree (01845) 523276

Stockton Road (A61); YO7 2NL Spacious low-ceilinged pub with three linked rooms and long back conservatory; ample choice of good honest food from sandwiches up including lunchtime/early evening two-course deal, three well kept beers, friendly staff; children welcome, tables on sloping lawn, five bedrooms, open (and food) all day Sun. *(Bob and Melissa Wyatt)*

SOWERBY BRIDGE SE0623

Hogs Head (01422) 836585

Stanley Street; HX6 2AH Brewpub in former 18th-c maltings; one large room with heavy beams, bare boards and big woodburner, brewery visible behind glass, five of their good beers and guests from well stocked bar, no food; open all day weekends, from 3pm Mon-Fri. *(Francis and Mandy Robertson)*

SOWERBY BRIDGE SE0523

Hollins Mill (01422) 647410

Hollins Mill Lane, off A58; HX6 2QG Large airy bare-boards pub in converted joinery workshop by Rochdale Canal; seating from pews to comfortable sofas, up to eight well kept ales including Phoenix and Timothy Taylors, craft beers, a couple of ciders and decent range of gins, good value pubby food from sandwiches and baked potatoes up, efficient young staff; music nights in big upstairs room; children and dogs welcome, disabled facilities, backyard (covered in poor weather), open all day, food all day weekends till early evening. *(Pat and Tony Martin)*

STANBURY SE0037

Old Silent (01535) 647437

Hob Lane; BD22 0HW Welcoming old moorland dining inn; enjoyable fairly priced home-made food (all day weekends), three or four local ales including one badged for them, attentive helpful service, character linked rooms with beams, flagstones, mullioned windows and open fires, restaurant and conservatory; free wi-fi; children and dogs welcome, eight bedrooms, closed Mon, otherwise open all day. *(Caroline and Oliver Sterling)*

STAVELEY SE3662

Royal Oak (01423) 340267

Signed off A6055 Knaresborough–Boroughbridge; HG5 9LD Popular pub in village conservation area under friendly new management; beams, panelling and open fires, broad bay windows overlooking small front garden, well kept Black Sheep, Timothy Taylors and two local guests, several wines by the glass, enjoyable fairly priced food in bar and restaurant; quiz nights; children and dogs welcome, closed Mon, otherwise open all day. *(Geoff and Anne Marston)*

STILLINGTON SE5867

Bay Tree (01347) 811394

Main Street; leave York on outer ring road (A1237) to Scarborough, first exit on left signposted B1363 to Helmsley; YO61 1JU Cottagey pub-restaurant in pretty village's main street; modern bar areas with comfortable cushioned wall seats and kitchen chairs around mix of tables, central gas-effect coal fire, real ales such as Black Sheep, several wines by the glass and extensive range of gins, good interesting food from chef-owner along with some pub favourites and lunchtime sandwiches, steps up to cosy dining area, larger conservatory-style back restaurant; background music; children and dogs (in bar) welcome, seats in garden and a couple of picnic-sets at front, closed Sun evening to Weds lunchtime. *(William and Sophie Renton)*

STOKESLEY NZ5208

White Swan (01642) 710263

West End; TS9 5BL Good Captain Cook ales brewed at this attractive 18th-c flower-decked local; L-shaped bar with three relaxing seating areas, log fire, assorted memorabilia and nice bar counter with carved panels, speciality pies; Weds quiz, regular live music and beer festivals; no children, dogs welcome, open all day. *(Adam Jones)*

SUTTON UPON DERWENT SE7047

★St Vincent Arms (01904) 608349

Main Street (B1228 SE of York); YO41 4BN Busy pub with seven well kept ales including Fullers, lots of wines by the glass and good popular food from lunchtime sandwiches/ciabattas up, friendly efficient service; parlour-style front bar with panelling, traditional high-backed settles, windsor chairs and cushioned bow-window seat, gas-effect coal fire, another lounge and separate dining room; children and dogs (in bar) welcome, garden tables, handy for Yorkshire Air Museum. *(Peter and Anne Hollindale)*

SUTTON-UNDER-WHITESTONECLIFFE SE4983

Whitestonecliffe Inn (01845) 597271

A170 E of Thirsk; YO7 2PR Well located 18th-c beamed roadside pub; enjoyable fairly priced food from traditional menu along with blackboard specials, three well kept ales including Black Sheep, friendly staff, log fire and some exposed stonework in bar, separate restaurant, games room with pool and darts; quiz nights; children and dogs welcome, six self-catering cottages, closed Weds lunchtime. *(Comus and Sarah Elliott, Tony and Wendy Hobden)*

TAN HILL NY8906

Tan Hill Inn (01833) 628246

Arkengarthdale Road, Reeth–Brough, at junction Keld/West Stonesdale Road;

DL11 6ED Basic old pub (Britain's highest) in wonderful bleak setting on Pennine Way, often snowbound; full of bric-a-brac and interesting photographs, simple sturdy furniture on flagstones and an ever-burning log fire with prized stone side seats, five well kept ales including one badged for them from Dent, good cheap pubby food, family room; live weekend music; dogs welcome, bedrooms, bunk rooms and camping, wandering ducks and chickens, Swaledale sheep show here last Thurs in May, open (and some food) all day, can get very crowded. *(Glen and Patricia Fuller)*

THIRSK SE4282

Golden Fleece (01845) 523108

Market Place; YO7 1LL Refurbished old brick coaching inn; good food from snacks and sharing plates up including pub staples and stone-baked pizzas, friendly helpful service, ales such as Black Sheep and Copper Dragon, craft beers and over 20 wines by the glass, good range of gins too, clean contemporary décor in bar and separate dining rooms, view across marketplace from bay windows; children and dogs (in some areas) welcome, part-covered back courtyard, 26 bedrooms, open (and food) all day. *(Jeremy King)*

THIXENDALE SE8461

Cross Keys (01377) 288272

Off A166 3 miles N of Fridaythorpe; YO17 9TG Unspoilt country pub in deep valley below the rolling wolds – popular with walkers; cosy and relaxed L-shaped bar with fitted wall seats, well kept Tetleys and a couple of guests, generous uncomplicated blackboard food; no children or dogs inside, views from big back garden, handy for Wharram Percy earthworks, comfortable bedrooms in converted stables, good breakfast, closed Mon-Thurs lunchtimes (unless pre-booked by walking group). *(Alf and Sally Garner)*

THOLTHORPE SE4766

New Inn (01347) 838329

Flawith Road; YO61 1SL Updated beamed village-green pub with log-fire bar and candlelit restaurant; good food (allergies catered for) from sandwiches and wood-fired pizzas up including popular Sun lunch, Fri evening fish and chips deal, John Smiths and a local guest, friendly helpful staff; small shop; children welcome, closed Mon and lunchtime Tues. *(Monica and Steph Evans)*

THORNTON SE0933

Ring o' Bells (01274) 832296

Hill Top Road, W of village, and N of B6145; BD13 3QL Modernised roadside dining pub in hilltop position with long views towards Shipley and Bingley; series of linked rooms including conservatory-like area, black beams and painted stone walls, banquettes and other pubby furniture on carpet or flagstones, highly rated interesting food including plenty of gluten-free choices, also some pub favourites and good value weekday set menu, beers such as Timothy Taylors Landlord from well stocked bar, friendly efficient service; children and dogs welcome, closed Mon otherwise open (and food) all day, kitchen shuts 6.30pm Sun. *(Gordon and Margaret Ormondroyd)*

THORNTON SE0832

White Horse (01274) 834268

Well Heads; BD13 3SJ Deceptively large country pub popular for its wide choice of good food including early bird menu (till 6.30pm Mon-Thurs), five well kept Timothy Taylors ales, pleasant helpful staff, four separate areas, two with log fires, busy bustling atmosphere; children welcome, upstairs lavatories (disabled ones on ground level), also disabled parking, open all day, food all day weekends (till 7.45pm Sun). *(John and Eleanor Holdsworth)*

THORNTON DALE SE8383

New Inn (01751) 474226

The Square; YO18 7LF Friendly early 18th-c beamed coaching inn (packed weekend evenings); three well kept ales such as Theakstons, good fairly traditional food cooked by landlord including evening specials and deals; children and dogs (in bar) welcome, courtyard tables, six bedrooms and self-catering cottage, pretty village on edge of Dalby Forest, open all day, food all day Sun. *(Freddie and Sarah Banks)*

THORNTON IN LONSDALE SD6873

Marton Arms (01524) 242204

Off A65 just NW of Ingleton; LA6 3PB Recently refurbished old pub opposite 13th-c church where Arthur Conan Doyle was married; half a dozen real ales and around 50 gins, generous helpings of enjoyable food from sandwiches, snacks and pub favourites up, friendly staff, opened-up interior keeping beams and some exposed stonework, built-in settles and mix of wooden table and chairs on polished wood floor, logburner; background and some live music, Tues quiz, free wi-fi; children and dogs welcome, picnic-sets on front terrace and back lawn, great walking country, 11 comfortable bedrooms, open all day, food all day Fri-Sun. *(John and Sylvia Harrop)*

THORNTON-LE-CLAY SE6865

White Swan (01653) 618286

Off A64 SW of Malton, via Foston; Low Street; YO60 7TG Updated 19th-c family-run village pub; well kept local ales, nice wines by the glass and enjoyable reasonably priced home-made food including daily specials and themed nights, friendly helpful young staff; live music and quiz nights; children welcome, large garden, attractive countryside nearby and Castle Howard, open all day Sun, closed Mon, Tues. *(Val and Malcolm Travers)*

THRESHFIELD SD9863

Old Hall Inn (01756) 752441

B6160/B6265 just outside Grassington; BD23 5HB Old creeper-clad village inn set back from the road; enjoyable food served by attentive friendly staff, good choice of beers and wines, flagstoned bar with dining rooms either side, open fires (one in fine blacked kitchen range), high beam-and-plank ceiling, cushioned wall pews; neat garden and pretty hanging baskets, seven comfortable bedrooms, self-catering cottage, open (and food) all day. *(Edward Edmonton)*

THRINTOFT SE3293

New Inn (01609) 771961

Thrintoft Moor Lane, off Bramper Lane; DL7 0PN Friendly 18th-c village local with good variety of generously served home-made food including popular Sun lunch, well kept Black Sheep and a guest such as nearby Walls County Town, restaurant, open fire and woodburner; occasional quiz nights, free wi-fi; children welcome, no dogs inside, disabled access, front garden with two quoits pitches, closed Mon lunchtime. *(Monica and Steph Evans)*

TIMBLE SE1852

★Timble Inn (01943) 880530

Off Otley–Blubberhouses moors road; LS21 2NN Smartly restored 18th-c dining inn tucked away in quiet farmland hamlet; good food from pub favourites up including well aged Nidderdale beef (booking advised), ales such as Copper Dragon, Ilkley and Theakstons; children welcome, no dogs at food times, good walks from the door, seven well appointed bedrooms, closed Sun evening to Weds lunchtime. *(Colin and Daniel Gibbs)*

TONG SE2230

Greyhound (0113) 285 2427

Tong Lane; BD4 0RR Traditional low-beamed and flagstoned local by village cricket field; distinctive areas including cosy dining room, generous helpings of enjoyable good value food, well kept regional ales and several wines by the glass, efficient friendly service; tables outside, open all day. *(David Appleyard)*

TOPCLIFFE SE4076

Angel (01845) 578000

Off A1, take A168 to Thirsk, after 3 miles follow signs for Topcliffe; Long Street; YO7 3RW Part of the West Park Inns group; softly lit bare-boards bar with log fire, real ales and good choice of wines by the glass, enjoyable food in carpeted grill restaurant including weekday early bird deal (till 6.30pm) and themed nights, cheerful helpful service; background music, comedy night (usually first Tues of month); children welcome, nice garden, 16 bedrooms, open all day (food all day Sun till 8pm). *(Rosie and John Moore)*

TOWTON SE4839

Rockingham Arms (01937) 530948

A162 Tadcaster–Ferrybridge; LS24 9PB Comfortable roadside village pub with enjoyable home-made food from lunchtime sandwiches up, efficient friendly service, ales such as Black Sheep and Theakstons, back conservatory; children and dogs welcome, garden tables, handy for Towton Battlefield, open all day, no food Sun evening. *(John and Eleanor Holdsworth)*

ULLESKELF SE5140

Ulleskelf Arms (01937) 835515

Church Fenton Lane; LS24 9DS Refurbished village pub under newish management; good home-made food (till 6pm Sun evening, not Tues) including daily specials and Mon pie night, four well kept ales such as Timothy Taylors Boltmaker, open-plan interior with mix of old and new furniture on laminate flooring; background music; children, walkers and dogs welcome (resident lurcher is Dexter), beer garden behind, open all day Sun, closed lunchtimes Mon and Tues. *(Nick Wilkinson)*

WAKEFIELD SE3417

Castle (01924) 256981

Barnsley Road, Sandal; WF2 6AS Popular roadside dining pub with good affordably priced food including set menu (till 6pm Mon-Sat), well kept Black Sheep and a couple of guests, friendly staff and pleasant relaxed atmosphere; unobtrusive background music; children welcome, dogs in bar, rattan-style furniture on paved back terrace overlooking bowling green, open (and food) all day. *(John and Eleanor Holdsworth)*

WAKEFIELD SE3320

Fernandes Brewery Tap (01924) 386348

Avison Yard, Kirkgate; WF1 1UA Owned by Ossett but still brewing Fernandes ales in the cellar, interesting guest beers, bottled imports and traditional ciders, ground-floor bar with flagstones, bare brick and panelling, original raftered top-floor bar has some unusual breweriana; occasional folk, open mike and quiz nights; dogs welcome, open all day Fri-Sun (when some lunchtime food available), from 4pm other days. *(Adam Jones)*

WAKEFIELD SE3220

Harrys Bar (01924) 373773

Westgate; WF1 1EL Cheery little one-room local with good selection of real ales and bottled beers, stripped-brick walls, open fire; live music Mon and Weds, free wi-fi; small back garden, open all day Sun from 5pm Mon-Thurs, 4pm Fri-Sat. *(Adam Jones, John Harris)*

WALTON SE4447

Fox & Hounds (01937) 842192
Hall Park Road, off back road Wetherby–Tadcaster; LS23 7DQ Popular dining pub with good reasonably priced food from sandwiches to specials (should book Sun lunch), early evening set menu Tues-Fri, well kept ales such as Black Sheep and Timothy Taylors, friendly thriving atmosphere; children welcome, handy A1 stop, closed Mon. *(Les and Sandra Brown)*

WALTON SE3517

New Inn (01924) 255447
Shay Lane; WF2 6LA Open-plan village pub with friendly uniformed staff and buoyant atmosphere; seven well kept mainly local ales such as Jolly Boys, decent wines by the glass and some premium gins, extensive choice of good reasonably priced food from sandwiches and sharing plates up, afternoon teas, new stylish dining area in building behind with own terrace; quiz nights Sun and Mon; children welcome, dogs in bar, seats out in front and in lawned garden, open (and food) all day. *(Michael Butler)*

WARLEY TOWN SE0524

Maypole (01422) 835861
Signed off A646 just W of Halifax; HX2 7RZ Popular and welcoming village dining pub; generous helpings of good reasonably priced food from fairly traditional menu including lunchtime/early evening set deal (Tues-Fri), well kept ales such as Black Sheep, efficient friendly young staff, comfortable open-plan interior with two-way woodburner; children welcome, open all day Fri-Sun, closed Mon lunchtime, food till 7.30pm Sun. *(Celia Caulkin)*

WASS SE5579

Stapylton Arms (01347) 868280
Back road W of Ampleforth; or follow brown sign for Byland Abbey off A170 Thirsk–Helmsley; YO61 4BE Refurbished whitewashed village pub; two bustling bars with log fires, ales from Helmsley and Theakstons, restaurant in 18th-c granary serving generous helpings of good freshly made food from lunchtime sandwiches to daily specials, friendly staff; children welcome, no dogs, pretty village and surrounding countryside, near ruins of Byland Abbey (EH), three comfortable well equipped bedrooms. *(Dr Peter Crawshaw)*

WATH SE3277

George (01765) 641324
Main Street; village N of Ripon; HG4 5EN Friendly refurbished village pub with several rooms; good range of enjoyable food from traditional choices up using local ingredients (some home-grown), ales such as Hambleton, Rudgate and Theakstons, decent choice of wines; a couple of picnic-sets out at front, more in back garden, five comfortable bedrooms, open all day weekends (food till 7pm Sun), closed lunchtimes Mon-Weds. *(Michael Butler)*

WATH-IN-NIDDERDALE SE1467

★**Sportsmans Arms** (01423) 711306
Nidderdale road off B6265 in Pateley Bridge; village and pub signposted over hump-back bridge, on right after a couple of miles; HG3 5PP Civilised and beautifully located restaurant with rooms run by long-serving owner; although most emphasis on the excellent food and bedrooms, it does have a proper welcoming bar with open fire, well kept Black Sheep and Timothy Taylors, Thatcher's cider, lots of wines by the glass (extensive list) and 40 or so malt whiskies, also a highly rated ploughman's and other bar food, helpful hospitable staff, elegant dining room; background music; children welcome, dogs in bar, benches and tables outside, pretty garden with croquet, own fishing on River Nidd. *(Hunter and Christine Wright)*

WEAVERTHORPE SE9670

Blue Bell (01944) 738204
Village signed off A64 Malton–Scarborough at Sherburn; Main Road; YO17 8EX Upscale country dining pub, quite ornate in parts, with good attractively presented food and fine choice of wines (many by the glass including champagne), well kept Tetleys and Timothy Taylors Landlord, cosy cheerful bar with unusual collection of bottles and packaging, open fire, intimate back restaurant, friendly attentive staff; 12 bedrooms (six in annexe), interesting village, closed Sun evening, Mon. *(Michael Butler)*

WEAVERTHORPE SE9771

Star (01944) 738346
Village signed off A64 Malton–Scarborough at Sherburn; YO17 8EY Modernised village pub with decent range of enjoyable fairly priced food including stone-baked pizzas and good Tues curry night, a couple of well kept Wold Top ales, friendly service, pleasant bar with woodburner and small area for darts, restaurant; children and dogs welcome, picnic-sets on front grass by little stream, five updated bedrooms, closed Mon and lunchtimes (apart from Sun). *(Michael Butler)*

WENSLEY SE0989

Three Horseshoes (01969) 622327
A684; DL8 4HJ Old whitewashed roadside pub with neat beamed and flagstoned bar;

All *Guide* inspections are anonymous. Anyone claiming to be a *Good Pub Guide* inspector is a fraud. Please let us know.

five well kept ales including Theakstons and Yorkshire Dales, enjoyable straightforward food at reasonable prices from sandwiches up, pizzas only Mon evening, friendly helpful service, woodburner and open fire; children and dogs welcome, lovely Wensleydale views from paved terrace, popular with walkers, open all day. *(Clive and Fran Dutson)*

WEST TANFIELD SE2678

Bruce Arms (01677) 470325

Main Street (A6108 N of Ripon); HG4 5JJ Smart dining pub (18th-c coaching inn) under same ownership as the nearby Bull; good restaurant-style food served by friendly attentive staff, well kept Theakstons and good range of wines, gins and malt whiskies; terrace tables, three comfortable bedrooms, good breakfast, closed Mon-Weds lunchtime. *(Julian Richardson)*

WEST TANFIELD SE2678

Bull (01677) 470678

Church Street (A6108 N of Ripon); HG4 5JQ Busy pub in picturesque riverside setting; simple décor in flagstoned bar and slightly raised dining area, popular fairly standard food (all day Sat, till 7pm Sun), well kept Black Sheep and Theakstons, friendly buoyant atmosphere; background and live music once or twice a month (Sun), free wi-fi; children (away from bar) and dogs welcome, tables on terraces in attractive garden sloping steeply to River Ure and its old bridge, five bedrooms, open all day. *(Michael Butler)*

WEST WITTON SE0588

★**Wensleydale Heifer** (01969) 622322

A684 W of Leyburn; DL8 4LS Stylish restaurant-with-rooms rather than pub, but can pop in for a drink; excellent food with emphasis on fish/seafood and grills (not cheap and best to book), also lunchtime/early evening set menu, sandwiches and snacks, good wines, cosy dining bar with Black Sheep and a house beer brewed by Yorkshire, much bigger and more formal restaurant, attentive helpful service; children welcome, dogs in some areas, 13 good bedrooms (back ones quietest), generous breakfast, open all day. *(John and Penny Wildon, John and Enid Morris, Ian Wilson)*

WESTOW SE7565

Blacksmiths Arms (01653) 619606

Off A64 York–Malton; Main Street; YO60 7NE Cleanly updated 18th-c family-run pub with attractive beamed bar, woodburner in brick inglenook and original bread oven, well kept beers such as Tetleys and good home-made food from sandwiches and pub favourites up (steaks a speciality), restaurant; picnic-sets on side terrace, open all day. *(Michael Heuck)*

WHITBY NZ8911

Abbey Wharf (01947) 600306

Market Place; YO22 4DD Steps up to airy modern bar-restaurant (former Burberry factory) with lots of glass and exposed timberwork; good selection of beers from well stocked tile-fronted bar, enjoyable food including signature fish/seafood and chargrills (they add a service charge), friendly staff, mezzanine floor with own bar; maybe weekend live bands; children and dogs welcome, small terrace overlooking harbour, open (and food) all day. *(Darren and Jane Staniforth)*

WHITBY NZ9011

Black Horse (01947) 602906

Church Street; YO22 4BH Small traditional two-room pub, much older than its Victorian frontage, and previously a funeral parlour and brothel; friendly and down to earth with five changing ales, continental beers and a proper cider, range of yorkshire tapas, tins of snuff for sale; dogs welcome, four cosy bedrooms, open all day. *(David and Leone Lawson)*

WHITBY NZ9011

Duke of York (01947) 600324

Church Street, Harbour East Side; YO22 4DE Busy pub in fine harbourside position, good views and handy for the famous 199 steps leading up to the abbey; comfortable beamed lounge bar with fishing memorabilia, five well kept ales such as Black Sheep and Caledonian, decent wines and several malt whiskies, enjoyable straightforward bar food at reasonable prices; background music, TV, games machine, free wi-fi; children welcome, bedrooms overlooking water, no nearby parking, open (and food) all day. *(Bob and Melissa Wyatt)*

WHITBY NZ8911

Station Inn (01947) 603937

New Quay Road; YO21 1DH Welcoming three-room drinkers' pub across from the station and harbour; eight well kept ales including Ossett, Timothy Taylors and Whitby, craft beers, Weston's cider and good wines by the glass, friendly mix of customers; background and regular live music, quiz Thurs, traditional games; dogs welcome, three bedrooms, open all day. *(Edward Edmonton)*

A star symbol before the name of a pub shows exceptional character and appeal. It doesn't mean extra comfort. And it's nothing to do with exceptional food quality, for which there's a separate star-on-a-plate symbol. Even quite a basic pub can win a star, if it's individual enough.

WHITBY NZ9011

White Horse & Griffin (01947) 604857 *Church Street; YO22 4BH* Historic 17th-c coaching inn; tall narrow front bar with bare boards and a couple of large chandeliers, ales such as Black Sheep and Timothy Taylors, good wines and over 30 gins, steps down to low-beamed bistro-style dining area with flagstones and log fire, well liked interesting food served by friendly staff; ten bedrooms, close to the 199 steps to the abbey, open all day. *(John Robinson)*

WIGHILL SE4746

White Swan (01937) 832217 *Main Street; LS24 8BQ* Fairly modern family-run village pub with two cosy front rooms and larger side extension; well kept Black Sheep Bitter, a house beer from Moorhouses and a guest, enjoyable interesting food, friendly staff; children welcome, no dogs inside, wheelchair access with help (steps down to loos), picnic-sets on side lawn, closed Mon, otherwise open all day. *(Michael Butler)*

WINTERSETT SE3815

Anglers Retreat (01924) 862370 *Ferry Top Lane; WF4 2EB* Unpretentious rural local by Anglers Country Park and popular with walkers, birders and anglers; small lounge and tiny flagstoned bar, three well kept ales including Acorn, no food, hospitable landlord and friendly cheerful atmosphere; pleasant side garden; children and dogs welcome, open all day Sat, otherwise closed evenings and all day Tues. *(Michael Butler)*

WITHERNWICK TA1940

Falcon (01964) 527925 *Main Street; HU11 4TA* Welcoming 18th-c beamed corner pub; popular good value food from fairly pubby menu, well kept Timothy Taylors and Tetleys; children welcome, a few seats outside, closed Mon and lunchtimes apart from Sun. *(David Appleyard)*

WOMBLETON SE6683

Plough (01751) 431356 *Main Street; YO62 7RW* Welcoming 15th-c village local with good home-made food (not Sun evening) including blackboard specials, ales such as Black Sheep, John Smiths, Tetleys and Theakstons, bar area and restaurant; tables outside, open all day Fri-Sun, closed Mon lunchtime. *(Michael Doswell)*

WORTLEY SK3099

Wortley Arms (0114) 288 8749 *A629 N of Sheffield; S35 7DB* 18th-c stone-built coaching inn with several comfortably furnished rooms; beams, panelling and large inglenook, enjoyable food (all day Sat) including decent vegetarian options, three well kept ales such as Bradfield and good range of gins; monthly live music and quiz nights; children and dogs (in bar) welcome, nice village about ten minutes from M1, open all day (till 8pm Sun). *(Simon and Sue Lamb)*

YORK SE6051

Black Swan (01904) 679131 *Peaseholme Green (inner ring road); YO1 7PR* Striking black and white Tudor building; compact panelled front bar, crooked-floored central hall with fine period staircase and black-beamed back bar with vast inglenook, good choice of real ales, decent wines and generous helpings of reasonably priced pubby food from sandwiches up; background music, Thurs folk club; children welcome, useful car park behind, bedrooms, open all day, no food weekend evenings. *(Alf and Sally Garner)*

YORK SE6051

★**Blue Bell** (01904) 654904 *Fossgate; YO1 9TF* Delightfully old-fashioned little Edwardian pub, very friendly and chatty, with well kept Bradfield Farmers Blonde, Rudgate Ruby Mild, Timothy Taylors Landlord and guests, some snacky food including good pork pies, tiny tiled-floor front bar with roaring fire, panelled ceiling and stained glass, corridor to small back room with hatch service, lamps and candles, pub games; soft background music; no children, dogs welcome, open all day (but maybe just for locals on busy nights due to its size). *(Stephen Postlethwaite)*

YORK SE5951

★**Brigantes** (01904) 675355 *Micklegate; YO1 6JX* Bar-bistro (Market Town Tavern) with shop-style frontage; wooden tables and chairs on bare boards, blue-painted half-panelling and screens forming booths, ten well kept mainly local ales (York Brewery is in street behind), plenty of bottled beers, decent wines and coffee, good food from fairly priced varied menu, cheerful service, upstairs function room; children and dogs welcome, open (and food) all day. *(Barry Collett)*

YORK SE6051

Golden Ball (01904) 652211 *Cromwell Road/Victor Street; YO1 6DU* Friendly co-operative-owned Edwardian corner pub with four well preserved rooms; up to seven well kept ales, no food apart from bar snacks, bar billiards, cards and dominoes; Sun folk night and other live music (first and third Thurs of month), quiz Tues, TV; lovely small walled garden, open all day weekends, closed weekday lunchtimes. *(Alf and Sally Garner)*

YORK SE6051

Golden Fleece (01904) 625171 *Pavement; YO1 9UP* Popular little city-centre pub with four well kept ales including Theakstons Old Peculier and enjoyable good value pubby food; long corridor from bar to comfortable back dining room (sloping floors – it dates from 1503), interesting décor and lots of ghost stories; background music and occasional folk evenings, sports TV; children allowed if eating, no dogs, four bedrooms (two with four-posters), open all day. *(Michael Butler)*

YORK SE6052

Guy Fawkes (01904) 466674

High Petergate; YO1 7HP Splendid spot next to the Minster; dark panelled interior with small bar to the left, half a dozen real ales including Timothy Taylors and York, enjoyable sensibly priced food (not Sun evening) from shortish menu plus blackboard specials, good helpful service, dining rooms lit by gas wall-lights and candles, open fires; courtyard tables, 13 bedrooms, open all day. *(Phil and Jane Villiers, Peter Smith and Judith Brown)*

YORK SE6052

House of Trembling Madness (01904) 640009

Stonegate; YO1 8AS Unusual place above own off-licence; impressive high-raftered medieval room with collection of stuffed animal heads from moles to lions, eclectic mix of furniture including cask seats and pews on bare boards, lovely old brick fireplace, cask and craft beers from pulpit servery, also huge selection of bottled beers (all available to buy downstairs), good knowledgeable staff, reasonably priced hearty food including various platters; two self-catering apartments in ancient courtyard behind, open (and food) all day. *(Stephen Postlethwaite)*

YORK SE6052

Lamb & Lion (01904) 612078

High Petergate; YO1 7EH Appealing Georgian inn next to Bootham Bar; five well kept local ales and nice choice of wines by the glass, good food from sandwiches and pub favourites to more restauaranty choices, friendly helpful staff, bare-boards bar and series of compact rooms off narrow corridors; steep steps up to attractive paved garden below city wall and looking up to the Minster, bedrooms, open all day. *(Phil and Jane Villiers)*

YORK SE6051

Phoenix (01904) 656401

George Street; YO1 9PT Friendly little pub next to the city walls; proper front public bar and comfortable back horseshoe-shaped lounge, five well kept ales from yorkshire brewers, decent wines and simple food; live jazz two or three times a week, bar billiards; beer garden, for Barbican, open all day. *(Alf and Sally Garner)*

YORK SE6051

Pivni (01904) 635464

Patrick Pool; YO1 8BB Old black and white pub close to the Shambles with small narrow bar; extensive range of foreign draught and bottled beers (some unusual choices), also good selection of local ales, friendly knowledgeable staff, some snacky food and good coffee, more seats upstairs; Mon quiz, juke box and occasional live music; dogs welcome, open all day. *(Lindy Andrews)*

YORK SE6051

Punch Bowl (01904) 655147

Stonegate; YO1 8AN Bustling 17th-c black and white-fronted pub with good choice of well kept ales, decent wines and sensibly priced Nicholsons menu, efficient friendly service, small panelled rooms off corridor, dining room at back with fireplace; background music; a couple of tables out by pavement, open (and food) all day. *(Alf and Sally Garner)*

YORK SE6052

Snickleway (01904) 656138

Goodramgate; YO1 7LS Interesting little open-plan pub behind big shopfront window; lots of antiques, copper and brass, cosy fires, six well kept ales, some lunchtime food (not Sun) including good sandwiches, cheery landlord and prompt friendly service, stories of various ghosts including Mrs Tulliver and her cat; open all day. *(John Harris)*

YORK SE6052

Star Inn the City (01904) 619208

Museum Street; YO1 7DR Restauranty place (sister to the Star at Harome) in wonderful central riverside setting – a former 19th-c pumping station with modern glass extension; very good but not cheap food (they also do a weekday set menu till early evening), beers including a house ale (Two Chefs) from Great Yorkshire and Pilsner Urquell dispensed from two large copper tanks, good range of wines by the glass and cocktails, afternoon teas, friendly service; open all day from 9.30am for breakfast. *(Stephen Postlethwaite)*

YORK SE6051

Swan (01904) 634968

Bishopgate Street, Clementhorpe; YO23 1JH Unspoilt 1930s pub (Grade II

Please tell us if any pub deserves to be upgraded to a featured entry – and why: feedback@goodguides.com, or (no stamp needed) The Good Pub Guide, FREEPOST RTXY–ZCBC–BBAZ, Stream Lane, Sedlescombe, Battle TN33 0PB.

listed) near the city walls; two small rooms either side of lobby bar, several changing ales and ciders, friendly knowledgeable staff; pleasant little walled garden, open all day Fri-Sun, from 4pm Mon-Wed, 3pm Thurs. *(Paul Faraday)*

YORK SE6052

Three Legged Mare (01904) 638246

High Petergate; YO1 7EN Light and airy bar with York Brewery ales and guests kept well, good range of belgian beers and other drinks, efficient friendly staff, no food, back conservatory; regular live music including Thurs open mike, Mon quiz; children (till 7pm) and dogs welcome, disabled loo (others down spiral stairs), back terrace, open all day till midnight (10.30pm Sun). *(Francis and Mandy Robertson)*

YORK SE6051

Walmgate Ale House (01904) 629222

Walmgate; YO1 9TX 17th-c city-centre pub on three levels; ground-floor bar with half a dozen yorkshire ales and good range of wines, snacks including sausages rolls and local cheeses, upstairs bistro with wide choice of enjoyable food including set menu choices and weekend brunch (from 9.30am), further loft dining area, good friendly service; children welcome, closed Mon, Tues lunchtime otherwise open (and food) all day. *(Martin Cooke)*

YORK SE5951

Whippet (01904) 500660

Opposite Park Inn Hotel, North Street; YO1 6JD Steak and alehouse in street set back from the river; good popular food including signature dry-aged steaks, small bar area with four well kept ales from yorkshire brewers, lots of wines by the glass, interesting cocktails and excellent range of gins, friendly well informed staff; no children, open all day. *(Pat Martin)*

YORK SE5951

York Tap (01904) 659009

Station, Station Road; YO24 1AB Restored Edwardian bar at York station; high ceiling with feature stained-glass cupolas, columns and iron fretwork, bentwood chairs and stools on terrazzo floor, button-back banquettes, period fireplaces, great selection of real ales from circular counter with brass footrail, also bottled beers listed on blackboard, good pork pies; seats out by platform, open all day. *(Stephen Postlethwaite)*

London

CENTRAL LONDON

Map 13

Admiral Codrington

(020) 7581 0005 – www.theadmiralcodrington.co.uk

Mossop Street; South Kensington tube; SW3 2LY

Long-standing Chelsea landmark with easy-going bar and pretty restaurant, popular food and seats outside

Our readers enjoy their visits to this tucked-away pub, all citing the friendly atmosphere and interesting food. A central dark-panelled bar has high red chairs beside the counter with more around equally high tables on either side of the log-effect gas fire, button-back wall banquettes with cream and red patterned seats, little stools and plain wooden chairs around a medley of tables on black-painted floorboards, patterned wallpaper above a dado and a shelf with daily papers. There are ornate flower arrangements, a big portrait above the fire, several naval prints and quiet background music. Helpful staff serve Marstons 61 Deep, Shepherd Neame Whitstable Bay and Wychwood Hobgoblin on handpump and good wines by the glass. The light and airy restaurant area is a total contrast: high-backed pretty wall seats and plush dining chairs around light tables, an open kitchen, fish prints on pale blue paintwork, a second fireplace and an impressive skylight. A back garden has chunky benches and tables under a summer awning.

Rewarding food includes sandwiches, sharing boards, twice-baked smoked haddock soufflé with white wine butter sauce, ham hock terrine with gribiche sauce, beer-battered haddock with triple-cooked chips, vegetable risotto with ricotta, peas and spinach, beef bavette with caramelised shallots and red wine jus, red snapper fillet with mango and pineapple salsa, cumin-marinated chicken with curried oyster mushrooms and chimichurri, and puddings such as chocolate torte and sticky toffee pudding with butterscotch sauce. *Benchmark main dish: burger with french fries £14.00. Two-course evening meal £22.00.*

Free house ~ Licensee Aurelien Durand ~ Real ale ~ Open 11.30-11.30 (1am Sat); 12-10 Sun ~ Bar food 12-10 ~ Restaurant ~ Children welcome ~ Dogs allowed in bar ~ Wi-fi

Recommended by Margaret McDonald, Tom Stone, Alister and Margery Bacon, Ian Duncan, Dr and Mrs A K Clarke, David Jackman, Chloe and Michael Swettenham

CENTRAL LONDON

Map 13

Alfred Tennyson

(020) 7730 6074 – www.thealfredtennyson.co.uk

Motcomb Street; Knightsbridge tube; SW1X 8LA

Bustling and civilised with good drinks choice, rewarding food and friendly, helpful service

Set out over four floors, there's plenty of space in this civilised pub for both drinking and dining. There are high stools around equally high shelf tables for chatting, cushioned wooden settles around dark tables on parquet flooring for dining and eclectic décor that encompasses Edward Lear illustrations and antique books on windowsills. Stools line the counter where friendly, helpful staff serve Hammerton N1 and Sharps Doom Bar on handpump, 20 malt whiskies, cocktails and 32 wines by the glass. The upstairs restaurant has plush upholstered chairs and wooden tables on more parquet, large house plants and a huge mirror above an open fire. Above that is a loft room that's used for drinks parties. Outside on the front pavement are tables and chairs beneath a striped awning; there's disabled access to the bar but no disabled loos.

Enjoyable food includes breakfasts (on the ground floor, 8-11.30am), salt squid with smoked chilli and lime, potted trout with horseradish and cucumber, warm root vegetable salad with baby spinach, pickled walnuts and pear dressing, dry-aged burger with onion relish and barbecue sauce, chicken with morels, lovage, jersey royals and jus, hake with baby gem, peas and tarragon velouté, a pie of the day, steak with fries and red wine jus, and puddings such as dark chocolate délice with candied peanuts and honeycomb and warm marmalade and ginger pudding. *Benchmark main dish: beer-battered fish and chips £15.00. Two-course evening meal £23.00.*

Cubitt House ~ Lease Tony Gualtieri ~ Real ale ~ Open 8am-11pm; 8am-11.30pm Fri; 9am-11.30pm Sat; 9am-10.30pm Sun ~ Bar food 8am-10pm Mon-Thurs; 9am-10.30pm Sat; 9am-9.30pm Sun; light meals 11.30am-midday ~ Children welcome ~ Dogs allowed in bar ~ Wi-fi *Recommended by Sam Cole, Stuart and Natalie Granville, Elisabeth and Bill Humphries, Jill and Dick Archer*

CENTRAL LONDON Map 13

Black Friar

(020) 7236 5474 – www.nicholsonspubs.co.uk

Queen Victoria Street; Mansion House or Temple tube, Blackfriars tube/rail; EC4V 4EG

Remarkable art nouveau décor, a fine choice of ales, friendly atmosphere and popular all-day food

This is a very special architectural gem that includes some of the best Edwardian bronze and marble art nouveau work to be found anywhere. The inner back room has big bas-relief friezes of jolly monks set into richly coloured Florentine marble walls, an opulent marble-pillared inglenook fireplace, a low vaulted mosaic ceiling, gleaming mirrors, seats built into rich golden marble recesses and tongue-in-cheek verbal embellishments such as Silence is Golden and Finery is Foolish. The other large room has a fireplace and plenty of seats and tables. Staff are helpful, efficient and friendly (despite the crowds) and serve a fantastic range of around ten real ales including their core three – Fullers London Pride, Nicholsons Pale Ale (named for the pub from St Austell) and Sharps Doom Bar – on handpump with guests from breweries such as Purity, Roosters, Sambrooks, Thornbridge, Titanic and so forth, and several wines by the glass. Background music. In warmer weather, people spill out on to the wide forecourt, near the approach to Blackfriars Bridge.

As well as their speciality sausage and chop menu (11 different sausages and six types of chop) the well thought-of food includes breakfasts, sandwiches, puy lentil and vegetable pie, chicken topped with bacon, cheese and barbecue sauce, beer-battered fish and chip, gammon and eggs, steak frites, and puddings such as salted caramel profiteroles with ice-cream and lemon tart with blackcurrant curd. *Benchmark main dish: beer-battered fish and chips £13.25. Two-course evening meal £19.00.*

Nicholsons ~ Manager John McKeone ~ Real ale ~ Open 10am-11pm; 9am-11pm Sat; 12-10.30 Sun ~ Bar food 10-10; 9am-10pm Sat; 12-9.30 Sun ~ Children welcome ~ Dogs allowed in bar ~ Wi-fi *Recommended by Giles and Annie Francis, Darrell Barton, Diana and Bertie Farr, Philip J Alderton, Cliff and Monica Swan, Alan and Linda Blackmore*

CENTRAL LONDON Map 13

Coach Makers Arms

(020) 7224 4022 – www.thecoachmakersarms.co.uk

Marylebone Lane; Bond Street tube; W1U 2PY

Restored three-level pub in Marylebone with plenty of room for both eating and drinking, imaginative food and a thoughtful choice of wines and spirits

This carefully restored pub occupies several floors and our readers have been quick to voice their enthusiasm. The bustling ground-floor bar is the heart of the place with button-back banquette wall seats, high chairs around equally high tables, striking ceiling lights and friendly staff who serve Beavertown Gamma Ray and Hammerton N1 on handpump, 32 wines by the glass and 20 malt whiskies; background music and TV. In the basement, the cosy cocktail bar has beams and panelled walls, red or green plush seats and wall banquettes by simple tables, some modern art and drinks that include a seasonally changing cocktail menu. On the first floor is the bright and airy dining room with a restful atmosphere, leather or elegant wooden chairs around a medley of tables on dark floorboards, oil portraits and old photographs on the walls and stained-glass windows overlooking the Marylebone streets below. Disabled access to the bar but not to the loos.

Particularly good food includes pork croquettes with cauliflower and rhubarb, juniper-cured trout with crab rémoulade, cucumber and sorrel, white asparagus and stuffed artichoke with smoked pine nuts, crumble and nasturtiums, home-made sausages with rosemary mash and apple and onion gravy, a pie of the day, pork with haricot beans, spinach and pickled shallots, hake with clams, broad beans and grilled baby gem, lamb with boulangère potatoes, garlic and thyme jus, and puddings such as apple pie with vanilla ice-cream and marmalade and ginger pudding with roasted pear and gingerbread ice-cream. *Benchmark main dish: burger with toppings and green peppercorn mayonnaise £16.00. Two-course evening meal £23.00.*

Cubitt House ~ Lease Tony Gualtieri ~ Real ale ~ Open 11.30-11; 11.30-11.30 Fri, Sat; 11.30-10.30 Sun ~ Bar food 12-10; 12-10.30 Fri, Sat; 12-9.30 Sun ~ Restaurant ~ Children welcome ~ Dogs allowed in bar ~ Wi-fi *Recommended by Georgia Egner, Lucia Halliwell, Lucy Spencer-Davidson, Elizabeth and Giles Hancock*

CENTRAL LONDON Map 12

Cross Keys

(020) 7351 0686 – www.thecrosskeyschelsea.co.uk

Lawrence Street; Sloane Square tube (some distance away); SW3 5NB

Popular pub with a friendly bar, airy back restaurant, real ales and modern bar food

There's always a chatty crowd filling this gently civilised pub, for both the up-to-date food and good choice of drinks. The central counter has bar areas to each side with simple furnishings: distressed panelled walls, some exposed brickwork, a couple of open fires, framed tobacco postcards and display cases of butterflies, mirrors, tankards on a rack, industrial-style ceiling lights, and a mix of cushioned wooden dining chairs, wheelbacks and plush stools around scrubbed tables on bare boards. At the back, the airy conservatory-style dining room has button-back wall seating and similar chairs and tables. On handpumps beside a stuffed rabbit holding a gun, friendly staff serve Brakspears Bitter, Trumans Swift and West Berkshire Good Old Boy plus seasonal cocktails and good wines by the glass; background music.

Pleasing modern food includes seared foie gras with rhubarb, tuna ceviche with lemongrass, ginger, chilli, sesame and lotus crisp, jerusalem artichoke risotto with confit mushroom and parmesan, burger with smoked cheese, celeriac rémoulade and skin-on chips, duck breast with salt-baked swede, crispy duck leg, wild garlic and port jus, roasted pollock with potato purée, cauliflower, samphire and kale, sirloin steak with anchovy butter and rocket and parmesan salad, and puddings such as raspberry and chocolate fondant with salted caramel ice-cream and gin pannacotta with rhubarb and granola. *Benchmark main dish: sausages and mash with red wine jus £16.00. Two-course evening meal £27.00.*

Free house ~ Licensee Nick Botting ~ Real ale ~ Open 12-11; 12-midnight Fri, Sat; 12-10.30 Sun ~ Bar food 12-3, 6-10; 12-4, 6-10 Sat; 12-9 Sun ~ Restaurant ~ Children welcome ~ Dogs welcome *Recommended by Dan and Belinda Smallbone, Sandra and Miles Spencer, James and Sylvia Hewitt, Sarah Kennewell, Shalaine Duffy*

CENTRAL LONDON — Map 13

Grazing Goat

(020) 7724 7243 – www.thegrazinggoat.co.uk

New Quebec Street; Marble Arch tube; W1H 7RQ

A good mixed crowd of customers, restful décor, a thoughtful choice of drinks and good interesting food; bedrooms

Goats really did graze here once, though it's hard to believe that now given the pub's proximity to Oxford Street and Marble Arch. This is a stylish place; the bar has a big gilt-edged mirror above an open fire and plenty of spreading dining space with white cushioned and beige dining chairs around pale tables on bare boards, sage green or oak-panelled walls, ceiling lamps and lanterns and some goat memorabilia dotted about. Efficient, friendly staff serve Beavertown Gamma Ray and Sharps Doom Bar on handpump, 32 wines by the glass, 17 malt whiskies and ten cocktails; background music. The upstairs restaurant is more formal. Glass doors open on to the street where there are a few wooden-slatted chairs and tables. The bedrooms are modern and well equipped, with good bathrooms. There is disabled access to the bar but not to the loos.

Pleasing food includes a house-cured charcuterie board with feta, pickles and sourdough, chilli salt squid with smoked chilli and lime dressing, black garlic dumplings with asparagus, sheep's yoghurt and nettle pesto, chicken with wild rice, avocado, grilled courgette, soft lettuce and balsamic dressing, salmon with crayfish, garlic and vermouth velouté, rare-breed pork with caramelised onions, samphire, lemon, sorrel and date chutney, grass-fed rib-eye steak with truffle and parmesan fries and béarnaise sauce, and puddings such as pineapple carpaccio with passion-fruit buttermilk pannacotta and meringue and vanilla crème brûlée with strawberries. *Benchmark main dish: burger with toppings £17.00. Two-course evening meal £24.00.*

Cubitt House ~ Lease Tony Gualtieri ~ Real ale ~ Open 7.30am-11pm (10.30pm Sun) ~ Bar food 7.30am-10pm (9.30pm Sun) ~ Restaurant ~ Children welcome ~ Dogs allowed in bar

~ Wi-fi ~ Bedrooms: £210/£250 *Recommended by Tim and Sarah Smythe-Brown, Charles Todd, Laura Reid, Dr and Mrs A K Clarke, Heather and Richard Jones, Andrew Lawson, Victoria and James Sargeant*

CENTRAL LONDON Map 13

Harp

(020) 7836 0291 – www.harpcoventgarden.com

47 Chandos Place; Leicester Square tube, Charing Cross tube/rail; WC2N 4HS

Ten real ales and lots of ciders and perries in bustling narrow pub

Set in the very centre of London, this busy little tavern is a favourite with many. The main draw, of course, is the choice of ten particularly well kept real ales on handpump: these change quickly but always include Harveys Best, Dark Star American Pale Ale and Hophead and Fullers London Pride, with guests sourced from all over the country. Also, around six farm ciders, a perry and quite a few malt whiskies. The pub pretty much consists of one long narrow, very traditional bar, with lots of high bar stools along the wall counter and around elbow tables, big mirrors on the red walls, some lovely stained glass and loads of interesting, quirkily executed celebrity portraits. If you're lucky, you may be able to snare one of the prized seats by the front windows. A little room upstairs is much quieter, with comfortable furniture and a window overlooking the road below. At any time of day, the pub is always packed; at peak times, customers are happy to spill out on to the pavement or the back alley. The hanging baskets are wonderful in summer.

Food – served at lunchtime only – consists of sandwiches, sausage rolls and pork pies. *Benchmark main dish: sausages £4.00.*

Free house ~ Licensee Paul Sims ~ Real ale ~ Open 10.30am-11.30pm; 10.30am-midnight Fri, Sat; 12-10.30 Sun ~ Bar food 12-2 ~ Wi-fi *Recommended by Edward and William Johnston, William Slade, Dr and Mrs A K Clarke, Miles Green, Nigel and Jean Eames, Charlotte Smyrk, Lucia Halliwell*

CENTRAL LONDON Map 13

Lamb & Flag £

(020) 7497 9504 – www.lambandflagcoventgarden.co.uk

Rose Street, off Garrick Street; Covent Garden or Leicester Square tube; WC2E 9EB

Historic yet unpretentious, full of character and atmosphere, with six real ales and pubby food

Many of the customers here (including ourselves) have been using this characterful old tavern for years, and, thankfully, nothing changes. The more spartan front room leads into a cosy, atmospheric, low-ceilinged back bar with high-backed black settles and an open fire. Fullers ESB, London Pride, Olivers Island and Seafarers plus a guest such as Dark Star Hophead on handpump, as well as 12 wines by the glass and 12 malt whiskies. The upstairs Dryden Room is often less crowded and has more seats (though a smaller choice of beers). There's a lively and well documented history: Dryden was nearly beaten to death by hired thugs outside, and Dickens made fun of the Middle Temple lawyers who frequented it when he was working in nearby Catherine Street.

Popular food is served upstairs: lunchtime sandwiches, duck pâté with caramelised onion jam, salt and pepper squid with nam jim dipping sauce, rigatoni pasta with tomato, spinach, rosemary and chilli breadcrumbs, pork in ale sausages with crispy leeks, mash and onion gravy, burger with toppings and chips, a pie of the day with red wine gravy, chicken breast with parsley potatoes and chorizo butter, scampi with triple-cooked chips, and puddings such as apple and blackberry crumble and vintage ale sticky toffee pudding with toffee sauce. *Benchmark main dish: beer-battered fish and chips £14.00. Two-course evening meal £20.00.*

Fullers ~ Manager Patrick Linn ~ Real ale ~ Open 11-11; 12-10.30 Sun ~ Bar food 12-9 (10 Fri, Sat) ~ Restaurant ~ Children in upstairs dining room only ~ Dogs allowed in bar ~ Wi-fi *Recommended by Philip J Alderton, Max Simons, Peter Brix, Lyn and Freddie Roberts, Georgia Egner*

CENTRAL LONDON Map 13

Old Bank of England

(020) 7430 2255 – www.oldbankofengland.co.uk

Fleet Street; Chancery Lane or Temple tube, Blackfriars tube/rail; EC4A 2LT

Dramatically converted former bank building, with gleaming chandeliers in impressive soaring bar, well kept Fullers beers and tasty food

This extraordinary Grade I-listed Italianate building rarely fails to impress first- (or even second-) time visitors. It was once a subsidiary branch of the Bank of England and the splendid spacious bar has three gleaming chandeliers hanging from an exquisitely plastered ceiling that soars above an unusually tall island bar counter crowned with a clock. The end wall has huge paintings and murals that look like 18th-c depictions of Justice, but, in fact, feature members of the Fuller, Smith and Turner families, who set up the brewery that owns the pub. There are well polished dark wooden furnishings, luxurious curtains swagging massive windows, plenty of framed prints and, despite the grandeur, some surprisingly cosy corners, with screens between tables creating an unexpectedly intimate feel. The quieter galleried section upstairs offers a bird's-eye view of the action; some smaller rooms (used mainly for functions) open off. Fullers ESB, London Pride nd Olivers Island and a guest such as Dark Star Hophead on handpump alongside a good choice of malt whiskies and a dozen wines by the glass. At lunchtime, the background music is generally classical or easy listening; it's louder and livelier in the evenings. There's also a garden with seats (one of the few pubs in the area to have one).

Pies have a long if rather dubious pedigree in this area: it was in the vaults and tunnels below the Old Bank and the surrounding buildings that Sweeney Todd butchered the clients destined to provide the fillings at his mistress Mrs Lovett's nearby pie shop. The popular food here does indeed include pies, and also sandwiches, tapas-style dishes, rigatoni pasta with tomato, spinach, rosemary and chilli breadcrumbs, burger with toppings and triple-cooked chips, haddock and salmon fishcakes with sauce gribiche, chicken breast with parsley potatoes and chorizo butter, and puddings such as chocolate brownie and vanilla ice-cream and raspberry and lime posset. *Benchmark main dish: pies £12.95. Two-course evening meal £18.00.*

Fullers ~ Manager Stuart Elseui ~ Real ale ~ Open 11-11; 12-8 Sat; closed Sun ~ Bar food 12-10; 12-4 Sat ~ Children welcome until 6pm ~ Wi-fi *Recommended by Dr and Mrs A K Clarke, Barry Collett, Nik and Gloria Clarke, Philip J Alderton, Louise and Anton Parsons, Kerry and Guy Trooper*

Please tell us if the décor, atmosphere, food or drink at a pub is different from our description. We rely on readers' reports to keep us up to date: feedback@goodguides.com, or (no stamp needed) The Good Pub Guide, FREEPOST RTXY–ZCBC–BBAZ, Stream Lane, Sedlescombe, Battle TN33 0PB.

THE GOOD PUB GUIDE

CENTRAL LONDON

Map 13

Olde Mitre £

(020) 7405 4751 – www.yeoldemitreholborn.co.uk

Ely Place; the easiest way to find it is from the narrow passageway beside 8 Hatton Garden; Chancery Lane tube, Farringdon tube/rail; EC1N 6SJ

Hard to find but well worth it – an unspoilt old pub with lovely atmosphere, unusual guest beers and bargain toasted sandwiches

You need to be in the know to find this unspoilt and tucked-away little place – it's a real refuge from the modern city nearby. The cosy small rooms have lots of dark panelling as well as antique settles and (particularly in the popular back room where there are more seats) old local pictures and so forth. It gets good-naturedly packed with the City suited-and-booted between 12.30pm and 2.15pm, filling up again in the early evening, but in the early afternoons and by around 8pm it's a good deal more tranquil. An upstairs room, mainly used for functions, may double as an overflow area at peak periods. Fullers London Pride, Olivers Island and Seafarers with guests from breweries such as Electric Bear and Pheasantry on handpump, and they hold three beer festivals a year; eight farm ciders and several wines by the glass. No music, TV or machines – the only games here are cribbage and dominoes. There's some space for outside drinking by the pot plants and jasmine in the narrow yard between the pub and St Etheldreda's church (which is worth a look). Note the pub doesn't open on weekends or bank holidays. The best approach is from Hatton Garden, walking up the right-hand side away from Chancery Lane; an easily missed sign on a lamp-post points the way down a narrow alley. No children.

Bar snacks, served all day, are limited to scotch eggs, pork pies, sausage rolls and really good value toasties.

Fullers ~ Manager Judith Norman ~ Real ale ~ Open 11-11; closed weekends and bank holidays ~ Bar food 11-10 ~ Wi-fi *Recommended by Margaret McDonald, Adam Jones, Max and Steph Warren, Alison and Michael Harper*

THE GOOD PUB GUIDE

CENTRAL LONDON

Map 13

Orange

(020) 7881 9844 – www.theorange.co.uk

Pimlico Road; Sloane Square tube; SW1W 8NE

London Dining Pub of the Year

Carefully restored pub with simply decorated rooms, thoughtful choice of drinks and up-to-date food; bedrooms

At the heart of this pub is the ground-floor bar with its bustling, chatty and easy-going atmosphere. There are high ceilings, wooden dining chairs around pale tables on bare boards, an open fire at one end and a big carved counter where friendly staff keep Beavertown Gamma Ray and Sharps Doom Bar on handpump, 32 wines by the glass, 17 malt whiskies and ten cocktails. The dining room to the right, usually packed with cheerful customers, is decorated with prints, glass bottles and soda siphons, big house plants and a few rustic knick-knacks. Upstairs, the linked restaurant rooms are similarly furnished with old french travel posters and circus prints on cream walls, more open fireplaces, big glass ceiling lights, chandeliers and quiet background music. Bedrooms are well equipped and comfortable and breakfasts are first class. There's disabled access to the bar but not to the loos.

Good, modern food includes seared yellowfin tuna with cauliflower, toasted rice, apple and caper dressing, beef bresaola with pickled strawberries, wood-fired pizzas, chicken croquettes with manouri cheese, broccoli, celery and walnut salad and dandelion honey, courgettes, pea fritters, fennel ragoût and toasted cashews, a pie of the day, poached chalk-stream trout with brown crab fritters, seaweed, gooseberries and sorrel hollandaise, grass-fed rib-eye steak with baked bone marrow and lovage pesto, and puddings such as carrot cake with passion-fruit cream cheese and walnuts and strawberry and custard fool with coconut sorbet. *Benchmark main dish: dry-aged burger with toppings and mustard mayonnaise £16.00. Two-course evening meal £24.00.*

Cubitt House ~ Lease Tony Gualtieri ~ Real ale ~ Open 8am-11.30pm; 8am-midnight Fri, Sat; 8am-10.30pm Sun ~ Bar food 8am-10.30pm; 8am-11pm Fri, Sat; 8am-9.30pm Sun ~ Restaurant ~ Children welcome ~ Dogs allowed in bar ~ Wi-fi ~ Bedrooms: £205/£240 *Recommended by Rosie and John Moore, Penny and David Shepherd, Elizabeth and Peter May, Ian Herdman, Michael Butler, Daisy Rutledge, Megan and Hallam Cunningham*

CENTRAL LONDON Map 13

Punchbowl

(020) 7493 6841 – www.punchbowllondon.com

Farm Street; Green Park tube; W1J 5RP

Bustling, rather civilised pub with good wines and ales, enjoyable food and helpful service

This is an enjoyable tucked-away Mayfair pub. Perhaps the nicest part is at the back where several panelled booths have suede bench seating, animal-decorated scatter cushions, some etched glasswork and church candles on tables. Elegant spoked chairs are grouped around dark tables on worn floorboards, a couple of long elbow shelves are lined with high chairs and one fireplace has a coal fire while the other is piled with logs. At the front it's simpler, with cushioned bench seating and pubby tables and chairs on floor tiles. All sorts of artwork from cartoons to oil paintings line the walls and the ceiling has interesting old hand-drawn street maps; background music. Caledonian Deuchars IPA, a beer named for the pub (also from Caledonian), and a changing guest beer on handpump, good wines by the glass and professional, friendly service. The smart dining room upstairs has plush furnishings, large artworks and a huge gilt mirror above an open fire; there are private dining facilities too.

Pleasing food includes a sandwich of the day, tapas-style nibbles, seared yellowfin tuna with radish, avocado and wasabi, chicken and pistachio terrine with apricot chutney, asparagus and wild garlic risotto with crispy black garlic, cumberland sausages with onion and thyme gravy, burger with toppings and chips, thai monkfish and prawn curry, coriander and pilau rice, roasted guinea fowl with squash and pearl barley risotto with red onion and basil, rib-eye steak with confit garlic, parmesan and chips, and puddings such as orange polenta cake with crème fraîche and orange marmalade and pear and chocolate tarte tatin with vanilla ice-cream. *Benchmark main dish: beer-battered fish and chips £16.00. Two-course evening meal £22.00.*

Free house ~ Licensee Hannah Bonnell ~ Real ale ~ Open 12-11 (10.30 Sun) ~ Bar food 12-3.30, 5.30-10; 12-10 Sat; 12-9 Sun ~ Restaurant ~ Children welcome if seated and dining ~ Dogs allowed in bar ~ Wi-fi *Recommended by Laura Reid, Jeff Davies, Maggie and Stevan Hollis, Samuel and Melissa Turnbull, Isobel Mackinlay, Belinda Stamp*

If we know a featured-entry pub does sandwiches, we always say so – if they're not mentioned, you'll have to assume you can't get one.

CENTRAL LONDON

Map 13

Seven Stars

(020) 7242 8521 – www.thesevenstars1602.co.uk

Carey Street; Chancery Lane, Holborn or Temple tube; WC2A 2JB

Fine pub dating from 1602 with cheerful staff, an interesting mix of customers and a good choice of drinks and food

A favourite haunt of lawyers, Church of England music directors and choir singers, this Grade II-listed pub faces the back of the law courts. Numerous caricatures of barristers and judges line the red-painted walls of the two main rooms and there are posters of legal-themed british films, big ceiling fans and checked tablecloths that add a quirky, almost continental touch. A third area, in what was formerly a legal wig shop next door, still retains its original frontage, with a neat display of wigs in the window. It's worth arriving early as they don't take bookings and tables get snapped up quickly. Adnams Broadside, Harveys Best, Sharps Doom Bar and Whitstable Native Bitter on handpump and six wines by the glass (the wine is imported from France); they do a particularly good dry martini. On busy evenings, customers overflow on to the quiet road in front; things generally quieten down after 8pm and there can be a nice, sleepy atmosphere some afternoons. The steep Elizabethan stairs up to the loos were recently covered with English Heritage-approved wrought oak, and two brass bars were added. The pub cat, who wears a ruff, is called Peabody. No children.

Cooked according to the landlady's fancy, the good, interesting food includes chicken liver pâté, black bean and sweetcorn soup, rabbit and chicken pie, merguez sausages with pilau rice, spiced lamb filo parcels and linguine with prawns and squid or cream and parmesan. *Benchmark main dish: soused herrings and potato salad £11.50. Two-course evening meal £20.00.*

Free house ~ Licensee Roxy Beaujolais ~ Real ale ~ Open 11-11; 12-11 Sat; 12-10 Sun ~ Bar food 12-9.30; 1-9 weekends ~ Wi-fi *Recommended by Philip J Alderton, Elise and Charles Mackinlay, Lucia Halliwell, Angela and Martin Kendall*

CENTRAL LONDON

Map 13

Star

(020) 7235 3019 – www.star-tavern-belgravia.co.uk

Belgrave Mews West, behind the German Embassy, off Belgrave Square; Hyde Park Corner or Knightsbridge tube; SW1X 8HT

Bustling local with restful bar, upstairs dining room, Fullers ales, well liked bar food and colourful hanging baskets

Outside peak times, there's a peaceful, local feel to this tucked-away pub in its cobbled mews. The small bar is pleasant, with sash windows, a wooden floor, stools by the counter, an open winter fire and Fullers ESB, London Pride and Olivers Island plus a couple of guest beers on handpump, nine wines by the glass and a few malt whiskies. An arch leads to the main seating area with well polished tables and chairs and good lighting; there's also an upstairs dining room. In summer, the front of the building is covered with an astonishing array of hanging baskets and flowering tubs. It's said that this is where the Great Train Robbery was planned.

As well as Saturday brunch (10.30-3), the well liked food includes lunchtime sandwiches, prawn cocktail, popcorn chicken with harissa and coriander mayonnaise, tomato and goats cheese tart with rocket, basil and fennel salad, burger with toppings and chips, lamb faggots with creamed potatoes, roasted shallot gravy and crushed peas, smoked mackerel with courgette, fennel, spelt, dill and pomegranate, chicken curry, dry-aged sirloin steak with béarnaise sauce, and puddings such as vintage ale sticky toffee pudding with toffee sauce and salted caramel ice-cream and apple and blackberry crumble with crème anglaise. *Benchmark main dish: steak in ale pie £12.50. Two-course evening meal £20.00.*

Fullers ~ Manager Ollie Coulombeau ~ Real ale ~ Open 11-11; 12-11 Sat; 12-10.30 Sun ~ Bar food 12-3, 5-10 weekdays; 12-10 Sat; 12-4, 5-10 Sun ~ Restaurant ~ Children welcome ~ Dogs welcome ~ Wi-fi *Recommended by Philip J Alderton, Phoebe Peacock, Caroline Prescott, Susan and John Douglas, Shalaine Duffy, Megan and Hallam Cunningham*

CENTRAL LONDON — Map 13

Thomas Cubitt

(020) 7730 6060 – www.thethomascubitt.co.uk

Elizabeth Street; Sloane Square tube, Victoria tube/rail; SW1W 9PA

Belgravia pub with a civilised and friendly atmosphere and enjoyable food and drink

At the heart of Belgravia, this is a stylish and busy place in well heeled Elizabeth Street. The ground-floor bar has miscellaneous Edwardian-style dining chairs around wooden tables on stripped parquet flooring, and architectural prints and antlers on panelled or painted walls; open fires and lovely flower arrangements. Attentive staff serve Beavertown Gamma Ray and Sharps Doom Bar on handpump, 32 wines by the glass, 17 malt whiskies and ten cocktails. The more formal dining room upstairs has smart upholstered wooden chairs around white-clothed tables, candles in wall holders, a few prints, house plants and window blinds; background music and TV. In warm weather, the floor-to-ceiling glass doors are pulled back to the street where there are cordoned-off tables and chairs on the pavement. Disabled access to the bar but not to the loos.

Tempting food in the bar includes potted trout with pickled cucumber and dill, rare-breed beef tartare with bone marrow and beef fat toast, cauliflower and blue cheese pie with chive mash, beer-battered fish and chips, chicken breast with spiced swede, broccoli and pomegranate dressing, grilled octopus salad with carrots, radicchio, blood orange and red onion, and puddings such as beetroot and cream cheese cake with praline ice-cream and spiced chocolate ganache with passion-fruit mousse and chocolate shortbread. *Benchmark main dish: beer-battered fish and chips £15.00. Two-course evening meal £22.00.*

Cubitt House ~ Lease Tony Gualtieri ~ Real ale ~ Open 12-11 (10.30 Sun) ~ Bar food 12-10 (9.30 Sun) ~ Restaurant ~ Children welcome ~ Dogs allowed in bar ~ Wi-fi *Recommended by Tim and Sarah Smythe-Brown, Peter and Emma Kelly, John Robinson, Barbara and Phil Bowie, Dave Braisted, Nigel and Sue Foster*

NORTH LONDON — Map 12

Holly Bush

(020) 7435 2892 – www.hollybushhampstead.co.uk

Holly Mount; Hampstead tube; NW3 6SG

Unique village local, with good food and drinks, and lovely unspoilt feel

A timeless old favourite, this was originally a stable block and is hidden away among some of Hampstead's most villagey streets. The old-fashioned front bar has a dark sagging ceiling, brown and cream panelled walls (decorated with old advertisements and a few hanging plates), open fires, bare boards and secretive bays formed by partly glazed partitions. The slightly more intimate back room, named after the painter George Romney, has an embossed red ceiling, panelled and etched glass alcoves, and ochre-painted brick walls covered with small prints; lots of board and card games. Fullers ESB, London Pride and Olivers Island plus a guest or two such as Adnams Ghost Ship and Liberation Ale on handpump, as well as 15 malt whiskies and 14 wines by the glass from a good wine list. The upstairs dining room has table service at the weekend, as does the rest of the pub on Sundays. There are benches on the pavement outside.

Popular food includes lunchtime sandwiches, chicken liver and smoked bacon on toast, soft shell crab with smashed avocado, sharing plates, wild mushroom lasagne, mussels in cider broth with chips, barnsley lamb chop with salsa verde, whole grilled poussin with garlic glaze, hot smoked salmon with a rock oyster and fennel and lemon risotto, and puddings such as peanut butter parfait with caramelised banana and chocolate popcorn and sticky toffee pudding with salted caramel ice-cream. *Benchmark main dish: beer-battered fish and chips £14.00. Two-course evening meal £24.00.*

Fullers ~ Manager Ben Ralph ~ Real ale ~ Open 12-11 (10.30 Sun) ~ Bar food 12-3.30 (4.30 weekends), 6-10 ~ Restaurant ~ Children welcome ~ Dogs welcome ~ Wi-fi
Recommended by Isobel Mackinlay, John and Mary Warner, John Wooll, Mark Morgan, Philip Chesington, Ben Lees

NORTH LONDON — Map 13

Lighterman

(020) 3846 3400 – www.thelighterman.co.uk
Granary Square, Regent's Canal; King's Cross or St Pancras tube/rail; N1C 4BH

Light and airy contemporary place with up-to-date décor and furnishings, a wide range of drinks, interesting all-day food and good, quick service

Ultra-modern and stylish, this is a bar-restaurant on three floors in the redeveloped plaza behind King's Cross station with views across the fountains in Granary Square and Regent's Canal. The ground-floor terrace and the wrap-around decking on the first floor have plenty of seats, benches and tables to make the most of this vista. Floor-to-ceiling windows and big folding doors in the open-plan bars keep it all very light and airy, while the minimalist, industrial-style décor takes in contemporary chairs, wall seats and tables on wood-strip floors. High chairs line the counters where efficient, friendly staff serve Brick Peckham Pale and Crate Golden and SIPA on handpump, 22 wines by the glass and seasonal cocktails; background music.

Rewarding food includes breakfasts, flatbreads with toppings, potted smoked salmon with apple and horseradish, pea and mint croquettes with mustard aioli, beetroot and goats cheese parcel with sorrel and watercress, chicken and leek pie, roasted chalk-stream trout with broad beans, peas and lemon butter sauce, beer-battered fish and chips, from the wood-fired grill marinated free-range chicken breast, yellowfin tuna steak and dry-aged sirloin steak all with a choice of sauce and sides, and puddings such as caramelised lemon tart with blackberry sorbet and warm chocolate brownie with salted caramel ice-cream. *Benchmark main dish: burger with toppings and skin-on fries £15.00. Two-course evening meal £27.00.*

Open House London ~ Real ale ~ Open 8am-11.30pm (midnight Fri); 9am-midnight Sat; 9am-10.30pm Sun ~ Bar food 8am-10.30pm (11.30 Fri); 9am-11pm Sat; 9am-9.30 Sun ~ Restaurant ~ Children welcome ~ Dogs allowed in bar ~ Wi-fi *Recommended by Brian Glozier, Maggie and Stevan Hollis, Adam and Natalie Davis, Robert and Diana Ringstone, Trevor and Michele Street*

NORTH LONDON

Map 13

Princess of Wales

(020) 7722 0354 – www.lovetheprincess.com

Fitzroy Road/Chalcot Road; Chalk Farm tube via Regents Park Road and footbridge; NW1 8LL

Friendly place with three different seating areas, enjoyable food, wide choice of drinks and funky garden

Spread over three floors, this bustling pub usefully offers some kind of food all day at weekends. The main bar, at ground level, is open-plan and light with big windows looking out to the street, wooden tables and chairs on bare boards and plenty of high chairs against the counter: Sambrooks Wandle and a beer named for the pub (also from Sambrooks) plus a changing guest ale on handpump, 16 wines by the glass, 11 malt whiskies and good cocktails. Upstairs, the smarter dining room has beige- and white-painted chairs, leather sofas and stools around wooden tables on more bare boards, big gilt-edged mirrors and chandeliers; two TVs. The Garden Room downstairs has a bar, three connected areas and access to the suntrap garden with its Bansky-style mural, framed wall mirrors and picnic-sets (some painted pink and purple) under parasols.

Good food includes sandwiches, salt fish croquettes with tartare sauce dip, buttermilk chicken in polenta and parmesan crumb with burnt lemon mayonnaise, chicken caesar salad, pizzas, seafood linguine with white wine and chive sauce, beer-battered fish and chips, barbecue pulled pork with apple slaw and skinny fries, half a roast chicken with french fries, a pie of the day, roasted salmon with gnocchi, broad beans, cucumber and lettuce fricassée with beetroot pesto, and puddings such as double chocolate and peanut butter brownie with salted caramel ice-cream and raspberry and passion-fruit cheesecake. *Benchmark main dish: burger with toppings and chips £13.50. Two-course evening meal £20.00.*

Free house ~ Licensee Lawrence Santi ~ Real ale ~ Open 11am-midnight; 10am-midnight Sat; 10am-11.30pm Sun ~ Bar food 12-3, 6-10; 12-10.30 weekends ~ Restaurant ~ Children welcome ~ Dogs allowed in bar ~ Wi-fi *Recommended by Laura Reid, Jamie Green, Alf and Sally Garner, Glen and Patricia Fuller, Ben Lees, Lucy Spencer-Davidson*

SOUTH LONDON

Map 12

Fox & Grapes

(020) 8619 1300 – www.foxandgrapeswimbledon.co.uk

Camp Road; [BR] Wimbledon; SW19 4UN

Wide mix of customers for very popular pub with enjoyable food and drink; bedrooms

This 18th-c pub is ideally placed on the edge of Wimbledon Common and is extremely popular with walkers at lunchtime. There's always a good mix of both drinkers and diners, and the efficient, friendly staff manage to keep things running smoothly, even at peak times. The spacious main bar, with a step between its two halves, has high ceilings with unusual chandeliers, all sorts of wooden and leather dining chairs around scrubbed or painted tables on stripped boards or parquet flooring, built-in wall seats and settles with pretty scatter cushions, a couple of large cartwheels and high black leather chairs against the counter. Here they keep Fullers London Pride and Wimbledon Common PA and Copper Leaf on handpump, 13 wines by the glass (plus two sparking ones) and a few malt whiskies; background music and TV. There's a cosy area with green-painted planked walls and an ornately carved mirror. The bedrooms are light, airy and pretty. This is sister pub to the Malt House in Fulham (West London) and the Victoria in East Sheen (South London) and is part of the Jolly Fine Pub Group.

As well as breakfasts (8.30-10.30am; not Sunday), the rewarding food includes tiger prawn cocktail, pork rillettes with piccalilli and sourdough toast, buffalo ricotta tortelloni with peas, broad beans, mint and parmesan, chicken caesar salad, beer-battered fish and triple-cooked fish, salt marsh lamb rump with tempura courgette flower, goats cheese, basil pesto and pine nuts, yellowfin grilled tuna steak with warm new potato and green bean salad, caper and tomato salsa and aioli, 28-day-aged rare-breed sirloin steak with truffle butter and triple-cooked chips, and puddings such as coconut and kaffir lime pannacotta with chilli and mango salsa and treacle tart with vanilla ice-cream. *Benchmark main dish: steak burger with toppings and triple-cooked chips £15.00. Two-course evening meal £25.00.*

Enterprise ~ Manager Jessica Chanter ~ Real ale ~ Open 8.30am-11pm (10.30pm Sun) ~ Bar food 12-9.30; 12-3, 4-9.30 Sat; 12-8.30 Sun ~ Children welcome ~ Dogs welcome ~ Wi-fi ~ Bedrooms: /£180 *Recommended by Nick Higgins, Daniel King, Julian Thorpe, Moira and Jon Weller*

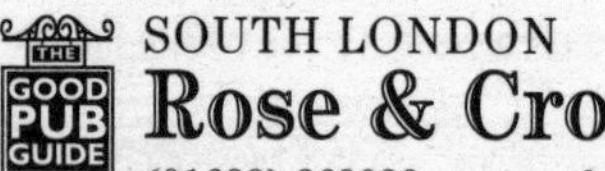

SOUTH LONDON — Map 12

Rose & Crown

(01689) 869029 – www.the-roseandcrown.co.uk

Farnborough Way (A21); Chelsfield rail (some distance away); BR6 6BT

Sizeable pub on the edge of London with large back garden, character bars, a wide choice of food and drink and cheerful service

The big garden behind this renovated pub is quite a surprise – it has colourful beach huts and cabanas, chairs and tables on a terrace, picnic-sets on grass and a sizeable children's play area. Inside, the open-plan, interconnected rooms (there are alcoves and smaller, cosier areas too) are interestingly furnished. There's every shape and size of Edwardian-style dining chairs, leather tub seats, upholstered stools and coloured button-back banquettes grouped around polished tables on rugs, bare boards or black and white tiles, and the walls are hung with frame-to-frame prints and pictures; also, house plants, church candles, lots of mirrors, hundreds of books on shelves and three log fires (one is a woodburner). Friendly, efficient young staff serve a beer named for the pub (from Youngs), Ringwood Razorback, Sharps Doom Bar, Westerham Summer Perle and Youngs Bitter and Special on handpump, and 16 wines by the glass.

Good, popular food includes sandwiches, salted cod fritters on curried cauliflower purée with leeks and tomato and chilli sauce, chicken liver parfait with red onion marmalade, three macaroni cheese with garlic bread, steak burger with toppings and skinny fries, chicken, bacon and leek pie, lamb shank osso bucco with soft polenta, sausages with bubble and squeak and onion and thyme gravy, sirloin steak with chips and béarnaise or cognac and green peppercorn sauce, and pudddings such as sticky toffee pudding with toffee sauce and pineapple upside-down cake with mango sorbet. *Benchmark main dish: salmon with caper and potato roulade, shaved fennel and grapefruit salad, red onion and tomato salsa £13.95. Two-course evening meal £20.00.*

Whiting & Hammond ~ Manager Andrew Roberts ~ Real ale ~ Open 11-11; 9am-11pm Sat; 9am-10.30pm Sun ~ Bar food 12-9.30 (9 Sun) ~ Restaurant ~ Children welcome ~ Dogs allowed in bar ~ Wi-fi *Recommended by Christian Mole, Lionel Smith, Daphne and Robert Staples, B and M Kendall, Philip Chesington, Mike Buckingham*

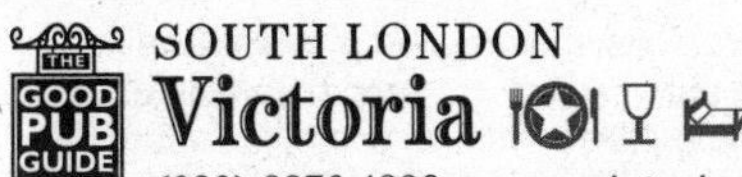

SOUTH LONDON Map 12

Victoria

(020) 8876 4238 – www.victoriasheen.co.uk

West Temple Sheen; Mortlake rail; SW14 7RT

Bustling pub serving all-day food and drink, with open fires in winter and a leafy garden in summer; comfortable bedrooms

Just a five-minute walk from Richmond Park, this bustling but informal pub serves customers all day. The bar rooms have button-back leather sofas and simple chairs and tables on bare floorboards, candles in lanterns, decorative bright pink or stag's head wallpaper, and stools against the blue-painted counter where friendly young staff serve Timothy Taylors Landlord, Twickenham Naked Ladies and Wimbledon Common PA on handpump, 18 good wines by the glass, summer home-made raspberry lemonade and elderflower cordial and winter mulled wine; board games and TV for sports. There's also a room with an open fire, chandeliers and a stag's head. Background music and board games. A conservatory-style dining room has comfortable, contemporary orange leather chairs around tables of varying sizes on pale floorboards, and doors that lead into the leafy walled (and heated) garden where good quality seats and tables sit under parasols and there's an outdoor kitchen and children's play area. The old stables have been converted into comfortable, contemporary bedrooms and breakfasts are good. Disabled access but no disabled loos. This is sister pub to the Fox & Grapes in Wimbledon (South London) and the Malt House in Fulham (West London) and is part of the Jolly Fine Pub Group.

Good, interesting food includes chicken liver parfait with red onion jam, asian prawn salad with edamame beans, bean shoots, pickled ginger, chilli and roasted peanuts, lunchtime sandwiches, spiced butternut, roasted pepper and apricot tagine with couscous, smashed avocado and toasted pitta, cumberland sausage and mash with crispy onions and ale gravy, steak with green peppercorns and rosemary pie, slow-cooked lamb breast with wild garlic polenta, hispi cabbage, crispy capers and lamb jus, chargrilled sea bass with fennel and kohlrabi salad and béarnaise sauce, and puddings such as chocolate fudge cake with chocolate ice-cream and lemon and lime cheesecake with blackcurrant sorbet; vegetarian day is Monday. *Benchmark main dish: hake wrapped in serrano ham with saffron and chorizo risotto, lemon and garlic £17.00. Two-course evening meal £22.50.*

Enterprise ~ Lease Lea Slobodnikova ~ Real ale ~ Open 8am-11pm; 12-10 Sun ~ Bar food 8am-10pm ~ Children welcome ~ Dogs allowed in bar and bedrooms ~ Wi-fi ~ Bedrooms: /£125 *Recommended by Jamie Green, Chris Stevenson, Jamie Dorman, Charlie Stevens, Mark and Mary Setting*

WEST LONDON Map 3

Bell

(020) 8941 9799 – www.thebellinnhampton.co.uk

Thames Street, Hampton; Hampton rail; TW12 2EA

Bustling pub by the Thames with seats outside, real ales, a good choice of food and friendly service

In warm weather, head for the garden of this friendly riverside pub, where you'll find plenty of contemporary chairs and tables plus booth seating, heaters, lighting and barbecues. Inside, a wide mix of customers create a good bustling atmosphere in the interconnected rooms: wooden dining and tub chairs around copper-topped or chunky wooden tables, comfortably upholstered wall seats with scatter cushions, mirrors, old photographs and lots of church candles. From the long panelled bar counter, helpful staff serve Sharps Atlantic and Doom Bar and guests such as Sambrooks Junction, Twickenham Naked Ladies and Windsor & Eton Windsor Knot on handpump, 20 wines by the glass, ten gins and cocktails. Background music.

Interesting food includes scallops and chorizo with pea purée, garlic and rosemary baked camembert with apple and ginger chutney, sharing boards, chargrilled, harissa-spiced lamb kebab salad with feta cheese, olives and yoghurt dressing, king prawn and crab linguine, crispy halloumi and chargrilled vegetable kebabs in pitta bread with sweet potato chips, 10oz rare-breed sirloin steak with crispy onions and a choice of sauce, and puddings such as a seasonal crumble with vanilla bean custard and dark chocolate brownie. *Benchmark main dish: cheese and bacon burger £12.00. Two-course evening meal £20.00.*

Authentic Inns ~ Lease Simon Bailey ~ Real ale ~ Open 11-11 (midnight Sat); 11am-10pm Sun ~ Bar food 12-3, 5-10; 12-10 Sat; 12-9 Sun ~ Restaurant ~ Children welcome ~ Dogs allowed in bar ~ Wi-fi ~ Live music Sat evening monthly *Recommended by Hilary and Neil Christopher, Carol and Barry Craddock, Maddie Purvis, Martin and Sue Neville, Fiona and Jack Henderson*

WEST LONDON Map 12

Brown Cow

(020) 7384 9559 – www.thebrowncowpub.co.uk

Fulham Road; Parsons Green tube; SW6 5SA

Busy pub with food and drink served all day by cheerful staff

This efficiently run dining pub is open (and serves food) all day, so there are always plenty of customers popping in and out. The open-plan bar is furnished and decorated in a minimalist style with wooden and cushioned dining chairs and leather-topped stools around rustic tables on bare boards, button-back wall banquettes, prints on pale painted walls, a few suitcases on racks, house plants and industrial-style ceiling lamps. From a small bar counter lined with stools, friendly staff serve Shepherd Neame Whitstable Bay and Wychwood Hobgoblin on handpump, good wines by the glass and a growing collection of gins; background music and TV. There are a couple of tables outside on a side road.

As well as offering weekend brunches, the enjoyable food includes chicken liver parfait with berry chutney, mussels with garlic and white wine, baby pumpkin, spinach, chestnuts and wild mushrooms, hake with boulangère potatoes, mussels and tarragon velouté, pork belly with truffled mash, kale and wholegrain mustard gravy, confit barbary duck leg with crispy kale, wild rice and pancetta, chargrilled flat-iron steak with sautéed mushrooms, a fried egg and triple-cooked chips, and puddings such as caramel affogato and chocolate brownie with butterscotch sauce. *Benchmark main dish: 28-day-dry-aged rib-eye steak £25.00. Two-course evening meal £27.00.*

Free house ~ Licensee Adam Byallas ~ Real ale ~ Open 12-midnight; 10am-midnight Sat; 12-10 Sun ~ Bar food 12-3, 6-10; 10-4, 6-10 Sat; 12-9 Sun ~ Restaurant ~ Children welcome ~ Dogs welcome ~ Wi-fi *Recommended by Gail and Arthur Roberts, Sally and Colin Allen, Julia and Fiona Barnes, Rosie and Marcus Heatherley, Mary and Douglas McDowell*

WEST LONDON Map 12

Colton Arms

(020) 3757 8050 – www.thecoltonarms.co.uk

Greyhound Road; Barons Court tube; W14 9SD

Extended and refurbished pub opposite the famous tennis courts, attractive bar and dining rooms, interesting décor, well liked food and seats outside

A cosy pub next to the tennis courts of the renowned Queen's Club, this has been refurbished by Hippo Inns. The small front Dot's Bar (named after the long-serving former landlady) has painted panelling, wooden stools and chairs and simple tables on bare floorboards, an open fire and friendly staff serving Fullers London Pride and Sambrooks Wandle on handpump and good wines by the glass. The extended sky-lit back dining room has striped and floral upholstered wall seating, all sorts of wooden or leather chairs and tables on floor tiles and some quirky decorative touches such as brightly coloured artificial birds in cages, taxidermy, an eclectic range of artwork and portraits, ornamental old cash registers and sawn-off antique tennis rackets acting as coat racks; background music. Glass doors lead into the terraced garden which is marked out and painted like a tennis court. Street parking is free at weekends and after 5pm on weekdays.

As well as Saturday brunch, the pleasing food includes crab, tomato and marjoram salad, mushroom pasta with parmesan, cheese, onion and cauliflower tart, monkfish, samphire and lemon with beurre blanc sauce, roasted lamb rump with minted peas, broad beans and roast garlic purée, free-range pork chop with fennel and red onion slaw, 35-day-aged rib-eye steak with a choice of sauce and triple-cooked chips, and puddings such as white chocolate pannacotta with gooseberry jam and lemon tart and raspberries. *Benchmark main dish: lamb rump with niçoise salad £20.00. Two-course evening meal £22.00.*

Hippo Inns ~ Managers Rupert and Jo Clevely ~ Real ale ~ Open 12-11; 10am-midnight Sat; 12-10.30 Sun ~ Bar food 12-3, 6-10; 10-10 Sat; 12-9 Sun ~ Restaurant ~ Children welcome ~ Dogs allowed in bar ~ Wi-fi *Recommended by Susan and John Douglas, William and Tasha Fraser, Elizabeth and Giles Hancock*

WEST LONDON Map 12

Dove

(020) 8748 9474 – www.dovehammersmith.co.uk

Upper Mall; Ravenscourt Park tube; W6 9TA

Character pub with a lovely riverside terrace, cosily traditional front bar and an interesting history

As ever, our readers love this old-fashioned riverside place and it gets packed at peak times – particularly the front snug which is in the *Guinness World Records* for having the smallest bar room – a mere 1.3 metres by 2.4 metres. The main bar is cosy, traditional and unchanging, with black panelling and red leatherette cushioned built-in wall settles and stools around assorted tables. It leads to a bigger, similarly furnished back room that's more geared to eating, which in turn leads to a conservatory. Fullers ESB, London Pride, Seafarers and a seasonal guest on handpump and 19 wines by the glass including champagne and sparkling wine. Head down steps at the back to reach the verandah with its highly prized tables looking over a low river wall to the Thames Reach just above Hammersmith Bridge; a tiny exclusive area, reached up a spiral staircase, is a prime spot for watching rowers on the water. The pub has played host to many writers, actors and artists over the years (there's a fascinating framed list on a wall); it's said to be where 'Rule Britannia' was composed and was a favourite with Turner, who painted the view of the Thames from here, and with Graham Greene. The street itself is associated with the foundation of the arts and crafts movement – William Morris's Kelmscott House (open certain afternoons), is nearby.

Pleasing food includes sandwiches, crispy squid with coriander and chilli jam, chicken liver parfait with apple and vanilla chutney, pasta with broccoli pesto, spinach, dried cherry tomatoes and pine nuts, battered fish and chips with crushed peas, burger with toppings and triple-cooked chips, pork rib-eye with warm pearl barley, green beans, spring onions and watercress and hazelnut salad, sea bass with grilled artichokes, roast tomatoes and spinach purée, harissa-spiced chicken with couscous, roasted peppers and yoghurt, and puddings such as strawberry pannacotta with strawberry ice-cream and chocolate and hazelnut mousse with blackcurrant mousse. *Benchmark main dish: lamb rump with burnt onion, pea purée, pistachios, black olives and anchovies £19.00. Two-course evening meal £22.00.*

Fullers ~ Manager Sonia Labatut ~ Real ale ~ Open 11-11; 12-10.30 Sun ~ Bar food 12-10; 12-9 Sun ~ Children welcome ~ Dogs welcome ~ Wi-fi *Recommended by Chantelle and Tony Redman, Belinda and Neil Garth, Gary and Marie Miller, Dave Chapman, B and M Kendall, Nicholas and Maddy Trainer*

WEST LONDON Map 12

Duke of Sussex

(020) 8742 8801 – www.thedukeofsussex.co.uk

South Parade; Chiswick Park rail; W4 5LF

Attractively restored Victorian local with interesting bar food, a good choice of drinks and a lovely big garden

On a warm day, the unexpectedly big garden behind this well run pub is a real treat – there are seats and tables under parasols, nicely laid out plants, carefully positioned lighting and (if it gets cooler in the evening) heaters. The classy, simply furnished bar has some original etched glass, chapel and farmhouse chairs around scrubbed pine and dark wood tables, and huge windows overlooking Acton Green. The big horseshoe-shaped counter, lined with high bar stools, is where hard-working, friendly staff keep four or five real ales from breweries such as Reunion, Sambrooks, Twickenham and Wimbledon on handpump, 30 wines by the glass and 15 malt whiskies. Off here is a dining room, again with simple wooden furnishings on parquet, but also six-seater booths, chandeliers, antique lamps, a splendid skylight framed by colourfully painted cherubs and a couple of big mirrors, one above a small tiled fireplace.

Highly thought-of food includes tapas such as salt cod croquetas, red cabbage, goats cheese, grapefruit and pine nut salad, chipirones (baby squid) with garlic, parsley and chilli and spanish cured meat plus vegetable paella, chicken pie (for two), squid ink, monkfish, clams and aioli with pasta, confit duck leg with charred gem, sautéed beetroot and walnut salad, fish and chips with pea purée, onglet steak with chips, watercress and chimichurri, and puddings such as treacle tart with clotted cream and chocolate brownie with chocolate sauce. *Benchmark main dish: seafood paella £17.00. Two-course evening meal £21.00.*

Greene King ~ Manager Andrew Taylor ~ Real ale ~ Open 12-11; 12-11.30 Fri, Sat; 12-10.30 Sun ~ Bar food 12-10 (9.30 Sun) ~ Restaurant ~ Children welcome ~ Dogs allowed in bar ~ Wi-fi *Recommended by Ben and Diane Bowie, Sophia and Hamish Greenfield, Philip J Alderton, Alexandra and Richard Clay, Peter Pilbeam*

Please keep sending us reports. We rely on readers for news of new discoveries, and particularly for news of changes – however slight – at the fully described pubs: feedback@goodguides.com, or (no stamp needed) The Good Pub Guide, FREEPOST RTXY–ZCBC–BBAZ, Stream Lane, Sedlescombe, Battle TN33 0PB.

WEST LONDON Map 12

Malt House

(020) 7084 6888 – www.malthousefulham.co.uk

Vanston Place; Fulham Broadway tube; SW6 1AY

Creative food and good drinks choice in refurbished Georgian pub, stylish bar and dining areas and hidden-away garden; bedrooms

Dating from 1729, this large refurbished corner pub has a good, bustling atmosphere in its U-shaped bar. There are big windows, high ceilings, wooden or tiled floors, green leather button-back wall seating and dark wooden dining chairs around pale-topped tables and groups of sofas and armchairs dotted here and there. Planked walls are hung with watercolours, there's a lot of cream paintwork throughout and some bookshelf wallpaper. Contemporary high chairs line the counter where helpful staff serve Brakspears Bitter and Oxford Gold and Ringwood Fortyniner on handpump, 14 wines by the glass, 11 malt whiskies and 17 gins; background music, TV and board games. The small paved back garden has pretty hanging baskets and bunting, candles in lanterns, cheerful scatter cushions and wooden tables and chairs. Bedrooms are comfortable and light and airy. This is sister pub to the Fox & Grapes in Wimbledon and Victoria in East Sheen (both in South London) and is part of the Jolly Fine Pub Group.

As well as breakfast (8.30-10.30am weekdays; brunch 10am-3pm Sat), the enjoyable food includes crispy squid with garlic mayonnaise, asian prawn salad with edamame beans, pickled ginger, chilli and roasted peanuts, stuffed pepper (piedmontese-style) with polenta fritters and black olive tapenade, red chicken curry, pressed ham hock with a fried duck egg, new potato salad and shaved fennel, moroccan-spiced lamb burger with tomato chilli jam, tzatziki and triple-cooked chips, grilled sea bass with courgettes, roasted cherry tomatoes, samphire and sorrel, rare-breed sirloin steak with a choice of sauce, and puddings such as buttermilk pannacotta with blackberries and honeycomb and chocolate nemesis with chocolate soil and crème fraîche. *Benchmark main dish: cheese burger with triple-cooked chips £15.00. Two-course evening meal £21.50.*

Brakspears ~ Lease Jessica Chanter ~ Real ale ~ Open 8.30am-11pm; 9am-11pm Sat; 9am-10pm Sun ~ Bar food 12-3, 6-10 ~ Restaurant ~ Children welcome ~ Dogs allowed in bar ~ Wi-fi ~ Bedrooms: /£130 *Recommended by Susan Eccleston, Sally and David Champion, Geoff and Ann Marston, Belinda Stamp, Elise and Charles Mackinlay*

WEST LONDON Map 12

Mute Swan

(020) 8941 5959 – www.brunningandprice.co.uk/muteswan

Palace Gate, Hampton Court Road; Hampton Court rail; KT8 9BN

Handsome pub close to the Thames with sunny seats outside, relaxed bar, upstairs dining room and imaginative food and drinks choice

Always busy and friendly, this well run pub is just yards from the River Thames (though there's no view). The light and airy bar has four big leather armchairs grouped around a low table, while the rest of the room has brown leather wall seats, high-backed Edwardian-style cushioned dining chairs around dark tables and rugs on bare boards. The walls are covered in interesting photographs, maps, prints and posters and there are sizeable house plants, glass and stone bottles on the windowsills and a woodburning stove. The atmosphere is informal and relaxed. Hogs Back TEA, Park Summer Pale, Red Cat Mr M's Porter, Twickenham Grandstand

Bitter and Windsor & Eton Kohinoor on handpump, a carefully chosen wine list with 30 by the glass, 42 gins, 75 malt whiskies and farm cider; staff are efficient and helpful. A metal spiral staircase – presided over by an elegant metal chandelier – leads up to the dining area where there are brass-studded caramel leather chairs around well spaced tables on bare boards or carpeting, and numerous photos and prints. The tables and chairs on the front terrace get snapped up quickly and the pub is opposite the gates to Hampton Court Palace. There are a few parking spaces in front, but you'll probably have to park elsewhere.

Rewarding, up-to-date food includes sandwiches (until 5pm), miso-glazed scallops with wasabi pea purée, squid ink tuile and grilled octopus, chicken liver pâté with spiced pear chutney, sweet potato, aubergine and kale curry with coconut rice, steak burger with toppings, coleslaw and chips, paprika-roasted poussin and seafood paella, braised lamb shoulder with dauphinoise potatoes and red wine sauce, salmon fillet with summer vegetables, baby gem sauce and salsa verde, and puddings such as hot waffle with caramelised banana, toffee sauce and salted caramel ice-cream and lemon meringue tart with raspberry sorbet. *Benchmark main dish: chicken, ham and leek pie £15.95. Two-course evening meal £24.00.*

Brunning & Price ~ Manager Sal Morgan ~ Real ale ~ Open 11-11; 11-midnight Fri, Sat; 11-10.30 Sun ~ Bar food 12-10 (9.30 Sun) ~ Restaurant ~ Children welcome in upstairs restaurant only ~ Dogs allowed in bar ~ Wi-fi *Recommended by Belinda May, Alf Wright, Miranda and Jeff Davidson, Andrew and Michele Revell, Charlotte Smyrk*

WEST LONDON Map 3

Old Orchard

(01895) 822631 – www.brunningandprice.co.uk/oldorchard

Off Park Lane, Harefield; Denham rail (some distance away); UB9 6HJ

Wonderful views from the front garden, a good choice of drinks and interesting brasserie-style food

Tables on the front terrace and in the garden provide stunning views down to the narrowboats on the canal way below and across to the lakes that are part of the conservation area known as the Colne Valley Regional Park – it's a haven for wildlife. Inside, the open-plan rooms have an attractive mix of cushioned dining chairs around all sizes and shapes of dark wooden tables, lots of prints, maps and pictures covering the walls, books on shelves, old glass bottles on windowsills and rugs on wood or parquet flooring. One room is hung with a large rug and some tapestries. There are daily papers to read, two cosy coal fires, big pot plants and fresh flowers. Half a dozen real ales on handpump served by friendly, efficient staff include Phoenix Brunning & Price Original, Dark Star Hophead, London Road Kodiak, Mighty Oak Oscar Wilde, Tring Side Pocket for a Toad and XT Eight; also, 20 wines by the glass, 80 gins, 140 malt whiskies and farm cider.

Good, modern food includes sandwiches (until 6pm), crispy chilli squid with watermelon, spring onion and coriander salad, pigeon with hazelnuts, curly kale, carrot purée and game jus, pumpkin tortellini with blue cheese sauce, walnuts and parmesan, steak burger with toppings, coleslaw and chips, tempura cod cheek with butternut squash purée, curried oil and wilted spinach, blackened cajun chicken with quinoa salad, lime greem yoghurt, mango and feta, 10oz rump steak with horseradish butter, trimmings and chips, and puddings such as chocolate brownie with chocolate sauce and vanilla ice-cream and crème brûlée. *Benchmark main dish: braised lamb shoulder with dauphinoise potatoes, roasted root vegetables and gravy £17.95. Two-course evening meal £25.00.*

Brunning & Price ~ Manager Alisha Craigwell ~ Real ale ~ Open 11.30-11; 12-10.30 Sun ~ Bar food 12-9.30; 12-10 Fri, Sat; 12-9 Sun ~ Children welcome ~ Dogs welcome ~ Wi-fi
Recommended by Nigel and Sue Foster, Trevor and Michele Street, Buster and Helena Hastings, Holly and Tim Waite, Colin and Daniel Gibbs

WEST LONDON — Map 12

Sands End

(020) 7731 7823 – www.thesandsend.co.uk
Stephendale Road; Imperial Wharf rail; SW6 2PR

Simply furnished, bustling pub in a quiet street with interesting food and a thoughtful range of drinks; seats outside

Busy and friendly with lots of young locals and visitors, this Fulham dining pub has an informal but gently civilised atmosphere. The open-plan bar features a mix of wooden dining chairs, the odd settle and cushioned wall seat and scrubbed pine, painted or polished wooden tables on bare boards; the dining area is quieter and more spacious. There's an open fire, large house plants, a few wall prints, a TV and background music. From the solid, central counter, efficient staff serve Brakspears Oxford Gold, Sambrooks Junction and Wandle and Sharps Doom Bar on handpump and good wines by the glass. Upstairs is a private dining room. Outside, there are seats and tables at the front on the quiet residential street.

Well regarded food includes scallops with peas, broad beans, roast shallots, mint and madeira jus, foie gras and chicken liver parfait with toasted brioche, pea and pecorino risotto with asparagus, preserved lemon, mascarpone and pine nuts, a charcuterie sharing board, slow-roast pork belly with pig head croquettes, burnt apple, hispi cabbage and hazelnuts, crab fettuccine with bisque, slow-roast tomatoes and coriander, halibut with roast leeks, cauliflower purée, coastal herbs and brown shrimp butter, and puddings such as morello cherry soufflé with pistachio ice-cream and tonka bean pannacotta with apricot compote. *Benchmark main dish: burger with toppings and chips £15.00. Two-course evening meal £25.00.*

Free house ~ Licensee Susan Carrol ~ Real ale ~ Open 12-midnight (11 Sun) ~ Bar food 12-4, 6-10; 12-9 Sun ~ Restaurant ~ Children allowed but no high chairs ~ Dogs welcome
Recommended by John and Claire Masters, Patricia and Anton Larkham, Lucy and Giles Gibbon, Nicola and Holly Lyons

WEST LONDON — Map 12

White Horse

(020) 7736 2115 – www.whitehorsesw6.com
Parsons Green; Parsons Green tube; SW6 4UL

Cheerfully relaxed local with big terrace, excellent range of carefully sourced drinks and popular food

On summer evenings and weekends, the front terrace – overlooking Parsons Green itself – has something of a continental feel with its many seats and tables; there are barbecues most sunny evenings. Inside, the stylishly modernised U-shaped bar has a gently upmarket and chatty atmosphere, plenty of leather chesterfield sofas and wooden tables, huge windows with slatted wooden blinds, flagstone and wood floors, and winter coal and log fires (one in an elegant marble fireplace). There's also an upstairs dining room with its own bar. The impressive range of drinks takes in real ales such as Harveys Best and seven constantly changing real ales on handpump, a fantastic choice of foreign bottled beers, several malt whiskies and up to 20 good wines by the glass. They have several festivals a year celebrating beers from around the world.

Much enjoyed food includes crab on toasted sourdough with avocado and capers, pork, chicken and pistachio terrine with sloe gin jelly, chicken caesar salad, sausages with creamy mash, crispy onions and red wine jus, burger with toppings and fries, sea trout with leeks, parsnip crisps and sage and onion pesto, côte de boeuf (to share) with triple-cooked chips and horseradish butter, venison steak with butternut squash, braised red cabbage and red wine jus, and puddings such as chantilly cream profiteroles with caramel sauce and sticky toffee pudding with vanilla ice-cream. *Benchmark main dish: beer-battered fish and chips £14.95. Two-course evening meal £21.00.*

Mitchells & Butlers ~ Manager Luke Swain ~ Real ale ~ Open 11am-11.30pm; 11am-midnight Thurs, Fri, Sat ~ Bar food 9.30am-10.30pm ~ Restaurant ~ Children welcome ~ Dogs welcome ~ Wi-fi *Recommended by Jim and Sue James, Jeff Davies, Mike Buckingham*

WEST LONDON — Map 12

Windsor Castle

(020) 7243 8797 – www.thewindsorcastlekensington.co.uk

Campden Hill Road; Notting Hill Gate tube; W8 7AR

Genuinely unspoilt, with lots of atmosphere in tiny, dark rooms and lovely summer garden

To enjoy the old-fashioned charm here, try to visit at lunchtime when it's quieter. Unchanging and full of character, the pub has a wealth of dark oak furnishings, sturdy high-backed built-in elm benches, time-smoked ceilings, soft lighting and a coal-effect fire. Three of the tiny unspoilt rooms have their own entrance from the street, but it's much more fun trying to navigate through the minuscule doors between them inside. The panelled and wood-floored dining room at the back overlooks the garden. Marstons Pedigree, St Austell Proper Job, Sharps Doom Bar and Timothy Taylors Landlord plus up to four guest beers on handpump, decent house wines, farm ciders, malt whiskies and jugs of Pimms. The garden, on several levels, has tables and chairs on flagstones and feels secluded thanks to the high ivy-covered walls; there are heaters for cooler evenings.

Good, popular food includes crab on toasted sourdough with avocado, pork, chicken liver and pistachio terrine with sloe gin jelly and golden beetroot piccalilli, miso-glazed aubergine with cashews, cavolo nero and jasmine rice, steak and smoked cheese pie with red wine jus, beef short rib with smoked brisket, chestnut mash and rioja and shallot sauce, beer-battered fish and chips, 28-day-aged rib-eye steak with horseradish butter and triple-cooked chips, and puddings such as warm chocolate brownie with hazelnut ice-cream and treacle pudding with vanilla ice-cream. *Benchmark main dish: sausages and spring onion mash with red wine jus £13.50. Two-course evening meal £20.00.*

Mitchells & Butlers ~ Manager Ian Constantine ~ Real ale ~ Open 12-11 (10.30 Sun) ~ Bar food 12-10 (9 Sun) ~ Restaurant ~ Children allowed in dining area ~ Dogs welcome ~ Wi-fi *Recommended by Neil Allen, Philip J Alderton, Sarah Kennewell, Justine and Neil Bonnett*

'Children welcome' means the pub says it lets children inside without any special restriction. If it allows them in, but to restricted areas such as an eating area or family room, we specify this. Places with separate restaurants often let children use them, and hotels usually let children into public areas such as lounges. Some pubs impose an evening time limit – let us know if you find one earlier than 9pm.

Also Worth a Visit in London

Besides the fully inspected pubs, you might like to try these pubs that have been recommended to us and described by readers. Do tell us what you think of them: feedback@goodguides.com

CENTRAL LONDON

EC1

Bishops Finger (020) 7248 2341 *West Smithfield; EC1A 9JR* Welcoming little pub close to Smithfield Market; Shepherd Neame ales including seasonal and enjoyable pubby food from bar snacks and sharing boards up, can eat in bar or upstairs room; children welcome, seats out in front, closed weekends and bank holidays, otherwise open all day and can get crowded, no food Fri evening. *(Alison and Michael Harper)*

Butchers Hook & Cleaver (020) 7600 9181 *West Smithfield; EC1A 9DY* Fullers conversion of bank and adjoining butcher's shop; their full range kept well and enjoyable pubby food including various pies, helpful efficient service, spiral stairs to mezzanine; background music, free wi-fi; closed weekends, otherwise open (and food) all day, gets busy with after-work drinkers. *(Fiona and Jack Henderson)*

Coach (020) 3954 1595 *Ray Street; EC1R 3DJ* Smartly revamped Clerkenwell dining pub (former Coach & Horses) with very good french-inspired cooking from chef-proprietor; traditional oak-panelled front bar serving Adnams, Timothy Taylors and well chosen wines by the glass, airy pitched-roof back dining room with floor-to-ceiling glass overlooking small garden, more dining space upstairs; open all day, kitchen closes 4pm Sun. *(Shalaine Duffy)*

Craft Beer Company (020) 7404 7049 *Leather Lane; EC1N 7TR* Corner drinkers' pub with excellent selection of real ales and craft beers plus an extensive bottled range, good choice of wines and spirits too, stools by high tables on bare boards, big chandelier hanging from mirrored ceiling, food limited to snacks, more room upstairs; closed Sun, otherwise open all day and can get very busy. *(Sarah Kennewell)*

Dovetail (020) 7490 7321 *Jerusalem Passage; EC1V 4JP* Fairly small and can get very busy with drinkers spilling into alleyway outside, specialises in draught/bottled belgian beers and serves popular food including some belgian and vegetarian/vegan dishes, efficient staff coping well at peak times; open (and food) all day Sun. *(Cliff and Monica Swan)*

Fox & Anchor (020) 7250 1300 *Charterhouse Street, by Smithfield Market; EC1M 6AA* Beautifully restored late Victorian pub/boutique hotel with fine art nouveau façade; long slender bar with unusual pewter-topped counter, lots of mahogany, green leather and etched glass, small back snugs, Youngs ales and guests, enjoyable food from good breakfast onwards, friendly efficient staff; individual well appointed bedrooms, open all day from 7am (8.30am Sat, 11am Sun). *(Alan and Linda Blackmore)*

Gunmakers (020) 7278 1022 *Eyre Street Hill; EC1R 5ET* Small Victorian pub under new ownership; renovated split-level bar with bare boards and modern artwork, a couple of changing ales and interesting asian-inspired food, more room upstairs including (at the top) a hairdressers/barbers offering cocktails; background music; back garden, open all day weekdays, closed weekends. *(Jill and Dick Archer)*

★**Hand & Shears** (020) 7600 0257 *Middle Street; EC1A 7JA* Traditional unspoilt Smithfield corner pub; three rooms and small snug arranged around central servery, up to six changing ales served by friendly staff, bare boards, panelling and a couple of gas fires, interesting prints and old photographs; closed weekends, otherwise open all day (bustling lunchtime/early evening). *(Megan and Hallam Cunningham)*

★**Jerusalem Tavern** (020) 7490 4281 *Britton Street; EC1M 5UQ* Atmospheric re-creation of a dark 18th-c tavern (1720 merchant's house with shopfront added 1810); tiny dimly lit bar with simple wood furnishings on bare boards, some remarkable old wall tiles, coal fires and candlelight, stairs to a precarious-feeling (though perfectly secure) balcony, plainer back room, St Peters beers tapped from the cask and in bottles, short choice of lunchtime food including good sandwiches, friendly attentive young staff; no children but dogs welcome, seats out on pavement (plastic glasses if you drink out here), open all day weekdays, closed weekends, bank holidays and 24 Dec-2 Jan; can get very crowded at peak times. *(Giles and Annie Francis)*

Ninth Ward (020) 7833 2949
Farringdon Road; EC1R 3BN
American-themed bar/grill (has sister restaurant in New York) with unusual New Orleans-inspired interior (quite dark), tasty food such as burgers and fried chicken, good range of craft and bottled beers, cocktails, friendly staff; background music; closed Sat lunchtime and Sun, otherwise open all day till late. *(Kerry and Guy Trooper)*

Old Fountain (020) 7253 2970
Baldwin Street; EC1V 9NU Popular traditional old pub in same family since 1964; long bar serving two rooms, excellent range of real ales and craft beers chalked on blackboard (some brewed in the cellar), friendly knowledgeable staff, enjoyable good value food from open kitchen, main carpeted part with wooden tables and chairs, padded stools and fish tank; function room for live music, darts; nice roof terrace; open (and food) all day. *(Tony Taylor)*

Old Red Cow (020) 7726 2595
Long Lane; EC1A 9EJ Cheerful little pub close to the Barbican and within sight of Smithfield Market; fine changing selection of cask, craft and bottled beers, tasters offered by friendly knowledgeable staff, nine wines by the glass, well liked food (not Mon) from sharing boards and home-made pies to good Sun roasts, modernised interior with larger room upstairs; open all day and popular with after-work drinkers. *(John Herbert)*

Viaduct (020) 7600 1863
Newgate Street; EC1A 7AA Opposite Old Bailey on site of Newgate Prison (a couple of cells surviving below), big copper lanterns outside, fine ornate high-ceilinged Victorian interior with three or four snug areas, Fullers ales and good selection of gins from horseshoe bar, snacky food such as toasties; popular with after-work drinkers; open (and food) all day weekdays, closed weekends. *(Charlotte Smyrk)*

EC2

Hamilton Hall (020) 7247 3579
Bishopsgate; also entrance from Liverpool Street station; EC2M 7PY
Showpiece Wetherspoons with flamboyant Victorian baroque décor mixing with contemporary bar counter and modern furniture; lots of real ales, decent wines and their usual food and competitive pricing, friendly staff coping well at busy times, good-sized comfortable mezzanine; silenced machines, free wi-fi, screens showing train times; good disabled access, café-style tables and chairs out in front, open all day from 7am, can get very crowded after work. *(Ben Lees)*

Lord Aberconway (020) 7929 1743
Old Broad Street; EC2M 1QT Victorian feel with high moulded ceiling, dark panelling, some red leather bench seating and drinking booths, six well kept ales and reasonably priced Nicholsons menu, dining gallery; handy for Liverpool Street station, gets busy with after-work drinkers, open all day (till 6pm Sun). *(Holly and Tim Waite)*

EC3

★ **Counting House** (020) 7283 7123
Cornhill; EC3V 3PD Spacious bank conversion retaining original Victorian character; impressive glass dome and grand ceiling, chandeliers, rich polished mahogany, mosaics, island bar topped with four-sided clock, gallery seating, Fullers beers kept well and enjoyable food including range of pies, efficient friendly service; wheelchair access, closed weekends, otherwise open (and food) all day. *(Ross Balaam)*

East India Arms (020) 7265 5121
Fenchurch Street; EC3M 4BR
Standing-room 19th-c corner pub popular with City workers; small single room with wood floor, half-panelling, old local photographs and brewery mirrors, well kept Shepherd Neame ales served by efficient staff; tables outside, closed weekends, otherwise open all day. *(Kerry and Guy Trooper)*

Hoop & Grapes (020) 7481 4583
Aldgate High Street; EC3N 1AL Originally 17th-c (dismantled and rebuilt 1983) and much bigger inside than it looks; long partitioned bare-boards bar with beams, timbers, exposed brickwork and panelling, mix of seating including some button-back wall benches, seven real ales and standard Nicholsons menu (popular lunchtime), friendly efficient service; muted sports TV; a few seats in front, closed Sun, otherwise open (and food) all day. *(Aiden)*

Jamaica Wine House
(020) 7929 6972 *St Michael Alley, Cornhill; EC3V 9DS* Red-stone 19th-c pub (site of London's first coffee house) in warren of small alleys; traditional Victorian décor with ornate coffered ceiling, oak-panelling, booths and bare boards, Shepherd Neame ales and wide choice of wines, friendly helpful service and bustling atmosphere (quieter after 8pm), food in bar or downstairs dining room; closed weekends. *(Georgie Egner)*

Lamb (020) 7626 2454
Leadenhall Market; EC3V 1LR Stand-up bar with friendly staff coping admirably with hordes of after-work drinkers; Youngs ales and good choice of wines, dark panelling, engraved glass and plenty of ledges and shelves, spiral stairs up to small carpeted gallery overlooking market's central crossing, corner servery for lunchtime food from sandwiches up, separate stairs to nice bright dining room, also basement bar with shiny wall tiles; tables out under splendid Victorian

market roof – crowds here in warmer months, open (and food) all day, closed weekends. *(Daisy Rutledge)*

Ship (020) 7929 3903
Talbot Court, off Eastcheap; EC3V 0BP Interesting Nicholsons pub tucked down alleyway; busy bare-boards bar with soft lighting and ornate décor, candles in galleried dining area, friendly efficient staff, several well kept ales including their house beer from St Austell, well liked good value food; closed Sun, otherwise open all day, till 6pm Sat. *(Lucia Halliwell)*

Ship (020) 7702 4422
Hart Street; EC3R 7NB Tiny one-room 19th-c City pub with ornate flower-decked façade; well kept Caledonian and a couple of guests, craft beers and eight wines by the glass, lunchtime food including selection of bar snacks and signature burgers, meal/drink deals, friendly staff, limited seating and can get packed, upstairs dining room; spiral stairs down to lavatories; closed weekends. *(John Herbert)*

Swan (020) 7929 6550
Ship Tavern Passage, off Gracechurch Street; EC3V 1LY Traditional Fullers pub with bustling narrow flagstoned bar; their well kept ales and lunchtime sandwiches/ burgers, friendly efficient service, neatly kept Victorian panelled décor, low lighting, larger more ordinary carpeted bar upstairs; silent TV; covered alley used by smokers, open all day Mon-Fri, closed weekends. *(Trevor and Michele Street)*

EC4

Cockpit (020) 7248 7315
St Andrews Hill/Ireland Place, off Queen Victoria Street; EC4V 5BY Plenty of atmosphere in this little corner pub near St Paul's Cathedral; as name suggests, a former cockfighting venue with surviving spectators' gallery; good selection of beers such as Adnams, St Austell and Shepherd Neame, lunchtime food; open all day. *(Moira and Jon Weller)*

Old Bell (020) 7583 0216
Fleet Street, near Ludgate Circus; EC4Y 1DH Dimly lit 17th-c tavern backing on to St Bride's Church; stained-glass bow window, heavy black beams, bare boards and flagstones, half a dozen or more well kept changing beers from island servery (tasting trays available), usual Nicholsons food, friendly helpful young staff, various seating nooks, brass-topped tables, coal fire; background music; covered and heated outside area, open all day. *(Lyn and Freddie Roberts)*

★**Olde Cheshire Cheese**
(020) 7353 6170 *Wine Office Court, off 145 Fleet Street; EC4A 2BU* Best to visit this 17th-c former chophouse outside peak times as it can be packed (early evening especially); soaked in history with warren of old-fashioned unpretentious rooms, high beams, bare boards, old built-in black benches, Victorian paintings on dark brown walls, big open fires, tiny snug and steep stone steps down to unexpected series of cosy areas and secluded alcoves, Sam Smiths beers, all-day pubby food; Coco the profane parrot – also look out for Polly (now stuffed) who entertained distinguished guests for over 40 years; children allowed in eating area lunchtime only, closed Sun evening. *(Jill and Dick Archer)*

Olde Watling (020) 7248 8935
Watling Street; EC4M 9BR Heavy-beamed and timbered post-blitz replica of pub built by Wren in 1668; interesting choice of well kept beers, standard Nicholsons menu, good friendly service, quieter back bar and upstairs dining room; open all day. *(B and M Kendall)*

Three Cranes (020) 3455 7437
Garlick Hill opposite Mansion House tube; EC4V 2BA Newly revamped City pub under same ownership as the Coach (EC1) and Hero of Maida (W9); blue panelled bar with beers such as Beavertown, Portobello and Timothy Taylors, good range of wines and other drinks, snacky food including sharing boards, full meals in upstairs grill room; open all day weekdays, closed weekends. *(Alan and Linda Blackmore)*

SW1

Antelope (020) 7824 8512
Eaton Terrace; SW1W 8EZ Pretty little flower-decked local in Belgravia; traditional interior with snug seating areas, bare boards, panelling and etched windows, mix of old and new furniture, interesting prints and gas-effect coal fire in tiled Victorian fireplace, well kept Fullers ales from central counter, upstairs dining room serving decent pubby food (all day weekends) including popular Sun roasts; TVs, free wi-fi, daily papers; children (if eating) and dogs welcome, open all day and can get crowded in the evening. *(Michael Butler)*

Buckingham Arms (020) 7222 3386
Petty France; SW1H 9EU Welcoming and relaxed early 19th-c bow-windowed local; Youngs ales and a guest from long curved bar, good range of wines by the glass and well liked pubby food from back open kitchen, elegant mirrors and dark woodwork, stained-glass screens, stools at modern high tables, some armchairs and upholstered banquettes, unusual side corridor with elbow ledge for drinkers; background music, TV; dogs welcome, handy for Buckingham Palace, Westminster Abbey and St James's Park, open all day, till 6pm weekends. *(Dr and Mrs A K Clarke)*

Cask & Glass (020) 7834 7630
Palace Street; SW1E 5HN Snug traditional one-room pub with friendly atmosphere; black panelling, button-back wall benches and old prints, good range of Shepherd Neame ales, lunchtime toasties; quiet corner TV, free wi-fi; a few tables outside under awning, handy for Queen's Gallery, open all day, till 8pm Sat, closed Sun. *(Cliff and Monica Swan)*

Cask Pub & Kitchen (020) 7630 7225
Charlwood Street/Tachbrook Street; SW1V 2EE Spacious simply furnished modern bar; excellent choice of draught beers with over 500 more in bottles, decent range of wines too, friendly knowledgeable staff, good burgers, bar snacks and Sun roasts, chatty atmosphere – can get packed and noisy in the evening; Sun live music, regular beer-related events such as Meet the Brewer; downstairs gents'; some outside seating, open all day, food all day weekends. *(Fiona and Jack Henderson)*

Clarence (020) 7930 4808
Whitehall; SW1A 2HP Popular beamed corner pub (Geronimo Inn) with cheerful quirky décor; Youngs and guests such as Twickenham, decent wines by the glass and good food from snacks up, quick friendly service, well spaced tables and varied seating including tub chairs and banquettes, upstairs dining area; pavement tables, open (and food) all day. *(Dr and Mrs A K Clarke, Jon Isherwood, Dave Braisted)*

★**Fox & Hounds** (020) 7730 6367
Passmore Street/Graham Terrace; SW1W 8HR Small flower-decked pub in backstreets below Sloane Square; well kept Youngs ales and interesting guests, warm red décor with lots of old pictures, prints and photographs, wall benches and leather chesterfields, coal-effect gas fire, back room with skylight; open (and snacky food) all day, can get crowded early evening. *(Alison and Michael Harper)*

★**Grenadier** (020) 7235 3074
Wilton Row; the turning off Wilton Crescent looks prohibitive, but the barrier and watchman are there to keep out cars; SW1X 7NR Steps up to cosy old mews pub with lots of character and military history, but not much space (packed 5-7pm); simple unfussy panelled bar, stools and wooden benches on bare boards, ales such as Greene King, Timothy Taylors and Woodfordes from rare pewter-topped counter, famous bloody marys, well liked pubby food in intimate back restaurant; children over 8 and dogs allowed, hanging baskets, sentry box and single table outside, open (and food) all day. *(Ben Lees)*

Grosvenor (020) 7821 8786
Grosvenor Road; SW1V 3LA Traditional pub across from river (no views), chatty and relaxed, with three well kept ales including Sharps and nice selection of wines, enjoyable reasonably priced pub food including good fish and chips and popular Sun roasts, friendly staff; some tables out by road, secluded beer garden behind, open (and food) all day. *(Shalaine Duffy)*

Jugged Hare (020) 7828 1543
Vauxhall Bridge Road/Rochester Row; SW1V 1DX Popular Fullers pub in former colonnaded bank; iron pillars, dark woodwork and large chandelier, old photographs of London, smaller back panelled dining room, stairs up to gallery, four well kept ales and straightforward reasonably priced food including range of pies, good friendly service; background music, TVs, silent fruit machine; open all day. *(Dr and Mrs A K Clarke, Nigel and Sue Foster)*

★**Lord Moon of the Mall**
(020) 7839 7701 *Whitehall; SW1A 2DY* Popular Wetherspoons bank conversion; elegant main room with big arched windows looking over Whitehall, old prints and a large portrait of Tim Martin (the chain's founder); through an arch the style is more recognisably Wetherspoons with neatly tiled areas and bookshelves opposite long servery, ten real ales and their good value food (from breakfasts up); children (if eating) and dogs welcome, open all day from 8am (till midnight Fri, Sat). *(Dr and Mrs A K Clarke, Dave Braisted)*

Morpeth Arms (020) 7834 6442 *Millbank; SW1P 4RW* Victorian pub facing the Thames with view over to MI6 headquarters from upstairs Spy Room; etched and cut glass, lots of mirrors, paintings, prints and old photographs (some of british spies), well kept Youngs ales and guests, decent choice of wines and fair value pubby food, welcoming efficient staff, built on site of Milbank Prison and cells remain below; background music; seats outside (and a lot of traffic), handy for Tate Britain and Thames Path walkers, open (and food) all day, can get very busy weekday evenings. *(Nigel and Sue Foster)*

Nags Head (020) 7235 1135
Kinnerton Street; SW1X 8ED Unspoilt and unchanging little mews pub with no-nonsense plain-talking landlord; low-ceilinged panelled front room with unusual sunken counter, log-effect gas fire in old range, narrow passage down to even smaller bar, well kept Adnams from 19th-c handpumps, uncomplicated food, theatrical mementoes and other interesting memorabilia including

We say if we know a pub has background music.

what-the-butler-saw machine and one-armed bandit; no mobiles, individual background music; well behaved children and dogs allowed, a few seats outside, open (and food) all day. *(Jess and Dan Holt)*

Red Lion (020) 7930 4141
Crown Passage, behind St James's Street; SW1Y 6PP Cheerful traditional little pub tucked down narrow passage near St James's Palace; dark panelling and leaded lights, upholstered settles and stools on patterned carpet, lots of prints, decorative plates and horsebrasses, well kept Adnams, St Austell and decent range of malt whiskies, friendly service, lunchtime sandwiches (no hot food), narrow overflow room upstairs; sports TV; colourful hanging baskets, closed Sun, otherwise open all day. *(Dr and Mrs A K Clarke)*

Red Lion (020) 7930 5826
Parliament Street; SW1A 2NH Victorian pub by Houses of Parliament used by Foreign Office staff and MPs; divided bare-boards bar with showy chandeliers suspended from fine moulded ceiling, parliamentary cartoons and prints, Fullers/Gales beers and decent wines from long counter, good range of food, efficient staff, also clubby cellar bar and upstairs panelled dining room; free wi-fi; children welcome, outside bench seating, open all day (till 9pm Sun). *(Dr and Mrs A K Clarke)*

★**Red Lion** (020) 7321 0782
Duke of York Street; SW1Y 6JP Pretty little flower-decked Victorian pub, remarkably preserved and packed with customers often spilling out on to the pavement; series of small rooms with profusion of polished mahogany, gleaming mirrors, cut/etched windows and chandeliers, striking ornamental plaster ceiling, Fullers/Gales beers and traditional lunchtime food; no children; dogs welcome, closed Sun and bank holidays, otherwise open all day. *(Revd R P Tickle)*

Speaker (020) 7222 1749
Great Peter Street; SW1P 2HA Bustling chatty atmosphere in unpretentious smallish corner pub (can be packed at peak times); well kept Timothy Taylors and guests, bottled beers and lots of whiskies, short choice of enjoyable simple food, friendly staff, panelling, political cartoons and prints, notes here and there on etiquette; no mobiles, background music or children; open (and food) all day weekdays, closed weekends. *(Dr and Mrs A K Clarke)*

★**St Stephens Tavern**
(020) 7925 2286 *Parliament Street; SW1A 2JR* Victorian pub opposite Houses of Parliament and Big Ben (so quite touristy); brass chandeliers hanging from lofty ceilings, tall windows with etched glass and swagged curtains, gleaming mahogany, division bell for MPs and lots of parliamentary memorabilia, also charming upper gallery bar (may be reserved for functions), four well kept Badger ales from handsome counter with pedestal lamps, fairly priced traditional food including burgers and pies, friendly efficient staff; open (and food) all day. *(Dr and Mrs A K Clarke)*

White Swan (020) 7828 2000
Vauxhall Bridge Road; SW1V 2SA Roomy split-level corner pub handy for Tate Britain and recently spruced-up by McMullens; their ales and guests, decent wines by the glass and enjoyable sensibly priced pubby food, friendly staff; background music, sports TV; open (and food) all day and can get very busy at peak times. *(Dr and Mrs A K Clarke)*

SW3

Coopers Arms (020) 7376 3120
Flood Street; SW3 5TB Recently refurbished 19th-c pub under new management, a useful bolthole for King's Road shoppers (so can get busy); comfortable bar with good mix of tables and chairs on stripped boards, large moose head on one wall, Youngs ales, guest beers and good selection of other drinks including over 20 wines by the glass and cocktails, decent food from fairly pubby menu; Tues quiz, projector for major sports; well behaved children till 7pm, dogs allowed in bar, courtyard garden, open (and food) all day. *(Lucy Spencer-Davidson)*

Hour Glass (020) 7581 2497
Brompton Road; SW3 2DY Under same ownership as nearby Brompton Food Market deli; compact wood-floored bar with open brick fireplace, leather banquette at each end, stools along drinking shelf overlooking street, Fullers London Pride and a couple of guests, proper cider, highly regarded interesting food from bar snacks up (not Mon, Tues), panelled upstairs dining room with open kitchen, friendly helpful service; children and dogs (in bar) welcome, handy for V&A and other nearby museums, open all day. *(Georgia Egner)*

Surprise (020) 7351 6954
Christchurch Terrace; SW3 4AJ Late Victorian Chelsea pub (Geronimo Inn) popular with well heeled locals; Sharps, Youngs and a house beer (HMS Surprise) from light wood servery, champagne and plenty of other wines by the glass, interesting food (all day weekends) including british tapas-style canapé boards, friendly service, soft grey décor and comfortable furnishings with floral sofas and armchairs on sturdy floorboards, stained-glass partitioning, a model ship or two, upstairs dining room, daily papers; open all day. *(Jamie Dorman)*

W1

★**Argyll Arms** (020) 7734 6117
Argyll Street; W1F 7TP Popular and individual Nicholsons pub with three interesting little front cubicle rooms (essentially unchanged since 1860s); wooden partitions and impressive frosted and engraved glass, mirrored corridor to spacious back room, around eight real ales from well stocked bar and good sensibly priced food, upstairs dining room overlooking pedestrianised street; background music, fruit machine; children welcome till 8pm, pavement tables, handy for the Palladium, open (and food) all day. *(B and M Kendall)*

Audley (020) 7499 1843
Mount Street; W1K 2RX Classic late Victorian Mayfair pub; opulent red plush, mahogany panelling and cut glass, clock in extravagantly carved bracket and chandeliers hanging from ornately corniced ceiling, long polished bar serving Greene King ales and guests, good choice of pub food (reasonably priced for the area), upstairs panelled dining room, cellar wine bar; quiet background music, TV, pool, free wi-fi; children till 6pm, pavement tables, open (and food) all day. *(Daisy Rutledge)*

Clachan (020) 7494 0834
Kingly Street; W1B 5QH Nicholsons corner pub behind Liberty (and once owned by them): ornate plaster ceiling supported by fluted pillars, comfortable screened leather banquettes, smaller drinking alcove up three or four steps, fine selection of real ales from handsome mahogany counter, dining room upstairs serving affordably priced food; open (and food) all day, can get very busy. *(Lucia Halliwell)*

Crown & Two Chairmen
(020) 7437 8192 *Bateman Street/Dean Street; W1D 3SB* Large main room with smaller area off to the right, different height tables on bare boards, four real ales along with craft beers, interesting up-to-date food from bar snacks up including weekday brunches and Sun roasts, upstairs dining room, good mix of customers (busy with after-work drinkers); free wi-fi; open (and food) all day. *(John Herbert)*

★**Dog & Duck** (020) 7494 0697
Bateman Street/Frith Street; W1D 3AJ Bags of character in this tiny Soho pub – best enjoyed in the afternoon when not so packed; unusual old tiles and mosaics (the dog with tongue hanging out in hot pursuit of a duck is notable), heavy old advertising mirrors and open fire, Adnams, Sharps and guests from unusual little counter and quite a few wines by the glass, enjoyable well priced food (including pre-theatre menu) in cosy upstairs dining room where children welcome; background music; dogs allowed in bar, open (and food) all day with drinkers often spilling on to the pavement. *(Ben Lees)*

Flying Horse (020) 7636 8324
Oxford Street, near junction with Tottenham Court Road; W1D 1AN Ornate late Victorian pub with long narrow bar, old tiling, mirrors, mahogany fittings and so forth, also three notable murals behind glass of voluptuous nymphs, dark floorboards and leather banquettes, half a dozen real ales, over 20 gins and enjoyable food from Nicholsons menu, friendly service, bar and dining room downstairs; background music, free wi-fi; children welcome until 9pm, can get very busy at lunchtime, open (and food) all day. *(Charlotte Smyrk)*

French House (020) 7437 2477
Dean Street; W1D 5BG Small character Soho pub with impressive range of wines, bottled beers and other unusual drinks, some draught beers but no real ales or pint glasses, lively chatty atmosphere (mainly standing room), theatre memorabilia, shortish choice of modern food (Mon-Fri till 3.30pm) in bar or upstairs restaurant, efficient staff; no music or mobile phones; can get very busy evenings with customers spilling on to the street, open all day. *(Sarah Kennewell)*

★**Grapes** (020) 7493 4216
Shepherd Market; W1J 7QQ Genuinely old-fashioned pub with dimly lit bar, plenty of well worn plush red furnishings, stuffed birds and fish in display cases, some old guns, wood floors, panelling, coal fire and snug back alcove, six ales including Fullers, Sharps and a house beer from Brains, good choice of authentic all-day thai food (some english dishes too), lots of customers (especially lunchtime and early evening) congregating out in the square; children till 6pm weekdays (anytime weekends), open all day. *(Richard Tilbrook)*

★**Guinea** (020) 7409 1728
Bruton Place; W1J 6NL Lovely hanging baskets and chatty customers outside this tiny 17th-c Mayfair mews pub, standing room only at peak times, a few cushioned wooden seats and tables on tartan carpet, side elbow shelf and snug back area, old-fashioned prints, planked ceiling, Youngs and a couple of guests from striking counter, good range of wines and whiskies, shortish choice of food (not Sat lunchtime, Sun evening) including sandwiches and famous steak and kidney pie, also smart (and expensive) Guinea Grill restaurant; no children; open all day (till 6pm Sun). *(Dr and Mrs A K Clarke)*

Running Horse (020) 7493 1275
Davies Street/Davies Mews; W1K 5JE Stylish 18th-c pub with open-plan bare-boards bar; appealing collection of dining chairs and cushioned settles around mix of tables, tartan armchairs in front of

green-tiled fireplace, horse-racing prints on plain or navy-painted panelling, ales such as Rebellion, lots of wines by the glass and good imaginative food from bar snacks up, friendly service, upstairs cocktail bar with button-back club chairs, brass chandeliers and more horsey prints; background music, projector showing live televised racing. free wi-fi; children and dogs welcome, contemporary wicker seats and tables out on the pavement, open all day (till 8pm Sun) from 9.30am for breakfast. *(Alison and Michael Harper)*

Shakespeares Head (020) 7734 2911
Great Marlborough Street; W1F 7HZ Taylor Walker corner pub dating from the early 18th c (though largely rebuilt in the 1920s); dark beams, panelling and soft lighting, well kept ales including Greene King, pubby food from sandwiches and pies up, dining room upstairs overlooking Carnaby Street; sports TV, free wi-fi; open (and food) all day. *(Fiona and Jack Henderson)*

Three Tuns (020) 7408 0330
Portman Mews S; W1H 6HP Large bare-boards front bar and sizeable lounge/dining area with beams and nooks and crannies, Greene King ales and guests, enjoyable reasonably priced pubby food, good friendly staff and buoyant atmosphere; regular quiz; open (and food) all day. *(Cliff and Monica Swan)*

W2 TQ2680

Leinster Arms (020) 7402 4670
Leinster Terrace; W2 3EU Small traditional flower-decked pub close to Hyde Park, friendly and busy, with Fullers London Pride, three guest beers and well liked pubby food at sensible prices; sports TV, free wi-fi; children and dogs welcome, a few pavement tables, open (and food) all day. *(Dr and Mrs A K Clarke)*

Mad Bishop & Bear (020) 7402 2441
Paddington station; W2 1HB Fuller's pub up escalator from concourse; their beers kept well and good choice of wines, reasonably priced standard food quickly served including breakfast from 8am (10am Sun); airy interior with ornate plasterwork and mirrored columns, high tables and chairs on light wood or tiled floors, raised carpeted dining area with some booth seating; background music, games machines and TVs (including train times); tables out at front, open all day till 11pm (10.30pm Sun). *(Ian Herdman, Dr and Mrs A K Clarke)*

★**Victoria** (020) 7724 1191
Strathearn Place; W2 2NH Well run bare-boards pub with lots of Victorian pictures and memorabilia, cast-iron fireplaces, gilded mirrors and mahogany panelling, brass mock-gas lamps above attractive horseshoe bar serving Fullers ales, guest beers and several wines by the glass, popular reasonably priced food from sandwiches and snacks up, friendly service and chatty relaxed atmosphere; upstairs has small library/snug and replica of Gaiety Theatre bar (mostly for private functions); quiet background music, TV; children and dogs welcome, pavement tables and pretty hanging baskets, open all day. *(Dr and Mrs A K Clarke, Michael Domeney)*

WC1

Bountiful Cow (020) 7404 0200
Eagle Street; WC1R 4AP Popular for its excellent burgers and steaks; informal bar with booth seating and raised area by the windows, chrome stools against counter serving ales such as Adnams and several wines by the glass, smallish upper room with wicker dining chairs around oak tables, larger downstairs dining room; background music, jazz nights, free wi-fi; children welcome, closed Sun, otherwise open all day. *(Patrick Chartham)*

Calthorpe Arms (020) 7278 4732
Grays Inn Road; WC1X 8JR Friendly early Victorian corner local with well kept Youngs ales and guests such as Sambrooks and Twickenham, short choice of enjoyable low-priced food including Sun roasts, carpeted bar with plush wall seats, upstairs overspill dining/function room; Sat folk night and regular film evenings, sports TV; dogs welcome, pavement tables, open all day, no food Sun evening. *(Ellie James)*

★**Cittie of Yorke** (020) 7242 7670
High Holborn; WC1V 6BN Splendid back bar rather like a baronial hall with extraordinarily extended counter, 1,000-gallon wine vats resting above gantry, bulbous lights hanging from soaring raftered roof, intimate ornately carved booths and triangular fireplace with grates on all three sides, smaller comfortable panelled room with lots of little prints of York, cheap Sam Smiths beers and reasonably priced bar food, lots of students, lawyers and City types but plenty of space to absorb the crowds; children welcome, closed Sun, otherwise open all day. *(Eddie Edwards)*

Harrison (020) 7278 3966
Harrison Street; WC1H 8JF Tucked-away 1930s red-brick corner pub; modernised bar with simple mix of tables and chairs on bare boards, sofas by woodburner, enjoyable generously served food from snacks up (plenty for vegetarians), good friendly service; regular live music (mainly folk),

We checked prices with the pubs as we went to press in summer 2018.
They should hold until around spring 2019.

comedy nights and cinema in basement; pavement picnic-sets, four bedrooms, closed Sat lunchtime, otherwise open all day. *(Jon Tickner)*

Lady Ottoline (020) 7831 0008
Northington Street; WCIN 2JF 19th-c Bloomsbury pub recently reopened after sympathetic refurbishment; original fitted benches together with modern high tables and stools on bare boards, woodburner, various artworks including portrait of Lady Ottoline Morrell who had associations with the Bloomsbury Set, enjoyable up-to-date food from short menu (not particularly cheap), four changing ales, over 40 gins and plenty of wines by the glass, attentive friendly service, upstairs dining rooms; background music, TV; children (till 6pm) and dogs allowed, open all day (till 5pm Sun). *(Jill and Dick Archer)*

★**Lamb** (020) 7405 0713
Lambs Conduit Street; WC1N 3LZ Authentic 19th-c Bloomsbury pub with green-tiled frontage; bank of cut-glass swivelling snob screens around U-shaped counter, sepia photographs of 1890s actresses on ochre-panelled walls, traditional cast-iron-framed tables and button-back wall benches on stripped boards, snug little back room, Youngs ales and guests kept well, good choice of wines and malt whiskies, decent food from sandwiches, sharing boards and pub favourites up, function room upstairs; Sun quiz; children welcome till 5pm, seats in small paved courtyard behind, Foundling Museum nearby, open all day (till midnight Thurs-Sat) and can get very busy. *(Tracey and Stephen Groves)*

Museum Tavern (020) 7242 8987
Museum Street/Great Russell Street; WC1B 3BA Ornate high-ceilinged Victorian pub facing British Museum; half a dozen well kept ales and several wines by the glass, standard Taylor Walker menu, friendly helpful staff; one or two tables out under gas lamps, open (and food) all day and busy lunchtime/early evening. *(Lyn and Freddie Roberts)*

★**Princess Louise** (020) 7405 8816
High Holborn; WC1V 7EP Splendid Victorian gin palace with extravagant décor – even the gents' has its own preservation order; gloriously opulent main bar with wood and glass partitions, fine etched and gilt mirrors, brightly coloured and fruit-shaped tiles, slender Portland stone columns soaring towards the lofty and deeply moulded plaster ceiling, open fire, good value Sam Smiths beers from long counter, competitively priced pubby food (not weekends) in quieter upstairs room; no children, open all day (till 6.45pm Sun) and gets crowded early weekday evenings. *(Barry Collett)*

Queens Head (020) 7713 5772
Acton Street; WC1X 9NB Small Victorian terraced pub attracting good mix of customers; wide ever-changing range of UK and European draught beers (plenty more in bottles), real ciders and extensive whisky choice, friendly knowledgeable staff, food such as pork pies and meat/cheese boards, traditional interior with several large mirrors, wood floors and skylit back part; piano, live jazz last Thurs of month; open all day. *(Shaun Flook, Heather Campbell, Mark Holmes)*

Queens Larder (020) 7837 5627
Queen Square; WC1N 3AR Cosy little Bloomsbury corner pub also known as the Queen Charlotte (it's where she stored food for her mad husband George III, who was being cared for nearby); character bare-boards bar with cast-iron tables, wall benches and stools around U-shaped counter, theatre posters on dark panelled walls, Greene King ales and decent pubby food, friendly service, upstairs function room; background music; dogs welcome, pavement picnic-sets. *(Alison and Michael Harper)*

Skinners Arms (020) 7837 5621
Judd Street; WC1H 9NT Richly decorated, with glorious woodwork, marble pillars, high ceilings and ornate windows, lots of London prints on busy wallpaper, interesting layout including comfortable back seating area, coal fire, Greene King and guests from attractive long bar, enjoyable home-made food; unobtrusive background music and muted TV; pavement picnic-sets, handy for British Library, closed Sun, otherwise open all day. *(Tracey and Stephen Groves, John E, Anthony Barnes)*

Union Tavern (020) 7278 0111
Lloyd Baker Street; WC1X 9AA Bare-boards Victorian corner pub with attractive period décor; much enjoyed food from varied menu including very good value lunchtime/early evening set deals, friendly helpful service, beers such as Curious, Sambrooks and Trumans, lots of wines by the glass and some premium gins; background music; children welcome, open all day, food most of the day too, weekend brunch from 10.30am. *(Fiona and Jack Henderson)*

WC2 TQ2980

Admiralty (020) 7930 0066
Trafalgar Square; WC2N 5DS Handsome naval-theme pub by Trafalgar Square; button-back leather seating booths by big windows, high stools and elbow tables, grand chandeliers and lots of interesting prints, flagstaff with white ensigns and union jacks, Fullers/Gales beers from traditional counter, grand steps up to mezzanine, also atmospheric vaulted cellar bar, standard pub food including speciality pies, efficient staff; children welcome, a few pavement tables,

open all day from 9am (10am Sun). *(Cliff and Monica Swan)*

Bear & Staff (020) 7930 5261
Bear Street; WC2H 7AX Traditional Nicholsons corner pub with six well kept changing ales and pretty standard food (including deals) from sandwiches up, friendly staff, upstairs dining room named after Charlie Chaplin who was a customer; open all day. *(Alan and Linda Blackmore)*

Coal Hole (020) 7379 9883
Strand; WC2R 0DW Well preserved Edwardian pub adjacent to the Savoy; original leaded windows, classical wall reliefs, mock-baronial high ceiling and raised back gallery, nine changing ales from central servery, standard Nicholsons menu, wine bar downstairs; sports TV; open all day and can get very busy. *(Dr and Mrs A K Clarke, Tony Scott)*

Cross Keys (020) 7836 5185
Endell Street/Betterton Street; WC2H 9EB Flower-decked Covent Garden pub with fascinating interior; masses of photographs, pictures and posters including Beatles memorabilia, all kinds of brassware and bric-a-brac from stuffed fish to musical instruments, well kept Brodies ales and couple of guests (usually smaller London brewers), decent wines by the glass, good lunchtime sandwiches and a few bargain hot dishes including Sun roast; fruit machine, gents' downstairs; sheltered outside cobbled area with flower tubs, open all day. *(Jill and Dick Archer)*

Edgar Wallace (020) 7353 3120
Essex Street; WC2R 3JE Spacious open-plan pub dating from the 18th-c; eight well kept ales and enjoyable good value traditional food from sandwiches up, friendly efficient service, half-panelled walls and red ceilings covered in beer mats, interesting Edgar Wallace memorabilia and lots of old beer and cigarette adverts, upstairs dining room; a few high tables in side alleyway, closed weekends, otherwise open all day. *(John Herbert)*

George (020) 7353 9638
Strand; WC2R 1AP Timbered pub near the law courts with long narrow bare-boards bar, plenty of real ales and a dozen wines by the glass, lunchtime food from sandwiches up, also upstairs Pig and Goose bar/restaurant; open all day. *(Dr and Mrs A K Clarke)*

Knights Templar (020) 7831 2660
Chancery Lane; WC2A 1DT Good well managed Wetherspoons in big-windowed former bank; marble pillars, handsome fittings and plasterwork, bustling atmosphere on two levels, ever-changing range of well kept/priced ales, good wine choice and enjoyable bargain food, friendly efficient service no matter how busy; free wi-fi; open all day Mon-Fri, till 6.30pm Sat, closed Sun. *(Dr and Mrs A K Clarke, Ian Herdman)*

Mr Foggs Tavern (020) 7581 3992
St Martins Lane; WC2N 4EA Themed around Jules Verne's Phileas Fogg; small Victorian-style bar with appropriate pictures and stuffed animals on panelled walls, masses of bric-a-brac hanging from ceiling including model boats, bird cages, brass instruments, even an old pram, craft beers and over a dozen wines by the glass from metal-topped servery, friendly staff in period dress, enjoyable food including bar snacks, sharing plates and range of pies, atmospheric upstairs re-creation of 19th-c salon/gin parlour, swagged curtains, chinese wallpaper and chaise longues, extensive selection of gins and cocktails; open all day, upstairs from 4pm (7pm weekends). *(Charlotte Smyrk)*

Nell Gwynne (020) 7240 5579
Bull Inn Court, off Strand; WC2R 0NP Narrow dimly lit old pub tucked down alleyway; character bare-boards interior with lots of pictures (some of Nell Gwynne) on papered walls, a few tables but mainly standing room and drinkers spill outside at busy times, ales such as St Austell Tribute, some interesting bottled beers including Camden Town and extensive range of spirits; good juke box, TV, darts; open all day. *(Ben Lees)*

Porterhouse (020) 7379 7917
Maiden Lane; WC2E 7NA London outpost of Dublin's Porterhouse brewery, their interesting beers along with guests and lots of bottled imports, good choice of wines by the glass and irish whiskeys, decent pubby food including pizzas; three-level labyrinth of stairs (lifts for disabled), galleries, gleaming copper ducting and piping, prominent open-work clock hanging from the ceiling and neatly cased bottled beer displays dotted about; background and live music, sports TVs (even in the gents'); tables on front terrace, open all day and can get packed evenings. *(Jamie Dorman)*

Salisbury (020) 7836 5863
St Martins Lane; WC2N 4AP Gleaming Victorian pub in the heart of the West End; a wealth of cut-glass and mahogany, wonderfully ornate bronze light fittings and etched mirrors, some interesting photographs including Dylan Thomas

enjoying a drink here in 1941, well kept ales and usual Taylor Walker menu from sharing platters up, cheerful staff; steep stairs down to lavatories; children allowed till 5pm, seats in pedestrianised side alley, open (and food) all day. *(Georgia Egner)*

Ship (020) 7405 1992
Gate Street; WC2A 3HP Tucked-away bare-boards pub with roomy minimally furnished bar, some booth seating, chesterfields by open fire, quite dark with leaded lights, panelling and plaster-relief ceiling, six changing ales, variety of gins and enjoyable bar food, upstairs restaurant with good separate menu, friendly service; background and some live music; open (and food) all day. *(David Hartshorne)*

★**Ship & Shovell** (020) 7839 1311
Craven Passage, off Craven Street; WC2N 5PH Unusually split between two facing buildings; well kept Badger ales and a guest, decent reasonably priced lunchtime food including wide range of baguettes, other bar snacks and pubby choices, good friendly service; one side brightly lit with dark wood, etched mirrors and interesting mainly naval pictures, plenty of tables, some stall seating and open fire; other side (across 'Underneath the Arches' alley) has a cosily partitioned bar; open all day, closed Sun. *(Kelly Simon)*

Temple Brew House (020) 7936 2536
Essex Street; WC2R 3JF Popular refurbished basement bar; fine range of beers including some from on-site microbrewery, lots of wines by the glass and well liked food from sandwiches, small plates and burgers up (own smokehouse), friendly service from enthusiastic knowledgeable young staff; open (and food) all day. *(Dr and Mrs A K Clarke)*

Wellington (020) 7836 2789 *Strand/ Wellington Street; WC2R 0HS* Long narrow traditional corner pub next to the Lyceum theatre; eight real ales including Adnams and Sharps, a couple of craft beers and several wines by the glass, usual Nicholsons menu, friendly staff, quieter upstairs bar/restaurant; sports TV; tables outside, open all day. *(Dr and Mrs A K Clarke)*

EAST LONDON

E1

Princess of Prussia (020) 7702 0723
Prescot Street; E1 8AZ Atmospheric pub keeping original Burton Brewery signage at front and a couple of large Victorian lanterns; cosy interior with lots of pictures and bits and pieces on shelves, open fire, four well kept Shepherd Neame ales and enjoyable thai food, friendly landlady and relaxed chatty atmosphere; nice terrace garden behind, open all day weekdays, closed weekends. *(Shalaine Duffy)*

★**Prospect of Whitby** (020) 3603 4041
Wapping Wall; E1W 3SH Claims to be oldest pub on the Thames dating from 1520 (although largely rebuilt after much later fire), was known as the Devil's Tavern and has a colourful history (Pepys and Dickens used it regularly and Turner came for weeks at a time to study the river views) – tourists love it; L-shaped bare-boards bar with plenty of beams, flagstones and panelling, five changing ales served from fine pewter counter, good choice of wines by the glass, bar food and more formal restaurant upstairs, cheerful helpful staff; children welcome (only if eating after 5.30pm), no dogs inside, unbeatable views towards Docklands from tables on waterfront courtyard, open all day. *(B and M Kendall)*

Town of Ramsgate (020) 7481 8000
Wapping High Street; E1W 2PN Interesting old-London Thames-side setting; long narrow dimly lit bar with squared oak panelling, Fullers, Harveys, Youngs and a guest, good choice of traditional food including daily specials and deals, friendly helpful service; background music, Mon quiz; children (till 8pm) and dogs welcome, restricted river view from small back terrace, open (and food) all day. *(Jess and Dan Holt)*

Water Poet (020) 7426 0495
Folgate Street; E1 6BX Large rambling Spitalfields pub with enjoyable food in bar and dining room including popular Sun roasts, good selection of real ales and craft beers, decent wines, friendly staff, comfortable leather sofas and armchairs on wood floor, basement bar/function room (comedy club), separate games room with two pool tables; sports TV, regular quiz nights; children allowed till 7pm, no dogs inside, enclosed outside area with 'barn' room and barbecue, open all day. *(Daisy Rutledge)*

Williams (020) 7247 5163
Artillery Lane; E1 7LS Busy Greene King pub with 14 real ales predominantly from smaller London brewers, proper ciders too, decent choice of well liked food from snacks up, comfortable seating areas, photographs of old London breweries on the walls; background and occasional live music, darts; open (and food) all day. *(Lucia Halliwell)*

We mention bottled beers and spirits only if there is something unusual about them – imported belgian real ales, say, or dozens of malt whiskies; so do please let us know about them in your reports.

E2

Carpenters Arms (020) 7739 6342
Cheshire Street; E2 6EG Welcoming neatly looked-after little corner pub just off Brick Lane and once owned by the Kray twins; well kept ales such as Timothy Taylors Landlord, enjoyable blackboard food; beer garden at back, closed Mon-Weds till 4pm, otherwise open all day. *(Paddy Bird)*

Sun (020) 7739 4097
Bethnal Green Road; E2 0AN Updated 19th-c bar with good choice of local craft beers and other drinks including cocktails, irish whiskeys and poitin, friendly helpful service, padded stools around copper-topped counter with lanterns above, bare boards, exposed brickwork and some leather banquettes, bar snacks and sharing boards; open all day (till 2am Thurs-Sat). *(Cliff and Monica Swan)*

E3

Palm Tree (020) 8980 2918
Haverfield Road; E3 5BH Lone survivor of blitzed East End terrace tucked away in Mile End Park by Regent's Canal; two Edwardian bars around oval servery, old-fashioned and unchanging under long-serving licensees, a couple of well kept ales, lunchtime sandwiches, good local atmosphere with popular weekend live music; no credit cards; open all day (till late Sat). *(Alan and Linda Blackmore)*

E7

Forest Tavern (020) 8503 0868
Forest Lane across from Forest Gate station; E7 9BB Part of the Antic group, relaxed and unsmart, with six real ales, craft beers and enjoyable food from pub favourites to more unusual choices, friendly staff; live music and DJ nights, Tues quiz, games including table football; children and dogs welcome, seats out on decking, open all day weekends (till 1am Fri and Sat), from 4pm other days. *(Jill and Dick Archer)*

E11

Red Lion (020) 8988 2929
High Road Leytonstone; E11 3AA Large 19th-c corner pub (Antic group) with plenty of quirky character; high-ceilinged open-plan interior with lots of pictures, mirrors, books and general bric-a-brac, ten changing ales, craft kegs and real ciders, enjoyable interesting food along with some pub staples, bar billiards and table football; weekend DJs and live music, Mon quiz, occasional comedy nights; children and dogs welcome, picnic-sets out at front and in good-sized back garden, open all day. *(Lyn and Freddie Roberts)*

E13

Black Lion (020) 8472 2351
High Street, Plaistow; E13 0AD Beamed 18th-c coaching inn surviving among 20th-c development; up to four real ales including Mighty Oak and enjoyable well priced pubby food, friendly staff; sports TVs; picnic-sets in spacious garden, open all day, no food weekends except on West Ham match days. *(David Jackman)*

E14

George (020) 3637 5993
Glengall Grove; E14 3ND Refurbished 1930s corner pub on the Isle of Dogs; two bars, snug and conservatory, traditional food from snacks up including pie, mash and liquor menu, four mainstream ales and over two dozen wines by the glass; background and some live music, sports TV, darts; children welcome, nice back garden with vine clad arbour, open (and food) all day. *(Steve Manning)*

★**Grapes** (020) 7987 4396
Narrow Street; E14 8BP Relatively unchanged since Charles Dickens used it as a model for his Six Jolly Fellowship Porters in Our Mutual Friend; a proper traditional tavern with friendly atmosphere and good mix of customers, partly panelled bar with prints of actors, old local maps and the pub itself, elaborately etched windows, plates along a shelf, larger back area leading to small deck looking over river towards Canary Wharf; Adnams, Black Sheep, Timothy Taylors and two guests, good value tasty bar food, upstairs restaurant with fine views; no children, dogs welcome, open all day, food all day Sat, kitchen closed Sun evening. *(B and M Kendall, Mike Buckingham)*

Gun (020) 7515 5222
Coldharbour; E14 9NS Dining pub with great views from riverside terrace of the O2 arena; smart front restaurant and two character bars – busy flagstoned drinkers' one with antique guns and log fire, cosy red-painted next-door room with leather sofas and armchairs, stuffed boar's heads and modern prints, Fullers ales, several wines by the glass and good modern food (not cheap); background music; children welcome till 8pm, open all day. *(Moira and Jon Weller)*

Narrow (020) 7592 7950
Narrow Street; E14 8DJ Stylish dining pub (part of Gordon Ramsay's chain) worth knowing for it's great Thames views from window seats and covered terrace; simple but smart bar with white walls and blue woodwork, mosaic-tiled fireplaces and colourful striped armchairs, beers such as Fullers London Pride, good wines, food from bar snacks to pricier restaurant meals, set menu Mon-Fri, dining room also white with matching furnishings, local maps, prints and a suspended boat; background and some live music; open all day. *(Holly and Tim Waite)*

E17

Queens Arms (020) 8520 9184
Orford Road; E17 9NJ 19th-c corner pub in Walthamstow village, spacious and comfortable, with well kept ales such as Timothy Taylors Landlord and numerous wines by the glass, good food from interesting changing menu, friendly service and good buoyant atmosphere; background music; children very welcome, seats outside, open all day. *(Michael Butler)*

NORTH LONDON

HA3

★**Hare** (020) 8954 4949
Brookshill/Old Redding; HA3 6SD Carefully renovated old pub with attractive contemporary décor in bar and linked dining rooms; long counter serving Sharps Doom Bar, Timothy Taylors Landlord and several wines by the glass, also extensive range of gins and cocktails, good interesting food including set menu till 6.30pm (not Sun), stylish brasserie with rugs on bare boards and woodburner, two other dining areas, one perfect for a small group, church candles and modern artwork throughout; children and dogs (in bar) welcome, some picnic-sets out at front, more seats in back garden with gazebo, open (and food) all day. *(Charles Todd)*

N1

Camden Head (020) 7359 0851
Camden Walk; N1 8DY Comfortably preserved Victorian pub in pedestrianised street; lots of fine etched glass and mahogany panelling, unusual clock suspended from ceiling, button-back leather wall seats and a few small booths, half a dozen well kept changing ales including Greene King from oval servery, fairly priced pubby food (order at the bar); free nightly comedy club upstairs; children welcome till 7pm, no dogs, chunky picnic-sets on front terrace, open (and food) all day. *(Kerry and Guy Trooper)*

Craft Beer Company
(020) 7278 4560 *White Lion Street; N1 9PP* Flower-decked Islington pub with extensive choice of interesting draught and bottled beers, good range of wines and spirits too; cosy and softly lit with dark green walls, wood-strip or red carpeted floors, a couple of ornate Victorian pillars, leather armchairs under a portrait of Churchill, high tables in main bar, low ones in adjacent areas, good mix of customers, burger menu (all day weekends); occasional live acoustic music; small side garden, open all day Fri-Sun, from 4pm other days. *(Alan and Linda Blackmore)*

★**Drapers Arms** (020) 7619 0348
W end of Barnsbury Street; N1 1ER Welcoming simply furnished Georgian townhouse in residential Islington; busy U-shaped bar with dark wooden tables and wheelback chairs on bare boards, gilt mirrors over fireplaces, sofa and some comfortable chairs in one part, Harveys, Sambrooks and Trumans, british draught lagers and 17 carefully chosen wines by the glass from bright green counter, good imaginative modern food, stylish upstairs dining room with striking chequerboard-painted floor; background music, free wi-fi; children welcome (must be seated and dining after 6pm), dogs allowed in bar, nice paved back terrace with zinc-topped tables under large parasols, open all day. *(Mrs Margo Finlay, Jörg Kasprowski)*

Duke of Cambridge (020) 7359 3066
St Peters Street; N1 8JT Well established as London's first organic pub; simply decorated busy main room with chunky wooden tables, pews and benches on bare boards, corridor past open kitchen to more formal dining room and conservatory, ales from small breweries, also organic draught lagers, ciders, spirits and wines, interesting bar food using seasonal produce (not cheap and they add a service charge), teas and coffees; children welcome, dogs in bar, open all day, food all day Sun. *(Jamie Dorman)*

Earl of Essex (020) 7424 5828
Danbury Street; N1 8LE One-room pub with great choice of beers on draught (listed on boards) and in bottles, decent range of other drinks too, varied menu from small plates up including suggested beer pairings, friendly knowledgeable staff; back walled garden, open (and food) all day. *(Sarah Kennewell)*

Hemingford Arms (020) 7607 3303
Hemingford Road; N1 1DF 19th-c ivy-clad pub filled with bric-a-brac; good choice of real ales from central servery, thai evening food plus Sunday roasts, open fire, upstairs bar/function room; live music including Mon bluegrass, quiz nights, sports TV, machines; picnic-sets outside, open all day. *(Shalaine Duffy)*

Islington Townhouse
(020) 3637 6424 *Liverpool Road; N1 0RW* Corner pub refurbished by Hippo Inns; stylish modern décor over three floors, good selection of beers and other drinks including cocktails and over 20 wines by the glass, enjoyable sensibly priced food from assorted small plates up, Sat brunch, friendly engaging staff; background music, quiz nights; children welcome, open (and food) all day. *(Jess and Dan Holt)*

★**Parcel Yard** (020) 7713 7258
King's Cross station, N end of new concourse, up stairs (or lift); N1C 4AH Impressive restoration of listed Victorian parcel sorting office; lots of interesting

bare-boards rooms off corridors around airy central atrium, pleasing old-fashioned feel with exposed pipework and ducting adding to the effect, back bar serving full range of well kept Fullers beers plus guests from long modern counter, plenty of wines by the glass, similar upstairs area with old and new furniture including comfortable sofas, railway memorabilia and some nice touches like Victorian-envelope wallpaper, food from bar snacks up, breakfast till 11.45am; power points to recharge phones/laptops, screens for train times, platform views; seats out at front, open all day from 8am (9am Sun). *(Susan and John Douglas)*

Wenlock Arms (020) 7608 3406
Wenlock Road; N1 7TA Friendly old-fashioned corner local with excellent choice of real ales, craft beers and ciders from central servery, plenty of foreign bottled beers too, simple food, alcove seating and coal fires; darts, free wi-fi; children (until 8pm) and dogs welcome, open all day. *(Megan and Hallam Cunningham)*

N6

Flask (020) 8348 7346
Highgate West Hill; N6 6BU Traditional Georgian pub with intriguing up-and-down layout; unusual sash-windowed bar hatch, panelling and bare-boards in snug lower area, log fires, Fullers beers and a guest, good variety of food from sandwiches and snacks up, barrel-vaulted flagstoned dining area; children and dogs welcome, picnic-sets out in front courtyard, handy for strolls around Highgate village or Hampstead Heath, open all day, food all day Sun till 7pm. *(Georgia Egner)*

Red Lion & Sun (020) 8340 1780
North Road (B519); N6 4BE 1920s Highgate Village dining pub with good variety of well liked food (can be pricey) including pub favourites, they also do takeaway fish and chips, three real ales such as Timothy Taylors, lots of wines by the glass (good list) and extensive range of whiskies, cheerful helpful service; well behaved children and dogs welcome, tables on leafy front terrace and in smaller back courtyard, open (and food) all day. *(Victoria Brooks)*

N16

Railway Tavern (020) 3092 3344
St Jude Street/King Henrys Walk; N16 8JT 19th-c bow-fronted single-bar pub; half a dozen well kept ales along with craft kegs and bottled beers, good authentic thai food (roasts on Sun), reasonable prices and friendly relaxed atmosphere, some railway memorabilia; Tues quiz, acoustic live music; children and dogs welcome, open all day weekends, from 4pm other days. *(Andrew Bosi)*

NW1

★**Chapel** (020) 7402 9220
Chapel Street; NW1 5DP Corner dining pub attracting equal share of drinkers (busy and noisy in the evening); spacious rooms dominated by open kitchen, smart but simple furnishings, sofas at lounge end next to big fireplace, a couple of Greene King ales and good choice of wines by the glass, coffees and teas, decent food from weekly changing menu, brisk friendly service; children and dogs welcome, picnic-sets in sizeable back garden, more seats on decking under heated parasols, open all day. *(Daisy Rutledge)*

Constitution (020) 7380 0767
St Pancras Way; NW1 0QT Traditional standalone 19th-c pub close to Camden Lock and a quieter alternative to the busy market area; four local beers and good selection of wines by the glass, pubby lunchtime food Mon-Fri, friendly staff and pleasant atmosphere; pool, darts and juke box, cellar bar for live music; barbecues in lovely sunny garden overlooking canal, open all day. *(Lucia Halliwell)*

★**Doric Arch** (020) 7388 2221
Eversholt Street; NW1 2DN Virtually part of Euston station (up stairs from the bus terminus) and a welcome retreat from the busy concourse; well kept Fullers ales, guest beers and enjoyable well priced pubby food from snacks and sharing plates to specials, friendly efficient service, compact bare-boards bar with railway memorabilia and pretty Victorian fireplace, some button-back bench seating and a cosy boothed alcove, steps up to carpeted back dining area; background music, TVs (including train times); open (and food) all day. *(John Herbert)*

Metropolitan (020) 7486 3489
Baker Street station, Marylebone Road; NW1 5LA Flight of steps up to spacious Wetherspoons in impressively ornate pillared hall (designed by Metropolitan Railway architect Charles W Clarke), lots of tables on one side, very long bar the other, ten or more real ales, good coffee and their usual food; free wi-fi; family area, open all day from 8am (10am Sun). *(Tony Hobden)*

Somerstown Coffee House
(020) 7691 9136 *Chalton Street (tucked away between Euston and St Pancras stations); NW1 1HS* Despite its name (there was a coffee house here in the

Virtually all pubs in this book sell wine by the glass. We mention wines if they are a cut above the average.

18th c) this is a busy pub with fine range of well kept ales including Wells and Youngs and enjoyable food from british tapas up, friendly service, spacious interior with main bar on the ground floor, basement cocktail bar (from 5pm) and upstairs private dining rooms; background music; children and dogs welcome, outside tables front and back, open all day from 8am (10am weekends) for breakfast. *(David Hunt, Anthony Barnes)*

Tapping the Admiral
(020) 7267 6118 *Castle Road; NW1 8SU* Friendly local with fine range of well kept ales mainly from London brewers, fairly priced home-made food including range of pies; quiz nights and live music, free wi-fi; children welcome till 7pm, heated beer garden, open all day. *(Sarah Kennewell)*

NW3

★**Flask** (020) 7435 4580
Flask Walk; NW3 1HE Bustling local with two traditional front bars divided by unique Victorian screen, smart banquettes, panelling and lots of little prints, attractive fireplace, Youngs and a guest, plenty of wines by the glass and maybe winter mulled wine, popular all-day food, good friendly service, dining conservatory; background music, TV; children (till 8pm) and dogs welcome, seats and tables in alley, open all day. *(Cliff and Monica Swan)*

Spaniards Inn (020) 8731 8406
Spaniards Lane; NW3 7JJ Busy 16th-c pub next to Hampstead Heath; attractive and characterful low-ceilinged rooms with oak panelling, antique winged settles, snug alcoves and open fires, up to five real ales, several craft beers and 18 wines by glass, decent food from sandwiches and sharing boards up, dining room upstairs; free wi-fi; charming garden with own bar (arrive early weekends as popular with dog walkers and families), car park also fills quickly and nearby parking difficult, open (and food) all day. *(Fiona and Jack Henderson)*

NW5 TQ2886

Bull & Last (020) 7267 3641 *Highgate Road; NW5 1QS*
Traditional décor with a stylish twist in this Victorian corner dining pub; single room with big windows, colonial-style fans in planked ceiling, bulls' heads and other stuffed animals, stone fireplace at one end along with collection of tankards and big faded map of London, much emphasis on their good imaginative food (not cheap), takeaways available including picnic hampers for Hampstead Heath, well kept changing ales and a house craft beer, good selection of wines, whiskies and gins, upstairs restaurant; children (away from bar) and dogs welcome, hanging baskets and picnic-sets by street, open all day. *(Michael Butler)*

Southampton Arms 07958 780073
Highgate Road; NW5 1LE Popular simply furnished drinkers' pub; one long room with big front window, wall seats and stools around tables on bare boards, up to ten changing beers and good range of ciders, bar snacks, no credit cards; live piano some evenings, Mon quiz; small garden at back, handy for Hampstead Heath, open all day. *(Tony Scott)*

SOUTH LONDON

SE1

Dean Swift (020) 7357 0748
Gainsford Street; SE1 2NE Comfortably updated corner pub tucked away behind Tower Bridge; well kept cask ales, lots of craft beers and several wines by the glass, friendly well informed staff, rewarding choice of food from bar snacks to Sun roasts, upstairs restaurant; sports TV; open (and food) all day. *(B and M Kendall)*

Fire Station (020) 7620 2226
Waterloo Road; SE1 8SB Unusual fire station conversion, busy and noisy, with two big refurbished knocked-through rooms, burger and pizza menu, craft beers such as Beavertown, Camden and Sambrooks, 11 wines by the glass and cocktails, friendly staff; background music; children welcome, a few tables out in front, handy for Old Vic theatre and Waterloo station, open (and food) all day from 7am (9am weekends) for breakfast. *(Dr and Mrs A K Clarke)*

Founders Arms (020) 7928 1899
Hopton Street; SE1 9JH Modern glass-walled building in superb location – outstanding terrace views along Thames and handy for South Bank attractions; plenty of customers including tourists, theatre- and gallery-goers spilling on to pavement and river walls, Youngs Bitter and a guest, lots of wines by the glass, food served all day, tea and coffee from separate servery; background music; children welcome (till 8pm) away from bar, dogs allowed on terrace, open till midnight Fri, Sat. *(Alison and Michael Harper)*

★**George** (020) 7407 2056
Off 77 Borough High Street; SE1 1NH Tucked-away 16th-c coaching inn mentioned in *Little Dorrit*, owned by the National Trust and beautifully preserved; lots of tables in bustling cobbled courtyard with views of the tiered exterior galleries, series of no-frills ground-floor rooms with black beams, square-latticed windows and some panelling, plain oak or elm tables on bare boards,

old-fashioned built-in settles, dimpled glass lanterns and a 1797 Act of Parliament clock, impressive central staircase up to a series of dining rooms and balcony, well kept Greene King ales and a beer badged for the pub, traditional food from sandwiches up; children welcome away from bar, open (and food) all day. *(Dr and Mrs A K Clarke)*

★**Kings Arms** (020) 7207 0784
Roupell Street; SE1 8TB Proper corner local tucked away amid terrace houses, bustling and friendly, with curved servery dividing traditional bar and lounge, bare boards, open fire and various bits and pieces including local road signs, nine well kept changing beers, good wine and malt whisky choice, welcoming helpful staff, enjoyable reasonably priced food from thai dishes to Sun roasts, big back extension with conservatory/courtyard dining area; background music; children till 7pm, open all day. *(Alan and Linda Blackmore)*

★**Market Porter** (020) 7407 2495
Stoney Street; SE1 9AA Properly pubby, no-frills place opening at 6am weekdays for workers at neighbouring Borough Market; up to ten unusual real ales (over 60 guests a week) often from far-flung brewers and served in top condition, particularly helpful friendly service, bare boards and open fire, barrels balancing on beams, simple furnishings, food in bar or upstairs lunchtime restaurant with view over market; background music; children allowed weekends till 7pm, dogs welcome, gets very busy with drinkers spilling on to the street, open all day. *(Mike Buckingham, Dr and Mrs A K Clarke)*

Rake (020) 7407 0557
Winchester Walk; SE1 9AG Tiny discreetly modern Borough Market bar with amazing bottled beer range in wall-wide cooler, also half a dozen continental lagers on tap and four real ales, light snacks available or you can bring your own food from the market, good friendly service; fair-sized covered and heated outside area. *(Jill and Dick Archer)*

★**Royal Oak** (020) 7357 7173
Tabard Street/Nebraska Street; SE1 4JU Bustling corner pub under new management; has the look and feel of an old-fashioned London alehouse with two little L-shaped rooms arranged around central servery, Harveys ales and a guest, Thatcher's cider, food has been good, patterned rugs on wood floors, plates on delft shelf, some black and white scenes or period sheet music on red-painted walls; children and dogs welcome, disabled access from the Nebraska Street entrance, open all day (till 9pm Sun). *(Tom Stone, Patricia Hawkins, Giles and Annie Francis, Dr and Mrs A K Clarke, Patricia and Gordon Tucker, B and M Kendall)*

Sheaf (020) 7407 9934
Southwark Street; SE1 1TY In cellars beneath the Hop Exchange (easy to miss); brick vaulted ceilings and iron pillars, button back benches, sofas and some high tables, lots of framed black and white photographs of former regulars, ten real ales and decent inexpensive pubby food; sports TVs; open all day. *(B and M Kendall)*

Wheatsheaf (020) 7940 3880
Stoney Street; opposite Borough Market main entrance; SE1 9AA Updated Youngs pub directly below new railway bridge; their well kept ales with guests such as Camden Town and Meantime, good choice of wines by the glass and decent food from sandwiches and snacks up, cheerful busy atmosphere; live music; heated outside area with campervan acting as servery, open (and food) all day from 9am (10 Sun, noon Mon). *(Dr and Mrs A K Clarke)*

White Hart (020) 7928 9190
Cornwall Road/Whittlesey Street; SE1 8TJ Backstreet corner pub near Waterloo station with friendly community bustle; interesting range of cask and craft beers, lots more in bottles and good selection of other drinks, sensibly priced up-to-date blackboard food along with pub standards, comfortable sofas on stripped boards, fresh flowers on tables; background music, free wi-fi; disabled facilities, open all day. *(B and M Kendall)*

SE5

★**Crooked Well** (020) 7252 7798
Grove Lane; SE5 8SY Popular early 19th-c restauranty pub in heart of Camberwell; button-back sofas, wall seats and variety of wooden dining chairs and tables on bare boards, good imaginative food including express lunch menu, plenty of wines by the glass and cocktails (happy hour 5-8pm), craft beers and a couple of real ales, welcoming helpful staff, private dining/function rooms upstairs; children welcome, pavement picnic-sets, closed Mon lunchtime, closed lunchtime Mon-Weds, otherwise open all day. *(Ben Lees)*

Union Tavern (020) 7091 0447
Camberwell New Road; SE5 0RR Stylish 19th-c pub with seperate dining and drinking areas, rustic furniture and open kitchen in restaurant, tall wooden tables and chairs in bar, popular food including keenly priced set menus, four changing ales, good choice of wines and gins, friendly efficient service; background music; children welcome (menu for them), open all day, 10.30am brunch menu on weekends. *(Fred)*

SE8

Dog & Bell (020) 8692 5664
Prince Street; SE8 3JD Friendly old-fashioned local tucked away on Thames Path; wood benches around bright cheerfully

decorated L-shaped bar, open fire, up to half a dozen well kept ales including Fullers, bottled belgian beers and reasonably priced pub food from sandwiches up, prompt friendly service, dining room; bar billiards, TV; tables out in courtyard, open all day. *(Jim Silver)*

SE9

Park Tavern (020) 8850 3216
Passey Place; SE9 5DA Traditional Victorian corner pub off Eltham High Street; eight well kept changing ales and 14 wines by the glass, log fire, friendly easy-going atmosphere, pizzas and pub snacks served lunchtime; background music; pleasant little garden behind, open all day. *(Charlotte Smyrk)*

SE10

★**Greenwich Union** (020) 8692 6258
Royal Hill; SE10 8RT More like a bar than pub with full Meantime craft range, over 150 bottled beers, unusual spirits and interesting choice of teas and coffees, enjoyable food from lunchtime sandwiches and traditional favourites up, friendly brisk service; long narrow stone-flagged room with simple front area, wooden furniture, stove and daily papers, comfortable part with sofas and cushioned pews, booth seating in end conservatory; free wi-fi; well behaved children and dogs welcome, paved terrace with teak furniture, old-fashioned lamp posts and end fence painted as a poppy field, open (and food) all day. *(Rupert Watson)*

★**Guildford Arms** (020) 8691 6293
Guildford Grove/Devonshire Drive; SE10 8JY Civilised bow-fronted Georgian dining pub in residential area; although emphasis is on their highly regarded imaginative food, there's also a small bar serving beers such as Brockley and Phipps, 17 wines by the glass and cocktails, stylish upstairs restaurant with abstract art on pale grey walls; background music, free wi-fi; children and dogs (in bar) welcome, tables under parasols in lovely back garden, closed Mon, otherwise open all day. *(Louise and Simon Peters)*

Pilot (020) 8858 5910
River Way, Blackwall Lane; SE10 0BE Early 19th-c pub surviving amid O2 development; opened-up interior on three levels with roof terrace overlooking park, well kept Fullers/Gales beers, good choice of food (all day Fri, Sat, till 6pm Sun) from pubby choices and charcoal grills to daily specials; background music, newspapers and free wi-fi; dogs welcome, picnic-sets outside in front, more seating in enclosed back garden, ten well equipped boutique bedrooms, open all day. *(Taff Thomas)*

Prince of Greenwich
(020) 8692 6089 *Royal Hill; SE10 8RT* Victorian pub under warmly welcoming Sicilian owners, good italian food from freshly made pizzas up, Fullers London Pride, Sharps Doom Bar and nice wines by the glass, quirky décor and unusual furnishings, lots of black and white jazz photos/posters (regular live jazz); italian film night Thurs; children and well behaved dogs welcome, closed Mon, open from 4pm Tues-Fri, 12.30pm weekends. *(David Northrop)*

Sail Loft (020) 8222 9310
Victoria Parade, Greenwich; SE10 9FR Airy modern Thames-side pub on two floors, excellent views over to Canary Wharf from floor-to-ceiling windows; Fullers/Gales beers and plenty of wines by the glass, short but varied choice of food from open kitchen; background music, free wi-fi; children and dogs welcome, terrace with covered seating booths taking in the view, open all day. *(Cliff and Monica Swan)*

SE11

Prince of Wales (020) 7735 9916
Cleaver Square; SE11 4EA Comfortably traditional little Edwardian pub in smart quiet Georgian square near the Oval; well kept Shepherd Neame ales and simple pub food from sandwiches up, warm friendly atmosphere; pavement seats, boules available to play in the square, open all day. *(Tracey and Stephen Groves)*

SE12 TQ3974

Lord Northbrook (020) 8318 1127
Burnt Ash Road; SE12 8PU Opened-up bare-boards Victorian corner pub, contemporary paintwork and lots of pictures, good mix of seating including a couple of chesterfields by Victorian fireplace, well kept Fullers/Gales beers, decent food from shortish menu (all day weekends), friendly staff, conservatory; children and dogs welcome, paved split-level back garden; open all day. *(Fiona and Jack Henderson)*

SE15 TQ3575

Ivy House (020) 7277 8233
Stuart Road; SE15 3BE Co-operative owned pub with eight real ales and good range of craft beers and ciders, well priced food (not lunchtimes Mon, Tues) including burgers, old-fashioned panelled interior, stage in back room for live music, comedy and theatre nights; children (till 8pm) and dogs welcome, rack for cyclists, open all day. *(Alison and Michael Harper)*

If you report on a pub that's not a featured entry, please tell us any lunchtimes or evenings when it doesn't serve bar food.

Old Nuns Head (020) 7639 4007
Nunhead Green; SE15 3QQ Popular open-plan 1930s brick and timber pub on edge of small green; half a dozen interesting changing beers and enjoyable food provided by pop-up kitchens including burgers and indian street food, just roasts on Sun, cheerful efficient staff; music, quiz and comedy nights; children (till 8.30pm) and dogs welcome, back garden and a few seats out in front, handy for fascinating gothic Nunhead Cemetery, open all day (till 1am Fri, Sat), food from 6pm weekdays, midday weekends. *(Sarah Kennewell)*

SE16

★**Mayflower** (020) 7237 4088
Rotherhithe Street; SE16 4NF Cosy old riverside pub in unusual street with lovely early 18th-c church; generous food including more upmarket daily specials, well kept Greene King Abbot and four guests, good value wines and decent coffee, friendly young staff, black beams, panelling, high-backed settle and coal fires, nautical bric-a-brac, great Thames views from upstairs candlelit evening restaurant; background music, Tues quiz; children welcome, fun jetty/terrace over water (barbecues), handy for Brunel Museum, open (and food) all day. *(Richard Tilbrook, Mike Buckingham)*

SW4

Abbeville (020) 8675 2201
Abbeville Road; SW4 9JW Popular dining pub in same small Three Cheers group as the Latchmere (Battersea); split-level interior including small mezzanine, bare boards, half-panelling and open fire, mix of old furniture, vintage prints and a stag's head, good food from short but varied menu, beers such as Meantime and Timothy Taylors, plenty of wines by the glass, cocktails, efficient friendly service; children and dogs welcome, pavement tables, open all day, food all day Sun. *(Jeremy Brodie)*

Clapham Tap (020) 7498 9633
Clapham Manor Street; SW4 6ED Friendly little end-of-terrace pub (former Craft Beer Co/Manor Arms); U-shaped bare-boards bar serving six well kept ales including Sharps, 16 craft beers and good range of gins and other spirits, enjoyable pubby food at reasonable prices; TVs, board games; seats out at front and in AstroTurf back garden with table tennis and other games, open all day weekends, from 4pm weekdays. *(Barry Manning)*

Windmill (020) 8673 4578
Clapham Common South Side; SW4 9DE Large bustling pub by the common; contemporary front bar with quite a few original Victorian features, pillared dining room leading through to conservatory-style eating area, popular varied choice of food, Youngs ales and decent wines by the glass; background music, live Sat (4-9pm), Sun quiz; children welcome, tables under umbrellas along front, more seats in side garden with 'burger shack', good bedrooms, open (and food) all day. *(Georgia Egner)*

SW11

Eagle Ale House (020) 7228 2328
Chatham Road; SW11 6HG Unpretentious backstreet local; seven well kept changing ales including southern brewers like Harveys, Surrey Hills and Westerham, welcoming efficient service, L-shaped carpeted bar with simple pubby furniture, shelves of books either side of Victorian fireplace; some live music, big-screen sports TV; children and dogs welcome, back terrace with heated marquee, open all day weekends, from 4pm Mon-Thurs, 3pm Fri. *(Jill and Dan Archer)*

Fox & Hounds (020) 7924 5483
Latchmere Road; SW11 2JU Victorian pub with good italian-influenced food (all day Sun, not Mon-Thurs lunchtimes), St Austell and two local ales, several wines by glass, spacious straightforward bar with big windows overlooking street, bare boards, mismatched tables and chairs, photographs on walls, fresh flowers, view of kitchen behind; background music, TV, daily newspapers; children and dogs welcome, terrace picnic-sets, open all day Fri-Sun, closed Mon lunchtime. *(Lyn and Freddie Roberts)*

Latchmere (020) 7223 3549
Battersea Park Road; SW11 3BW Popular Battersea corner pub with award-winning theatre upstairs; open-plan bare-boards interior, Edwardian-style dining chairs, two-sided banquettes and red leather wall seats around wooden tables, sofas either side of log fire, big mirrors, model yachts, animal prints and posters, stools by counter serving St Austell, Sharps and Timothy Taylors, 19 wines by the glass and cocktails, enjoyable food including pre-theatre set menu; children (till 7pm) and dogs welcome, heated terrace with booths down one side and plenty of other seating, open all day, food all day Sun. *(Donald Allsopp)*

Westbridge (020) 7228 6482
Battersea Bridge Road; SW11 3AG Draft House pub with interesting ever-changing choice of real ales, craft beers and ciders served by friendly knowledgeable staff, tasting trays available, good reasonably priced food from open kitchen, can eat in bar or restaurant; background music (often blues/jazz), sports TV; small garden, open (and food) all day. *(Moira and Jon Weller)*

Woodman (020) 7228 2968
Battersea High Street; SW11 3HX Busy village-feel pub tucked behind cobbled Battersea Square; enjoyable food from

sharing boards up, Badger ales and a dozen wines by the glass, good friendly service; children and dogs welcome, back garden with heaters and wood-fired pizza oven, open (and food) all day. *(Holly and Tim Waite)*

SW12

★**Nightingale** (020) 8673 1637 *Nightingale Lane; SW12 8NX* Early Victorian local, cosy and civilised, with small front bar opening into larger back area and attractive family conservatory, well kept Youngs and guests, decent wines and enjoyable sensibly priced bar food, friendly service, open fire; dogs welcome, nice secluded back beer garden with summer barbecues, open all day. *(David Seward)*

SW13

Bulls Head (020) 8876 5241 *Lonsdale Road; SW13 9PY* Imposing Victorian riverside pub famous for its live jazz in back music room (nightly and Sun afternoon); comfortable open-plan areas brightened up in Geronimo Inns usual colourful, modern style, three real ales including Sharps and Youngs from central servery, upstairs balconied restaurant; children welcome, open (and food) all day. *(Edward Mirzoeff)*

Red Lion (020) 8748 2984 *Castelnau; SW13 9RU* Roomy and comfortably refurbished 19th-c Fullers pub, their well kept ales and good range of wines from central counter, friendly staff, varied choice of popular attractively presented food including blackboard specials, lofty back dining part has most character with big arched windows, impressive Victorian woodwork and domed stained-glass ceiling light, also front snug with gas-effect coal fire; TV, free wi-fi; children and dogs welcome, disabled access/loo, spacious back garden with teak furniture on heated terrace, open (and food) all day. *(Edward Mirzoeff)*

White Hart (020) 8876 5177 *The Terrace; SW13 0NR* Imposing 19th-c Barnes dining pub with fine Thames views; well kept Wells and Youngs ales along with craft beers such as Camden Town and Meantime from island servery, good selection of wines by the glass, popular food in bar or upstairs restaurant with open kitchen and river-view balcony; more seats on side terrace, open (and food) all day. *(Moira and Jon Weller)*

SW15

Bricklayers Arms (020) 8789 0222 *Down cul-de-sac off Lower Richmond Road near Putney Bridge; SW15 1DD* Tucked-away little 19th-c local with well kept changing ales, proper cider/perry and good selection of english wines, efficient friendly staff, long L-shaped room with pitched-roof section, pine tables on bare boards, lots of pictures on painted panelling, log fire; background music, sports TV; open all day Fri-Sun, from 4pm other days. *(Holly and Tim Waite)*

Half Moon (020) 8780 9383 *Lower Richmond Road; SW15 1EU* Good long-standing music venue; Youngs and a couple of guests from elegant curved counter, food from burgers and hot dogs to more elaborate choices and a brunch menu; live music, comedy and quiz nights; open (and food) all day. *(Kerry and Guy Trooper)*

Jolly Gardeners (020) 8789 2539 *Lacy Road; SW15 1NT* Slightly quirky bare-boards pub in residential Putney; gardening theme with trowels and watering cans on walls, potted flowers and botanical prints, bucket lampshades, a reclining gnome and row of colourful heated sheds in the back garden; four changing ales and several other draught beers, good selection of wines, enjoyable varied choice of food from sandwiches and sharing boards up; quiz nights, sports TV, newspapers and free wi-fi; front fairy-lit terrace, open (and food) all day. *(Trevor and Michele Street)*

SW16

Earl Ferrers (020) 8835 8333 *Ellora Road; SW16 6JF* Opened-up Streatham corner pub with Sambrooks and several other well kept ales (tasters offered), interesting food along with pub standards including popular Sat brunch and Sun roasts, good friendly service; live music and quiz nights, pool and darts; children welcome, some tables outside with tractor-seat stools, open all day weekends, from 5pm weekdays. *(Alison and Michael Harper)*

Railway (020) 8769 9448 *Greyhound Lane; SW16 5SD* Busy Streatham corner local with two big rooms (back one for families); rotating ales from London brewers such as Belleville, Redemption and Sambrooks, good range of bottled beers and decent wines by the glass, enjoyable freshly made food (all day Sat), friendly staff, events including Tues quiz, weekend DJs and comedy nights; walled back garden, open all day (till 1am Fri, Sat). *(Linda Harper)*

SW18

Alma (020) 8870 2537 *York Road, opposite Wandsworth Town station; SW18 1TF* Corner Victorian pub-hotel with well kept Youngs ales and good choice of wines from island bar, sofas and informal mix of tables and chairs on wood floor, mosaic plaques and painted mirrors, wide range of good food from bar snacks up, back restaurant, friendly helpful staff; 23 bedrooms, open (and food) all day from 7am (8am weekends). *(Jules Sargent)*

Cats Back (020) 8617 3448
Point Pleasant; SW18 1NN Traditionally refurbished 19th-c Harveys corner pub; four of their ales along with bottled beers, enjoyable food from sandwiches to Sun roasts, friendly staff; upstairs events including live music, life drawing, film and comedy nights; partially covered beer garden with heaters, open all day. *(Lucia Halliwell)*

★**Earl Spencer** (020) 8870 9244
Merton Road; [U] Southfields; SW18 5JL Cheerful well run Edwardian pub with emphasis on good interesting food; cushioned wooden, farmhouse and leather dining chairs around all sorts of tables on bare boards, modern artwork and open fire, back bar with long tables, pews and benches, beers such as By the Horns, Sambrooks and Wimbledon Common from U-shaped counter, also, 20 wines by the glass, 50 gins, 12 british vodkas and 20 malt whiskies, efficient friendly service; children and dogs (in bar) welcome, picnic-sets on front terrace, open all day Fri-Sun, closed till 4pm other days. *(James Landor, Rona Mackinlay, Chantelle and Tony Redman)*

Jolly Gardeners (020) 8870 8417
Garrett Lane; SW18 4EA Bustling easy-going Victorian corner pub; L-shaped front bar; high-backed dining chairs around straightforward tables on pale floorboards, stools at high tables and at counter serving By the Horns, Sambrooks and a dozen wines by the glass, good modern food (not Sun evening), dining area with open fire, friendly chatty staff, simply furnished conservatory opening onto courtyard garden with heaters, summer barbecues; children and dogs (in bar) welcome, open all day, till 8pm Sun. *(Millie and Peter Downing, Edward Nile)*

SW19

Alexandra (020) 8947 7691
Wimbledon Hill Road; SW19 7NE Busy 19th-c Youngs pub with their well kept beers and guests from central servery, decent wine choice and enjoyable food from sandwiches and sharing boards to good Sun roasts, friendly attentive service, linked rooms with comfortable fairly traditional décor, more contemporary upstairs bar (burger menu); sports TVs; tables out in mews and on attractive popular roof terrace, open (and food) all day. *(Shalaine Duffy)*

Crooked Billet (020) 8946 4942
Wimbledon Common; SW19 4RQ Busy 18th-c pub popular for its position by Wimbledon Common (almost next door to the Hand in Hand); Youngs ales and guests, good choice of wines and generally well liked up-to-date food in open-plan bar or dining room, mix of wooden dining chairs, high-backed settles and scrubbed pine tables on oak boards, some interesting old prints, winter fire; Mon quiz board games; children (away from bar) and dogs welcome, plastic glasses for outside, open (and food) all day. *(Jess and Dan Holt)*

Hand in Hand (020) 8946 5720
Crooked Billet; SW19 4RQ Friendly Youngs local on edge of Wimbledon Common; their ales and guests kept well, enjoyable home-made pubby food (all day Fri-Sun), several areas off central bar with leather armchairs, sofas and built in wall seats, bookshelves, photos and prints on papered walls, stubby candles and a log fire; front courtyard, benches out by common, open all day. *(Megan and Hallam Cunningham)*

Sultan (020) 8544 9323
Norman Road; SW19 1BN Friendly 1950s red-brick drinkers' pub owned by Hop Back and hidden in a tangle of suburban roads; their well kept ales and a guest, some snacky food, big scrubbed tables, darts in public bar; nice walled beer garden with summer barbecues, open all day (from 3pm Mon-Weds). *(Lucy Black)*

WEST LONDON

SW6

★**Atlas** (020) 7385 9129
Seagrave Road; SW6 1RX Busy ivy-clad pub with long simple bar; panelling and dark wall benches, mix of old tables and chairs on bare boards, brick fireplaces, good if pricey italian influenced food (all day Sun), four well kept ales, lots of wines by the glass and decent coffee, friendly service; background music, summer quiz Tues; children (till 7pm) and dogs welcome, attractively planted side terrace, open all day. *(Georgia Egner)*

Eight Bells (020) 7736 6307
Fulham High Street/Ranelagh Gardens; SW6 3JS Friendly traditional local tucked away near Putney Bridge; Fullers London Pride, Sharps Doom Bar and a guest, good value standard pub menu (all day Sun); sports TV; dogs welcome, seats outside under awning, close to Bishop's Park, open all day and busy with away supporters on Fulham match days. *(Elliott Butler)*

Harwood Arms (020) 7386 1847
Walham Grove; SW6 1QP Popular bare-boards Fulham restaurant-pub (Michelin-

A star symbol before the name of a pub shows exceptional character and appeal. It doesn't mean extra comfort. Even quite a basic pub can win a star, if it's individual enough.

starred) with top notch food including set menu choices (not cheap), a couple of well kept changing ales and extensive wine list, opened-up informal bare-boards interior with all tables set for dining, stools at bar for drinkers; credit card required for booking (charge for late or no show); closed Mon lunchtime. *(Susan and John Douglas)*

SW7

★**Anglesea Arms** (020) 7373 7960
Selwood Terrace; SW7 3QG Very busy 19th-c pub, well run and friendly, with mix of cast-iron tables on wood-strip floor, central elbow tables, panelling and heavy portraits, large brass chandeliers hanging from dark ceilings, big windows and swagged curtains, several booths at one end with partly glazed screens, Greene King Abbott, IPA and four guests, around 20 malt whiskies and 15 wines by the glass, interesting bar food, steps down to dining room; children welcome, dogs in bar, heated front terrace, open all day. *(Moira and Jon Weller)*

Hereford Arms (020) 7370 4988
Gloucester Road, opposite Hereford Square; SW7 4TE Traditional Fullers pub with opened-up bar; wooden furniture including some high tables on bare boards, chequered tiles around carved U-shaped counter serving their ales and a couple of guests, good food from bar snacks to blackboard specials, friendly staff; free wi-fi; children welcome, disabled access, small outside drinking area, open (and food) all day. *(Holly and Tim Waite)*

Queens Arms (020) 7823 9293
Queens Gate Mews; SW7 5QL Popular Victorian corner pub with open-plan bare-boards bar; generous helpings of enjoyable good value home-made food, decent wines by the glass and good selection of beers including Fullers and Sharps, friendly helpful service; discreet background music and TV; children welcome, disabled facilities, handy for Royal Albert Hall, open all day. *(Kerry and Guy Trooper)*

W4

★**Bell & Crown** (020) 8994 4164
Strand on the Green; W4 3PF Fullers local with great Thames views from back bar and conservatory; good interesting food along with pub classics, efficient friendly service, panelling and log fire, lots of atmosphere and can get very busy weekends; children and dogs welcome, terrace and towpath seating, good riverside walks, open (and food) all day. *(Jamie Green)*

Bollo House (020) 8994 6037
Bollo Lane; W4 5LR Spacious 19th-c corner pub in residential Chiswick; four changing local ales and plenty of wines by the glass, cocktails (early bird deal Thurs), good variety of enjoyable food (service charge added), friendly relaxed atmosphere; background and occasional live music, Tues quiz; children and dogs welcome, tables out at front behind wooden planters, open all day, food all day weekends. *(Dr Martin Owton)*

Bulls Head (020) 8994 1204
Strand on the Green; W4 3PQ Cleanly updated old Thames-side pub (said to have served as Cromwell's HQ during the Civil War); seats by windows overlooking the water in beamed rooms, steps up and down, Greene King IPA and London Glory along with four guests, several wines by the glass and enjoyable food from pub favourites up, friendly efficient staff; background music; children and dogs (in bar) welcome, seats out by river, pretty hanging baskets, open (and food) all day. *(Susan and John Douglas)*

City Barge (020) 8994 2148
Strand on the Green; W4 3PH Attractively furnished old riverside pub; light modern split-level interior keeping a few original features such as Victorian panelling and open fires, good choice of ales/craft beers and wines by the glass (prosecco on tap), interesting food from open kitchen including good fish choice; background music; children and dogs welcome, waterside picnic-sets facing Oliver's Island, deckchairs on grass and more formal terrace, open all day, food all day weekends. *(Jamie Green)*

Roebuck (020) 8995 4392
Chiswick High Road; W4 1PU Popular relaxed Victorian dining pub with bare boards and high ceilings; front bar and roomy back dining area opening on to delightful paved garden, enjoyable well presented food (all day weekends) from open kitchen, daily changing menu, four real ales and good choice of wines by the glass; children and dogs welcome, open all day. *(Jamie Green)*

Swan (020) 8994 8262
Evershed Walk, Acton Lane; W4 5HH Cosy 19th-c local with good mix of customers and convivial atmosphere; well liked interesting food along with more pubby choices, friendly staff, a dozen or so wines by the glass, ales such as St Austell Tribute, two bars with wood floors and panelling, leather chesterfields by open fire; dogs very welcome, children till 7.30pm, picnic-sets on good spacious terrace, open (and food) all day weekends, from 5pm other days. *(Jamie Green)*

★**Tabard** (020) 8994 3492 *Bath Road; W4 1LW* Roomy Chiswick pub built in 1880 with arts and crafts interior (Grade IIH listed); up to ten real ales including Greene King, decent choice of wines and all-day pubby food, friendly efficient staff, lots of nooks and corners, period mirrors and high frieze of William de Morgan tiles; fringe theatre upstairs, free wi-fi; well behaved children and dogs welcome, disabled access, terrace tables by busy road, open all day (till midnight Fri, Sat). *(Jamie Green)*

W5

Ealing Park Tavern
(020) 8758 1879 *South Ealing Road; W5 4RL* Sizeable 19th-c bow-windowed corner pub; bare-boards bar with pendant lighting and some exposed brickwork, animal heads including a couple of large moose behind the counter, armchairs by log fire, own Long Arm ales, guest beers and plenty of wines by the glass, good attractively presented food prepared in open kitchen from lunchtime sandwiches and pub favourites up, oak-panelled dining room with high beamed ceiling, antlers above another open fire; Weds curry and quiz night, Thurs live music, sports TV; children welcome, cheerfully painted booths in AstroTurfed garden, open all day, food all day weekends. *(Jeff Davies)*

W6

★**Anglesea Arms** (020) 8749 1291
Wingate Road; W6 0UR Bustling Victorian corner pub with four changing ales and good range of wines by the glass, bare-boards panelled bar with open fire, good food from short but interesting menu (all day Sun), close-set tables in sky-lit bare-brick dining room; children and dogs welcome, tables out by quiet street, open all day Fri-Sun, closed Mon-Thurs lunchtimes. *(Sam Pullin)*

Blue Anchor (020) 8748 5774
Lower Mall; W6 9DJ Right on the Thames, a short walk from Hammersmith Bridge; two traditional linked areas with oak floors and panelling, four real ales including a house beer brewed by Nelsons, enjoyable food from light meals up (all day weekends), nice upstairs river-view dining room with balcony; quiz night Weds, TV; disabled facilities, waterside pavement tables, open all day. *(Charlie May)*

Carpenters Arms (020) 8741 8386
Black Lion Lane; W6 9BG Relaxed little corner dining pub in residential Hammersmith; highly regarded imaginative food including good value set lunch, fine too for just a drink with plenty of wines by the glass and a well kept beer such as Adnams, friendly staff and good mix of customers, simple bare-boards interior with open fire; dogs welcome, attractive garden, open all day. *(Duncan Milligan)*

Hampshire Hog (020) 8748 3391
King Street; W6 9JT Spacious Hammersmith pub with light airy interior; plenty of emphasis on food from interesting if not extensive menu, good choice of wines including 50cl carafes, cocktails, ales such as Adnams and Fullers, prices can be high; background music; nice big garden with some seats under cover, closed Sun evening, otherwise open all day from 8am (10am weekends) for breakfast/brunch. *(Jeff Davies)*

Latymers (020) 8748 3446
Hammersmith Road; W6 7JP Recently revamped 1990s corner pub; modern bistro-feel bar with wood floor and padded wall benches, feature mirrored ceiling, well kept Fullers ales from blue-painted counter, back restaurant serving good fairly priced thai food, friendly staff; background music, TV, free wi-fi; children and dogs welcome (pub dog is Roxy), pavement seating, open all day. *(Susan and John Douglas)*

Pear Tree (020) 7381 1787
Margravine Road; W6 8HJ Arts and crafts building (plenty of original features) tucked away behind Charing Cross Hospital; cosy softly lit interior with heavy drapes and open fires, cushions on well worn seating, fresh flowers, candles and crisp white evening tablecloths, good modern pub food from bar snacks up, well kept mainstream ales and good range of wines by the glass, efficient service; background music; dogs welcome, seats in small garden, open all day (from 3pm Mon). *(Charlie May)*

Queens Head (020) 7603 3174
Brook Green; W6 7BL Spacious Fullers pub dating from the early 19th c; cosy linked areas with beams and open fire, good menu from lunchtime sandwiches and bar snacks up, four well kept ales, craft beers and nice wines by the glass; Mon quiz; children and dogs welcome, big garden behind, open (and food) all day. *(Holly and Tim Waite)*

Thatched House (020) 8748 6174
Dalling Road; W6 0ET Corner pub (Youngs' first) with matt black exterior; their ales and guests from large grey-painted servery, spacious open-plan interior, rugs on bare boards, candles on mix of wooden tables, open fire, good imaginative food along with pub favourites, extensive wine list (many by the glass), efficient friendly service, back conservatory with raised log-effect gas fire; paved terrace, closed Mon, otherwise open all day (till 9pm Sun), food all day weekends. *(Simon King)*

W7

Fox (020) 8567 4021
Green Lane; W7 2PJ Friendly 19th-c open-plan local in quiet cul-de-sac near Grand Union Canal; several real ales including Fullers, St Austell and Timothy Taylors, craft beers and decent wines by the glass, popular well priced food, panelling and stained glass, farm tools hanging from ceiling; quiz Thurs; children and dogs welcome, food/craft market last Sat of month, towpath walks, open all day. *(Cliff and Monica Swan)*

W8

Britannia (020) 7937 6905
Allen Street, off Kensington High Street; W8 6UX Smartly presented Youngs pub with spacious front bar; pastel walls contrasting dark panelling, patterned rugs on bare boards, banquettes, leather tub chairs and sofas, steps down to back area with wall-sized photoprint of the demolished Britannia Brewery, dining conservatory beyond, good freshly prepared food including pub staples, spiral staircase up to overflow/function room; background and occasional live music, quiz nights, sports TV; children welcome, wheelchair access (side passage to back part), open (and food) all day. *(Jill and Dick Archer)*

★**Churchill Arms** (020) 7727 4242
Kensington Church Street; W8 7LN Bustling old pub dense with bric-a-brac: countless lamps, miners' lights, horse tack, bedpans and brasses hanging from ceiling, prints of american presidents and lots of Churchill memorabilia, a couple of interesting carved figures and statuettes behind central counter, well kept Fullers ales, 18 wines by the glass and good value thai food, spacious rather smart plant-filled dining conservatory; free wi-fi; children and dogs welcome, some chrome tables and chairs outside, stunning display of window boxes and hanging baskets, open (and food) all day. *(Margaret Macdonald)*

Princess Victoria (020) 7937 4534
Earls Court Road; W8 6EB Modern open-plan bar run by spanish landlady; upholstered wall benches and light wood tables on bare boards, cushioned stools along servery, good choice of wines and cocktails (happy hour Mon-Fri 5-7pm), well liked food in upstairs dining room including tapas; live music/DJs some weekends; wooden tables out at front, open all day. *(Neil Allen)*

Scarsdale (020) 7937 1811
Edwardes Square; W8 6HE Popular easy-going Georgian pub in leafy Kensington square; scrubbed pine tables, simple cushioned dining chairs, pews and built-in wall seats on bare boards, oil paintings in fancy gilt frames and old local photographs, heavily swagged curtains, coal-effect gas fires, Fullers ales and a guest such as Adnams, 16 wines by the glass and a dozen malt whiskies, fairly pubby food from lunchtime sandwiches up; free wi-fi; children (in dining area) and dogs welcome, seats and tables under parasols on attractive front terrace, open (and food) all day. *(Jeff Davies)*

W9

Hero of Maida (020) 3960 9109
Shirland Road; W9 2JD Victorian corner pub (former Truscott Arms) reopened under same owners as the Coach (EC1) and Three Cranes (EC4); nicely refurbished interior keeping original tiles, cornices, ceiling roses and so forth, high-ceilinged bare-boards bar with long blue-leather wall bench and other seats, lots of pictures, zinc-topped counter serving beers such as Adnams, Timothy Taylors and Tiny Rebel, carefully chosen wines by the glass and good range of other drinks, generally well liked food from anglo-french menu, upstairs dining room; courtyard garden, open all day, no food Sun evening. *(John Harris)*

Warwick Castle (020) 7266 0921
Warwick Place; W9 2PX Popular character pub in narrow street near Little Venice; open-fronted with a few pavement tables, comfortable Victorian-feel rooms, real ales including Greene King IPA, wide choice of food from sandwiches and pub standards up (all day Fri-Sun); quiz nights; children and dogs welcome, open all day. *(Holly and Tim Waite)*

W12

Oak (020) 8741 7700
Goldhawk Road; W12 8EU Large refurbished Victorian pub serving interesting italian-influenced food including speciality wood-fired pizzas, good range of beers and wine, friendly staff; open all day weekends, from 6pm other days. *(Max Simons)*

Princess Victoria (020) 8749 4466
Uxbridge Road; W12 9DH Imposing former gin palace attractively refurbished by new owners (Three Cheers); rather grand parquet-floored bar with groups of old prints on off-white walls, blue-painted panelling, comfortable leather wall seats and small 19th-c fireplace, ales such as Sambrooks and Timothy Taylors from handsome marble-topped horseshoe counter, also 120 gins, cocktails and plenty of wines by the glass, good food from snacks and pizzas up including weekday set lunch, friendly service, big dining room; Sun quiz, TV for major sports; children (till 8pm) and dogs (in bar) welcome, tables under large parasols on front cobbled terrace, also pretty back courtyard with white wrought-iron furniture, open all day. *(Mary King)*

W13

Duke of Kent (020) 8991 7820
Scotch Common; W13 8DL Large Ealing pub built in 1929 (Grade II listed) with warren of interesting linked areas; mix of old and new furniture on wood floors, panelling and coal fires, several Fullers ales and guests, good food from pub standards up including themed nights, friendly staff; live music Sun evening, free wi-fi; children and dogs welcome, steps down to big garden with partly covered terrace, picnic-sets and play area, open (and food) all day. *(Susan and John Douglas)*

W14

Crown & Sceptre (020) 7603 2007 *Holland Road; W14 8BA* Civilised Victorian corner pub with light airy interior; sofas, antique-style dining chairs and leather cube stools around wooden tables, rugs on bare boards, gas fire, Caledonian Golden XPA, Courage Directors and a guest, plenty of wines by the glass and extensive range of whiskies and gins, enjoyable food including pub favourites and range of burgers, friendly service, cosy cellar bar with banquettes, candles in bottles and big prints on rough wood walls; background music, TV, board games; children and dogs (in bar) welcome, pavement tables, comfortable bedrooms, handy for Olympia, open all day from 7.30am. *(Lyn and Freddie Roberts)*

★**Havelock Tavern** (020) 7603 5374 *Masbro Road; W14 0LS* Busy 19th-c corner dining pub with blue-tiled frontage; light airy L-shaped bar with plain unfussy décor, second smaller room behind, Sambrooks Wandle, Sharps and guests, wide choice of interesting wines by the glass, good imaginative food from short changing menu, friendly efficient service; free wi-fi; children and dogs welcome, picnic-sets on small paved terrace, open all day. *(Michael Robinson)*

OUTER LONDON

BARNET EN5

Black Horse (020) 8449 2230 *Wood Street/Union Street; EN5 4HY* Attractively updated 19th-c pub with eight real ales including own Barnet beers from back microbrewery, good range of food (all day weekends); children and dogs (in bar) welcome, terrace seating, open all day. *(Chris Stevenson)*

Gate (020) 8449 7292 *Barnet Road (A411, near Hendon Wood Lane); EN5 3LA* Comfortably opened-up with country pub feel; beams and log fires, good choice of enjoyable food and well kept ales such as Greene King and Sharps, friendly atmosphere; children welcome, open (and food) all day. *(Barbara Brown)*

Olde Mitre (020) 8449 6582 *High Street; EN5 5SJ* Small early 17th-c local (remains of a famous coaching inn); bay windows in low-beamed panelled front bar, back area on two slightly different levels, some bare boards and lots of dark wood, open fires, good choice of well kept ales including Adnams Southwold, Caledonian Deuchars IPA and Timothy Taylors Landlord, craft beers and decent wines, enjoyable pubby food, friendly service; Sun live music, sports TV; children and dogs welcome, nice heated courtyard garden behind, open all day (till 1am Fri, Sat). *(Gavin Conway)*

BECKENHAM BR3

George (020) 8663 3468 *High Street; BR3 1AG* Busy weatherboarded pub with half a dozen real ales and enjoyable food including deals, efficient staff; regular quiz nights (Mon, Tues); children welcome, side garden with terrace, open all day. *(Andrew Vincent)*

BEXLEYHEATH DA6

Robin Hood & Little John (020) 8303 1128 *Lion Road; DA6 8PF* Small 19th-c family-run local in residential area, welcoming and spotless, with eight well kept ales such as Adnams, Bexley, Fullers and Harveys, popular bargain pubby lunchtime food (not Sun); over-21s only, seats out at front and in back garden. *(Dan Huxley)*

BROMLEY BR1 TQ4069

Red Lion (020) 8460 2691 *North Road; BR1 3LG* Chatty backstreet local in conservation area; traditional dimly lit interior with wood floor, tiling, green velvet drapes and shelves of books, well kept Greene King, Harveys and guests, lunchtime food, good friendly service; tables out in front, open all day. *(Trevor and Michele Street)*

BROMLEY BR2

Two Doves (020) 8462 1627 *Oakley Road (A233); BR2 8HD* Popular Victorian local, comfortable and unpretentious, with cheerful staff and regulars, well kept Youngs and guests, snacky lunchtime food such as rolls and baked potatoes, modern back conservatory and lovely garden; open all day Fri-Sun. *(Philip Chesington)*

CHELSFIELD BR6

Five Bells (01689) 821044 *Church Road; just off A224 Orpington bypass; BR6 7RE* Chatty 17th-c white weatherboarded village local; two separate bars and dining area, inglenook fireplace, well kept Courage, Harveys and a couple of guests, reasonably priced food from lunchtime sandwiches up, evening meals Thurs-Sat only, Sun breakfast 9-11am; live music including jazz and open mike nights, Tues quiz, sports TV; children welcome, picnic-sets among flowers out in front, open all day. *(Mike Buckingham)*

CHISLEHURST BR7

Bulls Head (020) 8467 1727 *Royal Parade; BR7 6NR* Handsome refurbished pub-hotel (18th-c coaching inn); Wells and Youngs ales and lots of wines by the glass, good food from sandwiches and sharing boards up, afternoon teas, two bars and roomy restaurant; children welcome, plenty of tables in back garden, 15 bedrooms, open (and food) all day. *(Charlie Jamieson)*

Crown (020) 8467 7326
School Road; BR7 5PQ Imposing Victorian pub overlooking common; simple attractive interior with flagstoned bar and several dining areas, well kept Shepherd Neame ales and good quality food from sandwiches and traditional choices up, friendly helpful service; events including open mike night first Tues of month; children welcome, terrace tables, pétanque, seven bedrooms, open all day. *(B and M Kendall, Mike Buckingham)*

EASTCOTE HA5 TQ1089

Case is Altered (020) 8866 0476
High Road/Southill Lane; HA5 2EW Attractive 17th-c pub in quiet setting adjacent to cricket ground; main bar, flagstoned snug and barn seating/dining area, Rebellion, Oakham, West Berkshire and a couple of guests, draught and bottled craft beers, lots of wines by the glass (can be pricey) and good range of other drinks, enjoyable food from sandwiches and snacks to charcoal grills from open kitchen, friendly staff; background music, weekly quiz, free wi-fi; children and dogs welcome, nice front garden with outside bar (very popular in fine weather), handy for Eastcote House Gardens, open (and food) all day. *(Maureen Eaton)*

GREENFORD UB6

Black Horse (020) 8578 1384
Oldfield Lane; UB6 0AS Spacious pub on two levels by Grand Union Canal; well kept Fullers ales, a dozen wines by the glass and decent choice of enjoyable reasonably priced food from sandwiches and snacks up, efficient friendly service; weekend live music, sports TV, darts and machines; children and dogs welcome, balcony tables overlooking canal and big garden fenced from towpath, open all day, food all day Fri-Sun. *(Tony Hobden)*

HAMPTON TW12

Jolly Coopers (020) 8979 3384
High Street; TW12 2SJ Friendly end-of-terrace Georgian local; four or five well kept ales and good choice of wines, well liked freshly cooked food (all day Sat) in back restaurant extension including good evening tapas and Sun lunch till 5pm; pretty terrace with climbing plants and summer barbecues, open all day. *(Paul Scofield)*

HARROW HA1

Castle (020) 8422 3155
West Street; HA1 3EF Edwardian Fullers pub in picturesque part (steps up from street); their well kept ales and guests, decent food from lunchtime sandwiches up including Thurs pie and craft beer night, several rooms around central servery, rugs on bare boards, lots of panelling, open fires, collection of clocks in cheery front bar, more sedate back lounge; children welcome, nice garden behind with rattan furniture, open (and food) all day, weekend brunch from 10.30am. *(Nick Higgins)*

ISLEWORTH TW7

London Apprentice (020) 8560 1915
Church Street; TW7 6BG Large Thames-side Taylor Walker pub; reasonably priced food from sandwiches up, well kept ales and good wine choice, log fire, pleasant service, upstairs river-view restaurant; quiz nights; children welcome, attractive riverside terrace with tables under parasols, open (and food) all day. *(Maria and Henry Lazonby)*

KINGSTON KT2 TQ1869

Boaters (020) 8541 4672 *Canbury Gardens (park in Lower Ham Road if you can); KT2 5AU* Family-friendly pub by the Thames in small park; good selection of ales/craft beers, decent wines and varied choice of enjoyable food from changing menu, friendly staff coping well at busy times, comfortable banquettes in split-level wood-floored bar; Sun evening jazz, quiz nights; riverside terrace and balcony, parking nearby can be difficult, open (and food) all day. *(David and Sally Frost)*

Queens Head (020) 8546 9162
Richmond Road/Windsor Road; KT2 5HA Large refurbished red-brick Fullers pub; modern interior arranged around traditional wooden servery (rescued from another London pub), four real ales and good variety of enjoyable food from snacks up including some themed nights, helpful young staff; background music, free wi-fi; children welcome, part-covered front deck, paved back terrace with wooden planters and cabins, play area, ten bedrooms, open (and food) all day. *(David and Sally Frost)*

ORPINGTON BR6 TQ4963

★**Bo-Peep** (01959) 534457
Hewitts Road, Chelsfield; 1.7 miles from M25 junction 4; BR6 7QL Popular country-feel dining pub; old low beams and enormous inglenook in carpeted bar, two cosy candlelit dining rooms, airy side room overlooking lane and fields, well kept Sharps, Westerham and an Adnams house beer, good helpings of enjoyable food (all day Sat, not Sun evening) from traditional choices up, weekday afternoon teas, cheerful helpful staff; background music; children and dogs (in bar) welcome, picnic-sets on big brick terrace, open all day and a useful M25 stop. *(David Jackman, Alan Cowell)*

RICHMOND UPON THAMES TW9

Mitre (020) 8940 1336
Just off the Upper Richmond Road; TW9 1UY Refurbished Victorian local with ten changing ales and four draught ciders/perries (tasters offered), wood-fired pizzas, friendly staff and pub dog (others welcome), bare boards, leaded windows and woodburner; music nights; children allowed,

seats on small front terrace, open all day weekends, from 3pm other days. *(Sandra Hollies)*

Princes Head (020) 8940 1572
The Green; TW9 1LX Spacious open-plan pub overlooking cricket green, clean and well run, with low-ceilinged panelled areas off island servery, well kept Fullers ales, popular sensibly priced pub food from sandwiches up, friendly young staff and chatty locals, coal-effect fire; background music, TV and daily papers; children allowed in certain areas, circular picnic-sets outside, handy for Richmond Theatre, open (and food) all day. *(Charles Welch)*

Watermans Arms (020) 8940 2893
Water Lane; TW9 1TJ Friendly old-fashioned Youngs local with their well kept ales and a couple of guests from Twickenham, enjoyable thai food plus some standard english dishes, traditional layout with open fire, upstairs restaurant; handy for the river, open all day, no food Mon. *(Charles Welch)*

★**White Cross** (020) 8940 6844
Water Lane; TW9 1TH Lovely garden with terrific Thames outlook, seats on paved area, outside bar and boats to Kingston and Hampton Court; two chatty main rooms with local prints and photographs, three log fires (one unusually below a window), well kept Youngs and guests from old-fashioned island servery, a dozen wines by the glass and enjoyable fairly pubby food from 10am brunch on, also bright and airy upstairs room (children welcome here till 6pm) with pretty cast-iron balcony for splendid river view; background music, TV; dogs allowed, tides can reach the pub entrance (wellies provided), open (and food) all day. *(Michael Massey, Dave Chapman)*

White Swan (020) 8940 0959
Old Palace Lane; TW9 1PG Civilised little 18th-c pub with rustic dark-beamed bar, well kept Otter, St Austell, Sharps and Timothy Taylors, enjoyable food, coal-effect fires, back dining conservatory and upstairs restaurant; soft background music; children (till 6.30pm) and dogs welcome, some seats on narrow paved area at front, more in pretty walled back terrace below railway, open all day. *(Charles Welch)*

RICHMOND UPON THAMES TW10

New Inn (020) 8940 9444
Petersham Road (A307, Ham Common); TW10 7DB Attractive Georgian pub in good spot on Ham Common; unashamedly old-fashioned inside with very traditional décor, two open fires and a woodburner, well kept Adnams Broadside, Fullers London Pride, Theakstons Lightfoot and Youngs Bitter, decent pubby food including daily specials, friendly staff and good chatty atmosphere; children and dogs welcome, disabled facilities, picnic-sets out at front and in back courtyard, handy for Ham House (NT), open all day. *(Susan and John Douglas)*

ROMFORD RM1

Golden Lion (01708) 740081
High Street; RM1 1HR Busy former coaching inn – dates from the 16th c and is one of the town's oldest buildings; spacious beamed interior, four or five well kept ales, good value food from sandwiches, sharing plates and pub favourites up, friendly staff and good mix of customers; weekend live music, sports TV, free wi-fi; children welcome, open (and food) all day. *(Robert Lester)*

ROMFORD RM2

Ship (01708) 741571
Main Road; RM2 5EL Friendly black and white pub built in 1762; low beams, panelling and woodburner in fine brick fireplace, Greene King, Sharps, Timothy Taylors and guests, enjoyable good value food (not weekend evenings) from sandwiches and sharing boards up; quiz Thurs, live music Sat; children and dogs welcome, picnic-sets in back garden under parasols, open all day. *(Robert Lester)*

SURBITON KT6 TQ1767

Antelope (020) 8399 5565
Maple Road; KT6 4AW Double-fronted Victorian pub with excellent choice of cask and craft beers including own Big Smoke unfined range from on-site microbrewery, several ciders too, friendly knowledgeable staff, split-level bare-boards interior with comfortable mix of seating, grey-painted and tiled walls, lots of pump clips, open fire, tasty food (all day Sat) including range of burgers; background music from vinyl collection, board games; dogs welcome, paved back terrace, open all day. *(Rob Unsworth)*

TEDDINGTON TW11

Kings Head (020) 3166 2900
High Street; TW11 8HG Comfortably updated bare-boards front bar with easy chairs and button-back wall benches, modern artwork and photographs on vibrant walls, woodburners, well kept changing ales, lots of wines by the glass and cocktails, well separated back dining part with similar décor and open kitchen, enjoyable interesting food served by courteous staff; background music; children and dogs welcome, seats out at front and on enclosed back terrace, open (and food) all day. *(George Sanderson)*

If we know a pub has an outdoor play area for children, we mention it.

TWICKENHAM TW1

★**Crown** (020) 8892 5896
Richmond Road, St Margarets; TW1 2NH Popular Georgian pub with emphasis on good food from sandwiches and sharing plates to restauranty choices, several large dining areas including splendid Victorian back hall, also well kept ales, nice wines by the glass and good coffee, friendly efficient staff, open fire; newspapers and free wi-fi; children and dogs welcome, picnic-sets in sunny courtyard garden, open (and food) all day. *(Taff Thomas, David and Sally Frost, Michael Massey)*

White Swan (020) 8892 2166
Riverside; TW1 3DN Refurbished 17th-c Thames-side pub up steep anti-flood steps; bare-boards L-shaped bar with cosy log fire, river views from prized bay window, five real ales such as Fullers, Sharps and Twickenham, enjoyable fairly priced food (all day Sat, Sun till 6pm), friendly local atmosphere, board games; live acoustic music and quiz nights; children and dogs welcome, tranquil setting opposite Eel Pie Island with well used balcony and waterside terrace (liable to flooding) across quiet lane, open all day. *(Taff Thomas, Michael Massey)*

TWICKENHAM TW2 TQ1572

Sussex Arms (020) 8894 7468
Staines Road; TW2 5BG Traditional bare-boards pub with 15 handpumps plus ciders and perries from long counter, plenty in bottles too, simple food including good home-made pies, pizzas and burgers, friendly staff, walls and ceilings covered in beer mats and pump clips, open fire; some live acoustic music; large back garden with boules, open all day. *(Miles Green)*

SCOTLAND

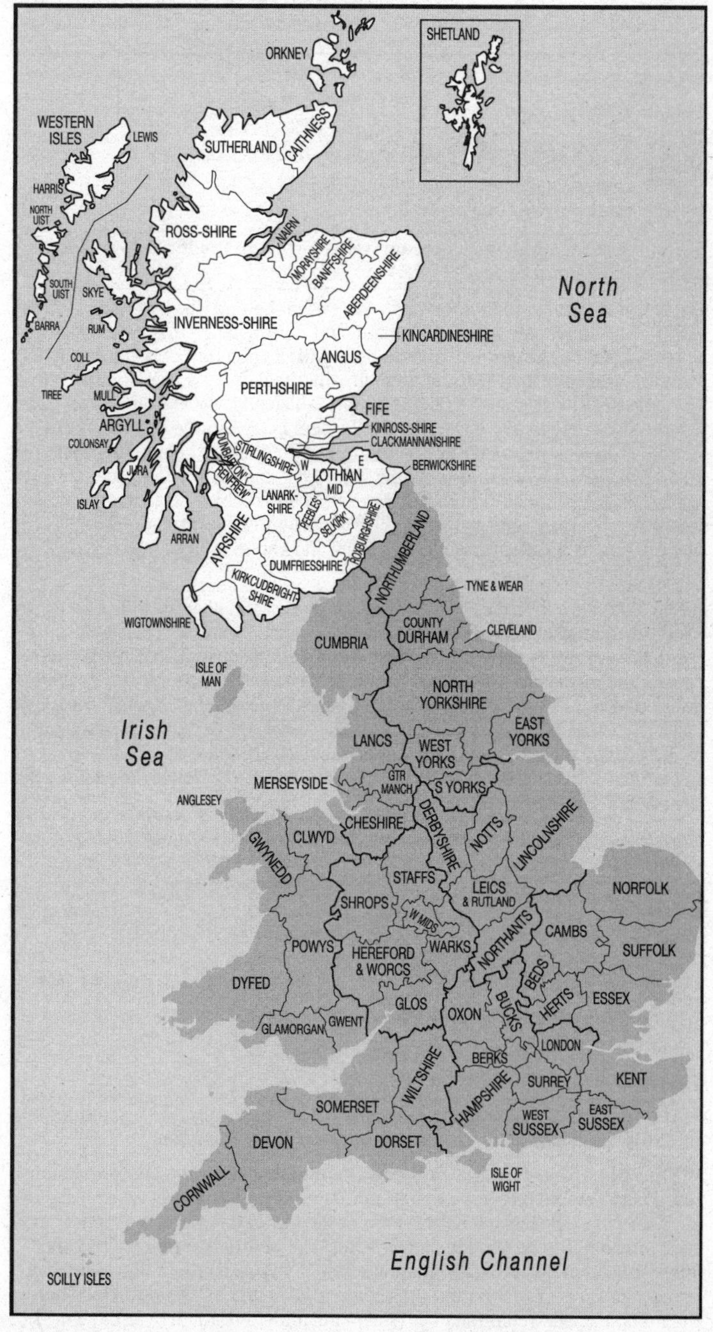

SHETLAND
ORKNEY
WESTERN ISLES
LEWIS
HARRIS
NORTH UIST
SOUTH UIST
BARRA
SKYE
RUM
COLL
TIREE
MULL
COLONSAY
JURA
ISLAY
ARRAN
SUTHERLAND
CAITHNESS
ROSS-SHIRE
NAIRN
MORAYSHIRE
BANFFSHIRE
ABERDEENSHIRE
INVERNESS-SHIRE
KINCARDINESHIRE
ANGUS
PERTHSHIRE
ARGYLL
FIFE
KINROSS-SHIRE
CLACKMANNANSHIRE
STIRLINGSHIRE
DUNBARTON
RENFREW
W
E
LOTHIAN
MID
BERWICKSHIRE
LANARK-SHIRE
PEEBLES
SELKIRK
ROXBURGHSHIRE
AYRSHIRE
DUMFRIESSHIRE
KIRKCUDBRIGHT-SHIRE
WIGTOWNSHIRE
North Sea
NORTHUMBERLAND
TYNE & WEAR
COUNTY DURHAM
CLEVELAND
CUMBRIA
ISLE OF MAN
NORTH YORKSHIRE
EAST YORKS
Irish Sea
LANCS
WEST YORKS
GTR MANCH
S YORKS
MERSEYSIDE
ANGLESEY
CHESHIRE
DERBYSHIRE
NOTTS
LINCOLNSHIRE
GWYNEDD
CLWYD
STAFFS
LEICS & RUTLAND
NORFOLK
SHROPS
W MIDS
NORTHANTS
CAMBS
SUFFOLK
POWYS
HEREFORD & WORCS
WARKS
BEDS
DYFED
GLOS
OXON
BUCKS
HERTS
ESSEX
GLAMORGAN
GWENT
LONDON
BERKS
WILTSHIRE
SURREY
KENT
SOMERSET
HAMPSHIRE
WEST SUSSEX
EAST SUSSEX
DEVON
DORSET
ISLE OF WIGHT
CORNWALL
SCILLY ISLES
English Channel

ANCRUM NT6224 Map 10

Cross Keys

(01835) 830242 – www.ancrumcrosskeys.com

Off A68 Jedburgh–Edinburgh; TD8 6XH

Friendly village pub with a deserved reputation for local ales and particularly good food

In warm weather, the picnic-sets in the garden behind this bustling 200-year-old pub are much in demand and there's a gate that leads down to Ale Water. The chatty bar, always busy with a good mix of regulars and visitors, has a dog or two by an open fire, minimal décor and is simply furnished with wall seats, straightforward tables and stools against the counter where they serve Born in the Borders Foxy Blonde and Flower of Scotland on handpump, several wines by the glass and a healthy number of malt whiskies; a side bar is for both drinking and eating. The blue-walled dining room has chunky tables and chairs on bare boards, an open kitchen and, again, minimal décor. Service is helpful and friendly. The view across the village green from a few tables and chairs in front of the stone building is lovely.

Much enjoyed food includes venison and smoked bacon terrine with pear chutney, smoked haddock and parmesan omelette, deep-fried polenta with goats cheese, peppers, aubergine and basil pesto, sea bass fillet with crushed potatoes, spinach and parsley and caper sauce, parmesan chicken with boulangère potatoes and grilled courgettes, slow-cooked treacle-cured beef with a herb crust, mustard mash and onion jus, local sirloin steak with onion rings and a choice of sauce, and puddings such as rhubarb custard and cream pastry stack and millionaire's chocolate mousse with mascarpone and hazelnut biscuit base. *Benchmark main dish: beer-battered fish and chips £12.00. Two-course evening meal £21.00.*

Free house ~ Licensee John Henderson ~ Real ale ~ Open 5-11; 12pm-1am Sat; 12-11 Sun; closed weekday lunchtimes ~ Bar food 5.30-8.30 Weds-Sun; 12-2.30, 5.30-8.30 weekends; no food Mon, Tues ~ Restaurant ~ Children welcome ~ Dogs allowed in bar ~ Wi-fi

Recommended by Alan and Alice Morgan, Elizabeth and Peter May, Molly and Stewart Lindsay, Mary and Douglas Kirkwood

APPLECROSS NG7144 Map 11

Applecross Inn

(01520) 744262 – www.applecross.uk.com

Off A896 S of Shieldaig; IV54 8LR

Isolated pub on famously scenic route on west coast, with particularly friendly welcome, real ales and good seafood; bedrooms

'This place is just magic,' says one of our enthusiastic readers about Judith Fish's remote but very popular inn. The exhilarating west coast drive to get here over the Bealach na Bà (Pass of the Cattle) is one of the highest in Britain and not to be tried in bad weather. The alternative route, along the single-track lane winding around the coast from just south of Shieldaig, has equally glorious sea loch (and then sea) views nearly all the way. Once here, the no-nonsense, welcoming bar (full of customers from all over the world) has a woodburning stove, exposed-stone walls, upholstered pine furnishings and a stone floor; Applecross Inner Sound, Red Rock and Sanctuary on handpump, over 50 malt whiskies, 20 gins and a good, varied wine list; background music and board games. Tables in the shoreside garden enjoy magnificent views and there's an outdoor eating area for summer use. If you wish to stay here, you'll have to book months ahead. Some disabled facilities.

Most people opt for the first class fresh local fish and seafood that includes squat lobsters, oysters, fresh haddock, langoustines, a seafood platter, king scallops and dressed crab with smoked salmon – but they also offer chicken liver parfait with grape chutney, pigeon breast salad with crispy bacon and pine nuts, linguine with provençale vegetables and crème fraîche, thai green chicken curry, local lamb rump with wild mushrooms and pancetta lardons, local Estate venison casserole, crispy-battered fresh haddock and chips, and puddings such as hot chocolate fudge cake and raspberry cranachan. *Benchmark main dish: local prawns in hot lemon and garlic butter £22.00. Two-course evening meal £25.00.*

Free house ~ Licensee Judith Fish ~ Real ale ~ Open 11am-11.30pm (midnight Sat); 12.30-11.30 Sun ~ Bar food 12-9 ~ Restaurant ~ Children welcome till 8.30pm ~ Dogs allowed in bar and bedrooms ~ Wi-fi ~ Bedrooms: £90/£140 *Recommended by Barry Collett, Neil and Angela Huxter, Mandy and Gary Redstone, Murray and Peggy Lindsay*

DALKEITH NR3264 Map 11

Sun

(0131) 663 2456 – www.thesuninnedinburgh.co.uk

A7 S; EH22 4TR

Family-run inn with charming bar and restaurant, local ale and delicious food and a leafy garden; comfortable, airy bedrooms

Surrounded by five acres of wooded grounds and close to the River Esk, you'd never believe Edinburgh is just 20 minutes away. This is very much a family-run business and the bars have been carefully renovated with walls stripped back to the original stone (or with hunting-theme wallpaper), bare floorboards and refurbished fireplaces. There are cushioned built-in settles, all sorts of wooden dining chairs around an appealing collection of tables, gilt-edged mirrors and high stools against the counter where friendly staff serve Inveralmond Lia Fail and Stewart Pentland IPA on handpump and good wines by the glass; background music. Seats on the covered courtyard overlook the garden where they hold popular summer barbecues, a new decked area overlooks the river and there's also a new coffee shop. Bedrooms are thoughtfully equipped and comfortable and breakfasts highly rated. Disabled access to restaurant only.

First class modern british food cooked by the landlord and his son, using the best ingredients from local producers, includes prawn and crayfish cocktail with bloody mary dressing, pig cheek with black pudding, crispy bacon and apple purée, aubergine stuffed with ratatouille topped with tomato sauce, gruyère and basil pesto, half a roast chicken with coleslaw, corn on the cob and skinny fries, whole dressed crab with lemon and dill aioli, venison loin with dauphinoise potatoes, cauliflower, granola and game jus, 35-day dry-aged 10oz rib-eye steak with toppings and a choice of sauce, a chilled seafood platter (for two people), and puddings such as black forest pannacotta with cherry sorbet and sticky toffee pudding with caramel sauce; they also offer an early bird menu (12-2, 6-7). *Benchmark main dish: beer-battered haddock and chips £15.00. Two-course evening meal £24.00.*

Free house ~ Licensee Bernadette McCarron ~ Real ale ~ Open 8am-11pm (midnight Sat) ~ Bar food 8-5, 6-9 ~ Restaurant ~ Children welcome ~ Wi-fi ~ Bedrooms: £75/£95 *Recommended by Laura Reid, Jeff Davies, Lance and Sarah Milligan, Molly and Stewart Lindsay, Julie and Andrew Blanchett, Lenny and Ruth Walters*

EDINBURGH NT2574 Map 11

Abbotsford £

(0131) 225 5276 – www.theabbotsford.com
Rose Street; E end, beside South St David Street; EH2 2PR

Busy city pub with period features, changing real ales, and bar and restaurant food

This is a handsome place with a lively atmosphere and an unchanging feel, and you'll usually find an eclectic mix of business people and locals occupying stools around the bar at lunchtime. Served from the hefty Victorian island bar (ornately carved from dark spanish mahogany and highly polished), the real ales come from breweries such as Atlas, Caledonian, Fyne, Harviestoun, Orkney and Stewart; there's also a selection of bottled american craft beers and around 70 malt whiskies. Long wooden tables and leatherette benches run the length of the high-panelled dark wood walls, while high above is a rather handsome green and gold plaster-moulded ceiling. The smarter upstairs restaurant is also impressive as well.

Bar food includes sharing platters, haggis, neeps and tatties, beef in ale pie, burgers with toppings, coleslaw and chips, a vegetarian risotto, grilled bass with fennel, pomegranate and orange salsa, and puddings such as lemon posset and sticky toffee pudding. *Benchmark main dish: breaded fish and chips £10.25. Two-course evening meal £16.00.*

Stewart ~ Licensee Daniel Jackson ~ Real ale ~ Open 11-11 (midnight Sat) ~ Bar food 12-3, 5.30-10; 12-10 Fri, Sat ~ Restaurant 12-2.15, 5.30-9.30 ~ Children over 5 allowed in restaurant *Recommended by Susan Eccleston, Lorna and Jack Musgrave, Charles and Maddie Bishop, Katherine Matthews*

EDINBURGH NT2574 Map 11

Bow Bar

(0131) 226 7667
West Bow; EH1 2HH

Cosy, enjoyably unpretentious pub with an excellent choice of well kept beers

The interior of this cheerful pub is unpretentious but warmly welcoming and it's a bastion of simple stand-up drinking. The splendid range of drinks – served by knowledgeable staff from the rectangular bar with its impressive carved mahogany gantry – includes eight well kept real ales dispensed from the tall 1920s founts on the counter: regulars such as Fallen Odyssey, Tempest Cascadian Blonde and Stewart 80/- and five quickly changing guests from breweries such as Cloudwater, Cromarty, Swannay and Wild Beer; they hold regular beer festivals. Also on offer are some 400 malts, including five 'malts of the moment', a good choice of rums, 60 international bottled beers and 20 gins. The walls are covered with a fine collection of enamel advertising signs and handsome antique brewery mirrors, and there are sturdy leatherette wall seats and café-style bar seats around heavy narrow tables on the wooden floor. No children allowed.

Lunchtime-only food is limited to pies.
Benchmark main dish: steak in ale pie £4.50.

Free house ~ Licensee Mike Smith ~ Real ale ~ Open 12-midnight; 12.30-11.30 Sun ~ Bar food 12-4; 12.30-4 Sun ~ Dogs welcome ~ Wi-fi *Recommended by Sarah and David Gibbs, Nicola and Holly Lyons, Jane Rigby, Frances Parsons*

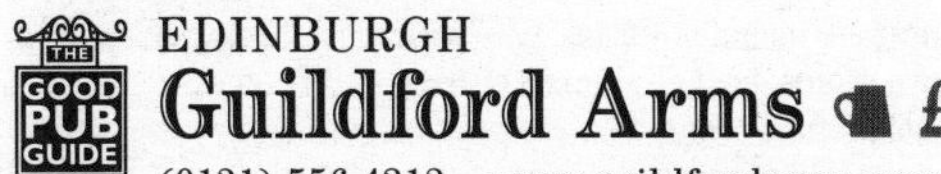

EDINBURGH NT2574 Map 11

Guildford Arms £

(0131) 556 4312 – www.guildfordarms.com

West Register Street; EH2 2AA

Busy and friendly with spectacular Victorian décor, a marvellous range of real ales and good food

The choice of ten well kept real ales is a big part of this bustling pub's appeal, but its chief glory is the splendid Victorian décor. Opulently excessive, this features ornate painted plasterwork on the lofty ceiling, dark mahogany fittings, heavy swagged velvet curtains and a busy patterned carpet. Tables and stools are lined up along towering arched windows opposite the bar, where knowledgeable, efficient staff serve quickly changing beers such as Fyne Ales Jarl, Loch Lomond Southern Summit, Orkney Dark Island, Stewart Pentland IPA, Swannay Orkney IPA and Wells Bombardier. Also, ten wines by the glass, 50 malt whiskies, a dozen rums and a dozen gins; TV and background music. The snug upstairs gallery restaurant, with contrasting modern décor, gives a fine dress-circle view of the main bar.

As well as lunchtime sandwiches and burgers, food includes Stornaway black pudding and bacon, crab and mackerel pâté, vegetarian wellington, haggis, neeps and tatties, sausages of the day, mussel and prawn linguine and steaks. *Benchmark main dish: steak in ale pie £12.95. Two-course evening meal £19.00.*

Stewart ~ Lease Steve Jackson ~ Real ale ~ Open 11-11; 11am-midnight Thurs- Sat ~ Bar food 12-2.30 (3 Sun), 5.30-9.30; 12-10 Sat; snacks throughout afternoon except Fri, Sat ~ Restaurant 12 (12.30 Sun)-2.30, 6-9.30 (10 Fri, Sat) ~ Children welcome in upstairs gallery if dining and over 5 ~ Dogs allowed in bar ~ Wi-fi ~ Live music during Edinburgh Festival *Recommended by Barry Collett, Charles Fraser, Rob Anderson, Len and Lilly Dowson, Louise and Anton Parsons*

EDINBURGH NT2574 Map 11

Kays Bar £

(0131) 225 1858 – www.kaysbar.co.uk

Jamaica Street West; off India Street; EH3 6HF

Cosy, enjoyably chatty backstreet pub with good value lunchtime food and an excellent choice of well kept beers

Surprisingly untouristy, this convivial small backstreet pub has an eclectic mix of customers and a wonderful choice of drinks. On handpump they keep around seven real ales with four constants such as Caledonian Deuchars IPA, Fyne Ales Jarl, Theakstons Best and Timothy Taylors Landlord, plus more than 50 malt whiskies aged from eight to 50 years old, 15 gins and half a dozen wines by the glass. There are long, curving, well worn, red plush wall banquettes and stools around cast-iron tables on red carpet, and red pillars supporting a red ceiling. Décor is simple with big casks and vats arranged along the walls, old wine and spirits merchants' notices and gas-type lamps. A quiet panelled back room (a bit like a library) leads off, with a narrow, plank-panelled pitched ceiling and a collection of books ranging from dictionaries to ancient steam-train books for boys; there's also a lovely coal fire in winter, and board games. In days past, the pub was owned by John Kay, a whisky and wine merchant: wine barrels were hoisted up to the first floor and dispensed through pipes attached to nipples that are still visible around the ceiling light rose. Dogs are allowed before midday and after 2.30pm.

Good value lunchtime-only food includes stovies, pâté with toast, haggis, neeps and tatties, warm brie or prawn salads, beef or chicken curries, chilli con carne, steak pie, and puddings such as chocolate fudge cake. *Benchmark main dish: haggis, neeps and tatties £4.50.*

Free house ~ Licensee Fraser Gillespie ~ Real ale ~ Open 11am-midnight; 11am-1am Fri, Sat; 12.30-11 Sun ~ Bar food 12-2.30; not Sun ~ Dogs allowed in bar ~ Wi-fi *Recommended by Rona Mackinlay, Molly and Stewart Lindsay, William and Tasha Fraser, Murray and Peggy Lindsay*

GLASGOW NS5965 Map 11

Babbity Bowster

(0141) 552 5055 – www.babbitybowster.com

Blackfriars Street; G1 1PE

A lively mix of traditional and modern with a continental feel too; bedrooms

With its mix of regulars and visitors, thoroughly convivial atmosphere and thoughtful choice of drinks and food, this 18th-c former tobacco merchant's house remains very much a Glasgow institution. The simply decorated, light-filled interior has fine tall windows, plush stools and cushioned ladder-back chairs around a mix of dark tables on bare boards, some wall bench seating, open fires and attractive plant prints on light paintwork. The bar opens on to a pleasant terrace with picnic-sets under parasols and there's another back terrace too. High chairs line the counter where they keep Caledonian Deuchars IPA and a couple of guests such as Fyne Ales Jarl and Kelburn Jaguar on air-pressure tall fount, and a remarkably impressive collection of wines and malt whiskies; good tea and coffee too. They hold traditional live music sessions on Wednesdays from 3pm and Saturdays from 4pm; boules. Simple, cosy bedrooms and the room rate includes tea or coffee with toast and home-made preserves.

Enjoyable food includes sandwiches, various croques, haggis, neeps and tatties, moules marinière, a daily vegetarian and fresh fish choice, chicken provençale, salmon fillet with creamy watercress sauce, saddle of highland venison with whisky sauce, duck breast with orange and star anise sauce, braised ox cheeks with port wine and mushroom sauce, and puddings such as seasonal fruit tart with crème anglaise and clootie dumpling with toffee sauce. *Benchmark main dish: cullen skink £6.25. Two-course evening meal £19.00.*

Free house ~ Licensee Fraser Laurie ~ Real ale ~ Open 11am-midnight; 12.30-midnight Sun ~ Bar food 12-10 ~ Restaurant ~ Children welcome if eating ~ Wi-fi ~ Live traditional music Weds afternoon, Sat early evening ~ Bedrooms: £55/£70 *Recommended by Rona Mackinlay, Barry Collett, Barry and Daphne Gregson, John Herbert, Elliott Kemp*

GLASGOW NS5965 Map 11

Bon Accord £

(0141) 248 4427 – www.bonaccordweb.co.uk

North Street; G3 7DA

Remarkable choice of drinks, a good welcome and bargain food

Knowledgeable staff serve the marvellous drinks in this convivial tavern and can help you decide what you want – which is just as well since the choice is huge. As well as 400 malt whiskies, there are daily changing real ales served from a swan-necked handpump and sourced from breweries all around Britain, including Caledonian Deuchars IPA and nine daily changing guests, continental bottled beers, a farm cider and, in a remarkable display behind the counter, 50 gins and lots of vodkas and rums. The several linked traditional bars are warmly understated with cream or terracotta walls, a mix of chairs and tables, a leather sofa and plenty of bar stools on polished bare boards or carpeting; TV, background music and board games. There are circular picnic-sets arranged on a small terrace, and modern tables and chairs set out in front.

Exceptionally good value food includes baguettes, peppered mushrooms with garlic bread, giant yorkshire pudding filled with sausages and onion gravy, chilli con carne, all-day breakfast, cajun chicken or burger with french fries, gammon and egg, and puddings such as clootie dumpling or apple pie with custard. *Benchmark main dish: fish and chips £6.95. Two-course evening meal £9.50.*

Free house ~ Licensee Paul McDonagh ~ Real ale ~ Open 11am-midnight; 12.30-midnight Sun ~ Bar food 11-8; 12.30-8 Sun ~ Children welcome until 8pm ~ Wi-fi ~ Quiz Weds evening *Recommended by Helena and Trevor Fraser, Dave Sutton, Edward and William Johnston, Sophia and Hamish Greenfield*

GLENELG NG8119 Map 11

Glenelg Inn

(01599) 522273 – www.glenelg-inn.com

Unmarked road from Shiel Bridge (A87) towards Skye; IV40 8JR

Outstanding Skye views from charming inn reached by a dramatic drive with an enjoyably pubby bar and good fresh local food

Glenelg is the closest place on the mainland to Skye, so this delightfully placed inn has lovely views across the water to the island. It's memorably reached by a single-track road climbing dramatically past heather-blanketed slopes and mountains with spectacular views to the lochs below. Feeling a bit like a mountain cabin (and still decidedly pubby given the smartness of the rest of the place), the unpretentious carpeted bar has a big fireplace, simple tables and chairs, black and white photographs on some walls, winter pool and maybe background music; you can be sure of a warm welcome from both locals and staff. Caledonian Deuchars IPA plus beers from the new Dun brewery (in the village) on handpump. The beautifully kept garden has plenty of tables and nearby walks are lovely. Some of the bedrooms have great views, and in summer there's a little car ferry across to Skye.

Cooked fresh daily, the tasty food includes cullen skink, crab claws with herb and lime dressing, heather-smoked pigeon with prunes and flowers, roast butternut squash with grains and pulses, fresh pasta with squat lobsters, hand-dived local scallops with samphire and lemon, pork belly stuffed with apricots and pistachios with an ale gravy, duck breast with herbed beans, beer-battered haddock and chips, cod fillet with chanterelle mushrooms and caper butter, and puddings. *Benchmark main dish: seafood sharing plate £20.00. Two-course evening meal £20.00.*

Free house ~ Licensee Sheila Crondie ~ Real ale ~ Open 11-11 (12.30am Sat); 12.30-11 Sun; 5-11 Thurs-Sun in winter; closed part of Jan/Feb ~ Bar food 12.30-2.30, 6.30-9 ~ Restaurant ~ Children welcome ~ Dogs welcome ~ Bedrooms: £85/£110 *Recommended by David Todd, Elliott Kemp, Sarah Roberts, William and Tasha Fraser*

ISLE OF WHITHORN NX4736 Map 9

Steam Packet

(01988) 500334 – www.thesteampacketinn.biz

Harbour Row; DG8 8LL

Waterside views from friendly, family-run inn with up to eight real ales and tasty food; bedrooms

On the tip of the south-west peninsula, this friendly, family-run inn is right on the quayside in a pretty fishing village; big picture windows overlook the bustle of yachts and inshore fishing boats, and if you stay, some of the bedrooms have the same view. The comfortable low-ceilinged bar is split into two: on the right, plush button-back banquettes and boat pictures, and on the left, stools around cast-iron-framed tables on big stone tiles, and a woodburning stove in the bare stone wall; TV, board games and pool. They brew their own ales here at the Five Kingdoms Brewery and also keep Belhaven IPA, Fyne Ales Highlander, Greene King Old Speckled Hen and guests from other breweries such as Kelburn and Orkney on handpump, plus 12 gins, 23 malt whiskies, nine wines by the glass and a couple of farm ciders. There's a lower beamed dining room with high-backed dining chairs around square tables on wooden flooring plus another woodburner, a small eating area off the lounge bar, and an airy conservatory leading into the garden. You can walk from here up to the remains of St Ninian's kirk, which is located on a headland behind the village.

Well liked food includes chicken liver pâté, vegetable curry, burger with toppings, onion rings and chips, seafood platter, sirloin steak with a choice of sauces, and puddings such as Drambuie crème brûlée and apple and blueberry crumble. *Benchmark main dish: fish and chips £11.95. Two-course evening meal £18.00.*

Free house ~ Licensee Alastair Scoular ~ Real ale ~ Open 8am-midnight ~ Bar food 12-2, 6.30-9 ~ Restaurant ~ Children welcome except in public bar ~ Dogs allowed in bar and bedrooms ~ Wi-fi ~ Folk music third Sun of month ~ Bedrooms: /£80 *Recommended by Jack Trussler, Mike Benton, Paddy and Sian O'Leary, Philip J Alderton, Victoria and Len Meadows, Tim and Sue Mulligan*

KILCHRENAN NN0323 Map 11

Kilchrenan Inn

(01866) 833130 – www.kilchrenaninn.co.uk

B845, by road to Ardanaiseig; PA35 1HD

Close to the banks of Loch Awe with good food from a well thought-out menu, scottish drinks, friendly owners and seats outside; bedrooms

To reach this refurbished 18th-c former trading post there's a lovely drive along Loch Awe and then on to Ardanaiseig Gardens. The stylish modern décor in the bar includes high chairs against the counter where they keep Fyne Ales Highlander and Jarl on handpump, eight wines by the glass, scottish gins and several malt whiskies, tartan-upholstered stools and wall seats around simple tables on bare floorboards and a woodburning stove. The atmosphere throughout is relaxed and friendly. A dining room leads off and is similarly furnished, with up-to-date lighting and local artwork on planked walls. Outside, in front of the inn are benches and tables with picnic-sets arranged on the grass opposite. Three character, contemporary bedrooms are warm and comfortable; one of them is suitable for families. Breakfasts are highly rated.

As well as all-day bar snacks, the enjoyable food cooked by the landlord from a sensibly shortish menu includes mussels and leeks in cider, duck liver pâté with pickled beetroot, pearl barley with girolle mushrooms, chestnuts and thyme, local venison pie with pickled cabbage, fried haddock and chips, duck breast with vegetables of the day, lambs liver and sage with mash and onion gravy, and puddings such as hazelnut terrine with chocolate sauce and apple and bramble crumble with ice-cream. *Benchmark main dish: braised oxtail hotpot £14.60. Two-course evening meal £19.70.*

Free house ~ Licensees Lesley and Jordan ~ Real ale ~ Open 12pm-1am; 12-midnight Sun; closed Tues, Weds Nov-Mar; closed last week Jan, first week Feb ~ Bar food 12-3, 6-9; 12.30-8 Sun ~ Restaurant ~ Children welcome ~ Dogs allowed in bar and bedrooms ~ Wi-fi ~ Bedrooms: /£95 *Recommended by Scott and Charlotte Havers, Nicholas and Lucy Sage, Maggie and Stevan Hollis, Philip Chesington*

MEIKLEOUR NO1539 Map 11

Meikleour Arms

(01250) 883206 – www.meikleourarms.co.uk

A984 W of Coupar Angus; PH2 6EB

Beautifully refurbished, charming 19th-c inn with genuinely welcoming, helpful staff and interesting food; lovely bedrooms

This enjoyable country inn is part of the Meikleour Estate and there's a lot to see and do nearby, including one of the best salmon beats in Scotland. The bar area has high chairs by the counter, painted chairs and sage green tweed banquettes by pale oak tables on flagstones, tree-pattern wallpapered or stone walls and a two-way woodburning stove; darts, board games and background music. Orkney Dark Island and Strathbraan Due South and Head East on handpump, a carefully and thoughtfully chosen wine list with 12 wines by the glass and a wine of the month, 20 gins and 50 malt whiskies. The main dining room has been newly built in the style of a barn with high rafters in an apex ceiling, old family portraits and fly fishing touches on leaf-pattern wallpapered or stone walls, and high-backed carved wooden dining chairs and wall seating around rustic tables on more flagstones. There's also a private dining room, a country-style sitting room for residents and a drying room and tackle area for anglers. Seats in the garden and on a small colonnaded verandah (with more on a sloping lawn) have distant Highland views. All the elegant bedrooms have been stylishly refurbished; three have four-posters and the downstairs rooms have wooden flooring and are dog-friendly. Do visit the spectacular beech hedge just 300 metres away which was planted over 250 years ago – it's the tallest in the world.

Using produce from the Estate (including venison) and some from their walled garden, their own eggs and local meat and game, the food includes moules marinière, black pudding scotch egg with tomato chutney, potato and celeriac rösti with mushroom ragoût, beer-battered fish and chips, steak in ale pie, pork belly with chickpeas, lentils, bacon and sun-dried tomatoes with carrot purée, seafood salad, chargrilled sirloin steak with a choice of sauce, and puddings such as dark chocolate mousse cake and lemon posset with lime curd. *Benchmark main dish: venison steak with a changing sauce £15.95. Two-course evening meal £20.00.*

Free house ~ Licensees Sam and Claire Mercer Nairne ~ Real ale ~ Open 11am-midnight ~ Bar food 11-9 ~ Restaurant ~ Children welcome ~ Dogs welcome ~ Wi-fi ~ Bedrooms: £90/£110 *Recommended by Patricia and Gordon Tucker, Jamie and Lizzie McEwan, Neil and Angela Huxter, Jeremy Snow, Anne Taylor*

MELROSE NT5433 Map 9

Burts Hotel

(01896) 822285 – www.burtshotel.co.uk

B6374, Market Square; TD6 9PL

Scotland Dining Pub of the Year

Comfortable town-centre hotel with imaginative food and a fine array of malt whiskies; bedrooms

On all counts this is a special place. It's a smart, family-run hotel right at the heart of an attractive border town and the bedrooms, though quite small, are immaculate, comfortably decorated and make a lovely base for exploring the area. Neat public areas are maintained with attention to detail and the welcoming red-carpeted bar has a warming fire, tidy pub tables between cushioned wall seats and windsor armchairs, scottish prints on pale green walls and a long dark wood counter serving Orkney Red MacGregor, Tempest Cascadian Blonde and Timothy Taylors Landlord on handpump, 12 wines by the glass from a good wine list, a farm cider and around 80 malt whiskies. The elegant restaurant with its swagged curtains, dark blue wallpaper and tables laid with white linen offers a smarter dining experience; background music. In summer you can sit out in the well tended garden. The abbey ruins are just a few steps away.

Beautifully presented and delicious food uses first class local produce: sandwiches (not Sunday), crab tian with tempura king prawns, sweetcorn relish and ginger and lime dressing, roulade of duck leg with fennel slaw, soya dressing and crispy wonton, chicken caesar salad, butternut and chickpea moroccan stew with almond and sultana rice and flatbreads, sea bass with smoked haddock and onion cake and shallot and gherkin vinaigrette, slow-cooked beef with breaded haggis and whisky and wholegrain mustard sauce, and puddings such as pineapple mousse with rum-infused pineapple, pineapple jelly and coconut sorbet and textures of chocolate with milk sorbet. *Benchmark main dish: roast rump of local lamb with celeriac and rosemary jus £17.95. Two-course evening meal £21.95.*

Free house ~ Licensees Graham and Nick Henderson ~ Real ale ~ Open 11-2.30, 5-11; 12-2.30, 6-11 Sun; closed one week Feb ~ Bar food 12-2, 6-9 ~ Restaurant ~ Children welcome ~ Dogs allowed in bar and bedrooms ~ Wi-fi ~ Bedrooms: £78/£145 *Recommended by Nick Higgins, Barbara and Phil Bowie, Dan and Belinda Smallbone, John Stephenson, Mike and Sarah Abbot, Justine and Neil Bonnett*

PLOCKTON NG8033 Map 11

Plockton Hotel ★

(01599) 544274 – www.plocktonhotel.co.uk

Village signposted from A87 near Kyle of Lochalsh; IV52 8TN

Neat little hotel with wonderful views, very good food with emphasis on local seafood and real ales; bedrooms

Our readers are as enthusiastic as they've always been about this charming family-run hotel which forms part of a long terrace of stone-built houses in a waterfront village owned by the National Trust for Scotland. Tables in the front garden look out past the village's trademark palm trees to a shore lined with colourful flowering shrubs and across the sheltered anchorage to rugged mountains. Inside, the welcoming, comfortably furnished lounge bar has window seats with views of the harbour boats, as well as antique dark red leather seating around neat Regency-style tables on a tartan carpet, and three model ships set into the woodwork and partly panelled stone walls. The separate public bar has pool, board games, TV, a juke box and background music. Cromarty Happy Chappy, Fyne Ales Jarl, Strathcarron Golden Cow and a guest beer on handpump, 20 malt whiskies, nine wines by the glass and ten scottish gins. Half the comfortable bedrooms have extraordinary water views, while the others, some with balconies, look over the hillside garden; breakfasts are good. Disabled access to one bedroom. There's a hotel nearby called the Plockton Inn, so don't get the two confused.

Fresh fish and shellfish play a big part here with dishes including hot garlic crab claws, queen scallops and smoked bacon with garlic, sole and salmon parcels with prawn thermidor sauce, sea bass with roasted butternut squash risotto, and seafood platter; they also offer bloomers and toasted paninis, a haggis and whisky starter, a vegetarian dish of the day, chicken breast stuffed with smoked ham and cheese with a sun-dried tomato, garlic and cream sauce, venison with cumberland sauce and chargrilled rib-eye steak with a choice of sauce, and puddings. *Benchmark main dish: local langoustines £22.00. Two-course evening meal £25.00.*

Free house ~ Licensee Alan Pearson ~ Real ale ~ Open 11am-midnight; closed first two weeks Jan ~ Bar food 12-2.15, 6-9 ~ Restaurant ~ Children welcome ~ Dogs allowed in bar ~ Wi-fi ~ Live traditional music May-Oct in back bar ~ Bedrooms: £75/£150 *Recommended by Laura Reid, Dr A McCormick, Philip Chesington, Amy and Luke Buchanan, Sophia and Hamish Greenfield*

RATHO NT1470 Map 11

Bridge

(0131) 333 1320 – www.bridgeinn.com

Baird Road; EH28 8RA

Canalside inn with cosy bar and airy restaurant, a thoughtful choice of drinks and enjoyable food; attractive bedrooms

In fine weather, seats on the terrace by this popular inn are quickly snapped up as they look over the Union Canal. Inside, the cosy bar has an open fire with leather armchairs to either side and a larger area with a two-way fireplace and upholstered tub and cushioned wooden chairs on pale boards around a mix of tables; a contemporary and elegant dining room leads off. A beer named for the pub (from Stewart), Orkney Red MacGregor and a guest beer on handpump, 36 wines by the glass and 50 malt whiskies. The main restaurant is light and airy with up-to-date pale oak settles, antique-style chairs and big windows overlooking the water. The individually decorated and well equipped bedrooms also have fine views and breakfasts are lovely.

Using home-grown produce, own-bred pork and free-range eggs from their flock of chickens and ducks, the interesting food includes lunchtime sandwiches, prawn cocktail with compressed cucumber and tomato with seaweed dressing, smoked ham terrine with piccalilli, cream and peas, sharing plates, mushroom risotto topped with blue cheese and peanut crumb, burger with toppings and french fries, a pie of the day, roe deer with king oyster mushrooms, butternut squash and blackberries, a trio of pork (braised cheek, crispy belly and truffle-scented fillet) with savoy cabbage, cod loin with curry flavours, cauliflower and mango, and puddings such as pannacotta with caramel and gingerbead and baked almond sponge with rhubarb. *Benchmark main dish: flat-iron steak with confit garlic and roast tomatoes £18.00. Two-course evening meal £20.00.*

Free house ~ Licensees Graham and Rachel Bucknall ~ Real ale ~ Open 9am-11pm; 9am-midnight Fri, Sat; 11-11 Sun ~ Bar food 12-3, 5-9; 12-4, 5-9 Sat; 12-4, 5-8 Sun ~ Restaurant ~ Dogs allowed in bar ~ Wi-fi ~ Bedrooms: /£130 *Recommended by Victoria and James Sargeant, Mr and Mrs P R Thomas, Angela and Steve Heard, Martin and Joanne Sharp, Jim and Sue James*

SHIELDAIG NG8153 Map 11

Tigh an Eilean Hotel

(01520) 755251 – www.tighaneilean.co.uk

Village signposted just off A896 Lochcarron–Gairloch; IV54 8XN

Wonderfully set hotel with separate contemporary bar, real ales and enjoyable food; tranquil bedrooms

The setting here is really exceptional, beneath the Torridon summits and looking down Loch Shieldaig, a haunt of otters and sea eagles. Separate from the hotel, the bright, attractive bar is on two storeys with an open staircase; dining is on the first floor and a decked balcony has a magnificent loch and village view. The place is gently contemporary and nicely relaxed with timbered floors, timber-boarded walls, shiny bolts through exposed timber roof beams and an open kitchen. A couple of changing ales from Strathcarron Golden Cow and Red Cow on handpump and up to a dozen wines by the glass; background music, TV, darts, pool and board games. Tables outside in a sheltered little courtyard are well placed to enjoy the gorgeous position. To preserve the peace and quiet, the comfortable bedrooms have no TVs and no telephones, though each has its own sitting area; good, ample breakfasts.

Food is reliably good and includes shellfish delivered fresh from the jetty: lunchtime sandwiches, seafood chowder, moules marinière, mediterranean vegetable and brie wellington, venison sausages with mash and onion gravy, haggis, neeps and tatties, hand-dived local scallops with chorizo, pizzas from the wood-fired oven, seafood platter, venison casserole with dumplings, rib-eye steak with pepper sauce and chips, and puddings such as crème brûlée and sticky toffee and date pudding with vanilla ice-cream. *Benchmark main dish: seafood stew £19.50. Two-course evening meal £20.00.*

Free house ~ Licensee Cathryn Field ~ Real ale ~ Open 11-11 (midnight Sat); 10am-11pm Sun ~ Bar food 12-2.30, 6.30-9 (8.30 in winter) ~ Restaurant ~ Children welcome ~ Dogs allowed in bar and bedrooms ~ Wi-fi ~ Traditional live folk music Fri or Sat in summer ~ Bedrooms: £72/£145 *Recommended by William Slade, Brian and Sally Wakeham, William and Ann Reid, Robert and Diana Ringstone, Daisy Rutledge, William and Tasha Fraser*

SLIGACHAN NG4930 Map 11

Sligachan Hotel

(01478) 650204 – www.sligachan.co.uk

A87 Broadford–Portree, junction with A863; IV47 8SW

Spectacularly set mountain hotel with walkers' bar and plusher side, all-day food and impressive range of whiskies

The huge, modern, pine-clad main bar in this stunningly set hotel on the Isle of Skye falls somewhere between a basic climbers' bar and the smarter, more sedate hotel side. It's spaciously open to the ceiling rafters and has geometrically laid-out dark tables and chairs on neat carpets; pool, TV and board games. As well as their own Cuillin Eagle, Old Bridge and Pinnacle, they keep a guest on handpump plus an incredible display of over 400 malt whiskies at one end of the counter. It can get quite lively in here some nights, but there's a more sedate lounge bar with leather bucket armchairs on plush carpets and a coal fire; background highland and islands music. The separate restaurant is in the hotel itself. The interesting little museum, well worth a visit, charts the history of the hotel and its famous climbers, with photographs and climbing and angling records. There are tables out in the garden and a big play area for children, which can be seen from the bar. The bedrooms are comfortable, bright and modern, and they also offer self-catering and have a campsite with caravan hook-ups. Some of the most testing walks in Britain are right on the doorstep.

Some sort of food is on offer all day: cullen skink, smoked duck with tomato and red pepper salad and crispy parma ham, three-bean chilli with sour cream, cod bites in filo pastry with asian slaw and fries, scallops with mango, chilli and red pepper salsa, lamb shank with parsley mash and rosemary jus, lemon and thyme chicken with new potatoes and jus, sea bream with lemon-infused mash, spinach and tomato and basil sauce, and puddings such as raw lemon and cashew cake and sticky toffee pudding with butterscotch sauce. *Benchmark main dish: beer-battered haddock and chips £12.95. Two-course evening meal £20.00.*

Own brew ~ Licensee Sandy Coghill ~ Real ale ~ Open 9am-12.30am; 12-9 in winter; closed early Jan-Mar ~ Bar food 11-9 ~ Restaurant ~ Children welcome ~ Dogs welcome ~ Wi-fi ~ Live ceilidh Sat evenings ~ Bedrooms: £90/£140 *Recommended by Charles Welch, Angus Light, Matthew and Elisabeth Reeves, Harry and Megan Evans, Ben Lees*

STEIN NG2656 Map 11

Stein Inn

(01470) 592362 – www.stein-inn.co.uk

End of B886 N of Dunvegan in Waternish, off A850 Dunvegan–Portree; OS Sheet 23 map reference 263564; IV55 8GA

Inn of character on Skye's Waternish peninsula with good, simple food and lots of whiskies; a rewarding place to stay

Skye's oldest inn boasts a prime waterfront spot in this untouched little hamlet, with views over the sea to the Hebrides; benches in front make the most of this. The unpretentious original public bar makes a particularly inviting retreat from the elements, with sturdy country furnishings, flagstones, a beam-and-plank ceiling, partly panelled stripped-stone walls and a warming double-sided stove between the two rooms. Caledonian Deuchars IPA and a couple of local guests such as Cairngorm Gold and Isle of Skye Red on handpump, ten wines by the glass, 130 malt whiskies and 18 gins. Good service from smartly uniformed staff. Pool, darts, board games, dominoes and cribbage in the games area, and maybe background music. There's a lively indoor play area for children and showers for yachtsmen. Warm bedrooms overlook the water and they also offer self-catering properties. Dogs are welcome in the inn but not during evening food service.

Good, wholesome food uses local fish, lamb, highland beef and wild venison: sandwiches (the crab is popular), black pudding with whisky and mustard dressing, peat-smoked local salmon, vegetarian, chicken or beef burger with toppings and fries, fresh local langoustines, venison casserole with chocolate, duck breast in garlic, cider and cream, salmon fillet with a cajun crust, slow-cooked lamb shank with mint gravy, and puddings such as lemon cheesecake and fruit crumbles. *Benchmark main dish: beer-battered haddock and chips £11.95. Two-course evening meal £18.00.*

Free house ~ Licensees Angus and Teresa Mcghie ~ Real ale ~ Open 11am-midnight; 12-11 Sun; 12-11 (midnight Sat) in winter; closed winter Mon ~ Bar food 12-4, 6-9.30; 12.30-4, 6-9 Sun ~ Children welcome ~ Dogs allowed in bar and bedrooms ~ Wi-fi ~ Bedrooms: £55/£83 *Recommended by Alison and Michael Harper, Rob Anderson, Daniel King, Angus Light, Molly and Stewart Lindsay, Stuart and Natalie Granville*

SWINTON NT8347 Map 10

Wheatsheaf

(01890) 860257 – www.wheatsheaf-swinton.co.uk

A6112 N of Coldstream; TD11 3JJ

Civilised place with small bar for drinkers, comfortable lounges, top quality food and drinks and professional service; appealing bedrooms

Although there's also quite an emphasis on the enjoyable food here, the attentive, friendly staff welcome customers into the little bar and informal lounges too. Here they keep Belhaven IPA on handpump alongside 30 malt whiskies and 18 wines by the glass. There are comfortable plush armchairs, several nice old oak settles with cushions, a little open fire, sporting prints and china plates on the bottle-green walls in the bar and small agricultural prints and a fishing-theme décor on the painted or bare-stone walls in the lounges. The dining room and front conservatory with its vaulted pine ceiling have carpet on the floor and high-backed slate-grey chairs around pale wood tables set with fresh flowers, while the more formal restaurant has black leather high-backed dining chairs around clothed tables; background music. To make the best of the surrounding countryside, why not stay in the well equipped and comfortable bedrooms; breakfasts are good and hearty. This is a pretty village just a few miles from the River Tweed.

Food includes traditional dishes but they also have creative choices such as local salmon with a crab bonbon and lemon gel, pigeon breast with tempura-battered courgette flower, black pudding and red onion jam, roasted aubergine with wild mushroom risotto, toasted pine nuts and grano padano shavings, steak burger with toppings, barbecue sauce, coleslaw and chips, steak and Guinness pie, roast chicken and haggis mousse ballotine with pancetta, roast parsnips and whisky sauce, seared cod fillet with mussels, white wine, garlic and cream, slow-cooked lamb shank with moroccan-style couscous, confit lemon and flatbread, and puddings such as vanilla crème brûlée and white chocolate mousse with popping candy base, chocolate soil and whisky gel. *Benchmark main dish: king prawn linguine £15.95. Two-course evening meal £25.00.*

Free house ~ Licensee Michael Lawrence ~ Real ale ~ Open 11-11 (midnight Sat); 11-11 Sun ~ Bar food 12-2, 6 (5.30 Thurs, Fri)-9 ~ Restaurant ~ Children welcome ~ Dogs allowed in bar and bedrooms ~ Wi-fi ~ Bedrooms: £99/£132 *Recommended by Rosie and Marcus Heatherley, Kerry and Guy Trooper, Mary and Douglas Kirkwood, Elliott Kemp*

THORNHILL NS6699 Map 11

Lion & Unicorn

(01786) 850204 – www.lion-unicorn.co.uk

Main Street (A873); FK8 3PJ

Busy, interesting pub with emphasis on its home-made food; friendly staff and bedrooms

Parts of this neatly kept and family-run inn date from 1635 and of the three log fires, one is in an original fireplace with a high brazier almost big enough to drive a car into. The pubby character back bar has some exposed stone walls, wooden flooring and stools lined along the counter where they keep An Teallach Ale and Caledonian Deuchars IPA on handpump and several wines by the glass. This opens to a games room with a pool table, juke box, fruit machine, darts, TV and board games. The more restauranty-feeling beamed and carpeted front room is traditionally furnished and set for dining; background music. Outside there are benches in a gravelled garden and a lawn with a play area.

Popular food includes sandwiches, chicken liver parfait with apple chutney, home-made haggis fritters with whisky, honey and grain mustard dip, leek, mushroom and parsnip crumble, beer-battered fresh haddock and chips, roast beef with yorkshire pudding and red wine gravy, chicken topped with haggis and wrapped in bacon with a whisky cream sauce, 10oz local rib-eye steak with trimmings and battered onion rings, and puddings such as sticky toffee pudding and assorted ice-creams. *Benchmark main dish: steak in ale pie £9.75. Two-course evening meal £16.00.*

Free house ~ Licensee Fiona Stevenson ~ Real ale ~ Open 12-midnight (1am Fri, Sat) ~ Bar food 12-9 ~ Restaurant ~ Children welcome ~ Dogs allowed in bar ~ Wi-fi ~ Bedrooms: £70/£85 *Recommended by Patricia Healey, Frances Parsons, Charles and Maddie Bishop, Charles Todd, Miranda and Jeff Davidson*

Also Worth a Visit in Scotland

Besides the fully inspected pubs, you might like to try these pubs that have been recommended to us and described by readers. Do tell us what you think of them: feedback@goodguides.com

ABERDEENSHIRE

ABERDEEN NJ9305

Grill (01224) 573530

Union Street; AB11 6BA Don't be put off by the exterior of this 19th-c granite building – the remodelled 1920s interior is well worth a look; long wood-floored bar with fine moulded ceiling, mahogany panelling and original button-back leather wall benches, ornate servery with glazed cabinets housing some of the 550 whiskies (a few from the 1930s, and 60 from outside scotland), five well kept ales including Harviestoun Bitter & Twisted, basic snacks; no children or dogs; open all day. *(Mary and Douglas Kirkwood)*

ABERDEEN NJ9406

★**Prince of Wales** (01224) 640597

St Nicholas Lane; AB10 1HF Individual and convivial old tavern with eight changing ales from very long counter; painted floorboards, flagstones or carpet, pews and screened booths, original tiled spittoon running length of bar, bargain hearty food; live acoustic music Sun evening, quiz Mon, games machines; children over 5 welcome if eating, open all day from 10am. *(Elliott Kemp)*

ABOYNE NO5298

★**Boat** (01339) 886137

Charlestown Road (B968, just off A93); AB34 5EL Busy welcoming country inn with fine views across River Dee; bare-boards bar with contemporary paintwork, scatter cushions on built-in wall seats, antlers, animal hides and scottish pictures, model train chugging its way around just below ceiling height, woodburner in stone fireplace, three well kept ales, decent wines and some 30 malt whiskies, particularly good food from 7.30am breakfast on, more elaborate seasonal evening menu, additional dining area; background music, games in public bar end; children and dogs welcome, comfortable well equipped bedrooms, open all day. *(Dr A McCormick, S G N Bennett)*

BALMEDIE NJ9619

Cock & Bull (01358) 743249

A90 N of Balmedie; AB23 8XY Friendly atmosphere and interesting décor in this country dining pub; good locally sourced food from sandwiches to daily specials, a well kept ale such as Burnside, obliging service, beamed log-fire lounge, restaurant and conservatory; children and dogs (in bar) welcome, refurbished bedrooms in converted cottage, open (and food) all day. *(Murray and Peggy Lindsay)*

OLDMELDRUM NJ8127

Redgarth (01651) 872353

Kirk Brae, off A957; AB51 0DJ Good-sized comfortable lounge with traditional décor; two or three well kept ales and interesting range of malt whiskies (village has a distillery), popular reasonably priced food, friendly attentive service, restaurant; children welcome, lovely views to Bennachie, six bedrooms (get booked quickly), open (and food) all day Sun. *(Philip Chesington)*

PENNAN NJ8465

Pennan Inn (01346) 561201

Just off B9031 Banff–Fraserburgh; AB43 6JB Whitewashed building in long row of old fishermen's cottages, wonderful spot right by the sea – scenes from the film Local Hero (1983) shot here; small bar with simple furniture and exposed stone walls, modern décor in separate restaurant, enjoyable sensibly priced food from shortish menu, at least one real ale; five bedrooms, at foot of steep winding road and parking along front limited, closed Tues and lunchtimes Wed-Fri. *(William and Tasha Fraser)*

ANGUS

BROUGHTY FERRY NO4630

★**Fishermans Tavern** (01382) 775941

Fort Street; turning off shore road; DD5 2AD Once a row of fishermen's cottages, this refurbished friendly pub is just steps from the beach; up to eight well kept changing ales (May beer festival) and good range of malt whiskies, comfortable lounge with coal fire, small snug and back dining area with another fire, popular fair-priced pubby food from sandwiches up; sports TV; children and dogs welcome, disabled facilities, tables on front pavement, more in secluded little walled garden, 14 bedrooms, open (and food) all day. *(Nicholas and Lucy Sage)*

CLOVA NO3273

Glen Clova Hotel (01575) 550350

B955 NW of Wheen; DD8 4QS Tucked-away 19th-c hotel's unpretentious climbers' bar; flagstones, bench seats and stone fireplace with woodburner, bric-a-brac and old photographs, a couple of well kept changing beers, 18 malts and plenty of wines by the glass, good food (same menu as their restaurant) using home-reared beef and lamb and venison from surrounding hills, friendly staff; children and dogs welcome, ten bedrooms, eight garden lodges and bunkhouse, glorious walks nearby, open all day. *(Maggie and Stevan Hollis)*

ARGYLL

ARDFERN NM8004

Galley of Lorne (01852) 500284
B8002; village and inn signposted off A816 Lochgilphead-Oban; PA31 8QN 17th-c drovers' inn on edge of Loch Craignish; cosy beamed and flagstoned bar with warming log fire, black panelling and unfussy assortment of furniture including settles, up to four real ales and 50 whiskies, good choice of food from lunchtime sandwiches up, lounge bar with woodburner and spacious picture-window restaurant; background music, small pool room, darts, games machine, sports TV; children and dogs welcome, good sea and loch views from sheltered terrace and deck, seven bedrooms in extension, open all day summer. *(David Todd)*

BRIDGE OF ORCHY NN2939

★**Bridge of Orchy Hotel**
(01838) 400208 *A82 Tyndrum–Glencoe; PA36 4AB* Spectacular spot on West Highland Way, very welcoming with good food in bar, lounge and smarter restaurant, decent choice of well kept ales, house wines and malt whiskies, interesting mountain photographs, open fires; free wi-fi; dogs welcome; good bedrooms, more in airy riverside annexe, open (and food) all day. *(Lorna and Jack Musgrave)*

CAIRNDOW NN1811

★**Cairndow Stagecoach Inn**
(01499) 600286 *Village and pub signed off A83; PA26 8BN* 17th-c coaching inn in wonderful position on edge of Loch Fyne; good sensibly priced food including local venison and fresh fish, ales from nearby Fyne and 37 malt whiskies (including a whisky of the month), friendly accommodating staff; children and dogs welcome, lovely peaceful lochside garden, comfortable bedrooms, some in modern annexe with balconies overlooking the water, good breakfast, open (and food) all day. *(David J Austin, Dr A McCormick)*

CONNEL NM9034

Oyster (01631) 710666
A85, W of Connel Bridge; PA37 1PJ 18th-c inn opposite former ferry slipway, lovely view across the water (especially at sunset); decent-sized bar (the Glue Pot) with friendly highland atmosphere, log fire in stone fireplace, Caledonian Deuchars IPA, good range of wines, gins and malts, enjoyable all-day food from pubby choices to local seafood, friendly attentive service; sports TV; modern hotel part with 11 bedrooms and separate evening restaurant (closed winter). *(Susan Eccleston)*

GLENCOE NN1058

★**Clachaig** (01855) 811252
Old Glencoe Road, behind NTS Visitor Centre; PH49 4HX 18th-c climbers' and walkers' inn surrounded by the scenic grandeur of Glencoe; Boots Bar with 14 scottish ales, some 300 malts and interesting range of artisan gins, vodkas and rums from across Scotland, slate-floored snug with whisky barrel-panelled walls and open fire, lounge (children allowed here) has mix of tables and booths, photos signed by famous climbers and local artwork, hearty food; background and live music, pool, free wi-fi; children (in lounge bar) and dogs welcome, 23 comfortable bedrooms in adjoining hotel plus self-catering cottages, open (and food) all day. *(Jeremy Snow)*

INVERARAY NN0908

★**George** (01499) 302111
Main Street East; PA32 8TT Georgian hotel (packed in high season) at hub of this appealing small town; pubby bar with exposed joists, bare stone walls, old tiles and big flagstones, antique settles, carved wooden benches and cushioned stone slabs along the walls, four log/peat fires, a couple of real ales and 100 malt whiskies, good food in bar and smarter restaurant, conservatory; children and dogs welcome, well laid-out terraces with plenty of seats, 17 bedrooms, Inveraray Castle and walks close by, open (and food) all day. *(Sarah Roberts)*

OBAN NM8530

Cuan Mor (01631) 565078
George Street; PA34 5SD Contemporary quayside bar-restaurant with over 100 malts, a couple of changing beers and wide choice of competitively priced food including set menus, Fri steak night and meat-free Mon, friendly service; children welcome, some seats outside, open all day. *(Susan Eccleston)*

OBAN NM8529

Lorne (01631) 570020
Stevenson Street; PA34 5NA Traditional Victorian pub tucked away behind the seafront; a well kept changing ale and good selection of whiskies and gins from island servery with ornate brasswork, reasonably priced food including burgers and fish/seafood, good service; weekend live music and DJs, Weds quiz, TVs; children and dogs welcome, café-style tables and chairs in sheltered beer garden, open (and food) all day. *(Susan Eccleston)*

OTTER FERRY NR9384

Oystercatcher (01700) 821229
B8000, by the water; PA21 2DH Refurbished pub-restaurant in old building in outstanding spot overlooking Loch Fyne; good food using local fish and shellfish, well kept ales including Fyne from pine-clad bar, decent wine list, friendly staff; dogs

welcome in bar; lots of tables out on spit, free moorings, open all day (closed Tues and Weds). *(Jeremy Snow)*

PORT APPIN NM9045

Pierhouse (01631) 730302

In Appin, turn right at the Port Appin/ Lismore Ferry sign; PA38 4DE Beautiful location overlooking Loch Linnhe to Lismore and beyond; smallish bar with attractive terrace, good range of wines and beers, 100 malt whiskies and over 30 gins (many scottish), excellent seafood (plus other bar food), picture-window restaurant enjoying the fine view, helpful friendly staff; children welcome, comfortable bedrooms, moorings for visiting yachts, open all day. *(Maggie and Stevan Hollis)*

TARBERT NR8365

West Loch Hotel (01880) 820283

A83, a mile S; PA29 6YF Friendly 18th-c inn overlooking sea loch; comfortably updated with exposed stone walls, pale-wood tables and dark high-backed dining chairs, relaxing lounges with fine views and warming fires, enjoyable food using local produce, Belhaven and good selection of whiskies and gins, helpful cheerful service; children and dogs welcome, bedrooms (some with loch view), handy for ferry terminal. *(Jeremy Snow)*

TAYVALLICH NR7487

Tayvallich Inn (01546) 870282

B8025; PA31 8PL Small single-storey bar-restaurant by Loch Sween specialising in good local seafood; pale pine furnishings on quarry tiles, local nautical charts, good range of whiskies and usually a couple of beers from Loch Ness, friendly atmosphere; background music (live first Fri of month); children and dogs welcome, a few rustic picnic-sets on front deck with lovely views over yacht anchorage, open all day. *(Lorna and Jack Musgrave)*

AYRSHIRE

DUNURE NS2515

Dunure (01292) 500549

Just off A719 SW of Ayr; KA7 4LN Busy place attractively set overlooking the little harbour; updated bar, lounge and restaurant, well liked food including fresh fish/seafood, good service, nice wines but no real ales; courtyard tables, bedrooms, not far from Culzean Castle (NTS), open all day. *(Sarah Roberts)*

SORN NS5526

Sorn Inn (01290) 551305

Village signed from Mauchline (A76); Main Street; KA5 6HU Restauranty pub in tiny conservation village; highly regarded imaginative food from brasserie dishes up in two restaurant areas, also smallish bar serving an Orkney ale, friendly staff; children and dogs (not in restaurant) welcome, four comfortable well appointed bedrooms, open (and food) all day weekends, closed Mon. *(Buster May)*

SYMINGTON NS3831

Wheatsheaf (01563) 830307

Just off A77 Ayr–Kilmarnock; Main Street; KA1 5QB Single-storey former 18th-c posting inn, charming and cosy, with good food (must book weekends) including lunchtime/early evening set menu, efficient friendly service, log fire; children welcome, circular picnic-sets outside, quiet pretty village, open (and food) all day. *(Sarah Roberts)*

BERWICKSHIRE

ALLANTON NT8654

★**Allanton Inn** (01890) 818260

B6347 S of Chirnside; TD11 3JZ Well run 18th-c stone-built village inn with attractive open-plan interior; very good fairly priced food with emphasis on fresh fish/seafood from daily changing menu, a couple of well kept ales such as Born in the Borders, good wine list and speciality gins, friendly efficient service, cosy bare boards bar with scatter cushions on bench seats, immaculate dining areas, log fire; background music; children welcome, no dogs inside, picnic-sets in sheltered garden behind, nice views, bedrooms, open all day. *(Mike and Sarah Abbot)*

AUCHENCROW NT8560

Craw (01890) 761253

B6438 NE of Duns; pub signed off A1; TD14 5LS Delightful little 18th-c pub in row of cream-washed cottages, friendly and welcoming, with enjoyable well presented food, changing ales from smaller brewers and good wine list, pictures on panelled walls, woodburner, more formal back restaurant; children welcome, tables out on village green and on decking behind, three bedrooms and self-catering annexe, open all day weekends. *(Jim and Sue James)*

LAUDER NT5347

Black Bull (01578) 722208

Market Place; TD2 6SR Comfortable white-painted 18th-c inn festooned with cheerful window boxes and hanging baskets; cosy rustic-feel bar with country scenes on panelled walls, quieter room off and restaurant, well kept Campbells Gunner and Stewart Edinburgh Gold, good sensibly priced food using local seasonal produce, friendly helpful service; background music, sports TV, free wi-fi; children and dogs (in bar) welcome, eight bedrooms, open (and food) all day. *(Mrs Lynda Kellman)*

BORDERS

AYTON NT9261

Hemelvaart Bier Café 07968 359917
High Street; TD14 5QL Welcoming village bar with plenty of community spirit; two real ales, six craft kegs and extensive range of bottled beers, interesting collection of gins too, friendly knowledgeable staff, enjoyable good value food including range of burgers and locally made pies, themed nights, also good coffee and home-made cakes; regular live music, comedy evenings and other events; children and dogs welcome, open from 5pm Mon, closed Tues and Weds, otherwise open all day (till midnight Fri, Sat). *(Katherine Matthews)*

DUMFRIESSHIRE

BARGRENNAN NX3576

House O' Hill (01671) 840243
Off A714, road opposite church; DG8 6RN Small pub on edge of Galloway Forest; decent food from fair-priced varied menu including daily specials, a couple of real ales and decent wine list, afternoon teas, friendly helpful staff; children and dogs (in bar) welcome, two comfortable bedrooms and self-catering cottage, open all day. *(Roddy Duncan)*

BEATTOCK NT0702

Old Stables (01683) 300134
Smith Way; 0.25 mile from M74 junction 15; DG10 9QX Turreted 19th-c pub at edge of the village; Belhaven beers and bargain home-cooked food, friendly staff, bar and second railway-themed room with memorabilia from the old Beattock line (famous for its steep gradients); live music, pool, darts, big-screen TVs and fruit machine; children and dogs welcome, covered outside seating area, bedrooms and parking for campervans, open all day. *(Mary and Douglas Kirkwood)*

DUMFRIES NX9776

★**Cavens Arms** (01387) 252896
Buccleuch Street; DG1 2AH Good generously served home-made food (not Mon) from pubby choices up, seven well kept interesting ales, traditional ciders and fine choice of malts, friendly attentive service, civilised front part with lots of wood, drinkers' area at back with bar stools, banquettes and traditional cast-iron tables, more recently added lounge/restaurant; discreet TV; no children or dogs, disabled facilities, small terrace behind, open all day and can get very busy. *(Philip Chesington)*

DUMFRIES NX9775

Globe (01387) 252335
High Street; DG1 2JA Proper town pub with strong Burns connections, especially in the dark-panelled 17th-century snug and little museum-like room beyond; main part is more modern in feel; ales such as Caledonian and Sulwath, plenty of whiskies and good value pubby food, friendly service; live music Mon, children welcome in eating areas, terrace seating, open all day. *(Philip Chesington)*

DUNBARTONSHIRE

ARROCHAR NN2903

Village Inn (01301) 702279
A814, just off A83 W of Loch Lomond; G83 7AX Friendly lochside inn with well kept ales such as Fyne and several dozen malts, wide choice of popular food in simple dining area including breakfasts, heavy beams, bare boards, panelling and roaring fire, steps down to unpretentious bar; background music, sports TV; children welcome in eating areas, tables out on deck and lawn with lovely loch and hill views, neat comfortable bedrooms (more spacious ones in converted barn), open all day. *(Mike and Sarah Abbot)*

LUSS NS3498

Inn on Loch Lomond (01436) 860678 *A82, about 3 miles N; G83 8PD* Large open-plan inn across the road from Loch Lomond; decent choice of enjoyable food including local fish in bar and restaurant, well kept beers, some 30 wines by the glass and good range of whiskies, friendly helpful staff; children welcome, private jetty with boat trips, bedrooms including eight in water's edge lodge, open (and food) all day. *(Dr A McCormick)*

EAST LOTHIAN

GULLANE NT4882

★**Old Clubhouse** (01620) 842008
East Links Road; EH31 2AF Single-storey building in nice position overlooking Gullane Links; cosy bar and more formal dining room, seating from wooden dining chairs and banquettes to big squashy leather armchairs and sofas, Victorian pictures and cartoons, stuffed birds, sheet music covers and other memorabilia, open fires, good choice of enjoyable home-made food, Caledonian Deuchars IPA, Timothy Taylors Landlord and a couple of guests, nice house wines, friendly helpful service; under-10s till 8pm, dogs welcome in bar, plenty of seats out at front, open (and food) all day. *(Maggie and Stevan Hollis)*

HADDINGTON NT5173

Victoria (01620) 823332
Court Street; EH41 3JD Popular bar-restaurant under new management; enjoyable local food, Belhaven ales and short

but decent wine list, prompt friendly service, mix of cushioned dining chairs and wall banquettes on wooden flooring or carpets, woodburning stove; five bedrooms, open (and food) all day. *(Scott and Charlotte Havers)*

FIFE

CULROSS NS9885

Red Lion (01383) 880225
Low Causeway; KY12 8HN Convivial old pub in pretty NTS village; wide choice of fair value food, a beer from Inveralmond and several wines by the glass, beams and amazing painted ceilings; seats outside, open (and food) all day. *(William and Tasha Fraser)*

CUPAR NO3714

Boudingait (01334) 654681
Bonnygate; KY15 4BU Bustling bar with captain's and cushion-seated chairs around dark tables on wood flooring, open fire, high chairs against counter serving a couple of changing ales, good choice of well liked traditional food at reasonable prices, afternoon teas, friendly helpful staff; quiz Weds, regular live music including folk; children welcome, open all day, food all day Fri-Sun. *(Roddy Duncan)*

ELIE NO4999

Ship (01333) 330246
The Toft, off A917 (High Street) towards harbour; KY9 1DT Attractively updated and in great position for enjoying a drink overlooking the sandy bay; bar and two restaurants (one upstairs), good seasonal food, friendly service; children and dogs welcome, seats on terrace (own bar) looking out to stone granary and pier, maybe beach cricket, six boutique-style bedrooms, open all day. *(Nell Attwood)*

INVERNESS-SHIRE

ARDGOUR NN0163

Inn at Ardgour (01855) 841225
From A82 follow signs for Strontian A861 and take Corran Ferry across loch to the inn; note that ferry does not sail over Christmas period; PH33 7AA Traditional fairly remote roadside inn by Corran Ferry slipway with fine Loch Linnhe views; enjoyable food and decent beer and whisky choice, friendly accommodating staff, restaurant; children and well behaved dogs welcome, a few tables outside, bedrooms, open all day in season (from 4pm winter). *(Dr A McCormick)*

AVIEMORE NH8612

Cairngorm (01479) 810233
Grampian Road (A9); PH22 1PE Large flagstoned bar in traditional turreted hotel, lively and friendly, with Cairngorm ales and good choice of other drinks, well priced food from wide-ranging menu using local produce, buffet night Thurs, prompt helpful service, tartan-walled and carpeted restaurant; daily live music (not Tues when there's a quiz), sports TV; children welcome, comfortable smart bedrooms (some with stunning views), open (and food) all day. *(Katherine Matthews)*

CARRBRIDGE NH9022

Cairn (01479) 841212
Main Road; PH23 3AS Welcoming traditionally furnished hotel bar; three well kept ales such as Cairngorm and good home-cooked food, old local pictures, warm coal fire, separate more formal dining room; pool and sports TV; children and dogs welcome, seats and tables out in front, seven comfortable bedrooms, open all day. *(Johnston and Maureen Anderson)*

DORES NH5934

★**Dores** (01463) 751203
B852 SW of Inverness; IV2 6TR Traditional country pub with exposed stone walls and low ceilings in delightful spot on the shore of Loch Ness; small attractive bar on right with two or three well kept changing scottish ales and several whiskies, two-part dining area to the left serving good food from pub favourites up, friendly staff; children and dogs welcome, sheltered front garden, lots of picnic-sets out behind taking in the spectacular view, open (and food) all day, closed Mon in winter. *(Elliott Kemp)*

FORT WILLIAM NN1274

Ben Nevis Inn (01397) 701227
N off A82: Achintee; PH33 6TE Roomy converted stone barn in stunning spot by path up to Ben Nevis; good mainly straightforward food (lots of walkers so best to book), ales such as Cairngorm and Isle of Skye, prompt cheery service, bare-boards dining area with steps up to bar; live music (Tues in summer, maybe first and third Thurs in winter); children welcome, no dogs, seats out at front and back, bunkhouse below, open all day Apr-Oct, otherwise closed Mon-Weds. *(Elliott Kemp)*

GLENFINNAN NM9080

Glenfinnan House (01397) 722235
Take A830 off A32 to Glenfinnan, turn left after Glenfinnan Monument Visitors Centre; PH37 4LT Beautifully placed 18th-c hotel by Loch Shiel; traditional bar with well kept ales and over 50 whiskies, good food including fish/seafood and local venison, restaurant; lawns down to the water, comfortable bedrooms, may close during the winter. *(Lorrie Penman)*

GLENUIG NM6576

Glenuig Inn (01687) 470219
A861 SW of Lochailort, off A830 Fort William–Mallaig; PH38 4NG Friendly bar set on picturesque bay; enjoyable locally sourced food including some from next-door

smokery, well kept Cairngorm ales and a scottish cider on tap, lots of bottled beers and good range of whiskies, dining room with woodburner; dogs welcome, bedrooms in adjoining block, also bunkhouse popular with walkers and divers, moorings for visiting yachts, open (and food) all day. *(Andrew Chetty)*

INVERMORISTON NH4216

Glenmoriston Arms (01320) 351206 *A82/A887; IV63 7YA* Small civilised hotel dating in part from 1740 when it was a drovers' inn; bare-boards bar with open fire and big old stag's head, a well kept beer such as Orkney and over 100 malt whiskies, good food here from lunchtime sandwiches up or in neatly laid-out evening restaurant with antique rifles, friendly staff; children welcome, handy for Loch Ness, ten bedrooms (three in converted outbuilding), open all day, from 4pm Nov-Mar. *(Philip J Alderton)*

INVERNESS NH6645

Black Isle (01463) 229920 *Church Street; IV1 1EN* Buzzy corner bar owned by Black Isle brewery, over 20 draught beers (listed on screens) plus extensive bottled range from slabby wood counter, long rustic tables, benches and mix of wooden chairs on bare boards, full-length windows at front, some colourful murals and high ceiling with exposed ducting, enjoyable wood-fired pizzas, friendly knowledgeable staff; barrel tables and seats made from pallets on part-covered terrace, new hostel-style bedrooms (private and shared), open (and food) all day. *(The Dutchman)*

INVERNESS NH6645

Number 27 (01463) 241999 *Castle Street; IV2 3DU* Busy pub opposite the castle, friendly and welcoming, with plenty of draught and bottled beers and good choice of well liked/priced food including Mon steak night, restaurant at back; children welcome, open (and food) all day. *(Elliott Kemp)*

INVERNESS NH6645

Phoenix Ale House (01463) 240300 *Academy Street; IV1 1LX* Much-liked 1890s bare-boards bar with fine oval servery, up to ten real ales and enjoyable reasonably priced food, neatly furnished adjoining dining room; sports TV; open (and food) all day. *(Elliott Kemp)*

MALLAIG NM6796

Steam (01687) 462002 *Davies Brae; PH41 4PU* Popular Victorian inn with good food including freshly landed fish/seafood (takeaway menu too), efficient friendly service, bar with open fire, split-level bare-boards restaurant; live music; children and dogs welcome (resident great dane), tables in back beer garden, five simple but comfortable bedrooms (no breakfast), open all day. *(Angus Light)*

WHITEBRIDGE NH4815

Whitebridge (01456) 486226 *B862 SW of village; IV2 6UN* Old-style hunting, shooting and fishing hotel set in the foothills of the Monadhliath Mountains, popular and cheerful, with good traditional food, well kept ales such as Cairngorm, Cromarty and Loch Ness and around 50 malts, two bars with woodburners, summer restaurant; well behaved dogs welcome, 12 bedrooms, open all day in summer, all day weekends winter. *(Lorrie Penman)*

KINCARDINESHIRE

FETTERCAIRN NO6573

Ramsay Arms (01561) 340334 *Burnside Road; AB30 1XX* Hotel with tartan-carpeted bar and smart oak-panelled restaurant; well kept ales and a dozen malts including the local Fettercairn, enjoyable fairly traditional food, friendly service; children welcome, picnic-sets in garden, attractive village (liked by Queen Victoria who stayed at the hotel), 12 bedrooms, good breakfast. *(Lorna and Jack Musgrove)*

STONEHAVEN NO8595

Lairhillock (01569) 730001 *Netherley; 6 miles N of Stonehaven, 6 miles S of Aberdeen, take the Durris turn off from the A90; AB39 3QS* Extended 200-year-old family-run inn; beamed bar with dark woodwork, panelled wall benches and mix of old seats, lots of brass and copper, nice open fire, Timothy Taylors Landlord and a guest, several wines by the glass, good malt whiskies, generally well liked food from lunchtime baguettes up, spacious lounge with unusual central fire, panoramic views from back conservatory; children and dogs (in bar) welcome, open all day. *(Stuart James)*

STONEHAVEN NO8785

Ship (01569) 762617 *Shore Head; AB39 2JY* Whitewashed 18th-c waterside inn with bustling local atmosphere, good selection of changing beers and over 100 whiskies, well liked food in bar or modern restaurant, friendly staff; sports TV; children (till 8pm) and dogs welcome, disabled access/loos, tables out overlooking pretty harbour, 11 bedrooms, open all day, food all day weekends. *(Dr A McCormick)*

KIRCUDBRIGHTSHIRE

CASTLE DOUGLAS NX7662

Sulwath Brewery (01556) 504525 *King Street; DG7 1DT* Convivial bar attached to this small brewery; six Sulwath ales in top condition and their bottled beers, Weston's cider, limited food (hot pies), stools and barrel tables, off-sales and souvenirs, brewery tours Mon and Fri at 1pm (unless by prior arrangement); dogs welcome, disabled access, open 10am-6pm Mon-Sat. *(Roddy Duncan)*

DALRY NX6281

Clachan (01644) 430241

A713 Castle Douglas–Ayr; DG7 3UW Cheerful traditional inn with plenty of character; beams, dark woodwork and open fires, some large stuffed fish in display cases and other interesting bits and pieces, two well kept changing ales and good selection of other drinks, popular affordably priced food from lunchtime sandwiches and pub favourites up, regular deals, friendly efficient service, woodburner in timbered restaurant with pitched ceiling; TV, fruit machine; children and dogs welcome, on Southern Upland Way, bedrooms, open all day. *(Phil Papworth)*

GATEHOUSE OF FLEET NX6056

Masonic Arms (01557) 814335

Ann Street; off B727; DG7 2HU Spacious recently refurbished 18th-c dining pub; comfortable two-room pubby bar with traditional seating, pictures on timbered walls and stuffed fish above brick fireplace, Caledonian Deuchars IPA, Sulwath Galloway Gold and good choice of malt whiskies, enjoyable freshly made food from lunchtime sandwiches up, restaurant and new sun room; background music (live Thurs), quiz Fri, pool, free wi-fi; children and dogs (in bar) welcome, picnic-sets under parasols in neatly kept sheltered garden, more seats in front, open all day (although may shut Mon, Tues in winter), food all day weekends. *(Michael and Sheila Hawkins)*

HAUGH OF URR NX8066

Laurie Arms (01556) 660246

B794 N of Dalbeattie; Main Street; DG7 3YA Welcoming 19th-c village pub with good local atmosphere; traditional furnishings and log fire in split-level carpeted bar, well kept changing ales, decent wines by the glass and enjoyable reasonably priced home-made food including good steaks, friendly service, restaurant, games room with darts and pool; quiz first Fri of month; children welcome, dogs in bar, tables out at front and on sheltered terrace behind, open (and food) all day weekends. *(Nicholas and Lucy Sage)*

KIRKCUDBRIGHT NX6850

Selkirk Arms (01557) 330402

High Street; DG6 4JG Comfortable well run 18th-c hotel in pleasant spot by mouth of the Dee; tartan-carpeted lounge with open fire, up to three real ales including a house beer from local Sulwath, 30 malt whiskies and 21 gins, cosy refurbished cocktail bar (open from 2pm), good variety of enjoyable food in bistro and evening restaurant from pub standards up, afternoon teas, friendly efficient service; background music; children and dogs (in Burns Room) welcome, tables under parasols in neat garden with 15th-c font, 16 renovated bedrooms, open all day. *(Michael and Sheila Hawkins, Philip J Alderton)*

LANARKSHIRE

BALMAHA NS4290

Oak Tree (01360) 870357

B837; G63 0JQ Family-run slate-clad inn on Loch Lomond's quiet side; beams, timbers and panelling, pubby bar with lots of old photographs, farm tools, stuffed animals and collection of grandfather clocks, log fire, good choice of enjoyable food from sandwiches and snacks up, own-brewed ales along with other scottish beers and over 50 whiskies, restaurant, coffee shop and ice-cream parlour, village shop; children welcome, plenty of tables out around ancient oak tree, popular with West Highland Way walkers, attractive bedrooms, cottages and bunkhouses. *(Rod Anderson)*

BIGGAR NT0437

Crown (01899) 220116

High Street (A702); ML12 6DL Friendly old pub with good choice of enjoyable food from tapas-style plates and pizzas up, meal deals and good value Sun carvery, two well kept changing ales (annual beer festival – see website), open fire in beamed front bar, panelled lounge with old local pictures, restaurant; live music every other Fri; children welcome, open (and food) all day. *(Murray and Peggy Lindsay)*

FINTRY NS6186

Fintry (01360) 860224

Main Street; G63 0XA Community-owned 18th-c village pub with friendly relaxed atmosphere; beers from on-site microbrewery and enjoyable fairly priced home-made food, modernised interior with beams and two-way woodburner; traditional music Weds evening, Sun afternoon and first Sat of the month, quiz last Mon; children welcome, dogs in pool room, suntrap back garden, open (and food) all day. *(Alice Wright)*

GLASGOW NS5767

Belle (0141) 339 2299

Great Western Road; G12 8HX Busy pub with wide mix of customers; leather-topped stools, modern and traditional chairs around all sorts of tables on polished wood floor, stags' heads and unusual mirrors on painted or exposed stone walls, open fire, american craft beers and European lagers; dogs welcome, tables out on pavement and in tiny leafy back garden, open all day. *(Elliott Kemp)*

GLASGOW NS5865

Drum & Monkey (0141) 221 6636

St Vincent Street; G2 5TF Busy Nicholsons bank conversion; lots of carved mahogany, granite pillars and ornate ceiling, island bar serving five real ales, over 20 gins and decent range of wines, good value food, quieter back area; open (and food) all day. *(Elliott Kemp)*

GLASGOW NS5865

Pot Still (0141) 333 0980
Hope Street; G2 2TH Comfortable and welcoming little pub with over 700 malt whiskies (good value whisky of the month); traditional bare-boards interior with raised back part, button-back leather bench seats, dark panelling, etched and stained glass, columns up to ornately corniced ceiling, four changing ales and interesting bottled beers from nice old-fashioned servery, friendly knowledgeable staff, food limited to range of good value pies; silent fruit machine; open all day and can get packed. *(Stuart James)*

GLASGOW NS5466

St Louis (0141) 339 1742 *Dumbarton Road, by the roundabout; G11 6RD* Relaxed bar-café with simple stylish décor; Williams beers and enjoyable reasonably priced food including sandwiches and range of burgers, friendly staff; live music Sat, quiz Tues, monthly poetry night; dogs welcome, open (and food) all day from 9am (10am weekends). *(Michael Butler)*

GLASGOW NS5865

State (0141) 332 2159
Holland Street; G2 4NG High-ceilinged bar with marble pillars, lots of carved wood including handsome oak island servery, half a dozen or so well kept changing ales, food from bargain lunchtime meals up, some areas set for dining, good atmosphere and friendly staff, armchairs among other comfortable seats, coal-effect fire in big wooden fireplace, old prints and theatrical posters; background music (live Tues and comedy night Sat), silent sports TVs, games machine; open all day, no food weekends. *(Elliott Kemp)*

GLASGOW NS5666

Tennents (0141) 339 7203
Byres Road; G12 8TN Big busy high-ceilinged Victorian corner pub near the university; ornate plasterwork, panelling and paintings, traditional tables and chairs, stools and wall seating, a dozen well kept ales and keenly priced wines, wide range of good value food including breakfast till midday; basement bar for weekend DJs, sports TVs; open all day from 10am. *(Eddie Gallacher)*

GLASGOW NS5666

Three Judges (0141) 337 3055
Dumbarton Road, opposite Byres Road; G11 6PR Traditional corner bar with eight quickly changing ales from small breweries far and wide (they get through several hundred a year), friendly staff will offer tasters; live jazz Sun afternoons, TV; dogs welcome, open all day. *(Stuart James)*

MIDLOTHIAN

EDINBURGH NT2574

★**Café Royal** (0131) 556 1884
West Register Street; EH2 2AA Wonderful Victorian baroque interior – floors and stairway laid with marble, chandeliers hanging from magnificent plasterwork ceilings, superb series of Doulton tilework portraits of historical innovators (Watt, Faraday, Stephenson, Caxton, Benjamin Franklin and Robert Peel), substantial island bar serving well kept Greene King IPA, Belhaven 80/-, Stewart Edinburgh Gold and four guests, several wines by the glass and 40 malts, very well liked food with emphasis on fresh seafood, good friendly service, the restaurant's stained glass is also worth a look (children welcome here); background music; open all day (till 1am Fri, Sat), can get very busy. *(Barry Collett)*

EDINBURGH NT2573

Doric (0131) 225 1084
Market Street; EH1 1DE Welcoming 17th-c pub-restaurant with plenty of atmosphere; simple furnishings in small bar with wood floor and lots of pictures, four cask ales and good range of bottled beers, 50 single malts, friendly young staff, interesting modern food (must book) in upstairs wine bar (children welcome) and bistro; handy for Waverley station, open all day. *(Archie)*

EDINBURGH NT2573

Ensign Ewart (0131) 225 7440
Lawnmarket, Royal Mile; last pub on right before castle; EH1 2PE Charming dimly lit olde-world pub handy for the castle (so gets busy); beams peppered with brasses, huge painting of Ewart capturing french banner at Waterloo, assorted furniture including elbow tables, well kept Caledonian ales and lots of whiskies, straightforward bar food; background and regular live music (not Tues, Thurs) games machine, keypad entry to lavatories; open all day. *(Colin McLachlan)*

EDINBURGH NT2472

Fountain (0131) 229 1899
Dundee Street; EH11 1AX Nicely updated pub with open-plan split-level interior; four or five draught beers from long well stocked bar, popular fairly priced home-made food including brunch, good friendly service; children and dogs welcome, open (and food) all day. *(Martin Day, Archie)*

EDINBURGH NT2573

★**Halfway House** (0131) 225 7101
Fleshmarket Close (steps between Cockburn Street and Market Street, opposite Waverley station); EH1 1BX Tiny one-room character pub off steep steps;

part carpeted, part tiled, with a few small tables and high-backed settles, lots of prints (some golf and railway themes), four well kept scottish ales and good range of malt whiskies, short choice of decent low-priced food, friendly staff; dogs welcome, open (and food) all day. *(Archie)*

EDINBURGH NT2473

Hanging Bat (0131) 229 0759
Lothian Road; EH3 9AB Modern bar on three levels with own microbrewery, six real ales, craft kegs and plenty of bottled beers, food such as ribs and hot dogs; children till 8pm, open (and food) all day. *(Archie, Sally Alton)*

EDINBURGH NT2573

Inn on the Mile (0131) 556 9940
High Street; EH1 1LL Centrally placed pub-restaurant-boutique hotel in former bank; long high-ceilinged bar with booth seating, good selection of drinks including cocktails, well priced pubby food, friendly efficient service; live music, projector for major sports, free wi-fi; children welcome, a few seats outside, nine bedrooms, open all day (till 1am Fri, Sat when can be lively). *(Sally Alton)*

EDINBURGH NT2573

Jolly Judge (0131) 225 2669
James Court, by 495 Lawnmarket; EH1 2PB Small comfortable basement bar with interesting fruit and flower-painted wooden ceiling, welcoming relaxed atmosphere, three changing ales and good range of malts, lunchtime bar meals, log fire; quiz night Mon; no children, open all day. *(Archie)*

EDINBURGH NT1968

Kinleith Mill (0131) 453 3214
Lanark Road (A70); EH14 5EN Refurbished old pub with contemporary bar; three well kept ales and enjoyable food including early bird deal for two, friendly staff; sports TV, darts; children and dogs welcome, suntrap back garden, open all day. *(Charles Todd)*

EDINBURGH NT2473

Oxford (0131) 539 7119
Young Street; EH2 4JB Friendly no-frills backstreet local with links to Ian Rankin and other scottish writers and artists; tiny bustling bar with a couple of built-in wall settles, steps up to quieter back room, four well kept regional beers and good range of whiskies, no food or children; TV; dogs welcome, open all day. *(Charles Todd, Archie)*

EDINBURGH NT2573

Sandy Bells (0131) 225 1156
Forrest Road; EH1 2QH Small unpretentious place popular for its nightly folk music; eight scottish ales and wide choice of whiskies, simple snacky food, good mix of customers and friendly atmosphere; open all day. *(Charles Todd)*

EDINBURGH NT2374

Scran & Scallie (0131) 332 6281
Comely Bank Road; EH4 1DT Well thought-of dining pub with very good traditional food including weekday set lunch and weekend breakfasts; bar has blue button-back walls seats, leather-topped stools and blue-painted chairs on bare boards, well kept Scottish ales, impressive collection of whiskies and house cocktails, sizeable dining area with painted brick walls, contemporary wallpaper and woodburner, helpful friendly service; TV; children and dogs welcome, open all day. *(Penny Barr, Belinda and Neil Garth)*

EDINBURGH NT2574

★**Starbank** (0131) 552 4141
Laverockbank Road, off Starbank Road, just off A901 Granton–Leith; EH5 3BZ Cheerful pub in a fine spot with terrific views over the Firth of Forth; long airy bare-boards bar with leather bench and tub seats, up to eight well kept ales and good choice of malt whiskies, interesting food from sharing plates up in conservatory restaurant; live music and quiz nights, sports TV, fruit machine; children welcome till 9pm if eating, dogs on leads, sheltered back terrace, parking on adjacent hilly street, open all day. *(Sally Alton)*

EDINBURGH NT2574

Stockbridge Tap (0131) 343 3000
Raeburn Place, Stockbridge; EH4 1HN Welcoming corner pub with traditional L-shaped interior, seven interesting beers and good reasonably priced food (not Mon or Tues); no children, dogs welcome, open all day. *(Charles Todd)*

EDINBURGH NT2676

Teuchters Landing (0131) 554 7427
Great Junction Street, Leith; EH6 6LU Interesting waterside pub in former ferry waiting room; great choice of whiskies and wines (listed on blackboard), half a dozen well kept ales such as Caledonian, Fyne, Inveralmond and Timothy Taylors, plus several craft beers, generous helpings of popular food (best to book, especially in summer for conservatory or floating terrace), friendly staff; TV for rugby; children and dogs welcome, open (and food) all day. *(Archie)*

MORAYSHIRE

FINDHORN NJ0464

Crown & Anchor (01309) 690243
Off A96; IV36 3YF Nice village setting adjacent to small sheltered harbour; enjoyable food including good fresh fish/seafood specials, a couple of real ales and plenty of whiskies, woodburner in cosy bar; sports TV; children welcome (under-14s

in conservatory and restaurant till 8pm), outside seating and smokers' shelter (the Smokooterie), seven bedrooms, sand dune walks and good boating in Findhorn Bay, open all day. *(John Evans)*

NAIRNSHIRE

CAWDOR NH8449

Cawdor Tavern (01667) 404777

Pub signed from B9090; IV12 5XP Popular dining pub in lovely conservation village near the castle; well kept Orkney ales, nine wines by the glass (comprehensive list) and good range of malt whiskies, enjoyable freshly cooked food from traditional choices up, friendly staff, oak-panelled lounge with log fire, pool in public bar, restaurant; children welcome, seats on front terrace, open (and food) all day in summer. *(The Dutchman, John Evans)*

PEEBLESSHIRE

INNERLEITHEN NT3336

★Traquair Arms (01896) 830229

B709, just off A72 Peebles–Galashiels; follow signs for Traquair House; EH44 6PD Old stone inn at heart of this pretty borders village; one of the few places serving Traquair ale (produced in original oak vessels in 18th-c brewhouse at nearby Traquair House), also Tempest Cascadian and Timothy Taylors Landlord, over 40 malt whiskies, enjoyable traditional food (all day weekends); main bar with warm open fire, another in relaxed bistro-style restaurant, good mix of customers; background music; children welcome, dogs in bar, seats out at front and in attractive back garden, 16 bedrooms and two self-catering cottages, open all day. *(Mark Morgan)*

PERTHSHIRE

BANKFOOT NO0635

Bankfoot (01738) 787243

Main Street; PH1 4AB Traditional coaching inn dating from 1760, two bars and restaurant, well kept local ales and enjoyable food cooked by landlady, friendly helpful staff, open fires; live folk night Weds; children and dogs welcome, comfortable bedrooms, open all day weekends, closed Mon lunchtime and all day Tues (food for residents only those days), check website for winter hours. *(Katherine Matthews)*

BLAIR ATHOLL NN8765

★Atholl Arms (01796) 481205

B8079; PH18 5SG Sizeable stone hotel with nice old-fashioned scottish feel; traditional beamed Bothy bar serving four local Moulin ales and good well priced food, quick friendly service, cosy lounges and grand dining room with suit of armour and stag's head; 31 good value bedrooms, self-catering cottages, lovely setting near the castle, open (and food) all day. *(Graham Smart)*

BRIG O' TURK NN5306

Byre (01877) 376292

A821 Callander–Trossachs, just outside village; FK17 8HT Refurbished and beautifully placed byre conversion; slate-floored log-fire bar and roomier high-raftered restaurant, good popular food including local game and fish, a couple of changing scottish ales and nice wines, friendly helpful staff; background music; children welcome, outside tables and boules piste, lovely walks, bike hire available (pre-book), open all day. *(Katherine Matthews)*

CALLANDER NN6208

Old Rectory (01877) 339215

Leny Road (A84); FK17 8AL Friendly 19th-c stone inn away from the town centre; cosy little bar with fine range of whiskies, well liked reasonably priced food in small adjoining restaurant including good Sun roasts, pleasant helpful staff; live folk music Weds and Sat, quiz second Tues of month, free wi-fi; dogs welcome, four bedrooms, handy for Trossachs National Park, open all day. *(John Evans)*

DUNBLANE NN7801

Tappit Hen (01786) 825226

Kirk Street; FK15 0AL Small welcoming drinkers' pub across close from cathedral, five changing ales and good range of malt whiskies, friendly busy atmosphere; sports TV, fruit machine; dogs welcome, open all day (till late Fri, Sat). *(Les and Sandra Brown)*

DUNKELD NO0243

Atholl Arms (01350) 727219

Atholl Street (A923); PH8 0AQ Sizeable 19th-c hotel with smallish bar and lounge, open fires, well kept ales such as Inveralmond, enjoyable food including burgers, pizzas and some vegan choices, attentive friendly service, restaurant; children and dogs welcome, garden across road running down to the River Tay, pavilion serving teas, coffees and cakes, 17 bedrooms (some with river views), open (and food) all day. *(Katherine Matthews)*

DUNNING NO0114

Kirkstyle (01764) 684248

B9141, off A9 S of Perth; Kirkstyle Square; PH2 0RR Character 18th-c streamside pub renovated and improved under present owners; log fire in snug bar, up to three real ales including one badged for them (Risky Kelt) and good choice of whiskies, enjoyable fairly priced home-made food, attentive friendly service, split-level stripped-stone back restaurant; background and live music (traditional session upstairs

Weds); children and dogs welcome, open all day weekends. *(Andrew Vincent)*

KENMORE NN7745

Kenmore Hotel (01887) 830205

A827 W of Aberfeldy; PH15 2NU Hotel dating from the 16th c in pretty Loch Tay village; comfortable traditional front lounge with warm log fire (there's a poem pencilled by Burns himself on the chimney breast), dozens of malts helpfully arranged alphabetically, friendly attentive staff, modern restaurant with balcony; also back bar and terrace overlooking River Tay with enjoyable food from lunchtime soup and sandwiches to grills, Inveralmond Ossian and decent wines by the glass; pool and winter darts, juke box, TV, fruit machine; children and dogs welcome, 40 bedrooms plus lodges, open all day. *(Jeremy Snow)*

KILMAHOG NN6008

★**Lade** (01877) 330152

A84 just NW of Callander, by A821 junction; FK17 8HD Lively family-run place with strong scottish theme – traditional weekend music, shop with over 190 bottled beers from regional microbreweries plus their own WayLade ales; plenty of character in several cosy beamed areas with panelling and stripped stone, highland prints and local artwork, 40 malt whiskies, good home-made food from bar snacks up (booking advised), big-windowed restaurant, friendly staff; background music; children and dogs (in bar) welcome, disabled access, terrace and pleasant garden with fish ponds, open all day (till 1am Fri, Sat, but may close early in winter if quiet). *(Jim and Sue James)*

KIRKTON OF GLENISLA NO2160

Glenisla Hotel (01575) 582223

B951 N of Kirriemuir and Alyth; PH11 8PH 17th-c coaching inn recently reopened after major refurbishment (same owners); high-ceilinged bar with woodburner, beamed lounge with another fire leading through to restaurant, two well kept changing scottish ales, eight wines by the glass and good selection of whiskies and gins, popular freshly made food from traditional choices up, good friendly service; children and dogs (not in restaurant) welcome, garden with gravel terrace, ten well appointed bedrooms, good walks from the door (on Cateran Trail), open all day, kitchen shuts 5-6pm. *(Jim and Sue James)*

PERTH NO1223

Greyfriars (01738) 633036

South Street; PH2 8PG Small comfortable local in old part of town; a couple of well kept changing ales and good collection of whiskies and gins enjoyable lunchtime food (not Sun) in bar or little upstairs dining room, friendly welcoming staff; live music; open all day. *(Roddy Duncan)*

PITLOCHRY NN9163

★**Killiecrankie Hotel** (01796) 473220

Killiecrankie, off A9 N; PH16 5LG Comfortable splendidly placed country hotel with attractive panelled bar and airy conservatory, well kept ales, over 40 malt whiskies and well chosen wines, good imaginative food in bar or more formal evening restaurant, friendly efficient service; children in eating areas, dogs welcome, extensive peaceful grounds with dramatic views, ten bedrooms. *(David Hall)*

PITLOCHRY NN9459

★**Moulin** (01796) 472196

Kirkmichael Road, Moulin; A924 NE of Pitlochry centre; PH16 5EW Attractive much-extended inn brewing its own good beers in stables across the street, decent wines by the glass too and around 45 malt whiskies, cheerfully busy down-to-earth bar in oldest part with traditional character, smaller bare-boards room and bigger carpeted area with booths divided by stained-glass country scenes, popular quickly served food, separate restaurant; bar billiards and 1960s one-arm bandit; children and dogs (in bar) welcome, picnic-sets on gravel looking across to village kirk, good nearby walks, 15 well appointed comfortable bedrooms and two self-catering cottages, open all day. *(Johnston and Maureen Anderson, Barry Collett, Philip J Alderton)*

PITLOCHRY NN9358

Old Mill (01796) 474020

Mill Lane; PH16 5BH Welcoming family-run inn (former 19th-c watermill) with enjoyable food from sandwiches and sharing plates up, four real ales including Strathbraan and good wine and whisky choice, quick friendly service; live music, free wi-fi; courtyard tables by Moulin Burn, comfortable well equipped bedrooms, open all day. *(Dr A McCormick)*

WEEM NN8449

★**Ailean Chraggan** (01887) 820346

B846; PH15 2LD There's plenty to do and see close to this little hotel; chatty bar with good mix of customers, local Strathbraan ales and around 100 malt whiskies, popular locally sourced food including Sun carvery, efficient friendly service, adjoining neatly old-fashioned dining room and a comfortable carpeted modern lounge; quiz nights; children and dogs (in bar) welcome, covered terrace and garden behind, views stretching beyond the Tay to Ben Lawers (the highest peak in this part of Scotland), four spacious bedrooms, open all day Thur-Sun, from 5pm other days. *(Neil and Angela Huxter)*

There are report forms at the back of the book.

ROSS-SHIRE

BADACHRO NG7873

★**Badachro Inn** (01445) 741255
2.5 miles S of Gairloch village turn off A832 on to B8056, then after another 3.25 miles turn right in Badachro to the quay and inn; IV21 2AA Superbly positioned by Loch Gairloch with terrific views from decking down to water's edge, popular (especially summer) with mix of sailing visitors (free moorings) and chatty locals; welcoming bar with interesting photographs, An Teallach, Caledonian and a guest ale, about 50 malt whiskies and eight wines by the glass, quieter eating area with big log fire, dining conservatory overlooking bay, fair-priced food including locally smoked fish and seafood; background music, free wi-fi; children and dogs welcome, one bedroom, open all day. *(Scott and Charlotte Havers)*

GAIRLOCH NG8075

Old Inn (01445) 712006
Just off A832/B8021; IV21 2BD Quietly positioned old drovers' inn by stream; own-brew beers and guests, decent wines by the glass and some 20 malt whiskies, enjoyable food (not Sun evening) including local fish and game, relaxed locals' bar with traditional décor and woodburner, bistro/restaurant; background music (live Fri), TV; children and dogs welcome, picnic-sets out by trees, bedrooms, open all day. *(Colin McLachlan)*

PLOCKTON NG8033

★**Plockton Inn** (01599) 544222
Innes Street; unconnected to Plockton Hotel (see Main Entries); IV52 8TW Close to the harbour in this lovely village, and a congenial bustling atmosphere even in winter; good fairly priced food with focus on local fish/seafood (some from own smokery), friendly efficient service, well kept changing beers and good range of malts, lively public bar with traditional music Thurs (also Tues in summer); children welcome, seats out on decking, 14 bedrooms (seven in annexe over road), good breakfast, open all day. *(Barry Collett, Scott and Charlotte Havers)*

SHIEL BRIDGE NG9319

Kintail Lodge (01599) 511275
A87, N of Shiel Bridge; IV40 8HL Large bar adjoining hotel nestled down by Loch Duich, convivial bustle in season, Isle of Skye Red and plenty of malt whiskies, good food here and in restaurant/conservatory with magnificent view to Skye, friendly efficient service; children and dogs welcome, 12 comfortable bedrooms, bunkhouse and moorings for visiting yachts, good breakfast, open all day from easter, ring for out of season hours. *(Buster May)*

ULLAPOOL NH1293

★**Ceilidh Place** (01854) 612103
West Argyle Street; IV26 2TY More arty café-bar than pub with gallery, bookshop and coffee shop; conservatory-style main area with mix of dining chairs around dark wood tables, cosy bar and other rooms filled with armchairs, sofas and scatter-cushioned wall seats, rugs on floors, woodburner, a beer from An Teallach, lots of wines by the glass and 75 malt whiskies, tasty food (something available all day); regular jazz, folk and classical music, art exhibitions; children welcome but must leave bar by 7pm, tables on front terrace looking over houses to distant hills beyond natural harbour, comfortable bedrooms, open all day. *(Scott and Charlotte Havers)*

ULLAPOOL NH1294

Morefield Motel (01854) 612161
A835 N edge of town; IV26 2TQ Modern family-run place, clean and bright, with cheerful L-shaped lounge bar, good food including local fish/seafood, well kept changing ales, decent wines and over 50 malt whiskies, large conservatory; background music, pool and darts; children welcome, terrace tables, bedrooms and bike lock-up, open all day. *(Johnston and Maureen Anderson)*

ROXBURGHSHIRE

KELSO NT7234

★**Cobbles** (01573) 223548
Bowmont Street; TD5 7JH Small comfortably refurbished 19th-c dining pub just off the main square; friendly and well run with good range of food from pub standards to more enterprising dishes, local Tempest beers and decent range of wines and malts, open fire and pubby furnishings in bar, elegantly furnished restaurant with overspill room upstairs; folk music Fri evening; children welcome, disabled facilities, open all day (till late Fri, Sat). *(Murray and Peggy Lindsay)*

KIRK YETHOLM NT8328

★**Border** (01573) 420237
Village signposted off B6352/B6401 crossroads, SE of Kelso; The Green; TD5 8PQ Popular inn facing village green and continuing well under new management; welcoming traditional locals' bar with beams, flagstones and log fire, snug side rooms, two or three real ales, decent wines by the glass and numerous whiskies, good home-made food from extensive menu, friendly service, spacious dining room, lounge with another fire and neat conservatory; background music; children and dogs (in bar) welcome, sheltered back terrace, five well appointed comfortable bedrooms, good breakfast, at end of Pennine Way and start of Scottish National Trail, open all day. *(Sara Fulton, Roger Baker)*

ST BOSWELLS NT5930

Buccleuch Arms (01835) 822243
A68 just S of Newtown St Boswells; TD6 0EW Civilised 19th-c sandstone hotel opposite village green; refurbished bar, comfortable lounge and bistro, good popular food from bar snacks up, prompt friendly service, two or three local ales, open fires; children and dogs welcome, tables in attractive garden behind, 19 bedrooms, open (and food) all day. *(Martin Day)*

SELKIRKSHIRE

MOUNTBENGER NT3324

Gordon Arms (01750) 82261
A708/B709; TD7 5LE Nice old inn – an oasis in these empty moorlands; a couple of real ales and enjoyable reasonably priced pubby food cooked by landlord; good regular traditional music (there's a recording studio on site), free wi-fi; children and dogs welcome, comfortable bedrooms, good walking country, open (and food) all day. *(Jeremy Snow)*

STIRLINGSHIRE

KIPPEN NS6594

★**Cross Keys** (01786) 870293
Main Street; village signposted off A811 W of Stirling; FK8 3DN Cosy and gently civilised 18th-c inn; log fires in two bars, exposed stonework, bare boards or carpeting, built-in wall seating, wooden dining chairs and stools against counter serving a couple of Fallen ales (one brewed for the pub), a guest beer, 20 malt whiskies and a dozen wines by the glass, very good food including lighter lunch menu, friendly staff; background music, live folk first and third Sun of month, free wi-fi; children (till 9pm) and dogs welcome, tables in garden looking across to the Ochil Hills, play area, three comfortable bedrooms, generous breakfast, open (and food) all day weekends. *(Giles and Suzie Nunn)*

STRATHCLYDE

CAIRNDOW NN1810

Stagecoach (01499) 600286
Just off and signed from A83; PA26 8BN Old inn run by same family for over 50 years in lovely setting overlooking Loch Fyne; good local fish and seasonal produce in bar and restaurant, Fyne ales and plenty of whiskies, efficient friendly service; live music and quiz nights; children welcome, garden picnic-sets, bedrooms (some in separate building with balconies taking in the view), open (and food) all day. *(Frances Parsons)*

SUTHERLAND

KYLESKU NC2333

★**Kylesku Hotel** (01971) 502231
A894, S side of former ferry crossing; IV27 4HW Remote but surprisingly busy hotel on shores of Loch Glendhu; pleasant tartan-carpeted bar facing glorious mountain and loch view, with seals and red-throated divers often in sight (tables outside too); wonderfully fresh seafood along with other good locally sourced food (booking advisable), friendly accommodating staff, well kept ales such as An Teallach, nice wines by the glass and numerous malt whiskies, more expensive restaurant extension overlooking loch; children welcome, comfortable bedrooms, good boat trips from hotel slipway, closed winter. *(Neil and Angela Huxter)*

LAIRG NC5224

★**Crask Inn** (01549) 411241
A836 13 miles N towards Altnaharra; IV27 4AB Remote whitewashed inn on single-track road through peaceful moorland, homely and welcoming, with basic but comfortable bar, large stove, interesting books and harmonium, a couple of Black Isle ales (more in bottles), good simple food cooked by landlord including own lamb, friendly helpful staff, separate dining room; church service third Thurs of month (the pub is church-owned); children and dogs welcome, four bedrooms, camping (no facilities), closed till 1pm Tues, otherwise open all day. *(Nicholas and Lucy Sage)*

LOCHINVER NC0922

Caberfeidh (01571) 844321
Culag Road (A837); IV27 4JY Delightful lochside position and lovely views; cosy bar, conservatory and more formal evening restaurant, two woodburners, good food (best to book) from changing blackboard menu with emphasis on local seafood (one or two large plates and a selection of smaller tapas-style dishes), a couple of well kept ales such as An Teallach, good choice of wines, whiskies and gins, friendly staff; children and dogs (in bar) welcome, small garden with view of the loch, open all day in summer apart from Mon lunchtime, in winter closed Mon-Weds and till 5pm (12.30pm Sun), but best to check website. *(Neil and Angela Huxter)*

WEST LOTHIAN

BO'NESS NS9981

Corbie (01506) 825307
A904 Corbiehall; EH51 0AS Neatly furnished pub with up to six well kept local ales including own Kinneil brewed behind, 70 malt whiskies (tasting evenings) and

quite a choice of enjoyable food at fair prices, friendly staff; children welcome, garden with play area, open (and food) all day. *(Donald Allsopp)*

LINLITHGOW NS0077

★**Four Marys** (01506) 842171
High Street; 2 miles from M9 junction 3 (and little further from junction 4) – town signposted; EH49 7ED Named after Mary, Queen of Scots' four ladies-in-waiting and filled with mementoes of the ill-fated queen – pictures and written records, pieces of bed curtain and clothing, even a facsimile of her death-mask; L-shaped room with traditional and more modern seating on wood-block floor, mainly stripped-stone walls (some remarkable masonry in the inner area), elaborate Victorian dresser serving as part of the bar, seven well kept ales (taster glasses available, May, Oct beer festivals), good range of malt whiskies and gins, enjoyable reasonably priced food (all day Sat), friendly staff, tartan carpeted dining area where children allowed (till 8pm); enclosed terrace, open all day. *(Philip Chesington)*

WIGTONSHIRE

BLADNOCH NX4254

Bladnoch Inn (01988) 402200
Corner of A714 and B7005; DG8 9AB Roadside pub across from Bladnoch distillery (tours) in nice riverside setting; cheerful neat bar with eating area, separate restaurant, tasty pubby food from sandwiches up including set menus and Sun carvery, a couple of changing real ales, friendly obliging service; background music; children and dogs welcome, four good value bedrooms, open all day Sun, otherwise from 4.30pm. *(George Sanderson)*

PORTPATRICK NW9954

Crown (01776) 810261
North Crescent; DG9 8SX Popular seafront hotel in delightful harbourside village; enjoyable reasonably priced food including notable seafood and local game, friendly prompt service, two changing ales such as local Portpatrick, several dozen malts and decent wines by the glass, warm fire in rambling traditional bar with cosy corners, sewing-machine tables, old photographs and posters, attractively decorated early 20th-c dining room opening through conservatory into sheltered back garden; background music, TV; children and dogs welcome, tables out in front, 12 bedrooms, open (and food) all day. *(George Sanderson)*

STRANRAER NX0660

Grapes (01776) 703386
Bridge Street; DG9 7HY Popular and welcoming 19th-c local; simple and old-fashioned, with a couple of well kept ales and over 60 malts, regular traditional music in bar or upstairs room; children and dogs welcome, courtyard seating, open all day. *(George Sanderson)*

Scottish Islands

ARRAN

CATACOL NR9049

Catacol Bay (01770) 830231
A841; KA27 8HN Unpretentious hotel rather than pub run by same family for 39 years; wonderful setting just yards from the sea looking across to Kintyre; simple bar with log fire, Timothy Taylors Landlord and a guest, all-day food (Sunday buffet until 4pm) and hearty breakfasts; pool, TV; tables outside and children's play area, six simple bedrooms with washbasins (ones at front have the view), own mooring, open all day in summer. *(William and Tash Fraser)*

BARRA

CASTLEBAY NL6698

Castlebay Hotel (01871) 810223
By aeroplane from Glasgow or ferry from Oban; HS9 5XD Comfortable cheerful bar next to the hotel; popular food from sandwiches up, keg and bottled beers, also two-level lounge/restaurant with great harbour view, pleasant young staff; live music and comedy nights; decent bedrooms. *(Roddy Duncan, Archie)*

BUTE

ROTHESAY NS0864

Black Bull (01700) 502366
W Princes Street; PA20 9AF Traditional comfortably furnished pub with enjoyable reasonably priced bar food, three well kept ales and good friendly service; weekend live music, TV; children welcome till 8pm, no dogs, opposite pier with its wonderfully restored Victorian gents', open all day, no food Mon, or evenings except Fri and Sat. *(Katherine Matthews)*

COLONSAY

SCALASAIG NR3893

★**Colonsay** (01951) 200316
W on B8086; PA61 7YP Extended stylish 18th-c hotel, a haven for ramblers, cyclists and birders; chatty bar is hub of the island and full of locals and visitors, comfortable sofas and armchairs on painted boards, pastel walls hung with interesting old islander pictures, log fires, Colonsay IPA, several wines by the glass and interesting selection of whiskies, relaxed informal

restaurant overlooking the harbour, good food using home-grown produce (own oyster farm) including pre-ferry two-course offer (from 5.30pm), friendly efficient service; children and dogs (in bar) welcome, nice views from garden, ten comfortable pretty bedrooms, backpackers' lodge and holiday cottages, closed Nov-Mar except Christmas and New Year, otherwise open all day (till 1am Sat). *(Nick Higgins)*

CUMBRAE

MILLPORT NS1554

Frasers (01475) 530518
Cardiff Street; KA28 0AS Small cheerful pub set just back from the harbour; bar with old paddle-steamer pictures and woodburner, back vaulted dining room, a couple of changing beers and enjoyable very reasonably priced pubby food, friendly staff; children welcome till 8pm, no dogs, tables in yard behind, open all day. *(Sandra Hollies)*

HARRIS

TARBERT NB1500

★**Harris Hotel** (01859) 502154
Scott Road; HS3 3DL Large hotel in same family for over a century; small welcoming panelled bar with Hebridean brewed ales and fine selection of malt whiskies including some rarities, interesting food using local game and seafood, morning coffee and afternoon teas, they can also provide packed lunches, friendly accommodating staff, smart (but relaxed) airy restaurant; 23 comfortable sea-view bedrooms (some up narrow stairs). *(Mr and Mrs P R Thomas)*

ISLAY

BOWMORE NR3159

★**Harbour Inn** (01496) 810330
The Square; PA43 7JR Attractively updated old inn opposite the distillery; lovely harbour/loch views from dining room and conservatory, good fish/seafood and other locally sourced food, nice wines and plenty of Islay malts including some rarities, traditional bar with unusual barrel counter, friendly helpful staff; children welcome, seven bedrooms with views. *(Sophia and Hamish Greenfield)*

PORT ASKAIG NR4369

Port Askaig (01496) 840245
A846, by port; PA46 7RD Family-run inn on Sound of Islay shore overlooking ferry pier; snug, tartan-carpeted bar with good range of malt whiskies, local bottled ales and popular food, neat sea-view restaurant and traditional first-floor residents' lounge; dogs welcome in bar, plenty of picnic-sets on waterside grass, 11 neat bedrooms and self-catering apartment, open (and food) all day. *(Mike and Sarah Abbot)*

PORT CHARLOTTE NR2558

★**Port Charlotte Hotel** (01496) 850360 *Main Street; PA48 7TU* Most beautiful of Islay's Georgian villages and in lovely position with sweeping views over Loch Indaal; exceptional collection of some 150 Islay malts including rarities, two changing local ales and decent wines by the glass, good food using local meat, game and seafood, civilised bare-boards pubby bar with padded wall seats, open fire and modern artwork, second comfortable back bar, neatly kept restaurant and roomy conservatory (overlooking beach); regular traditional live music; children welcome, garden tables, ten attractive bedrooms (most with sea view), open all day till 1am. *(Maggie and Stevan Hollis)*

PORTNAHAVEN NN1652

An Tighe Seinnse (01496) 860224
Queen Street; PA47 7SJ Friendly little end-of-terrace harbourside pub tucked away in this remote attractive fishing village; cosy bar with room off, open fire, fair-priced good food including local seafood, Belhaven keg beer and bottled Islay ales, good choice of malts; sports TV and occasional live music; can get crowded, open all day. *(Nick Higgins)*

JURA

CRAIGHOUSE NR5266

Jura Hotel (01496) 820243
A846, opposite distillery; PA60 7XU Family-run and in superb setting with views over the Small Isles to the mainland; bar, two lounges and restaurant, good food using local fish, seafood and game (breakfasts for non-residents if capacity allows), warm friendly service; garden down to water's edge, 17 bedrooms (most with sea view), camping. *(Sally and Jim Lazonby)*

MULL

DERVAIG NM4251

★**Bellachroy** (01688) 400314
B8073; PA75 6QW Island's oldest inn dating from 1608; pub and restaurant food including local seafood, afternoon teas and packed lunches, ales such as Isle of Mull and good choice of whiskies and wines, traditional bar with darts, attractive dining area, comfortable residents' lounge

We say if we know a pub allows dogs.

with games and TV; children and dogs welcome, covered outside area plus plenty of picnic-sets, nice spot in sleepy lochside village, six comfortable bedrooms, open all year. *(Caroline and Peter Bryant)*

FIONNPHORT NM3023

Keel Row (01681) 700458
A849; PA66 6BL Simply furnished bare-boards bar with exposed stone walls and woodburner, Caledonian Deurchars IPA and several whiskies, generous helpings of tasty pub food, friendly helpful staff, sea views over to Iona from dining room's big windows; TV, darts; children welcome, handy for ferry, open all day. *(David Eberlin)*

TOBERMORY NM5055

Mishnish (01688) 302500
Main Street – the yellow building; PA75 6NU Popular and lively place right on the bay; dimly lit two-room bar with cask tables, old photographs and nautical/fishing bric-a-brac, woodburner, little snugs, well kept Belhaven and Isle of Mull, enjoyable bar food, can also eat in next-door Mishdish or italian restaurant upstairs; background and live music, pool; beer garden behind, 14 attractive bedrooms (some with sea view), good breakfast, open all day till late. *(Andrew Caleya-Chetty)*

ORKNEY

DOUNBY HY3001

Merkister (01856) 771366
Russland Road, by Harray Loch; KW17 2LF Fishing hotel in great location on the loch shore; bar dominated by prize catches, good food here and in evening restaurant including hand-dived scallops and local aberdeen angus steaks, good friendly service; 16 bedrooms, open all day. *(Caroline and Peter Bryant)*

ST MARY'S HY4700

Commodore (01856) 781788
A961; KW17 2RU Modern single-storey building with stunning views over Scapa Flow; bar with well kept Orkney beers, pool and darts, good food using local produce in contemporary restaurant; only open Fri, Sat from 6pm. *(Caroline and Peter Bryant)*

WESTRAY HY4348

Pierowall Hotel (01857) 677472
Centre of Pierowall village, B9066; KW17 2BZ Comfortable pub-hotel under new ownership; enjoyable home-cooked food from sandwiches and snacks to good fresh fish, bottled Orkney beers and plenty of malts, lounge bar with warming stove, public bar and separate restaurant; six bedrooms (four ensuite) with bay or hill views; tables out on front grass, handy for ferry. *(Caroline and Peter Bryant, Sandra Hollies)*

SKYE

CARBOST NG3731

★**Old Inn** (01478) 640205
B8009; IV47 8SR Unpretentious waterside pub with stunning views and well positioned for walkers and climbers; simply furnished chatty bar with exposed stone walls, bare-board or tiled floors, open fire, Cuillin ales and a guest, traditional cider and quite a few malt whiskies, tasty fair priced food using local fish and shellfish and highland meat; background music (live Weds, Thurs, Fri), darts and pool; children and dogs welcome, picnic-sets on terrace by the water, bedrooms and family chalet also enjoying the views, Talisker distillery nearby, closed afternoons in winter, otherwise open (and food) all day, breakfast 7.45-9.30am. *(Shone and Jim McDuff)*

EDINBAINE NG3451

Edinbaine (01470) 582414
Just off A850, signed for Meadhan a Bhaile; IV51 9PW Friendly former farmhouse with simply furnished modernised bar, light wood flooring and woodburner in stone fireplace, well kept Isle of Skye beers, airy carpeted dining room serving good attractively presented food including local fish/seafood, friendly staff; live traditional music (Fri, Sun); children and dogs welcome, six refurbished bedrooms, open all day (but best to check winter hours). *(Shone and Jim McDuff)*

ISLE ORNSAY NG7012

★**Eilean Iarmain** (01471) 833332
Off A851 Broadford–Armadale; IV43 8QR Smartly old-fashioned 19th-c hotel in beautiful location looking over the Sound of Sleat; cosy traditional bar with panelling and open fire, well kept Isle of Skye and good choice of vatted (blended) malt whiskies including their own Gaelic Whisky Collection, good food here or in charming sea-view restaurant, friendly efficient service; traditional background and live music; children welcome, outside tables with spectacular views, 16 comfortable bedrooms, open all day. *(James and Sylvia Hewitt)*

SOUTH UIST

LOCH CARNAN NF8144

Orasay Inn (01870) 610298
Signed off A865 S of Creagorry; HS8 5PD Wonderful remote spot overlooking the sea (lovely sunsets); good local food including fish/seafood and beef from own herd, can eat in modern lounge or conservatory-style restaurant, friendly service, pleasant simply furnished public bar; seats outside on raised decked area, compact comfortable bedrooms (two with terraces), open all day in summer. *(Shone and Jim McDuff)*

WALES

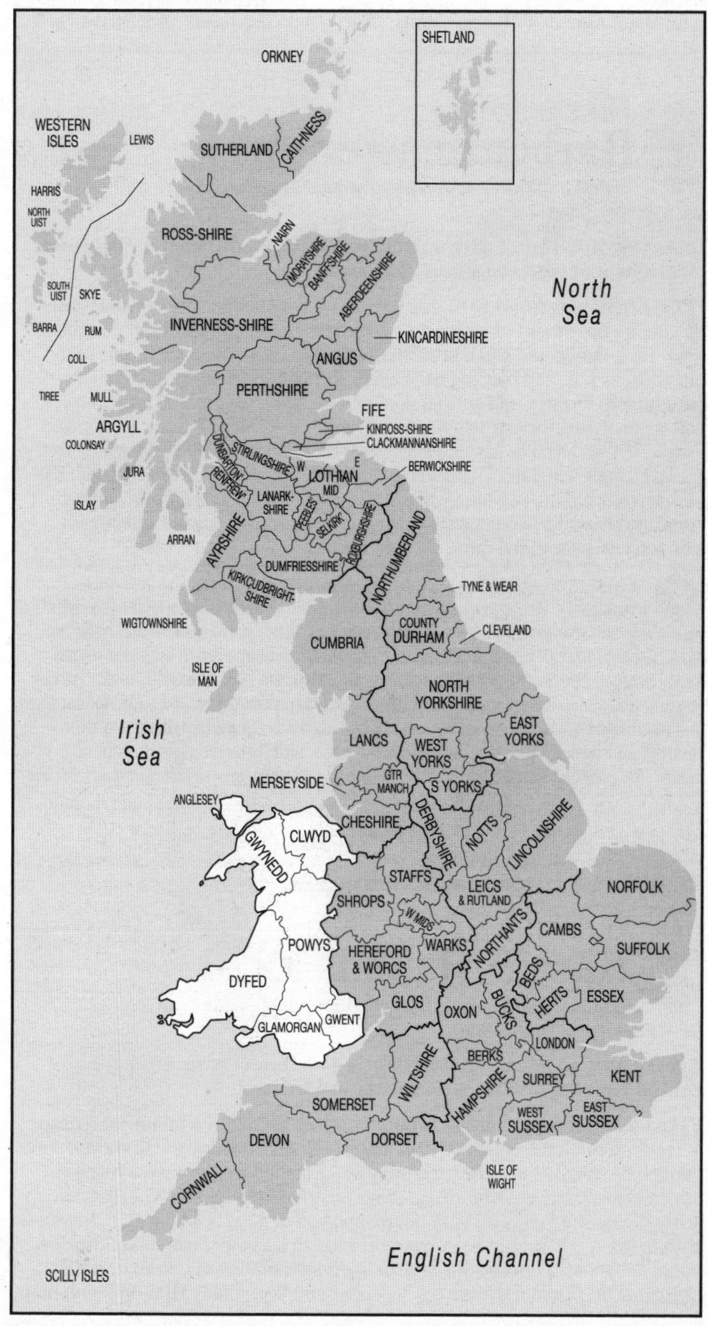
SHETLAND
ORKNEY
WESTERN ISLES
LEWIS
SUTHERLAND
CAITHNESS
HARRIS
NORTH UIST
ROSS-SHIRE
NAIRN
MORAYSHIRE
BANFFSHIRE
ABERDEENSHIRE
North Sea
SOUTH UIST
SKYE
BARRA
RUM
INVERNESS-SHIRE
KINCARDINESHIRE
COLL
ANGUS
TIREE
MULL
PERTHSHIRE
FIFE
ARGYLL
KINROSS-SHIRE
CLACKMANNANSHIRE
COLONSAY
STIRLINGSHIRE
DUMBARTON
W
E
LOTHIAN
BERWICKSHIRE
JURA
RENFREW
MID
LANARK-SHIRE
PEEBLES
SELKIRK
ROXBURGHSHIRE
ISLAY
ARRAN
AYRSHIRE
NORTHUMBERLAND
DUMFRIESSHIRE
KIRKCUDBRIGHT-SHIRE
TYNE & WEAR
WIGTOWNSHIRE
COUNTY DURHAM
CLEVELAND
CUMBRIA
ISLE OF MAN
NORTH YORKSHIRE
Irish Sea
EAST YORKS
LANCS
WEST YORKS
GTR MANCH
MERSEYSIDE
S YORKS
ANGLESEY
CHESHIRE
DERBYSHIRE
NOTTS
LINCOLNSHIRE
CLWYD
GWYNEDD
STAFFS
LEICS & RUTLAND
NORFOLK
SHROPS
W MIDS
NORTHANTS
CAMBS
POWYS
HEREFORD & WORCS
WARKS
SUFFOLK
BEDS
DYFED
GLOS
OXON
BUCKS
HERTS
ESSEX
GLAMORGAN
GWENT
LONDON
BERKS
WILTSHIRE
SURREY
KENT
SOMERSET
HAMPSHIRE
WEST SUSSEX
EAST SUSSEX
DEVON
DORSET
CORNWALL
ISLE OF WIGHT
English Channel
SCILLY ISLES

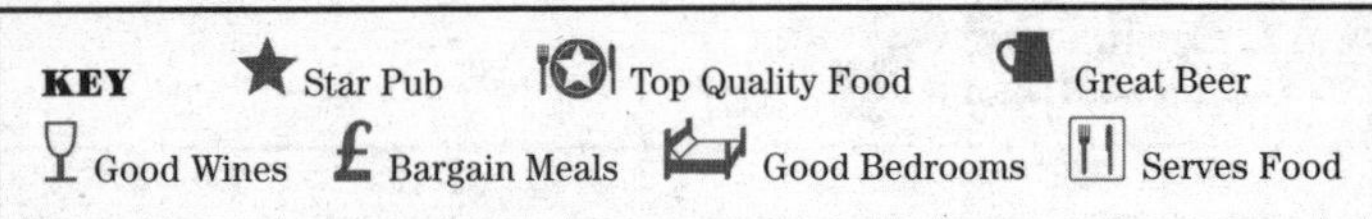

ABERAERON SN4562 Map 6

Harbourmaster

(01545) 570755 – www.harbour-master.com

Quay Parade; SA46 0BA

Charming little hotel with a lively bar, simply furnished dining room, local ales and first class food; bedrooms

The bright blue frontage of this former harbourmaster's office stands out among the other colour-washed buildings lining the yacht-filled harbour here. It's a handsome small hotel that our readers praise year in and year out without fail. The buzzing bar has all sorts of chairs around tables on bare boards, brown leather wall banquettes, some bright blue armchairs and stools lining the bar where friendly staff keep Mantle Rock Steady and Purple Moose Glaslyn Ale and HM Bitter on handpump, 17 good wines by the glass, 11 malt whiskies, cocktails and local farm cider. The dining room has blue leather chairs, sea-blue walls and seaside-inspired art. Bedrooms are comfortable and breakfasts are particularly good. You can sit outside on a bench and take in the view. Disabled access.

As well as breakfast (8-11.45am), the first class food, using the best local ingredients, includes crispy cockles with chilli vinegar, salmon fishcakes with lemon mayonnaise, pearl barley with kale, peppers, mint, pomegranate and halloumi, beer-battered haddock and skinny fries, liver, onion and bacon with leek and thyme mash, seafood risotto, burger with toppings and fries, sea bass fillet with roast chicken gnocchi and sauce vierge, guinea fowl breast with dauphinoise potatoes and mushrooms, and puddings such as lemon and orange baked alaska and vanilla pannacotta with rhubarb and rhubarb granita; they also offer a two- and three-course set evening menu. *Benchmark main dish: crab linguine £14.00. Two-course evening meal £27.50.*

Free house ~ Licensees Glyn and Menna Heulyn ~ Real ale ~ Open 8am-11pm ~ Bar food 12-2.30, 6-9 ~ Restaurant ~ Children welcome (must be over 5 in bedrooms) ~ Wi-fi ~ Bedrooms: £75/£120 *Recommended by Mr and Mrs P R Thomas, Anna and Mark Evans, Mike and Mary Carter, Harry and Megan Evans, Jan and Sally Jones*

ABERTHIN ST0075 Map 6

Hare & Hounds

(01446) 774892 – www.hareandhoundsaberthin.com

NE of Cowbridge; CF71 7HB

Excellent food in easy-going country pub, interesting drinks, helpful courteous service and seats in garden

First and foremost, this is a proper pub with plenty of regulars who drop in for a pint and a chat, though many are here to enjoy the first class food cooked by the chef-landlord. The simply furnished rooms have a relaxed, informal atmosphere, whitewashed walls, mate's chairs and wheelbacks around wooden tables on bare boards, posies of flowers in vases, a dresser with home-made preserves, a woodburning stove in an inglenook fireplace, bookshelves with cookbooks and an open kitchen. Brains Hancocks HB, Cotleigh Old Hooker, Gower Up 'n' Under and Wye Valley HPA on handpump, local cider, home-made seasonal drinks such as damson gin, and 18 wines plus sparkling ones by the glass from a thoughtful list; background music (restaurant only) and darts. The hanging baskets at the front of the building are pretty and there are benches and picnic-sets in the garden.

From a small, daily changing, seasonal menu using local and some home-grown produce and making everything in-house, the appetising food includes crispy pigs cheek with chicory, mustard and pickled apple, duck liver parfait with boozy damsons, potato and wild garlic gnocchi with watercress and violet artichoke, breast and leg of duckling with smoked bacon, garlic and potatoes, pigeon with smoked bacon, red cabbage and confit potato, stone bass with purple sprouting broccoli and langoustine sauce, and puddings such as buttermilk pudding with honeycomb and brandy and chocolate fondant with vanilla ice-cream; they also offer a two- and three-course set lunch. *Benchmark main dish: roast and braised local lamb £16.50. Two-course evening meal £20.00.*

Free house ~ Licensees Tom Watts-Jones, Alex Howells ~ Real ale ~ Open 12-midnight; 3-11 Mon, Tues; 12-10 Sun ~ Bar food 12-2.30, 6-9; 12-4 Sun ~ Restaurant ~ Children welcome but must leave bar by 7.30pm ~ Dogs allowed in bar ~ Wi-fi *Recommended by Susan and Callum Slade, Alister and Margery Bacon, Naomi and Andrew Randall*

BEAUMARIS SH6076 Map 6

Bull

(01248) 810329 – www.bullsheadinn.co.uk
Castle Street; LL58 8AP

Interesting historic inn with plenty of interest, a rambling bar, stylish brasserie and restaurant; well equipped bedrooms

Dating back to 1472 and located near the castle, this inn has been variously visited by such luminaries as Samuel Johnson and Charles Dickens. The charming rambling and beamed bar with its fine log fire still welcomes a wide mix of customers who are keen to see the interesting reminders of the town's past, such as a rare 17th-c brass water clock, a bloodthirsty crew of cutlasses and even an oak ducking stool tucked in the snug alcove. Seats range from comfortable low-seated settles and leather-cushioned window seats, there are lots of copper and china jugs, and courteous staff serve Bass, Brains Hancocks HB and guests such as Great Orme Orme, Purple Moose Ysgawen Ale and Sharps Doom Bar on handpump and around 28 gins with interesting tonics; board games. In contrast, the new contemporary and stylish restaurant has around 18 wines by the glass, while the exceptionally good upstairs restaurant is an elegantly smart choice for a more formal meal and has a wine list that runs to 120 bottles. The entrance to the pretty courtyard – which now contains their new outside restaurant – is an astonishing 3.3 metres wide and 4 metres high. Bedrooms are named after characters in Dickens' novels and are very well equipped; some are traditional, others more contemporary in style. They also have bedrooms in the Townhouse, an adjacent property with disabled access.

Delicious food is beautifully presented and includes lunchtime sandwiches, creamy arbroath smokies, beetroot-cured gravadlax with black caviar and lobster mayonnaise, malaysian sweet potato and tofu curry, boar and chorizo burger with toppings and chips, pasta with flaked confit lamb shoulder with mint pesto and artichoke, bacon chop with black pudding bonbon, leek mash and cider sauce, sea trout with crème fraîche, fine beans and vine tomatoes, 50-day himalayan salt-aged rib-eye beef with béarnaise sauce and chips, and puddings such as chocolate trio (chilled dark fondant, milk profiterole and white brûlée) and mascarpone and rhubarb cheesecake. *Benchmark main dish: local beer-battered cod and chips £14.50. Two-course evening meal £20.00.*

Free house ~ Licensees Kate and David Robertson ~ Real ale ~ Open 11-11 (10.30 Sun) ~ Bar food 12-2, 6-9; 12-9 weekends ~ Restaurant ~ Children welcome ~ Dogs allowed in bar ~ Wi-fi ~ Bedrooms: £85/£110 *Recommended by Andrew Vincent, Tim King, Donald Allsopp, Elizabeth and Andrew Harvey, Holly and Tim Waite, Daisy and Jonathan Spicer*

BODFARI SJ0970 Map 6

Dinorben Arms

(01745) 775090 – www.brunningandprice.co.uk/dinorbenarms

Off A541, near church; LL16 4DA

Cleverly extended village pub with interesting furnishings in open plan bars, a fine choice of drinks and rewarding food

The fine, far-reaching views here can be enjoyed from a spacious partly covered terrace with qood quality seats and tables and from a high tower; there are plenty of picnic-sets on grass too. Inside, the large open-plan bar has several cosier areas leading off, the oldest of which is heavily beamed and has antique settles, stone bottles on a delft shelf and a woodburning stove. There's a glassed-over well in one corner, a curved central counter, leather armchairs grouped around one open fire (there are others), all manner of wooden dining chairs around tables on rugs or bare boards, elegant metal chandeliers, hundreds of prints on pale-painted or exposed-stone walls, large house plants and sizeable gilt-edged mirrors. Brunning & Price Phoenix Original plus quickly changing guests from breweries such as Caledonian Deuchars, Castle Rock, Facers, Hafod, Purple Moose, Spitting Feathers and Timothy Taylors on handpump, lots of wines by the glass and a good choice of spirits.

Interesting food includes sandwiches, crispy baby squid with sweet chilli sauce, chicken liver pâté with carrot and apricot chutney, moroccan vegetable and chickpea pie with charred courgettes, baby peppers and toasted almonds, chicken in a basket with fries and barbecue sauce, chalk-stream trout with cockles, mussels, bacon, asparagus and white wine sauce, steak in ale suet pudding, seared duck breast and leg croquette with orange purée, rib-eye steak with dijon and tarragon butter and chips, and puddings such as crème brûlée and triple chocolate brownie with chocolate sauce. *Benchmark main dish: slow-braised lamb shoulder with dauphinoise potatoes and rosemary gravy £17.25. Two-course evening meal £21.00.*

Brunning & Price ~ Licensee John Unsworth ~ Real ale ~ Open 11-11; 12-10.30 Sun ~ Bar food 12-9.30 (10 Fri, Sat); 12-9 Sun ~ Restaurant ~ Children welcome ~ Dogs allowed in bar ~ Wi-fi *Recommended by Richard and Tessa Ibbot, Maggie and Stevan Hollis, Chloe and Michael Swettenham, Donald Allsopp, Andrew and Michele Revell*

COLWYN BAY SH8478 Map 6

Pen-y-Bryn

(01492) 533360 – www.brunningandprice.co.uk/penybryn

B5113 Llanwrst Road, on southern outskirts; when you see the pub, turn off into Wentworth Avenue for the car park; LL29 6DD

Spacious, open-plan, one-storey building overlooking the bay with brasserie-style all-day food, good range of drinks and obliging staff

Don't be put off by the bungalow-style building as it's rather special once you're inside. Extending around the three long sides of the bar counter, you'll find welcoming coal fires, oriental rugs on pale stripped boards, a mix of seating and well spaced tables, shelves of books, a profusion of pictures, big pot plants, careful lighting and dark green old-fashioned school radiators. A fine choice of drinks served by knowledgeable young staff includes

Phoenix Brunning & Price Original, Purple Moose Snowdonia Ale and Timothy Taylors Boltmaker plus three quickly changing guests on handpump, well chosen good value wines including 19 by the glass and 65 malt whiskies; board games and background music. The big windows at the back look over seats and tables on the terraces and in the sizeable garden and then out to the sea and the Great Orme. In summer, the award-winning flowering tubs and hanging baskets are lovely.

Attractively presented up-to-date food includes sandwiches, prawn cocktail, potted venison, rabbit and pigeon with sloe gin and blackberries, butternut squash, borlotti bean and aubergine lasagne, pork and leek sausages with mash and onion gravy, crispy duck salad with hoisin, watermelon and cashew nuts, sea bass fillet with mussels, fennel, samphire, saffron potatoes and bouillabaisse, chicken breast with cauliflower and squash biryani with red onion bhaji, 8oz rib-eye steak with tarragon butter and dijon mustard, and puddings such as passion-fruit and mango cheesecake with blood orange sorbet and belgian-style waffle with butterscotch sauce and rum and raisin ice-cream. *Benchmark main dish: braised lamb shoulder with dauphinoise potatoes and gravy £16.95. Two-course evening meal £21.00.*

Brunning & Price ~ Manager Andrew Grant ~ Real ale ~ Open 11.30-11; 12-10.30 Sun ~ Bar food 12-9.30 ~ Children welcome ~ Dogs allowed in bar ~ Wi-fi *Recommended by Tony Smaithe, Pauline and Mark Evans, Mike and Wena Stevenson, Fiona and Jack Henderson, Mike Kavaney, Joe and Belinda Smart*

CRICKHOWELL SO2118 Map 6

Bear ★

(01873) 810408 – www.bearhotel.co.uk

Brecon Road; A40; NP8 1BW

Convivial and interesting inn with a splendid, old-fashioned bar area warmed by a log fire and rewarding food; comfortable bedrooms

This is a particularly appealing place to stay with quite a choice of bedrooms: the older ones in the main building have antiques, others are in a country style and the luxury ones have hot tubs and four-poster beds. Breakfasts are excellent. It's a lovely old inn that's been run by the same welcoming family for many years and our readers are full of praise for the place. Customers of all ages mix happily together in the bustling bar which has heavy beams, little plush-seated bentwood armchairs and handsome old cushioned settles, fresh flowers on tables, and a window seat that looks down on the market square. Next to the great roaring log fire are a big sofa and leather easy chairs on oak parquet flooring with rugs and antiques including lots of pewter mugs and brassware, a longcase clock and interesting prints. Brains Rev James, Caledonian Deuchars IPA, Felinfoel Dragons Heart and Wadworths 6X on handpump, alongside 30 malt whiskies, local ciders, vintage and late-bottled ports and unusual wines (with 11 by the glass); disabled loos. Reception rooms are comfortably furnished, and there are seats in the small garden.

Using the best local produce, the enjoyable food includes sandwiches, confit duck leg and redcurrant terrine with cumberland sauce, cajun-spiced fishcake with lemon and sweet dipping sauce, wild mushroom risotto with ricotta, home-made faggots with onion gravy, sous vide rump of local beef with garlic mash and thyme and red wine sauce, fresh and smoked fish pie, chicken with wild mushrooms, marsala and peppercorn sauce and sautéed potatoes, seafood linguine with tomato, garlic, caper and parsley sauce, 30-day-aged local rib-eye steak with garlic butter and trimmings, and puddings such as mixed berry eton mess and triple chocolate and pistachio brownie with chocolate sauce. *Benchmark main dish: braised local lamb shank with spring onion mash and braising juices £16.50. Two-course evening meal £22.00.*

Free house ~ Licensee Stephen Hindmarsh ~ Real ale ~ Open 10am-11pm; 11-11 Sun ~ Bar food 12-10 (9.30 Sun) ~ Restaurant ~ Children welcome ~ Dogs allowed in bar and bedrooms ~ Wi-fi ~ Bedrooms: £90/£112 *Recommended by Lorna and Jack Mulgrave, Miranda and Jeff Davidson, B and M Kendall, Mike and Mary Carter, Sheila and Sam Thorpe, Martine and Derek Cotton*

DALE SM8105 Map 6

Griffin

(01646) 636227 – www.griffininndale.co.uk

B4327, by sea on one-way system; SA62 3RB

Friendly waterside pub with fresh fish and shellfish, local ales and a new extension

As well as a genuine welcome from the helpful licensees, you can be sure to get some delicious fresh fish and shellfish here. The two imaginatively decorated rooms have an easy-going atmosphere, open fires, wood panelling and traditional red quarry tiles; there's also a new modern extension with a stand-alone woodburning stove, up-to-date seats and tables and big glass windows and doors that take in the wonderful view. Brains Rev James, Cwrw Iâl Hâf Gwyn and Harbwr Tenby North Star on handpump, six wines by the glass, local cider and malt whiskies – including a welsh one; background music and board games. The pub is right by the water with a pontoon and a seawall, and seats on the rooftop terrace make the most of the lovely estuary view. There are fine coastal walks to either side.

The pub co-owns a local fishing boat and the menu offers prawns, lobsters, crab, razor clams, scallops, whole sea bream, hake, cod and haddock. Also, a changing pâté with sun-dried tomato chutney, goats cheese on toasted brioche with red onion marmalade, vegetable lasagne, beef in ale or chicken and leek pies, steak burger with onion rings and chips, gammon with free-range eggs, local rump steak with beer-battered onion rings and peppercorn sauce, and puddings. *Benchmark main dish: fresh fish dish of the day £19.95. Two-course evening meal £23.00.*

Free house ~ Licensees Sian Mathias and Simon Vickers ~ Real ale ~ Open 12-11; check website for times in winter ~ Bar food 12-2.30, 6 (5.30 school holidays)-8.30 ~ Restaurant ~ Children welcome ~ Wi-fi *Recommended by S and L McPhee, Simon Sharpe, Ted and Mary Bates, Roy and Gill Payne*

EAST ABERTHAW ST0366 Map 6

Blue Anchor £

(01446) 750329 – www.blueanchoraberthaw.com

Village signed off B4265; CF62 3DD

Character pub with cosy range of low-beamed little rooms, making a memorable spot for a drink

One of the oldest pubs in Wales, this lovely thatched place dates back to 1380. A warren of low-beamed and atmospheric little rooms lead off the central server with tiny doorways, open fires (including one in an inglenook with antique oak seats built into the stripped stonework) and other seats and tables worked into a series of small, chatty alcoves. The more open front bar still has an ancient lime-ash floor and keeps Brains Bitter, Theakstons Old Peculier, Wadworths 6X, Wye Valley HPA and a guest beer on handpump, as well as farm cider, ten malt whiskies and eight wines by the glass. Outside, rustic seats shelter peacefully among tubs and troughs of flowers, with stone tables on a newer terrace. The pub can get very full in the evenings and on summer weekends. A path from here leads to the shingle flats of the estuary.

Well liked food includes sandwiches, mussels in tomato, shallot and chilli sauce, greek salad with feta, vegetable curry, pheasant suprême with roasted garlic mash, thai green chicken curry, deep-fried line-caught cod with chips, pheasant meatloaf and red wine jus, venison haunch with roasted baby beetroot, potato bake and red wine jus, salmon suprême with potato and leek dauphinoise and herb crème fraîche, and puddings such as coffee crème brûlée and vanilla pannacotta with roasted pineapple and tarragon. *Benchmark main dish: pie of the day £11.95. Two-course evening meal £18.00.*

Free house ~ Licensee Jeremy Coleman ~ Real ale ~ Open 11-11; 12-10.30 Sun ~ Bar food 12-2, 6-9; 12-3.30 Sun ~ Restaurant ~ Children welcome ~ Dogs allowed in bar ~ Wi-fi *Recommended by Ian Duncan, Sandra and Miles Spencer, Monty Green, Alfie Bayliss, Katherine and Hugh Markham*

FELINFACH SO0933 Map 6

Griffin

(01874) 620111 – www.eatdrinksleep.ltd.uk

A470 NE of Brecon; LD3 0UB

Wales Dining Pub of the Year

Highly thought-of dining pub with exceptional food, a fine range of drinks and upbeat rustic décor; inviting bedrooms

The gently civilised but easy-going atmosphere, excellent food, super wine list and friendliness of the efficient staff all come in for high praise from our readers. The back bar is quite pubby in an up-to-date way, with four leather sofas around a low table on pitted quarry tiles by a high slate hearth with a log fire. Behind them are mixed stripped seats around scrubbed kitchen tables on bare boards, and a bright blue and ochre colour scheme with some modern prints; background music, board games and plenty of books. Efficient staff serve interesting drinks, many from smaller independent suppliers, including well chosen wines (18 by the glass and carafe and they have a wine shop), welsh spirits, cocktails, local bottled cider, locally sourced apple juice, non-alcoholic cocktails made with produce from their garden, unusual continental and local bottled beers and a range of sherries. Grey Trees Caradog, Montys Pale Ale and Wye Valley Butty Bach on handpump. The two smallish front dining rooms that link to the back bar are attractive. On the left: mixed dining chairs around mainly stripped tables on flagstones and white-painted rough stone walls, with a cream-coloured Aga in a big stripped-stone embrasure. On the right: similar furniture on bare boards, big modern prints on terracotta walls and smart dark curtains. Dogs may sit with their owners at certain tables while dining. There are seats and tables outside. The bedrooms are comfortable and tastefully decorated and the hearty breakfasts are nicely informal (you make your own toast and help yourself to home-made marmalade and jam). Good wheelchair access.

Using some home-grown and other local produce the imaginative food includes smoked pork rillettes with crispy pork and celeriac rémoulade, cider-cured trout with horseradish, pomegranate and pine nuts, hake with triple-cooked chips and tartare sauce, beef bourguignon with mash, silver mullet with confit potato, savoy cabbage, pancetta and almonds, lamb breast with white bean mash, salsa verde and sweetbreads, duck breast with chicory, duck fat mash, orange and anise, and puddings such as dark chocolate mousse with pecans and caramel and coconut and cardamom rice pudding with lime and mango. *Benchmark main dish: rib-eye steak with dripping chips, onion and gremolata £21.50. Two-course evening meal £25.00.*

Free house ~ Licensees Charles and Edmund Inkin and Julie Bell ~ Real ale ~ Open 11-11 (midnight Sat) ~ Bar food 12-2.30, 6-9 ~ Restaurant ~ Children welcome ~ Dogs allowed in bar and bedrooms ~ Wi-fi ~ Bedrooms: £110/£135 *Recommended by Brian and Sally Wakeham, Bernard Stradling, Barry Collett, Roger and Anne Mallard, Ian Herdman, Megan and William Revell*

THE GOOD PUB GUIDE GRESFORD SJ3453 Map 6

Pant-yr-Ochain

(01978) 853525 – www.brunningandprice.co.uk/pantyrochain

Off A483 on N edge of Wrexham: at roundabout take A5156 (A534) towards Nantwich, then first left towards the Flash; LL12 8TY

Particularly well run dining pub with good food all day, a very wide range of drinks and lovely lakeside garden

In warm weather the seats on the front terrace and the picnic-sets on the lawn in the flower-filled grounds (many are beside the small lake) are quickly snapped up. The place feels like a country house as it's reached down a long drive and the 16th-c inglenook fireplace merely adds to the atmosphere. Light and airy, the rooms are stylishly decorated with a wide range of interesting prints and bric-a-brac, and a good mix of individually chosen furnishings, including comfortable seats for relaxing as well as more upright ones for eating. One area is set out as a library with floor-to-ceiling bookshelves, while the popular dining conservatory overlooks the pretty garden; board games. An impressive line-up of drinks served by well trained staff includes Phoenix Brunning & Price Original and guests such as Hawkshead Windermere Pale, Merlin The Wizard, Purple Moose Snowdonia Ale, Rudgate Jorvik, Timothy Taylors Landlord and Weetwood Eastgate on handpump, a farm cider, 20 wines by the glass, around 80 malt whiskies, 50 gins and 30 rums. Good disabled access.

Brasserie-style food includes sandwiches, char siu pork belly with pak choi and pickled ginger salad, crispy baby squid with sweet chilli sauce, moroccan vegetable and chickpea pie with charred aubergine, baby peppers and toasted almonds, sausages with mash and onion gravy, sea bass with new potatoes, dill, spinach, tempura spring onions and lemon butter sauce, lemon and thyme marinated chicken salad with feta, cucumber and garlic lemon purée, roasted pork fillet wrapped in prosciutto with black pudding potato cake and calvados sauce, braised lamb shoulder with dauphinoise potatoes and rosemary gravy, and puddings such as cherry bakewell with custard and white chocolate and strawberry arctic roll with strawberry salad. *Benchmark main dish: steak burger with toppings, coleslaw and chips £12.95. Two-course evening meal £19.00.*

Brunning & Price ~ Licensee James Meakin ~ Real ale ~ Open 11-11 (10.30 Sun) ~ Bar food 12-9.30 (9 Sun) ~ Children welcome ~ Dogs allowed in bar ~ Wi-fi *Recommended by Miles Green, Sandra Morgan, Douglas Power, Mike and Wena Stevenson, Rosie Fielder, Trish and Karl Soloman, Georgia Egner, Lenny and Ruth Walters*

HAWARDEN SJ3266 Map 6

Glynne Arms

(01244) 569988 – www.theglynnearms.co.uk

Glynne Way; CH5 3NS

Golden-stone Georgian pub with simply furnished bars, imaginative food, four real ales and charming staff

A good mix of customers (many from the village) fill this handsome, early 19th-c stone coaching inn with chat and laughter. It's been nicely renovated and the interconnected character rooms have built-in blue or brown leather wall seats, dark pubby and other simple chairs around a mix of tables on bare boards or parquet, a few bright rugs, pale walls hung with mirrors and framed posters and bills, and three open fires. A few quirky touches include bobbins on a delft shelf, jelly moulds, antlers and crossed axes and log-end wallpaper. From the stripped and attractively panelled bar counter (lined by stools), friendly staff serve Big Hand Little Monkey, Facers This Spendid Ale, Mobberley Maori and Sandstone Sandstone Edge on handpump and eight wines by the glass; background music, board games and TV. The back courtyard has some picnic-sets. Sister business the Hawarden Estate farm shop is just a mile away.

Using Estate produce, interesting dishes include tapas-style choices such as buffalo chicken thighs with blue cheese dressing, baharat-spiced falafel with harissa and ginger, and crab cakes with sorrel, chive and salad cream, as well as thai green vegetable curry with egg noodles, sausages with champ mash, cabbage, bacon and mead gravy, sea bass with crab linguine, chilli and lime dressing and spring onions, pork chop with black pudding, roasted cauliflower, choucroute and sherry vinegar jus, and puddings such as hazelnut knickerbocker glory and lemon thyme and honey pannacotta with gooseberry compote. *Benchmark main dish: beer-battered fish and chips £13.00. Two-course evening meal £19.00.*

Free house ~ Licensee Alan Downes ~ Real ale ~ Open 11-11 (midnight Sat) ~ Bar food 12-9 ~ Restaurant ~ Children welcome ~ Dogs allowed in bar ~ Wi-fi *Recommended by Joe and Belinda Smart, Julian Richardson, Heather and Richard Jones, Michael Butler*

LITTLE HAVEN SM8512 Map 6

Swan

(01437) 781880 – www.theswanlittlehaven.co.uk
Point Road; SA62 3UL

Charming village pub with sea views from both inside and outdoor terrace, and enjoyable food and ales

Seats in the bay window of this quaint and unchanging little pub or on the heated terrace (where there are rattan-style chairs and tables) provide good views across a broad and sandy hill-sheltered cove to the sea, and it's right on the Pembrokeshire Coast Path. The traditional oak-floored bar has a mix of furniture including cask tables, a couple of leather armchairs by an open fire at one end, and a woodburning stove at the other, while the snug has a large table suitable for around ten diners. From the heavily panelled counter, helpful staff serve Brains Rev James and Sharps Doom Bar on handpump alongside two quickly changing guests such as Bluestone Bedrock Blonde and Harbwr Tenby MV Enterprise and ten wines by the glass from an extensive list; they hold a beer festival every August. There's a blue-painted dining room and a more contemporary upstairs restaurant. This is one of the prettiest coastal villages in west Wales.

Popular food includes local crab and scallops, panko chicken with sweet chilli and spring onion sauce, sweet potato and quinoa cakes with cauliflower purée, beer-battered fresh fish and chips, gressingham duck breast with spiced plum sauce, prosciutto-wrapped pork tenderloin with black pudding bonbon and cabbage, himalayan salt-aged sirloin steak with halloumi fritters and roast garlic cream, and puddings such as lemon posset and vegan coconut cheesecake. *Benchmark main dish: hake fillet with caper butter sauce £20.00. Two-course evening meal £22.00.*

Free house ~ Licensees Matt and Helen John ~ Real ale ~ No credit cards ~ Open 12-midnight; 12pm-1am Fri, Sat ~ Bar food 12-2.30, 6-8.30 ~ Restaurant Thurs-Sat evenings, also Weds evening in summer ~ Children welcome ~ Dogs allowed in bar ~ Wi-fi
Recommended by Nik and Gloria Clarke, Alison and Graeme Spicer, William and Sophia Renton, Mark Holmes, Simon Rowntree, David and Leone Lawson

LLANARMON DYFFRYN CEIRIOG SJ1532 Map 6

West Arms

(01691) 600665 – www.thewestarms.co.uk

End of B4500 W of Chirk; LL20 7LD

Former drovers' inn in an idyllic location with a public bar, lounge and separate restaurant, reliably good food and picturesque gardens; comfortable bedrooms

An inn since 1570 with fine walks all around, this friendly place makes a good base for exploring the area on foot, bike, car or horse, and the individually and comfortably furnished rooms offer character and some quirkiness. There's a small back bar and a beamed and timbered lounge with a friendly, informal atmosphere, antique settles and armchairs, an inglenook fireplace and original flagstones. Big Hand Apaloosa and Super Tidy and Weetwood Cheshire Cat and Eastgate Ale on handpump, bottled beers from their local microbrewery, 14 wines by the glass, 20 malt whiskies and 32 gins; background music. The restaurant is slightly more formal but still has a relaxed, traditional feel. In warm weather you can sit in the garden against a backdrop of the Ceiriog Valley and the Berwyn mountains.

Using local, seasonal produce, the highly regarded food includes lunchtime sandwiches, potted crab with sourdough bruschetta, cucumber and guacamole, honey roasted ham croquettes with mustard aioli, spinach tortellini with lemon ricotta and wild mushrooms, burger with toppings, coleslaw and chips, slow-cooked pork with spring onion mash and caramelised apple, rib-eye steak with chips and a choice of sauce, and puddings such as textures of lemon with sesame meringues and chocolate martini with tropical marshmallow and caramel churros. *Benchmark main dish: lamb glazed in honey and mustard with lamb pudding and herbed greens £18.00. Two-course evening meal £25.00.*

Free house ~ Licensees Nicky and Mark Williamson ~ Real ale ~ Open 11-11 ~ Bar food 12-2.30, 6.30-9 ~ Restaurant ~ Children welcome ~ Dogs welcome ~ Wi-fi ~ Bedrooms: /£115 *Recommended by Dave Sutton, Sally and David Champion, Dave Snowden*

LLANBERIS SH6655 Map 6

Pen-y-Gwryd

(01286) 870211 – www.pyg.co.uk

Nant Gwynant; at junction of A498 and A4086, ie across mountains from Llanberis – OS Sheet 115 map reference 660558; LL55 4NT

Atmospheric and unchanged mountaineers' haunt in the wilds of Snowdonia, run by the same family since 1947; bedrooms

With views across a striking mountain landscape, this much-loved Snowdonia institution is packed with items left by the climbing fraternity over the years. You can still make out the fading signatures scrawled on the ceiling by the 1953 Everest team who used this as a training base; on display is the very rope that connected Hillary and Tenzing on top of the mountain. One snug little room in the homely slate-floored log cabin bar has built-in wall benches and sturdy country chairs; from here you can look out to precipitous Moel Siabod beyond the lake opposite. A smaller room has a worthy collection of illustrious boots from famous climbs, while a cosy panelled smoke room has more fascinating climbing mementoes and equipment; darts, pool, board games, bar billiards and table tennis. Purple Moose Glaslyn and Madogs are on handpump and they have several malts. Staying in the comfortable but basic bedrooms can be quite an experience, and there's an excellent traditional breakfast (served

8.30-9am, though they may serve earlier). The inn has its own chapel (built for the millennium and dedicated by the Archbishop of Wales), sauna and outdoor natural pool.

The short choice of simple, good-value lunchtime food includes rolls, ploughman's, pies, salads and quiche of the day as well as daily specials such as roast beef or lamb. The hearty three- or five-course set meal in the evening restaurant is signalled by a gong at 7.30pm (if you're late, you'll miss it): maybe warm goats cheese and parma ham salad, smoked mackerel mousse, beef in ale pie, salmon fillet with hollandaise, peppered tenderloin of pork with wild mushroom and tomato risotto, cod in a leek, onion and butter sauce, and puddings such as sticky toffee pudding with toffee sauce and strawberry and vanilla cheesecake. *Benchmark main dish: roast leg of local lamb £9.50. Two-course evening meal £27.00.*

Free house ~ Licensee Nicholas Pullee ~ Real ale ~ Open 11-11; closed Jan, Feb ~ Bar food 12-2; evening meal 7.30pm ~ Restaurant evening ~ Children welcome ~ Dogs allowed in bar and bedrooms ~ Wi-fi ~ Bedrooms: £47.50/£95 *Recommended by Peter and Emma Kelly, Helena and Trevor Fraser, Anna and Mark Evans, John Herbert, William and Tasha Fraser*

THE GOOD PUB GUIDE

LLANDUDNO JUNCTION SH8180 Map 6

Queens Head

(01492) 546570 – www.queensheadglanwydden.co.uk

Glanwydden; heading towards Llandudno on B5115 from Colwyn Bay, turn left into Llanrhos Road at roundabout as you enter the Penrhyn Bay speed limit; Glanwydden is signed as the first left turn; LL31 9JP

Consistently good food served all day at comfortably modern dining pub

Modest from the outside it may be, but the food inside is extremely good and our readers have voiced their enthusiasm for it under the new owners – it's best to book a table in advance. The spacious yet intimate lounge bar is a mix of beams, rustic wooden tables and chairs, an open woodburning stove and fresh flowers. The little snug bar keeps Adnams Best, Conwy Clogwyn Gold and Timothy Taylors Landlord on handpump, 12 decent wines by the glass, several malt whiskies and good coffee; background music.There's a pleasing mix of seats and tables under parasols outside. Northern Snowdonia is within easy reach.

Particularly good food includes sandwiches (until 5pm), crab, king prawn and mussel bisque with tomato, brandy and saffron cream, smoked bacon and leek rösti with home-made black pudding, a fried duck egg and mustard dressing, butternut squash, sage and aubergine lasagne, steak in ale pie, calves liver and crispy bacon on creamy mash with onion gravy, moroccan-spiced chicken with sultana, pepper and almond couscous, coriander yoghurt and home-made flatbread, sea bass on crushed new potatoes, braised fennel, spinach and capers, brown shrimp and white wine sauce, braised lamb shoulder with dauphinoise potatoes and redcurrant and rosemary gravy, and puddings such as cherry bakewell tart and a fruit crumble of the day. *Benchmark main dish: beer-battered fish and chips £13.50. Two-course evening meal £21.00.*

Stange & Co Pub Group ~ Lease Dan McLennan ~ Real ale ~ Open 12-10.30 ~ Bar food 12-9 ~ Restaurant ~ Children welcome ~ Wi-fi *Recommended by Mike and Mary Carter, Harry and Megan Evans, Daisy and Jonathan Spicer, Millie and Peter Downing*

Bedroom prices are for high summer. Even then you may get reductions for more than one night, or (outside tourist areas) weekends. Winter special rates are common, and many inns reduce bedroom prices if you have a full evening meal.

LLANELIAN-YN-RHOS SH8676 Map 6

White Lion

(01492) 515807 – www.whitelioninn.co.uk

Signed off A5830 (shown as B5383 on some maps) and B5381, S of Colwyn Bay; LL29 8YA

Bustling local with bar and spacious dining areas, tasty food, real ales and helpful staff

This picturesque old village pub is tucked away at a crossing of narrow lanes in quiet hilly countryside above Colwyn Bay. There are two distinct parts linked by a broad flight of steps, and each has its own cheery personality. Up at the top is a very spacious and neat dining area, while at the other end is a traditional old bar with antique high-backed settles fitting snugly around a big fireplace, and flagstones by the counter. Marstons Saddle Tank, VOG South Island and Youngs London Gold on handpump, 15 wines by the glass, farm cider, several gins including welsh ones and ten malt whiskies are served by helpful staff. Off to the left is another dining room with jugs hanging from beams and teapots above the windows; background music and board games. There are tables in an attractive courtyard (also used for parking) next to the church. Though the present building is only a few centuries old, there's been some sort of place here for 1,200 years.

As well as lunchtime sandwiches and baguettes, the tasty food includes deep-fried goats cheese with red onion chutney, pâté of the week with granary toast, toad in the hole, a tart of the day, pork ribs in sticky barbecue sauce with coleslaw and chips, white fish, king prawn and sweet potato curry, beer-battered hake and chips, chicken in mushroom, rosemary, sage and cider sauce topped with bacon and cheese, sea bass with chilli and ginger, and puddings. *Benchmark main dish: roast beef and yorkshire pudding £11.95. Two-course evening meal £18.00.*

Free house ~ Licensee Simon Cole ~ Real ale ~ Open 11.30-3.30, 6-11; 11.30-11 Sat; 12-10.30 Sun; closed Mon except school and bank holidays ~ Bar food 12-2, 6-9; 12-2, 5-9 Fri, Sat; 12-8.30 Sun ~ Restaurant ~ Children welcome ~ Wi-fi *Recommended by George Sanderson, Darrell Barton, Patricia and Gordon Tucker, Louise and Anton Parsons, Alison and Michael Harper, Jill and Dick Archer*

LLANGOLLEN SJ2142 Map 6

Corn Mill

(01978) 869555 – www.brunningandprice.co.uk/cornmill

Dee Lane, very narrow lane off Castle Street (A539) just S of bridge; nearby parking can be tricky, may be best to use public car park on Parade Street/East Street and walk; LL20 8PN

Fascinating riverside building with fine views, personable young staff, super food all day and good beers

On a raised deck in front of this cleverly restored watermill, seats overlook the rushing mill race and rapids below; you can also watch steam trains arriving and leaving the station on the opposite riverbank. The interior is interestingly fitted out with pale pine flooring on stout beams, a striking open stairway with gleaming timber and tensioned steel rails, and mainly stripped-stone walls. Quite a lot of the old machinery is still in place, including the huge waterwheel (often turning) and there are good-sized dining tables, big rugs, thoughtfully chosen pictures (many to do with water) and several pot plants. One of the two serving bars, away from the water, has a much more local feel with regulars sitting on bar stools, pews on dark slate flagstones and daily papers. Phoenix Brunning & Price Original and

Facers DHB on handpump with guests such as Facers North Star Porter, Salopian Oracle and Stonehouse Sunlander, 20 wines by the glass, 50 malt whiskies and farm cider.

As well as sandwiches, the interesting menu includes sandwiches, korean chicken wings with kimchi salad, seared scallops with roasted butternut squash purée, crispy chorizo and lemon and caper dressing, poached smoked haddock on curried rice with a crispy egg, cauliflower, chickpea and almond tagine with apricot and date couscous, mustard-glazed ham and eggs, steak burger with toppings, coleslaw and chips, chicken with smoked pancetta and leek mash with wild mushroom and button onion sauce, sea bass with crab croquette, pea purée and oven-dried cherry tomato dressing, and puddings such as dark chocolate torte with Baileys ice-cream and raspberry and almond bakewell tart with custard. *Benchmark main dish: chicken, ham and leek pie £13.95. Two-course evening meal £22.00.*

Brunning & Price ~ Manager Andrew Barker ~ Real ale ~ Open 11-11 (10.30 Sun) ~ Bar food 12-9.30 (9 Sun) ~ Restaurant ~ Children welcome ~ ~ Dogs allowed in bar ~ Wi-fi
Recommended by Mike and Wena Stevenson, Andrew and Ruth Simmonds, Mark Hamill, Mike and Mary Carter, Colin and Daniel Gibbs, Sally Harrison

LLANMADOC SS4493 Map 6

Britannia

(01792) 386624 – www.britanniainngower.co.uk
The Gower, near Whiteford Burrows (NT); SA3 1DB

Fine views from seats behind this popular pub with more in the big garden, well liked food and ales

After enjoying one of the good, surrounding walks, come to this bustling pub for refreshment. The refurbished beamed bar has a woodburning stove and plenty of space to enjoy a pint of Gower Gold, Sharps Doom Bar and Wye Valley HPA on handpump and several wines by the glass served by friendly staff; background music, darts, TV and board games. The beamed restaurant has attractive modern wooden tables and chairs on a striped carpet, paintings on exposed-stone walls and another woodburning stove. Picnic-sets on the raised decked area at the back have marvellous views over the Loughor estuary and do get snapped up quickly; there are also tables out in front and in the big garden. They have a rabbit hutch and an aviary with budgies, cockatiels, quail and a parrot.

As well as lunchtime sandwiches, the rewarding food includes local mussels in white wine, garlic, chilli and tomato broth, fresh crab salad with roasted shell bisque, steak in ale pie, thai green vegetable curry, smoked haddock risotto with sauce vierge, free-range chicken ballotine with roast vegetable and pearl barley ragoût, butternut squash purée and crispy wings, venison with wholegrain mash, caramelised red cabbage and game jus, Tia Maria and espresso crème brûlée and sticky toffee pudding with caramel sauce; they also offer a two- and three-course set lunch. *Benchmark main dish: salt marsh lamb with dauphinoise potatoes and lamb jus £17.95. Two-course evening meal £21.00.*

Enterprise ~ Tenants Martin and Lindsey Davies ~ Real ale ~ Open 12-11 ~ Bar food 12-3, 6-9 ~ Restaurant ~ Children welcome ~ Dogs allowed in bar ~ Wi-fi
Recommended by Hugh Roberts, Trevor and Michele Street, Rosie and John Moore, I D Barnett

Real ale may be served from handpumps, electric pumps (not just the on-off switches used for keg beer) or – common in Scotland – tall taps called founts (pronounced 'fonts') where a separate pump pushes the beer up under air pressure.

MOLD SJ2465 Map 6

Glasfryn

(01352) 750500 – www.brunningandprice.co.uk/glasfryn

N of the centre on Raikes Lane (parallel to the A5119), just past the well signposted Theatr Clwyd; CH7 6LR

Busy, open-plan, bistro-style pub with inventive all-day food, nice décor and wide choice of drinks

On warm days, the wooden tables on the large front terrace here are a restful place to sit, providing sweeping views of the Clwydian Hills. The open-plan interior, with its lively, cheerful atmosphere and wide mix of customers, is cleverly laid out to create plenty of nice quiet corners with a mix of informal, attractive country furnishings: turkey-style rugs on bare boards, deep red ceilings (some high), shelves of books, house plants, a warming fire and plenty of close-hung homely pictures. Phoenix Arizona and Brunning & Price Original, Crouch Vale Brewers Gold, Hobsons Best, Purple Moose Snowdonia Ale, Stonehouse Sunlander and Timothy Taylors Boltmaker on handpump, 22 wines by the glass, 30 gins, 25 rums, 60 malt whiskies and farm cider; background music. Theatre Clwyd is just over the road.

Lovely, modern food includes sandwiches, smoked duck with chicory and candied walnut salad and raspberry vinaigrette, tempura king prawns with asian salad and thai green dressing, butternut squash, spinach, lentil and stilton pie with celariac purée and port sauce, steak burger with toppings, coleslaw and chips, braised lamb shoulder with fondant potatoes and gravy, seafood and sweetcorn chowder with prawns, mussels, salmon, haddock and sweetcorn dumplings, harrisa-spiced pork belly with couscous, pomegranate, almond, fig and mint salad, and puddings such as crème brûlée and Oreo and chocolate brownie cheesecake with white chocolate ice-cream. *Benchmark main dish: crispy beef salad with sweet chilli sauce and roasted cashews £13.95. Two-course evening meal £21.00.*

Brunning & Price ~ Manager Graham Arathoon ~ Real ale ~ Open 11.30-11; 12-10.30 Sun ~ Bar food 12-9.30 (9 Sun) ~ Children welcome ~ Dogs allowed in bar ~ Wi-fi *Recommended by Mike and Wena Stevenson, Molly and Stewart Lindsay, Chantelle and Tony Redman, Elliott Kemp, Daisy Rutledge*

NEWPORT SN0539 Map 6

Golden Lion

(01239) 820321 – www.goldenlionpembrokeshire.co.uk

East Street (A487); SA42 0SY

Attractive, friendly local, with tasty food and pleasant staff; well appointed bedrooms

Both regulars and visitors enjoy this cheerful pub and all get a genuine welcome from the attentive staff. The genuinely pubby bar has Sharps Doom Bar and a couple of guest ales from the nearby Bluestone Brewery on handpump, several malt whiskies, wines by the glass and Gwynt y Ddraig cider; background music, TV, pool, juke box, darts and games machine. There's also a cosy series of beamed rooms with distinctive old settles and the dining room has elegant blond oak furniture, whitewashed walls and potted plants. You can sit outside at the front and in a side garden. This coastal village makes a good base for exploring northern Pembrokeshire and the bedrooms are comfortable and fair value; good disabled access and facilities.

Highly thought-of food includes lunchtime sandwiches and platters, king prawns in chilli and garlic, creamy garlic mushrooms on toasted brioche, a pie of the day, thai green vegetable curry with sticky coconut rice, pork and chorizo burger with toppings and fries, lamb chops with rosemary and mint sauce, tandoori hake fillet with saag aloo potatoes and cucumber raita, black pepper and maple syrup chicken with thyme-roasted carrots and sautéed potatoes, rib-eye steak with peppercorn and brandy sauce, and puddings such as mixed berry eton mess and a crumble of the day with an almond and coconut topping and custard. *Benchmark main dish: beer-battered cod and chips £12.95. Two-course evening meal £20.00.*

Free house ~ Licensee Daron Paish ~ Real ale ~ Open 12pm-2am ~ Bar food 12-2.30, 6.30-9 ~ Restaurant ~ Children welcome ~ Dogs allowed in bar and bedrooms ~ Wi-fi ~ Live music Sat Sept-Mar ~ Bedrooms: £80/£100 *Recommended by Mark Hamill, Colin and Daniel Gibbs, Peter Brix, Frank Price, Frances Parsons, Matt and Hayley Jacob*

OLD RADNOR SO2459 Map 6

Harp

(01544) 350655 – www.harpinnradnor.co.uk

Village signposted off A44 Kington–New Radnor in Walton; LD8 2RH

Charming inn in beautiful spot, with cottagey bar, tasty food and well kept ales; comfortable bedrooms

Unanimously loved by our readers, this is a rather special 15th-c inn in perfect walking country overlooking the heights of Radnor Forest. Run by friendly, hands-on licensees it has a public bar with a great deal of character, high-backed settles, an antique reader's chair and other venerable chairs around a log fire; board games, cribbage, darts and quoits. The snug slate-floored bar contains a handsome curved antique settle, a log fire set in a fine inglenook and lots of local books, maps and guides for residents; a quieter dining area off to the right extends into another dining room with a woodburning stove. Brains Rev James and Wye Valley HPA on handpump, as well as five wines and prosecco by the glass, local cider and local gins, vodkas and whiskies. Tables outside make the most of the glorious view. The spic and span bedrooms are highly sought after and share the same lovely views; good breakfasts too. Do visit the impressive village church and look for its early organ case (Britain's oldest), fine rood screen and ancient font.

As well as simple pub dishes you'l find lunchtime sandwiches (Friday and Saturday only), mussels in garlic, cream and wine, tuna and mozzarella melt with pesto on toasted ciabatta, wild mushroom, leek and brie pasty with roast garlic mash and watercress cream, battered cod and chips, pork chop with welsh rarebit, sautéed potatoes and wholegrain mustard and cider cream, and puddings such as bitter chocolate pudding with marmalade ice-cream and banoffi pie with roasted banana ice-cream. *Benchmark main dish: sea trout fillet with champ mash and bloody mary tomato sauce £16.50. Two-course evening meal £20.00.*

Free house ~ Licensees Chris and Angela Ireland ~ Real ale ~ Open 6-11 Weds, Thurs; 12-3, 6-11 Fri, Sat; 12-3, 6-10.30 Sun; closed Mon except bank holidays, Tues ~ Bar food 12-2 Fri, Sat; 6-9 Weds-Sat ~ Children welcome ~ Dogs allowed in bar and bedrooms ~ Wi-fi ~ Bedrooms: £75/£105 *Recommended by Anne and Ben Smith, Alison and Michael Harper, P and J Shapley, Professor James Burke, Peter and Emma Kelly, Belinda and Neil Garth*

OVERTON BRIDGE SJ3542 Map 6

Cross Foxes

(01978) 780380 – www.brunningandprice.co.uk/crossfoxes

A539 W of Overton, near Erbistock; LL13 0DR

Terrific river views, contemporary food and an extensive range of drinks in bustling, well run pub

The raised terrace with oak chairs and tables has fine views over the River Dee below this substantial 18th-c coaching inn, while picnic-sets down on a lawn are even closer to the water; there's also a swing, a slide and a tractor. The ancient low-beamed bar has a red tiled floor, dark timbers, a log fire in a big inglenook and built-in old pews, and several dining areas are furnished with turkey rugs, big pot plants and frame-to-frame wall pictures; big windows in the airy dining conservatory look over the water. Board games and newspapers. A fine range of drinks includes 40 malt whiskies, 30 Armagnacs, 45 gins and lots of wines by the glass – plus Banks's Sunbeam, Brakspears Bitter, Exeter 'fraidNot and Marstons EPA on handpump and a farm cider. Service is friendly and efficient.

Interesting modern food includes sandwiches, potted smoked trout and crab with samphire, fennel and pickled cucumber salad, chicken liver pâté with carrot and apricot chutney, wild mushroom arancini with roast celeriac, fennel and hazelnut salad and tarragon dressing, steak burger with toppings, coleslaw and chips, goan king prawn and coconut curry with coriander rice and poppadums, braised lamb shoulder with dauphinoise potatoes, carrot mash and rosemary gravy, glazed duck breast and duck croquette with carrot and orange purée and red wine sauce, and puddings such as caramelised apple tart with vanilla ice-cream and butterscotch sauce and triple chocolate brownie with chocolate sauce. *Benchmark main dish: warm crispy beef salad with radishes and peppers £12.95. Two-course evening meal £20.00.*

Brunning & Price ~ Manager Ian Pritchard-Jones ~ Real ale ~ Open 11-11; 12-10.30 Sun ~ Bar food 12-9.30 (9 Sun) ~ Children welcome ~ Dogs allowed in bar ~ Wi-fi *Recommended by David Longhurst, Julie Swift, Christopher Mannings, Samuel and Melissa Turnbull, Nicholas and Lucy Sage, Edward Nile, John and Delia Franks*

PANTYGELLI SO3017 Map 6

Crown

(01873) 853314 – www.thecrownatpantygelli.com

Old Hereford Road N of Abergavenny; off A40 by war memorial via Pen Y Pound, passing leisure centre; Pantygelli also signposted from A465; NP7 7HR

Country pub in fine scenery, attractive inside and out, with good food and drinks

Reliably well run and warmly friendly, this pub is much enjoyed by our readers. The dark flagstoned bar, with sturdy timber props and beams, has a woodburning stove in a stone fireplace, a piano at the back with darts opposite, Bass, Rhymney Best, Wye Valley HPA and a guest such as Evan Evans Triumph on handpump from the slate-roofed counter, seven good wines by the glass, local organic apple juice and good coffees. On the left are four smallish, linked, carpeted dining rooms, the front pair separated by a massive stone chimneybreast; thoughtfully chosen individual furnishings and lots of attractive prints by local artists make it all thoroughly civilised. Background music, darts and board games. On the flower-filled front terrace, wrought-iron and wicker chairs look up from the lush valley to the hills and there's also a smaller back terrace surrounded by lavender.

Highly regarded food includes baguettes and ciabattas, prawn cocktail, a pâté of the day with home-made chutney, goats cheese tart with new potatoes, venison sausages and mash with red onion gravy, bubble and squeak with cold roast beef, chicken breast on tomato, potato, parma ham and asparagus with pesto dressing, sea bass fillet with truffled celeriac and potato purée, roast shallots and mussels, roast lamb rack in a herb crumb with fried potato gnocchi, feta salad and rosemary jus, and puddings such as chocolate tart with candied orange and crème fraîche and pineapple and vanilla pannacotta. *Benchmark main dish: steak in ale pie £11.50. Two-course evening meal £22.00.*

Free house ~ Licensees Steve and Cherrie Chadwick ~ Real ale ~ Open 12-2.30 (3 Sat), 6-11; 12-3, 6-10.30 Sun; closed Mon lunchtime ~ Bar food 12-2, 7-9; not Sun evening or Mon ~ Restaurant ~ Children welcome ~ Dogs allowed in bar ~ Wi-fi *Recommended by Julian Richardson, Tim King, R T and J C Moggridge, Liz and Martin Eldon*

PENNAL SH6900 Map 6

Riverside

(01654) 791285 – www.riversidehotel-pennal.co.uk

A493; opposite church; SY20 9DW

Carefully refurbished pub with tasty food and local beers, and efficient young staff; bedrooms

'What a pleasure it is to come here,' says one reader with enthusiasm, and many others agree. Of course, the pleasing food is at the top of the agenda but there's a thoughtful range of drinks too. The neatly furnished rooms have green and white walls, slate tiles on the floor, a woodburning stove, modern light wood dining furniture and some funky fabrics. High-backed stools are lined up along the stone-fronted counter where they serve Purple Moose Glaslyn, Salopian Golden Thread and Wye Valley Butty Bach on handpump, 30 malt whiskies, 45 gins, 12 wines by the glass and farm cider. There are seats and tables in the garden. As the pub is just inside the southern boundary of Snowdonia National Park, there are plenty of fine surrounding walks. They also run a Georgian guesthouse in the pretty village. Disabled access to restaurant (no disabled loos).

A wide choice of rewarding food includes sandwiches, deep-fried chilli and salt calamari, smoked salmon with spiced avocado salad, bean burger with halloumi, guacamole and sweet potato fries, plaice with a parmesan crust, king prawns, sautéed potatoes and salsa verde, gammon and egg, chicken breast with risotto and basil dressing, lamb steak with dauphinoise potatoes and red wine jus, and puddings such as apple and blackberry crumble with custard and white chocolate cheesecake; they also offer a two- and three-course set menu (Wednesday-Saturday lunch and Sunday-Friday evening). *Benchmark main dish: spiced mediterranean fish stew with king prawns and chorizo £14.00. Two-course evening meal £20.00.*

Free house ~ Licensees Glyn and Corina Davies ~ Real ale ~ Open 12-3, 6-11.30; 12-11.30 Sat, Sun; closed Mon and Tues Nov-Mar; two weeks mid Jan ~ Bar food 12-2 (2.30 Sun), 6-9; no food Mon except school holidays ~ Restaurant ~ Children welcome ~ Dogs allowed in bar and bedrooms ~ Wi-fi ~ Bedrooms: £60/£80 *Recommended by John Evans, Alf Wright, Mike and Wena Stevenson, Mike and Mary Carter, Shalaine Duffy, Mary and Douglas Kirkwood*

PONTYPRIDD ST0790 Map 6

Bunch of Grapes

(01443) 402934 – www.bunchofgrapes.org.uk

Off A4054; Ynysangharad Road; CF37 4DA

Unpretentious, bustling gastropub with a fine choice of drinks in friendly, relaxed bar, first class inventive food and a warm welcome for all

This particularly well run, 18th-c pub is known for its inventive food, but they also keep a fantastic range of drinks served by knowledgeable, friendly staff, too: Oakham Citra, Salopian Lemon Dream and Thornbridge Jaipur (and some from welsh microbreweries) on handpump, five local craft keg beers, local ciders and perries, nine wines by the glass and up to 15 gins (four are local). They hold six beer and music festivals a year. The cosy bar has an informal, relaxed atmosphere, comfortable leather sofas, wooden chairs and tables, a roaring log fire, newspapers to read and background music and board games. There's also a restaurant with elegant high-backed wooden dining chairs around a mix of tables and black and white local photo-prints taken by the landlord (an ex-professional photographer). There are seats outside on the suntrap decked area.

Using the best local, seasonal produce, the excellent food includes pork, venison and juniper terrine with beer and date relish, cockles with pancetta and laverbread, chickpea, chilli and coriander burger with chilli gremolata and citrus yoghurt, steak burger with bourbon whisky relish and crispy onion straws, wild boar sausages with cider-braised red cabbage and wild garlic pesto mash, cod with crushed new potatoes, a poached free-range egg and chive butter, pork loin chop in sage and brown butter with balsamic and red wine onions and caramelised apple, and puddings such as white chocolate panacotta with salted caramel and crushed meringue and rhubarb and vanilla trifle. *Benchmark main dish: lamb chump with parmesan and truffle oil risotto and jus £17.50. Two-course evening meal £19.50.*

Free house ~ Licensee Nick Otley ~ Real ale ~ Open 11am-11.30pm; 11.45am-11pm Sun ~ Bar food 12-3, 4.30-9.30; 12-9 Fri, Sat; 12-3.30 Sun ~ Restaurant ~ Children welcome ~ Dogs allowed in bar ~ Wi-fi *Recommended by Edward Edmonton, Barry and Daphne Gregson, Elizabeth and Peter May, Kerry and Guy Trooper, Philip J Alderton, Peter and Alison Steadman*

PUMSAINT SN6540 Map 6

Dolaucothi Arms

(01558) 650237 – www.thedolaucothiarms.co.uk

A482 Lampeter–Llandovery; SA19 8UW

Friendly new owners for enjoyable inn with simply furnished bar and dining room, local beers and riverside garden; bedrooms

At heart, this is a 16th-c drovers' inn and part of a cluster of stone cottages in a small village; it's part of the Dolaucothi Estate and owned by the National Trust. The chatty bar has three comfortable armchairs and a sofa, red and black floor tiles and a welcoming woodburning stove. There are stone and glass bottles on the mantelpiece, local artwork on the walls and books of local and historic interest; darts in both bars and a children's corner with colouring books and board games; background music. Evan Evans Cwrw and Warrior and Gower Gold on handpump, several wines by the glass, local farm cider and a range of malt whiskies and gins. The terracotta-painted dining room has another woodburning stove, traditional local furniture to include nice dining room chairs and tables on flagstones, and walls that are hung with local maps and old photos of the pub, the village and the Estate. Picnic-sets in a neat garden overlook the Cothi River where the pub has four miles of fishing rights. This is a warm and cosy place to stay, with simply furnished bedrooms (one is dog-friendly) complete with a half decanter of port and shortcake biscuits.

Popular food using local produce and herbs from the garden includes sandwiches, smoked mackerel and horseradish pâté, deep-fried brie with cranberry sauce and orange and walnut salad, pies and curries of the day, burgers with topping and chips, a fresh fish dish of the day, weekly specials, steaks with a choice of sauce, and puddings such as chocolate brownie with chocolate sauce and fruit crumbles with custard. *Benchmark main dish: pie of the day £11.00. Two-course evening meal £17.00.*

Free house ~ Licensees Karen Charles and Clare Perry ~ Real ale ~ Open 12-11; 12-8 Sun; 4-11 Tues-Thurs in winter; closed Mon ~ Bar food 12-2.30, 6-8.30 ~ Restaurant ~ Children welcome ~ Dogs allowed in bar ~ Wi-fi ~ Bedrooms: £60/£80 *Recommended by James Allsopp, Christine and Tony Garrett, Sara Fulton, Roger Baker, Buster and Helena Hastings, Ted and Mary Bates*

RAGLAN SO3609 Map 6

Clytha Arms

(01873) 840206 – www.clytha-arms.com

Clytha, off Abergavenny road – former A40, now declassified; 3 miles W of Raglan; NP7 9BW

Fine setting in spacious grounds, a relaxing spot for enjoying good food and impressive range of drinks; comfortable bedrooms

Extensive, well cared-for grounds on the edge of Clytha Park surround this civilised old country inn which is just a short stroll from the riverside path by the Usk; long heated verandahs and diamond-paned windows take in the garden views. There's a chatty, easy-going atmosphere and a wide array of customers, and the bar and lounge are comfortable, light and airy, with a good mix of nice old furniture, pine settles, window seats with big cushions, scrubbed wooden floors and open log fires; the contemporary restaurant is linen-set. A notable array of drinks includes Felinfoel Nut Brown Ale, Harbwr Tenby North Star, Untapped Monnow and Whoosh (from a little brewery just down the road) and Wye Valley Bitter on handpump, an extensive wine list with eight available by the glass, 20 malt whiskies, three farm ciders, their own perry and various continental beers; they hold a cider and beer festival over the late May Bank Holiday weekend. You'll also find darts, bar skittles, boules, board games and large-screen TV for rugby matches. The bedrooms are comfortable and the welsh breakfasts good. Dogs are welcome and the pub has its own labrador and collie.

Appetising food includes interesting choices such as snails with goats cheese and herb butter, shellfish bourride, moules frites, caribbean fruit curry, pork and wild mushroom faggots with black pudding mash, pie of the day, venison in rioja with chorizo dumplings, stuffed ham in cider sauce with garlic and rosemary potatoes, rump steak with pink peppercorn sauce and chips, and puddings such as raspberry and white chocolate cheesecake and treacle pudding with custard. *Benchmark main dish: wild boar and duck cassoulet £16.50. Two-course evening meal £20.50.*

Free house ~ Licensees Andrew and Beverley Canning ~ Real ale ~ Open 12-3, 6-11; 12-11 Fri, Sat; 12-9 Sun; closed Mon lunchtime ~ Bar food 12.30-2.15, 7-9.30; 12.30-2.30 Sun ~ Restaurant ~ Children welcome ~ Dogs allowed in bar and bedrooms ~ Wi-fi ~ Bedrooms: £70/£90 *Recommended by Heather and Richard Jones, Simon and Miranda Davies, Roy and Gill Payne, Terry Davis, Ian Herdman, Katherine Matthews*

STACKPOLE SR9896 Map 6

Stackpole Inn

(01646) 672324 – www.stackpoleinn.co.uk

Village signed off B4319 S of Pembroke; SA71 5DF

Busy pub, a good base for the area, with enjoyable food and friendly service; comfortable bedrooms

A friendly young couple run this bustling inn and our readers are enthusiastic with their praise on all aspects of the place. There's an area around the bar with pine tables and chairs but most of the pub, L-shaped on four different levels, is given over to diners, with neat light oak furnishings, ash beams and low ceilings to match; background music and board games. Brains Rev James, Felinfoel Double Dragon and Rhymney Bitter on handpump, 14 wines by the glass, 15 malt whiskies and two farm ciders. Attractive gardens feature colourful flower beds and mature trees and there are plenty of picnic-sets at the front. The four bedrooms are spotless and very comfortable and breakfasts are very good.

You can walk along the Pembrokeshire Coast Path and the two beaches nearby are stunning.

As well as daily fresh fish dishes (with a choice of sauce and double-cooked chips), the top quality food includes lunchtime rolls and ploughman's plus pork, smoked bacon and cranberry terrine with a caper and mustard dressing, moroccan butter bean and garlic hummus dip with spiced, toasted nuts and seeds and chargrilled pitta bread, local sausages with caramelised onion mash and cider gravy, cawl (lamb broth) with potatoes, swede, carrots and cheese, salmon fillet on chorizo, tomato and cannellini bean cassoulet, 28oz rib of beef (for two) with garlic and herb butter and red wine jus, and puddings such as tonka bean pannacotta with marinated cherries and belgian chocolate and orange brownie with honeycomb ice-cream. *Benchmark main dish: fresh fish dish of the day £15.00. Two-course evening meal £20.00.*

Free house ~ Licensees Gary and Becky Evans ~ Real ale ~ Open 12-3, 6-11; 12-11 Sat; closed Sun evening in winter ~ Bar food 12-2.15, 6.30-9 ~ Restaurant ~ Children welcome ~ Dogs allowed in bar ~ Wi-fi ~ Bedrooms: /£100 *Recommended by S and L McPhee, Mike Benton, Jamie Green, Alexander and Trish Gendall, Stephen Funnell, Guy Vowles, Ian Wilson*

TINTERN SO5300 Map 6

Anchor

(01291) 689582 – www.theanchortintern.co.uk

Off A466 at brown sign for Tintern Abbey; NP16 6TE

Wonderful setting for ancient inn next to Tintern Abbey ruins and river, historic features, plenty of space and good ales and food

From the picnic-sets on the terrace and in the front garden there are wonderful views of Tintern Abbey's magnificent ruins (floodlit at night). A refurbishment in early 2018 saw the opening up of a new restaurant with exposed-stone walls, flagstones and elegant wooden chairs and tables and the addition of a central fireplace with a woodburning stove and folding doors out on to the terrace. The bar counter has been moved but the central feature remains what was the horse-drawn cider press when the grounds were the abbey's orchards. Kingstone Tewdrics Tipple, Otter Amber and Wye Valley HPA on handpump, good wines by the glass and local ciders are served by hard-working, friendly staff. The existing orangery remains the best place for abbey views while the oldest part (once the ferryman's cottage and boat house and connected to the abbey's north wall) has kept its character and original features. The River Wye is just behind and there are plenty of surrounding walks.

Quite a choice of food includes sandwiches (until 5pm), wild boar terrine with apple compote, breaded brie with tomato and onion chutney, macaroni cheese with garlic bread, beef and mushroom in ale pie, lasagne, half a rack of barbecue ribs with coleslaw and chips, superfood salad, butter chicken curry, chargrilled 21-day-aged sirloin steak with a choice of sauce and chips, and puddings such as baked salted caramel cheesecake and raspberry pannacota with white chocolate sauce. *Benchmark main dish: beer-battered haddock and chips £10.50. Two-course evening meal £18.00.*

Free house ~ Licensee Niki Foreman ~ Real ale ~ Open 11.30-11.30 ~ Bar food 12-9; 12-4, 5-8 Sun ~ Restaurant ~ Children welcome ~ Dogs allowed in bar ~ Wi-fi *Recommended by Simon and Miranda Davies, Charles Todd, Julie Braeburn, Anna and Mark Evans, Roger and Donna Huggins, Alison and Tony Livesley, Martin and Sue Neville*

The details at the end of each featured entry start by saying whether the pub is a free house, or if it belongs to a brewery or pub group (which we name).

TY'N-Y-GROES SH7773 Map 6

Groes

(01492) 650545 – www.groesinn.com

B5106 N of village; LL32 8TN

Stacks of character in gracious, antiques-filled, 15th-c Snowdonia hotel with a good choice of drinks and lovely garden; bedroom suites

The views from the well equipped bedroom suites here (some have terraces or balconies) look over the Vale of Conwy and the peaks of Snowdonia; dogs are allowed in selected rooms. Past the woodburning stove in the entrance area, the rambling, low-beamed and thick-walled rooms are nicely decorated with antique settles, a sofa, old clocks, hats, portraits and tins hanging from the walls and fresh flowers. Built into one wall is a fine antique fireback, perhaps originally from the formidable fireplace in the back bar, which houses a collection of stone cats; background music. Lees Dragons Fire, MPA and a guest on handpump, quite a few malt whiskies and gins and wines by the glass. Several options for dining include an airy conservatory with a 30-year-old vine and a smart restaurant set with white linen. The idyllic back garden has flower-filled hayracks and a verdant outlook, and there are more seats on a narrow flower-decked roadside terrace.

Quite a choice of food includes sandwiches, chicken liver pâté with ale chutney, home-made duck spring rolls with carrot and cucumber salad and plum sauce, sharing boards, pearl barley risotto with butternut squash and a soft poached egg, gammon with pineapple and eggs, steak burger with toppings, coleslaw and skinny chips, coq au vin, pork chop with mushrooms, shallots and english mustard cream, beer-battered fish and chips, and puddings such as chocolate brownie with chocolate sauce and white chocolate ice-cream and glazed lemon tart with strawberries. *Benchmark main dish: braised lamb with fondant potatoes and jus £16.00. Two-course evening meal £20.00.*

Lees ~ Manager Andrew McGilvray ~ Real ale ~ Open 12-3, 6-11 (10.30 Sun) ~ Bar food 12-2, 6.30-9; 12-3, 6-8 Sun ~ Restaurant ~ Children welcome ~ Dogs allowed in bar and bedrooms ~ Wi-fi ~ Bedrooms: £100/£125 *Recommended by Dr Martin Owton, Rob Anderson, Pauline and Mark Evans, Charles Todd*

USK SO3700 Map 6

Nags Head

(01291) 672820 – www.nagsheadusk.co.uk

The Square; NP15 1BH

Traditional in style with a hearty welcome and good food and drinks

For more than half a century this handsome old coaching inn has been run by the Key family and you'll always be personally welcomed by one of them. The traditional main bar is cosy and friendly with well polished tables and chairs packed under its beams (some of these have farming tools, lanterns or horsebrasses and harness attached), as well as leatherette wall benches, and various sets of sporting prints and local pictures; look out for the original deeds to the pub. Tucked away at the front is an intimate little corner, while on the other side of the room a passageway leads to a dining area; background music. Brains Rev James and Sharps Atlantic and Doom Bar on handpump and several wines by the glass. There are seats outside at the front under fantastic hanging baskets. The church is well worth a look. The pub has no car park and nearby street parking can be limited.

Generous helpings of tasty food using local meat and seasonal game includes sandwiches, country pâté with toast, prawn cocktail, leek and bean casserole, faggots with mushy peas and onion gravy, gammon with eggs and pineapple, chicken with tomatoes, onions and mushrooms in red wine, guinea fowl with wine and figs, crispy half duck with orange and Cointreau sauce, and puddings such as treacle and walnut tart and sticky toffee pudding with toffee sauce. *Benchmark main dish: rabbit pie £10.50. Two-course evening meal £18.00.*

Free house ~ Licensee Key family ~ Real ale ~ Open 10.30-2.30, 5-11 ~ Bar food 11.30-2, 5.30-9 ~ Restaurant ~ Children welcome ~ Dogs welcome ~ Wi-fi *Recommended by Caroline Sullivan, M G Hart, Diana and Bertie Farr, Louise and Simon Peters, Amanda Shipley, Alison and Graeme Spicer*

Also Worth a Visit in Wales

Besides the fully inspected pubs, you might like to try these pubs that have been recommended to us and described by readers. Do tell us what you think of them: feedback@goodguides.com

ANGLESEY

ABERFFRAW SH3568

Crown (01407) 840222
Bodorgan Square; LL63 5BX Village-square pub with two well kept ales such as Lincoln Green Archer and Weetwood Southern Cross, good selection of gins and enjoyable home-made food including daily specials, quick friendly service; sports TV; well behaved children and dogs welcome, suntrap beer garden with sturdy furniture and views towards the dunes, open all day, food all day Sat, till 6pm Sun. *(Brian and Anna Marsden)*

MENAI BRIDGE SH5773

Gazelle (01248) 713364
Glyngarth; A545, halfway towards Beaumaris; LL59 5PD Hotel and restaurant rather than pub in outstanding waterside position looking across to Snowdonia, main bar with smaller rooms off, up to three Robinsons ales kept well and seven wines by the glass, decent bar food; children and dogs (in bar) welcome, steep garden behind (and walk down from car park), bedrooms including suites, slipway and mooring for visiting boats, open all day weekends. *(Alan McQuilan)*

MENAI BRIDGE SH5572

Liverpool Arms (01248) 712453
St Georges Road/Water Street; LL59 5EY Refurbished pub close to the quay and not far from the famous suspension bridge; ales such as Facers and Purple Moose, enjoyable home-made food (all day Fri-Sun) including daily specials and Mon steak night, quick friendly service; quiz Weds and Sun; children welcome, part-covered terrace, open all day weekends. *(Daisy and Jonathan Spicer)*

MOELFRE SH5186

Kinmel Arms (01248) 410231
Moelfre Bay; LL72 8LL Popular sea-view pub with nautical-theme interior, four Robinsons ales and generous helpings of enjoyable traditional food from sandwiches up, friendly service; dogs welcome, picnic-sets on paved front terrace, open all day. *(Brian and Anna Marsden)*

PENTRAETH SH5278

Panton Arms (01248) 450959
The Square; LL75 8AZ Welcoming roadside pub with spacious cleanly presented interior; enjoyable good value food and three well kept ales such as Purple Moose; free wi-fi; children and dogs (in bar) welcome, good-sized back garden with play area, open all day in summer, food all day weekends. *(Brian and Anna Marsden)*

RED WHARF BAY SH5281

Ship (01248) 852568
Village signed off A5025 N of Pentraeth; LL75 8RJ Whitewashed 18th-c pub right on Anglesey's east coast – fantastic views of miles of tidal sands; big old-fashioned rooms either side of servery, nautical bric-a-brac, long varnished wall pews, cast-iron-framed tables and open fires, three well kept ales including Adnams, 48 malt whiskies and decent choice of wines, enjoyable food (may ask for a card if you run a tab); background music; children welcome in room on left, dogs in bar, limited disabled access, numerous outside tables, open all day. *(Paul Humphreys)*

RHOSCOLYN SH2675

★**White Eagle** (01407) 860267
Off B4545 S of Holyhead; LL65 2NJ Remote place rebuilt almost from scratch on site of an old pub (same group as the Oystercatcher at Rhosneigr); airy

modern feel in neatly kept rooms, relaxed atmosphere and nice winter fire, Coach House, Conwy, Weetwood and guests from smart oak counter, several wines by the glass, extensive choice of good locally sourced interesting food, friendly helpful service, restaurant; children welcome, dogs in bar (biscuits for them), terrific sea views from decking and picnic-sets in good-sized garden, lane down to beach, open (and food) all day. *(Dave Snowden)*

RHOSNEIGR SH3272

Oystercatcher (01407) 812829
A4080; LL64 5JP Modern glass-fronted Huf Haus set in dunes close to the sea – same owners as the White Eagle at Rhoscolyn but not really a pub (created as a restaurant/chefs' academy); great views from upstairs restaurant and bar with good range of much enjoyed food, well kept ales such as Brimstage Oyster Catcher and Conwy Welsh Pride plus a house beer from Coach House, decent choice of wines by the glass, ground-floor coffee/wine bar serving lighter meals till 6pm; children, walkers and dogs welcome, upper terrace with rattan sofas and colourful beach huts, full wheelchair access, open all day. *(Brian and Anna Marsden)*

CLWYD

CARROG SJ1143

Grouse (01490) 430272
B5436, signed off A5 Llangollen–Corwen; LL21 9AT Welcoming little pub with superb views over River Dee and beyond from bay window and covered terrace; Lees ales, decent food from sandwiches up including vegetarian/vegan and gluten-free choices, reasonable prices, friendly helpful staff; background music; children, walkers and dogs welcome, handy for Llangollen steam railway; open (and food) all day. *(Gareth Evans)*

COLWYN BAY SH8579

Toad (01492) 532726
Promenade; LL28 4BU Steps up to seafront pub overlooking the prom and beach; enjoyable varied choice of food including fixed-price menu, good wine list and real ales such as Jennings, friendly efficient service; children welcome, tables on front terrace, open all day Sun. *(Paul Humphreys)*

GRAIG FECHAN SJ1454

Three Pigeons (01824) 703178
Signed off B5429 S of Ruthin; LL15 2EU Extended largely 18th-c beamed pub with good choice of enjoyable sensibly priced food (all day weekends) from sandwiches and light dishes up, OAP lunch deal Weds, four quickly changing ales, local cider and plenty of wines by the glass, friendly service, various nooks and corners, interesting mix of furniture and some old signs on the walls, great country views from restaurant; children and dogs (in bar) welcome, big garden with terrace and same views, good walks, two self-catering apartments, camping, open all day Sat, till 9.30pm Sun, closed Mon and lunchtime Tues (all day Tues in Jan). *(Mike and Wena Stevenson)*

LLANARMON DYFFRYN CEIRIOG SJ1532

★**Hand** (01691) 600666
B4500 from Chirk; LL20 7LD Peaceful former farmhouse at heart of Upper Ceiriog valley set against backdrop of the Berwyn Mountains; low-beamed bar with inglenook log fire, sturdy tables and a mix of seating including settles, wheelbacks and mate's chairs on carpet, old prints on the walls, ales such as Weetwood, seven wines by the glass and 17 malt whiskies, good popular food, woodburner in largely stripped-stone restaurant, quiet lounge and games room with darts and pool; children welcome (not in bar after 8pm), dogs in some areas, picnic-sets on crazy-paved front terrace, more tables in garden, not far from Pistyll Rhaeadr (Wales's highest waterfall), well equipped spacious bedrooms, good breakfast, open all day. *(Julie Braeburn)*

LLANFERRES SJ1860

Druid (01352) 810225
A494 Mold–Ruthin; CH7 5SN Extended 17th-c whitewashed inn set in fine walking country – Alyn Valley towards Loggerheads Country Park, or up Offa's Dyke Path to Moel Famau; views from broad bay window in civilised plush lounge and from bigger beamed back bar with two handsome antique oak settles, pleasant mix of more modern furnishings and quarry-tiled area by log fire, Marstons-related ales, 30 malt whiskies, reasonably priced traditional food; games room with darts and pool; background music, TV; children welcome, dogs in bar, bedrooms, open all day Fri-Sun. *(Sheila and Sam Thorpe)*

LLANFWROG SJ1158

Cross Keys (01824) 308081
B5105 just outside Ruthin; LL15 2AD Attractively refurbished old pub run by father and son team; sofas either side of woodburner in stone fireplace, tartan-upholstered chairs around wooden tables and against counter serving Hafod ales and good wines by the glass, wide choice of well liked food from sandwiches and sharing boards up, restaurant upstairs with high rafters, whitewashed walls and good quality furniture; different terrace areas in garden with fine country views; closed Mon lunchtime. *(Alison and Michael Harper)*

LLANGOLLEN SJ2142

Chainbridge (01978) 860215
2 miles W; LL20 8BS Refurbished 19th-c hotel in great position overlooking River Dee

rapids, chain bridge and renovated steam railway; bar, lounge, restaurant and good outside spaces, decent food from sandwiches and pubby choices up; children and dogs welcome, plenty of bedrooms (some with river-view balconies), good walks, open all day. *(Mike and Wena Stevenson)*

MINERA SJ2651

Tyn-y-Capel (01978) 269347

Church Road; LL11 3DA Ancient coaching inn with good locally sourced food and four real ales including one badged for them; regular live music, Sun quiz; children and dogs (in bar) welcome, lovely hill views from terrace, park opposite with play area, open (and food) all day, kitchen shut till 7pm Sun. *(Lenny and Ruth Walters)*

RUABON SJ3043

Bridge End (01978) 810881

Bridge Street; LL14 6DA Proper old-fashioned pub serving own McGivern ales (brewed here) alongside several guests and ciders, friendly staff and cheerful local atmosphere, some snacky food, black beams, open fires; Tues quiz, regular summer live music, beer festival Aug; children and dogs welcome, seats in garden, open all day weekends, from 5pm weekdays (4pm Fri). *(Katherine and Hugh Markham)*

ST GEORGE SH9775

★**Kinmel Arms** (01745) 832207

Off A547 or B5381 SE of Abergele; LL22 9BP The long-serving owners at this popular Main Entry pub are retiring – so expect some changes; bar with sofas either side of woodburner, mix of nice old tables and chairs on wood floor, ales such as Facers, Heavy Industry and Thwaites, good selection of wines and whiskies, food has been imaginative; children and dogs (in bar) welcome, plenty of picnic-sets for warm weather, and the surrounding countryside is stunning with good walks right from the door; comfortable bedrooms made up of contemporary suites with own decked areas, has closed Sun. *(Geoff and Ann Marston, Brian and Sally Wakeham)*

DYFED

ABERAERON SN4562

Cadwgan (01545) 570149

Market Street; SA46 0AU Small brightly painted late 18th-c pub opposite the harbour; fairly basic with friendly regulars, well kept Hancocks HB and a couple of guests, some nautical memorabilia and interesting old photographs, open fire, no food; sports TV; children and dogs welcome, pavement seats and little garden behind, closed Sun evening, Mon lunchtime, otherwise open all day. *(Sally Harrison)*

ABERCYCH SN2539

★**Nags Head** (01239) 841200

Off B4332 Cenarth–Boncath; SA37 0HJ Friendly tucked-away riverside pub with dimly lit beamed and flagstoned bar; stripped wood tables and woodburner in big fireplace, hundreds of beer bottles on shelves, clocks showing time around the world on stone wall, Mantle Cwrw Teifi and two guests from brick servery, enjoyable pubby food including specials, various other connecting rooms, one with a coracle hanging from ceiling; background music, darts; children and dogs welcome, benches (some under cover) in garden overlooking river (pub has fishing rights), play area with wooden castle, three comfortable bedrooms, closed lunchtimes Mon and Tues, otherwise open all day (till 7.30pm Sun). *(Michael Cecil)*

ABERGORLECH SN5833

Black Lion (01558) 685271

B4310; SA32 7SN Friendly accommodating new owners for this old pub in fine rural position; traditional stripped-stone and beamed bar, old flagstones, pubby seats and tables, woodburner, a couple of local ales, good, popular honest food, dining extension with farmhouse kitchen chairs around mix of tables on bare boards, local paintings, another woodburner; background music, free wi-fi; children and dogs welcome, lovely views of Cothi Valley from riverside garden. *(Mike and Anita Beach)*

ANGLE SM8603

Hibernia (01646) 641517

B4320; SA71 5AT Welcoming village pub with good reasonably priced home-made food and well kept changing ales, traditional bar with coal fire, more modern dining room; some live music, sports TV, pool; children and dogs welcome, one bedroom, open all day in high summer. *(Alec and Susan Hamilton)*

ANGLE SM8703

★**Old Point House** (01646) 641205

Signed off B4320 in village, along long rough waterside track; SA71 5AS Quaint simple place in idyllic spot overlooking sheltered anchorage; opened-up bar with wooden tables and chairs on stone floor, log fire, a couple of real ales, farm cider and several wines by the glass, enjoyable pubby food in carpeted lounge; outside lavatories; children and dogs welcome, picnic-sets on grass with charming views across the water, lovely surrounding walks (on Pembrokeshire Coast Path), open (and food) all day in summer, check website for winter hours; note

If you know a pub is ever open all day, please tell us.

that the road from Angle is unmade and gets cut off by spring tides about four times a year for a couple of hours. *(Jamie Green)*

BORTH SN6089

Victoria (01970) 871417

High Street; SY24 5HZ Stone-built pub backing on to the beach and popular with locals and tourists; five well kept ales including Sharps Doom Bar and Wye Valley, good variety of enjoyable reasonably priced food including well cooked fish, friendly accommodating staff even when busy, more space upstairs and sea-view balcony; live music, sports TV; children and dogs (in bar) welcome, tables on back deck with steps down to the shingle, open all day; for sale, so may be changes. *(Dave Snowden)*

BOSHERSTON SR9694

St Govans Country Inn

(01646) 661311 *Off B4319 S of Pembroke; SA71 5DN* Busy pub with big modernised open-plan bar, cheery and simple, with several changing ales and well priced pubby food, good climbing photographs and murals of local beauty spots, log fire in large stone fireplace; background music, TV, games machine and pool (winter only); children and dogs welcome, picnic-sets on small front terrace, four good value bedrooms (residents' parking), handy for water-lily lakes, beach and cliff walks, open all day in season (all day weekends at other times). *(Frances Parsons)*

BRECHFA SN5230

Forest Arms (01267) 202288

Opposite church (B4310); SA32 7RA Renovated stone-built village inn; well kept Rhymney General Picton and a summer guest, enjoyable reasonably priced food including daily specials and good vegetarian/vegan options, friendly helpful staff, two beamed bars, one with big inglenook and angling theme (pub can arrange fishing on River Cothi), the other in two sections, note Bob the stuffed raven, also dining/function room with pitched ceiling, chairs from St David's Cathedral and another log fire; children and dogs welcome, picnic-sets in back garden, good walks and mountain bike trails, three comfortable bedrooms and self-catering holiday cottage, open all day weekends, closed Mon. *(John and Delia Franks)*

BROAD HAVEN SM8614

★**Druidstone Hotel** (01437) 781221

N on coast road, bear left for about 1.5 miles then follow sign left to Druidstone Haven; SA62 3NE Cheerfully informal country house hotel in grand spot above the sea, individual, relaxed and with terrific views; inventive cooking using fresh local ingredients (best to book), helpful efficient service, cellar bar with a welsh ale tapped from the cask, country wines and other drinks, ceilidhs and folk events, friendly pub dogs (others welcome); attractive high-walled garden, all sorts of sporting activities from boules to sand-yachting, spacious homely bedrooms as well as self-catering cottages. *(Frances Parsons)*

CAIO SN6739

Brunant Arms (01558) 650483

Off A482 Llanwrda–Lampeter; SA19 8RD Comfortable unpretentious village pub; beams, old settles, china on delft shelving and nice log fire, a couple of ales such as Evan Evans, enjoyable home-made food from regularly changing menu, Tues steak night, friendly helpful staff, stripped-stone public bar with games including pool; some live music, sports TV; children and dogs welcome, small Perspex-roofed verandah and lower terrace, bedrooms, handy for Dolaucothi Gold Mines (NT), closed Sun evening, Mon. *(John and Delia Franks)*

CAREW SN0403

Carew Inn (01646) 651267

A4075 off A477; SA70 8SL Stone-built pub with appealing cottagey atmosphere; unpretentious small panelled public bar, nice old bentwood stools and mix of tables and chairs on bare boards, small dining area, lounge bar with low tables, warm open fires, two changing beers and enjoyable generously served food, some themed nights, two upstairs dining rooms with leather chairs at black tables; background music, dominoes, darts; children and dogs (in bar) welcome, enclosed back garden with play equipment, view of Carew Castle ruins and remarkable 9th-c celtic cross, new self-catering accommodation, open all day. *(Sally Harrison)*

CILYCWM SN7540

Neuadd Fawr Arms (01550) 721644

By church entrance; SA20 0ST Nicely placed 18th-c drovers' inn above River Gwenlais among lanes to Llyn Brianne; eclectic mix of old furniture on huge slate flagstones, woodburners, good seasonal food with interesting specials in bar or smaller dining room, one or two changing local ales, friendly helpful service and chatty locals; children and dogs welcome, open all day Sun, closed Mon-Thurs lunchtimes. *(John and Delia Franks)*

COSHESTON SN0003

Brewery Inn (01646) 686678

Signed E from village crossroads; SA72 4UD Welcoming 17th-c village pub with attractively furnished bar, flagstones and exposed stone walls, good choice of enjoyable generously served food including vegetarian options, a locally brewed house beer and guest, ten gins, helpful friendly service and buzzy atmosphere; weekly quiz, live music last Sat of month; children and dogs welcome, closed Sun evening, Mon. *(Stephen Funnell)*

CRESSWELL QUAY SN0506

★ **Cresselly Arms** (01646) 651210
Village signed from A4075; SA68 0TE
Simple unchanging alehouse overlooking tidal creek; plenty of local customers in two welcoming old-fashioned linked rooms, built-in wall benches, kitchen chairs and plain tables on red and black tiles, open fire in one room, Aga in the other with lots of pictorial china hanging from high beam-and-plank ceiling, third more conventionally furnished red-carpeted room, a house beer from Caffle along with Hancocks, Sharps and a rotating guest; no children or dogs, seats outside making most of view, you can arrive by boat if tide is right, open all day in summer. *(Frances Parsons)*

CWM GWAUN SN0333

★ **Dyffryn Arms** (01348) 881305
Cwm Gwaun and Pontfaen signed off B4313 E of Fishguard; SA65 9SE
Classic rural time warp known locally as Bessie's after the much-loved veteran landlady (her farming family have run it since 1840 and she's been in charge for well over a third of that time); basic 1920s front parlour with plain deal furniture and draughts boards inlaid into tables, red and black quarry tiles, woodburner, well kept Bass served by jug through sliding hatch, low prices, WWI prints and posters, a young portrait of the Queen and large collection of banknotes, darts; may be duck eggs for sale; lovely outside view and walks in nearby Preseli Hills, open more or less all day (may close if no customers). *(Giles and Annie Francis)*

FISHGUARD SM9537

★ **Fishguard Arms** (01348) 872763
Main Street (A487); SA65 9HJ Tiny unspoilt bay-windowed terrace pub with friendly community atmosphere and character landlord, front bar with unusually high counter serving well kept/priced Bass direct from the cask, rugby photographs and open fire, back snug with woodburner, traditional games and sports TV, no food; smokers' area out behind, open all day, closed Weds evening. *(Giles and Annie Francis)*

FISHGUARD SM9537

Royal Oak (01348) 218632
Market Square, Upper Town; SA65 9HA
Refurbished village pub with stripped beams, exposed stonework and slate flagstones, big picture-window dining extension, plaque commemorating defeat of bizarre french raid in 1797 (peace treaty was signed in the pub), well kept ales such as Bluestone, Evan Evans and Glamorgan, farm cider, good choice of well liked fairly priced pubby food, friendly prompt service; folk night Tues; children and dogs welcome, pleasant terrace with view down to Lower Town bay, open all day. *(Kevin Simms)*

FISHGUARD SM9637

Ship (01348) 874033
Newport Road, Lower Town; SA65 9ND
Old-fashioned 18th-c terrace-row pub near the old harbour; dark interior with beams and coal fire, lots of boat pictures, model ships and other memorabilia, well kept ales such as Felinfoel and Theakstons, no food; some live music; children and dogs welcome, front door directly on to the road (careful as you leave), open all day weekends, closed Mon, Tue and lunchtimes Weds-Fri. *(Giles and Annie Francis)*

JAMESTON SS0699

Tudor Lodge (01834) 871212
A4139, E of Jameston; SA70 7SS
Friendly refurbished inn close to the coast; two bars with open fire and woodburner, well kept ales such as Sharps Doom Bar and several wines by the glass, decent choice of enjoyable food including early bird deal (4-6pm), Tues curry and Thurs steak night, airy dining room with painted beams and high-backed chairs; children welcome, play area and plenty of picnic-sets outside, five stylish comfortable bedrooms, open (and food) all day weekends, from 4pm weekdays. *(Edward Nile)*

LITTLE HAVEN SM8512

St Brides Inn (01437) 781266
St Brides Road; SA62 3UN Just 20 metres from Pembrokeshire Coast Path; neat stripped-stone bar and linked carpeted dining area, traditional furnishings, log fire, interesting well in back corner grotto thought to be partly Roman, Banks's, Marstons and a guest, enjoyable bar food including fresh fish and other local produce, nice staff; background music and TV; children welcome, no dogs inside, seats in sheltered suntrap terrace garden across road, two bedrooms, open all day in summer. *(John and Enid Morris, Simon Rowntree)*

LLANDDAROG SN5016

★ **Butchers Arms** (01267) 275330
On back road by church; SA32 8NS
Ancient black-beamed local with three intimate eating areas off small central bar, popular food, Felinfoel ales tapped from the cask and nice wines by the glass, conventional pub furniture, gleaming brassware and open woodburner in biggish fireplace; background music; children welcome, tables outside and pretty window boxes, bedroom in converted stables, closed Sun, Mon. *(Jason Cummings)*

LLANDEILO SN6226

Angel (01558) 822765
Rhosmaen Street; SA19 6EN Town-centre local painted a distinctive pale blue; comfortably furnished front bar with ales such as Evan Evans from central servery, step up to popular back restaurant serving

very good food at reasonable prices including daily specials, friendly helpful staff; children welcome, walled beer garden behind, accommodation in refurbished cottage, closed Sun, Mon. *(Simon King)*

LLANDOVERY SN7634

Castle (01550) 720343

Kings Road; SA20 0AP Popular and welcoming hotel next to castle ruins; good attractively presented food from sandwiches to charcoal grills, afternoon teas, courteous efficient service, well kept ales; children and dogs welcome, picnic-sets out in front under parasols, comfortable bedrooms, open all day (till 6pm Sun). *(Sally Harrison)*

LLANDOVERY SN7634

Kings Head (01550) 720393

Market Square; SA20 0AB Early 18th-c beamed coaching inn; bar with patterned carpet, exposed stonework and large woodburner, three well kept ales including Evan Evans, enjoyable food from snacks and bar meals up, Fri steak night, friendly service; children and dogs welcome, nine bedrooms, open all day. *(Edward Nile)*

LLANFIHANGEL-Y-CREUDDYN SN6676

★**Y Ffarmers** 07890 581568

Village signed off A4120 W of Pisgah; SY23 4LA This popular and welcoming community pub suffered extensive fire damage at the beginning of 2018, but will hopefully be open again by late autumn; highly regarded food from pub favourites to more restauranty dishes, two changing ales, a craft beer, real cider and interesting selection of gins (several from welsh distillers), good friendly service; children and dogs welcome, back terrace with steps up to lawn, 13th-c village church opposite, open all day weekends (no food Sun evening), closed Mon and lunchtime Tues. *(Dr Simon Innes, B and M Kendall)*

LLANGRANNOG SN3154

Pentre Arms (01239) 654345

On the front; SA44 6SP Friendly old seafront pub beautifully placed in this pretty coastal village – magnificent sunset sea views from bar's picture window; well kept ales such as St Austell Tribute, fairly standard food including good steaks and often fresh fish, separate restaurant, pool room with games machines and TV; regular live music; children and dogs (in bar) welcome, seven bedrooms (some directly overlooking the small bay), staff will advise on dolphin-watching, handy for coast path, open all day. *(Sally Harrison)*

LLANGRANNOG SN3154

Ship (01239) 654510

Near the front, by car park entrance; SA44 6SL Just back from the bay with tables out by beachside car park; good generous food including local fish/seafood (booking advised weekends), friendly accommodating staff, well kept ales and good selection of gins, bare-boards bar with burnt-orange walls and big woodburner, further spacious upstairs eating area, local artwork for sale, games room with pool; weekend live music; children and dogs welcome, car parking charge refunded against food, open all day and can get very busy in summer. *(John and Delia Franks)*

LLANSTADWELL SM9404

Ferry House (01646) 600270

Hazelbeach, Church Road; SA73 1EG Neatly kept, traditionally furnished inn by the Cleddau waterway with great views; good food including local fish, Sharps Doom Bar and a guest beer, timber-framed dining conservatory making most of the view; children and dogs welcome, picnic-sets on waterside terrace, summer pontoon for visiting boats, six comfortable bedrooms, closed Sun evening. *(Dave Braisted)*

MATHRY SM8831

Farmers Arms (01348) 831284

Brynamlwg, off A487 Fishguard–St David's; SA62 5HB Popular pub with traditional beamed bar; well kept ales, several gins and ample helpings of enjoyable good value pubby food, friendly staff and locals, large vine-covered dining conservatory; background music, TV, games machine and pool; children welcome, dogs in bar, nearby campsite, open all day. *(Rock Dweller)*

NEWCHAPEL SN2239

Ffynnone Arms (01239) 841800

B4332; SA37 0EH Welcoming 18th-c beamed pub with enjoyable traditional food including popular Sun carvery, special diets catered for and some produce home-grown, a couple of changing ales, local cider and afternoon teas in season, two woodburners; darts, pool and table skittles; disabled facilities, picnic-sets in small garden, open all day Sun, from 5pm weekdays, 2pm Sat. *(Alfie Bayliss)*

NEWPORT SN0539

Castle (01239) 820742

Bridge Street; SA42 0TB Welcoming old pub with divided bar – one part panelled with open fire, the other with pool, darts, juke box and projector for major sports; enjoyable home-made food including Sun carvery, ales such as Wye Valley, pleasant service, restaurant; some live music; children and dogs welcome, three bedrooms, handy for Parrog estuary walk (especially for bird-watchers), open all day. *(Jason Cummings)*

NEWPORT SN0539

Royal Oak (01239) 820632

West Street (A487); SA42 0TA Sizeable 18th-c pub with good traditional food plus lots of authentic curries (takeaway service), well kept Felinfoel and a guest, friendly helpful staff, lounge with eating areas, separate stone and slate bar with pool and games, upstairs dining room; children welcome, no dogs, some tables outside, easy walk to beach and coast path, open (and food) all day. *(Heulwen and Neville Pinfield)*

PEMBROKE DOCK SM9603

Shipwright (01646) 682090

Front Street; SA72 6JX Little blue-painted end-of-terrace pub on waterfront overlooking estuary; enjoyable home-made food and a couple of well kept ales, friendly efficient staff, bare-boards interior with nautical and other memorabilia, some booth seating; children welcome, five minutes from Ireland ferry terminal. *(Jason Cummings)*

PENRHIWLLAN SN3641

Daffodil (01559) 370343

A475 Newcastle Emlyn–Lampeter; SA44 5NG Contemporary open-plan dining pub with comfortable welcoming bar; sofas and leather tub chairs on pale limestone floor, woodburner, Greene King Abbot, Hancocks HB and maybe a guest from granite-panelled counter, two lower-ceilinged end rooms with big oriental rugs, steps down to a couple of airy dining rooms, open kitchen serving particularly good food; background music; children and dogs (in bar) welcome, nicely furnished decked area outside with valley views, closed Sun evening and Mon. *(Kristin Warry)*

PONTRHYDFENDIGAID SN7366

Black Lion (01974) 831624

Off B4343 Tregaron–Devils Bridge; SY25 6BE Relaxed country inn run well by friendly landlord; smallish main bar with dark beams and exposed stonework, old country furniture on bare boards, woodburner and big pot-irons in vast fireplace, copper, brass and so forth on mantelpiece, historical photographs, well kept Felinfoel Double Dragon and a guest, several wines by the glass and enjoyable good value home-cooked food, quarry-tiled back restaurant, small games room with pool and darts; background music; children and dogs welcome, back courtyard and tree-shaded garden, bedrooms (some in converted stables), good walking/cycling country and not far from Strata Florida Abbey, open all day Sun, from 4pm other days. *(Edward Nile)*

PORTHGAIN SM8132

Sloop (01348) 831449

Off A487 St David's–Fishguard; SA62 5BN Busy tavern (especially holiday times) snuggled down in cove wedged tightly between headlands on Pembrokeshire Coast Path – fine walks in either direction; plank-ceilinged bar with lobster pots and fishing nets, ship clocks, lanterns and some relics from local wrecks, decent-sized eating area with simple furnishings, well liked bar food from sandwiches to good steaks and fresh fish, Brains, Felinfoel and Greene King, separate games room; seats on heated terrace overlooking harbour, self-catering cottage in village, open all day from 9.30am for breakfast, till midnight Sat. *(Heulwen and Neville Pinfield)*

RHANDIRMWYN SN7843

Royal Oak (01550) 760201

7 miles N of Llandovery; SA20 0NY Friendly 17th-c stone-built inn set in remote peaceful walking country, comfortable traditional bar with log fire, three well kept local ales, ciders and perries, good variety of popular sensibly priced food sourced locally, big dining area; children and dogs (in bar) welcome, hill views from garden and five cottagey bedrooms, handy for Brecon Beacons, closed Sun evening, Mon. *(Kevin Simms)*

ST DAVID'S SM7525

Farmers Arms (01437) 721666

Goat Street; SA62 6RF Bustling old-fashioned low-ceilinged pub by cathedral gate; cheerful and unpretentiously pubby, mainly drinking on the left and eating on the right, central servery with three well kept ales including Felinfoel Double Dragon, decent food (summer only) from sandwiches to specials, friendly staff and atmosphere; TV for rugby, pool, free wi-fi; children and dogs welcome, cathedral view from large tables on big back suntrap terrace, open all day in summer (best to check winter times). *(Sally Harrison)*

ST DOGMAELS SN1646

Ferry (01239) 615172

B4546; SA43 3LF Old whitewashed waterside pub with spectacular views of the Teifi estuary from attractively furnished picture-window dining extension, good freshly made food, Brains ales and several wines by the glass, pleasant attentive staff, character bar with pine tables and leather sofas, interesting old photographs and local artwork; background music; children, walkers and dogs welcome, plenty of room outside on linked decked areas, own jetty/moorings and at start of Pembrokeshire Coast Path, open all day. *(Frank Price)*

TREVINE SM8332

Ship (01348) 831445

Off A487 at Croes-Goch or via Penparc; Ffordd y Felin; SA62 5AX Well positioned traditional little pub just up from coast path; popular well priced food and a couple of interesting changing beers, friendly service, dining extension; children welcome, lovely view from back garden, open all day. *(Giles and Annie Francis)*

GLAMORGAN

BISHOPSTON SS5789

Joiners Arms (01792) 232658
Bishopston Road, just off B4436 SW of Swansea; SA3 3EJ Thriving 19th-c stone local with own good value Swansea ales along with well kept guests, ample helpings of enjoyable freshly made pub food (not Sun evening, Mon), friendly staff, unpretentious quarry-tiled bar with massive solid-fuel stove, comfortable lounge; TV for rugby; children and dogs welcome, open all day (from 3pm Mon and Tues). *(Stan Jeffries)*

BISHOPSTON SS5889

Plough & Harrow (01792) 234459
Off B4436 Bishopston–Swansea; SA3 3DJ Cleanly modernised and renovated old pub with L-shaped bar and restaurant; good imaginative food from chef-owner including good value two-course lunch deal, ales such as St Austell Tribute and plenty of wines by the glass, helpful courteous service; open all day Sun, closed Mon lunchtime. *(Stan Jeffries)*

CARDIFF ST1876

Cambrian Tap (029) 2064 4952
St Mary Street/Caroline Street; CF10 1AD Revamped city-centre corner pub popular for its good range of Brains cask and keg beers plus guests, several more in bottles, friendly knowledgeable staff, nice home-made pies; Mon open mike night, Tues comedy night; dogs welcome, open all day. *(Taff Thomas, Tony and Wendy Hobden)*

CARDIFF ST1876

City Arms (029) 2064 1913
Quay Street; CF10 1EA City-centre alehouse with four Brains beers and ten regularly changing guests (some tapped from the cask), tasting trays available, also plenty of draught/bottled continentals and real cider, friendly knowledgeable staff, no food; some live music, darts, free wi-fi; open all day (till 2am Fri, Sat), very busy on rugby match days. *(Colin and Daniel Gibbs)*

CARDIFF ST1776

Cricketers (029) 2034 5102
Cathedral Road; CF11 9LL Victorian townhouse in quiet residential area backing on to Glamorgan CC; well kept Evan Evans ales and enjoyable freshly made food (all day Fri, Sat, until 5pm Sun); children welcome, sunny back garden, open all day. *(Colin and Daniel Gibbs)*

COWBRIDGE SS9974

★**Bear** (01446) 774814
High Street, with car park behind off North Street; signed off A48; CF71 7AF Busy Georgian coaching house in smart village; well kept ales, decent house wines and enjoyable food from sandwiches/wraps up, lunchtime weekday set menu, friendly helpful service; three attractively furnished bars with flagstones, bare boards or carpet, some stripped stone and panelling, big hot open fires, barrel-vaulted cellar restaurant; children and dogs (in one bar) welcome, courtyard tables, comfortable quiet bedrooms, disabled parking, open all day. *(Joe and Belinda Smart)*

GWAELOD-Y-GARTH ST1183

Gwaelod y Garth Inn
(029) 2081 0408 *Main Road; CF15 9HH* Meaning 'foot of the mountain', this stone-built village pub has wonderful valley views and is popular with walkers on the Taff Ely Ridgeway Path; highly thought-of well presented food (all day Fri and Sat, not Sun evening), friendly efficient service, own-brew beer along with Wye Valley and guests from pine-clad bar, log fires, upstairs restaurant (disabled access from back car park); some live music Fri and Sat; table skittles, pool, juke box; children and dogs welcome, three bedrooms, open all day. *(Derek Stafford)*

KENFIG SS8081

Prince of Wales (01656) 740356
2.2 miles from M4 junction 37; A4229 towards Porthcawl, then right when dual carriageway narrows on bend, signed 'Maudlam, Kenfig'; CF33 4PR Ancient local with plenty of individuality by historic sand dunes; well kept ales including Bass, decent wines and good choice of malts, generous straightforward food served by friendly staff; chatty panelled room off main bar, log fires, stripped stone and lots of wreck pictures, restaurant and upstairs overspill room; TV for rugby; children allowed till 9pm, dogs in bar, handy for nature reserve (June orchids), open all day (from 4pm Mon), no food Sun evening, Mon. *(Gareth Owen)*

LLANBLETHIAN SS9873

Cross (01446) 772995
Church Road; CF71 7JF Welcoming former staging inn; enjoyable freshly made food from pubby choices up in bar or airy split-level restaurant, reasonable prices and various deals, well kept Wye Valley and guests, good choice of wines, woodburner and open fire; children welcome, dogs in bar, tables out on decking, open till 7pm Sun, shut Mon lunchtime, otherwise open all day. *(Sally Harrison)*

LLANCARFAN ST0570

Fox & Hounds (01446) 781287
Signed off A4226; can also be reached from A48 from Bonvilston or B4265 via Llancadle; CF62 3AD Comfortably modernised village pub with snug bar; good interesting food, local ales and nice choice of wines; tables on covered terrace (dogs allowed here), charming streamside setting by interesting church, comfortable bedrooms,

good breakfast, open all day (from 3pm Mon and Tues). *(Frances Parsons)*

MONKNASH SS9170

★**Plough & Harrow** (01656) 890209
Signposted 'Marcross, Broughton' off B4265 St Brides Major–Llantwit Major – turn left at end of Water Street; OS Sheet 170 map reference 920706; CF71 7QQ New people due to take over this previous Main Entry pub as we went to press – reports please; has had a fine range of real ales (some tapped from the cask), also local ciders and quite a few gins/whiskies, food has been fair value; the main bar with its massively thick stone walls used to be the scriptures room and mortuary (this was once part of a monastic grange and dates back nine centuries), heavily beamed ceiling with ancient ham hooks, broad flagstones and log fire in cavernous fireplace with huge bread oven, intriguing arched doorway at the back; picnic-sets in front garden, can walk from the pub through wooded Cwm Nash valley to spectacular coastline, has opened all day. *(Sandra King, Audrey and Paul Summers)*

MUMBLES SS6287

Pilot 07897 895511
Mumbles Road; SA3 4EL Friendly 19th-c seafront local with half a dozen well kept ales including some from own back microbrewery, slate-floored bar with boat suspended from planked ceiling, woodburning stove, no food; TV, free wi-fi; dogs welcome, open all day. *(Alison and Michael Harper)*

OLDWALLS SS4891

Greyhound (01792) 391027
W of Llanrhidian; SA3 1HA 19th-c pub with spacious beamed and dark-panelled carpeted lounge bar, well kept ales including own Gower brews (brewed at sister pub), decent wine and coffee, wide choice of popular food from sandwiches, baguettes and wraps up, friendly staff, hot coal fires, back dining room and upstairs overspill/ function room; children and dogs welcome, picnic-sets in big garden with terrace, play area and good views, open all day. *(Colin and Daniel Gibbs)*

PENARTH ST1771

Pilot (029) 2071 0615
Queens Road; CF64 1DJ End-of-terrace pub set high in residential area overlooking Cardiff Bay; good food including pub favourites from changing blackboard menu, four well kept ales, friendly welcoming staff; regular live music, cocktail evenings and summer beer/cider festival; children and dogs allowed, tables out in narrow front area, open (and food) all day. *(Edward Nile)*

PENDERYN SN9408

Red Lion (01685) 811914
Off A4059 at Lamb, then up Church Road (narrow hill from T junction); CF44 9JR Friendly old stone-built pub (former drovers' inn) set high in good walking country; dark beams, flagstones and blazing log fires, antique settles and interesting bits and pieces including some military memorabilia, good range of real ales and ciders tapped from the cask, also whiskies and other spirits from local Penderyn distillery, highly regarded imaginative food (not Mon lunchtime, best to book); children and dogs (in bar) welcome, great views from big garden, open all day weekends, closed Mon lunchtime. *(David Evans)*

PENTYRCH ST1081

★**Kings Arms** (029) 2089 0202
Church Road; CF15 9QF Up for sale as we went to press, this 16th-c longhouse has become well known for its top class food, but is also popular with regulars dropping in for a drink and a chat; the cosy bar has a log fire in sizeable brick fireplace and mix of seats on flagstones, Brains ales along with a guest beer and 14 wines by the glass, there's also a comfortable lounge and restaurant; children and dogs (in bar) welcome, plenty of seats on terrace, picnic-sets under parasols in the garden, open all day (till 8pm Sun). *(Sally and David Champion)*

REYNOLDSTON SS4889

King Arthur (01792) 390775
Higher Green, off A4118; SA3 1AD Cheerful pub-hotel with timbered main bar, country-style restaurant and nautically themed family dining area (games room with pool in winter); good fairly priced food from sandwiches and pub favourites up, Felinfoel and guests kept well, log fires and country house bric-a-brac, buoyant local atmosphere in the evening; background music; tables out on green, play area, bedrooms and self-catering cottage, open (and bar food) all day. *(Christian Mole)*

ST HILARY ST0173

Bush (01446) 776888
Off A48 E of Cowbridge; CF71 7DP Cosily restored 16th-c thatched and beamed pub; flagstoned main bar with inglenook, bare-boards lounge and snug, nice mix of old furniture, Greene King, Hancocks and guests, Weston's cider and good wines by the glass, enjoyable food including home-made pies and wellingtons, gluten-free diets catered for, friendly service, restaurant; children and dogs (in bar) welcome, some picnic tables out at front, garden behind, open all day Fri-Sun. *(Margo and Derek Peters)*

SWANSEA SS6492

Brunswick (01792) 465676
Duke Street; SA1 4HS Large rambling local with traditional pubby furnishings, lots of knick-knacks and local artwork for sale, good value popular weekday food till

7.30pm (also Sun lunch), half a dozen well kept ales tapped from the cask, friendly helpful service, regular live music, quiz night Mon; no dogs, open all day.
(Kevin Simms)

TAFFS WELL ST1283

Fagins (029) 2081 1800
Cardiff Road, Glan-y-Llyn; CF15 7QD
Terrace-row pub with interesting range of cask-tapped ales, friendly olde-worlde atmosphere, benches, pine tables and other pubby furniture on flagstones, faux black beams, woodburner, good value straightforward food (not Sun evening, Mon) from lunchtime baguettes up, restaurant; live music, sports TV; children and dogs welcome, open all day Sun (from 3pm Mon, 2pm Tues-Sat).
(Jan and Sally Jones)

THREE CROSSES SS5694

Poundffald Inn (01792) 931061
Tirmynydd Road, NW end; SA4 3PB
Refurbished 17th-c beamed and timbered pub; farmhouse, mate's and attractively upholstered chairs around wooden tables on patterned carpet, woodburner, changing real ales and enjoyable pubby food including deals, sports TV in separate bar; dogs welcome, picnic-sets under parasols on side terrace, open (and food) all day, apart from Sun when kitchen closes at 6pm. *(Chris Stevenson)*

GWENT

ABERGAVENNY SO2914

Angel (01873) 857121
Cross Street, by town hall; NP7 5EN Comfortable late Georgian coaching inn; good local atmosphere in two-level bar, rugs on flagstones, big sofas, armchairs and settles, some lovely bevelled glass behind counter serving real ales such as Wye Valley, proper cider and good choice of wines and malt whiskies, well liked food, friendly helpful staff, attractive lounge (popular afternoon tea) and smart dining room; free wi-fi; children and dogs (in bar) welcome, pretty candlelit courtyard, 35 bedrooms (some in other buildings), open all day. *(Donald Allsopp)*

ABERGAVENNY SO3111

★**Hardwick** (01873) 854220
Hardwick; B4598 SE, off A40 at A465/A4042 exit – coming from E on A40, go right round the exit system, as B4598 is final road out; NP7 9AA Restaurant-with-rooms and you'll need to book for owner-chef's highly rated imaginative food; drinkers welcome in simple bar with spindleback chairs around pub tables, stripped brickwork by fireplace and small corner counter serving Rhymney and Wye Valley, local perry and a dozen wines by the glass, two dining rooms, one with beams, bare boards and huge fireplace, the other in lighter carpeted extension, friendly service; background music; no under-8s in restaurant after 8pm, teak tables and chairs under umbrellas by car park, neat garden, bedrooms, open all day. *(Daisy and Jonathan Spicer)*

CAERLEON ST3490

Bell (01633) 420613
Bulmore Road; off M4 junction 24 via B4237 and B4236; NP18 1QQ Old stone coaching inn with good variety of enjoyable food including vegetarian choices and daily specials (some dishes served on boards or slates), three well kept changing ales and ten welsh ciders/perries, friendly helpful staff, linked beamed areas, big open fireplace; children and dogs (menu for them) welcome, pretty back terrace, open all day Fri and Sat, closed Mon and Tues lunchtime (all day Tues in winter). *(M G Hart)*

CHEPSTOW ST5394

Three Tuns (01291) 645797
Bridge Street; NP16 5EY Early 17th-c and a pub for much of that time; bare-boards interior with painted farmhouse pine furniture, a couple of mismatched sofas by woodburner, dresser with china plates, five local ales and ciders from nice wooden counter at unusual angle, very reasonably priced home-made lunchtime only bar food including speciality pies, friendly staff; background and regular live music, quiz nights; dogs welcome, wheelchair access, four bedrooms (one suitable for disabled customers), open all day. *(Tom and Ruth Rees)*

GROSMONT SO4024

Angel (01981) 240646
Corner of B4347 and Poorscript Lane; NP7 8EP Small welcoming 17th-c local; rustic interior with simple wooden furniture, Wye Valley Butty Bach, a couple of guests and local cider (regular summer beer/cider festivals), reasonably priced traditional food (not Mon), pool room with darts; TV for rugby, no lavatories – public ones close by; dogs welcome, seats out by ancient market cross on attractive steep street in sight of castle, back garden with boules, good local walks, open all day Sat, closed Sun evening, Tues and weekday lunchtimes.
(Gareth Evans)

LLANDENNY SO4103

★**Raglan Arms** (01291) 690800
Centre of village; NP15 1DL Well run dining pub with relaxed informal atmosphere; interesting freshly cooked food, Wye Valley Butty Bach and good selection of wines, friendly welcoming young staff, big pine tables and a couple of leather sofas in linked dining rooms leading to conservatory, log fire in flagstoned bar's handsome stone fireplace; children welcome, garden tables, closed Sun and Tues evenings, all day Mon.
(Sheila and Sam Thorpe)

LLANGATTOCK LINGOED SO3620

Hunters Moon (01873) 821499

Off B4521 just E of Llanvetherine; NP7 8RR Attractive tucked-away pub dating from the 13th c; beams, dark stripped stone and flagstones, woodburner, friendly licensees and locals, welsh ales tapped from the cask and enjoyable straightforward food, separate dining room; children and dogs welcome, tables out on deck and in charming dell with waterfall, glorious country on Offa's Dyke Path, four comfortable bedrooms, open (and food) all day. *(Alison and Michael Harper)*

LLANGYBI ST3797

White Hart (01633) 450258

On main road; NP15 1NP Friendly village dining pub in delightful 12th-c monastery building (part of Jane Seymour's dowry); pubby bar with roaring log fire, steps up to pleasant light restaurant, enjoyable food including daily specials and two-course weekday lunch deal, well kept mainly welsh ales and good choice of wines by the glass; children welcome, closed Sun evening and Mon, otherwise open all day (best to check winter hours). *(Lenny and Ruth Walters)*

LLANISHEN SO4703

Carpenters Arms (01600) 860812

B4293 north of Chepstow; NP16 6QH Old cottagey family-run pub with good food including blackboard specials, well kept changing and friendly welcoming staff, comfortable bar/lounge, coal fire, back games room with pool; flagstoned terrace and little side lawn up steps, self-catering cottage, closed Mon and lunchtimes Tues and Weds, no food Sun evening. *(Bob and Margaret Holder)*

LLANOVER SO2907

★Goose & Cuckoo (01873) 880277

Upper Llanover signed up track off A4042 S of Abergavenny; after 0.5 miles take first left; NP7 9ER Remote pub looking over picturesque valley just inside Brecon Beacons National Park; essentially one little rustically furnished room with woodburner in arched stone fireplace, small picture-window extension making most of the view, three well kept ales, 50 whiskies and generous helpings of simple tasty home-cooked food; live music, board games, cribbage and darts; children and dogs welcome, picnic-sets out on gravel below, bedrooms and self-catering, closed Mon, open all day Fri-Sun. *(Kevin Simms)*

LLANTHONY SO2827

★Priory Hotel (01873) 890487

Aka Abbey Hotel, Llanthony Priory; off A465, back road Llanvihangel Crucorney–Hay; NP7 7NN Magical setting for plain bar in dimly lit vaulted crypt of graceful ruined Norman abbey, lovely in summer with lawns around and the peaceful border hills beyond; well kept Felinfoel Double Dragon and a couple of summer guests, enjoyable good value food (more restauranty in the evening), efficient service; children welcome but not in hotel part (seven non-ensuite bedrooms in restored abbey walls), no dogs, open all day weekends Apr-Oct (all day July, Aug), closed in winter apart from Fri evening, Sat and lunchtime Sun. *(Ian Herdman, Mrs J Ekins-Daukes)*

LLANTRISANT FAWR ST3997

Greyhound (01291) 672505

Off A449 near Usk; NP15 1LE Prettily set 18th-c country inn with relaxed homely feel in three linked beamed rooms (steps between two), nice mix of furnishings and rustic decorations, enjoyable home cooking at sensible prices, efficient service, two or more well kept ales, decent wines by the glass, log fires, pleasant panelled dining room; muddy boots and dogs welcome in one bar, disabled access, attractive garden with big fountain, hill views, comfortable bedrooms in converted stable block, closed Sun evening, otherwise open all day. *(Matt and Hayley Jacob)*

LLANVIHANGEL CRUCORNEY SO3220

Skirrid (01873) 890258

Signed off A465; NP7 8DH One of Britain's oldest pubs, dating partly from 1110 and a former courthouse – plenty of atmosphere and ghostly tales (landlord is happy to give tours); ancient studded door to high-ceilinged main bar, exposed stone, flagstones and panelling, huge log fire, well kept ales and pubby food, separate dining room; children and dogs welcome, tables on terrace and small sloping back lawn, bedrooms, closed Sun evening, Mon lunchtime. *(Joe and Belinda Smart)*

MAGOR ST4287

Wheatsheaf (01633) 880608

A mile from M4 junction 23; Newport Road off B4245; NP26 3HN Welcoming white-painted pub with black beams and some exposed stonework, pubby furniture on wood, flagstone or quarry-tiled floors, woodburner in big fireplace, ales such as Rhymney and Sharps, decent wines and 20 gins, well priced food from bar snacks to full meals, good service, carpeted restaurant, pool and darts in tap room; live music, quiz nights; children and dogs welcome, wheelchair access (ramp for restaurant), open all day. *(Chris and Angela Buckell)*

MAMHILAD SO3004

Horseshoe (01873) 880542

Old Abergavenny Road; NP4 8QZ Old beamed country pub with slate-floor bar; traditional pubby furniture and a couple of unusual posts acting as elbow tables, original Hancocks pub sign, ornate woodburner in stone fireplace, local ale and Blaengawney cider, tasty fairly priced food from lunchtime baguettes up; children welcome, dogs away from dining area, lovely views particularly from tables by car park over road, open all day Fri-Sun. *(Joe and Belinda Smart)*

NEWPORT ST3188

Olde Murenger House (01633) 263977 *High Street; NP20 1GA* Fine 16th-c black and white timbered building; carefully restored split-level interior with ancient dark woodwork, panelled walls and leaded windows, traditional furniture including settles on bare boards or carpet, well kept/priced Sam Smiths ales and enjoyable straightforward home-made food; open all day. *(Donald Allsopp)*

PANDY SO3322

Old Pandy (01873) 890208 *A465 Abergavenny–Hereford; NP7 8DR* Welcoming 17th-c beamed roadside pub on edge of the Black Mountain and popular with walkers; good reasonably priced food from fairly traditional menu, well kept ales including Wye Valley, friendly service; pool and darts; children and dogs welcome, adjacent walkers' bunkhouse, closed Mon lunchtime, open (and food) all day Fri-Sun. *(Phil and Jane Hodson)*

PENALLT SO5209

Inn at Penallt (01600) 772765 *Village signed off B4293; at crossroads in village turn left; NP25 4SE* Welcoming 17th-c country inn with enjoyable freshly made food including Thurs wood-fired pizzas, welsh ales, ciders and gins, courteous efficient service, roaring woodburner in airy slate-floored bar, restaurant and small back conservatory (appealing Forest of Dean views); children and dogs welcome, big garden with terrace and play area, comfortable clean bedrooms, closed Mon, Tues. *(Frances Parsons)*

RAGLAN SO4107

Beaufort Arms (01291) 690412 *High Street; NP15 2DY* Pub-hotel (former 16th-c coaching inn) with two character beamed bars, one with big stone fireplace and comfortable seats on slate floor, well kept local ales, carefully sourced food (all starters and mains gluten-free) including good fish/seafood, light airy brasserie, friendly attentive service; background music, open mike night first Tues of month; children and dogs (in bar) welcome, terrace tables, 16 bedrooms, open all day from 7am. *(Stan Jeffries)*

REDBROOK SO5309

★**Boat** (01600) 712615 *Car park signed on A466 Chepstow–Monmouth, then 30-metre footbridge over Wye; or very narrow steep car access from Penallt in Wales; NP25 4AJ* Beautifully set riverside pub with well kept Wye Valley and guests tapped from the cask, lots of ciders, perries and country wines too, enjoyable fair value food (not Sun or Mon evenings) from baguettes and baked potatoes up, helpful staff, unchanging interior with stripped-stone walls, flagstones and woodburner; live bands Thurs evening; children and dogs welcome, home-built rustic seats in informal tiered suntrap garden with stream spilling down into duck pond, open all day (in winter closed Tues, and from 9pm Sun, Mon); for sale as we went press, so may be changes. *(Daisy and Jonathan Spicer)*

SKENFRITH SO4520

★**Bell** (01600) 750235 *Just off B4521, NE of Abergavenny and N of Monmouth; NP7 8UH* Elegant 17th-c coaching inn handy for nearby ruins of Skenfrith Castle (NT); main bar with inglenook fireplace and plenty of seating including comfortable sofas, bleached-oak counter serving ales such as Bespoke Wickwar and Wye Valley, bottled local cider/perry, 15 wines by the glass and good range of spirits, imaginative modern food using some home-grown produce, friendly helpful staff, restaurant; background music, free wi-fi; children and dogs (in one bar) welcome, disabled access, terrace with good solid tables under parasols, steps up to sloping lawn, orchard area and neat kitchen garden, comfortable well equipped bedrooms named after fishing flies, open all day (closed one week in both Jan and Nov). *(Gerry and Pam Pollard, Jennifer and Nicholas Thompson, Mrs J Ekins-Daukes)*

TALYCOED SO4115

Warwicks (01600) 780227 *B4233 Monmouth–Abergavenny; though its postal address is Llantilio Crossenny, the inn is actually in Talycoed, a mile or two E; NP7 8TL* Pretty 17th-c wisteria-clad pub under enthusiastic welcoming management; softly lit beamed bar with friendly locals, good log fire in stone fireplace, settles and mix of other old furniture, horsebrasses and assorted memorabilia, well kept ales such as Hancocks, good quality food cooked by landlady including daily specials, cosy little dining room; children welcome, dogs in bar, seats on front terrace and in neat garden, lovely countryside and surrounding walks, open all day Sun, closed Mon, Tues and lunchtime Weds. *(Derek Stafford)*

TRELLECK SO5005

Lion (01600) 860322 *B4293 6 miles S of Monmouth; NP25 4PA* Open-plan bar with one or two low black beams, nice mix of old furniture and two log fires, ales such as Wye Valley, wide range of fair-priced food including takeaway pizzas; background music, traditional games; children and dogs welcome, tables out on grass and side courtyard overlooking church, self-catering cottage, open (and food) all day, kitchen closes 6pm Sun. *(Gareth Evans)*

TRELLECK GRANGE SO5001

Fountain (01291) 689303

Minor road Tintern–Llanishen, SE of village; NP16 6QW Traditional 17th-c country pub under friendly family management; enjoyable local food from pub favourites to game specials, some themed nights, well kept welsh ales, farm cider/perry, roomy low-beamed flagstoned bar with log fire; dogs welcome, small walled garden, peaceful spot on small winding road, comfortable bedrooms (no children), camping, open all day weekends, closed Mon and lunchtimes Tues-Fri. *(Sheila and Sam Thorpe)*

USK SO3700

Kings Head (01291) 672963

Old Market Street; NP15 1AL Popular 16th-c family-run inn, chatty and relaxed, with generously served traditional food and well kept beers, friendly efficient staff, huge log fire in superb fireplace; sports TV; nine bedrooms, open all day. *(Alison and Michael Harper)*

GWYNEDD

ABERDARON SH1726

Ty Newydd Hotel (01758) 760207

B4413, by the sea; LL53 8BE Hotel right by sea with lovely views over Cardigan Bay; good choice of enjoyable food from bar snacks to Sun carvery, four real ales, friendly helpful staff; panoramic terrace within feet of the waves, 11 bedrooms, traditional welsh breakfast, open all day. *(Steve Parry, Dave Braisted)*

ABERDOVEY SN6196

★**Penhelig Arms** (01654) 767215

Opposite Penhelig station; LL35 0LT Fine harbourside location for this popular 18th-c hotel; traditional bar with warm fire in central stone fireplace, some panelling, Brains ales and a guest, good choice of wines and malt whiskies, enjoyable food including home-made pizzas and afternoon tea; children welcome, dogs allowed in bar and comfortable bedrooms (some have balconies overlooking estuary, ones nearest to the road can be noisy), open (and food) all day. *(Simon Sharpe)*

BETWS-Y-COED SH7955

★**Ty Gwyn** (01690) 710383

A5 just S of bridge to village; LL24 0SG Family-run restaurant-with-rooms rather than pub (you must eat or stay overnight to be served drinks), but pubby feel in character beamed lounge bar with ancient cooking range, easy chairs, antiques, old prints and bric-a-brac, highly regarded interesting food using local produce including own fruit and vegetables, some themed nights, well kept ales, friendly professional service; background music; children welcome, comfortable bedrooms and holiday cottage, closed Christmas and ten days in Jan. *(Lenny and Ruth Walters)*

BLAENAU FFESTINIOG SH7041

Pengwern Arms (01766) 762200

Church Square, Ffestiniog; LL41 4PB Unpretentious community-owned pub on village square; well kept/priced ales in panelled bar, dining area serving good value food (not Sun evening), friendly local atmosphere; games room, live music; dogs welcome, fine views from back garden, eight bedrooms, open all day weekends, from 6pm Mon-Thurs, 5pm Fri. *(Colin and Daniel Gibbs)*

CAERNARFON SH4762

Bar Bach (01286) 673111

Greengate Street, near the castle; LL55 2NF Tiny bar opposite Caernarfon Castle; simple furnishings, exposed stonework and small fire, three changing local beers, decent lunchtime food, friendly staff and regulars; sports TV; dogs welcome, open all day till 1.30am. *(Peter Meister)*

CAERNARFON SH4762

★**Black Boy** (01286) 673604

Northgate Street; LL55 1RW Busy traditional 16th-c inn with cosy beamed lounge bar, sumptuously furnished and packed with tables, additional dining room across corridor and dimly lit atmospheric public bar, up to four well kept ales, several wines by the glass and good generous food from sandwiches up (try the traditional 'lobsgows' stew), lunchtime set deal, good friendly service and lots of welsh chat; background music can be loud, TV, free wi-fi; disabled access (ramps) and loos, a few pavement tables, 16 bedrooms (ten in separate townhouse), open (and food) all day. *(Peter Meister)*

CAPEL CURIG SH7257

Bryn Tyrch (01690) 720223

A5 E; LL24 0EL Family-owned roadside inn perfectly placed for mountains of Snowdonia; bistro-bar with open fire and amazing picture-windows views, Conwy Welsh Pride and a guest, quite a few malt whiskies, comprehensive choice of good well presented food (not Mon lunchtime), second bar with big menu boards, leather sofas and mix of tables on bare boards; free wi-fi; children, walkers and dogs welcome, steep little side garden, more seats on terrace and across road by stream, 11 bedrooms including two bunk rooms, open all day in summer. *(Stuart Doughty)*

CAPEL CURIG SH7357

Tyn y Coed (01690) 720331
A5 SE of village; LL24 0EE Bustling community inn across from River Llugwy with good surrounding walks; enjoyable home-made food using local produce, well kept Purple Moose and two guests, pleasant quick service, beams and log fires, pool room; children and dogs welcome, small garden either side, renovated stagecoach over the road, comfortable bedrooms, cycle storage and drying room, open all day Fri-Sun, from 3pm other days. *(Jan and Sally Jones)*

CONWY SH7777

Albion (01492) 582484
Uppergate Street; LL32 8RF Interesting sensitively restored 1920s pub under collective ownership of four welsh brewers – Conwy, Great Orme, Nant and Purple Moose, their beers and guests kept well (tasting trays available), friendly staff, some snacky food including pies, three linked rooms with plenty of well preserved features including stained glass and huge baronial fireplace, back part with serving hatch is quieter; dogs welcome, open all day. *(Stuart Doughty)*

LLANDUDNO SH7882

Cottage Loaf (01492) 870762
Market Street; LL30 2SR Popular former bakery with three linked rooms; dark beams and timbers, rugs on pale flagstones or bare boards, good mix of tables, benches, cushioned settles and dining chairs, woodburners, decent home-made food from sandwiches up, well kept ales (often from local microbreweries), friendly service, big garden room extension; teak furniture on front and back terraces, children welcome, open (and food) all day. *(Simon Collett-Jones, David H Bennett)*

LLANFAETHLU SH3286

Black Lion (01407) 730718
A5025; LL65 4NL Renovated 18th-c inn with simple elegant décor, cosy bar with wooden tables and chairs on black slates, woodburner, oak-topped counter serving beers such as Bragdy Lleu, Purple Moose and Timothy Taylors, seven wines by the glass, welsh whisky and gin, high-raftered dining room with another woodburner, enjoyable food using Anglesey produce including meat from own farm; children and dogs (in bar) welcome, terrace with lovely views to Snowdonia, two spacious bedrooms, open all day weekends (no Sun evening food), closed Mon, Tues and lunchtime Weds, check website for opening hours outside school holidays. *(Brian and Anna Marsden)*

LLANUWCHLLYN SH8730

Eagles (01678) 540278
Aka Eryrod; A494/B4403; LL23 7UB Family-run and welcoming with good reasonably priced food using own farm produce, ales such as Purple Moose, opened-up slate-floor bar with log fire, beams and stripped stone, back picture-window view of mountains with Lake Bala in the distance; small general stores open from 7.30am; sports TV; children welcome, metal tables and chairs on flower-filled back terrace, caravan and camping park, open all day. *(Mike and Wena Stevenson)*

MAENTWROG SH6640

Grapes (01766) 590365
A496; village signed from A470; LL41 4HN Handsome 17th-c village inn; three bars and good-sized conservatory with views of steam trains on Ffestiniog Railway, enjoyable reasonably priced pubby food, ales such as Purple Moose, friendly helpful staff; children welcome, dogs in bar, seats on pleasant terrace, simply furnished clean bedrooms, open all day. *(Frances Parsons)*

PENMAENPOOL SH6918

George III (01341) 422525
Just off A493, near Dolgellau; LL40 1YD Attractive inn dating from 1650, lovely views over Mawddach estuary from partly panelled upstairs bar opening into cosy inglenook lounge, more basic beamed and flagstoned downstairs bar, three well kept ales and decent food including Sun carvery, restaurant; children and dogs welcome, sheltered terrace, 11 bedrooms (some in converted station – line now a walkway), open all day. *(John Evans)*

PORTH DINLLAEN SH2741

★**Ty Coch** (01758) 720498
Beach car park signed from Morfa Nefyn, then 15-minute walk; LL53 6DB Popular former 19th-c vicarage in idyllic location right on the beach with wonderful views, far from roads and only reached on foot; bar crammed with nautical paraphernalia, pewter, old miners' and railway lamps and other memorabilia, simple furnishings, coal fire, up to three real ales including Purple Moose and a craft beer (served in plastic as worried about glass on beach), simple lunchtime bar menu, friendly service; children and dogs welcome, open all day in season and school holidays (till 5pm Sun), in winter open all day Fri and Sat, 11-5pm Sun-Thurs. *(Peter Meister)*

PORTHMADOG SH5639

Australia (01766) 515957
High Street; LL49 9LR Purple Moose brewery tap with their well kept ales and guests, decent wines by the glass and tasty pub food, chunky contemporary wooden furniture, beer barrel tables and banquettes on bare boards; occasional quiz and live music nights; children welcome, seats outside, open all day. *(Mike and Eleanor Anderson)*

PWLLHELI SH3735

Whitehall (01758) 614091
Gaol Street; LL53 5RG Family-run pub-bistro in centre of this market town; local ales such as Llŷn and good choice of wines, popular freshly made food from lunchtime ciabattas up, friendly staff, spiral stairs to upstairs dining room; TV in bar; children welcome, open all day (till late Fri, Sat). *(Hefina Pritchard, Andrea Watts)*

RHYD DDU SH5652

Cwellyn Arms (01766) 890321
A4085 N of Beddgelert; LL54 6TL Simple and welcoming 18th-c village pub (same owners for over 30 years) not far below Welsh Highland Railway top terminus; up to nine real ales and good choice of popular seasonal food from home-baked rolls to blackboard specials, friendly helpful staff, two cosy bars with log fires and restaurant with woodburner; children, walkers and dogs welcome, spectacular Snowdon views from garden tables, babbling stream just over wall, campsite, bedrooms and bunkhouses, open all day. *(Mike and Eleanor Anderson, Adrian Johnson)*

TREFRIW SH7863

Old Ship (01492) 640013
B5106; LL27 0JH Well run old pub with nice staff and cheerful local atmosphere; much enjoyed home-made food from daily changing blackboard menu, Marstons-related beers and a local guest kept in top condition, good range of wines/malt whiskies and new gin corner with collection of 50, log fire and inglenook woodburner; picnic-sets outside by stream, children welcome, open (and food) all day weekends, closed Mon except bank holidays. *(Mike and Wena Stevenson, Martin Cawley)*

TREMADOG SH5640

Union (01766) 512748
Market Square; LL49 9RB Traditional early 19th-c stone-built pub in terrace overlooking square, cosy and comfortable, with quiet panelled lounge and carpeted public bar with exposed stone walls and woodburner, well kept ales such as Great Orme and Purple Moose, enjoyable pubby food including range of burgers, friendly staff, back restaurant; darts and TV; children and dogs welcome, paved terrace behind, closed weekday lunchtimes. *(Sally Harrison)*

TUDWEILIOG SH2336

Lion (01758) 659724
Nefyn Road (B4417), Llŷn Peninsula; LL53 8ND Cheerful village inn with traditional furnishings in lounge bar and two dining rooms (one for families, other with woodburner), enjoyable sensibly priced home-made food, changing real ales, dozens of malt whiskies and decent wines, quick friendly service; pool and board games in public bar; children and dogs welcome, pleasant front garden, bedrooms, open all day in season. *(Lenny and Ruth Walters)*

POWYS

BEGUILDY SO1979

Radnorshire Arms (01547) 510634
B4355 Knighton–Newtown; LD7 1YE 17th-c black and white beamed country pub with enjoyable good value food (not Sun evening), Ludlow, Stonehouse and a beer badged for them, friendly helpful service inglenook woodburner; pool; no dogs inside, beer garden, closed Mon. *(Colin and Daniel Gibbs)*

CILMERY SO0051

Prince Llewelyn (01982) 552694
A483; LD2 3NU Country pub under friendly newish licensees; plush dining chairs and button-back banquettes in dining room, woodburner in carpeted bar, a couple of real ales and enjoyable food using local produce; children and dogs welcome, lovely surrounding walks, closed Sun evening, Mon and till 6pm Tues, Wed. *(John and Delia Franks)*

CRICKHOWELL SO2118

Dragon (01873) 810362
High Street; NP8 1BE Welcoming old family-owned inn, more hotel-restaurant than pub, but with neat small bar serving Rhymney, stone and wood floors, sofas and armchairs by open fire, enjoyable traditional food including welsh choices in tidy dining room, steak night Thurs, good friendly service; 15 bedrooms; open (and food) all day. *(Gareth Owen)*

CRICKHOWELL SO1919

★**Nantyffin Cider Mill**
(01873) 810775 *A40/A479 NW; NP8 1SG* Former 16th-c drovers' inn facing River Usk in lovely Black Mountains countryside – charming views from tables on lawn; bar with solid furniture on tiles or carpet, woodburner in broad fireplace, well kept ales, proper ciders and several wines by the glass, open-plan main area with beams, standing timbers and open fire in grey stonework wall, striking high-raftered restaurant with old cider press, good home-made food from sandwiches to grills, packed lunches also available (must book); background music; children and dogs (in bar) welcome, play area in garden, handy for Tretower Court and Castle, closed Mon and Tues, open all day Thurs-Sun. *(Roger and Anne Mallard)*

DERWENLAS SN7299

★**Black Lion** (01654) 703913
A487 just S of Machynlleth; SY20 8TN Cosy 16th-c country pub with extensive range of good well priced food including children's menu and daily specials, friendly

staff coping well at busy times, Wye Valley Butty Bach and a guest, decent wines, heavy black beams and timbering, thick walls, carpet over big slate flagstones, good log fire; background music; garden behind with play area and steps up into woods, limited parking, bedrooms, closed Mon. *(Stan Jeffries)*

DINAS MAWDDWY SH8514

Red Lion (01650) 531247

Dyfi Road; off A470 (N of A458 junction); SY20 9JA Two small traditional front bars and more modern back extension, changing ales and decent food including popular pies and Sunday carvery, friendly efficient service, open fire, beams and lots of brassware; children welcome, simple bedrooms (four ensuite), pub named in welsh (Llew Coch). *(Kevin Simms)*

FELINFACH SO0933

Plough & Harrow (01874) 622709

Village and pub signed from A470, 4 miles N of Brecon; LD3 0UB Small village pub under welcoming long-serving licensees; simple bar, comfortable lounge area with woodburner and dining room, well kept Sharps Doom Bar and a guest, good reasonably priced home-made food; three bedrooms, open evenings only from 6pm (7pm Sun). *(Barry Collett)*

GLADESTRY SO2355

Royal Oak (01544) 370669

B4594; HR5 3NR Friendly old-fashioned village pub on Offa's Dyke Path; simple stripped-stone slate-floored walkers' bar, beams hung with tankards and lanterns, carpeted lounge, open fires, ales such as Wye Valley Butty Bach, uncomplicated home-made food from sandwiches up; may not accept credit cards; children welcome, dogs in bar, sheltered sunny back garden, four bedrooms, camping, closed Sun evening, Mon, Tues and lunchtimes Weds-Fri. *(Millie and Peter Dowling)*

GLASBURY SO1839

Harp (01497) 847373

B4350 towards Hay, just N of A438; HR3 5NR Welcoming homely old place with good value pubby food (not Mon) cooked by landlady including proper pies, curries and takeaway pizzas, well kept local ales, log-fire lounge with eating areas, black beamed bar, picture windows over wooded garden sloping to River Wye; live folk music and quiz nights, darts; more river views from picnic-sets on terrace and back bedrooms, good breakfast. *(Millie and Peter Dowling)*

HAY-ON-WYE SO2242

Blue Boar (01497) 820884

Castle Street/Oxford Road; HR3 5DF Old ivy-clad pub with character bar: cosy corners, dark panelling, pews and country chairs, open fire in Edwardian fireplace, four well kept ales including Brains Rev James and Timothy Taylors Landlord, organic bottled cider and several wines by the glass, decent food in long café/dining room with another open fire, friendly service; background music; children and dogs welcome, tables under parasols in beer garden, open all day from 9am for breakfast. *(Lionel Jenkinson)*

HAY-ON-WYE SO2342

Old Black Lion (01497) 820841

Lion Street; HR3 5AD 17th-c inn with comfortable low-beamed bar, original fireplace and old pine tables, good british/italian food using local organic produce, Wye Valley Butty Bach and Evan Evans, friendly helpful service; live jazz Fri evening; children and dogs (in one area) welcome, sheltered back terrace, character bedrooms (some above bar) with modern bathrooms, good breakfast, open all day. *(Rachel Hadley)*

KNIGHTON SO2872

Horse & Jockey (01547) 520062

Wylcwm Place; LD7 1AE Popular pub under new management; several cosy areas, one with wood burning stove, enjoyable good value food from traditional choices to daily specials, can eat in bar or adjoining restaurant, cheerful service, well kept beers; children and dogs welcome, tables in pleasant medieval courtyard, eight bedrooms, handy for Offa's Dyke Path, open all day. *(Joe and Belinda Smart)*

LIBANUS SN9926

Tai'r Bull (01874) 622600

A470 SW of Brecon; LD3 8EL Welcoming old roadside village pub under newish management; five well kept ales and enjoyable home-made food from sharing plates up, traditional bar with woodburner in large stone fireplace, airy restaurant; with high-backed leather chairs and white tablecloths; children welcome, great views of Pen-y-Fan from small front terrace, five bedrooms, open all day. *(Matt and Hayley Jacob)*

LLANBEDR SO2320

Red Lion (01873) 810754

Off A40 at Crickhowell; NP8 1SR Quaint old village local run by charming landlady; heavy beams, antique settles in lounge and snug, log fires, well kept ales, front dining area with fair value home-made food; good walking country (porch for muddy boots), open all day weekends, closed Mon and weekday lunchtimes. *(Stan Jeffries)*

LLANFIHANGEL-NANT-MELAN SO1958

Red Lion (01544) 350220

A44 10 miles W of Kington; LD8 2TN Stripped-stone and beamed 16th-c roadside pub; roomy main bar with flagstones and woodburner, carpeted restaurant, front sun porch, tasty reasonably priced food cooked by landlord including reduced helpings for OAPs, well kept changing ales, friendly service, back bar with another woodburner; children and dogs welcome, country views from pleasant garden, five bedrooms (three in annexe), handy for Radnor Forest walks and near impressive waterfall, closed Mon and Tues. *(Jan and Sally Jones)*

LLANGATTOCK SO2117

Horseshoe (01873) 268773
Off B4558; NP8 1PA Busy attractively refurbished old inn; bar with flagstones, exposed stonework and some beams, button-back leather wall banquettes and other traditional furniture, two woodburners, more seating in back pitched-ceiling room with bare boards and pine dresser, Wye Valley Butty Bach, Brains Rev James and a guest, well liked food, friendly helpful service; TV; children and dogs welcome, comfortable bedrooms, open all day, no food Sun evening. *(Gareth Evans)*

LLANGEDWYN SJ1924

Green Inn (01691) 828234
B4396 E of village; SY10 9JW Old country dining pub with various snug alcoves, nooks and crannies, good mix of furnishings including oak settles and leather sofas, woodburner, Brains, Sharps, Stonehouse and a guest, enjoyable well priced pubby food, friendly helpful staff; children and dogs welcome, attractive garden over road running down towards River Tanat, closed Mon lunchtime, otherwise open all day. *(Daisy and Jonathan Spicer)*

LLANGYNIDR SO1519

Coach & Horses (01874) 730245
Cwm Crawnon Road (B4558 W of Crickhowell); NP8 1LS Flower-decked country dining pub; well kept ales and enjoyable generously served food from chef-owner, beams, stripped stone and big log fire, restaurant; children and dogs (in some areas) welcome, picnic-sets and play area across fairly busy road in fenced sloping garden by lock of Monmouthshire & Brecon Canal, four bedrooms, open all day. *(Giles and Annie Francis)*

LLANIDLOES SN9584

Crown & Anchor (01686) 412398
Long Bridge Street; SY18 6EF Friendly largely unspoilt town-centre pub known locally as Ruby's after landlady who ran it for 50 years; well kept Brains Rev James and Wye Valley Bitter, chatty locals' bar, lounge, snug and two other rooms separated by central hallway; pool and games machine; open all day Fri-Sun, closed Mon, Tues and lunchtimes Wed-Thurs. *(Simon Day)*

LLANWRTYD WELLS SN8746

Neuadd Arms (01591) 610236
The Square; LD5 4RB Sizeable 19th-c hotel (friendly and by no means upmarket) brewing its own good value Heart of Wales beers in back stable block (up to ten on at a time), enjoyable straightforward home-made food, log fires in lounge and small tiled public bar still with old service bells, restaurant, games room; well behaved dogs welcome in bars, a few tables out at front, 20 bedrooms (front ones can be noisy), engaging very small town in good walking area, novel events such as bogsnorkelling and man v horse, open all day. *(Max Simons)*

MALLWYD SH8612

Brigands (01650) 511999
A470 by roundabout in village; SY20 9HJ Sizeable 15th-c beamed coaching inn with gently civilised atmosphere; well kept changing ales and enjoyable food from bar snacks up, popular afternoon teas, friendly efficient staff; children and dogs welcome, extensive lawns with lovely views, can arrange fishing on River Dovey, nine bedrooms, open all day. *(Margo and Derek Peters)*

MIDDLETOWN SJ3012

Breidden (01938) 570880
A458 Welshpool–Shrewsbury; SY21 8EL Part pub, part chinese restaurant with locals drinking two local ales and playing pool in one part and customers eating good asian food in the other; helpful, friendly staff, cheerful atmosphere; sports TV; children welcome, decent-sized garden with play area, open all day (closed Mon). *(Gareth Owen)*

PAINSCASTLE SO1646

★**Roast Ox** (01497) 851398
Off A470 Brecon–Builth Wells, or from A438 at Clyro; LD2 3JL Well restored pub with beams, flagstones and stripped-stone walls, appropriate simple furnishings and some rustic bric-a-brac, huge antlers above open fire, ales tapped from the cask and good range of ciders and malt whiskies, popular freshly made food including good fish and chips, friendly quick service; children and dogs welcome, picnic-sets outside, attractive hill country, ten comfortable neat bedrooms. *(Tony Hough)*

'Children welcome' means the pub says it lets children inside without any special restriction. If it allows them in, but to restricted areas such as an eating area or family room, we specify this. Places with separate restaurants often let children use them, and hotels usually let children into public areas such as lounges. Some pubs impose an evening time limit – let us know if you find one earlier than 9pm.

PENCELLI SO0925

Royal Oak (01874) 665396
B4558 SE of Brecon; LD3 7LX
Unpretentious country pub with two small bars; low beams and log fires, assorted furniture on flagstones, well kept Brains Rev James and a couple of guests, enjoyable home-made food including Sun roasts till 6pm, simple modern dining room; children and dogs welcome, terraces backing on to Monmouth & Brecon Canal (nearby moorings), lovely canalside walks and handy for Taff Trail, open all day. *(Giles and Annie Francis, Frank Price)*

PENYCAE SN8313

Ancient Briton (01639) 730273
Brecon Road (A4067); SA9 1YY Friendly opened-up roadside pub; log fire in bar, seven or more well kept ales from far and wide, local cider and enjoyable reasonably priced home-made food; children and dogs welcome, seats outside and play area, four bedrooms, campsite (good facilities including disabled loo and shower), handy for Dan-yr-Ogof caves, Henrhyd Waterfall and Craig-y-Nos Country Park, open all day. *(Margo and Derek Peters)*

RHAYADER SN9668

★**Triangle** (01597) 810537
Cwmdauddwr; B4518 by bridge over River Wye, SW of centre; LD6 5AR
Interesting little 16th-c pub with buoyant local atmosphere; good value home-made pubby food (best to book evenings) from shortish menu, well kept Brains Rev James, Hancocks HB and reasonably priced wines, friendly staff, dining area with nice view over to River Wye; darts; children and dogs (in bar) welcome, picnic-sets on small front terrace, self-catering cottage opposite, parking can be difficult, closed Mon in winter (Mon lunchtime in summer). *(Stan Jeffries)*

A little further afield

CHANNEL ISLANDS

GUERNSEY

FOREST

Deerhound (01481) 238585
Le Bourg; GY8 0AN Spacious roadside dining pub with modern interior; food including summer seafood menu can be good, Liberation ales, friendly service; free wi-fi; children welcome, sunny sheltered terrace with parasols, handy for the airport, open all day. *(Margaret McDonald)*

KING'S MILLS

★ **Fleur du Jardin** (01481) 257996
King's Mills Road; GY5 7JT
Lovely 15th-c country hotel in pretty walled garden; low-beamed bar with log fire, Liberation and guests, local cider and plenty of wines by the glass, very good attractively presented food, afternoon teas, friendly helpful service, restaurant; background music; children and small dogs welcome, plenty of tables on back terrace, solar-heated swimming pool, 15 stylish, contemporary bedrooms, open all day. *(Jeff Davies)*

ST MARTIN

Les Douvres (01481) 238731
La Fosse; GY4 6ER Sister hotel to the Fleur du Jardin at King's Mills; popular beamed bar with country pub feel, three changing ales and plenty of wines by the glass, decent range of enjoyable fairly priced food including burgers and pizzas, friendly helpful staff; live music Fri; garden with swimming pool, 19 elegant bedrooms, good breakfast, open all day. *(Charlie Walker)*

ST PETER PORT

Ship & Crown (01481) 721368
Opposite Crown Pier, Esplanade; GY1 2NB Bustling old town pub with bay windows overlooking harbour; interesting photographs (especially of World War II occupation, also boats and local shipwrecks), decent bar food from sandwiches up, Liberation ales and guests such as Sharps Doom Bar and Fullers London Pride, welcoming prompt service even when busy, more modern-feel Crow's Nest brasserie upstairs with good views; sports TVs in bar; open all day from 10am (midday Sun) till late. *(Richard, Margaret McDonald)*

VALE

Houmet (01481) 242214
Grande Havre; GY6 8JR Modern building overlooking Grande Havre Bay; front restaurant-bar with conservatory, good choice of reasonably priced popular food (best to book) including fresh fish and seafood, friendly service, a couple of real ales and several wines by the glass, back public bar with pool, darts and big-screen sports TV (dogs allowed here); quiz nights; children welcome, tables out on sheltered deck, open all day (not Sun evening). *(Margaret McDonald)*

JERSEY

ST AUBIN

Boat House (01534) 747141
North Quay; JE3 8BS Modern steel and timber-clad quayside building with great views (window tables for diners); bar serving well kept local ales and several wines by the glass, good food ranging from tapas to Josper grills, efficient young staff, airy upstairs restaurant (evenings, weekends, closed Mon); balcony and decked terrace overlooking harbour, open all day, breakfasts from 8.30am Sat, Sun. *(John Beeken)*

ST AUBIN

★ **Old Court House Inn**
(01534) 746433 *Harbour Boulevard; JE3 8AB* Attractively updated and prettily positioned harbourside inn; bustling bar with low beams and open fire, other rambling areas including bistro, popular generously served food from sandwiches and pubby choices to good fresh fish/seafood, well kept

Liberation ales and 15 wines by the glass, handsome upstairs restaurant with lovely views across the bay to St Helier, efficient service; children welcome, front deck overlooking harbour, more seats in courtyard behind, ten comfortable well equipped bedrooms, open all day (food all day in summer). *(Susan and John Douglas)*

ST AUBIN

Tenby (01534) 741224

Le Boulevard, towards St Helier; JE3 8AB Randalls pub overlooking the harbour; large bar and several other rooms, decent choice of food (all day Sun) from sandwiches and wraps to good seafood, a couple of real ales such as Skinners, helpful service; children welcome, disabled access/loos, seats out on small front deck under awning, more on paved side terrace, open all day. *(Tom and Lorna Harding)*

ST BRELADE

Old Smugglers (01534) 741510

Ouaisne Bay; OS map reference 595476; JE3 8AW Unpretentious pub just above Ouaisne beach; up to four well kept ales, proper cider and enjoyable traditional food, friendly service, black beams, built-in settles and log fires, restaurant; occasional live music, sports TV, darts, cribbage and dominoes; children and dogs welcome, sun porch with coast views, open all day in summer (food served all day weekends). *(John Beeken)*

ST HELIER

Cock & Bottle (01534) 722184

Royal Square; JE2 4WA Big lively outside eating area in Royal Square with lovely hanging baskets, rattan tables and chairs under parasols, heaters and blankets for cooler evenings; pleasantly old-fashioned and pubby inside with upholstered settles and small stools in front of large fireplace, wide choice of good food from sandwiches and wraps through pub favourites and bistro choices to summer seafood menu, well kept Liberation ales; open all day, no evening food Fri-Sun. *(Susan and John Douglas)*

ST HELIER

Halkett (01534) 732769

Halkett Place; JE2 4WG Modern pub-cum-bar close to tree-lined square, mix of traditional and contemporary décor and furnishings, Liberation ales, 17 wines by the glass and wide choice of food from pubby and brasserie dishes to summer seafood menu; very busy with visitors and locals; Fri and Sat DJs; open all day, no food Sun evening. *(Jeff Davies)*

ST HELIER

★**Lamplighter** (01534) 723119

Mulcaster Street; JE2 3NJ Small friendly pub with up to eight well kept ales, real ciders and more than 150 malt whiskies from pewter-topped counter, low-priced pubby food including good crab sandwiches and popular steak nights (Tues and Thurs), traditional décor with lots of pump clips on heavy timbers and some old gas light fittings; sports TV, can get very busy; wheelchair access (no disabled loos), interesting patriotic façade (the only union flag visible during Nazi occupation), open all day, no evening food Fri-Sun. *(Jeff Davies)*

ISLE OF MAN

DOUGLAS SC3875

Rovers Return

Church Street; IM1 3LX Lively old-fashioned pub tucked down alleyway attracting good mix of customers; several rambling bars, mainly Bushy ales but some mainland guests, generous straightforward lunchtime food, friendly staff, back room filled with Blackburn Rovers memorabilia (landlord is a supporter); rock juke box, TV, pool and darts; no children, tables outside, open all day. *(Dave Braisted)*

LAXEY SC4382

Shore (01624) 861509

Old Laxey Hill; IM4 7DA Friendly nautically themed village pub brewing its own Old Laxey Bosun Bitter, good value wines by the glass and enjoyable pubby lunchtime food (regular curry and steak nights); children welcome till 9pm, picnic-sets out by lovely stream, nice walk to Laxey waterwheel, two bedrooms, good breakfast, open all day. *(Peter and Caroline Waites)*

PEEL SC2484

Creek (01624) 842216

Station Place/North Quay; IM5 1AT In lovely setting on the ancient quayside opposite the House of Manannan heritage centre and very busy at peak times; wide choice of highly thought-of food including fish, crab and lobster fresh from the boats, good local kippers too, up to 15 well kept changing ales (always some from Okells), nautical-themed lounge bar with etched mirrors and mainly old woodwork; TVs and weekend live music in public bar; children welcome, tables outside overlooking harbour, open (and food) all day from 10am. *(Julie and Andrew Blanchett)*

PORT ERIN SC1969

Falcon's Nest (01624) 834077

Station Road; IM9 6AF Friendly family-run hotel overlooking the bay, enjoyable food including local fish/seafood and Sun carvery, up to five well kept ales and over 60 malt whiskies, two bars, one with open fire, conservatory and restaurant; sports TV; children welcome, 39 bedrooms, many with sea view, also eight self-catering apartments, handy for steam rail terminus, open all day. *(Louise and Anton Parsons)*

Pubs that serve food all day

We list here all the pubs (in the Main Entries) that have told us they plan to serve food all day, even if it's only one day of the week. The individual entries for the pubs themselves show the actual details.

Bedfordshire

Ireland, Black Horse

Berkshire

Peasemore, Fox

Sonning, Bull

White Waltham, Beehive

Buckinghamshire

Forty Green, Royal Standard of England

Cambridgeshire

Cambridge, Punter

Peterborough, Brewery Tap

Stilton, Bell

Cheshire

Aldford, Grosvenor Arms

Allostock, Three Greyhounds Inn

Aston, Bhurtpore

Bostock Green, Hayhurst Arms

Bunbury, Dysart Arms

Burleydam, Combermere Arms

Burwardsley, Pheasant

Chester, Architect

Chester, Mill

Chester, Old Harkers Arms

Cholmondeley, Cholmondeley Arms

Cotebrook, Fox & Barrel

Delamere, Fishpool

Macclesfield, Sutton Hall

Mobberley, Bulls Head

Mobberley, Church Inn

Mobberley, Roebuck

Mottram St Andrew, Bulls Head

Nether Alderley, Wizard

Thelwall, Little Manor

Warmingham, Bears Paw

Cornwall

Mylor Bridge, Pandora

Polgooth, Polgooth Inn

Cumbria

Cartmel Fell, Masons Arms

Crosthwaite, Punch Bowl

Elterwater, Britannia

Ings, Watermill

Levens, Strickland Arms

Lupton, Plough

Ravenstonedale, Black Swan

Derbyshire

Chelmorton, Church Inn

Fenny Bentley, Coach & Horses

Hathersage, Plough

Hayfield, Royal

Devon

Cockwood, Anchor

Iddesleigh, Duke of York

Postbridge, Warren House

Sidbury, Hare & Hounds

Dorset

Burton Bradstock, Three Horseshoes

Weymouth, Red Lion

Worth Matravers, Square & Compass

Essex

Feering, Sun

Fyfield, Queens Head

Little Walden, Crown

South Hanningfield, Old Windmill

Gloucestershire

Cheltenham, Old Courthouse

Didmarton, Kings Arms

Nailsworth, Weighbridge

Sheepscombe, Butchers Arms

Hampshire

Bransgore, Three Tuns

Cadnam, White Hart

Littleton, Running Horse

Hertfordshire

Barnet, Duke of York

St Albans, Prae Wood Arms

Isle of Wight

Fishbourne, Fishbourne Inn

Seaview, Boathouse

Kent

Chiddingstone Causeway, Little Brown Jug

Langton Green, Hare

Penshurst, Bottle House

Sevenoaks, White Hart

Shipbourne, Chaser

Stalisfield Green, Plough

Lancashire

Bashall Eaves, Red Pump

Bispham Green, Eagle & Child

Formby, Sparrowhawk

Great Mitton, Aspinall Arms

Great Mitton, Three Fishes

Manchester, Wharf

Nether Burrow, Highwayman

Pleasington, Clog & Billycock

Preston, Haighton Manor

Uppermill, Church Inn

Leicestershire

Lyddington, Marquess of Exeter

Swithland, Griffin

Lincolnshire

Kirkby la Thorpe, Queens Head

Stamford, George of Stamford

Norfolk

King's Lynn, Bank House

Larling, Angel

Morston, Anchor

Salthouse, Dun Cow

Thorpe Market, Gunton Arms

Woodbastwick, Fur & Feather

Northamptonshire

Ashby St Ledgers, Olde Coach House

Northumbria

Blanchland, Lord Crewe Arms

Carterway Heads, Manor House Inn

Newton, Duke of Wellington

Oxfordshire

Charlbury, Bull

Kingham, Plough

Oxford, Bear

Oxford, Punter

Wolvercote, Jacobs Inn

Woodstock, Woodstock Arms

Shropshire

Chetwynd Aston, Fox

Shipley, Inn at Shipley

Shrewsbury, Armoury

Somerset

Dunster, Luttrell Arms

Hinton St George, Lord Poulett Arms

Stanton Wick, Carpenters Arms

Wedmore, Swan

Staffordshire

Brewood, Oakley

Longdon Green, Red Lion

Salt, Holly Bush

Wrinehill, Hand & Trumpet

Suffolk

Chelmondiston, Butt & Oyster

Southwold, Harbour Inn

Stoke-by-Nayland, Crown

Waldringfield, Maybush

Surrey

Buckland, Pheasant

Chiddingfold, Swan

Chobham, White Hart

Elstead, Mill at Elstead

Englefield Green, Bailiwick

Milford, Refectory

Norwood Hill, Fox Revived

Sussex

Alfriston, George

Charlton, Fox Goes Free

Eridge Green, Nevill Crest & Gun

Friday Street, Farm at Friday Street

Horsham, Black Jug

Ringmer, Cock

Warwickshire

Birmingham, Old Joint Stock

Birmingham, Physician

Hunningham, Red Lion

Long Compton, Red Lion

Shipston-on-Stour, Black Horse

Shipston-on-Stour, George

Warmington, Falcon

Welford-on-Avon, Bell

Wiltshire

Bradford-on-Avon, Castle

Yorkshire

Beck Hole, Birch Hall

Blakey Ridge, Lion

Bradfield, Strines Inn

Broughton, Bull

Elslack, Tempest Arms

Grinton, Bridge Inn

Halifax, Shibden Mill

Hetton, Angel

Ledsham, Chequers

Linton in Craven, Fountaine
Welburn, Crown & Cushion
Widdop, Pack Horse
York, Judges Lodging

London

Central London, Black Friar
Central London, Coach Makers Arms
Central London, Old Bank of England
Central London, Olde Mitre
Central London, Seven Stars
Central London, Thomas Cubitt
North London, Holly Bush
North London, Lighterman
South London, Victoria
West London, Dove
West London, Duke of Sussex
West London, Mute Swan
West London, Old Orchard
West London, White Horse
West London, Windsor Castle

Scotland

Applecross, Applecross Inn
Edinburgh, Abbotsford
Edinburgh, Guildford Arms
Glasgow, Babbity Bowster
Glasgow, Bon Accord
Shieldaig, Tigh an Eilean Hotel
Sligachan, Sligachan Hotel
Thornhill, Lion & Unicorn

Wales

Colwyn Bay, Pen-y-Bryn
Gresford, Pant-yr-Ochain
Hawarden, Glynne Arms
Llandudno Junction, Queens Head
Llanelian-yn-Rhos, White Lion
Llangollen, Corn Mill
Mold, Glasfryn
Overton Bridge, Cross Foxes
Pontypridd, Bunch of Grapes

Pubs near motorway junctions

The number at the start of each line is the number of the junction. Detailed directions are given in the Main Entry for each pub. In this section, to help you find the pubs quickly before you're past the junction, we give the name of the chapter where you'll find the text.

M1

9: Redbourn, Cricketers (Hertfordshire) 3.2 miles

13: Woburn, Birch (Bedfordshire) 3.5 miles

18: Ashby St Ledgers, Olde Coach House (Northamptonshire) 4 miles

M3

1: Sunbury, Flower Pot (Surrey) 1.6 miles

3: West End, The Inn West End (Surrey) 2.4 miles; Chobham, White Hart (Surrey) 4 miles

5: North Warnborough, Mill House (Hampshire) 1 mile; Hook, Hogget (Hampshire) 1.1 miles

M4

9: Bray, Crown (Berkshire) 1.75 miles

13: Curridge, Bunk (Berkshire) 3 miles; Chieveley, Crab & Boar (Berkshire) 3.5 miles; Peasemore, Fox (Berkshire) 4 miles

14: Shefford Woodlands, Pheasant (Berkshire) 0.3 miles

M5

10: Coombe Hill, Gloucester Old Spot (Gloucestershire) 1 mile

13: Eastington, Old Badger (Gloucestershire) 1 mile

19: Clapton-in-Gordano, Black Horse (Somerset) 4 miles

M6

16: Barthomley, White Lion (Cheshire) 1 mile; Sandbach, Old Hall (Cheshire) 1.2 miles

18: Allostock, Three Greyhounds Inn (Cheshire) 4.7 miles

19: Mobberley, Bulls Head (Cheshire) 4 miles

33: Bay Horse, Bay Horse (Lancashire) 1.2 miles

36: Lupton, Plough (Cumbria) 2 miles; Levens, Strickland Arms (Cumbria) 4 miles

40: Yanwath, Gate Inn (Cumbria) 2.25 miles; Tirril, Queens Head (Cumbria) 3.5 miles

M11

9: Hinxton, Red Lion (Cambridgeshire) 2 miles

10: Duxford, John Barleycorn (Cambridgeshire) 1.8 miles; Whittlesford, Tickell Arms (Cambridgeshire) 2.4 miles

M25

5: Chipstead, George & Dragon (Kent) 1.25 miles

8: Walton on the Hill, Blue Ball (Surrey) 2.5 miles

18: Flaunden, Bricklayers Arms (Hertfordshire) 4 miles

21A: Potters Crouch, Holly Bush (Hertfordshire) 2.3 miles

M27

1: Cadnam, White Hart (Hampshire) 0.5 miles; Fritham, Royal Oak (Hampshire) 4 miles

M40

2: Hedgerley, White Horse (Buckinghamshire) 2.4 miles; Forty Green, Royal Standard of England (Buckinghamshire) 3.5 miles

12: Gaydon, Malt Shovel (Warwickshire) 0.9 miles

M42

5: Barston, Malt Shovel (Warwickshire) 3 miles

6: Hampton-in-Arden, White Lion (Warwickshire) 1.25 miles

M50

1: Baughton, Jockey (Worcestershire) 4 miles

3: Kilcot, Kilcot Inn (Gloucestershire) 2.3 miles

M60

13: Worsley, Worsley Old Hall (Lancashire) 1 mile

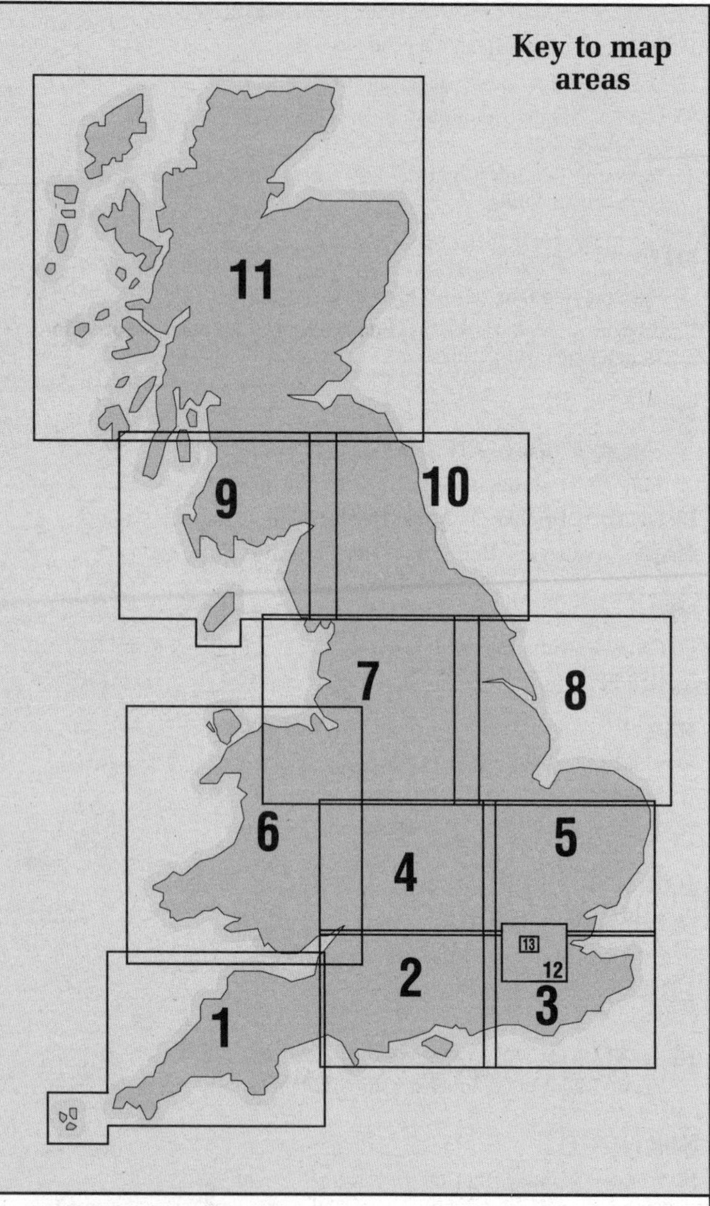

Reference to sectional maps

Motorway
Major road
County boundary
Main Entry
Main Entry with accommodation
Place name to assist navigation

MAPS

1

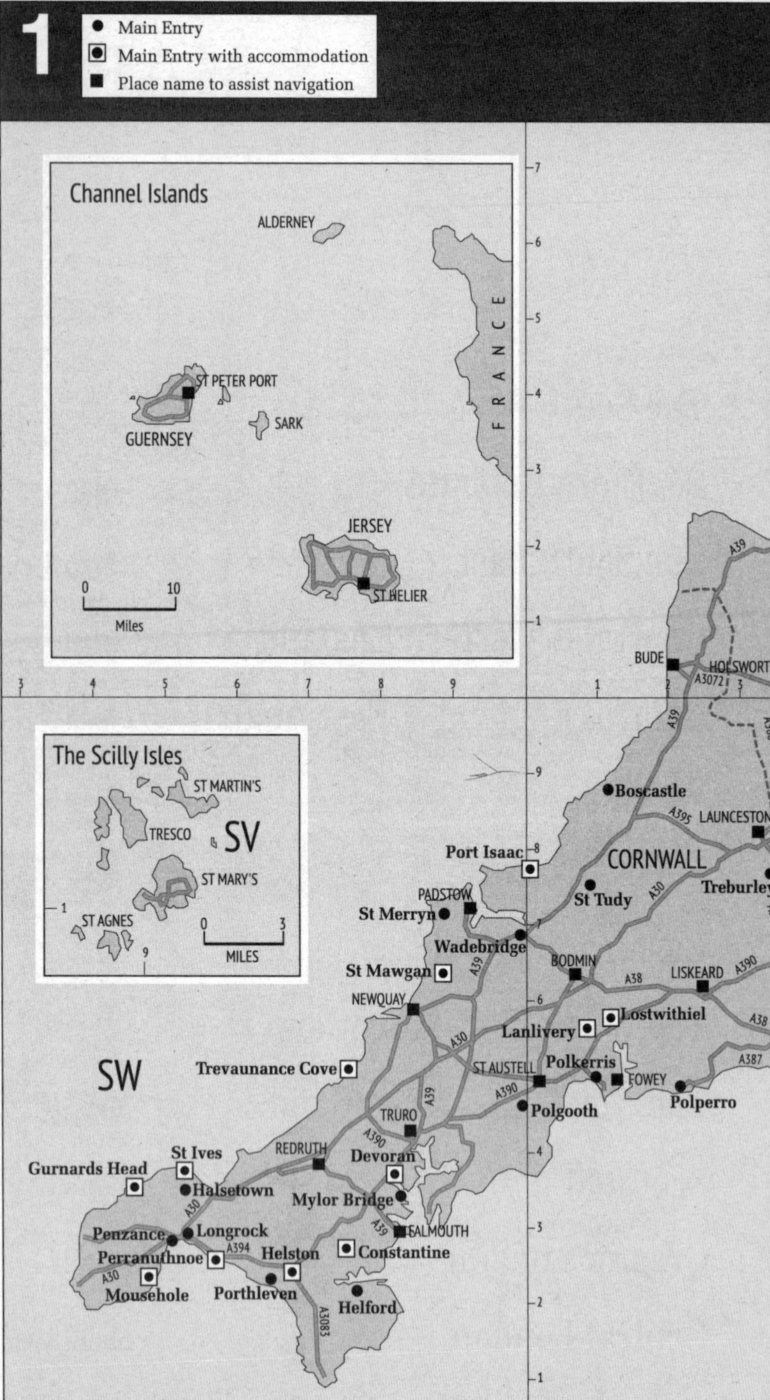

Main Entry
Main Entry with accommodation
Place name to assist navigation
Channel Islands
ALDERNEY
FRANCE
ST PETER PORT
GUERNSEY
SARK
JERSEY
ST HELIER
Miles
The Scilly Isles
ST MARTIN'S
TRESCO
SV
ST MARY'S
ST AGNES
MILES
SW
BUDE
HOLSWORTHY
Boscastle
LAUNCESTON
CORNWALL
Port Isaac
St Tudy
Treburley
PADSTOW
St Merryn
Wadebridge
BODMIN
LISKEARD
St Mawgan
NEWQUAY
Lostwithiel
Lanlivery
Trevaunance Cove
ST AUSTELL
Polkerris
FOWEY
Polperro
Polgooth
TRURO
REDRUTH
Devoran
St Ives
Gurnards Head
Halsetown
Mylor Bridge
FALMOUTH
Penzance
Longrock
Perranuthnoe
Helston
Constantine
Mousehole
Porthleven
Helford
A39
A3072
A388
A395
A30
A38
A390
A387
A394
A3083

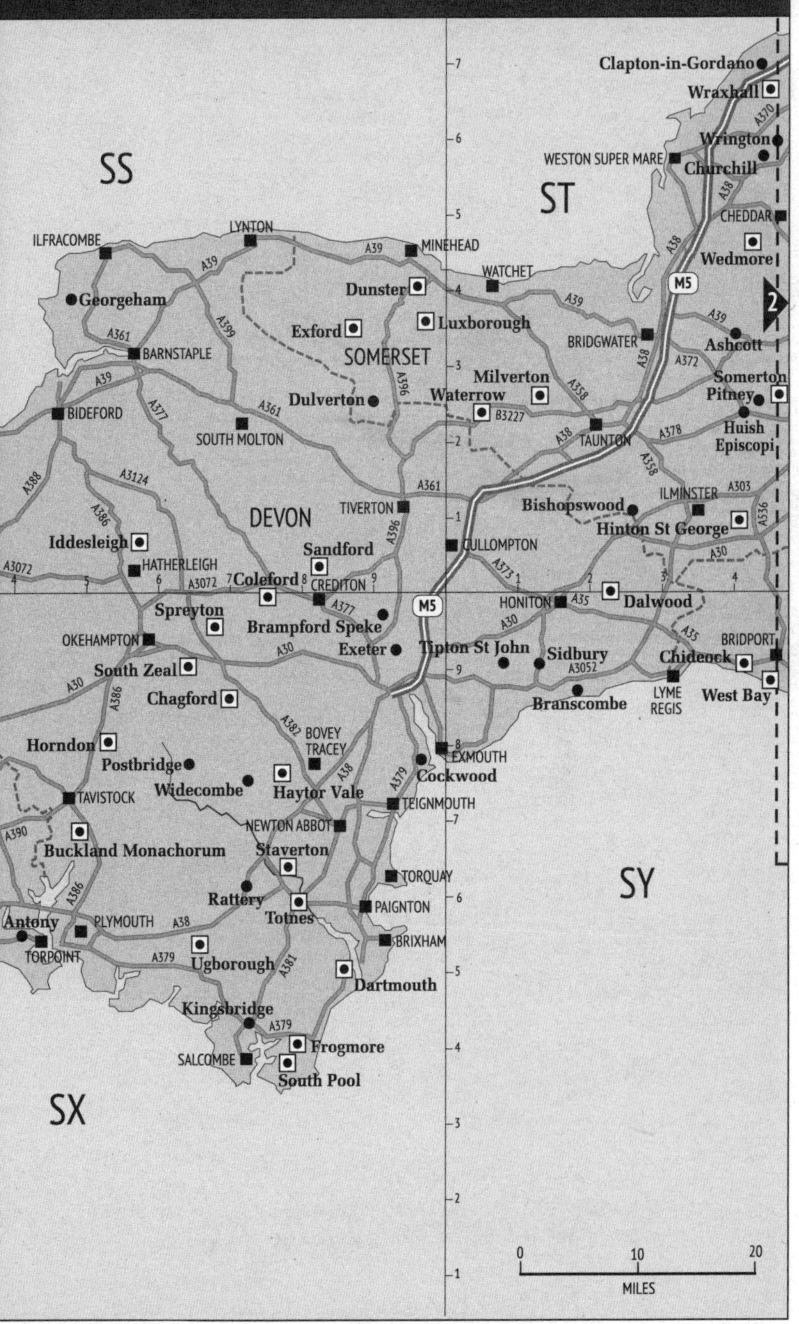
SS
ST
SX
SY
SOMERSET
DEVON
Clapton-in-Gordano
Wraxhall
Wrington
Churchill
WESTON SUPER MARE
CHEDDAR
Wedmore
M5
2
ILFRACOMBE
LYNTON
MINEHEAD
WATCHET
Georgeham
Dunster
Exford
Luxborough
BARNSTAPLE
BRIDGWATER
Ashcott
Milverton
Somerton
Pitney
Huish Episcopi
Dulverton
Waterrow
BIDEFORD
SOUTH MOLTON
TAUNTON
TIVERTON
Bishopswood
ILMINSTER
Hinton St George
Iddesleigh
HATHERLEIGH
Sandford
CULLOMPTON
Coleford
CREDITON
HONITON
Dalwood
Spreyton
Brampford Speke
OKEHAMPTON
Exeter
Tipton St John
Sidbury
BRIDPORT
Chideock
South Zeal
LYME REGIS
West Bay
Chagford
Branscombe
BOVEY TRACEY
Horndon
EXMOUTH
Postbridge
Cockwood
Widecombe
Haytor Vale
TAVISTOCK
TEIGNMOUTH
NEWTON ABBOT
Buckland Monachorum
Staverton
TORQUAY
Rattery
Totnes
PAIGNTON
Antony
PLYMOUTH
TORPOINT
BRIXHAM
Ugborough
Dartmouth
Kingsbridge
Frogmore
SALCOMBE
South Pool
0
10
20
MILES

2

- ● Main Entry
- ⊡ Main Entry with accommodation
- ■ Place name to assist navigation

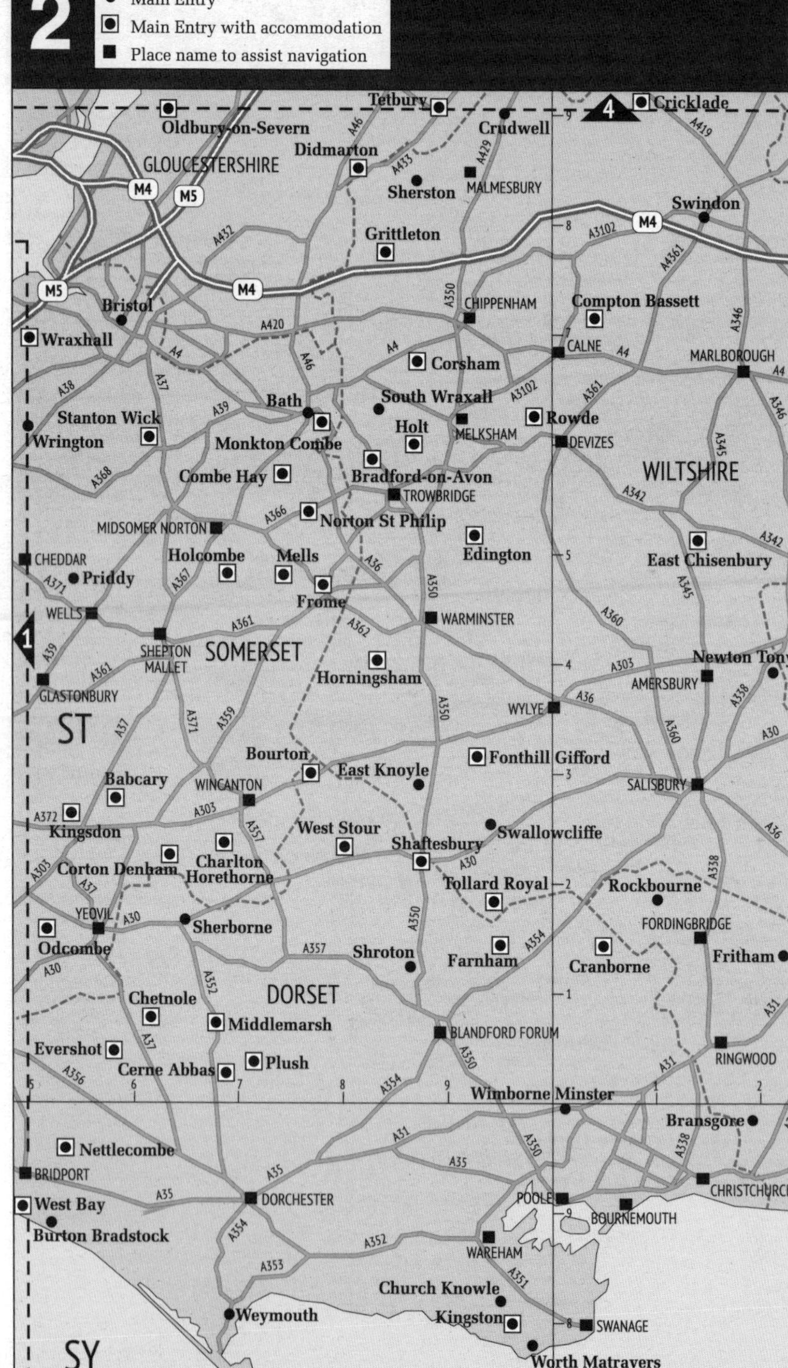

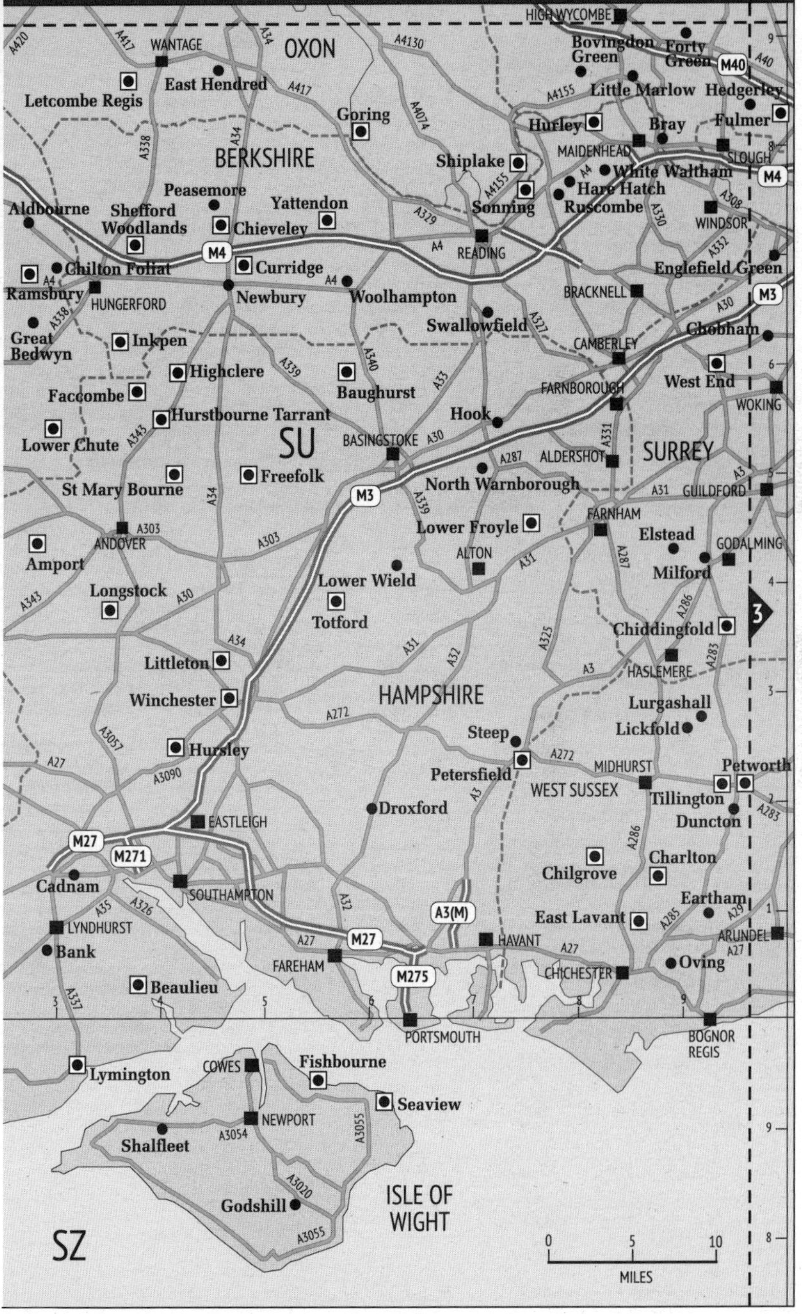
OXON
BERKSHIRE
SU
SURREY
HAMPSHIRE
WEST SUSSEX
ISLE OF WIGHT
SZ
HIGH WYCOMBE
WANTAGE
Bovingdon Green
Forty Green
Letcombe Regis
East Hendred
Little Marlow
Hedgerley
Goring
Hurley
Bray
Fulmer
MAIDENHEAD
SLOUGH
Shiplake
White Waltham
Peasemore
Hare Hatch
Sonning
Ruscombe
Yattendon
Aldbourne
Shefford Woodlands
Chieveley
WINDSOR
READING
Curridge
Chilton Foliat
Englefield Green
Ramsbury
HUNGERFORD
Newbury
Woolhampton
BRACKNELL
Swallowfield
Chobham
Great Bedwyn
Inkpen
CAMBERLEY
Highclere
West End
Baughurst
FARNBOROUGH
WOKING
Faccombe
Hook
Hurstbourne Tarrant
Lower Chute
BASINGSTOKE
ALDERSHOT
Freefolk
North Warnborough
St Mary Bourne
GUILDFORD
FARNHAM
Lower Froyle
Elstead
ANDOVER
GODALMING
Amport
ALTON
Milford
Lower Wield
Longstock
Totford
Chiddingfold
HASLEMERE
Littleton
Winchester
Lurgashall
Lickfold
Steep
Hursley
Petworth
Petersfield
MIDHURST
Tillington
Droxford
Duncton
EASTLEIGH
Charlton
Chilgrove
Cadnam
SOUTHAMPTON
Eartham
East Lavant
LYNDHURST
ARUNDEL
Bank
HAVANT
FAREHAM
CHICHESTER
Oving
Beaulieu
PORTSMOUTH
BOGNOR REGIS
Lymington
COWES
Fishbourne
Seaview
NEWPORT
Shalfleet
Godshill
M4
M3
M40
M27
M271
M275
A3(M)
0
5
10
MILES
3

3

- Main Entry
- Main Entry with accommodation
- Place name to assist navigation

BUCKS
M1
M11
5
Harefield (see West London section)
Hedgerley
GREATER LONDON
M25
A127
Horndon-on-the-Hill
A13
M40
Fulmer
UXBRIDGE
A128
M4
BERKS
M25
TILBURY
A30
Englefield Green
STAINES
DARTFORD
GRAVESEND
A2
A30
Sunbury
ROCHESTER
M3
Esher
Meopham
A2
M2
Chobham
A3
M25
M20
A227
A24
A228
A233
Walton on the Hill
A3
M25
M20
WOKING
Ripley
Chipstead
Chipstead
M26
A217
A22
MAIDSTONE
Mickleham
M25
Sevenoaks
A246
A24
Oxted
WESTERHAM
Buckland
Shipbourne
GUILDFORD
A25
A25
DORKING
REIGATE
A21
A227
A26
TQ
Chiddingstone
SURREY
A217
A23
TONBRIDGE
Shamley Green
A29
Norwood Hill
A22
Penshurst
M23
A264
Langton Green
Goudhurst
A23
Copthorne
Tunbridge Wells
A262
CRAWLEY
EAST GRINSTEAD
A281
Withyham
Eridge Green
A21
2
A24
A264
West Hoathly
Mark Cross
Horsham
A22
A26
A267
CROWBOROUGH
Ticehurst
Lower Beeding
Danehill
Warninglid
A275
A265
Salehurst
A29
Fletching
HAYWARDS HEATH
Uckfield
Robertsbridge
Petworth
A272
A272
A283
Dial Post
A23
BURGESS HILL
A267
EAST SUSSEX
A21
A26
A22
A24
A273
WEST SUSSEX
A275
A271
Ringmer
A29
LEWES
HAILSHAM
A27
Burpham
A27
A283
A27
A23
A259
A26
A22
ARUNDEL
A27
BEXHILL
A259
WORTHING
A259
BRIGHTON
NEWHAVEN
Alfriston
Friday Street
EASTBOURNE
TV

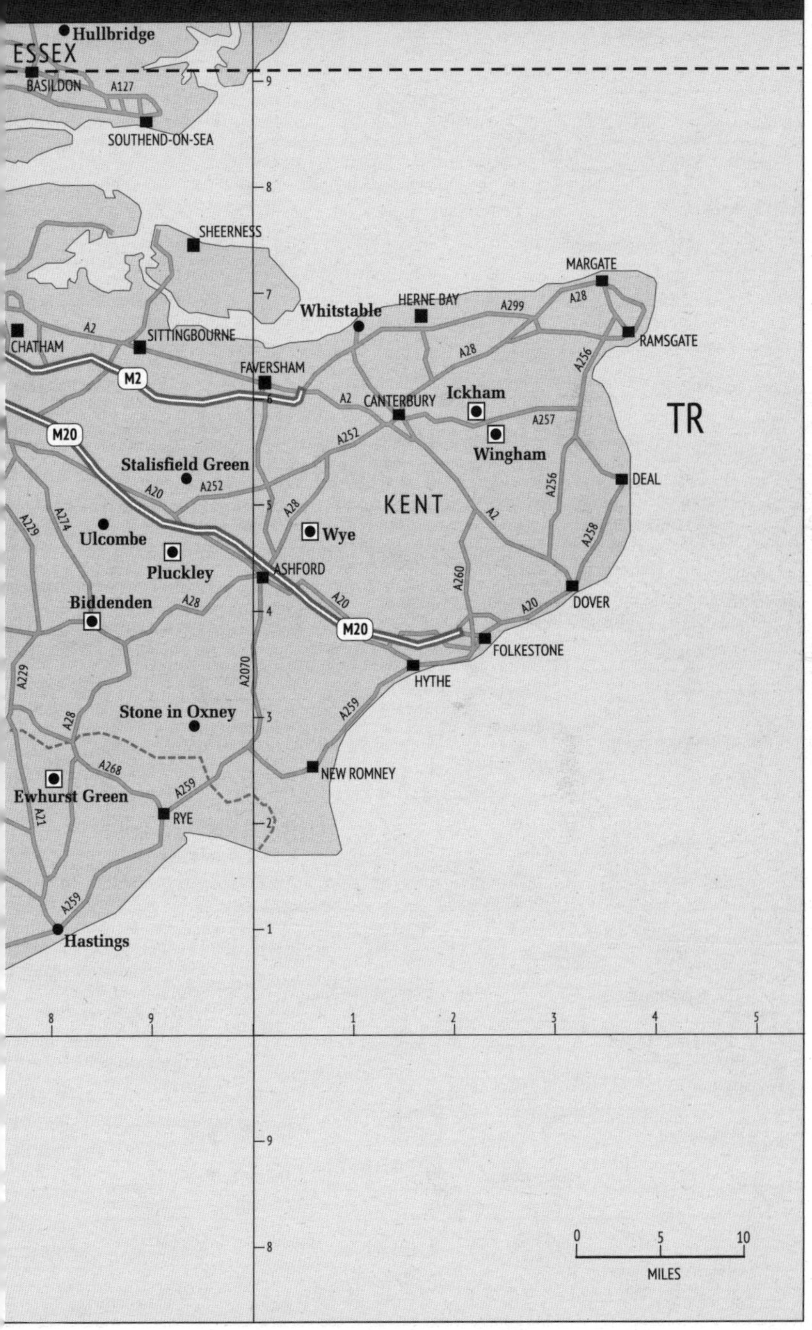
Hullbridge
ESSEX
BASILDON
A127
SOUTHEND-ON-SEA
SHEERNESS
MARGATE
HERNE BAY
A299
A28
Whitstable
RAMSGATE
A2
SITTINGBOURNE
CHATHAM
M2
FAVERSHAM
A256
A28
Ickham
A2
CANTERBURY
A257
TR
M20
A252
Wingham
Stalisfield Green
A252
DEAL
A20
A256
KENT
A28
A229
A274
Wye
A2
Ulcombe
Pluckley
A258
ASHFORD
A260
Biddenden
A28
DOVER
A20
A20
M20
FOLKESTONE
A229
A2070
HYTHE
Stone in Oxney
A259
A28
A268
NEW ROMNEY
Ewhurst Green
A259
A21
RYE
A259
Hastings
MILES

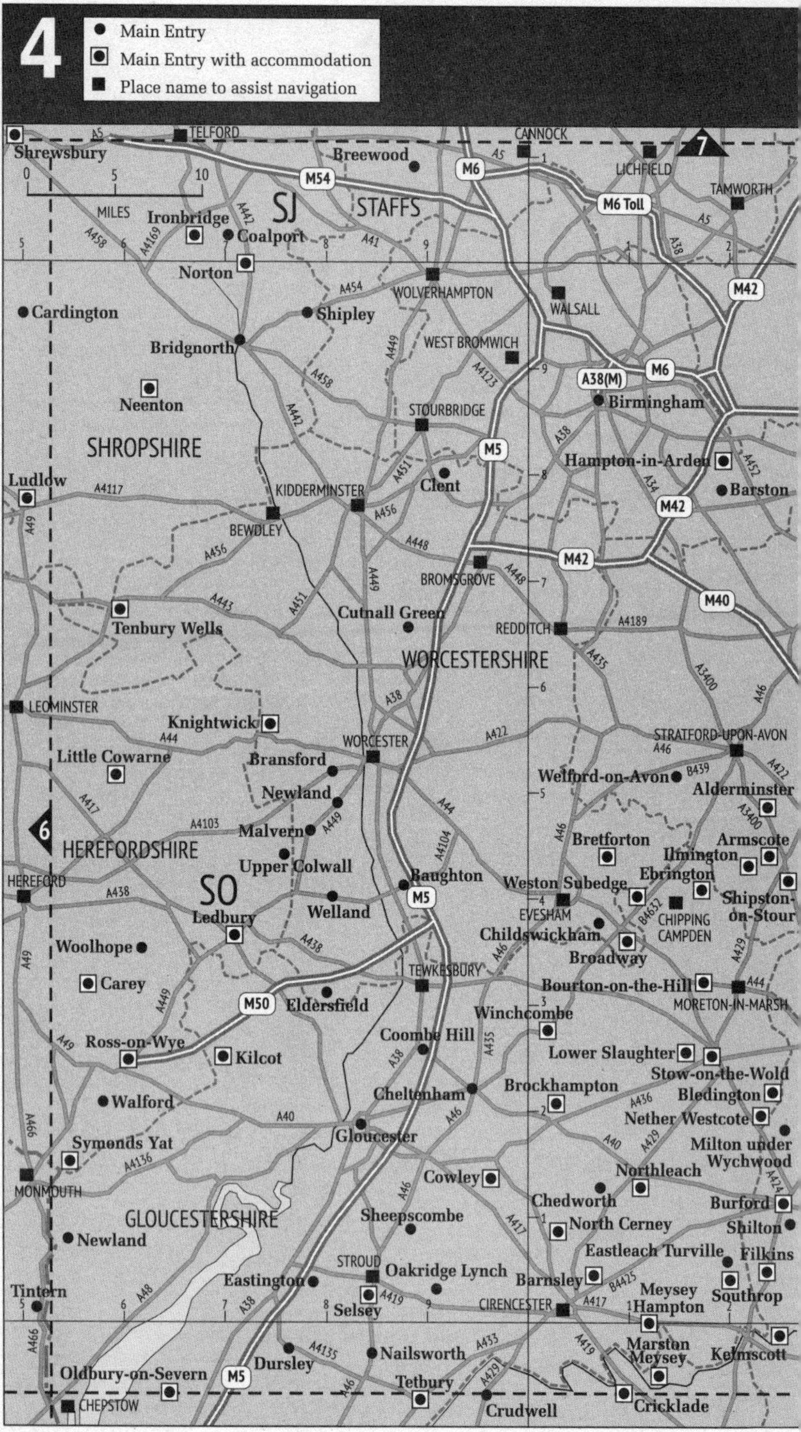
4
Main Entry
Main Entry with accommodation
Place name to assist navigation
Shrewsbury
TELFORD
CANNOCK
LICHFIELD
7
Breewood
M54
M6
M6 Toll
TAMWORTH
MILES
SJ
STAFFS
Ironbridge
Coalport
Norton
WOLVERHAMPTON
WALSALL
M42
Cardington
Shipley
Bridgnorth
WEST BROMWICH
A38(M)
Birmingham
Neenton
STOURBRIDGE
SHROPSHIRE
M5
Hampton-in-Arden
Ludlow
Clent
Barston
KIDDERMINSTER
BEWDLEY
BROMSGROVE
M40
Tenbury Wells
Cutnall Green
REDDITCH
WORCESTERSHIRE
LEOMINSTER
Knightwick
WORCESTER
STRATFORD-UPON-AVON
Little Cowarne
Bransford
Welford-on-Avon
Alderminster
Newland
6
Malvern
Bretforton
Armscote
HEREFORDSHIRE
Upper Colwall
Ilmington
Baughton
Ebrington
HEREFORD
SO
Weston Subedge
Shipston-on-Stour
Ledbury
Welland
EVESHAM
CHIPPING CAMPDEN
Woolhope
Childswickham
Broadway
Carey
TEWKESBURY
Bourton-on-the-Hill
MORETON-IN-MARSH
M50
Eldersfield
Winchcombe
Ross-on-Wye
Kilcot
Coombe Hill
Lower Slaughter
Stow-on-the-Wold
Walford
Cheltenham
Brockhampton
Bledington
Nether Westcote
Gloucester
Milton under Wychwood
Symonds Yat
Northleach
MONMOUTH
Cowley
Chedworth
Burford
GLOUCESTERSHIRE
Sheepscombe
North Cerney
Shilton
Newland
Eastleach Turville
Filkins
STROUD
Oakridge Lynch
Barnsley
Eastington
Meysey Hampton
Southrop
Tintern
Selsey
CIRENCESTER
Marston Meysey
Kelmscott
Nailsworth
Dursley
Oldbury-on-Severn
Tetbury
CHEPSTOW
Crudwell
Cricklade

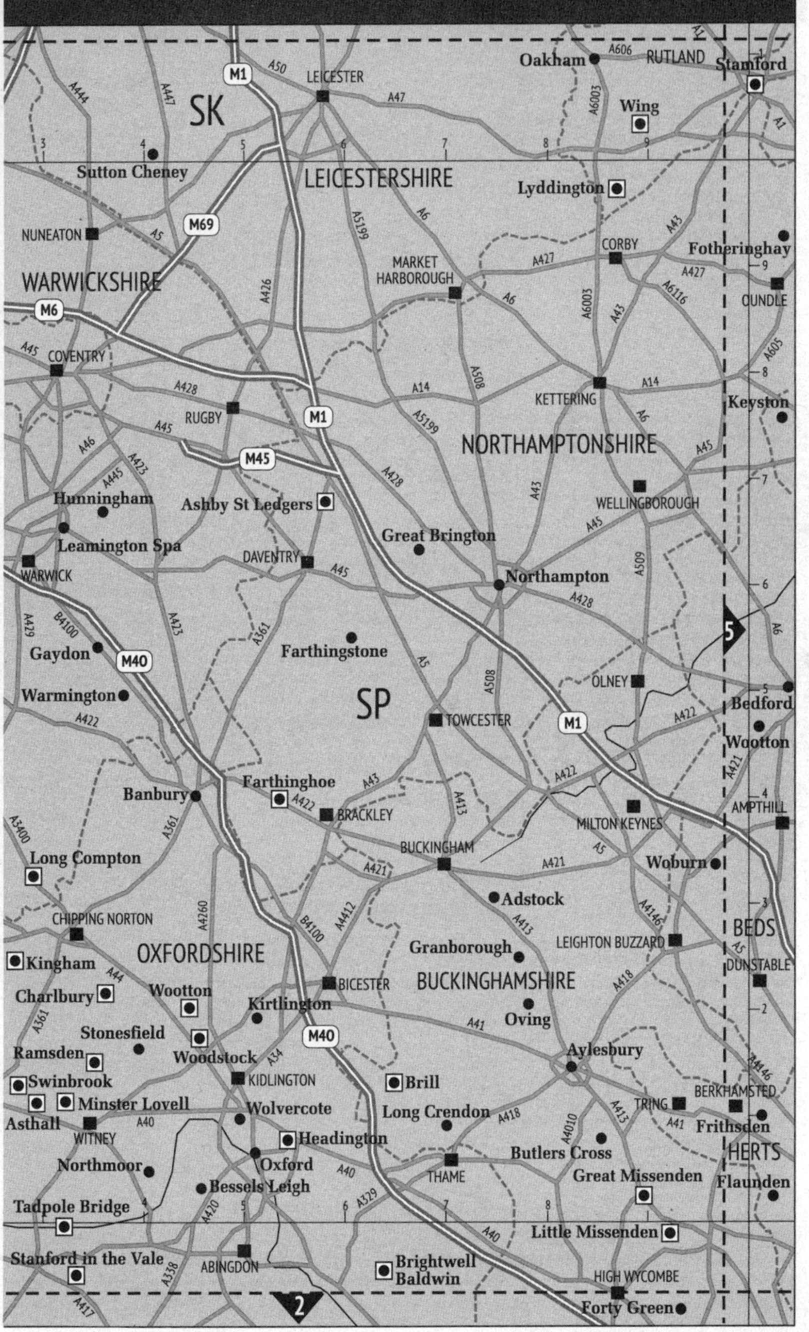

SK
SP
LEICESTERSHIRE
WARWICKSHIRE
NORTHAMPTONSHIRE
OXFORDSHIRE
BUCKINGHAMSHIRE
RUTLAND
BEDS
HERTS
Oakham
Stamford
Wing
LEICESTER
Sutton Cheney
Lyddington
NUNEATON
CORBY
Fotheringhay
MARKET HARBOROUGH
OUNDLE
COVENTRY
KETTERING
Keyston
RUGBY
Hunningham
Ashby St Ledgers
WELLINGBOROUGH
Leamington Spa
Great Brington
WARWICK
DAVENTRY
Northampton
Gaydon
Farthingstone
Warmington
OLNEY
Bedford
TOWCESTER
Wootton
Banbury
Farthinghoe
BRACKLEY
AMPTHILL
MILTON KEYNES
BUCKINGHAM
Long Compton
Woburn
Adstock
CHIPPING NORTON
LEIGHTON BUZZARD
Granborough
Kingham
DUNSTABLE
Charlbury
Wootton
BICESTER
Kirtlington
Oving
Stonesfield
Ramsden
Woodstock
Aylesbury
Swinbrook
KIDLINGTON
Brill
Minster Lovell
Wolvercote
Long Crendon
TRING
BERKHAMSTED
Asthall
WITNEY
Headington
Frithsden
Northmoor
Oxford
THAME
Butlers Cross
Bessels Leigh
Great Missenden
Flaunden
Tadpole Bridge
Little Missenden
Stanford in the Vale
ABINGDON
Brightwell Baldwin
HIGH WYCOMBE
Forty Green
M1
M69
M6
M45
M40
A1
A606
A50
A47
A444
A447
A6003
A5199
A6
A5
A43
A427
A426
A6116
A45
A428
A14
A508
A605
A46
A423
A445
A509
A429
B4100
A361
A422
A421
A413
A3400
A4260
A4412
A4146
A418
A44
A41
A34
A40
A4010
A420
A329
A338
A417
5
2

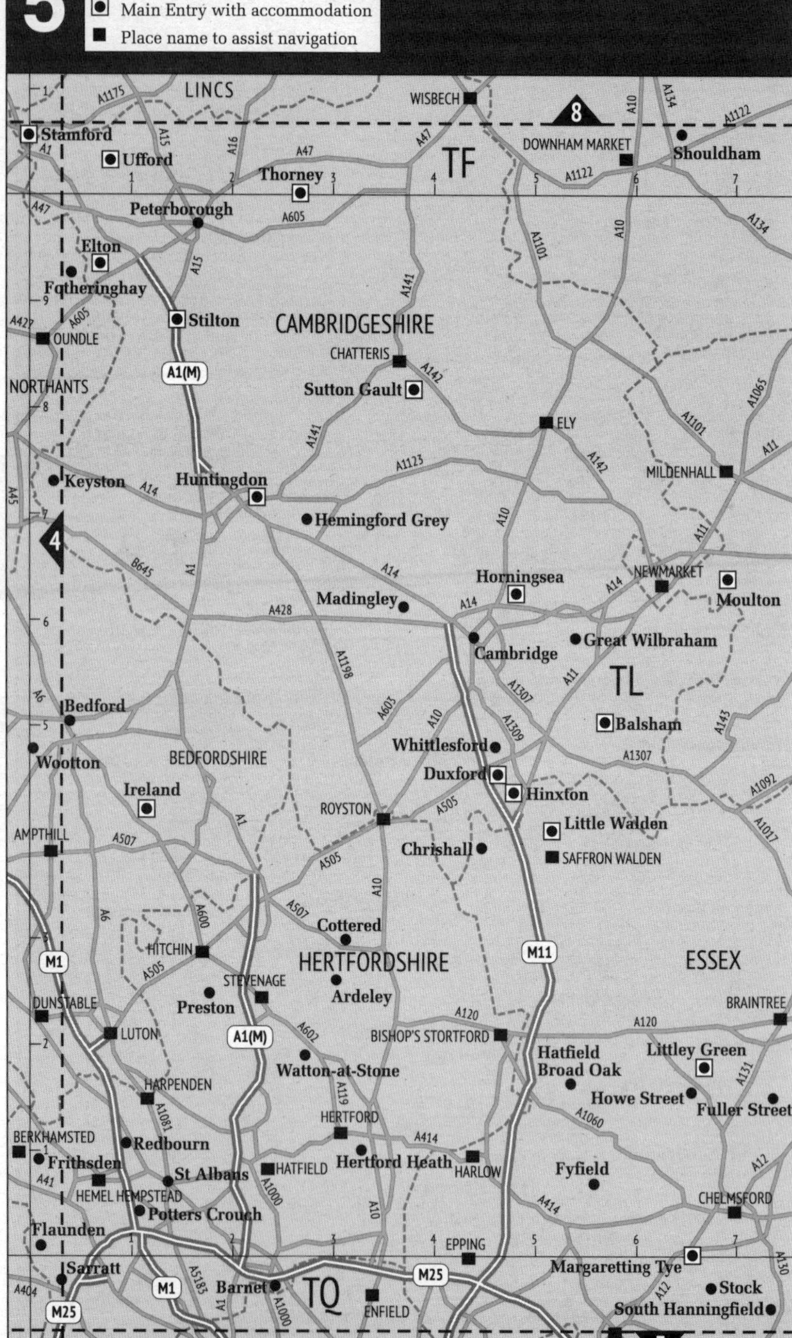
5
Main Entry
Main Entry with accommodation
Place name to assist navigation
LINCS
WISBECH
8
Stamford
Ufford
Thorney
TF
DOWNHAM MARKET
Shouldham
Peterborough
Elton
Fotheringhay
Stilton
CAMBRIDGESHIRE
OUNDLE
NORTHANTS
CHATTERIS
Sutton Gault
ELY
MILDENHALL
Keyston
Huntingdon
Hemingford Grey
4
Horningsea
NEWMARKET
Moulton
Madingley
Cambridge
Great Wilbraham
TL
Bedford
Balsham
Wootton
BEDFORDSHIRE
Whittlesford
Duxford
Hinxton
Ireland
ROYSTON
Little Walden
AMPTHILL
Chrishall
SAFFRON WALDEN
Cottered
HITCHIN
HERTFORDSHIRE
ESSEX
M1
M11
STEVENAGE
Preston
Ardeley
DUNSTABLE
BRAINTREE
LUTON
A1(M)
BISHOP'S STORTFORD
Watton-at-Stone
Hatfield Broad Oak
Littley Green
HARPENDEN
Howe Street
Fuller Street
HERTFORD
BERKHAMSTED
Redbourn
Frithsden
HATFIELD
Hertford Heath
HARLOW
Fyfield
HEMEL HEMPSTEAD
St Albans
Potters Crouch
CHELMSFORD
Flaunden
EPPING
Margaretting Tye
Sarratt
M25
Barnet
TQ
ENFIELD
Stock
South Hanningfield
BRENTWOOD
3

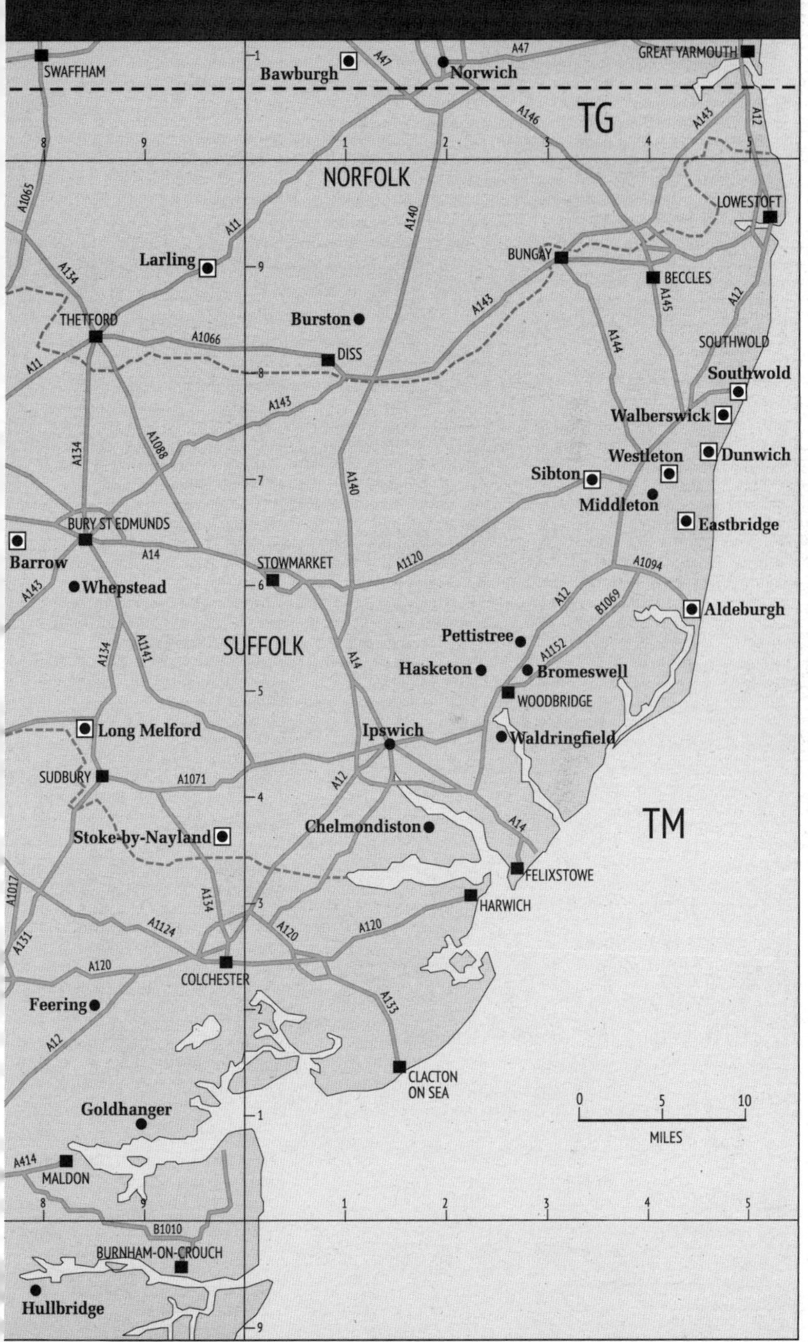
SWAFFHAM
Bawburgh
Norwich
GREAT YARMOUTH
TG
NORFOLK
LOWESTOFT
Larling
BUNGAY
BECCLES
THETFORD
Burston
DISS
SOUTHWOLD
Southwold
Walberswick
Westleton
Dunwich
Sibton
Middleton
Eastbridge
BURY ST EDMUNDS
Barrow
STOWMARKET
Whepstead
Aldeburgh
SUFFOLK
Pettistree
Hasketon
Bromeswell
WOODBRIDGE
Long Melford
Ipswich
Waldringfield
SUDBURY
TM
Chelmondiston
Stoke-by-Nayland
FELIXSTOWE
HARWICH
COLCHESTER
Feering
CLACTON ON SEA
0
5
10
MILES
Goldhanger
MALDON
BURNHAM-ON-CROUCH
Hullbridge

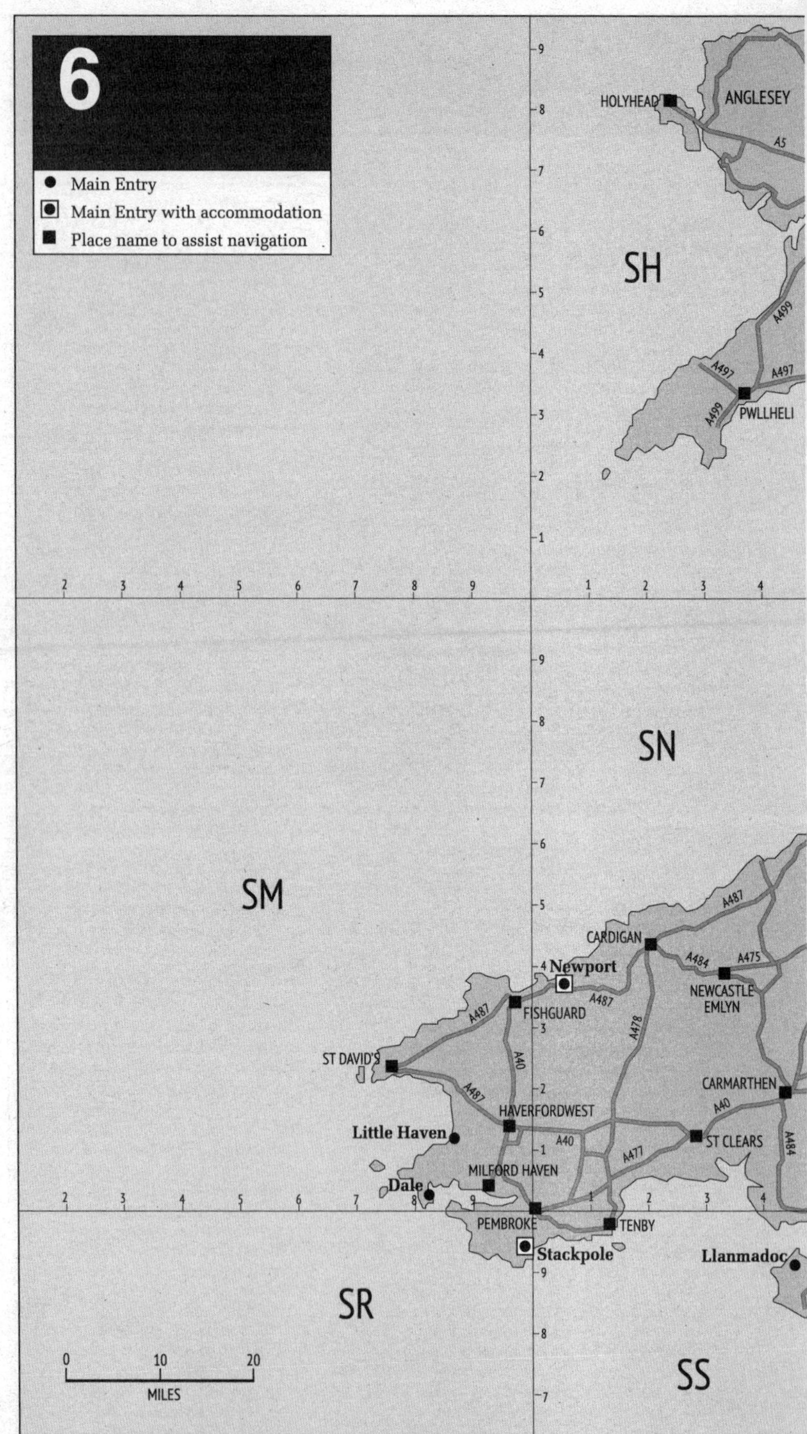

6
Main Entry
Main Entry with accommodation
Place name to assist navigation
HOLYHEAD
ANGLESEY
A5
SH
A499
A497
A497
A499
PWLLHELI
SN
SM
A487
CARDIGAN
A484
A475
Newport
NEWCASTLE EMLYN
A487
FISHGUARD
A487
A478
ST DAVID'S
A40
A487
CARMARTHEN
HAVERFORDWEST
A40
Little Haven
A40
A477
ST CLEARS
A484
MILFORD HAVEN
Dale
PEMBROKE
TENBY
Stackpole
Llanmadoc
SR
SS
0
10
20
MILES

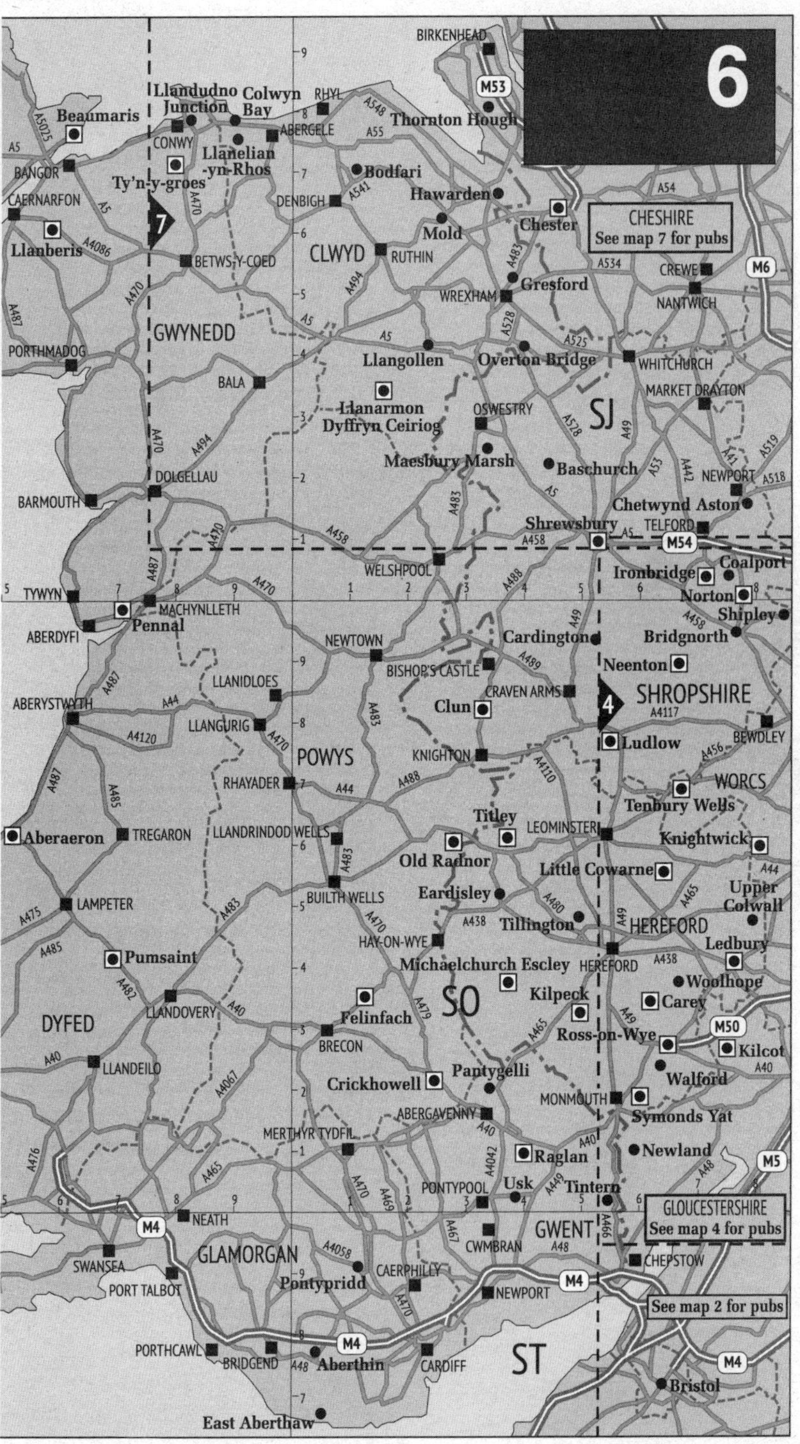

6
CHESHIRE See map 7 for pubs
GLOUCESTERSHIRE See map 4 for pubs
See map 2 for pubs
7
4
Birkenhead
M53
Thornton Hough
Llandudno Junction
Colwyn Bay
Rhyl
Beaumaris
Conwy
Llanelian-yn-Rhos
Abergele
A548
A55
Ty'n-y-groes
Bangor
Bodfari
Denbigh
A541
Hawarden
Chester
A54
Caernarfon
Llanberis
A4086
Mold
Clwyd
Ruthin
Betws-y-Coed
A494
A483
Gresford
Wrexham
Crewe
Nantwich
M6
A534
Gwynedd
A528
A525
Porthmadog
Llangollen
Overton Bridge
Whitchurch
Market Drayton
Bala
Llanarmon Dyffryn Ceiriog
Oswestry
SJ
Maesbury Marsh
Baschurch
Newport
Dolgellau
Barmouth
Chetwynd Aston
Shrewsbury
Telford
M54
A458
Welshpool
Ironbridge
Coalport
Norton
Shipley
Tywyn
Machynlleth
Pennal
Aberdyfi
Newtown
Cardington
Bridgnorth
Bishop's Castle
Neenton
Llanidloes
Craven Arms
Shropshire
Aberystwyth
Clun
A4117
Bewdley
Llangurig
Ludlow
Powys
Knighton
Worcs
Rhayader
Tenbury Wells
Titley
Leominster
Knightwick
Aberaeron
Tregaron
Llandrindod Wells
Old Radnor
Little Cowarne
Eardisley
Upper Colwall
Builth Wells
Lampeter
Tillington
Hereford
Hay-on-Wye
Ledbury
Pumsaint
Michaelchurch Escley
Woolhope
Kilpeck
Carey
Felinfach
SO
Llandovery
Dyfed
Ross-on-Wye
M50
Kilcot
Brecon
Walford
Llandeilo
Pantygelli
Crickhowell
Monmouth
Symonds Yat
Abergavenny
Merthyr Tydfil
Newland
Raglan
M5
Usk
Tintern
Pontypool
Neath
Gwent
M4
Cwmbran
Chepstow
Swansea
Glamorgan
Port Talbot
Pontypridd
Caerphilly
Newport
Porthcawl
Bridgend
Aberthin
Cardiff
ST
Bristol
East Aberthaw

7

Main Entry
Main Entry with accommodation
Place name to assist navigation
9
Ulverston
Lupton
Kirkby Lonsdale
Nether Burrow
BARROW-IN-FURNESS
MORECAMBE
LANCASTER
LANCASHIRE
SD
MILES
Bay Horse
Sawley
Whitewell
FLEETWOOD
Bashall Eaves
Downham
Great Mitton
BLACKPOOL
Mellor
BURNLEY
Preston
LYTHAM ST ANNE'S
Pleasington
BLACKBURN
SOUTHPORT
Bispham Green
ORMSKIRK
GREATER MANCHESTER
Formby
SKELMERSDALE
WIGAN
Worsley
MERSEYSIDE
LIVERPOOL
BIRKENHEAD
Thelwall
WARRINGTON
RUNCORN
Llandudno Junction
Colwyn Bay
RHYL
Thornton Hough
ELLESMERE PORT
CHESHIRE
Mobberley
CONWY
ABERGELE
Lower Peover
NORTHWICH
Ty'n-y-groes
Llanelian-yn-Rhos
St George
Bostock Green
Allostock
Bodfari
Delamere
DENBIGH
Hawarden
Swettenham
Chester
Cotebrook
SH
Mold
Aldford
Warmingham
RUTHIN
Sandbach
Burwardsley
Bunbury
BETWS-Y-COED
CLWYD
CREWE
Gresford
Barthomley
WREXHAM
Cholmondeley
NANTWICH
SJ
Aston
Wrinehill
GWYNEDD
Llangollen
Overton Bridge
Burleydam
WHITCHURCH
BALA
MARKET DRAYTON
Llanarmon Dyffryn Ceiriog
OSWESTRY
6
Maesbury Marsh
Baschurch
SHROPSHIRE
DOLGELLAU
NEWPORT
Chetwynd Aston
POWYS
Shrewsbury
TELFORD

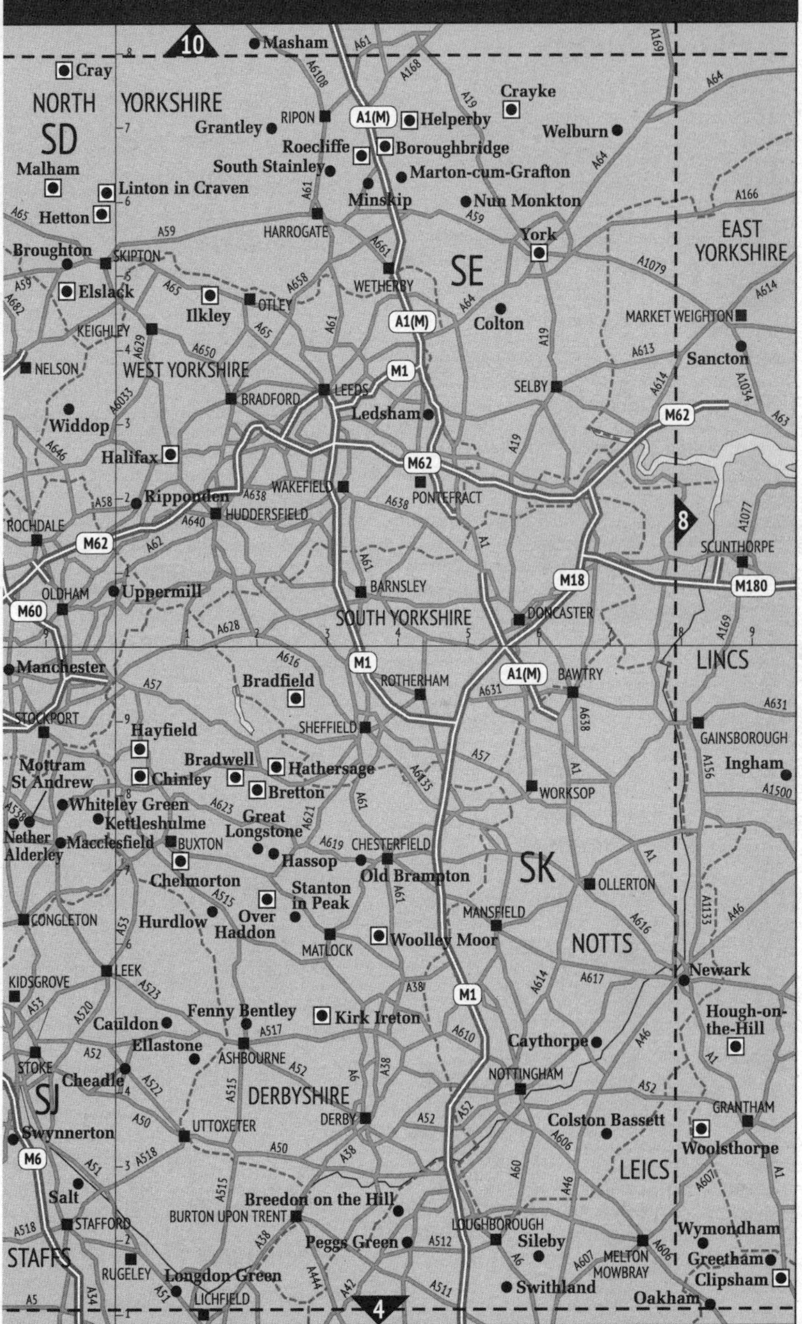
10
Masham
Cray
NORTH YORKSHIRE
SD
RIPON
A1(M)
Helperby
Crayke
Grantley
Welburn
Roecliffe
Boroughbridge
South Stainley
Marton-cum-Grafton
Malham
Linton in Craven
Minskip
Nun Monkton
Hetton
A166
HARROGATE
York
EAST YORKSHIRE
Broughton
SKIPTON
SE
WETHERBY
A1079
Elslack
Ilkley
OTLEY
Colton
MARKET WEIGHTON
KEIGHLEY
A614
NELSON
WEST YORKSHIRE
A613
Sancton
M1
SELBY
BRADFORD
LEEDS
Widdop
Ledsham
M62
Halifax
M62
WAKEFIELD
PONTEFRACT
Ripponden
HUDDERSFIELD
8
ROCHDALE
M62
SCUNTHORPE
M18
OLDHAM
Uppermill
BARNSLEY
M180
M60
SOUTH YORKSHIRE
DONCASTER
Manchester
LINCS
Bradfield
M1
ROTHERHAM
A1(M)
BAWTRY
STOCKPORT
Hayfield
SHEFFIELD
GAINSBOROUGH
Bradwell
Hathersage
Ingham
Mottram St Andrew
Chinley
Bretton
WORKSOP
Whiteley Green
Great Longstone
Kettleshulme
Nether Alderley
Macclesfield
BUXTON
CHESTERFIELD
Hassop
SK
Chelmorton
Old Brampton
OLLERTON
Stanton in Peak
CONGLETON
Hurdlow
Over Haddon
MANSFIELD
NOTTS
MATLOCK
Woolley Moor
LEEK
Newark
KIDSGROVE
M1
Hough-on-the-Hill
Fenny Bentley
Kirk Ireton
Cauldon
Ellastone
Caythorpe
ASHBOURNE
STOKE
Cheadle
NOTTINGHAM
SJ
DERBYSHIRE
GRANTHAM
DERBY
Colston Bassett
Swynnerton
UTTOXETER
Woolsthorpe
M6
LEICS
Salt
Breedon on the Hill
BURTON UPON TRENT
LOUGHBOROUGH
Wymondham
STAFFORD
Sileby
Peggs Green
MELTON MOWBRAY
Greetham
STAFFS
RUGELEY
Longdon Green
Clipsham
Swithland
LICHFIELD
Oakham
4

8

- ● Main Entry
- ◙ Main Entry with accommodation
- ■ Place name to assist navigation

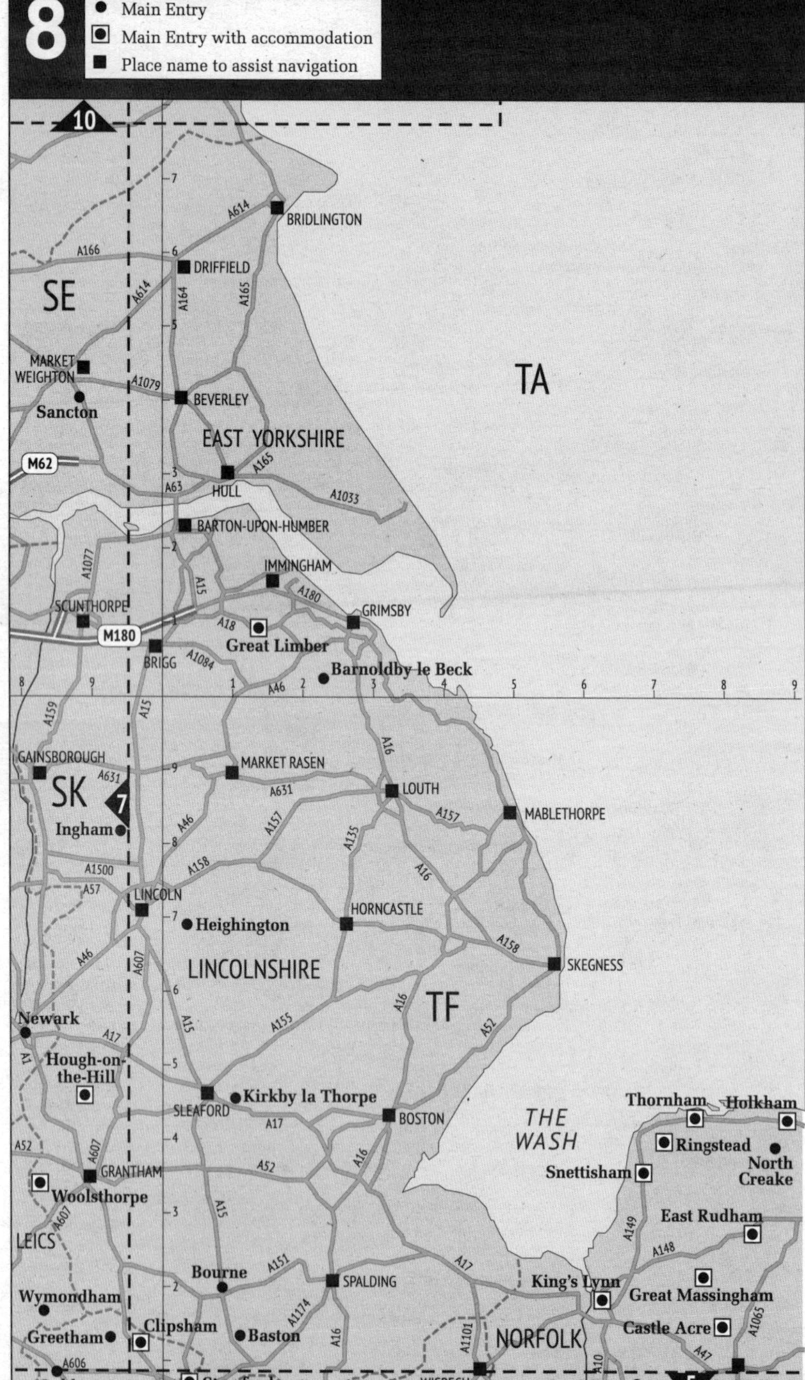

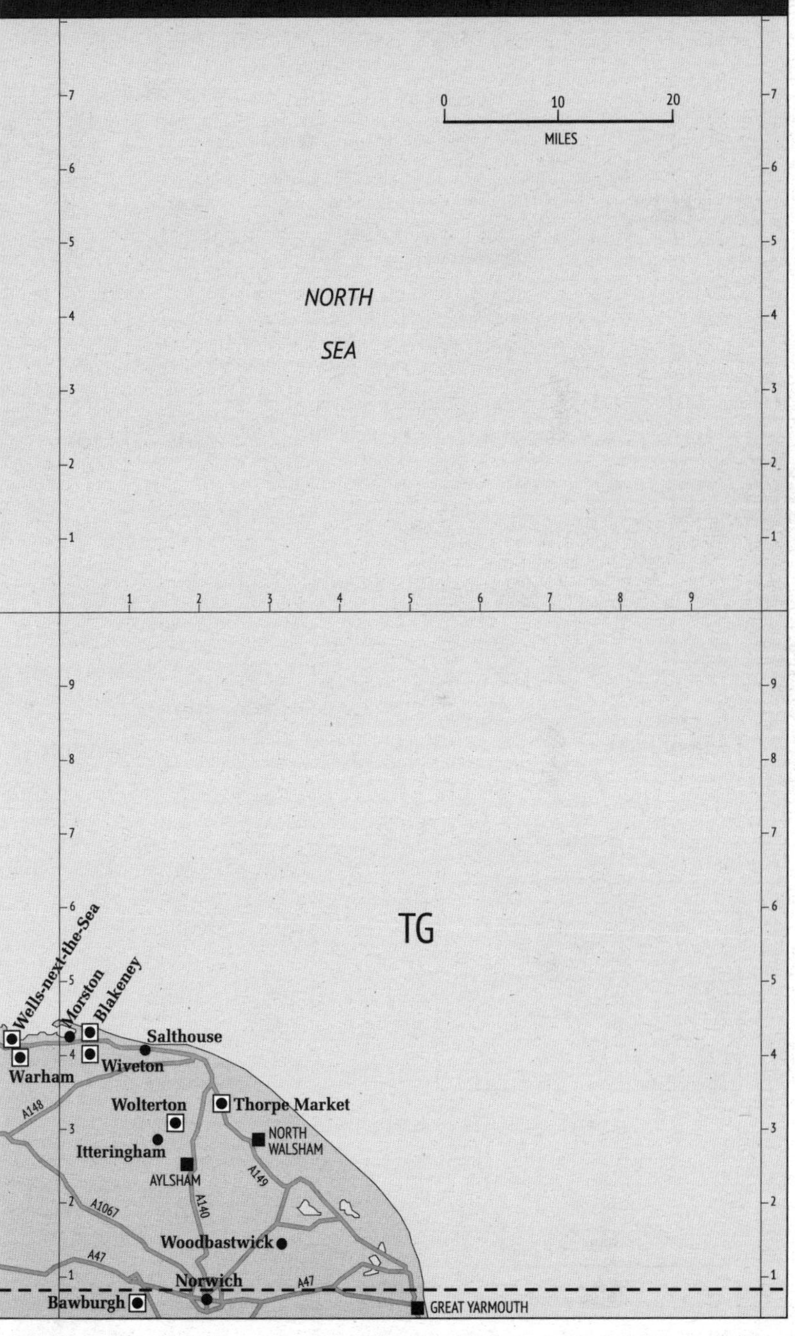
0
10
20
MILES
NORTH
SEA
TG
Wells-next-the-Sea
Morston
Blakeney
Salthouse
Warham
Wiveton
Wolterton
Thorpe Market
Itteringham
NORTH
WALSHAM
AYLSHAM
A148
A149
A140
A1067
Woodbastwick
A47
Norwich
Bawburgh
GREAT YARMOUTH

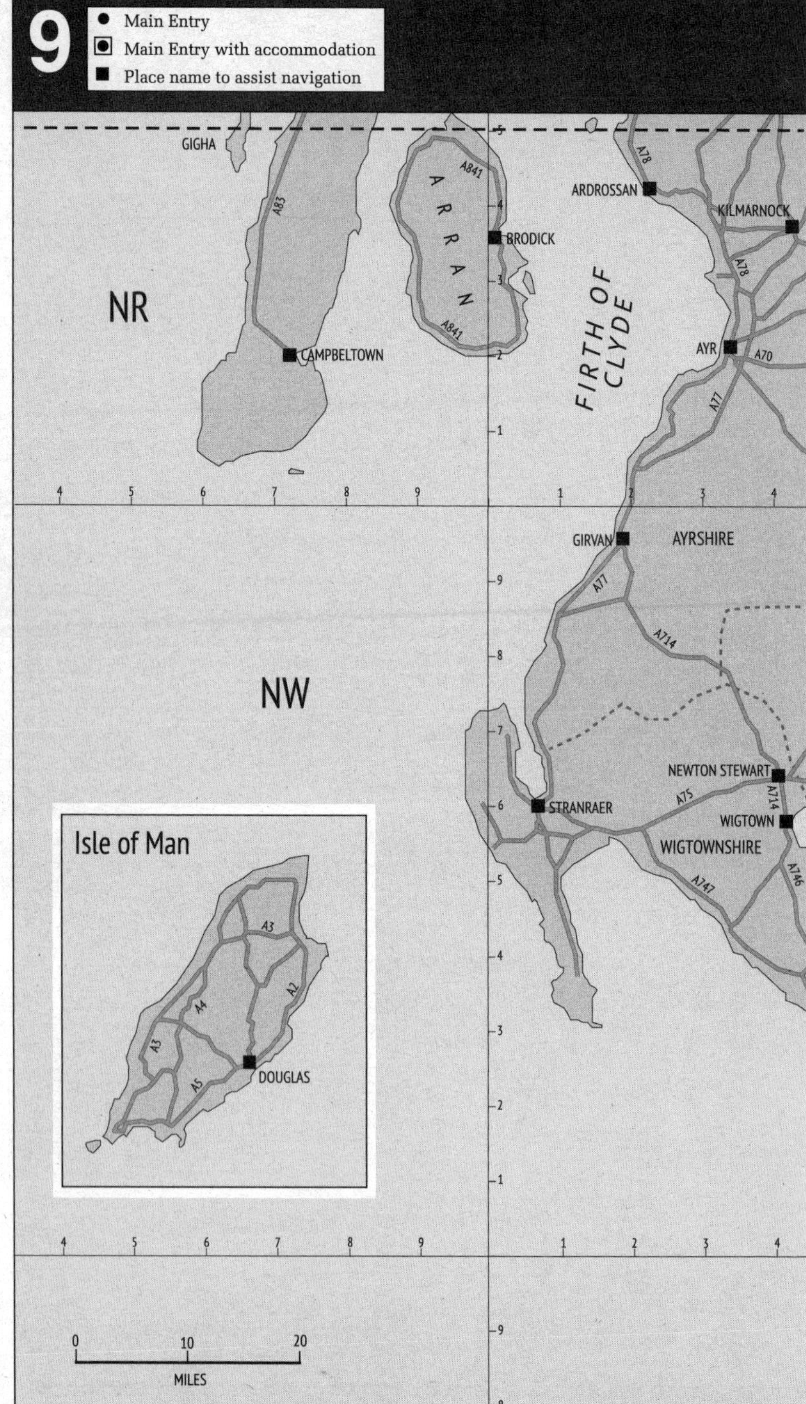

9
Main Entry
Main Entry with accommodation
Place name to assist navigation
GIGHA
NR
CAMPBELTOWN
ARRAN
BRODICK
ARDROSSAN
KILMARNOCK
FIRTH OF CLYDE
AYR
GIRVAN
AYRSHIRE
NW
NEWTON STEWART
STRANRAER
WIGTOWN
WIGTOWNSHIRE
Isle of Man
DOUGLAS
MILES

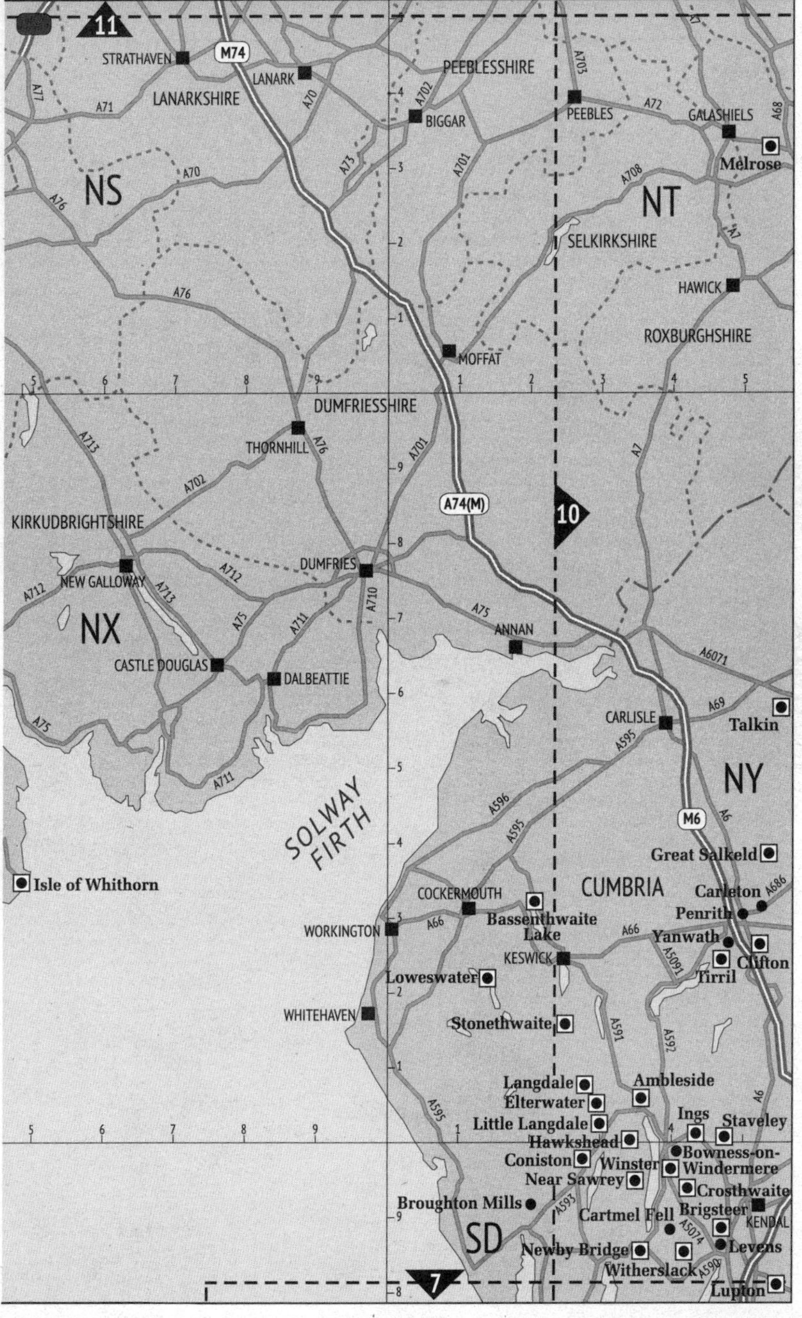
11
STRATHAVEN
M74
LANARK
LANARKSHIRE
PEEBLESSHIRE
BIGGAR
PEEBLES
GALASHIELS
Melrose
NS
NT
SELKIRKSHIRE
HAWICK
ROXBURGHSHIRE
MOFFAT
DUMFRIESSHIRE
THORNHILL
KIRKUDBRIGHTSHIRE
A74(M)
10
NEW GALLOWAY
DUMFRIES
NX
ANNAN
CASTLE DOUGLAS
DALBEATTIE
CARLISLE
Talkin
NY
M6
SOLWAY FIRTH
Great Salkeld
Isle of Whithorn
COCKERMOUTH
CUMBRIA
Carleton
Penrith
Bassenthwaite Lake
WORKINGTON
Yanwath
KESWICK
Clifton
Tirril
Loweswater
WHITEHAVEN
Stonethwaite
Langdale
Ambleside
Elterwater
Little Langdale
Ings
Staveley
Hawkshead
Coniston
Bowness-on-Windermere
Winster
Near Sawrey
Crosthwaite
Broughton Mills
Brigsteer
Cartmel Fell
KENDAL
SD
Newby Bridge
Levens
Witherslack
7
Lupton
A77
A71
A70
A76
A73
A702
A701
A703
A72
A68
A708
A7
A713
A712
A75
A711
A710
A6071
A69
A595
A596
A6
A686
A66
A5091
A591
A592
A593
A5074
A590

10

- ● Main Entry
- ◙ Main Entry with accommodation
- ■ Place name to assist navigation

11

BERWICKSHIRE
Swinton
BERWICK-UPON-TWEED
A703
A6112
A697
A1
A698
PEEBLES
A7
A68
GALASHIELS
A72
COLDSTREAM
A698
Melrose
KELSO
A708
NT
WOOLER
Seahouses
Ancrum
SELKIRKSHIRE
Ellingham
Newton-by-the-Sea
JEDBURGH
Craster
A697
HAWICK
A6088
A68
ALNWICK
A7
ROXBURGHSHIRE
A1
NORTHUMBERLAND
A68
OTTERBURN
A1068
DUMFRIESSHIRE
Stannersburn
A696
A68
MORPETH
9
Wark
Barrasford
A1
A19
A74(M)
A7
HAYDON BRIDGE
North Shields
Gilsland
Newton
NEWCASTLE UPON TYNE
A6071
BRAMPTON
A69
A69
HEXHAM
CORBRIDGE
A695
A69
Diptonmill
GATESHEAD
CARLISLE
Talkin
A686
Hedley on the Hill
A595
A689
A68
CONSETT
NY
Blanchland
Carterway Heads
ALSTON
A691
M6
A686
A6
Durham
A68
A689
DURHAM
Great Salkeld
Penrith
Carleton
A1(M)
A66
Yanwath
Clifton
BISHOP AUCKLAND
A167
KESWICK
Tirril
A688
Romaldkirk
Cotherstone
A167
A66
Stonethwaite
A67
CUMBRIA
BROUGH
A66
BARNARD CASTLE
DARLINGTON
A591
A592
Langdale
Elterwater
A6
A685
SCOTCH CORNER
Ambleside
M6
Moulton
Little Langdale
Ings
Staveley
Ravenstonedale
RICHMOND
A1
Hawkshead
Bowness-on-Windermere
A683
NORTH
Coniston
Winster
Crosthwaite
Grinton
Constable Burton
KENDAL
SEDBERGH
A684
Near Sawrey
Leyburn
Kirkby Fleetham
Cartmel Fell
Brigsteer
A5074
SD
A590
A590
Levens
A683
East Witton
Witherslack
Thornton Watlass
Newby Bridge
A6
7
Lupton
Masham
A6108
A1(M)

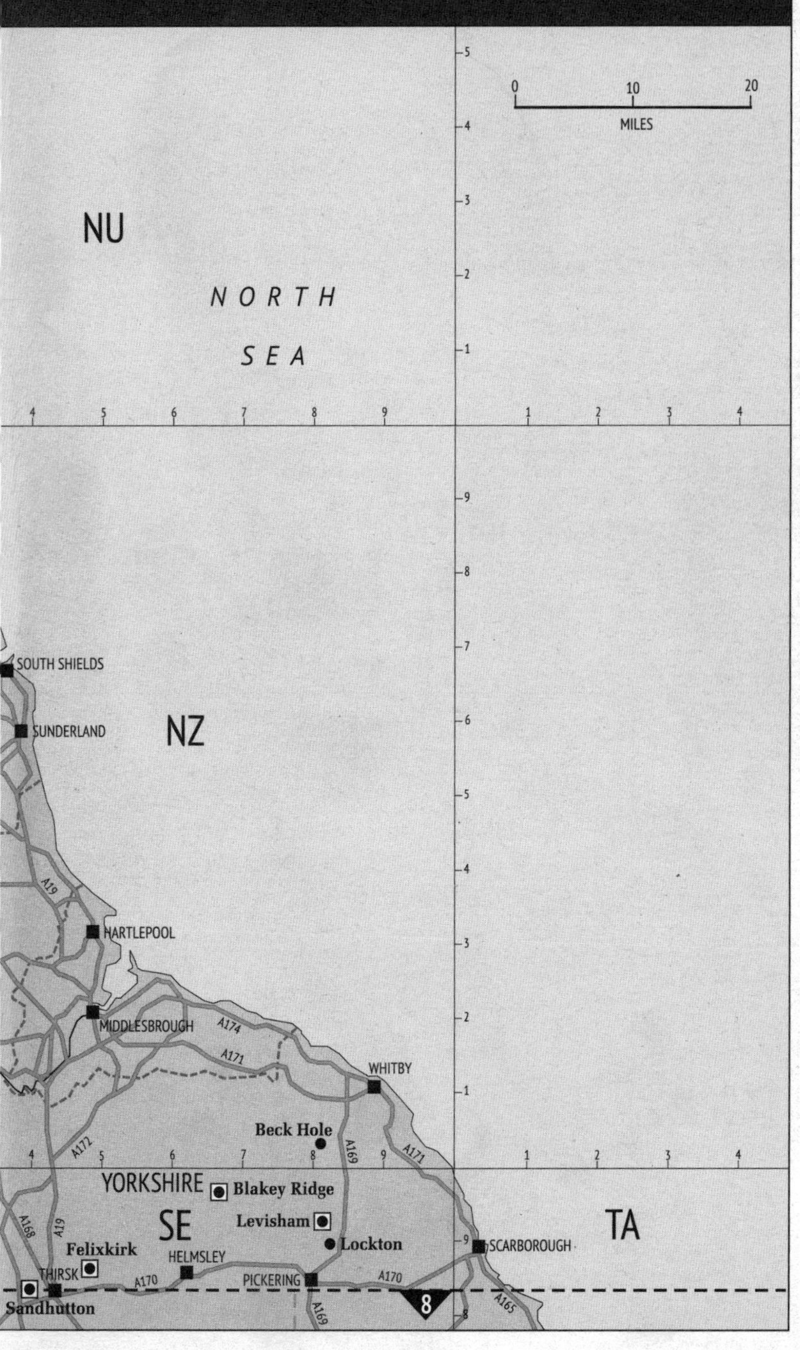

0
10
20
MILES
NU
NORTH
SEA
NZ
SOUTH SHIELDS
SUNDERLAND
HARTLEPOOL
MIDDLESBROUGH
A19
A174
A171
WHITBY
Beck Hole
A169
A172
A171
YORKSHIRE
Blakey Ridge
SE
Levisham
Lockton
Felixkirk
HELMSLEY
THIRSK
A170
PICKERING
A170
Sandhutton
A168
A19
A169
8
SCARBOROUGH
A165
TA

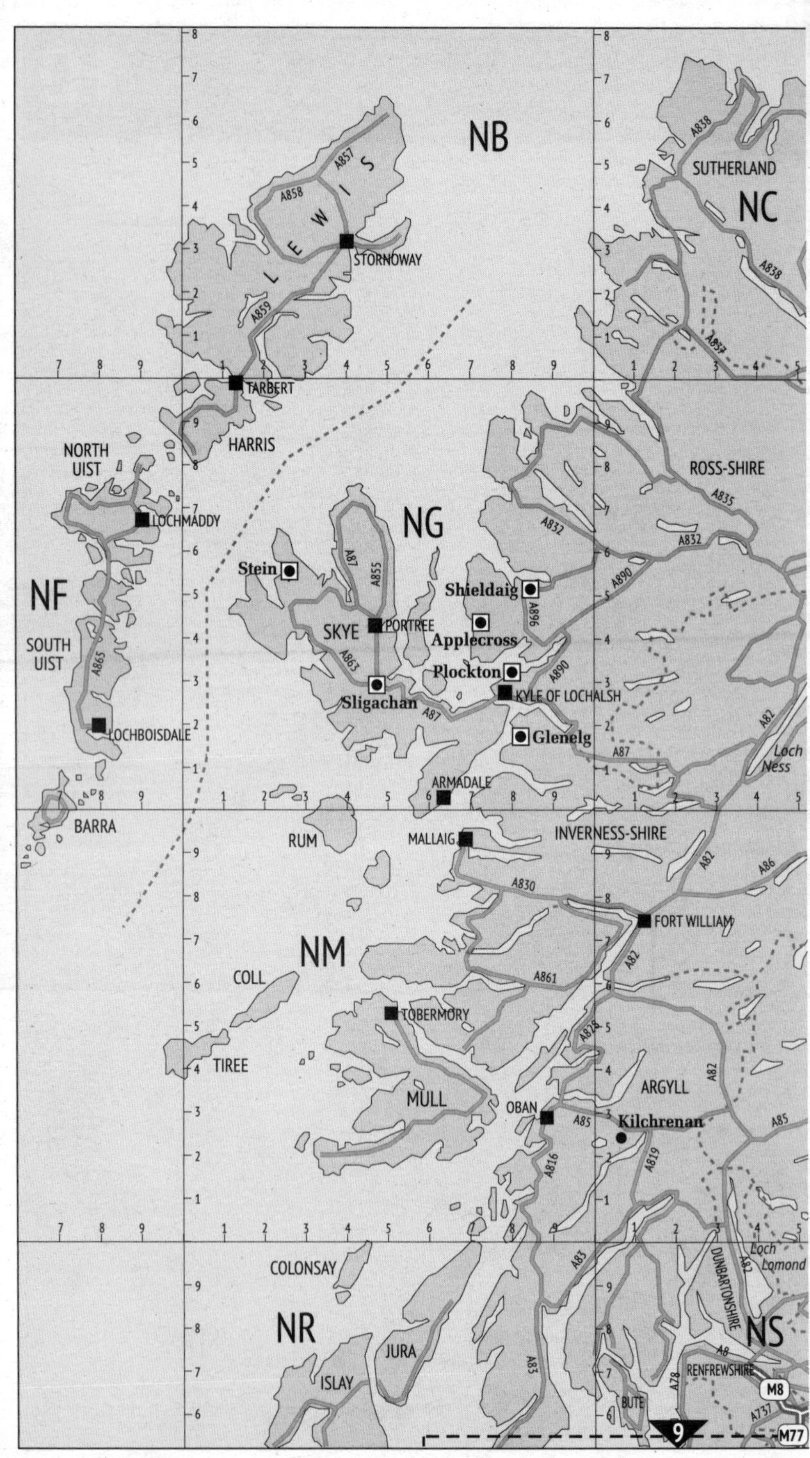

NB
LEWIS
STORNOWAY
TARBERT
HARRIS
NORTH UIST
LOCHMADDY
NF
SOUTH UIST
LOCHBOISDALE
BARRA
NG
Stein
SKYE
PORTREE
Sligachan
Shieldaig
Applecross
Plockton
KYLE OF LOCHALSH
Glenelg
ARMADALE
RUM
MALLAIG
INVERNESS-SHIRE
NM
COLL
TIREE
TOBERMORY
MULL
OBAN
Kilchrenan
ARGYLL
FORT WILLIAM
NC
SUTHERLAND
ROSS-SHIRE
Loch Ness
NR
COLONSAY
JURA
ISLAY
BUTE
DUNBARTONSHIRE
RENFREWSHIRE
Loch Lomond
NS
M8
M77
9
A857
A858
A859
A87
A855
A863
A865
A896
A890
A832
A835
A838
A837
A82
A86
A830
A861
A828
A85
A816
A819
A83
A8
A78
A737

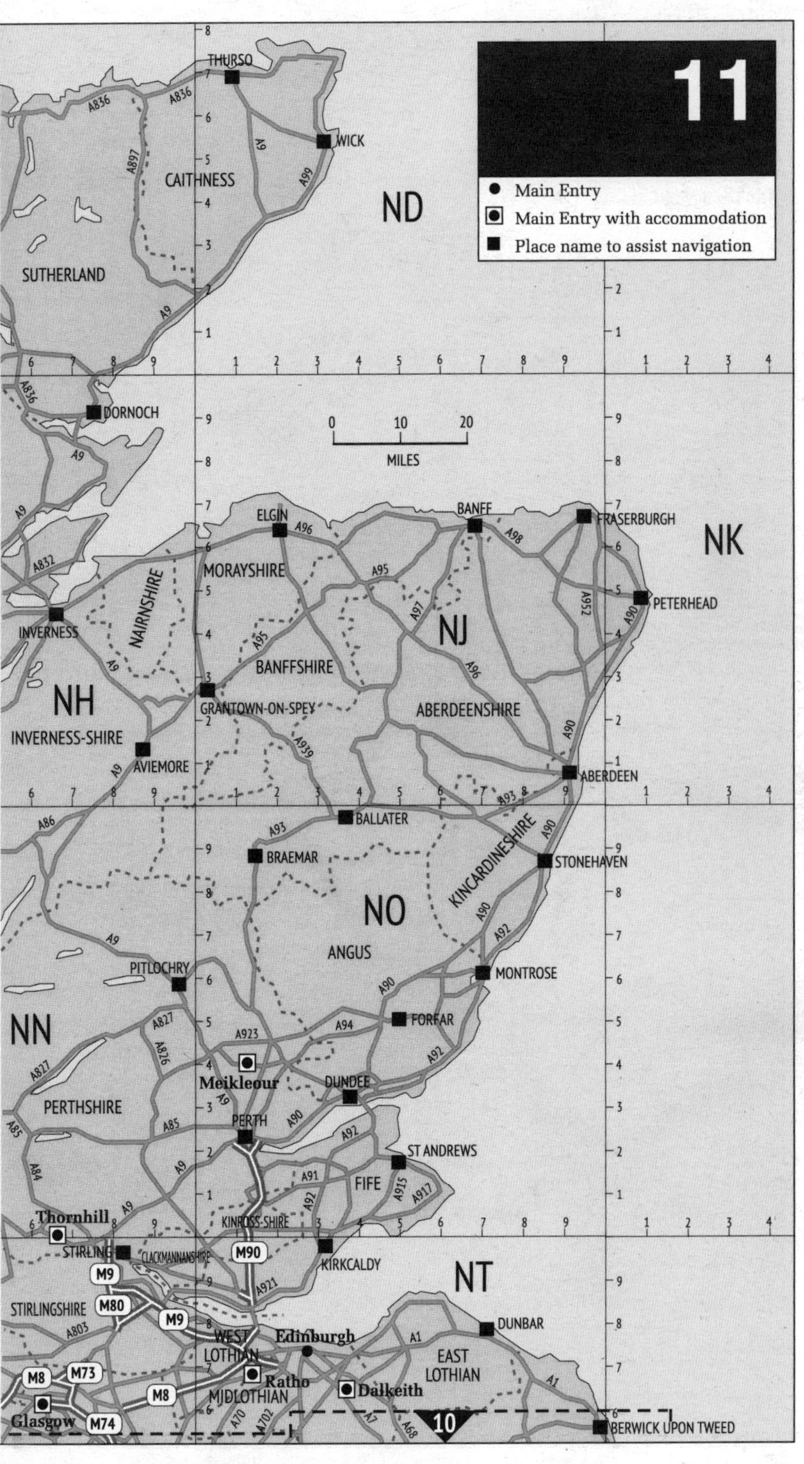
11
Main Entry
Main Entry with accommodation
Place name to assist navigation
ND
NK
NJ
NH
NO
NN
NT
THURSO
WICK
CAITHNESS
SUTHERLAND
DORNOCH
0 10 20
MILES
ELGIN
BANFF
FRASERBURGH
PETERHEAD
MORAYSHIRE
NAIRNSHIRE
INVERNESS
BANFFSHIRE
GRANTOWN-ON-SPEY
ABERDEENSHIRE
INVERNESS-SHIRE
AVIEMORE
ABERDEEN
BALLATER
BRAEMAR
KINCARDINESHIRE
STONEHAVEN
ANGUS
PITLOCHRY
MONTROSE
FORFAR
Meikleour
DUNDEE
PERTHSHIRE
PERTH
ST ANDREWS
FIFE
Thornhill
KINROSS-SHIRE
STIRLING
CLACKMANNANSHIRE
KIRKCALDY
STIRLINGSHIRE
DUNBAR
WEST LOTHIAN
Edinburgh
EAST LOTHIAN
Ratho
Dalkeith
MIDLOTHIAN
Glasgow
10
BERWICK UPON TWEED

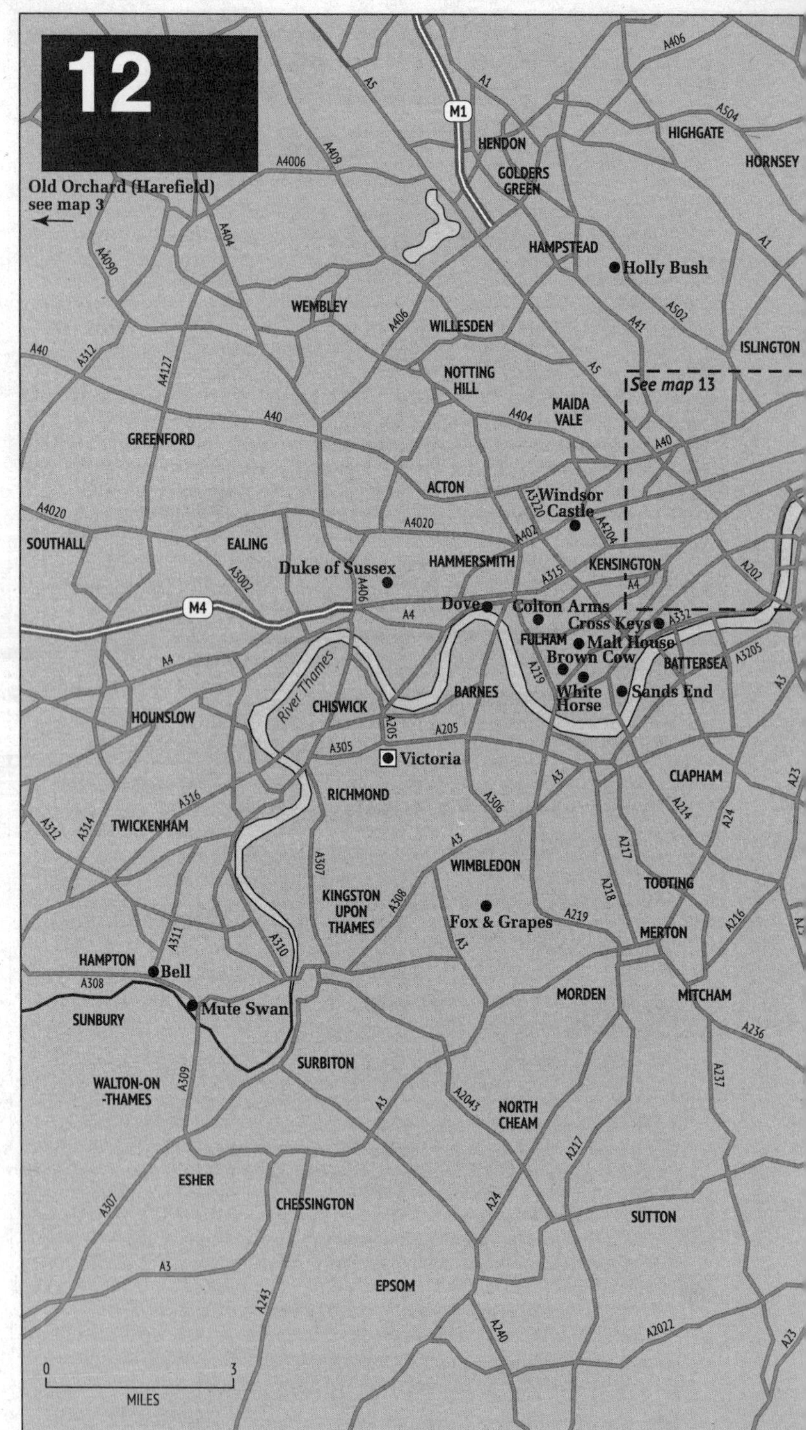
12
Old Orchard (Harefield)
see map 3
See map 13
HENDON
GOLDERS GREEN
HIGHGATE
HORNSEY
HAMPSTEAD
Holly Bush
WEMBLEY
WILLESDEN
ISLINGTON
NOTTING HILL
MAIDA VALE
GREENFORD
ACTON
Windsor Castle
SOUTHALL
EALING
Duke of Sussex
HAMMERSMITH
KENSINGTON
Dove
Colton Arms
Cross Keys
FULHAM
Malt House
Brown Cow
BATTERSEA
White Horse
Sands End
River Thames
CHISWICK
BARNES
HOUNSLOW
Victoria
CLAPHAM
RICHMOND
TWICKENHAM
WIMBLEDON
TOOTING
KINGSTON UPON THAMES
Fox & Grapes
MERTON
HAMPTON
Bell
Mute Swan
SUNBURY
MORDEN
MITCHAM
SURBITON
WALTON-ON-THAMES
NORTH CHEAM
ESHER
CHESSINGTON
SUTTON
EPSOM
MILES
0
3

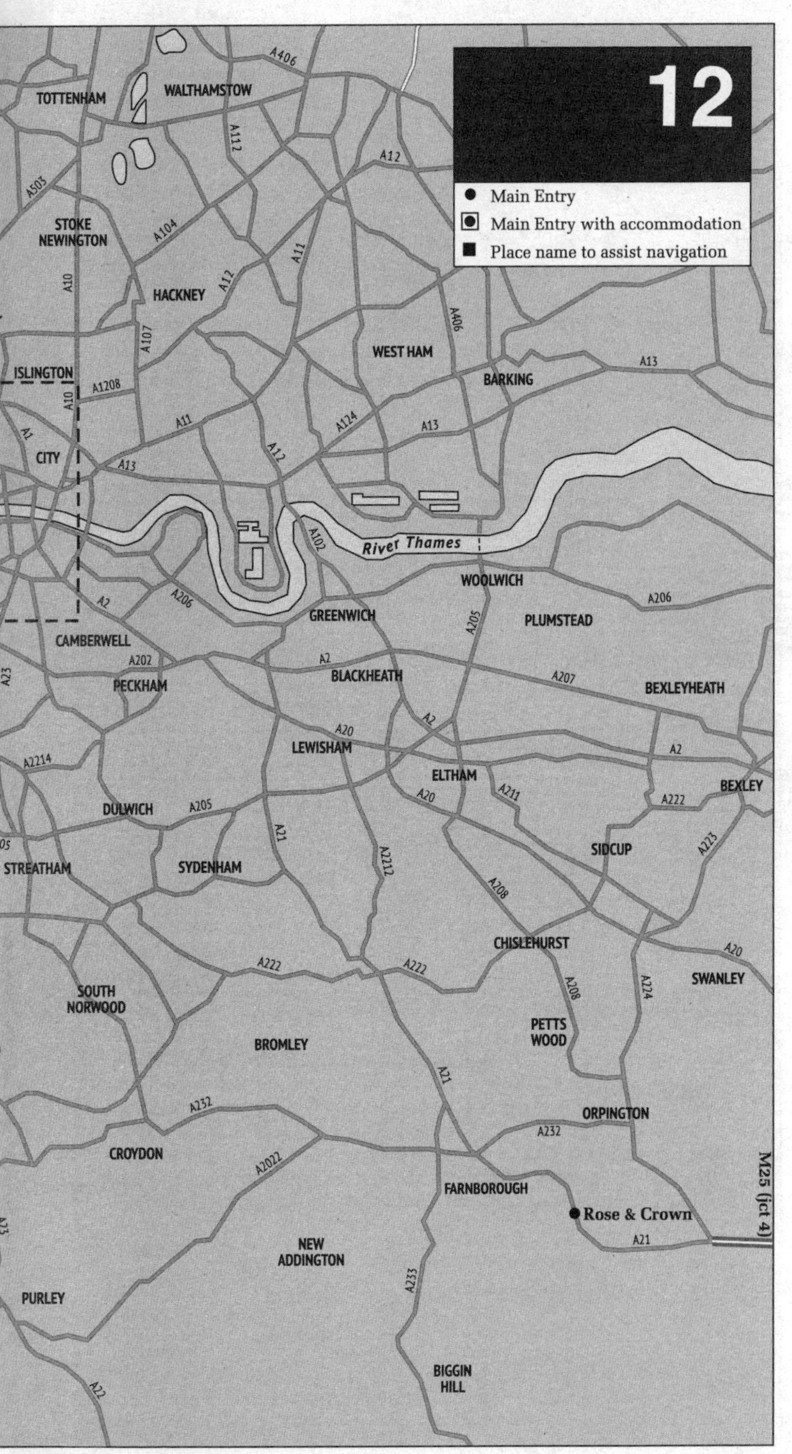
12
Main Entry
Main Entry with accommodation
Place name to assist navigation
TOTTENHAM
WALTHAMSTOW
STOKE NEWINGTON
HACKNEY
ISLINGTON
CITY
WEST HAM
BARKING
River Thames
WOOLWICH
GREENWICH
PLUMSTEAD
CAMBERWELL
PECKHAM
BLACKHEATH
BEXLEYHEATH
LEWISHAM
ELTHAM
BEXLEY
DULWICH
SIDCUP
STREATHAM
SYDENHAM
CHISLEHURST
SWANLEY
SOUTH NORWOOD
PETTS WOOD
BROMLEY
ORPINGTON
CROYDON
FARNBOROUGH
Rose & Crown
M25 (jct 4)
NEW ADDINGTON
PURLEY
BIGGIN HILL

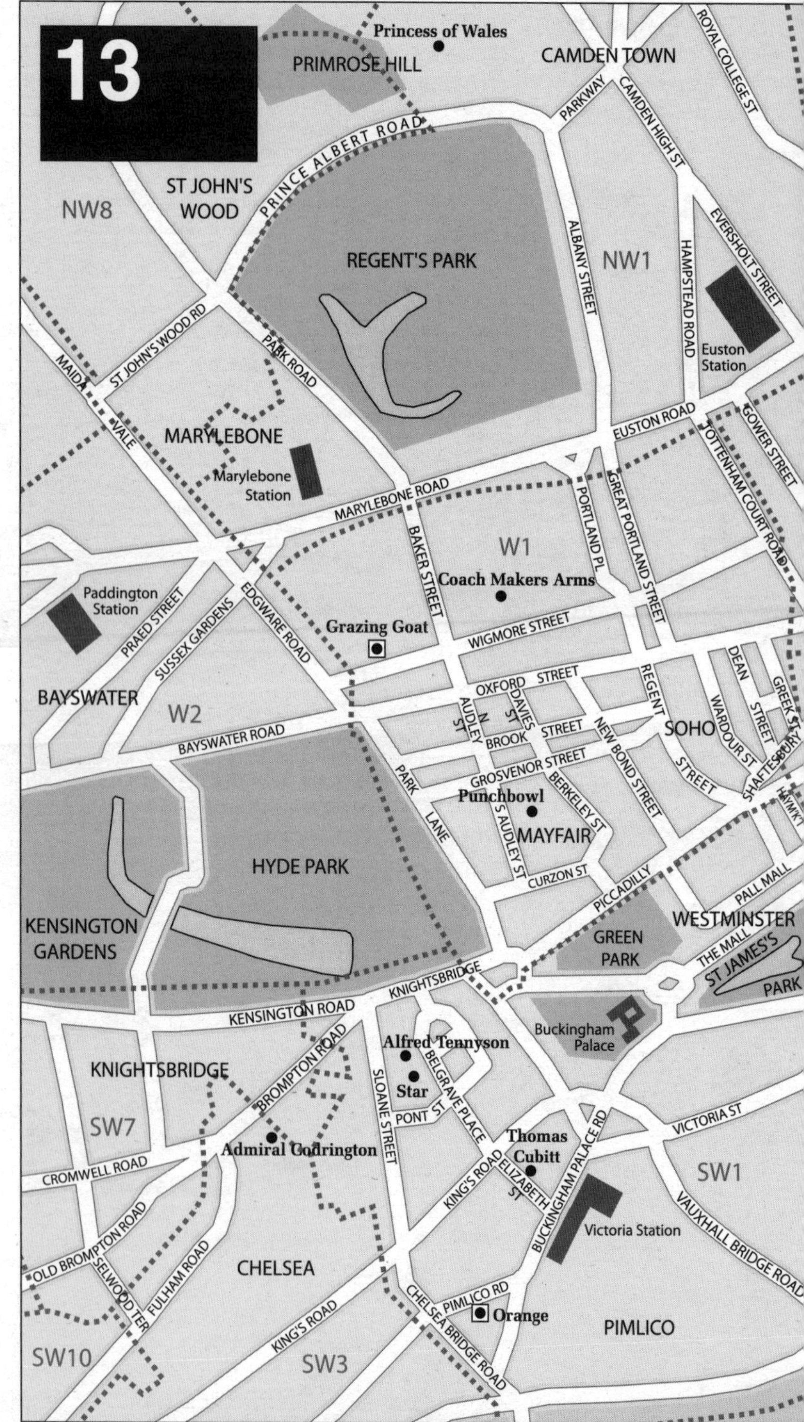

13
Princess of Wales
PRIMROSE HILL
CAMDEN TOWN
PRINCE ALBERT ROAD
PARKWAY
CAMDEN HIGH ST
ROYAL COLLEGE ST
ST JOHN'S WOOD
NW8
REGENT'S PARK
ALBANY STREET
NW1
HAMPSTEAD ROAD
EVERSHOLT STREET
Euston Station
ST JOHN'S WOOD RD
PARK ROAD
MAIDA VALE
MARYLEBONE
Marylebone Station
EUSTON ROAD
GOWER STREET
TOTTENHAM COURT ROAD
MARYLEBONE ROAD
PORTLAND PL
GREAT PORTLAND STREET
BAKER STREET
W1
Coach Makers Arms
Paddington Station
PRAED STREET
SUSSEX GARDENS
EDGWARE ROAD
Grazing Goat
WIGMORE STREET
OXFORD STREET
REGENT
DEAN STREET
GREEK ST
BAYSWATER
W2
N AUDLEY ST
DAVIES ST
BROOK STREET
NEW BOND STREET
SOHO
WARDOUR ST
BAYSWATER ROAD
PARK LANE
GROSVENOR STREET
BERKELEY ST
STREET
SHAFTESBURY
HAYM'KT
Punchbowl
S AUDLEY ST
MAYFAIR
HYDE PARK
CURZON ST
PICCADILLY
PALL MALL
KENSINGTON GARDENS
GREEN PARK
WESTMINSTER
THE MALL
ST JAMES'S PARK
KNIGHTSBRIDGE
KENSINGTON ROAD
Buckingham Palace
Alfred Tennyson
BROMPTON ROAD
BELGRAVE PLACE
Star
KNIGHTSBRIDGE
SW7
SLOANE STREET
PONT ST
VICTORIA ST
Thomas Cubitt
Admiral Codrington
BUCKINGHAM PALACE RD
CROMWELL ROAD
KING'S ROAD
ELIZABETH ST
SW1
VAUXHALL BRIDGE ROAD
Victoria Station
OLD BROMPTON ROAD
SELWOOD TER
FULHAM ROAD
CHELSEA
PIMLICO RD
Orange
PIMLICO
KING'S ROAD
CHELSEA BRIDGE ROAD
SW10
SW3

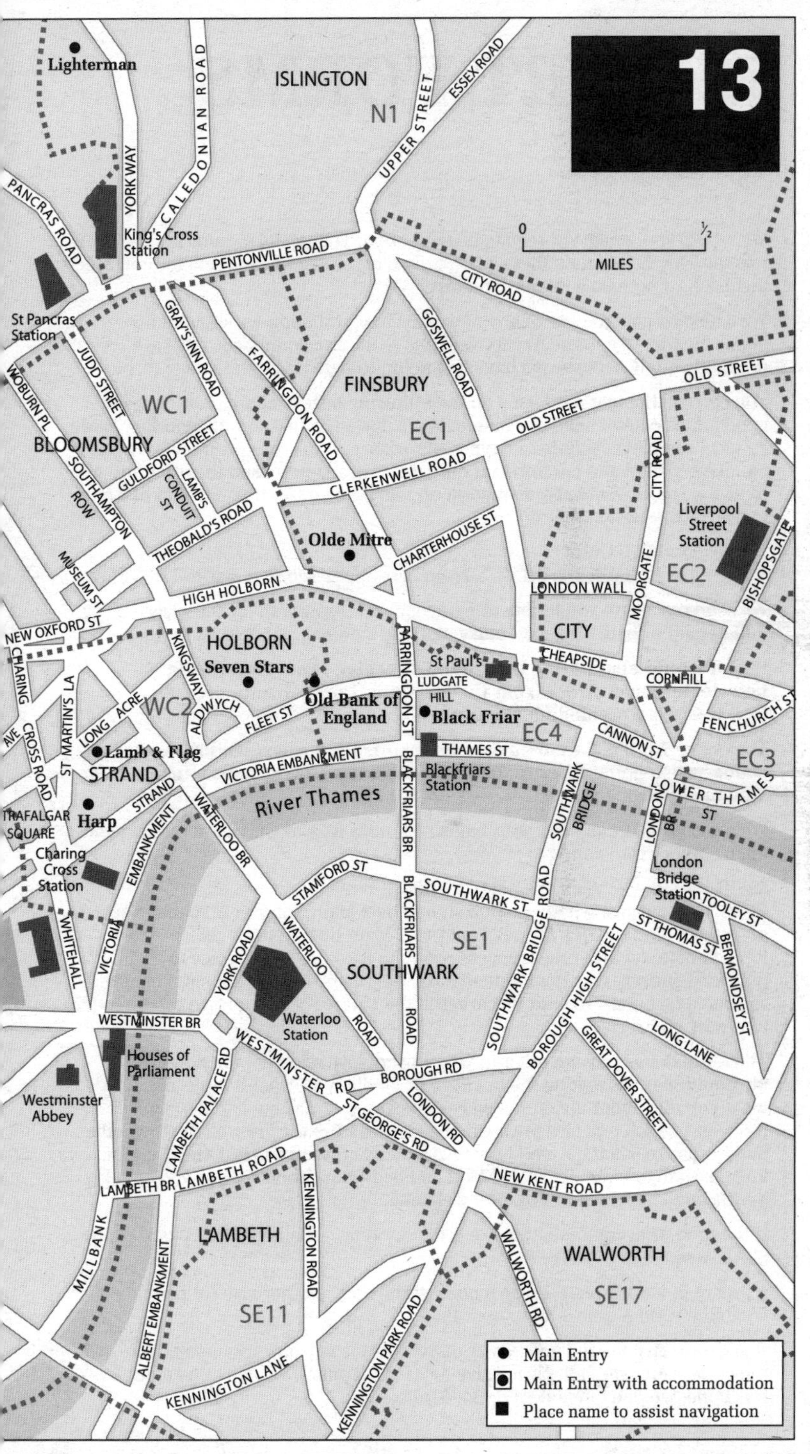
13
Lighterman
ISLINGTON
N1
0
½
MILES
King's Cross Station
St Pancras Station
WC1
BLOOMSBURY
FINSBURY
EC1
Olde Mitre
Liverpool Street Station
EC2
CITY
HOLBORN
Seven Stars
Old Bank of England
Black Friar
St Paul's
WC2
EC4
EC3
Lamb & Flag
STRAND
Harp
River Thames
Blackfriars Station
London Bridge Station
Charing Cross Station
SE1
SOUTHWARK
Waterloo Station
Houses of Parliament
Westminster Abbey
LAMBETH
SE11
WALWORTH
SE17
Main Entry
Main Entry with accommodation
Place name to assist navigation

REPORT FORMS

We would very much appreciate hearing about your visits to pubs in this *Guide*, whether you have found them as described and recommend them for continued inclusion or noticed a fall in standards.

We'd also be glad to hear of any new pubs that you think we should know about. Readers' reports are very valuable to us, and sometimes pubs are dropped simply because we have had no up-to-date news on them.

You can use the tear-out forms on the following pages, email us at feedback@goodguides.com or send us comments via our website (www.thegoodpubguide.co.uk) or app. We include two types of forms: one for you to simply list pubs you have visited and confirm that our review is accurate, and the other for you to give us more detailed information on individual pubs. If you would like more forms, please write to us at:

The Good Pub Guide
Freepost RTXY-ZCBC-BBAZ, Stream Lane, Sedlescombe, Battle TN33 0PB

We send out thank-you letters to everyone who reports to us, but please understand if there's a delay (particularly in summer, our busiest period).

If you would also like to continue to receive *Good Pub Guide* newsletters and offers from the Random House Group, please tick the box provided on the form.

The end of April is the cut-off date for reports for the next edition. We will, of course, use reports after this date, but your name will not appear in the *Guide* until the following year.

We'll assume we can print your name or initials as a recommender unless you tell us otherwise.

MAIN ENTRY OR 'ALSO WORTH A VISIT'?
Please try to gauge whether a pub should be a Main Entry or in the Also Worth a Visit section (and tick the relevant box). Main Entries need qualities that would make it worth other readers' while to travel some distance to them. If a pub is an entirely new recommendation, the Also Worth a Visit section may be the best place for it to start its career in the *Guide* – to encourage other readers to report on it.

The more detail you can put into your description of a pub, the better. Any information on how good the landlord or landlady is, what it looks like inside, what you like about the atmosphere and character, the quality and type of food, and which real ales are available and whether they're well kept, whether bedrooms are available, and how big/attractive the garden is. Other helpful information includes prices for food and bedrooms, food service and opening hours, and if children or dogs are welcome.

If the food or accommodation are is outstanding, tick the FOOD Award or the STAY Award box.

If you're in a position to gauge a pub's suitability or otherwise for people with disabilities, do please tell us about that.

If you can, give the full address or directions for any pub not currently in the *Guide* – most of all, please give us its postcode. If we can't find a pub's postcode, we don't include it in the *Guide*.

I have been to the following pubs in *The Good Pub Guide 2019* in the last few months, found them as described, and confirm that they deserve continued inclusion:

continued overleaf

PLEASE GIVE YOUR NAME AND ADDRESS ON THE BACK OF THIS FORM

Pubs visited continued.........

By returning this form, you confirm your agreement that the information you provide in your review may be used by The Random House Group Ltd (or its assignees and/or licensees) in any media or medium whatsoever. Any personal details which you provide from which we can identify you are held and processed in accordance with the General Data Protection Regulation (GDPR), and details on how we process this personal data can be found in our Privacy Policy (https://www.penguinrandomhouse.co.uk/PrivacyPolicy/). **Your details will not be passed on to any third parties for their marketing purposes.**

I would like to receive Good Pub Guide updates and offers from The Random House Group. ☐

Your own name and address *(block capitals please)*

....

....

....

Postcode...

Please return to

The Good Pub Guide
FREEPOST RTXY–ZCBC–BBAZ,
Stream Lane,
Sedlescombe, Battle
TN33 0PB

IF YOU PREFER, YOU CAN SEND US REPORTS BY EMAIL:

feedback@goodguides.com

I have been to the following pubs in *The Good Pub Guide 2019* in the last few months, found them as described, and confirm that they deserve continued inclusion:

continued overleaf

PLEASE GIVE YOUR NAME AND ADDRESS ON THE BACK OF THIS FORM

Pubs visited continued..........

By returning this form, you confirm your agreement that the information you provide in your review may be used by The Random House Group Ltd (or its assignees and/or licensees) in any media or medium whatsoever. Any personal details which you provide from which we can identify you are held and processed in accordance with the General Data Protection Regulation (GDPR), and details on how we process this personal data can be found in our Privacy Policy (https://www.penguinrandomhouse.co.uk/PrivacyPolicy/). **Your details will not be passed on to any third parties for their marketing purposes.**

I would like to receive Good Pub Guide updates and offers from The Random House Group. ☐

Your own name and address *(block capitals please)*

....

....

....

Postcode..

Please return to

The Good Pub Guide
FREEPOST RTXY–ZCBC–BBAZ,
Stream Lane,
Sedlescombe, Battle
TN33 0PB

IF YOU PREFER, YOU CAN SEND US REPORTS BY EMAIL:

feedback@goodguides.com

I have been to the following pubs in *The Good Pub Guide 2019* in the last few months, found them as described, and confirm that they deserve continued inclusion:

continued overleaf

PLEASE GIVE YOUR NAME AND ADDRESS ON THE BACK OF THIS FORM

Pubs visited continued..........

By returning this form, you confirm your agreement that the information you provide in your review may be used by The Random House Group Ltd (or its assignees and/or licensees) in any media or medium whatsoever. Any personal details which you provide from which we can identify you are held and processed in accordance with the General Data Protection Regulation (GDPR), and details on how we process this personal data can be found in our Privacy Policy (https://www.penguinrandomhouse.co.uk/PrivacyPolicy/). **Your details will not be passed on to any third parties for their marketing purposes.**

I would like to receive Good Pub Guide updates and offers from The Random House Group. ☐

Your own name and address *(block capitals please)*

....

....

....

Postcode ....

Please return to

The Good Pub Guide
FREEPOST RTXY–ZCBC–BBAZ,
Stream Lane,
Sedlescombe, Battle
TN33 0PB

IF YOU PREFER, YOU CAN SEND US REPORTS BY EMAIL:

feedback@goodguides.com

I have been to the following pubs in *The Good Pub Guide 2019* in the last few months, found them as described, and confirm that they deserve continued inclusion:

continued overleaf

PLEASE GIVE YOUR NAME AND ADDRESS ON THE BACK OF THIS FORM

Pubs visited continued.........

By returning this form, you confirm your agreement that the information you provide in your review may be used by The Random House Group Ltd (or its assignees and/or licensees) in any media or medium whatsoever. Any personal details which you provide from which we can identify you are held and processed in accordance with the General Data Protection Regulation (GDPR), and details on how we process this personal data can be found in our Privacy Policy (https://www.penguinrandomhouse.co.uk/PrivacyPolicy/). **Your details will not be passed on to any third parties for their marketing purposes.**

I would like to receive Good Pub Guide updates and offers from The Random House Group. ☐

Your own name and address *(block capitals please)*

....

....

....

Postcode...

Please return to

The Good Pub Guide
FREEPOST RTXY–ZCBC–BBAZ,
Stream Lane,
Sedlescombe, Battle
TN33 0PB

IF YOU PREFER, YOU CAN SEND US REPORTS BY EMAIL:

feedback@goodguides.com

I have been to the following pubs in *The Good Pub Guide 2019* in the last few months, found them as described, and confirm that they deserve continued inclusion:

continued overleaf

PLEASE GIVE YOUR NAME AND ADDRESS ON THE BACK OF THIS FORM

Pubs visited continued..........

By returning this form, you confirm your agreement that the information you provide in your review may be used by The Random House Group Ltd (or its assignees and/or licensees) in any media or medium whatsoever. Any personal details which you provide from which we can identify you are held and processed in accordance with the General Data Protection Regulation (GDPR), and details on how we process this personal data can be found in our Privacy Policy (https://www.penguinrandomhouse.co.uk/PrivacyPolicy/). **Your details will not be passed on to any third parties for their marketing purposes.**

I would like to receive Good Pub Guide updates and offers from The Random House Group. ☐

Your own name and address *(block capitals please)*

....

....

....

Postcode..

Please return to

The Good Pub Guide
FREEPOST RTXY–ZCBC–BBAZ,
Stream Lane,
Sedlescombe, Battle
TN33 0PB

IF YOU PREFER, YOU CAN SEND US REPORTS BY EMAIL:

feedback@goodguides.com

I have been to the following pubs in *The Good Pub Guide 2019* in the last few months, found them as described, and confirm that they deserve continued inclusion:

continued overleaf

PLEASE GIVE YOUR NAME AND ADDRESS ON THE BACK OF THIS FORM

Pubs visited continued..........

By returning this form, you confirm your agreement that the information you provide in your review may be used by The Random House Group Ltd (or its assignees and/or licensees) in any media or medium whatsoever. Any personal details which you provide from which we can identify you are held and processed in accordance with the General Data Protection Regulation (GDPR), and details on how we process this personal data can be found in our Privacy Policy (https://www.penguinrandomhouse.co.uk/PrivacyPolicy/). **Your details will not be passed on to any third parties for their marketing purposes.**

I would like to receive Good Pub Guide updates and offers from The Random House Group. ☐

Your own name and address *(block capitals please)*

....

....

....

Postcode...

Please return to

The Good Pub Guide
FREEPOST RTXY–ZCBC–BBAZ,
Stream Lane,
Sedlescombe, Battle
TN33 0PB

IF YOU PREFER, YOU CAN SEND US REPORTS BY EMAIL:

feedback@goodguides.com

I have been to the following pubs in *The Good Pub Guide 2019* in the last few months, found them as described, and confirm that they deserve continued inclusion:

continued overleaf

PLEASE GIVE YOUR NAME AND ADDRESS ON THE BACK OF THIS FORM

Pubs visited continued..........

By returning this form, you confirm your agreement that the information you provide in your review may be used by The Random House Group Ltd (or its assignees and/or licensees) in any media or medium whatsoever. Any personal details which you provide from which we can identify you are held and processed in accordance with the General Data Protection Regulation (GDPR), and details on how we process this personal data can be found in our Privacy Policy (https://www.penguinrandomhouse.co.uk/PrivacyPolicy/). **Your details will not be passed on to any third parties for their marketing purposes.**

I would like to receive Good Pub Guide updates and offers from The Random House Group. ☐

Your own name and address *(block capitals please)*

....

....

....

Postcode..

Please return to

The Good Pub Guide
FREEPOST RTXY–ZCBC–BBAZ,
Stream Lane,
Sedlescombe, Battle
TN33 0PB

IF YOU PREFER, YOU CAN SEND US REPORTS BY EMAIL:

feedback@goodguides.com

Report on (pub's name)

....

Pub's address

....

☐ YES MAIN ENTRY ☐ YES WORTH A VISIT ☐ NO don't include

Please tick one of these boxes to show your verdict, and give reasons, descriptive comments, prices and the date of your visit

☐ Deserves **FOOD Award** ☐ Deserves **STAY Award** 2019:1

PLEASE GIVE YOUR NAME AND ADDRESS ON THE BACK OF THIS FORM

✂ ....

Report on (pub's name)

....

Pub's address

....

☐ YES MAIN ENTRY ☐ YES WORTH A VISIT ☐ NO don't include

Please tick one of these boxes to show your verdict, and give reasons, descriptive comments, prices and the date of your visit

☐ Deserves **FOOD Award** ☐ Deserves **STAY Award** 2019:2

PLEASE GIVE YOUR NAME AND ADDRESS ON THE BACK OF THIS FORM

DO NOT USE THIS SIDE OF THE PAGE FOR WRITING ABOUT PUBS

Your own name and address *(block capitals please)*

By returning this form, you confirm your agreement that the information you provide in your review may be used by The Random House Group Ltd (or its assignees and/or licensees) in any media or medium whatsoever. Any personal details which you provide from which we can identify you are held and processed in accordance with the General Data Protection Regulation (GDPR), and details on how we process this personal data can be found in our Privacy Policy (https://www.penguinrandomhouse.co.uk/PrivacyPolicy/). **Your details will not be passed on to any third parties for their marketing purposes.**

I would like to receive Good Pub Guide updates and offers from The Random House Group. ☐

✂ ....

DO NOT USE THIS SIDE OF THE PAGE FOR WRITING ABOUT PUBS

Your own name and address *(block capitals please)*

By returning this form, you confirm your agreement that the information you provide in your review may be used by The Random House Group Ltd (or its assignees and/or licensees) in any media or medium whatsoever. Any personal details which you provide from which we can identify you are held and processed in accordance with the General Data Protection Regulation (GDPR), and details on how we process this personal data can be found in our Privacy Policy (https://www.penguinrandomhouse.co.uk/PrivacyPolicy/). **Your details will not be passed on to any third parties for their marketing purposes.**

I would like to receive Good Pub Guide updates and offers from The Random House Group. ☐

Report on (pub's name)

....

Pub's address

....

☐ YES MAIN ENTRY ☐ YES WORTH A VISIT ☐ NO don't include

Please tick one of these boxes to show your verdict, and give reasons, descriptive comments, prices and the date of your visit

☐ Deserves **FOOD Award** ☐ Deserves **STAY Award** 2019: 3

PLEASE GIVE YOUR NAME AND ADDRESS ON THE BACK OF THIS FORM

✂ ....

Report on (pub's name)

....

Pub's address

....

☐ YES MAIN ENTRY ☐ YES WORTH A VISIT ☐ NO don't include

Please tick one of these boxes to show your verdict, and give reasons, descriptive comments, prices and the date of your visit

☐ Deserves **FOOD Award** ☐ Deserves **STAY Award** 2019: 4

PLEASE GIVE YOUR NAME AND ADDRESS ON THE BACK OF THIS FORM

DO NOT USE THIS SIDE OF THE PAGE FOR WRITING ABOUT PUBS

Your own name and address *(block capitals please)*

By returning this form, you confirm your agreement that the information you provide in your review may be used by The Random House Group Ltd (or its assignees and/or licensees) in any media or medium whatsoever. Any personal details which you provide from which we can identify you are held and processed in accordance with the General Data Protection Regulation (GDPR), and details on how we process this personal data can be found in our Privacy Policy (https://www.penguinrandomhouse.co.uk/PrivacyPolicy/). **Your details will not be passed on to any third parties for their marketing purposes.**

I would like to receive Good Pub Guide updates and offers from The Random House Group. ☐

✂ ....

DO NOT USE THIS SIDE OF THE PAGE FOR WRITING ABOUT PUBS

Your own name and address *(block capitals please)*

By returning this form, you confirm your agreement that the information you provide in your review may be used by The Random House Group Ltd (or its assignees and/or licensees) in any media or medium whatsoever. Any personal details which you provide from which we can identify you are held and processed in accordance with the General Data Protection Regulation (GDPR), and details on how we process this personal data can be found in our Privacy Policy (https://www.penguinrandomhouse.co.uk/PrivacyPolicy/). **Your details will not be passed on to any third parties for their marketing purposes.**

I would like to receive Good Pub Guide updates and offers from The Random House Group. ☐

Report on (pub's name)

....

Pub's address

....

☐ YES MAIN ENTRY ☐ YES WORTH A VISIT ☐ NO don't include

Please tick one of these boxes to show your verdict, and give reasons, descriptive comments, prices and the date of your visit

☐ Deserves **FOOD Award** ☐ Deserves **STAY Award** 2019: 5

PLEASE GIVE YOUR NAME AND ADDRESS ON THE BACK OF THIS FORM

✂ ....

Report on (pub's name)

....

Pub's address

....

☐ YES MAIN ENTRY ☐ YES WORTH A VISIT ☐ NO don't include

Please tick one of these boxes to show your verdict, and give reasons, descriptive comments, prices and the date of your visit

☐ Deserves **FOOD Award** ☐ Deserves **STAY Award** 2019: 6

PLEASE GIVE YOUR NAME AND ADDRESS ON THE BACK OF THIS FORM

DO NOT USE THIS SIDE OF THE PAGE FOR WRITING ABOUT PUBS

Your own name and address *(block capitals please)*

By returning this form, you confirm your agreement that the information you provide in your review may be used by The Random House Group Ltd (or its assignees and/or licensees) in any media or medium whatsoever. Any personal details which you provide from which we can identify you are held and processed in accordance with the General Data Protection Regulation (GDPR), and details on how we process this personal data can be found in our Privacy Policy (https://www.penguinrandomhouse.co.uk/PrivacyPolicy/). **Your details will not be passed on to any third parties for their marketing purposes.**

I would like to receive Good Pub Guide updates and offers from The Random House Group. ☐

DO NOT USE THIS SIDE OF THE PAGE FOR WRITING ABOUT PUBS

Your own name and address *(block capitals please)*

By returning this form, you confirm your agreement that the information you provide in your review may be used by The Random House Group Ltd (or its assignees and/or licensees) in any media or medium whatsoever. Any personal details which you provide from which we can identify you are held and processed in accordance with the General Data Protection Regulation (GDPR), and details on how we process this personal data can be found in our Privacy Policy (https://www.penguinrandomhouse.co.uk/PrivacyPolicy/). **Your details will not be passed on to any third parties for their marketing purposes.**

I would like to receive Good Pub Guide updates and offers from The Random House Group. ☐

Report on (pub's name)

....

Pub's address

....

☐ YES MAIN ENTRY ☐ YES WORTH A VISIT ☐ NO don't include

Please tick one of these boxes to show your verdict, and give reasons, descriptive comments, prices and the date of your visit

☐ Deserves **FOOD Award** ☐ Deserves **STAY Award** 2019: 7

PLEASE GIVE YOUR NAME AND ADDRESS ON THE BACK OF THIS FORM

✂ ....

Report on (pub's name)

....

Pub's address

....

☐ YES MAIN ENTRY ☐ YES WORTH A VISIT ☐ NO don't include

Please tick one of these boxes to show your verdict, and give reasons, descriptive comments, prices and the date of your visit

☐ Deserves **FOOD Award** ☐ Deserves **STAY Award** 2019: 8

PLEASE GIVE YOUR NAME AND ADDRESS ON THE BACK OF THIS FORM

DO NOT USE THIS SIDE OF THE PAGE FOR WRITING ABOUT PUBS

Your own name and address *(block capitals please)*

By returning this form, you confirm your agreement that the information you provide in your review may be used by The Random House Group Ltd (or its assignees and/or licensees) in any media or medium whatsoever. Any personal details which you provide from which we can identify you are held and processed in accordance with the General Data Protection Regulation (GDPR), and details on how we process this personal data can be found in our Privacy Policy (https://www.penguinrandomhouse.co.uk/PrivacyPolicy/). **Your details will not be passed on to any third parties for their marketing purposes.**

I **would like to receive Good Pub Guide updates and offers from The Random House Group.** ☐

DO NOT USE THIS SIDE OF THE PAGE FOR WRITING ABOUT PUBS

Your own name and address *(block capitals please)*

By returning this form, you confirm your agreement that the information you provide in your review may be used by The Random House Group Ltd (or its assignees and/or licensees) in any media or medium whatsoever. Any personal details which you provide from which we can identify you are held and processed in accordance with the General Data Protection Regulation (GDPR), and details on how we process this personal data can be found in our Privacy Policy (https://www.penguinrandomhouse.co.uk/PrivacyPolicy/). **Your details will not be passed on to any third parties for their marketing purposes.**

I **would like to receive Good Pub Guide updates and offers from The Random House Group.** ☐

Report on (pub's name)

....

Pub's address

....

☐ YES MAIN ENTRY ☐ YES WORTH A VISIT ☐ NO don't include

Please tick one of these boxes to show your verdict, and give reasons, descriptive comments, prices and the date of your visit

☐ Deserves **FOOD Award** ☐ Deserves **STAY Award** 2019:9

PLEASE GIVE YOUR NAME AND ADDRESS ON THE BACK OF THIS FORM

✂ ....

Report on (pub's name)

....

Pub's address

....

☐ YES MAIN ENTRY ☐ YES WORTH A VISIT ☐ NO don't include

Please tick one of these boxes to show your verdict, and give reasons, descriptive comments, prices and the date of your visit

☐ Deserves **FOOD Award** ☐ Deserves **STAY Award** 2019:10

PLEASE GIVE YOUR NAME AND ADDRESS ON THE BACK OF THIS FORM

DO NOT USE THIS SIDE OF THE PAGE FOR WRITING ABOUT PUBS

Your own name and address *(block capitals please)*

By returning this form, you confirm your agreement that the information you provide in your review may be used by The Random House Group Ltd (or its assignees and/or licensees) in any media or medium whatsoever. Any personal details which you provide from which we can identify you are held and processed in accordance with the General Data Protection Regulation (GDPR), and details on how we process this personal data can be found in our Privacy Policy (https://www.penguinrandomhouse.co.uk/PrivacyPolicy/). **Your details will not be passed on to any third parties for their marketing purposes.**

I would like to receive Good Pub Guide updates and offers from The Random House Group. ☐

✂ ....

DO NOT USE THIS SIDE OF THE PAGE FOR WRITING ABOUT PUBS

Your own name and address *(block capitals please)*

By returning this form, you confirm your agreement that the information you provide in your review may be used by The Random House Group Ltd (or its assignees and/or licensees) in any media or medium whatsoever. Any personal details which you provide from which we can identify you are held and processed in accordance with the General Data Protection Regulation (GDPR), and details on how we process this personal data can be found in our Privacy Policy (https://www.penguinrandomhouse.co.uk/PrivacyPolicy/). **Your details will not be passed on to any third parties for their marketing purposes.**

I would like to receive Good Pub Guide updates and offers from The Random House Group. ☐

Report on (pub's name)

....

Pub's address

....

☐ YES MAIN ENTRY ☐ YES WORTH A VISIT ☐ NO don't include

Please tick one of these boxes to show your verdict, and give reasons, descriptive comments, prices and the date of your visit

☐ Deserves **FOOD Award** ☐ Deserves **STAY Award** 2019:11

PLEASE GIVE YOUR NAME AND ADDRESS ON THE BACK OF THIS FORM

✂ ....

Report on (pub's name)

....

Pub's address

....

☐ YES MAIN ENTRY ☐ YES WORTH A VISIT ☐ NO don't include

Please tick one of these boxes to show your verdict, and give reasons, descriptive comments, prices and the date of your visit

☐ Deserves **FOOD Award** ☐ Deserves **STAY Award** 2019:12

PLEASE GIVE YOUR NAME AND ADDRESS ON THE BACK OF THIS FORM

DO NOT USE THIS SIDE OF THE PAGE FOR WRITING ABOUT PUBS

Your own name and address *(block capitals please)*

By returning this form, you confirm your agreement that the information you provide in your review may be used by The Random House Group Ltd (or its assignees and/or licensees) in any media or medium whatsoever. Any personal details which you provide from which we can identify you are held and processed in accordance with the General Data Protection Regulation (GDPR), and details on how we process this personal data can be found in our Privacy Policy (https://www.penguinrandomhouse.co.uk/PrivacyPolicy/). **Your details will not be passed on to any third parties for their marketing purposes.**

I would like to receive Good Pub Guide updates and offers from The Random House Group. ☐

✂ ....

DO NOT USE THIS SIDE OF THE PAGE FOR WRITING ABOUT PUBS

Your own name and address *(block capitals please)*

By returning this form, you confirm your agreement that the information you provide in your review may be used by The Random House Group Ltd (or its assignees and/or licensees) in any media or medium whatsoever. Any personal details which you provide from which we can identify you are held and processed in accordance with the General Data Protection Regulation (GDPR), and details on how we process this personal data can be found in our Privacy Policy (https://www.penguinrandomhouse.co.uk/PrivacyPolicy/). **Your details will not be passed on to any third parties for their marketing purposes.**

I would like to receive Good Pub Guide updates and offers from The Random House Group. ☐